FAMOUS
FIRST FACTS

Also by Joseph Nathan Kane

Facts About the Presidents

The American Counties

Nicknames and Sobriquets
of U.S. Cities, States, and Counties
(with Gerard L. Alexander)

JOSEPH NATHAN KANE

FAMOUS FIRST

FACTS * A Record of

First Happenings, Discoveries,

and Inventions in American

History * *Fourth Edition*

Expanded and Revised

The H.W. WILSON COMPANY New York 1981

Copyright © 1933, 1935, 1950, 1964, 1981
by Joseph Nathan Kane

Copyright renewal © 1961, 1963, 1978
by Joseph Nathan Kane

First Edition 1933

Second Edition 1950

Third Edition 1964

Printed in the United States of America

Library of Congress Cataloging in Publication Data

Kane, Joseph Nathan, 1899-
    Famous first facts.

    Includes indexes.
    1. Encyclopedias and dictionaries.   I. Title.
AG5.K315   1981   031'.02   81-3395
ISBN 0-8242-0661-4   AACR2

Composition by Datapage, a division of Western Publishing Company, Inc.

Contents

Preface

More than half a century has elapsed since I submitted the manuscript for the first edition of *Famous First Facts* to Halsey W. Wilson. What was intended to be just another useful book has fortunately since become a standard reference book, the most extensive record of American firsts ever assembled.

Famous First Facts now includes more than 9,000 firsts in American history. These pertain to Americans and to events that have occurred in the United States.

A collection of this sort and size — and it is still growing — can evolve only from a relentless quest for information. Facts have been pursued in hundreds of libraries, ranging from one-room rural libraries and specialized collections to the Library of Congress.

Information has also been obtained from organizations and associations, government departments, public records, and directly from the achievers, many of whom I have been fortunate enough to meet. Sometimes many more sources have been consulted to establish a single fact from the mounds of conflicting data.

Much information concerning first events has emerged since the third edition of *Famous First Facts*. Incorporated in the fourth edition are not only new and newly discovered facts, but many previously unconfirmed or unknown details of events, as well as, in a few incidences, accounts that supersede material in earlier editions.

The facts are arranged alphabetically by subject, with extensive cross-references. There are four indexes to facilitate access. The Years and the Days of the Month indexes are arranged chronologically; the Personal Names index, which includes names of people directly or indirectly connected with an event, is arranged alphabetically; and the Geographical index is arranged alphabetically by states and municipalities within states.

To Bruce Carrick, Editor of General Publications; Kim Sinclair, Associate Editor; and Ethel Crockford, Assistant Editor, my thanks for their friendly cooperation in producing this book.

It is hoped that future editions of *Famous First Facts* will offer further data, for much is now being investigated for authenticity.

JOSEPH NATHAN KANE

July 1981

Famous First Facts

A

The First

ABDOMINAL OPERATION. *See* Surgical operation

ABERDEEN-ANGUS CATTLE IMPORTATION. *See* Animals: Cattle (Aberdeen-Angus) importation

ABOLITION NEWSPAPER. *See* Newspaper

ABOLITION SOCIETY was The Society for the Relief of Free Negroes Unlawfully Held in Bondage, formed April 14, 1775, in Philadelphia, Pa. The first president was John Baldwin. The society was reorganized in 1784, adopted a new constitution April 23, 1787, and was incorporated December 8, 1789, as the Pennsylvania Society for Promoting the Abolition of Slavery and for the Relief of Free Negroes Unlawfully Held in Bondage and for Improving the Condition of the African Race. *(Pennsylvania Magazine of History and Biography. Vol. 36, No. 1 January 1912)*

ABORTION LEGISLATION
   Abortion legalization law was signed April 25, 1967, by Governor John Arthur Love of Colorado. It permitted therapeutic abortions in cases in which a three-doctor board of an accredited hospital licensed by the Colorado State Department of Health agreed unanimously.

ABRASIVE for commercial use, to perform work that previously was possible only with diamond dust, was boron carbide (B_4C). It is lighter than aluminum and its density is 2.52 grams per cc. It was produced by the Research Laboratories of the Norton Company, Worcester, Mass., and introduced to the world through a technical paper read before the Electrochemical Society in New York on September 27, 1934.

ABSENTEE VOTING LAW. *See* Election law

ABSOLUTE MONARCH TO VISIT THE UNITED STATES. *See under* Visiting celebrities

ACADEMY was The Academy and College of Philadelphia, founded by Benjamin Franklin in 1749 in Philadelphia, Pa. Franklin drew up the constitution for the academy and on November 13, 1749, was appointed its president. The academy opened August 13, 1751. Seven men were graduated May 17, 1757, at the first commencement, 6 as Bachelors of Arts and 1 as Master of Arts. State legislation enacted September 13, 1791, united the University of the State of Pennsyl-

The First

vania with the College Academy and Charitable School of Philadelphia under the name of the Trustees of the University of Pennsylvania. The first meeting was held November 8, 1791, at Independence Hall, Philadelphia, Pa. Inasmuch as many of the academies were elementary schools and the title *academy* was used indiscriminately, there is considerable conflict as to which was the first academy. *(Ellwood Patterson Cubberley— The History of Education)*

ACADEMY AWARDS. *See under* Television—Telecast

ACADEMY OF ARTS AND LETTERS. *See* Arts and letters society

ACADEMY OF ARTS AND SCIENCE. *See* Arts and science society

ACADEMY OF DESIGN. *See* Art organization

ACADEMY OF POLITICAL AND SOCIAL SCIENCE. *See* Political science society: Political and social science society (national)

ACADEMY OF SCIENCE. *See* Arts and science society; Science association: National Academy of Sciences

ACCIDENT, AUTOMOBILE. *See* Automobile accident

ACCIDENT, RAILROAD. *See* Railroad accident

ACCIDENT INSURANCE. *See* Insurance

ACCIDENT REPORT
   Industrial accident reports required from employers were demanded by Massachusetts, under the Employers' Liability Act, Chapter 270 of the Acts of 1887 passed May 14, 1887, effective September 1, 1887, entitled "An act to extend and regulate the liability of employers to make compensation for personal injuries suffered by employees in their service." Section 3 of the act relates to the filing of notice.

ACCORDION PATENT was issued January 13, 1854, to Anthony Faas of Philadelphia, Pa., and bore patent No. 11,062.

ACCOUNTANCY DEGREE. *See* Degrees (academic and honorary): Doctor of Philosophy in Accounting degree

ACCOUNTANCY LAW (state) was Chapter 312, "an act to regulate the profession of public accountants," signed April 17, 1896, by Governor Levi Parsons Morton of New York. Charles Waldo Haskins was appointed the first chairman of the New York Board of Certified Public Accountant Examiners.

The First

ACCOUNTANT to be made a certified public accountant was Frank Broaker of New York City, who received certificate No. 1 on December 1, 1896, from the New York State Board of Certified Public Accountant Examiners. His name was first on the alphabetical list of 30 accountants certified on that date.

ACCOUNTANTS' SOCIETY

Accountants' society was the Institute of Accountants and Bookkeepers, organized July 28, 1882, in New York City. The name was changed on June 23, 1886, to the Institute of Accounts.

Accountants' society formed by a state group was the New York State Society of Certified Public Accountants, which was organized in New York City, March 30, 1897, following the passage of the New York State Certified Public Account Law of April 17, 1896 (Chapter 312). Charles Waldo Haskins was the first president. It was incorporated January 25, 1897.

Accountants' society to become a national organization was the American Association of Public Accountants, formed in New York City on December 22, 1886, although it was not incorporated until August 20, 1887. The first president was James Yalden.

ACE. See Aviation—Pilot: American ace; Aviation—Pilot: Naval ace

ACETYLENE

Acetylene chemical products full-scale commercial plant was completed in 1956 by the General Aniline & Film Corporation at Calvert City, Ky., at a cost of $6 million. It was patterned after a pilot plant operated by them at Linden, N.J., from 1947 to 1956.

Acetylene or carbide gas was made May 4, 1892, by Thomas Leopold Wilson of the Wilson Aluminum Company in Spray, N.C. He was experimenting to produce metallic calcium by fusing lime and coal tar in an electric furnace. The experiment was unsuccessful and when the molten slaglike mass was dumped into a nearby stream, it was seen that a gas was liberated. The gas which the carbide liberated on contact with water was recognized as acetylene. Shortly afterward acetylene was manufactured on a commercial scale. Acetylene had been made previously, however, on a laboratory scale. *(The Story of Carbide —National Carbide Sales Corporation)*

ACHROMATIC LENS. *See* Lens

ACIDOPHILUS MILK. *See* Milk

ACQUISITION OF LAND BY THE U.S. GOVERNMENT. *See under* Territorial expansion

ACTOR

Actor of American birth was John Martin, who appeared at the Old Southwark Theatre, Philadelphia, Pa., March 13, 1790, as Young Norval in

The First

a play entitled *Douglas. (Charles Durang—History of the Philadelphia Stage)*

Actor to have an exclusive contract. *See* Motion picture actor: Actor to have an exclusive contract

Actor to perform in two cities the same day was Nat C. Goodwin (Nathaniel Carr Goodwin), who left New York City on February 9, 1887, in the 11:30 P.M. sleeping car and arrived in Boston at 7:00 A.M. He acted in *Turned Up* at 11:30 A.M. on February 10, 1887, for the Boston Elk's Lodge and returned on the 1:00 P.M. train to New York City where he acted in *The Mascot* at the Bijou Theatre at 8:00 P.M.

Actor to receive curtain applause was Edmund Keene, who appeared in a group of special performances in Boston, Mass., in 1821. *(Eugene Tompkins—History of the Boston Theatre)*

Actress elected to Congress was Helen Gahagan Douglas, Democrat, of California, who served from January 3, 1945, to January 3, 1951.

American actor to appear abroad was James Henry Hackett, who made his English debut on April 5, 1827, at Covent Garden, London, England. His first appearance on the stage was in a small role in Newark, N.J., in 1816 when he was sixteen years of age, but his professional debut was made March 1, 1826, when he appeared as Judge Woodcock in *Love in a Village* at the Park Theatre, New York City. *(Montrose Jonas Moses—Famous Actor Families in America)*

English actor of note to perform in the United States was George Frederick Cooke of Covent Garden, London, England, who left Liverpool, England, October 4, 1810. He arrived in New York City, November 16, 1810, and made his debut November 21, 1810, as Richard the Third in the play of the same name at the Park Theatre, New York City, before two thousand people. His manager, Thomas Apthorpe Cooper, paid him $125 a week for ten months, a traveling fee of 25 cents per mile, and expenses. Cooke died in New York City, September 26, 1812. *(William Dunlap— Memoirs of George Frederick Cooke)*

Matinee idol was John Henry, an Irish actor who made his debut at Covent Garden, London England, in 1762. His American debut was made in Philadelphia, Pa., October 6, 1766, as Publius Horatius in *The Roman Father. (Arthur Hornblow —History of American Theatre)*

ACTORS' EQUITY ASSOCIATION. *See* Actors union

ACTORS' HOME was the Forrest Home, Philadelphia, opened October 2, 1876. The property consisted of 90 acres of farm land and 20 acres of lawn. The first superintendent was Joseph McArdle.

The First

ACTORS' NATIONAL PROTECTIVE UNION. See Actors' union

ACTORS' UNION was the Actors' National Protective Union, New York City, chartered by the American Federation of Labor, January 4, 1896. It combined with the White Rats (established June 1900) and the Actors' Equity Association (organized May 26, 1913) to form the Associated Actors and Artists of America (chartered August 28, 1919). A strike that was called August 7, 1919, in thirteen theaters in New York City and that spread to other cities was settled in the union's favor September 6, 1919. *(George Fuller Golden— My Lady Vaudeville and Her White Rats)*

ACUPUNCTURE TREATMENT CENTER. See Medical Clinic

ADAPTO CAR. See Railroad car: Freight car Adapto Car)

ADDING MACHINE

Adding machine absolutely accurate at all times was the "Comptometer," which was invented by Dorr Eugene Felt of Chicago, Ill. The model was constructed in November 1884, in Chicago. A patent was applied for in March 1887 and issued on October 11, 1887 (No. 371,496). Felt entered into partnership with Robert Tarrant on November 28, 1887. This firm was later incorporated on January 15, 1889, as the Felt & Tarrant Company. Up to 1902 this machine was the only multiple-order key-driven calculator on the market. *(J. A. V. Turck—Origin of Modern Calculating Machines)*

Adding machine successfully marketed was invented by William Seward Burroughs of St. Louis, Mo., who on August 21, 1888, obtained a patent (No. 388,118), for which he had applied January 10, 1885. In January 1886 he incorporated the business as the American Arithmometer Corporation of St. Louis, Mo., with an authorized capitalization of $100,000. This company was acquired on January 16, 1905, by the Burroughs Adding Machine Company, organized under the laws of Michigan with capital stock of $5 million. *(Burroughs Bulletin, March 9, 1929)*

Adding machine to employ depressible keys was made by Du Bois D. Parmelee of New Paltz, N.Y., who received patent No. 7,074 on February 5, 1850. He called his machine a "calculator." It was neither practical nor generally used. *(J. A. V. Turck—Origin of Modern Calculating Machines)*

Adding machine to print totals and subtotals was made in 1872 by Edmund D. Barbour of Boston, Mass., who obtained patent No. 133,188 on November 19, 1872. His machine, which was called a "calculating machine," was not practical.

ADDRESSOGRAPH was invented in 1892 by Joseph Smith Duncan of Sioux City, Iowa. The first model consisted of a hexagonal wood block upon which was glued rubber type torn from rubber stamps. The block revolved, advancing a new

The First

name and address to the printing point and inking the type simultaneously at each operation. This model was never marketed. The model "Baby 'O' " was put into production on July 26, 1893, in one small back room in the old Caxton Building on Dearborn Street in Chicago, Ill. Duncan obtained patent No. 558,936, April 28, 1896, on an "addressing machine."

ADHESIVE AND MEDICATED PLASTER

Adhesive and medicated plaster used in the treatment of fractures was reported in *Anatomy, Physiology and Diseases of the Bones and Joints,* by Samuel David Gross, published in 1830 in Philadelphia, Pa. *(American Journal of Medical Science. June 1897)*

Adhesive and medicated plaster patent was No. 3965, issued March 26, 1845, to Dr. Horace Harrel Day of Jersey City, N.J., and Dr. William H. Shecut. They dissolved rubber in a solvent, such as benzine, turpentine, and bisulphide of carbon, which they spread with a brush on fabric. They sold the process to Dr. Thomas Allcock, who introduced Allcock's Porous Plaster. *(American Journal of Pharmacy. Vol. 82, 1910)*

Adhesive and medicated plaster with a rubber base to be successfully manufactured was produced by Robert Wood Johnson and George J. Seabury in 1874 at East Orange, N.J. In 1886 Johnson separated from Seabury and formed Johnson & Johnson, New Brunswick, N.J., which introduced a full line of pharmaceutical plasters with an India rubber base.

ADHESIVE STAMP. See Postage stamp

ADJUTANT GENERAL. See Army officer

ADMIRAL. See Naval officer

ADMIRAL IN THE COAST GUARD. See Coast Guard (U.S.): Vice admiral in the Coast Guard

ADMIRAL IN THE MERCHANT MARINE. See Merchant Marine: Merchant Marine officer to hold the rank of rear admiral

ADMIRAL KILLED IN ACTION. See Naval officer: Admiral killed in action in World War II

ADMIRAL WHO WAS A GENERAL. See Army officer: General to become a rear admiral

ADVENTIST. See Seventh Day Adventist Church

ADVERTISEMENT

Advertisement appeared May 1–8, 1704, in the Boston *News-Letter.* Three ads occupied four inches in a single column. The only display was a two-line initial letter in the text and the word *Advertisement* above them. One offered "At Oysterbay on Long Island in the Province of New York . . . a very good Fulling Mill to be Let or Sold, as also a Plantation, having on it a large new Brick house, and other good house by it for a Kitchin and workhouse, etc." Another offered a reward for the capture of a thief and the return of certain

The First

ADVERTISEMENT—*Continued*

wearing apparel, and the third was a notice of the loss of two anvils. In the first issue, April 17–24, 1704, an announcement was made that advertisements would be published. *(James Melvin Lee—History of American Journalism)*

Advertisement to occupy a half page space in a periodical. *See* Double-column advertisement

Advertising or commercial radio broadcast. *See under* Radio broadcast

Automobile advertisement in a national magazine of general circulation appeared in the March 31, 1900, *Saturday Evening Post,* Philadelphia, Pa. The W. E. Roach Company, Philadelphia, featured its slogan, "Automobiles That Give Satisfaction." The *Scientific American,* however, on July 30, 1898, had published a one-column advertisement of the Winton Motor Car Co., Cleveland, Ohio, under the caption "Dispense with a Horse."

Double-column advertisement appeared in the New York *Weekly Journal,* New York City, July 18, 1743. "To be Seen. At Mr. Pacheco's Ware-House, in Marketfield Street, commonly known by the Name of Petticoat Lane, opposite the Cross Guns, near the Fort. A Curious Musical machine, arriv'd from England, the third Day of May last, which performs several strange and diverting Motions to the Admiration of the Spectators, viz. The Doors fly open of their own accord, and there appear six Ringers in white Shirts all busy pulling the Bell-Ropes, and playing several Tunes, Chimes and Changes: They first appear with black Caps and black Beards, at one Corner there is a Barbers Shop and a Barbers Pole hung out, and at the Shop Door stands the Barber's Boy, who, at the Word of Command, gives three Knocks at his Master's Door, out comes the Barber with his Rasor and Baton to shave the Ringers, then the Doors shut themselves whilst the Barber is Shaving them, then the Doors open themselves." Exhibitions were held at 4:00 P.M. and 7:00 P.M., 1 shilling 1 pence admission. The advertisement for this machine (which was the first automaton in this country) was also the first advertisement to occupy a half-page space in a periodical.

Magician's advertisement appeared March 18, 1734, in the New York *Weekly Journal* and announced that on March 18 Joseph Broome would "perform Wonders of the World by Dexterity of Hand" at the home of Charles Sleigh, on Duke Street, New York, and invited "all to be Spectators of his Ingenuity." The admission fees were 1s, 9d, and 6d. *(John Mulholland—Quicker Than the Eye)*

Newspaper advertisement printed on aluminum foil. *See under* Newspaper

The First

Newspaper with perfumed advertising page. *See under* Newspaper

Patent medicine advertisement appeared in the 1692 *Boston Almanack* printed by Benjamin Harris and John Allen: "That Excellent Antidote against all manner of Gripings called Aqua anti torminales, which if timely taken, it not only cures the Griping of the Guts, and the Wind Cholick; but preventeth that woful Distemper of the Dry Belly Ach; With printed directions for the use of it. Sold by Benjamin Harris at the London-Coffee House in Boston. Price three shillings the half pint Bottle."

Radio broadcasting contract for FM broadcasting. *See* Radio advertising: Radio advertising contract for frequency modulation broadcasts

Three-dimensional newspaper advertisement was published June 12, 1953, in the *Daily Freeman,* Waukesha, Wis. The Hale-Frame Associates decorators, used a full page to advertise carpets A cardboard cutout with a red and blue lens to see the third-dimensional effect was supplied with the newspaper. On consecutive days, starting July 13 1953, Bullock's Downtown used six full-page three-dimensional advertisements in the Los Angeles *Times.*

ADVERTISING AGENCY was opened by Volney B. Palmer in Philadelphia, Pa., in 1841, for the reception of advertisements. He thus became the first commercial advertising agent. *(V. B. Palmer—Business Men's Almanac for the year 1849)*

ADVERTISING COURSE. *See* Radio instruction Radio-advertising course

ADVERTISING LEGISLATION

Advertising legislation (state) was "an act to regulate the sale of merchandise and to prevent misleading and dishonest representations in connection therewith," Chapter 657 of the Laws of New York passed April 30, 1898. Those whose advertisements are "intended to have the appearance of an advantageous offer, which is untrue or calculated to mislead, shall be guilty of a misdemeanor."

Outdoor advertising legislation (state) was passed by New York March 28, 1865, amending Chapter 573, Laws of 1853, entitled "an act for the more effectual prevention of wanton and malicious mischief and to prevent the defacement of natural scenery." Painting and printing upon stones, rocks, trees, and the defacement of natural scenery in certain localities constituted a misdemeanor punishable by a fine not exceeding $250, or six months' imprisonment, or both. *(Chapter 222, Laws of 1865)*

ADVERTISING MAGAZINE was the *Advertising Agency Circular,* a monthly founded by George Presbury Rowell and published by George P. Rowell & Co., New York City. It was issued from 186. until December 1866, when the name was changed

The First

to the *Advertiser's Gazette.* On Thursday, April 1, 1875, it was first issued as a weekly. *(Advertiser's Gazette. Vol. 9, No. 1, April 1, 1875)*

ADVERTISING ORGANIZATION to combat business abuses by advancing truth and fair practice in business was the Vigilance Committee of the Advertising Club of New York, New York City, organized at a meeting called December 1911 by Lewellyn E. Pratt, program committee chairman. Investigation work commenced March 1912. On May 19, 1912, the Associated Advertising Clubs of America in convention at Dallas, Tex., formed a national committee with Harry D. Robbins as chairman. *(Hurnard Jay Kenner—The Fight for Truth in Advertising)*

ADVERTISING SCHOOL was established in 1920 by the Poor Richard Club in their clubhouse, Philadelphia. In 1923–1924, a diploma was awarded for the completion of the two-year course. In 1924, the name was changed to the Charles Morris Price School of Advertising and Journalism of the Poor Richard Club.

ADVERTISING SHOW (annual) was held May 3–9, 1906, at Madison Square Garden, New York City. Its slogan was "If your business isn't with advertising, advertise it for sale."

ADVERTISING STANDARDIZATION. *See* Billboard standardization

ADVISORY COMMITTEE FOR AERONAUTICS (national). *See under* Aviation

AERIAL CAMERA. *See* Camera

AERIAL FERRY BRIDGE. *See* Bridge

AERIAL FOREST PATROL. *See* Forest Service: Forest Service aerial patrol

AERIAL LIFT BRIDGE. *See* Bridge

AERIAL MOTION PICTURES. *See* Aviation: Airplane motion picture show

AERIAL PHOTOGRAPH. *See* Photograph

AERIAL POLICE OFFICER (WOMAN). *See* Police: Police officer (woman) on the aerial force

AERO CLUB OF AMERICA LICENSE. *See* Aviation—License

AEROCYCLE. *See* Helicopter

AEROLITE. *See* Meteorite

AERONAUTIC INTERNATIONAL EXPOSITION. *See* Aviation—Expositions and Meets

AERONAUTICAL BOARD. *See* Aviation: Air control municipal board

AERONAUTICAL ENGINEERING COURSE. *See under* Aviation—School

AERONAUTICAL STOWAWAY. *See under* Aviation

The First

AERONAUTICAL TROPHY. *See under* Aviation

AERONAUTICS. *See* Aviation

AERONAUTICS (civil) AUTHORITY (U.S.). *See* Civil aeronautics authority (U.S.)

AEROSOL PATENT. *See* Patent

AFRICAN CHURCH was the Bethel African Methodist Episcopal Church, founded in 1793 by Richard Allen, a black, at Sixth and Lombard Street, Philadelphia, Pa. It was opened for public worship July 17, 1794, and dedicated July 29, 1794, by Bishop Francis Asbury. On October 12, 1794, the Reverend Robert Blackwell announced from the pulpit that the congregation was received in full fellowship in the Methodist Episcopal Church. It was incorporated March 28, 1796, as the "Minister, Church, Wardens and Vestrymen of the African Episcopal Church of St. Thomas in the City of Philadelphia. *(Carter Godwin Woodson—History of the Negro Church)*

AFRICAN METHODIST EPISCOPAL CHURCH. *See under* Methodist Episcopal Church

AFRICANDER CATTLE. *See* Animals

AGENCY, ADVERTISING. *See* Advertising agency

AGRICULTURAL ADJUSTMENT ADMINISTRATION was authorized by act of Congress (H.R. 3835, 73rd Congress) "to relieve the existing national economic emergency by increasing purchasing power." The act, approved May 12, 1933 (48 Stat. L. 31), was known as the Agricultural Adjustment Act. The first administrator was George Nelson Peek of Moline, Ill., named May 4, 1933, who served under Henry Agard Wallace, Secretary of Agriculture, until December 15, 1933, when he was appointed President Franklin Delano Roosevelt's special adviser on commercial policy.

AGRICULTURAL APPROPRIATION by a state for carrying out extension training work along agricultural lines was made by New York, May 12, 1894, when Governor Roswell Pettibone Flower signed the act "to amend the agricultural law in relation to agricultural experiment stations within this state, and to make an appropriation therefor," Chapter 675. The appropriation was $16,000.

AGRICULTURAL "BOARD" (state) was provided for in New York State by a law passed April 7, 1819, but was not actually organized until January 20, 1820. It was made up wholly of agricultural society delegates and was a quasi-public organization. *(Edward Wiest—Agricultural Organization in the United States)*

AGRICULTURAL BOOK
Agricultural book was *The Husbandman's Guide: In Four Parts. Part First. Containing many Excellent Rules for Setting and Planting of Orchards, Gardens and Woods, the times to Sow*

The First

AGRICULTURAL BOOK—*Continued*
Corn, and all sorts of Seeds. Part Second. Choice Physical Receipts for divers dangerous Distempers in Men, Women and Children. Part Third. The Experienc'd Farrier. . . . Part Fourth. Certain rare Receipts to make Cordial Waters, Conserves, Preserves. . . . " It was a 107-page reprint of an English book and was published in 1710 for Eleazar Phillips by John Allen, Boston, Mass.

Agricultural book distinctly American was *Essays upon Field Husbandry in New England* by Jared Eliot. It consisted of six essays, originally printed separately, which were printed and sold by Edes and Gill in Boston, Mass., in 1760. The first essay appeared in 1748, the second in 1749, the third in 1751, the fourth in 1753, the fifth in 1754, and the sixth in 1759. *(Franklin Bowditch Dexter—Biographical Notices of the Graduates of Yale College 1701–1745)*

AGRICULTURAL DICTIONARY. *See* Dictionary

AGRICULTURAL ENCYCLOPEDIA was Anthony Florian Madinger Willich's *The Domestic Encyclopedia, or A Dictionary of Facts, and useful knowledge, comprehending a concise view of the latest discoveries, inventions and improvements, chiefly applicable to rural and domestic economy* . . . , a five-volume set, published in Philadelphia, Pa., in 1804 by William Young Birch and Abraham Small. It had originally appeared in England. *(Percy Wells Bidwell and John Ironside Falconer —History of Agriculture in Northern United States)*

AGRICULTURAL EXPERIMENT STATION
Agricultural experiment farm was ten acres set aside by Savannah, Ga., in 1735. A skillful botanist was appointed "to collect the seeds of drugs and dying-stuffs in other countries in the same climate, in order to cultivate such of them as shall be found to thrive well in Georgia." *(Collections of Georgia Historical Society. Vol. 1. 1840)*

State agricultural experiment station was the Connecticut Agricultural Experiment Station, established in Connecticut by Act approved July 20, 1875. Orange Judd, editor and proprietor of the *American Agriculturist*, offered $1,000, and the trustees of Wesleyan University at Middletown, Conn., offered the free use of the chemical laboratory of Orange Judd Hall on condition that the legislature appropriate $2,800 per annum for two years. The appropriation was made October 1, 1875, and work begun January 1, 1876. Professor Wilbur Olin Atwater was made the first director of this first regularly organized state experiment station and served until April 9, 1877. *(Bulletin 80. Office of Experimental Stations—U.S. Department of Agriculture)*

AGRICULTURAL FAIR. *See* Fair

The First

AGRICULTURAL IMPLEMENTS. *See* Plow Reaper

AGRICULTURAL JOURNAL
Agricultural journal was the *Agricultural Museum*, a sixteen-page octavo issued July 4, 1810 under the sponsorship of the Columbian Agricultural Society. It was edited by the Reverend David Wiley and printed by W. A. Rind at Georgetown, D.C. The first volume was semimonthly, but beginning with Volume 2 it was issued monthly. Subscription was $2.50 for 24 numbers. Publication ceased May 1812. *(Agricultural History. Vol. 2, No. 2. April 1928)*

Agricultural journal to attain prominence was the *American Farmer*, an eight-page quarto-size weekly, which was founded in Baltimore, Md., April 2, 1819, by John Stuart Skinner. It flourished under various names until 1897. *(William Edward Ogilvie—Pioneer Agricultural Journalists)*

Agricultural journal written directly from practical experience was the *Genesee Farmer and Gardener's Journal*, a weekly paper devoted to agriculture, horticulture and rural economy, edited by N. Goodsell and published by Luther Tucker & Company, Rochester, N.Y. The first issue was dated January 1, 1831, and consisted of eight pages. Subscription was $2.50 a year. One thousand copies were printed of the first issue.

AGRICULTURAL LAND GRANT proposal was made by Justin Smith Morrill. He advocated giving each state an allotment of land, the income from which should be used to support at least one agricultural college in each state. The bill was vetoed by President James Buchanan in 1857, but was signed by President Abraham Lincoln on July 2, 1862 (12 Stat. L. 503), after certain modifications had been made. It was known as the Morrill Act and its full title was an "Act donating public land to the several states and territories which may provide colleges for the benefit of agriculture and the mechanic arts." *(George Washington Atherton —The Legislative Career of Justin S. Morrill)*

AGRICULTURAL SCHOOL
Agricultural college (state) to be chartered was the Farmers High School of Pennsylvania, incorporated April 13, 1854. The charter was repealed and it was reincorporated February 22, 1855. The school opened February 16, 1859. In the first session, 119 students were admitted. The Bachelor of Scientific and Practical Agriculture degree (B.S.A.) was awarded to those who completed a four-year course and submitted a dissertation. The name was changed on May 6, 1862, to the Agricultural College of Pennsylvania.

Agricultural college (state) to open was the Agricultural College of Michigan, Lansing, Mich., which was chartered on February 12, 1855, and opened on May 13, 1857. On May 14, 1857, the faculty of six conducted classes for the 63 stu

The First

dents. The first president was Joseph Ricketson Williams. The school was later renamed the Michigan State College of Agriculture and Applied Science.

Vocational agricultural school with dormitory facilities that was a department of a state university was the School of Agriculture of the University of Minnesota, established October 18, 1888, at St. Anthony Park, St. Paul, Minn. The first principal was William Wirt Pendergast.

AGRICULTURAL SEED DISTRIBUTION (national) was undertaken in 1836–37 by the Commissioner of Patents, Henry Leavitt Ellsworth, at his own expense and without congressional authorization. In 1838 the cost of agricultural statistics and seeds was $126.40. In 1839 about 30,000 packets were distributed, the expense being about $1,000. Seed distribution was discontinued June 30, 1923.

AGRICULTURAL SOCIETY

Agricultural society on the American continent was the Philadelphia Society for the Promotion of Agriculture, which was organized on March 1, 1785. Meetings were scheduled every two months. The promotion of agriculture was undertaken as one of the functions of the New Jersey Society for Promoting Agriculture, Commerce and Arts, established in 1781. A meeting was held September 7, 1781, in Trenton, N.J. Samuel Witham Stockton was secretary. *(Early Development of Agricultural Societies in the U.S.—Agricultural Historical Society Papers)*

Agricultural society for dairymen was the Vermont Dairymen's Association, organized October 27, 1869, at Montpelier, Vt., "to improve the dairy interests of Vermont, and all subsidiary interests." *(Annual Report, 1875—Vermont Department of Agriculture)*

Agricultural society of national importance was the National Grange of the Patrons of Husbandry, which was organized in Washington, D.C., December 4, 1867, with William Saunders of the Department of Agriculture as master, and Oliver Hudson Kelley, a native of Boston, Mass., as secretary. This was the first important cooperation undertaken by farmers. The movements and meetings of the society were carried on in secret. *(Solon Justus Buck—The Granger Movement)*

AGRICULTURAL SOIL CONFERENCE of importance was the International Congress of Soil Science that met in Washington, D.C., June 13-22, 1917. Delegates were present from over twenty countries. *(International Congress of Soil Science —Proceedings and Papers of the First International Congress)*

AGRICULTURAL STATE COLLEGE. *See* Agricultural school

The First

AGRICULTURAL STATION. *See* Agricultural experiment station

AGRICULTURE

Crop limitation law was passed October 16, 1629, by the Virginia General Assembly. Act Five limited the planting of tobacco. *(William Waller Hening—Statutes at Large of Virginia. Vol. 1)*

Crop surplus destruction was ordered January 6, 1639, by the Virginia General Assembly: "Tobacco by reason of excessive quantities made, being so low that the planters could not subsist by it or be enabled to raise more staple commodities or pay their debts, enacted that the tobacco of that year be viewed by sworn viewers and the rotten and unmerchantable, and half the good to be burned, so the whole quantity made would come to 1,500,000 pounds without stripping and smoothing." *(William Waller Hening—Statutes at Large of Virginia. Vol. 1)*

Federal Crop Insurance Corporation. *See* Federal Crop Insurance Corporation

Grain Stabilization Corporation. *See* Grain Stabilization Corporation

AGRICULTURE BUREAU

Agriculture bureau (hitherto a section of the Patent Office) was made a separate entity on May 15, 1862, by an act "to establish a Department of Agriculture" (12 Stat. L. 387) and was administered by a Commissioner of Agriculture until February 9, 1889 (25 Stat. L. 659), when it was made the eighth executive department in the federal government. The first Superintendent of Agriculture under the Department of the Interior was Thomas Green Clemson, who served from February 3, 1860, to March 4, 1861. Isaac Newton was appointed Commissioner of Agriculture by President Abraham Lincoln on July 1, 1862, and served until June 19, 1867, at $3,000 a year. *(Records in Bureau of Plant Industry, U.S. Department of Agriculture, Washington, D.C.)*

Agriculture bureau scientific publication was *A Report on the Chemical Analysis of Grapes,* a four-page leaflet, by Charles Mayer Wetherill, Ph.D., M.D., dated October 15, 1862, printed by the Government Printing Office, Washington, D.C. *(Edgar Fahs Smith—Charles Mayer Wetherill)*

AGRICULTURE DEPARTMENT (state)

State department of agriculture was created by Georgia by act of February 28, 1874. The first commissioner was Dr. Thomas P. Janes, who served for six years.

AGRICULTURE DEPARTMENT (U.S.)

Agriculture Department distinguished service gold medal. *See under* Medal

Office of Markets was created May 16, 1913, by the Secretary of Agriculture under authority of March 4, 1913 (37 Stat. L. 854), which appropriated $50,000 for its operation. The first chief was

The First

AGRICULTURE DEPARTMENT (U.S.)—*Continued*
Charles John Brand, who served from May 16, 1913, to June 30, 1919. In the appropriation act of June 30, 1914 (38 Stat. L. 440), a similar paragraph was headed "Office of Markets" and the amount increased to $200,000. The Office of Markets and the Office of Rural Organization were combined on July 1, 1914, and the resulting unit was called the Office of Markets and Rural Organization. It was changed to the Bureau of Markets by the act of March 4, 1917 (39 Stat. L. 1162).

Secretary of the Department of Agriculture was Norman Jay Colman of Missouri, who was appointed February 13, 1889, by President Grover Cleveland and who served until March 5, 1889. Previously he had served as Commissioner of Agriculture from April 4, 1885, to February 12, 1889. *(William Lawrence Wanlass—United States Department of Agriculture, a Study in Administration)*

AGRICULTURE PROFESSOR in a college was Samuel Latham Mitchill, who was appointed by Columbia College, New York City, on July 9, 1792, as Professor of Natural History, Chemistry, Agriculture, and the other related sciences. Part of his course included the "theory of vegetation and application of its principles to practical agriculture, nutrition and food of plants, with the history of manures, multiplication, dissemination and habitations of plants. Chemical history of various vegetable products, Sap, Gum, Resin, Farina, etc., with their preparation and application to the uses of man. Vegetable colors, vegetable poisons, baking, brewing, tanning, etc." *(Alfred Charles True—History of Agricultural Education in the United States)*

AIR (compressed) for tunnel construction was employed in 1879. This method was introduced by Dewitt Clinton Haskin and was used in the construction of the famous Hudson River tunnel between Hoboken, N.J., and Morton Street, New York City. The tunnel plans called for two tubes, each 16 feet wide and 18 feet high. During the construction, on July 21, 1880, the compressed air blew a hole through the soft silt of the roof about 360 feet from the Hoboken shaft, flooding the tubes and drowning 20 workmen. Work was discontinued and the tunnel was not completed and opened until February 25, 1908. *(Archibald Black—The Story of Tunnels)*

AIR (liquid) was economically produced in 1895 by Charles Eastman Tripler of the Tripler Liquid Air Company, New York City. His invention reduced the cost of production from $500 a pint to $4 a gallon. *(New Hampshire Medical Society. Transactions. May 25, 1899—"Liquid air"—J. Milnor Coit)*

The First

AIR BOAT COMMERCIAL LINE SERVICE. *See* Aviation: Hydroplane commercial line service

AIR BRAKE was invented by George Westinghouse, Jr., of Schenectady, N.Y., who received patent No. 88,929 on April 13, 1869, on a "steam power brake." It was used on an experimental train carrying officials of the Panhandle Railroad. It immediately demonstrated its value. But inasmuch as it took longer for the air to reach the last cars of a train, each car stopped at a different time. A "triple air brake" which corrected this fault was patented by Westinghouse (No. 124,405) on March 5, 1872. He invented an automatic brake 15 years later. *(Bulletins of the Westinghouse Air Brake Co.)*

AIR BRUSH PATENT was No. 248,579, which was granted to Leslie L. Curtis of Cape Elizabeth, Me., on October 25, 1881, for his "atomizer for coloring pictures."

AIR-CONDITIONED AUTOMOBILE. *See* Automobile

AIR-CONDITIONED FACTORY. *See* Factory

AIR-CONDITIONED HOTEL. *See* Hotel

AIR-CONDITIONED OFFICE BUILDING. *See* Building

AIR-CONDITIONED RAILROAD CAR. *See* Railroad car

AIR-CONDITIONED THEATER. *See* Theater

AIR-CONDITIONED TRAIN. *See under* Railroad

AIR CONFERENCE (international). *See* Aviation—Expositions and Meets

AIR CONTROL MUNICIPAL BOARD. *See under* Aviation

AIR CORPS
    Air Corps (U.S. Army) was established by Act of July 2, 1926 (44 Stat. L. 780), which authorized a Chief of the Air Corps (major general), 3 assistants (brigadier generals), 1,514 officers (from second lieutenants to colonels), and 16,000 enlisted men. Frederick Trubee Davison of New York was sworn in July 16, 1926, as Assistant Secretary of War for Aviation.

AIR DEFENSE COMMAND (U.S.) was created February 26, 1940, with headquarters at Mitchel Field, Long Island, N.Y., pursuant to War Department Orders, dated February 26, 1940, for defense against air attack through the practical application of the coordinated effort of aviation, antiaircraft artillery, and aircraft warning agencies including fixed military and civilian installations. It was charged with the development of a system for unified air defense of an area and the determination of tasks within the capabilities of the various combinations of tactical units that might be assembled for the air defense of cities, continental bases, manufacturing and industrial areas, or

The First

of armies in the field. The first commander was Brigadier General James Eugene Chaney.

AIR FLIGHT ATTENDANT. *See under* Aviation

AIR FORCE
See also Air Corps
Air Force aviation unit equipped and trained for overseas duty was the Marine Aeronautic Company, comprised 12 officers and 133 enlisted men, which sailed on January 9, 1918, from Cape May, N.J., and landed January 21, 1918, at Ponta Delgada, Azores.

Air Force class trained to fire intercontinental missiles completed the course on December 17, 1957, at Northrop Aircraft, Inc., Hawthorne, Calif. Most of the 105 airmen were assigned to the Strategic Air Command's first operational long-range missile squadron.

Air service (military) under one command was effected on September 3, 1917, when Brigadier General William Lacy Kenly was made chief of the Air Service of The American Expeditionary Force in France, serving until February 1918.

Air Force Secretary was William Stuart Symington of Missouri, who was sworn in by Chief Justice Frederick Moore Vinson in Washington, D.C., on September 18, 1947. He served until April 24, 1950, when his successor, Thomas Knight Finletter, was sworn in.

AIR FORCE ACADEMY (U.S.)
Air Force Academy was authorized April 1, 1954 (68 Stat. L. 47). Temporary headquarters were established July 11, 1955, at the Lowry Air Force Base, Denver, Colo., when 306 candidates were sworn in. The first commandant was Lieutenant General Hubert Reilly Harmon. The first advisory board consisted of Dr. Arthur Holly Compton, Dr. Virgil Melvin Hancher, Dr. John Alfred Hannah, Kaufman Thuma Keller, Charles Augustus Lindbergh, and General Carl Andrew Spaatz. The $135 million academy at Colorado Springs, Colo., received its first cadets on August 29, 1958. The first graduating class (207 cadets) was commissioned June 3, 1959, the commencement address being delivered by James Henderson Douglas, Secretary of the Air Force. First in the graduating class was Bradley Clark Hosmer of Dunseith, N.Dak. The four-year course consisted of 1,548 hours of the humanities, 1,629 hours of science, and 2,178 hours of airmanship.

Air Force Academy graduate (American Indian) was Leo Johnson of Fairfax, Okla., who was one of the 297 graduates of the U.S. Air Force Academy, Colorado Springs, Colo., on June 6, 1962. President Lyndon Baines Johnson delivered the commencement address and presented the diplomas. Air Force Chief of Staff General Curtis E. LeMay presented the military commissions.

The First

Air Force Academy graduates (black) were Charles Vernon Bush, Isaac Sanders Payne, IV, and Roger Bernard Sims, who were graduated from the Air Force Academy, Colorado Springs, Colo., on June 5, 1963, and received the Bachelor of Science degree.

Air Force Academy woman officer was Captain Naomi M. McCracken of Redding, Calif., who took over her duties as assistant director of cadet records at the Air Force Academy temporary headquarters, Denver, Colo., on April 26, 1957.

Women students were admitted to the Air Force Academy at Colorado Springs, Colo., on June 28, 1976, when 155 women were enrolled. At the end of the first year, 138 remained.

AIR FORCE FLAG. *See* Flag

AIR FORCE OFFICER
Air Force Ace in Vietnam was Captain Richard Stephen Ritchie of Reidsville, N.C., who downed his fifth MIG-21 aircraft in North Vietnam on August 28, 1972, in an air-to-air missile battle southwest of Hanoi. He flew an F-4 Phantom of the 555th Tactical Fighter Squadron of the 432d Tactical Reconnaissance Wing based in Thailand. His other "kills" occurred May 10th, May 31st, and two on July 8, 1972.

Air Force chairman of the Joint Chiefs of Staff was General Nathan Farragut Twining, who was sworn in August 15, 1957, in Washington, D.C., by President Dwight David Eisenhower. On September 29, 1960, the day before Twining retired as chief of staff, President Eisenhower decorated him with the Distinguished Service Medal.

Air Force chaplain (woman) was Captain Lorraine Potter of Warwick, R.I., American Baptist minister, appointed September 26, 1973, to serve in San Antonio. She served at the West Webster United Church of Christ, Webster, N.Y., and completed an orientation course at Maxwell Air Force Base, Montgomery, Ala.

Air Force general (woman) was Brigadier General Jeanne Marjorie Holm of Portland, Ore., nominated December 12, 1970, by President John Fitzgerald Kennedy. On July 16, 1971, the silver stars were pinned on her shoulders by Air Force Secretary Robert Channing Seamans, Jr., and Lieutenant General James Dixon at the Pentagon, Washington, D.C. Holm had served since 1965 as Director of Women in the Air Force.

Air Force Surgeon General was Major General Malcolm Cummings Grow, who served from July 1, 1949, to November 30, 1949. Air Force General Order No. 35 of June 8, 1949, authorized the U.S. Air Force Medical Service and the Office of Surgeon General. Grow had previously served as air surgeon from January 1946 to July 1, 1949.

The First

AIR FORCE OFFICER—*Continued*

Brigadier general (black) in the Air Force was Benjamin Oliver Davis, Jr., of Washington, D.C., director of Operations and Training of the Far East Air Force, who was named October 27, 1954. He was the son of Brigadier General Benjamin Oliver Davis of the U.S. Army.

Chief Master Sergeant (black) of the Air Force was Thomas N. Barnes of Chester, Pa., who entered the U.S. Air Force in April 1949 and became a master sergeant on December 1, 1969, and Chief Master Sergeant of the Air Force on October 1, 1973, for a two-year term. The post of Chief Master Sergeant was established in 1967.

Judge Advocate General of the U.S. Air Force was Colonel Reginald Carl Harmon, who was nominated by President Harry S. Truman on September 8, 1948, for a four-year term as the first judge advocate general of the Air Force with the rank of major general.

Military engineer (woman) in the Air Force was Second Lieutenant Susanne M. Ocobock, who served from April 8, 1971, to August 15, 1972, as a industrial civil engineer at Kelly Air Force Base, Tex.

Nun in the Air Force Reserve was (Roman Catholic) Sister Nancy Ann Eagan, nurse, who became a lieutenant on May 5, 1970. She was assigned to the 932d Aeromedical Airlift Group, Scott Air Force Base, Ill.

AIR FORCE SURVIVAL SCHOOL. *See* Aviation—School

AIR GUN was the "Chicago" a wooden gun marketed in March 1886 by the Markham Manufacturing Company, Plymouth, Mich. It fired a size "BB" shot. In 1888, a metal gun was manufactured and on January 16, 1889, sales rights were granted to the Plymouth Iron Windmill Company.

AIR MAIL. *See* Airmail service

AIR MEDAL. *See* Medal

AIR MEET. *See* Aviation—Expositions and Meets

AIR PASSENGER INTERNATIONAL STATION. *See* Aviation—Airport

AIR PATROL (U.S.), CIVIL. *See* Civil air patrol (U.S.)

AIR RACE, INTERCITY. *See under* Aviation—Races

AIR RAID SHELTER

Air raid community shelter was the Highlands Community Shelter, Inc., Boise, Idaho, which was completed on July 1, 1961. It was designed to accommodate 1,000 people. Family membership cost $100. The shelter cost $142,000, of which $122,000 was government research funds obtained from the Office of Civil Defense.

The First

Air raid shelter was built by Howard Moyer Gounder at Fleetwood, Pa., R.F.D. #1, and completed November 1, 1940. Stone walls 18 inches thick set in concrete with 18-inch retaining walls built alongside a mountain boulder supported an 8-inch reinforced concrete roof, weather-conditioned with asphalt tar. Movable bunks on one wall accommodated six people. The floors were made of cement. Heavy double doors, one opening inward, the other outward, contained small windows. Electric wiring encased in iron pipes supplied illumination. A stove provided heating and cooking facilities, while ventilation was afforded by a protected chimney in the rear.

House with a built-in nuclear bomb shelter. *See under* Building

AIR-RAIL PASSENGER SERVICE. *See* Aviation: Air-rail passenger transcontinental service

AIR RIGHTS LEASE was made by the New York Central Railroad Company in February 1910 to the Grand Central Palace, New York City, for $30,000 a year. The Palace was permitted to build its structure over the New York Central Railroad tracks. The air rights idea was originated by Ira A. Place.

AIR SERVICE (U.S.). *See* Aviation: Air service of the United States Army

AIR SPRAY (paint). *See* Paint spraying device

AIR SQUADRON. *See* Aviation: Air squadron (complete); Navy: Air squadron of jets (U.S. Navy)

AIR STATION (COAST GUARD). *See* Aviation: Coast Guard air station

AIR STEWARDESS. *See* Aviation: Flight attendant (woman)

AIR TERMINAL. *See* Aviation—Airport

AIR-TO-AIR ROCKET. *See* Rocket

AIR TRAFFIC REGULATION COURSE. *See under* Traffic regulation course

AIR TRAINING SCHOOL (Naval). *See* Aviation—School: Naval air training school

AIRBOAT COMMERCIAL LINE SERVICE. *See* Aviation: Hydroplane commercial line service

AIRCRAFT BATTLE FORCE COMMANDER. *See* Naval officer: Naval officer designated commander, Aircraft Battle Force

AIRCRAFT CANNON. *See* Ordnance: Automatic aircraft cannon

AIRCRAFT CARRIER. *See* Ship

AIRCRAFT LIABILITY INSURANCE. *See* Insurance

AIRCRAFT OWNED BY U.S. FOREST SERVICE. *See under* Forest service

The First

AIRMAIL

Airmail pickup from a steamer at sea was made June 12, 1929, by Lieutenant Commander George R. Pond and L. V. Rawlings in a Fairchild monoplane equipped with a cable device to drop mail and pick up simultaneously, invented by Dr. L. S. Adams. The plane left Keyport, N.J., at 5:58 P.M. and contacted the S.S. *Leviathan,* 60 miles at sea, which had sailed at 3:30 P.M.

Dirigible to drop mail by parachute was the *Graf Zeppelin,* which flew over Washington, D.C., on October 15, 1928, for about 20 minutes and dropped a pouch and a postcard picture of Count Ferdinand von Zeppelin. The packet was held for postage, as no stamps were used. The zeppelin landed at Lakehurst, N.J., October 15, 1928, at 5:38 P.M., completing its 6,300-mile trip from Friedrichshafen, Germany.

AIRMAIL SERVICE

Airmail contractor (domestic) was the Varney Air Line, which operated a single-engine Swallow biplane on April 6, 1926, between Pasco, Wash., and Elko, Nev., where connections were made with the Post Office Department's transcontinental line. Chief pilot Leon Cuddeback took off from Pasco. Franklin Rose, who took off from Elko, Nev., crashed in the desert.

Airmail experimental route was flown May 15, 1918, between Washington, D.C., Philadelphia, Pa., and New York City by planes and pilots supplied by the War Department. Lieutenant Torrey H. Webb in a Curtiss JN-4 left Belmont Field, L.I., N.Y., with two sacks containing 2,457 pieces of mail and flew to Philadelphia. Lieutenant James Clark Edgerton continued the trip to Potomac Field, Washington, D.C., in a relief plane. The 218 miles were covered in 3 hours 20 minutes. A similar service started from Washington, with Lieutenant George L. Boyle flying east. A broken propeller forced his descent at Waldorf, Md. The mail was carried by motor truck to Philadelphia, then flown to New York City by Lieutenant H. Paul Culver.

Airmail flyer's medal of honor. *See under* Medal

Airmail long-distance night service was established on July 1, 1925, from New York City to Chicago, Ill., over a 774-mile course. The first plane, from Hadley Field, New Brunswick, N.J. (the New York area), was piloted by Dean C. Smith. It was followed by a second plane piloted by J. D. Hill. The first plane eastward was simultaneously dispatched from Chicago, was piloted by Shirley Short, and was likewise followed by a second plane carrying the surplus mail.

Airmail pilot was Earl Lewis Ovington, who was sworn in on September 23, 1911, at Garden City, Long Island, N.Y., as "air mail pilot number one." In his Blériot monoplane, *Dragonfly,* he delivered airmail from Postmaster General Frank

The First

Harris Hitchcock at Garden City to postmaster William McCarthy at Mineola, L.I., a distance of six miles, inaugurating the first official airmail service authorized by the Post Office Department. The first mail consisted of 640 letters and 1,280 postcards that bore the cancellation "Aeroplane No. 1, Garden City Estates, N.Y." Flights were made from September 23, 1911, to October 1, 1911, during the International Aviation Tournament held at the Airdrome, Garden City, L.I., N.Y., except for September 29 and October 1. This was not a regularly scheduled flight, since the service was performed without expense to the Post Office Department. *(Records in Division of Main Service. Post Office Department, Washington, D.C.)*

Airmail regular service was established August 12, 1918, by the Post Office Department between New York City and Washington, D.C. Ben B. Lipsner was the first superintendent of airmail. The pilots were Ed. V. Gardner, Maurice Newton, Max Miller, and Robert F. Shank.

Airmail regular service between New York and Chicago was scheduled to take off at 6:15 A.M. from Belmont Park, L.I., on December 18, 1918. Leon D. Smith, in a 450 h.p. de Havilland-Liberty, was unable to take off. At 7:30 A.M., he took off in another airplane, which was unable to fly farther than Bellefonte, Pa. The mail was then flown to Williamsport, Pa., where 266 pounds of mail was placed on a Chicago-bound train.

Airmail regular transcontinental through-service was established between New York City and San Francisco, Calif., July 1, 1924, when the airmail-railroad service was discontinued. The first westward flight of this service was made by Wesley Leland Smith, who flew from New York City to Cleveland, Ohio, and the first eastward flight by Claire K. Vance, who flew from San Francisco, Calif., to Reno, Nev. The service was daily including Sunday, with 14 stops en route.

Airmail service between North and South America was inaugurated May 14, 1929, from Miami, Fla.

Airmail service from ship to shore was inaugurated August 13, 1928, by the Trans-Atlantic Aerial Company when an amphibian was launched from the *Ile de France,* 400 miles at sea. Three sacks of mail, including two packages of films, were delivered at New York City 15 hours before the ship docked. Service was discontinued September 28, 1928.

Airmail service to a steamer at sea was made August 14, 1919, when an Aeromarine flying boat piloted by Cyrus Johnston Zimmermann dropped a bag of mail on the forward deck of the White Star liner *Adriatic,* an hour and a half after the ship had left the pier in New York City.

Airmail stamp. *See* Postage stamp

AIRMAIL SERVICE—Continued

Airmail transatlantic service was inaugurated on May 20, 1939, by the *Yankee Clipper*, a Pan American four-engine 41½ ton airplane that left Port Washington, N.Y., on 9:07:48 P.M., flew to Horta in 20 hours 16 minutes, and arrived in Lisbon, 6 hours 54 minutes later, on May 21, 1939, at 8:42 P.M. Arthur Earl La Porte was captain.

Airmail transcontinental flight was from San Francisco, Calif., to New York City. The plane left San Francisco at 4:30 A.M., February 22, 1921, and arrived at Hazelhurst Field, Long Island, N.Y., at 4:50 P.M. on February 23, 1921, 33 hours 20 minutes later. The actual flying time was 25 hours 16 minutes; the average speed for the 2,629 miles was 104 m.p.h.

Airmail transcontinental service (combination airplane-railroad) began on September 8, 1920, when 16,000 letters reached the West Coast in 22 hours less than the best train time. The mail was carried by planes during the day and by trains at night, a service of 63 hours for the flight west and 78½ hours for the eastward flight. The various sections and the dates of first service were: New York City to Cleveland, July 1, 1919; Cleveland to Chicago, May 15, 1919; Chicago to Omaha, May 15, 1920; and Omaha to San Francisco, September 8, 1920.

Airmail transport to be piloted by a woman. *See* Aviation—Pilot: Woman to pilot an airmail transport.

Airplane mail pickup by which planes snatch mail from the ground without landing was demonstrated on October 1, 1929, by Pennsylvania-Central Airlines at Washington, D.C. Despite rain, 253 successful pickups were made in 255 attempts. The pickup device was authorized by the Post Office Department for use on PCA, later known as Capital Airlines, and was used on regular schedules at Beaver Falls and Newcastle, Pa., and Youngstown, Ohio, on the Pittsburgh–Cleveland route.

Autogiro mail delivery direct to a post office took place May 25, 1935, in Philadelphia, Pa. Pilot Louis Levy landed an autogiro on the roof of the Market Street Post Office and handed a sack of mail from the Central Airport, Camden, N.J., to Postmaster General James Aloysius Farley. A few minutes later, pilot James Garrett Ray swooped down in another autogiro, took a sack of mail, and followed Levy back to the airport.

Autogiro mail delivery regular service began July 6, 1939, when Captain John MacDonald Miller flew an Eastern Air Line autogiro from the roof of the Philadelphia Post Office to the Central Airport, Camden, N.J., six miles away, in 6 minutes. The autogiro made the round trip to its starting place in 14 minutes.

Balloon flight carrying mail. *See under* Balloon

Helicopter airmail and express service was inaugurated in a Sikorski S-51 on October 1, 1947, by Los Angeles Airways, Inc., Los Angeles, Calif., to serve the San Fernando Valley area. On May 20, 1947, the company received the first Civil Aeronautics Board certificate, which covered a three-year period. Service was extended October 15, 1947, and January 8, 1948, to serve 42 communities. During the first three-year period, 200,000 flights were made and 13 million pounds of mail carried. Pilots on the first flight were Boyd Kesselering and John De Blauw.

Helicopter airmail and express service to carry passengers was Los Angeles Airways, Inc., which instituted the combined service on November 22, 1955, between Los Angeles and Long Beach, Calif.

Helicopter airmail delivery by commercial helicopter was made July 5, 1946, between the Bridgeport, Conn., post office and the airport. The pilot was D. D. ("Jimmy") Viner, chief pilot of Sikorsky Aircraft, Bridgeport, Conn.

Helicopter airmail experimental tests were made July 8, 1946, from the Lockheed Airport, Burbank, Calif., by the Post Office Department and the Army Air Force. For three weeks, two weekly trips were made to Long Beach, Calif., to the north, and to Santa Ana to the south, serving 24 post offices en route.

International airmail was inaugurated March 3, 1919, between Seattle, Wash., and Victoria, B.C., Canada (74 miles), by Edward Hubbard of the Hubbard Air Service, who piloted a Boeing Type C open cockpit biplane with pontoons. William Edward Boeing was a passenger on the flight. Regular service under contract began October 14, 1920, and continued under successive contracts until June 30, 1937.

Jet-propelled airplane to transport mail was a P-80 Shooting Star that on June 22, 1946, carried a letter addressed to President Harry S Truman. It was piloted by Captain Robert Atkinson Baird III of Clarksdale, Miss., who left the Schenectady County Airport, Schenectady, N.Y., and arrived at the National Airport, Washington, D.C. (370 miles), in 49 minutes. Another jet-propelled P-80, piloted by Major Kenneth Oscar Chilstrom of Elmhurst, Ill., left for Dayton, Ohio, with a letter for Orville Wright and, after a stopover at Wright Field, arrived at Chicago, Ill., in 2 hours 2 minutes.

Letter to encircle the world by commercial airmail flight. *See under* Postal service

Missile mail (official) was dispatched from the submarine U.S.S. *Barbero* (SSC-317), about 100 miles at sea off the Atlantic coast, to the Mayport Naval Auxiliary Station, near Jacksonville, Fla., on June 8, 1959. Bearing four-cent postage rather than seven-cent airmail stamps, 3,000 letters were shot in a 36-foot Regulus 1 winged missile at about

The First

600 m.p.h. The missile landed 22 minutes after being launched. The letters, signed by Postmaster General Arthur Ellsworth Summerfield, were addressed to President Dwight David Eisenhower and to other government officials and important personages. The project was under the supervision of Captain Arnold Schade.

Pacific airmail flight and the first air crossing from California to the Philippines was made by the *China Clipper* of Pan American Airways, Inc., commanded by Edwin Charles Musick. The plane left San Francisco, Calif., November 22, 1935, at 3:46 A.M. Pacific Standard Time and made stops at Honolulu, Midway, Wake, and Guam, landing at Manila, P.I., November 28, 1935, at 11:31 P.M., having covered 8,210 miles in 59 hours 48 minutes. It carried 58 sacks of mail containing 110,865 letters. The return trip started December 1, 1935, from Manila and was completed December 6, 1935, at 10:37 A.M. at San Francisco, Calif. The eastbound flight was made in 63 hours 24 minutes, the total flying time being 123 hours 12 minutes. *(William Stephen Grooch—From Crate to Clipper)*

Parcel post domestic air service was authorized June 29, 1948 (62 Stat. L. 1097), and began September 1, 1948. The country was divided into eight postal zones, the maximum rate being 80 cents for the first pound and 65 cents for each additional pound or fraction thereof.

Parcel post international air service was inaugurated March 15, 1948, between the United States and 21 countries in Europe and Africa. Service to South America was instituted on September 4, 1948, and to the Pacific area on September 11, 1948.

Rocket airmail flight was made February 23, 1936, at Greenwood Lake, N.Y., in the *Gloria,* an 11-foot rocket with a 15-foot wing spread. The fuel was liquid oxygen and alcohol. The inventors of the rocket were Willy Ley, Louis Goodman, and Hugh Franklin Pierce. The flight was sponsored by Frido W. Kessler. The rocket carried 4,323 letters and 1,826 postcards. Each cover was franked with special rocket stamps in addition to the regular postage stamps.

Rocket (steam-driven) to carry mail was launched May 24, 1969, from the Proving Grounds, Las Cruces, N. Mex. under the guidance of Professor John F. Porter of the Electrical Engineering Department of the Northrop Institute of Technology, Inglewood, Calif. The rocket was 85 inches tall, 6 inches in diameter, weighing 42 pounds at lift-off. It carried 400 first-day covers in a container 14 inches tall and 5½ inches in diameter. It rose to about 600 feet altitude. The steam was derived from heating 22 pounds of water to 475° Fahrenheit.

The First

AIRMAIL STAMP. *See* Postage stamp

AIRPLANE. *See* Aviation—Airplane

AIRPLANE-AUTOMOBILE COMBINATION. *See under* Automobile

AIRPLANE FLYING SCHOOL. *See* Aviation—School

AIRPLANE HIGH-SPEED TANK. *See* Aviation: Airplane high-speed tank to test airplanes

AIRPLANE INSTRUCTOR'S LICENSE. *See* Aviation—License

AIRPLANE LEGISLATION. *See* Aviation—Legislation: Aviation legislation

AIRPLANE MAIL PICKUP. *See* Airmail service

AIRPLANE PASSENGER (official). *See under* Aviation—Passenger

AIRPLANE PASSENGER (woman). *See under* Aviation—Passenger

AIRPLANE POST OFFICE. *See* Post office

AIRPLANE RACE. *See* Aviation—Races

AIRPLANE SALE. *See* Aviation—Airplane: Airplane sold commercially

AIRPLANE TELECAST. *See under* Television—Telecast

AIRPLANE TO RACE A TRAIN. *See under* Aviation—Races

AIRPLANE TORPEDO. *See* Torpedo

AIRPLANE TRANSCONTINENTAL PASSENGER (woman). *See* Aviation—Passenger

AIRPLANE WEDDING. *See* Wedding

AIRPORT (federally owned). *See* Aviation—Airport

AIRPORT HOTEL. *See under* Aviation—Airport

AIRPORT MANAGER (woman). *See under* Aviation—Airport

AIRSHIP. *See* Aviation—Airship

AIRSHIP BOMBING. *See under* Aviation—Airship

AIRSHIP DISASTER. *See under* Aviation—Airship

AIRSHIP (U.S. Navy). *See* Aviation—Airship

AIRWAYS ILLUMINATION. *See under* Aviation

ALARM. *See* Burglar alarm

ALARM CLOCK. *See* Clock

ALBANY REGENCY. *See* Political machine

ALBERT MEDAL. *See* Medal

ALCOHOL
Power alcohol plant was established by the Bailor Manufacturing Company, Atchison, Kans., which sold power alcohol October 2, 1936. Five

The First

ALCOHOL—*Continued*
percent of the total output was butyl alcohol and acetone, which were blended with ethyl alcohol, which in turn was blended with gasoline. Raw materials used were rye, oats, sweet potatoes, barley, milo, kafir corn, molasses, and rice.

ALCOHOL CONTROL ADMINISTRATION. *See* Federal alcohol control administration

ALFALFA is supposed to have been introduced into California in 1854 from Chile, but John Spurrier, in his book *The Practical Farmer,* dedicated to Thomas Jefferson and published at Wilmington, Del., in 1793, described alfalfa, which he called "lucerne." *(Joseph Elwyn Wing—Alfalfa Farming in America)*

ALGEBRA BOOK
See also Arithmetic

Algebra book was *Arithmetic, or the art of ciphering, according to the coins, measures and weights of New York, together with a short treatise on algebra (Arithmetica of Cyffer-Konst, Volgens de Munten Maten en Gewigten, te Nieu York, gebruykelyk als mede een kort ontwerp van de Algebra),* a Dutch textbook by Pieter Venema printed by J. Peter Zenger in 1730 in New York City. *(Lao Genevra Simons—Bibliography of Early American Textbooks on Algebra)*

Algebra book by a native-born American was Nicholas Pike's *A New and Complete System of Arithmetic, composed for the use of the citizens of the United States,* published in 1788 by John Mycall, Newburyport, Mass. It contained 512 pages, of which 39 were devoted to algebra. *(Lao Genevra Simons—Bibliography of Early American Textbooks on Algebra)*

ALIEN CITIZENSHIP. *See* Immigration: Alien registration

ALIEN DISCRIMINATORY LAW was the "act respecting aliens" over 14 years old passed July 6, 1798 (1 Stat. L. 577), which required that aliens "not actually naturalized shall be liable to be apprehended, restrained, rescued and removed as alien enemies."
See also Immigration

ALIEN REGISTRATION. *See under* Immigration

ALL-BLIND AIRPLANE FLIGHT. *See* Aviation—Flights

ALL-GLASS WINDOWLESS STRUCTURE. *See* Building

ALL-STEEL PASSENGER CAR. *See* Railroad car

ALL-STEEL RAILWAY BRIDGE. *See* Bridge

ALLERGY MAGAZINE. *See* Medical periodical

ALLIGATOR FARM was established in 1892 at Anastasia Island, St. Johns County, Fla., by George Reddington.

The First

ALMANAC
Almanac was *An Almanak for the Year of Our Lord, 1639, Calculated for New England,* by William Peirce, printed in 1638 at Cambridge, Mass., by Stephen Day's Cambridge Press. The months began with March. *(Clarence Saunders Brigham—An Account of American Almanacks)*

Almanac with a continuous existence was *The Farmer's Almanack, Calculated on a New and Improved Plan, for the Year of Our Lord 1793; Being the First After Leap Year, and Seventeenth of the Independence of America,* founded by Robert Bailey Thomas of Sterling, Mass., and printed at the Apollo Press in Boston, by Belknap and Hall in 1792. The price was 6 pence a copy, 4 shillings a dozen, 40 shilllings a gross. Three thousand copies were printed. In 1832, the title was changed to *The Old Farmer's Almanac.*

Almanac bibliography was *A Preliminary Check List of American Almanacs 1639–1800,* 160 pages, by Hugh Alexander Morrison of the Library of Congress, published in 1907 by the Government Printing Office, Washington, D.C. The entries were arranged geographically by states.

Nautical almanac was Samuel Stearns's *The Universal Kalendar, Comprehending the Landsman's and Seaman's Almanack for the Year 1783,* published December 29, 1782, in Boston, Mass., by Benjamin Edes and Son.

Patent medicine almanac was *Bristol's Free Almanac for 1844 being bissextile or leap year and of American Independence, the 68th containing astronomical calculations and other useful and entertaining matter,* calculated by Lucas Seaver and published at Batavia, N.Y., in 1843. It contained 24 pages, including 10 of testimonials, and was issued by C. C. Bristol, manufacturer of Bristol's Sarsaparilla, Buffalo, N.Y.

ALTERNATING-CURRENT POWER PLANT. *See* Electric power plant

ALTERNATING-CURRENT POWER TRANSMISSION. *See* Electric power plant: Alternating-current power plant

ALTERNATOR, ELECTRIC. *See* Electric alternator

ALUMINUM
Aluminum was produced in commercial quantities in November 1888 by the Pittsburgh Reduction Company (which later developed into the Aluminum Company of America). It was based upon the invention of Charles Martin Hall, completed on February 23, 1886. On July 9, 1886, Hall applied for a patent, which he obtained on April 2, 1889 (No. 400,766), on reducing aluminum by electrolysis. Hall produced aluminum electrically instead of chemically, greatly reducing its cost. He dissolved alumina in a bath of cryolite (the double fluoride of aluminum and sodium) and

The First

passed an electric current through the solution. *(Joseph William Richards—Aluminum)*

Aluminum girder-type highway bridge. *See* Bridge: Welded-aluminum girder-type highway bridge

Aluminum used commercially in a transmission conductor was employed November 30, 1899, by the Hartford Electric Light Company of Hartford, Conn., on a transmission from its waterpower plant at Tariffville, Conn., to Hartford, Conn.

Newspaper advertisement printed on aluminum foil. *See under* Newspaper

ALUMINUM-FACED BUILDING. *See* Building

ALUMINUM STREETCAR. *See* Streetcar

ALUMNI ASSOCIATION, COLLEGE. *See* College alumni association

AMALGAM FOR FILLING TEETH. *See under* Dentistry

AMATEUR FENCERS LEAGUE OF AMERICA. *See* Fencing

AMBASSADOR. *See* Diplomatic service

AMBASSADOR, JAPANESE. *See* Japanese ambassador

AMBULANCE
Hospital ambulance service was introduced by the Commercial Hospital (now the General Hospital), Cincinnati, Ohio, prior to 1865. The list of employees for the year ending February 28, 1866, names James A. Jackson, employee No. 27, as "driver of ambulance" at an annual salary of $360. A similar service was started in June 1869 by Bellevue Hospital, New York City, under the direction of Dr. Edward Barry Dalton.

Incubator ambulance service maintained for transportation of premature infants was instituted by the city of Chicago, Ill. The ambulance was ordered February 26, 1935, and made its first run March 21, 1935.

Mobile coronary-care ambulance was formed by St. Vincent's Hospital and Medical Center of New York, New York City, and went into operation October 1968. It brought doctors, nurses, and paramedics along with defibrillator, respirator, and electrocardiograph to the patient's side within moments after an attack. The concept of on-site treatment of cardiac cases was created by Dr. William Joseph Grace.

AMBULANCE AIR SERVICE. *See under* Aviation

AMBULANCE CORPS, ARMY. *See* Army ambulance corps

AMBULANCE SHIP. *See* Ship

The First

AMENDMENT TO THE CONSTITUTION. *See* Constitutional amendment (U.S.)

"AMERICA" (as a geographical designation) was first used by Martin H. Waldseemüller, also called Ilacomilus or Hylacomylus, in his *Cosmographiae Introductio*, published in April 1507, at St. Dié in the Vosges Mountains of Alsace. The first delineation of the New World was made in 1506 by Giovanni Matteo Contarini, an Italian, and the map was engraved by Francesco Roselli of Florence, Italy. *(Geographical Review. October 1930)*
See also Map: Globular map published showing the Western Hemisphere

"AMERICA" (the song) was first publicly sung July 4, 1832, in the Park Street Church, Boston, Mass., by the school children of Boston. The song was written on a scrap of paper in half an hour by Dr. Samuel Francis Smith, a Baptist minister. The original manuscript is in the Harvard University Library.

"AMERICAN" (as an adjective), to be used instead of "United States," was officially recommended by Secretary of State John Hay, who instructed American diplomatic and consular officers under date of August 3, 1904, to use "American" instead of "United States" as an adjective. In strictly formal documents and in notarial acts performed by consular officers, the adjective form of designation is not used but the full name of the country is given as, for example: Government of the United States of America, Embassy of the United States of America.

AMERICAN ACADEMY OF ARTS AND LETTERS. *See* Arts and letters society

AMERICAN ACADEMY OF ARTS AND SCIENCES. *See* Arts and science society

AMERICAN ACADEMY OF POLITICAL AND SOCIAL SCIENCE. *See* Political science society

AMERICAN ACE. *See* Aviation—Pilot

AMERICAN ANTIQUARIAN SOCIETY. *See* Historical society

AMERICAN ANTIVIVISECTION SOCIETY. *See* Antivivisection society

AMERICAN ASSOCIATION FOR THE ADVANCEMENT OF ATHEISM. *See* Atheism society

AMERICAN ASSOCIATION FOR THE ADVANCEMENT OF SCIENCE. *See* Science association

AMERICAN ASSOCIATION FOR THE HARD OF HEARING. *See* Deaf—Association: National social organization for the hard of hearing

AMERICAN ASSOCIATION OF PUBLIC ACCOUNTANTS. *See* Accountants' society

AMERICAN BANKERS ASSOCIATION. *See* Bankers association

AMERICAN BIBLE SOCIETY. *See* Bible society

AMERICAN BIRD BANDING ASSOCIATION. *See* Bird banding society

AMERICAN BOWLING CONGRESS. *See* Bowling tournament: Bowling convention

AMERICAN BRASS ASSOCIATION. *See* Trade association

AMERICAN CHEMICAL SOCIETY. *See* Chemical society

AMERICAN COLLEGE OF SURGEONS. *See under* Medical society

AMERICAN ECONOMIC ASSOCIATION. *See* Economics association

AMERICAN EXPEDITIONARY FORCE
   American Expeditionary Force to leave the United States (since the Mexican War) and the first to leave for a destination beyond the Western Hemisphere sailed May 25, 1898, from San Francisco, Calif., on the *Australia, City of Pekin,* and *City of Sydney,* bound for Manila, Philippines, a distance of 6,220 miles. The expeditionary force consisted of 115 officers and 2,386 enlisted men, commanded by General Wesley Merritt. They arrived off Manila, June 30, 1898, and landed July 1, 1898. Admiral George Dewey and General Merritt demanded the surrender of Manila, August 7, 1898, but the city did not comply until August 13, 1898.

   American Expeditionary Force Air Service chief was Colonel Mason Mathews Patrick, appointed May 29, 1918. On July 6, 1918, the Senate approved his nomination as major general. On June 26, 1923, at the age of 60, he qualified as a pilot at Bolling Field, Washington, D.C. *(Mason Mathews Patrick—United States in the Air)*

   American expeditionary force to land in Africa. *See under* World War II

   American expeditionary force to land on the European continent in World War II. *See under* World War II

AMERICAN FEDERATION OF LABOR. *See* Labor union: Labor union of importance

AMERICAN FLAG. *See* Flag

AMERICAN FORESTRY ASSOCIATION. *See* Forestry society

AMERICAN GEOLOGICAL SOCIETY. *See* Geological society (national)

AMERICAN GUERNSEY CATTLE CLUB. *See* Cattle club

AMERICAN HISTORICAL ASSOCIATION. *See* Historical society

AMERICAN HISTORY CHAIR. *See under* History instruction

AMERICAN HUMANE ASSOCIATION. *See* Humane Society

AMERICAN INDIAN CHURCH
   Church for American Indians in New England was established in Natick, Mass., by John Eliot in 1660. Six other praying towns were established before 1674. *(Daniel Gookin—Historical Collections of the Indians in New England)*

   Church organized by American Indians was the First American Church, incorporated October 10, 1918, with its principal seat of government and place of business at El Reno, Canadian County, Okla., by Mack Haag and Sidney White Crane of the Cheyenne tribe of Indians; Charles W. Dailey, George Pipestem and Charles N. Moore of the Oto tribe; Frank Eagle of the Ponca tribe; William Peawa and Manwat of the Comanche tribe; Kiowa Charlie of the Kiowa tribe; and Apache Ben of the Apache tribe—all residents of the state of Oklahoma.

AMERICAN INDIAN–ENGLISH DICTIONARY. *See under* Dictionary

AMERICAN INDIAN GRAMMAR. *See under* Grammar

AMERICAN INDIAN-LANGUAGE BIBLE. *See* Bible: Bible in an American Indian language

AMERICAN INDIAN-LANGUAGE MONTHLY. *See under* Periodical

AMERICAN INDIAN NEWSPAPER. *See under* Newspaper

AMERICAN INDIAN PLAY. *See* Play (drama): Play about an American Indian

AMERICAN INDIAN PRIMER. *See* Primer: Primer in an American Indian dialect

AMERICAN INDIAN RESERVATION
   American Indian reservation (federal) was established by the United States Government in 1786, but the first official notice of the removal of American Indians residing east of the Mississippi to reservations west of that river was contained in the act of March 26, 1804 (2 Stat. L. 283), "erecting Louisiana into two territories, and providing the temporary government thereof." Reservations established by executive order without an act of Congress were not held to be permanent before the general allotment act of February 8, 1887 (24 Stat. L. 388), an "act to provide for the allotment of lands . . . severally to Indians on the various reservations, and to extend the protection of the laws of the United States and the territories over the Indians."

   American Indian reservation (state) was established on August 29, 1758, when the New Jersey Legislature appropriated 1,600 acres of a tract of 3,044 acres in Indian Mills, Evesham township,

The First

Burlington County, N.J., to be used as a reservation for the American Indians of New Jersey. Governor Francis Bernard named the tract Brotherton. About 200 Indians, probably Lenapes and Unamis, located on it and John Brainard was appointed superintendent. In 1801, the land was sold and the Indians moved to the Lake Oneida Reservation. *(William Nelson—Indians of New Jersey)*

AMERICAN INDIAN SCHOOL

American Indian boarding school on a reservation was the Yakima Agency Boarding School, opened November 1860 with 25 pupils, in the buildings of old Fort Simco on the Yakima Reservation, Wash., under provision of Article 5 of the treaty with the Yakima Nation of June 8, 1855, proclaimed April 18, 1859 (12 Stat. L. 951). James H. Wilbur was appointed superintendent of teaching September 1, 1860.

American Indian school of prominence was opened November 1, 1879, at the old Army Barracks, Carlisle, Pa., with 147 students. It was supported by private funds until March 3, 1881, when Congress appropriated $1,000 to pay Captain Richard Henry Pratt's salary as director (21 Stat. L. 501). The schoolwork did not go above the eighth grade, but useful trades were taught. Students were assisted under the outing system to continue their studies under the supervision of the school. At the end of the first year 196 students were enrolled—139 boys and 57 girls. *(Eadle Keatah Toh. Vol. 1, No. 7. November 1880)*

American Indian school (permanent) in America was established in 1720 in Williamsburg, Va., through the generosity of Robert Boyle, the eminent English scientist and formulator of Boyle's Law. To house the school, the Brafferton Building was erected at the College of William and Mary in 1723. The building was named after Boyle's estate in Yorkshire, which provided revenue from rents to support the school. *(James Luther Kibler—Historic Virginia Landmarks)*

Catholic school for American Indians was the St. Regis Seminary, Florissant, Mo., which opened May 11, 1824, under the direction of Father Van Quickenborne. It was located in 3 buildings which cost about $2,000. There were 40 to 60 students. It closed June 30, 1831. *(Catholic Historical Review—Vol. 4, No. 4—Jan. 1919)*

AMERICAN INDIANS

American Indian chief (white woman). See Woman: White woman to become an American Indian chief

American Indian chief (woman) was Queen Anne, chief of the Pamunkey tribe of Virginia from about 1675 to 1715. She was the widow of Totopotomoi, chief of the tribe, who lost his life in 1654 while aiding the English to repel an invasion by other tribes. *(Frederick Webb Hodge—Handbook of the American Indians North of Mexico)*

The First

American Indian preacher of Christianity was Hiacoomes. Thomas Mayhew taught him how to read and write. He was ordained August 22, 1670, by John Eliot and John Cotton, and preached to his countrymen in a small church in Martha's Vineyard, Mass. *(Charles Edward Banks—The History of Martha's Vineyard)*

American Indian Protestant was Manteo, chief of the Hatteras Indians, who was baptized into the Church of England and into the Protestant Christian faith on August 13, 1587. He was invested by Sir Walter Raleigh with the power of Baron or Lord of Roanoke (and of Dasamonguepeuk) by members of what is now regarded as the "lost colony." There were, however, baptisms of Indians by the Roman Catholic priests in Florida prior to this time. *(Hakluyt's Voyages, Vol. VI)*

American Indian senator. *See under* Senator (U.S.)

American Indian superintendent of a Bureau of Indian Affairs agency was Shirley Plume, an Oglala Sioux, designated as acting superintendent of the Standing Rock Agency, Fort Yates, N. D., August 20, 1973, and appointed to that position on January 24, 1974.

American Indian tribal constitution under the Indian Reorganization Act of June 18, 1934 (48 Stat. L. 984), was signed October 28, 1935, in the office of the Secretary of the Interior, Harold Le Claire Ickes, in Washington, D.C. The signatories of the constitution affecting the Flathead Reservation at Dixon, Mont., were Roy E. Courville, chairman of the election board; Joseph R. Blodgett, president of the Tribal Council; Luman W. Shotwell, superintendent and ex-officio secretary of the Tribal Council; Martin Charlo of the Confederated Salish Tribe; and Paul Koos-ta-ta, chief of the Kootenai Tribe.

American Indian Vice President. *See under* Vice President (U.S.)

Catholic beatification of an American Indian. *See under* Catholic beatification

Citizenship statute for American Indians was enacted June 2, 1924 (43 Stat. L. 253). It provided that "all non-citizen Indians born within the territorial limits of the United States be, and they are hereby declared to be, citizens of the United States."

Indian Affairs Commissioner (U.S.) was Elbert Herring, appointed July 10, 1832, under the act of July 9, 1832, an "act to provide for the appointment of a Commissioner of Indian Affairs" (4 Stat. L. 564), at a salary of $3,000. He was subject to the President and the Secretary of War and had "the direction and management of all Indian affairs and of all matters arising out of Indian relations." He served until July 4, 1836. *(U.S. Bureau of American Ethnology—Handbook of American Indians North of Mexico)*

The First

AMERICAN INDIANS—*Continued*

Indian Affairs Commissioner (U.S.) who was an American Indian was Brigadier General Ely Samuel Parker (Do-Ne-Ho-Geh-Weh), a chief of the Tonawanda Seneca tribe, who was appointed commissioner of Indian Affairs on April 21, 1869, by President Ulysses Simpson Grant. He served until December 1871. *(Arthur Caswell Parker— The Life of General Ely Samuel Parker, Last Grand Sachem of the Iroquois and General Grant's Military Secretary—Buffalo Historical Society. Publication No. 23.)*

Indian war. *See* War (colonial): French and Indian War battle

League of American Indian nations in America was the Iroquois Confederacy, which was also known as the Five Nations and later as the Six Nations. The league was composed of the following tribes: Senecas, Cayugas, Onondagas, Mohawks, Oneidas, and later the Tuscaroras (in 1715). According to tradition the Confederacy was formed by Hiawatha about the beginning of the 15th century. *(Lewis Henry Morgan—League of the Ho-dé-no-sau-nee, or Iroquois)*

Massacre of white people by American Indians was at Jamestown, Va., on March 22, 1622, when 347 white people out of a population of 1,240 were slain.

Medals presented by colonists to friendly American Indians. *See under* Medal

Paper money issued by American Indians. *See under* Money

Scalping of American Indians by white men took place February 20, 1725. An Indian-hunting party of New Hampshire volunteers ran across a band of ten sleeping American Indians and scalped them all. The hunting party entered Dover in triumph with the ten scalps stretched on hoops and elevated on poles. A bounty of £100 for each scalp was paid in Boston out of the public treasury. Individual scalps had been brought in earlier. *(Jeremy Belknap—History of New Hampshire)*

Vaccination legislation for American Indians. *See under* Vaccination legislation

AMERICAN JERSEY CATTLE CLUB. *See* Cattle club

AMERICAN LANGUAGE

Book on Americanisms was John Pickering's *A Vocabulary, or Collection of Words and Phrases Which Have Been Supposed to Be Peculiar to the United States of America; to which is prefixed an essay on the present state of the English language in the United States,* a 206-page book published in 1816 by Cummings and Hilliard, Boston, Mass.

Legislation to establish the American language as an official language was the State of Illinois law enacted June 19, 1923, which stated that "the

The First

official language of the State of Illinois shall be known hereafter as the 'American' language."

AMERICAN LEAGUE. *See* Baseball league

AMERICAN LEGION. *See* War veterans' society

AMERICAN LIBRARY ASSOCIATION. *See* Library society

AMERICAN LUTHERAN CHURCH. *See* Lutheran Church

AMERICAN MEDICAL ASSOCIATION. *See* Medical society

AMERICAN METROLOGICAL SOCIETY. *See* Weights and Measures Standardization: National organization to improve systems of weights, measures, and moneys

AMERICAN NEWSPAPER PUBLISHERS ASSOCIATION. *See* Newspaper: Newspaper association

AMERICAN PARTY, or "Know-Nothing Party," was organized about 1854. The first national convention was held June 5, 1855, in Philadelphia, Pa. The party was really a secret organization rather than a political party. Membership was divided into three degrees. The first included members who were American-born and were wholly unconnected with the Roman Catholic Church. They were obliged to vote as the society determined. The second degree included members who were permitted to hold office inside the organization. The third degree was composed of members who were eligible for office outside the organization. On February 18, 1856, a convention held in Philadelphia, Pa., abolished the secret character of the organization and made presidential nominations —former President Millard Fillmore of New York for President and Andrew Jackson Donelson of Tennessee for Vice President. Fillmore received only eight electoral votes. The name American Party was used by organizations in 1874 and 1887, but each was a distinct and separate party.

AMERICAN PHARMACEUTICAL ASSOCIATION. *See* Pharmacy society (national)

AMERICAN PHILOLOGICAL ASSOCIATION. *See* Philological society

AMERICAN PHILOSOPHICAL SOCIETY. *See* Science association

AMERICAN PHYSICAL SOCIETY. *See* Physics: National physics association

AMERICAN PHYSIOLOGICAL SOCIETY. *See* Physiological society

AMERICAN POLITICAL SCIENCE ASSOCIATION. *See* Political science society

AMERICAN PSYCHOLOGICAL ASSOCIATION. *See* Psychological society

The First

AMERICAN RED CROSS was organized in Washington, D.C., on May 21, 1881, by Clara Barton, who became its first president. The constitution was adopted May 21, 1881, and the society was incorporated July 1, 1881, under the laws of the District of Columbia, and reincorporated April 17, 1893. The society was again incorporated, by act of Congress, June 6, 1900, as the American National Red Cross (31 Stat. L. 277), and again January 5, 1905 (33 Stat. L. 599). Jean Henri Dunant had proposed an international Red Cross organization agreed to by 16 nations at a preliminary conference October 26–29, 1863, and also at a convention August 22, 1864, at Geneva, Switzerland. The treaty was ratified March 16, 1882 (22 Stat. L. 940), by the U.S. Senate, making the United States the 32nd nation to join. *(Mabel Thorp Boardman— Under the Red Cross Flag)*

AMERICAN REPUBLICS CONFERENCE. *See* Conference

AMERICAN SOCIAL SCIENCE ASSOCIATION. *See* Social science society (national)

AMERICAN SOCIETY FOR THE PREVENTION OF CRUELTY TO ANIMALS. *See* Humane society

AMERICAN SOCIETY OF CIVIL ENGINEERS. *See* Engineering society

AMERICAN SOCIETY OF COMPOSERS, AUTHORS, AND PUBLISHERS. *See* Music society

AMERICAN SOCIETY OF DENTAL SURGEONS. *See* Dental society

AMERICAN SOCIETY OF MECHANICAL ENGINEERS. *See* Engineering society

AMERICAN SOCIOLOGICAL SOCIETY. *See* Sociological society

AMERICAN STATISTICAL ASSOCIATION. *See* Statistical society

AMERICAN THEOSOPHICAL SOCIETY. *See* Theosophical society

AMERICAN UNITARIAN ASSOCIATION. *See* Unitarian society

AMERICIUM. *See* Element: Element 95

AMMUNITION. *See* Ordnance

AMNESTY proclamation to citizens was issued by President Abraham Lincoln on December 8, 1863. He also issued another, similar proclamation, March 26, 1864. President Andrew Johnson issued supplementary proclamations May 29, 1865; September 7, 1867; July 4, 1868; and December 25, 1868. *(Henry Jarvis Raymond—Lincoln, His Life and Times)*

AMPHIBIOUS SEAPLANE GLIDER. *See* Glider

The First

AMPHIBIOUS VEHICLE

Amphibious vehicle was the Marsh Screw Amphibian designed and developed by the Chrysler Corporation's Defense Operations Division for the U.S. Navy Bureau of Ships under sponsorship of the Defense Department's Advanced Research Projects Agency. Two rotary aluminum pontoons fitted with spiral blades propel the amphibious craft forward, backward, and even sideways. It weighs 2,330 pounds without cargo or crew, is 13 feet 8 inches long, 8 feet 4 inches wide, with an overall height of 57 inches. Power is supplied by a modified Chrysler-built 225-cubic-inch Slant Six engine. It has an operational range of 10 continuous hours at full power and can carry 6 passengers plus the driver, or a cargo of approximately 1,050 pounds. It was first tested in March 1963 in Louisiana.

Steam-operated amphibious vehicle was the *Orukter Amphibolos*, or "amphibious digger," invented in 1805 by Oliver Evans of Philadelphia, Pa. He had been commissioned by the Philadelphia Board of Health to manufacture a scow, and he built a steam vehicle 30 feet long and 12 feet wide which was equipped with wheels so that it could be operated either on land or water. It was also equipped with a chain of buckets which brought up mud when it was employed as a scow. In July 1805 he propelled it a distance of about a mile and a half, from his shop to the Schuylkill River. There, by means of a stern paddle wheel, it was navigated down to the Delaware junction. *(Greville Bathe and Dorothy Bathe— Oliver Evans)*

AMUSEMENT DEVICES. *See* Carrousel; Ferris wheel; Loop-the-loop centrifugal railway; Railroad: Switchback railway

ANARCHIST was Josiah Warren, who was known as the "father of anarchy." He was of the intellectual type and was not an advocate of violence. In 1827 he opened a "time store" in Cincinnati, Ohio, to vindicate his theory of "labor for labor." He sold merchandise at cost, plus 7 percent for handling and a labor charge for the clerk's hire. He advocated the transference of government activities to private persons. *(William Bailie —Josiah Warren, The First American Anarchist)*

ANATOMY BOOK. *See* Medical book

ANATOMY LECTURES (Scientific). *See* Medical instruction

ANATOMY RESEARCH INSTITUTE. *See* Research institute

ANCIENT AND MODERN HISTORY CHAIR. *See* History instruction

ANCIENT ARABIC ORDER OF NOBLES OF THE MYSTIC SHRINE. *See* Freemasons

The First

ANCIENT MYSTICAL ORDER ROSAE CRUCIS, the Rosicrucian order, often abbreviated AMORC, a nonsectarian fraternity devoted to the investigation and study of the higher principles of life as found expressed in man and nature, was first established in America in 1694 by Magister Kelpius, appointed in England to become the first master of the order in America. The first lodge, temple, and laboratories of the order were erected in 1694 in what is now Fairmount Park, Philadelphia, Pa. The national headquarters of the Grand Lodge of the Rosicrucian Order of the North and South Jurisdiction is located at Rosicrucian Park, San Jose, Calif. Each jurisdiction is under the direction of an imperator who has a Supreme Council as an advisory board that charters lodges and chapters.

ANESTHESIA
Anesthetic (general) was sul-ether, used by Dr. Crawford Williamson Long of Jefferson, Ga., in December 1841 and January 1842. He removed a cystic tumor about half an inch in diameter from the back of the neck of James M. Venable on March 30, 1842, applying ether under a towel. His bill for the operation amounted to $2.25: for sulphuric ether 25 cents and for excising the tumor $2. This discovery antedates that of Morton by four years and that of Wells by two years. It was not reported, however, until 1852, when the Georgia State Medical Society was notified. *(Francis Randolph Packard—History of Medicine in the United States)*

Anesthetic in dentistry was used by Dr. Horace Wells, a dentist of Hartford, Conn., who discovered the anesthetic property of nitrous oxide (laughing) gas. On December 11, 1844, while under the influence of gas, he had one of his teeth extracted by Dr. John M. Riggs. The use of the gas was not successful, as he did not know it had to be combined with oxygen, a discovery that was not made until 24 years later. *(Yale Journal of Biology and Medicine. May 1933)*

Ether administered in childbirth was employed December 27, 1845, by Dr. Crawford Williamson Long during the delivery of his second child, Fanny (Long) Taylor, at Jefferson, Ga.

Painless surgery demonstration was given on October 16, 1846, at the Massachusetts General Hospital, Boston, Mass. Dr. John Collins Warren operated on Gilbert Abbott, who had a swelling on the right side of his jaw, and removed a tumor, using the drug of William Thomas Green Morton of Charleston, Mass. Morton was refused admission to hospitals until he divulged the name of the secret drug. Although he is credited with the discovery of anesthetics, eight or ten others have also claimed the honor.

Spinal anesthesia report was "The Growing Importance and Value of Local and Regional Anesthesia in Minor and Major Surgery," by Dr.

The First

Rudolph Matas of New Orleans, La., which was published in 1900 in the *Journal of the Louisiana State Medical Society*. On November 10, 1899, he anesthetized a patient by "spinal subarachnoid method." *(New Orleans Medical and Surgical Journal. February 1928)*

Trifluoroethyl vinyl ether given to a human was administered on April 10, 1953, to Dr. Max Samuel Sadove, Professor of Anesthesiology at the University of Illinois, by Dr. John Christian Krantz, Jr., Professor of Pharmacology of the University of Maryland, at the Research and Educational Hospitals of the University of Illinois, Chicago, Ill. This anesthetic takes effect in less time than standard ether.

ANGINA OPERATION. *See* Surgical operation

ANGLE IRON. *See* Iron

ANGLING BOOK. *See* Fishing treatise

ANIMAL BREEDING SOCIETY
Artificial animal breeding cooperative society was the artificial Breeding Unit No. 1 of the New Jersey Holstein-Friesian Cooperative Association, organized May 16, 1938, in Hunterdon, Somerset, and Warren Counties, N.J. Dr. James Arnold Henderson was in charge. The original membership consisted of 102 dairymen, who entered 1,050 Holstein cows.
See also Horse breeding society

ANIMAL GLUE FACTORY. *See* Glue factory (animal products)

ANIMAL HOSPITAL. *See* Veterinary hospital

ANIMAL HUSBANDRY
Animal husbandry federal appropriation. *See under* Animal Industry Bureau (U.S.)

Animal husbandry professor was John Alexander Craig of the Wisconsin Agricultural Experiment Station, University of Wisconsin, Madison, Wis., who served from 1890 to 1897. His specialty was sheep husbandry.

ANIMAL INDUSTRY BUREAU (U.S.)
Animal husbandry federal appropriation was approved April 23, 1904 (33 Stat. L. 281), an "act making appropriations for the Department of Agriculture for the calendar year ending June 30, 1905." For experiments in animal breeding and feeding in cooperation with state agricultural stations, $25,000 was appropriated, part of an appropriation of $1,362,880 to the Bureau of Animal Industry. The first expenditure was July 1, 1904.

Bureau of Animal Industry of the United States Department of Agriculture was established by act of Congress, May 29, 1884 (23 Stat. L. 31). The first chief of the Bureau of Animal Industry was Dr. Daniel Elmer Salmon, who served from May 31, 1884, to October 31, 1905.

Dairy division of the Bureau of Animal Industry was organized July 1, 1895. Major Henry Elijah Alvord was appointed the first chief. His original staff consisted of one assistant and two clerks. *(Ulysses Grant Houck—Bureau of Animal Industry)*

Pathology division of the Bureau of Animal Industry was established April 1, 1891. Dr. Theobald Smith was appointed the first chief. *(Ulysses Grant Houck—Bureau of Animal Industry)*

ANIMAL-INFECTING VIRUS TO BE CRYSTALLIZED. *See* Virus: Virus (human- or animal-infecting virus) to be crystallized

ANIMAL POUND. *See* Pound (enclosure for animals)

ANIMAL TRAPS. *See* Traps

ANIMAL VIVISECTION. *See* Antivivisection society; Vivisection

ANIMALS
Animal awarded a Distinguished Service Cross. *See* Medal: Distinguished Service Cross awarded to an animal

Animals fired into space and rescued from a rocket. *See under* Rocket

Aquatic mammals. *See* Aquatic mammals

Bear (white) brought to the United States was Ursa Major, a nine-month-old cub, caught in Davis Strait, on the western coast of Greenland, which was exhibited January 18, 1733, at Clark's Wharf, North End of Boston. It was brought by Captain Atkins from Greenland and kept in a large cage. It was shipped to London on February 27, 1734. *(Boston Weekly News Letter. Jan. 18, 1733)*

Birds. *See* Birds

Camel imported was an "African camel . . . 7 feet high and 12 feet long," exhibited in Boston, Mass., and advertised in the Boston *Gazette* of October 2, 1721.

Camels imported for commercial purposes were landed May 14, 1856, at Indianola, Tex. Lieutenant David Dixon Porter of Chester, Pa., left Smyrna February 15, 1856, on the *Supply*, a Navy storeship, and arrived at Powder Horn, 3 miles below Indianola, on May 1, 1856, but the camels were not landed until later. The shipment consisted of 34 camels—one more than left Smyrna. On March 3, 1855 (10 Stat. L. 639), Congress had appropriated $30,000 to the War Department for the purchase and importation of camels and dromedaries to be employed for military purposes. *(Bibliographical Society of America—Transactions. Vol. 46, 4th quarter.)*

Cattle (Aberdeen-Angus) importation was made in 1873 by George Grant, Victoria, Kans., who imported four bulls, two of which were ex-

hibited the same year at Kansas City, Mo. The bulls, imported from Scotland, were crossed with native longhorn Texas cattle.

Cattle (Africander cattle) arrived December 11, 1931, in New York City. Sixteen bulls and 13 cows and heifers left Capetown, South Africa, November 14, 1931, and were held in quarantine from December 12, 1931, to March 9, 1932, at the United States Department of Agriculture, Animal Quarantine Station, Clifton, N.J. William Henry Black, in charge of Beef Cattle Investigations, Bureau of Animal Industry, selected the cattle and had complete supervision until arrival at final destination, March 14, 1932, at King Ranch, Kingsville, Tex.

Cattle club. *See* Cattle club

Cattle exportation was made from Savannah, Ga. A shipment of 16 steers was exported in 1755; and in 1770, 28 steers and cows. In 1772, 136 steers and cows were shipped from that port, probably to the West Indies. It is possible that prior shipments were made, but there is no known record of them.

Cattle exportation to Great Britain is believed to have been made in 1868 by Nelson Morris, who shipped a few live cattle from Chicago, Ill., to London and Glasgow. The first large shipment was made in October 1876 by William Colwell, a cattle dealer of Boston, Mass., who shipped a cargo of 450 live cattle to Liverpool on the steamship *Istrian* of the Leyland Line. *(Rudolf Alexander Clemen—The American Livestock and Meat Industry)*

Cattle (Guernsey cattle) imported were one bull and two heifers that arrived at Boston, Mass., in 1831. They were taken to the farm of General Moody Adams Pillsbury at Guernsey Island, Lake Winnepesaukee, N.H.

Cattle importation law (U.S.) prohibiting the importation of diseased cattle from foreign countries was the "act to prevent the spread of foreign diseases among the cattle of the United States" passed December 18, 1865 (14 Stat. L. 1). The first application of the law took place on July 31, 1875, when meat, cattle, and hides from Spain were excluded on account of the presence of foot-and-mouth disease in that country.

Cattle importation of purebred shorthorns was effected by the Ohio Company for Importing English Cattle, which was organized at Chillicothe, Ohio, on November 2, 1833. The company issued 92 shares at $100 each, which were held by 48 persons, 28 of whom held one share each. To further purebred strains, the society sent Felix Renick to England to buy purebreds. On May 20, 1834, he purchased 7 bulls and 12 cows, which were shipped to Philadelphia, Pa., and driven overland to Chillicothe, Ohio, where they arrived in June 1834. Although cattle had been imported since 1624, this was the first society organized for

The First

ANIMALS—*Continued*

importing purebred stock. *(Ohio Archaeological and Historical Quarterly. Vol. 33. January 1924)*

Cattle (shorthorn) public auction sale was held October 29, 1836, at Felix Renick's Indian Creek Farm, Chillicothe, Ohio, when 43 head sold for $34,540, an average of $803.25 apiece.

Cattle tuberculosis test was made March 3, 1892, on a herd of cattle belonging to Dr. J. E. Gillingham, Claremont Farms, Villa Nova, Pa. The herd was tested with tuberculin brought from Europe by Dr. Leonard Pearson, Dean of the Veterinary Department of the University of Pennsylvania, Philadelphia.

Chinchilla farm that was successful was established February 22, 1923, at Los Angeles, Calif., by Mathias Farrell Chapman with 11 chinchillas imported from Peru and Chile. The farm, later moved to Inglewood, Calif., contained about 1,300 animals.

Cow flown in an airplane was Elm Farm Ollie, a Guernsey, who went aloft on February 18, 1930, with a corps of reporters. She was milked during the flight and the milk was sealed in paper containers and parachuted over St. Louis, Mo.

Cows were imported from Devon, England, in March 1624, by Edward Winslow, who on January 1, 1633, became governor of the Plymouth Colony (Mass.). In 1632 "no farmer was satisfied to do without a cow; and there was in New England, not only a domestic, but an export, demand from the West Indies, which led to breeding for sale. But the market was soon overstocked, and the price of cattle went down from fifteen pounds and twenty pounds to five pounds; and milk was a penny a quart." Cows were raised principally for their hides; secondly, for meat; and only very incidentally for their milk. *(Albert Sidney Bolles—Industrial History of the United States)*

Dog race. *See* Dog race

Dog show. *See* Dog show

Dogs trained to guide the blind were taught at The Seeing Eye, Nashville, Tenn., in 1928. The Seeing Eye was incorporated January 9, 1929, under the laws of Tennessee as an association not for pecuniary profit. Mrs. Harrison Eustis was the first president. The organization moved to Morristown, N.J., in May 1929 and was incorporated on April 30, 1932, under the laws of New Jersey. "Buddy," the first Seeing Eye dog to guide a blind man, was a shepherd dog brought over from Vevey, Switzerland, in June 1928 by Morris S. Frank, to whom it had been presented on April 25, 1928.

Dugong. *See under* Aquatic mammals

Elephant arrived on the *America*, April 13, 1796, at New York City from Bengal, India. She was two years old, six and a half feet high, and was exhib-

The First

ited by Jacob Crowninshield at the corner of Beaver Street and Broadway. The elephant's habits were described as follows: "It eats thirty pounds of rice besides hay and straw—drinks all kinds of wine and spirituous liquors, and eats every sort of vegetable; it will also draw a cork from a bottle with its trunk." *(New York Argus. April 23, 1796)*

Fishes. *See* Fishes

Fur-bearing animals raised commercially were minks reared in Oneida County, N.Y., in 1866 by H. Ressegue. Prices of skins were high, and live animals for breeding stock brought $30 a pair.

Gerenuk born in the United States was born September 30, 1963, at the Zoological Park, Bronx Park, New York City. Gerenuks, *Litocranius walleri*, are reddish-brown gazelle-like antelopes, that are indigenous to eastern Africa.

Giant panda was Su-Lin, imported from China by Mrs. William H. Harkness, Jr., on the *President McKinley*. It weighed about 5 pounds when it arrived at San Francisco, Calif., December 18, 1936. Su-Lin died April 1, 1938, in the Brookfield Zoo, Chicago, Ill., which had purchased it for $8,-750.44. The giant panda was discovered on November 9, 1936. Bearlike in appearance but related to the raccoon, it ranges in bamboo jungles on mountainous land between China and Tibet. Its head and neck are white. Splotchy black fur encircles its eyes, and its tiny ears are grayish black. Forelegs, chest, shoulders, and hind legs are black. Grayish white fur covers its back and sides. It eats shoots and roots of bamboo and grows to a weight of 300 pounds, a length of 5 feet, and a height of 3 feet. *(Ruth Harkness—The Lady and the Panda)*

Goat show. *See* Goat show (of milch goats)

Gorilla born in captivity was Colo, born December 22, 1956, at the Columbus, Ohio, zoo. She weighed 3¼ pounds and was the offspring of Baron (11 years old, 380 pounds) and Christiana (9 years old, 260 pounds).

Horse. *See* Horse

Leopard was exhibited February 2, 1802, by Othello Pollard, near the Columbian Museum, Boston, Mass. An admission fee of 25 cents was charged to see the "import from Bengal." *(Boston Independent Chronicle, No. 2177. Feb. 8, 1802)*

Lion was exhibited November 26, 1716, in Boston, Mass., by "Captain Arthur Savage, at his house in Brattle Street, where is to be shewn by William Nichols, a Lyon of Barbary, with many other rarities, the like never before in America." *(Boston News Letter, No. 659. Nov. 26–Dec. 3, 1716)*

Monkey trained to perform was "a creature called a Japanese, of about two feet high, his body resembling a human body in all parts except the feet and tail" exhibited February 25, 1751, at the house of Mr. Edward Willet, New York City. Admission of a shilling was charged for the performance, in which the monkey walked a tightrope, exercised a firelock (gun), and danced.

Mule was bred from a jack sent to President George Washington. The exportation of full-blooded jacks from Spain was prohibited, but Charles III of Spain, learning of Washington's interest, sent him two jacks, which arrived in Boston, Mass., on October 26, 1785. These were the first jacks to arrive in the United States. *(Paul Leland Haworth—George Washington, Country Gentleman)*

Musk ox born in captivity was a calf born September 5, 1925, at the Bronx Zoo, New York City.

Okapi was imported August 4, 1937, at New York City. It was 21 months old, weighed 235 pounds, and was 49 inches tall at the shoulder. It resembled a cross between a zebra and a giraffe, and had a mahogany-red body with white stripes on its buttocks and upper legs. It consumed 8 bananas, 4 heads of cabbage, 3 bunches of carrots, and 6 liters of condensed milk and water daily. It was captured in the Belgian Congo and shipped July 22, 1937, on the Red Star liner *Pennland,* under the personal care of Dr. William Reid Blair, director of the Bronx Zoo, New York City, to which it was delivered.

Platypus. *See* Aquatic mammals: Platypus (duckbill)

Porpoise. *See* Aquatic mammals: Porpoise born in captivity

Pronghorn antelope bred and reared in captivity was born in the City Park Zoo, Denver, Colo., in 1903. The event was noted by Theodore Roosevelt, who congratulated the zoo director, Alfred Hill.

Reindeer born in the United States was a jet-black calf born on May 31, 1929, at Lodgepole Ranch, the estate of Otis Emerson Dunham at North Beverly, Mass.

Rhinoceros was exhibited September 13, 1826, at Peale's Museum and Gallery of the Fine Arts, New York City. Advertisements stated that "its body and limbs are covered with a skin so hard and impervious that he fears neither the claws of the tiger nor the proboscis of the elephant; it will turn the edge of a scimitar and even resist the force of a musket ball." The exhibit, scheduled to close October 13, was extended to November 25.

Sheep were imported into America in 1609, when the London Company brought over a shipment to Jamestown, Va.

Sheep (Karakul fur sheep) imported were 5 rams and 10 ewes that arrived at New York City in 1908 from Russia on the S.S. *Esthonia.* They were placed in quarantine at Athenia, N.J.,

preparatory to shipment to the ranch of Dr. C. C. Young at Holliday, Tex. *(U.S. Department of Agriculture Yearbook, 1915)*

Sheep (Merino sheep) were imported in 1802 by Colonel David Humphreys, United States Minister to Spain, who shipped 100 of them from Lisbon to Derby, Conn. In 1809 they were valued at $1,500 each. It is also recorded that in 1793 three merino sheep were smuggled in by William Foster, but were eaten, their value being unknown at the time. *(Francis Little—Early American Textiles)*

Sheep (Merino sheep) exhibition was in 1807 at Pittsfield, Mass. by Elkanah Watson, a native of Plymouth, Mass. Two sheep were on display "under the great elm tree in the public square of Pittsfield." *(Louis George Connor—A Brief History of the Sheep Industry in the United States)*

Snakes (cobra). *See* Cobra: King cobra snakes

ANIMATED BOOK. *See* Flicker

ANIMATED CARTOON. *See under* Motion picture

ANIMATED CARTOON ELECTRIC SIGN. *See* Electric sign

ANIMATED CARTOONING SCHOOL. *See* Cartoon school

ANIMATED PHOTOGRAPHIC PICTURE PROJECTION. *See under* Motion picture

ANNEXATION OF TERRITORY. *See* Territorial expansion

ANNUAL was *Le Souvenir, or Picturesque Pocket Diary, Containing an Almanack, Ruled Pages for Memoranda, Literary Selections and a Variety of Useful Information for 1825* published at Philadelphia, Pa., by A. R. Poole in 1825. It was for 24 months and contained 108 pages, including a calendar for 1826. It was issued in a cardboard slip case. It preceded the *Atlantic Souvenir—Christmas and New Year's Offering 1826,* copyrighted October 3, 1825, edited by Henry D. Gilpin, published by [H. C.] Carey and [I.] Lea, Philadelphia, Pa. *(Ralph Thompson—American Literary Annuals and Gift Books)*

ANNULMENT

Annulment by court decree was passed December 3, 1639, at Boston, when "James Luxford, being psented for haveing two wifes, his last marriage was declared voyde, or a nullity thereof and to bee divorced, not to come to the sight of her whom hee last tooke, and hee to be sent away to England by the first opportunity; all that hee hath is appointed to her whom hee last married for here and her children; he is also fined 100 t. and to bee set in the stocks an houre upon a market day after the lecture, the next lecture day if the weather permit, or else the next lecture day after (3rd of the 10th month 1639)." *(Records of the Governor and Com-*

ANNULMENT—*Continued*
pany of the Massachusetts Bay in New England—.
Nathaniel B. Shurtleff, ed.)

ANNUNCIATOR was invented by Seth Fuller of
Boston, Mass., who obtained a patent on December 26, 1833. It was installed at the Tremont
House, Boston, Mass., and was known as "hanging bells." There were 140 bells, which occupied
a space 57 feet long, 6 feet high, and 1 foot deep.
A small hammer hitting a gong caused the sound
and vibrated a card showing a number corresponding with the room number. Each bell was in
a glass-enclosed box. They were placed in operation when the hotel opened, October 16, 1829.

ANSWERING SERVICE (telephone). *See* Telephone

ANTARCTIC EXPEDITION. *See* Discovery: Discovery of Antarctica

ANTARCTICA DISCOVERY. *See* Discovery

ANTELOPE (Pronghorn). *See* Animals

ANTENNA
   Master skyscraper antenna was erected at an
estimated cost of $30,000 by the Alfred Manufac-
turing Company, Boston, in 1965 on the 102nd
floor, at the 1,250 foot level of the Empire State
Building, New York City, in 1965. It enabled 17
frequency modulation stations to broadcast simultaneously. The first were WQXR-FM,
WHOM-FM, WLIB-FM, and WNCM-FM. Transmissions were made mid-October 1965. The transmitters were located on the 81st floor.

ANTHEM, NATIONAL. *See* National anthem

ANTHOLOGY (American) was *American Poems,
Selected and Original,* 304 pages, compiled by
Elihu Hubbard Smith, published in 1793 in Litch-
field, Conn., by [Thomas] Collier and [David]
Buel. (The two-volume work *Select Poems on
Various Occasions, Chiefly American,* printed by
S. Hall, Boston, Mass., in 1787, contained English
as well as American poems.)

ANTHRACITE COAL. *See* Coal

ANTHRAX VACCINE. *See* Vaccine

ANTHROPOLOGY DOCTORATE. *See* Degrees
(academic and honorary)

ANTHROPOLOGY LABORATORY was the
Laboratory of Anthropology that was formally
opened to the public on September 1, 1931, at
Santa Fe, N.Mex. Jesse Logan Nusbaum was in
charge. Dr. Alfred Vincent Kidder was chairman
of the board of trustees. *(American Civic Annual,
Vol. 3. 1931)*

ANTIDISCRIMINATION COMMISSION. *See*
Labor: Labor antidiscrimination commission
(state)

ANTILYNCHING STATUTE. *See* Lynch law
(state)

ANTI-MASONIC PARTY was formed in 1827 in
western New York. The first national convention
was held in a room in the District Court, Philadelphia, Pa., on September 11, 1830, and was attended by 96 delegates from 10 states. On
September 26, 1831, 113 delegates from 13 states
attended a convention at Baltimore, Md., at which
they voted for their first presidential candidates.
William Wirt of Maryland was nominated for
President and Amos Ellmaker of Pennsylvania for
Vice President. In the 1832 elections Wirt received
7 electoral votes as compared with 219 cast for the
Democratic nominee, Andrew Jackson. *(Proceedings of the United States Anti-Masonic Convention held at Philadelphia, Pa., September 11, 1830,
embracing the journal of proceedings, the reports,
the debates and the address to the people.)*

ANTI-MONOPOLY PARTY was formed May 14,
1884, at a convention held in Chicago, Ill. The
existence of "The Anti-Monopoly Organization of
the United States," as it was named, was of short
duration, as its members joined the People's
Party. General Benjamin Franklin Butler of Massachusetts was nominated for the presidency by
the Anti-Monopoly Party, and General Absolom
Madden West of Mississippi for the vice presidency; both were also nominated by the Greenback
Labor Party at its national convention. They received 175,370 votes as compared with 4,874,986
cast for Grover Cleveland of New York, the
Democratic candidate, in the election of November 4, 1884.

ANTIQUARIAN BOOKSTORE. *See* Bookstore
(antiquarian)

ANTIQUARIAN SOCIETY. *See* Historical society

ANTIQUITIES COLLECTION, EGYPTIAN. *See*
Egyptian antiquities collection

ANTI-SALOON LEAGUE. *See* Temperance society

ANTI–SIT–DOWN–STRIKE LEGISLATION. *See*
Strike: Anti–sit–down–strike legislation (state)

ANTISLAVERY BOOK was published in Boston
in 1833 by Allen & Ticknor. It was written by
Lydia Maria Francis Child and entitled *An Appeal
in Favor of That Class of Americans Called Afri-
cans.*

ANTISLAVERY MAGAZINE. *See under* Periodical

ANTISLAVERY PARTY was the Liberty Party
which held its first convention in Warsaw, New
York, November 13, 1839. James Gillespie Birney
of Kentucky was nominated for the presidency
and Francis Julius LeMoyne for the vice presidency. The nominations were confirmed on April 1
1840, despite the unwillingness of the candidate

The First

to accept, and in the Harrison–Van Buren election they polled 7,069 votes. The first national convention of the Liberty Party was held in New York City on May 12, 1841. *(Theodore Clarke Smith— The Liberty and Free Soil Parties in the Northwest)*

ANTISLAVERY SOCIETY. *See* Abolition society

ANTITOXIN LABORATORY was established in September 1894 by the New York City Department of Health. Dr. William Hallock Park was in charge. This was also the first antitoxin laboratory in the world established by a public health organization and the first to provide for the free distribution of antitoxin to the poor. *(Wade Wright Oliver—The Man Who Lived for Tomorrow)*

ANTITRUST LAW. *See under* Trust

ANTITUBERCULOSIS VACCINE. *See* Vaccine

ANTIVIVISECTION PLAY. *See* Play (drama)

ANTIVIVISECTION SOCIETY was the American Anti-Vivisection Society organized February 3, 1883, at Philadelphia, Pa. Its object according to its charter was "the restriction of the practice of vivisection within proper limits, and the prevention of the injudicious and needless infliction of suffering upon animals under the pretense of medical and scientific research." The founder of the society was Caroline Earle White. The first president was Dr. Thomas George Morton. The first annual meeting was held January 30, 1884, in Philadelphia, Pa. *(Anti-Vivisection Society—Annual Report, 1884)*

APARTMENT HOUSE. *See* Building

APARTMENTS SOLD BY A DEPARTMENT STORE. *See* Business: Department store to sell apartments

APOSTOLIC DELEGATE. *See* Catholic apostolic delegate

APOTHECARY. *See* Druggist

APPENDECTOMY. *See* Surgical operation

APPENDICITIS OPERATION. *See* Surgical operation

APPLE PARER was invented on February 14, 1803, by Moses Coats, a mechanic of Downington, Pa.

APPLES were imported from England in 1629 by John Winthrop, colonial governor of Massachusetts. The first apples grown in this country were probably obtained from trees planted in Boston, Mass., from which "ten fair pippins" were plucked on October 10, 1639. Governor John Endicott planted the first nursery of young fruit trees in Danvers, Mass. *(George Kirby Holmes— Progress of Agriculture in the United States: 1899 Yearbook, Department of Agriculture)*

The First

APPLIED CHEMISTRY PROFESSORSHIP. *See* Chemistry professor

APPORTIONMENT, CONGRESSIONAL. *See* Congressional apportionment

APPRENTICE CONTINUATION SCHOOL. *See* Continuation school

AQUARIUM
Aquarium for monsters of the deep was Marineland, 18 miles south of St. Augustine, Fla., built at an approximate cost of $500,000. Ground was broken May 15, 1937, and the dedication and formal opening took place June 23, 1938. The marine studios consisted of two adjacent open-air steel and concrete tanks (one rectangular, 100 feet by 40 feet, and 18 feet deep; the other circular, 75 feet in diameter and 11 feet deep) with 200 portholes.

Aquarium (inland saltwater) was installed in Chicago, Ill., for the 1893 Columbian Exposition by Marshall McDonald. Medals were conferred upon him by Belgium, Britain, France, Germany, and Russia for his efforts in increasing and bettering the hatching and propagation of fish.

AQUACULTURE SCHOOL
Fisheries college. *See* College: Fisheries college

AQUANAUT
Aquanaut to lose his life at work was Berry Louis Cannon, age 33, a civilian electronics engineer from Panama City, Fla., who descended at 5:00 A.M. P.S.T. on February 17, 1969, off San Clemente Island, Calif., while engaged in Project Sealab 3. His air-lung was not filled, and he suffered a seizure that resulted in his death.

United States Navy divers to submerge 10 days were Lieutenant Commander Robert E. Thompson of the Medical Corps, gunners mate first class Lester E. Anderson, chief quartermaster Robert A. Barth, and chief hospital corpsman Sanders W. Manning, who descended in the *Sealab 1* (a 40-foot compartment, 9 feet in diameter) on July 22, 1964, 30 miles off Hamilton, Bermuda, to a 192-foot depth and surfaced July 31, 1964. The air they breathed was a mixture of 80 percent helium, 4 percent oxygen, and 16 percent nitrogen at 86 pounds pressure. They spent one day in the compression center before being hoisted to the deck of the Argus steel tower.

AQUATIC MAMMALS
Dugong arrived at the Steinhart Aquarium, San Francisco, Calif., on November 16, 1955, and was on display until December 27, 1955, when it died. It belongs to the order Sirenia and is a sea mammal. The mammary glands are located under the forelimbs and not near or toward the hindquarters as in most other mammals.

Platypus (duckbill) *(Ornithorhynchus anatinus)* was publicly exhibited July 15, 1922, by the New York Zoological Society at Bronx Park, New York

The First

AQUATIC MAMMALS—*Continued*
City. It arrived at San Francisco, Calif., from Australia. The platypus is a small fur-bearing aquatic animal with webbed feet and a bill like that of a duck. Though a mammal, it is oviparous (egg-laying).

Porpoise born in captivity was born February 14, 1940, at Marineland, Fla. The porpoise was born dead.

Whale. *See* Whale; Whaling

AQUATIC PLAY. *See* Play

AQUEDUCT BRIDGE. *See* Bridge

ARABIC DAILY NEWSPAPER. *See* Newspaper

ARABIC MAGAZINE was *The Star of America (Kowkab America),* a weekly, edited by Abraham Mitrie Rihbany, which was published in New York City in 1892. *(Abraham Mitrie Rihbany—A Far Journey)*

ARBITRATION
Arbitration proceeding in the Hague Permanent Court of Arbitration was the Pious Fund Case of the Californias, a dispute between the United States and Mexico. The protocol of agreement was signed May 22, 1902, and the award of the court was made October 14, 1902. Mexico was forced to pay $1,420,682.67 in Mexican currency and $43,059.99 annually, beginning February 2, 1903. The issue was whether the claim of the United States for indemnity in behalf of the Roman Catholic Archbishop of San Francisco and the Bishop of Monterey was governed by the principle of *res judicata,* by virtue of the arbitral sentence of Sir Edward Thornton of November 11, 1875. The contention of the United States that the claim should be so governed was sustained by a unanimous court. The Pious Fund was money collected by Jesuits in Mexico for missions in California. After 1848, when Upper California was ceded to the United States, Mexico refused payment of income to churches in California. *(Charles Cheney Hyde—International Law)*

Arbitration tribunal was established by the Chamber of Commerce, New York City, N.Y., on May 3, 1768, and consisted of seven members to adjust "any differences between parties agreeing to leave such disputes to this Chamber." A different committee was appointed for each meeting. *(Joseph Bucklin Bishop—A Chronicle of One Hundred and Fifty Years: The Chamber of Commerce of the State of New York, 1768–1918)*

Colonial arbitration law was "an act for the more easy and effectually finishing of controversies by arbitration," passed at the legislative session held from October 11, 1753, to November 2, 1753, in New Haven, Conn. Each side appointed an arbitrator and the court appointed one. The court was granted power to levy and collect the awards. *(Charles Jeremy Hoadly—The Public*

The First

Records of the Colony of Connecticut from May 1751 to February 1757)

Federal arbitration law was "an act to make valid and enforceable written provisions or agreements for arbitration of disputes arising out of contracts, maritime transactions or commerce among the States or Territories or with foreign nations" (43 Stat. L. 883), approved February 12, 1925, to take effect January 1, 1926.

Federal Board of Mediation and Conciliation (labor relations only) was the United States Board of Mediation and Conciliation, authorized by the act of March 4, 1913 (37 Stat. L. 739), and giving the secretary of labor "power to act as mediator and to appoint commissioners of conciliation in labor disputes whenever in his judgment the interests of industrial peace may require it."

Interstate carrier arbitration law was the act of October 1, 1888 (25 Stat. L. 501), "an act to create boards of arbitration or commission for settling controversies and differences between railroad corporations and other common carriers engaged in interstate and territorial transportation of property or passengers and their employees." It provided for two methods of settling disputes namely, voluntary arbitration (not used in ten years) and investigation (applied only once, ineffectively, in the Pullman strike of 1894).

National Mediation Board. *See under* Labor relations

State arbitration law was Chapter 21, "An act for amending and declaring the law in the case therein mentioned," passed December 15, 1778, by the General Assembly of Maryland, at Annapolis which ruled "it shall be lawful to and for such court to give judgment upon the award of the person or persons to whom such submission and reference shall be made." *(Clement Dorsey—The General Public Statutory Laws and Public Local Law of the State of Maryland from the year 169 to 1939 inclusive with annotations thereto and copious index)*

State arbitration law (modern), under which an agreement to arbitrate controversies which may arise from a contract is recognized as valid and enforceable, was the "Arbitration Law" of New York, an "act in relation to arbitration constituting chapter seventy-two of the consolidated laws," Chapter 275 of the Laws of 1920, New York which became effective April 19, 1920, the day when it was signed by Governor Alfred Emanuel Smith. Many laws were passed between 1886 and 1920 by several states, but they were not effective.

State Board of Mediation and Arbitration was the New York Board of Mediation and Arbitration, organized June 1, 1886, under authority of an act of May 18, 1886. The commissioners were William Purcell, Gilbert Robertson, Jr., and Florence F. Donovan. On June 2, 1886, Massachusetts and thorized a state arbitration board "for the settlement of differences between employers and their employees."

Strike settlement. *See under* Strike

ARBITRATION ASSOCIATION

Arbitration association devoted exclusively to advancing principle and practice in this field was the Arbitration Society of America, Inc., formed at New York City on May 15, 1922. On January 29, 1926, the American Arbitration Association was formed by a merger of the Arbitration Society of America, Inc., the Arbitration Foundation, Inc., and the Arbitration Conference. The first officers of the American Arbitration Association were Anson W. Burchard, president; Lucius Root Eastman and Frances Keller, vice presidents; and J. Noble Braden, executive secretary.

ARBOR DAY. *See* Holiday

ARC LIGHT. *See* Electric lighting

ARCADE was the Philadelphia Arcade, which extended from Chestnut Street through to Carpenter Street between Sixth and Seventh streets, Philadelphia, Pa. It was erected by the Arcade Company, of which John Haviland was architect. The cornerstone was laid on May 3, 1826, and the building finished in September 1827. The cost of construction was $112,000; $42,500 was paid for the land.

ARCH BRIDGE, STEEL. *See* Bridge

ARCH RAILROAD BRIDGE, STONE. *See* Bridge

ARCHAEOLOGICAL SOCIETY

Archaeological society (national) was the Archaeological Institute of America, which was founded May 10, 1879, at Boston, Mass. The contitution was adopted May 17, 1879. The first annual meeting was held May 15, 1880, at Boston, Mass. It was incorporated by act of Congress, May 26, 1906. Its purpose was to promote and direct archaeological research. The first president was Charles Eliot Norton. *(First Annual Report of the Executive Committee of the Archaeological Institute of America)*

ARCHERY CLUB

Archery association (national) was the National Archery Association, formed January 23, 1879, in Crawfordsville, Ind., by representatives of eight archery clubs. The first president was Maurice Thompson. The first grand annual meeting and the first tournament were held August 12–14 in Chicago, Ill., at which 20 women and 69 men competed. High score was made by Will H. Thompson, who won with 172 hits and a score of 824. *(Robert Potter Elmer—American Archery)*

Archery club was the United Bowmen of Philadelphia, founded in 1825 by Franklin Peale; Titian Ramsey Peale; Robert E. Griffith, M.D.; Samuel P. Griffith, Jr.; Jacob M. Morris; and Thomas Sully. The club was not formally organized until 1828,

when membership was limited to 25. Members dressed in frock coats of Lincoln green, ornamented with gold braid, and wore broad straw hats with three black ostrich plumes.

ARCHITECT

Landscape architect was John Reid, gardener to Sir George Mackenzie of Rosebaugh, lord advocate under Charles II, who left Aberdeen, Scotland, August 28, 1683, on the *Exchange*, accompanied by his wife and three daughters. He landed at Staten Island, N.Y., December 19, 1683. *(New Jersey Historical Society Proceedings, January 1937)*

Woman architect to enter the architectural profession was Louise Blanchard Bethune, who opened an independent office in 1881 in Buffalo, N.Y. She was the first woman member of the American Institute of Architects, elected to full membership on September 15, 1890.

Woman graduate of the Webb Institute of Navel Architecture, Glen Cove, Long Island, N.Y., was Karen Hansen, who was graduated June 22, 1978, and received a position designing oil drilling platforms and ships at a salary exceeding $20,000.

ARCHITECTURE BOOK

Architecture book distinctly American was *The Country Builders' Assistant; containing a collection of new designs of carpentry and architecture,* by Asher Benjamin. It contained 30 plates and was printed in 1797 by Thomas Dickman, Greenfield, Mass.

Architecture book printed in America was Abraham Swan's *British Architect; or the Builders Treasury of Staircases,* published in 1775 by R [obert] Bell in Philadelphia, Pa., for J. Norman. It was a reprint of the edition published in London, England, in 1745.

ARCHITECTURE SCHOOL

Architecture school of collegiate rank was established February 20, 1865, by the Massachusetts Institute of Technology, Boston, Mass., which opened a Department of Architecture. William Robert Ware was the first head of the department and received the title of professor.

Landscape architecture course for women was offered September 15, 1901, by the Lowthorpe School of Architecture, Groton, Mass. The director of the school was Mrs. Edward Gilchrist Low. Degrees were not conferred, but certificates were given. First certificates were awarded June 10, 1903, to three students.

ARCHIVAL ADMINISTRATION comprehensive program for training of archivists was offered September 25, 1940, by the School of Public Affairs, American University, Washington, D.C. John Clarke Patterson was Director of the Graduate School and the School of Public Affairs.

The First

ARCHIVAL COURSE was "Archives and Historical Manuscripts," offered September 29, 1938, by Columbia University, New York City, under Dr. Solon Justus Buck, director of publications, National Archives, Washington, D.C.

ARCHIVIST OF THE UNITED STATES was Robert Digges Wimberley Connor, appointed October 10, 1934. The position was created by act of Congress (48 Stat. L. 1122) an "act to establish a National Archives of the United States Government," approved June 19, 1934, by President Franklin Delano Roosevelt, which established the Archives Bureau. Connor served from October 10, 1934, to September 15, 1941; his resignation was formally effective August 1, 1941. The archivist has an official seal and is chairman of a national publications committee.

ARCTIC EXPEDITION. *See* Expedition

ARCTICS. *See* Artics

ARITHMETIC
See also Algebra book

American Arithmetic by a native-born American was Isaac Greenwood's *Arithmetick—Vulgar and Decimal with the Application Thereof to a Variety of Cases in Trade and Commerce*, which was published in 1729 in Boston, Mass., by S. Kneeland and T. Green for T. Hancock at the Sign of the Bible and Three Crowns in Ann Street. It contained 158 pages, 4 pages of index, and 4 pages of advertisements. *(David Eugene Smith and Jekuthiel Ginsburg—History of Mathematics in America Before 1900)*

Arithmetic to be printed in the colonies was James Hodder's *Arithmetick; or that necessary art made most easy. Being explained in a way familiar to the capacity of any that desire to learn it in a little time*, printed by James Franklin, Boston, Mass., in 1719 for S. Phillips. It had originally been published in London in 1661. *(Louis Charles Karpinski—Bibliography of Mathematical Works Printed in America Through 1850)*

ARMED FORCES EXPEDITIONARY MEDAL.
See Medal

ARMENIAN CATHEDRAL
Armenian cathedral was the Armenian Cathedral of St. Vartan, New York City, consecrated April 28, 1968, by His Holiness Vasken I, Supreme Patriarch and Catholicos of All Armenians. The Most Reverend Torkom Manoogian was the first upon whom the Catholicos personally bestowed the rank of archbishop in the United States.

ARMISTICE DAY. *See* Holiday

ARMOR PLATE CONTRACT (U.S. NAVY) was awarded to the Bethlehem Iron Company, South Bethlehem, Pa., on June 1, 1887. Six thousand seven hundred tons were ordered at $536 a ton for the battleships *Maine* and *Texas* and the monitors *Puritan, Amphitrite, Monadnock,* and *Terror.*

The First

(American Iron and Steel Association—History of the Manufacture of Armor Plate for the United States Navy)

ARMOR-PLATED VESSELS. *See* Ship

ARMORED CAR. *See* Automobile

ARMORED COMMERCIAL CAR HOLDUP. *See* Automobile robbery

ARMORED TANK. *See* Army armored tank

ARMORY. *See* Arsenal

ARMY
American army division to cross the Rhine River. *See* World War I: U.S. Army division to cross the Rhine River

Armored division transported by airplanes to a foreign country was the Second Armored Division commanded by Major General Edwin Hes Hurba, who took off with 62 men of his staff on October 22, 1963, in a C-135 Stratolifter from the Bergstrom Air Force Base, near Austin, Tex., for the Rhein-Main Air Base in West Germany, as part of Operation Big Lift. In 63 hours and 20 minutes, 196 airplanes, including 23 jets, transported 15,268 combat-ready troops in 235 missions. The division returned to Texas from November 12 to 21, 1963. Major General Archie J. Old, Jr., of the Fifteenth Air Force was the overall commander of the flight.

Army aviator. *See* Aviation—Pilot

Army Engineering Department of the Continental Army was authorized by the Continental Congress, June 16, 1775. It established a separate engineering department in the army composed of 1 chief engineer, who received $60 a month, and 2 assistant engineers at $20 a month. The first chief engineer was Colonel Richard Gridley, who was appointed in June 1775 under the resolve of the Continental Congress of June 16, 1775. A formal Corps of Engineers was established March 11, 1779, but was disbanded November 3, 1783, upon the dissolution of the Revolutionary Army.

Army expeditionary force. *See* American expeditionary force

Army flag (official). *See under* Flag

Army Military Police school. *See* Police: Army Military Police school

Army organization under the Constitution was enacted April 30, 1789, (1 Stat. L. 119) "act for regulating the military establishment of the U.S." and provided for one regiment of infantry to consist of three battalions of four companies each, one battalion of artillery with four companies and a total strength not to exceed 1,216 non-commissioned officers, privates and musicians." The monthly authorized pay was lieutenant colonel commandant $60, majors $40, captains $30, lieu

The First

tenants $22, corporals $4, privates $3, musicians $3.

Army Veterinary Corps was established as part of the Medical Department of the Army by the National Defense Act of 1916 (39 Stat. L. 166) enacted June 3, 1916. The legislation authorized 2 officers for each regiment of cavalry, 1 for every 3 batteries of field artillery, and 1 for each mounted battalion of engineers.

Automobiles ordered for the U.S. War Department. *See under* Automobile

Ballistic missile operational unit was the 259th Field Artillery Missile Battalion, which completed training November 1954 at Fort Bliss, Tex. The unit was deployed to Europe in February 1955 to provide guided missile support for units in the U.S. Seventh Army.

Battle fought by U.S. troops. *See under* War

Brevet was authorized by the Continental Congress on July 20, 1776, for Jacques Antoine de Franchessin, a Knight of the Order of St. Louis, an experienced officer in the service of France, who received a brevet commission of lieutenant colonel.

Brevet conferred upon an American was authorized November 19, 1777, by the Continental Congress, which granted the rank of lieutenant colonel and a sword valued at $100, to Major Walter Stewart. *(James Barnet Fry—The History and Legal Effect of Brevets in the Armies of Great Britain and the United States)*

Cavalry unit was the Regiment of Dragoons, later known as the First Regiment of Dragoons, organized at Jefferson Barracks, Mo., in August 1833. Colonel Henry Dodge assumed command August 29, 1833. The designation of this organization was changed to the First Cavalry by act of Congress of August 3, 1861 (12 Stat. L. 287). On March 5, 1792, Congress gave the President power to raise a squadron of cavalry at his direction to serve for three years. *(Records in Adjutant General's Office, War Department, Washington, D.C.)*

Confederate general killed in the Civil War. *See under* Civil War

Dental Corps of the U.S. Army. *See under* Dental Corps (U.S. Army)

Doctor (woman) commissioned in the regular Army. *See* Army officer: Woman doctor commissioned in the regular Army

Engineer Corps of the United States Army was established by Act of March 16, 1802 (2 Stat. L. 132), "fixing the military peace establishments of the United States." The corps consisted of one engineer (major), two assistant engineers (captains), two other assistants (second lieutenants), and ten cadets. The first engineer in charge was Major Jonathan Williams, appointed April 13,

The First

1802. *(Jonathan Williams—Plan of Jonathan Williams for Fortifying the Narrows)*

Gas regiment of the United States Army was authorized August 15, 1917, by General Order 108, and organized by Colonel Earl James Atkisson. The first year it was known as the 30th Engineers, and later it was named the First Gas Regiment. The first battalion was organized October 16, 1917. Its first independent action took place June 18, 1918, against Germans in the Toul sector, France.

Helicopter battalion activated was the Eighth Transportation Battalion (helicopter), consisting of three helicopter companies and one maintenance company, formed April 1, 1954, at Fort Bragg, N.C., under command of Major Robert Kolb.

Law (federal) authorizing military service for blacks was introduced July 16, 1862, by Senator Henry Wilson of Massachusetts and signed July 17, 1862, by President Abraham Lincoln. It empowered the President to accept "persons of African descent, for the purpose of constructing intrenchments or performing camp competent." *(George Washington Williams—A History of the Negro Troops in the War of the Rebellion)*

Law (state) conferring military privileges and duties on blacks was chapter 24 of the Public Acts of Tennessee, passed June 28, 1861. The governor was authorized to receive "all male free persons of color between the ages of 15 and 50 . . . to do all such menial service for the relief of the volunteers."

Medical Corps of the U.S. Army is generally claimed to have been organized by the Reorganization Act of April 14, 1818 (end section—3 Stat. L. 426), under which Joseph Lovell was appointed surgeon general. Medical officers previously were generally appointed for special regiments. Richard Allison of Pennsylvania was appointed surgeon of a corps of 700 rank and file, which the first Congress had authorized on September 29, 1789. From this date to 1798, medical officers were appointed for regiments as they were authorized by Congress. The Act of May 28, 1798 (1 Stat. L. 558), provided for the appointment of a physician general, for which post James Craik of Virginia was selected. The Act of March 3, 1813 (2 Stat. L. 819), authorized the appointment of a physician and surgeon general. Dr. James Tilton of Delaware was appointed physician and surgeon general, and Francis Le Baron of Massachusetts was appointed apothecary general.

Military airplane. *See* Aviation—Airplane: Airplane in actual military operation

Military leader of the Puritan settlers. *See* Military leader

The First

ARMY—*Continued*

Motion picture for training soldiers. *See under* Motion picture

Newspaper published by soldiers in the field. *See under* Newspaper

Parachute fatality in the U.S. Army. *See* Aviation—Parachute: Parachute fatality in the U.S. Army

Railroad to carry troops. *See under* Railroad

Reserve Officers Training Corps was authorized by the National Defense Act of June 3, 1916 (39 Stat. L. 191), an "act for making further and more effectual provision for the national defense and for other purposes." Men were accepted for military training in times of peace to take the place of officers in time of war.

Reserve Officers Training Corps course in mountain and winter warfare was announced October 3, 1947, by President Homer Levi Dodge of Norwich University, Northfield, Vt. The course began in December 1947. The equipment included 150 pairs of skis, 130 pairs of snowshoes, 6 toboggans, and sleds.

Reserve Officers Training Corps units were infantry units established, under authority of War Department Bulletin No. 44, October 21, 1916, at the University of Arkansas, Fayetteville, Ark.; University of Maine, Orono, Me.; St. John's College, Annapolis, Md.; Agricultural and Mechanical College of Texas, College Station, Tex.; College of St. Thomas, St. Paul, Minn.; and the Citadel, Charleston, S.C. *(John Dickinson—The Building of an Army)*

Signal Corps was authorized as a separate branch of the U.S. Army by act of Congress March 3, 1863 (12 Stat. L. 753). The corps was established under act of June 1, 1860 (12 Stat. L. 66), which appropriated $2,000 "for the manufacture or purchase of apparatus and equipment for field signals" and the appointment of one signal officer. On June 27, 1860, Assistant Surgeon Albert James Myer was appointed signal officer, with the rank of major.

Soldier to receive 7 decorations at one time. *See under* Medal

Soldier to win the 3 highest-ranking decorations. *See under* Medal

Strike in which federal troops were called in peacetime. *See under* Strike

Wedding in the United States Occupation Forces in Korea. *See under* Wedding

Woman to become a member of the Women's Army Corps. *See under* Army auxiliary corps

Women's Army Medical Specialist Corps was authorized under the Army-Navy Nurses Act of 1947, April 16, 1947 (61 Stat. L. 41), which estab-

The First

lished a dietitians' section, a physical therapists' section, and an occupational therapists' section to consist of 24 majors and 385 captains and first and second lieutenants.

ARMY AMBULANCE CORPS

Army ambulance corps was established August 2, 1862, by Major General George Brinton McClellan, who issued General Order No. 147 authorizing one captain to each army corps as the commandant of the Ambulance Corps, a first lieutenant for a division, a second lieutenant for a brigade, and a sergeant for each regiment. The members of the corps wore a green band on the cap and a green half chevron two inches broad or each arm above the elbow. *(Medical and Surgical History of the War of the Rebellion, Vol. 2, Surgical History Part 3)*

Army Ambulance Corps established by congressional action was authorized by the "Act to Establish a Uniform System of Ambulances in the Armies of the United States," approved March 11 1864 (13 Stat. L. 20), which provided each army corps with two-horse ambulances in accord with their strength. Infantry regiments of from 200 to 500 men were entitled to two ambulances, while those of over 500 men were entitled to three. Cavalry regiments with fewer than 500 men were entitled to one ambulance, while those of over 500 were entitled to two.

ARMY ARMORED CAR UNIT in the United States Army was Troop A, First Armored Car Squadron, which was organized at Fort George G Meade, Md., in 1928. It was commanded by Captain Harold G. Holt.

ARMY ARMORED TANK. *See* Ordnance

ARMY AUXILIARY CORPS

Legion of Merit medal awarded a Women's Army Corps member. *See* Medal: Legion of Merit Medal awarded to a Women's Army Corps member

Woman to become a member of the Women's Army Corps, Regular Army, was Technician Third Grade Vietta M. Bates of Camden, N.J., who was sworn in July 8, 1948, in Washington, D.C., by General Omar Nelson Bradley, Army Chief of Staff. The ceremony was televised.

Women's Army Auxiliary Corps (WAAC) was authorized May 14, 1942 (56 Stat. L. 278), an "act to establish a Women's Army Auxiliary Corps for service with the Army of the United States, under the command of a director who was to receive $3,000 annually plus allowances. The director was Oveta Culp Hobby (Mrs. William Pettus Hobby), appointed May 15, 1942. She assumed command the following day, when she was sworn in by Secretary of War Henry Lewis Stimson. On September 30, 1943, the Women's Army Auxiliary Corps became the Women's Army Corps (WAC

The First

Women's Army Auxiliary Corps (WAAC) training course began July 20, 1942, at Fort Des Moines, Des Moines, Iowa, and concluded August 29, 1942, when 346 women were commissioned third officers.

ARMY AVIATOR. *See* Aviation—Pilot

ARMY BALLOON CORPS of the U.S. Army was the Balloon (Aeronautic) Corps of 5 balloons and 50 men under the command of Thaddeus Sobieski Coulincourt Lowe, chief aeronaut of the Army of the Potomac, formed October 1, 1861. Four balloons were ready for service November 10, 1861, and were used for reconnaissance and for directing artillery fire via telegraph in Virginia. *(Official Records of the Union and Confederate Armies, Series 1)*

ARMY BALLOON SCHOOL was established on April 6, 1917, by Major Albert Bond Lambert on ground leased at Grand and Meramec streets, St. Louis, Mo. When the first class (of 12) graduated, May 15, 1917, all the equipment was offered without compensation to the War Department, which operated it until November 1917, when winter quarters were opened at San Antonio, Tex. In May 1918 the school was transferred to Camp John Wise at San Antonio.

ARMY CAMP

Army camp for "limited service" selectees was opened at Camp McCoy, Wis. Company No. 1, consisting of 85 enlisted men, was activated July 19, 1942. The commanding officer was Major William Lutz Krigbaum.

Army Camp for training black officers was established June 15, 1917, at Fort Des Moines, Des Moines, Iowa, and was known as the 17th Provisional Training Regiment. On October 15, 1917, the first commissions were granted, 106 blacks being commissioned as second lieutenants.

Army Citizens' Military Training Camp was established in 1921 with an enrollment of 10,299. The camps were authorized by the amendment to the National Defense Act of June 4, 1920 (41 Stat. L. 759).

ARMY DENTAL CORPS. *See* Dental Corps (U.S. Army)

ARMY DENTIST. *See under* Dental Corps (U.S. Army)

ARMY "E" AWARD. *See* Navy "E" award: Army-Navy "E" awards

ARMY EXCLUSION LAW imposing a penalty for excluding soldiers in uniform from public places was Chapter 1562 passed May 5, 1908, by Rhode Island. The bill was sponsored by Theodore Francis Green. This act was amended from Section 32 of Chapter 283 of the General Laws of 1896.

The First

ARMY EXECUTION in the American Army occurred on June 27, 1776. A treacherous guard, Thomas Hickey, plotted with others to capture George Washington and deliver him to Sir William Howe. Hickey was tried, convicted, and formally executed in New York City. All the officers and men off duty belonging to the brigades of Spencer, Heath, Sterling, and Scott assembled under arms at their respective barracks and at ten o'clock marched to the grounds, a field near the Bowery Lane. Hickey was hanged in the presence of 20,000 persons.

ARMY FIELD HOSPITAL. *See* Hospital

ARMY FIELD RANGE, or "Moving Kitchen," drawn by horses, was introduced by Captain Daniel Frank Craig, Fourth Field Artillery, on a 21-day march in May 1908, while he was serving on the staff of Colonel Alexander Brydie Dyer at Vancouver, Wash. It was mounted on a two-wheeled truck or trailer and was drawn behind a rations wagon. It was never officially adopted by the War Department, although extensively used.

ARMY HELIPORT. *See* Heliport

ARMY HOSPITAL. *See* Hospital

ARMY INSIGNIA

Chevrons for noncommissioned army uniforms were authorized by General Regulations for the Army of the United States, 1847, which provided three bars and an arc for sergeant major, three bars and a tie for quartermaster sergeant, three bars and a lozenge for first sergeant, three bars for a sergeant, and two bars for a corporal. *(Henry Loomis Nelson—The Army of the United States)*

Corps badges systematically assigned to an entire army were adopted in March 1863 by the Army of the Potomac. The I Corps was assigned a circle or sphere, the II Corps a trefoil or shape commonly called a club, the III Corps a diamond shape, the IV Corps a triangle with two equal sides inside a larger triangle, the V Corps a cross pattée, etc. *(Evans E. Kerrigan—American Badges and Insignia)*

Service number (G.I. serial number) to an enlisted man was issued to Master Sergeant Arthur P. Crean, who received number ASN-1 on February 28, 1918. The first service numbers to officers were issued June 1921, the first number being issued to General John Joseph Pershing, Chief of Staff, who received No. O-1. Social Security numbers replaced all service numbers on dogtags on July 1, 1969. By 1972, a similar numbering system covered the Air Force, Navy, and Marine Corps.

Shoulder sleeve insignia, known as a shoulder patch, depicted a wildcat in a circle and was authorized October 19, 1918, for the 81st Division, nicknamed the Stonewall Jackson Division, the Bobcat Division, and the Wildcat Division.

The First

ARMY INSIGNIA—*Continued*

Shoulder sleeve insignia issued to an independent air unit was authorized July 20, 1937, for the General Headquarters Air Force. It consisted of an ultramarine-blue 3-bladed propeller outlined against an orange disk. (An independent air unit was one directly under the command of the War Department, not under a commander who in turn was under the War Department.)

Special insignia or marking to designate regiments was instituted by the Massachusetts Provincial Congress on July 5, 1775, which "resolved that thirteen thousand coats be provided . . . and one thereof given to each non-commissioned officer and soldier in the Massachusetts Forces . . . and that the Committee of Supplies . . . are to cause all the coats to be buttoned with pewter buttons, and that the coats for each regiment, respectively, have buttons of the same number stamped on the face of them."

Wound chevron was authorized, pursuant to General Orders No. 6, War Department, on January 2, 1918. It was a gold chevron, identical with that of war service, worn on the left sleeve.

ARMY LANGUAGE SCHOOL began courses in Japanese November 1, 1941, at Crissey Field, Presidio of San Francisco, Calif. It was deactivated, and activated as the Military Service Language School, Camp Savage, Minn., on June 1, 1942. It was moved to Fort Snelling, Minn., on August 15, 1944, and to the Presidio of Monterey, Calif., on June 11, 1946. The school was redesignated the Army Language School on September 1, 1947. In 1953 the school offered courses in 24 languages.

ARMY LODGE (Masonic). *See* Freemasons

ARMY MEDICAL BOOK. *See* Medical book

ARMY-NAVY FOOTBALL GAME. *See* Football game

ARMY NUCLEAR POWER PLANT. *See* Atomic reactor: Military nuclear power plant

ARMY NURSE CORPS (female) was established as a permanent organization of the Army by section 19, Act of February 2, 1901 (31 Stat. L. 753), to consist of one superintendent ($1,800 annual compensation) and nurses and reserve nurses who received $40 a month within the continental limits of the United States and $50 a month when on foreign service and transportation and necessary traveling expenses when traveling under orders. Quarters, subsistence, and medical attendance were also provided. The first superintendent was Mrs. Dita H. Kinney, who was appointed March 15, 1901, and who resigned July 31, 1909. Anita Newcomb McGee, acting assistant surgeon, United States Army, appointed August 29, 1898, had organized the nurses who remained with the Army after the Spanish-American War into a corps under the Surgeon General. She served until

The First

December 31, 1900. *(Julia Catherine Stimson—History and Manual of the Army Nurse Corps)*

ARMY OFFICER

Adjutant general in the Continental Army was Horatio Gates, whose commission was signed June 19, 1775, by John Hancock. He received $125 a month and the rank of brigadier general. The resolution to establish this office was passed June 16, 1775. Gates was chosen June 17, 1775, and on May 16, 1776, became a major general. He had a hectic military career, resigned from service, reentered it, was suspended, and was later reinstated *(Samuel White Patterson—Horatio Gates)*

Air surgeon of the War Department was Colonel David Norvell Walker Grant, chief of the Medical Division of the Office of the Air Corps, who was named to the post on October 24, 1941. He was rated a flight and air surgeon on July 3, 1942, and was assigned as chief surgeon under the commanding general of the Army Air Forces.

American general captured by the Germans *See under* World War II

American general killed in Vietnam by enemy action. *See under* Vietnam War

American general missing in action in World War II. *See under* World War II

American general to fly over enemy lines was Brigadier General William Lendrum Mitchell, who took off at 5:30 P.M. from La Cheppe, France, on April 24, 1917, in an airplane piloted by Lieutenant François Lafont and flew over the German lines at an altitude of 6,000 feet, returning at 7:00 P.M.

Army chaplain of Japanese ancestry was First Lieutenant Masao Yamada, a Congregational minister, assigned on June 9, 1943, to Camp Shelby, Miss., to preach to soldiers of Japanese ancestry.

Army Chief of Staff was Lieutenant General Samuel Baldwin Marks Young, who served from August 15, 1903, to January 9, 1904.

Army nurse awarded a Distinguished Flying Cross. *See* Medal: Distinguished Flying Cross awarded to a nurse

Army officer to occupy both the nation's highest military post and the highest nonelective civilian post was General George Catlett Marshall of Pennsylvania. He was Acting Chief of Staff on July 1, 1939; Chief of Staff with rank of major general on September 1, 1939, serving until November 20, 1945; Secretary of State from January 21, 1947 to January 20, 1949; and Secretary of Defense from September 21, 1950, to September 12, 1951.

Army officer to receive the three highest decorations was Captain Maurice L. Britt of Lonoke, Ark., infantry, the recipient of the Medal of Honor, the Silver Star, the Purple Heart with three Oak

The First

Leaf clusters, and the Military Cross of the British Empire, who was presented with the Distinguished Service Cross on December 7, 1944, by Major General Frank L. Walker for gallantry in action.

Army pilot (black) to down an Axis airplane. *See* Aviation—Pilot: Black pilot to down an Axis airplane

Army Dental Corps Major General. *See under* Dental Corps (U.S. Army)

Army Medical Specialist Corps male officer commissioned was Second Lieutenant Sheldon Saffren of Philadelphia, Pa., who was commissioned December 30, 1955, at the University of Pennsylvania Physical Therapy School, Philadelphia. The Army-Navy Nurses Act of April 16, 1947 (61 Stat. L. 4), was amended on August 9, 1955, by the Bolton Amendment (69 Stat. L. 579), which extended nurses' commissions to male personnel.

Army War College women graduates. *See* Army War College: Army War College women graduates

Brigadier general (black) was Benjamin Oliver Davis, commanding officer of Harlem's 369th Coast Artillery (National Guard), appointed October 25, 1940, to command a brigade in the Second Cavalry Division at Fort Riley, Kans.

Chaplain (black) of the U.S. Army was Henry McNeal Turner, pastor of the Israel African Methodist Episcopal Church, Washington, D.C. He was commissioned chaplain of the United States Colored Troops by President Abraham Lincoln in 1863. Turner enlisted in the First United States Colored Infantry, otherwise known as the First District Regiment of Columbia, and was present and active in all its military engagements. He was mustered out of service in September 1865 and was appointed a chaplain in the regular Army by President Andrew Johnson. *(Richard Robert Wright—Centennial Encyclopedia of the African Methodist Episcopal Church)*

Chaplain (Catholic) appointed by the President was the Reverend Francis Edward Boyle of the District of Columbia. He was appointed June 13, 1862, accepted June 16, 1862, and was assigned to tone Hospital, Washington, D.C.

Chaplain (Catholic) of the Continental Army was the Reverend Louis Eustace Lotbinière, appointed January 26, 1776, by General Benedict Arnold, to act as chaplain to the regiment of Colonel James Livingston. *(Peter Force, comp.—American Archives, Vol. 1)*

Chaplain (Catholic) of the U.S. Army was the Reverend Samuel H. Milley, who served as post chaplain at Monterey, Calif., from September 28, 1849, to February 1850. *(Aidan Henry Germain, comp.—Catholic Military and Naval Chaplains)*

The First

Chaplain (chief) of the U.S. Army was John Thomas Axton, a clergyman of the Congregational Church, appointed July 15, 1920, with the rank, pay, and allowance of colonel. He retired April 6, 1928. The office of chief of chaplains was established pursuant to Section 15 of an Act of Congress approved June 4, 1920 (41 Stat. L. 769).

Chaplain (Jewish) of the U.S. Army was the Reverend Jacob Frankel of Philadelphia, Pa., who was appointed September 10, 1862, and who accepted September 18, 1862. This appointment expired by constitutional limitation March 4, 1863. He was reappointed April 22, 1863, to the United States Hospital, Philadelphia, Pa., and was honorably mustered out of service July 1, 1865. Michael Mitchell Allen was regimental chaplain of the 65th regiment of the Fifth Pennsylvania Cavalry, resigning September 26, 1861, but he was not a "regularly ordained clergyman." *(U.S. War Department—Records of Chaplains Commissioned in 1862)*

Chaplain killed in action was Chaplain John Rosbrugh of Allen Township, Pa., who served as chaplain of Northampton County. He was commissioned December 26, 1776, and was killed at the battle of Assunpink, or the Second Battle of Trenton, on January 2, 1777. *(John Cunningham Clyde—Rosbrugh, a Tale of the Revolution)*

Chaplain of the U.S. Army was the Reverend John Hurt, who was appointed March 4, 1791, and who resigned April 30, 1794. He served during the Revolution as chaplain of the Sixth Virginia Infantry, beginning October 1, 1776. He became brigade chaplain on August 18, 1778, and served as such to the close of the war. *(Francis Bernard Heitman—Officers of the Continental Army, 1775–1783)*

Chemical warfare chief was Brigadier General Amos Alfred Fries, who served from July 16, 1920, to March 4, 1921, and from March 28, 1921, to March 27, 1929. On February 24, 1925, he was advanced to major general.

Chief engineer of the Continental Army was Colonel Richard Gridley, who served from June 17, 1775, to August 5, 1776. On June 16, 1775, the Continental Congress authorized one chief engineer at $60 a month, and two assistants at $20. *(Andrew Atkinson Humphreys—Historical Sketch of the Corps of Engineers)*

Commander-in-chief of the U.S. Army was Josiah Harmar, who served from September 29, 1789, to March 4, 1791, with the rating of lieutenant colonel of infantry. He was succeeded by Arthur St. Clair, Anthony Wayne, James Wilkinson, and George Washington, the fifth commander-in-chief, who served from July 3, 1798, to December 14, 1799, as lieutenant general and general.

Flight surgeon of the U.S. Army was Dr. John Patrick Kelly, who reported for duty at the Signal Corps School of Aviation, College Park, Md., on

The First

ARMY OFFICER—*Continued*
June 30, 1911, and who moved with the school to Augusta, Ga., on November 29, 1911.

General (American) to die in Vietnam. *See under* Vietnam War

General appointed from civilian rank was William Signius Knudsen, director general of Office of Priority Management, appointed a lieutenant general on January 16, 1942, by President Franklin Delano Roosevelt.

General (black) to lead an infantry brigade in combat was Major General Frederic Ellis Davison, who led the 199th Light Infantry brigade in the Tet offensive at Long Binh, Vietnam, in February 1968 in which 14 Americans and about 900 attacking troops were killed.

General (Continental Army) was George Washington, appointed June 15, 1775, by the Second Continental Congress assembled at the State House, Philadelphia, Pa., and served until December 23, 1783. Congress resolved "that five hundred dollars per month be allowed for the pay and expenses of the general." Washington was made general and commander in chief of the army of the United Colonies and served without pay. *(Douglas Southhall Freeman—George Washington: A Biography)*

General killed in World War II. *See* World War II: American general killed in World War II

General of the Armies of the United States was General John Joseph Pershing, whose appointment was unanimously confirmed by the U.S. Senate on September 4, 1919. The position was created by "act relating to the creation of the office of General of the Armies of the United States" (41 Stat. L. 283), approved September 3, 1919. Pershing's was the only appointment under the act.

General of the Armies of the United States with the rank of 6 stars was George Washington, whose posthumous promotion to General of the Armies was signed by President Gerald Rudolph Ford on October 19, 1976. The appointment was authorized by a joint congressional resolution enacted October 11, 1976 (90 Stat. L. 2078), to take effect July 4, 1976.

General of the U.S. Army was Ulysses Simpson Grant, appointed July 25, 1866. He served until March 4, 1869, when he was inaugurated President of the United States.

General to be consecrated a bishop was Major General William Richard Arnold, former chief of chaplains of the United States Army, in active service as a major general in the inspector general's office when consecrated titular bishop of Phocaea on October 11, 1945, in St. Patrick's Cathedral, New York City, by Archbishop Francis Joseph Spellman.

The First

General to become a rear admiral was Samuel Powhatan Carter, who organized the Tennessee Brigade and became a brigadier general of volunteers May 1, 1862. He was breveted major general March 13, 1865, for gallantry and meritorious service and was mustered out of volunteer service January 15, 1866. On June 23, 1865, he was a lieutenant commander in charge of the gunboat *Monocacy* on the Asiatic station. He was appointed rear admiral May 16, 1882, and retired August 6, 1882.

General to command the forces of the United Nations in Korea was General Douglas MacArthur, who served as commander-in-chief from July 4, 1950, to April 10, 1951. The resolution of July 7, 1950, at the 476th meeting authorized the unified command, at its discretion, to use the United Nations flag in the course of operations against North Korean forces concurrently with the flags of the various nations participating. Lieutenant General Matthew Bunker Ridgway replaced MacArthur on April 11, 1951, by order of President Harry S Truman.

General who rose from draftee was Keith L. Ware, who was drafted November 23, 1940. He attended Officer's Candidate School, Fort Benning, Ga., and rose to commander of U.S. First Infantry Division in Vietnam, becoming brigadier general on November 28, 1967. He, his staff of 3 and 4 helicopter crewmen were killed on September 13, 1968, when his helicopter was shot down about 60 miles north of Saigon during the battle of Locninh. He was the fourth general killed in the Vietnam War.

Generals who were brother and sister were Elizabeth Paschel Hoisington of Newton, Kansas, sworn in June 11, 1970, as a brigadier general and her brother, Perry Milo Hoisington, who had been made a brigadier general in March 1958. Their two brothers and their father were also officers.

General wounded in action in World War II. *See* World War II: American general wounded in action in World War II

Generals to wear the five-star insignia as Generals of the Army were Henry Harley Arnold, Dwight David Eisenhower, Douglas MacArthur and George Catlett Marshall, whose appointments were ratified December 15, 1944, by the Senate. The grade of General of the Army was established by Public Law No. 482, approved by Act of Congress, December 14, 1944 (58 Stat. 802).

Judge advocate of the Continental Army was Lieutenant Colonel William Tudor, who served from July 29, 1775, to April 9, 1777. On August 1, 1776, he was made lieutenant colonel with the rank of judge advocate general.

The First

Judge advocate of the U.S. Army was Captain Campbell Smith of the 4th Infantry, who served from March 3, 1797, to March 16, 1802.

Lieutenant general was George Washington, appointed July 11, 1798, by President John Adams under authorization of the act of May 28, 1798 (1 Stat. L. 558), as lieutenant-general and commander-in chief of all the armies raised or to be raised for the service of the United States. He served from July 3, 1798 to December 14, 1799, when he died. He was authorized to receive a salary of $250 monthly, $50 monthly allowance for forage, and 40 rations per day, or money in lieu thereof at the current price.

Major (black) was Martin Robinson Delany, who received his commission on February 8, 1865. On April 5, 1865, he was ordered to report to Charleston, S.C. *(Alrutheus Ambush Taylor—The Negro in South Carolina During the Reconstruction)*

Major general of the Continental Army, next in rank to George Washington, was Artemas Ward, who was appointed on June 17, 1775, by an act of the Continental Congress, and who served until April 23, 1776, when he resigned with the rank of major general. *(Charles Martyn—The Life of Artemas Ward)*

Male nurse commissioned was Second Lieutenant Edward L. T. Lyon of Kings Park, N.Y., who was sworn in October 6, 1955, by First Army Surgeon Brigadier General Harold Willard Glattly in the chapel of St. Cornelius the Centurion on Governors Island, N.Y. The Army-Navy Nurses Act (61 Stat. L. 41) of April 16, 1947, was amended on August 9, 1955, by the Bolton Amendment (69 Stat. L. 579), which extended nurses' commissions to male personnel.

Mother and son to enlist simultaneously were Michael Fleming (17) and his mother, Ethel Fleming (34), who enlisted October 15, 1975, in Merced, Calif., as transportation specialists.

Naval ship christened by an Army officer. *See under Ship*

Paymaster of the U.S. Army was Caleb Swan, appointed May 9, 1792. His office was authorized by act of May 8, 1792 (1 Stat. L. 271). He resigned June 30, 1808. He received $60 a month and was required "to reside near the headquarters of the troops of the United States." The first Pay Department, by that name, was organized under the Act of April 24, 1816 (3 Stat. L. 297).

Paymaster general of the Continental Army was James Warren of Massachusetts, appointed June 27, 1775. On June 16, 1775, the Continental Congress established a separate department in the Army to take care of payments to troops. The department consisted of the paymaster general, who received $100 a month, and a deputy at $50 a month. Warren resigned April 19, 1776. *(Massa-*

The First

chusetts Historical Society—Warren-Adams Letters)

Quartermaster of the Continental Army was Major Thomas Mifflin, who served from August 14, 1775, to November 7, 1777. *(Lancaster County Historical Society Papers, 1889)*

Regimental Jewish chaplain was Rabbi Elkan Cohen Voorsanger, commissioned as chaplain first lieutenant November 15, 1917, in Paris, France. He served with the American Expeditionary Forces and was promoted to the grade of captain on February 22, 1919. The act of June 3, 1916 (39 Stat. L. 176), authorized the appointment of one chaplain for each regiment of cavalry, infantry, field artillery, and engineers, and 1,200 of coast artillery. The act of October 6, 1917 (40 Stat. L. 394), authorized the appointment of 20 chaplains-at-large.

Secretary of the Army (black) was Clifford Leopold Alexander, Jr., named January 18, 1977, by President Jimmy Carter and sworn in February 14, 1977. He served in the 569th Field Artillery Battalion, New York National Guard, and separated from the Army at Fort Dix, N.J., in February 1953.

Sergeant major of the Army was William O. Wooldridge, a native of Shawnee, Okla., who served in the U.S. Army starting in 1940, fought in World War II, in Korea, and in Vietnam, and was sworn in July 11, 1966, to present the enlisted man's point of view to the Army Chief of Staff, General Harold Keith Johnson.

Surgeon general of the Continental Army was Benjamin Church, who served from July 27, 1775, to October 16, 1775. He held the position of director general and chief physician and received $4-a-day compensation. On November 1, 1775, he was jailed for treason. *(Allen French—General Gage's Informers)*

Surgeon general of the U.S. Army to whom the title was officially applied was James Tilton of Delaware, who was physician and surgeon general of the U.S. Army from June 11, 1813, until June 15, 1815, when he was honorably discharged. His office was established by act of March 3, 1813 (2 Stat. L. 819). Tilton, in 1813, wrote *Economical Observations on Military Hospitals*, which was published at Wilmington, Del., by J. Wilson. The first medical officer to fill the position now known as surgeon general of the Army was Joseph Lovell, who served from April 18, 1818, until his death, October 17, 1836. His salary was $2,500 per annum. The position was authorized by act of April 14, 1818 (3 Stat. L. 426), an "act regulating the staff of the Army." *(Francis Bernard Heitman—Historical Register and Dictionary of the U.S. Army)*

Woman army officer (other than those in the Medical Department) to be sworn in in the regular U.S. Army was Colonel Mary Agnes Hallaren, who took the oath of office December 3, 1948.

The First

ARMY OFFICER—*Continued*
After the oath, Secretary of the Army Kenneth Claiborne Royall announced her selection as director of the Women's Army Corps, Regular Army. The ceremony took place in the office of General Omar Nelson Bradley, Army chief of staff, the oath being administered by Major General Edward Fuller Witsell, adjutant general.

Woman assistant army surgeon was Dr. Mary Edwards Walker, who served as a contract surgeon from March 11 to August 23, 1864, and from September 22, 1864, to June 15, 1865. She wore male attire. The Congressional Medal of Honor awarded her, January 24, 1866, was, by adverse action of the Board of Medal Awards, stricken from the list February 15, 1917, nothing having been found in the records to show the specific act or acts for which the decoration was originally awarded.

Woman doctor commissioned in the regular Army was First Lieutenant Fae Margaret Adams of San Jose, Calif., sworn in March 11, 1953, in Washington, D.C. Previously, she had been a WAC reserve medical officer. She obtained her degree under the GI Bill of Rights.

Woman officer in the Judge Advocate General's Department was Captain Phyllis Ladora Propp, who was detailed May 3, 1944. She was a WAC officer and served on active duty from October 3, 1942, to September 21, 1949.

Woman to be appointed a regular army officer (colonel) was Florence Aby Blanchfield, who on July 9, 1947, was appointed lieutenant colonel in the U.S. Army with permanent rank under authority of the Army Nurses Law of April 16, 1947. The ceremony was held at the Pentagon, Washington, D.C. General Dwight David Eisenhower, Chief of Staff, presented her with her commission. On June 1, 1943, she had been appointed superintendent of Army Nurses.

Woman to command an Armed Forces Examining and Entrance Station was Lieutenant Colonel Mattie V. Parker of Mount Olive, N.C., who assumed command of the Army Recruiting Command's Armed Forces Examining and Entrance Station, Detroit, on May 31, 1975.

Woman with rank corresponding to colonel in the United States Army was Julia Otteson Flikke, Army Nurse Corps, who received the relative rank of colonel, Army of the United States, on March 13, 1942. She was appointed to the Army Nurse Corps, March 8, 1918.

Woman with rank corresponding to major in the United States Army was Julia Catherine Stimson, superintendent of the Army Nurse Corps. Relative rank was conferred by Act of Congress, June 4, 1920 (41 Stat. L. 767).

The First

ARMY PARACHUTE TROOPS consisted of a test platoon of 2 officers and 48 men from the 29th Infantry who started training July 1, 1940. The first United States Army Parachute Battalion was the 501st, organized October 1, 1940, at Fort Benning, Ga., under the command of Major William Maynadier Miley.

ARMY RADIO CAR. *See* Radio car (military)

ARMY SCHOOL
Army school was the Military Academy of the United States, established at West Point, N.Y., by Act of Congress (2 Stat. L. 132) of March 16, 1802 for the purpose of educating and training young men in the theory and practice of military science. The first superintendent was Jonathan Williams, who served from April 15, 1802, to June 20, 1803, with the rank of major. He resigned, but at the request of President Thomas Jefferson returned to the same position on April 19, 1805, and served as lieutenant colonel until July 31, 1812, when he resigned. During the interim following his first resignation, the senior officers assumed command of the academy.

Army school graduate (black) was Henry Ossian Flipper, born a slave March 29, 1856, in Thomasville, Ga. He was appointed a second lieutenant in the Tenth Cavalry on June 15, 1877, and remained in service until June 30, 1882, when he was dismissed for conduct unbecoming an officer and a gentleman. In December 1976, the Army reviewed his court-martial charge and changed his discharge record from dishonorable to honorable. He was a cadet from May 20, 1873, to June 14, 1877. The first black admitted to the army school was James Webster Smith, who was appointed by Congressman Solomon Lafayette Hoge and who reported on May 31, 1870. *(Henry Ossian Flipper—The Colored Cadet at West Point).*

Army school graduate (Jewish) was Simon Magruder Levy of Maryland, a cadet from March 2, 1801, to October 12, 1802, when he was graduated and commissioned a second lieutenant in the Corps of Engineers. He was appointed a cadet for his good conduct as orderly sergeant at the Battle of Maumee Rapids, August 20, 1794. He resigned from the Army September 30, 1805, and died in 1807 in Georgia.

Army school graduate killed in military action was George Ronan. In the War of 1812 with Great Britain, he was engaged in Captain Nathan Heald's desperate battle near Fort Chicago, Ill., August 15, 1812, against a vastly superior force of Indians, when he was struck down—not, however, before killing 2 Indians in a hand-to-hand fight and continuing the struggle, on his knees and weak from loss of blood, until the last moment. *(George Washington Cullum—Biographical Register of the Officers and Graduates of the U.S. Military Academy)*

The First

Army school graduates were Joseph Gardner Swift of Massachusetts and Simon Magruder Levy of Maryland. Both men were graduated from the United States Military Academy at West Point, New York, on October 12, 1802. That same day they were appointed to the rank of second lieutenant. Levy resigned from the Army on September 30, 1805, because of his ill health. Swift, on November 11, 1813, was brevetted a·brigadier general for his heroism in the battle at Chrystler's Field, Williamsburg, in upper Canada. On February 19, 1814, he was promoted to brigadier general for his meritorious service in the defense of New York in the War of 1812. Swift became head of the Military Academy in 1816 and retired from the Army on November 12, 1818. He died in 1865. Levy and Swift were the only students to graduate of the original class of ten, which consisted of five men from Massachusetts, and one each from Connecticut, Maryland, Missouri, New York, and Virginia. *(George Washington Cullum—Biographical Register of the Officers and Graduates of the U.S. Military Academy)*

Army School graduates (Chinese) were Ying Shing Wen and Ting Chia Chen, who enrolled at West Point June 15, 1905, and were graduated from West Point June 11, 1909. As they were foreigners, they were not commissioned.

Army training school to teach security troops, federal and state, was the First Corps Area Tactical School, opened June 13, 1942, at Concord, Mass., under General Sherman Miles, commander of the First Corps Area. The instructors included army officers, scouting experts, and Bert "Yank" Levy, author of *Guerilla Warfare.*

Graduate of the U.S. Military Academy (West Point) killed in action in World War I was First Lieutenant Stewart Whiting Hoover of Blackfoot, Iowa. An infantry officer acting as captain, he was killed in an American sector trench in Lorraine (near Toul), France, on March 1, 1918. He entered the academy on June 14, 1913, and was graduated April 20, 1917.

Instructor nongraduate was Infantry Major Courtney Hicks Hodges, who served as assistant instructor of tactics at West Point from December 4, 1920, to September 1, 1924. On June 11, 1946, he assumed the post of commanding general of the First Army.

Instructor (woman) was Elizabeth Matthew Lewis, whose course EN392 "Introduction to Fine Arts, including art history, appreciation and related activities" began at West Point on February ?, 1968. She had served since November 6, 1967, as fine arts librarian.

Jewish graduate of the U.S. Military Academy. *See* Army school graduate (Jewish), above

The First

Jewish woman graduate of the U.S. Military Academy (West Point) was Cadet Donna Maller of Cockeysville, Md., one of 13 Jewish cadets (831 men, 63 women) who were graduated and commissioned June 4, 1980.

Woman cadet to receive a commission was Ms. Hollen of Altoona, Pa., who rated tenth in the class of 1980. She was commissioned second lieutenant at the U.S. Military Academy graduation at West Point, N.Y., on May 28, 1980.

Women cadets of the U.S. Military Academy (West Point) were accepted for admission on March 9, 1976, and enrolled on July 7, 1976. The 1980 class of 1,480 included 119 women. As of January 31, 1979, 64 women remained, making the attrition rate 46 percent. On May 28, 1980, 62 women were commissioned second lieutenants.

ARMY SCHOOL FOR CHAPLAINS. *See* Chaplains' school

ARMY SCHOOL OF NURSING. *See* Nursing school

ARMY SECRET SERVICE BUREAU was inaugurated in 1861 by President Abraham Lincoln, who appointed Allan Pinkerton to be in charge. The identity of Pinkerton, who was the first chief of this bureau, was not revealed, and he served as "Major Allan." He was attached to the staff of General George Brinton McClellan.

ARMY SURGEON. *See* Army officer: Surgeon general

ARMY UNIFORM was standardized by order of the Continental Army in October 1779, when Washington, as the commander in chief, prescribed a uniform through a general order. The coat was blue. The facings for the infantry were varied—white, buff, red, and blue; the artillery and artificers' coats were faced with scarlet and had scarlet linings; and the light dragoons' coats were faced with white and had white buttons and linings.

ARMY VOTE was tabulated in 1864. The soldiers in the field were allowed to vote in the election of November 8, 1864. Of a total of 150,635 votes cast by the soldiers, 116,887 were for Abraham Lincoln, Republican, and 33,748 for George Brinton McClellan, Democrat.

ARMY WAR COLLEGE

Army war college was authorized by War Department general orders No. 155 on November 27, 1901, to furnish advanced military instruction to regularly commissioned army officers; $20,000 was authorized by Congress, May 26, 1900 (31 Stat. L. 209). The first class of 16 officers was convened November 1, 1904, and terminated May 31, 1905. The first president was Major General Sam-

The First

ARMY WAR COLLEGE—*Continued*

uel Baldwin Marks Young, who served from July 10, 1902, to August 15, 1903. The cornerstone of the War College, Washington, D.C., was laid February 21, 1903, and the building opened June 20, 1907. Quarters were rented until the building was completed.

Army War College women graduates were Lieutenant Colonel Frances V. Chaffin of Washington, D.C., and Lieutenant Colonel Shirley Rowell Heinze of Houston, Tex., of the Women's Army Corps, who were graduated June 16, 1969, in a class of 224, at Carlisle, Pa.

ARSENAL of the U.S. Government was the Springfield Armory, Springfield, Mass. (originally established in April 1778 as a laboratory for the preparation of all kinds of ammunition), established April 2, 1794 (1 Stat. L. 352), as a National Armory for the manufacture of small arms. The manufacture of small arms began in 1795. The first superintendent was David Ames and the master armorer was Robert Orr. The first gunlock was filed by hand by Alexander Crawford after a struggle of three days. It took a month to complete 20 muskets. Only 245 were completed the first year. *(Moses King—Handbook of Springfield)*

ART AUCTION IN A DEPARTMENT STORE. *See* Business: Department store to hold a public art auction

ART COMMISSION (federal). *See* Fine Arts Commission (federal)

ART COMMISSION (public) and the first important commission for a painting with more than one figure was *The Last Supper,* an oil on canvas, 117½ inches wide and 35 inches high, by Gustavus Hesselius, commissioned September 5, 1721, by the Vestry of St. Barnabas' Church, Queen Anne's Parish, Prince Georges County, Md. It was put in place as an altarpiece on November 26, 1722. Hesselius was paid "£17 currt. money" for the painting and installation. *(Philadelphia Museum of Art,—Gustavus Hesselius, 1682–1755)*

ART COURSE

Art course in true fresco painting was offered September 14, 1936, by the Department of Fine Art, Louisiana State University, University, La. Two courses, mural painting and advanced mural painting, were offered by Conrad Albrizio. Students were required to mix and put up their own plaster.

Industrial camouflage course met October 15, 1940, at Kansas City Art Institute, Kansas City, Mo. The instructor was Keith Martin. No points or credits were given for the 12-week course.

ART DEPARTMENT IN A COLLEGE. *See* Fine arts department: Fine arts department in a college

The First

ART GALLERY (WPA). *See* Works Progress Administration: Works Progress Administration Federal Art Project Gallery

ART ORGANIZATION

Art organization of importance was the Pennsylvania Academy of Fine Arts, which was established in Philadelphia, Pa., on December 26, 1805, "to promote the cultivation of the Fine Arts in the United States of America, by introducing correct and elegant copies from works of the first masters in sculpture and painting." It was incorporated March 28, 1806. The first president of the Academy was George Clymer.

Artists' society of importance was the New York Drawing Association, organized November 8, 1825, in New York City. On January 18, 1826, 15 of the membership were empowered to select 15 other artists to form the National Academy of Design, which was incorporated April 5, 1828. Samuel Finley Breese Morse was elected president and Thomas Seir Cummings, treasurer; both served from January 18, 1826, to May 14, 1845. On April 7, 1906, the Society of American Artists merged with the academy, their members automatically becoming members of the academy *(Thomas Seir Cummings—Historic Annals of the National Academy of Design . . .)*

ARTICLES OF CONFEDERATION were adopted November 15, 1777, and were formally engrossed July 9, 1778, in Philadelphia, Pa. South Carolina was the first state to ratify them, February 5, 1778, and Maryland was the last of the 13 states to accept them, January 30, 1781. The articles as ratified by the 13 states were formally announced to the public on March 1, 1781. *(Merrill Jensen— The Articles of Confederation)*

ARTICS were patented on February 2, 1858, by Thomas Crane Wales of Dorchester, Mass., who obtained patent No. 19,269 on waterproofing boots and gaiters. They were originally known as Wales Patent Artic Gaiter. They were made then as now, of rubber and cloth and were both water proof and coldproof.

ARTIFICIAL BREEDING. *See* Animal breeding society: Artificial animal breeding cooperative society

ARTIFICIAL EYE. *See* Eye

ARTIFICIAL FERTILIZER. *See* Fertilizer (artificial)

ARTIFICIAL HEART was a spirally coiled glass tube and pump invented in 1935 by Dr. Alexis Carrel, assisted by Colonel Charles Augustus Lindbergh. The apparatus consisted of a culture chamber and the electrically operated glass pump. An extirpated organ was suspended in the culture chamber and the main artery and vein connected with the glass tubes of the pump, which circulated a nutritive fluid through the organ and kept it alive. The experiments were carried on at

The First

Rockefeller Institute in New York City. *(Science Magazine. Vol. 81, June 21, 1935)*

ARTIFICIAL INSEMINATION. *See* Impregnation

ARTIFICIAL LEG. *See* Leg (artificial) patent

ARTIFICIAL LIGHTING. *See* Acetylene; Electric lighting; Gas

ARTIFICIAL LIGHTNING. *See* Lightning (artificial)

ARTIFICIAL SNOW. *See* Snow

ARTIFICIAL TEETH. *See* Dentistry: Patent for artificial teeth

ARTIST
   See also

Engraver	Pastelist
Etcher	Sculptor
Lithograph	

American artist of importance was John Singleton Copley, who sailed from Boston, Mass., in 1774 for England, where he painted the portraits of the king and queen. *The Death of Chatham* is one of his most widely known works. He is credited with more than 269 oil paintings, 35 crayons, and 14 miniatures. *(Augustus Thorndike Perkins—A Sketch of the Life and Some of the Works of John Singleton Copley, R.A.)*

American artist to win distinction was Benjamin West, who on March 24, 1792, became president of the Royal Academy of London, succeeding Sir Joshua Reynolds. His first discourse to the students of the Royal Academy was delivered December 10, 1792. Born October 10, 1738, near Swarthmore, Pa., he went to Italy in 1760, arriving in Rome on July 10. He studied there for three years and afterward remained abroad. *(Henry Ezekiel Jackson—Benjamin West, His Life and Work)*

Artist successful in commercial art was Mathew Pratt, who painted signboards in Philadelphia, Pa., in 1768. He sailed from Philadelphia, Pa., for London on June 24, 1764, and studied under Benjamin West. On March 20, 1768, he sailed from Bristol, England, and returned to Philadelphia. *(William Sawitzky—Matthew Pratt, 1734–1805: A Study of His Work)*

Artist to arrive in America was Jacques Le Moyne de Morgues, who accompanied the French expedition to Florida in 1564 under Laudonnière. They sailed from Havre de Grace, France, April 20, 1564, and reached Florida (New France) June 22, 1564, remaining until September 25, 1565. Le Moyne's work consisted principally of scenic and historical views. *(Narrative of Le Moyne. Translated by Fred B. Perkins from the Latin of De Bry and printed for William Appleton—Boston, 1874)*

English artist in territory now a part of the United States was John White, governor of Sir Walter Raleigh's Virginia Colony, and grandfather of Vir-

The First

ginia Dare the first white child born in America. His drawings were made in Virginia and Florida from 1585 to 1590 *(Theodore de Bry—America)*

Woman painter (and the first pastelist in America) was Henrietta Johnston. She worked with colored chalk, producing most of her paintings between 1707 and 1720. Her subjects were mostly women of South Carolina, but her best work is a likeness, *His Excellency Robert Johnson, Captain General, Governor and Commander-in-Chief in and over His Majesty's Province of Carolina*, which was made in 1718. *(The Antiquarian. September 1928)*

ARTS AND LETTERS SOCIETY

Arts and letters society (national) was the American Academy of Arts and Letters, founded April 23, 1904 (incorporated April 17, 1916—39 Stat. L. 51), as a section of the National Institute of Arts and Letters. The latter organization was founded in September 1898 (incorporated February 4, 1913—37 Stat. L. 600). The first membership of the American Academy of Arts and Letters comprised William Dean Howells, Augustus Saint-Gaudens, Edmund Clàrence Stedman, John La Farge, Samuel Langhorne Clemens, John Hay, and Edward MacDowell. The first member added to the original group was Henry James, January 7, 1905. *(American Academy of Arts and Letters—Proceedings in Commemoration of the Twenty-Fifth Anniversary)*

Arts and letters society (national) gold medal special award. *See* Medal: Arts and letters society (national) gold medal special award

Black member of the National Institute of Arts and Letters was Dr. William Edward Burghardt Du Bois, head of the Department of Sociology at Atlanta University, Atlanta, Ga., who was elected to membership on December 22, 1943.

National Institute of Arts and Letters gold medal. *See under* Medal

Woman elected to the American Academy of Arts and Letters was Julia Ward Howe, author of "The Battle Hymn of the Republic," who was elected January 28, 1908. *(Laura Elizabeth Richards and Maud Howe Elliott—Julia Ward Howe, 1819–1910)*

Woman elected to the National Institute of Arts and Letters was Julia Ward Howe, who was elected January 25, 1907.

ARTS AND SCIENCE SOCIETY

Arts and science society (national) was the American Academy of Arts and Sciences, founded in Boston, Mass., and chartered on May 4, 1780, "to cultivate every art and science which may tend to advance the interest, dignity, honor and happiness of a free, independent and virtuous people." The first president was James Bowdoin, who served from 1780 to 1790. *(American Acade-*

The First

ARTS AND SCIENCE SOCIETY—*Continued*
my of Arts and Sciences—Centennial Volume,
Memoirs VII)

**Woman elected to the American Academy of
Arts and Sciences** was Maria Mitchell, elected
unanimously May 30, 1848. At Nantucket, Mass.,
she had discovered a telescopic comet on October
1, 1847, for which King Frederick VI of Denmark
had also presented her with a gold medal. *(Proceedings, American Academy of Arts and
Sciences. May 1890)*

ASHKENAZIC JEWISH CONGREGATION. *See*
Jewish congregation

ASPHALT PAVEMENT. *See* Road: Sheet asphalt
pavement

ASSAY OFFICE BUILDING (federal) was authorized March 3, 1853 (10 Stat. L. 212), and erected on Wall Street, New York City, in 1854. The
first assayer in charge was John Torrey. An assay
office was opened in Philadelphia, Pa., in 1828 as
a department of the Mint and not as a separate
institution (4 Stat. L. 278). The assay offices of the
government were placed under the Bureau of the
Mint when the bureau was authorized (12 Stat. L.
424), on February 12, 1873, to control all the mints
and assay offices. The first director of the Mint
was Henry Linderman. *(Jesse Paul Watson—The
Bureau of the Mint)*

ASSEMBLY, LEGISLATIVE. *See* Legislative assembly

ASSOCIATE JUSTICE (woman). *See* Judge

**ASSOCIATION FOR THE ADVANCEMENT OF
SCIENCE.** *See* Science association

ASTRONAUT
American astronaut to orbit the earth was Lieutenant Colonel John Herschel Glenn, Jr., of New
Concord, Ohio, who was blasted off at 9:48 A.M.
E.S.T. on February 20, 1962, from Cape Canaveral,
Fla., in an *Atlas D*, 93 feet high, with a 16-foot
maximum base diameter. The bell-shaped capsule, which weighed 4,265 pounds at launch, 2,987
pounds at orbit insertion, and 2,422 pounds on
recovery, traveled around the earth three times,
covering 83,450 miles at an average speed of 17,-
400 m.p.h. The capsule came down at 2:43 P.M. in
the Atlantic Missile Range and Glenn was taken
aboard the U.S.S. *Noa* at 3:04 P.M.

Astronaut (American) to be launched into space
was Commander Alan Bartlett Shepard, Jr. (U.S.
Navy). His capsule, *Freedom 7*, launched on May
5, 1961, by a Mercury-Redstone 3 rocket from
Cape Canaveral, Fla., reached a height of 1165
miles. The flight was a suborbital trip of 302 miles
and lasted 15 minutes 22 seconds. It was the first
U.S. manned suborbital flight.

Astronaut (American) to become a general was
Colonel James Alton McDivitt (U.S. Air Force),
who was nominated December 12, 1970, by Presi-

The First

dent Richard Milhous Nixon and promoted to the
temporary grade of brigadier general effective
March 1, 1972, with date of rank February 17, 1972.
McDivitt was commander of the *Apollo IX* flight,
March 3-13, 1969.

Astronaut (American) to become an admiral
was Alan Bartlett Shepard, Jr., whose date of rank
was December 1, 1971.

**Astronaut (American) to converse with an
aquanaut** while each performed in his respective
field was Lieutenant Colonel Leroy Gordon Cooper (U.S. Air Force), who spoke from spacecraft
Gemini V (GT-5), 100 miles above the earth on
August 29, 1965, on its 117th orbit, to Commander
Malcolm Scott Carpenter (U.S. Navy) in *Sealab 2*,
a 12-by-58-foot steel capsule, 205 feet beneath the
surface of the Pacific Ocean, about 1,000 yards off
La Jolla, Calif.

Astronaut (American) to die was Air Force Captain Theodore Cordy Freeman of Haverford, Pa.
who was killed October 31, 1964, at 8:50 A.M. at
Ellington Air Force Base, Houston, Tex., in a T-38
jet trainer that crashed into a snow goose, which
clogged the air ducts of the two jet engines. He
was graduated from the U.S. Naval Academy on
June 5, 1953, and was named on October 18, 1963
to the astronaut program.

**Astronaut (American) to make a suborbital
flight twice** was Virgil Ivan Grissom, who made a
302.5-mile flight at an altitude of 118 miles in 15
minutes 37 seconds in the *Liberty Bell 7*, launched
by a Mercury Redstone 4 rocket from Cape
Canaveral, Fla., at 8:20 A.M. E.D.T. on July 21, 1961.
His second trip was made in *Gemini III* (nick
named "Molly Brown"), launched by a solid-fuel
Titan 2 booster rocket from Cape Kennedy, Fla. at
9:24 A.M. E.D.T. on March 23, 1965. Lieutenant
Commander John Watts Young (U.S. Navy) was
also on this trip.

**Astronaut (American) to maneuver outside a
satellite** was Major Edward Higgins White, II
(U.S. Air Force), who opened the hatch of *Gemini
IV* (GT-4) at 3:42 P.M. E.D.T. on June 3, 1965
stepped out into space at a 120-mile altitude at
3:45 P.M., and remained outside 20 minutes until
4:05 P.M. attached to the craft by a 25-foot tether.
A hand-held 7.5-pound oxygen jet propulsion gun
operated by pressure on a trigger gave him control
over his movements. Command Pilot Major James
Alton McDivitt remained inside *Gemini IV*. The
satellite was launched June 3, 1965, at 11:16 A.M.
E.D.T. from Cape Kennedy, Fla., made 62 revolu
tions in a 97-hour 56-minute flight, and touched
down on June 7, 1965, at 1:14 P.M. E.D.T. in the
Atlantic Ocean, 40 miles from the original target
ed point and 56 miles from the U.S.S. *Wasp*, on
which the astronauts were landed by helicopter
55 minutes later.

The First

Astronaut (American) to orbit the earth on two trips was Lieutenant Colonel Leroy Gordon Cooper (U.S. Air Force), whose first trip was made from Cape Canaveral, Fla., May 15–16, 1963, in *Faith 7* (Project Mercury), when he made 22 orbits in 34 hours 19 minutes 45 seconds. His second flight was made August 21–29, 1965, when he and Lieutenant Commander Charles Conrad, Jr. (U.S Navy), made a two-man spaceflight of 120 orbits in 190 hours 55 minutes 14 seconds in *Gemini V* (GT-5).

Astronaut (American) to orbit the earth six times was Walter Marty Schirra, Jr., who on October 3, 1962, made a 9-hour 13-minute flight from Cape Canaveral, Fla., in *Sigma 7*, launched by a 4,325-pound Mercury-Atlas rocket. The spacecraft had an apogee of 176 miles and a perigee of 100 miles. It landed at a predetermined point, 5 miles from target, in the Pacific Ocean, and Schirra and the spacecraft were aboard the carrier U.S.S. *Kearsarge* within 40 minutes.

Astronaut (American) to orbit the earth 22 times was Major Leroy Gordon Cooper (U.S. Air Force), launched on May 15, 1963, at 8:04 A.M. E.S.T. in *Faith 7*, a Mercury-Atlas IX project, from the Atlantic Missile Range, Cape Canaveral, Fla. The launch vehicle was a Atlas D with a 16-foot maximum base diameter, 93 feet high, with an approximate lift-off weight of 260,000 pounds. After a 34-hour 20-minute flight, it splashed down in the Pacific Ocean near Midway Island at 7:24 P.M. E.D.T. on May 16, 1963. The spacecraft was recovered at 8:00 P.M. E.D.T. and placed aboard the U.S.S. *Kearsarge.*

Astronaut (American) to travel over 700 hours in space was James Arthur Lovell, Jr. (U.S. Navy), who logged 715 hours 4 minutes 54 seconds in four flights; 330 hours 35 minutes 1 second in *Gemini VII*, December 4–18, 1965; 94 hours 34 minutes 31 seconds in *Gemini XII*, November 11–15, 1966; 147 hours 41 seconds in *Apollo VIII*, December 21–27, 1968; and 142 hours 54 minutes 41 seconds in *Apollo XIII*, April 11–17, 1970.

Astronaut (American civilian) to orbit the earth was Neil Alden Armstrong, who orbited for 10 hours 42 minutes in *Gemini VIII*, launched at 9:00 A.M., March 16, 1966, from Complex 14, Cape Kennedy, Fla. The satellite achieved the world's first docking in space and was hoisted aboard the U.S.S. *Leonard F. Mason* on March 17, 1966. Major David Randolph Scott, U.S. Air Force, accompanied him.

Astronaut (black) selected for the manned orbiting laboratory program at El Segundo, Calif., was Captain Edward Joseph Dwight, Jr. (U.S. Air Force), of Kansas City, Mo., who was appointed March 31, 1961.

The First

Astronaut (black) to qualify for the training course was (U.S. Air Force) Major Robert Henry Lawrence, Jr., of Chicago, Ill., selected June 30, 1967, by the Defense Department for the manned orbiting laboratory program at El Segundo, Calif. He was killed December 8, 1967, in a training trip in an F-104 that crashed on the runway at Edwards Air Force Base in California. Captain Edward Joseph Dwight, Jr. (U.S. Air Force), of Kansas City, Mo., had been selected March 31, 1963, but Lawrence was the first to qualify for the training course.

Astronaut international rescue agreement was the Agreement on the Rescue of Astronauts, the Return of Astronauts and the Return of Objects Launched into Outer Space signed by Secretary of State Dean Rusk at a ceremony held on April 22, 1968, and ratified by the Senate on October 8, 1968, by a vote of 66 to 0. President Lyndon Baines Johnson announced on December 3, 1968, that it was in force. The signatories were the United States, the United Kingdom, and the Union of Soviet Socialist Republics.

Astronauts chosen by the National Aeronautics and Space Administration for Project Mercury were trained at the Langley Research Center, Hampton, Va. The selection of the seven men was announced April 7, 1959. They were Air Force Captains Leroy Gordon Cooper, Jr., of Carbondale, Colo.; Virgil Ivan Grissom of Mitchell, Ind.; and Donald Kent Slayton of Sparta, Wis.; Navy Lieutenants Malcolm Scott Carpenter, of Boulder, Colo.; and Walter Marty Schirra, Jr., of Hackensack, N.J.; Navy Lieutenant Commander Alan Bartlett Shepard, Jr., of East Derry, N.H.; and Lieutenant Colonel of Marines John Herschel Glenn, Jr., of New Concord, Ohio.

Astronauts (American) in orbit to transfer from one spacecraft to another were Russell Louis Schweickart, civilian, and Colonel James Alton McDivitt (U.S. Air Force), who made an intravehicular transfer from "Gumdrop," the *Apollo IX* command ship, to "Spider," the lunar module on March 6, 1969, leaving Colonel David Randolph Scott (U.S. Air Force), the pilot, alone in the command ship. A Saturn 5 rocket launched the satellite at 11:00 A.M. on March 3, 1969, from Cape Kennedy, Fla. It redocked at 2:00 P.M. It made a 10-day orbit (241 hours 40 minutes 53 seconds) and landed March 13, 1969, in the Atlantic Ocean, 250 miles east southeast of Bermuda, where it was picked up by helicopter and transferred to the U.S.S. *Guadalcanal* 3 miles away.

Astronauts (American) on the moon to retrieve an object were U.S. Navy commanders Charles ("Pete") Conrad, Jr., and Alan La Vern Bean, who on November 19, 1969, recovered a piece of the unmanned Surveyor 3, which had landed on the Ocean of Storms of the Moon on April 19, 1967. They were two of the three astronauts on *Apollo*

The First

ASTRONAUT—*Continued*

XII—Commander Richard Francis Gordon, Jr. (U.S. Navy) remained in the command module. *Apollo XII* was launched November 14, 1969. It made the second astronaut lunar landing. Splashdown took place on November 24, 1969, after a 244-hour 36-minute 25-second flight.

Astronauts (American) to die in a spacecraft were Lieutenant Colonel Virgil Ivan Grissom (U.S. Air Force), Lieutenant Colonel Edward Higgins White, II (U.S. Air Force), and Lieutenant Commander Roger Bruce Chaffee (U.S. Navy), who died on January 27, 1967, when a flash fire caused by electrical arcing erupted inside the *Apollo I* spacecraft command module on the ground at the Kennedy Space Center, Cape Kennedy, Fla. The astronauts had been participating in a simulation of the *Apollo I* flight scheduled for February 21, 1967. (Astronauts Elliot See, Jr., and Charles Bassett, II, had been killed February 28, 1966, in a T-38 jet trainer that crashed into the roof of the McDonnell Aircraft Corporation building in St. Louis, Mo., injuring 12 workmen.)

Astronauts (American) to exceed 2,000 hours flight time were Lieutenant Colonel Gerald Paul Carr (U.S. Marine Corps), Dr. Edward George Gibson, civilian scientist, and Lieutenant Colonel William Reid Pogue, (U.S. Air Force), crew of *Skylab 4*, the third manned Skylab launch, whose flight time was approximately 2,017 hours 16 minutes (November 16, 1973–February 8, 1974) from Cape Canaveral, Fla.

Astronauts (American) to land at night were Colonel Frank Borman (U.S. Air Force), Captain James Arthur Lovell, Jr. (U.S. Navy), and Major William Alison Anders (U.S. Air Force), who took off at 7:51 A.M. (10:51 A.M. E.S.T.) from Cape Kennedy, Fla., on December 21, 1968, in satellite *Apollo VIII* and circled the moon 10 times in 20 hours. They plunged back into the atmosphere at 24,530 miles an hour and landed at 10:51 A.M. E.S.T. on December 27, 1968, when it was still dark, splashing down in the Pacific Ocean about 4 miles from the carrier U.S.S. *Yorktown*, about 1,000 miles southwest of Hawaii. They remained in their cone-shaped spacecraft 90 minutes and were on board 1 hour 14 minutes after contact. They were as close as 70 miles to the moon.

Astronauts (American) to land on the moon were civilian Neil Alden Armstrong, flight commander; Lieutenant Colonel Edwin Eugene Aldrin, Jr., lunar module *(Eagle)* pilot; and U.S. Air Force Lieutenant Colonel Michael Collins command module *(Columbia)* pilot. They were lifted off in *Apollo XI* at 9:32 A.M. E.D.T. by a Saturn 5 launch vehicle on July 16, 1969, from Kennedy Space Center, Fla. (Cape Canaveral). At 4:17:40 P.M., Sunday July 20, 1969, the four-legged lunar module *(Eagle)* touched down on the moon's Sea of Tranquility. At 10:56 P.M. Armstrong placed his

The First

foot on the moon and said: "That's one small step for man, one giant leap for mankind." He was joined on the lunar surface by Aldrin at 11:14 P.M. They placed a plaque on the moon and erected an 8-foot aluminum staff with a 3-foot by 5-foot nylon United States flag. Collins remained in the spacecraft. At 1:34 P.M., Monday, July 21, 1969, the *Eagle* lifted off the lunar surface. The *Columbia* splashed down at 12:50 P.M. E.D.T. on Thursday, July 24, in the Pacific Ocean, about 920 miles southwest of Hawaii. The astronauts were taken on board the *Hornet* at 2:12 P.M. and entered a Mobile Quarantine Facility where they remained until August 11th.

Astronauts (American) to orbit the earth 200 times were Major Frank Borman (U.S. Air Force) and Lieutenant Commander James Arthur Lovell, Jr., (U.S. Navy), in *Gemini VII* (GT-7), launched December 4, 1965, at 2:30 P.M. E.S.T., from Cape Kennedy, Fla. After a flight of 206 revolutions in 330 hours 35 minutes, they landed on December 18, 1965, at 9:06 A.M. E.S.T., about 700 miles southwest of Bermuda, only 7.6 miles from target and were taken aboard the carrier U.S.S. *Wasp*.

Astronauts (American) to orbit the moon were Colonel Frank Borman (U.S. Air Force), Captain James Arthur Lovell, Jr. (U.S. Navy), and Major William Alison Anders (U.S. Air Force), who made 10 lunar orbits in *Apollo VIII* (AS-503), launched by a three-stage Saturn 5 rocket from Pad 39A Complex 39, Cape Kennedy, Fla., at 7:51 A.M. E.S.T. on December 21, 1968. The spacecraft reentered the atmosphere and splashed down in the Pacific Ocean 147 hours 11 seconds later, approximately 5,100 yards from the U.S.S. *Yorktown*. They were picked up by a helicopter and were safe aboard the ship at 12:20 P.M. E.S.T. on December 27, 1968.

Astronauts (American) to participate in an international spaceflight were the commander Brigadier General Thomas Patten Stafford, docking module pilot Donald Kent ("Duke") Slayton, and command module pilot Vance Devoe Brand, who took off from Cape Kennedy, Fla., on July 15, 1975, at 3:30 E.D.T. and returned July 24, 1975, traveling 217 hours, 28 minutes, and 24 seconds, for the Apollo-Soyuz Test Project (ASTP). Their craft *(Apollo XVIII)* docked with the Russian spacecraft *(Soyuz XIX)*, manned by Aleksei Arkhipovich Leonov and Valery Nikolayevich Kubasov, on July 17, 1975.

Astronauts (American) to remain one day on the moon were U.S. Navy commanders Charles ("Pete") Conrad, mission leader, and Alan La Vern Bean, lunar landing pilot. With Commander Richard Francis Gordon, Jr., commander module pilot, they were blasted off in *Apollo XII* by a Saturn 5 rocket from Cape Kennedy, Fla., at 11:22 A.M. E.S.T. on Friday, November 14, 1969. At 11:40 P.M. on November 18, 1969, the lunar module *In-*

trepid pulled away from the command module and at 1:53 A.M., November 19, 1969, landed on the moon's Ocean of Storms. Conrad, followed by Bean, walked on the moon. At 3:21 A.M. on November 20, 1969, they reentered the lunar module. They took off at 9:23 A.M. on November 20, 1969, and rejoined *Apollo XII,* piloted by Commander Gordon, splashing down 400 miles from Samoa on November 24, 1969. The feat required 244 hours 36 minutes 25 seconds. The astronauts were picked up by helicopters and delivered on board the U.S.S. *Hornet.* At 9:10 A.M. E.S.T. on November 29, 1969, they were received at Ellington Air Force Base, Houston, Tex., where they were placed in quarantine.

Astronauts (American) to rendezvous in space were Captain Walter Marty Schirra, Jr., (U.S. Navy), and Major Thomas Patten Stafford (U.S. Air Force), who took off December 15, 1965, at 8:43 A.M. from Cape Kennedy, Fla., in *Gemini VI* (GT-6) to meet *Gemini VII* (GT-7) orbiting Major Frank Borman (U.S. Air Force) and Lieutenant Commander James Arthur Lovell, Jr. (U.S. Navy) The two *Geminis* flew in formation within 20 to 100 feet of each other for 5 hours 16 minutes, during which the astronauts photographed each other's craft, sighted a fire in Madagascar, and conversed. *Gemini VI* reentered the atmosphere and landed December 16, 1965, after 25 hours 52 minutes (16 revolutions), impacting in the Atlantic Ocean 7.6 miles from the aiming point. The capsule was hoisted aboard the U.S.S. *Wasp.*

Astronauts (American) to ride a vehicle on another planet were U.S. Air Force Colonel David Randolph Scott and Lieutenant Colonel James Benson Irwin, who on July 31, 1971, rode the four-wheeled electric cart Rover, a LRV (Lunar Roving Vehicle), alongside the 1,200-foot-deep canyon Hadley Hills on the moon. With Major Alfred Merrill Worden, they were launched on July 26, 1971, at 9:34 A.M. from Cape Kennedy, Fla., in *Apollo XV* and landed on August 7, 1971.

Astronauts (women) selected by the National Aeronautics and Space Administration (NASA) were announced on January 16, 1978. Six women were among the 35 selected from the 3,000 applications. The women were Anna L. Fisher of Rancho Palos Verdes, Calif.; Shannon W. Lucid of Oklahoma City, Okla.; Judith A. Reznik of Akron, Ohio; Sally K. Ride of Stanford, Calif.; Margaret R. Seddon of Memphis, Tenn.; and Kathryn D. Sullivan of Paterson, N.J.

Space flight by an American astronaut was made by Commander Alan Bartlett Shepard, Jr., whose 15-minute suborbital flight in a capsule rocketed by a Redstone missile with about 75,000 pounds of thrust took place on May 5, 1961. The capsule, weighing slightly more than 2,000 pounds, made a 302-mile trip downrange from Cape Canaveral, Fla., at a ground speed of 4,500

m.p.h.; it reached an altitude of 115 miles before reentering the earth's atmosphere. Shepard experienced a 5-minute period of weightlessness.

See also Medal: National Aeronautics and Space Administration Distinguished Service Medal

Space-to-ground news conference telecast took place at 7:30 P.M. E.S.T. on November 23, 1969, when the Yankee Clipper *Apollo XII* was 108,000 miles from earth traveling to earth at 3,670 m.p.h. Commanders Charles ("Pete") Conrad, Jr., Alan La Vern Bean, and Richard Francis Gordon, Jr. answered questions submitted in writing by reporters at the Manned Spacecraft Center, Houston, Tex., to Lieutenant Colonel Gerald P. Carr (U.S. Marine Corps), who read them to the astronauts. *Apollo XII* took off November 14, 1969, and splashed down on November 24, 1969, after a 244-hour 36-minute 25-second trip, and the astronauts were taken by helicopter to the U.S.S. *Hornet.*

Three-man spaceflight (American) was made by Captain Walter Marty Schirra, Jr. (U.S. Navy), Major Donn Fulton Eisele (U.S. Air Force), and Major Ronnie Walter Cunningham (U.S. Marine Corps), who flew 4.5 million miles, circling the earth 163 times in 260 hours 8 minutes 45 seconds in *Apollo VII.* The satellite was launched by a 1-B Saturn rocket at 11:03 A.M. E.D.T. on October 11, 1968, from Cape Kennedy, Fla., and orbited the earth every 90 minutes at an altitude of 140-183 miles at 17,500 miles an hour. It landed one third of a mile from the target point, 325 miles south of Bermuda, at 7:11 A.M. E.D.T. October 22, 1968. The descent required 29 minutes, and the capsule was picked up by a helicopter from the U.S.S. *Essex* about 8 miles away.

Two-man spaceflight (American) of 3 orbits was made March 23, 1965, by Lieutenant Commander John Watts Young (U.S. Navy) and Major Virgil Ivan Grissom (U.S. Air Force), in a *Gemini III* satellite (GT-3) nicknamed "Molly Brown," launched by a Titan 2 rocket from Cape Kennedy, Fla., at 9:24 A.M. E.S.T. They made three orbits of the earth in a 4 hour 53 minute flight. The Titan 2 was 89 feet high with a 10-foot diameter and a lift-off weight of 337,349 pounds. The bell-shaped payload weighed 7,136 pounds, and was 18 feet 5 inches high with a 10-foot base diameter. It impacted in the Atlantic Ocean, 58 miles short of goal and was picked up by helicopters and taken aboard the aircraft carrier U.S.S. *Intrepid.*

Two-man spaceflight (American) of 62 orbits was made by Command Pilot Major James Alton McDivitt (U.S. Air Force) and Pilot Major Edward Higgins White (U.S. Air Force), who took off June 3, 1965, at 11:16 A.M. E.D.T. in the *Gemini IV* (GT-4) from Cape Kennedy, Fla., and made 62 revolutions in 97 hours 56 minutes in a bell-shaped payload weighing 7,879 pounds, which was 18 feet 5

The First

ASTRONAUT—*Continued*
inches high with a 10-foot base diameter. The launching vehicle, Titan 2, was 89 feet high with a 10-foot diameter and a lift-off weight of 336,000 pounds. The apogee was 175 miles, the perigee 100 miles. The capsule landed June 7, 1965, at 1:13 P.M. E.D.T., 48 miles short of destination in the Atlantic Ocean, and McDivitt and White were hoisted aboard the carrier U.S.S. *Wasp* about 40 minutes later.

Two-man spaceflight (American) of 120 orbits was made by Lieutenant Colonel Leroy Gordon Cooper, Jr. (U.S. Air Force) and Lieutenant Commander Charles Conrad, Jr. (U.S. Navy), who took off August 21, 1965, in a *Gemini V* (GT-5) from Cape Kennedy, Fla., made 120 revolutions of the earth in 190 hours 56 minutes and landed at 8:56 A.M. E.D.T. August 29, 1965, in the Atlantic Ocean, about 760 miles east of Cape Kennedy, where they were picked up by helicopter and brought to the aircraft carrier U.S.S. *Lake Champlain*. The apogee was 217 miles, the perigee 101 miles. The total weight of the capsule was 7,947 pounds, which included the reentry and adapter modules.

ASTRONOMER
Astronomer of note in the American colonies was John Winthrop of Cambridge, Mass., who made sunspot observations on April 19, 20, and 22, 1739. No observations were made on April 21, as it was cloudy. The observations consist of one-page reports in the University Archives, Harvard University Library, and have never been published.

Astronomer to acquire fame after the Revolution was Nathaniel Bowditch, who in 1802 wrote *The New American Practical Navigator, being an epitome of navigation, containing all the tables necessary to be used with the nautical almanac in determining the latitude and the longitude by lunar observations, and keeping a complete reckoning at sea,* published in Newburyport, Mass. This book corrected over 8,000 errors in other works and was adopted by the U.S. Navy Department as the standard authority on navigation. *(Henry Ingersoll Bowditch—Sketch of the Life and Character of Nathaniel Bowditch)*

Astronomer to measure the size of a fixed star was Dr. Francis Gladheim Pease, who on December 13, 1920, at Mount Wilson Observatory, Mount Wilson, Calif., measured Betelgeuse, the bright red star in the right shoulder of Orion, by means of an inferometer designed by Professor Albert Abraham Michelson. He found the star to be 260 million miles in diameter. *(Astrophysical Journal. Vol. 53. 1921)*

Woman astronomer employed in the U.S. Naval Observatory was Eleanor Annie Lamson, a graduate of George Washington University, Washington, D.C., who was employed on July 20, 1900, and who served until her sudden death, July 27, 1932.

The First

She computed all the results for gravity determination made by Dr. Felix Andries Vening-Meinesz's observations on his submarine cruise to the West Indies and was working on the reports of his second expedition, the East Indian cruise, at the time of her death.

ASTRONOMICAL OBSERVATIONS BOOK was James Melville Gillis' *Astronomical Observations made at the Naval Observatory, Washington, under Orders of the Honorable Secretary of the Navy, Dated August 13, 1838.* It consisted of 671 pages and was a catalog of 1,248 stars. It was printed in Washington, D.C. *(National Academy of Science—Biographical Memoirs, Vol. 1)*

ASTRONOMICAL OBSERVATORY. *See* Observatory; Planetarium

ASTRONOMY
Meteoric display ("shooting stars") on record was observed by Andrew Ellicott on November 12, 1799, off the Florida Keys. The "whole heaven appeared as if illuminated with sky rockets, flying in an infinity of directions, and I was in constant expectation of some of them falling on the vessel. They continued until put out by the light of the sun after day break." *(Andrew Ellicott—The Journal of Andrew Ellicott)*

Motion picture of an eclipse of the sun taken from a dirigible. *See under* Motion picture

Planet (asteroid) named for an American President was Hooveria. It was discovered in March 1920 by Professor Johann Palisan of the University of Vienna, Austria, and named for Herbert Hoover, who at that time was engaged in feeding the distressed European peoples.

Planet found beyond Neptune was Pluto, discovered at the Lowell Observatory, Flagstaff, Ariz., February 18, 1930, by Clyde William Tombaugh, on plates made in a systematic long-continued search begun under the direction of the late Dr. Percival Lowell, who had mathematically predicted and located the planet many years before, almost exactly in the position where found. The announcement was withheld even after it had been observed many times and completely checked, until March 13, 1930, the anniversary of Lowell's birth (and of Herschel's discovery of Uranus). *(Scientific Monthly. Vol. 34. January 1932)*

ASTRONOMY EXPEDITION to record an eclipse of the sun consisted of Professors Samuel Williams, Stephen Sewall, James Winthrop, Fortesque Vernon, and six students, who were sent, October 9, 1780, from Harvard College, Cambridge, Mass., to Penobscot Bay. The Commonwealth of Massachusetts supplied a boat. Although the country was at war with Britain, the British officer in command at Penobscot Bay permitted the expedition to land and observe the eclipse of October 27, 1780, which lasted from

The First

11:11 A.M. to 1:50 P.M. *(American Academy of Arts and Sciences—Memoirs, 1785)*

ASTRONOMY MAGAZINE presenting a popular exposition of astronomy was *The Sidereal Messenger,* published by Ormsby MacKnight Mitchel, editor and director of the Cincinnati Observatory. It cost $3 a year. The first issue was published July 1846 by Derby Bradley & Company, Cincinnati, Ohio, and consisted of eight pages. Publication ceased October 1848.

ATHEISM SOCIETY of importance was the American Association for the Advancement of Atheism, the first society in the United States to use the word atheism or any of its forms as a title. The society was organized in New York City in October 1925, and was incorporated November 16, 1925, in New York State. The charter was at first denied by the Supreme Court. The first president of the association was Charles Smith. *(American Association for the Advancement of Atheism—Annual Report. Vol. 1)*

ATHLETE

Athlete presented with the Associated Press Athlete of the Year award was John Leonard ("Pepper") Martin of the St. Louis Cardinals for his performance against the Philadelphia Athletics in the World Series, October 1–10, 1931.

Athlete to win the James E. Sullivan Memorial Trophy of the Amateur Athletic Union of the United States. *See* Sports Trophy: Sports trophy for the outstanding amateur athlete of the year

Black to win the James E. Sullivan Memorial Trophy, the top award for United States amateur athletes, presented annually since 1930 by the Amateur Athletic Union, was Malvin Greston (Mal) Whitfield of the Los Angeles Athletic Club, a half-miler, who was the first choice on 252 of 657 ballots cast by a nationwide tribunal of sports authorities and tabulated on December 30, 1954. Whitfield set the Olympic record for 800 meters in London in 1948 and held the world 880-yard record and the 600-yard indoor record.

Black woman awarded the James E. Sullivan Memorial trophy was Wilma Rudolph Ward of Clarksville, Tenn., the amateur athlete who did the most to advance good sportsmanship throughout the year. The presentation was made February 23, 1962, at the New York Athletic Club, New York City. She was winner of three Olympic gold medals in track at the 1960 Olympic Games in Rome.

Two-time winner of the Associated Press Athlete of the Year award was J Donald ("Don") Budge on August 3, 1938 (for the year 1937) and on December 12, 1938 (for the year 1938). In 1938, he received 26 firsts (122 points) while Henry Armstrong, the boxer, received 19 firsts (104 points) in the voting.

The First

ATHLETIC ASSOCIATION. *See* Intercollegiate athletic association; Sports: Athletic club

ATHLETIC CLUB. *See under* Sports

ATHLETIC COMPETITIONS. *See* Sports; also *see under* specific headings, *e.g.,* Olympic games

ATHLETIC GAMES. *See* Sports; also *see under* specific headings

ATHLETICS DEPARTMENT. *See* Physical culture department

ATLANTIC CABLE. *See* Cable

ATLANTIC OCEAN BROADCAST. *See* Radio broadcast: Transatlantic broadcast

ATLANTIC OCEAN FLIGHT. *See* Aviation—Flights (transatlantic); Aviation—Pilot: Pilot to fly 100 times across the Atlantic Ocean

ATLANTIC OCEAN SCHEDULED AIR SERVICE. *See* Aviation—Flights (transatlantic)

ATLAS issued by a state was *The Atlas of the State of South Carolina, made under the authority of the Legislature; prefaced with a geographical statistical and historical map of the state.* It was prepared under the direction of Robert Mills and printed for the state in 1825 by John D. Toy, Baltimore, Md. It contained a map of the state of South Carolina and 28 district maps scaled 21 miles to the inch, which were engraved by H. S. Tanner and assistants. The atlas was 18 inches by 24 inches and included the location of the roads, rivers, bridges, ferries, factories, taverns, many of the plantations, etc.

ATOMIC BOMB

Atomic bomb detonation from a captive balloon telecast. *See under* Television—Telecast

Atomic bomb dropped from an airplane over water was released from *Dave's Dream,* an Air Force B-29 Superfortress, on June 30, 1946 (21:01 Greenwich Civil Time), over the Bikini Lagoon in the Pacific Ocean. The shot, designated "Able," was part of Operation Crossroads. It had a 520-foot height of burst and caused the sinking of 2 transports (the *Gilliam* and the *Carlisle*) and damage to 18 other ships, which were among a group of 73 vessels used as a target.

Atomic bomb explosion occurred July 16, 1945 (12:29:15 G.C.T.), in a desert area at Alamogordo Air Base, 120 miles southeast of Albuquerque, N.Mex. The shot, designated "Trinity," was part of Operation Trinity. It was a tower shot with 100-foot height of burst.

Atomic bomb explosion over enemy territory took place on August 6, 1945, over Hiroshima, Japan, from the *Enola Gay,* a B-29 airplane. The pilot was Colonel Paul Warfield Tibbets, Jr., of Miami, Fla., and the bombardier was Major Thomas W. Ferebee of Mocksville, N.C. *(William Leonard*

The First

ATOMIC BOMB—*Continued*
Laurence—Dawn Over Zero: The Story of the Atomic Bomb)

Atomic bomb underground explosion was detonated November 29, 1951 (19:59:59.7 G.C.T.), at Frenchman Flat, Nev., and witnessed by a group consisting of some members of Congress and some military officers headed by Chief of Staff General Joseph Lawton Collins. The explosion, which caused a hole about 800 feet in diameter and 100 feet deep, was designated as "Uncle," a part of Operation Buster-Jangle.

Atomic bomb underwater explosion took place July 24, 1946 (20:35 G.C.T.), in the Pacific Ocean, 3 miles off Bikini. The bomb was dropped from an airplane at a height of 7,000 feet and exploded 90 feet underwater. The shot, designated "Baker," was part of Operation Crossroads. It resulted in the sinking of ten vessels (including the battleship *Arkansas*) that were set up as a target.

Atomic explosion witnessed by troops as part of a war maneuver was designated "Dog." It was part of Operation Buster-Jangle, which took place November 1, 1951 (15:30:01.6 G.C.T.), in New Mexico. The 11th Airborne Division of Camp Campbell, Ky., witnessed the airdrop explosion.

Atomic fusion (thermonuclear or hydrogen) bomb was detonated October 31, 1952 (19:14:59.4 G.C.T.), and designated as "Mike" of Operation Ivy. It was a tower shot with a burst of 20 feet at the Elugelab Atoll at the Eniwetok Proving Ground, Marshall Islands.

Atomic fusion (thermonuclear or hydrogen) bomb dropped from an airplane exploded May 20, 1956 (17:50:38.7 G.C.T.) over Namu Atoll at the northwest edge of the Bikini Atoll. It was designated as "Cherokee," a part of Operation Redwing. It created a fireball four miles in diameter.

Rocket with an atomic warhead. *See under* Rocket

ATOMIC-BOMB-RESISTANT FEDERAL BUILDING. *See* Building

ATOMIC CANNON. *See* Ordnance

ATOMIC ELECTRIC-GENERATING STATION (full-scale). *See* Electric power plant

ATOMIC ENERGY
Atomic electric-generating station (full-scale). *See under* Electric power plant

Atomic energy peacetime production was undertaken by Clinton Laboratories, Chicago, which delivered one millicurie of carbon 14 to Barnard Free Skin and Cancer Hospital, St. Louis, Mo., on August 2, 1946. The radioactive carbon has a half-life of 10,000 to 25,000 years and gives off millions of beta particles. It was a white powder, in a quantity too small to be seen by the naked eye,

and was placed in aluminum and steel containers.

Atomic-powered cruiser. *See under* Ship

Atomic-powered merchant ship. *See under* Ship

Atomic-powered submarine. *See under* Submarine

Electric power from nuclear energy was obtained through the use of Experimental Breeder Reactor I (EBR-I), placed in operation during the summer of 1951 at the National Reactor Testing Station operated by the United States Atomic Energy Commission near Idaho Falls, Idaho. EBR-I is a fast breeder reactor designed and operated by the Argonne National Laboratory, Argonne, Ill. The core in use at the time of the first production of electricity enabled the reactor to produce 1,400 thermal kilowatts and 150 electrical kilowatts. On December 20, 1951, the reactor supplied steam to a turbo-generator which produced electrical energy of more than 100,000 watts to operate the pumps and other reactor equipment and to provide light and electrical facilities for the building in which the reactor was housed.

Electric power generated from atomic energy to be sold commercially. *See under* Electric power plant

Electric power generated from atomic energy to illuminate an entire town. *See under* Electric power plant

Self-sustaining nuclear chain reaction demonstration was made December 2, 1942, by Enrico Fermi and his staff at the Metallurgical Laboratory of the University of Chicago, Chicago, Ill., before approximately 40 persons, when energy of the atom was released and controlled. Atomic particles known as neutrons, spontaneously released by atoms of metallic uranium or uranium oxide, embedded in a suitable pattern throughout a block of graphite, were permitted to collide with neighboring atoms of uranium or uranium oxide, causing these neighboring uranium atoms to split. The uranium atoms thus split released additional neutrons, which caused further similar reactions with still other uranium atoms, and so on at a rapidly increasing rate.

ATOMIC ENERGY COMMISSION
Atomic Energy Commission was established by the Atomic Energy Act, approved August 1, 1946 (60 Stat. L. 755), which created a five-man commission of civilians to develop and utilize atomic energy toward improving the public welfare, increasing the standard of living, strengthening free competition in private enterprise, and promoting world peace. The commission, appointed October 28, 1946, by President Harry S. Truman and confirmed April 9, 1947, by the Senate, consisted of chairman David Eli Lilienthal, Robert Fox Bacher, Sumner Tucker Pike, Lewis Lichtenstein Strauss, and William Wesley Waymack. The first meeting was held November 13, 1946.

The First

Atomic Energy Commission black member was Dr. Samuel Milton Nabrit, a biologist, of Houston, Tex., who served from August 1, 1966, to August 1, 1967

Atomic Energy Commission Patent Compensation Board award was made November 21, 1951, to Cyril Elwin McClellan of Glen Burnie, Md., who was awarded $7,500 for a method of separating isotopes used at the Brookhaven National Laboratory, Upton, Long Island, N.Y. The invention was assigned to the Atomic Energy Commission. McClellan applied for a patent December 22, 1942. It was placed under security order but was removed February 18, 1949.

Atomic Energy Commission woman chairman was Dr. Dixy Lee Ray, marine biologist and educator, who became chairman on February 6, 1973. She had served as a commissioner from August 8, 1972. Ray was also the first woman to be named to a full term on the commission.

Atomic Energy Commission woman member was Dr. Mary Ingraham Bunting, a biochemist and president of Radcliffe College, who was sworn in June 29, 1964, at Washington, D.C., by President Lyndon Baines Johnson and served until June 30, 1965.

Hospital completely devoted to the study of the atom in the treatment of cancer. *See* Hospital: Hospital completely devoted to the study of the atom in the treatment of cancer

ATOMIC ENERGY MUSEUM. *See* Museum

ATOMIC POWER
Lighthouse (atomic powered). *See* Lighthouse: Lighthouse (atomic powered)

ATOMIC POWER CLOCK. *See* Clock

ATOMIC REACTOR
Atomic reactor for research and development designed to determine the feasibility of plutonium-containing fuels for power reactors reached criticality on November 25, 1960. This reactor was part of the Plutonium Recycle Program (PRP) conducted by the General Electric Company for the Atomic Energy Commission at the Hanford Atomic Products Operation, Richland, Wash. The use of plutonium-239 as an enrichment material instead of uranium-235 would permit the operation of enriched-fuel reactors without dependence on expensive uranium isotope separation facilities. It would increase the amount of energy recovered from a given amount of raw uranium and provide a way of utilizing for peaceful purposes plutonium not needed for weapons use.

Atomic reactor in medical therapy was the Atomic Energy Commissions' Brookhaven National Laboratory unit in Upton, near Brookhaven, N.Y., placed in operation February 15, 1951.

The First

Atomic reactor (large) to specifically produce power was the Submarine Thermal Reactor, placed in operation on May 31, 1953, at the U.S. Atomic Energy Commission's Idaho Operations Office near Idaho Falls, Idaho. It was a landlocked submarine hull, *Mark 1,* the prototype of the Nautilus engine, and was a joint development of the Westinghouse Electric Corporation and the Argonne National Laboratory.

Atomic reactor patent was No. 2,708,656 on May 17, 1955, granted to Enrico Fermi of Santa Fe, N.M., and Leo Szilard of Chicago, assigned to the United States of America as represented by the United States Atomic Energy Commission. The application was filed December 19, 1944.

Atomic reactor (privately operated) was the Raleigh Research Reactor, Raleigh, N.C., placed in operation September 5, 1953, by the North Carolina State College of Agriculture and Engineering and the University of North Carolina. Completely independent of the Atomic Energy Commission and other federal government financial support, the reactor is free of secret or classified data and is available without restriction to the general public for observation and to students and staff for study and research.

Atomic reactor system to be patented by a private company was a water-boiler type invented by John William Flora of Canoga Park, Calif., who on May 17, 1960, received U.S. patent No. 2,937,127, assigned to North American Aviation, Inc. The reactor, 8 feet high and 8 feet in diameter, was built by Atomics International, a division of North American Aviation, Inc. It was fueled by enriched uranium in solution.

Atomic reactor to produce plutonium was placed in operation in September 1944 at the Manhattan district, U.S. Army Corps of Engineers' Hanford Engineering Works, Richland, Wash. The Hanford plant was originally constructed and operated by the E. I. du Pont de Nemours Company and was valued at $347 million. Since 1946 the plant has been operated by the General Electric Company and has been expanded to represent an investment of $1,136,500,000.

Commercial atomic energy reactor was the $57 million Yankee Atomic Electric Company's plant at Rowe, Mass., on the Deerfield River, which produced power for distribution on November 10, 1960. The company was formed by 12 New England utility companies, which signed a contract on June 4, 1956, with the Westinghouse Electric Corporation, principal contractor. The reactor became critical on August 19, 1960. This pressurized light water reactor produced 135,000 kilowatts of atomic-fueled electricity.

Graphite reactor with a sizeable power output was an X-10 installed at the Oak Ridge National Laboratory, Oak Ridge, Tenn., on November 4,

The First

ATOMIC REACTOR—*Continued*

1943, principally for research and radioisotope production. (This was the second reactor constructed.)

Military nuclear power plant designed for air shipment of major components was dedicated at the U.S. Army Engineer Research and Development Laboratories, Fort Belvoir, Va., on April 29, 1957, by Secretary of the Army Wilber Marion Brucker. The Army Package Power Reactor, designated the SM-1, was the result of studies initiated in 1952 to determine the feasibility of applying nuclear power to military uses. The first plant, serving as a prototype, was a pressurized-water type producing 1,855 kilowatts of electricity. A single core loading operates the plant from 1½ to 2 years at a power factor of 0.8. The plant was designed and constructed by Stone and Webster Engineering Corporation and Alco Products, Inc.

Nuclear reactor built for private industrial research was a 50,000-watt research reactor (L-47) designed and built by Atomics International, a division of North American Aviation, Inc., which began operating June 28, 1956. The reactor is located on the campus of the Illinois Institute of Technology, Chicago, Ill., and is operated by the Armour Research Foundation. It is of the "solution" type, fueled by enriched uranium, with a reactor core surrounded by graphite bars arranged in a stack (8 feet by 5 feet by 5 feet) that acts as a reflector. The rate of fission in the reactor is controlled by four boron bars. The reactor produces neutrons and gamma rays and is not used to generate electrical power. It cost about $700,000. Twenty-four industrial companies contributed about $20,000 each toward the total cost. The first director of the project was Dr. Richard Franklin Humphreys.

Plutonium-fueled nuclear reactor to produce useful amounts of electricity was installed in the experimental reactor of the Argonne National Laboratory's Idaho division, near Idaho Falls, Idaho. It was announced June 30, 1963.

Sodium reactor (experimental) (SRE) was built by Atomics International, a division of North American Aviation, Inc., for the Atomic Energy Commission in the Santa Susana Mountains, about 30 miles northwest of Los Angeles, Calif. The atomic power reactor went critical on April 25, 1957. It generates about 6,000 kilowatts of electricity.

Submarine with two nuclear reactors. *See under* Submarine

Thorium-uranium reactor (privately owned) to supply light and power was designed and fabricated by the Babcock and Wilcox Company for the Consolidated Edison Company's Indian Point nuclear electric-generating station at Buchanan, N.Y., a 275,000 kilowatt plant built at a cost of

The First

$100 million. This was the first reactor designed to supplement fissionable uranium-235 with fertile thorium-232. Construction began January 28, 1958.

ATOMIC VESSELS. *See* Navy: Atomic submarine division; also *see under* Ship; Submarine

ATTACHÉ, NAVAL. *See* Naval officer

ATTORNEY GENERAL

Assistant attorney general (state) who was a woman was Ella Louise Knowles (later Mrs. Henry Joseph Haskell), who was admitted to the Montana bar on December 28, 1889. In 1892 she was a candidate for attorney general on the Populist ticket. She ran 5,000 votes ahead of her ticket in a state casting only 50,000 votes. Her Republican opponent, Henry Joseph Haskell, who won the election and whom she later married, appointed her assistant attorney general.

Attorney General of the United States was Edmund Jennings Randolph, who was appointed by President Washington on September 26, 1789, entered on his duties on February 2, 1790, and served till January 1, 1794. The office was created by act of Congress September 24, 1789 (1 Stat. L. 73), an "act to establish the Judicial Courts of the United States." His salary was $1,500 a year. He was required to provide his own quarters, law books, fuel, furniture, and stationery, and to pay a law clerk. In 1814, the attorney general became a member of the President's Cabinet. *(Albert George Langeluttig—Department of Justice of the United States)*

Attorney general (U.S.) to be incarcerated was John Newton Mitchell who entered the federal minimum security prison at Maxwell Air Force Base, near Montgomery, Ala., on June 21, 1977. He was the 25th person convicted for participating in the Watergate debacle.

Attorney general (U.S.) to plead guilty to a criminal offense was Richard Gordon Kleindienst of Arizona the 68th attorney general, who served from June 12, 1972, to April 30, 1973, when he resigned. He refused to tell the Senate investigating committee about presidential pressure affecting the International Telephone and Telegraph Corporation.

Attorney general (U.S.) whose father also served as attorney general was William Ramsey Clark of Texas, sworn in March 10, 1967, at Washington, D.C. His father, Thomas Campbell Clark of Texas, who served from June 30, 1945, to August 22nd, 1949, administered the oath to his son.

Black Assistant Attorney General (U.S.) was William Henry Lewis of Boston, Mass., who was appointed Assistant U.S. Attorney General by President William Howard Taft. Lewis served from March 26, 1911, to April 1, 1913.

The First

Opinion by a U.S. Attorney General was rendered by Edmund Randolph to the Secretary of the Treasury on August 21, 1791, the government at that time being in Philadelphia, Pa. The opinion held that interest on certificates issued pursuant to the Act of Congress passed August 4, 1790, was not allowable and the courts would embarrass a system of finance by a determination in favor of interest for the year 1791. *(U.S. Justice Department —Digest of the Official Opinions of the Attorneys General of the U.S., 1885)*

State attorney general (woman) was Anne X Alpern, commissioned attorney general of Pennsylvania at Harrisburg on January 20, 1959. She served to August 28, 1961. (X was her middle initial and middle name.)

ATTORNEY OF THE UNITED STATES

Attorney of the United States was Samuel Sherburne, Jr., of New Hampshire, who was appointed United States attorney in and for the New Hampshire District on September 26, 1789. Twelve other attorneys, one for each state district, were appointed on the same date.

United States attorney (black) was Cecil Francis Poole, who was sworn in July 6, 1961, at San Francisco, as U.S. attorney for the northern district of California. He retired February 3, 1970. Poole was the first black to hold the position in continental United States but was preceded by four others for the Virgin Islands.

AUCTION. *See* Book auction; Philatelic auction, etc.

AUCTION BRIDGE. *See* Bridge (game)

AUCTION OF ART OBJECTS BY A DEPARTMENT STORE. *See* Business: Department store to hold a public art auction

AUDIENCE PARTICIPATION TELECAST. *See* Television—Telecast

AUDION TUBE. *See* Radio Tube: Three-element vacuum tube

AUGER (screw auger) was manufactured in 1810 by Walter French in Seymour, Conn. He was also the first to put a screw point on augers. Previously, only pod augers without screws had been used and a gouge was required to start the hole before an auger could be made to work. *(Connecticut Magazine. July 1900)*

AUREOMYCIN

Aureomycin chlortetracycline, the first broad-spectrum antibiotic, was released to the American physician in November 1948. It was developed and produced by Lederle Laboratories, a division of American Cyanamid Company, Pearl River, N.Y. Discovered by Dr. Benjamin Minge Duggar, the antibiotic is a yellow crystalline substance obtained from a mold named *Streptomyces aureofaciens*. *(Annals of New York Academy of Sciences. Vol. 51, p. 175. November 1948)*

The First

AURORA BOREALIS display recorded in America took place in New England on December 11, 1719. "This evening, about eight o'clock, there arose a bright and red light in the E.N.E. like the light which arises from an house when on fire (as I am told by several credible persons who saw it, when it first arose) which soon spread itself through the heavens from east to west, reaching about 43 or 44 degrees in height, and was equally broad." *(Massachusetts Historical Society Collections, Vol. II)*

AUSTRALIAN BALLOT SYSTEM. *See under* Election law

AUTHOR

Author to win a Pulitzer Prize in both fiction and poetry was Robert Penn Warren, whose *All the King's Men* won the 1947 fiction award and whose *Promises: Poems 1954–1956* won the poetry award in 1958.

Author whose livelihood was obtained exclusively by writing was Charles Brockden Brown of New York and Philadelphia. His first book was *Alcuin, a Dialogue,* one of the earliest known works by an American championing the rights of women. It was published anonymously and was first announced April 28, 1798, by T. & J. Swords, New York City. His first novel was *Wieland, or the Transformation,* which was published in New York City in 1798. The scenes were set on the banks of the Schuylkill, and the complications were mainly created by ventriloquism. The book was the first American example of the Gothic horror novel. *(David Lee Clark—Charles Brockden Brown, Pioneer Voice of America)*

Sportswriter was Henry William Herbert, who used the nom de plume Frank Forester, and who acquired fame in 1834 as an authority on outdoor sports. *(David Wright Judd—Life and Writings of Frank Forester)*

Successful woman serial writer was Anna Sophia Winterbotham Stephens, whose poems "The Tradesman's Boast" and "The Polish Boy," published in 1834, brought her fame. She edited *Peterson's Magazine* and *Godey's Lady's Book,* and was the author of 30 books, many of which appeared as serials.

Woman author in America is claimed to be Anne (Dudley) Bradstreet, whose poems were printed in 1640 in a volume entitled *Several Poems, compiled with great variety of Wit and Learning, full of delight; wherein especially is contained a compleat Discourse and Description of the Four Elements, Constitutions, Ages of Man, and Seasons of the Year, together with an exact Epitome of the Three first Monarchies, viz; The Assyrian, Persian, and Grecian; and the beginning of the Roman Commonwealth to the end of their last King, with divers other pleasant and serious Poems; by a Gentlewoman of New England.* She

The First

AUTHOR—*Continued*
was the daughter of Governor Thomas Dudley and wife of Governor Simon Bradstreet, both of Massachusetts. *(Samuel Eliot Morison—Builders of the Bay Colony)*

Woman author to make writing a profession was Hannah Adams. Her income from this source was very limited. In 1784 her first book appeared, *Alphabetical Compendium of the Various Sects which Have Appeared from the Beginning of the Christian Era to the Present Day. (Dedham Historical Register, July 1896)*

AUTOBANK. *See* Bank

AUTOGIRO
Autogiro was a C8 Mark II designed and built by Juan de la Cierva, which was brought to this country by Harold Frederick Pitcairn and arrived at Bryn Athyn, Pa., on December 17, 1928. The first autogiro to be flown in America, the C8 Mark II, which was remodeled from an English biplane, was piloted by Pitcairn on December 19, 1928. Pitcairn formed the Pitcairn-Cierva Autogiro Company of America for licensing the manufacture of the autogiro in this country. On January 19, 1931, the name of the company became Autogiro Company of America. The plane was presented to the Smithsonian Institution on July 22, 1931. *(The Autogiro—Pitcairn-Cierva Autogiro Company of America)*

Autogiro licensed for commercial use was the Pitcairn PCA-2, built by the Pitcairn Aircraft Company, Inc., Willow Grove, Pa., which received Approved Type Certificate on April 2, 1931. It had two seats in tandem, the front one designed for two people. Its Wright Whirlwind 300 h.p. engine had a cruising speed of 24 m.p.h. The four-bladed rotor was 43 feet in diameter and each blade was fitted with a hydraulic damper. The plane had both drag and flapping hinges, and weighed 2,094 pounds empty, 2,598 pounds fully loaded.

Autogiro mail delivery. *See under* Airmail service

Autogiro manufactured in the United States was a Pitcairn-Cierva, equipped with Wright J5 motors, which was completed on October 28, 1929, by the Pitcairn-Cierva Autogiro Company of America under license. On January 19, 1931, the name of the company became the Autogiro Company of America. *(The Autogiro—Pitcairn-Cierva Autogiro Company of America)*

Autogiro manufactured with a closed cabin was the Kellett Convertible K2 model, powered with a 165 h.p. Continental engine, which was flown October 21, 1931, at the Philadelphia Municipal Airport, Philadelphia, Pa. It had a door which opened part of the roof, and a window on the pilot's side. It seated two passengers and could be transformed into an open model at will.

The First

Autogiro of the U.S. Government was the XOP-1, U.S. Navy experimental rotary wing aircraft, ordered at a cost of $29,500 from the Pitcairn Aircraft Company, Inc., Philadelphia, on January 22, 1931. It was delivered June 1, 1931, to Washington, D.C., and flown at the Anacostia Station, where it remained aloft 30 minutes. It had a 300 h.p. Wright J-6 motor, a speed of 123 m.p.h., and a ceiling of 16,400 feet. It was a two-seater and weighed 2,807 pounds.

Autogiro patent was U.S. Patent No. 2,155,409 on an "aircraft with autorotative wings" granted posthumously to Juan de la Cierva of Madrid, on April 25, 1939. It was assigned to the Autogiro Company of America. The patent was applied for on January 15, 1936.

Autogiro rotary-wing aircraft fellowship was the Juan de la Cierva Fellowship, established at the College of Engineering, New York University. The first recipient of the fellowship was Samuel B. Sherwin of New York City, who enrolled September 8, 1939.

Autogiro to land and take off from a ship (aircraft carrier) was an XOP-1 built by the Pitcairn Aircraft Company, Inc., Philadelphia. It made three successful landings and takeoffs on September 23, 1931, using the airplane carrier U.S.S. *Langley* off Norfolk and Cape Henry, Va., as its base. Lieutenant Alfred Melville Pride (U.S. Navy) of the experimental division of the Hampton Roads Naval Air Base made the first flight and three subsequent flights, each with a different passenger. No landing crew was required.

Autogiro to land on the White House lawn was a Pitcairn-Cierva piloted by James Garrett Ray of Philadelphia, Pa., who landed April 22, 1931. He was presented with the 1930 Collier Trophy by President Herbert Hoover.

Autogiro to land packages on a moving ship was piloted by James Garrett Ray of the Pitcairn Company, Philadelphia, Pa. He lowered several rolls of film to the *Ile de France* on April 30, 1931, as the departing steamer left New York City for Europe.

Autogiro to loop the loop publicly was demonstrated by John MacDonald Miller at the National Air Races, Cleveland, Ohio, August 27, 1932.

Autogiro to tow a glider was piloted by John MacDonald Miller at Valley Stream, L.I., N.Y., on May 23, 1933. The glider was piloted by Jack O'Meara.

Autogiro used commercially was the *Detroit News No. 2*, a Pitcairn PCA-2, powered by a Wright 300 h.p. motor, manufactured by the Pitcairn Aircraft Company, Inc., Willow Grove, Pa., which was flown on February 12, 1931, from Pitcairn Field, Willow Grove, Pa., to the *Detroit News*, Detroit. The autogiro was demonstrated publicly on February 15, 1931.

The First

Autogiro (wingless direct-control) for military purposes was the KD-1, a two-place open-cockpit tandem-type with dual controls, manufactured by the Kellett Autogiro Corporation, Philadelphia, Pa., in 1934. Control was accomplished by means of the rotor system, which was inclined by moving the control stick in conventional manner. The autogiro had a gross weight of 2,050 pounds and a cruising range of 3½ hours—361 miles. It was first flown December 9, 1934, at the Philadelphia Airport, Philadelphia, Pa.

Autogiro with side-by-side seating arrangement was a Kellett Autogiro K2 model with a 165 h.p. Continental engine. The design was planned January 13, 1931, and the ship was completed and tested April 17, 1931, at the Philadelphia Municipal Airport, Philadelphia, Pa.

Parachute jump from an autogiro. *See under* Aviation—Parachute

Pilot of an autogiro carrying a passenger was Amelia Earhart, who flew a PCA-2 Pitcairn Autogiro at Pitcairn Field, Willow Grove, Pa., on December 19, 1930. She made several trips with various passengers and flew until dark.

AUTOGIRO—FLIGHTS

Autogiro flight was at Pitcairn Field, Willow Grove, Philadelphia, on December 19, 1928. It was brought to this country by Harold Frederick Pitcairn, who formed the Pitcairn-Cierva Autogiro Company of America for licensing the manufacture of the autogiro in this country. On January 19, 1931, the name of the company became Autogiro Company of America. *(The Autogiro—Pitcairn-Cierva Autogiro Company of America)*

Autogiro solo flight by a woman was made by Amelia Earhart, who flew a PCA-2 Pitcairn Autogiro at Pitcairn Field, Willow Grove, Pa., on December 18, 1930.

Autogiro transcontinental flight made by a woman was made May 29, 1931, by Amelia Earhart (Amelia Earhart Putnam), who took off in a Pitcairn PCA-2 from Newark Airport, N.J., and landed at Los Angeles, on June 7, 1931.

Intercity autogiro flight was made by Harold Frederick Pitcairn, who flew a Cierva autogiro on May 13, 1929, from Philadelphia to Langley Field, Va., where it was exhibited and tested at the fourth annual meeting of the National Advisory Committee for Aeronautics.

Transcontinental autogiro flight was made by John MacDonald Miller, who left Pitcairn Field Willow Grove, Philadelphia, Pa., in *The Missing Link* (PCA-2) May 14, 1931. Many stops were made en route to California to exhibit the machine. The autogiro landed May 28, 1931, at the North Island Naval Air Station, San Diego, Calif.,

The First

and May 29, 1931, at Los Angeles Municipal Airport.

AUTOGRAPH TIME RECORDER. *See* Time recorder

AUTOMAT (restaurant). *See* Restaurant

AUTOMATED SUBWAY TRAIN. *See* Subway

AUTOMATIC AIRCRAFT CANNON. *See* Ordnance

AUTOMATIC COMPUTING SCALE. *See* Scale

AUTOMATIC HEADLIGHT CONTROL. *See under* Headlight

AUTOMATIC PARKING METER. *See* Parking meter (automatic)

AUTOMATIC PILOT. *See under* Aviation

AUTOMATIC RECORD CHANGER. *See under* Phonograph

AUTOMATIC RIFLE. *See* Ordnance: Semiautomatic rifle

AUTOMATIC TELEPHONE. *See* Telephone

AUTOMATIC TIMER
Prizefight timed by automatic timer. *See under* Prizefight

AUTOMATIC TOLL COLLECTOR. *See* Toll collector (automatic)

AUTOMATON
Automaton was imported from England on May 3, 1743, and was exhibited by Mr. Pacheco of New York City, who charged one shilling one pence admission. It performed "several strange and diverting motions to the admiration of the spectators" and was advertised in the *New York Weekly Journal* of July 18, 1743.

Automaton to operate by long-distance control, electronically geared to duplicate simultaneously the exact motions of a master machine at long distances, was the machine nicknamed Yes Man. The automaton was made by the General Electric Company's General Engineering Laboratory, Schenectady, N.Y., for the Aircraft Nuclear Propulsion Department under contract with the U.S. Air Force, and its manufacture was announced on May 23, 1956. It was designed to perform remote-control mechanical jobs in dangerously radioactive areas from any required distance.

AUTOMOBILE
Air-conditioned automobile was manufactured by the Packard Motor Car Company, Detroit, Mich., and publicly exhibited November 4–12, 1939, at the 40th Automobile Show, Chicago, Ill. Air in the car was cooled to the temperature desired, dehumidified, filtered, and circulated.

The First

AUTOMOBILE—*Continued*
Heat was provided in the winter. The refrigerating coils were located behind the rear seat in an air duct, with heating coils in another compartment of the same duct. The capacity of the unit was equivalent to 1.5 tons of ice in 24 hours when the car was driven at 60 m.p.h., or 2 tons at 80 m.p.h.

Armored car was designed by Colonel Royal Page Davidson in May 1898. A Colt automatic machine gun was mounted on the car, which was intended for military use. The automobile was manufactured by the Duryea Automobile Company of Peoria, Ill., and was used by the Northwestern Military and Naval Academy of Lake Geneva, Wis.

Armored commercial car was employed by Brink's Incorporated, Chicago, Ill., in 1918. It had one thickness of armor-plate steel, but was not of all-steel construction throughout.

Armored commercial car completely protected was put in service February 1, 1920, by Michael Francis Sweeney of the Sweeney Detective Bureau, Inc., St. Paul, Minn. Construction was started in March 1919 by the Boyd Auto Shops, Minneapolis, Minn. The side walls and roof were steel, welded-steel construction; no wooden walls or roof supports were used. The glass was "polished plate wired glass." Hinged steel plates were placed over the windshield and window glass. They were so arranged that the tripping of a catch caused the steel plates to cover the glass windows and windshield.

Army armored car. *See* Army armored car unit; Army armored tank

Artmobile was conceived and designed by the Virginia Museum of Fine Arts, Richmond, Va., and began its tours on October 13, 1953, at Fredericksburg, Va., with an exhibition of art objects. It was an all-aluminum trailer weighing over 5 tons, measuring 34 feet in length and 7 feet 10 inches in height on the inside. When set up for exhibitions, it required a space 60 by 35 feet.

Automobile-airplane combination was the Arrowbile, built by the Waterman Arrowplane Corporation, Santa Monica, Calif., completed for testing February 20, 1937. Delivery of five Arrowbiles was made August 15, 1937, to the Studebaker Corporation, South Bend, Ind. In the air, its top speed was 120 m.p.h. and its cruising speed was 105 m.p.h. It had a 6-cylinder Studebaker engine that developed 100 h.p.

Automobile exhibited at a circus. *See* Circus: Circus to feature an automobile as an attraction

Automobile (gasoline-electric combination) was placed in service about 1910. It was equipped with the Owen magnetic drive and a generator in a combined unit.

The First

Automobile (new-type gasoline-electric combination) was delivered on August 30, 1929, to Colonel Edward Howland Robinson Green by the General Electric Company of Schenectady, N.Y. It was capable of developing 60 h.p. and had no clutch or gear-shifting device. There were only two foot pedals, one at the left for the brake and the other at the right for acceleration. To start the car the driver stepped on the starting button and then fed the engine gas.

Automobile regularly made for sale was manufactured by the Duryea Motor Wagon Company, which was organized in Springfield, Mass., in 1895. Charles Edgar Duryea, America's pioneer automobile manufacturer, began building his automobile in August 1891. It was completed at his shop, 47 Taylor Street, Springfield, Mass., and successfully operated April 19, 1892.

Automobile slung beneath airplane fuselage in flight. *See* Aviation—Flights: Airplane flight with an auto slung beneath the fuselage

Automobile snow cruiser. *See* Snow cruiser (automobile)

Automobile to exceed the speed of a mile a minute was driven on November 16, 1901, by A. C. Bostwick on a straightaway course at Ocean Parkway, Brooklyn, N.Y., in a race sponsored by the Long Island Automobile Club. He covered the distance in 56 2/5 seconds. This record was held only a few minutes, as Henry Fournier lowered it to 51 4/5 seconds in a 40 h.p. gasoline automobile, and Foxhall Keene lowered it to 54 3/5 seconds. Both Fournier and Keene raced in French automobiles. Bostwick used a 40 h.p. Winton. *(Smithsonian Institution—Smithsonian Report for 1901)*

Automobile to exceed the speed of 200 m.p.h. was a 1,000 h.p. *Mystery Sunbeam* driven by Major Henry O'Neil de Hane Segrave on March 29, 1927, at Daytona Beach, Fla., at an average speed of 203.79 m.p.h. both ways. *(Henry O'Neil de Hane Segrave—The Lure of Speed)*

Automobile to exceed the speed of 300 m.p.h. was a Bluebird Special driven by Sir Malcolm Campbell, who on September 3, 1935, at Bonneville Salt Flats, Utah, drove a mile at the rate of 304.331 m.p.h., and made a return run at 298.013 m.p.h., an average speed of 301.1292 m.p.h.

Automobile to exceed the speed of 400 m.p.h. was a Railton Mobil Special, driven by John Rhodes Cobb on September 16, 1947, at Bonneville Salt Flats, Utah, on a 14-mile straightaway. His speed was 385.645 m.p.h. in the first test and 403.135 m.p.h. in the second.

Automobile with a circulating lubrication system was the Autocar model of 1904, manufactured at Ardmore, Pa.

The First

Automobile with left-hand steering was the Northern four-cylinder car of 1907, manufactured by the Northern Motor Car Company of Detroit, Mich. The automobile was also equipped with air brakes. The designer of these improvements was Charles Brady King, one of America's pioneer automobile inventors.

Automobiles ordered for the U.S. War Department were purchased in 1899 from the Woods Motor Vehicle Company of Chicago, Ill. "The automobiles were provided for ordinary horse transportation when they serve to furnish electrical power in the field for use of telegraphy, telephony, signal lights, etc., while, when circumstances permit, the same power is available for transportation itself."

Collection and delivery of mail in automobiles. *See under* Postal service

Diesel-engine automobile. *See* Diesel engine: Diesel-engine automobile trip

Electric storage battery automobile was designed by William Morrison and built by Morrison & Schmidt, Des Moines, Iowa, in the summer of 1891. It was powered by 24 storage battery cells, placed under the seats, which took 10 hours to charge, and could run continuously for 13 hours. It carried 12 people, had a 4 h.p. motor, and was capable of a speed of 14 m.p.h. It was sold to J. B. McDonald, president of the American Battery Company of Chicago, in 1892. *(Scientific American. January 9, 1892)*

Electric taxicabs were introduced in New York City in the spring of 1897 by the Electric Vehicle Company, whose office and garage were located at 1684 Broadway, New York City. *(Horseless Age. Vol. 3, No. 7. October 1898)*

Field hospital automobile with X-ray equipment was designed at Lake Geneva, Wis., by Colonel Royal Page Davidson and was first used in May 1915 at the Northwestern Military Academy, Lake Geneva, Wis. The necessary electric current was generated by the automobile motor.

Foreign automobile exhibited was displayed at the World's Fair in Chicago in 1893 by Karl Benz of Germany. It was built by Gottlieb Daimler of Germany and was named after his daughter, Mercedes.

Free-piston automobile was the XP-500, an advanced-design experimental model built by the research staff of the General Motors Corporation, Detroit, Mich. The first public announcement was made April 15, 1956; the first public display took place May 16, 1956, at the dedication of the GM Technical Center. The engine had two horizontal cylinders, each containing two opposed pistons. These cylinders and pistons served to produce hot gases which turned a turbine wheel geared to the rear wheels of the car. The engine generated 250 h.p.

The First

Front-wheel-drive subcompact American automobile was the World Car built by the Ford Motor Company's Fort Wayne, Mich., plant. The first car off the assembly line was driven on August 11, 1980, by John Barson, president of the United Auto Workers Local 900.

Gas-turbine automobile was the XP-21 Firebird, built by the General Motors Corporation, and tested by Mauri Rose in October 1953 at the GM Proving Ground, near Milford, Mich. Its first public appearance was January 21–26, 1954, at the GM Motorama, Waldorf Astoria Hotel, New York City. A 370 h.p. Whirlfire turbo-power jet was installed in the rear of the car. The total weight of the engine unit, including the gasifier and the power sections, was 775 pounds, the overall weight of the entire car being 2,500 pounds. It had a plastic body and accommodated only the driver. Its speed was 150 m.p.h., but it was believed capable of 235 m.p.h. Since it consumed fuel faster than conventional cars, it was not commercially produced.

Gas-turbine automobile operated on city streets was a 1955 Plymouth sedan that was first operated in Detroit, Mich., on April 19, 1955.

Miniature automobile manufactured in the United States was offered for sale by Powell Crosley, Jr., on April 28, 1939. It had an 80-inch wheelbase and was 10 feet long from bumper to bumper. It had 2 cylinders, 3 forward speeds and a reverse, 4-wheel mechanical brakes, a 4-gallon capacity tank, and safety glass. The 2-passenger convertible coupe and the 4-passenger convertible sedan sold for $325 and $350, F.O.B. Richmond, Ind. On June 19, 1939, the Crosley cars were put on sale in R. H. Macy's basement in New York City.

Mobile telephone commercial service. *See under* Telephone

Plastic automobile was manufactured by the Ford Motor Company, Dearborn, Mich., in August 1941. Fourteen plastic panels were mounted on a tubular welded frame; windows and windshield were of acrylic sheets, which resulted in approximately a 30 percent decrease in weight. On January 13, 1942, patent No. 2,269,451 was obtained by Henry Ford, Dearborn, Mich., on the automobile body construction, an auto body chassis frame made from steel tubes or pipes designed for use with automobiles made from plastics. *(Modern Plastics. September 1941)*

Plastic laminated fiberglass-body sports car was the Chevrolet Corvette, produced June 30, 1953, by the Chevrolet Motor Division of the General Motors Corporation plant at Flint, Mich. Two experimental models had been made in January 1953. The list price was $3,250, including a 1953 powerglide automatic transmission as standard equipment. The car was only 33 inches at the door (body height), 70 inches wide, and 167 inches long

The First

AUTOMOBILE—*Continued*
on a 102-inch wheelbase. Its curb weight was approximately 2,900 pounds.

President to ride in an automobile. *See under* President (U.S.)

Presidential candidate to ride in an automobile. *See* Presidential Candidate: Presidential candidate to ride in an automobile

Production of more than 100,000 passenger cars in one year was achieved in 1909, when 123,990 cars were manufactured. More than 1 million cars (1,525,578) were manufactured in 1916; more than 5 million cars (5,119,466) in 1949; more than 7 million cars (7,920,186) in 1955. *(Automobile Manufacturers Association—Automobile Facts and Figures)*

Production of more than one million passenger cars of one make in one year was achieved in 1949, when 1,109,958 Chevrolets were manufactured by the Chevrolet Motor Division of General Motors Corporation, Detroit, Mich.

Radio car (military). *See* Radio car (military)

Right-hand-drive automobile for the delivery of mail was a Crosley, placed in service in Cincinnati, Ohio, from December 27, 1951, to January 6, 1952, for special delivery service. On January 7, 1952, it was placed in service for letterbox delivery on a mounted route. It is possible that some of the early makes of automobile, that had right-hand drives, may have been used earlier.

Rocket vehicle to break the sound barrier on land was a 3-wheel rocket-powered vehicle driven 739.666 m.p.h. on a 3-mile test strip on December 16, 1979, by Stan Barrett, stunt rider, at Rogers Lake, Edwards Air Force Base, Calif. It cost about $800,000 and was powered by a 48,000 h.p. rocket engine boosted by a 12,000 h.p. Sidewinder missile. It was brought to a stop by drag parachutes.

Sedan-type automobile was the 1913 Hudson Sedan, manufactured by the Hudson Motor Car Company, Detroit, Mich. It was officially shown January 11, 1913, at the Thirteenth National Automobile Show, New York City. It carried all accessories as standard equipment.

Shaft-driven automobile was constructed in 1901 by the Autocar Company of Ardmore, Pa. It was driven in 6 hours and 15 minutes from Ardmore to Madison Square Garden, New York City, where it was exhibited in the New York Automobile Show of December 1901. The first 800 cars were equipped with steering levers, but the later ones were equipped with steering wheels. *(Autocar Messenger. Vol. 13, No. 10)*

Steam automobile was invented in 1866 by Henry Alonzo House. It was driven through the streets of Bridgeport, Conn., and surrounding towns for several months. On October 6, 1866,

The First

House and his brother, James A. House, coinventor, drove the car to Stratford, Conn., taking a party of men to a vessel launching.

Steam-operated amphibious vehicle. *See* Steam-operated amphibious vehicle

Sun-powered automobile was a 15-inch sunmobile built by William G. Cobb of General Motors Corporation and publicly demonstrated August 31, 1955, at the General Motors Powerama, Chicago, Ill. It had 12 photoelectric cells made of selenium which converted light into electric current. The current powered a tiny electric motor with a driveshaft connected to the rear axle by a pulley.

Transparent-top automobile in regular production was the Mercury Sun Valley, a sports coupe with transparent green-tinted plexiglass replacing the steel over the front section of the roof, announced December 7, 1953, by the Ford Motor Company, Detroit, Mich.

Two-way radio in an automobile. *See under* Radio telephone

AUTOMOBILE ACCIDENT occurred in New York City, May 30, 1896, when Henry Wells of Springfield, Mass., in a Duryea Motor Wagon collided with Evylyn Thomas, a bicycle rider, who was taken to the Manhattan Hospital. Her leg was fractured and Wells spent the night in jail awaiting the report as to the extent of the injuries. *(New York Daily Tribune. May 31, 1896)*
See also Automobile Fatality

AUTOMOBILE ADVERTISEMENT. *See* Advertisement

AUTOMOBILE-AIRPLANE COMBINATION *See under* Automobile

AUTOMOBILE BRAKE (four wheels) was invented by Otto Zachow and William Besserdich of Clintonville, Wis., who obtained patent No. 907,940, December 29, 1908, on "power applying mechanism."

AUTOMOBILE BUS
Automobile sightseeing bus was the Motor Tally-Ho owned and operated by Isaac Harris in Brooklyn's Prospect Park. It was operated by gasoline and had a 60 h.p. engine and 4 cylinder with a three-bearing crankshaft. It carried 1 passengers and the driver. It was built by the Mack Motor Truck Corporation, Brooklyn, N.Y., in 1900 and sold for approximately $3,000.

Bus night coach was built by the Pickwick Corporation in Los Angeles, Calif., and placed in service in July 1929 between Los Angeles and San Francisco, Calif. The car was of metal construction, chiefly of Duralumin, and provided sleeping and seating accommodation for 26 people. The bus had two lavatories, a kitchen, and pantry and carried a crew of 3: pilot, steward, and porter.

The First

Bus operated by a railroad for the transportation of passengers was used by the Spokane, Portland and Seattle Railway Company. The railroad organized the Spokane, Portland and Seattle Transportation Company, which was incorporated on July 23, 1924, and began its highway operations on August 25, 1924. *(American Bankers Association. Commission on Commerce and Marine—Automotive Transportation and Railroads)*

Bus with a double deck was imported from France and introduced on Fifth Avenue, New York City, by the Fifth Avenue Coach Company in 1906. The Di Dion Bouton type bus was used. An experimental model propelled by electricity supplied by a battery was tested in 1904. *(Motor Coach. June–July 1924)*

Bus with a double-deck body and chassis made in the United States was constructed in 1915 by the Fifth Avenue Coach Company of New York City.

Bus with cross seats was introduced by the Fifth Avenue Coach Company, New York City. The double-deck buses were fitted with cross seats on March 17, 1914, and the single-deck buses on August 27, 1915. All seats had been longitudinal before that. The single-deck buses seated 16 people; the double-deck, 44. *(Motor Coach. July 1928)*

Coast-to-coast through bus line was the Yelloway Bus Line, which began service on September 11, 1928, from Los Angeles, Calif., to New York City. Three 26-passenger buses departed daily from each terminal, covering 3,433 miles in 5 days and 14 hours.

Gas-turbine bus was the GM Turbocruiser, a modified GMC coach built by the research staff of the General Motors Corporation, Detroit, Mich., and publicly announced June 10, 1954, after it had already logged more than 2,000 miles. The engine used a single burner and two turbine wheels, one to drive the centrifugal compressor, the other to drive a transmission which was connected to the rear wheels of the bus.

Transcontinental no-change bus service was instituted September 8, 1953, by Continental Trailways, which started its through service at 9:00 P.M. from the Port Authority Bus Terminal, New York City, to San Francisco, Calif. The fare for the 3,154-mile trip was $56.70. The time was 88 hours 50 minutes, of which 77 hours 19 minutes was the actual riding time.

Two-way radio equipped bus. *See under* Radio telephone

AUTOMOBILE CATALOG was a one-sheet four-page circular, issued in 1895 by the Duryea Motor Wagon Company of 285 Main Street, Springfield, Mass. The retail price for a "two-seater" automobile was $1,000, for a "four-seater," $2,000. The automobile was described as follows: "It has two

The First

actual 3 horsepower motors. . . . It uses ordinary stove gasoline and costs less than ½ cent per mile. . . . It has 34-inch front and 38-inch rear wheels. . . . It weighs 700 pounds or about 300 pounds more than a similar common wagon. . . . It is steered by a sidewise motion of the lever and speeded by a vertical motion. . . . "

AUTOMOBILE CLUB was the American Motor League, which held its preliminary meeting November 1, 1895, in Chicago, Ill., with 60 members. On November 29, 1895, a constitution was adopted and officers elected. No president was selected, but 4 vice presidents—Charles Edgar Duryea of Illinois, Hiram Percy Maxim of Connecticut, Henry Gurney Morris of Philadelphia, and H. D. Emerson of Cincinnati, Ohio—were elected. Dr. Joseph Allan Hornsby was elected secretary and Charles Brady King, treasurer.

AUTOMOBILE COMPANY incorporated was the Duryea Motor Wagon Company of Springfield, Mass., incorporated September 21, 1895, under the laws of Maine.

AUTOMOBILE DRIVER (woman)

Woman automobile driver to exceed the speed of 300 m.p.h. was Lee Ann Roberts Breedlove (wife of auto racer Craig Breedlove) who drove the jet-powered *Spirit of America* on November 4, 1965, at Bonneville Salt Flats, Utah. She made two runs over the one-mile course at an average speed of 308.56 m.p.h.

Woman automobile driver was Genevra Delphine Mudge (Mrs. Eva Mudge Nelson), who drove a Waverly Electric in 1898 in New York City. On December 31, 1899, she participated in an automobile race in New York City, driving a Locomobile that skidded on the snow and knocked five spectators down.

AUTOMOBILE DRIVING COURSE in a high school, including both classroom work and behind-the-wheel training, was offered at State College High School, State College, Pa., from February 17, 1934, to June 11, 1934. The first instructor was Amos Earl Neyhart. Students who completed the course received Pennsylvania automobile operators' licenses.

See also Automobile school

AUTOMOBILE ELECTRIC SELF-STARTER

Automobile electric self-starter, applied commercially to an automobile, was offered to the public in May 1911 by the Cadillac Motor Car Company of Detroit, Mich. The self-starter was patented by Charles Franklin Kettering, who obtained patent No. 1,150,523 on August 17, 1915, on an "engine starting device."

Automobile electric self-starter patent was No. 745,157, which was granted on November 24, 1903, to Clyde Jay Coleman of New York City. He invented the self-starter in 1899, but the invention was impractical. The license was purchased by

The First

AUTOMOBILE ELECTRIC SELF-STARTER—
Continued
the Delco Company, which was taken over by the
General Motors Corporation.

AUTOMOBILE FATALITY was Henry H. Bliss, a
real estate broker, 68 years old, who was knocked
down and run over as he was alighting from a
southbound streetcar at Central Park West and
74th Street, New York City, on September 13,
1899. He was taken to Roosevelt Hospital, where
he died. Arthur Smith, the driver, was arrested
and held in $1,000 bail.

AUTOMOBILE FINANCE COMPANY was the
Bankers Commercial Corporation, New York
City, organized February 1915, an affiliate of the
Commercial Security Company, Inc. (formerly the
Fidelity Contract Company), Chicago, Ill.

AUTOMOBILE GARAGE. *See* Garage: Garage
(public)

AUTOMOBILE HILL-CLIMBING CONTEST was
sponsored by the Automobile Club of America
and held September 9, 1901, at Nelson Hill, just
outside Peekskill, N.Y., as one of the feature
events in the 500-mile test run from New York City
to Buffalo, N.Y. The Class A race was won by the
Grout brothers, automobile manufacturers of
Orange, Mass., who entered a steam-propelled
open Stanhope automobile of their own manufacture. The car weighed 920 pounds and seated two
people, including the driver. The climb took 2 minutes 45 seconds. The hill was 226 feet high and
2,372 feet long, with a slant varying from 12 to 17
degrees. *(Automobile Club of America—Five
Hundred Mile Endurance Contest)*

AUTOMOBILE INSURANCE. *See* Insurance

AUTOMOBILE LEGISLATION
    Automobile seat belt safety legislation requir-
ing automobiles to be equipped with attachments
(frame holes) to which seat belts could be fastened was enacted by Illinois on June 27, 1955,
and signed by Governor William Grant Stratton
on July 6, 1955. The law provided that on or after
July 1, 1956, no new motor vehicle could be registered unless equipped with seat belt attachments
conforming to the specifications of the Society of
Automotive Engineers.

    Federal motor carrier legislation was the act of
August 9, 1935 (49 Stat. L. 543), "to amend the
Interstate Commerce Act, as amended, by providing for the regulation of the transportation of passengers and property by motor carriers operating
in interstate or foreign commerce." *(Parker
McCollester—Federal Motor Carrier Legislation)*

    State motorcar legislation was passed by the
General Assembly of Connecticut, "An act regu-
lating the speed of motor vehicles," approved
May 21, 1901. Robert Woodruff of the town of
Orange, a representative in the Connecticut As-
sembly, presented the bill, which provided that

The First

the speed of all motor vehicles should not exceed
12 miles an hour on country highways and 8 miles
an hour upon highways within the limits of the
city. A substitute bill was presented, however,
which provided that "no motor vehicle shall run
on any highway or public place outside the limits
of the city at a speed to exceed fifteen miles an
hour . . . or within the limits of the city to exceed
twelve miles an hour. A person having charge of
a powerful vehicle shall have such vehicle under
their control and shall reduce the speed of such
vehicle until said crossing of such street or road
shall have been passed. Upon meeting or passing
any vehicle drawn by a horse, the person having
charge of the power of the vehicle shall reduce the
speed and if the horse drawing such vehicle appears to be frightened the person in charge of said
motor vehicle shall stop."

AUTOMOBILE LICENSE BOARD was the Board
of Examiners of Operators of Automobiles authorized July 6, 1899, by Chicago, Ill. It consisted
of Edward Beach Ellicott, city electrician, chairman; Dr. Arthur Rowley Reynolds, commissioner
of health; John Ericson, city engineer; and James
Furlong, secretary, appointed to ascertain the
qualifications of persons seeking licenses.

AUTOMOBILE LICENSE (federal)
    Common carrier license issued by the Interstate
Commerce Commission was MC-60785, granted
December 22, 1936, to Rodger's Motor Lines, Inc.,
Scranton, Pa., to become effective January 21,
1937.

    Contract carrier license issued by the Interstate
Commerce Commission was MC-81,751, issued
December 29, 1936, to Howard W. Juett, Carters-
ville, Ga., effective as of December 29, 1936. This
permit authorized his operations as a contract
carrier of certain specified commodities to and
from Cincinnati, Ohio, to points in the state of
Florida, as specified therein.

AUTOMOBILE LICENSE PLATES
    Automobile license plates were required by
New York State in 1901 under "an act to amend
the highway law, in relation to the use of highways by automobiles or motor vehicles and re
quiring the owners of such vehicles to register
with the Secretary of State." The act became a
law April 25, 1901, and took effect immediately
Registration was required within 30 days. Owners
of automobiles were obliged to register their
names and addresses and a description of their
machines. The registration fee was $1. In 1901 fees
totaling $954 were received, and in 1902, $1,082
The licenses bore the owners' initials and were
required to be over three inches in height.

    Permanent license plates were issued by Con
necticut and became effective March 1, 1937. The
plates, of plain aluminum, had black letters. A
changeable colored insert designated the year.

The First

Plastic license plate tabs were issued December 15, 1942, by the Massachusetts Department of Public Utilities for 1943 truck registrations. They were made of a laminated phenolic compound by the General Electric Company, Schenectady, N.Y. Printed resin-impregnated sheets of paper, backed by a suitable filler, covered by a translucent sheet, were bonded together under approximately 250° F. temperature and 1,500 pounds pressure.

AUTOMOBILE MAGAZINE was *The Horseless Age,* published November 1895 in New York City by Edward P. Ingersoll.

AUTOMOBILE MAIL DELIVERY. *See* Postal service: Collection and delivery of mail in automobiles

AUTOMOBILE MAIL WAGON built especially for mail collection service was constructed by the Winton Motor Vehicle Company of Cleveland, Ohio, in 1899. A test was made in Cleveland over a 22-mile route, when mail was collected from 120 boxes. Although the test was made in a severe snowstorm under adverse conditions, the trip took 2 hours 27 minutes, whereas the horse and wagon trip required 6 hours. The test was authorized by Mr. Dewston, Cleveland's postmaster. *Automobile Magazine. Vol. 1. February 1900)*

AUTOMOBILE PARADE was held at Newport, R.I., September 7, 1899. Society leaders of Boston, New York, and Philadelphia participated. The vehicles were all profusely decorated with flowers and flags. A prize was awarded to Mrs. Hermann Oelrichs, whose automobile was overhung with wisteria. Upon the radiator was a flock of pure white doves that appeared to be drawing the carriage. Nineteen cars were in the line. *(Automobile Magazine. October 1899)*

AUTOMOBILE PARKING REGISTER. *See* Parking meter (automatic)

AUTOMOBILE PATENT was No. 549,160, filed on May 8, 1879, by George Baldwin Selden, an attorney of Rochester, N.Y. It was granted to him on November 5, 1895, and embodied his claims to the original application of the internal-combustion hydrocarbon motor to a road vehicle.

AUTOMOBILE POLICE PATROL WAGON was designed by Frank Fowler Loomis of Akron, Ohio, and was placed in service by the Akron Police Department in June 1899. It had three speeds and made 16 m.p.h. It was operated by electric power and weighed 5,500 pounds, including the batteries. *(Automobile Magazine. May 1900)*

AUTOMOBILE RACE
Automobile race was held on November 28 (Thanksgiving Day), 1895, over snowy roads from

The First

Chicago to Waukegan, Ill., a distance of approximately 52 miles. Of the 80-odd entries, only 6 could start: 3 foreign cars, 2 American-made cars, and 1 American gasoline car. The race and the $2,000 prize offered by the Chicago *Times-Herald* were won by James Franklin Duryea, who drove an automobile invented by his brother, Charles Edgar Duryea. Arthur M. White, umpire, rode with him. Only one other entry finished, an American rebuilt Benz electric, which was pushed many miles. The Duryea entry had a water-cooled gasoline engine with a water pump, a bevel-gear transmission with three speeds forward and reverse, and electric ignition. It was equipped with a rigid front axle with steering knuckles at the ends. It was steered by a tiller handle, the up-and-down motion of which changed the speed. The average speed in the race was 7½ m.p.h.

Automobile race from New York to Paris via Seattle and Yokohama started February 12, 1908, from Times Square, New York City. Six automobiles were entered: three French cars, one Italian, one German, and one American. The race was won by George Schuster, driver, George J. Miller, mechanic, and Montague Roberts, assistant mechanic, in a car made by the E. R. Thomas Motor Company, Buffalo, N.Y. The elapsed time was 170 days, of which 88 were spent in actual driving. The average daily run was 152 miles; the longest daily run 420 miles. It was not necessary for the same mechanic or helpers to accompany the cars throughout the trip. The Thomas car arrived in Paris on August 1, 1908, and returned to New York City on the SS *Lorraine,* arriving August 15, 1908. The race was sponsored by the New York *Times* and the Paris newspaper *Le Matin. (George Schuster and Tom Mahoney—The Longest Automobile Race)*

Automobile race (long-distance) was held September 9–14, 1901, under the auspices of the Automobile Club of America, which sponsored a 500-mile race from its clubhouse, Fifth Avenue and 58th Street, New York City, to Buffalo, N.Y. The race was won by David Wolfe Bishop, who drove a Panhard automobile manufactured by Panhard-Levassor of Paris, France. The car carried one passenger and driver and was operated with gasoline. It weighed 2,800 pounds when fully equipped. The average speed was 15 m.p.h. There were 87 entries in the race, with 80 starters. The race was not a speed or endurance test but a reliability test. The exact mileage was 464.2 miles, divided into day trips with stops at Poughkeepsie, Albany, Herkimer, Syracuse, Rochester, and Buffalo. *(Automobile Club of America—Five Hundred Mile Endurance Contest)*

Automobile race on a track was held September 7, 1896, at Narragansett Park, Cranston, R.I., as a feature of the Rhode Island State Fair and

The First

AUTOMOBILE RACE—*Continued*
was witnessed by 40,000 spectators. Six gasoline and two electric automobiles raced, the winner being a Riker Electric Stanhope made by the Riker Electric Motor Car Co., Brooklyn, N.Y., with a speed of approximately 24 m.p.h. The driver was A. H. Whiting and the passenger was A. L. Riker, the owner. The time for the winner was 15 minutes 1¾ seconds. The race was for five heats of 5 miles each on a 1-mile dirt track, one heat to be raced each afternoon of the fair week. The prize offered was $1,000 each day.

Automobile race on a track (long-distance) took place May 30, 1911, at the Indianapolis Speedway, Indianapolis, Ind., and was won by Ray Harroun, 29 years old, who drove a 16-cylinder Marmon Wasp over the 2.5-mile oval course for a distance of 500 miles in 6 hours 41 minutes and 8 seconds, an average of 74.7 m.p.h. Only 38 of the 44 cars entered completed the race. One contestant was killed in an accident. The race was witnessed by 85,000 spectators.

Fifty-mile automobile cross-country road race was sponsored by the Automobile Club of America on April 14, 1900. It started at 10:24 A.M. at the junction of Merrick Road and Springfield Avenue, Springfield, L.I., N.Y., went to Babylon, L.I., and then returned to Springfield. There were 15 entries, 9 of whom started. They were dispatched at 30-second intervals. The race was won by Andrew Lawrence Riker in his electric automobile, the only electric entered. His time was 2 hours 3 minutes 30 seconds.

Transcontinental automobile race started June 1, 1909, from New York City and ended June 22, 1909, at Seattle, Wash., scene of the Alaska-Yukon Pacific Exposition. Mayor George Brinton McClellan fired the starting gun. There were six entrants: an Acme, an Itala, a Shawmut, a Stearns, and two model T Fords. The Stearns failed to start. The race was won by Bert W. Scott and C. James Smith, who drove one of the Ford cars. They received a silver prize and a $2,000 award from H. Robert Guggenheim.

Transcontinental automobile race (for a time record) was won by Dwight B. Huss of Detroit, Mich., who left New York City May 8, 1905, in *Old Scout*, an Oldsmobile runabout, and arrived at Portland, Oreg., on June 21, 1905. He was accompanied by Milford Wigle of Detroit. *(From Hell Gate to Portland—Olds Motor Works)*

Vanderbilt Cup Race started at Hicksville, L.I., N.Y., October 8, 1904, on a 10-lap course over a 30-mile circuit. Five Mercedes cars, three Panhards, two Fiats, two Pope-Toledos, and one each of Renault, De Dietrich, Clement-Bayard, Simplex, Packard, and Royal Tourist were entered. The race was concluded when two cars finished. The winner was George Heath in a Panhard, with an average speed of 52.2 m.p.h.

The First

Vanderbilt Cup Race to be won by an American was that of October 24, 1908. George H. Robertson won in a 90 h.p. Locomobile over a 23.46-mile circuit (distance 11 rounds, 258.06 miles) at the Motor Parkway, L.I., N.Y. His average speed was 64.3 m.p.h., his time 4 hours 48.2 seconds.

AUTOMOBILE RACER

Automobile racer to win $100,000 in a race was Roger Ward of Indianapolis, Ind., who drove a Leader Card Special on May 30, 1959, at an average speed of 185.857 m.p.h. for the 500-mile race at the Indianapolis Speedway.

Automobile racer to win over $200,000 in a race was Al Unser of Albuquerque, N.M., who won the 55th running of the Indianapolis 500, Indianapolis on May 29, 1971, in the P.J. Colt–Ford "Johnny Lightning Special" at 157.735 m.p.h. His prize, including payment for his crew, was $238,454. There were 33 entrants; 9 cars were wiped out in 4 accidents.

Automobile racer to win the Daytona 500 at Daytona Beach, Fla., six times was Richard Petty who on Feburary 18, 1979, drove an Oldsmobile an average speed of 143.977 m.p.h. for his sixth victory, winning $73,500. There were 13 drivers entered and the attendance was about 125,000.

Automobile racer to win the Indianapolis 500 three times (Indianapolis Motor Speedway, Indianapolis) was Louis Meyer of Huntington Park Calif., who drove a four-cylinder special. He won $25,000 at the Indianapolis Speedway on May 30 1928, in 5 hours 1 minute 35.75 seconds, averaging 99.482 m.p.h.; $12,000 on May 30, 1933, 4 hours 48 minutes 00.55 seconds, 104.162 m.p.h.; $35,000 on May 30, 1936, 4 hours 35 minutes 3.39 seconds 109.069 m.p.h.

Automobile racer to win the Indianapolis 500 four times (Indianapolis Motor Speedway, Indianapolis) was Anthony Joseph Foyt, Jr., whose speed was 139.130 m.p.h. on May 30, 1961; 147.35 m.p.h. on May 30, 1964; 151.207 m.p.h. on May 31 1967; and 161.331 m.p.h. on May 29, 1977, in hours 5 minutes 57.70 seconds, covering the 200 laps around the 21.5 mile rectangular course and winning about $260,000 of the record $1.12 million purse.

Woman driver to compete in the Indianapolis 500, International Speedway, Indianapolis, was Janet Guthrie, who qualified May 22, 1977, with an average speed of 188.403 m.p.h. for four consecutive laps. Her speed in the race, May 29, 1977, was 151.207 m.p.h. She was forced to make 8 pit stops and only completed 27 laps, finishing in 29th place (out of 33 entries).

AUTOMOBILE RACETRACK

Automobile racetrack (asphalt-covered) was opened on September 18, 1915, at the Narragansett Speedway, Cranston, R.I., where two world records were broken.

The First

Automobile speedway (board track) was the Los Angeles Motordrome, near Playa del Rey, Calif., started January 30, 1910. It was made of wood, "pie pan" in shape, with a circumference of 5,281 feet, and was under the direction of Fred Evans Moskovics. The motordrome was opened April 7, 1910, although trial races were held March 23, 1910.

AUTOMOBILE RIM. *See* Automobile tire: Demountable tire-carrying rim

AUTOMOBILE ROAD MAP. *See* Map

AUTOMOBILE ROBBERY

Armored commercial car holdup was staged March 11, 1927, by the Flatheads gang, about seven miles from Pittsburgh, Pa., on the Bethel Road on the way to Coverdale. An armored truck carrying a $104,250 payroll of the Pittsburgh Terminal Coal Company was dynamited while passing over a mine placed under the roadbed by the bandits. Five guards were badly injured.

AUTOMOBILE SCHOOL

See also Automobile driving course

Automobile school was established in 1903 by the Department of Education of the Young Men's Christian Association, Boston, Mass., to train chauffeurs, mechanics, and prospective owners of cars. The course consisted of lectures on the construction and operation of cars together with laboratory, machine shop, and repair work. Enrollment the first year was approximately 250 students.

Truck-driving training school was opened in June 1954 by the Bedford Motor-Transport Drivers Training Program, Inc., Bedford, Pa., and the first class was graduated July 31, 1954.

AUTOMOBILE SERVICE STATION

Drive-in service station was opened by the Gulf Refining Company on December 1, 1913, at the intersection of Baum Boulevard and St. Clair Street, Pittsburgh, Pa. The station remained open all night and provided free crankcase service. Only 30 gallons of gasoline were sold the first day. Frank McLaughlin was the first manager.

AUTOMOBILE SHOW was held at Madison Square Garden, New York City, November 3–10, 1900, under the auspices of the Automobile Club of America. There were 51 exhibitors, 31 of whom showed cars, and the others, accessories. A ramp was built to show the hill-climbing ability of the cars, and barrels were placed on the floor to show their steerability. Braking (stopping) contests and starting contests were held. Admission to the "horseless horse show" was 50 cents.

AUTOMOBILE SPEEDING ARREST

Driver arrested for speeding was Jacob German, operator of Cab No. 1,565 for the Electric Vehicle Company, who was arrested May 20, 1899, by Bicycle Roundsman Schuessler for driv-

The First

ing at a "breakneck speed" of 12 m.p.h. on Lexington Avenue, New York City. German was booked and jailed in the East 22nd Street station house.

AUTOMOBILE TIRE

Balloon tire production on a regular basis was introduced April 5, 1923, by the Firestone Tire and Rubber Company of Akron, Ohio. Earlier, on several occasions, large-section, thin-walled tires with small bead diameters were used experimentally or for special purposes. No prior commercial use, however, was made. *(India Rubber Review. February 1924)*

Clincher tire was manufactured in 1899 by B. F. Goodrich Company of Akron, Ohio, in sizes ranging from 28 by 2½ inches to 36 by 3 inches. The tire was of 19-ply construction.

Cord tire for commercial use was manufactured in 1910 by the B. F. Goodrich Company of Akron, Ohio.

Demountable tire-carrying rim was invented by Louis Henry Perlman of New York City, who applied for a patent May 21, 1906. Patent No. 1,052,-270 was granted February 4, 1913. *(James Rood Doolittle—The Romance of the Automobile Industry)*

Nonskid tire of the modern type was patented by Stacy G. Carkhuff of the Firestone Tire and Rubber Company, Akron, Ohio. The patent was applied for on September 4, 1908, and granted on April 14, 1914, as No. 1,093,310. The angle formation of the edges of the raised portions molded on the tire provided against skidding in all directions. The tires were manufactured in Akron, Ohio. *(Cycle and Trade Journal. Nov. 1, 1908)*

Pneumatic tire was made in 1895 by the Hartford Rubber Works, Hartford, Conn., owned by the Pope Manufacturing Company, now a subsidiary of the United States Rubber Company. It was used in March 1895 on the Duryea automobile that won the *Times-Herald* race November 28, 1895. *(Henry Clemens Pearson—Pneumatic Tires)*

Pneumatic tire patent was No. 488,494, awarded December 20, 1892, to Alexander T. Brown and George F. Stillman of Syracuse, N.Y.

Rubber tire patent. *See under* Rubber

Synthetic-rubber tire was commercially marketed by the B. F. Goodrich Company, Akron, Ohio, which exhibited on June 5, 1940, passenger car tires made of butadiene, synthesized from soap, gas, petroleum, and air. These tires were trademarked Ameripol.

Tubeless automobile tires were manufactured by the B. F. Goodrich Company, Akron, Ohio, which announced the manufacture on May 11, 1947. The tires automatically sealed themselves when punctured. They were marketed in Indiana, Kentucky, Ohio, and West Virginia before being offered for national distribution.

The First

AUTOMOBILE TIRE CHAIN was invented by Harry D. Weed of Canastota, N.Y., who obtained patent No. 768,495 on August 23, 1904, on a "grip-tread for pneumatic tires." Weed licensed manufacture to the Weed Chain Tire Grip Company, which later was acquired by the American Chain and Cable Company.

AUTOMOBILE TRACK. *See* Automobile race-track

AUTOMOBILE TRACTOR

Diesel-engine tractor with an American-built engine was assembled May 1930 by the Cummins Engine Company, Columbus, Ind. A Cummins model U4-cylinder, 4½-by-6-inch bore and stroke diesel engine, which developed 50 h.p. at 1,000 revolutions per minute and weighed 1,400 pounds, was placed in an Allis-Chalmers Track Type Tractor.

Diesel-powered tractor offered on the market was the Caterpillar Diesel Tractor, manufactured by the Caterpillar Tractor Company, Peoria, Ill. It was a track-type, weighed 24,390 pounds, and developed 68 maximum drawbar h.p. It was powered with a four-cylinder, four-cycle diesel engine, the first of which was delivered in October 1931. *(Caterpillar Tractor Company, Peoria, Ill.)*

Endless-chain tractor was invented by Charles Dinsmoor of Warren, Pa., who obtained patent No. 351,749 November 2, 1886, on a "vehicle." The endless-chain tractor, or track-type tractor, did not become a commercial and practical reality until Benjamin Holt of the Holt Manufacturing Company of Stockton, Calif., produced such a tractor in 1906 and proceeded to build and sell them in quantities. *(Scientific American. December 18, 1886)*

Gasoline tractor was manufactured in 1892, by John Froelich of Froelich, Iowa, who shipped one of his tractors on September 6, 1892, to Langford, S.Dak., where it was employed from September 24, 1892, to November 16, 1892, in threshing. It had a Van Duzen vertical single-cylinder gasoline engine mounted on wooden beams to operate a J. I. Case threshing machine. Froelich formed the Waterloo Gasoline Traction Engine Company, Waterloo, Iowa, January 10, 1893, incorporated for $50,000, and later acquired by the John Deere Plow Company.

Steam tractor was made by Daniel Best of San Leandro, Calif., in 1886. One of his Best tractors was loaded on a car at San Leandro, February 8, 1889.

AUTOMOBILE TRANSCONTINENTAL TRIP

Gas-turbine automobile to make a transcontinental trip was the Turbine Special, a 1956 stock four-door Plymouth sedan, which left New York City on March 26, 1956, at 9:45 A.M. E.S.T. and arrived at Los Angeles, Calif., on March 30, 1956,

The First

at 11:55 A.M. E.S.T., covering 3,020 miles in 95 hours 15 minutes elapsed time (74 hours 19 minutes driving time). It was driven by two-man teams of turbine research engineers under the direction of George John Huebner, Jr., executive engineer in charge of research for the Chrysler Corporation.

Transcontinental automobile group tour was begun June 26, 1911, when 10 Premier automobiles with 40 occupants, a pilot car, and a truck, left Atlantic City, N.J., on an "ocean to ocean" tour. They arrived at Los Angeles, Calif., on August 10, 1911, and concluded the trip August 13, 1911, at Venice, Calif., covering 4,617.6 miles.

Transcontinental automobile trip by a nonprofessional driver in his own car was made by Dr. Horatio Nelson Jackson of Burlington, Vt., a physician, with Sewell K. Crocker of Seattle Wash., as his mechanic. The car was a 20 h.p $2,500 Winton, manufactured by the Winton Motor Carriage Company of Cleveland, Ohio. Jackson and Crocker left San Francisco, Calif., on May 23, 1903, and arrived in New York City on July 26, 1903. The average daily run was 125 miles. The trip lasted 63 days, of which 44 were spent traveling and 19 awaiting supplies. *(Motor World July 23 and July 30, 1903)*

Transcontinental automobile trip by a woman was made by Alice Huyler Ramsey (Mrs. John R Ramsey) of Hackensack, N.J., and Nettie R. Powell, Margaret Atwood, and Hermine Jahns, who left New York City on June 9, 1909, in a 30 h.p Maxwell-Briscoe open car and arrived at San Francisco, Calif., on August 6, 1909. Mrs. Ramsey was president of the Women's Motoring Club of New York. *(Alice Huyler Ramsey—Veil, Duster and Tire Iron)*

Transcontinental family automobile trip requiring only a month was made by Mr. and Mrs. Jacob M. Murdock of Johnstown, Pa., and their children (Lillian, 18; Alice, 14; and Milton, 10), who left Los Angeles, Calif., on April 24, 1908, in a 4-cylinder 30 h.p. Packard. They arrived in New York City on May 26, 1908, having covered 3,693.8 miles in 31 days 5 hours 25 minutes. No distance was covered at night, on the 5 Sundays, on 1 rainy day, or on 1 day of visiting at Johnstown. Only 1 tire blowout occurred. The family was accompanied by a mechanic, Philip De May. (A similar trip made by family in 1906 had required 175 days.)

AUTOMOBILE TRUCK

Automobile truck was designed and built in Pittsburgh in 1898 and 1899 by Louis Semple Clarke and his associates. They were organized as the Pittsburgh Motor Vehicle Company and later incorporated as the Autocar Company. The first truck was pictured and described in Autocar's 1899 catalog as "a delivery wagon which can be made of any size or design, that will be fitted with five to eight horsepower motors. Complete

The First

with motors it will weigh from 900 to 1400 pounds —so simple in construction that any driver of ordinary intelligence can operate it with more safety than he could drive a horse." *(Twenty-Fifth Anniversary—Autocar Co.)*

Automobile truck completely streamlined from the ground up was introduced by the White Motor Company, Cleveland, Ohio, on September 4, 1935.

AUTOMOBILE TRUCKING SERVICE

Automobile intercity trucking service began October 29, 1904, when William B. Chenoweth placed a six-cylinder motor truck in service between Colorado City, Colo., and Snyder, Tex.

Automobile trucking service by railroad motor coaches was inaugurated on January 8, 1923, by the Baltimore, Chesapeake and Atlantic Railway between Cambridge, Salisbury, and Tyaskin, Md. It served six stations.

AUTOMOBILE TWO-WAY RADIO. *See* Radio telephone: Two-way radio in an automobile

AUTOMOBILE WRECKING CRANE. *See* Crane

AUTOMOTIVE ENGINEER (woman). *See under* Woman

AUTOPSY

Autopsy was performed in Florida in 1536 on Philippe Rougement (Felipe de Rojamón), 22 years old, a victim of the plague or scurvy. "On the chance that they might discover some remedy by examining the internal damage, they opened him. The heart was found to be extremely white, surrounded by date-colored water. All the black and putrid blood had backed up on the heart, and gushed forth when he was opened." (Andrés González de Barcia Carballido y Zúñiga—*Ensayo cronológico para la historia general de la Florida*)

Autopsy and verdict of a coroner's jury was recorded in Maryland on September 24, 1657. The surgeon received his fee of "one hogshead of tobacco" for "dissecting and viewing the corpse" of a black slave supposed to have been murdered by his master.

Autopsy by a woman physician on a male corpse was performed by Dr. Bethenia Owens-Adair at Roseburg, Ore., in 1870 and verified by 6 physicians. She attended 2 courses of medical lectures and completed the course of study at the Eclectic School of Medicine, Philadelphia, Pa.

Officially recorded autopsy took place at Salem, Mass., in September 1639. "This boy was ill-disposed, and his master gave him unreasonable correction and used him ill in his diet. After the boy gate a bruise on his head, so as there appeared a fracture in his skull, being dissected after his death." Marmaduke Perry of Salem, Mass., was arraigned for the death of his apprentice. *(John Winthrop—History of New England)*

The First

AVIATION

See also

Airmail service	Aviation—Flights
Autogiro	(transpacific)
Aviation—Airplane	Aviation—Flights
Aviation—Airplane	(world)
bombing	Aviation—Legislation
Aviation—Airport	Aviation—License
Aviation—Airship	Aviation—Magazine
Aviation—Exposi-	Aviation—Parachute
tions and Meets	Aviation—Passenger
Aviation—Flights	Aviation—Pilot
Aviation—Flights	Aviation—Races
(transatlantic)	Aviation—School
Aviation—Flights	Balloon
(transcontinental)	Glider
	Helicopter

Ace. *See* Aviation—Pilot: American ace; Aviation—Pilot: Naval ace

Admiral in uniform to ride in an airplane. *See under* Aviation—Passenger

Advisory Committee for Aeronautics (National) was established by act of Congress (U.S.C. title 50, sec. 151), approved March 3, 1915. The membership, appointed by the President, consisted of two representatives each from the aviation sections of the War and Navy departments, and one each from the Smithsonian Institution, Weather Bureau, and Bureau of Standards, and eight others "acquainted with the needs of aeronautical science, either civil or military, or skilled in aeronautical engineering or its allied sciences." The first chairman was Brigadier General George Percival Scriven. Naval Constructor Holden Chester Richardson was secretary. The committee was appointed April 2, 1915, and the organization meeting held April 23, 1915. *(National Advisory Committee for U.S. Aeronautics—Annual Report 1915)*

Aerial photography. *See* Photography: Demonstration of rapid aerial photography

Aerial policeofficer (woman). *See* Police: Policeofficer (woman) on the aerial force

Aeronautic international exposition. *See under* Aviation—Expositions and Meets

Aeronautical Division of the United States War Department was authorized August 1, 1907, by Brigadier General James Allen, chief signal officer of the Army, to take charge "of all matters pertaining to military ballooning, air machines and all kindred subjects." Captain Edward Ward and first class private Joseph E. Barrell were assigned to the division, which was headed by Captain Charles deForest Chandler.

Aeronautical elopement occurred October 26, 1912, when Arthur Smith, 19, and Aimée Cour, left Fort Wayne, Ind., in a biplane and flew to Hillsdale, Mich., where they landed on the campus of

The First

AVIATION—*Continued*
Hillsdale College. They flew 75 miles with one stop only for gasoline.

Aeronautical patent was granted October 28, 1799, to Moses McFarland of Massachusetts on a "federal balloon."

Aeronautical stowaway was William Ballantyne, a rigger, a member of the original crew of the British dirigible R-34. Ballantyne and two other men had been laid off in order to lighten the load for a transatlantic crossing to America, but Ballantyne stowed away on the flight. The R-34 left East Fortune, Scotland, 2:00 A.M., July 2, 1919, and arrived 9:54 A.M. at Roosevelt Field, L.I., N.Y., July 6, 1919.

Aeronautical trophy was awarded by the *Scientific American* in New York City in 1908. It was valued at $2,500. It was to become the property of the flyer taking it three years in succession, the conditions for winning to be changed each year according to the progress of aviation. Flights were to be made before official witnesses at a preannounced time and place. Glenn Hammond Curtiss was the first trophy winner. His first flight was made for the trophy on July 4, 1908, at Hammondsport, N.Y., at 7:30 P.M., in his *June Bug* at a speed of 40 m.p.h. The *June Bug* was equipped with an eight-cylinder air-cooled Curtiss engine with a six-foot propeller on the rear of its crankshaft. *(Scientific American. July 18, 1908)*

Air attack on Germany itself by the U.S. Army Air Forces. *See under* World War II

Air combat of an American organization in World War I. *See under* World War I

Air control municipal board was the San Diego, Calif., Board of Air Control, which was created by Municipal Ordinance No. 11,485 on December 19, 1927. Prior to its formation, aircraft operations were controlled by Municipal Ordinance No. 10,-035, adopted June 25, 1925.

Air defense command. *See* Air defense command (U.S.)

Air flight attendant (black woman) was Ruth Carol Taylor, a graduate nurse of Ithaca, N.Y., who made her first flight on February 11, 1958, from Ithaca to New York City on Mohawk Airlines.

Air flight attendant (woman) was Ellen Church, a nurse, of Cressbill, Iowa, who made her first flight between San Francisco, Calif., and Cheyenne, Wyo., on Boeing Air Transport, a forerunner of United Air Lines. Requirements for the job were that she be not older than 25, not taller than 5 feet 4 inches, and that her weight be 115 pounds or less. The salary was $125 a month for 100 hours of flying.

The First

Air passenger-mile traffic volume to exceed first-class rail traffic volume was recorded in 1951 when scheduled United States domestic, territorial, and local-service (feeder) carriers flew 10,556,-139,000 revenue passenger-miles, compared with parlor and sleeping car traffic on class one railroads of 10,225,525,000 miles.

Air-rail passenger transcontinental daily service began at 5:00 P.M. June 14, 1929, when a New York Central train left New York City, arriving at Cleveland, where the passengers continued by Universal Air Express Lines to Garden City, Kans (1,087 miles), where they boarded a Santa Fe Railroad train to Los Angeles, arriving at 9:15 A.M. on June 17, 1929, the elapsed time being 62 hours 15 minutes. For the occasion Mayor James John Walker of New York City sent a bottle of water to Mayor George Edward Cryer of Los Angeles.

Air service of the United States Army originally came into being on July 18, 1914, when the aviation section was created within the Signal Corp with an allotted strength of 60 officers and 260 men. The entire equipment consisted of six planes. War Department General Order 75 o December 14, 1913, prescribed a provisional aero squadron with 20 officers and 90 enlisted men.

Air squadron (complete) of American D.H. planes with Liberty motors crossed the German lines on an independent mission on August 7 1918. All the planes returned safely. The first American-built De Havilland airplane with a Liberty motor took to the air in France on May 17 1918.

Air squadron of the United States Army in World War I was Squadron No. 1, assigned to the front on April 8, 1918, for observation duty. The first combat action took place on April 12, 1918 when the First Aero Squadron was attacked while on a reconnaissance mission.

Aircraft carrier. *See under* Ship

Aircraft owned by the Forest Service. *See under* Forest Service

Airline to install rear-facing passenger seat aboard its planes was North American Airlines Burbank, Calif. The first flight of a plane equipped with these seats was made from Burbank, Calif to La Guardia Field, New York City, on June 1 1953.

Airmail stamps. *See under* Postage stamp

Airplane commutation tickets were placed o sale May 1, 1929, by the Colonial Division c American Airways, which inaugurated commuta tion tickets on the Newark–Boston line. Thes commutation tickets were for 10 and 50 trips.

Airplane diesel engine was manufactured b the Packard Motor Car Company of Detroi Mich., in 1928. The engine was an air-cooled 9 cylinder 225 h.p. radial engine and weighed 51

The First

pounds. It was used in a Stinson Detroiter airplane and made its first flight September 19, 1928.

Airplane disaster involving more than 100 persons occurred June 30, 1956, when a Trans World Airlines Super Constellation en route from Los Angeles to Kansas City collided over the Grand Canyon, Ariz., with a United Air Lines DC-7 from Los Angeles to Chicago and Newark, resulting in 128 deaths.

Airplane fatality. *See under* Aviation—Airplane fatalities

Airplane "fly-it-yourself" system was started by the Saunders Drive It Yourself Company on September 15, 1929, at the Fairfax Airport, Kansas City, Kans. The idea was not profitable and operations ceased on May 15, 1930.

Airplane high-speed tank to test airplanes was designed in 1929 and completed May 1931 by the National Advisory Committee for Aeronautics, Washington, D.C. It was the first towing tank in which the towing carriage ran with pneumatic wheels on steel rails and in which very large models could be tested at relatively high speeds. The dimensions were 2,020 feet (length) by 24 feet (width) by 12 feet (depth). Towing speeds up to 50 miles an hour could be obtained.

Airplane human pickup was accomplished September 5, 1943, when the pilot, Captain Norman Rintoul, picked up Paratrooper First Lieutenant Alexis Doster of Washington, D.C., with an airplane from which a hook was suspended from a 185-foot, ½-inch-thick nylon rope, at the Clinton County Army Air Base at Wilmington, Ohio. An electric reeling motor weighing 200 pounds was used to hoist the pickup.

Airplane loop-the-loop. *See under* Aviation—Flights

Airplane merchandise shipment was delivered to the Morehouse-Martens Company of Columbus, Ohio, by pilot Philip Parmelee. Five bolts of Rajah silk manufactured by Rogers and Thompson of New York City, valued at $600, were shipped from New York City to Dayton and taken from there to Columbus in a Wright biplane, which landed at the old Columbus Driving Park. The silk was cut up and stamped: "This silk is a piece of the first merchandise ever carried in an airplane—Dayton to Columbus, November 7, 1910." The distance of 60 miles was made in 56 minutes. The delivery was a publicity stunt for which $5,000 was paid. The shipping rate was 71.42 a pound.

Airplane motion picture show was given on October 8, 1929, by Transcontinental Air Transport, Inc., in a Ford transport plane 5,000 feet in the air. A current newsreel and two cartoon comedies were shown with the cooperation of the Universal Newsreel Company and the Duograph Company. The machine was installed by J. Frankenberg, its

The First

originator. The projector weighed about 8 pounds, the entire apparatus together with batteries less than 34 pounds. A delicate filament lamp specially designed to operate on low voltage was unaffected by the vibration of the motors.

Airplane rescue at sea was effected January 30, 1911, by the destroyer *Terry,* which picked up John Alexander Douglas McCurdy within 4 minutes after his 50 m.p.h. biplane en route from Key West, Fla., to Camp Columbia, Havana, Cuba, landed on the sea 10 miles from Havana as a result of a faulty oil connection. The plane's pontoons kept it afloat. The pilot had been in the air 2 hours and 8 minutes and had made the first sea flight out of sight of land.

Airplane rescue at sea effected by another airplane was made by Hugh Robinson on August 14, 1911, over Lake Michigan. Pilot Rene Simon dived down in his monoplane to wave to some motorboats. Unable to rise, he crashed into Lake Michigan. Robinson, in a Curtiss hydroplane, flew over to Simon and found him in his floating plane smoking a cigar. Robinson hailed several people in motorboats, and they towed Simon and his monoplane to the shore.

Airplane sleeping berths were introduced by American Airways of Chicago, Ill., in March 1933. The berths were made by folding two of the plane's chairs to form a cot. The first airplane with nonconvertible sleeping berths was placed in service October 5, 1933, by Eastern Air Transport between Atlanta, Ga., and New York City. The plane was a Curtiss-Wright Condor and was designed to contain eight berths and five seats, but on the initial trip only two berths were installed, an upper and a lower. The berths were 6 feet 5 inches long and 2 feet 4 inches wide. The first passengers to occupy the berths were Captain Edward Vernon Rickenbacker and Alexander Strong. The plane was equipped in the company's shops at the Atlanta Municipal Airport, where the first trip started.

Airplane takeoff from a hotel roof was made by a Curtiss biplane at 2:35 P.M., June 11, 1912. In a light rain, Silas Christoferson took off from the Multnomah Hotel, Portland, Oreg., on a 170-foot board runway built over obstructions. Christoferson, who had not yet won his pilot's license, crossed the Willamette and Columbia rivers on the flight.

Airplane tank discharger was patented by John Hays Hammond, Jr., Gloucester, Mass., who received patent No. 2,038,998, April 28, 1936, on a "gas tank discharger for airplanes." A cylinder of compressed carbon dioxide cut off the supply of gasoline to the carburetor and dumped it into space.

The First

AVIATION—*Continued*

Airplane to land on the White House lawn was the *Moth,* piloted by Harry Nelson Atwood, who landed on July 14, 1911, about 3 P.M., and was presented by President William Howard Taft with the gold medal of the Aero Club of Washington. Atwood circled the Capitol and the Library of Congress and flew down Pennsylvania Avenue and over the Washington Monument and the Executive Mansion.

"Airplane train." *See under* Aviation—Flights

Airways illumination was attempted August 21, 1923, when 42 landing fields on the Chicago–Iowa City–Omaha–North Platte–Cheyenne route were lit by 30 six-inch electric arc beacons which made complete revolutions 3 times a minute. The lights were of 5.3 million candlepower and were visible for 50 miles.

Ambulance air service to transport sick people by airplane to hospitals was organized on October 21, 1929, by the Colonial Flying Service and the Scully Walton Ambulance Company of New York.

Automatic pilot, an instrument which can be set to take over and relieve the pilot in flying modern aircraft, was developed by William Green and used on a Gates-Day Standard J5 airplane on October 8, 1929, at Cleveland, Ohio, in a Pennsylvania-Central Airlines (now Capital Airlines) plane flown by Captain Trow Sebree from Cleveland to Pittsburgh, Pa.

Aviation gasoline. *See under* Gasoline

Aviation trainer was the Link Trainer, an aircraftlike mechanical-electrical device complete with hooded cockpit, controls, and a full complement of flight instruments. The trainer behaves like an airplane but does not leave the ground. It was invented by Edwin Albert Link. The first sale was made in 1929 to the Link Flying School, Binghamton, N.Y. It was adopted by the U.S. Navy in 1931 and by the U.S. Army Air Corps in 1934.

Aviation trainer (jet) was the C-11, completed March 1949 by Link Aviation, Inc., Binghamton, N.Y., and shipped to Air Materiel Command Headquarters, Wright-Patterson Air Force Base, Dayton, Ohio, on March 16, 1949. Final inspection was accomplished and the trainer approved and accepted by the U.S. Air Force on October 3, 1949. Flight evaluation tests were held November 15–18, 1949. The trainer was put into service at Tyndall Air Force Base, Panama City, Fla., in September 1950. Production models of this trainer weighed 6,840 pounds and were 17 feet 9 inches long.

Battleship sunk by an airplane was the *Ostfriesland,* a former German battleship, which was sunk July 21, 1921, near Hampton Roads, Va., in a bombing demonstration conducted by General William Mitchell. Three direct hits were made out

The First

of five attempts, each of the five bombs weighing 1,000 pounds. Later, the Martin bombers dropped seven 2,000-pound bombs and sank the battleship within 21 minutes after the attack. Near-misses were preferred to direct hits, since the former would shake open the seams and cause the battleship to topple. These seven bombs caused the dreadnought to turn on her port side and sink stern first.

Caterpillar Club. *See* Caterpillar Club: Caterpillar Club member

Civil air patrol (U.S.). *See* Civil Air Patrol (U.S.)

Coast Guard air station was established March 24, 1920, at Morehead City, N.C. It operated until July 1, 1921, when it was decommissioned because of lack of funds.

Coast Guard aviation unit was formed under Act of Congress August 29, 1916 (39 Stat. L. 601), which authorized the Secretary of the Treasury "to establish, equip, and maintain aviation stations, not exceeding ten in number, for the purpose of saving life and property along the coasts of the United States and at sea contiguous thereto."

Floating seaplane ramp (municipally owned) was launched August 15, 1934, at the Brooklyn Navy Yard, N.Y. It was formally dedicated September 5, 1934, by Bernard Seymour Deutsch, president of the Board of Aldermen of the City of New York. The New York and Suburban Airlines Inc., a subsidiary of the National Aviation Corporation, operated the Bellanca Airbus on floats, furnishing a commuting service between the downtown area and Oyster Bay and adjacent points on Long Island, and weekend service to Martha's Vineyard and Nantucket, Mass. The first passenger flight was made July 16, 1934, from Oyster Bay to the foot of Wall Street in 19½ minutes. The landing was made at an improvised float.

Flying medical clinic. *See under* Medical clinic

Forest service aerial patrol. *See under* Forest Service

Gyroscope automatic stabilization for aircraft that was successful was demonstrated by Lawrence B. Sperry and Lieutenant Patrick Nelson Lynch Bellinger in August 1913 at Lake Keuka, Hammondsport, N.Y., in a Curtiss-F boat. Stabilization was longitudinal and lateral.

Hydroplane commercial line service started January 1, 1914, between St. Petersburg, Fla., and Tampa, Fla. The planes were built by the Benoist Aircraft Company and were operated by the St. Petersburg–Tampa Airboat Line. The first plane was piloted by Antony (Tony) Jannus. Mayor Abram Cump Pheil of St. Petersburg, Fla., paid $400 for the first round trip. Noel Mitchell paid $175 for the second trip. Two round-trip flights were made daily. The regular round-trip fare was

The First

$10. The planes flew 80 feet above the water across Tampa Bay, an air distance of 18 miles, in 23 minutes.

Hydroplane commercial line service (international) was established by Aeromarine Airways, Inc., on November 1, 1920, from Key West, Fla., to Havana, Cuba. The service employed two hydroplanes, each with the capacity to carry 3 people. The fare was $50. Mail was also carried.

Jet drone target missile was a Ryan Firebee pilotless jet plane made by the Ryan Aeronautical Company, San Diego, Calif., and first flown April 23, 1954, at Holloman Air Development Center, Alamogordo, N.Mex. It was powered by a 1,000-pound-thrust jet engine (Continental Turbojet J69-T19) and was able to fly at a speed of more than 600 m.p.h. at altitudes up to 42,500 feet. It was air- or ground-launched, pilotless, and flown by electronic remote control from a ground station. It was 17 feet 3 inches long, and 5 feet 10 inches high, had a wingspan of 11 feet 2 inches, and weighed 1,848 pounds gross.

Master of Arts degree in aeronautics. *See* Degrees (academic and honorary): Master of Arts degree in aeronautics

Motion picture from an airplane. *See under* Motion picture

Newspaper with an aviation section. *See* Newspaper: Newspaper with an aviation section

Physiological research laboratory of the U.S. Army Air Corps was completed January 1, 1937, at the Air Corps Materiel Division, Wright Field, Dayton, Ohio. Its purpose was to investigate and devise means to alleviate the distressing symptoms occurring during air travel and to furnish information to the engineer that would enable him to provide conditions aloft most favorable for the efficient functioning of the pilot and observer. *(Aviation Medicine. June 1937)*

President to fly. *See* President (U.S.): President to fly

President to fly in a helicopter. *See* President (U.S.): President to fly in a helicopter

President to fly in a twin-engined airplane. *See* President (U.S.): President to fly in a twin-engined airplane

President to fly in an airplane while in office. *See* President (U.S.): President to fly in an airplane while in office

Propeller blade of hollow steel made from a single piece of steel tubing was placed in mass production by the American Propeller Corporation, Toledo, Ohio, in June 1942. The process was developed at the Lycoming Division of the Aviation Corporation, Williamsport, Pa. Over 80,000 hollow steel propeller blades were made from tubing in three years.

The First

Radio broadcast from an airplane. *See* Radio broadcast: Radio broadcast sent from an airplane

Radio telephone communication between the ground and an airplane. *See under* Radio telephone

Refueling attempt in midair was made at Rockwell Field, Coronado, Calif., on June 27, 1923, at 4:43 A.M. in a De Havilland plane piloted by Captain Lowell Herbert Smith, Air Corps, with Lieutenant John Paul Richter, Air Corps, as receiver of fuel. A 40-foot steel-wire-encased hose was lowered to the fuel-receiving plane. They refueled in flight and remained aloft 37 hours 15 minutes 14.8 seconds. *(Records in Headquarters Rockwell Field, Office of the Commanding Officer, Coronado, Calif.)*

Secretary of the Air (U.S.). *See* Defense Department (U.S.)

Sermon from an airplane was delivered Sunday, April 16, 1922, by Belvin W. Maynard, the "Flying Parson," an ordained Baptist minister, who preached a sermon broadcast from his Fokker airplane. Listeners were asked to donate to the Veterans Mountain Camp, Tupper Lake, N.Y.

Telegram dispatched from an aerial station. *See under* Telegram

War night-flying scout group was the 185th Pursuit Squadron, which went to the front on October 5, 1918, assigned to the Meuse-Argonne sector in France.

Wedding in an airplane. *See* Wedding: Airplane wedding

Women's Auxiliary Ferrying Squadron (WAFS, later WASPS) to ferry training and liaison aircraft from factory to domestic airfields was under the supervision of Nancy Harkness Love of Newcastle, Del., whose appointment was announced September 10, 1942, by Lieutenant General Henry Harley Arnold. The pilots received civil service status and $3,000 a year.

AVIATION—AIRPLANE
See also

Autogiro	Glider
Aviation—Airship	Helicopter
Balloon	

Airplane catapulted. *See under* Aviation—Flights

Airplane (commercial) stabilized was the Curtiss Condor No. 5, built in 1931 by the Curtiss Aeroplane and Motor Company in its factory at Garden City, L.I., N.Y. The plane was powered by two liquid-cooled 12-cylinder engines, 650 h.p., and was equipped with both a Sperry stabilizer and an automatic pilot, which were placed in a box under the pilot's seat. The airplane carried 18 passengers, 2 pilots, and a hostess, and was oper-

AVIATION—AIRPLANE—*Continued*
ated by the Eastern Air Transport airlines between New York City and Miami, Fla.

Airplane equipped with radio to cross the Atlantic Ocean was the tri-motored Fokker monoplane *The America*, which took off from Roosevelt Field, N.Y., at 5:24 A.M. on June 29, 1927, with a four-man crew, Commander Richard Evelyn Byrd, pilots Bert Acosta and Lieutenant Bernt Balchen, and radioman Lieutenant George O. Noville. The plane landed July 1, 1927, near the shore at Ver-sur-Mer, France, after a 4,200-mile flight, in 43 hours and 21 minutes.

Airplane fatality. *See under* Aviation—Airplane fatalities

Airplane (heavier-than-air) to make any long-sustained flight. *See under* Aviation—Flights

Airplane in actual military operation by the United States Army was used in March 1916 when the First Aero Squadron, composed of 11 officers, 82 enlisted men, 1 civilian mechanic, and 8 JN airplanes, was ordered to proceed to Casa Grandes, Mexico, for active duty with the punitive expedition under General John Joseph Pershing. Airplanes had been previously used, however, in February 1913, when the Army Aviation School, then at Augusta, Ga., was transferred to Texas City, Tex., for the purpose of providing aviation for ground troops stationed on the Mexican border to prevent disorders. *(Records in Office of the Chief of the Air Corps, War Department, Washington, D.C.)*

Airplane outfitted with a machine gun was a Wright biplane flown at College Park, Md., May 7, 1912, by pilot Lieutenant Thomas de Witt Milling. Charles de Forest Chandler of the Army Signal Corps was in charge of a Lewis machine gun. *(Scientific American. July 6, 1912)*

Airplane owned by a large company for transportation of its executives was the *Stanolind*, a 600 h.p. trimotor monoplane, which had a complete set of double controls. It could accommodate 2 pilots, 1 mechanic, 8 passengers and could carry 4,000 pounds. It was sold by the Stout Metal Aircraft Division of the Ford Motor Company of Detroit, to the Standard Oil Company of Indiana for $47,709.48. The first flight was made May 21, 1927, from Detroit to Chicago. (Paul Henry Giddens— *History of the Standard Oil Company [Indiana], Oil Pioneer of the Middle West*)

Airplane patent. *See* Patent: Airplane patent

Airplane post office. *See under* Post office

Airplane purchased by the United States Government was a Wright biplane which was given its first official flight on July 30, 1909, and accepted from Orville and Wilbur Wright of Dayton, Ohio, on August 2, 1909. The purchase price was $25,-000, but a bonus of $5,000 was given because the

specified speed, 40 m.p.h. in still air, was exceeded. The plane, built at Dayton, Ohio, was powered by a 25 h.p. motor. It was 28 feet long, with a wingspan of 36 feet 4 inches, and weighed 740 pounds (gross weight, 1,200 pounds). Its top speed was 44 m.p.h. It was known as *Miss Columbia*. Lieutenant Frank Purdy Lahm and Wilbur Wright made the first flight under government ownership at College Park, Md., on October 8, 1909. *(Benjamin Delahauf Foulois—From the Wright Brothers to the Astronauts, the Memoirs of Major General Benjamin D. Foulois)*

Airplane smoke screen. *See* Smoke screen

Airplane sold commercially was the *Gold Bug*, delivered by Glenn Hammond Curtiss June 16, 1909, to the New York Aeronautical Society at Hammondsport, N.Y., for $5,000. Flying instructions were given to two members. *(Chelsea Curtis Fraser—Famous American Flyers)*

Airplane telecast. *See under* Television—Telecast

Airplane to carry 100 people on one flight across the Atlantic Ocean was *The Champ*, a four-engine Air Force C-74 Globemaster, 82 tons, built by the Douglas Company, Santa Monica, Calif. It was commanded by Captain John M. Kelly of West Palm Beach, Fla. The plane took off at 3:35 P.M. from Mobile, Ala., on November 17, 1949, with 103 persons (90 Air Force replacement personnel and a crew of 13) aboard. It landed at Marham, England, at 7:35 P.M. (3:35 P.M. E.S.T.) November 18, 1949: flying time, 23 hours.

Airplane to land at the U.S. Capitol, Washington, D.C., was piloted by Lawrence Burst Sperry of Garden City, N.Y., who landed it on the steps of the U.S. House of Representatives wing on March 23, 1922. It weighed 500 pounds and had a wing spread of 20 feet.

Airplane to receive national acclaim was constructed by the Wright brothers. On December 17, 1903, at Kitty Hawk, N.C., with Orville Wright at the controls, this machine "raised itself into the air in full flight, sailed forward without reduction in speed, and finally landed at a point as high as that from which it started." The plane, with the 179-pound four-cylinder engine, weighed 745 pounds. The engine made 1,200 r.p.m. and developed 12 h.p. The plane was launched from a monorail after a 35- to 40-foot run. Four flights were made against a 21-mile wind. The average speed developed was 31 m.p.h. The longest flight was 852 feet in 59 seconds. *(Century Magazine. 1908)*

"Airplane train." *See under* Aviation—Flights

Airplane used by a newspaper was a Canadian Curtiss 75-mile-an-hour biplane, piloted by Lieutenant William D. Tipton, which was placed in service by the *Evening Sun* of Baltimore, Md., on September 1, 1920, when it reported a railroad

The First

wreck at Back River. Two days later it flew out to sea and located the submarine S-5, in trouble off the Delaware Capes.

Airplane with a delta wing was the Convair, model 7002, built by the Consolidated Vultee Aircraft Corp. at Vultee Field division in Downey, Calif., and San Diego. It was 42 feet 5 inches long, 17 feet 8 inches high, and had a 31 foot 3 inch wingspan. The wing had a 60° sweepback on its leading edge and had elevons on its straight trailing edge. It was powered by a single-jet Allison J33-A 29 engine. It made its first flight September 18, 1948, at Muroc, Calif. (later Edwards Air Force Base). It was delivered to the Air Force on May 14, 1949, and designated XF 92A.

Airplane with ailerons was an 850-pound biplane that attained a speed of 40 m.p.h. The engine was in the rear and was connected to two large propellers by chain drive. It was built by William Whitney Christmas of Washington, D.C., who obtained Patent No. 1,095,548 on May 5, 1914, on a flying machine. It was assigned to the Christmas Aeroplane Company of Washington, D.C. On December 18, 1923, the U.S. Government paid $100,000 for the patent.

Airplane with eight engines was the Hercules, a Hughes Flying Boat, built by Howard Robard Hughes at Culver City, Calif., and first test-flown by him at Long Beach harbor, Calif., on November 2, 1947, when it flew a mile at an altitude of about 70 feet. The plane had eight 3,000 h.p. Pratt & Whitney R-4360 Wasp Major 28-cylinder radial engines, each driving a 4-blade propeller. It was 219 feet long, had a 320-foot wingspan, and its keel was 80 feet above the rudder. It was designed to carry 700 troops, or 350 stretcher cases, with doctors, nurses, and medical supplies, or a 60-ton tank, assembled and ready for action upon landing.

Airplanes to transport an armored division. *See* Army:Armored division transported by airplanes to a foreign country

Atomic-fusion (thermonuclear) bomb dropped from an airplane. *See under* Atomic bomb

Bomber (all-wing jet) was the Northrop Flying Wing XB-49, which had its taxi trial October 21, 1947, at Northrop Field, Hawthorne, Calif. It had a span of 172 feet and weighed in excess of 88,000 pounds. The eight-jet XB developed thrust equivalent to 32,000 h.p. "Clean" design obtained by eliminating the drag-producing tail surfaces and fuselage boosted the XB-49's speed and range over that of a comparable conventional model.

Bomber with the Flying Wing design was the Northrop XB35, built by Northrop Aircraft, Inc. which took off from Northrop Field, Hawthorne, Calif., on June 25, 1946, and made a successful flight of 85 miles to the U.S. Army Air Force Base at Muroc, Calif. It weighed 209,000 pounds in

The First

gross overload condition and had a 172-foot wingspan with a 53-foot overall length. It had an operational range of about 10,000 miles and could carry 56,000 pounds of bombs.

Catapulted airplane. *See* Aviation—Flights: Airplane catapulted

Child born in an airplane. *See under* Births

Cow flown in an airplane. *See under* Animals

Dirigible. *See under* Aviation—Airship

Fighter airplane was the Kirkham Fighter, designed by Charles Kirkham, manufactured by the Curtiss Aeroplane and Motor Company, Garden City, L.I., N.Y., and tested at Garden City, August 19, 1918, when it attained a speed of 162 m.p.h. It established a world's record on October 11, 1918, when it made a ceiling climb of 26,300 feet.

Fighter airplane carrying a cannon was the P-39 (Airacobra), tested by pilot Jimmy Taylor at Wright Field, Dayton, Ohio, on April 6, 1938. It was built by the Bell Aircraft Corporation at the Niagara Falls Airport, Niagara Falls, N.Y. The armament consisted of a 37 mm cannon located on the fuselage center line, the gun barrel projecting through the reduction gearbox and propeller hub; two .50 caliber machine guns in the forward fuselage; and four .30 caliber free-firing machine guns installed in pairs in each outer wing panel. *(Aviation. May 1943)*

Gas-turbine propeller-driven airplane was the XP-81, a fighter, designed and produced by the Vultee Field, Downey, Calif., division of Consolidated Vultee Aircraft Corporation and first flight-tested February 11, 1945, at an Army Air Force base in Muroc, Calif. Its wingspan was 50 feet 6 inches and its fuselage 44 feet 8 inches long. It weighed 19,500 pounds and traveled at a speed greater than 500 m.p.h. In the nose was a propeller-drive gas turbine type TG-100, built by the General Electric Company. Between the cockpit and the tail was a 1-40 jet engine, also built by the General Electric Company.

Hydroplane that was successful was the *Flying Fish,* which was flown by its inventor, Glenn Hammond Curtiss, at San Diego, Calif., on January 26, 1911. On September 29, 1909, Wilbur Wright had flown from Governors Island, N.Y., to and around the Statue of Liberty, and back, a distance of 19½ miles, in an airplane that carried a canoe.

Hydroplane flight to and from a ship. *See under* Aviation—Flights

Hydroplane of stainless steel built for commercial purposes was the Sea Bird, designed and constructed by Fleetwings, Inc., Bristol, Pa., with welding apparatus especially designed by the company. It was first flown experimentally by Daniel Johnson Brimm, test pilot, off the Delaware River at Bristol, Pa., on September 4, 1936. It

The First

AVIATION—AIRPLANE—*Continued*
weighed 2,320 pounds empty (gross load 3,425 pounds) and had a cruising speed of 135 m.p.h. (The Edward G. Budd Manufacturing Company of Philadelphia, Pa., had built an experimental stainless-steel plane in 1931 duplicating a Savois Marchetti design already existent in wood.)

Hydroplane with a multi-engine was the *America,* financed by Rodman Wanamaker and christened June 22, 1914, at Hammondsport, N.Y. It had two Curtiss 1,250 r.p.m., 90 h.p. engines and attained a speed of 65 mph. The *America* weighed 3,000 pounds empty (5,200 pounds fully loaded) and had five watertight compartments. Length overall was 34 feet. The upper wingspan was 74 feet, lower wingspan 46 feet. A third motor was added in July 1914 but was rejected.

Jet airplane to land on a ship was the FD-1 Phantom piloted by Lieutenant Commander James J. Davison, which landed July 21, 1946, on the deck of the carrier *Franklin D. Roosevelt,* 60 miles east of Cape Henry, Va. The plane was airborne after a 360-foot run. It was designed and built by the McDonnell Aircraft Corporation of St. Louis, Mo., and had a service ceiling over 7 miles and a top speed in excess of 500 m.p.h. It was a single-seat, low-wing monoplane of conventional monocoque design, with twin axial-flow Westinghouse turbo-jet engines built into the wing roots. Total weight with full combat load was less than 10,000 pounds. The wings folded electrically and when rigged for stowage the plane was 16 feet wide.

Jet magnesium airplane was an F-80C Shooting Star, flown June 11, 1955, at Mitchel Air Force Base, Long Island, N.Y., by Captain Richard Otto Ransbottom. It was designed and manufactured for the Air Research and Development Command of the U.S. Air Force by East Coast Aeronautics, Inc., Pelham Manor, N.Y., a subsidiary of the Barnum Steel Corporation. He made a 10-minute flight.

Jet-propelled airplane designed and built in the United States was the XP-59, an Airacomet, built by the Bell Aircraft Corporation, Buffalo, N.Y., and flown for the first time October 1, 1942, at a secret testing base in Muroc, Calif., by Robert Morris Stanley. It was rated over 400 m.p.h. and in excess of 40,000 feet. The higher the altitude (up to a certain maximum altitude) the faster it flew. It employed two turbojet engines built by General Electric Company, Lynn, Mass., from designs of the British inventor Group Captain Frank Whittle. The fuel was generally kerosene, although anything that burns could be used. There was no propeller.

Jet-propelled fighter plane to be accepted by the U.S. Army Air Force for combat purposes was the P-80 Shooting Star, designed by Clarence L. Johnson, and constructed in 143 days by the Lockheed

The First

Aircraft Corporation, Burbank, Calif. It had a wingspan of 38 feet 10½ inches, an overall length of 34 feet 6 inches, and a height of 11 feet 4 inches. The first flight was made January 1944, and in February 1945 it was announced by the Army as perfected for actual combat.

Jet-propelled fighter plane (four-engine) for the U.S. Army was the Curtiss XP-87, built by the Curtiss-Wright Corporation, Columbus, Ohio, and tested September 15, 1947. It had a 60-foot wingspan and an approximate overall length of 65 feet. The engines, built by the Westinghouse Electric Corporation, were placed in pairs in housings built into the wings. The plane was tested in flight at Muroc, Calif., on March 1, 1948.

Jet-propelled landing on an aircraft carrier was made November 6, 1945, by Ensign Jake C. West in an FR-1 Fireball on the escort aircraft carrier *Wake Island* (CVE), off San Diego, Calif. The Fireball, a Ryan-built navy fighter plane, was powered by both a turbojet and a conventional reciprocating engine, and normally used its reciprocating power plant for takeoff and landing, switching over to the jet as either an exclusive or a supplementary propulsive force once it was in the air. As West was landing, the reciprocating engine power failed and he landed using jet power.

Jet-propulsion four-engine bomber was the XB-45, built by North American Aviation, Inc., Los Angeles, Calif., which made its test flight March 6, 1947, at Muroc, Calif. It was flown by George Krebs. It had a wingspan of 89½ feet and was 74 feet long and 25 feet high from ground to tail top. The engines were arranged in pairs in single nacelles in each wing.

Jet transport commercial airplane built in the United States was the Boeing jet Stratoliner Model 707, first tested July 15, 1954, by Alvin M. ("Tex") Johnston at Renton, Wash., where it was built by the Boeing Airplane Company. It had four Pratt & Whitney J-57 engines with more than 10,000 pounds thrust. It weighed 190,000 pounds and cost about $20 million. It was designed to carry about 150 passengers across the Atlantic Ocean at a speed of 550 m.p.h. The first transport was delivered August 16, 1958, to Pan American Airways.

Letter to encircle the world by commercial airmail. *See under* Postal service

Molded-plywood airplane was the *Whistling Bill,* a two-place fighter, built in 1918 by the Curtiss Aeroplane and Motor Company, Garden City, L.I., N.Y. The fuselage was made of four 3/32-inch longitudinal sheets of Haskelite, three-ply birch plywood, steamed and formed to contour in a concrete die. The wings were not of plywood. The cooling radiators were of the tubular type, located on the sides of the fuselage. The plane was of 400 h.p., carried two .30 caliber machine guns, and

The First

had a sea-level speed of 170 m.p.h. It was designed by Charles Kirkham.

Monoplane (American) was the Walden III, invented by Dr. Henry W. Walden and test-flown at Mineola, L.I., N.Y., on December 9, 1909. It was equipped with a 1909 Anzani three-cylinder motor, which developed 22 h.p., and flew at a speed of 52 m.p.h. *(U.S. Naval Institute Proceedings. March 1934)*

Naval airplane was the Curtiss Amphibian Triad, delivered July 1911. It was equipped with dual controls, permitting two pilots to operate them in flight. It was tested at Lake Keuka, Hammondsport, N.Y. The first naval pilots were Lieutenants Theodore Gordon Ellyson and John Henry Towers. Funds were obtained from a $25,000 congressional appropriation passed March 4, 1911 (36 Stat. L. 1268), "for experimental work in the development of aviation for naval purposes."

Naval patrol bomber launched like a ship was the 140,000-pound Glenn L. Martin Company's XPB2M-1, christened *Mars,* November 8, 1941, in Baltimore, Md., by Mrs. Artemus Land Gates, wife of the assistant secretary for the Navy for Air. The keel was laid August 22, 1940. The bomber had a 200-foot wingspan and four engines each of 2,000 h.p. It was the first flying boat accorded Navy keel-laying and launching ceremonies.

Photograph from an airplane. *See under* Photograph

Plastic bonded airplane to be awarded a Type certificate by the Civil Aeronautics Administration was an open two-place tandem low-wing full-cantilever type monoplane built by the Timm Aircraft Corporation, Van Nuys, Calif., in July 1940. It was approved April 5, 1941. It was a training plane, the fuselage, wings, and all control surfaces of which were fabricated from a special material formed by binding several laminations of plywood with liquid plastic and pressing in a precision mold to the exact contour and size desired. The entire airplane structure contained less than 7 percent aluminum.

Police airplane-arrest. *See* Police: Police airplane-arrest

Postage stamps to picture an airplane. *See under* Postage stamp

Presidential airplane. *See under* President (U.S.)

Radio message sent from an airplane. *See* Radio broadcast: Radio broadcast sent from an airplane

Rocket airplane (military) was the MX-324, built by the Northrop Aircraft, Inc., Hawthorne, Calif., and flown July 5, 1944, by Harry Crosby, pilot. It had a prone cockpit in which the pilot lay flat to withstand the pull. An Aerojet XCAL-200 rocket motor was used with monoethylaniline as fuel. The craft was known as the Rocket Ram. It

The First

was originally tested as a glider on October 2, 1943, by John Myers.

Rocket plane built in the United States designed for supersonic flight to carry a human was the Army XS-1, manufactured by the Bell Aircraft Corporation, Buffalo, N.Y. The craft, which was an orange-colored needle-nose plane 31 feet long, with a 28-foot wingspan and a 210-pound engine, carried fuel that incorporated oxygen. After a series of glide tests, the XS-1 made its first powered flight on December 9, 1946, when it was released from a B-29 bomber at 25,000 feet. It remained aloft 19 minutes, 7 of which were under power. It carried both fuel and oxygen. The test pilot, Chalmers ("Slick") Goodlin of New Alexandria, Pa., landed the plane at Muroc Army Air Field, Calif.

Rocket to intercept an airplane. *See under* Rocket

Skyjack of a commercial American airplane was a National Airlines twin-engine Convair CV 440 en route from Miami to Key West, Fla. It left Marathon, Fla., at 3:23 P.M. E.S.T. May 1, 1961. Antillo Ortiz, using the name Elpirata Cofresi (The Pirate Cofresi), threatened the crew of 3 and the 8 passengers with a pistol and a knife. The crew comprised pilot Francis X. Riley, copilot J. T. Richardson and flight attendant Inez Barlow. The airplane was flown to Havana; it returned to Key West at 8:35 P.M. (4½ hours late).

Skyjack that was successful took place November 24, 1971, when D. B. Cooper commandeered a Northwest Airlines plane at 11:00 P.M. He parachuted near Woodland, Wash., into a raging thunderstorm with winds up to 200 m.p.h. and temperature 7 degrees below zero, wearing a light business suit. He escaped with 10,000 $20 bills. He was not brought to justice, and it is believed that he may have been killed.

Skywriting. *See* Skywriting

Symphony to call for an airplane propeller. *See* Symphony: Symphonic work to call for an airplane propeller

Telecast from an airplane. *See* Television—Telecast: Airplane telecast (network)

Telephone communication between the ground and an airplane. *See* Radio telephone: Radio telephone communication between the ground and an airplane

Three-motor airplane was an 8-passenger Curtiss Eagle which made its first public flight on July 24, 1919, at Garden City, L.I., N.Y., developing a top speed of 99 m.p.h. It had three 150 h.p. K-6 engines, a wingspan of 61 feet 4 inches, and a wing area of 770 square feet. Its gross weight was 7,450 pounds. On October 29, 1919, at Washington, D.C., this machine made 82 flights and carried 496 people, mostly prominent government officials.

The First

AVIATION—AIRPLANE—Continued

Transatlantic hydroplane flight. *See under* Aviation—Flights (transatlantic)

Transatlantic robot pilotless airplane was the Skymaster, a U.S. Army C-54, four-engine military transport which took off from Stephensville, Newfoundland, on September 22, 1947, and arrived 10 hours and 15 minutes later at Brise Norton, four miles from London, England (2,400 miles). The robot piloting device was not touched after the throttles were opened to start the airplane. The plane carried 14 persons, including Colonel James Milligan Gillespie, the pilot and commander.

Transport airplane designed especially for transoceanic service was the Pan American Clipper, a 19-ton flying boat powered by four Hornet air-cooled, geared, and super-charged engines, each developing 750 h.p. It was an all-metal monoplane, 68 feet long, with a wingspread of 118 feet 2 inches. It carried within its hull and in the wings and pontoons a fuel load of more than 8½ tons, adequate for a flight range of 3,500 miles. Under the command of Captain Edwin Charles Musick, the first Clipper took off April 16, 1935, at 6:50 P.M. from San Francisco, Calif., and arrived 12:59 P.M. on April 17, 1935, at Pearl Harbor, Honolulu, covering 2,301 air miles in 18 hours 39 minutes. The return trip was begun April 22, 1935, at 8:59 P.M. from Pearl Harbor, and the transport landed at Alameda Airport, Calif., April 23, 1935, at 5:59 P.M.

Turbine-propeller light airplane was flown November 5, 1952, at Wichita, Kans., by Hank Waring, who piloted the XL-19B Bird Dog, built by the Cessna Aircraft Company, Wichita. It was powered by a 250-pound Boeing turbine engine with a rating of 210 h.p. on takeoff and a cruise rating of 175 h.p. It utilized the exhaust gases from the jet power-producing section to drive a propeller shaft through a second-stage turbine wheel and a reduction gear system.

Twin-engine pressurized airplane was the Convair Liner, a 300 m.p.h., 40-passenger airliner, equipped with two Pratt and Whitney engines. Its wingspan was 91 feet 9 inches; its length 74 feet 8 inches; its height 26 feet 11 inches. The Convair's jet exhaust propulsion principle was used for added speed. The plane was produced at the Consolidated Vultee Aircraft Corporation's San Diego, Calif., plant. It was first test-flown on March 16, 1947.

Two-way conversation between a glider and the land. *See under* Radio telephone

AVIATION—AIRPLANE BOMBING

American bombing mission. *See under* World War II

Airplane bombing experiment was made June 30, 1910, under the auspices of the New York *World* by Glenn Hammond Curtiss over Lake Keuka, Hammondsport, N.Y. Curtiss released

The First

lead missiles attached to colored streamers from a height of 50 feet upon a target 500 feet by 90 feet. He scored ten hits and four misses. The tests were witnessed by Admiral William Wirt Kimball. *(Aeronautics. August 1910)*

Airplane bombing experiment with explosives was carried out by Philip O. Parmelee and Lieutenant Myron Sidney Crissy upon a test range at Tanforan Race Track, San Francisco, Calif., January 7–25, 1911.

Airplane bombing in the United States occurred on November 12, 1926, during a Prohibition feud between rival illicit beer and rum factions, the Sheltons and the Birgers, in Williamson County, Ill. A plane swooped low and dropped three bombs over the farmhouse of Charles Birger, but as they were crudely made, they failed to explode, a failure which probably saved the lives of Birger and his companions, for the marksmanship of the flyer was unusually good.

Airplane bombing raid by an American air unit was made by 6 Army airplanes of the 96th Aero Squadron Air Service. The unit left the airdrome at Amanty, in Breguet airplanes, on June 12, 1918. Five airplanes dropped 80 bombs on a railroad junction at Dommary-Baroncourt, about 40 miles inside enemy territory. Lieutenant Howard Grant Rath was the lead observer. *(Records in Office of the Chief of the Air Corps, War Dept. Washington, D.C.)*

Hydrogen bomb dropped from an airplane. *See* Atomic bomb: Atomic fusion (thermonuclear) bomb dropped from an airplane

AVIATION—AIRPLANE FATALITIES

Airplane fatality in a solo military airplane was Second Lieutenant George E. Maurice Kelly of the U.S. Signal Corps, who crashed to the ground in a Curtiss airplane about 7:30 A.M. May 10, 1911, in San Antonio. He suffered a fractured skull and was rushed to Fort Sam Houston Hospital, where he died one hour later.

Airplane fatality occurred on September 17, 1908, at Fort Myer, Arlington Heights, Va., when a propeller blade struck an overhead wire because of the wearing through of a fitting to which the guy wire was attached. Thomas Etholen Selfridge, U.S. Army, was killed as a result of a skull fracture and Orville Wright received multiple hip and leg fractures.

Airplane fatality (U.S. Navy) was Ensign William Devotie Billingsley of Winona, Miss., who was thrown out of a Navy hydro-airplane, a Wright biplane with attached pontoon, when a wind current hit his plane on June 20, 1913, four miles off Kent Island, Md., 1,600 feet over Chesapeake Bay. Lieutenant John Henry Towers, U.S. Navy, of Rome, Ga., was injured when the plane crashed in the water.

The First

Airplane fatality (woman) was Julia ("Julie") Clark of Denver, Colo., who was killed June 17, 1912, at the Illinois State Fair Grounds, Springfield, Ill., when her Curtiss biplane struck the limb of a tree and turned turtle while circling the field at 40 m.p.h. on her first flight. Her death was the 151st in a heavier-than-air craft.

Airplane fatality (woman pilot with passenger) was Harriet Quimby, who was thrown out of her Bleriot monoplane at a 1,000 foot altitude when it plunged to destruction on July 1, 1912, into Dorchester Bay at Boston, about 200 feet offshore. Her passenger, William A. P. Willard, also fell to his death. About 5,000 persons witnessed the tragedy.

AVIATION—AIRPORT

Air passenger international station was established at Meacham Field, Key West, Fla., the first flight being made by Pan American World Airways on October 28, 1927, to Havana, Cuba. The airport facilities consisted of a small frame building that served as the station. Maintenance facilities were housed in an old fort nearby and in a small frame structure that served as a radio shack. Federal Health, Customs, and Immigration officials came to the station when notified of the arrival or departure of a plane.

Air terminal (not located at an airport) was opened January 27, 1941, in New York City, for American Airlines, Eastern Airlines, Pan American Airways System, Transcontinental & Western Air, Inc., and United Airlines.

Airport (county owned) was the Kern County Airport, Bakersfield, Calif., developed in 1925 under the auspices of the Kern County Chamber of Commerce near Highway 99, about a mile west of the present site of Meadows Field.

Airport (federally owned and operated) (not Army) was the Washington National Airport, Washington, D.C., opened for regular traffic June 16, 1941. The cornerstone of the Terminal Building was laid by President Franklin Delano Roosevelt, September 28, 1940. The Civil Aeronautics Administration was in charge, and John Groves was the manager.

Airport hotel was the Oakland Airport Inn, in Oakland, Calif., built by the Board of Port Commissioners. It was opened July 15, 1929, and operated by the Interstate Company.

Airport manager (woman) was Laurette Schimmoler, appointed May 28, 1932, at Port Bucyrus, Ohio, at a salary of $510 a year. *(Charles E. Planck —Women With Wings)*

Airport municipal legislation was enacted at Modesto, Calif., July 8, 1910 (Article 3 Section 6), and ratified September 14, 1910, at a special election that authorized the city to acquire "aviation landings." An airfield was not erected within the city limits until 1918. *(California Laws, 39th Session, 1911)*

The First

Airport municipally owned was the Tucson Municipal Airport, east of Tucson, Ariz. The first plane landed on November 20, 1919, and was piloted by "Swede" Myerhofer. *(Arizona Yearbook. 1930)*

Airport to receive an A1-A rating from the Department of Commerce was the Pontiac, Mich., Municipal Airport, which obtained the rating on February 11, 1930. The field covers 240 acres.

AVIATION—AIRSHIP
See also
Aviation—Flights (transatlantic)
Aviation—Flights (transcontinental)
Aviation—Flights (transpacific)
Aviation—Flights (world)

Airship (American) lost to enemy action. *See under* World War II

Airship bombing was suggested by John Wise, an aeronaut, who petitioned Congress in 1851 for funds with which to carry out his plan. He wrote *A System of Aeronautics*, published in Philadelphia, Pa., in 1850.

Airship disaster occurred on May 23, 1908, at Berkeley, Calif., when the 450-foot cigar-shaped balloon invented by John A. Morrell collapsed and exploded, injuring the inventor and 15 passengers. It was 46 feet in diameter at the center and contained 6 gasoline engines, which generated 200 h.p. each.

Airship disaster resulting in more than 70 deaths occurred April 4, 1933, when the airship *Akron* (ZRS-4) crashed in a storm at sea off Barnegat Lightship, N.J., resulting in 73 deaths, including Rear Admiral William Adger Moffett, chief of the Navy Bureau of Aeronautics, and Frank C. McCord, commanding officer of the *Akron*. At the time the *Akron* was the largest airship in the world.

Airship filled with helium gas was the semirigid cigar-shaped dirigible C-7 of the U.S. Navy. It contained 181,000 cubic feet of gas and was powered by 2 motors. It was tested December 1, 1921, at Hampton Roads Base, Va., and on December 4, 1921, made a round trip from Hampton Roads to Washington, D.C. Lieutenant Commander R.F. Wood was the pilot.

Airship (lighter-than-air) was the British dirigible R-34. It was under the command of Major George Herbert Scott, who left East Fortune, Scotland, on July 2, 1919, and arrived at Roosevelt Field, N.Y., on July 6, having flown 3,130 nautical miles in 108 hours 12 minutes. The airship returned to Pulham, England, a few days later, flying 3,200 miles in 74 hours 56 minutes. *(Edward Maitland Maitland—The Log of H.M.A. R-34 Journey to America and Back)*

The First

AVIATION—AIRSHIP—*Continued*

Airship of the U.S. Navy was the DNI, a twin-engine nonrigid 115,000-cubic-foot dirigible. The envelope was built at New Haven, Conn., and the car at Boston, Mass. It was acquired under contract of June 1, 1915, at a cost of $45,636.25. It was too overweight to leave the ground and the twin engine was replaced with a single engine. The first flight was made at Pensacola, Fla., April 1917. Only three flights were made, as the airship was damaged in handling and did not justify repairing.

Airship of the U.S. Navy that was successful was the F1, built to U.S. Navy specifications under contract dated March 14, 1917, by the Goodyear Tire and Rubber Company, Akron, Ohio. The ship was assembled at a Chicago, Ill., amusement park and the first flight made from Chicago to Wingfoot Lake, near Akron, May 30, 1917.

Airship to land on a roof was the A4, a 160-foot dirigible with a 95,000-cubic-foot gas capacity, which took off from the Wingfoot Lake Naval Air Station, near Akron, Ohio, and landed on a 30-by-30-foot platform on the roof of the Statler Hotel, Cleveland, Ohio, on May 23, 1919. Two of the five passengers alighted, one of them Ralph Hazlett Upson, designer of the dirigible. The pilot was James Shade.

Airship with an enclosed cabin was the nonrigid dirigible *Pilgrim,* a 51,000-cubic-foot airship built by the Goodyear Tire and Rubber Company, Akron, Ohio. The car was fitted close to the envelope. The first flight was made June 3, 1925, with John Maloney Yolton as pilot.

Atlantic Ocean regular commercial airship service. *See under* Aviation—Flights (transatlantic)

Balloon. *See* Balloon

Catholic mass in an airship over the ocean. *See under* Catholic mass

Dirigible was designed and built by Caesar Spiegler. The flight was scheduled for July 3, 1878, with John Wise of Lancaster, Pa., as the pilot. The dirigible was of the cigar shape and supported a wicker-cage partition with a door and window.

Dirigible (American-built rigid) and the first of the Zeppelin type to use helium gas, the ZR1, was christened *Shenandoah*—"daughter of the stars" —by Mrs. Edwin Denby, on October 10, 1923. Commanded by Lieutenant Commander Zachary Lansdowne, it was destroyed in a storm on September 3, 1925, over Caldwell, Ohio. Lansdowne and 14 members of the crew were killed. It was launched August 20, 1923, and tested in flight September 4, 1923, at Lakehurst, N.J. *(Charles Emery Rosendahl—Up Ship)*

Dirigible balloon contracted for by the United States Government was built by Captain Thomas Scott Baldwin. Designed by Glenn Curtiss, it was 96 feet long, 19½ feet in diameter, carried 19,500

The First

cubic feet of hydrogen, and had a 10-foot wooden propeller and a 20 h.p. Curtiss engine. The body was covered by 2 layers of Japanese silk with vulcanized rubber. It was demonstrated to the government representatives at Fort Myer, Va., on August 18, 1908, Baldwin acting as pilot and Curtiss as engineer. It was subsequently purchased from Captain Baldwin and used by the Signal Corps at Omaha, Neb., for several years. Its engine, the first water-cooled engine that Curtiss made, is now in the National Museum. It averaged 19.61 m.p.h. and stayed aloft two hours. It was sold for $5,737.50.

Dirigible circular flight was made by *California Arrow,* 54-feet long, 17-feet wide, constructed by Captain Thomas Scott Baldwin, powered by a Curtiss motor that weighed 60 pounds. On August 3, 1904, at Oakland, Calif., it took off from Idora Park, circled, and returned.

Dirigible for private commercial operation was delivered on May 22, 1930, by the Goodyear Zeppelin Corporation of Akron, Ohio, to the New England Airship Company of Bedford, Mass. It was chartered by Bird & Son, Inc., of East Walpole Mass., and as a goodwill messenger made 1,380 flights, carrying more than 6,000 passengers in less than five months.

Dirigible landing and taking off from an ocean-going steamship was the nonrigid dirigible *Mayflower,* a blimp of the Goodyear Fleet. On July 31, 1930, as the S.S. *Bremen* reached New York City, the *Mayflower* lowered itself to the deck (which was 85 feet long by 36 feet wide) and picked up a passenger, Paul Weeks Litchfield, president of the Goodyear Tire and Rubber Company. The railings of the ship were covered with mattresses to prevent the puncturing of the sides of the dirigible. The *Mayflower* was 128 feet long and 37 feet wide and contained 86,000 cubic feet of gas.

Dirigible made completely of metal was the ZMC-2, which was constructed by the Detroit Aircraft Corporation, Detroit, Mich. It was tested at Grosse Ile Airport, Mich., August 19, 1929, and was manned by Captain William E. Kepner and a crew of four who stayed aloft 49 minutes 55 seconds. The ship was 149 feet 5 inches long and 52 feet 8 inches in diameter and had a displacement of 202,200 cubic feet of helium gas. Its weight, empty, was 9,115 lbs. It carried a total load of 12,242 pounds. On June 24, 1926, President Calvin Coolidge had signed House Resolution 9690 appropriating $300,000 toward its construction. The contract with the Navy had been signed on August 18, 1926, under the administration of the first Assistant Secretary of the Navy for Aeronautics Edward Pearson Warner. *(Detroit Aircraft Corporation—The Metalclad Airship)*

Dirigible merchandise shipment sent to the United States by air was a shipment of toys brought over in 1924 by the German dirigible LZ-

he First

26 (2,540,300 cubic feet), which took off from Frie-
lrichshafen, Germany, on October 13, 1924, and
anded at Lakehurst, N.J., on October 15, 1924.
*here it was renamed the *Los Angeles* (U.S. Navy
.R-3). It was manned by a crew of 33 men and
1ade the 50,000-mile trip in 81 hours 17 minutes.

Dirigible passenger transfer to an airplane. *See
nder* Aviation—Passenger

Dirigible telecast. *See under* Television—Tele-
.ast

Dirigible transfer of mail to a train was effected
n June 15, 1928, by an Air Corps blimp piloted by
ieutenant Karl S. Axtater and Lieutenant Ed-
.ard H. White, who flew directly over an Illinois
.entral train near Scott Field, Belleville, Ill., and
ipped low enough to permit the railroad mail
lerk to reach the sack of mail that was suspended
y means of a rope. The blimp was a "C" type
irigible, 210 feet long, with a crew of six.

President's wife to pilot a dirigible was Rosa-
.nn Smith Carter, who was a passenger on the
;oodyear dirigible *America,* which left Dulles
airport, Washington, D.C., in command of Cap-
ain Larry Chambers on her 51st birthday, August
B, 1978. She was invited to pilot the ship while
.ruising over northern Virginia.

**Radio distress signal resulting in an airship res-
.ue.** *See under* Radio distress signal

Stock order from a Zeppelin. *See under* Broker-
.ge

Transatlantic dirigible flight. *See under* Avia-
.on—Flights (transatlantic)

Transcontinental airship voyage. *See under
.viation—Flights (transcontinental)

**Wireless message sent from an airship over the
.tlantic Ocean.** *See under* Radio Broadcast

Woman airship passenger was Mary P. Miller,
.ho ascended at 8:00 P.M. on August 11, 1906, from
.ranklin, Pa., in the 40 h.p., 22,500-cubic-foot air-
.hip owned by her husband, Major Charles J. S.
.liller, and piloted by Leo Stevens, the inventor
.nd builder of the airship. It rose about 600 feet
.nd flew ⅛ mile before the engine stopped. The
.irship landed and Mary Miller alighted. Stevens
.en adjusted the engine, ascended again, and
.rossed the city in total darkness. He landed a
.ile from town.

Woman Zeppelin passenger. *See* Aviation—
.assenger: Woman Zeppelin passenger (paying)

VIATION—DIRIGIBLE

Dirigible to drop mail by parachute. *See* Air-
.ail: Dirigible to drop mail by parachute

VIATION—EXPOSITIONS AND MEETS

Aeronautic international exposition was held in

The First

New York City May 9–18, 1912, at the Grand Central Palace under the auspices of the Aero Club of
America. An invitation to attend was extended to
Rear Admiral Hugo Osterhaus on the opening day
by Robert Joseph Collier, president of the Aero
Club of America, who flew from Keyport, N.J., to
the U.S.S. *Washington* moored in the Hudson River. *(Aero Club of America—First Annual International Aeronautical Exhibition)*

Air conference (international) was held August
1-4, 1893, in Chicago, Ill. The opening address was
delivered by Octave Chanute. Other speakers
were Charles Edgar Duryea, Samuel Pierpont
Langley, and Professor Albert Francis Zahn of
Notre Dame University. *(Proceedings of the International Conference on Aerial Navigation, 1893)*

Aviation meet was held at Dominguez Field,
Los Angeles, Calif., January 10-20, 1910, under the
auspices of the Aero Club of California. American
planes had an opportunity of proving their power
in competition with foreign planes. Two Farman
biplanes and two Blériot monoplanes were foreign exhibits. Three Curtiss biplanes of American
manufacture were shown, piloted by Glenn Hammond Curtiss, Charles Keeney Hamilton, and
Charles Foster Willard. At the meet, Louis Paulhan broke the altitude record of the world with a
flight to 4,165 feet.

Intercollegiate air meet was held May 7, 1920, at
Mitchel Field, L.I., N.Y., under the auspices of the
Intercollegiate Flying Association, the U.S. Air
Service, and the American Flying Club. The Air
Service loaned the fliers Curtiss JN-4 planes. Yale
University won with nine points, Williams was
second with six points, and Princeton and Co-
lumbia tied for third place with five points each.
The other college entries were Cornell, Harvard,
Lehigh, Pennsylvania, Pittsburgh, Rutgers, and
Wesleyan.

AVIATION—FLIGHTS

Airplane altitude flight to exceed 28,000 feet
was made September 18, 1918, by Captain Rudolph William Schroeder, who reached an altitude of 28,900 feet at Wilbur Field, Fairfield, Ohio,
while flying a 300 h.p. Hispano-Suiza motor-pow-
ered Bristol fighter.

Airplane catapulted successfully was a Curtiss
hydro-airplane, catapulted from the Washington
Navy Yard, Washington, D.C., on November 12,
1912. The catapult was built under the direction of
Captain Washington Irving Chambers, assisted
by Naval Constructor Holden Chester Richardson
and Admiral Nathan Crook Twining of the Bureau
of Ordnance. The airplane was piloted by Lieutenant Theodore Gordon Ellyson. Similar attempts had been made previously at Annapolis,
Md., but were not successful. *(Aviation Magazine.
Feb. 28, 1921)*

The First

AVIATION—FLIGHTS—*Continued*

Airplane catapulted from a dirigible was a Vought two-seater observation plane that was released on May 20, 1930, from the airship *Los Angeles.* It was piloted by Lieutenant Commander Charles Ambrose Nicholson, who flew it to the carrier *Saratoga.*

Airplane endurance flight exceeding one hour was made September 9, 1908, by Orville Wright, who flew a Wright airplane with a Wright motor at Fort Myer, Va., for 1 hour 2 minutes 15 seconds.

Airplane endurance flight exceeding 400 hours was made by Dale Jackson and Forest O'Brine, who took off at 7:17 A.M. on July 13, 1929, in the *St. Louis Robin* from the Lambert–St. Louis Field, St. Louis, Mo., and landed there at 7:38:30 P.M. on July 30 after a flight of 420 hours 21 minutes 30 seconds. Each flier earned $15,672.50 for the flight, which was sponsored by the Curtiss-Robertson Airplane Manufacturing Company.

Airplane endurance flight exceeding 1,200 hours (50 days) was made by Jim Heth and Bill Burkhart, who took off from Garland-Dallas Airport, Dallas, Tex., at 7:01 P.M. on August 2, 1958, in a single-engine Cessna 172 with a Continental engine. The plane remained in the air 1,200 hours 18 minutes 30 seconds before landing at 7:18:30 P.M. on September 21, 1958.

Airplane flight was made August 14, 1901, near Bridgeport, Conn., by Gustave Whitehead, who made four flights, one of which covered a distance of a mile and a half, in his airplane *No. 21. (Stella Randolph—Lost Flights of Gustave Whitehead)*

Airplane flight (commercially scheduled) over a single route linking four continents was made by the 42½-ton *Dixie Clipper,* with 10 passengers and 11 in the crew. Commanded by Captain Harold Edwin Gray, the plane left La Guardia Field, New York City, February 1, 1941, on an 11,348-mile trip. Stops were made at Bermuda; Lisbon, Portugal; Bolama, Portuguese Guinea; Port of Spain, Trinidad; and San Juan, Puerto Rico. The plane returned to the starting field February 9, 1941. This was also the first airplane of commercial United States registry to land at an African airport.

Airplane flight from a ship was made on November 14, 1910, when Eugene Burton Ely, a civilian pilot of the Curtiss Company, took off from the bow of the scout cruiser *Birmingham,* anchored at the Hampton Roads Yacht Clubhouse at Willoughby Spit, and flew through fog and rain to Hampton Roads, Va. The runway was 83 feet long, with a 5-degree slope, allowing only a 26-foot takeoff, as the length of the plane was 57 feet. He won a $5,000 prize offered by John Barry Ryan.

Airplane flight to the deck of a carrier was made on January 18, 1911, by Eugene Burton Ely of San Francisco, Calif., who took off at 10:45 A.M. from

The First

Selfridge Field, Camp Selfridge, Calif., flew 1 miles, and landed on the sloped wooden platform 130 feet long and 50 feet wide, above the deck o the cruiser *Pennsylvania* in San Francisco harbor Ropes and sandbags were used to stop the air plane. His speed was 35 m.p.h. After lunch, h returned (at 12:30 P.M.) to Selfridge Field.

Airplane flight under a bridge was made o June 27, 1911, by Lincoln Beachey, who flew in th rain in a 60-h.p. Curtiss biplane from a baseba field on the American side of the Niagara Rive Niagara Falls, N.Y., crossed over the America Falls and Horseshoe Falls at an altitude of 2,00 feet and under the 168-foot high and 100-foot wid steel arch bridge, about 15 feet above the wate He flew down the gorge almost to the Whirlpoo Rapids at a speed of 60 m.p.h. and landed on th Canadian side. About 150,000 spectators wi nessed the flight, which was a stunt for the inte national carnival. He repeated the flight on Jun 29, 1911.

Airplane flight with an auto slung beneath th fuselage was made February 11, 1935, from Floy Bennett Field, N.Y., with Lou Reichers at the con trols. An Uppercu-Burnelli transport with a cabi 12 feet wide supported a Ford roadster fastene and braced with struts between the wheels of th landing gear. The test was made to demonstra the quick-starting ability of a branded gasolin but was valuable because it demonstrated th possibility of transporting tanks behind enem lines in battle.

Airplane (heavier-than-air) to make any lon sustained flight under its own power was Samu Pierpont Langley's model No. 5, which was teste May 6, 1896, on the shores of the Potomac Rive This unmanned model "aerodrome" weighed 2 pounds, was 16 feet in length, and had four cam bered single-tier wings, each about 14 feet fro tip to tip. It was driven by a 1 h.p. steam engin It was catapulted from a platform 20 feet abov the water and flew a distance of about ¾ mil remaining aloft 1½ minutes during one of i flights. As the fuel was exhausted, the plane de scended gently to the water. It was picked u dried off, refueled, and relaunched the same afte noon. Langley predicted that airplanes would b used to carry men, but his friends and the pre scoffed. *(Nature. May 28, 1896)*

Airplane loop-the-loop was made by Lincol Beachey at North Island, San Diego, Calif., o November 18, 1913. At a 1,000-foot level, h brought his machine up with a swoop and a m ment later was flying head downward. The loo was completed at a 300-foot level. On Novembe 28, 1913, he made a triple loop.

Airplane night scheduled passenger flight wa made April 1, 1927, when a three-engine Fokker the Colonial Air Transport Company took off f oston, Mass., from Hadley Field, N.J., then the nly lighted airport with a lighted runway.

Airplane round trip, made in one day between wo large cities, was made on June 13, 1910, when harles Keeney Hamilton, flying in a Curtiss bi-lane equipped with a Curtiss motor, made the ound trip between Governors Island, N.Y., and hiladelphia, Pa. He left Governors Island at 7:36 .M. and arrived at Front Street and Erie Avenue, hiladelphia, at 9:26 A.M. The average speed for is flight of 1 hour 50 minutes was 46.92 m.p.h. He ft Philadelphia at 11:33 A.M. and, after a detour, nded at South Amboy, N.J., at 12:54 P.M., in a wamp instead of on a green. He repaired a bro-en spark plug and reascended at 6:17 P.M. and nded at Governors Island at 6:40 P.M. The flying me for the round trip was 3 hours 34 minutes. For is accomplishment he won a $10,000 prize of-ed by the New York *Times* and the Philadelphia *edger. (Lyman J. Seely—Flying Pioneers of Ham-ondsport)*

Airplane to carry 100,000 pounds was an XC-99 onvair that took off from Carswell Air Base, Fort /orth, Tex., on April 15, 1949, with a cargo princi-lly of zinc alloy used in aircraft tooling. B. A. rickson was pilot and F. Keen was copilot. The ansport, built by the Convair division of General ynamics Corp., San Diego, was designed to rry 400 fully armed men or 300 litter patients ith their attendants.

Airplane to carry 3 passengers was a Curtiss plane flown August 14, 1910, at Mineola, N.Y., / Charles Foster Willard. The passengers were F. Patterson, A. Albin, and Harry Willard. The rplane weighed 650 pounds and the weight of ssengers totaled about 375 pounds.

Airplane to carry 300 passengers on one flight as the U.S. Navy Flying Boat *Caroline Mars,* hich transported 301 passengers and 7 crewmen Air Group 5 from the Naval Air Station, Alame-, Calif., to San Diego, a distance of approxi-ately 500 miles, on May 19, 1949, in 2 hours 54 inutes. Commander James G. Long of Mapleton, nn., piloted the four-engine craft.

Airplane to fly a distance greater than 500 miles as a 2-year-old obsolete Curtiss biplane that as flown a distance of 590 miles from Chicago, ., to Hornell, N.Y., on November 19, 1916, by th Law. She left at 8:25 A.M. and arrived at 2:10 ., in 5 hours 45 minutes' flying time. She landed d refueled and continued on to Binghamton.

Airplane to fly faster than 200 m.p.h. was pilot- by Lieutenant Lester James Maitland on Octo-r 14, 1922, at the national airplane meet at lfridge Field, Mount Clemens, Mich. Maitland w a Curtiss pursuit plane with a 375 h.p. engine, a speed of 216.1 m.p.h. for 50 kilometers.

Airplane to fly faster than 300 m.p.h. was flown

September 4, 1933, over Glenview, Ill., by James R. Wedell of Patterson, La., who won the Phillips Trophy Race. He made four consecutive runs over a 3 km course at an average speed of 304.980 m.p.h., in a monoplane of his own design (Wedell-Williams No. 44) fitted with 300 h.p. Wasp super-charged engine.

Airplane to fly faster than 600 m.p.h. was pilot-ed by Army Air Force Colonel Albert Boyd of Asheville, N.C., on June 19, 1947, at Muroc Air Field, Calif. He flew a jet-propelled Lockheed P-80R at 623.738 m.p.h., over a 1.86-mile course, flying four times, twice in each direction, and at one time attaining a speed of 632 m.p.h.

Airplane to fly faster than 800 m.p.h. was a North American F-100C Super Sabre Jet that reached 822.135 m.p.h. on August 20, 1955, over the Mojave Desert at Palmdale, Calif. It was pilot-ed by Colonel Horace Albert Hanes at a 40,000-foot altitude.

Airplane to fly faster than 1,300 m.p.h. was the D-558-2 Skyrocket, a jet built for the U.S. Navy by the El Segundo, Calif., division of the Douglas Air-craft Company. Piloted by Scott Crossfield of the National Advisory Committee for Aeronautics, it attained a speed of 1,327 m.p.h. in a 3-minute flight on November 20, 1953, over Edwards Air Force Base, Muroc, Calif. It was designed under the di-rection of chief engineer Edward H. Heinemann and first flew in 1947 at Muroc, Calif.

Airplane to fly faster than 4,000 m.p.h. was the X-15 flown November 9, 1961, by Major Robert White (U.S. Air Force) at Edwards Air Force Base, Calif. A speed of 4,093 m.p.h. (Mach 6.04) was sustained for 86 seconds. The outer panel of the right windshield cracked.

Airplane to fly faster than 4,500 m.p.h. was the X15-A2 flown by Major William J. ("Pete") Knight, U.S. Air Force. It was launched from the belly of a B-52 mothership on October 3, 1967, over Ed-wards Air Force Base, Calif. It achieved a speed of 4,534 m.p.h. (7,297 km), Mach 6.72.

Airplane to fly faster than the speed of sound and break the sound barrier was the Bell X-1, a U.S. Army rocket airplane, flown October 14, 1947, at Edwards Air Force Base, Muroc, Calif., by Air Force Major Charles Elwood (Chuck) Yeager. The rocket engine was built by Reaction Motors, Inc., Rockaway, N.J. The plane attained the speed of 967 m.p.h. and an altitude of 70,140 feet. The official announcement did not come, however, until released June 10, 1948, by Air Secretary Wil-liam Stuart Symington. Alcohol and liquid oxygen were used as fuel, forced into the burners by gase-ous nitrogen. The plane was equipped with rock-ets that could keep it in the air only 10 minutes. It had to be dropped from a bomber while at a high

The First

AVIATION—FLIGHTS—*Continued*
altitude. (At sea level, the speed of sound is 760 m.p.h.)

Airplane to fly faster than the speed of sound, flown by a civilian, was piloted by Herbert Henry Hoover of Knoxville, Tenn., chief test pilot in charge of the National Advisory Committee for Aeronautics, who on March 10, 1948, from Edwards Air Force Base, Calif., made a supersonic flight in a Bell X-1 rocket-propelled research airplane.

Airplane to fly higher than a mile in altitude was a Wright biplane flown by Walter Richard Brookins to an altitude of 6,234 feet on July 9, 1910, over Atlantic City, N.J. The gasoline gave out when he descended to 5,800 feet, and the engine stopped, but Brookins glided the airplane to safety. He was in the air 1 hour 2 minutes 35 seconds. For his feat he won a $5,000 prize offered by the Atlantic City Aero Club.

Airplane to land on the White House lawn. *See under* Aviation

"Airplane train" soared from Floyd Bennett Field, N.Y., August 2, 1934, at 10:44 A.M. It consisted of a Wright-Eaglerock airplane, piloted by Elwood Keim, which towed three gliders, piloted by Jack O'Meara, Dr. Roswell Earl Franklin, and Stanley Smith. The gliders were to be released from the train at Philadelphia, Baltimore, and Washington. The flight was arranged by the Lustig Sky Train Corporation, and each glider carried about 75 pounds of mail. Because of heavy winds, the air train was forced down at Philadelphia at 1:20 P.M.

Airship to exceed 200 hours in flight nonstop without refueling was made by a 342-foot U.S. Navy blimp ZPG-2, the *Nan.* The nonrigid blimp with 1,000,000 cubic feet of helium left the Naval Air Station, Lakehurst, N.J., at 6:32 A.M. on May 17, 1954, and flew to Bermuda, to Puerto Rico, and then to Key West, Florida, a distance of 2,660 miles in 200 hours 12 minutes, arriving on May 25, 1954. It used 2,400 gallons of gasoline, was powered by two 800 h.p. Wright Cyclone engines, and carried 14 persons. The commanding officer was Commander Marion H. Eppes of Pinson, Fla.

All-blind cross-country test of instrument or "blind" flying and landing was made on March 21, 1933, from College Park, Md., to Newark, N.J., by James Kinney, pilot, accompanied by Harry Diamond, U.S. Bureau of Standards scientist, who helped develop the instrument landing system, and William La Violette, radio technician.

All-blind distance flight by the U.S. Army was made April 6, 1940, by Major Carl B. McDaniel, assisted by Captain William A. Matheny, Lieutenant William P. Ragsdale, and four enlisted men, in a four-motored 22½-ton craft from Mitchel Field, L.I., N.Y., to Langley Field, Va. Two civilian pass-

The First

engers were carried in the 2-hour 2-minute fligh

All-blind flight was made September 24, 192 at Mitchel Field, L.I., N.Y., by Lieutenant Jame Harold Doolittle in a two-seater Consolidated Wright biplane. He made a complete flight in a enclosed cockpit without seeing the ground or an part of the airplane except an illuminated instru ment board. From takeoff to landing only fligh instruments were used. He was guided by a radi beacon. Lieutenant Benjamin Kelsey accom panied him in the event of an emergency.

All-blind solo flight by the U.S. Army was mad May 7, 1932, by Captain Albert Francis Hege berger at Patterson Field, Dayton, Ohio, in a Army Douglas BT-2 plane equipped with standar Air Corps instruments. He took off and landed th plane completely enclosed in the hooded cockp with no external vision from start to finish. *(U.. Air Forces. July 1932)*

Balloon flight. *See under* Balloon

California–Hawaii flight. *See under* Aviation-Flights (transpacific)

Glider flight. *See under* Glider—Flights

Helicopter flight. *See under* Helicopter—Fligh

Honolulu squadron flight. *See under* Aviation-Flights (transpacific)

Hydroplane flight to and from a ship was mac by Glenn Curtiss to the U.S.S. *Pennsylvania* in th Pacific Ocean on February 17, 1911, from Nor Island, San Diego, Calif. He landed alongside th ship and was hoisted aboard. Then the procedu was reversed. He received the Robert F. Colli Trophy in 1912 for outstanding contributions American aviation.

Intercity airplane flight by a U.S. officer wa made July 30, 1909, by Lieutenant Benjamin Del hauf Foulois, who flew with Orville Wright as th pilot from Fort Myer, Va., to Alexandria, Va. The traveled 10 miles at an altitude of 600 feet, avera ing 42 m.p.h., thereby establishing three wor records for distance, speed, and altitude.

Jet passenger commercial service. *See und* Aviation—Flights (transatlantic)

Jet passenger international trip was made Ap 18, 1950, in an Avro Canada Jetliner from Malt Airport, Toronto, Canada, to the Internation Airport, New York City, a distance of 359 miles 1 hour. Chief pilot was Donald Howard Roge Four Rolls-Royce Derwent jet engines we mounted in pairs in the 2 underslung nacell which also housed the main landing wheels. T plane carried 3 passengers, a crew of 3, and 15,0 airmail letters marked with an official Canadi government cachet, the first mail carried in a transport.

The First

Jet passenger trip was made January 10, 1951, when an Avro Jetliner four-engine turbojet piloted by Donald Howard Rogers took off from Chicago, Ill., at 11:07 A.M., and arrived at New York City in 1 hour 42 minutes, setting a new speed record of 342 m.p.h.

New York–Alaska flight, 4,345 miles each way, was made by four United States planes of the Alaskan Flying Expedition that left Mitchel Field, L.I., N.Y., July 15, 1920, and arrived at Nome, Alaska, August 25, 1920. The expedition left Nome, August 29, 1920, and returned to Mitchel Field, October 20, 1920, making 16 stops en route. The average flying speed of the trip was 80 m.p.h. The crew consisted of Captain St. Clair Streett, in command; First Lieutenant Clifford Cameron Nutt; Second Lieutenants Ross C. Kirkpatrick, Erik Henning Nelson, and Clarence E. Crumrine; Sergeants James Long and Joseph E. English; and Captain Howard Douglas, advance officer.

New York–Bermuda flight was made on April 1, 1930, by Captain Lewis Alonzo Yancey, navigator, William Alexander, pilot, and Zeh Bouck, radio operator, in the Stinson monoplane *Pilot,* equipped with a Wright Whirlwind motor. They landed 60 miles from their goal on the ocean and floated overnight. They resumed their flight and arrived at Hamilton, Bermuda, on April 2, 1930. Each member of the crew received $1,000 from the Bermuda Board of Trade.

New York–Chicago nonstop flight was made by Captain E. F. White, April 19, 1919, piloting a De Havilland-4 army biplane. He covered the 727 miles in 6 hours 50 minutes' flying time, an average speed of 106 m.p.h.

New York–Panama nonstop flight was made by Captain Roy W. Ammel of Chicago in his Lockheed-Sirius monoplane, the *Blueflash.* He left Floyd Bennett Field, Brooklyn, N.Y., at 2:10 P.M. November 9, 1930, and crash-landed at France Field, Panama, at 2:45 P.M., November 10, 1930, flying 3,189 miles.

Night flight was made by Walter Richard Brookins on April 18, 1910, at Montgomery, Ala.

North Pole flight was made by Lieutenant Commander Richard Evelyn Byrd, U.S.N. retired, and Floyd Bennett on May 9, 1926. In the *Josephine Ford,* a triple-engine Fokker monoplane, they flew from King's Bay, Spitzbergen, to the Pole and back, without stopping, covering 1,545 miles in 15 hours 30 minutes. *(Richard Evelyn Byrd—Skyward)*

North Pole flight in a single-engine airplane was made by Captain Charles Francis Blair, Jr., of Port Washington, L.I., N.Y., from Bardu Foss, Norway, to Fairbanks, Alaska, in 10 hours 29 minutes (nonstop), on May 29, 1951, in the *Excalibur III,* a converted flame-red Mustang fighter plane with a 12-cylinder V-type engine. The takeoff was at 4:02

The First

P.M. (11:02 A.M., New York time) and the landing was at 3:29 P.M. (9:29 P.M., New York time) at the Ladd Air Force Base. About 3,000 letters were carried on this airmail polar flight.

North Pole jet crossing was made September 20, 1951, in a six-jet medium Boeing B-47 Stratojet, which took off and returned to Eielson Air Force Base, near Fairbanks, Alaska. The plane was piloted by Colonel Richard Cox Neeley of Salt Lake City, Utah, and copilot Colonel John Gibbons Foster of New York City. The third member of the crew was radar operator-navigator Captain David Jacob Haney of Copperhill, Tenn.

North Pole landing by an airplane at the geographic pole was made by a U.S. Air Force skiwheeled C-47, which landed May 3, 1952. It took off from Fletcher's Ice Island, about 115 miles from the Pole, and carried 10 air force officials and scientists. It was piloted by Lieutenant Colonel William Pershing Benedict of San Rafael, Calif., and copilot Lieutenant Colonel Joseph Otis Fletcher of Shawnee, Okla.

Overwater flight was made by Glenn Hammond Curtiss, who on August 31, 1910, flew in his biplane from Euclid Beach Park, Cleveland, Ohio, to Cedar Point, Sandusky, Ohio, a distance of 70 miles over Lake Erie in 78 minutes nonstop. He flew at an altitude between 400 and 500 feet.

Overwater round-trip flight was made by Glenn Luther Martin in a biplane pusher type, on May 10, 1912. The trip was made in 37 minutes at an altitude in excess of 2,000 feet for an approximate distance of 31 miles over the Pacific Ocean from Newport Bay to Avalon, Santa Catalina Island, Calif. The return flight was from Santa Catalina Island via San Pedro and down the coast to Newport Bay, covering 45 miles in 51 minutes. An inflated tire tube on the fuselage served as a life preserver.

President to fly in a twin-engined airplane. *See under* President (U. S.)

President to fly in an airplane while in office. *See under* President (U. S.)

Sky-train international round-trip flight was made from Key West, Fla., May 14, 1935, at 1:40 P.M. to Havana, Cuba. The flight lasted 1 hour 45 minutes, the average speed being 64 m.p.h. The sky train consisted of an airplane and two gliders towed by the plane. The plane was piloted by Elwood Keim of New York City, and the gliders by E. Paul du Pont, Jr., of Wilmington, Del., and Jack O'Meara of New York City. The return flight was made from Havana, May 19, 1935.

South Pole flight was made in a Ford tri-motor airplane on November 28, 1929, by Lieutenant Commander Richard Evelyn Byrd, U.S.N. retired, from his base, Little America, in the Antarctic, at 10:29 P.M. (New York time). The crew consisted of Bernt Balchen, pilot; Harold I. June, radio opera-

The First

AVIATION—FLIGHTS—*Continued*

tor; and Captain Ashley C. McKinley, photographer. They reported that they reached the Pole about 8:55 A.M. (New York time) on November 29, 1929, and dropped a United States flag there, returning at 5:10 P.M. (New York time). *(Richard Evelyn Byrd—Little America)*

Stratoliner commercial flight was made July 8, 1940, by Transcontinental & Western Air, with a Boeing 307-B four-engine plane. It flew normally 4 miles above the earth. This was the first commercial flight to use supercharged cabins. It was a 33-passenger plane by day and a 25-passenger plane at night. The cabin was designed with 9 individual seats and 4 compartments, each of 6-passenger capacity. At night, these compartments were converted into sleepers of 4 berths each. The first eastbound transcontinental commercial flight was made in 12 hours 22 minutes (11 hours 55 minutes, flying time), and the westbound trip in 14 hours 17 minutes (14 hours, flying time). Stops were made at Kansas City. The terminals were La Guardia Airport, New York City, and the Lockheed Air Terminal, Burbank, Calif.

Women to fly in excess of 120 hours were Evelyn "Bobby" Trout and Edna May Cooper who took off from Glendale, Calif., on January 4, 1931, in the monoplane *Lady Rolph* and returned on January 9, 1931, at 5:20 P.M. P.S.T. after a flight of 122 hours and 20 minutes. They landed because their engine smoked.

AVIATION—FLIGHTS (transatlantic)

Air mail transatlantic service. *See under* Air-mail service

Airplane flight (commercially scheduled) over a single route linking four continents. *See under* Aviation—Flights

Atlantic Ocean regular commercial airship service was inaugurated by the *Hindenburg,* of the German Zeppelin Transport Company, which departed from Friedrichshafen, Germany, at 9:30 P.M. (Central European Time) on May 6, 1936, and landed May 9, 1936, at the United States Naval Air Station, Lakehurst, N.J., at 6:08 A.M. (Eastern Standard Time), completing the voyage of approximately 4,000 miles in 61 hours 38 minutes, an average speed of 65 m.p.h. Fifty-one passengers and 56 officers and crew made the flight. The ship was in the command of Captain Ernst August Lehmann, under the general direction of Dr. Hugo Eckener. *(Ernst August Lehmann—Zeppelin, The Story of Lighter-than-Air Craft)*

Atlantic Ocean scheduled air service was inaugurated by Pan American Airways on May 20, 1939, when the *Yankee Clipper,* a 4-engine, 4½-ton flying boat, took off from Manhasset Bay, Port Washington, L.I., N.Y., and arrived at Lisbon, Portugal, in 26½ hours (20 hours 16 minutes, actual flying time). It was commanded by Captain Ar-

The First

thur Earl La Porte and carried a crew of 14, 3 PA/ employees, and 1,680 pounds of mail.

Balloon Atlantic crossing attempt. *See unde* Balloon

Jet passenger commercial service was inaugu rated October 4, 1958, by the British Oversea Airways Corporation, whose jets crossed the A lantic Ocean in both directions. The flight fror New York City to London, piloted by Captai Thomas Butler Stoney, was made in 6 hours 1 minutes, with a stop at Gander, Newfoundlan The flight from London to New York was made i 10 hours 26 minutes with a 1-hour 10-minute sto at Gander, Newfoundland. The planes, Come IV's, averaged 580 m.p.h. and flew at an altitud of 34,000 to 40,000 feet. First-class passage wa $435.

Jet transatlantic flight west–east was made Ju 20, 1948, by 16 Lockheed P-80 Shooting Stars fror Mount Clemens, Mich., to Odiham, England (4,28 miles), in 10 hours 40 minutes, under the comman of Colonel David Carl Schilling, of Raleigh, N.C commander of the 56th Fighter Group. Stops we made at Goose Bay, Labrador; Bluie West Tw Greenland; Keflavik, Iceland; and Stornoway, the Outer Hebrides, off Scotland.

Jet transatlantic nonstop flight east–west wa made on September 22, 1950, by Colonel Davi Carl Schilling of Raleigh, N.C., commandir officer of the 31st Escort Wing, from Mansto England, to the Air Force Base, Limestone, M (3,300 miles), in a single-engine F-84E Republ Thunderjet. The flight took 10 hours 1 minut Schilling made three aerial refueling contac with Air Force tanker planes. Lieutenant Colon William D. Ritchie, who also took off in an F-8 was forced to bail out over Labrador.

Jet transatlantic nonstop flight west–east wa made by two Boeing B-47 Stratojets of the Strat gic Air Command's 306th Medium Bombardme. Wing, based at MacDill Air Force Base, Tamp Fla., on April 7, 1953. The flight was made fro Limestone, Me., to Fairford, England, in 5 hours minutes—a distance of 3,120 miles at an averag speed of 555 m.p.h. The lead plane was piloted I Colonel Michael Norman Wright McCoy; Lieute ant Colonel Michael Irwin Berkowitz, observe and Lieutenant Colonel George Purnell Birdson Jr., copilot. In the second plane were Colon Lloyd Dean Griffin, copilot, and Lieutenant Col nel Lawrence Harry Grant, observer.

Pilot to fly 100 times across the Atlantic Ocea *See under* Aviation—Pilot

Transatlantic dirigible flight was attempted I Walter Wellman on October 15, 1910, when I and his companions left Atlantic City, N.J., in nonrigid dirigible, *The America,* en route to Ir land. The dirigible was 228 feet long, with a 5 foot diameter. They were forced down after 71

he First

ours by storms and fogs after flying 1,008 miles. The entire crew was rescued about 375 miles east f Cape Hatteras, N.C.

Transatlantic foreign squadron flight to the nited States was led by General Italo Balbo, alian Air Minister, who was in command of a quadron of 24 Italian seaplanes manned by 98 en. The flight cost was approximately $3 million, cluding an estimated value of $56,000 for each ane. The planes covered 6,100 miles in 47 hours : minutes. The squadron left Orbetello, Italy, unday, July 2, 1933, at 12:40 A.M. and flew to Amerdam, Holland; Londonderry, North Ireland; eykjavik, Iceland; Cartwright, Labrador; Sheac, New Brunswick; and Montreal, Canada, efore landing in Chicago, Ill., at 7:00 P.M. on July ~. *(Italo Balbo—My Air Armada)*

Transatlantic hydroplane flight was made by mericans, but it was not a single nonstop flight. ne NC 4, commanded by Lieutenant Commander lbert Cushing Read, left Rockaway, L.I., N.Y., on ay 8, 1919, in company with the NC 1 and NC 3, t was the only plane to finish the trip. Stops ere made at Trepassey, Newfoundland; Horta id Ponta Delgada, in the Azores; and Lisbon, rtugal. The final destination, Plymouth, Engnd, was reached on May 31—a total distance of 500 miles. Read's crew was composed of Lieunants Elmer Fowler Stone, Walter Hinton, and mes Lawrence Breese; Ensign Herbert Charles dd; and Chief Machinist's Mate Eugene Saylor oads. *(George Conrad Westervelt—The Triph of the N.C.'s)*

Transatlantic nonstop flight from America was ade in a Vickers Vimy Bomber, a bimotored lls-Royce airplane with four-bladed propellers, hich was piloted by Captain John Alcock of the yal Air Force and navigated by Lieutenant Arur Whitten Brown of the Royal Flying Corps. ey left St. John's, Newfoundland, Saturday, ne 14, 1919, and arrived in Clifton, Ireland, 16 urs 12 minutes later, covering a distance of 60 miles at the average speed of 120 m.p.h. *(Arur Whitten Brown—Flying the Atlantic in Sixen Hours)*

Transatlantic nonstop flight from Europe to the nited States and the first flight from Europe to e mainland of North America was made by Capn Dieudonné Coste and his mechanic, Maurice llonte, in a red sesquiplane, *The Question Mark.* ey took off from Le Bourget Field, France and rived at Curtiss Airport, Valley Stream, N.Y., at 2 P.M. on September 2, 1930, completing the first nstop flight from France to the United States, a p which consumed 37 hours 18½ minutes. This p was the 14th conquest of the North Atlantic airplane and the 5th westward flight. *(Dieunné Coste—Paris–New York)*

The First

Transatlantic regular commercial airplane service, flying the "southern route," was undertaken by the 41½-ton *Dixie Clipper* of Pan American Airways, commanded by Captain Robert Oliver Daniel Sullivan, which left Port Washington, L.I., N.Y., June 28, 1939, at 1:59 P.M., with 12 crew members and 22 passengers. It was powered by four 1,550 h.p. Wright Cyclone engines. Stops were made at Horta, in the Azores, and at Lisbon, Portugal. The plane landed at Marseilles, France, June 30, 1939, at 8:21 A.M. The fare was $375.

Transatlantic round-trip flight from the United States was made in the *Lady Peace* by Richard Merrill and Harry Richman, who left Floyd Bennett Field, New York, September 2, 1936, at 4:37 A.M., and arrived September 3, 1936, about 10:30 A.M., in a forced landing at Llwyncelyn, Carmarthenshire, Wales, 175 miles from Croydon Airdrome. The return trip was made from Southport, England, September 13, 1936, and the plane crashlanded at Musgrave Harbor, Newfoundland, about 100 miles from Harbor Grace, Newfoundland, returning to New York City a week later.

Transatlantic solo flight was made by Charles Augustus Lindbergh on May 20, 1927, from New York to Paris. He flew about 3,610 miles in 33 hours 32 minutes in the *Spirit of St. Louis,* a Ryan monoplane equipped with a single 225 h.p. Wright Whirlwind motor. He left Roosevelt Field at 7:52 A.M. on May 20, 1927, and arrived at 5:24 P.M. (New York time) the following day at Le Bourget field, Paris. *(Charles Augustus Lindbergh—We)*

Transatlantic solo flight by a woman was made by Amelia Earhart Putnam, who left Harbor Grace, Newfoundland at 5:50 P.M. Friday, May 20, 1932, and arrived at Londonderry, Ireland, at 8:46 A.M. Saturday, May 21, 1932. Her flight was made exactly five years after Lindbergh's flight. Lindbergh flew 3,610 miles in 33 hours 32 minutes; Amelia Earhart flew 2,026 miles in 14 hours 56 minutes. *(Amelia Earhart—Fun of It)*

Transatlantic solo westward flight was made by James Allan Mollison. He left Portmarnock, Ireland, August 18, 1932, 6:33 A.M., and landed at 12:45 A.M., August 19, 1932, at Pennfield Ridge, N.B., Canada. He made the trip in *The Heart's Content,* a de Havilland Puss Moth with a Gipsy III inverted engine. Accompanied by his wife, Amy Mollison, he made another east–west flight across the Atlantic Ocean, thus becoming the first man to have twice crossed the Atlantic in a westward flight. He took off from Wales, July 22, 1933, in the *Seafarer,* a de Havilland Dragon plane, and landed July 23, 1933, at Stratford, Conn., where the plane crashed. *(James Allan Mollison—Death Cometh Soon or Late)*

Woman airplane passenger to cross the Atlantic Ocean. *See under* Aviation—Passenger

The First

AVIATION—FLIGHTS—*Continued*

Woman pilot to fly across the Atlantic Ocean. *See* Aviation—Pilot: Woman pilot to fly across the Atlantic Ocean east–west

AVIATION—FLIGHTS (transcontinental)

Airmail regular transcontinental through-service. *See under* Airmail service

Airmail transcontinental flight. *See under* Airmail service

Airmail transcontinental service. *See under* Airmail service

Jet passenger commercial transcontinental service began January 25, 1959, when a four-engine American Airlines Boeing 707 made the trip between Los Angeles, Calif., and New York City with 112 passengers and 8 in the crew in 4 hours 3 minutes 3 seconds. The plane was piloted by Captain Charles Macatee of Huntington, L.I., N.Y. Another flight from New York to Los Angeles was made in 6 hours 33 minutes. The fare was $158.85 one way plus tax and $301.90 round trip plus tax.

Stratoliner commercial flight. *See under* Aviation—Flights

Transcontinental airplane flight was made by Calbraith Perry Rodgers, who left Sheepshead Bay, N.Y., September 17, 1911, in his Burgess-Wright biplane and was 49 days en route to California, arriving in Pasadena on November 5, 1911. He was followed by a special train carrying spare parts. The distance was 3,417 miles (2,567 airline miles), which he covered in 70 hops. His actual flying time was 3 days 10 hours 14 minutes. His best day's coverage was 231 miles and his best single flight was 133 miles, from Stovall to Imperial Junction. Weather was responsible for the loss of 11 days, and 13½ days were consumed in making repairs. On November 12, at Compton, Calif., he crashed and was badly injured, but on December 10 he continued his journey to the Pacific and landed at Long Beach, Calif.

Transcontinental airplane flight by a woman was made by Laura Ingalls, who left Roosevelt Field, N.Y., on October 5, 1930, in a Moth biplane. She made nine stops before reaching Glendale, Calif., on October 9, 1930, in 30 hours 27 minutes' flying time. On October 18 she made a return flight in 25 hours 35 minutes.

Transcontinental airplane flight (eastbound) was made by Robert Grant Fowler, who left Los Angeles, Calif., on October 19, 1911, in a model B Wright biplane equipped with a 30 h.p. four-cylinder Wright engine. He made 65 landings en route in California, Arizona, New Mexico, Texas, Louisiana, Alabama, Georgia, and Florida, and landed at Jacksonville, Fla., on February 8, 1912.

Transcontinental airship voyage was made by the *Shenandoah,* a dirigible of the Zeppelin type, which left Lakehurst, N.J., October 7, 1924, under

The First

the command of Lieutenant Commander Zachar Lansdowne, and arrived at San Diego, Calif., O tober 11, 1924. The *Shenandoah* made the retur flight and arrived at Lakehurst October 25, 192 The airship was originally the ZR1. It made i maiden trip September 4, 1923, and was chri tened the *Shenandoah* October 10, 1923, at Lak hurst, N.J. It crashed at Caldwell, Ohi September 3, 1925.

Transcontinental autogiro flight. *See under* A togiro

Transcontinental commercial overnight tran port service was inaugurated August 1, 1934, b the Transcontinental and Western Air. A twi motored Douglas monoplane, the *Sky Chief,* pilo ed by Otis Frank Bryan, took off from Newa Airport, Newark, N.J., August 1, 1934, at 5:24 P. and arrived at Kansas City, Mo. Here the passe gers transferred to a plane piloted by M. O. Brow and flew to Glendale Airport, Los Angeles, Cali where they arrived at 7:13 A.M., August 2, 1934.

Transcontinental dirigible flight (nonrigid diri ble) was made by the C2, which left Langley Fiel Newport News, Va., on September 14, 1922, a arrived at Ross Field, Arcadia, Calif., on Septem ber 23, 1922. The dirigible was 192 feet long, feet wide, and 67 feet high and contained 172,0 cubic feet of hydrogen gas. It was powered by tv 150 h.p. Wright motors and commanded by Maj Harold A. Strauss and Captain George W. McE tire. On its return trip on October 17, 1922, the b ripped while being towed out of the hangar at S Antonio, Tex., causing an explosion which injur seven of the eight-man crew.

Transcontinental flight in 24 hours' flying tin was made by Lieutenant William Devoe Coney the 91st Aero Squadron, who took off from Roc well Field, San Diego, Calif., at 7:00 P.M., Februa 21, 1921. He was forced down at Bronte, Tex., a snowstorm. He completed his flight at Pab Beach, Jacksonville, Fla., on February 24, 1921, 7:27 A.M. He covered 2,079 miles in 36 hours minutes' elapsed time and 22 hours 27 minut flying time.

Transcontinental flight made by blacks in th own plane was made by Charles Alfred Anders of Bryn Mawr, Pa., holder of a transport licen and Dr. Albert Ernest Forsythe of Atlantic Ci privately licensed pilot. They took off from Bac Airport, Atlantic City, N.J., July 17, 1933, at 2 A.M. and arrived at Los Angeles, Calif., July 1933, at 5:30 P.M.

Transcontinental flight within 24 hours w made June 23, 1924, by Lieutenant Russell Low Maughan of the Army Air Service in a 12-cylinc Curtiss PW8 pursuit plane equipped with a 4 h.p. engine. The airplane weighed 2,230 poun (gross weight 3,599 pounds). The flight started 3:00 A.M. (New York time), from Mitchel Field, L N.Y., and concluded at Crissy Field, San Franc

The First

co, Calif., 2,670 miles, at 9:48 P.M. (Pacific time). Stops were made to refuel at Dayton, Ohio; St. Joseph, Mo.; North Platte, Neb.; Cheyenne, Wyo.; and Salduro, Utah. The elapsed time was 21 hours 48 minutes, and the total flying time was 18 hours 52 minutes.

Transcontinental glider flight. *See* Glider: Glider towed across the continent

Transcontinental nonstop east-west flight by a woman was made by Laura Ingalls in a Wasp-powered Lockheed Orion monoplane, the *Auto da Fé,* which left Floyd Bennett field, Brooklyn, N.Y., July 10, 1935, and arrived at Burbank, Calif., 18 hours 19½ minutes later.

Transcontinental nonstop eastward scheduled service was inaugurated October 19, 1953, when a Trans World Airlines Lockheed Super-Constellation took off from International Airport, Los Angeles, Calif., at 7:09 P.M. (10:09 P.M. New York time) and arrived at Idlewild, New York International Airport, New York City, at 6:26 A.M. (New York time), on October 20, 1953. On westward flights, a stopover at Chicago, Ill., was made.

Transcontinental nonstop flight was made by Lieutenants Oakley G. Kelly and John A. Macready, of the Air Service, U.S.N. On May 2, 1923, the pilots, flying a Fokker T2 monoplane equipped with a Liberty engine, took off from Roosevelt Field, N.Y., at 11:36 P.M., and arrived at Rockwell Field, Coronado Beach, Calif., at 12:26 P.M., the next day, covering a distance of 2,700 miles in 26 hours 50 minutes.

Transcontinental nonstop flight by a woman was accomplished by Amelia Earhart Putnam. She took off from Los Angeles, Calif., August 24, 1932, at 4:26 P.M. (New York time), in her red Wasp-powered Lockheed airplane, and arrived at the Newark, N.J., Metropolitan Airport, 11:32 A.M. (New York time). She flew approximately 2,600 miles in 19 hours 5 minutes.

Transcontinental regularly scheduled through air service was opened October 25, 1930, simultaneously from New York City and Los Angeles, Calif., by Transcontinental & Western Air, Inc., a merger of TAT-Maddux Airlines and Western Air Express. The westward flight required 39 hours, of which 25 hours 35 minutes were in actual flight. Ground time was consumed in stops at Philadelphia, Harrisburg, Pittsburgh, Columbus, Indianapolis, St. Louis, Kansas City (overnight), Wichita, Amarillo, Albuquerque, Winslow, and Los Angeles. The eastbound flight, operating on the same schedule of stations, including the overnight stop at Kansas City, required a total of 34 hours 18 minutes. Actual time aloft was 23 hours 43 minutes. The one-way fare was $200.

Transcontinental regularly scheduled two-way nonstop service was instituted November 29, 1953, by American Airlines, using Douglas DC-7s,

The First

between International Airport, Los Angeles, Calif., and Idlewild, New York International Airport, New York City. The eastbound flight was scheduled for 7 hours 15 minutes and the westbound flight for 7 hours 55 minutes. Preliminary test runs over the 2,540-mile course were made November 20, 1953.

Transcontinental round-trip airplane flight within one day was made June 12, 1946, when a jet-propelled P-80 Shooting Star fighter plane, piloted by Colonel Leon Gray of Casa Grande, Ariz., Major Robin Olds of Beverly Hills, Calif., and Lieutenant Jack Richardson of Oklahoma City, Okla., left March Field, Calif., and arrived at Andrews Field, Md., in 5 hours 31 minutes, with a 34-minute stop at Oklahoma City to refuel. They returned in 6 hours 45 minutes, with stops to refuel at Scott Field, Ill., and Midland, Tex. The trip of approximately 4,540 miles was made in 12 hours 15 minutes. Total elapsed time, including a drive to Washington, D.C., for luncheon and return to the field, was 14 hours 51 minutes.

Transcontinental round-trip solo flight between sunrise and sunset was made May 21, 1955, by First Lieutenant John M. Conroy of Van Nuys, Calif., who took off from Los Angeles, Calif., in the *California Boomerang,* an F-86 Sabre Jet airplane, at 5:59:45 A.M. (Pacific time), and covered 5,085 miles in 11 hours 18 minutes 27 seconds, elapsed time. On the eastbound flight, he made stops at Columbus, Ohio; Tulsa, Oklahoma; and Albuquerque, N.Mex. On the return flight, after a 32-minute stop at Mitchel Field, N.Y., he landed at Denver, Colo., and Springfield, Ill.

AVIATION—FLIGHTS (transpacific)

California–Hawaii flight began at 7:09 A.M., June 28, 1927, when Lieutenants Lester James Maitland and Albert Francis Hegenberger flew in the *Bird of Paradise,* a triple-engine Fokker monoplane from Oakland, Calif., and arrived at Wheeler Field, Oahu Island, Hawaii, June 29, 1927—2,400 miles in 25 hours 50 minutes. *(Lester James Maitland— Knights of the Air)*

Honolulu squadron flight was made by six U.S. Navy seaplanes under the command of Lieutenant Commander Knefler McGinnis. The planes, with 30 pilots, left San Francisco, Calif., January 10, 1934, 2:22 P.M. and arrived at Pearl Harbor, Hawaii, 2,408 miles distant, 24 hours 56 minutes later, crossing the ocean at an average speed of 100 m.p.h.

Jet transpacific nonstop flight was made July 29, 1952, by a four-jet RB-45 Tornado bomber from Elmendorf Air Force Base at Anchorage, Alaska, to Yokota Air Base, Japan, a distance of 3,460 miles, in 9 hours 50 minutes, at an average speed of 350 m.p.h. The plane was refueled twice in flight by B-29 tanker aircraft. The flight was under the command of Major Louis H. Carrington of Austin, Tex., Captain Wallace D. Yancey of Fort Worth,

The First

AVIATION—FLIGHTS (transpacific)—*Continued*

Tex., was copilot, and Major Frederic W. Shook of Fort Worth, Tex., was navigator.

Pacific airmail. *See* Airmail service; Pacific airmail flight

Transpacific nonstop flight was made by Clyde Pangborn and Hugh Herndon, Jr., who landed at Wenatchee, Wash., October 5, 1931, having covered the 4,458-statute-mile hop from Sabishiro, Japan, in 41 hours 13 minutes in a single-motored 425 h.p. Bellanca monoplane. This was the last lap of their round-the-world trip.

Woman pilot to fly solo across the Pacific Ocean. *See under* Aviation—Pilot

AVIATION—FLIGHTS (world)

Jet round-the-world nonstop flight was made by three B-52 Air Force Stratofortress bombers, which flew 24,325 miles in 45 hours 19 minutes at an average speed of 525 m.p.h., under the command of Major General Archie J. Old, Jr., of the 15th Air Force. The takeoff was from Castle Air Force Base, Merced, Calif., on January 16, 1957, and the landing was made at March Air Base, Riverside, Calif., on January 18, 1957. The planes were refueled in flight by KC aerial tankers. Each eight-engine jet carried a crew of nine. The route was via Newfoundland, French Morocco, Saudi Arabia, the coasts of India and Ceylon, the Philippines, and Guam.

Round-the-world civil air service began June 17, 1947, when a Pan American airplane, commanded by Hugh Gordon, left La Guardia Field, New York City, with 21 passengers and a crew of 10. The route, 22,297 miles, was via Gander, London, Istanbul, Karachi, Manila, Bangkok, Calcutta, Shanghai, Tokyo, Guam, Wake, Honolulu, and San Francisco. The first trip took 309 hours 21 minutes, with 101 hours 32 minutes' actual flying time. Round-trip fare for the world flight was $1,700.

Round-the-world flight over the North Pole on a regularly scheduled commercial air route began November 15, 1954, when the Scandinavian Airlines System, using DC-6B's, inaugurated simultaneous service in both directions between Copenhagen, Denmark, and Los Angeles, Calif. The eastbound flight with 40 passengers left International Airport, Los Angeles, Calif., at 8:23 P.M. (Greenwich Mean Time) and arrived at Copenhagen on November 16, 1954, at 8:18 A.M. (G.M.T.), an elapsed time of 23 hours 55 minutes (20 hours 38 minutes' flying time) for the 5,800 miles. The westbound flight was made in 24 hours 11 minutes' flying time (27 hours' elapsed time).

Round-the-world nonstop airplane flight was made in 94 hours 1 minute by a B-50 Superfortress, *Lucky Lady II,* under the command of Captain James Gallagher. The plane left Carswell Air

The First

Force base, Fort Worth, Tex., on February 26, 1949, at 11:21 A.M. It carried a crew of 14 and averaged 249 m.p.h. on its 23,452-mile trip. It was refueled four times in the air by B-29 tanker planes and landed March 2, 1949, at 9:22 A.M.

World flight was made by three of the planes that took part in the round-the-world flight of the U.S. Army Service: the *Chicago,* piloted by Lieutenant Lowell Herbert Smith; the *Boston,* piloted by Lieutenant Leigh Wade; and the *New Orleans,* piloted by Lieutenant Erik Henning Nelson. The *Chicago* and the *New Orleans* crossed the Atlantic from Kirkwall, Scotland, to Indian Harbor, Labrador, stopping at Iceland and Greenland, completing the first leg of the world flight. The flight began at Seattle, Wash., April 6, 1924, and ended there on September 28, 1924. The *Boston* was forced down near the Faroe Islands in the North Atlantic. This trip also marked the first crossing of the China Sea and the first crossing of the Atlantic via Iceland and Greenland. The flight was made in 57 hops, averaging 483 miles each and in circumnavigating the globe the pilot touched or traversed 21 countries, 25 states, and 1 territory of the United States. The distance flown was 26,103 miles, the total time 175 days, flying time 351 hours 11 minutes. *(Lowell Jackson Thomas—The First World Flight)*

World flight by a commercial airplane was made by the *Pacific Clipper,* of Pan American Airways, which left San Francisco, Calif., December 2, 1941, under Captain Robert Ford, with a 10-man crew, and returned to New York City, January 6, 1942, covering 31,500 miles in 209½ hours' flying time. The return trip from New Zealand, because of war conditions, was over the Coral Sea, Netherlands East Indies, Indian Ocean, Java Sea, Bay of Bengal, Arabian Sea, Persian Gulf, Red Sea, the Nile and Congo rivers, overland to West Africa, thence to Brazil, and finally to New York.

World solo airplane flight was made by Wiley Hardeman Post in a Lockheed Vega monoplane, the *Winnie Mae.* He took off from Floyd Bennett Field, New York City, Saturday, July 15, 1933, at 5:10 A.M. and landed in Berlin, Germany, at 6:55 A.M. the following day (25 hours 45 minutes). Other stops were at Koenigsberg, Moscow, Novosibirsk, Irkutsk, Rukhlovo, Khabarovsk, Flat, Fairbanks, and Edmonton. Post returned to Floyd Bennett Field, Saturday, July 22, 1933, at 11:59:30 P.M., making the round-the-world circuit of 15,596 miles in 7 days 18 hours 49 minutes, of which 115 hours 36 minutes 30 seconds was flying time. His airplane was equipped with a Sperry automatic pilot and a directional radio. Accompanied by Harold Gatty, Post had previously made a round-the-world flight in the *Winnie Mae.* Starting from Roosevelt Field, N.Y., on June 23, 1931, they covered a total of 15,474 miles at an average speed of 145.8 m.p.h. They returned July 1, 1931, after an elapsed time of 8 days 15 hours 51 minutes. This trip was 2

The First

ours 2 minutes longer than the later solo flight by Post, the first man to fly around the world twice. *Wiley Post—Around the World in Eighty Days)*

AVIATION INSTRUCTION. *See* Aviation—School

AVIATION—LEGISLATION

Airport municipal legislation. *See under* Aviation—Airport

Aviation legislation (municipal) was enacted August 1908 by the town of Kissimmee City, Fla., imposing a tax on airplanes of $100, on helicopters 150, on ornithopters $200, and on all other types of flying machines $300 plus a tax on their carrying capacity, etc., and authorized the purchase of an "aeroplane of approved modern type" for the marshal to enforce the provisions of the ordinance. No attempt was made to enforce the law.

Aviation legislation (national) dealing with the operation of civil aircraft was the Air Commerce Act of 1926 (44 Stat. L. 568), approved May 20, 926, "to encourage and regulate the use of aircraft in commerce, and for other purposes." It was he basis for the formation of the Aeronautics branch of the Department of Commerce. Legislation dealing with the Army Air Corps and Naval Aeronautics was passed prior to 1926.

Aviation legislation (state) was passed by Connecticut, June 8, 1911 (page 1348, Chapter 86, Public Acts of 1911). The act "concerning the registration, numbering, and use of air ships and the licensing of operators thereof" was recommended by Governor Simeon Eben Baldwin. It required all airships to be registered ($5 fee) and all applicants for a pilot's license to be tested (fee not over $25). A license to operate and direct airships was required by each pilot ($2 fee). The law also provided as penalty for nonobservance a 100 fine and six months' imprisonment. (Earlier, a 1905, Tennessee passed an act in statutory form that authorized a tax on aircraft, but it did not attempt to regulate or control aircraft.) On May 0, 1927, the legislature of Connecticut authorized the organization of the Connecticut Department of Aviation, the first independent state department for the control and regulation of aeronautics in the United States (Chapter 324). Offices were opened July 1, 1927, at Brainard Field, Hartford, Conn. The first commissioner of aeronautics was Clarence Moore Knox, who served until March 1931.

AVIATION—LICENSE

Airplane instructor's license issued under the Civil Aeronautics Authority created by the Civil Aeronautics Act approved June 23, 1938 (52 Stat. 973) was a rerated license issued to Arthur J. anks, Atlanta, Ga., September 27, 1939. The first woman licensed was Evelyn Pinckert Kilgore, San Bernardino, Calif., October 13, 1939. In the early ays, "instructor" could be written on a private lot's license after 200 hours of flight.

The First

Cargo airlines licensed by the Civil Aeronautics Board were the Flying Tiger Line, Inc.; Slick Airways, Inc.; United States Airlines; and Airnews, Inc., which were issued licenses on April 29, 1949, effective June 24, 1949.

Civil Aeronautics Administration honorary license was awarded to Orville Wright on August 19, 1940, under authority of act of Congress passed June 13, 1940 (54 Stat. L. 1283). It authorized the issuance to Orville Wright of "honorary aircraft pilot's certificate numbered one in recognition of the outstanding service rendered by him in advancing the science of aeronautics."

Glider license awarded a woman by the National Aeronautic Association was No. 10 Class "A" issued to Maxine Dunlap (Mrs. Bennett) on February 5, 1931. Requirements were a flight of one-minute duration with two S curves and a normal landing.

Glider license Class "C" issued by the National Aeronautic Association (for a flight above the starting point of at least five minutes or a flight of at least five minutes without loss of altitude recorded by a barograph) was license No. 1 issued February 5, 1931, to Commander Ralph Stanton Barnaby, U.S.N. The first woman to receive the license was Hattie Meyer Barnaby, Washington, D.C., who was awarded license No. 37, August 12, 1931.

Glider pilot's license issued by the National Aeronautic Association was awarded to Leonard A. Wiggins, Akron, Ohio, on October 7, 1930. He was the first to receive both the "A" license (for a flight of one-minute duration with two S curves and normal landing) and the "B" license (for a starting, 360-degree turn both to the left and the right).

Glider pilot's license (honorary) was No. 1, issued to Clarence Marshall Young, assistant secretary of commerce for aeronautics, on November 7, 1929. Licenses were issued for student, commercial, and noncommercial classes. *(Records in Aeronautics Branch, U.S. Department of Commerce, Washington, D.C.)*

Pilot's license granted to a woman by the U.S. Department of Commerce was issued to Phoebe Fairgrave Omlie, who, on June 30, 1927, obtained Transport License No. 199. *(Records in Aeronautics Branch, U.S. Department of Commerce, Washington, D.C.)*

Pilot's license issued by the Aero Club of America, the first society officially recognized by the Federation Aeronautique Internationale, was license No. 1, awarded to Glenn Hammond Curtiss on June 8, 1911.

Pilot's license issued by the U.S. Department of Commerce was Private Pilot's License No. 1, awarded on April 6, 1927, to William Patterson MacCracken, Jr., former assistant secretary of

The First

AVIATION—LICENSE—*Continued*
commerce for aeronautics. *(Records in Aeronautics Branch, U.S. Department of Commerce, Washington, D.C.)*

President to hold an airplane pilot's license. *See under* President (U.S.)

Woman pilot to pass the test of the Aero Club of America was Harriet Quimby of New York, who on August 1, 1911, successfully passed her license test (F.A.I. License No. 37). She was also the first woman to cross the English Channel in a plane.

AVIATION—MAGAZINE
Aviation magazine was *Aeronautics,* published from October 1893 to September 1894 by the *American Engineer and Railroad Journal,* New York City. It was edited by Matthias Nace Forney, and featured reports and articles about airplanes, gliders, and balloons. It contained 16 pages and sold for 10 cents a copy or $1 a year.

Aviation magazine devoted primarily to airplanes was *Fly,* published November 1908 in Philadelphia, Pa., by [Alfred William] Lawson and [John F.] Kelley. It contained 20 pages and sold for 10 cents a copy or $1 a year. The cover showed a girl seated on the back of an American eagle beckoning to the pilots flying the only 2 airplanes that could fly. (*The American Magazine of Aeronautics,* published in July 1907, was devoted to balloons, kites, etc., as well as to airplanes.)

AVIATION—MEDICINE
Aviation medicine book. *See under* Medical book

AVIATION—PARACHUTE
Motion picture actor to stage a parachute jump. *See* Motion picture actor: Stunt actor

Nylon-parachute jump was made June 6, 1942, from an airplane at Brainard Field, Hartford, Conn., by Adeline Gray, parachute rigger of the Pioneer Parachute Company, Manchester, Conn.

Parachute known as the "free parachute"—the type with which the operator jumps before pulling the rip cord—was developed by the Army Air Corps under the direction of Major Edward L. Hoffman. The first person to jump with the Army manually operated chute was Leslie Le Roy Irvin, who jumped on April 28, 1919, from a de Havilland DH-9 biplane at an altitude of 1,500 feet, flying at a speed of 100 m.p.h. over McCook Field, Dayton, Ohio. He broke his ankle when he struck the ground. Floyd Smith was at the controls. Later Irvin founded the Irving Air Chute Co. In error, his name was spelled *Irving* on the incorporation papers. *(Records in Air Corps Materiel Division, Wright Field, Dayton, Ohio)*

Parachute fatality in the U.S. Army occurred March 6, 1941, when Sergeant Floyd S. Beard, age 28, of Coleman, Ga., a parachutist of Company C

The First

of the 501st Parachute Battalion at Fort Benning Columbus, Ga., jumped 750 feet to his death a Columbus, Ga., when his parachute failed to func tion. He was participating in a mass jump with 3 others.

Parachute jump from a balloon was made b Charles Guille, who ascended August 2, 1819 from Vauxhall Gardens, New York City, in wicker basket decorated with flowers suspende from a 25,000-cubic-foot prepared-silk balloo that cost $3,000. Avoiding a squall, he jumpe from a height of 2 miles with an umbrella-shape parachute and fell 300 feet before it expanded. H drifted across the East River and in 15 minute was out of sight, landing at New Bushwick, L.I., miles from the city. He carried 2 phials of harts horn and cologne water to counteract dizziness

Parachute jump from an airplane was mad March 1, 1912, by Captain Albert Berry from Benoist Pusher plane, piloted by Antony Jannu at Jefferson Barracks, St. Louis, Mo. Berry jumpe from an altitude of 1,500 feet while the plane wa traveling 50 m.p.h.

Parachute jump from an airplane by a woma was made by Georgia ("Tiny") Broadwick, 1 years old, on June 21, 1913, over Griffith Field, Lo Angeles, Calif., from an airplane piloted by Glen Martin and flying at a 1,000-foot altitude and speed of 30 m.p.h. After a 100-foot drop, her "lif boat," an 11-pound silken parachute, opened an she landed in a barley field.

Parachute jump from an airplane from a 53,00 foot altitude was made by Colonel Jack D. Nol Deputy Commander for Maintenance, 4080 Strategic Wing (SAC) U.S. Air Force, who baile out of a U-2 jet airplane on September 26, 1957, 2:54 P.M., at a 53,000-foot altitude over Laughlin A Force Base, near Del Rio, Tex. He was in the a 22 minutes, although the fall should have lasted 3 minutes.

Parachute jump from an autogiro was mad November 15, 1931, by Frankie Hammond, a par chute jumper of West Paterson, N.J., from a Pi cairn Autogiro at an air circus at Curtiss Esse Airport Caldwell, N.J. The air show was for th benefit of the family of Victor Brooks, Keypo pilot, who was killed November 1, 1931, when h plane crashed during a race at Stanhope, N.J.

Parachute jumper snagged in midair w Charles M. Alexander, who jumped from a singl engine Cessna 180 airplane at 10,000 feet on A gust 29, 1966, above the Sussex County Airpo Georgetown, Del. While at 9,000 feet, his par chute was snagged by a C-122 transport piloted b Captain Arnold Olsen at 120 m.p.h. to demo strate a method of rescue for airmen who bail o over enemy territory. Alexander was a test par chutist for the Pioneer Parachute Co., Mancheste Conn. Following engagement by the C-122 air craft, Alexander was taken aboard safely.

The First

Parachute tower for training parachute jumpers was a free-drop tower built April 1935, at Hightstown, N.J., by the Safe Parachute Jump Company, Hightstown, N.J. The tower was 125 feet high, with a horizontal arm at the top capable of being rotated 360 degrees.

Parachute wedding. *See under* Wedding

Pilot to bail out of a disabled airplane was Lieutenant Harold R. Harris, chief of the flying section of McCook Field, Dayton, Ohio, who jumped from a Loening monoplane on October 20, 1922, 2,000 feet over North Dayton, Ohio, before his plane crashed.

Pilot to bail out of an airplane flying at supersonic speed was George Franklin Smith of Manhattan Beach, Calif., who was propelled into the air when his seat automatically detached itself from an F-100A Super Sabre Jet fighter on February 26, 1955, above the Los Angeles International Airport, Los Angeles, Calif. He was at an altitude of 6,500 feet at the supersonic speed of 777 m.p.h. His clothes were cut to ribbons, and his socks, helmet, and oxygen mask were stripped off. He felt deceleration of 40 G's, so that his organs weighed 40 times normal. He landed in the ocean and was rescued by a passing boat off Laguna Beach, Calif. He was hospitalized about 6 months.

AVIATION—PASSENGER

Admiral in uniform to ride in an airplane was Rear Admiral Bradley Allen Fiske, U.S.N., who flew over the Hudson River and New York City on May 10, 1912, in a plane piloted by Walter Brookins and Robert Joseph Collier. *(Bradley Allen Fiske—From Midshipman to Rear Admiral)*

Airplane passenger (official) was Lieutenant Frank Purdy Lahm, who flew 6 minutes 26 seconds at Fort Myer, Va., on September 9, 1908, in a Wright plane piloted by Orville Wright. The first passenger to fly was Charles W. Furnas, who went aloft May 14, 1908, with Wilbur Wright at the controls.

Dirigible passenger transfer to an airplane was effected on August 29, 1929, at the Cleveland, Ohio, Air Show. Lieutenant Adolphus W. Gorton of the U.S. Navy attached a hawser, stretched between two uprights on the top wing of his plane, to a hook attached to a ladder of metal girders lowered from the keel of the dirigible *Los Angeles.* Lieutenant Calvin Bolster then descended to the plane.

Woman airplane passenger was the wife of Captain Ralph Henry Van Deman of the General Staff of the U.S. Army, who made a 4-minute flight October 27, 1909, at College Park, Md., with Wilbur Wright at the tiller.

Woman airplane passenger to cross the Atlantic Ocean was Amelia Earhart, who rode as the passenger of Wilmer Stultz, the pilot, and Louis Gordon, the mechanic, in the *Friendship,* a

The First

tri-motored Fokker airplane. They left Trespassey, Newfoundland, on June 17, 1928, and in 20 hours 40 minutes arrived at Burry Port, Wales. Amelia Earhart (later Mrs. George Palmer Putnam) was the first American woman pilot to whom the International Aeronautic Federation awarded a pilot's license. The award was made in 1923. *(Amelia Earhart—Twenty Hours Forty Minutes)*

Woman airplane passenger (transcontinental) was Lillian Gatlin of Santa Ana, Calif., who in a U.S. Post Office de Havilland mail plane equipped with a 400 h.p. Liberty motor, left San Francisco, Calif., October 5, 1922. Stops were made at Reno, Salt Lake City, Rock Springs, Cheyenne, North Platte, Omaha, Iowa City, Chicago, and Cleveland. The flight covered 2,680 miles in 27 hours 11 minutes' flying time. The final lap from Cleveland, Ohio, to Mineola, N.Y., was made by pilot Elmer C. Leonhardt, who landed at Curtiss Field, October 8, 1922.

Woman flown in a U.S. Army plane from one country to another was Herminia Davila, wife of Carlos Davila, former President of Chile. She was ill and was taken on board on a stretcher December 7, 1939, at Mitchel Field, L.I., N.Y., and arrived at Santiago, Chile, on December 9, 1939.

Woman Zeppelin passenger (paying) was Clara Adams of Tannersville, Pa., who left Lakehurst, N.J., on Monday, October 29, 1928, in the *Graf Zeppelin* on its eastward return flight to Germany.

AVIATION—PILOT

Ace (jet). *See* Marine Corps: Marine Corps jet ace

American ace under American colors was Lieutenant Douglas Campbell, who shot down a German pilot on April 14, 1918. His fifth victory, which qualified him as an ace, occurred May 31, 1918.

American ace in World War II was First Lieutenant Boyd David ("Buzz") Wagner of Johnstown, Pa. While serving in the Army Air Corps in the Philippines, Wagner was attacked on December 12, 1941, by 5 Japanese pursuit planes. He shot 2 planes out of the air and machine-gunned 12 on the ground, leaving 5 burning. He was awarded the Distinguished Service Cross and mentioned by Lieutenant General Douglas MacArthur in one of his communiques.

American ace (jet) was Captain James Jabara, of Wichita, Kans., a member of the Fourth Fighter Interceptor Wing, who in an F-86 Sabre Jet airplane shot down his 5th and 6th Communist MiG jet airplanes on May 20, 1951, in battle over Sinuiju, northwest Korea. Later, he defeated his 15th Communist MiG over Korea, becoming the second triple jet ace, the first being Captain Joseph McConnell, Jr., who scored 16 MiG victories.

The First

AVIATION—PILOT—*Continued*

American Ace of Aces was Captain Edward Vernon Rickenbacker, of Columbus, Ohio, who was credited with 26 victories (22 airplanes and 4 balloons). His first victory took place in the Baussant region, in the Toul sector, France, April 29, 1918, and his last in the St. Juvin region, October 30, 1918. *(Sender Garlin—The Real Rickenbacker)*

American ace (triple jet) in Korea was Captain Joseph Christopher McConnell, Jr., who shot down 16 MiG-15s in his F-86 Sabre Jet. On May 18, 1953, he downed three in one day. He completed 106 missions in Korea, and on August 10, 1953, a residence known as Appreciation House was presented to him by his neighbors in Apple Valley, Calif., who built it in 45 hours. He was killed August 25, 1954, at Edwards Air Force Base, north of Rogers Dry Lake, Calif., while testing a new plane, an F-86 H.

American bombardier over German-occupied territory. *See under* World War II

American pilot killed while a pilot in the Lafayette Escadrille, an American flying squadron in the service of France, was Victor Emmanuel Chapman, who was shot down June 23, 1916, northeast of Douaumont in the Verdun sector. From August 1914 to August 1915 he had been in the Foreign Legion. *(Bert Hall—One Man's War: The Story of the Lafayette Escadrille)*

American pilot shot down in World War I was H. Clyde Balsley of the Lafayette Escadrille, who was attacked by a German squadron at a height of 10,000 feet above Verdun, France, on June 18, 1916. Although wounded, he managed to land his airplane within the Allied lines. He received the Military Medal and the War Cross for his bravery. *(Edwin C. Parsons—The Great Adventure: the Story of the Lafayette Escadrille)*

American pilot to shoot down a German fighter plane. *See under* World War II

Army pilot to solo was Second Lieutenant Frederic Erastus Humphreys, who on October 26, 1909, at College Park, Md., made 2 circuits of the field in 3 minutes. He was followed by Lieutenant Frank Purdy Lahm, who went 6 times around and made some small circles as well, remaining aloft 13 minutes. Lieutenant Humphreys then resumed his solo flying for 8 minutes. *(Scientific American. Nov. 13, 1909)*

Army pilot to win a victory over an enemy airplane was First Lieutenant Stephen W. Thompson, First Aero Squadron, whose victory is recorded as of February 5, 1918, at Saarbrucken, Germany, where he downed an Albatross pursuit plane.

Black airplane pilot on a scheduled passenger line was Perry H. Young of Orangeburg, S.C., who was hired as a flight crewman on December 17, 1956, by New York Airways. He started regular

The First

passenger flights on February 1, 1957, as a copilo in a 12 passenger S-58 helicopter between Nev York International, La Guardia, and Newark, N.J airports.

Black army pilot to down an Axis airplane wa First Lieutenant Charles Hall of Brazil, Ind., wh in a Warhawk in a fighter squadron escortin bombers shot down a German Focke-Wulf 19 over Sicily on July 2, 1943. Lieutenant Colone Benjamin Oliver Davis, Jr., of Washington D.C was squadron commander.

Black flier of the U.S. Naval Reserve was Jess Leroy Brown of Hattiesburg, Miss., who was com missioned ensign on April 15, 1949. He crashe December 4, 1950, near the Changjin Reservoir i. Korea, the first black flier killed in action in Kores

Jet plane combat victor in the Korean War wa First Lieutenant Russell John Brown of Pasadenæ Calif., who on November 8, 1950, while flying U.S. Air Force F-80, destroyed a MiG-15 ove North Korea in a jet-versus-jet combat.

Ensign (women) to fly solo was Gale Ann Gor don, 23, of Stow, Ohio, of the Medical Servic Corps at the Pensacola Naval Air Station, Per sacola, Fla., who flew a propeller-driven T-34 o March 28, 1966. She received her flight training a part of her course of instruction as an aviatio experimental psychologist.

Father and son commercial airline pilots wer Captain E. ("Ham") Hamilton Lee and his so First Officer Robert E. Lee. Captain Lee was en ployed July 1, 1927, by Boeing Air Transpor which on February 1, 1929, became known a United Air Lines. Robert E. Lee, was employed a a first officer on May 19, 1941. Both did their tear flying between San Francisco and Los Angeles.

Marine pilot. *See under* Marines

Medal of Honor awarded to a helicopter pilo *See under* Medal

Naval ace in Korea was Lieutenant Guy Borde on, who in a World-War-II-vintage propeller-driv en F-4U Corsair achieved his fifth victory on Jul 17, 1953. He was awarded a Navy Cross.

Naval ace in World War I was David Sinto Ingalls of the U.S. Naval Aviation Forces, wh while attached to the 213th Squadron of the Bri ish Royal Air Force "alone and in conjunctio with other pilots shot down at least four enem aeroplanes and one or more enemy balloons." H was awarded the Distinguished Flying Cross b the British Government on October 25, 1918, an the Distinguished Service Medal by the Unite States on November 11, 1920. He served as assi tant secretary of the navy for aeronautics fror March 16, 1929, to March 15, 1932.

Naval ace in World War II was Lieutenant E ward Henry O'Hare who, alone and single-hanc ed, attacked 9 twin-engine Japanese heav

The First

bombers, shot down 5, and damaged a 6th on February 20, 1942, in the southwest Pacific, in an action of about 5 minutes' duration.

Pilot (American) to establish an altitude record was Louis Paulhan, who flew a Farman biplane on January 12, 1910, to a height of 3,967 feet at an aviation meet at Aviation Camp, Los Angeles, Calif. About 50,000 spectators witnessed his flight, which lasted 50 minutes 46.2 seconds. His descent was made in 7 minutes 30 seconds.

Pilot (American Navy) shot down and captured in North Vietnam. *See under* Vietnam War

Pilot in an airplane to qualify as an astronaut by attaining a 50-mile altitude was Major Robert Michael White, U.S. Air Force, who piloted the X-15 rocket airplane to an altitude of 314,750 over Nebraska on July 17, 1962. He was awarded astronaut wings on July 18, 1962. He took off from Edwards Air Force Base, Calif., and was launched from a B-52. He landed on Rogers Dry Lake, the flight lasting about 11 minutes. White was the fifth to qualify as an astronaut, being preceded by Alan B. Shepard, Jr., Virgil Grissom, John H. Glenn, and Scott Carpenter.

Pilot to die because of a lack of oxygen was Captain Hawthorne C. Gray, U.S. Army Air Corps, who took off from Scott Field, Belleville Ill., on November 4, 1927, in a balloon that rose to 40,000 feet. Despite his oxygen mask, he lacked oxygen because of his inability to open a reserve oxygen cylinder. He was found near Sparta, Tenn., about 310 miles from Belleville, in the basket of his balloon.

Pilot to down two enemy fighter airplanes in one day in Korea was Air Force First Lieutenant Robert Earl Wayne of Garden City, L.I., N.Y., who in an F-80 jet airplane shot down two enemy airplanes over Korea on June 27, 1950. He was one of the flight leaders with the 35th Fighter Squadron of the 8th Fighter Group. He was also the first jet pilot to down an enemy aircraft.

Pilot to fire a gun from an airplane was Lieutenant Jacob Earl Fickel of the 29th Infantry, who fired rifle shots at a target on August 20, 1910, at the Sheepshead Bay Race Track, New York City, from a single-seater Curtiss plane piloted by Glenn Hammond Curtiss.

Pilot to fly a million miles in a jet airplane was Melvin C. Garlow of Alexandria, Va., who flew his millionth mile on March 7, 1959. His first jet flight was made January 1955 in a Capital Viscount.

Pilot to fly 100 times across the Atlantic Ocean was Captain Robert Oliver Daniel Sullivan, who completed his 100th trip on December 28, 1942, from New York to Lisbon, Portugal. His first flight across the Atlantic was made January 28–29, 1938, from New York to Marseilles, France.

The First

Pilot to receive the Congressional Medal of Honor, granted by the President with the approval of Congress, was Second Lieutenant Frank Luke, for extraordinary heroism in action at Murvaux, France, September 12–15, 1918. The award was made April 14, 1919, for the destruction of 8 enemy balloons in 4 days, and was posthumously presented at Phoenix, Ariz., on May 29, 1919, to his father, Frank Luke, Sr. Luke was a member of the 27th Aero Squadron when he was killed in action. He is officially credited with 18 victories, a record that was surpassed in World War I only by Captain Edward Vernon Rickenbacker, who was credited with 26 victories and who later also received the Medal of Honor. *(Norman Shannon Hall—The Balloon Buster, Frank Luke of Arizona)*

Woman pilot to fly across the Atlantic Ocean east-west was Amy Johnson Mollison, who, accompanied by her husband, James Allan Mollison, left Pendine, Wales, July 22, 1933, at 7:00 A.M. in the *Seafarer* on a nonstop flight. They crashed July 23, 1933, at 9:30 P.M. at Stratford, Conn., about 55 miles from their ultimate goal. They flew 3,190 miles in 38½ hours.

Woman pilot to fly an airmail transport on a regular schedule was Helen Richey, who flew from Washington, D.C., to Detroit, Mich., via Pittsburgh and Cleveland, on December 31, 1934. She was appointed a copilot by Central Airlines and flew a Tri-Motored Ford 12-passenger transport.

Woman pilot to fly an airplane faster than 300 m.p.h. was Margie Hurlburt of Painesville, Ohio, whose clipped-wing Navy Corsair reached a speed of 337.635 m.p.h. over a 3-kilometer standard course at Tampa, Fla., in the All-Woman Air Show, on March 16, 1947. She broke the old record of 292.71 m.p.h. set by Jacqueline Cochran in 1937.

Woman pilot to fly solo across the Pacific Ocean was Amelia Earhart Putnam. She left Wheeler Field, Honolulu, at 10:15 P.M. Friday, January 11, 1935, and arrived at the Oakland Airport, Oakland, Calif., at 4:31 P.M. Saturday, covering 2,408 miles in 18 hours 16 minutes at an average speed of 133 m.p.h. *(George Palmer Putnam—Soaring Wings: A Biography of Amelia Earhart)*

Woman pilot to make a public flight was Blanche Stuart Scott, a pupil of Glenn Hammond Curtiss, who made a solo flight October 23, 1910, at the Driving Park, Fort Wayne, Ind. She used an Ely machine, rose to a height of 12 feet, and sailed across the field. After the flight, she stated, "I believe I could have turned and circled the track, but Mr. Curtiss has absolutely forbidden me attempting the turns until I have mastered the straightway flights." *(Fort Wayne Journal-Gazette. Oct. 24, 1910)*

Woman test pilot to test standard production aircraft was Alma Heflin, who made her first pro-

AVIATION—PILOT—*Continued*
duction test flight November 12, 1941, for the Piper Aircraft Corporation, Lock Haven, Pa.

Woman to fly entirely around the world by commercial heavier-than-air plane was Marjorie Shuler (Mrs. Felix Charles), who left Southampton, England, on June 4, 1938, and flew across Europe, down into Africa, across Asia, to Australia, back to Bangkok, to Hongkong, and across the Pacific, and from San Francisco, Calif., to New York City. She took off from Port Washington, L.I., N.Y., June 17, 1939, and completed her trip at Marseilles, France, June 19, 1939, covering the last leg of her flight from New York to Marseilles, 4,650 miles, in 42 hours 28 minutes. *(Marjorie Shuler—A Passenger to Adventure)*

Woman to pilot an airplane faster than the speed of sound was Jacqueline Cochran (Mrs. Floyd Bostwick Odlum), who on May 18, 1953, flew a North American F-86 Canadair over Rogers Dry Lake, Calif., at the speed of 652.337 m.p.h.

AVIATION—RACES

Airplane passenger race around the world to test commercial flying routes started September 30, 1936, from Lakehurst, N.J. Three reporters, Dorothy Kilgallen, Herbert Roslyn Ekins, and Leo Kiernan, made the trip by different routes. The race was won by Ekins of the New York *World-Telegram*, who returned to Lakehurst, October 19, 1936, covering 25,654 miles in 18 days 11 hours 14 minutes 33 seconds. The average speed was 127 m.p.h. The total flying time was 8 days 10 hours 6 minutes. *(Dorothy Kilgallen—Girl Around the World)*

Airplane race (of importance) in which both men and women were contestants was the National Air Race, August 30–31, 1931, from Los Angeles, Calif., to Cleveland, Ohio, in which 36 men and 16 women competed. It was a handicap derby scored on the basis of comparative power of motor and speed of plane. It was won by Phoebe Fairgrave Omlie of Memphis, Tenn., to whom an award was given on August 31, 1931. She also won the grand prize and the prize for the women's division.

Airplane race won by an American in Europe was the First International Air Race held at Reims, France, during the week of August 22, 1909. The fastest time on the 20-km. course was 15 minutes 50.6 seconds. The race was won by Glenn Hammond Curtiss, in the *Golden Flyer* (length 31 feet 1 inch, wingspan 30 feet, height 11 feet). He was also the first to win the James Gordon Bennett trophy in aeronautics.

Airplane to race a train was piloted by Glenn Hammond Curtiss, who took off May 29, 1910, from Van Rensselaer Island, Albany, N.Y., at 7:02 A.M. At 8:30 A.M. he landed at Poughkeepsie, N.Y., where he refueled the plane with 8 gallons of gasoline and 1½ gallons of oil. Another stop was

made at 214th Street, New York City, before th landing at Governors Island, N.Y. The distance o 150 miles was covered in 4 hours 57 minutes, c which 2 hours 46 minutes was flying time. Th plane weighed 1,000 pounds and had a 30-foc length and a 30-foot wing spread. It was powere by an 8-cylinder, 40 h.p. V engine built by th Elbridge Engine Company, Rochester, N.Y. Cur tiss won a $10,000 prize offered by the New Yor *World.* Although this event had been schedule as a race, the train really served as an observatio train. *(Clara Studer—Sky Storming Yankee)*

Intercity airplane race was held August 5, 191 between New York City and Philadelphia, P. Three Curtiss machines with Curtiss engines le Governors Island, N.Y. The race was won by Lir coln Beachey, who covered the 83 miles in 1 hou 50 minutes. Hugh Robinson completed the trip i 2 hours 8 minutes 47 seconds, while Eugene Bu ton Ely was forced to land at Princeton, N.J.

Transcontinental air race was held October 1919. Fifteen planes left San Francisco, Calif., an 48 left Roosevelt Field, Mineola, N.Y., in a 5,40 mile race across the continent and back in th aerial derby sponsored by the American Flyin Club of New York. Lieutenant Belvin W. May nard, in a de Havilland-4 with a Liberty moto crossed the continent in 24 hours, 59 minutes, an 48.5 seconds' actual flying time. He left Mineol October 8, 1919, 9:24 A.M. and landed at the Pres dio, San Francisco, October 11, in the elapse time of 3 days 6 hours 4 minutes. He left the Pres dio, October 14, 1:19 P.M. and arrived at Roosevel Field, October 19, in the elapsed time of 3 days 2 hours 31 minutes. Maynard won by elapsed tim but in his actual flying time he was eclipsed b three others.

Women's cross-country air derby was the Pow der Puff Air Derby, which began August 18, 192 when 19 women pilots took off from Santa Mon ca, Calif., in 10 minute intervals. Overnight stop were made at San Bernardino, Calif.; Phoenix an Douglas, Ariz.; Midland and Abilene, Tex.; W chita, Kans.; East St. Louis, Ill.; and Columbu Ohio. On August 26, 1929, 15 women complete the trip at Cleveland, a distance of 2,350 mile The winner was Louise McPhetridge Thaden Pittsburgh, Pa., whose time was 20 hours 19 min utes 10 seconds. Second was Gladys O'Donnell Long Beach, Calif., in 21 hours 21 minutes; an third was Blanche Noyes of Cleveland, Ohi whose time was 24 hours 33 minutes 58 second

AVIATION—SCHOOL

Aeronautical engineering course (complete cc lege course) was given in 1913–14 under the D partment of Naval Architecture and Marir Engineering, Massachusetts Institute of Technol gy, Cambridge, Mass. Lectures in aeronauti were given in 1912 and 1913. The first regular i structor in aeronautical engineering was appoin d in 1913. The aerodynamic laboratory was laced in operation and a graduate course was stablished leading to the degree of Master of cience in Aeronautical Engineering in 1914.

Air Force Academy (U.S.) *See under* Air Force academy (U.S.)

Air Force survival school was conducted by the 904th Composite Wing, Strategic Air Command, a December 1949. It was moved to Stead Air orce Base, Reno, Nev., in 1952. Training began in uly 1952. The Stead Air Force Base and the surival school became a part of the Air Training ommand's Crew Training Air Force on September 1, 1954, at which time the 3635th Combat Crew raining Wing was activated. Colonel Burton E. IcKenzie assumed command of the Training Ving in July 1955. The course lasted 17 days and vas devoted to instruction in survival under adverse conditions with limited food supplies.

Airplane flying school was opened by the Curss Exhibition Company in September 1910. It ave military officers free instruction in flying at e field at Lake Keuka, Hammondsport, N.Y. Ilenn Hammond Curtiss was the instructor. The rst officer of the U.S. Army assigned to these ourses was Captain Paul N. Beck, who became e first "military aviator." The Navy Department lso sent officers for instruction in flying.

Airplane flying school operated by a woman vas the Stinson School of Flying, Stinson Field, an Antonio, Tex., owned and opened in 1914 by mma Beaver Stinson (mother of Jack, Eddie, larjorie, and Katherine Stinson). On January 20, 916, a field of about 200 acres was leased from e city of San Antonio for $5 a year.

Correspondence school in aviation was the Inrnational School of Aeronautics, New York ity, which offered three courses—spherical balons, dirigible balloons, and heavier-than-air achines—on January 1, 1908, for the instruction f amateurs in aerostatics and aviation. Albert C. riaca was the founder and director of the school, nd Lieutenant Colonel Espitallier of the French rmy prepared the lessons. (*Aeronautics*—March 908, p. 18)

High school aviation course was instituted by aaren High School, New York City, in September 1929 with 11 students under the direction of Villiam Arnheim. In September 1931 an aviation nnex was organized and the 833 boys enrolled in e aviation course were transferred to this buildg. In 1944, there were 3,500 students enrolled.

Naval air training school was the U.S. Navy eronautic Station, Pensacola, Fla., opened ecember 1, 1914, under the command of Captain enry Croskey Mustin. The first staff consisted of ree instructors and a dozen mechanics. The ame was later changed to the U.S. Naval Air tation. From 1911 to 1914, flight training was

given at a camp at Greensbury Point, near Annapolis, Md.

AVIATION BOOK
Aviation book was John Wise's *A System of Aeronautics, Comprehending Its Earliest Investigations, and Modern Practice and Art; Designed as a History for the Common Reader, and Guide to the Student of the Art,* 310 pages, published in three parts in 1850 at Philadelphia, by Joseph A. Speel.

AVIATION COMPANY
Airplane company to carry 100 million passengers was American Airlines, New York City, which selected Lieutenant General James Harold Doolittle, chairman of the board of Space Technology Laboratories, Inc., Los Angeles, as the national symbol of the 100,000,000th passenger and presented him on December 28, 1961, with a crystal bowl.

AVOCADO was imported by Henry Perrine in 1833 and planted at Santa Barbara, Calif. (*Wilson Poppenoe—Manual of Tropical and Subtropical Fruits*)

AWARD. *See under* name of award; *also under* Medal

AX manufacturing plant was erected in 1800 at Johnstown, N.Y., by William Mann. The business was continued by his family at various locations and was sold in 1890 to the American Axe and Tool Co.

AXMINSTER CARPETS. *See* Carpet loom: Carpet power loom to weave Axminster carpets

---

B

BABIES' HOSPITAL. *See* Hospital

BABY CARRIAGE was made by Charles Burton in 1848 in New York City. Protests were heard because the people wheeling them showed a tendency to hit pedestrians. Burton moved to England, where he opened a factory and obtained orders for his "perambulator" from Queen Victoria, Queen Isabella II of Spain, and the Pasha of Egypt. (*Chronicles of a Baby Carriage—F. A. Whitney Carriage Co.*)

BABY CARRIAGE FACTORY successfully operated was started in 1858 in Leominster, Mass., under the firm name of F. W. & F. A. Whitney. This later became the F. A. Whitney Carriage Company. The carriages had two wheels, with a long tongue and supporting standard in front, and were made of wood. The first year only 75 carriages were built.

BABY SHOW was held at Springfield, Ohio, October 5, 1854, more in a spirit of jest than with a serious object. It met with instant favor and 127

The First

BABY SHOW—*Continued*
babies were entered, the prize baby being the 10-month-old daughter of William Ronemus of Vienna, Ohio, who was awarded a silver plate service including a large salver worth $300. Three other prizes were awarded.

BABY-SITTERS' INSURANCE POLICY. *See* Insurance

BACHELOR TAXES. *See* Tax

BACHELOR'S DEGREES. *See under* Degrees (academic and honorary)

BACK-PEDAL BICYCLE BRAKE. *See* Bicycle: Bicycle with a back-pedal brake

BACTERIOLOGY INSTRUCTION. *See* Medical instruction

BACTERIOLOGY LABORATORY
　Bacteriology diagnostic laboratory, as an integral part of the work of a health department, was the Division of Pathology, Bacteriology and Disinfection, established by the Department of Health of New York City in 1892. The first director of the laboratory was Dr. Hermann Michael Biggs, who served from September 14, 1892, to February 3, 1902. *(Wade Wright Oliver—The Man Who Lived for Tomorrow)*

　Bacteriology laboratory was the Hoagland Laboratory, 335 Henry Street, Brooklyn, N.Y., incorporated February 21, 1887, and opened for experimentation in February 1889. The first director of Laboratory and Department of Bacteriology was Dr. George Miller Sternberg, who demonstrated the microbe of pneumonia in saliva. The laboratory is a privately endowed institution and retains its corporate identity although affiliated with the Long Island College of Medicine, Brooklyn, N.Y. (Private bacteriology laboratories had been established earlier by individual physicians.)

BACTERIOLOGY LECTURES. *See* Medical instruction

BACTERIOLOGY TEXTBOOK. *See* Medical book

BAGS (PAPER). *See* Paper bag manufacturing machine

BAHA'I HOUSE OF WORSHIP was opened at Wilmette, Ill., for public lectures and guided tours on May 1, 1931. The site was blessed by Abdu'l-Baha, son of Baha'u'llah, on May 1, 1912. The temple was dedicated for public worship on May 2, 1953.

BAKING POWDER MANUFACTURER was Benjamin Talbert Babbitt, whose Star Yeast Powder was introduced to the public in 1870.

BAKING SODA (bicarbonate of soda) commercial production was undertaken by John Dwight and Dr. Austin Church in 1846, in New York City.

The First

In 1847 they organized John Dwight & Company

BALL BEARING commercial installation was made October 30, 1794, on the weather vane topping the steeple of the Evangelical Lutheran Church of the Holy Trinity, Lancaster, Pa. The brick portion of the tower rises 86 feet and includes the bell chamber, above which rises a spire from an octagonal base to a height of 195 feet, on top of which is the weather vane. The bearings were of the antifriction roller type with a pin through them.

BALL-BEARING SKATE PATENT. *See under* Roller skate

BALL-POINT PEN. *See* Pen

BALLET
　Ballet was presented February 7, 1827, in *The Deserter,* at the Bowery Theatre, New York City. The danseuse, Madame Francisquy Hutin, who introduced the modern ballet, wore a dress of gauze, and "a sort of subdued expression of fear and terror simultaneously rose from the ladies present, and at the next instant, as if inspired by one idea, they fled from the house." *(New York Clipper, Nov. 23, 1872)*

　Ballet transmitted by satellite shown in the United States was the Royal Ballet's "The Royal Ballet Salutes the U.S.A.," hosted by Gene Kelly from Covent Garden, London and broadcast over WNEW-TV, New York City, at 8:00 P.M., July 22, 1978, and at 3:00 P.M., July 23, 1978. The program was a Metromedia Television-British Broadcasting Company television coproduction and was sponsored by the Irving Trust Company.

BALLET INSTRUCTION
　University to offer ballet technique instruction was Texas Christian University, Fort Worth, Texas. Eighteen students registered in the 1949 fall semester freshman class, taught by David Preston. The first graduate to receive the Bachelor of Fine Arts degree, a ballet-theater, major, was Doris Nolan, who received the degree on May 31, 1957.

BALLISTIC MISSILE. *See* Rocket

BALLISTIC MISSILE OPERATIONAL UNIT. *See under* Army

BALLISTIC MISSILE SUBMARINE. *See* Submarine

BALLOON
　See also Aviation—Airship

　Balloon Atlantic crossing attempt was made by the 300,000-cubic foot *Daily Graphic,* which was launched on October 6, 1873, in Capitoline Gardens, Brooklyn, N.Y. Instead of a basket, a lifeboat supported by two slings was used. The crew consisted of Captain Washington Harrison Donaldson, George Ashton Lunt, and a newspaperman, Alfred Ford. The balloon left the earth at 9:

M. Later the crew ran into a storm and jumped, ear New Canaan, Conn., at 1:15 P.M. *(Washing-n Harrison Donaldson—History of Donaldson's 'alloon Ascensions)*

Balloon carrier. *See under* Ship

Balloon corps (army). *See* Army balloon corps

Balloon destroyed by enemy gunfire was shot own by the Spanish July 1, 1898, at Santiago, :uba. It was piloted by Colonel George Derby of ie Army Engineer Department who advised the irmy as to the enemy's movements. The balloon vas above the American troops, and the soldiers rere glad that it was brought down, as it drew fire i their direction.

Balloon parachute descent. *See* Aviation—arachute: Parachute jump from a balloon

Balloon to land on a building was flown by A. oy Knabenshue on June 30, 1905. He flew a dis-ince of 3 miles in 25 minutes and landed on a 0-story building in Toledo, Ohio. After a 15-iinute pause, he returned the airship to its start-ig point.

Dirigible. *See under* Aviation—Airship

Japanese balloon casualties. *See under* World Var II

Stamp for balloon mail. *See* Postage Stamp: tamp for balloon mail

ALLOON—FLIGHTS
Balloon flight was made by Edward Warren, 13 ears old, on June 24, 1784, at Baltimore, Md., in eter Carnes's balloon, 35 feet in diameter and 30 :et high, made of silk of various colors. The air vas rarefied by a cylindrical stove of iron sus-ended under the balloon. Carnes attempted a ight on July 17, 1784, at Philadelphia, Pa., but the alloon burst into flames. *(Maryland Journal and 'altimore Advertiser. June 24, 1784)*

Balloon flight by a native-born American in the Jnited States was made by Charles Ferson Dur-nt, the first to make aeronautics a profession. On eptember 9, 1830, at Castle Garden, New York :ity, he gave an exhibition in a balloon that he onstructed at his own home and flew to Perth imboy, N.J. Durant was the first person to land on oard a ship, a feat that he performed in Chesa-eake Bay on the *Independence.* For his accom-lishment he was awarded a gold medal in 1836 y the American Institute. *(Eric Adolphus Dime—'harles Ferson Durant: America's First Aeronaut)*

Balloon flight carrying mail dispatched from a ost office and using postage stamps was made by >hn Wise in the *Jupiter* on August 17, 1859, from afayette, Ind. He carried 123 letters and 23 circu-irs in a pouch. His destination was New York :ity, but instead he landed at Crawfordsville, nd., about 27 miles south of the takeoff. On July , 1859, he endeavored to fly mail from St. Louis,

The First

Mo., to New York City, but he jettisoned it in a storm.

Balloon flight in which a presidential order was carried was a 40-minute flight made by Jean Pierre Blanchard of France, who left Philadelphia, Pa., at 10:16 A.M., January 9, 1793, in the presence of President George Washington and other officials. He was permitted the use of the Walnut Street Prison courtyard at Germantown, Philadelphia, and the roar of artillery announced the moment of his de-parture. President Washington presented him with an order "To all to whom these presents shall come" directing that he be allowed "to pass in such direction and to descend in such places as circumstances may render most convenient." The balloon reached about 1 mile in altitude. He land-ed in Deptford Township, Gloucester County, N.J., about 15 miles away. It was his 45th ascension. *(Jean Pierre Blanchard—Journal of My 45th As-cension, Being the First Performed in America)*

Balloon flight powered by solar energy was made at 8:30 A.M. E.S.T. on May 16, 1973, by Tracy Barnes, president of the Balloon Works, States-ville, N.C., from the soccer field of the University of North Carolina, Charlotte, N.C., and lasted about 10 minutes. It was made in the *Solar FireFly*, AX-10, a 203,129 cubic feet tetrahedron or invert-ed pyramid. It used only solar energy to fly and did not employ a lifting gas or heat-producing de-vice. The heat of the sun's rays was absorbed by the dark skin, and the solar energy dilated the air within the balloon, creating its buoyancy.

Balloon flight to rise higher than 40,000 feet was made by Captain Hawthorne C. Gray of the U.S. Army Air Service, who ascended on May 4, 1927, from Scott Field, Ill., in a free balloon 80,000 cubic feet in capacity, with sand ballast. He reached an altitude of 42,470 feet in a flight of 1 hour 57 min-utes. Trouble developed over Grayville, Ill., and the balloon descended too rapidly. Abandoning the balloon at an altitude of 8,900 feet, he para-chuted and landed at Golden Gate, Ill. (not an official record, since Gray was not in command of the balloon landing).

Balloon flight to rise higher than 70,000 feet was made November 11, 1935, by Captains Orvil A. Anderson and Albert William Stevens, U.S. Army Air Force, from Rapid City, S.Dak., in the *Explorer II*, which ascended to 72,394 feet. It landed 12 miles from White Lake, S.Dak., about 240 miles east of the starting point. The 3,700,000-cubic-foot-capacity free balloon was aloft 8 hours 13 min-utes.

Balloon flight to rise higher than 100,000 feet was made by the Winzen Research Balloon flown as part of project Manhigh from Crosby, Minn., on August 19, 1957. It descended at Elm Lake, S.Dak., August 20, 1957, having reached an altitude of 101,516 feet during its 32 hours in the stratosphere. For approximately 26 hours its altitude was over

The First

BALLOON—FLIGHTS—*Continued*

90,000 feet. Major David Goodman Simons, medical officer of the U.S. Air Force, was awarded the Distinguished Flying Cross for this flight on August 24, 1957.

Transcontinental nonstop balloon flight was made by Maxie Leroy Anderson and his son, Kris Anderson, of Albuquerque, N.M., who took off from San Francisco at 12:30 A.M. P.S.T. on May 8, 1980, in the *Kitty Hawk* a 75-foot-tall helium-filled plastic balloon bound for Kitty Hawk, N.C. They flew 3,100 miles—a straight distance of 2,817 miles —and landed May 11, 1980, outside Matane, Quebec, in the Gaspé peninsula.

BALLOON CORPS, ARMY. *See* Army balloon corps

BALLOON HONEYMOON

Balloon honeymoon was spent on June 20, 1909. Roger Noble Burnham of Brookline, Mass., married Eleanor Howard Waring, Sunday, June 20, 1909, at Woods Hole, Cape Cod, Mass. They ascended at 12:40 P.M. in the *Pittsfield,* a balloon piloted by William Van Sleet, and were obliged to land at 4:30 P.M. at Ralph Gilkey's orchard at Holbrook, Mass., 14 miles from Boston Common.

BALLOON RACE

Balloon cup race for the James Gordon Bennett Aeronautic Cup was won by Lieutenant Frank Purdy Lahm, pilot of the balloon *United States,* who on September 30, 1906, with Major Henry Blanchard Hersey, flew from Paris, France, to Whitby, England, covering 410 miles in 22 hours 17 minutes. Sixteen balloons from seven countries were entered. The first race in the United States was held October 21, 1907, at St. Louis, Mo., and won by the German balloon *Pommern,* which, with Oscar Erbslöh and Henry Holm Clayton as pilots, flew 880 miles to Asbury Park, N.J., in 39 hours 59 minutes 25 seconds. There were nine balloon entrants in the 1907 race.

Dirigible balloon race was held at St. Louis, Mo., October 4-9, 1909, at which time four dirigibles, all the existing dirigibles in the United States, flew from Forest Park and Clayton Road to Kingshighway and Lindell avenues and back. The first prize of $1,000 was won by Lincoln Beachey. Roy Knabenshue and Captain Thomas Baldwin were close runners-up. Cornwall Dixon, using foot power, was carried over the city and landed in East St. Louis. The four dirigibles were housed in improvised tents and were filled with hydrogen produced by a slow process with sulfuric acid and iron filings.

BALLOON SCHOOL, ARMY. *See* Army balloon school

BALLOON TIRE. *See under* Automobile tire

The First

BALLOON TROPHY

Balloon trophy to a woman was awarded by the Dayton Aviation Committee to Mrs. Clifford Burke Harmon, who made 4 ascensions on September 16, 1910, in Dayton, Ohio, including a flight of 60 miles in 3 hours.

BALLOT. *See* Election: Printed ballot

BALLOT SYSTEM, AUSTRALIAN. *See under* Election law

BANANA IMPORTATION was recorded in 1804 when the schooner *Reynard* brought 30 bundles of bananas from Cuba. *(Philip Keep Reynolds—The Banana)*

BAND

School band was formed in 1857 by the Boston Asylum and Farm School for Indigent Boys on Thompson Island in Boston Bay, Mass. Musical sounds were produced by singing through paper covered combs. Later, three violins, a bass violin saxhorn, cornopean, and drum were added. Since 1859 the band has participated in street parades in Boston and elsewhere. In 1860 they had 1 brass pieces and a bass drum. On June 10, 1907 the name of the school was changed to the Farm and Trades School and in 1956 to Thompson Academy. Thompson Academy is a private 4-year school supported largely by contributions rather than tuition. *(Raymond W. Stanley—The Four Thompsons of Boston Harbor)*

BAND SAWMILL. *See* Sawmill

BANDING, BIRD. *See* Bird banding

BANDWAGON utilized for the distribution of samples and advertising matter was employed in 1871 by Benjamin Talbert Babbitt, who used eight imported white Arabian stallions to pull the wagon. The band was seated on top of the wagon. His slogan, "For All Nations," appearing on advertising cards over the doors of the Broadway street cars, was prominently featured. (Babbitt had the distinction of being one of the first to advertise in cars and buses.) *(John William Leonard—History of the City of New York)*

BANJO CLOCK PATENT. *See under* Clock

BANK

See also Federal Reserve System

Autobank complete service was instituted November 12, 1946, by the Exchange National Bank of Chicago. Ten tellers' windows protected by heavy bulletproof glass and impregnable corrugated steel were equipped with automatic slide out drawers to enable motorists to transact business without leaving their automobiles.

Automated "tellerless" bank was the Surety National Bank's Civic Center branch, Los Angeles, which opened April 27, 1970. It contained telestations equipped by closed-circuit television and monitored by a teller. A "validator" provided

The First

istant validation of checks by code rather than y signature. A money machine dispensed cash in n envelope.

Bank chartered by Congress was the Bank of Jorth America in Philadelphia, Pa., which was rganized on November 1, 1781. It began business n January 7, 1782, with a total capital of $400,000, f which amount the government subscribed 250,000. Thomas Willing was elected president, nd Tench Francis, cashier. Later the bank en-ered the National Banking System. *(Laurence ewis—A History of the Bank of North America, he First Bank Chartered in the United States)*

Bank credit card. *See* Credit Card: Bank credit ard

Bank established in a foreign country by a Unit-d States bank was opened November 10, 1914, by ie National City Bank of New York in Buenos .ires, Argentina. The Federal Reserve Act (38 tat. L. 251) approved December 23, 1913, permit-ed American banks to establish branches broad.

Bank for blacks operated by blacks was the avings bank of the Grand Fountain of the United)rder of True Reformers, a special order founded y William W. Browne, which was incorporated a 1881 in Richmond, Va. The bank, chartered in 1arch 2, 1888, began operations April 3, 1889, /ith a paid-up capital of $4,000. The first day's eposits were $1,268.69. The board of directors 'as elected by the society. (The Freedman's Sav-igs and Trust Company, established in 1865, was ot a black bank, but a bank operated by whites or blacks.) *(New England Magazine. Vol. 32, 905.)*

Bank for blacks privately operated by blacks nd independent of fraternal connections was the :apitol Savings Bank of Washington, D.C., .orga-ized October 17, 1888, with a capital of $6,000. *Association for the Study of Negro Life and His-ory, Inc. Arnett Grant Lindsay, John Henry Har-ion, and Carter Godwin Woodson: The Negro as Business Man)*

Bank of the United States was sponsored by the ederalist Party and was chartered February 25, 791, by "an act to incorporate the subscribers to ie Bank of the United States" (1 Stat. L. 191), in 'hiladelphia, Pa. Although the charter made no pecific provision for the deposit of government inds, the Secretary of the Treasury, Alexander familton, used the bank as a fiscal agent. The harter expired in 1811 and was not renewed by :ongress because of the opposition of the Demo-ratic-Republicans. The closing of the bank was artly responsible for the panic of 1814. The sec-nd Bank of the United States was authorized on April 10, 1816 (3 Stat. L. 266) and was opened on anuary 7, 1817. It ceased functioning as a na-ional institution in March 1836. *(Louis Carroll 'oot—The First United States Bank)*

The First

Bank open day and night was the Night and Day Bank, New York City, opened May 1, 1906, with a capital of $200,000, a surplus of $200,000, and a reserve of $100,000. Oakleigh Thorne was the first president. The idea was originated by Thomas Benedict Clarke. The bank closed at midnight June 5, 1910. It later became the Harriman National Bank.

Bank payments to depositors of a closed insured bank were made by the Federal Deposit Insurance Company on July 3, 1934, to the depositors in the Fond du Lac State Bank, East Peoria, Ill., which suspended business May 28, 1934, and went into receivership June 25, 1934. The insured deposits were approximately $104,000.

Bank president (black woman) was Maggie Lena Walker, who founded the Saint Luke Penny Savings Bank, Richmond, Va., incorporated July 28, 1903. It had a paid-in capital of $25,000. The first day's deposits exceeded $8,000. *(Sadie Iola Daniel—Woman Builders)*

Bank to install an automatic teller was the Chemical Bank, New York City, which placed its first machine in operation at Rockville Center, Long Island, N.Y., on January 1969. A coded card inserted in an opening dispensed a package envelope containing a set sum.

Bank to operate a window in a subway station for the convenience of subway riders was the Bowery Savings Bank, New York City, which opened two tellers' windows in a glass-enclosed cubicle in the Grand Central Station of the Interborough Rapid Transit subway on September 26, 1955. The windows had bullet-resistant glass. A special receptacle for passing money and bankbooks permitted only one side to be open at a time.

Bank to provide motion pictures for its customers waiting in line to be served was the Chemical Bank, New York City, which on December 22, 1972 projected motion pictures on a four-by-five-foot screen at 3 different locations, 2681 Broadway, 86th Street and Lexington Avenue, and at 67 Broad Street.

Bank with deposits exceeding $70 million was the Bank of America National Trust and Savings Association, San Francisco, Calif., whose deposits on December 31, 1978, amounted to $76, 795,-474.

Bank with resources exceeding $90 million was the Bank of America National Trust and Savings Association, San Francisco, Calif., whose resources on December 31, 1978, amounted to $92,-987,034. Deposits were $76,795,474, making it the first bank with deposits exceeding $70,000,000.

Bank with resources exceeding 1 billion dollars was the National City Bank (later Citibank), New York City, whose assets on November 17, 1919, were $1,027,938,114.31.

The First

BANK—*Continued*

Checkmaster plan (checking account service with no minimum balance requirements) was introduced June 27, 1935, by the National Safety Bank and Trust Company, New York City. A charge of 5 cents was made for each check drawn and each item deposited.

Christmas savings club was originated by Merkel Landis, treasurer of the Carlisle Trust Company, Carlisle, Pa., in 1909, and placed in operation by that bank the same year. The first payment was received December 1, 1909.

Clearinghouse was the New York Clearing House, organized August 23, 1853, by 16 presidents, 1 vice president, and 21 cashiers representing 38 banks, at the Merchants Bank, New York City. The plan was presented August 31, 1853, and was adopted September 13, 1853. The exchange was opened October 11, 1853, at 14 Wall Street. Total clearings the first day were $22,648,109.87 and the balances $1,290,572.38. Clearings for the year ending September 30, 1854, were $5,750,455,-987.06; for the same period, ending in 1980, they were $38,220,657,325,683.42. The New York Clearing House Association charter, drawn by George Curtis, was adopted June 6, 1854. *(James Sloan Gibbons—The Banks of New York)*

Drive-in bank. See Autobank complete service, above

Export-Import Bank of Washington, D.C., was organized February 8, 1934, pursuant to Executive Order No. 6581 dated February 2, 1934, "to aid in financing and to facilitate exports and imports and the exchange of commodities" between the United States, its territories, insular possessions, and any foreign country or its agencies or nations. The bank is a District of Columbia corporation, the certificate of which was filed February 12, 1934. Officers were elected February 13, 1934. The first president was George Nelson Peek, the first secretary Warren Lee Pierson. The capital stock of the corporation was $1 million par value of common stock and $10 million par value of preferred stock.

Federal Home Loan Bank Board. See Federal Home Loan Bank Board

Federal reserve system was placed in operation on November 16, 1914, when the 12 Federal Reserve Banks were formally opened. The Federal Reserve Act, approved December 23, 1913 (38 Stat. L. 251), was an "act to provide for the establishment of Federal Reserve Banks, to furnish an elastic currency . . . to establish a more effective supervision of banking in the United States." The 12 regional district banks were under the supervision of a 7-member Board of Governors.

Freedmen's bank was the Freedman's Savings and Trust Company, for the Negro, chartered by Congress (13 Stat. L. 510) March 3, 1865. A central

The First

bank was established in Washington, D.C., with branches in 34 cities. The bank was in operation about eight years, during which time it received deposits amounting to $57 million. The depreciation in security values due to the panic of 1873 caused the trustees to vote to close the bank, the affairs of which were placed in the hands of three commissioners.

Joint stock land bank chartered was the Iowa Joint Stock Land Bank of Sioux City, Iowa. It was chartered April 24, 1917, and authorized to do business in the states of Iowa and South Dakota. The charter was granted under the Federal Farm Loan Act of July 17, 1916 (39 Stat. L. 360).

Major bank to lease personal property was the Bank of America, San Francisco, Calif., which instituted the service on July 22, 1963, under the direction of Robert D'Oyly Syer. James Joseph Saxon, comptroller of the currency, advised national banks on March 18, 1963, that they were permitted to lease personal property, buying equipment and leasing it directly to customers.

National bank under the national banking law of February 25, 1863 (12 Stat. L. 665), an "act to provide a national currency," was the first National Bank of Davenport, Iowa, now the Union Savings Bank and Trust Company. The application for the charter was mailed from Davenport, Iowa, on February 24, 1863, one day prior to President Abraham Lincoln's signing the bill. Charters were numbered in the order in which they were received in Washington, D.C. Davenport, being located some distance from Washington, received charter No. 15, dated June 22, 1863. Subscription books were opened on May 25, and in three days the capital stock of $100,000 had been subscribed. The first stockholders' meeting was held Saturday, May 30, and the first directors were elected June 6, 1863, to serve until January 12, 1864. The first president was Austin Corbin. The bank was opened on June 29, 1863. For two days the bank was the only national bank in operation under the new act.

National bank branch legally operated was the Pascagoula National Bank of Moss Point, Miss., Charter No. 8,593. This bank was a conversion of the Bank of Moss Point, a state association, with a branch at Scranton, Miss. (now known as Pascagoula). This branch was retained and operated by the Pascagoula National Bank of Moss Point under authority conferred by the Act of March 3, 1865 (13 Stat. L. 484), which provided that "any bank or banking association organized under state laws, and having branches, the capital being joint and assigned to and used by the mother bank and branches in definite proportions, may, if it becomes a national banking association in conformity with existing laws, retain and keep in operation its branches, or such one or more of them as it may elect to retain." The Pascagoula Na-

he First

onal Bank of Moss Point was chartered on
March 14, 1907, and is still in operation, together
with the branch at Pascagoula, Miss. The branch
t Pascagoula has operated continually since the
pening of the parent bank at Moss Point.

National bank chartered was the First National
ank of Philadelphia, Pa., Charter No. 1. This
ank, chartered on June 20, 1863, was no conver-
ion of a state bank into the national system, but
primary organization. It opened for business
uly 11, 1863.

National bank failure was the First National
ank of Attica, N.Y., placed in receivership April
4, 1865. The failure was due to injudicious bank-
ng and failure of large debtors. The receivership
vas terminated January 2, 1867.

National bank woman president was Frances
stelle (Mason) Moulton, who was elected Janu-
ry 11, 1938, as president of the Limerick National
ank, Limerick, Me., to fill the vacancy caused by
he death of her father, Jeremiah Miller Mason.

Postal savings bank was authorized by Presi-
ent William Howard Taft on June 25, 1910 (36
tat. L. 814), when he signed the "act to establish
ostal savings depositories for depositing savings
t interest," introduced by Senator Thomas Henry
arter of Montana on January 26, 1910, an act
vhich created a board of trustees consisting of the
ostmaster General, the Secretary of the Treas-
ry, and the Attorney General, severally, acting
x officio, for the control, supervision, and ad-
ninistration of the postal savings system. Postal
avings service was established initially at 48 sec-
nd-class post offices on January 3, 1911. The ser-
ice was gradually extended to other post offices.
ttention was drawn to postal savings by Post-
naster General John Angel James Creswell in
871, but no action was taken despite the fact that
0 such bills were introduced into Congress be-
ween 1873 and 1910. Deposits in 11 months
eached a total of $11,000,000, which was distrib-
ted among 2,710 national and state banks.

Savings bank was the Bank for Savings in the
ity of New York, which was conceived on
November 29, 1816, but for which the charter was
ot granted until March 26, 1819. The bank opened
or business on July 3, 1819. The deposits on the
irst day, received from 80 depositors, amounted
o $2,807. The statement for the first six months
howed a loss of $27 suffered as a result of the
ank's accepting counterfeit money and a short
hange loss of $23.92. *(Emerson Willard Keyes—
listory of Savings Banks)*

**Savings bank actually to receive money on
deposit** was the Philadelphia Saving Fund Soci-
ty, Seventh and Walnut streets, Philadelphia,
a., which opened for business on December 2,
816, in the office of George Billington, the secre-
ary-treasurer, on the west side of Sixth Street.
illington received a salary of $250 a year. The

The First

affairs of the bank were conducted by 12 managers. Andrew Bayard was the first president. The
bank was chartered February 25, 1819. Condy
Raguet, on November 25, 1816, suggested the idea
of the bank to four others.

Savings bank to become a corporation was the
Provident Institution for Savings in Boston, Mass.,
which was chartered December 13, 1816, and
opened for business on February 19, 1817. It paid
interest at the rate of 5 percent per annum and
was under the management of 1 president, 12 vice
presidents, and 24 other trustees, who had the
power to elect a treasurer and other officers. *(Edward Levi Robinson—One Hundred Years of Savings Banking)*

Savings bank with a half-billion-dollar deposit
was the Bowery Savings Bank of New York,
which, according to its statement of March 31,
1932, had more than $502 million, owned by 378,-
000 depositors.

Savings group to teach children to save their
money in a methodical manner was started March
16, 1885, by Professor John Henry Thiry of Long
Island City, N.Y., who established a system of
fund collections in schools and a school savings
bank. *(Edward Levi Robinson—One Hundred
Years of Savings Banking)*

**State bank wholly owned and operated by a
state** was the Bank of North Dakota, Bismarck,
N.D., established by special referendum election
June 26, 1919, under jurisdiction of the federal Industrial Commission, and opened July 28, 1919. It
was the only legal depository of all the state funds
and those of state institutions.

Trailer bank was the Meadow Brook National
Bank, West Hempstead, Long Island, N.Y., which
opened a branch trailer bank at Locust Grove,
Long Island, N.Y., on May 26, 1956, in a 46-foot
air-conditioned trailer. It had four tellers' windows opening out on one side of the trailer. The
first day, over $100,000 was received in deposits.
The trailer was used pending the erection of a
permanent structure adjacent to the trailer.

Traveler's checks. *See under* Check

Trust company permitted to do a trust business
was the Farmer's Fire Insurance and Loan Company of New York City, which was incorporated
February 28, 1822. It became the City Bank Farmer's Trust Company and later the First National
City Trust Company. The first company to use
"Trust Company" as part of its title was the New
York Life Insurance and Trust Company of New
York City. The company was chartered on March
9, 1830, with an authorized capital of $1 million.
The organization meeting was held on April 12,
1830, and William Bard was chosen the first presi-
dent. In 1922 it merged with the Bank of New York
and National Banking Association, forming the
Bank of New York and Trust Company. The first

The First

BANK—*Continued*

company organized to do a trust business exclusively was the United States Trust Company of New York, which was incorporated on April 12, 1853. The first president was Joseph Lawrence. *(American Institute of Banking—Study Course)*

World bank was the International Bank for Reconstruction and Development, which entered into force on December 27, 1945, when it was subscribed to by 21 countries, whose subscription amounted to $7,173 million. The United States subscription was $3,175 million. The first loan was made on May 9, 1947, to France—a 30-year loan of $250 million at 3¼ percent and $150 million at 3 percent.

BANK LEGISLATION

Bank guaranty legislation was the Glass-Steagall Act, the "Banking Act of 1933," which was passed by Congress, June 16, 1933 (48 Stat. L. 162) to provide for the safer and more effective use of the assets of banks, to regulate interbank control, to prevent the undue diversion of funds into speculative operation, effective January 1, 1934. It insured deposits up to $2,500 each in all Federal Reserve banks and, on July 1, 1934, deposits in approved banks—100 percent up to $10,000; 75 percent from $10,000 to $50,000; 50 percent over $50,000. "An act to provide for the sound, effective and uninterrupted operation of the banking system, and for other purposes" (49 Stat. L. 684) approved August 23, 1935, limited the insurance to $5,000 for any one depositor.

Bank legislation (state) to insure depositors was the Safety Fund Banking Law of New York, Chapter 94, "an act to create a fund for the benefit of the creditors of certain monied corporations," enacted April 2, 1829. Banking organizations were assessed ½ of 1 percent of the capital stock, until 3 percent was set aside for a bank fund. Three commissioners, known as Bank Commissioners of the State of New York, were appointed for two-year terms at an annual salary of $1,500. Banks, their officers, and servants were required to be examined under oath, at least once every four months.

National banking system was created by statute on February 25, 1863. This act provided for a Comptroller of Currency under the Treasury Department. The first incumbent was Hugh McCulloch, who served from May 9, 1863, to March 8, 1865. *(Amos Kidder Fiske—The Modern Bank)*

BANK ROBBERY occurred Saturday, March 19, 1831, when two doors of the City Bank, Wall Street, New York City, were opened by duplicate keys and the bank was robbed of $245,000. Edward Smith, an Englishman (alias Jones, alias James Smith, alias James Honeyman), was indicted by the Grand Jury and arraigned May 2, 1831, at the Court of General Sessions. On May 11, 1831, he was sentenced to five years at hard labor at

The First

Sing Sing. Over $185,000 of the loot was recov ered. *(New York Gazette. March 22, 1831)*

BANKERS' ASSOCIATION

Bankers' association formed by a state grou was the Texas Bankers' Association, which wa organized July 23, 1885, at Lampasas, Tex., wit an initial membership of 31. The first presiden was James Francis Miller and the first secretar Frank R. Malone.

National bankers' association was the Ameri can Bankers Association, which was organize on May 24, 1875. The first national conventio was held at Saratoga, N.Y., July 20-22, 1875, a which time Charles Bingley Hall was electe president. The objects of the association wer self-protection against frauds, standardization o rules, and bettering of conditions between th banks and their clients. *(Banker's Magazine. Au gust 1875)*

BANKRUPTCY ACT was the act of April 4, 180 (2 Stat. L. 20), "to establish a uniform system o bankruptcy in the United States." It contained 6 sections and applied to "any merchant or othe person residing within the United States, actuall using the trade of merchandise, by buying an selling in gross, or by retail, or dealing in ex change as a banker, broker, factor, underwriter o marine insurer." It was repealed in Decembe 1803. It did not permit voluntary bankruptcy an applied to traders only. *(Charles Warren—Bank ruptcy in United States History)*

BAPTISM

Baptism occurred in March 1540. Two India guides called Peter and Mark were baptized in th Ocmulgee River near Macon, Ga. *(John C. Butler–Historical Record of Macon and Central Georgia)*

Black child baptized in the English colonies i North America was William Tucker, baptized i 1624 at Jamestown, Va.

BAPTIST CHURCH

Baptist Church in America was probably estab lished by Roger Williams, "the Apostle of Reli gious Liberty," in Providence, R.I., in 1639. Th First Baptist Church of Newport, R.I., founded b Dr. John Clarke, its first pastor (now the First Bap tist John Clarke Memorial Church), was definitel called a Baptist Church in 1644. A church and meetinghouse, however, are believed to hav been erected as early as 1638. *(Edward Franci Rines—Old Historic Churches of America)*

Baptist Church (black) was established in 177 by a Mr. Palmer at Silver Bluff, S.C., a small settle ment opposite Augusta on the Savannah Rive George Galphin became a patron and permitte David George to be ordained for this special wor after having previously allowed George Liele t preach there. *(Carter Godwin Woodson—Histor of the Negro Church)*

The First

German Baptists (also known as Dunkards, Dunkers, and Tunkers) held their first immersion December 25, 1723, at Wissahickon Creek, Germantown, Philadelphia, Pa. The first chosen elder was Peter Becker and the first congregation was the Coventry Congregation, which met September 7, 1724. *(Martin Grove Brumbaugh—History of the German Baptist Brethren in Europe and America)*

Seventh Day Baptist Church was organized at Newport, R.I., in 1671, by Stephen Mumford, an English Sabbatarian Baptist. The first deacon was William Weeden. *(Albert Henry Newman—History of the Baptist Churches in the United States)*

BAR ASSOCIATION. *See* Lawyers' association

BARBED WIRE. *See* Wire

BAREKNUCKLE CHAMPIONSHIP FIGHT. *See* Prizefight: International fight with bareknuckles.

BARGE (concrete). *See* Ship: Concrete barge

BARLESS ZOO. *See* Zoological garden: Barless zoological garden of naturalistic rock construction

BARRAGE, MINE. *See* Mine barrage

BASEBALL

Baseball (yellow) was used April 27, 1938, in the Columbia-Fordham game, New York City. It was a regulation National League ball dyed yellow, with red stitches, and was developed by Frederic Rahr.

Cork-center baseball was invented by Benjamin F. Shibe of Bala, Pa., who obtained patent No. 924,696 on June 15, 1909. It was manufactured by A. G. Spalding & Bros., Chicago, Ill., and used in occasional league games in 1909 and in regular play in 1910. The ball was first used in World Series games on October 20, 22, and 23, 1910, in Chicago, Ill., between the Philadelphia (American League) and the Chicago (National League) teams.

BASEBALL BATTING AND FIELDING CAGE was built at Yale University, New Haven, Conn., in the fall of 1885 by Captain Philip Battell Stewart. The candidates for the team worked there during the winter of 1886. The building was about 70 feet long and 20 feet wide and had skylights protected by wire. It was the forerunner of the expensive cages and field houses so common in American colleges and universities.

BASEBALL BOOK was Robin Carver's *The Book of Sports,* published in 1834 in Boston, Mass., by Lilly, Wait, Colman, and Holden. It was based on an English edition of the *Boy's Own Book.* Similar rules applied to the game of rounders were published in 1829.

BASEBALL CATCHER'S MASK was invented by Frederick Winthrop Thayer of Waverly, Mass., captain of the Harvard University Baseball Club, who obtained Patent No. 200,358 on February 12, 1878, on a "face guard or safety mask." It was

The First

made by a Cambridge, Mass., tinsmith, tried out in the gymnasium in the winter of 1876–77, and used by James Alexander Tyng in a game with the Live Oaks at Lynn, Mass., April 12, 1877. Louis Trauschke, catcher of the Foster Baseball Club, Lawrence, Mass., who had been hurt by a pitched ball, adopted the mask. It was manufactured by Peck & Snyder, New York City. *(H Book of Harvard Athletics)*

BASEBALL CHEST PROTECTOR

Chest protector for catchers was invented by William Gray of Hartford, Conn., and used in 1878. He sold his rights in the 1880s to Albert Goodwill Spalding for $5,000.

BASEBALL COACH

Baseball coach (black) in the major leagues was John ("Buck") O'Neil of the Chicago Cubs (National League), hired May 29, 1962, as one of its 6 coaches. Previously he served the team in various other capacities.

BASEBALL "DICTATOR" was Judge Kenesaw Mountain Landis, elected November 12, 1920, for a seven-year term from 1921 to 1928. He received $42,500 a year and $10,000 expenses to rule the 16 American and National League Baseball Clubs. He served from January 12, 1921, to November 24, 1944. (He was reelected in 1925, 1935, and 1942.) He died November 24, 1944, and was succeeded by Senator Albert Benjamin ("Happy") Chandler of Kentucky, elected April 24, 1945, for a seven-year period at $50,000 a year.

BASEBALL GAME

All-star baseball game (major league) was played July 6, 1933, at Comiskey Park, Chicago. The American League defeated the National League 4-2. The American runs were batted in by Earl Douglas Averill, Vernon Louis ("Goofy," "Lefty") Gomez, and George Herman ("Babe") Ruth, who hit 2 runs, 1 of which was a homer in the third inning. The National runs were made by Johnny Leonard, Roosevelt ("Pepper") Martin (the "Wild Hoss of the Osage"), and Francis ("Frankie") Frisch (the "Fordham Flash"). Cornelius McGillicuddy ("Connie") Mack was the American manager, John Joseph McGraw, the National manager. The attendance was 49,200; receipts were $56,378.50.

American League 20-inning baseball game was played in the afternoon at Boston on July 4, 1905. The Philadelphia Quakers defeated the Boston Puritans 4-2. George Edward ("Rube") Waddell was the Philadelphia pitcher; Denton True ("Cy") Young, the Boston pitcher, did not give a base on balls the entire game. The playing time was 3 hours 31 minutes, the attendance 12,666. In the morning game Philadelphia defeated Boston 5-2. In the 20th inning the 2-2 tie was broken.

The First

BASEBALL GAME—*Continued*

Baseball is attributed to Colonel Abner Doubleday, who later became a general in the U.S. Army. In 1839 he laid out the first regular baseball diamond at Cooperstown, N.Y., and formulated the rules of play.

Baseball game at night was played June 2, 1883, at League Park, Fort Wayne, Ind., between a club of boys known as the M.E. College and the Quincy professionals. The score was Quincy 19, College 11. The field was illuminated by 17 lights of 4,000 candlepower each. Only 7 innings were played. The game was witnessed by 2,000 people. A preliminary test was made May 29, 1883, using 11 of the 16 lights then set up. The Quincy team was from Adams County, Ill. *(Fort Wayne Journal-Gazette. June 3, 1883)*

Baseball game at night by a regular league team took place in Grand Rapids, Mich., on July 8, 1909. It was played between the Grand Rapids and Zanesville teams in the Central League. Grand Rapids won 11 to 10.

Baseball game at night by major-league teams was played at Crosley Field, Cincinnati, Ohio, May 24, 1935, when the Cincinnati Reds defeated the Philadelphia Phillies 2 to 1 before a paid attendance of 20,422. President Franklin Delano Roosevelt, in Washington, D.C., pressed a button that turned on 363 lights (1,000 kilowatts each) on 8 giant towers for this National League game.

Baseball game broadcast with a play-by-play description. *See under* Radio broadcast

Baseball game for which admission was charged. *See* Baseball game: Baseball series

Baseball game in which one team scored more than 100 runs was played Sunday October 1, 1865. In a 9-inning game in Philadelphia, the Philadelphia Athletics defeated the Jersey City Nationals 114-2. About 500 women were among the 5,000 spectators.

Baseball game in which there were two triple-steals was played July 25, 1930, at Cleveland, Ohio, between the American League Philadelphia Athletics and the Cleveland Indians. In the first inning Aloysius Harry ("Al") Simmons scored, Edmund John ("Bing") Miller and Edwin Debbell ("Deb") Williams stole a base: in the fourth inning, Gordon Stanley ("Mickey") Cochrane scored, Max Frederick Bishop and Edmund John ("Bing") Miller stole a base. Philadelphia won 14-1.

Baseball game (major league) in which 49 runs were made in a 9-inning game was played August 25, 1922, in Chicago. The National League Chicago Cubs made 26 runs, the Philadelphia Phillies 23. Chicago used 5 pitchers, Philadelphia 2. The game lasted 3 hours 1 minute. There were 61 hits. Chicago made 10 runs in the second inning and 14 in the fourth.

The First

Baseball game (major league) in which 14 runs were scored in 1 inning was played July 6, 1920, at Washington, D.C., when the New York Yankees defeated the Washington Senators of the American League 17-0. In the fifth inning, the Yankees made 14 runs, as the result of 7 hits, 2 sacrifice hits, a base hit, 3 passes, 5 errors, and a wild pitch. Olaf Erikson was the losing Washington pitcher. (Chicago made 18 runs against Detroit in 1883, but this was not in a major league game.)

Baseball game (major league) in which 1 team scored 24 runs was played May 18, 1912, at Shibe Park, Philadelphia, when the American League Philadelphia Athletics defeated the Detroit Tigers 24-2 in a 1-hour 45-minute game attended by 15,-000 spectators. The Detroit team refused to play and Hugh ("Hughie") Ambrose Jennings, the manager, recruited a team on the field, offering each player $50 for his services. The scrub team wore the Detroit team's traveling uniforms.

Baseball game (major league) to last longer than 25 innings was the 26-inning game at Braves Field, Boston, on May 1, 1920, between the Boston Braves and the National League Brooklyn Robins. The game lasted 3 hours 50 minutes and was called on account of darkness, the score being 1-1. Leon Joseph ("Caddy") Cadore was the Brooklyn pitcher, Joseph Carl ("Joe") Oeschger the Boston pitcher. Both pitched all the innings.

Baseball game telecast. *See* Television—Telecast: Baseball game (collegiate) televised

Baseball game to attract more than 83,000 spectators was a double-header played May 30, 1938, at the Yankee Stadium, New York City. The New York Yankees defeated the Boston Red Sox 10-0 in the first game, and 5-4 in the second game. The attendance was 83,533 spectators; not included were 511 whose money was refunded for lack of seats. The gate receipts amounted to $91,610.75.

Baseball games under the code adopted on September 23, 1845, was played June 19, 1846, at Elysian Fields, Hoboken, N.J., when the Knickerbocker Club of New York team played the New York team. They were defeated 23-1. The game ended after 4 innings as 21 runs constituted a game. The umpire was Alexander Jay Cartwright.

Baseball game (World Series) broadcast. *See* Radio broadcast: Baseball World Series broadcast

Baseball play-off series for a National League pennant took place October 1, 1946, in St. Louis, Mo., and October 3, 1946, in Brooklyn, N.Y., after the Brooklyn Dodgers and the St. Louis Cardinals had tied on September 29, 1946, both teams having won 96 and lost 58 games for a .623 average in the National League. The Cardinals won the first two of the two-out-of-three series by the score of 4-2 and 8-4, thus winning the National League pen-

The First

nant and the right to play the Boston Red Sox of the American League in the World Series. The World Series opened October 6, 1946, in St. Louis, Mo. The Cardinals won 4 of the 7 games.

Baseball series was played July 20, August 17, and September 10, 1858, at the Fashion Race Course, L.I., N.Y., between teams representing Brooklyn and New York. New York won two of the three games with the Brooklyn Atlantics. The first time spectators were charged admission to see a baseball game was July 20, 1859, on which date 1,500 people paid a 50-cent admission fee. The players did not receive remuneration until 1858, when they received a share of the gate receipts. *(Seymour Roberts Church—Baseball. The History, Statistics and Romance of the American National Game from Its Inception to the Present)*

Double no-hit nine-inning baseball game in the major leagues was played May 2, 1917, at Weeghman Park, Chicago, Ill., by the Chicago Cubs (Jim Vaughn, pitcher) and the Cincinnati Reds (Fred Toney, pitcher). Both players pitched a full nine-inning game without allowing a hit. In the tenth inning, the Cincinnati team brought in a run. The score was Cincinnati 1, Chicago 0.

Home run in a World Series baseball game. *See* World Series home run, below.

Intercollegiate baseball game was played on July 1, 1859, between Amherst and Williams Colleges, in Pittsfield, Mass. The pitcher was 35 feet from the batter. Amherst won by a score of 73-32. The game, played on a 60-foot square, began at 11:00 A.M. and continued 4 hours without interruption. Each team had 13 players and the game lasted 26 innings. The captain of Amherst was James Fitzgerald Claffin, the Williams captain Humphrey Stevenson Anderson. *(Statistics of Intercollegiate Contests, Athletic Council, Williams College)*

Major-league game in which the majority of the players on one team were blacks was played July 17, 1954, between the National League Brooklyn Dodgers and Milwaukee Braves at Milwaukee, Wis. The Braves won 6 to 1. The black players on the Brooklyn team were Donald N. ("Don") Newcombe ("Newk"), pitcher; Roy Campanella, catcher; James William G. ("Jim") Gilliam ("Junior"), second base; Jack Roosevelt ("Jackie") Robinson, third base; and Edmundo Isasi ("Sandy") Amoros, left field.

National League 20-inning baseball game was played June 30, 1892, at Cincinnati, Ohio, before a crowd of about 1,200 spectators. The Chicago pitcher was Addison Courtney ("Ad") Gumbert, the Cincinnati pitcher Anthony John ("Tony") Mullane. At the end of the 5th inning, the score was even. The game was stopped because of

The First

darkness at the end of the 20th inning, the score being 7-7.

Night baseball game (major league) to last longer than 6 hours was played April 15, 1968, at the Astrodome, Houston, between the New York Mets and the Houston Astros, the latter winning 1-0. It was a 24-inning game and lasted 6 hours 6 minutes.The game was the longest scoreless game, until the 24th inning. The losing pitcher was Leslie Norvin ("Les") Rohr, the 8th hurler used by the Mets.

Night baseball game (major league) to last longer than 7 hours was the 25-inning game in which the St. Louis Cardinals defeated the New York Mets at Shea Stadium, New York City. The game began at 8:00 P.M. September 12, 1974, and concluded at 3:13 A.M., St. Louis winning, 4-3. About 13,460 spectators watched the 50 players.

Night baseball World Series game was played October 6, 1946, at Sportsman's Park, St. Louis, Mo. The American League Boston Red Socks defeated the National League St. Louis Cardinals 3-2 in a 10-inning game. The Cardinals won the series 4-3.

No-hit nine-inning baseball game was pitched by Joseph Emley Borden of the Philadelphia team of the National Association on July 28, 1875, in Philadelphia, Pa., against Chicago. The score was Philadelphia 4, Chicago 0.

No-run nine-inning baseball game was played May 11, 1875, at Red Stocking Park, St. Louis, Mo., between the Chicago White Stockings and the St. Louis Reds of the National Association. The score of the 1-hour 35-minute game was Chicago 1, St. Louis 0. Chicago made six base hits and scored one run; St. Louis made three base hits and did not score. George ("Charmer") Zettlein was the Chicago pitcher and Joseph Myles Blong the St. Louis pitcher.

Opening day no-hit major league baseball game was played April 16, 1940, in Chicago. Robert William Andrew ("Rapid Robert," "Bob") Feller of the American League Cleveland Indians retired 15 men in a row from the 4th to the 8th inning, against the Chicago White Sox.

President to pitch a ball to open the baseball season. *See* President: President to pitch a ball to open the baseball season

Shutout double-header games were played September 26, 1908, at Washington Park, Brooklyn, N.Y. Edward Marvin ("Big Ed") Reulbach of the National League Chicago Cubs defeated the Brooklyn Superbas 5-0 and 3-0. He allowed only 5 singles in the first game (1 hour 40 minutes) and 3 singles in the second game (1 hour 12 minutes).

Shutout game was the Chicago vs. Louisville game (National League) played April 25, 1876, at Louisville, Ky., before approximately 2,000 spec-

The First

BASEBALL GAME—*Continued*
tators. Albert Goodwill Spalding, Chicago White Stockings pitcher, pitched a 7-hitter and also made 3 of Chicago's 8 hits off James Alexander ("Jim") Devlin. The score was Chicago 4, Louisville 0.

Shutout World Series game was played October 13, 1905, at New York City, the fourth game in the 1905 series, between the New York Nationals and the Philadelphia Athletics of the American League. Joseph Jerome ("Iron Man") McGinnity of New York shut out the Philadelphia team 1-0. New York won the series 4-1.

Shutout World Series game (nonsanctioned) was played October 2, 1903, at Boston, when the Pittsburgh Nationals defeated the Boston Americans 3-0. Samuel W. ("Deacon") Leever was the Pittsburgh pitcher, and William Henry ("Big Bill") Dinneen was the Boston pitcher. Boston won the series 5-3, the best 5 out of 9 games. Although the series was not league sanctioned, it was official.

Triple play unassisted by a player in organized baseball was made May 8, 1878, by Paul Hines playing in center field on the Providence team. The game was played at Providence, R.I., between Providence and Boston, the former winning 3-1.

Triple play unassisted in a modern major-league game was made by shortstop Cornelius ("Neal") Ball, shortstop of the Cleveland American League team on July 19, 1909, at Cleveland, Ohio, in the second inning of the first game of a doubleheader against the Boston American League team. Ball caught Ambrose Moses ("Amby") McConnells' liner; touched second, retiring Charles F. ("Honus") Wagner, who was on his way to third; and tagged Garland ("Jake") Stahl as he came up to second. When Ball came to bat in the same inning, he hit a home run. Cleveland defeated Boston 6-1 in the first game. Boston defeated Cleveland 8-2 in the second game.

Triple play unassisted in a World Series was made October 10, 1920, in the fifth game of the series, at Cleveland, Ohio, by William Adolph ("Bill") Wambsganss, second baseman of the Cleveland American League team, in a game with the Brooklyn National League team. In the fifth inning, Wambsganss caught Otto Lowell Miller's drive, tagged Peter John ("Pete") Kilduff for a double play, ran to first, and tagged Clarence Elmer Mitchell. The Cleveland Indians defeated the Brooklyn Robins 8-1.

World Series baseball annual championship was played at the Polo Grounds, New York City, October 23–24–25, 1884. The Providence Grays of the National Association defeated the New York Metropolitans of the American Association, 3 games to none. Providence won the first game 6-0 in 2 hours on October 23rd, the second game 3-1 in 1 hour 35 minutes on October 24th, the third

The First

game 11-2 in 1 hour 20 minutes on October 25th. (A 2-game post-season duel between Cincinnati of the American Association and Chicago of the National League was played at Cincinnati, Ohio; on October 6, 1882. Cincinnati won 4-0; on October 7, 1882, Chicago won 2-0. The first game attracted 2,700 spectators, the second 4,500.)

World Series baseball game was played October 1, 1903, at Boston, when the National League Pittsburgh Pirates defeated the Boston Americans 7-3 before a crowd of about 16,200 people. Boston won 5 of the 9-game series: William Henry ("Big Bill") Dinneen, 3; Denton True ("Cy") Young, 2. Pittsburgh won 3 games. The final game was played October 13, 1903, at Boston; the Boston team defeated Pittsburgh 3-0.

World Series baseball game broadcast. *See* Radio broadcast: Baseball World Series broadcast

World Series baseball game in which a batter made 3 consecutive home runs in 1 game was the sixth game played October 18, 1977, at the Yankee Stadium, New York City. Reginald Martinez ("Reggie") Jackson of the American League New York Yankees hit home runs in the 4th, 5th, and 8th innings against the National League Los Angeles Dodgers. The pitchers were Burt Hooton (4th), Elia Sosa (5th), and Charley Hough (8th). The Yankees won 8-4.

World Series baseball game in which 3 home runs were made in 1 game was played October 6, 1926, at St. Louis, Mo., in which George Herman ("Babe") Ruth of the American League New York Yankees hit 3 home runs against the National League St. Louis Cardinals. He also hit 3 homers in 1 game for the Yankees against the Cardinals on October 9, 1928, at St. Louis, Mo. Both games were the fourth in the series. In 1926 the Yankees won 10-5; in 1928, 7-3.

World Series baseball game to draw more than 90,000 persons was the October 6, 1959, game at Los Angeles, when 92,706 people saw the Chicago White Sox of the National League defeat the Los Angeles Dodgers of the American League 1-0.

World Series baseball game to last longer than 9 innings was played October 8, 1907, at Chicago, when the Chicago Cubs of the National League and the Detroit Tigers of the American League played 12 innings resulting in a 3-3 tie. Chicago won the series 4-0.

World Series baseball games to gross $1 million were played October 10-15, 1923, in New York City between the New York Yankees of the American League (Miller James Huggins, "the Mighty Mite," manager) and the New York Giants of the National League (John Joseph McGraw, "the Little Napoleon," manager) at the Yankee Stadium and the Polo Grounds. Receipts were $1,-063,815, of which the players' share was

The First

$368,783.04. The Yankees won 4–2. *(Frank Graham —The New York Yankees)*

World series grand slam (American League) was hit by Elmer John Smith, right outfielder of the Cleveland Indians, who hit a grand slam home run on October 10, 1920, in the first inning of the fifth game against the Brooklyn Robins at Cleveland, Ohio. Cleveland won the series 5-2.

World Series grand slam (National League) was hit October 8, 1962, by Charles Joseph ("Chuck") Hiller, second baseman of the San Francisco Giants, who hit a grand slam at Yankee Stadium, New York, in the fourth game against the American League New York Yankees. The game score was New York 7, San Francisco 3. The series was won by New York 4-3.

World Series home run was made in the opening game, October 1, 1903, at Boston by James Dennison Sebring of the Pittsburgh team (National League), which defeated the American League Boston team 7-3. About 16,250 people witnessed the 1-hour 55-minute game.

BASEBALL GLOVE was worn by Charles ("Charlie") Waite, first baseman of Boston, in 1875. It was flesh color so as not to be conspicuous and had a large round opening at the back for ventilation. *(Albert Goodwill Spalding—America's National Game)*

BASEBALL HALL OF FAME. *See* Hall of fame

BASEBALL LEAGUE

American League was organized on January 29, 1900, in Philadelphia, and originally consisted of eight teams, Buffalo, Chicago, Cleveland, Detroit, Indianapolis, Kansas City, Milwaukee, and Minneapolis. The first president of the league was Byron Bancroft ("Ban") Johnson, who served from 1900 to 1927.

Baseball league association was the National Association of Professional Baseball Leagues, which was organized at the Leland Hotel, Chicago, Ill., on September 5-6, 1901, by seven presidents of the minor leagues: the Western League, the Western Association, the Pacific Northwest League, the Eastern League, the New York State League, the New England League, and the Three-I-League. The first president was Patrick Thomas Powers, and the first secretary was John H. Farrell of New York. The first annual meeting was held at the Fifth Avenue, Hotel, New York City, on October 23-25, 1902.

Baseball league of importance was the National Association of Professional Base-Ball Players, organized March 17, 1871, at Collier's Cafe, New York City. James N. Kerns of Troy, N.Y., was elected president. The member clubs were the Athletics of Philadelphia; the Mutuals of New York; the Kekiongas of Fort Wayne; the Olympics of Washington; the Haymakers of Troy; the Bostons of Boston; the White Stockings of Chicago;

The First

Cleveland; and Rockford. Each club paid an entry fee of $10. The first game was played May 4, 1871, at Fort Wayne, Ind. (The score was Fort Wayne 2, Cleveland 0.) The series consisted of three out of five games with the other teams. The champion team was the Athletics of Philadelphia (manager Elias Hicks Hayhurst), winning 22 games and losing 7 (.759). Chicago was second, winning 20 games and losing 9 (.690). Boston was third, winning 22 games and losing 10 (.688).

Juvenile baseball league was the Waynesburg, Pa., Juvenile Baseball League, formed in 1908 by 3 teams—the Colts, the North Side Cubs, and the Times Pirates (the last composed of carrier boys for the Waynesburg *Times*). An admission fee of 10 cents was charged for each game, the seasonal proceeds of $60 being donated to a library fund.

National League of Professional Base Ball Clubs was formed on February 2, 1876, in Grand Central Hotel, New York City, and consisted of 8 baseball teams: Boston, Chicago, Cincinnati, Hartford, Louisville, New York, Philadelphia, and St. Louis. The first game, Boston vs. Philadelphia, April 22, 1876, watched by 3,000 spectators at Philadelphia, was won by Boston 6-5. The Boston battery was Joseph Emley Borden, pitcher; Timothy S. McGinley, catcher—the Philadelphia battery, Alonzo P. ("Lon") Knight, pitcher; Wilbur K. Coons, catcher. The schedule called for 70 games for each team. The first president was Morgan Gardner Bulkeley, who served from February 2, 1876, to December 7, 1876.

BASEBALL MANAGER

Baseball manager to guide the same club on three different occasions was Stanley Raymond ("Bucky") Harris, who managed the American League Washington Senators from 1924 to 1928 (winning first place twice, third place once, and fourth place twice); from 1935 to 1942 (winning fourth place once, fifth place once, sixth place four times, and seventh place twice); and from 1950 to 1954 (winning fifth place three times, sixth place once, and seventh place once).

Baseball manager to win pennants in both leagues was Joseph Vincent ("Marse") McCarthy, nonplaying manager of the Chicago National League team, whose team on October 6, 1929, earned the pennant by winning 98 games and losing 54 games. As manager of the New York American League team he won the pennant on September 23, 1932, winning 106 games and losing 46 games. On October 2, 1932, the New York American League team also won the world championship, defeating the Chicago National League team in four straight games.

BASEBALL PARK

Baseball park (enclosed) was the Union Grounds, Brooklyn, N.Y., which opened May 15, 1862, on the site at Lee Avenue and Rutledge Street formerly used as a skating rink.

The First

BASEBALL PARK—*Continued*

Baseball park to charge admission was the New York Fashion Race Track course, Long Island, N.Y., which charged 50 cents on July 20, 1858, to pay expenses for rental of the track and other expenses. The New Yorker All Stars defeated the Brooklynites 22-18. A second game in the series was played August 19th; a third game, September 10th.

BASEBALL PITCHER

Baseball pitcher (major league) to strike out 19 batters in a night game was Stephen Norman ("Lefty") Carlton of the St. Louis Cardinals (National league) against the New York Mets in a night game on September 15, 1969, at St. Louis, Mo. He struck out 19 of the 38 batters and allowed 9 hits and 2 walks. He had 3 strike-outs in the first, second, and fourth innings. The Mets won the game 4-3.

Baseball pitcher (major league) to strike out 300 or more batters in each of 3 seasons was Sanford ("Sandy") Koufax of the Los Angeles Dodgers, who struck out 306 batters in 1963, 382 in 1965, and 307 in 1966. On September 29, 1966, he struck out 13 St. Louis Cardinal batters, bringing his score to 307.

Baseball pitcher (major league) to win 2 complete games in 1 day was Emil Henry ("Dutch") Levsen of the American League Cleveland Indians, who allowed 4 hits in each game against the Boston Red Sox on August 28, 1926, at Boston. Cleveland won 6-1 and 5-1. The first game ran 1 hour 29 minutes; the second game, 1 hour 40 minutes.

Baseball pitcher to curve a ball is reported to be William Arthur ("Candy") Cummings, who introduced this innovation in 1866. He played with the Excelsior Junior Nine and the Stars of Brooklyn. Others for whom the claim is made are Fred Goldsmith of the Chicago White Stockings and George McConnell.

Baseball pitcher to hit a grand slam in a World Series game was David Arthur ("Dave") McNally of the American League Baltimore Orioles. He pitched the Orioles to a 9-3 victory against the Cincinnati Reds on October 13, 1970, at Memorial Stadium, Baltimore, Md. In the 6th inning, he hit a home run with the bases loaded. (This was the 12th grand slam in a World Series game, the first by a pitcher.)

Baseball pitcher to pitch a no-hitter on opening day was Robert William Andrew ("Bob") Feller of the American League Cleveland Indians, who pitched against the Chicago White Sox on April 17, 1940, at Comiskey Park, Chicago, Ill. Cleveland won 1-0.

Baseball pitcher to pitch a perfect no-hit, no-run, no-walk World Series game was Donald James ("Don") Larsen of the American League

The First

New York Yankees. On October 8, 1956, in the fifth game of the World Series played with the National League Brooklyn Dodgers, at the Yankee Stadium, New York City, Larsen pitched a perfect game. The score was New York 2, Brooklyn 0.

Baseball pitcher to pitch three no-hit games was Lawrence J. ("Larry") Corcoran of the Chicago Nationals, who pitched a no-hitter against Boston on August 19, 1880, against Worcester on September 20, 1882, and against Providence on June 27, 1884.

Baseball pitcher to retire more than 40 batters in succession was Jim Barr of the National League San Francisco Giants, who struck out the last 21 Pittsburgh Pirates in the August 23, 1972, game at San Francisco, Calif., and the first 20 St. Louis Cardinals in the August 29, 1972, game at St. Louis, Mo.

Baseball pitcher to win 4 no-hitters was Sanford ("Sandy") Koufax, left-hander of the National League Los Angeles Dodgers. On June 30, 1962, he defeated the New York Mets 5-0 at New York City; May 11, 1963, the San Francisco Giants 8-0 in a night game at Los Angeles; June 4, 1964, the Philadelphia Phillies 3-0 in a night game at Philadelphia; September 9, 1965, the Chicago Cubs 1-0 at Los Angeles, Calif.

Baseball pitcher (world series) with 3 shutout games was Christopher ("Christy," "Big Six") Mathewson of the National League New York Giants, who defeated the American League Philadelphia Athletics 3-0 on October 9, 1905, the first game of the series and 9-0 on October 12, 1905, the third game of the series, both games at Philadelphia; and 2-0 on October 14, 1905, the fifth game of the series, in New York City. He pitched 27 innings without allowing a single run or a batter to reach third base. He struck out 16 batters and allowed only 15 hits. New York won the series 4 to 1.

Woman baseball pitcher engaged by an organized male baseball team was Virne Beatrice ("Jackie") Mitchell, 19 years old, who on April 1, 1931, was engaged by the Chattanooga Baseball Club of the Southern Association.

BASEBALL PLAYER

See also Baseball Pitcher

Baseball "Home Run King" to hit 25 home runs in one season was John ("Bucky") Freeman, outfielder of the Washington club of the National League, who hit 25 home runs and 27 triples in 1899.

Baseball pinch hitter was John Joseph Doyle, a substitute catcher, ordered to bat in the ninth inning by Oliver Wendell ("Patsy") Tebeau of the Cleveland Spiders in a game played June 7, 1892, in Brooklyn, N.Y., against the Brooklyn Ward's Wonders. John Joseph ("Jack," "Dirty Jack") Doyle made a single, advancing John Joseph

The First

("Jack") O'Connor from first to third base. The 1891 rules allowed substitutions anywhere at any time during a game.

Baseball player (major league) killed in a game was Raymond Johnson ("Ray") Chapman, shortstop of the American League Cleveland Indians, who was accidentally hit on the left side of his head by pitcher Carl William ("Willie") Mays of the American League New York Yankees in a game at the Polo Grounds, New York City, on August 16, 1920.

Baseball player (major league) to bat in 12 runs in a major league 9-inning game was James Le Roy ("Sunny Jim") Bottomley, first baseman of the National League St. Louis Cardinals, who defeated the Brooklyn Robins 17-3 at Ebbets Field, New York City. On September 16, 1924, he hit a single in the first, seventh, and ninth innings, a double in the second inning, and a home run in the fourth and sixth innings, bringing in 12 runs on 6 hits.

Baseball player (major league) to hit in 44 consecutive games was William Henry ("Wee Willie") Keeler, star outfielder of the National League Baltimore Orioles, who played from April 22, 1897, to June 18, 1897. He was at bat 201 times, made 53 runs, 82 hits, 11 two-base hits, and 8 three-base hits. His batting average was .408.

Baseball player (major league) to hit more than 60 home runs in 1 season was Roger Eugene Maris, outfielder of the American League New York Yankees, who hit his 61st home run at Yankee Stadium, New York City, on October 1, 1961, in the fourth inning of a game against the Boston Red Sox. The ball landed in right field. Evan Tracy ("Tracy") Stallard was the Boston pitcher. The Yankees won 1-0. The season was a 162-game season.

Baseball player (major league) to make nine hits in 1 game was John Henderson ("Johnny") Burnett, American League Cleveland shortstop, who hit 7 singles and 2 doubles in an 18-inning game at Cleveland, Ohio, between the Philadelphia Athletics and the Cleveland Indians on July 10, 1932. He was at bat 11 times. The score was Philadelphia 18, Cleveland 17.

Baseball player (major league) to make 7 consecutive hits in 7 times at bat in the same game was Cesar Dario ("Cocoa") Gutierrez, shortshop for the American League Detroit Tigers, who, in the second game of a doubleheader with the Cleveland Indians at Cleveland, Ohio, on June 21, 1970, hit a single in the first, third, fifth, eighth, tenth, and twelfth innings and a double in the seventh inning. Detroit beat Cleveland 9-8.

Baseball player (major league) to steal 6 bases in 1 game was Edward Trowbridge ("Cocky") Collins, Sr., second baseman of the American League Philadelphia Athletics, who stole 6 bases in a game against Detroit on September 11, 1912, in

The First

Detroit, Mich. Philadelphia won 9-7. He also stole 6 bases on September 22, 1912, at St. Louis, Mo., in a game that Philadelphia won 8-2 against St. Louis.

Baseball player to catch a ball dropped from the Washington Monument, Washington, D.C. (500-foot level) was William F. ("Billy," "Pop") Schriver of the Chicago National League club, who accomplished this feat on August 29, 1892, and again on August 25, 1895. Charles Evard ("Gabby") Street, catcher of the Washington club of the American League, caught a baseball dropped from the top of the monument on August 21, 1908.

Baseball player to hit a home run and a double in 1 inning was Thomas Everett ("Tommy") Burns, shortstop, National League Chicago White Stockings, who batted 3 times in the 7th inning on September 6, 1883, at Chicago, Ill. Nine batters went to bat 20 times in the inning, reaching 28 bases on hits and scoring 18 runs—11 of them earned runs. The game lasted 2 hours 25 minutes. The score was Chicago 26, Detroit 6.

Baseball player to hit a home run in an All-Star game was George Herman ("Babe") Ruth of the American League New York Yankees, who on July 6, 1933, at Comiskey Park, Chicago, Ill., hit a home run in the third inning of the first game of the annual series. The run brought in Charles Leonard ("Charlie") Gehringer of Detroit. The American League won 4-2. William Anthony ("Wild Bill") Hallahan was the National League pitcher and James Alger ("Jimmy") Wilson was the catcher, both of the St. Louis Cardinals.

Baseball player to hit four consecutive home runs in one game was Henry Louis ("Lou," "the Iron Horse") Gehrig of the American League New York Yankees, who hit home runs in the first, fourth, fifth, and seventh innings on June 3, 1932, in a game in Philadelphia, Pa., against the American League Philadelphia Athletics. The score was Yankees 20, Athletics 13. (Minor league players had performed the same feat earlier.)

Baseball player to hit four home runs in one 9-inning game was Robert Lincoln ("Link," "Bobby") Lowe, second baseman of the Boston National League team, who achieved this distinction in Boston, Mass., on May 30, 1894, in the third (two runs), fifth, and sixth innings in a game against Cincinnati. The score was Boston 20, Cincinnati 11.

Baseball player to hit in more than 50 consecutive games was the "Yankee Clipper" Joseph Paul ("Joltin' Joe") Di Maggio of the American League New York Yankees, who played in 56 consecutive games from May 15, 1941, through July 16, 1941. He batted 223 times, scoring 15 home runs, 4 three-baggers, 16 two-base hits, and 91 one-base hits. He batted in 55 runs and had an average of .408.

The First

BASEBALL PLAYER—*Continued*

Baseball player to hit 60 home runs in 2 different seasons was Joseph John ("Unser Choe") Hauser, who hit 63 home runs in 1930, Baltimore (International League) and 69 home runs in 1933, Minneapolis (International League).

Baseball player to play all 9 positions in 1 game was Blanco Dagoberto ("Bert") Campaneris of the American League Kansas City Athletics, who played all 9 positions in a 13-inning night game at Kansas City, Mo., on September 8, 1965. The Athletics were defeated by the California Angels 5-3.

Baseball player to play in more than 2,100 consecutive games was Henry Louis ("Lou") Gehrig, the Iron Horse, who played in 2,130 consecutive games from June 1, 1925, to April 30, 1939. He played first base for the New York Yankees.

Baseball player to score more than 4,000 hits was Tyrus Raymond ("Ty") Cobb who played in 3,033 games in 24 years (Detroit, American League, 1905–1926; Philadelphia, American League, 1927–1928), scoring 4,191 hits in his 11,429 times at bat.

Baseball player to steal more than 100 bases in a season was Maurice Morning ("Maury") Wills, shortstop for the National League Los Angeles Dodgers, who stole his first base on April 13, 1962, in game 4 against Milwaukee and his 100th on September 26, 1962, in the third inning against the Houston Colts at Los Angeles. Wills and left-fielder Thomas ("Tommy") Davis pulled a double steal. Will stole his 104th base in game 165 on August 3, 1962, against New York, 3 steals in 1 game.

Baseball player to win the Most Valuable Player Award three times was Stanley Frank ("Stan") Musial of the National League St. Louis Cardinals, who won the award for 1943, 1946, and 1948.

Baseball player who was an American Indian was James Madison ("Jim") Toy of the American Association, who played first base for the Cleveland team in 1887 and catcher for the Brooklyn and Baltimore teams in 1890.

Baseball players (brothers) to oppose each other in a World Series were Robert William ("Bob," "Long Bob") Meusel, American League New York Yankees, who played right field, and Emil Frederick ("Irish") Meusel, National League New York Giants, who played left field. The first game was on October 5, 1921, when the Yankees won 3-0; the eighth and last game was on October 13, 1921, when the Giants won 1-0.

Baseball players paid more than $6,000 for winning the World Series were the American League New York Yankees, who defeated the National League New York Giants in the first World Series game in Yankee Stadium in the October 10–15, 1923 series. The share of the winners was $6,143.49, that of the losers $4,112.89. The gross

The First

receipts were $1,063,815, the attendance 301,430. The final score was 4–2.

Baseball players to hit a home run were Roscoe Conkling ("Ross") Barnes of the National League Chicago White Stockings and Charles Wesley ("Baby") Jones of the National League Cincinnati Reds, on May 2, 1876, at Cincinnati, Ohio. Chicago won 15–9.

Baseball rookie to hit a grand slam home run in the World Series was Gilbert James ("Gil") McDougald of the American League New York Yankees, who played second and third base October 9, 1951, at the Polo Grounds, New York City. The slam was in the third inning of the fifth game in the 1951 series against the New York Giants. In 1950 he was with the Beaumont Club of the Texas League.

Black baseball player was Moses Fleetwood ("Fleet") Walker, catcher on the Northwestern League Toledo team who played with that team from 1883 to 1889. He played in 41 games in 1884 and hit .251. The team entered the American Association in 1884.

Black baseball player (American league) was Charles Grant, who played second base with the Columbia Giants. In 1901 he was hired by John Joseph McGraw and billed as Charles Tokohama, a full-blooded Cherokee Indian. At that time the American League had not yet been recognized as a major league. *(Lee Allen—The American League Story)*

Black baseball player on a white team was John Jackson, who played in 1872 on a white baseball team in New Castle, Pa., under the name of John W. ("Bud") Fowler. From 1872 to 1899 he usually played second base.

Black baseball player to hit a home run in a World Series was Lawrence Eugene ("Larry") Doby of the American League Cleveland Indians, who hit a 425-foot drive in the third inning into right field, on October 9, 1948, at Cleveland, Ohio. Cleveland defeated the National League Boston Braves 4-2.

Black major-league baseball player was Jack Roosevelt ("Jackie") Robinson of the National League Brooklyn Dodgers, who played in an exhibition game on April 11, 1947, against the New York Yankees. He played at first base in the exhibition game and during the season. *(Carl Thomas Rowan and Jackie Robinson—Wait Till Next Year)*

Hall of Fame (baseball) Jewish player. *See* Hall of Fame: Hall of Fame (baseball) Jewish player

Major-league baseball player to pitch two successive no-hit no-run games in a season was John Samuel ("Johnny") Vander Meer, "the Dutch Master," of the National League Cincinnati Reds, who on June 11, 1938, shut out Boston by 3-0 in

The First

Cincinnati, Ohio. Only three men reached first base, all on walks. On June 15, 1938, he defeated the Brooklyn Dodgers in New York City, 6-0.

"Most valuable player" award (major league) to a black was made to Jack Roosevelt ("Jackie") Robinson, second baseman of the National League Brooklyn Dodgers, who received 264 points on November 18, 1949, high score of the 24-man committee of the Baseball Writers Association, winning the Kenesaw Mountain Landis Memorial plaque for 1949.

"Most valuable player" award (major league) was made in 1911 to Frank ("Wildfire") Schulte, National League Chicago Cubs, and Tyrus Raymond ("Ty") Cobb, American League Detroit Tigers.

"Most valuable player" award (major league) to a black in the American League was made November 7, 1963, to Elston Howard, American League New York Yankee catcher, who received 15 of the 20 first-place votes.

"Most valuable player" in both major leagues was Frank Robinson, outfielder of the National League Cincinnati Reds. He was elected November 22, 1961, by the 16-man committee of the Baseball Writers Association, receiving 219 of a possible 224 points. On November 8, 1966, he was unanimously elected for services in the American League Baltimore Orioles.

Professional baseball player was Alfred James Reach, outfielder of the Philadelphia Athletics of the National Association from 1871 to 1875. He played in 82 games. In 1874 he received $1,000 for playing 14 games.

BASEBALL RULES

Baseball rule code was adopted September 23, 1845, by the Knickerbocker Club of New York. *(J. Austin Fynes—Athletic Sports in America)*

Baseball rules standardizing the game were adopted May 1858, in New York City by the National Baseball Association. The rules provided that the bat was not to exceed 2½ inches in diameter and the ball 10½ inches in circumference, the latter to weigh 6½ ounces. The game was to last innings or until one team won 21 runs. Previously each team had played under its own set of rules. Three delegates from each of the following clubs attended the meeting: Atlantic, Baltic, Bedford, Continental, Eagle, Empire, Excelsior, Eckford, Gotham, Harmony, Knickerbocker, Nassau, Olympic, Putnam, and Union.

BASEBALL STADIUM. *See* Stadium

BASEBALL STRIKE

Baseball strike took place May 18, 1912, at Shibe Park, Philadelphia, Pa., when 19 players of the American League Detroit Tigers refused to play the Athletics in sympathy for Tyrus Raymond ("Ty") Cobb, their outfielder, who was sus-

The First

pended by Byron Bancroft ("Ban") Johnson, president of the league, because he mauled a spectator who had cursed him at the Tiger-Yankee game in New York City. The strikers were fined $50 a day, $100 for 48 hours. Hugh A. ("Hughie") Jennings, the Detroit manager, recruited a scrub team that was defeated 24-2. There was not a regular Detroit player on the team.

Baseball strike of serious consequence took place April 1, 1972, and ended April 13, 1972, delaying the opening season until April 15, 1972, and postponing 86 games. The strike, staged by the Major League Baseball Players Association, was initiated over the issue of pensions.

BASEBALL TEAM

Baseball team was the Knickerbocker Club of New York, organized September 23, 1845, by Alexander Joy Cartwright, which played the New York Baseball Club at the Elysian Field in Hoboken, N.J., on June 19, 1846. Duncan F. Curry was the first president. The game lasted 4 innings and was won by the New York Baseball Club with the score of 23-1. At this date, there was no standard baseball, and as each home club supplied the ball it often varied in size, elasticity, and content. Three seasons later the Knickerbockers adopted a blue and white uniform and were the first team uniformly outfitted. *(By-Laws, Regulations and Rules of the Knickerbocker Base Ball Club of New York)*

Baseball team (black professional) was the Cuban Giants, organized in New York City by Frank P. Thompson in 1885. S. K. Govern was manager. The players received expenses and weekly salaries according to positions: pitchers and catchers, $18; infielders, $15; and outfielders, $12. The players also served as waiters during the summer season at the Argyle Hotel, Babylon, L.I., N.Y. *(Sol White—History of Colored Baseball)*

Baseball team (major league) to score 18 runs in 1 inning was the National League Chicago White Sox, who defeated Detroit 26-6 on September 6, 1883, at Chicago. Chicago scored 18 runs in the seventh inning when 23 players batted in 14 runs before Detroit manager Dan O'Leary changed pitchers; Dick Burns replaced George Weidman at the mound.

Baseball team to hit 4 consecutive runs in 1 inning was the National League Cincinnati Reds, which defeated the Milwaukee Braves 10-8 on June 8, 1961, in Cincinnati, Ohio. In the 7th inning, Joe Adcock and Hank Aaron each hit a home run (pitcher, Jim Maloney) and Eddie Mathews and Frank Thomas each hit a home run (Marshall Bridges, relief pitcher). The game lasted 3 hours 14 minutes and was witnessed by 5,149 spectators.

Baseball team to receive a regular salary for its services was the Red Stockings of Cincinnati, led by Harry and George Wright, which traveled in 1869 to various cities, engaging local teams.

The First

BASEBALL TEAM—*Continued*
Through 1869 and up to June 1870, they played without losing a game. A salary of $1,400 was paid to George Wright, shortstop; $1,200 to Harry Wright, captain and center field; $1,100 to Asa ("Count") Brainard, pitcher; $1,000 to Frederick A. ("Fred") Waterman, third base; and $800 each to the first and second baseman, the catcher, the left and right fielder, and the substitute.

Baseball team to tour was the Brooklyn Excelsiors, under the management of Captain Joseph B. Leggett, which left June 30, 1860, for Albany, N.Y. They played at Troy, Buffalo, and cities in the west and south.

Baseball team to win more than 20 World Series was the American League New York Yankees, who won the series in 1923, 1927, 1928, 1932, 1936, 1937, 1938, 1939, 1941, 1943, 1947, 1949, 1950, 1951, 1952, 1953, 1956, 1958, 1961, 1962, 1963, 1964, 1976.

Baseball team to win 30 pennants was the American League New York Yankees, who won their first pennant in 1921 and their thirtieth in 1976.

Baseball team to win three World Series in succession was the American League New York Yankees, which won the world championship October 6, 1936, and October 9, 1937, against the New York Giants; October 9, 1938, against the Chicago White Sox.

Baseball team to win five World Series in succession was the American League New York Yankees, managed by Charles Dillon ("Casey") Stengel, "the Old Professor," which won the world championship on October 9, 1949, from the Brooklyn Dodgers (4-1); on October 7, 1950, from the Philadelphia Phillies (4-0); on October 10, 1951, from the New York Giants (4-2); on October 7, 1952, from the Brooklyn Dodgers (4-3); on October 5, 1953, from the Brooklyn Dodgers (4 games-2).

Baseball teams to go on a world tour were the Chicago and All America teams. They started their world tour October 20, 1888, and returned April 20, 1889. They played 53 games of 4 innings and over, in Australia, Ceylon, Egypt, Italy, France, England, and the United States. Twenty-eight games were won by the All America team, 22 by the Chicago team, and 3 were tied. Their first game abroad was played December 10, 1888, in Auckland, New Zealand. *(Henry Clay Palmer—Athletic Sports in America)*

Baseball teams to travel beyond the confines of the United States were the Boston Red Stockings and the Philadelphia Athletic Blue Stockings, National Association teams that played a series of 15 exhibition games from July 30, 1874, to August 27, 1874, in England and Ireland. *(Henry Chadwick—De Witt's Base-Ball Guide for 1875)*

The First

Baseball (town ball) team was the Olympic Club of Philadelphia, Pa., which played "cat ball" or town ball from July 4, 1833, to the year 1860 when they changed to standard baseball. Town ball, a game similar to the British game of rounders, was the immediate forerunner of regular baseball in the United States.

Professional-league baseball team to win three pennants in succession was the Chicago Cubs of the National League, who won pennants in 1880, 1881, and 1882. In 1880 the team won 67 games, lost 17; in 1881 it won 56 games, lost 28; in 1882 it won 55 games, lost 29. Adrian Constantine ("Cap") Anson was the manager. *(Adrian Constantine Anson—A Ball Player's Career)*

Women's baseball team was organized in Peterboro, N.H., in 1868. The squad of 50 women wore short blue and white tunics reaching to the knees, white stockings, and straw hats. The captain of the senior team was Nannie Miller, who was also the catcher. Clara Mills was the pitcher; Mary Manning first base; Fran Richardson, second base; Bertha Powell, third base; Jennie Hand shortstop; Hattie Ferris, left field; Maggie Marshall, right field; and Mary Frothingham, center field.

BASEBALL TICKET
Baseball rain check was used in 1887 by Charles Abner Powell, manager of the New Orleans club, New Orleans, La., to prevent "crashers" from getting tickets to the next day's game.

BASEBALL UMPIRE
Baseball umpire (major-league) to wear eyeglasses was Edwin ("Eddie") Americus Rommel who wore them in the game between the New York Yankees and the Washington Senators on April 18, 1956, in Washington, D.C. He became an umpire in the American League in 1938.

Baseball umpire (major league) who was black was Emmett Littleton Ashford, purchased September 15, 1965, from the Pacific Coast League by the American League. His salary was $7,500 a year plus $27 daily for expenses. He umpired at third base at the opening game of the season at Washington, D.C., on April 12, 1966, between the Cleveland Indians and the Washington Senators.

Black umpire in organized baseball was Emmett Littleton Ashford of the Class C Southwestern International League, who was authorized as a substitute umpire on February 20, 1952, by president Les Powers.

BASILICA. *See* Catholic Church: Catholic church raised to the dignity of a basilica

BASKETBALL GAME
All-Star Game of the National Basketball Association was played March 2, 1951, at the Boston Gardens, Boston, before a crowd of 10,094 patrons. The East team, coached by Joe Lapchick

The First

defeated the West team, coached by John Kundla, by the score of 111-94.

Basketball was invented in 1892 by James Naismith, who introduced the game in the International Young Men's Christian Association Training School in Springfield, Mass. As the game was originally played, it was necessary for the players to use a ladder to get up and remove the ball from the basket. *(James Naismith and Luther Gulick—Basket Ball)*

Basketball collegiate team to win the National Invitation Tournament and the National Collegiate Athletic Association trophy was the Beavers of the City College of New York, coached by Nat Holman, who defeated Bradley University, Peoria, Ill., 69-61, on March 18, 1950, and 71-68 on March 28, 1950.

Basketball game at a large commercial sports arena was a benefit performance for the New York Relief Fund played January 19, 1931, at Madison Square Garden, New York City. Six college teams played; Columbia University defeated Fordham University 26-18, Manhattan College defeated New York University 16-14, and St John's University defeated City College 17-8. About 15,000 persons attended, and $22,854 was raised.

Basketball game telecast. *See* Television—Telecast: Basketball game to be televised

Basketball intercollegiate five-man-team game was played January 16, 1896, in Iowa City, Iowa. The University of Chicago team defeated the University of Iowa team 15-12. There were no substitutions. *(William G. Mokray—Ronald Encyclopedia of Basketball)*

Basketball intercollegiate game was played December 10, 1896, in New Haven, Conn., between Wesleyan University, Middletown, Conn., and Yale University, New Haven. Wesleyan won 4-3. Seven men were on each team.

Basketball played at a women's college was introduced in 1892 by Senda Berenson, director of physical education at Smith College, Northampton, Mass. Several intercollegiate games were played against other colleges.

Basketball player (professional) to score more than 15,000 points was Dolph Schayes of the Syracuse Nationals of the National Basketball Association. On January 12, 1960, in Philadelphia, Pa., Schayes tallied 34 points in a 127-120 triumph over the Boston Celtics, raising his score to 15,013 points. Schayes played professional basketball for 12 years.

Basketball team (college) was formed at Mount Union College, Alliance, Ohio. H. S. Jones introduced basketball as a collegiate game at the Morgan Gymnasium at Mount Union College in December 1892 and it was accepted as an intercollegiate sport.

The First

National Basketball Association black player was Charles Henry Cooper, all-star player, who was drafted April 24, 1950, by the Boston Celtics and who played his first game for that team on November 1, 1950, in Fort Wayne, Ind.

Olympic Games basketball championship. *See under* Olympic Games

BASKETBALL PLAYER

Basketball player (collegiate) to score more than 1,000 points in 1 season was John ("Johnny") O'Brien of South Amboy, N.J., scoring champion of the National Collegiate Athletic Association, who scored 1,051 points in 37 games for Seattle University, Seattle, Wash., in the 1951-1952 season. He achieved his score on February 28, 1952, when he made 30 points in the game against Portland University. Seattle won 79-75.

Basketball player (professional) to score more than 3,000 points in one season was Wilt Chamberlain of the Philadelphia Warriors of the National Basketball Association, who scored 32 points on March 10, 1961, against the Detroit Pistons at Fort Wayne, Ind., bringing his score to 3,033 points (1,251 goals, 531 field throws) for 79 games in the 1960-1961 season.

Basketball player (professional) to score more than 4,000 points in 1 season was Wilt Chamberlain of the Philadelphia Warriors of the National Basketball Association, who made 34 points on March 14, 1962, at Chicago, in a game against the Chicago Packers, bringing his total score to 4,029.

BASKETBALL RULES

Basketball rule book was *Rules for Basketball* by James Naismith, instructor in the International Young Men's Christian Association Training School, Springfield, Mass., published in 1892 by the Springfield Printing and Binding Company, Springfield, Mass. *(James Naismith—Basketball, Its Origin and Development)*

Basketball rules were published in the *Triangle Magazine,* Springfield, Mass., January 15, 1892.

BASKETBALL TEAM

Basketball team to score more than 10,000 points in 1 season was the Philadelphia Warriors of the eastern division of the National Basketball Association, who scored 10,035 points in the 1961-1962 season. In the 1966-1967 season the team scored 10,143 points.

BATHHOUSE

Bathhouses owned and operated by a municipality were the L Street baths of Boston, Mass., built in 1865. They were first opened to the general public in 1866 and were under the supervision of the Board of Bath Commissioners, which had charge of all baths and gymnasiums up to 1913. *(John Koren—Boston 1822 to 1922: The Story of Its Government and Principal Activities During One Hundred Years)*

The First

BATHHOUSE—*Continued*

Legislation concerning public baths which provided for the establishment of free public baths in cities, villages, and towns of 50,000 or over, in such number as determined necessary by local health boards, was Chapter 351, "An act to promote the public health and to amend chapter 473 of the laws of 1892 entitled 'An act to establish free public baths in cities, villages and towns,'" passed by New York State, April 18, 1895. The law required the baths to be kept open not less than 14 hours a day and to be provided with hot and cold water. This law was mandatory, whereas Chapter 473 of the laws of 1892 had permitted cities to erect free public baths if they desired to do so. *(William Paul Gerhard—On Bathing and Different Forms of Baths)*

Public bath- and washhouse was opened January 1, 1852, by the New York Association for Improving the Condition of the Poor in Mott Street, near Grand Street, New York City, now the Community Service Society. The first year 80,375 bathers and 10,038 washers availed themselves of the advantages.

Public baths with showers were provided by the People's Bath, New York City, formally opened August 17, 1891. The bath cost $25,922 and was operated by the Association for Improving the Condition of the Poor, now the Community Service Society. There was a charge of 5 cents for the use of a shower, including soap and towel. During the first 13½ months there were 69,944 bathers.

Steam baths for curing disease were advocated by Samuel Thomson, who in 1796 experimented with steam in the treatment of his daughter, whom physicians were unable to cure. He traveled on horseback through New Hampshire, Maine, Vermont, and Massachusetts, advocating treatment by steam as well as by the use of herbs. *(Samuel Thomson—A Narrative of the Life and Medical Discoveries of Samuel Thomson)*

Turkish bath was opened October 6, 1863, by Dr. Charles H. Shepard at 81 Columbia Heights, Brooklyn, N.Y. It was known as "The Hammam," the name used in the East. Admission was a dollar. Only 1 bather came the first day, and only 50 the first month. *(Journal of the American Medical Association. March 10, 1900)*

BATHROOMS (hotel). *See* Hotel: Hotel to install bathrooms

BATTERY

Battery to convert radioactive energy into electrical energy was a radioelectric cell invented by Philip Edwin Ohmart of Cincinnati, Ohio, which was announced on December 31, 1951. It consisted of two electrochemically dissimilar electrodes separated by a filling gas that was ionized by

The First

exposure to nuclear energy to produce an electrical current.

Solar battery to convert useful amounts of the sun's energy into electricity was invented by Gerald Leondus Pearson, Calvin Souther Fuller, and Daryl M. Chapin at the Bell Telephone Laboratories, New York City, and announced April 25, 1954. Made of specially treated strips of silicon, the battery needed no fuel other than the light of the sun. It had no moving parts, nothing in it was consumed or destroyed, and theoretically it was possible for it to last indefinitely.

Solar energy battery manufactured commercially was made by National Fabricated Products Inc., Chicago, Ill., in 1955. It consisted of a disc, the size of a half dollar, which was hermetically sealed. It generated a half volt from its two terminals. The battery was first advertised May 2, 1955, in *Electronic Design,* and the first shipment was made June 1, 1955.

BATTING AND FIELDING CAGE (baseball). *See* Baseball batting and fielding cage

BATTLE. *See* War; also *see under* names of various wars, e.g. Civil War

BATTLE OF GOLDEN HILL. *See* Revolutionary War: Attack on British soldiers

BATTLE OF MAKASSAR STRAIT

American naval counterattack against the Japanese. *See under* World War II

BATTLE OF MONMOUTH COURTHOUSE. *See* Revolutionary War: Conflict on equal terms between American regulars and British regulars

BATTLESHIP. *See* Ship

BATTLESHIP SUNK BY AN AIRPLANE. *See under* Aviation

BAUXITE was discovered in 1887 at a point a few miles northeast of Rome, Floyd County, Ga. A few fragments of the unknown mineral were picked up on the Holland lot, two miles north of the Ridge Valley Iron Company's furnace at Hermitage, Ga. Bauxite mining began in April 1888, when the deposits on the Holland property, Lot 61, 23rd district of Floyd County, were first opened and worked. The first shipments of the ore were made in May 1888 to the Pennsylvania Salt Company, Natrona, Pa., and to Greenwich Point, Pa. This ore is said to have been used for the manufacture of both alum and metallic aluminum. *(Geological Survey of Georgia. Bulletin No. 11)*

BAZOOKA ROCKET GUN. *See under* Ordnance

BEACON. *See* Lighthouse

BEACONS, RADIO. *See* Radio beacons

BEADS, GLASS. *See* Glass bead

The First

BEAR. *See under* Animals

BEATIFICATION, CATHOLIC. *See* Catholic beatification

BEAUTY PAGEANT
See also under Television—Telecast

Beauty pageant (national) was the Miss America Pageant held September 7–8, 1921, at a two-day carnival at Keith's Theatre on the Garden Pier, Atlantic City, N.J. The award to the most beautiful contestant was made to Margaret Gorman of Washington, D.C., 16 years old, whose measurements were: bust, 30 inches; waist, 25 inches; hips, 32 inches; weight, 108 pounds; height, 5 feet 1 inch. Howard Chandler Christie headed the board of judges.

Black contestant in the Miss America Pageant was Cheryl Adrenne Browne of Jamaica, Long Island, New York, a sophomore at Luther College, Decorah, Iowa, who was selected June 13, 1970, at Davenport, Iowa, to represent Iowa in the contest at Atlantic City, N.J., September 6–12, 1970.

BED
Box spring. *See under* Bedspring

"Concealed bed" was manufactured by the Murphy Door Bed Company in San Francisco, Calif., in 1909. The beds, known as In-a-door beds, operated on a pivot and could be swung out of sight behind doors or in closets.

Folding-bed manufacture was successfully accomplished in 1875–1876 at Sixth and Filbert Streets, Philadelphia, Pa., by the Hale and Kilburn Manufacturing Company, later known as Hale and Kilburn Company. The folding bed was invented by a man in the company's employ named Everett and was improved upon by H. S. Hale. The bed was designed because of the inception of the apartment house idea and the necessity of economy in space. The beds were equipped with "flexible spring" which afterwards developed into what was called a "sectional spring bed," or the ordinary bedspring divided into three sections, lengthwise, each being filled with springs and enclosed in a canvas covering. This spring developed into the box spring now in use.

BEDSPRING
Bedspring manufacturing patent was granted August 25, 1831, to Josiah French of Ware, Mass.

Box spring was imported from France in 1857 by James Boyle, Chatham Square, New York City, manufacturer of bedding. Made reversible, it was about 12 inches deep. The frame was made in 8 sections, 1¼-inch lumber boards joined together with strips of ticking. The center of the spiral was attached to the center of the frame, and then came the usual ties of twine.

The First

BEEF EXPORTS. *See under* Meat

BEER
Beer was brewed at the Roanoke Colony (Virginia) of Sir Walter Raleigh in 1587. According to Thomas Hariot's account, "Wee made of the same [pagatowr, or maize] . . . some mault, whereof was brued as good ale as was to bee desired. So likewise by the help of hops thereof may bee made as good beere." (*Thomas Hariot—A Briefe and True Report of the New Found Land of Virginia*)

Beer in cans. *See under* Cans

Lager beer was manufactured in Philadelphia, Pa., in 1840 by John Wagner, who had an eight-barrel kettle in his home. It was stored in a cellar under the brewhouse.

BEER, ROOT. *See* Root beer

BEET SUGAR. *See* Sugar

BELL. *See* Electric bell

BELLOWS
Bellows for smiths and furnace fires was invented by John R. Morrison of Springfield, Ohio, who was granted a patent on December 23, 1834.

BELLS. *See* Carillon; Chimes

BELT (cartridge belts). *See* Cartridge belt patent

BELT CONVEYOR SYSTEM
Belt conveyor more than four miles long was manufactured by the Goodyear Tire and Rubber Company, Akron, Ohio, for the Weirton mine of the National Mines Corporation to convey coal 10,900 feet from a West Virginia mine to the Monongahela River. The conveyor was installed in 1949 in a single loop of belting more than four miles in total circumference. It traveled at a speed of 300 feet a minute to deliver 300 tons of coal an hour.

Belt conveyor system was described by Oliver Evans in his book *The Young Millwright and Millers Guide* published in Philadelphia, Pa., in 1795. Evans illustrated a flat belt receiving material on its upper run and discharging it over the end, on a broad endless strap of thin pliant leather or canvas revolving over two pulleys in a case or trough. (*Greville Bathe and Dorothy Bathe— Oliver Evans: A Chronical of Early American Engineering*)

BELTING sold to manufacturers is recorded in the account books of Pliny Jewell, a leather dealer of Harford, Conn. There is an entry in 1826 of the sale of a leather belt three inches wide. Manufacturers who required belting usually bought skins, cut them to the desired thickness, and by nailing the ends of the pieces to the floor when wet, and driving wedges between the leather and floor, halfway between the ends, stretched them taut.

The First

BELTS OF LEATHER for transmitting power from shaft to shaft were devised by Paul Moody, who used them in the Appleton cotton mill in Lowell, Mass., in 1828. Up to this time all transmissions had been by means of iron gears. Belting, however, had previously been used in some mills to carry power from shafts that in turn were driven by gears from a waterwheel. *(Louis W. Arny—National Association of Leather Belting Manufacturers. Report. Nov. 20, 1918)*

BENEFIT PERFORMANCE. *See* Play (drama)

BENEVOLENT AND PROTECTIVE ORDER OF ELKS was organized February 16, 1868, in New York City from an older social and benevolent organization, the Jolly Corks. The presiding officer of the Jolly Corks at the time of adopting the B.P.O.E. title was Charles A. S. Vivian. The first exalted B.P.O.E. ruler was George W. Thompson. The Grand Lodge was incorporated on March 10, 1871, in New York and the first Grand Exalted Ruler was George J. Green. *(Charles Edward Ellis —An Authentic History of the Benevolent and Protective Order of Elks)*

BERKELIUM. *See* Element: Element 97

BESSEMER STEEL CONVERTER. *See under* Steel

"BEST SELLER." *See* Book: Best-seller novel

BETATRON
See also Bevatron

Betatron was built at the University of Illinois, Urbana, Ill., by Professor Donald William Kerst and placed in operation July 15, 1940. It had an output energy of 2.3 million electron volts. The betatron is a machine to accelerate electrons by the use of a magnetic field and can produce either a sharp beam of high-energy X rays or a free beam of high-energy electrons.

Mobile betatron was placed in operation on November 12, 1948, at the United States Naval Ordnance Laboratory, White Oak, Md. It was built by the General Engineering and Consulting Laboratory of the General Electric Company, Schenectady, N.Y., and was a 10-million-volt X-ray generator capable of penetrating 16 inches of steel.

Photograph of high-volt X rays. *See* Photograph: Photograph of a beam of 1-billion-volt X rays

BEVATRON was built for the Radiation Laboratory of the University of California at Berkeley, and placed in operation on February 15, 1954. It had a maximum beam energy of 6.25 billion volts. It was housed in a circular building 220 feet in diameter and 69 feet high.
See also Betatron

BIBLE
Bible for the blind in embossed form, the old

The First

line letter system, was issued in 1835 by th American Bible Society, New York City. This sc ciety was also the first to supply the blind with th Bible in New York Point, and in the more recen Braille.

Bible in an American Indian–language transla tion was finished in 1661 by John Eliot, the "Apos tle to the North American Indians." It was entitle "*The New Testament of Our Lord and Saviou Jesus Christ,*" and was dedicated in English t Charles II. It contained 130 printed leaves withou pagination and two title pages, one in English an the other in the Algonquin Indian dialect. The tex was in double columns with marginal reference In 1663 "*The Holy Bible, Containing the Old Tes tament and the New, Translated into the India Language*" was printed in quarto size. From Gene sis to the end of the Old Testament, it containe 414 leaves, and from St. Matthew to the end of th New Testament, 126 leaves. Both Bibles were "o dered to be printed by the Commissioners of th United Colonies in New England, at the charg and with the consent of the corporation in En land for the propagation of the gospel amongst th Indians in New England" and were printed Cambridge, Mass., by Samuel Green and Ma maduke Johnson. *(Samuel Eliot Morison—Builde ers of the Bay Colony)*

Bible in folio size to be illustrated was *The Ho Bible, containing the Old and New Testament With the Apocrypha. Translated out of the orig nal tongues and with the former translations di gently compared and revised by the speci command of King James I of England,* publishe in 1791 by I[saiah] Thomas, Worcester, Mass. was 8 7/8 by 11½ inches and contained 1,07 pages and about 50 plates. *(Edwin A. R. Rumba Petre—Rare Bibles)*

Bible printed in English was printed by Robe Aitken of Philadelphia, Pa., in 1782. The fronti piece read: "*The Holy Bible, containing the O and New Testaments—newly translated out the original tongues; and with the former transl tions diligently compared and revised. Print and sold by R. Aitken, at Pope's Head, Thre doors above the Coffee House, in Market Stree Philadelphia, Pa., 1782.*" It was a duodecimo of 3 pages without pagination. The venture, though a thorized by Congress, September 21, 1782, w unsuccessful financially. The New Testament w printed in 1781 by Aitken. *(Robert Rowla Dearden and Douglas Sloane Watson—The Bib of the American Revolution)*

Bible printed in German was printed by Chr toph Sauer (also spelled Saur or Sower), Germa town, Pa., in 1743 from the text of the 32nd Hal edition with type obtained from Frankfurt, G many. Its title was *Biblia Das ist; Die Heili Schrift Altes und Neues Testaments, Nach d*

The First

Deutschen Uebersetzung D. Martin Luthers, mit
edes Capitels Kurtzen Summarien, auch Beyge-
ügten vielen und richtigen parallelen; nebst
einem gewöhnlichen anhang des dritten und viert-
en buchs Esra und des dritten Buchs der Mac-
cabäer.

Bible translated into English in America was
*The Holy Bible, containing the old and new cove-
nant, commonly called the Old and New Testament; translated from the Greek,* issued in four
volumes with unnumbered pages. It was printed
in Philadelphia, Pa., by Jane Aitken in 1808. It was
copyrighted September 12, 1808, in the District of
Pennsylvania by the translator, Charles Thomson,
who had been Secretary to the Continental Congress.

Bible translation by a woman was made by
Julia Evelina Smith of Glastonbury, Conn., and
published in Hartford, Conn., in 1876 by the
American Publishing Company. Her knowledge of
Latin, Greek, and Hebrew enabled her to make
the translation. In the historical narratives, the
verbs were translated in the future tense. The Old
Testament consisted of 892 pages and the New
Testament of 276 pages. The full title was *The
Holy Bible, containing the Old and New Testa-
ments: translated literally from the original
tongues.*

Bibles in hotel rooms were placed there in October 1908, in the Superior Hotel, Iron Mountain
(now Superior), Mont., by the Gideons, the Christian Commercial Traveling Men's Association.
The organization was founded in 1899 at Bosco-
bel, Wis. The first president was Samuel Eugene
Hill. The work was extended to include distribution to hotels, hospitals, penal institutions, and
public schools.

Catholic Bible in English was a 990-page quarto
printed by Carey, Stewart & Co., Philadelphia, Pa.,
in 1790. It was printed from new type cast in the
foundry of John Baine, Philadelphia, and was intended to be issued in 48-page sections every
Saturday. The first section was issued December
2, 1789. The title was *The Holy Bible, translated
from the Latin Vulgate: diligently compared with
the Hebrew, Greek and other editions, in divers
languages; and first published by the English College at Douai, anno 1609. Newly revised and corrected, according to the Clementine edition of the
scriptures, with annotations for elucidating the
principal difficulties of Holy Writ.* It was based on
the New Testament published in 1582 in Reims,
France, and the Old Testament published in
Douai, Flanders, in 1609.

Greek Testament was *The New Testament in
Greek,* 478 pages, 16 mo., printed in 1800 by Isaias
[Isaiah] Thomas, Worcester, Mass.

The First

Hebrew Bible published in America was *Biblia
Hebraica,* printed in 1814 by Thomas Dobson,
Philadelphia, Pa., from type imported from Amsterdam, Holland. *(Publications of the Jewish Historical Society, 1926)*

Phonetic Bible was *The New Testament of Our
Lord and Saviour Jesus Christ, translated out of
the original Greek, and with the former translations diligently compared and revised,* 397 pages,
by Andrew Comstock, M.D., published in 1848 in
Philadelphia, Pa. Comstock used a character for
each of the 38 elementary sounds and 6 for compound letters. The text was set in double columns.

BIBLE CONCORDANCE

Bible concordance was a reprint of an edition
published in London in 1643. It was published in
Cambridge, Mass., in 1683. In 1720 it was published as the *Cambridge Concordance* by Samuel
Newman of Cambridge, Mass.

Welsh concordance of the Bible was Abel Morgan's *Cyd-Gordiad Egwyddorawl o'r Scrythurau:
Neu Daflen Lythyrennol o'r Prif Eiriau Yn y Bibl
Sanctaidd,* published [228p.] by Samuel Keimer
and Dafydd Harry in Philadelphia, in 1730.

BIBLE SCHOOL to train missionaries was the

Missionary Training College for Home and Foreign Missionaries and Evangelists, New York
City, founded 1882 and formally opened October
1, 1883, with an enrollment of four students. The
course consisted of one year of study, including
courses in English, Christian Evidences, Bible
Study and Interpretation, Church History, and
Christian Life and Work. The first commencement
was May 1884. The school was founded by Dr.
Albert Benjamin Simpson, who was the first president. The name was changed to the Missionary
Training Institute in April 1894. On October 24,
1897, opening exercises were held at South
Nyack, N.Y.

BIBLE SOCIETY

Bible society was the Bible Society of Philadelphia, organized December 12, 1808, at Philadelphia, Pa. The name was changed to the
Pennsylvania Bible Society in 1840. The Reverend
William White, D.D., was the first president and
B. B. Hopkins the first secretary. The society was
governed by 24 managers from whom were selected a president, 4 vice presidents, 2 secretaries,
and a treasurer. The initiation fee was $5 and the
dues $2 a year. Life membership was $50. *(An
Address of the Bible Society Established at Philadelphia to which is subjoined the constitution of
said society and the names of the managers)*

Bible society (national organization) was the
American Bible Society, formed by delegates from
35 Bible societies for the sole purpose of increasing the circulation of the Holy Scriptures. The
delegates met May 8, 1816, in New York City, and
organized the society on May 11, 1816. The first

The First

BIBLE SOCIETY—*Continued*
president was Elias Boudinot, who served from
1816 to 1821. In the first year, 6,140 Bibles were
distributed. *(American Bible Society—Bible Society Manual)*

BIBLICAL LITERATURE BIBLIOGRAPHY. *See*
Bibliography: Bibliography of theological and biblical literature

**BIBLICAL STUDENTS SUMMER CONFER-
ENCE** was organized by Dwight Lyman Moody,
July 7, 1886, at the Mount Hermon School,
Northfield, Mass. The conference, at which 250
students from 85 colleges in 22 states were
present, marked the beginning of the Student
Volunteer movement, which has sent thousands
of missionaries into all parts of the world. The
students devoted their time to a study of the Bible
and to methods of evangelical work. *(William Revell Moody—The Life of D. L. Moody)*

BIBLIOGRAPHY
Bibliography of Americana in English was *Bibliotheca Americana; or a Chronological Catalogue
of the most curious and interesting books, pamphlets, state papers, etc. upon the subject of North
and South America, from the earliest period to the
present in print . . .*, published in 1789 in London,
England, for J. Debrett. It contained 271 pages and
included an introductory study on the state of literature in North and South America.

Bibliography of theological and biblical literature was Cotton Mather's *Manuductio Ad Ministerium; directions for a candidate of the ministry,
wherein first, a right foundation is laid for his
future improvement, and, then, rules are offered
for such a management of his academical and
preparatory studies, and thereupon, for such a
conduct after his appearance in the world, as may
render him a skilful and useful minister of the
gospel.* The work was printed in 1726 for Thomas
Hancock and sold at his shop in Ann Street, Boston, Mass. It contained 151 pages and a catalog for
a young student's library.

BIBLIOGRAPHY COURSE was offered in 1878
by the University of Michigan, at Ann Arbor. Raymond Cazallis Davis, the librarian, gave a lecture
once a week during November and December.
(University of Michigan—Catalogue 1878–79)

BIBLIOGRAPHY SOCIETY (national) was the
Bibliographical Society of America, organized
October 18, 1904, in St. Louis, Mo., "to promote
bibliographical research and to issue bibliographical publications." The first officers were William
Coolidge Lane, president; Herbert Putnam, first
vice president; Reuben Gold Thwaites, second
vice president; and Wilberforce Eames, librarian.

BICAMERAL LEGISLATURE. *See* Legislature

The First

BICARBONATE OF SODA. *See* Baking soda

BICYCLE
Bicycle velocipedes or "swift walkers," as they
were then called, were imported in 1819. The first
one in New York City made its appearance on
May 21, 1819. The Common Council met on August 19, 1819, and in solemn session passed a law
"to prevent the use of velocipedes in the public
places and on the sidewalks of the city of New
York."

Bicycle with a back-pedal brake was patented
on December 24, 1889, by Daniel C. Stover and
William A. Hance of Freeport, Ill., who received
patent No. 418,142.

Bicycle with a rotary crank was patented (No.
59,915) on November 20, 1866, by Pierre Lallemont
of Paris, France. It was known as a "bone shaker."
He rode on it from Ansonia, Conn., to New Haven,
Conn. The fore wheel was axled to the jaws of a
depending bar, which was pivoted in the frame
and turned by a horizontal lever bar, which was
revolved by a treadle crank.

BICYCLE CLUB. *See* Bicycle society

BICYCLE CORPS (military) was organized in
1894 by Colonel Royal Page Davidson and was
made up of cadets in the Northwestern Military
Academy, Lake Geneva, Wis. It was composed of
16 bicycles, each equipped with special clips for
carrying rifles, etc. One of the feats of the corps
was a maneuver in which the riders put themselves and their bicycles, which with their military equipment weighed 54 pounds each, over a
16-foot wall in 2 minutes and 48 seconds. Numerous long cross-country trips were made. On June
7, 1897, 11 cadets left Chicago, Ill., carrying a message from Major General John R. Brooks of Fort
Sheridan, Ill., over the mountains and the National Pike to Washington, D.C., where it was
delivered to Russell Alexander Alger, Secretary
of War, on June 26, 1897. *(Bicycle World. July
1897)*

BICYCLE MAGAZINE was *The American Bicycling Journal,* published December 22, 1877, in
Boston, Mass. It contained 16 pages and cost 10
cents a copy. It appeared every other Saturday.
Frank William Weston was the editor and proprietor. It was absorbed by *Bicycling World and
Motor Cycle Review.*

BICYCLE MANUFACTURER
Bicycle factory was established by Colonel Albert Augustus Pope of Hartford, Conn., who saw
a bicycle at the 1876 Centennial Exposition, Philadelphia, Pa., and commissioned W. S. Atwell of
Boston, Mass., to build a 70-pound model for him
at a cost of $313. In 1878, he ordered 50, which he
sold promptly. The Weed Sewing Machine Company, Hartford, Conn., filled this first order, for
Columbia bicycles (originally called Standard

The First

Columbus), and he reordered, sold 10, and had back orders for 32.

BICYCLE PATENT

Bicycle patent was granted to William K. Clarkson, Jr., of New York City on June 26, 1819, for an "improved curricle." Bicycles were then known as "curricles," "velocipedes," or "swift walkers."

Water velocipede patent was No. 95,531, granted on October 5, 1869, to F. A. Spofford and Mathew G. Raffington of Columbus, Ohio.

BICYCLE RACE

Bicycle race telecast. *See under* Television—Telecast

Intercollegiate bicycle race was held May 27, 1896, at the Manhattan Beach Track, New York City, under the auspices of the Intercollegiate Association of Amateur Athletes of America. Five races were held—¼ mile, ½ mile, 1 mile, 1 mile tandem, and 5 miles. Contestants scored 5 points for each first place, 2 points for each second place, and 1 point for each third place. The score was Columbia 20, Yale 8, Pennsylvania 5, Columbian University of Washington 5, and Harvard 2.

International six-day bicycle race was held in Madison Square Garden, New York City, from midnight Sunday, October 18, 1891, to midnight Saturday, October 24, 1891, and was won by William ("Plugger Bill") Martin of Detroit, Mich., who rode a "high wheeler" bicycle. There were 40 contestants but only 6 finished. Martin covered 1,466 miles and 4 laps and won a $2,100 prize. Charles Ashlager rode 1,441 miles and won $1,500; William Lamb rode 1,462 miles and won $900; Albert Schrock rode 1,329 miles and won $720; J. Albert rode 1,308 miles and won $480; and W. M. Boyst rode 1,301 miles and won $300. The gate receipts were $26,000. Ten laps constituted a mile. The first two-man team event was held from February 12, 1899, to February 17, 1899, and was won by Charles Miller and Frank Waller, "the Flying Dutchman," who rode a combined total of 2,733.4 miles.

Motorcycle-paced bicycle race was a 100-mile race for a $1,000 prize held July 29, 1899, at the Manhattan Beach Track, Manhattan Beach, New York City. There were four entries: Harry Elkes, Frank Waller, Charles Miller, and Burns Pierce. Pierce covered the course in 3 hours, 27 minutes, and 5.4 seconds, beating the nearest competitor by 7 1/3 miles. The contestants were on bicycles. The motorcycle was used to pace them.

Paired six-day bicycle race was held at Madison Square Garden, New York City, December 9-14, 1901. The winners of the $1,500 team prize were Robert Walthour of Atlanta, Ga., and Archie McEachern of Toronto, Canada, who pedaled 2,555 miles. Sixteen professional riders from nine nations competed. Paired races were instituted

The First

because the law prohibited one man from being on the track more than 12 hours a day.

Women's six-day bicycle race was held February 11–16, 1889, at Madison Square Garden, New York City, under the management of William O'Brien. Tony Pastor officiated as the starter. The week's proceeds amounted to $10,212; $4,084.80 of that amount went to the winner, Lottie Stanley. The honesty of the competition was later questioned: a Troy, N.Y., promoter had entered 10 salaried riders.

BICYCLE RACER

Bicycle racer to attain the speed of a mile a minute was Charles Minthorn Murphy, known as Mile-A-Minute-Murphy, who on June 30, 1899, rode a mile in 57.8 seconds, riding behind a Long Island Railroad train from Farmingdale, L.I., to Maywood, L.I., N.Y., on a three-mile measured track. He followed the train, which was equipped with an extension top and sides so that he raced in a comparative vacuum.

Bicyclist to ride a mile in less than 2 minutes from a standing start was John Johnson of Minneapolis, Minn., whose speed on September 22, 1892, at Independence, Iowa, was 1:56 3/5.

Woman bicycle champion of the National Amateur Bicycle Association was Doris Kopsky of Belleville, N.J., who on September 4, 1937, in Buffalo, N.Y., covered a mile in 4 minutes 22.4 seconds.

Woman bicycle champion of the National Amateur Bicycle Association to win twice was Mildred Marie Dietz of St. Louis, Mo., who won at Humboldt Park, Chicago, Ill., on August 18-19, 1945, and at Columbus, Ohio on August 17, 1946.

BICYCLE RACETRACK OF WOOD was built by the Bay City Club, San Francisco, Calif., and placed in use July 1, 1893. The outer edges of the track were built on an incline.

BICYCLE RIDER

Bicycle rider to cross the continent in less than three weeks was Eugene McPherson, 22 years old, of Ohio State University, who left Santa Monica, Calif., on September 1, 1949, and arrived at New York City on September 21, 1949, covering 3,054 miles in 20 days 4 hours 29 minutes.

Bicycle rider to go around the world was Thomas Stevens, who started from San Francisco, Calif., on April 22, 1884, on a 50-inch bicycle (diameter of the large front wheel). He pedaled across the United States, arriving at Boston, Mass., on August 24, 1884. He left for Europe by ship and visited England, France, Germany, Austria-Hungary, Serbia, Bulgaria, Turkey, Persia, India, China, and Japan. On December 17, 1886, he landed at Yokohama, Japan, having actually wheeled about 13,500 miles. He left Yokohama on the *City of Peking* and arrived at San

The First

BICYCLE RIDER—*Continued*

Francisco January 7, 1887. *(Thomas Stevens—Around the World on a Bicycle)*

BICYCLE SCHOOL for velocipede riding was opened in New York City on December 5, 1868, at 932 Broadway, by Pearsall Brothers.

BICYCLE SOCIETY

Bicycle club was the Boston Bicycle Club, formed February 11, 1878, in Boston, Mass., by 14 members. George B. Woodward was president, Thatcher Goddard was captain, and Harry S. Mann was secretary and treasurer. The uniform was a gray jacket, shirt, breeches, and stockings and a blue Glengarry Scotch cap with a small visor in front. The first meet was held March 9, 1878. *(The Wheelman. March 1883)*

Bicycle society (national organization) was the League of American Wheelmen, formed May 31, 1880, at Newport, R.I., by 128 members representing 28 cycling clubs. The first officers were president Charles Ed Pratt of Boston, Mass.; vice president Thomas K. Longstreth of Philadelphia, Pa.; and Commander C. Kirk Munroe of New York City. *(Bicycling World. June 12, 1880)*

BICYCLE TIRE

Bicycle tire (cord) was invented by John F. Palmer of Chicago, Ill., who obtained patent No. 476,680 on June 7, 1892. The patent covered a self-healing tire in which the tread portion of the rubber was placed under compression, so that a puncture would tend to close rather than gape open. The tire was manufactured in 1892 by the B. F. Goodrich Company of Akron, Ohio, and was first exhibited at the Philadelphia Cycle Show in February 1893.

Bicycle tire (pneumatic) was made in the tire factory of the George R. Bidwell Cycle Company of New York City in April 1891 for use on its bicycles. *(William Chauncey Geer—Reign of Rubber)*

Rubber tire patent. *See under* Rubber

BICYCLE TRAFFIC COURT was held at Racine, Wis., June 18, 1936, under authority of Grover Cleveland Lutter, chief of police. The judges of the court were Sergeant Wilbur Hansen and Officer Alphonse Costabile of the Racine Police Department. Sessions were held Saturday mornings. Section 12.71 of Code of the General Ordinance of the City of Racine passed by Common Council May 4, 1937, approved May 8, 1937, required all bicycles to be registered with the police department.

BICYCLE TRIP

Bicycle trip of 100 miles sponsored by a club took place September 6, 1882, when the Boston Bicycle Club, Boston, Mass., sponsored a trip from Worcester, Mass., to Boston. The trip started at 4:38 A.M. and ended at 9:30 P.M. with frequent stopoffs for food, refreshments, and repairs. The elapsed time was 16 hours 52 minutes, of which 12

The First

hours 6 minutes was the actual riding time. Seven men covered the complete 102½ miles, but many others rode along for varying distances. The route was via South Framingham, Natick, Wellesley, Dedham, Stoughton, Brockton, Randolph, Braintree, Quincy, Mattapan, Waltham, and Newton.

BICYCLE TRIP (WORLD)

Bicycle trip around the world by a married couple was made by Dr. and Mrs. H. Darwin McIlrath of Chicago, who left Chicago on April 10, 1895 They wheeled to San Francisco on June 4, 1895 crossed the Pacific by ship to Japan, thence to China, Burma, India, Persia, Russia, Austria, Hungary, Germany, France, and Great Britain. They departed from Southampton, England, on the S.S Pennland, arrived in New York City on October 27, 1898, and completed their trip of approximately 28,000 miles at Chicago on December 1, 1898 The trip took 3 years, 7 months, 21 days, 2 hours, and 55 minutes.

Bicycle trip around the world by a woman was made by Annie Londonberry, who left June 26 1894, from the State House, Boston, and ended her trip September 12, 1895, at Chicago. She returned to Boston on September 24, 1895, to collect a $10, 000 bet for completing the trip within 15 months and $5,000 in lecture fees.

BIFOCALS. *See* Lens

BILL. *See* Money

BILL OF RIGHTS. *See* Constitutional amendment (U.S.): Constitutional amendments

BILLBOARD LEGISLATION. *See* Advertising law: Outdoor advertising legislation (state)

BILLBOARD STANDARDIZATION was attempted by the owners of outdoor advertising services who reorganized and formed the Associated Bill Posters and Distributors of the United State and Canada on July 15, 1891, in Chicago, Ill. At a meeting held in Kansas City, Mo., October 16-20 1925, the name was changed, to the Outdoor Advertising Association of America, Inc., by virtue of the absorption of the Painted Display Advertising Association. Billboards were usually from 50 to 100 feet in length. In 1912 the boards were divided into sections 25 feet long. The posters were all of the same height, 8 feet 10 inches, but their length varied. The 8-, 12-, 16-, and 24-sheet posters were in general use. The 24-sheet poster was 19 feet inches long. The difference between the size of the poster and the billboard allowed for the use of white border which tended to intensify the pictorial poster. At later dates the height of the billboard was changed until it was as high as 15 feet from the ground line, with 3 feet of lattice apron border at the base.

BILLIARD BALL of composition material resembling ivory was invented by John Wesley Hyatt the winner of a $10,000 prize offered by Phelan and Collender of New York City for the best sub

The First

stitute for an ivory ball. Hyatt obtained patent No. 50,359, October 10, 1865, on a billiard ball; patent No. 76,765, April 14, 1868, on a compound for billiard balls; patent No. 88,634, April 6, 1869, on a method of coating and painting; and patent No. 105,338, July 12, 1870, on celluloid. *(Journal of Industrial and Engineering Chemistry. Vol. 6. No. 2)*

BILLIARD BOOK was *Billiards Without a Master: a full and complete set of rules for the government of the game of billiards and the various games of pool, etc; hints to players, advice to amateurs, keepers of saloons, etc.,* by Michael Phelan, containing 127 pages and 50 copperplate diagrams. It was published in 1850 in New York City by D. D. Winant.

BILLIARD MATCH

Billiard match of importance was played May 3, 1854, for a $200 stake at Malcolm Hall, Syracuse, N.Y., by Joseph N. White of New York City and George Smith of Watertown, N.Y. It was a four-ball carom game, 500 points up, on a 6-by-12 four-pocket table. White won by a score of 500-84. The score of runs and averages was not kept. *(Michael Phelan—American Billiard Record)*

Billiard match to attain international prominence was played in Detroit, Mich., on April 12, 1859, between Michael Phelan of New York City and John Seereiter of Detroit for the championship of the world and a $15,000 purse. Phelan, known as the "father of billiards," won the championship by a score of 2,000 against his competitor's 1,904. The best run made by Phelan was 129 points. The game was played on a 6-by-12 four-pocket table with four balls. Pushing and crotching were allowed.

Billiard three-ball match on a 6-by-12 carom table was played for a $500 stake April 30, 1855, at San Francisco, Calif., between Michael Phelan, then of San Francisco, and M. Damon of Paris, France. Phelan conceded his opponent 20 points in 100, and won two out of three games. *(Brooklyn Daily Eagle Almanac, 1887)*

Intercollegiate billiard match was played July 5, 1860, in Worcester, Mass., when freshmen of Harvard and Yale engaged in a "grand trial of skill." A six-pocket, 6-by-12 table, was used. Four balls, white, spotted, light red, and dark red, each ⅜ inches, were used. Pushing and crotching were allowed. Benjamin Thompson Frothingham and William Stackpole of Harvard won with 800 points against 720 for George St. John Sheffield and Theodore C. Bacon of Yale. The best run was 5, made by Bacon. *(Michael Phelan—American Billiard Record)*

BILLIARDS

Billiard player to win a match in the first inning was Willie Mosconi of Philadelphia, Pa., who ran 50 balls on April 17, 1956, at Kinston, N.C., following the break by Jimmy Moore of Albuquerque, N.M., who played a safety shot.

The First

Mosconi won each of his 14 matches and scored a 150-0 victory in the final match of the world pocket billiards tournament.

Billiards were brought to America by the Spaniards who settled in St. Augustine, Fla., in 1565.

BINDER, BOOK. *See* Bookbinder

BINET-SIMON TEST. *See* Intelligence test

BIOGRAPHY COURSE

Biography department in a college was established at Carleton College, Northfield, Minn., in the college year 1919–20. It was organized by Dr. Ambrose White Vernon as a separate department of the college.

BIOLOGY

Biology course (general) offered in a college was conducted by Professor Edmund Beecher Wilson, professor of biology, at Bryn Mawr College, Bryn Mawr, Pa., beginning September 23, 1885. Five lectures were given weekly, with eight hours of laboratory practice. The students examined the structure of typical animals and plants, first of familiar species, then of unicellular organisms, working thence progressively upward and taking the higher animals and plants, and ending with the embryological development of the chick. An advanced class was engaged in the study of animal morphology. Lectures on specific phases of biology had, however, been given earlier.

Biology instruction. *See* Physiological laboratory

BIRD BANDING

Bird banding was done at Mill Grove Farm, Montgomery County, 24 miles northwest of Philadelphia, Pa., in 1803 by John James Audubon, who used silver wire to band a brood of phoebes *(Sayornis phoebe)* and was fortunate in obtaining two returns.

Bird banding by federal authorities was done by the United States Biological Survey. Bands were attached to different species of ducks and other water birds during the summer of 1914 by Dr. Alexander Wetmore, who was making investigations of the duck sickness at the Bear River marshes, Utah. *(U.S. Agricultural Bulletin No. 1145. May 1923)*

BIRD BANDING SOCIETY was the American Bird Banding Association, formed in New York City by 30 charter members on December 8, 1909. The society was dissolved in 1920, when records and effects were turned over to the Bureau of Biological Survey of the United States Department of Agriculture, Washington, D.C. *(The Auk. Vol. 38, 1921)*

BIRD LEGISLATION (international) was the Migratory Bird Treaty for the protection of migratory birds in the United States and Canada, signed August 16, 1916, by the United States and Great Britain at Washington, D.C. (39 Stat. L. 1702). It

The First

BIRD LEGISLATION (international)—*Continued* was signed by President Woodrow Wilson, September 1, 1916, and ratified by Great Britain October 20, 1916. Ratifications were exchanged in Washington, D.C., December 7, 1916, and the treaty proclaimed December 8, 1916.

BIRD MONUMENT. *See* Monument: Monument to a bird

BIRD PROTECTION AGENCY (federal) was begun on July 1, 1885, as a section of Economic Ornithology, Division of Entomology, Department of Agriculture. It became the Bureau of Biological Survey on July 1, 1905, was transferred to the Department of Interior on July 1, 1939, and consolidated with the Bureau of Fisheries on June 30, 1940, to form the present Fish and Wildlife Service.

BIRD REFUGE authorized by a state was established at Lake Merritt, Oakland, Calif., by authority of Chapter 109, Act of February 14, 1872.

BIRD RESERVATION (national) was established by Executive Order of President Theodore Roosevelt on March 14, 1903, at Pelican Island, situated in the Indian River near Sebastian, Fla. to protect a nesting colony of pelicans and herons. This wildlife refuge was enlarged by Executive Order of January 26, 1909, to include adjacent mangrove and other islands. *Records in Bureau of Biological Survey, U.S. Department of Agriculture, Washington, D.C.)*

BIRD SANCTUARY for wild birds was the Hawk Mountain Sanctuary, Drehersville, Pa., which received options on the area, August 29, 1934.

BIRDS
Bird for which a definite crossing of the Atlantic has been recorded is that of a common tern *(Sterna hirundo)* that was banded at Eastern Egg Rock, Me., on July 3, 1913, and found dead in August 1917 at the mouth of the Niger River, West Africa. *(Frederick Charles Lincoln—Migration of American Birds)*

Eagle depicted on a postage stamp. *See* Postage stamp: Postage stamps depicting the American eagle

Ostrich farm was established at South Pasadena, Calif., by Edwin Cawston in 1886. He imported 50 ostriches from Africa, 18 of which survived the trip and were landed at Galveston, Tex., in 1886. In order to discourage the exportation of ostriches from Africa, an export tax of $500 was placed on each ostrich and $25 on each egg, but this shipment escaped the tax, as the boat sailed from Africa a few hours before the tax became effective.

Partridge propagation was encouraged in 1790 when Richard Bache, son-in-law of Benjamin Franklin, stocked his plantation at Beverly, N.J. Four years previously, General Lafayette had sent

The First

a few partridges to George Washington. *(Technical Bulletin No. 61) (U.S. Department of Agriculture)*

Ptarmigan (Eskimo chicken) hatched and reared in captivity was hatched July 24, 1934, a Ithaca, N.Y., from one of ten eggs obtained from Churchill, Manitoba, Canada, by Arthur Augustus Allen, Professor of Ornithology, Cornell University, Ithaca, N.Y. The ptarmigan was 110 days old when it died of enterohepatitis (commonly called blackhead).

Quetzal bird (adult) *(Pharomacrus costaricensis)* was imported October 4, 1940, by Dr. Victor Wolfgang Von Hagen, New York City, who had captured it. It was acquired by the St. Louis Zoo, St. Louis, Mo., but was exhibited until October 7 1940, at the Bronx Zoo, New York City. It was a male, three years old, pigeon-sized, with a crimson breast. The back and head were emerald green with a gold trim. The wings were jet black and the tail black and white; over the tail was a green train about a yard long, and four additional feathers. On October 29, 1937, Dr. Von Hagen had brought back nine young quetzals, which were shown at the Bronx Zoo until April 1939, when the last one died. *(Victor Wolfgang Von Hagen—Jungle in the Clouds)*

Snow goose bred in captivity was hatched i 1934 in the City Park Zoo, Denver, Colo. This gosling was the first seen anywhere. Three eggs were laid; one hatched, one was destroyed, and one was given to the Colorado Museum of Natural History, in the City Park Zoo, Denver, Colo. Clyde E. Hill was the director of the zoo.

Sparrows were imported under the auspices of Nicholas Pike and other directors of the Brooklyn Institute in 1850 for the purpose of protecting shade trees from foliage-eating caterpillars. Eight pairs of English, or house, sparrows *(Passer domesticus)* were imported. The birds were kept in cages until liberated in the spring of 1851. They did not thrive, and in 1852 a larger number were imported. *(Frederick William Evans—English Sparrows)*

Whooping crane born in captivity was Dawn, six-inch-tall crane born May 28, 1975, at the Rare and Endangered Bird Research Center, Laurel Md.

BIRLING. *See* Log rolling (birling)

BIRTH CONTROL CLINIC. *See* Medical clinic

BIRTH REGISTRATION
Birth Registration Law (state) was passed by the state of Georgia, December 19, 1823. It required the "clerks of the court of ordinary, in each county respectively to enter and register in book" the dates of births of all persons upon proof made by affidavit or oath. The clerk was entitled to charge 25 cents for each registration

The First

Georgia Law, Extract General Appropriation Bill, p. 192, Approved December 19, 1823)

Birth registration uniform system for the numbering of birth certificates was adopted March 18, 1948, by the American Association of Registration Executives. The Council on Vital Records and Vital Statistics approved this resolution of the legislation executives at a meeting on August 30, 1948. The system was inaugurated January 1, 1949. Each state was assigned a number: 101 for Alabama, 102 for Arizona, 103 for Arkansas, etc. A second number refers to the year, and a third number to the order of the birth in the state's record. The lowest number in the classification was awarded to Leonard Blake Gunnells of Prattville, Ala., whose name was the first on the roll of the first county in Alabama's alphabetical county list. His number was 101-49-000001.

BIRTHS

Birth (human) to be televised. *See under* Television—Telecast

Child born in an airplane was the daughter of Mr. and Mrs. T. W. Evans, born on October 28, 1929, in a transport plane over the city of Miami, Fla.

Child born in the White House, Washington, D.C., was James Madison Randolph, the son of Thomas Mann Randolph and Martha (Jefferson) Randolph, the daughter of President Thomas Jefferson, born January 17, 1806. He died January 23, 1834. The Randolphs were married February 23, 1790. *(Robert Isham Randolph—The Randolphs of Virginia)*

Child born in the White House, Washington, D.C., the offspring of a President, was Esther Cleveland, born September 9, 1893. She was the second child of President Grover Cleveland and Frances Folsom Cleveland, who were married June 2, 1886, in the Blue Room of the White House, Washington, D.C. *(Gibson Willets—Inside History of the White House)*

Child born of English parents in America was Virginia Dare. She was born at Roanoke Island, North Carolina, on August 18, 1587, and was the daughter of Ananias Dare and Eleanor (White) Dare, and granddaughter of John White, governor of the colony sent out from England by Sir Walter Raleigh on May 8, 1587. Only the first 9 days of her life are known to history. On May 8, 1587, 3 vessels left England with 150 colonists, including 25 women and children. They landed at Cape Hatteras on July 22, cruised up what is now Pamlico Sound to the "iland called Roanoac." Two vessels returned immediately and the third with John White sailed on August 27 for more supplies. When he returned four years later, the colonists were all gone and the fort was in ruins. *(Major Graham Daves—Virginia Dare—North Carolina Booklet Vol. 1, No. 1, May 10, 1901)*

The First

Child born of English parents in New England was Peregrine White, born on board the *Mayflower* off Cape Code harbor on November 20, 1620. He was the son of Susanna and William White. He died at Marshfield, Mass., July 22, 1704.

Child born of European parents on American soil was Snorro, the son of Thorfinn Karlsefni and Gudrid, the widow of Thorstein Ericsson (Leif Ericsson's brother). About 160 Norse volunteers arrived in America in 1007 to form a settlement in Vinland, which may have been Nova Scotia or the coast of Maine. Snorro returned to Iceland and took an important part in its government.

Child born on a vessel passing through the Panama Canal was the child of Mr. and Mrs. M. Niezes of Panama. The baby was born on June 2, 1930, on the Dutch steamship *Baralt*, passing through Gatun locks.

President of the United States to be born in a hospital was Jimmy Carter (James Earl Carter, Jr.), the 39th President. The son of Lilian Gordy Carter and James Earl Carter, Sr., he was born October 1, 1924, in Wise Sanitarium in the small town of Plains, Georgia.

Quadruplets delivered by cesarean operation were Maureen, Kathleen, Eileen, and Michael Cirminello, born to Mr. and Mrs. Joseph Cirminello on November 1, 1944, in Philadelphia, Pa. The cesarean section was performed under spinal anesthesia. The obstetrician in charge was Dr. John Calvin Ullery of Upper Darby, Pa.

Quintuplets to live more than 5 years were 1 boy (James Andrew) and 4 girls (Mary Ann, Mary Catherine, Mary Magdalen, and Mary Margaret), born within the space of 63 minutes to Mr. and Mrs. Andrew J. Fischer of Aberdeen, S.D., on September 14, 1963, in St. Luke's Hospital. They weighed approximately 2½ to 4 pounds each. The physician was Dr. James Barbos.

Quintuplets were five boys born February 13, 1875, in Watertown, Wis., to Mrs. Edna Beecham Kanouse, wife of Edward Cole Kanouse. All five died within two weeks. (The birth of quintuplets in 1776 is claimed for Mars Bluff, S.C., and in 1800 for Monticello, Ill.)

Sextuplets were three boys and three girls born September 8, 1866, in Chicago, Ill., to James and Jennie A. Lewis Bushnell. The attending physician was Dr. James Edwards and the midwife was Priscilla Bancroft. One of the sextuplets—Lucy—died at the age of two months, and one—Laberto—died at eight months. Of the surviving four, one—Norberto—died at 68, and three—Alberto, Alice Elizabeth (Mrs. Hughes), and Alincia L. (Mrs. Parker)—were over 70 when they died. (According to the *Boston Medical and Surgical Journal* of 1847 (Vol. 35, p. 27), sextuplets were born on June

The First

BIRTHS—*Continued*

27, 1846, to a Mrs. Marr of Phipsburg, Maine, but the report may have been a hoax.)

Telecast (public) of a human birth. *See* Television—Telecast: Birth (human) to be televised for the public

Three million births in one year were recorded for 1943, when 3,104,000 births occurred, 22.7 per 1,000 population. In 1954, there were 4,078,000 births, 25.3 per 1,000.

White child of French Protestant parentage was born in 1565 in the French settlement of Fort Caroline, Fla., established in 1564 by René Goulaine de Laudonnière, a Huguenot. In August 1565 the original settlement was reinforced with the arrival of Captain Jean Ribaut's expedition, bringing women, children, agricultural implements, etc. *(Thomas Frederick Davis, Historic St. Johns Bluff, near Jacksonville, Fla.)*

World War baby was born on June 7, 1918, to Mrs. Kate Lewis, who married William Lewis of the American Expeditionary Force in London, England, on July 14, 1917.

BISCUIT. *See* Cracker

BISHOP, CATHOLIC. *See* Catholic bishop

BISHOP

General to be consecrated a bishop. *See* Army officer: General to be consecrated a bishop

BISHOP'S HERESY TRIAL. *See* Heresy trial of a bishop

BLACK

See also under names of churches, civil and military positions, organizations, professions, scholarships, schools, sports, etc.

Black woman college graduate was Lucy Ann Stanton (Mrs. Levi N. Sessions) of Cleveland, Ohio, who was graduated December 8, 1850, from Oberlin College, Oberlin, Ohio, receiving the Bachelor of Literature (L.B.) degree.

National convention for blacks assembled at Bethel Church, Philadelphia, Pa., on September 15, 1830, to better the condition of black people. It was attended by delegates from seven states. Bishop Richard Allen was elected the first president.

BLACK COMMUNITY OF CATHOLIC NUNS. *See* Catholic nuns: Catholic nuns (black community)

BLACKOUT

Blackout lighting demonstration was made May 14, 1941, when 12 specially designed blackout luminaries spaced 100 feet apart along Parkland Avenue, Lynn, Mass., were illuminated. Each lighting fixture used a 2½-watt Argon (gaseous) lamp and gave off light in the form of ultraviolet

The First

rays invisible to observers in planes at a height o 20,000 feet.

Blackout outdoor light control was instituted by Seattle, Wash., May 11, 1942, which required a outside types of lighting to be controlled by manu al control, master control wire, photoelectric cell or radio switch, and subject to permit.

BLANKET

Blanket factory was the Burleigh Blanket Mills established by Captain John H. Burleigh in 1854 on the Piscataqua River, Me. The factory wa located on the site originally selected by Fer dinando Gorges in 1620 for a grist mill, at what i now South Berwick, Me.

Blanket robe and carriage lap robe busines was successfully undertaken at Sanford, Me., i 1867 by Thomas Goodall. *(William Morrell Emer, —History of Sanford, Me.)*

Electric (electronic) blanket was manufacture by Simmons Company on October 9, 1946, in Pe tersburg, Va. Temperature was regulated by a "electronic" thermostatic control. It sold fo $39.50.

Horse blankets were manufactured by Thoma Goodall at Troy, N.H., in 1852. The only hors blankets then in use were imported and wer square in shape. Goodall cut them to fit and put o buckles. He sold out his interest in 1865 to a grou of financiers from Keene, N.H. *(M. T. Stone—His torical Sketch of the Town of Troy, N.H.)*

BLAST FURNACE. *See* Iron: Iron blast furnace

BLASTING, SAND. *See* Sandblasting

BLIND

Bible for the blind. *See under* Bible

Book for the blind. *See under* Book

Correspondence school for the blind to offer i struction in the Braille system of embossed pri was the Hadley Correspondence School for th Blind, Winnetka, Ill., which offered courses, August 1921, in English grammar, business corr spondence, and the study of Scriptures, as well instruction in the Braille system. The schoo founded by William Aaron Hadley, was inco porated in Illinois, January 2, 1922.

Dogs trained to guide the blind. *See under* Ar mals

Kindergarten for the blind. *See under* Kinde garten

Machine for reading printed matter aloud wa invented by Raymond Kurzweil and first demo strated publicly on January 13, 1976, and was tes ed by the National Federation for the Blind. camera controlling a computer scans pages a analyzes the letters. The machine, manufactur by the Kurzweil Computer Products, Inc., Ca bridge, Mass., converts ordinary printed mate ls, books, magazines, and typewritten correspondence directly into spoken English at 150 words per minute.

Magazine for the blind. *See under* Periodical

Music magazine published in Braille. *See* Music magazine: Music magazine published in Braille

School for blind blacks was the State School for the Blind and the Deaf opened in Raleigh, N.C., on January 4, 1869, with 26 pupils. *(Seventieth Anniversary of the State School for the Blind and the Deaf, Raleigh, N.C.)*

School for the blind was the New England Asylum for the Blind, Boston, Mass., incorporated March 2, 1829. The school was founded by Dr. John Dix Fisher and opened under Dr. Samuel Gridley Howe in August 1832 with six pupils. On April 1, 1839, the name was changed to the Perkins Institution and the Massachusetts Asylum for the Blind in honor of Thomas Handasyd Perkins, who in 1833 offered his Boston home with pen grounds around it for a school building. On October 3, 1877, the word "asylum" was dropped and the name changed to the Perkins Institution and Massachusetts School for the Blind. The present name of the school, now at Watertown, Mass., is the New England Institution for the Education of the Blind. *(Paul Monroe—Cyclopedia of Education)*

School for the blind to adopt the Braille system was the Missouri School for the Blind, St. Louis, Mo. In 1859 Dr. Simon Pollak, a trustee of the school, introduced the system direct from Paris, France. Three letters were changed and it was used in music, spelling, etymology, and other subjects.

State school for the blind was the Ohio Institution for the Blind, authorized April 3, 1837, and opened July 4, 1837, with 5 pupils, in the Presbyterian Church, Columbus, Ohio, in the presence of 900 people. Anson W. Penniman was the first teacher. The first superintendent was William Chapin, who served from May 1, 1840, to October 1846. On April 25, 1902, a law was enacted to change the name to the Ohio State School for the Blind.

Talking book. *See* Talking book

Telephone switchboard with Braille markings. *See under* Telephone

"BLIND" AIRPLANE FLIGHT. *See* Aviation—Flights: All-blind flight

BLOCK SIGNAL SYSTEM (railroad). *See* Railroad signal system

BLOCK TIN BUTTON. *See* Button

BLOCKADE was effected on April 30, 1778, from West Point, N.Y., to Constitution Island, N.Y. A huge chain was forged at the Sterling Iron Works, Orange County, N.Y., from ore mined in the same

county and was carried in sections to West Point, where it was joined and stretched across the Hudson to prevent British ships from passing. The chain weighed 180 tons and was 1,700 feet long; each link was 2½ inches wide and 30 inches long. It was placed in position April 16 and on April 30, 1778, was secured at both ends. In the summer of 1776, a chain of chevaux-de-frise and sunken ships had been extended between Fort Washington, N.Y., and Fort Lee, N.J., but the British passed it October 9, 1776, without firing a gun. *(Macgrane Coxe—The Sterling Furnace and the West Point Chain)*

BLOOD BANK

Blood bank to preserve by refrigeration blood for transfusions was established March 15, 1937, by the Cook County Hospital, Chicago, Ill. *(Journal of the American Medical Association. July 10, 1937)*

Blood serum (human, dried) was prepared by Dr. Earl William Flosdorf and Dr. Stuart Mudd of the School of Medicine, University of Pennsylvania, Philadelphia, Pa., on December 21, 1933, with glass apparatus made by them. The powdered dried blood serum was used successfully for transfusions for the prevention and treatment of children's diseases at a hospital at Philadelphia, Pa. The method was first described at a meeting of the American Chemical Society at St. Petersburg, Fla., in April 1934. More recently, the applications and uses of the dried blood serum have been greatly extended.

BLOOD GROUPING TEST. *See* Medical legislation: Blood grouping test laws (state)

BLOOD SERUM (dried). *See* Blood bank: Blood serum (human, dried)

BLOODSHED IN THE CIVIL WAR. *See under* Civil War

BLOOMERS were introduced at the First Woman's Rights Convention at Seneca Falls, N.Y., which met at Lyceum Hall on July 19, 1848, the name being derived from their sponsor, Mrs. Amelia Jenks Bloomer. The costume is supposed to have been devised by Mrs. Elizabeth Smith Miller. *(Dexter Chamberlain Bloomer—Life and Writings of Amelia Bloomer)*

BLOTTING PAPER was made in New Haven, Conn., by Joseph Parker & Son Company in 1856 at the West Rock Paper Mill on a Fourdrinier machine. Until this time only small quantities had been imported from England, as sandboxes were in general use. *(Paper World. Aug. 1881)*

BLOWPIPE was invented in 1801 by Professor Robert Hare of Philadelphia, Pa., who called it a "hydrostatic blowpipe." He reported his discovery to the Chemical Society of Philadelphia in *A Memoir of the Supply and Application of the Blow-Pipe, Containing an Account of the new method of supplying the Blow-Pipe either with*

The First

BLOWPIPE—*Continued*
common air or oxygen gas; and also of the effects
of the intense heat produced by the combustion of
the hydrogen and oxygen gases. (Edgar Fahs
Smith—Life of Robert Hare)

BLUE LAW

Blue law was enacted by the first legislative body assembled in America, the Virginia House of Burgesses, at its first session in 1619. The law provided that "all persons whatsoever upon the Sabbath days shall frequent divine service and sermons, both forenoon and afternoon." The Anglican Church was established by law and the creed of the church was the rule of the colony. *(Gustavus Myers—Ye Olden Blue Laws)*

Blue law regulating gambling was passed in 1624 by the Virginia Assembly. It specified that "Mynisters shall not give themselves to excesse in drinking or yette spend their tyme idelie by day or by night, playing at dice, cards or any unlawful game." *(Catherine Perry Hargrave—History of Playing Cards)*

Gambling legislation (colonial). *See* Gambling legislation (colonial)

BLUE SKY LAW. *See under* Trust

BOARD OF EDUCATION (state). *See* Education: State board of education

BOARDING SCHOOL FOR AMERICAN INDIANS. *See under* Indian school: American Indian boarding school on a reservation

BOARDWALK was dedicated June 26, 1870 at Atlantic City, N.J. To finance it, $5,000 was obtained by the sale, at a 10 percent discount, of scrip which could be used to pay taxes. The one-mile-long boardwalk rested on the sand and was 8 feet wide. It was built in 8-foot collapsible sections, which for 18 years were removed in September and stored for the winter. It was conceived by a hotel man, Jacob Keim, of the Chester County House, and Alexander Boardman, a railroad conductor on the Camden and Atlantic Railroad.

BOAT CLUB

Boat club was the Knickerbocker Boat Club of New York, organized in 1811. The club had a white boat, with green gunwales and gilt stripes, named the *Knickerbocker*, built by John Baptist. John Palmerton was coxswain, and William Cracker, John Burt, Thomas Dixon, and Thomas Palmerton were the oarsmen. The *Knickerbocker* raced the *Invincible*, built by John and William Chambers, from Harsimus, N.J., to the Battery, New York City. On the crew of the *Invincible* were William Chambers, coxswain, and John Chambers, James Rush, Peter Snider, and John Swinburn, oarsmen. The club disbanded in 1812. *(New York Mirror. July 15, 1837)*

The First

Boat club association of amateur clubs was the Castle Garden Amateur Boat Club Association which operated a boathouse at Castle Garden, N.Y., from 1834 to 1842. Annual regattas around Bedloe's Island and back were held, the last one on July 4, 1842. Some of the boats entered were the *Wave, Gull, Gazelle, Pearl, Cleopatra, Halcyon, Ariel, Minerva,* and *Gondola. (Robert F. Kelley—Amateur Rowing)*

BOAT RACE

See also Motorboat race; Rowing; Yacht race

Fisherman's boat race was held May 1, 1886 over a triangular course. The start was off the Boston Light, Little Brewster Island, Boston, to and around Davis Ledge buoy off Minot's Ledge thence to and around Half Way Rock off the Marblehead shore, and back to Boston Light. The *John H. McManus* won the first prize of $1,500, finishing two miles ahead of the *Sarah H. Prior,* which was a few minutes ahead of the *Gertie S. Windsor.* The pilot schooner *Hesper* won the race and the cup, but not the prize money, as it was not truly a fisherman's boat. *(Wesley George Pierce—Goin' Fishin')*

Intercollegiate boat race, in eight-oared boats took place August 3, 1852, between Yale and Harvard on a two-mile course on Lake Winnepesaukee, Centre Harbor, N.H. Harvard's lone entry, the *Oneida,* a 38-foot boat captained by Joseph Mansfield Brown, won by two lengths over Yale's *Shawmut,* followed by Yale's *Undine* and *Atlanta. (James Wellman—Story of the Harvard Yale Race 1852–1912)*

Intercollegiate regatta was held July 26, 1859, at Lake Quinsigamond, Worcester, Mass. Harvard defeated both Yale and Brown over a three-mile course. A regatta was scheduled July 23, 1858, at Springfield, Mass., but was postponed because a member of the Yale crew had drowned the day before.

International boat race was held August 27, 1869, from Aqueduct Bridge, Putney, to Ships Inn, Mortlake, on the River Thames, London, England, between Oxford and Harvard colleges. The shells were 44 feet long, 21 inches wide, and 8 inches deep. The 4¼-mile course was covered in 22 minutes 40.5 seconds. Oxford won by 4 lengths (6 seconds). The Oxonian (blue) team consisted of H. Hall, coxwain; F. Willan, J. C. Tinne, A. C. Yarborough; and S. D. Darbishire, bow. The Harvard (magenta or crimson) team included Arthur Burnham, coxwain; Alden Peter Loring, Sylvester Warren Rice, W. H. Simmons; and George Bass, bow.

International lifeboat race was held September 7, 1927, from the Statue of Liberty to Pier A, New York City, under the auspices of the Neptune Association. Eleven boats of different sizes, shapes and weights from seven different nations competed

e First

. A prize cup was presented to Captain John F.
lliken of the M.S. *Segundo* of Norway, whose
am of eight men covered the course in 15 mines 27 seconds. Second honors went to the crew
the M.S. *Titania* of Norway (16 minutes 27 sec-
ds) and third place to the crew of the *De Grasse*
France (17 minutes 7 seconds). Later races de-
loped uniform conditions.

Regatta. *See under* Yacht race

Yacht race (international). *See under* Yacht race

OATS. *See* Catamaran; Ferryboat; Lifeboat;
torboat; Ship

OBSLED COMPETITION

Four-man bob-team competition in the United
ates was held February 14–15, 1932, at the Third
ympic Winter Games at Lake Placid, N.Y., with
teams from 6 nations competing. First place
s won by the United States team of William L.
ke, driver, and Edward F. Eagan, Clifford B.
ay, and Jay O'Brien, brakemen, in a contest
ich covered the four heats in a total time of 7
nutes 53.68 seconds.

Two-man bob-team competition was held Feb-
ary 9–10, 1932 at the Third Olympic Winter
mes at Lake Placid, N.Y., with 15 teams from 8
tions entered in the competition. First place
s won by the United States (J. Hubert Stevens,
ver, and Curtis Stevens, brakeman) in 8 min-
s 14.74 seconds for the four heats.

OBSLED RUN of international specifications
s the Mountain Van Hoevenberg bobsled run
North Elba, N.Y., on the highway between Lake
cid and Elizabethtown, N.Y., designed by Sta-
aus Zentzytzki. It was built for the New York
te Olympic Winter Games Commission at a
t of more than $200,000 for the construction.
e run contained 26 curves and was 1.5 miles
g. About 29,000 gallons of water were needed
ry 24 hours to spray the run. Work was begun
gust 4, 1930, and the run was open to the public
cember 25, 1930.

HEMIAN-AMERICAN CHURCH was St. John
pomuk Church, St. Louis, Mo., opened April 20,
5, by the first pastor, Reverend Henry Li-
vsky, a former lieutenant in the Austrian
ny. The first solemn high mass was sung by
her de Smet, the famous Jesuit missionary
ong the Indians, on May 16, 1855, the patronal
st.

HEMIAN-AMERICAN DICTIONARY. *See*
tionary

HEMIAN NEWSPAPER (Czech). *See* News-
er: Czech-language newspaper

ILER

arbon monoxide boiler to achieve complete
version of waste gases into useful power was
igned and developed by the Sinclair Oil Cor-

The First

poration and placed in operation November 1953
at its Houston, Tex., refinery. Carbon monoxide
(CO) was converted into carbon dioxide (CO_2) by
injecting a stream of air into the waste gases from
the generator. The catalyst was regenerated in the
catalytic oil cracking process.

BOILER INSURANCE COMPANY. *See under* Insurance

BOILER LEGISLATION was the state boiler inspection law, approved July 9, 1864, by Connecticut. Chapter 67 authorized the governor to appoint
an "Inspector of Boilers" to check every steam
boiler used for manufacturing or mechanical purposes.

BOILER PLATES were made between 1816 and
1825 by Dr. Charles Lukens' mill, the Brandywine
Mill at Coatesville, Pa. The mill was originally
started at Rokeby, Pa., by Isaac Pennock in 1790
as the Federal Slitting Mill. Iron slabs were heated
in an open charcoal fire, rolled out into plates, and
then slit up into rods for general blacksmiths' use.
In 1810 Pennock purchased a sawmill at Brandywine, which he converted into the Brandywine
Iron Mill. The organization has remained in the
hands of Lukens' descendants, and is now known
as the Lukens Steel Company, one of the world's
largest plate mills.

BOLL WEEVIL. *See* Cotton-boll weevil

BOLT FACTORY. *See* Nut and bolt factory

BOLT MACHINE. *See* Nut and bolt machine

BOMB EXPLOSION (atomic). *See* Atomic bomb:
Atomic bomb explosion

BOMB SHELTER. *See* Air raid shelter; Building:
House with a built-in nuclear bomb shelter

BOMBER. *See* Aviation—Airplane

**BOMBING MISSION (AMERICAN) OVER ENE-
MY-OCCUPIED TERRITORY.** *See under* World
War II

**BOMBING ON CONTINENTAL AMERICAN
SOIL.** *See under* World War II

BOND

Bonds of the United States Government were
the interest-bearing obligations that were authorized by the Act of August 4, 1790 (1 Stat. L. 138),
for the refunding of the domestic debt and that
part of the state debt which was assumed by the
Federal Government. The total issue amounted to
$64,456,963.90; $30,088,397.75 drew interest at 6
percent; $19,719,237.39, at 3 percent; and $14,649,-
328.76 drew interest at 6 percent after 1800. Practically the entire issue was retired by 1836. *(U.S.
Treasury Dept. Commissioner of the public debt—
Liquidating the Revolutionary War)*

Bonds payable specifically in United States gold
coins were issued under authority of a financial
bill, an "act to define and fix the standard of val-

The First

BOND—*Continued*

ue, to maintain the parity of all forms of money issued or coined by the United States, to refund the public debt," March 14, 1900 (31 Stat. L. 45).

Confederate government bond was authorized by act of February 28, 1861, "to raise money for the support of the government and to provide for the defense of the Confederate States of America" not exceeding $15 million.

Liberty bond. *See* Loan: Liberty loan subscriptions

Treasury notes (interest-bearing) were authorized by the act of June 30, 1812 (2. Stat. L. 766). The President was authorized to issue treasury notes to an amount not exceeding $5 million. The act provided "that the said treasury notes shall be reimbursed by the United States, at such places, respectively, as may be expressed on the face of the said notes, one year, respectively after the day on which the same shall have been issued; from which day of issue they shall bear interest at the rate of five and two-fifths per centum a year, payable to the owner or owners of such notes, at the treasury, or by the proper commissioner of loans, at the places and times respectively designated on the face of said notes for the payment of principal." *(John Jay Knox—United States Notes, A History of the Various Issues of Paper Money by the Government of the United States)*

War bond. *See* War bond

BONDED WAREHOUSE. *See* Warehouse legislation

BONDING COMPANY. *See under* Insurance

BONDING LAW (state). *See under* Insurance

BONE BANK. *See under* Medicine

BONE BANK CENTER. *See* Deaf—Bone Bank: National temporal-bone bank center for ear research

BOOBY TRAP. *See* Land mines

BOOK

See also under specific type of book or subject, e.g.,

Agricultural book	Novel
Almanac	Pharmacopoeia
Aviation book	Social Register
Bible	

Best-seller (nonfiction) other than a text or purely theological work was *In His Steps, or What Would Jesus Do?* by the Reverend Charles Monroe Sheldon. It was written in the winter of 1896 and was a Utopian fantasy of what the world might be like if people lived literally according to Christ's teachings. It was read by the author a chapter at a time to his Sunday evening congregation in the Central Congregational Church, Topeka, Kans. He sold the story for $75 to the Chicago *Advance* and it was printed as a serial in 1897. As

The First

only parts of the serial were sent to the copyrig office, the copyright was declared defective. Ov 8 million copies in various editions were pu lished by different publishers. *(Charles Monr Sheldon—Charles M. Sheldon: His Life Story)*

Best-seller novel was *Charlotte, a Tale of Tru* by Mrs. Rowson (Susanna Haswell Rowson), actress of the New Theatre, Philadelphia, Pa., a author of *Victoria* (1786), *The Inquisitor* (178 *Rebecca, or the Fille de Chambre* (1792), etc. *Ch lotte* was printed by D. Humphreys for M. Car Philadelphia, Pa., in two volumes in 1794. English edition of *Charlotte* was printed in Lc don in 1790. Later it was entitled *Charlotte Te ple.* About 200 editions have been print *(American Antiquarian Society. Proceedings, V 42. April 1932)*

Book advance payment to exceed $3,000,0 was made by Bantam Books, New York City, w contracted with Crown Publishers for the pap back-rights edition of *Princess Daisy* for $3,20 000 on September 12, 1979, the second novel Judith Krantz, author of *Scruples.*

Book (American) made with American pap ink, type, etc., was the *Impenetrable Secr* printed and sold by Story & Humphreys in 1775 Philadelphia. It was advertised on June 23, 17 in the *Pennsylvania Mercury* as "just publish and printed with types, paper and ink manuf. tured in this Province." *(Lawrence Counselm Wroth—The Colonial Printer)*

Book bound with a preprinted offset cloth w Gertrude Stein's *Portraits and Prayers*, a 264-pa book published November 7, 1934, by Rand House, New York City. The cover showed a p trait of Gertrude Stein made at her home in Be nin, France, by Carl Van Vechten. The cloth w supplied by Columbia Mills, Inc., Syracuse, N

Book (cloth-covered) commercially bound v the fourth edition of Charlotte Anne Waldie ton's *Rome in the Nineteenth Century; contain a complete account of the ruins of the ancient c the remains of the middle ages, and the mo ments of modern times,* republished in 1827 b & J. Harper, New York City. It was first publish in 1820 in Edinburgh and reprinted in 1822, 18 and 1826.

Book entered for copyright was *The Ph delphia Spelling Book arranged upon a plan tirely new, adapted to the capacities of child and designed as an immediate improvement spelling and reading the English language, wh* was registered in the clerk's office of the first trict of Pennsylvania, June 9, 1790, by John Ba the author. It was printed in Philadelphia, Pa. 1790 by Carey, Stewart and Co. It was also iss as *The American Spelling Book.*

he First

Book for the blind was the *Gospel of St. Mark,* ublished in 1833 in Philadelphia, Pa., by the nnsylvania Institution for the Instruction of the ind. It was printed in embossed roman letters, per and lower case. Jacob Snider, Jr., recording cretary of the Pennsylvania Institute, proposed e publication and the funds were donated by athan Dunn and Edward Coleman. *(Pennsyl-nia Institution for the Instruction of the Blind—cond Annual Report. Mar. 2, 1835)*

Book (full-size) published in the colonies was ephen Day's (Steeven Daye's) *The Whole Booke Psalmes, Faithfully Translated into English etre whereunto is prefixed a Discourse declar-g not only the lawfulness, but also the necessity the heavenly ordinance of singing scripture almes in the Churches of God.* The book, 5½ by inches, contained 296 pages and was published July 1640 by the Cambridge Press, Cambridge, ass. It was a new metrical version of the psalms, revision of those of Sternhold and Hopkins. venteen hundred copies were printed and sold r 20 pence each, netting a profit of almost 0. *(George Emery Littlefield—The Early Massa-usetts Press)*

Book intended for circulation in the English lonies was Martin Luther's *Little Catechism,* nslated into the Algonquian Indian language in 56 by Johannes Campanius, a clergyman, who dicated it to King Karl X Gustav of Sweden. It ntained 132 pages of text and 27 pages of dictio-ry. About 600 copies of this 160-page book were inted in 1696, 40 years later, in Stockholm, Swe-n, by Thomas Campanius Holm, Campanius's andson. The title was *Lutheri Cathechismus os-rsatt pä American-Virginiste Språtet.* It was tended for missionary work among the Indians the colony of New Sweden and also contained small vocabulary in the Algonquin Indian lan-age.

Book list. *See* Book index

Book of Common Prayer in use in what is now e United States was the one used by the Rever-d Francis Fletcher, chaplain and chronicler of ake's ship, the *Golden Hind,* June 24, 1579. A eat stone cross in Golden Gate Park, San Fran-co, Calif., commemorates the event.

Book of Common Prayer (in the Mohawk Indian nguage) was *The morning and evening prayer, e litany, church catechism, family prayers, and veral chapters of the Old and New Testament, nslated into the Mahaque Indian language by wrence Claesse, interpreter to William An-ews, Missionary to the Indians from the Honou-ble and Reverend the Society for the opagation of the Gospel in Foreign Parts.* The ok contained 115 pages and was published in 15 by William Bradford in New York City.

The First

Book of folio size, other than laws, was Samuel Willard's *A Compleat Body of Divinity in Two Hundred and Fifty Expository Lectures on the As-sembly's Shorter Catechism wherein the doc-trines of the Christian religion are unfolded, their truth confirm'd . . . etc.,* published in 1726 in Bos-ton, Mass., by [Bartholomew] Green and [Samuel] Kneeland. It was published posthumously, and contained 1,000 pages printed in two columns. There is an error in pagination, as the work was printed by two presses.

Book (of size) completed entirely by one man was *Old Papermaking,* by Dr. Dard Hunter, pub-lished in 1923 by the author at Chillicothe, Ohio. It consisted of 140 pages, size 9 by 11½ inches, printed on handmade paper from linen and cotton cloth. Dr. Hunter not only was the author, but manufactured the paper, designed the book, cut and cast the type, printed the book, etc.

Book on cornstalk paper was *Farm Products in Industry,* by George McCullough Rommel, which was printed in June 1928 by Rae D. Henkle Co. Inc., New York City.

Book on microcards. *See under* Microcard

Book on vellum was George Allen's *The Life of Philidor, Musician and Chess Player,* published in 1863 by E. H. Butler & Co., Philadelphia, Pa. Only two copies of the regular edition were printed on vellum.

Book on the game of bridge by a championship team was *The Four Aces System of Contract Bridge,* 302 pages, published in 1935 by Random House, New York City. It contained an introduc-tion by Harold Stirling Vanderbilt and new inter-national contract bridge laws and scoring chart. The team of Four Aces, formed in August 1933, consisted of Oswald Jacoby, David Burnstine, Howard Schenken, and Michael T. Gottlieb who had won 11 of 13 major championship events.

Book (pamphlet) on vellum was *The First Ply-mouth Patent, Granted June 1, 1621,* a small quar-to, of 16 pages. It was edited by Charles Deane and published in 1854 in Cambridge, Mass. Only four copies were printed. It was bound in full brown levant morocco with a gilt border and fillets enclosing an ornamental inside border on the sides.

Book printed in the Indiana Territory was *Laws for the Government of the District of Louisiana, passed by the Governor and Judges of the Indiana Territory at their first session begun and held at Vincennes on Monday the first day of October 1804.* The book was published by territorial au-thority and printed by E. Stout in 1804 in Vin-cennes, Indiana Territory.

Book printed on American paper with Ameri-can-made plates and bound in America was Char-lotte (Turner) Smith's *Elegiac Sonnets and Other Poems,* printed in October 1795 by Isaiah Thomas,

The First

BOOK—*Continued*

Worcester, Mass. The five oval plates were by Joseph H. Seymour, Jr. The 126-page book was a reprint of an English edition.

Book privately printed was John Eliot's *Communion of Churches; or, The Divine Management of Gospel-Churches by the Ordinance of Councils, Constituted in Order According to the Scriptures,* printed in 1665 by Marmaduke Johnson, Cambridge, Mass. It contained 40 pages. It was not for general sale. *(Charles Evans—American Bibliography)*

Book review telecast. *See* Television—Telecast: Book review to be televised

Book series microfilmed. *See under* Microfilm

Book series of small size paperbacks was The Little Blue Books, 3½ x 5 inches, published in 1919 by (Emanuel) Haldeman-Julius Publications, Girard, Kans. The books, priced at 5 cents each, contained from 32 to 128 pages; most were 64 pages. The first 2 booklets were *The Rubaiyat of Omar Khayyam* and *The Ballad of Reading Gaol* by Oscar Wilde (Oscar Fingal O'Flahertie Wills Wilde). By 1931, 1,666 titles were printed. By 1974, more than 300,000,000 books had been sold. *(Emanuel Haldeman—The First Hundred Million)*

Book set by linotype was *The Tribune Book of Open Air Sports,* edited by Henry Hall and published in 1887 by the Tribune Association, New York City. The foreword states, "This book is printed without type—being the first product in book form of the Mergenthaler machine which wholly supersedes the use of movable type."

Book set by the Photon process. *See* Typesetting machine: Photographic type-composing machine

Book set into type completely by electronic composition was *The Long Short Cut,* a 192-page suspense novel by Andrew Garve, which was published by Harper and Row, Publishers, New York City, in April 1968. The type was composed and pages were produced by means of an electronic beam projected on the face of the high-resolution cathode ray tube at speeds of up to 600 characters per second. The book was produced by Haddon Craftsmen, Inc., of Scranton, Pa., who used an RCA Videocomp and computer system installed in Video Graphic Systems, Inc., of Hauppauge, Long Island, N.Y.

Book showing action photographs in action in sequence was *An Electro-Photographic Investigation of Consecutive Phases of Animal Movements,* by Eadweard Muybridge, begun in 1872, completed in 1885, published in 11 volumes under the auspices of the University of Pennsylvania, Philadelphia, Pa., in 1887. The 781 plates comprising 20,000 figures of men, women, and children; animals and birds; were printed by the Photo-Gravure Company of New York.

The First

Book with color plates was *The City of Phila delphia in the State of Pennsylvania North Amer ca as it appeared in the year 1800 consisting (twenty-eight plates drawn and engraved by W Birch and Son,* published December 31, 1800, ¡ Philadelphia, Pa. It was a large oblong folio coⁿ taining 26 separate views drawn and engrave and 2 preliminaries. It was originally issued in ¹ numbers (2 parts) in wrappers. It sold for $28.C uncolored, $41.50 hand-tinted in unbound board and $44.50 bound. *(Pennsylvania Magazine of Hi, tory and Biography. Vol. 73, No. 3. July 1949)*

Book written in America was *A True Relatic of Such Occurrences and Accidents of Noate ¡ Hath Happened in Virginia Since the First Plan ing of That Collony,* printed for I. Tappe in 1608 ¡ London. The author was Captain John Smith, wʰ used the pseudonym Th. Watson.

Comic books containing colored cartooⁱ which had been published previously in newsp pers were published in 1904 by Cupples & Leo New York City. The books were 10 inches hiₗ and 15 inches long, contained 40 pages, and r tailed for 75 cents. The titles of some of the booⁱ were *Alphonse and Gaston and Their Frier Leon,* by Frederick Burr Opper; *Happy Hooliga* by Frederick Burr Opper; *The Naughty Adve, tures of Vicious Mr. Jack,* by James Swinnertoⁱ *Tigers,* by James Swinnerton; *The Katzenjamm Kids;* and *Lulu and Leander.*

Contract bridge laws book was *Laws of Co tract Bridge 1927,* which was adopted and issuᵉ by the Whist Club [of New York]. It was publishᵉ by John C. Winston Co., New York City, and co tained 57 pages. The rules became effective (September 15, 1927. The game was invented 1925 by Harold Stirling Vanderbilt.

Hymnbook. *See under* Music book

Map made in the United States published in book. *See under* Map

Miniature book was William Secker's *A We ding Ring, Fit for the Finger, or the Salve of Divir ty on the Sore of Humanity. With directions those men that want wives, how to choose theⁱ and to those women that have husbands, how use them.* The book contained 92 pages and w published in 1705 in Boston, Mass., by T. Green ⁱ Nicholas Buttolph. The size was approximately by 3½ inches. It was a reprint of a work publishᵉ in 1658 in London, England.

Novel. *See* Novel

Profane poetry translation prepared in the col nies to be published was George Sandys' transl tion of Ovid's *Metamorphoses,* which w published in 1626 in London, England as *Ovi Metamorphoses Englished, Mytholized a, Represented in Figures.* A second edition w published in 1632 to which was added a transl tion of Virgil's *Aeneid.* Sandys was treasurer

he First

e Virginia Company. *(Richard Hooper—The Po-ical Works of George Sandys)*

Stereotyped book was *The Larger Catechism,* hich bore on the title page "The first book ever ereotyped in America. Stereotyped and printed J. Watts and Co., New York, June 1813." The ocess was introduced by John Watts and was a mbination of the systems of Firmin Didot and arles Mahon, Earl of Stanhope. *(George Adolf bler—A New History of Stereotyping)*

Translated classic published was Marcus Porci- Cato's *Moral Distichs Englished in Couplets,* hich was translated by James Logan, President the Council and Chief Justice of the Province of iladelphia. It was printed and sold in 1735 by njamin Franklin, Philadelphia, Pa. It consisted 24 pages of precepts of morality and moral apo- egms. It sold for one shilling and was an- unced in the *Pennsylvania Gazette* of cember 11 and December 18, 1735, "newly nslated into English verse. Very proper to be t into the Hands of Young Persons. Sold by the inter thereof. Price 1s."

Typewritten book manuscript. *See* Typewritten ok manuscript

Ultramicrofiche book collection of importance. e Microfiche: Ultramicrofiche book collection importance

OK AUCTION was authorized April 18, 1662, the Court of Burgomasters and Schepens of w Amsterdam: "Anna Claas Croezens, widow Daniel Litschoe, deceased, requests by petition be allowed to sell by the Baliff some books ich she has belonging to Sir Henry Moedy, as cording to obligation she has a claim on him for considerable sum." *(Records of New Amster- m from 1653 to 1674. Vol. 4. p. 64)*

OK AUCTION CATALOG
Book auction catalog was announced in the ston *News Letter,* Monday, May 18, 1713, No. 5: "On Thursday next, the 28th current being the y after the election, there will be exposed to le by public vendue or outcry at the house of Mr. nbrose Vincent, silk dyer in Wings Lane, Bos- n, a good collection of books, to be seen at the id house two days before the sale, etc. Cata- ues will be posted at public places." *(Clarence unders Brigham—History of Book Auctions in nerica)*

Book auction printed catalog was *A Catalog of rious and Valuable Books Belonging to the Late verend and Learned Mr. Ebenezer Pemberton, nsisting of Divinity, Philosophy, History, Po- y and Generally Well Bound,* which described books "to be sold by auction at the Brown ffee House in Boston, Mass." on July 2, 1717, at 0 P.M. The catalog was printed by B. Green in 17 and was obtainable gratis at the shop of nuel Gerrish, bookseller. *(George Leslie*

The First

McKay—American Book Auction Catalogues 1713–1934)

BOOK BINDER in America was John Ratliffe, who in 1663 was commissioned to bind Eliot's "Indian Bible" and "take care of the binding of 200 of them strongly and as speedily as may bee with leather, or as may bee most serviceable for the Indians." On August 30, 1664, he sent a letter to the Commissioners of New England stating that he was not well satisfied with the prices paid him for binding, and that 3 shillings 4 pence, or 3 shill- ings 6 pence was the lowest price at which he could bind books.

BOOK CATALOG
Book catalog containing the combined trade lists of American publishers in uniform size was *The American Bookseller's Complete Reference Trade List and Alphabetical Catalogue of Books Published in This Country with the Publishers' and Authors' Names and Prices Arranged in Classes for Quick and Convenient Reference,* which was compiled by Alexander Vietts Blake and published in 1847 by Simeon Ide, Claremont, N.H. It contained 232 pages, including 219 ar- ranged alphabetically by publishers, 3 pages ar- ranged by subjects, and a 6-page appendix by Peter T. Washburn entitled "Laws of the United States Now in Force Relating to Copy-rights With Notes and References to Adjudged Cases."

Book catalog of publishers was *The Uniform Trade List Annual, Embracing the Full Trade Lists of American Publishers, Together with Advertise- ments and Business Cards of Prominent Firms Connected with the Book and Stationery Trades,* published in October 1873 by *Publishers' Weekly,* 37 Park Row, New York City.

College book catalog was *Catalogus Eorum Qui in Collegio Harvardino . . . Alicujus Gradus Lau- rea Donati Sunt* printed in 1697 in Boston, Mass., by Bartholomew Green and John Allen.

Printed library catalog in book forms was com- piled in Latin by Joshua Gee, Harvard College librarian, Cambridge, Mass., and published in 1723 at Boston by B. Green. It was entitled *Catalo- gus Librorum Bibliothecae Collegij Harvardini Quod Est Cantabrigiae in Nova Anglia.* Only 300 copies were printed. It contained 106 pages and listed books according to size: folio, quarto, oc- tavo, duodecimo, etc., then alphabetically through the first letter of the entry word.

State library to publish a master book catalog of a major part of its holdings was the Oregon State Library, Salem, Ore., which published in 1974 a 25-volume master catalog, with two-column pages measuring 8½ by 11 inches, containing the entries from over 3,500 catalog drawers of the Oregon State Library's adult nonfiction holdings (mainly books), 190,000 separate titles in all, in an author, title, and subject catalog.

The First

BOOK CLUB

Book-of-the-Month Club was established in New York City, April 1926, by Harry Scherman, with Robert Haas as president. The original book judges were Dorothy Canfield, Heywood Broun, Henry Seidel Canby, William Allen White, and Christopher Morley. On April 16, 1926, the first book selection, *Lolly Willowes, or the Loving Huntsman*, by Sylvia Townsend Warner, published by Viking Press, was distributed to 4,750 members.

BOOK COLLECTORS' MAGAZINE. *See* Book Trade Magazine

BOOK COURSE was given in a college by Dr. Edwin Osgood Grover, Professor of Books, appointed in the fall of 1926 by President Hamilton Holt of Rollins College, Winter Park, Fla. The first instruction was given September 22, 1926. The idea of a "professorship of books" was suggested by Ralph Waldo Emerson in his essay "Books" *(Atlantic Monthly)*, Vol. 1, No. 3, Jan. 1858) and was advocated by the U.S. Bureau of Education in 1876, but no college accepted the idea until 1926.

BOOK FAIR was held in the Coffee House on Beaver Street, New York City, on June 1, 1802, to display offerings of publishers and booksellers. Hugh Gaines was chairman and Mathew Carey of Philadelphia was secretary. This literary fair was attended by 46 booksellers, and proved so successful that the following year a similar one was held in Philadelphia, Pa., after which the fairs alternated between those cities.

BOOK GUIDE

Book guide was *The American Bookseller's Guide*, published monthly by the American News Company, New York City. The first issue was dated January 7, 1869. It was issued free to every publisher, bookseller, news dealer, music dealer, and stationer in the United States and Canada. The price to librarians and others not engaged in the trade was $1 a year.

BOOK INDEX

Book index was the *American Book Circular*, published in 1843 by Wiley and Putnam, New York City. It contained 64 pages, of which 55 were devoted to a list of 1,172 original works in 2,474 volumes. It classified "some of the most important and recent American publications."

General catalog of books was *The Catalogue of All the Books Printed in the United States, with the prices and places where published. . . .* It was printed January 1804 for the booksellers of Boston, Mass., and contained 80 pages. It sold for 10 cents. The books were classified according to subjects: law, physic, divinity, Bibles, and miscellanies, schoolbooks, and singing books.

Government Publications Index. *See* Index of government publications

The First

Monthly cumulative index of books was th Cumulative Book Index, published February 189 by Morris & Wilson, Minneapolis, Minn. It liste 9 pages of books published during January 189 The cumulative feature was begun a few month later, when all the books listed in previous issue were cumulated in one alphabet.

BOOK JACKET

Book Jacket was designed by John Keep for *Th Keepsake; a Gift for the Holidays* published i 1833 in New York City. It was variously called book cover jacket, a book jacket, a dust cover, dust jacket, or a wrapper.

BOOK LIST. *See* Book index: Monthly cumulativ index of books

BOOK MATCHES. *See under* Match

BOOK PLATE by an American engraver of whic there is any record was made by Nathaniel Hu of Boston, Mass., in 1740 for Thomas Dering. *(D vid McNeely Stauffer—American Engravers up Copper and Steel)*

BOOK PUBLISHER of denominational boo was the Methodist Book Concern, organized at conference in the John Street Methodist Episcop Church, New York City, May 1789. The Reverer John Dickins advanced the capital, $600, from h private savings and started publishing in Phil delphia, Pa. The first book issued was *The Chr tian's Pattern*, Wesley's version of Thomas Kempis's *Imitation of Christ*. *(Henry C. Jennings-The Methodist Book Concern, a Romance of H tory)*

BOOK REVIEW

Book review editor was Sarah Margaret Full (later the Marchioness Ossoli), who was hired December 1844 by Horace Greeley for his Ne York *Tribune*. In addition to her salary, the co tract provided that she be given a home wi Greeley's family and allowed her the privilege writing when she desired. She wrote under t name of Margaret Fuller and served until Augu 1846, when she made a trip to Europe. *(Sarah Ma garet Fuller Ossoli—Memoirs of Margaret Full Ossoli)*

Book review newspaper supplement was t Book Review Supplement of the New York *Time* issued Saturday, October 10, 1896. It contained pages of 4 columns each, the last page devoted a full-page advertisement of the Sunday magazi supplement. The first editor was Francis Whiti Halsey. On January 29, 1911, it was issued on Su day as a 16-page supplement.

BOOK TRADE MAGAZINE

Book collectors' magazine was *The Philob lion, a Monthly Biographical and Literary Journ Containing Critical Notices of and Extracts fr Rare, Curious and Valuable Old Books*, publish on India paper by J. W. Bouton, New York Ci

e First

e first issue was dated December 1861. George ilip Philes was the editor.

Book trade magazine was the *Bookseller's Advertiser & Monthly Chronicle of Literary Enterprises*, also known as the *Bookseller's Advertiser Monthly Register of New Publications*, which peared January 1, 1834 (published by West & ow, New York City), and contained 8 printed arto pages. Subscription was $1 yearly. It listed 5 "Original American Works published in 1833" d American reprints of foreign works.

Successful book trade magazine was the nerican *Publishers' Circular and Literary Gatte,* a weekly for booksellers and libraries, issed September 1, 1855, by the New York Book blishers' Association, of which William Henry pleton was president; Alfred Smith Barnes, e president; and George Palmer Putnam, secre-y. It was absorbed by *Publishers Weekly.*

OOK WAGON. *See under* Library

OOKKEEPER. *See* Accountant

OOKS OF POSTAGE STAMPS. *See under* Post-e stamp

OOKSELLER of importance in the colonies was zekiah Usher, who started in business in Cam-idge, Mass., in 1639. He later had a monopoly on inting the laws of the General Court of Massa-usetts and superintended the publications of e London Society for the Propagation of the spel Among the Indians. *(Isaiah Thomas—His--y of Printing)*

OOKSELLERS' ASSOCIATION was the Ameri-n Company of Booksellers, organized June 7, 01, in New York City "to improve quality, to oid interference, to discontinue importations, to vor a literary fair, to recommend correspon-nce and to promote the general interest." The st president was Mathew Carey of Phila-lphia, Pa. *(Adolph Growall—Book Trade Bibli-raphy in the United States in the Nineteenth ntury)*

OOKSELLER'S CATALOG of first American itions of American authors was the *Catalogue First Editions of American Authors, Poets, ilosophers, Historians, Statesmen, Essayists, amatists, Novelists, Travellers, Humorists, etc.,* blished in 1885 by Leon and Brother, booksell-s, of New York City. It consisted of 58 pages and ted the various American authors in alphabeti-l order and the current prices for first editions their works. In addition to the regularly issued talog, there were also interleaved copies on ndmade paper.

OOKSTORE (antiquarian) was established July 1830, in Boston, Mass., by Samuel Gardner ake, who specialized in writing about Ameri-n Indians. *(Potter's American Monthly. October 75)*

The First

BOOSTER, LOCOMOTIVE. *See* Locomotive booster

BORAX was discovered by Dr. John A. Veatch, January 8, 1856, in mineral water from Tuscan Springs, Tehama County, Calif. Commercial production began at Borax Lake, Lake County, Calif., in 1864, when pure crystals were refined by immersion in solution and permitted to crystallize out again, thus disposing of an apparently very minute amount of impurities. This deposit supplied the United States until 1868, when larger deposits were found in Nevada. *(John Randolph Spears—Illustrated Sketches of Death Valley and Other Borax Deserts of the Pacific Coast)*

BORDER PATROL

Border patrol organization under the Immigration and Naturalization Service was established June 1, 1924, under authority of an act of May 28, 1924 (43 Stat. L. 240). It originally consisted of 427 men. William Walter Husband was commissioner general of Immigration, but there was no officer directly in charge of all the border patrol units, as they operated under the supervision of the various district heads.

Border patrol officer was Jefferson Davis Milton, United States Immigration and Naturalization Service, who served from April 13, 1904, to June 30, 1932. He was appointed under authority of annual appropriation acts before the border patrol was formally established by act of Congress on May 28, 1924, and patrolled the border to prevent the smuggling of Orientals across the Mexican border.

BOREALIS. *See* Aurora borealis

BORON CARBIDE. *See* Abrasive

BOTANIC GARDEN was planned and made by John Bartram, who laid out about five or six acres with his own hands in 1728. The garden is located at 43d and Eastwick streets, Philadelphia, Pa., on the banks of the Schuylkill River. Bartram at one time acted as botanist to George III. He corresponded with Linnaeus, who considered him the "greatest natural botanist in the world." *(William Jay Youmans—Pioneers of Science in America)*

BOTANIC SCIENTIFIC EXPEDITION to study and classify botanical species was made in the New England area by Manasseh Cutler, who set out from Ipswich, Mass., on July 19, 1784, for Mount Washington, N.H. He examined 350 species and classified them according to the Linnaean method. *(William Parker Cutler and Julia Perkins Cutler—Life, Journals and Correspondence of Rev. Manasseh Cutler)*

BOTANIST

Botanist to become a prominent landscape gardener was Andrew Jackson Downing of Newburgh, N.Y. In 1841 he wrote *A Treatise on the Theory and Practice of Landscape Gardening Adapted to North America,* the first serious dis-

The First

BOTANIST—*Continued*

cussion on the subject. *(Knickerbocker Magazine. October 1852)*

Woman botanist to distinguish herself in America was Jane Colden, daughter of Cadwallader Colden. She manifested her interest in botany in 1728, at the age of 4; and by the age of 34, in 1758, had described 400 plants according to the Linnaean method, using English terms. *(William Darlington—Memorials of John Bartram and Humphry Marshall)*

BOTANY BOOK

Botany book (elementary work) was *The Elements of Botany, or Outlines of the Natural History of Vegetables,* by Benjamin Smith Barton. It was illustrated with 30 plates. It was originally printed in Philadelphia, Pa., in 1803 and was reprinted in 1804 in London, England. Barton was appointed Professor of Natural History and Botany in the College of Philadelphia in 1789.

Botany book strictly American and the first treatise on American plants written by a native American and printed in this country was *Arbustrum Americanum; the American Grove, or an alphabetical catalogue of forest trees and shrubs, natives of the American United States . . . also some hints of their uses in medicines, dyes and domestic economy,* 174 pages, by Humphry Marshall of Chester County, Pa., published in 1785 by Joseph Crukshank, Philadelphia, Pa. *(William Darlington—Memorials of John Bartram and Humphry Marshall)*

BOTANY PROFESSOR was Adam Kuhn, who was appointed in January 1768 by the Philadelphia College, Philadelphia, Pa. He occupied his post for 21 years. His schooling was obtained in Sweden under Linnaeus. *(Eclectic Repertory. April 1818)*

BOTTLE

Bottle blown in America was made in a factory set up in the woods one mile from Jamestown, Va., in 1608, 12 years before the landing of the Pilgrims. The common glass bottle bears the distinction of being the first manufactured product exported from this country. This factory, the first glass factory in America, was destroyed in 1622 by the Indians who massacred the inhabitants of Jamestown. *(Fifty Years of Achievement—Illinois Glass Co.)*

Milk bottles were made by Louis Porter Whiteman, owner of the Warren Glass Works, Cumberland, Md., who manufactured the Warren Glass Works Glass Air Tight Milk Jars in 1879. They were used by the Echo Farms Dairy Company, New York City. To commemorate the event, the Pennsylvania State Agricultural Society presented a plaque to Whiteman.

The First

Screw-cap bottle with a pour lip was patente May 5, 1936, by Edward A. Ravenscroft, Glenco Ill., who received patent No. 2,039,345. The bottle were manufactured by the Abbott Laboratorie North Chicago, Ill.

BOTTLE CAP with the crown cork was invente in 1892, by William Painter, founder of the Crow Cork and Seal Co., Baltimore, Md., who obtaine U.S. Patent No. 468,226 on February 2, 1892. Th crown cork is a simple bit of tin with a corrugate rim or skirt into which is inserted a disc of natur or composition cork.

BOTTLER OF MINERAL WATER was Elie M gloire Durand, who also invented a machine f bottling it under pressure. Durand opened a dru store in 1825 at the corner of Sixth and Chestn Streets, Philadelphia, Pa., *(Thomas Meehan—Pr ceedings of the Academy of Natural Sciences Philadelphia, 1873)*

BOUNTY was granted under authority of Act 5 the General Assembly held at James City, V October 5, 1646. It was signed by Sir Willia Berkeley, Knight Governor, and provided th "what person soever shall after publication h reof kill a wolfe and bring in the head to a commissioner, upon certificate of said commu cation to the county court, he or they shall recei one hundred pounds of tobacco for so doing to raised out of the County where the wolfe killed." *(William Waller Hening—Virginia St utes at Large)*

BOWIE KNIFE, which is shorter than the regu sword, was invented by Colonel James Bowie Texas about 1835. It is variously claimed that made the first knife out of a file; that the weap was originally used by the Mexicans; and that an encounter with Mexicans his original swo broke to within 20 inches of the hilt, leaving t balance of the sword, which was the first Bov knife, easier to handle. The knife had but one ed and a curved point, which necessitated its bei carried in a sheath. *(Evelyn Brogan—James l wie; a Hero of the Alamo)*

BOWLER

Bowler to earn $100,000 in 1 year in tour ments was Earl Anthony of Tacoma, Wash., w won $8,000 at the Buzz Fazio Open at Ba Creek, Mich., on October 27, 1975, his seve victory of the Professional Bowlers Associati bringing his earnings to $100,890.

Bowler to make a perfect score of 300 in American Bowling Congress tournament w William Knox of Philadelphia, Pa., who rolle perfect game on March 10, 1913, in Toledo, O in the 13th international bowling tournament was the 14th perfect game recognized with a g medal.

e First

Bowler to roll two perfect games in a sanc-
ned league competition was Frank Caruana of
ffalo, N.Y., who rolled two perfect games in
ccession on March 5, 1924, in Buffalo, N.Y. He
d five strikes on a third game, rolling 29 strikes
 succession. His score for 4 games was 1,115
0, 300, 268, 247).

Bowler to win $10,000 in a tournament was
rry Smith (of St. Louis Falstaff team), who won
 19th annual All-Star match-game bowling
ampionship for men on January 15, 1960, at the
ic Auditorium, Omaha, Neb. He scored 13,399
s in 64 games plus 212 for various winnings.

Woman bowler to obtain a perfect score in a
ictioned competition under conditions of the
man's International Bowling Congress was
ma Fahning (Mrs. Charles Fahning) of the Ger-
in Cleaning Team, who bowled a perfect game
 March 4, 1930, in Buffalo, N.Y.

WLING

Bowling automatic scorer was the Brunswick
tomatic Scorer installed in September 1967 at
lage Lanes, a 16-lane bowling center in Chica-
It automatically records pinfall, ball by ball,
me by frame; computes and totals individual
d team scores; and, in a fraction of a second,
its scores on a permanent scorecard and proj-
s them onto an easy-to-view overhead screen.
onsole serves 4 lanes. It was first used in sanc-
ied league games on October 10, 1967.

Duckpins were introduced in the spring of 1900
he Diamond Bowling Alleys, Howard Street,
timore, Md., owned by Wilbert Robinson and
n Joseph McGraw at Schuetzen Park,
on Hill, N.J., on July 18, 1900, was won by
timore with 412 pins; the Stuyvesants of Brook-
were second with 373 pins.

WLING MAGAZINE was *Gut Holz* issued Au-
t 9, 1893, in New York City. It was originally
ated in German. On May 19, 1894, it became the
vlers' Journal.

WLING RULE STANDARDIZATION was un-
taken November 13, 1875, when 27 delegates
 at Germania Hall, New York City, and orga-
ed a National Bowling Association. The asso-
ion soon went out of existence, however, as
the American Amateur Bowling Union, which
 organized in 1890. The first important bowl-
convention to standardize rules was held by
American Bowling Congress, when it orga-
d September 9, 1895, in New York City.
*ierican Bowling Congress 1895–1945—Just
 Years)*

WLING TOURNAMENT

owling convention of importance was the
erican Bowling Congress held in New York
 September 9, 1895.

The First

Bowling match recorded is that of January 1,
1840, played at the Knickerbocker Alleys, New
York City.

**Bowling match in which white balls were used
on black lanes** was held Saturday May 23, 1959,
at the Neptune Lanes, Brooklyn, N.Y. The lanes
were coated with a formula of Brunswick-Balke
Collender Co. The match was televised on the
Major League Bowling Show.

Bowling tournament for women under the auspices of the Women's International Bowling Congress (organized November 29, 1916; incorporated
October 20, 1919) was held March 17, 1917, in St.
Louis, Mo. Eight five-woman teams, 16 two-wom-
an teams and 24 individuals participated. The individual high score was won by Mrs. M. Koester,
with an average of 162.

**Bowling tournament sponsored by the Ameri-
can Bowling Congress** convened in Chicago, Ill.,
January 8–11, 1901. Forty-one five-man teams, 79
two-man teams and 115 individuals participated
in the contest. The prize money was $2,500. The
individual winner was Frank ("Pop") Breill (or
Brill) of Chicago, Ill., with a score of 648. A two-
man team, J. Voorhies and C. K. Starr, of the Metropolitan Bowling Club of New York, rolled 1,203
points and won $80. The Standard Bowling Club
of Chicago rolled 2,720 points, defeating the Cres-
cents of Chicago, who had 2,692 points, and winning $200.

Gold medal award to a perfect-score bowler by
the American Bowling Congress was made in
1909. Three perfect scores were entered: Al Roth-
well of St. Louis on February 26, 1908, whose
claim was rejected as his league was not sanctioned; Homer Sanders of St. Louis on April 4,
1908; and A. C. Jellison on December 15, 1908. A
roll-off for the medal was held March 11, 1909, in
Pittsburgh, Pa., and was won by Jellison, who received a gold medal, while Sanders received a
silver medal. The awards were not for perfect
scores, but for high scores.

BOX SPRING. *See under* Bedspring

BOXING. *See* Prizefight

BOY SCOUTS OF AMERICA

Boy scout to become an eagle scout was Arthur
Rose Eldred of the Oceanside, L.I., N.Y., troop,
who received this distinction on August 21, 1912.
Others may have qualified at about the same time,
but his name is the first recorded.

Boy Scout uniformed troop was Troop No. 1,
organized at the Central YMCA, Troy, N.Y., in the
fall of 1911. The uniform was designed by Charles
M. Connally of Troy and has since become standard equipment. *(Rutherford Hayner—History of
Troy and Rensselaer County)*

The First

BOY SCOUTS OF AMERICA—*Continued*

Boy Scouts of America, an organization for boys from nine years upward, was incorporated in the District of Columbia, on February 8, 1910, and was granted a federal charter by an act of Congress of June 15, 1916. The motto of the organization is Be Prepared.

BOYCOTT LAW was passed September 26, 1903, by Alabama (Act No. 329), "to prohibit boycotting, unfair lists, picketting, or other interference with the lawful business or occupation of others, and to provide a penalty therefor." The law declared it a misdemeanor for two or more persons to conspire to prevent persons from carrying on a lawful business, to print or circulate stickers, cards, etc., and to use threats. The fine was not less than $50 nor more than $500, or imprisonment of not more than 60 days at hard labor. *(General Laws and Joint Resolutions of the Legislature of Alabama. Act No. 329, p. 281)*

BOYS' CAMP. *See* Camp for boys' outdoor recreation

BRAILLE

Braille Bible. *See* Bible: Bible for the blind in embossed form

Braille magazine. *See* Periodical: Magazine for the blind

Braille music magazine. *See* Music periodical: Music magazine published in Braille

Braille schools. *See* Blind: School for the blind

BRAKE. *See* Air brake; Automobile brake

BRAKE PATENT

Brake patent was granted August 29, 1828, to Robert Turner of Ward (now Auburn), Mass., on a "self-regulating wagon brake."

Railroad brake patent was issued September 19, 1838, to Ephraim Morris of Bloomfield, N.J., on "eccentric brakes for cars."

BRANDING

Branding punishment by a federal court was imposed by the U.S. Court at Pensacola, Fla., in 1844. Jonathan Walker, a ship captain, was convicted of stealing 7 slaves and carrying them in a schooner about 30 feet long. He started June 23, 1844, for Nassau, was captured by the U.S. steamer *General Taylor* and taken to Pensacola, Fla., on July 20, 1844, where he was imprisoned, tried in the District Court, and placed in the pillory on the public highway to be pelted with rotten eggs. He was sentenced to 1 year in jail for each of the 7 slaves, fined $600 for each slave and all the costs of the trial. The initials SS (slave stealer) were branded on the palm of his right hand. *(Frank Edward Kittredge—The Man With the Branded Hand)*

The First

BRANDING LEGISLATION was enacted February 5, 1644, by Connecticut. It provided that cattle and swine (but not horses) older than s months be earmarked or branded before May 1644, and that the marks be registered. The pen ty for violation was five shillings a head, two which were paid to informers.

BRASS was rolled in 1802 by Abel Porter & Co pany of Waterbury, Conn. The factory was own by Abel Porter and Levi Porter, who were also t first to make brass by the direct fusion of cop and zinc. *(Joseph Anderson—Town and City Waterbury, Vol. II)*

BRASS AND COPPER SEAMLESS TUBES we manufactured in 1851 by the American Tu Works at Somerville, Mass. The process was troduced by Joseph Fox. Previously strips rounded metal with brazed edges had been use *(Brass Pipe—80th Anniversary—American Tu Works)*

BRASS AND IRON FOUNDRY in America w opened at Lynn, Mass., in 1645, by Joseph Jen (or Jenks), who manufactured the first kitch utensils, tools, and machines in the New Wor

BRASS CLOCK WORKS. *See under* Clock

BRASS KETTLES were made in 1834 in Wolco ville, now Torrington, Conn., by Israel Coe, w organized the Coe Brass Company. They used so-called battery process.

BRASS ROD was drawn in 1873 by the Coe Br Company of Torrington, Conn.

BRASS SPINNING was invented by Hir Washington Hayden of Waterbury, Conn., v obtained patent No. 8589 on December 16, 1 on machinery for making kettles and articles like character from discs of metal. A disc v mounted in a chuck that was rotated at a unif speed. A tool was then pressed against the me which was thus shaped to the die. The proc was first attempted at Wolcottville (now Torri ton), Conn., and was later sold to the Waterb Brass Company. *(William Gilbert Lathrop— Brass Industry in the United States.)*

BRASS WIRE. *See* Wire

BRASS WIRE DRAWING AND TUBE-MAK MACHINERY was imported in 1831 from Engl by Israel Holmes for his firm, Holmes and Ho kiss, established in 1830 in Waterbury, Conn

BRAWL IN CONGRESS. *See* Congress (U.S House of Representatives: Brawl

BREACH OF PROMISE SUIT was instituted 14, 1623, in the Virginia Council of State, Cha City County, Va. The Reverend Greville Po brought suit against Cicely (Sysley) Jordan, widow of Captain Samuel Jordan, who had ji him in favor of William Ferrar (or Farrar). penalty for a third offense was either corp

he First

nishment, or fine, or otherwise. *(Alexander own—The First Republic in America)*

READ

Bread made from unbolted flour, which later ecame known as graham bread, was invented nd introduced by Sylvester Graham in 1847. Bak-s disliked the product and started riots, threat-ing Graham's life if he persisted in its anufacture. *(Franklin Bowditch Dexter—Bio-aphical Sketches of the Graduates of Yale Col-ge)*

Completely automatic bread plant was in-alled and opened July 1, 1910, by the Ward Bak-g Company, Chicago, Ill. The dough was not uched nor the bread handled except when it as placed on the wrapping machine.

Frozen bread was offered to stores November 3, 52, by Arnold Bakers, Inc., Port Chester, N.Y.

REAKFAST FOOD

Breakfast foods (ready to eat) were introduced incipally by Charles William Post, who pro-ced Grape Nuts in 1897. He manufactured Post asties in 1915, and Post's Bran in 1922. *(Prod-ts of General Foods. General Foods Corpora-n.)*

Shredded wheat biscuits were made by Henry Perky, and William H. Ford of Watertown, Y., who obtained patent No. 502,278 on August 1893, on a machine for making the shreds or aments of wheat. The Cereal Machine Compa-, Denver, Colo., was formed in 1893 to manufac-re them.

REECH-LOADING CANNON. *See* Ordnance: nnon (breech-loading)

REEDING SOCIETY, ANIMAL. *See* Animal eeding society

REVET. *See under* Army

REWERY to remain in business for 200 years s that of the Francis Perot's Sons Malting Com-ny of Philadelphia. The original concern was tablished in 1687 by Anthony Morris, 2d, in iladelphia, Pa., on the east side of Front Street, ow Walnut, facing the Delaware River, and s incorporated in 1887. The concern descended m father to son for eight generations. *(Histori-' Sketch of the Oldest Business House in Ameri-)*

ICK

3rick building. *See under* Building

3rick insulating was supplied to the trade by Armstrong Cork Company of Lancaster, Pa., in e 1913 under the trade name Nonpareil Insulat-Brick. This brick was used in high temperature uipment such as industrial furnaces, ovens, oil ls, blast furnaces, stoves, and similar ap-atus. Diatomaceous earth was pulverized, xed with finely ground cork, and a small quanti-

The First

ty of clay added for a binder. It was molded into brick form and then fired. The cork was con-sumed, leaving the finished brick terra-cotta in color and extremely cellular in structure. Because of the many small voids left when the particles of cork were burned out, and because of a large amount of noncirculating air, the ability of the brick to hold heat was exceptionally high.

Brick pavement. *See under* Road

Brick roofing tile. *See under* Tile

Fire brick was made by the Salamander Works of Woodbridge, N.J., in 1825. Although definite records are not obtainable, it is believed an at-tempt was made to manufacture fire bricks in 1812. *(Heinrich Ries and Henry Leighton—History of the Clay Working Industry in the United States.)*

Fire brick to withstand high heat was manufac-tured in 1841 by the Mount Savage Fire Brick Works of Mount Savage, Md., now the Union Min-ing Company of Allegany County, Md.

Lightweight brick was developed in 1927 by Charles Frederick Burgess of the C. F. Burgess Laboratories, Inc., Madison, Wis. It was porous, one fifth the weight of ordinary brick, and yet resistant to the entrance of water. It floated in water and had adequate compressive strength for use in all types of buildings for load-bearing walls.

Terra-cotta was manufactured by James Ren-wick in 1853 in New York City. He conceived the idea of introducing terra-cotta as a building mate-rial and substitute for cut stone work. *(Walter Geer—Story of Terra Cotta)*

Terra-cotta factory to be successful was estab-lished by J. N. Glover in Louisville, Ky., in 1867. After a series of successive changes of locale and management it gradually developed into the Northwestern Terra Cotta Co., Chicago, Ill.

BRICK KILN in America was established in Salem, Mass., in 1629.

BRICK MACHINE for the production of soft mud bricks was designed and built by Henry Martin in 1857 and installed in Hartford, Conn. The clay was pushed from the press box through a die or jack mold into sanded wooden molds by a process similar to the method of pressing the clay by hand into wood or steel molds.

BRIDGE

Aerial ferry was put in operation April 9, 1905, over the ship canal from Lake Avenue, Duluth, to Minnesota Point, Minn. The car was suspended in the air from a superstructure which had a clear height over Lake Superior of 135 feet. The truss in the center was 51 feet, making a total height at the highest part of the superstructure of 186 feet above water level. The width, center to center of trusses, was 34 feet, and the clear span was 393.75

BRIDGE—*Continued*

feet in length. The car platform was 34 by 50 feet, with room enough to accommodate six automobiles and two glassed-in cabins, each 7 by 30 feet, for passengers, and with a carrying capacity of 125,000 pounds. The platform was 12 feet above the water line. The round trip could be made in ten minutes. *(Henry Grattan Tyrrell—Transporter Bridges)*

Bridge was erected in 1634 over the Neponset River from Milton to Dorchester, Mass., by Israel Stoughton. Authority to build a bridge and mill was extended April 1, 1634, by the Massachusetts General Court. *(Albert Kendall Teele—History of Milton)*

Bridge named for a woman was the Betsy Ross Bridge, which spans 3 miles across the Delaware River, connecting Philadelphia and Pennsauken, N.J. It was officially opened on April 30, 1976. The construction cost about $105 million.

Bridge of flowers was instituted at the suggestion of Mrs. Walter Burnham in 1929, when a 400-foot five-arch concrete-span bridge over the Deerfield River between Shelburne and Buckland, Mass., was abandoned with the passing of the trolley line. The bridge at Shelburne Falls, Mass., was converted into a walk, both sides being lined with innumerable species of flowering plants and shrubs.

Bridge of importance was the West Boston Bridge, connecting Boston and Cambridge, Mass., begun July 15, 1792. It rested on 180 piers, was 3,483 feet long with a 3,344-foot causeway, and cost $76,000. Woodwork was undertaken April 8, 1793, and the bridge was opened for traffic on November 23, 1793. The distance from the end of the causeway to the first church in Cambridge was 7,810 feet. It was 40 feet wide with a railing on each side. The toll right was granted to the proprietors for 70 years.

Bridge to a foreign country. *See* Bridge: Railroad suspension bridge

Bridge with open-mesh steel flooring was the University Bridge, Seattle, Wash., opened for traffic April 7, 1933. The flooring, 80 percent open, self-cleaning and self-draining, was originated by Walter Edward Irving of the Irving Subway Grating Company, Inc., Long Island City, N.Y., who obtained patent No. 1,991,154 on February 12, 1935.

Bridge with piers sunk in the open sea was the Golden Gate suspension span, San Francisco, Calif. Actual construction was officially started January 5, 1933. Joseph Baermann Strauss was appointed chief engineer. The length of the main structure of the bridge was 8,940 feet, with towers 746 feet above water and a minimum clearance of 220 feet. The Golden Gate bridge was the first

built across the outer mouth of a major ocea? harbor.

Cantilever bridge was designed by Charle? Shaler Smith for the Cincinnati Southern Railroa? to cross the Kentucky River. It was built in 187? 1877, near Harrodsburg (Mercer County), Ky. ? contract for an iron-truss bridge was let to th? Baltimore Bridge Company on July 9, 1875, f? $377,500. Construction started October 12, 187? and was completed February 20, 1877. The brid? was tested April 20, 1877. It had three spans, eac? 375 feet long.

Cast-iron bridge was built in 1835 over Dunlap? Creek at Brownsville, Pa., by John Snowdon fro? the design of and under the direction of his for? man, John Herbertson. It had five tubular arch ri? of 85-foot span and was 25 feet wide. *(Engineerin? Record. June 6, 1908)*

Cast-iron girder bridge was built by Earl Trum? bull over the Erie Canal in 1840 at Frankfort, N.? It had a span of 77 feet. *(Wrought Iron Record. V? 1, No. 3. Wrought Iron Research Association)*

Concrete arch highway bridge was designed ? Carl A. Trik, Superintendent of Bridges, Bureau ? Highways, Philadelphia, Pa., and erected in 18? to carry Pine Road over Pennypack Creek, Phil? delphia. It consisted of two arched spans, each ? feet 4¾ inches wide, with a rise of 6 feet 6 inche? supported by concrete abutments and a concre? pier, built on a light skew. It was 34 feet wide a? carried a 26-foot-wide macadam roadway wi? two granite-paved gutters on concrete found? tions. The entire bridge, including the appurt? nances and the thorough renovation of t? retaining walls on both approaches, cost $9,288.? *(Report of 1893—Philadelphia Superintendent ? Bridges)*

Concrete cantilever bridge was erected over ? dian Creek at Marion, Iowa, in 1905 for the Mari? Street Railway Company. It had three 50-fo? spans with two longitudinal ribs 12 inches wi? supported on concrete columns and floor slabs ? transverse beams.

Double-deck bridge of importance was t? Queensboro Bridge, over the East River, N? York City, which was opened to traffic on Mar? 30, 1909. The Manhattan Suspension Bridge, al? a double-deck bridge over the East River, w? opened to traffic on December 31, 1909. The to? cost of the land and construction of the Quee? boro Bridge was approximately $17 million and ? the Manhattan Suspension Bridge about $31 m? lion. *(Records in the Department of Plants a? Structures, New York City)*

Hanging railroad bridge was built in 1879 a? location several miles east of Canon City, Co? where the Royal Gorge of the Arkansas Rive? only thirty feet wide and entirely filled by ? river. Sheer rock cliffs rise for more than 1,000 f?

he First

each side. The bridge was built above and
arallel to the river, one side imbedded in the rock
iff and the other suspended over the stream by
eans of overhead V-type beams. It was designed
/ Charles Shaler Smith.

Iron-truss bridge with parallel chords and open
eb was designed by Richard Osborne, chief en-
neer of the Reading Company. Construction of
usses began January 1845 at Pottstown, Pa., and
as completed in March. The bridge had a 34.2-
ot span, with a 4-foot space between tracks, and
as erected a half mile east of Flat Rock Tunnel,
rth of West Manayunk station. Erection was
gun Saturday night, May 3, 1845, and the bridge
as finished Sunday, May 4, 1845. It remained
til 1901 on the main line of the Philadelphia and
ading Railroad Company, now the Reading
mpany. *(Henry Gratton Tyrrell—History of
idge Engineering)*

Iron-wire suspension bridge was the Schuylkill
ver bridge at Philadelphia, Pa., designed and
nstructed by Erskine Hazard and Captain Jo-
ah White. It was 408 feet long, with a board floor
inches wide. It had a 33-foot sag and could not
pport more than six or eight persons at a time.
weighed 4,702 pounds, cost $125, and was
ened to traffic June 1816. A toll of a cent a per-
n was charged until the tolls defrayed the cost.
ngineering News. March 16, 1905)

Pile bridge was designed and constructed by
ajor Samuel Sewall and built across the York
ver at York, Me., in 1761. Thirteen bands of piles
re hammered upright, the ends protruding
ove the water, upon which a 270-foot wooden
idge was erected. *(George Alex Emery—An-
nt City of Gorgeana)*

Pontoon bridge was floated into place at Col-
s' Pond, Lynn, Mass., in 1804. The Board of Di-
ctors authorized Captain Moses Brown to
dge the pond, which was of great depth. The
nd had a soft, peaty bottom that did not permit
e use of any feasible means of constructing
dge piers. The pontoon bridge was 511 feet in
gth and 28 feet wide. It consisted of five layers
pine timber, each at right angles to the one
low it. The lowest course of logs hewn on
e side and the next three courses were about a
t square. The whole mass was secured togeth-
by 3-inch dowels. Including the top planking, it
s about 5 feet thick. *(Charles Jeptha Hill Wood-
ry—The Floating Bridge at Lynn. Historical
llection of the Essex Institute. Vol. 36)*

Pontoon bridge of reinforced concrete was the
ke Washington Floating Bridge, Seattle, Wash.,
gun December 29, 1938, and dedicated July 2,
0. It was composed of 25 pontoons bolted
ether, each having two or more 65-ton anchors.
total length was 34,021 feet. It was financed by
PWA grant of $3,794,000 and a bond issue of
500,000 to be repaid by toll charges.

The First

Railroad all-steel bridge was the Glasgow
Bridge, a 2,700-foot structure built by the Chicago
and Alton Railroad Company over the Missouri
River at Glasgow, Mo. The contract for steel was
dated October 12, 1878, and the bridge was placed
in service about November 1, 1879. *(Archibald
Black—The Story of Bridges)*

Railroad bridge across the Mississippi River
was the Rock Island Railroad Bridge, between
Rock Island, Ill., and Davenport, Iowa, built of
wood resting on stone piers. The piers were completed June 1854. The bridge was fully completed
and a locomotive sent across it on April 21, 1856.
On April 22, 1856, a train consisting of three
locomotives and eight passenger cars crossed as
a test.

Railroad suspension bridge was the Niagara
Falls Suspension bridge over the gorge at Niagara,
which was completed in 1854. It had a span of 825
feet and two decks, the lower one carrying a highway 15 feet wide, partially enclosed at the side by
timber stiffening trusses. The upper deck, 24 feet
wide and 245 feet above high water, had a single
railroad track in the center and was floored over
to separate it from the highway below. The bridge
was started in 1853 by Charles Ellet, who withdrew from the work. It was completed by John
Augustus Roebling. The first train crossed the
bridge March 8, 1855. *(John Augustus Roebling—
Memoir of the Niagara Falls and International
Suspension Bridge)*

Rolling lift bridge was the Van Buren Street
bridge, located over the Chicago River, Chicago,
Ill., which was opened to traffic February 4, 1895.
It consisted of two arms meeting at the center of
the river, which when open provided a clear channel 82 feet in width, measured along the line of the
stream. Each arm consisted of three trusses that
carried two roadways, each 18 feet wide, and two
sidewalks, each 8 feet wide. The bridge was operated by two 50 h.p. electric motors on each side of
the river. The total construction cost was $169,-
700. The bridge's construction was patented by
William Scherzer of Chicago, Ill.

Steel arch bridge was the Eads Bridge built
across the Mississippi River by James Buchanan
Eads. It was built from St. Louis, Mo., to East St.
Louis, Ill., at a cost of $6,536,729.29. Construction
started in 1869. The center span was 520 feet, the
two side spans 502 feet each. On May 24, 1874,
over 15,000 people paid a toll to walk across; on
June 3, 1874, the upper roadway was ready for
vehicles; and on July 4, 1874, President Ulysses
Simpson Grant made the formal dedication
speech. It was the first bridge in the building of
which pneumatic caissons were used. *(Henry
Grattan Tyrrell—History of Bridge Engineering)*

Stone arch railroad bridge in the world was the
Carrollton Viaduct of the Baltimore and Ohio
Railroad, spanning Gwynn's Falls at Baltimore,

BRIDGE—*Continued*

Md. It was named after Charles Carroll, who laid the last stone in the bridge several weeks prior to its official opening and inspection by the president and board of directors on December 21, 1829. It was 300 feet long and 70 feet high and had two arches: a large 80-foot span over the stream and a small arch through which, originally, a wagon road passed. The bridge was built by James Lloyd. *(Joseph Gurn—Carroll of Carrollton)*

Stone bridge (arch) in America was built in 1697–1698 at Pennepecka, near Germantown, Pa.—the Frankford Avenue bridge over Pennypack Creek, Philadelphia, Pa. William Penn wrote from Pennsburg on June 22, 1700, to "urge the justices about the bridge at Pennepecka and Poquessin forthwith for a carriage or I cannot come down" to attend a local meeting. *(Site and Relic of Germantown—Reports)*

Suspension bridge was erected in 1796 by James Finley across Jacob's Creek, Westmoreland County, Pa. It had a 70-foot span and cost $6,000. He patented his design in 1801. The bridge was on the turnpike between Uniontown, Pa., and Greensburg, Pa.

Suspension bridge of importance having steel towers instead of the customary masonry towers was the Williamsburg Bridge, connecting Brooklyn and Manhattan, New York City, which was opened on December 19, 1903. The cost was $24,100,000 for land and construction. *(Records in Department of Plants and Structures, New York City)*

Timber trestle pier of lattice construction was started in June 1840 at the Long Hollow Crossing, Shuman's Station, Pa., and was originally on the Little Schuylkill and Susquehanna Railroad, later the Catawissa Branch of the Reading Company. The pier was designed by James F. Smith and was 740 feet long and 122 feet high. The timber piers were later replaced with stone masonry; then the trusses with wooden trestles; then the wooden trestles with iron and steel viaducts. Finally all were replaced with concrete bridges and fill. *(Catawissa Railroad Company—Annual Report)*

Toll bridge was erected by Richard Thurlow (variously spelled Thorla, Thorlo, and Thurley) in 1654 over the Newbury River at Rowley, Mass. He built the bridge at his own cost and on May 3, 1654, the General Court of Massachusetts fixed a rate of toll for animals. Passengers were permitted free passage. The bridge remained a toll bridge until 1680. *(Joshua Coffin—History of Newbury)*

Tubular-plate girder bridge was built in 1841 by James Millholland for the Baltimore and Ohio Railroad Company near Bolton Depot, Md. The bridge had a 50-foot span. The sides and bottom were wholly of wrought iron, but the flange was reinforced with 12-by-12-inch timbers. The plates were 38 inches wide and 6 feet long. The whole

bridge weighed 14 tons and cost approximately $2,200. *(Henry Grattan Tyrrell—History of Bridge Engineering)*

Twin covered-bridges were built in 1849 by Peter Ent at Village Forks, Pa., over Huntington Creek at a cost of $750. They were the 60-foot-long East Paden Bridge (No. 120), a queen post form of truss, and the 92-foot-long West Paden Bridge (No. 121), a Theodore Burr design. They were constructed of wood with some iron reinforcing.

Welded-aluminum girder-type highway bridge was a four-span structure, 36 feet wide and 23 feet long, on Clive Road, about one mile north and one mile west of Urbandale, Iowa, erected for the Iowa State Highway Commission by the Jensen Construction Co. and the United Contractors of Des Moines, Iowa. It was completed September 24, 1958, at a cost of approximately $125,000.

Wire-cable suspension aqueduct bridge was built in Pittsburgh, Pa., across the Allegheny River by John Augustus Roebling. There were seven spans of 162 feet each, consisting of a wooden trunk to hold water, and supported by a continuous wire cable on each side, 7 inches in diameter. The length of the aqueduct without extension was 1,140 feet; the cables, 1,175 feet. The total weight of the water in the aqueduct was 2,100 tons. The cost of construction and removal of the old wooden bridge was $62,000. The bridge was completed in May 1845. *(Charles Beebe Stuart—Lives and Works of Civil and Military Engineers)*

Wire suspension bridge for general traffic was erected over the Schuylkill River at Fairmount, Pa., by Charles Ellet. The bridge was opened January 2, 1842. It had a 358-foot span, was supported by wire cables, five at each side, and had a width of 25 feet. It cost $35,000.

Wooden railroad bridge of a purely truss type was built in 1838 by Benjamin Henry Latrobe for the Baltimore and Ohio Railroad Company across the Patapsco River at Elysville (now Alberton), Md. It consisted of two spans, each about 150 feet in length. The bridge was completed in 1839 and the wooden trusses were replaced in 1852 by iron Bollman trusses. *(William Hubert Burr and Myron Samuel Falk—Design and Construction of Metallic Bridges)*

Wrought-iron lattice-girder railroad bridge was built by the New York Central across the Mohawk River at Schenectady, N.Y., in 1859. Howard Carroll was the engineer in charge. *(Wrought Iron Record. Vol. 1, No. 3)*

"Y" bridge was authorized by the General Assembly of Zanesville, Ohio, on January 21, 18__. The bridge, in the form of the letter Y, spanned the Licking and Muskingum rivers and was opened for traffic in 1814. The present concrete bridge, the fourth structure to have occupied the site. *(The Sohioan. August 1929)*

RIDGE (game)

Auction bridge championship (duplicate) was
ld July 9, 1914, at the Lake Placid Club, Lake
acid, N.Y. The four-man team of the New York
idge Whist Club defeated the team of the Knick-
bocker Whist Club of New York City by 7 tricks
48 boards to win the American Whist League's
amilton Trophy, symbolic of the whist cham-
onship of the United States and Canada.

Bridge hand in which each of the 4 players was
alt a perfect hand of 13 cards of the same suit
as on March 12, 1954, at Cranston, R.I. Irene
otta bid 7 hearts and won the bid.

Contract bridge laws book. *See* Book: Contract
idge laws book.

RIDGE (GAME) PLAYER

Bridge player to earn a lifetime total of 8,000
ints was Oswald Jacoby of Dallas, Tex., who
d earned 8,451 points by October 15, 1964.

Bridge player to win more than 1,000 master
ints in 1 year was Oswald Jacoby of Dallas,
x., who passed the 1,000 mark on November 15,
63, in a tournament held at Edgewater Park,
ss. His total points for 1963 were 1,034.

Father and son team to win national contract
idge championship was Oswald Jacoby of Dal-
s, Tex., and James Jacoby, 26 years old, at the
th annual American Contract Bridge League at
e Empress Hotel in Miami Beach, Fla., on
cember 1, 1955. About 1,500 contestants par-
ipated in the open team-of-four contest.

RIDGE (game) TABLE

Bridge table to shuffle and deal the cards by
ctricity was patented November 29, 1932, by
urens Hammond of Chicago, Ill., who obtained
ent No. 1,889,729 for a "card table with an au-
natic dealing device." The unshuffled cards are
ced in a sliding drawer which starts the mech-
ism and delivers thirteen cards to each player.
e entire mechanism is concealed in the table.
e table was manufactured by the Hammond
ock Company Chicago, Ill., which marketed it in
32.

IDGE WHIST. *See* Whist

IDGE WHIST TOURNAMENT. *See* Whist
urnament

IGADIER GENERAL (black). *See under* Army
cer

ITANNIA WARE was manufactured in 1824 in
unton, Mass., by Isaac Babbitt and William
ossman. On July 17, 1839, Isaac Babbitt of Bos-
, Mass., obtained patent No. 1,252 on a "wheel
x with anti-friction rollers." An act of Congress
August 29, 1842 (5 Stat. L. 547) authorized the
cretary of the Navy to pay $20,000 for the "right

to use Babbitt's anti-attrition metal." *(George
Sweet Gibb—The Whitesmiths of Taunton)*

**BRITISH PARLIAMENT MEMBER (American
woman).** *See* Woman: American-born woman to
become a member of Parliament

BRITISH SETTLEMENT. *See* Colonist: English
settlement in America (permanent)

BROAD JUMP. *See* Long jump

BROADCASTING. *See* Radio broadcast

BROADCLOTH was produced in Pittsfield,
Mass., in 1793 from fleeces of the merino sheep of
Arthur and John Scholfield. Soon after 1793 they
manufactured 24½ yards of broadcloth. *(Joseph
Edward Adams Smith—History of Pittsfield)*

BROADSIDE. *See* Newspaper

BROADWAY PLAY TO BE TELEVISED. *See*
Television—Telecast: Play to be televised with its
original Broadway cast

BROKERAGE

American Stock Exchange women members
(office brokers not on the floor) were Julia Montgomery Walsh, general partner of Ferris & Company, Washington, D.C., and Phyllis Kathryn Smith
Peterson, general partner of Sade & Company,
Washington, D.C., elected Nov. 18, 1965.

**Brokerage firm whose shares were traded by a
major stock exchange** was Merrill Lynch, Pierce,
Fenner and Smith Inc., symbol MER. The stock
opened on the New York Stock Exchange on July
27, 1971, at 38¼ and closed at 37. There were
47,500 shares traded the first day. Previous transactions had been made over the counter.

Clearinghouse for stocks and bonds was the
Philadelphia Clearing House, which was organized in Philadelphia, Pa., in August 1870 as an
adjunct of the Board of Brokers, Philadelphia
stock exchange.

Curb exchange in history to transact more business in a day than the New York Stock Exchange
was the New York Curb, on June 15, 1929, when
the volume for the Curb was 1,287,900 shares, as
compared with 1,260,400 for the Stock Exchange.

Exchange to specialize in mining securities was
the San Francisco Stock and Exchange Board,
September 11, 1862. Its name has twice been
changed—to San Francisco Stock Exchange and
then to San Francisco Mining Exchange. It was
organized by a group of 37 independent brokers
determined to establish fixed positive prices for
shares of the Comstock mining companies. The
Comstock Lode in Nevada in 1859 produced $680
million, enough to pay the entire cost of the Civil
War. The companies issued shares that were
widely traded at prices ranging from $1,000 to $2,-
000 each.

The First

BROKERAGE—*Continued*

Financial "corner" took place in New Amsterdam (New York) in 1666. Frederick Phillipse cornered the market in wampum by creating a shortage. He buried several hogsheads of it in order to force those who had to use this medium of exchange to purchase wampum from him at a higher price.

Investment trust is claimed to have been the New York Stock Trust, New York City, a general portfolio statutory trust, formed April 1, 1889, with 50,000 shares at $10 a share. *(John Francis Fowler, Jr.—American Investment Trusts)*

New York Stock Exchange black director was Dr. Jerome Heartwell Holland, retired U.S. ambassador to Sweden, 1 of the 10 public nominees on the 21-member board, who was nominated on June 6, 1972, elected on July 5, 1972, and attended the organization meeting on July 13, 1972.

New York Stock Exchange black member was Joseph Louis Searles, III, a partner in the brokerage firm of Newburger, Loeb and Company, New York City, whose admission was approved by the board of governors on February 13, 1969.

New York Stock Exchange woman governor was Dr. Juanita Morris Kreps, professor of economics and dean of the Women's College, Duke University, Durham, N.C., who was nominated on June 6, 1972, elected on July 5, 1972, and attended the organization meeting on July 13, 1972.

New York Stock Exchange woman seat owner was Muriel ("Mickie") Siebert who paid $445,000 plus a $7,515 initiation fee on November 18, 1967. She was admitted on December 28, 1967, as a full member with privilege to handle customers' orders on the floor.

Oceangoing brokerage office was opened on the French liner *Ile de France* on August 15, 1929, orders being taken as the boat left Le Havre. A special wireless station, independent of the ship's wireless equipment, was installed in a space adjoining the board room. Three radio channels, one to receive continuous quotations, the second to transmit orders to New York, and the third to receive executions, were available for use.

Stock exchange was the New York Stock Exchange, the outgrowth of an agreement signed on May 17, 1792, by 24 brokers to fix the rates of commission on stocks and bonds. The first meeting was held at the Merchants Coffee House, 2d and Gold streets, New York City. The first president was Matthew McConnell. This protective league existed until March 8, 1817, when the New York Stock and Exchange Board adopted its constitution, organized on its present lines. On January 29, 1863, the name was changed to the New York Stock Exchange. *(Edmund Clarence Stedman—History of the Stock Exchange)*

The First

Stock exchange at which more than a milli shares were traded in one day was the New Yo Stock Exchange, New York City, whose transa tions on December 15, 1886, totaled 1,096,5(shares.

Stock order from a zeppelin was radioed (August 8, 1930, from the *Graf Zeppelin*. The rad message was picked up at Tuckerton, N.J., and t order sent to Portland, Me., by telegraph. Tl order was sent by Alexander Godfrey of Bosto Mass.

Telegraph ticker used by a brokerage concer *See* Telegraph: Telegraph ticker used by a broke age concern

Visitor to open the New York Stock Exchan; was Leonard Ross, a ten-year-old boy from Ca fornia, who was introduced on April 24, 1956, Keith Funston, president of the exchange, a who pressed the button that activated the openi gong. Young Ross had won $100,000 on the telev sion show "The Big Surprise."

Woman brokerage office owner was Victor Claflin Woodhull, who, with her sister Tenness Celeste Claflin, opened offices in 1869 in the Ho man House, New York City. Their compar Woodhull, Claflin & Co., showed a net profit $750,000 for the first six weeks. A newspaper ca toon depicted them driving a chariot drawn two bullocks and two bears, with the heads of t largest financiers of the time. Tennessee w holding the reins while Victoria was whippi from right to left. The wheels of the chariot we crushing financiers while others embodied ducks, with crutches under their wings, were t ing to fly away. *(Theodore Tilton—Biographi Sketch of Victoria C. Woodhull)*

Woman director of a stock exchange was Ma Gindhart Roebling of the Trenton Trust Compai Trenton, N.J., who on October 28, 1958, becat one of the 32 governors of the American Stc Exchange, New York City. As a governor she w entitled to go on the floor of the exchange. S was one of the three so-called public members connected with the Wall Street community.

Woman president of a major stock brokera concern was Josephine Perfect Bay (Mrs. Char Ulrick Bay), who on December 1, 1956, becar chairman and president of A. M. Kidder & C Inc., New York City.

Woman stock exchange member (commod exchange) was Gretchen B. Schoenleber of Ambrosia Chocolate Company, Milwaukee, W who was admitted September 3, 1935, to memb ship in the New York Cocoa Exchange, Inc., N York City.

Woman to sell securities on the floor of the N York Curb Exchange, New York City, was moti picture actress Linda Darnell, who occupied P

The First

29 on November 19, 1941, to sell U.S. Defense Bonds and stamps.

BRONCHITIS TREATISE. *See under* Medical book

BRONZE EQUESTRIAN STATUE. *See under* Monument

BRONZE SKYSCRAPER. *See under* Building

BRONZE STAR. *See* Medal

BRONZE STATUE (full-length) was executed by Ball Hughes in 1847 and placed in the cemetery at Mount Auburn, Cambridge, Mass. It represented the astronomer Dr. Nathaniel Bowditch, seated and holding a copy of his translated work, La Place's *Mécanique Céleste,* with a globe and a quadrant beside him. The statue was imperfect and was recast by Gruet Jne. Fondeur of Paris, France, in 1886. *(Boston Courier. June 16, 1847)*

BRUSHES were manufactured at Medfield, Mass., in 1808 by Artemas Woodward in a shop that stood near the present site of the Orthodox parsonage. *(William Smith Tilden—History of the Town of Medfield)*

BUDDHIST TEMPLE was established July 15, 1904, in Los Angeles, Calif., in a meeting room. The chief priest was Rinban Izumeda. Most of the congregation belonged to the Shinshu Sect of Buddhism, a branch of the home Hompa Hongwanji Buddhist Temple.

BUDGET BUREAU (United States) was created by Act of Congress (42 Stat. L. 22) approved June 10, 1921. The bureau was then part of the Treasury Department, but under the immediate direction of the President. The first director of the budget was Brigadier General Charles Gates Dawes, who served until July 1, 1922. *(William Franklin Willoughby—National Budget System)*

BUDGET COMMISSIONER OF A STATE (Woman). *See* Woman: Woman state budget commissioner

BUILDING

See also specific types of buildings, e.g. Customhouse, Library, School, Stadium, Theater

Air-conditioned factory. *See under* Factory

Air-conditioned office building was the Milam Building, San Antonio, Tex., which opened January 1, 1928. The building was 21 stories high, contained nearly 3 million cubic feet of space, and had 247,779 square feet of gross floor area. It was the first air-conditioned office building in the world with the air conditioning a part of the original construction.

All-glass windowless structure was the Owens-Illinois Glass Company's packaging laboratory, Toledo, Ohio, completed January 15, 1936. Eighty thousand translucent water-clear hollow glass blocks weighing about 150 tons were used in the

The First

two-story building, which had 39 rooms and an aggregate floor area of 20,000 square feet. The blocks were manufactured at the company's Muncie, Ind., plant and were a part of the structural strength of the building.

Aluminum geodesic-dome civic center was the Virginia Beach Convention Center, Virginia Beach, Va., opened May 15, 1957. It was renamed the Alan B. Shepard Convention Center on July 28, 1961, but is referred to as the Civic Center.

Aluminum-faced building was the Alcoa Building, Pittsburgh, Pa., a 30-story, 410-foot skyscraper, completed August 1, 1953, for the Aluminum Company of America and dedicated September 15, 1953. The exterior walls were thin stamped aluminum panels, 6 by 12 feet, bolted to angles on the spandrel beams and backed up with 4 inches of perlite-concrete sprayed on slotted aluminum lath and reinforcing bars. It had 183,000 square feet of exterior wall area. About 3 million pounds of aluminum were used. The elevators were of all-aluminum construction, the electrical wiring and conductors all-aluminum, and the plumbing 65 percent aluminum.

Apartment house cooperative was the Gramercy, a 10-story apartment house at 34 Gramercy Park, New York City, constructed by James Campbell for the Gramercy Company, incorporated March 28, 1883, with a capital stock of $150,000. Each apartment was adjudged equal to a certain number of shares; apartments sold for from $4,500 to $8,000. The property was managed by 7 trustees, George R. Read serving as secretary. The building had 3 hydraulic elevators and a restaurant on an upper floor that was leased in October 1883 to Louis Sherry. The cooperative was ready for occupancy in September 1883.

Apartment house to occupy a square city block was the Belnord Apartment House, a 12-story building (then the largest apartment house in the world) containing 6 separate passenger elevators and 178 suites of from 7 to 11 rooms with 2, 3, and 4 baths each, between 86th and 87th streets (south and north) and Broadway and Amsterdam Avenue (west and east), in New York City. Ready for occupancy October 15, 1909, its area was 64,614 square feet with an interior court of 22,033 square feet. Every room was an outside room. Annual rentals ranged from $2,100 upwards. (Philip) Hiss and (H. Hobart) Weekes were the architects.

Apartment house with a modern layout was erected in New York City in 1869. It was known as the Stuyvesant Apartments and was located at 142 East 18th Street. It contained "four distinct suites of apartments" on each of the four floors. Each had a kitchen, dining room, parlor, and bedrooms—all separated from each other—plus a dumbwaiter and a servant's room. The fifth and top floor was arranged for artists' studios. The annual rental for the apartments varied from $1,-

The First

BUILDING—*Continued*
200 to $1,800 each; $200 was charged for the studios. The architect was Richard Morris Hunt; the owner, Rutherford Stuyvesant. *(Annual Report of the Superintendent of Buildings, New York, 1862–1869)*

Atom-bomb-resistant federal building was the laboratory for the Armed Forces Institute of Pathology, Walter Reed Army Medical Center, Washington, D.C., which was occupied March 13, 1955, and dedicated by President Dwight David Eisenhower on May 23, 1955. The 8-story reinforced concrete bomb-resistant building contained 8 floors, 5 above ground and 3 underground. It had a gross area of approximately 215,000 square feet and a net usable area of 130,000 square feet. It was constructed by the Cramer-Vollmerhousen Co., Inc., of Washington, D.C.

Brick building was erected in 1633 in New Amsterdam (New York City) as a residence for Wouter Van Twiller, the fifth Dutch governor. Several other brick structures were likewise erected within the fort. The bricks were imported from Holland. *(Charles Thomas Davis—Practical Treatise on the Manufacture of Bricks, Tiles and Terra Cotta)*

Bronze and glass skyscraper was a 519-foot structure, 38 stories high, at 375 Park Avenue, New York City. It contained 3,650,000 square feet of glass divided into 3,800 windows. The steel framework was put together by use of high-tensile steel bolts instead of steel rivets. Mies van der Rohe and Philip Johnson were the architects and Kahn & Jacobs the associated architects, with the George A. Fuller Company, the general contractors. The highest point of steel construction was reached on December 17, 1956. Named the Seagram Building, it was completed in November 1957.

Building built inside a factory completely ready for occupancy, and the first building floated across a river, was a 41-ton 5-room house and garage (32 by 42 feet), fully equipped with furnace, cooling system, laundry, and plumbing, and partly furnished. It was built by R[obert] G[ilmour] Le Tourneau, Inc., Peoria, Ill. It was towed across the Illinois River on its own bottom from Peoria to the Le Tourneau test farm in East Peoria, Ill., on September 17, 1938.

Building constructed wholly of cast iron was a factory five stories high that was built by James Bogardus at the corner of Centre and Duane streets in New York City in May 1848. *(John W. Thomson—Cast Iron Buildings: Their Construction and Advantages)*

Building containing 6.5 million square feet of usable space was the Pentagon, Arlington, Va., built of reinforced concrete faced with Indiana limestone, and completed on January 15, 1943, at a cost of about $83 million. It is 5 stories high; each

The First

facade is 921 feet long; and each floor has a different color scheme. It has five rings of buildings intersected by 10 corridors. The length of the corridors is 17½ miles. It covers 34 acres of land, with a 5-acre pentagonal court in the center and 204 acres of lawns and terraces. It accommodates the headquarters of the Department of Defense. It was designed by George Edwin Bergstrom of Los Angeles, Calif.

Building devoted entirely to highway traffic was erected by the Eno Foundation for Highway Traffic Control, Inc., at Saugatuck, Conn. Ground was broken July 18, 1938, the cornerstone laid August 29, 1938, and the building completed July 1, 1939. The organization was incorporated April 22, 1921, and affiliated with Yale University, New Haven, Conn., February 15, 1933.

Building erected by the Government in Washington, D.C., was the Executive Mansion. It was modeled after the palace of the Duke of Leinster in Ireland and was designed by James Hoban. The cornerstone was laid October 13, 1792. The Executive Mansion was first occupied by President John Adams in 1800, and the first New Year's reception was held there on January 1, 1801. The Executive Mansion was burned by the British in 1814 and only the four walls were left standing. It was restored in 1818 and, in order to obliterate the marks of fire, the stones were painted white. Since that time the Executive Mansion has been known as the White House. When Adams first took occupancy, there was only a path through an elder swamp leading from the President's house to the Capitol. *(Charles Hurd—The White House: A Biography)*

Building erected in the United States for public use, under the authority of the Federal Government, was a structure for the U.S. Mint. This was a plain brick edifice, on the east side of Seventh Street, near Arch, in Philadelphia, Pa. The mint was established by the Act of April 2, 1792 (1 Stat. L. 246), an "act establishing a mint and regulating the coins of the United States." The cornerstone was laid by David Rittenhouse, director of the Mint, on July 31, 1792.

Building for telephone directory compilation and printing was built for the General Telephone Directory Company, a subsidiary of the General Telephone Corp., in Des Plaines, Ill., and dedicated April 30, 1953. It had a total of 30,000 square feet of working area. The company then produced directories for 2,500 communities and 2 million telephones in 34 states.

Building heated by steam was the Eastern Hotel of Boston, Mass., erected in 1845. Small wrought-iron pipes conveyed the steam and the heat was diffused by coils of pipe.

The First

Building higher than 750 feet in height was the Woolworth Building, in New York City, measuring 791½ feet high, 947 feet above sea level at high tide. It was formally opened on April 24, 1913, at 7:30 P.M., when President Woodrow Wilson at the White House, Washington, D.C., pressed a telegraph key that rang a bell in the engine room and dining hall and lit the electric lights on the 55 floors. The architect was Cass Gilbert. At the time, it was the tallest structure in the world with the exception of the Eiffel Tower in Paris.

Building higher than 1,250 feet was the Empire State Building, New York City, 102 stories, dedicated May 1, 1931, by President Herbert Clark Hoover, who pressed a button in Washington, D.C. that switched on the lights. It was 1,250 feet high and cost about $52 million. The builder was Colonel William Aiken Starrett; the architect, William Frederick Lamb; the engineer, Homer Gage Balcom. Alfred Emanuel Smith, former governor of New York, was the president of Empire State, Inc. In 1950, a 222-foot television sending-tower was constructed on the roof.

Building higher than 1,400 feet in height was the 110-story Sears Building of Sears Roebuck & Company, measuring 1,454 feet high, located on Jackson Boulevard between Adams and Franklin streets in Chicago, which was topped out on May 4, 1973, and completed in 1974.

Building in all-Gothic architecture was Trinity Episcopal Church, New Haven, Conn., designed by Ithiel Town of New Haven in 1814. It had seam-faced traprock with brownstone trim. *(Roger Hale Newton—Town and Davis, Architects)*

Building in which wrought-iron beams were used was erected for Harper & Brothers in New York City in 1854. Wrought-iron beams were rolled for the first time in the United States in 1854 at the Trenton, N.J., Iron Works, of which Peter Cooper was the principal owner. These beams were intended for the Cooper Union building, but they were not ready in time, as it took two years to prepare them. They were 7 inches deep, weighed 81 pounds per yard, and were of the type known as deck beams. Previously cast iron beams had been used in construction work. *(More Than One Hundred Years of Publishing—Harper & Bros.)*

Building known as a Quonset hut was built in September 1941 at Quonset Point air station, Greenwich, R.I., for the U.S. Navy by the Great Lakes Steel Corporation, Stran-Steel Division, Detroit, Mich. The structures were built around a framework of Stran-Steel members, a light steel building material distinguished by a patented groove into which nails could be driven. They were officially designated by the U.S. Navy as U.S. Navy Arch-Rib Huts.

The First

Building known as a skyscraper was a ten-story steel-skeleton building erected by the Home Insurance Company of New York at La Salle and Adams streets, Chicago, Ill. Designed by Major William Le Baron Jenney, it was started on May 1, 1884, and completed in the fall of 1885. It was constructed of marble and flanked by four columns of polished granite supporting a marble balcony. Two additional stories were added to it later. A steel frame supported the entire weight of the walls instead of the walls themselves carrying the weight of the building. *(William Aiken Starrett —Skyscrapers and the Men Who Build Them)*

Building of fireproof construction was the Fireproof Building, which was designed and built by Robert Mills in 1822–1823 on Meeting Street, between Queen and Broad streets, Charleston, S.C. It was built for the preservation of the county records and was a stone and iron structure. Even the window sashes were made of iron. The building is still in use. *(Charleston Courier. Mar. 30, 1822)*

Building of pressed structural steel was a 2-story 14-room building designed and built in June 1907 by the Taft-Howell Co., of Cornwall Landing, N.Y., for the Tuxedo Park Association, Tuxedo Park, N.Y. The pressed steel, known by its trade name, Metal Lumber, was developed by Harry Merrill Naugle, chief engineer of the Berger Manufacturing Company, Canton, Ohio. The building had structural members substituting in every detail for what normally would be wood studs and joists in balloon frame construction for dwellings.

Building shaped like an elephant was James V. Lafferty's the Elephant, which was built in the form of an elephant with a covering of tin painted to resemble an elephant hide. It was built in 1882 in Cedar Grove in Atlantic City, N.J., as an attraction to promote his real estate surrounding it. The legs contained a spiral staircase that led into a large room handsomely fitted with carved wood displaying photographs and models of the property for sale. The front legs contained staircases leading to the eyes, through which the ocean was visible. It cost $25,000 to build. The howdah, which was 65 feet above the sand, served as an observation tower.

Building with a high steeple was Trinity Church, New York City, which was begun October 17, 1839, and dedicated May 21, 1846, Ascension Day. A small admission fee was charged visitors, who climbed the 308 steps to the Trinity steeple, "with suitable resting places provided" to a point 34 feet below the peak. The steeple was 284 feet above Broadway, and was the highest point until 1893, when the Manhattan Life Insurance Company erected its 17-story building and tower, which thrust its pinnacle 60 feet above the Trinity spire.

The First

BUILDING—*Continued*

Building with an all-marble dome was the Rhode Island State House, in Providence, R.I., occupied by the General Assembly and other state officers on January 1, 1901. Ground was broken September 16, 1895, and the cornerstone was laid on October 15, 1896. The architects were McKim, Mead and White, and the builders were Norcross Brothers, Worcester, Mass. The dome had 327,000 cubic feet of white Georgia marble, and was 94-feet high. The diameter of the dome below the top of the gallery was 70 feet; the diameter above the top of the gallery, 56 feet; and the diameter of the dome proper, 50 feet.

Building with its roof supported by cables was the J. S. Dorton Arena, in Raleigh, N.C., which was completed and dedicated in 1953. The metal/asbestos roof is suspended on a network of cables that extend crosswise from the 90-foot parabolic; it is saddle-shaped. The 14-foot-wide arches reach a maximum height of 90 feet. They cross each other at about 26 feet above ground, then extend into a tunnel below the surface at the east and west ends. The weight of the roof is equalized by tension cables, with 14 foot, 2 inch strands connecting each end of the parabola through the stress tunnel. The roof, is so suspended that it eliminates any necessity for structural steel supports and presents no obstructions of view from any seat.

Building with prefabricated walls of mosaic concrete was completed in February 1935. It is located on the Colesville Pike, north of Washington, D.C., and was built by the Earley Process Corporation, Washington, D.C. The walls of the house consisted of 32 panels, 2 inches thick, approximately 9 feet high, and from 4 to 10 feet wide, heavily reinforced with electrically welded steel mesh, fireproof, weatherproof, and waterproof. Color and texture were determined by the color of the crushed quartz and quartz sand used in the concrete.

Caisson-foundation building was the Manhattan Life Insurance Company building, New York City, opened May 1, 1894. The bridge caissons (made of steel in varying size, from 9.6 inches in diameter to 25 x 21 feet square fitted with concrete) were sunk by pneumatic process. The 16-story building with a 67-foot frontage had 5 hydraulic and 2 electric elevators. The architects were [Francis Henry] Kimball and [George Kramer] Thompson.

Capitol building. *See* Capitol

Circular office building was the Capitol Tower, Hollywood and Vine streets, Los Angeles, Calif., dedicated April 6, 1956. It was 150 feet high (13 stories), and had a diameter of 92 feet. Above the roof was a 90-foot spire from which a beacon light flashed the word *Hollywood* in Morse code. Welton Becket was the architect.

The First

Circular school building was St. Patrick Central High School, Kankakee, Ill., opened February 6, 1956. It was a two-story building, 200 feet in diameter, which housed classrooms and a gymnasium unit accommodating 2,000 spectators. It was connected to a small rectangular wing containing the administrative offices and library. The total cost of the school was $736,592. Belli and Belli of Chicago, Ill., were the architects.

Commercial building heated by the sun was the Solar Building, Albuquerque, N.Mex., a single-story building. The heating system, designed by Frank Hillman Bridgers and Donald Paxton, was completed August 1, 1957. One wall of the building, sheathed in glass tilted to face the sun, collected heat from the sun's rays and heated panels containing water, which flowed through a conventional heating system.

Elevator in an office building. *See under* Elevator

Elliptical-shaped office building was the $40 million Phoenix Mutual Building of the Phoenix Mutual Life Insurance Company, constructed as a part of the urban renewal project on Constitution Plaza, Hartford, Conn. It was designed by (Wallace Kirkman) Harrison and (Max) Abramovitz and completed in November 1963. It contained 13 floors, each about 13,000 feet; measured 225 feet from end to end, and 87 feet across at the widest point. George A. Fuller was the contractor.

Fire escapes for tenements. *See* Fire escapes for tenements

Fraternity house. *See under* Fraternity (Greek-letter)

House completely solar-heated was built in Dover, Mass., and occupied on December 24, 1948. The house trapped the sun's energy through a unit consisting of a black sheet-metal collector behind two panes of glass. The solar heat was stored in a "heat bin" containing an inexpensive sodium compound. Electric fans blew the stored heat through vents as desired. The experiments were sponsored by Amelia Peabody. The house was designed by Eleanor Raymond and the heating system was developed by Dr. Maria Telkes.

House with a built-in nuclear bomb shelter was exhibited May 24, 1959, at Hi-Tor Woods, Pleasant Hills, Pa. It was built by the Obie Construction Co., Pittsburgh, Pa., and contained a fully equipped underground integral shelter with bunks to sleep four persons, sanitary facilities, a food storage area and refrigerator, a transoceanic radio, a first-aid kit, a weather-warning device, a Geiger counter, a fire extinguisher, and other equipment. The main part of the shelter was 22 feet long and 8 feet wide. Another section contained an auxiliary power plant, heating equipment, an air filtering system, and an oxygen tank. The walls were made of concrete blocks 10 inches

The First

thick; lead was used for insulation against radiation. The shelter had a concrete escape tunnel.

Housing cooperative sponsored by a labor union was the Amalgamated Houses, originally called the Amalgamated Cooperative Apartments, built by the Amalgamated Housing Corporation, which opened 2 buildings on November 1, 1927, in The Bronx, New York City. Additional buildings were erected accommodating 1,495 families. The housing project was organized by Abraham Eli Kazan for the Amalgamated Clothing Workers of America.

Library building. *See under* Library

Marble building. *See* Marble building

Monolithic concrete building was the Milton House, Milton, Wis., a hotel built in 1845 by Joseph Goodrich on the corduroy road between Chicago, Ill., and Madison, Wis. It replaced a log house built in 1837 and a frame building of 1839. The walls were 18 inches thick. A hexagonal tower three stories high served as a lookout for Indians; the remaining portion was two stories high. *(Concrete Age. August 1924)*

Penitentiary building. *See under* Prison

Post office building (U.S.). *See under* Post office

"Presidential mansion." *See* "Presidential mansion"

Retractable roof (large) building was the Civic Area and Exhibit Hall, a stainless steel dome structure, in Pittsburgh, Pa., which was dedicated on September 17, 1961. The roof, which has no interior support, is divided radially into 8 leaves, 2 of which are stationary and 6 of which rotate about a pin at the top as they roll along curved rails laid on a reinforced concrete ring girder. The dome was constructed to open or close electrically in 2½ minutes. It is nearly circular, 415 feet in diameter, 136 feet high at center, and can accommodate 13,000 spectators at a basketball game and 15,000 at a rally. It occupies a five-acre site and cost $22 million. There are approximately 2,950 tons of structural steel in the roof. The first event held there was the Ice Capades, from September 18 to 30, 1961.

Solar-heated and radiation-cooled house was built by Raymond Whitcomb Bliss in Tucson, Arizona. The system, built at a cost of nearly $4,000 for labor and materials, was placed in operation January 15, 1955. A large slanting slab of steel and glass converted the sunlight into heat, which was brought into the house by ducts. The same fans, controls, ducts, etc., were used for summer cooling.

Split-level buildings were the Elfreth houses, 3 brownstone buildings, at 258–260–262 South Third Street, in Philadelphia, built in 1830. The rooms in the rear were higher than those in the front.

The First

"State House" located outside a state was the Florida House, Washington, D.C., a 3-story remodeled building originally erected in 1887, purchased by voluntary contributions in 1972, and opened October 26, 1973. It is maintained by tax-deductible contributions as a hospitality house for Floridians.

Steam-heated factory. *See under* Factory

Steel-frame building was the Tacoma Building in Chicago, Ill., completed in 1887. It was designed by Holabird & Roche and built by George Allon Fuller. This building embodied the principles upon which all modern skyscrapers are designed and erected.

Steel-frame residence was the Copper House, built in 1890, at Shore Road and 88th Street in the Bay Ridge section of Brooklyn, N.Y. The house was constructed with copper sheets riveted to the exterior. It was built by Niels Poulson, who resided in it from 1890 until his death in 1911. *(American Scandinavian Review. February 1931)*

Summer home was the manor house erected in 1769 on the 4,000–acre tract of John Wentworth, last royal colonial governor of New Hampshire (1767-1775). It served as his summer home and was located on the shore of Lake Wentworth, Wolfeboro, N.H.

Tenement house was built in New York City in 1833 on Water Street, on a site now within the limits of Corlears Park. It was four stories high, with arrangements for one family on each floor. This was the beginning of the system of grouping many homes under one roof. A tenement is any house, or part of a house, occupied by three or more families living independently of each other and doing cooking on the premises. The term generally refers to buildings less expensive than apartment houses, especially insofar as rents are concerned.

Theater. *See under* Theater

"White House." *See* Building: Building erected by the Government in Washington, D.C.

"White House of the Confederacy" was used as a residence by Jefferson Davis from February 18, 1861, to May 22, 1861. It is located at 626 Washington Street, Montgomery, Ala. Davis arrived at Montgomery on February 16, 1861, and remained at a local hotel for a few days.

Windowless factory. *See under* Factory

Woman to have her name placed on the cornerstone of a United States Government building. *See under* Woman

BUILDING AND LOAN ASSOCIATION was the Oxford Provident Building Association, which was organized on January 3, 1831, in Thomas Sidebotham's Tavern, 4219 Frankford Avenue, Frankford, Pa. The organizers were Jesse Castor,

The First

BUILDING AND LOAN ASSOCIATION—*Continued*

secretary, Samuel Pilling, treasurer, and Jeremiah Horrocks. The company was succeeded by the Decatur Building Association. The first loan was $500, made on April 11, 1801, to Comly Rich, a lamplighter at 4276 Orchard Street, Philadelphia, Pa. *(Robert Riegel—The Building and Loan Association)*

BULL MOOSE PARTY. *See* Progressive Party

BULLFIGHT
Bullfight was held July 4, 1884, in Dodge City, Kans. The first bull put up a good fight but was not killed. The next four bulls showed little inclination to fight and likewise were spared. To appease the crowd, the first bull was returned to the ring and was killed by Captain Gregorio Gallardo. Among the bulls were Ringtailed Snorter, Iron Gall, Sheriff, Rustler, Loco Jim, Ku Klux, and Eatem-up Richard. Another bullfight was held the following day. (On Saturday, July 31, 1880, at 5:00 P.M., a steer-baiting contest had been held in New York City before 4,000 spectators, but rubber caps had been placed on the bulls' horns and the matadors were not permitted to kill the bulls. The rosettes were not stuck into the bulls, but glued on.) *(Kansas Historical Quarterly. Vol 2, No.3. August 1933)*

Woman bullfighter (professional) was Patricia McCormick, of Big Spring, Tex., whose professional debut was made January 20, 1952, in Ciudad Juárez, Mexico. On that occasion she killed 2 bulls. In her first two years, she killed 80 bulls. *(Patricia McCormick—Lady Bullfighter)*

BUNTING manufacture was undertaken in 1838 by Michael Hodge Simpson at the New England Worsted Company, Saxonville, Mass.

BUREAU OF FOREIGN AND DOMESTIC COMMERCE. *See* Commerce Department (U.S.): Foreign and Domestic Commerce Bureau

BUREAU OF IDENTIFICATION. *See* Police: Police bureau of identification

BUREAU OF MEDICINE AND SURGERY (Naval). *See under* Navy

BUREAU OF NAVIGATION. *See* Navigation Bureau (U.S.)

BUREAU OF STANDARDS. *See* Standards Bureau (U.S.)

BURGLAR ALARM
Burglar alarm was installed by Edwin Thomas Holmes on February 21, 1858, in Boston, Mass. The releasing of a spring by the opening of a door or window made a contact that caused a short circuit of the wires. *(Edwin Thomas Holmes—A Wonderful Fifty Years)*

The First

Burglar alarm operated by ultrasonic or radio waves using the Doppler effect was the Alertronic, invented by Samuel Bagno of New York City, who obtained patent No. 2,655,645 on October 13, 1953, on a movement detection system for intruders or fire. It was manufactured by the Alertronic Corporation, Long Island City, N.Y., and first sold in June 1950. Reflected waves of 19,000 cycles a second, pitched too high for normal human ears, are recorded through a microphone into an alarm, generally stationed at a convenient location. The noise made by an intruder, having a slightly different frequency, causes the alarm gong to sound.

Burglar alarm system in which the protected premises were connected by wire to a central office system that was immediately apprised of entry was installed by the Holmes Burglar Alarm Company, New York City, in 1872. The alarms served safe cabinets and bank vaults specifically, instead of providing general protection for stores and houses.

BURIAL PLOT (Jewish). *See* Cemetery: Jewish burial plot

BURLESQUE SHOW. *See under* Play (drama)

BUS. *See* Automobile bus

BUSINESS
Chain store organization is ascribed to many, but the first of the existing chain stores was the Great Atlantic and Pacific Tea Company. George Huntington Hartford was in the hide and leather business in New York City in 1857 and in 1859 added tea to his merchandise. In 1864 he originated the Great American Tea Company, which in 1869 developed into the Great Atlantic and Pacific Tea Company, the presidency of which he kept until his death, August 29, 1917. Despite the name, the first store on the Pacific Coast was not opened until January 1930.

Commercial rating agency was established in New York City on August 1, 1841, as the Mercantile Agency, by Lewis Tappan, who founded the *Journal of Commerce* in 1828. The first place of business of the agency was at the corner of Hanover Street and Exchange Place, New York City. Branch houses were later opened, the first in Boston, Mass., in February 1843. On May 1, 1859, the firm was taken over by R. G. Dun & Company.

Corporation to have more than 3 million stockholders was the American Telephone and Telegraph Company (AT&T), New York City, which had 3,001,280 security owners on October 17, 1972.

Department store was the Zion's Co-Operative Mercantile Institution, created by Brigham Young in 1868 in Salt Lake City, Utah. In the beginning, each department was housed in its own store. One handled dry goods and carpets, another men's clothing. Groceries were carried in a different store; still another was a drugstore. In 1869, they were all assembled under one roof and on

The First

December 1, 1870, were incorporated. In 1876, a 100-by-365-foot lot was purchased and a new building constructed, which was occupied in October 1876. *(Edward W. Tullidge—History of Salt Lake City)*

Department store television sales demonstrations (large-scale). *See* Television—Telecast: Department store sales demonstrations (large-scale)

Department store to hold a public art auction was Gimbel Brothers, New York, City, on November 14 and 15, 1941, when 303 items were auctioned by the Kende Galleries, Inc. The sales totaled $12,066.

Department store to occupy a city block was A. T. Stewart & Co. (Alexander Turney Stewart) department store, 9th-10th streets, Broadway-Fourth Avenue, New York City, which opened in 1860.

Department store to sell apartments was Gimbel Brothers, Philadelphia, Pa., which on January 13, 1953, invited the public to the furniture floor to see full-size furnished duplicates of Philadelphia's first cooperative apartments. Over a million dollars' worth of apartments were contracted for the first day.

Department store to sell insurance of various types was Carson Pirie Scott & Co., Chicago, Ill. The first sale was made September 29, 1953, on a wedding present and personal effects floater for $2,500. The premium was $20.

Five-cent store was opened in Utica, N.Y., on February 22, 1879, by Frank Winfield Woolworth. The store was a great disappointment as its sales after a few weeks were as low as $2.50 a day. Woolworth moved his store in June 1879 to Lancaster, Pa., where it proved a success. His idea was developed on September 24, 1878, in Watertown, N.Y., when during the week of the country fair he originated a "five-cent table" in the store of Moore and Smith. The first joint venture of the Woolworth brothers in Harrisburg, Pa., was called "Great 5 Cent Store." *(F. W. Woolworth Co.—Fifty Years of Woolworth)*

Food-O-Mat was installed in the Grand Union Company store, Carlstadt, N.J., on May 24, 1945. It was invented by Lansing Peter Shield. The patented merchandise display fixture operated on a gravity-feed, rear-load principle. Stockmen working behind the unit placed cans, jars, and packages, label upright, on inclined runways. The items reached the shopper brand name uppermost. As the customer picked out an item, another slid in place by gravity.

Installment finance company to purchase installment contracts from retail dealers was the Fidelity Contract Company, Rochester, N.Y., which held its first directors' meeting April 7, 1904. The company, organized by Lee Richmond, Frederick Zoller, and George Gale Foster, became

The First

the Bankers Commercial Corporation of New York City.

Keedoozle store was opened in Memphis, Tenn., on May 15, 1937, by the Keedoozle Corporation of Memphis, Tenn., of which Clarence Saunders was president. Sample merchandise was displayed behind rows of tiny glass windows. The customer made purchases by inserting a notched rod into a keyhole beside the items desired. The mechanism automatically recorded the selections. The merchandise was automatically collected and wrapped when the insertion of the key in a final slot released the contents to a conveyor for wrapping. *Keedoozle* is a coined word for *key-does-all.*

Mail-order house was established by Aaron Montgomery Ward in 1872 in a 12-by-14 foot room at 825 North Clark Street, Chicago, Ill., with $2,400 capital, one third of which was advanced by George R. Thorne. The first catalog consisted of a single-sheet price list, 8 by 12 inches, without illustrations. The first catalog was issued August 18, 1872, and inaugurated a money-back policy. In 1873, the catalog was increased to 4 pages and listed 394 items. Afterward, catalogs with descriptive pictures were issued and a 15-cent charge made for them. The first free catalogs, more than 3 million weighing four pounds each, were mailed in 1904. *(History and Progress of Montgomery Ward and Co.—Montgomery Ward and Co.)*

Nurse employed by an industrial organization. *See under* Nurse

Retail store whose sales in one day exceeded $1 million was R. H. Macy Co., New York City, whose sales on December 7, 1944, exceeded $1 million. On December 14, 1957, they first exceeded $2 million; on December 18, 1965, $3 million; and on December 18, 1967, $4 million.

Sales meeting televised. *See under* Television—Telecast

Shopping center in a suburban business area planned to cater exclusively to the automobile trade was the Country Club Plaza, Kansas City, Mo., built by Jesse Clyde Nichols from the master plan drawn by Edward Buehler Delk on April 22, 1922. Construction began in November 1922, and the first tenant moved in March 1923. The center occupies 40 acres and has 150 stores, a 2,000-seat auditorium, and accommodations for 5,500 automobiles.

BUSINESS ECONOMICS COURSE, under the title "Commerce, Political Economy and Statistics," was established by the University of Louisiana (now Tulane University), New Orleans, La., in 1849; and was conducted by Professor James Dunwoody Brownson De Bow.

The First

BUSINESS EXPOSITION. *See* Fair: Industrial exposition

BUSINESS HISTORY CHAIR was the Isidor Straus Professorship of Business History, established in 1923 by the Graduate School of Business Administration, Harvard University, Cambridge, Mass. The first incumbent was Norman Scott Brien Gras, appointed in 1927.

BUSINESS LIBRARY. *See* Library

BUSINESS MACHINES. *See under* specific kinds of machine, e.g., Adding machine; Cash register; Postage meter; Telautograph

BUSINESS MANUAL was John Hill's *The Young Secretary's Guide; or a Speedy help to learning* . . . printed by B[artholomew] Green and J[ohn] Allen for S. Phillips in 1703 in Boston, Mass. It was based on an English work, contained 192 pages of instructions on writing business and social letters, punctuation rules, a dictionary of "hard words," and examples of bonds, bills, letters of attorney, deeds of sale, mortgage forms, warrants of attorney, deeds of gift, bills of sale, bills of exchange, assignments, etc. *(Louis Charles Karpinski—Bibliography of Mathematical Works Printed in America Through 1850)*

BUSINESS PUBLICATION
    Business publication was the *South-Carolina Price-Current,* a broadside, issued by Crouch and Gray, commission merchants, Charles-Town, S.C., on a sheet 6 by 12 inches, two columns wide. The first known copy, that of July 30, 1774, listed 168 commodities with their prices.

BUSINESS SCHOOL
    Business collegiate school was the Wharton School of Commerce and Finance in Philadelphia, Pa., established in 1881 by the University of Pennsylvania through a $100,000 gift of Joseph Wharton. *(Thomas Harrison Montgomery—A History of the University of Pennsylvania)*

    Business high school was the Washington Business High School, Washington, D.C., authorized June 11, 1889, by the Board of Education. It opened September 22, 1890, in an unused grade school building of seven rooms. Allan Davis was the first principal. *(Reports of the Board of Trustees of the Public Schools in Washington, D.C., 1885–1900)*

    Business school was opened in Rochester, N.Y., in 1842 by George Washington Eastman, and was known as the Eastman Commercial College.

    Commercial high school. *See* Commercial high school

BUSTLE was patented by Alexander Douglas of New York City, who obtained patent No. 17,082 on April 21, 1857, on an "improvement in bustles," making them adjustable so that the size could be increased or decreased.

The First

BUTTON
    Buttons of freshwater pearl were manufactured in Muscatine, Iowa, in 1890 by John F. Boepple, assisted by William Molis and R. Kerr. The pearl was obtained from domestic freshwater clam shells. *(U.S. Bureau of Fisheries. Vol. 36. 1917–18)*

    Cloth-covered buttons were made by hand in Easthampton, Mass., in 1826 by Mrs. Samuel Williston, who was the first to introduce their use commercially in the United States. Her husband formed a partnership with Joel Hayden, who invented the first machine for making covered buttons. The partnership lasted until 1848, when Williston bought out his partner and conducted the business alone.

    Gilt buttons to be commercially manufactured were produced in 1802 by Abel Porter & Company of Waterbury, Conn. The faces were all gilded, and gold was extensively used in the manufacture. This concern later developed into the Scovill Manufacturing Company of Waterbury, Conn. *(Henry Bronson—History of Waterbury)*

    Pewter or block tin buttons were manufactured in 1790 in Waterbury, Conn., by Henry, Silas, and Samuel Grilley, three brothers who established a small factory on Bunker Hill, an elevated section of the city. The buttons were cast in molds. The eyes were originally cast of the same material. Later, wire eyes were used. *(Homer Franklin Bassett—Waterbury and Her Industries)*

BUTTONHOLE SEWING MACHINE. *See* Sewing machine

C

CAB LOCOMOTIVE. *See* Locomotive

CABIN AIRSHIP. *See* Aviation—Airship: Airship with an enclosed cabin

CABINET (U.S.)
    Black sub-Cabinet member was James Ernest Wilkins of Chicago, Ill., who was appointed assistant secretary of Labor for International Affairs by President Dwight David Eisenhower on March 4, 1954, and sworn in March 18, 1954, in Washington, D.C. On August 18, 1954, with Secretary of Labor James Mitchell and Under Secretary Arthur Larson out of town, he was the first black representative of a department to attend a Cabinet meeting. (William Henry Lewis, a black Boston attorney, was special assistant attorney general from March 26, 1911, to April 1, 1913, but the "special" in his title deprived him of sub-Cabinet rank.)

    Cabinet was appointed by President George Washington during his first term, April 30, 1789, to March 3, 1793. Members of the Cabinet were Thomas Jefferson of Virginia, secretary of state;

The First

Alexander Hamilton of New York, secretary of the treasury; Henry Knox of Massachusetts, secretary of war; Samuel Osgood of Massachusetts, postmaster general; and Edmund Jennings Randolph of Virginia, attorney general. The seat of the federal government at that time was New York City. *(Henry Barrett Learned—The President's Cabinet)*

Cabinet appointee rejected by the Senate was Roger Brooke Taney of Maryland, appointed secretary of the treasury by President Andrew Jackson on September 23, 1833. This was a recess appointment, since Congress was not in session. Jackson submitted Taney's name on June 23, 1834, and it was rejected 28-18 on September 24, 1834. *(William Henry Smith—History of the Cabinet of the United States of America)*

Cabinet conference telecast was presented on June 3, 1953, from the White House, Washington, D.C. President Dwight David Eisenhower conferred for half an hour with Mrs. Oveta Culp Hobby, Secretary of Health, Education, and Welfare; George Magoffin Humphrey, Secretary of the Treasury; Ezra Taft Benson, Secretary of Agriculture; and Herbert Brownell, Attorney General. The telecast was carried by four networks.

Cabinet meeting attended by a foreign national was held April 20, 1965, at Washington, D.C. President Lyndon Baines Johnson had invited Aldo Moro, the visiting Italian premier, Amintore Fanfani, Italian foreign minister, and Dr. Sergio Fenoaltea, Italian ambassador to the United States, to attend.

Cabinet member (black) was Robert Clifton Weaver of Washington, D.C., nominated January 13, 1966, by President Lyndon Baines Johnson and sworn in January 18, 1966, as Secretary of Housing and Urban Development.

Cabinet member convicted of a crime committed while a member of a President's Cabinet was Albert Bacon Fall, who was tried in the District of Columbia Supreme Court. He was found guilty by Justice William Hitz on October 25, 1929, of receiving and accepting a bribe of $100,000 from Edward Laurence Doheny in connection with the Elk Hills Naval Oil Reserve in California, a bribe given with a view to influencing Fall, as Secretary of the Interior in President Warren G. Harding's Cabinet, to grant valuable oil leases to Doheny's Pan-American Petroleum and Transport Company. On November 1, 1929, Fall was sentenced to one year in prison and was fined $100,000.

Cabinet member to serve in 4 different capacities was Elliott Lee Richardson of Massachusetts, who was sworn in on June 24, 1970, as Secretary of Health, Education and Welfare (under Nixon); February 2, 1973, as Secretary of Defense (under Nixon); May 25, 1973, as Attorney General (under Nixon); and February 2, 1976, as Secretary of Commerce (under Ford).

The First

Cabinet member who was a brother of a President was Robert Francis Kennedy, who took office as Attorney General in the Cabinet of President John Fitzgerald Kennedy on January 21, 1961.

Cabinet member who was a Catholic was Roger Brooke Taney of Maryland, Attorney General in Andrew Jackson's Cabinet from July 20, 1831, until September 23, 1833, and Secretary of the Treasury from September 23, 1833, until June 25, 1834.

Cabinet member who was Jewish was Oscar Solomon Straus of New York, who was Secretary of Commerce and Labor during President Theodore Roosevelt's second administration. He was appointed on December 12, 1906, and served from December 17, 1906, to March 3, 1909. *(Oscar Solomon Straus—Under Four Administrations from Cleveland to Taft)*

Cabinet officer to address a joint session of Congress was Secretary of State Cordell Hull, who reported on November 18, 1943, that the tripartite conference at Moscow pointed toward the maintenance of peace and security in the postwar world. The two houses, being in recess, assembled to hear him, but technically it was not a "joint session."

Cabinet session held at a place other than the seat of the United States Government was held November 22, 1955, at President Dwight David Eisenhower's farm at Gettysburg, Pa. It was attended by the President, the Vice President, the ten Cabinet officers, and four other government officials.

Cabinet session telecast. *See under* Television —Telecast

Confederate to serve in the Cabinet was David McKendree Key, a senator from Tennessee, who served from March 12, 1877, to August 24, 1880, as Postmaster General in the cabinet of President Rutherford Birchard Hayes. He had been a lieutenant colonel in the 43rd Regiment of Tennessee and had been wounded and captured at Vicksburg.

Father and son to occupy the same Cabinet posts were Henry Cantwell Wallace, Secretary of Agriculture under Presidents Warren Gamaliel Harding and Calvin Coolidge, March 5, 1921, to October 25, 1924, and Henry Agard Wallace, Secretary of Agriculture under President Franklin Delano Roosevelt, March 4, 1933, to August 26, 1940.

Full Cabinet sworn in at the same time and place by the same official took office on March 4, 1933, when Justice Benjamin Nathan Cardozo of the Supreme Court of the United States swore in nine men and one woman as President Franklin Delano Roosevelt's Cabinet in the library on the second floor of the White House.

CABINET (U.S.)—*Continued*

German-born Cabinet member was Carl Schurz, born March 2, 1829, at Liblar, near Cologne, Prussia, who was appointed Secretary of the Interior by President Rutherford Birchard Hayes and served from March 12, 1877, to March 4, 1881.

Postmaster general of the United States to become a member of the President's Cabinet. *See under* Postmaster

Secretary of Health, Education, and Welfare was Oveta Culp Hobby (Mrs. William Pettus Hobby) of Houston, Tex., who was sworn in April 11, 1953, by Frank Kesler Sanderson, White House administrative officer, in President Dwight David Eisenhower's office, in the White House, Washington, D.C., as the tenth officer in the President's Cabinet. She was in charge of 37,500 workers in 550 offices in the country. Previously she had been administrator of the Federal Security Agency.

Secretary to the Cabinet and presidential assistant was Maxwell Milton Rabb of Boston, Mass., appointed November 22, 1954, by President Dwight David Eisenhower "to organize the work, keep the records, follow through on decisions, etc."

Vice President to preside over a Cabinet meeting. *See under* Vice President (U.S.)

Woman Cabinet member was Frances Perkins (Mrs. Paul Caldwell Wilson), appointed Secretary of Labor by President Franklin Delano Roosevelt. She served from March 4, 1933, to June 30, 1945. She had been Industrial Commissioner for New York prior to this appointment. *(U.S. Department of Labor—Frances Perkins, a Bibliographical List)*

Woman sub-Cabinet member was Annette Abbott Adams, who was appointed Assistant Attorney General on June 26, 1920, by President Woodrow Wilson. She resigned August 15, 1921. *(Arthur J. Dodge—Origin and Development of the Office of the Attorney General)*

CABLE (telegram)

Cable message sent around the world by commercial telegraph was "This message sent around the world" sent at 7:00 P.M., August 20, 1911, from the 17th floor of the New York Times building, New York City, by the New York *Times* and received at 7:16:30 P.M. over 28,613 miles and 16 relays via the the the Azores, Gibraltar, Bombay, Philippine Islands, Midway, Guam, Honolulu, and San Francisco.

News dispatch by cable was received August 26, 1858, and was published in the New York *Sun,* August 27, 1858. It stated that a treaty of peace had been concluded by China in which Britain and France obtained all their demands, including the establishment of embassies at Peking and indemnification for military expenses.

CABLE (telegraph)

Cable was an insulated copper wire laid October 18, 1842, by Samuel Finley Breese Morse in New York Harbor between the Battery and Governors Island. On the following day, while transmitting signals, the cable ceased to work because a vessel in raising its anchor had caught and wrecked 200 feet of the cable. Another cable was laid in New York Harbor for commercial use in 1843 by Samuel Colt. It was insulated with cotton yarn, beeswax, and asphaltum encased in a lead pipe, and connected New York City with both Fire and Coney Islands. *(Edward Wright Byrn— Progress of Invention in the Nineteenth Century; Samuel Irenaeus Prime—Life of S. F. B. Morse)*

Cable across the Atlantic Ocean was completed on August 5, 1858, through the efforts of Cyrus West Field. Two unsuccessful attempts had been made previously. On July 28, 1858, a splice was made in midocean, and on the following day two ships, belonging to Britain and the United States, paid out the cable as they sailed for home—the *Agamemnon* and *Valorous,* bound for Valentia, Ireland, and the *Niagara* and *Gorgon,* for Trinity Bay, Newfoundland, which were to be the terminals. The cable was 1,950 statute miles long and over two thirds of it was laid more than 2 miles deep. Introductory and complimentary messages were exchanged by President James Buchanan and Queen Victoria on August 16, 1858. The cable was weak and the current insufficient, and service was suspended September 1, 1858. *(Isabella Field Judson—Cyrus W. Field, His Life and Work)*

Cable across the Atlantic Ocean was paid out on August 6, 1857. The American frigate *Niagara* and the British warship *Agamemnon* attempted the task, but the cable broke and it was impossible to mend the break or complete the cable *(Henry Martyn Field—History of the Atlantic Telegraph)*

Cable across the Pacific Ocean was paid out on December 14, 1902, between San Francisco, Calif. and Honolulu, Hawaii, a distance of 2,277 nautical miles (2,620 miles), by the cableship *Silverton* and was landed on the beach near Honolulu, January 1, 1903. The first message was sent at 11:03 P.M. (San Francisco time) on that day. This cable was opened for public use on January 5, 1903.

Cable across the Pacific Ocean between Honolulu, Midway, Guam, and Manila was completed and spliced at Manila on July 3, 1903. After testing, the first official message was sent by President Theodore Roosevelt from his home at Oyster Bay, N.Y., at 10:50 A.M., July 4, 1903, to Governor William Howard Taft at Manila, who immediately answered it. Another message was sent westward across the Pacific and around the world to Clarence Hungerford Mackay, president of the Commercial Pacific Cable Company, who was with President Roosevelt at his home. The

The First

transmission time of the message was 11 minutes. The message was answered by Mr. Mackay, his message going eastward to London and over the system of the Eastern Telegraph Company to Manila, thence over the new Pacific cable and back to Oyster Bay, transmission time of the message being 9 minutes. The cable from San Francisco, Calif., to Manila via Honolulu was 7,876 nautical miles (9,060 miles).

Coaxial cable was invented by Lloyd Espenschied of Kew Gardens, N.Y., and Herman A. Affel of Ridgewood, N.J., whose application for a patent was filed May 23, 1929. They were awarded patent No. 1,835,031 on December 8, 1931, on a "concentric conducting system" which was assigned to the American Telegraph and Telephone Company, New York City.

Intercollegiate transatlantic chess match by cable. *See* Chess Tournament: Intercollegiate transatlantic chess match by cable

Submarine cable plow. *See under* Plow

Submarine telegraph cable that was practical was laid by Ezra Cornell, an associate of Samuel Finley Breese Morse. In 1845 he laid 12 miles of cable enclosed in lead pipes across the Hudson River connecting Fort Lee, N.J., with New York City. This cable was carried away by ice in 1846. Later a steel wire was suspended from high masts erected on opposite shores, but sleet and snow caused the wire to snap.) Before the cable was installed, messages for Philadelphia, Pa., and Washington, D.C., were carried across the Hudson by messengers in boats. *(Alonzo B. Cornell— True and Firm, Biography of Ezra Cornell)*

Submarine telegraph cable to be insulated with gutta-percha was made by Samuel T. Armstrong and Lorenzo Higgins at a factory on Water Street, Brooklyn, N.Y., in May 1848. It was laid across the North (Hudson) River for the Magnetic Telegraph Co. *(American Institute—Transactions, 1847)*

CABLE CAR. *See* Streetcar

CESAREAN OPERATION (successful). *See* Surgical operation: Cesarean operation (successful)

CAFETERIA was opened in 1895 in Chicago, Ill., on Adams Street between Clark and La Salle Streets by Ernest Kimball. In 1899 he moved it to the basement of the New York Life Building, where it was located until 1925.
See also Restaurant

CALCULATING MACHINE. *See* Adding machine

CALICO printery was established in Boston, Mass., by George Leason and Thomas Webber, who advertised in the Boston *News Letter,* April 21–28, 1712, that they had "set up a Callender-Mill and Dye House in Cambridge Street, Boston, near

The First

the Bowling Green where all gentlemen, Merchants, and others may have all sorts of Linnens, callicoes, stuffs or Silks Callendered: Prints all sorts of Linnens."

CALIFORNIA CONSUL. *See* Diplomatic Service: Consul to California

CALIFORNIA–HAWAII FLIGHT. *See under* Aviation—Flights (transpacific)

CALIFORNIA MISSION was dedicated and blessed by Father Junipero Serra on July 16, 1769. After high mass, the royal standard of Spain was unfurled over the mission, which was named in honor of San Diego de Alcala. The mission was the first of a chain of 21 that were erected. It is located in what is now San Diego, Calif. *(Trowbridge Hall—California Trails)*

CALIFORNIUM. *See* Element: Element 98

CALIPER (screw) was constructed by John Edson Sweet in 1874 in the shops of Sibley College (Cornell University), Ithaca, N.Y. The screw of the machine had 16 threads per inch and its divided circle had 625 readings, the calibration reading to 1/10,000 inch. The machine stood on three legs. *(Frederick Arthur Halsey—Methods of Machine Shop Work)*

CALL BOX (telegraph). *See* Telegraph: Telegraph call boxes

CALLIOPE was invented by Joshua C. Stoddard of Worcester, Mass., who on October 9, 1855, received patent No. 13,368 on a "new musical instrument to be played by the agency of steam or highly compressed air." He formed the American Steam Music Company in Worcester, Mass., in 1855. The first marine exhibition was held August 6, 1856, on the large side-wheel tugboat *Union.* *(John Harrison Morrison—History of American Steam Navigation)*.

CAMEL RACE took place April 7, 1864, at Agricultural Park, Sacramento, Calif. The proceeds obtained from the sale of tickets were used to aid the poor. *(May Humphreys Stacey—Uncle Sam's Camels)*

CAMELS. *See* Animals

CAMERA
Aerial camera (nine-lens) for large-scale mapping was designed by personnel of the U.S. Coast and Geodetic Survey in 1934 under the direction of Lieutenant Oliver Scott Reading and built under contract by the Fairchild Aerial Camera and Instrument Company, Jamaica, N.Y., in 1935. It was placed in operation in 1936. It was 29 inches wide, 27 inches fore and aft, 31 inches high, and weighed 306 pounds net. Gross weight with all equipment for photography was 750 pounds. The nine lenses photographed the terrain simultaneously on one piece of film. The camera was loaded with a strip of film 23 inches wide and 200 feet long, and could take 100 exposures without

The First

CAMERA—*Continued*
reloading. When flown at a height of 13,750 feet, the camera photographed 121 square miles at one exposure at a scale of 1 inch to 1,667 feet.

Camera to take, develop, and print pictures on photographic paper was the Polaroid camera, invented by Edwin Herbert Land and demonstrated on February 21, 1947, at a meeting of the Optical Society of America meeting at the Hotel Pennsylvania, New York City. The camera contained a specially prepared photographic paper with "pods" of developer and hypo sandwiched with the film. The turning of a knob squeezed open one of the pods, which developed the negative and made the print. The picture was produced in about one minute.

Filmpack camera was the Premo Film Camera, a box camera for a 3¼" x 4½" filmpack, introduced in 1903 by the Rochester Optical and Camera Company, Rochester, N.Y. It cost $4. Some cameras offered filmpack adapters. In 1905 the Premo Folding Film bellows camera was offered at $10.

Fluoro-record reflector camera. *See under* X ray

Motion picture camera (portable) was the Victor Cine Camera, manufactured by the Victor Animatograph Company, Inc., Davenport, Iowa, in 1923. It was 3 by 6 by 8 inches, weighed 5 pounds, and cost $55. It was advertised August 12, 1923.

Nonelectronic device for observing in total darkness was the Evaporograph, built by Baird Associates, Inc., Cambridge, Mass., an affiliate of the American Research and Development Corporation, and announced to the public on February 15, 1956. It cost $9,500 and was housed in a cabinet 18 by 14 by 11 inches. It was designed to observe radiation differences corresponding to temperature variations of one to several thousand degrees Fahrenheit.

Photo-finish camera (electric-eye) installed at a racetrack was placed in operation January 16, 1936, at the Hialeah Race Course, Hialeah, Fla.

Roll-film camera, which did not require a table or tripod for support, was Kodak No. 1, a fixed-focus box camera, announced in June 1888 by George Eastman of Rochester, N.Y. It weighed 22 ounces and had a lens fast enough to make instantaneous exposures. It used a roll of film of 100 exposures and took a round picture 2½ inches in diameter. It was covered by patent No. 388,850 dated September 4, 1888, and the name Kodak was registered on the same date.

Tintype camera was patented by Professor Hamilton Lamphere Smith, professor of natural sciences, Kenyon College, Gambier, Ohio, who obtained patent No. 14,300, on February 19, 1856, on "photographic pictures on japanned surfaces." The photographs were collodion positives on

The First

black or chocolate-colored iron plates. *(Rober Taft—Photography and the American Scene)*

CAMERA EXPOSURE METER. *See under* Pho tography

CAMERA EXPOSURE SCALE. *See* Photography Camera exposure scale

CAMOUFLAGE was undertaken as a scientifi study by Abbott Henderson Thayer, who pre sented a valuable treatise on protective colora tion entitled "The Law Which Underlie Protective Coloration," which appeared in th April 1896 issue of *The Auk,* an ornithologica journal, published in New York City.

CAMOUFLAGE COURSE. *See* Art course: Indus trial camouflage course

CAMP, ARMY. *See* Army camp

CAMP FIRE GIRLS organization was develope by Mrs. Luther Halsey Gulick at her camp at Lak Sebago, Maine. The name and ranks were sug gested by W. C. Langdon. The society, an organi zation for young girls, was made public March 17 1912. The watchword is "Wohelo," made from th first two letters of each of the words Work Health, and Love. *(Luther Halsey Gulick— Campfire Girls of America)*

CAMP FOR BOYS' outdoor recreation was Cam Comfort, Welch's Point, Milford, Conn., estab lished in August 1861, when Frederick Willian Gunn, founder of the Gunnery School, took 5 boys on a two-week camping trip. The camp wa organized again in August 1863 and in Augus 1865. In 1867 Gunn started another camp at Poin Beautiful on Lake Waramaug, Washington, Conn which was opened for a two-week period in Au gust for 12 successive years.

CAMP FOR CONSCIENTIOUS OBJECTORS. *Se* Conscientious objectors' camp

CAMP MEETING was held in 1803 by Jame M'Geary, William McGee (Presbyterian), an John McGee (Methodist) in a little log church o the Gaspar River in Logan County, Ky. *(G. W Gorham—Camp Meeting Manual)*

CAMPAIGN (political)
    Election campaign using radio. *See under* Radi Broadcast

    Political campaign telecast. *See under* Televi sion—Telecast

CAMPAIGN MEDAL. *See* Medal

CAMPAIGN (presidential) COMANAGE (WOMAN). *See* Woman: Woman presidentia campaign comanager

CANAL
    Canal was built around the falls of the Connect icut River at South Hadley Falls, Mass., in 1793. was chartered by "the Proprietors of the Uppe Locks and Canals on the Connecticut River in th

The First

County of Hampshire." The canal was two miles long and was opened to traffic in 1794. Benjamin Prescott was the engineer. Boats were run into movable cassons filled with water and were hauled by cables operated by water power. The canal had two levels connected by an incline, up and down which boats were raised or lowered in a tank of water and propelled by cables operated by water wheels. *(Alonzo Barton Hepburn—Artificial Waterways and Commercial Development)*

Canal for creating water power was dug by English settlers in 1639–1640 at Dedham, Mass., at Mill Creek, or Mother Brook as it is commonly called, and was used to run a mill. It conveyed water from the Charles River into the Neponset River. The order for the construction of the canal follows: "The 25th of ye 1 month, Commonly Called March. 1639. Assembled whose names are underwritten vizt. . . . Ordered y^t a Ditch shalbe made at a Common Charge through purchased Medowe vnto ye East Brooke. y^t may both be a ticon fence in ye same; as also may serve for a Course vnto a water mill." *(Early Records of the Town of Dedham, Mass. Dedham Historical Register. Vol. 6. No. 4)*

Canal of importance was the Erie Canal, which connected the waters of Lake Erie at Buffalo with the waters of the Hudson at Albany, N.Y. Lake Erie lies 550 feet above the level of tide water in the Hudson. The canal was 360 miles in length, 40 feet wide at the top and 28 feet wide at the bottom, and 4 feet deep. The canal was authorized on April 15, 1817, and construction started July 4, 1817. The first boat plied between Rome and Utica on October 22, 1819. The canal was opened for traffic on October 26, 1825. The original cost was approximately $9 million. *(Historical Catechism. 7th ed. Utica. 1835)*

Great Lakes to the Gulf waterway became an accomplished fact on June 21, 1933, upon arrival at Chicago, Ill., of the first tow from New Orleans, La. On June 1, 1933, the Federal Barge Line steamer *Vicksburg* with barges laden with coffee, sisal, and general merchandise left New Orleans, La. The tow was transferred to the *Hoover* at Memphis, Tenn.; to the *Sawyer* plying the Illinois River; and to the *Warner* at Ottawa, Ill., which brought it to Chicago. The completion of the Lakes to the Gulf Waterway was officially celebrated in Chicago, June 22, 1933.

St. Lawrence Seaway, 2,342 miles from the Atlantic Ocean to Duluth, Minn., was opened April 5, 1959. The first ship to enter the 400-mile system between Montreal and Lake Erie was the Canadian government ship *d'Iberville,* a 6,000-ton icebreaker; the first commercial ship was the *Simcoe* of the Canada Steamship Lines; the first oceangoing ship was the *Prins Willem George Frederik;* the first United States ship was the *Santa Regina*

The First

of the Grace Lines. The seaway was formally opened June 26, 1959, by Queen Elizabeth II and President Dwight David Eisenhower.

CANAL LOCKS made of concrete were built by the United States Government for the Illinois and Mississippi Canal (the Hennepin canal), which connected Lake Michigan at Chicago, Ill., with the Mississippi River, south of Rock Island, Ill. Excavation work commenced July 1892 and the first section, the Milan section, was opened to traffic on April 17, 1895. *(Illinois and Mississippi Canal: Annual Report of the Chief Engineer, 1908)*

CANCER CLINIC. *See* Medical clinic

CANCER HOSPITAL. *See* Hospital

CANCER LABORATORY, exclusively for the study of cancer, was the New York State Pathological Laboratory for the Study of Cancer established in May 1898 under a $10,000 appropriation made by the New York State legislature on April 29, 1898, Chapter 606, "for the faculty of the medical department of the University of Buffalo for the equipment and maintenance of a laboratory to be devoted to an investigation into the causes, nature, mortality rate and the treatment of cancer." Dr. Roswell Park was the first director and Dr. Harvey Russell Gaylord, associate. *(First Annual Report of the Director of the New York State Pathological Laboratory. 1899)*

CANCER RESEARCH FUND was the Collis P. Huntington Fund for cancer research established in 1902 by Mrs. Collis Potter Huntington. The fund, amounting to $100,000, was used by the New York Cancer Hospital, New York City. It enabled the hospital to administer X-ray treatments and install new equipment. *(Reports of the Collis P. Huntington Fund for Cancer Research of the General Memorial Hospital)*

CANDLE FACTORY for making spermaceti candles was established by Benjamin Crabb in Newport, R.I., in 1748. It was destroyed by fire in 1750.

CANE SUGAR. *See* Sugar

CANNING

See also Cans

Canning was introduced in 1819 by Ezra Daggett, and his nephew, Thomas Kensett, who canned salmon, oysters, and lobsters in New York City. On January 19, 1825, they obtained a patent to "preserve animal substances in tin." Cans were in use in 1825, but the real development of the canning industry did not start until after the Civil War. *(Henry Meech Loomis—The Canning of Foods)*

Salmon cannery was erected in 1864 at Washington, Yolo County, Calif., on the banks of the Sacramento River by Hapgood, Hume and Company. The firm consisted of Andrew S. Hapgood, George W. Hume, and William Hume. About 2,000 cases of salmon were canned the first year. Ap-

The First

CANNING—*Continued*

proximately 50 percent of the first production spoiled because the cans were not hermetically sealed. *(R. D. Hume—The Salmon of the Pacific Coast)*

Sardine cannery that was successful was established in 1876 in Eastport, Me., by Julius Wolff of Wolff and Reesing, New York City. The cans, as originally used, were made of three pieces, top, bottom, and side, which were soldered together. *(Frederick Clarence Weber—The Maine Sardine Industry. U.S. Department of Agriculture, Bulletin No. 908)*

CANNING BOOK was a translation of François Appert's *L'Art de Conserver, pendant plusieurs années, toutes les substances animales et végétales,* published in 1812 by [David] Longworth, New York City.

CANNON. *See* Ordnance: Cannon (breech-loading)

CANNON IN A FIGHTER AIRPLANE. *See* Aviation—Airplane: Fighter airplane carrying a cannon

CANOE ASSOCIATION was the American Canoe Association, formed August 3, 1880, by 25 canoeists at Crosbyside Park, Lake George, N.Y. The first commodore was William Livingston Alden and the first secretary Nathaniel Holmes Bishop. *(American Canoe Association Yearbook, 1895)*

CANOE CLUB was the New York Canoe Club founded in New York City in 1870. A clubhouse was built in 1879, during which year a regatta was held. The club was dissolved August 3, 1880. *(C. Bowyer Vaux—Canoe Handling)*

CANONIZATION

See also Saint (Catholic)

Canonization of a saint in the United States occurred November 1, 1964, when the Russian Orthodox Church Outside of Russia canonized the Reverend John Sergiev, known as Father John of Cronstadt, in a ceremony in the Cathedral of Our Lady of the Sign, New York City. The canonization ceremony was presided over by Metropolitan Philaret, primate of the Russian Orthodox Church Outside of Russia. (Father John died in 1909 at the age of 80.)

Canonization of North Americans took place in a three-day celebration commencing June 30, 1930. Each of those canonized was credited with having performed two miracles and having met a heroic death. The laymen were René Goupil and John Lalande. The Jesuit priests were Isaac Jogues, John De Brébeuf, Noel Chabanel, Anthony Daniel, Gabriel Lalemant, and Charles Garnier. The Pontifical Mass was celebrated at the Vatican by Archbishop Forbes of Ottawa, Canada.

The First

CANS

Beer in cans for retail sale was packed by the Krueger Brewing Company at Newark, N.J., and placed on sale in Richmond, Va., on January 24 1935.

Can (tin) with a key opener was invented by J. Osterhoudt of New York City who obtained patent No. 58,554 on October 2, 1866, for an "improved method of opening tin cans." The can had a projecting lip and key.

Disposable can for dispensing liquids unde pressure was invented by Julian Seth Kahn o New York City who received U.S. patent No. 2, 170,531 on August 22, 1939, for an "apparatus fo mixing a liquid with gas." Under controlled pres sure, with an inexpensive disposable valve mech anism, it dispensed such items as whipped cream paints, pharmaceuticals, and insecticides.

CANTALOUPE. *See* Melons

CANTILEVER BRIDGE. *See* Bridge

CANTOR

Jewish woman cantor was Betty Robbins (Mrs Sheldon Robbins) of Massapequa, Long Island N.Y., whose first service was sung on Septembe 15, 1955, the eve of Rosh Hashanah, the Jewisl New Year, at Temple Avodah, Oceanside, L.I N.Y.

School for cantors was the Hebrew Unio School of Education and Sacred Music, New Yorl City, which opened October 16, 1948. Cantor educator diplomas were awarded June 17, 1951, t the graduating class of ten men.

CAPITAL PUNISHMENT

See also Execution

Capital punishment authorized by federal lav made the killing of a federal officer a mandator capital offense. The law was enacted May 18, 193 (48 Stat. L. 780), and the first case to be tried wa that of *United States vs. John Paul Chase.* O March 25, 1935, Chase was convicted of first-de gree murder for the killing of Samuel Cowley, De partment of Justice agent, on November 27, 1934 in Barrington, Ill. Judge Philip Sullivan sentence Chase to life imprisonment on March 28, 1935, a the jury did not recommend the death penalt since he was not the principal in the matter. Th first execution was that of George W. Barrett, fc the murder of federal agent Nelson Bernard Klei in College Corner, Ind., on August 16, 1935. H was tried before U.S. District Judge Robert C. Bal zell, convicted December 14, 1935, and hange March 24, 1936, at the Marion County Jail, I dianapolis, Ind.

Death penalty was first abolished by Michiga law, enacted May 4, 1846, effective March 1, 184

The First

The gallows were still retained, however, for treason against the state. On April 22, 1794, Pennsylvania had abolished the death penalty except for murder in the first degree. *(Michigan History Magazine. Vol. 29, No. 1)*

Lethal-drug executions authorized were provided for by Chapter 41, enacted May 10, 1977, by the state of Oklahoma: "the punishment of death must be inflicted by continuous, intravenous administration of a lethal quantity of an ultrashort-acting barbiturate in combination with a chemical paralytic agent until death is pronounced by a licensed physician according to accepted standards of medical practice."

Woman judge to sentence a man to death. *See under* Judge

CAPITOL (state)

Capitol was a statehouse on Duke of Gloucester Street, Williamsburg, Va., in which the General Assembly met. The building was erected in 1698 by Governor Francis Nicholson, who was the first person to apply the term "capitol" to a government building.

CAPITOL (U.S.)

American flag made of American bunting to fly over the Capitol, Washington, D.C. *See under* Flag

Body to lie in state in the Capitol rotunda was Senator Henry Clay who died in Washington, D.C., at the age of 75 on June 29, 1852. His body was placed in the rotunda, where it was displayed July 1, 1852, prior to interment in Lexington Cemetery, Lexington, Ky.

Capitol (of the United States) was designed by Dr. William Thornton, whose plan was accepted as the most suitable one submitted in a national contest. On July 16, 1790, the site for the Capitol was chosen, and on January 24, 1791, George Washington directed a survey for the Capitol. The cornerstone of the Capitol was laid in Washington, D.C., on September 18, 1793. George Washington delivered an oration and the Grand Master of the Maryland Masons an appropriate address. After the laying of the cornerstone, the assembly retired to an extensive booth to enjoy a barbecue feast. George Washington laid the cornerstone on the southeast corner of the central (oldest) section. The central section is of Virginia sandstone painted white to make it harmonize with the Massachusetts marble of the two wings. *(Rufus Rockwell Wilson—Washington, the Capitol City)*

President's body to lie in state in the Capitol rotunda was Abraham Lincoln, whose body was placed on a catafalque where it was on view April 19-21, 1865. President Lincoln was shot April 14, 1865, and died the following day; interment was in Oak Ridge Cemetery, Springfield, Ill.

CAPTAIN. *See* Naval officer

The First

CAR. *See* Automobile; Railroad car; Streetcar

CARBIDE BORON. *See* Abrasive

CARBIDE FACTORY to manufacture commercial quantities of carbide was established in 1894 by Thomas Leopold Willson in Spray, N.C. He obtained United States patents No. 541,137 and No. 541,138 on June 18, 1895, on carbide (calcium carbide), a compound of calcium and carbide. He produced it by fusing calcium or lime with coke at a very high temperature. *(The Story of Carbide—National Carbide Sales Corp.)*

CARBIDE GAS. *See* Acetylene

CARBON MICROPHONE. *See* Radio microphone (carbon)

CARBON MONOXIDE BOILER. *See* Boiler

CARBON TETRACHLORIDE (CCl_4) was manufactured by Charles Ernest Acker who introduced his process in 1908. He also invented the Acker process of manufacturing caustic soda by the electrolysis of molten salt in 1896, for which he received the Elliott Cresson Gold Medal of the Franklin Institute in 1902. He was also the first to produce carbon and tin tetrachloride on a commercial scale.

CARBORUNDUM, a trademarked abrasive, to be used in place of emery, corundum, and other similar materials, was invented by Edward Goodrich Acheson in 1891 in Monongahela City, Pa. By running a current of electricity through a mixture of silica and carbon, he obtained a material hard enough for rough-polishing diamonds, rubies, sapphires, and other precious and semiprecious stones. He obtained patent No. 492,767 February 28, 1893, on the production of artificial crystalline carbonaceous materials. The first sale of this material was 10 carats at the rate of 40 cents a carat or $880 a pound. *(The Story of Carborundum—The Carborundum Co.)*

CARD, POSTAL. *See* Postal card

CARD TIME RECORDER. *See* Time recorder

CARDINAL (Catholic). *See* Catholic priest; Catholic priest to be elevated to the cardinalate

CARDING MACHINE. *See* Spinning, carding, and roping machines

CARDS, CHRISTMAS. *See* Christmas cards

CARGO SHIP. *See* Ship

CARGO SUBMARINE. *See* Submarine

CARGO VESSEL. *See* Ship

CARICATURE was Nathaniel Hurd's "The True Profile of the Notorious Doctor Seth Hudson," published in 1762 in Boston, Mass. It depicted Dr. Hudson in pillory and Howe, his assistant, at the whipping post, in punishment for forging the prov-

The First

inces' paper money. *(William Murrell—A History of American Graphic Humor)*
   See also Cartoon

CARILLON
   Carillon was installed in the belfry of the Old North Church (now Christ Church), Boston, Mass., in 1745. Eight bells were ordered in 1744 from Abell Rudhall's foundry, Gloucester, England, by Thomas Gunther, who put up a bond to guarantee payment. They were shipped on the *Two Friends* on March 9, 1745, the total cost being £560, 4 shillings, 10 pence. *(New England Historical and Genealogical Register. Vol. 58. 1904)*

   Carillon (modern) was installed in the Church of Our Lady of Good Voyage, Gloucester, Mass., and blessed by His Eminence Cardinal O'Connell on July 2, 1922. The bells and apparatus, weighing 28,000 pounds, were made and installed by John Taylor & Co., Loughborough, England, and consisted of 31 bells, the largest weighing 2,826 pounds. They were played for the first time by carillonneur George B. Stevens. *(William Gorham Rice—Carillon Music and Singing Towers of the Old World and the New)*

CARNEGIE HERO FUND COMMISSION was established on March 12, 1904, by Andrew Carnegie, who transferred to the Commission $5 million of first collateral 5 percent bonds of the United States Steel Corporation. The bylaws were adopted May 20, 1904, in Pittsburgh, Pa. The first award was a bronze medal that was presented to Louis A. Baumann, Jr., 17, a laborer, who saved Charles Stevick, 16, also a laborer, from drowning, near Wilkinsburg, Pa., July 17, 1904. Baumann dived into Sulphur Pond in water ten feet deep, and after three attempts, rescued Stevick, who was panic-stricken. In the first year, 248 cases were considered, and 3 silver and 6 bronze medals awarded.

CARPET FACTORY
   Carpet mill was founded in 1791 by William Peter Sprague in North Second Street, Philadelphia, Pa. He manufactured Axminster carpets on handlooms, and one of his earliest designs represented the aims and achievements of the new republic of the United States.

   Carpet mill to make ingrain carpets was established in 1810 by George M. Conradt in Frederick, Md. The carpets were produced on handlooms on a drum having rows of pegs, and were of two- or three-ply, the warp being worsted or cotton with a wool filling.

CARPET LOOM
   Carpet power loom was invented by Erastus Brigham Bigelow of West Boylston, Mass., who obtained patent No. 169 on April 20, 1837. It was employed by the Lowell Manufacturing Company of Lowell, Mass., in the weaving of carpets.

   Carpet power loom to weave Axminster carpets was invented in 1876 by Halcyon Skinner, em-

The First

ployed by the Alexander Smith & Sons Carpet Company of Yonkers, N.Y. Axminster carpets have a fluffy, thick pile with a linen or hemp warp and chenille filling. Skinner obtained patent No. 186,374 on January 16, 1877, jointly with Alexander Smith.

   Carpet power loom to weave ingrain carpets was used by the Lowell Manufacturing Company of Lowell, Mass. In 1841 the company adopted the power machinery invented by Erastus Brigham Bigelow, and within two years hundreds of the machines were in operation.

CARPET SWEEPER that was practical was invented in 1876 by Melville Reuben Bissell of Grand Rapids, Mich., who obtained patent No. 182,346 September 19, 1876. Although the idea had been introduced earlier, no practical sweeper was invented until he devised the "broom-action" principle by which, through variable pressure on the handle, a sweeper could be made responsive to the different grades of floor coverings. Bissell organized the Bissell Carpet Sweeper Company in Grand Rapids, Mich.

CARPETING
   Carpeting of tufted plastic was manufactured at La Fayette, Ga., by the E. T. Barwick Mills and offered for sale January 4, 1953, for April 1, 1953, delivery. The carpeting, made of Saran fibers, is immune to moths, mildew, and fungi and is almost completely resistant to ink and other stains. It will soften, char, and decompose in flame, but will not support combustion.

   Carpeting (velvet) and tapestry were manufactured in Newark, N.J., in 1855 by John Johnson.

CARRIAGE, BABY. *See* Baby carriage

CARRIAGE LAP ROBE. *See* Blanket: Blanket robe and carriage lap robe business

CARRIER, AIRCRAFT. *See* Ship

CARRIER (commercial electric power line). *See* Electric transmission: Electric power line commercial carrier

CARRIER SYSTEM. *See* Cash carrier system

CARROUSEL
   Carrousel patent was No.117,336, granted on July 25, 1871, to Willhelm Schneider of Davenport Iowa. It was a two-story carrousel and not very successful or practical.

   Carrousel with the jumping horse mechanism was invented by Charles Wallace Parker of the C W. Parker Amusement Company, Leavenworth Kan. He started manufacturing it in 1896 and completed it in April 1898 in Abilene, Kans. The first one was sold to his brother, William T. Parker.

   Portable carrousel was a "Carry-Us-All" manufactured in 1896 in Abilene, Kans., by the C. W. Parker Amusement Company. It weighed 20 tons and consisted of 16 sections.

he First

ARTEL. See Trust

ARTOON
See also Caricature

Cartoon awarded a Pulitzer prize was "On the oad to Moscow," by Rollin Kirby, which appeared August 5, 1921, in the New York *World.* he award of the $500 prize was announced on 1ay 21, 1922.

Democratic cartoon, in which the emblem of the arty was represented as a donkey appeared in *arper's Weekly,* New York City, January 15, 370. The drawing, by Thomas Nast, was entitled A Live Jackass Kicking a Dead Lion." The jackss was tagged "Copperhead papers" and the ead lion represented Edwin McMasters Stanton, incoln's Secretary of War. The background 1owed an eagle perched on a rock and in the far ackground the United States Capitol. *(Albert igelow Paine—"Th. Nast")*

Newspaper cartoon was "Join or Die" designed y Benjamin Franklin and published in Philaelphia, Pa., in his newspaper, the *Pennsylvania azette,* on May 9, 1754. It was printed in the first olumn of the second page and was 2⅞ by 2 inchs. It depicted a snake cut up into segments, each epresenting a colony. *(James Melvin Lee—Hisry of American Journalism)*

Newspaper cartoon strip was published September 11, 1875, in the New York *Daily Graphic* nd showed 17 successive pictures on one full age. It was entitled "Professor Tigwissel's Burar Alarm."

Newspaper Sunday comic section. *See under* ewspaper

Republican cartoon, in which the emblem of the arty was represented as an elephant, appeared Harper's Weekly,* New York City, November 7, 374. The drawing by Thomas Nast was entitled The Third-Term Panic" and referred to the possility that Grant might seek a third term. It depictd an ass labeled "N.Y. Herald" in a lion's skin beled "Caesarism," frightening numerous timid nimals labeled "N.Y. Times," "N.Y. Trib.," etc., hile a berserk elephant, labeled "Republican ote," about to fall into "Chaos," tossed platform lanks to right and left. The quotation, "An Ass aving put on the Lion's skin, roamed about the orest, and amused himself by frightening all the olish Animals he met with in his wanderings," ccompanied the title.

Uncle Sam cartoon appeared in the New York antern, a comic weekly, on March 13, 1852. It as called "Raising the Wind" and depicted the ruggle between a United States shipowner and e Cunard Company, with John Bull actively elping his line while Uncle Sam was an onlooker. he cartoonist was Frank Henry Temple Bellew. he original "Uncle Sam" was Samuel Wilson of ew Hampshire, who was the official inspector in

The First

Troy, N.Y., of provisions purchased for the United States troops in the War of 1812. All shipments as inspected were branded "U.S." by Wilson, whose nickname was "Uncle Sam." The coincidence of initials suggested the application of the nickname to the government.

CARTOON ELECTRIC SIGN. *See* Electric sign: Animated-cartoon electric sign

CARTOON SCHOOL giving courses in the production of animated cartoons was the Hastings School of Animation, New York City, organized February 1938. Instruction began April 1938.

CARTRIDGE. *See* Ordnance

CARTRIDGE BELT patent was No. 67,898 granted on August 20, 1867, to Anson Mills, Brevet Lieutenant Colonel, U.S. Army, Fort Bridger, Utah. Moisture had previously affected the cartridge belts. Mills invented a woven cartridge belt, and the machinery for making it, which was adopted by both the Army and Navy. *(Anson Mills—My Story)*

CARTRIDGE-LOADING MACHINE. *See* Ordnance: Cartridge-loading machinery

CASEIN FIBER was produced December 1935 by Earle Ovando Whittier and Stephen Philip Gould of Washington, D.C., who obtained patent No. 2,-140,274 on December 13, 1938, and dedicated it "to the free use of the people of the United States of America."

CASH CARRIER SYSTEM was invented by David Brown of Lebanon, N.J., who obtained patent No. 165,473 on July 13, 1875, on "an apparatus for transmission of goods, packages, etc." It had a wire rail with endless rope pulleys. William Stickney Lamson installed it in his ladies' furnishing store in Lowell, Mass., in February 1879. By means of two overhead wires, a small basket was conveyed from the salesman to the cashier. In the spring of 1881, he organized the Lamson Consolidated Store Service Company to manufacture these carriers for others and in January 1882 incorporated the Lamson Cash Railway Company. *(Frank Pierce Hill—Lowell Illustrated)*

CASH REGISTER was invented in 1879 by James J. (Jake) Ritty, a businessman of Dayton, Ohio, who while on a trip to Europe observed the workings of a recording device on the steamship which marked the revolutions of the ship's propeller and gave to its officers each day a complete and accurate record of the speed of the boat. He returned to the United States and invented a machine for registering receipts of cash and totaling them. He manufactured the machine in Dayton, but it was not accurate, and in the following year, 1880, he produced a machine that gave some evidence of being practical. James Ritty and John Ritty of Dayton obtained patent No. 221,360 on a "cash regis-

The First

CASH REGISTER—*Continued*

ter and indicator" on November 4, 1879. In 1884 the National Cash Register Company took over the business, which in five years' time had gone through three changes, and developed from a plant with 20 workmen to an organization with a staff of more than 15,000 persons. *(Brief History of the Cash Register—National Cash Register Co.)*

CAST-IRON BRIDGE. *See* Bridge

CAST-IRON BUILDING. *See* Building

CAST-IRON PIPES (city waterworks). *See* Iron: Cast-iron pipes used in a city waterworks system

CAST STEEL. *See* Steel

CASTER for furniture was patented by Philos Blake, Eli Whitney Blake, and John A. Blake, of New Haven, Conn. They were awarded patent No. 821 on June 30, 1838, on a "mode of constructing casters and applying them to bedsteads."

CAT SHOW

Cat Show was held at Madison Square Garden, New York City, from May 8, 1895, through May 11, 1895. Over 200 cats were exhibited in cages. The owners could take their cats home overnight upon payment of a $5 bond guaranteeing they would be brought back the following day. Prizes and money were awarded for each class—for example, the best litter of kittens, the best homeless cat. Caesar won the Angora class; Mete won the best short-haired tiger-marked class.

CATALOG, AUTOMOBILE. *See* Automobile catalog

CATALOG, FRATERNITY. *See* Fraternity catalog

CATALOG, STAMP. *See* Postage stamp catalog

CATALOG OF THE LIBRARY OF CONGRESS. *See under* Library catalog

CATALYTIC CRACKING PROCESS. *See* Gasoline: Aviation gasoline

CATAMARAN, a jointed boat, used principally by lifeguards at public beaches, was patented by Nathanael Greene Herreshoff of Providence, R.I., who received patent No. 189,459 on April 10, 1877, on two parallel hulls.

CATAPULTED AIRPLANE. *See* Aviation—Flights: Airplane catapulted

CATCHER'S MASK. *See* Baseball catcher's mask

CATERPILLAR CLUB

Caterpillar Club member was John Boettner, pilot of the *Wing Foot* balloon of the Goodyear Tire and Rubber Company, Akron, Ohio, who parachuted 1,200 feet to safety on July 21, 1919, while his balloon crashed into a building at La Salle Street and Jackson Boulevard, Chicago, Ill.

The First

The crash resulted in the death of 3 persons an injuries to 28. "Caterpillar Club" is a name use to designate those persons whose lives have bee saved by parachute jumps from aircraft in di tress. *(Office of the Chief of the Air Corps—Roste of the Caterpillar Club)*

Father and son Caterpillar Club members wer Paul Fisk Collins, who jumped November 19, 192 north of Brookville, Pa.; and Lieutenant Paul Lisk Collins, who jumped on February 11, 1944, 5 miles south of Fairbanks, Alaska.

Woman Caterpillar Club member was Mr Irene McFarland, who jumped from her plane Jur 28, 1925, over Grissard Field, Cincinnati, Ohi She tested a parachute that was packed in a co tainer fastened to the plane, so that when sh jumped her weight would cause the container break and permit the parachute to slip and blo out. Officials also required her to use an arm parachute. She jumped and her parachu jammed, suspending her under the fuselage, fro which she swung like a pendulum. She could n release herself and Lieutenant Watson, her pilc could not land. He motioned to her to release th army parachute, which she did, the force breakir the cords that held her tied to the airplane. Ha the original parachute worked, Mrs. McFarlan would not have been eligible for membership the Caterpillar Club.

CATGUT

Catgut substitute for medical use was Dexon, polyglycolic acid suture, a virtually nonirritati synthetic absorbable, produced in April 1966 t the Davis & Geck department of Lederle Laborat ries, Pearl River, N.Y., a division of the America Cyanamid Company. Work began in January 19 at Cyanamid's Central Research Laboratory Stamford, Conn.

CATHEDRAL

Armenian cathedral. *See* Armenian cathedra

Cathedral was the Cathedral of the Assumptie of the Blessed Virgin Mary, in Baltimore, Md., primatial see of the Catholic Church. The corne stone was laid July 7, 1806, and the building w dedicated May 31, 1821, by Archbishop Ambro Marechal. It was completed in 1851. In 1936, t Baltimore Cathedral was raised to the rank of minor basilica by Pope Pius XI. The first dioce (of Baltimore) was created by Pope Pius VI November 6, 1789.

Episcopal cathedral was the Cathedral of O Merciful Saviour, Faribault, Minn., built by tl Right Reverend Henry Benjamin Whipple, Fir Bishop of Minnesota, as his own church. Th cathedral was begun in 1862 and completed 1869 at a cost of $100,000. A tower was added 1902.

Serbian Orthodox cathedral. *See* Serbian C thodox cathedral

The First

CATHOLIC APOSTOLIC DELEGATE (permanent) was Monsignor Francesco Satolli, representative of Pope Leo XIII, who arrived January 24, 1893, in Washington, D.C. He was created Cardinal November 29, 1895, with the title of Santa Maria in Ara Coeli. *(Catholic University Bulletin. Vol. 16, No. 2. Feb. 1910)*

CATHOLIC BEATIFICATION
See also Saint (Catholic)

Catholic beatification of an American-born woman was of Elizabeth Ann Bayley Seton, who was beatified March 17, 1963, at the Vatican, Rome, by Pope John XXIII. She was born in New York City August 28, 1774, and died January 4, 1821, in Emmitsburg, Md. She was an Episcopalian, mother of five children, and a convert to Roman Catholicism in 1805. She was canonized September 14, 1975.

Catholic beatification of an American citizen (female) took place at St. Peter's Basilica, Rome, Italy, November 13, 1938, when Mother Frances Xavier Cabrini, founder of the Institute of the Missionary Sisters of the Sacred Heart, was beatified.

Catholic beatification of an American citizen (male) took place October 12, 1963, in St. Peter's Basilica, Rome, when Pope Paul VI proclaimed that John Nepomucene Neumann was Blessed. Neumann came to the United States from Bohemia in 1836, was ordained in St. Patrick's Cathedral, Mott Street, New York City, on January 25, 1836, and became a citizen of the United States in 1848. He became the fourth bishop of Philadelphia in 1852 and died in 1860. On June 19, 1977, he was canonized in Rome by Pope Paul VI. *See also* Saint (Catholic): American saint (male).

Catholic beatification of an American Indian took place on May 9, 1939, when the Cardinals of the Congregation of Rites in Rome, Italy, recommended the beatification of Kateri Tekakwitha, the "lily of the Mohawks," who was born in 1656 at Ossernenon, near Auriesville, N.Y. Their decision was sanctioned by Pope Pius XII on May 19, 1939.

CATHOLIC BIBLE. *See under* Bible

CATHOLIC BISHOP
See also Catholic priest

Black Catholic bishop who was American born was the Very Reverend Bishop Harold Robert Perry of Lake Charles, La., named auxiliary bishop of the Archdiocese of New Orleans. He was named on October 2, 1965, by Pope Paul VI to serve as auxiliary to the archbishop of New Orleans and consecrated in the Basilica of St. Louis, New Orleans, La., on January 6, 1966. He was the pastor of the New Orleans Parish of St. Theresa of the Child of Jesus, Society of the Divine Word.

Catholic bishop to exercise episcopal functions was Frai Juan Cabezas de Altamirano, son of Juan

The First

Cabezas and Doña Ana Calzado, appointed Bishop of Santiago de Cuba in 1603. He visited the Provinces of Florida in 1607 and at St. Augustine administered the sacrament of confirmation to many Spaniards and converted Indians.

Catholic bishop appointed to serve in the United States was the Right Reverend John Carroll, "Superior of the Missions in the thirteen United States of North America." A petition for appointment of a bishop was sent to Pope Pius VI on March 12, 1788, and was acted upon favorably June 23, 1788. Bishop Carroll received 24 of the 25 votes, and the result was confirmed by the Pope on November 6, 1789. The Right Reverend Charles Walmesley (Bishop of Rama and Vicar Apostolic of the Western District, England), consecrated John Carroll bishop August 15, 1790, in the chapel of Lulworth Castle, Dorset, England. On April 8, 1808, he became an archbishop. *(An Account of the Consecration by One Bishop of the First Romish Bishop in the United States)*

Catholic bishop (black) was Bishop James Augustine Healy, consecrated June 21, 1875, as Bishop of Portland, Me., with jurisdiction over Maine and New Hampshire. He was ordained a priest in 1854 in Paris, and was assigned to St. James' Church (white), Boston, Mass., in 1866. Bishop Healy was not known as a black. His father was an Irish immigrant and his mother a mulatto slave.

Catholic bishop (black) consecrated in the United States was Bishop Joseph Oliver Bowers, consecrated on April 22, 1953, by Francis Cardinal Spellman at the Church of Our Lady of the Gulf, Bay St. Louis, Miss.

Catholic bishop consecrated in present U.S. limits was Leonard Neale, who was consecrated bishop of Gortyna (Crete) in the procathedral of St. Peter's in Baltimore, Md., on December 7, 1800.

Catholic bishop of a diocese within the present territorial limits of the United States was Fray Suárez, a Franciscan, who was nominated bishop of Florida and Rio de las Palmas under the Bull of Julius II, the Catholic pope. He did not receive episcopal consecration. He reached Florida on Holy Thursday, April 14, 1528, arriving with Pánfilo de Narváez. *(The Catholic Historical Review. Vol. 4. 1919—Rev. Juan Juarez, O.F.M.—Florida's First Bishop)*

Native bishops of the South were the Right Reverend Domenic Manucy, Bishop of Mobile, and his cousin Anthony Domenic Ambrose Pellicier, Bishop of San Antonio, who were ordained August 15, 1850, in Mobile, Ala. They were born in St. Augustine and educated at Spring Hill College, Ala. *(Francis Xavier Reuss—Biographical Cyclopedia of the Catholic Hierarchy)*

CATHOLIC CHAPLAIN (U.S. Army). *See* Army officer: Chaplain (Catholic)

CATHOLIC CHURCH

Catholic church raised to the dignity of a basilica was the Sanctuary of Our Lady of Victory, Lackawanna, in the Diocese of Buffalo, N.Y. It was dedicated and consecrated on May 25, 1926, as Our Lady of Victory Shrine, and on July 28 by Apostolic Decree of Pope Pius XI it was dignified with the title of "Basilica of Our Blessed Lady of Victory."

Catholic eucharistic international congress in the United States was the 28th congress held in Chicago, Ill., on June 20, 1926, adjourning June 24th to Mundelein, Ill.

Catholic parish church for blacks was St. Francis Xavier's, Baltimore, Md., purchased October 10, 1863, and dedicated February 21, 1864.

Eucharistic Congress of the Catholic Church began October 2, 1895, at St. Patrick's Church, Washington, D.C., and transferred to Catholic University the following day. The celebrant of the mass was Monsignor Francesco Satolli, the Apostolic Delegate. The priests passed resolutions favoring strict Sunday observance.

CATHOLIC COLLEGE. *See* College

CATHOLIC CONVENT. *See* Convent

CATHOLIC DIOCESE was the Diocese of Baltimore, Md., established April 6, 1789, and raised to the dignity of the first Archdiocese in the United States, April 8, 1808. By a decree of the Sacred Congregation of the Propaganda, July 19, approved by Pius IX, July 5, 1858, prerogative of place was conferred on the Archdiocese of Baltimore, so that it is known as the Premier See of the country.

CATHOLIC FUNERAL

Catholic funeral attended by the U.S. Continental Congress was that of Philippe Charles Jean Baptiste Tronson du Coudray, French officer. On September 15, 1777, while crossing the Schuykill River at Middle Ferry on a ferry to join Washington's army, his horse became frightened and plunged overboard. Tronson du Coudray, who had assumed the post of inspector general of the American Army, was drowned. Congress resolved that he should be buried with military honors and that the members of Congress should attend his funeral, which was held in Philadelphia, Pa., September 17, 1777. *(John Thomas Scharf and Thompson Wescott—History of Philadelphia)*

CATHOLIC HOLY ORDERS were conferred by Don Gabriel Díaz Vara Calderón, Bishop of Santiago de Cuba, on a visit to St. Augustine, Fla., August 24, 1675. Minor orders were conferred on seven candidates.

CATHOLIC MAGAZINE. *See* Catholic periodic▮

CATHOLIC MASS

Catholic mass was celebrated June 1526 in th▮ present territory of the United States by th▮ Dominican Fathers Antonio Montesino and A▮ tonio de Cervantes, for the several hundred col▮ nists under the leadership of Lucas Vásquez d▮ Ayllón on the Atlantic coast. Masses may als▮ have been said for the earlier Norse explorers.

Catholic mass for night workers was held Ma▮ 5, 1901, at the Church of St. Andrew, New Yor▮ City. Father Luke J. Evers obtained special pe▮ mission from the Pope to institute this service, a▮ church law did not permit mass before sunrise.▮

Catholic mass in an airship over the ocean wa▮ conducted in the Zeppelin *Hindenburg* May ▮ 1936, the Feast of the Apparition of St. Michael th▮ Archangel, by Father Paul Schulte of the Oblate▮ of Mary Immaculate.

Catholic mass in an airship over the ocean by a▮ American priest was conducted in the Zeppeli▮ *Hindenburg* on August 6, 1936, by Father Jame▮ Renshaw Cox of St. Patrick's Church, Pittsburg▮ Pa.

Catholic mass in English (full English mass▮ was celebrated August 24, 1964, in Kiel Auditor▮ um, St. Louis, Mo., by Rev. Frederick Richar▮ McManus of the Catholic University of Americ▮ The Gloria, most of the responses, the Creed, an▮ the Agnus Dei (Lamb of God) prayer were i▮ English. Joseph Elmer Cardinal Ritter, the Arc▮ bishop of St. Louis, authorized the celebration t▮ mark the 25th annual Liturgical Week, attende▮ by about 11,000 bishops, priests, nuns, and la▮ men.

Catholic mass in English said for a Presiden▮ was the memorial mass for President John Fitz▮ gerald Kennedy at Holy Cross Cathedral, Bosto▮ Mass., on Sunday, November 22, 1964. Richar▮ Cardinal Cushing was the celebrant.

Catholic mass (midnight) telecast. *See* und▮ Television—Telecast

CATHOLIC NUNS

See also Convent

Catholic nuns (black community) were th▮ Oblate Sisters of Providence, founded by Jacque▮ Hector Nicholas Joubert de la Muraille on July ▮ 1829, in Baltimore, Md. Pope Gregory XVI ap▮ proved the order October 2, 1831.

Catholic nuns (cloistered community) were th▮ Magdalen Sisters at the Convent of the Goo▮ Shepherd, Baltimore, Md., founded April 24, 192▮

Nun in the Air Force Reserve. *See* Air For▮ Officer: Nun in the Air Force Reserve

Nun who professed her vows in the Unite▮ States was Sister St. Stanislas Hachard of th▮ Ursuline Convent, New Orleans, La., who took h▮

he First

oly vows March 15, 1729. *(The Ursulines in New Orleans and Our Lady of Prompt Succor)*

Nun who was born in the United States was Mary Turpin of Illinois, born in 1731, who entered the Ursuline Convent, New Orleans, La., in 1748. She began her novitiate July 2, 1749, and made her profession of faith January 31, 1752. She died November 20, 1761, at the age of 30.

CATHOLIC PARISH was the parish of St. Augustine, Fla., founded September 8, 1565, on the day of the Feast of the Nativity of the Blessed Virgin, by Don Pedro Menéndez de Avilés. The first parish register is also owned by this church and consists of 15 volumes beginning January 1, 1594, and continuing down to the time of the British occupation of Florida in 1763. The first parish priest was Don Martin Francisco López de Mendozo Grajales.

CATHOLIC PERIODICAL
Catholic magazine was the weekly journal *Courier de Boston*, which appeared on April 23, 1789, and continued publication weekly for six months. It was published in French in Boston, Mass., and was edited by Paul Joseph Guérard de Nancrède, instructor in French at Harvard University. *(Apollinaris William Baumgartner—Catholic Journalism)*

Catholic magazine in English was the *Michigan Essay or Impartial Observer*, a weekly, which was issued August 31, 1809. It was printed and published in Detroit, Mich., by James M. Miller and was only semi-Catholic in scope. The idea was advocated by the Reverend Gabriel Richard of Detroit. The weekly consisted of 4 pages, 9¼ by 16 inches, of which a small part was printed in French. The rates were $5 a year for subscribers living in the city; $4.50 in upper Canada; and $4 elsewhere. *(Paul J. Folk—Pioneer Catholic Journalism)*

CATHOLIC PRESIDENT. *See* President (U. S.): President who was a Catholic

CATHOLIC PRESIDENTIAL NOMINEE. *See* Presidential candidate: Presidential candidate who was a Catholic

CATHOLIC PRIEST
See also Catholic bishop

Black Catholic priest ordained to work in the United States was the Reverend Augustus Tolton. He was ordained at the College of Propaganda, Rome, Italy, on April 24, 1886, and opened a mission in Quincy, Ill., in the Diocese of Springfield (Ill.) *(John Thomas Gillard—The Catholic Church and the American Negro)*

Black Catholic priest ordained in the United States was Charles Randolph Uncles, who was ordained in the Baltimore Cathedral, Baltimore, Md., December 19, 1891, by Cardinal Gibbons.

The First

Catholic cardinal whose see was west of the Rockies was James Francis Cardinal McIntyre, Archbishop of Los Angeles, who was elevated to the Sacred College of Cardinals on January 12, 1953, by Pope Pius XII.

Catholic priest called to the Sacred Roman Rota, the Vatican Court of Appeals, from diocesan tribunals was Francis (James) Cardinal Brennan of Philadelphia, Pa., appointed August 1, 1940. He arrived in Rome, on November 5, 1940; was received by Pope Pius XII in private audience; and took his oath of office on November 18, 1940. Brennan served as judge until 1959 when, as senior member of the court, he became dean when a vacancy occurred. The Sacred Roman Rota is the church's court of appeals for matrimonial and some other cases.

Catholic priest ordained in the United States was Father Stephen Theodore Badin, ordained May 25, 1793, by Bishop John Carroll in Baltimore, Md. He was appointed to the Mission of Kentucky and held his first mass in Kentucky on the first Sunday of Advent, 1793, in the house of Dennis McCarthy in Lexington, Ky. *(Benedict Joseph Webb—Centenary of Catholicity in Kentucky)*

Catholic priest to be elevated to the cardinalate was John McCloskey who was preconized cardinal by Pope Pius IX in the Consistory of March 15, 1875. The investiture was made in the cathedral on Mott Street, New York City, on April 27, 1875. He was made a cardinal under the title of Santa Maria supra Minervam. *(John Murphy Farley—The Life of John, cardinal McCloskey, First Prince of the Church in America 1810–1885)*

Catholic priest to receive his full theological training in the United States was Demetrius Augustine Gallitzin (Dimitri Augustin Golitzyn) who was ordained a Catholic Bishop by Bishop John Carroll on March 18, 1795, in Baltimore, Md. *(Sarah M. Brownson—Life of Demetrius Augustine Gallitzin)*

Deacon (married) ordained was Rev. Michael George Cole, who was ordained June 1, 1969, by the Most Reverend Archbishop Fulton John Sheen at St. Augustine's Church, Rochester, N.Y., to officiate in the Roman Catholic diocese of Rochester, N.Y. at baptisms, weddings, funerals; to distribute holy communion; and to teach and preach; but not to say Mass. He was a former Anglican priest from England and director of the Family Life Bureau in the Rochester diocese. He left the Roman Catholic Diocese in April 1970 and became curate of St. Wilfrids' Anglican Church in Islington (near Toronto), Canada.

Native-born Catholic priest was Father Francisco de Florencia, who joined the Jesuit order in 1643. He was born in St. Augustine, Fla., in 1620. *(Francisco de Florencia—Origen de los Dos Célebres Santuarios de la Nueva-Galicia Obis-*

The First

CATHOLIC PRIEST—*Continued*
*pado de Guadalaxara en la América Septentrion-
al)*

Prelate born in the United States named to the
Roman Curia was Samuel Alphonsus Cardinal
Stritch, archbishop of Chicago, nominated March
1, 1958, by Pope Pius XII for Pro Prefect of the
Vatican's Sacred Congregation for the Propagation of the Faith to head one of the 12 congregations or departments of the Church's central
administration. He arrived in Rome on April 25,
1958, and on April 26, 1958, was admitted to the
Sanatrix Clinic, where he died on May 27, 1958,
before he could take up his post.

Roman Catholic priest to serve in Congress. *See
under* Representative (U.S.)

CATHOLIC PROVINCIAL COUNCIL of the
Roman Catholic Church convened in Baltimore,
Md., October 4, 1829, and consisted of 5 prelates.
Four bishops were unable to attend. The council
enacted 28 decrees. The first plenary session of
the National Council assembled in Baltimore,
Md., May 10, 1852, and consisted of 6 archbishops,
23 bishops, 40 theologians, and 18 other ecclesias-
tics. *(Henry Stanislaus Spalding—Catholic
Colonial Maryland)*

CATHOLIC SAINT. *See* Saint (Catholic)

**CATHOLIC SEMINARIANS (black) to be or-
dained to the priesthood by a black bishop** were
ordained on June 29, 1953, by Bishop Joseph
Oliver Bowers, S.V.D., at St. Augustine's Seminary, Bay St. Louis, Miss.

CATHOLIC SEMINARY
Catholic seminary for the education of black
priests was opened by the Missionaries of the
Society of the Divine Word, at Bay St. Louis,
Miss., and was dedicated September 16, 1923.

Catholic seminary was St. Mary's Seminary
and College, in Roland Park, Baltimore, Md. It was
established on July 10, 1791, when Francis Charles
Nagot, the first superintendent, arrived in Baltimore with Fathers John Mary Tessier, Anthony
Garnier, and Michael Levadoux, and 5 students;
Francis Tulloh, John Edward de Mondésir, Joseph
Perinault, John Edward Caldwell, and John Floyd.
It became a pontifical university on May 1, 1822,
when Pope Pius VII granted it the right and privilege of conferring degrees in divinity. The first
degrees were granted on January 24, 1824, to Fa-
thers Deloul, Damphoux, and Whitfield. *(Joseph
William Ruane—The Beginnings of the Society of
St. Sulpice in the U.S. 1791-1829—Catholic Uni-
versity of America. Studies in American Church
History, Vol. 22. 1935)*

CATHOLIC SETTLEMENT (permanent) was
made in 1565 in St. Augustine, Fla., where a
Catholic congregation was founded.

The First

See also Catholic mass

CATHOLIC STUDENT to seek admission to th
American College of the Roman Catholic Churc
of the United States, a pontifical college founde
in Rome, Italy, on December 8, 1859, was Micha
Augustine Corrigan. He was consecrated May
1873, in St. Patrick's Cathedral, Newark, N.J., a
Bishop of Newark. He was later made an arc
bishop, the palladium being conferred on him o
March 4, 1881.

CATHOLIC UNIVERSITY FOR BLACKS. S
College: University (Catholic) for blacks.

CATHOLIC WORK written by an America
Catholic was published in Annapolis, Md.,
1784. The author was John Carroll, whose artic
was entitled "An Address from the Roman Cath
lics of the United States of North America," ar
answered an attack made by an ex-Jesuit. *(Dani
Brant—Biographical Sketch of . . . John Carro
First Archbishop of Baltimore)*

CATTLE. *See* Animals

CATTLE BRANDING LEGISLATION (state). S
Branding legislation

CATTLE CLUB
Cattle club (Guernsey cattle) was the America
Guernsey Cattle Club, formed March 1, 1876,
the home of Augustus Ward, Farmington, Conn.
permanent organization was effected February
1877, when 11 men from five states met in Ne
York City. The first annual meeting was he
December 19, 1877.

Cattle club (Jersey cattle) was the America
Jersey Cattle Club, formed July 1868, at Newpo
R.I., by 43 dairymen who signed a tentative cons
tution. The first annual meeting was held April
1869, at the Astor House, New York City. It wa
incorporated May 25, 1880. Its object was
record and perpetuate the breed of Jersey cattl
The first president was Samuel J. Sharpless
Philadelphia, Pa. Colonel George E. Waring w
secretary, and Thomas J. Hand, treasurer. *(Robe
M. Gow—The Jersey)*

CAUCUS, CONGRESSIONAL. *See* Congressio
al caucus

CAVALRY UNIT. *See under* Army

CELESTIAL PHOTOGRAPH. *See* Photograph

CELLOPHANE
Cellophane was made in the early part of 19.
by the Du Pont Cellophane Company at its pla
in Buffalo, N.Y., with machinery manufactured
its own shops. Cellophane originally sold for $2.
a pound. *(Du Pont Magazine. Fall 1925)*

Cellophane transparent tape was invented
Richard Gurley Drew of St. Paul, Minn., who o
tained patent No. 1,760,820 on May 27, 1930,
"Adhesive Tape." The application was filed M
28, 1928. The patent was assigned to the M

The First

esota Mining and Manufacturing Company of St. aul, Minn., who manufactured the tape, which vas introduced September 8, 1930.

ELLULOID was invented by John Wesley Hyatt f Albany, N.Y., and Isaiah Smith Hyatt of Rockord, Ill., who obtained patent No. 91,341 on June 5, 1869. This invention won a $10,000 prize offred by Phelan & Collender of New York City for substitute for ivory in billiard balls. The invenors dissolved pyroxyline and camphor in alcohol, hen subjected the mixture to heat and pressure in olds. They began manufacturing it in 1872, orgaized the Newark Celluloid Manufacturing Comany, and obtained United States trademark egistration No. 1102 on January 14, 1873, on the vord "celluloid," which they derived from the ombination of *cellulose* and *-oid,* meaning "like." *Edward Chauncey Worden—Nitro-Cellulose Industry)*

ELLULOID PHOTOGRAPHIC FILM. *See* Photoraphic film

ELLULOSE NITRATE PATENT was No. 4,874, ssued to Christian Frederick Schoenbein of Basle, Switzerland, on December 5, 1846. It covred the use of cotton wool in an explosive comound. He obtained an English patent on October , 1846.

ELLULOSE SPONGE. *See* Sponge

EMENT
Cement was introduced into the United States rom England about 1870. Because of its weight it vas brought over as ballast. American portland ement was invented by David Oliver Saylor of llentown, Pa., who perfected a process for makng hydraulic cement from argillo-magnesium and rgillo calcareous limestone and received patent No. 119,413 on September 26, 1871. European cenent was regarded as superior and it was not ntil 1897 that the use of American cement exeeded importations from Europe. *(Portland Cenent Association—Cement and Concrete)*

Natural cement rock was discovered in 1818 by Canvas White near Fayetteville, Onondaga Couny, N.Y. He obtained a patent on a cement manuacturing process, which he sold to New York State for $10,000. *(Robert Whitman Lesley—Hisory of the Portland Cement Industry in the United States)*

EMENT STADIUM. *See* Stadium

EMETERY
Congressional cemetery was established in Washington, D.C., in a section of Christ Church nown as the Washington Parish Burial Ground. Records show that burials were made early in 804 but the date of the deed which is recorded is March 31, 1812. The cemetery at 18th and E treets, S.E., is more familiarly known as the Conressional Cemetery and occupies 30 acres alongide the Anacostia River.

The First

Federal cemetery in the United States to contain graves of both Union and Confederate soldiers was opened in Springfield, Mo., by act of Congress dated March 3, 1911 [36 Stat. L. 1077). The Confederate cemetery, which was maintained by the state of Missouri prior to 1911, was deeded to the federal government on June 21, 1911. A stone wall separates the graves of the Confederate troops from those of the Union soldiers. The cemetery contains over 3,100 graves. *(Jonathan Fairbanks and Clyde Edwin Tuck—Past and Present of Greene County, Mo.)*

Foreign servicewomen interred in the Arlington National Cemetery, Arlington, Va., were Section Officer Monica M. Daventry of Worcester, England, and Section Officer Ruth P. Watson of Hampstead, England, members of the British Women's Auxiliary Air Force, interred November 19, 1942. Returning from duty, they were killed in an automobile accident. American soldiers served as pallbearers and 12 Waves as honorary pallbearers.

Jewish burial plot was established by Congregation Shearith Israel in 1656. The plot occupied a piece of ground in the section now known as Chatham Square, New York City. It was consecrated February 22, 1656. *(American Jewish Historical Society Publications, Vol. 18)*

National cemeteries as they exist today were authorized by the Act of July 17, 1862 (12 Stat. L. 596). Prior to this act a number of cemeteries had been established for the burial of military dead, although it was not until later that they were designated "national cemeteries." Among these are the following: Mexico City (Mexico) National Cemetery, 1851; Fort Leavenworth (Kans.) National Cemetery, 1861; Loudon Park (Baltimore, Md.) National Cemetery, 1861; Lexington (Ky.) National Cemetery, 1861; Soldiers' Home (Washington, D.C.) National Cemetery, 1861; and Cypress Hills (Brooklyn, N.Y.) National Cemetery, 1862. The national cemetery in Mexico City was established in 1851 although it was not designated as a national cemetery until the Act of July 17, 1862. *(Records in Office of the Quartermaster General, U.S. War Dept. Washington, D.C.)*

President buried in the National Cemetery at Arlington. *See under* President

CENSORSHIP
State board of censorship on literature was appointed by Georgia in March 1953 under authority of an act approved February 19, 1953, "an act to provide for the creation, membership and compensation of a State Literature Commission; to provide for certain definitions; to provide for recommendations of prosecution by the commission; to provide for identification of 'literature'; to repeal conflicting laws; and for other purposes." The committee consisted of James Wesberry, chairman, Hubert Dyan, and William Boswell.

The First

CENSORSHIP—*Continued*
Newspapers were not subject to review or censorship.

CENSORSHIP BOARD (motion pictures). *See under* Motion picture censorship

CENSUS
Census compiled by machines was the 1890 census, which recorded a population of 62,979,766 on June 1, 1890.

Census compiled in part from statistics obtained by mail was the 19th decennial census, mailed on April 1, 1970.

Census in which the population of the United States exceeded 10 million was the fifth census, the census of 1830, which showed a population of 12,866,620. The tenth census, the census of 1880, listed the population as 50,155,783, the first over the 50 million mark.

Census in which the population of the United States exceeded 100 million was the census of 1920, which showed a population of 105,710,620. The first census over 150 million was that of 1950, which showed a population of 150,697,361.

Census in which the population of the United States exceeded 200 million was that of 1970, which showed a population of 203,184,772. That figure was later found to be incorrect and was revised by the U.S. Bureau of the Census to 203,-211,926. A public ceremony was held November 20, 1967, at the U.S. Department of Commerce, Washington, D.C., when the nation's population reached 200 million persons.

Census of the United States was authorized by act of March 1, 1790 (1 Stat. L. 101), "providing for the enumeration of the inhabitants of the United States." The census compilation cost $44,377 and utilized the services of 17 marshals and 650 assistants. Marshals received from $100 to $500 and assistants $1 for every 150 persons in county districts and $3 for every 300 in cities and towns. The enumeration, as of August 1, 1790, showed a population of 3,939,326 located in 16 states and the Ohio territory. Virginia, with 747,610, was the most populous state; Rhode Island, with 68,825, the least. New York City had a population of 33,-131, Philadelphia had a population of 28,522, and Boston had a population of 18,320. *(Simon Newton Dexter North—A Century Population Growth From the First Census to the Twelfth)*

Census that included the deaf, dumb, and blind was taken in 1830. Previously, those so afflicted were not enumerated at all.

City to exceed 1 million in population was New York City, whose population according to the census of 1880 was 1,206,299, not including Brooklyn, which was then an independent city. New York City was also the first with a population exceed-

The First

ing 5 million. The population of the five borough of New York City was 5,620,048 in 1920.

State to exceed 5 million in population wa New York State, with a population, according t the census of 1880, of 5,082,871. According to th 1920 census, New York State with 10,385,227 wa the first to exceed the 10 million mark.

States to exceed 1 million in population wer New York State, 1,372,812; Virginia, 1,065,366; an Pennsylvania, 1,049,456, according to the 182 census.

CENSUS BUREAU
Census Bureau permanent organization was es tablished by congressional act of March 6, 190: (32 Stat.L.51), which authorized the appointmer of a Director of Census at $6,000 a year to superir tend and direct the taking of the 13th Censu (1910). On February 14, 1902 (32 Stat. L. 826), th Census Bureau was transferred from the Depar ment of the Interior to the Department of Con merce and Labor. The bureau at that time ha 70,286 employees.

CENTENNIAL CELEBRATION. *See* Fair

CENTER-AISLE RAILROAD CAR. *See* Railroa car

CENTRAL HEATING. *See* Heating system

CENTRAL STATISTICAL BOARD (U.S.) wa created by Executive Order No. 6225, dated Jul 27, 1933, under authority vested in the Presider by the National Industrial Recovery Act "to for mulate standards for and to effect coordination c the statistical services of the Federal Governmer incident to the purposes . . . of the National Indus trial Recovery Act." It was organized August ! 1933, and was originally composed of eight mem bers. The first chairman was Winfield Willian Riefler. *(U.S. Budget Bureau—Statistical Star dards Division—Report for the Period July 2: 1933–February 12, 1934)*

CENTRIFUGAL LOOP-THE-LOOP RAILWAY *See* Loop-the-loop centrifugal railway

CENTRIFUGAL MILK SEPARATOR. *See* Crean separator

CERAMICS SCHOOL was started by Ohio Stat University, Columbus, Ohio, in 1894 under th guidance and direction of Professor Edward Or ton, Jr. *(Heinrich Ries and Henry Leighton—His tory of the Clay Working Industries in the Unite States)*

CERTIFICATES, GOLD. *See* Money

CERTIFIED-MAIL STAMP. *See* Postage Stamp

CERTIFIED PUBLIC ACCOUNTANT. *See* Ac countant

CERTIFIED SCHOOL PLAN FOR COLLEGE EN TRANCE. *See under* College

The First

CHAIN-STITCH SEWING MACHINE. *See* Sewing machine

CHAIN STORE ORGANIZATION. *See under* Business

CHAIN STORE TAX. *See* Tax

CHAIR
   Dental chair. *See* Dental chair

Folding theater chair was invented by Aaron H. Allen of Boston, Mass., who obtained patent No. 12,017 December 5, 1854, on an "improvement in seats for public buildings."

Recumbent-chair patent was No. 2,100, issued May 22, 1841, to Henry Peres Kennedy, a cabinetmaker and upholsterer of Philadelphia, Pa. A spiral spring was placed horizontally between the back rail of the seat and the front rail of the chair.

Rocking chair is believed to have been invented by Benjamin Franklin about 1760. This date is not verified and no authentic instance of a prior rocker has come to light. *(Walter Alden Dyer and Esther Stevens Fraser—The Rocking Chair: An American Institution)*

Steamer chair, or deck chair, was introduced in 1891 by Heinrich Conried, impresario of the Metropolitan Opera House, New York City. He built 100 chairs and formed the Ocean Comfort Company to distribute and rent them. At one time 5,000 chairs were on rental to steamship companies that did not provide their own chairs for the decks. The first rental contract was signed with Albert Ballin, general director of the Hamburg-American lines. *(Montrose Jonas Moses—Life of Heinrich Conried)*

CHAIR FACTORY was established by Lambert Hitchcock in Hitchcockville (now Riverton), Conn., in 1818. The chairs were generally hand-painted on the back. They were shipped "knocked-down" and sold extensively in the South.

CHAMBER MUSIC ORGANIZATION. *See under* Music

CHAMBER OF COMMERCE
   Chamber of Commerce of the United States of America was founded in 1912 by approximately 700 representatives of commercial organizations, trade associations, and individual establishments, who were invited to participate in a series of discussions by President William Howard Taft and Secretary of Commerce and Labor Charles Nagel. The headquarters of the Chamber of Commerce of the United States, one of the finest buildings in Washington, D.C., was dedicated May 20, 1925.

Chamber of commerce (state) was the New York Chamber of Commerce, formed April 5, 1768, by 20 merchants at a meeting at Fraunces Tavern, New York City. John Cruger was the first presi-

The First

dent, and Anthony Van Dam the first secretary. The preamble to a resolution adopted at that time reads: "Whereas Mercantile Societies have been found very useful in trading cities for promoting and encouraging commerce, supporting industry, adjusting disputes relative to trade and navigation, and procuring such laws and regulations as may be found necessary for the benefit of trade in general, etc. . . . " The Chamber of Commerce was incorporated March 13, 1770, under a royal charter from King George III. Its motto was "Non Nobis Nate Solum" (Not born for ourselves alone). *(Joseph Bucklin Bishop—A Chronicle of One Hundred and Fifty Years)*

Junior chamber of commerce was organized October 13, 1915, as the Young Men's Progressive Civic Association in St. Louis, Mo. The name was changed to the Junior Chamber of Commerce in 1918. On January 21, 1921, delegates from 24 cities assembled in St. Louis to establish the United States Junior Chamber of Commerce. The first national convention was held in St. Louis June 17–19, 1920. Henry Giessenbier, Jr., was elected president.

CHANDELIER. *See* Glass crystal chandelier

CHANNEL SWIMMER (American). *See* Swimmer: American swimmer to swim the English Channel; Woman: American woman to swim the English Channel

CHAPEL CAR. *See under* Railroad car

CHAPLAIN. *See under* Air Force officer; Army officer; Congress (U.S.)—House of Representatives; Naval officer

CHAPLAINS' SCHOOL
   Army school for chaplains was the Army Chaplain School, Fort Monroe, Va., organized February 9, 1918. Instruction was offered in military law, international law, and military science and tactics. The school was moved to Camp Taylor, Ky., on April 9, 1918.

Naval chaplains' school conducted by the U.S. Navy was the Chaplains' School, Naval Operating Base, Norfolk, Va., which held its first session February 23, 1942.

CHARITY BOARD (state) was the Massachusetts State Board of Charities established April 29, 1863 (Chapter 240—Acts of 1863). Five members and a general agent were sworn in October 7, 1863. Otis Norcross was the first chairman. The only compensation received by board members was traveling expenses.

CHAUTAUQUA ORGANIZATION was formed August 4, 1874, by the first Sunday School Teachers Assembly at a meeting held in Fair Point, N.Y., at the suggestion of John Heyl Vincent and Lewis Miller. On August 10, 1878, home study courses were offered and the name Chautauqua Literary

The First

CHAUTAUQUA ORGANIZATION—*Continued*
and Scientific Circle adopted. *(Rebecca Richmond —Chautauqua: An American Place)*
    See also Home study course

CHECK
    Check sent by radio across the Atlantic Ocean.
See Radio facsimile transmission: Check sent by radio across the Atlantic Ocean

    Traveler's checks were devised in 1891 by Marcellus Fleming Berry, who was then general agent of the American Express Company. In the first year only 248 checks amounting to $9,120 were sold. *(Alden Hatch—American Express)*

CHECK PHOTOGRAPHING DEVICE was the Checkograph, invented by George Lewis McCarthy, who received patent No. 1,748,489, February 25, 1930. Commercial manufacture was undertaken May 1, 1927, by the Eastman Kodak Company, Rochester, N.Y., which marketed the device as the Recordak and made the first installation May 1, 1928, at the Empire Trust Company, New York City. The machine photographs checks on 16 mm motion picture film. The first application of the machine, other than by banking institutions, was made in 1929 by the United States Treasury. The first application in libraries was made in 1935 when the New York *Times* and the New York Public Library cooperated in photographing copies of the New York *Times* of World War I period on microfilm.

CHECK PROTECTORS were manufactured in 1870 and consisted of punches that perforated figure holes in paper. These protectors were not certain proof against forgeries. In June 1899 Libanus McLouth Todd completed the model of a check protector in a woodshed at 384 Gregory Street, Rochester, N.Y. He filed his application August 8, 1899, and placed the machine, which he called a Protectograph, on the market in the fall of that year. The machine forced ink into the paper under pressure, making it part of the fiber of the document. He obtained patent No. 766,853, August 9, 1904. *(Jack W. Speare—Protecting the Nation's Money)*

CHECKMASTER PLAN. *See under* Bank

CHEESE
    Liederkranz-brand cheese of American origin was made in 1892 by Emil Frey in Monroe, N.Y. He was a cheesemaker for the Monroe Cheese Company, which was acquired in 1929 by the Borden Company. The cheese was named for the Liederkranz (wreath of songs) Club, New York City.

    Pineapple cheese was made in 1808 by Lewis Mills Norton of Troy, Pa. On April 17, 1810, he obtained a patent on a "vat for forming pineapple cheese."

The First

CHEESE FACTORY
    Cheese factory cooperative was established by farmers of Cheshire, Mass., in 1801. On July 20 1801, a cheese was pressed at the farm of Elisha Brown, Jr., which on August 20 weighed 1,23 pounds. It was placed on a wagon drawn by six horses and on January 1, 1802, presented to President Thomas Jefferson at the White House *(Agricultural History. Vol. 18, No. 4)*

    Cheese factory of consequence was established in Rome, N.Y., by Jesse Williams in 1851. It is referred to as the first permanent system of associated dairying in the United States. The first shipment of milk was received May 10, 1851. *(Benjamin Davis Gilbert—The Cheese Industry of the State of New York)*

CHEMICAL WARFARE CHIEF. *See* Army office

CHEMISTRY LABORATORY
    Chemical laboratory for instruction in chemical analysis and chemistry as applied to the arts was established in Philadelphia in 1836 by James Curtis Booth. Charles Thomas Jackson opened a similar laboratory in Boston in 1836 for instruction and research in analytical chemistry, but it did not last long.

    Chemical laboratory in a collegiate institution where instruction was offered to undergraduates was opened at Boylston Hall, Harvard University, Cambridge, Mass., in 1858. Josiah (Joseph) Parsons Cooke, author of numerous chemical books, was in charge of instruction.

CHEMISTRY LABORATORY MANUAL was James Woodhouse's *Young Chemist's Pocket Companion*, a 56-page book that contained about 100 experiments. It was published in 1797 in Philadelphia, Pa. *(Edgar Fahs Smith—James Woodhouse, a Pioneer in Chemistry)*

CHEMISTRY MAGAZINE was the *Memoirs of the Columbian Chemical Society of Philadelphia*, which was printed by Isaac Peirce, 3 South Fourth Street, Philadelphia, Pa., in 1813–1814. The first volume consisted of 221 pages. The society was founded in 1811.

CHEMISTRY NOBEL PRIZE WINNER. *See under* Nobel Prize

CHEMISTRY PROFESSOR
    Chemistry professor who taught chemistry only, in a regularly appointed position in an educational institution of recognized standing, was Benjamin Rush, one of the signers of the Declaration of Independence. He gave lectures in chemistry at the Philadelphia Medical School, Philadelphia, Pa., as early as 1769. *(Lyman Churchill Newell—Chemical Education in America from the Earliest Days to 1820. In Journal Chemical Education. Vol. 9. April 1932)*

Professorship of applied chemistry was granted by Yale University, New Haven, Conn., to Benjamin Silliman, Jr. in 1846, although the Yale Analytical Laboratory did not open its doors to students until 1847. The Yale Analytical Laboratory was afterward renamed the Sheffield Scientific School in honor of Joseph Earl Sheffield in recognition of his benefactions to the institution. *(Forris Jewett Moore—A History of Chemistry)*

CHEMISTRY TEXTBOOK

Chemistry textbook was Benjamin Rush's *Syllabus of a Course of Lectures on Chemistry* published in 1770 in Philadelphia, Pa. *(Harry Gehman Good—Benjamin Rush and His Services to American Education)*

CHEMISTS SOCIETY

Chemical society in the world was the Chemical Society of Philadelphia, founded in 1792 by James Woodhouse. *(Edgar Fahs Smith—James Woodhouse, a Pioneer in Chemistry)*

Chemical society (national) was the American Chemical Society, organized in New York City April 20, 1876, although many meetings to form the society had been held previous to that date. The first president was John William Draper. The society was chartered November 9, 1877, as a non-profit, nonstock corporation of the State of New York "for the advancement of chemistry and the promotion of chemical research." *(Henry Carrington Bolton—Chemical Societies of the Nineteenth Century)*

CHENILLE MANUFACTURING MACHINE was

made by William Canter of New York City, who obtained patent No. 37,415 on January 13, 1863.

CHESS

Chess match between players on different ships at sea was played at 2:30 P.M., June 11, 1902, by passengers on the American liner *Philadelphia* and the Cunard liner *Campania* about 70 miles apart. The moves were broadcast by wireless operators aboard the ships. About 100 moves were made. The match was not concluded, since the radio was required for navigational use.

CHESS BOOK was *Chess Made Easy—New*

Comprehensive Rules For Playing the Game of Chess with Examples from Philidor, Cunningham, etc. to which is prefixed a pleasing account of its origin; some interesting anecdotes of several exalted personages who have been admirers of it; and the Morals of Chess written by the ingenious Mr. Franklin. It consisted of 106 pages, including 8 pages of advertisements and a frontispiece, and was printed and sold in 1802 by James Humphreys of Philadelphia, Pa. Evidently it was a reprint of an English edition. *(Alfred C. Klahre—Early Chess in America)*

CHESS CHAMPION

Chess champion of the world (American-born)

was Paul Charles Morphy, 20 years old, of New Orleans, La., who won first place at the First Chess Congress held in New York City from October 6, 1857, to November 10, 1857. In the years 1857-59, he played 95 games: 68, win; 14, draw; 13 lose. He visited Europe and won the Grand Tournament of the First National Chess Association in England and France held from July 19, 1858, to August 22, 1858. He returned to New York City, May 11, 1859. Technically, the World Chess Championship did not formally exist at that time. The first to use the title was Wilhelm Steinitz, in 1866. *(Frederick Milne Eige—The Exploits and Triumphs in Europe of Paul Morphy)*

Chess champion to play more than 100 games simultaneously was Frank James Marshall of New York City, who met 105 local players at the National Press Club, Washington, D.C., on March 21, 1916. He won a total of 82 games, lost 8, and drew 15.

CHESS TOURNAMENT

Chess tournament of importance was held October 6, 1857, by the American Chess Congress at the Descoule's Rooms, 764 Broadway, New York City, under the sponsorship of the New York Chess Club. The victor of the Grand Tournament was Paul Morphy, who received the first prize, a silver service consisting of a pitcher, four goblets, and a salver. A national organization, the American Chess Association, was formed October 10, 1857, in New York City. A. B. Meek was elected president of the Congress and Daniel Willard Fiske the secretary. *(Daniel Willard Fiske—Book of the First American Chess Congress)*

Intercollegiate transatlantic chess match by cable was played April 21–22, 1899, at the Knickerbocker Athletic Club, New York City, when 6 players at 6 tables from Columbia, Harvard, Princeton, and Yale universities competed against 6 from Cambridge, Oxford, and London universities at the British Chess Club, in London, England, for a $1,000 trophy presented by Isaac L. Rice. The moves were cabled, 20 an hour. The British team won 3½ to 2½. The American players scored as follows: Meyer of Columbia 1, Cook of Yale 1, Falk of Columbia ½, Arensber of Harvard 0, Catchings of Harvard 0, and Young of Princeton 0.

CHEVRON. *See* Army insignia

CHEWING GUM

Chewing gum was the "State of Maine Pure Spruce Gum," manufactured in Bangor, Me., in 1848 by John Curtis and his brother on a Franklin stove. In 1850 they moved to Portland, Me., and made paraffin gums under the brands of Licorice Lulu, Four-in-Hand, Sugar Cream, Biggest and Best, and White Mountain; and also spruce gums, Yankee Spruce, American Flag, Trunk Spruce, and 200 Lump Spruce. *(George Thomas Little—Genealogical and Family History of the State of Maine, Vol. 2)*

The First

CHEWING GUM—*Continued*

Chewing gum patent was No. 98,304 issued on December 28, 1869, to William Finley Semple of Mount Vernon, Ohio, who claimed the "combination of rubber with other articles, in any proportions adapted to the formation of an acceptable chewing gum."

CHICKEN SHOW. *See* Poultry show

CHIEF ENGINEER (Continental Army). *See under* Army officer

CHIEF JUSTICE. *See* Supreme Court (U.S.): Chief Justice of the Supreme Court

CHILD BORN. *See* Births

CHILD DELINQUENCY LAW (state) was passed April 28, 1909, by Colorado. It defined as guilty, persons "who shall encourage, cause or contribute to the dependency, neglect or delinquency of a child."

CHILD HYGIENE BUREAU was established August 1908 in New York City with Dr. Sara Josephine Baker as director. It was "the first organization established under municipal control to deal with the health of children from birth to legal working age, in so far as a municipal Health Department may regulate and control the conditions of child life and health."

CHILD LABOR LAW

Child labor law (federal) was passed September 1, 1916 (39 Stat. L. 675), "an act to prevent interstate commerce in the products of child labor," the provisions of which were to be administered by the Children's Bureau. The government did not have the power to legislate directly in the field of labor, so the attempt was made to regulate child labor through its power to legislate on interstate commerce. The act became effective September 1, 1917, but on June 3, 1918, it was declared unconstitutional by the Supreme Court as an invasion of states' rights.

Child labor law regulating hours of employment was Chapter 60 of the laws of 1842 of Massachusetts, approved by Governor John Davis on March 3, 1842. Massachusetts prohibited children under 12 years of age from working more than 10 hours a day. Connecticut enacted a similar law, which prohibited children under 14 years of age working more than 10 hours a day. *(Massachusetts Acts and Resolves, 1842)*

Child labor law restricting the age of the worker was Pamphlet Law No. 278, approved March 28, 1848, by Governor Francis Rawn Shunk of Pennsylvania. The law prohibited children under 12 years of age from engaging in commercial labor. In 1849 the age limit was raised to 13 years. Similar legislation was enacted in 1853 by Rhode Island, in 1855 by Connecticut, and in 1866 by Massachusetts with age limits respectively of 12, 9, and 10 years.

The First

Child labor law to include educational provision was Chapter 245 passed by Massachusetts April 16, 1836, effective April 1, 1837. It required all children to attend school at least 3 months of the year until they came to the age of 15. Manufacturers were not allowed to hire children in their mills for more than 9 months a year, but the children were conveniently transferred from mill to mill so that this legislation was not effective. *(Miriam Elizabeth Laughran—Historical Development of Child Labor Legislation in the United States)*

Compulsory education law. *See under* Education

CHILD WELFARE CONGRESS. *See* Children's Welfare Congress (International)

CHILDBIRTH FEVER PAMPHLET. *See* Medical book

CHILDREN'S BOOK was John Cotton's catechism *Milk for Babes, Drawn out of the Breasts of Both Testaments, Chiefly for the Spiritual Nourishment of Boston Babes in either England: But may be of like use for any children,* printed by Stephen Day in Cambridge, Mass., 1641–45. No first edition has been located and the reprints (one printed in London, England, in 1646; and one printed for Hezekiah Usher in Boston, Mass., by S[amuel] G[reen], Cambridge Mass.) vary and appear with different subtitles. *(Paul Leicester Ford—The New England Primer)*

CHILDREN'S BUREAU (U.S.) was established in the Department of Commerce and Labor, by act of Congress, April 9, 1912 (37 Stat. L. 79) "to investigate and report . . . upon all matters pertaining to welfare of children and child life among all classes of our people." The first chief, Julia Clifford Lathrop, was appointed June 4, 1912, by President Woodrow Wilson and confirmed by the Senate, at a salary of $5,000 a year. *(James Alner Tobey—The Children's Bureau)*

CHILDREN'S CHURCH. *See* Church

CHILDREN'S CLINIC. *See* Medical clinic

CHILDREN'S COURT. *See* Court: Juvenile court

CHILDREN'S HOSPITAL. *See* Hospital

CHILDREN'S LIBRARY DEPARTMENT. *See* Library

CHILDREN'S MAGAZINE. *See under* Periodical

CHILDREN'S PLAYGROUND. *See* Playground for children

CHILDREN'S WELFARE CONGRESS (international) was the International Congress in America for the Welfare of the Child, held March 10–17, 1908, in Washington, D.C., under the auspices of the National Congress of Mothers. President Theodore Roosevelt addressed the congress.

The First

CHIMES and bells, as well as the first tower clocks, were manufactured by Benjamin Hanks, who came to America in 1699, settling in Plymouth, Mass.

CHINAWARE

Chinaware for restaurant use was made by the Greenwood Pottery Company of Trenton, N.J. in 1862. It combined the best qualities of both porcelain and earthenware.

Dishes (complete set) made in America for the Executive Mansion, Washington, D.C., were ordered by President Woodrow Wilson and delivered July 31, 1918. The set, consisting of 1,700 pieces bearing the seal of the President of the United States, was manufactured by Walter Scott Lenox of Lenox Incorporated, Trenton, N.J.

CHINCHILLA FARM. *See under* Animals

CHINESE-AMERICAN HOSPITAL. *See* Hospital

CHINESE-AMERICAN OFFICER IN MARINES. *See* Marine Corps: Marine officer of Chinese descent

CHINESE-AMERICAN PUBLIC SCHOOL. *See* Public school: Public school for Chinese-Americans

CHINESE-AMERICAN TELEPHONE EXCHANGE. *See* Telephone: Telephone switchboard or exchange for Chinese-American subscribers

CHINESE-AMERICAN WOMEN'S CLUB. *See* Women's club

CHINESE BROADCAST. *See* Radio broadcast

CHINESE-DESCENT MARINE OFFICER. *See* Marines

CHINESE EMBASSY was under the jurisdiction of Chen Lan-pin, who presented his papers as Envoy Extraordinary and Minister Plenipotentiary to President Rutherford Birchard Hayes, October 4, 1878, in Washington, D.C. Yung Wing was the associate minister, a title which was afterward abolished. Accompanied by 34 persons, Chen Lan-pin landed at San Francisco, Calif., on July 25, 1878.

CHINESE GRANTED CITIZENSHIP. *See under* Citizenship

CHINESE IMMIGRANTS. *See under* Immigration

CHINESE LABOR IMMIGRATION. *See* Immigration

CHINESE LANGUAGE AND LITERATURE LECTURESHIP was created by Yale University, New Haven, Conn., in 1877. Samuel Wells Williams, Commodore Oliver Hazard Perry's secretary and interpreter in Japan, was the lecturer.

CHINESE NEWSPAPER. *See* Newspaper

The First

CHINESE STUDENTS were brought to the United States by the Reverend Samuel Robbins Brown, head of the Morrison School, the first English school in China. Three Chinese arrived April 12, 1847, in New York City and entered the Monson Academy, Monson, Mass. One of them, Yung Wing, entered Yale University, New Haven, Conn., in 1850 and graduated June 13, 1854 with a B.A. degree, becoming the first Chinese to graduate in the United States. *(Yung Wing—My Life in China and America)*

CHINESE TELEPHONE EXCHANGE. *See* Telephone: Telephone switchboard or exchange for Chinese-American subscribers

CHINESE THEATER. *See* Theater

CHINESE THEATRICAL PERFORMANCE. *See* Play (drama)

CHINESE TONG. *See* Tong (Chinese secret society)

CHIROPODIST was Nehemiah Kenison, who was assisted by his brother and a cousin. They opened an office in 1840 directly opposite the Old South Church on Washington Street, Boston, Mass. They developed instruments and protective dressings that greatly aided in the relief of the pain caused by troublesome corns, etc.

CHIROPODY BOOK. *See* Medical book

CHIROPODY LAW. *See* Medical legislation

CHIROPODY SCHOOL

Chiropody school as a regular division of a university opened September 20, 1915, at Temple University, Philadelphia, Pa. The chiropody clinic at the Garretson Hospital, an annex to Temple Hospital, opened April 6, 1915. Four students completed the 34-week course June 1916 and received the degree of M.Cp. The course now covers four years and leads to the degree of D.S.C. (Doctor of Surgical Chiropody). Dr. Frank Adoniram Thompson was the first dean of the school, and Dr. W. Ashton Kennedy and Dr. James Richardson Bennie were the first professors of chiropody. *(Pedic Items. May 1915)*

Chiropody school of note was the New York School of Chiropody, organized in 1910 by members of the Pedic Society of the State of New York, incorporated June 3, 1895. On January 1, 1913, it became the First Institute of Podiatry, with Dr. Maurice J. Lewi as president. Its first graduating class in 1913 consisted of 13 men and 1 woman. On November 16, 1939, it became affiliated with Long Island University, awarding the degree of Pod.D. (Doctor of Podiatry).

CHIROPRACTIC SCHOOL was the Palmer School of Chiropractic, Davenport, Iowa, which opened in 1900. It was established by Daniel David Palmer.

The First

CHIROPRACTOR was Daniel David Palmer, who gave the first adjustment treatment of vertebrae on September 18, 1895, to Harvey Lillard in Davenport, Iowa. *(Bartlett Joshua Palmer—Science of Chiropractic)*

CHLORINE WATER PURIFICATION. *See* Water purification

CHLOROFORM was distilled in 1831 by Dr. Samuel Guthrie in Sackets Harbor, N.Y. He called it "chloric ether," and obtained it by distilling chloride of lime with alcohol in a copper still. He described it in "A New Mode of Preparing a Spirituous Solution of Chloric Ether." It is a colorless liquid known chemically as trichloromethane $(CHC1_3)$. *(Edgar Fahs Smith—Chemistry in America)*

CHLOROMYCETIN
Chloromycetin laboratory established exclusively to produce chloromycetin by chemical means was opened on March 13, 1952, by Parke Davis & Company, Holland, Mich. The main processing building was longer than a football field and had a 40-foot ceiling. Chloromycetin was the first antibiotic to be produced commercially by synthesis.

CHLOROPHYLL
Chlorophyll was patented by Dr. Benjamin Gruskin of Philadelphia, Pa., who obtained patent No. 2,120,667 on June 14, 1938, on a "therapeutic agent for use in the treatment of infection." His application was dated December 1, 1937. The patent was assigned to the Lakeland Foundation, Chicago, Ill.

Chlorophyll "a" was synthesized June 27, 1960, by Professor Robert Burns Woodward at the Converse Memorial Laboratory, Harvard University, Cambridge, Mass. The chlorophyll molecule is composed of 55 atoms carbon, 72 atoms hydrogen, 5 atoms oxygen, 4 atoms nitrogen, and 1 atom magnesium.

CHOCOLATE MILL was erected beside the Neponset River at Dorchester, Mass., in 1765 and was operated by John Hannan. In 1780 Dr. James Baker purchased the mill, originating the present Walter Baker and Co.

CHOLERA EPIDEMIC. *See* Epidemic

CHOP SUEY was concocted in New York City on August 29, 1896, by Chinese Ambassador Li Hungchang's chef, who devised this dish to appeal to both American and Oriental taste. Chop suey was unknown in China at the time. Li Hung-chang and his suite of 18, attended by 22 servants, 5 valets, 3 cooks, and a barber, arrived in New York City, August 28, 1896. He was greeted by President Grover Cleveland. *(Eng Ying Gong—Tong War)*

CHOREOGRAPHIC SCORE COPYRIGHTED. *See under* Copyright

The First

CHRISTIAN SCIENCE CHURCH was founded by Mary Baker Eddy in Boston, Mass., in 1879, following her founding of this religion, and her issuing of its textbook, *Science and Health, with Key to the Scriptures*, in 1875.

CHRISTMAS CARDS were 4½ by 6 inches, were printed in black on white paper with the message "A Merry Christmas and Happy New Year," and designed and produced by Richard H. Pease, engraver and lithographer, at Albany, N.Y., in 1851 The illustration showed a fanciful structure with a banner "Pease's Great Varety Store in the Temple of Fancy." (He misspelled *Variety*.) The cards were sent to his customers and friends. Louis Prang, an engraver at Roxbury, Mass., produced Christmas cards that he sold to England in 1874 and to the United States in 1875. *(Louis D. Chamberlain—The Romance of Greeting Cards)*

CHRISTMAS CAROLS ASSOCIATION (national) was the National Christmas Carols Association, organized January 20, 1947, in St. Louis Mo., with William Henry Danforth as president The first local club was the St. Louis Christmas Carols Association, organized with nine members in 1911 in St. Louis. The first president was Elizabeth Hitchcock. Numerous groups of carol singers had existed previously and club organization was purely secondary.

CHRISTMAS SAVINGS CLUB. *See under* Bank

CHRISTMAS SEAL. *See under* Seal

CHRISTMAS STAMP. *See* Postage Stamp

CHRISTMAS-STAMP ANNUAL SERIES. *See* Postage Stamp

CHRISTMAS TREE designated as the "Nation's Christmas Tree," was the General Grant Tree, in General Grant National Park, Calif., dedicated May 1, 1926, by Mayor Henry Leonard Suderman of Sanger, Calif., although a Christmas ceremony had been held at high noon Christmas Day 1925 The greatest horizontal diameter of the tree was 40.3 feet at the base, and at 200 feet above the ground the diameter was about 12 feet. The tree was 267 feet high and 3,500–4,000 years old.

CHRISTOPHER COLUMBUS MONUMENT. *See* Monument

CHROME TANNING. *See* Leather

CHROMIUM PLATING process (commercial) was invented in 1924 by Dr. Colin Garfield Fink at Columbia University, New York City. He obtained patent No. 1,581,188 on April 20, 1926. He also received patent No. 1,802,463 on April 28 1931, on a process of electro-depositing chromium and of preparing baths therefor which he assigned to the Chemical Treatment Co., Inc. *(Allen Gibb Gray—Modern Electroplating)*

The First

CHROMO was made in 1861 of John Banvard's painting *The Orison*—the interior of the St. Eustace convent in Italy. It was 16 by 24 inches and chromolithographed by Sarony, Major and Knapp. Proofs were $10, prints $5. *(South Dakota Historical Collections, Vol. 21. 1942)*

CHURCH

See also Cathedral; and, *under* names of religious organizations or sects, e.g., Buddhist temple, Catholic church, Federal Council of Churches, Mormon temple

Children's church built to scale and operated by children, was the Children's Church (Unitarian), Milton, Mass., dedicated November 14, 1937, by the Reverend Vivian Towse Pomeroy, pastor of the First Parish Unitarian Church, Milton, Mass. The miniature church was 18 feet by 32 feet, complete with steeple, belfry, organ, spire, and pews 2 feet 8 inches in height. It cost in excess of $5,000. The first pastor was the Reverend Mrs. Dorothy Pomeroy.

Church for the deaf. *See* Deaf—Church service: Church services for the deaf

Church services aired from another church were heard April 17, 1921, at the Herron Avenue Presbyterian Church, in Pittsburgh, Pa., which installed a loudspeaker and loop antenna in order to receive services broadcast from the Calvary Episcopal Church in Pittsburgh, because they were without a pastor.

Church without theology, creed, or dogma was organized by Richard Wolfe of Denver, Colo., in 1912. The First Liberal Church of Denver, the first of the new sect, was organized in 1922. Wolfe became the first bishop of the Liberal Church of America.

Floating church was moored in the East River at the foot of Pike Street, New York City. It was constructed in 1843 and known as the Floating Church of Our Saviour. The church was organized by the Young Men's Church Missionary Society, an auxiliary of the City Mission Society. The society dissolved in 1844 and deeded the church to the Protestant Episcopal Church Missionary Society for Seamen in the City and Port of New York, an organization that emanated from the original group. The first clergyman was the Reverend Benjamin Clarke Cutler Parker, who was called by the title of missionary, rather than clergyman. In 1906 the corporate title was changed to Seamen's Church Institute of New York. The work is now conducted in a large building at 15 State Street, New York City.

General Council of Congregational and Christian Churches was formed as the result of a merger of the National Council of Congregational Churches and the General Convention of Christian Churches held in Seattle, Wash., June 25–July

The First

3, 1931. The first executive secretaries were the Reverend Charles Emerson Burton of New York City and the Reverend Warren Hathaway Dennison of Dayton, Ohio.

Mariners' church was built June 4, 1820, by the New York Port Society, as a nonsectarian, interdenominational church. The society was organized in May 1818 and was chartered, April 13, 1819, as the Society for Promoting the Gospel Among Seamen in the Port of New York. The first pastor was the Reverend Ward Stafford, who preached from 1818 to 1821.

Universal chapel embracing eight faiths was dedicated April 8, 1956, in the Universalist Church of the Divine Paternity, New York City. On its altar is a globe of the earth representing "human unity" and the symbols of eight religions—Buddhism, Christianity, Confucianism, Hinduism, Judaism, Shinto, Taoism, and Zoroastrianism.

Woman moderator of the General Council of Congregational and Christian Churches was Helen Kenyon of New York City, who was elected June 17, 1948, in Oberlin, Ohio.

CHURCH MILITARY SCHOOL. *See* Military school

CHURCH OF ENGLAND

American bishop to become bishop of a British Church of England diocese was the Right Reverend Spence Burton, who was enthroned Bishop of the Church of England, diocese of Nassau, Bahamas, November 1, 1942, at Christ Church Cathedral, Nassau. He was suffragan bishop of Haiti, a missionary district of the Episcopal Church, from May 3, 1939, to September 1, 1942.

Church of England organized in New England was King's Chapel at the corner of Tremont and School Streets, Boston, Mass., built in 1686. The first minister was James Freeman, ordained November 17, 1785. *(Henry Wilder Foote—Annals of King's Chapel from the Puritan Age of New England to the Present Day)*

CHURCH OF JESUS CHRIST OF LATTER-DAY SAINTS

Black ordained to the priesthood (office of elder) by the Church of Jesus Christ of Latter-Day Saints was Joseph Freeman, Jr., who was ordained June 11, 1978, in Salt Lake City, Utah. He was a lay minister, a regular member of his congregation, not a pastor.

Church building of the Church of Jesus Christ of Latter-Day Saints. *See* Mormon temple

Church of Jesus Christ of Latter-Day Saints, more familiarly known as the Mormon Church, was organized on April 6, 1830, in Fayette Township, Seneca County, N.Y., in the home of Peter Whitmer. Joseph Smith, its main organizer, de-

The First

CHURCH OF JESUS CHRIST OF LATTER-DAY SAINTS—*Continued*

clared that an angel of God had brought him the law. The *Book of Mormon,* 588 pages of text, was printed in the spring of 1830 at a cost of $3,000. It was translated in June 1829 from the "plates" of gold from the divine source. *(Gordon B. Hinckley —Truth Restored, a short history of the Church of Jesus Christ of Latter-Day Saints)*

CHURCH OF THE UNITED BRETHREN IN CHRIST was formed on Pentecost Sunday, May 18, 1766, at a meeting in Isaac Long's barn, Lancaster, Pa., by the Reverend Martin Boehm and the Reverend Philip William Otterbein. The first conference was held in 1789 at Otterbein's home in Baltimore, Md. Otterbein and Boehm were elected to the office of bishop in September 1800 at a conference. The first general conference at which delegates were regularly elected was held June 6, 1815, in Mount Pleasant, Pa. *(Reverend Daniel Berger—History of the Church of the United Brethren in Christ)*

CHUTE. *See under* Postal service

CHUTE-THE-CHUTES. *See* Shoot-the-chutes

CIDER MILL was patented by Isaac Quintard of Stanfield, Conn., who obtained a patent April 5, 1806, on a cider and bark mill.

CIGAR BAND of special interest was prepared for cigars distributed at a dinner given by the Common Council of the City of New York on September 2, 1858, at the Metropolitan Hotel, New York City, to honor Cyrus West Field and the officers of the U.S. steam frigate *Niagara* and the British steamship H.B.M. *Gorgon* who had completed the laying of the Atlantic cable August 5, 1858. About 600 persons attended the dinner. The cigar bands, which were printed in black ink, depicted Field.

CIGAR FACTORY of importance was established by Simeon Viets in 1810 in West Suffield, Conn. He employed 15 women and a foreman. His popular brands were Windsors and Long Nines. *(General Executive Committee—Celebration of the 250th Anniversary of the Settlement of Suffield, Conn.)*

CIGAR LIGHTER PATENT was No. 121,049, granted to Moses F. Gale of New York City on November 21, 1871.

CIGAR ROLLING MACHINE that was practical was invented by Oscar Hammerstein of New York City, who obtained patent No. 272,958 on February 27, 1883.

CIGARETTE MANUFACTURING MACHINE was the Hook machine, which was invented by Albert H. Hook of New York City in 1872, but did not come into practical commercial use until 1882. As late as 1875 only 50 million cigarettes were made, according to revenue collection figures. The

The First

Hook machine was granted patent No. 184,207 on November 7, 1876. It produced a continuous cigarette of indefinite length, to be cut into separate cigarettes. Tobacco was fed to a ribbon of paper as it was drawn from a spool, the edges passing over a gummed wheel.

CIGARETTE TAX

Cigarette tax was levied by the United States under an act of June 30, 1864 (13 Stat. L. 302), but the system of placing stamps on each package was not inaugurated until ordered by an act of July 20, 1868 (15 Stat. L. 155).

Cigarette tax (state) was established April 11, 1921, when Iowa enacted a tax applicable only to cigarettes, cigarette papers, and cigarette tubes. The tax on cigarettes was one mill on each cigarette ($1 per 1,000) and was effective July 4, 1921. This act repealed the then existing law prohibiting the sale of cigarettes in that state. *(Alfred Grehee Buehler—General Sales Taxation, Its History and Development)*

CIRCUIT COURT JUSTICE (woman). *See* Judge

CIRCULAR OFFICE BUILDING. *See* Building

CIRCULAR SAW. *See* Saw (circular)

CIRCULAR SCHOOL. *See under* Building

CIRCULATING LIBRARY. *See* Library

CIRCULATION AUDIT (newspaper). *See* Newspaper audit

CIRCUS

See also Equestrian exhibition; Flea circus

Circus was owned by John Bill Ricketts and known as Ricketts' Circus. A building was erected especially for his use at 12th and Market streets, Philadelphia, Pa., where he gave exhibitions as early as 1792. President George Washington attended Ricketts' Circus, April 22, 1793. Ricketts erected a larger building called the Art Pantheon and Amphitheatre, which opened to the public October 19, 1795, and in 1797 he built an Amphitheatre on Greenwich Street in New York. In 1798 he exhibited in other towns as far north as Albany, N.Y. *(American Antiquarian Society Proceedings, April 1933)*

Circus telecast. *See under* Television—Telecast

Circus to feature an automobile as an attraction was Wheeler, Hatch & Hitchcock's Circus and Royal Hippodrome, which toured New York, Massachusetts, Connecticut, and Rhode Island, in 1864. It exhibited a "tremendous novelty, never seen before, of an ordinary road carriage driven over the common high-ways without the aid of horses or other draught animals, being beyond doubt the most simple, useful and ingenious piece of mechanism ever put into practical use."

The First

CIRCUS TIGHTS. *See* Tights (circus)

CITIZENS' MILITARY TRAINING CAMP. *See* Army camp

CITIZENSHIP
See also Immigration

Chinese granted citizenship, after the repeal of the Chinese exclusion act, was Edward Bing Kan of Chicago, Ill., interpreter of the United States Immigration and Naturalization Service, who filed his application December 18, 1943, and was naturalized January 18, 1944, in Chicago. On December 17, 1943, President Franklin Delano Roosevelt signed the Chinese Act (57 Stat. L. 600) "to repeal the Chinese exclusion acts, to establish quotas." This made Chinese residents eligible for naturalization and permitted the annual immigration of a quota of 105 Chinese. *(U.S. Department of Justice, Immigration and Naturalization Service—Monthly Review. Vol. 1, No. 10. April 1944)*

Citizenship (colonial) conferred by special grant was awarded by the General Assembly of Maryland at the session held November 1, 1784, to January 22, 1785, at Annapolis, Md. It provided that "the Marquis de Lafayette and his heirs male for ever, shall be, and they and each of them are hereby deemed, adjudged, and taken to be, natural born citizens of this state, and shall henceforth be entitled to all the immunities, rights and privileges, of natural born citizens thereof." *(Maryland, Acts of 1784, Chapter XII November session, William Paca, Governor)*

Citizenship granted to an alien on foreign soil was conferred December 4, 1942, in the Panama Canal Zone by Thomas Buckman Shoemaker, Assistant Commissioner of the Immigration and Naturalization Service, on Irish-born Private James Alexander Finnell Hoey. The Second War Powers Act of March 27, 1942 (56 Stat. L. 176), authorized the Commissioner of Immigration and Naturalization to designate a representative who shall have power to naturalize "any person entitled to naturalization, who while serving honorably in the military or naval forces of the United States is not within the jurisdiction of any court authorized to naturalize aliens."

Citizenship statute for American Indians. *See under* American Indians

Honorary citizenship authorized by the U.S. Congress was conferred on Sir Winston Churchill of Great Britain by proclamation of April 9, 1963, by President John Fitzgerald Kennedy under authority of the Act of April 9, 1963 (77 Stat. L. 5).

Japanese granted citizenship was Joseph Heco, naturalized June 30, 1858, in the United States District Court, Baltimore, Md., before the Hon. William Fell Giles. His witnesses were Beverly C. Saunders and Thomas Spicer, clerk of the court. *(Joseph Heco—The Narrative of a Japanese)*

The First

Naturalization act in the American colonies was provided for on March 12, 1664, in the letters patent of Charles II to James, the Duke of York, who was permitted to bring in subjects of the realm as well as "any other subjects who would become subjects." *(Joseph Willard—Naturalization in the American Colonies)*

CITIZENSHIP AND PUBLIC AFFAIRS SCHOOL was opened October 3, 1924, by Syracuse University, Syracuse, N.Y., through the generosity of George Holmes Maxwell. The first dean was William Eugene Mosher.

CITRON fruit grown commercially in any large quantity was raised by Edwin Giles Hart, who planted 6,000 trees at La Habra, Calif., in 1925.

CITY (incorporated) in the colonies was Georgeana, now York, Me. Sir Ferdinando Gorges on December 2, 1631, received a grant of 24,000 acres on both sides of the Agamenticus, or York, River and founded a town named after the river on April 10, 1641. It subsequently changed its name to Georgeana when it was incorporated on March 1, 1642. The name was later changed to York, Me. The charter embraced a territory of 21 square miles and the inhabitants were formed into a body politic. This was the first English charter for a city in America. Kittery, Me., was the first and oldest town in the state, whereas Georgeana was a city incorporate and not a town. *(George Alexander Emery—Ancient City of Georgeana and Modern Town of York, Me.)*

CITY (Lilliputian) was built under the direction of William H. Johnson upon a carefully prepared townsite of five acres, with avenues, electric lights, and water mains, all to a scale of one inch to a foot, in Grant Beach Park, Springfield, Mo., June 6, 1925. Ten thousand children helped to build Tiny Town, which had 1,200 miniature structures, covering every aspect of a modern city. The town was conducted under the manager-commission form of government, the officers being schoolchildren. Conceived and constructed as an incentive to building, Tiny Town boosted building permits from a $280 daily average for the 90 days preceding its exhibition to $1,843 per day for the 90 days immediately following. Six years before the townsite was selected, a miniature village was exhibited by Johnson on the floor of the convention hall in Springfield.

CITY COLLEGE. *See* College

CITY DIRECTORY. *See* Directory

CITY MANAGER was Charles Edward Ashburner of Richmond, Va., who on April 2, 1908, was elected general manager by the City Council of Staunton, Va. He opened his office April 15, 1908. His first year's salary was $2,000; the second year's, $2,500. His first report covered the period from March 1, 1909, to June 1, 1909. He served until July 1911.

The First

CITY MANAGER PLAN of government was adopted by Sumter, S.C. In June 1912, through a regular election, the voters adopted the commission–city manager form of government. The commission was composed of a mayor and two councilmen, all elected at large. The commission employed a city manager, and active administration of the affairs of the city was entrusted to him. He was, however, accountable to the commission, which was the final authority. Later the commission was composed of a mayor and four councilmen.

CITY MAP. *See* Map

CITY PLANNING INSTRUCTION was offered in 1909 by Harvard University, Cambridge, Mass., under James Sturgis Pray, professor of landscape architecture. Registration commenced September 30, 1909. In the fall of 1929, the Charles Dyer Norton Chair of Regional Planning was founded by a gift from James F. Curtis, and a separate School of City Planning was set up requiring a bachelor's degree for entrance and giving a Master of City Planning degree. The first degrees of Master in Landscape Architecture were conferred on June 18, 1925, and the first degrees of Master of City Planning on June 18, 1931.

CIVIC DESIGN CHAIR in a university was established by the University of Illinois, Urbana, Ill., in 1912 as part of the landscape development program inaugurated in 1897 by Joseph Cullen Blair, in charge of the Department of Horticulture. The first incumbent of the chair was Professor Charles Mulford Robinson, who served as professor of civic design from September 1, 1913, until his death, December 30, 1917.

CIVIL AERONAUTICS ADMINISTRATION HONORARY LICENSE. *See under* Aviation—License

CIVIL AERONAUTICS AUTHORITY (U.S.) was created by act of Congress passed June 23, 1938 (52 Stat. L. 973), "to create a Civil Aeronautics Authority and to promote the development and safety and to provide for the regulation of civil aeronautics." It was established as an independent agency composed of a five-member board named the Civil Aeronautics Authority, an administrator, and a three-member Air Safety Board.

CIVIL AERONAUTICS BOARD
Civil Aeronautics Board woman member was Elizabeth Ellery Bailey of Rumson, N.J., who was nominated to the 5-member board by President Jimmy Carter on July 7, 1977. The appointment was confirmed July 28, 1977, for the term expiring Dec. 31, 1983, as well as a full term.

CIVIL AIR PATROL (U.S.) was organized as a division of the Office of Civilian Defense on December 1, 1941. The first national commander was Major General John Francis Curry, appointed

The First

December 10, 1941. On April 29, 1943, it was transferred to the War Department by presidential order and became an auxiliary of the Army Air Forces. It was the only civilian organization permitted to use "U.S." on its insignia, and the letters appear on a shoulder emblem to identify the corps as prisoners of war, if captured, instead of civilians.

CIVIL DEFENSE
Civil defense test (nationwide) was held on June 14, 1954, in the continental United States, 10 provinces of Canada, Alaska, Hawaii, Puerto Rico, and the Virgin Islands from 10:00 A.M. to 10:10 A.M., when the all-clear signal was given.

CIVIL DEFENSE DIRECTOR was Paul J. Larsen, who assumed office on March 1, 1950, as director of the Office of Civilian Mobilization of the National Security Resources Board.

CIVIL ENGINEERING COURSE. *See under* Engineering college

CIVIL ENGINEERING NATIONAL SOCIETY *See under* Engineering society

CIVIL GOVERNMENT IN AMERICA was the Watauga Commonwealth, an independent civil government. By the treaty of Fort Stanwix in 1768 the Six Nations agreed to surrender all the lands between the Ohio and Tennessee rivers to the British. Inasmuch as there was some misunderstanding because the Iroquois had ceded land to which they had no legal right, the settlers organized a civil government in May 1772 and drew the "Articles of the Watauga Association," the first written constitution ever adopted by a community of American-born freemen. The settlers elected a representative assembly of 13 men which in turn elected a committee of 5, John Sevier, James Robertson, Charles Robertson, Zachariah Isbell, and John Carter, vested with judicial and executive authority. This was the first free and independent community established on the American continent. The area was in North Carolina and the mountains of Tennessee. (*Samuel Cole Williams—History of the Lost State of Franklin*)

CIVIL RIGHTS CHAIR was established at Lafayette College, Easton, Pa., through the gift of Fred Morgan Kirby. The first lectures were given in February 1921, by Professor Herbert Adams Gibbons. (*David Bishop Skillman—The Biography of a College*)

CIVIL RIGHTS LEGISLATION (federal)
Civil rights legislation (federal) was an "Act to Protect all Persons in the United States in their Civil Rights and Furnish the Means of Their Vindication" (14 Stat.L.27) enacted April 9, 1866, during the first session of the 39th Congress. The act conferred citizenship upon blacks.

The First

CIVIL SERVICE

Civil Service Commission was appointed by President Ulysses S. Grant in March 1871 and consisted of George William Curtis, Alexander Gilmore Cattell, Joseph Medill, D.A. Walker, Ezekiel Brown Elliott, Joseph H. Blackfan, and David C. Cox. An act of Congress of March 3, 1871 (16 Stat. L. 514) authorized the President to prescribe regulations for admissions of persons into the Civil Service. It became effective January 1, 1872. Congress refused to make any further appropriations and despite two direct appeals from President Grant, the Civil Service was abandoned in 1874. The Pendleton bill reestablishing the Civil Service was approved by President Chester A. Arthur, January 16, 1883 (22 Stat. L. 403). *(Carl Russell Fish—The Civil Service and the Patronage)*

Civil Service woman appointee was Mary Francis Hoyt (later Mrs. Brice J. Moses), who passed the examination and was appointed on September 5, 1883, to a $900-a-year clerkship in the Bank Redemption Agency of the Treasury Department. She held the position five years.

Woman Civil Service commissioner was Helen Hamilton Gardener of Washington, D.C., who was appointed by President Woodrow Wilson and sworn in in Washington, D. C., on April 13, 1920. She used the pen name Helen Hunt Gardner in her writings.

CIVIL WAR

Act that marked the inauguration of the War of 1861-1865 was the firing upon the *Star of the West*, a staunch merchant steam vessel chartered by the United States Government to convey supplies and men to reinforce Major Robert Anderson, at Fort Sumter, Charleston Harbor, although the announced destinations were Savannah, Ga., and New Orleans, La. It left New York harbor January 5, 1861, and when within two miles of Forts Sumter and Moultrie was fired upon from a detachment at Morris Island on January 9, 1861. Captain John McGowan retired from the scene after 17 shots had been fired at his ship, only 2 of which took effect. Major P. F. Stevens ordered Cadet George E. Haynesworth of Sumter, S.C., to pull the lanyard and fire the first shot. *(John Peyre Thomas—Historical Sketch of the South Carolina Military Academy 1783–1892)*

Attack in the Civil War was made on Fort Sumter, S.C. The first gun was fired on the morning of April 12, 1861, by Edmund Ruffin, a Virginian 75 years of age. There were no casualties. *(Edmund Ruffin—The Diary of Edmund Ruffin 1856–1861)*

Black regiment in the Civil War was the First Regiment, South Carolina Volunteers, organized in July and August 1862 by Major General David Hunter. There being no authority at that time for its muster into federal service, it was disbanded, then reorganized in October 1862 and mustered into federal service at Buford, S.C., January 31,

The First

1863. Its designation was changed February 8, 1864, to the 33d United States Colored Infantry. *(Records in Adjutant General's Office, U.S. War Department)*

Bloodshed in the Civil War occurred on April 19, 1861. When President Abraham Lincoln issued his state of insurrection proclamation and call for militia on April 15, 1861, Governor John Albion Andrew of Massachusetts sent five regiments of infantry, a battalion of riflemen, and a battery of artillery to Washington. While passing through Baltimore, they were stoned and fired upon by a mob of citizens. Four Union soldiers were killed and 20 injured. Nine casualties were reported among the mob.

Bloodshed north of the Mason-Dixon Line in the Civil War occurred in the battle of Hanover, Pa., June 30, 1863, between Brigadier General Judson Kilpatrick's Third Cavalry Division, Army of the Potomac, and Major General James Ewell Brown Stuart's Cavalry Division, Army of Northern Virginia. About 11,000 troops were in this cavalry and artillery engagement, in which the casualties were more than 300. This battle was one of the determining factors that enabled the North to win at Gettysburg, Pa.

Call for Union troops in the Civil War, a call for 75,000 volunteers, was made by President Abraham Lincoln on April 15, 1861, the day after the surrender of Fort Sumter, S.C.

Confederate cruiser to raid Union commerce. *See under* Ship

Confederate forts to surrender were Fort Clark and Fort Hatteras on Hatteras Island, N.C., guarding Pamlico Sound. They surrendered on August 29, 1861, to Flag Officer Silas H. Stringham and General Benjamin Franklin Butler. They had captured the garrison with 715 men, 31 heavy guns, and 1,000 stands of arms.

Confederate general killed in the Civil War was Robert Selden Garnett, a graduate of the United States Military Academy, who resigned from the United States Army on April 30, 1861, and was appointed a brigadier general of the Confederate States on June 6, 1861. He was killed July 13, 1861, at the battle of Corrick's (Carrick's) Ford, Va., now near Parsons, W.Va. *(Mark Mayo Boatner— A Civil War Dictionary)*

Confederate officer killed in the Civil War was Captain John Quincy Marr of Warrenton, Va., commander of the Warrenton Rifle Guards (designated Company K of the 17th Virginia Infantry Regiment), who was killed June 1, 1861, in a skirmish at Fairfax Court House, Va. Marr was actually a lieutenant colonel, having been commissioned May 2, 1861, but his letter of commission from Governor John Letcher had not been delivered to him. (*See also* Skirmish in the Civil War, below)

The First

CIVIL WAR—*Continued*

Conflict between ironclad vessels in the Civil War was that of the 172-foot *Monitor,* crew of 58, under the command of Lieutenant John Lorimer Worden, partially blinded by a shot while observing action and superseded by Lieutenant S. Dana Greene, and the 275-foot *Merrimac* (renamed the *Virginia*), crew of 300, under the command of Captain Franklin Buchanan, wounded and superseded by Lieutenant Catesby ap Roger Jones, at Hampton Roads, Va., March 9, 1862, a battle which was won by the Union's *Monitor. (Le Grand Bouton Cannon—Records of the Ironclads—Monitor and Merrimac—and Incidents of the Fight)*

Naval attack was made by the revenue cutter *Harriet Lane,* which left New York City April 8, 1861, and arrived off Charleston, S.C., on April 11, 1861. On April 12, 1861, she fired a shot across the bow of the *Nashville,* a merchantman that showed no colors. The *Nashville* hoisted a U.S. ensign and was allowed to proceed, even though it was a Confederate ship. The *Harriet Lane* was transferred to the U.S. Navy in 1858.

Naval chaplain killed in action. *See under* Naval officer

Naval engagement in the Civil War took place September 14, 1861, at Pensacola, Fla. Lieutenant John Henry Russell, with a detachment of the crew of the U.S.S. *Colorado,* descended upon the navy yard at Pensacola at 2:00 A.M. The steamer *Judah* (five guns), lying at anchor, was burned, and the only gun in the yard spiked. There were no Confederate casualties. Three of the Union troops were killed and four wounded. *(Union Army—Federal Publishing Co.)*

Naval officer (Union) killed in the Civil War was Captain James Harmon Ward of the *Thomas Freeborn,* who landed at Mathias Point, Va., on the Potomac River about 50 miles south of Washington, D.C., on June 27, 1861, with about 35 men and 250 sandbags to erect breastworks to unload a cannon. They were surprised by about 1,500 infantry who attacked them and drove them off. Ward was hit in the breast by a Minie ball and died from an internal hemorrhage. He had been appointed on May 16, 1861, to command the Potomac flotilla.

Regiment to respond to President Abraham Lincoln's proclamation of April 15, 1861, was the Ringgold Light Artillery of Reading, Pa., known as the First Defenders, commanded by Dr. John Keys. They reported to Governor Eli Slifer at Harrisburg, Pa., April 16, 1861. Their first engagement was September 24, 1861, at Hanging Rocks, W.Va. The other Pennsylvania regiments did not arrive in Harrisburg until April 17, 1861. Pennsylvania regiments were the first to arrive at Washington, D.C. *(Samuel Clarke Farrar, The 22nd Pennsylvania Cavalry and the Ringgold Battalion)*

The First

Serious engagement in the Civil War took place on Bull Run Creek, Va., July 21, 1861. The Confederate forces under General Joseph Eccleston Johnston defeated the Union forces under General Irvin McDowell. *(James Ford Rhodes—History of the United States from the Compromise of 1850 to the Final Restoration of Home Rule in the South in 1877)*

Skirmish in the Civil War took place on June 1, 1861, at Fairfax Court House, Va. Fifty men of Company B, Second United States Cavalry, under Lieutenant Charles H. Tompkins, were sent out to reconnoiter. They discovered a force much larger than their own and retreated. By exceeding his specific orders Tompkins frustrated a much larger movement which had been planned. One Union soldier was killed and 4 injured, while the Confederates suffered 1 killed and 14 wounded. The action at Philippi, W.Va., which has often been regarded as the first Civil War land battle, occurred June 3, 1861. The United States forces under Brigadier General Thomas Armstrong Morris routed the Confederate forces under Colonel George A. Porterfield. *(Union Army—Federal Publishing Co.)*

Union soldier killed by enemy action in the Civil War was Bailey Thornsberry Brown, Company B Second West Virginia Volunteer Infantry. On May 22, 1861, while engaged in obtaining recruits he was fired upon by Confederate pickets at Fetterman, near Grafton, W.Va. He was given a military funeral and buried in a temporary cemetery on upper Maple Avenue in Fetterman. In 1900 Reno Post No. 7, G.A.R., Grafton, erected a shaft to Brown's memory on Pearl Street in Grafton, and in 1928 the Betsy Ross Tent Daughters of the Union Veterans erected a monument in Fetterman on the spot where Brown fell. *(United States Army Register)*

CIVIL WAR MONUMENT. *See* Monument

CIVIL WORKS ADMINISTRATION (U.S.) was established November 9, 1933, with an allocation of $400 million. The first administrator was Harry Lloyd Hopkins. *(U.S. Federal Civil Works Administration—Rules and Regulations, 1933)*

CIVILIAN CONSERVATION CORPS (U.S.) was authorized by Act of Congress (48 Stat. L. 22), "an act for the relief of unemployment through the performance of useful public work, and for other purposes," signed by President Franklin Delano Roosevelt, March 31, 1933. On April 5, 1933, Robert Fechner of Boston was appointed first director Enrollment began on April 5 and the first camp was set up April 10, 1933. By July 4 the enrollment of all units, including veterans, was complete. The peak registration for the first period was 311,230 The first camp was Camp Roosevelt, near Luray Va., opened April 17, 1933.

The First

CLAIMS COURT. *See* Court

CLARINET made exclusively of metal was manufactured by Charles Gerard Conn of Elkhart, Ind., who obtained patent No. 410,072 on August 27, 1889, on a "clarionet." Previously, all clarinets had been made of wood. Conn's clarinet was made with double metal walls in the old Albert system.

CLAY PIGEON TARGET. *See under* Trapshooting

CLEARINGHOUSE. *See* Bank

CLEARINGHOUSE (stocks and bonds). *See* Brokerage

CLIMATOLOGY PROFESSOR was Robert De Courcy Ward, appointed in 1910 by Harvard University, Cambridge, Mass. He was assistant in meteorology, 1892–1895; instructor, 1895–1896; instructor in climatology, 1896–1900; assistant professor, 1900–1910; and professor, 1910–1931.

CLINCHER TIRE. *See* Automobile tire

CLINIC. *See* Medical clinic

CLINICAL INSTRUCTION. *See* Medical instruction

CLIPPER FOR CUTTING HAIR was manufactured by George Henry Coates of Worcester, Mass., in 1876. His product was so superior to those imported from England and France that he received an initial manufacturing order for 5,000 clippers.

CLIPPER SHIP. *See* Ship

CLIPPING BUREAU. *See* Press clipping bureau

CLOCK

Alarm clock was made by Levi Hutchins of Concord, N.H., in 1787. It was 29 inches high and 14 inches wide and had a pine case with a mirror in the door. The alarm rang at a specified time and could not be set or altered.

Banjo clock patent was obtained by Simon Willard of Boston, Mass., on February 8, 1802, for "an improvement in a time-piece."

Brass clock works were invented in 1837 by Chauncey Jerome of the Jerome Clock Company, Bristol, Conn. (later the New Haven Clock Company). Jerome's production of standardized parts of pierced brass plates from steel dies enabled him to sell an eight-day metal clock for $4 whereas one-day wooden clocks sold for $12.

Clock (one-day back-wind alarm clock) in a metal case was made in 1876 by the Seth Thomas Clock Company of Thomaston, Conn. The clock case was patented October 24, 1876, (No. 183,725) by Seth E. Thomas of New York City.

Clock patent was granted to Eli Terry of East Windsor, Conn., on November 17, 1797, on an equation clock. The clock had two minute hands,

The First

one of which showed the mean or true time, while the "other together with the striking part and hour hand showed the apparent time, as divided by the sun according to the table of the variation of the sun and clock for each day of the year." *(Penrose Robinson Hoopes—Connecticut Clockmakers of the Eighteenth Century)*

Clock to operate by atomic power was the Atomicron, made by the National Company, Inc., Malden, Mass., and exhibited October 2, 1956, at the Overseas Press Club, New York City. It was 84 inches high, 22 inches wide, and 18 inches deep, and was priced at $50,000. Its "pendulum" was the cesium atom, which oscillates at a never-changing frequency of 9,192,631,830 megacycles a second.

Clock to strike the hours was constructed in 1754 by Benjamin Banneker, a black man, at Elkridge Landing, near Baltimore, Md. At the age of 23, without any tools except a jackknife, and without ever having seen anything similar but a sundial and a watch, Banneker constructed this clock, made of wood, which kept time for more than 20 years. Banneker later became distinguished as a scientist. *(Journal of Negro History. Vol. 3, April 1918)*

Electric watch was made by the Hamilton Watch Company, Lancaster, Pa., and introduced to the public on January 3, 1957. The movement is powered by a small energy cell guaranteed to operate the watch for a year. It has no mainspring and has 35 percent fewer parts than an automatic or self-winding watch.

Electrical timing device. *See* Electric Timer: Electrical timing device

Electronic wristwatch (called Accutron) was produced by the Bulova Watch Company in its plant at Jackson Heights, New York City, and placed on sale October 25, 1960. In place of mainspring, hairspring, and related gears the watch had a precision tuning fork vibrating exactly 360 times per second, transistorized electronic circuitry, and a miniature power cell to move the hands and maintain timekeeping accuracy (less than one minute per month was lost or gained).

Self-winding clock was made by Benjamin Hanks of Litchfield, Conn., who made a "clock or machine that winds itself up by help of the air and will continue to do so without any other aid or assistance." On October 6, 1783, he applied for a 14-year exclusive patent right from Connecticut.

Watch (eight-day) was manufactured in 1850 by Aaron Lufkin Dennison. It was regarded, however, as impractical and inferior to the one-day watch. It was made in the factory of the American Horologe Company of Roxbury, Mass., later the Waltham Watch Company, Waltham, Mass. *(Charles Walden Moore—Timing a Century: History of the Waltham Watch Company)*

The First

CLOCK—*Continued*

Watch made by machinery was placed on the market in 1838 by James and Henry Pitkin of Hartford, Conn., the manufacturers. The movements were ¾ plate, slow train, and about the diameter of the modern 16-size. The factory was moved to New York, but in 1841 was closed down, being unable to meet the competition of the imported Swiss watches.

Watch movement to be electrically wound and synchronized was made by H. Chester Pond in Chicago in the fall of 1885. In the summer of 1886, 50 of these movements were made and set up in New York City as a system. A high-grade master clock transmitted an hourly signal to the various self-winding or "subsidiary" clocks, correcting them hourly, and thereby maintaining in each clock location the same high degree of time accuracy that was inherent in the master clock.

Watchmaker was Luther Goddard, who in 1809 opened a shop in Shrewsbury, Mass., his birthplace. He was aided by a law that forbade the importation of clocks and watches, and so was able to develop a small business. In reality, he assembled more watches from imported parts than he actually constructed. The real beginning of the watch industry came in 1849, when the American Horologe Company was formed in Roxbury, Mass., by three men, Aaron L. Dennison of Boston, who was an experienced watchmaker; Edward Howard of Bingham, Mass., who was skilled in making machinery for watches; and Samuel Curtis, who financed the enterprise, which later became the Waltham Watch Company. *(Henry G. Abbott—History of the Watch Factories of America)*

CLOCK LOCK. *See* Lock

"CLOSEUP" MOTION PICTURE. *See* Motion picture

CLOTH

Cloth mill was built in 1638 by John Pearson in Rowley, Mass. According to Captain Edward Johnson's book, *Wonder-Working Providences of Sion's Savior in New England,* published in London in 1654, "the Lord brought over the zealous affected and judicious servant of His, Master Ezekiel Rogers, who with an holy and humble people, made his progress to the northeastward and erected a town about six miles from Ipswich, called Rowley—they were the first people that set upon making cloth in this western world."

    Gingham factory. *See* Gingham factory

    Haircloth. *See* Haircloth

Jeans, fustians, everlastings, and coatings were made commercially by Samuel Wetherill, Jr., of Philadelphia, Pa. Prior to April 3, 1782, his products were sold at his dwelling house and factory on what was then South Alley, between Market and Arch streets.

The First

    Sailcloth factory was the Boston Sail Cloth Factory, Boston, Mass., established in 1788. It was 2 stories high and 180 feet long. In 1789, 30 women and girls worked 26 looms and turned out 40 yards each a week.

CLOTH-COVERED BUTTON. *See* Button: Cloth-covered buttons

CLOTURE RESOLUTION (SENATE). *See* under Congress (U.S.)—Senate

CLUBS. *See* Societies; *also* specific headings, e.g. Canoe club, Tennis club

CLUBWOMAN was Anne Hutchinson, the founder of the Antinomian party in the New England colonies. She left England and arrived in Boston, Mass., on September 18, 1634. She organized groups of women who met at her house and led them in the discussion of secular and theological questions. Her influence became so great and her views so pronounced that she was brought to trial on November 17, 1637, in Cambridge and was banished from the territory of Massachusetts. She left for Rhode Island in March 1638, accompanied by 70 followers. *(Edith Roelker Curtis—Anne Hutchinson)*

COACH (professional trainer). *See* Sports: Sports trainer (professional)

COACH (railroad). *See* Railroad car

COACH SERVICE. *See* Stagecoach intercity service

COACHING as a pastime was brought to the United States in 1875 by Colonel Delancey Astor Kane. A tallyho was built by Holland and Holland of London, England, and imported to New York. The first trip, May 1, 1876, started from the Hotel Brunswick, Fifth Avenue and 26th Street, New York City, and ended at the Arcubarius Hotel, Pelham, N.Y. The fare was $1.50 each way. The interest in the tallyho lasted 35 years. Some coaches had been imported earlier.

COACHING CLUB to encourage four-in-hand driving was the Coaching Club, formed by nine men December 3, 1875, at the Knickerbocker Club, New York City. The officers were William Jay, president; James Gordon Bennett, vice president; and William P. Douglas, secretary and treasurer. The first meet, at which six coaches participated, was held April 22, 1876. *(Reginald William Rives—The Coaching Club)*

COAL

    Anthracite coal was discovered accidentally in 1791 by Philip Ginter, a hunter, near Sharp Mountain, Carbon County, Pa. It was regarded as a species of black stone. Its value was not appreciated fully, as the coal was difficult to kindle and produced such a high heat that it endangered the old-time boilers, which were designed principally for burning wood. *(Fred Brenckman—History of Carbon County, Pa.)*

The First

Anthracite coal burned experimentally was used by Judge Jesse Fell in his home in Wilkes-Barre, Pa., February 11, 1808, much to the surprise of the populace, which regarded the coal as valueless. *(Wilkes-Barre—The Diamond City)*

Anthracite coal used commercially was successfully burned in 1812 in a heating furnace at White and Hazard's Fairmount Nail and Wire Works near Philadelphia, Pa. The coal was supplied by Colonel George Shoemaker of Pottsville, Pa., who loaded nine wagons from his mine at Centreville, Pa. A second wagonload was sold to Mellon & Bishop of the Delaware County Rolling Mill. The remaining seven loads were given away because no one would buy hard coal. *(William Jasper Nicolls—Story of American Coals)*

Anthracite coal used in smelting iron ore was used in a furnace in 1837 by the Lehigh Coal and Navigation Company at Mauch Chunk, Pa. The anthracite coal used was approximately 80 percent of the fuel consumed. On August 27, 1838, another blast furnace was erected in which anthracite was used exclusively. *(Walter Rogers Johnson—Notes on the Use of Anthracite)*

Coal is said to have been discovered by Father Louis Hennepin in 1673–1680 while on his exploration trips. It is asserted that he noticed coal on the bluffs of the Illinois River not far from Ottawa and La Salle, Ill. *(Louis Hennepin—A Discovery of a Large Rich and Plentiful Country in the North America)*

Coal hydrogenation chemicals pilot plant (large) designed specifically for converting coal into chemicals was opened May 8, 1952, in Institute, W.Va., by the Carbide and Carbon Chemicals Company. Coal was received, pulverized, and mixed with oil to form a paste, then converted under heat and pressure in combination with hydrogen gas into liquid chemical intermediate products. The $11 million plant had a capacity of 300 tons of coal a day. Some of the principal products were cresols, higher phenols, naphthalene, and aromatic hydrocarbon.

Coal pipeline loops (experimental) were built as a test at Library, Pa., on May 23, 1950, by the Research and Development Division of the Pittsburgh Consolidation Coal Company, Pittsburgh, Pa. Three other pipelines were also built. They had as their purpose the study of variables in the process of the delivery of solids by pipeline.

Coal pipeline unit (demonstration) began functioning on November 1, 1951, near Cadiz, Ohio, on the property of the Hanna Coal Division of the Pittsburgh Consolidation Coal Company. It carried approximately 9,000 tons daily through a 12¾-inch pipe. A fine size of coal was mixed with water to form a slurry, and this mixture was pumped through the pipeline under pressure.

The First

Commercial coal pipeline was completed September 12, 1956, and placed in commercial operation June 4, 1957. It extended 108 miles from the Georgetown Preparation Plant of the Hanna Coal Company, a division of the Pittsburgh Consolidation Coal Company, near Cadiz, Ohio, to the Eastlake Power Station of the Cleveland Illuminating Company, Eastlake, Ohio. The pipeline, 10¾ inches in diameter, was originally designed to move an equal mixture of coal and water at the rate of 150 tons of coal per hour.

COAL-BURNING LOCOMOTIVE. *See* Locomotive: Locomotive to burn coal (practical, American-made)

COAL CARS. *See under* Railroad car

COAL MINE
Coal mine designed for 100 percent mechanical operation was the Butler Consolidated Coal Company's Wildwood mine, Wildwood, Pa., which opened in October 1930. The drilling, crushing, loading, screening of sizes, mechanical cleaning, dumping, and transportation operations were accomplished mechanically. Rubber conveyor belts carried the coal.

Woman to die in a coal mine disaster was Marilyn J. McCusker, killed by falling rocks while working as a roof-bolter on October 2, 1979, in the Rushton Mining Company mine, Coalport, Pa.

COAL MINING CORRESPONDENCE COURSE. *See* Correspondence school

COAL OIL FACTORY to manufacture coal oil from coal tar was started in 1853 by the U.S. Chemical Manufacturing Company in Waltham, Mass. The light fractions from this coal oil distillation were called coal oil, and used for illuminating purposes. The oil made in connection with picric acid, benzol, and other products from coal tar was named Coup Oil by Luther Atwood, the inventor. When Edwin Drake demonstrated, in 1859, that petroleum could be secured by drilling, the coal oil industry died a natural death. *(Samuel Dana Hayes—History and Manufacture of Petroleum Products)*

COALING STATION, NAVAL. *See under* Navy

COAST GUARD (U.S.)
Coast Guard was created by an act of January 28, 1915 (38 Stat. L. 800), "an act to create the Coast Guard by combining therein the existing Life Saving Service and the Revenue Cutter Service." The Revenue Cutter Service had been organized by an act of August 4, 1790 (1 Stat. L. 145), "an act to provide more effectually for the collection of the duties imposed by law on goods, wares and merchandise imported into the United States and on the tonnage of ships and vessels." The Life Saving Service had been authorized by an act of June 18, 1878 (20 Stat. L. 163), "an act to organize the Life Saving Service." The motto of the Coast Guard is *Semper Paratus* (Always Ready).

The First

COAST GUARD (U.S.)—*Continued*

Coast Guard air station. *See under* Aviation

Coast Guard aviation unit. *See under* Aviation

Coast Guard commandant was Alexander V. Fraser, who served in the Revenue Cutter Service from February 1, 1842, to November 15, 1848. John Canfield Spencer, Secretary of the Treasury, appointed him commandant. His first report was submitted January 9, 1844. The Revenue Cutter Service was absorbed into the Coast Guard in 1915.

Coast Guard officers' training school was the Revenue Cutter Service School of Instruction (which later became the Coast Guard Academy). The school opened July 31, 1876, in New Bedford, Mass. The classes were held on board the Revenue Cutter *J.C. Dobbin,* which sailed on its first practice cruise May 25, 1877, commanding officer Captain J. A. Henriques, and arrived at New Bedford, Mass., on Oct. 15, 1877. In 1914 the name changed from School of Instruction to U.S. Revenue Cutter Academy, and later, with the creation of the Coast Guard, to the U.S. Coast Guard Academy. Hamilton Hall opened September 20, 1932.

Coast Guard women to serve aboard ships (other than hospital ships) were Ensign Beverly Gwin Kelley of Bonita Springs, Fla., assigned to the seagoing cutter *Morgenthau,* and third-class petty officer Debra Lee Wilson of San Jose, Calif., assigned to the seagoing cutter *Gallatin,* on June 22, 1977.

Coast Guard Women's Reserve (called SPARS, from the initials of the Coast Guard motto, *Semper Paratus*—Always Ready) was authorized November 23, 1942, and placed under the command of Lieutenant Commander Dorothy Constance Stratton. She assumed office November 24, 1942, became commander on January 1, 1944, and captain on February 1, 1944. The first recruit was Dorothy Edith Lorne Tuttle, who enlisted on December 7, 1942, as a yeoman third class.

Coastguardsman (black) was Michael A. Healy of Georgia, who was appointed on March 7, 1865, to the Revenue Cutter Service; appointed second lieutenant on June 6, 1866; advanced to first lieutenant on July 20, 1870, and to captain on March 3, 1883. He was commanding officer of the *Bear* from 1886 to 1895. He retired on September 22, 1903.

Inland U.S. Coast Guard station was opened November 3, 1881, when four surfmen were employed on Station No. 10 of the Ninth Life Saving District (embracing Lake Erie and Lake Ontario) at Louisville, Ky., near the falls of the Ohio River. The station was commanded by Captain William M. Devan. The first rescue was made November 7, 1881, when the 1,603-ton steamer *City of Baton Rouge* of St. Louis, Mo., valued at $125,000, with

The First

26 persons on board, was stranded on the left-hand reef of the falls. The vessel was finally floated off the rocks on November 24, 1881.

Mother of a coastguardsman killed in action to join the SPARS (Women's Coast Guard Reserve, from the Coast Guard Motto, *Semper Paratus*—Always Ready) was Mrs. James Munro of South Cle Elum, Wash., who was sworn in on May 27, 1943.

Woman airplane pilot in the Coast Guard was Ensign Janna Lambine, who was graduated on March 4, 1977, from the U.S. Naval Air Station, Whiting Field, Milton, Fla.

Woman to command a naval ship on regular patrol was Coast Guard Lieutenant (Junior Grade) Susan Ingalls Moritz, who assumed command of the U.S.S. *Cape Current* on June 8, 1979. The ship operated in the Straits of Florida, where smuggling of drugs and of immigrants was a constant problem. She served 17 weeks at Officer Candidate School at Yorktown, Va., in addition to taking general training courses.

COAST GUARD ACADEMY

Black graduate of the U.S. Coast Guard Academy was Merle James Smith, Jr., of Baltimore, Md., 82nd in the class of 113 graduated June 8, 1966. The ceremony was held at Jones Field, New London, Conn. His commission was presented to him by his father, a colonel in the regular Army.

Women graduates of the U.S. Coast Guard Academy, New London, Conn., were those of May 21, 1980. There were 14 women in a class of 156. The first of the women to be graduated was Jean Marie Butler of Hershey, Pa., since the graduates were called in alphabetical order.

Women students were admitted to the U.S. Coast Guard Academy, New London, Conn., on June 28, 1976, when 38 women were enrolled. Completion of the four-year course entitles them to receive the bachelor of science degree in engineering and commissions as ensigns and second lieutenants at a salary of $660 a month. Their admission was authorized by act of October 21, 1975, signed by President Gerald Rudolph Ford.

COAST GUARD OFFICER

Coast Guard Women's Reserve officer to serve overseas was Lieutenant Margaret Moon of Muskegon, Mich., who was assigned to Hawaii as a personnel officer on November 22, 1944, to prepare for arrival of SPARS in 1945.

Navy Cross to a Coast Guard officer. *See* Medal: Navy Cross awarded to a Coast Guard officer in World War II

Rear admirals who were twins nominated at the same time were Benjamin Franklin Engel, commander of the 14th Coast Guard District, Honolulu, Hawaii, and Arthur Bright Engel, Superintendent of the U.S. Coast Guard Academy.

The First

New London, Conn. They were nominated on December 15, 1966, by President Lyndon Baines Johnson and confirmed by the Senate on March 23, 1967. Each brother was graduated from the U.S. Coast Guard Academy with a B.S. degree and a commission as ensign on June 2, 1938.

Rear admirals who were twins to serve at the same time were Frank Terry Kenner and William Wilson Kenner, who were commissioned ensigns on October 17, 1924. Frank Kenner was appointed a rear admiral in May 1953 and retired in May 1957; William Kenner was appointed a rear admiral in June 1954 and retired on July 1, 1960.

Vice Admiral in the Coast Guard was Russell Randolph Waesche, commandant of the United States Coast Guard, who was appointed vice admiral on March 24, 1942.

Woman commander of a Coast Guard ship was Lieutenant (jg.) Beverly Kelley, who was appointed on April 16, 1979, to command the 95-foot long cutter *Cape Newagen,* with a crew of 14, based in Maalaea, Maui, Hawaii, to check search missions, boating safety, antipollution patrols, and law enforcement.

COAST SURVEY was authorized by act of Congress of February 10, 1807 (2 Stat. L. 413), "an act to provide for surveying the coasts of the United States," which appropriated a sum not exceeding 50,000.

COAST SURVEY BOOK was Captain Lawrence Furlong's *The American Coast Pilot, containing the courses and distance from Boston to all the principal harbours, capes and headlands included between Passamaquady and the Capes of Virginia with directions for sailing into, and out of, all the principal ports and harbours, with the sounding on the coast...,* 121 pages, printed March 1796 in Newburyport, Mass., by [Edward March] Blunt and [Angier] March.

COAST SURVEY SUPERINTENDENT was Ferdinand Rudolph Hassler, who was formally appointed August 3, 1816, by Alexander James Dallas, Secretary of the Treasury. Hassler received $3,000 a year and $2,000 for personal expenses in the field. The U.S. Coast Survey was authorized February 10, 1807, but the first appropriation was made July 10, 1832 (4 Stat. L. 570) an act to carry into effect the act to provide for a survey of the coast of the United States." The appropriation was not to exceed $20,000. *(Centennial Celebration of the U.S. Coast and Geodetic Survey)*

COASTAL SHIPPING SERVICE. *See under* Shipping

COAT

Tuxedo coat is said to have been introduced

The First

from England by Griswold Lorillard, who wore a tailless dress coat and waistcoat of scarlet satin at the Tuxedo Club, Tuxedo Park, N.Y., on October 10, 1886. *(Edwin Clark Kent—Story of Tuxedo Park)*

COAXIAL CABLE. *See under* Cable (telegraph): Coaxial cable

COBRA

King cobra snakes born in captivity in the United States were hatched July 4, 1955, at the New York Zoological Park (Bronx Zoo), New York City. The parent snakes were mated March 10, 1955, and on April 25, 1955, 41 eggs were laid. Nine eggs hatched, the first on July 4 and the last on July 12, 1955. The infant cobras were mottled white and brown and felt leathery to the touch.

COCKTAIL is said to have been served in 1776 by Betsy Flanagan, a barmaid at Halls Corners, Elmsford, N.Y., who decorated the bar with tail feathers. An inebriate called for a glass of "those cocktails," so she prepared a mixed drink, and inserted one of the feathers.

COCKTAIL, OYSTER. *See* Oyster cocktail

COD-LIVER OIL was described in Thomas Morton's *New English Canaan* in 1635. A "great store of traine oyle is mayd of the livers of the Codd, and is a commodity that without question will enrich the inhabitants of New England quicly and is therefore a principall commodity." His report was published in 1637 in a book printed by Jacob Frederick Stam in Amsterdam, Holland.

CODE CONVERTER. *See under* Telegraph

CODEBALL was played May 11, 1929, at the Lake Shore Athletic Club, Chicago, Ill. The game is a combination of golf and soccer football and was invented by Dr. William Edward Code of Chicago. A 6-inch ball, weighing 12 ounces, capable of withstanding a 600-pound pressure, is used. Codeball-in-the-court is played in an enclosed court and codeball-on-the-green is played in the open. Both games were adopted by the Amateur Athletic Union of the United States at St. Louis, Mo., on November 18, 1929.

CODIFICATION BOARD (U. S.) was created by act of June 19, 1937 (50 Stat. L. 304), "an act to amend the Federal Register Act (49 Stat. L. 500) approved July 26, 1935." Its purpose was "to supervise and coordinate the form, style, arrangement and indexing of codifications to be prepared by each agency of the administrative branch of the Federal Government which is empowered by Congress to exercise rule-making power." The board consisted of six members. The first chairman was Major Bernard Reilly Kennedy, appointed June 19, 1937. The first codification was filed July 1, 1938.

COEDUCATIONAL COLLEGE. *See* College

COEDUCATIONAL MEDICAL SCHOOL. *See* Medical school

COFFEE
   Freeze-dried coffee was marketed in 1964 and made available nationally in 1968 by General Foods, 250 North Street, White Plains, N.Y. This coffee is percolated and frozen at temperatures below zero. By sublimation, water passes under high vacuum directly from its solid icy state to vapor, bypassing entirely the liquid form.

COFFEE MILL PATENT was granted April 3, 1829, to James Carrington, Wallingford, Conn.

COFFEE PERCOLATOR PATENT was No. 51,741, granted to James H. Nason of Franklin, Mass., on December 26, 1865.

COG RAILROAD. *See* Railroad: Cog railroad

COIL STAMP. *See* Postage stamp

COIN. *See* Money

COINAGE. *See* Mint (U.S.)

COIN BOX for streetcars was invented about 1870 by Thomas Loftin Johnson in Louisville, Ky. He rose from clerk to owner of a street railway in Indianapolis and a large stockholder in railroad companies in New York, Cleveland, and Detroit. *(Thomas Loftin Johnson—My Story)*

COIN-OPERATED MAILBOX. *See under* Postal service

COIN-OPERATED TELEVISION RECEIVER. *See* Television receiver

COIN-OPERATED VENDING MACHINE. *See* Vending machine: Vending machine (coin-operated) to dispense postage stamps

COIN TELEPHONE. *See* Telephone

COKE used successfully as a blast-furnace fuel was demonstrated in 1835 by William Firmstone at the Mary Ann Furnace in Huntingdon County, Pa.

COLD STORAGE PLANT operated by mechanical refrigeration was opened in 1881 by the Mechanical Refrigerating Company at Boston, Mass. (In *U.S. Department of Agriculture Yearbook, 1900: The Influence of Refrigeration on the Fruit Industry, by William A. Taylor*)

COLLAPSIBLE TUBE. *See* Tube

COLLAR
   Collar (detached) was made in 1825 in Troy, N.Y., by Hannah Lord Montague, who, tired of washing her husband's shirts merely because the collar was dirty, took scissors and performed the amputation that created a new style in men's apparel. *(Rutherford Hayner—Troy and Rensselaer County, N.Y.)*

   Paper collar was invented by Walter Hunt o▮ New York City, who obtained patent No. 11,376▮ July 25, 1854. He used a thin white cotton musli▮ and coated both sides with a very thin white pa▮ per, a layer of paste interposed between them▮ The collars were then varnished with a colorles▮ bleached shellac that made them proof agains▮ perspiration; they could be wiped clean with ▮ damp cloth.

COLLAR FACTORY for the manufacture o▮ men's linen collars and shirt bosoms as a specia▮ business was established by Orlando Montagu▮ and Austin Granger, under the firm name of Mon▮ tague and Granger, in Troy, N.Y., in 1833. *(Arthu▮ James Weise—Troy's One Hundred Years, 1789▮ 1889)*

COLLAR MANUFACTURER of detachable co▮ lars was Ebenezer Brown, who started in Tro▮ N.Y., in 1829. He hired a number of women t▮ make, wash, and iron the collars, giving in pay▮ ment merchandise from his retail store, located a▮ 285 River Street. These collars, which wer▮ known as string collars because they were tie▮ about the neck with a string, were placed in pape▮ boxes 16 or more inches in length, and were sol▮ in his store. *(Arthur James Weise—Troy's On▮ Hundred Years, 1789–1889)*

COLLEGE
   For chairs, courses, departments, professo▮ ships, special colleges, and the like, *see und▮ name of specific subject or profession or type ▮ school, e.g., Agricultural school, Biograph▮ course, Language instruction, Law school, Norm▮ school, Political economy chair

   For college sports, *see under* name of game ▮ sport, e.g., Baseball, Boat race.

   See also Degrees (academic and honorary)

   Belly-dancing college course was "Body Cond▮ tioning Through the Art of Oriental Belly Dance▮ a noncredit course consisting of 6 lessons offere▮ August 1973 by the University of Texas at Arlin▮ ton, Tex. The instructor was Germaine Brow▮ known professionally as Chastity Fox. Sixty e▮ rollees paid the $25 fee.

   Catholic college was Georgetown Colleg▮ Washington, D.C., established January 23, 178▮ and opened November 15, 1791. The first stude▮ to register was William Gaston of Newberne, N.▮ Authority to grant degrees was authorized by a▮ of Congress of March 1, 1815 (6 Stat. L. 152). *(Col▮ man Nevils—Miniatures of Georgetown)*

   Catholic college for women was the College ▮ Notre Dame of Maryland, Baltimore, Md., whic▮ opened on September 2, 1895. It was incorporate▮ April 2, 1896. The first commencement was he▮ June 14, 1899, when four bachelor of arts and tw▮ bachelor of literature degrees were awarded ▮ six women. Charles Joseph Bonaparte, a grandn▮

The First

hew of Napoleon, was the commencement peaker, his subject being "The Significance of the achelor's Degree."

City college was the College of Charleston, Charleston, S.C., which was founded in 1770, hartered March 19, 1785, and opened in 1790. The everend Robert Smith was the first principal and erved until 1797. On December 20, 1837, it ecame a municipal university under municipal ontrol and opened April 1, 1838, with 16 students. he first president was the Reverend Dr. William heophilus Brantley, pastor of the Baptist Church, vho was appointed February 2, 1838, and who erved until his death in 1845. *(Roscoe Huhn Eck-lberry—History of the Municipal University)*

Coeducational college was Oberlin Collegiate nstitute, Oberlin, Ohio, which opened December , 1833, with 44 students, 29 men and 15 women. was incorporated February 2, 1834. The first ommencement was held October 29, 1834. Equal tatus was not granted to women, however, until eptember 6, 1837, when 4 women—Elizabeth mith Prall of New York City; Caroline Mary udd of Huntington, Conn.; Mary Hosford of berlin, Ohio; and Mary Fletcher Kellogg of imestown, N.Y.—and 30 men matriculated. In 341 the first 3 of these women graduated with the .A. degree, having pursued a classical course quivalent to that at Yale. On March 21, 1850, the ame of the school was changed to Oberlin Col-ge. It was the first school to advocate the aboli-on of slavery and to accept black men and omen on equal terms with white students.

College was Harvard College, established in 36. On September 8, 1636, the General Court of lassachusetts Bay appropriated £400 and in 1637 ppointed 12 of the principal men of the colony o take orders for a college at New Towne," and e name Cambridge was adopted. Reverend John arvard, who died September 24, 1638, left the llege about £800 and 300 books, and the name the college was changed in his honor. The first uilding, erected in 1637, was known as "The Indi-1 Collidge." It was made of brick and was 30 feet ng and 200 feet wide. The first commencement as held September 23, 1642, when the B.A. de-ee was conferred on 9 graduates: Tobias Bar-ard, Nathaniel Brewster, John Bulkley, Samuel ellingham, George Downing, William Hubbard, enry Saltonstall, John Wilson, and Benjamin 'oodridge. Nathaniel Eaton was appointed the rst master of the College. The first president was enry Dunster, who served from August 27, 1640, October 24, 1654. *(Samuel Atkins Eliot—A xetch of the History of Harvard College)*

College book catalog. *See* Book Catalog: Col-ge book catalog

College charter granted by a governor or acting overnor with only the assent of his council was sued October 22, 1746, to 12 trustees of the Col-

The First

lege of New Jersey (now Princeton University), Princeton, N.J., by Governor John Hamilton, president of His Majesty's Council. The college opened the fourth week of May 1747. The first commencement was held November 9, 1748. Reverend Jonathan Dickinson was the first president. *(John Maclean—History of the College of New Jersey)*

College charter granted by the Crown under the Seal of the Privy Council was "their Majesties Royal College of William and Mary," the charter for which was granted February 8, 1693. The first president of the college was Dr. James Blair, who was "created and established the first president during his natural life." *(College of William and Mary. Bulletin, No. 3, June 1930)*

College classes to combat the influence of communism were instituted December 4, 1935, by St. Joseph's College, Philadelphia, Pa. More than 1,200 students registered for the courses, the only charge being a registration fee of one dollar. College credits were not given but certificates of completion were issued. The president of the college was the Very Reverend Thomas Joseph Higgins.

College commencement exercises within a prison were held on January 20, 1975, in the Jackson State Prison, Jackson, Mich. Twenty associate degrees were conferred by Jackson Community College. In 1969 a pilot program of 5 classes was given at the prison on a tuition-free basis.

College comprehensive senior examination program was adopted on May 26, 1913, by the faculty of Whitman College, Walla Walla, Wash. Beginning with the class of 1914 every student who has graduated from Whitman College has passed successfully an examination, oral, or oral and written, given by a committee of the faculty in his or her department and covering the entire field of study in his or her major subject. The written examinations run from six to ten hours and the orals from one to three. *(Edward Safford Jones—Comprehensive Examinations in American Colleges)*

College cooperative. *See under* Cooperative

College course without Greek or Latin was established in 1824 by Geneva College (now Hobart College), Geneva, N.Y. The course, known as the "English Course," was designed "for the practical business of life by which the Agriculturist, the Merchant and the Mechanic may receive a practical knowledge of what genius and experience have discovered, without passing through a tedious course of Classical studies." The first course diploma, in English, was awarded in 1827 to Henry Smith Attwater. *(Journal of Higher Education. October 1933)*

College daily. *See under* Newspaper

College entrance "certified school plan" in which admission was based upon the examination of preparatory schools rather than upon the individual was "the Michigan System," originated

The First

COLLEGE—*Continued*

by Henry Simmons Frieze and introduced in September 1871 at the University of Michigan, Ann Arbor, Mich. A student who graduated from a regularly approved school was admitted without the necessity of taking individual examinations.

College entrance requirement other than Greek, Latin, and arithmetic was geography, which was required in 1807 for admission to Harvard College, Cambridge, Mass. *(Clarence Frank Birdseye—Individual Training in Our Colleges)*

College extension courses granting college credits were offered January 1, 1893, by the University Extension Division in the Class-Study Department of the University of Chicago, Chicago, Ill., "with credit . . . given in the books of the University to properly qualified students who completed any course of instruction." Twenty-five academic or secondary school courses and 40 college courses were given. Admission requirements were the same as those to other parts of the university. The first director of the Extension Division was George Henderson. *(Thomas Wakefield Goodspeed—History of the University of Chicago)*

College for women was Mount Holyoke Seminary, South Hadley, Mass., chartered February 11, 1836, and opened November 8, 1837, as the Mount Holyoke Female Seminary, with 80 students who paid $64 a year for tuition and board. The fee was eventually reduced to $60. They were required to do cooperative household tasks. The first principal was Mary Lyon, who served until 1849. Eunice Caldwell was the associate principal and Mary W. Smith and Amanda A. Hodgman were the teachers. The first graduation was held on August 23, 1838. The four women who graduated were Martha A. Abbott, Sarah Brigham, Abigail Moore, and Persis C. Woods. In 1893 the name was changed to Mount Holyoke College.

College for women to affiliate with a university was the H. Sophie Newcomb Memorial College, established October 11, 1886, in New Orleans, La. Dr. Brandt Van Blarcom Dixon was the first dean and served from October 11, 1886, until he retired at the end of the 1918–1919 session. The college affiliated with Tulane University, New Orleans, La., in October 1887.

College for women under Jewish auspices (degree-granting, liberal arts) was the Stern College for Women, New York City, which opened September 13, 1954, with 33 students. The first graduation was June 19, 1958, when 26 B.A. degrees were awarded. The first president was Dr. Samuel Belkin.

College foreign-language house in an American university was Deutsches Haus, a 4-story brick building at Columbia University, New York City, opened in 1911. The first director was Rudolph

The First

Tombs, Jr. The house was suggested by President Nicholas Murray Butler of Columbia University.

College library building. *See* Library: Library building (university)

College magazine. *See under* Periodical

College medical clinic. *See under* Medical clinic

College museum. *See under* Museum

College named after George Washington was Washington College in Washington College, Tenn. It was founded in 1780 by the Reverend Samuel Doak, and on April 24, 1783, it was chartered as Martin Academy by North Carolina (Tennessee was then a part of North Carolina). A second charter was received March 31, 1785, from the "Lost State of Franklin." A third charter, its present one, received July 8, 1795, changed the name to Washington College. The Reverend Dr. Doak was the first president of the new institution and served until 1818. The name, Washington College, was proposed to the legislature of "Territory of the United States South of the River Ohio" by General John Sevier. *(Howard Ernest Carr—Washington College)*

College orchestra. *See under* Orchestra

College president (black) of a major university predominantly white. *See* College President: College president (black) of a major university predominantly white

College principally for war veterans (G.I.s) was Champlain College, Plattsburg, N.Y., opened September 16, 1946. It was operated by the Associated Colleges of Upper New York, a corporation created by legislative act effective April 1, 1946. Two other colleges of the corporation were established, Mohawk, College, Utica, N.Y., opened October 16, 1946, and Sampson College, Sampson, N.Y., opened October 23, 1946. The president was Asa Smallidge Knowles. The deans of faculty were Dr. William H. Tenney of Champlain, Dr. Robert G. Dawes of Mohawk, and Dr. C. M. Loutt of Sampson.

College proposed was the College of William and Mary in 1617. In 1618 the London Company set aside 10,000 acres and on July 31, 1619, the General Assembly at Virginia petitioned to have workmen sent for "erecting of the university and college" at Henrico, Va. However, it was not incorporated as the College of William and Mary, Williamsburg, Va., until February 8, 1693, and instruction was begun about 1696. The first graduation exercises were held in 1700. James Blair was the first president. The college was second to Harvard College in actual operation.

College silver diploma was issued May 18, 193 by the Colorado School of Mines, in Golden, Col Made of sterling silver, measuring 4⅞ inches b 5¾ inches, 20 thousandths of an inch thick, th

The First

diplomas were signed with a stylus by the president, Dr. Melville Fuller Coolbaugh.

College summer school was established at Mount Union College, Alliance, Ohio. Lewis Miller of Akron, Ohio, presented the idea to the faculty in February 1870 and the summer school was started as a part of a four-term system in June 1870.

College to confer medals as prizes was the College of William and Mary at Williamsburg, Va. In 1770 Lord Botetourt, Governor of Virginia, presented two gold medals: one to be awarded to the best student in philosophy; the other, in classics.

College to dispense with the system of credits, hours, points, grades, etc., was Olivet College, Olivet, Mich. A new system was proposed by its president, Joseph Brewer, and was put in operation October 1, 1934. The college is divided into a Junior and a Senior Division. Candidates for the degree of Bachelor of Arts are required to pass both a preliminary examination and a final examination and to have had at least three years of instruction. Lectures are at all times open to all members of the college without distinction. Although tutors are assigned to guide the student's course, the responsibility for acquiring an education is the student's.

College to grant women absolutely equal rights with men was Mount Union College, Alliance, Ohio, a Methodist Episcopal school, founded by the Reverend Orville Nelson Hartshorn on October 20, 1846, as Mount Union Seminary. Women were granted degrees and permitted to stand on the platform on commencement day, a privilege not generally accorded elsewhere. The first nonsectarian college of high rank to grant equal privileges was Antioch College, Yellow Springs, Ohio (chartered May 14, 1852, opened October 5, 1853). Its first graduating class, July 1, 1857, had three women. Horace Mann was the first president. *Herald of Gospel Liberty. Feb. 10, 1916)*

College to have a full faculty, consisting of a president, six professors, usher, and writing master, was the College of William and Mary, Williamsburg, Va. On February 27, 1729, the college realty was transferred from the trustees to the faculty.

College to offer athletic scholarships to women was the University of Miami, in Coral Gables, Fla., which offered 15 full-tuition scholarships ($2,400 a year) to 15 athletes. The first recipient was Terry Williams of Homestead, Fla., on May 1973.

College to offer courses to commuters in traveling railroad cars was Adelphi University, in Garden City, Long Island, N.Y., which offered graduate courses in business statistics, microeconomic analysis, accounting, marketing, and the legal environment of business, on trains of the

The First

Long Island Railroad between Huntington and Hunters Point, New York City, on October 18, 1971. The commuting classrooms contained swivel chairs, audiovisual systems, blackboards, and microphones. The fee was the same as on the campus, $246 for the three-point course, plus train fare. The Master of Business Administration degree (MBA) was awarded upon completion of the 2-year course, which consisted of 3 classes a week for 8 weeks, or 2 a week for 12 weeks. The 66-minute class began at 5:56 A.M. from Huntington; the 77-minute return-trip class from New York City began at 5:56 P.M. The courses, for which Adelphi received a $20,000 grant from the Long Island Trust Company, were under the direction of Dr. Peter Berman and Dean Julius Liff.

College to prohibit discrimination because of race, religion, or color was Cooper Union for the Advancement of Science and Art, New York City, whose deed of trust, dated April 29, 1851, prohibited discrimination in the acceptance of students for reasons of race, creed, or color. Peter Cooper was the first president.

College to receive a coat of arms from the College of Heralds was the College of William and Mary at Williamsburg, Va., which was granted the seal May 14, 1694.

College whose tuition fees were based on family income was Beloit College, in Beloit, Wis., which adopted the plan on October 11, 1971, for the term beginning on September 5, 1972. Tuition varied for families with no other children in college in 1972–73 from $500 for those with an adjusted income of less than $7,000 to $1,650 for those with an adjusted income of $30,000 or more.

Dean of men was Benjamin Harrison Brown, professor of physics and chemistry at Whitman College, Walla Walla, Wash., who was appointed in 1901. At the same time, Dr. Louis Francis Anderson, Professor of Greek, was appointed dean of women. *(Stephen Beasley Linnard Penrose—Whitman)*

Dean of the faculty was Martha Carey Thomas, one of the four women Ph.D.'s in the world at that time, appointed at the January 1884 meeting of the trustees of Bryn Mawr College, Bryn Mawr, Pa.

Educational hosteling network was Elderhostel which offered actual week-long high-quality college-level courses at college campuses and other special sites for people over 60 years of age. The first program was offered June 8-14, 1975, at New England College, Henniker, N.H. The fee was $50 per person for room, board, courses, and extracurricular activities. Four other schools in New Hampshire participated in the program: Franconia College, the University of New Hampshire, Keene State, and Plymouth State. The founders of Elderhostel a private nonprofit organization were Martin P. Knowlton and David Bianco at the Uni-

COLLEGE—*Continued*
versity of New Hampshire. In 1979 the courses
were offered in all 50 states.

Educational institution exclusively for women,
which offered courses and granted degrees
equivalent to those in the best colleges for men,
was Elmira College of Elmira, N.Y. It was originally chartered in 1852 as Auburn Female University,
but opened in 1855 as the Elmira Female College.
The first class of 17 graduated with the A.B. degree in 1859. From the first, Elmira was "subject to
the visitation of the Regents of the University of
the State of New York, in the same manner and to
the same extent as the other colleges of the state."
The first chairman of the executive committee
was Samuel Robbins Brown. The first president
was Dr. Augustus Woodruff Cowles, who served
for 35 years. *(Addresses Made upon the Occasion
of the Seventy-Fifty Anniversary—June 6, 1930—
of the Founding of Elmira College)*

Elective system of study was introduced by the
College of William and Mary, Williamsburg, Va.
In 1779 students were permitted to choose the
subjects which they cared to pursue. *(Bulletin of
the College of William and Mary in Virginia)*

**Farmers' institute held by a land grant agricul-
tural college off its campus.** *See* Farmers' Institute:
Farmers' Institute held by a land grant college off
its campus

Farmers' institute sponsored by a college. *See*
Farmers' Institute: Farmers institute sponsored by
a college

Fellowship awarded a woman. *See* Fellowship:
Fellowship awarded a woman

**Fellowship (graduate) awarded by a women's
college.** *See* Fellowship: Fellowship (graduate)
awarded by a women's college

Fine arts department in a college. *See* Fine Arts
Department: Fine arts department in a college

**Fine arts department in a college to grant de-
grees.** *See* Fine Arts Department: Fine arts department in a college to grant degrees

Finnish college was Suomi College, in Hancock,
Mich., which opened on September 8, 1896.
Founded and supported by people of Finnish descent, it was operated by the Finnish Evangelical
Lutheran Church. The 2-year college opened with
11 students, in rented quarters, and the total first
semester enrollment was 15 men and 7 women.
Fees were $10 for the fall term and $15 for the
spring term; room and board cost $2 a week. The
first rector was Juho Kustra Nikander. In 1904
Suomi, whose purpose was to preserve Finnish
religious heritage and culture, became a theological seminary. The college is related to the Lutheran Church in America, which was formed by a
merger of the Finnish Evangelical Lutheran
Church and other Lutheran churches in 1962.

Fisheries college was the College of Fisheries
University of Washington, Seattle, Wash., estab
lished March 1919 when 76 students enrolled i
the first classes. A 4-year course leading to
Bachelor of Fisheries degree and short courses i
parctical training in fisheries were offered. Th
first dean was John Nathan Cobb.

Forestry school. *See* Forestry school: Forestr
school of collegiate character

Graduate school for women was Bryn Maw
College, Bryn Mawr, Pa., which was organized i
1884. The formal opening of the college took plac
October 23, 1885. From the first Bryn Mawr ha
offered graduate work leading to M.A. and Ph.
degrees. The first class graduated June 6, 188
and consisted of 24 candidates for bachelor's de
grees.

Greek college and orphanage. *See* Greek co
lege and orphanage

Group insurance for college students. *See* und
Insurance

Honor examination system. *See* Honor syste

Honors course offered by a university was he
September 1882 at the University of Michiga
Ann Arbor, Mich. The courses enabled studen
to take required work for two years and the
under faculty committee direction, to procee
within a limited range of subjects in a sort of sp
cialized course. Students who exhibited
thorough knowledge in their special fields we
given bachelor's degrees or master's degrees up
passing a cumulative examination and comple
ing a thesis.

**Intercollegiate Association of Amateur Athlet
of America.** *See* Intercollegiate Athletic Associ
tion

Intercontinental system of study was intr
duced by Boston University, Boston, Mass., whi
entered into reciprocal agreement on February
1875, with the National University, Athe
Greece, and the Royal University, Rome, Ital
Students could attend these universities witho
paying tuition and have their credits applied t
wards degrees at Boston University. *(Boston
Vol. 13)*

Italian instruction in a college. *See under* La
guage instruction

"Junior Year Abroad" was instituted by t
University of Delaware, Newark, Del. On July
1923, Professor Raymond Watson Kirkbride to
a group of eight students to France for work at t
University of Paris. The courses were given
Sorbonne professors.

Land grant college for blacks was the Alc
Agricultural and Mechanical College, which w
established by the state of Mississippi in 1871
Rodney, Miss. The original name was Alcorn U

The First

ersity. Mississippi received scrip for 210,000 acres under the Morrill Act of 1862, which it disposed of for $188,928. Three fifths of the sum went to Alcorn University and the remaining two fifths toward the support of the University of Mississippi. *(Survey of Land Colleges and Universities—U.S. Department of Education. Bulletin No. 9. 930)*

Lettermen's club. *See* College "Lettermen's lub"

Liberal arts college for police and corrections officers established by a city was the College of Police Science, in New York City, which was chartered in June 1964 and opened on September 0, 1965. The first president was Leonard E. Reisman, who was appointed on October 14, 1965. The college offered a broad selection of courses leading to both associate and baccalaureate degrees. Each course was offered by the same instructor in both the daytime and the evening to accommodate officers on shifting tours of duty. The name of the college was changed on December 19, 1966, to the John Jay College of Criminal Justice. The first graduation ceremonies were held on June 13, 966, at the Police Academy, New York City.

Masonic college was the Masonic College of Missouri, opened for enrollment May 12, 1844, near Philadelphia, Marion County, Mo. Tuition in the college was $15 a session ($10 for the preparatory department); board and washing, $25. Two sessions of five months each were offered. The maximum cost was not to exceed $85 a year for the college and $75 a year for the preparatory department. From 1847 to the close of the college year 1859, the college was located at Lexington, Mo. The first president was J. Worthington Smith, M., who was also professor of moral philosophy. *(First Annual Catalogue. Masonic College of Missouri. Sept. 30, 1845)*

Nondenominational college was Blount College, Knoxville, Tenn. (now the University of Tennessee), chartered September 10, 1794. The charter provided that the college "take effectual care that students of all denominations may and shall be admitted to the equal advantages of a liberal education and to the emoluments and honors of the college, so that they shall receive a like, fair, generous and equal treatment during their residence therein." The first president was Samuel Carrick. The next nondenominational college was Union College, Schenectady, N.Y., chartered February 25, 1795. It was required that the majority of the 24 trustees of Union College "shall not at any time be composed of persons of the same religious sect or denomination." The Reverend John Blair Smith assumed office as the first president on December 8, 1795.

Papal seminary was the Pontifical College Josephinum, Worthington, Ohio, a Roman Catholic institution immediately subject to the Holy See,

The First

established September 1, 1888. Thirteen students enrolled in the courses in liberal arts and general professional theology.

Planetarium owned by a university. *See* Planetarium: Planetarium owned by a university

School for the higher education of women was started by Emma Hart Willard in 1814 in her home in Middlebury, Vt., as the Middlebury Female Seminary. In 1819 she moved to Waterford, N.Y., and established the Waterford Academy. She had hoped for state aid, but no funds were appropriated. However, the citizens of Troy, N.Y., provided funds for a building, and in 1821 she moved to Troy and opened the Troy Female Seminary. The name was later changed and the school is now known as the Emma Willard School. Prior to the opening of Emma Willard's first school, girls were taught the merest rudiments of reading and writing, and accomplishments such as painting, embroidery, French, and singing.

State college for women was established in Columbus, Miss., by act of the Mississippi legislature, March 12, 1884. The original name of the college was the Mississippi Industrial Institute and College. The name was changed by act of the legislature in 1920 to the Mississippi State College for Women, since the word "Industrial" was misleading. The first session began October 22, 1885; the first graduation exercises took place in June 1889, at which time ten A.B. degrees were conferred. The first president was Dr. Richard Watson Jones.

State university chartered was the University of Georgia, Athens, Ga. Although it was chartered on January 27, 1785, it was not opened to students until 1801. The first state university actually opened was the University of North Carolina (Chapel Hill, N.C.) on February 13, 1795. *(Elwood Patterson Cubberley and Edward Charles Elliot—State and County School Administration)*

State university supported by a direct property tax was the University of Michigan, Ann Arbor, Mich. Act No. 59, Laws of Michigan, approved March 15, 1867, assessed all taxable property 1/20 of a mill on each dollar of taxable property, for the use, aid, and maintenance of the University of Michigan. The funds paid to the university in 1867 were $15,398.30.

State university to grant equal privileges to women was Indiana University, Bloomington, Ind. Sarah Parke Morrison, who was graduated in 1869, was the first woman to enter the school and the first to receive a degree from it. *(Samuel Bannister Harding—Indiana University 1820–1904)*

Technical college for women was Simmons College of Boston, Mass., which was chartered in 1899 by the provisions of the will of John Simmons, a Boston merchant who died in 1870. The college opened in 1902 and the first class gradu-

The First

COLLEGE—*Continued*

ated June 13, 1906. Thirty-two B.S. degrees were conferred. The first president was Henry Lefavour.

"Unit Cost Plan" was adopted by Rollins College of Winter Park, Fla. The plan, by which the operating expenses of the college are divided by the estimated number of students in order to ascertain the individual cost for each student, was recommended by President Hamilton Holt and was adopted in September 1933. Each student was required to pay $1,350 to cover the cost of board, room, and tuition for the year.

University extension summer meeting was held by the Society for the Extension of University Teaching at the University of Pennsylvania, Philadelphia, Pa., from July 5, 1893, to August 2, 1893. Edward T. Devine was director. Courses were offered in American history, European history, botany, biology, English literature, pedagogy, sanitation, harmony, sociology, political economy, and university extension organization. *(University Extension—October 1893)*

University for blacks was Lincoln University, which chartered by act of the Legislature of Pennsylvania April 29, 1854, as Ashmun Institute in Chester County, Pa., to give theological, classical, and scientific training to blacks. It was named after Jehudi Ashmun, the reorganizer of the colony of Liberia. It opened January 1, 1857. The first president was John Pym Carter, who served three years. The charter was amended April 4, 1866, changing the name to Lincoln University. *(Survey of Negro Colleges and Universities—U.S. Department of Education. Bulletin No. 7. 1928)*

University for blacks (Catholic) was Xavier University, New Orleans, La., which conferred 5 A.B. degrees on June 6, 1928. It opened September 27, 1915, as a high school and the first diplomas were issued June 15, 1917. A two-year normal department was opened September 24, 1917, the first diplomas being awarded June 20, 1919, to 11 graduates. The college department opened September 13, 1925, with Sister Mary Frances as the first dean. The first president was the Reverend Edward Brunner, S.S.J.

University for blacks to establish undergraduate, graduate, and professional schools was Howard University, Washington, D.C., founded November 20, 1866, as the Howard Theological Seminary. On January 8, 1867, the name was changed to Howard University. On May 1, 1867, the normal department and the preparatory department opened in a leased frame structure with five students, children of the trustees. It was incorporated March 2, 1867, by act of Congress (14 Stat. L. 438), which authorized the establishment of the normal and preparatory, collegiate, theological, medical, law, and agricultural departments. The first president was the Reverend Charles

The First

Brandon Boynton, who was elected January 8, 1867, and who served from March 19, 1867, to August 26, 1867. The first black president was Dr. Mordecai Wyatt Johnson of Charleston, W.Va. whose service began on September 1, 1926. *(Walter Dyson—Howard University)*

University founded by a federal land grant was Ohio University, Athens, Ohio, which was chartered February 18, 1804, and opened June 1, 1808, with three students. Governor Edward Tiffin presided at the first trustees' meeting. The first president was the Reverend Jacob Lindley. A contract dated October 27, 1787, between the Ohio Company of Associates and the Federal Government provided that the rental derived from the townships' land should be set aside for the support of a university.

University legally designated as a university was the University of the State of Pennsylvania, the name of the institution was changed on November 27, 1779, from the College of Philadelphia by the Pennsylvania legislature. Since 1791, the name has been University of Pennsylvania. It is a privately endowed institution, not a state university. Whether it was a university in fact before it was designated as one, and whether it was the first institution to merit being called a university, are questions of definition.

University on the Pacific Coast was Willamette University, Salem, Oreg., organized with the election of a board of trustees on February 1, 1842. The school opened August 13, 1844, with five students as the Oregon Institute, offering only elementary work. It was chartered January 12, 1853, as a university by the Oregon Territorial Legislature. The first officers under the new charter were elected March 19, 1853. The Oregon Institute continued as a preparatory school. *(Willamette University Alumnus—January 1927)*

University to adopt the preceptorial system was Princeton University, Princeton, N.J., which originated the system in 1905 under President Woodrow Wilson. Forty-seven new men were added to the staff with the rank of assistant professor and the special function of "preceptor." *(Varnum Lansing Collins—Princeton)*

University west of the Allegheny Mountains was the Transylvania Seminary, which was chartered in 1783 and located near Danville, Ky. The first classes were held at the home of the Reverend David Rice. It was moved in 1789 to Lexington, Ky., and consolidated with the Kentucky Academy. In 1915 its name was changed from Transylvania University to Transylvania College. *(The Register of the Kentucky State Historical Society—Vol. 33, No. 105. October 1935)*

Woman college professor accorded the same privileges as men professors was Rebecca Mann Pennell, professor of physical geography, drawing, natural history, civil history and didactics

The First

appointed in September 1852 by Antioch College, Yellow Springs, Ohio. She conducted classes when the college opened on October 5, 1853. In other institutions, women were not permitted to attend faculty meetings at that time.

Woman coxswain of a men's collegiate varsity team. *See under* Woman

Woman dean of a graduate school was Dr. Frieda Wunderlich, elected January 4, 1939, as dean of the Graduate Faculty of Political and Social Science organized under the New School for Social Research, New York City. Her term of office began September 15, 1939.

Woman professor at a first-class medical school was Dr. Florence Rena Sabin, who served at Johns Hopkins University School of Medicine, Baltimore, Md., as special fellow in anatomy 1901–1902, assistant in anatomy 1902–1903, associate in anatomy 1903–1905, associate professor of anatomy 1905–1917, and professor of histology 1917–25. She was the first woman to teach there and was the first woman member of the National Academy of Sciences.

Women's college (chartered) to confer on women "all such honors, degrees, and licenses as are usually conferred in colleges and universities" was Wesleyan College in Macon, Ga. The charter, 1836, called the new college the Georgia Female College. The first class of 11 women graduated July 16, 1840. The name was changed in 1843 to Wesleyan Female College, later to Wesleyan College. The first president was George Foster Pierce. The first graduate (alphabetically) was Miss Catherine E. Brewer. The first class was examined for graduation by the president of Emory College and by the governor of the state. (It is also claimed that the first chartered women's college was the Elizabeth Female Academy, Washington, Miss., named in honor of Elizabeth Roach. It opened in November 1818, was chartered on February 17, 1819, and remained in operation until 1843.) *(Thomas Woody—A History of Woman's Education in the United States)*

Women's volunteer college unit to serve overseas was the Smith College Relief Unit of Smith College, Northampton, Mass., which sailed August 12, 1917, on the S. S. *Rochambeau*. The unit consisted of 18 members, 17 of whom were graduates from the classes of 1888 to 1914, under the direction of Mrs. Harriet Boyd Hawes. *(Ruth Louise Gaines—Ladies of Grécourt)*

COLLEGE ACADEMIC COSTUME STANDARDIZATION was advocated by Gardner Cotrell Leonard of Albany, N.Y., in "The Cap and Gown in America," an article in the December 1893 issue of *University Magazine*. On May 16, 1895, a commission composed of representatives from colleges and universities assembled at Columbia University, New York City, and drew up a code. A Bureau of Academic Costume was chartered

The First

July 2, 1902, at Albany, N.Y., by the Regents of the University of the State of New York "to maintain a register of statutes, codes, and usages, designs and descriptions of the articles of academic costume and regalia with their correct color, materials, qualities, sizes, proportions and the arrangement thereof. . . . "

COLLEGE ALUMNI ASSOCIATION

College alumni association established for any considerable period without suspending operations was the Society of Alumni of Williams College, Williamstown, Mass., formed September 1821. The first president was Dr. Asa Burbank of the class of 1797, and the first secretary was Charles Augustus Dewey of the class of 1811.

College alumni association secretary (full-time paid position) was established June 30, 1897, by the University of Michigan, Ann Arbor, Mich., to foster service on the part of the alumni for the university. This office was supported by the regular alumni organization. The first secretary was Ralph C. McAllister.

COLLEGE DEGREE. *See* Degrees (Academic and honorary)

COLLEGE "LETTERMEN'S CLUB" for sports was established January 29, 1904, at the University of Chicago, Chicago, Ill., by Amos Alonzo Stagg. It was known as the "order of the 'C.' " Since then practically all colleges and high schools have established similar organizations. The practice of awarding blankets to lettermen who had completed their competition was initiated by Amos Alonzo Stagg at the University of Chicago following the football season of 1904. This practice has also been widely copied.

COLLEGE LITERARY SOCIETY

College literary society was the Cliosophic Society, founded at Princeton University, Princeton, N.J., in 1765. *(Charles Richard Williams—The Cliosophic Society, Princeton University)*

College literary society (coeducational) was the Alethezetean Society of Antioch College, Yellow Springs, Ohio, founded in December 1853. The society was disbanded in 1855 by vote of the faculty.

COLLEGE MAGAZINE. *See* Periodical: College magazine

COLLEGE OF SURGEONS. *See* Medical society

COLLEGE PRESIDENT

College president (black) of a major university predominantly white was Clifton Reginald Wharton, Jr., who assumed charge on January 2, 1970, as the 14th president of Michigan State University, East Lansing, Mich., which had an enrollment of about 44,000.

Woman college president was Frances Elizabeth Willard, professor of science at the Northwestern Female College, Evanston, Ill. When the reorganization took place and the name was

The First

COLLEGE PRESIDENT—*Continued*
changed to the Evanston College for Ladies in February 1871, she became president. All the members of the faculty and all the trustees were women. On June 25, 1873, the College for Ladies became the Woman's College of Northwestern University and Miss Willard became the dean of the Woman's College, which post she occupied until June 16, 1874. *(Lydia Jones Trowbridge— Frances Willard of Evanston)*

Woman college president of two colleges was Dr. Rosemary Park, inaugurated the 5th president of the Connecticut College for Women, New London, Conn., on May 17, 1947. She was inaugurated November 15, 1962, as the second president of Barnard College, New York City.

COLLEGE RADIO STATION. *See* Radio Station

COLLEGE SELF-GOVERNMENT ORGANIZATION was the Bryn Mawr Self-Government Association, chartered February 23, 1892, by the trustees, subjecting student conduct outside the classrooms at Bryn Mawr, Pa., to student rulings.

COLLEGE STUDENT
American Indian to graduate from college was Caleb Cheeshahteaumuck, a Narragansett, the son of a petty sachem of Holmes Hole in Martha's Vineyard, who was graduated from Harvard College in Cambridge, Mass., in 1665. After graduation, he returned to his tribe and shortly thereafter died of consumption.

Black woman college graduate was Lucy Ann Stanton (Mrs. Levi N. Sessions) of Cleveland, Ohio, who was graduated December 8, 1850, from Oberlin College, Oberlin, Ohio, receiving the Bachelor of Literature (L.B.) degree.

College graduate (black) was Edward A. Jones of Charleston, S.C., who was graduated from Amherst College, Amherst, Mass., on August 23, 1826, 11 days before John Brown Russwurm was graduated from Bowdoin College in Brunswick, Maine. *(Hugh Hawkins—First American Negro College Graduate.* In *School and Society. Nov. 4, 1961)*

College student to work his way through college was Zechariah Brigden, 14 years old, who graduated from Harvard College, Cambridge, Mass., in 1657. He earned money by "ringing the bell and waytinge."

Congressman to attend college after his term of office. *See under* Representative (U.S. Congress)

Jewish college graduate was Isaac Abrahams who was graduated from King's College (Columbia College), New York City, in 1774, receiving the A.B. degree. He delivered a Latin oration on Concord at the commencement exercises.

COLONIAL CITIZENSHIP. *See* Citizenship

The First

COLONIAL ELECTION. *See* Election

COLONIAL GOVERNMENT
Colonial council in America was held in Jamestown, Va., on May 13, 1607, and consisted of Bartholomew Gosnold, Edward Maria Wingfield, Christopher Newport, John Smith, John Ratcliffe, John Martin, and George Kendall. Edward Wingfield was chosen the first president for a year. King James I placed the names of the officers in a sealed box that was not to be opened until the colonists arrived in America. *(Edward Lewis Goodwin—Colonial Church in Virginia)*

Colonial government union was the United Colonies of New England, organized May 10, 1643, in Boston, Mass., by the colonies of Connecticut, Massachusetts, New Haven, and Plymouth for "a firm and perpetual league of friendship and amity for offence and defence, mutual advice and succor, upon all occasions, both for preserving and propagating the truth and liberties of the gospel, and for their own mutual safety and welfare." A board of eight commissioners, two from each colony, formed the "consociation." Issues could be referred to the general courts for appeal, if not approved by six votes. John Winthrop of Massachusetts was the first president. Massachusetts, the largest colony, gradually withdrew since it did not have proportional representation. *(Herbert Levi Osgood—American Colonies in the Seventeenth Century)*

Government on the Pacific Coast was authorized by the people of Willamette Valley at Champoeg, Oreg., May 2, 1843, when Americans and Canadians met in a field to consider the report of the Committee of Twelve on Organizations, appointed February 2, 1843. A committee of nine was chosen on July 5, 1843, to report a plan of civil government. An executive committee of three, Alanson Beers, David Hill, and Joseph Gale, was appointed for the year ending May 14, 1844. (A second executive committee, P. G. Stewart, Osborne Russell, and W. J. Bailey, served from May 14, 1844, to June 12, 1845.) The first governor was George Abernethy, who served from June 12, 1845, to March 3, 1849, when the United States took over jurisdiction of the Oregon Territory. *(John B. Horner—Oregon, Her History, Her Great Men and Her Literature)*

Independent government in any of the American colonies was formed in March 1776 in Charleston, S.C. John Rutledge was elected president, Henry Laurens vice president, and William Henry Drayton chief justice. An army and navy were created, privy council and assembly were elected, and the issue of $600,000 of paper money was authorized, as well as the issue of coin. *(The Centennial of the Incorporation of Charleston S.C.)*

The First

COLONIAL MISSIONARY SOCIETY. *See* Missionary society

COLONIAL PATENT. *See* Patent

COLONIAL POST OFFICE. *See* Post office

COLONIAL POSTMASTER GENERAL. *See under* Postmaster

COLONIAL REBELLION. *See* Rebellion

COLONIAL SUFFRAGE. *See* Woman suffrage: Colony to grant suffrage to women

COLONIAL TREATY. *See* Treaty

COLONIAL WARFARE. *See* War (colonial)

COLONIST
   Civilian settlement west of the Allegheny Mountains, other than forts and outposts, was led by Dr. Thomas Walker, a physician, and five companions, Ambrose Powell, Colby Chew, William Tomlinson, Henry Lawless, and John Hughes. They started from Charlottesville, Va., on March 6, 1750, for the Loyal Land Company of Virginia and on April 23, 1750, reached Barbourville, Ky., where they built a house that was completed April 30, 1750.

   Colonial white settlement (north of Florida) was on Neutral Island at Calais, Me., on the St. Croix River at the head of Passamaquoddy Bay. It was founded in 1604 by Pierre du Guast, Sieur de Monts, the French explorer. *(Isaac Case Knowlton —Annals of Calais, Me.)*

   Colonists to reach the Pacific coast left New York City on September 6, 1810, on the S.S. *Tonquin,* a 290-ton vessel captained by Jonathan Thorn. They rounded Cape Horn, December 25, 1810, landing April 12, 1811, at Cape Disappointment, Wash., a promontory at the mouth of the Columbia River. The enterprise was sponsored by John Jacob Astor. *(Elizabeth Louisa Gebhard— Life and Ventures of the Original John Jacob Astor)*

   English settlement in America (permanent) was established by the colonists who were sent out by the London Company on December 19, 1606, from Blackwell, England, and who arrived at Jamestown, Va., on May 13, 1607. One hundred and five colonists arrived on the *Susan Constant,* 100 tons, under Captain Christopher Newport; the *Godspeed,* 40 tons, under Captain Bartholomew Gosnold; and the *Discovery,* 20 tons, under Captain John Ratcliffe.

   Permanent white settlement in America was founded on September 8, 1565, by Don Pedro Menéndez de Avilés at St. Augustine, Fla. He left Cadiz, Spain, on July 28, 1565, and sighted land off the Florida coast August 28, 1565, St. Augustine's Day. *(Herbert Eugene Bolton—The Spanish Borderlands)*

The First

   Women to cross the continent were Narcissa Prentiss Whitman and Eliza Hart Spalding, who crossed the Continental Divide, South Pass, Wyoming, on July 4, 1836. They reached Fort Walla Walla, Wash., September 1, 1836, accompanied by their husbands, Marcus Whitman, M.D., and the Reverend Henry Harmon Spalding, Presbyterian missionaries sent by the American Board of Commissioners for Foreign Missions. *(Washington Historical Quarterly. January, 1917)*

COLOR MOVIES. *See* Motion picture: Colored motion pictures

COLOR ORGAN. *See* Organ

COLOR PHOTORADIO. *See under* Radio facsimile transmission

COLOR PLATE IN A BOOK. *See* Book: Book with color plates

COLOR PLATES. *See* Book: Book with color plates

COLOR TALKING FILM. *See* Motion picture

COLOR TELEVISION. *See under* Television— Telecast

COLORSCOPE public demonstration was made in New York City June 5, 1930. The colorscope, invented by Harold Horton Sheldon, of New York University, and Dr. Walter Arthur Schneider, is a photoelectric cell that reacts to colored light beams. It gives off infinitesimal electric currents capable of operating relays, which will start or stop machinery, operate graph needles, or perform other laboratory or shop service. It matches colors more exactly than is possible by the human eye.

COLUMBUS MONUMENT. *See* Monument

COMB of ivory was made at Centerbrook, Conn., by Andrew Lord in 1789. He cut the plates and teeth with a handsaw.

COMB-CUTTING MACHINE was invented by Phineas Pratt of Connecticut, who received a patent April 12, 1799, on a "machine for making combs." Phineas Pratt and Abel Pratt cut the plates with handsaws and the teeth with circular saws operated by a windmill and waterpower at Ivoryton, Conn. The firm is now Pratt, Read & Company. *(Perry Walton—Comb Making in America)*

COMB FACTORY on a commercial scale was undertaken by Enoch Noyes of West Newbury, Mass., in 1759. His combs were made from animal horns flattened out with their original color untouched. *(Perry Walton—Comb Making in America)*

COMBAT INFANTRY BADGE. *See* Medal

COMBUSTION ENGINE. *See* Engine

The First

COMET

Comet recorded was on November 1618; "that perspicuous bright blazing comet; anon after Sun set it appeared as they say in the South-west, about three houres, continuing in her horizon for the space of thirty sleepes (days)." *(Edward Johnson—Johnson's Wonder-working Providence 1628 –1651)*

COMIC BOOKS. *See under* Periodical

COMIC CHARACTER MONUMENT. *See* Monument

COMIC HISTORY. *See* History

COMIC MAGAZINE. *See* Periodical

COMIC OPERA. *See* Opera

COMIC SECTION IN A NEWSPAPER. *See under* Newspaper

COMIC WEEKLY. *See* Periodical

COMMANDER IN CHIEF OF THE CONTINENTAL NAVY. *See* Naval officer

COMMEMORATIVE COINAGE. *See* Money

COMMEMORATIVE POSTAGE STAMP. *See* Postage stamp

COMMERCE AND LABOR DEPARTMENT (U.S.) was authorized by act of February 14, 1903 (32 Stat. L. 825), an "act to establish the Department of Commerce and Labor." This department was to include a Bureau of Immigration (taken from the Treasury Department) and the former Labor department. The first secretary was George Bruce Cortelyou of New York, appointed February 16, 1903. The act of March 4, 1913 (37 Stat. L. 736), created the Department of Labor and changed the name of the Department of Commerce and Labor to the Department of Commerce. The Secretary of Commerce and Labor, William Cox Redfield, became the Secretary of Commerce and served until March 5, 1921. William Bauchop Wilson was made Secretary of Labor and served until November 1, 1919.

See also Commerce Department (U.S.)

COMMERCE CASE decided under the Constitution by the Supreme Court was the case of *Thomas Gibbons v. Aaron Ogden*, the opinion on which was written by Chief Justice John Marshall in February 1824. The decision determined that navigation from one state to another was interstate commerce and ruled, "This court is therefore of opinion that the decree of the Court of New York for the trial of Impeachments and the Correction of Errors, affirming the decree of the Chancellor of that State, which perpetually enjoins the said Thomas Gibbons, the appellant, from navigating the waters of the State of New York with the steam boats the 'Stoudinger' and the 'Bellona,' by steam or fire, is erroneous, and ought to be reversed, and the same is hereby reversed." *(Henry Wheaton—Reports of Cases Argued and*

The First

Adjudged in the Supreme Court of the United States, February Term. 1824)

COMMERCE COURT (U.S.). *See* Court

COMMERCE DEPARTMENT (U.S.)

See also Commerce and Labor Department (U.S.)

Commerce Department (U.S.) was established on March 4, 1913, by act of Congress, which authorized the division of the Department of Commerce and Labor into two departments. The Secretary of Commerce and Labor, William Cox Redfield, became the first Secretary of Commerce on March 5, 1913, and served until March 5, 1921.

Foreign and Domestic Commerce Bureau was created by the act of August 23, 1912 (37 Stat. L. 409), which provided that all duties of the Bureau of Manufactures and the Bureau of Statistic should be exercised by the Bureau of Foreign and Domestic Commerce.

COMMERCIAL ARTIST. *See* Artist

COMMERCIAL CORPORATION. *See* Corporation

COMMERCIAL HIGH SCHOOL

Commercial high school was established in Pittsburgh, Pa., in 1868, graduating a class of 14 in 1869. A school report covering the period 1869–1873 contains the following statement: "In August 1868, the Central Board decided to try the experiment of extending the usefulness of the school by creating a Normal Department and a Commercial Department. In the Commercial School the course of study embraces the same studies as are pursued in the best Commercial Colleges, and a diploma is issued to those who sustain satisfactory examination."

COMMERCIAL MUSEUM. *See* Museum

COMMERCIAL POLICY EXECUTIVE COMMITTEE, composed of representatives of the various departments, agencies and commissions of the government which are particularly concerned with trade relations with other countries, was organized November 21, 1933. George Nelson Peek Agricultural Adjustment Administrator, was designated head of this committee as special assistant to the President on American trade policy

COMMERCIAL RATING AGENCY. *See under* Business

COMMISSION FORM OF GOVERNMENT originated in Galveston, Tex., in 1901 as an emergency measure following the flood. The legislature granted Galveston a charter on April 19, 1901, and the system went into operation on September 1 1901. Under this form, large powers both legislative and executive are vested in a single group of officers, elected by the whole body of voters within the city without regard to political party. *(E*

The First

nest Smith Bradford—Commission Government in American Cities)

COMMODITY CREDIT CORPORATION (U.S.) was created by Executive Order No. 6340 dated October 16, 1933, in order to carry out efficiently and effectively the provisions of the emergency legislation approved and passed by Congress during 1932 and 1933. The Board of Directors consisted of eight members, with Lynn Porter Talley as president. The corporation was given authority to buy, sell, and deal in agricultural and other commodities and to loan and borrow thereon; to assist in crop reduction and marketing programs; and to store, handle, and process commodities of all kinds in connection with relief plans.

COMMON CARRIER LICENSE. *See under* Automobile license (federal)

COMMON PRAYER BOOK. *See under* Book

COMMUNICATIONS COMMISSION. *See* Federal Communications Commission

COMMUNICATIONS SATELLITE. *See* Satellite

COMMUNION CUP
   Individual communion cups to replace the single chalice were introduced May 1894 by the Central Presbyterian Church, Rochester, N.Y. One of the elders, Dr. Charles Forbes, urged the adoption of individual cups.

COMMUNIST LABOR PARTY OF AMERICA was formed August 31, 1919, in Chicago, Ill., to stand by the principles laid down by the Third Internationale formed in Moscow, Russia. The party adopted the emblem of a scythe and hammer surrounded by a wreath of wheat, and the motto "Workers of the World Unite." On September 1, 1919, the party held a convention in Chicago which was attended by 140 delegates representing 58,000 party members. The name was adopted September 2, 1919. Alfred Wagenknecht was made executive secretary.

COMMUNIST PARTY OF AMERICA was formed September 2, 1919, in Chicago, Ill. Members of the party adopted as an emblem the figure of earth in the center in white with gold lines and a red flag across the face bearing the inscription "All power to the workers." Their program was the seizure of political power, the overthrow of capitalism, and the destruction of the bourgeois state.

COMMUNISTIC SOCIETY
   Communistic nonreligious settlement was made at New Harmony, Ind., in 1825, by Robert Owen and his associates, who purchased for approximately $150,000 the development of George Rapp and his Rappites. It had about 1,000 members and existed until May 1827. *(Jacob Schneck and Richard Owen—The History of New Harmony, Ind.)*

The First

   Communistic society was a monastic group established in the colony of Ephrata, eight miles from Lancaster, Pa., in 1733 by Johann Conrad Beissel. A convent for sisters was similarly established. *(Julius Friedrich Sachse—The German Sectarians of Pennsylvania)*

COMMUNITY CHORUS. *See under* Music

COMMUNITY FOREST. *See* Forest

COMMUNITY HOSPITAL. *See* Hospital

COMMUNITY TELEVISION ANTENNA SYSTEM. *See under* Television

COMMUNITY TRUST was the Cleveland Foundation, Cleveland, Ohio, established January 2, 1914, by resolution passed by the board of directors of the Cleveland Trust Company, Cleveland, Ohio. A temporary survey committee was formed in February 1914, which served until 1917, conducting certain important community surveys. The first distribution committee of the foundation was appointed in May 1917, with Dr. James De Long Williamson as chairman. The first director of the Cleveland Foundation was Dr. Raymond Moley, serving under the Distribution Committee from 1919 to 1923. The community trust plan was conceived by Frederick Harris Goff, then president of the Cleveland Trust Company.

COMPANY NURSE. *See* Nurse

COMPARATIVE PHILOLOGY CHAIR. *See* Philology chair

COMPARTMENTIZER FREIGHT CARS. *See* Railroad car

COMPASS. *See* Gyrocompass; Radio compass

COMPENSATION (workmen's) *See* Insurance: Workmen's compensation insurance law (federal); Insurance (workmen's compensation law (state); Workmen's compensation

COMPOSER. *See* Musician

COMPOSER OF AN AMERICAN OPERA. *See under* Opera

COMPOSERS', AUTHORS', AND PUBLISHERS' ASSOCIATION. *See* Music society

COMPOSOGRAPH PHOTOGRAPH. *See under* Newspaper

COMPOTYPE was designed and patented on October 20, 1925, by Clifton Chisholm of Cleveland, Ohio, who obtained patent No. 1,557,754 on an "embossing machine." He assigned the patent to the Multigraph Sales Company of Cleveland, Ohio. The machine embosses characters on an aluminum strip from which printed material is produced.

COMPOUND LOCOMOTIVE. *See* Locomotive

The First

COMPRESSED AIR. *See* Air (compressed)

COMPRESSED PILL. *See* Pill

COMPRESSED YEAST. *See* Yeast

COMPTOMETER. *See* Adding machine: Adding machine absolutely accurate at all times

COMPTROLLER

Comptroller of the Currency was Hugh McCulloch, who served from May 9, 1863, to March 8, 1865, when he resigned to accept appointment as Secretary of the Treasury. His office was authorized February 25, 1863 (12 Stat. L. 665). The term was five years, at $5,000 a year. *(Thomas P. Kane —The Romance and Tragedy of Banking)*

Comptroller of the United States Treasury was Nicholas Eveleigh of South Carolina, who served from September 11, 1789, to April 16, 1791. The office was authorized September 2, 1789 (1 Stat. L. 65).

COMPTROLLER GENERAL of the United States was John Raymond McCarl, appointed by President Warren Gamaliel Harding on June 27, 1921. He served from July 1, 1921, to June 30, 1936. He was the first head of the General Accounting Office (GAO) created by the Budget and Accounting Act of June 10, 1921 (42 Stat. L. 23). The term was 15 years, without eligibility for reappointment, and the salary was $10,000 per annum.

COMPULSORY EDUCATION LAW. *See under* Education

COMPUTER

Electronic computer was the Electronic Numerical Integrator and Computer (ENIAC), designed and built under the direction of J. Presper Eckert, Jr., and John W. Mauchly of the Moore School of Electrical Engineering at the University of Pennsylvania, Philadelphia, Pa. Completed in 1946, the ENIAC subsequently was used at the Ordinance Department of the U.S. Army at Aberdeen, Md. It was housed in a room 30 by 50 feet, contained approximately 18,000 vacuum tubes, and required 130 kilowatts per hour.

Electronic computer (commercial) was the Univac I, manufactured by the Remington Rand Corporation, Philadelphia, Pa. It was demonstrated and dedicated at the U.S. Bureau of the Census at Philadelphia on June 14, 1951. It could retain a maximum of 1,000 separate numbers; accept information contained on magnetic tape at the rate of more than 10,000 characters per second; and add, subtract, multiply, divide, sort, and collate, and take square and cube roots as needed.

Electronic computer to employ Thin-Film memory was the Univac 1107, built by the Sperry Rand Corporation at St. Paul, Minn., and announced December 9, 1960. Its operational speed was measured in billionths of a second (nanoseconds), compared to speeds in most other computers measured in millionths of a second (microseconds).

The First

The computer consisted of a ferromagnetic film a few millionths of an inch thick formed by the deposit of vapors of iron, nickel, cobalt, or other materials on a suitable surface, such as a thin glass plate, a process generating incredible magnetic qualities that may be employed as computer memory. Memory could be accessed more than a million times a second.

Mobile computer center was established by Remington Rand Univac, a division of the Sperry Rand Corporation, New York City, which equipped a motor van with a Univac Solid-State 90 computer. The first assignment was undertaken on March 27, 1961, for the Douglas Aircraft Corporation, Charlotte, N.C.

Solid-state electronic computer was developed by Remington Rand Univac, a division of the Sperry Rand Corporation, at the company's Philadelphia, Pa., laboratories in 1958 and built at Ilion, N.Y. This computer, because of solid-state elements such as transistors, Ferractor amplifiers, and magnetic cores used in its construction, weighed only 3,500 pounds and occupied only 275 square feet of floor space. Though it had 100 times the capacity and 10 times the speed of the first electronic computer, it occupied about one sixth the space.

COMPUTER PUMP. *See* Pump

COMPUTING MACHINE. *See* Adding machine

COMPUTING SCALE. *See* Scale

CONCEALED BED. *See* Bed

CONCENTRATED MILK. *See* Milk

CONCERT. *See* Music

CONCHOLOGY REPORT by an American to appear in the United States was Thomas Say's *Descriptions of Land and Fresh-Water Shells of the United States*, which was published in Philadelphia, Pa., in 1817 in an American edition of William Nicholson's *British Encyclopedia, or Dictionary of Arts and Sciences*. It consisted of 15 pages and 4 plates, which were published in the second volume, and reprinted separately. *(Harry Bischoff Weiss and Grace M. Ziegler—Thomas Say)*

CONCILIATION COURT. *See* Court

CONCORDANCE OF THE BIBLE. *See* Bible concordance

CONCRETE BARGE. *See* Ship

CONCRETE BRIDGE. *See* Bridge

CONCRETE MONOLITHIC BUILDING. *See* Building

CONCRETE ROAD. *See* Road

CONDENSED MILK. *See* Milk

The First

CONDUCTOR-COMPOSER (woman). *See under* Musician

CONDUIT. *See* Water conduit

CONE, ICE CREAM. *See* Ice cream cone

CONFECTIONERY MACHINE for making "suckers," more familiarly known by the trade name "lollipops," supposed to be an exclusive name used by the Bradley-Smith Company of New Haven, Conn., was manufactured by the Racine Confectioners' Machinery Company, Racine, Wis., in 1908. Its capacity at that time was 40 lollipops a minute, a rate which manufacturers felt would produce more suckers in a week than they could sell in a year.

CONFEDERATE COINAGE. *See* Money

CONFEDERATE CRUISER. *See* Ship

CONFEDERATE CURRENCY. *See* Money

CONFEDERATE FLAG. *See* Flag

CONFEDERATE GENERAL KILLED. *See under* Civil War

CONFEDERATE STATES CONGRESS. *See* Congress of the Confederate States

CONFEDERATE STATES CONSTITUTION. *See* Constitution of the Confederate States of America

CONFEDERATE STATES PRESIDENT. *See* President of the Confederate States

CONFEDERATE STATES SEAL. *See* Seal

CONFEDERATE STATES WHITE HOUSE. *See under* Building

CONFERENCE
Conference of American Republics was the General Congress of South American States assembled March 14, 1826, at Panama. Convoked by Simon Bolivar, who sent invitations in December 1824, it was attended by delegates from Mexico, Colombia, Peru, and Central America. Richard Clough Anderson and John Sargeant were appointed delegates from the United States in July 1825, but their appointment was not confirmed until December 6, 1825, and the conference adjourned before they reached it.

Conference of great powers to be held on American soil and affecting American interests was the Conference on the Limitation of Armaments, which assembled in Washington, D.C., November 12, 1921, to February 6, 1922, at Memorial Continental Hall. Nine nations took part in the Conference: the United States, Great Britain, France, Italy, Japan, China, Holland, Belgium, and Portugal. The American delegation consisted of Secretary of State Charles Evans Hughes, Senators Oscar Wilder Underwood and Henry Cabot Lodge, and Elihu Root.

The First

Interstate legislative conference. *See* Legislative conference (interstate)

Pan American Conference in the United States opened in Washington, D.C., on October 2, 1889. It was called the First International Conference of American States and was initiated by James Gillespie Blaine, Secretary of State under President Benjamin Harrison. Ten nations signed an arbitration treaty. *(Russell Herman Conwell—Life and Public Service of James G. Blaine)*

CONGREGATION, JEWISH. *See* Jewish congregation

CONGREGATIONAL CHURCH
Congregational Church was founded in 1620 by 102 Pilgrim Separatists under the leadership of William Brewster, William Bradford, and Edward Winslow, upon their arrival at Plymouth, Mass. Ralph Smith was the first pastor. *(Albert Elijah Dunning—Congregationalists in America)*

Congregational Church council or synod met at Mr. Shepard's church, Cambridge (Newtowne), Mass., August 30, 1637, to condemn the preachings of Anne Hutchinson's party. Eighty-two errors of Mrs. Hutchinson's party were enumerated and condemned. The synod adjourned September 22, 1637. *(Williston Walker—A History of the Congregational Churches in the United States)*

Congregational woman minister. *See* Woman: Woman ordained a minister

CONGRESS (colonial)
Colonial congress met at Albany, N.Y., from June 19, 1754, to July 11, 1754, to form a plan of union and negotiate a treaty with the Six Nations of Indians (Iroquois). Seven colonies attended: Massachusetts Bay 4, New Hampshire 4, New York 4, Pennsylvania 4, Connecticut 3, Maryland 2, and Rhode Island 2.

CONGRESS (Continental). *See* Continental Congress

CONGRESS (U.S.)
Cabinet officer to address a joint session of Congress. *See under* Cabinet (U.S.)

Congress in session a full year was the third session of the 76th Congress, in session from January 3, 1940, to January 3, 1941 (366 days). The first session of the 77th Congress lasted 365 days from January 3, 1941, to January 2, 1942.

Congress in which 1,000 bills were introduced was the 22nd Congress, held from December 5, 1831, to July 16, 1832 (226 days), and December 3, 1832, to March 2, 1833 (91 days). There were 976 bills and 24 joint resolutions introduced (of which 462 were passed); 175 public acts and 16 resolutions; and 270 private acts and 1 resolution.

Congress of the United States met in New York City from March 4, 1789, to September 29, 1789. The 13 states were represented by 26 senators and

The First

CONGRESS (U.S.)—*Continued*
65 representatives. The largest number of representatives from any state was 10, from Virginia. The first quorum of the House of Representatives met April 1, 1789, when 30 members were present, and the first Senate quorum assembled on April 6, 1789. The final session in New York City was held August 12, 1790, when the capital was moved to Philadelphia, Pa. The first session was held in Philadelphia December 6, 1790, and the final session on May 14, 1800. The act of April 24, 1800 (2 Stat. L. 55) provided for the removal of the government to Washington, D.C., and on November 17, 1800, the second session of the Sixth Congress convened there. On February 27, 1801, Congress assumed jurisdiction over the District of Columbia.

Congress to appropriate $1 billion was the 52nd Congress (March 4, 1891 to March 3, 1893), which appropriated $507,376,397.52 in the first session for the fiscal year 1893 and $519,535,293.31 in the second session for the fiscal year 1894. The first session was held from December 7, 1891, to August 5, 1892 (251 days), and the second session was from December 5, 1892, to March 3, 1893 (89 days). The appropriations included appropriations for the postal service, payable from postal revenues, and estimated permanent annual appropriations, including sinking-fund requirements.

Congress to contain members of political parties other than Federalist, Whig, Republican, or Democrat was the 25th Congress (March 4, 1837, to March 3, 1839), which contained 242 members, of whom 10 were "others," 115 Whigs, and 117 Democrats.

Congress to enact over 1,000 laws was the 70th Congress, which met from March 4, 1927, to March 3, 1929. It enacted 1,722 acts; 1,037 public acts; 108 public resolutions; 568 private acts; and 9 private resolutions.

Congressional act was "An Act to regulate the Time and Manner of administering certain Oaths" which was approved by President George Washington on June 1, 1789 (1 Stat. L. 23). The first Congress (March 4, 1789-March 3, 1791) enacted 118 acts: 94 public acts, 14 public resolutions, 8 private acts, and 2 private resolutions.

Congressional act declared unconstitutional by the Supreme Court of the United States was the act of September 24, 1789 (1 Stat. L. 80, sec.13). This section authorized the Supreme Court to issue writs of mandamus "in cases warranted by the principles and usages of law, to any courts appointed, or persons holding office, under the authority of the United States." In a suit for a mandamus to the Secretary of State, the Court held that it had no jurisdiction, since the statute purported to extend it to cases not named in the Constitution.

The First

Congressional Budget Office, an independent agency, was authorized July 12, 1974 (88 Stat. L. 302). The first director was Georgianna Alice Mitchell Rivlin, who served from February 24, 1975, to January 3, 1979.

Congressional hearing witness (woman). *See* Woman: Woman congressional hearing witness

Congressional investigation was authorized March 27, 1792, when the House of Representatives by a vote of 44 to 10 resolved "that a committee [of seven] be appointed to inquire into the causes of the failure of the late expedition under Major General [Arthur] St. Clair; and that the said committee be empowered to call for such persons, papers and records as may be necessary to assist their inquiries." The committee headed by Thomas Fitzsimons, a Federalist of Pennsylvania, absolved St. Clair and ruled that his defeat on the Ohio-Indiana border on November 4, 1791, "can in no respect be imputed to his conduct either at any time before or during the action." *(Annals of Congress, Second Congress, First Session)*

Congressional library. *See* Library: Library of Congress

Congressional opening session to be televised. *See under* Television—Telecast

Congressional proceedings report. *See* Senate journal

Congressional session in air-conditioned Senate and House chambers was the second session of the 75th Congress, which opened November 15, 1937.

Congressional session proceedings telecast. *See under* Television—Telecast

Joint meeting of the Senate and the House of Representatives was held Monday April 6, 1789 in the Senate Chamber, New York City. The House of Representatives attended the opening and the counting by the Senate of the electoral votes for President and Vice President. The electoral votes were cast as follows: George Washington 69, John Adams 34, Samuel Huntingdon 2, John Jay 9, John Hancock 4, Robert H. Harrison 6, George Clinton 3, John Rutledge 6, John Milton 2, James Armstrong 1, Edward Telfair 1, and Benjamin Lincoln 1. Only ten states voted. Rhode Island, North Carolina, and New York did not vote. The first presidential election was held Wednesday, January 7, 1789, and on Wednesday, February 4, 1789, the electors elected the President and Vice President.

Nullification proceedings. *See* Nullification proceedings

Officer to preside over both of the branches of Congress was Schuyler Colfax of Indiana, who served as Speaker of the House of Representatives in the 38th, 39th, and 40th Congresses (March 4, 1863–March 3, 1869) and who as Vice

The First

President under President Ulysses Simpson Grant (March 4, 1869–March 3, 1873) presided over the Senate.

Page (female). *See under* Congress (U.S.)—House of Representatives

President elected by the House of Representatives. *See under* President (U.S.)

Prime Minister of Great Britain to address the Congress of the United States was Ramsay MacDonald, who delivered a short talk before the Senate on October 7, 1929.

Reigning queen to address a joint session of Congress was Queen Wilhelmina of the Netherlands, who made a brief address on August 6, 1942.

Special session was held May 15, 1797, in Philadelphia, Pa. President John Adams had issued a proclamation on March 25, 1797, for convening the Senate and the House of Representatives to consider the difficulty with France. *(Annals of Congress, Fifth Congress, First Session)*

Woman lobbyist. *See under* Woman

Woman private citizen to address the House of Representatives and the Senate was Mme Chiang Kai-shek of China, who spoke before both houses on February 18, 1943. (Reigning Queen Wilhelmina of the Netherlands was, however, the first woman to address a joint session of Congress.)

Woman witness at a congressional hearing. *See* Woman: Woman congressional hearing witness

CONGRESS (U.S.)—HOUSE OF REPRESENTATIVES

Black page of the House of Representatives was Frank Mitchell, age 15, of Springfield, Ill., who was appointed on August 14, 1965, by Representative Paul Findley, Republican, of Illinois.

Black preacher to deliver a sermon in the House of Representatives was the Reverend Dr. Henry Highland Garnet, pastor of the 15th Street Presbyterian Church, Washington, D.C. President Abraham Lincoln, with the unanimous consent of his Cabinet and the two congressional chaplains, arranged for the special Sunday morning service. The chaplain of the House, the Reverend William Henry Channing, extended an invitation to Dr. Garnet to preach a sermon commemorating the triumph of the Union Army and the deliverance of the country from chattel slavery. He delivered the sermon on Sunday, February 12, 1865, to a crowded chamber. He was, incidentally, the first black allowed in the House, as previously blacks had been forbidden to enter the grounds. *(James McCune Smith—Sketch of the Life and Labors of the Rev. Henry Highland Garnet)*

Brawl in the House of Representatives took place in Philadelphia, Pa., January 30, 1798, during the presidential administration of John Adams.

The First

Matthew Lyon of Vermont had an argument with Roger Griswold of Connecticut and spat in Griswold's face. A resolution was introduced to expel Lyon. Lyon acted as his own attorney and defended himself in the proceedings, which lasted from January 30 to February 12, 1798, and occupied practically all the attention of the House. The resolution was carried, 52-44, but Lyon was not expelled, the measure requiring a two-thirds vote. *(Annals of Congress, Fifth Congress, Second Session)*

Catholic chaplain of the House was Father Charles Constantine Pise, ordained in 1825, who served the 22nd Congress from March 4, 1831, to March 3, 1832.

Chaplain of the House of Representatives was Reverend William Linn, a Presbyterian minister, who served in the first congress from May 1, 1789, to December 10, 1790.

Clerk of the House of Representatives was John Beckley of Virginia, who served from April 1, 1789, to May 15, 1797, in the First to the Fifth Congresses, and from January 10, 1803, to October 26, 1807, in the Seventh to the Tenth Congresses.

Committee of the House of Representatives was the Committee on Elections, a standing committee, appointed April 2, 1789, to determine eligibility and rights of admission of those who had been elected. It was resolved "that a committee be appointed to prepare and report such standing rules and orders of proceedings as may be proper to be observed." *(Chester Harvey Rowell—A Historical and Legal Digest of all the Contested Election Cases in the House of Representatives)*

Congressional committee bilingual report was *Needs of the Hispanic Elderly, hearing before the Select Committee on Aging, House of Representatives, Ninety-Fifth Congress, second session* held March 28, 1978, at Miami, Fla., simultaneously printed in Spanish under the title *Las Necesidades de los Ancianos Hispanos,* a 215-page hearing.

Congressional committee headed by a woman was the District of Columbia Affairs Committee, of which Mary Teresa Hopkins Norton, a Democrat of Jersey City, N.J., became the chairperson on December 15, 1931. She served until June 22, 1937, when she became the chairperson of the House Committee on Labor.

Congressional standing committee headed by a black was the Committee on Expenditures in the Executive Departments to which William Levi Dawson of Chicago, Ill., was appointed on January 18, 1949.

Congressman. *See* Representative (U.S.)

Contested election in the House of Representatives was between David Ramsay and William Loughton Smith of South Carolina. Smith took his

The First

CONGRESS (U.S.)—HOUSE OF REPRESEN-TATIVES—*Continued*

seat April 13, 1789. On April 15, 1789, Ramsay presented a petition that Smith be declared ineligible, on the ground that he had not been "seven years a citizen of the United States," as he had studied abroad during that period. The dispute was referred to the Committee on Elections on April 18, 1789, which ruled that Smith was entitled to his seat. *(Matthew St. Clair Clarke and David A. Hall—Cases on Contested Elections in Congress, published by the House of Representatives, 1834)*

Filibuster of "dilatory tactics" occurred June 11, 1790, when Elbridge Gerry of Massachusetts and William Loughton Smith of South Carolina made long speeches in the House of Representatives during consideration of the resolution to change the seat of government. *(Annals of Congress, First Congress, Second Session)*

Foreign clergyman to open the House of Representatives with prayer was the Reverend Abraham de Sola, D.D., LL.D., professor of oriental history, McGill University, Montreal, Canada, who delivered the invocation January 9, 1872.

Gag rule was adopted May 26, 1836, by the House of Representatives, which voted 117 to 68 that "And, whereas it is extremely important and desirable that the agitation of this subject should be finally arrested, for the purpose of restoring tranquility to the public mind, your committee respectfully recommend the adoption of the following additional resolution: Resolved that all petitions, memorials, resolutions, propositions, or papers, relating in any way, or to any extent whatever, to the subject of slavery, or the abolition of slavery, shall without being either printed or referred, be laid upon the table, and that no further action whatever shall be had thereon." *(Register of Debates in Congress, Vol. 12)*

House of Representatives met in New York City, Wednesday, March 4, 1789, and was attended by four delegates from Massachusetts, three from Connecticut, four from Pennsylvania, one from Virginia, and one from South Carolina. Meetings were constantly called and adjourned inasmuch as no quorum was present. The first quorum gathered Wednesday, April 1, 1789, and the first business transacted was the balloting for Speaker of the House. Frederick Augustus Conrad Muhlenberg of Pennsylvania was elected. John Beckley was elected clerk. The first session of Congress held in Washington, D.C., convened from November 17, 1800, to March 3, 1801, the second session of the Sixth Congress.

Jewish rabbi to open the House of Representatives with prayer was Rabbi Morris Jacob Raphall, rabbi of Congregation B'nai Jeshurun, New York City, who delivered the invocation on Febru-

The First

ary 1, 1860 (first session of the 36th Congress). *(Congressional Globe. p. 648. Feb. 2, 1860)*

Joint meeting of the Senate and the House of Representatives. *See under* Congress (U.S.)

Officer to preside over both of the branches of Congress. *See* Congress of the United States: Officer to preside over both of the branches of Congress

Page (female) was Gene Cox, 13, daughter of Representative Edward Eugene Cox of Georgia, who served on the first day of the 76th Congress convening January 3, 1939, and received a check for $4 for her services.

President elected by the House of Representatives. *See under* President (U.S.)

Sergeant at Arms of the House of Representatives was Joseph Wheaton of Rhode Island, who served in the First to the Ninth Congresses, from April 8, 1789, to October 27, 1807.

Speaker of the House of the first Congress, 1789 –1791, was Frederick Augustus Conrad Muhlenberg. He served as a representative from Pennsylvania from March 4, 1789, to March 3, 1797, and as Speaker of the House in the First Congress from April 1, 1789, to October 23, 1791, and in the Third Congress from December 2, 1793, to December 6, 1795. *(Hubert Bruce Fuller—Speakers of the House)*

Speaker of the House of Representatives to serve longer than 10 years was Samuel Taliaferro ("Sam") Rayburn of Texas, elected to the 76th Congress on September 16, 1940, who served until the 83rd Congress, January 3, 1953—10 years 3 months 14 days with the exception of the 80th Congress from January 3, 1947, to December 19, 1947, when he was minority leader. Previous record was held by Henry Clay: 8 years 4 months 11 days.

Vice President to have served in the House of Representatives. *See under* Vice President (U.S.)

Vote recorded by electronic means in the U.S. House of Representatives. *See under* Voting Machine

Voting machine in the U.S. House of Representatives to record individual votes. *See under* Voting machine

CONGRESS (U.S.)—SENATE

Black page of the Senate was Lawrence Wallace Bradford, Jr., age 16, of New York City, who was appointed by Senator Jacob Javits of New York on April 13, 1965.

Broadcast from the Senate chamber, Washington, D.C., was made March 4, 1929, in connection with the inauguration ceremonies of President Herbert Clark Hoover and Vice President Charles

Curtis. The retiring Vice President, Charles Gates Dawes, and the incoming Vice President, Charles Curtis, were both heard.

Congressional open-session broadcast. *See under* Radio Broadcast

Contested election in the Senate was that of Abraham Alfonse Albert Gallatin of Pennsylvania. He presented his credentials as senator-elect on February 28, 1793. No action was taken during the Second Congress, which adjourned March 2, 1793, but on December 2, 1793, a petition was presented alleging that he had not been a citizen of the United States for the nine years required by the Constitution. The case began February 20, 1794, and on February 28, 1794, the Federalist Senate declared his election void. He was later elected as a Democrat to the Fourth, Fifth, and Sixth congresses and served from March 4, 1795, to March 3, 1801. *(John Austin Stevens—Albert Gallatin)*

Election in which 2 women contested for the same Senate seat was held November 8, 1960, in Maine. Incumbent Margaret Chase Smith, Republican, defeated Lucia Marie Cormier, Democrat, by a vote of 255,890 to 159,809.

Joint meeting of the Senate and the House of Representatives. *See under* Congress (U.S.)

Loudspeaker in the Senate, Washington, D.C., was installed for the impeachment proceedings of Federal Judge Harold Louderback, judge of the United States District Court for the northern district of California, held in the Senate from May 15, 1933, to May 24, 1933. He was acquitted.

Officer to preside over both of the branches of Congress. *See* Congress of the United States: Officer to preside over both of the branches of Congress

Parliamentarian of the Senate was Charles Lee Watkins, who was appointed July 1, 1937, although he had served as parliamentarian and journal clerk since July 1, 1935, and in other capacities in the Senate since July 16, 1914. He resigned January 1, 1965. He was designated parliamentarian emeritus of the Senate by Senate Resolution No. 4 on January 4, 1965.

Photograph (authorized) of the Senate in session. *See* Photograph: Photograph (authorized) of the Senate in session

President pro tempore of the United States Senate was John Langdon of New Hampshire, who held office on April 6, 1789, to count the vote for President and Vice President, a quorum of the Senate then appearing for the first time. John Adams, Vice President, appeared on April 21, 1789, and took his seat as President of the Senate. *(Clara Hannah Kerr—The Origin and Development of the United States Senate)*

President to address the Senate. *See* President (U.S.): President to address the Senate

President with a brother in the Senate. *See* President (U.S.): President with a brother in the Senate

Senate met in New York City, March 4, 1789. The only members present were Senators John Langdon and Paine Wingate of New Hampshire; William Samuel Johnson and Oliver Ellsworth of Connecticut; William Maclay and Robert Morris of Pennsylvania; Caleb Strong of Massachusetts; and William Few of Georgia. Various sessions were called but adjourned as no quorum was present. The first session of the Senate at which there was a quorum was held April 6, 1789, at which meeting John Langdon of New Hampshire was elected president pro tempore.

Senate cloture resolution was proposed by Senator Thomas Staples Martin of Virginia and passed March 8, 1917, by a vote of 76-3: "If at any time a motion, signed by sixteen senators, to bring to a close the debate upon any pending measure is presented to the Senate, the presiding officer shall at once state the motion to the Senate, and one hour after the Senate meets on the following calendar day but one, he shall lay the motion before the Senate. . . . " If it is passed by a two-thirds vote, debate is limited to one hour per individual. The resolution was first invoked November 15, 1919, by a vote of 78-16 on the Versailles Treaty discussion. *(U.S. Senate Journal, Sixty-fourth Congress, Second Session)*

Senate filibuster took place February 11–21, 1811, when discussion was held on the Bank of the United States. The filibuster was not continuous, as other business was transacted during the period. The charter was approved in an "act to incorporate the subscribers to the Bank of the United States," February 25, 1791 (1 Stat. L. 191). *(Annals of the Congress of the United States, Eleventh Congress, Third Session)*

Senate filibuster (continuous) extended from February 18, 1841, to March 11, 1841. The topic was the dismissal of the printers of the Senate (27th Congress) and the election of a public printer.

Senate hearing in which women, other than members of Congress, were permitted on the floor was held on November 22, 1929. Two women employees of the Tariff Commission, Ruth Peterson and Evelyn Southworth, testified as experts during the tariff debate on rayon.

Senate proceedings telecast. *See under* Television—Telecast

Senate session in which 2 women were seated was the 87th Congress, which convened January 3, 1961. The women senators were Margaret Chase Smith, Republican, of Maine, and Maurine Brown Neuberger, Democrat, of Oregon.

The First

CONGRESS (U.S.)—SENATE—*Continued*

Senate session to which the public was admitted was the trial of Abraham Alfonse Albert Gallatin, senator from Pennsylvania. It was argued that he had not been a citizen of the United States for the required nine years. On February 11, 1794, it was resolved "that the doors of the Senate be opened, and continue open, during the discussion upon the contested election of Albert Gallatin." A motion was passed February 20, 1794, during the second session of the Third Congress that the Senate chamber "be provided with galleries which shall be permitted to be open every morning so long as the Senate shall be engaged in their legislative capacity, unless in such cases as may in the opinion of the Senate require secrecy." *(Henry H. Gilfry—Precedents. Decision on Points of order, with Phraseology, in the United States Senate)*

Senate special session was held for one day, March 4, 1791, at the Senate Chamber, Philadelphia, Pa., and was summoned by President George Washington to nominate the several officers necessary to put the federal government into operation in the newly admitted state of Vermont, the supervisors of the several districts within the United States, and the officers for an additional military establishment of the United States. *(Annals of Congress, Second Congress, First Session)*

Senatorial controversy in which no candidate was seated after a recount followed the election of November 2, 1926, in Pennsylvania. William Bauchop Wilson, a Democrat, was defeated by William Scott Vare, a Republican, who presented his credentials as senator-elect for the term beginning March 4, 1927. The Senate, on December 6, 1929, by a vote of 58-22 decided that Vare was not entitled to the senatorial seat. He was not permitted to qualify and was unseated on December 6, 1929. Governor John Stuchell Fisher of Pennsylvania appointed Joseph Ridgway Grundy, a Republican, to the vacant seat. Grundy served from December 11, 1929, to December 1, 1930.

Whip was Senator James Hamilton Lewis of Illinois, who was appointed May 28, 1913, by the Democratic Party to see that Democrats were present or paired at every roll call. He was designated as assistant to Majority Leader Senator John Worth Kern of Indiana. The first whip of the Republican Party was Senator James Wolcott Wadsworth of New York, who served one week in 1915 until Senator Charles Curtis of Kansas was named his successor.

CONGRESS of the Confederate States held its first provisional session in Montgomery, Ala., from February 4, 1861, to March 16, 1861. The president of the Senate was Alexander Hamilton Stephens of Georgia; the president pro tempore, Robert Mercer Taliaferro Hunter of Virginia, and the Secretary of the Senate, James H. Nash of

The First

South Carolina. The House of Representatives under the permanent constitution met in Richmond, Va., February 18, 1861. Emmet Dixon of Georgia was elected clerk; and Thomas Salem Bocock of Virginia, speaker. The session adjourned April 21, 1862.

CONGRESSIONAL APPORTIONMENT under the Constitution was authorized by act of April 14, 1792 (1 Stat. L. 253), an "act for apportioning representatives among the several states according to the first enumeration." The first apportionment was made in 1793 based on the first decennial census (1790) and provided for 106 representatives, one for every 33,000 of population. The first Congress consisted of 65 representatives, one for every 30,000.

CONGRESSIONAL CAUCUS

Congressional caucus was held secretly in 1800 by the Federalist party at the instigation of Alexander Hamilton, who desired the reelection of President John Adams. The Democratic-Republicans later held a caucus and nominated Thomas Jefferson. Adams and Jefferson each received 73 electoral votes, whereupon the election was turned over to the House of Representatives, which, after 37 ballots between February 11 and 17, 1801, elected Thomas Jefferson of Virginia as President and Aaron Burr of New York as Vice President. *(Theodore Wells Cousens—Politics and Political Organizations in America)*

Congressional caucus (open, not secret) was held February 29, 1804, by the Democratic-Republicans, who nominated Thomas Jefferson of Virginia for President. Jefferson was elected, receiving 162 of the 176 electoral votes. George Clinton was elected Vice President.

CONGRESSIONAL CEMETERY. *See* Cemetery

CONGRESSIONAL DIRECTORY published by the United States Government was authorized by act of February 14, 1865 (13 Stat. L. 568), and published in 1865 for the first session of the 39th Congress. Compiled by Benjamin Perley Poore, it contained, in addition to a roster of congressmen, information about Washington banks, insurance companies, hotels, express offices, churches, railroads, steamboats, mails, etc. It contained 57 pages. *(Benjamin Perley Poore—Perley's Reminiscences)*

CONGRESSIONAL HEARING WITNESS (woman). *See* Woman: Woman congressional hearing witness

CONGRESSIONAL LIBRARY. *See* Library: Library of Congress

CONGRESSIONAL MEDAL. *See* Medal: Medal of Honor

CONGRESSMAN (U.S.). *See* Representative (U.S.)

The First

CONGRESSWOMAN (U.S.). *See* Representative (U.S.)

CONJURER

Conjurer of note was Richard Potter, who demonstrated "upward of one hundred curious but mysterious experiments with cards, eggs, money, etc." He was also a ventriloquist and performed at the Columbian Museum, Boston, Mass., in November 1811.

CONSCIENCE FUND was started in 1811 during President James Madison's administration by an unknown person who claimed to have defrauded the government and the Treasury of $5. Other deposits in that year increased the total to $250. No further deposits were received until 1827, when $6 was forwarded. Nothing was received in 1848. The largest amount collected in one year was received in 1950 when $370,285.47 was sent in. For statistical and accounting purposes, funds are listed as "Miscellaneous Receipts."

CONSCIENTIOUS OBJECTOR TO RECEIVE A MEDAL OF HONOR. *See under* Medal

CONSCIENTIOUS OBJECTORS to refuse to aid the country in time of war were led by Ann Lee. She and eight of her sect of Shakers left Liverpool, England, on the *Mariah,* May 19, 1774, arrived in New York City, August 6, 1774, and settled in Watervliet, N.Y., in 1776. Because of religious reasons, she and a group of Shakers refused to aid the colonies in the War for Independence with the result that they were accused of treason and imprisoned in the old fort in Albany, N.Y. They were placed in jail without the formality of a trial. Her disciples were released from prison on December 20, 1780. Ann Lee was transferred to the Poughkeepsie, N.Y., jail and was released shortly thereafter. *(The Life and Gospel Experience of [Mother] Ann Lee, Canterbury, Md.)*
    See also Shaker Society

CONSCIENTIOUS OBJECTORS' CAMP (class IV-3) was the Patapsco Camp–Civilian Public Service Camp, Relay Post Office, Md., opened May 15, 1941, when 26 men of various faiths and beliefs arrived. The director was Dr. Ernest Atkins Wildman, professor of chemistry, Earlham College, Richmond, Ind. Members worked in the neighboring Patapsco State Park and in the State Forestry Nursery. Similar camps were later opened by the National Service Board for Religious Objectors.

CONSCRIPTION

Colonial conscription legislation was enacted April 18, 1637, in Boston, Mass., by the Massachusetts Bay legislature, which provided "there shalbee 160 men pvided to be chosen out of the severall townes according to the portion underwritten," to be used in the war against the Pecoit Indians. The conscription call was as follows: Boston 26, Salem 18, Ipswich 17, Saugust 16, Watertowne 14, Dorchester 13, Charlestown 12,

The First

Roxberry 10, Newetowne 9, Newberry 8, Hingham 6, Waymothe 5, Meadfoarde 3, and Marbleheade 3. *(Nathaniel B. Shurtleff—Records of the Governor and Company of the Massachusetts Bay of New England 1628–1641)*

Conscription was authorized by the act of May 8, 1792 (1 Stat. L. 270), "effectually to provide for the National Defense by establishing a uniform militia throughout the United States." Every free able-bodied white male citizen between the ages of 18 and 45 was required to be enrolled in the militia of the United States and to supply himself with a gun and no fewer than 24 cartridges suited to the bore of his musket. There was no penalty for nonobservance. This law left the militia in the command of the states.

Peacetime conscription bill was passed September 14, 1940 (Senate: 47 for, 35 against; House: 232 for, 124 against), and called for a total of 900,-000 selectees to be trained in any given year. Registration was required of all men who attained the age of 21 and who had not reached the age of 36 on October 16, 1940. The drawing of numbers was made October 29, 1940, in Washington, D.C. The call for the first 75,000 men was made November 15, 1940. Dr. Clarence Addison Dykstra was confirmed as director of the draft on October 15, 1940. The first number, No. 158, was drawn by Secretary of War Henry Lewis Stimson.

Wartime conscription bill was passed March 3, 1863 (12 Stat. L. 731), "an act for enrolling and calling out the national forces, and for other purposes." It required men 20 to 45 years of age to be enrolled April 1, 1863, by provost marshals. Exemptions could be bought for $300. The first draft call was made July 7, 1863. A conscription bill had been passed November 10, 1814, by the Senate and another on December 9, 1814, by the House, but no compromise bill was enacted since the Treaty of Peace signed December 24, 1814, at Ghent, Belgium, terminated the war of 1812.

CONSERVATION CORPS. *See* Civilian Conservation Corps (U.S.)

CONSTITUTION

Constitution to state "the foundation of authority is in the free consent of the people" was the "fundamental orders," the first constitution of Connecticut, drawn by Roger Ludlow and adopted January 14, 1639, in Hartford, Conn., by representatives of Wethersfield, Windsor, and Hartford. Ludlow was influenced by a sermon delivered May 31, 1638, by Thomas Hooker at Center Church, Hartford, Conn. *(James Hammond Trumbull—Public Records of the Colony of Connecticut Prior to the Union with the New Haven Colony)*

Constitution of the Continental Congress. See Articles of Confederation

The First

CONSTITUTION—*Continued*
    State constitution. *See under* State

CONSTITUTION OF THE CONFEDERATE STATES OF AMERICA, adopted March 11, 1861, contained this preamble: "We the people of the Confederate States, each State acting in its sovereign and independent character, in order to form a permanent federal government, establish justice, insure domestic tranquility, and secure the blessings of liberty to ourselves and our posterity —invoking the favor and guidance of Almighty God—do ordain and establish this constitution for the Confederate States of America." It was adopted at Montgomery, Ala. *(Confederate States of America—The Statutes at Large of the Provisional Government of the Confederate States of America . . .)*

CONSTITUTION OF THE UNITED STATES
    Constitution (federal) was signed September 17, 1787, at the conclusion of the Constitutional Convention, which first met at Philadelphia, Pa., on May 25, 1787. The convention was scheduled for May 14, 1787, but a quorum of 7 states was not present until May 25, 1787, on which date the delegates elected George Washington president of the convention and William Jackson secretary. Sessions were held on 87 of the 116 days between May 25 and September 17. Of the original 55 delegates, only 41 remained to the conclusion. Three refused to sign the Constitution. The 9th state to ratify the Constitution, thus making it binding for the 13 former colonies, was New Hampshire, whose legislature approved by a vote of 57-47 on June 21, 1788.

    Constitution of the United States was first published in a newspaper in the September 19, 1787, *Pennsylvania Packet and Daily Advertiser,* Philadelphia, Pa., published by [John] Dunlap and [David C.] Claypoole.

    Printed copies of the Constitution of the United States of America, consisting of a preamble and seven articles, were printed from plates engraved by Jacob Shallus, assistant clerk of the Pennsylvania Assembly, who received $30 for the work. Sixty proof sheets were printed August 1-3, 1787, and laid before the Constitutional Convention on August 6, 1787. The constitution was adopted September 17, 1787, and ratified by the necessary nine states by June 21, 1788, but was not declared in effect until March 4, 1789.

    State to ratify the federal Constitution. *See under* State

CONSTITUTIONAL AMENDMENT (U.S.)
    See also Declaration of Rights

    Constitutional amendment submitted to the states for repeal was offered by the Blaine repeal resolution to void the 18th (Prohibition) Amendment. The bill was passed by the Senate, February 16, 1933, by a vote of 63-23, and by the House

The First

on February 20, 1933, which concurred by 289-121. The amendment was proposed to conventions of the states by the 72nd Congress on February 20, 1933. The first state to ratify was Michigan, April 10, 1933. The amendment was declared ratified December 5, 1933, by a proclamation of the Secretary of State, after the 36th state had ratified it.

    Constitutional amendments, known as the Bill of Rights, were drawn up by James Madison and were declared in force on December 15, 1791, having been passed by both Houses and ratified by the required number of states. Originally 12 amendments were passed by both houses, but 2 of them failed to secure the requisite number of state ratifications. The first of the 10 amendments established religious freedom, freedom of speech and press, and the right to assemble and to petition. The amendments were submitted to the states by the First Congress on September 25, 1789. The first state to ratify was New Jersey, which acted on November 20, 1789. *(Francis Newton Thorpe—Constitutional History of the American People)*

    Income tax amendment to the Constitution. *See under* Tax

    Proposed amendment to the Constitution was Article I, submitted 1789. It dealt with the proportionment of representatives and was not ratified. The second proposal concerned compensation. Both were defeated. Articles III to XII were ratified and became the first 10 amendments, known as the Bill of Rights.

    Proposed Constitutional amendment to bear the signature of a President was signed by President Abraham Lincoln on March 2, 1861, during the second session of the 46th Congress: "no amendment shall be made to the Constitution which will authorize or give to Congress, the power to abolish or interfere, within any State, with the domestic institutions thereof, including that of persons held to labor or service by the laws of said State." The proposal was not ratified. As the constitution provides that upon the concurrence of two-thirds of both Houses of Congress the proposal becomes law when ratified by three-fourths of the States, a presidential signature is not necessary or required.

    Woman suffrage amendment. *See under* Woman suffrage

CONSTITUTIONAL UNION PARTY was organized May 9, 1860, at a convention held in Baltimore, Md., the occasion on which the party may be said to have been definitely organized. This was the party's first and only convention. The platform declared for "the Constitution of the Country, the Union of the States and the Enforcement of the Laws." The delegates nominated John Bell of Tennessee for president and Edward Everett of Massachusetts for vice president. They received 12 electoral votes as compared with 180

The First

cast for Abraham Lincoln, the Republican nominee, in the election of November 6, 1860.

CONSULAR SERVICE. *See under* Diplomatic service

CONSULAR SERVICE FEE STAMPS. *See* Stamp

CONSUMER PROTECTION
   Consumer protection (federal law) was "an act forbidding the importation, exportation or carriage in interstate commerce of falsely or spuriously stamped articles of merchandise made of gold or silver or their alloys" enacted June 13, 1906 (34 Stat.L.260) and effective 1 year after passage.

CONSUMER TRANSACTION LAW. *See* Language: Plain language law

CONSUMERS' ADVISORY BOARD (U.S.) was authorized June 16, 1933 (48 Stat. L. 195) under the National Industrial Recovery Act. It was organized June 26, 1933. The first chairman was Mrs. Charles Cary Rumsey.

CONSUMERS' COOPERATIVE SOCIETY. *See under* Cooperative

CONSUMERS' COUNSEL (U.S.) was authorized June 16, 1933, under the Agricultural Adjustment Act. Frederic Clemson Howe was appointed the first counsel.

CONSUMPTIVES' HOSPITAL. *See* Hospital: Tuberculosis hospital

CONTACT LENS. *See* Lens

CONTEMPORARY NOVELS COURSE. *See* Novel course

CONTESTED ELECTION (Congress). *See under* Congress (U.S.)—House of Representatives; Congress (U.S.)—Senate

CONTINENTAL CONGRESS
   See also President of the Continental Congress

   Continental Congress assembled at Carpenters' Hall, Philadelphia, Pa., on Monday, September 5, 1774, and consisted of 44 delegates from 11 colonies. Delegates from Georgia and North Carolina did not attend until later sessions. The Congress adjourned October 26, 1774, recommending another session to begin May 10, 1775, at Philadelphia, Pa. *(Journals of the Continental Congress from 1774 to 1789)*

   Continental Congress to be opened with prayer was held on September 7, 1774. The Reverend Jacob Duche, an Episcopalian, rector of Christ Church, appeared in his canonicals, attended by his clerk. The morning service of the Episcopal Church was read, the clerk making the responses. The Psalter for the seventh day of the month includes the 35th Psalm, wherein David prays for protection against his enemies: "Plead my cause, O Lord, with them that strive with me; fight against them that fight against me." The rector concluded with an appeal so heartfelt that Con-

The First

gress gave him a vote of thanks. The session opened at 9 A.M. at Carpenters' Hall, Philadelphia, Pa. *(Thatcher's Military Journal)*

   Law (federal) prohibiting slavery in a territory of the United States. *See under* Slavery

CONTINENTAL CONGRESS CONSTITUTION. *See* Articles of Confederation

CONTINENTAL CONGRESS LOTTERY. *See* Lottery

CONTINENTAL CONGRESS MEDAL. *See* Medal

CONTINENTAL CONGRESS PENSION ACT. *See under* Pension

CONTINENTAL CONGRESS PRESIDENT. *See* President of the Continental Congress

CONTINENTAL MONEY. *See* Money

CONTINENTAL NAVY COMMANDER. *See* Naval officer

CONTINUATION SCHOOL
   Apprentice continuation school supported by a board of education from public funds was established in Cincinnati, Ohio, on August 30, 1909. Classes were conducted in the third story of a building at Twelfth and Jackson streets. Tool apprentices were given the opportunity of a technical education along practical lines.

   Continuation school established by state law was the Racine Continuation School, Racine, Wis., which opened November 3, 1911, to offer evening instruction to adults as well as to children from 14 to 16 years of age who had permits to work. It was authorized under Chapter 616 approved July 7, 1911, "an act relating to education in industrial, commercial, continuation and evening schools."

CONTRACEPTIVE CLINIC. *See* Medical clinic

CONTRACT CARRIER LICENSE. *See under* Automobile license (federal)

CONVENT
   Catholic convent to admit black women as sisters was the Sisters of Loretto, Loretto, Ky. The Reverend Charles Nerinck in May 1824 admitted to the novitiate five black women, who followed the same community exercises as the other sisters, but who lived apart from the white sisters.

   Convent permanently established was in New Orleans, La., in a two-story frame building, with six apartments on each floor, occupied August 6, 1727, by the Ursulines. On August 9, 1727, the Holy Sacrifice of the Mass was offered for the first time. The Superioress was Mother Marie (Tranchepain) of St. Augustine. *(Reverend Henry Churchill Semple—The Ursulines in New Orleans and Our Lady of Prompt Succor)*

The First

CONVENTION (political) BROADCAST. *See under* Radio Broadcast

CONVENTION (political) TELECAST. *See under* Television—Telecast

CONVEYOR BELT SYSTEM. *See* Belt conveyor system

CONVICT LABOR LAW. *See* Labor law

COOKBOOK
Cookbook was *The Compleat Housewife: or Accomplished Gentlewoman's Companion. Being a collection of upwards of Five Hundred of the most approved Receipts fit either for private Families, or such Publick-Spirited Gentlewomen as would be beneficent to their poor Neighbours.* It was modeled after one printed by Mrs. E. Smith in England. It was published in 1742 in Williamsburg, Va., by William Parks. *(Lawrence Counselman Wroth—William Parks)*

Cookbook of American authorship was Amelia Simmons's *American Cookery, or the Art of Dressing Viands, Fish, Poultry and Vegetables, and the Best Modes of Making Puff-Pastes, Pies, Tarts, Puddings, Custards and Preserves, and All Kinds of Cakes, from the Imperial Plumb to Plain Cake—Adapted to This Country, and All Grades of Life.* It was printed by Hudson and Goodwin in Hartford, Conn., in 1796 for the author and contained 46 pages.

COOKING EXPERIMENT, ELECTRIC. *See* Electric cooking experiment

COOKING SCHOOL was the New York Cooking School, which was opened in November 1876 by Juliet Corson at her residence in St. Mark's Place, New York City. In 1875 she gave cooking instruction in the Ladies' Cooking Class of the free Training School for Women, New York City.

COOLING TOWER HYPERBOLIC-SHAPED. *See under* Electric Power Plant

COOPERATIVE
College cooperative store was the Harvard Cooperative Society, Cambridge, Mass., the constitution for which was presented February 28, 1882. On March 15, 1882, it had 400 subscribers. The plan was proposed by Charles Hayden Kip. Frank Bolles was the first president. Merchandise was sold below prevailing retail prices to members. The store was managed by students of the university. *(Norman Scott Brien Gras—Harvard Co-operative Society—Past and Present 1892–1942)*

Consumers' cooperative society was organized in 1830 in New York City by William Bryan, treasurer of a cooperative in Brighton, England. He established a store in New York City which sold articles to members at prices generally below those prevailing at retail outlets.

The First

Cooperative cheese factory. *See* Cheese factory: Cheese factory cooperative

Cooperative operated entirely by women was the Montgomery Farm Women's Cooperative Market, Bethesda, Md., incorporated August 1932 by 29 women. The following year they built a market valued at about $50,000, the mortgage on which was paid off in January 1945.

Cooperative state law was an "act to authorize the formation of mechanics' and laboring men's cooperative associations," Act No. 288 of Michigan, approved and effective March 20, 1865, which allowed "any ten or more persons, who shall be desirous of uniting as mechanics and laboring men, in any cooperative association" to incorporate.

Group hospital-medical cooperative. *See under* Insurance

COOPERATIVES CONVENTION was held in Springfield, Ill., September 25–27, 1918, under the auspices of the Co-operative League of America. Dr. James Peter Warbasse, president of the league, presided over the 185 delegates. *(Report of the Proceedings of the First American Co-operative Convention Held at Springfield, Ill., September 25, 26, 27, 1918, under the Auspices of the Co-operative League of America)*

COPLEY MEDAL. *See* Medal

COPPER COINS. *See* Money

COPPER MINE known to have been worked was the Simsbury mine at Granby, Conn., with a history dating back to 1705. A company to mine the ore was formed in 1709 by John Winthrop, the younger, and was the first mining company chartered. The mine was also known as the Granby mine and was worked for several years by convicts in the Newgate prison established there. In 1737 the copper obtained from this mine was used in the manufacture of the "Granby coppers," among the earliest colonial coins minted. The mine was worked spasmodically until 1773. *(Charles Burr Todd—In Olde Connecticut)*

COPPER REFINERY FURNACE (to operate by the use of gaseous fuel) was constructed in 1878 by William Franklin Durfee for the Wheeler and Wilson Company in Ansonia, Conn.

COPPER TUBE. *See* Brass and copper seamless tubes

COPYRIGHT
Book entered for copyright. *See under* Book

Choreographic score copyrighted was presented in Labanotation (the Rudolf von Laban notation system) on microfilm by Hanya Holm, New York City, and registered February 25, 1952, as an unpublished dramatic-musical composition. It was a complete score of her choreography for Cole Porter's musical comedy *Kiss Me, Kate,*

The First

which opened December 30, 1948, at the Century Theater, New York City.

Motion picture film copyrighted consisted of 47 successive frames showing Fred Ott sneezing. The copyright was recorded as follows: "Edison Kinetoscopic Record of a Sneeze, January 7, 1894. Entered in the name of W. K. L. Dickson, under No. 2,887, January 9, 1894." On August 28, 1882, pictures in silhouette showing motion had been copyrighted by Eadweard J. Muybridge. They could not be projected but could be arranged to simulate movement when viewed in an electrical tachyscope.

COPYRIGHT LAW
Copyright law securing benefit of copyright was passed May 15, 1672, by the General Court of Massachusetts assembled in Boston, Mass., which granted John Usher, a bookseller, the privilege of publishing on his own account a revised edition of *The General Laws and Liberties of the Massachusetts Colony.* It was ordered "that for at least seven years, unless he shall have sold them all before that time, there shall be no other or further impression made by any person thereof in this jurisdiction." The penalty for violation of the copyright was treble the whole charges of printing and paper.

Copyright law of the United States was an act (1 Stat. L. 124) "for the encouragement of learning by securing the copies of maps, charts and books to the authors and proprietors of such copies during the times therein mentioned." The bill was signed by the Speaker and the President of the Senate, May 25; 1790, laid before President George Washington on May 27, 1790, and signed May 31, 1790. Rights were granted only to citizens of the United States, a policy which continued until 1891. Protection was extended over a 14-year period, renewal rights being granted only if the author was still alive.

Copyright law (state) was "an act for the encouragement of literature and genius," passed during the session of the General Court of Assembly of the Governor and Company of the State of Connecticut, held in Hartford, Conn., January 8–February 7, 1783. The law gave authors sole right of publication for 14 years with power of renewal. Massachusetts passed a law March 17, 1783, for a 1-year period. Both laws extended rights only to other states having reciprocal legislation. *(Richard Rogers Bowker—Copyright, Its History and Its Law)*

International copyright agreement was the Platt-Simonds Copyright Act, passed March 4, 1891 (26 Stat. L. 1107), effective July 1, 1891. Citizens of Switzerland, France, Belgium, and Great Britain were thus enabled to obtain copyright protection in the United States. The United States was represented by Boyd Winchester at the Bern International Copyright Convention, September 9,

The First

1886, but did not become a signatory to the convention. *(Thorvald Solberg—The United States and International Copyright)*

Photographic copyright law was enacted March 2, 1861 (12 Stat. L. 246), and signed on March 3, 1861, by President James Buchanan.

COPYRIGHTED BOOK. *See* Book

COPYRIGHTS REGISTER
Copyrights registrar of the United States was Thorvald Solberg, who served from July 1, 1897, to April 22, 1930.

Women Register of Copyrights was Barbara Alice Ringer, who was appointed on November 19, 1973. She had served as Assistant Register of Copyrights from August 1, 1966, to April 28, 1972.

CORAL REEF BARRIER (copy) of importance on exhibition was installed in the American Museum of Natural History, New York City, under the direction of Dr. Roy Waldo Miner. Its construction occupied five years and the reef, weighing 40 tons, was completed in July 1934.

CORD TIRE. *See* Automobile tire; Bicycle tire

CORFAM. *See* Leather substitute

CORK for steam pipe covering was manufactured in the United States in 1894 by Stone & Duryea of Brooklyn, N.Y. The company moved to Bridgeport, Conn., in 1896 and the following year produced cork covering for cold pipe lines. It was succeeded by the Nonpareil Cork Manufacturing Company, which in turn was purchased by the Armstrong Cork Company in 1904.

CORK-CENTER BASEBALL. *See* Baseball

CORK JACKET. *See* Life preserver: Life preserver of cork

CORK MANUFACTURER is said to have been William King, who opened a factory in Brooklyn, N.Y., where he produced cork products from 1850 to 1860.

CORKBOARD (IMPREGNATED) was made in 1900 by the Armstrong Cork Company of Pittsburgh, Pa. It was produced in a specially constructed plant in Beaver Falls, Pa. The business grew rapidly until the "composition" corkboard gave way entirely to pure corkboard insulation.

CORKBOARD PATENT to be issued on pure corkboard was No. 456,068, granted to John T. Smith of Brooklyn, N.Y., on July 14, 1891. Manufacture was begun in Brooklyn in 1894 by Stone and Duryea. Cork covering was produced first, and then the manufacture of pure corkboard followed within a very few years. *(Pearl Edwin Thomas—Cork Insulation)*

CORKSCREW PATENT, No. 27,615, was granted on March 27, 1860, to M. L. Byrn of New York City. It covered a gimlet screw with a "T" handle.

The First

CORN

Shipment of hybrid seed corn was sold to Samuel Ramsay, Jacobsburg, Ohio, on April 13, 1916, by Funk Brothers Seed Co., Bloomington, Ill. The price was $15 a bushel.

CORN (MAIZE)

Corn (Maize) found by British settlers was discovered on November 16, 1620 (Old Style), in Provincetown, Mass., by 16 Pilgrims led by Myles Standish, William Bradford, Stephen Hopkins, and Edward Tilley at a place they named Corn Hill.

CORN HUSKING CHAMPIONSHIP CONTEST

(national) was held December 1, 1924, on a farm near Alleman, Polk County, Iowa. There were six contestants. The winner was Fred Stanek of Webster County, Iowa, who husked 1,891 pounds, a net of 1,705 pounds, or 24.3 bushels, in 80 minutes.

CORNCOB PIPE. *See* Pipe

CORNSTALK-PAPER BOOK. *See* Book: Book on cornstalk paper

CORNSTARCH

Cornstarch patent was No. 2,000, issued March 22, 1841, to Orlando Jones of City Road, England, "for operating on farinaceous matters to obtain starch and other products," especially flour or powder produced from rice.

Starch made commercially from Indian corn was made by Thomas Kingsford, who produced a small quantity in 1842 in Jersey City, N.J. In 1846, he and his son, Thomas, Jr., erected a small cornstarch plant in Bergen, N.J., and a larger one in Oswego, N.Y., in 1848.

CORNSTONE, or Maizolith, a product harder than the hardest wood and several times stronger than the strongest wood, was first made at the Iowa State College, Ames, Iowa, in 1922. It is made principally from corncobs or cornstalks by means of specially designed machinery. It ranges in color from golden tan to ebony and is used principally as a structural material when great strength as compared with weight is desired, and when great abrasion and impact must be withstood. It has a specific gravity of 1.5 and modulus of rupture of about 35,000 pounds.

CORONATION

CORONATION on what was to become United States soil was on February 12, 1883, when King Kalakaua and Queen Kapiolani were crowned King and Queen of the Hawaiian Islands at Iolani Palace, Honolulu, Hawaiian Islands. The Legislative Assembly elected David Kalakaua on February 12, 1874. He ascended to the throne and served 9 years before the coronation.

CORPORATION

Commercial corporation was the New York Fishing Company, which was chartered January 8, 1675, by the Governor and Council of New York

The First

acting for the Duke of York "for settleing a fisher in these parts." Shares of the capital stock wer £10 each. *(New York Council—Minutes III, Par 2:10)*

Corporate body of more than temporary dura tion, excluding town incorporations, was th President and Fellows of Harvard College, Cam bridge, Mass., chartered May 30, 1650. It consiste of seven persons: Henry Dunster, president; fiv fellows, Samuel Mather, Samuel Danford, Jona than Michell, Comfort Starr, and Samuel Eator and Thomas Danford, treasurer. *(Nathaniel Brac street Shurtleff—Records of the Governor an Company of the Massachusetts Bay in New Eng land. Vol. 4)*

Corporate body chartered by a special act o Congress was the President, Directors and Con pany of the Bank of the United States, chartere on February 25, 1791 (1 Stat.L.192). It was char ered by "An Act to Incorporate the Subscribers i the Bank of the United States" until March 4, 181 by the First Congress (Session 3).

Corporation incorporated with a capitalizatio of $1 billion was the United States Steel Corpora tion. It was incorporated on February 25, 190 and was ready for business on April 1, 1901, wit an authorized capitalization of $1.4 billion. Th original member companies were the Carneg Company, Federal Steel Company, National Stee Company, National Tube Company, America Steel and Wire Company of New Jersey, Amer can Tin Plate Company, American Steel Hoo Company, American Sheet Steel Company, Lak Superior Consolidated Iron Mines, and America Bridge Company. The first president was Charle M. Schwab.

Corporation with a net income of more than $ billion in one year was the General Motors Corpo ration, Detroit, Mich., whose net income in 195 was $1,189,477,082 (9.6 percent of net sale amounting to $12,443,277,420). It exceeded $1 billion in 1963 with net income of $1,591,823,08 (9.7 percent of net sales of $16,494,818,184). In 196 net income exceeded $2 billion; the corporatio reported net income of $2,125,606,400 (10.3 percei of net sales of $20,733,982,295).

CORPORATION COURSE

Industrial corporation course was entitled "Pr vate Corporations; Origin, history and preser status of joint stock concerns, including rai roads." It was offered by Dr. Amos Griswol Warner, lecturer on political and econom science, at the University of Nebraska, Lincol Neb., in 1888–89.

CORPORATION TAX. *See* Tax

CORRESPONDENCE SCHOOL to achieve di tinction was started through the initiative Thomas Jefferson Foster, proprietor and editor the Shenandoah *Herald,* who issued a course

The First

coal mining as a means of educating workmen and safeguarding lives through a knowledge of the fundamentals of mine developing and operating. The first student of this organization, which is now known as the International Correspondence Schools, with headquarters at Scranton, Pa., was enrolled October 16, 1891. Instruction is now offered in a great variety of subjects. *(International Correspondence Schools Field Staff Training Course—International Textbook Press)*

See also Blind: Correspondence school for the blind; Forestry school: Forestry correspondence course; Home study courses

CORRUGATED LIFEBOAT. *See* Lifeboat

CORRUGATED PAPER. *See* Paper

CORRUPT ELECTION PRACTICES LAW. *See under* Election law

CORSET manufactured by a factory as a health item rather than a fashion article was made July 1874 by Warner Brothers, McGraw, N.Y., a partnership of Dr. Ira DeVer Warner and Dr. Lucien Calvin Warner. The corset combined three garments in one—a corset, a skirt supporter, and self-adjusting pads—and had shoulder straps. *(Lucien C. Warner—Always Starting Things Through Seventy Eventful Years)*

COSMIC RAY

Cosmic ray was discovered in 1925 by Robert Andrews Millikan at the California Institute of Technology, Pasadena, Calif. The formal announcement of the discovery was made on November 11, 1925, before the National Academy of Sciences assembled in convention at Madison, Wis. *(Robert Andrews Millikan—Cosmic Rays)*

Electric power generated by cosmic rays. *See* Electric Power: Electric power generated by cosmic rays

COSTUME MUSEUM. *See* Museum

COTTON

Cotton acreage reduction payment was made July 28, 1933, to William E. Morris of Nueces County, Tex., who was presented with a check for $517 by President Franklin Delano Roosevelt for having plowed under 47 acres of his cotton crop. In addition, he was given an option on 23½ bales of cotton at 6 cents a pound.

Cotton crop commercially produced entirely by machinery, from planting to baling, with the exception of a few incidental hours of hand labor, was grown during the year 1944 on 28 acres owned by Hopson Planting Company of Clarksdale, Miss. The soil was prepared, crop-seeded, and cultivated by machines, weeds eradicated by same, and the crop harvested with a mechanical picker.

The First

Cotton exported to England consisted of eight bales from Charleston, S.C., which were seized by the custom house in England in 1764 on the grounds that the American colony could not have produced so much.

Cotton fabric used on a road. *See under* Road

Cotton goods to be trademarked were made by the Beverly Cotton Manufactory, Beverly, Mass. On June 6, 1788, it was enacted "that all goods which may be manufactured by the said corporation, shall have a label of lead affixed to one end thereof, which shall have the same impression as the seal of the corporation, and that if any person shall knowingly use a like seal or label with that used by said corporation, by annexing same to any cotton or cotton and linen goods, not manufactured by said corporation with a view of vending or distributing thereof, as the proper manufacture of said corporation, every person so offending shall forfeit and pay treble the value of said goods to be sued for and recovered for the use of said corporation, by action of debt, in any court of record proper to try the same."

COTTON-BALE METALLIC TIE was invented by Frederick Cook of New Orleans, La., who obtained patent No. 19,490, March 2, 1858, on "a friction clasp or buckle for attaching the ends of iron ties or hoops for fastening cotton bales and other packages so that the ties are prevented from slipping by the friction against a certain portion of the buckle."

COTTON-BOLL WEEVIL, which has been so destructive to cotton crops, was introduced into the United States from Central America about 1892, probably through Brownsville, Tex. The weevil is a species of beetle, which because of its small size and immunity to most insecticides has become a serious problem.

COTTON GIN, which separated the seed from the cotton, was invented in 1792 by Eli Whitney of Mulberry Grove (near Savannah), Ga., who applied for a patent on June 20, 1793. His model was stolen and was manufactured by dishonest interests, before Whitney received a patent on March 14, 1794, on "a machine for ginning cotton." Whitney formed a partnership with Phineas Miller and manufactured cotton gins. The invention was so valuable that redress was unobtainable, and his patent was not renewed because of the power exerted by those who had been enriched by his invention. *(Denison Olmsted—Memoir of Eli Whitney, Esq.)*

COTTON MILL

Cotton mill (see rival claim—next paragraph) was established in Beverly, Mass., between August 1788 and July 1789 by a company of proprietors known as the Beverly Cotton Manufactory. The company was incorporated on February 3, 1789, and was visited October 30, 1789, by George

The First

COTTON MILL—*Continued*
Washington. The spinning jenny spun 60 threads at one time and the carding machine carded 40 pounds of cotton a day. *(Edwin Martin Stone— History of Beverly)*

Cotton mill was established on James Island, near Charleston, S.C., by Frances Ramage, widow of a South Carolina planter, in 1789. It was used in the weaving and spinning of cotton or linen yarns. An account of the mill is contained in the *City Gazette or Daily Advertiser* of Charleston, S.C., of February 24, 1789. *(South Carolina Histori- cal and Genealogical Magazine. Vols. 8 and 9)*

Cotton mill in the world in which the whole process of cotton manufacturing from spinning to weaving was carried on by power was that of the Boston Manufacturing Company, Waltham, Mass., incorporated February 23, 1813, with a capitalization of $100,000. The mill was erected later the same year in Waltham, whence it took its better-known name, the Waltham Company. Labor was paid a fixed wage and various groups were departmentalized. Nathan Appleton, Fran- cis Cabot Lowell, and Patrick Tracy Jackson were the prime sponsors of this organization. The ma- chinery was constructed by Paul Moody. *(Edmund Lincoln Sanderson—Waltham as a Precinct of Watertown and as a Town)*

Cotton mill to spin cotton yarn successfully was started on December 20, 1790, by Samuel Slater in Pawtucket, R.I. It was 40 feet long, 26 feet wide, and 2 stories high, with an attic. Power was ob- tained from the old fulling mill waterwheel in Ezekiel Carpenter's clothier's shop on the east bank of the Blackstone River at the southwest abutment of Pawtucket Bridge. Alexander Hamil- ton in his report as Secretary of the Treasury made on December 5, 1791, said, "The manufacto- ry at Providence has the merit of being the first in introducing into the United States the celebrated cotton mill, which not only furnishes materials for the manufactory itself but for the supply of private families, for household manufacturing." *(Frede- rick Lewis Lewton—Samuel Slater and the Oldest Cotton Machinery in America)*

COTTON PICKER (mechanical) of importance was the Rust Cotton Picker, a horse-drawn picker, built by John Daniel Rust in Weatherford, Tex., in 1928. In 1929 it was rebuilt into a self-propelled model powered by a Model T motor; in 1935 a tractor model was built and tested; and in 1937 an improved model picked 13 bales of cotton in one day.

COTTON SPINNING JENNY was put into opera- tion by Daniel Jackson, a coppersmith, of Provi- dence, R.I., in 1786. At first it was set up in a private house, but was afterward removed to the upper room in the Market House where it was operated. *(Edward Field—History of Rhode Is- land and Providence Plantations)*

The First

COTTON THREAD. *See* Thread

COTTON TWINE FACTORY was established in 1839 by Jacob Sloat of Sloatsburg, N.Y. The mill was opened in 1815 and produced cloth until 1839. Sloat invented a dressing and produced as much as 6,000 pounds a week of cotton twine in 1839.

COTTONSEED HULLING MACHINE was in- vented by John Lineback of Salem, N.C., and pat- ented by him on March 31, 1814.

COTTONSEED OIL was produced in 1768 through the efforts of Dr. Otto, a Moravian, o Bethlehem, Pa. He was able to get nine pints of oi from a bushel and a half of cotton seed.

COTTONSEED OIL MILL was established in Pe tersburg, Va., in 1829 by Francis Follet.

COUNCIL, COLONIAL. *See under* Colonial gov ernment

COUNTESS
American woman to become a countess wa Sarah Thompson, whose father, Benjami Thompson, an American physicist, born in Nort Woburn, Mass., was knighted February 23, 1784 as Count Rumford by King George III of Englan and was created a count of the Holy Roman Em pire in 1791, by Charles Philip Frederick, Duke o Bavaria. The daughter was received as the Count ess of Rumford with the privilege of residing i any country she chose and receiving half of he father's pension of 2,000 florins. *(George Edwar Ellis—Memoir of Sir Benjamin Thompson, Coun Rumford, With Notices of His Daughter)*

COUNTRY CLUB
Country club to remain in existence 80 year was the Country Club of Brookline, Mass., orga nized September 13, 1882, and incorporate November 7, 1882. Its purpose was the encourage ment of athletic exercise and the establishmen and maintenance of places for reading rooms an social meetings. In 1882 Clyde Park, the estate c Francis E. Bacon, was leased for five years, and i 1887 it was purchased. In 1883 the Myopia Clu organized in Winchester in 1879, was absorbed b the Country Club. *(Frederic Haines Curtiss an John Heard—The Country Club, 1882-1932)*

COUNTRY DAY SCHOOL was the Countr School for Boys of Baltimore, a private schoo (later the Gilman Country School for Boys, Rolan Park, Baltimore, Md.), which was opened Septem ber 1897. The first headmaster was Frederic Winsor.

COUNTY
County created by federal legislation was Lata County, Idaho, authorized by Chapter 251, enac ed May 14, 1888, during the first session of the 50t Congress. The "Act to create and organize th county of Latah" set aside a portion of Nez Perc County in Idaho for Latah County, with the coun seat at Moscow.

The First

COUNTY LIBRARY. *See* Library

COUPLER, RAILROAD. *See* Railroad coupler

COURSING CLUB was the American Coursing Club, which was organized at Topeka, Kans., on July 9, 1886, with Colonel Taylor of Emporia, Kans. as president, Dr. G. Irwin Royce of Topeka as secretary, and J. V. Brinkman of Great Bend as treasurer. There were 38 entries at the first inaugural meeting on October 10–23, 1886, at Great Bend. The first all-age stake winner was Midnight, owned by Colonel Taylor.

COURT

See also Supreme Court (state); Supreme Court (U.S.)

Bicycle traffic court. *See* Bicycle traffic court

Commerce court (U.S.) was established by act of Congress, June 18, 1910 (36 Stat. L. 539). A presiding judge and five associates were appointed by President William Howard Taft for terms that extended from one to five years. The court was organized February 8, 1911, and opened February 5, 1911, in Washington, D.C. Appeal of its decisions could be made only to the Supreme Court. Because of various abuses, the court was abolished December 31, 1913. *(Walker Downer Hines —United States Commerce Court)*

Conciliation tribunal for small claims was the Conciliation Branch of the Municipal Court of Cleveland, established March 15, 1913, in Cleveland, Ohio. The first case was filed March 17, 1913, and was heard by Judge Dan B. Cull on March 24, 1913. The complainant could not be represented by counsel but had to present his own case. Strict rules of evidence and procedure were waived. The judgment rendered had the same force and effect, and was as binding, as a judgment rendered in any court of record. *(American Judicature Society—Bulletin, No. 8. April 1915)*

Court of claims was established by an act "to establish a court for the investigation of claims against the United States" (10 Stat. L. 612), signed February 24, 1855, by President Franklin Pierce. It required the appointment of three judges with life tenure by the President with the consent of the Senate. President Pierce appointed Isaac Blackford of Indiana and John James Gilchrist of New Hampshire on March 3, 1855, and George P. Scarborough of Virginia on May 8, 1855. The judges received $4,000 annually. The court was organized May 11, 1855, with Judge Gilchrist as presiding judge. It was reorganized by act of March 3, 1863 (12 Stat. L. 765). Until March 3, 1887, it was the only court in which cases could be prosecuted against the government.

Court in which the judge presided in a city other than the one in which the lawyers appeared was the Federal Court of Claims, Washington, D.C. A three-judge court, composed of Byron Skelton, Robert Kuntzig, and Philip Nichols, Jr., on October 16,

The First

1975, heard a claim for damages in litigation for 15 years involving $270,000. The lawyers, Assistant Attorney General Rex E. Lee and Bruce Mayor, counsel for the Merritt-Chapmann & Scott Co., presented their arguments before a picturephone located in the Bell Telephone Picturephone Service, 393 Seventh Avenue, New York City.

Domestic relations court was established in Buffalo, N.Y., in 1909 by Simon Augustine Nash, Judge of Police Court, who privately heard domestic relations cases in his chambers instead of in open court. Chapter 570, Laws of New York State, approved May 29, 1909, established the City Court of Buffalo, and the domestic relations division was opened January 1, 1910. *(Station Probation Commission, Buffalo, 1928)*

Governor removed from office by a state supreme court. *See under* Governor

Juvenile court in the world was the Juvenile Court of Cook County, known as the Chicago Juvenile Court, authorized April 21, 1899, and opened July 1, 1899, with Richard Stanley Tuthill as judge. On March 3, 1913, cases involving girls were tried by a woman judge, Mary Margaret Bartelme. During the first year about 2,300 children's cases were heard. *(Timothy David Hurley—Origin of Illinois Court Law)*

Night court in the world was opened in New York City on September 1, 1907. The first night session of a magistrates' court, the Jefferson Market Court at Ninth Street and Sixth Avenue, was presided over by Charles Nathan Harris. Sessions were held from 8 P.M. to 3 A.M. until September 1, 1910, when cases against men were transferred to Yorkville Court, 153 East 57th Street. Cases against women were held in the same building as before. On June 28, 1911, the closing hour of both sessions was fixed at 1 A.M. On April 21, 1919, the sessions of the Women's Court were changed to day sessions. *(Records in City Magistrates' Courts, New York City)*

Small debtors' court established by state law was authorized March 15, 1913, by Chapter 20, Laws of Kansas, to take effect April 30, 1913. Plaintiffs and defendants appeared without legal representation. Judges served without fee, pay, or award and were not required to be lawyers. Appeals could be taken to the district court. Cases were tried involving not more than $20. The first court was at Topeka, Kan., with W. H. Kemper as judge. *(William Franklin Willoughby—Principles of Judicial Administration)*

State Supreme Court composed entirely of women was the Special Supreme Court of Texas appointed by Governor Pat Morris Neff on January 8, 1925. When an application for writ of error in the case of *W. T. Johnson, et al.* vs. *J. M. Darr, et al.,* from El Paso County (a Woodmen of the World case) reached the Supreme Court of Texas, the three members thereof found themselves dis-

COURT—*Continued*
qualified to consider it and immediately certified their disqualifications to the governor as required by law. Thereupon the governor appointed Hortense Ward of Houston as special chief justice, and Hattie L. Henenberg of Dallas and Ruth Brazzil of Galveston as special associate justices to hear and determine the cause of action. They were sworn in January 8, 1925. The case was finally decided by the Special Supreme Court on May 23, 1925, affirming the judgment of the Court of Civil Appeals.

United States case tried before the Permanent Court of Arbitration at the Hague. *See* Arbitration: Arbitration proceeding in the Hague Permanent Court of Arbitration

Woman clerk of a state supreme court. *See under* Woman

COURT-MARTIAL
Court-martial trial was held August 24, 1676, in Newport, R.I., by Governor Walter Clarke, Deputy Governor John Crayton, and assistants. Edmund Calverly was the Attorney General. Quanpen, an Indian sachem also known as Sowagonish, was found guilty of participation in King Philip's War against the colonists and ordered shot on August 26. Others who had participated in the war were sentenced to various penalties. *(Record of a Court Martial held at Newport, R.I., in August and September 1676 for the Trial of Indians charged with being engaged in Philip's designs)*

Court-martial trial at which enlisted men were allowed to sit as members of the court was convened at 8:30 A.M., on February 1, 1949, in Heidelberg, Germany. Pfc. Andrew D. Byrd of Orlando, Fla., and Pfc. Oscar B. Gannon of Hanging Rock, Ohio, charged with premeditated murder of a German civilian and assault on another on December 31, 1948, in a brawl, were tried by a military court of four sergeants and six officers. They were convicted on February 3, 1949, of manslaughter and sentenced to serve seven years at hard labor and to receive dishonorable discharges.

Court-martial trial in the United States at which enlisted men were allowed to sit as members of the court was convened February 3, 1949, at Fort Bragg, N.C., and consisted of four sergeants and five officers. Rudy F. Johnson, 19, was convicted of escaping from the guardhouse and sentenced to six months at hard labor and fined $50 a month for six months. On the same day, a trial was held at First Army Headquarters on Governors Island, N.Y. It consisted of three sergeants and five officers. Private Thomas F. Quinn of Brooklyn, N.Y., 21, was convicted of absence without leave and theft of government and private property and sentenced to one year at hard labor and a dishonorable discharge.

Court-martial trial of an officer for collaborating with his captors was held September 23, 1954, at Fort Sheridan, Ill. A court of eight colonels and three lieutenant colonels sentenced Lieutenant Colonel Harry Fleming, reserve officer, of Racine, Wis., to "involuntary discharge" for collaborating with Communists during the Korean War. On February 8, 1957, the United States Court of Military Appeals upheld the conviction and agreed with the court-martial and military board of review.

Military court-martial was held January 20, 1778, in Cambridge, Mass. Colonel David Henley, commanding officer of the American troops in Cambridge, was accused "of a general tenor of language and conduct heinously criminal as an officer, and unbecoming a man, of the most indecent, violent, vindictive severity against unarmed men, and of intentional murder." The trial was concluded on February 25, 1778, when Henley was found not guilty. Brigadier General John Glover was the presiding officer at the trial. *(Proceedings of a General Court-Martial, held at Cambridge, on Tuesday the 20th of January and continued by several adjournments to Wednesday, the 25th of February 1778; upon the trial of Colonel David Henley)*

COURT TENNIS. *See* Tennis

COW. *See* Animals

COWCATCHER. *See* Locomotive cowcatcher

COXSWAIN (woman). *See* Woman: Woman coxswain of a men's collegiate varsity team

CQD DANGER SIGNAL. *See* Radio distress signal

CRACKER
Cracker (sweet) of American manufacture was introduced to the public in 1865 by Belcher & Larrabee of Albany, N.Y., in competition with the English varieties which were imported in increasing quantities. These crackers were of the sweetened variety. Soda crackers and salt crackers had been made previously.

Hard water crackers were made by hand in 1801 by Josiah Bent in his home in Milton, Mass. They were made from the best winter wheat and pure cold water and baked in ovens heated by bundles of hardwood fagots. Bent peddled them around the country and in 1827 sold his business which became Bent & Company. *(Albert Kendall Teele—The History of Milton, Mass.)*

Meat biscuit was invented by Gail Borden, Jr., of Elizabethport, N.Y., who manufactured a desiccated soup bread formed of the concentrated extract of alimentary animal substances combined with vegetable flour or meal and baked as flat brittle cakes. Hot water and seasoning added to the biscuit produced a soup. Borden obtained patent No. 7,066 on July 30, 1850, on a "preparation of portable soup bread."

The First

See also Medal: Medal awarded to an American food producer

CRACKER BAKERY was that of Theodore Pearson of Newburyport, Mass., which started in 1792. His products appealed chiefly because they kept better than bread.

CRAFT LABOR UNION. *See* Labor union

CRANBERRY CULTIVATION was attempted about 1820 by Captain Henry Hall of Dennis, Barnstable County, Mass. Cranberries grew wild and, most likely, were eaten by the Pilgrims.

CRANBERRY TREATISE was B. Eastwood's *A Complete Manual for the Culture of the Cranberry, with a Description of the Best Varieties*, published in 1856 by C. M. Saxton & Co., New York City. It contained 120 pages and described the location of patches, preparation of soils, planting lines, diseases, picking, etc.

CRANE
Automobile wrecking crane was devised in 1917 by Robert E. Manley, who later formed the Manley Manufacturing Company, York, Pa., which in 1928 was absorbed by the American Chain and Cable Company, Inc. The wrecking car had a tilting beam which permitted adjustment of weight and overhang to suit various conditions and a swivel nose that permitted direct pull from any angle. The crane had six leverages and speeds and two sets of controls so that it could be operated from either side of the car.

Crane was manufactured by the Yale and Towne Manufacturing Company, Stamford, Conn., in 1883 for the Pittsburgh Bessemer Steel Company. This machine was a two-ton full-revolving, self-propelling steam crane mounted on a four-wheel standard-gauge truck.

Wrecking crane was built by the Industrial Brownhoist Corporation, Bay City, Mich., in 1883. It had a capacity of 20 tons, and was mounted on a nonpropelling car to operate on a standard-gauge track. In 1886 an adaptation of the revolving crane was developed. This was a 15-ton steam-railway-type crane in which the crane proper was mounted at one end of the car and the boiler at the other.

CRANIOSCOPY BOOK was Dr. Samuel George Morton's *Crania Americana; or A Comparative View of the Skulls of Various Aboriginal Nations of North and South America to Which Is Prefixed an Essay on the Varieties of the Human Species*, published in 1839 by J. Dobson, Philadelphia, Pa. It was a tall folio containing a 5-page preface, 297 pages of text, and 4 blank sheets. It had 71 full pages of lithograph plates.

CRAPS was introduced in New Orleans, La., about 1813 by Bernard Xavier Philippe de Marigny de Mandeville, who had seen the game played in France as "hazards." As the nickname for a

The First

Creole was Johnny Crapaud, the game became known as Crapaud's game, which later was abbreviated to Craps. Mandeville lost a fortune at the game. He owned considerable property through which he was obliged to cut a street and sell lots on both sides to obtain funds to pay his debts. Maps show this street named Craps Street, later changed to Burgundy Street. *(Edward Laroque Tinker—The Palingenesis of Craps)*

CREAM SEPARATOR
Centrifugal cream separator was made in 1879 by David M. Weston and Edward Burnett of Boston, Mass., whose experience was obtained with sugar centrifugals. The first machine was used on the Deerfoot Farm, Southborough, Mass. It made 1,600 revolutions a minute and had a 26-inch bowl. The machine had to be stopped to draw off the cream and skim milk after separation.

Centrifugal cream separator patent was No. 195,515, granted September 25, 1877, to Wilhelm C. L. Lefeldt and Carl G. O. Lentsch of Schoeningen, Germany, on an "improvement in centrifugal machines for creaming milk." It consisted of an electric rotator that forced the heavy milk to the base of the pan.

Continuous-flow centrifugal cream separator was invented by Carl Gustaf Patrik de Laval of Stockholm, Sweden, who applied for a patent on July 31, 1879, which was granted October 4, 1881, No. 247,804. The first machine of this type used in the United States was put in operation in 1881 by Theodore Augustus Havemeyer, sugar refiner and Jersey stock breeder, on his farm at Mahwah, N.J.

CREAMERY (commercial) was established by Alanson Slaughter at Wallkill, N.Y., in 1861.

CREDIT CARD
Bank credit card was issued by the Franklin National Bank, Franklin Square, N.Y., on April 15, 1952. Purchases were charged to the bank, which made the payments and then billed the card holders. The service was extended to its branches.

Nationally accepted bank-oriented credit card was originated in 1959 by the Bank of America, California. There was no membership fee or service charge. Full-scale services were offered to cardholders and merchants.

CREDIT INSURANCE. *See* Insurance

CREDIT PROTECTIVE GROUP was the Merchants' Vigilance Association, formed in 1842 by importers and commission houses in New York City. The association distributed reports prepared by Sheldon P. Church. William C. Dusenbury, who later formed the Mercantile Agency of Woodward & Dusenbury, was the secretary.

CREDIT REPORT BOOK was prepared by Sheldon P. Church and published anonymously in 1844 in New York City. It was distributed to subscribers only and contained commercial information

208 FAMOUS FIRST FACTS

The First

CREDIT REPORT BOOK—*Continued*
about merchants in southern and midwestern states.

CREDIT UNION ACT. *See* Federal credit union act

CREDIT UNION ASSOCIATION was founded by Alphonse Desjardins in Manchester, N.H., on December 16, 1908. It was known as "La Caisse Populaire Ste. Marie" and was chartered April 6, 1909. Ninety-nine percent of the depositors were French. *(Edson Leone Whitney—Cooperative Credit Societies, Credit Unions in America and Foreign Countries)*

CREDIT UNION LAW was sponsored by Pierre Jay, first bank commissioner of Massachusetts, and was passed by the Massachusetts legislature. It was approved May 21, 1909, by Governor Eben Sumner Draper. *(Chapter 419, Acts of 1909, Massachusetts)*

CREMATION
Cremation was that of Henry Laurens, who was born in Charleston, S.C., in 1724 and who died on December 8, 1792. He was a staunch patriot, and after the Revolutionary War became one of the ministers to make arrangements for peace. His will read as follows: "I solemnly enjoin it upon my son as an indispensable duty that, as soon as he conveniently can after my decease, he cause my body to be wrapped in twelve yards of tow cloth, and burnt until it is entirely consumed, and then, collecting my ashes, deposit them wherever he may see proper." *(John Storer Cobb—A Quarter Century of Cremation in North America)*

Vice President cremated. *See under* Vice President (U.S.)

CREMATORY
Crematory was erected by Francis Julius Le-Moyne on his own grounds in Washington, Pa., in 1876. It was the first and the only crematory in the United States until 1884. The first incineration was of the body of Baron Joseph Henry Louis de Palm on December 6, 1876. LeMoyne died of diabetes on October 14, 1879, and two days later was cremated in his own crematory. *(Howard Atwood Kelly and Walter Lincoln Burrage—Dictionary of American Medical Biographies)*

Crematory (state) was authorized by Chapter 341 of New York State on May 21, 1888, when $20,000 was appropriated to build and equip a crematory on Swinburne Island in New York harbor. It was built by Dr. Miles Lewis Davis of Lancaster, Pa. In 1889, those buried at the Quarantine cemetery (Sequine's Point) were disinterred and cremated. *(New York Quarantine Commissioners—Annual Report, 1889)*

CREPE was produced in France in 1912 and was introduced into New York City in the same year by Haas Bros., who registered the name Crepe Georgette in the United States Patent Office on

The First

December 30, 1913, and commenced production in the United States.

CREPE PAPER. *See* Paper

CRICKET CLUB
College cricket club team to tour England was the Haverford College team, captained by John Lester, which competed from July 17 to July 31, 1896, against Harrow School, Eton College, Cambridge University, and others. They won 4 games, lost 4 games, and drew 7 games. They returned to the United States on the *Belgenland* on August 5, 1896.

Cricket club was the Boston Cricket Club founded in 1809 in Boston, Mass. The first president was Andrew Allen.

Cricket club to own its own clubhouse was the Germantown Cricket Club, which in 1854 occupied Belfield, the home of William Wister, in Germantown, Pa. *(Site and Relic Society of Germantown—Reports)*

CRICKET MAGAZINE
CRICKET MAGAZINE was *The American Cricketer, a Journal Devoted to the Noble Game of Cricket,* 4 pages, which was first published on June 28, 1877, at Philadelphia, Pa. It was published weekly from May to November and monthly from November to May. The subscription price was $ a year for 33 issues.

CRICKET TOURNAMENT
Cricket game played by a college team is said to have been played at Haverford College, Haverford, Pa. The game was introduced in 1836 by William Carvill, the college gardener. The bat and balls were of home manufacture.

Cricket match was held in New York City, on the site of Fulton Market, on May 1, 1751, between the Londoners and the New Yorkers. The New Yorkers made 80 and 86 and the Londoners 43 and 47. Cricket had been played by local teams on the same site about five years earlier. *(William Rotc Wister—Some Reminiscences of Cricket in Philadelphia Before 1861)*

International cricket tournament was held October 3–5, 1859, at St. George's ground, Hoboken, N.J., between the All-England team, captained by George Parr, and the St. George's Cricket Club of New York, captained by J. Wisden. The American team was weak at bat and the English team won in 1 inning, by 64 runs: England 156, United States 92. A second game was played October 10, 1859, at Philadelphia, Pa., the English winning by wickets. The English team played two games in the United States and two in Canada. *(Fred. Lilly white—The English Cricketeers' Trip to Canada and the United States)*

CRIME INSURANCE FEDERAL POLICY. *See under* Insurance

he First

RIME PREVENTION AND DETECTION

Crime prevention commission for interstate ooperation was the New Jersey Commission on terstate Cooperation, established by Senate int Resolution No. 3, introduced and sponsored y Senator Joseph Gustave Wolber. The joint solution was passed and signed March 12, 1935, y Governor Harold Giles Hoffman, and the com- ission was immediately organized, with Judge ichard Hartshorne as the first chairman. The mmission consisted of 15 members, 5 each ap- inted by the senate, the assembly, and the gov- nor. The commission was responsible for eveloping cooperation between states on vari- us problems such as crime control, motor vehi- es, conflicting taxation, labor problems, and griculture.

Interstate crime pact was effected between ew York and New Jersey and signed September , 1833, in New York City by Benjamin Franklin tler, Peter Augustus Jay, Henry Seymour, Theo- re Frelinghuysen, James Parker, and Lucius uintius Cincinnatus Elmer. Article 6 related to iminal process for New Jersey and Article 7 for ew York. The New Jersey legislature ratified the ct on February 26, 1834, and New York on Feb- ary 5, 1834. The pact was ratified by act of Con- ess, June 28, 1834. *(U.S. Laws 1834. Chapter 126)*

National conference on crime was held October -12, 1935, in Trenton, N.J., with a roster of offi- al delegates from 41 states and from the federal vernment. Its purpose was to develop recipro- l legislation and interstate compacts between ates and to curb crime throughout the country. he conference developed a permanent organiza- on composed of one official representative from ch state in the union and one from the federal vernment and established for the purpose of rrying out the recommendations of the confer- ce.

RIMINAL

Woman on the "ten most wanted" list of the deral Bureau of Investigation was Ruth Eise- ann-Schier, accused in the abduction for ransom f Barbara Jane Mackle on December 17, 1968, om a Decatur, Ga., motel. She was arrested in orman, Okla., on March 5, 1969; tried at Decatur, a., and convicted and sentenced to a 7-year pris- term on May 29, 1969. Mackle was found alive out 80 hours after the abduction, buried in a box derground.

RIMINAL ALIEN INVESTIGATION BUREAU.
e Police: Police bureau of criminal alien investi- tion

RIPPLES

Hospital for crippled children. *See* Hospital: rippled children's hospital (state)

The First

Kindergarten for crippled children was opened at the Alta Settlement House, Cleveland, Ohio in 1900.

Orthopedic hospital. *See under* Hospital

Private school for cripples was planned in 1861 by a Miss Cornelia and Dr. James Knight. It was opened May 1, 1863, at the Hospital for the Rup- tured and Crippled, New York City, under the aus- pices of the New York Society for the Relief of the Ruptured and Crippled, incorporated March 27, 1863. *(Fenwick Beekman—Hospital for the Rup- tured and Crippled)*

Public school for cripples was the Tilden School, Chicago, Ill., opened in 1900, with Emma Haskell as teacher. A horse-drawn wagon was used to transport the children.

CROIX DE GUERRE. *See* Medal

CROPS. *See under* Agriculture

CROQUET LEAGUE was the National Croquet League, organized February 12, 1880, in Phila- delphia, Pa. The first president was George Wash- ington Johnson of the Lemon Hill Croquet Club. David Evans of the Pennsylvania Croquet Club was elected secretary and treasurer. Representa- tives from 18 clubs attended to standardize the game. Wickets were reduced in size and the balls reduced in diameter.

CROSSING GATE, RAILROAD. *See* Railroad crossing gate patent

CROSSWORD PUZZLE was prepared by Arthur Wynne and was published in the supplement of the New York (Sunday) *World* of December 21, 1913.

CROSSWORD PUZZLE BOOK was the *Cross- word Puzzle Book,* published by Simon and Schuster, Inc., New York City, on April 18, 1924. It was edited by [Albert] Prosper Buranelli, F. Gregory Hartswick, and Margaret Petherbridge. It was an anthology of 50 puzzles from the New York *World.*

CROUP REPORT. *See under* Medical Book

CRUDE OIL CARRIER. *See* Ship: Commercial crude-oil carrier

CRUISE SHIP. *See* Ship

CRUSHER, STONE. *See* Stone crusher

CRYOTRONS were developed by Dudley Allen Buck at the Massachusetts Institute of Technolo- gy, Cambridge Mass., and publicly reported on February 6, 1957. A cryotron is a superconductive switch designed for use in digital computers. A switching circuit containing large numbers of cryotrons operates at about four degrees above absolute zero.

The First

CRYPTOGRAPHY BOOK was *A Dictionary to enable any two persons to maintain a correspondence with a secrecy, which is impossible for any other person to discover,* a 48-page pamphlet published anonymously in 1805 in Hartford, Conn. *(James D. Volts and David Shulman—A Bibliography of Cryptography)*

CRYPTOGRAPHY CHART was P. R. Wouves's *A Syllabical and Steganographical Table,* a chart 27 by 19¼ inches, with a list of syllables and words in English and French intended for secret correspondence. It contained 62 alphabetical columns, 6138 two-letter combinations, numbered from 1 to 99 so that words could be converted into numerical figures. It had two title pages, one in English and one in French, and was published in 1797 by Benjamin Franklin Bache in Philadelphia, Pa.

CRYSTAL CHANDELIER. *See* Glass crystal chandelier

CUMULATIVE BOOK INDEX MONTHLY. *See* Book index: Monthly cumulative index of books

CURB EXCHANGE. *See under* Brokerage

CURFEW BELL was introduced by Wilhelm Kieft, the third governor of New Netherlands (New York). In 1638 he instituted the custom of ringing the church bell nightly at nine o'clock to announce the hour of resting; every morning and evening to call persons to and from labor; and on Thursdays to summon prisoners to court. *(Edmund Bailey O'Callaghan—History of New Netherland, or New York Under the Dutch)*

CURIUM. *See* Element: Element 96

CURLING CHAMPIONSHIP (national) competition was held March 28-30, 1957, at the Stadium, Chicago, Ill. The men's national curling championship was won by the Hibbing Curling Club, Hibbing, Minn. The team consisted of Harold Lauber, skip; Louis Lauber, Peter Beasy, Matt Brklich, and Irwin Akin, alternate. Ten teams competed. Hibbing won eight games and lost one game. Second place was won by the Chicago, Ill., Curling Club and the Minot, N.D., Curling Club.

CURLING CLUB was the Orchard Lake Curling Club, organized in the winter of 1831–1832, near the present site of Pontiac, Mich. Lacking genuine curling stones, the club improvised wooden blocks sawed from hickory and shaped with ax and chisel. *(T. Williamson—Curling in Detroit and Vicinity)*

CURLING RINK
Indoor curling rink devoted exclusively to curling was opened December 19, 1920, by the Country Club, Brookline, Mass. *(Frederic Haines Curtiss and John Heard—The Country Club, 1882–1932)*

The First

CURRENCY. *See* Money

CURRENCY COMPTROLLER. *See* Comptroll Comptroller of the currency

CURRENCY LEGISLATION. *See* Money: Dem netization of silver

CUSTOMHOUSE in colonial America was esta lished in Yorktown, Va. It was built about 1706 Richard Ambler, who occupied it as "Collector Ports for Yorktown in 1720." At this period Yor town was the port of entry for New York, Phi delphia, and other northern cities. A tombstone Hampton, Va., badly obliterated but decipher ble, reads "Peter Heyman, Collector of his Maje ty's custom, died April 29, 1700." He is presum to have been one of the early collectors of cu toms at Yorktown. *(Records in Bureau of Custom U.S. Treasury Department, Washington, D.C.)*

CUSTOMS BUREAU
Bureau of Customs receipts totaling over $3 b lion were in 1968, when national receipts amou ed to $3,179,762,090. This included payments fro 219,581,549 persons entering the United Stat who had paid $1,132,467,676 in duties, of whi $939,620,702 had been levied on imports by sh and $192,846,974 on imports by air.

CUSTOMS COURT JUDGE (black). *See* Judg Black judge of a customs court (U.S.)

CUSTOMS COURT JUDGE (woman). *See* Judg Woman associate justice on the federal bench

CUT GLASS. *See* Glass

CUTLERY FACTORY
Cutlery factory of importance was the Gre River Works of John Russell and Compa Greenfield, Mass., established about 1833 for manufacture of chisels and table cutlery. It dev oped into the J. Russell Cutlery Company and h a branch office in New York City in 1840. *(Fran McGee Thompson—History of Greenfield, Mas*

Cutlery factory for the manufacture of pock cutlery was started at Lakeville, Conn., by t Holley Manufacturing Company in 1845.

CUTLERY SHEARS were made in Elizabethpo N.J., in 1825 by Rochus Heinisch.

CYCLONE
Cyclone recorded occurred August 27, 1667, Jamestown, Va. It produced "such violence tha overturned many houses burying in the ru much goods and many people, beating to t grounds such as were any ways employed in fields, blowing many cattle that were near the s or rivers, into them, whereby unknown numbe have perished, to the great affliction of all peop .... the sea swelled twelve foot above the norm eight, drowning the whole country before it, w many of the inhabitants, their cattle and fee *(James Cornell—The Great International Disas Book)*

he First

YCLOTRON. *See under* Physics

YLINDER PAPER-MAKING MACHINE. *See*
aper-making machinery: Papermaking machine
ylinder)

YLINDER PRINTING PRESS. *See* Printing press

YSTOSCOPIC PHOTOGRAPHS IN COLOR.
ee Photograph

ZECH-LANGUAGE NEWSPAPER. *See* News-
aper

D

ACRON

Dacron men's suits were introduced May 8,
51, by Hart, Schaffner & Marx Co. They were
ade of 8-8½ ounce fabric, consisting of 55 per-
nt Dacron and 45 percent worsted, produced by
eering, Milliken & Co., New York City, under the
rand name of Visa.

AGUERREOTYPE. *See* Photograph: Photograph
ken in the United States

AILY NEWSPAPER. *See* Newspaper

AIRY DIVISION OF THE BUREAU OF ANI-
AL INDUSTRY. *See under* Animal Industry Bu-
au (U.S.)

AIRY LEGISLATION (state) was enacted by
assachusetts, "an act to punish fraud by the sale
adulterated milk," Chapter 222, signed May 30,
56, by Governor Henry Joseph Gardner.

AIRY SCHOOL of collegiate rank with an orga-
zed course was offered by the College of Agri-
lture, University of Wisconsin, Madison, Wis.,
ened January 3, 1890, to supplement courses in
sting milk and farm churning. The first instruc-
r in charge of dairying was Professor John
'right Decker. The first year the organized
urse was attended by only 2 students, but the
llowing year 70 registered from nine states and
anada. Dairy certificates were awarded to those
ho passed the full course and had been in practi-
l charge of a creamery or cheese factory for two
asons of not less than seven months each, one
which followed the period of completing the
urse.

AIRYMEN'S ASSOCIATION. *See* Agricultural
ciety: Agricultural society for dairymen

AM

Dam disaster of great consequence occurred on
ay 31, 1889, at Johnstown, Pa., when the South
rk Dam burst and flooded the city with a wall
water reaching 75 feet high and half a mile
ide, causing a loss of 2,205 lives. The property
amage was about $10 million. The dam held
ck the waters of Conemaugh Lake, which was

The First

about 2½ miles long, and 1½ miles wide, with an
average depth of 50 feet.

Needle-type dam was constructed in 1900
under the supervision of B. F. Thomas at Louisa,
Ky. It is located on the Levisa Fork of the Big
Sandy River, just below the junction of Tug River.
This needle dam was built from the West Virginia
side to the Kentucky side and creates a pool some
40 miles long.

Rock-filled dam was built at Castlewood, Colo.,
for the Denver Land and Water Company, and
opened in November 1890. The upstream and
downstream faces of the dam were built of dry or
mortar rubble masonry. The core of the dam consisted of loosely dumped rock. The maximum
height of the dam above the valley floor was
about 70 feet, and the length about 600 feet. There
was a spillway, located near the center of the
dam, consisting of an opening 4 feet deep and 100
feet long. The outlets through the structure consisted of eight 12-inch cast-iron pipes, placed in
pairs, at four different elevations, with valves in
a chamber built inside the dam. The reservoir
capacity was about 3,400 acre-feet.

Steel dam was the Ash Fork Dam in Johnson
Canyon, four miles east of Ashfork, Ariz., which
was built in 1898 by the Atchison, Topeka and
Santa Fe Railway Company. It was built of steel
with masonry abutments. The west abutment was
84 feet long, 16 feet high. The steel portion was 184
feet long. Height of the spillway crest above
present reservoir bottom was 30 feet; lowest be-
drock to spillway crest was 46 feet; width of canyon at stream bed was 40 feet; top of dam
(exclusive of spillway) was 300 feet. Water spills
over the crest of the dam were designed as an
overflow weir. The capacity of this reservoir at
spillway crest was 96.7 acre-feet. Area of surface
at spillway crest was 7.1 acres. This canyon
drained about 30 square miles. Water flow was
intermittent in the stream bed. *(Edward Wegmann
—The Design and Construction of Dams)*

DANCE COURSE

Belly-dancing college course. *See* College: Belly-dancing college course

Dance course with collegiate credit was approved November 11, 1926, by the Board of Regents, and offered in the Department of Physical
Education of Women, University of Wisconsin,
Madison, Wis. Margaret Newell H'Doubler (Mrs.
Wayne Claxton) was appointed chairman of the
course, known as the dance major. The department offered work in the dance in the summer of
1917 without collegiate credit.

DANCE MARATHON

Dance marathon began Saturday, March 31,
1923, at 6:57 P.M., at the Audubon Ballroom, New
York City, and continued until Sunday April 1,
1923, 9:57 P.M., when Alma Cummings concluded
27 hours of continuous dancing to a live band and

The First

DANCE MARATHON—*Continued*
phonograph music. She danced the fox-trot, one-step, and waltz and tired out six partners.

Dance marathon to exceed 200 hours was won by Bernie Brand of Dallas, Texas, who danced continuously for 217 hours at St. Louis, Mo. He outlasted the other 21 entrants, beginning on June 1, 1923, and ending on June 10, 1923.

DANGER SIGNAL (CQD). *See* Radio distress signal

DAVIS CUP TENNIS MATCH. *See* Tennis match

DAYLIGHT SAVING, sponsored by the National Daylight Saving Association, was put into operation in the United States on Easter Sunday, March 31, 1918, when clocks were set one hour ahead. The measure was introduced by Senator William Musgrave Calder of New York on April 17, 1917, but was defeated. It was later passed without a roll call on June 27, 1917.

DEAD LETTER OFFICE. *See under* Postal service

DEAF—ASSOCIATION
National social organization for the hard of hearing was the American Association for the Hard of Hearing formed February 27, 1919, in New York City. The first annual meeting was held in New York City March 12, 1920. The name was changed to the American Society for the Hard of Hearing on June 5, 1935, at a meeting held in Cincinnati, Ohio.

DEAF—BONE BANK
National temporal-bone bank center for ear research was established in January 1961 at the Department of Otolaryngology, University of Chicago, Chicago, Ill.

DEAF—CHURCH SERVICE
Church service telecast in sign language. *See under* Television—Telecast

Church services for the deaf were held by an Episcopal priest, the Reverend Thomas Gallaudet (son of Thomas Hopkins Gallaudet) on October 3, 1852, in the small chapel of New York University, New York City. Oral services were held in the morning, sign services in the afternoon. On September 11, 1854, St. Ann's Church for Deaf-Mutes was incorporated and property purchased in 1859. The first services in the new church building were held August 7, 1859. *(Thomas Gallaudet—Sermon preached at the 25th Anniversary, Oct. 7, 1879)*

Ordained deaf clergyman was the Reverend Henry Winter Syle, a deacon in 1876 and a priest in 1883. He founded All Souls' Church for the Deaf, Philadelphia, Pa., in 1885.

Prayers in the sign language of the deaf were offered in 1817 at the American Institution for the Deaf, Hartford, Conn., by the Reverend Thomas Hopkins Gallaudet, a Congregational clergyman and teacher of the deaf.

The First

DEAF—COMMUNICATION
Visible and oral communication by the dea over distance was accomplished October 13, 194 when Bertha O'Donnell and Adele Costa con versed in sign language through two-way telev sion sets at W2USA, New York World's Fa Amateur Television Booth, and W2HID, 220 Ea 42nd Street, New York City, eight miles away.

DEAF—HEARING AID
Electrical hearing aid produced commercial was the Acousticon, invented by Miller Rees Hutchinson of New York City in 1901. On April 2 1880, Francis D. Clarke and M. G. Foster secure patent No. 226,902 on a "device for aiding the de to hear" that made its own electricity and ope ated by bone conduction.

Hearing aid of interest other than ear trumpe was the Audiphone, a fanlike device held again the teeth, patented September 23, 1879, by Ric ard S. Rhodes of River Park, Ill., who obtaine patent No. 219,828.

Transistorized hearing aid was manufacture by the Sonotone Corporation, Elmsford, N.Y., ar offered for sale December 29, 1952. It weighed 3 ounces and measured 3 by ¾ by 19/32 inches.

DEAF—LIPREADING TOURNAMENT. *See* I preading tournament (national)

DEAF—SCHOOL
Institution in the world for the higher educati of the deaf was the National Deaf Mute Colleg Washington, D.C., a department of the Columb Institution for the Instruction of the Deaf, Dum and Blind, incorporated February 16, 1857 (11 St L. 161). On April 8, 1864, the Columbia Instituti for the Deaf was authorized by a special act Congress (13 Stat. L. 45) to confer degrees. T first degree was an honorary Master of Arts co ferred June 1864. The first graduate received diploma in 1866. The name of the institution w changed to the Columbia Institution for the De as the education of the blind was transferred els where. The name of the advanced departme was changed in 1894 to Gallaudet College honor of Thomas Hopkins Gallaudet, who was t first principal of the first school for the deaf America. Dr. Edward Miner Gallaudet (son Thomas Hopkins Gallaudet), served as preside of Gallaudet College from 1864 to 1910. *(Hen Winter Syle—A Biographical Sketch of Thom Hopkins Gallaudet)*

Instruction for the deaf was given by the Rev end John Stanford, Chaplain to the Humane a Criminal Institutions, in 1807 in the Almshou New York City. This instruction continued f about a year. Ten years later a meeting was he at his home to organize the New York Instituti for the Deaf, now the New York School for Deaf, which opened in 1818. *(Fred de Land—T Story of Lip Reading)*

he First

Lipreading instruction for the deaf was given by ºarah Warren Keeler, a teacher at the Institution ⁱr the Improved Instruction of Deaf Mutes in ºew York City, who advertised lipreading lessons ⁱr adults in 1882. She lectured on the subject in ß84 and published her method in 1894.

Lipreading school for adults (successful) was ºstablished by Lillie Eginton Warren in 1890 in ºew York City. In 1895 she published *Defective ƥeech and Deafness*, a 116-page book, and on .pril 28, 1903, obtained patent No. 726,484 on a ʍeans for teaching of the facial expressions ʰich occur in speaking."

Lipreading tournament. *See* Lipreading tourna-ʌent (national)

Lipreading was first referred to in print in Dr. ⱴilliam Thornton's essays *On the Mode of Teach-ⁱg the Deaf, or Surd, and Consequently Dumb, to ƥeak*, which appeared in the *Transactions of the ʌmerican Philosophical Society*, Philadelphia, ⁷93.

Oral instruction for the deaf (known as visible ƥeech) was used by the Horace Mann School in ʋoston, Mass., in 1871. Alexander Graham Bell ⁱstructed the teachers of this school in the sys-ºm which his father, Alexander Melville Bell, ⱳas advocating. Visible speech was phonetic ʳriting invented by Alexander Melville Bell to ⁱow graphically any sound made by the human ʋoice, and used to facilitate pronunciation of for-ⁱgn languages. In appreciation of his services the ʋoston School Committee provided a fund of $500 ⁱ pay for the services of Alexander Graham Bell ⁱuring the spring of 1871. Oral instruction had ºen used in England in the eighteenth century.

Oral school for the deaf (still existing) wàs the ɹlarke School for the Deaf, which was founded in ß67 in Northampton, Mass. The nucleus of this ɔhool was a small experimental school in ʰelmsford, Mass., founded by Harriet Rogers ß65. Miss Rogers was appointed principal. John ɹlarke, philanthropist, gave $50,000. An oral ɔhool was started at Cobbs, Chesterfield County, ⱥ., in 1815 by Colonel William Bolling with John ʳaidwood as instructor, but it lasted only two ºars.

School for the deaf (permanent) was the Con-ºcticut Asylum for the Education and Instruction ⁱ Deaf and Dumb Persons, Hartford, Conn., ʰich opened April 15, 1817, with seven pupils. It ⱳas incorporated May 1816. A grant of $5,000 was ⱥde by the Connecticut legislature October ß16. On May 5, 1819, the name was changed to ⱡe American Asylum. The school was financed ⱡrough the generosity of a few men, one of whom, ⱱr. Mason Fitch Cogswell, had a deaf daughter, ⱡice. Thomas Hopkins Gallaudet, the first princi-ⱥl, inaugurated the system of teaching with the ɔllaboration of the Frenchman Laurent Clerc.

The First

Sign language and finger spelling were the only means of communication. *(Henry Winter Syle—A Biographical Sketch of Rev. Thomas Hopkins Gallaudet)*

DEAF—STUDENTS' MAGAZINE
    Magazine for deaf students was the *Deaf Mute Casket*, a four-page monthly printed in a school for the deaf by the deaf and edited by William D. Cooke. It was published in 1851 by the State School for the Blind and the Deaf in Raleigh, N.C.

DEAN OF MEN. *See under* College

DEAN OF THE FACULTY. *See under* College

DEAN (woman) OF A GRADUATE SCHOOL. *See* College: Woman dean of a graduate school

DEATH PENALTY. *See* Capital punishment

DEATH PENALTY FOR KIDNAPPING. *See under* Kidnapping

DEBATE, RADIO. *See* Radio broadcast: Debate over the radio

DEBT
    Public debt of the United States to exceed $100 million was $127,334,933.74 on January 1, 1816. The first to exceed $500 million was $524,-176,412.13 on July 1, 1862. The first to exceed $1 billion was $1,119,772,138.63 on July 1, 1863. *(U.S. Treasury Department. Bureau of Statistics—Public Debt of the United States 1791–1896)*

DEBT LEGISLATION (federal) exempting debtors from prison on processes issuing from a United States court amounting to less than $30 was "an act for the relief of persons imprisoned for debt" passed May 28, 1796 (1 Stat. L. 482). On February 28, 1839, an act of Congress (5 Stat. L. 321) prohibited imprisonment for debt by a United States court in states in which imprisonment for debt had been abolished.

DEBTORS' COURT. *See* Court: Small debtors' court established by state law

DEBTORS' PRISON to be abolished by law was that of Kentucky, which passed "an act to abolish imprisonment for debt" on December 17, 1821. The act repealed all laws authorizing *capias ad satisfaciendum*. *(Chapter 229, Acts Passed at First Session Thirtieth General Assembly, Frankfort, Ky.)*

DECALCOMANIAS, or transfer papers, were imported in 1862 and used as playthings. The first commercial production for decorating buggies, sleighs, bicycles, sewing machines, etc., was undertaken in Philadelphia, Pa., in 1890 by Thomas Burke, who established the National Decalcomania Company. The company was incorporated in 1922.

DECATHLON CHAMPION (American). *See* Olympic Games: American decathlon champion

The First

DECIMAL SYSTEM OF MONEY. *See under* Money

DECK CHAIR. *See* Chair: Steamer chair

DECKED SHIP. *See* Ship

DECLARATION OF INDEPENDENCE, AMERICAN

Declaration of Independence was formally made on July 12, 1774, in the First Presbyterian Church in Carlisle, Pa., at a meeting of freeholders and freemen from the several townships. Various resolutions were passed. The Reverend John Montgomery presided. *(Conway Phelps Wing— History of the First Presbyterian Church of Carlisle)*

Declaration of Independence by a colony was made on April 12, 1776, when the Provincial Congress in session at Halifax, N.C., by unanimous action empowered the delegates to the Continental Congress to concur with delegates of other provinces in declaring independence from Great Britain. The Mecklenburg (N.C.) Declaration of Independence had been previously adopted on May 20, 1775, in Charlotte, Mecklenburg County, N.C., by citizens who formally declared independence from Great Britain. Less drastic actions of similar nature were advocated by Patrick Henry and others. *(William Henry Hoyt—The Mecklenburg Declaration of Independence.* See also conflicting statement by *James Hall Moore—Defense of the Mecklenburg Declaration of Independence)*

Declaration of Independence was first ordered "to be fairly engrossed on parchment" on July 19, 1776, and was signed in Philadelphia on August 2, 1776, by 50 members of the original 56 who voted for its adoption. The other 6 signed at various later times. The last signer was Thomas McKean, who originally voted for it, but had left Philadelphia to join the Army and was permitted to sign as late as 1781.

Declaration of Independence was first printed July 5, 1776, in Philadelphia, Pa., by John Dunlop in a folio broadside and distributed the same day. On July 4 Congress, acting as a Committee of the Whole, approved the Declaration and ordered that it be printed and that copies be "sent to the several assemblies, conventions and committees or counsels of safety and to the several commanding officers of the Continental troops that it be proclaimed in each of the United States and at the head of the army."

Declaration of Independence was first published in a newspaper on July 6, 1776. It was reprinted in Vol. II, No. 228, of the *Pennsylvania Evening Post* of Philadelphia, Pa.

Declaration of Independence was first read publicly on July 8, 1776, when Colonel John Nixon, delegated by the High Sheriff of Philadelphia, read it in the old State House yard (Independence Square). The "Liberty Bell" with the prophetic in-

The First

scription "Proclaim liberty throughout all the lan unto all the inhabitants thereof" was rung to ca the citizens together to hear the reading. *(Haro Donaldson Eberlein and Cortland Van Dyke Hu bard—Diary of Independence Hall)*

Declaration of Independence was signed fir by John Hancock of Massachusetts, President the Continental Congress, on July 4, 1776, in Phil delphia, Pa. It was also signed by Charles Thor son, secretary (but not a delegate). The parchmer copy was signed by the delegates on August 1776. *(John Sanderson—Biography of the Signe of the Declaration of Independence)*

DECLARATION OF RIGHTS was passed on O tober 14, 1774, and was known as the "Declar tion and Resolves of the First Continent Congress." It agreed, "That they [the colonist are entitled to life, liberty and property; and the have never ceded to any foreign power whatsoe er a right to dispose of either without their co sent." It was enacted in Philadelphia, P *(Worthington Chauncey Ford, ed.—Journals the Continental Congress, 1774–1789)*

DECORATION. *See* Medal

DECORATION DAY. *See under* Holiday

DEEP-FREEZE LOCKER. *See* Locker: Public loc er plant

DEFENSE COMMAND (U.S.). *See* Air Defen Command (U.S.)

DEFENSE DEPARTMENT (U.S.) was authorize July 26, 1947 (61 Stat. L. 495) by the Nation Security Act of 1947. It was formed on Septemb 17, 1947, when the War and Navy departmen were combined with James Vincent Forrestal chief. He was sworn in September 17, 1947, Supreme Court Justice Frederick Moore Vinso The following day John Laurence Sullivan w sworn in as Secretary of the Navy and Willia Stuart Symington as Secretary for Air. Kenne Claiborne Royall had been sworn in nine wee previously as Secretary of the Army. The depa ment was granted Cabinet status and was autho ized by the National Security Act of July 26, 19 (61 Stat. L. 495).

DEFENSE MERITORIOUS SERVICE MEDA *See* Medal

DEFENSE SUPERIOR SERVICE MEDAL. S Medal

DEGREES (academic and honorary)

American awarded honorary degrees fro three of England's leading universities was A bassador Robert Worth Bingham, recipient of honorary LL.D. (Doctor of Laws) from Lond University on November 25, 1933, and from Ca bridge University on October 22, 1934; and honorary Litt.D. (Doctor of Letters) from Oxfo University on November 21, 1936.

The First

Anthropology doctorate was conferred March 1892, by Clark University, Worcester, Mass., on Alexander Francis Chamberlain for his 84-page thesis on "The Language of the Mississagua Indians." *(American Anthropologist, Vol. 16, p. 337)*

Bachelor of Arts degree was conferred September 23, 1642, by Harvard College, Cambridge, Mass., on nine graduates: Tobias Barnard, Samuel Bellingham, Nathaniel Brewster, John Bulkley, George Downing, William Hubbard, Henry Saltonstall, John Wilson, and Benjamin Woodbridge.

Bachelor of Music degree was granted December 23, 1873, by Adrian College, Adrian, Mich., to Hattie Pease Lowrie, who completed a four-year course in vocal and instrumental music and theory. A Master of Music degree was authorized for musicians of recognized ability who paid the regular fee and passed the required examination.

Bachelor of Sacred Music degree was conferred June 10, 1953, by the Hebrew Union College Jewish Institute of Religion, New York City, on seven men who had completed the course.

Bachelor's degree awarded by a recognized institution without requiring a single college credit as a Bachelor of Science degree awarded on September 20, 1974, to Nicholas E. France of Albany, N. Y., who satisfied all requirements of the University of the State of New York, Albany, N.Y., by using examinations rather than college courses. He employed the Regents External Degrees Business Examinations especially designed for the business program he completed along with the College Level Examination Program's General Examinations.

Degree awarded a ventriloquist's dummy was conferred August 28, 1938, by the School of Speech of Northwestern University, Evanston, Ill., to Charlie McCarthy during the regular Edgar Bergen–Charlie McCarthy hour in the Chicago studios of the National Broadcasting Company. The degree of Master of Innuendo and Snappy Comeback was conferred by the dean, Ralph Dennis.

Degree conferred by radio was granted June 9, 1925, by the State University of Iowa, Iowa City, Iowa, to Clifford L. Lideen of Burlington, Iowa. The university broadcast the conferring of his B.A. degree. He was forced to leave the university in 1922 because of illness and completed his work through broadcasts given by station WOI, Ames, Iowa.

Doctor of Dental Surgery. *See* Dental school: dental college

Doctor of Laws honorary degree was awarded July 21, 1773, by Harvard College, Cambridge, Mass., to John Winthrop, Doctor of Laws *pro meritis.* *(Henry Herbert Edes—John Winthrop, the First Recipient from Harvard College of the Degree of Doctor of Laws)*

The First

Doctor of Medicine. *See* Physican

Doctor of Military Science degree was created by New York University, New York City, and conferred April 11, 1930, upon General John Joseph Pershing, the first recipient of such a degree in the United States.

Doctor of Music degree was conferred July 24, 1849, by Georgetown University, Washington, D.C., on Professor Henry Dielman of Mount St. Mary's, Emmitsburg, Md. The degree was awarded *honoris causa* at exercises attended by President Zachary Taylor. *(John Gilmary Shea—Memorial of the First Centenary of the Georgetown College)*

Doctor of Philosophy degree was awarded in 1861 by Yale University, New Haven, Conn., to three graduates, Eugene Schuyler, James Morris Whiton, and Arthur Williams Wright. The degree had been authorized July 24, 1860. *(Paul Monroe—Cyclopedia of Education)*

Doctor of Philosophy degree awarded to a black was granted to Edward Alexander Bouchet by Yale University, New Haven, Conn., in 1876, in physics. He was also the first black to be elected to Phi Beta Kappa, the national scholastic fraternity. He was graduated from Yale in 1874. His thesis was entitled "Measuring Refractive Indices."

Doctor of Philosophy degree awarded to a woman was granted by Boston University Boston, Mass., June 6, 1877, to Helen Magill (Mrs. Andrew Jackson White). The title of her dissertation was "The Greek Drama." She received her A.B. degree in 1875 from Swarthmore. *(Institute of Women's Professional Relations, Greensboro, N.C.)*

Doctor of Philosophy degree awarded to a woman by a women's college was granted on June 21, 1882, by Smith College, Northampton, Mass., to Kate Eugenia Morris (later Mrs. Charles Morris Cone). The subject of her dissertation in history was the German electoral college.

Doctor of Philosophy in Accounting degree was conferred June 12, 1939, on John Wood McMahan at the annual commencement of the University of Illinois, Urbana, Ill.

Doctor of Sacred Theology degree was granted to Increase Mather on September 5, 1692 by Harvard College, Cambridge, Mass. Two tutors, John Leverett and William Brattle, were awarded the Bachelor of Sacred Theology degree.

Doctor of Science degree earned by a woman was awarded to Caroline Willard Baldwin (later Mrs. Charles T. Morrison) on June 20, 1895, by Cornell University, Ithaca, N.Y. The title of her dissertation was "A Photographic Study of Arc Spectra."

The First

DEGREES (academic and honorary)—*Continued*
Doctor of Social Science degree was awarded to Helen Rankin Jeter in 1924 by the School of Social Science Administration of the University of Chicago, Chicago, Ill. Her thesis, "The Chicago Juvenile Court," was published by the Children's Bureau of the United States Department of Labor.

Honorary degree awarded a black woman by a southern white college was a Doctor of Humanities degree awarded Mary McLeod Bethune on February 21, 1949, by Rollins College, Winter Park, Fla.

Honorary degree granted George Washington was the degree of "Doctor of Laws, the Law of Nature and Nations, and the Civil Law," conferred by the Governing Board of Harvard College, April 3, 1776, in Cambridge, Mass. *(Colonial Society of Massachusetts. Publications, Vol. 7)*

Honorary degrees presented simultaneously to a President and his wife were awarded May 30, 1964, by the University of Texas, Austin, Tex. President Lyndon Baines Johnson was awarded the degree of Doctor of Laws, and Claudia Alta ("Lady Bird") Taylor Johnson the degree of Doctor of Letters.

Husband and wife awarded honorary degrees by an American university were Vice President and Mrs. John Nance Garner, recipients of Doctor of Laws degree from Baylor University, Waco, Tex., on November 21, 1936.

Law degree of LL.M. (Master of Laws) was conferred June 29, 1864, at the 110th annual commencement of Columbia University, held at the Academy of Music, New York City. It was also granted in 1865, but not again (by Columbia University) until 1894, after which it was conferred at intervals. During the last few years, however, it has been conferred regularly. *(Alfred Zantzinger Reed—Training for the Public Profession of Law)*

Master of Arts degree in aeronautics was awarded June 1, 1910, by Columbia University, New York City, to Grover Cleveland Loening, whose 40,000-word thesis was entitled "An Investigation of the Practice and Theory of Aviation." Although his area of concentration was aviation or aeronautics, he technically was a student in the Department of Physics, so that the M. A. was technically in physics rather than in aeronautics. *(Grover Loening—Our Wings Grow Faster)*

Master of Arts degree in Sacred Music was conferred June 6, 1956, by the Hebrew Union School of Education and Sacred Music, New York City, on two students who had concluded 30 full sessions and submitted approved theses. The recipients were Cantor Ben William Belfer of Rockville Centre, N.Y., and Cantor Arthur M. Wolfson of Temple Emanuel, New York City.

The First

Master of Hebrew Literature degree awarded woman was granted May 28, 1939, by the Jewish Institute of Religion, New York City, to Helen Hadassah Levinthal, the first Jewish woman to graduate from a recognized theological college having completed the full rabbinical course.

DELINQUENCY LAW. *See* Child delinquency law (state)

DELIVERY TUNNEL, FREIGHT. *See* Tunnel: Freight delivery tunnel system

DEMAND NOTE. *See under* Money

DEMOCRATIC CARTOON. *See* Cartoon

DEMOCRATIC NATIONAL CONVENTION was held May 21–23, 1832 in Baltimore, Md., under the name Republican Delegates from the Several States. Twenty-one states and the District of Columbia sent delegates, who nominated Andrew Jackson for President and Martin Van Buren for Vice President. The Democratic party received 687,502 votes in the election of November 6, 1832, and the National Republicans 530,189 votes. While the present Democratic party was officially known at the time as the Republican party—name that had come down from the time of Jefferson—it was becoming popularly known as the Democratic-Republican party. In the early national conventions *Democrat* and *Republican* were often used interchangeably, but in 1840 the word *Republican* was dropped entirely and the official title became the Democratic National Convention, although even then speakers employed the name *Republican* when referring to what now the Democratic party. *(Frank Richardson Kent—The Democratic Party)*

DEMOCRATIC PARTY
Woman major political party chairman. *See under* Woman

DEMOCRATIC NEWSPAPER. *See* Newspaper

DE MOLAY, ORDER OF. *See* Freemasons: Order of De Molay

DEMONETIZED CURRENCY. *See* Money: Trade dollar

DEMOUNTABLE TIRE-CARRYING RIM. *See under* Automobile tire

DENTAL BOOK
Book for dental hygienists (text) was *Mouth Hygiene,* compiled and edited by Dr. Alfred Civilion Fones and associate editors Robert Halloch Wright Strang and Edward Cameron Kirk. It was a course of instruction for dental hygienists and consisted of 530 pages with 278 illustrations and 7 plates. It was published by Lea & Febiger, Philadelphia and New York, in 1916.

Book on dental surgery was Dr. James Edmund Garretson's *A Treatise on the Diseases and Surgery of the Mouth, Jaws and Associate Parts,*

e First

J-page book published in 1869 by J. B. Lippincott Co., Philadelphia, Pa.

Book on dental technics of value was *The anual of Operative Technics: A Practical Trea- e On the Elements of Operative Dentistry,* pub- hed in Chicago, Ill., in 1894 by Thomas Edwin eeks, professor of operative dentistry and den- anatomy in the College of Dentistry, University Minnesota, Minneapolis, Minn.

Book on dentistry (strictly American) was Rich- d Cort Skinner's *A Treatise on the Human eth, Concisely Explaining Their Structure and use of Disease and Decay,* copyrighted in 1801 Johnson and Stryker, New York City. It con- ned 26 pages and sold for 30 cents. Originally blished in 1794, it claimed to obviate every dis- se incident to the teeth and gums. *(Fielding dson Garrison—An Introduction to the History Medicine)*

Book on dentistry to become popular was Jo- ıh Foster Flagg's *The Family Dentist: Containing Brief Description of the Structure, Formation, seases and Treatment of the Human Teeth, nted and published in 1822 in Boston, Mass., by ieph W. Ingraham. It contained 82 pages.

Dental textbook was *A System of Dental Sur- ry in three parts: 1. Dental surgery as a science; Operative dental surgery; 3. Pharmacy connect- with dental surgery,* by Samuel Sheldon Fitch, urgeon dentist of Philadelphia, Pa. The work, ıich contained 568 pages, was published in 1829 New York City by G. & C. H. Carvill.

Orthodontia treatise to be printed was *An say on the Importance of Regulating the Teeth Children Before the Fourteenth Year; or the riod of Life when the Second Set of Teeth come Perfectly Developed,* by Solyman Brown, D., which was printed in 1841 in New York City. ırnhard Wolf Weinberger—Orthodontics)*

NTAL CHAIR that provided such necessary veniences as a headrest and changes in height d position of the seat and back was designed by Waldo Hanchett of Syracuse, N.Y., who re- ved patent No. 5,711, on August 15, 1848. *(His- y of Dental and Oral Science in America)*

NTAL CODE OF ETHICS was proposed July 1865, by Dr. John Allen at the Fifth Annual nvention of the American Dental Association d in Chicago, Ill.

NTAL CORPS (U.S. Army)
Army Dental Corps major general was Major neral Robert H. Mills, Director of the Dental vision, whose appointment was made possible War Department Special Orders No. 280, Octo- 7, 1943. The date of his rank was September 1943.

The First

Dental Corps commissions were authorized by act of Congress of March 3, 1911 (36 Stat. L. 1054) which limited commissions to first lieutenant. The act of June 3, 1916 (39 Stat. L. 173), permitted the ranks of captain and major; the act of October 6, 1917 (40 Stat. L. 397), the ranks of lieutenant colo- nel and colonel; the act of January 29, 1938 (52 Stat. L. 8), the rank of brigadier general for the director of the Dental Division, one of the assist- ants to the surgeon general.

Dental Corps of the U.S. Army was authorized by the Army Reorganization Act, February 2, 1901 (31 Stat. L. 752), "an act to increase the efficiency of the permanent military establishments of the United States." It authorized the employment of contract dental surgeons "not to exceed one to every 30,000 of said army, and not to exceed 30 in all." The first three contract dental surgeons were Drs. John Sayre Marshall, Robert T. Oliver, and Robert W. Morgan, named by the surgeon general on February 11, 1901.

Dentist officially employed in the U.S. Army was Dr. W. H. Ware, an enlisted man in the Medi- cal Department, who served as a dental surgeon in the U.S. Army in the Philippine Islands in 1898.

DENTAL CORPS (U.S. Navy)
Admiral in the Dental Corps (U.S. Navy) was Dr. Alexander Gordon Lyle, appointed a rear ad- miral on March 13, 1943.

Dental Corps of the U.S. Navy was authorized by act of Congress of August 22, 1912 (37 Stat. L. 344), which provided for not more than 30 dental surgeons to be part of the Medical Department of the U.S. Navy and to provide professional service for navy personnel. They received the rank of lieutenant, junior grade.

DENTAL DISPENSARY
Dental dispensary was the City Dispensary for the Medical Relief of the Poor, New York City, which opened February 1, 1791. It was incorporat- ed April 8, 1795. Isaac Roosevelt was the first president. From February 1, 1791, to November 23, 1791, 310 patients were admitted. The fee for ex- tractions and filling cavities with silver or lead foil was 50 cents; filling cavities with gold or a good set of front teeth cost $1.

DENTAL DRILL, ELECTRIC. *See* Drill

DENTAL LEGISLATION
Legislation (state) regarding dental hygienists was the Public Acts of the State of Connecticut, passed by the January 1915 session, Chapter 316, Section 12, and approved May 19, 1915. The first examination for dental hygienists was given by the State Board in June 1918 since no hygienists had applied for license prior to that date.

Legislation (state) regarding dental surgery was passed December 31, 1841, by Alabama. It pro- vided that from and after the first Monday of December 1842 there should be "medical boards

The First

DENTAL LEGISLATION—*Continued*
of the state to examine and to issue a license to applicants to practice dental surgery under the same rules and regulations, and subject to the same restrictions as those who apply for license to practice medicine."

DENTAL MALLET
Dental mallet was invented by Dr. William Gibson Arlington Bonwill of Philadelphia, Pa., who obtained patent No. 170,045 on November 16, 1875, on "electro-magnetic dental pluggers" used to impact gold into cavities. He conceived the idea of a vibrating mallet on February 27, 1867, while watching the "sounder" of a telegraph key in operation at the Continental Hotel in Philadelphia. *(Dental Cosmos. Vol. 17, No. 12. December 1875)*

DENTAL OFFICE (mobile)
Mobile dental office self-contained operating unit (U.S. Navy). *See* Navy: Mobile dental office self-contained operating unit (U.S. Navy)

DENTAL PERIODICAL
Dental journal to be published was *The American Journal of Dental Science, Devoted to Original Articles, Reviews of Dental Publications, etc.,* 24 pages, which made its appearance July 1839. The publishing committee consisted of Dr. Eleazar Parmly, Dr. Elisha Baker, and Dr. Solyman Brown. Dr. Chapin Aaron Harris was the first editor. It was published in New York City.

Orthodontia magazine was the *International Journal of Orthodontia,* edited by Dr. Martin Dewey. The first issue was published January 1915 in St. Louis, Mo., and contained 44 pages. The title was changed to the *American Journal of Orthodontics and Oral Surgery* in January 1938.

DENTAL SCHOOL
Dental assistants' and nurses' course was given by the Ohio College of Dental Surgery, Cincinnati, Ohio, from October 3, 1910, to May 1, 1911. The tuition fee was $75. The course was introduced by Henry Tomlinson Smith, the dean. *(Ohio College of Dental Surgery, 1911–1912 Annual Announcement)*

Dental college was the Baltimore College of Dental Surgery, organized in Baltimore, Md., in 1839 and formally opened November 3, 1840, with 5 students. The college was incorporated February 1, 1840. The faculty consisted of H. Willis Baxter, M.D., professor of anatomy and physiology; Thomas E. Bond, Jr., M.D., professor of special pathology and therapeutics; Chapin Aaron Harris, M.D., professor of practical dentistry; and Horace Henry Hayden, M.D., professor of dental physiology and pathology. The C.D.D. degree *(Chirurgiae Dentium Doctor)* was conferred on March 9, 1841, on Robert Arthur and R. Covington Mackall. This college is now the School of Dentistry, University of Maryland, Baltimore, Md.

The First

Dental hygienists' course was inaugurated Dr. Alfred Civilion Fones, who established t Fones Clinic, Bridgeport, Conn. The cour started November 17, 1913, with 33 women, 27 whom graduated June 5, 1914.

Dental school of the U. S. Navy was the U. Naval Dental School, a department of the U. Naval Medical College, which opened February 1923. The first class, which comprised lieutenar J. W. Baker, W. C. Carroll, A. W. Chandler, R. Davis, and R. H. Fladeland, was graduated Ju 16, 1923.

Dental school permanently established by university, and the first associated with a medic school, was the Harvard School of Dental Me cine, Boston, Mass., established July 17, 1867. T first class began November 4, 1868, with 16 s dents. The first commencement exercises we held March 10, 1869, and the D.M.D. degree *(D. tariae Medicinae Doctor)* was awarded to dentists. Dr. Nathan Cooley Keep was the fi dean. He served from March 19, 1868, to Janua 12, 1872, and also served as the first professor mechanical dentistry.

DENTAL SOCIETY
Dental society (local) was the Society of S geon-Dentists of the City and State of New Yo which was formed December 3, 1834, with Eleazar Parmly as the first president and Dr. So man Brown as the first corresponding secreta This was a local society, as was the Dental Ass ciation of Western New York. *(American Journ of Dental Science. Vol. 1)*

Dental society of importance was the Americ Society of Dental Surgeons, organized August 1840, at a meeting held at the American Hot New York City. The first officers were Dr. Hora Henry Hayden of Baltimore, Md., president; Josiah Foster Flagg of Boston, Mass., Dr. Elea Parmly of New York City, and Dr. Emile B. G dette, vice presidents. The society disbanded 1856. *(Journal American Dental Association. V 27. March 1940)*

Orthodontists' society was the American So ety of Orthodontists, founded June 1900 in Louis, Mo. The first annual meeting was held Ju 11–13, 1901, in St. Louis. The constitution w adopted June 15, 1901. The first president was Edward Hartley Angle of St. Louis. The soci was incorporated February 23, 1917, in Penns vania, and the name changed April 21, 1937, to American Association of Orthodontists.

DENTIST
Dentist who was a native-born American w Josiah Flagg, who, at the age of 18, practiced d tistry in 1782 in Boston, Mass. In 1785 he adv tised as follows: "Dr. Flagg transplants tee cures ulcers and eases them from pain with drawing; fastens those that are loose; mends te

he First

ith foil or gold to be as lasting and useful as the
ound teeth . . . sells, by wholesale and retail,
entifrices, tinctures, chew-sticks, mastics, teeth
nd gum brushes, suitable for every age, com-
laint and climate, with directions for their use."
*Charles Rudolph Edward Koch—History of Den-
·l Surgery)*

**Dentist in the U.S. Navy to serve aboard a naval
hip** was Dr. Harry Edward Harvey, who was
ssigned to the hospital ship U.S.S. *Solace* on
March 5, 1913. He served until October 1915.

**Dentist in the U.S. Navy to serve at an overseas
ase** was Acting Assistant Dental Surgeon James
. Brown, who was ordered April 27, 1913, to the
.S. Naval Station, Guam.

Naval ship named for a dental officer. *See under*
hip

Woman dentist to maintain a dental office in-
ependently was Dr. Emeline Roberts Jones, who
egan practice in Danielsonville (now Danielson),
onn., in May 1855 as an assistant to her husband,
·r. Daniel Albion Jones. In 1859 she became his
artner and in 1864 carried on independently
vhen her husband died. *(James McManus—
ecord of Connecticut Dentists)*

Woman dentist in the U.S. Navy was Lieuten-
nt Dr. Sara Gdulin Krout, who reported to the
;reat Lakes Training Station, Great Lakes, Ill.,
nd served from June 1, 1944, to January 31, 1946.
he was appointed lieutenant February 25, 1944,
· rank from December 30, 1943, and retired as
ommander on December 1, 1961.

Woman dentist to obtain a D.D.S. degree from
dental college was Lucy B. Hobbs (Mrs. Taylor),
vho graduated February 21, 1866, from the Ohio
College of Dental Surgery, Cincinnati, Ohio. She
vas required to attend only one college session
ecause of credits allowed for previous practice.
Licenses to practice dentistry were not compul-
ory.) She was elected a member of the Iowa State
Iental Society on July 1865, the first woman mem-
·er of a dental society. *(Dental Cosmos. Novem-
er 1910)*

DENTISTRY
See also headings beginning with Dental

Amalgam for filling teeth was introduced by
Messrs. Crawcour and Sons, who advertised it in
he August 12, 1834, New York *Commercial Ad-
ertiser* as "Royal Mineral Succedaneum for
lling decayed teeth without the slightest pain,
.eat or pressure." They paid little attention to
aries and filled all cavities without treatment.
'heir work was unsatisfactory and they were
·bliged to flee the country.

Anesthetic in dentistry. *See under* Anesthesia

The First

Dental association. *See* Dental society: Dental
society

Dental hygienists' book. *See* Dental book: Book
for dental hygienists (text)

Dental hygienists' course. *See under* Dental
school

Gold crown tooth was made by Dr. William
Newton Morrison, corresponding secretary of the
Missouri State Dental Association, who de-
scribed his process in the May 1869 issue of the
Missouri Dental Journal.

Gold inlay was described by William H. Taggart, a Chicago dentist, before the New York
Odontological Society, January 15, 1907. He invented the method of casting gold inlays by the
inverted pattern procedure, using the ancient
principle of the "disappearing core." *(Dental Cosmos. November 1907)*

Gold used for the filling of dental cavities was
advocated by Dr. Robert Arthur. In 1855 he discovered the cohesive property of annealed gold
foil, a discovery which practically revolutionized
the dental profession. He described it in an article, "Sponge Gold," in the *Dental News Letter* of
October 1854, published in Philadelphia, Pa., and
in an 86-page book, *A Treatise on the Use of
Adhesive Gold Foil,* published in 1857 in Philadelphia.

Patent for a gold crown was No. 144,182 granted
November 4, 1873, to Dr. John B. Beers of San
Francisco, Calif., on "artificial crowns for teeth."
The technique of preparing the hollow metal
crown or shell is described in the September 1880
Dental Cosmos, published by S. S. White Dental
Manufacturing Company, Philadelphia, Pa.

Patent for artificial teeth was granted on March
9, 1822, to Charles M. Graham of New York City.

Porcelain teeth were introduced about 1785,
owing principally to the efforts of Dr. John Greenwood of New York City. He advertised "artificial
teeth set in so firm (without drawing stumps or
causing the least pain) as to eat with them, and so
exact as not to be distinguished from natural."
Greenwood also invented the foot-power drill.
One of his patients was George Washington.
(Dental Items of Interest—November 1943)

DEPARTMENT OF ENERGY (U.S.)
Department of Energy was created on August
4, 1977, when President Jimmy Carter signed Public Law 95-91, the Department of Energy Organization Act. James Rodney Schlesinger became the
first Secretary of Energy, with cabinet status, on
August 5, 1977. The formal opening was October
1, 1977, when approximately 20,000 employees of
the Federal Power Commission, the Federal Energy Administration, the Energy Research and Development Administration, and components of

The First

DEPARTMENT OF ENERGY (U.S.)—*Continued*
other departments and agencies were consolidated in the new department.

DEPARTMENT STORE. *See under* Business

DEPARTMENTAL POSTAGE STAMP. *See* Postage stamp

DEPARTMENTS (U.S.) *See* specific departments, e.g. Agriculture Department, Interior Department

DEPORTATION was effected by the Plymouth Colony in 1628. Thomas Morton, residing at Mare Mount (Merry Mount), Mass., with a licentious group and also accused of supplying guns to the Indians, was deported because of the general disapproval of his actions. He was sent to England June 9, 1628, in the custody of John Oldham. *(Massachusetts Historical Collections, III, Governor Bradford's Letter Book)*

DEPOSIT GUARANTY ACT. *See* Bank legislation: Bank guaranty legislation

DEPOSIT INSURANCE CORPORATION. *See* Federal Deposit Insurance Corporation

DEPRESSED-TROUGH ROAD. *See* Road: Road with a depressed trough

DERBY HAT. *See* Hat

DERMATOLOGY CHAIR. *See under* Medical instruction

DERMATOLOGY TREATISE. *See under* Medical book

DESERT HOMESTEAD ACT. *See* Homestead act: Homestead act (desert)

DESIGN PATENT. *See* Patent

DESK with roll top was invented about 1850 by Abner Cutler, who formed the Cutler Desk Company of Buffalo, N.Y. The original patent showed the top very similar to the roll top of today. Flexible wooden curtains had been used previously. Cutler improved upon their manufacture by using a strong fabric held between an outer row of moldings and an inner row of soft wood slats, which made it possible to operate rolls six feet long and four feet wide.

DESK TELEPHONE. *See* Telephone

DETECTIVE (woman). *See* Police: Woman detective

DETECTIVE STORY to achieve popularity was Edgar Allan Poe's "The Murders in the Rue Morgue," published April 1841 in *Graham's Magazine,* Vol. 18, No. 4, Philadelphia, Pa.

DETECTOR CAR. *See* Railroad car: Rail detector car

DETERGENT
   Synthetic detergent for use in the home was

The First

Dreft, marketed October 10, 1933. It was a sodiu alkyl sulfate made from chlorosulfonic acid and fatty alcohol by the Procter & Gamble Compan Cincinnati, Ohio.

DETONATING FUSE. *See* Fuse: Textile-wrappe detonating fuse

DEUTERIUM. *See* Water: Heavy water

DIAGNOSTIC BACTERIOLOGY LABORATO RY. *See* Bacteriology laboratory: Bacteriolog diagnostic laboratory

DIAL TELEPHONE. *See* Telephone

DIAL TIME RECORDER. *See* Time recorder

DIAMOND
   Diamonds in a meteorite were found in Ju 1891 by Dr. George Augustus Koenig, professor mineralogy and geology at the University of Pen sylvania, Philadelphia, Pa., while cutting a met orite found at Canon Diablo, Arizona. In vario cavities he found small black diamonds of litt commercial value which cut through polishe corundum. *(Science, July 8, 1892)*

   Diamonds in actual rock, peridotite, were fou in the matrix August 1, 1906, by John W. Huddl son at Murfreesboro, Pike County, Ark. He four 2 diamonds, each weighing about 3 cara *(George Frederick Kunz—Diamonds in Arkansa In American Institute of Mining Engineers. Tra sactions 1909, Vol. 39)*

   Pilot plant for the actual production of artifici diamonds was established by the General Ele tric Company in 1955. Scientists of the Gener Electric Research Laboratory, Schenectady, N.Y announced on February 15, 1955, that they ha succeeded in making diamonds 1/16 inch by su jecting carbonaceous compounds to pressures 1,500,000 pounds per square inch at temperatur up to 5,000° F. They used a special pressure vess in a large hydraulic press.

DIATHERMY MACHINE for medical use th was practical was constructed by Dr. Willis Ro ney Whitney, director of research for the Gener Electric Company, Schenectady, N.Y., in Decen ber 1928. Albert B. Page first used the set Februa 19, 1929, at the Ellis Hospital, Schenectady, N.Y and the first patient was treated February 2 1929, by Dr. Charles Milton Carpenter. *(Scienc May 2, 1930)*

DICE. *See* Craps

"DICTATOR," BASEBALL. *See* Baseball "dicta tor"

DICTIONARY
   Agricultural dictionary published in the Unite States was Samuel Deane's *The New Englan Farmer; or, georgical dictionary: containing compendious account of the ways and methods which the most important art of husbandry, in a*

e First

branches is, or may be practised to the greatest *dvantage in this country,* a 335-page double-col-∎n book, published in 1790 by Isaiah Thomas in 'orcester, Mass. It was copyrighted September ∎, 1790, in the Third Massachusetts District.

American dictionary was Noah Webster's *A ∎mpendious Dictionary of the English Language. which 5,000 words are added to the number ∎und in the best English compends; the orthogra-∎y is in some instances corrected: the pronuncia-∎ns marked by an accent or other suitable ∎ection; and the definitions of many words ∎nended and improved.* 408 pages published in ∎06 at New Haven, Conn., by Sidney's press for ∎dson and Goodwin.

American Indian–English dictionary was *A Key ∎o the Language of America, or an help to the ∎nguage of the natives in that part of America lled New England; together with briefe obser-∎tions of the customes, manners and worships, ∎c., of the aforesaid natives,* by "Roger Williams Providence in New England." Williams pre-∎red it on shipboard en route to Southampton, ∎gland, and it was published by Gregory Dexter, ∎ndon, England, in 1643. *(James Ernst—Roger 'illiams)*

Bohemian-American dictionary was the *Dictio-∎ry of Bohemian and English Languages,* com-∎ed by Karel Jonas and published in Racine, is., in 1876. It contained 626 pages. *(Fanny S. ∎ne—Racine, Belle City of the Lakes)*

Dictionary compiled by a woman was *The Lan-∎age of Fashion,* edited by Mary Brooks Picken, ∎blished February 2, 1940, in New York City. It ∎ntained 8,000 terms and 600 illustrations relat-∎g to wearing apparel.

Dictionary published in the United States was ∎e *Royal Standard English Dictionary; the First ∎merican Dictionary, Carefully Revised and Cor-∎cted, from the Fourth British Edition,* by Wil-∎m Perry, lecturer in the Academy at Edinburgh, ∎hich was printed in 1788 in Worcester, Mass., by ∎d for Isaiah Thomas. It sold for 7 shillings and ∎ntained 596 pages, of which pages 73-359 con-∎ined the dictionary proper and an appendix of ∎cripture Proper Names." There were 38 lines to ∎age, double column, and the definitions usually ∎nsisted of only one line, the same line as the ∎rd itself. The dictionary was dedicated to the ∎merican Academy of Arts and Sciences. *(The 'orcester Magazine. February 1788)*

Hebrew dictionary was Clement Clarke Moo-∎'s *A Compendious Lexicon of the Hebrew Lan-∎age in Two Volumes; Volume 1, containing an ∎planation of every word which occurs in the ∎alms with notes; Volume 2, being a lexicon and ∎mmar of the whole language,* printed and sold ∎1809 by [Isaac] Collins and Perkins, New York ∎ty.

The First

Law dictionary. *See* Law dictionary (American)

Medical dictionary (complete) was *A Dictio-nary of Medical Science,* by Robley Dunglison, published in 1833 in Philadelphia, Pa.

Medical slang dictionary was *Dictionary of Medical Slang and Related Esoteric Expressions,* which consisted of 207 pages, by Jacob Edward Schmidt, published in 1959 in Springfield, Ill.

Military dictionary was *A Military Dictionary, or explanation of the several systems of Disci-pline of different kinds of troops, infantry, artil-lery and cavalry, the principles of fortification and all the modern improvements in the science of tactics . . . ,* by William Duane, a retired lieutenant colonel, published in 1810 in Philadelphia, Pa. It contained 748 pages.

Mongolian-English English-Mongolian dictio-nary was *Mongolian Vocabulary (Modern Khalk-ha Language),* compiled by Dorothy A. Troxel of the Army Map Service and published in January 1953 as Army Technical Manual TM 30-537.

Phonetic dictionary was the *Phonetic Dictio-nary of the English Language adapted to the present state of literature and science, with pro-nouncing vocabularies of classical, scriptural and geographical names,* 776 pages, compiled by Dan-iel S. Smalley and published by Longley Brothers, phonetic publishers, Cincinnati, Ohio, in 1855.

Pocket dictionary was William Perry's *The Royal Standard English Dictionary, in which the words are . . . rationally divided into syllables, accurately accented, their parts of speech proper-ly distinguished . . . ,* 12mo, 596 pages, printed in 1788 by Isaiah Thomas, Worcester, Mass. It was dedicated to the American Academy of Arts and Sciences and was based upon a British edition.

Rhyming dictionary was *A Rhyming Dictionary, containing all the perfect rhymes of a different orthography, and allowable rhymes of a different sound, throughout the language, with authorities for the usage of them from our best poets,* pub-lished in 1823 by F. & R. Lockwood, New York City. It was an American edition of John Walker's *A Dictionary of the English language answering at once the purposes of rhyming, spelling and pro-nouncing on a plan not hitherto attempted,* first published in London, England, in 1775.

DIDACTICS COURSE

Didactics course in a college was offered in 1853 as an elective to the sophomore course at Antioch College, Yellow Springs, Ohio. The college was opened October 5, 1853. Professor Rebecca Mann Pennell, in charge of the course, was elected to a professorship September 15, 1852.

DIES FOR COINS. *See under* Money

The First

DIESEL-ELECTRIC FREIGHT LOCOMOTIVE.
See Locomotive

DIESEL-ELECTRIC TOWBOAT. *See* Ship: Tugboat (diesel-electric)

DIESEL ENGINE
See also Engine; Locomotive

Diesel-engine automobile trip was made by Clessie Lyle Cummins of the Cummins Engine Company, Columbus, Ind., with a stock model engine weighing 1,200 pounds, delivering 50 h.p. at 1,000 r.p.m. with four cylinders of 4½ by 6 inch bore, installed in a seven-passenger Packard sedan. He left Indianapolis, Ind., January 3, 1930, and arrived in New York City January 6, 1930, covering 792 miles at a total fuel cost of $1.38.

Diesel-engine speed record (official) was made March 20, 1930, by Clessie Lyle Cummins of the Cummins Engine Company, Columbus, Ind., in a Packard roadster chassis equipped with a four-cylinder marine-type diesel engine with a bore and stroke of 4½ by 6 inches and piston displacement of 381.5 cubic inches. The car was stripped of fenders, windshield, and spare tires and fitted with a fabric cover over the driver's compartment. Cummins averaged 80.398 miles per hour in the test at Daytona Beach, Fla.

Streamlined all-steel diesel motor train. *See under* Railroad

DIESEL-ENGINE TRACTOR. *See under* Automobile tractor

DIME. *See* Money: Silver coins

DINER. *See* Lunch wagon

DINING CAR. *See under* Railroad car

DIOCESE, CATHOLIC. *See* Catholic diocese

DIPLOMATIC SERVICE
Ambassador, according to the records of the Department of State, was Thomas Francis Bayard, who was appointed ambassador extraordinary and plenipotentiary to Great Britain on March 30, 1893. His letter of credence was dated April 14, 1893, and he arrived at his post on June 10, 1893, and presented his credentials on June 22, 1893. He left his post on March 17, 1897, and his letter of recall dated March 31, 1897, was presented by his successor on April 22, 1897. *(Charles Callan Tansill—The Foreign Policy of Thomas F. Bayard)*

Ambassador assassinated in office was John Gordon Mein, U.S. ambassador to Guatemala, who was attacked and killed in his automobile on August 27, 1968, about 10 blocks away from the American embassy in the downtown section of Guatemala City, Guatemala.

Ambassador (black woman) was Patricia Roberts Harris (Mrs. William B. Harris) who was sworn in July 9, 1965, at Washington, D.C., as am-

The First

bassador to Luxembourg by Secretary of State Dean Rusk. She arrived at her post on September 3, 1965, and assumed her duties on October 1965.

Ambassador to Canada was Ray Atherton, who was nominated as Ambassador Extraordinary and Plenipotentiary on November 18, 1943. He held this office until his resignation and mandatory retirement on August 31, 1948. Previously, on July 7, 1943, he had been confirmed as envoy extraordinary and minister plenipotentiary of the United States to Canada and to Denmark.

Ambassador to Great Britain. *See* Ambassador above

Ambassador to Israel was James Grover McDonald, who served from July 2, 1948, to January 14, 1951, as ambassador extraordinary and plenipotentiary to Israel. *(James Grover McDonald—My Mission in Israel)*

Ambassador to Nepal was Henry Endicott Stebbins of Milton, Mass., appointed August 2 1959. The nomination was approved September 1959. Previously the United States ambassador to India had served as envoy to Nepal.

Ambassador to the Union of Soviet Socialist Republics was William Christian Bullitt, who served from November 21, 1933, until August 2 1936. The first Soviet representative to the United States was Alexander Antonovich Troyanovsky who was accredited as Russian ambassador from January 8, 1934, to June 22, 1938. Recognition of the U.S.S.R. was effected November 16, 1933, between President Franklin Delano Roosevelt and Maksim Maksimovich Litvinov, the People's Commissar for Foreign Affairs.

Ambassador (woman) was (Helen) Eugenie Moore Anderson (Mrs. John Pierce Anderson) of Red Wing, Minn., who was nominated October 1 1949, and sworn in by President Harry S Truman in Secretary of State Dean Acheson's office Washington, D.C., October 28, 1949, as ambassador to Denmark.

Ambassador (woman) to a communist bloc nation was (Helen) Eugenie Moore Anderson (Mrs John Pierce Anderson) of Red Wing, Minn., who presented her credentials on August 3, 1962, Dimiter Ganev, chief of state, at Sofia, Bulgaria.

Ambassador (woman) to a major nation was Clare Boothe Luce, who was sworn in on March 3, 1953, in Washington, D. C. as ambassador Italy by Frederick Moore Vinson, chief justice of the United States. She resigned on November 1 1956, effective on appointment of her successor.

Ambassador (woman) to the Court of St. James (England) was Anne Legendre Armstrong (Mrs Tobin Armstrong), who was nominated January 14, 1976, confirmed January 28, 1976; sworn in February

he First

ary 19, 1976; and who presented her credentials
• Queen Elizabeth II on March 17, 1976.

Ambassadors in service to wed were Ellsworth
unker, 72, ambassador-at-large, who married
arol Clendening Laise, 49, ambassador to Nepal,
. Katmandu, Nepal, on January 3, 1967. The
eremony was performed by Rev. H. Norman Gib-
y of North Eastham, Mass.

American legation in which a woman assumed
harge was the American Legation at Stockholm,
weden. Frances Elizabeth Willis, third secretary
f the American Legation at Stockholm, assumed
harge while Minister John Motley Morehead was
n furlough. She became ex-officio American
hargé d'affaires ad interim October 12, 1932, until
ctober 29, 1932. Edwin S. Crocker, 2d, second
ecretary of the Legation, who had also been ab-
ent from Stockholm, returned on October 29,
932, and succeeded Miss Willis as chargé
'affaires ad interim.

Black consul was Ebenezer Don Carlos Bassett,
ho was made consul general to Haiti, where he
erved from April 16, 1869, to November 27, 1877.

Black delegate to the United Nations from the
Jnited States was Edith Spurlock Sampson, who
vas appointed August 24, 1950, alternate delegate
o the fifth General Assembly. Her first assign-
ent, on September 28, 1950, was to the Social,
lumanitarian and Cultural Committee.

Chief executive-elect of a foreign country to
erve in a diplomatic position in Washington,
).C., was Dr. Enrique Olaya Hererra, who arrived
pril 20, 1930. He was sworn in August 7, 1930, as
resident of Colombia. Previously he had served
s Colombian ambassador to the United States.

Consul general was appointed by authority of
he act of August 18, 1856 (11 Stat. L. 57), which
assed the House on August 15 and the Senate on
ugust 16. The act went into effect August 18,
856.

Consul to California was Thomas Oliver Lar-
in, who was appointed consul to Monterey,
alif., on May 1, 1843, and special agent on Octo-
er 17, 1845. His resignation from the position of
onsul was dated August 17, 1846. His successor
s special agent was appointed on August 2, 1849.
*Reuben Lukens Underhill—From Cowhides to
3olden Fleece)*

Consul to die in service was Colonel William
alfrey, paymaster general of the Continental Ar-
nies, who was elected consul to Paris, France, on
Jovember 4, 1780, by the Continental Congress at
• salary of $1,500 a year. He received his commis-
ion November 9, 1780. He sailed for his post in
'rance on the *Shillala,* an armed ship of 16 guns,
vhich stopped en route at the port of Wilmington,
)el., on December 23, 1780, and was lost at sea
fter it passed the Delaware capes. *(Jared Sparks*

The First

—*The Library of American Biography, Vol. 7, 2nd
Ser.)*

Consul under the Department of State was
Major Samuel Shaw of Massachusetts. Having
been appointed consul to Canton, China, on January 1, 1786, prior to the ratification of the Constitution, he was nominated on February 9, 1790, and
confirmed the following day as consul of the United States of America at Canton, China. *(Tracy
Hollingsworth Lay—The Foreign Service of the
U.S.)*

**Consular officer detailed for duty in the Depart-
ment of Foreign Affairs** of the Continental government was Thomas Barclay of Pennsylvania, who
was appointed vice consul to Paris, France, on
January 21, 1781, at a salary of $1,000 a year. Upon
the formation of the United States Government,
President George Washington appointed him consul to Morocco on March 31, 1791. *(American Foreign Service Journal—April 1929)*

**Consuls of the United States appointed after the
adoption of the Constitution** were Joseph Fenwick
of Maryland; Nathaniel Barrett, Sylvanus Bourne,
Burrell Carnes, and William Knox of Massachusetts; John Marsden Pintard of New York; and
James Maury and Fulwar Skipwith of Virginia, all
of whom were appointed June 7, 1790.

Foreign service committee was formed November 29, 1775, when the Continental Congress voted
"that a committee of five be appointed for the sole
purpose of corresponding with our friends in
Great Britain, Ireland and other parts of the
world." The members of this secret Committee of
Correspondence were William Samuel Johnson of
Connecticut, John Jay of New York, John Dickinson of Pennsylvania, Benjamin Harrison of Virginia, and Benjamin Franklin of Pennsylvania,
who was the chairman. *(Secret Journals of the
Acts and Proceedings of Congress, Vol. 2)*

Foreign Service of the United States was created on July 1, 1924, by the Rogers bill (43 Stat. L.
140), approved May 24, 1924, when the diplomatic
and consular services were merged under the Department of State.

Jewish ambassador was Oscar Solomon Straus,
who was appointed envoy extraordinary and
minister plenipotentiary to Turkey on March 24,
1887. He presented his letter of recall June 16,
1889. He was reappointed June 3, 1898. He left on
leave of absence December 20, 1899, and his letter
of recall was presented by his successor March
29, 1901. On May 17, 1909, he was again appointed
ambassador extraordinary and plenipotentiary to
Turkey and in September 1910 he left the post. His
successor presented his letter of recall on August
28, 1911. *(William Willard Howards—Oscar S.
Straus in Turkey)*

The First

DIPLOMATIC SERVICE—Continued

Jewish diplomatic representative was Manuel Mordecai Manuel Noah, who represented the United States as consul to Tunis from 1813 to 1816. He was a consul with diplomatic powers. (Isaac Goldberg—Major Noah, American-Jewish Pioneer)

Korean embassy was received by President Chester Alan Arthur on September 18, 1883, at the Fifth Avenue Hotel, 23rd Street, New York City. Min Yong Ik, the ambassador, presented his credentials. He was accompanied by Hong Yong Sik, the vice ambassador, and by his secretary, the foreign secretary, and five attaches. The Koreans were dressed in court robes and dropped upon their knees as they salaamed President Arthur and Secretary of State Frederick Theodore Frelinghuysen.

Minister plenipotentiary was Benjamin Franklin, who was elected by the Continental Congress on September 14, 1778, to the court of France. The Department of State accredits Thomas Jefferson of Virginia, who was appointed on March 10, 1785, as the first minister plenipotentiary after the Revolutionary War. He sailed July 5, 1785, on the Ceres and served until October 1789. He left Yarmouth, England, October 22, 1789, and arrived at Norfolk, Va., November 23, 1789. (Journals of the Continental Congress, Vol. 12)

Minister to Great Britain was John Adams, who on June 1, 1785, was introduced by the Marquis of Carmarthen to the King of Great Britain as ambassador extraordinary from the United States of America to the Court of London. The first minister plenipotentiary to Great Britain was Thomas Pinckney of South Carolina, who was appointed on January 12, 1792. Adams however, is not listed as an ambassador by the State Department, which reckons 1893 as the year of the first appointment of the first ambassador. (Samuel Willard—John Adams: A Character Sketch) (See also Ambassador, above)

Ministers plenipotentiary to South and Central America were appointed on January 27, 1823, by President James Monroe. His appointments were Caesar Augustus Rodney of Delaware to Argentina, Herman Allen of Vermont to Chile, and Richard Clough Anderson of Kentucky to Colombia. (Records in Department of State, Washington, D.C.)

Naval attaché. See under Naval officer

Pan American delegates (American) were Caesar Augustus Rodney, Theodore Bland, and John Graham, who were appointed in July 1817 by President James Monroe "to obtain information of the actual condition and political prospects of the Spanish provinces which were contending for independence." They served at Buenos Aires, Argentina, from February 1818 until April 30, 1818.

The First

(House Document 2, 15th Congress, 2nd Sessio.

Representative of a foreign country to the Uni ed States was Conrad Alexandre Gérard France, who arrived in July 1778. He was style minister plenipotentiary and also bore a commi sion as consul general. (Maryland Historic Magazine. Vol. 15. 1920)

Woman ambassador from a foreign count. was Her Excellency Shrimati Vijaya Lakshr Pandit, ambassador of India, who presented h letter of credence to President Harry S. Truman (May 12, 1949.

Woman career diplomat advanced to the rar of ambassador was Frances Elizabeth Willis, wl after 25 years in the foreign service was sworn as ambassador to Switzerland on August 10, 195 at a ceremony in the State Department, Washin ton, D.C.

Woman diplomat to represent the United Stat in the capacity of a minister was Ruth Brya Owen, who was appointed by President Frankl Delano Roosevelt on April 12, 1933, as envoy e traordinary and minister plenipotentiary to De mark and Iceland. Her nomination was confirm by the Senate on April 12, 1933, without even tl customary formality of reference to a committe Ruth Bryan Owen (Mrs. Börge Rohde) was tl eldest daughter of William Jennings Bryan. (Ru Bryan Owen—Leaves from a Greenland Diary,

Woman legation secretary was Lucille Atche son of Columbus, Ohio. She was appointed (December 4, 1922, and was recommissioned Foreign Service Officer of Class 8 on July 1, 192 serving thereafter as secretary of legation at Ber Switzerland, and at Panama, R.P. On May 2 1924, the diplomatic and consular services we amalgamated into the American Foreign Servi

Woman to serve the United Nations as a perm. nent ambassador of the United States was Marie ta Peabody Tree, who was sworn in on October 2 1964, to the Trusteeship Council of the United N tions. She had served since 1961 as a United N tions delegate.

Woman vice consul in the American Forei Service was Pattie Hockaday Field of Denve Colo. She was appointed Foreign Service offic unclassified on March 20, 1925, and as America vice consul. She was assigned to Amsterdar Holland, September 2, 1925. She resigned June 2 1929.

DIRECT-LIFT AIRCRAFT. See Helicopter: He copter (direct-lift aircraft)

DIRECTORY (city) was Macpherson's Director for the City and Suburbs of Philadelphia Exten ing to Prime Street, Southward; and Maide Street, Northward; and From the River Delawa to Tenth Street Westward, published October 1785, by John Macpherson. It was printed by Fra.

The First

is Bailey at Loick's Head, 65 Market Street, Philadelphia, Pa., and contained 6,250 names, of which 486 were subscribers. William Bradford of Philadelphia also published a directory of that city the same year. It contained 83 pages, 43 names to the page, making a total of 3,569 names. *(American Collector. August 1926)*

DIRIGIBLE. *See under* Aviation—Airship

DIRIGIBLE BALLOON RACE. *See under* Balloon race

DIRIGIBLE PASSENGER TRANSFER TO AN AIRPLANE. *See under* Aviation—Passenger

DISABLED. *See* Blind; Cripples; Deaf

DISBARRED LAWYER. *See* Lawyer: Lawyer disbarred

DISCIPLES OF CHRIST church was organized August 17, 1809, in Washington, Pa., when a group of Presbyterians headed by Thomas Campbell formed themselves into a religious association, the Christian Association of Washington. On May 4, 1811, a church was established in Brush Run, Pa., with Thomas Campbell as elder. Alexander Campbell, his son, was licensed to preach the gospel. John Dawson, George Sharp, John Foster, and William Gilchrist were chosen as deacons. No attempt at forming a separate and distinct denomination was made until 1823, when Alexander Campbell and several members of the Brush Run Church founded a church in Wellsburg, W.Va. The first convention of the Disciples of Christ was held August 1827, when the Mahoning Association met at New Lisbon, Ohio, and appointed Walter Scott as the general evangelist to go into Ohio to preach and establish churches. The first general convention was held in Cincinnati, Ohio, October 24, 1849, at which time the American Christian Missionary Society was organized. *Walter Wilson Jennings—Origin and Early History of the Disciples of Christ)*

DISCOVERY

American to land by air at the South Pole and the first American to set foot and plant a flag at the South Pole was Rear Admiral George John Dufek who, with a party of six as part of Operation Deepfreeze commanded by Admiral Richard Evelyn Byrd and undertaken in connection with the International Geophysical Year 1957–1958, landed October 31, 1956, in the *Que Sera Sera,* a Navy R4D transport plane. Dufek was in charge of logistic support for the scientific body of the expedition.

Discovery of Antarctica was made November 8, 1820, by Captain Nathaniel Brown Palmer in the *Hero,* a sloop of 44 tons, with a crew of six men including the captain and the mate. He sailed from Stonington, Conn., July 25, 1820, and returned May 8, 1821. His discovery was made at a point near latitude 64° S and longitude 60° W. *(John*

The First

Randolph Spears—Captain Nathaniel Brown Palmer. An Old Time Sailor of the Sea)

Discovery of land on the United States Pacific coast by actual contact with it was made by Juan Rodríguez Cabrillo, who landed September 28, 1542, at what is now known as Ballast Point, San Diego, Calif. He left Navidad, Mexico, on June 27, 1542. The Pacific Ocean had been discovered by Europeans previously, however—Balboa and Magellan, among others. *(George Montague Wheeler —Report upon U.S. Geographical Surveys West of the 100th Meridian)*

Discovery of New England by an Englishman was made by Captain Bartholomew Gosnold, who with his crew of 31 landed at South Dartmouth, near New Bedford, Mass., on May 15, 1602. Gosnold township, Mass., comprising the Elizabeth Islands, was named in his honor. Gosnold left Falmouth, England, on March 26, 1602, in the *Concord* and landed on the southern Maine coast, near Cape Porpoise. *(Massachusetts Historical Society—Collections, Vol. VIII. 1843)*

Discovery of the Mississippi River by a European was made by Hernando de Soto, who in May 1541, with his crew of adventurous Spaniards, arrived at a village called Chisca, where they erected a huge cross. Shortly afterward De Soto died and was buried in the "Father of Waters," the first European to be buried in the Mississippi. In 1519 Alonso Alvarez de Pineda, who was sent out by Francisco de Garay, governor of Jamaica, entered the mouth of the river, which he called the Rio de Espiritu Santo. *(John Dawson Gilmary Shea—Discovery and Exploration of the Mississippi Valley)*

Discovery of the North Pole was made on April 6, 1909, by Robert Edwin Peary, accompanied by Matthew Alexander Henson, a black assistant, and four Eskimos, who reached 90° N.

Northwest Passage, between the Atlantic and the Pacific oceans, was charted in the period from June to September 1957 by three United States Coast Guard cutters *(Bramble, Spar,* and *Storis)* led by the *Labrador,* a Canadian ice patrol ship, through Beloit Strait between Boothia Peninsula and Somerset Island. The commanding officer was Commander Harold L. Wood.

DISCRIMINATION LAW. *See* Army exclusion law

DISCRIMINATION LAW, LABOR. *See* Labor law: Labor discrimination law (state)

DISCRIMINATORY LAW, ALIEN. *See* Alien discriminatory law

DISCUS

Discus hurler to win 4 gold medals in 4 consecutive Olympic Games was Alfred A. ("Al") Oerter, of West Islip, N.Y., who won at the 1956 Olympic Games at Melbourne, the 1960 games at Rome, the

The First

DISCUS—*Continued*
1964 games at Tokyo, and the 1968 games at Mexico City. On October 14, 1968, in Mexico City, he established a record on his third throw of 212 feet 6½ inches, winning his fourth gold medal.

DISCUS throw to exceed 160 feet was made March 29, 1929, by Eric Krenz of Stanford University at Palo Alto, Calif., when he achieved the world discus mark by a throw of 163 feet 8-¾ inches. (The old mark was 158 feet 1-¾ inches)

Discus throw to exceed 200 feet was by Alfred A. ("Al") Oerter who established a world record of 200 feet 5½ inches (61.10m) on May 18, 1962, at Los Angeles, Calif.

Discus throwing as a competitive event was revived in 1896 at the Olympic Games in Athens, Greece. Robert Garrett of Princeton University, representing the United States, won with a record throw of 95 feet 7½ inches. *(The Olympic Games 776 B.C.–1896 A.D.—Official Report)*

DISEASE (distinctly American) was tularemia, an epizootic of wild rabbits and other animals, which was recognized in 1910 in ground squirrels of Tulare County, Calif., by Dr. George Walter McCoy. He and Dr. Charles Willard Chapin named the organism *Bacterium tularense*. Dr. Edward Francis of the U.S. Public Health Service, who named the disease, was awarded a gold medal by the American Medical Association for his research into this disease. *(Journal of the American Medical Association. April 25, 1925)*

DISHES. *See* Chinaware

DISPENSARY. *See under* Hospital

DISPENSARY, DENTAL. *See* Dental dispensary

DISPENSATORY. *See* Medical book

DISSECTION ESSAY. *See under* Medical book

DISTILLING BOOK was Michael August Krafft's *American Distiller, or The Theory and Practice of Distilling, according to the latest discoveries and improvements, including its most important methods of constructing stills and of rectification,* dedicated to Thomas Jefferson. It contained 219 pages and 6 plates and was printed in 1804 by Thomas Dobson, Philadelphia, Pa. The preface was dated May 25, 1804, Bristol, Pa.

DISTINGUISHED FLYING CROSS. *See* Medal

DISTINGUISHED SERVICE CROSS. *See* Medal

DISTINGUISHED SERVICE MEDAL. *See* Medal

DISTINGUISHED SERVICE MEDAL (Navy). *See* Medal

DISTRESS SIGNAL. *See* Radio distress signal

DISTRICT ATTORNEY (woman). *See under* Woman

The First

DISTRICT LAND OFFICE. *See under* Land gran▮

DISTRICT NURSE. *See* Nurse

DIVING SUIT (practical) for submarine diving was invented by Leonard Norcross of Dixfield Me., who obtained a United States patent on June 14, 1834, on a "water-dress." It consisted of an airtight rubber dress to which was attached a brass cap or helmet resting on the shoulders. The cap was connected to an air pump on the boat by means of a rubber hose. The feet were weighted with heavy lead shot. *(Niles Register. Sept. 27 1834)*

DIVINITY DEGREE. *See* Degrees (academic and honorary): Doctor of Sacred Theology degree

DIVINITY PROFESSOR was Edward Wigglesworth, appointed January 24, 1722, to the Thomas Hollis Professorship of Divinity at Harvard College, Cambridge, Mass. He served until his death January 16, 1765.

DIVINITY SCHOOL. *See* Theological school

DIVORCE
   DIVORCE was granted at a Quarter Court at Boston the fifth of the first month 1643/1644 "Anne Clarke, beeing deserted by Denis Clarke hir husband, and hee refusing to accompany with hir, she is graunted to bee divorced, his refusal was under his hand, and seale, which hee gave before Mr. John Winthrop, Junr. Mr. Emanuel Downing, Mr. Nehemiah Bo'ne (Bourne) and Richard Babington, alsoe hee confesseth hee liveth in adultery with one, by whom he hath had 2 and refuseth hir which hee had two children by. *(Records of the Court of Assistants of the Colony of the Massachusetts Bay—1630–1652)*

   "No fault" divorce law (state) was enacted by California on July 6, 1970, effective January 2 1971. Divorces were dissolved for incurable insanity and irreconcilable differences.

   One million divorces in 1 year were in 1975 when 1,036,000 divorces were granted, 4.9 percent per 1,000 population. The statistics were compiled by the National Center for Health Statistics, Public Health Service *(DHEW Publication 78-1120).*

DOCK
   See also Dry dock

   Containership facility was opened for business August 15, 1962, when Sea-Land Service's S.S *Elizabethport* docked in Newark Bay, Elizabeth New Jersey, on the south side of the Elizabeth Channel, south of Port Newark. During its first year, the facility handled 1,504,021 tons of cargo on 242 vessels and employed 730 people, wh earned a total of $4,015,000. The Elizabeth-Port Authority Marine Terminal is operated by the Port of New York Authority.

The First

State-owned docks were acquired by California by act approved April 24, 1863, chapter 306, "an act to provide for the improvement and protection of the wharves, docks and water front in the city and county of San Francisco." Three commissioners, one elected by the state, one elected by San Francisco, and one appointed by the Senate and Assembly at a joint session, formed the Board of State Harbor Commissioners "to construct new wharves, to keep in good repair seawalls, embankments, wharves, piers, landings and thoroughfares for the advancement of commerce." The first meeting of the board was held November 4, 1863, in San Francisco. Robert E. C. Stearns was the first secretary.

DOCTOR (Navy). *See* Naval officer: Naval doctor

DOCTOR OF MEDICINE. *See* Physician

DOCTOR'S DEGREE. *See* Degrees (academic and honorary)

DOCUMENT, PRINTED. *See* Printing: Document printed in America

DOCUMENTS CATALOG. *See* Index of government publications

DOG HOTEL. *See* Kennel

DOG LICENSE
Dog license law (state) was "an act for the better protection of lost and strayed animals and for securing the rights of the owners thereof," passed March 8, 1894, by New York State, Chapter 115. It authorized the American Society for the Prevention of Cruelty to Animals to carry out the provisions of the law and collect a $2 annual fee for dogs in cities with populations over 1,200,000. Unlicensed dogs were to be destroyed if not redeemed within 48 hours. Nonresidents and exhibitors were not required to obtain licenses for their dogs.

DOG RACE. *See* Greyhound racing association

DOG RACETRACK on which an imitation rabbit was used was erected by Owen Patrick Smith at Emeryville, Calif., and opened February 22, 1920. It was about 300 yards around and was designed by R. S. Hawley. A car was run through a housing which covered the trolley and track; the car had a slot on the track side through which the arm carrying the rabbit extended.

DOG SHOW of importance was held at the Hippodrome (Gilmore's Garden), 26th Street and Madison Avenue, New York City, May 8, 1877, under the auspices of the Westminster Kennel Bench Show of Dogs. Charles Lincoln was superintendent of this show, at which there were 1,191 entries. Dog shows were often held as features at fairs and circuses. A successful dog show was held May 8-12, 1862, at Barnum's American Museum, New York City.

The First

DOGS TRAINED TO GUIDE THE BLIND. *See under* Animals

DOGSLED MAIL. *See* Postal service: International dogsled mail

DOGSLED RACE on an Olympic demonstration program was held February 6-7, 1932, when the United States and Canada entered 13 teams. Contestants were required to cover the course of 25.1 miles on two consecutive days. First place was won by Emile St. Goddard of Canada, but the United States teams won 7 of the 12 points. The race was held at Lake Placid, N.Y.

DOLLAR. *See* Money: Fifty-dollar gold pieces

DOLLAR MARKS to be made in type were cast in 1797 by [Archibald] Binny & [James] Ronaldson, type-founders of Philadelphia, who started in business on November 1, 1796. *(Daniel Berkeley Updike—Printing Types)*

DOMESTIC AIRMAIL CONTRACTOR. *See* Airmail service: Airmail contractor (domestic)

DOMESTIC RELATIONS COURT. *See* Court

DOOR (revolving) was invented by Theophilus Van Kannel of Philadelphia, Pa., who obtained patent No. 387,571 on August 7, 1888, on a "storm door structure."

DOUBLE-DECK BRIDGE. *See* Bridge

DOUBLE-DECK BUS. *See under* Automobile bus

DOUBLE-DECK CAR. *See* Railroad car

DOUBLE-DECK ELEVATOR. *See* Elevator

DOUBLE-DECK STEAMBOAT. *See* Ship

DOUBLE EAGLE COINAGE. *See under* Money

DOUGHNUT CUTTER was invented by John F. Blondel of Thomaston, Me., who obtained patent No. 128,783 on July 9, 1872. A spring pushed the dough out of a center tube to provide the hole.

DRAFT LEGISLATION. *See* Conscription

DRAGOON REGIMENT. *See* Army: Cavalry unit

DRAMA. *See* Play (drama); Theater

DRAMA (full-length melodrama) BROADCAST. *See under* Radio broadcast

DRAMA TELECAST FOR A FULL HOUR. *See* Television—Telecast: Play to be televised as a full-hour program

DRAMA TO WIN A PULITZER PRIZE. *See under* Play (drama)

DRAMATIC CRITICISM COURSE. *See* Theatrical school: Theater and dramatic criticism course

DRAWBACK LEGISLATION was Sections 3 and 4 of the Tariff Act of July 4, 1789 (1 Stat. L. 26), which became effective August 1, 1789. Dutiable merchandise imported into the United States which was reexported within a year was entitled

The First

DRAWBACK LEGISLATION—*Continued*
to a refund of 99 percent of the duty paid. In lieu
of a drawback of the duties imposed on the importation of salt employed and expended in the fish
industry, an allowance of 5 cents was granted on
the exportation of every quintal of dried fish, and
on every barrel of pickled fish or salted provision.
From August 1, 1789, to December 31, 1790, drawback to the amount of $10,582 was allowed on
dried and pickled fish.

DREDGE. *See* Ship: Dredge (seagoing hopper)

DRIED BLOOD SERUM. *See* Blood bank: Blood
serum (human, dried)

DRIED MILK. *See* Milk

DRILL
    Dental drill was invented in 1790 by John
Greenwood of New York City. It was adapted
from the spinning wheel, power being obtained by
means of a foot treadle. *(Dental Items of Interest
November 1943)*

    Dental drill (electric) was invented by George F.
Green of Kalamazoo, Mich., who obtained patent
No. 159,028 on January 26, 1875, on "electro-magnetic dental tools" used for sawing, filing, dressing, and polishing teeth. He claimed the
application to dental instruments of an electro-
magnetic motor. The patent was assigned to Samuel S. White of Philadelphia, Pa. The engines were
too heavy and the batteries too expensive for general use.

    Oil-drill offshore rig was patented by Thomas F.
Rowland of Greenpoint, N.Y., who obtained patent No. 89,794 on May 4, 1869, on a "submarine
drilling apparatus."

    Oil drill seagoing rig (for drilling in over 100 feet
of water) was built in the Beaumont Yard of Bethlehem Steel Company for the C. G. Glasscock
Drilling Company. The rig could drive piles with
a force of 827 tons and could pull a pile with the
force of 942 tons. It was placed in service March
24, 1955.

    Percussion rock drill was patented March 27,
1849, by Joseph James Couch, who received patent No. 6,237 on "improved machinery for drilling
rocks." The drill was driven by steam power and
acted independently of gravity. The machine was
stationary and the drill was thrown against the
rock, the tool being seized at the end of the blow
by means of friction-grips.

DRILL MANUAL. *See* Military drill manual

DRINKING STRAW. *See* Straws (artificial) for
drinking

DRIVE-IN BANK. *See* Bank: Autobank complete
service

DRIVE-IN SERVICE STATION. *See under* Automobile service station

The First

DRIVE-IN THEATER. *See under* Motion picture
theater

DRIVE-UP MAILBOX. *See* Postal service: Mailbox (drive-up)

DRIVING COURSE. *See* Automobile driving
course

DROUGHT recorded occurred in New England in
1727. After the first week of April, with the excep-
tion of two showers in May, rain did not fall until
June. According to a report, no rain fell between
May 3, 1622, and the middle of July. *(Sidney Perley
—Historic Storms of New England)*

DRUG LEGISLATION. *See* Pure food law: Pure
food and drug legislation (national)

DRUG MILL was established in 1812 in Philadelphia, Pa., by Charles V. Hagner, who used waterpower for grinding, performing in one day work
which previously would have required months of
hand powdering in mortars. His first task of importance was the grinding of several tons of
cream of tartar, for which Dr. Haral, a druggist,
paid him three cents a pound. *(Philadelphia College of Pharmacy and Science—The First Century
of the Philadelphia College of Pharmacy)*

DRUGGIST to fill prescriptions other than his
own was Jonathan Roberts, who served from May
1754 to May 19, 1755, as apothecary in the Pennsylvania Hospital, Philadelphia, Pa. Previously
apothecaries had made up their own remedies
only. *(Benjamin Franklin—Some Account of the
Pennsylvania Hospital From Its First Beginning of
the Fifth Month, called May, 1754)*

DRY DOCK
    Dry dock was constructed by Robert Fulton in
1805 in front of his foundry on the corner of Green
and Morgan streets, in Jersey City, N.J. He
managed it until his death, February 24, 1815. A
block of ground was sold to him by the Associates
of the Jersey Company for $1,000, allowing him
five years on the purchase money without interest. The deed was dated November 3, 1804. A
drydock had been authorized by Charlestown,
Mass., October 30, 1677, to be constructed by
James Russell, John Heyman, Samuel Ballard, and
John Phillips. On May 30, 1679, it was voted that
the drydock be rate free for 30 years and that no
other drydock be authorized for the same period
provided it was kept in "good repair." The
Charlestown dock, however, was never built.
*(Records of the Governor and Company of the
Massachusetts Bay, Vol. 5. May 30, 1679)*

    Dry dock authorized for the United States Gov-
ernment was approved February 25, 1799 by an
act (1 Stat. L. 622) which provided that "two
docks, for the convenience of repairing the public
ships and vessels, be erected in suitable places,
under direction of the President of the United
States, and that the sum of $50,000 be appropri-
ated towards effecting this object, to be paid out

The First

of the monies in the Treasury of the United States, not otherwise appropriated." On December 15, 1802, an appropriation of $100,000 was made, but dry docks were not constructed, as the amount was insufficient.

Federal dry docks were constructed at Boston, Mass., and Norfolk, Va., under authority of act of Congress of March 28, 1827 (4 Stat. L. 243). They were designed by Colonel Loammi Baldwin of Boston, Mass., who was hired by Secretary of the Navy Samuel Southard. The drydocks were founded upon piles and were built entirely of stone faced with cut granite. Construction of the Boston dry dock was started June 1827, the cornerstone laid May 21, 1829, and the dry dock turned over to the commandant September 9, 1833. It cost $677,089.98. The Norfolk dry dock was begun November 1827 and completed March 15, 1834. It cost $943,676.73. *(American Society of Civil Engineers—Transactions, Vol. 41. June 1899)*

National ship in a federal dry dock was the *Delaware,* which docked June 17, 1833, at the Norfolk Dry Dock, Portsmouth, Va. The *Constitution* was received at the Boston Dry Dock, June 24, 1833. Both ships docked before the dry docks were completed. The pumping machine was operated by steam. *(Charles Beebe Stuart—Naval Dry Docks of the United States)*

Timber dry dock was erected at Buffalo, N.Y., in 1840 for Great Lakes ships. The excavation was lined entirely with wood secured to poles driven in the bottom and upon the slopes of the sides, and faced with longitudinal timbers forming steps or altars upon the sides. The first timber dry dock on the Atlantic coast was erected in 1854 at Boston, Mass., by J. E. Simpson and Co. The first construction cost for these dry docks was small, but they did not prove practical for long periods as they deteriorated rapidly. *(American Society of Civil Engineers—Transactions, Vol 41. June 1899)*

DRY DOCK PATENT was issued on December 13, 1816, to John Adamson of Boston, Mass. A floating dry dock was erected a few years later in Weehawken Cove, Hoboken, N.J., for the dry docking and repairing of canal boats. The patent was extended 14 years by act of Congress, March 2, 1831 (6 Stat. L. 458) *(Sven Anderson—Floating Drydocks)*

DRY GAS METER. *See* Gas: Gas meter (dry)

DRY ICE. *See* Ice

DRY LAUNDRY SERVICE. *See* Laundry service: Rough-dry laundry service

DUAL SEWAGE SYSTEM. *See* Sewage: Sewage "dual system"

DUCK STAMP. *See* Revenue stamp printed by the Post Office Department; Stamp: Hunting permit stamps (federal)

The First

DUCKPIN BOWLING. *See* Bowling

DUCTILE TUNGSTEN. *See* Tungsten

DUDE RANCHING COURSE. *See* Recreational ranching course

DUEL

   Duel of which there is any record took place on June 18, 1621, between two servingmen, Edward Leister and Edward Dotey, both servants of Stephen Hopkins, one of the leaders of the Plymouth Colony. Governor William Bradford's decision was rendered as follows: "The Second Offense is the first Duel fought in New England, upon a Challenge at Single Combat with Sword and Dagger between Edward Dotey and Edward Leister, Servants of Mr. Hopkins; Both being wounded, the one in the Hand, the other in the Thigh; they are adjudg'd by the whole Company to have their Head and Feet tied together, and so to lie for 24 hours, without Meat or Drink; which is begun to be inflicted, but within an Hour, because of their great Pains, at their own and their Master's humble request, upon Promise of better Carriage, they are Released by the Governor."

   Duel between representatives in Congress was held on the famous Bladensburg, Md., dueling field in 1808, when George Washington Campbell of Tennessee shot Barent Gardenier of New York through the body. Gardenier had accused Congress of being under the influence of France, which Campbell denied, at the same time assailing Gardenier with a torrent of personal abuse. Gardenier challenged him to a duel, was wounded, and after his recovery returned to his attacks with more animosity than before. (Campbell served in Congress from October 17, 1803, to March 3, 1809; Gardenier served from March 4, 1807, to March 3, 1811.) *(Edward L. Merritt—Barent Gardenier)*

   Duel in which a future President of the United States participated took place on May 30, 1806, at Harrison's Mills on the Red River, Logan County, Ky. Andrew Jackson shot and killed Charles Dickinson in a duel, one of a hundred duels and brawls in which Jackson is said to have participated. They stood 24 feet apart, pistols downward. Dickinson fired first and the shot broke a couple of Jackson's ribs and grazed his breastbone. Despite the injury, Jackson fired and killed Dickinson. Jackson served as President of the United States from March 4, 1829, to March 3, 1837.

   DUELING LEGISLATION (state) was an "act to prevent the evil practice of duelling" passed by the Fourth General Assembly held at Knoxville, Tenn., and signed November 10, 1801, by Governor Archibald Roane. *(Chapter 32, Act of Tennessee, 1801)*

The First

DUGONG. *See* Aquatic mammals

DUMMY, FOOTBALL. *See* Football dummy

DUMMY AWARDED A DEGREE. *See* Degrees (academic and honorary): Degree awarded a ventriloquist's dummy

DUNKARD. *See* Baptist Church: German Baptists

DUPLEX COMPOUND LOCOMOTIVE. *See* Locomotive

DUPLEX TELEGRAPH. *See* Telegraph

DUPLICATE AUCTION BRIDGE CHAMPION-SHIP. *See under* Bridge (game)

DUTCH REFORMED CHURCH. *See* Reformed Church (Dutch)

DWARF exhibited was a man, 53 years of age, 22 inches high, who was shown at the house of Widow Bignall, next door to King's Head Tavern, a little above Mr. Hancock's wharf in Boston, Mass. Admission was one shilling. His appearance was advertised in the Massachusetts *Spy,* August 22, 1771.

DYES
Dyestuff full-scale plant was the Albany Aniline and Chemical Company, Albany, N.Y., which opened in 1868. It later moved to Rensselaer, N.Y., and was acquired by the General Aniline & Film Corporation.

DYNAMITE was manufactured in San Francisco, Calif., in 1866, in what is now Golden Gate Park, at the approximate location of "Portals of the Past," by Julius Bandmann, using the Nobel patents, under the name of Bandmann Neilson & Company. In 1867 the Giant Powder Company grew out of this concern. *(Arthur Pine Van Gelder and Hugo Schlatter—History of the Explosives Industry in America)*

DYNAMO
Dynamo that was successful was Jumbo No. 1, a direct-current steam dynamo, which was built in 1881 at the Edison Machine Works, Goerck Street, New York City. It weighed 27 tons, of which the armature weighed 6 tons. Its capacity was 700 sixteen-candlepower lamps when the armature was air-cooled. Tested July 5, 1882, the dynamo was put in operation September 4, 1882. *(Eric Hodgins and Frederick Alexander Magoun—Behemoth, the Story of Power)*

Dynamo for a direct-current outdoor lighting system was built in 1875 at Cornell University, Ithaca, N.Y., by Professor William Arnold Anthony and a graduate student, George Sylvanus Moler. It was exhibited at the Philadelphia Centennial in 1876 and was made from designs of the original Gramme machine. It was used to supply the current to light the Cornell campus in 1875.

E

The First

E PLURIBUS UNUM. *See* Money: Coin (state) to use "E Pluribus Unum"

EAGLE SCOUT. *See* Boy Scouts of America: Boy scout to become an Eagle Scout

EARMUFF was invented in 1873 by Chester Greenwood of Farmington, Me., who commenced manufacturing them commercially the following year. He obtained patent No. 188,292, March 13, 1877, on his "ear mufflers."

EARTH SATELLITE. *See* Satellite

EARTHQUAKE
Earthquake of consequence was felt on August 31, 1886, throughout the eastern part of the United States. In Charleston, S.C., 41 lives were lost and property to the extent of $5 million damaged. The epicenter was 15 miles northwest of Charleston. The loss of lives in the entire area was about 100. In Charleston, 90 percent of 6,956 brick buildings were damaged and about 95 percent of 14,000 chimneys were broken off at the roof. *(Clarence Edward Dutton—Ninth Annual Report of the United States Geological Survey)*

Earthquake description is contained in Governor William Bradford's *History of the Plymouth Plantation.* The earthquake occurred Friday, June 1, 1638, at 2 P.M. at Plymouth, Mass., and is described in part as follows: "However, it was very terrible for ye time; and as ye men were set talking in ye house, some women and others were without ye doors, and ye earth shooke with ye violence as they could not stand without catching hold of ye posts and pails yt stood next them, but ye violence lasted not long. And about halfe an hower, or less, came an other noyse & shaking, but neither so loud nor strong as ye former, but quickly passed over, and so it ceased." In 1638 several Indians described to Roger Williams an earthquake which occurred in 1558 at Providence. No accurate record exists prior to this date, although it is evident that there must have been many earlier earthquakes. *(U.S. Coast and Geodetic Survey—Earthquake History of the United States.)*

EAST–WEST RAILROAD SERVICE. *See* Railroad: Railroad to run west out of Chicago

EASTER EGG ROLL was held April 2, 1877, at the Capitol grounds, Washington, D.C., during President Rutherford Hayes's administration. The custom was carried on by later Presidents until discontinued by President Franklin Delano Roosevelt in 1942. It was reinstated on April 6, 1953, during the administration of President Dwight David Eisenhower.

The First

ECLIPSE OF THE SUN
Motion picture of an eclipse of the sun. *See under* Motion picture

Photograph of an eclipse of the sun. *See Photograph* of an eclipse of the sun taken from the atmosphere

ECONOMIC COOPERATION ADMINISTRATION (U.S.)
Economic Cooperation Administration was authorized April 3, 1948 (62 Stat. L. 137) "to promote world peace and the general welfare, national interest, and foreign policy of the United States through economic, financial and other measures necessary to the maintenance of conditions abroad in which free institutions may survive and consistent with the maintenance of the strength and stability of the United States." The first administrator was Paul Gray Hoffman, who was sworn in April 9, 1948, at $20,000 a year. On April 19, 1949, $1.15 billion was authorized for the April-June 1949 period and $4.28 billion for the fiscal year commencing July 1, 1949. The first European Recovery Program relief purchases totaled $21 million for Italy, France, Greece, Austria, and the Netherlands.

Industrial guaranty contract of investment of American capital in ERP (European Recovery Program) countries was made October 27, 1948, between Godfrey L. Cabot, Inc., Boston, Mass., and the Export-Import Bank of Washington, D.C., as agent of the Economic Cooperation Administrator, under the guaranty provisions of the Foreign Assistance Act of 1948 (62 Stat. L. 137). The amount of the guaranty was $850,000, later increased to $2,025,000. Cabot Carbon Limited erected a plant at Ellesmere Port, England, which on July 27, 1950, produced carbon black, used for the compounding of natural and synthetic rubber. A prior contract was canceled with another company which did not proceed with an investment in Italy.

ECONOMIC OPPORTUNITY OFFICE (U.S.)

Office of Economic Opportunity was authorized by the Economic Opportunity Act of 1964, August 20, 1964 (78 Stat. L. 508), "to mobilize the human and financial resources of the Nation to combat poverty in the United States," to prepare for the responsibilities of citizenship, to increase the employability of men and women age 16 through 21. Robert Sargent Shriver, Jr. was sworn in October 16, 1964, as director.

ECONOMICS ASSOCIATION was the American Economic Association, founded September 9, 1885, in Saratoga, N.Y. The purpose of the association was to encourage "economic research and freedom of economic discussion." The first president was Francis Amasa Walker. *(American Economic Association—Publication No. 1)*

The First

ECONOMICS COURSE. *See* Business economics course

ECONOMICS MAGAZINE devoted exclusively to economics was the *Quarterly Journal of Economics,* published in Boston, Mass., for Harvard University. The first number appeared in October 1886.

EDITOR (newspaperwoman). *See* Woman: Woman newspaper editor

EDITORIAL APOLOGY (newspaper). *See under* Newspaper

EDITORIAL AWARD. *See under* Newspaper

EDUCATION
Chair in education permanently established was created by the University of Iowa, Iowa City, in 1873, and was called "Philosophy and Education." The Normal Department, established 1855, was absorbed by the Collegiate Department of Education in 1873. A temporary department of education had been created by New York University in New York City in 1832.

Compulsory education law was passed by Massachusetts June 14, 1642. It stated: "This Court, taking into consideration the great neglect of many parents and masters in training up their children in learning and labor and other impl[o]yments which may be profitable to the common wealth, so hereupon order and decree, that in every towne the chosen men appointed for managing the prudentiall affayers of the same shall henceforth stand charged with the care of the redresse of this evil . . . and for this end . . . they shall have power to take account from time to time of all parents and masters, and of their children, concerning their calling and impl[o]yment of their children." *(Records of the Governor and Company of Massachusetts Bay, Vol. 2)*

Compulsory school attendance law (state) was Chapter 240, Acts of 1852 approved May 18, 1852, by Governor George Sewall Boutwell of Massachusetts. It prescribed that children must attend school "between the ages of eight and fourteen years" for 12 weeks in the year, 6 of which must be consecutive.

State board of education was established by Massachusetts on April 30, 1837 (Chapter 241, Section 1, Laws of Massachusetts, 1837). The first secretary of the board, later designated as commissioner, was Horace Mann. He was appointed June 29, 1837, and received $1,000 a year. *(Massachusetts Statutes, General Laws and Resolves Relating to Public Instruction)*

War Orphans Education Law was enacted June 29, 1956 (70 Stat. L. 411), "to establish an educational assistance program for children of servicemen who died as a result of a disability or disease incurred in line of duty during World War One, World War Two, or the Korean conflict." It au-

The First

EDUCATION—*Continued*

thorized the Veterans Administration to pay subsistence up to $110 a month not in excess of 36 months to a son or daughter between the ages of 18 and 23. The first recipient was George A. Turner, 19, of Brooklyn, N.Y., who enrolled at the University of Oklahoma, Norman, Okla. He was the son of William G. Turner, who died in 1954 at the age of 43 from a disability incurred during the Normandy invasion.

EDUCATION ASSOCIATION

Educational association (local) was the Middlesex County Association for the Improvement of Common Schools, organized May 1799 in Middletown, Conn., by the Reverend William Woodbridge, who served as its first president. *(American Journal of Education. July 1856)*

Educational association (national) was the American Institute of Instruction, formed at a preliminary meeting March 15–19, 1830, and organized August 19–21, 1830, at a convention at Boston, Mass., attended by delegates from 15 states. A constitution was adopted August 24, 1830, and the association was incorporated March 4, 1831. The first president was Francis Wayland, Jr., president of Brown University. *(The Introductory Discourse and Lectures Delivered in Boston Before the Convention of Teachers and Other Friends of Education)*

EDUCATION BOOK was the Reverend Samuel Read Hall's *Lectures to Teachers on School Keeping,* which was published in 1829 in Boston, Mass., by Richardson, Lord and Holbrook. Ten thousand copies were purchased by the State of New York. *(David Brainard Hall—The Halls of New England)*

EDUCATION DEPARTMENT (U.S.)

Department of Education (U.S.) was created by act of March 2, 1867 (14 Stat. L. 434), an "act to establish a Department of Education," an agency "for the purpose of collecting such statistics and facts as shall show the condition and progress of education in the several states and territories, and of diffusing such information respecting the organization and management of school systems and methods of teaching as shall aid the people of the United States in the establishment and maintenance of efficient school systems and otherwise promote the cause of education." The first commissioner of education was Henry Barnard, appointed March 14, 1867, by President Andrew Johnson. He served until March 17, 1870. The act of July 28, 1868 (15 Stat. L. 106), effective June 30, 1869, abolished the Department of Education and established the Office of Education in the Department of the Interior. *(Darrell Hevenor Smith—Bureau of Education)*

Secretary of Health, Education, and Welfare. *See under* Cabinet (U.S.)

The First

EDUCATION PERIODICAL

Educational magazine was the *Juvenile Mirror or Educational Magazine* published in New York City. It was edited by Albert Picket and John W. Picket. The first issue appeared August 1811. It lasted less than a year.

Educational magazine to achieve success was the *Academician,* a 16-page semimonthly published from February 7, 1818, to January 29, 1820, in New York City. It was edited by Albert Picket and John W. Picket, president and corresponding secretary, respectively, of the Incorporated Society of Teachers, which published the magazine. It offered advice and comments on teaching, and cost $3 a year.

EDUCATIONAL ENDOWMENT in America was made by Benjamin Syms (or Symmes), "Founder of the first Free School in the American Colonies" in 1634. He donated "two hundred acres of land on Poquoson River with the milk and increase of eight cows for the maintenance of a learned and honest man to keep upon the said grounds a free school." The school became known as the Syms-Eaton Academy, located in Hampton, Va. In 1805 the name was changed to the Hampton Academy. *(James Luther Kibler—Historic Virginia Landmarks)*

EDUCATIONAL TRUST FUND established by a municipality was created by Burlington, N.J., in 1682. The assembly provided that a valuable tract of land situated in the Delaware River above Burlington, and known as Matinicunk Island, "remain to and for the use of the town of Burlington . . . for the maintaining of a school for the education of youth. *(Francis Bazley Lee—New Jersey as a Colony and a State)*

EGG INCUBATOR PATENT. *See* Incubator (eggs) patent

EGG ROLL. *See* Easter egg roll

EGYPTIAN ANTIQUITIES COLLECTION was imported in 1835 by Colonel Mendes I. Cohen of Baltimore, Md. It was not publicly displayed until 1884, when it was bequeathed to Johns Hopkins University, Baltimore. *(New-York Historical Society Quarterly Bulletin. April 1920)*

EIGHT-DAY WATCH. *See under* Clock

EIGHT-ENGINED AIRPLANE. *See under* Aviation—Airplane

EIGHT-HOUR-DAY LAW. *See* Labor law

EINSTEINIUM. *See* Element: Element 99

ELASTIC WEBBING was produced by power machinery in the plant of the Russell Manufacturing Company of Middletown, Conn., in 1841, through the efforts of Henry Griswold Hubbard. The concern was incorporated in 1834 with a capital stock of $40,000, nine tenths of which was owned by Samuel Russell and Samuel D. Hub-

The First

bard. Originally the company manufactured nonelastic webbing, a venture which was not profitable. The elastic webbing, however, proved very successful. *(Middletown, Conn.—Mercantile Publishing Company)*

ELECTION

See also Election law; Suffrage; Voting machine

Accredited colonial election in America was held on May 18, 1631, when John Winthrop was elected Governor of Massachusetts. It is believed that in 1619 the Virginia Assembly was selected by means of votes.

Black voter. *See* Election law: Black to vote under authority of the 15th Amendment

Election contested in the House of Representatives. *See* Congress (U.S.)—House of Representatives: Contested election

Election contested in the Senate. *See* Congress (U.S.)—Senate: Contested election

Election day uniformly observed was authorized by act of January 23, 1845 (5 Stat. L. 721), "an act to establish a uniform time for holding elections for electors of President and Vice President in all the states of the Union." "The Tuesday next after the first Monday in the month of November of the year in which they are to be appointed" was selected. The first election under the act was held November 7, 1848.

Election in defiance of the Royal Courts was held April 11, 1640, in Wethersfield, Conn. Matthew Mitchell was elected recorder. The King's Court at Hartford refused to recognize the election and penalized Wethersfield five pounds and the recorder forty nobles. The fines were not paid.

Election in Washington, D.C., was the primary election held on Wednesday, May 6, 1964, when Rev. Edward Franklin Jackson, a black Methodist minister, defeated Frank Daniel Reeves for the office of Democratic committeeman.

Federal election in the United States was authorized on Saturday, September 13, 1788, by the Constitutional Convention which "resolved that the first Wednesday in January next [January 7, 1789] be the day for appointing electors in the several states, which, before the said day, shall have ratified the said Constitution, that the first Wednesday in February [February 4] next be the day for the electors to assemble in their respective states, and vote for a President; and that the first Wednesday in March next [March 4] be the time, and the present seat of Congress [New York City] the place for commencing the proceedings under the said Constitution."

Mayor elected by popular vote in a city was Cornelius Van Wyck Lawrence, a Democrat, who defeated Gulian Crommelin Verplanck, a Whig, in the three-day election held April 8–10, 1834, in New York City. There were 34,988 votes cast, of

The First

which 17,573 were for Lawrence, 17,393 for Verplanck, and 22 for others. Seven other municipal officers were also elected. Previously mayors had been chosen by a board of the Common Council.

Presidential election. *See* Presidential election

Presidential election in which votes were tallied electronically. *See under* Voting Machine

Printed ballot was authorized by the "act to regulate the general elections within this commonwealth" enacted February 15, 1799, by Pennsylvania. Section ten provided that "every elector may deliver written or printed tickets." The ballots were prepared by political parties and were known as "vest pocket tickets." They contained only the names of the issuing party's candidates. *(Eldon Cobb Evans—History of the Australian Ballot System in the United States)*

Woman whose vote was recorded. *See under* Woman

ELECTION LAW

Absentee voting law for military personnel. *See* Army vote

Absentee voting law (state) was enacted by Vermont on November 24, 1896. It provided that a person, by showing a certificate that he was qualified to vote in the state, could vote for state officers at any election booth in the state. *(Helen Mitchell Rocca—A Brief Digest of the Laws Relating to Absentee Voting and Registration)*

Australian ballot system was adopted by Kentucky in February 1888 and approved by Governor Simon Bolivar Buckner on February 24, 1888. It applied only to the city of Louisville. The first state to adopt the Australian ballot was Massachusetts, which enacted legislation May 30, 1888. Allen Thorndike Rice advocated this system of voting in 1886. *(Eldon Cobb Evans—History of the Australian Ballot System in the United States.)*

Black to vote under authority of the 15th Amendment (March 30, 1870) was Thomas Peterson-Mundy of Perth Amboy, N.J., who voted March 31, 1870, in Perth Amboy, N.J., in a special election for ratification or rejection of a city charter. The charter was adopted and he was appointed to the committee to revise the charter.

Corrupt election practices law (federal) was passed January 26, 1907 (34 Stat. L. 864). It prohibited corporations from contributing toward campaign funds in national elections of President, Vice President, senators, and representatives. An act passed March 4, 1909 (35 Stat. L. 1088), effective January 1, 1910, further prohibited national banks and corporations from making financial contributions to campaign funds in connection with any election to any political office.

Corrupt election practices law (state) was passed by New York State and signed by Governor Theodore Roosevelt on April 4, 1890 (Chapter

The First

ELECTION LAW—*Continued*

94, New York State Corrupt Practices Act of 1890), "an act to amend title five of the Penal Code Relating to Crimes Against the Elective Franchise." Candidates were required to file itemized expense accounts of campaign expenditures under penalty of imprisonment and loss of office. *(James Kern Pollock, Jr.—Party Campaign Funds)*

Election law granting black males the right to vote was the act of January 8, 1867 (14 Stat.L.375) "act to regulate the elective franchise in the District of Columbia." Each and every male person 21 years of age, except paupers, and those under guardianship and those convicted of infamous crimes or who have given voluntary comfort to the rebels were given the right to vote. The bill was vetoed by President Andrew Johnson on January 5, 1867. The Senate voted on January 7, 1867, to override the veto (29 yeas, 10 nays); the House, on January 8, 1867, (112 yeas, 38 nays)—on which date the bill became law.

Election law permitting persons 18 years of age or older to vote was Act. No. 28, which was enacted March 3, 1943, to amend the Georgia state constitution. The constitutional amendment was approved by popular vote on August 4, 1943, by a 3-1 majority. The first vote under this law was on November 7, 1944.

Federal legislation enabling persons 18 years of age or older to vote was the 26th Amendment to the Constitution. It was passed on March 10, 1971, by the U.S. Senate by a vote of 94-0, and on March 23, 1971, by the House of Representatives by a vote of 400-19. The first state to ratify the amendment was Minnesota, on March 23, 1971. It was enacted June 30, 1971, when it was passed by Alabama, North Carolina, and Ohio, which were the 36th, 37th, and 38th states to ratify. President Richard Milhous Nixon certified the amendment on July 5, 1971.

Fraudulent election law (colonial) was passed May 22, 1649, by the General Court in Warwick, R.I., and provided that "no one should bring in any votes that he did not receive from the voters' own hands, and that all votes should be filed by the Recorder in the presence of the Assembly." A committee of four freemen was authorized to determine violations of the law and "to examine parties and present to this court what they find in the case." *(Samuel Greene Arnold—History of the State of Rhode Island and Providence Plantations)*

Fraudulent election law (state) was passed by the legislature of California and signed by Governor Frederick Low on March 26, 1866. It was an "act to protect the elections of voluntary political associations, and to punish frauds therein" (Chapter 359—Statutes of California—16th Session). *(Charles Edwin Merriam and Louisa Overacker—Primary Elections)*

The First

Preferential ballot system originated in the city of Grand Junction, Colo. The charter which contained the preferential ballot provision was adopted September 14, 1909, and the first election was held thereunder on November 2, 1909. Opposite the name of each candidate were three columns headed "First Choice," "Second Choice," and "Third Choice." Any person receiving more than half of all the votes cast for first choice was elected; if no one received more than half of the first choices, the lowest candidate was dropped and first and second choices were added together. If any remaining candidate received a majority of the combined votes, he was elected, but if not, then the lowest candidate was again dropped, and all choices for each candidate then added together, and the person receiving the largest total vote was elected. In case of a tie, priority in choice determined election.

Primary election law was passed by Minnesota April 20, 1899 (Chapter 349). It applied to candidates for city and county offices, judges, and elective members of school, library, and park boards in counties having a population of 200,000 or more. Hennepin County was the only one that had the required population when the law went into effect. *(William Watts Folwell—History of Minnesota)*

Primary election (statewide) was held September 4, 1906, in Wisconsin. The law authorizing the election had been passed in 1903, Chapter No. 451, and published June 3, 1903. The first governor nominated and elected under the primary system was James Ole Davidson. The Minnesota primary law of 1899 antedated the Wisconsin primary law, but was limited in its application to counties of 200,000 population or over.

Proportional representation election was held November 2, 1915, in Ashtabula, Ohio. On August 10, 1915, the Hare system was authorized under Ashtabula's manager-plan charter adopted November 3, 1914. As seven council members were to be elected, the votes were so counted that each group consisting of one seventh of all the voters secured a representative. *(National Municipal Review. January 1916)*

Registration law (state) was enacted by Massachusetts (Chapter 74) and signed March 7, 1801, by Governor Caleb Strong. *(Joseph Pratt Harris—Registration of Voters in the United States)*

ELECTIVE SYSTEM OF STUDY. *See under* College

ELECTORAL COLLEGE

Electoral college members invited to a presidential inauguration was the college that had elected Franklin Delano Roosevelt in 1932. The 531 electors, all but 59 of whom were Democrats, were officially invited to attend the inauguration or

The First

March 4, 1933. *(Compton Mackenzie–Mr. Roosevelt)*

Electoral vote cast contrary to instructions was that of Samuel Miles, a Pennsylvania Federalist, in the presidential election of 1796. Instead of voting for John Adams, the Federalist candidate, Miles voted for Thomas Jefferson, a Democratic-Republican. The electors were pledged, but not legally bound, to support a candidate belonging to their party.

Electoral vote for a woman was cast by Roger L. McBride of Charlottesville, Va., whose vote for Theodora Nathan of Oregon, vice presidential candidate of the Libertarian Party, was counted January 6, 1973.

State law requiring presidential electors to cast their ballots for presidential and vice presidential candidates of the political party for which the electors were chosen was enacted by Maine on March 25, 1969.

ELECTRIC ALTERNATOR in parallel successfully operated was installed in 1896 by the Hartford Electric Light Company in its station at Hartford, Conn. It was used in connection with a waterpower unit.

ELECTRIC ARC LIGHTS. *See under* Electric lighting

ELECTRIC ATTACHMENT PLUG (separable) was invented by Harvey Hubbell of Bridgeport, Conn., who obtained patent No. 774,250, November 8, 1904. The plugs were first manufactured by Harvey Hubbell, Inc., Bridgeport, Conn.

ELECTRIC AUTOMOBILE. *See* Automobile

ELECTRIC BELL was invented by Joseph Henry in 1831. He was the first to insulate iron for the magnetic coil and the first to work out the differing functions of two entirely different kinds of electromagnets, the one surrounded by numerous coils of no great length, the other surrounded by a continuous coil of very great length. Joseph Henry's invention of 1831 increased the lifting power of the magnet from 9 pounds to 3,500 pounds. Every electrical dynamo or motor uses the electromagnet in practically the same form in which Henry left it. *(William Bower Taylor—Historical Sketch of Henry's Contribution to the Electro-Magnetic Telegraph)*

ELECTRIC BLANKET. *See* Blanket

ELECTRIC BLOCK SYSTEM. *See* Railroad signal system (automatic electric block)

ELECTRIC CELL. *See* Photoelectric cell

ELECTRIC COMPANY

Electric company was the Edison Electric Light Company, 65 Fifth Avenue, New York City, incorporated October 15, 1878, and organized October 24, 1878. Three thousand shares with a par value of $100 each were issued for the express purpose of financing Thomas Alva Edison in his invention of the incandescent lamp. The Edison Electric Il-

The First

luminating Company was incorporated December 17, 1880, with a capitalization of $1 million for the purpose of furnishing electric light in New York City. The first president of the company was Dr. Norvin Green, who was chosen December 20, 1880.

Electric company organized to produce and sell electricity was the California Electric Light Company, Inc., San Francisco, Calif., organized June 30, 1879. In September 1879 it furnished current from a central generating station for lighting Brush arc light lamps. *(Charles M. Coleman—Pacific Gas and Electric, the Centennial Story of the Pacific Gas and Electric Company, 1852–1952)*

Electric station (central) to supply light and power was the Edison Electric Illuminating Company of 257 Pearl Street, New York City, which opened on Saturday evening, September 4, 1882. It had one engine, which generated power for 800 electric light bulbs. Within fourteen months, the service had 508 subscribers and 12,732 bulbs. *(Francis Trevelyan Miller—T. A. Edison)*

Three-wire central-station incandescent electric lighting plant was the Edison Electric Illuminating Company, Sunbury, Pa., incorporated April 30, 1883. Operations were begun on July 4, 1883. Two 110-volt direct-current generators were connected in series, raising the distribution voltage to 220 volts. This increase in voltage allowed more current (amperes) to be transported over a given size of wire for a given distance, or allowed an equal amount of current to be transported over a given size of wire for a greater distance than is possible when lower voltages are used. The station was constructed by Thomas Alva Edison who served in the triple capacity of chief electrical engineer, mechanical expert, and superintendent of construction.

ELECTRIC COOKING EXPERIMENT was performed by Benjamin Franklin, on the banks of the Schuylkill River, Philadelphia, Pa., in 1749. In a letter sent to Peter Collinson, Franklin stated: "A turkey is to be killed for our dinner by the electrical shock and roasted by the electrical jack, before a fire kindled by the electrified bottle; when the healths of all the famous electricians in England, Holland, France and Germany are to be drank in electrified bumpers, under the discharge of guns from the electrical battery." The letter was dated April 29, 1749. *(I. Bernard Cohen—Benjamin Franklin's Experiments)*

ELECTRIC DENTAL DRILL. *See* Drill

ELECTRIC DYNAMO. *See* Dynamo

ELECTRIC ELEVATED RAILROAD. *See* Elevated railroad

ELECTRIC ELEVATOR. *See* Elevator

The First

ELECTRIC ENGINE USED BY A RAILROAD. *See* Railroad: Railroad to use an electric engine

ELECTRIC EXECUTION. *See* Execution: Electrocution experiment

ELECTRIC-EYE CAMERA. *See* Camera: Photo-finish camera (electric-eye) installed at a racetrack

ELECTRIC EYE FOR HIGH-JUMPING STANDARDS. *See* High-jumping standards

ELECTRIC FAN was invented by Dr. Schuyler Skaats Wheeler, who in 1882 placed a fan or propeller on the shaft of an electric motor. In 1904 the Franklin Institute awarded him the John Scott medal for this invention.

ELECTRIC FIRE-ALARM SYSTEM. *See* Fire-alarm system (electric)

ELECTRIC FLATIRON was invented by Henry W. Seely of New York City, who received patent No. 259,054, on June 6, 1882.

ELECTRIC FREIGHT LOCOMOTIVE. *See* Locomotive

ELECTRIC GENERATOR

Hydrogen-cooled turbine generator was built by the General Electric Company, Schenectady, N.Y., and installed in the Millers Ford station of the Dayton Power and Light Company, Ohio. The generator was put into commercial operation October 12, 1937. It had a capacity of 25,000 kilowatts.

Hydrogen-cooled turbine generator for outdoor installation was built by the General Electric Company, Schenectady, N.Y., for the city of Glendale, Calif., at a cost of $391,669. It went into operation April 11, 1941. The normal rating of the turbo-generator was 20,000 kilowatts. The generator unit was located on an open deck and served with a traveling gantry crane.

Mercury boiler turbine was installed at the Dutch Point Station of the Hartford Electric Light Company, Hartford, Conn., and placed in service September 7, 1923. It generated about 1,500 kilowatts.

Wind turbine to generate energy for an alternating-current central power system was placed in service at Grandpa's Knob, Vt., on October 19, 1941, when it was phased into the Central Vermont Public Service Corporation's system. Synchronized operation continued for two hours, during which a maximum output of 800 kilowatts was delivered. The wind velocity indicated by the anemometers at this load was 26 miles an hour. Palmer Cosslet Putnam was the inventor. *(Power, June 1941)*

ELECTRIC GENERATOR (steam turbine). *See under* Electric Power Generator

The First

ELECTRIC HOME AND FARM AUTHORITY, INC., was authorized by Executive order No. 6,-514, December 19, 1933. It was incorporated January 17, 1934, under the laws of the State of Delaware with a capital of $1 million "to encourage the fullest possible utilization of the present productive capacity of industries—to avoid undue restriction of production." The directors of the corporation named in the executive order were Dr. Arthur Ernest Morgan, chairman; Dr. Harcourt Alexander Morgan; and David Eli Lilienthal. The first sale of electric ranges, refrigerators, and water heaters financed by the Electric Home and Farm Authority, Inc., was held at Tupelo, Miss., May 21, 1934. The corporation was dissolved and a new one incorporated August 1, 1935, under the laws of the District of Columbia.

ELECTRIC IRON. *See* Electric flatiron

ELECTRIC LIGHT PLANT MUNICIPALLY OWNED. *See* Electric power plant

ELECTRIC LIGHT SOCKET with pull chain was patented August 11, 1896 (No. 565,451), by Harvey Hubbell of Bridgeport, Conn. The sockets were manufactured by Harvey Hubbell, Inc., Bridgeport, Conn.

ELECTRIC LIGHTING

Electric arc lights for public streetlighting were made by Charles Francis Brush and were used in the Public Square, Cleveland, Ohio, April 29, 1879. Twelve lamps of the carbon variety—two carbon points slightly separated—were used. The current jumped from carbon to carbon, giving off "a dazzling white light." Women complained about these lamps because they lighted their complexions to disadvantage. *(Thomas Commerford Martin and Stephen Leidy Coles—Story of Electricity)*

Electric incandescent lamp of practical value was invented on October 21, 1879, by Thomas Alva Edison of Menlo Park, N.J. After 13 months of experimenting, he discovered carbonized cotton filaments and produced a light bulb that would burn 40 hours in a vacuum inside a glass bulb. The first demonstration was held on December 20, 1879. Patent papers on this invention were applied for on November 4, 1879, and were granted January 27, 1880 (No. 223,898). The first public demonstration was held December 31, 1879. The Pennsylvania Railroad Company ran special trains to Menlo Park, N.J., to enable the public to view the demonstration. *(William Andrew Durgin—Electricity in Its Development)*

Electric incandescent lamp factory was the Edison Lamp Works, Menlo Park, N.J., opened October 1, 1880. More than 130,000 bulbs had been manufactured by April 1, 1882, when the factory moved to Harrison, N.J.

Electric indirect lighting demonstration was made in Chicago, Ill., in October 1908 by Augustus Darwin Curtis before the Illuminating Engineering

The First

Society and the Ophthalmological Society. *(Jacob L. Stair—The Lighting Book)*

Electric light for household illumination was probably used by Professor Moses Gerrish Farmer at 11 Pearl Street, Salem, Mass. In July 1859 he arranged a series of lamps in his parlor, the current for which was generated by a galvanic battery of some three dozen six-gallon jars in his cellar. The lamps could be turned on individually. He invented an incandescent lamp which consisted of a strip of sheet platinum operating in air. *(John White Howell and Henry Schroeder—The History of the Incandescent Lamp)*

Electric light bulb frosted on the inside with sufficient strength for commercial handling was invented by Marvin Pipkin of the Incandescent Lamp Department of the General Electric Company at Nela Park, Ohio. On June 29, 1925, he applied for a patent, which was granted October 16, 1928 (No. 1,687,510). Inside-frosted bulbs have a number of distinct advantages over outside-frosted bulbs, among which are less absorption of light and less collection of dust. Pipkin found that bulbs frosted by previous methods were weak because the etched surface was made up of minute sharp-angled pits or depressions, and that he could strengthen the bulb by changing these into round-ed pits by treating the bulb with a weaker etching solution, or by using the strong solution for a shorter period of time.

Electric light from a power plant in a residence was generated by an independent plant installed in the home of James Hood Wright in Fort Washington, N.Y., before December, 1881. Other residences which were equipped with local generating power plants were those of William Henry Vanderbilt and John Pierpont Morgan of New York City.

Electric light in a store was installed in the Philadelphia, Pa., establishment of John Wanamaker on December 26, 1878, in the Grand Depot. Twenty-eight arc lamps were used, eight dynamos supplying the current.

Electric sterilamp was introduced in March 1938 by the Lamp Division of the Westinghouse Electric and Manufacturing Company, Bloomfield, N.J. It was designed to reduce the germ population of the air by bactericidal ultraviolet radiation.

Electric traffic signal light. *See under* Traffic light

Electrically lighted elevator. *See* Elevator: Elevator with an electric light

Electrically lighted train. *See under* Railroad

Fluorescent lighting installed on every street in a city in accordance with illuminating engineering code levels was that in Brookings, S. Dak. The project, started in 1953, was completed in 1958.

The First

Glass light bulb machine was invented by Benjamin D. Chamberlin of Washington, D.C., who received patent No. 1,551,935, September 1, 1925, for an "apparatus for gathering glass and the treatment thereof on blowpipes," assigned to the Hartford-Empire Company, Hartford, Conn. He filed his application on April 23, 1909, serial No. 491,812. The first commercial machine was the result of several individuals' work and went into regular use about 1914 at the main plant of the Corning Glass Works, Corning, N.Y.

Hotel to install electric lights. *See under* Hotel

Illuminated 9-hole regulation golf course. *See* Golf Course: Illuminated 9-hole regulation golf course

Klieg light lighting unit for the motion picture industry was invented by John Hugh Kliegl and Anton Tiberius Kliegl and placed in use in 1911. Two 35-ampere arcs operating in series were equipped with an automatic arc-feed arrangement, using the then new white flame carbons. It gave four times as much light as other available sources. The lights were first used by the Carlton Motion Picture Laboratory, Coney Island, N.Y.; the Lubin Manufacturing Co., Philadelphia, Pa.; and the Thomas A. Edison, Inc., Decatur Avenue Studio, New York City. The name was not adopted until later.

Mercury vapor lamp was invented by Peter Cooper Hewitt of New York City, who received eight patents on September 17, 1901. It consisted of an elongated vacuum glass tube having a mercury electrode at one end and an iron electrode at the other end, the light being obtained from the gas or vapor of the mercury, through which an electric current passed. The lamps lacked red rays. The lamps were manufactured by the Cooper Hewitt Electric Company in New York City in December 1902. *(Electrical World and Engineer. April 27, 1901)*

Newspaper plant to install electricity. *See* Newspaper: Newspaper plant to install electricity

Photograph taken by incandescent electric light. *See under* Photograph

School completely irradiated with germicidal lamps. *See under* School

School to have all classroom lights controlled by electric eyes. *See under* School

Sewing machine lamp holder. *See under* Sewing machine

Ship (steamboat) with electric lights. *See under* Ship

Sodium vapor lamps were installed June 13, 1933, on the Balltown Road, near Schenectady, N.Y., by the General Electric Company and the New York Power and Light Corporation. The lamps were monochromatic and glowed in one

The First

ELECTRIC LIGHTING—*Continued*
color, giving two and a half times the light output
of incandescent lamps of the same wattage. The
lamp wattage was about 80 to 90 watts and the
light output about 4,000 lumens, which was the
equivalent of the 400-candlepower Mazda lamp
consuming 215 watts.

Streetlight of an automatic system in which the
lights individually turn themselves on and off was
installed in New Milford, Conn., on March 2, 1949,
by the Connecticut Light and Power Co., New Milford, Conn. The electronic device used in each
streetlight was a joint development of the General
Electric Company and the Connecticut Light and
Power Company. The installation of 190 photoe-
lectric-controlled streetlights on approximately 7
miles of street was completed in November 1949.

Streetlighting (electric) by a municipality was
undertaken by Wabash, Ind., which appropriated
$100 on February 2, 1880, to the Brush Electric
Light Company of Cleveland, Ohio, to install a
light on the dome of the courthouse. On March 31,
1880, four lights, each over 4,000 candlepower,
were placed on a staff above the courthouse, and
on April 8, 1880, a further payment of $1,800 was
authorized.

Theater lighted by electric lights. *See under*
Theater

ELECTRIC LOCOMOTIVE. *See* Locomotive

ELECTRIC LOCOMOTIVE HEADLIGHT. *See*
Locomotive headlight

ELECTRIC MAGNET was invented by Joseph
Henry, who, in June 1828, exhibited one closely
wound with silk-covered wire about 1/39 inch in
diameter, before the Albany Institute, Albany,
N.Y. *(Ellis H. Crapper—Electric and Magnetic Circuits)*

ELECTRIC METER, indicating the amount of
electrical energy dispensed or applied, was invented by Oliver B. Shallenberger of Rochester,
Pa., who obtained patent No. 388,003 on August
14, 1888. Commercial production of the meters
was started in August 1888 by the Westinghouse
Electric and Manufacturing Company, Pittsburgh,
Pa.

ELECTRIC MOTOR
Electric motor (interpole direct current) was invented by Mathias Pfatischer of Philadelphia, Pa.,
who obtained patent No. 775,310 on November 22,
1904, on a "variable speed motor." The application was filed April 7, 1904.

Electric motor (single-phase alternating current)
of variable speed was first used in 1901 in interurban service. In 1907 the first steam railroad adopted it.

ELECTRIC ORGAN. *See* Organ

The First

ELECTRIC PORTABLE TYPEWRITER. *See*
Typewriter

ELECTRIC POWER
Electric power from nuclear energy. *See under*
Atomic energy

Electric power generated by cosmic rays was
used April 30, 1939, when rays were trapped by a
Geiger-Mueller counter at the Hayden Planetarium, New York City, and set up a current of electricity that was carried by wire to the Fair
Grounds, Flushing Meadows, New York City, and
actuated relays of local battery circuits each connected with a switch to turn on the colored lights
at the Lagoon of the Nations.

Electric power generated from atomic energy to
be sold commercially was delivered by the Atomic Energy Commission at West Milton, N.Y., to the
Niagara Mohawk Power Corporation, which supplied power on July 18, 1955, to homes and industry at three mills per kilowatt hour. The power
was obtained from a reactor, the prototype of the
reactor used in the submarine *Seawolf.* A capacity of about 10,000 kilowatts was integrated with
the regular current.

Electric power generated from atomic energy to
illuminate an entire town was obtained from the
Utah Power and Light Company's station at Arco
Idaho, on July 17, 1955. At 11:28 P.M. the station
released steam from a borax reactor into a turbine
which drove a 3,500 kilowatt-capacity generator
to supply current for 1,200 inhabitants of Arco
The power, which lasted only one hour, was the
sole source of the town's light. The news was
withheld until August 11, 1955, when it was announced at the Atoms for Peace Conference a
Geneva, Switzerland.

Electric power using municipal refuse as a boiler fuel was obtained by the Union Electric Com
pany's Meramec Plant, St. Louis, Mo., on April 4
1972. Refuse was shredded and burned with coa
to generate electricity. The first month 200,00
kilowatt hours of electricity were generated.

Warship propelled by electricity. *See unde*
Ship

ELECTRIC POWER GENERATOR
Steam-turbine electric generator was installe
and placed in operation in October of 1901 in th
Pearl Street Station of the Hartford Electric Ligh
Company, Hartford, Conn.

**ELECTRIC POWER LINE COMMERCIAL CAR
RIER.** *See under* Electric transmission

ELECTRIC POWER PLANT
Alternating-current hydroelectric power plan
to operate over a long distance was built by th
Willamette Falls Electric Company at Willamett
Falls, Oregon City, Oreg., and operated two 30
h.p. Stilwell & Bierce waterwheels belted to a sin
gle-phase generator rated at 720 kilowatts. O

The First

June 2, 1889, it supplied current to Portland, Oreg., a distance of 13 miles. *(Oregon Historical Quarterly. Vol. 31, No. 1. March 1930)*

Alternating-current power plant was placed in operation in Great Barrington, Mass., on March 6, 1886, and commercially operated on March 20, 1886. The transformers were built by William Stanley in the Great Barrington laboratory and were successfully operated for a considerable time, but an accident disabled the generators and the plant was discontinued. *(Charles James Taylor—History of Great Barrington)*

Alternating-current power plant commercially successful was built in Buffalo, N.Y., in November 1886, by the Westinghouse Electric and Manufacturing Company, Pittsburgh, Pa. The station, located on Wilkerson Street, Buffalo, was placed in operation on November 30, 1886, by the Brush Electric Light Company. *(Edward Dean Adams—Niagara Power)*

Atomic electric-generating station (full-scale) devoted exclusively to peaceful uses is the Shippingport Atomic Power Station, Shippingport, Pa., whose reactor attained criticality December 2, 1957. The plant produced its full rated capacity of 60,000 net kilowatts on December 23, 1957. It consists of a single pressurized water-type reactor and its associated systems, four steam generators heated by the reactor, a single turbine-generator and associated systems, a radioactive waste disposal system, laboratory, shops, and administrative facilities. The station was designed to supply an initial electrical output of 60,000 kilowatts net, enough to provide for the residential needs of a city of 250,000 people. To allow for increased output from future nuclear fuel loadings, the turbine generator was designed with a capacity of 1 million kilowatts. President Dwight David Eisenhower broke ground for the station by remote control from Denver, Colo., on September 6, 1954, and formally dedicated the plant by remote control from Washington, D.C., on May 26, 1958.

Cooling tower hyperbolic-shaped was placed in commercial service January 1, 1963, at Ashland, Ky. Its capacity was 120,000 gallons per minute at 22.7° F. It was owned and operated by the Kentucky Power Company of Ashland, Ky., an electric utility of the American Electric Power System Corporation.

Floating electric power plant was the *Jacona,* a 7,000-ton steam-driven cargo vessel (396 feet long, 53 feet wide), built in 1919 by the Todd Dry Dock and Shipbuilding Company, Tacoma, Wash., for the United States Shipping Board and rebuilt in 1930 at the Newport News Shipbuilding and Dry Dock Company, Newport News, Va., which installed two 10,000-kilowatt turbines. The *Jacona* was towed by tug to Bucksport, Me., where it supplied a paper mill with 24,121,000-kilowatt hours of power from November 1930 to March 1931, at

The First

which time power was obtained from the Central Maine Power Company's Wyman Dam. The idea for the floating power plant was conceived by Walter Scott Wyman and the design engineering done by Nepsco Services.

Hydroelectric power plant was opened September 30, 1882, in Appleton, Wis. A single dynamo of 180 lights, each of ten candlepower, was erected. Incandescent lighting was furnished. *(Thomas Commerford Martin—Forty Years of Edison Service)*

Hydroelectric power plant built by the federal government was the Minidoka Dam on the Minidoka Project, Snake River, Idaho, constructed by the Bureau of Reclamation, Department of the Interior. The first unit of the power plant was started on May 1, 1909, and had a capacity of 1,400 kilovolt amperes. The Theodore Roosevelt Dam on the Salt River Project in Arizona supplied power to the Phoenix Gas and Electric Company on September 30, 1909.

Hydroelectric power plant (commercial) to furnish arc lighting service was the Grand Rapids Electric Light and Power Co., Grand Rapids, Mich., organized March 22, 1880, incorporated March 30, 1880, and placed in operation July 23, 1880. The first president and organizer was William T. Powers. The first generating equipment was a 16-arc-light Brush generator installed in the factory of the Wolverine Chair Company, which was driven by a waterwheel to supply power to the factory. Seven organizations were supplied with electric light. In September 1880 a larger generator was installed at a different site and on August 1, 1881, a new building was occupied from which current was generated to supply street lighting. This plant furnished arc lighting service for the first four years of its operations. *(Michigan History Magazine. 1939)*

Hydroelectric power plant (county-owned) was placed in operation by the people of Crisp County, Ga., on August 1, 1930. The plant was 14 miles southwest of Cordele on the Flint River and was built under government license. Emmet Stephen Killebrew was the chief engineer. It had a capacity of 14,000 h.p. and produced 47 million kilowatt-hours per annum. *(America's First County-Owned Hydro-Electric Power Plant—Crisp County Power Commission)*

Hydroelectric power plant to produce a million kilowatts was Boulder Dam, Boulder City, Nevada, which reached this production peak in June 1943. The Bureau of Reclamation of the Department of the Interior awarded a contract on March 11, 1931, for a concrete arch-gravity type dam. The dam was dedicated September 30, 1935, by President Franklin Delano Roosevelt. The first of its four generators (N-2) was placed in operation October 26, 1936, to serve the Los Angeles area. In 1947 its name was changed to Hoover Dam.

The First

ELECTRIC POWER PLANT—*Continued*

Hydroelectric power plant to use a storage battery making it possible to supply the peak load requirements from waterpower that would otherwise have gone to waste during the periods of relatively small demands was installed by the Hartford Electric Light Company, Hartford, Conn., in 1896.

Hydroelectric power plant to use water pumped into a reservoir was constructed in 1927 by the Connecticut Light and Power Company, Waterbury, Conn., at Rocky River, Conn. The first pumping commenced February 1928. Two 8,100 h.p. centrifugal pumps delivered water into a reservoir 10 miles long and 1¾ miles wide at its widest point. The water was stored and then used for generating electricity as needed in a 33,000 h.p. turbine. *(American Institute of Electrical Engineers—Transactions, October 1928)*

Mobile electric power plant was delivered January 10, 1944, by the General Electric Company, Schenectady, N.Y., to the U.S. Navy Bureau of Yards and Docks, Navy Yard, Philadelphia, Pa. It consisted of six specially built railway cars housing a complete steam-turbine generating plant as well as the switchgear and transformer apparatus for controlling and distributing the 10,000 kilowatts of electric power it was capable of generating. The boilers were fired by oil. The unit had no motive power of its own but could be hauled over the rails at speeds up to 40 miles an hour and could be placed in operation within 24 hours.

Municipally owned electric power plant was purchased in 1882 by Fairfield, Iowa. It supplied 13 streetlights, and 6 Brush arc lamps of 2,000 candlepower which were situated on a 185-foot tower. City operation was supervised by Al Robb and James McQuiston. The illumination cost $70 annually per arc. A windstorm blew the tower down May 9, 1883.

Rotary converter power plant was operated by the Chicago Edison Company, Chicago, Ill., on May 16, 1896, for the purpose of inaugurating a 2,500-volt alternating transmission from the company's station at Harrison Street at the river, to its station at 27th Street and Wabash Ave.

Utility-operated plant for central heating and cooling was placed in operation by the Hartford Steam Service Company, a subsidiary of the Hartford Gas Company, Hartford, Conn., and dedicated June 25, 1962. The chilled water was metered and the customers paid for the amount used. The plant was built by F. H. McGraw & Co.

ELECTRIC POWER TRANSMISSION

Power line of 765,000 volts was built in Kentucky and placed in operation in 1969. The 68-mile line, part of nearly 1,400 miles of 765,000-volt lines, connected Kentucky Power's Big Sandy plant with facilities serving the former Atomic En-

The First

ergy Commission's (now DOE) gaseous diffusion project near Portsmouth, Ohio.

ELECTRIC PRINTING PRESS. *See* Printing press

ELECTRIC PROCESS WELDING. *See* Welding by the electric process

ELECTRIC RAZOR. *See* Razor

ELECTRIC SAWMILL. *See* Sawmill

ELECTRIC SELF-STARTER. *See* Automobile electric self-starter

ELECTRIC SEWING MACHINE. *See* Sewing machine

ELECTRIC SHAVER. *See* Razor

ELECTRIC SIGN

Animated-cartoon electric sign was displayed April 28, 1937, by Douglas Leigh on the front of a building on Broadway, New York City. It contained 2,000 bulbs and presented a four-minute show depicting a cavorting horse, ball-tossing cats, etc.

Electric sign flasher installed was the Motogram, placed in service on the four sides of the New York *Times* building, New York City, on November 6, 1928, with the flashing of election returns. The system was invented by Francis E. J. Wilde of Meadowmere Park, N.Y., who obtained patent No. 1,626,900 on May 3, 1927, on an "electric sign control" designed "to permit changing of sign without interruption." It was installed by the Motogram Corporation, New York City, and was 360 feet long and 5 feet high. It had 14,800 lamps, 88,000 soldered connections, 1,386,000 feet of wire, and 39,000 contact brushes which created 21,925,664 lamp flashes an hour.

Electric sign (large) was designed and constructed by the Edison General Electric Company and installed in June 1892 on the wall of a nine-story building near Broadway and 23rd Street, New York City. The sign occupied a surface area 60 by 68 feet and was composed of 107 galvanized iron boxes varying in height from 3 to 6 feet. The front of each box was cut out to form the desired letter. Inside the boxes were 1,457 sixteen-candle-power Edison bulbs in red, blue, green, and white frosted. The sign read: "BUY HOMES ON / LONG IS LAND / SWEPT BY OCEAN BREEZES / MANHATTAN BEACH / ORIENTAL HOTEL / MANHATTAN HOTEL / GILMORE'S BAND / BROCK'S FIREWORKS." Current was supplied by the Edison Electric Illuminating Company. The sign was illuminated from dusk to 11 P.M. One line went on at a time, until all the lights were on, then all the lights went out. *(Electrical World. Vol. 20 No. 2. July 16, 1892)*

Neon-tube advertising sign was installed on a marquee at the Cosmopolitan Theatre, 59th Street and Columbus Circle, New York City, in July 1923. This sign advertised the theatrical production *Little Old New York,* in which Marion Davies played

The First

the leading role. A United States patent on this tube was granted to George Claude of Paris. It was applied for on November 9, 1911, and issued on January 19, 1915 (No. 1,125,476).

ELECTRIC STARTING GATE (racetrack) was invented by Clay Puett, who installed a two-stall working model on May 8, 1939, at Hollywood Park, Inglewood, Calif. The first full-size gate was used at Bay Meadows Race Track, San Francisco, Calif., October 7, 1939. The gates were equipped with a bomb-release type of lock operated by solenoids. The front doors when closed formed a V and opened outward by means of springs.

ELECTRIC-STORAGE-BATTERY AUTOMOBILE. *See* Automobile

ELECTRIC STOVE
See also Electric cooking experiment

Electric range was invented by George B. Simpson of Washington, D.C., who received patent No. 25,532 on September 20, 1859, on an "electrical heating apparatus" which he termed an electro-heater. Heat was generated by passing currents of electricity over a coil or coils of platina or other metallic wire.

Electric stove was a one-ring spiral coiled conductor invented by William S. Hadaway, Jr., of New York City, who obtained patent No. 563,032 June 30, 1896. It provided a uniform surface distribution of heat.

ELECTRIC STREETCAR. *See* Streetcar

ELECTRIC TATTOO MACHINE. *See under* Tattoo

ELECTRIC TAXICAB. *See under* Automobile

ELECTRIC THIRD-RAIL SYSTEM. *See* Railroad: Railroad operated by an electric third-rail system

ELECTRIC TIMER
Electrical timing device was tested May 14, 1932, at Baker Field, New York City, in 3 events, when Columbia defeated Syracuse in a track meet 87½-47½. The results were not accepted as final.

ELECTRIC TOASTER
Electric toaster of the household automatic pop-up type was marketed in June 1926 by the McGraw Electric Company, Minneapolis, Minn., under the trademark Toastmaster. One lever lowered the bread into the toaster and another wound the timer. It received one slice of toast at a time. The retail price was $13.50.

ELECTRIC TORPEDO. *See* Torpedo

ELECTRIC TRAFFIC SIGNAL LIGHT. *See* Traffic light

ELECTRIC TRANSMISSION
Alternating-current power transmission installation was made in 1890 at Telluride, Colo., by the Westinghouse Electric and Manufacturing Company. A 100 h.p., 88 1/3 cycle, single-phase, 3,000-

The First

volt generator was driven by waterpower. A 3-mile transmission line was erected and a single-phase synchronous motor was installed at the end of the line. The motor lacked a starting torque, and a necessary adjunct was a starting motor to bring the unloaded synchronized motor to its normal speed. *(Francis Ellington Leupp—George Westinghouse)*

Electric power line commercial carrier was placed in operation December 6, 1922, by the Utica Gas and Electric Company, Utica, N.Y. The plant was built by the General Electric Company, Schenectady, N.Y., and consisted of the transmitters, the power lines, and the associated receivers. The transmission lines carried both voices and power. A single power line could carry several different carrier frequencies simultaneously, making possible distant supervisory control of various types of electric equipment.

Substation with a rotary converter completely unattended was the Rowena Substation of the Detroit Edison Company, Detroit, Mich., which went into service in April 1914. It consisted of a 500-kilowatt General Electric rotary converter, three 175-kilowatt step-down transformers, and the necessary equipment for balancing direct-current machine voltage against bus voltage at Rowena. Included also were the typical devices to protect against alternating-current failure, direct-current failure, reverse current, and overspeed. This equipment acted to convert three-phase alternating current at 4,600 volts to direct current at 250 volts. This station was fed and controlled from another substation about a mile distant, which was attended, and known as Station "I" (later called the Elizabeth Substation).

Three-phase alternating high-frequency current transmission for any considerable distance by a utility company was operated in March 1893 from the Rainbow Hydroelectric Station on the Farmington River to the State Street station of the Hartford Electric Light Company, Hartford, Conn. The power transmitted was 300 kilowatts, between 4,000 and 5,000 volts.

ELECTRIC TROLLEY. *See* Streetcar

ELECTRIC TURNSTILE. *See* Turnstile (electric)

ELECTRIC VOTE RECORDER. *See* Voting machine

ELECTRIC WASHING MACHINE. *See* Washing machine

ELECTRIC WATCH. *See under* Clock

ELECTRIC WELDING. *See* Welding by the electric process

ELECTRICAL CONTRACT by a city with the federal government for electrical power was signed by J. P. Nanney, mayor of Tupelo, Miss., and Arthur Ernest Morgan, chairman of the Tennessee Valley Authority, on November 11, 1933, and went

The First

ELECTRICAL CONTRACT—*Continued*
into effect February 7, 1934. The contract was for 20 years, and by it the city agreed to purchase electricity from TVA and to sell it to its customers at rates agreed upon with the Authority. The electricity cost the city of Tupelo about 5½ mills per kilowatt hour.

ELECTRICAL ENGINEERING COURSE *See under* Engineering college

ELECTRICAL HEARING AID. *See under* Deaf—Hearing aid

ELECTRICAL JOURNAL. *See* Periodical

ELECTRICAL SHOW was held in Philadelphia, Pa., September 2–October 11, 1884, and was known as the Electrical Exhibition and National Conference of Electricians. It was sponsored by the Franklin Institute and was held in the Pennsylvania Railroad Station, 32d and Market streets. There were 216 exhibitors and 282,779 paid admissions. *(Official Catalogue of the International Electrical Exhibition, 1884)*

ELECTRICALLY PROPELLED SHIP. *See* Ship

ELECTRICALLY WOUND CLOCK. *See* Clock: Watch movement to be electrically wound

ELECTROBASOGRAPH was invented by Dr. Russell Plato Schwartz of the University of Rochester Medical School, Rochester, N.Y., who exhibited it June 12, 1933, at the American Medical Association convention, Milwaukee, Wis. It was designed "to record the walking gait of individuals, to distinguish between actual and spurious limps in damage claims for injuries."

ELECTROCUTION EXPERIMENT. *See under* Execution

ELECTROCUTOR, INSECT. *See* Insect electrocutor patent

ELECTROMAGNETIC TELEGRAPH. *See* Telegraph

ELECTRON MICROSCOPE. *See* Microscope

ELECTRON TUBE to enable humans to see in the dark was invented by Dr. Vladimir Kosma Zworykin and Dr. George Arthur Morton and described January 2, 1936, at the American Association for the Advancement of Science meeting, St. Louis, Mo. The device was sensitive to ultraviolet and infrared rays. Light rays from motion pictures were converted into electrons.

ELECTRONIC BLANKET. *See* Blanket: Electric (electronic)

ELECTRONIC COMPUTER. *See* Computer

ELECTRONIC RANGE. *See* Stove

ELECTRONIC TELEVISION SYSTEM. *See under* Television

The First

ELECTRONIC WRISTWATCH. *See under* Clock

ELECTROPHOTOGRAPHY. *See* Radio facsimile transmission

ELECTRO-THERAPEUTIC BOOK was Dr. Alfred Charles Garratt's *Electro-Physiology and Electro-Therapeutics, showing the best methods for the medical uses of electricity,* 712 pages, published in 1860 by Ticknor and Fields, Boston, Mass.

ELECTROTYPE
Electrotype was produced from a wood engraving in 1839 in New York City by Joseph Alexander Adams. The electrotype was made by an impression taken in an alloy of soft metal, bismuth probably being the chief ingredient. Electrotypes were first published in 1840 in *Mapes Magazine. (Robert Francis Salade—Handbook of Electrotyping and Stereotyping)*

Electrotype manufacturing for commercial purposes was started in 1846 by John W. Wilcox in Boston, Mass. *(Robert Francis Salade—Handbook of Electroplating and Stereotyping)*

ELEMENT
Element 87, francium (symbol Fr, atomic weight 223), was discovered by Drs. Fred Allison and Edgar Jackson Murphy of the Alabama Polytechnic Institute at Auburn in samples of pollucite and lepidolite ores. The discovery was announced in a letter dated January 11, 1930, published in the *Physical Review. (Physical Review. Vol. 35, No. 3. Feb. 1, 1930)*

Element 93, neptunium (symbol Np, atomic weight 237), was discovered at the University of California at Berkeley by Professor Edwin Mattison McMillan and Philip Hauge Abelson and announced June 8, 1940.

Element 94, plutonium (symbol Pu, atomic weight 242), was discovered in 1940 at the University of California at Berkeley by Drs. Glenn Theodore Seaborg and Edwin Mattison McMillan, who received the 1951 Nobel Prize in chemistry on December 10, 1951, in Stockholm, Sweden.

Element 95, americium (symbol Am, atomic weight 243), was discovered by Glenn Theodore Seaborg, Ralph Arthur James, Leon Owen Morgan, and Albert Ghiorso late in 1944 and announced November 16, 1945. It was formed by intense neutron bombardment of plutonium in the chain-reacting uranium-graphite structures at Clinton, Tenn., and Hanford, Wash.

Element 96, curium (symbol Cm, atomic weight 242), was discovered by Glenn Theodore Seaborg, Ralph Arthur James, and Albert Ghiorso in the summer of 1944 and announced November 16, 1945. It was obtained by the helium-ion bombardment of plutonium, element 94, in the 60-inch cyclotron of the Crocker Radiation Laboratory of the University of California at Berkeley.

The First

Element 97, berkelium (symbol Bk, atomic weight 249), was identified by Stanley Gerald Thompson, Albert Ghiorso, and Glenn Theodore Seaborg in December 1949. It was produced by the bombardment of milligram amounts of americium with helium ions accelerated in the 60-inch cyclotron of the Crocker Radiation Laboratory of the University of California at Berkeley. It was the fifth element produced by the cyclotron's atomic particle bombardment.

Element 98, californium (symbol Cf, atomic weight 249), was identified and produced by Stanley Gerald Thompson, Albert Ghiorso, Kenneth Street, Jr., and Glenn Theodore Seaborg in January 1950 and announced March 17, 1950. It does not exist in nature and was produced by the bombardment of microgram amounts of curium with helium ions accelerated in the 60-inch cyclotron of the Crocker Radiation Laboratory of the University of California at Berkeley.

Element 99, einsteinium (symbol E, atomic weight 253), was identified by Albert Ghiorso, Stanley Gerald Thompson; Bernard George Harvey, and G. Bernard Rossi in December 1952. It was obtained by the bombardment of uranium 238, element 92, with a beam of positively charged nitrogen atoms from the 60-inch cyclotron at the University of California at Berkeley. It was found in the debris of a thermonuclear explosion carried out by the University of California Radiation Laboratory, the Argonne National Laboratory, and the Los Alamos Scientific Laboratory.

Element 100, fermium (symbol Fm, atomic weight 255), was identified by Albert Ghiorso and others early in 1953 in the debris of a thermonuclear explosion carried out by the University of California Radiation Laboratory, the Argonne National Laboratory, and the Los Alamos Scientific Laboratory.

Element 101, mendelevium (symbol Mv, atomic weight 256), was discovered by Albert Ghiorso, Bernard George Harvey, Gregory Robert Choppin, Stanley Gerald Thompson, and Glenn Theodore Seaborg in February 1955 and announced April 30, 1955. It was obtained by the bombardment of einsteinium with helium ions in the 60-inch cyclotron at the University of California at Berkeley.

Element 102, nobelium (symbol No, atomic weight 253), was discovered by Swedish, British, and American scientists who bombarded curium, element 96. The discovery was announced July 9, 1957, by the Argonne National Laboratory, Lemont, Ill.

Element 103, lawrencium, was produced on February 14, 1961, at the Lawrence Radiation Laboratory of the University of California, Berkeley, Calif., by Albert Ghiorso, Torbjørn Sikkeland, Almon E. Larsh, and Robert M. Latimer, who bombarded a target consisting of three millionths of a

The First

gram of californium, element 98, with boron ions of approximately 60 million electron volts energy. When a californium nucleus captures one of the boron nuclei, a new nucleus of 103 protons is instantaneously formed.

Element 104, rutherfordium, atomic weight 261, artificial element was discovered at Lawrence Radiation Laboratory of the University of California, Berkeley, Calif., in 1969. It was named for the English physicist Sir Ernest Rutherford. (Discovery of this element is also claimed by Russia.)

Element 105, hahnium, artificial element, atomic weight 260, discovered at Lawrence Radiation Laboratory of the University of California, Berkeley, Calif, by Dr. Albert Ghiorso and named for German physicist Otto Hahn. The discovery was announced April 27, 1970, at the American Physical Society meeting at Washington, D.C.

ELEPHANT. *See* Animals

ELEPHANT BUILDING. *See* Building

ELEVATED RAILROAD

Electric elevated railroad, and the first commercial electric line, was operated at the Chicago Railway Exposition in June 1883 by the Electric Railway Company of the United States. *The Judge,* a 15 h.p. electric locomotive, hauled the trains on a 3-foot-gauge track around the outer edge of a gallery of the main exhibition building, curving sharply at either end on a radius of 56 feet. The total length of the track was 1,553 feet. The trial trip was made June 2, 1883, but the line was not permitted to operate until June 9. It ceased operating June 23, having run 118¾ hours. It made 1,588 trips, carried 26,805 passengers, and ran 446.24 miles. *(Thomas Commerford Martin and Joseph Wetzler—The Electric Motor and Its Application)*

Electric elevated railroad (permanent) was the Metropolitan West Side Elevated Railway, which opened on May 17, 1895. It ran from Franklin Street to Logan Square, a distance of 5 miles, in Chicago, Ill.

Elevated railroad was opened for traffic on July 2, 1867, in New York City. Charles T. Harvey received authority for its construction and built the first ½-mile test section on single columns along the curb line of Greenwich Street, between Battery Place and Dey Street. The speed of the cars was from 12 to 15 miles an hour. The line was unsuccessful and was sold at a sheriff's sale. It was reorganized February 14, 1870, and placed in operation with steam power. Service was extended as far north as the New York Central Railroad Passenger station at 29th Street and Ninth Avenue. *(The Industrial Museum of New York, Vol. 1–2, Museum of the Peaceful Arts)*

The First

ELEVATOR

Double-deck elevator was installed January 1932 by the Otis Elevator Company in the Sixty Wall Tower, Inc., building, New York City. It served 30 floors and traveled at a speed of 1,000 feet a minute. Eight double-decked cars were installed, which stopped at two floors at the same time. The building was formally opened May 13, 1932.

Dual elevator, with two cars operated separately on different levels in the same shaftway, was made and placed in regular service by the Westinghouse Electric and Manufacturing Company in its main office building in East Pittsburgh, Pa., in 1931. The upper elevator was an express. When it was on the main floor, the local was in the basement. Precautions were taken to prevent a collision in the shaft. The service was announced on January 13, 1931. *(Westinghouse News Service)*

Electric elevator successfully operated was installed in 1889 by Otis Brothers & Company for the Demarest Building, Fifth Avenue and 33d Street, New York City.

Electronic-signal-control elevator commercial installation was completed by the Otis Elevator Company during April 1948 at the Universal Pictures Building, New York City, after several years of experiment and development. Eight elevators, four local and four express, served the building's 22 stories. When a passenger touched a landing button, the call was registered by an electronic tube, the light of which indicated that the call was registered. The stopping of the cars in response to these calls, the canceling of the calls as they were answered, and the operation of the cars were all controlled by means of electronic circuits.

Elevator was a platform-type elevator which was made by Henry Waterman in 1850 in his shop on Duane Street, New York City. The elevator was installed in a building owned by Hecker and Brother, millers, 203 Cherry Street, New York City, who used it to hoist barrels upstairs in their mill.

Elevator in a hotel was installed in the six-story Fifth Avenue Hotel, New York City, which opened on August 23, 1859. The elevator operated on the principle of an Archimedean screw. It was viewed and inspected by Albert Edward, Prince of Wales, on October 11, 1860.

Elevator in an office building was installed in the original Equitable Life Assurance Society building, located on lower Broadway, New York City, in 1868.

Elevator patent for a vertical-geared hydraulic electric elevator, was No. 123,761, granted February 20, 1872, to Cyrus W. Baldwin of Boston, Mass. The elevator was installed in the Stephens Hotel, at 11th Street near Broadway, New York City.

The First

Elevator (suspended) was a steam hoist which was installed in 1866 in the St. James Hotel, New York City.

Elevator with an electric light was installed in the Blue Mountain House, Blue Mountain Lake, N.Y., on July 12, 1882. The hotel was operated by M. T. Merwin.

Elevator with completely enclosed car for conveying passengers to the upper floor of a building was installed in 1857 by Elisha Graves Otis, at the store of E. V. Haughwout, at the corner of Broadway and Broome Streets, New York City.

Elevator with safety devices to prevent falling of the car in case the ropes should break was made by Elisha Graves Otis in 1853 and exhibited by him the same year at the Crystal Palace Exposition in New York City. The first was delivered September 20, 1853, to Benjamin Newhouse, 275 Hudson Street, New York City.

Grain elevator operated by steam in the transfer and storage of grain for commercial purposes was designed by Robert Dunbar and made by Jewett & Root for Joseph Dart, Buffalo, N.Y., in 1842. The first cargo of corn was unloaded June 22, 1843, from the *South America. (Publications of the Buffalo Historical Society, 1879)*

ELKS. *See* Benevolent and Protective Order of Elks

ELOPEMENT

Airplane elopement. *See* Aviation: Aeronautical elopement.

EMANCIPATED SLAVE. *See* Slavery: Slave emancipated

EMANCIPATION ACT (state) was passed July 2, 1777, by Vermont, which embodied the following provision in its constitution: "No male person born in this country, or brought here from over sea, ought to be holden by law, to serve any person as a servant, slave or apprentice, after he arrives to the age of twenty-one years, nor female in like manner, after she arrives and to the age of eighteen years, unless they are bound by their own consent, after they arrive at such age, or bound by law, for the payment of debts, damages, fines, costs, or the like."

EMANCIPATION PROCLAMATION (preliminary) was made by President Abraham Lincoln on September 22, 1862. He issued a further proclamation on January 1, 1863, freeing the slaves in all states then in rebellion except in certain districts in Louisiana and Virginia occupied by federal troops. *(Henry Watson Wilbur—President Lincoln's Attitude Toward Slavery and Emancipation)*

The First

EMBALMING BOOK was the *History of Embalming, and of Preparations in Anatomy, Pathology and Natural History; including an account of a new process for embalming,* 264 pages, by Jean Nicolas Gannal, published in 1840 in Philadelphia, Pa., by Judah Dobson. It was a translation by Richard Harlan, M.D., with notes and additions of Gannal's book, published in French in 1838 in Paris.

EMBARGO ACT was passed December 22, 1807 (2 Stat. L. 451), by vote of 82 - 44. The act, "laying an embargo on all ships and vessels in the ports and harbors of the United States," required all American ships to refrain from international commerce. It was approved December 22, 1807, by President Thomas Jefferson. The act was repealed March 1, 1809. A later act substituted nonintercourse with Great Britain and France. *(Annals of Congress, Tenth Congress, First Session)*

Embargo act (Continental Congress) was the nonimportation act enacted October 14, 1774. It stated: "After the first day of December next, there be no importation into British America, from Great Britian or Ireland, of any goods, wares or merchandize whatsoever, or from any other place of any such goods, wares or merchandize," *(Worthington Chauncey Ford, ed.–Journals of the Continental Congress, 1774-1789)*

EMBOSSED BIBLE. *See* Bible: Bible for the blind in embossed form

EMBOSSED INLAID LINOLEUM. *See* Linoleum

EMBOSSING PRESS was a standing hand-lever press built in New York City in 1838 by Bernard Sheridan. An object placed between the descending die and the bed was given a raised surface when pressure was applied. The press sold for $200.

EMERGENCY COUNCIL (U.S.). *See* National emergency council (U.S.)

EMERGENCY HOUSING CORPORATION (U.S.) was authorized October 28, 1933, through the powers delegated to the administrator under the act of June 16, 1933, which created the Public Works Administration. The corporation was organized November 18, 1933, under Delaware laws and was composed of five officers and five directors. The president of the corporation was Harold Le Claire Ickes, administrator of Public Works. The Federal Housing Administration was created by the National Housing Act approved June 27, 1934 (48 Stat. L. 1246), "to encourage improvement in housing standards and conditions, to provide a system of mutual mortgage insurance." Its first administrator was James Andrew Moffett, appointed for the four-year term at an annual salary of $10,000.

The First

EMERGENCY RELIEF ADMINISTRATION. *See* Federal Emergency Relief Administration

EMMY. *See* Television Award

EMPLOYEES' TIME RECORDER. *See* Time recorder

EMPLOYER'S LIABILITY ACT (federal). *See under* Insurance

EMPLOYMENT SERVICE

Employment service (U.S.) as a distinct and separate unit of the Department of Labor was inaugurated under an order promulgated January 3, 1918, by the Secretary of Labor in pursuance of an act approved October 6, 1917 (40 Stat. L. 376). Previously the employment service had functioned under authority of an act to establish a Division of Information in the Bureau of Immigration (section 40, Immigration Act of February 20, 1907, 34 Stat. L. 909) and by the provisions of the organic act creating the Department of Labor (March 4, 1913, 37 Stat. L. 783).

Employment service (U.S.E.S.) was created June 6, 1933 (48 Stat. L. 113), "to provide for the establishment of a national employment system and for cooperation with the states in the promotion of such a system." The first director was William Frank Persons, who received $8,500 annually. Within ten weeks, 3,220 local offices opened, which registered 9 million people. It was, in turn under the Department of Labor, the Social Security Board, and the War Manpower Commission.

Municipal employment office was authorized by Seattle, Wash., on March 5, 1894, by a vote of 2,058 for and 523 against. John Lamb, the first labor commissioner, opened an office April 1, 1894, in a rough board shanty containing one small room. The following year larger quarters were obtained in the City Hall. *(Seventh Annual Report of Labor Commissioner, Seattle, Wash.)*

State employment service was created April 28, 1890, in Ohio by act of legislature amending section 308 of the Revised Statutes. Authorization was given to establish public employment offices in cities of the first and second class, Cincinnati, Cleveland, Columbus, Dayton, and Toledo. The first office was opened June 4, 1890, in Toledo, with Charles W. Murphy as superintendent. The Commissioner of Labor Statistics, under whom the system of five offices was set up during the year 1890, was John McBride. *(Ohio Bureau of Labor Statistics—Fourteenth Annual Report, 1890)*

ENCLAVE

Enclave was established at Fairhope, Baldwin County, Ala., by the Fairhope Industrial Association, Inc., composed of seven men who purchased 135 acres in the town for $771 on January 5, 1895, and an additional 200 acres for $250 at a later date. The association was succeeded by the Fair-

The First

ENCLAVE—*Continued*

hope Single Tax Corporation, incorporated August 9, 1904, which owned about 4,000 acres, three fourths of which was under lease. The association paid all taxes, and leaseholders paid only rent for the land.

Municipal enclave of economic ground rent was authorized by the Collierville Enclave Act passed by Collierville, Shelby County, Tenn. Governor Hill McAlister signed the bill April 21, 1933, and it took effect immediately. The bill was drawn up by Abe D. Waldauer, City Attorney for Collierville, and approved by Mayor J. T. Patrick. *(Chapter 523, Private Acts of the General Assembly of Tennessee for 1933)*

ENCLOSED CABIN AIRSHIP. *See* Aviation—Airship

ENCLOSED CAR ELEVATOR. *See* Elevator

ENCLOSURE FOR ANIMALS (pound). *See* Pound (enclosure for animals)

ENCYCLOPEDIA

Agricultural encyclopedia. *See* Agricultural encyclopedia

American encyclopedia was the *Encyclopedia Americana,* edited by Francis Lieber. The set consisted of 13 volumes, the first of which was issued in 1829 and the 13th in 1833. It was published in Philadelphia, Pa.

Braille encyclopedia for the blind was the 19-volume (ink print) *World Book Encyclopedia,* copyrighted in 1959 by the American Printing House for the Blind, Louisville, Ky. The braille edition, comprising 30,467 pages, consisted of 145 volumes, which were issued between 1961 and 1972. The study guide (volume 19) was not reproduced. Relevant captions of illustrations were edited into the text.

Encyclopedia printed in the United States was a reproduction of the third edition of the *Encyclopaedia Britannica,* originally published in Edinburgh between the years 1788 and 1797. The American reprint, however, was not called Encyclopaedia Britannica, but "Encyclopaedia; or a Dictionary of Arts, Sciences, and Miscellaneous Literature." It consisted of 18 volumes and was completed in 1798 by Thomas Dobson in Philadelphia, Pa. The first volume appeared in 1790 and contained 799 pages and 31 plates.

ENDLESS-CHAIN TRACTOR. *See under* Automobile tractor

ENDOWED LECTURE SERIES. *See* Lecture series (endowed)

ENDOWED SCHOOL. *See* School

ENDOWMENT, EDUCATIONAL. *See* Educational endowment

The First

ENDOWMENT, SOCIAL SERVICE. *See* Social service endowment

ENDURANCE RUN, MOTORCYCLE. *See* Motorcycle endurance run

ENERGY DEPARTMENT (U.S.). *See* Department of Energy (U.S.)

ENGINE

See also

Diesel engine	Locomotive
Electric motor	Motor
Fire engine	Steam engine
Gas engine	

Diesel engine built for commercial service was a two-cylinder 60 h.p. unit built in September 1898 in the plant of the St. Louis Iron and Marine Works, St. Louis, Mo. The engine, which drove a direct-current generator, was erected and operated in the Second Street plant of the Anheuser Busch, Inc., brewery and was the first diesel engine in the world to be placed in commercial service. Adolphus Busch bought Dr. Rudolf Diesel's American patent rights in 1897 for a sum of approximately $250,000. The next engines were built for the Diesel Motor Company of America, which was formed by Busch. These engines were built in the plant of the Hewes and Philips Iron Works, Newark, N.J., about 1900, and were of one size. They had an 11-by-20-inch cylinder which when running 200 r.p.m. was intended to develop 20 h.p. *(Lacey Harvey Morrison—Diesel Engines)*

Diesel engine in a submarine was the Vickers air-injection type, four cycle, four cylinder, nonair starting and nonreversing units. Two were placed in the Submarines E-1 (launched May 27, 1911, commissioned February 14, 1912) and the E-2 (launched June 15, 1911, commissioned February 14, 1912), built by the New London Ship and Engine Company of Groton, Conn. *(American Society of Naval Engineers Journal. Vol. 37. August 1925)*

Internal-combustion engine was invented by Captain Samuel Morey of Orford, N.H., who received a patent April 1, 1826, "on a gas or vapor engine." His engine had two cylinders, 180-degree cranks, poppet valves, a carburetor, an electric spark, and a water cooling device. He employed the vapor of spirits of turpentine and common air. A small tin dish contained the spirits, and the only heat he used was from a common table lamp. By means of a crank and flywheel, a rotary movement was obtained, as in the steam engine. *(Katherine Goodwin and Charles Edgar Duryea—Captain Samuel Morey)*

Multiengine hydroplane. *See* Aviation—Airplane: Hydroplane with a multiengine

Outboard motor (commercially successful) was developed in Milwaukee, Wis., in 1909 by Ole Evinrude. It was a single cylinder two-port two cycle battery-ignited engine, developing 1½ h.p.

The First

at about 1,000 r.p.m. It weighed 46 pounds. *(Journal of the Society of Automotive Engineers. January 1931)*

Outboard twin-cylinder motor (light) was developed in Milwaukee, Wis., in 1921 by Ole Evinrude. This was the two-port two-cycle Elto, which developed 2½ h.p. at 1,400 r.p.m. It weighed 47 pounds.

ENGINEER, ARMY. *See* Army officer: Chief engineer

ENGINEER, NAVY. *See* Naval officer: Naval officer to become an engineer

ENGINEER, WOMAN. *See* Woman: Woman automotive engineer

ENGINEER CORPS. *See* Army: Army Engineering Department; Army: Engineer Corps

ENGINEERING BOOK was a translation of Louis André de la Mamie de Clairac's *L'Ingénieur de Campagne; or Field Engineer.* It contained 256 pages and a variety of copperplates. It was translated by Major Lewis Nicola and was published in 1776 by R[obert] Aitken, Philadelphia, Pa.

ENGINEERING COLLEGE
Aeronautical engineering. *See under* Aviation —School

Civil engineering course in a college was given in 1819 at Norwich University, now located in Northfield, Vt. The university was founded August 6, 1819, as the American Literary, Scientific and Military Academy by Captain Alden Partridge in Norwich, Vt. Courses in civil engineering included the construction of roads, canals, locks, and bridges, and architecture. The name was changed November 6, 1834, to Norwich University. In March 1866 the buildings were destroyed by fire and the college was moved to Northfield, Vt.

Electrical engineering course in a college was established September 21, 1883, by the College of Engineering, Cornell University, Ithaca, N.Y. A four-year course was given, leading to the degree of Bachelor of Science. Instruction was given in the theory of electricity; the construction and testing of telegraph lines, cables, and instruments; dynamo machines; civil and mechanical engineering, etc. Dr. Andrew White pledged his own resources for the school.

Engineering college was the Rensselaer School, Troy, N.Y., founded November 5, 1824, and opened January 3, 1825. It was incorporated March 21, 1826. The first class of ten students graduated April 26, 1826, with the degree of A.B. The first C.E. degree was awarded in October 1835. Amos Eaton was senior professor and the first director. He served from November 1824 to May 10, 1842. The name of the school was changed to Rensselaer Institute on April 26, 1832, and to Rensselaer Polytechnic Institute on April 8, 1861.

The First

ENGINEERING LABORATORY, MECHANICAL. *See* Mechanical engineering laboratory

ENGINEERING SOCIETY
Civil engineering national society was the American Society of Civil Engineers, founded as the American Society of Civil Engineers and Architects, November 5, 1852, in New York City for "the advancement of the sciences of engineering and architecture in their several branches, the professional improvement of its members, the encouragement of intercourse between men of practical science, and the establishment of a central point of reference and union for its members." The name of the society was shortened later. The first president was James Laurie and the first secretary was Robert Bennett Gorsuch.

Engineering society of importance was the Boston Society of Civil Engineers, organized at an informal meeting April 26, 1848, at the United States Hotel, Boston, Mass. The first regular meeting was held July 3, 1848. The society was incorporated April 24, 1851, for the purpose of "promoting science and instruction in the department of civil engineering." The first officers were James Fowle Baldwin, president; George Dexter Minot, vice president; John Harrison Blake, secretary; and William Pearce Parrott, treasurer. Attempts had been made to form engineering societies in 1836 by engineers of the Cincinnati & Charleston Railroad, in 1839 by engineers in Baltimore, Md., and in 1841 in Albany, N.Y., but these sporadic attempts were not successful.

Mechanical engineering national society was the American Society of Mechanical Engineers, founded February 16, 1880, by 40 men from 8 states who met at the office of the *American Machinist,* New York City, and elected Alexander Lyman Holley chairman. An organization meeting was held April 7, 1880, at the Assembly Hall of Stevens Institute of Technology, Hoboken, N.J. The first president was Robert Henry Thurston. The first annual meeting was held November 4–5, 1880, in New York City. *(William Frederick Durand—Robert Henry Thurston, Biography)*

Woman elected to the American Society of Civil Engineers was Nora Stanton Blatch, elected as a Junior on March 6, 1906. The grade of Junior was a temporary one, and the first woman elected as an Associate Member (one of the two grades of corporate membership) was Elsie Eaves, elected on March 14, 1927.

ENGLISH ACTOR OF NOTE. *See* Actor

ENGLISH BIBLE. *See* Bible

ENGLISH CHANNEL SWIMMER, AMERICAN WOMAN. *See* Woman: American woman to swim the English Channel

ENGLISH GRAMMAR. *See* Grammar

ENGLISH GRAND OPERA. *See* Opera: Grand opera sung in English

ENGLISH NOVEL COURSE. *See under* Novel course

ENGLISH SETTLEMENT. *See under* Colonist

ENGLISH STEAM PACKET TO ARRIVE IN THE UNITED STATES. *See* Ship: Packet line

ENGRAVER of record to practice his art in the American colonies was Peter Pelham. In 1727 he produced the first mezzotint engraving, a 13⅝ × 9⅞-inch portrait of Cotton Mather. *(David McNeely Stauffer—American Engravers upon Copper and Steel)*

ENGRAVING

Engraving was a woodcut made about April 22, 1669, by John Foster, of the Reverend Richard Mather prior to his death. Foster cut away from the surface of a flat wooden block those parts which were to appear white in the print, leaving the actual design in raised outline on the block. The print was five by six inches. *(Carl W. Drepperd—Early American Prints)*

Engraving of any artistic merit was a line-engraving copperplate portrait of Increase Mather, made in 1701 by Thomas Emmes, which was used as a frontispiece to a sermon, "The Blessed Hope," published in Boston, Mass., in 1701 by Timothy Green for Nicholas Boone. *(Arthur Mayger Hind—History of Engraving and Etching)*

Engraving to achieve popularity was *The Bloody Massacre Perpetrated in King Street, Boston, on March 5, 1770*, which was engraved, printed, and sold by Paul Revere.

Halftone engraving was made by Stephen Henry Horgan and appeared in the New York *Daily Graphic*, March 4, 1880. It depicted a "Scene in Shantytown, N.Y." A screen gradated from transparency to opacity was the basis of the invention. *(Inland Printer. March-April 1924)*

Historical print engraved in America was *A Prospective Plan of the Battle Fought Near Lake George*, which presented a bird's-eye view of the march of troops shown at the left, the camp and battle at the right, and Forts William Henry and Edward in the upper right-hand corner. It was an engraving in line, colored by hand, by Thomas Johnston after Samuel Blodget, and printed by Richard Draper, in Boston, Mass., in 1755.

Mezzotint engraving of an American maritime print was *The Boston Lighthouse* engraved in 1729 by William Burgis "To the Merchants of Boston, this View of the Light House is most humbly presented by their Humble Serv't Wm. Burgis."

Pamphlet produced from a steel plate engraving was [Jacob] Perkins' and [Gideon] Fairman's *Running Hand Stereographic Copies*, published in

1815 by Charles Whipple, Newburyport, Mass. It contains a title page and seven pages of text, 3-3/16 by 7-11/16 inches, which contain samples of handwriting. The plate measured 13 by 15-3/4 inches.

Wood engraving made with an engraving tool, the burin, making use of the intaglio "white line," was a tobacco stamp made by Alexander Anderson in June 1793 in New York City. The following year, he made a wood engraving for a book, *The Looking-Glass for the Mind; or Intellectual Mirror* by William Durell, translated from Arnaud Berquin's *L'Ami des Enfants*. *(Everet Augustus Duyckinck—A Brief Catalogue of Books Illustrated with Engravings by Dr. Alexander Anderson with a Biographical Sketch of the Artist)*

ENGRAVING AND PRINTING BUREAU (U.S.)

Bureau of Engraving and Printing (U.S.) began operations August 28, 1862. Signatures were to be engraved in facsimile and the seal of the treasury imprinted on the notes after they had been delivered to the engravers. Certain stamps, notes, and bills were printed by individuals under contract. The act of February 25, 1862 (12 Stat. L. 346) authorized the Bureau. *(Laurence Frederick Schmeckebier—The Bureau of Engraving and Printing)*

Souvenir card of the Bureau of Engraving and Printing was issued on March 13, 1954, for the Postage Stamp Design Exhibition, at the National Philatelic Museum, in Philadelphia, Pa. The card was inscribed "souvenir sheet designed, engraved and printed by members, Bureau, Engraving and Printing. Reissued by popular request." It depicted 4 monochrome views of Washington, D.C. A souvenir sheet was issued in 1938 by the Post Office Department.

ENTOMOLOGIST

Federal entomologist was Townend Glover, commissioned June 14, 1854. He was the "expert for collecting statistics and other information on seeds, fruits and insects of the United States." His first report, which appeared under the imprint of the Patent Office, was *Insects Injurious and Beneficial to Vegetation* printed in 1854. *(Charles Richards Dodge—The Life and Entomological Work of the Late Townend Glover)*

State entomologist (not official, but so designated) to be appointed was Asa Fitch. The New York State Legislature on April 15, 1854, made an appropriation of $1,000 to pay for an examination and description of the insects of New York State, particularly those injurious to vegetation. The New York State Agricultural Society, through its executive committee, meeting at the Astor House, New York City, on May 4, 1854, appointed Asa Fitch to do this work and instructed him at that time to make his first report relative to injurious insects affecting fruits. The report appeared in the Agricultural Society Report for 1855. *(Journal of*

The First

the New York State Agricultural Society. 1854–1855)

ENTOMOLOGY BOOK (comprehensive) was Thomas Say's *American Entomology, or Descriptions of the Insects of North America,* three volumes, published in Philadelphia, Pa., by Samuel Augustus Mitchell. The first volume was published in 1824, the second in 1825, and the third in 1828. Each contained 18 plates. In 1817 a portion of Volume I, containing 6 plates and 38 pages, was published.

ENTOMOLOGY MAGAZINE devoted to applied entomology was the *Practical Entomologist,* the first issue of which was published in Philadelphia, Pa., in October 1865 by the Entomological Society of Philadelphia. The original editors were Ezra Townsend Cresson, Augustus Radcliffe Grote, and James W. McAllister. The magazine ceased publication after two years. The Entomological Society was founded in 1859 and incorporated in 1862. It changed its name to the American Entomological Society on February 23, 1867.

ENTOMOLOGY PROFESSOR was Hermann August Hagen, who served at Harvard University, Cambridge, Mass., from 1870 to 1893.

ENVELOPE

Airmail letter sheet depicted an airplane in blue on white stock and was placed on sale January 12, 1929. The stamped sheet, issued by the Post Office Department, was designed to be folded and serve as an envelope. It cost 5 cents.

Commemorative envelope issued in 2 sizes by the U.S. Post Office Department was the 8-cent rose red "Salute to Bowling," designed by George Giusti. Depicting a bowling ball and pin, it was issued August 21, 1971, at Milwaukee, Wis., in honor of the Seventh World Tournament of the International Bowling Federation. The sizes were No. 6¾, 3⅝″ x 6½″; and No. 10, 4⅛″ x 9½.″

Envelope folding and gumming machine was patented on February 8, 1898, by John Ames Sherman of Worcester, Mass., who received patent No. 598,716 on a "mechanism for folding and sealing envelopes." It reduced the cost of a completely gummed envelope ready for market from 60 cents to 8 cents per 1,000.

Envelope folding machine that proved practical commercially was patented on January 21, 1853, No. 9812, by Dr. Russell L. Hawes of Worcester, Mass. It was not self-gumming, but nevertheless it enabled three girls to produce the finished product at the rate of about 25,000 envelopes in ten hours. *(U. S. Envelope Co.—An Early History of the Envelope)*

Envelope machine patent was No. 6,055, granted on January 23, 1849, to Jesse K. Park and Cornelius S. Watson of New York City on "an improvement in machines for making envelopes." Other patents on improved machines were grant-

The First

ed shortly thereafter, with the result that this patent had but little value.

Envelope with an outlook or window was patented by Americus F. Callahan of Chicago, Ill., who obtained patent No. 701,839 on June 10, 1902. It was first manufactured in July 1902 by the U.S. Envelope Company of Springfield, Mass., to which company the patent was leased.

Liberty Bell on an envelope was on the 2-cent Sesquicentennial Exposition envelope, which was issued in carmine on white July 27, 1926, at Philadelphia, Pa.

Stamped envelope (U.S.) *See under* Postage stamp

ENVELOPE MANUFACTURER was a Mr. Pierson of New York City, who manufactured envelopes in a little store on Fulton Street in 1839. Prior to the manufacture of envelopes, letters were folded and the name and address written on the blank side.

EPIDEMIC

Cholera epidemic occurred in 1832. Individual cases are said to have developed in several cities, but the real force of the epidemic was manifested in the larger cities like New York, Boston, and Philadelphia. The first case in New York City appeared June 28, 1832, and from July 5, 1832, to August 29, 1832, 5,835 cases developed, of which 2,251 resulted in death. On July 21, 1832, New York City reported 311 cases and 100 deaths. *(Edward Warren—Sketch of the Progress of the Malignant or Epidemic Cholera)*

Influenza epidemic occurred in 1733 and was most serious in Philadelphia and New York City. About three fourths of the entire population was affected. *(James Thacher—American Medical Biography. 1828)*

Medical record of an epidemic was Benjamin Rush's *An Account of the Bilious Remitting Yellow Fever, as It Appeared in the city of Philadelphia, in the year 1793.* The book, which had 363 pages, was printed in 1794 by Thomas Dobson in Philadelphia, Pa. About 4,000 people died between August and November 1793.

Poliomyelitis epidemic occurred in Vermont, when 123 cases appeared in Rutland and Wallingford between June 17, 1894, and September 1, 1894. *(New York Medical Record. Dec. 1, 1894)*

Smallpox epidemic of importance occurred in 1616–1617 and almost swept away the New England Indians from the Penobscot to Narragansett Bay. It reduced the fighting force from 3,000 to just 50 men. Smallpox broke out about May 26, 1721, principally affecting Boston, Mass., and the larger cities. The death rate varied from 12 percent to 24 percent of the population. *(Reginald Heber Fitz—Zabdiel Boylston, Inoculator and the Epidemic of Small Pox in Boston in 1721)*

The First

EPIDEMIOLOGIST was Noah Webster. In 1796 he published *A Collection of Papers on the Subject of Bilious Fevers, Prevalent in the United States for a Few Years Past,* which was printed in New York City by Hopkins, Webb & Co., and in 1799 a two-volume work, *A Brief History of Epidemics and Pestilential Diseases; with the Principal Phenomena of the Physical World, which Precede and Accompany Them, and Observations Deduced from the Facts Stated,* which was published by Hudson and Goodwin, Hartford, Conn.

EPISCOPAL CATECHISM. *See* Protestant Episcopal catechism

EPISCOPAL CATHEDRAL. *See* Cathedral

EPISCOPAL CHURCH. *See* Church of England; Protestant Episcopal Church

EQUAL PAY ACT. *See under* Labor legislation

EQUAL RIGHTS PARTY was formed in San Francisco, Calif., September 20, 1884, at a convention of the Woman's Rights Party of Female Suffragettes. Belva Ann Bennett Lockwood of the District of Columbia was nominated as the presidential candidate and Marietta Lizzie Bell Stow of California as the vice presidential candidate. On May 10, 1872, 500 delegates from 26 states and 4 territories had seceded from the National Woman Suffrage Association convention in New York City and met at Apollo Hall, where they nominated Victoria Claflin Woodhull of New York for President and Frederick Douglass for Vice President under the People's Party ticket (Equal Rights Party).

EQUESTRIAN EXHIBITION in America was given by John Sharp in Boston, Mass., in 1771. He rode 3 horses, standing with one foot upon each of the outside horses; 2 horses, at full speed, standing upon the tops of the saddles with one foot upon each. He gave other exhibitions in Salem, Mass., and other cities. A Mr. Pool was the first rider to introduce a clown to the American public. He advertised in the *Pennsylvania Packet* on August 15, 1785, that he would mount three horses and while standing on the saddles would leap a hurdle at full speed.

EQUESTRIAN STATUE, BRONZE. *See* Monument: Bronze equestrian statue

ERASER ATTACHED TO A PENCIL. *See* Pencil: Pencil with an attached eraser

ESCALATOR
Escalator was manufactured by the Otis Elevator Company of New York City in 1900 and placed on exhibit at the Paris Exposition the same year. It was returned to the United States and installed in 1901 in the Eighth Street building of Gimbel Brothers, Philadelphia, Pa. The trademark Escalator was registered May 29, 1900, and was renewed by the Otis Elevator Company in 1930.

The First

Escalator patent was obtained by Nathan Ames of Saugus, Mass., who obtained patent No. 25,076 on August 9, 1859, on an improvement in revolving stairs. Steps or stairs were arranged upon an inclined endless belt or chain.

ESKIMO CHICKEN (ptarmigan). *See* Birds: Ptarmigan (Eskimo chicken)

ESKIMO PIE, an ice cream confection containing a normally liquid material frozen to a substantially hard state and encased in a chocolate covering to maintain its original form during handling, was invented by Christian K. Nelson of Onawa, Iowa, who obtained patent No. 1,404,539 on January 24, 1922. Subsequent patents which have also been issued are controlled by the Eskimo Pie Corporation of New York City.

ESPERANTO
Esperanto, a new artificial universal language was proposed by Dr. Lazarus Ludwig Zamenhof, a Russian physician, in 1887. An attempt was made to introduce it into the United States but it received little favor.

Talking picture in Esperanto. *See under* Motion picture

ESPERANTO CLUB
Esperanto club was the Esperanto Association organized February 16, 1905, at Boston, Mass. John Fogg Twombly was the first secretary.

Esperanto club (national organization) was the Esperanto Association of North America, organized September 7, 1908, at Chautauqua Lake, N.Y. George Brinton McClellan Harvey was the first president.

Esperanto Congress in the United States was the Sixth International Congress of Esperantists held August 14–20, 1910, in Washington, D.C. It was attended by about 300 delegates from 35 nations.

ESPERANTO COURSE carrying college credit was offered by Clark University, Worcester, Mass., on September 16, 1908. Dr. Robert Mowry Bell taught the course, which offered "a brief outline of the grammar, and some practice in reading the new universal language."

ESPERANTO MAGAZINE was *L'Amerika Esperantisto,* "a monthly journal of Esperanto, the international language," published October 1907 at Oklahoma City, Okla. It contained 16 pages and a cover. Subscription was $1 a year.

ETCHER of skill was William Dunlap, whose success in 1830 inspired others to practice the art of etching. *(William Dunlap—History of the Rise and Progress of the Arts of Design in the United States)*

ETHER FOR CHILDBIRTH. *See under* Anesthesia

The First

ETHICAL CULTURE SOCIETY was the New York Society for Ethical Culture, founded in New York City in May 1876 by Dr. Felix Adler. Additional groups were formed and in 1886 the American Ethical Union was organized. *(Horace James Bridges—Aspects of Ethical Religion, Essays in Honor of Felix Adler on the Fiftieth Anniversary of His Founding of the Ethical Movement, 1876, by His Colleagues)*

ETHYL GASOLINE. *See* Gasoline

EUCHARISTIC CONGRESS, INTERNATIONAL. *See* International Eucharistic Congress

EUTHANASIA
"Right to Die" law was the Natural Death Act of California, enacted September 30, 1976, Chapter 1,439, to withhold life-sustaining procedures in terminal conditions and to permit the natural process of dying.

EUTHANASIA SOCIETY was the National Society for the Legalization of Euthanasia, formed January 14, 1938, in New York City with Reverend Charles Francis Potter as president, Dr. Harold Hays, secretary, and Charles Edward Nixdorff, treasurer. The society was incorporated as the Euthanasia Society of America on November 30, 1938.

EVANGELICAL AND REFORMED CHURCH was organized June 26, 1934, in Cleveland, Ohio, by the merging of the Reformed Church in the United States, organized by John Philip Boehm, October 15, 1725, in Falkner Swamp, Montgomery County, Pa., and the Evangelical Synod of North America, organized October 15, 1840, in Mehlville, St. Louis County, Mo. The first president of the new group was Dr. George Warren Richards, president of the Theological Seminary of the Reformed Church, Lancaster, Pa.

EVANGELICAL ASSOCIATION COUNCIL met at the house of John Walter, Bucks County, Pa., November 3, 1803, to found a separate ecclesiastical organization. The 14 representatives present ordained Jacob Albright.

EVANGELICAL CHURCH was founded in 1800 by Jacob Albright. The first annual conference was held in Lebanon County, Pa., in November 1807. Albright was elected bishop. *(Ammon Stapleton—Flashlights on Evangelical History)*

EVANGELICAL CHURCH BUILDING was the Evangelical Church erected in 1816 in New Berlin, Pa. It was dedicated March 2, 1817. The Reverend John Dreisbach preached the dedicatory sermon. The church was 34 by 38 feet.

EVANGELICAL CHURCH GENERAL CONFERENCE convened on the property of Abraham Eyer, at the house of Martin Dreisbach, in Buffalo Valley, Union County, Pa., October 14–17, 1816, at which time the denomination took the name

The First

Evangelical Association. Twelve delegates attended.

EVANGELICAL CONFERENCE was held at the house of Samuel Becker, November 15, 1807, in Mühlbach, Dauphin County (now Kleinfeltersville, Lebanon County), Pa. It was attended by all the officers of the church, 5 itinerant ministers, 3 local preachers, and 20 class leaders and exhorters. Jacob Albright was elected bishop and George Miller an elder.

EVANGELICAL UNITED BRETHREN CHURCH was formed November 16, 1946, in Johnstown, Pa., by approximately 500 delegates representing 4,832 churches, who united the Church of the United Brethren in Christ and the Evangelical Church. There were 9 active bishops. Bishop Arthur Raymond Clippinger of Dayton, Ohio, was the senior bishop.

EVAPORATED MILK. *See* Milk

EVENING SCHOOL. *See* School

EVOLUTION law (state), prohibiting the teaching of the theory of evolution, was proposed by John Washington Butler, passed by the Tennessee legislature, and signed March 23, 1925, by Governor Austin Peay. It provided that "it shall be unlawful for any teacher in any of the universities, normal and all other public schools of the state which are supported in whole or in part by the public school funds of the state to teach any theory that denies the story of the Divine creation of man as taught in the Bible, and to teach instead that man has descended from a lower order of animals." The first conviction under the act was that of John Thomas Scopes, who appealed the decision of the court. The Attorney General entered a *nolle prosse,* which ended the proceedings. *(John Thomas Scopes vs. State of Tennessee, 154, Tenn. 105, 1926)*

EXCESS PROFITS TAX. *See* Tax

EXCHANGE. *See* Brokerage

EXCHANGE AND SECURITIES COMMISSION. *See* Securities and Exchange Commission (U.S.)

EXCISE TAX. *See* Tax

EXCLUSION LAW. *See* Army exclusion law

EXECUTION
See also Capital punishment

Army execution. *See* Army execution

Electrocution experiment was performed in Philadelphia, Pa., by Benjamin Franklin, who described his findings in 1773 in a letter to Barbeau Dubourg and Thomas Francois Dalibard. Current from six Leyden jars was used to electrocute chickens, a ten-pound turkey, and a lamb.

Electrocution of a human being was that of William Kemmler, alias John Hart, on August 6, 1890, at Auburn Prison, Auburn, N.Y. The electric chair

The First

EXECUTION—*Continued*

used was invented by Dr. Alphonse David Rockwell. An autopsy was performed three hours after the execution under the direction of Dr. Carlos Frederick MacDonald. The execution was in accordance with the law governing first-degree murder. Kemmler had been convicted of the murder of Matilda Ziegler, a crime committed on March 29, 1889. *(Report of Carlos F. MacDonald, M.D. on the Execution by Electricity of William Kemmler, Alias John Hart)*

Execution (federal) for slave trading took place at the Tombs prison, New York City, on February 21, 1862, when Nathaniel Gordon, a native of Portland, Me., was hanged. He was tried and convicted of piracy under the law of May 15, 1820, which defined slave trading as piracy. Gordon was the captain of the *Erie,* a ship transporting 890 blacks, 600 of whom were boys and girls, to a slave market. The U.S. *Mohican* stopped his ship about 50 miles off the African coast, released the captives in Liberia, and brought Gordon's ship to New York City, where his trial was held.

Execution (federal) for the killing of a Federal Bureau of Investigation agent took place at Sing Sing Prison, Ossining, N.Y., August 12, 1954, when Gerhard Puff was electrocuted. He was convicted of the killing of FBI agent Joseph Brock in a gun battle in New York City on July 26, 1952. Puff was wanted for participating in the November 23, 1951, robbery of $62,650 from the Johnson County National Bank and Trust Company of Prairie Village, Kan. He was confined 15 months in the death house and his execution was postponed five times pending various appeals.

Execution for treason. *See* Treason: Citizen of the United States to be tried for treason, convicted, and hanged

Execution for treason in peacetime. *See under* Treason

Execution in America was that of John Billington, one of the signers of the Pilgrims' compact, who was hanged in Plymouth, Mass., September 30, 1630. He was "arraigned, and both by grand and petie jurie found guilty of willful murder, by plaine and notorious evidence, and was for the same accordingly executed. This, as it was ye first execution amongst them, so was it a matter of great sadness unto them. He way-laid a young man, one John Newcomin (about a former quarele), and shote him with a gune, whereof he dyed." *(Joseph Dillaway Sawyer—History of Pilgrims and Puritans)*

Execution of a woman by electrocution took place at Sing Sing Prison, Ossining, N.Y., March 20, 1899, when Martha M. Place of Brooklyn, N.Y., was electrocuted for the murder, on February 7, 1898, in Brooklyn, N.Y., of her stepdaughter Ida.

The First

Execution of civilians. *See* Treaty: Treaty violation

Lethal-gas execution was that of a Chinese, Gee Jon, on February 8, 1924, in Carson City, Nev. Gee Jon was convicted of killing a rival tong man. Lethal gas as a means of execution had been adopted by Nevada on March 28, 1921.

Witchcraft execution. *See* Witchcraft execution

EXECUTIVE COMMERCIAL POLICY COMMITTEE. *See* Commercial policy executive committee

EXECUTIVE ORDER, PRESIDENTIAL. *See* Presidential executive order

EXHIBITION. *See* Fair

EXPEDITION
See also Discovery

Arctic expedition was made by Elisha Kent Kane and crew, who left New York City, May 31, 1853, in the *Advance.* They arrived at Cape Constitution, where they remained for 21 months, being unable to free the ship, which had become frozen in the ice pack. As disease broke out on board, the crew made a 1,000-mile trek to the nearest Eskimo village. *(William Elder—Biography of Elisha Kent Kane)*

Arctic expedition to seek the Northwest Passage for the £20,000 reward offered by Parliament for proofs of its existence, sailed March 1753 from Philadelphia, Pa. Captain Charles Swaine made a voyage in the *Argo,* a 60-ton schooner. He encountered ice off Cape Farewell, and entered Hudson Strait in the latter part of June 1753. He returned in November 1753. He made a second voyage the following year. *(Justin Winsor—A Narrative and Critical History of America)*

Astronomy expedition. *See* Astronomy expedition

Botanic scientific expedition. *See* Botanic scientific expedition

Expedition of Englishmen to cross the Alleghe ny Mountains began August 27, 1650, from For Henry, at the falls of the Appomattox River, Va. and returned September 4, 1650. The party con sisted of Captain Abraham Wood and his servan Henry Newcombe; Edward Bland, merchant, and his servant Robert Farmer; Elias Pennant and Sackford Brewster; and two guides, Oyeocker, a Nottaway werowance (chief), and Pyancha, a Appamattuck war captain. *(Clarence Walworth Alvord and Lee Bidgood—First Explorations of the Trans-Allegheny Region by the Virginians)*

Expedition across the continent to the Pacifi coast was undertaken by Captains Meriwethe Lewis and William Clark, who left St. Louis, Mo. May 14, 1804, reached the mouth of the Columbia River November 8, 1805, and returned to St. Loui on September 23, 1806. The expedition consisted of 9 Kentucky men, 14 Army men, 2 French voya

The First

geurs, and a black servant. *(Elliot Coues—History of the Expedition Under the Command of Lewis and Clark)*

Exploration of the Grand Canyon of the Colorado by a white man was made by Major John Wesley Powell, who left Green River City, above the head of the Colorado proper, on May 24, 1869, and emerged from the lower end of the Grand Canyon, August 29, 1869, with five of the nine men who had started with him. The following year he was appointed chief of the U.S. Topographical and Geological Survey of the Colorado River of the West. (The discovery of the Grand Canyon was reported by Spanish explorers in 1540, and described by the Sitgreaves expedition in 1851, and in 1858 by the War Department, which explored navigable waters from the south, but which stopped at the foot of the canyon. *(John Wesley Powell—First Through The Grand Canyon)*

Naval expedition (colonial). *See under* Navy

Polar expedition of which a woman was a member was the Peary Expedition. Josephine Peary, wife of the North Polar explorer Robert Edwin Peary, sailed with her husband June 6, 1891, in the *Kite.* This expedition did not reach the Pole. The expedition which left on the *Roosevelt,* July 6, 1908, located the North Pole on April 6, 1909, but the discovery was not announced until September 6, 1909. Both expeditions started from New York City. *(Josephine Diebitsch Peary—My Arctic Journal: A Year Among Ice Fields and Eskimos)*

Scientific expedition was outfitted by the Commonwealth of Massachusetts in 1761. John Winthrop, a physicist, went to Newfoundland in a vessel in the Provincial Service. His expenses were defrayed by the colonial government, and he observed for the second time the transit of Mercury. *(John Winthrop—Two Letters on the Parallax and Distance of the Sun)*

Scientific expedition fitted out by the United States Government was authorized by Congress May 14, 1836 (5 Stat. L. 29). An appropriation of $150,000 was made for a surveying and exploring expedition to the Pacific Ocean and the South Sea. Instructions were received August 11, 1838. The expedition left Hampton Roads, Va., August 18, 1838, with Lieutenant Charles Wilkes in command, to explore the South Seas, and returned to New York City June 10, 1842. The explorers saw the Antarctic continent on January 16, 1840. *(Charles Wilkes—Narrative of the U.S. Exploring Expedition)*

EXPEDITIONARY FORCE (U.S.) *See* American Expeditionary Force

EXPERIMENT STATION, AGRICULTURAL. *See* Agricultural experiment station

The First

EXPERT INFANTRYMAN'S BADGE. *See* Medal

EXPLOSION, ATOMIC BOMB. *See under* Atomic bomb

EXPLOSION TELECAST. *See* Television—Telecast: Atomic explosion telecast

EXPORT
See also under specific subjects, e.g., Animals, Cotton, Furs, Meat

Export report by the federal government covered the fiscal year ending September 30, 1791. The exports for the year amounted to $19,012,041, of which $18,500,000 was for domestic merchandise and $512,041 for foreign goods. The imports for the same period amounted to $29,200,000, an excess of imports over exports of $10,187,959.

Exports from the United States to exceed the imports were for the fiscal year ending September 30, 1811, and amounted to an excess of $7,916,832 over imports. The exports of domestic merchandise were $45,294,042, and for foreign merchandise $16,022,790, making a grand total of exports of $61,316,832 whereas the imports amounted to $53,400,000.

EXPORT-IMPORT BANK. *See* Bank

EXPOSITION. *See under* specific type of exposition, e.g., Automobile show; Aviation—Expositions and Meets; Dog show; Fair

EXPOSURE METER. *See* Photography: Camera exposure meter

EXPRESS SERVICE was organized February 23, 1839, by William Frederick Harnden of Boston, Mass., who arranged for delivery service between Boston and New York. The service was advertised to begin on March 4, 1839. The first shipment was a few suitcases. Shipments were made via the Boston and Providence Railway and Long Island Sound Steamboat. *(Alexander Lovett Stimson—History of Express Companies and the Origin of American Railroads)*

EXTENSION COURSE. *See under* College

EXTENSION SUMMER MEETING *See* College: University extension summer meeting

EXTENSION TRAINING WORK, AGRICULTURAL. *See* Agricultural appropriation

EXTINGUISHER. *See* Fire extinguisher

EXTRADITION
Extradition was established by the New England Confederation of 1643, which provided for the extradition of criminals between the provinces of Massachusetts, Connecticut, Plymouth, and New Haven.

Extradition treaty with a foreign country was the Treaty of Amity, Commerce and Navigation (8 Stat. L. 116), popularly known as the Jay Treaty, with Great Britain, signed in London, England,

The First

EXTRADITION—*Continued*
November 19, 1794. Article XXVII provided for the apprehension and delivery of persons charged with certain crimes. The signatory for the United States was John Jay, and for Great Britain, William Wyndham Grenville, Baron Grenville of Wotton, one of His Majesty's Privy Council and His Majesty's Principal Secretary of State for Foreign Affairs. The treaty was ratified by the Senate on June 24, 1795, and signed by the President on October 28, 1795. The ratification was proclaimed February 29, 1796. *(Treaties and Other International Acts of the United States of America, Document 16)*

EYE
Artificial eyes were manufactured by Pierre Gougelman in 1851 at Van Dam Street, New York City, from glass imported from France. The business is conducted by his descendants under the name of Mager & Gougelman, Inc. It was originally believed that artificial eyes offered their wearers new vision.

Eye bank was opened May 9, 1944, through the efforts of Dr. Richard Townley Paton of Manhattan Eye, Ear and Throat Hospital and Dr. John McLean of New York Hospital. These hospitals cooperated to establish the joint project at New York Hospital, New York City. Nineteen other hospitals in the metropolitan area offered cooperation in obtaining and sending eyes to the bank.

Eye conservation class for the education of schoolchildren with seriously defective vision opened April 3, 1913, at the Thornton Street School, Boston, Mass. Helen L. Smith was the teacher.

Identification system, based upon the pattern formed by the veins and arteries of the retina of the human eye and the relation of the four veins—the superior temporal, the inferior temporal, the superior nasal, and the inferior nasal—with their various branches, was devised by Dr. Isidore Goldstein, ophthalmic surgeon of Mount Sinai Hospital, New York City, in collaboration with Dr. Carleton Simon, former Deputy Police Commissioner of New York. The system was presented before the annual convention of the International Association of Chiefs of Police, July 7, 1935, in Atlantic City, N.J.

EYE INFIRMARY. *See* Hospital

EYEGLASS BIFOCALS. *See* Lens: Bifocal contact lens; Lens: Eyeglass bifocals

---

F

FACSIMILE BROADCAST. *See* Radio facsimile transmission: Facsimile high-speed transmission

The First

FACSIMILE TRANSMISSION. *See* Radio facsimile transmission

FACTORY
Air-conditioned factory to be built was the Gray Manufacturing Company's Gastonia, N.C., plant, erected in 1905 with an air-conditioning system manufactured by Stuart W. Cramer of Charlotte, N.C. This equipment drew in fresh air from out-of-doors, filtered and washed it, heated or cooled it, corrected any variation in humidity, and completely changed the air in the factory about five times an hour.

Air-conditioned factory with temperature and humidity control was the Brooklyn, N.Y., plant of the Sackett-Wilhelms Lithographing and Publishing Company, which in 1902 installed a 30-ton fan-cooled dehumidifying unit designed by Willis Haviland Carrier. Its primary purpose was to check the expansion and contraction of paper caused by varying weather conditions. *(Margaret Ingels—Father of Air Conditioning, Willis Haviland Carrier)*

Factories operated by the United States Government in peacetime were a jersey cloth mill formerly operated by the Famb Knitting Company and a fairly large hall called Forester's Hall at Millville, Mass., in which the Federal Emergency Relief Administration of Massachusetts established sewing and stock rooms. The project was started June 4, 1934, by authority of Joseph P. Carney, Emergency Relief Administrator of Massachusetts, who detailed Thomas E. Wye as factory supervisor to organize and start the project. The products were not sold but were distributed to different welfare divisions of the cities and towns in Massachusetts.

Factory-built building. *See* Building: Building built inside a factory

Steam-heated factory was the Burlington Woolen Company at Winooski River, Burlington, Vt., built in 1846. The factory, sold at auction October 20, 1852, was described in an advertisement in the Burlington *Free Press:* "The factory building and dye houses were heated by steam conducted through iron pipes in the most modern and approved manner. This modern and up to date mill was built six years ago." The mill is now owned by the American Woolen Company, Inc.

Windowless factory was erected in Fitchburg, Mass., in 1930. The plant, one story high and consisting of one room, was illuminated by hundreds of 1,000-watt electric lamps containing a small percentage of healthful ultraviolet rays. The walls and ceilings were painted orange, blue, green, and white to increase visibility, and the floors were jet black. The building also lacked skylights. It was ventilated by a system that circulated fresh air of the proper temperature which had been washed, heated, and humidified throughout the building

The First

Ten million cubic feet of air were changed every ten minutes. The walls were soundproof, as cork pads were used to reduce the noise inside. The building was constructed by the Austin Company of Cleveland, Ohio, for the Simonds Saw and Steel Company at a cost of $1,500,000.

FACTORY INSPECTION LAW. *See under* Labor law

FACTORY MUTUAL INSURANCE. *See* Insurance: Mutual fire insurance company

FACTORY STANDARDIZATION OF PRODUCTION by the United States Government was required in 1813, when a contract specifying interchangeable parts was drawn up between the United States Government (Callender Irvine, commissary general of the United States) and Colonel Simeon North of Berlin, Conn., on April 16, 1813, in Middletown, Conn. The contract, for 20,000 pistols at $7 each to be produced within five years, stipulated that "component parts of the pistols are to correspond so exactly that any limb or part of one pistol may be fitted to any other pistol of the 20,000." Colonel North established his pistol factory in 1810 in Staddle Hill, a suburb of Middletown. The factory produced about 10,000 pistols a year. *(Simeon Newton Dexter North—Simeon North, First Official Pistol Maker of the United States)*

FAIR

Agricultural fair was held October 1, 1810, in Pittsfield, Mass. It was promoted by Elkanah Watson and was known as the Berkshire Cattle Show. There were 383 sheep, 20 bulls, and 15 yoke of oxen entered for premiums amounting to $70. After the fair, there was a grand procession a half mile long of 60 yoke of prime oxen. *(Elkanah Watson—History of the Rise, Progress and Existing State of the Berkshire Agricultural Society)*

Annual fair was authorized by the director and council of New Netherlands on September 30, 1641. They "ordained that henceforth there shall be held annually at Fort Amsterdam a Cattle Fair on the 15th of October; and a fair for Hogs on the 1st of November. Whosoever hath any things to sell or to buy can regulate himself accordingly." *(Laws and Ordinances of New Netherlands, 1638–1674)*

Centennial celebration was held at Lexington, Mass., and Concord, Mass., on April 19, 1875, to commemorate the 100th birthday of American liberty. President Ulysses Simpson Grant, Secretary of War William Worth Belknap, Secretary of the Navy George Maxwell Robeson, Secretary of Interior Columbus Delano, many state governors, and other distinguished citizens attended.

Centennial exhibition was the International Exhibition that occupied 236 acres in Fairmount Park, Philadelphia, Pa. It opened May 10, 1876, and was host to 76,172 cash customers and 110,-

The First

500 free customers. It closed November 10, 1876. It attracted 60,000 exhibitors and 9,010,916 visitors.

Industrial exposition of an international character was held in New York City in 1853, modeled after the World's Fair (1851) of London, England. On March 11, 1852, the "Association for the Exhibition of the Industry of all Nations" was chartered. On March 17, 1852, the directors elected Theodore Sedgwick president. The exposition was held at Reservoir Square, 40th-42nd Streets between Fifth and Sixth avenues, in a specially erected two-story building with an area of 249,691 square feet. The exposition was opened by President Franklin Pierce, July 14, 1853. Admission was 50 cents for a single ticket, $2.50 monthly, $10 per person; children under 12 were admitted for 25 cents each. The building was destroyed by fire October 5, 1858. *(Illustrated Record of the Exposition)*

Manufacturers' fair was held October 24, 1828, under the auspices of the American Institute in the Masonic Hall, New York City. The American Institute in the City of New York was incorporated May 2, 1829, to encourage and promote domestic industry in the United States in agriculture, commerce, manufacturing, and the arts. *(New York As It Is in 1833)*

Woman's World Fair was held in Chicago, Ill., April 18–25, 1925, at which time women's progress was shown in 70 industries. At the World's Fair of 1893 in Chicago, Ill., women's handicrafts had been featured only at the sewing exhibit. The Woman's World Fair was officially opened by Mrs. Calvin Coolidge.

World's Fair that was financially successful was the Century 21 Exposition held from April 21, 1962, to October 21, 1962, at Seattle, Wash. It was opened by remote control by President John Fitzgerald Kennedy in conjunction with his speech transmitted by telephone from Palm Beach, Fla. The fair paid for its entire operating expenses, had a surplus of about a million dollars, and left a number of very valuable buildings and improvements on the site of the present Seattle Center.

FAIR LABOR STANDARDS ACT. *See under* Labor legislation

FAIR TRADE ADVERTISING COMMITTEE. *See* Advertising organization

FAIR TRADE LAW. *See* Price regulation law

FALLOUT SHELTER. *See* Building: House with a built-in nuclear bomb shelter

FAN, ELECTRIC. *See* Electric fan

FARM (agricultural experiment farm). *See under* Agricultural experiment station

The First

FARM BOARD (federal) met July 15, 1929, and consisted of eight members appointed by the President and confirmed by the Senate, in addition to the Secretary of Agriculture, who was an ex officio member. It was organized "to protect, control and stabilize the currents of interstate and foreign commerce" by minimizing speculation, by preventing inefficient and wasteful distribution, by encouraging farmers' organizations, and by preventing surpluses through orderly production. The Agricultural Marketing Act (46 Stat. L. 11) passed by Congress June 15, 1929, authorized $500 million to be used as a revolving fund. The board was later designated as the Farm Credit Administration. *(U.S. Federal Farm Board—First Annual Report)*

FARM BOOK. *See* Agricultural book

FARM BUREAU, a department of a city chamber of commerce working in combination with the co-operative agencies—the U.S. Department of Agriculture, the state college of agriculture, county and local farmers' organizations—was the Broome County Farm Bureau, established March 20, 1911, in Binghamton, N.Y. John H. Barron began work in Broome County, N.Y., as an agent of the U.S. Department of Agriculture, cooperating with the State College of Agriculture at Cornell University, the Binghamton Chamber of Commerce, and the Delaware, Lackawanna and Western Railway. The agent was given an office with the Chamber of Commerce and made manager of a new department of this organization which was called a farm bureau. On May 24, 1913, an act appropriating $25,000 for assisting the farm bureaus was passed by New York State, the first state to pass an act of this kind. *(William Allison Lloyd—Status and Results of County Agent Work)*

FARM CREDIT ADMINISTRATION (U.S.) was authorized March 27, 1933, by executive order of President Franklin Delano Roosevelt under power granted by the 73rd Congress, special session "Economy Act." The administration "to provide a complete and coordinated credit system for agriculture by making available to farmers long-term and short-term credit" was organized by executive order No. 6,084, March 27, 1933, with Henry Morgenthau, Jr., as the first administrator. Several agencies were grouped under this department.

FARM JOURNAL. *See* Agricultural journal

FARM LOAN BOARD (federal) was created in the Department of the Treasury to administer the Federal Farm Loan Act, approved July 17, 1916 (39 Stat. L. 360). The first federal land bank was chartered March 1, 1917, and the first national farm loan association March 27, 1917. The first farm loan commissioner was George William Norris, who took the oath of office August 7, 1916. Executive Order No. 6084 of March 27, 1933, effective May 27, 1933, transferred its functions to the Farm

The First

Credit Administration. *(U.S. Federal Loan Bureau —First Annual Report from Organization to November 30, 1937)*

FARM PAPER. *See* Agricultural Journal

FARM SOCIETY. *See* Agricultural society

FARMER LABOR PARTY was organized at a convention assembled June 12, 1920, in Chicago, Ill., and emanated from the National Labor Party, which was formed in 1919. The first presidential candidate was Parley Parker Christensen of Utah and the vice presidential candidate Maximilian Sebastian Hayes of Ohio. They received approximately 265,000 votes.

FARMERS' INSTITUTE
Farmers' institute held by a land grant agricultural college off its campus was sponsored by Iowa State College, Ames, Iowa, at Cedar Falls, Iowa, on December 20, 1870. The institute course continued five days and consisted of day and evening lectures on stock breeding and management, fruit culture, farm accounts, and kindred topics, conducted by George William Jones, professor of mathematics; James Mathews, professor of pomology; and Adonijah Strong Welch, president of the college. Other institutes were held the same year at Council Bluffs, Washington, and Muscatine, Iowa. *(Homestead and Western Farm Journal. December 1870)*

Farmers' institute sponsored by a college was held November 14, 1868, by the Kansas State Agricultural College, now the Kansas State College of Agriculture and Applied Science, at the Riley County Courthouse, Manhattan, Kan. Local arrangements for the institute were made by the Riley County Agricultural Society.

Farmers' institute sponsored by a state was held by the Massachusetts State Board of Agriculture in Springfield, Mass. The institute opened December 8, 1863, and continued for four days. Lectures and discussions pertaining to agriculture occupied the meetings. *(Jay Brownlee Davidson— A Study of the Extension Service)*

FARRIERS' COURSE IN A COLLEGE was presented in 1930 by Jack MacAllan at the Michigan State College, East Lansing, Mich., as part of a course in horse management. It was open only to students enrolled either in the 16-week short course or the 4-year course in the School of Agriculture. In 1946 a special farriers' course was offered under Jack MacAllan in the winter term to those who wished to train as specialists.

FARRIER'S GUIDE was *The Husband-Man's Guide, in Four Parts—Part first, containing many excellent rules for setting and planting. Part second, choice physical receipts for divers dangerous distempers in men, women and children. Part third, the experienced farrier. Part fourth containing rare receipts.* The book contained 107 pages

The First

and was printed in Boston, Mass., in 1710 by John Allen for Eleazer Phillips.

FASHION PLATE. *See* Periodical: Magazine containing a fashion plate

FASHION SHOW TELECAST. *See under* Television—Telecast

FASHION WEEKLY. *See* Periodical

FASTENING

Hookless fastening was invented by Whitcomb L. Judson of Chicago, Ill., who obtained patent No. 504,038 on August 29, 1893, on a clasp locker or unlocker for shoes and patent No. 557,207 on March 31, 1896 (on a fastening for shoes, comprising two metal chains which could be fastened together by movement of a slider) assigned to Universal Fastener Company in Illinois. The application had been filed October 2, 1894. The fasteners were first manufactured in 1893 by the Automatic Hook and Eye Company of Meadville, Pa., through the efforts of Colonel Lewis Walker.

Hookless fastening for universal use was invented about 1906 by Gideon Sundback of Hoboken N.J., who obtained patent No. 1,063,378 on April 29, 1913 on "separable fasteners." This fastener was improved upon by patents No. 1,219,881 and No. 1,243,458, which Sundback obtained on March 20, 1917, and October 16, 1917, respectively. These patents were assigned to by the Hookless Fastener Company of Meadville, Pa., manufacturers of the Talon Slide Fastener. *(Talon Hookless Fastener Co.)*

Hooks and eyes were successfully manufactured in 1836 in Waterbury, Conn., by Holmes & Hotchkiss. *(Henry Bronson—History of Waterbury)*

FATHER'S DAY. *See* Holiday

FATHOMETER, a device to measure the depth of water, was invented by Herbert Grove Dorsey of the U.S. Coast and Geodetic Survey, who received patent No. 1,667,540 on April 24, 1928. By means of a series of electrical sounds and light signals, the depth of water could be easily ascertained.

FEATURE MOTION PICTURE. *See* Motion picture: Foreign feature film exhibited

FEDERAL ALCOHOL CONTROL ADMINISTRATION was authorized December 4, 1933, by executive order No. 6,474 issued by President Franklin Delano Roosevelt. Joseph Hodges Choate, Jr., was appointed director, Harris Emanuel Willingham assistant director, and Edward George Lowry, Jr., counsel.

FEDERAL BOARD OF MEDIATION AND CONCILIATION. *See under* Arbitration

FEDERAL BUILDING. *See* Building: Building erected by the government in Washington, D.C.

The First

FEDERAL BUREAU OF INVESTIGATION
Woman on the "ten most wanted" list. *See* Criminal: Woman on the "ten most wanted" list

FEDERAL BUREAU OF INVESTIGATION TRAINING SCHOOL. *See* Police: Police training school

FEDERAL CEMETERY. *See* Cemetery

FEDERAL COMMUNICATIONS COMMISSION
Federal Communications Commission was created by act approved June 19, 1934 (48 Stat. L. 1064) to provide for the regulation of interstate and foreign commerce by wire or radio and to centralize these duties and responsibilities with a view to more effective supervision of communication. A committee of seven was appointed July 11, 1934. The first chairman was Eugene Octave Sykes, who served until March 11, 1935. Successors to the original committee were to be appointed for seven years, unless appointed to fill an unexpired term.

Federal Communications Commission woman member was Frieda Barkin Hennock, named by President Harry S. Truman to succeed Commissioner Clifford Judkins Durr, who resigned. She was sworn in July 6, 1948, in Washington, D.C.

International broadcasting license. *See under* Radio license

FEDERAL COUNCIL OF THE CHURCHES OF CHRIST IN AMERICA was organized in Philadelphia, Pa., December 2, 1908. The first president of the Council was Bishop Eugene Russell Hendrix of the Methodist Episcopal Church. The first executive secretary was Elias Benjamin Sanford. The constitution of the council, which had been ratified prior to the first meeting by the constituent denominations, provided for approximately 400 official members named directly by the cooperating denominations. They were appointed to attend the first meeting held December 2, 1908, in Philadelphia, and were designated as charter members. *(Elias Benjamin Sanford—Origin and History of the Federal Council of the Churches of Christ in America)*

FEDERAL CREDIT UNION ACT was approved June 26, 1934 (48 Stat. L. 1216) "to establish a Federal Credit Union System, to establish a further market for securities of the United States and to make more available to people of small means credit for provident purposes through a national system of cooperative credit, thereby helping to stabilize the credit structure of the United States." Charter No. 1 was granted to the Morris Sheppard Federal Credit Union of Texarkana, Tex., named in honor of the sponsor of the law, which held its organization meeting, October 1, 1934.

FEDERAL CROP INSURANCE CORPORATION was established by the Federal Crop Insurance Act, part of the Agricultural Adjustment Act of 1938 (52 Stat. L. 72), approved February 16, 1938,

The First

FEDERAL CROP INSURANCE CORPORA-TION—*Continued*

to provide for insuring wheat yields against natural hazards such as drought, flood, hail, winterkill, lightning, insect infestation and plant diseases. The directors were Milburn Lincoln Wilson, Jesse Washington Tapp, and Rudolph Martin Evans. Roy M. Green was manager of the corporation. The first application was signed May 18, 1938, by M. L. Purvines, Panhandle, Tex., and the first indemnity payment was made April 14, 1939, to John F. Biggs, Floydada, Floyd County, Tex., a payment of $129.32 to compensate him for the total loss of his share in a 52-acre wheat crop.

FEDERAL DEPOSIT INSURANCE CORPORA-TION was created June 16, 1933 (48 Stat. L. 162) by the Banking Act of 1933, "to provide for the safer and more effective use of the assets of banks, to regulate interbank control, to prevent the undue diversion of funds into speculative operations." The management of the corporation was vested in a board of three directors, one of whom was the comptroller of the Currency. The first board was composed of chairman Walter Joseph Cummings of Chicago, Elbert Gladstone Bennett of Salt Lake City, and James Francis Thaddeus O'Connor, comptroller of the Currency. The first official meeting of the board of directors was held September 11, 1933. The system went into effect January 1, 1934. The first payment was one of $125,000 to 1,789 depositors of the Fond du Lac State Bank of East Peoria, Ill. The bank suspended business May 28, 1934, and receivership became final on June 25, 1935. Lydia Lobsiger, a widow, received the first insurance check, covering her deposit, July 3, 1934.

FEDERAL EMERGENCY RELIEF ADMINISTRA-TION was created by the Federal Emergency Relief Act of 1933 (48 Stat. L. 55), approved May 12, 1933, "to provide for cooperation by the federal government with the several states and territories, and the District of Columbia in relieving the hardships and suffering caused by unemployment." The Federal Emergency Relief Administration became operative ten days after approval of the act. The first Federal Emergency Relief Administrator was Harry Lloyd Hopkins, appointed by the President with the advice and consent of the Senate. He took office May 22, 1933.

FEDERAL FARM BOARD. *See* Farm board (federal)

FEDERAL FARM CREDIT ADMINISTRATION (U.S.) *See* Farm Credit Administration (U.S.)

FEDERAL FARM LOAN BOARD. *See* Farm loan board (federal)

FEDERAL FISH HATCHERY. *See* Fish hatchery (federal)

The First

FEDERAL FISH PROTECTION OFFICE. *See* Fish protection: Fish protection office (federal)

FEDERAL FOREIGN AID BILL was "an act for the relief of the citizens of Venezuela" (2 Stat. L. 730), enacted May 8, 1812. An appropriation of $50,000 was made to enable the President to obtain such provisions as he should deem advisable for the relief of the citizens of Venezuela "who have suffered by the late earthquake."

FEDERAL FREE TRADE POLICY. *See* Free trade policy (federal)

FEDERAL GRANT-IN-AID TO STATES FOR ROADS. *See under* Road

FEDERAL HIGHWAY. *See* Road

FEDERAL HOME LOAN. *See* GI Bill of Rights

FEDERAL HOME LOAN BANK BOARD was established July 22, 1932, by the Federal Home Loan Bank Act (47 Stat. L. 725) for the purpose of establishing and supervising the Federal Home Loan Banks as a permanent credit reserve system for savings and loan associations and similar local thrift and home financing institutions and for savings banks and insurance companies making long-term home mortgage loans. The board consisted of five members, Franklin William Fort, chairman, Dr. John Matthew Gries, William Edward Best, Nathan Adams, and Morton Bodfish, who took the oath of office and held the first meeting August 9, 1932.

FEDERAL JUDGE IMPEACHED. *See* Impeachment: Impeachment of a federal judge

FEDERAL LABOR ADVISORY BOARD. *See* Labor: Labor advisory board (federal)

FEDERAL LAW COMPILATION. *See* Lawbook: Lawbook containing the federal laws of the United States

FEDERAL MARITIME COMMISSION

Woman chairman of the Federal Maritime Commission was Helen Delich Bentley, of Maryland, sworn in by Vice President Spiro Agnew. She served from October 27, 1969, to November 15, 1975.

Woman federal regulatory agency chairman. *See under* Woman

FEDERAL MOTOR CARRIER LEGISLATION. *See* Automobile legislation

FEDERAL NARCOTICS SANATORIUM. *See* Narcotics: Narcotics sanatorium (federal) for drug addicts

FEDERAL PENITENTIARY. *See* Prison: Penitentiary building (national)

FEDERAL PLAY PRESENTATION. *See* Play (drama): Theatrical presentation sponsored by the federal government

The First

FEDERAL RADIO COMMISSION. *See* Radio Commission (U.S.)

FEDERAL REGISTER. *See* Periodical: Magazine of the United States Government

FEDERAL RESERVE SYSTEM

Federal Reserve System Board of Governors member (black) was Andrew Felton Brimmer, who was appointed to the board on May 9, 1966, and served through August 31, 1974.

Federal Reserve System Board of Governors member (woman) was Nancy Hays Teeters (Mrs. Robert D. Teeters), nominated August 28, 1978, by President Jimmy Carter and sworn in September 18, 1978, to serve until January 31, 1984.

FEDERAL ROAD AGENCY. *See under* Road

FEDERAL SAVINGS AND LOAN ASSOCIATION was authorized by the Home Owners Loan Act of June 13, 1933 (48 Stat. L. 128), to provide a convenient place for the investment of small or large sums and to lend money on first mortgages on homes in the area in which the association is located. The first association was the First Federal Savings and Loan Association of Miami, Fla., which received Charter No. 1 on August 8, 1933. The Federal Savings and Loan Insurance Corporation, created June 27, 1934 (48 Stat. L. 1255), was organized to insure investors against loss up to $5,000, which amount was later increased by law to $10,000.

FEDERAL SECURITY AGENCY was established by the President's Reorganization Plan 1 on April 25, 1939 (53 Stat. L. 1424), to place under one administration the agencies which had as their major purpose the promotion of social and economic security, educational opportunity, and health. The units were the U.S. Employment Service, the Office of Education, the Public Health Service, the National Youth Administration, the Social Security Board, and the Civilian Conservation Corps. The first administrator was Paul Vories McNutt, who took office on July 13, 1939, and who served until September 13, 1945. His salary was $12,000 a year. On April 11, 1953, the Federal Security Agency became the Department of Health, Education, and Welfare.

FEDERAL SHIP. *See* Ship: Ship constructed by the federal government

FEDERAL SURPLUS RELIEF CORPORATION was incorporated under the laws of the state of Delaware, October 4, 1933. The incorporators were Federal Emergency Relief Administrator Harry Lloyd Hopkins, president; Secretary of Agriculture Henry Agard Wallace, vice president; and Federal Emergency Administrator of Public Works Harold Le Claire Ickes, treasurer. *(U.S. Agriculture Department. Surplus Marketing Administration—First Report, October 4, 1933–December 31, 1934)*

The First

FEDERAL TRADE COMMISSION

Federal Trade Commission came into existence September 26, 1914, by Act of Congress (38 Stat. L. 717), "an act to create a Federal Trade Commission, to define its powers and duties." The commission was organized to regulate commerce and prohibit unlawful means of obtaining trade March 16, 1915, when five commissioners, George Rublee, Edward Nash Hurley, Will H. Parry, Joseph Edward Davies, and William Julius Harris, were appointed, each at an annual salary of $10,000. *(Gerald Carl Henderson—The Federal Trade Commission)*

Federal Trade Commission trade practice conference was held October 3, 1919, in Omaha, Neb., for the creamery industry. Representatives from six states met with Commissioner William Byron Colver to discuss unfair practice complaints in the industry.

FEDERAL TRANSPORTATION COORDINATION. *See* Transportation coordination

FEDERAL WOMEN EMPLOYEES. *See* Woman: Women to become federal government employees

FEDERAL WORKS AGENCY was established by President Franklin Delano Roosevelt July 1, 1939, under authority of act of April 25, 1939 (53 Stat. L. 1427, Reorganization Plan No. 1), as a consolidation of five governmental public works units, the Public Buildings Administration, the Public Roads Administration, the Public Works Administration, the Works Projects Administration, and the United States Housing Authority. The first Federal Works Administrator was John Michael Carmody, who received $12,000 per annum.

FEDERATION OF ORGANIZED TRADES AND LABOR UNIONS. *See* Labor union: Labor union of importance

FELLOWSHIP

Fellowship awarded a woman was the Sage Fellowship in Entomology and Botany, granted June 19, 1884, to Harriet Elizabeth Grotecloss by Cornell University, Ithaca, N.Y. The fellowship had a stipend of $400 per year payable in six installments and provided free tuition for graduate study.

Fellowship (graduate) awarded by a women's college was offered the graduating class of Bryn Mawr College, Bryn Mawr, Pa. The first award was made June 6, 1889, to Emily Greene Balch of Boston, Mass., for "prosecuting sociological studies."

Resident fellowship for women awarded by a women's college was offered by Bryn Mawr College, Bryn Mawr, Pa., which established five resident fellowships in 1884, prior to the actual opening of the college. The recipients, who received free tuition, a furnished room, and $350 annually, were Jane M. Bancroft, in history; Katherine Augusta Gage, in Greek; Mary Gwinn, in

The First

FELLOWSHIP—*Continued*
English; Effie A. Southworth, in biology; and Ella
C. Williams, in mathematics.

FELT HAT. *See* Hat: Soft felt hats for women

FELT manufacturing mechanical process was invented by Thomas Robinson Williams of Newport, R.I., in 1820. The wool is carded and placed
in layers until the desired thickness is obtained,
the outside rolls being the finest in texture. The
mass is placed between rollers, partly immersed
in water, and is beaten, pressed, and given an
oscillating movement at the same time. Dyeing
and finishing complete the process.

FEMALE PAGE. *See* Congress (U.S.)—House of
Representatives: Page (female)

FENCING
Fencing champion to win three titles in one year
was Charles G. Bothner of the New York Athletic
Club, who won three amateur fencing titles—foil,
épée, and saber—on May 1, 1897, at the Fencers
Club, New York City.

Fencing league (national) was the Amateur
Fencers League of America, organized May 6,
1891. The first officers were Dr. Graeme M. Hammond, president; Charles Tatham, vice president;
and W. Scott O'Connor, secretary and treasurer,
all of New York City. The first competition was
held in 1892. The winners were W. Scott O'Connor of the Fencers Club (men's foils) and Dr. B. F.
O'Connor and R. O. Haubold of the New York
Athletic Club (dueling swords and sabers, respectively).

Intercollegiate fencing championship competition was held by the International Fencing Association on May 5, 1894, at the Racquet & Tennis
Club, New York City. Harvard defeated Columbia
five matches to four and won the silver challenge
cup. Yale, the only other entry in the competition,
withdrew after an accident to one of the team.
Fitzhugh Townsend of Columbia had the highest
individual score.

International fencing championship competition was held at the Racquet Club, Washington,
D.C., on November 18–19, 1921. The United States
team defeated Great Britain 13–3 the first day. The
U.S. team lost 10–4 on the second day. The finals
were held November 21, 1921, at the Hotel Astor,
New York City, the score being 8–8. The United
States won 25 of the 46 matches to win the Colonel Robert M. Thompson International Trophy.

FENCING BOOK was Edward Blackwell's *A
Compleat System of Fencing; or the art of defence,
in the use of the small sword; wherein the most
necessary parts thereof are plainly laid down;
chiefly for gentlemen, promoters and lovers of
that science in North America*, printed in 1734 by
William Parks, Williamsburg, Va. It was based on
Henry Blackwell's *The English Fencing Master*,

The First

published in London in 1705. *(Robert William
Henderson—Early American Sport)*

FERMIUM. *See* Element: Element 100

FERRIS WHEEL was invented in 1892 by George
Washington Gale Ferris, stimulated by a prize for
an attraction like the Eiffel Tower of Paris. It was
erected on the Midway at the Columbian Exposition in Chicago, Ill., in 1893. It consisted of 36 cars,
each capable of holding 60 passengers. The highest point of the wheel was 264 feet. The total
weight of the wheels and cars was 2,100 tons, of
the levers and machinery 2,200 tons, and of the
passengers per trip 150 tons. *(The Ferris and Other
Big Wheels*—In *Cassier's Magazine. July 1894)*

FERRYBOAT
Double-deck ferryboat was launched October
25, 1888, at the Delmater Iron Works, Newburgh,
N.Y. She was called the *Bergen* and plied across
the Hudson River from New York City to Hobok-
en, N.J. She was 203 feet in length and 62 feet
wide, with a 10-foot draft, and was first piloted by
Captain G. Beckwith.

Double-deck ferryboat with the propeller-type
steel hull was the *Hamburg*, built in 1891 by
Thomas S. Marvel & Company of Newburgh, N.Y.
She weighed 1,266 tons gross, 833 tons net, was
219 feet long, 40 feet wide, with a 16-foot draft
and cost $180,843.02. Passengers could not be
taken on or discharged from the upper deck. In
1905 the ferry was altered so that both the upper
and lower levels could be used for receiving and
discharging passengers. The ferry plied between
Hoboken, N.J., and New York City. *(Harry J. Smith
and John M. Emery—The Romance of the Hobok-
en Ferry)*

Ferry (aerial). *See* Bridge: Aerial ferry

Ferryboat built exclusively for motor vehicle
transportation was the *Governor Moore*, a diesel
electric ferry placed in service November 8, 1926.
She was built by the New York Shipbuilding Company of Camden, N.J., from plans conceived by
Eads Johnson. Five other boats were built in 1926,
each with capacity for 46 automobiles. The boats
which were operated by Electric Ferries, Inc.,
originally plied between 23rd Street, New York
City, and Edgewater, N.J., and 23rd Street, New
York City, and Weehawken, N.J. *(Motorship,
December 1932)*

Municipally owned ferryboats were placed in
operation in New York City, October 25, 1905, between Whitehall Street, Manhattan, and St.
George, Staten Island. They were under the jurisdiction of the Department of Docks up to July 1,
1918. *(Records in Department of Plants and Structures, New York City)*

Steam-propelled ferryboat was the *Juliana*, operated October 11, 1811, by John Stevens and his
son, Robert Livingston Stevens. She plied between Hoboken, N.J., and New York City.

The First

Steel-hull ferryboat was the *Lackawanna*, built in 1881 at Newburgh, N.Y., by Ward Stanton at a cost of $76,000. She weighed 822 gross tons, 645 net tons, and was 200 feet long, 35 feet wide, with a 13-foot draft. The boat plied between Hoboken, N.J., and New York City. *(Harry J. Smith and John M. Emery—The Romance of the Hoboken Ferry)*

Streamlined ferryboat was the *Kalakala* (the name is taken from Chinook, is pronounced Kah-lock'-ah-lah, and means "Flying Bird"). She was 276 feet long, had a beam of 55 feet 8 inches and a draft of 13 feet, and was designed to carry 2,000 passengers and 110 automobiles. She was 97.75 percent steel in construction and was built at the Lake Washington Shipyards at Houghton, Wash. She was first placed in commercial operation on July 4, 1935, by the Puget Sound Navigation Company, Seattle, Wash., between Seattle and Bremerton, Wash., on Puget Sound, under the command of Captain Wallace H. Mangan.

FERTILIZER (artificial) was developed by Professor James Jay Mapes of Newark, N.J., who experimented in 1847 with fertilizers on his 20-acre farm at Newark, N.J. He applied for a patent in 1849 on a superphosphate of lime made from charred bone (waste products of sugar refineries) to which were added sulfate of ammonia and Peruvian guano. Patent No. 26,196 was granted November 22, 1859. *(Chemical Industries. October 1937)*

FERTILIZER LAW (state) was passed March 16, 1871 (Chap. 35) by Delaware. The law was unworkable and was amended April 8, 1881 (Chap. 348) and several times later.

FEVER THERAPY INTERNATIONAL CONFERENCE. *See under* Medical congress

FEVER TREATISE (typhus). *See* Medical book: Typhus fever treatise

FIBERGLASS. *See* Suture: Fiberglass sutures

FIBERGLASS AUTOMOBILE. *See* Automobile: Plastic-laminated fiberglass-body sports car

FICTION MAGAZINE. *See* Periodical

FIELD HOSPITAL. *See* Hospital

FIELD HOSPITAL AUTOMOBILE (X-ray). *See under* Automobile

FIELD RANGE.. *See* Army field range

FIELDING CAGE. *See* Baseball batting and fielding cage

FIFTY-DOLLAR GOLD PIECES. *See* Money

FIGHT. *See* Prizefight

FIGHTER AIRPLANE. *See under* Aviation—Airplane

FIGURE GLASS (stained). *See* Glass: Stained figure glass

The First

FIGURE SKATING. *See under* Ice skating tournament: Figure skating international championship tournament

FIGURE SKATING CHAMPION. *See* Ice skating champion: American world figure skating champion

FIGURE SKATING OLYMPIC CHAMPIONSHIP. *See under* Olympic Games

FILE FACTORY

File factory (hand cutting) to manufacture files was started by Broadmeadow & Company in Pittsburgh, Pa., in 1829. The files were made by hand. With this exception, file making in the United States was practically unknown until 1839.

File factory (machine cutting) to attain success was the Nicholson File Company, which was organized in Providence, R.I., in 1864 to manufacture files by machine. This company used a machine for cutting files which was patented by William Nicholson of Providence, R.I., April 5, 1864 (patent No. 42,216).

FILE MANUFACTURING MACHINE was invented by Morris B. Belknap in 1812 in Greenfield, Mass. As far as is known, the machine was not a success.

FILIBUSTER. *See under* Congress (U.S.)—House of Representatives; Congress (U.S.)—Senate

FILM. *See* Photographic film

FILM CAMERA. *See* Camera: Roll-film camera

FILM-DEVELOPING MACHINE. *See under* Photography

FILMPACK CAMERA. *See under* Camera

FILMS. *See* Motion picture

FILTRATION (water) SYSTEM. *See* Water purification: Municipal filtration system

FINANCE COMPANY. *See* Automobile finance company; Business: Installment finance company

FINANCIAL CORNER. *See under* Brokerage

FINANCIAL NEWS AGENCY. *See* News agency

FINE ARTS COMMISSION (federal)

Fine arts commission (federal) was established by act of May 17, 1910 (36 Stat.L.371), which authorized the appointment of 7 commissioners to serve 4-year terms and appropriated $10,000 for expenditures.

FINE ARTS DEPARTMENT

Fine arts department in a college was the School of Fine Arts, Yale University, New Haven, Conn., established in 1864. In 1869, John Ferguson Weir was appointed Professor of Painting and Design and the school formally opened with four students. Certificates were given to those who completed the three-year course, until 1891, when upon the fulfillment of more advanced require-

The First

FINE ARTS DEPARTMENT—*Continued*
ments Josephine Miles Lewis received a Bachelor of Fine Arts (B.F.A.) degree.

Fine arts department in a college to grant degrees was the College of Fine Arts, Syracuse University, Syracuse, N.Y., established June 24, 1873. Dr. George Fisk Comfort was the first dean of the College of Fine Arts.

FINE ARTS SOCIETY. *See* Art organization

FINGERPRINT SOCIETY (international) was the International Association for Criminal Identification, formed October 9, 1915, in Oakland, Calif. Harry Howard Caldwell of the Oakland Police Department was the first president. A. J. Renoe of Washington, D.C., was the first secretary. On June 11–14, 1918, the word "criminal" was eliminated from the title. *(Henry Pelousz de Forest—Evolution of Dactyloscopy in the United States)*

FINGERPRINTING
Community to fingerprint its citizens was Oskaloosa, Iowa, which acted upon the suggestion made by Police Chief Howard Ray Allgood on May 21, 1934. Although registration was not compulsory, a Personal Identification Bureau was established through which most of the town's residents had their fingerprints recorded.

Federal penitentiary fingerprinting was undertaken November 2, 1904, by the Bureau of Criminal Identification at the United States Penitentiary at Leavenworth, Kans. This work was carried on until October 1, 1924, when it was taken over by the Federal Bureau of Investigation.

Fingerprint conviction was recorded February 1, 1911, in the Criminal Court of Cook County, Ill., when Thomas Jennings, a black, was found guilty and sentenced to death for the murder of Clarence B. Hiller on September 19, 1910. The conviction was upheld by the Illinois Supreme Court on December 21, 1911, when the court ruled that fingerprint evidence was admissible. Jennings was hanged in the Cook County jail on February 16, 1912. *(Illinois Reports. Vol. 252, p. 534)*

High school to fingerprint its students was the Watertown Senior High School, Watertown, S.Dak. The fingerprinting was started on October 19, 1936, as an outgrowth of a talk by a member of the Federal Bureau of Investigation.

International exchange of fingerprints between the United States and Europe was made July 6, 1905, when the St. Louis (Mo.) Metropolitan Police Department obtained the fingerprints of John Walker, alias Captain John Pearson, a frequent offender, from New Scotland Yard, London, England. The prints were later forwarded to New Orleans, La., and introduced as part of his criminal record.

The First

Police department to adopt the fingerprinting system was the St. Louis (Mo.) Metropolitan Police Department, which on October 28, 1904, adopted the Henry method to fingerprint persons arrested on serious charges. John M. Shea was the first to qualify as a fingerprint expert connected with any police service. He became associated with the St. Louis Metropolitan Police Department, May 1, 1899, and was appointed Superintendent of the Bertillon System, September 14, 1903. He remained in office until his death, July 17, 1926. *(Charles Edward Chapel—Fingerprinting: A Manual of Identification)*

State prison to take fingerprints of its prisoners was Sing Sing Prison, Ossining, N.Y., which commenced taking impressions on March 3, 1903.

FIRE
Fire in a mine was chronicled by the Reverend Charles Beatty in 1765. He reported that a fire had been burning at least a year in a coal mine known as Spot Hill, the opening of which was somewhere between the Point Bridge and the Smithfield Street Bridge, on the south side of the Monongahela River in that part of Pittsburgh now known as Mount Washington. *(Pittsburgh and the Pittsburgh Spirit—Pittsburgh Chamber of Commerce)*

Fire of great destructive force took place in New York City on December 16, 1835, when 600 buildings were demolished, entailing a loss of over $20 million. *(Martha Joanna Reade Lamb—History of the City of New York)*

Fire of serious consequence in America occurred on November 27, 1676, when there "burned down to the ground 46 dwelling houses, besides other buildings, meeting house, etc.," in Boston, Mass. On August 8, 1679, also in Boston, 80 dwellings and 70 commercial buildings were destroyed, the damage amounting to almost $1 million. *(Reverend William Hubbard—A General History of New England from the Discovery to 1680)*

Oil well fire. *See under* Oil

Theater destroyed by fire. *See under* Theater

FIRE-ALARM SYSTEM (electric) was invented by William Francis Channing of Boston, Mass., and Moses Gerrish Farmer of Salem, Mass., who on May 19, 1857, received patent No. 17,355 for "a magnetic electric fire-alarm." The first city to adopt this system was Boston, which on June 1851 voted $10,000 to test the device.

FIRE BRICK. *See* Brick

FIRE DEPARTMENT
Fire department composed entirely of women was the Ashville Fire Department, Ashville, N.Y. In February 1943, 13 women replaced the male members who were serving in the armed forces or were working elsewhere. They served without pay, operated a 500-gallon-per-minute pumper

and were proficient in rescue work and other fire department procedures.

Fire department established by municipal action was organized in 1659 by Peter Stuyvesant, governor of New Amsterdam, later New York. He distributed 250 leather buckets and a supply of ladders and hooks which he imported from Holland. A tax of one guilder for every chimney was imposed for the maintenance of this equipment. The fire alarm was given by the twirling of a rattle, with the result that the firemen became known as the Rattle Watch. In 1669 the city appointed a "brent-master," who seems to have been the first fire chief in this country. *(Industrial Fire Chief—Foamite-Childs Corporation)*

Fire department to be paid was authorized in 1697 by New York City. Two fire wardens were authorized for every ward. A penalty of 3 shillings was imposed upon owners for neglecting to remedy defective flues and hearths. If a fire resulted after warning, the fine was 40 shillings. Half of the fee went to the wardens and half to the city.

Fire department to be paid a salary was established by Cincinnati, Ohio, on April 1, 1853, through the efforts of Miles Greenwood. Members of the company received $60 a year, lieutenants $100, captains $150, pipemen and drivers $365. The chief engineer received $1,000 a year and assistant engineers $300. *(Charles Theodore Greve —Centennial History of Cincinnati and Representative Citizens)*

FIRE ENGINE

Fire engine made in this country was built in 1654 by Joseph Jencks, an iron maker of Lynn, Mass. He made a contract with the Selectmen of Boston for an "Ingine" to carry water in case of fire. It was a clumsy pump worked by relays of men at the handles. Its cistern was supplied with water by lines of bucket passers. *(Arthur Wellington Brayley—History of Boston Fire Department)*

Fire engine that was practical was the Uncle Joe Ross, invented by Alexander Bonner Latta and manufactured by Latta, Shawk & Company in 1852 in Cincinnati, in the shops of John H. McGowan. It took nine months to build, cost $10,000, and was tested on January 1, 1853, the date it went into service. It weighed five tons, was drawn by four horses and its own power, and had a square firebox, like that of a locomotive boiler, with a furnace open at the top, upon which the chimney was placed. It ran on three wheels, the front one revolving in the center of the car. It threw from one to six streams of water. In a single stream 1¾ inches in diameter it threw water a distance of 240 feet. Its adoption was due principally to the efforts of Miles Greenwood. *(History of the Cincinnati Fire Department)*

Steam Fire engine was designed and built by Paul Rapsey Hodge, C.E., and publicly tested March 27, 1841, at the City Hall, New York. It was 14 feet long and weighed about 8 tons. It had two small wheels under the boiler in front and two huge wheels at the rear. Two horses were required to draw it on level ground. It was placed in service by Pearl Hose No. 28. It was too heavy and was abandoned because sparks poured from its stacks.

FIRE ESCAPES for tenements were required by New York State, April 17, 1860 (Laws of New York 1860, Chapter 470). A serious fire in Elm Street, New York City, February 2, 1860, in which 20 persons were suffocated or burned to death, showed the necessity for this legislation.

FIRE EXTINGUISHER using vaporized chemical was manufactured by the Pyrene Manufacturing Company, Newark, N.J., and introduced in 1905. The first model had a single-action pump, which had to be tilted down after each stroke, in order to suck up liquid for the next discharge stroke.

FIRE EXTINGUISHER PATENT was awarded to Alanson Crane of Fortress Monroe, Va., who obtained United States patent No. 37,610, February 10, 1863.

FIRE HOSE of rubber-lined cotton web to replace riveted leather hose was invented by James Boyd of Boston, Mass., who obtained a patent May 30, 1821, on a "new and useful improvement in the mode of manufacturing fire engine hose." In 1819 he established James Boyd & Sons in Boston, Mass., and manufactured Boyd's Patent Double Fire Engine Hose.

FIRE INSURANCE. *See* Insurance

FIRE LOOKOUT TOWER. *See* Forest fire: Forest fire lookout tower

FIRE PATROL

Fire patrol was "The Philadelphia Society for the Protection of Movable Property in Time of Fire," organized in Philadelphia in 1819, to prevent theft and to salvage articles in fires. The company had large baskets in which to place the articles saved and had vehicles for carrying the baskets away.

Fire patrol to receive a salary was organized in New York City in 1835 and consisted of four men, each of whom was paid a salary of $250 a year to protect property from theft and damage during fires.

FIRE PREVENTION LEGISLATION was enacted March 17, 1631, by Cambridge (Newtowne), Mass., as the result of a fire the previous day in Boston, Mass., which spread to an adjoining house. The legislation provided that "no man there shall build his chimney with wood, nor cover his house with thatch." *(Thomas Prince—A*

The First

FIRE PREVENTION LEGISLATION—*Continued*
Chronological History of New England in the Form of Annals)

FIRE STATION. *See* Firehouse

FIREARM. *See* Ordnance; Pistol

FIREBOAT
    Fireboat was used in New York City in 1800. It was a flat-bottom boat shaped like a scow and had a sharp bow and square stern. It was powered by 12 men who used oars. A hand-operated pump was mounted on the boat, which was stationed at the foot of Roosevelt Street on the East River, and patrolled the docks and waterfront of New York City. Two of these fireboats, called "floating engines," were imported from England at a cost of $4,000 each. They arrived in New York City on September 28, 1800. They were in the charge of Thomas Howell and were inspected on November 10, 1800. *(Our Firemen—New York City)*

    Fireboat with two-way radio equipment was placed in service in 1925 by Boston, Mass. Bids on four transmitting and receiving radio stations, one land station and three on boats, were opened August 29, 1923. The boats were licensed March 17, 1924, and assigned the call letters WEY. *(Annual Report of the Fire Department and Wire Division of the City of Boston for the year ending January 31, 1924)*

FIREHOUSE POLE
    Firehouse pole was installed on April 21, 1878, by Captain David B. Kenyon of Engine Company No. 21, New York City. A hole was cut in an upper floor and a 3-inch-wide greased pole extended to the floor below to enable the firemen to slide down the pole instead of using the stairs.

FIREPROOF BUILDING. *See* Building

FIREPROOF HOTEL. *See* Hotel

FIREPROOF SAFE. *See* Safe

FIREWORKS BOOK was *A System of Pyrotechny, comprehending the theory and practice with the application of chemistry, designed for exhibition and for war, adapted to the military and naval officer, the man of science and the artificer.* The book contained 612 pages, and a 44-page introduction. It was written by James Cutbush, acting professor of chemistry and mineralogy at the U.S. Military Academy, and published by Clara F. Cutbush in Philadelphia, Pa., in 1825.

FIREWORKS LEGISLATION
    Fireworks legislation enacted by a large city was Section I (1557-a) passed by Cleveland, Ohio, July 18, 1908. It provided that "no person, firm or corporation shall within the city, sell, offer for sale or have in his or its possession or custody any toy pistol, squib, rocket, cracker, Roman candle or fire balloon or other combustibles, or fireworks"

The First

under penalty of a $100 fine or 30 days imprisonment, or both. The Board of Public Service was permitted to give pyrotechnic displays when directed by the Council.

    Fireworks legislation (state) was Act No. 14, Public Laws of 1929, passed March 29, 1929, by Michigan. It prohibited the use of fireworks by the general public but allowed displays by approved or licensed operators. Other states had partially restrictive laws.

FIRST AID EMERGENCY ORGANIZATION was the Humane Society of Philadelphia, Philadelphia, Pa., which was organized in 1780. The society was incorporated January 23, 1793. Its object, according to the charter, was the "recovery of drowned persons, and of those whose animation may be suspended from other causes, as breathing air contaminated by burning charcoal, hanging, exposure to the choke-damp of wells, drinking cold water while warm in summer, strokes of the sun, lightning, swallowing laudanum, etc."

FIRST AID INSTRUCTION was given at the annual encampment of the New York State militia at Peekskill, N.Y., in 1885. The idea was proposed by George Ryerson Fowler. *(William Francis Campbell—In Memoriam Dr. George Ryerson Fowler)*

FIRST EDITIONS CATALOG. *See* Bookseller's catalog

FISH AND FISHERIES COMMISSIONER of the United States was Spencer Fullerton Baird, who served without pay from March 8, 1871, to August 17, 1887. An appropriation of $5,000 was made March 3, 1871 (16 Stat. L. 503) for expense in "prosecuting the inquiry authorized by law into the cause of the decrease of the food fishes of the coast and lakes." The first full-time salaried commissioner was Marshall McDonald, who served from February 18, 1888, to September 1, 1895. The office was known as the United States Fish Commission until 1903, when it was made the Bureau of Fisheries in the Department of Commerce and Labor. In 1913 when the departments were separated, the Bureau of Fisheries was placed under the jurisdiction of the Department of Commerce.

FISH COMMISSION (state) was authorized by Massachusetts on May 16, 1856, "to ascertain, and report to the next General Court, such facts respecting the artificial propagation of fish, as may tend to show the practicability and expediency of introducing the same into this Commonwealth under the protection of law." The commission consisted of R. A. Chapman, chairman, Henry Wheatland, and N. E. Atwood. It ceased to function when the task was completed. *(Report of Commissioners Appointed under Resolve of 1856 Chapter 58, Concerning the Artificial Propagation of Fish)*

The First

FISH HATCHERY

Fish hatchery to breed salmon was an experimental laboratory established in 1864 under the supervision of James B. Johnson. He imported from Europe salmon eggs, which were hatched in his New York City laboratory.

Fish hatchery (federal) was established at Bucksport, Me., in 1872 for the propagation of Atlantic salmon. It was a joint activity, with the cooperation of the states of Maine, Massachusetts, and Connecticut, and was a continuation of experiments initiated by these agencies in 1871. It was under the supervision of Charles Grandison Atkins and was permanently established at East Orland, Me. *(Records in Bureau of Fisheries, Department of Commerce, Washington, D.C.)*

Fish-hatching steamer (federal). *See under* Ship

Goldfish hatchery successfully operated was established in the summer of 1899 by Eugene Curtis Shireman at Martinsville, Ind. The hatchery started with 200 goldfish and eventually bred millions of goldfish annually. It was incorporated in 1924 as Grassyfork, Inc.

FISH PROTECTION

Fish legislation was an act for "preserving fish in fresh water ponds" enacted May 28, 1734, by New York City. Fishing by hoop-net, draw-net, purse-net, catching-net, cod-net, bley-net or with any other engine, machine, arts, ways and means whatsoever, other than by angling with angle-rod, hook and line only, was subject to a fine of 20 shillings.

Fish protection office (federal) was authorized by act of February 9, 1871 (16 Stat. L. 594). It empowered President Ulysses Simpson Grant to appoint "from among the civil officers or employees of the Government, one person of proved scientific and practical acquaintance with the fishes of the coast to be Commissioner of Fish and Fisheries to serve without additional salary." The first commissioner was Spencer Fullerton Baird, appointed March 8, 1871.

FISH WARDEN. *See* Game warden

FISHERMAN'S BOAT RACE. *See* Boat race

FISHERIES SCHOOL

Fisheries college. *See* College: Fisheries college

FISHERY (commercial) is believed to have been established at Medford, Mass. On April 17, 1629, the colonists were given instructions to let the fish "be well saved with the said salt, and packed up in hogsheads; and send it home by the 'Talbot' or 'Lion's Whelpe.' " The industry flourished and on May 28, 1639, received "salt, lines, hooks, knives, boots, etc., for the fishermen." Fishing had also been attempted elsewhere by the first colonists. *(Charles Brooks—History of the Town of Medford)*

The First

FISHES

See also Aquatic mammals

Goldfish industry is believed to have had its inception in 1878 when Rear Admiral Daniel Ammen, U.S.N., presented a group of goldfish that had been brought over from Japan to the United States Fish Commission, now the Bureau of Fisheries. *(U.S. Department of Commerce. Bureau of Fisheries—Economic Circular No. 68)*

FISHING BOOK. *See* Fishing treatise

FISHING CLUB of more than temporary existence was the Schuylkill Fishing Company, founded in 1732 in Philadelphia, Pa., with a limited membership of 25. *(William Milnor, Jr.—An Authentic History of the Schuylkill Fishing Company of the State in Schuylkill from Its Establishment on that Romantic Stream near Philadelphia in the Year 1732 to the Present Time)*

FISHING (FLY CASTING) TOURNAMENT. *See* Fly casting tournament

FISHING LINE FACTORY was established in 1859 in Harlem, New York City, by Henry Hall, who manufactured linen and silk lines. The company moved to Astoria, Long Island, N.Y., later operating under the trade name Henry Hall and Sons. *(Forest and Stream. Vol. 12. Feb. 13, 1879)*

FISHING MAGAZINE was the *American Angler*, issued October 15, 1881. It contained 12 pages, was published in Philadelphia, Pa., and was edited by William Charles Harris. It was increased to 16 pages and issued monthly until January 21, 1882. On January 28, 1882, it became a weekly.

FISHING REEL

Electric spinning reel was made by Old Pal, Inc., a subsidiary of Woodstream Corporation, Lititz, Pa., and introduced at the American Fishing Tackle Manufacturer's Show at Chicago, Ill., on August 15, 1967. It weighed 26½ ounces, had 3 lure-retrieve speeds, from slow- to high-speed, and retailed for about $150. Enough power was supplied by 2 rechargeable nickel-cadmium energy cells to last a whole day.

FISHING ROD of telescoping steel tubes was made by Everett Horton of Bristol, Conn., who obtained patent No. 359,153 on March 8, 1887, on a fishing rod in "tubular metallic sections."

FISHING TREATISE was a 22-page report, *A Discourse Utter'd In Part at Ammauskeeg Falls in the Fishing Season 1739*, by Joseph Seccombe ("Fluviatulis Piscator"), parish minister in Kingston, N.H., published in 1743 in Boston, Mass., by Samuel Kneeland and Timothy Green. It was dedicated "to the honourable Theodore Atkinson, Esq., and others, the worthy patrons of the fishing at Ammauskeeg."

The First

FIVE-CENT STORE. *See under* Business

FIVE-MASTED TOPSAIL SCHOONER. *See* Ship: Schooner (five-masted)

FLAG

Air Force flag was approved March 26, 1951, by General Hoyt Sanford Vandenberg, Chief of Staff, as the ceremonial flag of the United States Air Force. It is an ultramarine blue flag with a center design showing the coat of arms and the encircling thirteen white stars on the seal of the Department of the Air Force. On a scroll attached to the bottom of the shield are the words "United States Air Force."

American flag was formally adopted by Congress on June 14, 1777, as the National Standard, and except for the adding of a new star for each new state and changes in the arrangement of the stars, the flag displayed today is the same as the first flag. Claims have been made that the first flag was made by Betsy Ross (Elizabeth Griscom Ross) in her little shop at 239 Arch St., Philadelphia, Pa., at the request of George Washington, Robert Morris, and Colonel George Ross, for the Continental Congress. *(George Henry Preble— Our Flag: Origin and Process of the Flag of the United States of America)*

American flag displayed on a man-of-war was flown in Portsmouth Harbor, N.H., when a group of young women made a flag of cloth from their own and their mothers' gowns which they presented to Captain John Paul Jones, who raised it to the mast of his ship, the *Ranger,* on July 4, 1777. *(Ezra Green—Diary of Ezra Green, M.D.)*

American flag flown in battle was carried September 3, 1777, by a detachment of light infantry and cavalry under General William Maxwell which met an advance guard of British and Hessian troops under Generals Richard Howe, Charles Cornwallis, and Wilhelm von Knyphausen at Cooch's Bridge, Delaware. (The August 3, 1777, Fort Stanwix flag was not the Stars and Stripes.)

American flag flown in battle on the Pacific was carried by the frigate *Essex,* commanded by Captain David Porter. The *Essex* sailed around Cape Horn and was the first American ship of war in the Pacific. She entered the Pacific Ocean March 5, 1813, and docked March 15, 1813, at Valparaiso, Chile. Her first prize on this cruise was the *Nereyda,* a Peruvian cruiser which was captured March 25, 1813. The *Nereyda*'s armament was thrown overboard and she was dispatched to Callao with a letter to the Viceroy of Peru. *(George Henry Preble—First Cruise of the U.S. Frigate Essex)*

American flag flown in World War I over a band of fighting Americans was flown at the Perignon Barracks, Toulouse, France, on September 30, 1914. Although the United States was neutral at the time, the American flag was carried by Ameri-

The First

can members of the French Foreign Legion who were ready to entrain for the front. *(Paul Ayres Rockwell—American Fighters in the Foreign Legion)*

American flag flown over a fortress of the Old World was flown on April 27, 1805, when Lieutenant Presley Neville O'Bannon of the U.S. Marines raised the colors over the Tripolitan fortress at Derne, on the north coast of Africa. *(James Alfred Moss—The Flag of the U.S.)*

American flag made of American bunting to fly over the Capitol, Washington, D.C., was hoisted February 24, 1866. It was 21 feet by 12 feet and was made by the United States Bunting Company, Lowell, Mass. It was presented to the Senate by the company.

American flag on the high seas was carried by Captain Thomas Thompson of the American sloop *Raleigh,* who, on September 4, 1777, was engaged in an encounter with a British vessel.

American flag over a schoolhouse was flown in May 1812 over the log schoolhouse at Catamount Hill, Colrain, Mass. It was cut and made by Rhoda Shippee, Mrs. Lois Shippee, Mrs. Sophia Willis, and Mrs. Stephen Hale at the home of Captain Amasa Shippee, who instructed the women in the arrangement of the stars and stripes. *(Harlan Hoyt Horner—The American Flag)*

American flag raised in Japan was flown September 4, 1856, at Shimoda, on the southern tip of Izu Peninsula, southwest of Yokohama, by Townsend Harris, American Consul General. The treaty of Yedo (Tokyo), signed July 29, 1858, opened Japan to the outside world. *(Carl Crow— He Opened the Door of Japan: Townsend Harris and the Story of His Amazing Adventures)*

American flag saluted by a foreign nation was flown from the top mast of the *Ranger.* The *Ranger* sailed for France, November 1, 1777, with dispatches of Burgoyne's surrender. On February 14, 1778, the *Ranger,* commanded by Captain John Paul Jones, saluted the French flag in the harbor of Quiberon, France, with 13 guns, which salute was returned by Admiral La Motte Piquet with 9 guns, the same salute authorized by the French court to be given an admiral of Holland or of any other republic. *(Henry Ernest Dunnack—The Maine Book)*

American flag saluted by a foreigner was flown at St. Eustatius, Dutch West Indies, on November 16, 1776, when Governor Johannes de Graeff saluted the *Andrea Doria,* which was flying the Continental Union flag. The brig was captained by Nicholas Biddle, who had been sent to St. Eustatius to transport arms and ammunition for the American army. *(Schuyler Hamilton—History of the National Flag of the United States of America,*

The First

American Flag to orbit the earth was carried in the capsule of the satellite *Discoverer XIII* (1960 Theta), which was launched on August 10, 1960, by the U.S. Air Force at Vandenberg Air Force Base, Calif., by a Thor-Agena missile with a 108,-500-pound lift-off weight. A 300-pound reentry capsule was ejected on August 11, 1960, on the 17th orbit and recovered the same day by the U.S.S. *Haiti Victory*, whose frogmen used a helicopter. The flag was presented to President Dwight David Eisenhower on August 15, 1960. The orbital time of the satellite was 94.1 minutes; its perigee was 161 miles, its apogee 436 miles.

Army flag (official) was established by executive order No. 10,670, signed June 12, 1956, by President Dwight David Eisenhower. On June 13, 1956, Vice President Richard Milhous Nixon presented a silk flag at the Capitol Building, Washington, D.C., to Secretary of the Army Wilber Marion Brucker, who passed it to General Maxwell Davenport Taylor, Army Chief of Staff, who handed it to the Third Infantry Regiment from Fort Meyer, Va. Although the Army had been established 181 years previously and had served in 7 major wars and 145 campaigns, this was its first official flag. In the center of a white field is the design in ultramarine blue of the seal of the Department of the Army (without the Roman numerals) above a scarlet scroll with the designation "United States Army" in white; beneath the scroll are the Arabic numerals 1775. Official flags may carry streamers, each of which bears the name of the campaign and the year in which it occurred.

British flag capture. *See under* Revolutionery War

Confederate States flag legally established was the "Stars and Bars," adopted by the Convention of Confederated States at Montgomery, Ala., on March 4, 1861, the same day Lincoln became President of the United States. It was designed by Major Orren Randolph Smith of Louisburg, N.C., and was reported to the convention by William Porcher Miles, president of North Carolina College. The original flag consisted of three bars and a field of seven stars, one for each of the Confederate States at that time. A star was added for each additional seceding state. Later this design was changed, since it resembled that of the national flag. *(George Henry Preble—History of the Flag of the U.S.A.)*

Flag around the world. *See* Ship: Ship to carry the United States flag around the world

Flag at the North Pole. *See* Discovery: Discovery of the North Pole

Flag displayed from the right hand of the Statue of Liberty in honor of an individual was flown on June 13, 1927, designated as Lindbergh Day, in honor of Charles Augustus Lindbergh's flight. The flag was hoisted to the peak of the right arm of the

The First

Statue of Liberty in unison with the raising of the Post Flag and the discharge of the Morning Gun at Governors Island, and was lowered in unison with Post Retreat ceremonies.

Naval vessel of the United States to display the American flag around Cape Horn. *See under* Ship

Navy flag (official) was authorized by executive order signed on April 24, 1959, by President Dwight David Eisenhower. The flag adopted was dark blue, with its center in colors showing part of the seal of the Navy Department in a circle of yellow rope. A yellow scroll below was inscribed "United States Navy" in dark blue letters. It had a 2½-inch yellow fringe.

President's flag, with the President's seal in bronze upon a blue background and a large white star in each corner, was adopted May 29, 1916, by executive order No. 2390 of President Woodrow Wilson. Previously other Presidents had had flags but they were more or less individual emblems. President Harry S. Truman, by executive order No. 9646 of October 25, 1945, made several further changes and increased the number of stars to 48, one for each state. The flag now has 50 stars, as decreed by executive order No. 10,860 of February 9, 1960, effective July 4, 1960. *(10 Federal Register 13391)*

Ship to carry the United States flag around the world. *See under* Ship

Vice President's flag was established February 7, 1936, by executive order No. 7285. It contains the seal of the United States and a blue star in each corner, on a field of white. The Navy had previously created a flag for the Vice President, but its use by other departments was optional.

FLAG DAY. *See under* Holiday

FLAG LEGISLATION

Flag act officially to establish the American flag was passed April 4, 1818 (3 Stat. L. 415), "an act to establish the flag of the United States." It authorized a flag with 13 horizontal stripes, alternate red and white representing the 13 original states, and a union of 20 white stars in a blue field, one star to be added to the flag for each new state on the Fourth of July succeeding such admission.

Legislation authorizing changes in the American flag was passed by Congress on January 13, 1794 (1 Stat. L. 341), an "act making an alteration in the flag of the United States" and providing "that from and after the first day of May 1795, the Flag of the United States be fifteen stripes, alternate red and white; and that the union be fifteen stars, white, in a blue field." The change was made so that Vermont and Kentucky would be represented on the flag. A law was passed on April 4, 1818 (3 Stat. L. 415) reducing the number of stripes to 13 to represent the original 13 states as in the first American flag made, and providing one star for each state. A new star was to be

The First

FLAG LEGISLATION—*Continued*
added on the Fourth of July following the admission of each new state.

FLAG MONUMENT. *See* Monument: Monument to the American flag

FLASHER. *See* Electric sign: Electric sign flasher

FLASHLIGHT was manufactured by the American Electric and Novelty Manufacturing Company of New York City, which started in business in 1896. The first flashlight was produced about 1898. The model was a crude affair, and consisted only of a paper tube with metal fittings, a rough brass stamping used for a reflector, without any lens, and a spring contact switch. The lamp was handmade, as was also the battery. The company later changed its name to the American Eveready Company and subsequently became a part of the National Carbon Company, Inc.

FLASHLIGHT LAMP. *See* Photography: Photographic flashlight lamps

FLATIRON, ELECTRIC. *See* Electric flatiron

FLEA CIRCUS was an "Extraordinary Exhibition of the Industrious Fleas" at 187 Broadway, New York City, which opened January 1835. Admission was 50 cents and performances were given from 11 A.M. to 3 P.M. and from 5 P.M. to 9 P.M. A cold spell forced the exhibit to close to enable the exhibitor "to fill up the vacancies that grim death had made." It was reopened January 20, 1835, for one week. *(New York Commercial Advertiser. Jan. 20, 1835)*

FLEA LABORATORY was opened January 1, 1939, at the University of California's Hooper Foundation for Medical Research, San Francisco, Calif. It was a flea-tight, rodent-tight, two-story concrete building, air-conditioned at a constant temperature. The first director was Dr. Karl Friedrich Meyer.

FLEET (warship). *See* Ship: Warship

FLICKER, a series of successive drawings bound together in book form which appeared to show animation, was patented by Henry Van Hoevenbergh of Elizabeth, N.J., who obtained patent No. 258,164, May 16, 1882, on an "optical toy." On June 20, 1882, he obtained patent No. 259,950 on an improvement combining two or more series of superposed leaves. Alternate leaves were indented and cut.

FLIGHT. *See* Aviation—Flights; Aviation—Flights (transatlantic); Aviation—Flights (transcontinental); Aviation—Flights (transpacific); Aviation—Flights (world)

FLIGHT ATTENDANT. *See* Aviation: Air flight attendant (woman)

FLIGHT SURGEON (U.S. Army). *See under* Army officer

The First

FLINT GLASS FACTORY. *See* Glass factory

FLIP BOOK. *See* Flicker

FLIP SHIP. *See* Ship

FLOATING CHURCH. *See* Church

FLOATING HOSPITAL. *See* Hospital

FLOATING SEAPLANE RAMP. *See under* Aviation

FLOATING TABLEAUX PARADE. *See* Parade

FLOATING THEATER (showboat). *See* Theater: Showboat

FLOOD of which there is any known record was that of the Mississippi River in 1543. When Hernando de Soto was making an exploratory trip, he noted that on March 18, 1543, the Mississippi River began overflowing its banks and continued until reached its crest on April 20, 1543. By the end of May, the flood had receded. There had doubtless been many previous floods, but no records exist of them. *(Garcilaso de la Vega—La Florida del Inca)*

FLOOR TILES. *See* Tile: Wall and floor tiles

FLORAL MAGAZINE. *See* Horticultural magazine

FLORAL SOCIETY. *See* Horticultural society

FLOUR MILL
Flour mill equipped with elevators conveyors drills, and a "hopper boy" was designed by Oliver Evans in 1789. With this equipment the mill could be operated by one man instead of the four who were needed in the old-fashioned mills. The mill had an endless belt conveyor with buckets spaced a foot apart on the belt, each bucket holding a quart of grain.

Flour rolling mill was invented by John Stevens of Neenah, Wis., whose patent application of December 28, 1877, on a "grain crushing mill" was granted March 23, 1880, No. 225,770. His method increased production 70 percent and produced a superior flour which sold for $2 more a barrel *(State Historical Society of Wisconsin—Proceedings, 1907)*

FLOWERS
Tetraploid flower produced by the use of chemicals was publicly exhibited by David Burpee of the W. Atlee Burpee Company, Philadelphia, Pa. on January 29, 1940, at the New York City Flower Show. A marigold was treated with colchicine, a chemical extracted from the roots of the fall crocus, with the result that it was one and a half times as large in diameter as the Guinea Gold from which it started.

FLUORESCENT ILLUMINATED CAR. *See* Railroad car: Car with fluorescent lighting

FLUORESCENT MINERAL EXHIBIT was opened April 26, 1929, at the Academy of Natural Sciences of Philadelphia, Pa. Carbon arc lamps with Corning filters were used by Samuel George Gordon, associate professor of minerals, to activate a display of minerals.

FLUOROGRAPH. *See* X ray

FLUORSPAR commercial mining was attempted in 1837 at Trumbull, Conn. It was used with magnetic iron pyrite in the smelting of copper ores and sold for $60 a ton. *(Charles Upham Shepard—A Report on the Geological Survey of Connecticut)*

FLY CASTING TOURNAMENT
Cast to exceed 100 feet was made by R. C. Leonard, who cast 101 feet 6 inches, on March 17, 1897, at the Sportsmen's Exposition, Madison Square Garden, New York City.

Fly casting tournament was held June 18, 1861, in Utica, N.Y., by the New York State Sportsmen's Association. The "throwing the fly" competition was won by George Lennebacker of Utica, N.Y.

Indoor fly casting tournament was held March 15–20, 1897, under the auspices of the Sportsmen's Association at Madison Square Garden, New York City. Competitions were held in casting for distance, casting for accuracy and distance, bass fly casting, etc. *(Score Book of the First Indoor Fly Casting Tournament of the Sportsmen's Association)*

FLYING CROSS. *See* Medal

FLYING MEDICAL CLINIC. *See* Medical clinic

FLYING-WING BOMBER. *See* Aviation—Airplane: Bomber with the Flying Wing design

FOG DISPOSAL UNIT was accepted by test on March 29, 1949, by the Los Angeles Airport, Los Angeles, Calif. It consisted of 392 oil burners installed alongside runways. During World War II, the system was used in England and known as FIDO, Fog Investigation and Disposal Operation.

FOLDING BED. *See* Bed

FOLDING MACHINE to fold paper for books and newspapers was invented by Cyrus Chambers, Jr., of Kennet Square, Pa., who obtained patent No. 15,842 on October 7, 1856. It was for plain three-fold right-angle work and delivered a 16-page folded signature to the packing box. It was installed in the Bible printing house of Jasper Harding & Son, Philadelphia, Pa.

FOLDING THEATER CHAIR. *See* Chair

FOOD LEGISLATION. *See* Pure food law: Pure food and drug legislation (national)

FOOD-O-MAT. *See under* Business

FOODSTUFFS PRODUCER to achieve great commercial success was Henry John Heinz, who in 1869 opened a factory at Sharpsburg, Pa. His

first product was grated and prepared horseradish. His company, known as the H. J. Heinz Company, manufactures several hundred varieties of products. *(H. J. Heinz Co.—The Romance of the 57)*

FOOTBALL
Football with a rubber covering was made by the W. J. Voit Rubber Corporation, Los Angeles, Calif., in March 1936. The ball, which did not soak up water, was otherwise identical with conventional leather-covered footballs. It was also cheaper and longer-lasting.

Football with a rubber covering used in a major collegiate game was used October 13, 1951, at Grant Field, Atlanta, Ga., in a game in which Georgia Tech defeated Louisiana State University 25–7.

FOOTBALL BOOK was *American Football,* by Walter Chauncey Camp, published in 1891 by Harper and Brothers, New York City. It contained 175 pages with 31 portraits.

FOOTBALL CLUB
Football association (professional) was the American Professional Football Association, formed in Canton, Ohio, on September 17, 1920, by 11 clubs representing the following cities: Chicago, Decatur, and Rock Island, Ill.; Hammond and Muncie, Ind.; Rochester, N.Y.; Akron, Canton, Cleveland, Dayton, and Masillon, Ohio.

Football club was the Oneida Football Club, which was organized in 1862 by Gerrit Smith Miller at Epes Sargent Dixwell's School in Boston, Mass. The members played all comers from 1862 to 1865. They were never defeated, nor was their goal line crossed. *(Winthrop Saltonstall Scudder—An Historical Sketch of the Oneida Football Club of Boston 1862–1865)*

Intercollegiate football association was the Intercollegiate Football Association organized at the Massasoit House, Springfield, Mass., November 23, 1876, with Columbia, Harvard, and Princeton as its three charter members (Rutgers and Yale joined later). The association standardized the number of men on each team (15) and the area of the field (140 by 70 yards). *(Frank Presbrey—Athletics at Princeton)*

FOOTBALL DUMMY for tackling purposes was improvised by Amos Alonzo Stagg at Yale University, New Haven, Conn., in the fall of 1889. He used an old gymnasium mat for the purpose. *(Amos Alonzo Stagg and Wesley Winans Stout—Touchdown)*

FOOTBALL GAME
All-star football game was sponsored by Chicago Tribune Charities, Inc., a nonprofit organization, and was played on August 31, 1934, at Soldier Field, Chicago, Ill. The Chicago Bears, coached by George Halas, played the College All-Stars, coached by Noble Kizer of Purdue, to a 0-0

The First

FOOTBALL GAME—*Continued*
tie. The players each received $150 and expenses. Attendance was 79,432.

American Football League's first championship game was played January 1, 1961, at Houston, Tex. The Houston Oilers of the Eastern Division defeated the Los Angeles Chargers of the Western Division 24-16 at Houston. The Oilers received $1,025 per man and the Chargers $718. The attendance was approximately 32,200.

Army-Navy football game was played November 29, 1890, at West Point, N.Y. The Army (U.S. Military Academy) captain was Dennis Michie, '92, and the Navy (U.S. Naval Academy) captain was Charles Rulf Emerich, '91. The score was Navy 24, Army 0. *(Dean Hill—Football thru the Years)*

Coast-to-coast football-game broadcast originating on the West Coast. *See under* Radio broadcast

Football game at night was played September 29, 1892, at the Mansfield Fair, Mansfield, Pa., between the Mansfield Teachers College and the Wyoming Seminary of Kingston, Pa. Twenty electric lights of 2,000 candlepower were used with a Thompson & Huston Dynamo Machine. The game lasted 70 minutes, but only one half was played, neither team scoring.

Football game between black colleges was played January 1, 1897, at Brisbine Park, Atlanta, Ga., between Atlanta University and Tuskegee Normal and Industrial Institute. Atlanta won 10-0. Atlanta's captain was George F. Porter, and Tuskegee's captain was Clarence Matthews. *(Atlanta University Bulletin. January 1897)*

Football game championship (professional) broadcast on a network. *See under* Radio broadcast

Football game coast-to-coast telecast. *See under* Television—Telecast

Football game (collegiate) broadcast. *See under* Radio broadcast

Football game in which referees were permitted to use television instant replays was the Hall of Fame Philadelphia Eagles game, July 29, 1978, at Canton, Ohio, when the Eagles defeated the National Football League Miami Dolphins 17-3. The game was telecast on Channel 7.

Football game played in the United States to be broadcast in England was the Yale-Harvard game of November 22, 1930, played at New Haven, Conn. Harvard won with a score of 13-0. The game was broadcast by the British Broadcasting Corporation.

Football game (professional championship) telecast. *See under* Television—Telecast

Football game televised. *See under* Television—Telecast

The First

Football game to attract 100,000 spectators was played at Memorial Stadium, Berkeley, Calif. on November 22, 1924, by teams from the University of California and Leland Stanford University, both undefeated for the Pacific Coast championship. The score was 20 to 20. The stadium accommodated 76,000 spectators, and 24,000 more witnessed the game from "Tight Wad" hill.

Football game to gross $1 million was played December 31, 1961, when the Green Bay Packers defeated the New York Giants 37-0 for the National Football League championship at the Green Bay's City Stadium, Green Bay, Wis. There were 39,029 spectators, and the paid attendance amounted to $1,013,792. Each of the Packers received $5,195.44 and each of the Giants $3,339.99. The Packers scored 2 touchdowns, 3 field goals, 4 conversions.

Indoor football game was played by the Springfield (Mass.) Young Men's Christian Association against the Yale Consolidated Team, a team which had five of the Yale varsity players on it. The game was played as part of a three-day winter carnival at Madison Square Garden, New York City, after the close of the 1891 season. The score was 16-10 in favor of Yale. The Springfield team led 10-6 until the end of the game, when William Walter Hefflinger evened the score. In the try for goal, the ball struck the post, bounding back into the field of play. Josh A. ("Josh") Hartwell caught the ball as then allowed and charged to the five-yard line, where an additional touchdown was made, making the score 16-10. *(Amos Alonzo Stagg and Wesley Winans Stout—Touchdown)*

Indoor football game (large) was played in the Chicago Coliseum, 63rd Street, Chicago, Ill., on Thanksgiving Day, November 26, 1896. The game was played between teams representing the University of Chicago and the University of Michigan. Chicago won 7 points to Michigan's 6. The gate receipts were approximately $10,000. *(Amos Alonzo Stagg and Wesley Winans Stout—Touchdown)*

Intercollegiate football championship was won in the fall of 1876 by Yale under the captaincy of Eugene Voy Baker, '77. Although not a member of the Intercollegiate Football Association, Yale played and defeated Columbia, Harvard, and Princeton. The standing of the teams was Yale 2, Princeton 2, Harvard 1, Columbia 0.

Intercollegiate football contest in the world was played at Rutgers Field, New Brunswick, N.J., on November 6, 1869. Captain William Stryker Gummere, '70 of Princeton (later chief justice of New Jersey), challenged Captain William James Leggett of Rutgers to a friendly game. Each team consisted of 25 men. The first team to score 6 goals was Rutgers, which won with a score of 6 goals to Princeton's 4. Each goal constituted a game. Six games decided the match, which lasted one hour.

The First

International football game was played December 6, 1873, at New Haven, Conn. The Yale team defeated the Eton (England) team with a score of 2 goals to 1.

Professional football game was played September 3, 1895, at Latrobe, Pa., between the Latrobe Young Men's Christian Association and the Jeannette (Pa.) Athletic Club, the former winning 12-0. Latrobe's captain was Harry Ryan and Jeannette's captain was "Posie" Flowers. The regular quarterback being unable to play, John K. Brallier of Indiana, Pa., was paid $10 and expenses. The following year four men were paid, and in 1897 the entire team was paid.

Professional football game attended by 80,000 spectators was played December 29, 1968, at the Cleveland Stadium, Cleveland, Ohio. The Baltimore Colts defeated the Cleveland Browns 34-0. The attendance was 80,628; the player's share, Colts $9,265, Browns $5,963.

Professional football game in which 10 touchdowns were made took place at Temple Stadium, Philadelphia, Pa., on November 6, 1934, when the National Football League Philadelphia Eagles defeated the Cincinnati Reds, 64-0. Three touchdowns each were made by Homer ("Swede") Hanson and Joseph ("Joe") Carter; one each by Edward Matesic, Edward ("Ed") Storm, Marvin Ellstrom, and Roger ("Red") Kirkman.

Professional football game to last longer than 80 minutes was the American Football League divisional play-off game that had 3 halves (6 quarters) and lasted 1 hour 22 minutes 40 seconds. The Miami Dolphins defeated the Kansas City Chiefs, 27-24, on December 25, 1971, at Arrowhead Stadium, Kansas City, Mo. The Dolphins made 3 points in the 6th quarter, and George Yepremian made a 37-yard field goal in the 2nd quarter of overtime.

Professional football game with 16 touchdowns occurred on November 27, 1966, at Washington, D.C., in a National Football League game. The Washington Redskins made 10 touchdowns, the New York Giants 6. The score was Washington 72 (13-21-14-24), New York 41 (0-14-14-13).

Professional world championship football game was played December 17, 1933, at Wrigley Field, Chicago, Ill., when the Chicago Bears of the Western Division defeated the New York Giants of the Eastern Division of the National Football League 23-21. The purse was divided; 60 percent to the players, 15 percent to each club, and 10 percent to the league. The individual player's shares were $210.44 for the Bears and $140.22 for the Giants.

Rugby contest (international) was held May 14, 1874, at Jarvis Field, Cambridge, Mass., between Harvard and McGill (Montreal, Canada) universities. The games were played under the Harvard

The First

rules and Harvard won three games, the first two lasting about 5 minutes and the third about 12 minutes. It was considered a game under the Harvard rules as soon as either team scored. McGill arrived with 11 men and Harvard with 15, 4 of whom were dropped to equalize the teams. A second match was played the following day, and a third match was played in the fall in Montreal.

Super Bowl contest, between the National Football League and the American Football League for the world championship, was played January 15, 1967, at the Memorial Coliseum, Los Angeles, Calif., before 63,036 spectators, when the Green Bay Packers (NFL) defeated the Kansas City Chiefs (AFL) 35-10. The winning Packers received $15,000 each, the Chiefs $7,500 each.

FOOTBALL GOALPOST

Football goalpost was used in the contest between McGill University (Montreal, Canada) and Harvard University, played at Cambridge, Mass., May 14, 1874. At this game, admission was charged, the first instance in which an admission fee was charged at a collegiate sporting event. The proceeds were used for lavishly entertaining the McGill team.

Football goalposts of collapsible folding metal were manufactured by Fisher Metal Parts Manufacturing Company, New York City, and were installed in June 1936 at the Yankee Stadium, New York City.

FOOTBALL PLAYER

Athlete enshrined in 2 Halls of Fame. *See under* Hall of Famer

Black football player to win the Heisman Memorial Trophy as the outstanding college player in the United States was Ernest ("Ernie") Davis, halfback of Syracuse University, named on November 28, 1961, and presented with the award on December 6, 1961, at the Downtown Athletic Club, New York City.

Football player to punt 98 yards was Steve O'Neal, New York Jet rookie (NFL), who punted 98 yards against the Denver Broncos on September 21, 1969, at the Mile High Stadium, Denver, Colo. Denver won 21-19 before approximately 50,600 spectators.

Football player to score 50 points in 1 game was Clark Hinkle of Bucknell University of Lewisburg, Pa., who scored 50 points on November 28, 1929 at Lewisburg, Pa., against Dickinson College, Carlisle, Pa. He made 8 touchdowns and 2 extra points after the touchdown. Bucknell won 78-0.

Woman football player (professional) was Patricia Palinkas, 27 years old, of Tampa, Fla., who played with the Orlando Panthers of the Atlantic Coast League on August 15, 1970, in a game against the Bridgeport Jets at Orlando, Fla. She held the ball for 3 plays by Steve Palinkas, her

The First

FOOTBALL PLAYER—*Continued*
husband, the team's kicker. The Panthers won 26-7.

FOOTBALL RULES were formulated at a meeting held October 18, 1873, in New York City and attended by delegates from Columbia, Princeton, Rutgers, and Yale.

FOOTBALL TEAM
Football team (big league) to travel coast-to-coast was the Chicago Bears, who tied the Chicago Cardinals (0-0) on November 26, 1925, at Chicago, Ill. Harold ("Red") Grange, the "Galloping Ghost," gained a net of 40 yards in 14 plays and added 69 more in running back 3 points; this was his first professional game. The season concluded in January 1926 with Grange having played at New York, Providence, Pittsburgh, Detroit, Chicago, Tampa, Jacksonville, Maimi, New Orleans, Los Angeles, San Diego, San Francisco, Portland, and Seattle.

Football team to score more than 750 points in one season was Harvard College, Cambridge, Mass., which in the 1886 season scored 765 points in 14 games, the largest amount being 158 against Exeter. Harvard won 12 games and lost 2.

Midwestern football team to play on the Pacific Coast was that of the University of Chicago, Chicago, Ill. The game was played on December 25, 1894, at San Francisco, Calif., against Leland Stanford, Jr. University. The score was 24-4 in favor of the Chicago team.

FOOTBALL UNIFORM
Football uniforms worn in a game were used November 13, 1875, at New Haven, Conn., by teams from Yale and Harvard colleges. The Yale team wore dark trousers, blue shirts, and yellow caps, while the Harvard team wore crimson shirts and stockings and knee breeches. Harvard won the game, 4-0. The game at that time resembled rugby more than present-day football. Each team had 15 players.

FOOTBALL UNIFORM NUMERALS sewn on the players' uniforms to enable the spectators easily to distinguish the players were used by the University of Pittsburgh, Pittsburgh, Pa., on December 5, 1908, for the game against Washington and Jefferson. The score was 14-0 in favor of Washington and Jefferson.

FOREIGN AFFAIRS DEPARTMENT. (U.S.) *See* State Department (U.S.)

FOREIGN AID BILL. *See* Federal foreign aid bill

FOREIGN AND DOMESTIC COMMERCE BUREAU (U.S.) *See* Commerce Department (U.S.): Foreign and Domestic Commerce Bureau

FOREIGN FEATURE FILM. *See under* Motion picture

The First

FOREIGN MISSIONARY SOCIETY. *See* Missionary society

FOREIGN NEWSPAPER. *See* Newspaper

FOREIGN SERVICE. *See* Diplomatic service

FOREIGN SERVICE SCHOOL was the School of Comparative Jurisprudence and Diplomacy of George Washington University, Washington, D.C., which opened November 15, 1898. It was discontinued as a separate school in 1913, the courses being given, however, in Columbian College until September 1928, when training in foreign service and governmental theory and administration was reestablished as a separate branch under the School of Government.

FOREIGN SERVICEWOMEN INTERRED IN ARLINGTON CEMETERY. *See under* Cemetery

FOREIGN SQUADRON AIRPLANE FLIGHT. *See* Aviation—Flights (transatlantic): Transatlantic foreign squadron flight to the United States.

FOREIGN TREATY. *See* Treaty

FOREST
Community forest was established in 1710 in Newington, N.H. An area of 110 acres of pine trees was set aside as a "town forest." *(U.S. Department of Agriculture—Community Forests)*

National forest was the Shoshone National Forest in Wyoming established by President Benjamin Harrison on March 30, 1891, by presidential proclamation 17 (26 Stat. L. 1565).

National forest in the southern states was Ocala National Forest, Fla., established as a public reservation by proclamation of President Theodore Roosevelt on November 24, 1908 (35 Stat. L. 2206).

FOREST FIRE
Forest fire drenched by artificial rain, produced by seeding cumulus clouds with dry ice, was attacked October 29, 1947, at Concord, N.H. Seeders of the General Electric Company, Schenectady, N.Y., flew over the burning area in "rain-making" planes and caused rain to fall. The experiment was Project Cirrus, a joint weather research program of the United States Army Signal Corps and the Office of Naval Research. General rain caused by natural conditions followed, so it was impossible to determine the extent of artificial rainfall.

Forest fire lookout tower was a log cabin with flat roof erected by M. G. Shaw Lumber Company, Greenville, Maine, on Squaw Mountain, southwest of Moosehead Lake. The first watchman was William Hilton of Bangor, Maine, whose service started June 10, 1905.

Forest fire of consequence occurred on October 8, 1871, at Peshtigo, Wis., north of Green Bay, Wis. The fire, which was 8 to 10 miles wide, destroyed 1,280,000 acres of timberland. The forests were dry, since it had not rained for 3 months.

The First

FOREST HORSE. *See* Horse

FOREST MANAGEMENT on a professional scale was begun in 1891 in Asheville, N.C., on the Biltmore estate of George Washington Vanderbilt.

FOREST PLANTING (federal). *See* Forest Service: Federal planting of forests

FOREST RESERVE

Forest reserve (national) was the Yellowstone Park Timberland Reserve, which was so designated by act of Congress on March 30, 1891 (26 Stat. L. 1565), signed by President Benjamin Harrison. It was placed under the administration of the Land Office of the Department of the Interior. *(Jenks Cameron—The Development of Government Forest Control in the United States)*

Forest reserve (state) was the New York State Forest Preserve, designated May 15, 1885. Legislation prohibiting the sale of state lands in certain counties in the Adirondack area was passed February 6, 1883. Essentially this forest reserve is a state park, and in it logging and other commercial forms of exploitation are prohibited.

FOREST SERVICE

Aircraft owned by the Forest Service of the Department of Agriculture was placed in service August 17, 1938, at the Oakland, Calif., airport. It was a 450 h.p. green-coated fire-fighting plane with a cruising speed of 175 m.p.h. and flying range of 700 miles. It had a service ceiling of 22,000 feet and could carry a full load of 1,250 pounds.

Federal planting of forests was begun in 1891 in cooperation with private individuals in the sand hills of Nebraska. A small plantation of jack and Norway pines was established four miles west of Swan, Neb., for the purpose of holding the sand in place by the use of shelter belts. The land was acquired under authority of the act of March 3, 1891 (26 Stat. L. 1095), "an act to repeal timber culture laws, and for other purposes."

Forest commission (state) (permanent) was the Board of Forestry of California authorized by "act to create a state board of forestry," passed March 3, 1885. The first meeting was held April 1, 1885, in San Francisco, Calif. James V. Coleman was elected chairman; Charles M. Chase, treasurer; and Sands W. Forman, secretary. Dr. Albert Kellogg was the other member of the original board. New York State on May 15, 1885, authorized a state forestry commission, which held its first meeting September 23, 1885.

Forest Service aerial patrol was established by the Department of Agriculture on June 1, 1919. Two patrols a day were operated out of March Field, Riverside, Calif. Five routes were covered, for each of which there was one airplane. The expense was borne mainly by the Army. From June 1 to October 30 the airplanes flew 2,457 hours

The First

and covered 202,009 miles. The patrol was discontinued October 31, 1919.

Forest Service (U.S.) was organized as the Division of Forestry and received permanent statutory recognition by the act of June 30, 1886 (24 Stat. L. 103). Dr. Bernhard Eduard Fernow was the first chief and served until 1898. By the act of March 2, 1901 (31 Stat. L. 929), the Division of Forestry became the Bureau of Forestry. The act of February 1, 1905 (33 Stat. L. 628), signed by President Theodore Roosevelt, provided for the transfer of Forest Reserves from the Department of the Interior to the Department of Agriculture, opened natural resources of the forests to legitimate use, and stabilized principles of reserving for public purposes the federally owned forest lands. The Appropriation Act of March 3, 1905 (33 Stat. L. 872) designated the old Bureau of Forestry as the Forest Service, which is the present organization. *(Bernhard Eduard Fernow—Division of Forestry —Department of Agriculture—1897 Yearbook)*

Forestry inquiry commission (state) was appointed by Wisconsin under act of March 23, 1867, relating to the growth of forest trees. The state agricultural society and the state horticultural society were each authorized to appoint one person, these two to appoint a third, to constitute a committee "to inquire and make report in detail" on "increasing the growth and preservation of forest and other trees." The first commissioners were Increase Allen Lapham, Joseph Gillett Knapp, and Hans Crocker, who published a 104-page report in 1867 entitled *Report on the Disastrous Effects of the Destruction of Forest Trees.*

FORESTRY BOOK was Franklin Benjamin Hough's *Elements of Forestry; designed to afford information concerning the planting and care of forest trees for ornament or profit and giving suggestions upon the creation and care of woodlands with the view of securing the greatest benefit for the longest time, particularly adapted to the wants and conditions of the United States.* It contained 381 pages and was published in 1882 by R. Clarke & Co., Cincinnati, Ohio.

FORESTRY LEGISLATION

Colonial forestry legislation was the act of March 29, 1626, passed by the Plymouth Colony, which required the approval of the governor and the council to sell or transport lumber out of the colony. *(Jay P. Kinney—Forest Legislation in America Prior to March 4, 1789)*

Federal forestry legislation was the act of February 25, 1799 (1 Stat. L. 622), which authorized the President to direct a sum "not exceeding $200,000 to be laid out in the purchase of growing or other timber, or of lands on which timber was growing, suitable for the navy." On December 19, 1799, a tract of 350 acres on Grover's Island, Ga., was purchased for $7,500. *(Jenks Cameron—The De-*

The First

FORESTRY LEGISLATION—*Continued*
velopment of Governmental Forest Control in the United States)

Federal forestry supervision was attempted August 15, 1876. An appropriation for this purpose had been provided by an amendment to the act making appropriations for the legislative, executive, and judicial expenses of the government for the year ending June 30, 1877. The total appropriation for the Division of Forestry for the fiscal year 1877, March 3, 1877 (19 Stat. L. 360), was only $10,000 ($2,000 for salaries and $8,000 for the "purpose of enabling the Commissioner of Agriculture to experiment and to continue an investigation and report upon the subject of forestry and the collection and distribution of valuable economic forest-tree seeds and plants"). Dr. Franklin Benjamin Hough was placed in charge of the survey on August 30, 1876. *(Michigan Political Science Association. Publications, Vol. 5)*

FORESTRY SCHOOL
Forestry correspondence course in tree surgery was started in 1914 by the Davey Tree Expert Company to prepare the men who intended to join to the Davey Institute of Tree Surgery of Kent, Ohio. *(The Davey Bulletin. Vol. XVII, No. 1A. Jan. 1, 1929)*

Forestry course in a university was established in 1881 by the University of Michigan, Ann Arbor, Mich., as one of seven main subjects given in the curriculum of a newly established School of Political Science. It was given for four successive years, then discontinued until the reestablishment of the Department of Forestry in 1902. Lectures, however, had been given on forestry and tree culture at Yale University in 1873, and at Cornell University in 1874.

Forestry school dealing exclusively with problems of forestry was the Biltmore Forest School of Biltmore, N.C., a private institution, opened by Dr. Carl Alvin Schenck, September 1, 1898. Instruction was largely given by Dr. Schenck in class, and later in field work and on extensive tours both in the western part of this country and in European countries. The school ran until 1912, when Dr. Schenck returned to Germany.

Forestry school of collegiate character for training men in forestry was established September 19, 1898, at Cornell University, Ithaca, N.Y., as the New York State College of Forestry. It was under the leadership of Dr. Bernhard Eduard Fernow as Director and Dean. The law under which this school was established was signed by Governor Frank Swett Black on April 8, 1898. New York was therefore the first state to establish a forestry course. The Forest Engineer degree (F.E.) was awarded in 1900 to Ralph Clement Bryant. The activities of the school were suspended in 1903.

The First

Forestry school to give scientific training in the care and preservation of trees was a department of the Davey Tree Expert Company, Kent, Ohio, incorporated February 9, 1909. The school technically was not a forestry school, but devoted itself to shade trees and the specialized methods of caring for them. The first president was John Davey, who served from February 9, 1909, to November 8 1923.

FORESTRY SOCIETY
National forestry association was the American Forestry Association, organized September 10 1875, in Chicago, Ill. The first president was Robert Douglas and the first secretary was Professor Henry H. McAfee, professor of Horticulture and Forestry, Iowa State College. Douglas immediately resigned and Dr. John Aston Warder was elected in his place. The American Forestry Congress (organized in Cincinnati, Ohio, April 25, 1882 merged with the American Forestry Association at a meeting held June 29, 1882, in Rochester, N.Y It was incorporated January 25, 1897. *(American Forestry Association—American Conservation)*

State forestry association was the Minnesota Forestry Association, organized January 12, 1876 in St. Paul, Minn., to promote the planting of forest trees. E. F. Drake was president and Leonard B Hodges, secretary. On March 2, 1876, the state appropriated $2,500 to carry on the work (Chapter 110).

FORK brought to America was in a leather case with a bodkin and knife. Governor John Winthrop of Massachusetts introduced it into this country about 1630, following the style which Queen Elizabeth of England had introduced despite the flaming denunciations of many eminent clergymen.

FORTY-HOUR-WEEK LAW (federal). *See* Labor law

FOUNDRY, TYPE. *See* Type foundry

FOUNTAIN PEN that was practical was invented by Lewis Edson Waterman and was manufactured in 1884 by the L. E. Waterman Company in New York City. The first year about 200 fountain pens were manufactured. They were originally manufactured by hand. Waterman also invented the machinery to produce fountain pens in commercial quantities. *(L. E. Waterman Co.—Pens)*

FOUNTAIN PEN PATENT was awarded on May 20, 1830, to D. Hyde of Reading, Pa.

FOUR-MASTED SCHOONER. *See* Ship

FOURDRINIER PAPER-MAKING MACHINE *See* Papermaking machinery: Papermaking machine (cylinder)

FOX HUNTING CLUB was the Gloucester Fox Hunting Club, composed of residents of Philadelphia, Pa., and Gloucester County, N.J. A group of 27 dog owners met October 29, 1766, in Phila

The First

delphia, Pa., and decided to hold a meeting on December 13, 1766, to formulate rules for the club, which began its activities January 1, 1767. John Massey, huntsman, was appointed to keep the dogs. The club dissolved in 1818. *(William Milnor, Jr.—Memoirs of the Gloucester Fox Hunting Club near Philadelphia)*

FOXHOUND ASSOCIATION was the Masters of Fox Hounds Association, formed February 14, 1907, in New York City. The first president was W. Austin Wadsworth and the first secretary Henry G. Vaughan.

FOXHOUND MASTER (American) to become a Master of Foxhounds in England was Robert Early Strawbridge of Philadelphia, who on May 1, 1913, became Master of Fox Hounds of the Cottesmore Hounds, Oakham, Rutland, England, and served until May 1, 1915.

FRACTIONAL CURRENCY. *See* Money: Paper money fractional currency

FRANCIUM. *See* Element: Element 87

FRANKING PRIVILEGE. *See* Postal service: Mail franking privilege

FRATERNAL GROUP INSURANCE. *See* Insurance

FRATERNITY CATALOG was published in 1830 by the Kappa Alpha Society, founded November 26, 1825, at Union College, Schenectady, N.Y.

FRATERNITY (Greek-letter)
Fraternity house was occupied in 1839 by the Williams Chapter (Alpha Chapter of Massachusetts) of the Kappa Alpha Society at Williams College, Williamstown, Mass. The chapter was founded October 29, 1833, and used various quarters until 1839, when it hired a frame structure two stories high, an annex to the residence of Captain James Meachem. The first floor supplied space for the social gatherings and a banquet room. A winding stair led to the second story, planned expressly for the secret meetings.

Fraternity west of the Alleghenies was Beta Theta Pi, founded August 8, 1839, at Miami University, Oxford, Ohio.

Intercollegiate Greek-letter national fraternity for black men was Alpha Phi Alpha formed December 4, 1906, by members of a social study club formed in 1905. The first president was George B. Kelley. The first chapter was Alpha at Cornell University, Ithaca, N.Y. The first annual banquet was October 30, 1906. It was incorporated January 29, 1908. The first convention was held at Beta chapter, Howard University, Washington, D.C., in 1908. *(Charles Harris Wesley—The History of Alpha Phi Alpha)*

Interfraternity council was the National Interfraternity Conference, composed of 26 fraternities which met November 17, 1909, at the University

The First

Club, New York City, to discuss matters of general interest and welfare.

Professional fraternity was Theta Xi, founded April 29, 1864, at the Rensselaer Polytechnic Institute, Troy, N.Y. Membership was confined to students of engineering and science. The fraternity was an offspring of Sigma Delta, a local society at Rensselaer Polytechnic Institute. *(William Raimond Baird—Baird's Manual of American College Fraternities)*

Scholastic fraternity was Phi Beta Kappa, founded December 5, 1776, at William and Mary College, Williamsburg, Va., with a nucleus of 50 members. In December 1779 it authorized the establishment of branches at Yale and Harvard. *(Oscar McMurtrie Voorhees—History of Phi Beta Kappa).*

Scholastic fraternity chapter established at a black university was formed April 4, 1953, by Phi Beta Kappa at Fisk University, Nashville, Tenn. Goodrich Cook White, president of the United Chapters of Phi Beta Kappa, presented the charter to eight charter members and two foundation members, both Fisk alumni. On April 8, 1953, a chapter was established at Howard University, Washington, D.C.

Social fraternity was Kappa Alpha, established November 26, 1825, at Union College, Schenectady, N.Y. The first initiation was held December 3, 1825. The first presiding officer was David White. *(Kappa Alpha Record. Centennial Edition 1825–1925)*

FRATERNITY MAGAZINE
Fraternity journal which has had a continuous existence and which has always possessed the features and aims of the current fraternity periodical is the *Beta Theta Pi*. It was a monthly, first published December 15, 1872, in Alexandria, Va., and edited by the Reverend Charles Duy Walker, professor at Virginia Military Institute.

FRAUDULENT ELECTION LAW. *See* Election law

FRAUDULENT USE OF THE MAILS. *See* Postal service: Postal fraud order

FREE-FALL JUMP. *See* Aviation—Parachute: Parachute

FREE LUNCH
Free lunch was dispensed by Pierre Maspero of the City Exchange, St. Louis Street, New Orleans, La., in the fall of 1838. *(Herbert Asbury—The French Quarter)*

Free lunches to aid convalescents were provided by a kitchen which the New York Diet Kitchen Association opened on April 24, 1873, at 410 East 23rd Street, New York City, for the relief of the destitute sick. Beef tea, soup, milk-cooked rice, eggs, and oatmeal were served. The first officers were Mrs. A. H. Gibbons, president; Mrs.

The First

FREE LUNCH—*Continued*
William C. (Flora Payne) Whitney, secretary; and Mrs. Charles L. Tiffany, treasurer.

FREE MAIL DELIVERY. *See* Postal service: Free city delivery of mail

FREE PORT was opened February 1, 1937, at Stapleton, Staten Island, N.Y., under authority of act of Congress, "an act to provide for the establishment, operation and maintenance of foreign-trade zones in ports of entry of the United States, to expedite and encourage foreign commerce, and for other purposes," approved June 18, 1934 (48 Stat. L. 998). The port embraced an 18-acre tract around New York Municipal Piers Nos. 12, 13, 15, and 16, and was operated as a public utility by the Department of Docks, New York City, under the supervision of the U.S. Customs Service. Foreign merchandise was admitted in bond without payment of import duties. The first superintendent was Dock Commissioner John McKenzie.

FREE PUBLIC LIBRARY. *See* Library

FREE SOIL PARTY was organized at the National Free Soil Convention in Buffalo, N.Y., August 9–10, 1848. In the election of 1848 the party's presidential candidate was Martin Van Buren of New York and the vice presidential candidate Charles Francis Adams of Massachusetts. Van Buren received 291,263 popular votes as compared with 1,360,099 cast for Zachary Taylor, the Whig candidate. The Free Soil Party was formed by the antislavery element of the Democratic Party and was supported by the Liberty Party. The party's slogan was "Free Soil, Free Speech, Free Labor, Free Men."

FREE TRADE POLICY (federal) was in effect from 1775 to 1780, but imports were taxed by the various states. Trade was free in Massachusetts during 1774–1781, in South Carolina 1776–1783, in Maryland and Connecticut 1776–1780. Although there were no federal restrictions, this period was extremely complicated and taxes were different in practically every state. *(William Hill—First Stages of the Tariff Policy of the United States. In American Economic Association Journal, November 1893)*

FREEDMEN'S BANK. *See* Bank

FREEDMEN'S BUREAU (U.S.) was created by act of Congress, March 3, 1865 (13 Stat. L. 507), signed by President Abraham Lincoln. Its existence was scheduled to have terminated in one year but was extended to June 30, 1872. Its object was to establish schools and better the conditions of blacks. The first commissioner was General Oliver Otis Howard, who took office May 15, 1865. His salary was $3,000 a year. *(Paul Skeels Peirce—Freedmen's Bureau)*

The First

FREEDOM MEDAL. *See* Medal

FREEDOM OF INFORMATION ACT
Freedom of Information Act was approved July 4, 1966 (80 Stat.L.250), effective one year later, to clarify and protect the right of the public to information. It amended a preliminary act passed June 11, 1946 (60 Stat.L.238).

FREEMASONRY BOOK. *See* Masonic book

FREEMASONRY MAGAZINE. *See* Masonic magazine

FREEMASONS
See also Masonry

Ancient Arabic Order of Nobles of the Mystic Shrine was established June 16, 1871, at Masonic Hall, 114 East 13th St., New York City. It was founded by Dr. Walter Millard Fleming and Professor Albert Leighton Rawson. The first temple, Mecca, was instituted in New York City, September 26, 1872. Only Masons are eligible for membership.

Black Mason was initiated on March 6, 1775, in an Army lodge (No. 441) stationed at Castle William under General Thomas Gage in or near Boston, Mass. It operated under Irish constitutions. When the British evacuated Boston, Prince Hall and his fellow members were given a permit to meet as a lodge. Under it, African Lodge No. 1 was formed July 3, 1776. On June 30, 1784, after the Revolution, Prince Hall and others applied to the Grand Lodge of England for a warrant, which was issued September 29, 1784, to African Lodge No. 459, with Prince Hall as Master. The first meeting under the charter was held May 6, 1787, in Boston, Mass. The lodge was not recognized by American masonry. *(Harry E. Davis—A History of Freemasonry Among Negroes in America)*

Black Masonic lodge was the Alpha Lodge of New Jersey, No. 116 Free and Accepted Masons, the warrant for which was granted at the Annual Communication of the Grand Lodge in Trenton, N.J., January 19, 1871. The first regular communication was held January 31, 1871. The first worshipful master was Nathan Mingus. *(Harold Van Buren Voorhis—Negro Masonry in the United States)*

Grotto began in a committee in Hamilton Lodge (Masonic) No. 120, Hamilton, N.Y. It was formed for frolic, with Le Roy Fairchild as moving spirit. The first formal organization was effected September 10, 1889. The ritual was written by F. R. Riddell and George Beal. A central governing committee known as the Supreme Council of the Mystic Order of Veiled Prophets of the Enchanted Realm was instituted June 13, 1890, at Hamilton, N.Y., with Thomas Lemuel James, New York City, in the chair as Grand Monarch. The first charter was granted June 13, 1890, to Druid Grotto No. 1, changed July 5, 1890, to Mokanna.

The First

Knights Templar Grand Encampment was held January 22, 1814, in New York City, at which time De Witt Clinton was elected Grand Master, a position which he filled until 1827. The first reference to Knights Templar in the United States is found in the *Independent Journal* of New York, December 28, 1785.

Mason known to arrive in America was John Skene (or Skeen) of Burlington, N.J. He was a member of a Lodge in Aberdeen, Scotland, came to New Jersey in 1682, and later became deputy governor of West Jersey.

Mason (native-born) was Jonathan Belcher, a citizen of Boston, Mass., who was made a Mason in England in 1704. Belcher became royal governor of the Colony of Massachusetts Bay (1730 to 1741) and royal governor of New Jersey in 1745. *(Massachusetts Historical Society Collections, Vol. 6)*

Masonic college. *See under* College

Masonic Grand Lodge was organized at Williamsburg, Va., October 13, 1778, when the Grand Lodge of Virginia was established with Right Worshipful John Blair, past-master of Williamsburg Lodge No. 6, as the first grand master. *(Melvin Maynard Johnson—The Beginnings of Freemasonry in America)*

Masonic lodge organized in the Indian Territory was Cherokee Lodge No. 21, Tahlequah, Cherokee Nation, chartered November 8, 1848, by the Grand Lodge F. & A.M. of Arkansas (Grand Master David J. Baldwin). The first officers were Walter Scott Adair, Worshipful Master; Nathan Baron Dannenberg, Senior Warden; Joseph Coody, Junior Warden; David Carter, treasurer; and William Potter Ross, secretary; all Cherokee citizens. The lodge became Cherokee Lodge No. 10 when the Grand Lodge for the Indian Territory was formed.

Masonic lodge to work under a regular charter was St. John's Lodge, established July 30, 1733, in Boston, Mass. It was organized by Henry Price. The first written records of an American Masonic lodge are found in an account book of St. John's Lodge, Philadelphia, Pa., indicating that the lodge existed as early as 1730. Such a lodge had no warrant as we understand the term today, but was merely an assembly of Masons who foregathered according to ancient custom.

Military Masonic lodge was formed at Crown Point, N.Y., under authority granted April 13, 1759, by Provincial Grand Master Jeremy Gridley of Massachusetts. Abraham Savage, master of the first lodge in Boston, Mass., served as the first master.

Order of De Molay was founded by Frank Sherman Land and nine young men in Kansas City, Mo., in 1919. It was an organization for boys whose male relatives were Masons. The seven cardinal precepts of De Molay are Love of Par-

The First

ents, Reverence, Patriotism, Cleanliness, Courtesy, Comradeship, and Fidelity. In the 1920's membership was opened to young men between the ages of 14 and 21 who believe in God and have good character.

Provincial grand master (Masonic) was Daniel Coxe, who was deputized on June 5, 1730. His deputation included New York, New Jersey, and Pennsylvania. He visited the Grand Lodge of England, January 29, 1731, and was received as the "Provincial Grand Master of North America." He was a justice of the Supreme Court of the Province of New Jersey.

FREEZER, ICE CREAM. *See* Ice cream freezer

FREIGHT CAR. *See* Railroad car

FREIGHT DELIVERY TUNNEL. *See* Tunnel

FREIGHT GLIDER. *See* Glider: Glider commercial freight service

FREIGHT LOCOMOTIVE. *See* Locomotive

FREIGHT RAILROAD STATION. *See* Railroad station

FREIGHT TRANSPORTATION RAILROAD. *See* Railroad

FREIGHT YARD (RAILROAD) FULLY AUTOMATIC. *See* Railroad: Railroad freight yard fully automatic

FRENCH AND INDIAN WAR. *See* War (colonial): Bloodshed in the French and Indian war

FRENCH GRAMMAR. *See* Grammar

FRENCH INDOCHINA WAR. *See* War (French Indochina)

FRENCH INSTRUCTION. *See* Language instruction

FRENCH NEWSPAPER. *See* Newspaper

FREQUENCY MODULATION. *See under* Radio license

FRESCO PAINTING COURSE. *See* Art course

FRICTION MATCH. *See* Match

FRIGATE. *See* Ship

FROG JUMPING JUBILEE was held at Angels Camp, Calaveras County, Calif., May 19–20, 1928. Fifty-one frogs were entered in the contest. "The Pride of San Joaquin," a frog owned by Louis R. Fischer of Stockton, Calif., was the winner with a jump of 3 feet 4 inches. The affair, an annual one, is sponsored by the Angels Boosters Club and is held in commemoration of Mark Twain's famous story, "The Celebrated Jumping Frog of Calaveras County."

FRONTIER DAY. *See* Holiday

FROZEN BREAD. *See* Bread

The First

FRUIT CULTURE TREATISE was *A Treatise on the Culture and Management of Fruit Trees; in which a new method of pruning and training is fully described. Together with observations on the diseases, defects and injuries in all kind of fruit and forest trees,* by William Forsyth, published for J. Morgan in 1802 in Philadelphia, Pa. The book also contained *An Introduction and Notes Adapting the Rules of the Treatise to the Climates and Seasons of the United States* by William Cobbett.

FRUIT SPRAYING was done in 1878 when an apple grower in Niagara County, N.Y., sprayed his apple trees with Paris green for the control of canker worms. *(U.S. Department of Agriculture—1925 Yearbook)*

FRUIT TREE PATENT. *See* Patent

FUEL OIL LOCOMOTIVE. *See* Locomotive

FUGITIVE SLAVE LAW. *See under* Slavery

FULLER'S EARTH was discovered by John Olson in 1891 in Benton, Ark. It was used in cleansing (fulling) cloth, wool, and fur, and later in the bleaching, clarifying, or filtering of fats, greases, and oils. In 1878 it had been imported and used for refining edible oils and petroleum. *(Charles Lathrop Parsons—Fuller's Earth)*

FULLING MILL. *See under* Wool

FUNERAL, CATHOLIC. *See* Catholic funeral

FUNERAL PARLOR. *See* Mortuary

FUR-BEARING ANIMALS. *See* Animals

FUR TRADING POST was established by the Pilgrims of Plymouth Colony in Augusta, Maine, in 1628. Trade was carried on with the Norridgewock Indians. The pelts were principally exported to England, although some were retained for protection against the cold. *(James William North —History of Augusta)*

FURNACE, BLAST. *See* Iron: Iron blast furnace

FURNITURE CASTER PATENT. *See* Caster

FURS exported were shipped on the S.S. *Fortune* on December 13, 1621. Robert Cushman returned to England with a cargo valued at $2,450 consisting of furs, sassafras, clapboards, and wainscot. The boat was captured by the French and the cargo seized. *(Albert Christopher Addison—The Romantic Story of the Mayflower Pilgrims)*

FUSE
    Cordeau-Bickford detonating fuse was introduced in 1913 by the Ensign-Bickford Company, Simsbury, Conn., which started to manufacture it in 1915. It was a detonating fuse consisting of a lead tube carefully drawn to a uniform size, filled with trinitrotoluene (TNT). It functioned at a speed of 17,000 feet a second.

The First

    Safety fuse was manufactured in 1836 by (Richard) Bacon, (William) Bickford, (Joseph) Eales & Company, Simsbury, Conn., on a spinning bench machine with traveling jennies which drew and twisted the yarn. Powder was fed to the center of the twisting strands and the resulting fuse lengths were afterwards "countered" and coated with waterproof compounds. The machine was imported from England.

    Textile-wrapped detonating fuse was manufactured in 1936 by the Ensign-Bickford Company, Simsbury, Conn. It was known as Primacord and consisted of a core of pentaerythrite tetranitrate enclosed in textile wrappings suitably protected by waterproof coverings. It had a velocity of detonation of approximately 20,000 feet per second.

FUTURITY RACE. *See* Horse race

G

GI BILL OF RIGHTS
    Army Corps veteran (woman) to receive a loan under the GI Bill of Rights was Elizabeth M. Lutz of Pittsburgh, Pa., who obtained $7,500 to buy a house from the Scott Realty Company of Pittsburg, Pa. The loan was announced on February 16, 1945, by the Veterans Administration.

GI COLLEGE. *See* College

GI SERIAL NUMBERS. *See* Army Insignia: Service number (GI serial numbers)

GAG RULE. *See under* Congress (U.S.)—House of Representatives

GALLSTONE OPERATION. *See* Surgical operation

GAMBLING LEGISLATION. *See* Blue law: Blue law regulating gambling

GAMBLING LEGISLATION (colonial) was passed March 22, 1630, in Boston, Mass.: "It is . . . ordered that all persons whatsoever that have cards, dice or tables in their houses, shall make away with them before the next court under pain of punishment." *(Nathaniel Bradstreet Shurtleff— Records of the Governor and Company of the Massachusetts Bay in New England.*

GAME LAW
    Game law (colonial) was passed March 24, 1629, by Virginia and provided that "no . . . hide or skins whatever be sent or carried out of the colony upon forfeiture of thrice the value, whereof the half to the informer and the other half to public use."

    Game law (national) was approved May 19, 1796 (1 Stat. L. 470) "to regulate the trade and intercourse with the Indian tribes and to preserve peace on the frontiers." The penalty for crossing

The First

the line to hunt or destroy game within Indian territory was a fine of $100 and six months in jail. A later treaty with the Indians signed in 1832 is generally regarded as the first national game law.

Game law (state) was passed by Massachusetts in 1817. Other states quickly followed, but as there was some difference regarding the hunting seasons and importation of birds, feathers, etc., an act was passed by Congress on March 4, 1909 (35 Stat. L. 1138) prohibiting the transportation of birds, parts, etc. On March 4, 1913 (37 Stat. L. 847), the first law regulating the shooting of migratory birds was passed, which became known as the McLean Law.

Hunting license fee (state) was required by law of 1864, Chapter 426, passed April 30, 1864, by New York. Deer hunters in Suffolk County were obliged to pay $10 for a license, the money to be "paid over to the overseers of the poor of such town for the benefit of the poor thereof."

GAME MANAGEMENT CHAIR was established by the University of Wisconsin, Madison, Wis., in August 1933, at which time Aldo Leopold was appointed Professor of Game Management. The primary aim was to provide facilities for graduate research and a clearinghouse for the development of game production as a new use for Wisconsin land. Although this was the first chair, it was not the first venture in game management by a university. Michigan had established a School of Conservation in 1927 and Iowa had set up a Director of Game Research in 1932.

GAME MANUFACTURING COMPANY to make games and children's books was the McLoughlin Company, organized in New York City in 1828 by John McLoughlin. In 1850 his sons, John and Edmund, were taken into partnership and the firm name became McLoughlin Brothers. In 1920 the company confined its activities to manufacturing books and moved to Springfield, Mass.

GAME PRESERVE
Game preserve was established by Judge John Dean Caton of Ottawa, Ill., about 1860, on his own state. The preserve was well stocked with all kinds and species of American native game.

Game preserve appropriation (federal) assisting state wildlife restoration projects was "an act to provide that the United States shall aid the states in wildlife restoration projects" (50 Stat. L. 917), passed September 2, 1937. A million dollars was appropriated June 16, 1938 (52 Stat. L. 736). The federal government paid 75 percent of the costs and the state 25 percent. The first project was Utah's Fish and Game Commission's plan to stabilize the water levels on some 2,000 acres of and bordering Great Salt Lake, approved July 23, 1938, by the U.S. Fish and Wildlife Service.

The First

GAME PROTECTION SOCIETY was the New York Sportsmen's Club, founded May 20, 1844, in New York City. B. J. Meserole was president and James McGay secretary. On March 10, 1873, it became the New York Association for the Protection of Game. *(Forest and Stream. Dec. 26, 1889)*

GAME WARDEN (salaried game and fish warden) was William Alden Smith, of Grand Rapids, Mich., appointed for a four-year term at $1,200 annually and expenses under Act No. 28, Public Acts of Michigan, approved March 15, 1887, "an act to provide for the appointment of a game and fish warden and to prescribe his powers and duties to enforce the statutes of this state for the preservation of moose, wapiti, deer, birds and fish." Wisconsin approved Act No. 456 on April 12, 1887, authorizing appointment of four game wardens for two-year terms at an annual salary of $600 with a maximum of $250 for expenses. Only two wardens were appointed by Wisconsin in 1887.

GARAGE
Completely automatic push-button-controlled garage was the Park-O-Mat Garage, opened December 5, 1951, in Washington, D.C., by Parking Services, Inc. It had no ramps, no aisles, and no lanes and needed but one attendant. A car could be parked or returned in 50 seconds. The garage was an open building with 16 floors and 2 basement levels. Two elevators parked 72 cars on a lot 25 by 40 feet. It was not necessary for the attendant to enter the cars. The "vehicle parking apparatus" was patented October 14, 1947, by Richard L. Sinclair of Los Angeles, Calif., who obtained patent No. 2,428,856.

Garage (public) was established in Boston, Mass., on May 24, 1899, by W. T. McCullough, as the Back Bay Cycle and Motor Company. He advertised its opening as a "stable for renting, sale, storage and repair of motor vehicles." *(Horseless Age. July 1889)*

Hydraulic-lift parking device was the Sky-Park, manufactured by Simmons Industries, Inc., Albany, N.Y., the first unit being installed in October 1954 in Washington, D.C. A rigid central column with two hydraulically powered platforms operated by push-button control raised automobiles, singly or doubly, thus providing double the parking space.

Municipally owned parking building was designed by Hassel T. Hicks and opened September 1, 1941, in Welch, W.Va. It accommodated 232 cars and showed a profit the first year.

GARBAGE COLLECTION
City to discontinue garbage collection because of the installation of waste disposing units was Jasper, Ind., which discontinued service August 1, 1950. The reduction of taxes by a corresponding

The First

GARBAGE COLLECTION—*Continued*
amount helped homeowners amortize the cost of their disposal units.

GARBAGE DISPOSAL. *See* Incinerator

GARDEN, BOTANIC. *See* Botanic garden

GARDENER'S MANUAL was the *Young Gardener's Assistant, containing a catalogue of garden and flower seeds, with practical directions under each head, for the cultivation of culinary vegetables and flowers, also directions for cultivating fruit trees, the grape vine, etc.,* by Thomas Bridgeman, published in 1835 in New York City.

GAS
See also Helium

Gas company was the Gas Light Company of Baltimore, incorporated February 5, 1817. An ordinance was passed permitting Rembrandt Peale and others to manufacture and distribute gas "to provide for more effectually lighting the streets, squares, lanes and alleys of the city of Baltimore." Coal gas was used. The first street was lighted on February 17, 1817. The first engineer of the company was David Pugh. *(Baltimore Gas and Electric News. February 1929)*

Gas conservation legislation was enacted March 2, 1891, by the state of Indiana, Chapter 47, "making it unlawful to burn natural gas in what are known as flambeau lights." Violation was considered a misdemeanor subject to a fine not exceeding $25; a second offense was subject to a fine not exceeding $200.
See also Oil: Oil and gas conservation legislation

Gas meter (dry) to record the amount of gas used was a "gasometer" patented October 17, 1834, by James Bogardus of New York City. It operated on the principle of a bellows, alternately being filled with gas and emptied, the pulsations being counted on a register.

Gas ordinance (city) authorized the Gas Light Company of Baltimore, Md., to lay pipes in Baltimore. It was approved June 19, 1816, by Mayor Edward Johnson and by William Patterson and Henry Payson, presidents of the first and second branch of the City Council, respectively. *(Gas Age. July 1, 1916)*

Gas storage tank (waterless) was completed about February 3, 1925, and put into service on February 10, 1925, by the Northern Indiana Gas and Electric Company in Michigan City, Ind. It was 105 feet in diameter, and 160 feet high, with a capacity of 1 million cubic feet of gas. The top section did not slide up and down; instead, a steel piston inside the shell rose and fell as the amount of gas varied. The walls of the holder were made of steel plates 20 feet long and 32 inches wide.

The First

Gaslight in the White House, Washington, D.C. was turned on December 29, 1848, during the administration of President James Knox Polk.

Gaslights for display were introduced in Philadelphia, Pa., in August 1796. The inflammable gas was manufactured by Michael Ambroise & Company on Mulberry Street between Eighth and Ninth streets, Philadelphia. The light showed "a grand fire-work by means of light composed of inflammable air." The lights were disposed so as to form an Italian parterre and Masonic figures and emblems. The jets of light were made to issue from orifices in pipes bent into the requisite shapes. The gas was not used for illuminating purposes. *(John Fanning Watson—Annals of Philadelphia)*

Gaslights (street) were installed on Pelham Street in front of the residence of David Melville of Newport, R.I. in 1806. He patented his apparatus for making coal gas March 18, 1813, about which time several important installations were made. *(American Gas Light Journal. Vol. 1)*

Lighthouse fueled by natural gas. *See* Lighthouse: Lighthouse fueled by natural gas

Municipal gas plant was acquired by Wheeling, W.Va., which appointed a board of trustees on June 23, 1871, to operate the gasworks. It was incorporated March 18, 1850, as the Wheeling Gas Company and received a city franchise on April 13, 1850. The company was organized with a capital stock of $50,000, the city subscribing $15,000. After considerable litigation, the city acquired the gas plant in 1871. *(Charles A. Wingerter—History of Greater Wheeling and Vicinity)*

Natural gas corporation was the Fredonia Gas Light & Water Works Company, organized in Fredonia, N.Y., in 1865. *(Brief History of the Natural Gas Industry—Zwetsch Heinzelmann & Co.)*

Natural gas for manufacturing was used in Olean, N.Y., in 1870 and in Tidioute, Pa., an oil town. The first use of natural gas in ironworking occurred at the Leechburg, Pa., works of Rogers and Burchfield Iron Mill, where it was extensively used in 1873 in both iron and puddle mill furnaces.

Natural gas used as an illuminant was tried in Fredonia, N.Y., in 1824. A pipeline was laid from the well to the Taylor House where a reception was tendered to General Lafayette. He arrived at 2:00 A.M. on June 4, 1825. The house was "brilliantly illuminated" in his honor by natural gas, using about 30 burners (60 candlepower). The illumination by the gas was regarded as a great curiosity. In 1821 a well, dug to the depth of 27 feet near a gas spring, supplied sufficient gas for 30 lamps. It was later walled up because its odor was offensive.

The First

Pipeline (long-distance) for natural gas was a two-inch pipe five miles in length, extending from Newton Wells to Titusville, Pa. It was completed on August 1, 1872.

Theater lighted by gas. *See under* Theater

Water gas plant was built in 1874 in Phoenixville, Pa. It was the first apparatus of the superheated generator type and was covered by three patents granted August 13, 1872 (Nos. 130,381; 130,382; 130,383) to Thaddeus Sobieski Coulincourt Lowe of Norristown, Pa., the inventor and originator of water gas production. *(O. E. Norman—Romance of the Gas Industry)*

Water gas production which was practical, and its first successful commercial use, began with Thaddeus Sobieski Coulincourt Lowe of Norristown, Pa., who obtained patent No. 167,847 September 21, 1875, for an "improvement in processes and apparatus for the manufacture of illuminating or heating gas."

GAS (carbide). *See* Acetylene

GAS COMMISSION (state) was established by Massachusetts, Chapter 314, Acts of 1885, approved June 11, 1885, by Governor George Dexter Robinson. In 1885 a commission, now the Department of Public Works, was established by Massachusetts to regulate the industry, to supervise the issue of capital stock, to reduce after complaint and hearing the price of gas and electricity to consumers, and to require gas companies to file annual returns with the commission. The Department of Public Utilities which assumed these duties was quasi-judicial in character.

GAS ENGINE was invented by Stuart Perry of New York City, who received patent No. 3,597, May 25, 1844. He invented both air- and water-cooled types and used turpentine gases as fuel.

GAS LEGISLATION
Gas legislation (federal) was the Natural Gas Act (52 Stat. L. 821), effective June 21, 1938, "to regulate the transportation and sale of natural gas in interstate commerce."

GAS MASK
Gas mask resembling the modern type was patented by Lewis Phectic Haslett of Louisville, Ky., who received patent No. 6,529 on June 12, 1849, on an "inhaler or lung protector." It had a filter of woolen fabric or other porous substance to purify the air, remove dust, etc.

Gas mask with a self-contained breathing apparatus was patented on July 2, 1850, by Benjamin Lane of Cambridge, Mass., who received patent No. 7,476 on a "respiring apparatus."

GAS PIPELINE. *See* Gas: Pipeline (long-distance)

GAS-POWERED STREETCAR. *See* Streetcar

The First

GAS PRODUCTION COURSE. *See* Oil and gas production course

GAS REFRIGERATOR. *See* Refrigerator

GAS REGIMENT. *See under* Army

GAS-TURBINE AUTOMOBILE. *See* Automobile

GAS-TURBINE BUS. *See* Automobile bus

GAS-TURBINE ELECTRIC LOCOMOTIVE. *See* Locomotive

GAS-TURBINE HELICOPTER. *See* Helicopter

GAS-TURBINE PROPELLER-DRIVEN AIRPLANE. *See under* Aviation—Airplane

GASOLINE
Aviation gasoline (100 octane) obtained by the catalytic cracking method was commercially produced June 6, 1936, by the Socony-Vacuum Oil Company, Inc., Paulsboro, N.J., which used the process invented by Eugene Houdry.

Cracking process used to obtain gasoline from crude petroleum was invented by William M. Burton of Chicago, Ill., who obtained patent No. 1,049,667 on January 7, 1913, on the "manufacture of gasoline." His method of treating the residue of the paraffin group of petroleum by distillation and condensation of the vapors was used by the Standard Oil Company of Indiana, to whom the patent was assigned.

Ethyl gasoline was marketed in Dayton, Ohio, February 2, 1923. Tetraethyl lead, made from alcohol and lead, was found to influence the combustion rate of gasoline by Thomas Midgley, Jr., of the General Motors Research Laboratories, Dayton. During the seven years of experimenting in the development of ethyl gasoline at least 33,000 compounds were tested to determine their antiknock effect. *(Ethyl Gasoline Corporation—Information about Ethyl Gasoline)*

GASOLINE AUTOMOBILE. *See* Automobile: Automobile (gasoline-electric combination)

GASOLINE PUMP. *See* Pump

GASOLINE TAX
Gasoline tax (federal) was enacted June 6, 1932, by the Revenue Act of 1932 (47 Stat. L. 266) which placed a tax of one cent a gallon on gasoline and other motor fuel (effective June 21, 1932).

Gasoline tax (state) was levied February 25, 1919, when Oregon (chapter 159) placed a tax of one cent a gallon on all motor fuel. The funds collected were used for road construction and maintenance. *(Oregon, Laws of 1919)*

GASOLINE TRACTOR. *See* Automobile tractor

GASOLINE TRAIN. *See* Railroad: Gasoline-driven, stainless-steel, air-conditioned, pneumatic-tire, two-car train

GASTROENTEROLOGY BOOK. *See* Medical book

GAUGE. *See* Wire gauge

GAZETTEER
American gazetteer was compiled by Jedidiah Morse and was printed in 1795 in Boston, Mass., by Isaiah Thomas and Ebenezer T. Andrews. It was titled *American Universal Geography, or a View of the Present State of All the Empires, Kingdoms, States and Republics in the Known World, and of the United States of America in Particular.* It contained 7,000 different subjects, "exhibiting in alphabetical order a much more full and accurate account than has been given of States, Provinces, Counties, Cities, Towns, etc."

Gazetteer of the world was *Lippincott's Pronouncing Gazetteer of the World,* which was published in 1854 by Lippincott, Grambo and Company of Philadelphia, Pa. It contained 1,364 pages.

GEM-CUTTING MACHINE (or lapidary) was invented by Abel Buell of Killingworth, Conn., in 1766. He claimed that his "method of grinding and polishing crystals and other stones of great value, all the growth of the Colony" would effect a great saving in money. *(Lawrence Counselman Wroth —Abel Buell of Connecticut)*

GENE PHOTOGRAPH. *See* Photograph: Photograph of genes

GENEALOGY
Genealogical collective work was Farmer's *Genealogical Register of the First Settlers of New England,* published in 1829 by John Farmer in Lancaster, Mass.

Genealogy of an American family was a 24-page pamphlet published in Hartford, Conn., in 1771 by Ebenezer Watson. It was Luke Stebbins' *The Genealogy of the Family of Mr. Samuel Stebbins and Mrs. Hannah Stebbins, His Wife from the Year 1707 to 1771 with their names, time of their births, marriages, and deaths of those that are deceased.* In *The Memoirs of Captain Roger Clap,* 38 pages, published by Bartholomew Green in Boston, Mass., in 1731, there was a 10-page supplement by James Blake, Jr., containing "a short account of the author and his family. Written by one that was acquainted therewith." Clap's family consisted of his wife and their six children.

GENERAL. *See* Air Force Officer; Army officer

GENERAL COUNCIL OF CONGREGATIONAL AND CHRISTIAN CHURCHES. *See under* Church

GEODESIC DOME BUILDING. *See* Building

GEODETIC SURVEY was undertaken by Simeon Borden and completed by him in 1841. In 1830 he made an apparatus for measuring the base line of the trigonometrical survey required by Massa-

chusetts. The apparatus was 50 feet long and was enclosed in a tube. It was also fitted with four compound microscopes, everything being adjustable to permit movement in any direction. *(American Philosophical Society Proceedings, Vol. II 1841–1843)*

GEOGRAPHER OF THE UNITED STATES was Thomas Hutchins, appointed under an ordinance of May 20, 1785. He was the first and only incumbent of this office. He was in charge of the survey of the public land and was known as the "Geographer of the United States." *(Thomas Donaldson— The Public Domain)*

GEOGRAPHICAL SOCIETY
Geographical society director (woman) was Sarah Kerr Myers, who assumed directorship of the American Geographical Society, New York City, on June 16, 1976.

GEOGRAPHY was Jedidiah Morse's *Geography Made Easy being a short but comprehensive system of that useful and agreeable science,* a 214-page duodecimo published in 1784 in New Haven, Conn., by Meigs, Bowen and Dana.

GEOGRAPHY SCHOOL was the Clark Graduate School of Geography, Clark University, Worcester, Mass., which opened in the fall of 1921. Dr. Wallace Walter Atwood, president of the university, was appointed director of the Clark Graduate School of Geography and professor of physical and regional geography.

GEOLOGICAL MAP. *See* Geology book

GEOLOGICAL SOCIETY (national) was the American Geological Society, founded in 1819 at Yale College, New Haven, Conn. The society functioned until 1828. The first president was William Maclure. *(Herman Le Roy Fairchild—The Beginning of Geologic Science)*

GEOLOGICAL SURVEY
Geological survey appropriation (U.S.) was authorized June 28, 1834 (4 Stat. L. 702), when Congress appropriated $5,000 to be applied to geological and mineralogical survey and research. The funds were used in making a geological survey of the country between the Missouri and the Red Rivers. George William Featherstonhaugh was in charge of the survey.

Geological survey director (U.S.) (under the Department of Interior) was Clarence King, nominated March 21, 1879, confirmed April 3, 1879. He entered upon his duties May 24, 1879, and received a salary of $6,000 a year. His office was created by an "act making appropriations for sundry civil expenses of the government for the fiscal year ending June 30, 1880, and for other purposes," approved March 3, 1879 (20 Stat. L. 394). The survey was for the classification of the public land and examination of the geological structure, mineral resources, and products of the national domain. *(U.S. Geological Survey—The United States*

The First

Geological Survey, Its Origin, Development, Organization and Operations)

Geological survey (state) completed at state expense was undertaken by Edward Hitchcock, 1830–1833, for Massachusetts. *(George Perkins Merrill—Contributions to the History of American Geology)*

GEOLOGIST

Geologist to reach the moon was Dr. Harrison Hagan Schmitt, who accompanied Captain Eugene A. Cernan and Commander Ronald E. Evans, both of the U.S. Navy, in *Apollo XVII,* which was launched December 7, 1972, at 12:33 A.M. EST at Cape Kennedy, Fla. He stepped out onto the surface of the moon from the lunar landing module Challenger on December 11, 1972. He and Cernan spent 3 days on the surface of the moon gathering scientific data.

GEOLOGY

Woman graduate in geology was Lou Henry (Mrs. Herbert Hoover), who completed the geology course at Leland Stanford, Jr., University, Palo Alto, Calif. She received her degree in 1898, three years after Herbert Hoover received his A.B. degree in geology. With her husband, she translated Agricola's *De Re Metallica.*

GEOLOGY BOOK

Geology book of importance was *Observations on the Geology of the United States,* which was read by William Maclure on January 20, 1809 before the American Philosophical Society. It was published in revised form in 1817 in Philadelphia, Pa., and contained the first geological map of the eastern United States and one of the first geological maps in the United States.

Geology textbook was *The Index to the Geology of the Northern States* by Amos Eaton, which was published in 1818 in Leicester, Mass. *(John Milton Nickles—Geological Literature on North America 1785–1918)*

GEORGE WASHINGTON MONUMENT. *See* Monument: Monument to George Washington

GEORGETTE CREPE. *See* Crepe

GERENUK. *See under* Animals

GERMAN BAPTIST. *See under* Baptist Church

GERMAN BIBLE. *See* Bible: Bible printed in German

GERMAN BOOK

German book printed in America was Johann Conrad Beissel's *Das Buchlein vom Sabbath,* printed in Philadelphia, Pa., in 1728 by Andrew Bradford. *(Oswald Seidensticker—First Century of German Printing in America 1728–1830)*

German book printed in German type in America was *Der Hoch-Deutsche Amerikanische Calender, auf das Jahr nach der Gnadenreichen Geburth Unseres Herrn und Heylandes Jesu Christi 1739 . . . zum ersten mal herausgegeben,*

The First

published in 1739 by Christoph Saur in Germantown, Pa. (Philadelphia). It contained 36 pages.

GERMAN INSTRUCTION. *See* Language instruction

GERMAN NEW CHURCH SOCIETY. *See* Swedenborgian or New Church Temple

GERMAN NEWSPAPER. *See* Newspaper

GIANT exhibited as a theatrical attraction was Patrick Magee, "just arrived from Ireland," who went on exhibition October 6, 1825, at 13 Park, Park Exchange, New York City, from 7 A.M. until 10 P.M. A charge of 25 cents was made to see the giant, "conspicuous for the masculine beauty of his form and his surprising strength."

GIANT PANDA. *See* Animals

GILT BUTTONS. *See* Button

GIN, COTTON. *See* Cotton gin

GINGHAM FACTORY was opened in Clinton, Mass., by Erastus Brigham Bigelow in 1846. It was named Lancaster Mills and was capitalized at $500,000. On April 10, 1845, Bigelow received patent No. 3,987 for his invention of gingham manufacturing machinery. Previously, all gingham had been made by hand at home. *(Andrew Elmer Ford —History of the Origin of Clinton, Mass. 1653–1865)*

GIRDER BRIDGE (cast-iron). *See* Bridge: Cast-iron girder bridge

GIRL SCOUTS organization was the Girl Guides, founded March 12, 1912, in Savannah, Ga., by Juliette Gordon Low. They wore a blue uniform similar to the English Girl Guides. The name was changed to Girl Scouts in 1913 and a khaki uniform adopted in 1914. On June 10, 1915, the organization was incorporated under the laws of the District of Columbia. The first national council meeting was held in Washington, D.C., June 10–12, 1915. The first Girl Guide was Mrs. Low's niece, Daisy Gordon. The first president was Juliette Low, elected 1915; the first honorary president, Mrs. Woodrow Wilson, named October 1917; the first black president, Dr. Gloria Dean Scott, elected October 29, 1975. She served three years. *(Gladys Denny Shultz and Daisy Gordon Lawrence—The Lady from Savannah, the Life of Juliette Low)*

GIRLS' HIGH SCHOOL. *See* High school

GLASPHALT ROAD. *See* Road

GLASS

Cut glass made from pressed blanks was manufactured in 1902 by Henry Clay Fry, who organized the H. C. Fry Glass Company, Rochester, Pa. The glass was pressed into a mold, the marks of the iron plunger remaining on the inside of the glass. Previously, cut glass had been blown.

The First

GLASS—*Continued*

Glass skyscraper. *See* Building: Bronze and glass skyscraper

Invisible-glass installation was made in September 1935 at Marcus & Co., New York City. The glass window was bent at several different radius points. Mirrors flanked the window opening. The glass was covered by patent No. 1,911,881, granted May 30, 1933, to Gerald Brown of London, England, on a "means for nullifying or reducing window reflections," and patent No. 2,003,735, on June 4, 1935, to Gerald Brown and Edward Pollard of London on a "display window."

Milk bottle. *See under* Bottle

Photosensitive glass was made in November 1937 by the Corning Glass Works, Corning, N.Y., and announced publicly ten years later, on June 1, 1947. It is a crystal-clear glass in which submicroscopic metallic particles can be formed by exposure to ultraviolet light and subsequent heat treatment. Exposure through photographic negatives permits development of positive images within the glass in a variety of colors. The image is believed to be as permanent as the glass itself. Photosensitive glass is believed to be the most durable photographic medium extant.

Plate glass was manufactured about 1853 by James N. Richmond in the factory which he established in 1850 in Cheshire, Mass., for the production of window glass. The plate glass was about ½ inch in thickness and sold for 50 cents a square foot. To make 600 square feet of glass, one day's work, 2,800 pounds of sand, 500 pounds of soda ash and 800 pounds of lime were used. The factory operated about nine months a year, until 1856, when it went out of business. *(Ellen M. Raynor and Emma L. Petitclerc—History of the Town of Cheshire, Mass.)*

Plate glass produced on a large scale was manufactured in 1883 by the New York City Plate Glass Company in Creighton, Pa. The company was capitalized for $600,000 but was refinanced a few months later and the name was changed to the Pittsburgh Plate Glass Company. *(Pittsburgh Plate Glass Company: Its Foundation and Growth)*

Sheet-glass drawing machine was invented in 1899 by Irving Wightman Colburn, who obtained patent No. 696,007 on March 25, 1902. It was installed in 1899 in an experimental factory on Frankford Avenue, Philadelphia, Pa. The glass was not transparent.

Stained figure glass was made in 1844 by William Jay Bolton and John Bolton for Christ Church, Pelham Manor, N.Y., consecrated September 25, 1843. It depicted the Adoration of the Magi, over which was the legend "Behold the Lamb of God, which taketh away the sins of the world." It was placed in a window above the altar.

The First

Wire glass was invented by Frank Schuman of Philadelphia, Pa., in 1892. He obtained patent No. 483,020 on September 20, 1892. While the glass was still plastic, he pressed a wire netting into it, smoothing the abrased surface. This glass was better able to withstand heat and shattering.

GLASS BEAD was manufactured about 1608 in Jamestown, Va., for trade and commerce with the Indians. The London Company later sent Captain William Norton, accompanied by four Italians and two servants, to the disbanded Jamestown glass factory, which they revived on July 25, 1621. The work was of short duration because of the Indian massacre of 1622.

GLASS-BLOWING MACHINE was patented (No. 534,840) February 26, 1895, by Michael Joseph Owens of Toledo, Ohio. It operated five molds which circulated around the machine, each one surrounding the melted glass, which was placed in its proper position on the end of a pipe and simultaneously revolved so as to make a perfect article without seams or roughness.

GLASS CRYSTAL CHANDELIER consisted of "six lights and shower upon shower of rainbow casting prisms." It was cut by William Peter Eichbaum at Bakewell's, Pittsburgh, Pa., in 1810 and made in a ten-pot furnace. It sold for $300 to a Mr. Kerr, who hung it in his hostelry.

GLASS DRESS of spun glass was made in 1893 for Georgia Cayven, who ordered 12 yards of glass cloth at $25 a yard from the E. D. Libbey Glass Company, Toledo, Ohio, which produced it at its exhibit at the World Columbian Exposition, Chicago, Ill. The cloth was made into a dress, but was not practical for wearing purposes.

GLASS FACTORY

Flint glass factory that was successful was founded in 1807 by George Robinson and Edward Ensel. It was located on the Monongahela River at the foot of Ross Street, Pittsburgh, Pa. The first furnace held six 20-inch pots. The factory was sold to Bakewell & Page in 1808, and the name was later changed to Bakewell, Pears & Company.

Glass factory was established in Jamestown, Va., in October 1608. German and Polish mechanics were imported, eight in number, to start the new industry. The factory remained in operation spasmodically for about seven years and was then disbanded, owing principally to the fact that the workmen found it more profitable to grow tobacco to supply England's trade.

Glass factory west of the Allegheny Mountains was established in 1794 by Abraham Alfonse Albert Gallatin, later secretary of the United States Treasury, at what is now the site of New Geneva, Pa., about 90 miles south of Pittsburgh on the Monongahela River. It was an eight-pot window glass factory, with wood for fuel. The firm made its own alkali from wood ashes for making the glass. The name Gallatin & Company was subsequently changed to the New Geneva Glass Works. *(Henry Adams—Life of Albert Gallatin)*

Window glass factory of importance was the Boston Crown Glass Company of Boston, Mass. It was chartered in 1787 and the manufacture of crown window glass began in 1792. The glass was blown through a pipe into a huge bulb, which was opened, flared out into a disc, and then cut into panes. The legislature gave this company the sole right to manufacture glass in Massachusetts for a 15-year period and exempted the company from taxes and the workmen from military duty. *(Arthur E. Frowle—Flat Glass)*

GLASS INSURANCE. *See* Insurance: Plate-glass insurance

GLASS LIGHT-BULB MACHINE. *See under* Electric lighting

GLASS-LINED TANK CAR. *See* Railroad car

GLASS SLIDES. *See* Magic lantern: Magic lantern slides (glass plate)

GLASS WINDOWLESS STRUCTURE. *See* Building: All-glass windowless structure

GLASS WOOL and the machinery for its manufacture was invented by Games Slayter and John H. Thomas of Newark, Ohio, who obtained four patents on October 11, 1938. On November 1, 1938, the Owens-Corning Fiberglas Corporation was founded by the Owens-Illinois Glass Company and the Corning Glass Works to market the product, used extensively for industrial equipment and building insulation.

GLIDER

Amphibious seaplane glider was the XL-Q-1, manufactured by the Bristol Aeronautical Corporation, New Haven, Conn., and flown January 16, 1943, at the Navy Yard, Philadelphia, Pa. It was designed as a troop transport and cargo carrier by the National Aircraft factory under Commander Ralph Stanton Barnaby at the Navy Yard. The glider was taken aloft behind a Catalina seaplane and released. It had an all-wood body, was 40 feet long, with a 72-foot wingspan, and carried 12 men and equipment.

Glider (all plywood-plastic) built entirely of wood and other nonstrategic materials was Model BM-5, built by Bowlus Sailplanes, Inc., San Fernando, Calif. Mock-up tests were begun December 1, 1941; an Army Air Force contract was obtained January 20, 1942; and the prototype was flown May 1942. The contract was terminated prior to delivery of the finished models and construction thereon was suspended.

Glider commercial freight service was inaugurated April 24, 1946, by Winged Cargo, Inc., of Philadelphia, Pa. Colonel Fred Paul Dollenberg took off from Northeast Airport, Philadelphia, in a DC-3 Air Liner which towed a Waco glider at the

end of a nylon towrope. The plane carried 5,000 pounds of freight and the glider 3,500 pounds. The average speed of the flight was 150 miles per hour. The first stop was at Miami, Fla., others at Havana, Cuba, and San Juan, Puerto Rico. Paul Myers Aubin piloted the glider.

Glider released from a dirigible was piloted by Lieutenant Ralph Stanton Barnaby of the U.S. Navy. The glider was cast loose on January 31, 1930, at Lakehurst, N.J., from the *Los Angeles*, commanded by Lieutenant Commander Herbert Victor Wiley, at an altitude of 3,000 feet. A perfect landing was made in 12 minutes. *(Records in the Office of Naval Intelligence, Washington, D.C.)*

Glider towed across the continent was the *Eagle* (also known as the *Cloud-Hopping Choo Choo*) piloted by Captain Frank Monroe Hawks. On March 30, 1930, he took off from Lindbergh Field, San Diego, Calif., across San Diego Bay from the Naval flying base in a glider designed for the Texas Company by Professor Roswell Earl Franklin of the University of Michigan. The glider was attached by a towline to a single-motor biplane piloted by J. D. ("Duke") Jernigin, Jr. Stops were made at Tucson, Ariz.; Sweetwater, Tex.; Tulsa, Okla.; East St. Louis, Ill.; Columbus, Ohio; and Buffalo, N.Y. The glider landed in the rain before 15,000 people on April 6, 1930, at Van Cortlandt Park, New York City. Flying time was 36 hours, 47 minutes. *(Frank Monroe Hawks—Once to Every Pilot)*

Glider towed by an autogiro. *See* Autogiro: Autogiro to tow a glider

Glider two-way conversation. *See* Radio telephone: Two-way conversation between a glider and the land

Glider with cambered wings was invented in 1895 by Octave Chanute, who made about 2,000 glider flights without accident in 1896 and 1897 from his base at Miller's Station (near Chicago), Ill. *(Indiana Magazine of History. Vol. 32, No. 3. September 1936)*

Powered soaring glider commercially licensed was the *Dragonfly*, designed by William Hawley Bowlus and built by the Nelson Aircraft Corporation, San Fernando, Calif., which was licensed by the Civil Aeronautics Administration on October 15, 1946. It was a strut-braced high-wing monoplane with a 47-foot, 4-inch wingspan. It had a 4-cylinder 2-cycle pusher engine developing 25 h.p. at 3,900 rpm.

Seaplane glider to be piloted in the air was loosed from a seaplane on March 15, 1930, at Port Washington, L.I., N.Y. It was built at Roosevelt Field, L.I., and was fashioned after a flying boat. The first seaplane glider pilot was Frank Monroe Hawks, whose achievement was duplicated later the same day by Robert Atwater, flying a German-built converted glider.

The First

GLIDER—FLIGHTS

Glider flight was made by John Joseph Montgomery on March 17, 1884, from a hillock south of the valley of Otay, Calif. The weight of the first glider was only 30 pounds and that of its rider 130 pounds. It traveled about 600 feet. Although Montgomery did not receive full recognition for his work at the time, probably because of lack of publicity, he nevertheless gained the title of the "Father of Gliding."

Glider flight in an American-built glider to exceed 1 hour was made by William Hawley Bowlus at Point Loma, Calif., on December 11, 1929. The flight of 2 hours 47 minutes 13½ seconds broke the former record by 1 hour 20 minutes. He landed at 5:30 P.M., as it began to get dark.

Glider flight indoors in "dead air" was made on March 2, 1930. Harry Kuchins, a member of the St. Louis Glider Club, flew a glider inside the St. Louis Terminal building at a Boy Scout circus. The glider was the one which had been used by Colonel Charles Augustus Lindbergh in June 1929.

Rocket glider flight that was successful was made at Atlantic City, N.J., on June 4, 1931, by William G. Swan. The 200-pound glider was equipped with pontoons. When it was up in the air, the pilot turned on a switch to ignite the rockets. He made a 1,000-foot hop at a 100-foot altitude. The next day, June 5, 1931, he made an 8-minute flight at an altitude of 200 feet, using the full power of 12 rockets.

GLIDER LICENSE. *See* Aviation—License: Glider pilot's license

GLIDER PILOT COMBAT MEDAL. *See* Aviation —Pilot: Pilot to receive the Congressional Medal of Honor

GLOBE FACTORY to produce terrestrial and celestial globes was started in 1813 by James Wilson in Bradford, Orange County, Vt. A large globe was made in 1811 by Ira H. Hill of St. Albans, Vt., for the Fairfield Academy of St. Albans. *(Abby Maria Hemenway—Vermont Historical Gazetteer)*

GLOBULAR MAP. *See* Map

GLOVE, BASEBALL. *See* Baseball glove

GLOVES manufactured in commercial quantities in the United States were made in 1809, when Talmadge Edwards of Johnstown, N.Y., hired a few operators to help him in producing gloves. As the demand was larger than the capacity of his small shop, he employed stitchers who performed their work at home. *(Daniel Walter Redmond— The Leather Glove Industry in the United States)*

GLUCOSE made from potato starch was obtained in 1831 by Samuel Guthrie in a refinery at Sackets Harbor, N.Y. *(Benjamin Silliman, Jr.— America's Contributions to Chemistry)*

The First

GLUE FACTORY (animal products) was established in 1807 at Boston, Mass., by Roger Upton. It was absorbed by the American Glue Company of Boston, Mass., and later taken over by the Peter Cooper Corporation, Gowanda, N.Y.

GOALPOST, FOOTBALL. *See* Football goalpost

GOAT SHOW (of milch goats) was held September 15–27, 1913, at Exhibition Park, Rochester, N.Y., in connection with the sixth annual Rochester Industrial Exposition. Pedigreed goats were exhibited at the show, sponsored by the Standard Milch Goat Breeders' Association of North America, a group which was formed May 24, 1913, and which changed its name on September 22, 1913, to the New York Milch Goat Breeders' Association.

GOLD

Deposit of gold bullion. *See under* Money

Gold discovered in California was found near the San Fernando Mission in 1842, but no importance was attached to the discovery. On January 24, 1848, James Wilson Marshall found a nugget on property owned by John Augustus Sutter in a millrace on a branch of the Sacramento River near Coloma, Calif. This was the discovery which started the gold rush of the Forty-niners to California. *(John Shertzer Hittell—Marshall's Gold Discovery)*

Gold nugget was found in the Reed Mine, Cabarrus County, North Carolina, in 1799. For several years its nature was not known. The nugget was the size of a "small smoothing iron." Later one was found weighing 28 pounds. Gold in limited quantities was discovered elsewhere, however. In 1782, Thomas Jefferson described a lump of ore of about 4 pounds, found four miles below the falls on the north side of the Rappahannock in Virginia, which yielded 17 pennyweight of gold *(U.S. Geological Survey. Annual Report. Vol. XV, pt. 3, by George F. Becker. 1894)*

GOLD CROWN TOOTH. *See under* Dentistry

GOLD FILLINGS. *See* Dentistry: Gold used for the filling of dental cavities

GOLD INLAY. *See under* Dentistry

GOLD (money). *See* Money: Gold coinage

GOLD LEAF in roll form was patented on April 5, 1892, by Walter Hamilton Coe of Providence, R.I., who obtained patent No. 472,252. It was made by the W. H. Coe Manufacturing Company of Providence, in rolls 67 feet in length, 1/250,000 inch thick, varying in width from 1/16 inch to 3 1/ inches. *(Bookbinding Magazine. September 1932)*

GOLD MEDALLIONS (U.S.). *See under* Treasury Department (U.S.)

GOLDFISH HATCHERY. *See* Fish hatchery

The First

GOLDFISH INDUSTRY. *See under* Fishes

GOLF BOOK was *Golf in America,* a practical manual by James Parrish Lee, published May 25, 1895, by Dodd, Mead and Company, New York City. It consisted of 194 pages and a frontispiece.

GOLF CHAMPION

Family to win more than one national championship in 1 year did so in 1923. The Intercollegiate championship held June 30, 1923, at the Siwanoy Country Club, Bronxville, N.Y., was won by Dexter Cummings of Yale, and the National Women's Amateur championship by his sister, Edith Cummings, on October 6, 1923, at the Westchester Biltmore Country Club, Rye, N.Y. There were 196 entries in the latter championship games.

Golf champion (American-born) to win the United States Amateur Golf Championship was Herbert M. Harriman of the Meadow Brook Golf Club, Hempstead, Long Island, N.Y., who on July 3, 1899, defeated Findlay S. Douglas, the defending champion, by a score of 3-2. Ninety-eight entrants participated in the tournament, the fifth United States Championship, which was played at the Onwentsia Club, Lake Forest, Ill. Harriman's scores were 81 and 82.

Golf champion (American-born professional) to win the United States Open Tournament was John J. McDermott, who won the play-off of a triple tie on June 26, 1911, at the Chicago Golf Club, Wheaton, Ill., with a score of 80, 4 above par.

Golf champion to hold the four highest golf titles at one time was Robert Tyre (Bobby) Jones, who won the British Open Championship at Hoylake, England, June 20, 1930; the British Amateur at St. Andrews, Scotland, May 31, 1930; the United States Open at Minneapolis, Minn., July 12, 1930; and the United States Amateur at Philadelphia, Pa., September 27, 1930.

Golf champion to win the United States National Amateur Tournament two years in succession was Robert Tyre (Bobby) Jones of Atlanta, Ga., who won the amateur championship September 27, 1924, at the Merion Cricket Club, Ardmore, Pa., and September 5, 1925, at the Oakmont Country Club, Pittsburgh, Pa. He again became a two-year champion by winning on August 27, 1927, at the Minikahda course, Minneapolis, Minn., and on September 15, 1928, at the Brae Burn course, West Newton, Mass.

Golf champion to win the United States Open and the Professional was Gene Sarazen, who won the United States Open Golf Championship July 15, 1922, at the Skokie Country Club, Glencoe, Ill., with a score of 288 for 72 holes, defeating 320 starters. He won the Professional Golfers' Tournament at the Oakmont Country Club, Oakmont, Pa., on August 18, 1922, winning a diamond medal

The First

and a purse of $500. *(Gene Sarazen—Thirty Years of Championship Golf)*

Golfer to win both the United States Open and the United States Amateur in the same year was Charles ("Chick") Evans, Jr., who won the national open championship at the Minikahda Country Club, Minneapolis, Minn., on June 27th, 29th, and 30th, 1916, with a score of 286 (70, 69, 74, and 73) and the amateur championship at the Merion links, Philadelphia, Pa., on September 9, 1916, by defeating Bob Gardner 4 up 3 to play in the final round.

Woman golfer (American-born) to win the British Women's Amateur Golf Tournament was Babe Didrikson Zaharias, who defeated Jacqueline Gordon on June 12, 1947, at Kullane, Scotland, to win the championship.

GOLF CLUB

Golf association (national) of importance was the United States Golf Association, formed in New York City on December 22, 1894, by the following charter members: Newport Golf Club, Newport, R.I.; Shinnecock Hills Golf Club, Southampton, L.I., N.Y.; the Country Club, Brookline, Mass.; St. Andrews Golf Club, Mount Hope, N.Y.; and the Chicago Golf Club, Wheaton, Ill. Officers for 1894–1896 were President Theodore A. Havemeyer of the Newport Golf Club, Secretary Henry O. Tallmadge of the St. Andrews Golf Club, and Treasurer Samuel L. Parrish of the Shinnecock Hills Golf Club.

Golf club was formed in Charleston, S.C., in 1786. In 1793, the officers were Dr. Purcell, president; Edward Penman, vice president; James Gardner, treasurer and secretary. *(South Carolina and Georgia Almanac for 1793)*

Intercollegiate Golf Association was formed in January 1897 by representatives from Columbia, Harvard, Princeton, and Yale. The first tournament was held May 13–14, 1897, at the Ardsley Casino Golf Club, Ardsley-on-Hudson, N.Y. The team championship was won by Yale; the individual championship by Louis Pintard Bayard, Jr., of Princeton's class of 1898.

GOLF CLUBS (or golf sticks)

Golf clubs (or golf sticks) are mentioned in an account of the estate of William Burnet, governor of New York and Massachusetts, who died in 1729. Among his possessions were "Nine Golf clubs, one iron ditto and seven dozen balls." *(Esther Singleton—The Furniture of Our Forefathers)*

Steel shaft for a golf club was invented by Arthur F. Knight of Schenectady, N.Y., who obtained patent No. 976,267 on November 22, 1910, on a golf club with tapered and tempered steel tubing.

The First

GOLF COURSE
Eighteen-hole golf course was designed and constructed by Charles Blair Macdonald, for the Chicago Golf Club, at Wheaton, Ill. It was opened for play in 1893.

Golf course (nine holes) was completed at Brenton's Point, near Newport, R.I., in 1890. *(Herbert Warren Wind—The Story of American Golf)*

Illuminated 9-hole regulation golf course was the 3,230-yard course of the Tall Pines Golf Club, Sewell, N.J., illuminated August 23, 1963, by 121 Mercury flood lights of 1,000 watts each. It was a private course by day and open to the public at night.

Midget golf course is said to have been built in 1929 by John Garnet Carter near Chattanooga, Tenn. The greens were made of a compound of cottonseed hulls dyed green. Carter patented the name "Tom Thumb," which was the trade name of a midget golf course system which was leased and sold as an amusement game device. Small golf courses with fewer than nine holes and courses with short holes, however, had been established previously. The Tom Thumb system presented hazards, obstacles, etc. The game was played exclusively with a putter.

GOLF MAGAZINE
was *Golfing,* a weekly published in 1894 in New York City by William L. Dudley, editor and publisher. It contained 32 pages and cover, and sold for 10¢ a copy or $4 a year.

GOLF MATCH
Mixed foursome was played on March 30, 1889, at the St. Andrews Golf Club, Yonkers, N.Y., Grey Oaks Course. John B. Upham and Carrie Low played John Reid and Mrs. John G. Reid. Upham and Mrs. Reid scored 1½ points—a half point for each hole, halved.

GOLF TEE
was invented by George F. Grant of Boston, Mass., who obtained patent No. 638,920, December 12, 1899, on a wooden tee with a tapering base portion and a flexible tubular concave shoulder to hold the golf ball.

GOLF TOURNAMENT
Amateur golf tournament of the United States Golf Association in which a black contestant was entered was held July 18, 1896, at the Shinnecock Hills Golf Club, a 4,423-yard course, Southampton, N.Y. The first prize was $200, second prize $100, third prize $50, fourth prize $25, and fifth prize $10. The winner was James Foulis of Chicago, Ill., whose score was 152 (78 and 74). Horace Rawlins of the Sadequada Club was second with 155 (79 and 76). The black contestant was John M. Shippen, the 16-year old caddie of the Shinnecock club, whose score was 159 (78 and 81).

The First

Amateur golf tournament (official) under the rules of the United States Golf Association was played on October 12, 1895, at the Newport Country Club, Newport, R.I. There were 32 entries. The winner was Charles Blair Macdonald and the runner-up Charles E. Sands. *(Charles Blair Macdonald—Scotland's Gift: Golf)*

Amateur golf tournament (unofficial) was played on the old Grey Oaks course of the St. Andrews Golf Club, Yonkers, N.Y., on October 13, 1894. Thirty-two contestants played an 18-hole match. The winner was Lawrence B. Stoddard of St. Andrews Golf Club, one up, and the runner-up was Charles Blair Macdonald of Chicago, Ill.

Intercollegiate golf tournament. *See* Golf club Intercollegiate Golf Association

International golf match for the Walker Cup was held at the National Golf Links of America (18 holes; 6,650 yards), Southampton, N.Y., August 28–29, 1922. The United States team, captained by William Clark Fownes, Jr., obtained 8 points, 5 points in the singles and 3 points in the foursomes, while the team from Great Britain and Ireland, captained by R. Harris, obtained 4 points, 3 points in the singles and 1 point in the foursomes. The cup was presented by George Herbert Walker, president of the United States Golf Association. An informal competition had been held the preceding year.

National championship stroke-play golf match was held on September 3–4, 1894, at the Newport (R.I.) Country Club. The championship was won by W. G. Lawrence with a score of 188. The runner-up was Charles Blair Macdonald, whose score was 189.

Open championship (official) golf tournament of the United States Golf Association was held October 4, 1895, at the New Newport (R.I.) Country Club and was won by Horace Rawlins, age 19 of the club. His score was 173 for 36 holes (45-46-41-41). The runner-up was Willie Dunn of the Shinnecock Hills Golf Club, whose score was 175 (43-46-44-42). Rawlins defeated 10 professionals and 1 amateur. He won $150 and a gold medal.

Professional Golfers Association tournament was won on October 14, 1916, at the Siwanoy Golf Club, Mount Vernon, N.Y., by James ("Long Jim") Barnes of the Whitemarsh Country Club, Philadelphia, Pa., who defeated runner-up Jock Hutchinson at medal play, one up. Barnes won the Rodman Wanamaker trophy, $500, a diamond-studded gold medal, and custody of a huge silver cup. There were 31 players in the 36-hole tournament held from October 10 to October 14, 1916.

Professional open championship match under the rules of the United States Golf Association was held June 14, 15, and 17, 1901, at the Myopia Hunt Club, Hamilton, Mass. Willie Anderson and Alex Smith tied for first place with 331 for 72

holes. An 18-hole play-off was won by Anderson 85 to 86.

Women's tournament golf championship (amateur—unofficial) was won by Mrs. Charles R. Brown in November 1895 at the Meadow Brook Golf Club, Westbury, L.I., N.Y. There were 13 entries. Mrs. Brown scored 132 for 18 holes. The runner-up was Nan C. Sargent.

GOLFER

Golfer to break 60 for 18 holes in a major tournament was Samuel Jackson ("Sam") Snead, who shot a 59 (31 out, 28 coming home), 11 strokes under par, in the third round of the Sam Snead Festival golf tournament at White Sulphur Springs, W.Va., on May 16, 1959. He had a score of 196 for 54 holes and won $4,500. The tournament was originally named the Greenbrier Open.

Golfer to break 60 in a Professional Golfers Association tour was Allen L. Geiberger of California, who shot a 59 on June 10, 1977, in the second round of the Danny Thomas Memphis Open at the Colonial Country Club course (7,249 feet; par 72). His score was 273 and he won $40,-000.

Golfer to earn $100,000 in a contest was Miller Barber of Texas, who won the first prize of $100,-000 in 144 strokes in the World Open at Pinehurst, N.C., November 8-17, 1973.

Golfer to earn over $100,000 in one year in regular tournaments was Arnold Daniel Palmer, whose winnings in 1963 were $130,835 (20 official events, $128,230; 9 unofficial events,$2,605).

Golfer to earn over $200,000 in one year in regular tournaments of the Professional Golfers Association was William Earl ("Billy") Casper, whose winnings in 1968 were $205,168.67.

Golfer to play 180 holes in 1 day was Edward Styles who started the marathon contest at 5:53 A.M. on July 11, 1919, at the Old York Road Country Club, Philadelphia, Pa., played 180 holes, 10 rounds of golf, in 796 strokes, and finished playing at 8:32 P.M. The average time per round was 1 hour 19 minutes, the total playing time was 13 hours 10 minutes. He walked nearly 40 miles and took time out 3 times for a change of shoes and for refreshments. His average score was 79 3/5ths strokes per round.

Golfer to play 24 hours continuously on a regulation course was James J. Johnson of Fort Worth, Tex., who played 363 holes at the 6,101-yard course of the Abilene Country Club, Abilene, Tex., on October 14-15, 1959. Rules enabled him to walk or run.

Golfer to shoot below his age on a Professional Golfers Association Tour was Samuel Jackson ("Sam") Snead, age 67, who shot a 66 on the fourth day of the Quad Cities Open tournament at Coal

City, Ill., on July 22, 1979. His score was 277 (70, 67, 74, and 66).

Golfer (woman) to play 150 holes continuously was Katherine Murphy of Los Angeles, Calif., who played 156 holes on June 19, 1967, on the 6,130-yard course (now 7,300 yards) at the San Luis Rey Golf Club, Bonsall, Calif.

Woman to win the United States Women's Amateur Championship was Beatrice Hoyt, who won by 7 strokes at the Morris Country Club, Morristown, N.J., on October 7-9, 1896; by 6 strokes at the Essex Golf Club, Manchester, Mass., on August 24-26, 1897; and by 8 strokes at the Ardsley Golf Club, Ardsley, N.Y., on October 11-16, 1898.

Holes in one by a father and son in the same game were shot by Charles H. Calhoun, Sr. and Jr., on August 24, 1932, at the third hole of the Washington Golf Club, Washington, Ga., while the two were playing in a foursome.

GOOSE, SNOW. *See* Birds

GORILLA. *See* Animals

GOTHIC-STYLE BUILDING. *See* Building

GOVERNMENT BUREAU OF STANDARDS. *See* Standards Bureau (U.S.)

GOVERNMENT—CABINET. *See* Cabinet (U.S.)

GOVERNMENT—CONGRESS. *See* Congress (U.S.)

GOVERNMENT (Commission form). *See* Commission form of government

GOVERNMENT DEPARTMENTS. *See under* title of departments, e.g. Commerce; Interior; Labor; Treasury

GOVERNMENT EMPLOYEE (woman). *See* Woman: Women to become federal government employees

GOVERNMENT EMPLOYMENT SERVICE. *See* Employment service

GOVERNMENT HOME LOAN. *See* GI Bill of Rights

GOVERNMENT INSURANCE. *See* Insurance

GOVERNMENT MINT. *See* Mint (U.S.)

GOVERNMENT-OPERATED FACTORY. *See* Factory

GOVERNMENT OPERATION OF RAILROADS. *See under* Railroad

GOVERNMENT PRINTING OFFICE

Government Printing Office was created as an independent establishment by an act of Congress of June 23, 1860 (12 Stat. L. 117) to provide printing and binding for Congress and the federal departments, bureaus, and independent offices. On February 19, 1861 (12 Stat. L. 132) $135,000 was appropriated for the purchase of the printing plant of Joseph T. Crowell, Washington, D.C. It was

The First

GOVERNMENT PRINTING OFFICE—*Continued*
purchased March 2, 1861, and began to function March 4, 1861. The first Superintendent of Public Printing was John Dougherty Defrees of Indiana, appointed March 23, 1861, by President Abraham Lincoln. *(Robert Washington Kerr—History of Government Printing Office)*

Superintendent of Documents under the Government Printing Office was authorized by act of January 12, 1895 (28 Stat. L. 610) to take charge of the preparation of official catalogs and indexes of the government, and the distribution and sales of government publications. F. A. Crandall, the first superintendent, served from March 26, 1895, to November 17, 1897. Sales were small to the end of the fiscal year June 30, 1895, but from June 30, 1895, to June 30, 1896, 3,581 publications were sold yielding a revenue of $889.09.

GOVERNMENT PUBLICATIONS INDEX. *See* Index of government publications

GOVERNMENT RECLAMATION SERVICE. *See* Reclamation Service (federal)

GOVERNOR
See also Lieutenant governor

Black governor (acting) was Pinckney Benton Stewart Pinchback, who was lieutenant governor of Louisiana from 1871 to 1872. During Governor Henry Clay Warmoth's impeachment, he acted as governor of Louisiana, from December 11, 1872, to January 14, 1873.

Black governor appointed by the President of the United States was William Henry Hastie, whose appointment by President Harry S. Truman as governor of the U.S. Virgin Islands was confirmed by the Senate on May 1, 1946. He was inaugurated May 7, 1946, at Charlotte Amalie, V.I.

Brothers to serve simultaneously as governors of their respective states were Governor Levi Lincoln, Jr., a Whig, who was sworn in as governor of the Commonwealth of Massachusetts on May 27, 1825, and who served until January 21, 1834, and Governor Enoch Lincoln, a Whig, who served as governor of Maine from January 4, 1827, until his death, October 8, 1829.

Catholic governor was Edward Douglass White, who resigned from the United States House of Representatives on November 15, 1834, and served as Governor of Louisiana from 1835 to 1839. He returned to the House of Representatives and served from March 4, 1839, to March 3, 1843. He died April 18, 1847, and was buried in St. Joseph's Catholic Cemetery at Thibodaux, La.

Governor granted almost dictatorial power was Paul Vories McNutt of Indiana. The Democrat-controlled legislature empowered him in February 1933 to organize the state government, then scattered in 168 boards and commissions, into nine

The First

departments, Executive, State, Audit, Treasury, Law, Education, Public Works, Commerce, and Industry. He was authorized to hire and fire all state employees and to raise or lower salaries as he saw fit. His power was limited by legislative appropriations and by the authority of the courts to review and void his decisions.

Governor impeached. *See* Impeachment: Impeachment and removal from office of a state governor

Governor of a territory and a state was John White Geary, who served as governor of the Kansas territory from September 9, 1856, to March 4, 1857, and as governor of Pennsylvania from January 15, 1867, to January 21, 1873.

Governor removed from office by a state supreme court decision was William Augustus Barstow, Democrat, of Wisconsin, who served the term from January 2, 1854, to January 7, 1856. He was installed for a second term on January 7, 1856. On March 20, 1856, the supreme court held that Coles Bashford, Republican, was entitled to the office because of irregularities in the election charged to Barstow. On March 21, 1856, Barstow resigned, and the lieutenant governor, Arthur MacArthur, was sworn in. MacArthur withdrew from office March 25, 1856. The state assembly recognized Bashford on March 27, 1856.

Governor to appoint two United States senators in one year for interim terms was Governor Robert Crosby of Nebraska, who appointed Eve Bowring (sworn in April 26, 1954) to replace Senator Dwight Palmer Griswold (deceased April 12, 1954) and Samuel Williams Reynolds (sworn in July 7, 1954) to replace Senator Hugh Alfred Butler (deceased July 1, 1954). Hazel Hempel Abel was elected to fill out the remaining time in Griswold's term and Roman Lee Hruska was elected to fill out the remaining time in Butler's term.

Gubernatorial election in which two brothers were the opposing candidates was held November 2, 1886, in Tennessee. Robert Love Taylor, the Democratic candidate, received 125,151 votes, defeating his brother, Alfred Alexander Taylor, the Republican candidate, who obtained 109,837 votes. Robert Love Taylor served as governor from January 17, 1887, to January 19, 1891, and from January 21, 1897, to January 16, 1899. Alfred Alexander Taylor defeated Albert Houston Roberts on November 2, 1920, and served as governor of Tennessee from January 15, 1921, to January 16, 1923.

Impeachment proceedings against a state governor. *See under* Impeachment

Jewish governor was David Emanuel of Georgia, who served from March 3, 1801, to November 7, 1801, after the resignation of Governor James Jackson. It is not entirely clear whether he became governor by virtue of the fact that he

The First

was president of the senate when Governor Jackson resigned, or whether he was regularly elected. The first Jewish governor elected for a full term was Moses Alexander of Idaho, a Democrat, who served from January 4, 1915, to January 6, 1919, as the 11th governor of Idaho. *(American Jewish Historical Society Publication No. 17)*

Native-born governor of New England was Josiah Winslow of Plymouth, Mass. He was elected governor of Massachusetts in 1673 and served until his death in 1680. *(Joseph Dillaway Sawyer—History of Pilgrims and Puritans)*

Woman governor elected without succeeding her husband was Ella (Rosa Giovanna Olivia Tambussi) Grasso, a Democrat, elected November 5, 1974, and sworn in January 8, 1975, as the 83rd governor of Connecticut. She was reelected in November 1978 for a second term, which, because of illness, she did not complete. On December 4, 1980, Grasso announced that she would resign on December 31. She died on February 5, 1981.

Woman governor of a state was Nellie Tayloe Ross who was elected governor of Wyoming on November 4, 1924, to fill the unexpired term of her husband, William Bradford Ross. She assumed her duties on January 5, 1925. Miriam Amanda ("Ma") Ferguson of Texas was inaugurated governor of Texas on January 10, 1925.

GRADUATE FELLOWSHIP. *See* Fellowship

GRADUATE SCHOOL. *See* College

GRAIN ELEVATOR. *See* Elevator

GRAIN STABILIZATION CORPORATION was authorized February 10, 1930, under act of Congress (46 Stat. L. 15) approved June 15, 1929. It was organized in February 1930 and was composed of 28 members. The first president was George Sparks Milnor.

GRAMMAR

English grammar by an American was *A Short English Grammar, an Accidence to the English Tongues,* by Hugh Jones, professor of mathematics at the College of William and Mary. It was published in London, England in 1724. *(Rollo La Verne Lyman—English Grammar in American Schools Before 1850)*

English grammar by an American published in America was Samuel Johnson's *The First Easy Rudiments of Grammar, Applied to the English Tongue. By one who is extremely desirous to promote good literature in America, and especially a right English Education. For the Use of schools.* It was published in 1765, in New York City by "J. Holt, near the Exchange in Broad Street." The grammar consisted of 36 pages. Dr. Johnson was the first president of King's College (now Columbia University). *(Charles Evans—American Bibliography)*

The First

French grammar written and printed in America was *A New French and English Grammar, wherein the principles are methodically digested, with useful notes and observations, explaining the terms of grammar, and further improving its rules* by John Mary, instructor at Harvard College. It was printed in 1784 by J[ohn] Norman, Boston, Mass., and sold by the author.

Hebrew grammar was *A Grammar of the Hebrew Tongue, being an essay to bring the Hebrew Grammar into English, to facilitate the instruction of all those who are desirous of acquiring a clear idea of this primitive tongue by their own studies,* by Judah Monis, an instructor in Hebrew at Harvard College, published in 1735 in Boston, Mass. It consisted of 94 pages and was dedicated to "His Excellency Jonathan Belcher, Esq: Governour in Chief of His Majesty's Province of the Massachusetts Bay in New England, and the Rest of the Honourables and the Reverend Overseers of Harvard College, and to the Reverend Mr. Benjamin Wadsworth, President and the Rest of the Honourable and Reverend Corporation of Said College." *(Lee Max Friedman—Early American Jews)*

Indian grammar was John Eliot's *The Indian Grammar Begun; or, An Essay to Bring the Indian Language into Rules, for the Help of Such as Desire to Learn the Same, for the Furtherance of Gospel Among Them,* published in Cambridge, Mass., in 1666 by Marmaduke Johnson. It was written in the language of the Massachusetts Indians and consisted of 66 pages of text. About 500 copies were printed.

Latin grammar textbook was *A Short Introduction to the Latin Tongue. For the use of the lower forms in the Latin School. Being the Accidence abbridg'd and compiled in that most easy and accurate method, wherein the famous Mr. Ezekiel Cheever taught and which he found the most advantageous by seventy years' experience.* It was prepared by Ezekiel Cheever, master of the Boston Latin School, and published in 1709 in Boston, Mass., by "B[artholomew] Green for Benj. Eliot at his shop under the Town-house." It contained 64 pages and was 3 by 6 inches. *(Elizabeth Porter Gould—Ezekiel Cheever, Schoolmaster)*

Spanish grammar was *A Short Introduction to the Spanish Language; to which is added a vocabulary of familiar words for the more speedy improvement of the learner: with a preface shewing the usefulness of this language particularly in these parts,* by Garrat Noel, printed in New York City by James Parker in 1751.

GRAMMAR INSTRUCTION IN A COLLEGE was offered in 1795 at the University of North Carolina, Chapel Hill, N.C. "The English language [was] taught grammatically on the basis of Webster's and South's *Grammar.*" *(Kemp Plummer Battle—History of the University of North Carolina)*

The First

GRAND AMERICAN TRAPSHOOT TOURNAMENT. *See* Trapshooting tournament

GRAND ARMY OF THE REPUBLIC. *See under* War veterans' society

GRAND CANYON EXPLORATION. *See* Expedition: Exploration of the Grand Canyon of the Colorado

GRAND JURY FOREMAN (woman). *See* Jury: Woman grand jury foreman

GRAND MASTER (Masonic). *See* Freemasons: Provincial grand master (Masonic)

GRAND OPERA IN ENGLISH. *See* Opera

GRANGE. *See* Agricultural society: Agricultural society of national importance

GRANITE was quarried in Quincy, Mass., in 1820 for the Bunker Hill Monument, Boston, Mass. About 9,000 tons in blocks 2 feet 6 inches square and 12 feet long were transported by the Granite Railway Company from the Quincy quarry to the wharf at Charlestown, Mass.

GRAPHITE was produced commercially in 1840 at Ticonderoga, N.Y., and became the center of the graphite industry of the United States. Graphite occurs associated with igneous and metamorphic rocks.

GRAPHITE REACTOR. *See* Atomic Reactor

GRAPHOPHONE. *See* Phonograph: Phonograph that was practical

GREAT LAKES COMMERCIAL VESSEL. *See* Ship

GREAT LAKES TO THE GULF WATERWAY. *See* Canal

GREAT POWERS CONFERENCE. *See* Conference

GREAT SEAL OF THE UNITED STATES GOVERNMENT. *See under* Seal

GREEK COLLEGE AND ORPHANAGE was the Monastery of St. Stephanos in Gastonia, N.C., dedicated September 18, 1932, by Archbishop Athenagaros of the Greek Orthodox Church in North and South America to the "oncoming generations of Greek youth."

GREEK DAILY NEWSPAPER. *See* Newspaper

GREEK LETTER SOCIAL SOCIETY. *See* Fraternity (Greek-letter): Social fraternity

GREEK ORPHANAGE. *See* Greek college and orphanage

GREEK ORTHODOX CHURCH
   Greek Orthodox Archdiocesan Council women members of the Greek Orthodox Archdiocese of North and South America were Katharine (Mrs. John C.) Pappas of Milton, Mass.; Lila (Mrs. Theodore) Prountis of New York City; Zoe (Mrs. Thomas) Cavalaris of Charlotte, N.C.; Christine

The First

(Mrs. Paul) Peratis of Los Angeles, Calif.; and Dr. Georgia Stathis of San Bernardino, Calif. The appointments were announced November 9, 1974, by Archbishop Iakovos, Primate of the Greek Orthodox Church and president of the Archdiocesan Council.

   Greek Orthodox Church bishop who had converted from the Roman Catholic Church was the Very Reverend Paul de Ballester, a Spaniard, who was elevated to bishop at the Cathedral of the Holy Trinity, New York City, on March 15, 1970. He had been archdiocesan vicar of the church for Mexico.

   Greek Orthodox Church was the Holy Trinity Church, 1222 N. Dorgenois Street, New Orleans, La., founded in 1867. The first pastor was Paisios Ferentinos. *(Seraphim G. Canoutas—Hellenism in America)*

GREEK PLAY. *See* Play (drama)

GREEK TESTAMENT. *See under* Bible

GREENBACK LABOR PARTY (formed by members of the Labor Reform and old Greenback party) was organized February 22, 1878, in Toledo, Ohio. The first national convention was held June 9–11, 1880, in Chicago, Ill. James Baird Weaver of Iowa was the nominee for President, Benjamin J. Chambers of Texas for Vice President.

GREENBACK PARTY (or Independent Party) was organized November 25, 1874, in Indianapolis, Ind., and the first convention was held there, May 16–18, 1876. The first presidential candidate was Peter Cooper of New York, who received 81,-737 votes in the 1876 election. Samuel Fenton Cary of Ohio was the vice presidential candidate. The party platform advocated the payment of the national debt of the government in greenbacks.

GREENHOUSE was erected by James Beekman in New York City in 1764. It is claimed that Andrew Faneuil erected a glass house at Boston, Mass., prior to 1737. *(Florists' Exchange. 1859)*

GREYHOUND RACING ASSOCIATION was the International Greyhound Racing Association, formed March 3, 1926, in Miami, Fla., to systematize efforts and to conduct the races on the highest possible standard. The association was incorporated as a nonprofit organization. The first high commissioner was Owen P. Smith.

GROTTO. *See under* Freemasons

GROUP HOSPITAL INSURANCE PLAN. *See under* Insurance

GROUP INSURANCE. *See* Insurance

GUANO was imported from Peru in 1832 for fertilizer use. Guano is the deposits of droppings of sea birds and bats, found in caves or above ground in areas where there is little or no rain. *(American Fertilizer Handbook, 1936)*

The First

GUARANTY BANK BILL. *See* Bank legislation: Bank guaranty legislation

GUERNSEY CATTLE. *See* Animals

GUERNSEY CATTLE CLUB. *See* Cattle club

GUIDED MISSILE CRUISER. *See* Ship

GUIDED MISSILE DESTROYER. *See* Ship

GUIDED MISSILE SUBMARINE. *See* Submarine

GUM. *See* Chewing gum

GUN. *See* Air gun; Ordnance; Pistol

GUNPOWDER MILL. *See under* Ordnance

GUTTA-PERCHA was imported from Calcutta in 1840 by William Bartlett as supercargo of the *Mary Parker.* Bartlett presented a whip made of gutta percha to William Rider of New York City, who organized William Rider and Brothers to handle the new commodity. Improvements of processes were constantly made. On June 1, 1852, John Rider obtained patent No. 8,992 on "vulcanized rubber," and in 1855 the North American Gutta Percha Company, New York City, was formed by the Rider brothers with a capitalization of $500,000. *(United States Magazine. April 15, 1855)*

GYMNASIUM to offer systematic instruction was started by the Round Hill School, Northampton, Mass., which was opened October 1, 1823, by John Green Cogswell and George Bancroft. Charles Beck was the instructor in Latin and gymnastics. Gymnastics was scheduled from 5 P.M. to 7 P.M. *(Old and New—July 1872)*

GYMNASTICS BOOK was *Gymnastics for Youth; or a practical guide to healthful and amusing exercises for the use of schools,* by Johann Christoph Friedrich Guts Muths, translated from the original work in German, but erroneously credited to Christian Gotthelf Salzmann. It was published in 1802 by William Duane, Philadelphia, Pa. It was illustrated with copper plates and contained 432 pages.

GYMNASTICS INSTRUCTION

Gymnastics instruction at a college was offered in 1826 at Harvard University, Cambridge, Mass. Charles Theodore Christian Follen, professor of German, was appointed superintendent of the gymnasium. He introduced Friedrich Ludwig Jahn's system of gymnastics. *(Fred Eugene Leonard—A Guide to the History of Physical Education)*

Gymnastics instruction at a college for women was offered in 1862 by Mount Holyoke College, South Hadley, Mass. The first teacher of gymnastics was a Miss Evans. During the first year, the course was optional, and the instruction was given "in the long storeroom over the wood and coal shed at the northwest corner of the court." A gymnasium was erected in 1865. Courses in calis-

The First

thenics, however, had been introduced in 1835, but were replaced by the Dio Lewis system of gymnastics. *(Persis Harlow McCurdy—The History of Physical Training at Mount Holyoke College. In American Physical Education Review. March 1909)*

GYROCOMPASS

Gyrocompass installed on an American naval vessel was placed on the U.S.S. *Delaware* and tested at sea August 28, 1911. The installation consisted of a master gyrocompass, employing the meridian seeking properties of a pendulous gyro. The master compass was designed to be installed in a protected station, with repeaters which followed the movements of the master located suitably for steering and taking bearings.

GYROPILOT. *See* Shipping: Automatic stearing gear

GYROSCOPE

Gyro-stabilized ship. *See* Ship: Gyro-stabilized American liner; Gyro-stabilized vessel to cross the Atlantic Ocean

Gyro stabilizer installed on an American naval vessel was placed on the U.S.S. *Worden* in April 1913 by the Sperry Gyroscope Company, Brooklyn, N.Y.

Gyroscopes (commercially manufactured) were made by the Holbrook Apparatus Company, Hartford, Conn., in June 1857. They were made of iron, sold for $2, and used as toys.

Gyroscopic automatic stabilization. *See under* Aviation

Gyroscopic stabilizer was patented by Elmer Ambrose Sperry and Harry Laurence Tanner of Brooklyn, N.Y., who obtained patent No. 1,236,993 on August 14, 1917, on a "gyroscopic stabilizer." The patent was assigned to the Sperry Gyroscope Company of Brooklyn, N.Y. The application was filed July 14, 1914.

GYRO-STABILIZED AMERICAN LINER. *See* Ship

H

HABEAS CORPUS

Habeas corpus suspension order was issued May 3, 1861, by President Abraham Lincoln, authorizing the commander of the military forces on the coast of Florida to suspend the writ of habeas corpus, if necessary. John Merryman was arrested May 25, 1861, by the military authorities and was refused the writ of habeas corpus. There was considerable agitation and on September 15, 1863, Lincoln issued a proclamation to the effect that in times of military strife the writ of habeas corpus could be suspended. *(Henry Jarvis Raymond—Lincoln, His Life and Times)*

The First

HABEAS CORPUS—*Continued*

Habeas corpus writ in America was obtained about 1707 in behalf of the American historian Robert Beverley.

HAFLINGER HORSE. *See* Horse

HAGUE ARBITRATION CASE. *See* Arbitration: Arbitration proceeding

HAHNIUM. *See* Element: Element 105

HAIL INSURANCE. *See* Insurance

HAILSTONE SHOWER

Hailstone shower of importance recorded occurred May 8, 1784, at Winnsborough, S.C., when "an extraordinary shower of hail, attended with thunder and lightning, killed several Negroes, sheep, lambs, geese, birds." *(Gazette, Charleston, S.C.—May 8, 1784)*

HAIR CLIPPERS. *See* Clipper for cutting hair

HAIRCLOTH was manufactured at Rahway, N.J., in 1813, the process for which was covered by patents granted to William Shotwell and Arthur Kinder of New York City on July 23, 1813. It was called Taurine cloth and was a coarse fabric made from the hair of cattle with a mixture of wool.

HALF CENT. *See* Money

HALFTONE ENGRAVING. *See* Engraving

HALL OF FAME

Hall of fame (baseball) was conceived in 1935, erected at Cooperstown, N.Y., during 1938, and dedicated June 12, 1939, as the National Baseball Museum and Hall of Fame. On January 29, 1936, the first group of five was elected to the Baseball Hall of Fame: Tyrus Raymond ("Ty") Cobb, George Herman ("Babe") Ruth, John Peter ("Honus") Wagner, Christopher ("Christy") Mathewson, and Walter Perry ("Big Train") Johnson.

Hall of fame (football) was the National Professional Football Hall of Fame, Canton, Ohio. Ground was broken August 11, 1962; the building was dedicated September 7, 1963. The first selection of members was made January 29, 1963.

Hall of fame (national) was National Statuary Hall, formerly the Hall of the United States House of Representatives in the Capitol at Washington, D.C., which was established by act of Congress of July 2, 1864 (13 Stat. L. 347). Each state was invited to contribute marble or bronze statues of its most distinguished citizens.

Hall of fame (university) was the Hall of Fame, which was dedicated May 30, 1901, on the University Heights campus of New York University, New York City. Twenty-nine tablets were unveiled. The oration was delivered by Senator Chauncey Mitchell Depew. The idea originated with Dr. Henry Mitchell MacCracken, chancellor of the university, who was aided in the project by a

The First

$250,000 endowment from Helen Miller Gould (Mrs. Finley Johnson Shepard). *(Robert Underwood Johnson—Your Hall of Fame)*

Walk of fame. *See* Walk of fame

HALL OF FAMER

Athlete enshrined in 2 Halls of Fame was Robert ("Cal") Hubbard, who was elected on April 4, 1963, to the Professional Football Hall of Fame, Canton, Ohio, and on August 9, 1976, to the Baseball Hall of Fame, Cooperstown, N.Y.

Hall of Fame (baseball) Jewish player was Henry ("Hank") Greenberg, first baseman and outfielder of the Detroit Tigers during the years 1933–1941 and 1945–1946, elected January 25, 1956, receiving 164 of the 193 ballots. He had a lifetime batting average of .313 with 1,628 hits in 1,394 major league games.

Hall of Fame (university) black was Booker Taliaferro Washington, who received 57 of the 93 votes cast and was 1 of 4 selected from 130 candidates. The announcement was made October 31, 1945.

HAMBLETONIAN. *See* Horse race

HAMMER (pneumatic) was invented by Charles Brady King of Detroit, Mich., in 1890. Brady applied for a patent on May 19, 1892; it was granted January 30, 1894 (No. 513,941). The hammer was exhibited at the World's Columbian Exposition in Chicago, Ill., in 1893.

HAMMER THROW

Hammer throw to exceed 231 feet was made July 21, 1962, at Palo Alto, Calif., by Harold Connolly of Santa Monica, Calif., who threw the 16-pound hammer 231 feet 10 inches.

HAMMERED IRON. *See* Iron

HANDBALL national championship match for amateurs was staged at the Jersey City Handball Club, Jersey City, N.J., on January 7–8, 1897, and was won by Michael Eagan.

HANDICAPPED. *See under* specific handicaps, e.g. Blind, Cripples, Deaf

HANGING RAILROAD BRIDGE. *See* Bridge

HARD PORCELAIN. *See* Porcelain (hard)

HARD WATER CRACKER. *See* Cracker

HARNESS RACE. *See* Horse race

HAT

Derby hat was manufactured by James Henry Knapp of Knapp and Gilliam of South Norwalk, Conn., in 1850. The first derbies were sold to New York jobbers, Henderson and Bird, who sold one and a half dozen each of brown and black to a retail store on Broadway and Ninth Street, New York City. An English clerk suggested "Derby" (pronounced "darby"), after the famous English horse race, as the name of the hat, which, through

The First

a difference in pronunciation, became known as "derby."

Soft felt hats for women were introduced in New York City in 1851 by John Nicholas Genin. Prior to this women wore bonnets. When Lajos (Louis) Kossuth, the Hungarian patriot, arrived in New York City on December 5, 1851, on board the *Mississippi,* Genin took low-crowned soft black hats and fastened the left side of the brim of each to the crown and ornamented it with a black feather, starting a new style in honor of the distinguished visitor. *(John Nicholas Genin—An Illustrated History of the Hat)*

Straw hats were made in June 1798 by 12-year-old Betsey Metcalf (later Mrs. Baker) of Providence, R.I. She plaited seven strands of oat straws into braid which she fashioned into bonnets and trimmed with ribbons. The hats were lined with pink satin and sold for $1 to $1.25. *(Harper's Magazine. October 1864)*

HAT BLOCKING AND SHAPING MACHINE was patented by Rudolph Eickemeyer and G. Osterheld of Yonkers, N.Y. Patent No. 52,661 was granted on April 3, 1866.

HAT FACTORY is believed to have been established in Danbury, Conn., in 1780 by Zadoc Benedict. He employed one journeyman and two apprentices whose total output was about 18 hats a week. They were fur hats made from rabbit or beaver fur, and sold for $6 to $10 apiece. They are described as being "without elegance, being heavy, rough and unwieldy." *(James Montgomery Bailey—History of Danbury)*

HATCHERY. *See* Fish hatchery

HAY FEVER BOOK. *See* Medical book

HEAD TAX, IMMIGRATION. *See under* Immigration

HEADLIGHT
   Automatic headlight control was the Autronic-Eye," developed by the Guide Lamp Division of General Motors Corporation, Anderson, Ind., and offered to the public on January 25, 1952. Headlights automatically dimmed at the approach of an oncoming car and flashed back to bright when traffic passed.

HEADLIGHT, LOCOMOTIVE. *See* Locomotive headlight

HEALTH BOARD
   See also Public health

   Health board (local) was appointed by Governor Thomas Sim Lee in 1792 for Baltimore, Md. Dr. John Ross was appointed quarantine physician for land and Dr. John Worthington for sea. On September 12 and 17, 1793, a quarantine was proclaimed against Philadelphia, Pa., which had a yellow fever epidemic and Governor Lee interdicted all direct commerce. Beginning April 24,

The First

1795, the Board of Health was elected instead of appointed. *(John Russel Quinan—Medical Annals of Baltimore from 1608–1880)*

   Health board (municipal) armed with sufficient powers for all emergencies was the Metropolitan Board of Health established in New York City by act of New York State Legislature passed February 26, 1866 (19th section, Chapter 74, Laws of 1866), "an act to create a Metropolitan Sanitary District and Board of Health for the preservation of life and health therein, and to prevent the spread of disease therefrom." The first meeting of the board was held March 5, 1866, and presided over by Jackson Smith Schultz. The other members of the board were Drs. James Crane, Willard Parker, and John Osgood Stone.

   Health board (state) was the Massachusetts State Board of Health and Vital Statistics established in 1869 by an "act to establish a State Board of Health" (Chapter 420, Acts of 1869, approved June 21, 1869). The first chairman was Henry Ingersoll Bowditch and the first secretary George Derby. Seven persons were appointed to serve terms ranging from one to seven years so that one term expired every year. The normal term of office was seven years.

   Health board (state) to regulate quarantine was a joint city and state board of health "to establish quarantine for the protection of the state," authorized by Louisiana (Section 2 of Act No. 336) and approved March 15, 1855, by Governor Paul Octave Hebert. The board consisted of nine "competent citizens," six appointed by the governor with the consent of the senate and three elected by the council of New Orleans. The first president of the health board was Dr. A. Forster Axson.

HEALTH DEPARTMENT
   County health department organized on a full-time basis was the Jefferson County, Ky., Health Department established January 7, 1908. The first full-time county health officer was Dr. Benjamin Wilson J. Smock, who received $150 a month. Office space was acquired January 21, 1908. The first health board was composed of County Judge Arthur Peter, Drs. M. Knox Allen, Emmett T. Grasser, A. David Wilmoth, and chairman Thomas M. Baker.

HEALTH DEPARTMENT (U.S.) *See* Cabinet (U.S.): Secretary of Health, Education, and Welfare

HEALTH INSTRUCTION in connection with the schools was undertaken by New York City in October 1902, when the Board of Estimate and Apportionment voted $30,000. The work was undertaken in cooperation with the Henry Street Nursing Service, New York City. Nurses were assigned to certain schools so that the children would not be absent from school for minor illnesses. The first staff of municipal school nurses in the United States was employed in November

The First

HEALTH INSTRUCTION—*Continued*
1902 by the New York City Department of Health.
(Lillian D. Wald—The House on Henry Street)

HEALTH INSURANCE. *See* Insurance

HEALTH INSURANCE, FEDERAL. *See* Medicare

HEALTH LABORATORY
Health laboratory (municipal) was established January 1, 1888, in Providence, R.I., although some experimental work had been undertaken in December 1887. Dr. Charles Value Chapin was in charge. Dr. Gardner Taber Swarts was the medical inspector.

Health laboratory (state) for the examination of sputa to diagnose diseases for physicians was established September 1, 1894, in Providence, R.I., by the Rhode Island Department of Public Health. The laboratory was supervised by Drs. Gardner Taber Swarts and Jay Perkings. During the first six months, 115 tests were made.

HEALTH MUSEUM not connected with another institution was the Cleveland Health Museum, Cleveland, Ohio, opened November 12, 1940, to give accurate understanding of the body and knowledge of how it functions and how to care for it. The museum was incorporated December 28, 1936. The first director was Dr. Bruno Gebhard.

HEALTH ORDINANCE prohibiting spitting on the sidewalks or in other public places was passed May 12, 1896, by the New York City Department of Health. *(Sanitary Code of the Board of Health of the Health Department of the City of New York)*

HEALTH SOCIETY for the promotion of national health, composed of physicians and laymen, was the National Tuberculosis Association, organized June 6, 1904, in Atlantic City, N.J. It had about 400 members. The first annual meeting was held May 18–19, 1905, in Washington, D.C. The first president was Dr. Edward Livingston Trudeau.

HEARING AID. *See* Deaf—Hearing aid

HEART, ARTIFICIAL. *See* Artificial heart

HEART OPERATION. *See* Surgical operation

HEATER. *See* Stove

HEATING SYSTEM
Heating system from a central station was installed in Lockport, N.Y., in 1877 by Birdsall Holly. He dug a trench and ran a steam line for a distance of 100 feet from his house to an adjoining property and found that the heat was not lost by being carried through pipes. He formed the Holly Steam Combination Company, Ltd.; the first plant was located at Elm and South streets, Lockport, N.Y. The company was later operated by the New York State Electric and Gas Corporation, Lockport division.

The First

Heating system (steam) was installed by Walworth & Nason in 1844 in Boston, Mass. James Jones Walworth and Joseph Nason organized a company for the purpose of "warming and ventilating buildings by means of steam and hot water apparatus." They had formed a company in New York City in 1841 and established a plant in Boston in 1842. At first they used hot water for the system, converting to steam in 1844. The company was later known as the Walworth Company. *(W. C. Mattox—Walworth Manufacturing Company: Its History and Traditions)*

HEAVY WATER. *See under* Water

HEBREW BIBLE. *See* Bible

HEBREW BOOK
Hebrew book all in Hebrew published in America was *Abne Yehoshua (Stones of Joshua)* by Joshua Ben Mordecai ha-Cohen Falk, published in 1860 in New York City. It consisted of 108 pages.

Hebrew Spelling Book was *The Hebrew Reader: Hebrew and English Designed as an Easy Guide to the Hebrew Tongue for Jewish Children and Self-instruction,* by Isaac Leeser, printed by Haswell, Barrington and Haswell at Philadelphia, Pa., in 1838. It contained 48 pages.

HEBREW DICTIONARY. *See* Dictionary

HEBREW GRAMMAR. *See* Grammar

HEBREW LITERATURE DEGREE. *See* Degrees (academic and honorary): Master of Hebrew Literature degree awarded a woman

HEBREW NEWSPAPER. *See* Newspaper

HEBREW PLAY BY PROFESSIONAL ACTORS. *See* Play: Hebrew professional acting troupe

HEBREW TYPE was used in Stephen Day's (Steeven Daye's) *The Whole Book of Psalmes, Faithfully Translated into English Metre . . . ,* issued in 1640 by the Cambridge Press, Cambridge, Mass.

HEEL, RUBBER. *See under* Rubber

HELICOPTER
Aerocycle was built by De Lackner Helicopters, Inc., Mount Vernon, N.Y., and tested at Camp Kilmer, N.J., by the U.S. Army, which bought 12 on December 29, 1955. The aerocycle weighs about 200 pounds, carries a load of about 300 pounds, has a top speed of 65 mph and a range of about 150 miles. Handlebars control the ascent and descent, the pilot steering by leaning in the direction he wants to go. The machine has helicopter blades, rises vertically, and is powered by a 41 h.p. outboard motor mounted above pontoons.

Gas-turbine helicopter (turborotor) was the U.S. Navy K-225, built by the Kaman Aircraft Corporation, Bloomfield, Conn., and tested December 10, 1951, at Bradley Field, Windsor Locks, Conn. It

The First

was powered by a Boeing 502-2 gas turbine developing 175 h.p. for continuous operation; the turbine was manufactured by the Boeing Airplane Company, Seattle, Wash.

Helicopter airmail. *See under* Airmail service

Helicopter battalion. *See under* Army

Helicopter commercially designed was the S-51, a four-passenger helicopter, designed and built by the Sikorsky Aircraft Division of the United Aircraft Corporation, Bridgeport, Conn., which made its initial flight February 16, 1946. It received its Approved Type Certificate from the Civil Aeronautics Authority on March 26, 1946. It cruises at 80 m.p.h. and has a range of 150 miles with pilot, 3 passengers, and 70 pounds of baggage.

Helicopter (direct-lift aircraft) that was successful was the VS-300, constructed in October–November 1939 by Vought-Sikorsky Aircraft, Stratford, Conn. A flight of 15 minutes and 3 seconds was made July 18, 1940, by Igor Ivan Sikorsky at Stratford, Conn., with a single main rotor, powered by a 70 h.p. Franklin engine. The helicopter had three auxiliary tail rotors for control, one turning in a vertical plane for rudder control and the other two turning in a horizontal plane on outriggers on either side of the tail.

Helicopter fully operated by remote control was the HTK-1, built by the Kaman Aircraft Corporation, Bloomfield, Conn. In July 1953, at Windsor Locks, Conn., it took off and landed; flew backward, sideward, and forward; and hovered at varying altitudes, speeds, and distances in compliance with commands from a remote-control station. The signals were sent by radio from a ground station to controls in the drone.

Helicopter licensed for commercial use by the Civil Aeronautics Administration was a Bell 47B able to cruise at speeds of 1 to 100 m.p.h.; fly forward, backward, or sideways; ascend or descend vertically or hover stationary. License No. 1 was granted March 8, 1946, to the New York *Journal-American,* New York City, which used the helicopter for news coverage and photo delivery.

Helicopter passenger service was instituted by New York Airways Inc., on July 9, 1953, at 9:15 A.M., with two passengers flying between La Guardia Airport and Idlewild Airport, both in New York City. Twelve passengers were transported the first day. The captain was Jack S. Gallagher and the flight attendant was Neils Johnson. (Freight service had been inaugurated October 1, 1947, by Los Angeles Airways, Inc., which carried mail in the San Fernando Valley, Calif.)

Helicopter pilot awarded a Medal of Honor. See Medal: Medal of Honor awarded to a helicopter pilot

The First

Helicopter rescue of an American pilot behind enemy lines was effected in Korea on September 4, 1950, by First Lieutenant Paul Van Boven of San Mateo, Calif., and hospital corpsman Corporal John Fuentz of Kansas City, Mo., who rescued Captain Robert Earl Wayne of Garden City, Long Island, N.Y., shot down on his 95th mission.

Helicopter to deliver material across a picket line was used on March 9, 1947, by the Cornell-Dubilier Electric Corporation, New Bedford, Mass. Seven hourly landings were made with supplies of raw materials. The helicopter was hired from the New England Helicopter Service.

Helicopter with a fully servo-controlled intermeshing rotor was the K-125, built by the Kaman Aircraft Corporation, Bloomfield, Conn. It made its initial flight in January 1947 at Windsor Locks, Conn.

Helicopter with a twin engine was the XHJD-1, built by the McDonnell Aircraft Corporation, St. Louis, Mo., and tested March 1946, at the Lambert-St. Louis Municipal Airport. Two 450 h.p. Pratt and Whitney Wasp Jr. engines, mounted midway on the pylons extending from the fuselage, turned two 40-foot blade rotors in opposite directions. The helicopter could carry a 3,000-pound load, operating on either one or both of the engines. It could take off or land vertically, hover motionless, fly forward, backward, or sideways. The span from rotor tip to rotor tip was 81 feet.

President to fly in a helicopter. *See under* President (U.S.)

Ramjet helicopter was the Little Henry, built by the McDonnell Aircraft Corporation, St. Louis, Mo., for the U.S. Air Force and tested May 5, 1947, by Charles Raymond Wood, Jr., at Lambert Field, St. Louis. It weighed 310 pounds and had a two-blade rotor, two tip ramjets weighing 10 pounds each, a small rudder, and an open steel-tube structure supporting the pilot, fuel tanks, and controls. It had a 50 mph forward speed and a 300-pound lifting capacity.

Twin gas-turbine helicopter (turborotor) was the HTK-1 helicopter, built by the Kaman Aircraft Corporation, Bloomfield, Conn., and flown March 26, 1954, at Bloomfield. It had two 190 h.p. Boeing 502-2 gas turbines manufactured by the Boeing Airplane Company, Seattle, Wash. They produced 380 h.p. and could be used separately or simultaneously.

HELICOPTER—FLIGHTS

Helicopter flight of importance was made June 16, 1922, by Henry Adler Berliner at College Park, Md., before representatives of the U.S. Bureau of Aeronautics. The machine raised itself three times to the height of seven feet. It had two lifting propellers in the front, the forward motion being obtained by tilting a propeller in the rear of the fuselage.

The First

HELICOPTER—FLIGHTS—*Continued*

Helicopter flight (cross-country) was made in a two-place XR-4 Air Force helicopter designed by Igor Ivan Sikorsky, which took off May 13, 1942, from Stratford, Conn. It flew at low altitudes and landed at Wright Field, Dayton, Ohio (761 miles), May 17, 1942, making 16 stops en route. Actual flying time was 16 hours 10 minutes. Charles Lester Morris, test pilot of Sikorsky Aircraft Division of the United Aircraft Corporation, was the pilot.

Helicopter flight from water was made April 17, 1941, by Igor Ivan Sikorsky at Stratford, Conn., in a Vought-Sikorsky helicopter (VS-300) mounted on rubber bags so that it could land and take off on either land or water.

Helicopter flight of one-hour duration was made April 15, 1941, by Igor Ivan Sikorsky, who hovered aloft in a Vought Sikorsky VS-300 for 1 hour 5 minutes 14.5 seconds over Sniffen's Point, Stratford, Conn. The main lift was supplied by a three-bladed propeller 28 feet in diameter. On May 6, 1941, the helicopter hovered over a tennis court for 1 hour 32 minutes 26.1 seconds.

Helicopter pilot awarded a Medal of Honor. *See* Medal: Medal of Honor awarded to a helicopter pilot

Helicopter refueling flight (successful) was accomplished at Fort Rucker, Ala., August 14, 1956, when an Army twin-rotary H-21 helicopter manufactured by the Vertol Aircraft Corporation, Morton, Pa., was refueled from a fixed-wing tanker.

Helicopter transatlantic flight was made by the U.S. Air Force Air Rescue Service in two H-19 (S-55) helicopters which left Westover Air Force Base, Mass., July 15, 1952, and arrived at the U.S. Air Force base at Wiesbaden, Germany, on August 4, 1952, in 51 hours 55 minutes, elapsed flight time. Leader of the flight was Captain Vincent Howard McGovern of Springfield, N.J., who with copilot Harry Celestine Jeffers of Newark, Ohio, piloted the project ship, *Hop-A-Long*. The accompanying aircraft, *Whirl-O-Way*, was piloted by First Lieutenant Harold W. Moore of Cincinnati, Ohio, and copiloted by Major George Okie Hambrick of Carter, Okla. The 3,410-mile Atlantic crossing was made in 42 hours 25 minutes. *(American Helicopter. August 1952)*

Transcontinental nonstop helicopter flight was made from Miramar Naval Air Station, San Diego, Calif., on August 23, 1956, to Washington, D.C., a distance of 2,610 miles in 31 hours 40 minutes, by a twin-rotored H21. Refueled four times in flight (Wink, Tex.; Abilene, Tex.; Maxwell Air Force Base, Ala.; and Fort Benning, Ga.) and while hovering over El Paso, Tex., and Shreveport, La., the helicopter landed August 24, 1956. The crew consisted of Major Hugh Gaddis of Tulsa, Okla.; Warrant Officer Joseph K. Givens of Stanford, Ky.; Captain James E. Bowman of Amboy, Ind.; Spe-

The First

cialist Robert M. Price of St. Louis, Mo.; and Pfc. Carl D. Herrington of Tulsa, Okla. The helicopter, produced by the Vertol Aircraft Corp., of Morton, Pa., weighed 3,300 pounds.

HELIPORT

Heliport commercial base in a major city was Heliport No. 1 at Pier 41, New York City, leased from the Department of Marine and Aviation by the Metropolitan Aviation Corporation, formerly operating from Teterboro, N.J. The seadrome was 161 by 60 feet. The first flight was May 18, 1949, the official opening of service, when pilot George Callahan and passenger Deputy Mayor John James Bennett flew in a Bell 47-B with a 605 payload capacity.

Hotel to establish a heliport. *See under* Hotel

Military heliport was the Fort Eustis Heliport, Felker Field, Fort Eustis, Va., dedicated December 7, 1954. The field was named for Warrant Officer Alfred Charles Felker, a graduate of the first army helicopter pilot course who was killed in an airplane flight in February 1953. The heliport was built in the shape of a huge wheel with 600-foot runways forming the spokes and a circular taxiway composing the rim. The first commanding officer was Lieutenant Colonel Robert C. Spiedel, Jr.

HELIUM

Helium was discovered as a constituent of natural gas in 1905 by Professor Hamilton Perkins Cady and Dr. David Ford McFarland of the University of Kansas. They tested the residuum from a gas well at Dexter, Cowley County, Kan., and found that it had a 1.84 percent helium content. *(On the Occurrence of Helium in Natural Gas.* In *American Chemical Society. Proceedings, 1906)*

Helium-filled balloon. *See* Balloon: Balloon filled with helium gas

Helium plant of the United States was the United States Production Plant, Fort Worth, Texas, completed in April 1921 under the cognizance of the Navy Department. It used the Linde Air Products Company process and was operated by that company. The Bureau of Mines assumed the supervision of this plant, July 1, 1925, and operated it until 1929, when it was closed on account of insufficient gas supply. *(Willard A. Pollard—Public Works of the Navy—Bulletin No. 31—United States Helium Production Plant)*

Helium plants (experimental) were those of the Linde Air Products Company, the Air Reduction Company, and the Jeffries-Norton Corporation, erected in 1917 and operated under the Bureau of Mines, Department of the Interior. One of these plants was erected at Petrolia, Tex., and the other two at Fort Worth, Tex. About 200,000 cubic feet of helium was produced by them in their experimental runs of which 147,000 cubic feet, compressed in steel cylinders, was on the dock at New

The First

Orleans, La., ready for shipment to France when the armistice was signed. *(Andrew Stewart—Production of Helium for Use in Airships—U.S. Bureau of Mines—1919)*

HEMOPHILIA TREATISE. *See* Medical book

HEMP EXPORTATION was made to England in 1730. It consisted of 50 hundredweight of hemp raised in New England and Carolina, and 3 hundredweight from Virginia.

HERBAL BOOK was Samuel Stearns's *The American Herbal or Materia Medica wherein the virtues of the mineral, vegetable and animal productions of North and South America are laid open*, printed in 1801 in Walpole, N.H., by D[avid] Carlisle for Thomas and Thomas and the author. It contained 360 pages.

HERD BOOK for livestock was the *American Herd Book, containing pedigrees of short horn cattle to which is prefixed a concise history, of English and American short horns*, 240 pages, edited by Lewis Falley Allen and published in 1846 in Buffalo, N.Y.

HEREDITY CLINIC. *See* Medical clinic

HERESY TRIAL of a bishop was held in 1925. William Montgomery Brown, Protestant Episcopal Bishop of Arkansas, author of *Communism and Christianity*, was deposed for heresy at New Orleans, La., on October 12, 1925. The deposition was imposed by the Right Reverend Ethelbert Talbot, D.D., presiding officer of the House of Bishops of the Protestant Episcopal Church. The Secretary of the House, Dr. Charles Laban Pardee, drew a line through Brown's name on the record. He was not excommunicated.

HERO FUND COMMISSION. *See* Carnegie Hero Fund Commission

HEROINE. *See under* Woman

HIGH-DEFINITION TELEVISION. *See under* Television—Telecast

HIGH JUMP over seven feet was made June 29, 1956, at the Coliseum, Los Angeles, Calif., by Charles Dumas, a 19-year-old Compton College freshman, who jumped 7 feet ⅝ inch and was credited with 7 feet ½ inch.

HIGH-JUMPING STANDARDS using electric eye detectors were constructed by Lyle Hudson Bennett Peer of the General Electric Research Laboratory and others, and were used May 31, 1941, at the Schenectady Patrolmen's Association interscholastic track meet, Schenectady, N.Y. A series of four parallel beams of light, one inch apart, recorded the height of each jump.

HIGH SCHOOL
Commercial high school. *See* Commercial high school

The First

County high school was the Dickinson County Community High School, Chapman, Kan., opened in September 1889. The first building was constructed entirely of limestone at a cost of $12,000. Enrollment the first year was 137. S. M. Cook, who taught mathematics, Latin, and Greek, was the first principal.

High school was opened in May 1820 in Boston, Mass., known as the English Classical School. The name was changed in 1824 to the English High School. Admittance was open to boys at least 12 years of age who were required to be "well acquainted with reading, writing, English grammar in all its branches, and arithmetic, as far as simple proportions." *(Josiah Quincy—Municipal History of the Town and City of Boston)*

High school aviation course. *See under* Aviation—School

High school business school. *See* Business school: Business high school

High school for girls was established in 1826 in Boston, Mass., but was abolished in 1828. Instead the course of study in the elementary schools was advanced. *(Alexander James Inglis—The Rise of the High School in Massachusetts)*

High school to fingerprint its students. *See under* Fingerprinting

Junior high school was the Indianola Junior High School, Columbus, Ohio, opened September 7, 1909. On July 6, 1909, the Columbus Board of Education directed Superintendent of Schools Jacob A. Shawan "to organize the new Indianola School primarily as a junior high school, with the 7th, 8th, and 9th grades as a unit, and only to admit such of the first six grades as might be necessary to relieve the neighboring districts." The ninth grade offered courses in English, German, algebra, elementary science, and physical geography, manual training, domestic science, general history, and government of Ohio.

Junior high school system was comprised of the McKinley and the Washington High Schools of Berkeley, Calif., authorized December 21, 1909, based on the recommendations made November 30, 1909, by Frank Forest Bunker. They were known as "introductory high schools." The McKinley School housed the seventh, eighth, and ninth grade pupils in a separate building with a reorganized curriculum and a separate administration, and opened the new term January 2, 1910, with Charles Louis Biedenbach as principal. The Washington High School opened on the same date with G. W. Monroe as principal. *(Frank Forest Bunker—The Junior High School Movement: Its Beginnings)*

Public high school to specialize in the performing field was the School of Performing Arts, a division of the Metropolitan Vocational High School, New York City, opened September 13,

HIGH SCHOOL—*Continued*
1948. Dr. Franklin J. Keller was the first principal. The school was conducted on the usual secondary school basis. However, half the time was given to practical work in the arts (music, dance, theater, and broadcasting) and the other half to college preparatory academic courses, with a diploma at the end of three years to those who had come from junior high schools and at the end of four years of study to those from eight-year elementary schools.

Vocational high school for girls was the Trade School for Girls, Boston, Mass., opened July 1904 as a summer experiment in training. Subjects taught were plain sewing, advanced sewing, dressmaking, millinery, machine operating, trade design, and domestic science. Florence M. Marshall was principal.

HIGH SCHOOL LEGISLATION authorizing night classes was enacted by Ohio (Section XVI of Act passed by the Legislature of Ohio, March 16, 1829). Accordingly there were opened in Cincinnati, Ohio, in November 1840, three evening schools for boys. In 1855, schools for girls were also opened. *(Paul Monroe—Cyclopedia of Education)*

HIGHWAY. *See* Road

HIGHWAY BRIDGE. *See* Bridge

HIGHWAY LEGISLATION (colonial). *See under* Road

HIGHWAY TRAFFIC BUILDING. *See* Building: Building devoted entirely to highway traffic

HIGHWAY TUNNEL. *See* Tunnel: Subaqueous highway tunnel

HIJACK LEGISLATION
Hijack legislation (federal) was "an act to amend the Federal Aviation Act of 1958 to provide for the application of federal criminal law to certain events occurring on board aircraft in air commerce" enacted September 5, 1961 (75 Stat. L. 466), and signed by President John Fitzgerald Kennedy. It made hijacking punishable by death or not less than 20 years imprisonment. Carrying a concealed or dangerous weapon was subject to a fine of $1,000 or imprisonment of not more than one year, or both.

HILL-CLIMBING CONTEST. *See* Automobile hill-climbing contest; Motorcycle hill-climbing contest

HILLSIDE SHRINE, RELIGIOUS. *See* Religious hillside shrine

HINDU WOMAN TO RECEIVE A DOCTOR OF MEDICINE DEGREE. *See under* Physician

HISTORICAL PRINT ENGRAVING. *See* Engraving

HISTORICAL SOCIETY
Historical society (general) was the American Historical Association, founded September 10, 1884, in Saratoga, N.Y., for the "promotion of historical studies, the collection and preservation of historical manuscripts." Its first report was transmitted to Congress June 16, 1890, and was published as Senate Miscellaneous Document No. 170. The first president was Andrew Dickson White. The society was incorporated by act of Congress January 4, 1889. *(American Historical Association. Papers, Vol. 1)*

Historical society (national) was the American Antiquarian Society, founded in Worcester, Mass., by Isaiah Thomas, the first printer of Worcester. Incorporated October 24, 1812, it was the first national historical society and had the first great American historical collection. The first meeting was held November 19, 1812, at the Exchange Coffee House, Boston, Mass. The first president was Isaiah Thomas, and the first vice presidents were Aaron Bancroft and Timothy Bigelow.

Historical society (state) was the Massachusetts Historical Society, organized August 26, 1790, in Boston, Mass., by five persons under the leadership of the Reverend Jeremy Belknap. Their next meeting, held on January 24, 1791, was attended by ten people. The main purpose of the society, incorporated February 19, 1794, was to gather manuscript material to be preserved and used for its publication for general use and to establish a library which would carry on the founders' plan. *(Massachusetts Historical Society. Collections, Vols. II and III)*

HISTORY
American history of importance written by a woman was a three-volume narrative history of the Revolutionary War entitled *History of the Rise, Progress, and Termination of the American Revolution, Interspersed with Biographical, Political and Moral Observation,* by Mercy Otis Warren. It was published in Boston, Mass., in 1805. *(Alice Brown—Mercy Warren)*

Comic history of the United States was *A Diverting History of John Bull and Brother Jonathan,* a 135-page book, by Hector Bull-Us [James Kirke Paulding], published in 1812 in New York City by Inskeep and Bradford.

History of a colony was *A True Relation of such occurrences and accidents of noate as hath hapned in Virginia since the first planting of that Collony, which is now resident in the south part thereof, tille the last return from thence* by Th. Watson, A Gent. (actually Captain John Smith) for J. Tappe, published London, England, 1608

History of New England published in the colonies was *New England's Memoriall, or a Brief Relation of the Most Memorable and Remarkable*

The First

Passages of the Providence of God, Manifested to the Planters of New England in America: With Special Reference to the First Colony Therefore, Called New Plimouth,"* published by Nathaniel Morton, secretary to the court for the Jurisdiction of New-Plymouth. It was printed in 1669 in Cambridge, Mass., by "S. G[reen] and M. J[ohnson]," for John Usher of Boston, Mass. Edward Johnson's *A History of New-England From the English Planting in the yeere 1628 untill, the yeere 1652, Declaring the Form of Their Government, Civil, Military and Ecclesiastique,* a 236-book also known as *The Wonder-Working Providence of Sions Saviour in New England,* was published in London, England, in 1654.

Political history was *A Political and Civil History of the U.S.A. from the year 1763 to the close of the administration of President Washington in March, 1797 including a summary view of the political and civil state of the North American colonies, prior to that period,* by Timothy Pitkin. It was published in two volumes by Hezekiah Howe and Durrie and Peck in 1828 at New Haven, Conn.

Printing history. *See* Printing history

Theater history. *See* Theater history

Woman to win 2 Pulitzer Prizes in history. *See under* Pulitzer Prize

HISTORY INSTRUCTION

American history chair was established by the University of Pennsylvania, Philadelphia, Pa., in 1850. The first incumbent was William Bradford Reed, who remained in the post until 1856.

Ancient and modern history chair was the McLean professorship endowed in 1823 under the will of John McLean. It was established at Harvard College, Cambridge, Mass., in 1838. The first incumbent (1838–1849) was Professor Jared Sparks.

History course (integrated) in a women's college was given by Professor Woodrow Wilson at Bryn Mawr College, Bryn Mawr, Pa., in 1885. The histories of Greece and Rome were taken as representative of ancient history, and of France and England as representative of medieval and modern history. The object was to "keep the student mindful of the broad views of history in which the events in the lives of individual nations stand related." *(Herbert Baxter Adams—The Study of History in American Colleges and Universities)*

History seminar was established by the University of Michigan at Ann Arbor, in 1869, under the leadership of Charles Kendall Adams. *(Andrew Ten Brook—American State Universities and the University of Michigan)*

School of modern history affiliated with a college was established at the College of William and Mary, Williamsburg, Va., in 1803.

The First

HISTORY OF MEDICINE DEPARTMENT. *See under* Medical instruction

HISTORY OF SCIENCE SOCIETY. *See under* Science association

HOCKEY

Hockey game telecast. *See under* Television—Telecast

Hockey team (U.S.) to win the Stanley Cup was the Seattle (Wash.) Metropolitans of the Pacific Coast League of Canada, which defeated the Montreal Canadiens of the National Hockey League on March 21, 24, and 27, 1917, winning three of the four games played to decide the series.

Professional hockey team was the Portage Lake Hockey Club of Houghton, Mich., formed 1896/1897. It became professional in 1903 under the leadership of Dr. J. L. Gibson, a dentist. In 1903 the team won 24 of the 26 games played.

HOCKEY PLAYER

Black player in organized hockey was Arthur Dorrington, who signed with the Atlantic City Seagulls of the Eastern Amateur League on November 15, 1950, Atlantic City, N.J., and played for them in 1950 and 1951.

Professional hockey player (black) was William Eldon ("Willie") O'Ree, forward, of the National Hockey League Boston Bruins, who played against the Montreal Canadiens at the Forum, Montreal, Canada, on January 18, 1958, which Boston won 3-0. He participated in 2 games in 1957–1958 and 43 games in 1960–1961, when he scored 14 points (4 goals, 10 assists).

Professional hockey player (defenseman) to score 100 points in 1 season was Robert Gordon ("Bobby") Orr of the National Hockey League Boston Bruins, who scored two goals and a pair of assists on March 15, 1970, at Boston, Mass., against the Detroit Red Wings, bringing his score to 101 points. He scored 120 points in the 1969–70 season in 76 games (33 goals, 87 assists).

Professional hockey player to reach a score of more than 1,000 points was Gordon ("Gordie") Howe of the National Hockey League Detroit Red Wings, who made 2 goals on November 27, 1960, at Detroit, Mich., in a game against the Toronto Maple Leafs, bringing his score to 1,001 points. In his NHL career Howe scored 786 goals and made 1,023 assists, for a total of 1,809 points.

Professional hockey player to score 50 goals in 1 season was Joseph Henri Maurice ("Rocket") Richard of the National Hockey League Montreal Canadiens, who scored his 50th goal on March 18, 1945, in the 17th minute 45th second of the third and last period against the Boston Bruins at the Boston Garden, Boston, Mass. He retired in 1960 with 544 goals in 16 regular seasons.

The First

HOCKEY PLAYER—*Continued*

Professional hockey player to score more than 100 points in 1 season was Gordon ("Gordie") Howe of the National Hockey League Detroit Red Wings, who scored 103 points (44 goals, 59 assists) in the 1968/69 season.

Professional hockey player to score 6 goals in 1 game was Syd Howe of the National Hockey League Detroit Red Wings, who scored 6 goals on February 3, 1944, in the game with the New York Rangers at the Olympia Stadium, Detroit, Mich. The score was Red Wings 12, Rangers 2.

HOIST. *See* Crane

HOLDUP OF AN ARMORED CAR. *See* Automobile robbery: Armored commercial car holdup

HOLDING COMPANY authorization (state) was enacted by New Jersey on April 4, 1888, "an act concerning corporations of this state, and of other states, doing business in this state." It provided that it was "lawful for any corporation of this state, or of any other state, doing business in this state and authorized by law to own and hold shares of stocks and bonds of corporations of other states, to own and hold and dispose thereof in the same manner and with all the rights, powers and privileges of individual owners of shares of the capital stock and bonds or other evidences of indebtedness of corporations of this state."

HOLE-IN-ONE GOLF CHAMPION. *See under* Golfer

HOLIDAY

Arbor Day celebration was held on April 10, 1872, in Nebraska. Governor Julius Sterling Morton suggested the holiday and helped celebrate it by causing trees to be planted throughout the state. Arbor Day did not become a legal holiday in Nebraska until April 22, 1885, Morton's birthday.

Armistice Day was celebrated simultaneously in many cities on November 11, 1919. Two California redwood trees were planted in Lafayette Square, opposite the White House, Washington, D.C., in the presence of Cabinet officers, General Pershing and other military and federal officials. Armistice Day, dedicated to the cause of world peace, was made a legal holiday on May 13, 1938 (52 Stat. L. 351). On June 1, 1954 (68 Stat. L. 168), the name *Armistice Day* was changed to *Veterans Day*.

Decoration Day celebration was held May 30, 1868. One year after the Civil War, April 26, 1866, the women of Columbus, Miss., strewed flowers on the graves of both the Confederate and Union soldiers at Friendship Cemetery. In May 1868, Adjutant General Norton Parker Chipman suggested to National Commander John Alexander Logan of the Grand Army of the Republic that this organization inaugurate the custom of spreading flowers on the graves of Union soldiers at periodic inter-

The First

vals. General Logan appointed May 30, 1868, as the date "for the purpose of strewing with flowers or otherwise decorating the graves of comrades who died in defense of their country during the late rebellion and with the hope that it will be kept up from year to year." The custom of decorating graves of soldiers, however, had often been locally observed previously. On August 1, 1888, an act of Congress (25 Stat. L. 353) proclaimed Decoration Day a holiday in the District of Columbia.

Father's Day celebration was held on June 19, 1910. The idea originated with Mrs. John Bruce Dodd, and the holiday was launched by the Ministerial Association and the YMCA of Spokane, Wash. It is now generally observed on the third Sunday in June.

Flag Day remembrance took place in 1877. The Government requested that the flag be flown from all public buildings on June 14, 1877, in commemoration of the 100th anniversary of the adoption of the American flag. Flag Day was made a legal holiday by Pennsylvania on May 7, 1937 (Act No. 155). It established June 14 as Flag Day and provided that the holiday be celebrated on Monday when it falls on Sunday.

Flag Day federal legislation was enacted by congressional joint resolution on August 3, 1949 (63 Stat. L. 492), which designated Flag Day as June 14th. The holiday had been proclaimed by President Woodrow Wilson in 1916 and by President Calvin Coolidge in 1927. President Harry S. Truman, however, officially designated June 14 as Flag Day in 1949.

Frontier Day holiday was celebrated by Cheyenne, Wyo. The first Cheyenne Frontier Day celebration was held at the Fair Grounds, Cheyenne, on Thursday, September 23, 1897. From a one-day exhibition, the celebration has grown to a six-day spectacle of ranch and range sports, Indian games and dances, military maneuvers by soldiers of the U.S. Army and races requiring the utmost skill in horsemanship. Other cities have similar celebrations under different names. *(Cheyenne Chamber of Commerce— Cheyenne Frontier Days)*

Indian Day observance was held on May 13, 1916, sponsored by the Society of American Indians. The purpose was to recognize and honor the American Indians and to improve their conditions. Indian Day is not a universal holiday.

Labor Day holiday was inaugurated December 28, 1869, by the Knights of Labor, an organization formed in Philadelphia, Pa. Annual observance was sponsored by the American Federation of Labor which resolved in convention at Chicago, Ill., on October 7, 1884, "that the first Monday in September be set aside as a laborer's national holiday."

The First

Labor Day holiday (federal) was officially declared by act of Congress of June 28, 1894 (28 Stat. L. 96), "an act making Labor Day a legal holiday." It designated the first Monday in September a legal holiday for federal employees and for the District of Columbia. There are no national holidays created for the nation, as each state declares for its own jurisdiction the holidays to be observed, either by legislative enactment or by executive proclamation.

Labor Day holiday parade was held September 5, 1882, in New York City under the auspices of the Central Labor Union. Ten thousand workmen, accompanied by bands of music, paraded carrying placards, "Less Work and More Pay"; "Less Hours More Pay"; "Labor Pays All Taxes"; "Labor Creates All Wealth"; "To the Workers Should Belong the Wealth"; "The Laborer Must Receive and Enjoy the Full Fruit of His Labor," etc. *(American Federationist, October 1897)*

Labor Day law (state) making Labor Day a state holiday was passed February 21, 1887, by Oregon. Colorado passed a similar law March 15, 1887, and New York, May 6, 1887.

Mardi Gras of New Orleans, La., had its inception in 1827 when a group of young men returned from Paris and introduced the French carnival idea. Mardi Gras is always on the Tuesday before Ash Wednesday, the day which marks the beginning of the Lenten season.

Maritime Day was established by joint resolution of Congress, May 20, 1933 (48 Stat. L. 73) as May 22, the anniversary of the sailing of the steamship *Savannah* from Savannah, Ga., on May 22, 1819. The resolution authorized and requested the President "annually to issue a proclamation calling upon the people of the United States to observe National Maritime Day by displaying the flag."

Memorial Day. *See* Decoration Day, above

Monday holidays legislation (federal) was enacted by Public Law No. 363 (82 Stat. L. 250) June 28, 1968, effective January 1, 1971, for federal employees and residents of the District of Columbia. It established new days for the observance of Washington's Birthday (the third Monday in February), Memorial Day (the last Monday in May), Labor Day (the first Monday in September), Columbus Day (the second Monday in October), and Veterans Day (the fourth Monday in October). Many states have adopted similar legislation.

Mother-in-Law Day was celebrated March 5, 1934, at Amarillo, Tex. The honored mother was Mrs. W. F. Donald, the mother-in-law of Gene Howe, part owner and editor of the Amarillo *Daily News* and the Amarillo *Globe*, who was responsible for the celebration.

The First

Mother's Day was suggested by Miss Anna Jarvis, of Philadelphia, Pa., at a public meeting in 1907. She proposed wearing a carnation on the second Sunday of May. The first city to adopt the plan was Philadelphia, which designated May 10, 1908, as the first Mother's Day. A joint resolution of Congress (J.R. No. 13) on May 8, 1914, established the second Sunday in May as Mother's Day (38 Stat. L. 770) and on May 9, 1914, President Woodrow Wilson proclaimed the date (38 Stat. L. 1996) as a national holiday, the first celebration being May 10, 1914.

National holiday was April 30, 1889, authorized by act of Congress March 21, 1889 (25 Stat. L. 980), to observe the centennial of the inauguration of George Washington. The day was "hereby declared to be a national holiday throughout the United States." A committee of five senators and five representatives of the 51st Congress was appointed to arrange an appropriate celebration in Congress on December 11, 1889, at which Chief Justice Melville Weston Fuller was the guest speaker.

Navy Day was suggested by Mrs. William Hamilton to the Secretary of the Navy, and celebrated October 27, 1922, the anniversary of the birth of President Theodore Roosevelt. Celebrations in commemoration were held in various parts of the United States.

Saturday half holiday was inaugurated by George Westinghouse, the inventor and manufacturer of the air brake, who established the custom in his factory in Pittsburgh, Pa., in June 1871. *(Francis Ellington Leupp—George Westinghouse, His Life and Achievements)*

Thanksgiving Day designated by presidential proclamation was November 26, 1789. On October 3, 1789, President George Washington issued a proclamation appointing November 26, 1789, as a day of general thanksgiving for the adoption of the Constitution. *(Howard Sylvester Jackson Sickel—Thanksgiving)*

Thanksgiving Day celebration (nationwide, colonial) was held Thursday, December 18, 1777, commemorating the surrender of Lieutenant General John Burgoyne on October 17, 1777, at Schuylerville, N.Y. On October 31, 1777, the Continental Congress appointed Samuel Adams, Richard Henry Lee, and Daniel Roberdeau to draft a recommendation "to set apart a day of thanksgiving for the signal success lately obtained over the enemies of the United States." The resolution was accepted November 1, 1777, and on November 7, 1777, it was voted "that a duplicate of the recommendation of Congress to the several states to set apart a day of thanksgiving signed by the president be sent to the respective states, and to General Washington and General Gates." *(Journals of the Continental Congress 1774–1789, Vol. 9)*

The First

HOLIDAY—*Continued*

Thanksgiving Day national proclamation was made on October 3, 1863, by President Abraham Lincoln, who set the fourth Thursday in November, a date which has since been generally nationally observed. Special thanksgiving days had been previously set aside for specific occasions of thanks. On April 10, 1862, Lincoln requested the nation "to implore spiritual consolation . . . at their next weekly assemblages in their accustomed places of public worship." On July 15, 1863, he designated Thursday, August 6, 1863, "to subdue the anger which has produced and so long sustained a needless and cruel rebellion."

Thanksgiving Day sermon (west of the Alleghenies) was given by the Reverend Charles Beatty, a Presbyterian minister, on November 26, 1758. He delivered a sermon entitled "A Clarion of Calvinism," at Duquesne (now Pittsburgh), Pa.

Thanksgiving Day service was held August 9, 1607, at Phippsburg, Maine, by colonists on "The Gift of God" and the "Mary and John" under the leadership of George Popham, who landed at "St. Georges Illand." Services were held by the Reverend Richard Seymour, "gyvinge God thanks for our happy metinge & saffe aryval into the country." *(Henry Otis Thayer—The Sagahadoc Colony)*

HOLY MASS, CATHOLIC. *See* Catholic mass

HOLY ORDERS. *See* Catholic holy orders

HOME LOAN. *See* GI Bill of Rights

HOME LOAN BANK BOARD. *See* Federal Home Loan Bank Board

HOME OWNERS' LOAN CORPORATION was authorized by the Home Owners' Loan Act of 1933, approved by President Franklin Delano Roosevelt, June 13, 1933 (47 Stat. L. 736), "to grant long term mortgage loans at low interest rates to those in urgent need of funds for the protection, preservation or recovery of their homes who were unable to procure the needed financing through normal channels." The Federal Home Loan Bank Board, consisting of five members, was organized under the Federal Home Loan Bank Act, approved July 22, 1932, to establish and supervise the 12 Federal Home Loan Banks according to the provisions of the act. Franklin Fort was appointed chairman of the Federal Home Loan Bank Board on July 22, 1932. The Federal Home Loan Bank System is a permanent system which makes loans to members of home financing institutions for home-financing purposes. The Home Owners' Loan Corporation was a temporary emergency corporation loaning directly to home owners who were threatened with foreclosure and were unable to obtain the money for refinancing through private channels.

The First

"HOME RUN KING". *See* Baseball player: Baseball "Home Run King"

HOME STUDY COURSE of a serious nature was offered by the Literary and Scientific Circle of the Chautauqua Institution which was organized August 10, 1878. In harmony with the plan of the first work of the Assembly, the correspondence School of Theology was organized and in 1881 received its charter. On March 30, 1833, the Chautauqua College of Liberal Arts was given a charter by the legislature of the State of New York, conferring full authority to grant diplomas and to confer the usual college and university degrees.

HOMEOPATHIC COLLEGE. *See* Medical school

HOMEOPATHIC HOSPITAL. *See* Hospital

HOMEOPATHIC MAGAZINE. *See* Medical periodical

HOMEOPATHIC MEDICAL SOCIETY. *See* Medical society

HOMEOPATHIC PHARMACY. *See* Pharmacy

HOMEOPATHY was brought to New York City in 1825 by Dr. Hans Burch Gram. In 1828 Gram was elected a member of the New York Medical and Philosophical Society, and in 1829 became its president. *(Thomas Lindsley Bradford—The Pioneers of Homeopathy)*

HOMEOPATHY TREATISE. *See* Medical book

HOMES, INSTITUTIONAL. See Old Age Home for pioneers; Soldiers' homes (national)

HOMESTEAD under the Homestead Act was taken by Daniel Freeman, a Union soldier, on January 1, 1863, near Beatrice, Neb.

HOMESTEAD ACT

Homestead act was "an act to secure homesteads to actual settlers on the public domain," passed by both houses of Congress on May 19, 1862, and approved on May 20, 1862 (12 Stat. L. 392) by President Abraham Lincoln. It went into effect on January 1, 1863. Under this law any man or woman of 21 could secure title to 160 acres of public land by living on it for five years, making certain improvements, and paying fees of approximately $18.

Homestead act (desert) was enacted on March 3, 1875 (18 Stat. L. 497), "to sell the desert land in Lassen County, Calif., at $1.25 an acre." This act differed from the Homestead Act of May 20, 1862 (12 Stat. L. 392) in that the owner was not required to reside on the land and that he could purchase four times the quantity of land permitted under the Homestead Act.

HONOLULU SQUADRON FLIGHT. *See under* Aviation—Flights (transpacific)

HONOR SYSTEM of conducting examinations was introduced by the College of William and

The First

Mary, Williamsburg, Va., in 1779, *(Bulletin of the College of William and Mary in Virginia)*

HONORS COURSE. *See under* College

HOOKLESS FASTENER. *See* Fastening: Hookless fastening

HOOKS AND EYES. *See under* Fastening

HORIZON CURVATURE PHOTOGRAPH. *See* Photograph: Photograph showing the lateral curvature of the horizon

HORMONE. *See* Pituitary hormone

HORSE

Forest horse born in the United States was Pepin, sired by Charlemagne and foaled by Siegling, May 18, 1956, at the Chicago Zoological Park, Brookfield, Ill. This extinct forest breed had been re-created by a program of crossbreeding that involved more than 300 Iceland ponies, Shetland ponies, Dartmoor ponies, Norwegian duns, Hanover coach horses, feral horses from Patagonia, and Koniks of Poland. Forest horses were first imported into the United States in 1955.

Haflinger horse was imported by Tempel Smith of Spring Grove, Ill., who imported 17 horses (10 mares, 3 stallions, 2 fillies, and 2 colts) on August 18, 1958. They arrived in New York Harbor from Austria. The Haflinger is compactly built, longer than tall, with a height of 140-150 centimeters at the withers.

Horse farm operated by the United States Government was the United States Morgan Horse Farm, Middlebury, Vt., established in 1907 on 400 acres donated by Colonel Joseph Battell of Middlebury, Vt. The first 270 acres of land were deeded to the United States by Battell, February 1, 1907. Horse breeding under the Bureau of Animal Industry began in December 1904, a cooperative enterprise with the Colorado Experiment Station to develop an American utility horse. *(U.S. Department of Agriculture—The Preservation of Our Native Types of Horses—Circular 137)*

Horse race. *See* Horse race

Horse show. *See* Horse show

Horse (thoroughbred) to defeat 2 triple-crown winners in the same race was Exceller, who defeated Seattle Slew (1977 winner) and Affirmed (1978 winner) on October 14, 1978, in the Jockey Club Gold Cup $300,000 Stakes at Belmont Park Raceway, Elmont, N.Y. (The Triple-Crown award goes to the winner of the following 3 events: Kentucky Derby, Preakness Stakes, and Belmont Stakes.)

Horse to pace 1 mile in better than 2:00 was Star Pointer, in harness at Readville, Mass., on August 28, 1897. The time was one mile in 1:59¼. The Tennessee-bred light-harness stallion was owned by James A. Murphy and driven by Dave

The First

McCleary. *(Hamilton Busbey—The Trotting and the Pacing Horse in America)*

Horse to trot a mile in less than 2 minutes was Lou Dillon, a 5-year-old chestnut mare, which established a record of 1:58½ on August 24, 1903, at Readville, Mass. She was driven by Millard F. Sanders and paced by 2 horses in a special exhibition against time. She took 2¼ seconds off the record. *(Henry Troth Coates—A Short History of the American Trotting and Pacing Horse)*

Horse to trot a mile in less than 3 minutes was Yankey, a gelding of unknown ancestry, from New Haven, Conn., who trotted 1 mile in 2 minutes 59 seconds on a half mile track at the Harlem Lane, Harlem, New York City, on June 10, 1806. The course was located at what is now the western foot of Mount Morris Park, between 125th Street on the north and Seventh Avenue on the west.

Horse to trot 100 miles in less than 9 hours was Conqueror, who trotted in 8 hours 56 minutes 1 second, driven by George Spicer on November 12, 1853, to win a $4,000 wager. Conqueror died a few days later.

Horse to win $1 million in races was Citation, a 6-year-old bay colt born and owned by Calumet Farms, which won the $100,000 Hollywood Gold Cup Handicap at Hollywood Park, Inglewood, Calif., on July 14, 1951, bringing his total earnings in 1947–1948 and 1950–1951 in 45 starts (32 firsts, 10 seconds, 2 thirds, 1 unplaced) to $1,085,760.

Horse to win the Triple Crown, the "Big Three," for three-year-olds, was Sir Barton. In 1919 he won a total of $57,275—on May 1, $20,825 in the Kentucky Derby, Churchill Downs, Ky.; on May 14, $24,500 in the Preakness, Pimlico, Md., and on June 11, 1919, $11,950 in the Belmont Stakes, Belmont Park, L.I., N.Y. At Belmont a new track record was set for the mile and three-furlong course.

Horse (trotting horse) was Messenger, a gray horse 15 hands 3 inches high, foaled in 1780. He was imported from England and arrived at Philadelphia, Pa., in May 1788. He was buried with military honors January 28, 1808. *(John Hervey—Messenger, The Great Progenitor)*

Horse whose total purses exceeded $100,000 was Miss Woodford, foaled 1880. She won 37 of 48 races between 1882 and 1886 for a purse of $118,270.00. The mare was the entry of the Dwyer Brothers (Michael and Philip).

Horses were imported into the colonies about April 17, 1629, by the Massachusetts Bay Colony. The agreement made by Matthewe Cradock, first governor of the company, required that "such cattle, both horses, mares, cowes, bulls, and goates, as are shipped by Mr. Cradock, are to bee devyded in equall halfes twixt him & the Companie." *(Nathaniel Bradstreet Shurtleff—Records of the*

The First

HORSE—Continued
Governor and Company of the Massachusetts Bay in New England. Vol. 1)

Morgan horse was named after its owner, Justin Morgan. It was foaled in 1789 in Randolph, Vt., and got by True Briton, also known as Beautiful Bay. It died in 1821. *(Joseph Battell—The Morgan Horse and Register)*

Pacer to win $1 million was Cardigan Bay, a New Zealand–bred 12–year–old gelding that won $7,500 in the Freehold Special at Freehold Raceway, Freehold, N.J., on September 14, 1968, bringing his earnings to $1,000,671. Stanley Dancer was the driver; 2 minutes 1 second, the time for the mile race.

Percheron (horse) importation was attempted by Edward Harris of Moorestown, N.J., in 1839. Four horses were obtained from France, but only a mare survived the trip. Two stallions and two mares were subsequently imported, one of the stallions (Diligence) being credited with 400 foals. *(Ellis McFarland—Brief History of the Percheron Horse)*

Thoroughbred horse is claimed to be Bulle Rock, who was imported into Virginia in 1730. He was foaled in 1717 and was a son of Darley Arabian and the mare Byerly Turk. It is also claimed that the first thoroughbred horse was Spark, who was presented to Lord Baltimore by the Prince of Wales, the father of George III. Lord Baltimore gave Spark to Governor Samuel Ogle of Maryland about 1750. *(John Gilmer Speed—The Horse in America)*

Trotter triple-crown winner (for 3-year olds) was Scott Frost, which won the Hambletonian at Good Time Park, Goshen, N.Y., $86,863 on August 3, 1955; the Yonkers Futurity, Yonkers, N.Y., $73,-840 on September 1, 1955; the Kentucky Futurity, Lexington, Ky., $62,702 on October 6, 1955. Sol Camp was the owner; Joe O'Brien, the driver.

Two stable-mate trotters to break a world record the same day were owned by the Arden Homestead Stable, Goshen, N.Y. At the Du Quoin Grand Circuit program at Du Quoin, Ill., on August 29, 1952, Florican, a 6-year old, with Del Miller driving, lowered the old record from 1:57 3/5 to 1:57 2/5; Star's Pride driven by Harry Pownal in the sulky covered the distance in 1:57 1/5.

HORSE BLANKET. *See* Blanket

HORSE BREEDING SOCIETY was the Massachusetts Society for Encouraging the Breed of Fine Horses, formed in Boston, Mass., in 1810. Annual trials and competitions were held October 23–25, at the Washington course, Boston, Mass. Rules provided that "every driver shall be dressed at starting neatly with a jockey cap, silk jacket with sleeves." etc.

The First

HORSE CAR. *See* Streetcar

HORSE FARM. *See under* Horse

HORSE MOTEL. *See* Motel

HORSE RACE
See also Horse; Jockey

American-bred horse to win a major race abroad was Prioress, a four-year-old bay mare, winner of the Cesarewitch Handicap at Newmarket, England, on October 13, 1857. There were 37 starters, of whom 3 tied. In the runoff after the regular daily program, Prioress won by a length and a half (4 minutes 15 seconds for the 2-mile 468-yard course). The odds were 100 - 1. Her owner was Richard Ten Broeck. *(Spirit of the Times. November 7, 1857)*

American-bred horse to win the English Derby was Iroquois, a three-year-old, owned by Pierre Lorillard, winner of the Epsom Derby at Epsom Downs, England, on June 1, 1881. There were 14 competitors. Fred Archer was the jockey.

Father and son harness drivers to gross more than $1 million each in 1 season were Billy Haughton (age 54) and Peter Haughton (age 23), whose winnings in 1977 were $1.16 million and $1.01 million respectively.

Filly to win the Kentucky Derby at Churchill Downs, Louisville, Ky., was Regret, Harry Payne Whitney's chestnut filly. She ran the mile and a quarter in 2:05 2/5 on May 8, 1915, to win the 41st Kentucky Derby. There were 16 starters.

Futurity race was held October 10, 1843, at Nashville, Tenn., and known as the Peyton Stakes. Out of 30 nominations, only 4 faced the starter. Four one-mile heats were held. Glumbalditch, a filly owned by Thomas Kirkham of Nashville, Tenn., won the third and fourth heat, thereby winning the race and a purse of $35,000. She was later renamed Peytona.

Harness driver (American) to score 300 victories in 1 year was Bob Farrington of Richwood, Ohio, who scored with Liza Volo ($20) in the 2nd race, Syndicate ($12.40) in the 6th race, and Dark Flash ($16.40) in the 9th race on November 21, 1964, at Washington Park, Chicago, Ill., bringing his victories to 300. *(New York Times. Nov. 22, 1964, Sec. 7, page 3.)*

Harness horse race (Hambletonian) for three-year-olds was won by Guy McKinney, a four-year old, winner of $45,868.42 of the $73,451.32 purse in 2:05¼ at the initial stake, August 30, 1926, at the New York State Fair, Syracuse, N.Y. The horse was owned by Henry B. Rea of Pittsburgh, Pa., and driven by Nat Ray. The first driver to win the Hambletonian twice was Benjamin Franklin White, who won August 16, 1933, with Mary Reynolds and on August 12, 1936 with Rosalind (at Goshen, N.Y.) *(Elizabeth Sharts—Cradle of the Trotter)*

The First

Harness race driver to win the Hambletonian four times was Benjamin Franklin White, who won the 18th stake on August 11, 1943, at the Empire City Track, Yonkers, N.Y. There were 11 starters and 8 recalls. White won on Volo Song, a bay colt owned by W. H. Strang. His other victories were on Mary Reynolds, August 16, 1933; Rosalind, August 12, 1936; and The Ambassador, August 12, 1942—all at Goshen, N.Y.

Horse race run on a regular basis was held on the Newmarket Course, Hempstead Plains, L.I., N.Y., in 1665, when Governor Richard Nicolls, the first English governor of New York, established the course. He issued the order to measure off a mile course on the level prairie near the village and gave a cup to reward the owner of the swift-est-running horse, "not so much for the divertisement of youth as for encouraging the bettering of the breed of horses, which through neglect has been impaired." *(Farmer's Home Journal. August 1930)*

Horse race (American Derby) was held at Washington Park Club, Chicago, Ill., on June 28, 1884. The race for three-year-olds was won by Modesty (Isaac Murphy, jockey) whose time for the 1½-mile course was 2:42¾. He won $10,700 in a field of 12. *(Goodwin's Annual Turf Guide for 1884)*

Horse race for a purse of more than $1 million was the All American Futurity for quarter horses held September 4, 1972, at Ruidoso Downs, Ruido-so, N.Mex., won by Possumjet, a chestnut filly two-year-old quarter horse owned by Jack Byers of Blanchard, Okla. Pete Herrera was the jockey. Possumjet won $336,629.70 (the richest first prize awarded) of the $1,035,900 purse and returned $44.60, $16, and $7.20 across the boards. The time for the 400 yards was 20:04 seconds. Attendance was 14,338.

Horse race for a purse of more than $2 million was the Woodrow Wilson purse for two-year olds on August 6, 1980, at the Meadowlands, East Rutherford, N.J., won by Land Grant (Del Insko, driver), a 69-1 shot. He earned $1,005,500 of the $2,011,000 purse. The pari-mutuel paid $141.80, $40.20, and $17. In the exacta, No. 9 and No. 11 paid $1,549. Armbro Wolf was second, Nero's BB third. The time for the mile was 1:56 4/5.

Horse race in which the British Royal Silks participated was the third running of the Washington, D.C., International, the seventh race, at Laurel, Md., on November 3, 1954. Queen Elizabeth II entered Landau, a three-year-old carrying the royal purple, gold, and scarlet silks. The jockey was Willie Snaith. The horse finished last. The $50,000 first prize in the $65,000 event was won by Eddie Arcaro riding Fisherman.

The First

Horse race (Kentucky Derby) was run May 17, 1875, at the Churchill Downs Course at Louisville, Ky. There were 15 starters. Aristides (jockey, Oliver Lewis) won a $2,850 purse covering the mile-and-a-half course in 2:37¾. Volcano was second, Verdigris third.

Horse race (Kentucky Derby) telecast in color. *See under* Television—Telecast

Horse race of 1,000 miles started 5:30 P.M., June 13, 1893, at Chadron, Neb., each contestant being allowed two race horses, one to ride and one to follow. The destination was Chicago, Ill., via Long Pine, Oneill, and Wausa, Neb.; Sioux City, Galva, Fort Dodge, Iowa Falls, Waterloo, Manchester, and Dubuque, Iowa; and Freeport, De Kalb, and Chicago, Ill. The winner, John Berry on Poison, arrived June 27, 1893, at 9:30 P.M., followed on June 28, by Emmet Albright at 11:15 A.M., and Joe Gillespie at 1:31 P.M.

Horse race on a stage in a theater was incorporated in *Herne, the Hunter*, a play presented February 18, 1856, in the Old Broadway Theatre, 326-328 Broadway, New York City. The theater had 4,000 seats (no backs) and room for 500 standees. Admission was 25 cents. A chariot pulled by 6 horses was used. Many injuries occurred: 1 horse caused the collapse of a platform, another fell off the proscenium onto spikes, and there were many similar mishaps.

Horse race (pace race) for a purse of more than $1 million was the Meadowland, a 1-mile race for 3-year-old thoroughbred or standard-bred horses, held July 18, 1980, at the Meadowland Race Track, East Rutherford, N.J. It was won by Niatross (Clint Galbraith, driver; Elsie Berger, owner) in 1:53:1. The purse was $1,011,000. The pari-mutel paid $2.80, $2.20, and $2.60. Storm Damage was second, Tyler B third. It was the richest race for thoroughbreds or standardbreds. Niatross won $505,500; Storm Damage, $252,750; Tyler B, $121,-320.

Horse race pari-mutuel with an entire field of women jockeys was the 6-furlong Lady Godiva $10,000 handicap at Suffolk Downs, Boston, Mass. $115.044 was wagered on April 19, 1969, on the third race. It was won by Penny Ann Early on Royal Fillet, which paid $5.40. Second place was won by Diane Crump on Destiny's Twist, third place by Tuesee Testa on Critical. Other jockies were Brenda Wilson, Robyn Smith, Barbara Ader, and Connie Hendricks.

Horse race prohibition legislation was enacted June 4, 1674, by Massachusetts. It provided "that whatsoeuer p'son shall run a race with any horse in any street or Comon road shall forfeite fiue shillings in Mony forthwith to be leuied by the Constable or set in the stockes one houre if it be not payed." *(David Pulsifer—Records of the Colony of New Plymouth in New England)*

The First

HORSE RACE—*Continued*

Horse-race telecast shown in a theater. *See* Television—Telecast: Horse-race telecast shown on a large screen in a theater

Horse to win a $100,000 purse in one race was Whichone, a two-year-old, son of Chicle and Flying Witch, winner of the 40th Belmont Futurity at Belmont Park Race Track, Elmont, Long Island, N.Y., on September 14, 1929. The time was 1:19 3/5 for 6¾ furlongs (approximately ⅞ mile). The purse was $105,730. Harry Payne Whitney was the owner and Sonny Workman the jockey. There were 17 starters in the race.

Mutuel ticket to pay more than $1,000 was made June 17, 1912, when Wishing Ring, a 4-year-old colt, at Latonia track, Covington, Ky., paid $1,885.50 to win, $744.40 to place, and $172.40 to show. Only four $2 tickets were sold. The colt was owned by J. S. Respess and won the sixth race; the odds were 900-1.

Night harness race was held at the Beacon Track, Hoboken, N.J., on October 5, 1843. The winner of the 2-mile race for the $300 purse was Dutchman (driver Hiram Woodruff), who won in 5:19. Americus (George Spicer, driver) was second; and Lady Suffolk (Dave Bryan, driver) was third, having previously run a dead heat. *(Hiram Woodruff—The Trotting Horse of America)*

Perfecta, or Exacta (in which bettors select the first 2 horses in the same race), paid $30.40 for a $2 winning ticket on Wednesday, June 30, 1965, at Monticello Raceway, Monticello, N.Y. Bayard, No. 8, was first; Sonny Ardin, No. 1, was second. There were 481 winning tickets; $17,242 was bet.

Racetrack at which more than $5 million was bet in one day was Belmont Park, Long Island, N.Y. On September 22, 1945, bets amounting to $5,016,745 were placed by 46,614 people, setting four records: a world mark for a daily double—$210,982; a world record for betting in one day—$5,016,745; a national record for a jumping race—$404,230; and a New York mark for a single race—$769,171.

Stakes race triple dead heat was the 46th running of the Carter Handicap, the sixth race at Belmont Park, Elmont, L.I., N.Y., on June 10, 1944. It was a ⅞th-of-a-mile race for 3-year-olds and upwards. The time for the 7 furlongs was 1:23 2/5. The $11.700 purse was split equally between Eric Guerin on Joe W. Brown's Brownie, Jimmy Stout on Belair Stud's Bossuet, and G. L. Smith on William Ziegler, Jr.'s Wait-A-Bit.

Steeplechase. *See* Steeplechase

Three-hundred-mile endurance run was held on October 15, 1919, from Fort Ethan Allen, Burlington, Vt., to Camp Devens, Mass. Ramela, owned by W. R. Brown, president of the Arab Club, and ridden by Albert W. Harris of Chicago, Ill., won the $1,000 prize and the United States Mounted

The First

Service challenge cup. The horse won 23 34/60 points of a possible 25, covering the distance in 51 hours 26½ minutes. Kingfisher was second and won the $500 prize. There were 14 starters. Points were determined by rating the condition of the horses, the food consumption, etc. Entrants were required to cover 60 miles a day and were ridden not less than 10 hours and not more than 15 hours a day, carrying weights from 200 to 245 pounds.

Trotting course was established at Jamaica, Long Island, N.Y., in 1825 by the New York Trotting Club. On May 16, 1825, the main race was won by Screwdriver.

Trotting futurity was the Spirit of the Times stake, a sweepstake for three-year-old trotting colts and fillies in 1866. The entrance fee was $250, of which $100 was paid on registration and $150 before the race. A one-mile harness race was held October 12, 1869, at Prospect Park Pleasure Grounds, Brooklyn, N.Y. Seventeen horses were entered. The race was won by Isaiah Rynder's Aberdeen (son of Hambletonian and Widow Machree) in 2 minutes 46 seconds. The first prize was $2,000, the second prize $500, and third prize $250. *(Spirit of the Times. Nov. 16, 1867, and Oct. 16, 1869)*

HORSE REGISTER

Pacing register was the *American Race-Turf Register, Sportsman's Herald and General Stud Book; containing the pedigrees of the most celebrated horses, mares, and geldings that have distinguished themselves as pacers on the American turf,* 602 pages, by Patrick Nisbett Edgar, published in 1833 in New York City.

Trotting register was John Hankins Wallace's *American Trotting Register, containing all that is known of the pedigrees of trotting horses, their ancestors and descendants, with a full record of all published performances in which a mile was trotted or paced in 2.40 or less, from the earliest dates till the close of 1868,* a 504-page book published in 1871 in New York City.

HORSE SHOW

Horse show was the Upperville Colt and Horse Show, Upperville, Va., established in 1853 by Colonel Richard Hunter Dulany. Shows were held annually in June until the Civil War. The first show after the war was held November 10, 1869. The show is still held annually.

Horse show of national scope was held at Madison Square Garden, New York City, October 22–26, 1883, by the National Horse Show Association of America. There were 187 exhibitors with 623 entries. Cornelius Fellowes was president of the association from its organization in 1883 until 1909.

HORSEBACK RIDER (woman) TO MAKE A SOLO CONTINENTAL TRIP. *See* Woman

The First

Woman horseback rider to make a solo transcontinental trip

HORSESHOE MANUFACTURING MACHINE was patented on November 23, 1835, by Henry Burden of Troy, N.Y., who received subsequent patents in 1843, 1857 and 1862. His machine produced a completed horseshoe from a rod of iron that was fed into it. It produced shoes more rapidly and uniformly than the hand production method which had been used prior to this invention. *(Margaret Burden Proudfit—Henry Burden, His Life, and a History of His Inventions)*

HORSESHOE PITCHERS' ASSOCIATION (national) was the Grand League of the American Horseshoe Pitchers Association organized May 16, 1914, in Kansas City, Kan. Rules were standardized. Pegs were raised to 8 inches and spaced 38½ feet apart. Ringers counted 5 points and leaners 3 points. The first championship tournament was held October 23, 1915, in Kellerton, Iowa. Frank Jackson won the championship winning 24 out of 25 games.

HORSESHOE PITCHING CONTEST (international) open to all was held in Bronson, Kan., in the summer of 1909. The contest was held on dirt courts; pegs were 2 inches high and were spaced 38½ feet apart. Frank Jackson of Blue Mound, Kan., was awarded the World's Championship belt with miniature horseshoes attached to it.

HORTICULTURAL MAGAZINE was the *Floral Magazine and Botanical Repository,* published May 1832 in Philadelphia, Pa., by D[avid] & C[uthbert] Landreth, nurserymen and seedsmen. Publication ceased after 80 pages and 31 colored lithograph prints had been issued.

HORTICULTURAL SOCIETY

Horticultural society was the New York Horticultural Society, founded in 1818 and incorporated March 22, 1822. It existed about 15 years.

Horticultural society (permanent) was the Pennsylvania Horticultural Society, organized November 24, 1827, in Philadelphia, Pa., with a membership of 53. Horace Binney was the first president. The first exhibition open to the public was held June 6, 1829. It is the oldest horticultural society still in existence. *(James Boyd—History of the Pennsylvania Horticulture Society)*

HOSE, FIRE. *See* Fire hose

HOSE, NYLON. *See under* Nylon

HOSPITAL

Ambulance ship. *See under* Ship

Ambulatory surgical facility independently operated and separate from a hospital designed exclusively for minor surgical procedures was Surgicenter, Phoenix, Ariz., opened February 12, 1970, for various kinds of surgical procedures in the categories of orthopedic surgery, urological, gynecological, ophthalmological, otolaryngological, and other surgical specialties. Surgicenter is owned and operated by John Laurence Ford, M.D., and Wallace Allison Reed, M.D.

Animal hospital. *See* Veterinary hospital

Army field hospital was a tent hospital established by Brigadier General Bernard John Dowling Irwin of the Army Medical Corps at Shiloh, Tenn., prior to the battle of April 6–7, 1862, when the Union army suffered more than 13,000 casualties.

Babies' hospital designed exclusively for infants was the Babies Hospital of the City of New York, which was chartered on June 23, 1887. The hospital opened in a house at 161 East 36th Street, New York City, with a total of eight beds. *(Twenty-Fifth Annual Report, Babies Hospital of the City of New York)*

Black hospital and asylum, founded by whites solely for blacks, was chartered December 24, 1832, as the "Georgia Infirmary, for the relief and protection of aged and afflicted Negroes," of Savannah, Ga. The organization meeting was held at the Exchange, January 15, 1833, and the first president was Richard F. Williams. *(Short History of the Georgia Infirmary—1933)*

Cancer home for incurables (free) was established in a room in a flat on Scammel Street, New York City, on September 15, 1896, by Rose Hawthorne Lathrop (later Sister Mary Alphonsa, O.D.) afterward assisted by Alice Huber (later Sister Mary Rose, O.D.). They organized the Servants of Relief for Incurable Cancer and on May 1, 1899, opened St. Rose's Free Home for Incurable Cancer in New York City, with accommodations for 15 patients. On June 1, 1901, a building in the country was acquired which carried on the work under the name of Rosary Hill Home at Sherman Park (now Hawthorne), N.Y.

Cancer hospital was the New York Cancer Hospital, 106th Street and Central Park West, New York City. The hospital had its beginning at a preliminary meeting held February 7, 1884, at the residence of Mrs. Elizabeth Hamilton Cullum and was incorporated May 31, 1884, "to establish, maintain and conduct a cancer hospital." It was opened for patients December 7, 1887, and by special act of March 6, 1899, of the legislature, its name was changed to the General Memorial Hospital for the Treatment of Cancer and Allied Diseases. On March 22, 1916, a court order was obtained to drop "General" from the title, effective April 26, 1916, and its name became the Memorial Hospital for the Treatment of Cancer and Allied Diseases. The first attending surgeons were Dr. James Bradbridge Hunter, Dr. Clement Cleveland, and Dr. William Tillinghast Bull. The first president was John E. Parsons. The hospital is now part of Memorial Sloan-Kettering Cancer Center and is located at 1275 York Avenue, New York City. *(Milestones of Memorial Hospital)*

The First

HOSPITAL—*Continued*

Cancer hospital (municipal) was the New York City Cancer Institute on Welfare Island (now Roosevelt Island), New York City, dedicated August 1, 1923. The first patient was admitted August 23, 1923. Dr. Isaac Levin was the first director.

Children's hospital was established in 1854 in New York City and was known as the Nursery and Child's Hospital. It originated from a society founded by Sarah Platt Doremus and Mrs. Cornelius Du Bois "for the maintenance and care of the children of wet-nurses, and the daily charge of infants whose parents labor away from home." *(New York Nursery and Child's Hospital—106th Annual Report. 1928)*

Children's hospital solely for research and treatment of catastrophic childhood diseases was St. Jude Children's Research Hospital, Memphis, Tenn., which opened February 4, 1962. It was founded by actor Danny Thomas, its first president. There are no charges to patients for treatment, hospitalization, or consultation.

Chinese-American hospital was the Chinese Hospital, Jackson Street, San Francisco, Calif., opened April 18, 1925. The first board of directors included B. S. Seid, president; B. S. Fong, vice president; Yee Y. Ng, secretary; and Chow King, treasurer.

Community hospital was the Community Hospital, Elk City, Okla., established by Dr. Michael Abraham Shadid. The organization meeting was held October 20, 1929. The hospital was dedicated August 13, 1931. *(Michael Abraham Shadid, A Doctor for the People)*

Consumptive hospital. *See* Hospital: Tuberculosis hospital

Crippled children's hospital (state) was the Gillette State Hospital for Crippled Children, St. Paul, Minn., authorized April 23, 1897 (Chapter 289, Laws of 1897) by "an act to provide for the care and treatment of crippled and deformed children." Five thousand dollars was appropriated. The hospital was named in honor of Dr. Arthur Jay Gillette.

Dispensary established for the specific purpose of furnishing free medicine to the needy was the Philadelphia Dispensary, instituted on April 12, 1786, by Bishop William White. It was chartered April 15, 1796, and was governed by 12 managers elected annually. It was not, however, the first to do free outpatient work, as the Pennsylvania Hospital treated indigent outpatients as early as December 13, 1752. The Philadelphia Dispensary affiliated with the Pennsylvania Hospital in 1922. *(Thomas George Morton and Frank Woodbury— The History of the Pennsylvania Hospital)*

The First

Eye hospital (permanent) was the New York Eye Infirmary, a two-room hospital on the second floor at 45 Chatham Street, New York City, which was opened August 14, 1820, and incorporated March 29, 1822. The chief surgeons were Dr. Edward Delafield and Dr. John Kearney Rodgers. The first officers were William Few, president; Henry I. Wyckoff, first vice president; John Hone, second vice president; John Delafield, treasurer; and James I. Jones, secretary. By January 1, 1822, the infirmary had treated 1,120 cases and cured 801. On April 30, 1864, the name was changed to the New York Eye and Ear Infirmary. *(Alvin Allace Hubbell—Development of Ophthalmology in America)*

Eye infirmary was established in New London, Conn., in 1817 by Elisha North. He studied at the University of Pennsylvania Medical School but did not obtain his M.D. degree. In appreciation of his interest and effort in behalf of medicine, he was later awarded an M.D. degree in Connecticut. *(Johns Hopkins Hospital Bulletin. October 1908)*

Floating hospital was the *Emma Abbott*, which made her trial trip July 19, 1875. The ship cost $20,000, was 215 feet long with a 40-foot breadth of beam, and had three decks, one of which served as a dining room. It was known as the "poor children's yacht" and was operated by St. John's Guild, New York City (organized October 19, 1866, and incorporated December 14, 1877). The ship served until 1902, when it was replaced with a more modern ship. In the summer of 1873, the guild hired a barge and gave 2 excursions for sick children, and in 1874, 18 similar excursions, accommodating 15,202 sick children and mothers. So noticeable was the health benefit that the guild decided to operate its own floating hospitals. *(St. John's Guild—Sixty-seventh Annual Report)*

General hospital to adopt the Social Security account number as a numbering system for medical records was the Altoona Hospital, Altoona, Pa., which began this method of numbering patients on January 20, 1967. The identification was discontinued since pseudo-numbers had to be issued for newborns and about one-third of the patients.

Group hospital-medical cooperative. *See under* Insurance

Homeopathic hospital was the Homeopathic Hospital of Pennsylvania, Philadelphia, Pa., incorporated September 20, 1850. Vincent L. Bradford was the first president. In 1852, a hospital with 30 beds was opened which served for about two years.

Hospital completely devoted to the study of the atom in the treatment of cancer was the Argonne Cancer Research Hospital, Chicago, Ill., operated for the Atomic Energy Commission by the Univer

The First

sity of Chicago as part of the university's South Side Cancer Research Center. The hospital, which was opened March 13, 1953, contained eight floors, two of which were underground. Bed space was limited to two floors to accommodate 56 patients. Other floors were devoted to equipment and laboratories. The first director was Dr. Leon Orris Jacobson. The cost of the building and equipment was about $4 million.

Hospital for the military and naval forces was the Army and Navy Hospital, Hot Springs, Ark., opened for the reception of patients on January 17, 1887. The appropriation was authorized by act of Congress of June 30, 1882 (22 Stat. L. 121). The hospital had five separate buildings, which were connected by verandas. *(Charles Cutter—Guide to the Hot Springs of Arkansas)*
See also Army field hospital, above; Marine hospital (U.S.) *and* Naval hospital, below

Hospital in America was the Pennsylvania Hospital, opened in Philadelphia February 11, 1752, through the efforts of Benjamin Franklin and Dr. Thomas Bond. A temporary hospital was erected in 1751 in a private house on High (now Market) Street. The care of the sick, however, had been undertaken earlier by both secular and religious agencies. St. Augustine, Fla., set aside six beds in a home for the poor in 1565; the Dutch West India Company on December 20, 1656, appointed Master Jacob Hendrickszen Varrevanger surgeon in New Amsterdam to look after the sick; the Ursulines of New Orleans, La., opened an infirmary without restrictions July 17, 1734, with Sister Xavier Herbert as the chief infirmarian. *(Thomas George Morton and Frank Woodbury— The History of the Pennsylvania Hospital)*

Hospital ship. *See under* Ship

Inebriates' asylum was the United States Inebriate Asylum, "for the reformation of the poor and destitute inebriates," incorporated April 15, 1854, and organized May 15, 1854, in Binghamton, N.Y., by Dr. James Edward Turner. In 1857 the name was changed to the New York State Inebriate Asylum. The cornerstone was laid September 24, 1858. John D. Wright was president of the corporation. N. A. Prince was registrar and Dr. James Edward Turner treasurer. *(James Edward Turner —History of the First Inebriate Asylum in the World)*

Insane detention home is credited to the Religious Society of Friends, which erected it in 1709 in Philadelphia, Pa. The opening of the Pennsylvania Hospital in February 1752 inaugurated a new epoch in the treatment of the insane in this country. They were received as patients, mentally diseased, and were to be subjected to such treatment as their cases required with a view to their ultimate restoration to reason, instead of being confined as malefactors.

The First

Insane hospital (state) for the care of the mentally disordered and insane was the Publick Hospital for Persons of Insane and Disordered Minds, incorporated in Williamsburg, Va., in 1768. It was opened October 12, 1773, and received as its first patient Zachariah Mallory of Hanover County, Va. The hospital was maintained by the colony from the beginning and later became known as the Eastern State Hospital. *(Eastern State Hospital—Annual Report)*

Interracial hospital was the Provident Hospital, Chicago, Ill., incorporated January 23, 1891, and opened May 4, 1891, with a grand opening party. Although primarily for blacks, there was no racial barrier as to the admission of patients or staff appointments of physicians. Frank Billings was chief consulting physician; Christian Fenger, chief consulting surgeon; and Drs. Ralph N. Isham and Daniel Hale Williams, attending surgeons. A nursing school, the Provident Hospital Training School Association, was connected with the hospital. *(Helen Buckler—Doctor Dan, Pioneer in American Surgery)*

Jewish hospital was Mount Sinai Hospital in New York, organized and incorporated January 15, 1852, as the Jews' Hospital in New York City for "benevolent, charitable and scientific purposes." The founder and first president was Sampson Simson. The first patients were received June 5, 1855, in a small building (25 beds) on West 28th Street, New York City. Julius Raymond was the first superintendent. Dr. Mark Blumenthal was the attending and resident physician. On April 17, 1866, a special act of the New York legislature changed the name to Mount Sinai Hospital of the City of New York.

Leper hospital was the Louisiana Leper Home, Carville, La., founded in 1894 by an act of the Louisiana legislature. It consisted of a plantation of about 200 acres, on which were seven cottages, an elevated pavilion, dining hall, kitchen, and quarters for the Sisters of Charity of the order of St. Vincent de Paul, four of whom took care of the lepers. The home accommodated 25 patients, and was controlled by a Board of Officers. The president was M. D. Lagan and the resident physician was Dr. Elihu Morgan Hooper. The home was purchased by the federal government from the state of Louisiana, January 3, 1921, to be operated by the U.S. Public Health Service under the Treasury Department. It was reopened June 8, 1921, and was known as the United States Marine Hospital or the National Leper Home. It accommodated over 300 persons. Surgeon Oswald Evans Denney was appointed Medical Officer in Charge. The Sisters of Charity continued to furnish the nursing care. *(Public Health Reports, Reprint No. 1,440)*

Marine hospital (U.S.) was authorized by act of Congress of July 16, 1798 (1 Stat. L. 605), an "act for the relief of sick and disabled seamen" which

The First

HOSPITAL—*Continued*

empowered the President to appoint medical officers at ports and elsewhere to give medical treatment to disabled seamen. Funds were obtained by a tax of 20 cents a month deducted from the pay of those employed on American vessels. On January 20, 1798, the Virginia legislature authorized the governor to offer its Marine Hospital (built in 1787). On April 20, 1801, Governor James Monroe of Virginia deeded the Norfolk Naval Hospital, Norfolk, Va., to the United States. *(Richard Cranston Holcomb—A Century with the Norfolk Naval Hospital)*

Military hospital on the modern pavilion plan was proposed in August 1861 by Dr. Alpheus Benning Crosby, division surgeon on the staff of General Charles Pomeroy Stone, to Surgeon Charles Stuart Tripler. A hospital was built in Poolesville, Md., which on October 21, 1861, was ready to receive the wounded from the battle of Ball's Bluff, Va. *(Josiah Whitney Barstow—In Memoriam, A Tribute to the Memory of Alpheus Benning Crosby, M.D.)*

Municipal veterinary hospital. *See under* Veterinary hospital

Narcotics sanatorium. *See under* Narcotics

Naval hospital was authorized by act of Congress "establishing Navy hospitals," February 26, 1811 (2 Stat. L. 650), which appropriated $50,000. On April 2, 1827, the cornerstone was laid for the first naval hospital at Portsmouth, Va. One wing was ready for occupancy in July 1830, and the building was completed and dedicated in 1833. *See also* Hospital for the military and naval forces, above

Orthopedic hospital was the Hospital for Ruptured and Crippled, opened May 1, 1863, in New York City by the New York Society for the Relief of the Ruptured and Crippled, organized December 18, 1862, and incorporated April 13, 1863. Dr. James Knight was the resident physician and surgeon. During the first year, treatment was given to 828 patients. The hospital's name was changed in 1940 to the Hospital for Special Surgery.

Psychiatric hospital (private) was founded April 14, 1813, as The Asylum for the Relief of Persons Deprived of the Use of Their Reason, in Philadelphia, Pa., by the Religious Society of Friends. The constitution was adopted June 1813. The grounds were located 5 miles from Philadelphia and 1 mile west of Frankford and covered 52 acres, 30 of which were cultivated, the balance in woodland. No manacles, handcuffs, iron grates, or bars were used. The name was changed in 1888 to the Friends Asylum for the Insane, and in 1914 to Friends Hospital.

Psychiatric ward associated with a general hospital fulfilling the function of actual therapeutic treatment, besides detention, was Pavilion F of

The First

Albany Hospital, Albany, N.Y., opened in 1901 "for the detention and care of persons afflicted with nervous mental disorders." The first patient was admitted February 1902. Dr. Jesse Montgomery Mosher was placed in full charge of the pavilion. *(Albert Deutsch—The Mentally Ill in America)*

Tuberculosis home for the care of consumptives was the Channing Home, Boston, Mass., opened May 1857 through the benevolence of Harriet Ryan. The home accommodated 12 patients and was not a sanatorium. It also accommodated patients with other chronic diseases.

Tuberculosis hospital to provide medical and surgical care for needy consumptives on a free, nationwide, nonsectarian basis, was the National Jewish Hospital, Denver, Colo., which opened December 10, 1899, with 58 beds, under the auspices of the B'nai Brith. It was incorporated October 31, 1900. An attempt had been made by the Jewish Hospital Association of Colorado (incorporated April 8, 1890) to establish a hospital earlier. The cornerstone was laid October 9, 1892, but the funds raised were not sufficient to build the hospital. *(Milton Louis Anfenger—The Birth of a Hospital)*

Tuberculosis hospital (municipal) for consumptive poor was the Branch Hospital (now Hamilton County Tuberculosis Hospital) under the jurisdiction of the Cincinnati Hospital (now Cincinnati General Hospital) which opened July 8, 1897, in Cincinnati, Ohio, with a capacity of 20 beds. John Fehrenbach was the superintendent and Dr. Benjamin Lyle the chief physician.

Tuberculosis hospital operated by the government for consumptives was opened at Fort Stanton, N.Mex., on April 27, 1899. The first patient was received November 18, 1899. It was suggested and established by Walter Wyman. It was not exclusively for men in military service but afforded care and treatment to all beneficiaries of the U.S. Public Health Service, most of whom at that time were seamen.

Tuberculosis preventorium for children was established in 1909 in Lakewood, N.J., through the efforts of Nathan Straus.

Tuberculosis sanatorium (modern) inaugurating present methods of treating tuberculosis, was the Trudeau Sanatorium, sometimes called the Adirondack Cottage Sanatorium, a one-room cottage 14 by 18 feet with two cot beds, heated by a wood stove, built at Saranac Lake, N.Y., for Dr. Edward Livingston Trudeau at a cost of $400. It was opened February 1, 1885. *(Edward Livingston Trudeau—An Autobiography)*

Tuberculosis sanatorium (private) was the Mountain Sanatorium for Pulmonary Diseases, opened in 1875 in Asheville, N.C., by Dr. William

The First

Gleitsmann. *(Philadelphia Medical and Surgical Reporter. February 1876)*

Tuberculosis sanatorium (state) was the Massachusetts Hospital for Consumptives and Tuberculosis Patients, Rutland, Mass., completed September 23, 1898. It received its first patient October 3, 1898. Dr. Walter John Marcley was the first medical director. *(State Sanatorium at Rutland, Mass.—Annual Report 1899)*

Vaccine institution. *See* Vaccine institution

Veterinary hospital. *See under* Veterinary hospital

Women's hospital in the world, founded by women for the exclusive use of women, was the Woman's Hospital of New York City. On February 10, 1855, a constitution was adopted by 30 women who termed themselves the Woman's Hospital Association. The Woman's Hospital was opened with 40 beds on May 4, 1855, in a hired building at Madison Avenue and 29th Street, New York City, with Dr. James Marion Sims as Resident Surgeon. The present building on 110th Street, between Columbus and Amsterdam avenues, New York City, was opened December 5, 1906. *(James Riddle Goffe—Historical Sketch of the Woman's Hospital in the State of New York)*

Women's infirmary staffed by women physicians was the New York Infirmary for Women and Children, New York City, incorporated December 13, 1853, "to provide for poor women the medical advice of competent physicians of their own sex." A one-room infirmary was opened in Tompkins Square. On May 12, 1857, a hospital was opened. The physicians were Dr. Elizabeth Blackwell, Dr. Emily Blackwell, Dr. Marie Elizabeth Zakrzewska.

HOSPITAL AMBULANCE SERVICE. *See under* Ambulance

HOSPITAL AUTOMOBILE, FIELD. *See under* Automobile

HOSPITAL INSURANCE. *See* Insurance: Health insurance law (state)

HOSPITAL-MEDICAL COOPERATIVE. *See* Insurance: Group hospital-medical cooperative

HOSPITAL PHARMACOPOEIA. *See* Pharmacopoeia: Pharmacopoeia prepared by a hospital staff

HOSPITAL RECORD system was introduced at the Bellevue Training School for Nurses, New York City, in 1874 by the head nurse, Linda Richards. The superintendent of the school was Sister Helen of All Saints' Hospital. Record was made of symptoms, diagnosis, medication, temperature, and pulse rate for all patients in the hospital. *(David Allyn Gorton—History of Medicine)*

The First

HOSPITAL SHIP. *See* Ship

HOSPITALIZATION GROUP INSURANCE. *See* Insurance: Group hospital insurance plan

HOSTEL, YOUTH. *See* Youth hostel

HOTEL

    See also Motel

    Airplane takeoff from a hotel roof. *See under* Aviation

    Airport hotel. *See under* Aviation—Airport

    Airship to land on a roof. *See* Aviation—Airship

    Bibles in hotel rooms. *See under* Bible

    Fireproof hotel was the Palmer House, Chicago, Ill., opened in November 1873 by Potter Palmer. The building cost approximately $2 million, the land $1 million, and the furnishings $500,000. It replaced the Palmer House opened October 1, 1870, and destroyed by fire October 8, 1871. A new Palmer House was completed in 1925.

    Hotel definitely recognized as a modern first-class hotel was the Tremont House in Boston, Mass., which celebrated its opening with an elaborate dinner on October 16, 1829. It contained 170 rooms; the rate was $2 a day, including four meals. Travelers were permitted to rent a single room instead of having to double up with strangers. (Previously when guests retired for the night they did not know whom they might find beside them in the morning. Frequently three or four slept in one bed "spoon fashion." Women were sometimes "roomed" with men.) Other innovations at the Tremont House were a key for each room, a washbowl, a pitcher, and a free cake of soap for every guest, gaslights, and a fine supply of running water in the eight "bathing rooms" in the basement. *(A Description of the Tremont House. 1830)*

    Hotel built for strictly hotel purposes was the City Hotel, of 70 rooms, opened in 1794 on Broadway, just below Wall Street, New York City. *(Jefferson Williamson—The American Hotel)*

    Hotel for dogs. *See under* Kennel

    Hotel for women was the Women's Hotel, New York City, founded by Alexander Turney Stewart and inspected by 20,000 visitors on the opening day, April 2, 1878. The 9-story building of brick, iron, and stone, was 197 feet by 205 feet, and 155 feet high. It had 5 steam elevators and was built around a courtyard. It had 115 rooms (16 x 17) at $12, 34 rooms (16 x 10) at $10, and 354 rooms (16 x 8½) at $7 a week, board included. The main dining room accommodated 600 diners and also supplied meals to be taken out. Breakfast was 35 cents, lunch 25 cents, dinner 50 cents. There were 250 servants. Ground was broken January 1, 1869. The cost of the hotel was $3.7 million—any profit was to be used to reduce the rates and any deficit was covered by a fund. On Saturday, June 8, 1878,

The First

HOTEL—*Continued*

it became a commerical hotel accommodating both sexes.

Hotel (large) built over a pier was the Flagship Hotel, Galveston, Tex., opened June 30, 1965. The hotel, containing 240 rooms, was built on a pier 1,500 feet long, 340 feet wide, extending into the Gulf of Mexico.

Hotel to establish a heliport was the Western Hills Hotel, Fort Worth, Tex. The heliport, 150 feet by 190 feet, surfaced with asphalt paving, was formally opened May 20, 1953, with 250 members of the national Aviators Writers Association present. It was privately owned but was intended for public use and was licensed by the city of Fort Worth on May 20, 1953, and approved by the Civil Aeronautics Administration. It was built by the E. M. Moore Construction Co., Fort Worth.

Hotel to install bathrooms and toilets was the Tremont House, Boston, Mass., designed by Isaiah Rogers, which opened October 16, 1829. It covered 12,849 square feet and contained 170 rooms. It had eight water closets, "privies," and eight bathing rooms in the basement, to which there was a separate entrance. The kitchen and laundry had running cold water. Each of the two cisterns in the attic contained three hogsheads of rainwater, one for the baths and the other for various outlets. The plumbers were Thomas Philpott and Thomas Pollard. The cornerstone of the hotel was laid July 4, 1828, by Samuel Turell Armstrong, president of the Massachusetts Charitable Mechanic Association. *(Description of the Tremont House, Boston, 1830)*

Hotel to install electric lights was the Prospect House, Blue Mountain Lake, N.Y. In 1881 the electric installation was made, but the lights were not entirely dependable. On October 12, 1882, the Duke of Veranga and his party arrived after dark, to celebrate Columbus Day. As they were shown to their rooms the lights went out, but after a slight delay the lights went on again. The hotel was owned by Howard M. Durant and operated by George Tunnicliffe. The name was later changed to the Eutowana.

Hotel to install radio reception with two selective channels was Hotel Statler of Boston, Mass., which on May 10, 1927, broadcast programs free to guests from a central control room. Thirteen hundred rooms were originally equipped with individual headsets. Later, loudspeakers were placed in the rooms.

Hotel transported was the Brighton Beach Hotel, Brooklyn, N.Y., which was moved 600 feet inland, the operation taking from April 3, 1888, to July 29, 1888. The hotel was jacked up on railroad cars on 24 parallel tracks and moved by 6 locomotives in 2 teams of 3 each. The building, which was 500 feet long and weighed 6,000 tons, was moved 124 feet the first day.

The First

Hotel with all-foam-rubber mattresses, pillows, and furniture cushions was the Western Hills Hotel, Fort Worth, Tex., partially opened on July 11, 1951, and completed and formally opened on October 7, 1951. It cost approximately $2 million and had 200 rooms, no two of which were furnished alike.

Hotel with individually controlled air conditioning and heating in every room was the St. Regis Hotel, New York City, opened September 4, 1904. Six dynamos operated 6 metallic fans, each 7 feet in diameter. The building cost approximately $4 million, $5.5 million when equipped.

Hotel with safe deposit boxes was the New England Hotel, Boston, Mass. In 1866 Lambert Maynard, the manager, purchased a Salamander safe into which he installed compartments with individual locks. *(Jefferson Williamson—The American Hotel)*

HOTEL ADMINISTRATION COLLEGE COURSE was offered by Cornell University, Ithaca, N.Y., in the fall of 1922, and included courses in accounting, administration, economics, engineering, food preparation, housekeeping, languages, etc. The course required four years and led to a B.S. degree. Professor Howard Bagnall Meek was the first Professor of Hotel Administration. *(Cornell University—Announcement of Department of Hotel Administration)*

HOTEL ELEVATOR. *See* Elevator

HOTHOUSE. *See* Greenhouse

HOUSE. *See* Building

HOUSE OF DAVID was established on May 1, 1903, in Benton Harbor, Mich., by Benjamin Purnell as a commonwealth according to apostolic plan. The first church building was opened on May 1, 1903, and the first minister was Benjamin Purnell.

HOUSE OF REPRESENTATIVES (U.S.). *See* Congress (U.S.)—House of Representatives

HOUSING CORPORATION (U.S.). *See* Emergency Housing Corporation (U.S.)

HUBBARD MEDAL. *See* Medal: National Geographic Society gold medal

HULLING MACHINE. *See* Cottonseed hulling machine

HUMAN BLOOD, DRIED. *See* Blood bank: Blood serum (human, dried)

HUMAN-INFECTING VIRUS TO BE CRYSTALLIZED. *See* Virus: Virus (human- or animal-infecting virus to be crystallized)

HUMAN PICKUP BY AN AIRPLANE. *See* Aviation: Airplane human pickup

The First

HUMANE SOCIETY

Humane association national organization was the American Humane Association, which was organized October 9, 1877, in Cleveland, Ohio, adopted its constitution on November 14, 1878, in Baltimore, Md., and was incorporated under the laws of the District of Columbia November 12, 1903, as a federation of societies for the prevention of cruelty to animals, with the primary purpose of preventing cruelty in the transportation of livestock. The first president was Edwin Lee Brown of Chicago, Ill., and the first secretary was Abraham Firth of Massachusetts.

Humane society was the American Society for the Prevention of Cruelty to Animals, founded in New York City by Henry Bergh, formerly of the American Legation at St. Petersburg, Russia, who was appalled by the beatings which droshky-moujiks administered to their horses. When he returned to the United States he organized the A.S.P.C.A., incorporated April 10, 1866, patterned after the Royal S.P.C.A. of London. *(Chapter 469, Laws of New York City 1866)*

HUMANIST SOCIETY was established January 13, 1929, in Hollywood, Calif., "to humanize religion, disseminate science, stimulate thought and promote good will." The first director was the Reverend Theodore Curtis Abell. The first Humanist National Assembly was held in New York City, October 10–11, 1934.

HUMANITARIAN SERVICE MEDAL. *See* Medal

HUMORIST (woman). *See under* Woman

HUNGARIAN DAILY NEWSPAPER. *See* Newspaper

HUNTING LICENSE. *See* Game law: Hunting license fee (state)

HUNTING PERMIT STAMPS. *See* Stamp

HURRICANE recorded occurred August 15, 1635, when a cyclonic storm ravaged the Plymouth colony vicinity. A severe storm on October 28, 1858, at Apalachee Bay, Fla., may have been a hurricane. *(Thomas Morton—New England Canaan)*

HUSBAND AND WIFE AWARDED DEGREES. *See under* Degrees (academic and honorary)

HUSBANDMAN'S GUIDE. *See* Agricultural book

HUSBANDRY. *See* Animal Industry Bureau (U.S.): Animal husbandry federal appropriation

HUSKING CHAMPIONSHIP. *See* Corn-husking championship contest (national)

HYBRID SEED CORN. *See* Corn: Shipment of hybrid seed corn

HYDRAULIC ELEVATOR. *See* Elevator

The First

HYDRAULIC-LIFT PARKING GARAGE. *See* Garage

HYDRO-ELECTRIC POWER STATION. *See* Electric power plant

HYDROGEN BOMB. *See* Atomic bomb: Atomic fusion (thermonuclear or hydrogen) bomb

HYDROGEN-COOLED TURBINE GENERATOR. *See under* Electric generator

HYDROPHOBIA BOOK. *See* Medical book

HYDROPLANE. *See under* Aviation—Airplane

HYDROPONICS. *See* Soilless culture of plants

HYDROTHERAPY BOOK. *See* Medical book

HYDROTHERAPY CHAIR was established in the Department of Materia Medica, College of Physicians and Surgeons, Columbia University, New York City in 1907. Dr. Simon Baruch was appointed Professor of Hydrotherapy in March 1907 and served until May 1913.

HYGIENE BUREAU. *See* Child hygiene bureau

HYGIENE INSTRUCTION

Hygiene and physical education professorship was established by the trustees of Amherst College, Amherst, Mass., in 1860. Dr. John Worthington Hooker, the original incumbent, resigned after less than a year of service and was succeeded by Dr. Edward Hitchcock of the class of 1849, who served continuously from 1861 until his death on February 16, 1911. *(Edward Hitchcock—A Report of Twenty Years' Experience in the Department of Physical Education and Hygiene in Amherst College)*

Hygiene and public health school was established in 1916 at Johns Hopkins University, Baltimore, Md., under an endowment from the Rockefeller Foundation "for the advancement of knowledge and the training of investigators, teachers, officials and other workers" in the general field of hygiene and public health. This school was opened October 1, 1918, with Dr. William Henry Welch as its first director.

Hygiene lectures. *See under* Medical instruction

Physiology and hygiene courses offered by a liberal arts college were given in 1853 at Antioch College, Yellow Springs, Ohio. The college opened October 5, 1853. Instruction was supervised by Professor Rebecca Mann Pennell and Acting Professor John Wesley Hoyt, M.D.

School Department of Hygiene to aid in instructing children in the fundamental laws of health and generally to improve health conditions was established in Boston, Mass., in 1907. The department was in charge of physical training and athletics, as well as the newly organized nursing program. Physical culture, however, had been introduced in 1864, and Boston had ruled as early as

The First

HYGIENE INSTRUCTION—*Continued*
1853 that "every scholar shall have daily in the forenoon and afternoon some kind of physical exercise."

HYGIENE PROFESSOR. *See* Medical instruction: Public hygiene professor

HYGIENISTS' TEXTBOOK. *See* Dental book: Book for dental hygienists (text)

HYMNBOOK. *See under* Music book

I

ICE
Commercial artificial-ice manufacturing plant was the Louisiana Ice Manufacturing Company, built in 1868 on Delachaise Street and the Mississippi River, in New Orleans. The process was kept secret and the factory was guarded.

Commercial transportation of ice was effected in 1799. The ice was cut on Canal Street, New York City, and shipped to Charleston, S.C.

Dry ice manufactured commercially was made by the Prest-Air Devices Company of Long Island City, N.Y., in 1925, through the efforts of Thomas Benton Slate. Dry ice is solid carbon dioxide. When compressed and cooled, it changes to a liquid, then to a solid. Its temperature is 109 degrees below zero. It does not melt but turns to gas. Dry ice was first used by Schrafft's, 181 Broadway, New York City, in July 1925 to keep ice cream from melting. The first large sale of dry ice was made later in the year to the Breyer Ice Cream Company of New York City.

Export of ice was shipped in August 1805 by Frederick Tudor, who sent 130 tons on the brig *Favorite* from Boston to the West Indies (Martinique). His business increased, and in 1833 he commenced making shipments to Madras, Bombay, and Calcutta, India. *(Business Historical Society—Bulletin. February 1935)*

ICE CREAM
Ice cream was made commercially by Mr. Hall of 76 Chatham Street (now Park Row), New York City, who advertised it on June 8, 1786. A record of a purchase for "a cream machine for ice" is contained in George Washington's expense ledger under date of May 17, 1784. *(Grover Dean Turnblow and Lloyd Andrew Raffeto—Ice Cream)*

Ice cream wholesale dealer was Jacob Fussel, a milk dealer in Baltimore, Md. In 1851, as a means of using up his surplus cream, he started manufacturing ice cream, which sold at 60 cents a quart.

ICE CREAM CONE
Ice cream cone is said to have originated at the Louisiana Purchase Exposition in St. Louis, Mo., in 1904. Charles E. Menches, a young ice cream

The First

salesman, gave an ice cream sandwich, as well as flowers, to the young lady he was escorting. Lacking a vase for the flowers, she took one of the layers of the sandwich and rolled it in the form of a cone to act as a vase. The remaining layer was also rolled similarly, with the result that the ice cream cone was invented. Similar claims have been made by other concessionaires.

Ice cream cone-rolling machine was invented by Carl Rutherford Taylor of Cleveland, Ohio, who obtained patent No. 1,481,813 on January 29, 1924, on a "machine for spinning or turning a waffle."

ICE CREAM FREEZER was patented by William G. Young of Baltimore, Md., who received patent No. 5,601, May 30, 1848, on an "improvement in ice cream freezers."

ICE CREAM SODA is supposed to have been introduced by Robert M. Green, the founder of Robert M. Green & Sons, manufacturers of soda fountains in Philadelphia, who added ice cream to plain soda water. The first demonstration of the new beverage was made at the Semi-Centennial Celebration at Franklin Institute, Philadelphia, Pa., in the summer of 1874.

ICE CREAM SUNDAE is said to have originated about 1897 in the Red Cross Pharmacy, State Street, Ithaca, N.Y., directly opposite the barroom of the Ithaca Hotel. As the barroom was closed on Sunday, thirsty patrons went to the drugstore, where a distinctive drink was sold as a sundae.

ICE HOCKEY. *See* Hockey

ICE LOADING MACHINERY for icing refrigerator railway cars was operated in May 1917 by the William Metz Ice Company of Pittsburgh, Pa. The machines were manufactured by the Thomas Wright Company, Inc., of Jersey City, N.J. Wright obtained patent No. 1,059,511, April 22, 1913, on a "body elevating mechanism." It consisted of a truck with an extension top adjustable to any position to enable ice to be placed in the uppermost section of the car, making it possible for one man to do all the loading without the help of assistants.

ICE SKATING CHAMPION
American world figure skating champion was Tenley Albright of Newton Center, Mass., who won the title February 15, 1953, at Davos, Switzerland. She was 17 years old.

Ice skater to cover 100 miles in less than 6 hours was Kirt Barnes, whose time on February 26, 1971, for 100 miles at the Fuller ice skating rink, Ann Arbor, Mich., without a pause, was 5 hours 34 minutes 1.45 seconds.

National women's figure skating four-time winner was Carol Elizabeth Heiss of Ozone Park, Queens, New York, who won her first title on March 15, 1957, at Berkeley, Calif.; her second and

The First

third, in 1958 and 1959; and her fourth consecutive title, January 29, 1960, at Seattle, Wash.

Skating champion (ice) was Charles June of Newburgh, N.Y., who defeated recognized English contestants in 1849.

ICE SKATING CLUB

Ice skating club was the Skaters' Club of the City and County of Philadelphia, formed December 21, 1849, at Stigman's Hotel, Philadelphia, Pa. It was formally organized on January 4, 1850. The first election was held January 8, 1850; the officers elected were James Page, president; Josiah Evans, vice president, William H. Jones, secretary; and Edward W. Bushnell, treasurer. *(Nigel Bruce—Ice-Skating)*

ICE SKATING RINK

Ice skating rink (artificial) of Olympic size was formally opened by Vice President Richard Milhous Nixon on February 18, 1960, at Squaw Valley, Calif., for the 8th Olympic Winter Games, in which 740 athletes from 30 nations competed. The competition began February 19, 1960, with paired figure skating and ended February 28, 1960. Freezing brine was piped into the rink via 70 miles of steel tubing. It had 300 feet of roof floating on cables suspended from 80-foot steel and concrete pillars.

Ice skating rink (indoor) was built by Thomas L. Rankin at Madison Square Garden, New York City in 1879. It had 6,000 square feet of surface. On February 12, 1879, a gala carnival was presented.

ICE SKATING TOURNAMENT

Figure skating international championship tournament was held March 20, 1914, at the Arena Ice Rink, New Haven, Conn., under the rules of the Skating Union of America. The ladies' championship was won by Theresa Weld of the Skating Club of Boston, Mass., the men's by Norman Scott of the Winter Club of Montreal, Canada. Other events were pair skating to music and waltzing.

ICE YACHT was built by Oliver Booth at Poughkeepsie, N.Y., in 1790 and consisted of a square box mounted on three runners covered with iron, a sail, a rudder post, and a wooden tiller.

ICE YACHT CLUB was the Poughkeepsie Ice Yacht Club of Poughkeepsie, N.Y., which was organized in 1861. Regattas and races were held on the Hudson River.

ICEBOX. *See* Refrigerator

ICONOSCOPE. *See* Television: Electronic television system

IDENTIFICATION BUREAU (police). *See* Police: Police bureau of identification

IDENTIFICATION SYSTEM BASED ON THE EYES. *See under* Eye

The First

ILLUMINATED AIRWAYS. *See* Aviation: Airways illumination

ILLUMINATING GAS. *See* Gas: Natural gas used as an illuminant

ILLUSTRATED BIBLE. *See* Bible: Bible in folio size to be illustrated

ILLUSTRATED NEWSPAPER. *See* Newspaper

ILLUSTRATED WEEKLY. *See* Periodical

IMMIGRATION

Alien registration was authorized under the Alien Registration Act of 1940 (54 Stat. L. 670), approved June 28, 1940, "to amend certain provisions of law with respect to the admission and deportation of aliens; to require the fingerprinting and registration of aliens." The registration was conducted by the Alien Registration Division of the Immigration and Naturalization Service. Earl Grant Harrison was the director in charge of registration. During the period August 27, 1940, to December 26, 1940, the number of noncitizens who registered was 4,741,971.

Border patrol. *See* Border patrol: Border patrol organization

Chinese immigrants were two men and a woman who arrived in San Francisco, Calif., in 1848, on the brig *Eagle*. *(Dr. Harley Farnsworth McNair—The Chinese Abroad)*

Chinese labor immigration was arranged through the efforts of William Kelly of Pittsburgh, Pa., who in 1854 induced 12 Chinese to work in his foundries. The Chinese were willing to work for extremely low wages.

Chinese labor immigration act restricting the admission of Chinese laborers was passed May 6, 1882, suspending Chinese immigration for a ten-year period and forbidding naturalization. A treaty between China and the United States, concluded November 17, 1880, approved May 5, 1881, by the Senate, was signed May 9, 1881 by President Chester Alan Arthur. Ratifications were exchanged July 19, 1881, and proclaimed October 5, 1881 (22 Stat. L. 826). It was agreed that the United States could "regulate, limit or suspend" the immigration of Chinese labor, but not prohibit it altogether. The Chinese exclusion acts were repealed December 17, 1943 (57 Stat. L. 600).

Citizenship granted to an alien on foreign soil. *See under* Citizenship

Immigration act requiring the recording of data pertaining to the arrival of aliens in the United States was the act of June 25, 1798 (1 Stat. L. 570), which required the master or commander of a vessel to make a written report to the customs officer in charge of the port of entry, giving the names of all arriving aliens, and other prescribed data pertaining to them. *(Records in Bureau of Immigration, Department of Labor, Washington, D.C.)*

The First

IMMIGRATION—*Continued*

Immigration bureau superintendent was William D. Owen, whose appointment on June 15, 1891, was confirmed by the Senate December 16, 1891. His salary was $4,000 a year. The office of Superintendent of Immigration authorized by act of March 3, 1891 (26 Stat. L. 1085) was under the Treasury Department at that time. Owen resigned March 20, 1893.

Immigration head tax was levied in accordance with the federal law of August 3, 1882 (22 Stat. L. 214). Each immigrant was required to pay 50 cents. In 1903 the fee was $2; in 1907, $4; and in 1918, $8.

Immigration quota act was the act of May 19, 1921 (42 Stat. L. 5), which became effective on June 3, 1921, and as amended on May 11, 1922 (42 Stat. L. 540), was effective until July 1, 1924. It limited immigration to 3 percent of the number of foreign-born persons of any given nationality in the United States as shown in the 1910 census. Not more than 20 percent of any country's quota was permitted to arrive in one month.

Japanese national to receive an immigration visa was Sozaburo Kujiraoka of Tokyo, Japan, who was given a visa on February 22, 1953, under the [Patrick A.] McCarran-[Francis Eugene] Walter "Immigration and Nationality Act" (66 Stat.L.163) of June 27, 1952, which allowed an annual quota of 100.

Japanese to enter the United States was Nakahama Manjiro, a 15-year-old boy, shipwrecked and rescued by American sailors, who in 1841 brought him to Fairhaven, Mass., where he attended school for six years. He returned to Japan and was beaten for having left his country. When Perry went to Japan in 1853, Manjiro acted as interpreter. *(Biographical Dictionary of Japan)*

Naturalization act. *See* Naturalization act

Refugee to arrive under the Refugee Relief Act of 1953 (67 Stat. L. 400), enacted August 7, 1953, "for the relief of certain refugees and orphans, and for other purposes" was Stamatoula Roumanis, a 12-year-old Greek girl, who arrived at Idlewild Airport, New York City, on January 1, 1954. (Idlewild is now JFK International Airport.)

IMMUNOLOGY SOCIETY. *See under* Medical society

IMPEACHMENT

Impeachment was that of Nicolas More, who in 1685 was Chief Justice of Philadelphia. He fell under such displeasure that the assembly on May 15, 1685, presented 10 charges of impeachment against him to the council; among other offenses he was charged with "assuming to himself an unlimited and arbitrary power in office." He was expelled on June 2, 1685, but the council refused to sanction the impeachment proceedings. *(Penn-*

The First

sylvania Magazine of History and Biography, Vol. 4)

Impeachment and removal from office of a state governor was that of William Woods Holden, the 39th governor of North Carolina. On December 20, 1870, impeachment proceedings were brought against him in which he was charged with "high crimes and misdemeanors." The trial was conducted by Chief Justice Richmond Mumford Pearson. On March 22, 1871, he was ordered to be removed from office, two thirds of the state Senate having found him guilty of six of the eight charges brought against him. *(Trial of William Woods Holden, Governor of North Carolina. Published in 1871 by order of the Senate of North Carolina.)*

Impeachment of a federal judge was that of Judge John Pickering, judge of the United States District Court for the district of New Hampshire, who was convicted and removed from office for drunkenness, profanity, and violence on the bench. The vote was 19 guilty, and 7 not guilty. The trial was held from March 3, 1803, to March 12, 1804. *(Annals of the Congress of the United States, Eighth Congress, Vols. 13-14: Impeachment of John Pickering)*

Impeachment proceedings against a justice of the Supreme Court of the United States were instituted in 1804 when, for political reasons, the Democratic Party brought charges against Samuel Chase. The trial was held from November 30, 1804, to March 1, 1805. Chase was acquitted and served until his death, June 19, 1811, at the age of 70. *(Charles Warren—The Supreme Court in U.S. History)*

Impeachment proceedings against a President of the United States were instituted against Andrew Johnson, the 17th President. The House of Representatives on February 24, 1868, voted to impeach him because he had dismissed Edwin McMasters Stanton, Secretary of War, and declared several laws unconstitutional. The charges were usurpation of the law, corrupt use of the veto power, interference at elections, and misdemeanors. The trial was held in the Senate from March 13 to May 16, with Chief Justice of the United States Salmon Portland Chase presiding. Fifty-four senators took oaths as jurors. Johnson was acquitted. The vote was 35 to 19 against Johnson, one short of the necessary two thirds. *(David Miller De Witt—The Impeachment and Trial of Andrew Johnson)*

Impeachment proceedings against a state governor were brought against Charles Robinson, the first governor of Kansas. He was indicted for treason and conspiracy on a charge by the proslavery party. He was acquitted in 1862 by the federal grand jury and completed his term as governor. *(Frank Wilson Blackmar—Charles Robinson, the First Free-state Governor of Kansas)*

The First

Impeachment proceedings against a United States senator were instituted against William Blount, United States senator from Tennessee, who served from August 2, 1796, until July 8, 1797, when he was expelled. The trial was held from December 17, 1798, to January 14, 1799, when the Vice President announced the decision of the High Court of Impeachment that the charges were dismissed for want of jurisdiction. Blount was accused of entering into a conspiracy with British officers to divert part of Louisiana from Spain to Great Britain, "a high misdemeanor, entirely inconsistent with his public trust and duty as a Senator." While the trial was in progress in Washington, Blount was elected by Tennessee to serve in the state senate, and at the opening session (December 3, 1797) was chosen president of the state senate. *(Marcus Joseph Wright—Some Account of the Life and Services of William Blount)*

Impeachment proceedings attempt against a President of the United States was made January 10, 1843, in the House of Representatives by John Minor Botts of Virginia, who introduced a resolution charging "John Tyler, Vice President acting as President" of corruption, malconduct in office, high crimes and misdemeanors. The nine charges were rejected and the resolution was not accepted: 83 ayes, 127 nays. *(Congressional Globe, Jan. 10, 1842)*

IMPERFORATED STAMP. *See* Postage stamp

IMPREGNATED CORKBOARD. *See* Corkboard (impregnated)

IMPREGNATION
Impregnation (artificial) resulted from experiments by Dr. Gregory Pincus of Clark University, Worcester, Mass., conducted at Harvard University, Cambridge, Mass., in November 1939 under the auspices of the Dazian and Josiah Macy, Jr., Foundation. Pincus produced a rabbit (born in October 1939) by removing an egg from the ovary of a female rabbit and fertilizing it with a salt solution. The egg was then transferred to the uterus of a second rabbit which acted as an "incubator." He exhibited the young rabbit November 1, 1939, at the 12th annual Graduate Fortnight at the New York Academy of Medicine.

Impregnation (human) by means of artificial insemination was made in 1866 by Dr. James Marion Sims, gynecologist and chief of the Woman's Hospital, New York City. Sims gave 54 other injections in 1866 and 1867.

Legalization of artificial insemination for humans was enacted by the state of Oklahoma and signed May 18, 1967, by Governor Dewey Follett Bartlett. The state operated birth control centers for all persons regardless of financial condition. A similar law restricted to welfare recipients was enacted earlier.

The First

"IN GOD WE TRUST". *See* Money: Coin to use "In God We Trust"

INAUGURAL BALL. *See* Presidential inaugural ball

INAUGURATION (presidential). *See* President (U.S.): President inaugurated

INCANDESCENT LAMP. *See* Electric lighting: Electric incandescent lamp

INCINERATOR that was successful was established in 1897 in St. Louis, Mo., by a private contractor who had a contract with the city for the collection and disposal of garbage. The Merz process was used. The water was drained off, cans, bottles, and rags were taken out, and grease was extracted by means of naphtha. *(American Society of Civil Engineers—Transactions, Vol. LIV, Pt. E)*

INCLINED RAILWAY. *See under* Railroad

INCOME TAX. *See* Tax: Federal income tax

INCORPORATED CITY. *See* City (incorporated)

INCUBATOR AMBULANCE SERVICE. *See under* Ambulance

INCUBATOR (eggs) PATENT was No. 3,019, awarded March 30, 1843, to Napoleon E. Guerin of New York City for a "mode of distributing steam heat, purifying air, etc." for hatching chickens by artificial heat.

INCUBATOR FOR INFANTS was constructed by order of Dr. Allan M. Thomas by Dr. William Champion Deming, in charge of the maternity ward of the State Emigrant Hospital, Ward's Island, New York City, in 1888. It was called a "hatching cradle" and was 3 feet square and 4 feet high and built in two sections, one of which contained 15 gallons of water. The first child placed in it was Edith Eleanor McLean, who weighed two pounds seven ounces when born on September 7, 1888. *(Morning Journal. Oct. 14, 1888)*

INDELIBLE PENCIL. *See* Pencil

INDEPENDENCE DECLARATION. *See* Declaration of Independence (American)

INDEPENDENT CHRISTIAN CHURCH. *See* Universalist Church of America (Independent Christian Church, Universalist)

INDEPENDENT PARTY. *See* Greenback Party (or Independent Party)

INDEX OF BOOKS. *See* Book index: Monthly cumulative index of books

INDEX OF GOVERNMENT PUBLICATIONS was *A Descriptive Catalogue of the Government Publications of the U.S.—Sept. 5, 1774–March 4, 1881,* compiled by order of Congress. The work was given to Benjamin Perley Poore on March 1, 1883, and finished in 1885. It was arranged chronologically with a general index and was published

The First

INDEX OF GOVERNMENT PUBLICATIONS—
Continued
by the Government Printing Office, Washington,
D.C.

INDEX OF NEWSPAPERS. *See* Newspaper index

INDIAN. *See* American Indian

INDIAN (AMERICAN INDIAN) CHURCH. *See*
American Indian Church

INDIAN (AMERICAN INDIAN) DAY. *See* Holiday

INDIAN (AMERICAN INDIAN) TREATY. *See*
Treaty: Treaty entered into by the United States
with Indian tribes

INDIAN CORN. *See* Maize

INDIAN-ENGLISH DICTIONARY. *See* Dictionary: American Indian–English dictionary

INDIAN GRAMMAR. *See* Grammar: American
Indian grammar

INDIAN-LANGUAGE BIBLE. *See* Bible: Bible in
an American Indian language

INDIAN-LANGUAGE MONTHLY. *See* Periodical: American Indian–language monthly

INDIAN NEWSPAPER. *See* Newspaper: American Indian newspaper

INDIAN PLAY. *See* Play (drama): Play about an
American Indian

INDIAN PRIMER. *See* Primer: Primer in an
American Indian dialect

INDIANS. *See* American Indians

INDIGO was planted and harvested in South
Carolina prior to 1690, when a petition was presented by Governor Seth Sothell to the Lords Proprietors asking that the inhabitants of South
Carolina might be allowed to "pay their rents in
the most valuable and merchantable produce of
their lands" and enumerating such products as
silk, cotton, rice, and indigo.

INDUSTRIAL ACCIDENT REPORT. *See* Accident report

INDUSTRIAL ADVISORY BOARD (federal). *See*
under Industry

**INDUSTRIAL AND LABOR RELATIONS
SCHOOL** was the New York State School of Industrial and Labor Relations, Cornell University,
Ithaca, N.Y., opened for registration on November
2, 1945. Edmund Ezra Day was president of the
university and Irving McNeil Ives dean of the
school. The first semester began November 5,
1945.

INDUSTRIAL ATOMIC REACTOR. *See* Atomic
reactor: Atomic reactor for research and development

The First

INDUSTRIAL CAMOUFLAGE COURSE. *See*
under Art course

INDUSTRIAL CORPORATION COURSE. *See*
Corporation course

INDUSTRIAL EXPOSITION. *See* Fair

INDUSTRIAL INSURANCE. *See* Insurance:
Group insurance policy

INDUSTRIAL MUSEUM. *See* Museum

INDUSTRIAL ORGANIZATION NURSE. *See*
Nurse

INDUSTRIAL PARK
  Industrial park was a planned industrial complex of 700 acres near the 70-foot waterfalls above
and below the Great Falls of the Passaic River,
Paterson, N.J., opened in 1792. It was sponsored
by Alexander Hamilton, who formed the Society
for Establishing Useful Manufactures in 1791.

INDUSTRIAL RECOVERY ACT
  **Code under the National Industrial Recovery
Act** was the tentative code of the cotton textile
trade which was submitted to President Franklin
Delano Roosevelt June 16, 1933, and approved July
9, 1933. It became effective July 17, 1933.

  **Compliance board under the National Industrial
Recovery Act** was announced as officially established by Office Order No. 40, issued October 26,
1933, and signed by Alva Brown, Executive Officer, National Recovery Administration. It consisted of the National Compliance Director, one
member of the Industrial Advisory Board, and one
member of the Labor Advisory Board. The board
undertook to further attempts at adjustment,
recommend exceptions, and remove the Blue Eagle, the official insignia for full compliance, when
and where necessary. General Hugh Samuel Johnson acted as first director of the Compliance
Board, then designated Colonel Robert Wentworth Lea to act temporarily, until November 24,
1933, when William Hammatt Davis was officially
appointed director.

  Conviction under a National Industrial Recovery Code was obtained December 2, 1933, against
the Hercules Gasoline Filling Stations, Inc., 711
Bedford Ave., Brooklyn, N.Y. The defendants
pleaded guilty to working their employees in excess of the hours allowed by the Petroleum Code,
and failing to display their gasoline prices properly. The case was tried before Judge Clarence G.
Galston in the United States District Court of the
Eastern District of New York. As the defendants
pleaded guilty, there was no decision on the merits of the case. They were fined a total of $400. The
defendants had not signed the Petroleum Code.
The decision showed that the signing of an NRA
code was not a requisite to its binding force upon
the members of an industry. *(United States Law
Week. Dec. 5, 1933)*

The First

Industrial Recovery Act (national) was passed by Congress June 16, 1933 (48 Stat. L. 195), and signed by President Franklin Delano Roosevelt. Its purpose was "to encourage national industrial recovery, to foster fair competition, and to provide for the construction of certain useful public works, and for other purposes." General Hugh Samuel Johnson was appointed by Executive Order No. 6,173 as the first administrator June 17, 1933, and served until October 15, 1934. On May 27, 1935, the Supreme Court of the United States declared the act unconstitutional, holding that the code-making provisions of the act constituted an invalid delegation by Congress of its legislative authority to persons wholly unconnected with the legislative functions of the government. *(U.S. National Recovery Administration—Bulletin No. 1)*

Postage stamps commemorating the National Recovery Act were sold August 15, 1933, in Washington, D.C., by Postmaster General James Aloysius Farley, who went behind the grille at the Post Office and sold 100 NRA stamps to Recovery Administrator Hugh Samuel Johnson.

State to place all its employees under the blanket code of the National Recovery Act Code was West Virginia. On July 27, 1933, Governor Herman Guy Kump issued an executive order decreeing that all state departments, boards, agencies, and commissions should adjust their work in conformity with President Franklin Delano Roosevelt's program.

INDUSTRIAL RESEARCH LABORATORY was the General Electric Research Laboratory, Schenectady, N.Y., opened in September 1900. It was supervised by Dr. Willis Rodney Whitney, former instructor at the Massachusetts Institute of Technology, who was appointed by Edwin Wilbur Rice, Jr., vice president and technical director of the General Electric Company. *(Laurence Ashley Hawkins—Adventure into the Unknown: The First Fifty Years of the General Electric Research Laboratory)*

INDUSTRIAL SCHOOL. *See under* Manual training

INDUSTRY

Industrial Advisory Board (federal) was authorized by President Franklin Delano Roosevelt, June 16, 1933, under the National Industrial Recovery Act. He stated that "it will be responsible that every affected industrial group is fully and adequately represented in an advisory capacity and any interested industrial group will be entitled to be heard through representatives of its own choosing." The board was organized June 26, 1933, and was at first composed of seven members. The first chairman was Walter Clark Teagle.

Prisoners (federal) employed in industry. *See under* Prison

The First

INEBRIATES' ASYLUM. *See under* Hospital

INFANTILE PARALYSIS EPIDEMIC. *See* Epidemic: Poliomyelitis epidemic

INFANTRYMAN'S BADGE (EXPERT). *See* Medal

INFLUENZA EPIDEMIC. *See* Epidemic

INFORMATION AGENCY (U.S.)

Woman to head an area office in the U.S. Information Agency was Dr. Dorothy Dillon, who was assistant director (USIA) in charge of the agency's activities in Latin America from August 1973 through April 1976.

INFORMATION SERVICE (U.S.) was created by the National Emergency Council as a directing center for all government activities under authority of Executive Order No. 6433-A and in conformity with statement issued by the White House, December 6, 1933. During the organization period from January 18, 1934, to March 7, 1934, Sarah Lee Fain served as chief. The office was officially opened March 15, 1934, with Harriet Maria Root as chief.

INFRARED PHOTOGRAPH. *See* Photograph

INGRAIN CARPETS. *See* Carpet loom: Carpet power loom to weave ingrain carpets

INHERITANCE TAX. *See* Tax

INITIATIVE AND REFERENDUM legislation was South Dakota's Joint Resolution No. 101, passed January 27, 1897, by the House and February 27, 1897, by the Senate. The amendment was submitted to the voters November 8, 1898, and passed with 23,816 votes for the amendment and 16,483 against the amendment. On June 2, 1902, Oregon adopted an amendment to the state constitution authorizing both initiative and referendum on legislation, by popular vote. *(Charles Austin Beard and Birl Earl Shultz—Documents on the Initiative, Referendum and Recall)*

INK

Ink was manufactured by the Thaddeus Davids Ink Company, established by Thaddeus Davids in New York City in 1825. The ink was bottled in various sizes and sold at retail. The first year only a few hundred bottles were manufactured. *(Thaddeus Davids—History of Ink)*

Ink paste was invented by Frank Buckley Cooney of Minneapolis, Minn., who obtained patent No. 1,479,533 on January 1, 1924. The paste, known as Cooney's Ink Paste, was manufactured February 10, 1923, by the Standard Ink Manufacturing Company, Minneapolis, Minn. The inventor sold rights to manufacture to the American Crayon Co.

Invisible ink used in diplomatic correspondence was employed by Silas Deane in 1776. As a member of the Committee of Secret Correspondence, organized November 29, 1775, "for the sole

The First

INK—*Continued*

purpose of corresponding with our friends in Great Britain, Ireland, and other parts of the world," he left Philadelphia, Pa., March 5, 1776, and arrived in France on May 4, 1776, with instructions to purchase military supplies on credit. His correspondence with John Jay was interlined with invisible ink, invented by Sir James Jay in 1776. Deane sent the first authentic account which Congress received of the determination of the British Ministry to reduce the colonies to unconditional surrender. The writing was done with a solution of tannic acid. To make the ink visible, the paper was sponged with ferrous sulfate, or copperas. The iron in the copperas combined with the tannic acid to form a dark compound easily visible.

Printer's ink. *See* Printer's Ink

INLAID LINOLEUM (embossed). *See* Linoleum

INOCULATION. *See* Vaccination

INSANE DETENTION HOME. *See under* Hospital

INSANE HOSPITAL. *See* Hospital

INSANE PATIENT'S MAINTENANCE ACT is found in the records of the Upland Court, Delaware County, Pa., in 1676. The act reads: "Jan Cornelissen of Amesland, Complayning to ye Court that his son Erick is bereft of his naturall Senses and is turned quyt madd and yt; he being a poore man is not able to maintaine him; Ordered: that three or four persons bee hired to build a little blockhouse at Amesland for to put in the said madman, and at the next Court, order will be taken yt; a small Levy be Laid for to pay for the building of ye house and the maintaining of ye said madman according to the laws of ye Government."

INSECT ELECTROCUTOR PATENT was No. 974,785, granted November 8, 1910, to William M. Frost of Spokane, Wash.

INSECT MONUMENT. *See* Monument: Monument to an insect

INSEMINATION. *See* Impregnation: Impregnation (human) by means of artificial insemination

INSPECTOR, NAVAL (woman). *See* Naval officer: Woman naval inspector

INSTALLMENT SALES LAW to protect consumers in practically all types of time sales was signed by Governor William Averell Harriman of New York on April 17, 1957, to become effective October 1, 1957. It placed a limit on credit service charges, required all charges to be clearly itemized, and prohibited fine print in the contracts.

INSULATING BRICK. *See* Brick: Brick insulating

The First

INSURANCE

See also Medicare

Accident insurance company was the Travelers Insurance Company of Hartford, Conn., chartered June 17, 1863, through the efforts of James Goodwin Batterson. The charter provided for the issuance of accident insurance to cover travel accidents only. In 1864 this was amended to include accidents of every description.

Accident insurance policy was issued by the Travelers Insurance Company of Hartford, Conn., to James Bolter of Hartford for $1,000 in 1864. The policy covered only the period he spent walking from the post office to his home on Buckingham Street. The premium was two cents. The agreement was oral.

Accident insurance policy (printed) was issued on April 1, 1864, by the Travelers Insurance Company of Hartford, Conn., to James Goodwin Batterson and covered only accidents of travel. The first policy covering general accidents, also issued to Batterson, was policy No. 1164, dated July 1, 1864.

Aircraft liability and property damage insurance was issued by the Travelers Insurance Company of Hartford, Conn., to a New York manufacturer in 1919.

Automobile compulsory insurance act (state) was "an act requiring owners of certain motor vehicles and trailers to furnish security for their civil liability on account of personal injury caused by their motor vehicles and trailers" (Chapter 346, Acts of Massachusetts), approved May 1, 1925, which became effective January 1, 1927. Automobiles were required to carry $5,000 and $10,000 liability.

Automobile insurance policy was issued by the Travelers Insurance Company of Hartford, Conn., on February 1, 1898, to Dr. Truman J. Martin of Buffalo, N.Y. The premium was $11.25, covering $5,000 to $10,000 liability.

Baby-sitters' insurance policy was issued on January 26, 1950, by the American Associated Insurance Companies, St. Louis, Mo., and covered sitters available through the Missouri State Employment Service, who were bonded up to $2,500 each for fraud and dishonesty.

Black-owned insurance company was the African Insurance Company of Philadelphia organized in 1810 with a capital stock of $5,000 in $50 shares. It specialized in insuring blacks. Joseph Randolph was president; Carey Porter, treasurer; and William Coleman, secretary. The company was not incorporated but was a voluntary association. *(William Edward Burghardt Du Bois—Economic Co-operation Among Negro Americans)*

The First

Boiler insurance company was the Hartford Steam Boiler Inspection and Insurance Company, of Hartford, Conn., chartered in June 1866. The first president of the company was Enoch Roberts. The first policy was issued February 14, 1867. *(Austin J. Lilly—The Institution of Insurance)*

Bonding company (exclusive) was the American Surety Company, New York City, incorporated December 7, 1881. It began business April 15, 1884.

Bonding law (state) for the bonding of all officers, deputies, and state employees was enacted by North Dakota (Chapter 194, sections 199–200A), approved March 1, 1913, effective January 1, 1914. The law was declared unconstitutional in 1914. Another law was passed (Chapter 158) and approved March 5, 1919. The premiums were 25 cents a year for each $100 of the required bond. A State Bonding Fund was created which in the first year showed a net income of $63,172.04. The fund was under the State Commissioner of Insurance. A. L. Carey was the first commissioner. The first claim was filed August 4, 1919, by Riggin Township, Benson County, for $1,000 for misappropriations of funds, and paid February 4, 1920.

Credit insurance was attempted in New York State in 1887, but the first company which operated for any length of time was the U.S. Credit System Company of New York, organized in 1889. *(Saul Benton Ackerman and Joseph William Neuner—Credit Insurance)*

Crime insurance federal policy was issued August 2, 1971, by George Romney, secretary of Housing and Urban Development; George Kaskel Bernstein, federal insurance administrator; and James McKinley Rose, Jr., assistant administrator for crime insurance. The policy was issued to William Early, proprietor of the Aida TV Sales and Service, Washington, D.C. The premium was $50 a thousand, $60 for 2 thousand, $70 for 3 thousand, and $80 for 5 thousand. It posited a deductible of $100 or 5%, whichever was greater.

Department store to sell insurance. *See under* Business

Employer's Liability Act (federal) was passed June 11, 1906 (34 Stat.L.232), but was declared unconstitutional by the Supreme Court in the Employer's Liability Cases (1908) (207 U.S. 463, 52 L.Ed. 297, 28 S.C.R.141) because its provisions extended to include the employees of interstate carriers even when such employees were not themselves engaged in any of the processes of interstate commerce. A revised act was passed April 22, 1908 (35 Stat.L.65).

Federal Deposit Insurance Corporation. *See* Federal Deposit Insurance Corporation

The First

Fire and tornado insurance fund (state) was established by Chapter 159 of the laws of North Dakota and began to function July 1, 1919. For the first five months, the gross income was $28,908.78 and the losses paid were $3,773.32. The net income, after expenses were paid, amounted to $24,143.70. The first loss was $1,500, paid on October 23, 1919, to Conway, S.Dak., No. 64, to compensate for damage caused by an overheated furnace. The law provided that no policy over $100,000 could be written. When necessary, additional insurance was obtained from private companies. *(Frederick Ludwig Hoffman—Windstorm and Tornado Insurance)*

Fire insurance agent is said to have been John Copson of High Street, Philadelphia, Pa., who inserted an advertisement on May 25, 1721, in the *American Weekly Mercury* to the effect that he would open an office for insurance on "vessels, goods and merchandise." *(John A. Fowler—History of Insurance in Philadelphia for Two Centuries)*

Fire insurance company was organized in 1735 in Charleston, S.C., as "The Friendly Society for the Mutual Insurance of Houses Against Fire," and received subscriptions beginning January 1, 1735. This company issued policies and conducted business over a period of about six years, as evidenced by advertisements and notices in the *South Carolina Gazette* from November 15, 1735, to February 19, 1741. On November 18, 1740, there was a conflagration which consumed half the town and probably ruined the society, as the last advertisement, which appeared on February 19, 1741, stated that "the bonds given by the members will be put in suit unless paid."

Fire insurance company to receive a charter was the Philadelphia Contributionship for the Insurance of Houses from Loss by Fire, Philadelphia, Pa. This was granted by the Lieutenant Governor and Proprietaries of the province of Pennsylvania on February 20, 1768, and was subsequently confirmed by George III, King of Great Britain, upon the advice of his Privy Council at the Court of St. James, London. On April 13, 1752, 12 directors and a treasurer had been elected, 16 years before the charter was obtained. The first name subscribed to the Deed of Settlement or Articles of Association was that of James Hamilton, the Lieutenant Governor of the Province under the Proprietaries. The first private name was that of Benjamin Franklin. At the first meeting of the directors, held May 11, 1752, a seal for the company "was ordered, being four Hands united." The marks were of lead, mounted upon a wooden shield, and were put up on all houses insured. The first fire insurance policy was issued on June 1, 1752, to John Smith of Philadelphia, who for £1 insured his house valued at £1,000. Smith was the first treasurer of the company. *(At the*

The First

INSURANCE—*Continued*
Sign of the Hand-in-Hand—Philadelphia Contributionship for the Insurance of Houses)

Fire insurance joint-stock company was the American Fire Insurance Company, organized February 28, 1810, in Philadelphia, Pa. The first president was Captain William Jones, who later became Secretary of the Navy under President James Madison. The first secretary of the company was Edward Fox. *(American Fire Insurance Company—Fire Insurance in America)*

Fraternal group insurance of consequence was issued in 1869 by the Metropolitan Life Insurance Company, New York City, to the Hildise Bund, an organization of German-American wage earners, which collected weekly premiums from its members. The premiums are said to have amounted at one time to about $7,500 a week.

Government insurance was enacted by the Plymouth Colony in 1636. The legislation provided that "if any [man] shalbee sent forth as a souldier and shall returne maimed, hee shalbee maintained competently by the Collonie of New Plymouth during his life." The act applied particularly to the soldiers engaged in the Pequot Indian War concluded on November 20, 1637. *(David Pulsifer—Records of the Colony in New England: Laws 1623–1682)*

Group hospital insurance plan was effected by Baylor University Hospital, Dallas, Tex., on December 21, 1929. The plan was inaugurated by Dr. Justin Ford Kimball, executive vice president of Baylor University. The first group insured was the Dallas Public School teachers.

Group hospital-medical cooperative was the Group Health Association, Inc., Washington, D.C., authorized February 24, 1937. The clinic opened November 1, 1937.

Group insurance contract of importance was made on July 1, 1912, between Montgomery Ward & Company of Chicago, Ill., and the Equitable Life Assurance Society of the United States, whereby 3,000 persons were insured as a group for approximately $6 million without medical examination.

Group insurance policy was written by William J. Graham of the Equitable Life Assurance Society of the United States on June 1, 1911, under one blanket contract. Without medical examination, 121 employees of the Pantasote Leather Company of Passaic, N.J., were insured as a group for $87,030. Each employee was given insurance protection amounting to a year's salary and a funeral benefit of $100.

Group insurance policy for college students covering medical, surgical, and hospital expenses was issued February 1, 1936, by the Ocean Accident and Guarantee Corporation, Ltd., to Vassar College, Poughkeepsie, N.Y. The plan was sponsored by the college for voluntary participation,

The First

and 565 students were included at a premium of $12 each for the year. Known as the Students' Reimbursement Plan, it was organized and managed by A. W. G. Dewar, Inc., of Boston, Mass., whose Tuition Refund Plan in 1929 had first introduced the insurance of school fees in American private schools.

Hail insurance on growing tobacco crops was written in 1880 by the Tobacco Growers' Mutual Insurance Company of North Canaan, Conn., incorporated in Connecticut, March 24, 1880. This company went out of business in 1887. *(U.S. Department of Agriculture, Bulletin No. 912)*

Hail insurance law (state) was enacted by the legislature of North Dakota in 1911 and approved by Governor John Burke, March 18, 1911. The number of policies issued the first year was 1,011, representing risks of about $1 million. The losses during the first year exceeded the premiums by nearly 18 percent, and the losses, as adjusted, had to be prorated at 70 percent. *(North Dakota Hail Insurance Department—Annual Report, 1912)*

Health insurance clause in a labor contract was put into effect on August 25, 1941, by the International Ladies Garment Workers Union with Waist and Dress Manufacturers Association of Philadelphia, setting aside 2½ percent of the payroll to establish a system of weekly sick benefits and a medical clinic to supervise the health of the workers. About 10 thousand cotton-dress and -blouse workers in Philadelphia, Pa., were covered.

Health insurance company was the Massachusetts Health Insurance Company of Boston, Mass., organized April 21, 1847. It was incorporated in 1847 under Chapter 214 of the Massachusetts General Law. The company existed for a very short period. *(George Edwin McNeill—A Study of Accidents and Accident Insurance)*

Health insurance law (state) was the Rhode Island Cash Sickness Compensation act, approved April 29, 1942, effective May 10, 1942. It required employers to collect 1 percent from employees after June 1, 1942, on salaries up to $3,000 paid in any calendar year, and granted benefits ranging from $6.75 to $18 a week. The board members supervising the fund were Chairman Mortimer W. Newton, Arthur P. Patt, and Tom Howick.

Insurance agency was opened by Israel Whelan in New York City in 1804. He was a representative of the Phoenix Fire Office of London, England. *(Harry Chase Brearley History of the National Board of Fire Underwriters)*

Insurance board (state) was the New Hampshire Insurance Department, established July 1, 1851, by New Hampshire Laws (1851, Chapter 1111), which authorized the governor to appoint three suitable persons, residents of the state, for a term of one year, whose duty it was to examine personally each year the affairs of all insurance

The First

companies and report to the legislature. The first board consisted of Albert S. Scott, Jacob E. Ela, and Timo Hoskins. *(Edwin Wilhite Patterson— The Insurance Commissioner in the United States)*

Insurance company to exclusively insure the lives of animals was the Animal Insurance Company of America, New York City, founded August 1, 1957, by Milton M. Weiss. Coverage was extended only to pedigreed dogs and cats until May 1958, at which time the company added insurance for livestock classes of horses and cattle. Policies on animals, however, were previously written by general insurance companies.

Insurance department (state) charged with the execution of the laws relating to insurance was the New York Insurance Department, which was established in 1859, by Chapter 366, approved April 15, 1859, effective January 1, 1860. The first superintendent was William Barnes, appointed January 11, 1860. *(First Annual Report of the Superintendent of the Insurance Department, New York State)*

Insurance policy to be illustrated was issued April 8, 1947, by the Allstate Insurance Company, Chicago, Ill.

Insurance rate standardization was effected July 18, 1866, in New York City by the National Board of Fire Underwriters, an organization of 75 fire insurance companies. The first annual meeting was held February 20, 1867, in New York City, and the first president was James McLean. *(Harry Chase Brearley—History of the National Board of Fire Underwriters)*

Insurance regulation (state) was enacted by Massachusetts, Chapter 46, approved February 13, 1799, "an act in addition to an act entitled, 'an act to incorporate sundry persons by the name of the Massachusetts Fire Insurance Company.'" It required that the company "shall, when and as often required by the legislature of the Commonwealth, lay before them such a statement of their affairs as the said legislature may deem it expedient to require, and submit to an examination hereon under oath."

Insurance service offered by a newspaper to its subscribers was instituted by the St. Louis *Star,* St. Louis, Mo., on April 14, 1919. Policies on a deferred payment plan were also offered. The first policy was furnished by the American Bonding and Casualty Company of Sioux City, Iowa, and was a peculiar affair resembling an old-style theater program.

Life insurance by a general insurance company was offered by the Insurance Company of North America, organized in Philadelphia, Pa., on December 10, 1792, with a capital of $600,000 and chartered on April 14, 1794. The first policy was issued on December 15, 1792. Only six policies

The First

were written in five years, and in 1804 the life insurance feature was discontinued. The first president was John Maxwell Nesbitt and the first secretary Ebenezer Hazard. *(Joseph Brotherton Maclean—Life Insurance)*

Life insurance company was the "Corporation for the Relief of Poor and Distressed Presbyterian Ministers and of the Poor and Distressed Widows and Children of Presbyterian Ministers," incorporated January 11, 1759, Philadelphia, Pa. The first officers were the Reverend Robert Cross, president; William Allen, treasurer; and Francis Alison, secretary. The first policy was issued May 22, 1761, to Francis Alison. Survivor annuities were granted at the death of the policyholder, the beneficiary receiving £10 to £35 for the duration of his or her life. The annual premium required was one fifth of the annuity.

Marine insurance law (state) was enacted in Massachusetts in 1818 (Chapter 120, Acts of 1818, approved February 16, 1818). An act was passed defining the powers, duties, and restrictions of insurance companies. It applied only to companies writing marine insurance and provided for annual publication by the president and directors of the amount of their stock, the risks against which they meant to insure, and the amounts of the single risks. They were also required to report to the legislature whenever so directed and were forbidden to write in any risk a sum exceeding 10 percent of the capital stock of the company.

Mutual fire insurance company for insuring factories was the Manufacturers' Mutual Fire Insurance Company of Rhode Island, located in Providence, R.I., and incorporated October 31, 1835. The first policy was issued December 3, 1835, to Zachariah Allen for $2,500 at a cash premium deposit rate of 60 cents a year. At the expiration of the policy a 51 percent dividend was declared, resulting in an insurance cost of 29.4 cents per $100 for the year. *(Journal of American Insurance. Vol. 1, No. 2)*

Mutual liability insurance company was the American Mutual Liability Insurance Company, Boston, Mass., incorporated March 30, 1887, formally organized April 21, 1887, and opened for business October 1, 1887, when 22 policies were written covering liability of employers to injured workers. The rate was 30 cents per $100 of payroll. The first officers were William Croad Lovering, president; Josiah Caleb Bartlett, first manager; Sydney Augustus Williams, secretary; and Charles Edward Hodges, bookkeeper and clerk. *(Charles Edward Hodges—The First American Liability Insurance Company, Pioneer in Loss Prevention, Since 1887)*

Mutual life insurance company to be chartered was the New England Mutual Life Insurance Company of Boston, Mass., which was chartered April 1, 1835. The first president was Judge Willard Phil-

The First

INSURANCE—*Continued*

lips. The company was not actually organized for business until December 1, 1843. The first policy was issued February 1, 1844.

Mutual life insurance company to operate was the Mutual Life Insurance Company of New York, which was chartered on April 12, 1842. The first policy was issued February 1, 1843, to Thomas N. Ayres. The first president was Morris Robinson. Policyholders were entitled to a share in the management through the election of directors. All profits belonged to the policyholders. *(Shepherd Bancroft Clough—A Century of American Life Insurance: A History of the Mutual Life Insurance Company of New York—1843–1943)*

No-fault automobile insurance law (state) was Chapter 670, Acts of Massachusetts, "an act providing for compulsory personal injury protection for all registered motor vehicles, defining such protection, restricting the right to claim damages for pain and suffering in certain actions of tort, regulating further the premium charges for compulsory automobile insurance and amending certain laws relating thereto." The act was approved by Governor Francis Williams Sargent, August 13, 1970. Section 6 became effective upon passage; it permitted policyholders to collect up to $2,000 for medical expenses and "out-of-pocket" costs including wages, to be paid directly by the insurance company, irrespective of fault. All other sections became effective on January 1, 1971. (A similar law had been enacted previously by Puerto Rico.)

Nonforfeiture insurance law (state) was enacted by Massachusetts in 1861 (Chapter 186, Acts of 1861, approved April 10, 1861). It was sponsored by Commissioner Elizur Wright. This law required domestic companies to use four fifths of the reserve to continue a policy as extended term insurance beyond the date of lapse. In event of death during the term period, the company had the right to deduct from the claim the premiums that would have been paid had the policy continued in force, plus interest.

Nonforfeiture insurance policy was issued by the New York Life Insurance Company of New York City, August 13, 1860, about eight months prior to the enactment of the "nonforfeitable" legislation in Massachusetts. This plan was not made retroactive. Although this was the first policy issued providing for nonforfeiture, nonforfeiture had in fact been granted for some time prior thereto, but was not provided in the policy.

Numerical system of insurance rating was originated by the New York Life Insurance Company of New York City about 1903. Values were assigned to various factors affecting the insurability of an applicant for insurance so as to aid a company in determining under its rules whether the applicant was insurable, and if insurable, at what

The First

rates of premium, i.e., whether the life is "standard" or "substandard," and if the latter, to what extent.

Plate-glass insurance was written by the United States Plate Glass Insurance Company of Philadelphia, Pa., incorporated April 12, 1867, with an original capital of $20,000. The first president was John Van Dusen.

Savings bank life insurance was launched by act of the Massachusetts legislature, June 26, 1907. The plan was originated by Louis Dembitz Brandeis, then a Boston lawyer, and later Associate Justice of the United States Supreme Court. The first savings bank to establish an insurance department was the Whitman Savings Bank in Whitman, Mass. The department was established June 18, 1908, and the first policy written June 22, 1908. Savings bank life insurance is legal reserve insurance that is sold "over the counter" by certain mutual savings banks. No solicitors are employed. *(General Laws—Massachusetts. Chapter 178, section 6)*

Social security. *See* Social Security Act (U.S.)

Substandard life insurance policy was issued July 1, 1896, by the New York Life Insurance Company of New York City. A substandard policy is one issued on a life which because of a medical impairment, hazardous occupation, or some other reason is "substandard" and therefore not insurable at "standard," or normal, rates of premium.

Teachers' death benefit. *See* Teachers' death benefit

Teachers' pension fund. *See* Teachers' pension funds

Teachers' sick benefit fund. *See* Teachers' sick benefit fund

Title guaranty insurance company was the Real Estate Title Insurance and Trust Company, organized in Philadelphia, Pa., on March 31, 1876. It offered security against errors in titles. The original capital was $250,000, half of which was paid in. The first president was Joshua H. Morris and the first secretary, Joseph S. Siddall.

Unemployment insurance act passed by a state was enacted by Wisconsin, January 28, 1932, and signed by Governor Philip La Follette. Every employer of ten or more was required to put 2 percent of the payroll aside until a fund accrued equaling $75 per eligible worker, which the employee could draw against in time of unemployment at the rate of $10 a week for a maximum of ten weeks. The first payment was made August 17, 1936. The chairman of the Industrial Commission which regulated the department was Voyta Wrabetz.

War Risk Insurance Bureau was established by act of Congress, September 2, 1914 (38 Stat. L. 711), to insure American vessels against war risks. The act was amended on June 12, 1917, and

The First

October 6, 1917, to provide yearly renewable term insurance against total disability and death to those in active military or naval service. Provision was made for policy conversion to other forms of life insurance. The bureau was under the general direction of the Secretary of the Treasury and directly supervised by William C. De Lanoy. Policy No. 1 was issued October 17, 1917, to Cope Flannagan, who received a $10,000 policy payable, in case of death or permanent disability, in monthly installments of $57.50. *(U.S. Veterans Bureau—Laws Governing the Organization and Administration of the Bureau of War Risk Insurance)*

Workers' compensation insurance law (federal) was approved May 30, 1908 (35 Stat. L. 556). It became effective August 1, 1908, and was applicable to certain classes of federal employees in the United States: artisans or laborers in any manufacturing establishment, arsenal, or navy yard and employees in the construction of river and harbor fortifications, in hazardous employment on construction work in the reclamation of arid lands, and in hazardous employment under the Isthmian Canal Commission.

Workers' compensation insurance law (state) to go into effect was passed by Wisconsin, May 3, 1911 (Chapter 50), and went into effect the same date. Washington passed a compensation insurance law (Chapter 74) which was approved on March 14, 1911, but which did not go into effect until October 1, 1911. New Jersey also passed a law (Chapter 95) which was approved April 4, 1911, and which went into effect July 4, 1911. Laws which were later declared unconstitutional had, however, been passed previously: Maryland, 1902; Montana, 1909; New York, 1910.

INSURANCE BOOK
Insurance proposal of importance published in America was *Ways and Means for the Inhabitants of Delaware to Become Rich, wherein the several growths and products of these countries are demonstrated to be a sufficient fund for a flourishing trade,* 65 pages, printed in Philadelphia, Pa., in 1725, by S. Keimer. The author was Francis Rawle, who advocated the establishment by the legislature of an insurance office in Philadelphia for the purpose of providing marine insurance for merchants. *(Philadelphia Contributionship—Franklin and Fires)*

INSURANCE MAGAZINE was *Tuckett's Monthly Insurance Journal,* published in 1852 in Philadelphia, Pa. *(Journal of American Insurance. Vol. 1, No. 3)*

INSURANCE TREATISE on the law of insurance was a reprint of the English *A System of the Law of Marine Insurances; with three chapters on bottomry, on insurance on lives and on insurances against fire,* by Sir James Alan Park, published in Philadelphia, Pa., in 1789.

The First

INSURED-BANK PAYMENTS. *See* Bank: Bank payments to depositors of a closed insured bank

INTEGRATED HISTORY COURSE. *See* History instruction: History course (integrated) in a women's college

INTELLIGENCE TEST used in a school for the feeble-minded was the Binet-Simon Test. It was introduced in August 1908 by Dr. Henry Herbert Goddard, director of research in the New Jersey Training School for Feeble-Minded Boys and Girls in Vineland, N.J., to determine the degree of subnormality of children in the institution. *(Alfred Binet and Theodore Simon—The Development of Intelligence in Children)*

INTER-AMERICAN HIGHWAY APPROPRIATION. *See under* Road

INTERCOLLEGIATE AIR MEET. *See under* Aviation—Expositions and Meets

INTERCOLLEGIATE ATHLETIC ASSOCIATION of importance was the Intercollegiate Association of Amateur Athletes of America, organized in Saratoga, N.Y., in June 1876, when a track meet was held. The charter members were Amherst, Bowdoin, Brown, City College of New York, Columbia, Cornell, Dartmouth, Harvard, Pennsylvania, Princeton, Trinity, Union, Wesleyan, Williams, and Yale. A preliminary meeting was held in Saratoga, N.Y., December 4, 1875. In 1873 James Gordon Bennett offered a cup to the best track athlete, the contestants for which were the members of the crews who participated in the Springfield, Mass., rowing races. The association was formed as a result of these meetings.

INTERCOLONIAL WAR. *See under* War (colonial)

INTERCONTINENTAL SYSTEM OF STUDY. *See under* College

INTERFRATERNITY COUNCIL. *See under* Fraternity (Greek-letter)

INTERIOR DEPARTMENT (U.S.)
Interior Department Secretary was Thomas Ewing of Ohio, who was appointed by President Zachary Taylor on March 8, 1849, and who served until July 23, 1850.

Interior Department (U.S.) was created by act of March 3, 1849 (9 Stat. L. 395), titled "an act to establish the Home Department."

INTERLOCKING MACHINE (railroad). *See* Railroad signal system: Railroad signal system of interlocking signal apparatus

INTERMEDIATE-RANGE BALLISTIC MISSILE. *See under* Rocket

INTERNAL-COMBUSTION ENGINE. *See* Engine

INTERNAL REVENUE ACT was passed by Congress, March 3, 1791 (1 Stat. L. 202). It established 14 revenue districts, one for each state, and

The First

INTERNAL REVENUE ACT—*Continued*
placed a tax on distilled spirits varying from 11
cents to 30 cents a gallon.

INTERNAL REVENUE COLLECTOR (woman).
See under Woman

INTERNAL REVENUE COMMISSIONER was
George Sewall Boutwell of Massachusetts, who
served from July 17, 1862, to March 4, 1863, under
the U.S. Bureau of Internal Revenue in the Treasury Department. The Bureau was created by act of
Congress July 1, 1862 (12 Stat. L. 432). The first
commissioner of the revenue was Tench Coxe of
Pennsylvania, who was assistant to the Secretary
of the Treasury in charge of internal revenue from
September 11, 1789, to May 8, 1792. He was designated commissioner on May 8, 1792.

INTERNAL REVENUE TAX. *See* Tax

**INTERNATIONAL AGREEMENTS, INSTITU-
TIONS, AND EVENTS.** *See under* specific sub-
jects, e.g., Automobile race, Copyright law,
Hospital, Weights and measures standardization

**INTERNATIONAL BUREAU OF WEIGHTS
AND MEASURES.** *See under* Weights and measures

**INTERNATIONAL EUCHARISTIC CONGRESS
in America** met in Chicago, Ill., June 20–24, 1926.
Although this was the 28th international session,
it was the first in the United States. Cardinal John
Bonzano was installed as the Papal Legate to preside for Pope Pius XI. Services were held at the
Cathedral of the Holy Name, Chicago.

INTERNATIONAL GOLF MATCH. *See* Golf
Tournament

**INTERNATIONAL GREYHOUND RACING AS-
SOCIATION.** *See* Greyhound Racing Association

INTERNATIONAL RAILROAD. *See* Railroad

INTERNATIONAL SKI MEET. *See* Ski meet (international)

INTERNATIONAL YACHT RACE. *See* Yacht
race

INTERRACIAL HOSPITAL. *See* Hospital

INTERSTATE CARRIER ARBITRATION. *See*
Arbitration

INTERSTATE COMMERCE ACT establishing
the Interstate Commerce Commission was approved February 4, 1887 (24 Stat. L. 379), and was
popularly known as the Cullom Act. Its terms,
effective April 5, 1887, provided for the appointment of five commissioners from January 1, 1887,
for terms of two, three, four, five, and six years. Its
principal objects were "to secure just and reasonable charges for [railroad] transportation; to prohibit unjust discrimination in the rendition of like
services under similar circumstances and conditions; to prevent undue preferences to persons,
corporations or localities; to inhibit greater com-

The First

pensation for shorter than for longer distances
over the same lines; and to abolish combinations
for the pooling of freights." The commission was
organized March 31, 1887, and started to function
April 5, 1887, with 38 persons on the payroll. The
first commissioners were Aldace Freeman Walker, Augustus Schoonmaker, Walter Lawrence
Bragg, Thomas McIntyre Cooley, and William
Ralls Morrison, appointed March 22, 1887, by
President Grover Cleveland. *(Isaiah Leo Sharf-
man—The Interstate Commerce Commission)*

INTERSTATE COMMERCE COMMISSION
Independent administrative agency of the federal government woman member was Virginia
Mae Brown (Mrs. James V. Brown), Democrat, of
Pliny, W.Va., a Charleston lawyer, who was appointed March 4, 1964, by President Lyndon
Baines Johnson and sworn in May 25, 1964. She
became vice chairman in 1968, and served as
chairman January 1, 1969, – December 31, 1969.

Woman independent federal administrative
agency chairman. *See under* Woman

**INTERSTATE   COMMERCE   COMMISSION
MEDAL.** *See* Medal

INTERSTATE CRIME PACT. *See under* Crime

INTERSTATE LEGISLATIVE CONFERENCE.
See Legislative conference (interstate)

INTERSTATE RAILROAD. *See* Railroad

INTERURBAN STREETCAR. *See* Streetcar

INVESTITURE OF ORDERS. *See* Knighthood

INVESTMENT FINANCE COMPANY. *See under*
Business

INVESTMENT TRUST. *See under* Brokerage

INVISIBLE GLASS. *See* Glass

INVISIBLE INK. *See* Ink

IRISH MAGAZINE was *The Shamrock or Hibernian Chronicle,* published December 15, 1810, in
New York City. It was edited by Edward Gillespy.
Publication was suspended three times. On June
18, 1814, it was revived as *The Shamrock. (Apollinaris William Baumgartner—Catholic Journalism)*

IRON
Angle iron was rolled in 1819 by Samuel Leonard at the Union Rolling Mill, on the Monongahela
River, at Pittsburgh, Pa. The mill had four pud-
dling furnaces.

Anthracite coal used in smelting iron ore. *See
under* Coal

Cast-iron bridge. *See under* Bridge

Cast-iron pipes used in a city waterworks system were installed by Philadelphia, Pa., in 1817.
The pipeline was 400 feet long and 4½ inches in
diameter. The pipes were imported from England
and were so much superior to the old wooden

water pipes that the Watering Committee decided, according to its report of January 23, 1817, to adopt them. In 1818 the committee resolved to make all future installations with cast-iron pipe.

Exportation of iron was made in 1650. In "1650 —Sam Hutchinson, merchant, shipped on the 'Charles' 3½ tunne, 172 bars of iron for acco. of Ri. Hutchinson, of London." This iron was probably made in Lynn, Mass. *(Stephen Lincoln Goodale— Chronology of Iron and Steel)*

Hammered iron was made in 1842 at the Weymouth Iron Works on the Great Egg Harbor River, N.J., founded in 1754. The iron was hammered at the forge by two great trip hammers operated by waterpower. Stephen Colwell received a medal from the Academy of Natural Sciences for developing the machinery used in this plant.

Iron blast furnace successfully to use anthracite coal was the Pioneer furnace in Pottsville, Pa., which was blown October 19, 1839, by Benjamin Perry. About 28 tons of foundry iron were produced a week. The furnace was built by William Lyman of Boston, Mass.

Iron bridge. *See under* Bridge

Iron casting is credited to Joseph Mallinson of Dusboro, Pa., who introduced it in 1739 and received a grant of 200 acres of unimproved land in recognition of his services. *(James Moore Swank —History of the Manufacture of Iron)*

Iron castings (malleable) were produced in Newark, N.J., July 4, 1826, by Seth Boyden. At first the iron was melted in crucibles, with lime used as a flux and heated in charcoal or hard coal fires.

Ironclad ships. *See* Ship: Ironclad naval vessels

Iron foundry. *See* Brass and iron foundry

Iron-hull ship. *See* Ship: Iron vessel

Iron lifeboat. *See* Lifeboat: Lifeboat (corrugated)

Iron mill to puddle and roll iron was the Plumstock Rolling Mill on Redstone Creek between Connellsville and Brownsville, Pa., in Fayette County, put into operation September 15, 1817, by Isaac Meason. It was wrecked by floods in 1824 and was not rebuilt. *(Western Pennsylvania Historical Survey: Guide to Historical Places in Western Pennsylvania)*

Iron patent was No. 3,605, granted January 6, 1844, to S. Broadmeadow of Woodbridge, N.J., for a process "to obtain malleable iron direct from iron ore."

Iron pile lighthouse. *See under* Lighthouse

Iron rail. *See* Railroad track: Railroad rails of iron

Iron slitting mill, for slitting railroads, was established in Milton, Mass., in March 1710 by Jonathan Jackson.

Iron sloop yacht. *See under* Ship

Iron steamship. *See under* Ship

Iron window sash. *See* Sash: Wrought-iron window sash installation

Iron-wire suspension bridge. *See under* Bridge

Iron yacht. *See* Ship: Iron sloop yacht

Ironworks was erected at Falling Creek, Va. (near Richmond), in 1619 by the Virginia Company. It operated only a short time, however, because of Indian troubles, and its charter was revoked in 1624. John Berkeley was in charge of operations. *(American Institute of Mining Engineering—Transactions, Vol. XX)*

Ironworks (successful) was constructed in 1643 by John Winthrop, Jr., and ten others. It was known as the Company of Undertakers for the Iron Works and was established near the Saugus River, near Lynn, Mass. It produced eight tons of iron per week from the neighboring bog ore. It was managed by Captain Robert Bridges and Thomas Dexter. A forge was later installed. *(Robert Charles Winthrop—Life and Letters of John Winthrop, Governor of the Massachusetts Bay Company at Their Emigration to New England 1630)*

Rolling mill was the Sarum ironworks, established in 1746 by John Taylor in Chester, Pa. Three stacks worked full blast.

Wrought-iron beams used in a building. *See* Building: Building in which wrought-iron beams were used

IRON LUNG RESPIRATOR. *See* Respirator (iron lung)

IROQUOIS CONFEDERACY. *See* American Indians: League of American Indian nations

IRRIGATION LEGISLATION (federal) was the act of July 26, 1866 (14 Stat. L. 251), which ruled that control of waterways was a matter of state control subject to "local customs, laws and decisions of the court." *(Ray Palmer Teele—Irrigation in the United States)*

ISLAND PRISON (military). *See* Prison: Military prison of the United States

ISLAND TERRITORIAL ACQUISITION. *See* Territorial expansion: Island territory

ISOTOPE

Radioactive isotope medicine was phosphorus 32, artificially produced in a 37-inch cyclotron. It was administered December 24, 1936, to a 28-year-old woman with chronic leukemia by Dr. John Hunsdale Lawrence, director of the Donner Laboratory at the University of California at Berkeley.

The First

ISOTOPE—*Continued*

Radioactive isotopes exported were produced from phosphorus 31 at the Oak Ridge National Laboratory, Oak Ridge, Tenn., and flown to San Francisco, Calif., for further flight to Canberra, Australia, where they arrived September 11, 1947. They were a by-product of a chain-reacting uranium pile and were used in the Australian commonwealth's X-ray and medical laboratory. (The Oak Ridge National Laboratory was operated by the Union Carbide Corporation for the United States Atomic Energy Commission.)

ITALIAN INSTRUCTION. *See* Language instruction

ITALIAN NEWSPAPER. *See* Newspaper

ITALIAN OPERA. *See* Opera

IVORY COMB. *See* Comb

J

JAI ALAI, the pelota game, was played at the Louisiana Purchase Exposition, St. Louis, Mo., in 1904 in the Jai-Alai Building—not on the World's Fair grounds but near the main entrance. *(Badminton Magazine. Vol. 51, 1919)*

JAIL. *See* Prison

JAMES E. SULLIVAN MEMORIAL TROPHY. *See under* Sports trophy

JAPANESE AMBASSADOR to the United States was Niimi Buzennokami. He and his staff of 74 men left Japan, January 22, 1860, on the U.S.S. *Powhatan* under Captain Josiah Tattnall and arrived in San Francisco, Calif., March 9, 1860. They arrived in Washington, D.C., via Panama on April 25, 1860, and were received by President James Buchanan, April 28, 1860. They arrived in New York City, May 28, 1860. On June 13, 1860, the party went back to Japan on board the American battleship *Niagara* via the Cape of Good Hope. The first Japanese legation was established in Washington, D.C., in October 1870, and on January 7, 1906, the legation was raised to the rank of embassy. E. Hicki was appointed charge d'affaires ad interim, and was succeeded by Shuzo Aoki, who was appointed the first Japanese ambassador Plenipotentiary on April 24, 1906. *(Masakiyo Yanagawa—First Japanese Mission to America)*

JAPANESE-AMERICAN REPRESENTATIVE IN CONGRESS. *See* Representative (U.S.): Representative of Japanese ancestry elected to the House of Representatives

JAPANESE CITIZEN. *See* Citizenship: Japanese granted citizenship

The First

JAPANESE IMMIGRANT. *See* Immigration: Japanese to enter the United States

JAPANESE LAWYER. *See* Lawyer

JAPANESE MIDSHIPMAN. *See* Naval academy: Japanese midshipman in the U.S. Naval Academy

JAZZ MUSIC COMPOSER. *See* Musician: Composer of jazz music

JEANS AND FUSTIANS (cloth). *See under* Cloth

JELLY PETROLEUM. *See* Petroleum jelly

JENNY, COTTON. *See* Cotton spinning jenny

JERSEY CATTLE. *See* Cattle club: Cattle club (Jersey cattle)

JET ACE. *See* Aviation—Pilot: American ace (jet)

JET-PROPELLED AIRPLANE. *See under* Aviation—Airplane

JETWAY

Jetway was installed July 29, 1959 at International Airport, San Francisco, Calif. It is a self-powered telescopic corridor that extends from 44 to 107 feet and swings smoothly into place to connect the terminal with aircraft. Designed to protect enplaning or deplaning jet passengers from wind and weather, it can be extended from the terminal building to the aircraft door in less than 60 seconds.

JEWELERS' SUPPLY HOUSE of importance was established in 1794 by Nehemiah Dodge, silversmith, goldsmith, and watch repairer, in a shop on North Main Street, Providence, R.I. In addition to his retail business he sold gold plate made of a thin sheet of gold united with a thicker sheet of copper to manufacturing jewelers.

JEWISH BOOK

Jewish book of Jewish authorship published in America was a 1719 reprint of the third edition of *The Wars of the Jews; in two books, with the most deplorable history of the siege and destruction of the City of Jerusalem epitomized from the works of Flavius Josephus,* published in London in 1717. The reprint was published by Samuel Kneeland and Nicholas Buttolph in Boston.

Jewish prayer book published in the United States was *Prayers for Shabbath, Rosh-Hashanah and Kippur, or the Sabbath, the beginning of the year and the Day of Atonements; with the Amidah and Musaph of the Moadim, or Solemn Seasons according to the order of the Spanish and Portuguese Jews,* translated by Isaac Pinto and printed for him in 1766 (the year 5526 according to the Hebrew calendar) by John Holt, New York City. The book contained 196 pages.

JEWISH COLLEGE

Jewish college was Maimonides College, Philadelphia, Pa., which opened October 28, 1867. It was sponsored by the Hebrew Educational Society of Philadelphia and the Board of Delegates of

The First

American Israelites. It offered a five-year course leading to Bachelor and Doctor of Divinity degrees. Tuition was $100, and board and lodging $200 per year. Of the eight students approved for matriculation the first year, only two remained the entire year. Dr. Marcus Jastrow was provost, and the Reverend Isaac Leeser, professor of homiletics, belles lettres, and comparative theology, was president of the faculty. The college closed in 1873. *(Bertram Wallace Korn—Eventful Years and Experiences)*

Jewish college of liberal arts and sciences under Jewish auspices was the Yeshiva College, Amsterdam Avenue and 186th Street, New York City, chartered March 29, 1928, by the Board of Regents of the University of the State of New York. The cornerstone was laid May 1, 1927. The first graduating class, consisting of 19 members, received B.A. degrees on June 16, 1932. The college offers courses leading to the degrees of B.A. and B.S. and awards honorary degrees of Doctor of Laws and Doctor of Humane Letters. The first president was Dr. Bernard Revel. On November 16, 1945, it became Yeshiva University and was authorized to establish new graduate and undergraduate schools and to confer 15 kinds of degrees.

Jewish college to train men for the rabbinate was Hebrew Union College, established October 3, 1875, in Cincinnati, Ohio, through the efforts of Dr. Isaac Mayer Wise, who served as president from 1875 to 1900. The first graduation was held July 11, 1883, when Israel Aaron, Henry Berkowitz, Joseph Krauskopf, and David Philipson were ordained.

Jewish nonsectarian college was Dropsie College for Hebrew and Cognate Learning of Philadelphia, Pa., chartered June 6, 1907. The college was founded in accordance with the will of Moses Aaron Dropsie, who directed "that in the admission of students there shall be no distinction on account of creed, color or sex." The first president of the college was Dr. Cyrus Adler. *(Dropsie College Register, 1918–1919)*

JEWISH CONGREGATION

Jewish congregation was Shearith Israel (Remnant of Israel) established in 1655 in New Amsterdam (later New York City) by Sephardic Jews who had fled from the inquisition in Portuguese Brazil. Saul Brown was the first rabbi. The foundation stones of the first synagogue were laid on Thursday, September 8, 1729, and the building was consecrated April 8, 1730. The building was located on Mill Street, now South William Street. The present synagogue is located at Central Park West and Seventieth Street, New York City. *(David de Sola Pool—The Mill Street Synagogue)*

Jewish congregation (Ashkenazic) was Congregation Rodeph Shalom of Philadelphia, Pa., founded October 10, 1802. *(Edward Davis—History of Rodeph Shalom)*

The First

Jewish congregation (Reform) was the Reformed Society of Israelites, organized November 21, 1824, by 12 members of the Congregation Beth Elohim of Charleston, S.C. This body desired a modified form of worship and started a new congregation. The organization lasted eight years and was without a rabbi, because of lack of funds. *(David Philipson—Reform Movement in Judaism)*

Jewish congregation to call a woman to exercise a rabbi's function was Temple Beth Israel, Meridian, Miss., which installed Mrs. Paula Ackerman, widow of Rabbi William Ackerman, on January 26, 1951, as spiritual leader with the duties and authority of a rabbi.

Jewish mobile synagogue was the Circuit Riding Rabbi Bus dedicated March 27, 1955, at the Amity Country Club, Charlotte, N.C. It was placed in operation April 4, 1955, in North Carolina communities and was the project of the North Carolina Association of Jewish Men. The first rabbi was Harold A. Friedman. The bus was equipped with desks, blackboards, maps, a projection machine, a record player, and a library.

JEWISH MUSEUM. *See* Museum

JEWISH PRAYER BOOK. *See under* Jewish book

JEWS

See also under

Army officer	Play (drama)
Cemetery	Representative (U.S.)
Diplomatic service	Senator (U.S.)
Governor	Sunday school
Hospital	Supreme Court
Naval officer	(U.S.)
Normal school	Women's club
Physician	

Jew known to have arrived in America was Jacob Barsimson, who landed at New Netherlands on August 22, 1654. He left the Netherlands on the *Pearboom* (or *Peartree*) on July 8, 1654, and paid 36 guilders for his passage. A month later, 23 more Jews arrived, but were temporarily denied admission by Governor Peter Stuyvesant as "hateful enemies and blasphemers of the name of Christ." They were later allowed to enter provided "the poor among them should not become a burden to the Dutch West Indies Company or the community, but be supported by their own nation." *(Charles Daly—Settlement of Jews in North America)*

Jew killed in the American Revolution was Francis Salvador, known as the Southern Paul Revere for having warned of the approach of the British fleet at Charleston, S.C. While he was leading the militia under the command of Major Andrew Wilkinson, Indians and Tories ambushed them near Esseneka (Seneca) on August 1, 1776. Salvador was shot through the body and the left

The First

JEWS—*Continued*

leg and was scalped by a group of Cherokee Indians who sided with the British Tories.

Jew to win all the rights and perform all the duties of citizenship was Asser Levy of New Amsterdam. The Council of New Amsterdam passed a law denying Jews the privilege of standing guard and keeping watch, compulsory for all other citizens, and taxed them for the exemption. Asser Levy and Jacob Barsimson objected to the discrimination and a decision was rendered against them. They appealed and on April 20, 1657, equal privilege was granted. *(Leon Huhner—Asser Levy, A Noted Jewish Burgher of New Amsterdam)*

Jewish fraternal society was the B'nai B'rith (Sons of the Covenant), founded October 13, 1843, in New York City by Henry Jones and 11 others. Jones was appointed chairman. The first lodge was formed on November 12, 1843, at which time Isaac Dittenhoefer was elected president.

Jewish Rabbinical Conference met in Cleveland, Ohio, October 17, 1855. Isidor Kalisch, who preached reform Judaism, was instrumental in assembling this meeting, the purpose of which was "to better the spiritual conditions of the Jews in America; to strip the Jewish divine services of heathenism and idolatrous customs; to weed out senseless and useless prayers, and to establish a uniform divine service throughout the land."

Jewish woman cantor. *See under* Cantor

JOCKEY

See also Horse race

Jockey (American-born) to win 3,000 races was Eddie Arcaro, who won the third race, riding Ascent, at Arlington Park, Chicago, Ill., on June 24, 1952. In 21 years, he rode 15,327 mounts, which won $12,265,455.

Jockey to ride 400 winners in one year was Willie Shoemaker, a 22-year-old of Arcadia, Calif., who brought in his 485th winner, Mercenary, at Santa Anita Park, Arcadia, Calif., on December 31, 1953, in 255 days of riding. He beat the 1952 record of Tony De Spirito by 95 winners. He participated in 1,683 races: 485 win, 302 place, 210 show, 686 unplaced.

Jockey to win 4,000 races was English-born Johnny Longden, who on Fleet Driver won his 4,000th race on May 15, 1952, at Hollywood Park, Inglewood, Calif.

Jockey to win more than $3 million in purses in 1 year was William ("Bill") Hartack, Jr., who won $3,060,501 in 1957 on 1,283 mounts: 341 firsts, 208 seconds, 178 thirds. He was also the first to win $2 million in purses in one year when he won $2,343,955 in 1956 on 1,387 mounts: 347 firsts, 252 seconds, 184 thirds.

The First

Jockey to win more than $5 million in purses in 1 year was Steve Cauthen of Kentucky, whose purses on October 24, 1977, amounted to $5,009,692.

Jockey to win one hundred $100,000 stakes was Willie Shoemaker, who rode Miss Musket, a 3-year-old filly, in the Fantasy Stakes at Oaklawn Park, Hot Springs, Ark., on March 30, 1974. His time for the 1 1/16 miles was 1:44 4/5. His earnings for that race were $79,740.

Jockey to win 7 consecutive races in 1 day was Leroy Moyers, who rode 7 straight winners at Suffolk Downs, Boston, Mass., on July 4, 1967, including Four Fingers in the $11,525 Mayflower Stakes.

Jockey to win 7 races in one day was Joseph Sylvester, who on October 18, 1930, at Ravenna, Ohio, won seven out of eight races, with purses totaling $1,800, and third place in the third race.

Jockey to win the Kentucky Derby 3 times (1½ miles) was Isaac Murphy, who on May 16, 1884, rode Buchanan (2:40¼) to earn $3,990; on May 14, 1890, rode Riley (2:45) to earn $5,460; and on May 13, 1891, rode Kingman (2:52¼) to earn $4,680—in the 10th, the 16th, and the 17th Kentucky Derby at Churchill Downs, Louisville, Ky. In 1896 the distance run was changed to 1¼ miles.

Jockey to win the Kentucky Derby 5 times was Eddie Arcaro, who at Churchill Downs, Louisville, Ky., rode Lawrin (2:04 4/5) on May 7, 1938, to win $47,500 (64th derby); Whirlaway (2:01 2/5) on May 3, 1941, to win $61,275 (67th derby); Hoop Jr. (2:07) on June 9, 1945, to win $64,850 (71st derby); Citation (2:05 2/5) on May 1, 1948, to win $83,400 (74th derby); and Hill Gail (2:01 3/5) on May 3, 1952, to win $96,300 (78th derby).

Jockey to win the national riding championship four times was Willie Shoemaker, who was champion in 1950, 1953, 1954, and 1958. On December 31, 1958, he won four races at Santa Anita Park, Arcadia, Calif., including the $17,650 Los Feliz Stakes, scoring 347 victories for the year.

Jockey to win the Triple Crown twice was Eddie Arcaro, who rode Whirlaway in 1941 and Citation in 1948 to win the "Big Three": the Kentucky Derby at Churchill Downs, Ky., the Preakness at Pimlico, Md., and the Belmont Stakes at Belmont Park, Elmont, N.Y. The combined purses amounted to $150,410 in 1941, and $324,090 in 1948. The date of the last event was June 12, 1948, at Belmont Park.

Jockey (woman) to ride in a Kentucky Derby was Diane Crump of Oldsman, Fla., who rode Fathom on May 2, 1970, in the 1¼ mile 96th Kentucky Derby, Churchill Downs, Ky. In the 17-horse race, she finished fifteenth.

Jockey (woman) to ride in a pari-mutuel race on a flat-track was Diane Crump of Woodmont, Conn., who rode Bridle n' Bit in the 7th race, 1 1/8

The First

miles, at Hialeah, Fla., on February 7, 1969. Odds against her were 48 to 1. She finished 10th in a race of 12. Her first win was March 1, 1969, on Bridle n' Bit in the 8th race at Florida Downs, Tampa, Fla., 1 mile 70 yards; it paid $6.80 win, $3.80 place, $2.80 show.

Jockey (woman) to ride 2 winners in 1 day was Barbara Jo Rubin of Miami Beach, Fla., who won by 3 lengths in the 5½-furlong race on Co Zipper in the second race and the 5-furlong race on Cohesian in the eleventh race at Waterford Park, Chester, W.Va., on March 8, 1969. Both horses were owned by D. Forrest Lawson.

Jockey (woman) to win a major stakes race at a major track was Robyn Smith, who won the Paumanauk Handicap ($27,450), six furlongs, on March 1, 1973. She rode North Sea, a 4-year-old colt, winning by 4 lengths at the Aqueduct Race Track. Aqueduct, L.I., N.Y. The horse, owned by Alfred Gwynn Vanderbilt, paid $26.20 on a $2 ticket.

Jockey (woman) to win on a regular pari-mutuel flat track was Barbara Jo Rubin of Miami Beach, Fla., who rode Cohesian in the 9th race (6½ furlongs), on February 22, 1969, at the Charles Town Race Track, Charles Town, W.Va., in 1:20 1/5. She received a temporary West Virginia license on February 18, 1969.

JOHN SIMON GUGGENHEIM MEMORIAL FOUNDATION AWARD.
Photographer to receive a John Simon Guggenheim Memorial Foundation award *See* Photographer: Photographer to receive a John Simon Guggenheim Memorial Foundation award.

JOURNAL. *See* Periodical

JOURNALISM COURSE
History of journalism course was offered in 1879–1880 at the University of Missouri, Columbia, Mo. Professor David R. McAnnally, Jr., for five years taught "the history of journalism . . lectures with practical explanations of daily newspaper life. The *Spectator,* the London *Times,* the New York *Herald."*

Journalism course was given in 1869 by Professor Willard Fiske at Washington University, later Washington and Lee University, Lexington, Va. The idea was introduced by General Robert Edward Lee. A knowledge of phonography (shorthand) and telegraphy and practical experience in the university printing office were required. (*Horatio Stevens White—A Sketch of the Life and Labors of Professor Willard Fiske)*

Journalism school offering a degree in journalism was opened September 14, 1908, at the University of Missouri, Columbia, Mo. Enrollment for the school year 1908–1909 was 97: 84 men and 13 women. The first degree, a B.S.J. (Bachelor of Science in Journalism), was awarded in 1909 to Charles Arnold. The following year 5 men and 1

The First

woman were graduated. The first dean was Walter Williams, whose title was Dean and Professor of the History and Principles of Journalism.

JUDGE
Black chief justice of a federal court was Chief Justice James Benton Parsons of the Illinois Supreme Court, who became chief justice on April 18, 1975.

Black judge of a circuit court of appeals was William Henry Hastie, former governor of the U.S. Virgin Islands, who was unanimously confirmed by the Senate on July 19, 1950, for a recess appointment to the Third Judicial Circuit (Pennsylvania, New Jersey, Delaware, and the Virgin Islands). He was sworn in by Chief Judge John Biggs, Jr., in Philadelphia, Pa.

Black judge of a customs court (U.S.) was Irvin Charles Mollison of Chicago, Ill., sworn in and inducted as a judge of the United States Customs Court on November 3, 1945, in New York City.

Black judge of a district court (U.S.) in the continental United States was Judge James Benton Parsons, who was sworn in September 22, 1961, at Chicago, Ill., as a U.S. district judge for the Northern District of Illinois. His appointment had been confirmed by the U.S. Senate on August 30, 1961.

Black woman judge elected was Edith Spurlock Sampson, elected associate judge of the Municipal Court of Chicago, Ill., on November 8, 1962, and sworn in December 3, 1962. She became an associate judge of the Circuit Court of Cook County, Chicago, Ill., on January 1, 1964.

Black woman judge of a federal district court was Constance Baker Motley, nominated by President Lyndon Baines Johnson on April 4, 1966, confirmed August 30, 1966, by the Senate Judiciary Committee and sworn in at the United States Court House, Foley Square, New York City on September 9, 1966. She served in the Southern District of New York.

Black woman judge of the U.S. Court of Appeals was Amalya Lyle Kearse of New York City, who was sworn in June 27, 1979, by Chief Judge Irving Robert Kaufman at the U.S. Court of Appeals, New York City.

Chief justice (woman) of a state supreme court was Lorna Elizabeth Lockwood, who was selected by unanimous vote of the other justices on January 8, 1965, as chief justice of the Arizona Supreme Court.

Impeachment proceedings. *See* Impeachment: Impeachment of a federal judge

Judge who had served time in prison was Robert A. ("Bob") Young, who was elected to serve the term from January 3, 1977, to December 31, 1983, as judge of the Justice Court, Loomis, Calif. He had been convicted at the age of 19 for stealing a credit card out of the mail and had served 20

The First

JUDGE—Continued

months in federal prison and 4 years on parole. He was graduated from law school in 1970 and after a 2-year investigation was admitted to the bar.

Supreme Court justice. *See under* Supreme Court (U.S.)

Woman associate justice of a state supreme court was Florence Ellinwood Allen of Cleveland, Ohio, who was elected on December 16, 1922, to the Ohio Supreme Court. *(Florence Ellinwood Allen—This Constitution of Ours)*

Woman associate justice of the circuit court of appeals was Florence Ellinwood Allen, nominated March 6, 1934, by President Franklin Delano Roosevelt to fill the vacancy brought about by the death of Judge Smith Hickenlooper. She was sworn in April 9, 1934. The oath was administered by Presiding Judge Charles Moorman in the presence of his two associates on the bench, Judge Xen Hicks of Knoxville, Tenn., and Judge Charles Caspar Simons of Detroit, Mich. She served in the sixth judicial court. *(Florence Ellington Allen—To Do Justly)*

Woman associate justice on the federal bench was Genevieve Rose Cline of the U.S. Customs Court, New York, who was appointed on May 4, 1928, by President Calvin Coolidge.

Woman judge (black) was Jane Matilda Bolin, who on July 22, 1939, was appointed judge of the Court of Domestic Relations by Mayor Fiorello La Guardia of New York City.

Woman judge of a juvenile court was Kathryn Sellers, judge of the Juvenile Court of the District of Columbia, Washington, D.C., who was appointed October 15, 1918, and reappointed for a second term on March 6, 1925, and who served until her successor was confirmed by the Senate on February 15, 1934. From 1913 to 1923 Mary Margaret Bartelme was assistant to the judge of the Juvenile Court of Cook County, Chicago, Ill., but she was not appointed as a judge of the juvenile court until later.

Woman judge of the Surrogates Court was Marie Macri Lambert, elected November 8, 1977, who began serving January 1, 1978, in the New York County Surrogates Court, New York City.

Woman judge to sentence a man to death was Florence Ellinwood Allen, a judge of the Court of Common Pleas of the County of Cuyahoga, Cleveland, Ohio. She tried Frank Motto, who had been indicted on a charge of murder in the first degree, and who, after being convicted by a jury on May 14, 1921, was sentenced by Judge Allen to be electrocuted August 20, 1921. The sentence was carried out.

Woman justice of the peace was Esther Hobart Morris of South Pass City, Wyo., who was appointed February 17, 1870, by the county commis-

The First

sioners. She served 8½ months. *(Pacific Northwest Quarterly—Vol. 44, No. 2—April 1953)*

Woman trial judge of the U.S. Court of Claims was Charlotte P. Murphy of Bethesda, Md., sworn in August 6, 1973, by Associate Justice Lewis Franklin Powell, Jr., of the Supreme Court of the United States.

JUDGE ADVOCATE. *See* Air Force officer: Judge advocate general of the U.S. Air Force; Army officer: Judge advocate; Naval officer: Judge advocate of the Navy

JUMP. *See* High jump; Long jump

JUNCTION TRANSISTOR. *See* Transistor

JUNIOR CHAMBER OF COMMERCE. *See under* Chamber of Commerce

JUNIOR HIGH SCHOOL. *See under* High school

"JUNIOR YEAR ABROAD." *See under* College

JURY

Grand jury convened September 1, 1635, at Newe Towne (now Cambridge), Mass., to investigate accusations against persons charged with crime and indict them for trial before a petit jury if there was sufficient evidence.

Jury composed of women was ordered by the Generall Provinciall Court at the session held September 22, 1656, at Patuxent, Md. The jury was composed of seven married women and four single women who tried Judith Catchpole for the murder of her child. The order read: "Whereas Judith Catchpole being brought before the Court upon Suspicion of Murdering a Child which She is accused to have brought forth, and denying the fact or that She ever had Child, the Court hath ordered that a Jury of able women be Impannelled and to give in their Verdict to the best of their Judgment whether She the said Judith hath ever had a Child or not." The jury's verdict was "not guilty" and the court ordered that "the said Judith Catchpole be acquitted of that charge unless further evidence appear." *(Maryland Archives. Vol. 10)*

Mixed jury (white and black) was the grand jury that indicted Jefferson Davis. The petit jury in this case was the second mixed jury. Davis, his wife, and their four children were captured at Irwinville, Ga., May 10, 1865, by Lieutenant Colonel Benjamin Dudley Pritchard, commanding the Fourth Michigan Cavalry. Davis was placed in jail and indicted for treason. In 1867 he was released on bond. The case was finally brought to trial on December 3, 1868, in the Circuit Court of the United States at Richmond, Va., before Judges Salmon Portland Chase and John Curtiss Underwood. The case was dismissed because of President Andrew Johnson's general amnesty proclamation, December 25, 1868. The charge was dropped by the district attorney on February 15, 1869. *(John William Jones—Memorial Volume of Jefferson Davis)*

The First

Woman grand jury foreman was Julia Isabelle Sims of Newark, N.J., who served on the Federal Grand Jury in the United States District Court for the District of New Jersey in session at Newark from April 6, 1937, to October 19, 1937. Judge William Clark, judge of the United States District Court, District of New Jersey, presided.

JURY SCHOOL

Jury school was opened January 16, 1937, by Federal Judge William Clark, United States District Court, District of New Jersey, in the Post Office Building, Newark, N.J. The first class was attended by 150 men and women. About 2,500 persons, mostly women, attended the course, designed to acquaint citizens with courtroom procedure and duties of jurors in considering evidence. The school was disbanded December 10, 1937.

JUSTICE, SUPREME COURT (U.S.). *See under* Supreme Court (U.S.)

JUSTICE DEPARTMENT (U.S.) was created June 22, 1870, by an act (16 Stat. L. 162) to establish a Department of Justice with the Attorney General as its head. The office of the Attorney General was created by act of September 24, 1789 (1 Stat. L. 73). The department was organized July 1, 1870, and all the law offices of the government placed under one head. *(Albert George Langeluttig—The Department of Justice of the United States)*

JUSTICE OF THE PEACE. *See* Judge

JUSTICE OF THE SUPREME COURT (impeachment proceedings). *See* Impeachment: Impeachment proceedings against a justice of the Supreme Court of the United States

JUTE CULTURE was introduced by the U.S. Department of Agriculture in 1869–1870. A quantity of seed was imported from France and India and planted from the Carolinas to Texas. *(Charles Richards Dodge—Fiber Investigations, 1896. Report No. 8)*

JUVENILE COURT. *See* Court

JUVENILE COURT JUDGE (woman). *See* Judge

JUVENILE REFORMATORY. *See* Prison: Reformatory for juvenile delinquents under legislative control

---

K

KAPOK was commercially introduced by the Netherlands, May 1, 1893, at the formal opening of the World's Columbian Exposition, Chicago, Ill. *(Stephen J. Zand—Kapok)*

KARAKUL SHEEP. *See* Animals: Sheep (Karakul fur sheep)

The First

KEEDOOZLE STORE. *See under* Business

KENAF FIBER planting of commercial importance was attempted in July 1951 at Belle Glade, Fla., by the American Kenaf Fiber Corporation. One and a half million pounds were harvested that year and sold at 30 cents a pound to the Commodity Credit Corporation for the Munitions Board. Kenaf is a ten-foot plant whose soft fibers are a substitute for jute and burlap. *(Fortune. December 1951)*

KENNEL

Hotel for dogs was the Kennelworth, 116 rooms, opened November 12, 1975, in New York City, by Leo Wiener. The rooms have different color schemes and are built around a circular court. They measured 28, 37, and 55 feet square and rented for $10, $12, and $14 a day, respectively. They are air conditioned, the air changing several times every hour. Proof of distemper and rabies shots was required.

KENNEL SHOW. *See* Dog show

KENTUCKY DERBY. *See* Horse race

KEROSENE. *See* Oil

KETTLE, BRASS. *See* Brass kettles

KIDNAPPING

Death penalty for kidnapping was mandated by the Circuit Court of Kansas City, Mo., on July 27, 1933. Walter H. McGee was found guilty by a jury of having kidnapped Mary McElroy, daughter of the city manager of Kansas City. The prosecutor was Assistant County Prosecutor Michael W. O'Hern. The congressional act of May 18, 1934 (48 Stat. L. 781), "whosoever shall knowingly transport or cause to be transported in interstate or foreign commerce . . . shall be convicted of death" was held to apply to kidnapping.

Kidnapping is recorded in a letter dated July 8, 1524, addressed to Francis I, king of France, by Giovanni da Verrazano, the Florentine explorer. It chronicled his discoveries in America and was sent from Dieppe, France. Verrazano relates that in 1524 his crew "tooke a childe [Indian] from . . . [an] olde woman to bring into France, and going about to take . . . [a] young woman which was very beautiful and of tall stature, they could not possibly, for the great outcries that she made, bring her to the sea; and especially having great woods to pass through and being farre from the ship, we purposed to leave her behinde, beareing away the childe only." *(James Carson Brevoort—Verrazano the Navigator)*

Kidnapping for ransom occurred July 1, 1874, in Germantown, Pa. Charles Brewster Ross, a four-year-old, was kidnapped and held for $20,000 ransom. *(Edward Dean Sullivan—The Snatch Racket)*

KIDNEY TRANSPLANTING. *See* Surgical operation

KILN, BRICK. *See* Brick kiln

KINDERGARTEN

American kindergarten was established in Boston, Mass., in 1868 by Elizabeth Palmer Peabody, who employed the Friedrich Froebel system of education as used in Germany. A kindergarten group had been formed in December of 1856 by Margarethe Meyer Schurz, wife of General Carl Schurz, in her home at Watertown, Wis. The first group consisted of 6 children, 2 of whom were her own. *(Nina Catherine Vandewalker—The Kindergarten in American Education)*

Free kindergarten was the Florence Kindergarten, which opened January 3, 1876, in Florence, Mass., in the home of its founder, Samuel Lapham Hill. The school is now known as the Hill Institute. *(Hill Institute Bulletin, 1930–1931)*

Kindergarten for crippled children. *See under* Cripples

Kindergarten for the blind was established by the Perkins Institution and Massachusetts School for the Blind in Roxbury, Mass. The kindergarten was authorized March 15, 1887, and was incorporated as a separate department of the school on March 30, 1887. The kindergarten was dedicated April 19, 1887, and was opened May 2, 1887, with ten children. The plan was proposed by Michael Anagnos, who became the first director. *(First Annual Report of the Kindergarten for the Blind, September 30, 1887)*

Nursery school was established in New York City in 1827 by the Infant School Society of the City of New York, founded May 23, 1827, "to relieve parents of the laboring classes from the care of their children while engaged in the vocations by which they live, and provide for the children a protection from the weather, from idleness and the contamination of evil example besides affording them the means of early and efficient education." Children from 18 months to 5 years of age were accommodated, 448 receiving attention in two years. Joanna Bethune was the first directress and Hannah L. Murray, the first directress and Hannah L. Murray, the first treasurer.

Public school kindergarten that was successful was authorized August 26, 1873, by the St. Louis, Mo., Board of Education and opened September 1873 with an enrollment of 42 in the Des Peres School. Susan Elizabeth Blow was the teacher. Dr. William Torrey Harris was the superintendent of schools. *(Annual Report of the Board of Education of St. Louis for the Year 1878–1879)*

KINDERGARTEN MANUAL was Edward Wiebe's *The Paradise of Childhood: A Manual for Self-Instruction in Friedrich Froebel's Educational Principles, and a Practical Guide to Kinder-Gartners,* printed in 1869 by Milton Bradley &

Company, Springfield, Mass. It was intended primarily for kindergarten teachers. Much of the material was translated from the German of Froebel, Marenholtz, Goldammer, and Morgenstern. The manual contained 86 pages and 74 full-page plates of illustrations.

KING

King and Queen of Great Britain to visit the United States. *See* Visiting celebrities: King and Queen of Great Britain

King born in the United States was Bhumibol Adulyadej (Phumiphon Aduldet), King of Thailand, born December 5, 1927, at Mount Auburn Hospital, Cambridge, Mass. He was crowned May 5, 1950, as King Rama IX. He was the son of Prince Mahidol.

King (reigning) to visit the United States. *See under* Visiting celebrities

"King" to exercise the authority of king and high priest in the United States was James J. Strang, a Mormon elder, who settled in 1847 in St. James on Big Beaver Island, Beaver Islands, Mich. In 1852 he was elected to the Michigan legislature. The colony he established was attacked by a mob of fishermen, and Strang was assassinated, or June 16, 1856.

KING COBRA SNAKES. *See under* Cobra

KLIEG LIGHT LIGHTING UNIT. *See under* Electric lighting

KNIFE, BOWIE. *See* Bowie knife

KNIGHTHOOD

Knighthood conferred in America was awarded Major General Jeffery Amherst for his campaign against the French and for his capture of Montreal on September 8, 1760. He was awarded the thanks of Parliament, and on May 26, 1761, George II made him a knight of the Bath, Sir Charles Cotterel-Dormer serving as his proxy. Major Robert Monckton, governor of New York, conferred the award in a special ceremony October 25, 1761, at Staten Island, N.Y. *(Lawrence Shaw Mayo—Jeffery Amherst)*

Knighthood conferred on a native-born American was awarded at Windsor Castle, London, England, on June 28, 1687, by King James II to William Phips [Phipps] for his fair distribution of 34 tons of silver, gold and jewels valued at $1,350,000 which he salvaged from a Spanish ship sunk near the Bahama Islands that had lain in the sea for 44 years. His share amounted to $72,000. He was born February 2, 1651, at Pemaquid (now Bristol), Maine. *(Alice Lounsberry—Sir William Phipps)*

Knighthood conferred on a native-born American for military leadership was awarded on September 23, 1745, to Sir William Pepperell, noted American general. He was made a baronet by Great Britain because of his military exploit of

The First

April 29, 1745, when he undertook the siege and reduction of Louisburg, a French fortress on the island of Cape Breton, Nova Scotia, built at a cost of $6 million. The siege lasted 49 days and the fortress capitulated June 16, 1745. *(Massachusetts Historical Society, Pepperell Papers)*

KNIGHTS OF COLUMBUS originated under a special charter granted by Connecticut on March 29, 1882. It was founded as a fraternal benefit association for Catholic men by the Reverend Michael Joseph McGivney and nine parishioners of St. Mary's Roman Catholic Church in New Haven, Conn., on January 16, 1882.

KNIGHTS OF LABOR. *See* Labor union: Labor organization to admit workmen other than craft workmen

KNIGHTS OF PYTHIAS brotherhood was founded in Washington, D.C., by Justus Henry Rathbone and 12 associates on February 19, 1864, Washington Lodge No. 1 being the first lodge organized. The Grand Lodge of the District of Columbia was formed April 8, 1864, with Joseph Theophilus Kirk Plant as grand chancellor. The Supreme Lodge of the Knights of Pythias of the World was convened August 11, 1868, in Washington, D.C., and the constitution adopted November 10, 1868, in Wilmington, Del. It was incorporated August 5, 1870, in the District of Columbia. The order is founded on the classical story of Damon and Pythias and advocates toleration in religion, obedience to law, and loyalty to government. *(Joseph Dame Weeks—History of the Knights of Pythias)*

KNIGHTS TEMPLAR. *See* Freemasons

KNITTING MACHINE (power) was put into operation in 1832 in Cohoes, N.Y., by Egberts and Bailey. The firm consisted of Egbert Egberts, Timothy Bailey, and his brother, Joshua Bailey, and was in operation until 1843 when the partnership dissolved. Timothy Bailey continued in the old plant, dividing his time between manufacturing knit goods and knit-goods machinery. *(Arthur Haynsworth Masten—History of Cohoes N.Y.)*

KNOW-NOTHING PARTY. *See* American Party

KONEL metal alloy was announced on September 9, 1929, by Dr. Erwin Foster Lowry of the research department of the Westinghouse Electric and Manufacturing Company of Pittsburgh, Pa. While the konel was red-hot, a test hammer "bounced off" the new metal, whereas steel would have been deformed under similar conditions. Konel is a combination of cobalt and nickel, from which it derives its name, and ferrotitanium, and is used among other things as a substitute for platinum in radio tubes.

KOREAN CONFLICT. *See* War (Korean)

The First

KOREAN EMBASSY. *See under* Diplomatic service

KU KLUX KLAN was established in 1865 in Pulaski, Tenn., as a social order, but became an organization for enforcing white supremacy by means of intimidation and violence, at the time black men were granted suffrage. The first grand wizard was General Nathan Bedford Forrest. Several attempts have been made to reorganize the Klan. *(Stanley Fitzgerald Horn—Invisible Empire)*

L

LABADIST COMMUNITY was established at Bohemia Manor, Md., in 1683, by the followers of Jean de Labadie, who held many tenets similar to those of the Dutch Reformed Church. The first Labadists were P. Vorstman and J. Shilders, who arrived September 23, 1679, in New Netherlands on the *Charles.* *(Jasper Danckaerts—Journal of our Voyage to New Netherland begun in the name of the Lord and for His Glory, the 8th of June 1679 and undertaken in the small flute-ship called the "Charles")*

LABEL (union label). *See* Labor union label

LABEL PATENT. *See* Patent

LABOR

See also Labor legislation; Labor relations

Chinese labor immigration. *See* Immigration: Chinese labor immigration

Labor Advisory Board (federal) was authorized June 16, 1933, under the National Industrial Recovery Act, which empowered the President to set up such administrative agencies as might be necessary to effectuate the purpose of the act. It was organized June 20, 1933, and was composed of nine members. The first chairman was Leo Wolman.

Labor antidiscrimination commission (state) was the New York State Commission Against Discrimination, appointed July 1, 1945, "to formulate policies to eliminate and prevent discrimination in employment because of race, creed, color or national origin, either by employers, labor organizations, employment agencies or other persons." It consisted of five commissioners at $10,000 a year whose terms ranged from one to five years, to be replaced upon expiration by appointments for five-year periods. The first chairman was Henry C. Turner. The commission was authorized by act of March 12, 1945 (chapter 118), signed by Governor Thomas Edmund Dewey.

Labor Board (national). *See under* Labor relations

The First

LABOR—*Continued*

Labor bureau (federal) was authorized by act of June 27, 1884 (23 Stat. L. 60), "an act to establish a Bureau of Labor." The first chief of the bureau, established in the Department of Interior, was Carroll Davidson Wright, whose title was commissioner of labor. He received $3,000 per annum. He was appointed January 31, 1885, by President Chester Alan Arthur and served until January 31, 1905. *(Gustavus Adolphus Weber—Bureau of Labor Statistics, U.S. Department of Labor)*

Labor bureau (state) was the Massachusetts Bureau of Statistics of Labor, established by Chapter 102, Acts of 1869, approved June 23, 1869, by Governor William Claflin. The duties of the bureau, under a chief and deputy, were "to collect, assort, systematize and present in annual reports to the Legislature . . . statistical details relating to all departments of labor in the Commonwealth." Henry Kemble Oliver was appointed chief July 31, 1869, at a salary of $2,500 a year. George E. McNeill was the first deputy, at a salary of $2,100 a year. *(Charles Ferris Gettemy—Massachusetts Bureau of Statistics)*

Labor congress (national) was the First Industrial Congress of the United States, which convened in New York City October 12, 1845. William E. Wait of Illinois was elected president. Although a few local meetings had been called national organizations, this was the first national congress of importance. Annual meetings were held regularly until 1856. *(New York Times. June 7, 1856)*

Labor Day. *See under* Holiday

Labor Relations Act (national). *See under* Labor relations.

National Mediation Board. *See under* Labor relations

Strike. *See under* Strike

Woman labor delegate to a national convention. *See under* Woman

LABOR BOARD. *See under* Labor relations

LABOR DAY. *See* Holiday

LABOR DEPARTMENT (U.S.)
See also Commerce and Labor Department (U.S.)

Labor Department (U.S.) was the Department of Labor, created by act of Congress of March 4, 1913 (37 Stat. L. 736). The first secretary was William Bauchop Wilson, who received $12,000 per annum. The Children's Bureau, the Bureau of Immigration, the Bureau of Naturalization, and the Bureau of Labor Statistics were all incorporated into the department. In 1913 the department was given Cabinet rank. Earlier, the congressional act of June 13, 1888 (25 Stat. L. 182), had authorized a Department of Labor under a commissioner of labor, who received $5,000 per annum.

The First

Native-born Secretary of Labor was William Nuckles Doak, who was appointed by President Herbert Hoover and sworn in December 9, 1930. He was the first secretary who was not a member of the American Federation of Labor, and the first secretary from any state except Pennsylvania. (He was born in Virginia.) *(Roger Ward Babson—Washington and the Depression Including the Career of W. N. Doak)*

Woman Secretary of Labor was Frances Perkins (Mrs. Paul Caldwell Wilson), who served from March 4, 1933, to June 30, 1945, the only Cabinet member to serve throughout the terms of Franklin Delano Roosevelt's administration.

Women's Bureau of the Labor Department was permanently organized by act of Congress on June 5, 1920 (41 Stat. L. 987), "an act to establish in the Department of Labor, a bureau to be known as the Women's Bureau." Its purpose was to formulate standards and policies to promote the welfare of wage-earning women, improve their working conditions, increase their efficiency, and advance their opportunities for profitable employment. The first director was Mary Anderson, who received an annual compensation of $5,000. *(Gustavus Adolphus Weber—The Women's Bureau)*

LABOR LAW. *See* Labor legislation

LABOR LEGISLATION
See also Labor relations

Child labor law (federal). *See under* Child labor law

Convict labor law was Act 29 of the Laws of Virginia, passed March 2, 1642, by the "Grand Assemblie at James Citty." It stated: "Be it also enacted that no person or persons whatsoever for any offence already committed or to be committed shall be hereafter adjudged to serve the collony." *(William Waller Hening—Statutes at Large of Virginia)*

Eight-hour day was advocated by local unions, such as the Machinists and Blacksmiths Union, the Molders Union, etc., in 1860. The first unified action was taken on August 20, 1866, in Baltimore, Md., by the National Labor Union at its first congress, which was attended by 77 delegates from 13 states. Industry, however, did not accede to the terms.

Eight-hour day for government laborers and mechanics was authorized by act of Congress of June 25, 1868 (15 Stat. L. 77), signed by President Andrew Johnson. It provided, among other things, that "eight hours shall constitute a day's work for all laborers, workmen, and mechanics who may be employed by or on behalf of the Government of the United States."

Factory inspection law was passed April 30, 1879, by Massachusetts, Chapter 305, Acts of 1879. It provided that the governor appoint two or more

The First

of the district police to act as inspectors of factories and public buildings. *(Public Document No. 52, Report of the Chief of the Massachusetts District Police for the year ending December 31, 1885, including the result of the Inspection of Factories and Public Buildings)*

Forty-hour-week law (federal) was the Public Contract Act of 1936 "to provide conditions for the purchase of supplies and the making of contracts by the United States" (49 Stat. L. 2036), approved June 30, 1936. Workers on government contracts over $10,000 (after September 28, 1936) were required to receive overtime compensation at the rate of not less than time and one half for hours worked in excess of 40, also overtime in excess of 8 hours in any one day, if such compensation yielded a greater amount than on the weekly 40-hour basis. Workers were not to be paid less than the prevailing minimum wage of industry and locality. The act was known as the [David Ignatius] Walsh-[Arthur Daniel] Healy Act.

Labor discrimination law (state) prohibiting the employer from discriminating in matters of employment against members of trade unions was "an act in relation to the employment of labor by corporations," Chapter 222, Laws of 1894 of New Jersey, approved May 15, 1894. Violation was subject to a fine not to exceed $500 or three months' imprisonment.

Labor law prohibiting discrimination in the payment of wages because of sex was the Equal Pay Act of 1963, enacted June 10, 1963 (77 Stat.L.56), "to prohibit discrimination on account of sex in the payment of wages by employers engaged in commerce or in the production of goods for commerce."

Labor law prohibiting the employment of women was "An act providing for the health and safety of persons employed in coal mines," passed and approved by Illinois, May 28, 1879, effective July 1, 1879. It prohibited the employment of women in mines in Illinois. *(Session Laws of Illinois of 1879. Section 6, p. 206)*

Labor law regulating fair labor standards was "an act to provide for the establishment of fair labor standards in employment in and affecting interstate commerce" enacted June 25, 1938 (52 Stat. L. 1060). It was known as the Fair Labor Standards Act of 1938. One of the act's provisions established the first federal minimum wage law.

Labor law regulating the working hours of women was passed by Ohio, March 29, 1852 (Ohio Laws, Volume 50, page 187). It regulated "the hours of manual labor of children under eighteen, and women." This law fixed ten hours per day as the maximum number of working hours. It was repealed in 1887, when a new code relative to women and children was adopted.

The First

Labor Relations Act (national) *See under* Labor relations

Minimum wage law was enacted by Massachusetts, June 4, 1912 (Acts and Resolves, 1912, Chapter 706, pages 780–84), to take effect July 1, 1913. It established a Minimum Wage Commission of three, one of whom might be a woman, to be appointed by the governor with the advice of the Council. Although Massachusetts passed the first act, Oregon in advance of all other states set up an administrative body to carry out the provisions of an act of February 17, 1913, which provided for the appointment, within 30 days, of a Welfare Commission to consist of three members, one representing the employer, one the employee and one the public (Sessions Laws of Oregon, 1913, Chapter 62, pages 92-9). *(U.S. Department of Labor—Development of Minimum Wage Laws in the United States 1912–1927)*

Minimum wage law (city) for public contract work enacted by a municipality was the City Contracts Minimum Wage law that was approved by Mayor Robert Ferdinand Wagner of New York City on December 29, 1961. It became effective January 28, 1962. It applied to "every contract for or on behalf of the city for the manufacture, furnishing or purchase of supplies, material or equipment, or for the furnishing of work, labor or services, and entered into by public letting founded in sealed bids."

Minimum wage law (federal). *See* Labor law regulating fair labor standards, above

National Mediation Board. *See under* Labor relations

Ten-hour-day law was section 20 of Chapter 488, Laws of 1847 of New Hampshire, which stated that "in all contracts relating to labor, ten hours actual labor shall be taken to be a day's work unless otherwise agreed by the parties." It was passed July 9, 1847, by a majority of 144, and went into effect September 15, 1847. As a result of the bargaining provision, the law was ineffective. *(Florence Patteson Smith—Chronological Development of Labor Legislation for Women in the United States)*

Women's equal employment legislation was passed by Illinois and approved by Governor John McAuley Palmer on March 22, 1872. The act, which went into effect July 1, 1872, provided that "no person shall be precluded or debarred from any occupation or employment (except military) on account of sex; Provided that this act shall not be construed to affect the eligibility of any person to an elective office. Nothing in this act shall be construed as requiring any female to work on streets or roads, or serve on juries. All laws inconsistent with this act are hereby repealed." *(Public Laws of the State of Illinois, 27th General Assembly, 1871–72)*

The First

LABOR ORGANIZATION. *See* Labor union

LABOR PAPER was *The Man,* published in New York City, February 18, 1834, by George Henry Evans. He advocated free homesteads, equal rights for women, and abolition of all laws governing collection of and imprisonment for debt. The *Daily Sentinel,* published February 15, 1830, in New York City was sympathetic to labor.

LABOR PARTY (political)
See also Farmer Labor Party; Greenback Labor Party

Labor party (national) was the Labor Reform Party, which was formed at a national convention held at Columbus, Ohio, February 22, 1872. The presidential candidate was David Davis of Illinois, who received but one electoral vote in the 1872 election. Joel Parker of New Jersey was the vice presidential candidate. Both candidates declined to run, but received popular votes nevertheless. *(Harry Edward Pratt—David Davis)*

Labor party (state) was the Workingmen's Party, which was organized in Philadelphia, Pa., in July 1828. The first convention was held on August 25, 1828. Only local Pennsylvania candidates were nominated at a meeting which was held in October of the same year. *(Philadelphia Gazette, Aug. 27, 1828)*

LABOR REFORM PARTY. *See* Labor party (political); Labor party (national)

LABOR RELATIONS
See also Arbitration; Strike

Labor Board (national) was authorized August 5, 1933, under authority of the National Industrial Recovery Act (48 Stat. L. 195), June 16, 1933, "to encourage national industrial recovery, to foster fair competition and to provide for the construction of certain public works." The board was organized August 5, 1933, and was originally composed of seven members. It ceased to exist July 9, 1934. The first chairman was Senator Robert Ferdinand Wagner. Its purpose was to mediate disputes or controversies between employers and employees arising through different interpretations of the President's Reemployment Agreement.

Labor dispute in which the Taft-Hartley law was invoked was between the American Federation of Labor Atomic Trades and Labor Council and the Oak Ridge National Laboratory, Oak Ridge, Tenn. President Harry S. Truman invoked the law. On March 19, 1948, Federal Judge George Caldwell Taylor at Knoxville, Tenn., issued an injunction to the Justice Department that restrained 900 members of the union from leaving their jobs on a walkout for an 80-day period, thus averting a strike by a difference of 7 hours.

The First

Labor Relations Act (national) was approved July 5, 1935 (49 Stat. L. 449), "to diminish the causes of labor disputes burdening or obstructing interstate and foreign commerce, to create a National Labor Relations Board, and for other purposes." The board consisted of Joseph Warren Madden, chairman, John Michael Carmody, and Edwin Seymour Smith, appointed August 24, 1935, and confirmed by the Senate August 27, 1935. The first meeting was held September 4, 1935.

National Labor Relations Board black member was Howard Jenkins, Jr., of Colorado, sworn in August 29, 1963, at Washington, D.C., by Supreme Court Justice Arthur Joseph Goldberg.

National Labor Relations Board woman chairman was Betty Southard Murphy of Virginia, who was appointed by President Gerald Rudolph Ford on January 8, 1975, and sworn in on February 18, 1975, at Washington, D.C., for the five-year term.

National Mediation Board was created by an act to amend the Railway Labor Act approved June 21, 1934 (48 Stat. L. 1185), to take the place of the U.S. Board of Mediation provided for by the act of May 20, 1926 (44 Stat. L. 577). The new board was organized July 21, 1934, "to avoid any interruption to commerce or to the operation of any carrier engaged therein, . . . to provide for the prompt and orderly settlement of all disputes concerning rates of pay, rules or working conditions." Dr. William Morris Leiserson was the first chairman.

LABOR RELATIONS SCHOOL. *See* Industrial and labor relations school

LABOR UNION
See also Trade association; also *see under* specific profession, e.g., Actors' union, Librarians union

Craft labor union contract between employer and organized labor was effected in 1799 by the Federal Society of Journeymen Cordwainers (shoemakers) of Philadelphia, Pa. After a strike of ten weeks, the employers acceded to their demands. *(Augusta Emile Galster—Labor Movement in the Shoe Industry)*

Craft labor union (local) was that of Philadelphia shoemakers. They organized in 1792, but the union existed for so short a period that its name is not even known. The shoemakers again organized in Philadelphia in 1794 and formed the Federal Society of Journeymen Cordwainers. They maintained their existence as such until the date of their trial in 1806 for conspiracy. *(John Rogers Commons—History of Labour in the United States.)*

Labor organization was authorized on October 18, 1648, when the "shoomakers of Boston" were permitted "to assemble and meete together in Boston, at such time and times as they shall appoynt, who being so assembled, they, or the great

The First

est number of them, shall have powre to chuse a master and two wardens, with fowre or six associats, a clarke, a sealer, a searcher, and a beadle. . . . " Similar permission was also extended to coopers. *(Nathaniel Bradstreet Shurtleff— Records of the Governor and Company of the Massachusetts Bay in New England)*

Labor organization to admit workmen other than craft workmen was the Noble Order of the Knights of Labor, a secret society which admitted "sojourners" on October 20, 1870. It was founded in Philadelphia, Pa., on December 9, 1869, by six men, one of whom was Uriah Smith Stevens, a tailor, who became its first Master Workman. Membership was originally restricted to garment cutters. Six candidates were proposed and elected on December 30, 1869. The first regular officers were elected January 6, 1870. The first annual report, on January 5, 1871, showed 69 members. *(Terence Vincent Powderly—Thirty Years of Labor 1859–1889)*

Labor union legalization (state) was "an act relative to persons combining and encouraging other persons to combine," Chapter 28, Laws of 1883, of New Jersey, approved February 14, 1883. It provided that combinations organized to persuade workers to enter or leave employment were not unlawful.

Labor union (national) of importance was the American Federation of Labor, which was organized in Pittsburgh, Pa., in 1881 under the name of "The Federation of Organized Trades and Labor Unions." It adopted the present title December 8, 1886, in Columbus, Ohio, at a meeting attended by 25 officers of national craft unions representing over 300,000 members. *(George Gorham Groat— An Introduction to the Study of Organized Labor in America)*

Labor union to nominate its own political candidates was the Mechanics Union, which nominated candidates for the New York State Assembly in 1784.

Labor union to nominate its own political candidates and win an election was the New York Working Men's Party, whose candidate, Ebenezer Ford, president of the Carpenter's Union, was elected to the New York State Assembly on November 7, 1829. Ford polled 6,166 votes. A meeting to form a Mechanic and Working Men's Ticket was held April 28, 1829. *(Working Man's Advocate. Nov. 7, 1829)*

Union organization of trades in a city was the Mechanics Union of Trade Associations, which was organized in Philadelphia, Pa., in 1827. Invitations to join were sent to "those trades who are as yet destitute of trade societies." They were also urged to "organize and send delegates as soon as possible." *(Earl Everett Cummins—Labor Problem in the United States)*

The First

Woman labor delegate. *See under* Woman

Women's labor organization was the United Tailoresses Society of New York, a protective association formed by women tailors in 1825 in New York City. In June 1831 they went on strike for an increase in wages. About 600 women remained out four or five weeks.

Women's labor organization (national) was the Daughters of St. Crispin, an organization of women shoe operators. Their first convention was held at Lynn, Mass., July 28, 1869. The first president was Carrie Wilson of Lynn, Mass., and the first secretary was Allie Jacques, also of Lynn. When 5,000 male shoe operators struck at Lynn in March 1860, their ranks were augmented by 1,000 women shoe workers.

LABOR UNION LABEL was adopted by the Cigar Makers' International Union and first came into use in San Francisco, Calif., in 1874. The label was adopted to combat the menace to free native labor of the Chinese coolies that were being brought into the state of California. This label was furnished free to all native manufacturers. The present blue label of the Cigar Makers' International Union was adopted in 1880 at the 13th convention of the organization held in Chicago, Ill. This label is issued free of charge to all manufacturers who operate strictly union factories. In 1869 the Carpenters' Eight Hour League of San Francisco stamped the lumber produced by planing mills working eight hours to differentiate it from that produced by the ten-hour mills. *(I. M. Ornburgh— History of Union Labels, Shop Cards and Service Buttons)*

LABORATORY. *See under* specific type of laboratory, e.g., Chemical laboratory, Health laboratory, Zoological laboratory

LABORATORY MANUAL, CHEMICAL. *See* Chemical laboratory manual

LABORSAVING DEVICE approved by a labor organization was the Autoplate stereotype platemaking machine, invented by Henry Alexander Wise Wood, which was approved in 1900 by the Stereotypers' Union. It dispensed with the handling of large quantities of molten metal type containing poisonous antimony and lead.

LACROSSE ASSOCIATION (intercollegiate) was the Intercollegiate Lacrosse Association, organized March 11, 1882, in Princeton, N.J., with Columbia, Harvard, New York University, and Princeton as charter members. Each college team was scheduled to play one game with every other member. George William Gilmore of Princeton was president and Dunbar Ferdinand Haasis of Columbia vice president. *(Frank Presbrey—Athletics at Princeton: A History)*

The First

LAFAYETTE ESCADRILLE AVIATOR KILLED. *See* Aviation—Pilot: American pilot killed while serving in the Lafayette Escadrille

LAGER BEER. *See* Beer

LAMINATED AUTOMOBILE. *See* Automobile: Plastic laminated fiberglass-body sports car

LAMP
Electric lamp. *See under* Electric lighting

Oil lamp for burning kerosene was developed in 1857 by A. C. Ferris and Company, later the Tarentum Oil, Salt and Coal Company.

LAND ANNEXATION. *See* Territorial expansion: Annexation of territory

LAND BANK. *See* Bank: Joint stock land bank

LAND GRANT
District land office opened July 2, 1800, in Steubenville, Ohio, with David Hoge as the first registrar. It was established under the act of May 10, 1800, which also authorized other district land offices in Cincinnati, Chillicothe, and Marietta, Ohio.

Land grant was authorized by the act of the Continental Congress of August 14, 1776. The act offered to make citizens of deserters from the British Army (Hessians and British) and tendered each deserter, or his heirs, to be held by him or them in absolute property, 50 acres of unappropriated land in certain states. On August 27, 1776, a similar act was passed offering terms to officers to encourage them to desert the British forces.

Land grant college for blacks. *See under* College

Land grant legislation. *See* Agricultural land grant

Land grant to schools by the Continental Congress was authorized by an ordinance of May 20, 1785: "There shall be reserved the lot No. 16 of every township for the maintenance of public schools within said township." This applied to the Western Reserve and other unsurveyed lands to the west. A new system of surveying was established, the land being laid out in townships 6 miles square and the townships subdivided into 36 numbered sections, each a mile square. Section No. 16 was popularly known as the "school section."

Land subsidy for internal improvements was granted April 30, 1802 (2 Stat. L. 173), "an act to enable the people of the eastern division of the territory northwest of the river Ohio to form a constitution and state government, and for the admission of such state into the union on an equal footing with the original states." It authorized Ohio to appropriate 1/20 of the net proceeds of the funds received from the sale of public lands to the laying out and making of public roads.

The First

Railroad land grant of importance was authorized by act of September 20, 1850 (9 Stat. L. 466), "an act granting the right of way and making a grant of land to the states of Illinois, Mississippi and Alabama in aid of the construction of a railroad from Chicago to Mobile." Illinois received 2,595,133 acres of land, which were transferred to the Illinois Central Railroad Company. The Illinois Central Railroad broke ground on December 23, 1851, and completed the first 60-mile section on May 16, 1853, from La Salle to Bloomington, Ill. *(Howard Gray Brownson—History of the Illinois Central Railroad to 1870)*

Special land grant to an individual was the act of May 17, 1796 (1 Stat. L. 464), "an act providing for the sale of the lands of the United States in the territory northwest of the River Ohio, and above the mouth of the Kentucky River." Congress granted Ebenezer Zane three tracts of land in Ohio, each one mile square, to operate ferries—one on the Muskingum River, one on the Sciota, and one on the Hockhocking. These grants were confirmed and patented to Zane on February 14, 1800, in return for his activities in opening Zane's "trail" or "trace" in 1797, about 200 miles long from Wheeling, W.Va., through Ohio to Maysville, then known as Limestone, Kentucky.

Special land grant to a foreigner was enacted on March 3, 1803 (2 Stat. L. 236), and authorized the Secretary of War to issue land warrants to Major General Lafayette (Marie Joseph Paul Yves Roch Gilbert du Motier, Marquis de Lafayette) for 11,520 acres which at his option were to be located, surveyed, and patented in conformity with the provisions of the act regulating the grants of land appropriated for military services.

State aid to railroads. *See under* Railroad

University founded by a federal land grant. *See under* College

LAND MINES or "booby traps" were invented by Captain Gabriel Jones Rains and were used against the Seminole Indians in 1840. They were also employed in the retreat from Yorktown, May 3, 1862, by Rains's Brigade under Major General John Bankhead Magruder, but "land torpedoes" were not considered "a proper or effective method of war" and were outlawed. They were permitted at river defenses where use of torpedoes was "clearly admissible." *(Douglas Southall Freeman —Lee's Lieutenants)*

LAND OFFICE
General Land Office (federal) was established in the Department of the Treasury by act of April 25, 1812 (2 Stat. L. 716). The salary of the commissioner was $2,250 a year.

Land Office was established in 1789 by Oliver Phelps and Nathaniel Gorham, who purchased 2,-600,000 acres in the "Great American Wilderness" at Canandaigua, N.Y., for resale to settlers. Wil-

The First

liam Walker was the agent. *(Charles Francis Milliken—History of Ontario County)*

LAND PREEMPTION ACT (federal) was enacted March 3, 1801 (2 Stat. L. 112), giving the right of preemption to certain persons who had contracted with John Cleves Symmes, or his associates, for lands lying along the Miami River. These persons were living upon the lands once within the Symmes tract but were not included in the patent for the reduced area, which he finally obtained. Settlers received preference over persons desiring to purchase and hold for investment or speculation. *(Thomas Corwin Donaldson—The Public Domain)*

LAND RESERVATION. *See* Forest reserve

LAND SALE ORDINANCE (general) for the sale of national land, was passed May 20, 1785, and provided for the sale of land in the Northwest Territory. *(Burke Aaron Hinsdale—The Old Northwest)*

LANDSCAPE ARCHITECT. *See* Architect

LANDSCAPE ARCHITECTURE COURSE FOR WOMEN. *See under* Architectural school

LANGUAGE
See also American language

Plain language law was "an act to amend the general obligations law, in relation to plain language requirements for certain agreements involving consumer transactions or to which a consumer is a party for the lease of space to be occupied for residential purposes (for personal family or household purposes)" enacted May 31, 1978, by the state of New York, effective November 2, 1978. *(State of New York. 1978 Session Laws —Chapter 199)*

LANGUAGE INSTRUCTION
Foreign-language course broadcast. *See under* Radio broadcast

French instruction was offered in 1733 at Harvard College, Cambridge, Mass. Louis Langloiserie was appointed instructor. *(Benjamin Pierce—A History of Harvard University)*

German instruction in a college was given by William Creamer, at the University of Pennsylvania, Philadelphia, Pa., from 1754 to July 11, 1755.

Italian instruction in a college was given at the College of William and Mary, Williamsburg, Va., in 1799 by Carlo Bellini, professor of modern languages. *(William and Mary Quarterly. October 1905)*

Modern-language school in a college was established by the College of William and Mary, Williamsburg, Va., in 1779. *(Bulletin of the College of William and Mary in Virginia)*

The First

LANTERN SLIDE. *See* Magic lantern: Magic lantern slides (glass-plate)

LAPIDARY. *See* Gem-cutting machine

LARYNGOLOGICAL SOCIETY (national). *See* Medical society

LARYNGOLOGY CLINIC. *See* Medical clinic

LARYNGOLOGY INSTRUCTION. *See* Medical instruction

LARYNGOLOGY PERIODICAL. *See* Medical periodical

LARYNGOPHONE (throat microphone) commercially manufactured was made by the Western Electric Company, New York City, in 1941, sale being confined exclusively to the armed forces of democratic powers. Patents were not applied for on the newer models. *(Philips Technical Review. Vol. 5, No. 1. January 1940)*

LASERS
Patent on lasers was No. 2,929,922 granted March 22, 1960, on "masers and maser communication system" to Arthur L. Schawlow of Madison, N.J., and Charles Hard Townes of New York City and assigned to the Bell Telephone Laboratories, Inc., New York City. The application was filed July 30, 1958. (*Maser* is an acronym for microwave amplification by stimulated emission of radiation.)

LATERAL CURVATURE OF THE HORIZON PHOTOGRAPH. *See* Photograph: Photograph showing the lateral curvature of the horizon

LATHE used for fashioning irregular forms was a profile lathe, patented by Thomas Blanchard of Middlebury, Conn., on September 6, 1819, a "machine for manufacturing gun stocks." The lathe did the work of 13 operators and made possible a great reduction in woodworking prices. *(Asa Holman Waters—Biographical Sketch of Thomas Blanchard)*

LATIN BOOK written in New England was *Responsio ad totam quaestionum syllogen a clarissimo viro domino Guilielmo Apollonio, ecclesiae middleburgensis pastore, propositam,* written by John Norton and published in 1648 in London, England. The preface was by John Cotton.

LATIN GRAMMAR. *See* Grammar

LAUNDRY
Commercial power laundry came into existence in 1851 when the Contra Costa Laundry was established in Leona Heights, Oakland, Calif. A 10 h.p. donkey engine bought from a ship captain served as a crude form of washing machine. *(California Journal of Development. Vol. 25. July 1935)*

Laundry was established in 1835 by Independence Starks, a manufacturer of Troy, N.Y., at 66 North Second Street, to wash and press the products of his own factory and of nearby collar mak-

The First

LAUNDRY—Continued
ers. *(Arthur James Weise—Troy, One Hundred Years 1789–1889)*

Rough-dry laundry service was started by W. M. Barnes in 1892 in Philadelphia, Pa., and in 1893 in Pittsburgh, Pa.

Washing machine for public use (washateria). *See under* Washing machine

LAW CODIFICATION (state) was the Louisiana Code of 1825, *A System of Penal Law, Divided into Code of Crimes and Punishments, Code of Procedure, Code of Evidence, Code of Reform and Prison Discipline, Beside a Book of Definitions.* On March 14, 1822, the legislature appointed L. Moreau Lislet, Edward Livingston, and Pierre Derbigny to remodel the code of 1808. The code was approved April 12, 1824 and promulgated June 13, 1825. *(Charles Havens Hunt—Life of Edward Livingston)*

LAW DEGREES. *See under* Degrees (academic and honorary)

LAW DICTIONARY (American) was John Bouvier's *A Law Dictionary Adapted to the Constitution and Laws of the United States of America and of the Several States of the American Union With References to the Civil and Other Systems of Foreign Law.* It was published in two volumes in Philadelphia, Pa., in 1839. *(Frederick Charles Hicks—Materials and Methods of Legal Research)*

LAW DIGEST was *An Abridgement of the Laws of the United States or a complete digest of all such acts of Congress as concern the United States at large, to which is added an appendix containing all existing treaties, the Declaration of Independence, the Articles of Confederation, the rules and articles for the government of the army and the ordinance for the government of the territory north-west of Ohio.* It was edited by William Graydon and published in Harrisburg, Pa., in 1803; it contained 650 pages.

LAW PERIODICAL
Law magazine was the *American Law Journal,* which was published in Baltimore, Md., from 1808 to 1817. It was edited by John Elihu Hall. *(Henry Simpson—The Lives of Eminent Philadelphians)*

Law review editor (woman). *See* Woman: Woman editor in chief of a law review

LAW REPORTS were Ephraim Kirby's *Reports of Cases Adjudged in the Superior Court of the State of Connecticut from the year 1785 to May 1788 with some determinations in the Supreme Court of Errors,* published in 1789 by Collier and Adam, Litchfield, Conn. It consisted of 456 pages of text, 12 pages of index, and a 5-page list of subscribers. Volume 1 of Harris and McHenry's *Maryland Reports,* published in 1809, reported cases as far

The First

back as 1658. *(Western Reserve and Northern Ohio Historical Tract No. 58. January 1883)*

LAW SCHOOL
Doctor of Laws honorary degree. *See under* Degrees (academic and honorary)

Law instruction in a college was offered by King's College (now Columbia University), New York City, in 1755. The fourth year of study was described as containing among other things "the Chief Principles of Law and Government together with History, Sacred and Profane." *(Edwin Grant Dexter—A History of Education in the United States)*

Law school was opened in Litchfield, Conn., in 1784 by Judge Tapping Reeve. He conducted it alone in a building near his home. The session was from 14 to 18 months, for which a tuition fee of $100 was charged for the first year and $60 for the balance of the course. From 10 to 20 students were enrolled the first year. Reeve conducted the school alone until 1798. *(Samuel Herbert Fisher—Litchfield Law School)*

Law school in a college was established in 1779 at the College of William and Mary, Williamsburg, Va. Professors did not receive a stipulated amount from the college but were paid by the students attending the course. The first professor was George Wythe, who was appointed to the Professorship of Law and Police on December 4, 1779. *(Chamber of Commerce of the United States —A Historic Old Virginia Pilgrimage)*

Law school of collegiate rank permanently organized was the Harvard College School of Law, Cambridge, Mass., which was opened in 1817. Courses in law, however, had been given previously at Harvard College as well as in many other colleges. The General Assembly of Maryland in 1812 authorized the College of Medicine of Maryland to establish a Faculty of Law. David Hoffman was elected professor of law but no regular school of instruction in law was opened until 1823. *(Josiah Quincy—History of Harvard University)*

Law school (university) to admit women was the St. Louis Law School, now the School of Law, Washington University, St. Louis, Mo. In 1869 two women students matriculated. Only one was graduated from the school (Phoebe W. Couzins of St. Louis, on June 15, 1871), although both eventually became members of the bar.

Law school where the faculty was 65 years of age or over was the Hastings College of the Law, University of California, San Francisco, Calif., founded in 1878, which engaged the first overage professor in 1940 on an emergency basis and made 2 other appointments in the mid-40s before the present policy was finally established as a firm policy in 1948. Except for the administrative officers, who are also members of the faculty, the full-time faculty consists only of individuals wh

The First

have attained the age of 65 and have retired elsewhere.

LAWN TENNIS. *See* Tennis

LAWBOOK

Compilation of colonial laws published was *The Book of the General Lauues and Libertyes concerning the inhabitants of the Massachusets, collected out of the records of the General Court for the several years wherein they were made and established and now revised by the same Court and disposed into an Alphabetical order and published by the same Authoritie in the General Court held at Boston the fourteenth of the first month Anno 1647.* The work was published in Cambridge, Mass., in 1648 and sold by Hezekiah Usher in Boston, Mass.

Law compilation of federal session laws (without regard to validity at time of publication) was *Acts passed at a Congress . . . begun and held . . . March 4–September 29, 1789, First Congress, First session . . .* , printed in 1789, in New York City and Philadelphia, Pa., by three independent publishers.

Law compilation of United States laws codifying the laws in force was *The Public Statutes at Large of the United States of America, from the organization of the government in 1789 to March 3, 1845, arranged in chronological order with references to the matter of each act and to the subsequent acts on the same subject, and copious notes of the decisions of the Courts of the United States construing those acts and upon the subjects of the laws with an index to the contents of each volume. . . .* The first volume, containing 777 pages, was published in 1845 in Boston, Mass., by Charles C. Little and James Brown. It was edited by Richard Peters. Publication was authorized by act of March 3, 1845 (5 Stat. L. 798), "a resolution to authorize the Attorney General to contract for copies of a proposed edition of the laws and treaties of the United States."

Lawbook published was William Penn's *The Excellent Privilege of Liberty and Property being the birth-right of the free-born subjects of England. Containing 1. Magna Charta, with a learned comment upon it. 2. The confirmation of the charters of the Liberties of England and of the Forrest, made in the 35th year of Edward the first. 3. A statute made the 34 Edw. 1. commonly called De Tallageo non concedendo; wherein all fundamental laws, liberties and customs are confirmed. With a Comment upon it. 4. An abstract of the pattent granted by the king to William Penn and his heirs and assigns for the province of Pennsylvania. 5. And lastly, the charter of liberties granted by the said William Penn to the freemen and inhabitants of the province of Pennsylvania and territories thereunto annexed, in America.* A

The First

16mo book containing 83 pages, it was printed by William Bradford in Philadelphia, Pa., in 1687.

Lawbook containing the federal laws of the United States was *Acts passed at a Congress of the United States of America, begun and held at the City of New York, on Wednesday the fourth of March 1789, being the acts passed at the first session of the First Congress of the United States,* to wit, New Hampshire, Massachusetts, Connecticut, New York, New Jersey, Pennsylvania, Delaware, Maryland, Virginia, South Carolina and Georgia, which eleven states ratified the Constitution of Government for the United States. The book contained 486 pages and was published in Hartford, Conn., in 1791 by [Barzillai] Hudson & [George] Goodwin.

Lawbook containing the federal laws of the United States of more than one session of Congress (without regard to whether or not they had been subsequently repealed prior to publication) was *The Laws of the United States of America. Vol 1. Containing the Federal Constitution; the Acts of the Three Sessions of the First Congress; The Treaties Existing Between the United States and the Foreign Nations, and the Several Indian Tribes. Also the Declaration of Independence and Sundry Resolves and Ordinances of Congress Under the Confederation. The whole collated with and corrected by the original rolls in the Office of the Secretary of State, agreeably to a resolve of Congress, passed February 18, 1791. To which is added a complete index,* 592 pages, printed in 1791 and sold by Francis Childs & John Swaine, New York City.

Lawbook (text) was George Caines' *An Enquiry into the Law-Merchant of the United States; or Lex Mercatoria Americana; on Several Heads of Commercial Importance,* a 648-page book published in 1802 by Abraham and Arthur Stansbury, New York City.

LAWYER

Attorney of the United States. *See under* Attorney of the United States

Black lawyer formally admitted to the bar was Macon B. Allen, who passed his legal examination in Worcester, Mass., and was admitted May 3, 1845. He had practiced for two years previously in Maine, where no license was required. *(John Daniels—In Freedom's Birthplace)*

Black lawyer to practice before the United States Supreme Court was John S. Rock, who was admitted to practice on February 1, 1865. His admittance was moved by Senator Charles Sumner of Massachusetts. Chief Justice Salmon Portland Chase presided. *(The Independent. Vol. 17, No. 845. Feb. 9, 1865)*

Black woman lawyer was Charlotte E. Ray, admitted to the Supreme Court of the District of Columbia, April 23, 1872. She received an LL.B.

The First

LAWYER—*Continued*
degree from the School of Law, Howard University, Washington, D.C., on February 27, 1871.

Black woman lawyer to practice before the United States Supreme Court was Violette Neatly Anderson of Chicago, Ill., who was admitted January 29, 1926.

Japanese lawyer to receive legal training in the United States was Takeo Kikuchi, who received an LL.B. degree from Boston University, Boston, Mass., on June 5, 1877.

Japanese woman lawyer was K. Elizabeth Ohi, admitted to practice in Illinois, June 10, 1937. She received the degrees of LL.B. February 6, 1937, and J.D., June 25, 1938, from the John Marshall Law School, Chicago, Ill.

Lawyer disbarred was Thomas Lechford, who was engaged by William and Elizabeth Cole in the summer of 1639 for the prosecution of an action against Mrs. Cole's brother, Francis Doughty of Taunton, Mass. In a Quarter Court held in Boston the 3rd day of the 7th month A.D. 1639 (September 3, 1639), Lechford was disbarred by the General Court of Massachusetts. The records state that "M. Thomas Lechford, for going to the Jewry, pleading with them out of Court, is debarred from pleading any man's cause thereafter, unless his owne, and admonished not to presume to meddle beyond what hee shalbee called to by the Courts." Lechford was pardoned, but a year later was again disbarred for the same offense, and again pardoned. *(Nathaniel B. Shurtleff—Records of the Governor and Company of the Massachusetts Bay in New England)*

Lawyers admitted to the Supreme Court of the United States were Elias Boudinot of New Jersey, Thomas Hartly of Pennsylvania, and Richard Harrison of New York, who were admitted on February 5, 1790. The requirements for admittance were "membership for three years past in the Supreme Court of the State in which they respectively belong, and that their private and professional character shall appear to be fair." *(Charles Warren—Supreme Court in United States History)*

Public defender's office. *See* Public defender's office

Woman lawyer was Arabella A. Mansfield of Mount Pleasant, Iowa, who was admitted to practice law in June 1869. She had studied in a law office and at home. Section 1610 of the Iowa Code of 1851, effective July 1, prevented women from being admitted to the bar by statute providing admission to "any white male person. . . . " The section was repealed by an act approved January 5, 1853. The court held that "the affirmative declaration that male persons may be admitted is not an implied denial to the right of females." Mrs. Mansfield was admitted to practice and on March

The First

8, 1870, the words "white male" were omitted from the statute. *(Green Bag. January 1890)*

Woman lawyer graduated from a law school was Ada H. Kepley of Effingham, Ill., who was graduated from the Union College of Law, Chicago, Ill., on June 30, 1870. *(Records in the Clerk's Office, Supreme Court of the United States, Washington, D.C.)*

Woman lawyer to become a member of the American Bar Association was Mary Florence Lathrop, who was admitted in 1917. She received her LL.B. degree from the University of Denver, Denver, Colo.

LAWYERS' ASSOCIATION
Lawyers' association (national) was the American Bar Association, organized August 21, 1878, at an informal meeting in Saratoga, N.Y., proposed by Judge Simeon Eben Baldwin. At the close of the meeting, the membership consisted of 291 lawyers from 29 states. The first president was James Overton Broadhead of St. Louis, Mo. *(James Grafton Rogers—Fifty Years of the American Bar Association)*

Lawyers' association (state) was the New York Bar Association, New York City, which operated from 1747 to 1770. Its purpose was to develop collective opinion on the economic issues prior to the Revolutionary War and to control admission to practice. *(Charles Warren—A History of the American Bar)*

Lawyers' association (state) woman president was Marie M. Lambert, who served from June 30, 1974, to June 30, 1976, as president of the New York State Trial Lawyers Association.

LEAD was mined and smelted in 1620 near Falling Creek, Va., to supply the local demand for bullets and shot. Mining operations ceased after John Berkeley and 20 workmen were massacred by Indians in May 1622. *(William Henry Pulsifer—Notes for a History of Lead)*

LEAD, WHITE. *See* White lead manufacturer

LEAD PENCIL FACTORY. *See* Pencil factory

LEAGUE OF AMERICAN WHEELMEN. *See* Bicycle society

LEAGUE OF NATIONS, INDIAN. *See* under American Indians

LEAGUE OF NATIONS representative (unofficial) was Grace Abbott, Chief of the Children's Bureau of the Department of Labor, who was appointed in an unofficial capacity on October 13 1922, by President Warren Gamaliel Harding to attend the League's Advisory Committee on the Traffic in Women and Children.

LEAPING SUBMARINE. *See* Submarine

The First

LEATHER

Chrome tanned leather successfully marketed was produced in 1890 by Robert Herman Foerderer of Philadelphia, Pa., who devised a method by which the fibrous and gelatinous matter in the natural article could be prepared to receive tanning agents, then another method to overcome the brittle effect. He registered his trademark, a horseshoe with seven nails, each nail standing for a letter of his trade name, Vici Kid.

Chrome tanning process for tanning hides and skins through the action of a metallic salt was invented by Augustus Schultz of New York City, who filed patent papers on May 31, 1883. He was granted patents No. 291,784 and No. 291,785 for tawing hides and skins on January 8, 1884. His process enabled leather to be tanned thinner and stronger than by vegetable tanning.

Leather-splitting machine to split leather to any thickness was invented by Samuel Parker of Billerica, Mass., who received patents on July 9, 1808, and April 26, 1809, on "currying and finishing leather." This invention doubled the use of leather.

Leather tanning in America is credited by many to the American Indians. The first of the known white tanners was Experience Miller who came to Plymouth, Mass., on the *Ann* in 1623. *(American Leather Producers, Inc.—Romance of Leather)*

Leather tanning by the "oil tan" method of preparing buckskin and other leathers was originated by Talmadge Edwards in Johnstown, N.Y., in 1810.

Patent leather was tanned in 1819 in Newark, N.J., by Seth Boyden at the tannery which he had established in 1813. At first the varnish was dried in the sun, but later it was dried in a warm room. Still later, in 1820, he made an oven to hold 16 skins.

LEATHER BELTING. *See* Belts of leather

LEATHER SUBSTITUTE

Artificial leather shoe upper was Corfam, a durable and permeable poromeric material that looks and feels like leather, introduced by E. I. du Pont de Nemours & Company, Wilmington, Del., to the press on October 2, 1963, and to stores in 20 cities on January 27, 1964.

LECTURE SERIES (endowed)

was given in 1866 at the Union Theological Seminary, New York City, by Professor Arnold Guyot, Ph.D., LL.D., on "The First Chapter of Genesis." A committee of the Board of Directors founded the Morse Lectureship on the Relationship of the Bible to Any of the Sciences, named in memory of the founder's father, Samuel Finley Breese Morse, on May 20, 1865. On May 8, 1865, an endowed series known as the Elias P. Ely Lectureship on the Evidences of Christianity had been established by the same institution, but lectures were not given until 1867.

The First

The Reverend Albert Barnes, D.D., LL.D., was the lecturer.

LECTURER

Lecturer of royal blood to speak for personal profit was Prince Vilhelm of Sweden, who toured the country twice, arriving in New York City on January 5, 1927, and again on October 3, 1927. He was the second son of King Gustaf V of Sweden.

LEG (artificial) patent was No. 4,834, granted to Benjamin F. Palmer of Meredith, N.H., on November 4, 1846. The leg had a pliable joint that worked noiselessly and preserved its contour in all positions. Artificial legs had been used previously. Howland & Co., of Brookfield, Mass., exhibited one in 1837 at the Massachusetts Charitable Mechanics Association.

LEGAL TENDER. *See* Money

LEGATION. *See* Diplomatic service

LEGION. *See* War veterans' society: American Legion

LEGION OF MERIT MEDAL. *See* Medal

LEGISLATIVE ASSEMBLY in America met at the Old Church, a wooden structure 50 by 20 feet, in Jamestown, Va., on July 30, 1619. The men sat with their hats on. It was decided that the new governor, Sir George Yeardley, was to summon a "General Assembly" elected by the inhabitants, every free man voting. The assembly was to consist of 22 members, 2 from each borough. The speaker was Master John Pory. The session was opened with prayer by a Mr. Bucke. The first laws were enacted against idleness, drunkenness, and gambling. *(John Esten Cooke—Virginia)*

LEGISLATIVE CONFERENCE (interstate) assembled in Washington, D.C., February 3, 1933, under the auspices of the American Legislators' Association. The conference was attended by 100 state legislators and tax experts from 32 states who discussed double taxation, overlapping and conflicting of federal and state taxes, etc. Only the legislators were entitled to vote.

LEGISLATOR (state)

Black legislator (state) to represent a constituency where the majority were white was Bishop Benjamin William Arnett of the African Methodist Episcopal Church, Greene County, Ohio, who served in the lower house of the Ohio State Legislature from 1885 to 1887. He served in the 66th session, which convened January 6, 1885, and adjourned May 4, 1885, and the 67th, which convened January 4, 1886, and adjourned May 19, 1886. *(Booker Taliaferro Washington—The Story of the Negro)*

Black representatives to sit in any state legislature were Edwin Garrison Walker and Charles Lewis Mitchell of Boston, Mass., who in 1866 were

The First

LEGISLATOR (state)—*Continued*
elected to the Massachusetts House of Representatives.

Black woman state legislator was Crystal Bird Fauset of Philadelphia, Pa., elected November 8, 1938, to the Pennsylvania House of Representatives. Her term of office began December 1, 1938, and she was sworn in and assumed her seat January 3, 1939.

Homosexual (avowed) elected to a state office was Elaine Noble, a Democrat, elected November 5, 1974, to the Massachusetts State Legislature. She received 1,730 of the 2,931 votes cast and represented the Sixth Suffolk, Boston's Fenway-Back Bay district.

Husband and wife simultaneously elected to both chambers of a state legislature were Richard Lewis Neuberger, state senator, and Maurine Brown Neuberger, state representative, both Democrats, elected to the Oregon legislature November 7, 1950. Richard Neuberger had served previously as state senator, having been elected November 2, 1948, to represent the 13th district. *(Richard Lewis Neuberger—Adventures in Politics)*

Woman speaker of a state house of representatives was Mrs. Minnie Davenport Craig of Esmond, N.Dak. On January 3, 1933, she was elected Speaker of the North Dakota House of Representatives. She was a Republican and served for one session from January 3, 1933, to March 31, 1933.

LEGISLATURE
Legislature with two chambers convened in Massachusetts in 1644. "An Act of the Generall Court at Boston, March 7/17, 1644," established one house for magistrates and another for deputies. *(Records of the Governor and Company of Massachusetts Bay, Vol. 2)*

Unicameral legislature (state), after the formation of the United States, was adopted by constitutional amendment by Nebraska on November 6, 1934. A body of 43 members replaced a House of 100 and a Senate of 33. The first president was Walter Herman Jurgensen and the Speaker was Charles Joseph Warner. The first session was opened January 5, 1937, by United States Senator George William Norris. The first bill, passed January 21, 1937, appropriated $10,000 for mileage, postage, and incidental expenses for the members. All states adopted bicameral systems at the formation of the United States, except Pennsylvania, Georgia, and Vermont, which changed after 4, 12, and 58 years, respectively. *(Harrison Boyd Summers—Unicameral Legislatures)*

LENS
Achromatic lenses were made in 1844 in Cambridgeport, Mass., by Alvan Clark. *(William Wallace Payne—The Life and Achievements of Alvan Clark)*

The First

Bifocal contact lens was developed by Newton K. Wesley, O.D., of the Eye Research Foundation and the Plastic Contact Lens Company, Chicago Ill., and officially introduced in May 1958. Distant vision prescriptions were ground in the center of the lens, and reading prescriptions were ground on the outer circle. The cost of a pair varied from $200 to $400.

Contact lenses were imported for commercial purposes in New York City in 1924 from Jena Germany, where they were manufactured by Carl Zeiss, Inc. The lenses were ground, rather than blown. They were thin saucer-shaped shells of optical glass which were worn under the eyelid in direct contact with the eye itself.

Eyeglass bifocals were invented by Benjamin Franklin, who, annoyed at having to carry two pairs of glasses, fashioned a single pair of glasses each lens of which consisted of two parts with different focusing powers. On May 23, 1785, from Passy, France, he wrote to George Whatley, "I have only to move my eyes up and down as I want to see distinctly far or near." Inasmuch as ordinary spectacles in the colonies cost as much as $100 each, his invention did not receive a ready popular response. *(Nathan Gerson Goodman—The Ingenious Dr. Franklin)*

Lens to provide zoom effects without requiring the camera to be moved toward or away from the object televised was the Zoomar lens, invented by Dr. Frank Gerard Back of New York City, who received patent No. 2,454,686 on November 23 1948, on a "varifocal lens for cameras" adjustable for closeups or long-distance shots. It was demonstrated April 16, 1947, by the National Broadcasting Company in New York City.

Plastic lens for cataract patients was fitted March 18, 1952, at Wills Eye Hospital, Philadelphia, Pa., by Dr. Warren Snyder Reese, who performed the [Frederick Thomas] Ridley operation, the insertion of a plastic lens approximately 8 mm in diameter.

LEOPARD. *See* Animals

LEPER HOSPITAL. *See* Hospital: Leper hospital

LEPERS' CHURCH (Protestant). *See* Protestant church: Protestant church for lepers

LEPROSARIUM. *See* Hospital: Leper hospital

LETHAL-GAS EXECUTION. *See* Execution

LETTER
Letter descriptive of America was probably written by Christopher Columbus, admiral of the ocean fleet, who sailed August 3, 1492, from the harbor of Palos, Spain, with three small caravels and about 90 men, and returned 224 days later, on March 14, 1493, to Lisbon, Portugal, where he dispatched two letters of identical content, one to Raphael Sanchez and the other to Luis de Santangel. *(The First Letter of Christopher Columbus to*

The First

the Noble Lord Raphael Sanchez Announcing the Discovery of America)

Letters written in English in America which have been recorded are claimed to be the four letters of Ralph Lane, the first commander of Raleigh's first colony, which were written on August 12, 1585, from Porte Ferdynando. The letters were not published until 1860. *(Francis Lister Hawks— History of North Carolina)*

LETTER BOX. *See* Postal service: Mailbox locker

LETTER CARRIER'S UNIFORM. *See under* Postal service

LETTER TO ENCIRCLE THE WORLD. *See under* Postal service

LETTERMEN'S CLUB, COLLEGE. *See* College "Lettermen's club"

LEVEES were built along the Mississippi River at New Orleans, La., in 1724. They extended 18 miles above and 18 miles below New Orleans, but they were rudimentary dikes compared with the present mighty embankments. Sieur le Blond de la Tour, a knight of St. Louis and chief engineer of the colony, began construction of a levee in 1718. It was completed in 1727. *(Henry Rightor—Standard History of New Orleans)*

LEWISITE was developed in February 1918 by Dr. Winford Lee Lewis, Washington, D.C. Production of this explosive compound of chloro-vinyl-dichloro-arsine was undertaken at Nela Park, Cleveland, Ohio, in the autumn of 1918 and amounted to ten tons a day in November 1918.

LIBERAL ARTS RADIO COURSE. *See* Radio instruction: Radio college course

LIBERAL REPUBLICAN PARTY convention was held in Cincinnati, Ohio, on May 1, 1872, at which meeting the party was formed. Horace Greeley of New York was the presidential candidate and Benjamin Gratz Brown of Missouri was the vice presidential candidate. In the election held November 5, 1872, Greeley (who was also the Democratic candidate) received 2,834,079 votes, as compared with 3,597,132 cast for Ulysses Simpson Grant, the Republican candidate. *(Proceedings of Liberal Republican Party Convention, 1872)*

LIBERTY ACT, RELIGIOUS. *See* Religious liberty act (colonial)

LIBERTY LOAN. *See* Loan

LIBERTY PARTY. *See* Antislavery party

LIBERTY SHIP. *See* Ship

LIBRARIAN
    Librarian to be paid for his services was Louis Timothee, a young French immigrant, who was hired November 14, 1732, and received three pounds sterling every trimester. He worked every Wednesday from two to three o'clock and every

The First

Saturday from ten to four in the Library Company of Philadelphia, the library which, was started in 1731 by Benjamin Franklin. *(George Maurice Abbot—A Short History of the Library Company of Philadelphia)*

Librarian of Congress was John James Beckley of Virginia, clerk of the House of Representatives, appointed January 29, 1802. He served until his death, April 8, 1807. His salary was not to exceed $2 per diem for every day of necessary attendance. The Library of Congress was established by authority of the act of April 24, 1800 (2 Stat. L. 56) appropriating $5,000 "for the purchase of such books as may be necessary for the use of both Houses of Congress." Until 1815, when George Watterston was appointed, the librarians were the clerks of the House of Representatives. *(Lucy Salamanca—Fortress of Freedom)*

LIBRARIANS' CONVENTION was held September 15–17, 1853, at the University of the City of New York, New York City. It was called to order by Charles Folsom of the Boston Athenaeum and was attended by 82 delegates from 47 libraries in 13 states. Charles Coffin Jewett, librarian of the Smithsonian Institution, served as president.

LIBRARIANS' UNION affiliated with the American Federation of Labor was the Library Employes' Union No. 15,590 of New York City, chartered May 15, 1917. The first secretary was May Walker and the first president was Tilloah Squires. The union was suspended November 20, 1929.

LIBRARY
    Bookwagon traveling library was started at the Washington County Free Library, Hagerstown, Md. Mr. Thomas, the janitor, drove a wagon through the county, making three trips a week beginning in April 1905. The wagon had shelves on the outside so that the books were visible. The inside of the wagon had been used for gathering eggs, butter, and country produce prior to library use. *(Mary Lemist Titcomb—The Story of the Washington County Free Library)*

    Business library supported by taxes was a branch of the Newark Public Library opened October 1, 1904, at 16 Academy Street, Newark, N.J. The first librarian of the business branch was Sarah B. Ball. John Cotton Dana was librarian of the Newark Public Library. The budget for the year 1904 was approximately $1,500.

    Children's department in a library is said to be that of the Minneapolis Public Library, opened in December 1889. The children's books were separated from those of the adults. In 1892 children were served from a special desk in the lower corridor in a separate room. In the fall of 1893 a children's department was opened, the whole corridor being equipped for their sole use.

LIBRARY—*Continued*

Circulating library in America was set up by the Library Company of Philadelphia, organized in 1731 by Benjamin Franklin through his society, the Junto. The instrument of association of the company was dated July 1, 1731. The first meeting was held November 8, 1731, at the house of Nicholas Scull. Fifty persons contributed 40 shillings each for purchasing the first parcel of books and 10 shillings per annum charges. The first books were ordered March 31, 1732. An agreement to hire Louis Timothee as librarian was made November 14, 1732. *(George Maurice Abbot—A Short History of The Library Company of Philadelphia)*

County library successfully conducted was the Brumback Library of Van Wert County, Van Wert, Ohio, which was organized in 1898. Actual work throughout the county was started in 1901, when the present building was opened to the public. Funds were secured from the County Commissioners through a tax levy.

Free public library was the Juvenile Library of Dublin, N.H., established in 1822.

Free public library (town-supported) maintained by a public tax and controlled and managed by vote of the town was established in Peterborough, N.H., April 9, 1833.

Library was established in Charleston, S.C., in 1698 through the efforts of Thomas Bray (later representative in Maryland of the Bishop of London), who in 1696 forwarded religious books to the clergy. On November 16, 1700, Charleston passed an act "for securing the Provincial Library of Charlestown, by which commissioners and trustees were appointed for its preservation." The act authorized any inhabitants to "have liberty to borrow any book out of the said provincial library, giving a receipt." *(Edward McCrady—History of South Carolina Under the Proprietary Government, 1670–1719)*

Library building used exclusively as a library was a frame house erected by James Logan on the west side of Sixth Street, between Chestnut and Walnut streets, Philadelphia, Pa., in 1725. It was available to the public for reading purposes by written permission from James Logan. On March 8, 1745, he turned over this property and 2,000 books to the city, but the library did not start to function as a public library until November 8, 1760. Upon the death in 1776 of his son, William Logan, who was the first librarian, the library was closed for several years. On March 31, 1792, the Loganian Library was incorporated with the Library Company of Philadelphia. *(Austin Kayingham Gray—First American Library)*

Library building (university) was the library of the University of South Carolina, Columbia, S.C., completed May 6, 1840. The first librarian of the university was Elisha Hammond, who began to

serve in 1805. The first librarian in the separate building was Dr. Thomas Park.

Library for seamen was inaugurated March 1829 by the American Seamen's Friend Society of New York City, which supplied traveling libraries to ships soon after its organization May 5, 1828, when Smith Thomson was elected president. Loan libraries were placed on board American ships, Coast Guard, and naval vessels, and in life-saving stations.

Library newspaper-room was opened November 7, 1859, in the reading room in the great hall on the third floor of Cooper Union for the Advancement of Science and Art, Astor Place, New York City. It contained 12 New York dailies and 16 other dailies. The section was 125 feet long, 82 feet wide, and 32 feet high and was open from 8:00 A.M. to 10:00 P.M., free to all persons (male and female) of good moral character, for the use and instruction of the working classes. The attendance was about 3,000 a week, 10 percent of which was female.

Library of Congress was established by act of April 24, 1800 (2 Stat. L. 56), which appropriated $5,000 "for the purchase of such books as may be necessary for the use of Congress at the said city of Washington and for fitting up a suitable apartment for containing them and for placing them therein." The first library catalog, dated April 1802, listed 964 volumes and 9 maps. The first librarian was clerk of the House of Representatives John James Beckley of Virginia.

Library of Congress catalog. *See under* Library catalog

Library of Congress librarian. *See under* Librarian

Mechanics' library was opened in New York City in 1820 by the General Society of Mechanics and Tradesmen of the City of New York and was known as the "Apprentice's Library." The name was changed in 1898 to the "Free Library of the General Society of Mechanics and Tradesmen." The Free Quakers in 1820 opened an apprentices' library at Carpenters' Hall, Philadelphia, Pa., holding the first public meeting and adopting a constitution on February 28, 1820. The library was opened June 3, 1820, at 100 Chestnut Street, Philadelphia. Horace Binney was the first president and Daniel B. Smith, the secretary. *(One Hundred and Forty-fifth Annual Report, General Society of Mechanics and Tradesmen of the City of New York; also Watson's Annals of Philadelphia)*

Mercantile library was the Mercantile Library Association of the City of New York, organized at 49 Fulton Street, New York City, November 9, 1820, with 150 sponsors in attendance. The constitution was adopted November 27, 1820. The library was founded to assist clerks and others engaged in mercantile business to enjoy the use of

The First

reading facilities. It opened February 12, 1821. Its present building is located at 17 East 47th Street, New York City. The first president was Lucius Bull, who served from November 27, 1820, to December 17, 1823. *(Mercantile Library Association of the City of New York—First Annual Report, November 6, 1821)*

Youth's library was established in January 1803 in Salisbury, Conn., through the generosity of Caleb Bingham of Boston, a native of Salisbury. He donated 150 volumes, the nucleus of the Bingham Library for Youth.

LIBRARY CATALOG

Catalog of the Library of Congress was *A Catalogue of Books, Maps, and Charts, Belonging to the Library of the Two Houses of Congress,* printed in 1802 by William Duane, Washington, D.C.

Union catalog of books in libraries in the United States was begun in 1901, when the Librarian of Congress authorized the exchange of Library of Congress printed catalog cards for cards printed by other libraries for books for which no Library of Congress cards were available. The catalog combines all holdings of the Library of Congress together with the holdings of over 600 other libraries in one author alphabet. More than 15 million card entries have been made, 9 million of which represent books located in libraries in the United States and Canada other than the Library of Congress.

Union catalog of books in a state library was undertaken in 1909 by the California State Library, Sacramento, Calif. At first cards for periodical files only were collected. The catalog was later extended to include books as well as periodicals in California libraries. *(Robert Bingham Downs—Union Catalogs in the United States)*

LIBRARY CHAIR endowed in a library school was the Melvil Dewey Professorship of Library Service, established by trustees' vote of April 4, 1938, as of July 1, 1938, at the Columbia University School of Library Service, New York City, through an endowment of $150,000 made by the Carnegie Corporation of New York. The first incumbent was Ernest James Reece, Professor of Library Service. *(Columbia University Quarterly. June 1938)*

LIBRARY LEGISLATION

Federal aid to libraries was the Library Services Act June 19, 1956 (70 Stat. L. 293), "to promote the further development of public library service in rural areas." It authorized the appropriation for the fiscal year ending June 30, 1957, and for each of the four succeeding fiscal years, of the sum of $7,500,000 to be used for making payments to states.

Library law enacted by a state was Chapter 861 of the Laws of 1849 of New Hampshire, approved July 7, 1849, "an act providing for the establish-

The First

ment of public libraries." It provided that "the inhabitants of any school district in any city or town, and of any city or town not divided into school districts, in this Commonwealth, may, at any meeting called for that purpose, raise money for the purchase of libraries, in the same manner as school districts may raise money for erecting and repairing school houses in their respective districts ... and that every public library established under provision of this act shall be open to the free use of every inhabitant of this town." *(William Frederick Yust—Library Legislation)*

LIBRARY LOAN made by a state library to a community was made on February 8, 1892, by the New York State Library. The law of April 27, 1892 (Chapter 378, section 36) permitted the loan of books for a period not exceeding six months to libraries or communities not yet having a public library, provided they were available to the public without charge for either reference or circulation. *(New York State Library—76th Annual Report for Year Ending September 30, 1893)*

LIBRARY PERIODICAL

Library periodical was the *Library Journal,* the monthly journal of the American Library Association, published by F. Leypoldt, New York City. The managing editor was Melvil Dewey; the general editor, Richard Rogers Bowker. The subscription price was 50 cents an issue, $5 a year. The first issue, September 30, 1876, contained 42 pages.

LIBRARY SCHOOL. *See* Library training (systematic)

LIBRARY SERVICES ACT. *See under* Library legislation

LIBRARY SOCIETY

Library association (national) was the American Library Association, organized October 6, 1876, at a meeting in Philadelphia, Pa., attended by 103 librarians. The association was incorporated December 10, 1879, under the laws of Massachusetts. The first president was Dr. Justin Winsor, and the first secretary was Melvil Dewey. Executive offices are maintained in Chicago, Ill. The first annual convention was held September 4, 1877, in New York City.

Library society (local) was the New York Library Club, formed June 18, 1885, at a meeting held at Columbia University, New York City, "to promote acquaintance and fraternal relations among librarians and those interested in library work and advance the interests of the libraries of New York and its vicinity." On September 11, 1885, the executive committee selected the first permanent officers: Richard Rogers Bowker, president, and C. Alexander Nelson, secretary. The first general meeting was held November 12, 1885.

The First

LIBRARY SOCIETY—Continued

Melvil Dewey medal was awarded June 24, 1953, to Ralph Robert Shaw, librarian of the U.S. Department of Agriculture, who received the medal and a citation at the 72nd annual conference of the American Library Association held at Los Angeles, Calif., for his work in applying "electric brain" equipment and other machines to library work. *(New York Times. 39:3. June 25, 1953)*

State librarians' society was the National Association of State Libraries, formed November 16, 1898, in Washington, D.C. William Elmer Henry of Indiana was chairman and Pauline L. Jones of Tennessee was secretary.

State library society was the New York Library Association "to promote library interests of the state of New York," organized by 43 persons on July 11, 1890, at the New York State Library, Albany, N.Y. The first president was Melvil Dewey and the first secretary-treasurer was George B. Gallup.

Woman to become president of the American Library Association was Theresa Hubbell West Elmendorf of the Buffalo (N.Y.) Public Library, who served from May 24, 1911, to July 2, 1912. *(Bulletin of the American Library Association. Vol. 6, No. 4)*

LIBRARY TRAINING (systematic) was introduced by the School of Library Economy at Columbia University, New York City, which opened January 5, 1887, through the efforts of Melvil Dewey. The school was transferred on April 1, 1889, to Albany, N.Y., and its name changed to the New York State Library School. It was placed under the direction of the University of the State of New York. The first session was held April 10, 1889. The first public commencement and conferring of degrees took place July 8, 1891. The first summer session was held from July 7 to August 10, 1896. In 1926 the school was returned to Columbia University, where it was united with the Library School of the New York Public Library to form the School of Library Service, Columbia University. It is a charter member of the Association of American Library Schools. *(Columbia University. School of Library Economy—First Annual Report)*

LIBRETTO published was Andrew Barton's *The Disappointment, or The Force of Credulity,* a two-act comic opera satire with prologue and epilogue, published in 1767 in New York City. It depicted the popular notion of the time concerning the treasure supposed to have been buried by Blackbeard, the pirate. *(Oscar George Theodore Sonneck—Early Opera in America)*

LICENSE, AVIATION. *See* Aviation—License

LICENSE PLATES, AUTOMOBILE. *See* Automobile license plates

The First

LIE DETECTOR used as evidence in a court of law for consideration by a jury was the Keeler Polygraph, invented by Leonarde Keeler of the Scientific Crime Detection Laboratory, Northwestern University School of Law, Chicago, Ill. Keeler conducted a test February 2, 1935, in Portage, Wis., and produced graphs of the test in the case of *Wisconsin State vs. Cecil Loniello and Tony Grignano.* Both defendants were found guilty of assault and sentenced by Judge Clayton F. Van Pelt of the Circuit Court of Columbia County, Wis. Tests of a similar nature, however, had been used in minor civil and criminal cases as early as 1924, when blood pressure readings were made with a Tycos sphygmomanometer. *(Journal of Criminal Law and Criminology. July 1935)*

LIEDERKRANZ CHEESE. *See* Cheese

LIEUTENANT GENERAL. *See* Army Officer

LIEUTENANT GOVERNOR

Black lieutenant governor was Oscar James Dunn, nominated at the Louisiana Republican nominating convention held at New Orleans, La., on January 14, 1868. He was elected April 22, 1868. He died November 22, 1871, of "congestion of the brain."

Woman lieutenant governor was Consuelo Northrop Bailey, Republican, of South Burlington, Vt., who was elected November 2, 1954, by a majority of 8,200 votes and sworn in January 6, 1955, at Montpelier, Vt.

LIFE INSURANCE. *See* Insurance

LIFE PRESERVER

Life preserver of cork was invented by Napoleon E. Guerin of New York City, who obtained patent No. 2,359 on November 16, 1841, on "an improvement in buoyant dresses or life-preservers." It was a jacket or waistcoat containing 18 to 20 quarts of rasped or grated cork.

Life preserver of cork approved by the Board of Supervising Inspectors was the Neversink Cork Jacket, formed of granulated cork compressed under pressure. It was invented by David Kahnweiler of New York City and tested in 1872 in the Potomac River. Patent No. 192,832 was issued on July 10, 1877. Life preservers of this type, used on board the S.S. *San Francisco* of the Pacific Mail Steamship Company, saved the lives of 287 persons when the ship was wrecked in the Pacific Ocean in 1877.

LIFEBOAT

Lifeboat was built in Nantucket, Mass., by William Raymond under the supervision of Captain Gideon Gardner and was completed in 1807. It was built for the Humane Society of the Commonwealth of Massachusetts and cost $1,433.11. An additional $160 was used for a shed in Cohasset, Mass., where the lifeboat remained until 1813. *(John Cameron Lamb—The Life Boat and Its Work)*

The First

Lifeboat (corrugated) was patented by Joseph Francis of New York City, who obtained patent No. 3,974 on March 26, 1845, on "making boats and other vessels of sheet iron and other materials." His "life car," built in 1850 by Stillman, Allen & Company, New York City, was 33 feet long and made of four sheets of hard rolled copper pressed into shape. It was used to rescue 201 persons on January 12, 1850, from the British ship *Ayreshire,* wrecked off Squan Beach, Monmouth County, N.J. *(Life Saving Appliances of Joseph Francis)*

Lifeboat race. *See* Boat race: International boat race

LIFESAVING MEDAL. *See* Medal

LIFESAVING SERVICE
Lifesaving service was introduced in 1871 by Sumner Increase Kimball. An act of Congress of June 18, 1878 (20 Stat. L. 163), an "act to organize the Life Saving Service," formally authorized the Life Saving Service as a separate and distinct service in the Treasury Department. This service and the Revenue Cutter Service were merged on January 28, 1915, to form the Coast Guard.

First Aid Emergency Organization. *See* First Aid Emergency Organization

LIFESAVING STATIONS FOR DISTRESSED MARINERS were established in 1787 by the Humane Society of the Commonwealth of Massachusetts (incorporated February 23, 1791). Huts were erected at a cost of $40 each at Scituate Beach, Nantucket, Mass., and at the west end of Lovell's Island, Mass. *(Mark Antony De Wolfe Howe—The Humane Society of the Commonwealth of Massachusetts, 1785–1916)*

LIFT BRIDGE. *See* Bridge: Rolling lift bridge

LIGATURES. *See* Suture: Silk suture

LIGHT BEAM COMMUNICATION from a dirigible was made May 19, 1932, from the U.S. Navy dirigible *Los Angeles.* The ship "fired" a searchlight beam at a 30-inch target atop the General Electric building at Schenectady, N.Y. As long as the light beam was on the target, communication was maintained.

LIGHT, ELECTRIC. *See* Electric lighting: Electric incandescent lamp

LIGHT OPERA. *See* Opera

LIGHTER-THAN-AIR AIRSHIP. *See* Aviation— Airship: Airship (lighter-than-air)

LIGHTHOUSE
See also Lightship

Iron pile lighthouse was built between 1847 and 1849 at Minot's Ledge, Mass., by William Henry Swift. The lamp was lit January 1, 1850, by Isaac Dunham, the keeper. The lighthouse was swept away in the gale of April 16, 1851, and two keepers were lost at sea. A lightship was placed in service

The First

in 1854. Construction of the stonework for a new lighthouse started July 1, 1855. It was completed June 29, 1860, and the light placed in operation November 15, 1860. *(Edward Rowe Snow—The Story of Minot's Light)*

Lighted beacon on the Pacific coast was the Spanish lighthouse erected in 1855 at Ballast Point on Point Loma, San Diego, Calif.

Lighthouse in America was a conical masonry tower erected by the Province of Massachusetts in 1716 on Little Brewster Island at the entrance to Boston Harbor at a cost of £2,285 17s 8½d. The lighthouse was authorized by act of July 23, 1715, and the light was first kindled September 14, 1716. It had 16 spermaceti oil lamps, in groups of four. A levy of a penny per ton was placed on all incoming and outgoing vessels except those engaged in coastal service. The lighthouse was rebuilt in 1783 and is still in service. The first lighthouse keeper was George Worthylake.

Lighthouse (atomic powered) was the Baltimore Light in Chesapeake Bay, Baltimore Harbor, Md., which went into operation May 20, 1964. A 60-watt radioisotope nuclear generator, 34½ inches high, 22 inches in diameter, weighing 4,600 pounds (including shielding), was developed and produced by the Martin Company's Nuclear Division, Baltimore, Md., a division of the Martin Marietta Corporation, to supply a continuous flow of electricity for 10 years without refueling. It was designated SNAP-7B (systems for nuclear auxiliary power). One-hundred twenty pairs of lead telluride thermo couples converted heat from radioactive strontium titanate, a safe form of strontium-90, into electricity.

Lighthouse built after American independence was located at Cape Henry, Va., at the entrance of Chesapeake Bay. On August 7, 1789, an act (1 Stat. L. 53) was passed "for the establishment and support of lighthouses, beacons, buoys and public piers," and on March 31, 1791, a contract for the erection of the Cape Henry Lighthouse was made with John McComb, Jr., It was finished in 1792. The first lighthouse keeper was Laban Goffigan. Fish oil was used for illumination. Then followed, in order, whale oil, colza oil, lard oil, kerosene, gas, and finally, electricity.

Lighthouse fueled by natural gas was the 35-foot stone lighthouse at Barcelona Harbor, N.Y., on Lake Erie, 17 miles southwest of Fredonia, N.Y., which was in operation from 1830 to 1859. It had eleven burners. The gas was transported three-fourths of a mile through a log pipeline from a gas spring on nearby Tupper Creek.

LIGHTING BLACKOUT. *See* Blackout: Blackout lighting demonstration

LIGHTNING (artificial) demonstration of 10 million volts of artificial lightning was conducted June 10, 1932, in Pittsfield, Mass., by the General

The First

LIGHTNING (artificial)—*Continued*
Electric Company. Five million volts had been the previous maximum voltage attained in the laboratory.

LIGHTNING DEMONSTRATION showing the relationship between lightning and electricity was made June 15, 1752, in Philadelphia, Pa., by Benjamin Franklin. His letter to Peter Collison, dated October 19, 1752, describing his experiments, was read before the Royal Society of London in December 1752. *(Benjamin Franklin—New Experiments and Observations on Electricity Made in Philadelphia in America)*

LIGHTNING-FLASH PHOTOGRAPH. *See* Photograph

LIGHTNING OBSERVATORY was erected during the summer of 1935 on top of the Pittsfield Works, the General Electric Company's building in Pittsfield, Mass. It was built almost entirely of metal and enclosed a circular area 14 feet in diameter. Within was a lightproof room 7 feet square which contained a periscope with a brilliantly silvered area reflecting lightning flashes from any direction and sending their images to a mirror set at an angle of 45 degrees. A 12-lens motor-operated high-speed camera recorded on a moving strip of film any flash of lightning within range.

LIGHTNING ROD was invented in 1749 by Benjamin Franklin, who installed it on his house at 141 Market Street, Philadelphia, Pa. He described his experiments in his "Opinions and Conjectures concerning the Properties and Effects of the Electrical Matter, and the means of preserving Buildings, Ships, etc., from Lightning, arising from Experiments and Observations made at Philadelphia, 1749." *(Oliver Joseph Lodge—Lightning Conductors and Lightning Guards)*

LIGHTSHIP was placed in the Elizabeth River off Craney Island, Va., on July 14, 1820. The displacement was 70 tons. The ship was built at a cost of $6,000. *(Records in Bureau of Lighthouses, U.S. Department of Commerce, Washington, D.C.)*

LIGHTWEIGHT BRICK. *See* Brick

LILLIPUTIAN CITY. *See* City (Lilliputian)

LIME was manufactured on January 27, 1662, in Providence, R.I. Thomas Hackelton was granted liberty by the town to burn lime at a certain place on the commons. On October 27, 1665, the town ordered that the lime rocks about the limekiln should remain in common ownership. *(Sidney Smith Rider—The Lands of Rhode Island)*

LIMITED-SERVICE ARMY CAMP. *See* Army camp: Army camp for "limited service"

LINEN THREAD FACTORY (successful) was established in Paterson, N.J., in 1865 by William Barbour and Sons of Lisburn, Ireland. The mill was driven by waterpower. The thread was used principally by shoe manufacturers and harness makers.

The First

cipally by shoe manufacturers and harness makers.

LINOLEUM
  Embossed inlaid linoleum was introduced in 1925 by the Armstrong Cork & Insulation Company of Lancaster, Pa. The company manufactured the linoleum and then placed it under an embossing press in which parts of the design were compressed, so that the tile blocks or other portions of the pattern stood out in relief. *(Armstrong Cork Co.—A Story of Floors)*

  Linoleum was manufactured in 1873 by the American Linoleum Manufacturing Company, Richmond, Staten Island, N.Y. *(Frederick Walton —The Infancy and Development of Linoleum Floorcloth)*

  Linoleum machine (fully automatic) for manufacturing straight-line linoleum was installed in 1911 by Congoleum-Nairn, Inc. at its Kearny, N.J., plant. *(Frederick Walton—The Infancy and Development of Linoleum Floorcloth)*

LINOTYPE
  Newspaper page set by linotype. *See* Newspaper: Newspaper page set by linotype

LINOTYPE MACHINE. *See* Typesetting

LINOTYPE-SET BOOK. *See* Book

LION. *See* Animals

LIPREADING INSTRUCTION FOR THE DEAF. *See under* Deaf—School

LIPREADING TOURNAMENT (national) was held June 23, 1926, in Philadelphia, Pa., during the seventh annual meeting of the American Federation of Organizations for the Hard of Hearing.

LIQUID AIR. *See* Air (liquid)

LIQUID FIRE EXTINGUISHER. *See* Fire extinguisher

LIQUID-FUEL ROCKET. *See* Rocket

LIQUID HEAT in actual installation was employed in the laboratories of the Pierce Foundation, Summit, N.J., on January 7, 1942. The system was operated by Orion O. Oaks, director of Heating, Ventilating and Sanitation Research of the John B. Pierce Foundation. Liquid heat is the designation given to the utilization of a chemical which, among other novel characteristics, has a boiling point of 800° F. and still is fluid at 40° below zero.

LIQUID SOAP. *See* Soap

LIQUOR BOARD MEMBER (woman). *See under* Woman

LIQUOR REFORM MOVEMENT was undertaken by the Dutch Reformed Church on Manhattan Island in 1623. It maintained a strong position against liquor, particularly with regard to exces-

The First

sive use. *(Edward Tanjore Corwin—Manual of the [Dutch] Reformed Church in America)*

LIQUOR STORES (state) were established by Pennsylvania in 1933. An act was passed by a special session of the legislature and signed by Governor Gifford Pinchot on November 29, 1933. On January 2, 1934, 90 stores were opened in various parts of the state, stocked and ready to do business.

LITERACY qualification for voting was required by Massachusetts. An amendment was passed May 1, 1857, by a vote of 23,833 for and 13,746 against, providing that "no person shall have the right to vote, or to be eligible to office under the constitution of this commonwealth, who shall not be able to read the constitution in the English language, and write his name," excepting those unable to qualify because of physical disability or those over sixty years of age. *(Chapter 20, Laws of 1857, Massachusetts)*

LITERARY SOCIETY, COLLEGE. *See* College literary society

LITERATURE PRIZE WINNER (Nobel Prize). *See* Nobel Prize: Nobel Prize in literature

LITHOGRAPH was *A Water Mill,* by Bass Otis of Philadelphia, Pa., published July 1819 in the *Analectic Magazine. (Harry Twyford Peters—America on Stone)*

LITHUANIAN CHURCH was St. Casimir's Lithuanian Church, Plymouth, Pa., organized October 27, 1889. The first pastor was the Reverend Alexander Burba.

LITTER LEGISLATION
Litter legislation (state) affecting containers of soft drinks and beer was enacted by Oregon on July 2, 1971, effective October 1, 1972. The bill outlawed pull-tab cans and nonreturnable bottles.

LIVESTOCK AUCTION
Auction of livestock broadcast. *See under* Radio broadcast

LIVESTOCK MARKET PAPER was the *Drover's Journal* published by Harvey L. Goodall at the Chicago Union Stock Yards, Chicago, Ill. The first issue was dated January 11, 1873. On January 19, 1877, it became a daily.

LOAN
See also Bonds

Liberty loan subscriptions were taken from May 2, 1917, to June 15, 1917, during which time approximately 4 million people subscribed for $3,035,226,850 in bonds to yield 3½ percent. The first loan was authorized by act of April 24, 1917 (40 Stat. L. 35), "an act to authorize an issue of bonds to meet expenditure for the national security and defense, and for the purpose of assisting in the prosecution of the war, to extend credit to foreign

The First

governments and for other purposes." A subscription of $2,000,000,000 was required.

Loan for war purposes by a central governmental agency was negotiated with France by the Continental Congress. A resolution of December 23, 1776, authorized the loan of $181,500 (1 million livres), which was used for the purchasing of supplies and construction of cruisers. The length of the loan was indefinite. Bonds were sold at par. The rate of interest was 5 percent, payable annually. The loan was received on June 4, 1777. The final redemption was made on December 31, 1793, when the balance due was merged into the general account of the French debt. *(Rafael Arroyo Bayley—The National Loans of the United States from July 4, 1776, to June 30, 1880)*

Loan to the United States was negotiated by Alexander Hamilton, who obtained, from the Bank of New York and the Bank of North America, between September 13, 1789, and February 17, 1790, $191,608.81, inclusive of $8.81 overcharge in their interest account. It was known as the Temporary Loan of 1789 and was obtained without authority of law. The money was used to pay salaries of the President, senators, representatives, and officers of the first Congress during the first session under the Constitution. The interest rate was 6 percent. The final redemption of the loan was made June 8, 1790.

State loan was authorized December 10, 1690, by the Massachusetts Bay Colony, which issued tax anticipation certificates which did not have a maturity date or bear interest. They were not redeemable in metal and were not considered legal tender.

War loan made by the United States Government to a war ally was a loan of $200 million at 3.5 percent made to Great Britain on April 25, 1917.

LOAN ASSOCIATION (building and loan). *See* Building and loan association

LOBBYIST (woman). *See under* Woman

LOBOTOMY (prefrontal). *See* Surgical operation

LOCK
Lock ("clock") superseding the keyhole lock and the first double locks (two locks within one case) were invented in 1851 by Linus Yale of Newport, N.Y., who obtained patent No. 8,071, May 6, 1851, on a lock and key. *(Henry Robinson Towne, Locks and Builders' Hardware)*

Mortised lock was introduced in 1835 by Philos Blake and Eli Whitney Blake of Blake Brothers, Westville, Conn.

Time lock was manufactured by [James] Sargent & [Halbert] Greenleaf, Rochester, N.Y., and installed May 1874 on the vault of the First National Bank of Morrison, Ill. James Sargent of Rochester, N.Y., obtained patent No. 165,878 on

The First

LOCK—*Continued*

July 20, 1875, on a "time-lock" and patent No. 195,-539 on September 25, 1877, on "combined time-locks, and bolt-works for safes."

LOCKER

Locker (coin vendor) was invented by Willis S. Farnsworth of Petaluma, Calif., who received patent No. 985,989 on March 7, 1911, which he assigned to the Coin Controlled Lock Co. He also secured a patent jointly with Wm. H. Reed on a coin receptacle "magazine-hinge and conveyor" on the same date, which bore No. 985,990. The insertion of a coin in a slot provided a key to open and close the locker.

Public locker plant was established in 1903 by A. G. Eames of the Chico Ice and Cold Storage Company, Chico, Calif. Individual lockers, each with a lock and key, were rented to the public. The company was purchased in 1913 by the Union Ice Company of San Francisco, Calif.

LOCKS, CANAL. *See* Canal locks

LOCKSTITCH SEWING MACHINE. *See* Sewing machine

LOCOMOTIVE

Diesel-electric freight locomotive was constructed by the New York Central Lines in January 1928. It was placed in operation in June 1928. A diesel-oil–electric passenger locomotive was first used in March 1929.

Diesel-electric locomotive was No. 1000, a 300 h.p. locomotive placed in service December 17, 1924, by the Central Railroad of New Jersey at the Bronx terminal, New York City. The diesel engine was built by the Ingersoll-Rand Company, Phillipsburg, N.J., the electrical components by the General Electric Company, Elmira, N.Y., and the locomotive structure by the American Locomotive Company, Schenectady, N.Y. The locomotive remained in service until June 13, 1957.

Duplex compound locomotive (Mallet) was built in 1904 at the Schenectady, N.Y., plant of the American Locomotive Company for the Baltimore and Ohio Railroad. The engine, locomotive No. 2400, used bituminous fuel and had a driving-wheel diameter of 56 inches. Its weight on drivers was 334,500 pounds.

Electric freight locomotive was built by the Pullman Car Company at Pullman, Ill., in 1888 for the Ansonia, Derby and Birmingham Electric Line, now a part of the Connecticut Company and thus a part of Conrail (New Haven Division). The locomotive weighed 17.5 tons and was capable of hauling a train weighing about 35 tons at less than 10 m.p.h. The first trial took place May 1, 1888. *(Along the Line. Vol. 6, No. 2. September 1929)*

Electric locomotive made a trial roundtrip on April 29, 1851, on the Washington branch of the Baltimore and Ohio Railroad from Washington,

The First

D.C., to Bladensburg, Md., five miles each way. It was designed by Charles Grafton Page of Salem, Mass. It was 15 feet long, 6 feet wide, and had a platform truck of four wheels under the forward end, and two 5-foot driving wheels under the rear end. It attained a speed of 19 m.p.h. It was operated by "galvanism" storage batteries, but was not practical as it did not run any appreciable distance. *(Edward Hungerford—Story of the Baltimore and Ohio Railroad)*

Gas-turbine–electric locomotive was track-tested November 15, 1948, at Erie, Pa. It was built by the American Locomotive Company for the Union Pacific Railroad Company and publicly demonstrated June 16, 1949. The locomotive weighed 500,000 pounds and had a continuous tractive effort of 68,500 pounds at 20.4 mph. It was 83 feet 7½ inches long inside of knuckles. Power from the generator was supplied to eight traction motors, each of which drove an axle. It was geared for 79 miles an hour, the locomotive carrying enough fuel for 12 hours of operation at 4,500 h.p. The gas turbine power was rated at 4,800 h.p.

Gas-turbine propane-fueled locomotive was placed in service on June 8, 1953, by the Union Pacific Railroad to haul freight between Los Angeles, Calif., and Las Vegas, Nev. It delivered 4,800 h.p., more than three diesel units operated together. The locomotive was built by the General Electric Company. Propane burns without leaving carbonlike deposits on the turbine blades.

Locomotive bid was solicited by the Baltimore and Ohio Railroad Company in a series of advertisements which first appeared January 4, 1831, in the Baltimore, Md., *American.* For the most approved engine of American manufacture $4,000 was offered, and $3,500 for the one adjudged the next best. The *York,* built by Phineas Davis of York, Pa., was selected. It weighed 3.5 tons and attained velocity by gearing, a spur wheel and pinion being on one of the axles of the wheels.

Locomotive built in the United States to pull passengers was the *Tom Thumb,* designed and built by Peter Cooper in Baltimore, Md. It weighed 6 tons and had a 30-inch driving wheel. Its gauge was 4 feet 8½ inches. On Saturday, August 28, 1830, it carried 26 passengers 13 miles over the tracks of the Baltimore and Ohio Railroad in 1 hour 15 minutes. It returned with 30 passengers in 61 minutes, including a 4-minute stop to take on water. Another American locomotive, the *Best Friend,* built at the West Point Foundry for use on the Charleston and Hamburg Railroad, made its initial trip November 2, 1830, but it was derailed. *(Edward Hungerford—The Story of the Baltimore and Ohio Railroad)*

Locomotive for railroad use was the *Stourbridge Lion* built by Foster, Rastrick & Co. of Stourbridge, England. The diameter of the driving wheel was 48 inches. The gauge was 4 feet 3 inch-

The First

es. Horatio Allen was sent to England by the Delaware and Hudson Railroad Company to purchase it. The engine weighed seven tons and traveled at the speed of 10 m.p.h. Its first run in the United States took place on August 9, 1829, on the tracks of the Delaware and Hudson between Carbondale, a coal mining center, and Honesdale, the canal terminus in Pennsylvania. The locomotive was too heavy for the track. The centenary of this run was celebrated at Honesdale, Pa., and Mrs. Russell D. Lewis of Orange, N.J., a granddaughter of Horatio Allen, the first engineer of the *Stourbridge Lion,* unveiled a statue in commemoration of the event.

Locomotive owned by an industrial company was ordered June 1890 by the Whitin Machine Works, Whitinsville, Mass. from the Thomson-Houston Electric Co., Lynn, Mass., and placed in service May 11, 1892, hauling freight cars to the plant. It could haul 60 tons at a speed of 7 m.p.h. *(Thomas B. Navin—The Whitin Machine Works Since 1831)*

Locomotive (super-giant) to carry the weight of 1,000,000 pounds on drivers was the Class EL-2B No. 125, a 6,800 h.p. electric locomotive built by the General Electric Company, Erie, Pa., and placed in operation on January 27, 1948, by the Virginian Railway Company, Norfolk, Va., between Roanoke, Va., and Mullens, W.Va. It had 16 driving axles and an overall length of 150 feet 8 inches.

Locomotive to attain a speed of less than 1 mile a minute was a No. 10 locomotive, built at Altoona, Pa., which covered 1 mile in 58 seconds and another mile in 59 seconds during a 34-mile run from Huntingdon, Pa., to Harrisburg, Pa., completed in 44 minutes on March 17, 1881.

Locomotive to attain the proved speed of 112.5 miles an hour was the New York Central's famous locomotive 999, the *Empire State Express,* built at the West Albany shops of the New York Central and Hudson River Railroad. The coupled wheels were 7 feet 2 inches in diameter. The time was clocked May 10, 1893.

Locomotive to burn coal (practical, American-made) was the *York,* built at York, Pa., invented by Phineas Davis, a watchmaker. Its first trial took place on February 19, 1831. It was the first locomotive which had coupled wheels and a double instead of a single pair of drivers. The only accident in which it was involved occurred on September 27, 1835, when as the result of a defective track Phineas Davis was killed riding on the locomotive. *(John C. Jordan—An Historical Citizen: The Career of Phineas Davis)*

Locomotive to pull a train on a track was a steam locomotive which was built by John Stevens October 23, 1824. When he was 76 years old, Stevens designed a locomotive which he operated on a circular track 220 feet in circumference on his

The First

estate at Hoboken, N.J. It was moved by means of a large gear wheel engaging a toothed rack placed on the ties between the rails. To keep it from running off the track—the wheels had no flanges—little horizontal friction rollers, fixed to posts like table legs on the underside chassis, pressed and rolled along the inner vertical face of the wooden beams used for rails. The locomotive could pull a 1,000-pound load at 12 m.p.h. *(Carl Weaver Mitman—The Beginning of the Mechanical Transport Era in America)*

Locomotive to use oil fuel was the *Young America,* an eight-wheeled wood-burning locomotive equipped with an oil burner from a San Francisco steamboat in 1879 by the Central Pacific Railroad. The fuel supply consisted of one barrel of crude oil mounted on a tender and connected to the burner with five hose lines.

Locomotive with a cab for the engineer and crew was the *Samuel D. Ingham,* built in 1835–1836 in Philadelphia, Pa., for the Beaver Meadow Railroad (now the Lehigh Valley). It was of the eight-wheel type and had a peculiar valve motion, the reversing being done by a block sliding on the valve seats. It was designed by Andrew Eastwick. Abner Houston was the engineer, and Stephen Maxwell and "Squire Longshore" were the spragmen who pressed the brake blocks against the wheels to lessen speed.

Locomotive with a four-wheeled front truck was the *Experiment,* designed by John Bloomfield Jervis for the Mohawk & Hudson River Railroad, the first railroad operated in New York State, and later a part of the New York Central. The *Experiment* was tried out in August 1832.

Locomotive with six or eight driving wheels, the axles of which were placed parallel to each other, was patented by Ross Winans on October 1, 1834. Winans was also the first to introduce eight-wheel cars in railroading. The first car was the *Columbus,* which was first used by the Baltimore and Ohio Railroad Company July 4, 1831. *(John Langdon Sullivan—On the Baltimore Rail-road Carriage Invented by Ross Winans)*

Narrow-gauge locomotive was constructed in Philadelphia by the Baldwin Locomotive Works. It was known as Engine No. 1, the *Montezuma,* and was first used by the Denver and Rio Grande Western Railroad Company on July 3, 1871. It had a 3-foot gauge, a length of 30 feet, and a total weight of 25,000 pounds.

Race between a locomotive and a horse-drawn vehicle took place on August 25, 1830, between Relay and Baltimore, Md., a distance of nine miles. The horse won, as the *Tom Thumb,* the locomotive of the Baltimore and Ohio Railroad, driven by Peter Cooper, was involved in an accident.

LOCOMOTIVE—*Continued*

Rack-rail diesel-electric locomotive was built by the General Electric Company, Schenectady, N.Y., for the Manitou and Pike's Peak Railway, the highest cog railroad in the world, and placed in service July 16, 1939. It pushed the 50-passenger car up the 16 percent grade, and on the downward trip backed down the grade in front of the car. Dynamic braking assisted in holding the car at a safe speed in descending the steep slopes.

Streamlined electric engine was No. 4800, type GG1, placed in service by the Pennsylvania Railroad Company on January 28, 1935, in a test run between Washington, D.C., and Philadelphia, Pa. The engine was 79½ feet long, of all-steel construction, and weighed 230 tons. It operated on an 11,000-volt, 25-cycle, single-phase system, the current fed by overhead wires through a pantograph. The electric engine was placed in passenger service February 10, 1935.

Streamlined steam locomotive was introduced by the New York Central Lines December 14, 1934, between Albany, N.Y., and Karner, N.Y. It was named the *Commodore Vanderbilt,* after the founder of the New York Central Lines and was 96 feet long and weighed 228 tons. It developed 4,075 h.p. and was built in West Albany, N.Y.

LOCOMOTIVE BOOSTER was used on a New York Central locomotive in July, 1918. This is a device to aid the locomotive when starting and on grades.

LOCOMOTIVE COWCATCHER was invented by Isaac Dripps and used in 1833 on the Camden & Amboy Railroad between Bordentown and Hightstown, N.J. It consisted originally of a small attachment on two wheels with projecting points, but since the prongs impaled animals, a heavy bar at right angles to the rails replaced it. *(John Elfreth Watkins—The Camden and Amboy Railroad)*

LOCOMOTIVE HEADLIGHT

Electric locomotive headlight was patented by Leonidas G. Woolley of Mendon, Mich., who obtained patent No. 241,112 on May 3, 1881. It was a polygonal lamp frame suspended in position by a series of opposing springs which neutralized the jarring.

Locomotive illumination was devised by Horatio Allen for the Charleston and Hamburg Railroad in 1831. He placed a little square flat car, about five feet long, in front of the locomotive and spread a layer of sand several inches deep, on top of which he built a fire of pinewood knots. The device was impractical because of the frequent fires ignited by sparks blowing into and against the cars when the train was in motion. *(Horatio Allen—The Railroad Era: The First Five Years of Its Development)*

Talking headlight was installed November 6, 1934, on a Union Pacific six-car streamlined train, and was demonstrated the following day at Schenectady, N.Y. The operator on the train aimed the beacon of his projector at a concave mirror on the platform which enabled persons aboard the train to speak over the beam of light to those on the platform. The installation was made by the General Electric Company of Schenectady, N.Y. The talking headlight was used principally to demonstrate the effectiveness of such a communication system on railroads, even in daylight.

LOCOMOTIVE STEAM WHISTLE was made by the Rogers Locomotive and Machine Works, Paterson, N.J., and used October 6, 1837, on *The Sandusky,* a locomotive with a four-wheeled truck under the forward part of the engine. The whistle was so overworked on its run from Paterson, N.J., to New Brunswick, N.J., on the Paterson and Hudson River Railroad that it affected the supply of steam. The locomotive was sold to the Mad River and Lake Erie Railroad Company for $6,750 and on October 14, 1837, was packed in boxes and shipped by schooner. *(Charles Frederick Carter—When Railroads Were New)*

LOG ROLLING (BIRLING) NATIONAL CHAMPIONSHIP was held September 9, 1898, on the lagoon at the Trans-Mississippi Exposition, Omaha, Neb., on Lumbermen's Day, by the Lumbermen's Association of America. There were six entries. The winner was Tommy Fleming of Eau Claire, Wis.

LOGANBERRY was introduced in 1881 by Judge James Harvey Logan in Santa Cruz, Calif., and given to the public in 1893 by the University of California. The loganberry is a cross between a California wild blackberry and a red raspberry. *(Edward James Wickson—California Fruits and How to Grow Them)*

LOGIC BOOK was William Brattle's *Compendium Logicae Secundum Principia, D. Renati Cartesii Plerumque Efformatum, et Catechistice Propositum* published in Boston, Mass., in 1735. It was published in Latin and contained 64 pages.

LOLLIPOP MACHINE. *See* Confectionery machine

LONG-DISTANCE TELEPHONE CALL. *See under* Telephone

LONG JUMP

Broad jump to reach more than 25 feet was made July 23, 1921, by Edward O. Gourdin (black athlete) of Harvard College, who jumped (broad long jump) 25 feet 3 inches during the International Meet at Harvard Stadium, Cambridge, Mass. The participants at the meet represented Harvard, Yale, Oxford, and Cambridge.

The First

LOOKOUT (forest fire). *See* Forest fire: Forest fire lookout tower

LOOP-THE-LOOP, AIRPLANE. *See under* Aviation—Flights

LOOP-THE-LOOP, AUTOGIRO. *See* Autogiro: Autogiro to loop the loop publicly

LOOP-THE-LOOP CENTRIFUGAL RAILWAY was invented by Edwin Prescott of Arlington, Mass., who obtained patent No. 609,164, August 16, 1898, on a roller coaster, and patent No. 667,-455, February 5, 1901, on a centrifugal railway. It was known as Boyton's Centrifugal Railway and was installed at Coney Island, N.Y., in 1900. It had a 75-foot incline and a 20-foot-wide loop.

LOTTERY
Daily state lotteries with the same winning daily number occurred on October 3, 1977, when number 92 won top prize in the Pick It Game of New Jersey (paying $411.50) and that of Pennsylvania (paying $250). On October 31, 1979, the New Jersey Pick-It and the Connecticut Daily had the same winning number: 728.

Lottery of importance was held on June 26, 1614, by the Virginia Company. The first Great Prize was 4,500 crowns. This method of obtaining funds was used by the colonies and the Continental Congress.

Lottery held by the Continental Congress was held April 10, 1777, in Philadelphia, Pa., for the purpose of obtaining funds. On November 1, 1776, a lottery was approved and a committee appointed which rendered a report, November 18, 1776. Seven managers were appointed to conduct the lottery. Treasury bank notes were awarded as prizes payable at the end of five years. Funds were obtained by lottery by the individual colonies at various times prior to this national lottery.

Lottery in which the top prize was $1 million was conducted by New York State and won by George Ashton, his wife Genevieve, and his son Glenn, of West Hempstead, Long Island, N.Y. on October 8, 1970, based on a horserace at the Belmont Track on September 24, 1970. The sale of lottery tickets amounted to $16,724,931.

Lottery legislation (national) hostile to lotteries was the act of March 2, 1827 (4 Stat. L. 238), which provided "that no postmaster or assistant postmaster shall act as agent for lottery offices or under any color of purchase, or otherwise, send lottery tickets; nor shall any postmaster receive free of postage or frank lottery schemes, circulars or tickets."

Lottery (state regulated) in which 3 zeros made up the winning number was the New Jersey lottery drawing held September 13, 1976, which paid $96. On August 16, 1977, 450 of the 700,000 players held 000, which returned $388 on a 50-cent ticket.

The First

(New York Times. Sec. II, p. 3, column 1. Aug. 17, 1977).

Lottery to guarantee a minimum of $1,800,000 to the winner was the "1776 Instant Lottery Drawing" of New Jersey, drawn January 27, 1976, at Montclair State College, Montclair, N.J. The winner was Eric C. Leek, hair stylist of North Arlington, N.J., who had the option of $1,776 a week for life; $92,352 a year for himself and heirs in 10 years of payments; or a guaranteed minimum of $1,800,000.

LOUDSPEAKER IN U.S. SENATE *See under* Congress (U.S.)—Senate

LOUISIANA PURCHASE. *See* Territorial expansion: Annexation of territory

LUCITE (polymethyl methacrylate) production (commercial) was begun by E. I. du Pont de Nemours & Company, Wilmington, Del., on May 21, 1936. Lucite is a plastic which is low in moisture absorption, highly nonconducting, and crystal clear, and which possesses the interesting property of bending light rays as they pass through it.

LUNCH, FREE. *See* Free lunch

LUNCH WAGON was introduced in Providence, R.I., in 1872 by Walter Scott. He drove a wagon to a location on Westminster Street where he sold coffee, sandwiches, pies, and cakes. This was the first "lunch car" or Night Owl, the forerunner of the dining lunch cars. In order to comply with Board of Health regulations and to secure running water, the operators of the wagons obtained desirable vacant sites where they hooked up to a water supply. Individual wagons were constructed until 1887, when they were commercially manufactured in Providence, R.I., by Ruel B. Jones, who also operated a chain of lunch wagons. *(Franklin Pierce Rice—Dictionary of Worcester)*

LUNG REMOVAL. *See* Surgical operation

LUTHERAN CHURCH
American Lutheran Church was organized in Toledo, Ohio, August 11, 1930, through the merger of the Lutheran Synod of Buffalo (organized June 25, 1845), the Evangelical Lutheran Synod of Iowa and other states (organized August 24, 1854), and the Evangelical Lutheran Joint Synod of Ohio and other states (organized September 14, 1818).

Lutheran Church building was dedicated by the Reverend Johannes Campanius at Christina (Tinicum Island), near the present site of Essington, Pa., September 4, 1645. Governor Johan Printz had erected Fort Göteborg and a small blockhouse in which Campanius had conducted services previous to the erection of the church.

Lutheran pastor was Reorus Torkillus from Mölndal, Sweden, who came over on the *Kalmar Nyckel (Key of Kalmar)* with Governor Peter Hollander Ridder, landing on April 17, 1640, at Fort Christina, Del. He died of the plague in 1643.

The First

LUTHERAN CHURCH—*Continued*
(Christopher Ward, New Sweden on the Delaware)

Lutheran pastor ordained in America was Justus Falckner, ordained in Gloria Dei Church at Wicaco, Philadelphia, Pa., November 24, 1703, with Andrew Rudman, Erick Biörck, and Andrew Sandel as officiating clergymen. *(Julius Friedrich Sachse—Justus Falckner)*

Lutheran services in English were held in 1694 in Germantown and Philadelphia by Heinrich Bernhard Koester. The first Lutheran synod in America, the Evangelical Lutheran Ministerium of Pennsylvania and adjacent states, was held on August 26, 1748, through the efforts of Henry Melchior Muehlenberg.

LYCEUM was organized by Josiah Holbrook in Millbury, Mass., in October 1826. Its purpose was to afford adults an opportunity for mutual improvement through association and study, stimulate an interest in the schools, and contribute to the training of teachers and the dissemination of knowledge through libraries and museums. The American Lyceum Association was organized May 4, 1831, in New York City by delegates from Maine, Massachusetts, and New York. The Millbury Lyceum became the Millbury Lyceum No. 1, branch of the American Lyceum. *(Centennial History of Millbury, Mass.)*

LYNCH LAW (state) was an antilynching statute approved December 20, 1893, by Georgia, "an act to prevent mob violence in this state, to prescribe a punishment for the same, to provide a means for carrying this act into effect, to punish a failure to comply with its requirements, and for other purposes" (No. 347 Part 1—Title 10, Misc.). Violators were guilty of a felony punishable by imprisonment of 1 to 20 years. If death resulted, a murder charge could be instituted.

M

MACADAM ROAD. *See* Road

MACARONI FACTORY was established by Antoine Zerega in Brooklyn, N.Y., in 1848. It consisted of a small mill with crude mechanical equipment for grinding raw materials.

MACHINE GUN. *See* Ordnance

MACHINE GUN IN AIRPLANE. *See* Aviation—Airplane: Airplane outfitted with a machine gun

MACHINE PATENT. *See* Patent

MADSTONE is supposed to have come from Chicago, Ill., in 1804. It was sold by Dr. Parker to Benjamin Milam of Winona, Miss., who used it to perform "miraculous cures." A madstone is a light porous stone of greenish color said to possess the

The First

property of drawing poison from the bite of a dog.

MAGAZINE. *See* Periodical; *also under* specific languages, occupations, religious and fraternal organizations, sciences, sports, trades, e.g., Agricultural journal, Book trade magazine, Catholic magazine, Masonic magazine, Welsh magazine

MAGIC LANTERN
Magic lantern book was *The Expositor, or Many Mysteries Unravelled; delineated in a series of letters between a friend and his correspondent, comprising the learned pig, invisible lady and acoustic temple, philosophical swan penetrating spy glasses, optical and magnetic, and various other curiosities on similar principles; also a few of the most wonderful feats as performed by the art of legerdemain, with some reflections on ventriloquism,* by William Frederick Pinchbeck. Printed in Boston, Mass., in 1805, it consisted of 100 pages.

Magic lantern feature show was *Miss Jerry,* previewed October 9, 1894, at the Carbon Studio, New York City. Alexander Black was the author, scenario writer, director, camera man, and titler. The leads were taken by Blanche Bayliss, who played Jerry, William Courtenay as the hero, and Ernest Hastings as the villain. Slides were shown at the rate of five a second.

Magic lantern slides (glass-plate) known as Hyalotypes were invented by Frederick Langenheim of Philadelphia, Pa., who obtained patent No. 7,784 November 19, 1850, on an "improvement in photographic pictures on glass."

MAGICIAN'S ADVERTISEMENT. *See* Advertisement

MAGNESIUM
Magnesium commercially produced from seawater was extracted on January 21, 1941, by the Dow Chemical Company, Freeport, Tex. It sold for approximately 23 cents a pound.

MAGNESIUM AIRPLANE. *See* Aviation—Airplane: Jet magnesium airplane

MAGNET. *See* Electric magnet

MAGNETIC TAPE RECORDER. *See* Tape Recorder

MAIL CAR. *See under* Railroad car

MAIL CHUTE. *See under* Postal service

MAIL FRANKING PRIVILEGE. *See under* Postal service

MAIL-ORDER HOUSE. *See under* Business

MAIL SERVICE. *See* Airmail service; Postal service

MAIL WAGON, AUTOMOBILE. *See* Automobile mail wagon

The First

MAILBOX. *See under* Postal service

MAIZE, or Indian corn, produced in quantity by people of English blood, of which there is any authentic record, was grown on a 40-acre tract planted in the Jamestown colony, Va., in 1609. Maize is indigenous to America, and records of its growth and use were made by both Columbus and Verrezano. *(Philip Alexander Bruce—Institutional History of Virginia in the 17th Century)*

MAIZOLITH. *See* Cornstone

MAJOR GENERAL. *See* Army officer

MALLET, DENTAL. *See* Dental mallet

MALLET LOCOMOTIVE. *See* Locomotive: Duplex compound locomotive (Mallet)

MALTED MILK. *See* Milk

MANGANESE STEEL. *See* Steel

MANILA PAPER. *See* Paper

MANUAL-BLOCK RAILROAD SIGNAL SYSTEM. *See* Railroad signal system: Railroad signal system (manual block)

MANUAL FOR KINDERGARTENS. *See* Kindergarten manual

MANUAL TRAINING
Industrial school on the Fellenberg plan was established in 1819 in Derby, Conn., by Josiah Holbrook. The boys paid a portion of their tuition by laboring on the farm. In 1824, with the cooperation of the Reverend Truman Coe, Holbrook established an Agricultural Seminary. Neither of these enterprises was successful. *(U.S. Department of Agriculture—History of Agricultural Education in the United States—Miscellaneous Publication No. 36)*

Industrial school for girls was organized in Lancaster, Mass., the funds being obtained by subscription undertaken in April 1854. The school was incorporated as a state institution, August 27, 1856, with Bradford K. Pierce as the first superintendent. This school was administered by the Department of Public Welfare.

Manual training institute was the Fellenberg Manual Labor Institute opened in 1829 in Greenfield, Mass., by James Henry Coffin. *(John Cunningham Clyde—Life of James H. Coffin)*

Manual training school entirely financed by public taxes was the Baltimore Manual Training School, established in Baltimore, Md., in 1884 under authority of municipal ordinance of October 20, 1883. Instruction and practice were given in the use of tools embracing the fields of carpentry, wood turning, pattern making, chipping and filing, forge work, molding, soldering and brazing, etc.

The First

School to offer courses in manual training was organized in Talbot County, Md., in 1750 by the Reverend Thomas Bacon, who named it "A Charity Workers' School." It opened December 1, 1751, with an enrollment of six boys. It was financed through funds from a series of concerts given in Maryland and Virginia. *(Oswald Tilghman—History of Talbot County, Md.)*

Vocational high school for girls. *See under* High school

MANUFACTURERS' ASSOCIATION of diversified industries (national) was the National Association of Manufacturers of the United States, organized on January 22, 1895, at a convention held in Cincinnati, Ohio. The first president elected was Thomas P. Dolan.

MANUFACTURERS' FAIR. *See* Fair

MAP
Automobile road map was published and distributed in 1914 by the Gulf Oil Company, Pittsburgh, Pa. William B. Akin conceived the idea, and 10,000 maps were distributed showing roads and routes in Allegheny County, Pa.

Geological map. *See* Geology book

Globular map published showing the Western Hemisphere and the first map to use the description "America" was printed in April 15, 1507 at St. Die in the Vosges Mountains of Alsace. It was designed in 12 connected globular segments, presumably intended to be cut out, mounted on heavy paper, and shaped into globular form. It was made by Martin Waldseemüller, a German cartographer, from a single wood block 9½ by 15 inches.

Map made in the United States published in a book appeared in the Reverend William Hubbard's *The Present State of New England being a narrative of the troubles with the Indians in New England, from the first planting thereof in the year 1607 to 1677*, published by John Foster, Boston, Mass., in 1677. It was a topographical woodcut folding map and was known as the "Wine Hills' Map" since the English edition had "Wine Hills" instead of the "White Hills" of New Hampshire. It bore the inscription "Being the first that ever was here cut, and done by the best Pattern that could be had, which being in some places defective, it made the other less exact, yet doth it sufficiently shew the Scituation of the Countrey and conveniently well the distance of places." The name of the cartographer is unknown. *(Emerson David Fite and Archibald Freeman—A Book of Old Maps)*

Map of a city within the present limits of the United States is a line-engraving map of St. Augustine, Fla., which appeared in *Expeditis Francisco Draki Eqvitis Angli in Indias Occidentalis—1588.* This illustrated map may not have been the first, but it is the earliest known.

The First

MAP—*Continued*

Map of the United States engraved in America was a wall map, 41 by 46.5 inches, made by Abel Buell in New Haven, Conn., in 1783, after the Treaty of Peace. It was a line engraving, and was advertised for sale in the *Connecticut Journal* of March 31, 1784: "As this Map is the effect of the compiler's long and unwearied application, diligence and industry, and as perfection has been the great object of his labors, and it being the first ever compiled, engraved, and finished by any one man, and an American, he flatters himself, that every patriotic gentleman, and lover of geographical knowledge, will not hesitate to encourage the improvement of his country. Every favour will be most gratefully acknowledged, by the public's most obedient and very humble servant." *(Leonard Mackall—Abel Buell)*

Mosaic map of the contiguous 48 states from scenes transmitted from a satellite measured 10 feet by 16 feet and consisted of 595 photographs selected from 200,000 taken by the Hughes-built multispectral scanner (MSS). The map was assembled in November 1974 by the U.S. Department of Agriculture's Soil Cartographic Unit, Hyattsville, Md. It took 2 men 5-6 months to construct the Earth Resources Technology photomosaic. The photographs were taken from a 560-mile altitude from the ERTS-1 mission (now *Landsat*) launched July 23, 1972.

Relief map was of the Island of San Domingo, made in 1871, by Edwin Eugene Howell. In 1876, he made a relief map of the Grand Canyon of the Colorado as part of the Government Exhibit at the Philadelphia Centennial Exposition, Philadelphia, Pa.

Road map was *A Survey of the Roads of the United States of America* published in 1789 in New York City by Christopher Colles. It contained 86 plates and detailed the routes near New York City.

Road map for public use was printed in *Tulley's Almanac* of 1698 published in Boston, Mass., by John Tulley. The almanac showed a list of towns, roads, and distances from Boston. Later editions gave the names of the tavern keepers.

War map to appear in America was published in the December 24, 1733, issue of John Peter Zenger's *New York Weekly Journal*. A map of the harbor and fortifications of Louisburg, Nova Scotia, were shown. *(Willard Grosvenor Bleyer—History of American Journalism)*

MAPPING CAMERA. *See* Camera: Aerial camera (nine-lens) for large-scale mapping

MARATHON DANCE. *See* Dance marathon

MARATHON RACE (annual) was the American Marathon Race, 26 miles 385 feet, from Hopkinton, Mass. (through Ashland, Framingham, Natick, Wellesley, and Newton) to Exeter Street,

The First

Boston, Mass., on April 19, 1897. It was won by John J. McDermott of the Pastime Athletic Club of New York City whose time was 2 hours 55 minutes 10 seconds. *(Boston Daily Globe. April 20, 1897)*

MARBLE BUILDING of importance was the Bank of the United States, Philadelphia, Pa., incorporated February 25, 1791. The building was designed by Samuel Blodget, although he was not an architect, and built in 1791.

MARBLE QUARRY was operated in 1785 by Isaac Underhill on land owned by Reuben Bloomer in Dorset, Vt. The quarry was first worked for stone for fire jambs, chimney backs, hearths, and lintels. A quarry was also opened in Rutland, Vt., in 1785. Marble used before 1785 had been obtained from exposed marble ledges. *(Report of Marble, Slate and Granite Industries of Vermont—George H. Perkins, state geologist)*

MARBLE STATUARY GROUP executed by an American was *The Chanting Cherubs* designed in 1830 by Horatio Greenough for James Fenimore Cooper. The subject was suggested by a portion of a Raphael painting but incurred hostility because of the nudity of the figures. *(Henry Theodore Tuckerman—A Memorial of Horatio Greenough)*

MARDI GRAS. *See* Holiday

MARGARINE. *See* Oleomargarine

MARIAN CONGRESS. *See under* Servite Church

MARINE BATTLE. *See under* War (colonial)

MARINE CORPS

American Marines were organized on November 10, 1775, under authority of the Continental Congress. The first Marine officer was Samuel Nicholas, a Philadelphia Quaker, commissioned captain on November 28, 1775, at $32 a month. They were called the First and Second Battalions of American Marines, and were commanded by 1 colonel, 2 lieutenant colonels, 2 majors, etc. The Marines were under the jurisdiction of the War Department until April 30, 1798, when Congress created the Navy Department. The present U.S. Marine Corps was created by act of July 11, 1798 (1 Stat. L. 594), "an act for the establishing and organizing a Marine Corps," which authorized 1 major, 4 captains, 16 first lieutenants, 12 second lieutenants, 48 sergeants, 48 corporals, 32 drums and fifes, and 720 privates, including enlisted men." The first major was William Ward Burrows of South Carolina, who was appointed July 12, 1798, and served nearly 6 years. *(Clyde Hill Metcalf—History of the U.S. Marine Corps)*

Black commissioned officer in the regular U.S. Marine Corps was John Earl Rudder, a midshipman in the regular Naval Reserve Officers' Training Corps at Purdue University, Lafayette, Ind. who was commissioned June 8, 1948, as a second lieutenant. He served as an enlisted man in the

The First

Marine Corps Reserve from July 24, 1943, to June 26, 1946.

Commando raid was made February 16, 1804, by Lieutenent Stephen Decatur (U.S. Marine Corps), who led 74 volunteers, including 8 Marines under Sergeant Solomon Wren, in a 20-minute raid to burn the U.S.S. *Philadelphia,* which had been captured by the Tripolitans and was lying under the protection of their shore guns. The raiders killed or captured all the enemy but two and set the *Philadelphia* afire.

General (black) of the Marines was Colonel Frank E. Petersen, Jr., of Topeka, Kans., nominated February 23, 1979, for brigadier general by President Jimmy Carter. (He was the 30th black to achieve the rank of general or admiral.)

General (4 stars) of the Marines was Major General Thomas Holcomb, commandant of the Marine Corps, who was advanced to Lieutenant General on January 20, 1942. When he retired on January 1, 1944, he was placed on the retired list, and his rank was raised to that of full general.

General (4 stars) of the Marines on active duty to become a full general was Lieutenant General Alexander Archer Vandegrift, appointed April 4, 1945, with date of rank from March 21, 1945.

General (woman) in the Marine Corps was Brigadier General Margaret Ann Brewer, nominated April 6, 1978, by President Jimmy Carter and sworn in May 11, 1978, as director of the division of information by Commandant of the Marine Corps General Lóuis Hugh Wilson, Jr.

Marine band was authorized by act of Congress of July 11, 1798 (1 Stat. L. 594), to appoint a drum major, a fife major, and 32 drummers and fifers. William Farr was leader of the Marine band from January 21, 1799, to November 22, 1804. The first President to review the band from his residence was John Adams on January 1, 1801.

Marine corps was organized in 1740 when three regiments were recruited in New York to serve under the British flag. They wore green swallow-tail coats faced with red, white waistcoats, buff trousers, crossed white belts, and three-cornered hats. *(Richard Strader Collum—History of the U.S. Marine Corps)*

Marine Corps jet ace in the Korean War was Major John F. Bolt of Sanford, Fla., who led a 4-plane Saber flight on his 37th mission and downed his 5th and 6th MIG-15 in an attack on 4 MIGs east of Sinuiju, Korea, on November 18, 1950. In World War II, he qualified as an ace, when he shot down 6 Zekes between September 23, 1943, and January 4, 1944, while serving with Boyington's Black Sheep Squadron.

Marine engagement in battle. *See under* War (colonial)

The First

Marine officer killed in service was John Fitzpatrick, a second lieutenant in the Continental Marines, who was killed April 6, 1777, when the *Alfred,* a 24-gun frigate under command of Captain Samuel Nicholas was attacked off Block Island by the 20-gun H.M.S. *Glasgow.*

Marine officer of Chinese descent in the U.S. Marine Corps was Wilbur Carl Sze, commissioned a second lieutenant on December 15, 1943. He was born in Washington, D.C., and at the age of 5 went to China, where he remained 11 years before returning to the United States.

Marine officer to orbit the earth was Marine Lieutenant Colonel John Herschel Glenn of New Concord, Ohio, who on February 20, 1962, in *Friendship 7* orbited the earth 3 times in the first manned space capsule and was the first to fly at supersonic speed.

Marine pilot was Lieutenant Alfred Austell Cunningham, assigned for training and instruction to the Navy Aviation Camp, Annapolis, Md., on July 9, 1912. He made his first solo flight August 1, 1912, received seaplane license certificate No. 2, and became naval aviator No. 5. From November 17, 1919, to December 12, 1920, he served as director of Marine Corps Aviation.

Marine pilot to fly over the Antarctic continent was Captain Alton U. Parker, U.S. Marine Corps Reserve, who was the pilot on the *Floyd Bennett,* the airplane of the First Byrd Antarctic Expedition, which took off from Little America on December 5, 1929.

Marine regiment in France was the 5th Regiment of Marines, commanded by Colonel Charles A. Doyen, which embarked June 14, 1917, at New York City on the *Henderson, De Kalb,* and *Hancock.* The entire regiment arrived at St. Nazaire, France, by July 2, 1917. The regiment ws detached for service in France by executive order of May 25, 1917.

Woman in the U.S. Marine Band was Staff Sergeant Ruth Johnson, who joined the band on May 17, 1973. She played the French horn.

Woman marine was Lucy Brewer, alias George Baker and Louisa Baker, who concealed her sex and served on board the *Constitution* in its battle with the *Guerrière,* August 19, 1812. *(Lucy Brewer —Affecting Narrative)*

Woman marine (enlisted) to christen a naval ship. *See* Ship: Naval ship (destroyer) christened by an enlisted woman marine

Woman marine major was Ruth Cheney Streeter of Morristown, N.J., appointed January 29, 1943, and sworn in February 12, 1943, as a major in the U.S. Marine Corps Women's Reserve. She was advanced to lieutenant colonel November 22, 1943, and to colonel February 1, 1944. She served as director of the Marine Corps Women's Reserve

The First

MARINE CORPS—*Continued*
from February 13, 1943 to December 7, 1945, when she resigned.

Woman marine reserve was Mrs. Opha May Johnson, who enrolled August 13, 1918, as a private and was assigned to duty as a clerk at Headquarters, Quartermaster Corps, U.S. Marine Corps, Washington, D.C. On August 12, 1918, Secretary of the Navy Josephus Daniels had granted authority "to enroll women in the Marine Corps Reserve for clerical duty at Headquarters, U.S. Marine Corps, Washington, D.C., and at other Marine Corps offices in the United States." She was appointed sergeant (provisional) September 11, 1918, and was honorably discharged February 28, 1919.

Woman unit commander to direct 2,000 men was Colonel Mary E. Bane of Normal, Ill., who on December 10, 1973, was named commanding officer of Headquarters and Service Company, Camp Pendleton, Oceanside, Calif., which had an enrollment of 2,150 men and women.

MARINE HOSPITAL. *See* Hospital

MARINE INSURANCE LAW (state). *See under* Insurance

MARINE TERMINAL. *See* Dock

MARINERS' CHURCH. *See* Church

MARINER'S MEDAL. *See* Medal

MARITIME DAY. *See* Holiday

MARITIME DISTINGUISHED SERVICE MEDAL. *See* Medal: Distinguished Service Medal (Merchant Marine)

MARITIME MUSEUM. *See* Museum

MARITIME SCHOOL
Woman graduate of a 4-year maritime school was Deborah B. Doane of Essex, Conn., who was graduated on May 1, 1976, from the Maine Maritime Academy, Castine, Me.

MARKETS, OFFICE OF (U.S.). *See* Agriculture Department (U.S.): Office of Markets

MARRIAGE. *See* Wedding

MARRIAGE COURSE in a college was given by Professor Ernest Rutherford Groves in 1924 at the University of North Carolina, Chapel Hill, N.C. *(Ernest Rutherford Groves—Marriage)*

MARSHAL
Marshals of the United States (women) were Jacqueline P. Balley, of Washington, D.C., and Joanne Neely, of Oxon Hill, Md., sworn in November 21, 1973, at Washington, D.C., by Wayne B. Colburn, director of the U.S. Marshals Service. Before assuming active service, they completed a 12-week course of instruction.

The First

MARTYR
Christian martyr on U.S. soil was Fray Juan de Padilla, Spanish Franciscan missionary who was murdered by the Kansas Indians in 1542 near Lyon, Kans. He accompanied Francis Vasquez Coronado into New Mexico (1540-1542).

MASK. *See* Baseball catcher's mask; Gas mask

MASKING TAPE. *See* Tape, Masking

MASONIC BOOK was printed and published by Benjamin Franklin in Philadelphia in 1734. It was advertised from May 9 to May 30, 1734, in the *Pennsylvania Gazette.* It was an American edition of Anderson's *Constitutions of the Freemasons; containing the History, Charges, Regulations, etc., of that most Ancient and Right Worshipful Fraternity.*

MASONIC COLLEGE. *See* College

MASONIC MAGAZINE was *Free-Masons Magazine and General Miscellany,* a monthly, published April 1811 by Levis and Weaver, Philadelphia, Pa. It was edited by George Richards. *(American Lodge of Research—Transactions, Vol. 3)*

MASONRY
See also Freemasons

Black Masonic Grand Lodge (not Free and Accepted Masons) was the Provincial Grand Lodge organized June 24, 1791, in Boston, Mass., with Prince Hall as Grand Master.

MASS, CATHOLIC. *See* Catholic mass

MASSACRE. *See* American Indians: American Indian massacre of white people

MASTER'S DEGREE. *See under* Degrees (academic and honorary)

MASTOID OPERATION. *See* Surgical operation

MASTSHIP. *See* Ship: Ship equipped with a masthead sea anchorage for a dirigible

MATADOR. *See* Bullfight: Woman bullfighter

MATCH
"Book matches" were made by the Diamond Match Company at its Barberton, Ohio, factory in 1896 under patent No. 483,166 granted September 27, 1892, to Joshua Pusey of Lima, Pa. *(Herbert Manchester—Fifty Years of Match Making)*

Friction matches were made in Springfield, Mass., in 1834 in a small establishment in the "L" of the Frederick Chapin house on Chicopee Street, Chicopee (then a part of Springfield). Daniel M. Chapin and Alonzo Dwight Phillips of East Hartford produced matches which were known as the Chapin-Phillips matches. The business was finally sold to Byam and Carlton of Boston, Mass., and the product was thereafter known as the Boston Match. Previous to 1834 the only match in use had been a slender sulfur splint which was ignited by

The First

being drawn quickly through a double fold of sandpaper.

Match patent on phosphorous friction matches was patent No. 68 on "manufacturing of friction matches" awarded on October 24, 1836, to Alonzo Dwight Phillips of Springfield, Mass. The constituents of the "head" were chalk, phosphorus, glue, and brimstone. *(Herbert Manchester—The Romance of the Match)*

MATERIA MEDICA BOOK. *See* Medical book: Therapeutics and materia medica book

MATERNITY BOOK was *Letters to Married Women on Nursing and the Management of Children* by Dr. Hugh Smith, published in 1792 in Philadelphia, Pa., by Mathew Carey. It contained 167 pages (15 chapters), devoted to birthmarks, miscarriages, mother's milk, suckling, weaning, etc. It was printed from the sixth London edition.

MATINEE IDOL. *See* Actor

MATRON, PRISON. *See under* Prison

MAYOR

Black mayor of a major city was Carl Burton Stokes, a Democrat, elected November 7, 1967, by the citizens of Cleveland, Ohio. He was sworn in November 13, 1967, in the City Council Chamber.

Socialist mayor of a large city was Emil Seidel, who served as mayor of Milwaukee, Wis., from April 1910 to April 1912.

Woman mayor was Susanna Medora Salter, elected mayor of Argonia, Kans., on April 4, 1887. Her name was submitted without her knowledge by the Woman's Christian Temperance Union, and she did not know that she was a candidate until she went to the polls and found her name listed on the ballot. Although only 27 years of age, she received a two-thirds majority of the votes. She served one year for $1.

Woman mayor elected by a city west of the Rocky Mountains was Clara Munson, who served as mayor of Warrenton, Ore. from January 6, 1913, to December 1, 1913.

Woman mayor elected with an all-woman council was Mrs. Mary D. Lowman, elected April 1888 in Oskaloosa, Kans. Her council consisted of Sadie Balsley, Millie Golden, Emma Hamilton, Carrie Johnson, and Hannah Morse.

Woman mayor of a city of over 200,000 population was Patience Sewell Latting, sworn in April 13, 1971, as mayor of Oklahoma City, Okla. Her salary was $2,000 a year. The city's population then exceeded 366,000.

Woman mayor of a major city (over 500,000 population) was Janet Gray Hayes of San Jose, Calif., elected November 6, 1974, on the Democratic ticket.

The First

MEASURES STANDARDIZATION. *See* Weights and measures standardization

MEASURING MACHINE. *See* Caliper (screw)

MEAT

Beef export was from Savannah, Ga., in 1755, when 40 barrels of beef were shipped out; in 1770, 639 barrels of beef and 4,985 pounds of tallow were exported.

Beef exported to England was shipped October 1, 1875, by Timothy C. Eastman of New York City. It was known as "dead meat" and was sampled by Queen Victoria. *(Rudolf Alexander Clemen—History of the American Livestock and Meat Industry)*

Railroad shipments of dressed beef. *See* Railroad: Railroad shipments of dressed beef (year-round long-distance)

MEAT BISCUIT. *See under* Cracker

MEAT INSPECTION LEGISLATION (federal) was approved August 30, 1890 (26 Stat. L. 414), and provided for the inspection of salted pork and bacon intended for export, and the inspection of export swine, cattle, sheep, and other ruminants. *(Ulysses Grant Houck—Bureau of Animal Industry)*

MEAT PACKER was William Pynchon, who established a warehouse at Warehouse Point, Springfield, Mass., in 1636. He dealt in mutton, tallow, and wool, but his chief business was pork packing. He also sold beaver skins. Competition was keen and "merchants encreased so many that it became little worth, by reason of their out-buying one another, which caused them to live on husbandry." *(Proceedings of Connecticut Valley Historical Society, Vol. 2)*

MECHANICAL COTTON PICKER. *See* Cotton picker (mechanical)

MECHANICAL ENGINEERING LABORATORY for research work was established at Stevens Institute of Technology at Hoboken, N.J., in 1874. It was proposed by Robert Henry Thurston, professor of mechanical engineering, who on January 30, 1874, outlined the usefulness of the laboratory to the community in a letter which he sent to the trustees of the school. *(William Frederick Durand—Robert Henry Thurston, a Biography)*

MECHANICAL ENGINEERS' SOCIETY. *See* Engineering society: Mechanical engineering national society

MECHANICS' LIBRARY. *See* Library

MECHANICS' MAGAZINE. *See under* Periodical

MECHANICS TEXTBOOK was *The Elements of Analytical Mechanics*, 445 pages, by William Holmes Chambers Bartlett, professor of natural and experimental philosophy at the United States

The First

MECHANICS TEXTBOOK—Continued
Military Academy, published by A. S. Barnes &
Co., New York City, in 1853.

MECHANIZED SHOOTING GALLERY. *See*
Shooting gallery (mechanized)

MEDAL

**Admiral to receive the Congressional Medal of
Honor** was Rear Admiral Frank Friday Fletcher,
who was awarded the medal on December 4, 1915,
"for distinguished conduct in battle, engagements
of Veracruz, April 21 and 22, 1914." He was commander of American fleet off Mexico.

**Agriculture Department distinguished service
gold medal** was awarded November 12, 1947, to
five individuals—Dr. Hugh Hammond Bennett,
William Ashby Jump, and Milburn Lincoln Wilson
of Washington, D.C.; Dr. James Fitton Couch of
Wyndmoor, Pa.; and Lewis B. Holt of Clearwater,
Idaho—and to two units, the Northern Regional
Research Laboratory, Peoria Penicillin Group, Peoria, Ill., and the Orlando Florida Laboratory, Orlando, Fla.

**Agriculture Department distinguished service
gold medal presented to a woman** was awarded
May 25, 1950, to Lucy Maclay Alexander of Beltsville, Md., "for outstanding achievement in applying fundamental scientific principles to meat and
poultry cookery; for relating cooking shrinkage to
chemical composition and to method of producing
and processing for market; for formulating pre-
cise, practical directions for cooking meat and
poultry; and for designing and sponsoring a practical meat thermometer."

**Air Force Medal of Honor for action in the Ko-
rean War** was awarded posthumously to Major
Louis J. Sebille of Chicago, Ill., who was killed
August 5, 1951, in an F-51 Mustang which he dived
into the ground amid a group of enemy armored
vehicles near Hamchang, Korea. The award was
presented to his widow, Mrs. Elizabeth J. Sebille,
on August 24, 1951, at March Air Force Base, Riverside, Calif., by General Hoyt Sanford Vandenberg, Chief of Staff of the Air Force.

Air Mail Flyer's Medal of Honor was presented
to Mal Bryan Freeburg, December 13, 1933, by
President Franklin Delano Roosevelt. On April 12,
1933, while Freeburg was flying a trimotor plane,
an outward propeller broke and the vibration
loosened a motor, which lodged in a wing strut
and damaged the landing gear. He flew over the
Mississippi River, banked his plane, and shook
the motor free so that it would fall in the river and
not endanger anyone. He then flew 25 miles to an
emergency field and landed safely. The Air Mail
Flyer's Medal was authorized February 14, 1931
(46 Stat. L. 1110).

Air Medal (U.S.) awarded to a woman was presented to Second Lieutenant Elsie S. Ott, Army
Nurse Corps, at Bowman Field, Louisville, Ky.,

The First

March 26, 1943, by Brigadier General Fred S.
Borum, First Troop Carrier Command, "for
meritorious achievement while participating in an
aerial flight." She served as nurse for five patients
evacuated from India to Washington, D.C., January 17–23, 1943.

**Albert Medal presented to a native-born Ameri-
can** was awarded June 10, 1884, to James Buchanan Eads for his plan for deepening the Mississippi
River as far as the mouth of the Ohio River by
jetties. The Albert Medal was established in 1862
in memory of Prince Albert, consort of Queen Victoria, and was awarded by the (British) Society
for the Encouragement of Arts, Manufactures and
Commerce for distinguished merit in promoting
arts, manufactures, or commerce. *(Louis How—
James B. Eads)*

**American Academy of Arts and Letters and the
National Institute of Arts and Letters gold medal,**
a joint award, was awarded to Charles Ephraim
Burchfield on May 8, 1942, in the Academy
Auditorium, New York City, for his watercolors of
American scenes.

Armed Forces Expeditionary Medal was established December 4, 1961, by President John Fitzgerald Kennedy (Executive Order No. 10,977). The
first awards were for service in Lebanon from July
1, 1958, to November 1, 1958; in the Taiwan Straits
from August 23, 1958, to January 1, 1959; and in the
Quemoy and Matsu Islands from August 23, 1958,
to June 1, 1963. The medal was to be issued only
when a nonspecific medal was needed for actions
after July 1, 1958, in U.S. military operations, U.S.
operations in direct support of the United Nations,
and U.S. operations of assistance to friendly foreign nations.

**Arts and letters society (national) gold medal
special award** was presented by the American
Academy of Arts and Letters, New York City, on
January 27, 1916, to Charles William Eliot, president emeritus of Harvard University, in recognition of "special distinction."

Bronze Star was established by Executive
Order No. 9419 dated February 4, 1944. It was
authorized for those who while serving in any
capacity with the Army, Navy, Marine Corps or
Coast Guard distinguished themselves on or after
December 7, 1941, "by heroic or meritorious
achievement or service, not involving participation in aerial flight." Airmen were eligible, but not
for deeds performed in the air. The ribbon worn
with the medal was red with a vertical blue stripe
in the center. Both the blue stripe and the ribbon
ends were piped in white.

Bronze Star presented to a woman was awarded to First Lieutenant Cordelia E. Cook, an Army
nurse of Fort Thomas, Ky., who served in direct
support of combat operations from November
1943 to January 1944, when she was wounded.
Despite her wounds, she carried on her hospital

The First

duties. The award was presented in May 1944 by Major General Geoffrey Keys of the Fifth Army. Lieutenant Cook also received the Purple Heart, thus qualifying as the first woman in World War II to win two decorations.

"Campaign medal" was the "Dewey Medal," authorized by act of Congress of June 3, 1898 (30 Stat. L. 746), to be presented to all officers and men under the command of Commodore George Dewey, who on May 1, 1898, participated in the Battle of Manila Bay. Unlike medals suspended from ribbons, this bronze medal is suspended from a bar which bears the design of an American eagle with its wings spread over the sea.

Chaplain to win a Congressional Medal of Honor. *See under* Naval officer

College to confer medals as prizes. *See under* College

Combat decoration for army personnel who participate in a combat parachute jump, a combat glider landing, or an initial assault landing on a hostile shore, was authorized December 22, 1944, for action after December 7, 1941. Its design featured a bronze Indian arrowhead one quarter of an inch high, worn in a vertical position with the point upward on the service ribbon indicating the theater in which it was earned.

Combat infantry badge was authorized November 4, 1943, to be awarded to those "whose conduct in combat is exemplary, or whose combat action occurs in a major operation."

Congressional Medal of Honor. *See* Medal of Honor, below

Copley Medal awarded to an American was presented to Benjamin Franklin in 1753 for his "curious experiments and observations on electricity." The medal, the highest distinction given by England for scientific research, was awarded by the Royal Society of London. *(Bernard Fay—Franklin, the Apostle of Modern Times)*

Croix de Guerre awarded to a black in the American Army was given to Private Henry Johnson, 369th Infantry, 93d Division, on May 24, 1918, with the following citation: "Being on double sentry duty at night, was attacked by twelve Germans. He shot one and seriously wounded two others with his bayonet. Even though he had been three times wounded at the beginning of the action by revolver bullets and grenades, he went to the assistance of his wounded comrade, who was about to be carried off by the enemy, and continued the combat until he put the Germans to flight. It was a splendid example of courage and energy." *(Emmett Jay Scott—American Negro in the World War)*

Defense Meritorious Service Medal was authorized by Executive Order No. 12,019 on

The First

November 3, 1977, for members of the Armed Services of the United States who have rendered outstanding noncombatant achievement or service while assigned to the office of the Secretary of Defense, the organization of the Joint Chiefs of Staff, a specified or unified command, or a Defense Agency.

Defense Superior Service Medal was created by Presidential Executive Order No. 11,904 dated February 6, 1976, to be issued "to any member of the Armed Forces of the United States who has rendered superior meritorious service in a position of significant responsibility with the Office of the Secretary of Defense, the organization and the Joint Chief of Staff, or specified or unified command or Defense Agency or such other joint activity as may be designated by the Secretary of Defense."

Distinguished Flying Cross was awarded to Lieutenant Basil G. Bradley, Sergeant Charles W. Rucker, Lieutenant Lawson H. Sanderson, and Major Thomas C. Turner of the U.S. Marine Corps for their flight in 2 DH-4Bs from Bolling Field, Washington, D.C., March 29, 1921, to Santo Domingo, Dominican Republic, and return on April 22, 1921. The flight covered 2,421 miles each way—elapsed time: 46 hours 17 minutes; flying time: 24 hours plus return trip (22 hours 6 minutes).

Distinguished Flying Cross (Air Corps) was authorized July 2, 1926 (44 Stat. L. 789), "for heroism or extraordinary achievement while participating in an aerial flight," to be awarded to members of the Air Corps of the Army of the United States, including the National Guard and organized reserves since April 6, 1917.

Distinguished Flying Cross awarded to a nurse was given posthumously to Lieutenant Aleda E. Lutz of the Army Nurse Corps, on December 28, 1944. She was killed on a flying mission to evacuate wounded personnel from forward areas.

Distinguished Flying Cross in the Korean War was awarded to First Lieutenant Robert Earl Wayne on July 14, 1950, by Advanced Headquarters, Fifth Air Force (General Orders No. 2).

Distinguished Service Cross (Army) was authorized by Congress July 9, 1918 (40 Stat. L. 870), for persons who "while serving in any capacity with the Army of the United States distinguish themselves by extraordinary heroism in connection with military operations against an armed enemy."

Distinguished Service Cross awarded in enemy-occupied territory was presented by Brigadier General Carl Andrew Spaatz, chief of the U.S. air forces in Europe on July 11, 1942, to Captain Charles C. Kegelman of El Reno, Okla., for "his heroism, his flying skill, his intimate knowledge of his equipment and his great coolness and judgment in action" against the enemy on July 4, 1941.

The First

MEDAL—*Continued*
Although one motor was shot to pieces, the tail riddled with bullets, and a hole made in the cabin, he saved his aircraft and his crew. His rank was raised to that of major on July 9, 1942.

Distinguished Service Cross awarded to an animal was authorized under General Orders 79 of the 3rd Infantry Division dated October 24, 1943, and conferred by Major General Lucian Truscott on Chips, a half-shepherd and half-husky dog owned by Mr. and Mrs. Edward Wren of Pleasantville, N.Y., for "courageous action in singlehandedly eliminating a dangerous machine-gun nest and causing surrender of the crew." The award, however, was rescinded February 3, 1944, in General Orders 17 of the unit, as the award of decorations to animals was prohibited by a War Department circular of January 19, 1944.

Distinguished Service Medal (Army) was authorized by act of Congress approved July 9, 1918 (40 Stat. L. 870), for persons who while serving in any capacity with the Army of the United States distinguish themselves by exceptionally meritorious service in a duty of great responsibility. The medal bears the coat of arms of the United States in bronze surrounded by a circle of dark-blue enamel bearing the inscription "For Distinguished Service." The name of the recipient is inscribed on the reverse on a scroll upon a trophy of flags and weapons. It is worn suspended from a white ribbon separated from red ends by a narrow blue band.

Distinguished Service Medal (Army) awarded to a woman was presented to Oveta Culp Hobby, director of the Women's Army Corps, on December 31, 1944. It was formally presented to her by Secretary of War Henry Lewis Stimson in his office in Washington, D.C., in the presence of General George Catlett Marshall, Chief of Staff, and General Henry Harley Arnold, General of the Army.

Distinguished Service Medal awarded to a woman was presented to Evangeline Booth, commander of the Salvation Army, on October 19, 1919, by Major General David Carey Shanks as personal representative of President Woodrow Wilson and Secretary of War Newton Diehl Baker.

Distinguished Service Medal (Coast Guard) was established August 4, 1949 (63 Stat. L. 535), for any person who, while serving in any capacity with the Coast Guard, distinguished himself by exceptionally meritorious service to the government in a duty of great responsibility. The obverse of the medal showed the *Massachusetts* in full sail in the center with a gold rim inscribed with the words *U.S. Coast Guard* above and *Distinguished Service* below. The reverse showed the Coast Guard seal upon crossed anchors and the recipient's name. The ribbon was light blue moiré edged

The First

in black with a narrow white stripe towards each edge.

Distinguished Service Medal (Merchant Marine) was authorized April 11, 1942 (56 Stat. L. 217), "to provide decorations for outstanding conduct or service in the line of duty" to persons who, on or after September 3, 1939, have distinguished themselves serving in the American Merchant Marine. The first presentation was made by President Franklin Delano Roosevelt at the White House in the presence of Rear Admiral Emory Scott Land, chairman of the United States Maritime Commission and administrator of the War Shipping Administration, on October 8, 1942, to Edwin Fox Cheney, Jr., of Yeadon, Pa., who, on March 12, 1942, had swum under blazing oil to save six shipmates from the torpedoed tanker *John D. Gill.*

Distinguished Service Medal (Navy) was authorized by act of Congress dated February 4, 1919 (40 Stat. L. 1056), for presentation to persons who while in the Naval Service of the United States since April 6, 1917, have distinguished themselves by "exceptionally meritorious service to the government in a duty of great responsibility." The medal is gold, bronze, and enamel. The obverse had the picture of an American eagle surrounded by a blue enameled band bearing the inscriptions "United States of America" and "Navy." The reverse is a trident encircled by olive branches around which is a band of blue enamel on which is inscribed "For Distinguished Service." It is worn suspended from a blue ribbon with a stripe of gold. On November 11, 1920, the Secretary of the Navy approved 150 awards.

Distinguished Service Medals of the Army, Navy, and Air Force presented to one person at the same time were presented by President Lyndon Baines Johnson on July 11, 1969, to General Lyman Louis Lemnitzer, former supreme U.S. and allied commander in Europe, in a ceremony at the White House, Washington, D.C.

Doctor to receive a congressional medal. *See under* Physician

Expert Infantryman's Badge of the U.S. Army was awarded March 29, 1944, at Fort Bragg, N.C., to Technical Sergeant Walter L. Bull of the 100th Division by Lieutenant General Lesley James McNair, commanding general of the Army Ground Forces. The badge, three inches long and a half inch wide, consists of a miniature silver rifle mounted on an infantry blue field with a silver border.

Humanitarian Service Medal was authorized January 19, 1977, for "members of the Armed Forces of the United States who after April 1, 1975, distinguish themselves by meritorious participation in a military act or operation of a humanitarian nature."

The First

Interstate Commerce Commission Medal of Honor was a bronze medal awarded December 5, 1905, to George H. Poell of Grand Island, Neb. On June 26, 1905, while a fireman on the St. Joseph and Grand Island Railway, he climbed out on the pilot of his engine and rescued a child on the tracks. Poell was seriously injured and one foot had to be amputated. The medal was authorized by act of Congress of February 23, 1905 (33 Stat. L. 743), for presentation to those "who shall hereafter, by extreme daring, endanger their own lives in saving, or endeavoring to save lives from any wreck, disaster or grave accident, or in preventing or endeavoring to prevent" accidents. Four degrees were established: chief commander, commander, officer, and legionnaire.

Legion of Merit Medal was authorized July 20, 1942 (56 Stat. L. 662), in four degrees for presentation to the personnel of the armed forces of this and friendly foreign nations, who since the proclamation of an emergency by the President on September 8, 1939, had distinguished themselves by meritorious conduct in the performance of outstanding services. The first presentation was made to Captain Ralph B. Praeger for services in the Philippine Islands, December 1941–March 1942. The award was presented posthumously in 1943.

Legion of Merit Medal awarded to a foreign national was presented on November 7, 1942, when the Legion of Merit, Degree of Commander, was conferred upon General Amaro Soares Bittencourt, military attaché of the Brazilian Embassy at Washington, D.C. The presentation was made at the U.S. Army parade grounds at the Air Force Technical Training Command, Miami Beach, Fla. An announcement of the award was made October 22, 1942, at a luncheon given in honor of the recipient. The first Legion of Merit, Degree of Chief Commander, presentation was made in China on July 7, 1943, to Generalissimo Chiang Kai-shek, commander in chief of the Chinese military forces, by Lieutenant General Joseph W. Stilwell.

Legion of Merit Medal awarded to a Women's Army Corps member was presented to Lieutenant Colonel Westray Battle Boyce on September 27, 1944, for outstanding services in the North African Theater of Operations from August 12, 1943, to August 8, 1944, in obtaining maximum utilization of WAC personnel.

Legion of Merit Medal to a Coastguardsman in World War II was presented by Rear Admiral Stanley V. Parker of the Coast Guard to Seaman Second Class John Cornelius Cullen of the Amagansett Life Saving Station, L.I., N.Y., in New York City on November 9, 1943. Cullen reported the landing on June 13, 1942, of 6 German spies.

The First

Legion of Merit Medal to a Women's Army Corps (WAC) member in the European Theater of Operations was awarded to Lieutenant Colonel Anna M. Wilson, WAC director in the ETO, on October 20, 1944, by Lieutenant General John C. H. Lee in Paris, France.

Lifesaving medal awarded by the Treasury Department was authorized by act of June 20, 1874 (18 Stat. L. 127), to "persons who should thereafter endanger their own lives in saving or endeavoring to save the lives of others from the perils of the sea within the United States or upon any American vessel." It was awarded in two classes, a gold medal worn from a red ribbon and a silver medal worn from a blue ribbon. The first award was a silver medal to Lucian M. Clemons, keeper of the United States Lifesaving Service Station at Marblehead, Ohio, on June 19, 1876, for saving men from the schooner *Consuelo* on May 1, 1875.

Mariner's medal was authorized "to any person who, while serving on any vessel in the American Merchant Marine during the war period, is wounded, suffers physical injury or suffers through dangerous exposure," by the War Shipping Administration on May 10, 1943 (57 Stat. L. 82).

Marines to win the Navy and Marine Corps Medal were Sergeant Norman C. S. Pearson, of Minneapolis, Minn., and Corporal Gordon Miller, of Cincinnati, Ohio, who risked their lives to save a gunner sergeant imprisoned in a fallen and burning airplane. They were specially commended on September 21, 1942, by Lieutenant General Thomas Holcomb, commandant of the Marine Corps, and promoted a grade.

Medal awarded by the Continental Congress was granted to General George Washington for his exploit of March 17, 1776, in compelling the British forces to evacuate Boston, Mass. The date of the resolution authorizing the medal was March 25, 1776. It was struck in Paris, and showed the profile of George Washington on the obverse. The reverse showed George Washington and his officers on horseback viewing the town of Boston in the distance with the British fleet in view under sail. Although this medal, the first authorized, was granted in 1776, it was not presented to Washington until 1786. *(Joseph Floumond Loubat—Medallic History of the U.S.A.—1776–1876)*

Medal awarded by the Continental Congress to a foreigner was a silver medal presented to Lieutenant Colonel Francois Louis Teisseidre de Fleury, who commanded the first of the storming parties in the assault upon Stony Point, July 15, 1779. He was the first man to enter the main fort and strike the British flag with his own hands. Fleury, who had been in the French military service, joined the Continental Army in 1777. The date of the congressional resolution was July 26,

The First

MEDAL—*Continued*
1779, and the presentation was made October 1, 1779.

Medal awarded to an American food producer was the Great Council Medal, which was awarded in 1851 to Gail Borden at the Great International Exposition in London, England, for his invention of the meat biscuit. A one-pound meat biscuit contained a nutrient value of five pounds of meat and ten ounces of flour and retained its original flavor and value for years. The biscuit was eagerly accepted by explorers, travelers, troops, etc., who needed rations packed as compactly as possible. *(The Borden Eagle. 1922)*
See also Cracker: Meat biscuit

Medal of Freedom was established on July 6, 1945, by executive order No. 9,586 of President Harry S. Truman for award to civilians for a meritorious act or service against an enemy or enemies on or after December 7, 1941, and for which an award of another United States medal or decoration is considered inappropriate. It is not awarded to a member of the armed forces of the United States or for service performed within the continental limits of the United States. The obverse depicted the head of "Freedom." In the lower portion in an arc was the inscription "Freedom" and on the reverse the "Liberty Bell" without carriage, within a circle composed of the words "United States of America." The ribbon had five red and four white stripes alternating. The original order was amended by President John Fitzgerald Kennedy (executive order No. 11,-085) on February 22, 1963, and the first presentation of medals was made in November 1963, to those "who contribute significantly to the quality of American life."

Medal of Freedom awarded to a black woman was presented to Marian Anderson on December 6, 1963, by President Lyndon Baines Johnson in the State Dining Room of the White House, Washington, D.C.

Medal of Freedom awarded to a husband and wife was announced by President Gerald Rudolph Ford on January 1, 1977, and presented on January 10, 1977, at ceremonies in the White House, Washington, D.C., to Will and Ariel Durant, 1968 Pulitzer Prize winners in general nonfiction for *The Story of Civilization.*

Medal of Freedom awarded to a woman was presented to Anna Rosenberg, a member of the Advisory Board of the Office of War Mobilization and Reconversion, on October 29, 1945, by Secretary of War Robert Porter Patterson in his office in Washington, D.C.

Medal of Honor action took place February 13–14, 1861, at Apache Pass, Arizona, when Colonel Bernard John Dowling Irwin, assistant surgeon, "voluntarily took command of troops and attacked and defeated the hostile Indians (Chirica-

The First

hua) he met on the way." This action occurred before the medal was authorized on July 12, 1862. The award was made January 21, 1894.

Medal of Honor (Army) was authorized July 12, 1862 (12 Stat. L. 623), to be given in the name of Congress "to such non-commissioned officers and privates as shall most distinguish themselves by their gallantry in action and other soldier-like qualities during the present insurrection." The first award was made to 6 members of a raiding party of 20 who in 1862 penetrated the Confederate lines for more than 200 miles and destroyed bridges and tracks between Chattanooga and Atlanta. A congressional act of March 3, 1863 (12 Stat. L. 751), authorized the award to commissioned officers. It is conferred upon those who have distinguished themselves in actual conflict with the enemy by gallantry and intrepidity at the risk of life beyond the call of duty. *(Theophilus Francis Rodenbough—Uncle Sam's Medal of Honor)*

Medal of Honor (Army) earned by a black was issued May 23, 1900, to Sergeant William Harvey Carney for his bravery on July 18, 1863, while a member of Company C, 54th Massachusetts Colored Infantry at Fort Wagner, S.C. He enlisted February 17, 1863. He was wounded twice while planting the flag on a parapet and removing it when the troops fell back under a fierce fire in which he was severely wounded. He was discharged June 30, 1864, with disability.

Medal of Honor awarded in the Korean War was presented on September 30, 1950, by President Harry S. Truman to Major General William Frische Dean of Berkeley, Calif., commanding general of the 24th Infantry Division, who at the battle for Taejon on July 20–21, 1950, personally and alone attacked an enemy tank while armed with only a hand grenade. Other recipients at the ceremony were Private First Class Melvin L. Brown of Mahaffey, Pa., and First Lieutenant Frederick F. Henry of Clinton, Okla. Posthumous awards were also made to Sergeant Charles W. Turner of Boston, Mass., and Master Sergeant Travis E. Watkins of Gladewater, Texas.

Medal of Honor awarded in World War I was presented by Secretary of the Navy Josephus Daniels in Washington, D.C., on May 21, 1919, to Ernest August Janson, gunnery sergeant, who served under the name of Charles F. Hoffman, of Brooklyn, N.Y., in the 49th Company, 5th Regiment, 2nd Division, U.S. Marine Corps. On June 6, 1918, near Chateau-Thierry, France, he saw 12 enemy soldiers with light machine guns and bayoneted two of them, forcing the others to flee and abandon their guns.

Medal of Honor awarded in World War II was presented on February 10, 1942, by Major General Walter H. Frank, commander of the Third Air Force, at Tampa, Fla., to Alexander Ramsey Nin-

The First

inger posthumously for Second Lieutenant Alexander Ramsey ("Sandy") Nininger, Jr., for heroism in action in the vicinity of Abucay, Bataan, Philippine Islands, on January 12, 1942.

Medal of Honor awarded to a black in the Korean War was posthumously awarded to Private First Class William Henry Thompson of Brooklyn, N.Y., who was mortally wounded by an enemy grenade August 6, 1950, while serving with Company M, 24th Infantry Regiment, 25th Infantry Division against enemy forces near Masan, Korea. The medal was presented to his mother, Mrs. Mary Elizabeth Henderson on June 21, 1951, by General Omar Nelson Bradley in Washington, D.C.

Medal of Honor awarded to a black in the Spanish American War was issued June 23, 1899, to Private George Henry Wanton, Troop M, 10th U.S. Cavalry, who voluntarily went ashore at Tayabacoa, Cuba, on June 30, 1898, "in the face of the enemy and aided in the rescue of his wounded comrades, this after several previous attempts at rescue had been frustrated."

Medal of Honor awarded to a chaplain was presented to Reverend Timothy O'Callahan, of Cambridge, Mass., on January 23, 1946, by President Harry S Truman at Washington, D.C. He gave the last rites, organized rescue parties, and carried ammunition when the U.S.S. *Franklin* was set afire by an aerial bomb by Kamikaze pilots on March 19, 1945, off the Japanese coast.

Medal of Honor awarded to a conscientious objector was presented on October 12, 1945, by President Harry S. Truman to Private First Class Desmond T. Doss of Lynchburg, Va., for outstanding bravery as a medical corpsman on Okinawa in specific acts between April 29 and May 21, 1945.

Medal of Honor awarded to a helicopter pilot was conferred posthumously upon Lieutenant (Junior Grade) John Kelvin Koelsch of Hudson, N.Y., on April 8, 1955, and presented to his next of kin on August 3, 1955. On July 3, 1951, Koelsch and Aviation Machinist Mate George M. Neal volunteered, took off without fighter escort, and rescued James V. Wilkins in North Korea. The helicopter was shot down and the three men were captured a few days later. Koelsch died of malnutrition and dysentery in a Korean prisoner-of-war camp on October 16, 1951.

Medal of Honor awarded to a Jewish soldier was conferred upon Sergeant Leopold Karpeles of Springfield, Mass., of Company E, 57th Massachusetts Infantry, who while color bearer rallied the retreating troops at the Battle of the Wilderness, Va., on May 6, 1864, and induced them to check the enemy's advance. The award was authorized July 12, 1864, and the date of issue was April 30, 1870.

The First

Medal of Honor awarded to a Marine was presented to Sergeant John Freeman Mackie by Commander Henry Rolando under authorization of General Order No. 17 dated July 10, 1862, for "gallant conduct and services, signal acts of devotion to duty . . . [He] fearlessly maintained his musket fire against the rifle pits along the shore and, when ordered to fill vacancies at guns caused by men wounded and killed in action, manned the weapon with skill and courage." During the attack on Fort Darling at Drewrys Bluff, James River, Va., on May 15, 1862, Mackie rallied the Marine Guard on the U.S.S. *Galena* after the entire Third Division, manning four 10-inch Dahlgren guns and 100-pound rifles, was killed or wounded. He cleared the deck and resumed the action without awaiting orders.

Medal of Honor awarded to a Marine in the Korean War was presented to Lieutenant Henry Alfred Commiskey of Hattiesburg, Miss., who on September 20, 1950, near Yongdungpo, outside Seoul, Korea, armed with a pistol, killed seven enemy soldiers in hand-to-hand combat. The medal, the 30th medal award of the Korean War, was presented on August 1, 1951, by President Harry S. Truman at the White House, Washington, D.C.

Medal of Honor awarded to a Marine in World War II was presented posthumously to First Lieutenant George ("Ham") Hammon Cannon of Ann Arbor, Mich., battery commander of Battery H, 6th Defense Battalion Fleet Marine Force, U.S. Marine Corps, on March 14, 1942. He was mortally wounded by shell fire on December 7, 1941, at the bombardment of Sand Island, Midway Islands, by Japanese forces, and refused to be evacuated from his post until after his own men who had been wounded by the same shell were evacuated, directing the reorganization of his command post until forcibly removed. He died from loss of blood.

Medal of Honor awarded to a member of the Naval Service was authorized by act of Congress, December 21, 1861 (12 Stat. L. 330), which authorized 200 medals for gallantry in action and other seamanlike qualities during the Civil War. The first awards were made to 36 recipients by General Order No. 11 of April 3, 1863. The first heroic deed for which the Medal of Honor was awarded was performed by John Williams, captain of the maintop of the U.S.S. *Pawnee* during an attack on Matthias Point on June 26, 1861. The act of March 3, 1915 (38 Stat. L. 931), extended the provisions to include the Navy, the Marine Corps, and the Coast Guard.

Medal of Honor awarded to a Nisei (American of Japanese parentage) in U.S. service was conferred upon Private First Class Sadao S. Munemori of Co. A, 100th Infantry Battalion, 442nd Combat Team, for action near Seravezza, Italy, on April 5, 1945, when he knocked out two machine

The First

MEDAL—*Continued*

guns with grenades and saved the life of two of his companions by diving on an exploding grenade. The medal was presented posthumously on March 13, 1946, to his mother, Mrs. Nawa Munemori.

Medal of Honor awarded to a Nisei in the Korean War was awarded August 26, 1953, to Sergeant Hiroshi Hershey Miyamura of Gallup, N.Mex., for his heroism in covering the retreat of his squad on April 25, 1951, and holding a position at Imjin River while he was attached to the Third Regiment of the Seventh Division. He was captured and held a prisoner for 28 months. He was repatriated from a prisoner-of-war camp in Korea to Freedom Village, Korea, where the award was made by Brigadier General Ralph Osborne. The medal was presented on October 27, 1953, by President Dwight David Eisenhower at ceremonies held at the White House, Washington, D.C.

Medal of Honor awarded to a pilot. *See* Aviation—Pilot: Pilot to receive the Congressional Medal of Honor

Medal of Honor awarded to a Seabee was presented posthumously by President Lyndon Baines Johnson on September 13, 1966, in Washington, D.C., to Marvin Glen Shields, of Port Townsend, Wash., for heroism in the 14-hour battle at Dongzoal, Vietnam, on June 10, 1965, during which he saved the lives of many of his companions. The medal was accepted by his widow Joan Elaine Shields.

Medal of Honor awarded to a soldier who already had received a Distinguished Service Cross in World War II was presented to Gerry Kisters of Bloomington, Ind., by President Franklin Delano Roosevelt on June 21, 1943, for heroism in the Sicily campaign. The Distinguished Service Cross had been awarded to him by General George Catlett Marshall in May 1943, for bravery in Africa.

Medal of Honor awarded to a woman was authorized for Dr. Mary Edwards Walker, army surgeon, January 24, 1866. On February 15, 1917, the award was stricken from the list by adverse action of the Board of Medal Awards, nothing having been found in the records to show the specific act or acts for which the decoration had originally been awarded.

Medal of Honor in the Vietnam war was presented in the East Room of the White House, Washington, D.C., on December 5, 1964, by President Lyndon Baines Johnson to U.S. Army Captain Roger Hugh Donlon, of Saugerties, N.Y. He was wounded 4 times (in the stomach, leg, shoulder, and face) at Nam Dong, about 20 miles from the Laotian frontier. The award was the first since the Korean War, the first in counterinsurgency effort, and the first to a soldier with a friendly foreign force engaged in an armed conflict in which the United States was not a belligerent.

The First

Medal of Honor in the Vietnam war awarded to a chaplain was presented November 19, 1968, by President Lyndon Baines Johnson in the East Room of the White House, Washington, D.C., to Roman Catholic Chaplain Captain Angelo Joseph Liteky of Jacksonville, Fla., for his heroism in rescuing over 20 wounded on December 6, 1967, while serving with Company A, 4th Battalion, 12th Infantry, 199th Light Infantry Brigade, in a search and destroy operation near Phuoc-Loc, Bien Hoa province, Republic of Vietnam.

Medal of Honor in the Vietnam war awarded to a Marine was presented on December 6, 1966, by President Lyndon Baines Johnson in Austin, Tex., to Robert Emmett O'Malley, of Woodside, Queens, L.I., N.Y., who was wounded 3 times in an engagement in 1965.

Medal of Honor (posthumous) in the Vietnam war to a black was awarded to Private First Class Milton Lee Olive, 3rd, of Company B, 503rd Infantry, 173rd Airborne Brigade, who was killed October 22, 1965, when he grabbed an enemy hand-grenade and fell on it to save the life of 4 companions. The presentation was made to his father by President Lyndon Baines Johnson in Washington, D.C., on April 21, 1966.

Medal of Honor in the Vietnam war awarded to a Marine (black) was posthumously awarded to Private First Class James Anderson, Jr., of Compton, Calif., who smothered an enemy grenade with his body on February 28, 1967, northwest of Cam Lo, Vietnam, and saved his companions from its full effect. On August 21, 1968, Secretary of Navy Paul Robert Ignatius presented the medal to Anderson's parents. The citation was read by General Leonard F. Chapman, Jr., commandant of the Marine Corps.

Medal of Honor (posthumous) to a Coastguardsman killed in action in World War II was awarded to Signalman First Class Douglas Albert Munro of South Cle Elum, Wash., who was killed September 27, 1942, while leading 5 Higgins boats from the seaplane tender *Ballard* to the beach to engage in the evacuation of a battalion of 500 Marines trapped by enemy forces at Point Cruz, Guadalcanal. The medal was presented by President Franklin Delano Roosevelt on May 27, 1943, to Munro's mother, Mrs. James Munro.

Medal of Honor winner to receive 2 awards was Thomas W. Custer, Second Lieutenant, Company B, 6th Michigan Cavalry, who was awarded the medal on May 3, 1865, for the capture of a flag at Namozine Church, Va., on May 10, 1863, and a second medal on May 26, 1865, for his heroism at Sailors Creek, Va., on April 6, 1865, when he jumped his horse over the enemy's works and captured 2 stands of colors despite the fact that his horse was shot under him and he received a severe wound.

The First

Medals known to have been presented by the colonists to friendly American Indians were authorized in Virginia by the Act of 1661 which authorized "silver and plated placques to be worn by the Indians when visiting the settlements." One of these has a crude representation of a tobacco plant and scrolls, above which is "Ye King Of" on the obverse, while on the reverse is a similarly engraved plant and the word "Patomeck" with the *e* overlined. The surface edges were engraved to represent scrolls and foldings, while the medal was holed for suspension. On December 2, 1662, an act "prohibiting the entertainment of Indians without badges" was passed by the Assembly at James City, Va. *(Harrold Edgar Gillingham—Indian and Military Medals)*

Melvil Dewey medal. *See under* Library society

Meritorious Service Medal was established by Presidential Executive Order No. 11,448 on January 16, 1969. It was a noncombat award to members of the Armed Forces, ranking between the Legion of Merit Medal and the Service Commendation Medal, and was only outclassed in significance by the Distinguished Service Medal.

National Aeronautics and Space Administration Distinguished Service Medal was presented by President John Fitzgerald Kennedy in Washington, D.C., on May 8, 1961, to astronaut Alan Bartlett Shepard, Jr., for making America's first space flight. Shepard's flight, 302 miles down the Atlantic missile range from Cape Canaveral, Florida, at an altitude of 115 miles, was made on May 5, 1961.

National Geographic Society gold medal was the Hubbard medal, presented December 15, 1906, in Washington, D.C., by President Theodore Roosevelt to Commander Robert Edwin Peary for Arctic explorations. (On December 15, 1909, Peary also received a medal for his discovery of the North Pole on April 6, 1909.) The Hubbard medal was first awarded to a woman on January 30, 1934, when the designee was Anne Morrow Lindbergh, copilot and radio operator of the Charles A. Lindbergh Aerial Survey. The medal was presented to Mrs. Lindbergh on March 31, 1934, in Washington, D.C., by Dr. Gilbert Grosvenor, president of the National Geographic Society.

National Geographic Society special gold medal was presented by President Herbert Clark Hoover at Constitution Hall, Washington, D.C., on June 21, 1932, to Amelia Earhart Putnam (Mrs. George Palmer Putnam) who on May 20–21, 1932, was the first woman to achieve a solo transatlantic flight.

National Institute of Arts and Letters gold medal was awarded posthumously on November 20, 1909, to Augustus Saint-Gaudens for his meritorious achievements in sculpture. *(American Academy of Arts and Letters—Public Meeting of the American Academy and the National Institute*

The First

of Arts and Letters at the Fine Arts Society, New York, November 20, 1909 . . .)

National Medal of Science was authorized by Act of Congress of August 25, 1959 (73 Stat.L.431), for outstanding contributions in the physical, biological, mathematical, and engineering sciences on the basis or recommendation of the National Academy of Sciences. The first presentation was made by President John Fitzgerald Kennedy at the White House on February 17, 1963, to Hungarian-born aerodynamicist Dr. Theodor von Karman.

National Security Medal was established January 19, 1953, by Presidential Executive Order No. 10,431, for "any person regardless of nationality who on or after July 26, 1947, contributed to the national intelligence effort of the United States." It was an oval medal with a dark blue ribbon with a gold diagonal ladder pattern in the center and was designed by the U.S. Mint. The obverse was of blue enamel–the words *United States of America* appeared across the top and *National Security* at the bottom, the whole enclosed within a laurel wreath of gold-finished bronze surmounted by an American bald eagle standing with wings raised facing left.

Navy chaplain to win the silver star in Vietnam. *See* Naval Officer: Naval chaplain to win the silver star in Vietnam

Navy Cross awarded to a Coast Guard officer in World War II was presented on June 4, 1942, to Lieutenant Maurice D. Jester in command of the 165-foot Coast Guard *Icarus* off the Carolina coast, which sank an enemy submarine, captured the commanding officer, his first mate, and 31 members of the crew and brought them as prisoners to Charleston, S.C.

Navy Cross 3-time winner was Lieutenant Noel Arthur Gaylor of Bremerton, Wash., who received the 3rd presentation on September 9, 1942, from Secretary of the Navy Frank Knox for destroying 2 Japanese airplanes and damaging 2 others on May 7–8, 1942, during the Battle of the Coral Sea. His first cross was received for shooting down 1 Japanese bomber and destroying 2 others on February 20, 1942; his second, for destroying an enemy seaplane and bombing 2 destroyers on March 10, 1942, in action at New Guinea.

Navy Expert Pistol Shot Medal awarded to a woman was presented to Ensign Rosalie Thorne of the Bureau of Aeronautics who qualified August 4, 1943, as a pistol expert by making 211 out of a possible 240 points.

Navy–Marine Corps Medal for Heroism awarded to a woman was presented on August 7, 1953, to Staff Sergeant Barbara Olive Barnwell, of Pittsburgh, Pa., U.S. Marine Corps Reserve, by General Lemuel Cornick Shepherd, Jr., Commandant of the U.S. Marine Corps, in Washington, D.C. She saved Private First Class Frederick G. Romann from

The First

MEDAL—*Continued*
drowning on June 7, 1952, at Onslow Beach, Camp Lejeune, N.C.

Navy Unit Commendation decoration for heroism in action against the enemy and for extremely meritorious military service not involving combat, but not sufficient to justify award of the Presidential Unit Citation, was established December 20, 1944. Members of units winning this award (for performing as a unit service of a character comparable to that which would merit the award of a Silver Star Medal or a Legion of Merit to an individual) are entitled to wear a ribbon having a wide myrtle-green stripe in the center with smaller cardinal red, Spanish yellow, and royal blue stripes extending to the edge in that order on either side. The first award of the Navy Unit Commendation to a ship or unit was granted on March 11, 1945, to the light cruiser *Helena:* "Her brave record of combat achievement is evidence of the 'Helena's' intrepidity and the heroic fighting spirit of her officers and men." The *Helena* was lost July 1943 in Kula Gulf.

Order of the Purple Heart, a decoration for "military merit," was established by George Washington on August 7, 1782, at Newburgh, N.Y., and was the first honor badge for enlisted men and noncommissioned officers. The first recipients of this honor "for singularly meritorious action" were Sergeants Daniel Bissell, William Brown, and Elijah Churchill of Connecticut regiments, decorated May 9, 1783. They were entitled "to wear on facings over the left breast, the figure of a heart in purple cloth or silk, with narrow lace or binding."

Order of the Purple Heart awarded in the Korean War was presented by Major General Edgar Erskine Hume, chief surgeon of the Far East Command, on July 8, 1950, in Tokyo, Japan, to Sergeant Leroy Deans, 22, of Alice, Tex., for an eye injury received June 28, 1950, when a Han River bridge was blown up.

Order of the Purple Heart awarded to a nurse was conferred on Captain Annie G. Fox "for outstanding performance of duty and meritorious acts of extraordinary fidelity and essential service" during the attack on Hickam Field, Hawaii, on December 7, 1941.

Pilot to receive the Congressional Medal of Honor. *See under* Aviation—Pilot

Platinum medal made by the United States Mint was presented to President Herbert Hoover on December 1, 1932, by the George Washington Bicentennial Commission, of which he was chairman. The medal was made in the Federal Mint in Philadelphia, Pa., and was three inches in diameter. It contained enough platinum for 120 wedding rings.

The First

Presidential citation to an entire division was made March 15, 1945, to the 101st Airborne Division, the heroes of Bastogne, by General Dwight David Eisenhower, somewhere on the western front. From December 18 to December 27, 1944, the division withstood tremendous odds. *(Samuel Lyman Atwood Marshall—Bastogne: The First Eight Days)*

Presidential Citizen Medal was established by Executive Order No. 11,494 on November 13, 1969, by President Richard Milhous Nixon for "citizens of the United States of America who have performed exemplary deeds of service for their country or their fellow citizens." President Nixon presented the first medal on May 14, 1973, to the widow of Roberto Walker Clemente, star outfielder of the Pittsburgh Pirates, who was killed December 31, 1972, in the crash of a DC-7 4-engined cargo plane off San Juan (Puerto Rico) International Airport while delivering aid to victims of the earthquake in Managua, Nicaragua.

Presidential Unit Citation award in peacetime was made by President Dwight David Eisenhower on August 8, 1958, under the command of William Robert Anderson to the crew of the submarine *Nautilus* (SSN-571) for its voyage from June 8, 1958, to August 5, 1958, across the top of the world from the Bering Sea to the Greenland Sea, passing submerged beneath the geographic North Pole. Her crew was entitled to wear a citation ribbon and a special clasp in the form of a golden *N.*

Presidential Unit Citation (Army) was authorized November 22, 1943, by Executive Order No. 9,396 (for action after Dec. 7, 1941).

Presidential Unit Citation (Navy) was authorized February 6, 1942, by President Franklin Delano Roosevelt (Executive Order No. 9,050), to any ship, aircraft, or other naval unit (for action after October 16, 1941).

Recipient of the four highest decorations awarded by the United States was Lieutenant Colonel William Joseph ("Wild Bill") Donovan, who received the Medal of Honor, the Distinguished Service Cross, and the Distinguished Service Medal for meritorious conduct in combat in 1918 in France, and the National Security Medal on April 4, 1957, for his service as director of the Office of Strategic Services from June 13, 1942, to October 1, 1945.

Representative who had a Medal of Honor. *See under* Representative (U.S. Congress)

Reserve Officers Association medal was presented on January 15, 1953, to President Harry S Truman, who retired as a colonel after 30 years of service. The medal, with two clusters, was presented in the Rose Garden of the White House by Brigadier General Fred Marshall Warren of Fort Thomas, Ky., vice president of the association.

The First

Silver Star Army Medal awarded to a civilian was presented by General Douglas MacArthur to Vern Haugland, Associated Press correspondent, on October 3, 1942. He was a passenger on an army airplane forced to descend in New Guinea. After 43 days in the jungle, he reached civilization.

Silver Star Medal awarded to a civilian by the U.S. Navy in World War II, presented to Tony Duenas, a Guam native, was approved March 3, 1945. The second award, approved May 22, 1945, was made to Donald H. Russell of Orange, Conn., for gallantry aboard the carrier *Franklin* when it was hit off Kyushu. He was a technician assigned to keep the Corsair planes in fighting condition. The presentation was made by Rear Admiral Monroe Kelly.

Soldier to receive seven decorations at one time was Llewellyn M. Chilson of Berwyn, Pa., a technical sergeant in the 45th Division, who was presented with the Distinguished Service Cross with two Oak Leaf clusters, the Silver Star and one Oak Leaf cluster, the Legion of Merit, and the Bronze Star by President Harry S. Truman on December 6, 1946, in Washington, D.C.

Soldier to win the three highest-ranking decorations for valor in combat in one war was Maurice Lee Britt of Lonoke, Ark., who received the Silver Star for action at Acerno, Italy, September 1943; the Medal of Honor for action November 7-12, 1943, at Mount Rotundo, Italy; and the Distinguished Service Cross (DSC) for heroism in action on January 24, 1944, near Campo Morto, Italy. He also received the Purple Heart with three Oak Leaf clusters, the Military Cross of the British Empire, the Combat Infantryman Badge, and a Distinguished Unit Badge awarded his unit, the Third Battalion. The DSC was presented to him on December 7, 1944, by Major General Fred L. Walker, commander of the Infantry School, Fort Benning, Ga., at a ceremony on the steps of the New York Public Library, New York City.

Soldier's Medal awarded to a woman was conferred on nurse Edith Greenwood June 21, 1943, for heroism in saving the lives of her patients in a fire in a station hospital near Yuma, Ariz., on April 17, 1943.

Soldier's Medal awarded to a Women's Army Corps member was presented November 17, 1943, to Private Margaret Helen Maloney of Rochester, N.Y., by Major General Everett Strait Hughes at Allied Headquarters, Algiers, for rescuing Private Kenneth J. Jacobs from a pool of burning gasoline.

Vietnam Service Medal was authorized July 8, 1965, by President Lyndon Baines Johnson's Executive Order No. 11,231 for members of the United States Armed Forces who served in Vietnam or contiguous waters or air space after July 31, 1961.

The First

Woman to have her likeness on a medal issued by the United States Mint was Nellie Tayloe Ross. The obverse of the three-inch medal showed her profile and the date when she became director of the Mint, 1933. The reverse, with the seal of the Mint at the top, showed her seated with assay balances, coins, bullion, and coining press. The medal was designed by John Ray Sinnock and was issued in June 1935.

Women's Army Corps Service Medal was authorized by Executive Order No. 9,365 on July 29, 1943, for the Women's Army Auxiliary Corps (between July 20, 1942, and August 31, 1943) and the Women's Army Corps (between September 1, 1943, and September 2, 1945). It was a 1¼-inch bronze medal worn on a silk moiré ribbon of old gold and moss-tone green. On the obverse was the head of Pallas Athene superimposed on a sheathed sword crossed with oak leaves and a palm branch within a circle.

MEDAL OF SCIENCE, NATIONAL. *See* Medal

MEDIATION. *See* Labor relations: National Mediation Board

MEDIATION AND CONCILIATION BOARD (federal). *See* Arbitration: Federal Board of Mediation and Conciliation

MEDIATION AND CONCILIATION BOARD (state). *See* Arbitration: State Board of Mediation and Arbitration

MEDICAL ALMANAC. *See* Almanac: Patent medicine almanac

MEDICAL BOOK

Anatomy book was *A Compendious System of Anatomy* (an extract from the American edition of the *Encyclopedia Britannica*) which was published in 1792 by Thomas Dobson in Philadelphia, Pa. It contained 438 pages and 12 anatomical plates and was divided into six parts covering osteology, the muscles, the abdomen, the thorax, the brain and nerves, and the senses.

Anatomy book (American) was *A System of Anatomy for the Use of Students of Medicine*, by Dr. Caspar Wistar, professor of anatomy at the medical school of the University of Pennsylvania from 1808 to 1818. The book contained 422 pages and was published in 1811 by Thomas Dobson in Philadelphia, Pa.

Aviation medicine book was *Aviation Medicine*, 241 pages, by Dr. Louis Hopewell Bauer, commandant of the School of Aviation Medicine. The book was published by Williams & Wilkins Co., Baltimore, Md., in 1926.

Bacteriology textbook was *Bacteria*, by Dr. Antoine Magnin, translated from the French by George Miller Sternberg, M.D., surgeon of the United States Army. The 227-page book was published in 1880 by Little, Brown & Co., Boston,

MEDICAL BOOK—*Continued*
Mass. *(Martha L. Sternberg—George Miller Sternberg)*

Bronchitis treatise was published in 1846 by Horace Green, professor of theory and practice of medicine at the New York Medical College, and was entitled *Treatise on the Diseases of the Air Passages comprising an Inquiry into the History, Pathology, Causes and Treatment of those affections of the Throat called Bronchitis, Chronic Laryngitis, Clergyman's Sore Throat. (Johann Hermann Baas—Outlines of the History of Medicine)*

Chiropody book was *Surgical and Practical Observations on the Diseases of the Human Foot* by Issachar Zacharie, published in 1860 in New York City.

Croup report (printed) was published in 1781 by H[ugh] Gaine, New York City. It consisted of a report made to William Hunter, M.D., by Richard Bayley, surgeon, N.Y., entitled "Cases of the Angina Trachealis with the Mode of Cure." He reported that his observances dated from April 1774.

Dermatology treatise was *The Atlas of Skin Diseases* by Dr. Louis Adolphus Duhring, professor of skin diseases at the medical school of the University of Pennsylvania. The first section was published in 1876 in Philadelphia, Pa.

Dispensatory was the *American Dispensatory, Containing the Operations of Pharmacy, Together With the Natural, Chemical, Pharmaceutical and Medical History of the Different Substances Employed in Medicine,* by John Redman Coxe. It was printed in 1806 in Philadelphia, Pa., by A. Bartram for Thomas Dobson. It was a simplified arrangement of Dr. Duncan's *Edinburgh New Dispensatory,* and contained 787 pages and 6 plates.

Dispensatory (American) was the *Dispensatory of the United States of America,* 1092 pages, published in 1833 in Philadelphia, Pa., by Grigg and Elliot. It was prepared by Dr. George Bacon Wood, professor of materia medica and pharmacy, and Dr. Franklin Bache, professor of chemistry, at the Philadelphia College of Pharmacy.

Dissection essay appeared in 1750. It was a report by Dr. John Bard and Dr. Peter Middleton, who in 1750 in New York City dissected the body of Hermanus Carroll, a criminal executed for murder. *(Dr. James Thacher—American Medical Biography. 1828)*

Gastroenterology treatise was *An Experimental Inquiry into the Principles of Nutrition and the Digestive Processes,* a 48-page graduation thesis submitted by John Richardson Young at the University of Pennsylvania, Philadelphia, Pa. It was published by Eaken & Mecum, Philadelphia, Pa., in 1803.

Hay fever book was Morrill Wyman's *Autumnal Catarrh—Hay Fever,* published in 1872 by Hurd & Houghton, New York City. It was dedicated to Jeffries Wyman, professor of anatomy, Harvard University School of Medicine, and contained 173 pages and 3 maps. Hay fever was known as Catarrhus Autumnalis.

Hemophilia treatise was prepared by Dr. John Conrad Otto of Philadelphia, Pa., who stated that the hemorrhagic tendency was transmitted through the females to the males but that the females were not susceptible themselves. His report appeared in 1803 in the *Medical Repository & Review of American Publications on Medicine and Surgery,* and was entitled "An Account of an Haemorrhagic Disposition Existing in Certain Families." The magazine was published in New York City. *(Francis Randolph Packard—History of Medicine in the U.S.)*

Homeopathic treatise was Christian Friedrich Samuel Hahnemann's *Geist der Homöopathischen Heil-Lehre,* translated by Dr. Hans Birch Gram and published as a 24-page pamphlet entitled *The Characteristic of Homöopathia.* The book was issued in December 1825 by J. & J. Harper, New York City.

Hydrophobia book was James Thacher's *Observations on Hydrophobia, Produced by the Bite of a Mad Dog or Other Rabid Animal,* published in 1812 by Joseph Avery at Plymouth, Mass.

Hydrotherapy book (American) was *On Baths and Mineral Waters* by Dr. John Bell, printed in 2 volumes in 1831 in Philadelphia, Pa. Volume 1 (374 pages) was "a full account of the hygienic and curative powers of cold, tepid, warm, hot and vapour baths and of sea bathing." Volume 2 (158 pages) was "a history of the chemical composition and medicinal properties of the chief mineral springs of the United States and Europe."

Hydrotherapy book in English was *The Curiosities of Common Water; or, the advantages thereof, in preventing and curing many distempers. Gather'd from the writings of several eminent physicians, and also from more than forty years experience to which are added some rules for preserving health by diet,* by John Smith, C.M., printed in London in 1712, reprinted in 1723 by Samuel Keimer, Philadelphia, Pa. It contained 47 pages.

Medical book for army medical use was *A Journal of the Practice of Medicine, Surgery and Pharmacy in the Military Hospitals of France,* published by order of the King. Reviewed and digested by M. De Horne, under the inspection of the Royal Society. Only one volume appeared. The 120-page octavo book, printed in 1790 by J. M. McLean & Co., New York City, was translated from the French by Joseph Browne. The French

The First

edition, consisting of seven volumes, was published from 1782 to 1788.

Medical catalog was *A Short Treatise of the Virtues of Dr. Bateman's Pectoral Drops: The Nature of the Distemper They Cure, and the Manner of Their Operation.* It contained 36 pages (pages 22-36 consisted of testimonials of users in the first person). It also contained a 4-page abstract: "An Abstract of the Patent granted by his Majesty King George to Benj. Okell, the inventor of a Medicine, call'd Dr. Bateman's Pectoral Drops, and to J.Cluer, R. Raikes and W.Dicey, the persons concerned with the said Inventor, that they enjoy the sole Benefit of the said Medine." The catalog was originally printed by J.Cluer in Bow-Churchyard, London; then it was reprinted by John Peter Zenger in New York, 1731. The medicine was sold by James Wallace of New York City, who sold the drops wholesale and retail in America, "for the rheumatism, stone and gravel pains, colds, agues, and fevers, gout, jaundice, ailments of the breast, and asthmas."

Medical dictionary (complete). *See* Dictionary: Medical dictionary (complete)

Medical education book was printed by William Bradford, Philadelphia, Pa., in 1765. It contained 63 pages of text and was entitled *A Discourse Upon the Institution of Medical Schools in America,* by John Morgan, M.D., professor of the theory and practice of medicine in the College of Philadelphia. The discourse was delivered at a public anniversary commencement held in the College of Philadelphia, May 30 and 31, 1765, and had a preface, containing among other things, The Author's Apology for attempting to introduce the regular mode of practicing Physic in Philadelphia.

Medical encyclopedia was the *American Cyclopedia of Practical Medicine and Surgery; A Digest of Medical Literature,* edited by Isaac Hays, surgeon to Wills' Hospital and physician to the Philadelphia Orphan Asylum, published by Carey, Lea & Blanchard, Philadelphia, Pa. Only two volumes of the work were published, covering "A to Azygores": Volume 1, 1834, 560 pages, and Volume 2, 1836, 589 pages.

Medical ethics book was *A Discourse Upon the Duties of a Physician, with Some Sentiments on the Usefulness and Necessity of a Public Hospital, delivered before the President and Governors of King's College at the commencement held on the 16th of May, 1769. As advice to those gentlemen who then received the first medical degrees conferred by that university,* by Samuel Bard, M.D., and printed by A. & J. Robertson, New York City, in 1769. It consisted of 18 printed pages.

Medical history was printed in New York City in 1769 by Hugh Gaine. It was entitled *A Medical Discourse, or An Historical Inquiry into the ancient and present State of Medicine: The Substance of which Was delivered at opening the*

The First

Medical School in the City of New York, by Peter Middleton, M.D., and Professor of the Theory of Physic in King's College. It contained a 2-page dedication and 72 pages of text.

Medical jurisprudence treatise (authoritative) was Theodoric Romeyn Beck's *Elements of Medical Jurisprudence,* a two-volume work published in 1823 in Albany, N.Y.

Medical pamphlet in America was published on January 21, 1677. It was a treatise on smallpox entitled *Brief Rule to Guide the Common People of New England how to Order themselves and theirs in the Small Pocks or Measles.* It was published in Boston, Mass., by Thomas Thacher and consisted of a single sheet of 15½ by 10½ inches. *(Fielding Hudson Garrison—History of Medicine)*

Medical slang dictionary. *See* Dictionary: Medical slang dictionary

Mental diseases book was *Medical Inquiries and Observations upon the Diseases of the Mind,* by Benjamin Rush, published in Philadelphia, Pa., in 1812. *(William Staughton—An Eulogium in Memory of the Late Dr. Benjamin Rush)*

Neurasthenia book was George Miller Beard's *A Practical Treatise on Nervous Exhaustion (Neurasthenia); Its symptoms, nature, sequences and treatment.* It contained 198 pages and was published in 1880 by M. Wood & Company, New York City. Beard's first article on this subject appeared April 29, 1869, in the *Boston Medical and Surgical Journal.*

Neurology textbook was Dr. William Alexander Hammond's *The Diseases of the Nervous System,* divided into five sections covering diseases of the brain, spinal cord, cerebrospinal system, nerve cells, and peripheral nerves. It was published in 1871 in New York City and was edited by Dr. Thaddeus M. B. Cross. The book consisted of Hammond's lectures delivered at the New York State Hospital for Diseases of the Nervous System and Bellevue Hospital Medical College, New York City.

Obstetrics book was Samuel Bard's *A Compendium of the Theory and Practice of Midwifery,* a 239-page book published in 1807 by Collins & Perkins, New York City. It contained "practical instructions for the management of women during pregnancy, in labor, and in child-bed, calculated to correct the errors, and to improve the practice of midwives as well as to serve as an introduction to the study of this art for students and young practitioners."

Ophthalmology book was *A Treatise on the Diseases of the Eye; Including the Doctrines and Practice of the Most Eminent Modern Surgeons, and Particularly those of Professor [George Joseph] Beer,* by Dr. George Frick, ophthalmic surgeon to the Baltimore General Dispensary, Baltimore, Md. It was published by Fielding

The First

MEDICAL BOOK—*Continued*
Lucas, Jr., and printed by John D. Toy in Baltimore, Md., in 1823; it consisted of 320 pages.

Pathology textbook was *A Treatise on Pathological Anatomy* which was published in Philadelphia, Pa., in 1829. It contained 460 pages. The author was William Edmonds Horner, who in 1831 was appointed professor of anatomy in the medical school of the University of Pennsylvania, Philadelphia, Pa.

Pediatrics book was *The Maternal Physician; A Treatise on the Nurture and Management of Infants, from the Birth until Two Years Old, Being the Result of Sixteen Years' Experience in the Nursery,* published in Philadelphia, Pa., in 1810 by "An American Matron."

Pediatrics book of importance was Dr. Luther Emmett Holt's *The Care and Feeding of Children, a Catechism for the Use of Mothers and Children's Nurses,* 66 pages, published in 1894 by D. Appleton & Company, New York City. It was dedicated to Mrs. Chapin, "the founder of the first training school for nurses of infants in America." *(Robert Luther Holt and L. Emmett Holt, Jr.—L. Emmett Holt, Pioneer of a Children's Century)*

Pediatrics monograph was Charles Caldwell's *An Attempt to Establish the Original Sameness of Those Phenomena of Fever, (Principally confined to Infants and Children) Described by Medical Writers Under the Several Names of Hydrocephalus Internus, Cynanche Trachealis and Diarrhoea Infantum,* a thesis presented May 17, 1796, for a degree at the University of Pennsylvania Medical School, Philadelphia, Pa. It was published in Philadelphia, Pa., by Thomas Dobson. *(Transactions of the American Pediatric Society, Vol. 9. 1897)*

Pharmacopoeia. *See* Pharmacopoeia

Pleurisy book was John Tennent's *An Essay on the Pleurisy,* 46 pages printed in 1736 by William Parks, Williamsburg, Va.

Psychiatry book was *Medical Inquiries and Observations Upon the Diseases of the Mind,* by Benjamin Rush, M.D., which was copyrighted October 26, 1812, published by Kimber and Richardson, Philadelphia, Pa., in 1812. This comprehensive book on mental illness contained 367 pages plus 4 pages listing books issued by the publishers. Dr. Rush was a professor of the Institutes and Practice of Medicine and of Clinical Practice in the University of Pennsylvania.

Psychological medicine modern textbook was *A Manual of Psychological Medicine,* by John Charles Bucknill and Daniel Hack Tuke, published in Philadelphia, Pa., in 1858. It contained 536 pages. The chapters on history, nosology, description, and statistics were written by Tuke; the chapters in the last half of the book on diagnosis,

The First

pathology, and treatment of insanity, and the appendix of cases, by Bucknill.

Puerperal fever pamphlet was *The Contagiousness of Puerperal Fever,* by Oliver W[endell] Holmes, M.D., prepared and written in 21 days and read before the Boston Society for Medical Improvement. It was published in the April 1843 issue of the *New England Quarterly Journal of Medicine and Surgery* and consisted of 28 pages.

Scarlet fever report was *The Practical History of a New Epidemical Eruptive Military Fever, with an Angina Ulcusulosa which prevailed in Boston, New-England in the years 1735 and 1736* a 24-page thesis by William Douglass, M.D., printed and sold by Thomas Fleet at the Sign of the Heart and Crown in Cornhill [Boston] in 1736. "This distemper did emerge 20th May 1735 in Kingston Township, fifty miles eastward from Boston, and affected one-fourth of the inhabitants."

Surgery manual was *Plain, Concise Practical Remarks on the Treatment of Wounds and Fractures; to which is added a short appendix on camp and military hospitals; principally designed for the use of young military surgeons in North America,* 92 pages, printed in 1775 by John Holt, New York City. The author was Dr. John Jones, professor of surgery in King's College (now Columbia University), New York City. *(American Journal of Surgery. December 1934)*

Therapeutics and materia medica book was *Discourses on the Elements of Therapeutics and Materia Medica,* published in 1817 in Philadelphia, Pa., by Nathaniel Chapman. *(Samuel David Gross—Lives of Eminent American Physicians and Surgeons)*

Tuberculosis circular. *See* Tuberculosis circular

Typhus fever treatise was Elisha North's *History of the Typhus Petechialis, or the Malignant petechial or Spotted Fever, as it appeared in Goshen, Conn., during the winter 1807-1808 with such remarks as may tend to elucidate its nature and to establish the best method of care,* which appeared in 1809 in *The Philadelphia Medical Museum,* published in Philadelphia, Pa. *(Philadelphia Medical Museum. Volume 6)*

MEDICAL CHEMISTRY COURSE. See under Medical instruction

MEDICAL CLINIC
Acupuncture treatment center was the Acupuncture Center of New York opened July 12, 1972. Due to legal complications it closed and then reopened December 27, 1972, as the Acupuncture Center of Washington, Washington, D.C.

Birth control clinic was opened on October 16, 1916, at 46 Amboy Street, Brooklyn, N.Y., by Fania Mindell, Ethel Byrne, and Margaret Sanger. A dodger circular announcing its opening was

The First

printed in English, Yiddish, and Italian. *(Margaret Sanger—My Fight for Birth Control)*

Cancer clinic (traveling) was established on February 14, 1946, by the Oklahoma Division, American Cancer Society of Oklahoma City, Okla. A school bus was remodeled to convey equipment and instruments necessary for establishing four examination rooms, which were presided over by an internist, a dermatologist, a gynecologist, and a surgeon. All services were rendered free of charge, and both physicians and nurses serving on the staff donated both time and expenses. Clinics were usually set up in church classrooms. The first clinic was set up in Tonkawa, Kay County, Okla.

Cancer prevention clinic for children was the Kate Depew Strang Foundation Prevention Clinic opened January 3, 1947, in the Prevention Clinic of Memorial Hospital, New York City.

Children's clinic was established in 1862 by the Medical Faculty of the University of the City of New York under the leadership of Dr. Abraham Jacobi. *(Solomon Robert Kagan—Leaders of Medicine)*

College medical clinic was established in 1840 by Dr. Willard Parker, Professor of Surgery in the College of Physicians and Surgeons, New York City. He opened a dispensary where outpatients were brought to be examined and treated in the presence of the medical students. Clinics were held one day a week, but the service was later extended. *(John Call Dalton—History of the College of Physicians and Surgeons)*

Contraceptive clinic (state) was opened March 15, 1937, in Raleigh, N.C., when the North Carolina State Board of Health officially introduced a program setting up contraceptive clinics for indigent married women in the regular maternity and child health services as locally administered. The director was Dr. George Marion Cooper of the Division of Preventive Medicine. Roberta Pratt, a Raleigh nurse, was employed to cooperate with the health officers.

Flying medical clinic left the United States in January 1930 to attend the Pan American Medical Association convention in Panama City, Panama. It was composed of physicians who demonstrated the latest methods in surgery and medicine in local hospitals in Guatemala, Nicaragua, Panama, Colombia, Venezuela, and other Latin American countries. The first demonstration of an operation was made on January 25, 1930, by Dr. Fred Houdlett Albee.

Heredity clinic was opened November 12, 1941, by the Department of Human Heredity, a research unit of the Laboratory of Vertebrate Genetics, University of Michigan, Ann Arbor, Mich., under the direction of Dr. Lee Raymond Dice. It secured data on the role that heredity plays and furnished

The First

advice to families about matters in which heredity is a factor.

Laryngology clinic was established in March 1863 by the Medical Faculty of the University of the City of New York under the supervision of Dr. Louis Elsberg. *(Laryngoscope. Vol. 15. 1905)*

Medical clinic (general) of importance was opened by the Johns Hopkins Medical School, Baltimore, Md., in October 1889. The Johns Hopkins Hospital was opened in May 1889. Sir William Osler, regius professor of medicine at Oxford, was the first physician in chief of the Johns Hopkins Hospital and professor of medicine at the Johns Hopkins Medical School. In this dual role, he was the director of the medical clinic, but he was without that title. *(William Henry Welch—Johns Hopkins Medical School)*

Ophtalmology clinic was opened by the Fifth Avenue Hospital, New York City, in September 1932. The clinic was devoted to the treatment of ocular muscle imbalances (including some types of cross-eye). The clinic was under the direction of Le Grand Haven Hardy, M.D., director of Eye Service.

Vasectomy outpatient service was opened October 3, 1969, by the Margaret Sanger Research Bureau, Inc., New York City, under the direction of Dr. Aquiles Jose Sobrero, director of the Sanger Bureau. The clinical director was Dr. Joseph Edward Davis.

MEDICAL COLLEGE. *See under* Medical school

MEDICAL CONGRESS

Cancer institute (convention) was attended by 530 persons, September 7-8, 1936, at the University of Wisconsin, Madison, Wis. The Wisconsin Alumni Research Foundation made available the necessary funds to finance the institute. Dr. William Shainline Middleton, dean of the medical school, served as chairman. The institute was opened by Dr. Glenn Frank, president of the University of Wisconsin. The conference emphasized the need for cooperation between medical authorities and public health departments to reduce cancer incidence.

Fever Therapy International Conference was held March 29-31, 1937, at the College of Physicians and Surgeons, Columbia University, New York City, and attended by physicians from 16 countries.

Mental Hygiene International Congress opened May 4, 1930, in Washington, D.C., with Dr. William Alanson White presiding. The sessions were attended by 3,000 persons from 53 countries, workers in mental hygiene and related fields.

MEDICAL CORPS (Army). *See under* Army

MEDICAL ENCYCLOPEDIA. *See* Medical book

The First

MEDICAL INSTRUCTION
See also Medical school

Anatomy lectures (scientific) to medical students were given by Dr. William Shippen at the College of Philadelphia, Pa., from 1762 to 1765. Public lectures on anatomy were given in Boston, Mass., in 1789 by John Jeffries, but public opinion was so much against his policy of dissecting that at the second lecture a mob invaded the lecture room and carried off the body of a convict on which he was demonstrating. Further lectures were stopped as a result of public animosity. *(Casper Wistar—Eulogium on Dr. William Shippen)*

Bacteriology courses in a college were given by the Hygienic Laboratory of the University of Michigan, Ann Arbor, Mich. The laboratory was established in 1887, and the first class in bacteriology was instituted by Dr. Victor Clarence Vaughan and Dr. Frederick George Novy in January 1889. Classes were in session four hours daily for three months. In 1890–1891 bacteriology became a required course for medical students.

Bacteriology lectures in a medical school were given in 1885 by Harold Clarence Ernst at the Harvard Medical School, Cambridge, Mass. *(Journal of Medical Research. 1903)*

Clinical instruction and bedside demonstration were introduced in 1818 by Alexander Hodgdon Stevens. It is said that in his operations as surgeon of the New York Hospital he often purposely avoided the neatness deemed so essential by other surgeons, in order to show his students that it was not essential to the recovery of the patient, provided the surgeon's skill and rapidity of manipulation were great enough. *(John Glover Adams—Discourse Commemorative of the Life and Character of Alexander Hodgdon Stevens, M.D., LL.D)*

Dermatology chair was founded by Harvard University, Cambridge, Mass., in 1871, when Dr. James Clarke White was made professor of dermatology. He was a lecturer in the medical school, 1863–64; adjunct professor of chemistry, 1866–71; instructor in medical chemistry, 1871–72. He was the first president of the American Dermatological Association founded in 1876.

History of medicine department with a full salaried professor and staff was the Institute of the History of Medicine, inaugurated October 18, 1929, by Johns Hopkins University, Baltimore, Md. Dr. William Henry Welch was the first professor of the history of medicine and Dr. Stephen d'Irsay was associate. *(Bulletin of the Johns Hopkins Hospital. Vol. 46. 1930)*

Hygiene lectures offered by a college were delivered in 1818 by Dr. James Jackson, Hersey professor of the theory and practice of physic, at Harvard College, Cambridge, Mass. The committee decided on October 8, 1818, "that he be required to deliver a number of lectures on subjects relating to the care and preservation of health, and that they be this year delivered to the members of the two upper classes, at the hour appointed on Friday for a public lecture to those classes."

Instruction for nurses. *See under* Nursing school

Laryngology instruction was offered regularly by the Medical Department of the University of the City of New York in the autumn of 1861. Dr. Louis Elsberg was a lecturer on the laryngoscope and diseases of the throat and larynx 1863–64. From 1869 to 1873 he was clinical professor of diseases of the throat and from 1873 to 1881 professor of diseases of the throat and laryngology. *(American Laryngological Association—Transactions, Vol. 1. 1879)*

Medical chemistry course (systematic) was offered in 1871 by Dr. Edward Stickney Wood, Assistant Professor of Chemistry, at the Harvard Medical School, Cambridge, Mass.

Medical jurisprudence course was given by Dr. James Stringham, professor of medical jurisprudence at the College of Physicians and Surgeons, Columbia University, New York City, from 1813 to 1817. Prior to this appointment he served as professor of chemistry.

Medical research chair in an American university was the John Herr Musser chair, established in 1910 by the School of Medicine, University of Pennsylvania, Philadelphia, Pa. The first incumbent was Professor Richard Mills Pearce. *(Medical Research and Education. 1913)*

Midwifery professor was Dr. John Van Brugh Tennent, appointed Professor of Midwifery at King's College (now Columbia University), New York City, in 1767. He held this post until his death in 1770.

Ophthalmology course (regular) was established in 1823 at the Ophthalmic Clinic, Baltimore General Dispensary, University of Maryland, Baltimore, Md.

Ophthalmology professor was Elkanah Williams, who was appointed by the Miami Medical College of Cincinnati, Ohio, in 1865.

Orthopedics chair was established by Bellevue Hospital Medical College, New York City in 1861. The first incumbent was Dr. Lewis Albert Sayre. *(New England Medical Monthly. June 1884)*

Pathology chair was established at Harvard University, Cambridge, Mass., in 1847, when John Barnard Sweet Jackson was appointed professor of pathological anatomy and curator of the Warren Museum. The professorship was endowed by George Cheyne Shattuck in 1854. The first chair of modern pathology (after the field had been revolutionized by Louis Pasteur and his successors) was established in 1883 by Johns Hopkins University,

Baltimore, Md. The first incumbent was Professor William Henry Welch.

Pediatrics professor was Dr. Abraham Jacobi, who lectured in 1857 at the College of Physicians and Surgeons (now the College of Physicians and Surgeons of Columbia University), New York City, and became clinical professor of pediatrics in 1870. He held the post until 1899. *(Medical Life. October 1926)*

Plastic surgery professor in any medical school or hospital was Dr. Joseph Eastman Sheehan who was appointed in 1926 to that post by the New York Postgraduate Medical School and Hospital, New York City. *(Joseph Eastman Sheehan—A Manual of Reparative Plastic Surgery)*

Psychiatric institute, organized for research and the training of physicians, was the Pathological Institute, New York City, established by Chapter 545 of the Laws of 1896 of New York State, passed May 12, 1896, effective July 1, 1896. Dr. Ira Van Gieson was appointed the first director and served until June 1901. It was reorganized by Dr. Adolf Meyer, who took office December 1902. The name was changed to the New York State Psychiatric Institute and Hospital by a decision of the State Commission in Lunacy and announced in the report for the year 1908–1909, but the name was first used officially in the commission's handbook for 1909. In 1927 it became the Psychiatric Department of the Columbia University-Presbyterian Hospital Medical Center and was housed in a new building dedicated December 3-4, 1929.

Public hygiene professor was Dr. Thomas Bevan, appointed in 1868 by Northwestern University, Chicago, Ill. In 1869, the title was changed to professor of hygiene, and the chair was held by Dr. Bevan until 1875. From 1858 to 1867 the departments of pathology and public hygiene were combined.

State medicine and public hygiene professorship was established in 1882 by Northwestern University, Chicago, Ill. The first incumbent was Dr. Oscar Coleman De Wolf.

MEDICAL JOURNAL. *See* Medical periodical

MEDICAL JURISPRUDENCE BOOK. *See* Medical book

MEDICAL JURISPRUDENCE COURSE. *See under* Medical instruction

MEDICAL LEGISLATION

Blood grouping test laws (state) were passed by New York State in 1935. Two bills, amending the civil practice act and the inferior criminal courts act, to empower the court to order the making of blood tests, were introduced by Assemblyman Charles H. Breitbart on January 9, 1935, as well as a bill on February 15, 1935, to amend the domestic relations law. The three bills, Chapter 196, 197,

and 198, laws of 1935, were signed by Governor Herbert Henry Lehman on March 22, 1935, to take effect immediately.

Chiropody law governing the study of chiropody was passed in New York City in 1895. It is difficult to ascertain which was the first school established, for the law required only the passing of an examination and demanded no prescribed course of study. For this reason many individuals "coached" prospective applicants for licenses, and those "schools" that did exist taught the theory of chiropody as a sideline of beauty culture.

Chiropractic legislation (state) was Chapter 291 enacted March 18, 1913, by the state of Kansas. It regulated the practice of chiropractic, provided for licensing and examination of chiropractors, and created a board of 3 people for examination and regulation. Applicants were required to be graduates of a chartered chiropractic school or college having a course of 3 years with actual attendance of more than 6 months each year.

Law (state) requiring marriage license applicants to undergo medical tests was enacted by New York. Chapter 640, Laws of 1938, "to amend the domestic relations law in relation to examinations and serological tests of applicants for a marriage license and effectual duration of the license for preventing the spread of syphilis," was signed April 12, 1938, by Governor Herbert Henry Lehman. The bill, known as the Demond-Breitbart Law, became effective July 1, 1938.

Law (state) requiring serological blood tests of pregnant women was Chapter 133, Laws of 1938, New York, the [Jeremiah F.] Twomey-[William Allan] Newell bill signed by Governor Herbert Henry Lehman on March 18, 1938, on which date it became effective.

Law to license the practice of medicine was New Jersey's law of September 26, 1772. The act was effective for a five-year period. It authorized a licensing board consisting of two judges of the Supreme Court of New Jersey and a third individual appointed by them, and forbade the practice of medicine without a license. Very severe fines were imposed upon violators, but the law did not apply to those who drew teeth, bled patients, or gave medical assistance for which they received no fee or compensation.

Law to regulate the practice of medicine (actually enforced) was an "act to regulate the practice of Physick and Surgery in the City of New York," passed June 10, 1760. It provided that "no person whatsoever shall practice as a physician or surgeon ... before he shall first have been examined in physick or surgery and approved of and admitted by one of His Majesty's Council, the Judges of the Supreme Court, the King's Attorney General and the Mayor of the City of New York for the time being or by any three or more of them." Violators were subject to a penalty of five pounds,

The First

MEDICAL LEGISLATION—*Continued*
one half of which went to the informer and the remainder to the poor funds.

Law to regulate the practice of medicine (colonial) was enacted May 3, 1649, in Massachusetts. "Physicians, chirurgians, midwives or others" were forbidden "to exercise or put forth any act contrary to the known rules of art, nor exercise any force, violence, or cruelty upon or towards the bodies of any, whether young or old." The act was "not intended to discourage the lawful use of their skill but to encourage and direct them in the right use thereof and to inhibit and restrain the presumptious arrogance of such as . . . exercise violence upon . . . bodies." *(Colonial Laws of Massachusetts)*

Medical law was passed by Virginia, October 21, 1639, an "act to compel physicians and surgeons to declare on oath the value of their medicines." *(William Waller Hening—Statutes at Large of Virginia. Vol. 1)*

Premature-baby health law was passed March 5, 1935, by Chicago, Ill., requiring physicians to report the birth of all premature babies within an hour after birth. A supplemental item was added to the official birth certificate to show whether or not a baby was born prematurely.

Sterilization legislation. *See* Sterilization legislation

MEDICAL PAMPHLET. *See under* Medical book

MEDICAL PERIODICAL
Allergy magazine was the *Journal of Allergy*, published November 1929 in St. Louis, Mo. It was edited by Dr. Harry Louis Alexander, and the first issue contained 112 pages.

Black medical journal was the *Medical and Surgical Observer*, 32 pages and cover, published in Jackson, Tenn., in December 1892. It appeared regularly for 18 months. The first editor was Vandahurst Lynk, M.D.

Homeopathic magazine was the *American Journal of Homeopathia*, 48 pages, issued February 1835. It was edited by Drs. John F. Gray and Amos Gerald Hull and published by Moore and Payne, New York City. Subscription was $4 a year. Only four issues were printed, February, April, June, and August, 1835.

Laryngology magazine was the *Archives of Laryngology*, a 108-page quarterly, published in New York City in March 1880. It was edited by Dr. Louis Elsberg of New York City, Dr. George Morewood Lefferts of New York City, Dr. Jacob Solis-Cohen of Philadelphia, Pa., and Dr. Frederick Irving Knight of Boston, Mass.

Medical magazine was published in New York City on August 8, 1797, and was called *The Medical Repository*, a "depository of facts and reasonings relative to Natural History, Agriculture and

The First

Medicine." Printed by T. & J. Swords, printers to The Faculty of Physicians of Columbia College, it was published quarterly and appeared until 1824. It was also the first scientific periodical published in the United States. The first editor was Dr. Samuel Latham Mitchill, who continued in this capacity for 16 years. Drs. Edward Miller and Elihu Hubbard Smith were also active in the founding of this journal.

Medical periodical devoted to diseases of women and children was the *American Journal of Obstetrics and Diseases of Women and Children*, a quarterly, started May 1868 in New York City. It was edited by Dr. Emil Jacob Noeggerath and Dr. Benjamin Frederick Dawson. The first issue contained 96 pages, including an article by Dr. Abraham Jacobi on "The Pathology and Treatment of the Different Forms of Croup."

Optometry magazine was *The Optician*, a 16-page monthly, edited and published by Frederick Boger, New York City, January 1891. Subscription was 50 cents a year. In May 1892 the name was changed to *The Optician and Allied Interests* and in October 1892 to *The Optician and Jeweler*.

Osteopathy magazine was the *Journal of Osteopathy*, which was started in May 1894 by the American School of Osteopathy in Kirksville, Mo. The first editor was Dr. Jenette Hubbard Bolles.

Physiology magazine. *See* Physiology magazine

MEDICAL RESEARCH CHAIR. *See under* Medical instruction

MEDICAL "ROGUES' GALLERY" listing medical quacks, manufacturers of spurious "cure-alls," peddlers of nostrums, "inventors" of diet, exercise, and other worthless systems, and others who prey on the ill and the gullible was started in January 1930 by the New York City Department of Health and is said to be the first of its kind in the world. The "gallery" was compiled by the National Better Business Bureau, Inc., at the suggestion of Special Deputy Health Commissioner Edward Fisher Brown.

MEDICAL SCHOOL
See also Medical instruction

Coeducational medical school was the Boston University School of Medicine, which was founded in 1873 (originally as a homeopathic school). When the New England Female Medical College was merged with it in 1874, the Boston University School of Medicine became the first coeducational medical school in the world.

Homeopathic college was the Homeopathic Medical College of Pennsylvania, Philadelphia, Pa., incorporated April 8, 1848. Preliminary instruction was given October 16, 1848. The regular course started with 15 students on November 6, 1848, and concluded on March 1, 1849. Six students graduated at the commencement exercises

The First

March 29, 1849. Dr. Walter Williamson was the dean of the college.

Homeopathic school was the North American Academy of the Homeopathic Healing Art, founded April 10, 1835, in Allentown, Pa. The cornerstone was laid May 27, 1835. Chartered on June 17, 1836, the school was known as the Allentown Academy. The degree of Doctor of Homoeopathia was conferred upon graduates. Instruction was in German. Constantine Hering, who came to Philadelphia in 1832 from Germany, became the first president and principal instructor. *(William Harvey King—History of Homeopathy and Its Institutions in America)*

Institute for research. *See under* Research institute

Medical center devoted to teaching, treatment, and research was the Columbia-Presbyterian Medical Center, 168th Street west of Broadway, New York City, opened March 6, 1928. The formal dedication was held October 12, 1928. It had a library of 100,000 books and was designed to serve 600 students (now approximately 350,000 books; 6,000 students). William Darrach was dean of the faculty of medicine (1919-1930).

Medical college was the College of Philadelphia Department of Medicine, now the University of Pennsylvania School of Medicine, which was established in Philadelphia, Pa., on May 3, 1765, principally through the efforts of Dr. William Shippen, Jr., and Dr. John Morgan, who became professor of the theory and practice of physick and professor of anatomy and surgery, respectively. The school was started in a wooden building known as Surgeons' Hall. The first commencement was held June 21, 1768, and the first medical diplomas (Bachelor of Medicine) issued in America were presented to the ten members of the graduating class.

Medical college (Jewish sponsored) was the Albert Einstein College of Medicine of Yeshiva University, New York City, which offered instruction on September 12, 1935, to 56 men and women, although only 1½ floors of the 6-story building were completed. It had a faculty of 200. Dr. Marcus David Kogel was the first dean.

Medical college on the Pacific Coast was the Medical Department of the University of the Pacific, opened at Santa Clara, Calif., in 1858 by Dr. Elias Samuel Cooper. *(University of the Pacific— 1859 Announcement of Lectures)*

Medical school based upon water-cure principles was the American Hydropathic Institute, New York City. Two terms, each 3 months long, were held March 15 and September 15, 1851. Instruction was $50. The instructors were Thomas L. Nichols, M.D., and Mary S. Nichols.

The First

Medical school professor (woman). *See* College: Woman professor at a first-class medical school

Medical summer school was opened at the Medical College of South Carolina, Columbia, S.C., in 1853 by John Julian Chisholm. *(Centennial Memorial of the Medical College of the State of South Carolina)*

Naval medical school was the Naval Laboratory and Department of Instruction opened August 1, 1893, at the United States Naval Hospital, Brooklyn, N.Y. The first director was Henry M. Wells, appointed August 21, 1893, with the relative rank of captain.

Naval medical school (unofficial) was authorized May 19, 1823, and opened at the Navy Yard Hospital, Philadelphia, Pa., under the direction of Dr. Thomas Harris of the Pennsylvania Hospital, Philadelphia, Pa., who taught naval hygiene, military surgery, customs and usage of the naval service, etc. The Secretary of the Navy appropriated $400 for the support of the school, the expenses being paid by Dr. Harris from his own income. The school was discontinued by order of January 31, 1843.

Osteopathy school was the American School of Osteopathy, chartered in Kirksville, Mo., on May 10, 1892. It opened October 3, 1892, in a little frame cottage. It had an enrollment of about 20 students. Eighteen diplomas were granted to the first graduating class on March 2, 1894. Its purpose, according to the articles of incorporation, was "to improve our system of surgery, midwifery, and treatment of general diseases—the adjustment of the bones is the leading feature of this school." The founders were Dr. Andrew Taylor Still and Dr. William Smith. *(Andrew Taylor Still—Autobiography)*

Women's medical school was the Boston Female Medical School, which was organized through the initiative of Samuel Gregory on November 1, 1848, with 12 pupils and 2 teachers, Enoch Carter Rolfe and William Mason Cornell. Rolfe was the first lecturer. On May 24, 1856, the school was incorporated as the New England Female Medical College, with power to confer degrees. In 1874 it was absorbed by the Boston University School of Medicine, which thus became the first coeducational medical school in the world. *(Frederick Clayton Waite—History of the New England Female Medical College 1848–1874)*

Women's medical school (still in existence as an independent institution), the Female Medical College of Pennsylvania, was organized in 1850. It was chartered in March 1850 and began holding classes on October 12, 1850. The first class was graduated on December 30, 1851. In 1867 the name was changed to the Woman's Medical College of Pennsylvania and in 1970 to the Medical College

The First

MEDICAL SCHOOL—*Continued*
of Pennsylvania. Male students were admitted in
1969.

MEDICAL SOCIETY
 American College of Surgeons was incorporated November 25, 1912, in Springfield, Ill., and was
organized in Washington, D.C., May 5, 1913, "to
elevate the standard of surgery, to establish a
standard of competency and of character for practitioners of surgery, and to educate the public and
the profession to understand that the practice of
surgery calls for special training." The first annual
convocation for the admission of fellows took
place in Chicago, Ill., November 13, 1913. Dr. John
Miller Turpin Finney of Baltimore, Md., was the
first president. *(American College of Surgeons—
Yearbook, 1913)*

 **Black doctor to become a member of a medical
association.** *See* Physician: Black doctor to
become a member of a medical association

 **Black member of the American College of Sur-
geons** was Dr. Daniel Hale Williams, admitted
November 13, 1913, at the convention held at
Chicago, Ill.

 First aid emergency organization. *See* First aid
emergency organization

 Homeopathic medical society was the Hah-
nemann Society, organized April 10, 1833, in
Philadelphia, Pa., by Drs. Carl Ihm, George H.
Bute, Charles F. Matlack, Constantine Hering, and
William Wesselhoeft.

 Immunology society was the American Association of Immunologists, organized in Minneapolis, Minn., June 19, 1913, with Dr. Gerald Bertram
Webb as temporary chairman. The first annual
meeting was held June 22, 1914, in Atlantic City,
N.J. The original conception of the society was to
bring together vaccine therapists, but in 1915 it
developed into a scientific organization covering
the whole field of immunology. Its purpose was to
study problems of immunology and its application
to clinical medicine.

 Laryngological society (national) was the
American Laryngological Association, founded
June 3, 1878, in Buffalo, N.Y. The first president
was Dr. Louis Elsberg; the first secretary and trea-
surer was Dr. George Morewood Lefferts. The first
annual meeting was held June 10, 1879, in New
York City. *(American Laryngological Society—
Transactions, 1879)*

 Laryngological society (state) was the Laryngological Society of New York, organized in New
York City in October 1873. Robert Fulton Weir
was president; Clinton Wagner, vice president;
and Woolsey Johnson, secretary. *(Fielding Hudson Garrison—An Introduction to the History of
Medicine)*

The First

 Medical society was founded in Boston, Mass.,
prior to 1735, and functioned until 1741. It was not
very effective and was only local in character.

 Medical society for blacks was the Medico-Chi-
rurgical Society of the District of Columbia, organized April 24, 1884, at the office of Dr. Robert
Reyburn, Washington, D.C. Reyburn was the first
president. The society was revived and incorporated January 15, 1895. Three of the eight incorporators were white. *(William Montague
Cobb—The First Negro Medical Society; a History of the Chirurgical Society of the District of
Columbia 1884–1939)*

 Medical society (national) of real permanence
was the American Medical Association, which
was organized May 5, 1847, in Philadelphia, Pa., in
the Hall of the Academy of Natural Sciences. It
was an outgrowth of the National Medical Association, which had been organized a year before,
on May 5, 1846. Dr. Jonathan Knight was the first
president. This meeting was the first national convention of the medical profession. Two hundred
and fifty delegates attended, representing 22
states, 28 medical schools, and 40 medical societies.

 Medical society (state) of consequence was the
Massachusetts Medical Society, which was incorporated in Boston November 1, 1781. Membership
was limited to 70 Fellows. Temporary officers
were chosen on November 28, 1781. The first
president was Dr. Edward Augustus Holyoke
(1782-1784), the first vice president Dr. James
Pecker (1782-1785), the first treasurer Dr. Aaron
Dexter (1782-1783), the first corresponding secretary Dr. John Barnard Swift (1782-1787), the first
recording secretary Dr. Nathaniel Walker Appleton (1782-1792). The charter was signed by Samuel Adams as president of the Senate, and by John
Hancock as governor of the Commonwealth.
*(Massachusetts Medical Society—A Catalogue of
the Officers and Fellows and Licentiates, 1781)*

 **Woman member of the Association of Ameri-
can Physicians** was Dr. Helen Brooke Taussig,
who was elected May 3, 1950, at the 63rd annual
meeting, held in Atlantic City, N.J.

 **Woman physician admitted to the American In-
stitute of Homeopathy,** Philadelphia, Pa., was Dr.
Mercy Bisbee Jackson, who was accepted in 1871.
*(Egbert Cleave—Biographical Cyclopedia of
Homeopathic Physicians and Surgeons)*

 **Woman physician elected a member of the
American Medical Association** was Dr. Sarah
Hackett Stevenson, who graduated from the
Woman's Medical College of Chicago in 1874. She
was elected to membership in the AMA in 1876 at
the Philadelphia meeting, having been sent there
as a delegate from the Illinois State Medical Society. *(Sarah Hackett Stevenson—The Physiology*

The First

of Woman Embracing Girlhood, Maternity and Mature Age)

Woman president of a major medical society was Dr. Emma Sadler Moss of the Charity Hospital, New Orleans, La., who was installed as president of the American Society of Clinical Pathologists on October 13, 1955, at the 34th annual meeting.

Woman president of a state medical society was Dr. Leslie Swigart Kent of Eugene, Oreg., who was elected president of the Oregon Medical Society at a meeting held September 18, 1948, in Medford, Oreg.

Women members of the American College of Surgeons were Dr. Alice Gertrude Bryant of Boston, Mass., a graduate (1890) of the Woman's Medical College of New York, and Dr. Florence West Duckering, also of Boston, a graduate (1901) of Tufts College Medical School, who became fellows of the society when 1,065 candidates were admitted at the second annual convocation held June 22, 1914, in Philadelphia, Pa.

Women's medical society was the Female Medical Educational Society of Boston, Mass., organized November 23, 1848, with six members "to provide and promote the education of midwives, nurses and female physicians, and to diffuse among women generally a knowledge of physiology and the principles and means of preserving and restoring health." Timothy Gilbert was president; Samuel Gregory, secretary; and John P. Jewett, treasurer. Membership was not confined to the professions.

MEDICARE

Health insurance federal plan was Medicare, authorized by Public Law 89-97 enacted July 30, 1965. The national government contributed from the general revenue an amount equal to that of the person enrolled. The first payments were made July 1, 1966. Under the extended care benefit provision of the statute the first payments for skilled nursing facilities were made January 2, 1967.

Medicare indentification card was card No. 1, presented to former President Harry S. Truman on January 20, 1966, by President Lyndon Baines Johnson at the Truman Library, Independence, Mo. Card No. 2 was given to Elizabeth ("Bess") Wallace Truman, at the same time.

MEDICARE INDENTIFICATION CARD. *See under* Medicare

MEDICATED PLASTER. *See* Adhesive and medicated plaster

MEDICINE

See also branches of medicine; phrases beginning with the word Medical, e.g. Medical books, Medical school; names of drugs; hospitals and types of hospitals; *and* names of diseases

The First

Atomic reactor in medical therapy. *See under* Atomic Reactor

Blood bank. *See under* Blood bank

Bone bank was established in April 1946 by Dr. Leonard Franklin Bush and Dr. Clarence Zent Garber at the New York Orthopaedic Hospital and Dispensary, New York City, and by Dr. Philip Duncan Wilson at the Hospital for Special Surgery, New York City.

Tissue bank, applying the freeze-dried principle to the storage of human tissue grafts, was undertaken in 1954 at the United States Naval Medical School, National Naval Center, Bethesda, Md. It was under the supervision of Lieutenant Commander George William Hyatt. Tissues were procured for storage in a centralized unit.

MEDICINE BALL was invented by Robert Jeffries Roberts, physical education director of the Boston Young Men's Christian Association, in 1895, and first used in Boston, Mass. *(Benjamin Deane Brink —The Body Builder: Robert J. Roberts)*

MEDICINE (patent) ADVERTISEMENT. *See* Advertisement

MEDIUM. *See* Spiritualist

MELODEON PATENT was No. 6,543, granted to C. Austin of Concord, N.H., on June 19, 1849. The melodeon was a small kind of reed organ and employed a suction bellows worked by treadles which drew the air through the reeds.

MELONS and cantaloupes were grown in Germantown, Pa., at the residence of E. B. Gardette on Wissahickon Avenue. The seed was brought over from Tripoli by Commodore James Barron in 1818.

MEMBER OF PARLIAMENT (American-born woman). *See* Woman: American-born woman to become a member of Parliament

MEMORIAL DAY. *See* Holiday: Decoration Day

MEMORIAL STAMP. *See* Postage stamp

MENDELEVIUM. *See* Element: Element 101

MENNONITES

Mennonite church meetinghouse was built in 1708 on the east side of Germantown Avenue, above Herman Street, Germantown, Pa. It was succeeded in 1770 by a stone building which is still in use. The first minister was William Rittenhouse (Rittinghuysen), who served for two years. *(John Thompson Faris—Old Churches and Meeting Houses In and Around Philadelphia)*

Mennonites arrived October 6, 1683, on the *Concord* from Crefeld, Germany. Thirteen families were induced to come to America through the generosity of William Penn, who offered them land in Germantown, Pa., and freedom from religious persecution.

The First

MENTAL DISEASES BOOK. *See* Medical book

MENTAL HYGIENE INTERNATIONAL CONGRESS. *See* Medical congress

MERCANTILE LIBRARY. *See* Library

MERCHANT MARINE
Merchant Marine Distinguished Service Medal. *See* Medal: Distinguished Service Medal (Merchant Marine)

Merchant Marine officer to hold the rank of rear admiral was Albert Borland Randall, commissioned rear admiral in the U.S. Naval Reserve as of February 1, 1942. He was appointed commandant of the U.S. Maritime Service effective March 31, 1943. He was released from active duty on April 30, 1945, because of poor health, and died December 1, 1945.

MERCHANT MARINE ACADEMY
Merchant Marine Academy (U.S.) at Kings Point, N.Y., was dedicated September 30, 1943, when President Franklin Delano Roosevelt's message was read to 5,000 guests. The dedicatory address was delivered by Captain Edward Macauley, Maritime Commissioner. The course of instruction was 18 months. Previously, training had been held aboard ship and in temporary shore establishments.

Merchant Marine Cadet Corps (U.S.) was established March 15, 1938, following the passage of the Merchant Marine Act of June 29, 1936 (49 Stat. L. 1985). The first class, started January 28, 1942, had an enrollment of 74 cadets. The first B.S. degree was awarded June 21, 1950, to 220 graduates. Degrees were subsequently awarded retroactively to all classes, beginning with the class of December 1947. *(Irving Crump—Our Merchant Marine Academy)*

Women were admitted to the Merchant Marine Academy on Acceptance Day, August 31, 1974, after having undergone, after July 16, 1974, two weeks of indoctrination and one month of general training at the Kings Point, N.Y., institution. The class of 1978 consisted of 15 women and 333 men of the 965 in the school. Upon completion of 3 years at the Academy and 1 year at sea, the "midshipmen" received a Coast Guard license as Third Assistant Engineer or Third Mate, a Bachelor of Science (B.S.) degree, or a commission as ensign in the Naval Reserve, U.S. Merchant Marine Academy.

MERCHANT SHIP. *See* Ship

MERCURY BOILER TURBINE. *See under* Electric generator

MERCURY VAPOR LAMP. *See under* Electric lighting

MERGER, RAILROAD. *See under* Railroad

The First

MERINO SHEEP. *See* Animals

MERITORIOUS SERVICE MEDAL. *See* Medal

MERRY-GO-ROUND. *See* Carrousel

MESH STEEL FLOORING BRIDGE. *See* Bridge: Bridge with open-mesh steel flooring

METAL CARTRIDGE. *See* Ordnance

METAL PURCHASED FOR COINAGE. *See under* Money

METAL SKATE. *See* Skate (all-metal)

METEORIC DISPLAY. *See under* Astronomy

METEORITE
Meteorite containing a diamond. *See* Diamond: Diamonds in a meteorite

Meteorite known to have struck a woman crashed through the roof of a house at Sylacauga, Ala., on November 30, 1954, and struck Mrs. Elizabeth Hodges. It was a sulfide meteorite, weighed eight and a half pounds, and was seven inches long at its longest. It is on display in the University of Alabama Museum of Natural History, Moundville, Ala.

Meteorite whose landing was recorded fell at 6:30 A.M., December 14, 1807, at Weston (now Easton), Conn., making a hole 5 feet long and 4½ feet wide.

Photograph on which a meteor was found. *See* Photograph: Photograph (taken in the United States) on which a meteor was found.

METER, ELECTRIC. *See* Electric meter

METER MAIDS. *See* Police

METHODIST CHURCH
Bishop (woman) was Rev. Marjorie Swank Matthews of Traverse City, Mich., elected bishop of the United Methodist Church on July 17, 1980, at Dayton, Ohio. She was consecrated July 18, 1980, at Selinsgrove, Pa. Rev. Emerson Colaw of Cincinnati, Ohio, was also elected and was consecrated on July 18, 1980.

Black Methodist minister of an all-white congregation was the Reverend Simon Peter Montgomery of Pineville, S.C., who assumed the pulpit of the Old Mystic Methodist Church, Old Mystic, Conn., on October 2, 1955.

Black minister with two white congregations was the Reverend Joseph Reed Washington, who on June 3, 1958, served as minister of the Methodist Church of Newfield and the Congregational Church of West Newfield, Maine, three miles apart.

Methodist bishop was Francis Asbury, who was appointed in 1784 by Thomas Coke, to whom the title really belonged. They were known as the joint bishops of the Church in North America. Bishop Asbury was elected by the first General Conference, called the Christmas Conference,

The First

which met December 24, 1784, in the Light Street Church, Baltimore, Md. *(Ezra Squier Tipple—Francis Asbury)*

Methodist chapel, or meetinghouse, was the Wesley Chapel, 42 by 60 feet, at 42 John Street, New York City, dedicated by Philip Embury, the first minister, October 30, 1768. It was a small frame house, one and a half stories high, built in antique Dutch style. It accommodated 700 people. *(Jesse Lee—A Short History of the Methodists in the United States)*

Methodist missionary was Ebenezer Brown, sent out by the Methodist Missionary Society. In 1819 he was assigned a residence in New Orleans, La., to preach to the French people of Louisiana. *(Christian Advocate. January 1899)*

Methodist missionary bishop was Francis Burns. In September 1834 he sailed to Liberia with the Reverend John Seys. At the Liberia Annual Conference, January 1858, Burns was elected the first bishop. He returned to the United States and was ordained October 14, 1858, at the Genesee Conference by Bishops Janes and Baker.

Methodist preacher was Philip Embury, who arrived August 11, 1760, in New York City on the *Perry,* which carried 70 passengers, half of whom were Methodists. With the assistance of Barbara Heck, he organized the first Methodist Society in America in 1776. *(New York Mercury. Aug. 18, 1760)*

Methodist Society in America was organized by Reverend Philip Embury with the assistance of Barbara Heck in 1776 in New York City.

METHODIST COLLEGE was Cokesbury College, Abingdon, Md., named in honor of the two bishops Thomas Coke and Francis Asbury. The building was 108 feet long, 40 feet wide, and 3 stories high. The first headmaster was the Reverend Mr. Heath. The foundation sermon was delivered June 5, 1785, and the building was opened December 6, 1787. *(George W. Archer—An Authentic History of Cokesbury College)*

METHODIST CONFERENCE was held July 16, 1773, in Philadelphia, Pa. It was called together by Thomas Rankin. In 1773 there were 1,160 Methodists in America whose spiritual care was administered by ten preachers. *(J. B. Eakeley—Lost Chapters Recovered from the Early History of American Methodism)*

METHODIST EPISCOPAL CHURCH

African Methodist Episcopal Church was established April 9, 1816, in Philadelphia, Pa., by Bishop Richard Allen, who led the black Methodists to separate from the white church because of disturbances due to color discrimination. The first general convention of the African Methodist Episcopal Church was held in Philadelphia, Pa., April 9-11, 1816. Richard Allen was ordained April 11, 1816, as the first bishop by General Conference,

The First

and consecrated by five regularly ordained ministers. *(Richard Robert Wright—Centennial Encyclopedia of the African Methodist Episcopal Church)*

Scandinavian Methodist Episcopal Church was organized in Cambridge, Wis., in April 1851 by the Reverend Christian B. Willerup with an initial membership of 52. The Church was incorporated May 3, 1851, and a stone building, costing $4,000, was dedicated in the summer of 1852. This church is the oldest Methodist Episcopal church built by Scandinavians in this or any other country.

METRIC SYSTEM LEGALIZATION. *See* Weights and measures standardization

MEXICAN WAR. *See* War (Mexican)

MEZZOTINT. *See* Engraver

MICA

Mica was obtained from the Ruggles mine, Isinglass Mountain, Grafton, N.H., in 1803. *(Douglas B. Sterrett—Some Deposits of Mica in the United States—United States Geological Survey)*

Synthetic mica commercial production was undertaken by the Synthetic Mica Corporation, Caldwell Township, N.J., and offered for sale May 17, 1956, under the trade name of Synthamica. It was a chemically pure synthetic fluor-phlogopite mica capable of withstanding sustained temperatures as high as 2000° F. without physical or electrical failure. Research on synthetic mica was begun in 1947 by the Bureau of Mines in Norris, Tenn.

MICROBIOLOGY LABORATORY (devoted exclusively to the field) was the Institute of Microbiology, Rutgers University, New Brunswick, N.J., dedicated June 7, 1954. The cost of the building was approximately $3,050,000 and that of the equipment $450,000. Classroom and seminar instruction was offered to graduate students. The first director was Dr. Selman Abraham Waksman.

MICROCARD

Book on microcards was Fremont Rider's *The Scholar and the Future of the Research Library,* put on microcards by the Microcard Corporation, La Crosse, Wis., in the fall of 1947. The 236-page book was reproduced on 3-by-5-inch cards containing about 80 pages to a card. These cards were not offered for sale but were given away to various individuals and institutions.

MICROFICHE

Ultramicrofiche book collection of importance was *The Library of American Civilization* prepared by Library Resources Inc., a subsidiary of the Encyclopaedia Britannica, Inc., Chicago, Ill. Costing more than $5 million to produce, it consisted of more than 19,000 bibliographic volumes —6,500,000 pages covering the American experience up to 1914. The ultramicrofiche are 3 inches by 5 inches in size and contain up to 1000 pages

The First

MICROFICHE—*Continued*
reduced from 55 to 90 times depending on the size of the original material. They were first delivered to subscribers in July 1971.

MICROFILM
Book series microfilmed was *A Short Title Catalogue of Books Printed in England, Scotland and Ireland and of English Books Printed Abroad 1475–1640,* compiled by [Alfred William] Pollard and [Gilbert Richard] Redgrave, 609 pages, published in London in 1926. It was microfilmed by University Microfilms, Ann Arbor, Mich., in 1935 from negatives made by the British Museum.

Check photographing device. *See* Check photographing device

Magazine on microfilm offered to subscribers was *Newsweek,* published in New York City, which offered a microfilm and microcard service to subscribers on June 1, 1949, for $15 a year. The microcard editions were printed on 3-by-5-inch cards. The microfilm editions were on 35mm reels in 100-foot lengths, 26 issues to a roll. Both editions were available in March and September of each year.

Microfilm machine to project enlarged images on ceilings for the use of bedridden patients was made by University Microfilms, Ann Arbor, Mich., and Argus Cameras, Inc., Ann Arbor, Mich., in 1945. The first machine was installed on March 21, 1946, at the Percy Jones Hospital, Battle Creek, Mich.

Microfilm reading device was invented by Bradley Allen Fiske of Washington, D.C., who applied for a patent on November 17, 1920, and received patent No. 1,411,008 on March 28, 1922, on a "reading machine." It was known as a Fiskeoscope and could be carried in the pocket. A 2½-inch newspaper column was reduced to ¼ inch and 100,000 words were contained on a 40-inch tape.

Microfilms of U.S. Government publications or documents offered as a regular service was offered by University Microfilms, Ann Arbor, Mich., in April 1952. The price was $900 for *Hearings, Reports, Committee Prints for the 82nd Congress.*

Newspaper to microfilm its current issues was the New York *Herald Tribune,* which began the service with the issue of January 1, 1936.

Newspaper to microfilm its past issues was the New York *Times,* whose microfilms of the issues from 1914 to 1927 were received in November 1935.

MICROGROOVE RECORD. *See* Phonograph record: Long-playing microgroove records

MICROPALEONTOLOGY COURSE. *See* Paleontology course

The First

MICROPHONE (throat microphone). *See* Laryngophone

MICROPHONE, CARBON. *See* Radio microphone (carbon)

MICROSCOPE
Electron microscope was invented by Dr. Vladimir Kosma Zworykin of the RCA Laboratory, Camden, N.J., and was first publicly demonstrated by Dr. Ladislaus Morton on April 20, 1940, at the American Philosophical Society convention, Philadelphia, Pa. The instrument was 10 feet high, weighed about 1,000 pounds and magnified up to 100,000 diameters.

Microscope for examining structure of materials with ability to block dangerous radiations from radioactive specimens was built by the American Optical Company's division, Buffalo, N.Y., and installed in September 1951 at the Knolls Atomic Power Laboratory, Schenectady, N.Y., which is operated by the General Electric Company for the Atomic Energy Commission. The microscope includes a camera, periscopes, and an illuminating system to permit light to get in and out through the thick walls of the test chamber.

MICROWAVE TELEVISION STATION. *See* Television station

MIDGET. *See* Dwarf

MIDGET GOLF COURSE. *See* Golf course

MIDWIFERY PROFESSOR. *See under* Medical instruction

MIGRATORY DUCK STAMP. *See* Revenue stamp printed by the Post Office Department

MILESTONES were set by the directors of an insurance company known as The Philadelphia Contributionship for the Insurance of Houses from Loss by Fire. On February 17, 1761, they agreed "to apply their fines (a forfeiture of one shilling for not meeting precisely at the hour appointed, and two shillings for total absence) in purchasing Stones to be erected on the Road leading from Philadelphia toward Trenton, the distance of a mile one from another with the Number of miles from Philadelphia, to be cut in each stone, and Tho. Wharton and Jacob Lewis are requested to Contract for the same." On May 15, 1764, at 5 o'clock in the morning, the two men started at Front and Market streets, taking with them the Surveyor General of the Province, and at the distance of every mile planted one of the stones. Within four chains from the edge of the Delaware River, they planted the 29th milestone, and having gained by accurate measurement two miles in the estimated distance, they gave the two additional stones, numbered 30 and 31, to be planted on the Jersey side of the road to New York. *(At the Sign of the Hand-in-Hand—Philadelphia Contributionship for the Insurance of Houses from Loss by Fire)*

The First

MILITARY ACADEMY (U.S.). *See* Army school

MILITARY AIRPLANE. *See* Aviation—Airplane: Airplane in actual military operation

MILITARY BICYCLE CORPS. *See* Bicycle corps (military)

MILITARY COURT-MARTIAL. *See* Court-martial

MILITARY DECORATION. *See* Medal

MILITARY DICTIONARY. *See* Dictionary

MILITARY DRILL MANUAL
Military drill manual was Baron von Steuben's *Regulations for the Order and Discipline of the Troops of the United States*, 154 pages, printed in 1779 in Philadelphia, Pa., by [Melchior] Styner and [Charles] Cist.

Military drill manual devoted to field strategy was Roger Stevenson's *Military Instructions for Officers detached in the field, containing a scheme for forming a corps of a partisan, illustrated with plans of the manoeuvres necessary in carrying on the Petite Guerre.* The 232-page book was printed in 1775 by Robert Aitken, Philadelphia, Pa.

MILITARY EXECUTION. *See* Army execution

MILITARY HELIPORT. *See* Heliport

MILITARY HOSPITAL. *See* Hospital

MILITARY INSIGNIA. *See* Army insignia

MILITARY LEADER of the Puritan settlers was Miles Standish, one of the Mayflower Pilgrims, who in 1621 was unanimously chosen military captain of the colony. *(Tudor Jenks—Captain Myles Standish)*

MILITARY MASONIC LODGE. *See under* Freemasons

MILITARY NUCLEAR POWER PLANT. *See under* Atomic reactor

MILITARY ORDER OF FOREIGN WARS. *See under* War veterans' society

MILITARY ORGANIZATION
See also War veterans' society

Military organization in an American colony was the Ancient and Honorable Artillery Company. It was chartered in Boston, Mass., on March 13, 1638, at which time it assumed legal rights. At the first elections, June 1638, Captain Robert Keayne was elected commander; Daniel Haugh (Howe), lieutenant; and Joseph Weld, ensign. *(Zechariah Gardner Whitman—History of the Ancient and Honorable Artillery Company)*

Military organization (anti-British) was the Light Horse of the City of Philadelphia, Pa., organized November 17, 1774, by 28 gentlemen, 3 of whom were members of the Committee of Correspondence of the first Congress of America, to resist the aggressions of the British crown. They

The First

elected their officers, and all swore to uphold the interests of the American colonists. The present First Troop Philadelphia City Cavalry is the continuation of the Light Horse of Philadelphia. *(Philadelphia City Cavalry First Troop—History of the First Troop—Philadelphia City Cavalry from its Organization 1774 to 1874)*

MILITARY PRISON (U.S.). *See* Prison

MILITARY RADIO CAR. *See* Radio car (military)

MILITARY SCHOOL
Church military school was the Catonsville Military Academy, founded in 1845 by Libertius Van Bokkelen in Catonsville, Md., and affiliated with St. Timothy's Protestant Episcopal Church.

Military school was the American Literary, Scientific and Military Academy founded by Captain Alden Partridge in Norwich, Vt., August 6, 1819. The students (cadets) were required to "dress in uniforms" and received instruction in fencing, military drawing, topography, "the Laws of Nations, Military Law . . . the construction of Marine Batteries, Artillery duty, the Principles of Gunnery . . . etc." The first class entered September 4, 1820. The first cadet enrolled was Cyril Pennock of Hartford, Vt. No specific time for completing the course was required, but the enrollment period varied from one to six years according to the student's ability. The name was changed, November 6, 1834, to Norwich University. In March 1866, the buildings were destroyed by fire and the school was removed to Northfield, Vt.

State military school was the Virginia Military Institute, Lexington, Va., established as an independent school at the Lexington Arsenal by act of March 29, 1839. It was governed by a board of visitors, appointed by the governor, subject to approval by the state senate. The first corps of 28 cadets was mustered into service November 11, 1839, and later increased by three others. The first superintendent was Professor (later Major General) Francis Henney Smith, who served until January 1, 1890. *(Virginia Military Institute Catalogue. Vol. 15, No. 3)*

MILITARY SCIENCE DEGREE. *See* Degrees (academic and honorary)

MILITARY SERVICE FOR BLACKS. *See* Army: Law (federal) authorizing military service for blacks

MILITARY TRAINING CAMP. *See* Army camp: Army Citizens' Training Camp

MILITARY UNIFORM. *See* Army uniform

MILITIA
Militia was established by the Court of Assistants of the Massachusetts Bay Colony, Boston, which ordered on April 12, 1631 "that there shalbe a watch of 4 kept [every] night att Dorchester and another of 4 att Waterton, the watches to begin att sunset." *(Records of the Governor and Company*

The First

MILITIA—*Continued*
of the Massachusetts Bay in New England—*Vol. 1, 1628-1641—p. 85)*

MILITIA, NAVAL. *See* Navy: Naval militia (state)

MILK

Acidophilus milk was devised early in 1920 by Dr. Leo Frederick Rettger and Harry Cheplin at Yale University, New Haven, Conn. Commercial production was undertaken by the Fairlea Farms Company, Orange, Conn., in February 1922 under the supervision of Dr. Rettger.

Concentrated milk was Sealtest, which was sold November 30, 1950, by the Clover Dairy Company, Wilmington, Del., as a test. Two parts of water were added to one part fluid milk. The Clover Dairy Company was a division of the National Dairy Products Corporation.

Condensed milk (commercial) was produced in 1851 by Gail Borden of Brooklyn, N.Y., who applied for a patent on May 14, 1853, which was granted August 19, 1856—patent No. 15,553 on an "improvement in concentration of milk." The patent office doubted the value of the invention. The first condensery was established at Wolcottville, Conn., in 1856. It was not successful, and another attempt was made at Burrville, Conn., in May 1857, but that was also a failure. A third attempt was made with an enlarged factory at Wassaic, N.Y., in June 1861. This venture was successful and later developed into the Borden Company, with factories throughout the country. *(The Borden Eagle. January 1922)*

Dried milk patent was obtained by Samuel R. Percy of New York City, who obtained patent No. 125,406, April 9, 1872, on a "process for the simultaneous atomizing and desiccating of fluids and solid substances" (spray-drying of various liquid products). It was never used commercially in its original form.

Evaporated milk was produced by John B. Meyenberg of St. Louis, Mo., who received patent No. 308,421 on November 25, 1884, for an "apparatus for preserving milk." On February 14, 1885, Meyenberg formed the Helvetia Milk Condensing Co., of Highland, Ill. Evaporated milk is milk from which approximately 60 percent of the water has been removed by evaporation. *(Theodore R. Gamble—Seventy-Five Years of the Pet Milk Company)*

Malted milk was invented in 1882 or 1883 by William Horlick of Racine, Wis., who coined the name in 1886. It was originally known as Diastoid. He dried whole milk and combined it with extract of wheat and malted barley in powder or tablet form. This was the first whole dried milk that would keep.

The First

Milk delivery in glass bottles was made in 1878 in Brooklyn, N.Y., by Alexander Campbell.

Milk pasteurized commercially was processed in Bloomville, N.Y., in 1895 by the Sheffield Farms Company of New York City. It was flash pasteurization, very slow, and quite expensive on account of the large quantity of ice used. Lewis Benjamin Halsey used two Champion coolers, one for the heating medium and the other for the cooling.

MILK BOTTLE. *See* Bottle

MILK INSPECTORS were required by Massachusetts under law of April 6, 1859. An Inspector of Milk was appointed August 10, 1859, by Boston, Mass., "to prosecute before the proper tribunal all such violations as shall come to his knowledge."

MILK SALE REGULATIONS were passed by the New York City Department of Health in 1896. The sale of milk without a permit was prohibited. This regulation has since been generally adopted by health authorities. The department of health, in June 1906, was also the first to organize a group of milk inspectors to undertake the inspection of dairies located beyond the political boundaries of the city which offer milk for sale in the city.

MILK STATION (municipal) to ensure clean, raw, tuberculin-tested milk for children during July and August and to raise the standard of the milk supply was established in 1897 in Rochester, N.Y., through the efforts of Dr. George Washington Goler. *(John Walter Kerr—History, Development and Statistics of Milk Charities in the United States)*

MILK TESTER of value for determining the percentage of butterfat in milk and cream was invented in 1890 by Stephen Moulton Babcock, professor of agricultural chemistry, University of Wisconsin, Madison, Wis. He did not apply for a patent. Prior to this invention, the amount of butterfat in milk and cream was determined by a method that could be used only in a chemical laboratory and was entirely unsuitable for use in a creamery or milk plant. *(University of Wisconsin. Agricultural Experiment Station—A New Method for the Estimation of Fat in Milk, Especially Adapted to Creameries and Cheese Factories—Bulletin No. 24. July 1890)*

MILKING PLATFORM (rotating) was invented by Henry W. Jeffers and housed on November 13, 1930, in the lactorium of the Walker Gordon Laboratory Company, Inc., at Plainsboro, N.J. It permitted 1,680 cows to be milked in seven hours by means of a revolving platform that brought them into position with the milking machines. It was called a Rotolactor. *(Walker Gorden News)*

MILL. *See* Cotton mill; Silk mill; Windmill

MIMEOGRAPH was invented by Thomas Alva Edison of Menlo Park, N.J., who obtained patent No. 180,857 August 8, 1876, on a "method of pre-

The First

paring autographic stencils for printing." On February 17, 1880, he obtained patent No. 224,665 for an improved model.

MIMEOGRAPHED DAILY NEWSPAPER. *See* Newspaper

MINE, COAL. *See* Coal mine

MINE, LAND. *See* Land mines

MINE, TORPEDO. *See* Torpedo

MINE BARRAGE was the invention of David Bushnell, who conceived the idea of floating kegs containing explosives which would ignite upon contact with ships. In August 1777 he attached a series of mines together in Black Point Bay, near New London, Conn. Members of the crew of the British frigate *Cerberus,* commanded by Captain J. Symons (or Simmons), noticed a rope alongside their ship. They hauled it in, not realizing that a mine was attached to the other end. They hoisted the mine on board and it exploded, killing three of the crew and blowing a fourth into the water. The mines were equipped with a gunlock with hammer which exploded upon collision contact. *(Royal Bird Bradford—History of Torpedo Warfare)*

MINE FIRE. *See* Fire: Fire in a mine

MINELAYER. *See* Ship: Minelayer; Ship: Navy vessel constructed as a minelayer; Ship: Navy vessel equipped to lay mines

MINERAL EXHIBIT, FLUORESCENT. *See* Fluorescent mineral exhibit

MINERAL SEGREGATION by flotation, the process that causes particles of the same metal to cling together, was demonstrated by Francis Edward Elmore in 1898. Employment of the law of gravitation was the main principle of the process. The first commercial operation was begun in 1911 by James M. Hyde in the Butte and Superior Mining Company's plant at Butte, Mont.

MINERAL WATER BOTTLER. *See* Bottler of mineral water

MINERALOGY INSTRUCTION (systematic) was given in 1786 by Dr. Benjamin Waterhouse at the Rhode Island College, Providence, R.I. *(Benjamin Waterhouse—A Journal of a Young Man of Massachusetts)*

MINERALOGY MAGAZINE was the *American Mineralogical Journal,* founded by Archibald Bruce, the first number of which was printed in New York City in January 1810. This was followed by three other issues, the last of which appeared in 1814. These four numbers, comprising 270 pages, constitute the first and only volume that was published.

MINERALOGY TEXTBOOK

Mineralogy textbook was *An Elementary Treatise on Mineralogy, being an introduction to the study of these sciences, and designed for the use*

The First

of pupils,—for persons attending lectures on these subjects,—and as a companion for travellers in the United States of America, by Parker Cleaveland, professor of mathematics and natural philosophy of Bowdoin College, published in 1816 by Cummings and Hilliard, Boston, Mass., and printed by Hilliard and Metcalf at the University Press, Cambridge, Mass. The book contained 668 pages and 6 illustrated plates.

MINES BUREAU (U.S.) was established in the Department of the Interior, by act of Congress (36 Stat. L. 369), an "act to establish in the Department of the Interior, a Bureau of Mines," approved May 16, 1910, and effective July 1, 1910. The first director was Dr. Joseph Austin Holmes. On July 1, 1925, the Bureau was transferred to the Department of Commerce. *(Fred Wilbur Powell—Bureau of Mines)*

MINES SCHOOL was opened November 15, 1864, in the basement of the Columbia University building on East 49th Street, New York City. The first professor of mines and metallurgy was Thomas Egleston, who was appointed February 1, 1864. It was through his efforts that the plan of the school was proposed and carried out. *(Joshua Lawrence Chamberlin—Universities and Their Sons)*

MINIATURE BOOK. *See* Book

MINIATURE GOLF. *See* Golf course

MINIATURE TELEVISION TUBE. *See* Television tube

MINIMUM WAGE LAW. *See under* Labor legislation

MINING SECURITIES EXCHANGE. *See* Brokerage: Exchange to specialize in mining securities

MINING TUNNEL. *See* Tunnel

MINISTER (diplomat). *See under* Diplomatic service

MINISTER (religious). *See under* specific religious denominations

MINISTER PLENIPOTENTIARY. *See under* Diplomatic service

MINKS. *See* Animals: Fur-bearing animals

MINSTREL SHOW TROUPE was the Virginia Minstrels, organized by Daniel Decatur Emmett, composer of "Dixie." Performances were given at the Chatham Theatre, New York City (constructed in 1842), which was located on Chatham Street between Roosevelt and James Streets. Frank Brower played the bones, Richard Pelham the tambourine, Daniel Emmett the violin, and William Whitlock the banjo. On January 31, 1843, they played at a benefit performance at the Chatham Theatre and on February 6, 1843, they were engaged to appear at the Bowery Amphitheatre. They wore white trousers, striped calico shirts, and long blue calico swallowtail coats; and they

The First

MINSTREL SHOW TROUPE—*Continued*
blackened their faces. Their popular songs included "Old Dan Tucker," "Happy Uncle Tom," and "The Raccoon Hunt." *(Carl Wittke—Tambo and Bones)*

MINT (U.S.)
See also Money

Assay office building (federal). *See* Assay office building (federal)

Coins minted for a foreign government were produced by the U.S. Mint, Philadelphia, Pa., during the fiscal year ending June 30, 1876, when 2 million 2½-centavo coins and 10 million 1-centavo coins were struck for Venezuela. The coins were composed of copper, nickel, and zinc and had a diameter of 23 millimeters and 19 millimeters respectively. The act of January 29, 1874 (18 Stat. L. 6), authorized coinage to be executed for foreign countries at the mints of the United States.

Mint of the United States was at Philadelphia. Robert Morris, as head of the Finance Department of the United States Government, laid a plan for American money coinage before Congress on January 15, 1782. Through his efforts and the cooperation of Thomas Jefferson and Alexander Hamilton, an act "establishing a mint and regulating the coins of the United States" (1 Stat. L. 246) was approved by both houses and signed by George Washington on April 2, 1792. The cornerstone was laid July 31, 1792; construction was completed September 7, 1792.

Mint (U.S.) director was David Rittenhouse, who was appointed by President George Washington April 14, 1792, and who remained in charge of the Mint at Philadelphia until June 1795, when he resigned because of illness. *(Jesse Paul Watson —The Bureau of the Mint)*

Private mint authorized by the United States Government was the Moffat Assay Office, Mount Ophir, Mariposa County, Calif., built in 1850 by John L. Moffat. The mint manufactured $50 hexagonal gold ingots used as legal tender to replace gold dust and nuggets. Beginning on February 20, 1851, the ingots were made under the supervision of the United States Assayer, and on July 3, 1852, Congress passed an "act to establish a branch of the mint of the United States in California" (10 Stat. L. 11). Augustus Humbert of New York was appointed United States Assayer to place the government stamp upon the ingots produced by Moffat and Company. In 1852 it became the United States Assay Office. *(Newell D. Chamberlain— The Call of Gold)*

Woman director of the Mint was Nellie Tayloe Ross, who assumed office May 3, 1933. *(Records in Office of the Director of the Mint, U.S. Treasury Department, Washington, D.C.)*

The First

MISS AMERICA PAGEANT. *See* Beauty pageant

MISSILE. *See* Rocket

MISSILE MAIL. *See under* Airmail service

MISSION, CALIFORNIA. *See* California mission

MISSIONARY
Black missionary to the American Indians was John Marrant, of New York, ordained May 15, 1785, as a Methodist minister in London, England. Among his converts were the king of the Cherokees and his daughter. *(William Aldridge—A Narrative of the Lord's Wonderful Dealings with John Marrant, a Black)*

Methodist missionary. *See under* Methodist Church

MISSIONARY SOCIETY
Foreign missionary society was the American Board of Commissioners for Foreign Missions, organized June 29, 1810, by the General Association of Massachusetts at its annual meeting in Bradford, Mass. The board received its charter in 1812 from Massachusetts.

Foreign missionary society organized by women to send unmarried missionaries to the Orient was the Woman's Union Missionary Society of America for Heathen Lands, organized November 1860 in Boston, Mass., by Ellen H. B. Mason (Mrs. Francis B. Mason) and nine other women. In May 1861, a similar society was formed in Philadelphia, Pa., which united with the former to form the Woman's Union Missionary Society for Heathen Lands, which received its charter April 11, 1861. The first president was Sarah B. Doremus (Mrs. Thomas C. Doremus). The first missionary was Sarah H. Marston, who sailed November 1861 for Tounghoo, Burma.

Missionary society (colonial) was the New England Protestant Missionary Society, chartered July 1649 by the British Parliament to propagate the gospel. Missionary work among the Indians, however, had been carried on earlier by John Eliot, John Cotton, Henry Dunster, and others.

Missionary society organized in the United States was the Society for the Propagation of Christian Knowledge Among the Indians of North America, which was founded in 1762 in the Massachusetts Bay Colony. The Archbishop of Canterbury persuaded King George III to cancel the charter, fearing it might become a non-Episcopal channel of influence.

MISSISSIPPI RIVER RAILROAD BRIDGE. *See* Bridge: Railroad bridge across the Mississippi River

MOBILE COMPUTER CENTER. *See under* Computer

MOBILE POWER PLANT (electric). *See* Electric power plant

The First

MOBILE TELEPHONE. *See* Telephone

MOBILE TELEVISION STATION. *See* Television
—Mobile unit

MODEL SCHOOL. *See* School

MODELS' TRAINING SCHOOL, for the systematic training of young women to be models and mannequins, was officially opened in 1928 in Chicago, Ill., and was known as *L'École de Mannequins,* the School of Modeling. Training was based upon the principles of mental control over physical action and expressions of bodily movements, a correct understanding of balance, poise, and control toward grace, and personality development for a definite purpose.

MODERATOR OF THE UNITED PRESBYTERIAN CHURCH. *See under* Presbyterian church

MODERN-LANGUAGE SCHOOL. *See* Language instruction

MOHAIR was commercially manufactured by the Arlington Mills, Lawrence, Mass., in 1872.

MOLAY, DE, ORDER OF. *See under* Freemasons

MOLDED-PLYWOOD AIRPLANE. *See under* Aviation—Airplane

MOLYBDENUM
Molybdenum centrifugal casting was made November 4, 1958, when a hollow molybdenum cylinder 4½ inches wide and 8 inches long was cast at the Albany Metallurgy Research Center of the U.S. Bureau of Mines, Albany, Oreg. The cast metal weighed about 10 pounds. Although molybdenum had previously been arc-melted in water-cooled copper crucibles to form cylindrical ingots, this was the first reported production of a shaped casting obtained from poured metal.

MONARCH TO VISIT THE UNITED STATES. *See* Visiting celebrities: Absolute monarch

MONASTERY
Zen Buddhist monastery was Zenshinji or Zen Mountain Center officially opened in July 1967 at Tassajara Springs, Calif. The first abbot was Shunryu Suzuki; the first director, Richard Baker.

MONEY
Battleship depicted on a bill was on the two-dollar note issued by the Federal Reserve Bank of Boston in 1918. The reverse side showed the head of Thomas Jefferson. The note bore the signatures of government officials Houston B. Teehee, Register of the Treasury, and John Burke, Treasurer of the United States, and of bank officials Bullen and Morse.

Bill bearing the portrait of a woman was the one-dollar silver certificate, series of 1886, delivered by the Bureau of Engraving and Printing to the United States Treasurer during September 1886. It had a portrait of Martha Washington. The reverse was in green, covered with ornamental

The First

lathe work. Each certificate carried the signature of the Register and the United States Treasurer. (The following individuals' names were used: William Starke Rosecrans and J. Fount Tillman, registers; Conrad N. Jordan, James W. Hyatt, James N. Huston, Enos H. Nebeker and Daniel N. Morgan, treasurers.)

Bill of $100,000 denomination was the gold certificate bearing the portrait of Woodrow Wilson and delivered by the Bureau of Engraving and Printing in January 1935 to the Department of the Treasury. These bills were not issued for general circulation and bore serial numbers from A 00 000 001 A through A 00 042 000 A. They were used within the Federal Reserve System.

Bill to depict both the face and the reverse side of the Great Seal of the United States was the one-dollar silver certificate, series of 1935, issued December 18, 1935. The steel plates from which the bills were printed did not carry the signature of the Secretary of the Treasury or the Treasurer. The signatures were printed in a blank space on the face of bills at the same time that the bills were numbered and sealed.

Coins bearing dates other than the year of issue were authorized July 23, 1965 (79 Stat.L.256). The statute provided that "any coins minted after the enactment of the Coinage Act of 1965 from .900 fine coin silver shall be inscribed with the year 1964." The first of these coins were issued November 1, 1965, at the mint in Philadelphia, Pa.

Coin bearing the portrait of a black American was the fifty-cent silver commemorative, honoring Booker Taliaferro Washington, authorized August 7, 1946. The first coin was presented to President Harry S Truman on December 17, 1946. The obverse showed the head of Booker T. Washington and the reverse a stylized Hall of Fame, under which were the words *From Slave Cabin to Hall of Fame.* Centered under this wording was a slave cabin, to the left of which was *In God We Trust,* and to the right, *Franklin County, Va.* Around the rim was *Booker T. Washington Birthplace Memorial—Liberty.* The coin was designed by Isaac Scott Hathaway.

Coin bearing the portrait of a foreign monarch was the Isabella silver quarter issued for the World's Columbian Exposition in Chicago, Ill. The coin was authorized March 3, 1893 (27 Stat. L. 586) and issued in June 1893. It bore on its obverse a crowned bust of Queen Isabella, facing left, with "1893" to the right in the field. About the center design was the inscription "United States of America." On the reverse, a spinner was pictured kneeling to the left, holding a distaff in her left hand and a spindle in her right. Below was the inscription "Columbian Quar. Dol."

The First

MONEY—*Continued*

Coin bearing the portrait of a living person was the 1921 Alabama Centennial commemorative half dollar, of which 70,000 were struck at the mint at Philadelphia, Pa. The obverse showed the heads of William Wyatt Bibb, the first governor of Alabama, and Thomas Erby Kilby, governor in office at the time of the centennial. The reverse depicted an American eagle.

Coin bearing the portrait of a living President was the 1926 Sesquicentennial half dollar, the obverse of which bore the heads of Presidents George Washington and Calvin Coolidge. The reverse depicted the original Liberty Bell. The net coinage was 141,120 pieces, struck at the mint at Philadelphia, Pa.

Coin bearing the portrait of a President was the 1909 Lincoln penny, a copper cent, designed by Victor David Brenner and based on a photograph of President Abraham Lincoln taken in 1864 by Mathew B. Brady. The design was adopted in April 1909 and in May 1909 coinage began at the Mint in Philadelphia, Pa. The first delivery of the coins was made June 30, 1909, to the Cashier of the Mint. No coins were paid out until after the close of the fiscal year, distribution beginning on August 2, 1909. The reverse was redesigned in 1959 to show the Lincoln Memorial.

Coin (state) to use "E Pluribus Unum" as a motto was the New Jersey cent issued in 1786, the obverse of which showed a horse's head above a plow with the date of coinage and the name of the state in Latin, *Nova Caesarea.* The reverse showed a heart-shaped shield of the United States and the national motto "E Pluribus Unum."

Coin to use "In God We Trust" was the two-cent piece of 1864. Salmon Portland Chase, Secretary of the Treasury, addressed a letter to the director of the Mint at Philadelphia stating that our coinage should bear a motto expressing in the fewest words that no nation can be strong except in the strength of God. Congress established the motto by act of April 22, 1864 (13 Stat. L. 54), which authorized the director of the Mint to fix the shape, mottoes, and devices to be used. On July 11, 1955, Congress enacted a law (69 Stat. L. 290) to provide that "all United States currency (and coins) shall bear the inscription 'In God We Trust.' " *(American Journal of Numismatics. Vol. 35. 1901. Boston)*

Coin (United States) to use "E Pluribus Unum" as a motto was the half eagle, authorized by act of April 2, 1792 (1 Stat. L. 248), and coined in 1795. The obverse showed the draped bust of Liberty facing right, with long, loose hair, and a liberty cap; above, "Liberty" and fifteen stars; below, "1795." The reverse displayed an eagle, bearing the shield of the United States on its breast; arrows in right claw and olive branch in left; in its beak, a scroll inscribed "E Pluribus Unum"; above

The First

the head, 16 stars; beneath, an arch of clouds. The coin had a reeded edge and weighed 135 grains.

Coins manufactured for a foreign government by the United States Mint were authorized January 29, 1874 (18 Stat. L. 6), and provided for 10 million pieces of "un centavo" of the nominal value of $100,000 and 2 million pieces of "dos y medio centavos" (nominal value, $50,000), the charge to equal the expenses, including labor and use of machinery. They were manufactured for Venezuela in 1876. The bill provided that their production was not to interfere with the required coinage for the United States. *(Report of the Director of the Mint for the Fiscal Year Ending June 30, 1876)*

Coins minted for a foreign government. *See* Mint (U.S.): Coins minted for a foreign government

Coins produced by steam power were coined in 1836 on a machine invented by M. Thonnelier of France in 1833. Previously all the work at the mint had been done by hand or horsepower.

Coins with a double mint mark were the silver dollars produced by the U.S. Mint at Carson City, Nev., from 1882 to 1884, which bore the mint mark *CC.*

Commemorative coinage was the Columbian silver half dollar authorized by the act of August 5, 1892 (27 Stat. L. 389), for the World's Columbian Exposition held in Chicago, Ill. It was first issued in November 1892. The Isabella silver quarter, issued for the same exposition, was authorized by the act of March 3, 1893 (27 Stat. L. 586). Charles E. Barber designed the obverse; George T. Morgan, the reverse.

Confederate coinage was a silver half dollar produced at the New Orleans mint in 1861. Only four pieces were minted. On the obverse was the Confederate shield with a liberty cap and a wreath of sugar cane and cotton branches. On the reverse side was the regular United States die. *(John Smith Dye—Coin Encyclopedia)*

Confederate currency was issued under the Confederate States Act of March 9, 1861, at Mobile, Ala., authorizing $1 million in Treasury Notes in denominations of $50, $100, $500, and $1,000. The $50 note featured three blacks in a field, two of them hoeing; the $100 note, a train of cars at a depot, at the right, and Liberty standing, at the left; the $500 note, a rural scene with cattle wading in a brook; and the $1,000 note, busts of Andrew Jackson and John Caldwell Calhoun.

Continental coin was the copper Fugio or Franklin cent, designed by Benjamin Franklin and authorized July 6, 1787. One side showed 13 circles linked together to form a circle around the edge; a small circle in the middle bore the words *United States* around it and in the center *We are one.* The other side showed a dial with hours on

The First

the face and a meridian sun above; on the left was the word *Fugio* (I fly) and on the right the year 1787; below the dial were the words *Mind Your Business.* A contract for the manufacture of 300 tons of the coins was awarded James Jarvis, who manufactured them in New Haven, Conn. The dies were made by Abel Buell, also of New Haven.

Continental money was a $3,000,000 issue, of which $2,000,000 was issued on June 22, 1775, and $1,000,000 on July 25, 1775. A second issue of $3,-000,000 was authorized November 29, 1775. The largest share of the original issue, $434,244, was given to Massachusetts; seconded by $372,208 awarded to Pennsylvania. Only 12 states were granted money. Georgia was not included as it was not represented in the Congress. *(William F. De Knight—History of the Currency of the Country and of the Loans of the United States)*

Copper cents minted by a state were issued by Vermont. On June 15, 1785, the state granted authority to Reuben Harmon, Jr., to make these coins for two years, beginning July 1, 1785. The copper coins were to be one third of an ounce each, troy weight. Harmon established a mint at Rupert, Vt., where he lived. In October 1785 Connecticut authorized the coinage of 10,000 pounds of copper cents. The mint at New Haven was operated by Samuel Bishop and John Goodrich of New Haven and Joseph Hopkins of Waterbury, Conn. *(Sylvester Sage Crosby—The Early Coins of America)*

Copper coins were made from copper obtained from the Şimsbury mine in Granby, Conn., by John Higley in 1737. They were stamped upon planchets of the pure copper, and, in consequence, were in demand by goldsmiths for alloy. The obverse side showed a standing deer, facing left, occupying the whole field, with the legend, "Value me as you please." The reverse side showed three hammers, each bearing a crown upon the head with the legend "I am good copper—1737." *(Richard H. Phelps—Newgate of Connecticut)*

Copper coins made by the United States Mint were one cent and half cent issues, of which there were four designs, the "chain cent," the "wreath cent," the "flowing hair," and the "liberty cap," which were authorized by congressional act "establishing a mint regulating the coins of the United States" (1 Stat. L. 246), approved April 2, 1792. The cent equaled 1/100 part of a dollar and contained 11 pennyweights of copper, while the half cent contained 5 pennyweights of copper. This issue was discontinued by act of February 21, 1857. *(Guttag Bros.—Coins of the Americas)*

Decimal system of money, with the dollar as a unit, was adopted July 6, 1785, by the Continental Congress, which established "that the money unit of the United States of America be one dollar; that the smallest coin be of copper, of which two hundred shall pass for one dollar; that the several

The First

pieces shall increase in a decimal ratio." On August 8, 1786, it was voted "that the standard of the United States of America for gold and silver, shall be eleven parts fine and one part alloy." *(Journals of the Continental Congress, 1774–1789)*

Demand notes were issued under the authority of an act of Congress of July 17, 1861 (12 Stat. L. 259), which provided that each note should be signed by the First or Second Comptroller or the Register of the Treasury and countersigned by such officer or officers as might be designated by the Secretary of the Treasury. *(Laurence Frederick Schmeckebier—The Bureau of Engraving and Printing)*

Demonetization of silver (abolishing bimetallism and making gold the sole monetary standard) was effected by the act of February 12, 1873 (17 Stat. L. 424), known as "the Crime of '73," which stopped the coinage of the old standard silver dollar of 412½ grains and authorized the coinage of the trade dollar of 420 grains for export. The trade dollar, not intended for circulation in the United States, but inadvertently made legal tender up to $5, was deprived of its legal tender feature by joint resolution of July 22, 1876 (19 Stat. L. 215), and dropped from the list of coins March 3, 1887 (24 Stat. L. 635). *(John Smith Hanson—Coin and Currency)*

Deposit of gold bullion for coinage was made by Moses Brown, a merchant of Boston, Mass., on February 12, 1795. It was of gold ingots worth $2,276.72, which were paid for in silver coins. *(George Greenlief Evans—Illustrated History of the U.S. Mint)*

Deposit of silver for coinage was made by the Bank of Maryland on July 18, 1794. It consisted of coins of France worth $80,715.73 as silver bullion. The first return of American silver coins to the Treasury was made on October 15, 1794.

Dies for coins in America were made in 1652 by Joseph Jencks at the Iron Works of Lynn, Mass., for the General Court of Massachusetts, which established a mint house in Boston on May 27, 1652. The dies were for silver coins worth 3, 6, and 12 pence, "forme flatt," with "N.E. Anno 1652" and a Roman numeral denoting the value on the obverse side. On the reverse were "Massachusetts" and a pine tree. The date was not changed annually. John Hull was the mint master. *(Noble Foster Hoggson—Epochs in American Banking)*

Double eagle coinage ($20) was authorized by act of Congress on March 3, 1849 (9 Stat. L. 397), an "act to authorize the coinage of gold dollars and double eagles." The first double eagles were coined in 1850. They were designed by James Longacre and weighed 516 grains. Production was discontinued January 30, 1934, by the Gold Reserve Act (48 Stat. L. 340), which stated "no gold shall hereafter be coined."

The First

MONEY—*Continued*

Fifty-dollar gold pieces were manufactured on February 20, 1851, by the Moffat Assay Office, Mount Ophir, Mariposa County, Calif. They were octagonal, with an eagle in the center surrounded by "United States of America," above the eagle "887 thous" indicating the fineness of the gold, and at the bottom "50 D C." On the reverse a number of radii extended from a center in which was stamped in small figures "50." Around the edge was "The United States Assayer." *(Newell D. Chamberlain—Call of Gold)*

Fifty-dollar gold pieces minted by the United States Government were coined June 15, 1915, for the Panama Pacific International Exposition. They were designed by Robert Aitken and about 3,000 were produced at the mint at San Francisco, Calif. Half were octagonal and half were round. The main design was a bust of Minerva with crested helmet.

Gold certificates were authorized by the act of Congress of March 3, 1863 (12 Stat. L. 709). Gold certificates of one- and two-year notes, and of compound interest notes, and certificates under the fifth section of the act were used for clearinghouse purposes soon after the passage of the national bank act. They were issued November 13, 1865, and were authorized to be received at par in payment of duties. *(John Jay Knox—United States Notes)*

Gold coinage was authorized April 2, 1792 (1 Stat. L. 248) when eagles ($10), half eagles ($5), and quarter eagles ($2.50) were authorized. On March 3, 1849, the coinage of double eagles ($20) and one-dollar gold pieces was authorized, and on February 21, 1853, three-dollar gold pieces were authorized. The minting of the one-dollar and three-dollar gold pieces was discontinued September 26, 1890 (26 Stat. L. 485). *(David Kemper Watson—History of American Coinage)*

Gold price fixed by Congress was $19.39 an ounce, authorized on April 2, 1792 (1 Stat. L. 248), which value remained firm except for the period between August 1814 and February 1817. On June 28, 1834 (4 Stat. L. 700), the value of an ounce of gold was raised to $20.67, which price remained firm until May 29, 1933, except during the panics of 1837 and 1857 and from February 25, 1862, to January 1, 1879.

Gold standard abrogation was authorized by the House May 29, 1933, and by the Senate June 3, 1933. The bill was signed by President Franklin Delano Roosevelt June 5, 1933 (48 Stat. L. 112), and provided that all obligations which gave the obligee the right to require payment in gold or any particular kind of currency were against public policy and that payment could be made dollar for dollar in any currency that was legal tender at the time of payment. Previous to this legislation, President Roosevelt had issued an order on April

The First

5, 1933, forbidding the hoarding of gold and on April 20, 1933, had placed an embargo on gold exports, which was modified on August 28, 1933, to permit the exportation of mined gold.

Half cent of the United States was authorized by the act of April 2, 1792 (1 Stat. L. 246). The obverse depicted "Liberty" facing left, over the date 1793. The reverse bore the inscription "United States of America" and a wreath of olive branches enclosing "half cent," below which was 1/200. It was size 14, weighed 132 grains, and was designed by the engraver Robert Scot. On the edge appeared "Two hundred for a dollar." Coinage was discontinued by act of February 21, 1857.

Legal tender was authorized by act of February 25, 1862 (12 Stat. L. 345), Chapter 331, "an act to authorize the issue of United States notes and for the redemption or funding thereof, and for funding the floating debt of the United States." This was known as the Legal Tender Act and authorized the issuance of greenbacks up to $150 million.

Metal purchased for coinage was six pounds of old copper at one shilling and three pence per pound, which was coined and delivered to the Treasurer in 1793.

Mint of the United States. *See under* Mint (U.S.)

Nickel, or five-cent piece, was authorized May 16, 1866 (14 Stat. L. 47). It weighed 77.16 grains and was composed of 75 percent copper and 25 percent nickel. The obverse side showed a United States shield surmounted by a cross, an olive branch pendant at each side; in back of the base of the shield were two arrows, only the heads and feathers visible; beneath, "1866"; above in the field, "In God We Trust." The reverse showed the figure "5" within a circle of 13 stars and rays, and "United States of America."

Notes wholly engraved and printed at the Bureau of Engraving and Printing, Washington, D.C., were those of the fractional currency authorized by the act of March 3, 1863 (12 Stat. L. 711). Over 3 million sheets of this currency, with a monetary value of over $13 million, had been printed by November 26, 1864. *(Laurence Frederick Schmeckebier—The Bureau of Engraving and Printing)*

Paper money in America was issued by the colonists. On February 3, 1690, Massachusetts established a provincial bank and issued money in denominations from two shillings to five pounds to pay the soldiers who served in the war with Quebec. Other states also issued paper money without any basis, so that in 1780 the ratio of paper to silver was 40 to 1. *(Adolphus M. Hart—History of Issues of Paper Money in the American Colonies)*

Paper money fractional currency was issued from August 21, 1862, to May 27, 1863, in denominations of 5 cents, 10 cents, 25 cents, and 50 cents. The bills were originally issued with perforated edges, but later were cut plain. They were also known as "postage currency" as they depicted postage stamps. They were receivable in payment for all dues to the United States less than five dollars and were exchangeable for United States notes by any assistant treasurer or designated United States Depository in sums not less than $5.

Paper money issued by the American Indians is believed to have been issued about 1840 or 1850 by the Arapahos in Oregon. A later specimen bears the following inscription: "Office of Discount at Arrapahos Way in the Far West. The President and Directors of the Oregon State Bank promise to pay five dollars on demand." The only known specimen of paper money of the Cherokee Nation in Oklahoma is a one-dollar note, on which is inscribed in ink, June 18, 1862, and #592. It reads in part, "Lewis Ross—Cherokee Nation" and is payable "in notes of the Confederated States at Tahlequah." It also bears numerous Cherokee symbols.

Paper money issued by the Government of the United States was authorized by the acts of July 17, 1861 (12 Stat. L. 259), and August 5, 1861 (12 Stat. L. 313), the amount authorized being $50 million. The notes were first issued March 10, 1862. The denominations were $5 (Hamilton), $10 (Lincoln), and $20 (Liberty). They were called "demand notes" because they were payable on demand at certain designated subtreasuries. They were not legal tender when first issued but afterwards were made so by act of March 17, 1862 (12 Stat. L. 370). *(American Institute of Banking—Study Course)*

Paper money of the present small size was issued on July 10, 1929. At that time there was outstanding a total of $4,997 million in old size currency, about 823 million pieces.

Return of coins to the treasury took place on July 31, 1795, and consisted of 744 half eagles. The first return of eagles took place on September 22, 1795, and consisted of 400 pieces. The first return of silver coins to the treasury took place on October 15, 1794. *(George Greenlief Evans—Illustrated History of the U.S. Mint)*

Scrip money to be self-liquidating was issued March 8, 1933, by the Franklin Chamber of Commerce, Franklin, Ind. The method of liquidating was that of placing a two-cent stamp on each dollar every time it circulated. Twenty-four hundred dollars of scrip was issued, of which nine hundred dollars was paid out. The full amount would have been paid had the banks not reopened.

Silver coins were the half dollar, quarter dollar, dime, and half dime authorized April 2, 1792 (1 Stat. L. 248). Other coins were authorized as follows: three-cent piece March 3, 1851; trade dollar February 12, 1873; twenty-cent piece March 3, 1875 (18 Stat. L. 478); Columbian half dollar Au-

gust 5, 1892; and Columbian quarter dollar March 3, 1893. The three-cent piece and half dime were discontinued February 12, 1873; the trade dollar, March 3, 1887; and the twenty-cent piece, May 2, 1878. *(David Kemper Watson—History of American Coinage)*

Silver dollar was coined in Philadelphia, Pa., at the Mint in 1794, under the act of April 2, 1792 (1 Stat. L. 246), which established the Mint and provided for the coinage of silver dollars. Under this act, all gold and silver coins struck at the Mint were full tender. *(Alonzo Barton Hepburn—History of Coinage and Currency in the United States)*

Silver half dimes were authorized April 2, 1792, and coined at the Mint in Philadelphia, Pa., on October 9, 1792. George Washington in his November 6, 1792, address to Congress reported: "There has been a small beginning in the coinage of silver half dimes; the want of small coins in circulation calling the first attention to them." *(John Smith Dye—Coin Encyclopedia)*

Trade dollar was authorized by act of February 12, 1873 (17 Stat. L. 427), and was not intended for circulation in the United States, but for export to China. When its coinage was authorized it was inadvertently made legal tender to the amount of five dollars, but this was repealed July 22, 1876 (19 Stat. L. 215). The trade dollar was discontinued March 3, 1887. It weighed 420 grains, 900 fine. *(Monetary Units and Coinage Systems of the Principal Countries of the World—Director of the Mint, Treasury Department)*

Trade tokens were issued in 1789 by William and John Mott, manufacturers and dealers in watches and jewelry, Water Street, New York City. They were smaller in size than the ordinary copper cent and beautifully engraved. On the obverse was a regulator supported by two columns, and surmounted by a small eagle. The inscription read, "Motts, N.Y. Importers, Dealers, Manufacturers of Gold and Silver Ware." On the reverse was an eagle, with expanded wings, facing to the left, holding an olive branch in one talon and three barbed arrows in the other, the shield of the United States upon its breast. The date "1789" was above the eagle, while below was the inscription "Watches, Jewelry, Silver Ware, Chronometers, Clocks." *(Charles Ira Bushnell—An Arrangement of Tradesmen's Cards, Political Tokens; also Election Medals, etc.)*

Treasurer of the United States to sign currency with 2 names. See under Treasury Department (U.S.)

Woman commemorated on a circulating U.S. coin was Susan Brownell Anthony, whose likeness appeared on a copper-nickel-clad dollar. The coin was authorized by Act of Congress, October 10, 1978, and was issued December 13, 1978, at the Philadelphia Mint, Philadelphia, Pa. The coin,

The First

MONEY—*Continued*

which was round, featured an 11-sided frame on both sides, within which was depicted a profile of Anthony on the obverse side and an eagle symbolizing the Apollo 11 spacecraft (dubbed *The Eagle*) landing on the moon on the reverse side. The weight was .3 oz., the diameter 1.04 inches. Also produced at the Denver and San Francisco mints, the coin was placed in circulation on July 1, 1979.

Treasury notes. *See under* Bond

Wooden money was issued at Tenino, Wash., in February 1932. When the Citizens Bank of Tenino closed its doors December 5, 1931, the town was without ready cash to do business. The Tenino Chamber of Commerce, through three trustees and the State Supervisor of Banking, devised the assignment of scrip. By this plan a depositor could assign to the Chamber a certain amount of his own proven deposit in exchange for a similar amount of scrip, which the Chamber guaranteed to redeem when the liquidation paid them the necessary funds. The first scrip was printed on lithographed sheets in denominations of 25 cents, 50 cents, $1, $5, and $10 by the *Thurston County Independent* in December 1931. In February 1932 wooden money in denominations of 25 cents, 50 cents, and $1 was printed on three-ply sitka spruce wood. Red cedar and Port Orford cedar were used afterward.

MONEY-ORDER SYSTEM. *See under* Postal service

MONKEY TRAINED TO PERFORM. *See under* Animals

MONOLITHIC CONCRETE BUILDING. *See* Building

MONOPLANE. *See* Aviation—Airplane

MONOTYPE. *See* Typesetting machine

MONUMENT

Bronze equestrian statue was Clark Mills's statue of General Andrew Jackson unveiled January 8, 1853, at Lafayette Park, Washington, D.C. It was cast from cannons captured by Jackson in the War of 1812. *(Charles Edwin Fairman—Art and Artists of the Capitol of the United States)*

Bronze statue. *See* Bronze statue

Marble statuary group. *See* Marble statuary group

Monument by a woman ordered by the U.S. Government was a life-size model of Abraham Lincoln. An act of Congress of July 28, 1866 (14 Stat. L. 370), authorized the Secretary of Interior to enter into contract with the sculptor Vinnie Ream (later Mrs. Richard Leveridge Hoxie). A contract was signed August 30, 1866, to pay her $10,000, half upon presentation of the model in plaster and the balance upon completion of the

The First

marble statue. The statue was unveiled January 25, 1871, in the Rotunda of the U.S. Capitol.

Monument to a bird was unveiled October 1, 1913, at Salt Lake City, Utah. It was designed by Mahonri Young, a grandson of Brigham Young, to commemorate the sea gulls from the Great Salt Lake which attacked a devouring horde of black crickets, or grasshoppers, which were destroying the wheat fields of the Mormon settlers in May 1848.

Monument to a comic character was the Popeye statue in Popeye Park, Crystal City, Tex., unveiled March 26, 1937, during the Second Annual Spinach Festival. It was six feet tall, made of concrete, and colored to represent Elzie Crisler Segar's cartoon character "Popeye."

Monument to a woman financed by women was dedicated May 10, 1894, to "Mary, the Mother of Washington" over the grave of Mary Ball Washington, Fredericksburg, Va. The National Mary Washington Memorial Association, chartered February 22, 1890, raised a fund of $11,500 to replace a neglected monument, the cornerstone of which had been laid May 7, 1833. The new monument, a 40-foot monolith on bases and plinth 10 feet high, was designed and built by a Mr. Crawford. The cornerstone was laid October 21, 1893. *(Susan Riviere Hetzel—The Building of a Monument)*

Monument to an American poet was a full-length bronze statue of Fitz-Greene Halleck. It was the work of Wilson MacDonald and was presented to New York City by a committee of private citizens. It was unveiled in Central Park, New York, May 15, 1877, ten years after the death of Halleck, by President Rutherford Birchard Hayes. *(William Cullen Bryant—Life and Writings of Fitz-Greene Halleck)*

Monument to an insect was dedicated December 11, 1919, at Enterprise, Ala. It was erected by the citizens of Enterprise, Coffee County, Ala., "in profound appreciation of the Boll Weevil and what it has done as the herald of prosperity." The deadly destruction of the weevil had caused the farmers to diversify their crops, with the result that their income shortly jumped to triple the amount received in the best cotton years.

Monument to Christopher Columbus was the Columbus Monument, dedicated October 12, 1792, in Baltimore, Md., 300 years after his discovery of this continent. *(Maryland Historical Magazine—September 1906)*

Monument to commemorate the Civil War was a plain brownstone shaft designed by Nelson Augustus Moore and dedicated in Kensington, Conn., on July 25, 1863, two years before the end of the war, at a cost of $350. It was "erected to commemorate the death of those who perished in suppressing the Southern Rebellion," and finally

The First

carried the names of 16 men. *(Connecticut Magazine—September–October 1900)*

Monument to George Washington was a cairn-like monument, 54 feet in circumference at its base and 15 feet high. The monument was built by Isaac C. Lutz in Boonsboro, Md., on July 4, 1827. The wall of the monument was composed of huge stones, many weighing upward of a ton. A flight of steps ran to the top, which was also used as an observation tower. There is some dispute as to whether or not this cairn should be called a monument. It was completed before the Baltimore monument which had been started several years earlier. *(Historical Sketch of the First Monument to Washington—Washington County Historical Society)*

Monument to George Washington (city or state) was the Washington monument of Baltimore, Md., the cornerstone of which was laid on July 4, 1815, with Masonic ceremony. The monument was not completed until October 19, 1829. The Baltimore monument has a shaft 180 feet high and is surmounted by a 16-foot statue of George Washington. The site was donated by General John Eager Howard and the funds were raised by lottery.

Monument to George Washington (national) was the Washington Monument in Washington, D.C., completed in 1884. It is a white marble obelisk 555 feet in height and 55 feet square at the base. The cornerstone was laid July 4, 1848. The capstone with the aluminum tip was set in place December 6, 1884. The monument was dedicated February 21, 1885, by George Winthrop, who had delivered the formal address at the cornerstone ceremonies 37 years earlier. The public was admitted to the monument October 9, 1888.

Monument to the American flag was dedicated June 14, 1927, the 150th anniversary of the United States adoption of the Stars and Stripes as the national banner, at Schenley Park, Pittsburgh, Pa. It was designed by Harvey A. Schwab, dedicated by William T. Kerr, founder of the American Flag Day Association, and unveiled by Florence Bent of the Bellefield High School, Pittsburgh, Pa.

Monument to the memory of the soldiers and sailors of the Spanish-American War was unveiled in Monroeville, Ohio, on Thursday, September 29, 1904.

Monument to the Unknown Soldier (national) was built to honor the large number of unidentified American soldiers who lost their lives in World War I. The Unknown Soldier was buried on November 11, 1921, in the National Cemetary at Arlington, Va. President Warren Gamaliel Harding, accompanied by practically every prominent government officer, attended the services and the unveiling of the national shrine.

The First

National monument was the Devils Tower, a massive fluted column of volcanic rock 865 feet tall in the Black Hills at Belle Fourche River, Wyoming. The base of this gray igneous rock is 1,700 feet in diameter. President Theodore Roosevelt signed a bill on September 24, 1906, establishing 1,153 acres as a national monument.

National monument dedicated to a black American was the George Washington Carver National Monument, authorized July 14, 1943, officially established June 14, 1951, and dedicated July 14, 1953. It consists of 210 acres about two and a half miles southwest of Diamond in Newton County, Mo. It is administered by the National Park Service of the United States Department of the Interior.

Obelisk to be brought to the United States was loaded in Alexandria June 12, 1880, and arrived in New York City July 20, 1880, on the U.S.S. *Dessoug* under Commander Henry Honeychurch Gorringe, U.S.N. A hole was cut in the starboard bow of the ship to accommodate the massive object. William Henry Vanderbilt bore the expenses of its removal. The obelisk was 90 feet high, and weighed 443,000 pounds. It was built in Heliopolis, Egypt, between 1591 and 1565 B.C. and was removed about 22 B.C. to Alexandria, where it stood until it was brought to the United States. It was presented to the United States by the Khedive of Egypt. The cornerstone was laid with masonic services on October 9, 1880, and the obelisk was erected on its pedestal in Central Park, New York City, January 22, 1881. On February 22, 1881, it was officially presented to the City of New York by William Maxwell Evarts, Secretary of State, on behalf of the United States Government and received by William Russell Grace, mayor of New York City. It is popularly known as "Cleopatra's Needle." *(Henry Honeychurch Gorringe—Egyptian Obelisks)*

Statue cast by the United States Government was a bronze of Admiral David Glasgow Farragut. On January 28, 1875, George Maxwell Robeson, Secretary of the Navy, awarded a $20,000 contract to the sculptor Vinnie Ream (later Mrs. Richard Leveridge Hoxie). It was cast at the Washington Navy Yard, Washington, D.C., and the mechanical work was performed by artisans employed by the Government. It was accepted April 25, 1881, by President James Abram Garfield. The base of the monument is formed of three tiers of uncut granite, the lower tier measuring 20 feet. The figure is of heroic size, standing in an easy position with one foot resting upon a pulley block around which a cable is coiled. In the hands is a telescope. The statue is located at Farragut Square, Washington, D.C.

Statue of a woman in National Statuary Hall, the Capitol, Washington, D.C., was the figure of Frances Elizabeth Willard, educator, editor, and

The First

MONUMENT—*Continued*
temperance reformer, erected by Illinois and dedicated February 17, 1905.

Statue officially sanctioned by Rome was the figure of Our Lady of Prompt Succor—the Patroness of Louisiana—which was blessed by Archbishop Janssens in the name of Pope Leo XIII on November 10, 1895, at the Ursulines Convent, New Orleans, La.

Statue presented by a foreign country to America was Liberty Enlightening the World, popularly called the Statue of Liberty, which stands on Liberty Island (formerly Bedloe Island) in New York harbor. The statue, designed by the French sculptor Frédéric Auguste Bartholdi, was a gift of the people of France in commemoration of the hundredth anniversary of American independence. The right hand and torch of the statue were exhibited at the Centennial Exhibition in Philadelphia in 1876. The statue was put in place in 1885 and unveiled on October 28, 1886. It is 151 feet high and stands on a granite pedestal 155 feet high which was provided by popular subscription in the United States.

Statue to commemorate literary characters was the Tom Sawyer and Huck Finn statue, a bronze group by Frederick Cleveland Hibbard, donated by Mr. and Mrs. George Addison Mahan and their son, Daniel Dulany Mahan. It was erected on a base of red granite on May 27, 1926, at Hannibal, Mo.

MOON PHOTOGRAPH. *See* Photograph: Celestial photograph

MORAVIAN to come to America was George Boehnisch, an Evangelist, who accompanied a group of Schwenkfelders to Pennsylvania. He arrived September 22, 1734.

MORAVIAN BISHOP was David Nitschmann, who came to Georgia in 1736. He was the first bishop of the Renewed Unitas Fratrum and was consecrated on March 13, 1735, in Germany, by Bishop Daniel Ernst Japlonsky with the written concurrence of Bishop Christian Sitkovius of Lissa. Nitschmann ordained Anton Seiffert, the first pastor of the Savannah group, which was the first ordination by a Protestant bishop in America.

MORAVIAN CHURCH was built in 1735 in Savannah, Ga., where General James Edward Oglethorpe had given 600 acres of land for a colony of Moravians. Their leader was Bishop August Gottlieb Spangenberg. *(Adelaide Lisetta Freis—The Moravian Church)*

MORAVIAN EASTER SERVICE was probably held in Bethlehem, Pa., in 1742, although it is possible that an earlier service was held either in Savannah, Ga., or in Nazareth, Pa. A group of Moravians had lived temporarily in Nazareth before settling permanently in Bethlehem in 1741.

The First

MORGAN HORSE. *See* Horse

MORMON CHURCH. *See* Church of Jesus Christ of Latter-Day Saints

MORMON TEMPLE was built in Kirtland, Ohio, in 1833-6, by Joseph Smith and was dedicated on March 27, 1836. Joseph Smith, who was the first prophet and founder of the church which became known as the Church of Jesus Christ of Latter-Day Saints, claimed that an angel visited him in 1820 in Manchester, N.Y. He started the new cult with 50 families. They moved to Kirtland, Ohio, where they resided for about seven years. Opposition to the cult increased and they were again obliged to move westward. Joseph Smith and his brother, Hyrum Smith, were murdered June 27, 1844, in Carthage, Ill. The temple, whose cornerstone was laid on July 23, 1833, measured 59 by 79 feet and was 50 feet high. It had a tower 110 feet high.

MORTUARY to operate on the cooperative plan was the Collingwood Memorial, Toledo, Ohio, which opened September 15, 1930. The expenses of operation were divided equally by the concerns using the building, thereby enabling funeral services to be provided more cheaply.

MOSAIC CONCRETE PREFABRICATED WALLS. *See* Building: Building with prefabricated walls of mosaic concrete

MOSAIC PAVEMENT. *See under* Road

MOSQUE of importance was the Islamic Center, Washington, D.C., whose cornerstone was laid January 11, 1949. It has a minaret 160 feet above the street level from which calls to prayer may be announced through a loudspeaker. A colonnade cloister joins the mosque to two wings which house an institute containing a library, a museum, classrooms for study, and administration offices. An auditorium in the basement of the mosque was designed to accommodate 300 people. The first director was Dr. Mahmoud Hoballah.

MOTEL
Horse motel was opened June 10, 1967, by Wayne Biggs at Marshfield, Mo. It was 100 feet long and 89 feet wide, with an addition of 24 by 48 feet on the back side. The price was $7 a night with feed and care, or $5 for lodging. About 40 horses could be accommodated in 1 night.

Motel was the Motel Inn built in 1924 on Neil Cook's property on the north side of San Luis Obispo and opened December 12, 1925. Arthur S. Heineman was the architect. Flashing lights alternated the letters *H* and *M* preceding the letters *otel* to spell out motel and hotel. It had accommodations for 160 guests in individual chalets with garage, bathroom, and telephones. (Small cabins often were known as motels.)

MOTHER-IN-LAW DAY. *See* Holiday

The First

MOTHER'S DAY. *See* Holiday

MOTION PICTURE
See also

Motion picture actor   Motion picture "studio"
Motion picture cen-   Motion picture theater
  sorship
Motion picture pro-
  jector

Academy of Motion Picture Arts and Sciences annual awards. *See under* Television—Telecast

Airplane motion picture show. *See under* Aviation

Animated cartoon was James Stuart Blackton's *Humorous Phases of Funny Faces,* containing about 8,000 drawings showing a man rolling his eyes and blowing smoke at a girl, a dog jumping over a hoop, etc. The final scene was a chalk-type drawing which the artist started as a sketch of one object, but which ended as a sketch of another. The film was released by Vitagraph in 1906. *(Journal of the Society of Motion Picture Engineers. September 1933)*

Animated cartoon in color was *The Debut of Thomas Kat,* the story of a kitten, taught by his mother to catch mice, who confidently and tragically tackled a rat. The cartoon was produced by the Bray Pictures Corporation, New York City, and was released in 1916 by Paramount. The drawings were made on transparent celluloid, the colors painted on the reverse side, and then photographed with a regular color camera. The Brewster color process was used.

Animated cartoon in color (Technicolor) of feature length with sound was Walt Disney's *Snow White and the Seven Dwarfs,* based on Grimm's fairy tale, first exhibited December 21, 1937, at the Carthay Circle Theatre, Los Angeles, Calif. The running time was 75 minutes.

Animated cartoon (present technique) was *The Artist's Dream,* also known as *The Dachshund,* released June 12, 1913, by Pathé Frères. The cartoon showed John Randolph Bray drawing a dachshund. The dog ate sausages until he exploded. It was produced by John Randolph Bray of New York City, who filed an application for a patent on January 9, 1914, which was granted August 11, 1914, No. 1,107,193.

Animated cartoon talking picture was Walt Disney's *Steamboat Willie,* produced in Hollywood, Calif., depicting the antics of Mickey Mouse. It was shown September 19, 1928, at the Colony Theatre, New York City.

Animated cartoon (technical), visualizing "unseeable" phenomena such as the flow of invisible gases, and radio waves, was produced in 1916 by the Bray Pictures Corporation of New York City.

The First

Animated photographic picture projection before a theater audience was shown February 5, 1870, at the Ninth Annual Entertainment of the Young Men's Society of St. Mark's Evangelical Lutheran Church of Philadelphia, at the Academy of Music, Philadelphia, Pa., by Henry Renno Heyl. Heyl used his Phasmatrope, a converted projecting lantern in front of which was a revolving disc containing 16 openings near the edge on which photographic plates were placed. The first plate showed dancers who appeared to move as the revolving wheel showed successive motions. The pictures were continuous and did not change. *(Motion Picture Magazine, November 1914)*

Animated three-dimensional cartoon in Technicolor (modern) was Walt Disney's *Melody,* distributed by RKO Radio Pictures. Its world premiere took place May 28, 1953, at the Hollywood Theatre and the Downtown Paramount Theatre, Los Angeles, Calif.

Bank to provide motion pictures for its customers waiting in line to be served. *See* Bank: Bank to provide motion pictures for its customers waiting in line to be served

Black-oriented talking picture (all-talking, all-singing) by a major company was the William Fox Movietone feature *Hearts In Dixie,* a musical comedy drama of the South, with 200 entertainers from the levees and cotton fields, shown February 27, 1929, at the Gaiety Theatre, New York City. It was a Paul Sloane production, written and directed by Eugene Walter, with story and dialogue by Walter Weems. The featured actor was Stephen ("Stepin' ") Fetchit, who played Gummy. All the cast were black, with the exception of the doctor.

Colored motion pictures were exhibited December 11, 1909, at the Madison Square Garden Concert Hall, New York City. They were run through red and green screens at about twice the present speed and were very hard on the eyes. The presentation was of about ten minutes' duration and was composed of short subjects and views. The pictures used the Kinemacolor films of Charles Urban and G. Albert Smith of England. American rights to manufacture were acquired by Gilbert Henry Aymer and James Klein Bowen, both of Allentown, Pa., who formed the Kinemacolor Company of America. In September 1895 Thomas Alva Edison exhibited colored motion pictures at the Cotton States Exposition, Atlanta, Ga. One of them was *Annabelle, the Dancer.* The film was hand-colored at West Orange, N.J., in 1894.

Foreign feature film exhibited was *Queen Elizabeth,* shown to an invited audience July 12, 1912, at the Lyceum Theatre, New York City, and commercially exhibited August 12, 1912, at the Powers Theater, Chicago, Ill. It was a four-reel feature made in France which starred Sarah Bernhardt as Queen Elizabeth and Lou Tellegen as Robert

The First

MOTION PICTURE—*Continued*
Devereux, Earl of Essex. It was released by Famous Players Film Co., of which Adolph Zukor was president and Daniel Frohman managing director.

Magic lantern show. *See under* Magic lantern

Motion picture camera. *See under* Camera

Motion picture closeup was made February 2, 1893, at the Edison studio, West Orange, N.J., by William Kennedy Laurie Dickson and showed Fred Ott sneezing. *(Antonia and William Kennedy Laurie Dickson—Edison's Invention of the Kineto-Phonograph)*

Motion picture contract. *See* Motion picture actor: Actor to have an exclusive contract

Motion picture featuring a black actor was *Natural Born Gambler,* produced by Biograph in 1916. It starred Bert Williams, leading comedian of the Ziegfeld Follies from 1909 to 1919.

Motion picture film. *See under* Photographic film

Motion picture film copyrighted. *See under* Copyright

Motion picture film exhibition was held May 9, 1893, before 400 persons at the Department of Physics, Brooklyn Institute, Brooklyn, N.Y. Thomas Alva Edison's Kinetograph was used. An optical lantern projector showed moving images of a blacksmith and his two helpers passing a bottle and forging a piece of iron. Each filmstrip had 700 images, each image being shown 1/92 second. The equipment which was to have provided sound accompaniment failed to operate at this showing. *(Scientific American. May 20, 1893)*

Motion picture film exhibition in a theater was held April 23, 1896, in Koster and Bial's Music Hall, 34th Street, New York City, when Thomas Alva Edison's Vitascope depicted a series of shorts of a ballet scene, a burlesque boxing match, surf breaking on the shore, a comic allegory entitled *The Monroe Doctrine,* etc. The images were about one-half of life size and were shown in conjunction with other acts. The audience called for Edison, but he did not appear and refused to take a bow.

Motion picture film transmitted by telephone wire. *See under* Radio facsimile transmission

Motion picture for training soldiers utilized by the U.S. Army was *School of the Soldier,* produced by the Bray Pictures Corporation of New York City at West Point, N.Y., in 1917.

Motion picture from an airplane was taken February 16, 1912, by Frank Trenholm Coffin in a hydroplane over Governors Island on a flight over lower Manhattan, New York City, to the Statue of Liberty, Bedloe Island. Still photographs were

The First

shown on a full page of the New York *Times* of February 18, 1912.

Motion picture (full length) telecast. *See under* Television—Telecast

Motion picture of a complete grand opera was Fortune Gallo's production of Leoncavallo's *I Pagliacci,* shown February 20, 1931, at the Central Park Theatre, Seventh Avenue and 59th Street, New York City. A symphony orchestra of 75 was featured with the San Carlo Grand Opera Company of 150. The part of Nedda was sung by Alba Novella, Canio by Fernando Bertini, Tonio by Mario Vaili, and Silvio by Giuseppe Interranti.

Motion picture of a prizefight (heavyweight championship) was taken March 17, 1897, at Carson City, Nev., by a 38-millimeter Veriscope. Robert ("Bob") L. Fitzsimmons, 167 pounds, knocked out James John ("Gentleman Jim") Corbett, 183 pounds, in 1 minute 45 seconds of the 14th round to win a purse of $15,000. George Siler was the referee.

Motion picture of a real pugilistic encounter taken at night was made by the Biograph Company November 3, 1899, at the Coney Island Athletic Club, Coney Island, N.Y. Illumination was furnished by 400 arc lamps over the ring. The contestants were James (Jim) Jackson Jeffries and Tom Sharkey. The bout was a bona fide fight of 25 rounds. Jeffries won on points. Sharkey was not knocked out. George Silver was the referee.

Motion picture of a staged prizefight was made by the Kinetoscope Exhibition Company in its Black Maria studio, West Orange, N.J., in July 1894, and showed Michael Leonard defeating Jack Cushing. The pictures were shown in six peep machines, each showing one round of the fight, at 83 Nassau Street, New York City.

Motion picture of an eclipse of the sun taken from a dirigible was taken from the U.S. Navy dirigible *Los Angeles* on January 24, 1925, when it was about 4,500 feet in the air at a point about 18¾ miles east of Monauk Point, L.I., N.Y. The total eclipse of the sun (2 minutes 4.6 seconds) was recorded by four astronomical cameras, two moving picture cameras, and one spectrograph. *(United States Naval Observatory Publications. Vol. 13)*

Motion picture of an eclipse of the sun taken from an airplane was made April 28, 1930, by Lieutenant Leslie Edward Gehres and Chief Photographer J. M. F. Haase of the U.S. Navy, flying approximately 18,000 feet over Honey Lake, Calif. The flight was sponsored by the United States Naval Observatory. The totality of the eclipse was 1½ seconds. An attempt to take similar pictures had been made September 10, 1923, at Santa Catalina, Calif., by Captain Albert Ware Marshall, Lieutenant Ben Harrison Wyatt, and Chief Photographer J. M. F. Haase of the U.S. Navy, but

The First

the pictures were of little value as it was cloudy. *(Popular Astronomy. October 1930)*

Motion picture of the inside of a living heart (of a dog) showing the opening and closing of the mitral valve (a structure often crippled by rheumatic fever) was made at Montefiore Hospital, New York City, by Dr. Elliott Samuel Hurwitt, Dr. Adrian Kantrowitz, and Anatol Herskovitz (photographer). The official title of the 9½-minute color film was *A Cinematographic Study of the Function of the Mitral Valve in Situ*, and it was first shown October 16, 1951, at the clinical session of the New York Academy of Medicine Post Graduate Fortnightly held at Montefiore Hospital.

Motion picture of the planets was made of Mars in October 1926 and of Jupiter in September 1927 by William Hammond Wright at the Lick Observatory, Mount Hamilton, Calif., with the aid of the Crossley telescope. Exposures were made every three minutes, so that at the rate of 32 frames a minute, movement of the planets took as many seconds on the screen as it does hours in the sky. The photographs were taken in several colors, ranging from ultraviolet to infrared. They illustrated the alterations in the appearance of the planets when the color by which they are viewed is changed.

Motion picture of the sun (other than of eclipses) was taken by Robert Raynolds McMath at the McMath-Hulbert Observatory of the University of Michigan at Lake Angelus, Pontiac, Mich., on June 19, 1934, with the Spectroheliokinematograph. The pictures, which showed solar prominences or sunspots in motion as well as activity in connection with sunspot groups, were first shown publicly before the American Astronomical Society on September 10, 1934, at Connecticut College New London, Conn.

Motion picture on film shown on a screen was exhibited by Woodville Latham, who demonstrated his Pantoptikon at 35 Frankfort Street, New York City, on April 21, 1895. A continuous roll of film, with hole perforations on the sides for spokes of the sprocket, reeled in front of an electric light contained in a magic-lantern type projector. A bout of four minutes' duration between Young Griffo and Battling (Charles) Barnett was staged May 5, 1895, by Otway Latham on the roof of Madison Square Garden, New York City. The film was exhibited May 20, 1895, at 153 Broadway, New York City, after which it was shown in a tent at Surf Avenue, Coney Island, N.Y., for the rest of the summer.

Motion picture premiere telecast. *See under* Television—Telecast

Motion picture premiere telecast on 2 successive nights. *See under* Television—Telecast

The First

Motion picture presented simultaneously in major cities throughout the world was *On the Beach*, an adaptation of the novel by Nevil Shute, which had its premiere December 17, 1959, at the Astor Theatre, New York City, and 17 other cities. The 134-minute film was produced by Stanley Kramer and written by John Paxton. It starred Gregory Peck, Ava Gardner, Fred Astaire, and Anthony Perkins.

Motion picture sex shocker was *A Daughter of the Gods*, directed by Herbert Brenon, music by Robert Hood Bowers, shown at the Lyric Theatre, New York City, on October 17, 1916. It featured Annette Kellerman, about whom a reviewer wrote that she "wanders disconsolately . . . through the film, all undressed and nowhere to go."

Motion picture (successful) projected to a paying audience was shown at Koster & Bial's Music Hall, New York City, on April 23, 1896, by Thomas Armat in association with Thomas Alva Edison.

Motion picture to gross $50 million was *The Clansman, or The Birth of a Nation*, 12 reels, produced by David Wark Griffith, starring Henry Walthall and Lillian Gish with a cast of 18,000 people and 3,000 horses. It was based on *The Clansman* by Thomas Dixon and was shown February 8, 1915, at Clune's Auditorium, Los Angeles, Calif. Two performances were presented daily; matinees at 2:30 P.M., admission 25 cents and 50 cents; evenings at 8:00 P.M., admission 25 cents, 50 cents, and 75 cents.

Motion picture to gross more than $70 million was Metro Goldwyn Mayer's production *Gone With The Wind*, based on the book by Margaret Mitchell. The premiere was held December 15, 1939, at Loew's Grand, Atlanta, Ga. The cast included Clark Gable as Rhett Butler, Leslie Howard as Ashley Wilkes, Vivien Leigh as Scarlett O'Hara, Olivia De Havilland as Melanie Hamilton, and Hattie McDaniel as Mammy.

Motion picture with a plot was *The Great Train Robbery*, produced by the Edison Company in the fall of 1903. It was staged and directed by Edwin Stanton Porter. The scenes were filmed in New Jersey. The cast included George Barnes, Broncho Billy Anderson (Max Aronson), Marie Murray, and A. C. Abadie. The film was printed on tinted celluloid: yellow for the dancehall, bluish green for the woods. *(Terry Ramsaye—A Million and One Nights)*

Motion picture with scent was *Behind the Great Wall*, a travelogue of modern China, presented December 8, 1959, at the De Mille Theatre, New York City. The film depicted a tiger hunt, fishing with cormorants, a May Day parade in Peiping, and other scenes. The scent was forced through ceiling vents by the Aromarama process.

The First

MOTION PICTURE—*Continued*

Newsreel was the Pathé Weekly, later known as Pathé News, which was first operated in November 1910. Herbert Case Hoagland was the editor. Moving pictures of historic events had, however, been taken earlier. Films of the McKinley inaugural parade of 1896, the funeral procession in Colón, Cuba, of the *Maine* victims in 1898, the embarkation of Theodore Roosevelt's Rough Riders, etc., had been made. *(International Photographer. Vol. 5, No. 8. September 1933)*

Newsreel in color was a Warner Brothers-Pathé Newsreel taken January 1, 1948, of the Tournament of Roses and the Rose Bowl Game, Pasadena, Calif. It was made by Cinecolor process and released January 5, 1948.

Peep show in which film was used in a vending machine or cabinet was exhibited by Andrew M. Holland of the Holland Brothers at 1155 Broadway, New York City, on April 14, 1894. The machine was invented by Thomas Alva Edison, who utilized the film prepared by George Eastman. The films were made in the Edison laboratories. The pictures were viewed directly, and not reflected, and were visible to only one person at a time. Annie Oakley, Sandow, Buffalo Bill, Ruth St. Denis, and other celebrities were shown. *(Frederick William Wile—A Century of Industrial Progress)*

Peep show machine was patented by Samuel D. Goodale of Cincinnati, Ohio, who obtained patent No. 31,310 on February 5, 1861, on a stereoscope machine. It was called the Mutoscope and was operated by hand. Pictures were placed on leaves fastened by one edge to an axis in such a way that they stood out like spokes. As the shaft revolved, different images were seen in motion.

Photographic attempt to show motion was made by Dr. Coleman Sellers of Philadelphia, Pa., who obtained patent No. 31,357, February 5, 1861, on the Kinematoscope, an "improvement in exhibiting stereoscopic pictures of moving objects." A series of still pictures with successive stages of action was mounted on blades of a paddle and viewed through slits passed under the lens of a stereoscope revolved at right angles. The pictures were not reflected on a screen, and were visible only in the cabinet. The whole of the picture was not seen at once, but only by degrees as the cylinder revolved. *(International Photographer. February 1933)*

Presidential candidate shown in motion pictures was William Jennings Bryan, who was filmed receiving congratulations after his nomination on July 10, 1908, at his residence at Fairview, Neb. The film was shown July 12, 1908, at Hammerstein's Roof, 42nd Street and Broadway, New York City, having been developed on the train heading east.

The First

Serial motion picture with installments longer than one reel was *The Adventures of Kathlyn,* issued by [William N.] Selig's Polyscope Company, Chicago, Ill., on December 29, 1913. The first installment was a two-part drama, "The Unwelcome Throne," in three reels, featuring Kathlyn Williams, Tom Santochi, Charles Clary, William Carpenter, and Goldie Caldwell. Twelve other installments of two reels each followed. F. J. Grandon was the director. The film was adapted by Gilson Willets from Harold MacGrath's story which appeared in the Hearst newspapers in 1913 and which was published in book form by the Bobbs-Merrill Company, Indianapolis, Ind., in 1914.

Six-reel feature-length comedy was *Tillie's Punctured Romance,* released December 21, 1914, by the Alco Film Corporation. It took four weeks to produce. The director was Mack Sennett and the stars were Marie Dressler, Mabel Normand, Charles Chaplin, and Mack Swain. *(Moving Picture World. Nov. 14, 1914)*

Sound motion picture featuring a black was *Snappy Tunes,* featuring Noble Sissle and Eubie Blake, in 1923. It used the Phonofilm system invented by Dr. Lee De Forest.

Sound-on-film motion picture was Dr. Lee De Forest's Phonofilm, demonstrated March 12, 1923, for the press and on April 4, 1923, before the New York Electrical Society at the Engineering Society's building, New York City. Pictures were shown with music, but no voices were heard. The pictures were later shown to an invited audience April 15, 1923, at the Rivoli Theatre, New York City. Presented on the film were "The Gavotte" (a man and woman dancing to old-time music); "The Serenade" (four musicians playing on wind, percussion, and string instruments); and an Egyptian dancer. The sound occupied a narrow margin of the film on which the pictures appeared.

Talking picture was presented on August 5, 1926, at an invitation performance at the Warner Theatre, New York City. On August 6, a gala premiere was held at which seats sold for $10, plus tax. The film depicted Will Hays, who welcomed Vitaphone; Mischa Elman, who played "Humoresque"; Marion Talley, who sang "Caro Nome"; Giovanni Martinelli, who sang "Vesti la Giubba" from *I Pagliacci;* Efrem Zimbalist, violinist, assisted by Harold Bauer, played variations and Beethoven's "Kreutzer Sonata"; the Cansinos and marimba band; and several other short features. The feature picture was *Don Juan,* a film of 10,018 feet, in which John Barrymore, Mary Astor, Warner Oland, Estelle Taylor, Myrna Loy, and other well-known stars took part. The musical score was played by the New York Philharmonic Orchestra of 107 men. The picture was directed by Alan Crosland. The film itself had no sound recorded on it but was synchronized with dis

The First

phonograph records (Vitaphone) of the musical score.

Talking picture entirely in color was Warner Brothers' Vitaphone Technicolor film *On With the Show*, exhibited May 28, 1929, at the Winter Garden, New York City. The cast included Betty Compson, Joe E. Brown, and Ethel Waters. It was directed by Alan Crosland and was based on a story by Humphrey Pearson.

Talking picture in Esperanto was a four-minute film made July 13, 1929, in the Paramount studio, New York City. The actors were Germaine Chomette and Henry W. Hetzel. Donald E. Parrish, secretary for the United States section of the Universal Esperanto Association with headquarters in Geneva, Switzerland, delivered an address and salutation to accompany the film at the 22nd annual convention of the Esperanto Society of North America. The film was exported to 16 countries.

Talking picture taken outdoors (full-length) was *In Old Arizona*, a film version of O. Henry's "The Caballero's Way," a Fox Movietone with sound recorded on the film. It was an all-talking drama, 8,724 feet, and was released January 20, 1929. Nine tenths of the entire production was taken on location in Zion National Park and Bryce Canyon, in Utah; on the Mohave desert; and at the old mission of San Fernando in California. It was directed by Raoul Walsh and Irving Cummings and featured Edmund Lowe as Sergeant Mickey Dunn, Warner Baxter as the Cisco Kid, and Dorothy Burgess as Tonia Maria.

Talking picture whose footage exceeded 6,000 feet was *The Lights of New York*, which was produced by Warner Brothers and released July 21, 1928. The principal players were Helene Costello, Mary Carr, Cullen Landis, Gladys Brockwell, and Wheeler Oakman. A gala performance was presented at midnight on Friday, July 6, 1928, at the Strand Theatre, New York City. The sound was on film (Vitaphonic). The picture was based on an original story by F. Hugh Herbert and Murray Roth.

Talking pictures of presidential candidates were taken August 11, 1924, by Theodore W. Case and Lee De Forest, of President Calvin Coolidge on the grounds of the White House and of Senator Robert Marion La Follette on the steps of the Capitol, Washington, D.C. John William Davis was photographed at Locust Valley, N.Y. The newsreel was shown in various theaters in September 1924.

Technicolor motion picture really successful was *The Toll of the Sea*, released December 3, 1922, at the Rialto Theatre, New York City. The process was developed by Dr. Herbert Thomas Kalmus, president and general manager of Technicolor Motion Picture Corporation from its inception until 1959.

The First

Three-dimensional feature motion picture was *Bwana Devil*, produced, directed, and written by Arch Oboler (Arch Oboler Productions) and released by United Artists in 1953. It was a Natural Vision-Magnetic Sound Track picture requiring Polaroid viewers. It opened February 18, 1953, at Loew's State Theatre, New York City, and featured Robert Stack, Barbara Britton, Nigel Bruce, and Ramsay Hill. It was the story of a British engineer who tracked two man-eating lions that had disrupted the construction of the first railroad in East Africa at the turn of the century.

Three-dimensional feature motion picture in color produced by a major studio was *The House of Wax*, starring Vincent Price, first exhibited April 10, 1953, at the Paramount Theatre, New York City. It was a remake of the 1933 *Mystery of the Wax Museum*. *The House of Wax* was in Warnercolor and was seen through Polaroid viewers.

Three-dimensional feature motion picture produced and released by a major company was *Man in the Dark*, which had its world premiere at the Globe Theatre, New York City, on April 8, 1953. It was produced by Columbia Pictures in sepia and starred Edmond O'Brien and Audrey Totter.

X-ray motion pictures. *See under* X ray

MOTION PICTURE ACTOR

Actor to have an exclusive contract for a single appearance in a moving picture was James John Corbett, engaged by the Kinetoscope Exhibition Company to appear in a six-round fight, one minute each round, with Pete Courtney of Trenton, N.J., in August 1894. *(Terry Ramsaye—A Million and One Nights)*

Black actor featured in a motion picture. *See* Motion Picture: Motion picture featuring a black actor

Black actor to win an Oscar for best actor was Sidney Poitier, who depicted an itinerant construction worker in *Lilies of the Field*. The presentation was made April 13, 1964, at the 36th annual Oscar ceremonies at Santa Monica, Calif.

Black woman to win an Oscar from the Academy of Motion Picture Arts and Sciences was Hattie McDaniel, who played Scarlett O'Hara's "mammy" in the movie adapted from Margaret Mitchell's *Gone With the Wind*. The award was presented February 29, 1940, in Hollywood, Calif., for the best performance by a supporting actress.

Husband and wife Oscar winners, (of the award of the Academy of Motion Picture Arts and Sciences) were Sir Laurence Olivier, who received the award March 24, 1949 (for 1948), for his performance in *Hamlet*, and his wife, Vivien Leigh, whom he married on August 30, 1940. She received the award on February 29, 1940 (for 1939), for her performance as Scarlett O'Hara in *Gone With the Wind*. On March 20, 1952, she re-

The First

MOTION PICTURE ACTOR—Continued

ceived a second Oscar for her part as Blanche du Bois in *A Streetcar Named Desire* (1951).

Motion picture actor and son to receive Oscars were Walter Huston, as the best supporting actor, and his son, John Huston, as the best director, for *The Treasure of Sierra Madre*. (The film also received the best screen play award.) The presentations were made in Hollywood, Calif., on March 24, 1949, by the Academy of Motion Picture Arts and Sciences.

Motion picture actors to receive Oscars, the award of the Academy of Motion Picture Arts and Sciences, were Emil Jannings *(The Last Command, The Way of All Flesh)* and Janet Gaynor *(Seventh Heaven, Street Angel, Sunrise)*, who received Oscars in Hollywood, Calif., on May 16, 1929, "for the best acting in pictures released in Los Angeles, Calif., between August 1, 1927, and July 31, 1928." Ten similar awards and two special awards were presented to others for excellence in allied fields, such as cinematography, art direction, engineering effects, and direction.

Motion picture actress depicted on a postage stamp was Grace Kelly, whose marriage to Prince Rainier III of Monaco on April 19, 1956, was commemorated by a series of eight Monacan stamps (1, 2, 3, 5, 15, 100, 200, and 500 francs), sold only on the wedding day.

Motion picture performer (woman) to win the Life Achievement Award of the American Film Institute was Bette Davis, who was presented the award by George Stevens, Jr., president of the Institute on March 1, 1977, at Beverly Hills, Calif., for work over a lifetime that stood the test of time.

Motion picture star was Max Aronson, known as Broncho Billy, Max Anderson, and Gilbert M. Anderson. His first film appearance was in 1903 in *The Great Train Robbery*, in which he played the roles of the bandit, the brakeman, and the passenger who was shot. His first starring role was in *The Messenger Boy's Mistake*, for which he was paid 50 cents an hour. *(Terry Ramsaye—A Million and One Nights)*

Motion picture star (female) was Florence Lawrence, whose first performance in films was in 1907 for the Edison company. She then worked for the Vitagraph Company. In 1909 she went to the Biograph Company and was featured as "The Biograph Girl." Later she became known as "The IMP Girl," working for the Independent Moving Picture Company.

Stunt actor was Frederick Rodman Law, a steeplejack, who staged a parachute jump from the Statue of Liberty on Bedloe Island in New York harbor on February 2, 1912, for Pathé News. On April 14, 1912, he jumped from the Brooklyn Bridge, and on November 12, 1912, from a dynamited balloon into the Hudson River.

The First

MOTION PICTURE CENSORSHIP

Motion picture censorship board (national) was the National Board of Censorship of Motion Pictures, organized March 1909 (by the People's Institute of New York City, founded May 15, 1897, by Charles Sprague Smith, its first executive chairman). Producing companies agreed to prorate a review charge among their member companies on the basis of $3.50 for a negative reel of 1,000 feet. The fund was applied to the office expense of the board. In 1916 the name was changed to the National Board of Review of Motion Pictures.

Motion picture censorship board (state) was the State Board of Censors created in Pennsylvania by act of June 19, 1911. No appropriation was made until April 4, 1913, when $7,500 was provided. Censors were appointed February 1, 1914. Ohio approved an act May 3, 1913, providing for a motion picture censorship board of three, who were appointed in 1913. Kansas approved an act March 13, 1913, effective April 1, 1913, but no provisions to enforce it were made until 1915. The United States Supreme Court in February 1915 held the Ohio and Kansas censorship laws unconstitutional.

Motion picture censorship regulation (federal) was the act of July 31, 1912 (37 Stat. L. 240), "to prohibit the importation and the interstate transportation of films or other pictorial representations of prize fights." The penalty for violation was not more than $1,000, or one year at hard labor, or both.

MOTION PICTURE MACHINE

Machine to show animated pictures was the Zoetrope, the Wheel of Life, patented April 23, 1867, No. 64,117, by William E. Lincoln of Providence, R.I., who assigned it to Milton Bradley & Company, Springfield, Mass. It consisted of a horizontal wheel with a series of animated drawings showing successive steps at right angles to the circumference. The drawings were viewed through a slit and, when the wheel revolved, appeared to show animation.

MOTION PICTURE PROFESSORSHIP

Motion Picture Professorship was established by the Washington Square College of Arts and Sciences of New York University, New York City, on May 26, 1941, when the appointment of Robert Gessner as assistant professor of motion pictures was approved for the term beginning September 1, 1941. The title for the position was variously changed to Professor of Television, Motion Pictures and Radio, and to Professor of Cinema.

MOTION PICTURE PROJECTOR

Motion picture projector patent was awarded O. B. Brown of Malden, Mass., who obtained patent No. 93,594 on August 10, 1869, on an "optical instrument." It combined the principles of the phenakistoscope and the magic lantern.

The First

Motion picture projector (portable) was invented by Dr. Herman Adolf De Vry and produced in 1913 in Chicago, Ill. It weighed approximately 26 pounds, cost $200, and was known as "the projector in a suitcase."

MOTION PICTURE "STUDIO" was a frame cabin covered with black roofing paper located on the Edison lot in West Orange, N.J., in 1892. The structure was built so that it could be pivoted to enable the stage to secure the maximum sunlight. It was a "revolving photographic building" and was completed February 1, 1893, at a cost of $637.67. It was nicknamed Black Maria.

MOTION PICTURE THEATER
Drive-in motion picture theater was opened June 6, 1933, on a ten-acre plot on Admiral Wilson Boulevard, Camden, N.J., by Richard Milton Hollingshead, Jr., and Willis Warren Smith of Riverton, N.J. Two shows were presented nightly on a screen 40 by 50 feet. Nine rows of inclined planes with aisles 45 feet deep accommodated 500 cars. The sound equipment was supplied by the RCA-Victor Company, Camden, N.J.

Motion picture theater was the Electric Theater, 262 South Main Street, Los Angeles, Calif., a circus front tent-show called a "black top," which was opened April 2, 1902, by Thomas Lincoln Tally. Among the first pictures shown were *The Capture of the Biddle Brothers* and *New York in a Blizzard.* The show lasted about one hour; the admission was ten cents. *(Frederick William Wile —A Century of Industrial Progress)*

Theater built especially for the rear projection of motion pictures was the Trans-Lux Theatre at 58th Street and Madison Avenue, New York City, which was opened March 14, 1931. The first rear-projection screen of theater size had been installed March 11, 1927, for the opening night of the Roxy Theatre, New York City. It was a Trans-Lux screen 18 by 22 feet which at first was used only for silhouette work, because the lens of the projector was imperfect.

Theater in the world devoted exclusively to the exhibition of motion pictures was the Nickelodeon, which was opened in June 19, 1905, by Harry Davis in an empty store at 433-435 Smithfield Street, Pittsburgh, Pa. It had 96 seats taken from Davis's theaters. Among the first films shown were *Poor But Honest* and *The Baffled Burglar.* A profit of over $1,000 was netted the first week. John Paul Harris was general manager and Isaac Lisbon manager.

MOTION PICTURE TRAILER. *See under* Television—Telecast

MOTOR, ELECTRIC. *See* Electric motor

MOTOR BUS. *See* Automobile bus

The First

MOTOR TRUCK. *See* Automobile truck

MOTORBOAT
Motorboat was invented by James Rumsey and exhibited by him in September 1784 on the Potomac River, in the presence of George Washington. It worked against the stream by mechanical means. He subsequently gave his attention to steam as a motive power and in March 1786 propelled a boat on the Potomac by a steam engine which produced motion by a pump at the stern. In December 1787 the experiment was successfully repeated on a larger scale. *(Ella May Turner— James Rumsey, Pioneer in Steam Navigation)*

Motorboat pleasure craft was produced in 1885 by F. W. Ofeldt and manufactured by the Gas Engine and Power Company, New York City. The boat contained a 2 h.p. engine, propelled by naphtha, which developed a speed of 5 to 7 knots. She was 21 feet long, had a 64-inch beam, and a draft of 22 inches.

Storage battery motorboat was the *Magnet* which was operated by one motor revolving a two-blade screw 18 inches in diameter. The battery was of 56 storage cells. A 10-hour charge ran the boat for 60 to 70 miles at a speed of 10 miles an hour. The *Magnet* was built in Newark, N.J., in 1888 and was owned by Anthony and Frederick Reckenzaun. She was 28 feet long, with a 6-foot beam, and was 3 feet deep amidships.

MOTORBOAT SPEED
Motorboat to travel at a speed of more than 40 m.p.h. was the *Furlong,* built and owned by Victor Emerson, Alexandria, Va., which made 42.5 m.p.h. on May 27, 1911, on the Potomac River. It had a 1,200-pound hull, was 26 feet long, had a 5-foot beam, and had a 250 h.p. gasoline engine with 2 propellers that revolved in opposite directions. *(New York Times. Sec. IV, p. 13, column 1. May 28, 1911)*

Motorboat to travel at a speed of 216.2 m.p.h. was the jet-powered *Bluebird,* piloted by Donald M. Campbell. Its speed was 216.2 m.p.h. (239.5 m.p.h. one way, 193 m.p.h. on return) on November 16, 1955, on Lake Mead, near Las Vegas, Nev. (at Boulder City, Nev.).

Motorboat to travel at a speed of more than 285 m.p.h. was the jet-powered *Hustler,* piloted by Lee Taylor, Jr., of Downey, Calif., on Lake Guntersville, Ala., on June 30, 1967. It attained the speed of 285.2127 m.p.h. under surveillance of the American Power Boat Association (288.1216 m.p.h. on the north run, 282.3039 m.p.h. on the return run). It reached 299.181 m.p.h. in an unofficial test.

MOTORBOAT ENGINE. *See* Engine: Outboard twin-cylinder motor (light)

The First

MOTORBOAT RACE

Motorboat race (ocean) under the Union of International Motorboating rules was the Sam Griffith Memorial Race, 172 miles, from Miami, Fla., to Bimini, Bahamas, and return, February 22, 1966. Although 31 boats started from Biscayne Bay, only 4 reached Bimini because of a 20-knot crosswind, and only 2 attempted the return trip. The *Thunderbird*, a 32-foot aluminum boat powered by two 500 h.p. United Aircraft gas turbine engines, with Jim Wynne and Walt Walters as codrivers made the trip in 4 hours 45 minutes 23 seconds, an average speed of 37 m.p.h. The *Thunderbird* was declared experimental and ineligible for the $3,000 prize. The award was made to Jerry Langer of the *No. 10* which returned 2½ hours after the *Thunderbird.*

Motorboat race under organized rules was held June 23-24, 1904, under the jurisdiction of the Columbia Yacht Club, 86th Street and Hudson River, New York City. A 32-mile race was held for the Gold Cup of the Challenge Cup Series, from the clubhouse to a point 16 miles north and back. The trophy was won by C. C. Riotte in the *Standard*, 100 h.p., 59 feet long, average speed 22.57 statute miles (19.67 nautical miles) per hour. The contest was decided by a point system and the rules were formulated on April 22, 1903, by the American Power Boat Association, which was organized by seven yacht clubs on January 20, 1903. *(American Power Boat Association: Story of Its Origin and Its Development)*

MOTORBOAT STAMPS. *See* Stamp

MOTORBOATING MAGAZINE

Motorboating magazine was *Motor Boat* (devoted to all types of power craft) published by The Motor Boat Publishing Company, New York City. The first issue, Vol. 1 No. 1, was dated April 10, 1904. It contained 40 pages plus a cover and sold for 10 cents a copy.

MOTORCYCLE

Motorcycle (practical) was manufactured by the E. R. Thomas Motor Company of Buffalo, N.Y., in 1900. A single-cylinder gasoline engine was attached to the transverse bar of an ordinary bicycle and a flat belt ran to a concentric pulley on the rear wheel.

Motorcycle (steam-driven) was a two-wheeled vehicle invented by William A. Austin of Winthrop, Mass., in 1868. The steam boiler was suspended amidships. The vehicle had a very limited traveling radius because of the small amount of steam generated.

Motorcycle (twin-cycle) was an Indian, made in 1905 in Springfield, Mass. It had a spring-front fork, battery ignition, and a gravity-feed oiling system. The machine was started by pedaling. The gas tank was mounted on the rear fender.

The First

Motorcycle with built-in gas engine especially designed was manufactured in Springfield, Mass., by George M. Hendee, who formed the Hendee Manufacturing Company, which began to market the Indian motorcycle in 1901. Previously, motorcycles had been ordinary bicycles to which motors were attached. In 1901 three motorcycles were built, and in 1902 production was increased to 143. The motors were made by the Aurora Machine Co., Aurora, Ill., and were assembled to the frames in Springfield, Mass., where they were built. The machines were first publicly demonstrated June 1, 1901, in a hill-climbing exhibition.

MOTORCYCLE ASSOCIATION was the Federation of American Motorcyclists, organized September 7, 1903, at Manhattan Beach, N.Y. The first president was R. G. Betts of the New York Motor Cycle Club. About 200 delegates attended the first meeting.

MOTORCYCLE ENDURANCE RUN was held July 4-5, 1902, covering a distance of 254 miles from Boston to New York City, through South Framingham, Worcester, Warren, Springfield, Hartford, Meriden, New Haven, Bridgeport, and Greenwich. Of the 32 entries, 31 started and 13 finished, and 7 made a perfect score of 1,000 points.

MOTORCYCLE HILL-CLIMBING CONTEST was staged in Riverdale, N.Y., on May 30, 1903, and was won by Glenn Hammond Curtiss, who received a gold medal from the New York Motorcycle Club. The race created quite a sensation because it was not believed that a motorcycle had much power.

MOTORCYCLE POLICE. *See* Police

MOTORCYCLE RACE

Motorcycle distance race (4 hours) was won by George N. Holden of Springfield, Mass., who covered 150 miles 73 yards on September 5, 1903, at the Manhattan Beach track, Manhattan Beach, New York City, defeating 13 competitors. A tire burst and he was thrown, but he returned to his motorcycle and continued the race.

Motorcycle race (250 miles) was sponsored by the Metropole Cycling Club of New York. Thirty-two riders took off at 8:00 A.M., July 4, 1902, from Copley Square, Boston, Mass., during the rain, for 60th Street and Broadway, New York City. Thirteen riders finished. First to arrive was George N Holly of Bradford, Pa., who arrived at 5:18 P.M. July 5, 1902. He was closely followed by N. P. Bernard of Hartford, Conn. (5:18½ P.M.). The route was via Worcester, Springfield, Hartford, New Haven, and Bridgeport, with an overnight stop at Hartford. *(New York Times. 2:7. July 6, 1902)*

Motorcycle race (300 miles) was held July 4 1914, at Dodge City, Kans., on a 2-mile dirt track about 2½ miles from the city. Of the 36 starters 18 finished, 6 completing 150 laps. The first-place

The First

prize of two gold medals and $600 was won by Glen R. ("Slivers") Boyd of Denver, Colo., in an Indian motorcycle. His time was 4 hours 24 minutes 58 seconds, with an average of 67.92 m.p.h.

Motorcycle to exceed 200 miles an hour was ridden by Wilhelm Herz, who rode a measured mile over the salt flats at Wendover, Utah, on August 4, 1956, at a speed of 210 m.p.h.

MOTORCYCLE TRIP

Motorcycle transcontinental trip was made by George A. Wyman of San Francisco, Calif., on a Yale-California motorcycle built by L. W. Leavitt and Company, San Francisco. Wyman left San Francisco May 16, 1903, and arrived in New York City July 6, 1903. The motorcycle was a 3½ h.p. single-cylinder machine with a belt drive. *(Motorcycle Magazine. August 1903)*

Motorcycle transcontinental trip by women was made by Adleina and Augusta Van Buren, who left New York City on July 5, 1916, and arrived in San Diego, Calif., on September 12, 1916, via Buffalo, Chicago, Omaha, Denver, and Salt Lake City.

MOTORCYCLIST

Woman professional motorcyclist licensed by the American Motorcycle Association was Kerry Kleid, 21 years of age, of Rye, N.Y., who received license No. 143B on August 22, 1971. Her debut was made October 17, 1971, in the Mt. Peter motocross, 6 miles north of Greenwood Lake, N.Y., for a $2,000 purse.

MOTTO OF THE UNITED STATES—"In God We Trust"—was authorized by act of July 30, 1956 (70 Stat. L. 732), a joint resolution "to establish a national motto of the United States" signed by President Dwight David Eisenhower.

MOURNING STAMP. *See* Postage stamp

MOVABLE CHURCH was the Chapel of the Transfiguration (Episcopal), which was consecrated June 3, 1899, at Conanicut Island, R.I. It was 27 feet long and 18 feet wide and contained 14 benches, 20 chairs, a platform, and an altar. The interior, including the pews, prayer desk, and altar, was made of oak. The church was built on a wooden chassis with four wheels and was drawn from place to place by horses. The first preacher was the Reverend Charles E. Preston of St. Matthew's Church. The first service was held April 23, 1899. *(Charles E. Preston—The First Movable Church)*

MOVING PICTURE. *See* Motion picture

MOVING SIDEWALK. *See* Sidewalk (traveling): Two-way moving walk

MOVING STAIRWAY. *See* Escalator

MOWER (horsepower) was patented on December 4, 1812, by Peter Gaillard of Lancaster, Pa.

The First

(Robert L. Ardrey—American Agricultural Implements)

MULE. *See* Animals

MULTIGRAPH was invented by Harry Christian Gammeter of Cleveland, Ohio, who obtained patent No. 722,404, March 10, 1903, on a "duplicating machine." It was the first successful machine designed to simplify the printing processes, so that the ordinary layman could print from type, either with ribbon or with ink. Commercial manufacture was undertaken December 12, 1902, by the American Multigraph Sales Company of Cleveland, Ohio.

MULTIPLE TELEPHONE SWITCHBOARD. *See under* Telephone

MUNICIPAL BATHHOUSE. *See* Bathhouse: Bathhouse owned and operated by a municipality

MUNICIPAL CANCER HOSPITAL. *See* Hospital

MUNICIPAL FILTRATION SYSTEM. *See under* Water purification

MUNICIPAL MILK STATION. *See* Milk station (municipal)

MUNICIPAL RAILROAD. *See* Railroad

MUNICIPAL STADIUM. *See* Stadium

MUNICIPAL THEATER. *See* Theater

MUNICIPAL UNIVERSITY. *See* College: City college

MURDER-TRIAL TELECAST. *See under* Television—Telecast

MUSEUM

Children's museum was the Brooklyn Children's Museum, Brooklyn Avenue and Park Place, New York City (in the Brower Park Building in the Crown Heights area). It opened December 16, 1899.

College art museum was the Yale University Art Gallery at 1111 Chapel Street, New Haven, Conn., founded in 1832. It was known as the Trumbull Art Gallery of Yale University.

College museum was the College of Charleston Museum, Charleston, S.C. The old Charleston museum building was torn down and the museum moved to the College of Charleston, where it was greatly enlarged and rechristened the College of Charleston Museum. On August 29, 1850, the city council ratified an "Ordinance to provide for the appointment of a Curator for the Museum of the College of Charleston" and on November 25, 1850, Francis Simmons Holmes was elected. On December 28, 1850, he was appointed professor of geology and paleontology at the college and on May 6, 1855, professor of natural history. *(Charleston Museum Bulletin)*

The First

MUSEUM—*Continued*

Commercial museum was the Philadelphia Commercial Museum, organized by city ordinance approved June 15, 1894. It was developed by Dr. William Powell Wilson, who conceived the idea of the institution and who served as its director and executive head from the first meeting of the board of directors on June 20, 1894, until his death May 12, 1927. The Philadelphia Commercial Museum comprised the museum proper, the Department of Visual Education, the Foreign Trade Bureau, the Library, and the Exhibition Hall with its convention hall. *(Report of the Philadelphia Commercial Museum: A Resolution in Memory of William P. Wilson, Sc.D.)*

Costume museum was the Museum of Costume Arts, New York City, incorporated April 28, 1937, to develop "cultural education in connection with those arts and industries which function in conjunction with design in form of apparel and accessories by applying to this field the ways and means now commonly used or applied by fine arts and industrial museum associations and foundations and musical societies of various kinds in their respective fields."

Health museum. *See* Health museum

Industrial museum was established by the Association for the Establishment and Maintenance for the People of the City of New York of a Museum of Peaceful Arts. It was incorporated February 26, 1914, and the name was changed in 1931 to the New York Museum of Science and Industry.

Maritime museum devoted exclusively to maritime affairs worldwide in scope was the Mariners' Museum, Newport News, Va., established June 2, 1930, by Archer Milton Huntington. The first board of trustees was composed of Mr. Huntington, Anna Hyatt Huntington, Homer Lenoir Ferguson, Charles Franklin Bailey, and Frederick Henry Skinner.

Museum devoted exclusively to atomic energy was the American Museum of Atomic Energy, Oak Ridge, Tenn., opened to the public on March 19, 1949, the anniversary of the removal of the security fence from the city of Oak Ridge. The museum is operated for the Atomic Energy Commission as a service to the public by the Oak Ridge Institute of Nuclear Studies, a nonprofit educational organization.

Museum devoted exclusively to papermaking was the Dard Hunter Paper Museum of the Massachusetts Institute of Technology, Cambridge, Mass., which opened June 5, 1939. The curator was Dr. Dard Hunter, who personally collected the material in every papermaking country of the world over a period of about 40 years.

Museum especially constructed as a museum and art gallery was Peale's Baltimore Museum and Gallery of the Fine Arts, operated by Rem-

The First

brandt Peale, son of Charles Willson Peale. It was a three-story building at 225 North Holliday Street, Baltimore, Md., and was designed by Robert Cary Long, Sr. The opening was advertised for August 15, 1814. The building was sold in 1830 to the City of Baltimore, which used it as its first City Hall.

Museum to install refrigerated vaults with automatic temperature control for the preservation of valuable specimens of furs and similar articles was the University of California Museum of Vertebrate Zoology, Berkeley, Calif. The museum was thus equipped when it was moved into the Life Science Building in March 1930.

Outdoor museum (or nature trail) was established in 1925 by Dr. Frank Eugene Lutz at the Station for the Study of Insects located in the Ramapo Mountains in Tuxedo Park, N.Y. This nature trail was developed under the auspices of the American Museum of Natural History, New York City, with the cooperation of the Palisades Interstate Park Commission. It consisted of two trails, each a half mile long, the Training Trail and the Testing Trail, which were posted with signs describing the trees, shrubs, flowering plants, insects, etc.

Public museum in America was the Charleston Museum of Charleston, S.C. It was organized on January 12, 1773, at the annual anniversary meeting of the Charleston Library Society. The first curators of the museum were Charles Cotesworth Pinckney, Esquire; Thomas Heyward, Esquire; Alexander Baron, physician; and Peter Fayssoux, physician. In 1915 the museum was incorporated as the Charleston Museum. *(Charleston Museum Quarterly. Vol. 1, No. 1. 1923.)*

Semitic museum was the Harvard University Semitic Museum, Cambridge, Mass., formally opened February 5, 1903, in the Peabody Museum of Archeology and Ethnology. It was founded by a donation from Jacob Henry Schiff and had been opened to students and the public on May 13, 1891. Its collection included Syrian, Arabic, and Hebrew manuscripts.

Waxworks museum. *See* Waxworks museum

Wine museum was the Finger Lakes Wine Museum opened July 1967 on Bully Hill Road, Hammondsport, N.Y. The name was changed in 1972 to the Greyton H. Taylor Wine Museum in honor of one of its founders.

MUSIC

Black to conduct the Metropolitan Opera House orchestra, New York City, was Henry Lewis, who conducted Giacomo Puccini's *La Bohème* on October 16, 1972.

Chamber music organization was the Mendelssohn Quintette Club of Boston, Mass. Its first concert was given at Chickering Hall, December 14, 1849.

Community chorus was established in 1912 in Rochester, N.Y., by Harry Barnhart, who appeared by permission of the mayor of Rochester at a band concert at the Convention Hall, where he introduced the idea of community singing.

Concert reported was "a concert of music on sundry instruments" held at six o'clock at Mr. (Peter) Pelham's "great room" near the Sun Tavern in Boston, Mass., on December 30, 1731. Tickets were five shillings. *(Boston News-Letter. Dec. 16-23, 1731)*

Libretto. *See* Libretto

Long-distance telephone concert was held March 31, 1877, at Steinway Hall, New York City. Music played in Philadelphia, Pa., was heard by means of Elisha Gray's so-called Transmission of Music by Telegraph. The audience heard "Home, Sweet Home," "The Last Rose of Summer," "Yankee Doodle," and other songs.

Music convention was attended by 96 men and 42 women singing teachers from 10 states and was held August 16-25, 1838, in Boston, Mass. Colonel Asa Barr of New Braintree, Mass., was president.

Music festival is claimed to have been given to celebrate the signing of the Treaty of Ghent, between the United States and Great Britain, on December 25, 1814. The news reached Boston, Mass., February 13, 1815, and a concert of sacred music was played February 16, 1815, at the Reverend Dr. Baldwin's, in Boston, Mass. The first part of Haydn's *Creation*, parts of Handel's *Judas Maccabeus*, the Dettingen *Te Deum*, Ode to St. Cecilia's Day, and the "Hallelujah Chorus" were presented. *(William Arms Fisher—Music Festivals in the United States)*

Music printed in a magazine was "The Hill Tops, a New Hunting Song" printed in the April 1774 issue of the *Royal American Magazine or Universal Repository of Instruction and Amusement*, published by Isaiah Thomas, in Boston, Mass.

Music publishers (exclusive) were [John C.] Moller & [Henri] Capron of Philadelphia, Pa., established in 1790. They also had a music store and offered musical instruction. *(Robert A. Gerson—Music in Philadelphia)*

Musical comedy broadcast. *See under* Radio broadcast

Musical comedy telecast. *See under* Television—Telecast

Musical instrument. *See under* specific instruments

Musical instrument dealer was Michael Hillegas, who opened a shop in Philadelphia, Pa., in 1759. On December 13, 1759, he advertised instru-

ments, music, and musical supplies in the *Pennsylvania Gazette*. Musical instruments, however, had been sold previously and were advertised for sale at a dancing school in Boston, Mass., in 1716. *(William Arms Fisher—One Hundred and Fifty Years of Music Publishing in the United States)*

Musical play to win a Pulitzer Prize. *See under* Play (drama)

Opera telecast. *See under* Television—Telecast

Operetta telecast. *See under* Television—Telecast

Orchestral song printed contained parts for a first viol, a second viol, a first clarinet, a second clarinet, E-flat horns, etc., and was tipped in after page 186 of the *Massachusetts Magazine* published in Boston, Mass., in March 1791. The song was "The Death Song of an Indian Chief," by Hans Gram of Boston. It was based upon *Ouabi*, an Indian tale in four cantos by "Philenia, a lady of Boston" (Sarah Wentworth Apthorp Morton). *(John Tasker Howard—Our American Music)*

Parade in which all the marching music was supplied by transistor radio receivers. *See* Parade: Parade in which all the marching music was supplied by transistor radio receivers

Patriotic American song was "The Liberty Song" (In Freedom We're Born) published by John Mein and John Fleming in July 1768 in Boston, Mass. The lyrics were by John Dickinson, set to the tune of "Hearts of Oak" by William Boyce of London. The words were published in the Boston *Gazette* of July 18, 1768. *(Frank Moore—Songs and Ballads of the American Revolution)*

Program theme song. *See under* Radio broadcast

Public school opera studio. *See under* Public school

Radio concert from an airplane. *See under* Radio broadcast

Saengerfest was held in Cincinnati, Ohio, in 1849. It was the first meeting of the several midwestern German singing societies, and as a result the North American Sängerbund was formed. Only one concert was given. The choir consisted of 118 singers.

Secular song by a native American composer was "My Days Have Been So Wondrous Free," composed in 1759 by Francis Hopkinson. It was based on a poem by Thomas Parnell. Despite its popularity, it was not published until the twentieth century.

Secular song hit with words and music by an American was "The Ministrel's Return from the War," by John Hill Hewitt, composed in Greenville, S.C., in 1825. It was published in 1827 by James L. Hewitt & Co., Boston, Mass., but was not copyrighted, as its importance was not anticipat-

The First

MUSIC—*Continued*
ed. *(Harry Dichter and Elliott Shapiro—Early American Sheet Music)*

Singing contest in America took place in 1790 in Dorchester, Mass., between the singers of the First Parish of Dorchester and the singing society of Stoughton. The Stoughtonians began with Jacob French's "Heavenly Vision," the author of which was their fellow townsman. When they finally sang Handel's "Hallelujah Chorus" without books, the Dorchestrians gave up the contest and gracefully acknowledged defeat. *(The Old Stoughton Musical Society: An Historical and Informative Record of the Oldest Choral Society in America)*

Symphony. *See* Symphony

Taps. *See* Taps

War song was "Chester," composed in 1778 by William Billings of Boston, Mass. The song was published in Billings's *The Singing Master's Assistant, or Key to Practical Music,* printed by Draper and Folsom, Boston, in 1778. "Chester" contains the following chorus: "Let tyrants shake their iron rod; / And Slav'ry clank her galling chains, / We fear them not; / We trust in God, / New England's God forever reigns." *(American Mercury.* May 1928)

War song of the Confederate States to achieve popularity was "I Wish I Was in Dixie's Land" (now known as "Dixie"), written and composed by Daniel Decatur Emmett, a Northerner, expressly for Bryant's Minstrels, who performed at 472 Broadway, New York City. It was announced as a plantation song and dance. According to some sources it was based on a song of lament of slaves owned by a Dutch tobacco planter named Dixye, who was unable to harvest tobacco in Harlem, New Amsterdam (New York), and who sold his slaves to a farmer in Piedmont County, South Carolina. The song was first introduced by Emmett on April 4, 1859, at Mechanics Hall, New York City. It was published by Firth Pond & Co., New York City. The song was sung at the inauguration of Jefferson Davis as President of the Confederate States on February 18, 1861.

MUSIC BOOK
Children's music book was the *Juvenile Lyre: or Hymns and Songs, Religious, Moral and Cheerful, set to appropriate music, for the use of primary and common schools,* by Lowell Mason, published in 1831 by Richardson, Lord and Holbrook, Boston, Mass. It contained 61 songs and was copyrighted February 1, 1831, in the District of Massachusetts.

German songbook published in America was *Ausbund, das ist: Etliche schöne Christliche Lieder wie sie in dem Gefängnüss zu Bassau in dem Schloss von den Schweitzer-Brüdern und von anderen rechtglaubigen Christen hin und her ge-*

The First

dichtet worden. Allen und Jeden Christen welcher religion sie seyen unpartheyisch fast nutzlich. Published by Christoph Saur, Germantown, Pa., in 1742, it contained 812 pages, plus an appended section.

Hymnbook was Stephen Day's (Steeven Daye's) *The Whole Booke of Psalmes, Faithfully Translated into English Metre whereunto is prefixed a discourse declaring not only the lawfullness, but also the necessity of the heavenly ordinance of singing scripture psalmes in the Churches of God,* 296 pages, published July 1640 in Cambridge, Mass.

Hymnbook with music was the ninth edition of *The Psalms, Hymns & Spiritual Songs of the Old and New Testament; Faithfully Translated into English Meetre. For the Use, Edification and Comfort of the Saints in publick and private especially in New England,* 420 pages, printed in 1798 by Bartholomew Green and J. Allen, Boston, Mass., for Michael Perry. The book contained 13 tunes.

Lutheran hymnbook (English) created in America was Johann Christoff Kunze's *A Hymn and Prayer Book for the Use of Such Lutheran Churches as Use the English Language,* printed and sold by Hurlin and Commardinger, 450 Pearl Street, New York City, 1795. Its 300 pages contained 240 hymns, 70 of which were of English origin. Kunze was the Senior of the Lutheran clergy in New York state.

Lutheran hymnbook (German) published in America was *Erbauliche Lieder-Sammlung zum Gottesdienstlichten Gebrauch in den Vereinigten Evangelisch-Lutherischen Gemeinken in Nord-America,* containing 707 hymns (361 in *Geistreiches Gesangbuch,* 236 in *Marburger Gesang-Buch,* 109 in others), compiled by Rev. Henry Melchior Muhlenberg and published in 1786 in Germantown, Pa. It was copyrighted October 2, 1786, by Peter Leibert and Michael Billmeyer.

Music book by a native-born American was *Urania; or a Choice Collection of Psalm-Tunes, Anthems, and Hymns, in Two, Three and Four parts; the whole peculiarly adapted to the use of churches and private families—to which are prefix'd the plainest and most necessary rules of Psalmody,* by James Lyon, A.B. It was published in 1761 in Philadelphia and contained 198 songs in its 220 pages.

Music book printed from type to be published in the United States was *The Psalms of David, with the ten commandments, creed, Lord's prayer etc. In Metre, also the catechism, confession of faith, liturgy etc.,* printed by James Parker, New York City, in 1767. It had 479 pages and contained 150 psalms translated from the Dutch for the use of the Reformed Protestant Dutch Church of the City of New York. It was edited by Francis Hopkinson and had a prefatory note by Johannes Rit-

The First

zema. The type for the music notes was obtained from Amsterdam, Holland.

Music book printed with bars was *The Grounds and Rules of Musick Explained; or, an Introduction to the art of singing by note. Fitted to the Meanest Capacities. Recommended by Several Ministers,* by the Reverend Thomas Walter of Roxbury, Mass. It was an oblong book containing 19 pages of songs with the reverse pages blank, and was printed in 1721 by J[ames] Franklin, Boston, Mass.

Music composition book was *The New England Psalm-Singer or American Chorister containing a number of psalm tunes, anthems, and canons in four and five parts,* composed by William Billings. It was printed by Edes and Gill, Boston, Mass., in 1770, consisted of 112 pages, and sold for eight shillings. *(Louis Charles Elson—History of American Music)*

Ragtime instruction book was Ben Harney's *Rag-Time Instructor,* published by M. Witmark & Sons, New York City, in 1897. It was "the only work published giving full instructions how to play rag-time music on the piano," contained 12 pages, and cost fifty cents. Harney was the composer of "Mister Johnson Turn Me Loose," "You've Been a Good Old Wagon, But You've Done Broke Down," etc. *(Isaac Goldberg—Tin Pan Alley)*

Secular songbook was Alexander Reinagle's *A Selection of the Most Favorite Scots Tunes,* published in August 1787 by Thomas Dobson, Philadelphia, Pa.

Secular songbook by a native-born American composer was Francis Hopkinson's *Seven Songs for the Harpsichord or Forte Piano,* which was dedicated to George Washington and published in 1788 by Thomas Dobson, Philadelphia, Pa. It was advertised in the *Federal Gazette:* "These songs are composed in an easy familiar style, intended for young practitioners on the harpsichord or forte piano, and is the first work of this kind attempted in the U.S."

Vocal instruction book was *A Very Plain and Easy Introduction to the Art of Singing Psalm-tunes; with the cantus or trebles of twenty-eight psalm-tunes, contrived in such a manner as that the learner may attain the skill of singing them, with the greatest ease and speed imaginable,* by John Tufts, pastor of Newburyport, Mass. It was printed by J[ames] F[ranklin] for S. Gerrish in Boston, Mass., in 1721. Letters took the place of notes on the staff. F, S, L, were used for fa, sol, la, etc. *(Frank Johnson Metcalf—American Writers and Compilers of Sacred Music)*

MUSIC DEGREES. *See under* Degrees (academic and honorary)

The First

MUSIC INSTRUCTION

College music chair was established at Harvard University, Cambridge, Mass., on August 30, 1875, when John Knowles Paine was appointed professor of music. On March 29, 1862, he had been appointed instructor in music and on June 2, 1873, assistant professor. He served until his death, April 25, 1906.

Music instruction (public school) was conducted by Lowell Mason in November 1837 at the Hawes School, South Boston, Mass. On August 28, 1838, the school board voted that a committee on music be instructed to contract with a teacher of vocal music for the several public schools of Boston. Lowell Mason was appointed and served from 1838 to 1841. He was in charge of four assistants. *(Edward Bailey Birge—History of Public School Music in the United States)*

Music school authorized to confer degrees was established about 1835 by Oramel Whittlesey in Salem, Conn. It was successively known as Mr. Whittlesey's Music School, Music Vale Seminary, and the Normal Academy of Music. The first degree was conferred about 1849. *(Frances Hall Johnson—Music Vale Seminary 1835–1876)*

Musical pedagogy school was the Boston Academy of Music, Boston, Mass., founded January 8, 1833. Samuel Atkins Eliot was the first president. The faculty consisted of Lowell Mason and George James Webb. The Pestalozzian method of teaching vocal music in classes was advocated.

State Supervisor of Music was Paul Eugene Beck, appointed July 1, 1915, by Pennsylvania. He served until August 1921.

MUSIC PERIODICAL

Music magazine was the *American Musical Magazine,* which was published in May 1786 in New Haven, Conn. It was issued regularly and was a collection of tunes and hymns. It was published and sold by Amos Doolittle and Daniel Read. The first issue of six pages contained the selection "The Seasons Moralized." *(Frank Luther Mott—History of American Magazines)*

Music magazine published in Braille was *The Musical Review for the Blind,* the first issue of which appeared in January 1930. It was published by the American Braille Press for War and Civilian Blind.

MUSIC SOCIETY

Music society for the literary protection of composers and authors was the American Society of Composers, Authors and Publishers, which was formed February 13, 1914, in New York City. The object of the society was to protect the copyrighted musical compositions of its members against illegal public performance for profit and other forms of infringement, and to collect license fees in respect of authorized performances in public

The First

MUSIC SOCIETY—*Continued*
amusement establishments for distribution among its members. The society is an unincorporated voluntary association and is affiliated with similar societies functioning in some 25 foreign countries. George Maxwell was the first president.

Music society of importance (local) was the St. Cecilia Society of Charleston, S.C., organized in 1737 as an amateur concert society. It was formally organized in 1762 and with the exception of a few years has given annual concerts and balls ever since.

MUSIC SUPERVISOR (state). *See* Music instruction: State Supervisor of Music

MUSICAL INSTRUMENTS. *See under* name of specific instrument, e.g., Piano, Saxophone

MUSICIAN
Composer (native-born American) was Francis Hopkinson, one of the signers of the Declaration of Independence, who graduated in 1757 from the College of Philadelphia. His first important song was "My Days Have Been So Wondrous Free," composed in 1759, and is one of the earliest secular compositions extant. In 1763, his *A Collection of Psalm Tunes, with a few anthems and hymns, some of them entirely new, for the use of the United Churches of Christ Church and St. Peter's Church in Philadelphia* was printed by W. Dunlop, Philadelphia, Pa. *(Quarterly Magazine of the International Musical Society. Vol. 5)*

Composer of jazz music was William Christopher Handy, the black composer of the "Memphis Blues," which he wrote in 1912. He was known as the "father of the blues," having composed numerous other pieces in the same idiom, among them "St. Louis Blues" and "Beale Street Blues." *(John Tasker Howard—Our American Music)*

Musician (native-born American) to achieve European fame was Louis Moreau Gottschalk, who in 1852 gave concerts in the leading music centers of the world. He exhibited a fondness for music at the age of four and when but six years old played an organ in church. In April 1845 he appeared in Paris, in 1846–47 in Italy, and in 1850 in Switzerland. *(Graham's Magazine. January 1853)*

"Negro-song" popularizer was Johann Christian Gottlieb Graupner, the "father of Negro songs." On December 30, 1799, at the Federal Street Theatre, Boston, Mass., he sang "The Gay Negro Boy" in the second act of *Oroonoko*. He accompanied himself on the banjo. He was well received and thereafter he specialized in popularizing this type of material. *(Memorial History of Boston, Vol. 4. 1883)*

The First

Orchestra leader to conduct without using a baton was George James Webb, who instituted this practice in Boston in 1843.

Woman conductor-composer to write an opera and conduct it in a major opera house was Ethel Leginska (Ethel Legins) whose opera *Gale* was sung November 23, 1935, by the Chicago City Opera Company, Chicago, Ill. It was a one-act arrangement of a Cornish legend adapted from "The Haunting" (1922) by Mrs. Catharine Amy Dawson-Scott. It was performed by an all-American cast including John Charles Thomas, Frank Forest, Julia Peters, and Helen Bertush.

MUSKET. *See* Ordnance

MUSTARD was manufactured by Benjamin Jackson, who established the Globe Mills on Germantown Road, Philadelphia, Pa., and sold his product in glass bottles with his label on them. He advertised in the *Pennsylvania Chronicle*, February 15, 1768, that he was "the original establisher of the mustard manufactory in America, and . . . at present the only mustard manufacturer on the continent. I brought the art with me into the country."

MUTINY (naval officer condemned). *See under* Naval officer

MUTUAL INSURANCE. *See* Insurance

MUTUEL TICKET. *See under* Horse race

MYSTERY RAILROAD EXCURSION. *See* Railroad excursion

MYSTIC SOCIETY PARADE. *See* Parade: Street parade held by a mystic society

N

NAIL CUTTING AND HEADING MACHINE was patented December 12, 1796, by George Chandler of Maryland.

NAIL MACHINE (wire) was built under the supervision of Major Thomas Norton by Adolph and Felix Brown of New York City and used in 1851 by William Hassall of New York City.

NAILS
Nails were cold-cut in 1777 and were manufactured by Jeremiah Wilkinson of Cumberland, R.I. "They were first cut by a pair of shears from an old chest lock and afterward headed in a smith' vice. Sheet iron was afterward used and the process extended to small nails." *(Samuel Greene Arnold—History of the State of Rhode Island)*

Steel-cut nails were manufactured in 1883 by the Riverside Iron Works of Wheeling, W.Va.

The First

NARCOTICS

Narcotics sanatorium (federal) for drug addicts was the United States Narcotics Farm at Lexington, Ky., which covered 11 acres of a 1,050-acre plot. The cornerstone was laid July 29, 1933, and the building was dedicated May 25, 1935, by Surgeon General Hugh Smith Cumming of the United States Public Health Service. The first occupants were received on May 29, 1935. Dr. Lawrence Kolb was the first director.

Narcotics sanatorium for minors offering full-scale long-term treatment was the Riverside Hospital, North Brother Island, New York City, which was converted for the purpose in November 1951. The first patients were received on July 1, 1952. The first superintendent was Dr. Jerome Louis Leon.

Narcotics tariff was enacted by the Tariff Act of August 30, 1842 (5 Stat. L. 558), which placed a levy of 75 cents a pound on opium. Prior to this act, opium was exempted from duty by the act of July 14, 1832 (4 Stat. L. 583), and the act of March 2, 1833 (4 Stat. L. 629).

NARCOTICS LEGISLATION

Narcotics prohibition act (federal) was Section 1 of the act of February 9, 1909 (35 Stat. L. 614): "After the first day of April 1909, it shall be unlawful to import into the United States, opium in any form or any preparation or derivative thereof . . . other than smoking opium for medicinal purposes."

Narcotics regulation (federal) was enacted by Congress as part of the McKinley Tariff Act on October 1, 1890 (26 Stat. L. 567). This act provided for an internal revenue tax of $10 a pound upon all smoking opium manufactured in the United States for smoking purposes, and limited the manufacture to United States citizens. It further provided for the bonding of manufacturers, the keeping of books, rendering of returns, etc. *(Records in Bureau of Narcotics, Treasury Department, Washington, D.C.)*

Narcotics regulation (state) was adopted March 10, 1933, by Nevada.

Narcotics prohibitory legislation (state) was chapter 160 enacted by Nevada on March 19, 1965. It stated that "the possession of dangerous drugs without a prescription is punishable as a gross misdemeanor upon first and second conviction and is punishable as a felony upon third conviction, and exempting physicians, dentists, chiropodists, veterinarians, pharmacists, manufacturers, wholesalers, jobbers and laboratories, and exempting ranchers under certain conditions."

NARROW-GAUGE LOCOMOTIVE. *See* Locomotive

The First

NATIONAL ACADEMY OF SCIENCES. *See under* Science association

NATIONAL ADVISORY COMMITTEE FOR AERONAUTICS. *See* Aviation: Advisory Committee for Aeronautics (National)

NATIONAL AERONAUTICS AND SPACE ADMINISTRATION. *See* Space Agency (U.S.)

NATIONAL AERONAUTICS AND SPACE ADMINISTRATION DISTINGUISHED SERVICE MEDAL. *See* Medal

NATIONAL ANTHEM was the "Star-Spangled Banner," designated by act of Congress (46 Stat. L. 1508), approved by President Herbert Hoover, March 3, 1931. The words were written by Francis Scott Key while a prisoner on the British warship *Supreme* during the British attack on Fort McHenry, Baltimore, Md., September 13, 1814. The verses were set to the air of "Anacreon in Heaven." The song was originally known as "The Defense of Fort McHenry," and printed on a handbill September 15, 1814, without the name of Francis Scott Key. *(Veterans of Foreign Wars—The Star-Spangled Banner)*

NATIONAL ARCHERY ASSOCIATION. *See* Archery club: Archery association (national)

NATIONAL ASSOCIATION OF BASEBALL PLAYERS. *See* Baseball league: Baseball league of importance

NATIONAL ASSOCIATION OF MANUFACTURERS. *See* Manufacturers' association

NATIONAL ASSOCIATION OF PROFESSIONAL BASEBALL LEAGUES. *See* Baseball league: Baseball league association

NATIONAL BANK. *See* Bank

NATIONAL BANKING SYSTEM. *See under* Bank legislation

NATIONAL BIBLIOGRAPHIC SOCIETY. *See* Bibliography Society (national)

NATIONAL CEMETERY. *See* Cemetery

NATIONAL CHRISTMAS CAROLS ASSOCIATION. *See* Christmas carols association (national)

NATIONAL CONVENTION FOR BLACKS. *See under* Black

NATIONAL EMERGENCY COUNCIL (U.S.) was authorized November 17, 1933, under Executive Order No. 6433A "for the purpose of coordinating and making more efficient and productive the work of the numerous field agencies." Frank Comerford Walker was appointed the executive director. He was also appointed executive secretary of the executive council of 23 members which was established July 11, 1933. *(United States National Emergency Council—Informational Handbook)*

The First

NATIONAL GEOGRAPHIC SOCIETY GOLD MEDAL. *See* Medal

NATIONAL GRANGE OF THE PATRONS OF HUSBANDRY. *See* Agricultural society: Agricultural society of national importance

NATIONAL HALL OF FAME. *See* Hall of fame

NATIONAL HOLIDAY. *See* Holiday

NATIONAL INDUSTRIAL RECOVERY ACT. *See* Industrial Recovery Act

NATIONAL INSTITUTE OF ARTS AND LETTERS. *See* Arts and letters society: Arts and letters society (national)

NATIONAL INSTITUTE OF SOCIAL SCIENCES. *See* Social science society (national)

NATIONAL LABOR BOARD. *See* Labor: Labor Advisory Board (federal)

NATIONAL LABOR PARTY. *See* Labor Party (political): Labor Party (national)

NATIONAL LABOR RELATIONS BOARD. *See* Labor relations: Labor Relations Act (national)

NATIONAL LEAGUE. *See under* Baseball league

NATIONAL MEDAL OF SCIENCE. *See* Medal

NATIONAL MEDIATION BOARD. *See under* Labor relations

NATIONAL PARK. *See* Park: Park (national)

NATIONAL PIKE. *See* Road: Federal highway

NATIONAL PLANNING BOARD (U.S.) to advise on preparation of a comprehensive program of public works was organized July 30, 1933, and was composed of three members: Frederic Adrian Delano, chairman, Wesley Clair Mitchell, and Charles Edward Merriam. The board was later abolished and its work delegated to other committees. *(United States National Resources Commission—National Planning)*

NATIONAL PROHIBITION SOCIETY. *See* Temperance society: Women's temperance society (national)

NATIONAL RADIO CONFERENCE. *See* Radio conference

NATIONAL RESEARCH COUNCIL. *See under* Science association

NATIONAL SECURITY COUNCIL (U.S.)
National Security Council was established by the National Security Act of 1947 (61 Stat. L. 496), July 26, 1947, to advise the President with respect to the integration of domestic, foreign, and military policies relating to the national security. The council's members are the President, the Vice President, the Secretary of State, and the Secretary of Defense. The council staff is headed by a civilian executive secretary appointed by the President.

The First

National Security Council meeting held outside Washington, D.C., was held September 13, 1954, in Denver, Colo.

Vice President to preside at a National Security Council. *See under* Vice President (U.S.)

NATIONAL SECURITY MEDAL. *See* Medal

NATIONAL SOLDIERS' HOME. *See* Soldiers' homes (national)

NATIONAL STATUARY HALL MONUMENT TO A WOMAN. *See* Monument: Statue of a woman in National Statuary Hall

NATIONAL TUBERCULOSIS ASSOCIATION. *See* Health society

NATIONAL UNION FOR SOCIAL JUSTICE originated November 1934 in Royal Oak, Mich. The first national convention was held August 14, 1936, at the Public Auditorium, Cleveland, Ohio, and the vote was 8,153-1 to support William Lemke and Thomas Charles O'Brien as candidates for President and Vice President of the United States.

NATIONAL UNITARIAN CONVENTION. *See* Unitarian Church convention (national): National organization of the Unitarian Churches of the United States and Canada

NATIONAL WOMAN'S RIGHTS CONVENTION. *See* Woman suffrage: Woman suffrage associations (national)

NATIVE AMERICANS. *See* American Indians

NATURAL CEMENT ROCK. *See under* Cement

NATURAL COLOR PHOTOGRAPH. *See* Photograph: Photograph in natural colors taken in the air

NATURAL GAS. *See under* Gas

NATURAL GAS ACT. *See under* Gas legislation

NATURAL SCIENCE SUMMER SCHOOL. *See* Science school

NATURALIZATION
Naturalization ceremony in the White House, Washington, D.C., was held November 23, 1968, when 54 immigrants from 26 nations (the youngest, an 8-year-old Filipino girl; the oldest, a 72-year-old Chinese laundry worker) became citizens.

NATURALIZATION ACT
Naturalization act of the United States Government was that of March 26, 1790 (1 Stat. L. 103), authorizing courts of record to "entertain the applications" of alien free white persons who had resided in the United States for two years or more, one year of which should be in a particular state, on proof of good character and on their taking an oath or affirmation to support the Constitution.

The First

Naturalization act (colonial). *See* Citizenship: Naturalization act

NATURE TRAIL. *See* Museum: Outdoor museum

NAUTICAL ALMANAC. *See* Almanac

NAUTICAL SCHOOL
See also
Naval Academy
Naval Officers' Train
    ing School
Naval War College

Nautical municipal school was the Nautical School of the Port of New York, opened January 11, 1875, in New York City on board the *St. Mary,* a 150-foot, 3-masted, full-rigged vessel known as a sloop of war. It was built in 1844 to chase slavers. The main deck was less than 144 feet above the water line. The officers were Commander Robert Lees Phythian, Lieutenant Commander George Henry Wadleigh, Lieutenants George Washington De Long and William Henry Jaques, all U.S. Naval Academy graduates. From July 22, 1875, to October 8, 1875, a Long Island Sound cruise was conducted. The school was authorized by Chapter 288, Laws of New York State, passed April 24, 1873, and was supported by state funds.

Nautical school was established May 29, 1827, in Nantucket, Mass., and was known as Admiral Sir Isaac Coffin's Lancasterian School. It was conducted by William Coffin, Jr., and Miss A. Meach and was located in a wooden schoolhouse. Courses on shipboard to train sailors had been offered previously.

Nautical state school was established by Massachusetts, Chapter 402, Act of June 11, 1891, an "act to establish a Nautical Training School" which authorized three commissioners to serve one, two, and three years for the Massachusetts Nautical Training School. On February 17, 1891, legislation authorized the governor to petition the United States Secretary of the Navy for a suitable vessel, and on October 28, 1892, the steam sloop *Enterprise* was transferred to Massachusetts.

NAVAL ACADEMY
See also
Chaplains' school
Nautical School
Naval Officers' Train
    ing School
Naval War College

Black midshipman in the United States Naval Academy was James Henry Conyers of South Carolina, who attended from September 21, 1872, to November 11, 1873. He did not graduate. *(Annual Register of U.S. Naval Academy, 1874–1875)*

Black midshipman in the United States Naval Academy to graduate was Wesley Anthony Brown of Washington, D.C., who graduated June 3, 1949, and received his commission as ensign.

The First

Japanese midshipman in the United States Naval Academy was Zun Zow Matzmulla, admitted December 8, 1869, under act of Congress, July 27, 1868 (15 Stat. L. 261), authorizing the Secretary of the Navy "to receive for instruction not exceeding six persons to be designated by the government of the Empire of Japan." Matzmulla completed the course in 1873 and stood 28th in a class of 29.

Naval Academy (U.S.) was established on a nine-acre site at Windmill Point, Fort Severn, Annapolis, Md., transferred on August 15, 1845, by the War Department to the Navy Department for the purpose of establishing a naval school. It was known as the Naval School and officially opened October 10, 1845, with 47 matriculating students, 8 non-matriculating. The first superintendent was Commander Franklin Buchanan, appointed September 3, 1845. The first class was graduated in July 1846. On July 1, 1850, the name was changed to the U.S. Naval Academy. As most of the midshipmen had already served some time at sea or otherwise in the Navy, the course of instruction varied in length, depending upon the dates of their appointments. A 4-year course began in 1851 and the first official graduation was held June 10, 1854. The academy was transferred to Newport, R.I., May 9, 1861, and was returned to Annapolis, Md., September 9, 1865, when Rear Admiral David Dixon Porter assumed charge. *(James Russell Soley—Historical Sketch of the U.S. Naval Academy)*

Naval Academy graduate to attain the rank of rear admiral was Edward Simpson, No. 00008, who was graduated in 1846 in the first class and became a lieutenant April 18, 1855; a lieutenant commander in 1862; a commander March 3, 1865; a commodore in April 1878; and a rear admiral in 1884. (He retired March 3, 1886, and died December 1, 1888.)

Representative who had a Medal of Honor and was graduated from the U.S. Naval Academy. *See* Representative (U.S. Congress): Representative who had a Medal of Honor and was graduated from the U.S. Naval Academy

Women students were admitted to the United States Naval Academy, Annapolis, Md., on July 6, 1976, when 80 women were admitted.

NAVAL "ACE." *See under* Aviation—Pilot

NAVAL AIR TRAINING SCHOOL. *See* Aviation —School

NAVAL ATTACHÉ. *See* Naval officer

NAVAL CHAPLAIN. *See* Naval officer

NAVAL CHAPLAINS' SCHOOL. *See* Chaplains' school

The First

NAVAL COALING STATION. *See under* Navy

NAVAL DENTAL OFFICE (Mobile)
Mobile dental office self-contained operating unit (U.S. Navy). *See* Navy: Mobile dental office self-contained operating unit (U.S. Navy)

NAVAL DENTAL SCHOOL. *See* Dental School

NAVAL DOCTOR. *See* Naval officer

NAVAL ENGAGEMENT IN THE CIVIL WAR. *See under* Civil War

NAVAL EXPEDITION (colonial). *See under* Navy

NAVAL HOSPITAL. *See* Hospital

NAVAL INSPECTOR (woman). *See* Naval officer: Woman naval inspector

NAVAL MAIL SERVICE. *See* Postal service: Navy mail service

NAVAL MILITIA. *See under* Navy

NAVAL NURSES' CORPS. *See under* Navy

NAVAL OFFICER
Admiral (four stars) who did not attend the U.S. Naval Academy was Ben Moreell, deputy coal mine administrator, who was nominated Vice Admiral on June 7, 1946, by President Harry S Truman and was confirmed on June 11, 1946. He retired September 18, 1946, from active duty, effective September 30, 1946.

Admiral in the Dental Corps. *See under* Dental Corps (U.S. Navy)

Admiral in uniform to ride in an airplane. *See under* Aviation—Passenger

Admiral killed in action in World War II was Rear Admiral Isaac Campbell Kidd, staff aide to Admiral Husband Edward Kimmel, commander in chief of the United States Fleet, killed December 7, 1941, when the U.S.S. *Arizona* blew up during the Japanese attack on Pearl Harbor, Hawaii.

Admiral to receive the Congressional Medal of Honor. *See* Medal: Admiral to receive the Congressional Medal of Honor

Admiral who was a black was Samuel Lee Gravely, Jr., whose date of rank was July 1, 1972.

Admiral who was Jewish was Rear Admiral Adolph Marix, who was advanced to the rank of rear admiral by President William Howard Taft on July 4, 1908. He entered the service as midshipman on September 26, 1864, served as master, lieutenant, lieutenant commander, and commander.

Admirals who were brothers were rear admirals Augustus Joseph Wellings, U.S. Naval Academy graduate No. 5370, who retired July 1, 1954; Timothy Francis Wellings, graduate No. 5851, who retired July 1, 1952; and Joseph Harold Wellings, graduate No. 7948, who retired August 1, 1963.

The First

Black captain in the U.S. Navy was Thomas David Parham, Jr., of Newport News, Va., a Presbyterian chaplain, whose rank was raised from commander to captain on February 1, 1966.

Black commissioned officer in the Naval Reserve was Bernard Whitfield Robinson, a medical student at Harvard University, Cambridge, Mass., who was commissioned ensign on June 18, 1942.

Black commissioned officer in the regular U.S. Navy was Ensign John W. Lee of Indianapolis, Ind., who was commissioned March 15, 1947, and assigned to the U.S.S. *Kearsarge.*

Black nurse in the Navy Reserve Nurse Corps was Phyllis Mae Daley, a registered nurse of New York City, who was sworn in March 8, 1945, as an ensign at the office of the Naval Officer Procurement, New York City.

Captain in the U.S. Navy who was a woman was Captain Sue Sophia Dauser, superintendent of the Nurse Corps, U.S.N., who received the rank of captain on February 26, 1944, and served until November 9, 1945. Previously she had held the relative rank of captain authorized by Public Law No. 828, the Pay Bill, effective December 22, 1942. She entered the service on September 15, 1917, when she was appointed a naval reserve nurse.

Captain in the U.S. Navy who was Jewish was Uriah Phillips Levy, whose rank of captain was effective March 29, 1844. He joined the service as a sailing master on October 21, 1812, became a lieutenant on March 5, 1817, and a commander on February 9, 1837. *(American Jewish Historical Society—Publications—1909)*

Chaplain to win a Congressional Medal of Honor was Lieutenant Commander Joseph Timothy O'Callahan, who received the award from President Harry S. Truman on January 23, 1946, at Washington, D.C., for his heroism on board the aircraft carrier *Franklin* when it was bombed off Kobe, Japan, in March 1945.

Commander in chief of the Continental Navy was Esek Hopkins, who served from December 22, 1775, to January 2, 1778. *(Edward Field—Esek Hopkins, Commander-in-Chief of the Continental Navy During the American Revolution)*

Commander of a combat ship who was a black was Lieutenant Commander Samuel Lee Gravely, Jr., of Richmond, Va., who on January 31, 1961, assumed command of the destroyer escort U.S.S. *Falgout* (150 crew, 13 officers), one of the vessels of Escort Squadron 5 on duty with the barrier Pacific force.

Electrician (woman) in the Navy was first class electrician Abby Putnam Morrison, who enlisted October 24, 1917, and was assigned to the Radio Bureau of Navigation. *(New York Times. 8:2. Oct. 27, 1917)*

The First

Engineer inspector (woman) was Jean Hales of Berkeley, Calif., appointed junior inspector August 24, 1942, by the 12th Naval District to test various metals to determine yield and tensile strength.

Judge advocate of the Navy was William Eaton Chandler of New Hampshire, who on March 6, 1865, was appointed by President Abraham Lincoln to be solicitor and naval judge advocate general under act of March 2, 1865 (13 Stat. L. 468). His salary was $3,500 a year. *(Leon Burr Richardson—William E. Chandler, Republican)*

Naval attaché was Lieutenant Commander French Ensor Chadwick. He was sent to London, England, November 15, 1882, and he remained there until April 3, 1889. *(French Ensor Chadwick —The American Navy)*

Naval chaplain was William Balch, a Congregationalist. He received his commission from President John Adams on October 30, 1799, and served until May 10, 1801.

Naval chaplain (black woman) was Lieutenant Junior Grade Vivian McFadden, Methodist, of John's Island, S.C., sworn in September 8, 1974, at the Naval Air Station, Atlanta, Ga., by Rear Admiral Francis Leonard Garrett, Chief of Chaplains.

Naval chaplain (Continental Navy) known to have served was the Reverend Benjamin Parks, a Congregationalist, appointed October 28, 1788, with the relative rank of lieutenant. Possibly others preceded him, but their identities are unknown.

Naval chaplain killed in action was Chaplain John L. Lenhart, who was commissioned chaplain on February 27, 1847. At that time chaplains did not hold naval rank and were known simply as chaplains. On March 8, 1862, the Confederate ironclad *Merrimac* encountered the Union frigate *Cumberland* off Hampton Roads, Va. The *Merrimac* crushed the *Cumberland* by driving her iron prow through the side of the *Cumberland,* at the same time pouring in a fire of shells. Chaplain Lenhart died with his sinking ship.

Naval chaplain to win the silver star in Vietnam was Lieutenant Richard M. Lyons, a Roman Catholic priest, who braved enemy fire to administer last rites to wounded marines during the battle for Hue, South Vietnam. The award for gallantry was presented April 18, 1968, by Brigadier General John W. Williams, commanding general Fleet Marine Force, Atlantic.

Naval chaplain who was Catholic was the Reverend Charles Henry Parks, who was commissioned chaplain, U.S. Navy, on April 30, 1888, with the relative rank of lieutenant. He was advanced to the rank of lieutenant commander on March 3, 1899, and resigned January 25, 1900. (Actual rank was not given chaplains until March 3, 1899.) He died in New York City on March 31, 1907.

The First

Naval chaplain who was Jewish was the Reverend David Goldberg of Corsicana, Texas, who was appointed chaplain, U.S. Navy, with the rank of lieutenant junior grade on October 30, 1917. He was the only Jewish chaplain who served in World War I. He was advanced to lieutenant commander on January 1, 1938, and retired March 1, 1941. *(Clifford Merrill Drury—U.S. Navy Chaplains 1778–1945)*

Naval chaplain (woman) was Lieutenant Florence Dianna Pohlman, of La Jolla, Calif., a Presbyterian, who was sworn in July 2, 1973, at Newport, R.I., and later assigned to the Naval Training Center, Orlando, Fla.

Naval doctor was Dr. Joseph Harrison, appointed in 1775 in Philadelphia, Pa., to serve on the *Alfred. (John Cropper Wise—Evolution of the Naval Medical Service and the Naval Medical School)*

Naval line officer (woman) assigned to sea duty (MSTS) was Lieutenant Charlene Ida Suneson, who was appointed July 7, 1961, and reported for duty December 8, 1961, on the Military Sea Transport Service (MSTS) ship U.S.S. *General W. A. Mann* (T-AP 12) at the Oakland Army Terminal, Oakland, Calif. She served until December 7, 1962, as assistant passenger officer. Two navy nurses and the wives of servicemen were also aboard. The MSTS is a passenger and freight service operated by the Navy for the three military services, but it is not a part of the Navy.

Naval medical officer to write a book was Edward Cutbush, whose *Observations on the Means of Preserving the Health of Soldiers and Sailors; and on the Duties of the Medical Department of the Army and Navy; with remarks on hospitals and their internal arrangement* was printed by Thomas Dobson, Philadelphia, Pa., in 1808. It contained 336 pages and a 14-page supplement by Dr. Benjamin Rush. *(Annals of Medical History. Vol. 5, No. 4)*

Naval nurses' corps (woman member) to receive the Distinguished Service Medal was Captain Sue Sophia Dauser, who received the decoration December 14, 1945, from Secretary of the Navy James Forrestal.

Naval officer commissioned was Captain Hopley Yeaton of New Hampshire appointed March 21, 1791, by George Washington to command "a cutter in the service of the United States of America." He was assigned to the *Scammel,* built at Portsmouth, N.H.

Naval officer condemned for mutiny was Midshipman Philip Spencer, son of the Secretary of War, who with Boatswain Samuel Cromwell and Seaman Elisha Small was hanged December 1, 1842, from the yardarm of the U.S.S. *Somers,* a brig of war, while at sea in the West Indian waters. They were convicted, at a court-martial held on shipboard, of conspiring to organize a mutiny,

The First

NAVAL OFFICER—*Continued*
murder the officers, and turn the ship into a pirate cruiser. The commander of the *Somers* was Alexander Slidell Mackenzie, who was exonerated at a court of inquiry and court-martial of charges. *(Case of the "Somers" Mutiny—Report at Court-martial of A. S. Mackenzie held at the Navy Yard, Brooklyn, N.Y.)*

Naval officer designated commander, Aircraft Battle Force, was Henry Varnum Butler, whose appointment was made March 5, 1935, effective April 1, 1935, with the rank of vice admiral.

Naval officer killed in the Spanish-American War. *See under* Spanish-American War

Naval officer to become a commodore was John Barry, senior officer in the navy, who was appointed in 1794 after the reorganization of the navy. *(Martin Ignatius Joseph Griffin—History of Commodore John Barry)*

Naval officer to become Admiral of the Navy was Admiral George Dewey, who served from March 3, 1899, until his death, January 16, 1917. The rank was conferred by act of Congress, passed March 2, 1899 (30 Stat. L. 995).

Naval officer to become an admiral was David Glasgow Farragut, who received his appointment on July 25, 1866. Previously by act of Congress, on July 16, 1862 (12 Stat. L. 583), Farragut had been given the rank of rear admiral, with rank comparable to major general in the Army, at a compensation of $5,000 a year at sea, $4,000 on shore duty and leave of absence, or $3,000 awaiting orders. On December 13, 1864, he had received the title of vice admiral. The office of vice admiral was authorized by act of December 21, 1864 (13 Stat. L. 420), an "act to establish the grade of Vice Admiral." The pay was $7,000 at sea, $6,000 on shore duty, and $5,000 when awaiting orders. On July 25, 1866 (14 Stat. L. 231), the Navy was authorized to have 10 rear admirals, 1 vice admiral, and 1 admiral. *(Joel Tyler Headley—Farragut and Our Naval Commanders)*

Naval officer to become an engineer in the U.S. Navy was Charles Haynes Haswell. He was commissioned February 19, 1836, by Secretary of the Navy Mahlon Dickerson, and appointed to design steam-power equipment. He was made chief engineer on July 12, 1836, and engineer-in-chief on October 3, 1844. *(American Society of Civil Engineers—Transactions, 1908. Vol. 61)*

Naval officer to serve as chairman of the Joint Chiefs of Staff was Admiral Arthur William Radford, who served from August 15, 1953, to August 15, 1957.

Naval officer (Union) killed in the Civil War. *See* Civil War: Naval officer (Union) killed

The First

Naval officers to wear the five-star insignia as Admirals of the Fleet were Ernest Joseph King, William Daniel Leahy, and Chester William Nimitz, whose appointments were ratified December 15, 1944, by the Senate. The grade of fleet admiral of the U.S. Navy was established by Public Law No. 482, approved by act of Congress, December 14, 1944.

Naval ship named for a sailor killed at Pearl Harbor. *See under* Ship

Naval surgeon of the U.S. Navy was Dr. George Balfour, who was ordered in 1801 to take charge of the first marine hospital established in Norfolk, Va. He entered the Army, April 11, 1792, and was transferred to the Navy, March 9, 1798. He resigned on April 12, 1804, to enter private practice. *(Richard Cranston Holcomb—A Century with the Norfolk Naval Hospital)*

Petty officer (woman) was Loretta Walsh, age 18, of Philadelphia, Pa., who was sworn in as chief yeoman on March 21, 1917, by Lieutenant Commander Payne at the United States Naval Home. She assumed office March 22, 1917, and was in charge of recruiting for the Naval Coast Defense Reserve. This rank is signified by a pair of crossed pens with 3 red chevrons and a spread eagle. *(New York Times. 2:2. Mar. 17, 1917)*

Pilot (American Navy) shot down and captured in North Vietnam. *See under* Vietnam War

Prisoner of war to head the Naval War College. *See under* War prisoner

Surgeon general of the Navy was Dr. William Maxwell Wood, appointed chief of Medical Bureau and Surgery, June 28, 1869. He served until October 25, 1871, although he had been placed on the retired list for age on May 27, 1871. The Naval Appropriations Act of March 3, 1871 (16 Stat. L. 532), provided that the chief of the bureau have the title Surgeon General *(Annals of Medical History. Vol. 6, No. 4)*

Woman dentist in the U.S. Navy. *See* Dentist: Woman dentist in the U.S. Navy

Woman doctor in the regular U.S. Navy was Dr. Frances Lois Willoughby of Pitman, N.J., appointed a lieutenant commander on October 15, 1948. During World War II, women were accepted in the Navy Medical Corps Reserve on a temporary basis.

Woman doctor in the WAVES (Women Accepted for Volunteer Emergency Service) was Dr. Cornelia Jane Gaskill, of Peekskill, New York, commissioned lieutenant junior grade on September 7, 1942, at Northampton, Mass., and enrolled in the indoctrination course on November 13, 1942, at the National Naval Medical Center, Bethesda, Md.

The First

Woman medical officer assigned to a naval vessel was Lieutenant Commander Bernice Rosenthal Walters, Medical Corps, U.S. Naval Reserve, of New York, who was assigned on March 8, 1950, to the Hospital Ship U.S.S. *Consolation*, reporting for duty on July 13, 1950. She entered the U.S. Naval Reserve on July 12, 1943, and served during World War II at the U.S. Naval Shipyards, Boston, Mass.; the U.S. Naval Air Station, Weymouth, Mass.; and the U.S. Naval Hospital, Bainbridge, Md.

Woman member of the Navy's Hurricane Hunters was Lieutenant Judith Ann ("Judy") Neuffer, who flew a 4-engine P-3 Orion into Carmen on September 1, 1974, encountering 120-knot winds. She flew into the western Caribbean—140 NM east of Belize and 115 NM north of the Honduras coast.

Woman naval inspector was Jean Hales of Berkeley, Calif., appointed August 24, 1942, by the Twelfth Naval District as junior inspector of engineering to test bars of metal to determine yield and tensile strength.

Woman naval officer commissioned in the U.S. Naval Reserve was Mildred Helen McAfee, who accepted an appointment as Lieutenant Commander on August 3, 1942, to serve as Director of the Women's Reserve, U.S. Naval Reserve, nicknamed WAVES (Women Accepted for Volunteer Emergency Service). The oath of office was administered by Secretary of the Navy Frank Knox; Admiral Ernest Joseph King and Rear Admiral Randall Jacobs, chief of the Bureau of Navy Personnel, attended. Miss McAfee, on November 13, 1943, became the first woman line officer to hold the rank of captain.

Woman naval officer to hold a major navy command was Captain Robin Lindsay Quigley, who assumed command on May 17, 1973, of the Navy Service School, San Diego, Calif., supervising 30,000 students.

Woman physician in the Medical Corps Reserve of the U.S. Navy was Dr. Hulda Thelander of San Francisco, Calif., who received a direct commission as a Lieutenant Commander MC-V (S) U.S.N.R. on April 19, 1944, in accordance with the existing laws. She was assigned to Headquarters, U.S. Marine Corps, Department of the Pacific, San Francisco, Calif.

Woman to preside as law officer of a general court-martial in the Navy was Lieutenant Commander Mary Lou McDowell of Annandale, Va., appointed February 11, 1957. She presided in March 1957.

Women sworn into the regular U.S. Navy took their oaths of office as administered by Rear Admiral George Lucius Russell on July 7, 1948, in Washington, D.C. They were Frances Teresa Devaney, Ruth Flora, Kay Louise Langdon, Wilma

The First

Juanita Marchal, Doris Roberta Robertson, and Edna Earle Young, all of whom were transferred from the Naval Reserve.

Women technicians in medicine assigned to the National Naval Medical Center, Bethesda, Md., were Lieutenant Kathryn Hyde, a medical artist of Los Angeles, Calif., and Lieutenant Dorothy Osborne of New York City, a medical technician. They reported for duty on November 13, 1942, after completing the 30-day course at the U.S. Naval Training School at Smith College, Northampton, Mass. (*New York Times. 9:5. Nov. 14, 1942*)

NAVAL OFFICERS' TRAINING SCHOOL
See also
Naval Academy
Naval War College

Dental school of the U.S. Navy. *See* Dental school: Dental school of the U.S. Navy

Naval officers' training school was established in Boston, Mass., December 10, 1815, at the Navy Yard, Charlestown. It was under the guidance of Commodore William Bainbridge, whose courage as a naval leader had been demonstrated in the war with Tripoli.

NAVAL PATROL BOMBER. *See under* Aviation—Airplane

NAVAL POST OFFICE. *See* Post office

NAVAL RADIO STATION. *See* Radio station

NAVAL SEAPLANE TENDER. *See* Ship

NAVAL SHIP. *See* Ship

NAVAL UNIFORM. *See under* Navy

NAVAL WAR COLLEGE
Black officers to attend the Naval War College, Newport, R.I., were Commander Samuel Lee Gravely, Jr., of Richmond, Va., who attended the School of Naval Warfare for senior officers, and Lieutenant Commander George Irwin Thompson of Los Angeles, Calif., who attended the School of Naval Command and Staff for mid-career officers at the Naval War College, Newport, R.I., from August 16, 1963, to June 17, 1964.

Naval War College was at Coaster's Harbor Island, Newport, R.I., and was established October 6, 1884, by General Order No. 325 of the Secretary of the Navy. Commander Stephen Bleecker Luce had been appointed superintendent on September 13, 1884. The college opened September 3, 1885, with a 1-month course for a class of eight. Naval officers were offered an 11-month course in military science, the art of naval warfare, and marine international law. On January 11, 1889, the college was consolidated with the Torpedo Station on Goat Island in Newport harbor. (*Albert Gleaves—Life and Letters of Rear Admiral Stephen B. Luce*)

The First

NAVAL WAR COLLEGE—*Continued*
Prisoner of war to head the Naval War College.
See under War prisoner

NAVEL ORANGES. *See* Oranges (seedless navel)

NAVIGATION ACT
Navigation Act affecting the American colonies was passed by the English Parliament in 1651, by which all merchandise for the English-American plantations were exempted from duty for three years on the condition that no colonial vessel be suffered to lade any goods of the growth of the plantations and carry them to a foreign port. Except for intercolonial trade, all goods were to be carried in English bottoms.

Navigation Act (U.S.) was approved July 20, 1789 (1 Stat. L. 27). It imposed a duty on the tonnage of vessels. *(Lloyd Milton Short—The Bureau of Navigation, Its History, Activities and Organization)*

NAVIGATION BUREAU (U.S.) was established under the Treasury Department by act of Congress, July 5, 1884 (23 Stat. L. 118), and permanently organized July 1, 1885. The Bureau was directed by the Deputy Commissioner of Navigation appointed by the President. *(Lloyd Milton Short—The Bureau of Navigation, Its History, Activities and Organization)*

NAVY
Air squadron of jets (U.S. Navy) was Fighter Squadron 17-A, which received its first jet airplane, a McDonnell FH-1 Phantom, at the Naval Air Station, Quonset Point, Rhode Island, on July 23, 1947. On May 5, 1948, at the close of three days of operations aboard the U.S.S. *Saipan,* the squadron became the first U.S. Navy jet squadron to qualify aboard a carrier.

All-nuclear task force voyage around the world without refueling or other logistic support was made by Task Force One consisting of the attack carrier U.S.S. *Enterprise,* the guided missile cruiser U.S.S. *Long Beach,* and the guided missile frigate U.S.S. *Bainbridge,* which left Norfolk, Va., on July 31, 1964, and returned October 3, 1964, completing "Operation Sea Orbit" a 30,000-knot trip that included 18 cities in 10 countries, going around the Cape of Good Hope and Cape Horn. The crew of 6,000 men was under the command of Rear Admiral Bernard Max Strean.

American sailor to lose his life in World War I. *See under* World War I

Armor plate contract (U.S. Navy). *See* Armor plate contract (U.S. Navy)

Atomic submarine division was Atomic Submarine Division 102, formed March 31, 1958, at New London, Conn. under command of Commander Robert Glennwood Black, who served from March 31 to July 1, 1958, when he was replaced by Captain Eugene Parks Wilkinson. The

The First

division consisted of the atomic submarines *Nautilus, Sea Wolf,* and *Skate,* and the conventional submarines *Hardhead, Bang,* and *Halfbreak.*

Bureau of Medicine and Surgery of the U.S. Navy was authorized by act of Congress, August 31, 1842 (5 Stat. L. 579). It was organized in 1842 by Dr. William Paul Crillon Barton, who served as Chief from September 2, 1842, to April 1, 1844. He was the first chief and the senior surgeon of the Navy at the time of his death. *(Military Surgeon. Vol. 46)*

Japanese homeland bombardment by the U.S. Navy. *See under* World War II

Large-scale assignment of women (other than nurses) to sea duty were 8 ensigns who reported for duty on November 1, 1978. They were Mary Pat Carroll of Roanoke, Va., and Jo Anne Carlton of Lynchburg, Va., assigned to the repair ship *Vulcan* at Norfolk, Va.; Linda M. Day of Gallipolis, Ohio, and Linda L. Crockett of Paterson, N.J., to the submarine tender *L.Y. Spear;* Elizabeth W. Bres of Alexandria, La., to the destroyer tender *Puget Sound;* Charlene Albright of Easton, Md., to the guided missile ship *Norton Sound* at Long Beach, Calif.; Roberta L. McIntyre of Charlotte, N.C., and Macushla M. McCormick of Selah, Wash.

Mobile dental office self-contained operating unit (U.S. Navy) was placed in operation February 18, 1945, by the 8th Naval District, U.S. Navy. Ten units and a prosthetic unit were built.

Naval coaling station on foreign soil was completed by the Navy in Baja California, Mexico, in April 1901.

Naval expedition (colonial) was undertaken in 1613 against a French settlement in Nova Scotia. It consisted of 11 vessels carrying a total of 14 light guns, commanded by Samuel Argall of Virginia. Argall captured Mount Desert, St. Croix, and Port Royal, Nova Scotia. *(Massachusetts Historical Society—Proceedings, November 1884)*

Naval expedition to the South Pole landed at 8:30 A.M. Greenwich time, October 31, 1956, in *Que Sera Sera,* a twin-engine Douglas R4D Skytrain. Rear Admiral George John Dufek, commander of the Naval Support Force, Antarctica, with 6 officers and the crew, made the flight.

Naval fleet was authorized on October 13, 1775, when the Continental Congress authorized two cruisers, one of 10 guns and another of 14 guns, and appointed a Marine Committee, consisting of John Adams, John Langdon, and Silas Deane, from its members to be in complete control of naval affairs. Although open hostilities began April 19, 1775, no consideration was given to protection by sea until October 5, 1775, when news was received that a British naval fleet would arrive. The

The First

Continental Navy was organized December 22, 1775, and consisted of two 24-gun frigates, the *Alfred* (Captain Dudley Saltonstall) and the *Columbus* (Captain Abraham Whipple) and two 14-gun brigs, the *Andrea Doria* (Captain Nicholas Biddle) and the *Cabot* (Captain John Burroughs Hopkins), and the schooners *Hornet* (10 guns), the *Wasp* (8 guns) and the *Fly* (8 guns). Esek Hopkins was commissioned commander of the fleet and received $125 a month. Sailors received $8 a month.

Naval legislation standardizing nomenclature for naval vessels was a congressional resolution passed March 3, 1819 (3 Stat. L. 538), a "resolution declaring the manner in which the vessels comprising the Navy of the United States shall be named." It provided that "the Secretary of the Navy shall name ships of the first class for states, of the second class for rivers, and of the third class for cities and towns."

Naval man to reenlist while under the North Pole was James Robert Sordelet, U.S.N., of Fort Wayne, Ind., electrician's mate first class on the submarine *Nautilus*, who reenlisted on August 3, 1958.

Naval militia (state) was the Massachusetts Naval Battalion, organized under Executive Order of March 18, 1890, carried into effect by General Order No. 6, A.G.O. Massachusetts of the same date, authorizing the formation of four companies to be lettered A, B, C, and D. The companies were formed March 25, 1890, with Thomas A. DeBlois, William M. Paul, William M. Wood and John W. Weeks, all of Boston, commanding companies A, B, C, and D, respectively. On May 7, 1890, John Codman Soley, a graduate of the United States Naval Academy, was commissioned Lieutenant Commander of the Naval Battalion.

Naval militia (state) to have a hydroplane was the Illinois Naval Reserve. Stewart MacDonald and commodore A. M. Andrews presented the *Alice*, a Curtiss flying boat, which had a 100-hp. engine and developed a speed of 70 m.p.h. It was christened May 22, 1915, by Mona Dunne, daughter of Governor Edward Fitzsimons Dunne of Illinois, at ceremonies in government hangars at the foot of Washington Street, Chicago Ill. *(Aerial Age Weekly—June 7, 1915)*

Naval nurses' corps was established May 13, 1908 (35 Stat. L. 146), in the Medical Department, U.S. Navy. Navy nurses received the same pay allowances, emoluments and privileges as the nurse corps (female) of the Army. The first superintendent was Esther Voorhees Hasson, who served from August 18, 1908, to January 16, 1911.

Naval protection was afforded by the Revenue Cutter Service, which was organized August 4, 1790 (1 Stat. L. 145), under an act of Congress, approved by President George Washington. It op-

The First

erated under the general direction of the Secretary of the Treasury. For 6 years and 11 months the revenue cutters formed the only armed force of the United States afloat. Commissions were granted March 21, 1791, to captains to command "a cutter in the Service of the United States of America" under the United States Revenue Cutter Service (now Coast Guard).

Naval Task Force assembled for foreign service was Task Force 19, consisting of 25 ships commanded by Rear Admiral David McDougal Le Breton; formed at Argentina, it sailed July 1, 1941. It included the battleships *Arkansas* and *New York*, the light cruisers *Brooklyn* and *Nashville*, plus destroyers.

Naval uniforms (standardized) were adopted by the Marine Committee on September 5, 1776. The uniform of captains in the Navy consisted of a coat of blue with red lapels, slashed cuffs, a stand-up collar, flat yellow buttons, blue breeches, and a red waistcoat with yellow lace. The sailors or mariners were to have green coats faced with white, round cuffs, slashed sleeves and pockets, with buttons around the cuff, a silver epaulet on the right shoulder, shirt collars turned back, buttons to match the facings, white waistcoats and breeches edged with green, black gaiters, and garters. The men were also to have green shirts, "if they can be procured."

Navy Day. *See under* Holiday

Navy Department (U.S.) was established by act of Congress approved April 30, 1798 (1 Stat. L. 553). The conduct of naval affairs was under the Secretary for the Department of War under act of Congress approved April 7, 1789. His salary was $3,000 a year, payable quarterly.

Navy man to reenlist while under water was Torpedoman's Mate First Class Billie L. Coffman, of Willimantic, Conn., one of the 10 divers in the U.S.N. *Sealab 2*, a 12 x 58 foot steel cylinder, 205 feet below the surface, 1,000 yards offshore, in the Pacific Ocean off La Jolla, Calif. He reenlisted August 31, 1965, and was sworn in by Captain George F. Bond, medical director of the project, and Captain Walter F. Mazzone.

Navy parachute school opened September 1, 1924, at the Naval Air Station, Lakehurst, N.J., to train personnel, and to care for, maintain, operate, and test parachutes.

Navy Secretary of Aviation was Edward Pearson Warner, sworn in July 12, 1926, as assistant secretary of the Navy in charge of aviation, to supervise naval aeronautics and the coordination of its activities with other governmental agencies. He served to March 15, 1929. The office was established by act of Congress of June 24, 1926 (44 Stat.L.767).

Navy yard acquired after the establishment of the Navy Department, April 30, 1798, was the

The First

NAVY—*Continued*
Portsmouth Navy Yard, N.H., which was purchased June 12, 1800, from William Dennet and his wife for $5,500. It embraced 58.18 acres and had previously been used in the building of men-of-war.

Podiatry Section of the Navy was established on November 3, 1953, under the Navy Medical Service Corps. The first podiatrist assigned was Ensign Richard Stuart Gilbert of New York City, who was assigned to the Naval Training Center, Bainbridge, Md., on June 3, 1954.

Prize money awarded by the U.S. Navy was granted to the U.S.S. *Delaware,* commanded by Captain Stephen Decatur, Sr., which captured the French schooner *Croyable* in June 1798 off the Delaware Capes during the undeclared naval war with France (1798–1801). By act of Congress, June 28, 1798 (1 Stat. L. 574), cases involving captured ships were tried in U.S. District Courts. The act provided that after condemnation the part accruing to the United States was to be paid into the public treasury, and the amount due the officers and crews to be distributed among them in the proportions which the President should direct. Prize money, however, had been awarded as early as the Revolution to men on the vessels of the Continental and state navies and privateers.

Secretary of the Navy was Benjamin Stoddert of Maryland, who was appointed by President John Adams, May 18, 1798. He was commissioned May 21, 1798, entered upon his duties June 18, 1798, and served until March 3, 1801. His salary was $3,000 a year. George Cabot of Massachusetts had been nominated on May 1, 1798, and commissioned May 3, 1798, but on May 11, 1798, had declined to serve. Appointments were made under the act of April 30, 1798 (1 Stat. L. 553), which established the Navy Department. *(Henry Cabot Lodge—Life and Letters of George Cabot)*

Shot fired by the American Navy in World War I. *See under* World War I

Task force to fight undersea craft was Alfa, which consisted of an aircraft carrier with group of antisubmarine aircraft, a helicopter squadron, destroyers, shore-based patrol planes, and submarines. The task force was created March 24, 1958, under the command of Rear Admiral John Smith Thach and placed in operation in April 1958.

Women (other than nurses) assigned to regular shipboard duty were Ensign Rosemary Elaine Nelson (assistant supply officer) and Lieutenant (Junior Grade) Ann Kerr (personnel officer) respectively assigned August 11, 1972, and October 25, 1972, to the hospital ship U.S.S. *Sanctuary.*

NAVY "ACE." *See under* Aviation—Pilot

NAVY CROSS. *See* Medal

NAVY DAY. *See* Holiday

The First

NAVY DENTAL CORPS. *See* Dental Corps (U.S. Navy)

NAVY DISTINGUISHED SERVICE MEDAL. *See* Medal

NAVY "E" AWARD
Army-Navy "E" awards were made to 20 war production plants, the first presentation ceremonies being held August 10, 1942. The award was granted to 4,283 concerns, approximately 5 percent of those engaged in war work. In July 1942, the Navy "E," the Army "A," and the Army-Navy Munitions Board "star" awards were all merged into the Army-Navy "E."

Navy "E" certificates of meritorious service were granted to 14 companies on July 25, 1941, by the Bureau of Ordnance, U.S. Navy.

Navy "E" certificates of meritorious service presented to an institution of higher learning was awarded by Lieutenant Holman Faust to Dr. Clarence Addison Dykstra, University of Wisconsin, Madison, Wis., on June 1, 1942, in recognition of the university's contribution of more men to naval aviation than any other similar institution.

NAVY EXPERT PISTOL SHOT MEDAL. *See* Medal

NAVY MAIL SERVICE. *See* Postal service

NAVY RESERVE NURSE CORPS. *See* Navy: Naval Nurses' Corps

NAVY SHIP. *See* Ship

NAVY TORPEDO STATION. *See* Torpedo: Torpedo manufacturing station

NAVY UNIT COMMENDATION DECORATION. *See* Medal

NAVY YARD. *See under* Navy

NEEDLE-TYPE DAM. *See* Dam

NEEDLES (machine-made) for sewing were manufactured by the Excelsior Needle Company of Wolcottville, Conn., which was organized March 2, 1866, with $20,000 capital. By means of the cold swaging process, needles of a uniform size and shape were made at a cost very much lower than that of the crude needles previously made. *(Samuel Orcutt—History of Torrington, Conn.)*

NEGRO. *See* Black

NEON-TUBE ADVERTISING SIGN. *See* Electric sign

NEOPRENE. *See* Rubber: Synthetic rubber (neoprene)

NEPTUNIUM. *See* Element: Element 93

NERVOUS DISEASES RESEARCH INSTITUTE. *See* Research institute: Institute for research in nervous diseases

The First

NETWORK TELEVISION DISTANCE DEMON-STRATION. *See* Television—Telecast: Television network demonstration (distant)

NEURASTHENIA BOOK. *See* Medical book

NEUROLOGICAL INSTITUTE. *See* Research institute: Institute for research in nervous diseases

NEUROLOGY TEXTBOOK. *See* Medical book

NEUTRALITY PROCLAMATION was made by President George Washington on April 22, 1793: "Whereas it appears that a state of war exists between Austria, Prussia, Sardinia, Great Britain and the United Netherlands on the one part and France on the other" citizens of the United States will be "liable to punishment or forfeiture under the law of nations by committing, aiding or abetting hostilities against any of the said powers."

NEUTRALITY REGULATION, governing the actions of citizens, was passed by act of Congress, June 5, 1794 (1 Stat. L. 381). The act provided that any citizen who "accepts and exercises a commission to serve a foreign prince, state, colony, district or people, with whom the United States are at peace shall be fined not more than $2,000 and imprisoned not more than three years." The first conviction was that of Isaac Williams of Norwich, Conn., who accepted a commission in a French armed vessel and served against Great Britain. He was tried in September 1799 in the Circuit Court of the United States for the Connecticut District, at Hartford, Conn., found guilty under two counts, and sentenced to a fine of $1,000 and imprisonment for four months, on each charge. *(Francis Wharton—State Trials of the United States)*

NEW CHURCH TEMPLE. *See* Swedenborgian or New Church Temple

NEW YORK STOCK EXCHANGE. *See under* Brokerage

NEWS AGENCY
Financial news agency was the Kiernan Financial News Agency, established in 1869 by John James Kiernan at 21 Wall Street, New York City. In 1882, the service was extended to include results of athletic contests, arrivals of steamships, commodity quotations abroad, etc.

News agency for gathering news was established in Boston, Mass., about 1811. Local papers were issued weekly and the current news was discussed at the coffeehouses, the principal one of which was Gilbert's Coffee House and Marine Diary. In 1814 Samuel Topliff became the owner of this establishment, the name of which he changed to the Merchant's Reading Room. The local newspapers published news "from Mr. Topliff's correspondent." Topliff kept a record of the news for his own patrons and supplied the papers with news articles which he collected from his correspondents in foreign countries. *(Ethel Stanwood*

The First

Bolton—"Memoir of Samuel Topliff" in Topliff's Travels)

Teletypesetter circuit operated by a news agency. *See under* Teletypesetter

NEWS CORRESPONDENT
Black news correspondent was Joel Augustus Rogers, who was sent to Addis Ababa, Ethiopia, by the Pittsburgh, Pa., *Courier,* in October 1935. He returned April 21, 1936.

Black news correspondent accredited to the White House was Harry McAlpin, representing the Atlanta, Ga., *Daily World* and the press service of the Negro Newspaper Publishers Association. He attended his first White House press conference February 8, 1944.

Black news correspondent admitted to the House of Representatives and Senate press gallery was Percival L. Prattis, representative of *Our World,* New York City, who was accredited on February 3, 1947.

News reporter tried as a spy was Thomas Wallace Knox, staff war correspondent of the New York *Herald,* tried February 5, 1863, at Young's Point, La., before a military court (a brigadier general, four colonels, and a major). He was charged with giving information to the enemy, being a spy, and with disobedience of orders. He was found guilty on the first two charges and not guilty on the third, in the 14-day trial, and was banished from General Grant's and General Sherman's theatre of war. The sentence was revoked by President Abraham Lincoln.

Washington correspondent of importance was James Gordon Bennett (the elder), whose articles first appeared January 2, 1828, in the New York *Enquirer,* later the *Courier and Enquirer. (Oliver Carlson—The Man Who Made News)*

White House reporter was William W. (Bill) Price, employed by the Washington, D.C., *Star* from April 24, 1897, to February 17, 1917. Starting with President Theodore Roosevelt's administration (1901–1909), he interviewed celebrities at the Executive Mansion, instead of at Capitol Hill.

Woman news correspondent accredited to the White House was Mrs. Emily Edson Briggs, correspondent for the Philadelphia, Pa., *Press,* who used the pseudonym "Olivia" for her "Olivia Letters," published January 1866 to January 7, 1882, during the administration of Presidents Johnson, Grant, Hayes, and Garfield. *(Emily Edson Briggs—The Olivia Letters)*

Woman news reporter at a political convention was Mary Ashton Rice Livermore, one of the editors of the *New Covenant,* who covered the Republican National Convention, May 12–18, 1860, at the Chicago Wigwam, Chicago, Ill., which nominated Abraham Lincoln. *(Edith Horton—A Group of Famous Women)*

The First

NEWS DISPATCH BY CABLE. *See under* Cable (telegraph)

NEWS DISPATCH BY TELEGRAPH. *See under* Telegram

NEWS DISPATCH BY TELEPHONE. *See under* Telephone

NEWS PHOTOGRAPH. *See* Photograph

NEWSBOY was Barney Flaherty, a ten-year-old who answered the advertisement, "To the Unemployed—A number of steady men can find employment by vending this paper. A liberal discount is allowed to those who buy to sell again," inserted in the New York *Sun*, New York City, on September 4, 1833, by Benjamin Day, the publisher.

NEWSPAPER

Abolition newspaper was the *Philanthropist*, published and edited by Charles Osborn, which appeared in Mount Pleasant, Ohio, on August 29, 1817. It published "An Appeal to Philanthropists" by Benjamin Lundy, which is said by some to be the most powerful abolition appeal ever made. *(Ohio State Archaeological and Historical Society. Publications, Vol. 31)*

American Indian newspaper was the *Cherokee Phoenix*, a weekly newspaper in English and Cherokee published from February 21, 1828, to October 1835 in New Echota, Ga. (the capital of the Cherokee nation). The Cherokee alphabet was invented by Sequoyah, son of Mastahangan. The paper was edited by Elias Boudinot, a Cherokee who was educated at the foreign mission school in Cornwall, Conn., at the instance of the philanthropist whose name he was allowed to adopt. *(Frederick Webb Hodge—Handbook of American Indians)*

Arabic daily newspaper in the United States was *Al-Hoda*, founded February 22, 1898, in Philadelphia, Pa., as a weekly by Naoum Anthony Mokarzel. On August 25, 1902, it started publication as a daily in New York City. Mokarzel was editor in chief and owner until his death in 1932.

Black newspaper edited by blacks for blacks was *Freedom's Journal*, a four-page weekly published in New York City from March 16, 1827, to March 28, 1829, and edited by John Brown Russworm and Samuel E. Cornish. *(Frederick German Detweiler—The Negro Press in the United States)*

Chinese daily newspaper was the *Chung Sai Yat Po (The Chinese Western Daily Paper)* of San Francisco, Calif., the first issue of which appeared February 16, 1900. It was 15 by 22 inches and consisted of four pages. The founder of the paper was Ng Poon Chew, Litt.D., who was the president and managing editor until his death, March 13, 1931.

The First

College daily was the *Yale News*, which was published in New Haven, Conn., on January 28, 1878. In that issue it was stated that the paper would be published daily during the college term.

Colored comic section. *See* Newspaper Sunday comic section, below

Composograph photograph in a newspaper was published November 25, 1925, in the *Evening Graphic*, New York City. It purported to depict a scene in the private chambers of Justice Morschauser at White Plains, N.Y., showing Alice Jones and her husband, Leonard Kip Rhinelander. A model was used and the photograph was pasted in true perspective to form a composite layout.

Constitution of the United States first published in a newspaper. *See* Constitution of the United States: Constitution of the United States was first published in a newspaper

Czech-language newspaper was the *Slovan Amerikansky*, a small folio weekly sheet edited by Frank Korizek and first issued January 1, 1860, in Racine, Wis. *(Fanny S. Stone—Racine, Belle City of the Lakes)*

Daily newspaper was the *Pennsylvania Packet and Daily Advertiser*, published by David C. Claypoole and John Dunlap in Philadelphia, Pa., which appeared September 21, 1784, as a daily. It sold for fourpence a copy. Previously, it had been the *Pennsylvania Packet and General Advertiser*, founded in 1771 as a weekly. The claim of being the first daily newspaper is also made for the *Pennsylvania Evening Post and Daily Advertiser*, whose title was changed in 1783 from the *Pennsylvania Evening Post and Public Advertiser*. It originally appeared on Tuesday, Thursday, and Saturday as a triweekly from June 24, 1775, until January 7, 1779, when it became a semiweekly. Benjamin Towne was editor and publisher.

Declaration of Independence first published in a newspaper. *See under* Declaration of Independence

Democratic newspaper using the word "Democratic" in its title was the Philadelphia, Pa., *Democratic Press*, published three times a week from March 27, 1807 until June 29, 1807, when it appeared as a daily, *The Democratic Press for the Country*. The editor was John Binns. *(Pennsylvania Historical Commission—A Checklist of Pennsylvania Newspapers)*

Editorial award of a Pulitzer Prize in journalism and letters was a $500 prize awarded on June 4, 1917, to the New York *Tribune* for a May 7, 1916, editorial by Frank Herbert Simonds, which was published on the first anniversary of the sinking of the *Lusitania*.

European edition of an American newspaper was the Paris edition of the New York *Herald*, published October 4, 1887. It consisted of four six-

The First

column pages, the last page being devoted to advertisements. *(Al Laney—Paris Herald, The Incredible Newspaper)*

French daily newspaper was the *Courrier Français* of Philadelphia, Pa., established April 15, 1794. It became a triweekly August 24, 1795, but was restored to a daily October 26, 1795. It was discontinued July 3, 1798.

French daily newspaper (successful) was the *Courrier des États Unis,* which appeared June 10, 1851, in New York City, with Paul Arpin as editor. It was originally started as a weekly by E. William Hoskin, the founder and first editor, and the first issue appeared March 1, 1828.

French newspaper was the *Courier de l'Amérique* of Philadelphia, published from July 27, 1784, to October 26, 1784.

German daily newspaper was the *New Yorker Staats-Zeitung* published in New York City on January 26, 1850. It had originally been a weekly paper, the first issue of which appeared December 24, 1834. The first editor was Gustav Adolf Neumann.

German newspaper was published on May 6, 1732 by Benjamin Franklin in Philadelphia, Pa., and was entitled *Philadelphische Zeitung.* It was a small sheet printed in German, four pages, 6½ by 9 inches, text in double columns and in Roman type. He intended to issue the paper weekly when 300 subscribers were assured. The second issue appeared on Saturday, June 24, 1732. Christopher Sauer's German newspaper *Der Hoch-Deutsch Pennsylvanische Geschichts-Schreiber, oder Sammlung wichtiger Nachrichten aus dem Natur-und-Kirchen-Reich,* "The High German Pennsylvania Recorder of Events or Collection of Important News from the Kingdom of Nature and of the Church," which is generally credited as the first newspaper, was first published on August 20, 1739. *(Pennsylvania Magazine of History and Biography. April 1902. "The First German Newspaper in America")*

Greek newspaper was the *Atlantis,* issued March 3, 1894, from 2 Stone Street, New York City as a four-page weekly of tabloid size, and afterwards two and three times a week. On January 3, 1905, it became a full-sized four-page daily. It was the first Greek publication in America and the first publication in the world to use typesetting machinery for the Greek alphabet. Its founder and first editor was Solon John Vlasto.

Hebrew newspaper was the *Ha-Zofeh ba-Arez ha-Hadashah* published in New York City from 1871 to 1876.

Hungarian daily newspaper was the *Amerikai Magyar Népszava,* published October 18, 1904, in New York City. Its founder and editor in chief was Geza David Berko. It was originally established in March 1899 as a weekly, and then was issued

The First

twice a week until October 18, 1904, when it became a daily.

Illustrated daily newspaper was the New York *Daily Graphic,* an illustrated evening newspaper that sold for 5 cents a copy. It was issued March 4, 1873, from 41 Park Place, New York City, and consisted of 8 pages printed by chromolithography using zinc plates.

Illustrated tabloid was the *Illustrated Daily News* of New York City, which appeared on June 26, 1919. It was published by Robert Rutherford McCormick and Joseph Medill Patterson. *(Willard Grosvenor Bleyer—History of American Journalism)*

Index. *See* Newspaper index separately published

Insurance service offered by a newspaper. *See under* Insurance

Italian newspaper was *Il Progresso Italo-Americano,* issued in New York City in September 1880. The first owner and editor was Charles Barsotti.

Jointly published newspaper was issued September 1923 during the newspaper strike and bore on its masthead the names: New York *American,* New York *Herald, The Journal of Commerce, The Daily News, The Morning Telegraph,* The New York *Times,* The New York *Tribune,* The *World,* The New York *Staats Zeitung, Il Progresso Italo,* and the *Americand.*

Labor newspaper. *See* Labor paper

Large-type weekly for persons with impaired vision was the *New York Times Large Type Weekly,* consisting of 28 pages, first published March 6, 1967. It was printed in New York City in 18-point type and was priced at $29 a year.

Line drawing of a current subject appeared in the New York *Sun,* New York City, on January 15, 1840, which issued a 4-page supplement with a drawing under the 5-column heading "Steamboat Lexington Burnt!! One Hundred and Fifty Lives Lost."

Livestock market paper. *See* Livestock market paper

Mimeographed daily newspaper was the *Kellogg Daily Reminder,* published July 25, 1923, by Eaton's Letter Shop, Kellogg, Idaho. The founder and first editor was Marson M. Eaton, Jr. The first issue was only one sheet printed on both sides.

Newspaper was a broadside. One of the earliest of the broadsides and in some ways the most important was *The Present State of the New English Affairs.* It was published "to prevent false reports" in 1689 by Samuel Green in Cambridge, Mass., and consisted of a single sheet printed in two columns, newspaper style, folio size, 8 by

The First

NEWSPAPER—*Continued*

14½ inches. *(Isaiah Thomas—History of Printing in America)*

Newspaper advertisement. *See* Advertisement: Advertisement

Newspaper advertisement printed on aluminum foil appeared in the *Sentinel,* Milwaukee, Wis., on March 18, 1958. It was a lamination of Reynolds aluminum foil on one side and paper on the other. The foil side was printed in seven colors at the gravure plant of the Reynolds Metal Company in St. Louis, Mo., while the paper side was printed by the *Sentinel* in one color and black.

Newspaper association was the American Newspaper Publishers Association, organized November 17, 1886, in Detroit, Mich. The call was made by William Henry Brearley of the Detroit *News.* The first convention was held February 16-17, 1887, in Rochester, N.Y., and was attended by 51 delegates.

Newspaper cartoon. *See under* Cartoon

Newspaper color-page was in the New York *Recorder,* whose issue of Sunday, April 2, 1893, carried a full-page advertisement of R.H. Macy, 14th Street and 6th Avenue, New York City, on page 13, and showed a large star printed in red.

Newspaper colored supplement was issued by the New York City *World* Sunday, November 19, 1893, and consisted of a four-page section, the outside pages of which were printed in five colors. Two half-page drawings in color featured "A Scene in Atlantic Gardens, Saturday Night," and "The Cathedral at Eleven O'Clock Mass." The inside pages were printed in black.

Newspaper daily railroad delivery service was instituted by the *Morning News* of Dallas, Tex., on October 1, 1885, when a special train was leased on the Texas and Pacific Railway to carry newspapers from Dallas to Fort Worth, Texas.

Newspaper delivery train was operated by the International Great Northern Railroad over the Galveston, Houston and Henderson Railroad, in 1883 to deliver the Galveston *News* to subscribers located between Galveston and Houston, Tex. The *News* paid $500 a month for the exclusive lease of the train.

Newspaper editorial apology appeared in the *American Weekly Mercury* of April 20, 1721. It stated: "N.B. In our last week's *Mercury* [April 13] No. 70, there is an account inserted from a private Letter sent to Boston, dated the 20th of September last, That the Government of Pennsilvania is Surrendered to the Crown, etc. These are to give Notice that we have now Letters from London, of a later Date, by which we find that the said Report concerning the Province of Pennsilvania is false and groundless and therefore was both by them

The First

and us too rashly inserted." This newspaper was published in Philadelphia, Pa.

Newspaper page set by linotype was the New York *Daily Tribune,* whose editorial page was set by linotype on Saturday, July 3, 1886.

Newspaper plant to install electricity was the New York *Times,* New York City, which turned on the current on September 4, 1882. The current was supplied by the Edison Electric Illuminating Company's central station, 257 Pearl Street, New York City. The editorial room had 27 electric lights, the counting room 25. The composing rooms and the press room were equipped later.

Newspaper printed atop a mountain was *Among The Clouds,* a daily published by Henry M. Burt during the summer at the old Summit House, Mount Washington, N.H. The first issue was that of July 20, 1877. There were 8 pages, approximately 9½ by 12¾ inches. Single copies were 10 cents; subscription for the season, $2.50.

Newspaper printed on a train was the *Weekly Herald,* a single sheet printed on both sides, approximately 7 by 8 inches. It was issued by Thomas Alva Edison and distributed on the train between Port Huron and Detroit, Mich. The first known issue was dated Port Huron, Mich., February 3, 1862.

Newspaper printed on bagasse newsprint (waste fiber left after grinding sugar cane) was the *Daily World* of Opelousas, La., printed February 11, 1954. Several test rolls were printed previously.

Newspaper printed on pine-pulp paper was the *Soperton News,* Soperton, Ga., of March 31, 1933, a four-page, six-column newspaper. The pines were grown in Treutlen County, Ga., and the paper was obtained from the Charles Holmes Herty-Savannah Pulp and Paper Laboratory, now the Herty Foundation Laboratory.

Newspaper printed on pine-pulp paper in color was the *News* of Dallas, Tex., a daily, which printed a pine-paper edition March 31, 1937.

Newspaper printed on wood-pulp paper was the Boston *Morning Journal* of Boston, Mass., published January 15, 1863. It was a four-page, eight-column newspaper and sold for three cents a copy.

Newspaper published at sea was the illustrated *Atlantic Telegraph,* printed on board the cable-laying *Great Eastern,* captained by James Anderson. It sold for five shillings for the series. Issues were published Saturday, July 29, 1865, August 5, 1865, and August 12, 1865. *(Isabella Field Judson—Cyrus W. Field—His Life and Work)*

Newspaper published at sea (daily) to carry world news was the *Cunard Daily Bulletin,* inaugurated by Guglielmo Marconi in October 1902 on the S.S. *Campania* and the S.S. *Lucania,* at

The First

that time "the crack liners of the fleet." The news was obtained from the wireless stations at Poldhu, Cornwall, England, and Glace Bay, Canada.

Newspaper published at sea (radio news service) was the *Transatlantic Times,* a four-page newspaper, which was issued on November 15, 1899, on board the American liner *St. Paul,* by Guglielmo Marconi and two engineers. It sold for $1 a copy, and the proceeds were donated to the Seaman's Fund. The news was obtained by wireless from the Needles Station, Isle of Wight.

Newspaper published by soldiers in the field was the *United States American Volunteer,* published May 21, 1861, at De Soto, Mo., by members of Company A, Fifth Regiment, Missouri Volunteers, commanded by Captain Nelson Cole. The issue consisted of a single page, the reverse being the first page of the abandoned *Jefferson County Herald.*

Newspaper published on the Pacific Coast was the *Oregon Spectator,* a semimonthly issued in Oregon City, Oreg., February 5, 1846. Its slogan was "Westward the star of empire takes its way." The newspaper was published by the Oregon Printing Association and was nonpolitical. The first editor was Colonel William G. T'Vault. The first California newspaper was the *Californian,* published August 15, 1846, in Monterey, Calif., by Robert Semple and the Reverend Walter Colton. *(John B. Horner—Oregon History and Early Literature)*

Newspaper published south of the Potomac River was the *Virginia Gazette,* containing "the freshest advices both Foreign and Domestick." It was established by William Parks and began its regular publication in Williamsburg, Va., August 5, 1736. It was a single sheet folded so as to have four pages. The subscription price was fifteen shillings a year.

Newspaper published west of the Alleghenies was the *Pittsburgh Gazette,* which was first issued on July 29, 1786. It was founded by John Scull and Joseph Hall and was printed in a log house on the Monongahela River, Pittsburgh, Pa. *(Pittsburgh and the Pittsburgh Spirit—Pittsburgh Chamber of Commerce)*

Newspaper publisher was Benjamin Harris, "the father of American newspapers." His paper, *Publick Occurrences, Both Foreign and Domestic,* issued from the London Coffee House, Boston, Mass., was printed by R. Pierce, on September 25, 1690. It was promptly suppressed because of certain "reflexions" distasteful to Governor Simon Bradstreet of Massachusetts. Harris had intended to issue it monthly "or if any Glut of Occurrances happen, oftener," but only the one issue appeared. It was a one-sheet paper folded to present four pages, containing news in double columns. The last page was blank. There were no advertise-

The First

ments. *(George Emery Littlefield—Early Massachusetts Press)*

Newspaper reproduced commercially and regularly by radio facsimile was the San Francisco edition of *The Wall Street Journal,* which had normally been prepared by conventional methods. Experimental editions, not distributed to the public, first appeared on April 10, 1962. Regular daily operations began on May 28, 1962. Page proofs were telecast to Riverside, Calif., by coaxial cable through microwave circuits where they were photographed preparatory to etching on zinc plates.

Newspaper room (library). *See* Library: Library newspaper room

Newspaper rotogravure sections were simultaneously instituted by seven newspapers on March 29, 1914, when an eight-page supplement showing 13 masterpieces of the Altman Collection in the Metropolitan Museum of Art, New York City, was included with the New York *Times,* the Boston *Sun-Herald,* the Philadelphia *Public Ledger,* the Chicago *Tribune,* the Cleveland *Plain Dealer,* the St. Louis *Post-Dispatch,* and the Kansas City *Star.*

Newspaper serial story in an American newspaper appeared in Samuel Keimer's *Pennsylvania Gazette* in Philadelphia in 1729. It was entitled "Religious Courtship" and was written by Daniel Defoe, author of *Robinson Crusoe.* It was reprinted from his book of the same title published in 1722 in London.

Newspaper (successful) was the Boston *News-Letter,* the first issue of which was dated April 17-24, 1704. The editor was John Campbell, a New England postmaster, who earned the distinction of being America's first vendor of news. It was printed by Bartholomew Green in a back room of his home. The page size was 7½ by 12½ inches. The text was set in small pica type. The paper was without competition for 15 years and reached a circulation of 300 copies.

Newspaper Sunday comic section was published by the New York *World* in 1893. The drawings were made by Richard Felton Outcault and depicted a humorous set of characters under the title of "Hogan's Alley." On November 18, 1894, the newspaper published the first of his six-box cartoon series "The Origin of a New Species," and later "The Yellow Kid." This was the first successful colored section.

Newspaper to appear on Sunday was the Sunday *Monitor,* Baltimore, Md., published by Philip Edwards, which appeared December 18, 1796. It consisted of four pages, 10¼ by 17 inches.

Newspaper to be microfilmed. *See* Check photographing device

The First

NEWSPAPER—*Continued*

Newspaper to insert an aluminum foil sheet to be used as a household wrapping was the *Sentinel*, Milwaukee, Wis., whose April 2, 1957, issue contained an insert featuring an advertisement of the Aluminum Corporation of America.

Newspaper to microfilm its current issues. *See under* Microfilm

Newspaper to microfilm its past issues. *See under* Microfilm

Newspaper to operate a radio station was the *News* of Detroit, Mich., whose station WWJ, Detroit, (as 8 MK) began operating on August 20, 1920.

Newspaper to use an airplane. *See* Aviation—Airplane: Airplane used by a newspaper

Newspaper 12-page advertising supplement featured "The Christmas Store of A Million Gifts," Gimbel Bros., Broadway and 33rd Street, New York City, issued as Section VI of the New York *Times* of December 7, 1913.

Newspaper whose input was derived from a communications satellite was the *Wall Street Journal*, set in type at Chicopee, Mass., and sent to Orlando, Fla., via the Westar communications satellite at 3½ minutes per page. Dedication ceremonies for the new system were held November 20, 1978.

Newspaper with a full page of woodcut engravings was the *Weekly Herald*, New York City, of Saturday June 28, 1845, which printed 6 woodcuts depicting the grand funeral procession of Andrew Jackson.

Newspaper with an aviation section was the Philadelphia, Pa. *Inquirer*, whose issue of June 7, 1908, devoted 5 columns on page 2A to "News from the Aeronautic Sphere." The heading was later changed to "In Aeronautic Sphere."

Newspaper with an illustrated color-page was the New York *World* of Sunday, May 21, 1893. One large sheet, printed in color and folded once, made up 4 pages. Page 29 showed a Walt McDougall cartoon in color, "Broadway Cable Car Possibilities." Pages 30 and 31 were printed in black. Page 32 was a full-page color reproduction of a painting of the Spanish ship *The Santa Maria*.

Newspaper with perfumed advertising page was issued March 25, 1937, by the *Daily News*, Washington, D.C. It contained a page advertisement of the Peoples Drug Stores featuring flowers.

Newspaper wrappers. *See under* Postal service

Norwegian-American newspaper was *Nordlyset* ("The Northern Light"), first published July 29, 1847, in Muskego, Wis. James De Noon Reymert was the first editor.

The First

Offset-printed daily newspaper that was successful was the daily *World* of Opelousas, La., which began operations on December 24, 1939. It was printed on a sheet-fed offset press. John Richmond Thistlewaite was editor and publisher.

Penny daily newspaper was *The Cent*, which was published in Philadelphia, Pa., in 1830 by Dr. Christopher Columbus Conwell, but the first successful penny paper was the New York *Sun*, published by Benjamin Henry Day, which appeared on September 3, 1833. *(George Henry Payne—History of Journalism in the United States)*

Periodical on microfilm. *See* Microfilm: Magazine on microfilm offered to subscribers

Political newspaper of national importance was the *Gazette of the United States*, the political organ of Alexander Hamilton, edited by John Fenno. The first issue appeared in New York City, April 15, 1789. When the government moved its headquarters to Philadelphia, the *Gazette* followed. The first issue printed in Philadelphia was that of April 14, 1790. The *New York Weekly Journal* was established November 5, 1733, by John Peter Zenger as a political organ to expose Governor Cosby. Zenger was arrested and imprisoned November 17, 1734, defended by Andrew Hamilton, a Philadelphia lawyer, and acquitted. His newspaper is often termed the first political paper. *(Merritt Way Haynes—Student's History of Printing)*

Pulitzer Prize award to a newspaper was presented June 5, 1918, to the New York *Times* at the graduation ceremony at Columbia University, New York City.

Radio facsimile newspaper was transmitted by KSTP, St. Paul, Minn., on December 17, 1937. It consisted of a roll of sensitized paper nearly five inches wide, with perforations at the sides, which issued from a receiving set.

Radio facsimile newspaper (daily) was transmitted December 7, 1938, by the *Post-Dispatch*, St. Louis, Mo., over Station W9XZY on an ultra-high frequency. Nine pages, each 8½ inches long, four columns to a page, printed in seven-point type, issued from a receiving set. About 15 minutes was required to transmit each page.

Religious weekly newspaper. *See under* Religious publication

Single copy delivered by a vending machine. *See* Vending Machine: Newspaper vending machine to deliver a single copy

Spanish newspaper was *El Redactor*, published July 1, 1827, in New York City. The first editor was Juan José de Lerena.

Three-dimensional newspaper advertisement. *See under* Advertisement

The First

Trademark controversy involving a newspaper. *See under* Trademark lawsuit

Transoceanic newspaper was the *Daily Mail,* a weekly digest of the London, England, *Daily Mail,* dated January 5, 1944. It was made up and edited in London, microfilmed, and flown to New York City, where it was enlarged and printed. It contained 12 pages, 9 by 12 inches, four columns wide.

Ukrainian daily newspaper was the *Ukrainian Daily News,* established January 31, 1920, in New York City. The first editor was M. Tkach.

Woman newspaper editor. *See under* Woman

Yiddish daily newspaper was the *Yiddishes-Tageblatt* or *Jewish Daily News,* which was founded in New York City in 1885 by Kasriel Hersch Sarasohn.

NEWSPAPER AUDIT

Newspaper circulation audit was made by a group of advertisers who organized the Association of American Advertisers to verify circulation figures. On August 21, 1914, the Audit Bureau of Circulations was formed in Chicago, Ill., with headquarters in that city as a cooperative, non-profit-making organization. Membership was composed of advertisers, advertising agencies, and publishers. Of the 25 directors, 4 were from daily newspapers, 2 from magazines, 2 from business papers, 2 from farm papers, 2 from advertising agencies, and 13 from among advertisers.

NEWSPAPER INDEX separately published was *The Index to the New York Times for 1865,* published in 1866 by Henry J. Raymond & Company, New York City. It contained 182 pages. Earlier indexes had been printed primarily for staff use.

NEWSPAPER PREMIUM

Newspaper premiums were offered by the New York *Recorder,* New York City, whose issue of March 25, 1893, printed the first of a series of coupons offering 17 by 25 inch color reproductions of celebrated paintings. Ten different subjects were offered, any one of which could be had for 20 coupons. Coupons and bonus prizes were also offered for ad insertions: a $10 goldpiece, 5 silver watches, and 10 plush ottomans. Similar coupons were also inserted in plug-cut tobacco packages by tobacco vendors.

NEWSPAPER PRINTING PRESS. *See* Printing press: High-speed newspaper printing and folding machine

NEWSPAPER REPORTER

See also News correspondent

Newspaper reporter to become a U.S. senator was [Arthur Edson] Blair Moody, Democrat, who served the Washington Bureau of the Detroit *News* for 18 years (1933–1951). He was appointed on April 23, 1951, by Governor Gerhard Mennen Williams of Michigan and was sworn in on April

The First

25, 1951, on which date Vice President Alben William Barkley called upon him to preside over the U.S. Senate.

Newspaper reporter to receive a Pulitzer Prize for newspaper reporting was Herbert Bayard Swope of the New York *World* for his stories on the internal situation in the German Empire. The award was announced by Columbia University, New York City, on June 4, 1917.

NEWSPAPER SYNDICATE

Newspaper syndicate to supply articles, stories, etc., was started on November 8, 1884, but was postponed until November 15, 1884, by Samuel Sidney McClure of New York City, who organized the McClure Syndicate. Because the syndicate offered larger payment than individual newspapers, a better class of writers endeavored to write for the daily press, their articles being syndicated throughout the country. *(Samuel Sidney McClure —My Autobiography)*

Press syndicate facsimile transmission. *See under* Radio facsimile transmission

Syndication of newspaper material was attempted by Moses Yale Beach of New York City, who printed President John Tyler's message, delivered December 7, 1841, to the second session of the 27th Congress. Sales were made to the Albany, N.Y., *Advertiser;* the Troy, N.Y., *Whig;* the Salem, Mass., *Gazette;* the Boston, Mass., *Times;* etc. Each newspaper printed its own name in the blank space provided for that purpose. *(Alexander Gurdon Abell—Life of John Tyler)*

NEWSREEL. *See under* Motion picture

NEWSREEL THEATER. *See* Theater

NIAGARA FALLS

Person to cross Niagara Falls on a tightrope was Jean Francois Gravelet, a Frenchman better known by his professional name, Émile Blondin, whose first exhibition took place on June 30, 1859, before a crowd of 5,000 people. Wearing pink tights and a spangled tunic of yellow silk, he crossed a cable about 2 inches in diameter strung 151 hundred feet high. A 1,100-foot rope was stretched below the suspension bridge with a series of parallel ropes alongside. In 1859 and 1860 Blondin gave a series of "ascensions." On August 19, he carried a man on his back across the cable, trundled over a loaded wheelbarrow, and walked across in a sack. On July 14, 1859, dressed as an ape, he pushed a wheelbarrow across. He usually carried a long pole which aided him to balance himself and which could also serve as a guard in case he fell, since it would be supported by the parallel ropes and thus prevent him from falling into the river. *(George Washington Holley—The Falls of Niagara)*

The First

NIAGARA FALLS—*Continued*

Person to go over Niagara Falls in a barrel was Anna Edson Taylor, who, on October 24, 1901, went over the Horseshoe Falls on the Canadian side in a barrel 4½ feet high and 3 feet in diameter. A leather harness and cushions were placed inside the barrel to protect her.

Person to go over Niagara Falls in a rubber ball was Jean Lussier, who made the descent July 4, 1928, in a ball of his own construction weighing 750 pounds and costing $1,485. It was equipped with oxygen tanks and reinforced with cushions. It was set adrift from a launch and went over the Horseshoe Falls. *(Wide World Magazine. Vol. 26, No. 370. January 1929)*

Utilization of Niagara Falls waterpower was made in 1757 by Chabert Joncaire, who dug a ditch so that the water would operate an overshot waterwheel to drive a crude sawmill. In 1879 the water turned a small dynamo which fed 16 arc lights in Prospect Park. In Niagara Falls, N.Y., on December 1881, an arc light machine was installed in a papermill on the cliff.

Utilization of Niagara Falls waterpower (large-scale) was made by the Niagara River Hydraulic Tunnel Power and Sewer Company, incorporated March 31, 1886. The name was changed to the Niagara Falls Power Company November 11, 1889. The Cataract Construction Company, incorporated June 13, 1889, under the general laws of the state of New Jersey, was the agent of the Niagara Falls Power Company in building and putting the project into operation. It ceased to exist in 1899. Ground was broken October 4, 1890. On October 24, 1893, a contract was executed with the Westinghouse Electric and Manufacturing Company of Pittsburgh, Pa., for three 5,000 h.p. generators delivering two-phase currents at 2,200 volts, 25 cycles. The first 5,000 h.p. turboalternator unit was completed within 18 months. On August 26, 1895, power was first transmitted commercially, the current being employed by the Pittsburgh Reduction Company in the reduction of aluminum ore. Buffalo received its first power for commercial purposes November 15, 1896. The three 5,000 h.p. generators at first installed were changed to 11,000-volt machines after 25 years of service, and these are still in use. Prior to the installation of the 5,000 h.p. generators, 1,000 h.p. was the capacity of the largest generator. *(Edward Dean Adams— Niagara Power)*

NICKEL COIN. *See* Money

NICKEL PLATING was invented by William H. Remington of Boston, Mass., who obtained patent No. 82,877 on October 6, 1868, on a "process of electroplating with nickel." He used a solution prepared by dissolving refined nickel in nitric acid, then precipitating the nickel by the addition of carbonate of potash, washing the precipitate

The First

with water, dissolving it in a solution of salammoniac, and filtering it.

NICKEL SILVER SPOONS. *See* Spoons

NICKELODEON. *See* Motion picture theater: Theater in the world devoted exclusively to the exhibition of motion pictures

NIGHT BASEBALL GAME. *See* Baseball game: Baseball game at night

NIGHT-COACH BUS. *See* Automobile bus: Bus night coach

NIGHT COURT. *See* Court

NO-FAULT INSURANCE. *See* Insurance

NO-HIT BASEBALL GAME. *See under* Baseball game

NO-RUN NINE-INNING BASEBALL GAME. *See under* Baseball game

NOBEL PRIZE

Black to win the Nobel Peace Prize was Dr. Ralph Johnson Bunche, whose mediations in 1949 between Israel and its warring Arab neighbors resulted in an armistice settlement. On December 10, 1950, at Oslo, Norway, he received the Nobel Medal and diploma and a cash award equivalent to $31,674.08.

Husband and wife in the United States to receive a joint Nobel Prize award were Dr. Carl Ferdinand Cori and Dr. Gerty Theresa Cori of the Washington University School of Medicine, St. Louis, Mo., who discovered how sugar in the human system is converted into glycogen through an enzyme or biological catalyst called phosphorylase. The award was announced October 23, 1947. A cosharer of the medicine award was Dr. Bernardo Alberto Houssay of the Buenos Aires Institute of Biology and Experimental Medicine for work on the relation between the pancreas and the pituitary gland.

Nobel Peace Prize awarded an American woman was granted to Jane Addams of Chicago, Ill., who received the award jointly with Dr. Nicholas Murray Butler, president of Columbia University, New York City. It was accepted for them at Oslo, Norway on December 10, 1931, by Hoffman Phillips, United States Minister to Norway. Jane Addams was the second woman recipient, the 1905 award having been made to Bertha von Suttner of Austria.

Nobel Prize awarded to an American was granted in 1906 to President Theodore Roosevelt for his service in the cause of peace in concluding the treaty between Russia and Japan at the end of the Russo-Japanese War.

Nobel Prize in chemistry awarded to an American was granted in 1914 to Theodore William Richards of Harvard University, Cambridge, Mass., "in recognition of his accurate determi

The First

nation of the atomic weight of a large number of chemical elements." The prize of 146,900 Swedish kroner was presented November 12, 1915, in Stockholm.

Nobel Prize in literature awarded to an American was granted in 1930 to Sinclair Lewis "for his great and living art in painting life, with a talent for creating types with wit and humor."

Nobel Prize in medicine and physiology awarded to an American was granted in 1912 to Dr. Alexis Carrel of the Rockefeller Institute for Medical Research "for his work on vascular ligature and on the grafting of blood vessels and organs."

Nobel Prize in physics awarded to an American was granted in 1907 to Albert Abraham Michelson of the University of Chicago "for his optical instruments of precision, and the spectroscopic and metrologic investigations which he carried out by means of them." *(Scientific Monthly. January 1939)*

Nobel Prize for peace to a professional soldier was awarded to General George Catlett Marshall on December 10, 1953, at Oslo University, Oslo, Norway. Gunnar Jahn, president of the Nobel Prize committee presented him with a 10-ounce gold medal, a scroll, and $33,840 in prize money. Marshall was the Chief of Staff of the United States Army during World War II and the sponsor of the European Recovery Program.

Nobel Prize in literature to a woman was awarded to Pearl Sydenstricker Buck, author of *The Good Earth* and other novels about China. The presentation of the 1938 medal and award of 155,077 kroner ($37,975) was made by King Gustaf of Sweden on December 10, 1938, at the Concert House, Stockholm.

Nobel Prize 2-time winner in the same field was John Bardeen, physicist, of Champaign, Ill., who received the Nobel Prize for physics, a medal, diploma, and $38,700 at Stockholm, Sweden, on December 10, 1956 (with Dr. William Shockley and Dr. William Houser Bralton, for their investigations on semiconductors and the discrepancy of the transistor effect). Bardeen also shared the 1972 prize (worth $98,100), with Leon N. Cooper and John Robert Schrieffer, for their explanation of superconductivity leading to more efficient transmission of electrical power.

Nobel Prize winners all of one country in 5 categories were from the United States: William Nunn Lipscomb, Jr., chemistry; Saul Bellow, literature; Milton Friedman, economics; Baruch Samuel Blumberg and Daniel Carleton Gajdusek, medicine; Burton Richter and Samuel Chao Chung Ting, physics. On December 10, 1976, in Stockholm, King Carl XVI Gustaf of Sweden presented the 7 Americans with the 5 prizes. The Nobel Prize

The First

for peace in that year went to Mairead Corrigan and Betty Williams of Northern Ireland.

Recipient of 2 full Nobel prizes was Dr. Linus Carl Pauling of the California Institute of Technology, who was presented the award for chemistry on December 10, 1954, at Stockholm, Sweden, and the Nobel Peace Prize for 1962 at Oslo University, Oslo, Norway, on December 10, 1963. The awards were worth $35,000 and $50,000 respectively.

NOBELIUM. *See* Element: Element 102

NOISE LEGISLATION

Noise-control statewide comprehensive legislation was New Jersey's Noise Control Act of 1971 signed January 24, 1972, by Governor William Thomas Cahill. The act, relating to the control and abatement of noise, empowered the state Department of Environmental Protection to promulgate codes, rules, and regulations for such purposes, created a Noise Control Council, and made a $100,000 appropriation.

NOMINATING CONVENTION. *See* Political convention

NONDENOMINATIONAL COLLEGE. *See* College

NONELECTRONIC DEVICE FOR OBSERVING IN TOTAL DARKNESS. *See under* Camera

NONFORFEITURE INSURANCE POLICY. *See under* Insurance

NONIMPORTATION ACT. *See* Embargo Act

NONRELIGIOUS COMMUNISTIC SETTLEMENT. *See* Communistic Society: Communistic nonreligious settlement

NONSKID TIRE. *See* Automobile tire

NORMAL SCHOOL
    See also College

Normal school established exclusively for the preparation of teachers was the Concord Academy, Concord, Vt., opened on March 11, 1823, by the Reverend Samuel Read Hall, who conducted it as a teachers' seminary until 1830.

Normal school instruction course given at a university was offered December 1, 1841, when Alfred Saxe was appointed Professor of Normal Instruction at Wesleyan University, Middletown, Conn., for a term of two years "to prepare teachers more perfectly for the business of instruction." No tuition charge was made for the course, which was a one-year program of study.

Normal school instruction offered by a college was given at the "model school" established at Lafayette College, Easton, Pa., by Dr. George Junkin, who paid $2,230.22 of his own money to erect a three-story building known as West College. A commemorative marble dial was inserted at the laying of the cornerstone on July 4, 1838, to give

The First

NORMAL SCHOOL—*Continued*
the latitude, longitude, and magnetic variations of
the college. *(David Bishop Skillman—The Biography of a College)*

Normal school (state) was the Normal School,
Lexington, Mass., which opened July 3, 1839, with
only three pupils. Free tuition was offered to those
who completed the one-year course and planned
to teach in Massachusetts. Cyrus Pierce was the
first principal. Edmund Dwight of Boston offered
$10,000 on condition that the Commonwealth appropriate the same amount to be expended by the
Board of Education in qualifying teachers for common schools. On April 19, 1838, the council appropriated the $10,000 to be used as required. On
December 15, 1853, the school moved to Framingham, Mass., where it is now located. *(Samuel Joseph May—Memoir of Cyrus Pierce, First
Principal of the First State Normal School in the
United States)*

Normal school (state) at which students actually conducted classes was the Oswego Training
School for Primary Teachers, Oswego, N.Y., established May 1, 1861, with an enrollment of 9
students. Dr. Edward Austin Sheldon, who served
from 1861 to 1897, was the first principal. The first
class, 39 students, was graduated in 1862. On
March 4, 1863, the New York legislature passed
"an act for the support of a training school for
primary teachers" which appropriated $3,000 for
two years calculated on an attendance of 50
pupils. On April 7, 1866, New York passed the
Normal School Act, and on March 27, 1867, acquired the school as a state normal school and
changed its name to the Oswego State Normal
and Training School. *(Ned Harland Dearborn—
The Oswego Movement in American Education)*

Teachers' training school (Jewish) was Gratz
College, Philadelphia, Pa., which offered a series
of general lectures in 1895. Nine trustees were
elected February 17, 1895. They selected from
their number Moses Aaron Dropsie as president,
Charles Joseph Cohen as treasurer, and David
Sulzberger as secretary. Regular instruction did
not commence until 1897.

Woman principal of a normal school was Anna
Callender Brackett, who on January 5, 1863, took
charge of the St. Louis Normal School, St. Louis,
Mo. Sarah M. Platt acted as her assistant. Miss
Platt and Miss Ann J. Forsyth were temporarily in
charge of the school until the principalship was
granted to Miss Brackett. *(Report of the St. Louis
Public Schools, 1862–1863)*

NORTH POLE. *See* Aviation—Flights; Discovery;
Expedition

NORTHERN LIGHTS. *See* Aurora borealis

NORTHWEST PASSAGE. *See under* Discovery

The First

NORTHWEST TERRITORY. *See* Territorial expansion: Acquisition of land by the federal government

NORWEGIAN-AMERICAN NEWSPAPER. *See*
Newspaper

NOVEL
American novel published in America was *The
Power of Sympathy or the Triumph of Nature
Founded in Truth,* dedicated "to the young ladies
of America." It was printed in 1789 in Boston,
Mass., by Isaiah Thomas & Co., and sold at the
company's bookstore, 45 Newbury Street. Publication was announced in the *Independent Chronicle* of January 21, 1789. It appeared in two
volumes of 138 and 158 pages. The story deals
with seduction. The author used the nom de plume
"Philenia." Authorship is attributed to Mrs. Sarah
Wentworth Apthorp Morton of Boston, Mass.,
and to William Hill Brown. *(Emily Pendleton and
Milton Ellis—Philenia, or the Life and Works of
Sarah Wentworth Morton)*

American novel republished in England was
Royall Tyler's *The Algerine Captive; or the Life
and Adventures of Doctor Updike Underhill; Six
Years a Prisoner among the Algerines,* originally
published in 1797 in Walpole, N.H.

Novel by a black was William Wells Brown's
*Clotel, or the President's Daughter, a Narrative of
Slave Life in the United States,* the story of an
efficient black woman represented as the
housekeeper of Thomas Jefferson. In the novel
one of the woman's two daughters drowns herself
in the Potomac River to elude pursuing slavers.
The book was published in London, England, in
1853, and reprinted with slight changes in 1864 in
Boston, Mass., under the title of *Clotelle, A Tale
of the Southern States.* It was published by James
Redpath of Boston, Mass., contained 104 pages,
and sold for ten cents.

Novel (full length) was *Theron, Paulinus and
Aspasio; or, Letters and Dialogues, upon the Nature of Love to God, Faith in Christ, Assurance of
a Title to Eternal Life, Containing Some Remarks
and Sentiments of the Rev'd Messieurs Hervey
and Marshal on These Subjects.* It consisted of
227 pages of text, written in the form of letters and
dialogues by Joseph Bellamy, A.M., Minister of
the Gospel at Bethlehem in New England, and
was printed and sold in 1759 by S. Kneeland, Boston, Mass. The first letter was dated, New England, December 15, 1758. It was undoubtedly
fiction despite its religious coloring.

Novel (full length) translated into a foreign language was *Adventures of Alonso: Containing
Some Striking Anecdotes of the Present Prime
Minister of Portugal* (Sebastião José de Carvalho
e Mello, Marquis de Pombal) by "A Native of
Maryland, some years resident in Lisbon." The
work is attributed to Thomas Atwood Digges of

The First

Warburton Manor, Md. The original edition consisted of two volumes, 148 pages and 129 pages, and was printed for John Bew in London in 1775. It was published in Leipzig in 1787 by Schwickert as *Alonzo's Abenteur [Abentheur]*, in two parts. *(American Literature. Vol. 12, No. 4. January 1941)*

Novel (pamphlet) was a 16-page pamphlet by Francis Hopkinson, entitled *A Pretty Story, Written in the Year of Our Lord 2774 by Peter Grievous, Esquire, ABCDE. Velunti in Speculo.* It was a political satire on the administration of the British colonies in North America and the causes of the American Revolution. It was printed in Williamsburg, Va., in 1774 by John Pinkney, for the benefit of Clementine Rind's children.

Novel to win the Pulitzer Prize in letters was *His Family*, by Ernest Poole, published in 1917 by the Macmillan Company, New York City. It was about Roger Gale, a New York man, and his three daughters, Edith, Deborah, and Laura. The award was announced June 3, 1918, by President Nicholas Murray Butler of Columbia University, New York City.

Pulitzer prize award to a woman for a novel was announced May 29, 1921, by Columbia University and presented to Edith Newbold Jones Wharton for her novel *The Age of Innocence*, published in 1920 by D. Appleton & Co.

Two-time winner of the Pulitzer Prize for a novel was Booth Tarkington, who won the 1918 award, announced by Columbia University on June 2, 1919, for *The Magnificent Ambersons* and the 1921 award, announced May 21, 1922, for *Alice Adams*.

NOVEL COURSE

Course on the contemporary novel, exclusively, was given by Professor William Lyon Phelps at Yale University, New Haven, Conn., in the academic year 1895–96. The course was called "Modern Novels" and was elected by 250 juniors and seniors.

Lecture course on the English novel offered by a university was given in 1889 by Professor Felix Emmanuel Schelling at the University of Pennsylvania, Philadelphia. It consisted of two one-hour lectures known as English Literature 2. *(Catalogue of the University of Pennsylvania, 1889–1890)*

NUCLEAR BOMB SHELTER. *See* Building: House with a built-in nuclear bomb shelter

NUCLEAR ENGINEERING COLLEGE COURSE

fully organized was established by the North Carolina State College of Agriculture and Engineering of the University of North Carolina, Raleigh, under the direction of Dr. Clifford Keith Beck, head of the physics department. The first students were accepted and enrolled June 12, 1950.

The First

NUCLEAR FISSION. *See* Atomic energy: Self-sustaining nuclear chain-reaction demonstration

NUCLEAR REACTOR. *See* Atomic reactor

NUCLEAR UNDERGROUND BLAST. *See* Atomic bomb: Atomic bomb underground explosion

NUDIST ORGANIZATION was the American League for Physical Culture, organized by 3 men, December 5, 1929, in New York City. The first nudist summer camp was that of the American League at Central Valley, N.Y., which opened in June 1930. There were approximately 30 members at the first summer camp.

NUGGET. *See* Gold: Gold nugget

NULLIFICATION PROCEEDINGS to offset federal congressional legislation were the Kentucky Resolutions introduced by John Breckinridge. They were adopted by the Lower House of Kentucky on November 10, 1798, and by the Upper House on November 13, 1798, and approved by Governor James Garrard on November 16, 1798. Objection was taken to the "act concerning aliens," June 25, 1798 (1 Stat. L. 570), and an "act for the punishment of certain crimes against the United States," July 14, 1798 (1 Stat. L. 596). *(Edward Payson Powell—Nullification and Secession in the United States)*

NUMBERING SYSTEM OF INSURANCE RATING. *See* Insurance: Numerical system of insurance rating

NUNS. *See* Catholic nuns

NURSE

Army Medical Specialist Corps male officer. *See under* Army Officer

Army Nurse Corps (female). *See* Army Nurse Corps (female)

Army nurse (male). *See* Army Officer: Male nurse

District nurse was employed by the Woman's Branch of the New York City Mission Society, New York City in 1877. *(William Raymond Jelliffe—One Hundred Years of City Mission and Tract Society)*

Naval nurses. *See under* Naval officer; Navy

Nurse appointed to a university professorship was Mary Adelaide Nutting, who was appointed professor of household administration, Teachers College, Columbia University, New York City, and who served from 1906 to 1910. From 1910 to 1923, she served as professor of nursing education, and from 1923 to 1925 as professor of nursing education at the Helen Hartley Foundation. She retired July 1, 1925, and was appointed professor emeritus of nursing education.

Nurse employed by an industrial organization to attend to the health of its employees, was Ada

The First

NURSE—Continued

Stewart, who was employed by the Vermont Marble Company of Proctor, Vt., in 1896.

Nurses' registration law (state) was ratified March 3, 1903, by North Carolina (Chapter 359, Public Laws of 1903). It provided voluntary registration with the county clerk of the Superior Court of any licensed trained nurse, after January 1, 1904, and for an examining and licensing board composed of two physicians and three registered nurses.

Order of the Purple Heart awarded to a nurse. *See under* Medal

Trained nurse was Linda Ann Judson Richards, first in a class of 5 to register as a pupil nurse in the Training School of the New England Hospital for Women and Children, Roxbury, Mass. Courses were given in medical, surgical, and obstetric nursing. The course began September 1, 1872, and concluded September 1, 1873. She served as night superintendent at Bellevue Hospital, New York City, from October 1, 1873, to October 15, 1874, and as Superintendent of the Training School of the Massachusetts General Hospital, Boston, Mass., from November 1, 1874, to April 1877. *(Linda Richards—Reminiscences of Linda Richards, America's First Trained Nurse)*

NURSERY SCHOOL. *See* Kindergarten

NURSES' CORPS, NAVAL. *See under* Navy

NURSES' MAGAZINE was *The Nightingale*, "a paper in the interests of the methodical nursing of the sick," which appeared March 6, 1886, in New York City. The first issue consisted of four pages. It was a monthly, subscription $2 a year, edited by Sarah [Sara] E. Post of the Graduate Training School for Nurses, Bellevue Hospital, New York City.

NURSES' SOCIETY

Nurses' society (local) was the Philomena Society, organized November 24, 1885, in New York City. It disbanded in 1887. *(Historical Sketch of the American Nurses Association)*

Society for superintendents of nursing schools was the American Society of Superintendents of Training Schools for Nurses, founded at the Hall of Columbus, Chicago, Ill., June 15-17, 1893. The first officers were Anna Alston, president; L. Darche, secretary; and L. L. Drown, treasurer. The first national convention was held January 10, 1894, in New York City. *(First and Second Annual Convention of American Society of Superintendents of Training Schools for Nurses)*

NURSING SCHOOL

Army School of Nursing was authorized May 25, 1918, by Secretary of War Newton Diehl Baker, as a division of the Surgeon General's Office under the Medical Department of the Army. The first class of 402 graduates completed the course

The First

at Walter Reed Hospital, Washington, D.C., on June 16, 1921. A three-year course of study was prescribed, but advanced credits were offered to graduates of approved courses. The first dean of the school was Annie Warburton Goodrich. The school was discontinued August 12, 1931, by Secretary of War Patrick Jay Hurley.

Instruction for nurses (systematic) was given by Dr. Valentine Seaman of the New York Hospital, New York City, who gave lectures on anatomy, physiology, the care of children, and midwifery from 1798 to 1817. The first class consisted of 24 nurses. *(Minnie Goodnow—Nursing History in Brief)*

School for nurses to award a diploma was the School of Nursing of the Woman's Hospital of Philadelphia, chartered March 22, 1861. The first diploma was awarded in 1865. The first nurse known to have received the diploma was Harriet N. Phillips.

Training school for black nurses was the Spelman Seminary, Atlanta, Ga., founded in 1881 by Sophia Booker Packard and Harriet E. Giles of Boston, Mass., as the Atlanta Baptist Female Seminary. In 1884 the name was changed to Spelman Seminary and in 1924 to Spelman College, the name by which it is now known. A nurses' training department was established in 1886 in a two-room frame building set apart for an infirmary and known as the Everts Ward. The first nurse received her certificate in 1888.

University school of nursing established as an integral part of a university was the School of Nursing, University of Minnesota, Minneapolis, authorized by the Board of Regents October 1, 1908, and established March 1, 1909, through the efforts of Dr. Richard Olding Beard. The first director of the school was Bertha Erdmann. The first graduation took place June 13, 1912, four students completing the training.

NUT AND BOLT FACTORY was established by Micah Rugg and Martin Barnes, in Marion, Conn., in 1840, although they began making bolts and nuts for the market in 1838 in Rugg's blacksmith shop. Their factory was a one-story wooden building, 30 feet by 20 feet, designed especially to carry on the business started two years before. They employed six operators, and the capacity production was 500 bolts a day. Prior to 1838, when they started making bolts commercially, these articles were hammered out and hand-finished by a blacksmith as needed from time to time. *(W. R. Wilbur—History of the Bolt and Nut Industry of America)*

NUT AND BOLT MACHINE was invented by David Wilkinson of Rhode Island, who obtained a patent December 14, 1798. The first machine of importance for trimming the heads of nuts and bolts was invented by Micah Rugg, who obtained patent No. 2,766, August 31, 1842.

The First

NYLON

Nylon was invented by Dr. Wallace Hume Carothers, who on February 16, 1937, obtained patent No. 2,071,250, which was assigned to E. I. du Pont de Nemours & Company, Inc. The patent covered synthetic linear condensation polymers capable of being drawn into pliable strong fibers, as well as the process for making them.

Nylon bristle filament production for toothbrushes began at Arlington, N.J., on February 24, 1938, by E. I. du Pont de Nemours & Company, Inc.

Nylon hose was placed on sale May 15, 1940, at stores throughout the country.

Nylon stretch yarn was introduced from Switzerland by Heberlein Patent Corporation, New York City. The first licensee to process Helanca stretch yarn was the Duplan Corporation, New York City, which supplied yarn to the Marion Knitting Company, the Chester H. Roth Company, and the Interwoven Stocking Company, which introduced men's stretch socks in August 1952.

Nylon yarn manufacture (commercial) was begun by E. I. du Pont de Nemours & Company, Inc., at Seaford, Del., on December 15, 1939. The yarn was distributed to hosiery mills, which knitted it into women's hosiery. This was the first use of nylon for apparel. Nylon stockings went on sale commercially for the first time in May 1940.

O

OAT-CRUSHING MACHINE was patented November 30, 1875, by Asmus J. Ehrrichson of Akron, Ohio, who obtained patent No. 170,536, on "an improvement in oatmeal machines." A hopper with a perforated bottom and a series of horizontal knives were the basis of his invention. It converted hulled kernels of oats into a cereal meal, thus superseding the old method of crushing grain with burrs or millstones, which produced a product of inferior quality and reduced the grain to a fine flour of less value than the coarse meal.

OBELISK. *See* Monument

OBJECTORS, CONSCIENTIOUS. *See* Conscientious objectors

OBSERVATION CAR. *See* Railroad car: Railroad car with an observation dome

OBSERVATION CARS (superdome). *See under* Railroad car

OBSERVATORY

See also Planetarium

Observatory (astronomical) connected with an institution of learning was built in 1830 by Joseph Caldwell, president of the University of North Carolina, Chapel Hill. It contained a meridian

The First

transit telescope, a zenith telescope, a refracting telescope, an astronomical clock, a sextant, a reflecting circle, and a Hadley's quadrant. The observatory was completed in 1831, having been built with Caldwell's own funds at a cost of $430.29. Caldwell was eventually reimbursed by the trustees of the college. *(Kemp Plummer Battle —History of the University of North Carolina)*

Observatory (lightning). *See* Lightning observatory

Observatory (national) was established by the Navy on December 6, 1830, in Washington, D.C. The first instrument installed was a 30-inch portable transit, which was made by Richard Patten of New York. Lieutenant Louis Malesherbes Goldsborough was appointed the first officer in charge of the observatory and served until 1833.

OBSTETRICS BOOK. *See* Medical book

OCCUPATIONAL THERAPY COURSE in a college was given in 1913 by the Milwaukee-Downer College of Milwaukee, Wis. The subjects included psychology, physiology, sociology, design, metal work, leather work, and textile craft. Two students enrolled. The form of treatment called occupational therapy "includes any occupation, mental or physical, which is definitely prescribed and guided for the distinct purpose of contributing to, or hastening recovery from diseases or injury."

OCCUPATIONAL THERAPY TREATMENT (systematic) was given by Susan Edith Tracy, author of *Studies in Invalid Occupation*, at the Training School for Nurses of the Adams Nervine Asylum, Jamaica Plain, Boston, Mass., which had been established under the will of Seth Adams, who died December 7, 1873. The school was incorporated March 16, 1877, and the first patients admitted in April 1880.

OCEANGOING BROKERAGE OFFICE. *See under* Brokerage

OCEAN MAIL CONTRACTS. *See under* Postal service

OCEAN PIER. *See* Pier

OCEANOGRAPHY INSTITUTION was the Scripps Institution of Oceanography of the University of California, located at La Jolla, Calif. It developed from the Scripps Institution for Biological Research of the University of California, which was established in 1912. The present name of the institution was adopted in October 1925. Its investigations cover the circulation of the waters in the ocean and the interrelation of the sea and the atmosphere, the chemistry of ocean water, the sediments on the sea floor, and marine organisms in their manifold interrelations with one another and with other conditions in the sea. *(University of California Register, 1929–1930)*

The First

ODD FELLOWS LODGE was Washington Lodge No. 1 established April 26, 1819, in Baltimore, Md. It was organized by Thomas Wildey, and acted under a charter obtained from the Duke of York Lodge of England. In 1821 Wildey organized the Grand Lodge of Maryland and the Grand Lodge of the United States, and became grand master of the Grand Lodge of Maryland and the grand sire of the Grand Lodge of the United States. *(James L. Ridgley—History of American Odd Fellowship)*

OFFICE-BUILDING ELEVATOR. *See* Elevator

OFFICE OF MARKETS (U.S.). *See under* Agriculture department (U.S.)

OFFICERS' RESERVE CORPS. *See* Army: Reserve Officers' Training Corps

OFFICERS' TRAINING CAMP FOR BLACKS. *See* Army camp for training black officers

OFFICERS' TRAINING SCHOOL (Coast Guard). *See* Coast Guard (U.S.): Coast Guard officers' training school

OFFICERS' TRAINING SCHOOL (Navy). *See* Naval officers' training school

OFFSHORE RADAR WARNING STATION. *See under* Radar

OIL
Offshore oil wells successfully drilled in the ocean were drilled at Summerland, Santa Barbara County, Calif., in 1896.

Oil and gas conservation legislation was enacted by Oklahoma, May 17, 1913, Chapter 207. It provided for a chief deputy inspector of oil and gas wells and of pipe lines and for necessary traveling and maintenance expenses to supervise the use and operation of natural gas wells and the drilling for and production of oil and gas.

Oil and gas magazine was the *Oil Investors' Journal,* a semimonthly whose first issue was published May 24, 1902, at Beaumont, Tex. Holland S. Reavis was the founder and editor. The first issue contained 16 pages and the subscription price was $1 a year. The last issue was Vol. 8 No.24, May 20, 1910. On June 16, 1910, it became the *Oil and Gas Journal* (Vol. 9 No.1).

Oil company was the Pennsylvania Rock Oil Company, incorporated December 30, 1854, in New York City by George H. Bissell of New Haven, Conn., with a capital stock of $250,000 (10,000 shares at $25). He owned 12,000 shares. George Henry Bissell and Jonathan G. Eveleth were the two principal trustees, each owning 1,200 shares. *(Paul Henry Giddens—Beginnings of the Petroleum Industry)*

Oil exported. *See* Petroleum exported to Europe

Oil (kerosene) from bituminous shale and cannel coal for illuminating purposes was obtained by Dr. Abraham Gesner, who secured U.S. patent

The First

No. 12,612 on March 27, 1855, covering his process. The product was called kerosene and was manufactured by the North American Kerosene Gaslight Company at Newton Creek, L.I., N.Y. Gesner obtained patents No. 11,203, 11,204, and 11,205 on June 27, 1854, on a process for obtaining kerosene by heat distillation. *(Raymond Foss Bacon and William Allen Hamor—American Petroleum Industry)*

Oil pipeline of importance to transport crude petroleum successfully was completed October 9, 1865, by Samuel Van Syckel of Titusville, Pa. It was about 5 miles long and extended from Miller's Farm on Oil Creek to Pithole, Pa. Wrought iron pipes 2 inches in diameter were laid underground in 15-foot sections. Two pumping stations supplied the power. *(David Talbot Day—Handbook of the Petroleum Industry)*

Oil pipeline within the oil regions was laid in 1862 by Barrows & Co., under the direction of J. L. Hutchins at the James Tarr farm at Oil Creek, Pa., a distance of 2½ miles to the Humboldt refinery at Plumer, Pa., on Cherry Run. The pipeline had a two-inch diameter; the sockets were of lead. It was completed February 19, 1863, but was abandoned because of leakage. *(Titusville Morning Herald. March 6, 1866)*

Oil platform offshore with a radioisotope generator was a 60-watt unit installed by the Phillips Petroleum Company in one of its platforms in the Gulf of Mexico. It went into unattended operation in June 1965.

Oil refinery was started by Dr. Samuel M. Kier, a druggist of Pittsburgh, Pa., to refine petroleum. He built a small refinery in 1855 using the oil, which he called Kier's Rock Oil, for medicinal purposes. A little later, he distilled the oil in his drugstore with laboratory equipment, bottled the product, and sold it for 50 cents a half pint. He also discovered that the light fractions from the crude oil would burn and the heavy fractions or bottoms were good for cleaning wool. *(Charles E. Bowles—The Petroleum Industry)*

Oil refinery (commercial) was erected by William Barnsdall and William Hawkins Abbott in Oil Creek Valley, Pa., June 1860. The only product saved was the kerosene. The small amount of gasoline manufactured was run into Oil Creek. The kerosene was sold in competition with whale oil and rock oil for use in lamps. In 1864 this refinery and some oil property on the Parker farm were sold for $50,000 to Jonathan Watson, William F. Hansell, Standish F. Hansell, Charles B. Keen, John C. Gillett, and Henry E. Rood, who organized an oil company.

Oil spring of record in America was marked on a map of territory near Cuba, N.Y., in 1627 by François Dollier de Casson and René de Brehant de Galinée, missionaries of the Order of St. Sulpice. The map was sent by them to Jean Talon,

The First

Intendant of Canada. A description of the oil spring is contained in a letter written by the Franciscan missionary Joseph de la Roche d'Allion dated July 18, 1627, reproduced in Gabriel Sagard-Théodat's *Histoire du Canada et Voyages que les Frères Mineurs Recollects y ont Faicts pour la Conversion des Infidelles,* published in 1636.

Oil tank cars were introduced by Charles P. Hatch of the Empire Transportation Company, Philadelphia, Pa., in 1864–1865 and used on the Oil Creek Railroad, the Warren and Franklin Railroad, etc. Cars with three wooden tanks containing 3,500 gallons were used, but rain dissolved the glue coating and caused leakage. Later, riveted iron tanks mounted horizontally were used. On September 1, 1865, Amos Densmore used two wooden tanks, one on each end over the trucks of a flat-car, and shipped oil from Miller's Farm to New York City over the Atlantic and Great Western Railroad. The shipment consisted of two cars, each car with two tanks, and each tank containing about 40 barrels.

Oil well commercially productive was discovered August 27, 1859, at Titusville, Pa. It produced from a depth of 69½ feet about 400 gallons a day. E. B. Bowditch and Edwin Laurentine Drake of the Seneca Oil Company, organized March 23, 1858, bored through the rock at Titusville in a section known as Oil Creek. William A. Smith and his son, Samuel B. Smith, were to do the work. Edwin Drake was the first to tap petroleum at its source and to offer proof of the occurrence of oil in reservoirs beneath the earth's surface. *(Raymond Foss Bacon and William Allen Hamor—American Petroleum Industry)*

Oil well drilled by torpedoes, as an experiment, was the Ladies' Well on Watson Flats near Titusville, Pa., on January 21, 1865. The method had been advocated in 1862 by Colonel Edward A. L. Roberts of New York City, who received patent No. 47,458 on April 25, 1865, on "exploding torpedoes in artesian wells." *(Charles Austin Whiteshot—The Oil Well Driller)*

Oil well fire occurred April 17, 1861, when the Little and Merrick well on the Buchanan farm near Rouseville, Pa., at Oil Creek, caught fire, shortly after it gushed. It burned for three days and 19 persons lost their lives. The well produced about 3,000 barrels a day.

Oil well (flowing) was drilled unintentionally in 1818 at the mouth of Troublesome Creek, on the Big South Fork of the Cumberland River, 28 miles southeast of Monticello, Ky., by Martin Beatty, who was seeking brine. The drillers, Marcus Huling and Andrew Zimmerman, searching for salt, drilled a 5-inch hole with pole and auger to a depth of 536 feet. The oil had no known value and sand was thrown down the well to plug it up. The "devil's tar," as Beatty called the oil, was allowed to flow into the Cumberland River and covered its

The First

surface for a distance of 35 miles. The oil became ignited and an enormous conflagration ensued which destroyed trees along the banks of the river and the salt works. *(Augusta Phillips Johnson—A Century of Wayne County, Kentucky, 1800–1900)*

Plastic pipeline to transport oil cross-country was placed in service October 19, 1953, by the C. C. Thomas Company between Williston Basin, near Poplar, Mont., and the storage tanks to a car siding of the Great Northern Railway, a distance of 9 miles. Its capacity was 2,500 barrels a day. A 20-foot section of the smooth flexible 3-inch pipe of Tenite butyrate plastic produced by the extrusion process weighed 13 pounds compared to 153 pounds of steel pipe. It withstood a pressure of 90 p.s.i (pounds to the square inch).

OIL AND GAS PRODUCTION COURSE at an institute of collegiate character was offered by the School of Engineering, University of Pittsburgh, Pittsburgh, Pa., in the university year 1912–1913. The course was given by Professor Roswell Hill Johnson.

OIL-FUEL LOCOMOTIVE. *See* Locomotive: Locomotive to use oil fuel

OIL LAMP. *See* Lamp

OIL-TAN LEATHER. *See* Leather: Leather tanning by the "oil tan" method

OIL TANKER. *See* Ship

OILCLOTH FACTORY (successful) was erected in 1845 in Winthrop, Maine, by Ezekiel Bailey. It was known as C. M. Bailey Sons & Company and within ten years did an annual business of $200,000. *(David Thurston—History of Winthrop)*

OILED SILK PATENT was granted February 1, 1793, to Ralph Hodgson, Lansingburg, N.Y., on "manufacturing oiled silk and linen."

OKAPI. *See* Animals

OLD AGE COLONY was dedicated October 23, 1936, at Roosevelt Park, Millville, N.J., by Senator Arthur Harry Moore. The project, which was completed January 1, 1937, contained seven houses for couples, which rented for $7 a month; six houses for single people, which rented for $5; and a community house. The city of Millville supplied the land, which had been taken over for taxes; the WPA supplied $34,571. The city collected rent and agreed to keep the houses in repair. Residents received $15 monthly from the state under the Old Age Assistance Act. The plan was originated by Effie Morrison, Deputy Director of Cumberland County Welfare Board, and was realized through William H. J. Ely, state WPA administrator, and George R. Swinton, WPA director for Cumberland, Atlantic, and Cape May counties.

OLD AGE HOME FOR PIONEERS was the Home for Aged and Infirm Arizona Pioneers, Prescott, Ariz., authorized by Chapter 23, Session Laws of

The First

OLD AGE HOME FOR PIONEERS—*Continued*
the 25th Legislative Assembly of the Territory of
Arizona, approved March 10, 1909. Residents of
Arizona not less than 35 years or over 60 years of
age, citizens of the United States for at least 5
years prior to the date of application, who were
active in the development in Arizona and who
were unable to provide themselves with the
necessities and comforts of life because of adverse circumstances or failing health, could apply
for admission. It was opened for guests February
6, 1911. The first superintendent was Major A. J.
Doran.

OLD AGE PENSION. *See* Pension

OLEOMARGARINE
Oleomargarine legislation (federal) was "an act
defining butter, also imposing a tax upon and
regulating the manufacture, sale, importing and
exporting of oleomargarine," passed August 2,
1886 (24 Stat. L. 209). It placed a $600 tax on manu-
facturers, $400 on wholesalers, and $48 on retailers, and levied a manufacturing stamp tax of two
cents a pound.

Oleomargarine legislation (state) was "an act
for the protection of dairymen and to prevent
deception in sales of butter," passed June 5, 1877
(Chapter 415) by New York State.

Oleomargarine manufacturer (successful) was
Alfred Paraf of New York City, who organized the
Oleo-Margarin Manufacturing Company in 1871.
On April 8, 1873, he obtained patent No. 137,564
on his process for purifying and separating fats.
*(Henry Augustus Mott—The Complete History
and Process of the Manufacture of Artificial But-
ter)*

Oleomargarine patent was No. 110,626, granted
January 3, 1871, to Henry W. Bradley, Binghamton, N.Y., on a "compound for culinary use," composed of lard, vegetable butter, or shortening.

OLYMPIC GAMES
American athlete to place in 4 events in 1 year
was Alvin C. Kraenzlein of Pennsylvania, who
won the 110-meter hurdles in 15.4 seconds, placed
second in the 60 meters in 7.0 seconds, third in the
long (broad) jump with a leap of 23 feet 6⅞ inches
and fourth in the 200-meter low hurdles in 25.9
seconds at the Olympic Games in Paris in 1900.
*(Richard Schaap—An Illustrated History of the
Olympics)*

American athlete to win four medals in one year
at the Olympic Games was Jesse Owens. In the
Olympic Games held in Germany in 1936, he won
the 100-meter run (10.3 seconds) on August 3; the
broad jump (26 feet 5⅜ inches) on August 4; the
200-meter run (20.7 seconds) on August 5; and the
400-meter relay (39.9 seconds) on August 9. The
relay team consisted of Jesse Owens, Ralph Met-
calfe, Foy Draper, and Frank Wykoff. *(John Kieran*

The First

*and Arthur Daley—The Story of the Olympic
Games)*

American athlete to win ten medals at the
Olympic Games was Ray Ewry, who won the
standing high jump and the standing broad jump
at the games held in Paris in 1900, in St. Louis in
1904, in Athens in 1906, and in London in 1908. At
the Paris and St. Louis Games, he won the hop,
step, and jump (now triple jump). *(John Kieran and
Arthur Daley—The Story of the Olympic Games)*

American decathlon champion was Harold M.
Osborne of the Illinois Athletic Club, who won
7,710.775 points on July 12, 1924, at the Olympic
Games, Paris. The ten events in the decathlon are
the 100-meter dash, the 400-meter run, the 1,500-
meter run, the 110-meter hurdle, the broad jump,
the high jump, the shot put, the discus throw, the
pole vault, and the javelin throw.

American Olympic competition winner was
James Brendan Connolly of the Suffolk Athletic
Club of South Boston, Mass., who represented the
United States in the hop, skip, and jump (now
triple jump) contest on April 6, 1896, at the Olympiad in Athens, Greece. His jump of 45 feet exceeded that of his nearest competitor by 3 feet 3
inches. He left the United States on the tramp
steamer *Fulda* from New York City on March 20,
1896, disembarked at Naples on April 1, 1896, and
competed on April 6, 1896. The American team of
ten men won 9 of the 12 events.

Black American athlete in the Olympic Games
to place was George C. Poage of the Milwaukee
Athletic Club, Milwaukee, Wis., who placed 3rd
in the 400-meter hurdles on August 31, 1904, and
3rd in the 200-meter hurdles on September 1, 1904,
at the Third Olympiad at St. Louis, Mo., during the
Louisiana Purchase Exposition.

Black American athlete to win an individual
event in the Olympic Games was William DeHart
Hubbard of the University of Michigan, who won
first place with a jump of 24 feet 5⅛ inches in the
running long jump on July 8, 1924, in the Colombes
stadium in Paris.

Dog sled race on an Olympic demonstration
program. *See under* Dog race

Figure skating Olympic champion (American)
was Richard (Dick) Button of Englewood, N.J.,
who earned the title February 5, 1948, at the Fifth
Winter Olympic Games, St. Moritz, Switzerland.

Olympic celebration in the United States was
the Third Olympiad, held in St. Louis, Mo., May
14, 1904, to August 1, 1904. The games were first
awarded to Chicago, Ill., but later they were given
to St. Louis to be staged in connection with the
World's Fair. The games were not popular, as
there were few entrants other than Americans in
the 14 events. In the field competitions, the American athletes made a clean sweep of all the events

The First

with the exception of lifting the bar and throwing the 56-pound weight.

Olympic Games basketball championship was won by a team from the United States, which defeated a Canadian team, 19-8, on August 14, 1936, in Berlin, Germany. The United States was the gold medalist, Canada the silver medalist, and Mexico the bronze medalist.

Ski tournament (international). *See* Ski tournament (international)

Winter Olympic Games competition was held at Lake Placid, N.Y., during which 307 athletes from 17 nations participated. Governor Franklin Delano Roosevelt of New York opened the games on February 4, 1932.

Woman (American) to win an Olympic competition was Ethelda Bleibtrey, who, at the Seventh Olympiad, held in Antwerp, Belgium, won the 100-meter free-style swim (1 minute 13 3/5 seconds) on August 25, 1920, and the 300-meter free-style swim (4 minutes 34 seconds) on August 26, 1920. *(Bill Henry—An Approved History of the Olympic Games)*

Woman slalom Olympic champion (American) was Gretchen Fraser of Vancouver, Wash., who won second place on February 5, 1948, in the Alpine Combination in the Olympic ski race at the Fifth Winter Olympic Games, St. Moritz, Switzerland.

ONE-STOP TRANSCONTINENTAL FLIGHT. *See* Aviation—Flights (transcontinental): Transcontinental flight in 24 hours' flying time

ONE-WAY TRAFFIC. *See under* Traffic regulation

OPEN-AIR POST OFFICE. *See* Post office

OPEN-HEARTH FURNACE. *See under* Steel

OPEN-MESH STEEL FLOORING BRIDGE. *See* Bridge: Bridge with open-mesh steel flooring

OPEN-SEA BRIDGE. *See* Bridge: Bridge with piers sunk in the open sea

OPERA

Black prima donna of an opera company was Caterina Jarboro, who appeared July 22, 1933, as Aida, the Ethiopian slave, in Giuseppe Verdi's opera *Aida,* presented by Alfredo Salmaggi's Chicago Opera Company at the New York Hippodrome, Sixth Avenue and 43rd Street, New York City.

Black singer of the Metropolitan Opera was Marian Anderson, contralto, who was the fortune teller Ulrica in Giuseppe Verdi's *Un Ballo in Maschera* ("The Masked Ball"), a three-act opera presented January 7, 1955, at the Metropolitan Opera House, New York City.

The First

Black to sing a white role with a white cast in an opera company was Robert Todd Duncan, a baritone of Washington, D.C., who first appeared as Tonio in *I Pagliacci* on September 28, 1945, and as Escamillo in *Carmen* on September 30, 1945, in the New York City Opera Company's presentation at the City Center of Music and Drama, New York City. Both operas were included in the 1945 fall season (September 27-December 17). *I Pagliacci* was performed five times and *Carmen* seven.

Grand opera sung in English was *Der Freischutz* ("The Free Shooter"), in three acts, billed as *The Wild Huntsman of Bohemia.* It was presented at the Park Theatre, New York City, on March 2, 1825. The music was by Karl Maria von Weber and the libretto by Johann Friedrich Kind. Mr. Lee appeared as Baron Ottocar; Mr. Woodhull as Conrad; Mr. Clarke as Caspar; Mr. Keene as Wilhelm. The opera commenced at 6:45 P.M. and at its conclusion was followed by a farce, *A Rowland for an Oliver.*

Light opera presented in 2 cities on the same day was Gilbert and Sullivan's *The Gondoliers or the King of Barataria,* presented by Francis Wilson's Company in Philadelphia, Pa., and in New York City, on April 17, 1890. The company left Philadelphia in the morning and arrived at the theatre in New York City before one o'clock, where they gave a performance, and returned to Philadelphia at 4:00 P.M. in time for the evening performance at the Broad Street Theatre. The musical instruments and the costumes were hand carried. The troupe featured Francis Wilson as Giuseppe Palmieri, Hubert Wilke as Marco Palmieri, Charles Plunkett as Luiz, H. Macdonough as Don Alhambra del Bolero, George H. Carr as Antonio, and James Glisson as Franceso.

Motion picture of a complete grand opera. *See under* Motion picture

Opera at the Metropolitan Opera House, New York City, was Charles François Gounod's *Faust,* sung in Italian on October 22, 1883. Augusto Vianesi was the conductor. Faust was sung by Italo Campanini, Mephistopheles by Franco Novara, Valentin by Giuseppe Del Puente, Wagner by Ludovico Contini, Siebel by Sofia Scalchi, Marthe by Louise Lablache, and Marguerite by Christine Nilsson. Admission was priced at $6 for orchestra stalls, $3 balcony, and $2 family circle. (The opera had, however, been performed in the United States in 1863.)

Opera at the Metropolitan Opera House, New York City, conducted by a woman was *La Traviata* by Giuseppi Verdi, conducted by Sarah Caldwell on January 13, 1976. The cast included Beverly Sills as Violetta, Stuart Burrows as Alfredo, and William Walker as Germont.

The First

OPERA—*Continued*

Opera broadcast in its entirety was presented Thursday May 19, 1921, at 8:15 P.M. during Music Week from the Auditorium, Denver, Colo. A municipal chorus of 150 voices presented *Martha* over station 9ZAF (now KLZ). Martha was sung by Ruth Hammond Theiss, Nancy by Florence Lamont Abramowitz, Plunkett by L. R. Hinman, Lionel by Robert H. Edwards, and the Sheriff of Richmond by B. H. Gilbert.

Opera broadcast in its entirety by a professional cast was Camille Saint-Saëns' *Samson et Dalila,* broadcast Monday, November 14, 1921, the opening night of the season of the Chicago Opera Company, over station KYW, Chicago, Ill., from the Chicago Auditorium. Lucien Muratore was Samson; Marguerite D'Alvarez was Dalila. Giorgio Polacco conducted.

Opera broadcast in its entirety by the Metropolitan Opera Company was Engelbert Humperdinck's opera *Hansel and Gretel,* presented on December 25, 1931, through the National Broadcasting Company, New York City. Editha Fleischer was Hansel; Queena Mario was Gretel; Karl Riedel conducted.

Opera broadcast in part from the stage of the New York City Metropolitan Opera Company was heard on January 13, 1910, when Enrico Caruso and Emmy Destinn sang arias from *Cavalleria Rusticana* and *I Pagliacci,* which were "trapped and magnified by the dictograph directly from the stage and borne by wireless Hertzian waves over the turbulent waters of the sea to transcontinental and coastwise ships and over the mountainous peaks and undulating valleys of the country." The microphone was connected by telephone wire to the laboratory of Dr. Lee De Forest. *(New York Times. Jan. 14, 1910)*

Opera broadcast over a national network from an American opera house was the third-act garden scene from Gounod's *Faust,* which was broadcast January 21, 1927, from the stage of the auditorium in Chicago by the Chicago Civic Opera Company. The "Flower Song," "Le Roi de Thulé," the "Invocation," and Marguerite's song at the window were sung by Edith Mason, soprano (Marguerite); Charles Hackett, tenor (Faust); Vanni-Marcoux, bass (Mephistopheles); Richard Bonelli, baritone (Valentin); and others. Fifteen microphones were used to pick up the opera from various places in the opera house. Giorgio Polacco was the director.

Opera by an American composer was *The Archers, or the Mountaineers of Switzerland,* which was performed in New York City on April 18, 1796. It dealt with the exploits of William Tell. The libretto was by William Dunlap and the music by Benjamin Carr.

The First

Opera by an American composer (important) was *Leonora,* a lyrical drama in three acts with a libretto by Joseph Reese Fry and music by William Henry Fry, which was performed June 4, 1845, at the Chestnut Street Theatre, Philadelphia, Pa. The plot was based on Bulwer-Lytton's *The Lady of Lyons.* It was sung in English and had a chorus of 75 and an orchestra of 50. *(Genealogical Society of Pennsylvania—Publications, Vol. 14, October 1943)*

Opera by an American composer performed at the Metropolitan Opera House of New York was *The Pipe of Desire,* by Frederick Shepherd Converse, which was produced March 18, 1910. The libretto was by George Edward Barton. The cast included Riccardo Martin as Iolan; Louise Homer Naoia; Clarence Whitehill, the Old One; Leonora Sparkes, the First Sylph; Lillia Snelling, the First Undine; Glenn Hall, the First Salamander; and Herbert Witherspoon, the First Gnome. The opera had been previously produced in Boston in 1906.

Opera (comic) to be prepared for the American stage was Andrew Barton's *The Disappointment or The Force of Credulity,* a satirical comedy in two acts with a prologue and epilogue, inspired by "the infrequency of dramatic compositions in America, the necessity of contributing to the entertainment of the city, and to put a stop (if possible) to the foolish and pernicious practice of searching after supposed hidden treasures." The satire was directed against the seekers of the treasure supposed to have been buried by the pirate Blackbeard. The opera contained 18 songs and was arranged with 7 scenes in the first act and 5 in the second. A performance was scheduled to take place on April 20, 1767, in Philadelphia, Pa., but at the last moment the work was withdrawn for fear of offending. *(George Overcash Seilhamer—History of American Theatre)*

Opera composed by a woman performed at the Metropolitan Opera House was *Der Wald,* in one act, by Ethel Mary Smyth, performed March 11, 1903, in New York City. Alfred Hertz was the conductor. Johanna Gadski sang Roschen, and Georg Anther was Heinrich. Others in the opera were Luisa Reuss-Belce, David Bispham, Robert Blass, Adolph Mühlmann, and Eugene Dufriche.

Opera house municipally owned was the War Memorial Opera House of San Francisco, Calif., which was opened on October 15, 1932, with a performance of *Tosca* by the San Francisco Opera Company.

Opera (Italian) to be produced in the United States in Italian, with Italian singers, was Gioacchino Antonio Rossini's *Il Barbiere di Siviglia* performed on November 29, 1825, at the Park Theatre, New York City. The libretto was by Cesare Sterbini. The singers were Manuel del Populo Vicente, De Rosich, Manuel Crivelli, Maria Felicita Garcia, and Manuel Garcia, Jr. The

The First

orchestra of 25 musicians was conducted by Nathaniel De Luce. Performances were given at 7:30 P.M. The prices were listed as follows: boxes, $2.00; orchestra, $1.00; and gallery, 25 cents. Twenty-three performances were given. The largest receipts for a single performance were $1,962, and the smallest $250.

Opera matinee at the Metropolitan Opera House, New York City, was on December 3, 1932, when *Elektra,* music by Richard Strauss, was performed. Artur Bodansky was the conductor. The book in German was by Hugo von Hofmannsthal. Gertrude Kappel sang the Elektra role and Karin Branzell, Klytemnestra.

Opera of a serious nature produced in America was James Hewitt's *Tammany, or The Indian Chief,* based on the book by Mrs. Anne Julia Kemble Hatton. The opera was produced on March 3, 1794, by Charles Ciceri, under the auspices of the Tammany Society, by the Old American Company at the John Street Theatre, New York City.

Opera performed by a professional visiting troupe was *The Beggar's Opera,* a three-act burlesque by John Gay, performed December 3, 1750, by the Walter Murray and Thomas Kean Company at the Nassau Street Theatre, a two-story-high gabled structure between John Street and Maiden Lane, New York City. It had 10 box seats at 8 shillings each, 161 pit seats at 5 shillings each, and 121 gallery seats at 3 shillings each. The principal songs were "Let Us Take to the Road," "Lillibulleru," "Green Sleeves," "Hither Dear Husband," and "When a Wife's in a Pout." Entertainment was presented between the acts. *(Phoebe Fenwick Gaye—John Gay)*

Opera performed in America was Colley Cibber's ballad opera *Flora, or Hob in the Well,* presented Tuesday, February 18, 1735, at the Courtroom, Charleston, S.C. It was advertised in the *South Carolina Gazette* and was shown with a pantomime entertainment billed as *The Adventure of Harlequin Scaramouche. (Oscar George Theodore Sonneck—Early Opera in America)*

Opera singer (American) to sing in an Italian opera in Italian was Julia Wheatley, who sang in Rossini's *Eduardo e Cristina* on November 25, 1834, at the Italian Opera House, New York City.

Opera singer to sing two major roles on the same day at the Metropolitan Opera House, New York City, was Hermann Jadlowker, who on March 22, 1911, sang the role of Turiddu in Mascagni's *Cavalleria Rusticana* and substituted for Riccardo Martin as Canio in Leoncavallo's *I Pagliacci.*

Opera telecast. *See* Television—Telecast: Opera (complete) to be televised

The First

Orchestra used in conjunction with an opera. *See under* Orchestra

Pay television opera. *See* Television—Telecast: Pay television presentation of an opera

OPERATION, ABDOMINAL. *See* Surgical operation

OPERETTA TELECAST. *See* Television—Telecast

OPHTHALMOLOGY BOOK. *See* Medical book

OPHTHALMOLOGY CLINIC. *See* Medical clinic

OPHTHALMOLOGY PROFESSOR. *See under* Medical instruction

OPTOMETRY INSTRUCTION

Optics and optometry courses offered by a university were given at Columbia University, New York City, which offered a two-year course beginning September 28, 1910, following enactment of legislation by New York State on March 31, 1909 (Chapter 134), which required licenses for optometrists. The work in optometry was given by Andrew Jay Cross (instructor in theoretic optometry) and Frederick Albert Woll; also, Charles F. Prentice (instructor in practical optics). Members of the university departments of physics and mathematics gave instruction in those subjects to the optometry students.

Optometry school was the Illinois College of Optometry, Chicago, Ill., founded in 1872 by George W. McFatrich, M.D., author of *Correction for Myopia,* who taught refraction. In 1907, Dr. William B. Needles founded the Needles Institute of Optometry, Kansas City, Mo. These schools merged under the name of the Northern Illinois College of Optometry, chartered 1927 under the Chicago College of Optometry in 1955 and becoming the Illinois College of Optometry.

OPTOMETRY LEGISLATION (state) was signed April 13, 1901 (Chapter 269, Laws of 1901), by Governor Samuel Rinnah Van Sant of Minnesota. *(George Ole Virtue—Government of Minnesota)*

OPTOMETRY MAGAZINE. *See* Medical periodical

OPTOMETRY SOCIETY

Optometry society (national) was the American Association of Opticians organized October 10, 1898, by 183 charter members from 31 states and Canada, in the Broadway Central Hotel, New York City. The officers elected were Charles Lembke of New York City, president; Henry Borsch of Chicago, first vice president; William Bohne of New Orleans, second vice president; Frederick Boger of New York, secretary; and Charles A. Longstreth of Philadelphia, treasurer. The name was changed in 1910 to the American Optical Association and in 1919 to the American Optometric Association.

The First

ORAL INSTRUCTION FOR THE DEAF. *See under* Deaf—School

ORANGES (seedless navel) grown in the United States were from a dozen budded sapplings brought from Bahia, Brazil, in 1871 by William Saunders, horticulturist of the United States Department of Agriculture. Two of the trees, which were secured by Jonathan and Eliza C. Tibbets in 1873, started the industry in Riverside, Calif. Other types of oranges, however, had been grown earlier in Florida. *(John Raymond Gabbert—History of Riverside, City and County)*

ORATORIO
Oratorio by an American was John Knowles Paine's *Oratorio of St. Peter,* performed June 3, 1873, at the City Hall, Portland, Maine, by the Haydn Society of Portland, assisted by eminent artists from abroad and the Harvard orchestra of Cambridge, Mass. (41 members). *(Daily Eastern Argus. June 4, 1873)*

Oratorio performance (complete) was a presentation of the *Messiah* on December 25, 1818, by the Handel and Haydn Society, Boylston Hall, Boston, Mass., with a chorus of approximately 200 singers. The soloists were the Misses Sumner and Bennett, Mr. J. Sharp, and Master White. Benjamin Holt was president of the society and, as was customary, conducted the concert.

ORCHESTRA
College orchestra was founded at Harvard University, Cambridge, Mass., March 6, 1808. The minutes record that "at a meeting held on March 6, 1808, by a number of students of Harvard University, they unanimously agreed to institute a society for their mutual improvement in instrumental music." It was known as the Pierian Sodality, as it was not the custom for any extracurricular activities to assume the name of the college. The orchestra is now known as the Harvard University Orchestra.

Municipal orchestra supported by taxes was the Baltimore Symphony Orchestra, Baltimore, Md., formed in 1915 with a Board of Estimate appropriation of $6,000. It was managed by Frederick R. Huber, who took office July 13, 1915, as the Municipal Director of Music. The first concert master was J. C. van Hulsteyn; the first soloist, Mabel Garrison; the first conductor, Gustav Strube. The first concert was presented February 11, 1916.

Orchestra was founded about 1810–1811 in Boston, Mass., by Johann Christian Gottlieb Graupner. This orchestra is believed to have been the original Philharmonic Orchestra. The last concert was given at the Pantheon, Boylston Square, Boston, on November 24, 1824. *(Frederic Louis Ritter—Music in America)*

The First

Orchestra (American) to make a European tour was the Symphony Society of New York, which sailed for Europe April 22, 1920. Under the leadership of Walter Johannes Damrosch, 34 concerts were given in 21 cities in France, Italy, Belgium, Holland, and England. The first concert was given on May 4, 1920, at the Paris Opera House. The last in the tour was given on June 20, 1920, at the Royal Albert Hall, London. The Symphony Society merged with the New York Philharmonic on March 30, 1928, to form the Philharmonic Society of New York, with Arturo Toscanini as conductor in chief.

Orchestra in a theater was employed in the Nassau Street Theater, between John Street and Maiden Lane, New York City, in 1750. The instruments used were German flutes, horns, and drums. The theater, two stories high, opened March 5, 1750, with a presentation of Shakespeare's *King Richard III*. It was illuminated by a chandelier, made of a barrel hoop through which a dozen nails were driven to serve as candle holders. The stage was set five feet above the floor level. *(Thomas Allston Brown—A History of the New York Stage)*

Orchestra (symphony), full size, devoted exclusively to radio broadcasting was the National Broadcasting Company (NBC) Symphony Orchestra, Arturo Toscanini conductor, formed November 13, 1937. Its debut was made at 10:00 P.M. December 25, 1937, over stations WEAF and WJZ, New York City, of the National Broadcasting Company. The program consisted of the first symphony of Johannes Brahms, Wolfgang Amadeus Mozart's G minor symphony, and Antonio Vivaldi's Concerto Grosso.

Orchestra used in conjunction with an opera was employed in 1752 when the Kean and Murray Company of London opened the new theatre in Upper Marlborough, Md., with *The Beggar's Opera*.

Radio orchestra was the Detroit News Orchestra, a 16-piece symphonic ensemble, which began broadcasting May 28, 1922. It was composed principally of members of the Detroit Symphony Orchestra. Otto Krueger, piccolo player, was conductor and Maurice Warner, first violinist, was concertmaster. The broadcasts were sponsored by the Detroit Bank on station WWJ, Detroit, Mich.

Symphony orchestra was the Collegium Musicum of Bethlehem, Pa., formed in 1744. There were 14 players—2 first violins, 2 second violins, 2 violas, 2 flutes, 2 trumpets, 2 French horns, one cello, and 1 double bass. *(Raymond Walters—Bethlehem, Long Ago and Today)*

ORCHESTRA LEADER. *See under* Musician

The First

ORCHESTRAL SONG. *See under* Music

ORDER OF DE MOLAY. *See under* Freemasons

ORDER OF THE PURPLE HEART. *See* Medal

ORDINANCE OF SECESSION. *See* Secession: Secession act

ORDNANCE

Airplane outfitted with a machine gun. *See under* Aviation—Airplane

Army armored tank operated by United States troops in the U.S. Army was the French Renault tank used in the Battle of St.-Mihiel on September 12, 1918. The first chief of the Tank Corps was Brigadier General Samuel Dickerson Rockenbach, appointed June 1919. No American-built tanks were used in World War I. *(Records in Office of the Chief of Infantry, War Department.)*

Atomic cannon was Atomic Annie or Amazon Annie, a 40-foot, 85-ton cannon, electronically fired at 8:30 A.M., May 25, 1953, at Frenchman Flat., Nev., at a target 7 miles away. A 280-millimeter projectile, 11 inches by 3 feet, was loaded by a crew of nine from the 52nd Field Artillery Group, Fort Sill, Okla. The shot produced an eight-second fireball visible 65 miles away despite the bright sunshine. The charge was touched off by scientists of the Atomic Energy Commission, 10 miles away, and the explosion was witnessed from points 3 to 7 miles from the target area by Defense Secretary Charles Erwin Wilson, Admiral Arthur William Radford, Army Secretary Robert Stevens, Army Chief of Staff Joseph Lawton Collins, and 100 members of Congress.

Automatic aircraft cannon of 20 mm was manufactured by the Eclipse Machine Division of the Bendix Aviation Corporation, Elmira, N.Y., and was delivered to the U.S. Army, May 16, 1941.

Bazooka rocket gun was produced on June 14, 1942, by the General Electric Company, Bridgeport, Conn. It weighed 12 pounds and was operated by a 2-man team. It consisted of a steel tube, about 50 inches long and 2½ inches in diameter, open at both ends. Attached to the tube were a shoulder stock and front and rear grips for the gunner, together with sights and an electric battery which set off the rocket-propelled charge when the launcher trigger was squeezed. The rocket was nearly 2 feet long. It fired about 300 yards. The first sample gun was produced in 4 days from plans, development was completed in 3 weeks, and production of 5,000 rocket guns completed within 30 days. It was known as Launcher, Rocket AT, M-1.

Cannon (breech-loading) was invented by Benjamin Chambers, Sr., who obtained patent No. 6,612 on July 31, 1849, on "an improvement in movable breeches for fire-arms and the locks and appurtenances of the same." His wooden model was

The First

discovered in an old smithy and is now in the possession of the Virginia Historical Society.

Cannon (steel, breech-loading, rifled) was made in 1854 by James Richards Haskell. He sold 25 to the Mexican Government.

Cartridge-loading machinery was invented by G. Moore Peters of Xenia, Ohio, who received patents No. 321,848 and No. 321,849 on July 7, 1885, for a round table loading machine, one of which was later installed at his factory, the Peters Cartridge Company, King Mills, Ohio.

Fighter airplane carrying a cannon. *See under* Aviation—Airplane

Gun (revolving) was made by John Gill of Newberne, N.C., in 1829. It had 14 chambers and was a percussion gun. It was never patented. The first patent for this type of gun was granted to David G. Colburn of Canton Canal, N.Y., on June 29, 1833.

Gun (rifled) was made in 1834 by Cyrus Alger. The first perfect bronze cannon was made by him in 1827 at the South Boston Iron Company's foundry for the U.S. Ordnance Department.

Gunpowder mill was operated by Edward Rawson, to whom the General Court of Massachusetts granted 500 acres of land at Pecoit, Mass., on June 6, 1639, on which to erect it. *(Arthur Pine Van Gelder and Hugo Schlatter—History of the Explosives Industry in America)*

Machine gun was invented by Charles E. Barnes of Lowell, Mass., who obtained patent No. 15,315 on July 8, 1856, on an "improved automatic cannon." It was operated by a crank, the speed of firing depending upon the speed with which the crank was turned.

Machine gun (rapid-fire) was invented by Richard Jordan Gatling of Indianapolis, Ind., who obtained patent No. 36,836 on November 4, 1862, on "an improvement in revolving battery guns." The first gun, which fired 250 shots a minute, was made in Indianapolis. *(Gatling's System of Fire-Arms, with Official Reports of Recent Trials and Great Success, Descriptions, General Directions, etc.)*

Metal cartridge successfully produced was made by Daniel Baird Wesson of the Smith & Wesson Company, Springfield, Mass., in 1857, based upon patent No. 11,496 granted him August 8, 1854. In 1860, additional patents were granted on a cartridge in which the fulminate was enclosed in the hollow annular projecting case. Metal cartridges revolutionized the firearms industry and made the breech-loading rifle possible.

Muskets produced at a government arsenal were made in 1795 at the Springfield Armory, Springfield, Mass., under the direction of David Ames, the first superintendent, and Robert Orr, a master armorer. The first gunlock was filed by

The First

ORDNANCE—*Continued*
Alexander Crawford, after a struggle of three days. Richard Beebe stocked it by hand. In the first year 245 muskets were produced.

Pistol. *See* Pistol

Polaris missile firing to be witnessed by a President. *See* President (U.S.): President to witness the firing of a Polaris missile

Revolving gun turret, used on the ironclad *Monitor* which defeated the Confederate *Merrimac* on March 9, 1862, at Hampton Roads, Va., was invented by Theodore Ruggles Timby, who was also the first to advocate the use of iron in the construction of ships. In April 1841 he showed the War Department an ivory model of a revolving battery and filed a caveat in 1843 for "a revolving tower for offensive and defensive warfare to be used on land and water." His idea, which he adapted from the shape of Castle Williams, N.Y., was not accepted until 20 years afterward. He obtained patents No. 35,846 and No. 35,847 on July 8, 1862, for his revolving battery tower. *(Francis Brown Wheeler—The First Monitor and Its Builders)*

Rifle. *See* Gun (rifled) above; Semiautomatic rifle, below

Seacoast gun carriage made of wrought iron was constructed in 1855 by James Gilchrist Benton, instructor in ordnance and gunnery at the United States Military Academy. It was immediately adopted by the United States Government. *(James Gilchrist Benton—The Fabrication of Small Arms for the United States Service)*

Semiautomatic rifle adopted as standard by the U.S. Army was the U.S. Rifle Caliber .30, M1, the Garand Semi-Automatic Shoulder Rifle, a service shoulder weapon adopted January 9, 1936. It was invented by John C. Garand of Somerset, Md., who obtained patent No. 1,603,684 on October 19, 1926, on an "automatic gun." *(Julian Sommerville Hatcher—The Book of the Garand)*

Shot tower used by an American manufacturer of ammunition was erected in 1895 by the Peters Cartridge Company at Kings Mills, Ohio. The factory was organized by G. Moore Peters and was incorporated on January 24, 1887.

Submachine gun was the Thompson Submachine Gun ("Tommy Gun"), invented by Brigadier General John Taliaferro Thompson, who organized the Auto-Ordnance Company in 1915 to build lightweight semiautomatic infantry shoulder rifles. The first model was proof-fired at the Warner & Swasey Company, Cleveland, Ohio, where the first gun was built. The gun weighed approximately 10 pounds and had a cyclic rate of fire of between 600 and 800 shots a minute.

The First

Tank (heavy 60-ton) built in the United States for the U.S. Army was constructed by the Baldwin Locomotive Works, Eddystone, Pa., and presented by William Henry Harman, vice president of the company, to Brigadier General Gladeon Marcus Barnes, Army Ordnance Department, on December 8, 1941. It had a 75 mm (3-inch) cannon in the turret.

Tank with a turbine engine was the XM-1 (the Abrams tank) powered by an AVCO Lycoming rotary diesel-fuel turbine engine that was rolled out February 29, 1980, at Chrysler Corporation's Lima, Ohio, factory. It had Chobham-type armor and a laser range-finder on its main gun, could attain 20 m.p.h. in 6 seconds, and could cruise at 45 m.p.h. It cost $1.5 million. The first unit recipient was H Company, 2nd Squadron, 6th Armored Cavalry Lightning Brigade. (On November 12, 1976, both Chrysler and General Motors had been awarded contracts to build a pilot tank. The G.M. tank had a diesel internal-combustion engine.)

OREGON TRAIL. *See* Road: Overland wagon road across the Rocky Mountains

ORGAN
Color organ was invented by Bainbridge Bishop of New Russia, N.Y., who obtained patent No. 186,298 on January 16, 1877, on an "attachment for key-board musical instruments" for typifying musical sounds by the display of colors.

Electric organ was built by Hilborne Lewis Roosevelt in 1876, and installed in Chickering Hall, Fifth Avenue and 18th Street, New York City. It was operated by storage batteries. It had 31 ranks, 10 in the great organ, 8 in the swell organ, 5 in the solo organ, 3 in the echo organ, and 5 in the pedal organ.

Organ built in the United States was constructed by Johann Gottlob Klemm (John Clemm) of Philadelphia, Pa., who proposed building an organ on June 1, 1739, for Trinity Church, New York City. His proposition was accepted, and in May 1740 the pipe organ was installed in the West Gallery. It had 3 manuals and 26 stops (10 in the great organ, 10 in the choir, and 6 in the swell) and cost about £520. *(Arthur Henry Messiter—A History of the Choir and Music of Trinity Church, New York City)*

Organs imported were brought into the United States in 1700, by the Episcopal Church, Port Royal, Pa., and the Gloria Dei Church (Swedish Lutheran, dedicated July 2, 1700) in Philadelphia, Pa. Priority is claimed for each. *(Bishop William Meade—Old Churches, Ministers and Families of Virginia)*

Pipeless organ was invented by Laurens Hammond, who received patent No. 1,956,350, April 24, 1934, covering 74 claims. The organ was manufactured by the Hammond Clock Company, Chicago, Ill., and was first exhibited at the Industrial Arts

The First

Exposition, New York City, on April 15, 1935. The organ consisted of a two-manual console with pedal clavier and a power cabinet. It had neither reeds, pipes, nor vibrating parts. It weighed 275 pounds and cost less than one cent an hour to operate.

ORGAN SCHOOL was the Guilmant Organ School, New York City, established in 1899 by Dr. William Crane Carl and Dr. Howard Duffield. The first classes met in the First Presbyterian Church, New York City. The school was named for the French organist Alexandre Guilmant.

ORGANISTS' SOCIETY

Organists' society (national) was the American Guild of Organists, organized April 13, 1896, and incorporated December 17, 1896. One hundred and forty-five organists, called founders, were enrolled by December 31, 1896. The first convention was held December 29-30, 1914, in New York City. Gerrit Smith was the first warden and Dr. Henry Granger Hanchett, inventor of the third pedal, the first secretary. The first branch chapter was organized in Philadelphia, Pa., on June 10, 1902.

ORPHANAGE

See also Greek College and Orphanage

Orphanage was established in New York City (New Amsterdam) in June 1654. Fifty orphan children were sent from Holland in order to help populate Manhattan Island. They arrived on the *Pereboom* and the *Gelderse Blom.* A resolution was passed and signed by Peter Stuyvesant, November 9, 1654, "to hire the house of Mr. [Isaac] Allerton and lodge there the children sent over by the Poor-masters." This orphanage also received the orphan children of the early colonists. *(New York Colonial Documents, Vol. 14)*

Orphanage with a continuous existence was founded in Savannah, Ga., by the Reverend George Whitefield in 1740. It was known as the Bethesda Home (house of mercy). The site was selected by James Habersham, the first superintendent. Whitefield was a Church of England curate in the colony, but there is nothing in the records to show that Bethesda was ever sectarian. At first both boys and girls were admitted. The home, which is now under the care of the Union Society, organized 1750, is known as the Bethesda Home for Boys. Girls are cared for in the Savannah Female Orphan Asylum and the Episcopal Home for Girls.

ORRERY. *See* Planetarium

ORTHODONTIA MAGAZINE. *See* Dental periodical

ORTHODONTIA TREATISE. *See* Dental book

ORTHODONTISTS' SOCIETY. *See* Dental society

The First

ORTHOPEDIC HOSPITAL. *See* Hospital

ORTHOPEDICALLY DISABLED. *See* Crippled

ORTHOPEDICS CHAIR. *See under* Medical instruction

OSCAR AWARDS. *See under* Motion picture actor

OSTEOPATHIC PHYSICIAN. *See* Physician

OSTEOPATHY MAGAZINE. *See* Medical periodical

OSTEOPATHY SCHOOL. *See* Medical school

OSTRICH FARM. *See under* Birds

OUTBOARD MOTOR. *See under* Engine

OUTDOOR ADVERTISING LEGISLATION (state). *See* Advertising legislation

OUTDOOR BLACKOUT LIGHTING CONTROL. *See* Blackout: Blackout outdoor light control

OUTDOOR MUSEUM. *See* Museum

OUTER-SPACE BROADCAST. *See under* Radio broadcast

OUTLOOK ENVELOPE. *See* Envelope: Envelope with an outlook or window

OVERLAND MAIL SERVICE. *See* Postal service

OVERLAND ROAD. *See* Road

OVERSHOES (Artics). *See* Artics

OVERWATER FLIGHT. *See* Aviation—Flights

OXIDIZED CELLULOSE (sponge). *See* Sponge

OYSTER COCKTAIL is attributed to a miner who appeared at a California bar about 1866 and ordered a whiskey cocktail and a plate of California raw oysters. After drinking the cocktail, he placed the oysters in the same glass with some tomato catsup, Worcestershire sauce, and pepper sauce, and ate them with great gusto. The bartender, seizing the idea, marketed a new product which sold for "four bits" per glass and which has since been called oyster cocktail.

OYSTER PROPAGATION (state) began in Rhode Island, which in June 1779 set aside part of the public domain for the cultivation and propagation of oysters. *(William Keith Brooks—The Oyster)*

P

PACER. *See* Horse: Horse to pace one mile in better than 2:00

PACIFIC AIR MAIL FLIGHT. *See under* Airmail service

PACIFIC CABLE. *See* Cable

The First

PACIFIC COAST DISCOVERY. *See* Discovery

PACIFIC COAST GOVERNMENT. *See* Colonial government: Government on the Pacific Coast

PACIFIC COAST MAIL. *See* Postal service: Overland mail service

PACIFIC COAST NEWSPAPER. *See* Newspaper

PACIFIC COAST UNIVERSITY. *See* College: University on the Pacific Coast

PACING REGISTER. *See under* Horse register

PACKAGE DELIVERY SERVICE. *See* Express service

PACKAGE STORES. *See* Liquor stores (state)

PACKER, MEAT. *See* Meat packer

PACKET LINE. *See under* Ship

PAGE (female). *See under* Congress (U.S.)— House of Representatives

PAGING SERVICE BY RADIO. *See* Radio paging service

PAINLESS SURGERY DEMONSTRATION. *See under* Anesthesia

PAINT

Paint prepared from standard formulas for floors, woodwork, furniture, walls, etc., was manufactured by the Sherwin-Williams Company of Cleveland, Ohio, in 1880. Stains, enamels, varnishes, and varnish stains were later produced under uniform production methods.

Paint (ready-mixed) was manufactured by the Averill Paint Company of New York City using as a basis patent No. 66,773, granted on July 16, 1867, to D. R. Averill of Newburg, Ohio. The concern went out of business about 1900. It was unable to maintain a "standard" paint.

PAINT SPRAYING DEVICE commercially manufactured was made in 1909 by the De Vilbiss Company of Toledo, Ohio. Employment of the same principle used in the De Vilbiss medical atomizer combined with compressed air started a revolution in painting and spraying. *(Spray Painting System—De Vilbiss Co.)*

PAINTER. *See* Artist

PALEONTOLOGY CHAIR in a college was established by Yale University, New Haven, Conn., in 1866, and was held by Professor Othniel Charles Marsh from that date to 1899. He was the first professor of vertebrate paleontology.

PALEONTOLOGY COURSE

Micropaleontology course was given by Professor Jesse James Galloway at Columbia University, New York City, starting on September 25, 1924. It covered the principles of paleontology, classification and nomenclature, the use of paleontological literature, and the identification of small forms with the microscope.

The First

PALEONTOLOGY REPORT was prepared in 1713 by the Reverend Cotton Mather and read before the Royal Society of London in 1714. He regarded three teeth and a 17-foot thigh bone which were unearthed in Albany, N.Y., in 1705 as the remains of a race of giants. He was elected a member of the Royal Society of London, the first American to receive this distinction. *(Abijah Perkins Marvin—Life and Times of Cotton Mather)*

PAMPHLET PRINTED ON VELLUM. *See* Book: Book (pamphlet) on vellum

PAN AMERICAN CONFERENCE. *See* Conference

PAN AMERICAN DELEGATES. *See under* Diplomatic service

PAN AMERICAN UNION was the International Bureau of American Republics, established on April 14, 1890, by the First International Conference of American States, which met at Washington, D.C., from October 2, 1889, to April 19, 1890, and was presided over by James Gillespie Blaine, United States Secretary of State. The name of the bureau was changed by resolution of August 11, 1910, to the Pan American Union. The first director of the Bureau was William Eleroy Curtis, who was appointed August 26, 1890, and who served until May 17, 1893. *(Bulletin of the Pan American Union. April 1930)*

PANAMA CANAL. *See* Ship: Steamboat to pass through the Panama Canal

PANDA. *See* Animals

PANORAMA SHOW. *See under* Theater

PAPER

Blotting paper. *See* Blotting paper

Corrugated paper was invented by Albert L. Jones of New York City, who received patent No. 122,023, December 19, 1871, on an "improvement in paper for packing." His patent covered corrugated sheets only and made no mention of backing or facing sheets. Later a facing sheet was applied to one side, and then to both sides, making single-face and double-face corrugated cardboard. Jones assigned his patent to Thompson & Norris Company of Brooklyn, N.Y., which was the first manufacturer of corrugated paper in the United States. Corrugated paper boxes came into use about 1890.

Crepe paper was manufactured in 1890 by Charles T. Bainbridge's Sons, Brooklyn, N.Y. It was made of rag paper with only one ratio of stretch. It was made in a variety of colors and sold to the trade for 50 cents a roll, 20 inches wide and 10 feet long.

Manila paper was invented by John Mark and Lyman Hollingsworth of South Braintree, Mass., partners under the firm name of J. M. & L. Hollingsworth, who received patent No. 3,362 on

The First

December 4, 1843. They manufactured it from hemp sails, canvas, and rope. *(Lyman Horace Weeks—History of Paper Manufacturing)*

Perforated wrapping paper was patented July 25, 1871, by Seth Wheeler of Albany, N.Y., who received patent No. 117,355. The paper was wound into rolls and was torn off at the perforations. It was claimed that "the fibers left between the perforations [were] sufficient for holding the sheets together as wound into a roll."

Sandpaper. *See* Sandpaper patent

Straw paper was made from straw and grass in 1829 by George Augustus Shryrock of Philadelphia, in the Hollywell mill near Chambersburg, Pa. He also invented a machine for producing it.

Toilet paper was unbleached pearl-colored pure manila hemp paper made in 1857 by Joseph C. Gayetty of New York City, whose name was watermarked on each sheet. It sold at 500 sheets for 50 cents and was known as "Gayetty's Medicated Paper—a perfectly pure article for the toilet and for the prevention of piles."

Wallpaper. *See* Wallpaper

Wood-pulp and rag paper for printing was manufactured by William Orr, of Troy, N.Y., in 1854. He made paper, the composition of which was three-fourths rag and one-fourth wood fiber, in his Troy paper mill. *(Arthur James Weise—City of Troy and Its Vicinity)*

Wood-pulp paper was made of basswood by John Beardsley of Buffalo, N.Y. He exhibited three samples of it on December 26, 1854, to the editor of the Buffalo *Democrat.*

PAPER BAG MANUFACTURING MACHINE

Paper bag manufacturing machine was invented by William Goodale of Clinton, Mass., who obtained patent No. 24,734 on July 12, 1859.

Square-bottom paper bag machinery was invented by Luther Childs Crowell of Boston, Mass., who obtained patents No. 123,811 and 123,812 on February 20, 1872, on an "improvement in paperbag machines." The bags produced by the machine had two longitudinal inward folds.

PAPER COLLAR. *See* Collar

PAPER-FOLDING MACHINE. *See* Folding machine

PAPER MILL was built in 1690 by William Rittenhouse, Samuel Carpenter, Robert Turner, Thomas Tresse and William Bradford in Germantown, Pa., on a rivulet called Paper Mill Run, about two miles above the junction of the Wissahickon with the Schuylkill. The mill was built on 20 acres of land leased from Samuel Carpenter at an annual rental of five shillings. The paper was made by hand, each sheet separately. Linen rags were pounded into pulp in stone mortars. The production rate was about 250 pounds a day. *(An Histo-*

The First

rie for Young & Olde About the Beginnings of Paper-making—Eastwood Wire Corporation)

PAPER MONEY. *See* Money

PAPER PATTERNS that were practical for dresses and other garments were manufactured by Ebenezer Butterick in 1863 in Sterling, Mass. Four years later he formed E. Butterick & Company, with offices on lower Broadway, New York City.

PAPER PENCIL. *See* Pencil

PAPER TWINE machinery was patented December 17, 1895, by George Loomis Brownell of Worcester, Mass., who obtained patent No. 551,615 on a "machine for making paper twine." It twisted strips or ribbons of paper into cord which was as strong as any known steel.

PAPER WATERMARK. *See* Watermark

PAPERMAKING MACHINERY

Papermaking machine (cylinder) was made by Thomas Gilpen in August 1817 and used in his paper mill at Brandywine, Del. The mill manufactured the first machine-made paper in the United States. Previously paper had been handmade and in small sizes because of limited facilities and molds, but this machine permitted paper to be made in unlimited lengths and as wide or narrow as desired. *(Joel Munsell—Chronology of Paper and Papermaking)*

Papermaking machine (Fourdrinier) made in the United States was manufactured in 1829 in South Windham, Conn., by James Phelps and George Spafford, who formed the firm of Phelps and Spafford. Aided by Charles Smith, they produced a machine which was set up in May 1829 in the mill of Amos H. Hubbard of Norwich Falls, Conn. The machine had no driers. The paper was run off wet and hung up to dry. The firm name of Phelps and Spafford was changed to Smith, Winchester & Company in 1837, and later to the Smith and Winchester Company.

Papermaking machine (Fourdrinier) imported was purchased in December 1827 by Joseph Pickering and set up in his shop in North Windham, Conn., January 1828 by George Spafford of South Windham, Conn. Henry and Sealy Fourdrinier of London purchased the patent of Nicholas Louis Robert and developed a machine for making paper in an endless web.

PAPERMAKING MUSEUM. *See* Museum: Museum devoted exclusively to papermaking

PAPRIKA MILL was the Carolina Paprika Mills, Inc., Dillon, S.C., incorporated March 25, 1941. The president was Robert Robich.

PARACHUTE

Dirigible to drop mail by parachute. *See* Airmail: Dirigible to drop mail by parachute

The First

PARACHUTE—*Continued*
Parachute. *See under* Aviation

PARACHUTE-JUMP COMBAT DECORATION.
See Medal: Combat decoration

PARACHUTE-JUMPING CONTEST
Parachute-jumping contest was held October 12, 1923, at Mitchel Field, N.Y. Two men on a Martin bomber and 2 men on a de Havilland jumped from a 4,500-mile height and landed 400 feet from each other, one and a half minutes apart. The first to land was Staff Sergeant Theodore Schieuming of Brooklyn, N.Y. One thousand spectators witnessed the jump.

PARACHUTE WEDDING. *See* Wedding

PARACHUTIST
Parachutist to make 124 jumps in one day was Neal Stewart of Birmingham, Ala., a paratrooper on 30-day leave from Fort Bragg, N. C., who made 124 jumps at Grand Praire, Tex., out of a small plane. His first jump was at 2:16 A.M., July 4, 1952, and the last on July 5, 1952, from an altitude of approximately 500 feet.

PARADE
Automobile parade. *See* Automobile parade

Labor Day parade. *See under* Holiday

Parade in which all the marching music was supplied by transistor radio receivers was held from 11:00 A.M. to 12:00 A.M. on July 4, 1977, at Streamwood, Ill. The marchers carried portable transistor radios that were all tuned to receive the program of music broadcast by radio station WRMN (1410 AM), Elgin, Ill. The parade was witnessed by thousands and telecast over channel 2 and channel 5.

Parade, with float tableaux was held in Mobile, Ala., on the evening of Mardi Gras day, February 24, 1868. The Order of Myths produced the first pageant. Next day followed the Infant Mystics and their pageant, then the Knights of Revelry. These are the original mystic societies of the South, and all still parade in Mobile's pageants. *(History of Mardi Gras—Mobile Carnival Association)*

Street parade held by a mystic society was held by the Cowbellian de Rakian Society, organized on December 31, 1830, in Mobile, Ala. The peculiar feature of this society and those which followed later was that absolute secrecy was maintained about their membership, the members never appearing except in costume and in mask. Parades were held annually on New Year's Eve, the first, December 31, 1830, being an impromptu raid on a hardware store staged by a score of young bloods, who were led, according to tradition, by Michael Krafft. On March 5, 1867, Mobilians abandoned the New Year's Eve celebration in favor of daylight parades which were held on Mardi Gras, literally Fat Tuesday, or Shrove

The First

Tuesday, the day preceding Ash Wednesday and the penitential season of Lent as observed in Catholic and Episcopal liturgy. *(Erwin Craighead —Mobile: Facts and Tradition)*

PARCEL POST. *See* Postal service

PARCEL POST DOMESTIC AIR SERVICE. *See* Airmail service

PARCEL POST STAMP. *See* Postage stamp

PARENT-TEACHER ASSOCIATION
Parent-teacher association (local) was the Froebel Society of Brooklyn, N.Y., founded in 1884 to further the "advancement of educational interests and the promotion of self-culture." It was named for the German educator Friedrich Wilhelm August Froebel.

Parent-teacher association (national) was the National Congress of Mothers, organized February 17, 1897, in Washington, D.C., by Alice McLellan Birney and Phoebe Apperson Hearst at a meeting attended by 2,000 persons. At the annual meeting of March 9, 1908, the name was changed to the National Congress of Mothers and Parent-Teacher Associations. On May 9, 1924, the name was changed to the National Congress of Parents and Teachers.

PARISH, CATHOLIC. *See* Catholic parish

PARK
Park land purchased by a city was Elm Park, containing 27 acres, which was sold to Worcester, Mass., on March 17 and March 20, 1854, by Levi Lincoln and John Hammond.

Park (national) was the Yellowstone National Park, Wyo., authorized March 1, 1872 (17 Stat. L. 32), by "an act to set aside a certain tract of land (2,142,720 acres) lying near the headwaters of the Yellowstone River as a public park." The first superintendent was Nathaniel Pitt Langford. Yellowstone Park now consists of 2,213,205 acres in the following states: Wyoming, 2,039,216 acres; Montana, 142,501 acres; Idaho, 31,488 acres. Hot Springs National Park in Arkansas, consisting of 911 acres with 46 hot springs, was established as a reservation by an act of Congress on April 20, 1832 (4 Stat. L. 505). It was not until March 4, 1921 (41 Stat. L. 1407), that it was designated as the Hot Springs National Park. Therefore, although it is the oldest national park, it was not the first one to be so called.

Park (national) in which there was an active volcano was the Lassen Volcanic National Park in the Sierra Nevada in California. It was established by an act of Congress approved August 9, 1916 (39 Stat. L. 443). It contains 104,526 acres, including the famous Lassen Peak, 10,453 feet high.

Park (national) east of the Mississippi and the first located on an ocean is the Acadia National Park, on the island of Mount Desert, about a mile

The First

south of Bar Harbor, Maine. It was established by President Wilson, July 8, 1916 (39 Stat. L. 1785), as the Sieur de Monts National Monument and February 26, 1919 (40 Stat. L. 1178), as the Lafayette National Park. The name was changed January 19, 1929 (45 Stat. L. 1083), to Acadia National Park. It contains 27,871 acres. *(George Bucknam Dorr— Acadia National Park, Its Origin and Background)*

State park was the Yosemite Valley park in California, an area embracing the valley itself and the Mariposa Grove of Big Trees some miles south of it. It was granted to the state of California by act of Congress, June 30, 1864 (13 Stat. L. 325), but actual control of the area and its development were delayed some ten years by the adverse claims of settlers in the area. The Yosemite National Park was created in 1890, and in 1905 the California State Legislature passed an act of retrocession by which the valley and grove were returned to the federal government to be included in the national park. *(Carl Parcher Russell—One Hundred Years in Yosemite)*

Underseas park (federal) was the Key Largo Coral Reef Preserve, 21 miles long and 3½ miles wide, lying in the Atlantic Ocean off Key Largo, Fla., established March 15, 1960, by presidential proclamation No. 3,339 of President Dwight David Eisenhower. This wildlife refuge contains 40 of the 52 known coral species. Previously, it had been the John Pennekamp Coral Reef State Park, the title to which had been obtained December 3, 1959, by the Florida Board of Parks and Historic Monuments. *(Federal Register. March 19, 1960)*

PARK, INDUSTRIAL. *See* Industrial Park

PARK SERVICE (national) was created by act of August 25, 1916 (39 Stat. L. 535), "to establish a National Park Service, and for other purposes" to promote and regulate the use of the federal areas known as national parks, monuments and reservations. The Secretary of the Treasury appointed Stephen Tyng Mather director at $4,500 per annum and Horace Marden Albright as assistant director at $2,500 a year. *(Jenks Cameron—The National Park Service)*

PARKING GARAGE. *See* Garage: Hydraulic-lift parking garage

PARKING METER

Parking meter (automatic) was the Park-O-Meter, which was installed in Oklahoma City, Okla., on July 16, 1935, by the Dual Parking Meter Company of Oklahoma City. Twenty-foot spaces were painted on the pavement and a nickel-in-the-slot parking meter was installed at each space so that it would be opposite the hood of the car parked there. The machines, devised by Carlton Cole Magee, were sold outright to the city, funds being obtained from their earnings.

The First

Parking-meter enforcement division. *See* Police: Parking-meter enforcement division

PARLIAMENT MEMBER (American-born woman). *See* Woman: American-born woman to become a member of Parliament

PARLIAMENTARY RULES OF ORDER were Thomas Jefferson's *A Manual of Parliamentary Practice, for the Use of the Senate of the United States,* a 199-page book, printed in 1801 by Samuel Harrison Smith in Washington, D.C.

PARLOR CAR. *See* Railroad car

PARTIES, POLITICAL. *See under* name of specific party, e.g. American Party, Equal Rights Party, People's Party

PARTRIDGE PROPAGATION. *See under* Birds

PASSENGER CAR. *See* Automobile

PASSENGER CONVEYOR. *See* Sidewalk (traveling)

PASSENGER STATION, RAILROAD. *See* Railroad station

PASSPORT

Passport recorded in the Passport Division of the State Department is dated July 8, 1796. The passport was issued to Francis Maria Barrere, "a citizen of the United States having occasion to pass into foreign countries about his lawful affairs," and was signed by Thomas Pickering, Secretary of State. *(American Passport: Its History—U.S. State Department, Washington, D.C.)*

Passport Division chief (woman). *See* Woman: Woman Passport Division chief

Passport fee was levied under the Internal Revenue Act of July 1, 1862 (12 Stat. L. 472), "to provide internal revenue to support the government and to pay interest on the public debt." It fixed a fee of $3 for "every passport issued in the office of the Secretary of State." Prior to this time, consuls in foreign countries charged a fee, not exceeding $1, for passports which they issued, but passports which were issued in the United States were gratis.

Passport issued to a President of the United States in office was made out on November 27, 1918, to President Woodrow Wilson. He left the United States on Wednesday, December 5, 1918, on the 25,576-ton U.S. transport *George Washington* and arrived at Brest, France, on December 13, 1918.

Passport photographs were required by a regulation effective November 20, 1914.

PASTE INK. *See* Ink: Ink paste

PASTELIST was Henrietta Johnston of Charlestown, S.C., whose artistic endeavors were produced between 1707 and 1720. She worked with colored chalk; her subjects were principally

The First

PASTELIST—*Continued*
colonial women of South Carolina. In 1718 she executed her best piece of work, a likeness of "His Excellency Robert Johnson Captain General, Governor and Commander-in-Chief in and over His Majesty's Province of Carolina." She also has the honor of being the first American woman painter. *(Margaret Simons Middleton—America's First Pastellist)*

PASTEURIZED MILK. *See* Milk: Milk pasteurized commercially

PATENT
Aerosol patent was No. 34,894, issued April 8, 1862, to John D. Lynde of Philadelphia, Pa., on an "improved bottle for aerated liquids." It had a valve, complete with dip tube for dispensing an aerated liquid from a bottle.

Airplane patent was No. 821,393, on "new and useful improvements in Flying-Machines," awarded to Orville Wright and Wilbur Wright of Dayton, Ohio, May 22, 1906.

Black to obtain a patent was Henry Blair of Glenross, Md., who obtained a patent on October 14, 1834, on a corn planter. Two years later, on August 31, 1836, he was also given a patent on a cotton seed planter.

Design patent was issued November 9, 1842, to George Bruce of New York City, under authority of an act of August 29, 1842 (5 Stat. L. 544). Design patent No. 1 was on a type face. Design patent No. 2 was on a design impressed on metal and was issued on February 24, 1843, to Waterman L. Ormsby of Bristol, Conn.

English patent granted to a resident of America was No. 401, issued November 25, 1715, to "Thomas Masters, Planter of Pennsylvania, for an invention found out by Sibylla his wife for cleaning and curing the Indian Corn growing in several colonies in America." *(Records in the Patent Office, London, England)*

Fruit tree patent was plant patent No. 7, which was issued February 16, 1932, to James E. Markham, and assigned to the Stark Bros. Nurseries & Orchards Company of Louisiana, Mo. The patent was obtained on a peach tree, the fruit of which ripens later than ordinary peaches.

Label patent was issued August 1, 1874, to the Baltimore Pearl Hominy Company of Baltimore, Md. Label patent No. 1 was for a breakfast hominy label to be attached to the sack, barrel, or box in which the hominy was to be sold.

Machine patent granted by the colonies was issued March 6, 1646, to Joseph Jencks by Massachusetts: "The Cort, considring ye necessity of raising such manufactures of engins of mils to go by water, for speedy dispatch of much worke with few hands, & being sufficiently informed of ye ability of ye petitionr to pforme such workes,

The First

grant his petition, (yt no othr pson shall set up or use any such new invention or trade for fourteen yeares, without ye licence of him, ye said Joseph Jenkes,) so farr as concernes any such new invention, & so as it shalbe alwayes in ye powr of this Corte to restraine ye exportation of such manufactures, & ye prizes of them, to moderation, if occasion so require." *(Nathaniel Bradstreet Shurtleff—Records of the Governor and Company of the Massachusetts Bay in New England)*

Numbering system for patents was introduced July 13, 1836. Previous to that, 9,957 unnumbered patents had been issued. Patent No. 1 under the consecutive numbering system was issued July 13, 1836, to John Ruggles of Thomaston, Maine, for "traction wheels for locomotive steam-engine for rail and other roads." Ruggles was chairman of the Committee on Patents of the United States Senate.

Patent granted by the colonies was awarded to Samuel Winslow in 1641 by Massachusetts for a new method of extracting salt: "Whereas Samuel Winslow hath made a proposition to this Court to furnish the contrey with salt at more easy rates then otherwise can bee had, & to make it by a meanes & way which hitherto hath not bene discovered, it is therefore ordered, that if the said Samuel shall, within the space of one yeare, set upon the said worke, hee shall enjoy the same, to him & his associates, for the space of ten yeares, so as it shall not bee lawfull to any other pson to make salt after the same way during the said yeares; pvided, nevthelesse, that it shall bee lawfull for any pson to bring in any salt, or to make salt after any othrway, dureing the said tearme." *(Nathaniel Bradstreet Shurtleff—Records of the Governor and Company of the Massachusetts Bay in New England, Vol. 1)*

Patent granted by the United States Government was issued to Samuel Hopkins of Vermont on July 31, 1790, for a process of making potash and pearl ashes. The document bore the signatures of George Washington, President; Thomas Jefferson, Secretary of State; and Edmund Randolph, Attorney General. Only three patents were issued that year. In May 1802 the Patent Office was organized and Dr. William Thornton was made Superintendent "to have charge of the issuing of patents." In 1833 the head of the Patent Office wanted to resign because "everything seems to have been done," although only about 9,000 patents had been issued. By 1960 nearly 3 million had been granted. *(George Whitfield Evans—The Birth and Growth of the Patent Office)*

Patent granted jointly to a father and son was awarded August 2, 1791, to Samuel Briggs, Sr. and Jr., of Philadelphia, Pa., on a machine for making nails.

The First

Patent issued by the Confederate States of America was No. 1, issued August 1, 1861, to James J. Van Houten of Savannah, Ga., on a breech-loading gun.

Patent law (national) was an "act to promote the progress of useful arts," approved April 10, 1790 (1 Stat. L. 109). The board in charge of granting patents styled itself the Patent Board, the Patent Commission, or the Commissioners for the Promotion of Useful Arts. Its first members were Thomas Jefferson, Secretary of State; Henry Knox, Secretary of War; and Edmund Randolph, Attorney General. The responsibility for administering the patent laws was given to the Department of State. The name was changed to the Patent and Trademark Office on January 2, 1975 (93 Stat. L. 596), by act of Congress. *(U.S. Department of Commerce—The Story of the American Patent System 1790–1940)*

Patent on a "solar airplane vehicle" was obtained by Elmer G. Johnson of Fairborn, Ohio, who received patent No. 3,089,670 on May 14, 1963. His application was filed September 25, 1957.

Patent reissue was granted January 9, 1838, to Julius Hatch of Great Bend, Pa. Patent reissue No. 1 was on a "machine for sowing plaster, ashes, seed and other separable substances," which had been patented August 17, 1835. A reissue is an amended claim and does not extend the life of a patent.

Patentee to obtain more than one patent from the United States Patent Office was Samuel Mulliken of Philadelphia, Pa., who was granted four patents on March 11, 1791. They were on a "machine for threshing grain and corn," a "machine for breaking and swingling hemp," a "machine for cutting and polishing marble," and a "machine for raising a nap on cloths."

Plant patent was awarded to Henry F. Bosenberg of New Brunswick, N.J., on August 18, 1931. Plant patent No. 1 covered a climbing rose named New Dawn which blooms successively throughout the season instead of in June only, as does its parent, Dr. Van Fleet. The application for the patent was filed on August 6, 1930.

President who had received a patent. *See under* President (U.S.)

Print patent was issued March 7, 1893, to the H. J. Heinz Company of Pittsburgh, Pa. The application was filed October 31, 1892. Print patent No. 1 was for "Heinz's Preserves, Celery Sauce, Ketchup" in the shape of a pickle with three designs in circles. A patented print cannot be used as a trademark but only in advertisements.

Woman granted a patent. *See under* Woman

The First

PATENT COMMISSIONER was Henry Leavitt Ellsworth, who was appointed on June 15, 1835, by President Andrew Jackson. Prior to that time the Patent Office had been directed by the Superintendent of Patents. Ellsworth resigned on April 30, 1845, to act as land agent in Lafayette, Ind., for the purchase and settlement of public lands. *(Henry Leavitt Ellsworth—A Digest of Patents Issued by the United States from 1790 to January 1, 1839)*

PATENT EXAMINER

Woman examiner-in-chief of the Patent Office and Trademark Office was Brereton Sturtevant of Wilmington, Del., nominated by President Richard Milhous Nixon on July 2, 1971, confirmed by the Senate on July 29, 1971, and sworn in August 24, 1971.

Woman patent examiner was Anna R. G. Nichols of Melrose, Mass., a clerk in the United States Patent Office, who satisfactorily passed a scientific examination and took office July 1, 1873, as an assistant examiner in the Patent Office.

PATENT LEATHER. *See* Leather

PATENT LIST was the *Official Gazette of the U.S. Patent Office,* issued weekly, which gave the numbers, titles, and claims of the patents issued during the week immediately preceding, together with the names and addresses of the patentees. The first issue was dated January 3, 1872.

PATENT MEDICINE ADVERTISEMENT. *See* Advertisement

PATENT MEDICINE ALMANAC. *See* Almanac

PATHOLOGY CHAIR. *See under* Medical instruction

PATHOLOGY DIVISION (Animal Industry Bureau). *See under* Animal Industry Bureau (U.S.)

PATHOLOGY TEXTBOOK. *See* Medical book

PATRIOTIC AMERICAN SONG. *See under* Music

PATROL. *See* Border patrol; Fire patrol

PATROL BOMBER, NAVAL. *See under* Aviation —Airplane

PATROL WAGON, POLICE. *See* Automobile police patrol wagon

PATTERNS, PAPER. *See* Paper patterns

PAVEMENT. *See* Road: Mosaic pavement

PAWNBROKING ORDINANCE was passed July 13, 1812, by New York City. *(Minutes of the Common Council of the City of New York 1784–1831)*

PAY STATION (telephone). *See under* Telephone

PAY TELEVISION. *See under* Television—Telecast

The First

PAYMASTER (U.S. Army). *See under* Army officer

PEACE CORPS
Woman director of the Peace Corps was Dr. Carolyn Robertson Payton, nominated September 7, 1977, by President Jimmy Carter, to head 6,200 volunteers and trainees in 62 developing nations. She resigned November 25, 1978.

PEACE PRIZE, NOBEL. *See* Nobel Prize

PEACE SOCIETY was the New York Peace Society, which was organized August 16, 1815. David Low Dodge was its first president. Similar societies were formed elsewhere, and on May 8, 1828, the New York Peace Society became a member of a national organization called the American Peace Society, which held its first annual meeting May 13, 1829, in New York City. *(Edson Leone Whitney—Centennial History of the American Peace Society)*

PEACETIME CONSCRIPTION BILL. *See under* Conscription

PEARL BUTTON. *See* Button: Buttons of freshwater pearl

PEDAGOGY BOOK. *See* Teaching methods book

PEDAGOGY CHAIR
Pedagogy chair (permanent) in a college requiring the occupant to give all his time to the subject was established by the University of Michigan, Ann Arbor, Mich., in 1879. The first incumbent was Professor William Harold Payne. The professorship was called the Science and the Art of Teaching. Although this was the first chair of pedagogy, it was not the first attempt at instruction in pedagogy, as Brown University had given instruction in the subject in 1850, and Antioch College had offered an elective course in the subject in 1853.

PEDIATRIC BOOK. *See* Medical book

PEDIATRIC CLINIC. *See* Medical clinic

PEDIATRICS PROFESSOR. *See under* Medical instruction

PEEP SHOW. *See under* Motion picture

PEEP-SHOW MACHINE. *See under* Motion picture

PEGGING MACHINE, SHOE. *See* Shoe pegging machine

PELLAGRA EXPERIMENT. *See under* Public health

PELOTA. *See* Jai alai

PEN
See also Fountain pen

Ball-point pen patent was No. 392,046, awarded October 30, 1888, to John J. Loud of Weymouth, Mass., on a pen having a spheroidal marking point

The First

capable of revolving in all directions. The application was filed February 4, 1888.

Pen with truly erasable ink was the Eraser Mate pen announced in January 1979 and available to consumers in April 1979. It was a refillable ball-point pen, a product of the Paper Mate Division of the Gillette Company. The ink was 1 million times thicker than water. Patent No. 4,097,290, issued on June 27, 1978, for "ball-point instruments writing with improved transitorially erasable trace and ink compositions therefor" to Frank Andrew Miller of West Los Angeles and Henry Peper, Jr., of Pacific Palisades, Calif., and assigned to the Gillette Company, Boston, Mass. The application was filed March 26, 1976. The pen was produced in Santa Monica, Calif.

Steel pen patent was obtained by Peregrine Williamson of Baltimore, Md., on November 22, 1809, on "a metallic writing pen."

Steel pens commercially produced were manufactured by Richard Esterbrook, who in 1858 established a factory in Camden, N.J. He produced steel pens which met with great success. His company is still producing pens and is now known as the Esterbrook Steel Pen Manufacturing Company.

PENCIL
Indelible pencil was invented by Edson P. Clark of Northampton, Mass., who obtained patent No. 56,180 on July 10, 1866. It had a "filling composed of silver, black lead, calcined gypsum and lampblack or asphaltum" which was shellacked to the groove in the wood.

Paper pencil was invented by Frederick E. Blaisdell of Philadelphia, Pa., who obtained patent No. 549,952 on November 19, 1895, as well as patent No. 550,212 on the same date on a machine for manufacturing paper pencils.

Pencil with an attached eraser was patented by Hyman L. Lipman of Philadelphia, Pa., who received patent No. 19,783 on March 30, 1858. The pencil had a groove at one end into which was "secured a piece of prepared rubber, glued in at one end."

PENCIL FACTORY was established by William Monroe of Concord, Mass., in June 1812. He manufactured about 30 lead pencils of unfinished cedar, unpolished, very thin, with square leads, which he sold to Benjamin Adams, a hardware dealer of Union Street, Boston, Mass. Adams then contracted to purchase all the pencils Monroe could produce.

PENITENTIARY. *See* Prison

PENNY DAILY NEWSPAPER. *See* Newspaper

PENNY RESTAURANT. *See* Restaurant

The First

PENSION

Old age pension laws (state) were enacted March 5, 1923, by Montana and Nevada, whose respective governors signed their pension measures the same hour on the same day. Montana, however, had the first statewide mandatory system. It granted pensions of $25 a month to people who were over 70 years of age and who had been citizens and residents of the state for the previous 15 years. The funds were derived from the counties. *(Abraham Epstein—Challenge of the Aged)*

Pension act was passed by the Plymouth Pilgrims, who enacted a regulation in 1636 providing that whosoever should set forth as a soldier and return maimed should be competently maintained by the colony for the rest of his life. *(David Pulsifer —Records of the Colony of New Plymouth in New England, Vol. II, p. 106)*

Pension act of the Continental Congress was passed August 26, 1776. It provided "that every commissioned officer, non-commissioned officer, and private soldier who shall have lost a limb in any engagement, or be so disabled in the service of the United States of America as to render him incapable afterwards of getting a livelihood, shall receive, during his life or the continuance of such disability, one half of his monthly pay from and after the time that his pay as an officer or soldier ceases." As the resources of the Continental Congress were meager, the states were asked to make the payment: "That it be recommended to the assemblies or legislative bodies of the several States to cause payment to be made of all such half pay or other allowances as shall be adjudged due to the persons aforenamed on account of the United States." *(William Henry Glasson—History of Military Pension Legislation in the United States)*

Pension for a President. *See under* President (U.S.)

Pension plan was offered to some 20,000 employees of the American Telephone and Telegraph Company during the presidency of Theodore Newton Vail and put into effect on January 1, 1913. The plan included coverage of employees 60 years of age with more than 20 years employment, accident and disability benefits with full pay for 13 weeks or half-pay up to 6 years, sickness disability (for those employed more than 10 years) paying full pay for 13 weeks or half-pay for 39 years, and a life insurance policy with a maximum value of $5,000.

Pension to the widow of a President was authorized by an "act granting a pension to Mary Lincoln," July 14, 1870 (16 Stat. L. 653). She received $3,000 per annum. An act of February 2, 1882 (22 Stat. L. 647), increased the annual pensions to $5,000 for the three widows then living and made a special grant of $15,000 to Mary Lincoln.

The First

Pensions paid by the United States Government were those paid under the act of September 29, 1789 (1 Stat. L. 95), which took up the obligation of paying the pensions granted under the provisions of the pension laws enacted by the Continental Congress and appropriated money for payments to invalids who were wounded and disabled during the Revolutionary War for one year from March 4, 1789. The act of July 16, 1790 (1 Stat. L. 121), continued the payment of pensions for one year from March 4, 1790. The act of April 30, 1790 (1 Stat. L. 121), provided for pensions to those wounded or disabled in the line of duty, and the act of March 23, 1792 (1 Stat. L. 245), provided for pensions of those suffering wounds or disabilities known to be of service origin. The act of March 18, 1818 (3 Stat. L. 410), was the first universal service pension act and was not limited to those who could prove their disabilities to be of service origin. *(William Henry Glasson—History of Military Pension Legislation in the United States)*

Pensions paid by the United States Government to workers in private industry were mailed July 13, 1936, when checks totaling $901.56 were sent to 18 retired railroad employees, in accordance with the Railroad Retirement Act of August 29, 1935 (49 Stat. L. 967), which appropriated $46,685,-000 "to establish a retirement system for employees of carriers subject to the Interstate Commerce Act, and for other purposes."

Teachers' pensions. *See* Teachers' pension fund

PENSIONS COMMISSIONER (U.S.) was James L. Edwards, appointed under the provisions of the act of March 2, 1833 (4 Stat. L. 622). He served as Commissioner of Pensions under the War Department from March 3, 1833, to November 1850, and received $2,500 a year. Previously he had been a clerk in the office of the Secretary of War and had been in charge of pension work since 1816.

PEOPLE'S PARTY (formed by members of the Farmers' Alliance and other industrial unions) was organized and the name adopted at a national convention held in Cincinnati, Ohio, May 19, 1891. At the second national convention, held July 2–5, 1892, in Omaha, Neb., James Baird Weaver of Iowa was nominated as the presidential candidate and James Gaven Field of Virginia for vice president. The People's Party developed into the Populist Party later.

PERAMBULATOR. *See* Baby carriage

PERCHERON HORSE. *See* Horse

PERCOLATOR. *See* Coffee percolator patent

PERCUSSION ROCK DRILL. *See* Drill

PERFORATED PAPER (wrapping). *See* Paper

PERFORATED POSTAGE STAMP. *See* Postage stamp

The First

PERFUMED ADVERTISING PAGE. *See* Newspaper: Newspaper with perfumed advertising page

PERIODICAL

See also under specific languages, occupations, religious and fraternal organizations, sciences, sports, trades, e.g., Agricultural journal, Book trade magazine, Catholic periodical, Welsh magazine

All-fiction pulp magazine was the October 1896 *Argosy*, 192 pages, size 7 by 10 inches. It was an outgrowth of an 8-page illustrated weekly for boys and girls edited by Frank Andrew Munsey entitled *The Golden Argosy*, which was first issued December 2, 1882, bearing the date December 9, 1882. It became the *Argosy* on December 1, 1888. It was published in New York City.

American Indian–language monthly was the *Siwinowe Kesibwi* ("The Shawnee Sun"), printed February 24, 1835, at the press of Jotham Meeker, a missionary at the Shawnee Baptist Mission in Kansas. The first issue was dated March 1835. Johnston Lykins, a Baptist missionary, was editor. *(Kansas Historical Quarterly. Vol. 2, No. 4. November 1933)*

American Jewish magazine (successful) was *The Occident and American Jewish Advocate*, a monthly periodical devoted to the diffusion of knowledge on Jewish literature and religion, edited by Isaac Leeser, published at Philadelphia, Pa. The first issue, 60 pages, was dated April 1843 (Nissan 5603).

Antislavery magazine was *The Emancipator*, issued monthly April 30–October 31, 1820. Edited and published by Elihu Embree, it cost $1 a year.

Art magazine of merit was *The Illustrated Magazine of Art* "containing selections from the various departments of painting, sculpture, architecture, history, biography, art-industry, manufactures, scientific inventions and discoveries, local and domestic scenes, ornamental works, etc." It was published by Alexander Montgomery in New York City, from January 1853 to December 4, 1854. The first issue contained 60 pages.

Black periodical was *The Mirror of Liberty*, a quarterly of 16 pages, edited and published in New York City by David Ruggles. The first issue was dated July 1838.

Children's magazine was published in Hartford, Conn., by [Barzillai] Hudson and [George] Goodwin, and was called the *Children's Magazine: Calculated for the Use of Families and Schools*. Only four issues were printed from January to April 1789, each containing 48 pages, an "abridgement of geography, essays on morality, religion, manners, etc., familiar letters, dialogues and select pieces of poetry."

Children's magazine with literary merit was *The Juvenile Miscellany*, founded by Lydia Maria Frances Child in 1826. It was a bimonthly and appeared from September 1826 to January 1829. It

The First

was published by Putnam & Hunt in Boston, Mass. The first issue contained 108 pages. *(Letters of Lydia Maria Child)*

College magazine was the Yale *Literary Cabinet*, published November 15, 1806, in New Haven, Conn. It was an 8-page biweekly and was edited by three college seniors. It sold for $1 a year and continued for a year only. *(Anonymous—Four Years at Yale—Henry Holt & Co. 1871)*

Comic magazine was *The Wasp*, edited by Robert Rusticoat, Esq. ("Rusty-Turncoat"), and printed by Harry Crosswell, Hudson, N.Y. Volume 1, No. 1 dated July 7, 1802, consisted of 4 pages and lampooned politics and politicians.

Comic weekly was *The John Donkey*, 16 pages, published by G. B. Zieber & Company of Philadelphia, Pa., from January 1, 1848, to October 21, 1848. It cost 6 cents a copy or $3 a year. It was edited by Thomas Dunn English and George G. Foster and was illustrated by Felix Octavius Carr Darley and Henry Louis Stephens.

Electricity journal was *The Electro-Magnetic and Mechanics Intelligencer*, which appeared on January 18, 1840. This was the first magazine printed on a printing press operated by electricity. It was printed in New York City on a press "propelled by electro-magnetism." The editor of the magazine and the inventor of the electrical printing press was Thomas Davenport.

Factory workers' magazine published was *The Lowell Offering*, "a repository of original articles on various subjects, wholly written, edited and published by females operatives employed in the mills," a bimonthly, 6¼ cents a copy, published October 1840 by Powers and Bagley.

Fashion weekly was *Harper's Bazar*, "a Repository of Fashion, Pleasure and Instruction," whose first issue, which contained 16 pages, was published on November 2, 1867, by Harper & Bros in New York City. It cost 10¢ a week or $4.00 a year. Ladies in the country were "supplied gratuitously, through the mails with the first six numbers of Harper's Bazar upon written application to the publishers." The magazine was edited by Mary Louise Booth and appeared as a weekly from November 1867 to April 1901 and then, beginning in May 1901, as a monthly. Within 10 years it had a circulation of 80,000.

Gas magazine was the *American Gas-Light Journal*, a monthly devoted to light, water supply, and sewerage, published by John B. Murray & Co., New York City, at $3 a year. The first issue, July 1, 1859, contained 16 pages. It listed 183 gaslight companies in the United States and 5 in Canada. The second issue, August 1, 1859, was larger in size and was described as the Representative of Light, Water, and the Public Health. In 1917 the name was changed to *American Gas Engineering Journal* and in 1921 to *American Gas Journal*.

The First

Illustrated weekly was *Brother Jonathan, a Weekly Compend of Belles Lettres and the Fine Arts, Standard Literature and General Intelligence,* issued January 1, 1842. It consisted of 28 pages and a 32-page supplement containing the installment "Adventures of Tom Stapleton," by John M. Moore. It was founded by Benjamin Henry Day and Nathaniel Parker Willis and was published by Wilson & Company, New York City. It was not the first magazine, however, to contain an illustration.

Jewish monthly magazine was *The Jew,* "a defence of Judaism against all adversaries, and particularly against the insidious attacks of *Israel Advocate,*" published in New York City from March 1823 to March 1825. Solomon Henry Jackson was the editor.

Jewish weekly (German-American) was the *Israels Herold,* 8 pages, published in New York City on March 30, 1849. It was printed every Friday and sold for $1.50 semi annually and 75¢ quarterly. A 12-line advertisement cost 50 cents, 3 insertions for $1. It ceased publication on June 15. Isidor Busch was editor. *(Historia Judaica—Oct. 1940)*

Jewish weekly published in English was *The Asmonean,* an 8-page family journal of commerce, politics, religion, and literature, devoted to the interests of the American Israelites, first issued October 26, 1849, in New York City. It was published by Robert Lyon and sold for $3 a year. It was 8 pages long, 3 columns on a page.

Large-type weekly. *See* Newspaper: Large-type weekly

Magazine containing a fashion plate was *The Port Folio,* published by Bradford and Inskeep, Philadelphia, Pa., and Inskeep and Bradford, New York City. The June 1809 issue contained two engravings, one page showing a full dress and one showing the front and back views of "Fontarabian robes of Saragossa brown net."

Magazine for the blind was the *Student's Magazine, a Periodical for the Blind,* published January 1837 by the Pennsylvania Institution for the Instruction of the Blind, Philadelphia, Pa. Embossed raised capital letters were used. It was a monthly and cost $3 a year. *(Pennsylvania Institution for the Instruction of the Blind—Sixth Annual Report. 1839)*

Magazine for women to continue publication for more than five years was the *Ladies' Magazine,* which was founded in Boston, Mass., in 1828 by Sarah Josepha Hale *(Frederic Hudson—Journalism in the United States)*

Magazine of the United States Government was the daily *Federal Register,* issued March 14, 1936. The masthead was decorated with the eagle shield and a Latin motto "Littera Scripta Manet" ("The Written Word Endures"). It was published in Washington, D.C. by the National Archives

The First

under Federal Register Act approved July 26, 1935 (49 Stat. L. 500), and contained 16 two-column pages. The administrative committee consisted of the archivist or acting archivist, an officer of the Attorney General, and the public printer or acting public printer. The magazine publishes federal laws, orders and reports and is not limited in scope like the *Congressional Record.*

Magazine published for mental patients was the *Illuminator,* written and published in 1843 by patients in Pennsylvania Hospital, Philadelphia, Pa. The first issue appeared April 1, 1843, and contained 24 three-column pages, each in Spencerian handwriting. Volume 1 consisted of three issues, April, May, and June; volume 2 contained two issues, July and August.

Magazine published in America was *The American Magazine, or a Monthly View of the Political State of the British Colonies,* the first issue probably appearing February 13, 1741, in Philadelphia, Pa. It was published by Andrew Bradford and edited by John Webbe. The first number contained 50 pages. It was published monthly for three months. On the title page was an illustration of the Philadelphia waterfront. It appeared probably about three days prior to Benjamin Franklin's *The General Magazine and Historical Chronicle for All the British Plantations in America. (Lyon Norman Richardson—A History of Early American Magazines)*

Magazine to contain a phonograph record was the November 1955 issue of *Pageant,* published in New York City, which went on sale October 10, 1955. It contained a 78 r.p.m. acetate recording of "If You Don't Want My Love," sung by Jaye P. Morgan to the accompaniment of Hugo Winterhalter's orchestra. Approximately 1,100,000 copies were issued.

Mechanics' magazine was *The American Mechanics' Magazine,* "containing useful original matter, on subjects connected with manufactures, the arts, and sciences; as well as selections from the most approved domestic and foreign journals," first published in New York City, by J.V. Seaman, February 5, 1825, to February 11, 1826. From 1826 to 1828 its title was *The Franklin Journal and American Mechanics' Magazine,* and later it became *The Journal of the Franklin Institute.*

Music printed in a magazine. *See under* Music

Photoengraved magazine was the *Literary Digest,* published in New York City, October 18, 1919. It consisted of 80 pages and cover. The material was typewritten and photoengraved. A strike of printers at the time made it impossible to issue regularly printed issues of the magazine without great difficulty.

The First

PERIODICAL—*Continued*

Quarterly magazine was *The American Review of History and Politics and General Repository of Literature and State Papers,* edited by Robert Walsh and published in Philadelphia, Pa. The first issue, January 1811, contained 200 pages and a 60-page appendix. Subscription was $6 a year, to be paid on the delivery of the second number of every year. The last issue was published October 1812.

Sectarian magazine was *The Christian History,* "containing accounts of the revival and propagation of religion in Great Britain and America." It consisted of 8 pages, printed for Thomas Prince by Samuel Kneeland and Bartholomew Green, Boston, from March 5, 1743, to February 23, 1745.

Sectarian magazine (German) was *Ein Geistliches Magazien; oder, Aus den Schätzen der Schrifftgelehrten zum Himmelreich gelehrt, dargereichtes altes und neues,* edited by Christoph Saur (or Sower), which appeared irregularly from 1764 to 1771 at Germantown, Pa. Fifty copies were printed and distributed gratis as an addendum to the *Germantauner Zeitung.*

Sectarian magazine printed in rotogravure was *Catholic Missions,* issued October 1, 1934, by the Society for the Propagation of the Faith, New York City. It was issued quarterly and sold for a penny a copy. Its editor was the Right Reverend Monsignor William Quinn.

Spanish magazine published by students was *El Estudiante Comercial,* founded in 1917 at the High School of Commerce, New York City. Philip Leonard Green was its first director and Irving B. Simon its first editor.

Trade journal was the *Rail-road Advocate,* published biweekly from July 4, 1831, to June 14, 1832, in Rogersville, Tenn., by "an association of gentlemen." The first issue contained 8 pages measuring 12½ by 9¾ inches. Its main objects were "to advocate railroads and other internal improvements that would connect East Tennessee with markets for its surplus produce" and "end its isolation from the rest of the country," and to collect and publish "all the information that can be collected on this interesting subject."

PERIODICAL INDEX was *An Alphabetical Index to Subjects Treated in the Reviews and Other Periodicals to Which No Indexes Have Been Published,* which was edited by William Frederick Poole and issued in 1848 by George Palmer Putnam, New York City. This was the forerunner of the famous *Poole's Index to Periodical Literature* first shown in September 1853 at a library convention in New York City.

PERISCOPE was invented by Thomas Doughty, acting chief engineer of the United States Navy in 1864. During Nathaniel Prentiss Banks's Red River expedition Doughty was on the turreted monitor

The First

Osage. Annoyed by bushwhackers and snipers who could not be seen yet did deadly work, Doughty rigged up a sheet iron tube extending from a few feet above the deck to the engine room below, with openings near the top and bottom, and by an arrangement of mirrors he could see the shore. When attacked, he would signal the gunners to fire. Admiral David Dixon Porter officially thanked him for his invention.

PERITONITIS

Peritonitis preventive (successful) was amniotic fluid, first used to prevent postoperative peritonitis and adhesions in 1922 by Dr. Herbert Lester Johnson of Boston, Mass. The first fluid was of human origin, from cesarean operations, but the widespread use of this new principle of preventive medicine resulted in a commercial preparation known as Amniotic Fluid Concentrate, made from bovine amniotic fluid.

PERMALLOY was developed June 7, 1913, at the Bell Telephone Laboratories, New York City, by Gustaf Waldemar Elmen. It was first applied commercially in 1924 when it was used in the New York–Azores submarine telegraph cable and increased the transmission rate from 300 to 2,000 letters a minute. Permalloy was used in the form of a thin tape, six-thousandths of an inch thick, which was wound around the conductor. Its extraordinarily high magnetic permeability at very low magnetizing forces permitted the high inductance necessary for high-speed transmission.

PERMIT MAIL. *See* Postal Service: Permit mail

PETROLEUM
See also Oil

Petroleum exported to Europe was shipped in barrels on the *Elizabeth Watts,* a 224-ton brig captained by Charles Bryant. On November 12, 1861, Messrs. Peter Wright and Sons of Philadelphia chartered this brig from Messrs. Edmund A. Sander and Co., and the shipment was made from Philadelphia, Pa., on November 19, 1861, and arrived at the Victoria Docks, London, England, on January 9, 1862, with 1,329 barrels of oil. Since it was not easy to recruit a crew (the men would not work above a cargo of oil), a crew was shanghaied. *(James Dodds Henry—Thirty-five Years of Oil Transport)*

Petroleum refining course of a collegiate grade was offered by the School of Mines, University of Pittsburgh, Pittsburgh, Pa., in the university year 1922–1923 under the direction of Dr. Warren Fred Faragher.

PETROLEUM JELLY was manufactured in 1870 by Robert Augustus Chesebrough who coined the word Vaseline and registered it May 14, 1878, as a trademark to identify his particular brand. On May 10, 1880, he organized the Chesebrough Manufacturing Company, New York City, of

The First

which he became president, holding this office until May 6, 1909.

PEWTER BUTTON. *See* Button

PHARMACIST

Pharmacist (woman) was Elizabeth Marshall (1768–1836), a daughter of Charles Marshall, who served as president of the Philadelphia College of Pharmacy (1821–1824). She became manager of the apothecary originally established by her grandfather, Christopher Marshall, in 1729 in Philadelphia, Pa. She served from 1804 until 1825, when the store was sold.

Pharmacist (woman graduate) was Susan Hayhurst of St. Michael's, Md., who graduated March 16, 1883, from the Philadelphia College of Pharmacy, Philadelphia, Pa., with the Ph.G. degree. The subject of her thesis was "Dispensary Work." She graduated on February 28, 1857, from the Female Medical College of Pennsylvania, receiving an M.D. degree. She was also the first woman physician to graduate from a pharmacy college.

PHARMACOPOEIA

Pharmacopoeia was the 32-page work of Dr. William Brown, Physician-General to the Hospitals of the United States, written especially for army usage and published in Philadelphia, Pa., in 1778 for the use of the Military Hospital of the U.S. Army located at Lititz, Pa. It was entitled *Pharmacopoeia simpliciorum et efficaciorum, in usum nosocomii militaris,* etc., and was printed entirely in Latin. The size of the type page was 4¼ by 2½ inches.

Pharmacopoeia (general) was *The Pharmacopoeia of the United States of America.* It was published December 15, 1820, in both English and Latin by Wells & Lilly of Boston, Mass., and copyrighted by Ewer & Bedlington of Boston. It listed 217 drugs. It consisted of 274 pages printed on rather porous paper, 6 by 10 inches, and was recommended by the New York County Medical Society. The chairman in charge of the work was Dr. Lyman Spalding, who had proposed the work on January 8, 1817, to the medical society. *(Dr. James Alfred Spalding—Dr. Lyman Spalding)*

Pharmacopoeia prepared by a hospital staff was the *"Pharmacopoeia Nosocomii neoeboracensis, or the Pharmacopoeia of the New York Hospital,"* published under the authority of the physicians and surgeons of that institution, to which was added an appendix containing a general dosage table. The work consisted of 180 pages prepared by Dr. Valentine Seaman and Dr. Samuel Latham Mitchill. It was printed by A. Paul and published in 1816 by Collins & Company, New York City.

Pharmacopoeia prepared by a medical association for the use of its members was authorized October 3, 1805, by the Massachusetts Medical Society, Boston, Mass. It contained 286 pages and

The First

was edited by Dr. James Jackson and Dr. John Collins Warren. It was published in 1808 in Boston, Mass., as *The Pharmacopoeia of the Massachusetts Medical Society.*

PHARMACY

Homeopathic pharmacy was established by J. G. Wesselhoeft in 1834 at 9 Broad Street, Philadelphia, Pa. In 1835 he opened a branch at 498 Greenwich Street, New York City, which was purchased by William Radde, his clerk. Dr. Francis E. Boericke acquired the business and in 1869 formed a partnership with Adolph J. Tafel as Boericke and Tafel.

PHARMACY COLLEGE

Pharmacy college was the Philadelphia College of Apothecaries, established February 23, 1821, at a meeting presided over by Stephen North at Carpenters' Hall, Philadelphia, Pa. Charles Marshall was elected president of the college on March 27, 1821. On April 23, 1821, Dr. Samuel Jackson was appointed professor of materia medica and pharmacy, and Dr. Gerardt Troost professor of chemistry. The first class was held November 9, 1821. The school was incorporated March 30, 1822, at which time it was renamed the Philadelphia College of Pharmacy. The Ph.G. degree was conferred November 28, 1826, on 3 graduates, Charles Hazard Dingee, Charles H. McCormick, and William Sharp. They completed two full courses. (This was not the first time, however, that degrees had been granted to pharmacists. The University of Pennsylvania on April 5, 1821, had awarded honorary Master of Pharmacy degrees to 16 practicing apothecaries.) *(Joseph Winters England—The First Century of the Philadelphia College of Pharmacy)*

Pharmacy college to make analytical chemistry a required course was the Maryland College of Pharmacy (now part of the University of Maryland), Baltimore, Md. The chair of analytical chemistry was established on March 20, 1872, and Dr. William Simon was the first professor appointed thereto. The Maryland College of Pharmacy was incorporated January 27, 1841. The first graduation took place June 19, 1842, when three students received degrees.

PHARMACY LEGISLATION (state) requiring graduation from a pharmacy course was enacted May 3, 1904, by New York, effective January 1, 1905 (Chapter 554). Four years of practical experience and two years of schooling in pharmacy were required.

PHARMACY MAGAZINE was *The Journal of the Philadelphia College of Pharmacy,* which appeared in December 1825. Its first editor was Daniel B. Smith, who served from 1825 to 1828. The magazine contained 32 pages of "original and selected papers on subjects connected with pharmacy and chemistry," and sold for 25 cents.

The First

PHARMACY PROFESSOR

Pharmacy professor was Dr. Samuel Powel Griffitts, appointed professor of materia medica and pharmacy in 1789 at the Medical School of the College of Philadelphia, Pa. He continued in 1791, when the school merged with the University of Pennsylvania, and served until 1796.

Pharmacy professorship in which the holder gave full time to instructing the students in the theory and practice of pharmacy was established in 1844 by the Maryland College of Pharmacy (now part of the University of Maryland), Baltimore, Md. David Stewart was appointed to the chair of theory and practice of pharmacy, which he held from April 24, 1844, to April 28, 1846. *(Eugene Fauntleroy Cordell—University of Maryland 1807–1907)*

PHARMACY SOCIETY (national) was the American Pharmaceutical Association, organized October 6, 1852, in Philadelphia, Pa. Daniel B. Smith was elected president and William Procter, Jr., corresponding secretary. The first annual meeting was held in Boston, Mass., August 24, 1853. A preliminary meeting, held October 15, 1851, at the New York College of Pharmacy, New York City, led to the organization of the association.

PHILATELIC AGENCY. *See under* Postal service

PHILATELIC AUCTION was held May 28, 1870, from 6:00 P.M. to 9:00 P.M. at the Clinton Hall Book Sales Rooms and Art Galleries, New York City, by Leavitt, Streibeigh & Co., auctioneers. About 14,-000 stamps in 269 lots were offered for sale. The highest price for a single lot was $38 for 1,800 stamps; the highest price for a single stamp was $11, the lowest 35 cents. The bid for the first lot, 100 foreign stamps, started at 25 cents and closed at 60 cents. The total receipts for the day were approximately $500.

PHILATELIC MAGAZINE

Philatelic magazine (club organ) was *The American Journal of Philately,* the journal of the New York Philatelic Society, published March 1, 1868, at New York, N.Y. It consisted of 16 pages and was edited by John Walter Scott.

Philatelic magazine was the *Stamp Collector's Record,* which consisted of 4 pages, 5½ x 8¼, 2 columns to a page, published December 15, 1864, at Albany, N.Y., by Samuel Allan Taylor. It was issued on the 15th of every month and sold for 50 cents per annum. The rate for advertising was 15 cents a line. Issue No. 9 was published Oct. 1865 at Boston, Mass.

PHILATELIC SOCIETY

Philatelic Society was the New York Philatelic Society, organized March 21, 1867, in New York City, by 8 collectors of postage stamps. A constitution was adopted January 19, 1868. The first officers were Rev. J. A. Morley, D.D., LL.D., president; H. Grafton, M.D., and Willard K. Freeman,

The First

vice-presidents; John Walter Scott, treasurer; Charles Watson, secretary; George H. Earl and G. P. Ten Broeck, directors.

PHILOLOGICAL SOCIETY

National philological society was the American Philological Association, organized in New York City on November 13, 1868, to promote the advancement and diffusion of philological knowledge. The first convention was held July 27, 1869, in Poughkeepsie, N.Y., and the first president was William Dwight Whitney. *(American Philological Association—Transactions, Vol. 50. 1919)*

PHILOLOGY CHAIR

Comparative philology chair was established by Lafayette College, Easton, Pa., in 1856. The first professor was Francis Andrew March.

PHILOSOPHY BOOK

Philosophy book (American) was *Elementa Philosophica: Containing Chiefly, Noetica, or Things Relating to the Mind or Understanding. and Ethica, or Things Relating to the Moral Behaviour.* Written by Samuel Johnson, it consisted of 103 pages and was printed in 1752 at Philadelphia, Pa., by Benjamin Franklin and D. Hall.

PHILOSOPHY DEGREE. *See* Degrees (academic and honorary)

PHONETIC BIBLE. *See* Bible

PHONETIC DICTIONARY. *See* Dictionary

PHONOGRAPH

Phonograph was invented by Thomas Alva Edison of Menlo Park, N.J., who secured patent No. 200,521 on February 19, 1878, on a "phonograph or speaking machine." His original idea had been to invent a telegraph repeater, directions for the building of which he had given to one of his mechanics, John Kreusi, on August 12, 1877. The first cylinder, operated by a hand crank, was wrapped in tin foil with which two needles fastened to diaphragms made contact. The first verse recorded on the new instrument was "Mary Had a Little Lamb." A clock spring motor and waxlike record were invented some ten years later.

Phonograph that was practical was the Graphophone, manufactured by Bell & Tainter. On May 4, 1886, Chichester Bell and Charles Sumner Tainter received United States patent No. 341,214 a fundamental and basic patent, "for recording and reproducing speech and other sounds." Patents No. 341,212 on "reproducing sounds from phonograph records" and No. 341,213 on "transmitting and recording sounds by radiant energy" were also received on May 4, 1886, jointly with Alexander Graham Bell.

Phonograph with an automatic record changer was introduced by the Victor Talking Machine Company, Camden, N.J., in March 1927. It played twelve 10-inch records or twelve 12-inch records

The First

and stopped automatically after the last record had been played.

Phonograph with an enclosed horn in the cabinet was the Victor Victrola, manufactured August 22, 1906, by the Victor Talking Machine Co., Camden, N.J. It was in a mahogany cabinet (4 feet high, 20 inches wide, and 22 inches deep), cost $200, and was advertised September 1906.

PHONOGRAPH RECORD

Instantaneous phonograph recording was made October 22, 1934, of the balloon flight of Professor Jean Picard and his wife that took off from Ford Airport, Detroit, Mich., at 6:58 A.M. E.S.T. and made an 8-hour flight, 2 hours of which were in the stratosphere. The balloon crossed Lake Erie and landed in a treetop at Cadiz, Ohio.

Long-playing microgroove records that were successful were made by Columbia Records, Bridgeport, Conn., a division of the Columbia Broadcasting System, Inc., and introduced to the public on June 21, 1948, at the Waldorf-Astoria Hotel, New York City. The records were made of nonbreakable Vinylite plastic and were played at a speed of 33 1/3 r.p.m. One side of a 12-inch record played for 23 minutes, compared to 4 minutes on one side of a standard 78 rpm record.

Magazine to contain a phonograph record. *See under* Periodical

Phonograph record of a stage performance by the original cast was a ten-inch single-face disc record of "Old Folks at Home" ("Swanee River"), sung in Act I of the spectacular military operetta *When Johnny Comes Marching Home,* recorded in 1904 and released as No. M2931 by the Victor Talking Machine Company, Camden, N.J. The libretto was by Stanislaus Stange, the music by Julian Edwards, and the production by the Whitney Opera Company of which F. C. Whitney was the proprietor and manager. W. H. Thompson took the role of Major William Walker and Miss Quinn was Kate Pemberton.

PHONOGRAPH TRADE MAGAZINE was *The Phonogram,* "official organ of the phonograph companies of the United States," edited by V. H. McRae, which was published monthly in New York City from January 1891 to January 1893. The first issue contained an article by Thomas Alva Edison entitled "How Sound Is Reproduced."

PHOTO-FINISH CAMERA. *See* Camera

PHOTOELECTRIC CELL

Photoelectric cell or tube was publicly demonstrated on October 21, 1925, by the Westinghouse Electric and Manufacturing Company at the Electrical Show at Grand Central Palace in New York City. At this demonstration the photoelectric cell, which is sensitive to light, was used to count objects as they interrupted a light beam in passing, to open doors as a person or car approached, and to perform similar functions.

The First

Photoelectric cell installed commercially for operating doors was in Wilcox's Pier Restaurant, West Haven, Conn. The Stanley Works of New Britain, Conn., had completed the installation on June 19, 1931, of the "magic eye" which provided fully automatic control and operation of swinging doors between the main dining room and kitchen.

PHOTOENGRAVED MAGAZINE. *See* Periodical

PHOTOGRAPH

Aerial photograph was "Boston as the Eagle and the Wild Goose See It," taken October 13, 1860, by Samuel Archer King (navigator) of Providence, R.I., and James Wallace Black (photographer) of Boston, Mass., in a balloon, *The Queen of the Air,* held by a cable 1,200 feet above the city. Eight pictures were taken, only one of which was good. It showed an area bounded by Brattle Street on the north, the harbor on the east, Sumner Street on the south, and Park Street on the west. Wet plates were used, which were prepared in the balloon before each exposure.

Celestial photograph was a daguerreotype of the moon taken December 18, 1839, by John William Draper, professor of chemistry at New York University, New York City. He exposed the plate 20 minutes. The image was one inch in diameter. He presented the photographs on March 23, 1840, to the Lyceum of Natural History of New York City. *(George Frederick Barker—Memoir of John William Draper)*

Class photograph was taken by Professor Samuel Finley Breese Morse on August 18, 1840, of the Yale College class of 1810 at their 30th reunion, New Haven, Conn. He made 35 daguerreotypes, each a half-inch square.

Color photo sent by radio. *See* Radio facsimile transmission: Color photoradio news photograph transmitted by radio for publication

Color transparency (35 mm) magnified 516 times was a Colorama taken by Ernst Haas and exhibited from February 22 to March 28, 1977, by the Eastman Kodak Company, Rochester, N.Y., at Grand Central Station, New York City. It was 18 by 60 feet and consisted of 20 panels, 18 feet high by 3 feet wide, which were spliced together and placed on an 18-foot spiral. It depicted a herd of impala grazing in a field in Kenya.

Comet photograph taken from space was made of the comet Kohoutek on December 29, 1973, by Dr. Edward George Gibson and Lieutenant Colonel Gerald Paul Carr, U.S. Marine Corps, from *Skylab 3.*

Composograph photograph. *See under* Newspaper

Cystoscopic photographs in color publicly exhibited were shown March 11–13, 1940, at the Postgraduate Surgical Assembly of the Southeastern Surgical Congress, Birmingham, Ala. The pic-

The First

PHOTOGRAPH—*Continued*

tures were taken by Drs. Edgar Garrison Ballenger, Harold Paul McDonald, and Reese Clinton Coleman of Atlanta, Ga., and were printed in the *Southern Surgeon,* June 1940.

Infrared photograph of a large group of people taken in the dark with a short exposure was made in the Eastman Kodak Research Laboratories in Rochester, N.Y., on October 7, 1931. A photograph was taken with a one-second exposure, in apparently total darkness, of a group of 50 visitors to the laboratories. The room was flooded with invisible infrared rays, and a new photographic emulsion sensitive to infrared was used.

Moon close-up photographs were taken July 31, 1964, by 6 RCA-TV cameras aboard the *Ranger VII,* launched July 28, 1964, from Cape Kennedy, Fla., travelling to the moon, 240,000 miles away, and were received by the National Aeronautics and Space Administration's receiving station in the Mojave Desert, Calif. In 17 minutes, 4,316 close-up still pictures were taken–68 hours, 36 minutes after takeoff–before *Ranger VII* crashed in the area northwest of the Sea of Clouds.

News photographs of distinction were made by Mathew B. Brady of New York City who, with the permission of President Abraham Lincoln and the U.S. Secret Service, had followed the Union Army and photographed it in action. He took more than 7,000 pictures, 2,000 of which were purchased by the Government for $25,000. Brady's studio at Broadway and Fulton Street in New York City was opened in 1844 as Brady's Daguerrian Miniature Gallery. *(Roy Meredith—Mathew B. Brady: Mr. Lincoln's Camera Man)*

Passport photograph. *See under* Passport

Photograph (authorized) of the Senate in session was taken September 24, 1963, by National Geographic Society photographers for the U.S. Capitol Historical Society, Washington, D.C. It showed 97 of the 100 senators seated. The nuclear test ban treaty was approved by a 80-19 vote.

Photograph bounced off a satellite was a photograph of President Dwight David Eisenhower which on August 18, 1960, was beamed 1,000 miles up to the satellite Echo I from a "dish" antenna by the Collins Radio Co., Cedar Rapids, Iowa. It was received on standard Associated Press Wirephoto equipment by the Alpha Corporation near Dallas, Texas.

Photograph bounced off the moon was received on January 28, 1960, at Washington, D.C., having been transmitted by the U.S. Navy from Hawaii.

Photograph from an airplane was taken by Major H. A. ("Jimmie") Erickson on January 10, 1911, in a Curtiss biplane piloted by Charles Hamilton over San Diego, Calif.

The First

Photograph from an airplane at night was taken November 20, 1925, over Rochester, N.Y., by Lieutenant George Goddard in cooperation with the Eastman Kodak Company, which supplied a photometer by which the intensity of light was measured. The photographs were taken from a 3,000-foot altitude and showed about 3 square miles of the city's area. A light bomb was dropped which made a flash lasting but one twentieth of a second.

Photograph in color of the earth from outer space was taken December 1, 1959, from the nose cone of a Thor missile launched from Cape Canaveral, Fla. The camera was found February 16, 1960, in the data capsule on the beach of Mayaguana Island, Bahama Islands, approximately 1,700 miles from the takeoff point.

Photograph in natural colors taken in the air was made by Melville Bell Grosvenor, Assistant Chief of Illustrations Division of *National Geographic* magazine, in July 1930, and published in the September 1930 issue.

Photograph of a beam of 1-billion-volt X rays, made by William Morris and Hubert Luckett in October 1946, showed the rays emanating from the betatron of the General Electric Company, Schenectady, N.Y. The beam did not cause a glowing of the air through which it passed, but was made visible to the camera by the placement of a fluorescent screen in its path. The camera exposure was made through a three-foot concrete wall in which an opening was made for the lens.

Photograph of a former President of the United States was taken by (Albert Sands) Southworth and (Josiah) Hawes Studio, Tremont Street, Boston, Mass. It was a photograph of John Quincy Adams taken in 1843 at his home in the town of Braintree (now Quincy), Mass. In 1845, Mathew B. Brady photographed Andrew Jackson at the Hermitage, Nashville, Tenn.

Photograph of a lightning flash was taken by W.C. Gurley of the Marietta Observatory, Marietta, Ohio, on the evening of May 4, 1884, about 3 miles away.

Photograph of a President (in office) was made of President James Knox Polk on February 14, 1849, by Mathew B. Brady in New York City. Former President John Quincy Adams sat for three photographs on November 13, 1843, while in Cincinnati, Ohio.

Photograph of a star (other than the sun) was that of Vega, which was made at the Harvard College Observatory, Cambridge, Mass., July 17, 1850, by Whipple, a professional photographer, under the direction of William Cranch Bond, the first director of the observatory. A 15-inch telescope was used as a camera lens and the daguerreotype plate was set up at the eye end.

The First

Photograph of a stellar spectrum showing the dark lines was one of Vega, Alpha Lyrae, made in 1872 by Dr. Henry Draper at Hastings-on-Hudson, N.Y. *(George Frederick Barker—Memoir of Henry Draper)*

Photograph of a total solar eclipse was taken August 7, 1869, by Professor Edward Charles Pickering at Mount Pleasant, Iowa. Using a portrait lens, he made the first successful photographs of the corona. The eclipse crossed America diagonally from Alaska to North Carolina. *(Samuel Alfred Mitchell—Eclipses of the Sun)*

Photograph of an eclipse of the sun taken from the atmosphere was made November 12, 1966, when *Gemini XII* was in direct line with the solar eclipse at 7:49 P.M. E.S.T., for 7 seconds. It took off at 2:08 P.M. E.S.T. on November 11, 1966, from Cape Kennedy, Fla., with astronauts Captain James Arthur Lovell, Jr. (U.S.Navy), and Major Edwin Eugene Aldrin, Jr. (U.S.Air Force). They circled the earth 59 times, in a flight of 94 hours 34 minutes 31 seconds.

Photograph of genes, the particles which transmit physical characteristics from one generation to another, was taken by Drs. Daniel Chapin Pease and Richard Freligh Baker at the University of Southern California, Los Angeles, Calif., and announced January 7, 1949. The tissue sections were magnified 120,000 times.

Photograph sent by radio across the Atlantic. *See under* Radio facsimile transmission

Photograph sent by radio across the continent. *See under* Radio facsimile transmission

Photograph showing action (not motion pictures) was taken in 1872 on a stock farm of Leland Stanford at Palo Alto, Calif., by Eadweard Muybridge. He used a series of twelve clocks for breaking electric circuits connected with camera shutters, thus taking a series of photographs at regular intervals, in rapid succession, of a racehorse in action.

Photograph showing air in motion across aerofoils or wings of airplanes was taken by Colonel Rutherford B. Harts during the winter of 1918–1919 at Bolling Field, Washington, D.C., under the auspices of the Division of Military Aeronautics and the invention secretary of the general staff of the U.S. Army. Three miles of film showed that no flying power whatever is exerted for about 30 percent of a flight on the wings of an aircraft by the air flow produced by the air screws and that rarefication, which produces the lifting power of an airplane, is not continuous but is exerted in intermittent or pulsating air waves. *(Aerial Age Weekly. June 2, 1919)*

Photograph showing motion. *See* Motion picture: Photographic attempt to show motion

The First

Photograph showing the lateral curvature of the horizon taken in the United States was made by Captain Albert William Stevens from the gondola of the stratosphere balloon *Explorer 11,* sent up November 11, 1935, by the National Geographic Society and the U.S. Army Air Corps. The photograph was made from an altitude of 72,395 feet, or 13.71 miles, above sea level. It was the first photograph of the horizon taken from such a great altitude; the first photograph the line of sight of which was entirely in the stratosphere; and the first photograph showing the extreme top of the "dust sphere" which marks the dividing line between the lower atmosphere with its clouds and dust and the stratosphere, which is clear. The balloon took off from Rapid City, S.Dak., and landed 8 hours 13 minutes later at White Lake, S.Dak.

Photograph taken by incandescent electric light was the portrait of Charles Batchelor, made in December 1879 in Menlo Park, N.J.

Photograph taken from the moon of the earth was made from Lunar Orbiter 1, which took off August 10, 1966. On August 14, 1966, it became the first United States probe to achieve lunar orbit and it photographed all 9 primary Apollo landing sites on 11 areas on the back side of the moon. A total of 207 frames (sets) of photographs were taken and relayed back to earth on August 23, 1966. Lunar Orbiter 1 was crashed into the moon's far side on October 29, 1966, to make way for the next launch.

Photograph taken in the United States was a daguerreotype, a form of image recording invented by Louis Jacques Mandé Daguerre of France on August 19, 1839. The first published description of the method appeared in the London *Globe,* which arrived in the United States on September 20, 1839, on the *British Queen.* Among those who are credited with taking the first daguerreotype are Samuel Finley Breese Morse, Amasa Holcomb, Robert Cornelius (a Philadelphia lamp maker), and Joseph Saxton (a balance maker at the Philadelphia mint). Dr. John William Draper took a picture of his sister Dorothy Catherine Draper in the summer of 1840, which is believed to be the first daguerreotype portrait. He used a 6-minute sunlight exposure.

Photograph (taken in the United States) on which a meteor was found was taken on August 10, 1889, by the Harvard College Observatory, Harvard University, Cambridge, Mass. The photograph of the meteor showed a straight dense line. The exposure, 13 hours 50 minutes, was taken by a Gundlach camera strapped to an 11-inch telescope. *(Annals, Harvard College Observatory, Vol. 87, Part 3)*

Photograph to gain world fame was a daguerreotype panorama of Niagara Falls, N.Y., taken in July 1845 by William and Frederick Langenheim of the Philadelphia Daguerrotype Establishment,

The First

PHOTOGRAPH—*Continued*
Philadelphia, Pa., from a site near the Clifton House on the Canadian side. Sets were made and presented to Louis Jacques Mandé Daguerre, President James Knox Polk, Queen Victoria, the kings of Prussia, Saxony, and Wurtemberg, and the Duke of Brunswick. *(Beaumont Newhall— Photography 1839–1939)*

Photograph transmitted by wire or wireless. *See* Radio facsimile transmission

Photographs in color of the heavens published in a magazine appeared in the May 1959 issue of the *National Geographic* magazine, Washington, D.C., and showed The Great Nebula in Orion, The Crab Nebula, and The Veil Nebula in Cygnus, the Swan. They were taken by William C. Miller, research photographer of the Mount Wilson and Palomar Observatories, using Super Anscochrome film and the 200-inch Hale telescope on Palomar Mountain.

Photographs taken on Mars were transmitted on July 20, 1976, to the *Viking* mother ship in orbit around Mars, which sent them to the Jet Propulsion Laboratory, Pasadena, Calif., via a radio telescope in Spain. The 1,300-pound, 10-foot *Viking I* lander carried 2 cameras; it landed on Chryse Planitia (Plain of Gold). The 340-degree panorama was telecast and copied. *Viking I* was launched August 20, 1975, entered Mars orbit June 19, 1976, and landed July 20, 1976.

Photographs taken under the sea which were successful were obtained by John Ernest Williamson at Chesapeake Bay, Va., in 1913 with the use of the Williamson Submarine Tube and Photosphere. *(John Ernest Williamson—Twenty Years Under the Sea)*

Photographs taken under the sea in natural colors were made for *National Geographic* magazine off the Tortugas of the Florida Keys, on July 16, 1926, and were published in the January 1927 issue of the magazine. The work was carried out by Dr. William Harding Longley of Goucher College and Charles Martin, Chief of the National Geographic Society's photographic laboratory. The camera used in making these autochromes was enclosed in a brass case with a plate-glass window in front of the lens. A supplementary hood was fitted above the regulation reflector and by means of an acute-angle mirror the photographer was able to focus his instrument.

Photographs used in surveying were taken by Edward Anthony of New York City, who took a complete daguerreotype outfit to survey the northeast boundary of the United States with Canada in dispute with Great Britain. He delivered them in 1839 to Daniel Webster of the Joint Boundary Commission, who submitted them to Alexander Baring, 1st baron Ashburton. The treaty was ratified at Washington, D.C., on August 20, 1842.

The First

Planet close-up photographs taken from above Earth's turbulent atmosphere were taken July 14, 1965, by the 550-pound *Mariner IV* for 8 hours. It took 8½ hours to transmit them the 134-million-mile distance. *Mariner IV* was launched November 28, 1964.

Portrait (life-size) of a human in a newspaper was a photograph of Larry Quinn, a 14-pound 7-ounce baby, 21½ inches high, published November 14, 1935, in the *Call-Bulletin,* San Francisco, Calif. The infant was born November 12, 1935, at Mary's Help Hospital, San Francisco, Calif.

Satellite to transmit photographs. *See under* Satellite

Solar-eclipse photograph was made March 25, 1857, by Frederick Langenheim of Philadelphia, Pa., who took 8 pictures in sequence of an eclipse of the sun.

Ultraviolet pictures of the sun were taken March 13, 1959, by a camera at an altitude of 123 miles from an Aerobee-Hi research rocket at White Sands, N.Mex., under the direction of the U.S. Naval Research Laboratory. A camera with spectroscopic mirrors reflected out the visible light of the sun, leaving only the Lyman-Alpha radiation to fall on the special film.

X-ray photograph. *See* X ray

PHOTOGRAPHER
Photographer to receive a John Simon Guggenheim Memorial Foundation award was Edward Weston of Los Angeles, Calif., who received a $2,500 grant for the making of a series of photographic documents of the West. Announcement of the award was made March 28, 1937. The photographs, taken by an 8 by 10 camera using panchromatic film, illustrated *California and the West,* by Charis Wilson Weston and Edward Weston, published by Duell, Sloan & Pearce, New York City, and copyrighted in 1940.

PHOTOGRAPHIC COPYING MACHINE. *See* Photostat

PHOTOGRAPHIC FILM
Celluloid photographic film and the process for producing it were invented by the Reverend Hannibal Williston Goodwin of Newark, N.J., who applied for a patent on May 2, 1887, and received patent No. 610,861 on September 13, 1898, on "nitro cellulose transparent flexible photographic film pellicles." He received an order from Thomas Alva Edison for one roll at $2.50 on September 2, 1889.

Color film (35 mm) telecast. *See under* Television–Telecast

Motion picture film (commercial) was manufactured March 26, 1885, by the Eastman Dry Plate & Film Company of Rochester, N.Y., which was also the first to produce, manufacture, and market

The First

films in continuous strips on reels. *(The Home of Kodak—Eastman Kodak Co.)*

Roll film for cameras was patented by David Henderson Houston of Cambria, Wis., who obtained patent No. 248,179, October 11, 1881 for a "photographic apparatus." He had a camera with a receptacle or box at its inner end containing a "roll of sensitized paper or any other suitable tissue, such as gelatine or any more durable material that may be discovered, and an empty reel, upon which the sensitized band is wound as rapidly as it has been acted upon by the light." The purpose of the camera was "to facilitate taking a number of photographic views successively in a short time."

Transparent paper-strip photographic film was invented in February 1884 by George Eastman of Rochester, N.Y., who obtained patent No. 306,594 on October 14, 1884. The film consisted of paper coated with an insoluble sensitive gelatin emulsion.

"V" mail film. *See under* Postal service

PHOTOGRAPHIC GLASS SLIDES. *See* Magic lantern: Magic lantern slides (glass-plate)

PHOTOGRAPHIC PAMPHLET was Francois Fauvel-Gouraud's *Description of the Daguerrotype Process, or a Summary of M. Gouraud's Public Lectures, According to the Principles of M. Daguerre, with a Description of a Provisory Method for Taking Human Portraits,* 16 pages and cover, printed in 1840 in Boston, Mass., by Dutton and Wentworth.

PHOTOGRAPHIC PATENT
Aerial photography patent was No. 510,758, awarded December 12, 1893, to Cornele Berrien Adams of Augusta, Ga., on a "method of photogrammetry." By means of photographs of the same tract taken from different points, a topographic effect was obtained.

Photographic patent was No. 1,582, granted to Alexander S. Wolcott of New York City on May 8, 1840, for "a method of taking likenesses by means of a concave reflector and plates so prepared that luminous or other rays will act thereon." The photographs, 1¾ by 2½ inches, were not reversed as were daguerreotypes with refracting lenses.

PHOTOGRAPHIC STUDIO
Commercial photography studio was opened March 4, 1840, in New York City by [Alexander S.] Wolcott and [John] Johnson. Wolcott took his first photograph on October 7, 1839. *(William Welling—Photography in America, The Formative Years)*

PHOTOGRAPHY
Camera exposure meter was invented in 1931 by William Nelson Goodwin, Jr., of the Weston Electrical Instrument Corporation, Newark, N.J., who obtained patent No. 1,407,147, February 21,

The First

1932, on a thermal ammeter. The first one, manufactured in February 1932, was called the Photronic Photoelectric Cell, although popularly known as a camera exposure meter. It contained a dial calculating device for translating brightness values into camera aperture settings. It required no battery for its operation, as it changed light energy directly into electrical energy.

Camera exposure scale was prepared by D. W. Seager and published in the March 1840 issue of the *American Repertory of Arts, Sciences, and Manufactures.* The shortest tabulated exposure was 5 minutes at noon on a very brilliant and clear day; the longest 50-70 minutes at 3:00 P.M. on a cloudy day.

Camera multiple flashbulb device, known as Flashcubes, were made by the Sylvania Electric Company, Montoursville, Pa., and introduced July 8, 1965, at a press conference at the Waldorf Astoria Hotel, New York City. Four flash bulbs were set in a single socket. A sleeve of 3 cubes retailed for $1.95. The cubes were presented jointly by the Sylvania Electric Products, Inc., and the Eastman Kodak Company.

Demonstration of rapid aerial photography was made September 5, 1925, before the U.S. General Staff and Command School. Lieutenant George Goddard, director of photography of the Air Corps Technical School, U.S. Army, took photographs of the Fort Leavenworth area in the "Flying Laboratory." These were developed and finished and dropped to the ground within eight minutes from the time of exposure. A photographic transmitting set sent the picture to Governors Island, where it was in the hands of General Charles Pelot Summerall within 27 minutes after it had been taken in Kansas, 1,700 miles away. Copies were also sent to General William Sidney Graves in Chicago, Ill., and General Charles Thomas Menoher in San Francisco, Calif.

Film-developing machine (fully automatic) was the Photomaton, invented by Anatol M. Josepho, who constructed the first model in a loft building on 125th Street, New York City. He applied for a patent March 13, 1925; patent No. 1,656,522 was issued January 17, 1928, on an apparatus for developing photographic film strips. It is said that the inventor received $1 million for this invention. The first Photomaton studio was opened to the public at 1659 Broadway, New York City, in September 1926.

Photographic flashlight bulbs, fireless, smokeless, odorless, and noiseless, similar to incandescent lamp bulbs, were made by the General Electric Company of Schenectady, N.Y., on August 1, 1930, under patent No. 1,776,637, awarded on September 23, 1930, to Johannes Ostermeier of Althegnenberg, Germany, for a "flash lamp." A small filament in the bulb, when connected to a source of electricity, became heated and ignited

The First

PHOTOGRAPHY—*Continued*

the foil and oxygen, causing a flash of light of high intensity and short duration. The bulb, a No. 20, was the size of a 150-watt incandescent bulb.

PHOTOGRAPHY BOOK

Photography book was *The History and Practice of the Art of Photography: or, the Production of Pictures Through the Agency of Light, Containing All the Instructions Necessary for the Complete Practice of the Daguerrean and Photogenic Art, Both on Metallic Plates and on Paper,* by Henry Hunt Snelling, published by G. P. Putnam, New York City, in 1849. It contained 139 pages of text.

PHOTOGRAPHY MAGAZINE

Photography magazine was the *Daguerreian Journal;* devoted to the Daguerreian and Photogenic Arts, also embracing the Sciences, Arts and Literature, a 32-page octavo fortnightly published November 1, 1850, in New York City. It sold for 25 cents a copy, $3 a year. S. D. Humphrey was the editor and publisher, and William S. Dorr, the printer.

PHOTORADIOGRAPHY. *See* Radio facsimile transmission

PHOTOSENSITIVE GLASS. *See* Glass

PHOTOSTAT

Photographic copying machine known by the trade name Photostat was commercially manufactured in 1910 by the Eastman Kodak Company, Rochester, N.Y., under the supervision of John S. Greene of the Photostat Corporation. It photographed the subject to be copied directly upon a roll of sensitized paper and eliminated the necessity for the use of any glass plate or film negative. It was capable of making a print 11½ by 14 inches. The process was not new, but was simplified.

PHOTOTELEGRAPHY. *See* Radio facsimile transmission

PHOTOTRANSISTOR. *See* Transistor

PHRENOLOGIST of importance to visit the United States was Johann Gaspar Spurzheim, an associate of Dr. Franz Joseph Gall, the German physician who originated the theory of phrenology. Spurzheim arrived in New York City on August 6, 1832. On August 20 he went to Boston, Mass., to give a series of 18 lectures at Athenaeum Hall, and on September 17 to Cambridge, Mass., for an additional series. He died on November 10, 1832. His funeral was attended by the Boston Medical Association as a group, and the oration was delivered by Charles Follen, Professor of German Literature, Harvard University.

PHRENOLOGY BOOK was the *Outlines of Phrenology* by Johann Gaspar Spurzheim, M.D., of the universities of Vienna and Paris, and a licentiate of the Royal College of Physicians of London. It was published in 1832 by Marsh, Capen & Lyon,

The First

Boston, Mass. It was divided into three sections covering general principles of phrenology, special facilities of the mind, and the usefulness of phrenology.

PHRENOLOGY MAGAZINE was published by Nathan Allen in October 1838 in Philadelphia, Pa. It was entitled the *American Phrenological Journal and Miscellany* and enjoyed a good circulation until its discontinuance in January 1911. (*William Lewis Montague—Biographies of Recent Alumni of Amherst*)

PHYSICAL CULTURE. *See* Health instruction

PHYSICAL CULTURE DEPARTMENT established by a university on a par with other departments was at the University of Chicago, Chicago, Ill. Amos Alonzo Stagg was made assistant professor and director of the Department of Physical Culture and Athletics and a regular member of the faculty in 1892. In 1901 he was granted a full professorship. Previously, in the East, Midwest, and South, athletics had been under the control of a student athletic association, and on the Pacific Coast under what is now known as the Associated Students. After the establishment of the department, the coaching of all athletic teams at the University of Chicago was done by members of the department. An Athletic Fund was established with the gate receipts placed in the hands of the comptroller of the university, but disbursed only with the consent of the director of the department.

PHYSICAL EDUCATION PROFESSORSHIP. *See* Hygiene instruction: Hygiene and physical education professorship

PHYSICALLY DISABLED. *See* Blind; Cripples; Deaf

PHYSICIAN

See also individual specialties *under* Medical instruction

American-born doctor who had graduated from a medical school abroad was Dr. William Bull, of Charleston, S.C. He had received his degree from Leyden University, Leyden, Netherlands, on August 18, 1734. The title of his thesis was "Colica pictonum."

Autopsy by a woman physician on a male corpse. *See* Autopsy: Autopsy by a woman physician on a male corpse

Black doctor was James Derham of Philadelphia, who settled in New Orleans, La., before 1790. Dr. Benjamin Rush said of him: "I thought I could give him information concerning the treatment of diseases, but I learned more from him than he could expect from me." (*John Andrew Kenney—The Negro in Medicine*)

Black doctor to become a member of a medical association was Dr. John Vancerlle De Grasse, who was admitted to the Massachusetts Medical

The First

Society in 1854. He graduated from Bowdoin and the Hampton Medical College, and practiced in New York City. *(Massachusetts Medical Society —A Catalogue of Its Officers and Fellows)*

Black member of the American College of Surgeons. *See under* Medical Society

Black woman awarded a medical degree was Rebecca Lee, who received an M.D. degree on March 1, 1864, from the New England Female Medical College, Boston, Mass. She completed a 17-week course to earn the Doctress of Medicine degree. Prior to May 28, 1856, the College had been known as the Female Medical Education Society. *(Frederick Clayton Waite—History of the New England Female Medical College 1848–1874)*

Capitol physician was Dr. George Wehnes Calver, a retired rear admiral, who reported for duty at the Capitol, Washington, D.C., on December 8, 1928, in response to a resolution, H.R. 253 of the 70th Congress, passed December 4, 1928, requesting the Secretary of the Navy to detail a medical officer to be in attendance at the sessions of Congress. His title was "the attending physician."

Captain (black) in the U.S. Navy Medical Corps was Dr. Paul Stewart Green of San Diego, Calif., commissioned July 12, 1968. He was one of the 3 black captains among the 380 officers on active duty in the Navy.

Chinese woman to receive a doctor of medicine degree was Dr. Mary Stone (Shih Mai-yu), who graduated from the Medical School of the University of Michigan, Ann Arbor, Mich., on June 22, 1896. She founded the Women's Hospital at Kiukiang, China, under the auspices of the Methodist Foreign Mission and served as its head for 25 years.

Doctor in New England was Dr. Samuel Fuller, one of the signers of the Compact on board the *Mayflower* on November 21, 1620. He arrived December 21, 1620. For some time he was the sole physician in the colony. In a letter dated June 28, 1630, written at Salem, Mass., to Governor William Bradford, he described one of the customary treatments, in which he "let some twenty of these people blood." *(Mayflower Descendants. Vol. 7. 1905)*

Doctor in the colony of Virginia was Lawrence Bohune, who arrived in the first half of 1610. He was the first physician of the London Company. He was killed on March 19, 1622, on board the *Margaret and John* when the vessel was attacked by Spanish ships. *(Wyndham Bolling Blanton— Medicine in Virginia in the 18th Century)*

Doctor to practice in space was U.S. Navy commander Dr. Joseph Peter Kerwin, of *Skylab 2*, which took off from Cape Kennedy, Fla., on May 25, 1973, and splashed down June 22, 1973, in the Pacific Ocean, about 840 miles southwest of San

The First

Diego, Calif. The duration of the flight was 28 days 49 minutes 49 seconds. Kerwin made daily routine medical tests on his fellow astronauts, Charles ("Pete") Conrad and Paul Weitz.

Doctor to receive a Bachelor of Medicine degree was John Archer, who graduated with nine others on June 21, 1768, from the University of Pennsylvania, Philadelphia, Pa. His name was the first alphabetically and he was therefore known as the first graduate. Four of these ten graduates returned to the university three years later (1771) and received the degree of Doctor of Medicine. Three years had to elapse before this M.D. degree could be obtained. At King's College, New York City (now Columbia University), the first M.D. degree was awarded in 1770. This school required only one year to elapse before a student could return and get his M.D. degree. At both schools, the applicant for the higher degree was required to write a thesis in Latin or an inaugural dissertation and defend it satisfactorily before the faculty in order to obtain the degree.

Doctor to receive a medal from Congress was Frederick Henry Rose of the British Navy. In April 1858, in Jamaica, yellow fever broke out on the U.S.S. *Susquehanna*. Rose offered his services and sailed to New York with the stricken crew. On May 11, 1858, Congress authorized a gold medal to be presented to him (11 Stat. L. 369) "for kindness and humanity to officers and crew of the U.S.S. 'Susquehanna.' "

Doctor to receive an honorary medical degree was Daniel Turner, who received a degree of Honorary Doctor of Medicine from Yale University, New Haven, Conn., on September 11, 1723, as a reward for valuable monetary contributions to the college. It was awarded by the Reverend Timothy Woodbridge, rector pro tempore. Turner never practiced in America. *(Annals of Medical History, 1919. Vol. 2, No. 4)*

Doctor's strike against long working hours in hospitals began at 7:00 A.M., March 17, 1975, when 21 of New York City's 91 voluntary and municipal hospitals were struck by interns and resident physicians demanding reduction in work hours, not to exceed 40 hours.

Hindu woman to receive a doctor of medicine degree was Anandibai Joshee, who arrived in the United States on June 4, 1883, and graduated from the Woman's Medical College of Pennsylvania, Philadelphia, Pa., on March 11, 1886, at the age of 21. She returned to her native city, Poona, India, where she died February 26, 1887. *(Ramabai Sarasvati—The High-Caste Hindu Woman)*

Jewish doctor was Jacob Lumbrozo, who settled in Maryland, January 24, 1656. He was a native of Lisbon, Portugal. He died in May 1666. *(Solomon Robert Kagan—Contributions of American Jews to Medicine)*

The First

PHYSICIAN—Continued

Physician (Jewish) to head an insane asylum was Dr. John de Sequeyra, a Portugese physician educated in Holland, who was appointed in 1770 at Williamsburg, Va.

Naval doctor. See under Naval officer

Naval medical officer. See under Naval officer

Ophthalmologist of note was Dr. Edward Delafield, who in 1864 became the first president of the American Ophthalmological Society. In 1818 he formulated a plan to establish the New York Eye Infirmary, which opened in 1820 in two rooms at 45 Chatham Street, treating 436 patients in the first seven months. *(Alvin Allace Hubbell—The Development of Ophthalmology in America)*

Orthopedics chair. See under Medical instruction

Osteopath (woman) was Jenette Hubbard Bolles, who graduated March 1, 1894, from the American School of Osteopathy, Kirksville, Mo. Two other women who graduated at the same time, Mamie B. Carter and Lou J. Kern, share the distinction.

Osteopathic physician was Dr. Andrew Taylor Still of Macon, Mo., who cured a case of "flux" on June 22, 1874. He was instrumental in founding both a college and a magazine devoted to osteopathy. *(Missouri Historical Review. Vol. 19)*

Pediatrics professor. See under Medical instruction

Physician with a mobile medical office for his private patients was Dr. Huerta Cortez Neals, cardiovascular specialist of the Jersey City Medical Center, who placed a motor home in service on June 23, 1970, in Jersey City, N.J., equipped with a bathroom, refrigerator, heating unit, air conditioner, 30-gallon water tank, electrocardiograph, blood-pressure apparatus, scale, blood Auto-Analyzer, etc.

Physicians in the Medical Corps of the Army and Navy were authorized by act of April 16, 1943 (57 Stat.L.65), which provided for "the appointment of female physicians and surgeons in the medical corps of the Army and Navy" with "the same pay and allowances, and entitled to the same rights, privileges and benefits as members of the Officers' Reserve Corps of the Army and the Naval Reserve of the Navy with the same grade and length of service."

Physiologist. See Physiologist

Surgeon general (Army). See under Army officer

Surgeon general (Navy). See under Naval officer

The First

Surgeon to substitute radium treatment for surgery for the treatment of cancer was Dr. Robert Abbe, who published his conclusions in the June 1904 *Yale Medical Journal.* He held professorships of surgery in the Women's Medical College and the New York Post Graduate School of New York City. *(City College Alumnus. January 1929)*

Woman appointed personal physician to the President was Dr. Janet Graeme Travell (Mrs. John Powell) of New York City, whose appointment was announced January 25, 1961, by President John Fitzgerald Kennedy. Dr. Susan Ann Edson, who was graduated from the Cleveland, Ohio, Homeopathic Medical College in 1854 had been "Head Nurse" to President James Abram Garfield from July 2, 1881, to September 19, 1881, when he died.

Woman assistant army surgeon. See under Army officer

Woman doctor commissioned in the regular Army. See under Army officer

Woman doctor in the WAVES. See Naval Officer: Woman doctor in the WAVES

Woman physician was Dr. Elizabeth Blackwell, a native of Bristol, England, who came to the United States in her youth and received her M.D. degree from the Medical Institution of Geneva, N.Y., on January 23, 1849, having attended "two full courses of Medical Lectures." On October 20, 1847, the entire medical class decided "that the application of Elizabeth Blackwell to become a member of our class meets our entire approval." The school is now the College of Medicine, Syracuse University. *(Elizabeth Blackwell—Pioneer Work in Opening the Medical Profession to Women)*

Woman physician admitted to the American Institute of Homeopathy. See under Medical society

Woman physician elected a member of the American Medical Association. See under Medical society

Woman physician in the Medical Corps of the U.S. Navy. See under Naval officer

Woman surgeon was Dr. Mary Harris Thompson, who received her M.D. degree in 1863 from the New England Medical College, Boston, Mass. In May 1865 she founded the Mary Thompson Hospital in Chicago, Ill., to care for widows and children of the poor, to sustain a free dispensary, and to train competent nurses. The hospital had 14 beds. It was destroyed by fire October 9, 1871, but the patients were removed to another location and operation resumed the same day. The hospital is now the Women's and Children's Hospital, Chicago, Ill.

The First

Woman's infirmary staffed by women physicians. *See under* Hospital

PHYSICS

Cyclotron, spiral atom smasher, was developed by Professor Ernest Orlando Lawrence, University of California, Berkeley, in 1934, to study the nuclear structure of the atom. A magnetic whirling machine using an 80-ton magnet produced 10-million- to 15-million-volt rays, and sent a stream of high-energy bullets from the nuclei of helium gas atoms or alpha particles in the form of a beam of light a foot from the machine. Professor Lawrence was assisted by Dr. Milton Stanley Livingston. *(Wilfred Basil Mann—The Cyclotron)*

National physics association was the American Physical Society for the advancement and diffusion of the knowledge of physics, formed May 20, 1899, at Columbia University, New York City, by physicists from 17 institutions. The first officers were Henry Augustus Rowland, president; Albert Abraham Michelson, vice president; Ernest Merritt, secretary; and William Hallock, treasurer. The first year 59 fellows were admitted.

Positron, a positively charged particle with the same mass and energy as the electron, was recognized in 1934 by Dr. Carl David Anderson at the California Institute of Technology, Pasadena. While working with cosmic rays, he noticed a line which curved in the wrong direction, a trailing vapor in a "cloud expansion chamber." In 1936 Anderson received a Nobel Prize in physics.

Radioactive substance produced synthetically was radium E, made by Dr. John Jacob Livingood of the University of California, Berkeley, on February 4, 1936. Radium E is one of the intermediary products in the slow deterioration of radium. Synthetic radium E was obtained through the bombardment of common inert bismuth with deuterons at an energy of approximately $5\frac{1}{2}$ million volts. Radiobismuth made synthetically is theoretically identical with natural radium E.

PHYSICS NOBEL PRIZE WINNER. *See* Nobel Prize: Nobel Prize in physics

PHYSIOLOGICAL LABORATORY was established in the Sheffield Scientific School at Yale University, New Haven, Conn., in 1874 under the direction of Russell Henry Chittenden. (Two rooms had been set aside in the Harvard Medical School, Boston, Mass., in 1871 for experimental medicine. Dr. Oliver Wendell Holmes was professor of physiology and anatomy.)

PHYSIOLOGICAL RESEARCH LABORATORY OF THE U.S. ARMY AIR CORPS. *See under* Aviation

PHYSIOLOGIST of note was Dr. William Beaumont, whose *Experiments and Observations on the Gastric Juice and the Physiology of Digestion* was published in 1833 in Plattsburg, N.Y. He

The First

achieved fame by his treatment of Alexis St. Martin (Samata, San Maten), who was shot in the stomach on June 6, 1822, at Fort Mackinac trading post. Dr. Beaumont was able to watch the digestive process through the aperture in the stomach wall and to find by experiment the effect of different foods and medicines. He found that gastric juices were secreted only when there was food in the stomach and that simple irritation of the mucous membrane would not initiate a flow of gastric juices. *(Jesse Shire Myer—Life and Letters of Dr. William Beaumont)*

PHYSIOLOGY AND HYGIENE COURSE. *See under* Hygiene instruction

PHYSIOLOGY AND MEDICINE NOBEL PRIZE WINNER. *See* Nobel Prize: Nobel Prize in medicine and physiology

PHYSIOLOGY MAGAZINE was *The American Journal of Physiology,* 144 pages, the first issue of which was dated February 1898. It was published by Ginn and Company, Boston, Mass.

PHYSIOLOGY SOCIETY

Physiological society was the American Physiological Society, organized February 11, 1837, in Boston, Mass., by 124 men and 39 women who signed the constitution. The object was to acquire and diffuse a knowledge of the laws of life and of the means of promoting human health and longevity. Dues were $1 per year. The first monthly meeting was held March 7, 1837. The first officers were William Andrus Alcott, president; David Campbell, corresponding secretary; John Kilton, recording secretary; and Nathaniel Perry, treasurer. This was a local organization. *(Bulletin of Institute of History of Medicine. Vol. 5, No. 8. October 1937)*

Physiological society (national organization) was the American Physiological Society, organized in New York City on December 30, 1887 with Silas Weir Mitchell of Philadelphia as president and Henry Newell Martin, professor of biology at Johns Hopkins University, as secretary. Their proceedings, the *American Journal of Physiology,* were first published on January 3, 1898.

PIANO

Piano was made by John Harris. It was called a spinet and was described in the *Boston Gazette* of September 18, 1769. It had only three or four octaves and differed from the modern piano in that it had no hammers to strike the strings. Instead, each jack was provided with a little spur of goose-quill which plucked the thin wire, almost as a mandolin player plucks a string with a pick. *(Alfred Dolge—Pianos and Their Makers)*

Piano frame of iron, designed to resist the tremendous tension of the modern piano without allowing the wires to deflect from pitch, was made in 1837 in Boston, Mass., by Jonas Chickering. *(Richard Green Parker—A Tribute to the Life and Character of Jonas Chickering)*

The First

PIANO—*Continued*

Piano patent was granted James Sylvanus McLean of New Jersey, on May 27, 1796, for an "improvement in piano fortes."

PIANO PLAYER

Piano player was invented by John McTammany, Jr., of Cambridge, Mass., who filed a caveat September 7, 1876, and received patent No. 242,-786 on June 14, 1881, on a "mechanical musical instrument." He constructed a mechanism for automatic playing of organs using narrow sheets of perforated flexible paper which governed the notes to be played.

Piano player (completely automatic) to be manufactured was the Angelus, made by the Wilcox & White Company, Meriden, Conn., in February 1897. It was invented by Edward H. Leveaux of Surrey, England, who obtained a British patent on February 27, 1879, and who filed an application for a U.S. patent on August 29, 1881. U.S. patent No. 247,993 was granted to Leveaux on October 4, 1881, for an "apparatus for storing and transmitting motive power."

Pneumatic piano player that was practical was the Pianola, invented in 1896 by Edwin S. Votey, of Detroit, Mich., who applied for a patent January 25, 1897; No. 650,285 was granted on May 22, 1900. His original model was larger than the piano to which it was attached. The patent was for an attachment of practical and economical construction which could be applied to and removed from any piano. It was introduced by the Aeolian Company.

PIANO WIRE. *See* Wire

PICKUP BY AIRPLANE. *See* Aviation: Airplane human pickup

PIER

Ocean pier was built by Colonel George W. Howard of Washington, D.C., at Atlantic City, N.J., in 1881. It was known as Howard's Pier and extended 650 feet seaward from the foot of Kentucky Avenue. On July 12, 1882, the opening celebration was held. It was destroyed in September 1882 by a severe storm and was rebuilt to 865 feet, but was again destroyed and washed away by a severe storm on January 9, 1884. *(Frank Butler—Book of the Boardwalk)*

Ocean pier of steel was erected at Atlantic City, N.J. It was half a mile long, devoted exclusively to amusements, and was opened to the public on June 18, 1898. It was owned by the Atlantic City Steel Pier Company, of which Kennedy Crossan was president. The pier was designed by Frank A. Souder and built by John T. Windram, architect.

"PIGGYBACK" RAILROAD OPERATION. *See under* Railroad

The First

PILE BRIDGE. *See* Bridge

PILE DRIVER

Pile driver was patented March 10, 1791, by John Stone of Concord, Mass., who obtained his patent on "driving pile for bridges."

Steam pile driver patent was No. 5,172 awarded June 26, 1847, by the U.S. Patent Office to James Nasmyth of Patricroft, England, on a "steam pile driver."

PILL

Compressed pills or tablets commercially manufactured, were made in 1863–1864 by Jacob Dunton, a wholesale druggist of Philadelphia, Pa., who employed a machine in their manufacture. The formulas that were sold in tablet form consisted principally of simple chemicals such as potassium chlorate, ammonium chloride, etc. Dunton sold his products to dispensing druggists and did not attempt to market them under his own name until 1869. His entire production from 1869 to 1876 was less than that now made daily in the laboratories of this country. *(Journal of the American Pharmaceutical Association. 1914, p. 820)*

Patented pills were introduced in 1796 by Samuel Lee, Jr., of Conn., and known as Lee's Windham Pills and Lee's New London Bilious Pills. On April 30, 1796, he obtained a patent on a "composition of bilious pills."

PILOT, AUTOMATIC. *See under* Aviation

PILOT LICENSE. *See* Aviation—License

PILOT TO RECEIVE THE CONGRESSIONAL MEDAL OF HONOR. *See under* Aviation—Pilot

PIN

Machine for manufacturing pins that was practical was invented by John Ireland Howe of Derby, Conn., who obtained a patent on it June 22, 1832. The machine was exhibited at the American Institute Fair in New York, and Howe received a silver medal for his contribution to manufacturing. In December 1835, he formed the Howe Manufacturing Company, New York City. He obtained patent No. 2,013 on March 24, 1841, for an improved model.

Machine "for sticking pins into paper" was patented September 30, 1841, No. 2,275, by Samuel Slocum of Poughkeepsie, N.Y. A sliding hopper deposited the pins in grooves.

Pins manufactured with a solid head were made in 1838 by Samuel Slocum of Rhode Island, who invented the machine to manufacture them. He did not obtain a patent on it. One man tending two machines could produce 100,000 pins in 11 hours. He formed the firm of Slocum, Jilson & Company, Poughkeepsie, N.Y., in 1839. His products were known as "Poughkeepsie pins." *(Journal of the American Institute. June 1839)*

The First

Safety pin was invented by Walter Hunt of New York City who obtained patent No. 6,281, April 10, 1849. Within the short period of three hours, he conceived the idea, made a model, and sold his patent rights for $100. The pins were manufactured in New York City.

PINBALL GAME

Pinball game machine was the Whoopee Game, manufactured in 1930 by In & Outdoor Games Company, Chicago, Ill. It was 24 inches wide and 48 inches long and had adjustable legs. It sold for $175. The fee for playing was 5 cents for ten balls. The game was modeled after the children's game known as Bagatelle.

Pinball game machine (toy) was the Caille Log Tavern built in 1910 by Adolph Caille of Caille Brothers Company, Detroit, Mich. The machine, which was placed flat on a table, had a slightly inclined board with pins on it. Marbles were shot up the board through an alley to top position, and would then roll down into scoring positions.

Pinball legislation enacted by a major city prohibiting the machines was the ordinance, approved June 19, 1939, by Atlanta, Ga., entitled "an ordinance to prohibit the operation of pin ball machines and similar machines in the city of Atlanta," signed by Mayor William Berry Hartsfield. The act, effective July 1, 1939, provided that any person convicted of a violation of this ordinance be subject to a fine not to exceed $20 and a sentence to the public works of the city for a period of 30 days, any part of either one or both at the discretion of the recorder.

"PINCH HITTER." See Baseball player: Baseball "pinch hitter"

PINE-PAPER NEWSPAPER. See Newspaper

PINEAPPLE CHEESE. See Cheese

PINNACE. See Ship

PIPE

Corncob pipe commercial manufacture was undertaken in 1869 by Henry Tibbe of Washington, Mo., who used plaster of paris to fill uneven surfaces in the pipe. He obtained patent No. 205,816 on July 9, 1878, on a "smoking pipe made of corncob, in which the interstices are filled with a plastic self-hardening cement." In 1872 his son, Anton A. Tibbe, assisted him, and later they incorporated as the Missouri Meerschaum Company.

PIPELESS ORGAN. See Organ

PIPELINE

Pipeline (gas). See Gas: Pipeline (long-distance)

Pipeline (interstate) to transport ethylene, a petroleum chemical used in the manufacture of plastics and synthetic rubber, was constructed between Lake Charles, La., and Orange, Tex., a distance of 30 miles, and placed in operation September 6, 1958. This 6⅝-inch pipeline transported

The First

ethylene to the E. I. du Pont de Nemours & Company plant at Orange, on September 6, 1958, and to the Spencer Chemical Company, also at Orange, on September 9, 1958.

Pipeline (oil). See Oil: Oil pipeline of importance

PIRACY LEGISLATION

Piracy legislation was "an act to protect the commerce of the United States and punish the crime of piracy" enacted March 3, 1819 (3 Stat. L. 510). Offenders upon conviction before a circuit court could be punished by death.

PIRATE on the Atlantic seaboard was Dixie Bull, who looted Bristol, Maine, in 1632. Previously he had received a grant of land at York, Maine. In June 1632, while Bull was in Penobscot Bay, a French pinnace arrived and seized his shallop and stock of "coats, ruggs, blanketts, bisketts, etc." Angered at this, he revenged himself by in turn becoming a pirate.

PISTOL

Government contract for pistols was authorized May 4, 1798, when Congress appropriated $800,-000 for guns, pistols, etc. The first contract was made March 9, 1799, with Simeon North, Berlin, Conn., for 500 horse pistols at $6.50 each. A second contract for 1,500 additional pistols of the same type was signed February 6, 1880. (Simeon Newton Dexter North—Simeon North, First Official Pistol Maker of the United States)

Pistol with a revolving cylinder was invented in 1830 by Samuel Colt while on the S.S. Corlo. With a pocket knife he whittled a wood model. He obtained a patent from England in 1835 and patent No. 138 from the United States on February 25, 1836, on "an improvement in revolving fire-arms." He formed the Patent Arms Manufacturing Company of Paterson, N.J., capitalized at $230,000, which was incorporated March 5, 1836. The first revolvers commercially manufactured were .34 caliber Texas models.

Revolver that was self-cocking was the Rider model, which was invented by John Rider and manufactured in 1856 by E. Remington and Sons of Ilion, N.Y.

PISTOL SHOOTING TOURNAMENT (international). See Revolver shooting tournament (international)

PISTON AUTOMOBILE. See Automobile: Free piston automobile

PITCHER, BASEBALL. See Baseball pitcher

PITUITARY HORMONE

Pituitary hormone isolated in chemically pure crystalline form was announced July 23, 1937, in Science by Drs. Abraham White, Hubert Ralph Catchpole, and Cyril Norman Hugh Long of the Laboratories of Physiological Chemistry and Physiology, Yale University School of Medicine, New Haven, Conn.

The First

PITUITARY HORMONE—*Continued*

Polypeptide hormone synthesized was oxytocin, a proteinlike compound made up of eight amino acids which stimulates uterine contractions and starts the flow of milk. Dr. Vincent du Vigneaud, biochemist, Cornell University Medical College, New York City, and his co-workers isolated oxytocin and synthetically reproduced the hormone. The announcement of the synthesis was made in the fall of 1953. On November 2, 1955, Dr. du Vigneaud was awarded the Nobel Prize in chemistry for this and other work on the chemistry and metabolism of sulfur compounds.

PLAGUE. *See* Epidemic

PLANET. *See under* Astronomy

PLANET (photographed in motion pictures). *See* Motion picture: Motion picture of the planets

PLANETARIUM
See also Observatory

Planetarium open to the public was the Adler Planetarium and Astronomical Museum, presented to the city of Chicago by Max Adler, at a cost of $1 million. Under the direction of Professor Philip Fox, the museum was opened to the public on May 10, 1930. The planetarium is a complex instrument for reproducing on an elaborate scale the planets of the' solar system and the 5,400 stars visible to humans. (Philip Fox, *Adler Planetarium and Astronautical Museum: An Account of the Optical Planetarium and a Brief Guide to the Museum*)

Planetarium or orrery was imported from England in 1732 and was presented by Thomas Hollis to Harvard College, Cambridge, Mass. It was built by Joseph Page and was "a very costly orrery, an instrument that this, or any other part of America, as far as we can learn, has never before been favored with." *(Boston News-Letter. Sept. 14, 1732)*

Planetarium or orrery built in America to represent the motion of the celestial bodies was constructed in 1743 by Thomas Clap, president of Yale College, New Haven, Conn. In the center was a globe 3 inches in diameter, from which 12 wooden arms about 7 feet long extended. The sun, planets, satellites, etc., were represented. The orrery was operated by hand as it had no gear work. *(American Magazine and Historical Chronicle. January 1744)*

Planetarium owned by a university was the Morehead Planetarium, University of North Carolina, Chapel Hill, opened May 10, 1949. It was the gift of John Motley Morehead. The first director was Dr. Roy Kenneth Marshall.

PLANK ROAD. *See* Road

The First

PLANNING BOARD (U.S.). *See* National Planning Board (U.S.)

PLANT PATENT. *See* Patent

PLANT QUARANTINE. *See* Quarantine

PLASTER, ADHESIVE AND MEDICATED. *See* Adhesive and medicated plaster

PLASTIC

Expandable polystyrene production (commercial) was undertaken by the Koppers Company, Kobuta, Pa., in 1954, with 17 tons valued at $20,000. Full production was not attempted until April 1958. Polystyrene is produced in small beads, which when heated in molds expand to take the shape of the enclosure.

Thermosetting artificial plastic was developed in 1906 by Dr. Leo Hendrik Baekeland of Yonkers, N.Y., who succeeded in controlling the reaction of phenol and formaldehyde. This reaction was explained in patent No. 942,699, application July 13, 1907, granted December 7, 1909, on "an improvement in methods of making insoluble condensation products of phenol-formaldehyde," commonly referred to as the "heat and pressure" patent. He also received patent No. 942,700 on December 7, 1909, on a "condensation product of phenol and formaldehyde and a method of making the same."

PLASTIC AIRPLANE. *See* Aviation—Airplane: Plastic-bonded airplane

PLASTIC AUTOMOBILE. *See* Automobile: Plastic-laminated fiberglass-body sports car

PLASTIC CARPETING. *See* Carpeting: Carpeting of tufted plastic

PLASTIC GLIDER. *See* Glider: Glider (all-plywood-plastic)

PLASTIC LENS. *See* Lens

PLASTIC LICENSE PLATE. *See* Automobile license plates

PLASTIC SURGERY PROFESSOR. *See under* Medical instruction

"PLATE FULCRUM" RAILWAY TRACK SCALE. *See* Scale: Platform scale

PLATE GLASS. *See* Glass

PLATE-GLASS INSURANCE. *See* Insurance

PLATFORM (national political party). *See* Political platform (national)

PLATFORM ELEVATOR. *See* Elevator

PLATFORM SCALE. *See* Scale

PLATINUM MEDAL. *See* Medal

PLATOON SCHOOL was the Central School, Bluffton, Ind., established September 1899, under the direction of William Wirt. The curriculum was arranged so that specific time was allotted to

The First

study, work, and play. In September 1902 the system was extended to the three elementary schools in the city. *(Roscoe David Case—The Platoon School in America)*

PLATYPUS. *See* Aquatic mammals

PLAY (drama)
See also Theater

Antivivisection play, *Woven Dreams,* written by Nina Halvey, winner of the International Humanitarian Prize of 1931, was presented October 4, 1932, in Philadelphia, Pa., under the auspices of the American Anti-Vivisection Society.

Aquatic play was *The Pirate's Signal, or The Bridge of Death,* presented July 4, 1840, at the Bowery Theatre, New York City. At the end of the fifth act, at the upper entrance of the stage, a full-rigged ship floated on water down to the footlights, turned, and went up the stage and off at the upper entrance. *(Thomas Allston Brown—A History of the New York Stage)*

Benefit performance was given January 7, 1751, at the Theatre on Nassau Street, New York City, for Walter Murray, one of the managers. It was advertised in the December 31, 1750, issue of the *Weekly Post-Boy:* "By his Excellency's Permission (for the benefit of Mr. Murray). On Monday, the seventh of January, will be performed, a comedy, called, 'A Bold Stroke For A Wife,' (being the last time of its being perform'd this season) to which will be added, an Entertainment called The Devil To Pay, Or, The Wives Metamorphos'd.' . . . "

Broadway play telecast. *See* Television—Telecast: Play to be televised with its original Broadway cast

Burlesque show of importance was *The Black Crook,* an original magical and spectacular drama in four acts by Charles M. Barras, with the scene laid in and around the Hartz Mountains about 600. It opened September 12, 1866, at Niblo's Garden, New York City, with the "Great Parisienne Ballet Troupe." Betty Regal of the Grand Opera, Paris, was the prima donna and soloist. It closed January 4, 1868, after playing 475 performances and grossing $1,300,000. *(Arthur Hornblow—A History of the Theatre in America)*

Chinese theatrical performance in America was offered by the Tong Hook Tong Dramatic Company under the management of Mr. Likeoon, Norman Assing, and Tong Chick at the American Theatre, Sansome Street, San Francisco, Calif., on October 18, 1852. The company consisted of 123 performers and musicians who were shareholders in the theatrical enterprise. The performance consisted of (1) "The Eight Genii Offering Their Congratulations to the High Ruler Yuk Hwang on His Birthday," (2) "Too Tsin Made High Minister by the Six States," (3) "Parting at the Bridge of Par-

The First

kew of Kwan Wanchang and Tsow," and (4) "Defeated Revenge."

Current Broadway play to be telecast with its original cast. *See under* Television–Telecast

Drama broadcast. *See under* Radio broadcast

Drama (full-length melodrama) broadcast. *See under* Radio broadcast

Drama to win a Pulitzer Prize was Jesse Lynch Williams' *Why Marry?,* a three-act comedy produced by Selwyn & Co., which opened December 25, 1917, at the Astor Theatre, New York City. It starred Nat C. Goodwin as Uncle Everett, Lotus Robb as Jean, Edmund Breese as John, and Harold West as Rex. It was originally written as a novel in 1914 entitled *And So They Were Married.* The Pulitzer award was announced June 3, 1918, by President Nicholas Murray Butler, president of Columbia University.

Full-length play by a black performed in New York City was *Appearances,* by Garland Anderson, a 3-act protest against lynch law, produced October 13, 1925, at the Frolic Theatre atop the New Amsterdam Theatre, New York City. It was produced by Lester W. Sager and lasted only 23 performances. *(Lindsay Patterson–Anthology of the American Negro in the Theatre)*

Greek play produced in Greek was *Oedipus Tyrannus* by Sophocles. It was presented at Harvard University, Cambridge, Mass., in May 1881. George Riddle played the part of Oedipus.

Hebrew professional acting troupe was the Hebrew Opera and Dramatic Company, which gave performances at the Bowery Garten Theater, 113 Broadway, New York City. It was directed by Leon Golubok, a 17-year-old comic who played the 80-year-old witch in *Die Hexe* (The Sorceress), by Arthur Firzer (nom de plume), on Saturday, September 25, 1880, and Monday, September 27, 1880. An advertisement of August 12, 1882, stated that a performance would be given for the benefit of ten poor Russian immigrant families. *(George Clinton Densmore Odell—Annals of the New York Stage, Vol. 11)*

Light opera. *See* Opera: Light opera presented in 2 cities on the same day

Musical comedy broadcast. *See under* Radio broadcast

Musical comedy by a black for black talent was *A Trip to Coontown,* a musical comedy in 2 acts by Bob Cole and Billy Johnson, produced at the Third Avenue Theatre (at 31st Street) in New York City on April 4, 1898. It was pretested in theatres in the neighboring towns. Bob Cole played the part of Willie Wayside, the tramp; and Billy Johnson played Jim Flimflammer, the bunco steerer. (New York *Dramatic Mirror—April 9, 1898)*

The First

PLAY (drama)—*Continued*

Musical (full-length), written, produced, directed, and performed as a Broadway (New York City) production was Bob Cole's *A Trip to Coontown.* It was a musical comedy in 2 acts with a cast of 18 and opened April 4, 1898, at the Third Avenue Theatre, New York City. It starred Bob Cole as Willie Wayside, Billy Johnson as Jim Flimflammer, and Sam Lucas. Try-outs had been held in smaller neighboring cities prior to the New York opening. It was also the first musical comedy written by a black for black performers.

Musical play to win a Pulitzer Prize was the two-act comedy *Of Thee I Sing,* by George Simon Kaufman, Morrie Ryskind, George Gershwin, and Ira Gershwin, awarded a Pulitzer Prize on May 2, 1932. It was produced by Sam H. Harris at the Music Box Theatre, New York City, on December 26, 1931, and starred Victor Moore as Alexander Throttlebottom and William Gaxton as John P. Wintergreen. It played for 441 performances.

Musical to run for more than 3,000 performances was *Fiddler on the Roof,* music by Jerry Bock, lyrics by Sheldon Harnick, book by Joseph Stein based on stories by Sholom Aleichem. It opened September 22, 1964, at the Imperial Theatre, New York City, ·and ran 3,242 performances. Zero Mostel took the part of Tevye. It was presented by Harold Prince and choreographed by Jerome Robbins.

Musical with an American theme and original score was *Evangeline, the Belle of Acadia,* performed at Niblo's Theatre, New York City, on July 27, 1874. It was based on Henry Wadsworth Longfellow's poem. The book and lyrics were by J. Cheever Goodwin. It ran for two weeks and featured bare-legged dancing. George K. Fortesque was the female impersonator playing the ponderous Catherine.

Native American play successfully acted on a regular stage by an established company was Royall Tyler's *The Contrast,* in five acts, produced April 16, 1787, at the John Street Theatre, New York City, by the American Company under the management of [Lewis] Hallam and [John] Henry. It depicted the contrast between meretricious standards of the fashionable world and simple, straightforward ideals of the true American. The play was published in 1790 for Thomas Wignell in Philadelphia, Pa., by Prichard & Hall. *(Dramatic Magazine. May 1880)*

Play about an American Indian written by an American was James Nelson Barker's *The Indian Princess, or La Belle Sauvage,* a three-act operatic melodrama, based on Captain John Smith's *General History of Virginia,* which was produced April 6, 1808, at the Chestnut Street Theatre, Philadelphia, Pa. *(Democratic Press. April 5, 1808)*

The First

Play acted by professional players was given at the New Theatre, December 6, 1732, in New York City. It was George Farquhar's *The Recruiting Officer.* The part of Worth was played by Thomas Heady, a barber. *(Arthur Hornblow—A History of the American Theatre)*

Play given by nonprofessional actors was *Ye Bare and Ye Cubb,* by Philip Alexander Bruce, performed August 27, 1665, at Accawmack, Va. The actors, Cornelius Watkinson, Philip Howard, and William Darby were summoned to appear in court on November 16, 1665, "in those habiliments that they then acted in and give a draught of such verses or other speeches and passages which were then acted by them." They were found not guilty of sedition and Edward Martin "who had informed on them" was ordered "to pay all the expenses of the presentment." *(Jennings Cropper Wise—Ye Kingdome of Accawmack)*

Play of note written by an American and acted in America was *Gustavus Vasa,* a tragedy by Benjamin Colman. Harvard students gave a performance of it in 1690 in Cambridge, Mass. *(Oscar Wegelin—Early American Plays)*

Play performed 1,000 times was *The Gladiator,* a five-act blank verse tragedy set in Rome and other parts of Italy about 73 B.C. It was written by Dr. Robert Montgomery Bird and was first performed September 26, 1831, at the Park Theatre New York City, with Edwin Forrest as Spartacus. By 1853 it had been performed 1,000 times. *(Clement Edgar Foust—The Life and Dramatic Works of Robert Montgomery Bird)*

Play telecast in color with its original cast. *See under* Television—Telecast

Play televised. *See under* Television—Telecast

Play written by a black woman to reach Broadway was *Raisin in the Sun,* by Lorraine Hansberry, which opened March 11, 1959, at the Ethel Barrymore Theatre, New York City. It was a story about a black family living in the south-side area of Chicago and starred Sidney Poitier, Ruby Dee and Claudia McNeil.

Printed American play was Governor Robert Hunter's *Androboros,* a biographical ("bographical") farce in three acts, "viz, the senate, the consistory and the apotheosis," printed in 1714 by William Bradford in New York City ("Monoropolis"). The work consisted of 3 preliminary leaves 27 pages, quarto size. "Androboros" means "man eater" and "Monoropolis" means "Fool's town" (otherwise, New York City). *(Frank Pierce Hill—American Plays Printed 1714–1830)*

Puppet show. *See* Puppet show

Puppet show televised. *See under* Television—Telecast

The First

Shakespearean play given in America is supposed to have been *King Richard III,* which was presented at the Nassau Street Theatre, New York City, on March 5, 1750, by Walter Murray and Thomas Kean. The play was "altered" by Colley Cibber. The performance began at 6:30 P.M. Admission to the pit was 5 shillings and to the gallery 3 shillings.

Theatrical presentation sponsored by the federal government was *The Family Upstairs,* produced January 30, 1934, by a cast of players operating under the Civil Works Administration at the Central School of Business and Arts, New York City. An appropriation of $28,000 for wages only was made January 12, 1934. The project was under the direction of Margaret Smith. Other plays were also presented later the same day. By March 25, 1934, 864,000 persons had witnessed 576 performances of 17 plays in 107 schools, clubs, and museums.

Vaudeville show. *See* Vaudeville

Wild West Show. *See* Wild West Show

PLAYER PIANO. *See* Piano player

PLAYGROUND for children was erected in Boston, Mass., in 1886 in the yard of the Children's Mission. "Three piles of yellow sand" were brought there. The first Boston school appropriation for playgrounds was made in 1899.

PLAYOFF BASEBALL SERIES. *See* Baseball game: Baseball playoff series

PLAYWRIGHT

Playwright (professional) was William Dunlap, who wrote or adapted 63 dramatic pieces. His first comedy, *Modest Soldier, or Love in New York,* was written in a few weeks in 1787. Five years previously, Dunlap had written *The History of The American Theatre.* (William Dunlap—The Diary of William Dunlap)

Playwright to win a Pulitzer Prize 4 times for drama was Eugene Gladstone O'Neill, who was awarded the prize by the committee for the 4th time on May 6, 1957, for his play *Long Day's Journey Into Night.* His other awards were in 1920 for *Beyond The Horizon,* in 1922 for *Anna Christie,* and in 1928 for *Strange Interlude.* (Robert Emmet Sherwood won 3 prizes for drama: *Idiot's Delight* in 1936, *Abe Lincoln in Illinois* in 1939, and *There Shall Be No Night* in 1941; and in 1949 he won the biography prize for *Roosevelt and Hopkins: An Intimate History.*)

PLOW

Cast steel for plows. *See under* Steel

Plow for pulverizing the soil was patented by George Page of Washington, D.C., who received patent No. 5,218 on August 7, 1847. Page designed a revolving single disk on the side of a peculiar form of plow. (Robert L. Ardrey—American Agricultural Implements)

The First

Plow patent was granted June 26, 1797, to Charles Newbold, a farmer of Burlington County, N.J. This plow was the first cast-iron plow to be used. It was of solid cast-iron (excepting handles and beam) and consisted of a bar, sheath, and moldplate. The invention did not meet with great success, as farmers believed that the iron poisoned the land, reduced fertility, and promoted the growth of weeds, and that the point would soon wear off. (Agriculture of the United States in 1860—U.S. Census Office)

Plow with interchangeable parts was patented by John Jethro Wood of Poplar Ridge, N.Y., September 1, 1819. His plow substituted cast iron for the wooden moldboard, landside, and standard. In this it was similar to the solid cast-iron plow which had been patented in 1797 by Charles Newbold. (Robert L. Ardrey—American Agricultural Implements)

Steel plow with a steel moldboard was made in 1837 by John Deere, a blacksmith, who tested it on the farm of Lewis Crandall, near Grand Detour, Ill. Deere used steel from a broken saw blade. In 1843 he imported rolled steel from England, which cost about $300 a ton. In 1847 he began manufacturing the plows in Moline, Ill., using steel produced by the Jones & Quiggs Steel Works, Pittsburgh, Pa. The company was incorporated in 1868 as Deere and Company.

Submarine cable plow was patented January 12, 1937, by Chester S. Lawton of Ridgewood, N.J., and Captain Melville H. Bloomer of Halifax, Nova Scotia, Canada, who obtained patent No. 2,607,-717, which they assigned to the Western Union Telegraph Company. The plow dug a trench in the bed of the ocean and simultaneously fed cable into the furrow. The plow could be used in depths as great as half a mile. The first transatlantic cable of a high-speed permalloy was buried June 14, 1938.

PLUG, ELECTRIC. *See* Electric attachment plug

PLUMBING

State plumbing legislation, enacted May 30, 1881, by Illinois, was "an act for the regulation and inspection of tenement and lodging houses or other places of habitation." In cities of 50,000 population, plumbers were required to receive a written certificate of instruction from the commissioner or commissioners before commencing work on buildings and to proceed according to plan. Violations were punishable by a fine of not less than $100 for the first offense and $10 a day for noncompliance.

PLUTONIUM. *See* Element: Element 94

PLUTONIUM PRODUCTION BY AN ATOMIC REACTOR. *See* Atomic reactor: Atomic reactor to produce plutonium

The First

PLYWOOD

Douglas fir plywood commercial production was undertaken by the Portland Manufacturing Company, Portland, Oreg., in 1905 at St. Johns (now Portland), Oreg. They sold Oregon pine panels, and later Columbian pine and Douglas fir. Plywood contains an odd number of veneer sheets bonded together, with the grain of each at right angles to the one above and below. Laminated sheets, all having the grain in the same direction, had been made earlier. *(Robert M. Cour—The Plywood Age)*

PLYWOOD AIRPLANE, MOLDED. *See under* Aviation—Airplane

PLYWOOD GLIDER. *See* Glider

PNEUMATIC HAMMER. *See* Hammer (pneumatic)

PNEUMATIC PLAYER PIANO. *See under* Piano player

PNEUMATIC SUBWAY. *See* Subway

PNEUMATIC TIRE. *See* Automobile tire; Bicycle tire

POCKET DICTIONARY. *See* Dictionary

PODIATRIST. *See* Chiropodist

POEM

Poem by an American to receive recognition at home and abroad was "Thanatopsis," written in 1810 by William Cullen Bryant. Washington Irving received recognition as the first American author. In both cases, the contemporaries were many, but the fame rests with these two men. This subject is one of constant dispute with those who prefer other authors. *(Parke Godwin—A Biography of William Cullen Bryant)*

Poem (printed) was "The Seminary at Quebeck," 4 lines published in Latin on December 24, 1705, in the Boston *News Letter*. It described a fire whose flames engulfed a church: *Gallica crux aequam flammam sentive coacta est.*

Poem to win national acclaim was Henry Wadsworth Longfellow's *Song of Hiawatha*, printed October 2, 1855, and published in book form on November 10, 1855, by Ticknor and Fields, Boston, Mass. In 4 weeks 10,000 copies were sold, in 18 months, 30,000. *(Jacob Blanck—Bibliography of American Literature, v5, 1969)*

POET

See also Author

American poet recognized as such was Benjamin Tompson. He graduated from Harvard College, Cambridge, Mass., in 1662 and produced many poems. His principal work, the first collection of American poems published in America, was *New Englands Crisis, or a Brief Narrative of New Englands Lamentable Estate at present,*

The First

compar'd with the former (but few) years of Prosperity. Occasioned by many unheard of Crueltyes practised upon the Persons and Estates of its united Colonyes, without respect of Sex, Age or Quality of Persons, by the Barbarous Heathen thereof." This work, a 31-page book of poems about King Philip's War, was published in 1676 in Boston, Mass. It was printed and sold by John Foster. Tompson's selection of subject matter was of greater importance than his literary style. *(Howard Judson Hall—Benjamin Tompson: His Poems)*

Black poet to be employed to teach creative writing by a university for blacks was James Weldon Johnson, author of *God's Trombones, The Book of American Negro Spirituals,* etc. He was appointed in January 1932 by Fisk University, Nashville, Tenn., to the Adam K. Spence Chair of Creative Literature and Writing, founded in memory of a Fisk professor who had taught those subjects. *(James Weldon Johnson—Along This Way: The Autobiography of James Weldon Johnson)*

Black woman poet was Phillis Wheatley (Phillis Peters), born 1753, whose first poem, "An Elegiac Poem on the Death of George Whitefield," was published in 1770. Her first book, *Poems on Various Subjects, Religious and Moral,* was published in London in 1773 and dedicated to the countess of Huntingdon. *(Charles Fred Heartman—Phillis Wheatley (Phillis Peters) Poems and Letters)*

Black woman to win the Pulitzer Prize for poetry was Gwendolyn Brooks of Chicago, who received the award May 1, 1950, for *Annie Allen,* a collection of poems about a woman as daughter, wife, and mother.

Poet to win a Pulitzer Prize 4 times was Robert Frost, who was awarded the prize by the committee on May 3, 1943, for *A Witness Tree.* His other awards were in 1924 for *New Hampshire: A Poem With Notes and Grace Notes,* in 1931 for *Collected Poems,* and in 1937 for *A Further Range.*

POETRY ANTHOLOGY. *See* Anthology (American)

POETRY BOOK. *See* Book: Profane poetry translation prepared in the colonies to be published

POETRY COLLECTION BY AN AMERICAN. *See* Poet: American poet

POET'S MONUMENT. *See* Monument: Monument to an American poet

POLAR EXPEDITION. *See* Expedition: Arctic expedition

POLARIS MISSILE. *See* Ship: Ship to fire a Polaris missile

POLE VAULT

Pole vault jump indoors over 16 feet was made February 2, 1962, by John Uelses, a Marine corporal, at the Millrose Games, New York City. Uelses

The First

cleared the bar at 16 and ¼ inch. The next night, at the Boston Athletic Association games, Boston, Mass., he exceeded his record by ½ inch.

Pole vault higher than 17 feet was made by John Pennel, who cleared the bar at 17 feet and ¾ inch on August 24, 1963, at the Florida Gold Coast Amateur Athletic Union meet at the University of Miami, Miami, Fla. He used a fiberglass pole.

Pole vault indoors higher than 17 feet was made March 6, 1966, by Bob Seagren of Glendale City College, Glendale, Calif., when he cleared the bar at 17 feet and ¼ inch in the National Amateur Athletic Union track and field championships at Albuquerque, N.Mex.

Pole vault indoors higher than 18 feet was made by Steve Smith of the Pacific Coast Club, who jumped 18 feet and ¼ inch on January 26, 1973, at the Millrose games at Madison Square Garden, New York City. He used a fiberglass pole.

Pole vault higher than 18.5 feet was made by Dave Roberts of Conroe, Tex., representing the Florida Track Club, whose jump of 18 feet 6½ inches on March 28, 1975, at the Florida Relays at the University of Florida, Gainesville, Fla., established a world's record.

POLE VAULTER

Pole vaulter to clear the bar at 15 feet, was Cornelius Warmerdam of the San Francisco Olympic Club, who established this record on April 13, 1940, at the triangular meet of Washington State College, the Olympic Club of San Francisco, and the University of California, at Berkeley, Calif. In 33 meets, 8 indoors and 25 outdoors, he duplicated or bettered this mark 43 times from 1940 through 1944.

POLICE

See also Border patrol; Fingerprinting; Secret Service

Army Military Police school was authorized December 19, 1941, and opened January 15, 1942, at South Post, Fort Myer, Va., with a faculty of 29 officers. The first class had 215 students. The first commandant was Colonel Robert B. Brown, who served from December 19, 1941, to May 29, 1942.

Execution (federal) for the killing of a Federal Bureau of Investigation agent. *See under* Execution

Motorcycle police were Anthony L. Howe and Eugene Case of the Police Department of the City of New York, who were assigned respectively to the police headquarters in the Bronx and Manhattan. They received official status on December 10, 1904, although experimental tests were made 2 years previously.

Parking-meter enforcement division was appointed June 1, 1960, by Mayor Robert Ferdinand

The First

Wagner of New York City. The "meter maids" underwent about 2 weeks training and received salaries ranging from $3,150 to $4,830 a year. The first summons was issued June 6, 1960.

Police airplane-arrest was simulated May 6, 1919, at Police Day at the Pan American Aeronautical convention at Atlantic City, N.J.

Police bureau of criminal alien investigation was started by the New York City Police Department December 23, 1930. The purpose was to bring to the attention of the United States Immigration authorities the undesirable aliens who are subject to deportation under the Immigration Law, because of either their criminal records or their illegal entry into the United States. *(Spring 3100. New York Police Department Magazine. April 1932)*

Police bureau of identification was established by Captain Michael Patrick Evans on January 1, 1884, for the Chicago Police Department. At its inception, only photographs were used. On June 1, 1887, the Bertillon system of identification was adopted, and on November 1, 1904, the Sir E. R. Henry system of fingerprinting was added. Evans was in charge of the Bureau of Identification from the time of its organization until the time of his death, October 6, 1931.

Police car radio. *See* Radio broadcast: Radio police system (two-way three-way)

Police department to adopt the fingerprinting system. *See under* Fingerprinting

Police officer (woman) killed in the line of duty was Gail A. Cobb of Washington, D.C., of the Metropolitan Police Force, murdered September 20, 1974, in an underground garage at 20th and L Streets in Washington by a robbery suspect.

Police officer (woman) on the aerial force was Cora Sterling, who was given a special commission as Seattle's first aerial policewoman by Mayor Charles Louis Smith. Her appointment to the aerial force was made July 13, 1934, and the commission by the Seattle Police Force was given in December 1934. She was only 20 years old and the holder of a Transport License.

Policeofficer (woman) to be appointed was Marie Owen, a patrolman's widow. In 1893 she was appointed to the Detroit Bureau of Police by Morgan A. Collins, Superintendent of Police.

Police officer (woman) under civil service was Alice Stebbins Wells of Los Angeles, Calif., who was appointed September 2, 1910, by the Department of Police, Los Angeles, Calif., and served until retirement on November 1, 1940.

Police patrol wagon (automobile). *See* Automobile police patrol wagon

The First

POLICE—*Continued*

Police training school of the Federal Bureau of Investigation, U.S. Department of Justice, was initiated on July 29, 1935, when 21 state and city policemen attended courses in the Federal Police Training School, under direction of John Edgar Hoover, head of the Division of Investigation. The courses, similar to those given in the training school for newly appointed special agents of the bureau, provide a program of training for local and state law enforcement officials and include subjects under the following headings: scientific and technical; statistics, records and report writing; firearms training and first aid; investigations, enforcement and regulatory procedure; police administration and organization. The course of training lasts for a period of 12 weeks and is given without cost to those enrolled. The first class consisted of 23 representatives of local and state law enforcement agencies, who received diplomas on October 19, 1935.

Police training school Federal Bureau of Investigation field officer chief (black) was Special Agent John D. Glover appointed February 16, 1979, to supervise the Milwaukee, Wis., office.

Police training school women graduates of the Federal Bureau of Investigation were Susan Lynn Roley of Long Beach, Calif., who was assigned to Omaha, Neb., and Joanne E. Pierce of Niagara Falls, N.Y., who was assigned to St. Louis, Mo. (Pierce had been employed by the FBI in Washington, D.C., in a clerical capacity from March 23, 1970.) They were graduated with 45 men from the 14-week training course at Quantico, Va., on October 25, 1972. The starting salary was $15,000 a year.

Police uniforms were authorized by the Common Council of New York, July 8, 1693, which ordered that the mayor should provide the police "with a coat of ye citty livery, with a badge of ye citty arms, shoes and stockings, and charge it to ye account of the city." *(Augustine E. Costello— Our Police Protectors)*

Prohibition enforcement officer. *See under* Prohibition

Radio system (police). *See* Radio broadcast: Radio police system (two-way three-way)

Special agents (women) of the police training school of the Federal Bureau of Investigation Academy were 6 women who completed the 14-week course on September 11, 1972, at Quantico, Va. The salary was $15,000 a year. There were 45 men in the course.

State police were the Texas Rangers, who were authorized by the General Council of the Provisional Government of Texas to organize three Ranger companies in 1835. On November 9, 1835, G. W. Davis was commissioned to raise 20 more men for this new service. *(Walter Prescott Webb —Texas Rangers)*

The First

State police class of women to complete training were 30 women of 104 who underwent a 20-week training course and were graduated June 27, 1980, at Sea Girt, N.J., to become members of the New Jersey State Police at a salary of $14,932 a year. They were assigned to 17 different barracks in the state.

State police officer (women) were appointed by the Division of State Police, Department of Public Safety, Mass., on April 18, 1930. They were Lotta Caldwell, who served to April 13, 1940, and Mary Ramsdell, who served to April 18, 1950.

Traffic police squad was the famous old "Broadway Squad" of New York City, organized in 1860. This was the first unit of the Police Department to have special functions in the field of traffic regulation. The members of the squad were stationed on the sidewalks along Broadway, from Bowling Green to 59th Street, at the intersections of the cross streets. It was their purpose to escort pedestrians across the streets and to stop traffic while so doing. The pavement of Broadway was of cobblestones and most of the traffic consisted of slow-moving horse-drawn vehicles.

Woman chief of police was Dolly Spencer, who was appointed in 1914 by the Mayor of Milford, Ohio.

Woman detective was Isabella Goodwin, who was appointed as acting detective sergeant, first grade, on March 1, 1912, by the Police Department of New York City. She had served as a police matron since May 15, 1896. On October 31, 1924, she retired.

Woman employed at a high level within a men's maximum security facility was Katherine Tripp who was employed as an assistant classification officer at the Maine State Prison, Thomaston, Me. September 11, 1974. The position was equivalent to a line lieutenant within the chain of command

POLIOMYELITIS EPIDEMIC. *See* Epidemic

POLIOMYELITIS VACCINE. *See* Vaccine

POLITICAL CONVENTION

Black delegate to a national political convention was Frederick Douglass of Rochester, N.Y. who attended the National Loyalists' Loyal Union Convention at Philadelphia, Pa., on September 6 1866. He paired with Theodore Tilton of New York City in the street parade. *(Frederick Douglass—Life and Times of Frederick Douglass)*

National committee of a political organization was formed May 22, 1848, at the Democratic Convention held May 22–26, in Baltimore, Md. At the convention, Lewis Cass of Michigan was nominated for President and William Orlando Butler of Kentucky for Vice President. They received 1,220,544 popular votes (127 electoral votes). The Whig Party candidates, Zachary Taylor and Millard Fillmore, were elected (1,360,099 popular votes 163 electoral votes).

The First

National nominating convention presided over by a black, held by a major political party, met in the Exposition Building, Chicago, Ill., on June 3, 1884. John Roy Lynch, a black, three times congressman from Mississippi, was nominated for temporary chairman of the Republican Party by Henry Cabot Lodge. The nomination was supported by Theodore Roosevelt and George William Curtis, and was carried by a vote of 424 for Lynch to 384 for Powell Clayton. John Brooks Henderson was the permanent chairman. The convention nominated James Gillespie Blaine for President and General John Alexander Logan for Vice President. *(Proceedings of the Eighth Republican National Convention Held at Chicago, Ill., June 3, 4, 5, and 6, 1884)*

National nominating convention to propose blacks for the offices of both President and Vice President was the 35th Democratic convention held August 26-29, 1968, at Chicago, Ill. On August 28, 1968, Rev. Channing Emery Phillips of Washington, D.C., received 67½ of the 2,622 votes cast by the delegates for President. On August 29, 1968, Julian Bond of Atlanta, Ga., was nominated but declined, as he did not fulfill the necessary age requirement. (Hubert Horatio Humphrey received 1,761 ¾ votes and won the nomination.)

Nominating convention (state) assembled at Utica, N.Y., in 1824 for the purpose of nominating candidates for governor and lieutenant governor. The number of delegates corresponded with the number of representatives in the assembly. De Witt Clinton was nominated by the Democratic-Republican Party and was elected November 3, 1824. He served as governor from January 1, 1825, to February 11, 1828, when he died. He had previously served as governor from January 1, 1818, to December 31, 1822.

Political convention broadcast. *See under* Radio broadcast

Political convention telecast. *See under* Television—Telecast

Political nominating caucus was held by the Democratic-Republican Party in New York City on September 15–16, 1812. President James Madison was nominated for a second term, and Elbridge Gerry of Massachusetts was nominated for the vice presidency, the latter office being vacant as a result of the death of George Clinton of New York. The Federalists nominated De Witt Clinton of New York and Jared Ingersoll of Pennsylvania. In the election, Madison received 128 electoral votes against 89 for Clinton and was elected President. Gerry received 131 electoral votes against 86 for Ingersoll. The votes were counted February 10, 1813.

Political nominating caucus attended by party leaders to designate presidential candidates was held February 25, 1804, by the Democratic-Repub-

The First

licans in Washington, D.C. Thomas Jefferson of Virginia was nominated for a second term as President and George Clinton of New York was nominated to serve as Vice President. The Federalists did not hold a caucus but supported Charles Cotesworth Pinckney of South Carolina for President and Rufus de Vane King of New York for Vice President. In 1800 certain leaders met in secret session.

Permanent chairman (woman) of a major political party was Frances Jean Miles Westwood of West Jordan, Utah, elected chairman July 14, 1972, at the Democratic National Committee meeting, Miami Beach, Fla., attended by 303 members from 50 states.

Presidential candidate to fly to a political convention. *See under* Presidential candidate

Presidential candidate to make a speech of acceptance at a nominating convention. *See under* Political convention

Presidential convention (national) addressed by a woman was the Republican National Convention in Cincinnati, Ohio, at which Sara Andrews Spencer spoke on June 15, 1876, against the disfranchisement of women and presented a memorial of the National Woman Suffrage Association stating "that the right to use the ballot inheres in the citizens of the United States."

Two-thirds rule, requiring a candidate for nomination to receive two thirds of the votes of the delegates, was adopted by the Democratic-Republican Convention, May 21–22, 1832, at the Athenaeum, Baltimore, Md. Robert Lucas of Ohio was chairman of the convention, which nominated Andrew Jackson for President and Martin Van Buren for Vice President. It was resolved "that the delegates from each state be entitled to as many votes in the selection of the candidates for the office of Vice President of the United States as such state may be entitled to in the Electoral College for the choice of this officer equally to the apportionment bill, recently passed by Congress; and that two thirds of the whole number of the votes given be required for a nomination, and on all questions therewith." *(Proceedings of a Convention of Republican Delegates from the several states in the Union, for the purpose of nominating a candidate for the office of the Vice President of the United States)*

Unit rule was adopted by the Whig Convention at Harrisburg, Pa., December 4, 1839. The state delegates selected a committee of three from their membership which was to assemble with other committees from other states similarly selected to form a Committee of the Whole. The state delegates meeting separately gave instructions to the members of their committee, who later voted as a unit in the Committee of the Whole. At the 1840 convention, the first at which the unit rule was applied, the final vote for presidential nominee

The First

POLITICAL CONVENTION—*Continued*

was 148 for William Henry Harrison of Ohio, 90 votes for Henry Clay, and 16 votes for Winfield Scott. John Tyler of Virginia was nominated for Vice President. *(Joseph Bucklin Bishop—Presidential Nominations and Elections)*

Political party national delegates (women) were alternates Therese A. Jenkins of Cheyenne, Wyo., and Cora G. Carleton of Hilliard, Wyo., who attended the 10th Republican Party convention at Minneapolis, Minn., June 7-10, 1892.

Woman delegate to make a seconding speech was Elizabeth Cohn of Utah, delegate at the Democratic National Convention at Kansas City, Mo., who seconded the nomination of William Jennings Bryan of Nebraska on July 5, 1900. *(New York Times. Sec. 1, page 6. July 6, 1900)*

POLITICAL ECONOMY COURSE

College chair of political economy was established at Columbia College, New York City, in 1818. Professor John McVickar occupied the chair of moral philosophy and political economy from 1818 to 1825.

Political economy chair, exclusively devoted to that subject, was established at Harvard University, Cambridge, Mass., in 1871. The first professor was Charles Franklin Dunbar.

Political economy course was given at the College of William and Mary of Williamsburg, Va., in 1784.

POLITICAL HISTORY. *See* History

POLITICAL MACHINE

that was well organized was the Albany Regency, made up of a group of Democrats who, from 1820 to 1854, exercised a controlling influence over the politics of New York State. Their headquarters were in Albany, N.Y., but their power extended into national politics. Prominent among them were Martin Van Buren, William Learned Marcy, Silas Wright, and John Adams Dix.

POLITICAL NEWSPAPER. *See* Newspaper

POLITICAL NOMINATING CAUCUS. *See under* Political convention

POLITICAL PARTY. *See* name of party, e.g. American Party, Equal Rights Party, Quids, Whig Party

POLITICAL PLATFORM (national) was adopted May 11, 1832, by a group of 295 Democratic-Republican delegates from 16 states and the District of Columbia who assembled in Washington, D.C., and drew up a list of resolutions for a platform. At the convention, on December 12, 1831, in Baltimore, Md., Henry Clay was nominated for President and John Sergeant for Vice President. *(Proceedings of National Republican Convention of Young Men Assembled May 7, 1832, at Washington, D.C.)*

The First

POLITICAL SCIENCE SOCIETY

Political and social science society (national) was the American Academy of Political and Social Science, organized in Philadelphia, Pa., December 14, 1889, for the purpose of promoting the political and social sciences. The first president was Professor Edmund Janes James; the first corresponding secretary, Roland Post Falkner; the first treasurer, Stuart Wood. The first annual meeting was held in Philadelphia, March 21, 1890. The academy was incorporated April 4, 1891.

Political science association was the American Political Science Association, founded in New Orleans, La., December 30, 1903, for the encouragement of the scientific study of politics, public law, administration, and diplomacy. The first president was Professor Frank Johnson Goodnow. *(American Political Science Association. Proceedings, Vol. 1)*

POLO

Intercollegiate indoor polo championship was won by Princeton University, which defeated Yale University, 10½-½, on March 18, 1922, at Squadron A Armory, New York City. Each team consisted of three players.

International polo series was played at Newport, R.I., August 25, 1886, between teams representing England and America. England won the series of two games with scores of 10-4 and 14-2. The American team consisted of Captain Thomas Hitchcock, Raymond Belmont, Foxhall P. Keene and W. K. Thorne. *(Frank Gray Griswold—The International Polo Cup)*

Polo was introduced by James Gordon Bennett upon his return from England in 1876. He imported polo balls, mallets, etc. The horses were brought up from Texas by Harry Blassan, a New York riding master. The first polo games were played in Dickel's Riding Academy, at the northeast corner of Fifth Avenue and 39th Street, New York City. On Thursday, May 11, 1876, a team captained by James Gordon Bennett played Lord Mandeville's team at Jerome Park, Westchester County, New York. *(Thomas Francis Dale—Polo, Past and Present)*

Polo game played outdoors at night took place on July 2, 1931, at Homewood Field, Baltimore, Md., between the Maryland Polo Club and the 110th Field Artillery. The first game was played with four men on each side. Homewood Field was amply lighted for the event.

POLO CLUB

Polo association (national) was the United States Polo Association, formed June 6, 1890, in New York City, by the Meadow Brook Club (Westbury, L.I., N.Y.), Philadelphia Country Club (Bala, Pa.), Rockaway Hunting Club (Cedarhurst, L.I., N.Y.), and the Westchester Polo Club (Newport, R.I.). The first chairman was H. L. Herbert

The First

and the first secretary-treasurer was Douglas Robinson.

Polo club was the Westchester Polo Club, organized in New York City in 1876. Matches were played at the Jerome Park racetrack in Westchester County, New York. *(Newell Bent—American Polo)*

POLYGAMY LEGISLATION (federal), enacted July 1, 1862 (12 Stat. L. 501), was "an act to punish and prevent the practice of polygamy in the territories of the United States and other places, and disapproving and annulling certain acts of the legislative assembly of the territory of Utah." Little effort was made to enforce it. The first important legislation was the act of March 22, 1882 (22 Stat. L. 30), the [George Franklin] Edmunds law, which defined simultaneous marriages as bigamy and prescribed loss of citizenship as an additional penalty for bigamists. It legitimized children born in polygamy before January 1, 1883.

POLYMETHYL METHACRYLATE PRODUCTION. *See* Lucite (polymethyl methacrylate) production (commercial)

POLYPEPTIDE HORMONE SYNTHESIZED. *See under* Pituitary hormone

POLYSTYRENE, EXPANDABLE. *See* Plastic: Expandable polystyrene production (commercial)

PONTIFF TO HAVE VISITED THE UNITED STATES. *See under* Visiting celebrities

PONTOON BRIDGE. *See* Bridge

PONY EXPRESS MAIL. *See* Postal service

POOL (game). *See* Billiards

POOL (swimming). *See* Swimming pool

POORHOUSE (state) to be replaced by a state home was closed by Delaware in 1933. On October 11, 1933, the State Welfare Home at Smyrna, Del., replacing three almshouses, was dedicated by Governor Clayton Douglass Buck. The first guests were admitted September 25, 1933, prior to the dedication. Dr. Alan Victor Gilliland was the first superintendent and served from August 1, 1933, to June 1, 1943. *(Delaware State Board of Welfare—Annual Report 1934)*

POPCORN was introduced to the English colonists at their first Thanksgiving dinner February 22, 1630, by Quadequina, brother of Massasoit. As his contribution to the dinner he offered a deerskin bag containing several bushels of the "popped" corn.

POPULAR VOTE FOR PRESIDENT. *See* Presidential popular vote

POPULIST PARTY. *See* People's Party

PORCELAIN (hard) to be manufactured successfully was made about 1825 by William Ellis Tucker at the American China Manufactory at the southwest corner of Sixth and Chestnut Streets,

The First

Philadelphia, Pa. *(Walter Alden Dyer—Early American Craftsmen)*

PORCELAIN TEETH. *See under* Dentistry

PORPOISES. *See* Aquatic mammals

PORT, FREE. *See* Free port

PORTABLE TYPEWRITER. *See* Typewriter

PORTLAND CEMENT. *See* Cement

POSITRON. *See under* Physics

POST OFFICE

Airplane post office was Flagship Station 1, officially opened and dedicated May 15, 1938, by Mrs. Franklin Delano Roosevelt during National Air Mail Week. It consisted of an American Airlines sleeper plane which, with wings removed, was set up as a special post office on Pennsylvania Avenue, Washington, D.C. Stamps were to have been sold in the plane, but this was found impractical and a station was set up in an adjoining building. The plane was exhibited and viewed by 78,636 people during the week it was open.

Colonial post office. *See* Postal service: Parliamentary act to establish a post office

Naval post office aboard a naval vessel was established August 20, 1908, on the U.S.S. *Nebraska*.

Open-air post office was opened October 1, 1917, in St. Petersburg, Fla. It had a roof, but no sides or enclosing walls. A lobby 18 feet wide extended around three sides of the building. The floor was made of pink natural colored stone resembling sandstone.

Post office act. *See* Postal service: Parliamentary act to establish a post office

Post office building (U.S.) built for that purpose was the Custom House and Post Office in Newport, R.I., built in 1829 and occupied in 1830. An act of Congress approved May 24, 1828 (4 Stat. L. 303), authorized the erection of the building. The title to the site was vested in the government on November 12, 1828.

Post office (colonial) for the collection of mail was established by order of the General Court of Massachusetts on November 5, 1639, in Boston at the house of Richard Fairbanks for "all letters which are brought from beyond the seas, or are to be sent thither." He was allowed a penny for the transmission of each letter and was accountable to the authorities in charge of the colony.

Post Office Department of the United States was temporarily established by act of September 22, 1789 (1. Stat. L. 70), which also created the office of postmaster general. The act of February 20, 1792 (1. Stat. L. 234), was the first to provide in detail for the Post Office Department and the postal service generally. The Post Office Department became an executive department by act of June 8,

POST OFFICE—*Continued*
1872 (17 Stat. L. 283), although it had been known as a department for many years. The change of status was made during the term of Postmaster General John Angel James Creswell of Maryland, who served from March 5, 1869, to March 17, 1873.

Post office fully mechanized was opened October 20, 1960, in Providence, R.I. A $20 million experimental installation designated Project Turnkey and built by Intelex Systems, Inc., a subsidiary of the International Telephone and Telegraph Corporation, was leased to the Post Office Department for 20 years. Letters were electronically faced and canceled and automatically transported to 300 destination bins at the rate of 18,000 per hour.

Self-service post office was an unattended unit installed in the Wheaton Plaza Regional Shopping Center at Wheaton, Md., on October 17, 1964. Located on a concrete island in the parking area, it dispensed stamps, envelopes, and postal cards at the same price as at stamp windows. It had a machine to make change for coins and bills, a scale for weighing letters and parcels up to fifty pounds, and a zone map for calculating parcel postage.

POSTAGE METER. *See under* Postal service

POSTAGE STAMP
Adhesive stamps were used by the City Despatch Post, established February 15, 1842, by Alexander M. Greig, with principal office at 46 William Street, New York City. They were engraved by Rawdon, Wright & Hatch, New York City, and printed in sheets of 42. They were a 3-cent denomination and sold for $2.50 a hundred stamps. Local delivery service was authorized by act of Congress July 2, 1836 (5 Stat. L. 80), "an act to change the organization of the Post Office Department." On August 1, 1842, the City Despatch Post was acquired by the United States government for $1,200 and was named the United States City Despatch Post. Alexander Greig was appointed a clerk in the new service and served until November 24, 1844. *(Elliott Perry and Arthur G. Hall—100 Years Ago, February 1842–August 1842: Centenary of the First Adhesive Postage Stamps in the United States)*

Airmail stamps were issued May 13, 1918, and consisted of three denominations, 6-cent orange, 16-cent green, and 24-cent carmine, rose, and blue, all with airplanes depicted on them. The 24-cent stamp was placed on sale May 13, 1918; the 16-cent on July 11, 1918; and the 6-cent on December 6, 1918.

American woman whose likeness appeared on a U.S. stamp was Martha Washington, shown on the 8-cent violet-black postage stamp issued December 6, 1902.

Black American depicted on a U.S. postage stamp was the educator Booker Taliaferro Washington, whose likeness was on the 10-cent brown stamp first placed on sale April 7, 1940, at Tuskegee Institute, Ala. The stamp was one of the Famous American Commemorative series issue of 1940. A 3-cent deep blue stamp depicting the log cabin in which he lived had been issued April 5, 1936.

Block-of-four postage stamps combined in 1 design in which each stamp is an entity were the multicolored Cape Hatteras National Seashore stamps issued April 5, 1972, at Hatteras, N.C., second in the series marking the 100th anniversary of the national parks. The upper left stamp in the block showed a ship's hulk pounded by the Atlantic Ocean; the upper right, the Cape Hatteras lighthouse. The two bottom stamps showed seagulls perched on driftwood. Combined, the 4 two-cent stamps paid the basic domestic first-class surface rate.

Books of postage stamps were issued April 16, 1900, as follows: books containing twelve 2-cent stamps, priced at 25 cents; twenty-four 2-cent stamps, 49 cents; and forty-eight 2-cent stamps, 97 cents. *(Records in Division of Stamps, Post Office Department, Washington, D.C.)*

Brothers to be pictured on individual postage stamps were John Fitzgerald Kennedy, 35th President of the United States, whose likeness appeared on the 5-cent blue-gray placed on sale May 29, 1964, and the 13-cent brown, on sale May 29, 1967, at Brookline, Mass., and Robert Francis Kennedy, U.S. senator from New York, whose likeness was on the 15-cent blue issued January 12, 1979.

Certified-mail stamp was issued June 6, 1955, at Washington, D.C. It was a vertical 15-cent red stamp that pictured a uniformed letter carrier on a light graduated background. It was for use on first-class mail, in addition to regular service, on which proof of mailing and delivery was desired at a cost less than registered mail. No indemnity value could be claimed.

Christmas-stamp annual series depicting both a religious and nonreligious subject was the 8-cent series issued November 10, 1971, at Washington, D.C. The religious stamp, multicolored with gold, was an adaptation of Giorgione's *Adoration of the Shepherds*, designed by Bradbury Thompson. The nonreligious stamp was dark green, red, and multicolored, designed by Jamie Wyeth and printed by rotogravure on the Andreotti rotary press. It was entitled *A Partridge in a Pear Tree.*

Christmas-stamp regular issue was placed on sale November 1, 1962, at Pittsburgh, Pa. It was a 4-cent red and green stamp printed on white paper, showing burning candles and an evergreen wreath with a red bow and the inscription Christmas 1962. It was designed by Jim Crawford, printed by the Giori press, 400 subjects to a sheet, in 4 panes of 100 each. On the first day, there were 491,312 covers canceled. The issue consisted of a billion stamps.

Coil multicolored postage stamp was the 6-cent American flag issued May 30, 1969, in Chicago, Ill., in connection with the Combined Philatelic Exhibition of Greater Chicago (COMPEX). It was printed on the 9-color Huck press by the Bureau of Engraving and Printing, Washington, D.C., in coils of 100 stamps.

Commemorative postage stamps issued by the Post Office Department were the Columbian series of 1893, which depicted incidents in the discovery of America by Columbus. The stamps were of sixteen denominations and ranged in value from 1 cent to $5. They were issued January 2, 1893, with the exception of the 8-cent stamp, which was issued March 3, 1893. The World's Commemorative Exposition at Chicago, Ill., was held from May 1, 1893, to October 30, 1893, to celebrate the 400th anniversary of the discovery of America by Christopher Columbus.

Departmental postage stamps were authorized by act of Congress of March 3, 1873 (17 Stat. L. 542), to be issued July 1, 1873, but they were placed in use May 24, 1873. The various departments had special colors assigned to them: Agriculture, yellow; Executive, carmine; Interior, vermilion; Justice, mauve; Navy, blue; Post Office, black; State, green; Treasury, brown; War, dull rose. The denominations were 1 cent, 2 cents, 3 cents, 6 cents, 7 cents, 10 cents, 12 cents, 15 cents, 24 cents, 30 cents, and 90 cents.

Dual-purpose postage stamp was the Air Post Special Delivery 16-cent stamp used for prepayment of the 6-cent air postage and the 10-cent special delivery fee. This horizontal stamp bore a reproduction of the great seal of the United States of America and was printed in blue ink. It was offered for sale on August 30, 1934, at the American Air Mail Society Convention Station, Chicago, Ill.

Encased postage stamps were introduced by John Gault of Boston, Mass., who obtained U.S. patent No. 1,627 on August 12, 1862. He inserted an unused postage stamp in a circular brass disc faced on one side by a transparent sheet of mica that allowed the value to be seen. The denominations of the stamps were 1-cent and 30-cent Franklin; 5-cent Jefferson; and 3-cent, 12-cent, 24-cent and 90-cent Washington. On the reverse side was advertising of the issuing firm. Due to the coin scarcity, these discs became popular and served in place of coins. They were sold to stores, bars, etc. at up to 20 percent above face value. They were produced by the Scovill Button Works, Waterbury, Conn.

First-day special cancellation was prepared for the Virginia Dare commemorative stamp released August 18, 1937, at Manteo, N.C. The 1-inch-square blue 5-cent stamp commemorated the 350th anniversary of her birth.

Flag (American) depicted on a postage stamp was shown on the 50-cent blue and carmine stamp issued May 15, 1869, which depicted an eagle with outstretched wings, facing to the left, resting on a shield with flags grouped on either side.

Flag series honoring countries overrun by Axis forces was printed by the American Bank Note Company, New York City and Chicago, and issued June 22, 1943, at Washington, D.C. The first country honored in the multicolored Overrun Nations Series was Poland. The other stamps in the series, which were issued at a later date, commemorated Czechoslovakia, Norway, Luxembourg, the Netherlands, Belgium, France, Greece, Yugoslavia, Albania, Austria, Denmark, and Korea—all of which were invaded and controlled by Axis powers during World War II.

Fluorescent-coated (or -tagged) postage stamp was the 8-cent fire-red stamp depicting a jet airplane soaring past the dome of the Capitol, issued August 1, 1963, at Dayton, Ohio. Under fluorescent light, the stamp glowed an orange red. The stamp was the regular airmail stamp issued December 5, 1962, at Washington, D.C., to meet the new postal rates in effect January 7, 1963.

Fractional-denomination postage stamp was the 1½-cent light brown Warren Gamaliel Harding stamp placed on sale March 19, 1925, at Washington, D.C. With the exception of the numeral, the stamp was the same as the 2-cent memorial stamp issued September 1, 1923. A ½-cent Nathan Hale stamp was placed on sale April 4, 1925, at New Haven, Conn., and Washington, D.C.

Gravure-printed postage stamp was a horizontal 5-cent stamp printed by the Bureau of Engraving and Printing, Washington, D.C., and issued November 2, 1967, at Washington D.C. It was printed with red, yellow, blue, and black inks and featured a photographic reproduction of Thomas Eakins' oil painting *The Biglin Brothers Racing* surrounded by a gold frame. The original picture, which depicts a sculling scene on the Schuylkill River near Philadelphia, Pa., hangs in the National Gallery of Art, Washington, D.C.

Imperforated ungummed sheet of postage stamps was the Byrd stamp souvenir sheet made for the National Stamp Exhibition at Rockefeller Center, New York City. The stamps were issued on February 10, 1934 and contained six 3-cent blue "Little America" stamps. Each plate contained 150 subjects in 25 panes of six stamps each.

Jew depicted on a postage stamp was Samuel Gompers, whose likeness was on the 3-cent bright red violet postage stamp issued January 27, 1950,

The First

POSTAGE STAMP—*Continued*
at Washington, D.C., to commemorate the centenary of his birth. The stamps were printed by rotary press, 70 stamps to the pane. Gompers (1850–1924) had served as president of the American Federation of Labor from 1886 to 1894 and 1896–1924.

Memorial stamp was the Lincoln 2-cent memorial issue commemorating the 100th anniversary of the birth of Abraham Lincoln and placed on sale February 12, 1909. This stamp was red, the size and shape of the regular issue of postage stamps. It depicted a profile of the head of Lincoln from Saint-Gaudens's statue in an oval with the words "1809 Feb. 12 1909" on a ribbon below. *(Records in Office of Third Assistant Post Master General, Post Office, Washington, D.C.)*

Moon cancellation was made July 20, 1969, by a die proof with the words *Moon Landing, U.S.A. —July 20, 1969.* A 10-cent airmail commemorative showed Neil Alden Armstrong stepping onto the moon from *Apollo XI.* The stamps were 1.05 by 1.80 inches and were issued in panes of 32. The plates used for printing the stamp were made from a master steel die that had been on board the *Apollo XI* landing module and had made the round-trip journey to the moon.

Mourning stamp was the 15-cent black postage stamp issued June 17, 1866, which depicted President Abraham Lincoln. A 10-cent and a 12-cent black stamp showing portraits of George Washington were issued on July 1, 1847, and July 1, 1851, but these were not "mourning" stamps.

Motion picture actress depicted on a postage stamp. *See under* Motion picture actor

Native American pictured on a postage stamp was the Nez Perce warrior Chief Joseph. The likeness was based on an oil painting by Cyrenius Hall in the National Portrait Gallery, Washington, D.C. The 6-cent vertical stamp was first placed on sale November 4, 1968, at Washington, D.C., to commemorate the opening of the National Portrait Gallery, Washington, D.C. Chief Joseph's garb was red, yellow, blue, and black, shown on a brown background. The stamp was designed by Robert J. Jones. This 5-color vertical stamp required 3 passes—2 by offset, 1 by Giori. The warrior's hair is printed black by intaglio with blue tones by offset.

Newspaper stamps were issued September 1865, under act of February 27, 1861 (12 Stat. L. 168), for prepayment of postage on bulk shipments. The stamps were a 5-cent blue Washington, a 10-cent green Franklin, and a 25-cent red Lincoln, on unwatermarked paper, without gum, typographed by the National Bank Note Company. The stamps were 2 by 3¾ inches and were discontinued July 1, 1898.

The First

Nonpictorial postage stamp was the 5-cent ultramarine Toward United Nations stamp issued April 25, 1945, at San Francisco, Calif., to commemorate the opening session of the United Nations at San Francisco in 1945. It was designed by Victor S. McCloskey and was printed on a rotary press, in sheets of 200 stamps, 4 panes of 50 each.

Nurse (individual) depicted on a postage stamp was Clara Maass, commemorated by a 13-cent stamp issued August 18, 1976, at Belleville, N.J. It was printed on the 7-color gravure press of the Bureau of Engraving and Printing, in colors of yellow, magenta, cyan, black, blue line, and black line

Offset-printed postage stamps were the 1-cent gray green issued December 24, 1918, the 2-cent rose carmine issued March 15, 1920, the 3-cent violet issued March 22, 1918. Each bore the profile of George Washington and were unwatermarked.

One-color one-size series of postage stamps was the parcel post issue of 12 red values: the 1-cent, 2-cent, 5-cent, and 25-cent issued on November 27, 1912; the 10-cent, on December 9; the 4-cent, on December 12; the 15-cent and 20-cent, on December 16; the 75-cent, on December 18, 1912; the $1, on January 3, 1913; the 50-cent, on March 15, 1913; and the 3-cent, on April 5, 1913. They were printed 45 to the page, 180 to the sheet.

One-dollar-valuation postage stamp was the salmon color $1 stamp depicting Isabella Pledging Her Jewels, after the painting by Antonio Muñoz Degrain, issued January 2, 1893. The issue ceased April 12, 1894.

Paintings depicted on postage stamps were placed on sale January 2, 1893. They were the 2-cent brown violet Landing of Columbus, after the painting by John Vanderlyn in the rotunda of the Capitol, Washington, D.C., and the 15-cent dark green Columbus Announcing His Discovery, after the painting by R. Balaca.

Parcel post postage-due stamps were authorized by act of August 24, 1912. The stamps were printed in dark green and issued in sheets of 180 stamps, 4 panes of 45 each, the 1-cent and 5-cent on November 27, 1912; the 2-cent on December 9, 1912; the 10-cent on December 12, 1912; and the 25-cent on December 16, 1912.

Parcel post stamps were the series of 1912–1913, placed on sale January 1, 1913, with the inauguration of the parcel post service. The issue consisted of twelve red stamps, from 1 cent to $1, prepared in three groups of four stamps each. The working personnel of the Postal Service was depicted on the first group, the transportation of mail on the second group, and the manufacturing and agricultural interests of the country on the third group.

The First

Perforated postage stamp was the 1-cent blue Benjamin Franklin, perforation 15, issued February 24, 1857. Originally issued in sheets July 1, 1851, the stamp bore the inscriptions "U.S. Postage" and "One Cent." The picture on the stamp was modeled after the bust of Franklin by Jean Jacques Caffieri. All U.S. postage stamps issued previously were imperforate, as were many after 1857.

Perforated postage stamps were contracted for February 6, 1857, and were delivered to the government February 24, 1857. The designs were the same as the 1851–1855 issue with the addition of three new values, the 24-cent portrait of Washington, the 30-cent profile bust of Franklin, and the 90-cent portrait of Washington. The stamps were printed by Toppan, Carpenter and Co. of Philadelphia, Pa. Previously imperforate stamps had been used.

Phosphorescent-impregnated postage stamp was the 4-cent red violet Abraham Lincoln of the Liberty issue, reproduced from a portrait by Douglas Volk in the Mellon collection, National Gallery of Art, Washington, D.C. It was placed on sale November 19, 1954, at New York City, without impregnation. The tagged stamp, which had a brief afterglow when exposed to ultraviolet light, was issued November 2, 1963.

Postage-due stamps were authorized March 3, 1879, and were issued in light brown May 9, 1879, in 1-cent, 2-cent, 3-cent, and 5-cent denominations. On September 19, 1879, the 10-cent, 30-cent, and 50-cent denominations were issued. The stamps were printed by the American Bank Company on unwatermarked paper, 1 by 25/32nd of an inch upright rectangles.

Postage stamp featuring a work of art in true color was the 4-cent stamp placed on sale October 4, 1961, at Washington, D.C., to commemorate the 100th anniversary of the birth of Frederic Remington, artist of the West. Shown on the stamp is a portion of Remington's oil painting *The Smoke Signal*, which is the property of the Amon Carter Museum of Western Art, Fort Worth, Tex. The stamp was printed on Giori presses in gradations of red, blue, and yellow on white paper.

Postage stamp in 3 colors printed in 1 passing of each sheet through the press was the American flag stamp—horizontal, in red, white, and blue, with a dark frame—first offered for sale at Washington, D.C., on July 4, 1957. The stamps were printed on the Giori press, which had 3 ink fountains and printed 3 different colors simultaneously.

Postage stamp issued jointly by 2 countries was the 4-cent green and rose Mexican Independence stamp commemorating the 150th anniversary of Mexican Independence, issued by the United States and Mexico on September 16, 1960, at Los

The First

Angeles, Calif. It was designed by Leon Helguera and Charles Chickering.

Postage stamp issued on the date of the event it commemorated was the Project Mercury commemorative of 1962, placed on sale throughout the nation on February 20, 1962. This 4-cent dark blue and yellow stamp showed the spaceship in which Colonel John Glenn orbited the earth. Three million covers were canceled the first day at Cape Canaveral, Fla.

Postage stamp of the United States having the same design as that of another country (Canada) was issued June 26, 1959. The inscriptions, denominations, and sizes differed, however. The denomination of the United States stamp was 4 cents, that of the Canadian stamp 5 cents. The design featured two interlocking links superimposed on a map of the Great Lakes with the St. Lawrence leading from them toward the sea. Within the left link was a maple leaf, Canada's emblem, and within the right link was a bald eagle, the United States emblem. The stamps commemorated the opening of the St. Lawrence Seaway.

Postage stamp on which was inscribed the name of a living American was the issue of 1927, a 10-cent blue stamp which pictured the *Spirit of St. Louis*, Colonel Charles Augustus Lindbergh's airplane, in flight, with "Lindbergh Air Mail" above it. In the background to the left appeared the coastline of the North American continent with the words "New York" in small dark letters, and to the right the coastline of Europe showing Ireland, Great Britain, and France, with the word "Paris" in small dark letters. A dotted line connected the two cities, showing the route of the flight. The stamp was first placed on sale June 18, 1927, in St. Louis; Detroit; Little Falls, Minn.; and Washington, D.C. The issue included special booklets of six stamps which represent the first and only airmail stamps issued in this form.

Postage stamp printed on the 9-color Huck press was the 6-cent multicolored Christmas stamp depicting a portion of the *Annunciation*, the painting by the Flemish artist Jan van Eyck, issued November 1, 1968, at Washington, D.C.

Postage stamp to honor a black woman was the Harriet Tubman stamp issued February 1, 1978, at Washington, D.C.

Postage stamp to picture an airplane was the 20-cent parcel post stamp "Aeroplane Carrying Mail," issued on December 16, 1912, and placed on sale January 1, 1913, the date of the inauguration of the parcel post service.

Postage stamps commemorating the National Recovery Act. *See under* Industrial recovery act

The First

POSTAGE STAMP—*Continued*

Postage stamps depicting scenes were the series of 1869, issued from March 1, 1869, to April 9, 1870. The designs were furnished by the National Bank Note Company of New York City, which received a contract on December 12, 1868, for furnishing the stamps. There were ten denominations. The 2-cent depicted a post horse and rider; the 3-cent brown a locomotive; the 12-cent ultramarine blue, milori green, a steamboat; the 15-cent Prussian blue, the landing of Columbus; and the 24-cent light green, the signing of the Declaration of Independence. The 1-cent ocher, the 6-cent ultramarine blue, and the 90-cent black and carmine stamps carried portraits of Franklin, Washington, and Lincoln respectively; the 10-cent orange and 30-cent carmine and blue stamps pictured an eagle resting on a shield.

Postage stamps depicting the American eagle were the 1-cent carrier's stamps in blue issued November 17, 1851.

Postage stamps in coils were issued February 18, 1908, and were coarsely perforated, 8½ holes to two centimeters. They were printed by the Bureau of Engraving and Printing, Washington, D.C., for the Post Office Department. In 1902 sheets of 400 stamps were cut into strips of 20 and spliced together into rolls which were prepared for vending and affixing machines by commercial organizations. These stamps were perforated on two sides only, either horizontally or vertically, two sides being imperforate.

Postage stamps issued by the Post Office Department were authorized by act of Congress of March 3, 1847 (9 Stat. L. 201), and first placed on sale in New York City on July 1, 1847. The issue consisted of two stamps, a 5-cent red-brown stamp depicting Benjamin Franklin, and a 10-cent black stamp bearing the likeness of George Washington. They were printed by Rawdon, Wright, Hatch and Edson of New York City. They were withdrawn from use on June 30, 1851. The issue consisted of 3,712,200 of the 5-cent denomination and 891,000 of the 10-cent denomination. The Bureau of Engraving and Printing began the printing of stamps with the 1894 issue of the "triangle" design stamps. *(U.S. Post Office Department—A Description of United States Postage Stamps)*

Postage stamps (U.S.) issued in a foreign country prior to sale in the United States were offered at the Canadian International Philatelic Exhibition (CAPEX), Toronto, Canada, on June 10, 1978. The minisouvenir sheet had eight 13-cent stamps. The complete uncut sheet consisted of 6 souvenir sheets (48 stamps) and sold for $6.24. The stamps depicted wildlife: 4 birds and 4 mammals that share the U.S.-Canadian border. The issue was offered for sale in the United States on August 28, 1978, at the Philatelic Bureau, Washington, D.C.

The First

Postage stamps to picture a woman were the Columbian commemorative stamps of 1893. Queen Isabella was depicted on three varieties which were placed on sale January 2, 1893. The 5-cent stamp (35,248,250 issued) was in chocolate brown and depicted "Columbus Soliciting the Aid of Isabella"; the $1 stamp (55,050 issued) was in rose salmon and showed "Isabella Pledging Her Jewels"; and the $4 stamp (26,350 issued) was in carmine, with portraits of Columbus and Isabella. Women were also shown as characters in group scenes in this set, but their identity was not given. The first American woman's portrait on a stamp was that of Martha Washington on an 8-cent dark-lilac stamp issued December 6, 1902. The portrait was after the painting by Gilbert Stuart.

Postage stamps to picture the coat of arms of the United States were the 10-cent yellow and the 30-cent blue and carmine stamps of the issue of 1869, on sale from March 1, 1869, to April 9, 1870.

Postage stamps without a denomination were the Christmas stamps printed in plates of 200 subjects in 4 panes of 50 each and issued October 14, 1975, in Washington, D.C. The stamps sold for 10 cents each and were printed before the postage rate was increased to 13 cents. One was based upon a painting by Domenico Ghirlandaio (c. 1470) in the National Gallery of Art, Washington, D.C.; the other, upon a Christmas greeting card produced by Louis Prang in Boston in 1878.

Postage stamps without the words United States or initials U.S. were the Pilgrim Tercentenary issue placed on sale December 18, 1920, at Provincetown and Plymouth, Mass. They were designed by C.A. Huston and issued in sheets of 280 stamps in 4 panes of 70 each. There were 3: the 1-cent green stamp, *The Mayflower* (137,978,207 stamps issued); the 2-cent red *Landing of the Pilgrims;* and the 5-cent blue *Signing of the Compact* (11,321,607 stamps issued).

Precanceled stamps printed on rotary presses at the Bureau of Engraving and Printing were issued April 21, 1923. This initial order embraced 1-cent stamps of the 1923 series. One-cent precanceled stamps in coils were first issued January 7, 1924. Prior to the addition of precanceling devices to rotary presses, the Bureau of Engraving and Printing precanceled 1-cent stamps in sheets for a limited number of post offices with electrotype plates containing 400 stamps each. The records indicate that Bureau precanceled stamps of this style were first issued to the New Orleans, La.; Augusta, Maine; and Springfield, Mass., post offices in January 1917.

President's wife depicted on a commemorative postage stamp was Anna Eleanor Roosevelt (Mrs. Franklin Delano Roosevelt) whose picture appeared on the 5-cent light purple stamp issued October 11, 1963, at Washington, D.C., on the anniversary of her birthday. (Martha Washington's likeness was shown on the 8-cent dark lilac regular issue placed on sale December 6, 1902.)

Pressure-sensitized-adhesive postage stamp was the 10-cent Dove of Peace precancelled Christmas stamp issued November 15, 1974, at New York City. It depicted a dove weather vane.

Printed matter on the reverse side of postage stamps was the Postal People special set consisting of 10 different 8-cent stamps printed on the same sheet in yellow, red, blue, black, and green, in panes of 50, on the Andreotti press and issued simultaneously on April 30, 1973, at more than 4,000 post offices and branches throughout the country during the observation of Postal Week. Each sheet contained 200 subjects in 4 panes of 50 each.

Public exhibition of postage stamps was held from May 10, 1876, to November 10, 1876, in the United States Building at the Centennial Exhibition at Fairmount Park, Philadelphia, Pa. It was arranged by John Walter Scott. The first important exhibit by collectors opened March 11, 1889, at the Eden Musee, New York City; 31 exhibitors showed 272 sheets of stamps from 161 countries, valued in excess of $200,000.

Registry stamp was a 10-cent, light blue stamp issued December 1, 1911, to prepay registry fees and not valid for postage. The design showed an eagle perched upon a rock, with wings extended. Issuance was discontinued on May 28, 1913.

Seal of the United States on a postage stamp was on the 16-cent dark blue special-delivery airmail stamp first offered for sale at the American Air Mail Society Convention Station, Chicago, Ill., on August 30, 1934. On February 10, 1936, the same stamp appeared as a bicolor: the border in red and the seal, the central design, in blue.

Sheet of souvenir postage stamps was the White Plains Commemorative issued to commemorate the 150th anniversary of the Battle of White Plains. The sheet consisted of twenty five 2-cent horizontal rectangle stamps printed in red ink. The margins of each sheet bore the inscription "International Philatelic Exhibition, October 16 to 23, 1926, New York, N.Y., U.S.A." The sheets were placed on sale October 18, 1926, and were not issued to postmasters for sale to the general public. They were printed in sheets of 100 subjects in 4 panes of 25 stamps each separated by 1-inch gutters with central guidelines. The stamps were 2-cents each, perforated 11. On the same date the regular sheets containing 100 stamps were also placed on sale.

Sheet of postage stamps to contain more than one variety of stamps was placed on sale May 9, 1936, in a temporary post office at Grand Central Palace, New York City, during the Third International Philatelic Exposition, May 9–May 17. The sheet consisted of four purple ungummed imperfo-

rate 3-cent stamps—one of the San Diego Exposition issue of 1935, one Texas Centennial issue of 1936, one Connecticut Tercentenary issue of 1935, and one Michigan Centenary issue of 1935—surrounded by a white border on which was lettered "Printed by the Treasury Department, Bureau of Engraving and Printing" at the left; "Under Authority of James A. Farley, Postmaster General" at the top; "In Compliment to the Third International Philatelic Exhibition of 1936" at the right; and "New York, N.Y., May 9–17, 1936," at the lower edge. About two thirds of the total issue of 2,809,039 sheets was sold during the exposition.

Special delivery stamp was a 10-cent dark blue oblong depicting, in an arched panel, a mail messenger running; the description alongside read: "Secures immediate delivery at a special delivery office." Service was authorized March 3, 1885 (23 Stat. L. 388), in 555 post offices, in places with 4,000 or more in population, and put into operation October 1, 1885. The stamps were printed by the American Bank Note Company and were available at all post offices on August 4, 1886. Service was extended to all post offices on September 6, 1888.

Special-handling stamps were authorized February 28, 1925, and placed on sale April 11, 1925, at Washington, D.C. They were printed in dark green, value 25 cents, and intended for use on 4th-class mail.

Stamp collecting agency. *See* Postal service: Philatelic agency

Stamp for balloon mail was engraved by Mrs. J. H. Snively and privately issued by John F. B. Lillard for use on mail carried June 18, 1877, on the balloon *Buffalo* from Nashville Tenn., to Gallatin, Tenn. Only 23 of the 300 stamps were used. They sold for 5 cents each.

Stamp to depict a living American was the multicolored 10-cent moon stamp, size 1.05 by 1.80 inches, issued September 9, 1969, to commemorate the moon landing of *Apollo XI* on July 20, 1969. The mission was carried out by astronauts Neil Alden Armstrong, Colonel Edwin Eugene Aldrin, Jr., and Lieutenant Colonel Michael Collins, with Armstrong in command—and it was Armstrong who first set foot on the moon. The stamp was printed in sheets of 128 and panes of 32 stamps, instead of the usual sheets of 200 and panes of 50, and was a horizontal stamp.

Stamp (U.S.) cancelled by a foreign country was the 5-cent multicolored postage stamp commemorating the 100th anniversary of Canada's achievement of federation, issued May 25, 1967, at the United States Pavillion at Expo 67, Montreal, Canada. The date of issue and cancellation coincided with President Lyndon Baines Johnson's visit to Ottawa and Montreal. The stamp was designed by Ivan Chermayeff of New York City and

The First

POSTAGE STAMP—*Continued*
showed a symbolic depiction of the scenic grandeur of Canada.

Stamped envelope (phosphor coated luminescent tagged) was the 5-cent bright purple eagle regular issue of January 5, 1965. It was tagged on August 15, 1967, at Washington, D.C. A 1″ by ⅜″ vertical block of phosphorous ink glowed red on airmail envelopes and green on regular mail envelopes when under lights.

Stamped envelopes issued to commemorate an event were the 3-cent green stamped envelopes printed on a Hartford press set up in the Post Office Department in the Government Building at the Centennial Exposition in Philadelphia, Pa., between May 10 and November 10, 1876. A shield design showed the initials "U.S.," a man on horseback above a locomotive pulling cars, the dates 1776 and 1876, and the words "three cents." *(Annual Report of the Third Assistant Postmaster General for the Fiscal Year Ending June 30, 1876)*

Stamped envelopes (U.S.) were issued in June 1853, under act of August 31, 1852 (10 Stat. L. 141), and were manufactured by George F. Nesbitt & Company of New York City under a contract dated October 25, 1852. They showed the profile of George Washington in an oval, the value above, and "cents" below. They were printed on white and buff paper. The first series included a 3-cent red, a 6-cent red and green, and a 10-cent green. *(Thomas Doane Perry—Guide to the Stamped Envelopes and Wrappers of the United States)*

Stamped envelopes with the identical design issued in various denominations were the 1932 Washington Bicentennial envelopes isued at Washington, D.C., on January 1, 1931, in commemoration of the 200th anniversary of the birth of George Washington on February 22, 1932. The denominations showing his residence at Mount Vernon, Va., were 1-cent olive green, 1½-cent brown, 2-cent carmine, 4-cent black, and 5-cent blue. The 3-cent envelope, stamped in bright purple, was issued June 16, 1932.

Twin postage stamps were issued September 29, 1967, and first placed on sale at the Kennedy Space Center, a branch of the Orlando, Fla., post office. A single horizontal design picture was perforated through the center. Each section or half was of the 5-cent denomination and could be used separately. The pair could be used as a 10-cent stamp. The stamp on the left depicted an astronaut in space and the stamp on the right showed the Gemini spaceship with the earth in the background. It was designed by Paul Calle of Stamford, Conn. Each sheet contained 200 subjects in 4 panes of 50 each.

The First

Two-color postage stamp produced by the rotary process at the Bureau of Engraving and Printing, Washington, D.C., was the 3-cent deep blue and carmine International Red Cross issue released November 21, 1952, in New York City. The stamps were printed 200 subjects in 4 panels of 50 stamps each.

United Nations postage stamps in U.S. denominations were placed on sale October 24, 1951, on United Nations Day in New York City. Six stamps were issued on that date: 1-cent magenta, 1½-cent blue green, 3-cent magenta and blue, 5-cent blue, 25-cent olive gray and blue, and $1 red; 5 denominations on November 16, 1951: 2-cent purple, 10-cent chocolate, 15-cent violet and blue, 20-cent dark brown, and 50-cent indigo. The stamps were only valid for use from United Nations Headquarters.

Vice President of the United States depicted on the postage stamp of a foreign country was Vice President Richard Milhous Nixon. The stamp was a green 2-sucre postage stamp issued by Ecuador on May 15, 1958. It bore Nixon's likeness and the flags of the United States and Ecuador.

Watermarked postage stamp was the 1-cent blue-green Benjamin Franklin stamp issued April 29, 1895. The initials *USPS* were watermarked in double-lined capital letters, each letter 16 mm high. These initials appear 90 times on each pane of 100 stamps. (This was the same stamp that was issued October 10, 1894, on unwatermarked paper.)

POSTAL CAR (steel). *See* Railroad car: Mail car (steel)

POSTAL CARD
Airmail postal card was the 4-cent card issued January 10, 1949. It depicted an eagle in flight, printed in orange-red on buff stock.

Airmail postal card commemorative was the 6-cent multicolored card issued March 31, 1967, at Charlotte Amalie, Virgin Islands, to commemorate the 50th anniversary of the purchase of the Islands from Denmark by the United States.

Commemorative postal card depicted the uplifted arm of the Statue of Liberty holding a flaming torch. It was issued May 4, 1956, at New York City to commemorate the Fifth International Philatelic Exhibit (FIPEX) at the Coliseum, New York City, from April 28 to May 6, 1956. It was a 2-cent deep carmine and dark blue triangular design on buff stock.

International postal card was the 7-cent single and identical 14-cent reply-paid postal card designed by Suren H. Ermoyan and placed on sale at New York City on August 30, 1963. It depicted a map of North America, highlighting Alaska and the United States and was printed on white stock by offset. It bore the slogan, "World vacationland,

The First

USA" against a bright blue background to publicize the Visit USA program.

Paid-reply postal card was the 1-cent black on buff reply-card attached to a 1-cent black on buff message card issued October 25, 1892, as a souvenir of the Columbian Exposition, depicting President Ulysses Simpson Grant. It was sold as two unsevered cards, 1 for the message and 1 for the reply. The message card had originally been issued as a single card on December 16, 1891.

Pictorial postal cards printed by the Government Printing Office, Washington, D.C., were issued June 29, 1972, at Boston, Mass., in observance of Tourism Year of the Americas. There were 5 pictorial cards, each 6 x 4¼ inches printed in black and dull orange on beige stock: three 6-cent cards for regular domestic surface mail; a 9-cent airpost card for domestic airmail, including Canada and Mexico; and a 15-cent card for international airmail beyond Canada and Mexico. Each featured 4 outstanding tourist attractions on the reverse side.

Postal card was issued May 1, 1873, under act of Congress of June 8, 1872 (17 Stat. L. 304). A 1-cent stamp printed on the upper right-hand corner showed a profile of the Goddess of Liberty looking to the left and surrounded by a lathework border with the words "U.S. Postage" inserted above, and "One Cent" below. The body of the card was light buff, the printing velvet-brown. The size of the card was 3 x 5⅛ inches. The cards were made by the Morgan Envelope Company, Springfield, Mass. The first known cancelation was May 12, 1873.

Postal card depicting other than the Liberty head showed the 1-cent brown on buff portrait of Thomas Jefferson and was issued August 24, 1885.

Statue of Liberty depicted on a postal card was the 4-cent deep red and ultramarine on buff stock issued November 16, at the American Stamp Dealers' Association National Postage Stamp Show, New York City, held November 16-18, 1956. It showed the Statue of Liberty with the inscription In God We Trust.

Street scene was the 4-cent dull blue and red designed by Gerald N. Kurtz, issued September 26, 1964, at Washington, D.C., to publicize the U.S. Social Security System in connection with the International Social Security Association conference at Washington, D.C.

POSTAL DIRECTORY was *A List of Post Offices in the United States with the Names of the Postmasters on the first of July 1855, also the Principal Regulations of the Post Office Department*, compiled by Daniel Tompkins Leech of the Post Office Department and printed by George S. Gideon, Washington, D.C., in 1855. It contained 146 pages of directory, 48 pages of regulations, and 6 pages of miscellaneous material.

The First

POSTAL FRAUD ORDER. *See under* Postal service

POSTAL ROUTE. *See under* Postal service

POSTAL SAVINGS BANK. *See* Bank

POSTAL SAVINGS STAMPS were issued December 22, 1910. Five denominations were issued in accordance with the authority conferred upon the Post Office Department by act of Congress of June 25, 1910 (36 Stat. L. 814), establishing postal savings depositories. Their use was discontinued on September 23, 1914. *(Edwin Walter Kemmerer—Postal Savings, An Historical and Critical Study of the Postal Savings System of the United States.)*

POSTAL SERVICE
Airplane mail pickup. *See under* Airmail service

Autogiro mail delivery. *See under* Airmail service

Automobile mail wagon. *See* Automobile mail wagon

Balloon flight carrying mail. *See under* Balloon

Coin-operated mailbox was the Mailomat, combining a postage meter with a United States letter box. Manufactured by Pitney-Bowes, Inc., Stamford, Conn., the first machine was installed at the General Post Office, New York City, on May 17, 1939. It was covered by patent No. 2,290,920, granted July 28, 1942, to Linden A. Thatcher of Stamford, Conn. Coins were dropped in slots, the desired stamp denomination was dialed, and the letter was inserted in a letter slot. The machine did the rest automatically—printed meter stamp with postmark and date of mailing and held the letter for scheduled collection. It provided postage from 1 cent to 33 cents, including airmail, special delivery, etc. It obviated the need of ordinary adhesive stamps, operated day or night as "a selfservice postoffice," and speeded mail because metered mail needs no post office "facing," canceling, or postmarking.

Collection and delivery of mail in automobiles owned by the government were made October 19, 1914, in Washington, D.C.

Dead letter office of the Post Office Department was organized in 1825 in Washington, D.C.

Dirigible transfer of mail to a train. *See under* Aviation—Airship

First-day special cancellation. *See under* Postage Stamp

Free city delivery of mail was authorized by act of March 3, 1863 (12 Stat. L. 705). City delivery service was placed in operation July 1, 1863, in 49 cities with 440 carriers at an annual cost of $300,-000. On January 3, 1887, free delivery service was extended to cities of over 50,000 population and

The First

POSTAL SERVICE—Continued
permitted in places having a population of at least 10,000 and postal receipts of $10,000.

Highway Post Office Service was approved July 11, 1940. The first route was established February 10, 1941, between Washington, D.C., and Harrisonburg, Va. Mail was transported in large bus-type vehicles equipped with facilities for sorting, handling, and dispatch of mail.

International airmail. *See under* Airmail Service

International dogsled mail left Lewiston, Maine, on December 20, 1928, with Alden William Pulsifer, postmaster of Minot, Maine, in charge and arrived January 14, 1929, at Montreal, Canada. A regular 8-foot mushing sled weighing 200 pounds was pulled by 6 blackhead Eskimo dogs. They averaged 9 miles an hour (7 to 8 on bare ground) and covered from 40 to 60 miles a day. The mail pouch contained 385 letters which were placed in government stamped canceled envelopes. The trip was not an official one. The sled returned to Lewiston on February 2, 1929, having passed through 118 cities, and having covered 600 miles, of which 90 percent was bare of snow.

Jet-propelled airplane to transport mail. *See under* Airmail service

Legislation permitting postage stamps of the United States to be illustrated in color was enacted June 20, 1968 (82 Stat.L.240). Previously, stamps could be shown only in black and white.

Letter carriers' uniforms were authorized by act of Congress of July 27, 1868 (15 Stat. L. 197), which authorized the Postmaster General "to prescribe a uniform dress to be worn by the letter-carriers." On October 31, 1868, Postmaster General Alexander Williams Randall approved a standard uniform.

Letter to encircle the world by commercial airmail was dispatched from New York City on April 19, 1937. It was routed via San Francisco, Hong Kong, Penang, Amsterdam, and Brazil and was returned to New York on May 25, 1937.

Mail chute (such as those used in office buildings, hotels, apartment houses, and other structures at which mail is dropped from the upper stories) was installed in 1883 in the Elwood Building, Rochester, N.Y., after plans prepared by James Goold Cutler, the architect of the building, who received patent No. 284,951, on September 11, 1883. The device was later developed and suited to the requirements of the Post Office and public use by Joseph Warren Cutler, under a series of about 30 patents issued to him.

Mail delivery by steamboats was authorized by act of Congress of February 27, 1813 (2 Stat. L. 805). The postmaster general was granted the power to transport mail "in any steamboats or boats . . . the pay not [to] be at a greater rate,

The First

taking into consideration distance, expedition and frequency, than is paid for carrying the mail by stages on the post road, or roads, adjacent to the course of such steamboats."

Mail franking privilege was granted to members of Congress and private soldiers in service on November 8, 1775. Regulations of January 9, 1776, provided that soldiers' mail was to be franked by the officer in charge. On April 3, 1800 (2 Stat. L. 19), free franking of mail during her natural life was granted to Martha Washington. *(Edward Stern—History of Free Franking of Mail in the United States)*

Mail fraud legislation was enacted June 8, 1872 (17 Stat.L.322), forbidding "fraudulent lottery, gift enterprise, or scheme for the distribution of money, or of any real or personal property, by lot, chance, or drawing of any kind, or in conducting any other scheme or device for obtaining money through the mails by means of false or fraudulent pretenses, representations, or promises. . . ." *(Chapter 335—42nd Congress, session 2. 1872)*

Mailbox (drive-up) to enable automobilists to post letters without moving from the seat of their cars was installed in July 1927 at Houston, Tex. The box had metal handles 8 to 10 inches long and was tilted 4 inches. The boxes were known as "courtesy collection boxes."

Mailbox locker was invented in 1810 by Thomas Brown, who was governor of Florida from 1849 to 1853. His mailboxes consisted of a series of numbered pigeonholes with glass fronts that enabled people to see whether there was any mail for them in their respective boxes.

Missile mail (official). *See under* Airmail service

Money order system was established on November 1, 1864, in order to promote public convenience and ensure safety in the transfer by mail of small sums of money. Foreign service was authorized July 27, 1868. The first agreement was made with Switzerland effective September 1, 1869. Service was extended to Great Britain on October 2, 1871, and to Germany on October 1, 1872. *(U.S. Post Office Department—Official Postal Guide)*

Navy mail service was established May 27, 1908, when an appropriation was made for the year ending June 30, 1909 (35 Stat. L. 417), to designate enlisted men of the Navy as naval mail clerks and assistant naval mail clerks to receive $500 and $300 extra respectively. The U.S.S. *Illinois, Prairie,* and *Rhode Island* were the first vessels afforded postal facilities, naval post offices having been established thereon August 15, 1908.

Newspaper wrappers were issued in October 1861 under act of February 27, 1861 (12 Stat. L. 167), in manila and buff, bearing a 1-cent blue stamp with the head of Franklin. In 1863 a 2-cent

The First

wrapper was added, bearing a black stamp with the head of Jackson.

Ocean mail contracts were authorized by act of March 3, 1845 (5 Stat. L. 732, chap. 43), "to provide for the transportation of the mail between the United States and foreign countries." The first contract was made in 1847, with the Ocean Navigation Company, for the transportation of United States mail once a month between the ports of New York City; Southampton, England; and Bremen, Germany, the compensation to be $16,666 for each round trip. The *Washington,* pioneer of American ocean steamers, started this service June 1, 1847. The contract expired June 1, 1857.

Overland mail service to the Pacific Coast was begun on September 15, 1858, by the Overland Mail coaches, the old John Butterfield stage line. Stages left Tipton, Mo., and San Francisco, Calif., simultaneously every Monday and Thursday. The route was operated under government contract authorized by act of March 3, 1857 (11 Stat. L. 189), for six years at a cost not to exceed $300,000 per annum for a semimonthly service, $450,000 for a weekly service, and $600,000 for a semiweekly service. The contract was signed on September 16, 1857, at $600,000 a year for six years, for semiweekly trips in both directions, in "good four-horse post coaches or spring wagons suitable for the convenience of passengers as well as safety and security of the mails." The specified running time for the 2,800 miles was to be not more than 25 days. The first trips were made in a few hours less than 24 days. *(Le Roy R. Hafen—Overland Mail, 1849–1869)*

Parcel post convention was negotiated with Jamaica, British West Indies, July 22, 1887 (25 Stat. L. 1393), and upon the adoption of the treaty, a feathered fan was sent to Mrs. Grover Cleveland by Jamaica officials.

Parcel post domestic air service was begun September 1, 1948. Overnight delivery of packages was planned. Service was authorized June 29, 1948 (62 Stat. L. 1097). The country was divided into 8 postal zones, the maximum rate being 80 cents for the first pound and 65 cents for each additional pound or fraction thereof.

Parcel post service was authorized August 24, 1912 (37 Stat. L. 559), when appropriations were made for the service that started January 1, 1913. Previously the weight limit of mail had been four pounds. The rates of the parcel post service depended upon the weight of the package and the distance carried.

Parliamentary act to establish a post office in the American colonies was passed in April 1692. A royal patent had been granted to Thomas Neale, February 17, 1691, by the sovereigns William and Mary, with "full power and authority to erect, settle and establish within the chief parts of their Majesties' colonies and plantations in

The First

America, an office or offices for the receiving and dispatching of letters and pacquets, and to receive, send and deliver the same under such rates and sums of money as the planters shall agree to give, and to hold and enjoy the same for the term of 21 years." Neale did not come to America but named Andrew Hamilton as postmaster general, an appointment which was confirmed April 4, 1692, by the British Postmaster General.

Permit mail was authorized April 28, 1904, and went into use October 1, 1904. Order No. 1,052, dated September 20, 1904, signed by Postmaster General Henry Clay Payne, permitted 2,000 or more identical pieces of 3rd or 4th class mail to be mailed without stamps affixed. The denomination of the postage, the place of mailing, and the permit was printed in the place of where the stamp would be affixed, and the fee paid in money.

Philatelic agency of the Post Office Department was placed in operation December 1, 1921, under Percy Warder Gibbon. Sales for the fiscal year were $20,906.50.

Pony Express mail left St. Joseph, Mo., and Sacramento, Calif., simultaneously April 3, 1860, carried by Henry Wallace riding west and John Roff riding east. The westbound packet was delivered in ten days, the eastbound in eleven and a half. (According to some accounts, the first rider westward was William [Billy] Richardson or John Frey, and the first rider eastward was Samuel Hamilton, who rode 20 miles in 59 minutes.) The route was through Fort Kearney, Fort Laramie, Fort Bridger, Salt Lake City, Camp Floyd, Carson City, Washoe Silver Mines, and Placerville. Until the service was discontinued on October 24, 1861, a rider left St. Joseph at noon and Sacramento at 8 A.M. every day except Sunday. It was a private enterprise under a charter granted by the state of Kansas to the Central Overland and Pike's Peak Express Co. The charge was $5 a half ounce. *(Waddell F. Smith—Story of the Pony Express)*

Postage-canceling machine patent was issued to Marcus P. Norton of Troy, N.Y., who obtained patent No. 25,036 on August 9, 1859, on a postmarking stamp to blot, cancel, and efface with cancellation showing date and post office of cancellation.

Postage meter was officially set at Stamford, Conn., November 16, 1920. Although the idea of metered mail originated in 1900 when the American Postage Meter Company of Chicago, Ill., was organized for that purpose, it was not until September 1, 1920, that the Post Office Department approved of it. The acting assistant postmaster general informed the Pitney Bowes Postage Meter Company of Stamford, Conn., that its machine would be acceptable to the department. About $2 million was spent on research and development of the machine. *(Metered Mail—Postage Meter Co.)*

The First

POSTAL SERVICE—*Continued*

Postal directory. *See* Postal directory

Postal fraud order was authorized by the act of Congress of June 8, 1872 (17 Stat. L. 322). The act granted the postmaster general, in cases in which fraud was practiced, the right to stamp mail, registered mail, and money orders "fraudulent" and return them to the sender instead of making the delivery to the addressee.

Postal route was between New York City and Boston, Mass. On December 10, 1672, Governor Francis Lovelace of New York announced that monthly service would be inaugurated January 1, 1673. The first trip was made January 22, 1673.

Postal service act under the Constitution was signed by President Washington, February 20, 1792 (1 Stat. L. 232). This act set the rates at 6 cents for letters to be carried not more than 30 miles, 8 cents between 30 and 60 miles, 10 cents between 60 and 100 miles, and 12½ cents between 100 and 150 miles.

Postmen's uniforms. *See* Postal Service: Letter carriers' uniforms

President's wife to frank mail. *See under* President (U.S.)

Railroad post office was tested July 7, 1862, and placed in operation July 28, 1862, on the Hannibal and St. Joseph (Mo.) Railroad during the administration of Postmaster General Montgomery Blair. The idea was originated by William Augustine Davis and the mail car built at Hannibal, Mo. *(J. L. Bittinger—The Railway Postal Service)*

Railroad post office for the general distribution of mail was tested July 1, 1864, regular service commencing August 28, 1864, on the Chicago & Northwestern Railway between Chicago, Ill., and Clinton, Iowa. George Buchanan Armstrong, one of the two special agents commissioned on December 20, 1864, to superintend postal matters, was appointed general superintendent of the Railway Mail Service on April 4, 1869.

Registration of letters was authorized by act of Congress of March 3, 1855 (10 Stat. L. 642). The system was placed in operation July 1, 1855. The fee was 5 cents.

Right-hand-drive automobile for the delivery of mail. *See under* Automobile

Rocket airmail flight. *See under* Airmail service

Rocket (steam-driven) to carry mail. *See under* Airmail Service

Rural free delivery was established October 1, 1896. Three routes were designated in West Virginia, one from Charles Town, one from Uvilla, and one from Halltown.

The First

Rural free delivery appropriation was made through the efforts of Thomas Edward Watson, a member of Congress from Georgia, 1891–93. Watson was the Populist Party's nominee for Vice President, and later its choice for President. Representative Watson's bill was introduced in 1893. *(U.S. Department of Agriculture—Yearbook, 1900 —"Free Delivery of Rural Mails," by C. H. Greathouse)*

Special delivery service was authorized by act of March 3, 1885 (23 Stat. L. 388). The service was established October 1, 1885, and at first was restricted to free delivery offices in towns of 4,000 or more inhabitants. An additional charge of 10 cents a letter was made for this service, and a blue special delivery stamp was issued on October 1, 1885. On August 4, 1886, the service was extended to all free delivery offices. *(Louis Melius—American Postal Service)*

Street letter box was invented by Albert Potts of Philadelphia, Pa., who obtained patent No. 19,-578 on March 9, 1858, on "a mode of attaching metallic letter-boxes." The box had a center hole through which the shaft of an ordinary cast-iron lamppost was placed. Boxes were erected on August 2, 1858, in Boston and New York City. *(American Gas Light Journal. Oct. 1, 1869)*

Strike of postal employees. *See under* Strike

"V" mail film was dispatched overseas from New York to London on June 22, 1942. It consisted of a partial roll of film on which there were only 212 individual letters. A complete roll of film contained 1,600 letters.

Vending machine (coin-operated) to dispense postage stamps. *See* Vending machine: Vending machine (coin-operated) to dispense postage stamps

Woman railway postal clerks were Maude and Mary Olson, daughters of a Galva, Ill., postmaster, who substituted for Colonel Charles Northrop, who was taken ill in September 1896. They served on the "Dolly," the Galva and Burlington Railroad Railway Post Office, later known as the Galesburg and Burlington Railway Post Office.

Zone numbers (two-digit postal zoning system) were put into use by the Post Office Department on May 1, 1943, at Pittsburgh, Pa. and later in 125 of its large-volume offices. The five-zone-number system, commonly referred to as the Zip (Zone Improvement Plan) Code, was inaugurated in July of 1963.

POSTCARD

Postcard (private mailing card) was authorized May 19, 1898 (30 Stat. L. 419), for use after July 1, 1898. Private mailing cards of the same form, quality, and weight as the government stamped postal card with a written message could be mailed for 1 cent. (The postcard was privately printed; the postal card with the monetary impression was

The First

produced by the government and required no additional postage stamp.)

POSTMASTER

Postmaster general appointed from the ranks was Jesse Monroe Donaldson, appointed by President Harry S. Truman on November 24, 1947, to take office December 1, 1947. The son of a postman, he became a letter carrier in 1908 and rose to first assistant postmaster general, an office to which he was appointed July 6, 1945.

Postmaster general (colonial) was Andrew Hamilton, appointed April 4, 1692, by the postmaster general of Great Britain, under an act of Parliament of April 1692 establishing post offices in the American colonies.

Postmaster general of the United States was Samuel Osgood, who was appointed by President George Washington and who served from September 26, 1789, to August 19, 1791. His office was authorized by act of Congress of September 22, 1789 (1 Stat. L. 70), which gave the general supervision of the post office to a postmaster general under the direction of the President. Other postmasters under Washington's administration were Timothy Pickering, appointed in 1791, and Joseph Habersham, in 1797. *(Daniel Calhoun Roper—The U.S. Post Office)*

Postmaster general of the United States to become a member of the President's Cabinet was William Taylor Barry, appointed by President Andrew Jackson, who served from April 6, 1829, to April 30, 1835. Barry resigned under congressional charges of inefficiency and corruption. Previously, the postal service had been under the Treasury department.

Postmaster general under the Continental Congress was Benjamin Franklin, who was appointed July 26, 1775, by the Second Continental Congress at a salary of $1,000 a year and who served until November 7, 1776. He served the crown as deputy postmaster at Philadelphia, Pa., from 1737 to 1753, and as deputy postmaster general for the colonies from 1753 to 1774. *(Ruth Lapham Butler—Dr. Franklin, Postmaster General)*

Woman postmaster appointed after the adoption of the Constitution was Sarah De Crow, who was made postmaster at Hertford, N.C., on September 27, 1792. She was the only woman among 195 postmasters.

Woman postmaster (colonial) was Mary Katherine Goddard, appointed postmaster at Baltimore, Md., in 1775. She served until November 14, 1789.

POSTMEN'S UNIFORMS. *See* Postal service: Letter carriers' uniforms

POSTMORTEM EXAMINATION. *See* Autopsy

The First

POTATO

Potato is believed by some authorities to have been introduced in December 1621 or January 1622. Imported from Bermuda by Virginia colonists, the first potatoes are said to have been used for food rather than for planting. *(Journal of Heredity. Vol. 16, No. 4. April 1925)*

Potato cultivation was undertaken in 1719 at Londonderry Common Field (now Derry), N.H., by Scotch-Irish immigrants who settled there and planted crops of their native Ireland.

POTATO CHIPS were introduced by a black chef about 1865. The first plant constructed for the exclusive manufacture of potato chips was erected in Albany, N.Y., in 1925 by A. A. Walter & Company. It is claimed that they were first made in 1853 by George Crum, an American Indian, at Moon's Lake House, Saratoga Springs, N.Y., and were known as Saratoga Potato Chips.

POTTER is believed to have been John Pride of Salem, Mass., who operated a pottery from 1641 to 1647. He made red earthenware from common brick clay. *(Joseph B. Felt—Annals of Salem, Mass.)*

POTTERY

See also Chinaware

Pottery was established by Dr. Daniel Coxe in Burlington, N.J., in 1680. It produced white and "chiney" ware for the local trade and also for export to Jamaica and Barbados. The factory was sold in 1691. He was governor of West New Jersey, from 1687 to 1692, but never came to America. *(Francis Bazley Lee—History of Trenton, N.J.)*

Pottery to make sanitary ware was founded in Trenton, N.J., in 1853 by Milington & Astbury. On April 4, 1873, they consolidated with Thomas Maddock & Sons.

POULTRY SHOW was the Grand Show of Domestic Poultry and Convention of Fowl Breeders and Fanciers held November 15–16, 1849, at the Public Garden, Boston, Mass., with 1,423 specimens in 219 cages. More than 10,000 persons attended. *(Report of the Committee of Supervision of the First Exhibition of Domestic Poultry)*

POUND (enclosure for animals) was authorized by section 48, Connecticut Code of 1650, passed May 1650, which decreed "that there shall be one sufficient pound or more made and maintained in every town and village within this jurisdiction, for the impounding of all swine and cattle as shall be found in any cornfield or other inclosure." *(Public Records of the Colony of Connecticut prior to the union with the New Haven Colony)*

POWDER MILL. *See* Ordnance: Gunpowder mill

The First

POWDERED SOAP. *See* Soap: Soap powder in packages

POWER ALCOHOL PLANT. *See under* Alcohol

POWER LINE CARRIER (electric power). *See* Electric transmission: Electric power line commercial carrier

POWER PLANT, ELECTRIC. *See* Electric power plant

POWER PRESS. *See* Printing press: Power or steam printing press

POWERBOAT RACE. *See* Motorboat Race

POWERED GLIDER. *See* Glider: Powered soaring glider commercially licensed

PRAYER BOOK (Book of Common Prayer). *See* Book: Book of Common Prayer

PRAYER BOOK (Unitarian). *See* Unitarian prayer book

PREACHER. *See under* name of specific religious denomination

PREACHER, AMERICAN INDIAN. *See under* American Indians

PRECANCELED STAMP. *See* Postage stamp

PRECEPTORIAL SYSTEM (university). *See* College: University to adopt the preceptorial system

PREEMPTION LAND ACT. *See* Land preemption act (federal)

PREFABRICATED BUILDING. *See* Building: Building with prefabricated walls of mosaic concrete

PREFABRICATED SHIP. *See* Ship: Prefabricated ship

PREFERENTIAL BALLOT. *See under* Election law

PREFRONTAL LOBOTOMY. *See* Surgical operation

PREMATURE-BABY HEALTH LAW. *See under* Medical legislation

PREMIUM
Premiums given by publishers were offered between 1870 and 1881 by the *Christian Union,* edited by Henry Ward Beecher. The paper's subscription jumped from 10,000 to 100,000. The premiums usually given to subscribers were chromos.

Premiums given with merchandise were successfully introduced by Benjamin Talbert Babbitt in 1865. When he first introduced wrapped soap, people felt that they were paying for the wrappers, so he printed the word "coupon" on them, and gave a "beautiful lithograph picture" for ten of them. This slowly developed into the operating of a premium department, which carried as many as a thousand different items in stock. *(Laurence*

The First

A. Johnson—Over the Counter and on the Street)

PREMIUM, NEWSPAPER. *See* Newspaper premium

PRESBYTERIAN CHURCH
Moderator (black) of the United Presbyterian Church in the U.S.A. was the Reverend Edler Garnet Hawkins, who assumed office May 21, 1964, at the 176th General Assembly at Oklahoma City, Okla. The moderator was the church's chief executive.

Moderator of the United Presbyterian Church in the United States was the Reverend Theophilus Mills Taylor, elected May 28, 1958, in Pittsburgh, Pa. Earlier the same day, this church was formed by a merger of the Presbyterian Church in the United States of America and the United Presbyterian Church of North America. A communion service was held to mark the occasion.

Presbyterian Church was established in 1611 in Virginia. The Reverend Alexander Whitaker was installed as pastor of the church, which was governed by him and a few of the most religious men of the colony.

Presbyterian Church of America was formed June 11, 1936, at a meeting of Presbyterians assembled in Philadelphia, Pa. The first General Assembly was held June 11–14 in Philadelphia and was attended by 35 ministers and 22 elders. The first two of its presbyteries was established in New York and Philadelphia. The first convener of the New York Presbytery was the Reverend Craig Long, and the convener of the Philadelphia Presbytery was Hall McAllister Griffiths.

Woman ordained a minister in the Presbyterian Church was the Reverend Margaret Ellen Towner, ordained October 24, 1956, in her home church in Syracuse, N.Y. She assumed the position of minister of Christian education of the First Presbyterian Church, Allentown, Pa. On May 25, 1954, she received a Bachelor of Divinity degree from Union Theological Seminary, New York City.

Woman ordained a minister in the Presbyterian Church in the United States (South) was Dr. Rachel Henderlite of Richmond, Va., ordained May 12, 1965, in All Souls Presbyterian Church, Richmond, Va.

PRESBYTERIAN ELDER (woman). *See under* Woman

PRESBYTERIAN GENERAL ASSEMBLY, the governing body of the church, met on May 22, 1789, at the Second Church of Philadelphia.

PRESBYTERIAN PRESBYTERY met in Philadelphia, Pa., in 1705 and was composed of seven ministers—Francis Makemie, John Hampton, George McNish, Samuel Davis, Nathaniel Taylor, John Wilson and Jedidiah Andrews—and 34 others. The first known ordination, which took place

The First

in 1706, was that of John Boyd, who settled in Freehold, N.J. *(Presbyterian Handbook—1936)*

PRESERVE. *See* Game preserve

PRESIDENT OF A BLACK AFRICAN COUNTRY TO VISIT THE UNITED STATES. *See under* Visiting celebrities

PRESIDENT OF A SOUTH AMERICAN COUNTRY BORN IN THE UNITED STATES was Galo Plaza Lasso, president of Ecuador (1948–52), who was born in the Greenwich Village section of New York City on February 17, 1906, the son of General Leonidas Plaza, Ecuadoran minister to the United States and later president of Ecuador for two terms.

PRESIDENT OF AN AFRICAN COUNTRY BORN IN THE UNITED STATES was Joseph Jenkins Roberts, who was born in Virginia in 1809. On January 3, 1848, he was inaugurated president of the Free and Independent Republic of Liberia, which had become an independent republic on July 26, 1847.

PRESIDENT OF THE CONFEDERATE STATES of America was Jefferson Davis of Mississippi, who was elected February 9, 1861. He was inducted into office February 18, 1861, and delivered his inaugural address on the steps of the State Capitol at Montgomery, Ala. Alexander Hamilton Stephens of Georgia was sworn in as Vice President February 11, 1861.

PRESIDENT OF THE CONTINENTAL CONGRESS was Peyton Randolph, a delegate from Virginia, who was elected September 5, 1774, the day the Congress assembled. He resigned October 22, 1774, to attend the Virginia State Legislature, and his place was taken on the same day by Henry Middleton of South Carolina. *(Edmund Cody Burnett—The Continental Congress)*

PRESIDENT OF THE REPUBLIC OF TEXAS was Sam Houston, who was elected September 5, 1836, and who took the oath of office on October 22, 1836 in Columbia, Tex. David Gouverneur Burnett served as Provisional President of Texas. Houston served until December 10, 1838, and was succeeded by Mirabeau Buonaparte Lamar. Houston was reelected and served from December 14, 1841, to December 9, 1844. Upon the admission of Texas on December 29, 1845, as the 28th state of the United States, Houston was elected as a Democrat to the United States Senate, where he served from February 21, 1846, to March 3, 1859. *(Rupert Norval Richardson—Texas, the Lone Star State)*

PRESIDENT (U.S.)

Administration office of the President was the Office of Administration authorized January 2, 1979, by President Jimmy Carter's Executive Order No. 12,112. The description of the official seal reads: "on a blue seal, the Arms of the United States proper above the inscription, Office of Ad-

The First

ministration, in gold raised letters, all within a white border edged gold and inscribed Executive Office of the President of the United States in blue raised letters. Dark blue suggested by the Seal of the President denotes the direct organizational link with the Presidential office."

Brother of a President to receive a Cabinet appointment. *See* Cabinet (U.S.): Cabinet member who was a brother of a President

Coin bearing the portrait of a President. *See under* Money

Duel in which a future President of the United States participated. *See under* Duel

Legislation passed over a President's veto. *See under* Veto

Pension for Presidents was enacted by Congress August 25, 1958. The act provided a pension of $25,000 for former Presidents and $10,000 to their widows.

Pension to the widow of a President. *See under* Pension

Photograph of a President. *See under* Photograph

Planet named for an American President. *See under* Astronomy

President and President's wife to die during the term for which he had been elected were Warren Gamaliel Harding, who died August 2, 1923, in San Francisco, Calif., and Florence Kling De Wolfe Harding, who died November 21, 1924, in Marion, Ohio. The term for which Harding had been elected was March 4, 1921–March 3, 1925.

President born a citizen of the United States was Martin Van Buren, the eighth President (1837 –1841). He was born December 5, 1782, in Kinderhook, N.Y. *(William Lyon Mackenzie—Life and Times of Martin Van Buren)*

President born beyond the boundaries of the original 13 states was Abraham Lincoln, the 16th President (1861–1865). He was born near Hodgenville, Ky., February 12, 1809.

President born on Independence Day was Calvin Coolidge, the 30th President (1923–1929). He was born July 4, 1872, in Plymouth, Vt.

President born posthumously was Andrew Jackson, the seventh President (March 4, 1829–March 3, 1837). He was born March 15, 1767, in Union County, N.C., a few days after the death of his father.

President buried in the National Cemetery at Arlington, Va., was William Howard Taft, the 27th President (1909–1913). He was buried March 11, 1930.

President buried in Washington, D.C., was Woodrow Wilson, the 28th President. He was buried February 5, 1924, in the National Cathedral,

The First

PRESIDENT (U.S.)—*Continued*
the Protestant Episcopal Cathedral of Sts. Peter
and Paul. *(Josephus Daniels—Life of Woodrow
Wilson)*

President elected under the Constitution was
George Washington, who was inaugurated in the
Federal Building on Wall Street in New York City,
and served from April 30, 1789, to March 4, 1797.
However, after the adoption of the Articles of
Confederation in 1781, the presidents of the ses-
sions of the Continental Congress signed them-
selves "President of the United States in Congress
Assembled." The first president of the Continen-
tal Congress was Thomas McKean of Delaware.

**President elected by the House of Representa-
tives** was Thomas Jefferson, the third President
(1801–1809). The electoral vote stood as follows:
Thomas Jefferson 73, Aaron Burr 73, John Adams
65, Charles Cotesworth Pinckney 64, and John Jay
1. The House assembled on February 11, 1801, and
on the 36th ballot elected Jefferson. Delaware and
South Carolina cast blank ballots, with the result
that the vote was 10 states for Jefferson and 4 for
Burr. *(Henry Stephens Randall—Life of Thomas
Jefferson)*

President elected for a fourth term was Franklin
Delano Roosevelt, the 32nd President (1933–1945).
He was also the first President of the United
States to be elected for a third term. He had received 27,241,939 popular votes in November
1940, against Wendell Lewis Willkie's 22,304,755,
when running for a third term; and 25,603,152
votes in November 1944 against Thomas Edmund
Dewey's 22,006,616 when running for a fourth
term. He served only a few months of the fourth
term, from January 20, 1945, until his death on
April 12, 1945.

President elected for two nonconsecutive terms
was Grover Cleveland, the 22nd President (1885–
1889) and the 24th President (1893–1897).

President inaugurated in the city of Washington
was Thomas Jefferson. He was inducted in the
Senate Chamber and sworn in by Chief Justice
John Marshall on March 4, 1801. *(Edward Channing—The Jeffersonian System: 1801–1811)*

President inaugurated on January 20, in accordance with the 20th Amendment to the Constitution, was Franklin Delano Roosevelt. The
amendment was ratified on February 6, 1933, and
President Roosevelt was inaugurated for his second term on January 20, 1937, in Washington, D.C.

President inaugurated on March 5 because
March 4 fell on Sunday was James Monroe, the
fifth President (1821–1825). He was inaugurated in
Washington, D.C., on March 5, 1821. President
Zachary Taylor was inaugurated on March 5,
1849, and Rutherford Birchard Hayes on March 5,
1877. Since 1877, whenever March 4 has fallen on
a Sunday, the oath of office has been administered

The First

in a private ceremony on March 3 or March 4 and
repeated in a public ceremony on March 5.

President married in the White House. *See
Wedding: White House wedding of a President*

President married while in office was John Tyler, the tenth President (1841–1845). He married
Julia Gardiner, daughter of a New York State
senator, on June 25, 1844, at the Church of
Ascension, New York City. His first wife, Letitia
Christian Polk, whom he married March 29, 1813,
died September 10, 1842, in the White House.
*(John Robert Irelan—The Republic, or, A History
of the United States of America in the Administrations)*

President on television. *See under* Television—
Telecast

President telecast in color was Dwight David
Eisenhower, who addressed the 40th reunion of
the class of 1915 of the United States Military
Academy at West Point, N.Y., on June 6, 1955. The
telecast was on June 7, 1955, from 11:00 A.M. to
12:00 A.M. on the *Home Show* on NBC-TV.

President to address the Senate was Harry S
Truman, who had served as the 33rd President of
the United States (1945–1953) and earlier as senator from Missouri (1935–1945). His presence in the
Senate, in Washington, D.C., was acknowledged
on May 8, 1964, his 80th birthday. He responded
with a 68-word speech.

**President to attend the launching of a manned
spaceflight** was Richard Milhous Nixon, who
viewed the launching of *Apollo XII* at 11:22 A.M. on
November 14, 1969, from Pad A at Cape Kennedy,
Fla. The crew consisted of Commander Charles
Conrad, Jr.; Richard Francis Gordon, Jr. (in command of the module pilot); and Alan La Vern
Bean. The total flight time was 244 hours 36 minutes 25 seconds. All mission objectives were successfully accomplished.

**President to attend the swearing-in of an Asso-
ciate Justice of the Supreme Court,** Washington,
D.C. was President Harry S. Truman, who appeared at the ceremony of his appointee Justice
Harold Hitz Burton on October 1, 1945.

President to be assassinated was Abraham Lincoln. He attended a performance of *Our American
Cousin* on April 14, 1865, at Ford's Theatre, Washington, D.C., where he was shot by John Wilkes
Booth. He died the following day, April 15, 1865.
*(Thomas Mealey Harris—Assassination of Lin-
coln, A History of the Great Conspiracy)*

**President to become a congressional represen-
tative.** *See* Representative (U.S.): Representative
who had been a President of the United States

**President to become a godfather to a member of
the British royal family** was Franklin Delano
Roosevelt. On August 4, 1942, the Duke of Kent,
youngest brother of King George VI, served as

The First

proxy for President Roosevelt at the christening of his son, Michael George Charles Franklin, Prince George of Kent, born July 4, 1942.

President to become a senator was Andrew Johnson, the 17th President (1865–69). Johnson was an unsuccessful candidate for election to the Senate in 1869 and an unsuccessful independent candidate for election to the House of Representatives in 1872. He was elected in 1875 and served as senator from Tennessee from March 4, 1875, until his death, July 31, 1875. *(Robert Watson Winston—Andrew Johnson, Plebeian and Patriot)*

President to become Chief Justice of the United States after serving as President was William Howard Taft. He was appointed Chief Justice June 30, 1921. He resigned on February 3, 1930, a few weeks before his death. *(Francis McHale—President and Chief Justice, the Life and Public Services of William Howard Taft)*

President to broadcast a presidential message. *See* Radio broadcast: Presidential message to be broadcast

President to broadcast by radio was President Warren Gamaliel Harding, the 29th President (1921–1923). His speech at the dedication of the Francis Scott Key Memorial at Fort McHenry, Baltimore, Md., on June 14, 1922, was broadcast by WEAR (now WFBR), Baltimore, Md. His voice was carried over telephone lines to the studio and broadcast from there. His World Court speech on June 21, 1923, at St. Louis, Mo., was transmitted over KSD, St. Louis, and WEAF, New York City. On November 5, 1921, a message from President Harding had been broadcast from Washington, D.C., to 28 countries. It was sent in code over the 25,000-volt RCA station at Rocky Point (near Port Jefferson), L.I., N.Y.

President to broadcast from a foreign country was Franklin Delano Roosevelt, whose speech at Cartagena, Colombia, on July 10, 1934, was relayed to New York and transmitted over the combined WEAF, WJZ, and WABC networks.

President to broadcast from the White House. *See under* Radio broadcast

President to broadcast in a foreign language was Franklin Delano Roosevelt, who addressed the French people on November 7, 1942, from Washington, D.C., at the same time that the American Army was taking part in the invasion of French territorial possessions in Africa.

President to celebrate his silver wedding anniversary at the White House was Rutherford Birchard Hayes, the 19th President (1877–81). The Reverend Dr. Lorenzo Dow McCabe of Ohio Wesleyan University, who had united him in marriage with Lucy Webb on December 30, 1852, again performed the ceremony on December 31, 1877. Mrs. Hayes wore her wedding gown of white flowered

The First

satin. *(Charles Richard Williams—Life of Rutherford Birchard Hayes)*

President to conduct ministerial services as commander-in-chief of the Navy was Franklin Delano Roosevelt, who read from the Book of Common Prayer of the Episcopal Church on Easter Sunday, April 1, 1934, while on the quarterdeck of Vincent Astor's yacht *Nourmahal* (PG), east of Key West, Fla. The services were attended by the crew of the *Nourmahal* (PG) and the U.S.S. *Ellis* (DD), a destroyer.

President to die in Washington, D.C., was William Henry Harrison, the ninth President, who died in the White House, April 4, 1841. President Harrison served only from March 4, 1841, to April 4, 1841. *(Benjamin Fisk Barrett—A Discourse . . . Suggested by the Death of William Henry Harrison)*

President to face enemy gunfire while in office, and the first President actively to use his authority as Commander in Chief was James Madison, the fourth President (1809–17). He assumed command August 25, 1814, of Commodore Joshua Barney's battery, known as Barney's Battery, stationed a half mile north of Bladensburg, Md. *(Mary Barney —A Biographical Memoir of the Late Commodore Joshua Barney)*

President to fly was Theodore Roosevelt, the 26th President (1901–1909). He was a passenger in a 4-minute flight in a Wright biplane piloted by Archibald (Archie) Hoxsey at St. Louis Aviation Field, St. Louis, Mo., on October 11, 1910, more than a year after he had ceased to be President. *(Henry Ladd Smith—Airways: History of Commercial Aviation in the United States)*

President to fly in a helicopter was Dwight David Eisenhower, the 34th President (1953–1961). On July 12, 1957, he flew in a three-seat Bell Ranger H-47J piloted by Major Joseph E. Barrett from the White House to an undisclosed site chosen for relocation of the White House during an atomic attack drill. He had previously flown in a helicopter while he was Supreme Allied Commander of the North Atlantic Treaty Organization.

President to fly in a twin-engined airplane was Dwight David Eisenhower, who made a 146-mile round-trip flight from Washington, D.C., to his farm at Gettysburg, Pa., on June 3, 1955. The trip to Gettysburg was made in 32 minutes and the return flight in 22 minutes. The airplane, a blue and white Aero Commander 560 (AF-2), was manufactured by the Aero Design and Engineering Company of Bethany, Okla., and cost approximately $70,000. It was flown by Lieutenant Colonel William Grafton Draper. (Before this flight, security regulations had required four-engine planes for presidential flights.)

The First

PRESIDENT (U.S.)—*Continued*

President to fly in an airplane while in office was Franklin Delano Roosevelt, who in January 1943 flew 5,000 miles in a four-engine Boeing Flying Boat from Miami, Florida, to the west coast of French Morocco for the Casablanca Conference with British Prime Minister Winston Churchill (January 14–23, 1943).

President to go through the Panama Canal while President was President Franklin Delano Roosevelt. He passed through the canal July 11, 1934, on the U.S.S. *Houston* destined for Hawaii and was greeted at Balboa, Panama, by President Harmodio Arias and Foreign Secretary Arosemena of Panama.

President to hold an airplane pilot's license was Dwight David Eisenhower, who was issued pilot's license No. 93,258 on November 30, 1939, by the Civil Aeronautics Administration. He learned to fly in 1939 when he was a lieutenant colonel on General Douglas MacArthur's staff in the Philippines.

President to invite the President-elect to discuss governmental problems was Herbert Clark Hoover, the 31st President (1929–1933). On November 12, 1932, Hoover invited President-elect Franklin Delano Roosevelt to confer with him with regard to the request made by Great Britain for suspension of payments of its war debt. The installment due on December 15, 1932, was $95 million. Roosevelt, then governor of New York, called on President Hoover on November 22, 1932. *(Vernon Boyce Hampton—Breasting World Frontiers: Herbert Hoover's Achievements)*

President to pitch a ball to open the baseball season was President William Howard Taft. On April 14, 1910, he threw the baseball which opened the American League Washington-Philadelphia game. Washington won 3-0. Pitcher Walter Johnson held the visitors to one hit. The crowd, 12,226 paid admissions, broke all previous attendance records.

President to receive fewer popular and electoral votes than an opponent was John Quincy Adams, the sixth President (1825–1829). In the November 1824 elections Andrew Jackson had received 153,-544 popular and 99 electoral votes; Adams had received 108,740 popular and 84 electoral votes; and William Harris Crawford and Henry Clay had received 42 and 37 electoral votes, respectively. Since no candidate had a majority of the electoral votes, it devolved upon the House of Representatives to choose from the highest three. In the meantime Crawford had become ill and was practically eliminated, and Clay as fourth agreed to use his influence to have Adams elected provided he would be appointed Secretary of State under Adams. The House of Representatives elected Adams by a vote of 13 states for Adams, 7 for Jackson, and 4 for Crawford.

The First

President to receive the unanimous vote of the presidential electors was George Washington, who received all of the 69 votes cast by the electors from the ten states which voted on February 4, 1789. In the election for the ninth term, 1821–1825, James Monroe of Virginia received 231 of the 232 votes cast by the electors from 24 states. The dissenting vote was cast by William Plumer of New Hampshire.

President to reside in Washington, D.C., was John Adams, the second President (1797–1801). On June 3, 1800, he resided at the Union Tavern, Georgetown, D.C., and in November 1800 moved into the President's House, the Executive Mansion.

President to resign was Richard Milhous Nixon, the 37th President, who submitted his resignation to Secretary of State Henry Alfred Kissinger on August 8, 1974, and announced at 9:04 P.M., via radio and television, his intention to resign at noon on Friday, August 9, 1974.

President to rest in state in the United States Capitol rotunda was Abraham Lincoln who died April 15, 1865. His body was removed to the White House where it remained April 15-18, after which it was removed to the Capitol rotunda, where it was kept April 19-20. On April 21 it was taken to the railroad station where it was conveyed to Springfield, Ill. Lincoln was buried May 4, 1865, in Oakland Cemetery, near Springfield, Ill. *(Ida Minerva Tarbell—Life of Abraham Lincoln)*

President to review the military forces at his residence was Thomas Jefferson. On July 4, 1801, on the White House grounds, he reviewed the Marines, led by the Marine Band.

President to review the U.S. Marine Band was John Adams. He reviewed the band from his residence on January 1, 1801.

President to ride in an automobile was Theodore Roosevelt, who rode in a purple-lined Columbia Electric Victoria August 22, 1902, at Hartford, Conn. He was accompanied by Colonel Jacob Lyman Greene. Twenty carriages followed the presidential car during the tour of the city.

President to ride on a railroad train was Andrew Jackson, who on June 6, 1833, took the stagecoach to Ellicott's Mills, where he boarded the Baltimore and Ohio train for Baltimore, Md., on a pleasure trip. John Quincy Adams, however, had made a trip on the same line a few months earlier, but after he had left the presidency.

President to serve as an official of the Confederate States was John Tyler, who became a delegate to the Provisional Congress of the Confederate States on August 1, 1861. He was elected a member of the House of Representatives of the permanent Confederate Congress on November 7, 1861, but died on January 18, 1862, before taking his seat. He had been President of the United States

The First

from 1841 to 1845. *(Journals of the Confederate Congress, Vol. 1)*

President to telephone to the moon. *See* Radio telephone: Telephone call to the moon

President to tour the country was George Washington, who traveled through the New England states from October 15 to November 13, 1789. He traveled in a hired coach accompanied by Major William Jackson, his aide-de-camp, and Tobias Lear, his private secretary, six servants, nine horses, and a luggage wagon. He went as far north as Kittery, Maine (then part of Massachusetts). As Rhode Island and Vermont had not joined the new government, he did not visit those states. Washington's first tour of the southern states was made from April 7 to June 12, 1791, during which time he left Mount Vernon, Va., on a 1,887-mile trip through Philadelphia, south through Virginia and the Carolinas into Georgia, and back to Mount Vernon.

President to translate a German book was John Quincy Adams. The book, originally written by Christoph Martin Wieland (1733–1813), was *Oberon; a Poetical Romance in twelve books,* translated from the German of Wieland (1799–1801) by John Quincy Adams; edited with an introduction and notes by A. B. Faust. A limited edition containing 340 pages, was published by F.S. Crofts & Co., New York City, in 1940.

President to travel underwater in a captured enemy submarine was Harry S. Truman, the 33rd President (1945–1953). He embarked at Key West, Fla., on November 21, 1946, in the U-2513, a captured German submarine. At sea off Key West, the vessel engaged in exercises during which it submerged. (President Theodore Roosevelt had submerged in the *Plunger,* an American submarine, on August 25, 1905.)

President to use a radio was President Warren Gamaliel Harding, who had a vacuum-tube detector and 2-stage amplifier receiving set installed in a bookcase in his study on the 2nd floor of the White House, Washington, D.C., on February 8, 1922.

President to use a telephone was James Abram Garfield, the 20th President (1881). He had a telephone installed in 1878 while he was a member of Congress.

President to visit a European country while President was Woodrow Wilson. He left Washington, D.C., December 4, 1918, on the S.S. *George Washington* and arrived at Brest, France, December 13, 1918. He returned to Boston, February 24, 1919. Wilson made a second trip, leaving Hoboken, N.J., March 5 and arriving at Brest March 13, 1919. He returned to Hoboken July 8, 1919. *(Gerald White Johnson—Woodrow Wilson)*

The First

President to visit a foreign country in wartime was Franklin Delano Roosevelt, who flew from Miami, Fla., to Trinidad, B.W.I., on January 10, 1943, then to Belém, Brazil; Bathurst, Gambia; and Casablanca, Morocco, arriving there on January 14. He returned by plane via Natal, Union of South Africa; Belém; Trinidad; and Miami. He arrived in Washington, D.C., by train on January 31, 1943.

President to visit a foreign country while President was Theodore Roosevelt, who sailed on the U.S.S. *Louisiana* for Panama, where he remained from November 14 to 17, 1906, after which he went to Puerto Rico. (While on a fishing trip Grover Cleveland once passed beyond the three-mile limit.) *(Harold Howland—Theodore Roosevelt and His Times)*

President to visit Alaska and Canada while President was Warren Gamaliel Harding, who visited Metlakahtla, Alaska, July 8, 1923, and Vancouver, B.C., July 26, 1923. He sailed on the U.S. naval transport *Henderson.*

President to visit Hawaii while President was Franklin Delano Roosevelt, who landed July 25, 1934, at Hilo, Hawaii. He was officially welcomed by Governor Joseph Poindexter on board the cruiser U.S.S. *Houston.*

President to visit South America while President was Franklin Delano Roosevelt, who stopped off at Cartagena, Colombia, July 10, 1934. Prior to his visit, he received President Enrique Olaya Herrera of Colombia at a formal visit on board the cruiser U.S.S. *Houston.* President Roosevelt returned President Herrera's visit on July 10.

President to witness the firing of a Polaris missile was President John Fitzgerald Kennedy, who on November 16, 1963, aboard the U.S.S. *Observation Island,* 32 miles off Cape Canaveral, Fla., watched the submerged nuclear submarine U.S.S. *Andrew Jackson* fire a Polaris A-2 missile, which broke through the surface of the water and headed on a 1,500-mile flight into the Caribbean.

President who had been a senator was James Monroe, who served as senator from Virginia from November 9, 1790, to May 27, 1794, filling the vacancy caused by the death of William Grayson on March 12, 1790.

President who had received a patent was Abraham Lincoln. On March 10, 1849, in Springfield, Ill., he applied for a patent for "buoying vessels over shoals," a device for lifting vessels over shoals by means of inflated cylinders. His application was granted and on May 22, 1849, he obtained patent No. 6,469. *(Sven Anderson—Floating Drydocks)*

President who had used a telephone for campaigning was William McKinley, the 25th President (1897–1901). He called 38 of his campaign managers in as many states from Canton, Ohio, in

The First

PRESIDENT (U.S.)—*Continued*
1896 during the presidential campaign which resulted in his election.

President who was a bachelor was James Buchanan, the 15th President (1857–1861).

President who was a Catholic was John Fitzgerald Kennedy, who was inaugurated January 20, 1961, in Washington, D.C., as the 35th President.

President who was a "dark horse" candidate was James Knox Polk, the 11th President (1845–1849). His name appeared for the first time on the eighth ballot at the Democratic convention on May 29, 1844. On the ninth ballot, amid great confusion, the convention stampeded for him. *(Frank van der Linden—Dark Horse)*

President whose assassination was attempted was Andrew Jackson. On January 30, 1835, Richard Lawrence snapped two pistols at President Jackson as he attended the funeral of Representative Warren Ransom Davis of South Carolina at the Capitol in Washington, D.C. Fortunately the weapons missed fire. *(Niles' Weekly Register. February 1835)*

President whose grandson became President was William Henry Harrison, the ninth President (1841). His grandson, Benjamin Harrison, was the 23rd President (1888–1893).

President whose mother lived at the Executive Mansion, Washington, D.C., was James Abram Garfield, the 20th President (March 4, 1881–September 19, 1881). His mother, Eliza Ballou Garfield, lived in the White House with her son. *(John Clark Ridpath—The Life and Work of James A. Garfield)*

President whose mother saw her son inaugurated President of the United States for a second term was Franklin Delano Roosevelt, whose mother, Sarah Delano Roosevelt, saw him take his second oath of office on January 20, 1937.

President whose son became President was John Adams, the second President (March 4, 1797–March 3, 1801), father of John Quincy Adams, the sixth President (March 4, 1825–March 3, 1829).

President whose wife was not born in the United States was John Quincy Adams. Mrs. Adams was the former Louisa Catherine Johnson, born February 12, 1775, in London, England, the daughter of Joshua Johnson of Maryland, first United States Consul in London. On July 26, 1797, they were married at the Church of the Parish of All Hallows, Barking, England. At the time Adams was United States Minister to Holland.

President with a brother in the Senate was President John Fitzgerald Kennedy, whose brother Edward Moore Kennedy was elected November 6, 1962, to fill JFK's unexpired term.

The First

Presidential address to be televised. *See under* Television—Telecast

Presidential airplane was the *Sacred Cow*, a four-engine Skymaster C-54 built at the Douglas Aircraft Company's Santa Monica, Calif., plant and delivered June 1944 to the Air Transport Command. Its first mission outside the United States was to fly Henry Lewis Stimson, Secretary of War, from Washington, D.C., to Naples, Italy, a distance of 4,200 miles, in 24 hours.

Presidential airplane (turbo-compound-powered) was the Air Force *Columbine III*, a Lockheed Super Constellation V C 121 E, christened November 24, 1954, at the National Airport, Washington, D.C., by Mrs. Dwight David Eisenhower. It cruised at 335 mph and could fly faster than 370 mph. It was powered by four Wright turbo-compound 3250 h.p. engines turning three-bladed Hamilton Standard propellers. It had a wingspan of 123 feet, a fuselage length of 116 feet, and a maximum gross takeoff weight of 133,000 pounds. It had accommodations for a crew of 18 and 28 passengers during daytime flight. The first official trip was made November 24, 1954, from Washington, D.C., to Augusta, Ga., with British Field Marshal Viscount Bernard Law Montgomery, and Ellis Slater, George Allen, Colonel Thomas Belshe, and their wives. (Mrs. Eisenhower had flown in the plane on a trip to New York City before November 15.)

Presidential amnesty proclamation. *See* Amnesty

Presidential campaign comanager (woman). *See* Woman: Woman presidential campaign comanager

Presidential citation. *See under* Medal

Presidential debate between an incumbent President and a candidate for his office. *See under* Television-Telecast

Presidential election in which votes were tallied electronically. *See under* Voting Machine

Presidential flag. *See* Flag: President's flag

Presidential impeachment proceedings. *See* Impeachment: Impeachment proceedings against a President of the United States

Presidential inauguration broadcast. *See under* Radio broadcast

Presidential message broadcast. *See under* Radio broadcast

Presidential news conference filmed for television and newsreels. *See under* Television—Telecast

Presidential nomination notification ceremony telecast. *See under* Television—Telecast

Presidential press conference recorded on tape was held January 25, 1951, at the White House, Washington, D.C. Portions were released by consent of President Harry S Truman. It was recorded for the White House archives by the Signal Corps

The First

unit of the United States Army permanently attached to the White House to handle communications.

President's car. *See under* Railroad car

President's child born in the White House. *See* Births: Child born in the White House, Washington, D.C., the offspring of a President

President's flag. *See under* Flag

President's widow to receive a pension. *See* Pension: Pension to the widow of a President

President's wife to frank mail was Martha Washington. On April 3, 1800, an "act to extend the privilege of franking letters and packages to Martha Washington" (2 Stat. L. 19) was passed. This privilege was granted her "for and during her life."

President's wife to travel in an airplane to a foreign country was Eleanor Roosevelt who on March 6, 1934, left Miami, Fla., in a commercial airplane, visited Puerto Rico; the Virgin Islands; Port au Prince, Haiti; and Nuevitas, Cuba, in a 2,836-air-mile trip, and returned to the United States on March 16, 1934.

Veto message read by a President. *See under* Veto (presidential)

Vice President to become President automatically. *See under* Vice President (U.S.)

PRESIDENTIAL CANDIDATE

Black presidential candidate nominated in a political convention was Frederick Douglass of Rochester, N.Y., who received one complimentary vote on June 23, 1888, on the fourth ballot at the Republican convention opened in Chicago, Ill., June 19, 1888. (On June 25, on the eighth ballot, the convention nominated Benjamin Harrison, who was elected as the 23rd President.) Douglass was later appointed United States minister to Haiti. *(Official Proceedings of the Republican National Convention Held at Chicago, June 19, 20, 21, 22, 23 and 25, 1888)*

Black presidential candidate proposed by a major political party was Rev. Channing Emery Phillips of Washington, D.C., proposed August 28, 1968, at the Democratic convention, Chicago, Ill.

Presidential candidate assassinated was General Joseph Smith of Nauvoo, Ill., whose candidacy was advocated on January 12, 1844, by the Council of Twelve of the Church of Jesus Christ of Latter-Day Saints. The National Reform Party confirmed the nomination in a state convention at Nauvoo on May 17, 1844, and Sidney Rigdon of Pennsylvania was confirmed as the vice presidential candidate. Joseph Smith was killed on June 27, 1844, when a mob broke into the jail at Carthage, Ill., where he kept for safekeeping after surrendering for trial upon charges preferred against him by

The First

his personal enemies and by seceders from the church he had founded.

Presidential candidate assassinated while campaigning was Senator Robert Francis Kennedy of New York, assasinated by Sirhan Bishara Sirhan on June 6, 1968, at the Biltmore Hotel, Los Angeles, Calif., during R.F.K.'s campaign for the nomination of the Democratic Party.

Presidential candidate debate series on television was the Richard Milhous Nixon–John Fitzgerald Kennedy debate series during the 1960 presidential campaign. The first of four debates was held September 26, 1960, in a Chicago studio; the second, October 7, 1960, in a Washington, D.C., studio; the third, October 13, 1960 (Kennedy in New York City, Nixon in Hollywood, Calif.); and the fourth, October 21, 1960, in a New York City studio.

Presidential candidate nominated at a caucus was Thomas Jefferson. The Democratic-Republican Party held a caucus on February 25, 1804, in Washington, D.C., at which Thomas Jefferson of Virginia was unanimously nominated for President, and George Clinton of New York for Vice President. Without holding a caucus, the Federalists supported Charles Cotesworth Pinckney of South Carolina for President and Rufus King of New York for Vice President. At the election in November 1804, Jefferson received 162 electoral votes and Pinckney 14.

Presidential candidate nominated at a national convention was Andrew Jackson. The Democrats at their national convention in Baltimore in 1832 nominated Andrew Jackson of Tennessee for President, and Martin Van Buren of New York for Vice President. *(Edgar Eugene Robinson—The Evolution of American Political Parties)*

Presidential candidate (Republican) renominated after a defeat was Thomas Edmund Dewey of New York, who was nominated by the Republican convention at Philadelphia, Pa., June 24, 1948. He was defeated in the November 7, 1944, election by President Franklin Delano Roosevelt.

Presidential candidate shown in motion pictures. *See under* Motion Picture

Presidential candidate to broadcast a political speech. *See under* Radio broadcast

Presidential candidate to campaign and make speeches in a foreign language was James Abram Garfield, who made several political speeches in German. He was elected the 20th President and was sworn in March 4, 1881. *(Emma Elizabeth Brown—Life and Public Services of James A. Garfield)*

Presidential candidate to fly to a political convention to make an acceptance speech was Franklin Delano Roosevelt, then governor of New York, who chartered a ten-passenger trimotor

The First

PRESIDENTIAL CANDIDATE—*Continued*

plane for himself and his party on July 2, 1932, and flew from Albany, N.Y., to Chicago, Ill.

Presidential candidate to make a speech of acceptance at a nominating convention was Franklin Delano Roosevelt, who on July 2, 1932, flew from Albany, N.Y., to Chicago, Ill. to address the Democratic Convention.

Presidential candidate to receive the greatest number of popular and electoral votes and yet fail of election was Andrew Jackson on November 2, 1824. He received 153,544 popular and 99 electoral votes, while John Quincy Adams received 108,740 popular and 84 electoral votes, William Harris Crawford 47,136 popular and 41 electoral votes, and Henry Clay 46,618 popular and 37 electoral votes. Since no candidate received a majority of the electoral votes, the decision went to the House of Representatives, which elected Adams after Clay, who in fourth place was out of the running, had thrown his votes to Adams.

Presidential candidate to ride in an automobile was William Jennings Bryan, who, accompanied by his wife, was given a ride in 1896 at Decatur, Ill., in an automobile made by the Mueller Manufacturing Company. There were only 10 automobiles in the United States at that time.

Presidential candidate who was a Catholic was Charles O'Conor of New York, who, on September 3, 1872, was nominated at the Democratic Convention at Louisville, Ky., by a wing of Democrats who refused to accept the nomination of Horace Greeley made at Baltimore, Md. O'Conor declined the nomination, but his name nevertheless was listed and he received approximately 30,000 votes from 23 states. *(American Irish Historical Society, Vol. 27. 1928)*

Presidential debate between an incumbent President and a candidate for his office. *See under* Television-Telecast

Talking pictures of presidential candidates. *See under* Motion picture

Woman presidential candidate was Victoria Claflin Woodhull, who was nominated by the National Radical Reformers at a meeting held May 10, 1872 at Apollo Hall, New York City. She was nominated by Judge Carter of Cincinnati, Ohio. Frederick Douglass was the vice presidential nominee. The National Radical Reformers seceded from the National Woman Suffrage Association, which met May 9–11, 1872, at Steinway Hall, New York City. *(Theodore Tilton—Biographical Sketch of Victoria C. Woodhull)*

Woman presidential candidate of a major political party was Margaret Chase Smith of Maine, who was nominated by Senator George David Aiken of Vermont on July 15, 1964, at the Republican National Convention at San Francisco, Calif.

PRESIDENTIAL CENSURE was passed in the form of a resolution by the United States Senate

The First

on March 28, 1834, by a vote of 26 - 20. The resolution declared that President Andrew Jackson "in the last executive proceedings in relation to the public revenue, has assumed upon himself authority and power not conferred by the constitution and laws, but in derogation of both." He incurred displeasure by his handling of the Bank of the United States matter. *(Gales and Seaton—Register of Debates in Congress, 23rd Congress, First Session)*

PRESIDENTIAL CITIZEN MEDAL. *See* Medal

PRESIDENTIAL COMMISSION

President requested by Congress to justify the creation of a presidential committee was John Tyler. The House of Representatives on February 7, 1842, passed a resolution "that the President of the United States inform this House under what authority the commission, consisting of George Poindexter and others, for the investigation of the concerns of the New York Custom House was raised, what were the purposes and objects of said commission . . . and out of what fund the said expenditures have been or are to be paid." Tyler, in a letter, dated February 9, 1842, cited the "authority vested in the President of the United States 'to take care that the laws be faithfully executed and to give to Congress from time to time information on the state of the Union.' "

Presidential commission was appointed by President George Washington to deal with the rebellious elements in Washington and Allegheny counties, Pa. In his proclamation to Congress on August 7, 1794, Washington stated: "I do hereby command all persons, being insurgents as aforesaid, on or before the first day of September next to disperse and retire peacefully to their respective abodes." In his sixth annual address, on November 19, 1794, he declared: "The report of the commissioners marks their firmness and abilities, and must unite all virtuous men, by shewing that the means of conciliation have been exhausted."

PRESIDENTIAL ELECTION

Presidential election in which candidates had been nominated for the vice presidency was held on November 6, 1804. Prior to the adoption of the 12th Amendment to the Constitution on September 25, 1804, the candidate for President receiving the second-highest number of votes became Vice President. In 1804 Thomas Jefferson was elected President and George Clinton Vice President.

Presidential election in which more than one candidate declared for the presidency was the election of 1797. John Adams received 71 electoral votes and was elected President. Thomas Jefferson, his opponent, received 68 electoral votes, and was elected Vice President. In the elections of 1789 and 1793 George Washington was the only avowed presidential candidate.

The First

PRESIDENTIAL ELECTORAL COLLEGE. *See* Electoral College

PRESIDENTIAL EULOGY, in which George Washington was termed "first in war, first in peace and first in the hearts of his countrymen," was delivered on December 26, 1799, before both Houses of Congress by Henry Lee of Virginia. *(Henry Lee—Funeral Oration on the Death of General Washington)*

PRESIDENTIAL EXECUTIVE ORDER to be numbered was issued by President Abraham Lincoln on October 20, 1862: "I do hereby constitute a provisional court, which shall be a court of record, for the State of Louisiana, and I do hereby appoint Charles A. Peabody of New York to be a provisional judge to hold said court." Peabody's annual compensation was $3,500. (Lincoln's order was not the first executive order issued by a President; it is the first one in the files of the Department of State.) *(James Daniel Richardson—A Compilation of the Messages and Papers of the Presidents)*

PRESIDENTIAL INAUGURAL BALL was held Thursday, May 7, 1789, at the Assembly Rooms, on the east side of Broadway, a little above Wall Street, New York City. A medallion portrait of President George Washington in profile on a fan was presented as a souvenir to the ladies.

"PRESIDENTIAL MANSION" was No. 1 Cherry Street, the Franklin House, corner of Franklin and Cherry streets, now Franklin Square, New York City, which was occupied by President and Mrs. George Washington from April 23, 1789, to February 23, 1790. It originally was the home of Samuel Osgood. *(New-York Historical Society Quarterly Bulletin. Vol. 23, 1939)*

PRESIDENTIAL NEWS CONFERENCE ON TELEVISION. *See under* Television—Telecast

PRESIDENTIAL POPULAR VOTE was recorded in the election of November 2, 1824, in which 356,-038 votes were cast. In 6 states the electors were chosen by the state legislatures, and in 18 states by popular vote (in 13 by general ticket and in 5 by districts). Andrew Jackson received 153,544 votes (99 electoral votes); John Quincy Adams, 108,740 votes (84 electoral votes); William Harris Crawford, 47,136 votes (41 electoral votes); and Henry Clay, 46,618 votes (37 electoral votes). None of the candidates having an electoral majority, the election went, on February 9, 1825, to the House of Representatives, which chose from the highest three. Clay was excluded and his strength went to Adams, who carried 13 of the 24 states and was elected. The candidates represented different factions of the Jeffersonian Republican party. Those in the Adams-Clay wing were known as National Republicans, and those in the Jackson wing as Democratic-Republicans or Democrats.

The First

PRESIDENTIAL PROTEST was signed April 15, 1834, by Andrew Jackson. He protested against the Senate resolution censuring the President for his course in the bank controversy.

PRESIDENTIAL SUCCESSION ACT passed March 1, 1792 (1 Stat. L. 239). It read: "In case of the removal, death, resignation, or disability of both the President and Vice-President of the United States, the President of the Senate, pro tempore, and in case there shall be no President of the Senate, then the Speaker of the House of Representatives for the time being shall act as President of the United States until such disability be removed or until a President be elected."

PRESIDENTIAL UNIT CITATION AWARD. *See* Medal

PRESS CLIPPING BUREAU was opened at 60 Ann Street, New York City, on April 15, 1884, by Samuel Leavitt. The business was absorbed by Henry Romeike, who had established a similar service in June 1881 in London, England. It was known as Henry Romeike's Press Cuttings.

PRESSING MACHINE (steam-operated) was invented by Adon J. Hoffman, who applied for a patent December 1, 1904, which was granted July 13, 1909, No. 928,199. The machine was equipped with a "buck," or lower pressing surface. The "head," or upper pressing surface, was heated by gas and it was necessary to lay a damp press cloth over the goods, as when pressing with a hand iron. The machine was marketed first in 1907 by the United States Hoffman Company of Seattle, Wash.

PRICE REGULATION AGREEMENT *See* Trust: Manufacturers' price regulation agreement

PRICE REGULATION LEGISLATION

Price regulation law (colonial) was "an act to prevent monopolies and oppression by excessive and unreasonable prices for many of the necessaries and conveniencies of life, and for preventing engrossers, and for the better supply of our troops in the army with such necessaries as may be wanted," enacted by Rhode Island, at Providence, on December 31, 1776, effective January 8, 1777. The law regulated prices on farm labor, beef, hides, shoes, cotton, sugar, salt, coffee, cheese, butter, beans, peas, potatoes, pork, wool, flannel, towcloths, flax, tallow, rum, molasses, oats, stockings, wheat, rye, Indian corn, salted pork, etc. Fines equivalent to the value of the merchandise were applied equally to the state and to informers.

Price regulation law (federal) was enacted by the Emergency Price Control Act of 1942, approved January 30, 1942 (56 Stat. L. 23), which created the Office of Price Administration as an independent agency under the direction of the price administrator. The Office of Price Administration and Civilian Supply was created by Executive Order No. 8,734 on April 11, 1941. Its name

The First

PRICE REGULATION LEGISLATION—*Continued*

was shortened to Office of Price Administration by Executive Order No. 8,875 on August 28, 1941.

Price regulation law (state) was Act No. 128 of Louisiana, "to prohibit unfair commercial discrimination between different sections, communities, cities, or localities in the State of Louisiana or unfair competition therein and providing penalties therefor," approved July 2, 1908, by Governor Jared Young Sanders. It became effective July 29, 1908.

Resale price maintenance law (state) was the California "Fair Trade Act" approved May 8, 1931 (Statutes 1931, chapter 278, effective August 14, 1931), which provided "that the buyer will not resell such commodity except at the price stipulated by the vendor." The title of the act is "an act to protect trade-mark owners, distributors and the public against injurious and uneconomic practices in the distribution of articles of standard quality under a distinguished trade-mark, brand or name."

PRIEST, CATHOLIC. *See* Catholic priest

PRIMA DONNA (black). *See* Opera: Black prima donna of an opera company

PRIMARY ELECTION LAW. *See* Election law

PRIME MINISTER OF GREAT BRITAIN TO ADDRESS THE CONGRESS OF THE UNITED STATES. *See under* Congress (U.S.)

PRIMER

See also Schoolbook

Primer in an American Indian dialect was *The Indian Primer; or, The Way of Training Up of Our Indian Youth in the Good Knowledge of God, in the Knowledge of the Scriptures and in an Ability to Read,* by John Eliot. It was printed in the Massachusetts Indian language and was published in Cambridge, Mass., in 1669 by Marmaduke Johnson. A similar edition by Eliot is believed to have been published in 1653–1654 by Samuel Green, Cambridge, Mass., but no known copies are in existence.

Typewriting primer was *Ted and Polly,* by Ralph Haefner, published in November 1933 by the Macmillan Company, New York City, and intended for use in first and second grades by children from five to eight. The material in the book had been tried out two years previously in various schools.

PRINCE OF WALES TO VISIT THE UNITED STATES. *See* Visiting celebrities

PRINT PATENT. *See* Patent

PRINTED AMERICAN PLAY. *See* Play (drama)

The First

PRINTED BALLOT. *See under* Election

PRINTER (woman). *See* Woman: Woman printer

PRINTER'S INK was successfully manufactured in America by Charles Eneu Johnson, who began manufacturing inks in Philadelphia, Pa., in 1804. His concern has been in continuous operation at the same location ever since. It is now part of the United Carbon Company.

PRINTING

Document printed in America (known to have been printed) was the "Oath of a Free Man," printed in March 1639 by the Stephen Day Press, Cambridge, Mass. It was a one-page sheet: "I doe solemnly bind myself in the sight of God, that when I shall be called to give my voice touching any subject of this State, in which Freemen are to deal, I will give my vote and suffrage as I shall judge in mine own conscience may best conduce and tend to the publick weal of the body, without respect of persons, or favour of any man." *(Lawrence Counselman Wroth—The Oath of a Free Man)*

PRINTING HISTORY was Isaiah Thomas's *History of Printing in America, with a Biography of Printers, and an Account of Newspapers,* published in two volumes in 1810 in Worcester, Mass.

PRINTING INSTRUCTION

Printing instruction was given in the social community school founded by Robert Owen in New Harmony, Ind., in 1826. Printing, lithography, and engraving were the subjects studied. *(Indiana Magazine of History. Vol. 33, No. 4. December 1937)*

Printing lecture course in a college was "An introduction to the technique of printing," offered February 1911 by the Graduate School of Business Administration, Harvard University, Cambridge, Mass. The course was given by Daniel Berkeley Updike. *(Daniel Berkeley Updike—Printing Types, Their History, Forms and Use)*

PRINTING MAGAZINE (professional) was the *Typographic Advertiser,* a quarterly, published by L. Johnson & Co., Philadelphia, Pa., which appeared April 1855.

PRINTING OFFICE (U.S.). *See* Government Printing Office

PRINTING PRESS

Cylinder and flatbed combination printing press was manufactured in 1844 by R. Hoe & Co., New York City. It was invented by Robert Hoe, who obtained patent No. 3,551 on April 17, 1844. The circumference of the cylinder was equivalent to the entire travel of the bed forward and backward. The cylinder made one revolution for each impression in printing without stopping.

The First

Cylinder printing press was made by R. Hoe & Co., New York City, in 1831 and was operated by hand power. Later steam was employed. It was used to print the *Temperance Recorder,* a monthly first published on March 6, 1832, in Albany, N.Y., and devoted exclusively to the cause of temperance. *(Merritt Way Haynes—Student's History of Printing)*

High-speed newspaper printing and folding machine, utilizing the gathering cylinder with a rotary folding cylinder, was installed in 1876 on the presses of the Philadelphia, Pa., *Times.* It printed and folded a four-page sheet at the rate of 400 a minute. The press was shown in operation at the Philadelphia Centennial Exposition in 1876.

Power or steam printing press was made by Daniel Treadwell of Boston in 1822. It was based upon the principle of the Washington hand press. Only three or four were manufactured.

Power printing press capable of fine book work was the Adams Press, invented by Isaac Adams of Boston, Mass., who obtained a patent October 4, 1830, on a "power printing press." He improved it and received an additional patent on the improvements on March 2, 1836.

Printing press was imported from England by the Reverend Jesse (Jose) Glover of Sutton, England, in the summer of 1638 on the ship *John* of London, together with printers skilled in its operation. Glover contracted with Stephen Day on June 7, 1638, to sail to America. They were accompanied by Day's wife, Rebecca, his sons, Stephen and Matthew, and William Boardman. Glover died on board the ship. The press was set in operation in March 1639, at Cambridge, Mass. *(Robert F. Roden—The Cambridge Press)*

Printing press for polychromatic printing was invented by Thomas F. Adams of Philadelphia, Pa., who obtained patent No. 3,744 on September 17, 1844. Different color rollers, operating in parallel, were used to produce linear work.

Printing press for printing "paper hangings" (wallpaper) in color was invented by Peter Force of Washington, D.C., who patented it August 22, 1822.

Printing press invented in America was the Columbian Press. In 1816 George E. Clymer of Philadelphia, Pa., devised an iron hand-printing press which was operated by a combination of compound levers instead of a screw to give the downward pressure. *(Wilbur Fisk Cleaver—Five Centuries of Printing)*

Printing press invented in America that was practical and successful was the Washington Press, invented in 1827 by Samuel Rust of New York City. This type of press is still used for taking fine proofs. Rust obtained patents on May 13, 1821; March 2, 1826; and April 17, 1829.

The First

Printing press operated by electricity was invented by Thomas Davenport of Brandon, Vt., and used in 1839 in New York City. An engine weighing less than 100 pounds operated a rotary printing press. The *Electro-Magnet and Mechanics Intelligencer* issued January 18, 1840, by Davenport was one of the periodicals printed by this press. He obtained patent No. 132 on February 25, 1837, on an "electrical motor."

Printing press to use a continuous web or roll of paper was the Bullock Press, produced by William Bullock of Pittsburgh, Pa., in 1865. It was the first machine built especially for curved stereotype plates. It printed both sides of the sheet, and cut it either before or after printing. U.S. patent No. 38,200 was granted April 14, 1863. The press was first used by the New York *Sun.*

Quadruple newspaper press was constructed in 1887 by R. Hoe & Co., New York City, for the New York *World* plant, where it was installed in 1891. It produced an 8-page newspaper at a running speed of 48,000 per hour or 10, 12, 14, or 16 pages at a running speed of 24,000 an hour. The papers were cut and folded, ready for delivery.

Rotary printing press with a continuous-roll feed to be perfected was produced in 1871 by R. Hoe & Company, New York City, and utilized the first gathering and delivery cylinder patented by Stephen D. Tucker of New York City. The press was installed in the New York *Tribune* plant and produced as many as 18,000 newspapers an hour.

Rotary type printing press was the double-cylinder machine invented by Richard March Hoe, of New York City. It was first used in the *Ledger* office in Philadelphia in 1846. The bed was of such length that the form of type passed backward and forward under both cylinders. The central cylinder was placed in a horizontal position. The output was 2,000 sheets per hour for each of four feeders. Patent No. 5,199 was obtained July 24, 1847. *(Robert Hoe—Short History of the Printing Press)*

Rotogravure press was imported in November 1904, by the American Photogravure Company of Philadelphia. It was built in Ramsbottom, England, by John Wood. *(Pennell's 1931 Annual of Photography)*

Sextuple printing press was constructed by R. Hoe & Co., New York City, and installed in 1891 at the New York *Herald* plant. It took 18 months to construct, weighed 58 tons, and was composed of 16,000 pieces. The form and impression cylinders were placed parallel instead of at right angles. It could print and fold 90,000 four-page newspapers an hour.

Web-fed four-color rotary printing press was made in 1890 by Walter Scott & Co., Plainfield, N.J., for the Chicago, Ill., *Inter-Ocean.* It was placed in operation in 1892. Curved stereotype

The First

PRINTING PRESS—*Continued*

plates, cast to fit the cylinders, were used in printing on a two-page-wide roll of paper.

PRISON

American imprisoned in the Tower of London was Henry Laurens of Charlestown, S.C., President of the Continental Congress from November 1, 1777, to December 10, 1778, who was confined from October 6, 1780, to December 31, 1781, on suspicion of high treason. Laurens sailed from Philadelphia, Pa., on August 13, 1780, on the brigantine *Mercury* en route to Holland to serve as United States minister and negotiate the Lee–Van Berkel loan and treaty but was captured three weeks later by the British off Newfoundland. He threw his papers overboard, but they were recovered and led to the British declaration of war against Holland on December 20, 1780. Imprisoned in the Tower, he was forced to pay for his room, board, and guard. He was released in exchange for Lord Cornwallis. Laurens, with Benjamin Franklin and John Jay, drew up the preliminary treaty of peace with Great Britain on November 30, 1782, to terminate the Revolutionary War.

College commencement exercises within a prison. *See* College: College commencement exercises within a prison

Debtors' prison. *See* Debtors' prison

Federal penitentiary fingerprinting. *See under* Fingerprinting

Military prison of the United States on an island was Fort Jefferson, Monroe County, Fla. Construction was begun in 1846 on an island in the Gulf of Mexico, 60 miles from Key West. It was a six-sided masonry structure with a huge courtyard in the center. The sides were 1,000 feet long, 80 feet high, and 60 feet thick. On January 19, 1861, it was garrisoned for the first time by Brevet Major Lewis Golding Arnold, 2d U.S. Artillery, with 4 officers and 62 men. At that time the fort had not been completed and was hardly defensible. A prison for the confinement of U.S. military prisoners was established at Fort Jefferson in 1863. The prison, often called Dry Tortugas, was maintained during the Civil War.

Organization of a prison into "community" groups was tried out in 1914 at Auburn Prison, Auburn, N.Y. A Mutual Welfare League, consisting of prisoners, was created to assume the responsibility of discipline in the prison. *(Louis Newton Robinson—Penology in the United States)*

Penitentiary building (national) authorized to be built was the Federal Penitentiary, Leavenworth, Kansas, authorized March 3, 1891 (26 Stat. L. 839). It was completed February 1, 1906. The Federal Penitentiary, Atlanta, Georgia, although authorized in 1899, two years after work had

The First

begun at Leavenworth, was completed in January 1902.

Prison was constructed in 1676 in Nantucket, Mass. The court hired William Bunker on November 16, 1676, to keep the prison for one year and agreed to pay him "foeur pounds, halfe in wheat, the other in other graine."

Prison built for women and managed exclusively by women was the Indiana Reformatory Institution for women and girls, Indianapolis, Ind., which received its first prisoners, 17 women, on October 8, 1873. The first superintendent was Sarah J. Smith, who served from June 10, 1873, to December 1, 1883. In 1907 the name was changed to the Indiana Women's Prison. Since January 1877 members of the Board of Trustees have all been women.

Prison (federal) exclusively for women was the Federal Industrial Institution for Women, Alderson, W. Va., established by act of Congress 1926 and opened the same year. The first superintendent was Dr. Mary Belle Harris, sworn in March 12, 1925. She served to 1941. Seventeen 2-story brick dormitories, each designed to accommodate 30, were built on the college plan. They cost over $2 million and occupied 500 acres of land. There were no prison walls or guards. *(New York Times. p. 18. March 26, 1925; Sec. VII, p. 11. Aug. 22, 1926)*

Prison matrons were appointed in 1845 through the efforts of the American Female Guardian Society. Four were assigned to Blackwell's Island, N.Y., and two to the City Prison, New York City.

Prison to have individual cells for prisoners was the Walnut Street prison in Philadelphia, Pa., built in 1773, which was remodeled in 1790 (in accordance with the act of April 5, 1790, of the Pennsylvania General Assembly) to contain 24 solitary cells each 6 feet wide, 8 feet long, and 7 feet high. The prisoners were kept in solitary confinement and not allowed to leave their cells. The prison held about 110 prisoners. *(Negley King Teeters—The Cradle of the Penitentiary; the Walnut Street Jail at Philadelphia 1773–1835)*

Prisoners (federal) employed in industry produced cotton duck for mail bags, etc., at the Cotton Duck Mill, United States Penitentiary, Atlanta, Ga., whose first loom started July 11, 1919. The building covered an area of almost three acres. The first year 386,414 yards of duck were produced. The mill was authorized by act of Congress of July 10, 1918 (40 Stat. L. 896), which appropriated $650,000 for equipment and $150,000 as working capital. A wage system for inmates established April 29, 1921, set up a wage fund of 2 cents per yard which was divided among the inmates in proportion to their number of hours of service.

The First

Reformatory for boys (state) was the reformatory school at Westborough, Mass., now the Lyman School for Boys. It was authorized April 9, 1847 (chapter 165). *(Hastings Hornell Hart—Juvenile Court Laws in the United States)*

Reformatory for juvenile delinquents under legislative control was the New York House of Refuge, New York City, officially opened January 1, 1825, with three boys and six girls. It was under the supervision of the Society for the Reformation of Juvenile Offenders in the City of New York and was incorporated March 29, 1824. The first president was Cadwallader David Colden; the first superintendent, Joseph Curtis. On April 9, 1825, the state authorized a grant of $2,000 annually for the next five years. *(First Annual Report of the Managers of the Society for the Reformation of Juvenile Offenders in the City of New York)*

Reformatory (state) conducted for women was the Reformatory Prison for Women, Sherborn, Mass., opened November 7, 1877. By an act of legislature, chapter 181, March 22, 1911, the name was changed to the Reformatory for Women. The first superintendent was Eudora Clark Atkinson. She resigned September 1, 1880 and was succeeded by Dr. Eliza Maria Mosher, who had been resident physician from the opening of the institution. In 1925 the part of Sherborn in which the reformatory was located was annexed to the town of Framingham, Mass. *(Massachusetts Bureau of Prisons—Annual Report, 1915)*

Representative elected who served time in prison. *See under* Representative (U.S.)

State prison to take fingerprints. *See under* Fingerprinting

Woman prison guard in a maximum security prison for men was Joan Wyatt Stewart of Burlington, Iowa, who was appointed Correction Officer on Feburary 1, 1973, in the Iowa State Penitentiary, Fort Madison, Iowa.

PRISON REFORM SOCIETY to bring about changes in prison administration was the Philadelphia Society for Alleviating the Miseries of Public Prisons, formed May 8, 1787, in the German School House on Cherry Street, Philadelphia, Pa., by Philadelphia Quakers. The first president was William White. A similar organization for war prisoners was the Philadelphia Society for Relieving Distressed Prisoners Owing to the War of Independence, organized February 7, 1776, which ceased operations in September 1777. *(Gustave de Beaumont and Charles Alexis Clérel de Tocqueville—Penitentiary System in the United States)*

PRISON SYSTEM
Woman to direct a prison system was Anna Moscowitz Kross sworn in January 1, 1954, as Commissioner of Correction, New York City. She served until March 30, 1966.

The First

Woman to direct a state Bureau of Corrections was Ward E. Murphy, who became Director of the Bureau of Corrections under the Department of Mental Health and Corrections at Augusta, Me., in July 1970. The Bureau encompasses adult and juvenile institutions as well as Probation and Parole. She was Superintendent of the Women's Correctional Center at Skowhegan, Me., from 1961 to 1970.

PRIVATE RAILROAD CAR. *See* Railroad car

PRIVATE SCHOOL FOR CRIPPLES. *See under* Cripples

PRIZE MONEY AWARDED BY THE U.S. NAVY. *See under* Navy

PRIZEFIGHT
Championship heavyweight title won in the first round was on April 6, 1900, when James Jackson ("Jim") Jefferies, 250 pounds, knocked out John ("Jack") Finnegan, 180 pounds, of Pittsburgh, Pa., in 55 seconds of the first round at Detroit, Mich.

Championship prizefight decided on a foul took place June 12, 1930, at the Polo Grounds, New York City, when Jack Sharkey fouled Maxmillian Adolph Otto Siegfried ("Max") Schmeling in the 4th round. The New York Boxing Commission awarded the heavyweight championship to Schmeling on June 19, 1930, by a 2-1 vote. The referee was Jim Crowley.

International fight, with bare knuckles, was held on the outskirts of St. Louis, Mo., June 15, 1869. Mike McCoole, American champion, fought Tom Allen of England and won on a questionable foul in the ninth round. *(Alexander Johnston—Ten —And Out)*

Motion picture of a prizefight. *See* Motion picture: Motion picture of a staged prizefight

Open-air arena especially built for a prizefight was constructed at Carson City, Nevada, for the James John Corbett–Robert Prometheus (Bob) Fitzsimmons fight held March 17, 1897. Fitzsimmons knocked Corbett out in the 14th round to win the world heavyweight championship. George Silver was the referee.

Prizefight arena was built near Worcester, Mass. for the fight between Tom Springs and Jack Langan, the Irish champion, on January 7, 1824. It had about 4,000 seats and room for 22,000 standees. Admission was 10 shillings ($2.50), half of which went to the fighters.

Prizefight at which admission tickets sold at $100 was the Joe Louis-Billy Conn world heavyweight championship fight at the Yankee Stadium, New York City, on June 19, 1946. It was promoted by the Twentieth Century Sporting Club, of which Mike Jacobs was president. Louis won in the eighth round. The attendance was 45,266.

The First

PRIZEFIGHT—*Continued*

Prizefight fatality on record occurred in a bare-knuckle fight on September 13, 1842, at Hastings, N.Y. Christopher ("Chris") Lilly, an Englishman, age 23, weighing 140 pounds, fought Thomas ("Tom") McCoy, an Irish-American, age 21, weighing 137, for a purse of $200. The fight lasted 2 hours 41 minutes (120 rounds). The round ended only when one man was unable to reach a line in the middle of the ring. McCoy suffocated from his own blood and died from the inflicted blows. (Earlier, in 1834, a French heavyweight fought Andy Marsden, a British heavyweight, in New Orleans, La., fracturing his skull. Marsden was taken to a hospital, where he died the next morning.)

Prizefight (heavyweight) to last longer than 100 rounds took place on September 9, 1841, at Caldwell's Landing, N.Y. Tom Hyer, son of fighter Jacob Hyer, defeated George McChester ("Country McChester") in a 2-hour 55-minute match that lasted 101 rounds.

Prizefight of importance under the Marquis of Queensberry rules was the heavyweight championship fight between John Lawrence Sullivan and James John Corbett on September 7, 1892, at the New Orleans Olympic Club, New Orleans, La., for a winner-take-all purse of $25,000 and an outside bet of $10,000. Five-ounce gloves were used. Corbett won in the 21st round. A previous contest under the Marquis of Queensberry rules had been held August 29, 1885, at Chester Park, Cincinnati, Ohio, between Sullivan and Dominick F. McCaffery of Pittsburgh, Pa. "Six rounds to decide the Marquis of Queensberry glove contest for the championship of the world" were presented. Billy Tate of Toledo, Ohio, was the referee. Sullivan was the winner but "ascribed his failure to knock the youngster out to the latter's get-away tactics and to the restrictions of the Marquis of Queensberry Rules." *(Commercial Gazette. Cincinnati, Ohio. Aug. 30, 1885)*

Prizefight of 110 rounds took place April 6, 1893, before thousands of spectators at the Olympic Club, New Orleans, La., when Andy Bowen fought Jack Burke for 7 hours 19 minutes for a $2,500 purse. Professor John Duffy, the referee, called it a "no contest", not a "draw," and divided the purse as the fighters refused to continue. Burke was leading until he broke his wrist in the 14th round and continued fighting in spite of that.

Prizefight timed by automatic timer used to time a 3-minute round and sound a gong at the expiration was used May 21, 1891, at the California Athletic Club, San Francisco, Calif., when Peter Jackson, a black Australian, and James John Corbett met in a 61-round fight that ended in a draw.

Prizefight to attract 100,000 spectators was the Jack Dempsey–Gene Tunney fight held September 23, 1926, at the Sesquicentennial Stadium, Phila-

The First

delphia, Pa. The attendance was 120,757 and the gate receipts were $1,895,733. Tunney defeated Dempsey in a ten-round fight under the point system.

Prizefight to gross $1 million was held July 2, 1921, at Jersey City, N.J. Approximately 75,000 persons paid $1,626,580 in gate receipts to see William Harrison ("Jack") Dempsey fight Georges Carpentier. Dempsey won "the battle of the century" by a knockout in the 57th second of the fourth round. He received $300,000 and Carpentier $200,000 as purses. *(Jack Dempsey—Round by Round)*

Prizefight to gross more than $5 million in sales was the Muhammed Ali (Cassius Marcellus Clay)–Leon Spinks 15-round-decision fight at the Louisiana Superdome, New Orleans, La., on September 15, 1978, which Muhammad Ali won in a 13-round unanimous decision. Spinks earned $3.73 million and Ali $3.25 million. Three other fights were on the program: Mike Rossman of New Jersey won a technical knockout over Victor Galindez, Danny Lopez of California won in the 2nd round over Juan Malvarez of Argentina, and Jorge Lujan of Panama won a unanimous decision over Alberto Davila of the United States.

Prizefight to gross $2 million was a 10-round return match on September 22, 1927, at Soldier Field, Chicago, Ill., between James Joseph ("Gene") Tunney, 189½ pounds, and William Harrison ("Jack") Dempsey, 192½ pounds—the latter was attempting to regain his title. Tunney won the decision. The gate receipts were $2,658,660, the attendance 104,943. Dave Barry was the referee, George Lytton and Commodore Sheldon Clark the judges. Tunney had won the title from Dempsey on September 23, 1926, in a 10-round decision.

Prizefight with a purse of $4.5 million was the 15-round fight on March 8, 1971, at Madison Square Garden, New York City, between Joe Frazier and Muhammad Ali Haj (Cassius Marcellus Clay). Frazier floored Ali in the 15th round. The gate at the door was $1,352,951 with a possible gross of $25 million. Arthur Mercante was the referee; and Bill Recht and Arthur Aidala, the judges.

Radio broadcast of a heavyweight championship prizefight. *See* Radio broadcast: Prizefight (heavyweight championship) broadcast

State legislation concerning prize fighting was Louisiana's Act No. 25, Laws of 1890, passed May 12, 1890, "an act defining the crime of prize fighting, and to provide for the punishment thereof in and out of the State of Louisiana." Although prizefighting was prohibited, the act did not "apply to exhibitions and glove contests between human beings, which may take place within the rooms of regularly chartered athletic clubs."

The First

Telecast of a prizefight. *See under* Television—Telecast

PRIZEFIGHT REFEREE

Heavyweight-championship-prizefight black referee was Zack Clayton of Philadelphia, Pa., who refereed the Joe ("Jersey Joe") Walcott (Arnold Raymond Cream)– Ezzard Charles fight at Municipal Stadium, Philadelphia, Pa., on June 5, 1952. Walcott outpointed Charles in the 15th round and retained his title.

Woman prizefight referee (licensed) was Belle Martell of Van Nuys, Calif., granted a license (No. 209), on April 30, 1940, by the California State Athletic Commission. She also held an announcer's license and a timekeeper's license. Her first assignment was a complete show of eight bouts in San Bernardino, Calif., on May 2, 1940. She retired the following month, on June 24, 1940, after an assignment in Los Angeles, Calif.

Woman to judge a heavyweight championship fight was Eva Shain, who refereed the 15-round Muhammad Ali–Earnie Shavers prizefight on September 29, 1977, at Madison Square Garden, New York City. She voted 9 rounds for Ali, 6 for Shavers. She had been licensed by the New York State Athletic Commission on January 6, 1975.

PRIZEFIGHTER

American lightweight champion of the world was Kid Lavigne of Saginaw, Mich., who defeated the British lightweight, Dick Burge, in the 17th round on June 1, 1896, at the National Sporting Club, London.

American to win distinction in the prize ring was Bill Richmond, a black, born in Richmond, Staten Island, N.Y., August 5, 1763, the son of a slave owned by the Reverend Charlton. On July 8, 1805, Richmond knocked out Jack Holmes, alias Tom Tough, in the 26th round at Cricklewood Green, a short distance from Kilburn Wells, England. On October 8, 1805, he was defeated by Tom Cribb at Hailsham, Sussex. He never fought in the United States. *(Henry Downes Miles—Pugilistica)*

Bareknuckle world heavyweight champion (American) was Paddy Ryan, who won an undisputed title by knocking out Joe Goss of England in the 85th round on June 1, 1880, near Colliers, W. Va., about 300 yards from the Pennsylvania boundary. The fight, which lasted 1 hour 27 minutes, was witnessed by 300 spectators. The prize was $2,000. Schell Fairchild was the referee.

Black heavyweight champion of the world was Jack Johnson, who defeated Tommy Burns at Sydney, Australia, on December 26, 1908, in 14 rounds, technically winning the championship. The actual title was earned July 4, 1910, when he defeated James Jackson (Jim) Jeffries in 15 rounds at Reno, Nevada. Johnson lost his title April 5, 1915, at Havana, Cuba, to Jess Willard in 26 rounds.

The First

Pugilist to hold three titles simultaneously was Henry Jackson Armstrong, who became featherweight champion October 29, 1937, by defeating Petey Sarron, at Madison Square Garden, New York City; welterweight champion by defeating Barney Ross on May 31, 1938, at Madison Square Garden Bowl, Long Island City, N.Y.; and lightweight champion by defeating Lou Ambers at Madison Square Garden, New York City, on August 17, 1938.

Pugilist to win a world championship 5 times in the same weight division was Sugar Ray Robinson (original name, Walker Smith), middleweight, who defeated Jake La Motta in 13 rounds in Chicago, Ill., on February 14, 1951; lost the title and won it back from Randy Turpin in 10 rounds in New York City on September 12, 1951; lost it again and won it back from Carl ("Bobo") Olson in the 2nd round in Chicago, Ill., on December 9, 1955; lost it again and won it back from Gene Fullmer in the 5th round in Chicago on May 1, 1957; and lost it once again, only to win it back from Carmen Basilio by a split decision in the 15th round in Chicago on March 25, 1958.

Pugilist to win and lose a championship in the first round was Abraham ("Al") Singer of New York, who knocked out Sammy Mandell in 1 minute 32 seconds of the first round on July 17, 1930, at Yankee Staduim, New York City, before a crowd of approximately 35,000, who paid $160,-000. Lightweight champion Singer was knocked out on November 14, 1930 by Tony Canzoneri in 1 minute 6 seconds at Madison Square Garden, New York City, before 14,600 spectators, who paid $69,700.

Pugilist to win the heavyweight championship 3 times was Muhammad Ali (Cassius Marcellus Clay), who defeated Sonny Liston by a knockout in the 7th round on February 25, 1964, at Miami Beach, Fla.; George Foreman by a knockout in the 8th round on October 30, 1974, at Kinshasa, Zaire, Africa; and Leon Spinks in a 13-round unanimous decision on September 15, 1978, at New Orleans, La. A fourth attempt was made October 2, 1980, by Ali, who was defeated by Larry Holmes at Reno, Nev. Ali did not answer the bell for the 11th round and this was recorded as an 11th round knockout.

Pugilist to win three world championships was Robert Prometheus (Bob) Fitzsimmons, who became middleweight champion by defeating Jack Dempsey (known as "The Nonpareil") in 13 rounds at New Orleans, La., on January 14, 1891; heavyweight champion by knocking out James John Corbett in 14 rounds at Carson City, Nev., March 17, 1897; light heavyweight champion by outpointing George Gardner in a 20-round decision at San Francisco, Calif., November 25, 1903. Prior to this fight, Fitzsimmons had lost the heavyweight championship to James Jackson (Jim) Jeff-

The First

PRIZEFIGHTER—*Continued*

ries, who knocked him out in the eighth round at San Francisco, Calif., on July 25, 1902.

World heavyweight champion to regain his crown was Floyd Patterson, who knocked out Ingemar Johansson of Goteborg, Sweden, in 1:51 minutes of the 5th round of a 15-round scheduled fight (a rematch) on June 20, 1960, at the Polo Grounds, New York City. On November 30, 1956, in the Chicago Stadium, Chicago, Ill., Patterson knocked down Archie Moore twice in the 5th round before the referee stopped the fight and he won the title that had been relinquished by Rocky Marciano, who had retired undefeated. Patterson subsequently lost the title to Ingemar Johansson in the 3rd round on June 26, 1959, in the Yankee Stadium, New York City. Johansson knocked Patterson down 7 times in that round, winning by a technical knockout.

PROBATE LEGISLATION

Probate law eliminating red tape was enacted June 22, 1973, by the state of Wisconsin, an "act relating to establishing a procedure for informal administration of estates," signed by Governor Patrick Joseph Lucey, which became effective October 1, 1973. It did not require laws to probate wills. *(Laws of Wisconsin, Chapter 39, 1973)*

PROBATION

Probation legislation for juvenile delinquents was enacted by the state of Massachusetts on June 23, 1869. The law required the governor to appoint a visiting agent at $2,500 a year to work for the welfare and redemption of delinquents, rather than for their punishment. The visiting agent or his deputies were directed to visit all children maintained wholly or in part by the Commonwealth of Massachusetts once every three months.

Probation system, without restrictions as to age, in any country in the world, was legally established as a judicial policy by Boston, Mass., in 1878 and Massachusetts in 1880.

PROCEDURE CODE. *See* Lawbook

PRODUCTION STANDARDIZATION. *See* Factory standardization of production

PROFESSIONAL ASSOCIATIONS. *See under* specific sports, trades, etc.

PROFESSIONAL BASEBALL LEAGUE. *See* Baseball league

PROFESSIONAL CLUB (women's). *See* Women's club; Women's professional club

PROFESSIONAL FRATERNITY. *See under* Fraternity (Greek-letter)

PROFESSIONAL GOLF TOURNAMENT. *See* Golf tournament: Professional open championship

The First

PROFESSOR. *See* specific subjects, such as Agriculture professor; Chemistry professor

PROFESSOR (woman). *See* College: Woman college professor

PROGRAM THEME SONG. *See under* Radio broadcast

PROGRESSIVE PARTY was organized June 19, 1912, by seceding members of the Republican Party. The first national convention, held August 6, 1912, at the Coliseum, Chicago, Ill., was attended by 1,800 delegates who on August 7, 1912, nominated Theodore Roosevelt of New York for President and Hiram Warren Johnson of California for Vice President. Roosevelt received 4,-126,000 popular votes (88 electoral votes); William Howard Taft, the Republican candidate, 3,487,922 (8 electoral votes); and Woodrow Wilson, the Democratic candidate, 6,297,099 (435 electoral votes). The party was nicknamed the Bull Moose Party. *(George Edwin Mowry—Theodore Roosevelt and the Progressive Movement)*

PROHIBITION

Prohibition amendment to the Constitution was the 18th Amendment, which prohibited the manufacture, sale, or transportation of intoxicating liquors within the United States. The amendment was submitted to the legislatures of the states on December 18, 1917. Mississippi was the first state to ratify it (January 8, 1918) and Nebraska the 36th (January 16, 1919). On January 29, 1919, the Secretary of State proclaimed the amendment effective as of January 16, 1920.

Prohibition bureau (federal) was authorized by act of Congress of March 3, 1927 (44 Stat. L. 1381), "to create a Bureau of Customs and a Bureau of Prohibition in the Department of the Treasury." The prohibition amendment became part of the Constitution on January 29, 1919, but did not become effective until January 16, 1920. The first commissioner was John Franklin Kramer, of Mansfield, Ohio, appointed November 17, 1919, by Secretary of the Treasury Carter Glass.

Prohibition enforcement officers were authorized by proclamation of Sir Francis Wyatt, Governor of Virginia, on June 21, 1622: "We do ordaine an officer for that purpose to be sworne in every plantacion, to give information of all such, as shalbe so disordered: the moiety of the forfeitures to be given the sd officer so informing, or for default in him to any other that shall informe, and the other to the. publique Threasury." *(William and Mary College Quarterly Historical Magazine. Vol. 7, Ser. 2, No. 4. October 1927)*

Prohibition law (national) forbidding the sale of intoxicating liquors, except for export, was the Wartime Prohibition Act passed November 21, 1918 (40 Stat. L. 1050). The prohibition of the sale of liquor containing more than one half of one percent was enacted by act of Congress passed

The First

October 28, 1919 (41 Stat. L. 305), the [Andrew John] Volstead Prohibition Act.

Prohibition state was Tennessee, which passed an "act to repeal all laws licensing tippling houses" on January 26, 1838. It provided that "all persons convicted of the offense of retailing spirituous liquors shall be fined at the discretion of the court" and that the fines and forfeitures be used for the support of common schools.

Prohibition vote which showed the House of Representatives with a dry majority was taken on December 22, 1914. The representatives voted 197 –189 in favor of a resolution to provide a constitutional amendment banning the manufacture and sale of intoxicating beverages. The resolution, offered by Representative Richmond Pearson Hobson of Alabama, failed to win the necessary two-thirds majority.

Repeal of prohibition amendment. *See* Constitutional amendment (U.S.): Constitutional amendment submitted to the states for repeal

PROHIBITION PARTY (national) was organized on September 12, 1869, at a convention in Chicago, Ill, attended by 194 delegates from 9 states. The party was organized because neither of the major political parties had put a prohibition plank in its platform. The first national convention met in Columbus, Ohio, February 22, 1872, and nominated James Black of Pennsylvania and John Russell of Michigan as the Prohibition candidates for President and Vice President respectively. The platform advocated prohibition, woman suffrage, a direct popular vote for President and Vice President, a sound currency, the encouragement of immigration, and a reduction of transportation rates. Black received 5,608 votes in the 1872 election, as compared with Grant, who received 3,597,132 votes. The organ of the party was *The Voice*, a magazine published in Chicago, the first issue of which appeared September 25, 1884.

PROHIBITION REFORM MOVEMENT. *See* Liquor reform movement

PROHIBITIONIST REPRESENTATIVE IN CONGRESS. *See* Representative (U.S.): Representative elected by the prohibitionists

PROJECTION OF PICTURES ON A SCREEN. *See* Motion picture: Animated photographic picture projection before a theater audience

PROJECTOR (portable). *See* Motion picture projector

PRONGHORN ANTELOPE. *See* Animals

PROPAGANDA COURSE (college) was given by Professor Harold Dwight Lasswell of the Department of Political Science, University of Chicago, Chicago, Ill., in 1927 and was entitled "Political Opinion and Propaganda."

The First

PROPANE-FUEL LOCOMOTIVE. *See* Locomotive: Gas-turbine propane-fueled locomotive

PROPELLER BLADE (hollow steel). *See under* Aviation

PROPELLER RESEARCH TUNNEL. *See* Wind tunnel

PROPELLER (twin-screw). *See* Ship: Steamboat with a twin-screw propeller

PROPERTY DAMAGE INSURANCE. *See* Insurance: Aircraft liability and property damage insurance

PROPERTY TAX. *See* Tax

PROPORTIONAL REPRESENTATION ELECTION LAW. *See* Election law

PROSTITUTE is recorded as "this goodly creature of incontinency" in Thomas Morton's *New English Canaan*, published in England in 1637. Morton was condemned by the Pilgrim fathers of the Plymouth colony as "the lord of misrule." In 1627, the Pilgrims, incensed at the licentiousness of his group at "Merry Mount," in what is now Quincy, Mass., cut down a Maypole he erected "upon the festival day of Philip and Jacob" when he regaled the natives with a "barrel of excellent beer." *(Thomas Morton—New English Canaan, Third Book, Chapters IX and XIII)*

PROTACTINIUM OXIDE. *See* Chemical element to be isolated in the United States

PROTESTANT, AMERICAN INDIAN. *See under* American Indians

PROTESTANT CHILD BORN IN AMERICA. *See* Births: White child of French Protestant parentage

PROTESTANT CHURCH

Protestant church west of Pennsylvania was built in 1772–73 at Schoenbrunn, Ohio. The first communion service was held June 9, 1772, but the church was not finished until September 19, 1772. A larger church was built and was dedicated October 24, 1773. The Reverend David Zeisberger was the first preacher. *(Joseph E. Weinland—The Romantic Story of Schoenbrunn)*

Protestant church for lepers was the Community Church dedicated at Carville, La., June 14, 1915. The sermon was "A merry heart doeth good like a medicine." The church was served by ministers who came in turn from Baton Rouge and New Orleans, La., a different minister coming each week for several years. There was no settled pastor until the summer of 1922, when the Reverend Henry Thomas Cousins was called.

Protestant church formed by the amalgamation of 4 churches of different denominations was the United Church of Schellsburg, Pa., formed November 22, 1964. The first minister was Rev. Daniel Griswold Kratz. The cooperating churches were St. Matthews Lutheran, Schellsburg Methodist,

The First

PROTESTANT CHURCH—*Continued*
Schellsburg Presbyterian, and St. Johns Reformed
(United Church of Christ).

Reformed Dutch Church black pastor was the
Reverend Dr. James Joshua Thomas, who on
November 14, 1954, was installed as minister of
the Mott Haven Reformed Church, the Bronx,
New York City.

PROTESTANT EPISCOPAL BISHOP
Black suffragan in the Episcopal church was the
Reverend Edward Thomas Demby, who was appointed suffragan among the blacks in Arkansas
and the southwest on September 29, 1918. Suffra-
gans or assistants, unlike diocesans, are not in full
charge of a diocese.

Black to administer a diocese was the Venerable John Melville Burgess, archdeacon of the Boston Episcopal Church of Boston, Mass., who was
elected suffragan bishop of the Protestant Episcopal Diocese of Massachusetts on September 22,
1962. He was consecrated December 9, 1962, at
Trinity Church, Boston, Mass. His area comprised
about 146,000 baptized Episcopalians. He was
chosen 12th bishop of the Episcopal Diocese of
Massachusetts on June 7, 1969, and installed on
Jan. 16, 1970, at St. Paul's Cathedral, Boston.

Protestant Episcopal bishop was Samuel Seabury, consecrated November 14, 1784, at Aberdeen, Scotland, by the Scottish bishops Robert
Kilgour, Arthur Petrie, and John Skinner. He was
rector of St. James Church, New London, Conn.,
and Bishop of Rhode Island and Connecticut from
that date until his death on February 25, 1796.

Protestant Episcopal bishop (black) of the
American church was the Reverend Samuel
David Ferguson, who was elected to the House of
Bishops of the Protestant Episcopal Church in
1884. He was consecrated June 24, 1885, at Grace
Church, New York City, as the successor of the
Missionary Bishop of Liberia.

**Protestant Episcopal bishop consecrated in a
Roman Catholic church** was Rev. Canon Robert
Bracewell Appleyard, D.D., consecrated bishop
coadjutor of the Episcopal Diocese of Pittsburgh
on February 10, 1968, in St. Paul's Cathedral in
Pittsburgh, Pa.

**Protestant Episcopal bishop consecrated in the
United States** was the Reverend Thomas John
Claggett, founder of the Trinity Episcopal Church,
Upper Marlboro, Md. He was consecrated Sep-
tember 17, 1792, at Trinity Church, New York City,
by the Bishops Seabury, White, Provoost, and
Madison. *(George Burwell Utley—The Life and
Times of Thomas John Claggett)*

PROTESTANT EPISCOPAL CATECHISM
Episcopal catechism published after the separation of the American synod from the British

The First

church was *The ABC with the Church of England
Catechism. To which are annexed, prayers used
in the academy of the Protestant Episcopal
Church in Philadelphia. Also a Hymn on the
Nativity of our Saviour; and another for Easter-
day* (12 pages, printed in 1785 by Young, Stewart
and M'Cullough, Philadelphia, Pa.). Only the
verses of the hymns were printed. On page 6 instead of the words "king" and "him," dotted lines
were printed so that the title of the head of government could be written in.

PROTESTANT EPISCOPAL CHURCH
Christian religious service in English on the Pa-
cific coast was the Holy Communion from the
Book of Common Prayer of the Church of England
conducted by the Reverend Francis Fletcher of Sir
Francis Drake's ship the *Pelican* on June 24, 1579,
St. John the Baptist's Day, at Drakes Bay, Calif.
Drake named the place Nova Albion, Latin for
New England. A 57-foot marble cross commemo-
rates the event in Golden Gate Park, San Francis-
co, Calif.

Priests (husband and wife) ordained together
were Rev. Michael Coburn and Rev. Ann Struthers Coburn, who were consecrated on December
17, 1977, in St. James Church, Danbury, Conn. The
vows were administered by his father, Right Rev.
John B. Coburn, an Episcopal bishop of Massachusetts.

Protestant Episcopal Church was established in
1607. On April 29, 1607, Captain Gabriel Archer,
Christopher Newport, George Percy, Bartholomew Gosnold, Edward Maria Wingfield, and
25 others planted a cross at Cape Henry. The Reverend Robert Hunt celebrated the Eucharist for
the first time in America at Cape Henry, Va., on
May 9, 1607. The event was reported as follows:
"We did hang an awning (which is an old saile) to
three or four trees, to shadow us from the sunne,
our walles were railes of wood, our seats un-
hewed trees till we cut plankes; our Pulpit a bar
of wood nailed to two neighboring trees." The first
parish was started June 21, 1607, at Jamestown.
*(Edward Lewis Goodwin—The Colonial Church
in Virginia)*

PROTESTANT SCHOOL FOR GIRLS. *See*
School: School for Protestant girls

PROTOCOL CHIEF. *See under* State Department
(U.S.)

PROVINCIAL COUNCIL, CATHOLIC. *See*
Catholic provincial council

PSYCHIATRIC ASSOCIATION was the Association of Medical Superintendents of American
Institutions for the Insane, formed October 16,
1844, in Philadelphia, Pa., by 13 members. The first
president was Samuel B. Woodward, the first vice
president Samuel White, and the first secretary-

The First

treasurer Thomas Story Kirkbride. The name of the association was changed in 1892 to the American Medico-Psychological Association and in 1921 to the American Psychiatric Association.

PSYCHIATRIC HOSPITAL. *See* Hospital

PSYCHIATRIC INSTITUTE. *See under* Medical instruction

PSYCHIATRIC WARD. *See under* Hospital

PSYCHOLOGY LABORATORY was established at Johns Hopkins University, Baltimore, Md., in 1881 by Granville Stanley Hall. It was discontinued in 1888 when Dr. Hall was appointed president of Clark University. A larger laboratory was established in 1904 by Professor George Malcolm Stratton, also at Johns Hopkins University.

PSYCHOLOGY MAGAZINE was the *American Journal of Psychology,* a quarterly first published in Baltimore, Md., in November 1887 under the editorship of Granville Stanley Hall. The subscription price was $3 a year.

PSYCHOLOGY PROFESSOR was James McKeen Cattell, who was appointed professor of psychology at the University of Pennsylvania, Philadelphia, and who served from 1888 to 1891.

PSYCHOLOGY SOCIETY

Psychology society (national organization) was the American Psychological Association, organized July 8, 1892, at Clark University, Worcester, Mass., and incorporated January 2, 1925, in Washington, D.C. Professor Granville Stanley Hall was the first president and Dr. Joseph Jastrow the first secretary and treasurer. The first scientific meeting was held December 27, 1892, at the University of Pennsylvania, Philadelphia, Pa. The official statement of purpose in the certificate of incorporation read: "The object of this society shall be to advance psychology as a science." *(Psychological Review. Vol. 1)*

PTARMIGAN (Eskimo chicken). *See* Birds

PUBLIC ACCOUNTANT. *See* Accountant

PUBLIC AFFAIRS SCHOOL. *See* Citizenship and public affairs school

PUBLIC ART COMMISSION. *See* Art commission (public)

PUBLIC BATH AND WASHHOUSE. *See* Bathhouse

PUBLIC BATHS LEGISLATION. *See* Bathhouse: Legislation concerning public baths

PUBLIC BUILDING (federal). *See* Building: Building erected in the United States for public use

PUBLIC BUILDINGS ADMINISTRATION was established as a part of the Federal Works Agency under the provisions of Reorganization Plan 1, section 303, pursuant to the provisions of the Reorganization Act of 1939, approved April 3, 1939 (53 Stat. L. 561). The first commissioner was Win-

The First

chester Englebert Reynolds, who served from July 1, 1939, to July 1, 1949. Congress enacted Public Law 152, which became effective July 1, 1949, creating the General Services Administration, and Reynolds continued as Commissioner of the Public Buildings Service, GSA, until July 1, 1954.

PUBLIC DEBT. *See* Debt

PUBLIC DEFENDER

Public defender (state) was Peter Murray, appointed director of the Office of State Public Defender by Governor Richard Joseph Hughes of New Jersey on June 20, 1967, for a 5-year term beginning July 1, 1967. A deputy public defender was appointed for each of New Jersey's 21 counties.

PUBLIC DEFENDER'S OFFICE was created by Los Angeles County, Calif., on June 13, 1913. The first public defender was Walton J. Wood, who assumed his duties on January 7, 1914. His salary was $200 a month. He had three deputies, one secretary, and one assistant secretary.

PUBLIC DOCUMENTS CATALOG. *See* Index of government publications

PUBLIC GARAGE. *See* Garage (public)

PUBLIC HEALTH

Medical system of inspection of schoolchildren was established by the Board of Health, Boston, Mass., in 1894. Eighty inspectors examined pupils sent to them by teachers, and advised with regard to medical and surgical treatment. They also provided for exclusion and isolation in cases of contagious diseases and imposed the conditions of readmission to school. In June 1915, this work was transferred to the School Committee, which commenced to function November 22, 1915. *(Dr. Burke —Hygiene in the Boston Public School. National Education Association. 1909)*

Pellagra experiment of note was made by Dr. Joseph Goldberger of the United States Public Health Service at the Mississippi State Penitentiary, eight miles east of Jackson, Miss. Twelve convicts agreed to submit to a restricted-diet test in exchange for an offer of pardon made by Governor Earl LeRoy Brewer. The test was held from February 4, 1915, to April 19, 1915. Six of the 11 convicts (1 was excused) developed pellagra, confirming conclusions that a deficiency of vitamin B "P-P" (pellagra-preventative) in the diet caused the disease. *(Joseph Goldberger—Experimental Pellagra in the Human Subject Brought About by a Restricted Diet)*

Public health school. *See* Hygiene instruction: Hygiene and public health school

Public health service (U.S.) was established by the act of July 16, 1798 (1 Stat. L. 605-6), and provided that after September 1, 1798, the master of every American ship arriving from a foreign port should pay to the Collector of Customs the sum of

The First

PUBLIC HEALTH—*Continued*
20 cents a month for each seaman, which amount he was authorized to deduct from the seaman's wage. This act referred only to merchant seamen. The money collected was spent for health service only in the district in which it was collected. The Public Health Service was reorganized under the act of June 29, 1870 (16 Stat. L. 169). Dr. John Maynard Woodworth was appointed supervising surgeon in April 1871. The department was placed under the Secretary of the Treasury.

Public health service (U.S.) assistant surgeon general (woman) was Lucile Petry (Mrs. Nicholas Charles Leone) of Lewisburg, Ohio, appointed June 7, 1949, with the pay, privileges, and gold braid of an admiral. She took office the same day.

PUBLIC HYGIENE PROFESSOR. *See under* Medical instruction

PUBLIC LIBRARY. *See* Library

PUBLIC MUSEUM. *See* Museum

PUBLIC SCHOOL
See also High School; School

Public school classes for epileptic children were organized January 1935 in a small school building in Detroit, Mich. In 1936 the courses were transferred to the White School, designated the White Special School, one of the divisions of Special Education of the Detroit Public Schools. The first teachers were Alice Mortimore and Edith Sargent.

Public school for Chinese-Americans supported by a municipality was established September 1859 in the basement of the Chinese Chapel, San Francisco, Calif. James Denman was the superintendent of schools. The school had an enrollment of 67 boys and 8 girls, but it had an average attendance of only 12. The school was suspended in June 1860, but later opened as an evening school. *(William Warren Ferrier—Ninety Years of Education in California)*

Public school for cripples. *See under* Cripples

Public school kindergarten. *See under* Kindergarten

Public school music instruction. *See* Music instruction: Music instruction (public school)

Public school opera studio for stage, radio, and screen was at the Los Angeles Junior College, part of the school system of Los Angeles, Calif., which offered courses in October 1937 under the direction of Dr. Hugh Strelitzer. Instruction was not individual but in groups.

Public school supported by direct taxation or by assessment on the inhabitants of the town was established by vote of Dorchester, Mass., on May 20, 1639: "It is ordered the 20th of May 1639, that there shall be a rent of twenty pounds a year for ever imposed upon Tomsons Island to be paid by every person that hath property in the said island

The First

according to the proportion that any such person shall from time to time enjoy and possess there." *(Committee of the Dorchester Antiquarian and Historical Society—History of the Town of Dorchester, Mass.)*

Public school with a continuous existence, the Boston Public Latin School for boys, was established February 13, 1635. The first schoolmaster was Philemon Pormort. Originally its purpose was training for the ministry and its objective was to enable students to "obtain a knowledge of the Scriptures and by acquaintance with the Ancient Tongues qualify them to discern the true sense and meaning of the original, however corrupted by false glosses." The school was originally supported by voluntary contributions. *(Henry Fitch Jenks—The Boston Public Latin School)*

PUBLIC SPEAKING DEPARTMENT in a university was established December 1892 at the University of Michigan, Ann Arbor, with Thomas Clarkson Trueblood as professor of elocution and oratory from 1892 to 1908. Similar courses had been given in 1887, but without departmental status.

PUBLIC WORKS ADMINISTRATION (U.S.) was authorized June 16, 1933, by President Franklin Delano Roosevelt. Full organization was not effective until July 8, when Harold Le Claire Ickes, Secretary of the Interior, was appointed administrator of the Public Works Administration. The Special Board of Public Works was composed of nine members, and the first chairman of the board was Harold Le Claire Ickes.

PUBLICITY MAN. *See* Theatrical advance publicity man

PUBLISHER (denominational). *See* Book publisher

PUBLISHER (newspaper). *See under* Newspaper

PUBLISHING SOCIETY was the Seventy-Six Society, organized September 5, 1854, in Philadelphia, Pa. Its *Collections* dealt solely with subjects pertaining to the American Revolution. Henry J. Williams was president; Henry Penington, secretary; and William Duane, treasurer. Other societies published tracts, religious papers, etc., but in conjunction with other activities and interests

PUGILIST. *See* Prizefight

PULITZER PRIZE
Woman to win 2 Pulitzer Prizes in history was Margaret Leech, who was awarded the 1941 prize on May 4, 1942, for *Reveille in Washington* and the 1959 prize on May 2, 1960, for *In the Days of McKinley.*

PULITZER PRIZE AWARDED TO A NEWSPAPER REPORTER. *See under* Newspaper Reporter

The First

PULITZER PRIZE IN JOURNALISM. *See under* Newspaper

PULITZER PRIZE IN LETTERS. *See under* Novel; Playwright; Poet

PULL-CHAIN ELECTRIC SOCKET. *See* Electric light socket

PULLMAN CAR. *See* Sleeping car

PULP NEWSPAPER. *See* Newspaper: Newspaper printed on pine-pulp paper

PULP PAPER. *See* Paper: Wood-pulp paper

PUMP

Computer pump was marketed by the Wayne Company, Fort Wayne, Inc., on November 1, 1932. The pump was invented by Robert Joseph Jauch, Ivan Richard Farnham, and Ross Harper Arnold, who received patent No. 1,888,533 on November 22, 1932, on a "liquid dispensing apparatus." The pump accurately computed and indicated exact quantity delivered in gallons and the price in dollars and cents as delivery was made. Total gallons dispensed and cash received were recorded by two totalizers.

Gasoline pump was manufactured in a barn by Sylvanus F. Bowser of Fort Wayne, Ind., in 1885. The first pump and tank were delivered September 5, 1885, to Jake D. Gumper of Fort Wayne. The tank had marble valves and wooden plungers and had a capacity of one barrel. Bowser's invention, for which patent No. 372,250 was issued on October 25, 1887, to Sylvanus F. Bowser and Augustus Bowser, Fort Wayne, Ind., became popular, and he organized S. F. Bowser and Co., Inc., of Fort Wayne.

Independent single direct-acting steam power pump was invented in 1840 by Henry Rossiter Worthington of New York City, who obtained patent No. 3,677, July 24, 1844, on a steam engine auxiliary for the purpose of supplying a steam boiler with water. The following year, with William H. Baker as partner, he started the firm of Worthington and Baker at Brooklyn, N.Y., later the Worthington Pump and Machinery Corporation, Harrison, N.J.

PUMPING PLANT. *See* Water: Water-pumping plant

PUNCHBOARDS were manufactured by Charles A. Brewer & Sons, Chicago, Ill. They were patented January 17, 1905 (No. 780,086), as "vending devices" by Charles A. Brewer and Clinton G. Scannell of Chicago, Ill.

PUPPET SHOW to which admission was charged was held February 12, 1738, in Mr. Holt's room (a room 39 feet long, 19 feet wide, and 9 feet high) at Broad and Pearl streets, New York City. The show was entitled *The Adventures of Harlequin and Scaramouche, or The Spaniard Trick'd.* Admis-

The First

sion was five shillings. *(New York Gazette, January 29–February 6, 1738)*

PUPPET SHOW TELECAST. *See under* Television—Telecast

PURE FOOD LEGISLATION

Pure food and drug legislation (national) to prevent the importation of adulterated drugs was passed June 26, 1848 (9 Stat. L. 237), an "act to prevent the importation of adulterated and spurious drugs and medicines." It was enforced by the Treasury Department through the Customs Service. Although it has never been repealed, it has been superseded by the Federal Food and Drug Act of June 30, 1906 (34 Stat. L. 768), effective January 1, 1907. *(U.S. Compiled Statutes, 1901. Vol. 2)*

Pure food and drug legislation (state) was "an act to prevent the adulteration of food or drugs," passed May 28, 1881, by New York to take effect August 27, 1881. Violators were guilty of a misdemeanor, subject to a fine up to $50 for the first offense and not exceeding $100 for each subsequent offense. Laws prohibiting the adulteration of specific products had been passed earlier, however.

PURPLE HEART. *See* Medal: Order of the Purple Heart

PUSHBALL played with a huge six-foot ball, was invented by M. G. Crane of Newport, Mass., in 1894. It found favor the following year at Harvard, but never became a major sport.

PUZZLE, CROSSWORD. *See* Crossword puzzle

PYTHIAN BROTHERHOOD. *See* Knights of Pythias

Q

QUACKS. *See* Medical rogues' gallery

QUADRANT that was practical was invented in 1730 by Thomas Godfrey, who called it a "reflecting quadrant." It was used on vessels plying between the West Indies and the Colonies in 1731–32. The invention was credited to John Hadley of England, but the Royal Society sent £200 to Godfrey to make amends. *(Pennsylvania Magazine of History and Biography. Vol. 51. 1927)*

QUADRUPLE NEWSPAPER PRESS. *See* Printing press

QUADRUPLETS DELIVERED BY CESAREAN OPERATION. *See under* Births

QUADRUPLETS TO COMPLETE A COLLEGE COURSE were the Keys sisters, Leota, Mary, Mona, and Roberta, who received B.A. degrees from Baylor University, Waco, Tex., on May 31, 1937. They were born June 4, 1914.

The First

QUAKERS

Quaker college was the Haverford School, Haverford, Pa., which opened October 28, 1833, under the sponsorship of members of the Society of Friends. The first superintendent was Samuel Hilles. The name was changed to Haverford College in 1856.

Quakers' annual meeting was held in Scituate, Mass., in 1660. The first monthly meeting is believed to have been held in Sandwich, Mass., on June 25, 1672. It is possible that earlier meetings were held, but no records of them have been preserved. *(Allen Clapp Thomas—History of the Friends in America)*

Quakers to arrive in America were two women, Ann Austin and Mary Fisher, who landed at Boston, Mass. July 11, 1656, from Barbados. They were subject to rigid examination and five weeks' imprisonment to ascertain if they were witches before admittance to the colony. The examining officers searched their trunks and their books "were by an order of council burned in the market place by the hangman." *(Allen Clapp Thomas— History of the Friends in America)*

Synod of Quakers was held at Cambridge, Mass., from September 9, 1637, to October 2, 1637 (24 days). "Eighty-two opinions" were discovered and declared to be "some blasphemous, othere erroneus and all unsafe." *(Rufus Matthew Jones— The Quakers in the American Colonies)*

QUARANTINE

Plant quarantine legislation (national) was the act of August 20, 1912 (37 Stat. L. 315), directed against dangerous plant diseases and injurious insect pests "new to or not theretofore widely prevalent or distributed within and throughout the United States." The quarantine provisions of Section 7 of the act became immediately effective as to the white-pine blister rust, potato wart, and Mediterranean fruit fly. Except as noted, the act did not become effective until October 1, 1912. The first quarantine under the authority of this act, directed against white-pine blister rust, was issued September 16, 1912. *(Leland Ossian Howard—A History of Applied Entomology)*

Plant quarantine legislation (state) was passed by California, March 4, 1881. Quarantine rules and regulations for the protection of fruit and fruit trees covering both intrastate and interstate shipments were issued November 12, 1881. The quarantine was particularly designed against an insect known as *Phylloxera vastatrix*, which in 1873 attacked the cultivated grapevines in the Sonoma Valley, and against the San Jose scale and codling moth, which in 1875 had caused serious damage to tree fruits. *(Records in California Department of Agriculture, Sacramento, Calif.)*

The First

Quarantine legislation (colonial) was passed by the General Court of Massachusetts March 1647. An epidemic, which raged in Barbados and the other islands of the West Indies and took over 6,000 lives, caused the court to publish an order that all ships which came from the West Indies should stay at the Castle at the entrance to the harbor and not land any passengers or goods without a license from three of the council, under a severe penalty. A like penalty was imposed upon any person visiting such quarantined vessel without permission. The act was repealed May 2, 1649. The first Quarantine Act passed by the General Assembly of Pennsylvania was "An act to prevent sickly vessels coming into this government," passed November 27, 1700. *(Pennsylvania Statutes at Large, Vol. 2. p. 80)*

Quarantine legislation (national) was passed by Congress on February 25, 1799 (1 Stat. L. 619). It was "an act respecting quarantines and health laws" requiring federal officers to aid and assist the enforcement of state and municipal regulations.

Ship permitted to enter port without stopping for quarantine. *See under* Ship

QUARRY. *See* Marble quarry

QUARTER DOLLAR. *See* Money: Silver coins

QUARTERLY MAGAZINE. *See* Periodical

QUARTERMASTER (U.S. Army). *See* Army officer

QUARTZ MERCURY ARC LAMP. *See* Electric lighting: Mercury vapor lamp

QUEEN TO VISIT THE UNITED STATES. *See* Visiting celebrities

QUETZAL BIRD. *See* Birds

QUIDS were organized during President Thomas Jefferson's administration and were led from 1804 to 1808 by John Randolph of Roanoke, Va. They believed in extreme states' rights and were also opposed to Jefferson's attempts to acquire West Florida. They ran James Monroe against James Madison in 1808. The name is derived from the Latin *tertium quid* ("a third thing"), indicating separation from both existing political parties, or from both administration and opposition forces. *(James Albert Woodburn—Political Parties and Party Problems in the United States)*

QUININE

Quinine was manufactured in 1822 by John Farr and Abraham Kunzi in Philadelphia, Pa.

Quinine sulfate was manufactured commercially in 1823 by Powers and Weightman of New York City. *(Samuel Hazzard Cross, Quinine-Production and Marketing)*

The First

Synthetic quinine was produced April 10, 1944, by Dr. Robert Burns Woodward and Dr. William von Eggers Doering at the Converse Memorial Laboratory, Harvard University, Cambridge, Mass. It consists of 20 atoms carbon, 24 atoms hydrogen, 2 atoms oxygen, and 2 atoms nitrogen.

QUINTUPLETS. *See under* Births

QUONSET HUT. *See* Building: Building known as a Quonset hut

QUOTA ACT, IMMIGRATION. *See under* Immigration

R

RABBI
Husband-and-wife rabbinical and cantorial team engaged by a synagogue was Rabbi Stuart Alan Gertman and Cantor Sarah Jean Sager, who began their service at Ansche Chesed Congregation-Fairmount Temple, Cleveland, Ohio, July 1, 1980.

Woman rabbi was Sally Jane Priesand, who was ordained June 3, 1972, in the Isaac M. Wise Temple, Cincinnati, Ohio. On August 1, 1972, she became assistant rabbi at the Stephen Wise Free Synagogue, New York City. She was graduated from the Hebrew Union College-Jewish Institute of Religion, Cincinnati, Ohio, on June 2, 1972, receiving the Master of Arts in Hebrew Letters (MAHL) degree.

RABBINICAL CONFERENCE. *See under* Jews

RABBINICAL SCHOOL. *See* Jewish college

RACING
See under Aviation—Races; Locomotive; and *also under* specific types of races:

Automobile	Dog
Bicycle	Horse
Boat	Motorcycle
Camel	Yacht

RACETRACK
Harness track to handle more than $300 million in bets in 1 year was Yonkers Raceway, Yonkers, N.Y., where a total of $300,973,393 was reached on December 8, 1969. When the season closed on December 13, 1969, a total of $311,776,286 had been wagered.

Harness track to handle more than $3 million in bets in 1 night was the Yonkers Raceway, Yonkers, N.Y., where 34,475 bettors wagered $3,191,020 on 9 races on November 30, 1962. The greatest amount wagered that night was on the 6th race, the $4,000 paced-mile race: $398,413. This race was won by Firesweep, which paid $6.10, $3.90, and $2.90.

The First

Racetrack to install an electric-eye camera. *See* Camera: Photofinish camera

RACETRACK STARTING GATE (electric). *See* Electric starting gate

RACING SHELL. *See* Ship

RACK-RAIL DIESEL-ELECTRIC LOCOMOTIVE. *See* Locomotive: Rack-rail diesel-electric locomotive

RADAR
Battleship equipped with radar was the U.S.S. *New York*, which was tested during battle maneuvers at sea in the months of January, February, and March of 1939. This radar set operated on a wavelength of a meter and a half, detecting destroyers at a distance of approximately eight miles. The first set to be installed on the *New York* was constructed at the Naval Research Laboratory at Washington, D.C.; the first contract was awarded in October 1939 to the Radio Corporation of America for the manufacture of six sets of aircraft detection equipment.

Offshore radar warning station was built by the Bethlehem Steel Company's shipbuilding division at Fore River, Quincy, Mass., for the Continental Air Defense Command. The keel was laid January 10, 1955, and the station was launched May 20, 1955. Known as a Texas Tower, it served as a weather collecting and reporting station, and consisted of a triangular 6,000-ton platform resting on three legs 87 feet above the water level. It was turned over to the First Naval District of the U.S. Navy on December 2, 1955.

Passenger ship equipped with radar was the flagship *New York* of the Hamburg-American Line. Two circular appendages three feet in diameter were installed atop the pilothouse of the ship. The equipment was placed in service February 26, 1938.

Radar detection of airplanes was accomplished June 24, 1930, by Dr. Albert Hoyt Taylor and Leo C. Young of the Naval Aircraft Radio Laboratory, Anacostia, D.C., who noted that airplanes, even though above the transmitter and receiver, rather than between them, reflected radio waves.

Radar for commercial and private planes was developed by Howard Robard Hughes and the electronic engineers of the Hughes Aircraft Corporation, Culver City, Calif., and demonstrated May 1, 1947, at Culver City on a TWA (Transcontinental & Western Air, Inc.) plane. A brilliant red light on the instrument panel and a horn in the cockpit warned the pilot whenever he came too close to an obstacle.

Radar installation aboard a commercial carrier. *See under* Ship

RADAR—*Continued*

Radar observations were made September 27, 1922, by Dr. Albert Hoyt Taylor and Leo C. Young of the Naval Aircraft Radio Laboratory, Anacostia, D.C., who reported to the U.S. Navy that radio detection equipment placed on any two ships could detect the passage of any vessel between them despite fog, darkness, or smoke screen, and that tall buildings reflected radio signals.

Radar signal bounced off the sun was transmitted on April 7, 1959, at Stanford University, Stanford, Calif., by Professor Von Russel Eshleman, Lieutenant Colonel Robert Charles Barthle, and Dr. Philip Benjamin Gallagher, who used a 40,000-watt transmitter. The signals reached the sun's corona about a half million miles above the visible part of the sun. The signals required 1,000 seconds for transmission in both directions. The signals consisted of a series of dots and dashes that were detected by an electronic computer even though they were much weaker than the radio noise from the sun.

Radar signal to the moon was beamed by the Army Signal Corps on January 10, 1946, from the Evans Signal Laboratories, Belmar, N.J. The experiment was supervised by Lieutenant Colonel John H. De Witt. An echo was received 2.4 seconds later which consisted of a 180-cycle note of a quarter-second duration.

Radar used to detect enemy airplanes was employed at Pearl Harbor, Hawaii. At 7:20 A.M., December 7, 1941, Private Joseph L. Lockard of Williamsport, Pa., reported to his superiors that he heard the approach of planes. The planes were assumed to be friendly, proper precautions were not taken, and a great disaster resulted. On February 8, 1942, Lockard received the Distinguished Service Medal and was sent to Officer Training School, Fort Monmouth, N.J.

RADIATION-COOLED HOUSE. *See* Building: Solar-heated and radiation-cooled house

RADIO ADVERTISING

Radio advertising contract for frequency modulation broadcasts was signed December 9, 1940, by the Longines Watch Company and provided for the broadcasting of Longines time signals by W2XOR, New York, for 26 weeks beginning January 1, 1941. On April 1, 1941, the experimental license was replaced with commercial license W71NY, and the station was operated from 8:30 A.M. to 11:30 P.M. on a frequency of 47,100 kilocycles.

Radio-advertising course. *See under* Radio instruction

RADIO BEACONS were originally known as radio fog signals. The first successful radio beacons, which sent out signals by radio in all directions around the horizon, as do lighthouses by

means of light beams, were established by the United States Lighthouse Service at three stations in the approaches to New York Harbor: on the Ambrose Channel Lightship, Fire Island Lightship, and Sea Girt Lighthouse, N.J. They were placed in regular operation May 1, 1921. Tests of radio fog signal transmitting sets leading to the installation of these stations were begun in 1916–1917 at Navesink Light Station, Atlantic Highlands, N.J., by the Lighthouse Service and the Bureau of Standards. The tests were interrupted when the United States entered World War I but were resumed in the fall of 1919 and lasted until September 1920. *(George Rockwell Putnam—Radio Beacons)*

RADIO BROADCAST

Advertising or commercial radio broadcast was sponsored by the Queensboro Realty Corporation, Jackson Heights, New York City, on August 28, 1922, over station WEAF, the experimental station of the American Telephone and Telegraph Company, New York City. The commercial rate was $100 for ten minutes. H. M. Blackwell spoke for ten minutes about Hawthorne Court, a dwelling in Jackson Heights.

All-Chinese commercial radio program was broadcast April 22, 1940, by KSAN, San Francisco, Calif. Thomas Tong, of the Golden Star Radio Company, San Francisco, was the director and the sponsor.

Auction of livestock broadcast was December 18, 1924, by WLS, Chicago, Ill., on 345-meter wavelength, of the national shorthorn and hereford sale of pigs, sheep, lamb, and cattle at the International Livestock Exposition, Chicago, Ill.

Baseball game broadcast with a play-by-play description was aired August 5, 1921, by KDKA, Pittsburgh, Pa., the field being connected by wire to the broadcasting station. The National League Pittsburgh Corsairs defeated Philadelphia, 8–5, at Pittsburgh, for their third straight victory.

Baseball World Series broadcast was effected by WJZ of the Westinghouse Electric and Manufacturing Company, Newark, N.J., which broadcast a play-by-play account of the National League New York Giants–American League New York Yankees series October 5, 1921, to October 13, 1921. Sandy Hunt, reporter on the Newark *Call*, telephoned the plays to Thomas H. ("Tommy") Cowan, who announced them from the radio shack atop the Westinghouse Building in Newark, N.J. The series was won by the Giants, who won five of the scheduled nine games; the Yankees won three.

Chain broadcast was accomplished October 7, 1922, when WJZ and WGY transmitted a World Series game from the field. Ordinary telegraph lines from Newark, N.J., and Schenectady, N.Y., were connected with the Polo Grounds, New York City, where a single microphone connected to these lines completed the requirements. It was not

The First

possible to transmit highest and lowest frequencies. Graham McNamee was the announcer. On January 4, 1923, WEAF of New York City and WNAC of Boston, Mass., had repeater points, and amplifiers were provided for faithful reproduction and transmission of both music and speech.

Church services aired from another church. *See* Church: Church services aired from another church

Circus broadcast was made from the menagerie of the Ringling Brothers Barnum and Bailey circus in the basement of Madison Square Garden, New York City, on April 10, 1924. Lew Graham was the circus announcer; the broadcast was from station WJZ, Aeolian Hall, New York City, to station WGY, Schenectady, N.Y. The roar of the animals at feeding time and the music of the calliope were broadcast.

Coast-to-coast football-game broadcast originating on the West Coast was the Rose Bowl Game, Pasadena, Calif., on January 1, 1927, in which the University of Alabama, of University, Ala., tied Stanford University, of Stanford, Calif., 7-7. There were about 60,000 spectators.

Coast-to-coast hookup took place February 8, 1924, when General John Joseph Carty, vice president and chief of research of the Bell Telephone system, spoke from the meeting of the Bond Men's Club at the Congress Hotel, Chicago, Ill. It is estimated that the speech—broadcast by WJAR, Providence, R.I.; WEAF, New York City; WCAP, Washington, D.C.; WMAQ, Chicago, Ill.; KLX, Oakland, Calif.; and KTO, San Francisco, Calif.—was heard by 50 million people.

Congressional open-session broadcast was the first session of the 68th Congress broadcast by radio station WRC, Washington, D.C., from the Senate on December 3, 1923, from 12:00 P.M. to 12:45 P.M. The president pro tempore of the Senate was Albert Baird Cummins of Iowa; the Speaker of the House of Representatives was Frederick Huntington Gillett of Massachusetts. The newly elected senators—Alva Blanchard Adams (Democrat, Colorado), Magnus Johnson (Farmer-Labor, Minnesota), and Porter Hinman Dale (Republican, Vermont)—were sworn in alphabetically and the session adjourned in memory of the recently deceased senators whose seats they were taking —Samuel Danford Nicholson (Republican), Knute Nelson (Republican), and William Paul Dillingham (Republican), respectively.

Cooperative radio show was "Thirty Minutes in Hollywood," broadcast October 10, 1937, by KHJ, Hollywood, Calif., over the Mutual Broadcasting System. It was broadcast for 26 weeks in 72 cities, the cost being borne by 48 commercial sponsors on a pro rata cost basis. The orchestra was conducted by Tommy Tucker; the masters of ceremonies were George Jessel and Norma Talmadge (Mrs. George Jessel). The guest star on the first

The First

program was Eddie Cantor.

Debate over the radio was held May 23, 1922, over station WJH of the White and Boyer Company, Washington, D.C. The affirmative, "Resolved, That daylight saving is an advantage," was taken by Calvin Ira Kephart, representing the Miller Debating Society, and the negative by Thomas E. Rhodes, representing the Alvey Debating Society, both of the National University Law School, Washington, D.C. The audience was requested to act as judge.

Degree conferred by radio. *See under* Degrees (academic and honorary)

Dinner broadcast around the world was broadcast by short wave from 2XAF, Schenectady, N.Y., on April 20, 1927, to London, Paris, Honolulu, and Tokyo. The dinner was held at the Waldorf-Astoria Hotel, New York City, and was broadcast by WEAF, New York City. The toastmaster was Dr. George Edgar Vincent, president of the Rockefeller Foundation, and the principal speaker was Dr. James Rowland Angell, 14th president of Yale University. Chief Justice William Howard Taft's speech from Washington, D.C., was telephoned to New York City and broadcast. The broadcast opened an appeal by Yale University for $20 million. It was estimated that the proceedings reached 18 million people over two radio networks in 200 cities in the United States and foreign lands.

Double radio wedding. *See under* Wedding

Drama broadcast from a regular stage with full scenery and a cast in costume was *Roses and Drums*, a dramatic story of the unsuccessful Union attempt in 1864 to capture Jefferson Davis and free the Union prisoners from Libby Prison. It was presented by WABC, New York City, September 24, 1933.

Drama broadcast from a ship at sea was heard over the WABC Columbia network, July 1, 1933, when an air version of a new motion picture was presented from the main salon of the Furness-Bermuda liner *Queen of Bermuda* on a weekend cruise to the mid-Atlantic. The picture from which the radio version was prepared was *Lady for a Day*, adapted from the short story by Damon Runyon.

Drama (full-length melodrama) broadcast was *The Wolf*, by Eugene Walter, broadcast August 3, 1922, by WGY, Schenectady, N.Y. The 2½-hour performance was directed by Edward H. Smith.

Editorial broadcast over a network was made from 8:00 P.M. to 8:15 P.M. on August 26, 1954, when Dr. Frank Stanton appealed over the Columbia Broadcasting System (CBS) network for permission to cover the hearings to censure Senator Joseph Raymond McCarthy (Republican, Wisconsin), which began August 31, 1954.

The First

RADIO BROADCAST—*Continued*

Election campaign using radio was undertaken by Senator Harry Stewart New, Republican of Indiana, who waged an unsuccessful campaign for reelection in 1922. He used radio the last 5 days of the campaign, from October 27 to November 2, 1922, and hired several halls in which loud speakers were placed. He was defeated November 7, 1922, by Samuel Moffett Ralston, the Democratic candidate.

Election returns broadcast took place on August 31, 1920, when WWJ of Detroit, Mich., broadcast the results of congressional and county primaries. On November 2, 1920, Leo H. Rosenberg of KDKA of Pittsburgh, Pa., broadcast the results of the Harding-Cox presidential election. (An experimental station, the De Forest Radio Laboratory in the Highbridge section of the Bronx, New York City, broadcast bulletins from the New York *American* on the results of the Wilson-Hughes election for approximately six hours beginning after dark on November 7, 1916. The broadcasters signed off about 11 P.M., with the announcement that Hughes had been elected.)

Football game championship (professional) broadcast on a network was played December 8, 1940, at Griffith Stadium, Washington, D.C. The Mutual Broadcasting System paid $25,000 for the rights to the game, which was broadcast by "Red" (Walter Lanier) Barber. The Washington Redskins defeated the Chicago Bears 73-0 and won the Ed Thorp Memorial Trophy.

Football game (collegiate) broadcast was presented November 25, 1920, by WTAW of College Station, Tex. The game was played on Thanksgiving Day between Texas University and the Agricultural and Mechanical College of Texas at College Station. At that time the station was operating under an experimental license and had the call letters 5XB. A spark transmitter was used and the transmission was in code. This was the first play-by-play broadcast of a football game.

Football game (collegiate) coast-to-coast broadcast was presented October 28, 1922, by WEAF, New York City, from Stagg Field, Chicago, Ill. The Princeton Tigers defeated the Chicago Maroons 21-18. Long-distance telephone lines carried the announcer's voice to New York City, from where it was broadcast. In addition to broadcasting, the station equipped a truck at Park Row, New York City, with a public address system.

Football game played in the United States to be broadcast in England. *See under* Football game

Foreign-language course broadcast took place on March 21, 1924, when WJZ, New York City, operating on a 455-meter wavelength, offered French lessons in cooperation with the Berlitz School of Languages.

The First

Musical comedy broadcast with specially composed music, was *The Gibson Family*, sponsored by Procter and Gamble Company of Cincinnati, Ohio, and introduced over the National Broadcasting Company network, September 15, 1934. The comedy was composed by Arthur Schwartz and the lyrics were written by Howard Dietz. The musical comedy was booked for a 39-week period and was broadcast from WEAF, New York City.

Network broadcast received on the Pacific Coast was the speech of President Calvin Coolidge on October 23, 1924, at the dedication of the Chamber of Commerce of the United States building, Washington, D.C. The 45-minute speech was broadcast by 23 stations, including stations in Los Angeles, Calif.; Portland, Oreg.; and Seattle, Wash.

Network sponsored broadcast was "The Eveready Hour" broadcast February 12, 1924, from station WEAF, New York City, to WCAP, Washington, D.C., and WJAR, Providence, R.I., under the sponsorship of the National Carbon Company.

News program was broadcast August 31, 1920, by station 8MK, owned by the Detroit, Mich., *News*. The call letters were changed later to WWJ. The station had begun operating on August 20, 1920.

News program (cooperative) was broadcast in November 1937 by Fulton Lewis, Jr., from WOL, Washington, D.C., under the direction of William B. Dolph. Individual sponsors in different cities bore the expenses on a cooperative basis.

News program (daily) was broadcast September 1, 1922, by WBAY, American Telegraph and Telephone Company, New York City, between 4:30 P.M. and 5:30 P.M. It was known as "The Radio Digest" and was edited by George F. Thompson. Questions and answers concerning radio were also broadcast.

Opera broadcast. *See under* Opera

Outer-space broadcast was made December 19, 1958, when a tape recording of the voice of President Dwight David Eisenhower delivering his Christmas greetings was broadcast on frequencies of 107.97 and 107.94 megacycles from a rocket revolving around the earth.

Police broadcast was made by WIL, St. Louis, Mo., September 4, 1921.

Political convention broadcast took place on June 10, 1924, when the Republican Convention assembled at Cleveland, Ohio, nominated Calvin Coolidge of Massachusetts and Charles Gates Dawes of Illinois for President and Vice President respectively. Graham McNamee was the announcer for the program, which was carried by 15 stations of the National Broadcasting Company from Boston, Mass., to Kansas City, Mo.

The First

Political speech by a President on radio was made by Calvin Coolidge on February 12, 1924, at the 38th annual Lincoln Day dinner of the National Republican Club held at the Hotel Waldorf-Astoria, New York City. He discussed tax reduction, oil, and other problems. About 5 million people heard his speech over stations WJZ and WEAF, New York City; WGY, Schenectady, N.Y.; WCAR, Washington, D.C.; and WJAR, Providence, R.I.

President to broadcast. *See* President (U.S.): President to broadcast by radio

President to broadcast from the White House was Calvin Coolidge, whose address on George Washington's Birthday, transmitted from his study in the White House, Washington, D.C., on February 22, 1924, was heard on 42 stations from coast to coast.

Presidential inauguration was broadcast March 4, 1925, from Washington, D.C., over 24 stations. Calvin Coolidge and Charles Gates Dawes took the oath as President and Vice President, respectively. On March 4, 1921, Harold W. Arlin of KDKA, Pittsburgh, Pa., who had received an advance copy of President Warren Gamaliel Harding's inaugural address, read it at the same time that President Harding was delivering it. Harding's 41-minute address was carried by 24 stations and heard by an audience estimated at 22,800,000.

Presidential message to be broadcast was heard on December 6, 1923, when President Calvin Coolidge delivered his message to a joint session of Congress held in the House of Representatives, Washington, D.C. It was broadcast by KSD, St. Louis, Mo.; WCAP, Washington, D.C.; WDAF, Kansas City, Mo.; WEAF, New York City; WFAA, Dallas, Tex.; and WJAR, Providence, R.I. His voice was received over telephone wires. On March 4, 1925, he broadcast his inaugural address.

Presidential nomination ceremony broadcast was made from Leland Stanford Junior University Stadium, Palo Alto, Calif., on August 11, 1928, and carried by over 107 stations. Herbert Hoover was formally notified of his nomination for the presidency by the Republican Party and accepted.

Presidential phone-in was presented on March 5, 1977, on the Columbia Broadcasting System (CBS) network. Walter Cronkite served as the moderator of the "Ask President Carter" show, in which President Jimmy Carter in the Oval Office in the White House, Washington, D.C., replied to 42 listeners from 26 states who phoned in questions on the nationwide radio broadcast.

Prizefight broadcast was the Jack Dempsey–Billy Miske fight at Benton Harbor, Mich., broadcast September 6, 1920, by WWJ, Detroit, Mich. Miske

The First

was knocked out in the third round of the scheduled ten-round fight.

Prizefight broadcast from the ringside was presented December 22, 1920, from Madison Square Garden, New York City. Joe Lynch of New York City defended his bantamweight title against Peter Herman of New Orleans in a 15-round fight.

Prizefight (heavyweight championship) broadcast was the Jack Dempsey–Georges Carpentier fight on July 2, 1921 at Boyle's Thirty Acres, Jersey City, N.J., in which Carpentier was knocked down in the fourth round. The fight was broadcast by Major J. Andrew White through WJY, Hoboken, N.J.

Program theme song—"How do you do everybody, how do you do?"—was broadcast October 21, 1921, by Billy Jones and Ernie Hare. It was the theme song introducing "The Happiness Boys" program.

Radio broadcast demonstration was made by Nathan B. Stubblefield in 1892. He was the first person to transmit the voice by air without the aid of wires. He gave a public exhibition of his invention on January 1, 1902; and on May 30, 1902, in Fairmont Park, Philadelphia, Pa., his voice was heard a mile away from the transmitter. He obtained patent No. 887,357 on May 12, 1908, but because of his idiosyncrasies he did not permit knowledge of his invention to be spread abroad. Inability to obtain a fabulous sum for his invention, as well as fear of imparting its secret before the patent was granted, deprived him of the fame which by right of priority should have been his. *(Kentucky Progress Magazine. Vol. II. No. 7)*

Radio broadcast from a moving train, of a regular program on a national network, was made by WABC, at 9 P.M., March 27, 1932, from a Baltimore and Ohio train. Pickup points were at Beltsville, Md., and Laurel, Md. The transmitter was operated on a frequency of 1542 kilocycles, employing high-percentage modulation and running on 50 watts power. Belle Baker and Jack Denny's orchestra were featured on the program.

Radio broadcast from a tape recording. *See under* Tape recording

Radio broadcast heard in both the Arctic and the Antarctic regions was effected September 23, 1934, by W2XAF, the short-wave station of the General Electric Company, Schenectady, N.Y. Admiral Richard Evelyn Byrd with his second expedition at Little America heard the program sent to Rockwell Kent, who was near Labrador, broadcast by the New York Coffee House.

Radio broadcast sent from an airplane was dispatched August 27, 1910, by James A. Macready from an airplane above the racetrack, Sheepshead Bay, N.Y. The message was "Another chapter in aerial achievement is hereby written in the receiving of this first message ever recorded from

The First

RADIO BROADCAST—*Continued*

an airplane in flight." *(United States Air Services, March 1926)*

Radio broadcast (two-way) from an airplane was accomplished August 14, 1924, in New York City by WJZ. A conversation was broadcast between Major William Nicholas Hensley, Commandant of Mitchel Field, in a plane, with Major Lester Durand Gardner on the ground in Central Park, New York City. *(Aviation. Sept. 8, 1924)*

Radio concert from an airplane was broadcast April 14, 1922, from a Fokker airplane over New York City. The plane was piloted by Belvin W. Maynard, an ordained Baptist minister. Jeanette Vreeland, a lyric soprano, sang to raise money for the Veterans Mountain Camp, Tupper Lake, N.Y., a home for tubercular ex-servicemen. She was introduced by Thais Magrane, chairman of the American Legion Auxiliary. The program was relayed by telephone to the camp's New York offices at the Hotel Astor.

Radio police system (two-way three-way) from headquarters to the cars, cars to headquarters, and from car to car, was installed by Radio Engineering Laboratories, Inc., Long Island City, N.Y., which contracted with Eastchester Township, N.Y., on May 8, 1933, to install one transmitter and receiver for police headquarters (20 watts, W2XCT) and two for police cars (4.5 volts, W2XCS and W2XEL). The cars were placed in operation July 10, 1933, and were under the direction of Sergeant William E. Robinson. (On October 22, 1932, Bayonne, N.J., made formal application for a construction permit; it was granted December 22, 1932, but the installation was not completed until July 31, 1933.)

Radio program broadcast was sent by Professor Reginald Aubrey Fessenden on December 24, 1906, from Brant Rock, Mass. The general call "CQ" was heard, followed by a song, the reading of verse, a violin solo, a speech, and an invitation to report on the kind of reception. A 40 h.p. steam engine driving a 35-kilowatt, 125-cycle alternator, with rotary spark at a frequency of 250 per second, was used. The antenna consisted of a single straight tube, 36 inches outside diameter, 429 feet high, in 8-foot sections bolted together. *(Gleason Leonard Archer—History of Radio to 1926)*

Radio program simultaneously transmitted over 24 AM and FM stations, and telecast over 5, was presented on March 20, 1948, when a sustaining feature, the NBC Symphony, was broadcast. The first commercial program similarly aired was "The Voice of Firestone" on March 22, 1948. The New York City outlet was WNBC.

Recorded coast-to-coast broadcast was made on May 6, 1937, by Herbert Morrison, who described the explosion of the dirigible *Hindenburg* at Lakehurst, N.J. The recording was flown to New York City. It was broadcast over both the Red and

The First

Blue networks of the National Broadcasting Company, from New York City.

Religious service broadcast was made January 2, 1921, when the Calvary Episcopal Church of Pittsburgh, Pa., broadcast its services through KDKA. The preacher was the Reverend Edwin Jan Van Etten.

Round-the-world broadcast was accomplished in one eighth of a second on June 30, 1930, by a series of radio relays. Clyde Decker Wagoner spoke into a short-wave microphone from W2XAD, Schenectady, N.Y. His voice was relayed to Holland, to Java, to Australia, across the Pacific Ocean to North America, and back to Schenectady.

Senate chamber broadcast. *See* Congress (U.S.) —Senate: Broadcast from the Senate chamber

Ship-at-sea broadcast from an ocean liner was made March 25, 1930, from the 49,746-ton German steamship *Europa* in quarantine in New York harbor. Speeches made in the chart room were sent out by short wave, received on the New Jersey coast, and rebroadcast by stations WEAF and WJZ, New York City. Commodore Nicolaus Johnson announced that the maiden trip of the *Europa* was made in 4 days 17 hours 6 minutes from Cherbourg to the Ambrose Lightship.

Ship launching broadcast was presented April 7, 1925, when several stations broadcast the launching of the airplane carrier U.S.S. *Saratoga*, christened by Mrs. Curtis Dwight Wilbur, wife of the Secretary of the Navy, at the New York Shipbuilding Corporation Yard, on the Delaware River, Camden, N.J.

Simultaneous broadcast on all 3 major networks (CBS, NBC, and Mutual) was that from the Radio City Music Hall, New York City, from midnight to 2:00 A.M. on February 11, 1937, for the benefit of the flood relief fund of the American National Red Cross. The master of ceremonies was Major Edward Bowes, assisted by Noel Coward and others.

Singer to broadcast was Eugenia H. Farrar, whose voice was broadcast by Lee De Forest December 16, 1907, from the Brooklyn Navy Yard, Brooklyn, N.Y., on the occasion of the departure of Admiral Robley Dunglison Evans ("Fighting Bob Evans") on a cruise with the fleet.

Solar power 2-way-radio coast-to-coast conversation was effected June 23, 1960, by the U.S. Army Signal Corps, when Colonel Leon J. D. Rouge at Fort Monmouth, N.J., conversed with Sheldon Stern at the transmitter on the roof of the Hoffman Electronics plant at El Monte, Calif. Each terminal station had a 20-foot square panel with 7,800 individual solar cells.

The First

Speaker to address an organization by radio was Dr. Weir Carlyle Ketler, president of Grove City College, Grove City, Pa., who addressed the Rotary Club of New Castle, Pa., 25 miles away, on April 20, 1920. The talk was received by Station 8HA, which amplified it to the audience. Rex Patch of New Castle, Pa., was in charge of the radio reception and amplification. *(Radio News. May 1920)*

Stereophonic sound program broadcast by separately owned stations was broadcast November 5, 1955, from 6:30 P.M. to 8 P.M. by KYW, Cleveland, Ohio, of the Westinghouse Broadcasting Company and WFLN of the Franklin Broadcasting Corporation from the High Fidelity Music Show at the Benjamin Franklin Hotel, Philadelphia, Pa. It was entitled "Sounds of Tomorrow" and was a cooperative undertaking. Listeners were advised to tune in KYW on AM and WFLN on FM, and arrange their sets about 12 feet apart with equal volume to obtain the stereophonic sound.

Submarine (submerged) broadcast was made October 5, 1919, from the U.S.S. *Nautilus* (SS-29) while in the Hudson River. The demonstration was conducted by Lieutenant C. Clark Withers and communication could be received within 50 miles. The *Nautilus* was laid down March 23, 1911.

Tennis match broadcast was the Davis Cup match between Australia and Great Britain, broadcast August 4, 1921, from the Allegheny Country Club, Sewickley, Pa., by KDKA, Pittsburgh, Pa.

Transatlantic broadcast (not experimental) was sent in code January 19, 1903, between Cape Cod, Mass., and Cornwall, England. Greetings were exchanged between King Edward VII and President Theodore Roosevelt.

Transatlantic broadcast of a voice was that of Dr. Harry Phillips Davis, vice president of the Westinghouse Electric and Manufacturing Company, Pittsburgh, Pa., broadcast December 31, 1923, by KDKA, Pittsburgh, via short wave. It was received by 2AZ, a station operated by the Metropolitan Vickers Company, Manchester, England, and rebroadcast to London.

Transatlantic radio message of the regular westward service was sent by Privy Councillor Lord Avebury, formerly Sir John Lubbock, to the New York *Times* from Clifden, Ireland, via Glace Bay, Nova Scotia, October 17, 1907, on regular Marconi transatlantic service. The message sent in code was:

IB Lr Sn Dh & 53 Collect D, PR, Land Lines London Via Marconi Wireless Glace Bay N. S., Oct. 17.

Times, New York

The First

"This message marks opening transatlantic wireless handed Marconi Company for transmission Ireland Breton limited 50 words only send one many messages received Times signalize event quote Trust introduction wireless more closely unite people states Great Britain who seem form one Nation though under two Governments and whose interests are really identical. Avebury Marshall 12:10 A.M. Oct. 17."

Transatlantic radio program from England was transmitted from 8 stations in England: Bournemouth, Cardiff, Glasgow, Birmingham, Newcastle, Manchester, Aberdeen, and Liverpool. It was sent to London and rebroadcast. The programs were received at Garden City, L.I.; Chatham, Mass; Quincy, Mass.; and Tarrytown, N.Y., from 10:00 P.M. to 10:30 P.M. E.S.T., on Sunday, November 25, 1923, when the words *Hello America* and piano selections were heard. All stations in the United States went off the air during this period to enable the broadcast to be heard.

Transatlantic radio signal was sent from Poldhu, Cornwall, by Guglielmo Marconi and was received at St. Johns, Newfoundland. The letter *S* was repeatedly sent by Morse code at stated time intervals and was faintly received by Percy Wright Paget, and by G. S. Kempon, December 11, 1901, and again on December 12, 1901.

Transpacific conversation broadcast was transmitted October 6, 1911, from the steamer *Chive Maru* to the wireless station on Hokkaido (Hokushu) island, northern part of Japan, and received at the Hillcrest station, San Francisco, Calif., approximately 6,000 miles away. The operators exchanged messages.

Underwater transatlantic radio conversation took place October 2, 1965, when aquanauts in Sealab 2, at a depth of 205 feet in the Pacific Ocean off La Jolla, Calif., spoke to French divers in Conshelf 3, at a depth of 330 feet in the Mediterranean Sea off Cape Ferrat, France.

Volcano eruption broadcast via short wave was transmitted by KGU, Honolulu, Hawaii, whose wires extended 3.5 miles from the mouth of the Mount Kilauea volcano to the transmitter. The broadcast was picked up at San Francisco, Calif., and relayed, being heard at 4:15 P.M. on December 28, 1931, by WJZ, New York City, which relayed the broadcast. Thomas A. Jaggar, volcanologist, likened the sound of the erupting volcano to the roar of Niagara and reported that in 6 days about 260,000 cubic feet of lava had been disgorged.

Weather broadcasts for the United States government were made April 26, 1921, by Station WEW, St. Louis, Mo.

Wireless message from an airship over the Atlantic Ocean was sent October 15, 1910, from the dirigible *America* piloted by Walter Wellman. The message—Good start. Everything working

The First

RADIO BROADCAST—*Continued*

well, and have fresh north winds. Fog still thick. Wellman—was sent by Jack Irwin, the wireless operator by Marconi Wireless to the New York *Times* and received at 10:50 A.M.

Yacht race broadcast was made in code October 16, 17, and 20, 1899, off Sandy Hook, N.J. The *Columbia* under Commander John Pierpont Morgan of the New York Yacht Club defeated the *Shamrock* under Sir Thomas Lipton of the Royal Ulster Yacht Club, in three races held for the International Yacht Race trophy (11th contest). The news was transmitted to coast stations and relayed by land wires to the Associated Press. *(Oliver Gramling—AP. The Story of News)*

Zoo broadcast took place at 3:30 P.M. on April 21, 1930, from the Bronx Zoo, New York City. Dr. Claude Willard Leister, curator of educational activities, was master of ceremonies of the program broadcast by National Broadcasting Company radio station WEAF, New York City.

RADIO CAR (military) was designed in 1911 by Colonel Royal Page Davidson at Lake Geneva, Wis., and was equipped with telescopic masts for radio broadcasting. Current for the operation of the radio was generated by the automobile motor. The radio car was also equipped with rapid-fire machine guns and two powerful electric searchlights with helix shutters for flashlight signaling.

RADIO CHURCH was established November 27, 1921, when services of the Radio Church of America were broadcast by Walter J. Garvey from his home, 2000 University Avenue, the Bronx, New York City. Hospitals, military installations, and radio operators were alerted to the program. The sermon was preached by Richard Jay Ward, assisted by Dr. M. H. Leventhal. Solos were sung by Clara Brookhurst and Adele Lauriat Barrow.

RADIO COMMISSION (U.S.) was created on February 23, 1927 (44 Stat. L. 1162), and consisted of five members, Henry Adams Bellows, Admiral William Hannum Grubb Bullard, U.S.N. Ret., Orestes Hampton Caldwell, John Forrest Dillon, and Eugene Octave Sykes, who were granted authority to license broadcasting stations for one year, to determine to whom licenses should be granted and to fix wave lengths and hours of operation. The organization meeting was held March 15, 1927. On March 15, 1928, this authority was placed under the Secretary of Commerce, the commission becoming an appellate body. *(Laurence Frederick Schmeckebier—The Federal Radio Commission)*

RADIO COMPASS on a naval airplane was used July 7, 1920, when a Curtiss F-5-L naval seaplane flew from Norfolk, Va., to the battleship *Ohio*, 95 miles at sea, and returned, guided entirely by radio signals.

The First

RADIO CONFERENCE

National Radio Conference convened in Washington, D.C., on February 27, 1922. It was called by Secretary of Commerce Herbert Clark Hoover to discuss regulations necessary for the industry and was attended by government officials, radio representatives, and radio amateurs.

RADIO CONTEST was held by the United Wireless Telegraph Company in Philadelphia, Pa., February 23, 1910. The American Morse telegraphic code was used in a test of speed and accuracy in receiving and transmitting signals. The winner was Robert F. Miller of the United Wireless Company; Harvey Williams of Western Union was the runner-up.

RADIO DISTRESS SIGNAL

Radio distress signal was the CQD signal which was established January 7, 1904, by General Order Circular No. 57 of the Marconi Company to become effective February 1, 1904. The CQ really meant "Stop sending and listen," while the D was later interpreted as "Danger." The popular interpretation of the call was "Come quick—danger." The SOS distress signal was adopted November 22, 1906, at the International Radio Telegraphic Convention in Berlin, Germany, and superseded the CQD call in July 1908.

Radio distress signal (CQD) from an American ship was sent December 7, 1903, by Ludwig Arnson from the *Kroonland* of the Red Star line, bound from Antwerp to New York City. Heavy seas struck the rudder and broke the tiller on which the steering engine was mounted, leaving the ship out of control. The call, sent out 130 miles west of Fastnet on the Irish coast, was received by the British H.M.S. *Kent*, which arrived about two hours later and towed the disabled ship to Queenstown (now Cobh), Ireland.

Radio distress signal resulting in an airship rescue was sent by Jack K. Irwin, wireless operator of the Wellman dirigible *America*. The Royal Mail steamship *Trent* responded at 7:00 A.M. on October 18, 1910, and rescued the crew of 6 in a lifeboat about 400 miles off Hatteras, N.C. The radio equipment was designed by Archie Frederick Collins. The *America* had taken off from Atlantic City, N.J., October 15, 1910, bound for Europe.

Radio SOS from an American ship was transmitted by Theodore D. Haubner, operator of the Clyde liner *Arapahoe*, a single-screw freight and passenger steamer of some 3,000 tons bound for Charleston and Jacksonville, from New York City. Her engines were disabled 21 miles southeast of Diamond Shoals, off Cape Hatteras, at 3:45 P.M., August 11, 1909. Both the SOS and the CQD signals were sent. The SOS was first heard and acknowledged by R. J. Vosburg, wireless operator at station HA, at Cape Hatteras. Foreign registry ships had used SOS signals earlier.

The First

RADIO FACSIMILE TRANSMISSION

Check sent by radio across the Atlantic Ocean was transmitted on April 20, 1926. It was drawn by General James Guthrie Harbord in London, England, against the Bankers Trust Company of New York City to the amount of $1,000 payable to the Radio Corporation of America.

Color photoradio news photograph transmitted by radio for publication was a photograph of President Harry S. Truman, Generalissimo Josef Stalin, and Prime Minister Clement Richard Attlee, taken at the Potsdam Conference in Germany and transmitted on August 3, 1945, by radiotelephoto to Washington, D.C. A one-shot camera exposed three negatives simultaneously. From the negatives, three black and white prints were made and each placed on a cylinder representing one of the three basic colors, red, blue, and yellow.

Drawing sent by radio across the Atlantic was a sketch of Ambassador Alanson Bigelow Houghton, drawn April 30, 1926, by Augustus John, which was transmitted from London, England, to the New York *Times,* New York City, on May 2, 1926, in 58 minutes.

Facsimile broadcast in ultra-high frequencies was made December 19, 1933, by station W9XAF, Milwaukee, Wis., on frequencies of 42,000–56,000 kilocycles and 60,000–86,000 kilocycles.

Facsimile high-speed transmission was demonstrated October 21, 1948, by the Radio Corporation of America at the Library of Congress, Washington, D.C., using Ultrafax, a system capable of transmitting a million words a minute. The first message was handwritten by Brigadier General David Sarnoff, president and chairman of the board of RCA. Margaret Mitchell's *Gone With the Wind,* 457,000 words, 1,047 pages, was transmitted from WNBW, Washington, D.C., to the Library of Congress, a distance of three miles, in 2 minutes and 21 seconds.

Facsimile transmitted to a moving train as a public demonstration was sent June 4, 1946, by Robert Emmet Hannegan, postmaster general of the United States, from the law library in the Capitol, Washington, D.C., and received on a test car moving from Baltimore, Md., to Washington, D.C., on the Baltimore and Ohio Railroad. The message, "What hath God wrought," written and signed by Margaret Truman, daughter of President Harry S. Truman, was the same as the telegraph message inaugurating commercial service over the same route. It was sent over WCBM, Baltimore, Md.

Motion picture film transmitted by telephone wire was a 2-hour transmission from Chicago, Ill., of 10 feet of film of Vilma Banky received April 4, 1928, at the American Telephone and Telegraph Company's New York studio. The negatives were

The First

placed between glass plates, rephotographed, and reassembled. There were only 8 telephonic sending-and-receiving stations in the United States. The feat had been attempted 2 years earlier, but the images received were blurred.

Photograph sent by radio across the Atlantic was a picture of Charles Evans Hughes, Secretary of State, transmitted on July 6, 1924, from the RCA Laboratories, New York City, by phototelegraphy to New Brunswick, N.J., then by radio to Brentwood, England, by wire to London, England, whence it was relayed back by wire to Carnarvon, Wales, then by radio to Riverhead, L.I., N.Y., and by wire to New York City, where it was recorded in the same room from which it was originally transmitted. It was not recorded in England, as there were no recording sets there at that time.

Photograph sent by radio across the Atlantic as a public demonstration was transmitted on November 30, 1924, from the Marconi offices in the Strand, London, England, and were received at 66 Broad Street, New York City. Pictures were sent of President Calvin Coolidge; Prime Minister Stanley Baldwin; Secretary of Foreign Affairs Austen Chamberlain; Secretary of State Charles Evans Hughes; the Prince of Wales; Owen D. Young; the Oxford team winning a relay race at Cambridge; the steamship *Reclamation* aground in the Thames River; and a photograph of the Chinese proverb "One picture is worth ten thousand words." The pictures were published December 1, 1924, in the New York *Herald Tribune.* Other pictures were sent of Queen Alexandria; Ambassador Frank Billings Kellogg; and of Donald Gordon Ward, sending the pictures from London.

Photograph sent by radio across the Atlantic from Europe was a photograph of Pope Pius XI, transmitted June 11, 1922, from Rome by Dr. Arthur Korn, a German physicist. It was published in the New York *World* on Sunday, June 11, 1922. The picture, a halftone 7 by 9½ inches, was received 40 minutes after transmission by Chief Radioman Edmund H. Hansen, U.S.N., at Bar Harbor, Maine. Light falling on a selenium cell produced a group of shaded dots which formed a halftone. *(Terry Korn and Elizabeth M. Korn— Trailblazer to Television)*

Photograph sent by radio across the Atlantic inaugurating commercial service was transmitted from London, England, on April 30, 1926, at 7 P.M. New York Daylight Saving Time. A photograph of the Pilgrims' Society dinner addressed to the New York *Times* was transmitted in 1 hour 25 minutes and reproduced in the May 1, 1926, issue. The operation was under the direction of Richard Howland Ranger. Three other photographs were transmitted. The following day, ten pictures were transmitted from London, among them four fashion plates. Transmission from New York to Lon-

The First

RADIO FACSIMILE TRANSMISSION—*Continued*

don commenced at midnight April 30, 1926. On May 1, 1926, nine pictures were sent.

Photograph sent by radio across the continent was a photograph of President Calvin Coolidge's inauguration on March 4, 1925, taken in Washington, D.C. One picture was sent every 12 minutes, the actual time for transmission being seven minutes. Nine photographs were sent to New York, Chicago, and San Francisco by the American Telegraph and Telephone Company.

Photograph sent by radio across the continent (commercial) was sent April 18, 1925, from San Francisco, Calif., and received in New York City by the American Telegraph and Telephone Company. The photograph, taken in Culver City, Calif., showed Marion Davies receiving a gift of a make-up box from Louis Burt Mayer of Metro-Goldwyn-Mayer Pictures.

Photograph sent overland by radio to a distant point was transmitted March 3, 1923, from radio station NOF, Anacostia, D.C., to the *Evening Bulletin*, Philadelphia, Pa. Photographs were transmitted of President Warren Gamaliel Harding, Secretary of Commerce Herbert Clark Hoover, Governor Gifford Pinchot of Pennsylvania, and others. *(Philadelphia Evening Bulletin. March 3, 1923)*

Photographs sent over a city telephone were transmitted on October 3, 1922, by Charles Francis Jenkins from 1519 Connecticut Avenue, Washington, D.C., to United States Navy Radio Station NOF at Anacostia, D.C., in the presence of Commander Albert Hoyt Taylor, U.S.N., and James Clark Edgerton of the Post Office Department. The signals were recorded on a photographic plate at 5502 16th Street, N.W., Washington, D.C. *(Charles Francis Jenkins—Vision by Radio, Radio Photographs)*

Press syndicate facsimile transmission direct to newspaper offices was an 8-by-10-inch air view of an American Airlines Curtiss Condor transport plane which had crashed in the Adirondack Mountains, 10 miles from Newhouseville, N.Y., on a flight from Cleveland, Ohio, to Boston, Mass. The facsimile was transmitted to newspapers in 24 cities by the Wirephoto service of the Associated Press on January 1, 1935. The picture was transmitted simultaneously to the newspapers over a leased wire in eight minutes.

Radio facsimile broadcasting on the regular broadcast band was instituted February 4, 1938, by WHO (Central Broadcasting Company), Des Moines, Iowa. The facsimile was on 1,000 kilocycles from 12:00 (midnight) to 12:36 A.M.

Radio facsimile long-distance transmission of a medical subject was made on May 28, 1925, when the American Telegraph and Telephone Company

The First

transmitted stethogram and electrocardiogram pictures or graphs showing heartbeats from its New York office to Chicago, Ill. Dr. James Richard Greer of Chicago diagnosed the charts, his report being heard by the American Medical Association in convention at the Steel Pier, Atlantic City, N.J. *(Journal of the American Medical Association. Vol. 84, No. 24. June 13, 1925)*

Radio facsimile newspaper. *See* Newspaper radio facsimile newspaper

Radio facsimile patent was No. 785,803, awarded March 28, 1905, to Cornelius D. Ehret of Rosemont, Pa., for "the art of transmitting intelligence." He also received patent No. 785,804 the same day for "a system of transmitting intelligence."

Transpacific and transcontinental facsimile transmission was made May 6, 1925, from Honolulu, Hawaii, to Kahuku by wire; to Marshall, Calif., by radio; to Bolinas, Calif., by radio; to Riverhead, L.I., N.Y., by radio; to New York City, by wire—a total distance of 5,136 miles. Pictures of war games, of Major General John Leonard Hines, of Rear Admiral Robert Edward Coontz, and of Governor Wallace Rider Farrington were transmitted by Alfred J. Koenig, using the transmitter designed by Captain Richard Howland Ranger.

RADIO FOG SIGNAL. *See* Radio beacons

RADIO IMPULSE TRANSMISSION (wireless) was accomplished by Joseph Henry in Princeton, N.J., in December, 1840. Current obtained from a group of Leyden jars was passed through a wire which by means of a magnetized needle produced a vibration on another line about 100 feet away. The lines were not connected with each other; the transmission was the result of induction.

RADIO INSTRUCTION

Radio-advertising course in a college was instituted by the School of Business and Civic Administration of the City College of New York September 28, 1930, under the direction of Frank Atkinson Arnold, director of development of the National Broadcasting Company. Lectures on the technique of broadcasting as applied to the preparation of programs, both sponsored and sustaining, were given. The class consisted of 62 students. Two college credits were given for the 14-week course of 2-hour lectures on Mondays; 45 minutes of each lecture was devoted to questions and answers and informal discussions. *(Broadcasting Magazine. Oct. 15, 1931)*

Radio college course was a four-year combined program in liberal arts and radio with full college credit leading to the degree of Bachelor of Arts, offered by New York University in September 1939 in the Washington Square College of Arts and Science. The course consisted of writing for radio, speaking on the radio, the use of music on

The First

the radio, announcing, the planning of radio programs, production, news broadcasting, broadcasting of special events, etc.

RADIO LEGISLATION (national) was the Wireless Ship Act of June 24, 1910 (36 Stat. L. 629), effective July 1, 1911, which required wireless equipment on all passenger vessels carrying 50 or more persons as passengers or crew.

RADIO LICENSE
Experimental radio license issued by the Department of Commerce following the International Radio Convention and Radio Act of 1912 (37 Stat. L. 302), August 13, 1912, was serial No. 1, granted St. Joseph's College, Philadelphia, Pa. (3XJ, 2 kilowatts).

Frequency modulation (FM) construction permit was granted August 18, 1937, to W1XOJ, the Yankee Network, Inc., Paxton, Mass. It went on the air with scheduled programs in May 1939 and subsequently operated with the highest output power (50 kilowatts) granted previous to World War II. Call letters were changed to W43B, and later to WGTR. The programs were fed from the studios in Boston, Mass., by an FM circuit.

Frequency modulation transmitter to receive a commercial license was W47NV, Nashville, Tenn., which operated on a frequency of 44,700 kilocycles with a power of 20,000 watts, licensed to cover a 16,000-square-mile radius. It began operations March 1, 1941, with full commercial status and presented the commercial of Standard Candy Company, Nashville, Tenn.

International broadcasting license issued by the Federal Communications Commission was granted October 15, 1927, to the Experimenter Publishing Company, New York City. The frequency was 9,700 kilocycles and the power 500 watts. The station was taken over in 1929 and subsequently moved to Boston, Mass., where it was operated as W1XAL by the World Wide Broadcasting Corporation.

Radio license issued in the United States was granted George Hill Lewis of Cincinnati, Ohio, in 1911.

Radio station licensed was KDKA, Pittsburgh, Pa., licensed October 27, 1920. At that time broadcasting was not recognized as such. When broadcasting stations received licenses, WBZ, of the Westinghouse Electric and Manufacturing Company, Springfield, Mass., a 1,500-watt station operating on 360 meters, was awarded license No. 224 on September 15, 1921, by the Bureau of Navigation, Department of Commerce.

RADIO MAGAZINE was *Modern Electrics*, published April 1908 by Hugo Gernsback, Modern Electrics Publication, New York City. The first issue contained 36 pages and cover. Subscription was $1 a year.

The First

RADIO MICROPHONE (carbon) for radio broadcasting was employed by Dr. Lee De Forest in 1907 in his laboratory at the Parker Building, 19th Street and Fourth Avenue, New York City. It was of the ordinary telephone variety. *(Georgette Carneal—A Conqueror of Space, an Authorized Biography of the Life and Work of Lee De Forest)*

RADIO ORCHESTRA. *See* Orchestra

RADIO PAGING SERVICE was instituted October 15, 1950, in the New York City area by Aircall, Inc., New York City. The first call was for a doctor who was on a golf course 25 miles away. An experimental license was issued by the Federal Communications Commission on September 8, 1948, for station K2XAQ, operating on five frequencies in the 72-73 megacycle range. On October 18, 1949, license KEA627 was granted for operation in the New York City area on 43.58 megacycles. Subscribers equipped with six-ounce Aircall pocket radio receivers could hear their call numbers repeated in numerical sequence on the air at least once per minute within a 30-mile area.

RADIO PATENT of importance was patent No. 465,971, granted December 29, 1891, to Thomas Alva Edison of Menlo Park, N.J., on a "means for transmitting signals electrically." In the patent, he claimed that "signalling between distant points can be carried on by induction without the use of wires connecting such distant points." His application was filed May 23, 1885.

RADIO RECEIVER
Hotel to install radio reception. *See under* Hotel

Parade in which all the marching music was supplied by transistor radio receivers. *See* Parade: Parade in which all the marching music was supplied by transistor radio receivers

Radio receiver advertised was the Telimco (an acronym of The Electro Importing Company), a $7.50 outfit announced in a one-inch advertisement in the January 13, 1906, issue of the *Scientific American* inserted by Hugo Gernsback of the Electro Importing Company of New York. The advertisement offered a "complete outfit comprising one inch spark coil, balls, key, coherer with auto decoherer and sounder, 50 ohm relay, 4 cell dry battery, send and catch wires and connections with instructions and diagrams. Will work up to one mile. Unprecedented introduction prices. Agents wanted. Illustrated pamphlet."

Radio receiver with an auxiliary silicon unit to convert the rays of the sun into electrical power was the Sun Power Pak, made by the Admiral Corporation, Chicago, Ill., which was first developed in October 1955 and offered for sale on April 16, 1956. The radio weighed 5¼ pounds and contained 6 transistors in place of vacuum tubes. It was 2⅞ inches thick, 8¾ inches high and 10⅜ inches long and cost $59.95. It was operated by six ordinary flashlight batteries lasting from 700 to

The First

RADIO RECEIVER—*Continued*

1,000 hours. The auxiliary Sun Power Pak, which converted energy into power, cost $185 additional. It had a 32 silicon "solar cell element" to pick up rays from the sun or from an incandescent bulb.

Transistor radio receiver mass-produced was the Regency Radio, manufactured by the Regency Division of Industrial Development Engineering Associates, Inc., Indianapolis, Ind. The first shipments to dealers were made in October 1954. The receiver was 3 inches by 5 inches by 1¼ inches and weighed 12 ounces. It had no tubes but instead contained four transistors. It was powered entirely by a 22½ volt B battery.

RADIO RECEIVING CONTEST

Radio receiving contest in which a speed of more than 50 words a minute was recorded was held May 7, 1922, at the Boston Radio Show, Boston Mass. Theodore R. McElroy, Boston *Herald* telegraph operator, recorded 51½ words a minute, transmitted by an automatic sending machine, typing for 3 minutes without making a mistake. In a contest on May 24, 1922, at the New York Radio Show, 71st Regiment Armory, New York City, May 22-27, 1922, he typed perfect copy for 2 minutes at 50½ words a minute, and won a silver cup inscribed Presented to the Champion Radio Code Operator of the World.

Radio receiving contest was held October 8, 1921, at the New York Electrical Show, 71st Armory, New York City. The open championship was won by B. G. Seutter, wireless operator of the transatlantic receiving division of the New York *Times*, who received from Major Andrew White the National Amateur Wireless Association award cup donated by the New York Edison Company. Seutter received code at 44-1/3 words a minute with no mistakes.

RADIO SEXTANT was made by the Collins Radio Company, Cedar Rapids, Iowa, and announced publicly July 14, 1954, although it had been used in February 1952 as a secret device on naval ships. It determined the sun's position automatically and continuously through reception of microwave energy emitted from the sun.

RADIO SOCIETY was the Wireless Association of America, formed in New York City, November 1908, with Dr. Lee De Forest as president, Dr. John Stone, vice president, William Mauver, Jr., secretary, and Hugo Gernsback, chairman and business manager. There were no dues and no obligations. Within a few months, more than 3,000 members were enrolled.

RADIO STATION

All-local network was formed May 15, 1950, by five local stations: WARL, Arlington, Va., 1,000 watts; WGAY, Silver Spring, Md., 1000 watts; WPIK, Alexandria, Va., 1,000 watts; WBCC, Bethesda, Md., 250 watts; and WFAX, Falls Church,

The First

Va., 250 watts. The time on all five stations was offered at $300 an hour.

All-news radio station was WINS, New York City, which broadcast news round-the-clock on April 19, 1965, on 1010 AM. Previously, it had broadcast rock 'n' roll.

Black network was the National Negro Network, formed January 20, 1954. The first program was "The Story of Ruby Valentine," starring Juanita Hall, broadcast January 25, 1954, on 40 stations. It was sponsored five days a week alternately by Philip Morris & Co., Ltd., and Pet Milk Company. The New York outlet was WOV.

College radio station was WRUC, Union College, Schenectady, N.Y., which went on the air on October 14, 1920, and instituted a series of weekly programs on October 15, 1920, consisting of vocal and instrumental phonograph records. The programs were broadcast from 8:00 P.M. to 8:30 P.M. with a 3-minute interval. They were initially heard within a 50-mile radius; this increased under favorable weather conditions. A five 50-watt U-tube transmitter was used. Frederic L. Ganter was president of the Radio Club of Union College; Wendell W. King, the chief engineer; and Francis J. Campbell, the chief operator. The station was owned by the trustees of the college.

Commercial radio station was 8MK licensed August 20, 1920 (now WWJ, Detroit, Mich.), which instituted daily service on August 20, 1920, with the program "Tonight's Dinner." Local election returns were broadcast August 31, 1920. KDKA, Pittsburgh, Pa., offered a semiweekly broadcast from November 2, 1920, to December 1, 1920. KDKA was licensed October 27, 1920.

Educational radio station licensed was WOI, Iowa State College of Agriculture and Mechanical Arts, which received the call letters 9Y1 (375 meters frequency, using 100 watts) on November 21, 1921. On April 28, 1922, the station was granted a license to broadcast on 360 meters (834 kc) using 1,000 watts.

Municipal radio station was WRR, Dallas, Tex. (50 watts), established in 1920 to broadcast fire alarms. So that owners of radio receivers could check to determine whether they were tuned to the station, phonograph records were played. In 1925 the station began selling time to sponsors.

Municipal school-owned ultra-high-frequency radio station to receive a license from the Federal Communications Commission was station WBOE, Cleveland, Ohio, granted license No. 1, November 21, 1938, to operate (500 watts, 41,500 kilocycles). Regular classroom lessons and music were broadcast Monday through Friday from 8:30 A.M. to 4:30 P.M. The station became an FM station in February 1941.

The First

Naval radio station was established in 1903 at the Highlands of Navesink, N.J. Chief Radioman Jack Scanlin was in charge.

Newspaper to operate a radio station. *See* Newspaper: Newspaper to operate a radio station

Radio station operating a 50-kilowatt transmitter was 2XAG, Schenectady, N.Y., using the 379.5 meter wave band, the same length as WGY, Schenectady, N.Y. The station was tested July 25, 1925, and placed in operation July 29, 1925.

Radio station operating a 100-kilowatt transmitter was 2XAG, Schenectady, N.Y., which was granted a 30-day permit to operate between the hours of 1 and 2 A.M. It went on the air August 4, 1927. Harry Hadenwater was in charge of broadcasting.

Radio station owned and operated by blacks was WERD, 1,000 watts, Atlanta, Ga., opened October 3, 1949. It was owned by Radio Atlanta, Inc., of which Jesse Bee Blayton was president.

Radio station with 500,000-watt power was KDKA, Pittsburgh, Pa., authorized to use call letters W8XAR from June 12, 1936, to May 1, 1938, to test high-power equipment (50 kw to 500 kw) from 1 A.M. to 6 A.M. on an experimental basis.

Seagoing radio broadcasting station was the 5,-800-ton, 338-foot Coast Guard cutter *Courier,* commissioned February 15, 1952, at Hoboken, N.J., and dedicated March 4, 1952, by President Harry S. Truman at a pier on the Potomac River, Washington, D.C. The ship had a 150,000-watt medium-wave transmitter and two 35,000-watt shortwave transmitters. It was used to broadcast the Department of State's "Voice of America" program to Eurasian areas. The first official test was made April 2, 1952, off the coast of Colombia, South America, and the first broadcast from European waters September 7, 1952, off the island of Rhodes, Greece. The *Courier* was a 1945 Navy cargo ship converted and equipped at a cost of over $2 million. The first captain was Oscar Cottman Buckingham Wev.

RADIO TELEPHONE
See also Telephone

Military portable superregenerative receiver and transmitter, known as the "Walkie-Talkie," was built in 1933 at the Signal Corps Engineering Laboratories, Fort Monmouth, N.J. The personnel principally concerned with this project were John Hessel, radio mechanic; C. W. Hayhurst, mechanical design engineer; and John Reid, shop mechanic. Commercial production was undertaken in 1934 by the Allen D. Cardwell Company, Brooklyn, N.Y.

The First

Radio telephone communication between the ground and an airplane took place July 2, 1917, at Langley Field, Va., where speech of good volume and quality was received from a transmitting plane two miles away. On July 4, 1917, speech from the ground was received by L. M. Clement of the Western Electric Company in a plane several miles away. On August 18 the first two-way communication was established between a plane and the ground, and on August 20, 1917, between two planes, all at Langley Field.

Radio telephone communication (one-way) was established April 4, 1915, by Bell System engineers from Montauk Point, L.I., N.Y., to Wilmington, Del., a distance of 250 miles.

Radio telephone concert transcontinental was broadcast by General Electric Company, Schenectady, N.Y. on March 25, 1922 on a 360 meter wave length and heard at the Rock Ridge station at Oakland, Calif.

Radio telephone conversation between someone on the ground and a person in a dirigible took place May 16, 1925, when Arthur Atwater Kent on board the dirigible *Los Angeles* conversed with his wife, who was in an automobile in Philadelphia, Pa. A single wire 300 feet long trailed from the airship.

Radio telephone marine demonstration of wireless telephony was held on board the steamer *Bartholdi* on the Potomac River, March 20, 1902. The apparatus and equipment used were the inventions of Nathan B. Stubblefield of Murray, Ky.

Radio telephone service (commercial) was inaugurated July 16, 1920, between Los Angeles and Santa Catalina Island, Calif. The radio link to telephone land lines was between Long Beach, Calif., and the town of Avalon on the island. The service was maintained by the Bell Telephone System for three years until it was replaced by cable because "speech-scrambling" devices had not yet been developed and the messages could be picked up by anyone capable of tuning a receiving set.

Radio telephone ship-to-shore commercial service was inaugurated December 8, 1929, when Walter Sherman Gifford, president of the American Telephone and Telegraph Company, lifted a receiver in New York City and spoke to Commodore Harold A. Cunningham of the S.S. *Leviathan.* The first personal call was made by William Hector Rankin, a New York advertising man, to Sir Thomas Lipton, aboard the liner. The rate varied from $7 to $11 a minute, depending upon the zone. *(American Telephone and Telegraph Co.— The Magic of Communication)*

The First

RADIO TELEPHONE—*Continued*

Radio telephone ship-to-shore conversation (radiophone noncommercial) took place May 6, 1916, over the regular telephone network to demonstrate a way of mobilizing the telephone and telegraph in case of war. Captain Lloyd Horwitz Chandler of the battleship *New Hampshire,* while at sea off Hampton Roads, Va., reported and received orders from Secretary of the Navy Josephus Daniels and Admiral William Shepherd Benson in Washington, D.C.

Telephone call to the moon was made by President Richard Milhous Nixon on July 20, 1969, to Neil Alden Armstrong and Edwin E. Aldrin, Jr., on *Apollo XI,* which had been launched July 16, 1969.

Transatlantic radio telephone message was transmitted October 21, 1915, from Arlington, Va., to Paris. The voice of B. B. Webb was heard by Herbert E. Shreeve and Austen M. Custis of the American Telephone and Telegraph Company and by Lieutenant Colonel Ferrie of the French government at the receiving station installed in the Eiffel Tower by Bell System engineers.

Transcontinental radio telephone demonstration was given September 29, 1915, when speech was transmitted from New York City to Arlington, Va., and thence by radio telephone to Mare Island at San Francisco, Calif., 2,500 miles away, and also to Honolulu that night.

Two-way conversation between a glider and the land was effected August 12, 1932, at 2:40 P.M. over the WEAF radio network by Jack O'Meara, a gliding champion, who was circling over the Empire State Building, New York City, in the *Chanute,* at an altitude of more than 5,000 feet, and Edward Thorgeson, a radio announcer. A test message was sent August 9, 1932, over Coney Island and Manhattan, New York City.

Two-way radio conversation between a brakeman in a caboose of a moving freight train and an engineer in the cab of a locomotive, a mile and a quarter away, was demonstrated June 15, 1927, by engineers of the General Electric Company, Schenectady, N.Y. Caboose and engine carried identical apparatus, a transmitter and a receiver. Communication was established at either end of the train by the simple act of removing a receiver and pressing a button.

Two-way radio conversation between a submerged submarine and another vessel was held October 5, 1919, between the U.S. submarine H-2, commanded by Lieutenant Commander Clark Withers, and the destroyer *Blakely.* The submarine was submerged in the Hudson River off 96th Street, New York City.

Two-way-radio-equipped bus was placed in service by the Arnold Lines (the Washington, Virginia and Maryland Coach Company, Inc.) on September 8, 1945. Tests were made July 8, 1945,

The First

and a permanent Federal Communications Commission license to operate was granted November 13, 1945.

Two-way radio in an automobile was installed by the Chalmers-Detroit Company in an automobile of its manufacture in March 1910 in New York City. The sending set contained two storage cells, a ten-inch spark coil, two Leyden jars, and a high and low voltage battery, a seven-foot aerial, etc. Successful demonstrations were made from the moving automobile in Central Park, New York City, to the Terminal Building, 42nd Street and Park Avenue, New York City, at distances varying from one to three miles. *(Scientific American. May 14, 1910)*

RADIO TELEVISION. *See* Television

RADIO TUBE

Radio tube made of metal was announced April 1, 1935, by the General Electric Company, Schenectady, N.Y. Metal tubes are smaller than the less-sturdy conventional glass tubes and provide their own shielding. They are particularly advantageous in the field of shortwave reception because the metal shell is a better heat conductor and radiator than glass.

Three-element vacuum tube was announced to the public by Dr. Lee De Forest of New York City at the October 20, 1906, meeting of the American Institute of Electrical Engineers held in New York City. The first three-element tube (filament and two plate electrodes), described as an amplifier of feeble electrical currents, was patented by Dr. Lee De Forest, January 15, 1907, No. 841,387 on a "device for amplifying feeble electrical currents." The first public description of the grid electrode tube was contained in another one of his patents, No. 879,532, February 18, 1908. The name "audion" was given to the tube by Clifford D. Babcock. *(Georgette Carneal—A Conqueror of Space: An Authorized Biography of the Life and Work of Lee De Forest)*

RADIOACTIVE ISOTOPE (medicine). *See under* Isotope

RADIOACTIVE SUBSTANCE PRODUCED SYNTHETICALLY. *See under* Physics

RADIOGRAPH. *See* X ray

RADIOPHOTOGRAPHY. *See* Radio facsimile transmission

RAG PAPER. *See* Paper: Wood pulp and rag paper

RAGTIME INSTRUCTION BOOK. *See under* Music book

RAIL-DETECTOR CAR. *See* Railroad car

RAILROAD
   See also

Railroad accident	Railroad legislation
Railroad apprentice	Railroad passenger

The First

school	Railroad signal sys-
Railroad car	tem
Railroad charter	Railroad station
Railroad commission	Railroad technical
(state)	report
Railroad coupler	Railroad track
Railroad crossing	Railroad train rob-
gate patent	bery
Railroad excursion	Railroad treatise
Railroad guide	

Air-conditioned train was installed by the Baltimore and Ohio Railroad Company, which began this service on the *Columbian* on Sunday, May 24, 1931, in both directions between Washington and New York. The westbound train left New York City at 3:57 P.M. and the eastbound train left Washington at 4 P.M. Each train was made up of the following cars, all of which were air-conditioned and air-cooled: individual-seat smoking car, individual-seat coach, lounge car, colonial dining car, one Pullman parlor car, and one observation sunroom parlor car. The train was drawn by one of the President series of twenty locomotives. *(The First Air Conditioned Train in History, B. & O. Railroad)*

Air-rail passenger service. *See* Aviation: Air-rail passenger transcontinental service

Auto-train to transport passengers and their automobiles on the same train was Auto-Train, which began daily service on December 6, 1971, between Lorton, Va. (outside Washington, D.C.), and Sanford, Fla. (north of Orlando, Fla.). At full complement, it consisted of 13 auto-carriers, 2 buffet-movie cars, 5 coaches, 4 bedroom cars, 2 locomotives, a steam-generator car, and a kitchen car. Automobiles were loaded on 2-level, enclosed, piggyback cars. Passengers rode in bilevel domed coaches; bedroom accommodations at an extra charge. One-way fare was $190 for an automobile and up to 4 people, with charge of $15 for each additional passenger up to the legal maximum of the shipped auto's capacity. A buffet dinner, late-evening snacks, a continental breakfast, and movies were included in the charge. The train could transport 100 cars and 400 people.

Cog railroad in the world was the Mount Washington Cog Railway, which ran to the summit of Mount Washington, N.H. The railway was invented by Sylvester Marsh of Littleton, N.H. Work was begun in May 1866 and the first public demonstration was made at the base on August 29, 1866, on a half-mile section. The railway was completed in July 1869 at a cost of $139,500. *(Guy Roberts and Frank Hunt Burt—Mount Washington; Its Past and Present)*

Daily railroad service to the Pacific Coast, with a change at Omaha, was established in 1887. On November 17, 1889, through service without a change was inaugurated between Chicago and Portland, Oreg., and between Chicago and San

The First

Francisco, Calif., by the Union Pacific Railroad Company. This train was the *Overland Limited.*

Dirigible transfer of mail to a train. *See under* Aviation—Airship

Electrically lighted train was the *Pennsylvania Limited* of the Pennsylvania Railroad Company, placed in service June 1887, between Chicago and New York. Steam from the engine was carried to a turbine in the forward compartment of the baggage car, where it drove an electric generator supplying current to the entire train. *(Pennsylvania Railroad Information Bulletin. June 1928)*

Gasoline-driven, stainless-steel, air-conditioned, pneumatic-tire, two-car train was built by the Edward G. Budd Manufacturing Co. of Philadelphia, Pa., in 1933 and was delivered to the Texas and Pacific Railway Company at Dallas, Tex., November 4, 1933. The overall weight was 104,000 pounds. The car was equipped with two 240 h.p. engines. It was placed in service between Fort Worth and Texarkana, Tex., making one round trip a day, a total distance of 490 miles.

Government operation of railroads began January 1, 1918. A proclamation was made by President Woodrow Wilson, December 26, 1917, and William Gibbs McAdoo, Secretary of the Treasury, was appointed director general. The railroads were returned to private ownership March 1, 1920.

Hotel transported. *See* Hotel: Hotel transported

Inclined railroad was erected in 1764 at Lewiston, N.Y., by British soldiers under the command of Captain John Montresor, for transporting supplies between the Niagara portage and the lower Niagara River, 300 feet below. The road consisted of two sets of parallel logs laid up the banks on stone piers from the ship wharf below to the portage above. The logs were deeply grooved to receive the wheels of two cradle cars. The cars were joined by heavy ropes passed around a revolving drum to balance when one car was at the bottom, and the other at the top. Originally, the road was used solely for military purposes by the troops, but later it was used for transporting merchandise.

International railroad was the Atlantic and St. Lawrence Railroad, construction of which began July 4, 1846. The first trains ran from Portland, Maine, to Montreal, Canada, on July 18, 1853, covering 292 miles in less than 12 hours. On August 5, 1853, the line was leased to the Grand Trunk Railway of Canada for 999 years. *(Edward Everett Chase—Maine Railroads)*

Interstate railroad was the Petersburg Railroad, chartered by special act of the General Assembly of Virginia on February 10, 1830, and by special act of the North Carolina Legislature on January 1, 1831. It was opened in 1833 from Petersburg, Va., to Blakely, N.C., a distance of 59 miles along the north bank of the Roanoke River. On Novem-

The First

RAILROAD—*Continued*
ber 21, 1898, it became part of the system now known as the Atlantic Coast Line Railroad Company.

Loop-the-loop railway. *See* Loop-the-loop centrifugal railway

Municipal railroad was the Cincinnati Southern Railway, whose regular passenger service began July 23, 1877, between Cincinnati, Ohio, and Ludlow and Somerset, Ky. Freight service started August 13, 1877. Construction was authorized by the Ohio legislature, May 4, 1869, with an "act to authorize cities of the first class to build railroads and to lease or operate the same." Freight service between Cincinnati and Chattanooga, Tenn., was inaugurated February 21, 1880, and through passenger trains on March 5, 1880. The railroad was leased on October 12, 1881, to the Cincinnati, New Orleans and Texas Pacific Railway Company for five five-year periods. *(Henry Paine Boyden—The Beginnings of the Cincinnati Southern Railway)*

Newspaper delivery train. *See under* Newspaper

"Piggyback" railroad operation began January 5, 1885, on the Long Island Rail Road Company when a produce train, consisting of eight flatcars for carrying farmers' wagons, eight cars to carry their horses, and a coach for teamsters, left Albertson's Station, Long Island, N.Y., and arrived at Long Island City at 6:30 A.M. At 7 A.M., a ferry carried the wagons across the East River to New York City.

Pullman sleeping car. *See under* Sleeping car

Railroad bridge. *See under* Bridge

Railroad car. *See* Railroad car

Railroad for commercial transportation of passengers and freight was the Baltimore and Ohio Railroad Company. It was incorporated in the state of Maryland February 28, 1827. The incorporation was confirmed by the state of Virginia, March 8, 1827. Stock was subscribed to provide funds for its execution April 1, 1827. The first board of directors was elected April 23, 1827, with Philip E. Thomas as president. The company was organized April 24, 1827. Construction began at Baltimore, Md., July 4, 1828. The first passenger revenue was obtained January 7, 1830. Tickets were 9 cents each or three tickets for 25 cents for a ride from Pratt Street to the Carrollton Viaduct. Passengers rode at first primarily for the novelty and experience. *(The Fair of the Iron Horse—B. & O. Railroad)*

Railroad for freight transportation was a tramroad built in 1809 by John Thompson for Thomas Leiper to carry stone from his quarries on Crum Creek to Ridley Creek, Pa., a distance of about three fourths of a mile. Wooden rails rested on sleepers eight feet apart. The cars had grooved

The First

wheels and were pulled by horses. The service was in operation for 19 years.

Railroad for freight transportation to celebrate its centenary was the Granite Railway Company of Massachusetts, which was incorporated by Massachusetts on March 4, 1826, for the "conveyance of stone and other property" with a capital of $1 million. The first president was Thomas Handasyd Perkins. Work on the road was begun April 1, 1826, and was completed October 7, 1826. The tracks were five-foot gauge, and the rails were pine, a foot deep and covered with oak plate and then with flat bars of iron. The cost was about $50,000. Horses and oxen supplied the power. The railroad was constructed by Gridley Bryant and was used to carry heavy blocks of granite for the building of the Bunker Hill Monument from the quarries at Quincy, Mass., to the docks about three miles away at Milton, Mass. It was also the first American railroad to cover the wooden rails with iron plates.

Railroad freight yard fully automatic was the Elgin, Joliet and Eastern Railway Company's Kirk Yard at Gary, Ind., which began operating under manual control on January 25, 1952, and changed to fully automatic operation on December 17, 1954. Radar and electronic brain circuits were used to sort out and assemble freight cars by destination, weigh them automatically, and couple them into trains. The equipment was installed by the General Railway Signal Company, Rochester, N.Y. *(Modern Railroads. October 1953)*

Railroad merger of importance was the agreement of May 17, 1853, in which ten companies consolidated under the title of New York Central Railroad Company with an aggregate capital of $23,085,000. On April 2, 1853, an act was passed by the New York legislature "to authorize the consolidation of certain railroad companies." Thirteen directors were selected on July 6, 1853, and on August 1, 1853, the company began to operate under its own officers. The equipment consisted of 187 first-class passenger coaches; 55 second-class coaches; 65 baggage, mail, and express cars; and 1,702 freight cars. There were 298 miles of main line, 236 miles of branch line, and 29 miles of leased road.

Railroad operated by an electric third-rail system was the Lackawanna & Wyoming Valley Railroad Company (Laurel Company), which commenced operations in Scranton, Pa., May 25, 1903. After the system had been tried out successfully in Scranton, the elevated railway in New York City was electrified with a third rail.

Railroad operated by the federal government was the Alaska Railroad acquired under the Alaska Railroad Enabling Act, March 12, 1914 (38 Stat.L.305), from various private railroad companies. The golden spike was driven by President Warren Gamaliel Harding at Nenana, Alaska, on

The First

July 15, 1923. The railroad, which operates 478 miles of single mainline-track, is under the control of the Federal Railroad Administration within the U.S. Department of Transportation.

Railroad shipments of dressed beef (year-round, long-distance) were made in 1877 by Gustavus Franklin Swift of Swift & Company, who shipped meat from Chicago in ten refrigerated cars built to his own specifications. The beef was hung from racks, and the floor was covered with boxes and cases.

Railroad to be completely equipped with diesel-electric engines was the New York, Susquehanna and Western Railroad. The first diesel unit was placed in service December 27, 1941, and on May 25, 1945, the last of a fleet of 16, completely dispensing with other types of engines, was put in operation. The diesels were built by the American Locomotive Company, New York City, and the General Electric Company, Schenectady, N.Y.

Railroad to carry troops was the Baltimore and Ohio Railroad Company, which on June 30, 1831, transported Brigadier General George H. Steuart, First Division Maryland Guards, and about 100 volunteer troops to Sykes Mills (now Sykesville), Md., where they quelled a riot of railroad workmen by arresting about 50 of them who were striking for back pay due.

Railroad to install gasoline-mechanical cars in regular service was the Pennsylvania Railroad Company, which placed them in operation in February 1923 on the Berwick, Flemington and Bustleton branches in the Philadelphia district. These cars superseded local passenger trains whose operation was unprofitable. They were replaced in 1926 by gasoline-electric cars.

Railroad to install track water tanks for trains to take water on the run was the Pennsylvania. A track tank was placed in the northbound track at Sang Hollow on the Pittsburgh division during the early months of 1870. In the same year a 1,200-foot tank was put down in the southbound track at the same location. In the same year, the New York Central installed track tanks between Montrose and Albany.

Railroad to run trains to Washington, D.C., was the Baltimore and Ohio Railroad. On July 1, 1835, the president, directors, and other officers of the road made a trial run from Baltimore to Washington and back. *(The Story of the Centenary Pageant of the B & O. Railroad Co.)*

Railroad to run west of the Mississippi River was the Pacific Railway of Missouri, incorporated March 12, 1849. Ground was broken at St. Louis, Mo., on July 4, 1851. On December 2, 1852, Charles Williams, the chief machinist of the company, made a test run; on December 9, 1852, the president and director of the company with a company of 50 officials and friends rode a distance of five

The First

miles in ten minutes to Cheltenham Sulphur Springs, where a party was held. The return trip was made in the afternoon. On December 23, 1852, the railroad began its passenger service. The name was changed to the Missouri Pacific Railway Company on October 20, 1876. (It later became part of the Missouri Pacific Lines.)

Railroad to run west out of Chicago was the Galena and Chicago Union Railroad, a constituent company of the Chicago and North Western Railway, whose first train was hauled by *The Pioneer,* a ten-ton wood-burning locomotive, which left Chicago, Ill., on October 25, 1848, for Oak Park, five miles away. The North Western rails reached the Missouri River at Council Bluffs in 1867, and when the last spike was driven by Senator Leland Stanford for the Union Pacific at Promontory, Utah, May 10, 1869, service between the East and the West coasts was available for the first time. The western roads were the Chicago & North Western, the Union Pacific, and the Central Pacific, now a part of the Southern Pacific.

Railroad to use an electric engine for a short distance in place of steam engines was the Baltimore and Ohio, which ran its first train with an electric engine through the Baltimore tunnel for a distance of 3.6 miles, supplanting the steam engine for that distance. The regular use of electric engines for freight trains for this distance was begun on August 4, 1894, and for passenger trains on May 1, 1895. *(Baltimore and Ohio 69th Annual Report for Year Ending June 30, 1895)*

Railroad train operated exclusively by women was placed in service June 6, 1979, by the Long Island Rail Road. It started from Port Washington, N.Y., at 4:35 P.M. and arrived at Pennsylvania Station, New York City, at 5:07 P.M. The train's conductor was Deirdre Hickey, the first woman to qualify in yard, freight, and passenger service. Doreen Boyle was the fare collector; Beverly Terrillion and Eileen Denn, the brakemen.

Railroad train to run 1,000 miles nonstop was the Chicago, Burlington and Quincy's streamlined train *Zephyr,* powered by a 660 h.p. diesel engine. The *Zephyr* left Union Station, Denver, Colo., at 6:04 A.M. Central Daylight Time on May 26, 1934, and arrived at the Halsted Street station, Chicago, Ill., a distance of 1,015 miles in 13 hours 5 minutes 44 seconds. The average speed was 77.6 m.p.h. and the top speed 112 m.p.h. There were 65 persons aboard.

Railroad tunnel. *See under* Tunnel

State aid to railroads was granted by Illinois, which was empowered by Congress on March 2, 1833 (2 Stat. L. 662), to sell land it had acquired from the federal government for canal land on March 2, 1827 (2 Stat. L. 234), and to use the proceeds to aid in the construction of railroads. This grant did not become effective and was not used by the state.

The First

RAILROAD—*Continued*

State-owned railroad was the Philadelphia and Columbia Railway, constructed under the act of March 24, 1828, P.L. 221, Section 5, Pennsylvania, which authorized and required the canal commissioners to build a railroad from Philadelphia to Columbia by way of Lancaster, and extending to the west end of York. The first locomotive trip was made April 2, 1834, from Lancaster to Columbia. This line was completed in 1834 from Philadelphia to Pittsburgh, in four divisions, the first of which was the Columbia Railroad. The construction and regulation of this road was imposed upon the Pennsylvania Board of Canal Commissioners, who built and operated it until August 1, 1857, when the Pennsylvania Railroad purchased it from the state and the road came under private management and control. *(Slason Thompson—Short History of American Railroads)*

Streamlined all-steel diesel-motor train was the *Zephyr*, 196 feet long, and 208,061 pounds in weight, built by the Edward G. Budd Manufacturing Company of Philadelphia, Pa., for the Chicago, Burlington and Quincy Railroad for service between Kansas City, Mo., and Lincoln, Neb. It was driven by a Winton 660 h.p. high-compression two-cycle, 8-inch-by-10-inch, eight-in-line diesel-electric motor. The first trip, on November 11, 1934, was a run from Lincoln to Kansas City, via Omaha, and back the same day.

Streamlined lightweight high-speed three-car passenger train was operated by the Union Pacific System, March 2, 1934, west from Omaha, Neb. It was designed by E. E. Adams, vice president, who conducted the research and development work under the direction of Carl Raymond Gray and William Martin Jeffers, president and executive vice president, respectively, of the Union Pacific System. The train was constructed of aluminum alloys having three times the strength of steel and therefore requiring one third of the material to obtain equivalent strength. The train was tubular in shape. The equipment was designed for a maximum speed of 110 m.p.h., with a sustained speed on straight and level track of 90 m.p.h. The train of three cars weighed 80 tons, the weight of one old-style Pullman sleeping car. The train was fully air-conditioned; windows were sealed and forced ventilation was used to heat the train in winter, to cool it in summer, and to filter all dirt and dust from the air as it was brought into the train.

Streamlined Pullman train (six cars) was the Union Pacific *Streamliner*—M-10001 which left Los Angeles, Calif., October 22, 1934, at 10 P.M. and drew into Grand Central Terminal, New York City, at 9:55 A.M. October 25, 1934, covering 3,259 miles in 56 hours 55 minutes. The average speed was a trifle under 60 m.p.h. The train was constructed of aluminum alloy for strength and lightness and streamlined into a smooth, low-slung

The First

tube. It was powered by a 900 h.p. V-type diesel of 12 cylinders which provided energy for the four electrical traction motors. The train was made up of the power car, a combination mail-baggage car, 3 Pullman sleeping cars, and a coach-buffet.

Streamlined railroad train was invented by the Reverend Samuel R. Calthorp of Roxbury, Mass., who obtained patent No. 49,227, on August 8, 1865, on an "air resister train." He gave "to the exterior surface of a railway train a form tapering from the center of the train toward either end, for the purpose of diminishing the atmosphere resistance." The front and rear ends of the train were pointed, and the wheels were enclosed in casing, the only projection being the smokestack. The tender was attached to the locomotive by an accordion hood.

Switchback railway was invented by La Marcus Adna Thompson and put in operation in June 1884 by the L. A. Thompson Scenic Railway Company at Coney Island, N.Y. It was 450 feet long. The cars started from a peak and ran downgrade, the momentum carrying the cars up an incline. The passengers got out, the attendants pushed the train over a switch to a higher point on a second track, and the passengers returned. The highest drop was only 30 feet. Thompson obtained patent No. 310,966 on January 20, 1885, on a roller-coasting structure and patent No. 332,762 on December 22, 1885 on a gravity switch-back railway. *(Oliver Pilat and Jo Ranson, Sodom by the Sea, History of Coney Island)*

Telegraph in railroading. *See under* Telegraph

Telephone service (commercial station) on railroad trains for passengers. *See* Telephone: Commercial telephone service on railroad trains for passengers

Telephone used by a railroad company. *See under* Telephone

Transcontinental through sleeping car. *See* Sleeping car: Transcontinental through Pullman sleeping car service

RAILROAD, ELEVATED. *See* Elevated railroad

RAILROAD ACCIDENT occurred July 25, 1832, on the Granite Railway, Quincy, Mass. Four visitors, after seeing the process of transporting large and weighty loads of stone, were invited to ascend the inclined plane in one of the vacant returning cars. The cable chain snapped and they were precipitated over a cliff, a distance of 30 to 40 feet. One man was killed and the others seriously injured. *(Granite Railway Company, The First Railroad in America)*

RAILROAD APPRENTICE SCHOOL for railway mechanics was established by the New York Central Railroad at Elkhart, Ind., in 1872.

RAILROAD AUTO TRUCKING SERVICE. *See* Automobile trucking service

The First

RAILROAD BRAKE PATENT. *See under* Brake

RAILROAD BRIDGE. *See* Bridge

RAILROAD BUS. *See* Automobile bus: Bus operated by a railroad

RAILROAD CAR

Air-conditioned car was tried in 1854 by the New York and Erie Railroad, which installed a funnel-shaped opening at the top and sides of a railroad car to catch the air, which was then passed through a water tank underneath the car to the interior of the car. In winter, the air was heated by a stove. An opening in the rear of the car enabled the air to escape. *(Scientific American. Vol. 9. No. 28. Mar. 25, 1854)*

Air-conditioned cars were installed by the Atchison, Topeka and Santa Fe Railway Company. Fifteen new dining cars were built in 1914, cars No. 1441 to No. 1455, in service on the *California Limited* between Chicago, Ill., and Los Angeles, Calif. The system was known as the Duntley Air Washer and consisted of a motor-driven spray wheel partially submerged in ice water. Fresh air was drawn through the spray and delivered into the car by means of a fan and air ducts along the deck of the car. This system was successful inasmuch as it washed the air and lowered the temperature of the cars a few degrees, but the capacity was inadequate.

Car with a center aisle was *The Columbus*, introduced July 4, 1831, by the Baltimore and Ohio Railroad Company. It was designed by Ross Winans and built at Baltimore, Md. It was feared that it would become one long spittoon. *(William Henry Brown—History of the First Locomotive in America)*

Car with an observation dome was placed in service July 23, 1945, by the Chicago, Burlington & Quincy Railroad. It was a standard Budd stainless-steel coach into which a Vista Dome was built at the Burlington's Aurora, Ill., shops. The Vista Dome car had three decks, an upper deck in the center with a curved double glass roof, an intermediate deck at the usual floor level, and a lower deck beneath the dome section. The Vista Dome section was 19½ feet long and extended the full width of the car. It seated 24 passengers, their heads and shoulders above the normal roof line of the train.

Car with fluorescent lighting was New York Central coach 1472, placed in service September 2, 1938. The *Twentieth Century Limited* streamliner used the first fluorescent tail sign June 15, 1938.

Chapel car was the *Evangel*, dedicated May 23, 1891, in Cincinnati, Ohio. The dedicatory address was delivered by Dr. Wayland Hoyt. The car was fitted out for religious services and was used on the Northern Pacific Railroad's tracks. Experimental services were held in St. Paul and Minneapolis, Minn., and after several months of

The First

prospecting work, the car was committed for the winter to the Reverend and Mrs. E. G. Wheeler, who conducted services in it on the Pacific Coast.

Coal cars with roller bearings were placed in service on the Wheeling and Lake Erie Railroad in December 1925. There were two 50-ton hopper cars, the trucks of which were placed under the existing car bodies by the Timken Roller Bearing Company. The cars were placed in coal service operating between mines in Ohio and Lake Erie. *(William C. Sanders—Railway Roller Bearings)*

Compartmentizer freight cars were developed jointly by the Western Pacific Railroad Company and the Pullman Standard Car Company and placed in service on September 12, 1952, between Chicago, Ill., and San Francisco, Calif. Four gates were installed in each car to separate the contents into sections and to prevent shifting and crushing.

Complete train of coal cars with roller bearings was placed in service during the early part of January 1930 by the Pennsylvania Railroad Company and consisted of 100 hopper cars of 70 tons capacity each. The cars were used between the Cresson Division and the Eastern Seaboard. The trucks, made by the Timken Roller Bearing Company, were placed under the regular standard cars.

Dining car ever operated in the world was the *Delmonico*, built in 1868 by the Pullman Palace Car Company, Pullman, Ill., and placed in service between Chicago, Ill., and St. Louis, Mo., by the Chicago & Alton Railroad Company. The Philadelphia, Wilmington and Baltimore Railroad in 1863 operated two remodeled day refreshment coaches, 50 feet long, fitted with an eating bar, steam box, etc., on the Philadelphia-Baltimore run. Food prepared at the terminals was sold. *(First in All Travel Conveniences—Chicago & Alton Traffic Department)*

Dining car (all-electric) was the *Cafe St. Louis*, built in Chicago, Ill., and placed in service March 9, 1949, between Chicago and St. Louis, Mo., by the Illinois Central Railroad. It had a self-contained electric power unit which developed approximately 50,000 watts, supplying the power for two broilers, two ranges, hot food table, coffee urn, plate and cup warmers, deep fry kettle, dish washer, glass washer, mixers and fruit juice extractors, refrigerators, garbage disposal system, etc.

Double-deck railroad coaches were built by Richard Imlay in August 1830 and used on the Baltimore and Ohio Railroad. The Improved Passenger Cars accommodated 12 passengers, while outside seats at the end accommodated 6 persons, including the driver. On top of the carriages was a double sofa which accommodated 12 additional passengers. An iron framework supported an awning that protected those on the upper deck.

The First

RAILROAD CAR—*Continued*

The coaches were placed in service between Baltimore, Md., and Ellicott's Mill, Md.

Freight car (Adapto Car) was built by the American Car and Foundry Division of ACF Industries, Inc., at Berwick, Pa., and placed in service on July 24, 1956, by the Chicago, Rock Island and Pacific Railroad Company between St. Louis, Mo., and Wichita, Kans. Sections of various shapes and sizes were made to fit above the chassis of a flatcar. The sections could be removed with their contents to allow reuse of the car without the delay generally attendant upon unloading.

Glass-lined tank car for transporting milk was built in 1910 by the Pflaudler Company, Rochester, N.Y., for the Whiting Milk Company, Boston, Mass. It was used on the Boston and Maine Railroad to collect milk from the country for city consumption.

Mail car (steel) was built by the Standard Steel Car Company, Pittsburgh, Pa., and exhibited May 4–13, 1905, at the International Railway Congress, Washington, D.C. It was lighted with acetylene gas and lined with fireproof composite board. The inside length was 65 feet 2 inches. It was framed of steel posts and girders, covered with steel plates, and insulated with hair felt. It was placed in service June 7, 1905, by the New York, Salamanca and Chicago Railroad Company. *(Erie Railroad Employes' Magazine. July 1905)*

Observation cars (superdome) were built by the Pullman-Standard Car Manufacturing Company, Chicago, Ill., in 1952. Ten cars were placed in service January 1, 1953, by the Chicago, Milwaukee, St. Paul and Pacific Railroad (Milwaukee Railroad). They were 85 feet overall, 10 feet wide, 15 feet 6 inches from top to rail. The dome section contained 625 square feet of curved safety glass in sections 3 feet wide and 5 feet high. The laminated glass consisted of polished plate glass and layers of plastic.

Oil tank cars. *See under* Oil

Parlor car was the *Maritana*, built by George Mortimer Pullman and placed in operation in 1875. The chairs were "richly upholstered," fitted with adjustable backs, and revolved on swivels.

Passenger car (ACF-Talgo) was built by the American Car and Foundry Division of ACF Industries, Inc., Berwick, Pa., for export to Spain. A complete train was tested on March 3, 1949. Coach height was 4 feet lower than that of conventional coaches. Floors were 3 feet closer to the rails than those of conventional coaches. The train weighed two thirds less than trains then in use, as it was made of aluminum and other lightweight material. It used about 40 percent less fuel, and cost 45 percent less than conventional equipment.

The First

Passenger car (ACF-Talgo for use in the United States) was built by the American Car and Foundry Division of ACF Industries, Inc., Berwick, Pa., and completed on April 22, 1955. The first train was the *Jet Rocket*, placed in service on February 11, 1956, by the Chicago, Rock Island and Pacific Railroad Company between Peoria and Chicago, Ill.

President to ride on a railroad train. *See under* President (U.S.)

President's car, owned by the government for the exclusive use of the President of the United States, is U.S. Car No. 1, formerly known as the *Ferdinand Magellan,* built in 1942 by the Association of American Railroads. It was purchased for a nominal fee by the government and assigned to the White House. It weighed 285,000 pounds, was built on extra heavy trucks, and was sheathed throughout with armor plate ⅝ inch thick. It had bulletproof glass 3 inches thick in all of the windows and doors. The car had a lounge-observation compartment, a dining room seating 12 persons (it also served as a conference room), a special galley where all the meals were prepared, and 4 bedrooms. It carried no identification marks other than the presidential seal on the brass-railed rear platform. (A private car was built for President Abraham Lincoln, but it was never accepted by him or assigned to the White House. It was, however, used to bear his remains from Washington, D.C., to Springfield, Ill.)

Private railroad car was outfitted for Jenny Maria Lind Goldschmidt (Jenny Lind, the "Swedish Nightingale"), who made her first appearance September 11, 1850, at Castle Garden, New York City. The car was used on her tour of the country.

Pullman sleeping car. *See under* Sleeping car

Pullman train completely equipped with roller bearings was the *Pioneer Limited* of the Chicago, Milwaukee, St. Paul and Pacific Railroad. Regular service was inaugurated May 21, 1927, between Chicago, Ill., and St. Paul–Minneapolis, Minn., a distance of 421 miles. *(The Military Engineer. September 1930)*

Rail detector car was invented by Dr. Elmer Ambrose Sperry and tested June 13, 1928, at Beacon, N.Y. It enabled railroads to locate internal flaws in railroad tracks. It was demonstrated September 13, 1928, near Poughkeepsie, N.Y., before representatives of the American Railway Association and various railroads. The first car, car No. 101, which traveled at 10 miles an hour, enabled only one rail to be examined at a time.

Rail detector car in commercial service was placed in service by the Wabash Railroad on November 15, 1928, at Montpelier, Ohio. It was a double-unit car, with one unit for towage and one for equipment. The first test, 155 miles, required 14

The First

consecutive days and revealed 14 defects a day.

Railroad coach modeled after those in use in England was built at the Old Colony South Boston (Boston, Mass.) shops for the Fall River Line, and placed in service on May 19, 1847.

Railroad shipments of dressed beef. *See under* Railroad

Refrigerator car patent was No. 71,423, granted to J. B. Sutherland of Detroit, Mich., November 26, 1867, and covered an insulated car constructed with ice bunkers in each end and ventilated by air admission above the ice and gravity circulation. "Hanging flaps" created and maintained constant circulation in the car by means of differences of temperature in the air. The air was admitted at the top, passed through the ice chamber, and then discharged into the cooling room near the bottom to reduce its temperature. *("Railway Refrigeration."* In *Ice and Refrigeration. September 1891)*

Refrigerator car shipment of fresh fruit was made by Parker Earle of Cobden, Ill., who in 1866 built and shipped chests of strawberries on the Illinois Central Railroad. The chests had three layers of board and were airtight and watertight. They held 100 pounds of ice and 200 quarts of strawberries, which brought $2 a quart. In 1872 Earle shipped a full carload from Anna, Ill., to Chicago, Ill. *(Carlton Jonathan Corliss—Main Line of Mid-America)*

Remote-control railroad passenger car was put in operation December 1, 1955, between New Rochelle, N.Y., and Rye, N.Y., on 7.5 miles of the New York, New Haven and Hartford system. The car was started, stopped, and speeded up to 70 m.p.h., and was operated from a control panel at Larchmont, N.Y. The tests were conducted by the Union Switch and Signal Division of the Westinghouse Air Brake Company.

Sleeping car. *See* Sleeping car

Steel passenger railroad coach was built in 1902 by the Pennsylvania Railroad Company in its shop at Altoona, Pa. It was completed in December 1903. It had a steel underframe and superstructure, a composite roof, and wooden window frames and sills. On December 23, 1907, the first all-steel passenger railroad coach was completed.

Train with fluorescent lights was the *General Pershing Zephyr*, a stainless-steel streamlined train operated by the Chicago, Burlington and Quincy Railroad. Its first run, on April 30, 1939, was between St. Louis, Mo., and Kansas City, Mo. Coaches, parlor-lounge, dining car, rear car, dressing rooms, and lavatories were all equipped with fluorescent lights. *(Railway Age. April 29, 1939)*

RAILROAD CHARTER was granted by New Jersey on February 6, 1815, when "an act to incorporate a company to erect a rail-road from the river

The First

Delaware, near Trenton, to the river Raritan, at or near New Brunswick" was passed in Trenton, N.J. The railroad, advocated by John Stevens of Hoboken, N.J., was not completed. James Ewing, Pearson Hunt, and Alner Reeder were appointed to receive subscriptions (not more than 5,000 shares at $100).

RAILROAD COACH. *See under* Railroad car

RAILROAD COMMISSION (state) was established July 1, 1869, under chapter 408 of the Acts of 1869 by the state of Massachusetts. It is now the Department of Public Works. The first three commissioners appointed were James C. Converse, Edward Appleton, and Charles Francis Adams, Jr.

RAILROAD COUPLER with which every railroad car in the United States, Canada, and Mexico is equipped was invented by Eli Hamilton Janney of Alexandria, Va., who obtained patent No. 138,405 on an "improvement in car-couplings" on April 29, 1873. *(Carl Weaver Mitman—The Beginning of the Mechanical Transport Era in America)*

RAILROAD CROSSING GATE PATENT was No. 68,306, which was awarded August 27, 1867, to J. Nason and J. F. Wilson of Boston, Mass.

RAILROAD EXCURSION

Railroad excursion (mystery) was run by the Missouri Pacific Railroad May 21, 1932. The trip was from St. Louis to Arcadia, Mo., a distance of 92 miles, but the passengers were not told in advance where they were going. The round trip fare was $2.50, which included a barbecue at Arcadia.

Railroad excursion rates originated in 1849 when Josiah Perham of Boston, Mass., persuaded railroads to grant a one-day excursion rate to Boston to persons desirous of viewing the panorama of the Saguenay, St. Lawrence, and Niagara Falls exhibited in Boston. The low rates stimulated travel. *(Charles Frederick Carter—When Railroads Were New)*

Railroad excursion (transcontinental) of an organization was made by the Boston Board of Trade, which left Boston May 23, 1870, in eight Pullman cars pulled by the locomotives *Meteor* and *William Penn*. The excursionists carried their own printing press and published a daily newspaper titled *Trans-Continental*. They arrived at San Francisco, Calif., on May 31, 1870, and returned to Boston on July 2, 1870.

RAILROAD GUIDE

Railroad guide was *The Traveller's Guide Through the State of New York, Canada, etc., embracing a general description of the city of New York; the Hudson River Guide, and the fashionable tour to the springs and Niagara Falls: with steam-boat, rail-road, and stage routes, accompanied by correct maps* (72 pages, published in 1836 by J. Disturnell, New York City). It contained a folded map of New York State and one of the

The First

RAILROAD GUIDE—*Continued*

Hudson River vicinity; a list of canal routes; stage and railroad routes from Albany to Buffalo, Albany to Boston, etc.; a list of railroads, cemeteries, monuments, colleges, museums, hotels, amusements, etc.; and a general description of New York City.

Railroad guide that printed the time schedule of the arrival and departure of trains at the various stops along the route and at the terminal points was Doggett's *United States Railroad and Ocean Steam Navigation Guide, illustrated with a map of the United States, showing the working lines of Railroad,* published September 1847 by John Doggett, Jr., of New York City. It contained 132 pages, and a folding map. It sold for 12½ cents.

RAILROAD LAND GRANT. *See* Land grant

RAILROAD LEGISLATION

Railroad legislation (federal) was the Safety Appliance Act, passed March 2, 1893 (27 Stat. L. 531), "an act to promote the safety of employees and travelers upon railroads by compelling common carriers engaged in interstate commerce to equip their cars with automatic couplers and continuous brakes and their locomotives with driving wheel brakes, and for other purposes."

Railroad legislation (state) was passed by the state of Georgia, March 5, 1856 (General Law 103). The state law making railroad companies liable for injuries caused by negligence to employees and others was "an act to define the liability of the several railroad companies of this state for injuries to persons or property, to prescribe in what counties they may be sued, and how served with process." *(John W. Duncan—Acts of the General Assembly of the State of Georgia passed in Milledgeville at Bi-ennial Session in November, December, January, February and March 1855–1856)*

RAILROAD LOCOMOTIVE. *See* Locomotive

RAILROAD MAGAZINE. *See* Periodical: Trade journal

RAILROAD MOTOR-COACH TRUCKING. *See* Automobile trucking service

RAILROAD PASSENGER

Railroad honeymoon trip was made by Mr. and Mrs. Henry L. Pierson of Ramapo, N.Y., who on January 15, 1831, while in Charleston, S.C., on their wedding trip, took a ride on the South Carolina Railroad from Charleston, S.C., to Hamburg, S.C., six miles away. The locomotive was *The Best Friend of Charleston* and Nicholas W. Darrell was the engineer. *(Charles Frederick Carter—When Railroads Were New)*

RAILROAD POST OFFICE. *See under* Postal service

The First

RAILROAD SIGNAL LIGHT

Atomic-powered signal light was manufactured by the United States Radium Corporation, Morristown, N.J., and shipped to the Denver and Rio Grande Western Railroad in November 1956. It was 1-foot square with 4 sides (2 red and 2 green).

RAILROAD SIGNAL SYSTEM

Railroad interlocking machine was placed in service at Spuyten Duyvil, N.Y., in 1874 by the New York Central & Hudson River Railroad. Levers, operated from a central location, controlled an arrangement of switch and signal appliances, providing a safe path for the movement of trains through switches, junctions, grade crossings, and terminal stations, and over drawbridges.

Railroad signal system (automatic electric block) was invented by Thomas S. Hall of Stamford, Conn., in 1867 and was installed on the New York and Harlem Railroad. Hall obtained patent No. 103,875 on June 7, 1870, for his electromagnetic railway signal apparatus. The wheels of the locomotive struck a lever fastened to the rail and this in turn set the signal at danger until the train was out of the block.

Railroad signal system (manual block) was installed in 1863 between Philadelphia (Kensington), Pa., and Trenton, N.J., on the Philadelphia and Trenton Railroad, a division of the Camden and Amboy Railroad, now a part of the Pennsylvania Railroad System. Installation was made by Robert Stewart, Superintendent of Telegraph and Train Dispatcher of the Camden and Amboy Railroad, under instructions of Ashbel Welch, President of the Camden and Amboy Railroad. The system was extended to New Brunswick, N.J., in 1864.

Railroad signal system of continuous cab signals was used by the Pennsylvania Railroad. On July 11, 1923, cab signals were installed experimentally in locomotives hauling trains between Lewiston Junction and Sunbury, Pa. These cab signals, located on the locomotives where the engineman and fireman could readily see them, were actuated by electric currents in track circuits of the track on which the locomotive was located. This was accomplished by coding the electric circuits to reflect the conditions on the track ahead of the locomotive.

Railroad signal system of interlocking signal apparatus operated by compressed air was installed by the Union Switch and Signal Company in 188 at Bound Brook, N.J., at the crossing of the Central Railroad of New Jersey with the Pennsylvania railroad.

RAILROAD STATION

Railroad station (passenger and freight) was the Baltimore and Ohio Railroad depot on Poppleton Street, south of Pratt Street, Baltimore, Md. The original two-story building, erected in 1830

The First

still stands, and is now a museum. *(First Passenger and Freight Station—Baltimore and Ohio Railroad Co.)*

Union passenger station was the Union Station at Indianapolis, Ind., opened September 20, 1853, for the trains of five railroad companies. The depot was 100 feet wide and 420 feet long, and contained five tracks inside and through the depot, two tracks outside and north of the depot. The building contract was let in May 1852. The constructing engineer was Colonel T. A. Morris. Edwards and Copeland were the general contractors. The depot was owned and operated by the Indianapolis Union Railway Company, which ran the union station, the union tracks, and the Indianapolis Belt Railroad.

RAILROAD TECHNICAL REPORT was William Strickland's *Reports on Canals, Railways, Roads and Other Subjects made to the Pennsylvania Society for the Promotion of Internal Improvement,* a 51-page pamphlet containing 72 engraved plates, published in 1826 by H. C. Carey and I. Lea, Philadelphia, Pa.

RAILROAD TIMETABLE. *See* Timetable (railroad)

RAILROAD TRACK

Manganese steel for railroad tracks. *See under* Steel

Railroad rails of Bessemer steel were rolled at the North Chicago rolling mill May 24, 1865, from ingots made at the experimental steel works at Wyandotte, Mich. The rails were rolled in Chicago, Ill., and their manufacture witnessed by members of the American Iron and Steel Association who were assembled in conference at Chicago.

Railroad rails of iron were rolled in 1844 at the Mount Savage Rolling Mill, Allegany County, Md., and weighed 42 pounds a yard. Five hundred tons of the inverted U type rails were rolled in 1845. They were laid between Mount Savage and Cumberland, Md., a distance of approximately nine miles. This rolling mill also produced T rails, which weighed 50 pounds a yard. *(James Walter Thomas and Thomas John Chew Williams—History of Allegany County, Md.)*

Railroad rails of steel were used by the Pennsylvania Railroad. The rails, which weighed 56 pounds a yard, were placed in service in 1864 between Altoona and Pittsburgh, Pa.

Railroad rails of T shape were invented in 1830 by Robert Livingston Stevens, president and engineer of the Camden and Amboy Railroad. They were made of malleable iron, weighed 36 pounds a yard, and were used by his railroad. Their adoption was very slow, as the type of rail then preferred was the flat rail which was nailed to the ties. *(Robert Henry Thurston—History of the Growth of the Steam Engine)*

The First

Railroad track (practical) was made of wood laid on a steep grade of 1½ inches to the yard, in Philadelphia, Pa., and was 180 feet in length. On July 31, 1809, a carriage with four grooved wheels was placed on the track at the lower end and a single horse walking on the loose dirt between the tracks pulled 10,696 pounds up the slope. *(Du Pont Magazine, June 1925)*

Railway track scale. *See under* Scale

RAILROAD TRAIN ROBBERY

Railroad train robbery of a disabled train took place on May 5, 1865, when an Ohio and Mississippi railroad train en route from St. Louis, Mo., to Cincinnati, Ohio, overturned at North Bend, Ohio, 14 miles from Cincinnati, and was robbed by looters.

Railroad train robbery of a train en route took place January 6, 1866, when a safe in the iron express car of the Adams Express Company was robbed of about $500,000 in bonds, specie, and government securities, while en route from New York City to Boston, Mass., on the New Haven Railroad. The loss was discovered when the train arrived at New Haven, Conn. At the trial in Bridgeport, Conn., before Judge Butler, Augustus ("Gus") Tristam pleaded guilty and was sentenced on February 14, 1866, to serve 3 years 6 months in the Connecticut Penitentiary. Thomas Clark was convicted on the fourth count.

Railroad train robbery of a train in motion took place on October 6, 1866, when Frank Sparks, John Reno, and Simeon Reno boarded an Ohio and Mississippi Railroad baggage and express car while it was getting into motion and threw off two safes, one containing $15,000 and the other $30,-000. The latter was recovered. The bandits were arrested, freed on bail, and never tried, although later convicted of other crimes and punished. *Robert William Shields—Seymour, Indiana, and the Famous Story of the Reno Gang*

RAILROAD TREATISE was John Stevens's *Documents Tending to Prove the Superior Advantages of Rail-ways and Steam-Carriages Over Canal Navigation,* printed in 1812 by T. and J. Swords, 160 Pearl Street, New York City. Stevens proposed to build a railroad from Albany to Buffalo, N.Y., laying the track on wooden stringers capped with wrought-iron plate. *(Magazine of History. Extra No. 54)*

RAILROAD TUNNEL. *See* Tunnel

RAILROAD UNION

Railroad union was formed when 68 engineers from 45 different railroads in 13 states met in Baltimore, Md., November 6-10, 1855, and organized the National Protective Association of the Brotherhood of Locomotive Engineers of the United States "to protect ourselves, the traveling public and our employers from the injurious effects re-

The First

RAILROAD UNION—*Continued*
sulting from persons of inferior qualifications being employed as locomotive engineers."

RAIN (artificial) to drench a forest fire. *See* Forest fire: Forest fire drenched by artificial rain

RAIN CHECK
Baseball rain check. *See* Baseball ticket: Baseball rain check

RAMJET HELICOPTER. *See* Helicopter

RANGE (army field range). *See* Army field range

RANGE (electric). *See* Electric stove: Electric range

RANSOM KIDNAPPING. *See* Kidnapping: Kidnapping for ransom

RAT EXTERMINATION (citywide) to avert bubonic plague was accomplished in San Francisco, Calif., in 1907–1908 by the Public Health Service, which saved the city and perhaps the nation by destroying the rats and ground squirrels which carry plague-bearing fleas. *(San Francisco—Citizens' Health Committee Report, March 31, 1909)*

RATE STANDARDIZATION (insurance). *See* Insurance: Insurance rate standardization

RATING AGENCY (commercial). *See* Business: Commercial rating agency

RATTLESNAKE MEAT in cans was packed in March 1931 by George Kenneth End of Arcadia, Fla. On April 9, 1931, canned rattlesnake meat was served at a dinner to American Legionnaires at the Hillsboro Hotel, Tampa, Fla. End founded and became president of the Floridian Products Corporation, which made its first sale of canned rattlesnake May 22, 1931.

RAY, COSMIC. *See* Cosmic ray

RAYON
Rayon was commercially produced by the American Viscose Company in Marcus Hook, Pa., on December 19, 1910. Production in 1911 amounted to 362,000 pounds. The patents were acquired from the General Artificial Silk Company, Lansdowne, Pa., which started in 1901. The term "rayon" was adopted in 1924 to replace "artificial silk" and similar names. *(Mois Herban Avran—The Rayon Industry)*

Rayon patent on spinning of artificial silk from cellulose acetate was granted William H. Walker, Newton, Mass., Dr. Arthur D. Little, Brookline, Mass., and Harry S. Mork, Boston, Mass., who obtained joint patent No. 709,922, September 30, 1902, "on making cellulose esters." They also received patent No. 712,200, October 28, 1902, on artificial silk, which they assigned to the Chemical Products Company, Boston, Mass.

RAZOR
Electric dry shaver was manufactured by

The First

Schick, Inc., Stamford, Conn., and delivered March 18, 1931. Colonel Jacob Schick obtained patents on a "shaving implement" on November 6, 1928 (No. 1,721,530).

Safety razor was the Star Safety Razor, made by Kampfe Brothers, New York City in 1880. It consisted of a short portion of a hand-forged blade of a barber's straight razor inserted in a frame with full safety features.

Safety razor to be successfully marketed was invented by King Camp Gillette. In 1895 he invented a razor equipped with a flexible and movable blade which could be thrown away. The blades were punched out of thin steel instead of being forged. The original Gillette Company was incorporated September 28, 1901. Twenty people paid $250 each for 500 shares of stock. In 1903 only 51 razors were sold. In 1906 the first dividend was paid, amounting to $130,000. *(Gillette Safety Razor Co.—Gillette's Decade of Development)*

READING DEVICE (microfilm). *See* Microfilm

REAPER
Reaper patent was granted to Richard French and John F. Hawkins of New Jersey on May 17, 1803. *(R. L. Ardrey—American Agricultural Implements)*

Reaper that actually worked was invented by Henry Ogle in 1826. It consisted of a straight scythe blade which moved against a series of triangular fingers, and cut the grain, which fell upon a collecting board. *(Merritt Finley Miller—The Evolution of Reaping Machines)*

Reaper that was practical was built by Cyrus Hall McCormick, who obtained a patent on June 21, 1834. His father, Robert McCormick, had also experimented with reapers but was unsuccessful and abandoned the work. The younger McCormick, using a new principle, built a reaper which he demonstrated in 1831 at a public trial in a field near Walnut Grove, Va. The owner of the field feared that the machine would rattle the heads off his wheat and stopped the demonstration. Another neighbor, whose ground was more level, invited McCormick to his field, and there the machine worked splendidly, cutting six acres of wheat in half a day—as much as six men would have done. The reaper was very difficult to popularize, and it was not until 1841 that McCormick was able to sell two machines. *(Herbert Newton Casson—The Romance of the Reaper)*

REAR-FACING AIRPLANE SEATS. *See* Aviation: Airline to install rear-facing passenger seats

REBELLION
See also
Civil War
Revolutionary War
War

The First

Insurrection of black slaves. *See under* Slavery

Rebellion against the federal government. *See under* War

Rebellion (colonial) was attempted in 1607 at the Jamestown colony, Va. George Kendall, one of the original first council appointed in England, "was put off from being of the Council, and committed to prison; for that it did manyfestly appear he did practize to sew discord between the President and Council." He was shot tó death for mutiny. *(Edward Maria Wingfield—A Discourse of Virginia)*

Rebellion of colonists against the English was led by Marcus Jacobson, "The Long Finne," who claimed to be the son of the Swedish general Konigsmark. He advocated an uprising against the English and was trapped and turned over to the English commandant. On December 20, 1669, he was condemned for insurrection in the first trial by jury in Delaware. He was lashed in public, branded with the letter *R,* and sold in chains as a slave in Barbados for having opposed the governmental authority of Governor Francis Lovelace.

RECLAMATION SERVICE (federal) was the United States Reclamation Service, a bureau of the Department of Interior, created by act of Congress of June 17, 1902 (32 Stat. L. 389), for reclamation of arid and semiarid lands. It was an outgrowth of the United States Geological Survey, authorized on March 30, 1888 (25 Stat. L. 63).*(Institute for Government Research—United States Reclamation Service: Its History, Activities and Organization)*

RECONSTRUCTION FINANCE CORPORATION was created by the Reconstruction Finance Corporation Act, approved January 22, 1932 (47 Stat. L. 5), "to provide emergency financial facilities for financial institutions, to aid in financing agriculture, commerce and industry, and other purposes." The act authorized the corporation to create, in any of the 12 Federal Land Bank Districts, intermediate credit corporations to assist farm stockmen. Interest at 7 percent was charged for the loans, which included all costs of inspection. The original capital of the corporation was set at $500 million. It was authorized to have up to three times its subscribed capital outstanding. The corporation was organized February 2, 1932 and managed by the United States Secretary of the Treasury and six directors.

RECORDED RADIO PROGRAM. *See* Radio broadcast: Recorded coast-to-coast broadcast

RECORDING DEVICE FOR TELEPHONE CONVERSATIONS. *See* Telephone: Telephone recording devices

RECREATIONAL RANCHING COURSE in a college, often referred to unofficially as a dude ranching course, was offered by the College of Agriculture of the University of Wyoming, Laramie. The first Bachelor of Science degree awarded

The First

by the College of Agriculture for the completion of the optional program known as "recreational ranching" was conferred June 6, 1938, on Donald Ellsworth Smith, who completed the four-year course.

RECUMBENT CHAIR. *See* Chair

RED CROSS SOCIETY. *See* American Red Cross

REFEREE, PRIZEFIGHT. *See* Prizefight referee

REFEREE (woman). *See* Prizefight referee: Woman prizefight referee (licensed)

REFERENDUM. *See* Initiative and referendum

REFINERY. *See* Copper refinery furnace; Oil refinery; Sugar refinery

REFLECTING TELESCOPE. *See* Telescope

REFORM CONGREGATION (Jewish). *See* Jewish Congregation: Jewish congregation (reform)

REFORMATORY. *See* Prison

REFORMED CHURCH (Dutch) was established in 1628 in New Amsterdam, N.Y., under the West India Company and the Church of Holland. *(Edward Tanjore Corwin—Manual of the Reformed Church in America)*

REFRIGERATED CAR. *See* Railroad car: Refrigerator car patent; Railroad car: Refrigerator car shipment of fresh fruit

REFRIGERATION (mechanical). *See* Cold storage plant

REFRIGERATOR

See also Ice cream freezer

Gas refrigerator (household) to be successfully introduced into the American market was the Electrolux, which was sponsored in 1926 by the Electrolux Refrigerator Sales Company of Evansville, Ind. A tiny gas flame and a tiny flow of water in the refrigerator took the place of all moving parts, circulating a liquid refrigerant which was hermetically sealed in rigid steel. The first patent issued to the Electrolux Servel Corporation on an absorption refrigerating apparatus was No. 1,609,-334, granted December 7, 1926, to Baltzar Carl von Platen and Georg Munters of Stockholm, Sweden.

Household refrigerating machine patent was No. 630,617, granted to Albert T. Marshall of Brockton, Mass., on August 8, 1899, for "an automatic expansion-valve for refrigerating apparatus." *(E. H. Parfitt—Home Refrigerator)*

Ice-making machine of the vapor compression type to be made in commercial quantities was invented in 1834 by Jacob Perkins, an American living in London, who obtained British patent No. 6,662, on August 14, 1834, on an "apparatus for producing ice and cooling liquids." Perkins showed that vapors or gases which do not ordinarily exist in liquid state may be liquefied upon being subjected to high pressure.*(James Ambrose Moyer and Raymond Underwood Fittz—Refrigeration)*

The First

REFRIGERATOR—*Continued*

Mechanical refrigerator patent was No. 8,080, granted Dr. John Gorrie of Apalachicola, Fla., May 6, 1851, on an "improvement in the process for the artificial production of ice." At a dinner on July 14, 1850, at the Mansion House, Apalachicola, Gorrie produced blocks of ice the size of bricks. He installed his system in the United States Marine Hospital in Apalachicola.

Refrigerator was invented in 1803 by Thomas Moore of Baltimore, Md. It consisted of two boxes, one inside the other, separated by insulating material. Ice and food were stored in the inner box. Licenses were granted for manufacture, but permission was extended without charge to the poor. The invention was described in a 28-page pamphlet, "An essay on the most eligible construction of ice houses, also, a description of the newly invented machine, called the Refrigerator."

REFRIGERATOR CAR. *See under* Railroad car

REFUELING IN AIR. *See* Aviation: Refueling attempt in midair

REFUGE, BIRD. *See* Bird refuge

REFUNDING ACT (federal) was approved August 4, 1790 (1 Stat. L. 138), "an act making provision for the [payment of the] debt of the United States," which provided that state, domestic, and foreign debts be consolidated and refinanced by three classes of bonds.

REFUSE DISPOSAL. *See* Incinerator

REGATTA. *See* Boat race; Yacht race

REGIMENT TO RESPOND TO LINCOLN'S PROCLAMATION. *See under* Civil war

REGIMENTAL JEWISH CHAPLAIN. *See* Army officer

REGISTRATION LAW (state). *See under* Election law

REGISTRATION OF ALIENS. *See* Immigration: Alien registration

REGISTRATION OF LETTERS. *See under* Postal service

REGULATION OF TRAFFIC (printed regulations). *See* Traffic regulation pamphlet: Printed traffic regulations

REINDEER. *See* Animals

RELIEF ADMINISTRATION (federal). *See* Federal Emergency Relief Administration; Federal Surplus Relief Corporation

RELIEF MAP. *See* Map

RELIGIOUS HILLSIDE SHRINE similar to those in European Catholic countries was "The Way of the Cross," built in New Ulm, Minn., in 1884. Connected with the shrine were the Loretto Hospital and the St. Alexander Home for the Aged.

The First

RELIGIOUS LIBERTY ACT (colonial) passed by an established legislature was the Tolerance Act of Maryland enacted in April 1649. It ordered toleration for all who professed faith in Jesus Christ and subscribed to the orthodox interpretation of the Trinity but prescribed the death penalty for Aryan heretics, atheists, and Jews. It stated that "Whatsoever person or persons within this province and the islands thereunto belonging shall from henceforth blaspheme God or deny our Saviour Jesus Christ to be the Son of God, or shall deny the Holy Trinity, the Father, Son and Holy Ghost, or the Godhead of any of these said persons of the Trinity, or the unity of the Godhead, shall be punished with death and forfeiture of all his or her lands and goods to the Lord Proprietary."

RELIGIOUS PUBLICATION

Religious journal was *The Christian History*, published weekly in Boston, Mass., by Samuel Kneeland and Timothy Green for Thomas Prince, Jr., editor, from March 5, 1743, to February 23, 1745.

Religious review was *The Herald of Gospel Liberty*, which was issued September 1, 1808, by the Reverend Elias Smith. In the beginning it was issued "every other Thursday," and in 1816 it was issued only on "the first of every other month." It was published in Portsmouth, N.H.

Religious weekly newspaper in the world with a continuous publication record was *The Religious Remembrancer*. It was first issued in Philadelphia, Pa., on September 4, 1813, by John Welwood Scott. In 1840 the name was changed to *The Christian Observer*. In 1869 the offices were moved to Louisville, Ky., where it is still published. *(Christian Observer—Converse and Co.)*

RELIGIOUS ROTOGRAVURE MAGAZINE. *See* Periodical: Sectarian magazine printed in rotogravure

RELIGIOUS SERVICE BROADCAST. *See* Radio broadcast

RELIGIOUS SERVICE TELECAST. *See* Television—Telecast

RELIGIOUS SOCIETY OF FRIENDS. *See* Quakers

RELIGIOUS TRACT SOCIETY. *See* Tract society

REPORTER. *See* Newspaper reporter

REPORTER (woman) accredited to the White House. *See* News correspondent: Woman news correspondent accredited to the White House

REPRESENTATIVE (U.S.)

Actress elected to Congress *See* Actor: Actress elected to Congress

Associate Justice of the Supreme Court who had been a representative in Congress. *See under* Supreme Court (U.S.)

The First

Black representative in the House of Representatives was Joseph Hayne Rainey (Republican) of Georgetown, S.C. He was sworn in December 12, 1870, to fill the vacancy caused by the action of the House of Representatives in declaring the seat of Benjamin Franklin Whittemore vacant. Rainey served ten years, in the 41st–45th congresses, until March 3, 1879.

Black representative (Democrat) to serve in Congress was Arthur Wergs Mitchell of the First District, Illinois, who served from January 3, 1935 to January 3, 1943 (74th–77th congresses).

Black representative from the North was Oscar Stanton De Priest, a Republican, of Chicago, Ill., who served in the House of Representatives from March 4, 1929, to January 3, 1935.

Black representative to head a committee. *See* Congress (U.S.)—House of Representatives: Congressional standing committee headed by a black

Black representative (woman) to serve in Congress was Shirley Anita St. Hill Chisholm, a Democrat, elected by the 12th District, New York (in the Bedford-Stuyvesant section of Brooklyn), on November 5, 1968, to the 91st Congress. She served from January 3, 1969, and was reelected to the 92nd, 93rd, 94th, 95th, and 96th congresses.

Catholic representative was Thomas FitzSimons of Pennsylvania, who was elected as a Federalist to the First, Second, and Third congresses. He served from March 4, 1789, to March 3, 1795. Charles Carroll of Maryland, who was a Catholic, also served in the First Congress. *(American Catholic Historical Society of Philadelphia. Records 1889, Vol. 2)*

Chief Justice of the United States who had been a representative in Congress. *See under* Supreme Court (U.S.)

Congressional candidate elected while "missing" was Thomas Hale Boggs, Democrat of Louisiana, elected November 7, 1972, for the term beginning January 3, 1973. He had disappeared on October 16, 1972, while on an airplane flight with representative-at-large Nick Begich, Democrat of Alaska, Russell Brown, and the pilot, Don E. Jonz. Boggs was House majority leader and was reelected to begin his 15th term. He was declared dead, and his wife, Corinne Claiborne ("Lindy") Boggs, was elected in his stead on March 20, 1973.

Duel between representatives. *See under* Duel

Father and daughter to serve in the same Congress. *See* Mother elected to Congess, below

Grandmother to serve in Congress was Millicent Hammond Fenwick, a Republican of New Jersey, who was elected to the 94th Congress, serving from January 3, 1975, and reelected to the 95th and 96th congresses. She was born February 25, 1910, and was first elected on November 5, 1974. She had 8 grandchildren.

The First

Italian-American representative was Francis Barretto Spinola, Democrat from New York, who served in the 50th, 51st, and 52nd congresses, from March 4, 1887, to April 14, 1891.

Japanese-American woman Representative was Patsy Takemoto Mink, Democrat, of Hawaii, who served from January 4, 1965, to January 3, 1975 in the 89th, 90th, 91st, 92nd, and 93rd congresses.

Jewish representative was Israel Jacobs, who was elected by Pennsylvania to sit in the Second Congress. He served from March 4, 1791, to March 3, 1793. (As there were two men named Israel Jacobs from Pennsylvania, this statement may be open to contradiction; confusion exists as to which one served.) The next Jewish congressman was Lewis Charles Levin, representative from Pennsylvania, elected as a candidate of the American Party to the 29th, 30th, and 31st congresses. He served from March 4, 1845, to March 3, 1851.

Mother and son simultaneously elected to Congress were Ohio Republicans elected November 4, 1952, to serve in the 83rd Congress beginning January 3, 1953. Oliver Payne Bolton, 35, represented Ohio's 11th District. His mother, Frances Payne Bolton, 67, represented Ohio's 22nd District, and had served since February 27, 1940, having been elected to fill the vacancy caused by the death of her husband, Chester Castle Bolton.

Mother elected to Congress was Winnifred Sprague Mason Huck (Mrs. Robert Wardlow Huck), a Republican, of Chicago, Ill., who was elected November 7, 1922, to fill the vacancy caused by the death of her father, William Ernest Mason on June 16, 1921. She served from November 20, 1922, to March 3, 1923, in the 67th Congress.

Polish-American Representative was Barbara Ann Mikulski, a Demoract, of Maryland, who was elected November 2, 1976, reelected November 7, 1978, and began service January 4, 1977.

Representative appointed to a presidential cabinet was James Madison of Virginia, who served in Congress from March 4, 1789, to March 3, 1797, and as Secretary of State from May 2, 1801, to March 3, 1809, under President Thomas Jefferson.

Representative-elect to be refused a seat was John Bailey, Independent, of Canton, Mass., elected in 1823 to the 18th Congress (March 4, 1823, to March 3, 1825). He was excluded on the ground that he was not a resident of the district he purported to represent. (House Resolution, March 18, 1824.) Later he was elected to fill the vacancy caused by his exclusion and was seated on December 13, 1824, in the 2d Session of the 18th Congress. He was reelected to the 19th, 20th, and 21st congresses and served to March 3, 1831.

The First

REPRESENTATIVE (U.S.)—*Continued*

Representative elected by the prohibitionists was Kittel Halvorson, born in Telemarken, Norway, who was elected as the candidate of the Farmers' Alliance and the prohibitionists. He served as a representative from Minnesota from March 4, 1891, to March 3, 1893, in the 52nd Congress.

Representative in office elected President of the United States was James Abram Garfield of Ohio, who was elected President on November 4, 1880. He served as Representative of Ohio from March 4, 1863, to November 8, 1880, when he resigned. He was elected to the Senate on January 13, 1880, for the term beginning March 4, 1881, but resigned on December 23, 1880, because he was elected President of the United States for the term beginning March 4, 1881.

Representative of Asian ancestry was Dalip Singh Saund, a Democrat, representing the 29th district of California, who was born in Amritsar, India. He was elected to the 85th Congress on November 6, 1956, sworn in January 3, 1957, and reelected in 1958 and 1960.

Representative of Japanese ancestry elected to the House of Representatives was Daniel Ken Inouye, 34, Democrat, who was elected July 28, 1959, by Hawaii, the 50th state. He was sworn in on August 24, 1959, by Sam Rayburn, Speaker of the House. Inouye lost an arm fighting in World War II.

Representative of Puerto Rican ancestry was Herman Badillo, a Democrat, of New York, born August 21, 1929, in Caguas, Puerto Rico. He was elected on November 3, 1970, by the 21st district of New York and was sworn in on January 21, 1971. He served in the 92nd, 93rd, 94th, and 95th congresses and resigned on December 31, 1977.

Representative reelected after serving a prison term was Thomas Joseph Lane, a Democrat of Massachusetts, who was elected to the 77th Congress at a special election on December 30, 1941. He was sentenced to 4 months in jail for income tax evasion and served from May 7, 1956, to September 4, 1956, when he was released from the Federal Correctional Institution, Danbury, Conn. He was subsequently elected on November 6, 1956, by the 7th Congressional District to serve his 9th term.

Representative sworn in before 8:00 A.M. was James Jarrell ("Jake") Pickle, a Democrat from Texas, elected December 17, 1963, at a special election to fill the vacancy caused by the resignation of Homer Thornberry. The December 24, 1963, session opened in the House of Representatives at 7:00 A.M. for the discussion of the foreign aid bill and at 7:15 A.M. Pickle was sworn in as a member of the 88th Congress.

Representative to attend college after his term of service was George Arthur Bartlett, a Demo-

The First

crat, representative from Nevada, who served from March 4, 1907, to March 3, 1911, in the 60th and 61st congresses. He enrolled as a freshman on August 18, 1911, in the University of Nevada, Reno, Nev. Previously, he was graduated from the law department of Georgetown University, Washington, D.C.

Representative to die was Theodoric Bland of Virginia, born March 21, 1742, who died June 1, 1790, in New York City. He was buried in Trinity Churchyard, New York City. His body was reinterred in the Congregational Cemetery, Washington, D.C., on August 31, 1828.

Representative to give birth while holding office was Yvonne Braithwaite Burke (Mrs. William Burke), age 41, Democrat of California, who gave birth to a daughter, Autumn Roxanne Burke, in Los Angeles, Calif., on November 23, 1973. She was elected to the 93rd Congress on November 7, 1972, and reelected to serve in the 94th and 95th congresses.

Representative to serve as Associate Justice of the Supreme Court. *See* Supreme Court (U.S.): Associate Justice of the Supreme Court who had been a representative in Congress.

Representative to serve before his 25th birthday in contravention of the 25-years-of-age requirement was William Charles Cole Claiborne of Tennessee, a Jeffersonian Democrat, who served from March 4, 1797, to March 3, 1801, in the 5th and 6th congresses. He was born in Sussex County, Va., in 1775.

Representative to serve 56 years was Carl Trumbull Hayden, who upon the admission of Arizona as a state into the Union was elected as a Democrat to the 62nd Congress and the 7 succeeding congresses, serving in the House of Representatives from February 19, 1912, to March 3, 1927, and then was elected to the U.S. Senate serving there from March 4, 1927, through May 1968.

Representative to serve 1 day was George Augustus Sheridan of Lake Providence, La., elected as a Liberal on November 5, 1872, to the 43rd Congress (March 4, 1873, through March 3, 1875). He finally took his seat on March 3, 1875, after an unsuccessful contest by Pinckney Benton Stewart Pinchback.

Representative who had a Medal of Honor and was graduated from the U.S. Naval Academy was Willis Winter Bradley, Jr., who served as a Representative from the 18th District, California, from January 3, 1947, to January 3, 1949, in the 80th Congress. He was graduated September 12, 1906, and served as lieutenant on the U.S.S. *Pittsburgh*, rescuing a sailor and extinguishing a fire in the explosives section on July 23, 1917.

Representative who had been a President of the United States was John Quincy Adams. He served as President from March 4, 1825, to March 3, 1829, and represented the Plymouth, Mass., district in

The First

Congress as a Whig from March 4, 1831, to February 23, 1848, when he died. He served in the 22nd and the 8 succeeding congresses 17 years less 10 days. *(John Quincy Adams—The Diary of John Quincy Adams)*

Representative who had lost both legs in World War II was Charles Edward Potter, Republican, of Michigan, who served in the House of Representatives from August 26, 1947, to November 4, 1952, and in the Senate from November 5, 1952, to January 3, 1959. He enlisted as a private in the Infantry and was discharged from service as a major on July 10, 1946. He suffered the loss of his lower limbs at Colmar, France, on January 31, 1945.

Representative (woman) elected to the United States House of Representatives was Jeannette Rankin. She was elected as a Republican by Montana and served from March 4, 1917, to March 4, 1919, and from January 3, 1941, to January 3, 1943. She was the first representative to vote twice against entry into war, on April 6, 1917, and December 8, 1941. *(Hannah Josephson—Jeannette Rankin)*

Representative (woman) elected to serve in the place of her husband was Mae Ella Nolan of the Fifth District of California. She was a Republican and filled the vacancy in the House of Representatives caused by the death of her husband, John Ignatius Nolan. She served from January 23, 1923, to March 3, 1925.

Representative (woman) to head a committee. *See* Congress (U.S.)—House of Representatives: Congressional committee headed by a woman

Representative (woman) to preside over the House of Representatives was Alice Mary Robertson of Oklahoma. At a special session of the 67th Congress on June 20, 1921, Representative David Walsh of Massachusetts asked her to take the chair. She merely announced the vote, which was 209 yeas and 42 nays on an appropriation of $15,000 for a commission to represent the United States at the Peruvian Centennial of Independence exhibition. *(Chronicles of Oklahoma, Vol. 10)*

Representative (woman) to vote twice against the entry of the United States into war was Mrs. Jeannette Rankin of Montana, whose votes were cast April 6, 1917, and December 8, 1941.

Representatives (brothers) to serve simultaneously were the Washburn brothers, each representing a different state: Israel Washburn, Jr., of Maine (Whig, 32nd–33rd congresses, Republican, 34th–36th congresses, March 4, 1851, to January 1, 1861); Elihu Benjamin Washburne of Illinois (spelled with an *e*) (Whig, 33rd and 8 succeeding congresses, March 4, 1853, to March 6, 1869); and Cadwallader Colden Washburn of Wisconsin (Republican, 34th–36th congresses, March 4, 1855, to March 3, 1861). The three brothers served si-

The First

multaneously as congressmen from March 4, 1855, to January 1, 1861. Another brother, William Drew Washburn of Minnesota (Republican, 46th–48th congresses), served from March 4, 1879, to March 3, 1885.

Representatives to marry each other were Martha Elizabeth Keys (Democrat, Kansas) and Andrew Jacobs, Jr. (Democrat, Indiana), both elected November 5, 1974, to the 94th Congress. They were married on January 3, 1976 at Topeka, Kan. He had first been elected November 3, 1964, and had served in the 89th, 90th, 91st, and 92nd congresses; and he was elected subsequently to the 95th and 96th congresses. She was reelected to serve in the 95th Congress.

Roman Catholic priest to serve in Congress was Father Gabriel Richard, 56 years old, who served as a nonvoting Delegate from Michigan Territory in the 18th Congress from March 4, 1823, to March 3, 1825. He was ordained a priest in France on October 15, 1790, and served as a missionary in Detroit, Mich.

Socialist representative was Victor Louis Berger of Wisconsin, who served from March 4, 1911, to March 3, 1913, in the 62nd Congress. He was elected to the 66th and 67th congresses, but was not permitted to hold a seat therein. He was elected to the 68th, 69th, and 70th congresses and served from March 4, 1923, to March 3, 1929. *(Victor L. Berger—Voice and Pen of Victor L. Berger)*

Woman representative who was not sworn in was Elizabeth ("Bessie") Hawley Gasque, a Democrat, of Florence, S.C., who was elected to the 75th Congress to fill the vacancy caused by the death of her husband Allard Henry Gasque. She served from September 13, 1938, to January 3, 1939. She was not sworn in because Congress was not in session.

Woman to serve 18 terms in Congress was Edith Frances Nourse Rogers, Republican, representing the 5th District of Massachusetts, who served in the 69th through the 86th congress, from December 7, 1925, to September 10, 1960. Her husband, John Jacob Rogers, who died on March 28, 1925, served from March 4, 1913, to his death (63rd to 69th congress inclusive).

Woman to serve in both the House of Representatives and the Senate was Margaret Chase Smith of Skowhegan, Me., a Republican, elected to the 76th Congress to fill the vacancy caused by the death of her husband, Representative Clyde Harold Smith on April 8, 1940. She was reelected to the 77th and the 3 succeeding congresses and served from June 3, 1940, to January 3, 1949. She was elected to the Senate for the term beginning January 3, 1949, and served to January 3, 1973, having been defeated for reelection in 1972.

REPUBLICAN CARTOON. *See* Cartoon

The First

REPUBLICAN PARTY

Republican Party meeting (local) was held on February 22, 1854, when the antislavery factions of the Whig and Free Democratic parties of Michigan held a preliminary organization meeting. The name Republican was suggested by Alvan Earle Bovay at a meeting in Ripon, Wis., on March 20, 1854; at a previous meeting in Ripon, on February 28, the new party had been organized in protest against the Kansas-Nebraska bill. The first convention formally organized under the name of Republican Party met in Strong, Maine, on August 7, 1854.

Republican Party meeting (national) was held in Pittsburgh, Pa., February 22, 1856, in response to a call issued on January 17, 1856, by David Wilmot of Pennsylvania, Lawrence Bainard of Vermont, William W. White of Wisconsin, A. P. Stone of Ohio, and J. Z. Goodrich of Massachusetts. The purpose of the meeting was to perfect the national organization and to arrange for a national convention of the new party to nominate candidates for President and Vice President for the coming election. *(Frank C. Harper—Pittsburgh of Today)*

Republican Party national convention was held at Music Fund Hall, Philadelphia, Pa., on June 17, 1856; at that convention the first Republican National platform was adopted. The first presidential candidate was John Charles Fremont and the vice presidential candidate William Lewis Dayton.

Woman Republican national committee chairman. *See under* Woman

RESALE PRICE MAINTENANCE LAW. *See* Price regulation law

RESEARCH COUNCIL. *See* Science association: National Research Council

RESEARCH INSTITUTE

Anatomy research institute was the Wistar Institute of Anatomy and Biology, which was established in Philadelphia, Pa., on July 20, 1891, by General Isaac Jones Wistar through a $20,000 fund in memory of Caspar Wistar. It was incorporated April 22, 1892. The first building was dedicated on May 21, 1894. *(Methods and Problems of Medical Education. Seventeenth series. Rockefeller Foundation)*

Institute for research in nervous diseases was the Neurological Institute of New York, incorporated April 5, 1909, which opened its hospital October 1, 1909, in New York City. The first superintendent was Alexander H. Candlish.

RESEARCH LABORATORY, INDUSTRIAL. *See* Industrial research laboratory

RESEARCH REACTOR. *See* Atomic reactor

The First

RESERVATION. *See* American Indian reservation; Bird reservation

RESERVE, FOREST. *See* Forest Reserve

RESERVE OFFICERS ASSOCIATION MEDAL. *See* Medal

RESERVE OFFICERS TRAINING CORPS. *See under* Army

RESIDENT FELLOWSHIP. *See* Fellowship

RESPIRATOR (iron lung) was invented by Professor Philip Drinker and Louis Agassiz Shaw, who made the original model in April 1927, adapted only for laboratory use. It consisted of a cheap galvanized iron box with a bed made from "garage creepers" and two household vacuum cleaners with hand-operated valves as the source of alternate positive and negative pressure. The Consolidated Gas Company of New York donated $7,000 to Harvard University, Cambridge, Mass., and a second model was manufactured, which was first used October 12, 1928, at the Children's Hospital, Boston, Mass., on a little girl suffering from respiratory failure caused by poliomyelitis. The machine was manufactured by Warren E. Collins, Inc., Boston, Mass. *(Journal of the American Medical Association. May 18, 1929)*

RESTAURANT

Cafeteria. *See* Cafeteria

Penny restaurant where most items were sold for 1 cent was opened by Bernarr Adolphus Macfadden at 487 Pearl Street, New York City, in the winter of 1900. In 1901 he opened a larger one and continued opening branches, until 30 were in operation in 1906. They were known as the Macfadden Physical Culture Restaurants.

Restaurant with an automatic arrangement for vending food was the Automat Restaurant, which was opened by the Horn & Hardart Baking Company at 818 Chestnut Street, Philadelphia, Pa., on June 9, 1902. The mechanism was imported from Germany, the patents having been acquired there from their Swedish originators. These original mechanisms differed materially from those later used in the Automat restaurants, which were of the company's own patent and manufacture.

Revolving restaurant was The Top of the Needle (The Space Needle) located at the 500-foot level of the 600-foot-high steel and glass tower dedicated May 22, 1961, at the Century 21 Exposition, Seattle, Wash. It contained 260 seats and revolved 360 degrees in an hour. Above the restaurant was an observation deck and above that a beacon. It was designed by John Graham & Company. The Seattle World's Fair on the 74-acre Fair Grounds was opened by remote control by President John Fitzgerald Kennedy from Palm Beach, Fla., on April 21, 1962.

The First

Self-service restaurant was opened September 4, 1885, at 7 New Street, New York City, opposite the New York Stock Exchange. It was called the Exchange Buffet.

RESTAURANT CHINA. *See* Chinaware

RETAIL PRICE LAW (state). *See* Price regulation legislation: Price regulation law (state)

REVENUE BUREAU. *See* Internal revenue act

REVENUE COLLECTOR (woman). *See* Woman: Woman internal revenue collector

REVENUE CUTTER. *See* Ship

REVENUE STAMP printed by the Post Office Department was the "Federal duck stamp," a $1 stamp required of all waterfowl hunters over 16 years of age, to be attached to game licenses as required by the Migratory Bird Conservation Act of March 16, 1934 (48 Stat. L. 451). The stamp went on sale August 14, 1934, and was the same size as the special delivery postage stamps. It depicted a male and female mallard coming to rest on a marshland and was drawn by Jay Norwood ("Ding") Darling, chief of the Bureau of Biological Survey of the Department of Agriculture. Stamps of this class, as well as all other revenue stamps, had previously been issued by the Treasury Department. Although sold through the Post Office Department, the proceeds went to the Department of Agriculture, where 10 percent was used for the expense of printing and selling the stamps and the balance to lease or purchase marsh areas for waterfowl sanctuaries.

REVIVAL MEETING of importance was known as the Great Awakening and was inspired by the Reverend Jonathan Edwards, noted theologian and metaphysician, pastor of the Congregational Church, Northampton, Mass. He was instrumental in bringing about the wave of religious hysteria which swept the country from 1735 to 1740.

REVOLUTIONARY WAR
American casualties occurred March 5, 1770, at Boston, Mass., when British soldiers of the 29th Regiment of Foot fired at a taunting crowd resulting in the deaths of Crispus Attucks, James Caldwell, Patrick Carr, Samuel Gray, and Samuel Maverick. The incident became known as the Boston Massacre. John Adams and Josiah Quincy, Jr., defended the murder charge instituted in October. Colonel Thomas Preston was acquitted, 6 soldiers were found not guilty, 2 soldiers were found guilty, branded on the hand and discharged.

Armed conflict in the Revolutionary War was a skirmish at Lexington, Mass., April 19, 1775, between the Minutemen under Captain John Parker and the British Regulars under Major John Pitcairn.

The First

Attack on British soldiers was made in New York City on January 18, 1770, by the Sons of Liberty, a group of citizens, who attacked from 40 to 50 soldiers because they had cut down the "Liberty Poles" that the citizens had erected. The soldiers used their bayonets and dispersed them. No one was killed, but several were seriously injured on both sides. The mob fight has been termed the Battle of Golden Hill.

Bayonet charge in the Revolutionary War occurred July 16, 1779, when General "Mad Anthony" Wayne with 1,200 men charged the British Garrison at Stony Point, N.Y., and forced it to surrender. He was slightly wounded. The British loss was 63 killed and 553 wounded; the American loss 15 killed and 83 wounded.

British flag capture was made by Brigadier General Richard Montgomery, who with 83 men attacked the 7th (Royal Fusiliers) Regiment of Foot and captured Fort Chambly, Canada, on October 18, 1775. He sent the captured flag to the Continental Congress.

Conflict on equal terms between American regulars and British regulars was the Battle of Monmouth Courthouse, Freehold, N.J., June 28, 1778. The Americans under General George Washington lost 69 killed and 160 wounded; the British under Sir Henry Clinton lost 300 killed and 100 wounded and prisoners. *(Trevor N. Dupuy— People and Events of the American Revolution)*

Incident in the Revolutionary War occurred December 13, 1774, when Major John Sullivan of the Granite State Volunteers, later a major general in the Continental Army, and 400 patriots attacked Fort William and Mary at New Castle, N.H., in Portsmouth harbor. They bound the commander of the fort and frightened the soldiers away, capturing 100 casks of powder and small arms. This attack took place some four months before the battle of Lexington. *(Thomas Coffin Amory—The Military Services and Public Life of Major General John Sullivan)*

Martyr in the Revolutionary War was Christopher Snider, an 11-year-old boy, who was killed February 22, 1770, in Boston, Mass., when Ebenezer Richardson fired upon a mob which attacked his house because he had removed the marks set against the house of Theophilus Lille, who had violated the merchants' agreement against importing. Sammy Gore was also shot by Richardson but did not die. On the day of the funeral, shops and schools closed. Richardson was convicted of murder and sentenced to two years in prison. *(Boston Evening Post. Feb. 26, 1770)*

Military action occurred May 10, 1775, when Ethan Allen and 83 men (the Green Mountain Boys) crossed Lake Champlain from Vermont in scows, entered Fort Ticonderoga, N.Y., through the south gate and swarmed into the barracks

The First

REVOLUTIONARY WAR—*Continued*
while the soldiers were asleep. Allen demanded the surrender of the fort "in the name of the Great Jehovah and the Continental Congress." The fort commanded by Captain William Delaplace and Lieutenant Jocelyn Feltham was captured with 78 guns, 6 mortars, 3 howitzers, thousands of cannon balls, 30,000 flints, and other supplies.

Naval attack was made June 9, 1772, against the British revenue cutter schooner *Gaspee* commanded by Lieutenant William Duddingston, which ran aground while chasing the packet *Hanna* off Namquit Point, Providence, R.I., in Narragansett Bay. During the night, 8 longboats captained by Abraham Whipple carried merchant John Brown and others who boarded the *Gaspee* and set it on fire. *(J. R. Bartlett—The Destruction of the Gaspee in Narragansett Bay)*

Naval battle of the Revolution took place June 12, 1775, when Captain James Moore of the British schooner *Margaretta* arrived in the harbor of Machias, Maine, and ordered the citizens to take down a liberty pole which they had erected. The citizens, led by Jeremiah and John O'Brien, set out in a confiscated sloop, *Unity,* and in a hand-to-hand encounter captured the *Margaretta,* confiscated her cannons, captured the crew, and marched them overland to Cambridge, Mass., where they were turned over to General Washington. The American loss was four killed and eight wounded. *(Andrew Magoun Sherman—Life of Captain Jeremiah O'Brien)*

Revolutionary war volunteer detachment to arrive in Cambridge, Mass., was the Reading Riflemen of Reading, Pa., which arrived July 18, 1775. The Riflemen of York, York, Pa., arrived July 25, 1775. *(American Archives. 4th Series. Vol. 12, p. 1722)*

REVOLVER. *See* Pistol

REVOLVER SHOOTING TOURNAMENT (international) was held June 16, 1900, between teams representing the United States and France. Each contestant had 30 shots at targets placed at 150 feet and 52½ feet. The American team won by 61 points. Out of a possible score of 6,000 points, the Americans received 4,889 and the Frenchmen 4,828 points. The contest was held at the shooting range in Armbruster Park, Greenville, N.J., and Gastinne-Renett's pistol range, Paris. The scores were cabled to the opposing teams.

REVOLVING DOOR. *See* Door (revolving)

REVOLVING GUN. *See* Ordnance

RHINOCEROS. *See* Animals

RHODES SCHOLAR
  American Rhodes scholar to be killed in action was William Alexander Fleet of Virginia, who died on May 18, 1918.

The First

  Black to win a Rhodes scholarship was Alain Le Roy Locke of Pennsylvania, who "attended Hertford [Oxford University] 1907–1910, read Philosophy." He received his A.B. degree in 1908 from Harvard University. *(Rhodes Scholarships, Records of Past Scholars)*

  Rhodes Scholars took up their residence at Oxford University, England, in 1904. Under the last will of Cecil Rhodes, dated July 1, 1899, annual awards of 3-year scholarships at Oxford were available to 2 American students from each state. Until World War I, 1 man was appointed from each state each year for 2 years, and all appointments were omitted the 3rd year. The first year 43 awards were made to students, each from a different state. The first award alphabetically went to Stanley Royal Ashby of Texas; the first award alphabetically to the first state alphabetically went to James Holtzclaw. During World War I the awards were suspended. Later the system was changed so that now the United States is divided into 6 districts of 6 states each and 2 of 7 states, from which 32 scholars are chosen each year, 4 from each district. The total number of scholars in residence at one time is the same under the two systems. *(Laurence Alden Crosby—Oxford of Today: A Manual for Prospective Rhodes Scholars)*

RHUBARB was shipped from London, England on January 11, 1770, by Benjamin Franklin to John Bartram in Philadelphia, Pa.

RHYMING DICTIONARY. *See* Dictionary

RICE was imported by Sir William Berkeley, governor of Virginia, in 1647. He directed that a half bushel of seeds be planted. The yield was 16 bushels. *(Amory Austin—Rice, Its Cultivation, Production and Distribution in the United States and Foreign Countries)*

RIDING CHAMPION (jockey). *See* Jockey: Jockey to win the national riding championship four times

RIFLE. *See* Ordnance: Gun (rifled); Ordnance: Semiautomatic rifle

RIFLE ASSOCIATION
  Rifle association (national) was the National Rifle Association, organized and chartered November 24, 1871, in New York City with 35 members. The first shooting meet was held April 25, 1873, at Creedmoor, L.I., N.Y. Nine regiments of the New York National Guard, one regiment of the New Jersey National Guard, the U.S. Engineers, and a squad of regular servicemen from Governors Island competed. The first officers of the association were president, General Ambrose Everett Burnside; vice president, Colonel William Conant Church; secretary, Captain George Wood Wingate; corresponding secretary, Frederick M. Peck; and treasurer, General John Blackburne Woodward.

The First

Rifle tournament (international) of consequence was held September 26, 1874, at Creedmoor, L.I., N.Y., between an American team commanded by Colonel George Wood Wingate, and an Irish team, commanded by Captain Arthur Blennerhassett Leech, which was the challenger. Each team was composed of six men who fired 15 shots each at targets at a distance of 800, 900, and 1,000 yards. The targets had square bull's-eyes and scores were rated at 4, 3, and 2 according to position. The maximum score possible was 1,080 points. The Americans represented by the Amateur Rifle Club of New York used American breechloaders and won the contest, 934-931 points. Captain Leech of the Irish team presented a cup to the National Rifle Association. In 1875 Princess Louise, on behalf of Queen Victoria, presented the association with the Wimbledon Cup, which has been the trophy since that date. *(A. H. Weston—The Rifle Club and Range)*

RIM (automobile). *See* Automobile tire: Demountable tire-carrying rim

RINK. *See* Ice skating rink; Roller skating rink

RIVET production (commercial) was attempted by Josiah Gilbert Pierson, who invented a "cold-header machine" on which he obtained a patent on March 23, 1794. His heading machine was a massive affair, with a heavy framework anchored to the floor. A large flywheel was provided and operated on the toggle principle. His factory was located on the present site of the New York Produce Exchange.

RIVETLESS CARGO VESSEL. *See* Ship

ROAD

Border-to-border national highway was Interstate 75, which extended 1,564 miles from Canada to the Gulf of Mexico. The final section was dedicated December 22, 1977.

Brick pavement was laid in Charleston, W.Va., in 1870 by a private citizen at his own expense. In 1873 the city extended the paving to include several streets.

Brick pavement on a rural road was the 7.93-mile project begun in 1893 on the Wooster Pike, now U.S. Route 42, leading out of Cleveland, Ohio. An 8-foot brick pavement was laid on a 6-inch broken stone base and edged with stone curbs. Completed in 1895, it extended from the York Road to the Lunn Road, then in the countryside outside the city.

Coast-to-coast paved road was the Lincoln Highway. Carl Graham Fisher proposed a 3,300-mile highway and on July 1, 1913, the Lincoln Highway Association was formed with Henry Bourne Joy as president. The proclamation of the opening of the road from New York City to San Francisco, Calif., was made September 10, 1913. The highway traversed 13 states—New York, New Jersey, Pennsylvania, Ohio, Indiana, Illinois,

The First

Iowa, Nebraska, Colorado, Wyoming, Utah, Nevada, and California—and cost about $10 million. The first complete coast-to-coast run over the official route was made by Neil Patterson. The association disbanded December 31, 1927.

Concrete road was built in Bellefontaine, Ohio, in 1892 on the west side of Main Street. A strip 10 feet wide and 220 feet long was put down. In 1893–94 the remainder of Main Street and also Columbus, Opera, and Court streets were paved on the four sides of the public square.

Concrete rural road was laid in Wayne County, Mich., in July of 1909. One mile of concrete pavement 18 feet wide and 6½ inches deep was laid on Woodward Road between Six Mile and Seven Mile roads near Detroit, at a cost of $13,534.59.

Cotton fabric used on a road was placed on a short stretch of experimental bituminous double-surface pavement on Route 2 between Chapin and Prosperity, Newberry County, S.C., in 1926. The fabric, classed as Cider Duck, was laid on the road in longitudinal strips overlapping each other two or three inches, after a coat of tar prime had been applied. Hot asphalt was then applied and covered with coarse sand and crushed rock.

Divided highway was Savery's Avenue, a half-mile dirt road in Carver, Mass., which was built in 1861–1862 and presented to the public by William Savery. Trees were left standing between the roads "for shade and ornament for man and beast." Both roads were macadamized in 1907.

Electronic highway system was conceived by Dr. Vladimir Kosma Zworykin at the RCA Laboratories, David Sarnoff Research Center, Princeton, N.J. Demonstrations were given in June 1953 with a controlled miniature car and on June 3, 1960, with a standard automobile. Wire cables buried under the pavement conveyed impulses to electronic circles in the automobiles in order to reduce speed automatically and thus prevent collisions.

Federal grant-in-aid to states for roads was the Federal Aid Road Act, "to provide that the United States shall aid the states in the construction of rural post roads, and for other purposes," passed July 11, 1916 (39 Stat. L. 355). For the fiscal year ending June 30, 1917, $5 million was appropriated, which amount was increased $5 million every year until the appropriation in 1921 was $25 million. The first project was in Contra Costa County, Calif., between the Alameda–Contra Costa boundary and the city limits of Richmond, Calif. Bids were opened June 26, 1916, and the contract awarded July 10, 1916, for the 2.55 miles. The work cost $53,938.85, of which $24,246.56 was the federal appropriation. The project statement was submitted September 1, 1916, and approved October 18, 1916, by David Franklin Houston, Secretary of Agriculture.

The First

ROAD—*Continued*

Federal highway built with funds from the national treasury was the Great National Pike, also known as the Cumberland Road, built in sections from 1806 to 1840 between Cumberland, Md., and Vandalia, Ill. A Congressional act of March 29, 1806 (2 Stat. L. 357), "to regulate the laying out and making a road from Cumberland, in the state of Maryland, to the state of Ohio" appropriated $30,-000. The first construction contracts were let April 16 and May 8, 1811. The last appropriation was made May 25, 1838 (5 Stat. L. 228), the total appropriation being $6,821,246. In 1856 the road was turned over to the states through which it passed. Some of the money obtained from the sale of public lands, however, was appropriated for state road work. *(Thomas B. Searight—The Old Pike)*

Federal road agency, known as the Office of Road Inquiry, was established in the Department of Agriculture by statute approved March 3, 1893 (27 Stat. L. 737), "to make inquiries in regard to the systems of road management throughout the United States, to make investigations in regard to the best method of road making, to prepare publications on this subject suitable for distribution." General Roy Stone was appointed head of the new organization as special agent and engineer for Road Inquiry.

Hard-surfaced road extended about 100 miles from the Pahaquarry Mines, N.J., to Kingston, N.Y., through Warren and Sussex counties, N.J. It was completed by the Dutch in 1663.

Highway legislation (colonial) was Act No. 50, passed by the Virginia legislature at the September 4, 1632, session at James City. It provided that "Highways shall be layd out in such convenient places as are requisite accordinge as the Governor and Counsell or the Commissioners for the monthlie corts shall appoynt, or accordinge as the parishoners of every parish shall agree." *(William Waller Hening—The Statutes at Large being a Collection of all the Laws of Virginia from the First Session of the Legislature in the Year 1619, Vol. 1)*

Highway planning surveys (nationwide) were authorized by Congress in the Hayden-Cartwright Act (48 Stat. L. 993), approved June 18, 1934. The surveys were designed to obtain traffic volume and load-weight and other information needed for the rational planning of a nationwide system of interstate highways. The surveys were to be made by the Bureau of Public Roads of the United States Department of Agriculture, in cooperation with the several state highway departments.

Inter-American highway appropriation was made by Congress March 26, 1930 (46 Stat. L. 115), when $50,000 was authorized for extending a route through the Central American republics connecting Panama City, Panama, with the United States.

The First

Interchange structure of 4 levels was built in Los Angeles, Calif., and connected the Hollywood, Harbor, Santa Ana, and the Arroyo Seco (now Pasadena) Freeways. All sections were opened and in operation September 22, 1953.

Law regarding state aid for roads was "an act to provide for the more permanent improvement of the public roads of this state," passed April 14, 1891, by New Jersey and signed by Governor Leon Abbett. It placed the administration of state aid under the direction of the president of the State Board of Agriculture, who served without fee or reward for two and a half years. On March 29, 1892, the act was amended and provided for the appointment of a commissioner of Public Roads. The first commissioner was Edward Burroughs, appointed May 17, 1894, by Governor George T. Werts. *(First Annual Report of the Commissioner of Public Roads for the year ending December 31, 1894)*

Macadam road was the Lancaster Turnpike, 62 miles long, connecting Philadelphia and Lancaster, Pa. Work was begun in February 1793 by the Philadelphia and Lancaster Turnpike Railroad Company, chartered April 9, 1792, of which William Bingham was the first president. The road was completed December 1795 at an approximate cost of $7,500 a mile, a total of $465,000, which was provided by individual investors. The first two miles of the road were surfaced with coarse gravel. The remainder, surfaced with "pounded" or broken stone, was 24 feet in width, 18 inches deep in the center, and 12 inches deep at the edge. Paralleling the main stone-surfaced road was a summer or side road 13 feet in width which was used in good weather as it was easier on the horses' feet than the angular crushed stone.

Mosaic pavement similar to old mosaics was laid on Canal Street, New Orleans, La. The mosaic effect was secured by mixing chipped metronite, crown point spar, and mica with the cement, then pouring the mixture into diamond-shaped brass-stripped forms, sanding it down, and polishing it. The work was completed on February 4, 1930, and was part of the project referred to as the "Beautification of Canal Street."

Overland wagon road across the Rocky Mountains to the Pacific coast was the Oregon Trail. It followed Indian and buffalo trails, and was blazed by many, but it may be considered to date from 1842 when John Charles Fremont made a survey of it for the government prior to the great covered-wagon expeditions. The Oregon Trail began at Westport Landing or Independence Landing on the Missouri River, followed the Sante Fe trail for a short distance, then extended for some 2,000 miles across Missouri, Kansas, Nebraska, Wyoming, Idaho, and Oregon to Vancouver on the north side of the Columbia River, in what is now the state of Washington.

The First

Plank road was completed July 18, 1846, by the Salina and Central Square Plank Road Company between Syracuse and Central Square, N.Y. Trenches were dug slightly below the level of the road and a single track of hemlock planks about 4 inches thick and 8 feet long was placed at right angles to the road. The track was covered with dirt as protection against horses' hoofs.

Road paved with glasphalt, a combination of crushed waste glass and a paving material, ¾ th of an inch thick, was completed August 6, 1971, on 15th Street, from Dodge Street to Capitol Avenue, Omaha, Neb. by J. J. Parks Company of Omaha at a cost of $13 a ton.

Road pavement was laid at Pemaquid, Maine, in 1625. It was 33 feet wide and consisted of stones, rocks, and cobblestones. *(John Henry Cartland—Twenty Years at Pemaquid)*

Road with a depressed trough was constructed on the Meridian Highway No. 2 between Temple and Belton, Tex., at a cost of approximately $50,-000 a mile. It was opened to traffic on December 15, 1925, but did not prove satisfactory. *(Records in State Highway Department, Austin, Tex.)*

Route numbering system (nationwide) was adopted March 2, 1925, by the Joint Board of State and Federal Highway officials appointed by the Secretary of Agriculture. To eliminate confusion caused by the motley array of signs in various localities the board adopted the familiar U.S. shield numbered marker.

Sheet asphalt pavement was laid on William Street, Newark, N.J., on July 29, 1870, by Professor Edward Joseph De Smedt of the American Asphalt Pavement Company, New York City. It was known as French asphalt pavement. On May 31, 1870, De Smedt obtained patents (Nos. 103,581 and 103,582), which he assigned to the New York Improved Anthracite Coal Company. *(Scientific American. Mar. 5, 1870)*

State highway metric-distance-marker system was instituted by the Ohio Department of Transportation, which began the erection of 4 signs on February 12, 1973, on Interstate 71 between Cincinnati and Columbus, and Columbus and Cleveland. The signs showed the distance in both miles and kilometers.

State road appropriation of a specific sum was made by Kentucky on December 19, 1795, when $2,000 was appropriated for the purpose of opening a wagon road from Crab Orchard to Cumberland Gap. *(Lewis Collins—History of Kentucky)*

State road authorization was made by Kentucky December 14, 1793, when Daniel Weisiger, Bennett Pemberton, and Nathaniel Sanders were appointed "commissioners to receive subscriptions in money, labor or property, to raise a fund for clearing a wagon road from Frankfort, Ky., to Cincinnati, Ohio."

The First

Stone pavement was laid in New York City in 1657 on Brouwere (Brewer Street), the location of many breweries. On January 24, 1858, Isaaq de Foreest and Jieronimus Ebbingh were authorized to contract for paving stones and to assess each house in the street. Cobble stones were used and the street was consequently known as Stone Street.

Synthetic rubber in an asphaltic concrete resurfacing mixture was used in Akron, Ohio, on September 7, 1948, when work commenced on the resurfacing of one mile on Exchange Street. Seven to 11 pounds of rubber powder were used to each ton of asphaltic concrete. A small test section was resurfaced in 1947.

Toll road was the Little River Turnpike in Virginia, which led from Alexandria to Snicker's (Snigger's) Gap, a pass through the Blue Ridge Mountains, leading into the Shenandoah Valley in the northwest part of the state. The General Assembly in October 1785 appointed nine commissioners to erect a chain of toll gates to collect tolls to "keep in repair the said roads." The receipts were to be applied to clearing and repairing this road and the road between Alexandria and Georgetown. The road was not surfaced and by 1795 was so completely worn out that complainants charged that the road needed "an artificial bed of pounded or broken stone." *(Joseph Austin Durrenberger—Turnpikes)*

Walk of fame. *See* Walk of Fame

ROAD MAP. *See* Map: Automobile road map; Map: Road map

ROBBERY, BANK. *See* Bank robbery

ROBOT PILOTLESS AIRPLANE. *See* Aviation—Airplane: Transatlantic robot pilotless airplane

ROCK DRILL. *See* Drill: Percussion rock drill

ROCK-FILLED DAM. *See* Dam

ROCK WOOL FACTORY was the Crystal Chemical Works, Alexandria, Ind., opened June 1, 1897, by Charles Corydon Hall, who melted limestone rock in a specially designed water-jacketed cupola. The rock was blown by steam pressure into fine wool-like threads for use as insulating material. The Johns Manville Corporation acquired the works in 1929.

ROCKET
See also Satellite

Air-to-air rocket was the *Mighty Mouse,* created by the Navy's Bureau of Ordnance for use by interceptor planes to destroy bombers. The rocket, which was placed in production in October 1951, was 4 feet long, weighed 18 pounds, and had a diameter of 2.75 inches. The rockets could be fired one at a time or in salvos of 6, 12, 18, or 24.

The First

ROCKET—*Continued*

American spacecraft to impact the moon was *Ranger VI* launched January 30, 1964, at 10:49 A.M. E.S.T. from the Atlantic Missile Range, Cape Canaveral, Fla. It impacted the moon at 4:24 A.M. E.S.T. February 2, 1964. The launch vehicle was an Atlas-Agena B, 102 feet high with a 16 foot base diameter and a lift-off weight of 275,000 pounds. The payload weighed 803.7 pounds and carried 6 TV cameras, earth and sun sensors, 200 data point engineering instrumentation with telemetry system. The rocket impacted the moon at 9.39 degrees north latitude and 21.51 degrees east longitude (selenographic coordinates), on the western side of the Sea of Tranquility. The cameras failed to work.

Animals fired into space and rescued from a rocket were Able and Baker, two one-pound female monkeys, one a rhesus, the other a spider monkey, who survived a 15-minute flight in separate containers in the nose cone of a Jupiter rocket launched on May 28, 1959, from Cape Canaveral, Fla. The cone was shot 300 miles into space and recovered about 90 minutes after firing off the island of Antigua, about 1,500 miles away, by U.S. Navy frogmen from the tug *Kiowa*. A previous attempt made December 13, 1958, had been unsuccessful.

Ballistic missile was the Corporal, fired May 22, 1947, at White Sands Proving Grounds, N.Mex. It responded accurately to guidance commands and reached a range of 63 miles.

Intermediate-range ballistic missile was a Jupiter, fired May 31, 1957, from the Atlantic Missile Range, Cape Canaveral, Fla. The firing was conducted by the Jet Propulsion Laboratories and the Army Ballistic Missile Agency.

Launching silos for Atlas F missiles were built by General Dynamics-Astronautics and turned over to the Strategic Air Command on September 13, 1962. Twelve underground silos, 175 feet deep, surround Salina, Kans. The complex cost about $150 million. The missiles have a range of 6,000 miles. *(New York Times. 7:6. Sept. 14, 1962)*

Liquid-fuel rocket flight was made March 16, 1926, at Auburn, Mass., under the direction of Professor Robert Hutchins Goddard. Pressure was produced internally by an outside pressure tank, and after launching by an alcohol heater on the rocket. The rocket traversed 184 feet in 2.5 seconds, making speed along the trajectory about 60 miles an hour. The flight was reported to the Smithsonian Institution, May 5, 1926. Working under a grant from Clark University, Worcester, Mass., Professor Goddard, as early as 1920, demonstrated the lifting force of rockets using liquid oxygen and ether. *(Smithsonian Institution. Miscellaneous Collection, Vol. 95)*

The First

Liquid-fuel rocket patent was No. 1,103,503, granted July 14, 1914, to Professor Robert Hutchins Goddard of Worcester, Mass. It covered what was later termed a rocket motor.

Rocket cone recovery was accomplished August 8, 1957, when the cone of a Jupiter-C ballistic missile, fired from the Atlantic Missile Range, Cape Canaveral, Fla., was recovered. It was fired by the Army Ballistic Missile Agency and the Jet Propulsion Laboratories.

Rocket patent was granted Andrew Lanergan of Boston, Mass., who on June 21, 1859, received patent No. 24,468 on an "improvement in exhibition rockets."

Rocket to attain a 100-mile altitude was a captured German V-2 rocket fired July 30, 1946, from the White Sands Proving Grounds, N.Mex. It descended 69 miles north of the launching platform, having attained an altitude of 104 miles.

Rocket to exceed a 150-mile altitude was a Viking XI, a test missile released by the Navy containing instruments to record weather conditions. On May 24, 1954, it rose to a height of 158 miles over the White Sands Proving Grounds, N.Mex.

Rocket to intercept a low-flying airplane was a Hawk missile, fired in May 1958, which engaged an F80 jet target flying at treetop level at the White Sands Proving Grounds, N.Mex.

Rocket to intercept a supersonic target missile was a Nike Hercules missile, fired in November 1958, which destroyed a supersonic target missile traveling faster than 1,500 m.p.h. at an altitude greater than 60,000 feet.

Rocket to intercept an airplane was a Nike, fired November 27, 1951, at the White Sands Proving Grounds, N.Mex., at an aerial target. The missile detonated about 25 feet from the target, which was flying at a range of about 15 miles, an altitude of 33,000 feet, and a speed of 300 miles an hour.

Rocket to pass the sonic barrier was Rocket No. 4, flown September 9, 1934, at Marine Park, Staten Island, N.Y., by the American Rocket Society. It climbed 400 feet and traveled 1,600 feet horizontally, reaching a speed of 700 m.p.h.

Rocket to reach a speed of 700 m.p.h. was the American Rocket Society's ARS-4, launched September 9, 1934, at Marine Park, Staten Island, N.Y. It reached an altitude of 400 feet and traveled 1,600 feet at a speed of 700 m.p.h.

Rocket to reach outer space was a two-stage rocket—a Wac Corporal set in the nose of a German V-2—fired February 24, 1949, from the White Sands Proving Grounds, N.Mex., by a team of scientists under Dr. Wernher von Braun. It reached an altitude of 250 miles.

The First

Rocket with an atomic warhead was an MB-I, known as the *Genie*, fired July 19, 1957, at Yucca Flat, Nev. It was an air-to-air rocket and contained a built-in guidance mechanism. It was made by the Douglas Aircraft Company, Santa Monica, Calif., and was fired from a jet F89 Scorpion.

Ship from which a long-range rocket was launched. *See under* Ship

Ship to fire a Polaris missile. *See under* Ship

Submarine to fire a Polaris missile. *See* Submarine: Submerged submarine to fire a Polaris missile

ROCKET AIRMAIL FLIGHT. *See under* Airmail service

ROCKET AIRPLANE. *See under* Aviation—Airplane

ROCKET GLIDER FLIGHT. *See under* Glider

ROCKET GUN. *See* Ordnance: Bazooka rocket gun

ROCKET SLED

Rocket-driven sled on rails was tested March 19, 1954, by Air Force Lieutenant Colonel John Paul Stapp, chief of the Aero Medical Field Laboratory of the Holloman Air Development Center at the Holloman Air Force Base, Alamogordo, N.Mex. It was known as the "abrupt deceleration vehicle" and was designed by Northrop Aircraft, Inc., to determine the effect upon fliers of bailing out at very high altitudes at supersonic speeds. Six rockets propelled the sled at 421 m.p.h. Later experiments increased the speed to over 3,000 m.p.h. The sled moved along heavy rails mounted in concrete. It was halted by water scooped in vents in the bottom of the sled. The water trough was 5 feet wide and 18 inches deep.

ROCKET VEHICLE. *See under* Automobile

ROCKING CHAIR. *See* Chair

ROCKING TREADLE SEWING MACHINE. *See* Sewing machine: Sewing machine equipped with a rocking treadle or double treadle

ROD, BRASS. *See* Brass rod

RODENT EXTERMINATION. *See* Rat extermination (citywide) to avert bubonic plague

RODEO competition was held July 4, 1888, at the racetrack at Prescott, Ariz. Juan Leivas was awarded a medal "for roping and tieing steer." With a 100-yard start, his time was 1.175 seconds. This rodeo developed into an annual competition. Previously, ranchers often held competitions among the ranchhands on a single ranch or with neighboring ranches, in impromptu tests of working skills.

The First

RODEO TELECAST. *See under* Television—Telecast

ROLL-FILM CAMERA. *See* Camera

ROLL FILM FOR CAMERAS. *See* Photographic film

ROLL-ON, ROLL-OFF CARRIER. *See* Ship

ROLL-TOP DESK. *See* Desk

ROLLER-BEARING COAL CAR. *See* Railroad car: Coal cars with roller bearings

ROLLER-BEARING PULLMAN TRAIN. *See* Railroad car: Pullman train completely equipped with roller bearings

ROLLER DERBY. *See under* Roller skating

ROLLER SKATE

Ball-bearing skate patent was patent No. 308,-990, awarded to Levant M. Richardson of Chicago, Ill., on December 9, 1884.

ROLLER SKATING

Roller derby was the Transcontinental Roller Derby, which opened August 13, 1935, at the Coliseum, Chicago, Ill., under the direction of Leo A. Seltzer. Fifty contestants, paired two to a team, endeavored to skate and race a distance equal to that from New York to California.

ROLLER SKATING RINK

Roller skating rink (public) was opened at Newport, R.I., in 1866 under the auspices of James Leonard Plimpton of Boston, Mass., the inventor of the Plimpton skate. The skating rink was located in the Atlantic House, corner of Bellevue Avenue and Pelham Street, on the site later occupied by the Elks' Home.

ROLLING LIFT BRIDGE. *See* Bridge

ROLLING MILL (flour). *See* Flour mill: Flour rolling mill

ROLLING MILL (iron). *See* Iron: Iron mill to puddle and roll iron: Iron: Rolling mill

ROMAN CATHOLIC CHURCH. *See* entries beginning with the word *Catholic*

ROOFING TILE, BRICK. *See* Tile

ROOT BEER was manufactured by Charles Elmer Hires, a student at the Jefferson Medical College, Philadelphia, Pa., in cooperation with Dr. William Simpson and Dr. Henry Leffman in 1866. In 1869 Hires opened a drugstore in Philadelphia and placed a sign over his fountain: "Hires Root Beer 5¢." In 1876, he started a national business selling root beer.

ROPE SKI TOW. *See* Ski tow (rope)

ROPING MACHINE. *See* 'Spinning, carding, and roping machines

The First

ROSE TOURNAMENT. *See* Tournament of Roses

ROSICRUCIAN SOCIETY. *See* Ancient Mystical Order Rosae Crucis

ROTARY CLUB was founded February 23, 1905, in Chicago by a lawyer, Paul Percy Harris, who induced three friends of his—a coal dealer, a tailor, and a mining engineer—to join. Meetings were held in each member's place of business in rotation, so that each could obtain some knowledge of the others' businesses. A national association was formed by a convention of 16 clubs in August 1910 in Chicago. An international association was formed in August 1912 in Duluth, Minn., to provide charters for Winnipeg, Canada, and London, England. The constitution was revised at the Los Angeles convention, June 6, 1922, and Rotary International adopted as the new name. *(Paul Percy Harris—This Rotarian Age)*

ROTARY CONVERTER POWER PLANT. *See* Electric power plant

ROTARY CRANK (bicycle). *See* Bicycle: Bicycle with a rotary crank

ROTARY-MOTION WASHING MACHINE. *See* Washing machine

ROTARY PRESS. *See* Printing press: Rotary-type printing press

ROTOGRAVURE PRESS. *See* Printing press

ROTOGRAVURE SECTARIAN MAGAZINE. *See* Periodical: Sectarian magazine printed in rotogravure

ROTOGRAVURE SECTIONS (newspaper). *See* Newspaper: Newspaper rotogravure sections

ROTOLACTOR. *See* Milking platform (rotating)

ROTOR SHIP. *See* Ship

ROTOR WINDMILL. *See* Windmill

ROUGH-DRY LAUNDRY SERVICE. *See under* Laundry

ROUTE NUMBERING SYSTEM. *See under* Road

ROWING
　Boat race. *See* Boat race

　College to feature rowing as a sport was Yale, which in 1844 held races between various classes and students.

　Racing shell. *See under* Ship

　Transatlantic solo trip by rowboat was made by John Fairfax, who left Las Palmas, Canary Islands, on January 20, 1969, in the *Britannia*, a 22-foot rowboat. He was swept down to the Cape Verde Islands off the West African coast and landed in the surf at Hollywood, Fla., at 1:48 P.M. on July 19, 1969, a 180-day voyage.

The First

　Transatlantic trip by rowboat was accomplished by George Harbo and Frank Samuelson, who left Battery Park, New York City, June 6, 1896, in a cedar boat 5 feet wide, 18 feet 4 inches long, both ends pointed, with air tanks at both ends. It had oak timbers but no masts or sails. Provisions consisted of 60 gallons of water, 100 pounds of bread and canned meat, 6 gallons of oil, 2 gallons of signal oil, and one dozen night signals. Harbo and Samuelson arrived at St. Mary's, the Scilly Isles, off southwest England, on August 1, 1896, where they made a 2-day stopover. They reached Le Havre, France, August 7, 1896, ending a 3,250-mile voyage.

　Woman coxswain of a men's collegiate varsity team. *See under* Woman

ROYAL ARCANUM was founded in Boston, Mass., June 23, 1877, by Darius Wilson. It was a fraternal mutual assessment beneficiary and benevolent society with the motto "Mercy, Virtue and Charity." *(Royal Arcanum Supreme Council. Official Bulletin, Vol. 1. 1893)*

RUBBER
　Football with a rubber covering. *See under* Football

　Rubber company was the Roxbury India Rubber Company of Roxbury, Mass., which manufactured various rubber products in 1832. It was incorporated February 11, 1833, by Lemuel Blake, Luke Baldwin, Edwin M. Chaffee, and Charles Davis, Jr. Inasmuch as the rubber was affected by heat and cold and had a disagreeable odor, the company was unable to create an outlet for its products.

　Rubber company west of the Allegheny Mountains was founded in 1870 by Dr. Benjamin Franklin Goodrich in Akron, Ohio. *(Wonder Book of Rubber—Goodrich Rubber Co.)*

　Rubber heel was made in Lowell, Mass., by Humphrey O'Sullivan. He obtained a patent on January 24, 1899, No. 618,128, on a "safety-heel."

　Rubber patent was granted to Jacob Frederick Hummel of Philadelphia, Pa., on April 29, 1813 on a "varnish of elastic gum to render water-proof" shoes and other objects.

　Rubber patent of importance was No. 240, granted to Charles Goodyear on June 17, 1837, for a method of destroying the adhesive properties of rubber by superficial application of nitric acid with copper, or bismuth, etc. *(Bradford Kinney Peirce—Trials of an Inventor: Life and Discoveries of Charles Goodyear)*

　Rubber shoe manufacturer was Leverett Candee, who established the L. Candee Shoe Factory in Hamden, Conn., in 1842. He used the Goodyear vulcanizing patent. Prior attempts had been made in 1823 and 1831 to manufacture rubber footwear out of gum elastic, but the shoes were not service-

The First

able. They melted and produced offensive odors.

Rubber tire patent was No. 5,104, awarded May 8, 1847, to Robert William Thomson of Adelphi, Middlesex County, England, on "an improvement in carriage wheels." It was granted on the application of elastic bearings around the rims of carriage wheels. This was based on a similar patent obtained June 10, 1846 (No. 10,990), in England.

Synthetic rubber was made by Lucas Petrou Kyrides and Dr. Richard Blair Earle in 1913 for the Hood Rubber Company, East Watertown, Mass. They prepared a number of polymerized hydrocarbons having rubberlike qualities, of which dimethyl butadiene had the most likely commercial possibilities. *(Chemical and Engineering News. Oct. 10, 1943)*

Synthetic rubber in an asphaltic concrete resurfacing mixture. *See under* Road

Synthetic rubber (neoprene) was produced April 10, 1930, by Dr. Arnold M. Collins, who isolated chloroprene and observed its polymerization. In 1931, it was commercially manufactured in Deepwater, N.J., by the Du Pont Company.

Synthetic rubber produced on a commercial scale in competition with natural rubber was Du Prene, manufactured by the Du Pont company, Wilmington, Del., November 2, 1931. Chemists working under Dr. Elmer K. Bolton discovered that vinylacetylene could be treated by chemical reaction with other substances to produce a chemical called chloroprene from which synthetic rubber was made. The first commercial production of various articles made from Du Prene began in May 1932, when the Manhattan Rubber Manufacturing Division of Raybestos-Manhattan, Inc., of Passaic, N.J., made oil hose from Du Prene and offered it for sale to oil companies. Experimental tires were made of this material in February 1934 by the Dayton Rubber Manufacturing Company of Dayton, Ohio.

Vulcanized rubber was successfully produced by Charles Goodyear of New York City who obtained patent No. 3,633 on June 15, 1844, on an "improvement in india-rubber fabrics." *(Ralph Frank Wolf—India Rubber Man; the Story of Charles Goodyear)*

RUBBER-BALL CROSSING OF NIAGARA FALLS. *See* Niagara Falls: Person to go over Niagara Falls in a rubber ball

RUBBER-LINED COTTON HOSE. *See* Fire hose: Fire hose of rubber-lined cotton

RUBBERS (Artics). *See* Artics

RUGBY CONTEST (international). *See under* Football game

RULES OF ORDER. *See* Parliamentary rules of order

The First

RUNNER

Runner (American) to run a mile in less than four minutes was Don Bowden of the University of California, who on June 1, 1957, ran the mile in 3 minutes 58.7 seconds at the Pacific Amateur Athletic Union Meet at Stockton, Calif. He was the 11th man in the world to better the four-minute mile.

Runner (professional) to run a mile in less than 4 minutes was Jim Ryun, who was clocked at 3:59 in an 11-lap race on April 13, 1973, at Cobo Arena, Detroit, Mich.

Runner to run a mile indoors in less than 4 minutes was James Tully ("Jim") Beatty of the Los Angeles Track Club, who ran the mile in 3 minutes 58.9 seconds, in the Los Angeles *Times* indoor track and field meet at the Los Angeles Memorial Sports Arena, Los Angeles, Calif., on February 10, 1962.

Runner to run a mile under four minutes (in the United States) was Jim Bailey, a University of Oregon student from Australia, who ran the mile on May 5, 1956, in 3 minutes 58.6 seconds at the Los Angeles Coliseum, Los Angeles, Calif.

Runner (woman) to run a marathon in less than 2.5 hours was Grete Waitz, who ran the 26 miles 345 yards in the New York City Marathon on October 21, 1979, in 2 hours 27 minutes 33 seconds. She placed 69th in the competition, in which 10,677 of the 11,533 starters (including 1,800 women) completed the run.

Runner (woman) to run a mile in less than 4.5 minutes was Mary Decker of Eugene, Oreg., who competed in the Brooks Meet of Champions at Franklin Field, Philadelphia, Pa., on June 30, 1979. Her time was 4 minutes 23.5 seconds. On January 26, 1980, she established a new world record of 4 minutes 21.7 seconds at Mount Smart Stadium in Auckland, N.Z.

Transcontinental foot race started from Ascot Park, Los Angeles, Calif., on March 4, 1928, with 275 runners and ended May 26, 1928, on its 84th day, inside Madison Square Garden, New York City, where a final 20-mile race was held. Fifty-five runners completed the race. The first prize of $25,000 was won by Andrew Payne, a Cherokee Indian of Claremore, Okla., whose time for the 3,422.3 miles was 573 hours 4 minutes 34 seconds. The runner-up and winner of the $10,000 prize was Long John Salo of Passaic, N.J., whose time was 588 hours 40 minutes 13 seconds. Philip Granville was third and won $5,000; Mike Joyce, fourth, won $2,500. Six additional prizes of $1,000 each were awarded. The time of the first lap from Los Angeles to Puente, Calif., was 1 hour 38 minutes for the 16 miles.

RUNNING. *See* Track Meet

The First

RUNNING CHAMPIONSHIP (cross-country). *See* Sports: Cross-country championships

RUNNING MEET (intercollegiate). *See* Track meet (intercollegiate)

RURAL FREE DELIVERY. *See under* Postal service

RUSSIAN SETTLEMENT was established March 15, 1812, at Cazadero, 18 miles north of Bodega Bay on the Russian River in California. The party consisted of 95 Russians and 80 Aleut hunters from Sitka, Alaska. Under the command of Ivan Alexandrovich Kuskof they built Fort Rumiantzof, consisting of 9 buildings in an area 300 by 280 feet, surrounded by a 12-foot stockade surmounted by spikes, and 50 other buildings outside the stockade. The fort was dedicated September 11, 1812. On April 15, 1839, the Russians decided to abandon it, and it was sold to John Augustus Sutter for $30,000. The bill of sale, signed by the Russian American Company, was delivered on December 12, 1841, by Commandant Alexander Rotcheff and registered at Yerba Buena the next day. The Russians evacuated the fort in December and sailed from San Francisco on January 1, 1842. The Spaniards called the settlement Fuerto de los Rusos, the Americans, Fort Ross. *(California Historical Society Quarterly. Vol. 12, No. 3. September 1933)*

RUTHERFORDIUM. *See* Element: Element 104

S

SOS. *See* Radio distress signal: Radio SOS from an American ship

SABOTEURS
   Saboteurs executed were 6 Nazis who were electrocuted August 8, 1942, in a District of Columbia jail. They were tried by a military commission of 7 generals and found guilty of landing via rubber boats from enemy submarines, with explosives, incendiaries, fuses, detonators, timing devices, acids, etc. Four saboteurs landed June 13, 1942, at Amagansett, Long Island, N.Y., and 4 on June 17th, 1942, at Ponte Vedra Beach near Jacksonville, Fla. The Long Island saboteurs were discovered by John C. Cullen, seaman 2nd class of the Amagansett Coast Guard Station. The two other saboteurs were sentenced: George John Dasch for 30 years and Ernest Peter Burger for life.

SACCHARIN was discovered by Constantine Fahlberg, working under the direction of Professor Ira Remsen at Johns Hopkins University, Baltimore, Md. Fahlberg submitted an article "On the Liquid Toluenesulphochloride" on February 27, 1879, to the *American Chemical Journal. (American Chemical Journal. Vol. 1, No. 2-3. June 1879)*

The First

SACRED THEOLOGY DEGREE. *See* Degrees (academic and honorary): Doctor of Sacred Theology degree

SAENGERFEST. *See under* Music

SAFE DEPOSIT BOXES (hotel). *See* Hotel: Hotel with safe deposit boxes

SAFE DEPOSIT VAULT was opened June 5, 1865, by the Safe Deposit Company of New York, 140-146 Broadway, New York City. Four vaults were located on the ground floor of the building and were constantly guarded. One of the vaults was devoted exclusively to the reception of deposits of valuable articles for which the rates ranged from $1.50 to $2.50 per year for every $1,000 represented. The three other vaults contained individual safe deposit vaults the rate on which varied from $30 to $40 annually. Each subscriber was provided with an individual key to open his vault box.

SAFE (fireproof) worthy of the name was the Salamander Safe, invented by Charles A. Gayler of New York City, who obtained a patent April 12, 1833 on a "fire-proof iron chest." It consisted of two chests, one within the other with a space between to "inclose air or any non-conductors of heat."

SAFETY CONGRESS
   Safety congress, together with a public exhibition of safety appliances, was held January 28, 1907, under the auspices of the American Institute of Social Science at the American Museum of Natural History, New York City.

   Safety congress (national) was the Cooperative Safety Congress held September 30–October 5, 1912, in Milwaukee, Wis. At the second congress, September 23–25, 1913, in New York City, the name was changed to the National Council for Industrial Safety, and on October 13–15, 1914, in Chicago, Ill., at the third congress, to the National Safety Council.

SAFETY FUSE. *See* Fuse

SAFETY PIN. *See* Pin

SAFETY RAZOR. *See* Razor

SAILCLOTH FACTORY. *See under* Cloth

SAILING
   Woman to sail alone across the Pacific Ocean was Sharon Sites Adams, who sailed from Yokohama, Japan, on May 12, 1969, in a 31-foot fiberglass ketch, the *Sea Sharp* and arrived at San Diego, Calif., on July 25, 1969, 74 days 17 hours 15 minutes later, having covered a distance of approximately 5,620 miles.

SAILING VESSEL. *See* Ship

SAILORS' CHURCH. *See* Church: Mariners' church

The First

SAILORS' LIBRARY. *See* Library: Library for seamen

SAINT (Catholic)
See also Catholic canonization

American saint (male) was John Nepomucene Neumann, born in Prachatice, Bohemia (now Czechoslovakia), March 28, 1811, who arrived in New York City in 1836 and was ordained there that year. He died January 5, 1860, and was declared Venerable in 1896. In 1963 he was beatified, and on June 19, 1977, he was canonized in Rome by Pope Paul VI.

Saint (native-born Catholic) was Elizabeth Ann Bayley Seton, born August 28, 1774, in New York City, who was canonized September 14, 1975. She married William Magee Seton, founded the Society for the Relief of Poor Widows with Small Children in 1797, made her profession of faith in St. Peter's Church, Barclay Street, New York City, on March 14, 1805, and died January 4, 1821. She was beatified March 17, 1963.

Saint (Catholic) who was an American citizen was Frances Xavier Cabrini, born July 15, 1850, in Italy. She came to the United States in 1889 and became a citizen. She died December 22, 1917, was declared venerable in November 1937, and was beatified November 13, 1938. On June 13, 1946, she was voted upon favorably and on July 7, 1946, Pope Pius XII participated in the formal rites held at St. Peter's Church, Rome, at which she was canonized. *(Lucille Papin Borden—Francesca Cabrini)*

ST. LAWRENCE SEAWAY. *See under* Canal

SALES MACHINE. *See* Vending machine

SALES TAX. *See* Tax

SALMON CANNERY. *See under* Canning

SALMON HATCHERY. *See* Fish hatchery

SALT
Salt well drilled west of the Alleghenies, was bored, tubed, rigged, and operated by David Ruffner and his brother Joseph in 1808 at the Great Buffalo Lick, six miles above Charleston, W.Va., on the Big Kanawha. They started drilling on November 1, 1807, and on January 15, 1808, had an ample flow of brine. With the most primitive instruments they bored through 40 feet of rock before they were successful.

Salt works was established in America in 1630 by Governor John Harvey of Virginia, who designed and established a factory for obtaining salt by evaporation of seawater. The factory was erected at Accomac on the eastern shore of Chesapeake Bay. *(Geoffrey Martin—Salt and Alkali Industry)*

SALT TRUST. *See* Trust

The First

SALT WATER AQUARIUM. *See* Aquarium

SALUTE (complimentary) fired by Great Britain in honor of an officer of the United States and virtually the first salute to the United States, was fired May 8, 1783. General George Washington and Governor George Clinton boarded the British ship *Ceres*, commanded by Sir Guy Carleton, in New York harbor to arrange for the British evacuation, and were saluted on their arrival. When they departed, 17 guns were fired in honor of Washington's rank. New York was evacuated by the British November 25, 1783. *(Magazine of American History. Annual 1880, Vol. 5. p. 108)*

SALVATION ARMY
Salvation Army, which had been founded by William Booth in London, England, in 1865 under the name of the East London Mission and later had changed its name to the Christian Mission, started in the United States in March 1880. Commissioner George Scott Railton and seven black-coated women arrived on the *Australia*, landed at the Battery, New York City, March 10, 1880, and proceeded to Castle Garden, New York City, where the first services were held. Services were held also between performances of *Uncle Tom's Cabin* at Harry Hill's Gentleman's Sporting Theatre, as well as at street meetings. *(George Scott Railton—Twenty-one Years' Salvation Army)*

Woman bell ringer was Amelia Devine, a native of Johnstown, Pa., who in December 1901 used a small bell whose tinkle attracted pedestrians in New York City to her Christmas kettle.

Woman commander of the Salvation Army was General Elizabeth Booth, daughter of the army's founder, who was elected its fourth general on September 3, 1934, in London, England on the fourth ballot. She was 69 years of age.

SANATORIUM, NARCOTICS. *See under* Narcotics

SANCTUARY, BIRD. *See* Bird sanctuary

SANDBLASTING, the process of cleaning, engraving, cutting, and boring glass, stone, metal, and other hard substances, was invented by Benjamin Chew Tilghman of Philadelphia, who received patent No. 108,408 on October 18, 1870, for "cutting and engraving stone, metal, glass, etc." with "sand used as a projectile."

SANDPAPER PATENT was granted to Isaac Fischer, Jr., of Springfield, Vt., on June 14, 1834. His invention was covered by four different patents, all issued on the same date.

SANITARY DISTRICT was the Sanitary District of Chicago, Ill., authorized November 5, 1889, by referendum vote to construct and operate the sewage system for the protection of the public water supply. A special election of trustees was held December 12, 1899, at which Murray Nelson

The First

SANITARY DISTRICT—*Continued*
was chosen president; Lyman Edgar Cooley, chief
engineer; and Charles Bary, secretary. The first
business meeting was held on January 18, 1890.

SANITARY FAIR STAMPS. *See* Seal: Seals for
raising funds

SANITARY WARE. *See* Pottery: Pottery to make
sanitary ware

SANTA CLAUS SCHOOL was opened September 27, 1937, in Albion, N.Y., with an enrollment of
six students for the one-week course. It was conducted by Charles Willis Howard to train men to
play the part of Santa Claus.

SARDINE CANNERY. *See under* Canning

SARRUSOPHONE was manufactured in 1921 by
C. G. [Charles Gerard] Conn Company, Ltd., Elkhart, Ind. It is an instrument of the oboe class with
a metal tube.

SASH
  Wrought-iron window sash installation of importance was made in 1929 by the Mesker Brothers Iron Company of St. Louis, Mo., which placed
70,000 square feet of sash in the new plant of the
Pittsburgh Plate Glass Company in Crystal City,
Mo.

SATELLITE
  Animal fired into space to orbit the earth was
Enos, a 37.5-pound, 5½-year-old male chimpanzee, sent aloft at 1:28 P.M. on November 29, 1961,
from Cape Canaveral, Fla., in the *Mercury-Atlas 5*
satellite (1961 Alpha Iota 1). The satellite orbited
the earth twice in a 3-hour 21-minute flight at a
speed of 17,500 m.p.h. It landed near Puerto Rico
and was recovered by the U.S.S. *Stormes* 1 hour
25 minutes later, after a water landing.

  American satellite to reach the moon was the
Ranger IV, launched April 23, 1962, at 3:50 P.M.
E.S.T. from the Atlantic Missile Range, Cape
Canaveral, Fla. It was launched by an Atlas-Agena B, 102 feet high, with a 16-foot base diameter and a lift-off weight of 275,000 pounds. It traveled an estimated 229,541 miles and impacted the
moon at 7:49:53 A.M. E.S.T. on April 26, 1962. The
velocity at lunar impact was 5,963 miles per hour.

  Ballet transmitted by satellite. *See* Ballet: Ballet
transmitted by satellite

  Biosatellite *(Biosatellite I)* was launched
December 14, 1966, from Cape Kennedy, Fla. It
weighed 936.5 pounds, including a 275-pound capsule containing 13 biological experiments. It was
scheduled for reentry on December 17, 1966, but
retrofire did not occur. A biosatellite is a research
satellite that carries small life forms (animal and
vegetable) to be exposed to cosmic rays for examination of effects.

The First

  Biosatellite (successful) was *Biosatellite II*,
launched from Cape Kennedy, Fla., on September
7, 1967. It weighed 940 pounds and included a
cylindrical cone 72 inches high and 56 inches in
diameter, containing 13 radiation and general biology experiments, e.g. 10,000 vinegar gnats; 1,000
flour beetles; 560 wasps; 120 frog eggs; 875 amoeba; 13,000 bacteria cells; 78 wheat seedlings; 10
million spores of orange head mold; 64 blue wild
flowers.

  Communications earth satellite to transmit telephone, television, teleprint, and facsimile signals
between the United States and England, Italy, and
Brazil was *Relay 1* (1962 Beta Upsilon), launched
3:30 P.M. Pacific Standard Time (6:30 P.M. E.S.T.) on
December 13, 1962, by a Thor-Delta rocket from
the Atlantic Missile Range, Cape Canaveral, Fla.
The rocket was 87 feet high with an 8-foot maximum base diameter and had an approximate lift-off weight of 114,000 pounds. It had 8,215 solar
cells, 3 nickel cadmium batteries, and 5 external
antennas. The payload weighed 172 pounds and
was 33 inches high with a 29-inch diameter. The
perigee was 817.7 miles, the apogee 4,610.9 miles.
The first test patterns were not transmitted until
January 3, 1963, when the solar cells had built up
sufficient battery charge.

  Communications satellite was a 26½-inch magnesium sphere, *Echo I*, launched by a Thor Delta
rocket, 92 feet high, with a 112,000-pound lift-off
weight, launched August 12, 1960, at 5:39 A.M. from
Cape Canaveral, Fla. The satellite went into orbit
at 7:45 A.M. after the three stages of the rocket had
been fired successfully. A taped message was
transmitted from Goldstone, Calif., bounced off
the satellite, and received by the Bell Telephone
laboratory at Holmdel, N.J.

  **Communications satellite successfully placed
in orbit** was a *Courier 1B*, a delayed repeater satellite weighing 500 pounds that was launched at
1:50 P.M. E.D.T. on October 4, 1960, from Cape
Canaveral, Fla., by a 2-stage Thor-Able-Star
launch vehicle. On its second orbit it received and
recorded from Fort Monmouth, N.J., a transcribed
message by President Dwight David Eisenhower
to Secretary of State Christian Archibald Herter
at the United Nations in New York City, who
delivered it to Frederick Henry Boland, president
of the General Assembly. The first launching attempt had exploded August 18, 1960. Early communications satellites were for testing purposes
only.

  Geodetic satellite was *Anna 1B*, 350 pounds,
launched by a Thor-Able-Star rocket at 3:08 A.M.
E.S.T. on October 31, 1962, from Cape Canaveral,
Fla. It had 4 flashing lights that gave off 5 flashes
spaced 5.6 seconds apart. It had an apogee of 727
miles and perigee of 670 miles. Distances were
computed by various stations by triangulation.

The First

The name Anna is an acronym for Army, Navy, NASA, and Air Force.

International satellite was the United States-United Kingdom *Ariel 1* (S-51) launched 1:00 P.M. E.S.T. on April 26, 1962, from the Atlantic Missile Range, Cape Canaveral, Fla., by a Thor-Delta booster, 90 feet high with an 8-foot-diameter base and a 112,000 pound lift-off weight. The 132-pound cylinder payload was 23 inches in diameter and 10 11/16 inches long. It carried 6 British experiments: 3 to measure electron density, temperatures, and composition of positive ions in the ionshere; 2 to monitor intensity of radiation from the sun; and 1 to measure cosmic rays. Its apogee was 754.2 miles and its perigee 242.1 miles.

Man-made object to orbit another planet was *Mariner 9*, an unmanned American spacecraft, which entered its Martian orbit at 7:33 P.M. E.S.T. on November 13, 1971, to return mapping photographs of 70 percent of the surface, and to study the planet's thin atmosphere, clouds, and hazes and its surface chemistry and seasonable changes.

Manned docking of 2 spacecraft was effected by *Gemini VIII* (GT-8) on March 16, 1966, which made a rendezvous and docking on its 4th orbit (6½ hours after launching), with a 26-foot Agena target vehicle launched from Complex 14 at 9:00 A.M. E.S.T., the same day. *Gemini VIII* was launched from Complex 19, Cape Canaveral, Fla., at 10:41 A.M. E.S.T. by a 2-stage Titan II that developed 430,000 pounds of thrust. It made 7 orbits in 10 hours 42 minutes flight time, landing in the Pacific Ocean at 10:23 P.M. E.S.T. near Okinawa, where it was picked up 3½ hours after splashdown and hauled on to the deck of U.S.S. *Leonard F. Mason* at 1:38 A.M. on March 17, 1966. Its apogee was 164 miles, its perigee 99 miles. Neil Alden Armstrong was the command pilot and Major David Randolph Scott (U.S. Air Force) the pilot.

Multisatellite launching (2 satellites in 1 shot) was made at 1:54 A.M. E.D.T., June 22, 1960, from Cape Canaveral, Fla., by a Navy Thor-Able-Star rocket. The satellite, designated *Transit 2-A*, carried 2 instrumented payloads, Eta 1, a 36-inch sphere that weighed 223 pounds, and Eta 2, a 20-inch sphere that weighed 42 pounds.

Multisatellite launching (3 satellites in 1 shot) was made June 29, 1961, by a 70-foot Thor-Able-Star rocket from the Atlantic Missile Range, Cape Canaveral, Fla. Designated 1961 *Omicron 1*, it had 3 payloads: Transit 4-A, 1,175 pounds, equipped with an atomic radioisotope-powered battery of the Snap series; Injun, 40 pounds, to gather data on the radiation belts; and Greb 3, 55 pounds, to gather data on X-ray radiation from the sun.

Multisatellite launching (5 satellites in 1 shot) was made by the Navy's *Composite 1* launched January 24, 1962, from the Atlantic Missile Range, Cape Canaveral, Fla. It failed to achieve orbit

The First

when the second stage of the Thor-Able-Star booster rocket misfired.

Multisatellite launching (8 satellites in 1 shot) was made March 9, 1965, by a Thor-Agena D from Vandenberg Air Force Base, Calif. The satellites were Greb 6 and Solrad to measure solar radiation, GGSE 2 and GGSE 3 to test stabilization for future spacecraft, Secor 3 to be used in geodesy, Oscar 3 to transmit radio broadcasts for ham operators, and 2 Surcal satellites to help calibrate tracking networks.

Navigational satellite was *Transit 1-B* (1960 Gamma), launched April 13, 1960, by a Thor-Able-Star from Cape Canaveral, Fla. The payload, weighing 265 pounds, included 2 ultrastable oscillators, 2 telemetry transmitters and receivers, batteries, and solar cells.

Nuclear reactor in orbit was *SNAP 10A* (Systems for Nuclear Auxiliary Power) launched April 3, 1965, by an Atlas-Agena from Vandenberg Air Force Base, Calif., at 1:25 P.M. Pacific Standard Time (4:25 P.M. E.S.T.). Ten-foot long, cone-shaped, and weighing 970 pounds, it circled the globe every 112 minutes. The reactor was placed in operation 3 hours 40 minutes after launching, by radio signal. Its electricity was stored in small quick-charge nickel cadmium batteries. The 500 watt power it developed was 20 times that previously attained. *SNAP 10A* was developed by Atomics International division of North American Aviation, Inc. at Canoga Park, Calif.

Orbiting geophysical observatory was *OGO 1*, launched September 4, 1964, at 9:23 P.M. E.D.T. from Cape Kennedy, Fla., by an Atlas-Agena B. The satellite was 108 feet high including payload shroud, 10 feet in diameter, and had a lift-off weight of 276,000 pounds. The payload weighed 1,073 pounds and was 6 feet long and 3 feet wide. The satellite carried 13 protruding appendages, had 32,250 solar cells and two 28-volt nickel cadmium batteries. Its velocity varied from 1,124 m.p.h. at apogee of 92,827 miles and 23,180 m.p.h. at perigee of 175 miles.

Orbiting solar-observatory satellite was *OSO 1* launched by a Thor-Delta booster on March 7, 1962, at 11:06 A.M. from Cape Canaveral, Fla. It was 37 inches tall and weighed 458 pounds. It transmitted data on solar flares and was stabilized and sun oriented, so that the instruments always pointed towards the sun. Its apogee was 370 miles, its perigee 340 miles.

Photograph bounced off a satellite. *See under* Photograph

Privately-owned satellite was *Telstar 1*, an active relay-communications satellite, designed and built by the Bell Telephone Laboratories for the American Telephone and Telegraph Company. An application permit was filed October 21, 1960, and an experimental license was granted January

The First

SATELLITE—*Continued*

19, 1961. The satellite was launched July 10, 1962, at 4:35 A.M. E.D.T. (3:35 A.M. E.S.T.) from Cape Canaveral, Fla., by the National Aeronautics and Space Administration, using a 3-stage Thor-Delta rocket, 90 feet high with an 8-foot base diameter and a lift-off weight of approximately 112,000 pounds. The satellite payload was a sphere 34½ inches in diameter that weighed 170 pounds. The perigee was 593 miles and the apogee 3,503 miles; orbit time 157.8 minutes.

Satellite fueled by liquid hydrogen successfully orbited was *Centaur II,* launched by an Atlas-Centaur at 2:03 P.M. E.S.T. on November 27, 1963, from the Atlantic Missile Range, Cape Canaveral, Fla. The lift-off weight was 300,000 pounds. *Centaur II* was 109 feet high with a 10-foot diameter and had a payload 28.5 feet high, 10 feet in diameter, weighing 10,164 pounds. Its apogee was 1,050 miles, its perigee 340 miles. (On May 8, 1962, a Centaur test flight had exploded 55 seconds after launching).

Satellite in orbit built by private citizens was *Discoverer XXXVI* (1961 Alpha-Kappa 1), launched by a Thor-Agena B December 12, 1961, by the U.S. Air Force from Vandenberg Air Force Base, Calif. In addition to its payload, it carried a piggyback 10-pound *Oscar I* (orbiting satellite carrying amateur radio) that transmitted "HI" in Morse code (4 dots and 2 dots) 90 minutes after launching. The capsule returned to earth 98 hours 24 minutes after launching and landed in the Pacific Ocean near Hawaii, where it was found by the 76th Air Rescue Squadron based at Hickham Air Force Base near Honolulu and brought aboard the U.S.S. *Renshaw.*

Satellite launched from another heavenly body was *Surveyor 6,* launched November 7, 1967, by an Atlas-Centaur from Cape Kennedy, Fla., which made a soft-landing in Sinus Medii, a dark plain in the center of the face of the moon, on November 9, 1967. The flight was initiated by Pasadena's Jet Propulsion Laboratory. The triangular 3-legged frame, 10 feet high and 14 feet between the legs, had 3 vernier engines that burned only 2.5 seconds and exerted 150 pounds of thrust to lift the 616-pound spacecraft about ten feet on November 17, 1967, and landed it laterally about 8 feet away. The satellite weighed 2,219 pounds. It transmitted 30,065 TV pictures during its first day.

Satellite placed in orbit by the United States was *Explorer 1* (1958 Alpha), launched January 31, 1958, from Cape Canaveral, Fla., by a Jupiter C Army missile. It was a bullet-shaped tubular rocket 80 inches long and weighed 30.8 pounds (weight of satellite proper, 18.13 pounds; final stage of rocket after burnout, 12.67 pounds). The satellite was airborne at 10:48:16 A.M. and went into orbit around the earth at 10:55 A.M. E.S.T., traveling at a speed ranging from 18,000 to 19,000 m.p.h.

The First

Satellite placed in orbit by an all-solid-propellant rocket was *Explorer IX* (1961 Delta), launched February 16, 1961, from the National Aeronautics and Space Administration Wallops Station at Wallops Island, Va. The satellite weighed 80 pounds. It contained a 15-pound sphere and 65-pounds of ejection, inflation, telemetry, and other equipment. Its velocity at perigee was 17,866 m.p.h. and at apogee 13,976 m.p.h.

Satellite placed in solar orbit to investigate interplanetary space between the orbits of Earth and Venus was *Pioneer V* (1960 Alpha), launched March 11, 1960, from Cape Canaveral, Fla. It was launched by a three-stage Thor-Able IV rocket, 90 feet high and 8 feet in diameter with a lift-off weight of approximately 105,000 pounds. The payload was a 26-inch sphere plus four vanes covered by 4,800 solar cells with a total weight of 94.8 pounds, including approximately 40 pounds of instruments. The satellite orbited the sun in 311.6 days. Its velocity at the third-stage burnout was 24,689 m.p.h. It was 74.9 million miles from the sun in perigee and 92.3 million miles in apogee. The last message was received on June 26, 1960, when it was 22.5 million miles from earth and had transmitted data for 138.9 hours.

Satellite to transmit a close-up photograph of Mars was *Mariner 4,* a 574-pound satellite, launched at 9:22 A.M. E.S.T. on November 28, 1964, from Cape Kennedy, Fla., by a 2-stage Atlas-Agena D booster-rocket. On July 14, 1965, when the satellite was 134 million miles away from earth and 10,500 miles from Mars, it transmitted 8.3 dots a second of varying darkness for 8½ hours depicting the planet Mars' regions known as Cebrenia, Arcadia, and Amazonis.

Satellite to transmit colored photographs of the full earth face was *Dodge,* a truncated octahedron, launched from Cape Kennedy, Fla., July 1, 1967, by a Titan 3C. It weighed 430 pounds and had an apogee of 20,925 miles and a perigee of 20,685 miles.

Satellite to transmit data from Venus was *Mariner 2,* a 447-pound spacecraft launched August 27, 1962, at 2:53 A.M. E.D.T. from Cape Canaveral, Fla., by an Atlas-Agena B. On December 14, 1962, it passed within approximately 21,600 miles of the planet Venus and measured and returned temperatures and other characteristics of the Venusian surface and its atmosphere, telemetry signals, etc.

Satellite to transmit lunar-orbit photographs was *Lunar Orbiter 1* launched by an Atlas-Agena D from Cape Kennedy, Fla., on August 10, 1966. Its total weight was 853 pounds. Its apogee was 1,152 miles, its perigee 119 miles. It achieved lunar orbit on August 14, 1966, and on October 29, 1966, crashed into the far side of the moon.

The First

Satellite to transmit lunar-surface close-up pictures was *Ranger VII,* launched July 28, 1964, from Cape Kennedy, Fla. The payload weighed 806 pounds, was 8.25 feet high with a 5-foot diameter, and included 6 RCA-TV cameras. It impacted in the area northwest of the moon's Sea of Clouds (240,000 miles) at 9:25 A.M. E.D.T. on July 31, 1964, after taking 4,316 pictures of the moon's surface. The total elapsed flight time to the moon was 68 hours 36 minutes.

Satellite to transmit photographs of the earth was *Explorer VI* (1959 Delta), launched August 7, 1959, from the Atlantic Missile Range, Cape Canaveral, Fla. The pictures, received in Hawaii, took 40 minutes to transmit. They were released September 28, 1959, by the U.S. National Aeronautics and Space Administration. They depicted a crescent shape of part of the earth in sunlight taken about 19,500 miles over Mexico from a position facing the Pacific Ocean. The velocity of the satellite at perigee was 23,031 m.p.h. The perigee was 156 miles and the apogee 26,357 miles. The lift-off weight of the Thor-Able rocket was 105,000 pounds, and the payload weight was 142 pounds, which included four solar vanes or paddles, each carrying 2,000 solar cells.

Satellite to use a fuel cell was *Gemini V* (GT-5), launched from Cape Kennedy, Fla., on August 21, 1965, at 10:00 A.M. E.D.T. It had a lift-off weight of 336,000 pounds, was 89 feet high, and had a 10-foot diameter. The bell-shaped payload was 18 feet 5 inches high with a 10-foot base diameter and weighed 7,879 pounds. It made 120 orbits of the earth in 190 hours 55 minutes and landed at 8:56 A.M. E.D.T., August 29, 1965, in the Atlantic Ocean about 760 miles east of Cape Kennedy. The spacecraft, carrying Lieutenant Colonel Leroy Gordon Cooper, Jr. (U.S. Air Force) and Lieutenant Commander Charles Conrad, Jr. (U.S. Navy) was recovered by helicopter and placed aboard the U.S.S. *Lake Champlain.*

Satellite with a nuclear power device was *Transit IV-A,* which weighed 1,175 pounds and was launched June 29, 1961, by a 79-foot Thor-Able Star rocket from the Atlantic Missile Range, Cape Canaveral, Fla. A Snap battery, atomic-radioscope-powered, 4¾ by 5 inches, weighing 4.7 pounds, built by the Martin Company, Baltimore, Md., was placed atop the drum-shaped craft to provide 2.7 watts of electricity for five years.

Satellite with a nuclear reactor to orbit the earth was *Snapshot I,* a 970-pound satellite, 12 foot long with a 5-foot diameter base, launched by an Atlas-Agena booster from Vandenberg Air Force Base, Calif., on April 3, 1965. It contained a System for Nuclear Auxiliary Power reactor *(SNAP 10A),* 15½ inches high and 9 inches in diameter, which weighed 250 pounds and generated 500 watts of power after it was in stable orbit. The reactor operated 43 days, until May 16, 1965, and

The First

produced 500,000 watt-hours of electricity. It orbited the earth every 112 minutes at an apogee of 820 miles and a perigee of 788 miles.

Satellite with an electrostatic (ion) engine to produce thrust in space was *SERT 1* (Space Electric Rocket Test), 375 pounds, launched July 20, 1964, from Wallops Island, Va. The rocket climbed 2,500 miles and after a 48-minute suborbital flight fell 2,000 miles away from the launch site. The mercury-propelled engine performed in space for 16 minutes, generated .0055 pounds of thrust, making backup flight unnecessary.

Satellite with spring-folded wings to intercept bombardment of tiny meteoroids was *Pegasus 1,* launched February 16, 1965, from Cape Kennedy, Fla., by a Saturn 1 launch-vehicle. The lift-off weight was 1,128,000 pounds, with a height of 188 feet and a diameter of 21.4 feet. The payload weighed 3,260 pounds and was 96 feet long and 14 feet high. The apogee was 451 miles, the perigee 309 miles. The instrumentation consisted of 416 capacitor panels of 3 different thicknesses, each 20 by 40 inches, for registry of meteoroid impacts. The center contained a motor that unfolded electrically-charged panels sensitive to the bombardment of tiny particles. The power supply contained 25,200 solar cells and 47 nickel cadmium batteries.

Space capsule recovered from an orbiting satellite was located August 11, 1960, in the Pacific Ocean. It was recovered from *Discoverer XIII* (1960 Theta), a satellite launched from Vandenberg Air Force Base, Calif., on August 10, 1960, by means of a Thor-Agena rocket 78 feet high, with an 8-foot base and a lift-off weight of approximately 108,500 pounds. The 350-pound capsule, 27 by 33 inches, was ejected from the satellite during its 17th polar orbit at a height of 200 miles over latitude 70° north. The descent of the capsule was slowed down by a parachute, which opened at about 50,000 feet. It was recovered by a Navy frogman, Boatswain's Mate third class Robert W. Carroll of Keene, N.H., who dived from a helicopter which took off from the U.S. Navy's *Haiti Victory.*

Space capsule recovered in midair from an orbiting satellite was a 300-pound capsule ejected from the satellite *Discoverer XIV* (1960 Kappa) and retrieved on August 19, 1960. The capsule dropped back to earth by parachute and was snatched at 8,000 feet by a U.S. Air Force C-119 aircraft, piloted by Captain Harold E. Mitchell, about 360 miles southwest of Honolulu, Hawaii. *Discoverer XIV* was launched on August 18, 1960, from Vandenberg Air Force Base, Calif. The launch vehicle was a Thor-Agena rocket 78 feet high, with an 8-foot base diameter and a lift-off weight of approximately 108,500 pounds. Its velocity was 17,658 m.p.h.

The First

SATELLITE—*Continued*

Surveillance satellite that was successful was *Midas II* (122 feet long, 5 feet in diameter, weight 5,000 pounds), launched May 24, 1960, at 12:37 P.M. E.S.T. from Cape Canaveral, Fla. The first stage was implemented by a standard Atlas ICBM, 77 feet long (including its adapter section), with a thrust of 360,000 pounds. The second stage booster was an Agena, separated by a 15,000-pound thrust liquid fuel rocket engine. *Midas II* circled the earth every 94.34 minutes. Its apogee was 292 miles, its perigee 322 miles. The payload approximated 3,300 pounds with a height of 21.66 feet. *(New York Times. 1:8. May 25, 1960)*

Synchronous satellite was *Syncom 2,* launched 10:33 A.M. E.D.T. on July 26, 1963, from the Atlantic Missile Range, Cape Canaveral, Fla., under the direction of the National Aeronautics and Space Administration. It was conceived and designed by the Hughes Aircraft Co. It had a lift-off weight of 114,000 pounds and was 90 feet high with an 8-foot base diameter. The cylinder was 28 inches in diameter and 15½ inches high and weighed 147 pounds. Its orbital period was 23.9 hours; its apogee 22,239 miles and its perigee 22,230 miles, almost equal to the time required for the earth to rotate once on its axis so that it seems to stand still in space.

Weather-observation satellite to provide cloud-cover photography was *Tiros 1* (Television and Infra Red Observatory Satellite), launched by a Thor-Able rocket on April 1, 1960, from Cape Kennedy, Fla. It took photographs of the earth's cloud-cover from an altitude of 450 miles. The last transmission was June 17, 1960.

Weather satellite to provide high-resolution nighttime cloud-cover pictures was *Nimbus 1* launched into polar orbit August 28, 1964, from the Western Test Range, Point Arguello, Calif., by a Thor-Agena B. It was 95 feet high, had an 8-foot base diameter, and weighed 126,400 pounds. The conical payload was 10 feet tall, 57 inches in diameter, and it weighed 830 pounds. On its first day in orbit, *Nimbus 1* obtained pictures of Hurricane Cleo, and later hurricanes Dora, Ethel, and Florence in the Atlantic, and pictures of typhoons Ruby and Sally in the Pacific. It viewed Hurricane Dora and Typhoon Ruby in complete darkness. The satellite returned 27,000 photographs and ceased operating September 23, 1964.

SATURDAY HALF-HOLIDAY. *See under* Holiday

SAVINGS AND LOAN ASSOCIATION, FEDERAL. *See* Federal savings and loan association

SAVINGS BANK. *See* Bank

SAVINGS BANK LIFE INSURANCE. *See* Insurance

The First

SAVINGS GROUP. *See* Bank

SAVINGS STAMP, POSTAL. *See* Postal savings stamps

SAW (circular) is supposed to have been produced by Benjamin Cummins in Bentonsville, N.Y., about 1814. His saws were originally used for cutting the teeth of clock wheels, and were later used for cutting wood. *(Edward Henry Knight—Mechanical Dictionary)*

SAWMILL

Band sawmill was operated in 1867 by Hoffman Brothers of Fort Wayne, Ind., who employed a band saw 40 feet in length, the ends of which were joined so as to revolve continuously. The saw blades, from 4 to 5 inches wide, were obtained from Sweden. Jacob Rosecrans Hoffman of Fort Wayne, Ind., obtained patent No. 92,191, July 6, 1869, on a "sawmill."

Electrically driven sawmill to operate successfully was designed and operated in 1896 by the Allis-Chalmers Manufacturing Company for the American River Land and Lumber Company, Folsom, Calif.

Sawmill engine that was portable was built in 1858 by Francis Wedge, designer for the H. & F. Blandy Company of Zanesville, Ohio. It was horizontal and mounted on a horizontal boiler.

SAXOPHONE production was undertaken in 1888 by Charles Gerard Conn, Elkhart, Ind. The instruments were made of brass, had two octave keys, and descended only to B-flat. Originally they were used only by military bands.

SCALE

Automatic computing pendulum-type scales were invented by Allen De Vilbiss, Jr., of Toledo, Ohio, who applied for a patent on the fan-type automatic computing scale on January 24, 1899. The patent was granted May 22, 1900, No. 649,915. In 1899 he organized the De Vilbiss Scale Company, which later developed into the Toledo Scale Company of Toledo, Ohio. This company was the first to produce an adjustable automatic indicator controller for bringing the hand to a quick stop. It was also the first to produce a commercially successful computing scale of the gravity type; first to invent and patent a cylinder-type platform scale, replacing the hanging cylinder-type scale; first to produce a commercially successful automatic-dial portable scale; first to produce auto truck scales having the lever pivots all on the same plane to permit the use of a shallow pit; first to produce a double-pendulum counterbalance with a floating fulcrum; first to produce a built-in, automatic, electric lighting system with a ribbon switch which does not hold the scale off zero; and first to produce a device for locking the pendulum and tare beam lever for safety in loading the scale.

Coin-operated scale was invented by John Glas Sandeman and Percival Everitt of London, England, who obtained patent No. 323,213 on July 28, 1885, on an apparatus for automatically delivering prepaid goods, such as postcards, stamped envelopes, and cigarettes to accord with the price therefor. The application was filed January 19, 1884.

Coin-operated weighing machine was invented by Percival Everitt of London, England, who obtained U.S. patent No. 336,042 on February 9, 1886, on a coin-operated weighing machine and Patent No. 336,043 on a recorder for a weighing machine. (Previously, he had obtained a patent in England, No. 16,433 on December 13, 1884.)

Computing scales were manufactured by Edward Canby in a small shop in the rear of the Callahan Building on Main Street, Dayton, Ohio. On March 20, 1891, the Computing Scale Company was incorporated, the first computing scale company in the world. In 1895 it produced and brought out the first successful computing scale.

Platform scale was built in St. Johnsbury, Vt., in 1830 by Thaddeus Fairbanks. It was patented June 30, 1831, by Erastus and Thaddeus Fairbanks of St. Johnsbury. Previously even-balance and steel-yard types of scales had been used.

Railway track scale was introduced by E. and T. Fairbanks and Company of St. Johnsbury, Vt., which operated under patent No. 16,381, granted January 13, 1857, to Thaddeus Fairbanks.

SCALPING (of American Indians). *See under* American Indians

SCANDINAVIAN METHODIST EPISCOPAL CHURCH. *See under* Methodist Episcopal Church

SCHOLASTIC FRATERNITY. *See under* Fraternity (Greek-letter)

SCHOOL

See also Academy; Education; *also* type of school or subject taught, e.g., Agricultural school, Army War College, Art course, Commercial high school, Jewish college, Naval War College

Air-conditioned public elementary school was the Belaire School, San Angelo, Tex., which was opened in October, 1955. The school, containing eight classrooms, was completely air-conditioned.

Black school (state) was the Snowden School of Alexandria, Va. It was authorized by act of legislature July 11, 1870, and was under the guidance of William Frank Powell. Its existence was of short duration.

Circular school building was St. Patrick Central High School, Kankakee, Ill., opened February 6, 1956. It was a two-story building, 200 feet in diameter, which housed classrooms and a gymnasium unit accommodating 2,000 spectators. It was connected to a small rectangular wing containing the

administrative offices and library. The total cost of the school was $736,592. Belli and Belli of Chicago, Ill., were the architects.

Endowed school was the "Free Schoole in Roxburie," which was established in Roxbury, Mass., in 1645. It was incorporated in 1789 as the "Grammar School in the Easterly Part of the Town of Roxbury." The school is still in existence and is known as the Roxbury Latin School. *(Charles Knapp Dillaway—A History of the Grammar School, or the Free Schoole of 1645 in Roxburie)*

Evening school was established in New Amsterdam (New York City) in 1661. Fees and regulations for instruction are contained in a report, *Instructions and Rules for Schoolmaster, Evert Pietersen,* which was drawn up by the burgomasters on November 4, 1661. *(Minutes of the Orphan Masters of New Amsterdam)*

Evening school (free, public) developed in New York City directly and naturally from the evening school controlled by philanthropic agencies and partly supported by public funds. The schools opened in 1833 in New York City were free, and in a sense public, for they were supported in part by public funds. *(Paul Monroe—Cyclopedia of Education, Vol. II)*

Land grant to schools. *See under* Land grant

Model school or laboratory school of practice for teachers was opened October 31, 1838, by Lafayette College, Easton, Pa., and was known as West College. Its cost of $2,230.22 was defrayed by President George Junkin of Lafayette College. *(David Bishop Skillman—Biography of a College)*

Professional school for exclusively training potential circus clowns was the "clown college" established September 1, 1968, at Venice, Fla., by Irvin Feld, president and producer of the Ringling Bros. and Barnum & Bailey Combined Shows. The 8-week tuition-free course was given during September, October, and November from 9:00 A.M. to 6:00 P.M. and included slaps and falls, juggling, stilt-walking, plate-spinning, makeup, mime and pantomine, acrobatics, equilibrium, elephant riding, etc.

Public school. *See* Public school

Public school built in conjunction with an apartment house was a 2-story building at University Avenue and West 166th Street, in the Bronx, New York City, containing 88,000 square feet, opened September 13, 1971. It is owned and operated by the Board of Education of the City of New York and houses Public School 126. The adjoining apartment house, 26 stories high, has 400 apartments and is operated by a real estate company.

School completely irradiated with germicidal lamps was the Cato-Meridian Central School, Cato, N.Y. The lamps, made of special glass to permit ultraviolet bactericidal wave lengths to

The First

SCHOOL—*Continued*

pass through, were made by the General Electric Company, Schenectady, N.Y., and were installed January 3, 1945. *(American School and University. 1946)*

School for black freedmen was established by the American Missionary Association at Fortress Monroe, Va., on September 17, 1861. The teacher was Mary S. Peake, a black woman.

School for Protestant girls was a boarding school established by Countess Benigna von Zinzendorf at Germantown, Pa., in 1742, exclusively for girls of the Moravian Church. By 1800 this had become a noted seminary. It is now the Moravian College for Women. Earlier the Ursulines had opened a convent for girls in New Orleans, La.

School for the mentally retarded was the Massachusetts School for the Idiotic and Feeble-Minded Youth, created through the efforts of Dr. Samuel Gridley Howe and established by a legislative resolution, approved May 8, 1848, which appropriated $2,500 a year for three years. The first students were received on October 1, 1848. The school was incorporated April 4, 1850. Later the name was changed to the Massachusetts School for the Feeble-Minded. The institution is now operated as the Walter E. Fernald State School, named for Dr. Walter Elmore Fernald, the first resident superintendent. *(Albert Deutsch— The Mentally Ill in America)*

School for unmarried, pregnant, teen-age girls to continue their education was the Educational Center of District 12 opened June 23, 1967, in the Lincoln Hospital Neighborhood Maternity Center, New York City. The school opened with approximately 75 students and had a staff of 1 administrator, 1 guidance counselor, and 5 subject teachers. It was organized and started by project coordinator Martha Neilson for the Board of Education of the City of New York.

School in America was established by the Dutch West India Company on Manhattan Island in 1633. (It is possible that instruction given a group of pupils by Pilgrim settlers may have constituted an earlier school.) The Dutch school was established in New Amsterdam (New York City) with Adam Roelantsen as its first master. Instruction was given in Dutch prior to 1775. In 1783 the school became known as the Collegiate School, the oldest school still in existence in the United States. *(Henry Webb Dunshee—History of the School of the Collegiate Reform Dutch Church in the City of New York)*

School supported by local taxation was opened in St. Petersburg, Fla., on May 20, 1832, and closed on October 7, 1832. An appropriation of $1,100 was made for 3 teachers for 1 year.

The First

School to fly an American flag. *See* Flag: American flag over a schoolhouse

School to have all classroom lights controlled by electric eyes was the Glenn H. Curtiss Memorial and Central Rural School, Hammondsport, N.Y., which placed the lights in operation on January 4, 1936. Paul William Seagers was the principal. *(American School and University. 1946)*

School to install a teletypesetter. *See* Teletypesetter: Teletypesetter installed in a school

School to operate on the one-class-to-a-room basis was established in 1846 in Quincy, Mass. *(Massachusetts Board of Education. Reports, Vol. 10)*

Technical school for American Indians was the Southwestern Indian Polytechnic Institute, Albuquerque, N.Mex., dedicated August 21, 1971. It opened September 16, 1971. It consisted of 12 buildings on a 164-acre campus and cost $13 million. It was coeducational and opened with 700 American Indian students from 64 tribes. John L. Peterson was the first superintendent.

Trade school for girls was the Manhattan Trade School for Girls, New York City, opened in November 1902. The first director was Professor Mary Schenck Woolman, director of the domestic art department of Teacher's College, Columbia University, New York City. Her staff consisted of an executive secretary, 6 supervisors, 6 instructors and forewomen, 6 assistants and 4 occasional workers. Twenty pupils enrolled the first day for courses in the use of the needle, the paint brush, and the foot- and electric-power sewing machine. Night classes were begun in 1903. *(Mary Schenck Woolman—The Making of a Trade School)*

Underground school was the Abo Elementary School, Artesia, N.Mex., built underground in 1976 for safety from radiation and the effects of fallout. The roof is at ground level. It is heated and air conditioned during school hours. It has 16 teaching stations, a large library media center and a multiuse room with tables and seats that fold up into the wall. There are no distractions or outside noises, the lighting is near perfect, and the acoustics are excellent.

SCHOOL ATTENDANCE LAW. *See* Education: Compulsory school attendance law (state)

SCHOOL COMMITTEE in America was elected in Dorchester, Mass., in 1645. The members were elected for life, although the town reserved the right to remove any of them for "weighty reasons." They had charge of everything which pertained to the betterment of the school.

SCHOOL DEPARTMENT OF HYGIENE. *See under* Hygiene instruction

The First

SCHOOL LAND GRANT. *See* Land grant

SCHOOL LEGISLATION

School law (compulsory) was passed November 11, 1647, by Massachusetts. It "ordered that every township in this jurisdiction, after the Lord hath increased them to the number of fifty householders, shall then forthwith appoint one within their town to teach all such children as shall resort to him to write and read, whose wages shall be paid either by the parents or masters of such children, or by the inhabitants in general." Towns of 100 families were required to "set up a grammar school, the master thereof being able to instruct youths so far as they may be fitted for the university." *(Records of Massachusetts Bay Colony, Vol. II)*

School law (state) to end de facto segregation was "an act providing for the elimination of racial imbalance in the public schools," Chapter 641 of the General Laws of Massachusetts, enacted August 18, 1965.

SCHOOL OF MODERN LANGUAGES. *See* Language instruction: Modern-language school

SCHOOL STADIUM. *See* Stadium

SCHOOL SUPERINTENDENT

School superintendent (city) was Roswell Willson Haskins, who was appointed "city superintendent of common schools" in 1836 by Buffalo, N.Y. He resigned before the end of the year as the law was imperfect and restrictions hampered his work. In 1837 Louisville, Ky., appointed Samuel Dickinson superintendent with the title "agent of the board."

School superintendent (state) was Gideon Hawley, who was appointed state superintendent of common schools by New York State in 1812. He served from January 14, 1813, until February 22, 1821. An act was passed April 15, 1814, making him secretary of the New York State Board of Regents at a salary of $400 a year. He was removed in 1821 because of political influence (Chapter 249 of 1821), and the secretary of state was authorized to act ex officio as superintendent. In 1854 New York again created a superintendent of Public Instruction. *(Proceedings of University Convocation, Albany, N.Y., Aug. 2, 1870)*

SCHOOL TAX

Public school tax enacted by a state was "an act providing for the establishment of free schools" enacted January 15, 1825, by the state of Illinois (4th General Assembly). It provided for a common school in each county open to every class of white citizens between the ages of 5 and 21 years and allotted a tax of $2 of every $100 and 5/6 of the interest from the school fund for the purpose.

SCHOOLBOOK was the *New England Primer* of 1689–90. It was "printed by R. Pierce for, and sold by Benjamin Harris, at the London Coffee-House," Boston, Mass. It was reprinted in 1691

The First

and was used mostly by the Dissenters and the Lutherans.

SCHOOLHOUSE west of the Allegheny Mountains was started in Schoenbrunn, Ohio, December 22, 1772, and completed July 29, 1773, by Moravian missionaries. The first teacher was the Reverend David Zeisberger. *(Joseph E. Weinland —The Romantic Story of Schoenbrunn)*

SCHOONER. *See* Ship

SCHWENKFELDER to immigrate to America was George Schultz, who arrived at Philadelphia, Pa., in 1731. The Schwenkfelders were a religious sect, followers of the Silesian nobleman Kaspar von Schwenkfeld (Caspar Schwenkfeld von Ossig). In 1734, 180 Schwenkfelders exiled from Silesia landed in Pennsylvania. They formally organized a church in 1782. *(Samuel Kriebel Brecht —General Records of the Schwenkfelders)*

SCIENCE ADVISORY BOARD was authorized July 31, 1933, under Executive Order No. 6238, to appoint committees to deal with specific problems in the various departments of the federal government. The nine-member board held its first meeting August 21, 1933. The first president was Dr. Karl Taylor Compton, president of the Massachusetts Institute of Technology.

SCIENCE ASSOCIATION

History of science society was organized in Boston, Mass., January 12, 1924, and incorporated under the laws of the District of Columbia, January 30, 1925, "to encourage and maintain active interest in the history of science and the various sciences in particular." The first president was Lawrence Joseph Henderson.

National Academy of Sciences was incorporated by act of Congress approved by President Abraham Lincoln, March 3, 1863 (12 Stat. L. 806), with the stipulation that "the Academy shall, whenever called upon by any department of the Government, investigate, examine, experiment, and report upon any subject of science or art, the actual expense of such investigations, examinations, experiments, and reports to be paid from appropriations which may be made for the purpose, but the Academy shall receive no compensation whatever for any services to the Government of the United States." The first president of the National Academy of Sciences was Alexander Dallas Bache, who held that position from 1863 to 1867. *(National Academy of Sciences. Report, 1864)*

National Research Council was established in 1916 by the National Academy of Sciences at the request of President Woodrow Wilson "to bring into co-operation existing governmental, educational, industrial and other research organizations, with the object of encouraging the investigation of natural phenomena, the increased use of scientific research in the develop-

The First

SCIENCE ASSOCIATION—*Continued*

ment of American industries, the employment of scientific methods in strengthening the national defense, and such other applications of science as will promote the national security and welfare." The original membership numbered 44, including 10 officers of the United States Government assigned by President Wilson. The council held its first meeting September 20, 1916, in New York City. *(Annual Report of the National Academy of Sciences for the Year July 1, 1933–June 30, 1932)*

Scientific society was the Boston Philosophical Society, which was founded by Increase Mather in 1683 in Boston, Mass. He wrote that it was "a philosophical society of agreeable gentlemen who met once a fortnight for a conference upon improvements in philosophy and additions to the stores of natural history." *(Ralph Samuel Bates— Scientific Societies in the United States)*

Scientific society (national organization) was the American Association for the Advancement of Science, organized September 20, 1848, in Philadelphia, Pa., for the purpose of advancing science in every way. The first president was William Charles Redfield. *(American Association for the Advancement of Science—A Brief History of the Association from its Founding in 1848 to 1940)*

Scientific society of importance was the American Philosophical Society, organized in 1743 in Philadelphia, Pa., by Benjamin Franklin. On May 14, 1743, he issued a broadside, "A Proposal for Promoting Useful Knowledge Among the British Plantations in America," as a prospectus. The organization was an outgrowth of the Junto, a Philadelphia society which he had organized in 1727. *(American Philosophical Society. Proceedings, Vol. 22)*

Woman elected to the National Academy of Sciences was Dr. Florence Rena Sabin, elected on April 29, 1925. At the time she was professor of histology at Johns Hopkins University, Baltimore, Md.

SCIENCE MEDAL, NATIONAL. *See* Medal

SCIENCE PERIODICAL

Science magazine was the *American Journal of Science and Art*, printed in New York City, and issued in July 1818. It was edited by Benjamin Silliman. The first volume of four numbers contained 448 pages. *(American Journal of Science. Series 4, Vol. 46. July 1918)*

Science magazine (popular) to report news of laboratory and workshop in popular terms was *Popular Science Monthly*, published by D. Appleton & Co., New York City, and first issued in May 1872. The first editor was Edward Livingston Youmans. The monthly contained 128 pages and sold for 50 cents. Some of the articles in the first issue were "Early Superstitions of Medicine," "The Study of Sociology," "The Causes of Dyspepsia,"

The First

"Disinfection and Disinfectants," and "Science and Immortality."

SCIENCE SCHOOL

Natural science summer school was opened on the island of Penikese, Buzzard's Bay, Mass., in 1873, when Professor Louis Agassiz and Professor Nathaniel Southgate Shaler established the Anderson School. Forty-three students attended the first session. *(Jules Marcou—Life, Letters and Works of Louis Agassiz)*

SCIENTIFIC EXPEDITION. *See* Botanic scientific expedition; Expedition

SCOUTS. *See* Boy Scouts of America; Girl Scouts

SCREW

Screw factory was established in 1810 by Aborn and Jackson at Bellefonte, R.I. Originally, screw manufacturing was a complicated matter. A blank was forged and the head of the screw was pinched between dies while hot, after which the threads were made by filing.

Screw machine to make the manufacture of pointed screws practical was devised by Cullen Whipple of Providence, R.I., who obtained patent No. 15,502 on June 3, 1856. Prior to this invention, the threaded end of the screw being blunt, it was necessary to bore a hole for its insertion. *(Wood Screws—American Screw Co.)*

Screw patent in connection with a machine for making screws was granted December 14, 1798, to David Wilkinson of Rhode Island.

SCREW AUGER. *See* Auger (screw auger)

SCREW CALIPER. *See* Caliper (screw)

SCREW-CAP BOTTLE WITH A POUR LIP. *See* Bottle

SCREW WRENCH. *See* Wrench: Pipe or screw wrench (practical)

SCRIP MONEY. *See* Money

SCULPTOR

Sculptor (American) of merit was Hiram Powers, whose chief works were undertaken from 1835 to 1873. In addition to his statues of *Eve*, the *Greek Slave*, *Proserpine*, *Il Penseroso*, *A Californian*, and *An American*, he made busts of Washington for Louisiana, of Calhoun for South Carolina, and of Daniel Webster for Boston. He made busts also of John Quincy Adams, Andrew Jackson, Chief Justice Marshall, Martin Van Buren, and other distinguished Americans. *(Lorado Taft—History of American Sculpture)*

Sculptor (American) to obtain a federal commission was John Frazee. A federal appropriation for $400 was granted March 2, 1831 (4 Stat. L. 474), for a bust of John Jay for the Supreme Court, Washington, D.C. *(Charles Edwin Fairman—Art and Artists of the Capitol of the U.S. of A.)*

The First

Woman sculptor. *See* Monument: Monument by a woman ordered by the U.S. Government; Monument: Statue cast by the U.S. Government; Woman: Woman sculptor honored by membership in the National Academy of Design

SCULPTURE

Stainless-steel bas relief (large size) was created by Isamu Noguchi and unveiled April 29, 1940, over the entrance to the Associated Press Building, New York City. It was 17 by 22 feet and depicted 5 figures, 1 using a pad and pencil, and the other 4 using a teletype, telephone, wirephoto, and a camera, respectively.

SEA BATTLE. *See* Revolutionary War: Naval battle of the Revolution; Spanish-American War: Ship captured in the Spanish-American War; War (1812): Frigate action of importance in the War of 1812; World War I: Shot fired by the American Navy in World War I; World War II: American destroyer torpedoed, American destroyer torpedoed and sunk while on convoy duty, Japanese submarine sunk by an American ship

SEACOAST GUN CARRIAGE. *See* Ordnance

SEAL

Christmas seals of the modern variety, sold to raise funds to fight tuberculosis, were designed in 1907 by Emily Perkins Bissell of Wilmington, Del., who proposed the idea, drew the design, and had the seals printed. They were first placed on sale December 9, 1907, in the post office, Wilmington, Del. They were issued in sheets of perforated seals, 228 seals to a sheet (19 horizontal, 12 vertical), in two types: "Merry Christmas" and "Merry Christmas and a Happy New Year." Lithographed by Theo. Leonhardt & Son, Philadelphia, Pa., they were sold by the Delaware chapter of the American National Red Cross. About $3,000 was realized. *(Leigh Mitchell Hodges—The People Against Tuberculosis)*

Great Seal of the United States Government was designed by William Barton and adopted June 20, 1782. The seal is composed of a spread eagle, the emblem of strength, bearing on its breast an escutcheon with 13 stripes, alternate red and white. In its right talon is an olive branch, the emblem of peace, and in its left 13 arrows, emblematic of the 13 states, ready for war should it be necessary. In its beak is a ribbon bearing the legend "E Pluribus Unum" (From many, one). Over the head of the eagle is a golden light breaking through a cloud surrounding 13 stars forming a constellation on a blue field. *(U.S. State Department—History of the Seal of the United States)*

Great Seal of the United States Government was impressed on September 16, 1782, on the upper left corner of a document authorizing General George Washington to negotiate and sign an agreement with the British for the exchange, subsistence, and better treatment of prisoners of war.

The First

The document bore the signatures of John Hanson, president of the Continental Congress, and Charles Thomson, secretary.

Great Seal on a bill. *See* Money: Bill to depict both the face and the reverse side of the Great Seal of the United States

Seal of the Confederate States of America was authorized April 30, 1863, at the third session of the first Congress of Confederate States with the resolution "that the seal of the Confederate States shall consist of a device representing an equestrian portrait of Washington (after the statue which surmounts his monument in the capital square at Richmond), surrounded with a wreath composed of the principal agricultural products of the Confederacy (cotton, tobacco, sugar cane, corn, wheat and rice) and having around its margin the words 'The Confederate States of America, twenty-second February, eighteen hundred and sixty-two' with the motto 'Deo vindice.'" *(James M. Matthews, ed.—The Statutes at large of the Confederate States of America Passed at the Third Session of the First Congress, 1863)*

Seals for raising funds (forerunners of the modern Christmas seals and tuberculosis stamps) were the Sanitary Fair Stamps. Eight days after the first gun was fired on Fort Sumter, April 12, 1861, a group of women in Cleveland, Ohio, formed an organization for aiding wounded soldiers. Five days later another group formed in New York City. The idea spread and fairs were held in various parts of the country to raise funds, notably in Chicago, New York, Albany, Boston, and Stamford. Special offices were established in these cities to sell stamps now known as the Sanitary Fair Stamps.

State seal designed by a woman was the Idaho State seal designed by Emma Sarah Edwards, who won the competition sponsored by the First Legislative Assembly. Governor Norman Bushnell presented her with the prize on March 5, 1891. The seal was adopted by an act of the first state legislature on March 14, 1891. It was the first and only seal designed by a woman.

SEAMEN'S LIBRARY. *See* Library

SEAPLANE GLIDER. *See* Glider

SEAPLANE RAMP, FLOATING. *See under* Aviation

SEAPLANE TENDER. *See* Ship

SEAT-BELT LEGISLATION. *See* Automobile legislation: Automobile-seat-belt safety legislation

SEATRAIN. *See under* Ship

SEAWATER CONVERSION PLANT. *See under* Water

The First

SECESSION

Secession act (the Ordinance of Secession) was passed by South Carolina, December 20, 1860, in the following form: "We, the people of the State of South Carolina, in convention assembled, do declare and ordain, that the ordinance adopted by us in convention on the 23d day of May, in the year of our Lord 1788, whereby the Constitution of the United States was ratified, and also all acts and parts of the General Assembly of this State ratifying amendments of the said Constitution, are hereby repealed; and that the Union now subsisting between South Carolina and other States, under the name of the United States of America, is hereby dissolved." On December 24, 1860, the South Carolina delegation in Congress offered its resignation, but it was not accepted by the Speaker, and the names of its members were called regularly throughout the entire session. The new state constitution was ratified on April 3, 1861. The vote was 114 yeas and 6 nays. At the close of the Civil War, on May 29, 1865, a provisional government was established. *(David Franklin Houston—A Critical Study of Nullification in South Carolina)*

Secession convention was held December 15, 1814, at Hartford, Conn., by delegates from Connecticut, Massachusetts, New Hampshire, Rhode Island, and Vermont, who opposed the war of 1812 and planned secession from the United States.

Secession was first mentioned in Congress on June 4, 1811, when Representative Josiah Quincy of Massachusetts declared, in a debate on the proposal to create a state from the Orleans Territory: "It will be the right of all and the duty of some [of the states] definitely to prepare for a separation; amicably, if they can; violently, if they must." Representative Poindexter of Mississippi called Quincy to order, as did the Speaker of the House; but on appeal the Speaker's decision was reversed, and Quincy was sustained by a vote of 53 ayes to 56 nays on the point of order. *(Edmund Quincy—Life of Josiah Quincy)*

SECOND ADVENT BELIEVERS General Conference convened October 14–15, 1840, in the Chardon Street Chapel, Boston, Mass. Henry Dana Ward was elected chairman. *(William Miller—Life of William Miller)*

SECRET SERVICE

Executive Protective Service woman agent was Phyllis Frances Shantz of Rome, N.Y., sworn in September 15, 1970, by Eugene Telemachus Rossides, Assistant Secretary (Enforcement and Operations) of the Department of the Treasury, to serve in the newly established Executive Protective Service (EPS), a uniformed security force supervised by the Secret Service to protect the White House, the President and members of his

The First

immediate family, and diplomatic missions in the metropolitan area of Washington, D.C.

Secret Service (colonial) was organized by Aaron Burr and Major Benjamin Tallmadge in June 1778 for the United Colonies. It was known as the Headquarters Secret Service and developed into the first organized intelligence department of the Army of the United Colonies. On July 4, 1778, General George Washington in a special order made Burr head of the Department for Detecting and Defeating Conspiracies and ordered him "to proceed to Elizabeth Town to procure information of movements of the enemy's shipping about New York." Information about the activities of the British had, however, been secretly gathered previously by patriotic individuals and societies.

Secret Service (federal) under the Treasury Department was created by act of June 23, 1860 (12 Stat. L. 102), to suppress counterfeiting in U.S. coins. The act was extended to include counterfeiting of notes, obligations, and securities of the government by act of July 11, 1862 (12 Stat. L. 533), and an appropriation act approved July 2, 1864. Since the death of President Lincoln, one of the duties of the Secret Service has been to guard the President and his family. The Federal Bureau of Investigation was created in 1908 under the Department of Justice to supplement the work of the Secret Service.

Secret Service female special agent killed in the line of duty was Julie Yvonne Cross who was involved in a counterfeit surveillance when fatally wounded on June 4, 1980, in Los Angeles, Calif.

Secret service (U.S. Army). *See* Army Secret Service Bureau

Secret Service women agents were Laurie B. Anderson, Sue A. Baker, Kathryn I. Clark, Holly A. Hufschmidt, and Phyllis Frances Shantz, former agents of the Executive Protective Service, who were sworn in as Special Agents on December 15, 1971, by Eugene Telemachus Rossides, Assistant Secretary (Enforcement and Operations) of the Department of the Treasury at Washington, D.C. Special agents are charged with the protection of the President and his immediate family, the Vice President, the President-elect, the Vice President-elect, a former President and his wife during his lifetime, the widow of a former President until her death or remarriage, minor children of a former President until they reach 16 years of age, major presidential and vice presidential candidates, visiting heads of foreign states or foreign governments, and, at the direction of the President, official representatives of the United States performing special missions abroad.

SECRET SOCIETY. *See* Tong (Chinese secret society); Women's club; Women's secret society

The First

SECTARIAN MAGAZINE. *See* Periodical

SECULAR SONG. *See* Music

SECULAR SONGBOOK. *See* Music book

SECURITIES AND EXCHANGE COMMISSION (U.S.) was created pursuant to section 4 of the Securities Exchange Act of 1934, approved by President Franklin Delano Roosevelt June 6, 1934 (48 Stat. L. 881). The first meeting was held July 2, 1934, to provide for regulation and control of transactions and practices of security exchanges and over-the-counter markets. Five members were appointed June 30, 1934. The first chairman was James McCauley Landis.

SEDAN AUTOMOBILE. *See* Automobile

SEED BUSINESS regularly established was organized January 7, 1784, by David Landreth at High Street, Philadelphia, Pa. The location is now covered by the buildings at 1210 and 1212 Market Street. Previously seeds had been imported from Europe. The firm, incorporated in 1904 as the D. Landreth Seed Company, later became a subsidiary of the Robert Buist Company, founded in Philadelphia in 1828.

SEED DISTRIBUTION. *See* Agricultural seed distribution (national)

SEEDING MACHINE PATENT was granted January 25, 1799 to Eliakim Spooner of Vermont on "a machine for planting." The seeds were fed by gravity. The machine was not practical.

SEEDING MACHINE (practical) was invented by Joseph Gibbons of Adrian, Mich., who received patent No. 1,731 on August 25, 1840. His machine was a grain drill with cavities to deliver seed and a device for regulating the volume. *(Robert L. Ardrey—American Agricultural Implements)*

SEEDLESS NAVEL ORANGE. *See* Oranges (seedless navel)

SEISMOGRAPH was installed at the Lick Observatory, University of California, Mount Hamilton, Calif., and exhibited at the formal opening of the building June 1, 1888. The equipment consisted of a three-component Ewing seismograph, a Gray seismograph, and a Duplex seismograph. *(Royal Society of London—Proceedings, Vol. 31)*

SELF-GOVERNMENT COLLEGE ORGANIZATION. *See* College self-government organization

SELF-SERVICE RESTAURANT. *See* Cafeteria; Restaurant: Self-service restaurant

SELF-STARTER. *See* Automobile electric self-starter

SELF-SUSTAINING NUCLEAR CHAIN-REACTION DEMONSTRATION. *See under* Atomic energy

The First

SELF-WINDING CLOCK. *See* Clock

SEMAPHORE TELEGRAPH SYSTEM was invented in 1799, by Jonathan Grout of Belchertown, Mass., who installed a series of towers, each within sight of the next, between Boston and Martha's Vineyard, Mass., 90 miles distant. By means of a combination of the semaphore and flag systems, he was able to ask a question and receive an answer within ten minutes. This system did not involve the use of an electric telegraph line.

SEMIAUTOMATIC RIFLE. *See* Ordnance

SEMINARY, CATHOLIC. *See* Catholic seminary

SEMITIC MUSEUM. *See* Museum

SENATE JOURNAL was the *Journal of the First Session of the Senate of the United States. Begun and Held at the City of New York, March 4, 1789,* published in 1789 in New York City.

SENATE (state)
Woman secretary of a state senate. *See under* Woman

Woman state senator was Martha Hughes Cannon, elected to the second session of the Utah Senate November 3, 1896. She served from January 11, 1897, through March 11, 1897, and was reelected to serve in the third session, which convened January 8, 1889, and adjourned March 9, 1899. She was a Democrat and represented the Sixth Senatorial District comprising Salt Lake County.

SENATE (U.S.). *See* Congress (U.S.)—Senate

SENATOR (U.S.)
American-Indian senator was Charles Curtis of Kansas, who served from January 23, 1907, to March 3, 1913, and from March 4, 1915, to March 3, 1929, when he resigned to assume the vice presidency under President Herbert Clark Hoover.

Black senator was Hiram Rhodes Revels of Mississippi, who was elected January 20, 1870, by the legislature of Mississippi to the United States Senate for the unexpired term beginning March 4, 1865, and ending March 3, 1871. He was sworn in February 25, 1870.

Black senator elected by popular vote was Edward William Brooke, Massachusetts attorney general, who was elected November 8, 1966, by a plurality of approximately 439,000 votes. He was seated January 10, 1967 (90th Congress).

Black senator to preside over the Senate was Blanche Kelso Bruce, Republican from Mississippi (March 4, 1875, to March 3, 1881), who presided on February 15, 1879, at which time he voted. *(Congressional Record containing the Proceedings and Debates of the 45th Congress, 3rd session, Vol. 8)*

The First

SENATOR (U.S.)—*Continued*

Black senator to serve a full term was Blanche Kelso Bruce of Mississippi, who served from March 4, 1875, to March 3, 1881.

Cabinet appointee rejected by the Senate. *See under* Cabinet (U.S.)

Catholic senator was Daniel Carroll, a Federalist of Maryland, who served from March 4, 1789, to March 3, 1791. His brother was John Carroll, the first Catholic bishop in the United States. *(American Catholic Historical Society—Records, 1941. Vol. 2)*

Father and son senators at the same session were Henry Dodge (father) of Wisconsin and Augustus Caesar Dodge (son) of Iowa, who sat together from December 7, 1848, to February 22, 1855 (30th-33rd congresses). Previously they had served as delegates to the House of Representatives in the 27th and 28th congresses from March 4, 1841, to March 3, 1845, prior to the statehood of their territories. Henry Dodge served in the Senate until March 3, 1857.

Father whose 3 sons were senators was Joseph Patrick Kennedy. His son, John Fitzgerald Kennedy, was sworn in January 3, 1953; Edward Moore Kennedy, January 9, 1963; and Robert Francis Kennedy, January 3, 1965.

Impeachment proceedings against a senator. *See under* Impeachment

Jewish senator was David Levy Yulee, a Democrat from Florida, who served from July 1, 1845, to March 3, 1851, and from March 4, 1855, to January 21, 1861. Prior to the admission of Florida as a state, he had been a delegate to the 27th and 28th congresses, serving from March 4, 1841, to March 3, 1845. *(American Jewish Historical Society— Publications, 1917)*

Senator appointed by a governor was John Walker of Virginia, who was appointed March 31, 1790, by Governor Beverley Randolph. Walker was appointed to the Senate to fill the vacancy caused by the death of William Grayson. He produced his credentials, took his seat April 26, 1790, and served until November 9, 1790, when James Monroe was elected to fill the unexpired term ending March 3, 1791. *(Biographical Directory of the American Congress, 1774–1927)*

Senator appointed (not seated) was Kensey Johns, who was appointed on March 19, 1794, by Governor Joshua Clayton of Delaware to fill the vacancy caused by the resignation of George Read on December 18, 1793, during the recess of the state legislature. On Monday March 24, 1794, Kensey Johns presented his credentials to the Senate, which maintained that the Delaware legislature had met in January and adjourned in February 1794 and that Johns was appointed on March 19, 1794, subsequent to the adjournment. It was ruled on March 28, 1794, that Johns was not

The First

entitled to his seat because a session of the legislature intervened between the resignation of the said George Read and the appointment of the said Kensey Jones. *(Annals of the Congress of the United States. 3rd Congress, 1793–1795)*

Senator censured was Timothy Pickering, a Federalist of Massachusetts, (20 yeas, 7 nays) on January 2, 1811, by the 3rd session of the 11th Congress, which stated that Pickering, who "read from his place certain documents confidentially communicated by the President of the United States to the Senate, the injunction of secrecy having been removed, has, in so doing, committed a violation of this body." He served in the Senate from March 4, 1803, to March 3, 1811, and in the House of Representatives from March 4, 1813, to March 3, 1817.

Senator elected by a write-in vote was J(ames) Strom Thurmond, a Democrat, of South Carolina, who was elected on November 2, 1954, for the term ending January 3, 1961. Thurmond received 139,106 votes, defeating Edgar Brown, the state Democratic Executive Committee nominee, who received 80,956 votes.

Senator elected by popular vote after the passage of the Seventeenth Amendment was incumbent Augustus Octavius Bacon, Democrat of Georgia, who was elected July 15, 1913, and sworn in July 28, 1913.

Senator elected on an antislavery ticket was John Parker Hale of New Hampshire, who was elected June 9, 1846, for the six-year term which began March 4, 1847. Previously he had served as a Democrat in the House of Representatives from March 4, 1843, to March 3, 1845.

Senator expelled. *See* Impeachment: Impeachment proceedings against a U.S. senator

Senator in military uniform to address the Senate was Edward Dickinson Baker, Republican, of Oregon, who on August 11, 1861, was drilling his regiment at Meridian Hill when he was summoned to refute Senator John Breckinridge, Democrat, of Kentucky, who was speaking against sending troops against the South. He did not have time to change into civilian attire but removed his sword prior to delivering his speech. He was killed at the Battle of Balls Bluff, Va., October 21, 1861.

Senator of Asian ancestry was Hiram Leong Fong, a Republican of Chinese-American ancestry, who was elected July 29, 1959, by Hawaii, the 50th state. He was sworn in on August 24, 1959, by Vice President Richard Milhous Nixon.

Senator returned to the Senate after being defeated for the presidency was Henry Clay of Kentucky, who was returned to the Senate on March 4, 1849. He had been the presidential candidate of the Whig Party and had been defeated in the presidential election of November 5, 1844.

The First

Senator to act in the movies was Everett McKinley Dirksen of Illinois, who appeared in *The Monitors,* a satire released October 9, 1969, rated "M" for mature audiences. It was a 91-minute film produced by Bell & Howell Productions in association with Commonwealth United Entertainment, Inc. The film featured Ed Begley as the President, Keenan Wynn as the general, and Larry Storch as the colonel. It depicted a pacifistic nonviolent United States dominated from the White House down by a horde of robot-like young men in bowlers.

Senator to become President. *See* President: President who had been a senator

Senator to filibuster for more than 24 hours was Senator Strom Thurmond, a Democrat of South Carolina, who spoke 24 hours 18 minutes against Civil Rights legislation on August 28-29, 1957.

Senator to preside over a Senate session directly after being sworn in as a senator was Arthur Edson Blair Moody, former Washington correspondent of the Detroit *News,* who was appointed senator by Michigan Governor Gerhard Mennen Williams to serve the unexpired term of Arthur Hendrick Vandenberg. Moody was sworn in April 25, 1951, by Vice President Alben William Barkley, who invited him to preside over the session. Moody served from April 25, 1951, to January 3, 1953.

Senator to receive a mileage allowance for a trip which he did not make was George Evans of Maine, who served from March 4, 1841, to March 3, 1847. It was not necessary for him to travel because he was already in Washington, D.C., having served in Congress as a representative from Maine in previous sessions, including the 2nd Session of the 26th Congress, December 7, 1840–March 3, 1841.

Senator to serve in contravention to the age limit was Henry Clay of Kentucky, who served from November 19, 1806, to March 3, 1807. He was born April 12, 1777, in Hanover County, Va., and was 29 years 221 days old when he took office, although Article 1 Section 3 of the Constitution of the United States states "no person shall be a Senator who shall not have attained to the age of thirty years."

Senator to serve three states was James Shields of Illinois, Minnesota, and Missouri. He was elected as a Democrat to serve Illinois in the 33rd Congress for the term commencing March 4, 1849. His election was declared void as he had not been a citizen the requisite number of years. He was reelected for the same term and served October 27, 1849, to March 3, 1855. He represented Minnesota in the 35th Congress and served from May 12, 1858, to March 3, 1859. He was elected by Missouri January 22, 1879, to fill the vacancy caused by the death of Lewis Vital Bogy and served in the

The First

44th Congress from January 27, 1879, to March 3, 1879.

Senator to win a seat which had been occupied by his father and his mother was Russell Long of Louisiana, who was elected November 2, 1948, and sworn in December 31, 1948, for the term expiring January 2, 1951. His father, Huey Pierce Long, was elected November 4, 1930, and took the oath of office January 25, 1932. His mother, Rose McConnell Long, was appointed January 31, 1936, serving until January 2, 1937.

Senator unseated after a recount was Smith Wildman Brookhart, a Republican of Iowa, presumed winner of the November 4, 1924, election. He presented his credentials as a senator-elect for the term commencing March 4, 1925, and served until April 12, 1926, when he was ousted by a Senate vote of 45-41. He was succeeded by Daniel Frederic Steck, a Democrat, who served from April 12, 1926, to March 3, 1931, having been found entitled to the senatorial seat.

Senator who served a term of less than 6 weeks was Pierre Soulé of New Orleans, La., elected as a State Rights Democrat to fill the vacancy caused by the death of Alexander Barrow, serving from January 21, 1847, to March 3, 1847. He was elected again and served from March 3, 1849, to April 11, 1853, when he resigned to become United States Minister to Spain (1853–1855).

Senator who was an astronaut was John Herschel Glenn of New Concord, Ohio, elected as a Democrat on November 5, 1974. He was the pilot of Mercury spacecraft (capsule 13) *Friendship* launched February 20, 1962, by an Atlas booster. He made 3 orbits in 4 hours 55 minutes and landed east of the Bahamas in the Atlantic Ocean.

Senator who had been President. *See* President: President to become a senator

Senators censured were Benjamin Ryan Tillman of South Carolina and John Lowndes McLaurin of South Carolina. Tillman charged that McLaurin had been bribed to vote for the Treaty of Paris terminating the Spanish-American War. McLaurin declared the accusation was "a willful, malicious and deliberate lie" and a fist fight ensued on the Senate floor on February 22, 1902 (57th Congress, 1st Session). Both were censured. They apologized and were permitted to retain their seats. Tillman served as senator from March 4, 1895, to July 3, 1918, and McLaurin from June 1, 1897, to March 3, 1903.

Senators collectively "elected by the people at a general election" were chosen November 4, 1913. Section 3, Article 1 of the Constitution provided for the election of senators by the state legislatures. The 17th Amendment was passed in the House, April 13, 1912, and by the Senate, June 12, 1912. The 36th state to ratify the amendment was Wisconsin, May 9, 1913, and the amendment

The First

SENATOR (U.S.)—*Continued*
was declared in force May 31, 1913. *(Charles Austin Beard—American Government and Politics)*

Senators-elect not seated were William Blount and William Cocke of Tennessee, elected by the Tennessee legislature, who presented their credentials May 9, 1796. They were refused seats as Tennessee was not admitted to the Union until June 1, 1796. They were elected again on August 2, 1796, and took their seats on December 6, 1796.

Vice President elected by the Senate. *See under* Vice President (U.S.)

Woman elected to the Senate was Hattie Ophelia Wyatt Caraway, a Democrat, of Jonesboro, Ark., widow of Senator Thaddeus Horatio Caraway. Before being elected she had received a temporary appointment from Governor Garvey Parnell on November 13, 1931, to fill the vacancy caused by the death of her husband. She was elected January 12, 1932, and reelected in 1938, serving until January 3, 1945.

Woman senator elected for a third and a fourth term was Margaret Chase Smith of Maine, a Republican, who was elected November 2, 1948, and served from January 3, 1949, to January 3, 1973. She was elected in 1960 for her third term and in 1966 for her fourth.

Woman senator elected without having previously served an appointed term was Margaret Chase Smith, a Republican of Maine, who was elected to the 81st Congress on September 13, 1948. She had been elected as a representative to the 76th Congress on June 3, 1940, to fill the vacancy caused by the death of her husband, Clyde Harold Smith.

Woman senator to preside over the Senate was Hattie Wyatt Caraway, Democrat of Arkansas, who on October 19, 1943, opened the proceedings and presided as president pro tempore in the absence of Vice President Henry Agard Wallace (78th Congress, 1st Session). On May 9, 1932 (75th Congress, 1st Session), while Senator Carter Glass held the floor, she had occupied the president's chair for a brief period, but no question of procedure arose.

Woman senator to succeed a woman senator was Hazel Hempel Abel, a Republican, of Nebraska, who replaced Eve Bowring, also a Republican, on November 8, 1954. Mrs. Abel was elected November 2, 1954, for the balance of a two-month term.

Woman to occupy a seat in the Senate was Rebecca Latimer Felton, a Democrat, who was appointed by Governor Thomas William Hardwick of Georgia to the Senate on October 3, 1922, to fill the vacancy caused by the death of Thomas Edward Watson. She attended two sessions of the Senate (November 21 and November 22, 1922) before a successor was elected. *(John Erwin Tal-*

The First

madge—Rebecca Latimer Felton, Nine Story Decades)

SEPARATOR. *See* Cream separator

SERBIAN ORTHODOX CATHEDRAL was the Cathedral of St. Sava, New York City, elevated June 11, 1944, from a pro-cathedral. On the same day Bishop Dionisije [Dionisije Milivojevich] conferred the Gold Cross and the title Stravrophor on Rector Doushan Jefta Shoukletovich and elevated him to dean. The cathedral was the diocesan headquarters of the Serbian Orthodox Church in Canada and the United States.

SERIAL MOTION PICTURE. *See* motion picture

SERIAL STORY. *See* Newspaper: Newspaper serial story

SERIAL WRITER (woman). *See* Author: Successful woman serial writer

SERMON PRINTED (American) was "The Sin and Danger of Self-Love, a Discourse" based on the text from I Cor. 10:24, "Let no man seek his own; But every man another's wealth." It was delivered December 9, 1621, by Robert Cushman in Plymouth, Mass., in "an assembly of His Majesty's faithful subjects, there inhabiting" and was printed in London, England in 1622. It was reprinted by S. Kneeland, Boston, Mass. in 1724. *(Robert Cushman—The First Sermon Ever Preached in New England)*

SEROLOGICAL BLOOD TESTS. *See* Medical legislation: Law (state) requiring serological blood tests of pregnant women

SERVICE STATION, AUTOMOBILE. *See* Automobile service station

SERVITE CHURCH
Marian Congress was held at the Sanctuary of Our Sorrowful Mother, Portland, Oreg., August 12–15, 1934, under the auspices of the Servite Fathers. A Marian Congress is similar to a Eucharistic Congress, except that the Blessed Virgin is the object of devotion rather than the Holy Eucharist.

Servite Church in America was established in August 1870 at Menasha, Wis., under the direction of the Very Reverend Austin Morini, O.S.M., a Servite of the Italian Province.

SESSION LAWS (U.S.). *See* Lawbook: Law compilation of federal session laws

SETTLEMENT. *See* Colonist: Colonial white settlement (north of Florida)

SETTLEMENT BY EUROPEAN COLONISTS. *See* Colonist: Permanent white settlement in America

SETTLEMENT HOUSE was the University Settlement, established by Stanton Coit in 1886 in a Forsythe Street tenement, New York City, "to raise not only the standard of living but the standard of living-together." Playgrounds were pro-

The First

vided for children, instruction was given in English to foreigners, and other educational programs were established. The idea was that intellectuals would "settle" in a slum area and by living and working with tenement neighbors would be able to help them raise standards.

SEVEN-MASTED STEEL SCHOONER. *See* Ship

SEVENTH DAY ADVENTIST CHURCH was the Adventist church in Washington Center, N.H., which began to keep the seventh day as Sabbath in the spring of 1844. The first Adventist minister to accept the seventh day as the Sabbath was Frederick Wheeler, of the Washington Center Church, in March 1844. The first general conference of Seventh Day Adventists was organized May 21, 1863.

SEVENTH DAY BAPTIST CHURCH. *See* Baptist Church

SEWAGE

Separate system of sewage disposal was started in Memphis, Tenn., under the direction of George Edwin Waring on January 21, 1880. Within four months, a system comprising 18 miles of pipe, with 152 flush tanks and 4-inch connecting drains, was installed. The pipes were for sewage only and were kept constantly cleansed and well ventilated, always being kept half full of water. Six-inch vitrified pipes emptied into larger pipes, which in turn emptied into increasingly larger ones until 20-inch pipes were used. An independent and separate set of pipes was provided for disposing of storm water. The total cost of 20 miles for the two main sewers, including labor, materials, engineering, superintending, and incidentals, was about $137,000. A similar system was also adopted by Pullman, Ill. (now a part of Chicago, Ill.). *(John Preston Young—History of Memphis, Tenn.)*

Sewage disposal by chemical precipitation was undertaken by Worcester, Mass., in 1890. Six chemical precipitation settling basins, each 66 2/3 by 100 by 7 feet, were used. The raw sewage was screened and then treated with milk of lime. It was passed through a mixing channel into the six settling basins in series. The detention period was approximately six hours. After being quiescent for a few hours the top water was drawn off, and the sludge run to a 6-inch centrifugal pump and discharged into lagoons.

Sewage "dual system" was built in Brooklyn, N.Y., in 1857 by Colonel Julius Adams. The size and capacity were scientifically calculated to care for a rainfall intensity of one inch per hour. *(Leonard Metcalf and Harrison Prescott Eddy— Sewerage and Sewage Disposal)*

Underground comprehensive sewer system (city) was undertaken by Chicago, Ill., in 1856 on the grid pattern. The sewers were of circular cross sections ranging from 3 to 6 feet in diameter and

The First

had brick walls 8½ inches thick. Branch sewers were 2 feet in diameter, and the hose drains were 4- and 6-inch pipes or boxes made of wood planks. Manholes were provided every 100 feet, and in general the slope or gradient was 1 foot in 500. By June 30, 1860, about 46 miles had been completed. Single uncoordinated sewers had been used earlier.

SEWING MACHINE

Chain-stitch single-thread sewing machine (practical) was invented by James Edward Allen Gibbs of Mill Point, Va., who received patent No. 17,427 on June 2, 1857.

Electric sewing machine was manufactured by the Singer Manufacturing Company in 1889 at its factory, Elizabethport, N.J.

Lock-stitch sewing machine was made in 1832–34 by Walter Hunt of New York, whose machine used two threads, one below the cloth and the other coming down through the cloth, thus interlocking with each other. As he made no attempt to patent his machine until June 27, 1854, his original application was refused on the ground of abandonment. Elias Howe obtained patent No. 4,750 on a lock-stitch machine on September 10, 1846.

Sewing machine equipped with a rocking treadle or double treadle was invented by Isaac Merritt Singer of New York City, who obtained patent No. 8,294, August 12, 1851. He used a treadle similar to that employed in the old spinning wheel and attached it by means of a pitman to the handle on the driving gear of the machine.

Sewing machine lamp holder was introduced by the Singer Sewing Machine Company in 1876. It "quite obviated the difficulty experienced by operators when sewing at night" because the lamp would not "jar off the table or upset" and it could "be moved without soiling the fingers." It was patented by Ludwig Martin Nicolaus Wolf of Avon, Conn., who obtained patent No. 138,831 on May 13, 1873, on a "lamp bracket for sewing."

Sewing machine manufacturer who was successful was Isaac Merritt Singer, who began business at 19 Harvard Place, Boston, Mass., in 1851, on a capital of $40 supplied by George B. Zieber. His first machine was made in 11 days in the machine shop owned by Orson C. Phelps.

Sewing machine motor patent was No. 13,661, which was granted on October 9, 1855, to Isaac Merritt Singer of New York City. It covered a spring and cone pulley device.

Sewing machine patent of which there is any record was granted on February 21, 1842, (No. 2,466) to John James Greenough of Washington, D.C. It was a short-thread machine, the needle being threaded with short lengths of thread as in hand sewing.

The First

SEWING MACHINE—*Continued*

Sewing machine to sew curving seams was patented (No. 12,116) by Allen Benjamin Wilson of Watertown, Conn., on December 19, 1854. The machine operated with four-motion feed, which made it possible to sew a curved seam on a sewing machine. Wilson received his first patent on a sewing machine on November 12, 1850 (patent No. 7776).

Sewing machine to stitch buttonholes was a machine patented by Charles Miller of St. Louis, Mo., on March 7, 1854. He obtained patent No. 10,609.

SEX DISCRIMINATION

State to ban sex discrimination was Washington, which enacted legislation on May 17, 1971, effective July 1, 1971, relating to discriminating practices and prohibiting discrimination based on sex. The law declared that it was illegal "to refuse to hire any person because of such person's age, sex, marital status, race, creed, color or national origin."

State that declared unconstitutional a ban against girls competing with boys in athletic events on a state level was Pennsylvania, whose Pennsylvania Commonwealth Court on March 19, 1975, upheld a law by a five-to-three decision opening "interscholastic practice and competition to girls in all high school sports, including football and wrestling," and declaring "unconstitutional the ban against girls competing with boys in the bylaws of the Pennsylvania Interscholastic Athletic Association."

SEX SHOCKER MOVIE. *See* Motion Picture

SEXTANT, RADIO. *See* Radio sextant

SEXTUPLE PRINTING PRESS. *See* Printing press

SEXTUPLETS. *See under* Births

SHADE. *See* Venetian blinds

SHAFT-DRIVEN AUTOMOBILE. *See* Automobile

SHAKER SOCIETY, a celibate religious community, was founded by Ann Lee of Manchester, England, and eight others who left Liverpool on the *Mariah* and arrived in New York City on August 6, 1774. The first Shaker "Family" was formed in Watervliet, N.Y., in 1776, and the first organized Shaker Community was established in 1788 in New Lebanon, N.Y. New Lebanon became Mount Lebanon in 1861. The ministers were the spiritual leaders of the Society and the Elders of Families. As the rules of the Society stated, "The head of the Shaker Order is Christ, Represented in a Dual Order of Leaders, Ministry, Elders and Trustees." *(Frederick William Evans—Compendium of the Origin, History, Principles, Rules and Regulations, Government, and Doctrines of the United Society of Believers in Christ's Second Appearing)*

The First

SHAKESPEAREAN PLAY. *See* Play (drama)

SHALLOP. *See* Ship: Prefabricated ship

SHAVER, ELECTRIC. *See* Razor

SHEARS. *See* Cutlery shears

SHEEP. *See* Animals

SHEET ASPHALT PAVEMENT. *See under* Road

SHEET GLASS. *See* Glass

SHEET MILL. *See* Steel: Continuous-sheet steel mill

SHELTER. *See* Air raid shelter; Building: House with a built-in nuclear bomb shelter

SHEPHERD DOG TO GUIDE THE BLIND. *See* Animals: Dogs trained to guide the blind

SHIP

See also Submarine

Air-conditioned naval ship (fully conditioned) was the cruiser *Newport News,* laid down October 1, 1945, by the Newport News Shipbuilding and Drydock Company, Newport News, Va. It was launched March 6, 1947, christened by Mrs. Homer Lenoir Ferguson, and commissioned January 29, 1949. It had a 75 1/6-foot beam, was 716½ feet long, and mounted nine 8-inch guns in three turrets. The first captain was Captain Roland Nesbit Smoot.

Air-conditioned ship was the *Mariposa,* 18,152 tons, built for the Matson Navigation Company at the Fore River plant of the Bethlehem Shipbuilding Corporation, Quincy, Mass. The keel was laid May 17, 1930, and the ship launched July 18, 1931. Only the dining room was air-conditioned. It left New York City on January 16, 1932, for the South Seas, Australia, and New Zealand.

Aircraft carrier wholly designed and built as such was the *Ranger,* constructed by the Newport News Shipbuilding and Drydock Company, Newport News, Va. Its keel was laid September 26, 1931, and it was launched February 25, 1933. Its was commissioned at Norfolk, Va., and formally delivered June 4, 1934. The first Captain was Arthur Leroy Bristol.

Aircraft carrier (American) sunk in World War II. *See under* World War II

Aircraft carrier (atomic-powered) was the *Enterprise,* CVA (N) 65, ordered August 16, 1957, laid down February 4, 1958, launched September 24, 1960, and completed December 20, 1961. It was 1,101 feet long and 252 feet wide, with a 133-foot beam, a 75,700-ton standard displacement and an 85,350-ton full-load displacement, and a draft of 37 feet. The carrier, built by the Newport News Shipbuilding and Dry Dock Company, Newport News, Va., had a complement of 440 officers and 4,160 enlisted men. It was equipped with eight pressurized water-cooled nuclear reactors and capable of steaming for five years without refueling. Its flight deck was large enough to accommodate four football fields, and its four propellers were the height of two-story buildings. It was christened by Mrs. William Birrell Franke, wife of the Secretary of the Navy.

Aircraft carrier escort was the *Long Island* (CVE-1) laid down July 7, 1939, launched January 11, 1940, acquired March 6, 1941, for $2,956,346, and converted at the Newport News Shipbuilding & Dry Dock Company, Newport News, Va. The ship was commissioned June 2, 1941; its first captain was Donald B. Duncan. It was 492 feet long, its breadth 69 feet 6 inches, its draught 25 feet 8 inches. Built at the Sun Shipbuilding & Dry Dock Company, Chester, Pa., it was placed in commercial service as the *Mormacmail* for the Moore McCormack Line, Inc.

Aircraft carrier to sail around Cape Horn was the U.S.S. *Oriskany,* which passed Cape Horn at 8:30 A.M. on June 29, 1952. It left New York City on March 30, 1952, and arrived at San Diego, Calif., at 6:20 P.M. on July 21, 1952, and at San Francisco, Calif., on August 7, 1952, calls having been made at Rio de Janeiro, Brazil; Valparaiso, Chile; and Callao, Peru. The commanding officer was Captain John Osgo Lambrecht, U.S.N.

Aircraft carrier with an angle deck was the supercarrier U.S.S. *Forrestal* (CVA-59), authorized in March and contracted for July 12, 1951, and laid down July 14, 1952. It was launched December 11, 1954, by the Newport News Shipbuilding & Drydock Company at Newport News, Va., and christened by Mrs. James Vincent Forrestal, wife of the first Secretary of Defense, for whom the ship was named. It was commissioned October 1, 1955. The first captain was Captain Roy Lee Johnson. It cost $198 million, was 1,045⅞ feet long and 252 feet wide, and carried a crew of 3,500 including its own air group. Its height from keel to top of mast was equal to that of a 25-story building, and its flight deck had an area of nearly four acres. The carrier's displacement was 65,000 tons.

Airmail service to a steamer at sea. *See under* Airmail service

Airplane flight from a ship. *See under* Aviation —Flights

All-welded self-propelled seagoing petroleum carrier was the motorship *White Flash,* launched September 10, 1931, at the Sun Shipbuilding & Dry Dock Company, Chester, Pa., and placed in service by the Atlantic Refining Company on September 14, 1931.

Ambulance ship was the U.S.S. *Solace,* of 5,700 tons, in service April 14, 1898, and used in naval warfare in the war with Spain. Formerly the S.S. *Creole,* it was purchased April 7, 1898. The *Solace* was the creation of Admiral William Knicker-

bocker Van Reypen. It was fitted out under the terms of the Geneva Convention and was undoubtedly the first designated ambulance ship—used for transporting as well as caring for the sick and wounded—and the first to carry the Geneva Cross flag at the fore. It was removed from the Navy list August 6, 1930, and sold November 6, 1930. The first hospital ship, as distinguished from an ambulance ship, was the *Red Rover,* converted to a hospital ship in 1862.

Ambulance ship designed and built as a hospital for the transportation of sick and wounded naval men was the U.S.S. *Relief.* Congress authorized the construction of the *Relief* August 29, 1916, and the contract for its construction was signed August 29, 1916; on July 4, 1917, its keel was laid, and the frame was erected May 15, 1918. The vessel was launched December 23, 1919, christened by Mrs. William G. Braisted, and delivered to the Navy, December 28, 1920. The overall length of the *Relief* was 484 feet and it had a displacement of 9,750 tons and a speed of 16 knots. The hospital capacity was 515 beds in 14 wards and 15 officers' rooms.

Ambulance ship for first aid to boaters and pleasure craft was the *Star of Life No. 1,* a 31-foot Uniflite boat owned by Fairfield Medical Products Corporation of Stamford, Conn., christened April 2, 1976, at the Yacht Haven East Marina No. 9. Its equipment consisted of a Fairfield Heart Defibrillator, coronary surveillance unit, and resuscitator (oxygen and aspirator) vacuum systems. The on-board equipment was equal to a typical hospital-emergency room. The fire retardant, highspeed, fiberglass Uniflite Cruiser was capable of a top speed exceeding 35 m.p.h. It was used in patrol and rescue duty on Long Island Sound between Greenwich and Norwalk and Glen Cove and Port Jefferson, covering more than 150 square miles.

American Army troopship torpedoed by the Germans. *See under* World War I

American destroyer torpedoed. *See under* World War II

American flag displayed on a man-of-war. *See under* Flag

American ship lost in World War I. *See under* World War I

American ship sunk by a U-boat. *See under* World War II

Atomic-powered cruiser was the *Long Beach,* CG (N) 9, 721 feet long, beam 73 feet, draught 26 feet, 14,000 tons standard, 18,000 tons full load. The cost of construction was about $320 million. The keel was laid December 2, 1957, and the ship christened by Mrs. Craig Hosmer at the launching July 14, 1959, at the Fore River Shipyard of the Bethlehem Steel Company's shipyard at Quincy, Mass. The ship, which had two nuclear reactors, attained a speed of 30 knots.

The First

SHIP—*Continued*

Atomic-powered merchant ship was the N.S. *Savannah,* 595 feet, 21,000 tons, authorized July 30, 1956 (70 Stat. L. 731). It was built by the New York Shipbuilding Corporation, Camden, N.J., for the U.S. Maritime Commission. The pressurized waterpower reactor was built by Babcock & Wilcox Co., New York City. The keel was laid May 22, 1958, and the ship christened July 21, 1959, by Mrs. Dwight David Eisenhower.

Ballistic-missile test ship was the *Compass Island* (EAG 153), acquired from the Merchant Marine by the U.S. Navy on March 29, 1956, tested at sea November 19, 1956, and commissioned December 3, 1956, at the New York Naval Shipyard, Brooklyn, N.Y. The ship was 529½ feet long, 76½ feet wide, with a 29-foot depth and a displacement of 17,600 tons. It was built by the New York Shipbuilding Corporation, Camden, N.J., and launched October 24, 1953, as the *Garden Mariner.*

Balloon carrier was the U.S.S. *Fanny,* an armed transport which John La Mountain used August 3, 1861, to transport a balloon attached to a windlass at the stern. At a height of 2,000 feet, the balloon was used to observe military positions at Fortress Monroe, Va.

Barge to transport liquid sulfur was *F.S. No. 7* owned by the Freeport Sulphur Company, placed in service on a 10-mile canal between the Grande Ecaille mine and the Port Sulphur shipping point in Louisiana on February 23, 1948.

Battleship built on the Pacific coast was the *Nebraska,* 441 feet 3 inches long, extreme beam 76 feet 3 inches, normal displacement 14,948 tons. The ship was authorized March 3, 1899, and built by the Moran Company, Seattle, Wash. Its keel was laid July 4, 1902. Commissioned July 1, 1907, the ship was launched October 7, 1904. The first captain was Reginald Fairfax Nicholson.

Battleship equipped with radar. *See under* Radar

Battleship (major) built on the Pacific coast was the armored cruiser *California* (BB-44), authorized March 3, 1915. The keel was laid October 25, 1916, and the ship launched November 20, 1919, at the Mare Island Navy Yard, Calif., and commissioned August 10, 1921. It was 624 feet 6 inches long, 97 feet 4 inches in breadth, with a displacement of 32,300 tons and carried a complement of 57 officers and 1,026 enlisted men. Captain Henry Joseph Ziegemeier was in command.

Battleship of importance was the U.S.S. *Maine,* authorized by act of Congress of August 3, 1886 (24 Stat. L. 215). It was built at the Brooklyn Navy Yard, Brooklyn, N.Y. Its keel was laid October 17, 1888, and it was launched November 18, 1890. It was commissioned September 17, 1895. Its length was 319 feet, beam 57 feet, mean draft 21 feet 6

The First

inches, displacement 6,682 tons. On the night of February 15, 1898, the *Maine* was mysteriously destroyed by explosion in Havana harbor, Cuba. Only 16 of the total crew of 354 wholly escaped injury. *(Charles Dwight Sigsbee—The Maine)*

Battleship sunk by an airplane. *See under* Aviation

Battleship to use fuel oil exclusively was the U.S.S. *Nevada* (BB-36), laid down by the Fore River Shipbuilding Co., Quincy, Mass., on November 4, 1912, and launched July 11, 1914. It was commissioned March 11, 1916. The ship was 583 feet long, 85 feet 3 inches in breadth, with a 27,500-ton displacement. It carried a complement of 864. Captain William Sowden Sims was in command.

Battleship to visit an inland city was the U.S.S. *Mississippi* (length, 375 feet; draft 24.8 feet; extreme breadth 77 feet; displacement 13,000 tons), which sailed 300 miles up the Mississippi River to Natchez, Miss., on May 20, 1909, and departed for New Orleans, May 24, 1909. It was built by William Cramp and Sons, Philadelphia, Pa., and was commissioned February 1, 1908.

Boat race. *See* Boat race: Intercollegiate boat race

Cargo ship fully automated and flying the American flag was the 12,000 ton S.S. *Mormacargo,* whose keel was laid April 22, 1963, at Ingalls Shipbuilding Corp., Pascagoula, Miss. Launched January 25, 1964, the ship's first run was August 28, 1964, from Pascagoula to Boston and its first transatlantic trip September 11, 1964, from New York City. It was 550 feet 9 inches long overall, with a beam of 75 feet and a displacement of 19,800 tons. It had a bridge console with electronic control of speed, boiler temperatures, and reefer temperatures, and other automatic devices. Instead of the normal crew of 49, the crew numbered 32, each having a private room. The *Mormacargo* cost in excess of $10 million and is operated by the Moore-McCormack Lines, Inc. Kenneth L. Chambers was the first captain.

Catamaran. *See* Catamaran

Child born on a vessel passing through the Panama Canal. *See under* Births

Clipper ship was the *Ann McKim,* launched June 3, 1833 for Isaac McKim by Kennard & Williamson of Fells Point, Baltimore, Md. It was 143 feet long, 31 feet wide, and of 493 tons register. The first master was Joseph Martin. Many other claims are made, since definitions vary as to what constitutes a clipper ship. *(Arthur Hamilton Clark—The Clipper Ship Era)*

Commercial crude-oil carrier was the *Brooklyn* built at the Brooklyn Navy Yard, New York City, by the Seatrain Shipbuilding Corporation and christened June 30, 1973, by Mary Harrison Lindsay, wife of John Vliet Lindsay, the mayor of New

The First

York City. The first test trip was made October 22, 1973, in the East River. The ship was 1,094 feet long with a 226,200-ton displacement and cost $80 million. It could carry 1½ million barrels of crude oil and could unload in 14 hours.

Commercial ship to conquer the Northwest Passage was the 1.005 ice-breaking oil tanker *Manhattan,* which left Chester, Pa., August 24, 1969, took off from Halifax, Nova Scotia, on August 29, 1969, and returned to Halifax on November 8, 1969. On September 14, the ship passed through the Prince of Wales strait to the Amundsen Gulf in the Beaufort Sea; the captain was Roger Steward. The ship was chartered from Seatrain Lines by the Humble Oil & Refining Company.

Concrete barge was the barge *Socony 200,* which was also the first reinforced-steel concrete barge for carrying oil in bulk. It was built to specifications for the Standard Oil Company of New York and was 98 feet long, 31 feet wide, and 9 feet 6 inches deep. The vessel was launched July 27, 1918, and placed in commission August 12, 1918. It was built by the Fougner Shipbuilding Company, Flushing Bay, New York.

Concrete seagoing ship was the *Faith,* built by the San Francisco Shipbuilding Company at Redwood City, Calif., and launched March 14, 1918, six weeks after the pouring of the concrete had started. It cost $750,000 and was the first concrete ship to cross the Atlantic Ocean. The ship was 8,000 tons burden, 320 feet long, 44.6 feet wide, and 30 feet deep. The builder and owner was W. Leslie Comyn, president of the San Francisco Shipbuilding Company. The engineers were Allan MacDonald and Victor Poss.

Concrete ship built for the United States Shipping Board Emergency Fleet Corporation was the *Atlantus,* launched December 4, 1918, and delivered November 11, 1919. The first ship delivered was the *Polias,* launched May 22, 1919, and delivered October 23, 1919. These ships were launched at Brunswick, Ga., and built by the Liberty Shipbuilding Company, Brunswick.

Confederate cruiser built in England, the *Oneto,* sailed from Liverpool, England, March 22, 1862, bound for the Bahamas. The ship was transferred to Captain John Newland Maffitt of the Confederate Navy, who took rank as commodore. The guns and stores were sent in another ship which followed.

Confederate cruiser to raid Union commerce was the *Sumter,* commanded by Captain Raphael Semmes. The *Sumter* was a merchantman which had been fitted out in 1861 at New Orleans, La., with five small guns. Semmes on the *Sumter* captured 18 vessels, of which 8 were burned. *(Raphael Semmes—Memoirs of Service Afloat During the War Between the States)*

The First

Confederate ship surrendered was the *Planter,* a 313-ton side-wheel-steamer armed dispatch boat, seized May 12, 1862, off Charleston harbor by Robert Smalls, a black slave who was its pilot. While the captain was ashore, he and the black crew took charge. Flying the Confederate flag, they saluted the forts on their voyage northward. When out of reach of ammunition. Smalls hoisted a white flag of truce and turned over the ship to the U.S.S. *Onward.* In appreciation, a special act of Congress was passed May 30, 1862, awarding Smalls and his black partners one half the value of the *Planter* and its cargo.

Conflict between ironclad vessels in the Civil War. *See under* Civil War

Cruise ship to circumnavigate the world was the Cunard liner *Laconia,* which left New York City on November 21, 1922, with 440 passengers on a 130-day cruise and returned March 30, 1923. An earlier world cruise was made by the *Cleveland* of the Hamburg-American Line, which departed February 6, 1912, from New York City, rounded Cape Horn and reached Hamburg, Germany, on May 17, 1912, via Honolulu, Yokohama, Kobe, Nagasaki, Hong Kong, Manila, Batavia, Singapore, Rangoon, Calcutta, Colombo, Bombay, Suez, Port Said, Naples, Gibraltar, and Southampton.

Decked ship built in America was completed and launched on the Hudson River near the Battery in the summer of 1614 by Adrianen Blok, a native of Holland. He named it the *Onrust* (the *Restless*). It was a 16-ton ship, 38 feet on the keel, 44½ feet overall, and 11 feet in the beam. (The year and the spelling of Blok's name vary in the records.)

Destroyer of the U.S. Navy named for a Confederate officer was the *Buchanan* (DD-131), named for Admiral Franklin Buchanan, ranking officer in the Confederate Navy. The ship was 314 feet 5 inches long, 31 feet 8 inches in breadth. It was launched at the Bath Iron Works, Bath, Me., on January 2, 1919, and commissioned on January 20, 1919. Lieutenant Howard Hartwell James Benson was the first in command. *(Charles Lee Lewis— Admiral Franklin Buchanan)*

Diesel-and-gas-turbine combined-propulsion plant in a major ship was installed in the U.S. Coast Guard's twin-screw 2,800-ton cutter *Alexander Hamilton* (WHEC-715), launched December 18, 1965, at the Avondale Shipyards, New Orleans, La. The ship's length was 378 feet 3 inches overall, the beam 42 feet, the draft 20 feet. It had two 35,000 h.p. Fairbanks Morse diesel engines and two 18,000 h.p. Pratt & Whitney gas turbines, and it cost $14.5 million. It was commissioned March 18, 1967. The crew consisted of 15 officers and 137 men; the commanding officer was Captain William Francis Adams.

The First

SHIP—*Continued*

Diesel-engine passenger ship was *The City of New York,* built by the Sun Shipbuilding Company, Chester, Pa., under the Merchant Marine Act of May 22, 1928, and tested January 11, 1930, on the Delaware River. The ship was 470.8 feet long, 61.6 feet in the beam, with a 26-foot draft. It carried 61 first-class passengers and had a 10,000-ton deadweight tonnage. Propelled by Sun-Doxford diesel engines, the ship made 13 knots. The first direct voyage left Brooklyn, N.Y., February 1, 1930, for Capetown, Union of South Africa, for the American South African Line (now Farrell Lines).

Dirigible landing and taking off from an ocean-going steamship. *See under* Aviation—Airship

Drama broadcast from a ship at sea. *See under* Radio broadcast

Dredge (seagoing hopper) was the *General Moultrie,* a steam dredge, built by William Colyer, New York City, in 1855. The 365-ton dredge was 150 feet long, 26 feet 8 inches wide, and 10 feet 3 inches in depth. Originally a commercial steamer, it was converted into a dredge by the installation of centrifugal dredging pumps, piping, etc., and the construction of bins in the holds. The machinery was furnished by C. H. De Lamater, New York City. The dredge was used in the Charleston, S.C., harbor.

Dual sponsorship of a U.S. Navy ship occurred January 15, 1962, when Margaret Denham and Jane Halsey, granddaughters of Fleet Admiral William Frederick ("Bull") Halsey, broke 2 bottles of champagne on the bow of the guided-missile frigate *Halsey* (DLG-23) at the launching ceremony at Hunter's Point Naval Shipyard, San Francisco, Calif. The keel was laid August 26, 1960, and the ship commissioned July 20, 1963. It was 533 feet long, 54 feet 10 inches in breadth, with a displacement of 7,515 tons, and had a complement of 377. H. H. Anderson, U.S. Navy, was the captain.

Eagle boat was the patrol craft *Eagle No. 1* (PE-1), whose keel was laid May 7, 1918. The ship was launched July 11, 1918, at Highland Park, Detroit, Mich., and commissioned October 27, 1918. It was 200 feet 9 inches long, with a breadth of 33 feet 1 inch and a 615-ton displacement. It had a complement of 5 officers and 56 enlisted men.

Electrically propelled ship of the U.S. Navy was the U.S.S. *Jupiter,* built as a collier at the Navy Yard, Mare Island, Calif. Its keel was laid October 16, 1911, and it was launched August 24, 1912. It was commissioned April 7, 1913. Its conversion to an aircraft carrier was authorized July 11, 1919 (41 Stat. L. 133), when $2,500,000 was appropriated. Its name was changed from *Jupiter* to *Langley* on April 21, 1920.

Federal steamer named for a woman was the *Harriet Lane,* named after a niece of President James Buchanan. A side-wheeler of 500 tons with

The First

8 guns, the *Harriet Lane* was 270 feet long, with a 22-foot beam. It was designed as a Treasury Department Revenue cutter and was built by William Henry Webb in 1857 in New York City. During the Civil War it fired a shot, April 12, 1861, near the bow of the steamer *Nashville* to force the *Nashville* to show her true colors—the first shot fired from a U.S. vessel in the war. On January 1, 1863, the *Harriet Lane* was captured in Galveston Bay after desperately resisting boarding parties from four rebel cotton-clads. *(Fletcher Pratt—The Navy, a History)*

Ferryboat. *See* Ferryboat

Fireboat. *See* Fireboat

Fish hatching steamer (federal) was the *Fishhawk,* authorized by Congress March 3, 1879 (20 Stat. L. 383), with an appropriation of $45,000. The vessel was designed by Charles W. Copeland, built by the Pusey and Jones Company of Wilmington, Del., launched December 13, 1879, and turned over to the U.S. Fish Commission on February 23, 1880. It was of 441 gross tonnage and 156 feet 6 inches long overall, with a 27-foot beam. The hull below the main deck was iron, sheathed with yellow pine. When commissioned, it was equipped with a very compete hatchery as well as a laboratory, a hoisting engine, dredges, trawls, deep-sea thermometers, etc. Lieutenant Zera Luther Tanner, U.S.N., was the first commanding officer. *(Records in Department of the Interior, Bureau of Fisheries, Washington, D.C.)*

FLIP ship (floating instrument platform) was developed by the U.S. Navy and the Marine Physical Laboratory of the Scripps Institution of Oceanography, University of California, San Diego, Calif., with financial support from the Office of Naval Research, and built at Gunderson Brothers Engineering Corporation yard in Portland, Ore. It was launched June 22, 1962. The ship towed like a log and could turn on end with only 55 of its 355 feet length above water. It weighed about 750 tons and cost under $600,000. Accepted August 6, 1962, it was placed in service in September 1962. Commander Earl D. Bronson (U.S. Navy, Retired) supervised construction and developed operating techniques.

Frigate was the *United States,* which was built by Joshua Humphreys at what was formerly the Association Battery, Philadelphia, Pa., and launched May 10, 1797. President John Adams attended the launching. The vessel was of 1,576 tons and was first captained by Commodore John Barry. It was scuttled and sunk April 20, 1861, when the Federal forces abandoned the Norfolk Navy Yard.

Frigate (American-built, steam-driven) to cross the Atlantic Ocean was the U.S. Steam Frigate *Missouri,* which left Norfolk, Va., August 5, 1843, with 384 persons. Under the Command of Captain John Thomas Newton, it arrived at Gibraltar, Au-

The First

gust 25, 1843. The following day it caught fire and became a total loss. *(William Bolton—A Narrative of the Last Cruise of the U.S. Steam Frigate Missouri)*

German ship captured in World War II. *See under* World War II

Great Lakes commercial vessel was *Le Griffon,* a two-masted armored square-rigger built in 1679 by Robert Cavelier, Sieur de La Salle, at Cayuga Creek, near the Niagara River. The keel was laid January 26, 1679. Its first voyage was made August 7, 1679. It was of 60 tons burden and sailed lakes Erie and Michigan. It sank on September 18, 1679, in a gale in Mackinaw Strait and is believed to be resting in Mississagi Strait, Manitoulin Island, Canada. *(Edward Channing and Marion Florence Lansing—Story of the Great Lakes)*

Guided missile cruiser was the *Boston,* CAG 1, converted November 1, 1955, and recommissioned at the U.S. Naval Base, Philadelphia, Pa. The cruiser, 13,600 tons standard, 17,200 tons full load, was laid down June 30, 1941, launched August 26, 1942, at the Bethlehem Steel Company, Quincy, Mass., and commissioned June 30, 1943. Its superstructure was entirely remodeled, one of the two stacks being removed to accommodate twin launchers capable of firing Terrier missiles. The ship was 673½ feet long and had a 71-foot beam and a draft of 26 feet. Captain Charles Bowling Martell was the first commanding officer of the converted cruiser.

Guided-missile escort ship was the *Brooke* (DEG 1), laid down December 10, 1962, and launched July 19, 1963, at the Lockheed Shipbuilding and Construction Company (formerly the Sound Bridge & Dry Dock Company), Seattle, Wash. The ship was 414.5 feet long with a 44.2 foot beam and a displacement of 3,425 tons full load and 2,640 tons standard. The *Brooke* carried 44 Tartar missiles. The first commanding officer was Commander Robert Levi Walters, the ship's complement 225 enlisted men and 16 officers. It was commissioned March 12, 1966.

Gyro-stabilized American liner was the S.S. *Mariposa* of the Matson Lines, christened October 16, 1956, in Portland, Oreg., by Electa Sevier. It sailed on its maiden voyage on October 26, 1956, from Los Angeles, Calif., to Australia and the South Seas. Fins made by the Sperry Gyroscope Company were built into the hull, below the surface of the sea, to remove up to 90 percent of ship roll.

Gyro-stabilized vessel to cross the Atlantic Ocean was the *Conte di Savoia* of the Italian Line, which arrived in New York City on December 7, 1932. The captain was Antonio Lena.

Gyro stabilizer installed on an American naval vessel was placed on the U.S.S. *Worden* in April

The First

1913 by the Sperry Gyroscope Company, Brooklyn, N.Y.

Gyrocompass installed on an American naval vessel. *See* Gyrocompass: Gyrocompass installed on an American naval vessel

Hospital ship of the U.S. Navy was the U.S.S. *Red Rover,* which had been captured from the Confederate forces on September 20, 1862. On December 26, 1862, it was converted into a hospital ship, and it remained in service until August 12, 1865. The first ambulance ship (used for transporting as well as caring for the sick and wounded) was the U.S.S. *Solace,* in service in 1898.

Ice yacht. *See* Ice yacht

Intercollegiate boat race. *See under* Boat race

Iron sloop yacht was the *Vindex,* built in 1871 at Chester, Pa., by Reany, Son and Company. It was 54 gross tons, 36 net tons, 62.5 feet long, 17.3 feet wide, and had a depth of 7.9 feet and a draft of 8.95 feet. Robert Center was the first owner. It was abandoned June 30, 1898. *(Howard Irving Chapelle—History of American Sailing Ships)*

Iron steamship built for transatlantic service was the *Bangor,* constructed by Betts, Harlan and Hollingsworth at Wilmington, Del., for the Bangor Steam Navigation Company and launched in May 1844. It was 120 feet long with 231 tons burden. It was schooner-rigged, had three wooden masts, and carried eight sails. *(Francis Burke Brandt—The Majestic Delaware)*

Iron vessel was the *John Randolph,* 122 tons, which was built in 1834 at Savannah, Ga., by John Caut for Gazaway Bugg Lamar. The plates were made by John Laird of Birkenhead, England, and shipped in sections to Savannah, where they were riveted together. The vessel was owned in and operated from Savannah. According to record, the *John Randolph* was not enrolled until July 2, 1842, although it may have been enrolled earlier. In 1836 John Caut also built the *Chatham,* 198 tons, which was enrolled on August 1, 1837, and in 1838 John Wade built the *Lamar,* 196 tons, which was enrolled on December 4, 1838. These three iron vessels were all built in Savannah of iron manufactured in England.

Iron vessel built for the U.S. Navy was an iron side-wheel steamer, the *Michigan,* built in Erie, Pa., under authority of act of Congress of September 9, 1841 (5 Stat. L. 460). Construction began in 1842 with the building of sections in Pittsburgh, Pa. These sections were transported to Erie, where the ship was completed and launched December 5, 1843. The cost of the ship was $165,000. Its hull was designed and built by Stockhouse and Tomlinson, Pittsburgh. Its displacement was 685 tons; length 163 feet, 3 inches; breadth 27 feet, 1½ inches; depth of hold 13 feet, 9 inches. It was renamed the *Wolverine* on June 17, 1905, and loaned to the city of Erie on July 19, 1927, by act

The First

SHIP—*Continued*

of Congress of December 21, 1926 (44 Stat. L. 923). She was officially stricken from the navy list on March 12, 1927.

Iron vessel built of American iron was the *De Rosset* of 186 tons, which was built in 1839 at Baltimore, Md., by Langley B. Culley. The *De Rosset* was registered at Baltimore on April 4, 1839. *(Records in Bureau of Navigation. Department of Commerce, Washington D.C.)*

Iron vessel (sheet iron) was the steamboat *Codorus*, built by John Elgar at York, Pa., and tested November 14, 1825, on the Susquehanna River. The sheet iron was riveted with iron rivets. The 5-ton vessel, built at a cost of about $3,000, had a 60-foot keel and a 9-foot beam, and drew about 7 inches of water. It had a cylindrical 8 h.p. coal- and wood-burning engine. The boiler weighed two tons. The *Codorus* was completed and loaded on an eight-wheeled wagon, to which ropes were attached, and on November 14, 1825, it was drawn from the foundry west of the Codorus Creek to the Susquehanna River, 12 miles distant. *(Alexander Crosby Brown—The Sheet Iron Steamboat Codorus)*

Ironclad naval vessels were the *Benton* and the *Essex* (1,000 tons each), and seven others (of 512 tons each), delivered at St. Louis, Mo., where they were accepted for the government by Captain Andrew Hull Foote on January 15, 1862. They were constructed under contract with James Buchanan Eads at Mound City and Cairo, Ill., and added to the Western Flotilla, also known as the Gunboat Flotilla on Western Waters, or the Mississippi Squadron, which was organized October 1, 1862.

Ironclad turreted vessel in the U.S. Navy was the U.S.S. *Monitor*, designed and built by John Ericsson, the contract for which was signed October 4, 1861, by Gideon Welles, Secretary of the Navy. The terms of the contract provided that the ship was to be completed within 100 days. The keel was laid October 22, 1861, and the ship was launched at Greenpoint, L.I., N.Y., on January 30, 1862. It was completed February 19, 1862, and the trial trip and delivery were made to the Navy on February 20, 1862. It had two 11-inch guns in the turret that fired a solid shot weighing 180 pounds. It left New York City, March 6, 1862, with Lieutenant John Lorimer Worden in command, and arrived at Hampton Roads, Va., on March 8, 1862, where it participated the next day in the engagement against the former Federal ship *Merrimac* (renamed the *Virginia* by the Confederates). *(Ebenezer Pearson Dorr—A Brief Sketch of the First Monitor and Its Inventor)*

Ironclad warship for service at sea was the *Galena*, built by Cornelius Scranton Bushnell and H. L. Bushnell of New Haven, Conn., and launched February 14, 1862, at the Maxson and Fish Yard, Mystic, Conn. The *Monitor*, a single-

The First

turreted vessel, was launched January 30, 1862, New York City, but it was not a seagoing ironclad, merely a floating battery for harbor defense.

Japanese submarine sunk by an American ship. *See under* World War II

Liberty ship in World War II was the *Patrick Henry*, launched September 27, 1941. It was built by the Bethlehem-Fairfield Shipbuilding Company, Baltimore, Md., in 244 days and delivered December 30, 1941, at Baltimore, Md., to the United States Maritime Commission, which transferred it to the Lykes Bros. Steamship Company, Inc., of New Orleans, La. It had an overall length of 441 feet 6 inches, a beam of 57 feet, a depth of 37 feet 4 inches, a total displacement of 14,100 tons, and a general cargo capacity of 9,146 tons. It had single-screw steam reciprocating propulsion and on her first voyage (to Alexandria, Egypt) her average speed was 11.19 knots. It was sponsored by Mrs. Henry Agard Wallace, wife of the Vice President. The first captain was Richard Gailard Ellis.

Lifeboat. *See* Lifeboat

Lightship. *See* Lightship

Liquid-bulk-chemical carrier was the *Marine-Dow Chem* a 16,500-ton oil tanker, 351 feet long, built by the Bethlehem Steel Company, shipbuilding division for the Marine Transport Lines, Inc., New York City, and under charter to the Dow Chemical Company. The ship arrived at New York City on its first run, April 13, 1954, from Freeport, Tex.

Mail delivery by steamboat. *See under* Postal service

Merchant ship formally blessed at a launching ceremony was the *Rio Hudson* of the Moore-McCormack Lines, Inc., blessed on November 27, 1940, by the Right Reverend Francis Taitt, bishop of the Pennsylvania Protestant Episcopal Diocese, at the yards of the Sun Shipbuilding and Drydock Company, Chester, Pa. It had a 17,500-ton displacement and carried 197 passengers.

Merchant ship of the United States commanded by a black captain was the *Booker T. Washington*, a Liberty ship launched by the California Shipbuilding Corporation at Wilmington, Del., September 29, 1942. It was commanded by Captain Hugh Mulzac, the first black to hold an unlimited mariner's license. It arrived at its first port, London, England, February 12, 1943. *(John Beecher— All Brave Soldiers; the Story of the S.S. Booker T. Washington)*

Minelayer was a 32-foot steam launch used August 1872 at the Engineer School of Application. It made eight knots and carried a dozen men. *(Henry Larcom Abbot—Material of the Submarine Mining Service of the U.S.A.)*

The First

Motorboat. *See* Motorboat

National ship in a federal dry dock. *See under* Dry dock

Naval post office aboard a naval vessel. *See under* Post office

Naval ship christened by a Marine Corps Women's Reserve member was the *Bucyrus,* built at Henry John Kaiser's Permanette Metals Corporation Yard No. 1 at Richmond, Calif., and launched October 31, 1944. The ship was christened by Sergeant Eleanor Segley of Bucyrus, Ohio, and was the 611th vessel launched by Kaiser. It was 455 feet long with a 62-foot breadth. Transferred to the U.S. Navy on November 29, 1944, and commissioned the same day, the ship was placed under the command of Lieutenant F. A. Geissert.

Naval ship christened by an Army officer was the *Colhoun* (DD-801), a destroyer launched April 10, 1944, by Todd-Pacific Shipbuilding Corporation, Seattle, Wash. and commissioned July 8, 1944, under Commander G. R. Wilson. It was named for Rear Admiral Edmund Ross Colhoun and christened by his great grandniece Captain Kathryn Kuntz Johnson of the Women's Army Corps. The ship was 376 feet 6 inches long with a breadth of 39 feet 8 inches and a displacement of 2,050 tons.

Naval ship designed to carry the DASH drone (drone antisubmarine helicopter) was the U.S.S. *Belknap,* a guided-missile frigate, launched July 19, 1963, at Bath, Me., by the Bethlehem Shipbuilding Corp., Quincy, Mass.

Naval ship (destroyer) christened by an enlisted woman Marine was the *Basilone* (DDE-824), a destroyer escort named for Sergeant John Basilone (U.S. Marine Corps), launched December 21, 1945, by Consolidated Steel Corp., Orange, Tex., and christened by his widow, Sergeant Lena Mae Basilone (U.S. Marine Corps Women's Reserve). The destroyer was reclassified January 28, 1948, and commissioned July 26, 1949, under Commander M. E. Dennett. It was deactivated and converted at the Quincy Yard of the Bethlehem Steel Company, Quincy, Mass.

Naval ship christened by an enlisted woman Marine was the *Basilone* (DDE-824), a destroyer escort named for Sergeant John Basilone (U.S. Marine Corps), launched December 21, 1945, by Consolidated Steel Corp., Orange, Tex., and christened by his widow, Sergeant Lena Mae Basilone (U.S. Marine Corps Women's Reserve). The destroyer was reclassified January 28, 1948, and commissioned July 26, 1949, under Commander M. E. Dennett. It was deactivated and converted at the Quincy Yard of the Bethlehem Steel Company, Quincy, Mass.

Naval ship christened by a woman not a U.S.

The First

citizen was the *Canberra* (CAGO2), a heavy cruiser, 673 feet 5 inches long, breadth 70 feet 10 inches, weighing 13,600 tons, built by the Bethlehem Steel Company, Quincy, Mass. She was launched April 19, 1943, by Lady Alice Crossland Dixon, wife of Sir Owen Dixon, Australian Minister to the United States, and was commissioned October 14, 1943. Captain A. R. Early was in command.

Naval ship named for a black naval officer was the destroyer escort *Jesse L. Brown,* a Knox-class ocean escort launched March 18, 1972, at the Avondale Shipyards, Westwego, La. The ship was named for ensign Jesse Leroy Brown of Hattiesburg, Miss., the Navy's first Naval Reserve black aviator killed in combat. On December 4, 1950, Brown lost his life in his airplane near the Changjin Reservoir, Korea.

Naval ship named for a dental officer was the torpedo boat destroyer *Osborne* (DD 295), laid down September 23, 1919, and launched December 29, 1919, by the Bethlehem Shipbuilding Corp., Squantum, Mass. It was commissioned May 17, 1920, with Lieutenant Dennis L. Ryan in command. The ship was named for Lieutenant (Junior Grade) Weedon E. Osborne, U.S. Dental Corps (6th Regiment, U.S. Marines). He was killed June 6, 1918, while carrying a wounded officer to safety during the advance on Bouresches, France. The Medal of Honor and the Distinguished Service Cross were awarded posthumously.

Naval ship named for a sailor killed at Pearl Harbor was the *England* DE-635, destroyer escort, named for John Charles England, ensign in the U.S. Naval Reserve, killed on the *Oklahoma* on December 7, 1941, during the bombing of Pearl Harbor, Hawaii. The *England* was launched September 26, 1943, by the Bethlehem Steel Company, San Francisco, Calif., and commissioned December 10, 1943. The ship was 306 feet long, 37 feet in breadth, with a draft of 9 feet 5 inches and a speed of 24 knots. The ship's complement was 186. The *England* sank 6 Japanese submarines in 12 days in May 1944.

Naval ship named for an enlisted man was the *Osmond Ingram* (DD-255), a destroyer named for Osmond Kelly Ingram of Pratt City, Ala., gunner's mate first class on the destroyer *Cassin,* who was blown overboard on October 16, 1917, when a torpedo from a German submarine hit his ship in the stern while he was attempting to throw a depth charge overboard. The *Osmond Ingram* was laid down October 15, 1918, by the Bethlehem Shipbuilding Company, Quincy, Mass., launched February 23, 1919, and commissioned June 28, 1919, at Boston, Mass.

Naval ship of the United States with a crew of mixed nationalities was the *Claude V. Ricketts* DDG-5, a 3,370-ton guided-missile armed destroyer, named for Admiral Claude Vernon Ricketts. The ship sailed January 4, 1965, from Norfolk, Va., on a 3-week cruise to the Caribbean Sea with a

The First

SHIP—*Continued*

7-nation crew (336 officers and men, half of them American and half, foreign) for the North Atlantic Treaty Organization. The ship was laid down by the New York Shipbuilding Corporation on May 18, 1959, launched June 4, 1960, and completed August 18, 1962. She was originally the *William P. Biddle* and was renamed on July 28, 1964.

Naval ship to surrender in peacetime without a fight was the 24-year old U.S.S. *Pueblo* (AGEK-2), an electronic intelligence ship that on January 23, 1968, was surrounded by three 50-knot torpedo boats and 2 subchasers while in 180 feet of water and brought into Wonsan, North Korea. The *Pueblo* had been launched April 16, 1944, at Kewaunee, Wis., by the Kewaunee Shipbuilding and Engineering Corporation. Commander Lloyd Mark Bucher and several of the crew were wounded and fireman Duane D. Hodges of Creswell, Ore., was killed when the subchaser fired 57 mm cannons. Commander Bucher and 82 surviving crew members were released on December 22, 1968, but the ship was held.

Naval ship with a plural name was the destroyer *The Sullivans,* launched April 4, 1943, at San Francisco, Calif. It was named for the five Sullivan brothers of Waterloo, Iowa—George Thomas, Francis Henry, Joseph Eugene, Madison Abel, and Albert Leo—who enlisted January 3, 1942, and were lost when the cruiser *Juneau* was sunk November 15, 1942, in a battle off Guadalcanal in the Solomon Islands.

Naval vessel of the United States to display the American flag around Cape Horn was the *Essex,* a frigate commanded by Captain David Porter, which left the Delaware capes on October 27, 1812, with a crew of 287 and 32 marines, and arrived at Valparaiso, Chile, on March 14, 1813. The ship had been launched September 30, 1799, by Enos Briggs, Salem, Mass., presented to the United States, and accepted by Captain Edward Preble on December 17, 1799. It was sold at public auction on June 6, 1837. *(George Henry Preble— Essex Institute Historical Collections 1870—The First Cruise of the U.S. Frigate Essex) (David Porter—Journal of a Cruise Made to the Pacific Ocean by Captain David Porter in the United States Frigate "Essex" in the Years 1812, 1813, and 1814)*

Naval vessel of the United States to sail around the Cape of Good Hope to the west coast of the United States was the *Constellation,* which left Boston, Mass., December 1840. Stopping first at Rio de Janeiro, it proceeded to the Cape of Good Hope, and thence to China. On the return voyage, it anchored in Monterey Bay, Calif., September 15, 1843.

Naval vessels to sink an enemy submarine in the Atlantic were the U.S.S. *Fanning* and the U.S.S. *Nicholson.* On November 17, 1917, at 4:10 P.M. in latitude 57°37′ N., longitude 8°12′ W., the

The First

U.S.S. *Fanning* while in convoy sighted the periscope of a submarine. The *Fanning* headed for the spot and dropped depth charges. The U.S.S. *Nicholson,* one of the vessels of the convoy, speeded to the spot and also dropped depth charges. The German submarine U-58 came to the surface. The *Nicholson* fired three shots from her stern while the *Fanning* headed for the submarine and fired its bow gun. After three shots the crew of the submarine came on deck and surrendered. The submarine sank shortly afterward. The commanding officer of the *Fanning* at the time was Lieutenant Commander Arthur Schuyler Carpenter, and the commanding officer of the *Nicholson* was Lieutenant Commander Frank Dunn Berrien.

Navy ship with a male-female company was the U.S.S. *Sanctuary* (AH-17), a 520-foot hospital ship with a hospital staff and ship's company of 70 officers and 460 enlisted personnel, including 2 women naval officers and 60 enlisted women. The ship was laid down as the U.S.S. *Marine Owl* by the Sun Shipbuilding and Dry Dock Company, Chester, Pa., on August 15, 1944. It was authorized by Chief of Naval Operations Admiral Elmo Russell Zumwalt, converted and commissioned on June 20, 1945. On November 18, 1972, the ship was recommissioned at Hunter's Point Naval Shipyard, San Francisco, Calif.

Navy vessel constructed as a minelayer was the U.S.S. *Terror* (CM-5), whose keel was laid September 3, 1940. It was launched June 6, 1941, at the Philadelphia Navy Yard, Philadelphia, Pa., and commissioned July 15, 1942. The ship displaced 5,875 tons standard, 8,640 at load speed, and had an overall length of 454 feet 10 inches, beam of 60 feet 2 inches. It cruised at 20 knots and mounted four 5-inch .38 caliber dual purpose guns and two twin 40 mm anti-aircraft guns. Howard W. Fitch was the commander.

Navy vessel equipped to lay mines was the cruiser *Baltimore,* which was commissioned January 7, 1890. It was built by William Cramp & Sons, Philadelphia, Pa., and its keel laid May 5, 1887. It was 252 feet 4 inches long. The captain was Winfield Scott Schley. The *Baltimore* served during the Spanish-American War as a cruiser. After being decommissioned, it was converted into a minelayer and recommissioned as such on March 8, 1915. During World War I it saw considerable service in this assignment.

Newspaper published at sea. *See under* Newspaper

Nuclear ship named for a black was the *George Washington Carver* (SSBN-656), whose keel was laid by the Newport News Shipbuilding and Dry Dock Company, Newport News, Va., on August 24, 1964. The ship (a nuclear-powered submarine) was launched August 14, 1965, and commissioned June 15, 1966.

The First

Oceangoing brokerage office. *See under* Brokerage

Oil tanker was the *Charles* of Antwerp, Belgium, which plied between the United States and Europe from 1869 to 1872. It contained 59 iron tanks, arranged in rows at the bottom of its hold in the 'tween decks. Its bulk capacity was 7,000 barrels (794 tons). *(Victor Ross—Evolution of the Oil Industry)*

Packet line, and the best known, was the Black Ball Line, out of New York to Liverpool. It began in 1816 with sailings on the first of each month. The original ships were the *Amity, Courier, Pacific,* and *James Monroe* of 400 tons each. Additional sailings were added later for the 16th of each month. During the first 9 years, ships of this line averaged 23 days for the transatlantic crossing. *(Arthur Hamilton Clark—The Clipper Ship Era)*

Post office aboard a naval vessel. *See* Post office: Naval post office aboard a naval vessel

Prefabricated ship was a shallop, a small, open boat, fitted with oars or sails, assembled in April-May 1607 at the entrance to Chesapeake Bay. It was completed and launched May 18, 1607. It was finally moored in 6 fathoms of water for settlement in Jamestown, Va. Captain John Smith wrote: "So next day [April 17, 1627] we began to build our shallop, which had been shipped in portions easy to be fitted together." *(John Smith—The Adventures and Discourses of Captain John Smith)*

Racing shell was *The Harvard,* a six-oared 40-foot rudderless round-bottom white pine boat built in 1857 by James Mackay of Brooklyn, N.Y., for the Harvard Boat Club of Harvard College, Cambridge, Mass. It was 26 inches wide and weighed 50 pounds. *(James Wellman, The Story of the Harvard-Yale Race 1852–1912)*

Radar installation aboard a commercial carrier operated by an American company was installed April 27, 1946, on the S.S. *African Star* of the American South African Line, Inc., and placed in operation on May 1, 1946, at which time the ship made its maiden voyage from New York City. The equipment, supplied by the General Electric Company, Schenectady, N.Y., was known as the Mariner.

Radio broadcast of a drama from a ship at sea. *See* Radio broadcast: Drama broadcast from a ship at sea

Radio telephone ship-to-shore conversation. *See under* Radio telephone

Revenue cutter was the *Massachusetts,* the keel of which was laid in 1791 in the yard of [William] Searle and [Joseph] Tyler at Newburyport, Mass. It had one deck and two masts and cost $1,440. It was one of ten revenue cutters author-

The First

ized August 4, 1790 (1 Stat. L. 175), at a cost of $10,000, to be paid out of the duties on goods imported. The master was John Foster Williams and the first mate Hezekiah Welch, both of whom were appointed March 21, 1791. *(Horatio Davis Smith—Early History of the U.S. Revenue Marine Service or U.S. Revenue Cutter Service)*

Revenue cutter and Navy cooperation took place July 10, 1798, when the *Governor Jay,* 14 tons and 70 men, and the *General Greene,* 10 guns and 54 men, of the revenue cutter service were placed under the command of Commodore John Barry of the Navy, who was cruising between Nantucket, Mass., and Cape Henry, Va. *(Horatio Davis Smith —Early History of the U.S. Revenue Marine Service or U.S. Revenue Cutter Service)*

Rivetless cargo vessel was built by the Charleston Dry Dock and Machine Company, Charleston, S.C., for the Texas Oil Company and was launched February 1930. The entire hull was put together by the arc welding process under a new system of dovetailed lock-notched plates, and only 11,000 pounds of welding wire was used instead of 18,000 pounds of rivets. A 20 percent to 25 percent saving in hull construction cost was effected by the use of the welding process. The ship had a 10-foot draft and a cargo capacity of 120 by 23 feet.

Rocket-tracking ship was the *Vanguard,* a World War II tanker cut apart and fitted with a new mid-body at the Electric Boat Division of General Dynamics Corporation at the shipyard in Quincy, Mass. It was 595 feet long and was used as an Apollo Instrumentation Ship by the U.S. Navy's Military Sea Transportation Service for the National Aeronautics and Space Administration. The ship completed initial builder's trials in the Atlantic Ocean off Boston, Mass., on Jan. 31, 1966, and was then placed in service.

Roll-on, roll-off carrier especially designed and built was the *Searoad,* placed in service September 1, 1955, between Hyannis and Nantucket Island, Mass., by the Searoad Transport Company, Inc., Hyannis, Mass. It was 64 feet long, had a superstructure 14 feet high, and drew only 6½ feet of water. Its 220 h.p. General Motors diesel engine attained a speed of 9 knots. It was built by the Blount Marine Corporation of Warren, R.I., and cost $65,000 to build and $25,000 to equip. The first skipper was Morris Johnson.

Rotor ship to dock in an American port was the *Baden-Baden,* which arrived in New York Harbor May 9, 1926, under the command of Captain Peter Callsen. It was equipped with two 45-foot towers, 9 feet in diameter, which rotated at 120 revolutions per minute maximum speed. The ship was invented by Anton Flettner and sailed from Hamburg, Germany, via the Canary Islands. It attained a speed of 9½ knots. *(Anton Flettner—Story of the Rotor)*

The First

SHIP—*Continued*

SOS from a ship. *See* Radio distress signal

Schooner built in America was launched at Gloucester, Cape Ann, Mass., in 1714. It was built by Henry Robinson. *(John James Babson—History of Gloucester, Mass.)*

Schooner (five-masted) was the *David Dows*, built at the Bailey Brothers Shipyard, Toledo, Ohio, and launched April 21, 1881. It had a keel length of 260 feet and a length overall of 275 feet. Its breadth of beam was 37½ feet, with an average depth of hold of 18 feet. It had five masts with top masts, 162 feet high, a gross tonnage of 1,418 tons, and a 1,347 net tonnage. It was owned by M. D. Carrington, Toledo, Ohio, and the first captain was Joseph Skeldon. It was lost off Whiting, Ind., on Thanksgiving Day 1889. *(Henry Hall—Report on the Shipbuilding Industry of the U.S.)*

Schooner (four-masted) to be built was the *William J. White*, which was launched at Bath, Maine, in June 1880.

Schooner (seven-masted, steel) was the *Thomas W. Lawson*, built at Quincy, Mass., by the Fore River Ship and Engine Company for the Coastwise Transportation Company of Boston, Mass. The contract was signed January 25, 1901, and the keel laid November 1, 1901. The ship was launched July 10, 1902. Its overall length was 403 feet 4 inches, its beam 50 feet, and its depth 35 feet 3 inches. Its sail area was 40,617 square feet. The masts alone weighed about 17 tons apiece, excluding the rigging of three tons for each. Its tonnage was 4,914 net and 5,218 gross, and its carrying capacity 8,100 tons.

Schooner (six-masted) was the *George W. Wells*, built by Holly Marshall Bean at Camden, Maine, and launched July 1, 1900. It was 340 feet overall, with a beam of 48 feet 6 inches, and a depth of 23 feet. It had a net tonnage of 2,745 and cost $125,000. The captain was John G. Crowley. *(Reuel Robinson, History of Camden and Rockport, Maine)*

Seaplane tender designed and built for the U.S. Navy was the U.S.S. *Curtiss*, authorized by Congress, July 30, 1937 (50 Stat. L. 544). Its keel was laid April 25, 1938, and it was launched April 20, 1940, at the New York Shipbuilding Corporation Yard, Camden, N.J. It was 527 feet 4 inches overall and had a standard displacement of 8,625 tons. Its contract price was $9,943,000. Three other vessels had been used earlier as seaplane tenders: the U.S.S. *Wright*, originally a lighter-than-air craft tender, and the U.S.S. *Jason* and U.S.S. *Langley*, both originally fleet colliers.

Seatrain was built in 1928 by the Sun Shipbuilding Company of Chester, Pa., for the Seatrain Lines, Inc., which inaugurated a service on January 12, 1929, between New Orleans, La., and Havana, Cuba. Loaded freight cars were hoisted

The First

from the railroad rails and placed aboard the seatrain, which accommodated 95 railroad cars. The seatrains have been named after the cities they serve—New York, New Orleans, etc.

Ship (American) attacked by a German submarine was the *Nantucket Chief*, from Port Arthur, Tex. (christened *Gulflight* in 1913). The 5,189-ton tanker, 3,262 net tonnage, 360 feet long, carrying a cargo of oil bound for Rouen, France, was torpedoed May 1, 1915, by the German submarine U-30 off the Scilly Isles.

Ship (American) to surrender to the Japanese was the 370-ton shallow-draft river gunboat *Wake* (PR-3), which carried two 3-inch pieces. It surrendered December 8, 1941, at Shanghai, the only U.S. ship to surrender during the war. Scuttle attempts failed as the attack was a surprise assault. The ship had been commissioned in 1927 as the *Gaum*, renamed *Wake* in 1941, and was renamed *Tataru* by the Japanese. It was surrendered by the Japanese to the United States in 1945 and turned over to the Republic of China Navy, who in turn renamed the ship *Tai Yuan*. It subsequently fell into the hands of the Chinese Communists during the civil war in China and was added to their navy.

Ship-at-sea broadcast. *See under* Radio broadcast

Ship brokerage office. *See* Brokerage: Oceangoing brokerage office

Ship built by the English in the American colonies was the *Virginia of Sagadahock*, launched in Maine from the banks of the Sagadahock River (now the Kennebec) by the Popham colonists in 1607. A ship of 30 tons, it was 30 feet long, had a beam of 13 feet, and drew 8 feet. Moss was used for calking and shirts were used for its sails. *(Henry Ernest Dunnack—The Maine Book)*

Ship built on the Pacific coast was the *Northwest America*, a schooner of 40 tons, begun June 11, 1788. It was built, launched, and equipped at Friendly Cove in King George's Sound (now Nootka Sound) abreast of the village of Nootka, British Columbia, Canada. Robert Funter was master. The ship was captured June 9, 1789, by Spain. *(John Meares—Voyages Made in the Years 1788 and 1789 from China to the North West Coast of America)*

Ship built to cross the Atlantic Ocean was a pinnace, a light sailing ship, built by the Huguenots of Jean Ribaut's expedition at Port Royal, S.C., in 1562. In the winter of 1562–1563 about 30 of them endeavored to return to France. They ran out of food and water and killed La Chere, one of their crew, whose "flesh was divided equally among his fellows." They reached the French coast but were rescued by an English ship which took them to Queen Elizabeth. *(Francis Parkman—France and England in North America)*

The First

Ship captured by American forces in the Spanish-American War. *See* Spanish-American War: Ship captured in the Spanish-American War

Ship completed in less than 2 weeks was the *Joseph N. Teal,* built by Henry John Kaiser's Oregon Shipbuilding Corp., at Portland, Ore. It made a trial run September 27, 1942, and was turned over to the Maritime Commission, 13 days 23½ hours after the laying of the keel. The previous record had been 29 days.

Ship constructed by the federal government was the *Chesapeake,* built at the Navy Yard, Gosport, Va., under an act of March 27, 1794, "to provide a naval armament" (1 Stat. L. 350). The President was authorized to obtain six ships by purchase or otherwise, equip and employ four ships to carry 44 guns each and two ships to carry 36 guns each, to protect commerce from the Algerines. The marine yard was lent to the government by Virginia, and Captain Richard Dale was appointed its superintendent. Construction started in 1794, but as peace was concluded in 1796, the work was discontinued. Work was again undertaken in 1797, after materials on hand had been sold, with Commodore Samuel Barron as superintendent of the yard. The *Chesapeake* was launched in December 2, 1799. *(Edward Phelps Lull—History of the United States Navy Yard at Gosport, Va.)*

Ship equipped with a masthead sea anchorage for a dirigible was the U.S.S. *Patoka.* While the *Patoka* rode at anchor on August 15, 1925, off Newport News, Va., the ZR1 *Shenandoah* "landed" and was towed about 20 miles.

Ship equipped with radar. *See* Radar: Passenger ship equipped with radar

Ship from the Atlantic coast to anchor in a California port was the *Otter* of Boston, commanded by Captain Ebenezer Dorr. She carried six guns and 26 men and arrived October 29, 1796, at Monterey, where she remained until November 6, 1796. *(Herbert Howe Bancroft—History of California)*

Ship from which a long-range rocket was launched was the airplane carrier *Midway.* On September 6, 1947, a captured German V-2 rocket was fired from the flight deck while the ship was several hundred miles off the east coast of the United States. The rocket traveled about six miles. Rear Admiral John Jennings Ballentine commanded the task group of which the U.S.S. *Midway,* commanded by Captain Albert Kellogg Morehouse, was the flagship.

Ship in motion on which packages were landed by autogiro. *See* Autogiro: Autogiro to land packages on a moving ship

The First

Ship launching broadcast. *See under* Radio broadcast

Ship named for a Seabee was the *Marvin Shields* (DD 1066), a destroyer escort named for Marvin G. Shields, construction mechanic third class with Seabee Team 1104, who was killed June 10, 1965, at Dong Xoai, South Vietnam. The ship was laid down April 12, 1968, at the Todd Shipyard Corporation, Seattle, Wash., launched in November 1969, and commissioned in 1971. It was 438 feet long, 47 feet in breadth, with a 4,000-ton displacement, and carried a complement of 230.

Ship-of-the-line was the *America,* authorized by the Continental Congress on November 20, 1776. It was designed by Joshua Humphreys and laid down May 1777 in John Langdon's shipyard, Portsmouth, N.H. John Paul Jones was elected commander. On September 3, 1782, the *America* was presented to Louis XVI in appreciation of French assistance during the Revolutionary War and sailed for France on June 24, 1783. *(Journals of the Continental Congress, Vol. 6—Oct. 9-Dec. 31, 1776)*

Ship outfitted for hurricane research was the *Crawford,* a 125-foot converted cutter, which was placed in service July 3, 1956, by the Oceanographic Institution, Woods Hole, Mass., to study how hurricanes originate. It carried a crew of 14 and 8 scientists. The first captain was David Casiles.

Ship permitted to enter port without stopping for quarantine procedure was the British S.S. *Cameronia,* which arrived February 1, 1937, at the port of New York. Ships which complied with certain health requirements were permitted to enter under a system of radio pratique for passenger vessels. During the first six months, 84 vessels of 9 nationalities representing 19 lines used radio pratique 471 times. Originally the arrangement applied only to New York; later it was extended to include Boston, Mass.

Ship sunk by a submerged German submarine was the S.S. *Frederick R. Kellogg* (7,127 tons), owned by Pan-American Petroleum and Transportation Company, from Tampico, Mex. A torpedo struck the engine room, hitting at 5:10 P.M. on August 13, 1918, twelve miles north of Barnegat Light, N.J. The ship sank in 15 seconds.

Ship to capture an enemy ship after the Revolution was the U.S.S. *Constellation,* a 36-gun frigate of 1,265 tons, authorized by Congress March 27, 1794 (1 Stat. L. 350), and launched September 7, 1797, at the Sterrett Shipyard, Baltimore, Md. The ship was 164 feet long, 40½ feet in the beam, 13½ feet deep in the hold. On February 9, 1799, off the island of Nevis, West Indies, the 36-gun *Constellation,* under the command of Commodore Thomas Truxton, met the 40-gun French frigate *Insurgente,*

The First

SHIP—*Continued*
inflicting 70 casualties and suffering only 4 herself.

Ship to carry the United States flag around the world was the *Columbia*, a 212-ton vessel which sailed from Boston, Mass., September 30, 1787, under Captain Kendrick. It was accompanied by the sloop *Washington*, under Captain Robert Gray, who exchanged commands with Captain Kendrick, and completed the trip, returning to Boston on August 9, 1790. The trip took three years and covered a distance of 41,899 miles. The crew explored the Queen Charlotte Islands and discovered the straits of Juan de Fuca and the mouth of the Columbia River. *(Rupert Sargent Holland—Historic Ships)*

Ship to circumnavigate the North American continent was the Coast Guard cutter *Spar*, of the Military Sea Transport Service task unit, based at Bristol, R.I., which sailed to Seattle, Wash., where it was joined by the *Bramble* and the *Storis*, all of which completed the Northwest Passage on September 7, 1957. They followed the *Labrador*, a Canadian ice-patrol ship which cleared Bellot Strait, the keystone of the Northwest Passage.

Ship to circumnavigate the world with but one in the crew was manned by Captain Joshua Slocum. He sailed from Boston, Mass., on April 24, 1895, in a little sloop called *The Spray*. It was 36 feet 9 inches long, 14 feet 2 inches wide, and 4 feet 2 inches in depth. Its tonnage was 9 tons net and its cost $553.62. The round trip of 46,000 miles was completed on July 3, 1898, when Captain Slocum sailed into Fairhaven, Mass., harbor, where the ship had been built. *(Captain Joshua Slocum—Sailing Alone Around The World)*

Ship to fire a Polaris missile was the *Observation Island* (EAG 154), commissioned December 5, 1958. It was 563 feet long overall, had a beam of 76 feet, a full load displacement of 16,100 tons, a draft of 24 feet, and a speed of 20 knots. It was commanded by Captain Leslie Slack. Formerly, it had been the S.S. *Empire State Mariner* (YAG 57), a cargo-type merchant ship that had been launched August 15, 1953, by the New York Shipbuilding Corporation, Camden, N.J., and transferred to the U.S. Navy on September 10, 1956. On August 27, 1959, a Polaris missile was launched from the *Observation Island* seven miles off Cape Canaveral, Fla. The missile, fired by compressed air, ignited successfully at 70 feet and sped 700 miles to the target area. It was a solid-propellant two-stage missile, 28 feet long and 4 feet 6 inches in diameter.

Ship to pass both ways through the Northwest Passage was the U.S. Coast Guard icebreaker *Northwind* (WAGB 282), an escort icebreaker that accompanied the oil tanker *Manhattan* in 1969. Built by the Western Pipe and Steel Company, San Pedro, Calif., the icebreaker was launched

The First

February 25, 1945. It was 250 feet long, with a full load displacement of 6,515 tons.

Ship-to-shore airmail service. *See* Airmail service: Airmail service from ship to shore

Ship-to-shore commercial telephone service. *See* Radio telephone: Radio telephone ship-to-shore commercial service

Ship-to-shore telecast. *See under* Television—Telecast

Ship to transport fresh orange juice in stainless-steel tanks was the S.S. *Tropicana*, 8,000 tons, which left Port Canaveral, Fla., on February 16, 1957, and arrived February 19, 1957, at Whitestone, L.I., N.Y., 56 hours later. The first shipment was made by Fruit Industries, Inc., of Bradenton, Fla., and consisted of 650,000 gallons.

Ship to use coal-derived oil to power its engines was the U.S. Navy's World War II destroyer, U.S.S. *Johnston*, which made a 1-day test cruise on November 15, 1973, from Philadelphia, Pa. The coal was crushed and decomposed by heat to produce a synthetic oil. Roughly, 1 ton of coal produced 1 barrel of oil.

Ship transported overland across the Rocky Mountains was the destroyer escort *Brennan*, which was prefabricated in Denver, Colo., and shipped in sections by rail to the Mare Island Naval Shipyard, Calif., where it was assembled and launched on August 22, 1942, as the H.M.S. *Bentinck* (BDE-13). The ship was transferred to the U.S. Navy and commissioned as the *Brennan* (DE-13). On January 20, 1943, Lieutenant Commander H. A. Adams, Jr., was placed in temporary command. The *Brennan* was 289 feet 5 inches long with a breadth of 35 feet 1 inch and a displacement of 1,146 tons. The ship's complement was 156.

Side-wheeler transpacific steamer was the *Celestial Empire*, built by William Henry Webb for the Pacific Mail Steamship Company. The steamer's keel was laid January 13, 1866, and the ship launched December 8, 1866. It made its trial trip June 4, 1867, and sailed for Panama and San Francisco, Calif., on July 1, 1867. The *Celestial Empire* was 360 feet long (370 feet overall) with a 47.4-foot beam (49-foot extreme beam), 23.3 feet in depth, and a weight of 3,386 tons. It burned 45 tons of coal daily. The name was later changed to *China*. The ship accommodated 1,200 passengers.

Speedboat to exceed 200 miles an hour was the jet-powered *Bluebird*, piloted by Donald Malcolm Campbell, which averaged 216.2 m.p.h. on November 16, 1955, on a measured kilometer course on Lake Mead, Nev. The speed for one leg of the course was 239.5 m.p.h.

Steam-propelled frigate was the *Demologos*, or *Fulton, the First*, of 2,475 tons, built by Robert Fulton for the U.S. Navy. Its keel was laid June 20,

The First

1814, and it was launched October 29, 1814, without engines, at Brown's Ship Yard, New York City. It was made of wood 5 feet thick and had a center-wheel propulsion. Its length was 156 feet on deck, breadth of beam 56 feet, and depth 20 feet. It drew 8 feet of water. The hull was built by A. & N. [Adam and Noah] Brown. It cost $320,000. It carried thirty 32-pound carronades and two columbiads, the latter each carrying a 100-pound red-hot ball. The guns were mounted in a battery protected by massive wooden sides. On June 1, 1815, it was propelled by its own steam and machinery. *(Charles Beebe Stuart—The Naval and Mail Steamers of the U.S.)*

Steam whaler was the *Pioneer,* whose first trip was made April 28, 1866, to November 14, 1866, under Captain Ebenezer Morgan. It had been converted in 1865 by Thomas W. Williams of New London, Conn., from a government transport. It was crushed in the ice in 1867. *(Clifford Warren Ashley—The Yankee Whaler)*

Steam whaler built as a whaleboat was the *Mary and Helen,* 420.5 tons, built at Bath, Maine, in 1879, registered September 8, 1879, from New Bedford, Mass., under the command of M. V. B. Millard. Its length was 138 feet 2 inches; breadth 30 feet 3 inches; and depth 16.06 feet.

Steamboat was built by William Henry in 1763. He built an engine and model stern-wheel boat which was tested on the Conestoga Creek at Lancaster, Pa. The trials demonstrated that the invention was unsuccessful. John Fitch invented a successful steam engine in 1787, and in 1807 Robert Fulton built the *Clermont,* which made the first run from New York City to Albany. *(Alex Harris—Biographical History of Lancaster County, Pa.)*

Steamboat built in America to cross the Atlantic Ocean was the *Savannah,* a 350-ton full-rigged wooden boat, designed by Daniel Dod of Elizabeth, N.J. It was built at Corlear's Hook, New York, at the shipyards of Crocker and [Francis] Fickett and launched August 22, 1818. It had one inclined direct-acting low-pressure engine of 90 h.p. The trial trip from New York City to Savannah, Ga., was made March 28, 1819. The *Savannah* sailed May 22, 1819, from Savannah, Ga., and arrived at Liverpool, England, June 20, 1819. Steam power was used for only 80 hours during the trip. Moses Rogers was the captain and Steven Rogers the first officer. The ship had 32 staterooms, but no passengers dared make the trip. *(John Elfreth Watkins—The Log of the Savannah —Smithsonian Report. 1890)*

Steamboat built on the Pacific coast for the government was the 453-ton side-wheel steamer *Saginaw,* outfitted with sails that was laid down September 16, 1858, and launched March 3, 1859, as the *Toucey* at the Mare Island Navy Yard, Vallejo, Calif. The engine was installed by the Union Iron and Brass Foundry at Peter Donahue's yard,

The First

San Francisco, Calif. The ship, renamed *Saginaw* and commissioned January 5, 1860, with James F. Schenck as captain, sailed March 8, 1860, from San Francisco and arrived May 12, 1860, at Shanghai, China. *(Arnold S. Lott—A Long Line of Ships, Mare Island's Century of Naval Activity in California)*

Steamboat (double-decked) was the steam-powered, stern-wheel flat boat *Washington,* built by Captain Henry Miller Shreve at the mouth of Wheeling Creek, Wheeling, Va. (now W.Va.). Its keel was laid September 10, 1815, and it was launched June 4, 1816. It arrived at its first destination, New Orleans, La., on October 7, 1816. Previously, engines had been placed in the hull. Shreve placed the machinery on the deck in a horizontal position, instead of in an upright position. Since that left no room on the deck for passengers, he added another deck above it to carry the horizontal boilers and passengers. He built two high-pressure engines, 24-inch cylinder, 6-foot stroke, unconnected, each one operating a side wheel, so that the pilot could go ahead on one wheel and reverse on the other, thus turning the boat around in its own length, 148 feet. The ship was the first of the Mississippi steamboats. *(Florence L. Dorsey —Master of the Mississippi)*

Steamboat engine built in America for a screw-propelled vessel was installed in the *Vandalia,* launched December 1, 1841, and enrolled April 14, 1842, at the port of Oswego, N.Y. It was designed by John Ericsson and built by Captain Sylvester Doolittle. It had two vertical cylinders, 14 inches in diameter, the stroke of which was 22 inches. Ericsson had previously built two engines which were installed in British ships. The *Vandalia* was 91 feet long, its beam was 20 feet 2 inches, and its depth of hold 8 feet 3 inches. Its displacement was 138 tons. It was the first screw-propelled vessel on the Great Lakes. *(Robert Dollar—One Hundred and Thirty Years of Steam Navigation)*

Steamboat on the Great Lakes was the *Walk-in-the-Water,* 135 feet long, 388 tons gross tonnage, built at Black Rock, Buffalo, N.Y., for McIntyre & Stewart and launched April 4, 1818. The first trip was on October 10, 1818, when it left Buffalo, N.Y., with 100 passengers, bound for Detroit, Mich. The *Frontenac,* built by Teabout and Chapman, launched September 7, 1816, plied only Lake Ontario.

Steamboat on the Pacific coast was the *Beaver,* tested May 16, 1836 under steam at Vancouver, Washington. It entered the Willamette River, Oregon, May 31, 1836, on its maiden voyage, ran down the river under steam, and entered the lower reaches of the Columbia River near Vancouver. It was 101.4 feet long, 20 feet in the beam, with a depth of 11 feet, and a tonnage of 109.12. The engines, built by Bolton & Watt of England, were not installed when the ship left Gravesend, Eng-

The First

SHIP—*Continued*

land, on August 27, 1835, shortly after completion. *(Robert Carlton Clark—History of the Willamette Valley, Oregon)*

Steamboat patent was issued by the state of Georgia to Isaac Briggs and William Longstreet on February 1, 1788, through the General Assembly at Augusta, Ga. This was the first and only patent issued by Georgia, authority having been vested by the Articles of Confederation, which were then in effect. The steamboat worked but was not practical. It was equipped with a boiler, two cylinders, and a condenser.

Steamboat service (regular) across the Atlantic was started by the *Great Western* and *Sirius*. Both ships arrived in New York City on April 23, 1838, the *Sirius* having completed the trip from London in 19 days and the *Great Western* from Bristol in 15 days. They were built by Isambard Kingdom Brunel, the celebrated English engineer. *(New York Albion—April 28, 1838)*

Steamboat service (regular) to California via Cape Horn was established by the Pacific Mail Steamship Company in 1849. The S.S. *California*, 1,050 tons, left New York October 6, 1848. It stopped at Rio de Janeiro, Brazil; Valparaiso, Chile; and Callao and Paita, Peru. On February 1, 1849, it arrived at Panama, where it took on 350 passengers. Further stops were made at Acapulco, San Blas, and Mazatlán, Mexico, and at San Diego and Monterey, Calif. On February 28, 1849, she reached San Francisco, where most of the crew deserted to work in the gold fields. Captain Cleveland Forbes was in command. This trip started a semimonthly mail service between New York and Panama and a monthly service between Panama and Oregon. *(Theodore Henry Hittell—History of California)*

Steamboat service around-the-world (regular passenger service) was inaugurated by the S.S. *President Harrison* of the Dollar Steamship Line, which sailed from San Francisco, Calif., February 1924. Cruise steamers, however, had made trips previously, usually one trip a year.

Steamboat to carry a man was built by John Fitch. On August 27, 1787, his boat plied up and down the Delaware River at the speed of three miles an hour. The boat was propelled by 12 large wooden paddles, 6 in tandem fashion along each side of the boat, alternately dipping into and drawing out of the water. The action of the paddles was the same as that used by the Indians in paddling a canoe. *(Carl Weaver Mitman—The Beginning of the Mechanical Transport Era)*

Steamboat to employ electric lights was the *Jeannette*, owned by James Gordon Bennett, acquired by act of Congress of February 27, 1879 (20 Stat. L. 323), which authorized the Secretary of the Navy "to accept for the purpose of a voyage of exploration by way of Bering Straits the ship

The First

'Jeannette' tendered by James Gordon Bennett for that purpose" at no government expense. It sailed from San Francisco, Calif., July 8, 1879, under command of Lieutenant Commander George Washington De Long, U.S.N. Unsuccessful attempts were made to use an electric system to light the sixty 16-candlepower lamps from October 14 to 30, 1879. On September 16, 1879, the *Jeannette* had begun to drift uncontrollably. On January 19, 1880, it sprang a leak from pressure of ice, and on June 13, 1881, it sank. *(George Washington De Long—The Voyage of the Jeannette)*

Steamboat to employ electric lights successfully was the *Columbia* (length 309 feet; beam, 38 feet 5 inches; hold, 23 feet 3 inches; net tonnage, 1,746 tons) of the Oregon Railway and Navigation Company, built at Chester, Pa. The *Columbia* plied between San Francisco, Calif., and Portland, Oreg. An "A" type dynamo, placed in operation on May 2, 1880, illuminated the passenger rooms and main salons. It operated successfully for 15 years, until a larger dynamo was installed.

Steamboat to make an ocean voyage was the *Phoenix*, 100 feet long, built at Hoboken, N.J., by Robert Livingston Stevens with his father, John Stevens. On June 10, 1809, it went from New York City to Philadelphia, Pa., by sea, navigating the Atlantic from Sandy Hook, N.J., to Cape May, N.J., under the command of Moses Rogers. *(Richard Cornelius McKay—South Street)*

Steamboat to make regular trips was designed by Robert Fulton. Under his supervision the hull of the *Clermont* was built by Charles Brown, a shipbuilder of New York. A Boulton & Watt engine was installed, and the boat made ready for its trial trip on August 7, 1807. It made a trip to Albany, a distance of 150 miles, in 32 hours and returned in 30 hours. *(Robert Henry Thurston—Robert Fulton, His Life and Its Results)*

Steamboat to pass through the Panama Canal was the craneboat *Alex. La Valley*, a self-propelled steamer, on January 7, 1914. Commercial traffic was inaugurated August 15, 1914. The first passage of commercial cargo took place on May 18–19, 1914. The first vessel to make a direct continuous voyage from ocean to ocean through the canal was the tug *Mariner*, on May 19, 1914. The first regular merchant vessel to transit the canal in commercial service was the *Ancon*, on August 15, 1914. The first merchant vessel to use the canal on a voyage between ports beyond the canal terminal was the *Arizonan*, on August 15–16, 1914. The first army transport to transit the canal was the *Buford*, on September 9, 1914, en route from San Francisco, Calif., to Galveston, Tex. *(Darrell Hevenor Smith—The Panama Canal, Its History, Activities and Organizations)*

Steamboat to sail down the Mississippi was the *New Orleans*, which left Pittsburgh, Pa., in September 1811 under the ownership and guidance of

Nicholas J. Roosevelt. It arrived at New Orleans, La., October 1, 1811. The crew consisted of a captain, engineer, pilot, six sailors, two female servants, a waiter, and a cook. Mr. and Mrs. Roosevelt were the only passengers. The *New Orleans* cost $38,000. *(John Hazlehurst Boneval Latrobe—The First Steamboat Voyage on the Western Waters—Maryland Historical Society Fund Publications, No. 4)*

Steamboat with a twin-screw propeller was built by John Stevens at Hoboken, N.J., in 1803. He patented the engine on April 11, 1803, and successfully navigated in New York harbor in 1804. The boat was 25 feet long and 4 feet wide and had two 5-foot screw propellers with four blades set at an angle of 35°. It was operated by a double direct-acting noncondensing engine with a 4½-inch cylinder and a 9-inch stroke. *(George Henry Preble—A Chronological History of the Origin and Development of Steam Navigation)*

Steamship passenger line between United States ports and Europe to fly the American flag was the Ocean Steam and Navigation Company; service began with the sailing of the *Washington* from New York City on June 1, 1847, for Bremen, Germany, with 120 passengers. The 1,700-ton *Washington* had four decks, three masts, and a full-length effigy of George Washington as a figurehead. It was 260 feet long and had a 39-foot beam and a 31-foot-depth hold. It was launched in 1847 from the East River yard of Wesstervelt & Mackary. The cost of the ship was $390,000. The *Hermann* was later added to the service. *(U.S. Department of Commerce—Shipping and Shipbuilding Subsidies—Trade Promotion Series, No. 129)*

Steamship to cross the Atlantic Ocean in less than 5 days was the *Rex* of the Italian Line, which sailed at 6:30 P.M., August 11, 1933, from Gibraltar and arrived off Ambrose Light 4 days 13 hours 58 minutes later, a distance of 3,181 miles. The ship carried 1,118 passengers and maintained an average speed of 28.92 knots. The captain was Francesco Tarabotto.

Steel sailing vessel was the *Dirigo,* built by Arthur Sewall & Co., Bath, Maine, and launched February 3, 1894. George W. Goodwin was the first captain. The *Dirigo* had a gross tonnage of 3,004 tons, and a net tonnage of 2,855 tons. Its length was 310 feet, its width 45.15 feet, and its depth 25.6 feet. It had two full decks and carried 13,000 square yards of canvas. *(Mark William Hennessy—The Sewall Ships of Steel)*

Steel vessels of the U.S. Navy were the cruisers *Atlanta, Boston,* and *Chicago* and the dispatch boat *Dolphin,* authorized by Congress March 3, 1883 (22 Stat. L. 477). The hulls were built by John Roach and Sons, Chester, Pa., and the machinery at the New York Navy Yard. The *Atlanta* and the *Boston* were 270 feet 3 inches long and 42 feet

wide, and had horizontal back-acting engines and cylindrical tubular boilers. The *Chicago* was 325 feet long and 48 feet 2 inches wide. The *Atlanta* was launched October 9, 1884, and commissioned July 19, 1886; the *Boston* was launched December 4, 1884, and commissioned May 2, 1887. *(Report of the Secretary of the Navy for 1883, Vol. 1)*

Streamlined steamship to arrive in the United States was the *Arctees,* of British registry, which sailed from Nicolaieff, Russia, on April 17, 1934, and arrived at Boston, Mass., on May 14, 1934.

Submarine chaser was the *SC-1,* 110 feet long, breadth 14 feet 8¾ inches, built at the Naval Station, New Orleans, La., and commissioned October 1, 1917. It had an 85-ton displacement and a complement of 2 officers and 25 enlisted men. It operated on gasoline fuel and had an 18-knot speed.

Tanker (automated) under the U.S. flag was the *Texaco Rhode Island,* a 25,413-ton tanker, 575 feet long with a 78-foot depth (604 feet 7 inches overall), 68 feet wide, 33 feet 10 inches in draft, built by the Bethlehem Steel Company, Inc. at Sparrows Point, Baltimore, Md., for Texaco, Inc., Wilmington, Del., and launched July 2, 1964. It had a centralized engine-room control system. An oil burner fueled the 2-cylinder steam turbine.

Telephone communication with a ship at sea. *See* Radio telephone: Radio telephone ship-to-shore conversation

Torpedo boat, worthy of the name, was the *Lightning,* built in 1876 at Bristol, R.I., by John Brown Herreshoff and Nathanael Greene Herreshoff. It was 58 feet long and had a speed of about 20 knots. *(U.S. Navy Department—Report of the Secretary, 1902)*

Torpedo boat of importance was the U.S.S. *Cushing* (TB-1), authorized August 3, 1886 (24 Stat. L. 215), launched January 23, 1890, and commissioned April 22, 1890, as seagoing torpedo boat No. 1, with Lieutenant C. M. Winslow in command. It was 140 feet long, of steel, with a normal displacement of 116 tons, and was built at a cost of $82,750. Its keel was laid in 1888 by the Herreshoff Manufacturing Company, Bristol, Pa., and it was commissioned April 22, 1890, as seagoing torpedo boat No. 1. *(Lewis Francis Herreshoff—Captain Nat Herreshoff)*

Trading ship sent to China was the *Empress of China,* a 360-ton privateer that was commanded by Captain John Green. It left New York February 22, 1784; arrived in Canton, China, August 28, 1784; left China on the return voyage December 28, 1784; and returned to New York May 11, 1785. Its owners made a profit of $30,727 on a $120,000 investment, which was financed by Robert Morris, Peter Whiteside, and William Whiteside. *(Foster Rhea Dulles—The Old China Trade)*

The First

SHIP—Continued

Transatlantic trip by rowboat. *See under* Rowing

Transoceanic newspaper published on a ship. *See* Newspaper: Newspaper published at sea

Triple launching of Liberty ships was made on July 4, 1942, at the Bethlehem Fairfield Shipyard, Baltimore, Md., when the *Joseph Stanton, William Wirt,* and *Luther Martin* were launched.

Triple-screw cruiser was the *Columbia,* launched July 26, 1892, by William Cramp & Sons Ship & Engine Building Company, Philadelphia, Pa., and commissioned April 23, 1894. Captain G. W. Sumner was in command. The *Columbia* (the fourth cruiser with that name) was 413 feet 1 inch long and 58 feet 2 inches in the beam, with a 7,475-ton displacement. The ship's complement was 475.

Troopship torpedoed. *See* World War I: American army troopship in World War I torpedoed by the Germans

Tugboat (diesel-electric) was placed in service in 1929 on the Warrior River, Ala., by the Tennessee Coal, Iron and Railroad Company. The power plant included two 550 h.p. diesel engines. Each propeller was driven by a double motor rated at 400 h.p. The length of the tow was limited to seven barges.

Tugboat (steam) was the *Rufus King,* built in 1825 by Smith and Dimon for the New York Dry Dock Company to tow vessels to and from the railway at the foot of East Tenth Street, New York City. It was 102 feet long and 19 feet wide and had a square engine of 34-inch cylinder by 4-inch stroke. *(John Harrison Morrison—American Steam Navigation)*

Turbine-propelled oceangoing merchant vessel (constructed in the United States) was the *Governor Cobb,* launched April 21, 1906, and delivered October 17, 1906, to the Eastern Steamship Line for service between Boston, Mass., and St. John, New Brunswick, Canada. It was 2,522 gross tons and 289 feet 1 inch long. The turbine was built by the W. A. Fletcher Company (now owned by the Bethlehem Steel Company) at Hoboken, N.J.

Turbine-propelled ship of the U.S. Navy was the *Chester,* a scout cruiser, launched July 26, 1907, and commissioned April 25, 1908. It was built at the Bath Iron Works Company, Bath, Maine. The contract price for the hull and machinery was $1,688,000. The *Chester,* which was equipped with four Parsons turbines, had an overall length of 423 feet 1 inch and a displacement of 3,750 tons. Its trial speed was 26.52 knots.

Turreted frigate in the U.S. Navy was the U.S.S. *Roanoke,* originally a wooden screw steam frigate built at the Norfolk Navy Yard under authorization of Act of Congress of April 6, 1854. It was

The First

launched December 13, 1855, and made its trial trip in 1857. It was altered to an ironclad in 1862–63 by the Novelty Iron Works, New York, and transferred to the New York Navy Yard, April 16, 1863. It had three revolving turrets of the Ericsson type and two pilothouses, and its battery on July 9, 1863 consisted of two 15-inch, two 11-inch, and two 150-pounder rifle guns. The alteration was not found satisfactory, the hull not being strong enough to sustain the weight. It was sold in 1883.

Two-way radio between a submarine and a ship. *See* Radio telephone: Two-way radio conversation between a submerged submarine and another vessel

Union ship captured in the Civil War was the U.S.S. *Fanny,* an Army steam tug grounded on a shoal and captured October 1, 1861, in Pamlico Sound (North Carolina) en route to Chicomacomica, the encampment of the 20th Indiana Regiment. The pilot and deckhand escaped by swimming ashore. Also captured by the Confederate naval forces were the *Raleigh,* a small iron-hull propeller-driven towing steamer; the *Junaluska,* 79 tons; and the *Culew,* 260 tons.

Vessel built by Europeans in America was a crude flatboat constructed by the Pánfilo de Narváez expedition between April 14 and sometime in September 1528 near what is now the town of St. Marks, Fla. The expedition reached the western shore of Florida on April 14, 1528, traveled inland and were unable to return to their supply ship. They spent six weeks building 5 boats, each 33 feet long. About 250 men embarked to reach the Spanish settlement on the Panuco River in Mexico, but only 4 reached civilization. *(Woodbury Lowery—Spanish Settlements Within the Present Limits of the United States, 1513–1561).*

Victory ship launched was the *United Victory,* launched January 12, 1944, at the yard of Henry J. Kaiser's Oregon Shipbuilding Corporation, at Portland, Ore., christened by Mrs. Thomas Beck, wife of the president of the Crowell-Collier Publishing Company. The Victory ships made 15 knots, which was faster than Liberty ships, and had 3 times as much power.

Warship (American) captured overseas was the 86-foot brigantine *Lexington* (formerly the *Wild Duck,* purchased February 1776). The ship was 24 feet 6 inches in breadth and carried a complement of 110. Out of ammunition and becalmed, Captain Henry Johnson surrendered the ship September 20, 1777, in the English Channel to the British cutter H.M.S. *Alert,* commanded by Lieutenant John Bazely.

Warship (American-built) to enter European waters was the 16-gun brig *Reprisal,* which on December 4, 1776, under the command of Captain Lambert Wickes, conveyed Benjamin Franklin, who was traveling incognito to Auray, France, to obtain French assistance. On the way over, it cap-

The First

tured two British vessels, and two others in the Bay of Biscay, one of which was the King's packet plying between Falmouth and Lisbon. This was the first capture by the American colonists of a ship in enemy waters and the first attempt to block and destroy British commerce at the source.

Warship builder was Joshua Humphreys, "father of the American Navy," appointed June 28, 1794, by General Henry Knox as constructor or master builder at an annual salary of $2,000. On March 27, 1794, Congress passed an "act to provide a naval armament" (1 Stat. L. 350), which authorized four ships of 44 guns and two of 36 guns. In 1794 Humphreys constructed the first of the naval war vessels, the *Constitution, Constellation, Chesapeake, President, The United States,* and numerous other ships. Humphreys served until October 26, 1801. *(Edward Phelps Lull—History of the United States Navy Yard at Gosport, Va.)*

Warship built on inland waters was the torpedo boat *Ericsson* (Torpedo Boat No. 2), launched on the Mississippi River May 12, 1894, by the Iowa Iron Works, Dubuque, Iowa, and commissioned February 18, 1897. It was a triple-screw steam vessel of 120 tons and carried 3 guns and a crew of 23. Lieutenant Nathaniel R. Usher was in command. The ship was 150 feet long, with an extreme beam of 15.62 feet, and cost $113,500.

Warship captured by a commissioned officer of the U.S. Navy was the British warship *Edward.* Captain John Barry of the 16-gun brig *Lexington* met it April 17, 1776, off the Virginia coast, captured it, and conveyed it to Philadelphia, Pa. *(William Bell Clark—Gallant John Barry)*

Warship convoy across the Atlantic Ocean. *See under* World War II

Warship docked in a government drydock. *See* Dry dock: National ship in a federal dry dock

Warship fleet to circumnavigate the globe left Hampton Roads, Va., on December 16, 1907, under the command of Rear Admiral Robley Dunglison Evans, who relinquished his command on May 9, 1908, to Rear Admiral Charles Stillman Sperry. The fleet left San Francisco, Calif., on July 7, 1908, and returned to Hampton Roads on February 22, 1909, stopping at Honolulu, Auckland, Sydney, Melbourne, Manila, Yokohama, Amoy, Colombo, Suez, and Gibraltar en route. The fleet was made up of the *Connecticut, Vermont, Kansas, Minnesota, Georgia, Nebraska, New Jersey, Rhode Island, Louisiana, Virginia, Missouri, Ohio, Wisconsin, Illinois, Kentucky, Kearsarge,* and several auxiliary vessels. *(U.S. Navy—Information Relative to the Voyage of the U.S. Atlantic Fleet Around the World)*

Warship named for a black was the U.S.S. *Harmon* (DE-72), a destroyer escort named for Leonard Roy Harmon, mess attendant, who was killed

The First

in action aboard the *San Francisco* during the naval battle of Guadalcanal, November 12-13, 1942. He was posthumously awarded the Navy Cross. The *Harmon* was laid down April 12, 1943, by the Bethlehem-Hingham Shipyard, Inc., Hingham, Mass. It was assigned to the United Kingdom on June 10, 1943, and was launched as the *Aylmer* on July 10, 1943, after which it was transferred to the Royal Navy on September 30, 1943, and eventually returned November 5, 1945. The *Harmon* was 306 feet long, 37 feet in breadth, with a displacement of 1,400 tons. The sponsor was Harmon's mother, Naunita Harmon Carroll of Cuero, Tex.

Warship propelled by electricity was the U.S.S. *New Mexico,* which was built at the Navy Yard, New York. The keel was laid on October 14, 1915. It was launched April 23, 1917, and commissioned May 20, 1918. The *New Mexico* was 624 feet in length, displaced 30,000 tons, and carried twelve 14-inch guns and twelve 5-inch guns. *(Records in Office of Naval Intelligence, Navy Department, Washington, D.C.)*

Warship regularly commissioned, by authority derived from the United Colonies with definite orders to attack the enemy, was the 78-ton schooner *Hannah,* commanded by Captain Nicholson Broughton of Marblehead, Mass. His order was dated September 2, 1775. The crew consisted of a detachment of soldiers from the Essex County Regiment of Marblehead, Mass. They sailed September 5, 1775, from Beverly, Mass., and on September 6, 1775, captured the 260-ton *Unity* en route from Portsmouth to Boston. *(William Bell Clark—George Washington's Navy)*

Warship sunk by an underwater torpedo mine was the ironclad Union gunboat *Cairo,* 175 feet long with a beam of 51 feet 2 inches, built by James Eads & Co., Mound City, Ill., and commissioned January 25, 1862. It had a 512-ton displacement and carried a crew of 251 officers and men. While clearing mines from the Yazoo River, near Vicksburg, Miss., the ship struck a bottle containing cannon powder floating beneath the surface and sank on December 12, 1862, in 30 feet of water, within 12 minutes. The crew was rescued by the gunboat *Queen of the West.* *(Edwin Cole Bearss—Hardluck Ironclad, the Sinking and Salvage of the Cairo)*

Warship to circumnavigate the globe was the 3-masted U.S.S. *Vincennes,* a 16-gun sloop of war of 700 tons burden, which left New York August 31, 1826, for the Pacific by way of Cape Horn, under the command of Commander William Bolton Finch (afterward known as William Compton Bolton). The ship was 127 feet long and had a beam of 34 feet. It returned in 1829 by way of the Cape of Good Hope, arriving at New York on June 8, 1830. *(U.S. Naval Institute—Early Voyages of*

The First

SHIP—*Continued*
American Vessels to the Orient. Proceedings, Vol. 36)

Warship with propelling machinery below the waterline and out of reach of hostile shot was the screw-warship *Princeton,* which was designed by John Ericsson in 1841. Its length on deck was 164 feet; beam 30½ feet; displacement 954 tons. Its wooden hull was built at the U.S. Navy Yard under the supervision of Captain Robert Field Stockton, and the machinery by Merrick and Towne, Philadelphia, Pa. It was launched December 10, 1843, at the Navy Yard, Philadelphia, Pa., and cost $212,615.00. It carried two long 225-pound wrought-iron guns and twelve 42-pound carronades. On February 28, 1844, while the ship was on a demonstration run, one of its guns exploded, killing several of the distinguished visitors. *(Samuel John Bayard—A Sketch of the Life of Commodore Robert F. Stockton)*

Whaleback steamer to cross the Atlantic was the S.S. *Charles W. Wetmore,* which sailed from Duluth, Minn., on June 11, 1891, with a cargo of grain for Liverpool, England. It was 265 feet long and 38 feet in the beam, with a 24-foot hold, a net tonnage of 1,075, and a dead capacity of 3,000 tons.

Woman to sail solo across the Atlantic Ocean was Ann Davidson, who in a 23-foot sailboat, the *Felicity Ann,* left Plymouth, England, on May 18, 1952, and arrived at Miami, Fla., on August 12, 1953. It made stops en route at Douarnenez, France; Vigo, Spain; Gilbraltar; and Dominica, Antigua, Nevis, St. Thomas, and Nassau, British West Indies.

Yacht was the *Jefferson,* a 22-ton sloop. She was constructed in Salem, Mass., in 1801 by Christopher Turner for Captain George Crowninshield. It was 35 feet 10 inches long and 12 feet 4 inches wide, and had a 6-foot depth. It was rigged first as a schooner, afterward as a sloop. *(Arthur Hamilton Clark—History of Yachting)*

Yacht to circumnavigate the world was the *North Star* (about 2,000 tons), which started its first voyage on May 21, 1853, from New York City. It went on the rocks at Corlears Hook and returned to drydock for minor repairs, after which the trip was resumed. The ship made leisurely stops at Southampton, Copenhagen, Le Havre, Malaga, Leghorn, and Rome. It was not allowed to moor at Naples because the authorities did not believe it possible for a single individual to own the ship and feared a sinister design. Further stops were made at Malta, Constantinople, Gibraltar, Tangier, and Madeira. The *North Star* returned to New York City on September 23, 1853, after a more than 15,000-mile trip. Asa Eldridge was the captain; Cornelius Vanderbilt, the owner. The only untoward incident on the voyage was the death of Robert Ogden Flint, quartermaster, who

The First

was accidently knocked overboard and drowned.

SHIP MOTION SIMULATOR
Ship motion simulator was built and installed in 1958 at the Cape Canaveral (later Cape Kennedy) Missile Testing Center, Cocoa Beach, Fla., to test and aid in the development of ballistic missiles fired from shipboard. It could simulate 3 important sea movements: roll, pitch, and vertical undulation or heave. It was designed by Loewy-Hydropress, now a division of Baldwin-Lima-Hamilton Corporation.

SHIP SUBSIDY. *See under* Shipping

SHIPPING
Automatic steering gear for ships, or Gyro-Pilot, called Metalmike, was installed on the *John D. Archibold* of the Standard Oil Company of New Jersey and tested April 7, 1922.

Coastal shipping service was established in 1831 by Thomas Lowery Servoss. He outfitted five packet ships that ran regularly between New York and New Orleans.

Embargo. *See* Embargo act

Ship subsidy was established "to provide for the transportation of the mail between the United States and foreign countries, and for other purposes." The act of Congress (5 Stat. L. 739), approved March 3, 1845, authorized the Postmaster General to make contracts with citizens of the United States for the carrying of mail in American vessels, by American citizens. The rate paid per letter for mail to Mexico and the West Indies was 10 cents a half ounce, 20 cents an ounce, and 5 cents for each additional half ounce; for ports not less than 3,000 miles away the rate was 24 cents a half ounce, 48 cents an ounce, and 15 cents for each additional half ounce. *(Royal Meeker—History of Shipping Subsidies)*
See also Postal Service: Ocean mail contracts

United States Shipping Board was established by the Shipping Act of September 7, 1916 (39 Stat. L. 728), "to regulate carriers by water in the foreign and interstate commerce of the U.S." On December 22, 1916, five commissioners were nominated, Bernard Nadel Baker, William Denman, John A. Donald, John Barber White and Theodore Brent, all of whose nominations were confirmed by January 23, 1917. *(Darrell Hevenor Smith and Paul Vernon Betters—The United States Shipping Board)*

SHIRT FACTORY of importance was established in Boston, Mass., in 1848 by Oliver Fisher Winchester.

SHOE
Rubber shoe manufacturer. *See under* Rubber

Shoe was manufactured in 1628 by Thomas Beard, who came over on the *Mayflower.* Prior to that date, shoes were imported from England. The colonists also learned from the Indians how to

The First

make moccasins, which were so well liked that as early as 1650 they were exported to England.

SHOE MANUFACTURING MACHINE was the McKay stitching machine, which revolutionized shoe manufacturing methods. It was invented by Lyman Reed Blake of Abington, Mass., who obtained patents No. 29,561 and 29,775, July 6, 1858. The upper was lasted upon the insole by means of tacks driven through the insole and clinched against the steel bottom of the last. The outsole was then attached to the insole and upper by the McKay sewing machine, which made a chain stitch through and through to the inside of the shoe. The surface of the insole was then covered by a lining. The machine was introduced in the factory of William Porter & Sons, Lynn, Mass., in 1861. It was probably operated by foot power. *(Frederic Augustus Gannon—Short History of American Shoemaking)*

SHOE MEASURING STICK was introduced as early as 1657. A dispute arose in court with regard to sizes and the court was informed that William Newman of Stamford, Conn., "hath an instrument in his hand, which he brought out of England, which is thought to be right to determine the question between the buyer and the seller." The court "did ordain that the said instrument should be procured and sent to New Haven."

SHOE PEG was invented by Joseph Walker of Hopkinton, Mass., in 1818. Prior to his invention, all shoe soles were sewn.

SHOE PEGGING MACHINE was operated by Charles D. Bigelow at his shop in Jacob Street, New York City, in the "Swamp" district, in 1852.

SHOOT-THE-CHUTES was built by Captain Paul Boyton and opened July 6, 1895, at Coney Island, N.Y. Each passenger toboggan held 16 persons. The inclined railway was 80 feet high with a 50 percent grade to the surface of a large body of water. *(Edo McCullough—Good Old Coney Island)*

SHOOTING GALLERY (mechanized) that was fully automatic was invented in 1890 by Charles Wallace Parker of Abilene, Kans., whose first sale was made to Leon Brownie of Houston, Texas.

SHOOTING STAR. *See* Astronomy: Meteoric display

SHORTENING

Shortening made by the hydrogenation process from vegetable oils was introduced as Crisco by the Procter & Gamble Company, Cincinnati, Ohio, on August 15, 1911. It was a creamy-white all-vegetable shortening, odorless and tasteless, made from cottonseed oil.

SHORTHAND BOOK was printed in 1728 by S. Keimer in Philadelphia, Pa., and was offered as a premium to anyone purchasing three shillings'

The First

worth of useful books. *(Charles Evans—American Bibliography)*

SHORTHAND MAGAZINE was the *American Phonographic Journal*, 16 pages, edited and published by Dyer & Webster, Philadelphia, Pa., which appeared in July 1848. It sold for 10 cents an issue or $1 a year. The first volume contained only eight issues, none being published in November and December 1848 or January and February 1849. It resumed publication in March 1849 (Vol. 2, No. 1), with E. Webster as the publisher.

SHORTHAND REPORT of a trial was made by John Llywellin, Clerk of the Council, who was instructed by Lord Baltimore to record the proceedings held in the Provinciall Court, St. Johns, Md., on November 15, 1681. The Justices Tailoor, Stevens, and Diggens found Josias Fendall guilty of mutiny on March 26, 1681, and sentenced him to pay "40,000 pounds of Tobacco for a fine, Be kept in safe custody at [his] own proper costes and charges until [he] shall have paid the same and after the same is paid to be for ever banished out of this Province." *(Maryland Archives. Vol. 5)*

SHORTHORN CATTLE AUCTION SALE. *See* Animals: Cattle (shorthorn) public auction sale

SHOT PUT

Shot-put to cover a distance of more than 70 feet was made May 8, 1965, when Randy Matson of Texas Agricultural and Military College tossed the 16-pound shot 70 feet 7 inches at the Southwest Conference track meet at College Station, Tex.

Shot-put to cover a distance of more than 71 feet was thrown at College Station, Tex., by Randy Matson of Texas Agricultural and Mechanical College at College Station, Tex., on April 22, 1967. The throw was 71 feet 5½ inches.

Shot-put toss over 60 feet was made May 8, 1954, when Parry O'Brien, formerly of the University of Southern California, tossed the 16-pound shot 60 feet 5¼ inches at the University of California at Los Angeles–Southern California Pacific Coast Conference dual meet held in Los Angeles.

SHOT TO LAND ON AMERICAN SOIL. *See under* World War I

SHOT TOWER. *See* Ordnance

SHOULDER PATCH. *See* Army insignia: Shoulder sleeve insignia

SHOVEL

See also Steam shovel

Shovel (steel) was manufactured in 1774 by Captain John Ames in West Bridgewater, Mass.

Two-handed shovel was used May 16, 1940, at the Niagara Falls, N.Y., bridge-dedication ceremonies by Mayor Ernst W. Mirrington, Jr., of Niagara Falls, N.Y., and Mayor George B. Ingles of Niagara

The First

SHOVEL—*Continued*
Falls, Ontario, Canada, who simultaneously held the shovel, each holding one handle.

SHOW. *See* Exposition, Fair, Magic lantern, Theater, and entries *under* the following types of show:

Automobile show	Horse show
Baby show	Milch goat show
Dog show	Poultry show

SHOWBOAT. *See under* Theater

SHOWERS IN PUBLIC BATHS. *See* Bathhouse: Public baths with showers

SHREDDED WHEAT BISCUIT. *See under* Breakfast food

SHRINERS. *See* Freemasons

SHUFFLEBOARD CHAMPIONSHIP
  Shuffleboard championship tournament was won by Carroll L. Bailey of Richmond, Va., who defeated 25 state champions at St. Petersburg, Fla., on March 27, 1931, to win the U.S. shuffleboard title.

SIAMESE TWINS
  Siamese twins were first brought to Boston, Mass., by Robert Hunter on August 16, 1829. They were known as Chang and Eng (Bunker). They were born April 15, 1811, in Bangesau, Siam, of a Chinese father and a Sino-Siamese mother. They were joined at the waist by a cartilaginous band about 4 inches long and 8 inches in circumference. They grew to be about 5 feet 2 inches in height, and, since they faced in the same direction, could walk, run, and swim. They were exhibited throughout the United States and later in Europe. They were married in April 1843 to the Misses Sarah and Adelaide Yates. Chang had ten children and Eng nine children. They died within three hours of each other on January 17, 1874.

  Siamese twins separated successfully by surgery were pygopagus twins whose lower intestines were connected and whose lower spinal bone structure and dural membrane were joined. The twins, Carolyn Anne and Catherine Anne, daughters of Ashton and Rosa Mouton, were born in Lafayette, La., on July 22, 1953. On September 17, 1953, 15 doctors worked 2¼ hours at the Ochsner Foundation Hospital, New Orleans, La., to separate them, and on October 14, 1953, they were discharged from the hospital.

  Siamese twins to survive a separation operation and live for one year were Nancy and Ellen, born December 14, 1952, in Cleveland, Ohio. They were joined at the base of the breastbone by a band of tissue ½ inch wide and 1½ inches long. The separation operation was performed by Dr. Jac Sidney Geller at the Mount Sinai Hospital, Cleveland, Ohio. The operation was a superficial one—the cutting of a layer of skin or cartilage that joined the babies at the chest.

The First

SIDEWALK (traveling)
  Sidewalk (traveling) was installed at the Columbian Exposition in Chicago in 1893 to convey passengers from one part of the fairgrounds to the other. It traveled at two speeds, three and six miles an hour, and accommodated 5,610 persons

  Sidewalk (traveling) in a railroad station was placed in operation May 24, 1954, by the Hudson and Manhattan Railroad Company at its Erie station, Jersey City, N.J. It cost $75,000. Made of rubber and canvas, it was 227 feet long and 5½ feet wide, and traveled up a 10 percent grade at 1½ miles per hour.

  Two-way moving walk was placed in service January 30, 1958 at Love Field Air Terminal, Dallas, Tex. It consisted of three loops and totaled 1,435 feet of moving walkway. In each loop a continuous rubber carpet was attached to an endless train of wheeled pallets, flexibly interconnected so that they could follow vertical or horizontal curves as required. The walk was also known as a moving sidewalk and passenger conveyor.

SIEVE
  Sieve was produced in 1768 in Philadelphia, Pa., by John Sellers. His sieves were used principally by millers.

  Wire sieves were manufactured commercially in 1834 by Edwin Gilbert of Gilbert, Bennett & Company at Georgetown, Conn. *(One Hundred Years of Progress—Gilbert and Bennett Manufacturing Co.)*

SIGHT-SEEING BUS. *See* Automobile bus: Automobile sight-seeing bus

SIGN FLASHER. *See* Electric sign: Electric sign flasher

SIGN-LANGUAGE RELIGIOUS SERVICE. *See* Deaf—Church service: Prayers in the sign language of the deaf

SIGNAL CORPS (U.S. Army). *See under* Army

SIGNAL LIGHT
  Electric traffic signal lights. *See under* Traffic light

SILK
  Silk culture was started about 1623 in Virginia. The Colonial Assembly directed the planting of mulberry trees. In 1656 an act was passed in which silk was described as the most profitable commodity for the country, and "a penalty of ten pounds of tobacco . . . imposed upon every planter who should fail to plant at least ten mulberry trees for every hundred acres of land in his possession." *(Linus Pierpont Brockett—Silk Industry in America)*

  Silk dyers to achieve success were Edward Vallentine and Lewis Leigh, who emigrated from England in 1838. They began business at Gurleyville, Conn., and achieved fame by producing a

The First

permanent black. *(Albert Henry Heusser—History of the Silk Dyeing Industry in the U.S.)*

Silk exportation took place in 1735 when eight pounds of raw silk was exported from Savannah to England. The Trustees of Georgia reported in 1736: "The raw silk from Georgia, organized by Sir Thomas Lombe, was made into a piece of silk and presented to the queen." This entry appears in the manuscript book of the trustees. It is possible that some silk may have been sent previously from Virginia, where silk cultivation was first introduced. *(Letter from the Secretary of the Treasury Regarding the Growth and Manufacture of Silk, Washington, D.C., Feb. 7, 1828)*

Silk loom of importance was the Gem Silk Loom, built in 1887 by the Knowles Loom Works, Worcester, Mass. On April 23, 1887, three 40-inch, 20-harness, 4-by-4 box loom machines were ordered by the Empire Silk Company, Paterson, N.J. Crepes, chiffons, or fancy pattern material requiring up to 20 harnesses could be woven on this loom.

Silk mill was erected for the Mansfield Silk Company by Rodney and Horatio Hanks in Mansfield, Conn., in 1810 in a building 12 by 12 feet. An effort was made to make sewing silk and twist by the machinery they had invented and manufactured.

Silk power loom, the figure or pattern of the cloth being made on a chain, was invented by William Crompton of Taunton, Mass., who obtained patent No. 491 on November 25, 1837, on a figure power loom. *(American Silk Journal, Thumbnail History of the Broad Silk Industry in the United States. November 1931)*

Silk suture. *See under* Suture

Silk thread. *See under* Thread

SILO (of record) was constructed by Fred L. Hatch in 1873 in McHenry County, Ill. *(Thomas Ross Pirtle—History of the Dairy Industry)*

SILOS, MISSILE. *See under* Rocket

SILVER BULLION DEPOSIT. *See* Money: Deposit of silver for coinage

SILVER COIN. *See* Money

SILVER DEMONETIZATION. *See* Money: Demonetization of silver

SILVER DOLLAR. *See* Money

SILVER HALF DIME. *See* Money

SILVER HALF DOLLAR. *See* Money: Silver coins

SILVER MILL to treat silver ore successfully and the first reducing mill to treat ore-bearing quartz was established by the Washoe Gold and Silver Mining Company, No. 1, near Virginia City, Nev., formed March 1860. The mill, operated by water-power, was built by Almarin B. Paul, who began the construction work May 25, 1860, and complet-

The First

ed it August 9, 1860. It consisted of 24 stamps which began to crush ore on August 11, 1860. *(U.S. Department of the Interior—Monographs of the U.S. Geological Survey, 1883. Vol. 4)*

SILVER MINE was the Silver Hill Mine, discovered in 1838 about ten miles from Lexington, N.C. The company was incorporated January 7, 1839, for $500,000. *(Richard Cowling Taylor—Reports on the Washington Silver Mine)*

SILVER PLATING FACTORY (successful) was Rogers Brothers, Hartford, Conn., established in 1847 by three brothers, William, Asa, and Simeon S. Rogers. In 1862, their factory was moved to Meriden, Conn., and they associated themselves with the Meriden Britannia Company, which in 1898 was succeeded by the International Silver Company. Silver plate consists of a hard metal which is plated or coated with silver. The base metal is usually nickel-silver, a combination of copper, zinc, and nickel. Prior to the introduction of silver-plated ware, silverware had been made from coin silver.

SILVER STAR. *See* Medal

SILVER WIRE SUTURE. *See* Suture

SILVERITES, who favored silver as a monetary standard, held their first national convention in St. Louis, Mo., July 22, 1896, and endorsed the Democratic candidates, William Jennings Bryan for President and Arthur Sewall for Vice President. The temporary chairman of the convention was Francis Griffith Newlands of Nevada, and the permanent chairman was William Pope St. John of New York. *(Wayne Cullen Williams—William Jennings Bryan)*

SIMPLIFIED SPELLING. *See* Spelling reform advocate

SIMULCAST. *See under* Television—Telecast

SINGER OF OPERA IN ITALIAN. *See* Opera: Opera (Italian)

SINGING CONTEST. *See under* Music

SINGING TELEGRAM. *See* Telegram

SINGLE-PHASE ALTERNATING-CURRENT MOTOR. *See* Electric motor: Electric motor (single-phase alternating-current)

SINGLE TAX

City to adopt the single tax for local revenue purposes was Hyattsville, Md., which operated under this system from July 1892 to March 1893. The Maryland legislature empowered the Board of Commissioners to make such deductions or exceptions from or addition to the assessment made by the assessors as they might deem just. The acts were declared unconstitutional and the law abrogated. *(Arthur Nichols Young—The History of the Single Tax Movement in the United States)*

The First

SINGLE TAX—Continued

Single tax national conference assembled September 1, 1890, in New York City and adopted a platform September 3. Five hundred delegates from 30 states formed a national organization, the Single Tax League of the United States, with a national committee composed of one member from each state, and an executive committee of which William T. Croasdale was the chairman. The first noted advocate of a single tax, on land, was Henry George, who in 1871 propounded the idea in *Our Land and Our Land Policy. (Joseph Dana Miller—Single Tax Year Book)*

Single tax political ticket was presented to the voters of Delaware in 1896. In September a full state ticket was drawn up, with Dr. Louis N. Slaughter nominated for governor. In the election of November 6, 1896, the single tax party polled only 855 votes. The symbol or device of the party was "The Earth." *(Arthur Nichols Young—The History of the Single Tax Movement in the United States)*

SINGLE-THREAD SEWING MACHINE. *See* Sewing machine: Chain-stitch single-thread sewing machine

SIT-DOWN STRIKE. *See* Strike: Modern sit-down strike

SIX-DAY BICYCLE RACE. *See* Bicycle race: International six-day bicycle race

SIX-MASTED SCHOONER. *See* Ship: Schooner (six-masted)

SIX-REEL COMEDY. *See under* Motion picture

SKATE (all-metal) was marketed by Everett Hosmer Barney. In 1864 he started business in Springfield, Mass., as Barney & Berry. On November 29, 1904, the firm was incorporated under the laws of the state of Massachusetts. In 1919 the capital stock was purchased by the Winchester Repeating Arms Company, which in 1922 moved the manufacturing business to its plant in New Haven. Barney was the first to conceive and execute the idea of fastening shoes to skates by means of metal clamps. He obtained patent No. 52,301, covering his invention of a screw-clamp skate, on January 16, 1866.

SKATING. *See* Ice skating; Roller skating

SKATING CHAMPION

Figure skating Olympic champion. *See under* Olympic Games

Skating champion (ice). *See* Ice skating champion

SKATING RINK. *See* Ice skating rink; Roller skating rink

SKATING TOURNAMENT. *See* Ice skating tournament

The First

SKEE-BALL ALLEY was built in 1914 by the National Skee-Ball Company of Coney Island, N.Y., and the first battery was operated by William A. Norwood in April 1914 at Coney Island.

SKEET

College skeet tournament was held November 12, 1928, in Princeton, N.J. A five-man team from Yale defeated Princeton 221–202. Bob Rosien of Yale scored a perfect 50.

National skeet tournament sponsored by the National Skeet Association was won by Lovell S. Pratt of Indianapolis, Ind., who led a field of 114 in Solon, Ohio, on August 31, 1935, to win the national all-bore with a score of 244 out of a possible 250. Second place was won by Phip Conway of Green Village, N.J., with 242 points. The women's title was won by Esther Abbie Ingalls of Hot Springs, Va., with a score of 95 out of 100.

SKI CAROUSEL

Ski carousel was the Doppelmayr Carousel of Austria placed in service in November 1975 at Stratton Mountain, Vt. It consisted of 4 twenty-foot metal arms extending from a revolving hub powered by a small motor. Skiers holding the arms were rotated at various speeds to simulate skiing conditions. The carousel cost about $5,500 and was imported from Austria.

SKI CLUB

Ski club association was the Central Organization, formed by ten clubs in 1891. The first meeting and tournament were held at Ishpeming, Mich. January 16, 1891. The National Ski Association of America was formed at Ishpeming, February 21 1904, with Carl Tellefsen of Ishpeming as president.

Ski club (local) was the Nansen Ski Club of Berlin, N.H., formed January 15, 1882.

Ski club (local) that was active was the Aurora Ski Club, organized January 19, 1886, by 28 men at Red Wing, Minn., with Christ Boxrud as the first president. Its first ski classic was held February 8 1887, with two great Norwegian skiers, Mikkel Hemmestvedt and Torjus Hemmestvedt, participating.

SKI JUMP (steel) was built in November 1908 at Chippewa Falls, Wis. It was 98 feet high, with a concrete foundation above the ground to make it 100 feet. In 1910 the national ski tournament was held on this jump.

SKI LIFT

Aerial tramway was the Cannon Mountain Tramway at Franconia, N.H., a 5,410-foot suspension ride. It was suspended by giant cables 40 feet above the trees, from the base to a peak of Cannon Mountain, N.H. It had 2 cars, each accommodating 27 persons, which made the trip up or down in 8 minutes at the speed of a thousand feet a minute. It was authorized June 17, 1937; opened June 17, 1938; and dedicated June 28, 1938.

The First

Tramway state legislation was Chapter 299, approved September 17, 1959, effective November 16, 1959, "an act relative to the operation of passenger tramways. . . . to register all ski lift devices and establish reasonable standards of design and operational practices" enacted by the state of New Hampshire. It required the registration, inspection, and approval of all ski-lift devices and established a tramway safety board of 4 appointive members and the commissioner of public works and highways.

SKI MEET (international) of importance was held February 10–13, 932, at Lake Placid, N.Y., during the Olympic Games. Finland and Sweden each won an event and Norway won two events.

SKI SCHOOL
Indoor ski school was the Bob Johnson Ski Center, opened October 16, 1939, in the Wells Memorial Building, Boston, Mass. About 300 square feet were covered with a special form of crystal plastics, patented by Robert H. Johnson of Boston, Mass., who received patent No. 2,558,759 on July 3, 1951. He subsequently opened a larger school of 7,000 square feet, at Framingham, Mass.

SKI SLOPE
Ski slope indoors was the Ski-Dek Center, Buffalo, N.Y., which opened January 17, 1962. It was constructed in a former moving picture theater. It consisted of a hugh bank of endlessly moving slopes treated to simulate 2 inches of powdered snow on a firm base. It had 9 slopes and could accommodate 144 skiers. Anything that can be done on skies (schuss, stem christie, slalom, jump turns, wedelns) can be done in this indoor slalom.

SKI TOW
Ski tow (rope) was built by Robert Royce and placed in operation January 28, 1934, at Woodstock, Vt. About 900 yards of ⅞-inch manila rope was spliced together, passed over pulleys and around a wheel attached to a tractor, and extended up the hill 300 yards. *(Ski Bulletin. Vol. 4, No. 7. Feb. 2, 1934)*

SKIMOBILE was invented in 1937 by George Morton of Goodrich Falls, N.H., and a 3,000-foot section was placed in operation December 27, 1938, by Cranmore Skimobiles Inc., at North Conway, N.H. One hundred and fifty toy cars, each seating one or two persons, were conveyed up a wide wood and steel trestle by a 6,000-foot endless steel cable, ⅞ inch in diameter, which was propelled by electric motors. On August 1, 1939, another 2,000-foot unit was added to propel 60 cars from the halfway station to the summit of Cranmore Mountain. The system had a capacity of 1,000 passengers per hour. The vertical lift from bottom to top was 1,367 feet.

The First

SKIN GRAFTING. *See* Surgical operation

SKY MARSHAL
Sky marshals were appointed in accordance with President Richard Milhous Nixon's Presidential Directive of October 28, 1970, because of the proliferation of hijackings of commercial airplanes. The Treasury Law Enforcement Officers Training School graduated 46 marshals on December 23, 1970, and 81 marshals, including 4 women, on April 9, 1971.

SKYDIVING. *See* Parachute—Jumping

SKYJACK. *See* Aviation—Airplane

SKY-TRAIN FLIGHT. *See under* Aviation—Flights

SKYSCRAPER. *See* Building: Building known as a skyscraper

SKYWRITING
Skywriting at night was exhibited by Andy Stinis of the Skywriting Corporation of America over New York City on September 18, 1937, when he wrote "Green River" for Oldtyme Distillers, Inc. The material used was the same as in the daytime and showed only when the moon was bright.

Skywriting exhibition was held at noon time over Times Square, New York City, on November 28, 1922, by Captain Cyril Turner, Royal Air Force, who spelled out in letters a half mile high at a 10,000-foot altitude the message "Hello, U.S.A. Call Vanderbilt 7200," which resulted in 47,000 telephone calls in 2½ hours. The letters were written upside down and in white smoke released from the rear of the airplane. The vapors formed when the oil hit the hot exhaust pipe. They were controlled by levers.

SLALOM OLYMPIC CHAMPION. *See* Olympic Games: Woman slalom Olympic champion (American)

SLANDER PROCEEDINGS were instituted September 17, 1607, by John Robinson, who accused Edward Maria Wingfield, the first governor of the Jamestown, Va., colony "of having said he, with others, consented to run away with the shallop to Newfoundland." A verdict was rendered in favor of Robinson. *(Edward Maria Wingfield—A Discourse of Virginia)*

SLATE used for roofing material was obtained from Delta, Pa., and Cardiff, Md., in 1734 by William and James Reese. *(Mining World. July 30, 1910)*

SLAVERY
Antislavery book. *See* Antislavery book

Antislavery magazine. *See under* Periodical

SLAVERY—*Continued*

Antislavery newspaper. *See* Newspaper: Abolition newspaper

Antislavery party. *See* Anti-slavery Party

Antislavery senator. *See* Senator (U.S.): Senator elected on an antislavery ticket

Antislavery society. *See* Abolition society

Fugitive slave law (federal) was passed February 12, 1793 (1 Stat. L. 302). It provided for the return of fugitives from justice and from labor: "No person held to service or labor in one state, under the laws thereof, escaping into another, shall, in consequence of any law or regulation therein, be discharged from such service or labor, but shall be delivered up on claim of the party to whom such service or labor may be due."

Insurrection of black slaves occurred in 1739 in South Carolina, where they greatly outnumbered the whites. The riot was promptly quelled by Lieutenant Governor William Bull. *(South Carolina Historical and Genealogical Magazine. January 1900)*

Law abolishing slavery in the District of Columbia was an "act for the release of certain persons held to service or labor in the District of Columbia" enacted April 16, 1862 (12 Stat. L. 376). It stated that those persons held "by reason of African descent are hereby discharged and freed from all claim to such service or labor;. . . . neither slavery nor involuntary servitude . . . shall hereafter exist in said district."

Law (federal) prohibiting slavery in a territory of the United States was prepared by Nathan Dane of Massachusetts and enacted July 13, 1787, by the Continental Congress for the Northwest Territory, a region east of the Mississippi, north of the Ohio, south and west of the Great Lakes, and west of Pennsylvania. The law prohibited slavery forever within the borders of the Northwest Territory.

Law regulating slavery was one of several "Acts and Orders made at the General Court of Election held at Warwick, R.I., this 18th day of May, anno 1652." It contained the following provision: "No blacke mankind or white . . . [may be] forced by covenant bond or otherwise to serve any man or his assignes longer than ten years, or until they come to be 24 years of age, if they be taken in under 14, from the time of their coming within the Liberties of the Collonie, and at the end or terme of ten years . . . [are to be set] free, as is the manner with the English servants. And that man that will not let them goe free, or shall sell them away elsewhere, to that end that they may be enslaved to others for a long time, he or they shall forfeit to the Collonie forty pounds."

Nonimportation of slaves act was passed June 13, 1774, by the Rhode Island General Assembly in Newport, R.I. It provided that "No Negro or mulatto slave shall be brought in to this colony, and in case any slave shall be brought in, he or she shall be, and are hereby, rendered immediately free, so far as respects personal freedom, and the enjoyment of private property, in the same manner as the native Indians." *(Records of the Colony of Rhode Island and Providence Plantations, Vol. 7)*

Slave emancipated was Elizabeth Freeman ("Marm Bett"), owned by Colonel Ashley of Sheffield, Mass., in 1780. Mrs. Ashley endeavored to strike her sister with a red-hot poker. The slave interfered, received the blow, and ran away. Judge Theodore Sedgwick of Stockbridge, Mass. defended her in a trial in Great Barrington, Mass. He granted her freedom. She died in 1829 and was buried in the Sedgwick plot.

Slavery protest of importance was made February 18, 1688, by the German Friends at a meeting in Germantown, Pa. They protested against the "traffic in the bodies of men" and considered the question of the "lawfulness and unlawfulness of buying and keeping Negroes." Some of the protestants were Francis Daniel Pastorius, Dirck op den Graeff, Abraham op den Graeff, and Gerhard Hendricks. *(Rufus Matthew Jones—The Quaker in the American Colonies)*

Slaves were introduced in Jamestown, Va., in August 1619 by a Dutch man-of-war which sold 20 "Negars" to the planter colonists as slaves.

State to abolish slavery was Vermont, whose constitution of July 2, 1777, provided that "no male person born in this country or brought from over sea, ought to be holden by law, to serve any person as a servant, slave or apprentice, after he arrives to the age of twenty-one years, nor female in like manner, after she arrives to the age of eighteen years, unless they are bound by their own consent, after they arrive to such age, or bound by law, for the payment of debts, damages, fines, costs or the like."

SLED (rocket). *See* Rocket sled: Rocket-driven sled on rails

SLED RUN. *See* Bobsled run

SLEEPING BERTHS, AIRPLANE. *See* Aviation: Airplane sleeping berths

SLEEPING CAR

Pullman sleeping car was *Old No. 9*, built by Ben Field and George Mortimer Pullman in 1859 in Chicago, Ill., and placed in service September 1, 1859, on the Chicago and Alton Railroad between Bloomington, Ill., and Chicago, Ill. It was a reconstructed day coach, little more than half the length of present coaches. Except for wheels and axles it was constructed almost entirely of wood. The roof was flat and so low that a tall man was likely

The First

o bump his head. The seats were adamantine. Two small woodburning stoves furnished heat. The illumination was furnished by candles. There was a small lavatory at each end. The drinking faucet supplied water to a nonenclosed washbasin. There were ten upper and ten lower berths with mattresses and blankets but not sheets. The upper berth was suspended about halfway between the floor and ceiling at night, and by day was drawn up to the ceiling by pulleys. *(Pullman Company—Pullman Progress)*

Pullman sleeping car made entirely of steel was manufactured in 1907 and complied with the regulations of the Hudson and Manhattan Railroad System which specified that no combustible equipment be used in the Hudson River tubes. The 4-foot-long car, which was manufactured in Pullman, Ill., had a steel-sheeted exterior and electric light obtained from an axle device. It had a low-pressure vapor heat system. *(Pullman Company—Evolution of the Pullman Car)*

Pullman sleeping car that was comfortable was *The Pioneer,* built by George Mortimer Pullman in 1865 in Chicago, Ill., at a cost of $18,000. It rested on 16 wheels, an experiment later abandoned in favor of 12, the present standard. The car was longer, higher, and wider than its predecessors and had the first raised upper deck and folding upper berth. It was heated by hot air furnaces under the floor, lighted with candles, and ventilated through deck windows. It was fully carpeted, and the seats were covered with French plush upholstery. *(Pullman Company—A Pioneer's Centennial)*

Sleeping car was *The Chambersburg* used in 1836 by the Cumberland Valley Railroad between Harrisburg and Chambersburg in Pennsylvania. It included four sleeping sections, each section with three bunks. No bedding was provided, and it was common for persons traveling to carry shawls which they drew over themselves when lying down in their clothes on the bunks. *(August Mencken—The Railroad Passenger Car)*

Sleeping car patent was granted to Henry B. Myer of Buffalo, N.Y., on September 19, 1854 (No. 11,699), for a "mode of converting the backs of car seats into beds or lounges."

Transcontinental through Pullman sleeping car service (standard, daily, without change of cars) was inaugurated March 30, 1946, between New York City and Los Angeles, Calif. The *Imperial Forest,* an all-room sleeping car of the *Twentieth Century Limited,* left at 5:30 P.M. and arrived at Los Angeles April 3, 1946, 11:50 A.M., attached to the Santa Fe *Chief.* The hookup and transfer were made at Chicago, Ill. Similar service started from Los Angeles. The first car arriving in New York City was the Pullman *Moencopi.* This service was discontinued April 27, 1958.

The First

SLEEVE INSIGNIA (U.S. Army). *See* Army insignia: Shoulder sleeve insignia

SLICING MACHINE was patented November 4, 1873, by Anthony Iske of Lancaster, Pa., who obtained patent No. 144,206 on a "machine for slicing dried beef." It employed an oblique knife in a vertical sliding frame.

SLIDE PROJECTOR. *See* Magic lantern

SLIDE RULE BOOK

Slide rule book was Thomas Abel's *Subtensial Plain Trigonometry, Wrought with a Sliding-Rule, with Gunter's Lines: and also arithmetically in a very concise manner. And this method apply'd to Navigation and Surveying, to which is added, 1. Mensuration of masons work, 2. A solution of rota, or Aristotle's wheel. 3. A brief discourse upon gravity,* printed in 1761 by Andrew Stuart, Philadelphia, Pa. It contained 86 pages and 7 folding plates.

SLITTING MILL, IRON. *See* under Iron

SLOT MACHINE

Slot machine payoff of $275,000 was October 29, 1978, when James Schelich of Washington, Mo., lined up 5 sevens on the bottom row of a dollar progressive jackpot slot machine at the Flamingo Hilton Hotel, Las Vegas, Nev.

SMALL CLAIMS COURT. *See* Court: Small debtors' court established by state law

SMALL DEBTORS' COURT. *See* Court

SMALLPOX EPIDEMIC. *See* Epidemic

SMALLPOX INOCULATION. *See* Vaccination for smallpox

SMOG CHAMBER

Smog chamber built by an industrial organization for air pollution research was placed in operation July 1962 by General Motors Research Laboratories, Warren, Mich. The cylindrical chamber contained 300 cubic feet of space irradiated by 247 fluorescent lamps simulating noonday sunlight.

SMOKE SCREEN used for concealing the movement of troops and ships was invented in 1923 by Thomas Buck Hine. It was first demonstrated publicly on September 5, 1923, during naval bombing tests off Cape Hatteras, N.C.

SNAKE (cobra). *See* Cobra

SNOW

Artificial snow from a natural cloud was produced November 13, 1946, by Vincent Joseph Schaefer of the General Electric Company who flew in an airplane over Mount Greylock, Mass. He dispensed small dry-ice pellets over a tract about 3 miles long from a height of about 14,000 feet. Snow fell an estimated 3,000 feet, but because of the dry condition of the atmosphere beneath the cloud it evaporated before reaching the

The First

SNOW—*Continued*

ground. Previously, on July 12, 1946, Schaefer had produced snow in a cold chamber.

SNOW CRUISER (automobile) for antarctic travel was designed by the staff of the Research Foundation of the Armour Institute of Technology, Chicago, Ill., under the direction of Dr. Thomas Charles Poulter. Built at a cost of $150,000, it was 55 feet 8 inches long and 19 feet 10½ inches wide and contained living quarters, a combination galley and darkroom, a two-way radio station, an engine room, a scientific laboratory, a machine shop, and a control room. It moved for the first time under its own power October 22, 1939, in Chicago. On October 24, the Snow Cruiser was driven to Boston, Mass., where it arrived November 12, 1939, to sail November 15, 1939, on the *North Star* for the Antarctic.

SNOW GOOSE. *See* Birds

SNOW-MELTING APPARATUS

Snow-melting apparatus was patented by Nicholas H. Borgfeldt of New York City, who obtained patent No. 88,693 on April 6, 1869. The device combined a sieve and a heated surface. A mass of snow was subdivided into flakes by a sieve and then melted by a heated surface.

Snow-melting apparatus (practical) with pipe imbedded in the sidewalk was tested December 8, 1946, and in actual operation during a blizzard on December 26, 1946. Best & Company, a department store in New York City, installed a system of 15 coils comprising 4,530 feet of pipe. A solution of about 67 percent water and 33 percent Zerex by volume was circulated as protection against freezing temperatures as low as 5 degrees below zero.

SNOWMOBILE

Snowmobile patent was obtained by Carl J. E. Eliason of Sayner, Wis., who received patent No. 1,650,334 on November 22, 1927, on a "vehicle for snow travel."

Snowmobile to exceed a speed of 125 m.p.h. was a 1972 Ski-Doo Blizzard X2R driven by Yvon Duhamel of Valcourt, Quebec, Canada, whose speed at the Boonville Airport, Boonville, N.Y., was 127.3 m.p.h. on February 11, 1972.

SNOWSHOE production for commercial purposes was undertaken in 1862 in Norway, Maine, by Alanson Millen Dunham, Jr. *(Charles Foster Whitman—History of Norway)*

SOAP

Cakes of soap of uniform weight and individually wrapped were manufactured by Jessie Oakley of Newburgh, N.Y., about 1830. Cakes had been sold to grocers in large blocks from which pieces were cut as desired. Oakley prepared one-pound packages. *(Ignatius Valerius Stanley Stanislaus and P. B. Meerbott—American Soap Maker's Guide)*

The First

Packaged soap. *See* Premium: Premiums given with merchandise

Soap in liquid form was patented August 22 1865, by William Sheppard of New York City, who was granted patent No. 49,561. It was made by mixing 1 pound of common soap with 100 pound of ammonia solution or spirits of hartshorn. The soap was dissolved in water or by steam to the consistency of molasses.

Soap powder in packages was introduced by Benjamin Talbert Babbitt about 1845. Rather than remelt the waste shavings of soap, he packaged the shavings in boxes ranging in contents from 1½ to 2 pounds. This innovation met with instantaneous success at laundries and hotels.

Soap to float was made in 1878 by the Procter & Gamble Company, Cincinnati, Ohio. It was known as White Soap until October 1879, when it was renamed Ivory Soap. A trademark was obtained July 18, 1879, and on December 21, 1882, the slogan "99 44/100% Pure" was introduced.

SOAP MANUFACTURER to render fats in his plant for soap stock was William Colgate, who opened a factory in 1806 at 6 Dutch Street, New York City. He had learned his trade at 50 Broadway, New York City, in the plant of John Slidell & Company. *(Ignatius Valerius Stanley Stanislaus and P. B. Meerbott—American Soap Maker's Guide)*

SOAP OPERA. *See* Television—Telecast: Serial daytime soap opera

SOCCER

Soccer game before 77,000 spectators was played August 14, 1977, at Giants Stadium, Meadowlands Sports Complex, East Rutherford, N.J., before 77,691 fans. The New York Cosmos defeated the Fort Lauderdale Strikers 8-3 in the quarter final game of the North American Soccer League.

Soccer game in which 12 points were scored by 1 player was played August 10, 1976, at Yankee Stadium, New York City. Giorgio Chinaglia of the New York Cosmos scored 12 points (5 goals and 2 assists—2 points for each goal, 1 for each assist) The game score was New York Cosmos 8, Miami Toros 2.

SOCIAL DEMOCRACY OF AMERICA PARTY was formed by the Brotherhood of the Cooperative Commonwealth, organized by Julius Augustus Wayland and members of the American Railway Union. The first national convention was held June 7, 1898, in Chicago, Ill.

SOCIAL-DEMOCRATIC PARTY OF AMERICA was formed in 1898 by Eugene Victor Debs, Victor Louis Berger, and Seymour Stedman, dissenters from the Social Democracy of America Party. The first convention was held in Rochester, N.Y., January 27, 1900. Eugene Victor Debs was the president

The First

dential candidate and Job Harriman the vice presidential nominee. The party received a popular vote of less than 100,000, compared with 7,200,-000 cast for William McKinley of Ohio, the Republican candidate.

SOCIAL FRATERNITY. *See under* Fraternity (Greek-letter)

SOCIAL REGISTER published was the *Society List and Club Register for the Season of 1886–7,* compiled by the Society List Publishing Company, New York City. It cost $3 and contained 381 pages, 276 pages being devoted to a list of marriages, deaths, subscription balls, and a directory of clubs and names, and 105 pages to advertisers and advertisements.

SOCIAL SCIENCE DOCTORATE. *See* Degrees (academic and honorary): Doctor of Social Science degree

SOCIAL SCIENCE SOCIETY (national) was the American Social Science Association, founded in 1865 and incorporated by act of Congress of January 28, 1899 (30 Stat. L. 804). An outgrowth of it was the National Institute of Social Sciences, organized in 1912 as a department, Hamilton Wright Mabie serving as president from October 1912 to October 1915. The first annual meeting was held March 20, 1914, in New York City. The federal charter was amended by act of Congress, June 16, 1926 (44 Stat. L. 751). Since then the National Institute of Social Sciences has operated as the main organization.

SOCIAL SECURITY ACT (U.S.) was approved by President Franklin Delano Roosevelt August 14, 1935 (49 Stat. L. 620). It authorized the appointment of a Social Security Board of three members. The first appointments were those of John Gilbert Winant, chairman (six years); Arthur Joseph Altmeyer (four years); and Vincent Morgan Miles (two years). The board administered grants-in-aid to the states which approved plans for assistance to the needy aged, the blind, and dependent children; approved state unemployment compensation laws for tax credit and for administrative grants; and administered a federal system of old-age benefits. The first unemployment compensation law approved by the Board was enacted November 15, 1935, by the District of Columbia. Several groups of unemployment insurance cards were issued simultaneously, so that it is not known to whom the first social security card was issued. The first beneficiary of monthly social security payments was Ida M. Fuller of Ludlow, Vt., who received check No. 00-000-001 for $22.54, dated January 31, 1940. Payments of various amounts had been made previously to individuals who did not have sufficient quarters of coverage or who did not qualify for monthly benefits.

The First

SOCIAL SERVICE ENDOWMENT was the White-Williams Foundation, established in February 1800 as the Magdalen Society, a Home for Girls, for the purpose of "providing more normal opportunities of development and inculcating good habits and to ameliorate the distressed condition of those unhappy females who have been seduced from the paths of virtue, and are desirous of returning to a life of rectitude." The society was incorporated March 23, 1802. On September 16, 1918, the corporate name was amended to the White-Williams Foundations for Girls, and again to the White-Williams Foundation, by decree of July 6, 1920. *(Frederick Paul Keppel, The Foundation)*

SOCIALIST REPRESENTATIVE IN CONGRESS. *See under* Representative (U.S.)

SOCIALIST LABOR PARTY OF NORTH AMERICA was formed July 4, 1874, as the Social Democratic Workmen's Party of North America. The name was changed in December 1877. The first national convention was held in Newark, N.J., on December 26, 1877. Simon Wing of Boston, Mass., and Charles Horatio Matchett of New York, the party's first presidential and vice presidential candidates, received 21,512 votes in the election held November 8, 1892. Grover Cleveland, the Democratic candidate, received 5,550,000 votes.

SOCIALIST PARTY was formed March 25, 1900, in Indianapolis, Ind., by a group of secessionists from the Socialist Labor Party, led by Morris Hillquit, who united with the Social-Democratic Party led by Eugene Victor Debs and Victor Louis Berger. The first national convention was held in Indianapolis, May 1, 1904.

SOCIETIES. *See under* names or types of organizations, e.g., academic, athletic, charitable, fraternal, professional, religious, scientific, service

SOCIETY FOR THE RELIEF OF FREE NEGROES UNLAWFULLY HELD IN BONDAGE. *See* Abolition society

SOCIETY OF THE CINCINNATI. *See* War veterans' society

SOCIOLOGY PROFESSOR was Albion Woodbury Small, appointed professor and head of the Department of Sociology at the University of Chicago, Chicago, Ill., effective October 1, 1892. Small held the position until his retirement on October 1, 1925. (He was also dean of the Graduate School of Arts and Literature from 1905 to 1923.) A course in sociology had been offered at Bryn Mawr in 1892 by Franklin Henry Giddings, associate professor of political science.

SOCIOLOGY SOCIETY

Sociological society (national) was the American Sociological Society, organized in Baltimore, Md., in December 1905, for the "encouragement of sociological research and discussion, and the pro-

The First

SOCIOLOGY SOCIETY—*Continued*
motion of intercourse between persons engaged in the scientific study of society." The first president was Lester Frank Ward. The first annual meeting was held in Providence, R.I., December 27–29, 1906. *(American Sociological Society. Papers and Proceedings 1906, Vol. 1)*

SOCIOLOGY TREATISE was *A Treatise on Sociology; Theoretical and Practical* (292 pages), by Henry Hughes of Mississippi published in Philadelphia, Pa., in 1854. *(Mississippi Valley Historical Association Proceedings, 1914–1915)*

SODA, ICE CREAM. *See* Ice cream soda

SODA FOUNTAIN
Ornamented soda fountain was made of white Italian marble and produced in 1858 by Gustavus D. Dows of Lowell, Mass. Typically American in design, it was adorned with spread eagles perched on the syrup cocks. In 1862 Dows invented the double-stream draft arm and cock, which allowed the use of a large or small stream. In 1863 Dows embarked on the manufacture of these fountains, which he sold for $225 each. His first patent was No. 99,170, which he obtained January 25, 1870.

Soda fountain patent was granted April 24, 1833, to Jacob Ebert of Cadiz, Ohio, and George Dulty of Wheeling, W.Va. *(Journal of the Franklin Institute. Vol. 16)*

SODA WATER
Soda water was prepared by Townsend Speakman of Philadelphia, Pa., who carbonated water for Dr. Philip Syng Physick. In 1807 Speakman added fruit juices to make it more palatable. The first soda water was dispensed regularly to patients from fountains at $1.50 a month for one glass a day.

Soda water commercially bottled was a carbonated water prepared in 1835 by Elias Durand at Philadelphia, Pa. *(First Century of the Philadelphia College of Pharmacy)*

Sugar-free soft drink was NoCal introduced in 1952 by Hyman Kirsch of Kirsch Beverages, Inc., College Point, N.Y.

SODA WATER MACHINE MANUFACTURER was John Matthews, who opened an establishment in New York City in 1834 exclusively for the manufacture of soda water apparatus. Various types of machines for making carbonated beverages had been made previously, however.

SODIUM REACTOR. *See* Atomic reactor

SODIUM VAPOR LAMPS. *See under* Electric lighting

SOFT FELT HATS FOR WOMEN. *See* Hat

SOFTBALL
Softball (indoor baseball game) was played

The First

November 30, 1887, at the Farragut Boat Club, Chicago, Ill. The game was invented by George W. Hancock, who devised a set of rules that gradually developed as the game progressed. A broomstick was used for the bat and a boxing glove for the ball. The game was known variously as Diamond Ball, Fast Ball, Kitten Ball, Playground Ball, Recreation Ball. It was named softball by Walter C. Hakanson. *(George W. Hancock—Indoor Baseball Guide)*

Softball game of 365 innings was played at Summerville Field, Monticello, N.Y., August 14–15, 1976, between Gager's Diner team and Bend n' Elbow Tavern. The game began at 10:00 A.M. Friday and continued to 4:00 P.M. Saturday, when it was called because of rain and fog. About 70 players including 20 women participated. About $4,-000 was raised for the construction of a new softball field and for the Community General Hospital. The Gagers made 832 hits and scored 491 runs; the Elbows, 738 hits, scoring 467 runs. There were 31 home runs. *(New York Times. 26:4. Aug. 16, 1976)*

SOIL CONFERENCE. *See* Agricultural soil conference

SOILLESS CULTURE OF PLANTS
Commercial hydroponicum built on the roof of a building was erected in 1936 in Seattle, Wash., by George O. Brehm.

Commercial hydroponicum (large) was established in Montebello, Calif., on December 5, 1935, by Ernest Walfrid Brundin and Frank Farrington Lyon, who installed a circulating system. They obtained patent No. 2,062,755 on December 1, 1936, on a "system of water culture" and incorporated the company October 19, 1937, as the Chemi-Culture Company.

Commercial production of plants in water instead of soil was undertaken by the firm of Vetterle and Reinelt of Capitola, Calif., in February 1934. They constructed a greenhouse 100 by 33 feet, with 100 tanks. The first planting consisted of about 2,000 begonias, which, as a result of exact regulation of humidity and food supply, grew more rapidly than if soil-planted. On October 12, 1935, tomato plantings were made which grew to 15 feet in height within six or eight months.

Hydroponic description was William Frederick Gericke's "Aquaculture, A Means of Crop Production," published December 1929 in the *American Journal of Botany* (Vol. 16, No. 10, p. 862). The term "hydroponics" for soilless crop production was first used in Gericke's article "Hydroponics—Crop Production in Liquid Culture Media," published February 12, 1937, in *Science* (Vol. 85, No. 2198, p. 177). Previously, crops had been grown in sand beds, mounted over nutrient solutions held

The First

in tanks. *(A. H. Phillips—Gardening Without Soil)*

Private soilless garden to grow vegetables and flowers was created in 1931 by William Frederick Gericke at his home in Berkeley, Calif. *(New York Times Mid-Week Pictorial, Oct. 8, 1932)*

SOLAR BATTERY. *See* Battery

SOLAR ENERGY

Balloon flight powered by solar energy. *See* Balloon—Flights: Balloon flight powered by solar energy

Solar energy battery. *See under* Battery

SOLAR-HEATED BUILDING

Solar-heated and radiation-cooled house. *See under* Building

SOLAR MOTION PICTURES. *See* Motion picture: Motion picture of the sun

SOLAR ORBIT. *See* Satellite: Satellite placed in solar orbit

SOLAR POWER PLANT

Solar-cell power plant was dedicated June 7, 1980, by Governor Scott Matheson at Natural Bridges National Monument, Utah. The $3 million photovoltaic system had 266,029 solar cells mounted in 12 long rows producing a 100-kilowatt output that supplied current for 6 staff residences, maintenance facilities, a water sanitation system, and the visitor's center. It was a joint venture of the National Park System, the Department of Energy, and the Massachusetts Institute of Technology's Lincoln Laboratory. It was 38 miles from the nearest power line.

SOLDERING GUN

Soldering gun was invented by Carl E. Weller of Easton, Pa., who received patent No. 2,405,866 on August 13, 1946, on an "electrical heating apparatus." The patent was assigned to the Weller Manufacturing Co., Easton, Pa. The application was filed July 14, 1941, and reissued (No. 23,619) on February 10, 1953, on a "soldering appliance for intermittent use." Other electrically heated soldering irons were on the market at that time.

SOLDIER VOTE. *See* Army vote

SOLDIERS' HOME

Soldiers' homes (national) put into operation in 1867 were the Eastern Home, Togus, Maine; the Central Home, Dayton, Ohio; and the Northwestern Home, Milwaukee, Wis. These were authorized by act of Congress of March 21, 1866 (14 Stat. L. 10), an "act to incorporate a national military and naval asylum for the relief of the totally disabled officers and men of the volunteer forces of the United States." *(Records in the Bureau of National Homes, Veterans Administration Bureau, Washington, D.C.)*

Woman admitted to a soldiers' home was Private First Class Regina C. Jones, of the Women's Army Corps (WAC), who was admitted to the

The First

U.S. Soldiers' and Airmen's Home, Washington, D.C., on September 2, 1955, as an applicant and on September 16, 1955, granted permanent admission. Except for a brief period, she was a resident until June 18, 1962.

SOLDIERS' MEDAL. *See* Medal

SOLICITOR GENERAL (U.S.)

Solicitor general of the United States was Benjamin Helm Bristow, who was appointed October 4, 1870, by President Ulysses Simpson Grant and who served until November 12, 1872. *(David Willcox—Memorial of B. H. Bristow)*

Solicitor General of the United States who was a black was Thurgood Marshall, who was nominated by President Lyndon Baines Johnson on July 13, 1965. His first case before the Supreme Court of the United States was tried October 13, 1965.

SOLO AIRPLANE FLIGHT AROUND THE WORLD. *See* Aviation—Flights (world): World solo airplane flight

SONG. *See* National anthem; also, *see under* Music

SORORITY

Black sorority was the Alpha Kappa Alpha sorority, founded January 15, 1908, at Howard University, Washington, D.C., by Ethel Hedgeman Lyle. The first officers were Lucy Slowe, president; Ethel Hedgeman Lyle, vice president; Marie Woolfolk, secretary; and Anna Brown, treasurer. On January 29, 1913, the sorority was incorporated in the District of Columbia.

Sorority (women's Greek-letter society) was Kappa Alpha Theta, which was founded January 27, 1870, at Indiana Asbury University, now De Pauw University, in Greencastle, Ind. Kappa Kappa Gamma Sorority of Monmouth, Ill., was organized in March 1870, but was not brought to public notice until October 13, 1870. *(William Raimond Baird—American College Fraternities)*

Women's secret society. *See under* Women's club

SOS. *See* Radio distress signal

SOUND-ABSORBING MATERIAL (rigid insulating board) perfected for use in buildings was invented by Carl Gebhard Muench of St. Paul, Minn., who obtained patent No. 1,153,512 on September 14, 1915, on a "thermo non-conductor" known as Insulite. The invention consisted of a rigid thermal insulation with groundwood screenings as a fiber source. The first board machine built to make a fibrous board in one thick continuous layer was installed in International Falls, Minn., where production was started May 15, 1914. Sugar-cane bagasse was also found to be a satisfactory fiber for making insulation board, and its manufacture was begun on August 10, 1921

The First

SOUND-ABSORBING MATERIAL—*Continued*
in Marrero, La., by the Celotex Corporation of
Chicago, Ill., under the trade name of Celotex.

**SOUND MECHANISM TO CREATE SPEECH
SOUNDS.** *See* Voice mechanism: Voice mechanism capable of creating the complex sounds of
speech

SOUND-ON-FILM MOTION PICTURE. *See* Motion picture

SOUP COMPANY to introduce and market
"finished" or "liquid" soups was the Franco-
American Food Company of New York City,
which was organized in November 1886 by Alphonse Biardot and his sons, Ernest and Octave.

SOUSAPHONE was manufactured by the C. G.
[Charles Gerard] Conn Company, Ltd., Ekhart,
Ind., from designs suggested by John Philip Sousa.
The first model was the "bell up" type. The first
"bell front" instrument, such as those used today,
was made in 1908.

SOUTH POLE FLIGHT. *See under* Aviation—
Flights

SOUTH POLE LANDING. *See* Discovery: American to land by air at the South Pole

SOUTH POLE NAVY EXPEDITION
    Naval expedition to the South Pole. *See* Navy:
Naval expedition to the South Pole

SOYBEAN PROCESSING PLANT (commercially
successful) was built by Augustus Eugene Staley
in Decatur, Ill., in 1922. The beans were run
through an expeller, the oil removed to within 4
percent, and the residue or cake sold to the feed
industry for use in commercial feeds or to farmers,
who mixed the meal with other ingredients as a
protein supplement.

SPA opened to the public was deeded to the colony of Virginia in 1756 by Thomas Fairfax, sixth
Baron Fairfax, "to be forever free to the publick
for the welfare of suffering humanity." (George
Washington had visited the mineral springs on
March 18, 1748.) The spa was located in Bath,
Berkeley County, Va. (now Berkeley Springs,
Morgan County, W.Va.), and was chartered in October 1776. (*Bulletin of the History of Medicine.
Vol. 11, No. 2. February 1942*)

SPACE AGENCY (U.S.) was the National
Aeronautics and Space Administration, authorized by the National Aeronautics and Space Act
of July 29, 1958 (72 Stat. L. 426). It was controlled
by a civilian administrator, who received a salary
of $22,500, and a deputy administrator, who received $21,500. On August 19, 1958, Thomas Keith
Glennan was sworn in at Washington, D.C. as
administrator and Hugh Latimer Dryden as deputy administrator. The agency was organized October 1, 1958.

The First

SPACE CABIN was the space cabin simulator, a
hermetically sealed cabin with equipment which
supplied oxygen, removed waste products by
chemical means, and recirculated waste body moisture
to cool the cabin. It was used at the School of
Aviation Medicine, U.S. Air Force, Randolph Air
Force Base, Tex. Simulated in the cabin were the
same climatic conditions that an astronaut would
meet in the sealed cabin of a rocket ship in space.
The first person to spend 24 hours within the cabin, living in outer-space conditions, was Dalton F.
Smith of New Orleans, La., an aeromedical technician, who was observed through glass ports
from 3 P.M. on March 31, 1956, to 3 P.M. on April 1,
1956.

SPACE FLIGHT. *See under* Astronaut

SPACE ORBIT CAPSULE. *See* Satellite: Space
capsule recovered from an orbiting satellite

SPACECRAFT. *See under* Rocket; Satellite

SPANISH-AMERICAN WAR
    **Army officer killed in battle in the Spanish-
American War** was Captain Allen Kissam Capron, who was killed in action on June 24, 1898, at
Las Guásimas, Cuba.

    Balloon destroyed by enemy gunfire. *See under*
Balloon

    **Naval officer killed in the Spanish-American
War** was Ensign Worth Bagley, executive officer
of the torpedo boat U.S.S. *Winslow,* commanded
by Lieutenant John Baptiste Bernadou. The *Winslow,* which had been sent to the wharves at Cardenas, Cuba, for a closer inspection of the docks,
was fired upon May 11, 1898, simultaneously by a
shore battery and a Spanish gunboat. (*John Randolph Spears—Our Navy in the War with Spain*)

    Ship captured in the Spanish-American War
was the Spanish *Buena Ventura,* which was taken
April 22, 1898, by the gunboat *Nashville.* Spain
declared that war existed with the United States
on April 24, three days after United States Minister Stewart Lyndon Woodford's passports had
been returned to him. On April 25 (30 Stat. L. 364)
Congress declared that a state of war had existed
since April 21. Sentiment against Spain was inflamed by the destruction of the battleship *Maine,*
which had blown up mysteriously on February 15
in the harbor of Havana, Cuba, with a loss of
about 260 American crewmen. (*French Ensor
Chadwick—Relations of the United States and
Spain*)

    Soldier killed in the Spanish-American War
was George Burton Meek, who lost his life in action on board the torpedo boat *Winslow* May 11,
1898. A monument was erected to his memory in
the McPherson Cemetery, Clyde, Ohio. (*Records
in Office of Naval Records and Library. Department of the Navy*)

The First

Spanish-American land engagement took place June 24, 1898, at Las Guásimas, Cuba, in which the First Cavalry, the Tenth Cavalry, and the Rough Riders, all unmounted, took part. Juragua was captured and 11 Spanish dead were left on the field. Sixteen Americans were killed and 52 wounded. *(Herbert Howland Sargent—Campaign of Santiago de Cuba)*

SPANISH-AMERICAN WAR MONUMENT. See Monument: Monument to the memory of the soldiers and sailors of the Spanish-American War

SPANISH MAGAZINE PUBLISHED BY STUDENTS. *See* Periodical

SPANISH NEWSPAPER. *See* Newspaper

SPARROW. *See* Birds

SPARS. *See* Coast Guard (U.S.): Coast Guard Women's Reserve

SPAY AND NEUTER CLINIC. *See* Veterinary Hospital: Municipal veterinary hospital

SPEAKER (House of Representatives). *See under* Congress (U.S.)—House of Representatives

SPECIAL DELIVERY SERVICE. *See* Postal service

SPECIAL DELIVERY STAMP. *See* Postage Stamp

SPECTROPHOTOMETER was invented by Professor Arthur Cobb Hardy of Wellesley, Mass., who received patent No. 1,987,441 on January 8, 1935, on a "photometric apparatus." This electronic device detected 2 million different shades of color and produced for permanent records a chart of each color. The patent was assigned to the General Electric Company, Schenectady, N.Y., which sold the first machine May 24, 1935. *(Journal of the Optical Society of America. February 1929)*

SPECULATORS, TICKET. *See* Ticket speculators

SPEEDBOAT. *See* Ship

SPEED LAW. *See* Traffic regulation: Traffic law

SPEEDING ARREST. *See* Automobile speeding arrest

SPELLING BOOK

Hebrew spelling book. *See* Hebrew Book: Hebrew spelling book

Spelling book was printed by Stephen Day in 1643 in Cambridge, Mass.

SPELLING REFORM ADVOCATE was Benjamin Franklin, who in 1768 wrote *A Scheme for a New Alphabet and Reformed Mode of Spelling; with Remarks and Examples.* He advocated dropping C, J, Q, W, X, and Y from the alphabet and substituting six other characters so "that there be no distinct sounds in the language without letters to express them." *(Noah Webster—Dissertations on the English Language)*

The First

SPERM WHALE. *See* Whale

SPERMACETI CANDLE FACTORY. *See* Candle factory

SPINAL ANESTHESIA REPORT. *See under* Anesthesia

SPINET. *See* Piano

SPINNING, BRASS. *See* Brass spinning

SPINNING, CARDING, AND ROPING MACHINES were manufactured in 1786 by Hugh Orr with the help of Robert Barr and Alexander Barr in their workshop in Bridgewater, Mass. On November 16, 1786, the Senate granted them £200 for their ingenuity and afterward granted them a further compensation of six tickets in the land lottery of that period. *(Nahum Mitchell—History of the Early Settlement of Bridgewater, Mass.)*

SPINNING JENNY. *See* Cotton spinning jenny

SPIRITUALIST was John D. Fox of Hydeville, Wayne County, N.Y., whose house in 1848 was the mecca of the curious who wanted to hear spirit knockings and rappings. Fox's daughters, Margaret and Catherine, continued his work and acted as mediums. *(Buffalo Medical Journal. March 1851)*

SPITTING LEGISLATION. *See* Health ordinance

SPLIT-SCREEN IMAGE. *See under* Television—Telecast

SPLITTING MACHINE FOR LEATHER. *See under* Leather

SPOILS SYSTEM was introduced by President Andrew Jackson as a reward to Simon Cameron of Pennsylvania and other supporters for their political assistance. Jackson served as President from March 4, 1829, to March 3, 1837. *(Thomas Edward Watson—Life and Times of Andrew Jackson)*

SPONGE

Oxidized cellulose (sponge) was made in 1936 by Dr. William Orlin Kenyon of the Tennessee Eastman Company, Kingsport, Tenn., a division of the Eastman Kodak Company, Rochester, N.Y.

Oxidized cellulose (sponge) for medical and surgical use was marketed by Parke Davis & Company, Detroit, Mich., under the trademark Oxycel, on June 5, 1946. It was a hemostatic material in the form of surgical dressings, which, when left in contact with incised body tissues, converted to an absorbable form. *(Industrial and Engineering Chemistry. Vol. 41. January 1949)*

SPOONS

Nickel silver spoons were manufactured by Robert Wallace of Wallingford, Conn., in 1835. Spoons previously had been made of silver or pewter. Nickel silver or German silver consisted

The First

SPOONS—*Continued*
of two parts copper, one part nickel, and one part zinc fused together.

SPORTS
See also under names of specific games and sports, e.g., Baseball, Boat race, Polo; and *under* the following subjects: Olympic Games, Radio, and Television—Telecast

Amateur athletic competition (interclub) was held September 27, 1879, by the National Association of Amateur Athletes of America at the New York Athletic Club's grounds in Mott Haven, N.Y. Twenty games were on the program. *(Frederick William Janssen—A History of American Amateur Athletics and Aquatics)*

Amateur indoor athletic games were held November 11, 1868, by the New York Athletic Club at the Empire City Skating Rink at 63rd Street and Third Avenue, New York City. Some of the events were the 75-yard race, the 220-yard race, the 440-yard race, the half-mile race, the one-mile walk, the standing broad jump, the standing high jump, the running broad jump, the running high jump, the shot put, and standing three-jumps. During the intermissions, Dodsworth's Band played. The York Athletic Club was formed September 8, 1868. The rink was 350 feet long, 170 feet wide, 70 feet high, and had accommodations for 10,000 spectators.

Amateur outdoor athletic games were held October 21, 1871, by the New York Athletic Club on its grounds at 130th Street and the Harlem River. This site was used afterward for the foundations of the Harlem Bridge.

Athletic club was the New York Athletic Club, which was organized September 8, 1868, at the Knickerbocker Cottage, Sixth Avenue and 28th Street. The club was incorporated April 4, 1870.

Cross-country championships were run November 6, 1883, under the auspices of the New York Athletic Club. *(New York Athletic Club, 1929)*

Sports trainer (professional) was Bob Rogers, who was engaged by the New York Athletic Club on May 1, 1883. Previous to this he was with the London Athletic Club.

Sportswriter. *See under* Author

Wheelchair national games. *See* Wheelchair athletics

SPORTS BOOK of importance was *The Sportsman's Companion, or, an essay on shooting; illustratiously shewing in what manner to fire at birds of game, in various directions and situations— and, directions to gentlemen for the treatment and breaking their own pointers and spaniels.* The book was published in 1783 in New York City.

The First

SPORTS MAGAZINE was the *American Turf Register and Sporting Magazine,* published in Baltimore, Md., by John Stuart Skinner. The first issue appeared in September 1829 and contained 56 pages. Its purpose was "to serve as an authentic record of the performances and pedigrees of the bred horse." *(Benjamin Perley Poore—Biographical Sketch of John Stuart Skinner)*

SPORTS TROPHY
See also Athlete

Sports trophy for the outstanding amateur athlete of the year was the James E. Sullivan Memorial Trophy of the Amateur Athlete Union of the United States awarded December 16, 1930, to golfer Robert Tyre ("Bobby") Jones of Atlanta, Ga., who received 1,625 votes—more than twice that of the runner-up. The selecting committee of 600 considered 150 nominations. The award was presented to Jones on February 26,1931, at the Medinah Athletic Club in Chicago, Ill. *(New York Times. 33:1. Dec. 17,1930; 24:4. Feb. 27, 1931)*

SPOTTED FEVER TREATISE. *See* Medical book: Typhus fever treatise

SPRAYING DEVICE. *See* Paint spraying device

SPRING, OIL. *See under* Oil

SPRING MANUFACTURER was Edward Lucian Dunbar, whose factory in Bristol, Conn., opened in 1845, and who specialized in coiled clock springs. They were tempered by a process invented by Silas Burnham Terry. At the time, weights were generally used in clocks, except smaller clocks, in which imported springs were used.

SPRING WINDING MACHINE, in which the size of the spring helix was determined solely by the angle at which the wire was forced between guides, was developed and built in 1892 by Clinton S. Marshall of the Washburn and Moen Manufacturing Company, Worcester, Mass.

SPRINKLER
Sprinkler to be used was the perforated pipe system invented by James Bichens Francis. The first installation was made in 1852 at the plant of the Proprietors of the Locks and Canals on the Merrimack River at Lowell, Mass. *(American Academy of Arts and Sciences. Proceedings, Vol. 28)*

Sprinkler head was invented by Henry S. Parmelee of New Haven, Conn., who obtained patent No. 154,076, August 11, 1874. It consisted of a perforated head containing a valve which was held closed against water pressure by a heavy spring made of low fusing material. *(Gorham Dana—Automatic Sprinkler Protection)*

The First

Sprinkler system patent was No. 131,370, granted to Philip W. Pratt of Abington, Mass., September 17, 1872. The system operated by means of a valve to which cords and fuses were attached. When the cords and fuses melted, the valve opened, releasing a stream of water.

SPUN-GLASS DRESS. *See* Glass dress of spun glass

SPY. German spy to receive a death sentence from the American forces during World War I. *See under* World War I

Peacetime death sentence for espionage was imposed April 5, 1951, by Judge Irving Robert Kaufman, U.S. District Court, who sentenced Ethel Rosenburg and her husband Julius Rosenberg. They were electrocuted June 19, 1953, at Sing Sing prison, Ossining, N.Y. The trial began March 6, 1951, and the jury rendered its verdict of guilty on March 29, 1951, at which time Morton Sobell was also convicted. He was sentenced to 30 years in a federal penitentiary.

SQUASH CLUB

Squash tennis organization (national) was the National Squash Tennis Association, formed by 14 charter members March 20, 1911, at the Harvard Club of New York City. The officers were John W. Prentiss, president; Josiah O. Low, vice president; Dr. Alfred Stillman, secretary, and C. M. Bull, treasurer. *(National Squash Tennis Association Official Handbook 1912)*

SQUASH RACQUETS CHAMPION

Squash racquets champion to win the U.S.A. Squash Racquets Singles championship was John A. Miskey of the Overbrook Golf Club, Philadelphia, Pa., who won the championship in 1907.

Woman to win the U.S.A. Women's Squash Racquets Singles championship was Eleanora R. Sears of the Harvard Club, Boston, Mass., who won at the Round Hill Club, Greenwich, Conn., January 16–19, 1928. Forty players entered. Miss Sears won three of four matches with Miss A. Boyden of Boston, Mass.

SQUASH TOURNAMENT sponsored by the National Squash Tennis Association was held at the Harvard Club, New York City, April 8-10, 1911. Forty entries from 13 clubs played. The champion was Dr. Alfred Stillman, 2d, who defeated John W. Prentiss on April 10, 1911, by scores of 15-5 and 17-15.

STABILIZED AIRPLANE. *See* Aviation—Airplane: Airplane (commercial) stabilized

STADIUM

Adjustable stadium was the Aloha Stadium, Honolulu, Hawaii, dedicated September 12, 1975. It has seating accommodations for 50,000 people in six 147-foot-high grandstand sections, 2 of which (the north and the south) are fixed and 4 others of which (the east and west) are remova-

The First

ble. Each section weights 1,750 tons and is about 14 stories high. Three large compressors force air into 416 discs, making it possible for hydraulic jacks to move any of the 4 sections, as desired, a distance of 180 feet in 25 minutes. It was designed by Charles Luckman Associates, Los Angeles, Calif.

Baseball stadium (fireproof) built of concrete and steel was Forbes Field, Pittsburgh, Pa., opened June 30, 1909, when the National League Pittsburgh Pirates defeated the Chicago Cubs 3-2 before a paying crowd of 30,338 spectators. The first game of the 1909 World Series was played there; the National League Pittsburgh Pirates defeated the American League Detroit Tigers 4-3. The stadium was named after Brigadier General John Forbes, the British officer who commanded the expeditionary force that captured Fort Duquesne at what is now Pittsburgh.

Cement stadium was the Harvard Stadium, Cambridge, Mass., constructed by the Aberthaw Construction Company, Boston, Mass., under the direction of Professor Lewis Jerome Johnson and Joseph Ruggles. The general architectural design was worked out by George Bruns de Gersdorff. The outer walls measured 527 by 420 feet and were divided into 37 reinforced concrete sections. The stadium was completed in the spring of 1904. Its capacity was 40,000. The colonnade was added in 1910 and the steel stands in 1929. The first football game played there was the Harvard-Dartmouth game of November 14, 1903, won by Dartmouth, 11-0.

Domed, fully-enclosed sports arena was the Harris County Domed Stadium, the Astrodome, Houston, Tex. Ground was broken for the building on January 3, 1962, and construction work started March 18, 1963. The overall cost was $35.5 million. The building has a permanent, translucent roof (with a clear span of 642 feet) covered with 4,596 plastic skylights, and an air-conditioning system of 6,600 tons. The distance to the top of the dome is 208 feet. The arena can accommodate 66,000 people at conventions and 48,000 at baseball games. The playing field is 466 feet by 288 feet, an area of 405,000 square feet—710 feet outside diameter, 516 feet inside diameter. It is 420 feet from homeplate to center field. The first baseball game was played April 9, 1965, at night; the National League Houston Astros defeated the American League Houston New York Yankees 2-1 in a 12-inning exhibition game attended by President Lyndon Baines Johnson. Governor John Connally of Texas threw the first ball. The first football game was played September 11, 1965, when the University of Tulsa defeated the University of Houston 14-0. The first polo game was played January 29, 1966, when the National All-Stars defeated the Texas All-Stars 3-2.

The First

STADIUM—*Continued*

Municipal stadium was the Golden Gate Park Stadium, San Francisco, Calif., completed in 1907. It was oval shaped and covered a 30-acre field. It had two entrances, one on the north and one on the south side, through tunnels 20 feet wide and 10 feet high under a ¾-mile trotting track 60 feet wide that encircled the stadium. Bicycle races were held November 29, 1906, before completion.

School stadium was built in Tacoma, Wash., and was dedicated June 10, 1910. It was 250 feet wide at the narrowest point next to the curve and 400 feet wide at the open ends. It cost $150,000, of which $100,000 was borne by the School District and $50,000 was obtained through the sale of five-year passes at $10 each. Frederick Heath was the architect and L. A. Nicholson the engineer.

STAGECOACH INTERCITY SERVICE was inaugurated November 9, 1756, between Philadelphia, Pa., and New York City by John Butler, Francis Holman, John Thompson, and William Waller.

STAINED GLASS. *See* Glass: Stained figure glass

STAINLESS-STEEL HYDROPLANE. *See* Aviation—Airplane: Hydroplane of stainless steel

STAIRWAY, MOVING. *See* Escalator

STAMP

See also Postage Stamp

Consular service fee stamps were authorized by Congress April 5, 1906 (59 Stat. L. 102), effective June 30, 1906, to show the payment of prescribed fees. The denominations were 25-cent green, 50-cent carmine, $1 dark violet, $2 brown, $2.50 dark blue, $5 brown red, and $10 orange. Congress discontinued their use June 28, 1955 (69 Stat. L. 187), effective September 30, 1955.

Hunting permit stamps (federal) were the Migratory Bird Hunting Stamps showing mallards alighting, issued to licensed hunters in 1934. They were blue, sold for $1, and were issued by the U.S. Department of Agriculture. This issue was void after June 30, 1935.

Motor boat stamps were required after April 1, 1960, on applications for certification of motorboats of more than 10 h.p. A $3 blue stamp with red numbers covered the fee for a 3-year period, and the $1 rose red stamp with black numbers covered the fee for reissuance of lost or destroyed certificates.

Revenue stamp of $10,000 denomination was the bright green stock transfer revenue stamp issued in 1944 without gum. It was overprinted in black "series of 1944-1945."

STAMP, TRADING. *See* Trading stamp

STAMP ACT REPUDIATION was made on November 23, 1765, by the Court of Frederick County, Frederick, Md. The British Stamp Act of

The First

March 22, 1765, levied by England under King George III had placed a tax of one shilling on every pack of playing cards, ten shillings on every pair of dice, etc. These 12 "immortal judges" strenuously opposed England's impost legislation by declaring that "all proceedings shall be valid and effectual without the use of stamps." *(Souvenir of Historic Frederick—Marken and Bielfeld, Inc.)*

STAMP CATALOG

Postage stamp catalog was compiled by A. C. Kline, 824 Walnut Street, Philadelphia, Pa., in 1862. It listed 1,500 varieties of stamps and was published in Philadelphia. Its title was *The Stamp Collector's Manual, Being a complete guide to the collectors of American and Foreign postage and despatch stamps.*

STAMPED ENVELOPE. *See* Postage stamp: Stamped envelopes (U.S.)

STANDARD TIME. *See* Time, Standard

STANDARDIZATION OF PRODUCTION. *See* Factory standardization of production

STANDARDS BUREAU (U.S.) was established by act of Congress of March 3, 1901 (31 Stat. L. 1449), effective July 1, 1901, which made the office of Standards, Weights and Measures a separate bureau. The first director was Samuel Wesley Stratton, whose annual salary was $5,000. Prior to this, the office of Standard Weights and Measures was a unit of the United States Coast and Geodetic Survey in the Treasury Department. On July 1, 1913, it became the National Bureau of Standards under the Department of Commerce.

STAR PHOTOGRAPH. *See* Photograph: Photograph of a star

"STAR-SPANGLED BANNER." *See* National anthem

STARTING GATE, ELECTRIC. *See* Electric starting gate

STATE

Noncontiguous overseas state was Hawaii, 2,090 miles across the Pacific from San Francisco, Calif. Voted into the Union by Congress March 12, 1959 (323 for, 89 against), Hawaii was admitted as the 50th state by proclamation of President Dwight David Eisenhower on August 21, 1959. A star was added to the American flag on July 4, 1960.

Noncontiguous state was Alaska, which was admitted as the 49th state on January 3, 1959, by proclamation of President Dwight David Eisenhower (73 Stat. L. 16). Alaska had become a territory August 24, 1912 (37 Stat. L. 512). A constitution was approved by popular vote on April 24, 1956. It was ratified by the United States Congress on July 7, 1958 (72 Stat. L. 339). Voters approved statehood on August 26, 1958, and the first state election was held November 25, 1958.

The First

State admitted to the Union after the ratification of the Constitution by the original 13 colonies was Vermont, on March 4, 1791. Statehood was authorized by Act of Congress of February 18, 1791 (1 Stat. L. 191). Vermont was formed from the New Hampshire Grants, over which both New York and New Hampshire claimed jurisdiction. In 1777 it had declared itself an independent commonwealth, the Republic of Vermont, and elected Thomas Chittenden as the first governor. He was also the first state governor, serving to 1797. *(Hinland Hall—History of Vermont)*

State admitted to the Union on the Pacific coast was California on September 9, 1850. The first state governor was Peter Hardeman Burnett, a Democrat, who served from 1849 to 1851. *(Hubert Howe Bancroft—History of California)*

State admitted to the Union west of the Mississippi River was Missouri, on August 10, 1821. The first governor of the new state was Alexander McNair, a Democrat, who served from 1820 to 1824. (Louisiana, the 18th state, admitted April 30, 1812, is both east and west of the Mississippi.) *(Perry Scott Rader—The History of Missouri)*

State constitution was that of Massachusetts, which was adopted on May 16, 1775, by the Provincial Congress of Massachusetts. The motto of the state was *Ense petit placidam sub libertate quietem*—"With the sword she seeks peace under liberty." The constitution was temporary. A new constitution was framed in Boston, September 1, 1779, and was completed March 2, 1780. It was ratified by a two-thirds vote. John Hancock served as the first governor under it. *(James Quayle Dealey—Our State Constitutions)*

State denied admission into the Union was Franklin formed August 23, 1784, when it seceded from North Carolina. It was formed by 3 counties between the Bald Mountains and the Holston River. It established a senate and a house of commons at Jonesborough and elected Thomas Talbot as clerk of the senate; Landon Carter, speaker; and John Sevier, governor, for a 4-year term with an annual salary of £200 or 1,000 deerskins. Sevier, arrested on charges of high treason, was freed, returned as state senator from his own county, and became the first governor of the state of Tennessee.

"State House" located outside a state. *See* Building: "State House" located outside a state

State named for a native-born American was Washington, the 42nd state, admitted into the Union on November 11, 1889 (26 Stat. L. 1552). The first governor was Elisha Peyre Ferry, Republican, who served from 1889 to 1893.

State readmitted to the Union after the Civil War was Tennessee, on July 24, 1866. A new constitution was adopted on January 9, 1865, and ratified on February 22, 1865. *(James Welch Patton*

The First

—Unionism and Reconstruction in Tennessee 1860–1869)

State to abolish both entail and primogeniture was Georgia, whose constitution of February 5, 1777, abrogated those two bulwarks of the ancient regime. *(Virginius Dabney—Liberalism in the South)*

State to abolish slavery. *See* Emancipation Act (state)

State to provide universal manhood suffrage. *See under* Suffrage

State to ratify the federal Constitution was Delaware, on December 7, 1787. The constitution was ratified December 6, 1787, and signed December 7, 1787, by all 30 members of the convention. Thomas Collins, who was president of Delaware at that time, automatically became the first state governor. *(George Herbert Ryden—Delaware, the First State in the Union)*

State to repudiate a debt was Mississippi in 1842. The sovereign state of Mississippi sold $5 million worth of bonds in June 1838 to pay for 50,000 shares in the Union Bank of Mississippi. The bank became hopelessly insolvent in 1840, and in 1842 the legislature denied that the state was under legal or moral obligation to pay the bonds in question. *(William Amasa Scott—The Repudiation of State Debts)*

State to secede from the Union. *See* Secession: Secession act

States admitted to the Union simultaneously were North and South Dakota. The Admission Act was signed February 22, 1889, by President Grover Cleveland. Each state held a constitutional convention beginning July 4, 1889 and both held the ratifying election October 1, 1889. President Benjamin Harrison signed the proclamations of admission without knowing which was which. Both states were admitted to the Union November 3, 1889. The first governor of North Dakota was John Miller, and of South Dakota Arthur Calvin Mellette, both Republicans. Washington and Montana were admitted by the same enabling act, but the proclamations were not signed until a few days later.

STATE ATLAS. *See* Atlas

STATE BOUNDARY DECISION. *See* Supreme Court (U.S.) decision: Supreme Court decision in a state boundary case

STATE CAPITOL. *See* Capitol

STATE COLLEGE FOR WOMEN. *See* College

STATE COLLEGE OF AGRICULTURE. *See* Agricultural school: Agricultural college (state) to be chartered

The First

STATE DEPARTMENT (U.S.)

Army officer to occupy the nation's highest military post and the highest nonelective civilian post. *See* Army Officer: Army officer to occupy both the nation's highest military post and the highest nonelective civilian post

Consul under the Department of State. *See under* Diplomatic service

Protocol chief (woman) was Shirley Temple Black, who was appointed by President Gerald Rudolph Ford and served from July 20, 1976, to January 20, 1977, in the State Department with the rank of ambassador.

State Department (U.S.) was established by an "act for establishing an executive department to be denominated the Department of Foreign Affairs," approved July 27, 1789 (1 Stat. L. 28). The name was ordered changed to the Department of State by act approved September 15, 1789 (1 Stat. L. 68).

State Department (U.S.) black official was Dr. Ralph Johnson Bunche, who was appointed January 4, 1944, as divisional assistant, Division of Political Studies, Department of State. On July 1, 1946, Dr. Bunche went on leave without pay from the Department of State to work with the United Nations. On March 23, 1947, he was transferred from the Department of State to the United Nations.

State Department (U.S.) Secretary was Thomas Jefferson, who was appointed by President George Washington. John Jay, who served as Secretary for Foreign Affairs for the Continental Congress from December 21, 1784, was held over without appointment or commission and continued, though not officially, to superintend the department under the Constitution until Thomas Jefferson took office as Secretary of State on March 22, 1790. *(Gaillard Hunt—The Department of State of the United States)*

Woman acting assistant Secretary of State was Florence Kirlin of Indiana, who assumed the post on September 3, 1955, and served through November 30, 1955, during the absence of Thruston Ballard Morton, assistant Secretary of State for Congressional Relations.

STATE LAW CODE. *See* Law codification (state)

STATE LEGISLATOR. *See* Legislator (state)

STATE MEDICINE AND PUBLIC HYGIENE PROFESSORSHIP. *See under* Medical instruction

STATE MILITARY SCHOOL. *See* Military school

STATE PARK. *See* Park

STATE POLICE. *See* Police

STATE REFORMATORY FOR BOYS. *See* Prison: Reformatory for boys (state)

The First

STATE SEAL. *See* Seal

STATE TAX. *See* Tax

STATE THEATER. *See* Theater

STATE UNION CATALOG. *See* Library catalog: Union catalog of books by a state library

STATE UNIVERSITY. *See* College

STATISTICAL BOARD, CENTRAL. *See* Central Statistical Board (U.S.)

STATISTICAL SOCIETY of importance was the American Statistical Association, organized November 27, 1839, in Boston, Mass., "to collect, preserve and diffuse statistical information in the different departments of human knowledge." A constitution was adopted December 11, 1839, and the association incorporated February 5, 1841. The first president was Richard Fletcher, who served from December 1839 to January 1844. The first annual meeting was held February 5, 1840, in Boston. *(John Korene—History of Statistics)*

STATUARY GROUP. *See* Marble statuary group

STATUE. *See* Bronze statue; Monument

STATUS OF FORCES TREATY. *See* Treaty

STEAM AUTOMOBILE. *See* Automobile

STEAM BATHS. *See under* Bathhouse

STEAM DISTRIBUTION PLANT of importance was the New York Steam Corporation, 16 Cortlandt Street, New York City, formed July 26, 1880. The first boiler plant was erected in the block bounded by Cortlandt, Dey, Greenwich, and Washington streets, and contained 48 boilers of 250 h.p. each. It had a chimney 225 feet high. On September 19, 1881, the company was consolidated with the Steam Heating and Power Company of New York, a smaller organization. The first distribution of steam from a central plant in New York City was made March 3, 1882, to the United Bank Building, 88-92 Broadway. Within nine months, the service had been extended to 62 customers. *(New York Steam Corporation—Fifty Years of New York Steam Service)*

STEAM-DRIVEN MOTORCYCLE. *See* Motorcycle: Motorcycle (steam-driven)

STEAM ELEVATOR. *See* Elevator: Elevator (suspended)

STEAM ENGINE

Steam engine was imported from England. It was brought over by Josiah Hornblower, who has been recognized as America's first steam engineer. Hornblower left London on the S.S. *Irene* June 6, 1753, and arrived in New York City September 9, 1753. The engine was delivered to the copper mine of Colonel John Schuyler in New Barbadoes Neck, now North Arlington, N.J., September 25, 1753. Its only use was to pump water from the mine. It was assembled, installed, and placed

The First

in service on March 12, 1755. *(Leonor Fresnel Loree—First Steam Fire Engine in America)*

Steam engine that was practical was manufactured by Oliver Evans of Philadelphia in 1795. In 1799 he introduced a high-pressure engine which because of its lightness and cheapness was ideally suited to the needs of the simple colonial industries. *(Journal of the Franklin Institute. July 1886)*

STEAM FIRE ENGINE. *See* Fire engine

STEAM FRIGATE. *See* Ship: Steam-propelled frigate

STEAM-HEATED BUILDING. *See* Building: Building heated by steam

STEAM-HEATED FACTORY. *See* Factory

STEAM HEATING SYSTEM. *See* Heating system

STEAM LOCOMOTIVE. *See* Locomotive: Streamlined steam locomotive

STEAM-OPERATED AMPHIBIOUS VEHICLE. *See* Amphibious vehicle

STEAM PRESSING MACHINE. *See* Pressing machine

STEAM-PROPELLED FERRYBOAT. *See* Ferryboat

STEAM-PROPELLED FRIGATE. *See* Ship

STEAM SHOVEL was invented in 1838 by William S. Otis of Philadelphia, Pa., who obtained patent No. 1,089 on February 24, 1839, on a crane for excavating and removing earth. It was first used on the Western Railroad in Massachusetts. *(Civil Engineer and Architect's Journal. April 1843)*

STEAM THRESHING MACHINE. *See* Thresher: Threshing machine to employ steam

STEAM TRACTOR. *See under* Automobile tractor

STEAM TUGBOAT. *See* Ship

STEAM TURBINE. *See* Turbine

STEAM-TURBINE ELECTRIC GENERATOR. *See under* Electric Power Generator

STEAM WHALER. *See* Ship

STEAM WHISTLE, LOCOMOTIVE. *See* Locomotive steam whistle

STEAMBOAT. *See* Ship

STEAMBOAT INSPECTION SERVICE (U.S.) was established by act of Congress, July 7, 1838 (5 Stat. L. 304), for the "better security of the lives of passengers on board of vessels propelled in whole or in part by steam." Inspectors were appointed by district judges of U.S. Courts and received $5 for each inspection. They gave the owners a certificate stating the age of the boat and soundness of the vessel. An annual inspection was required.

The First

(Lloyd Milton Short—Steamboat Inspection Service)

STEAMER CHAIR. *See* Chair

STEAMSHIP. *See* Ship

STEEL
    Armor plate contract (U.S. Navy). *See* Armor plate contract (U.S. Navy)

Bessemer steel converter used commercially was erected by the Eureka Iron and Steel Works in 1864 in Wyandotte, Mich., on the site of what is now the public library. The steel was made in a 2½-ton experimental converter by William Franklin Durfee by means of the Kelly-pneumatic process.

Bessemer steel track. *See* Railroad track: Railroad rails of Bessemer steel

Building of pressed structural steel. *See under* Building

Cast steel for plows was made by William Woods at the steel works of Jones and Quigg, Pittsburgh, Pa., in 1846. The plows were made by John Deere at Moline, Ill. *(James Moore Swank—History of the Manufacture of Iron in All Ages)*

Continuous-sheet steel mill was designed by John Butler Tytus and built by the American Rolling Mill Company, Ashland, Ky., in 1922. The mill consisted of an arrangement of machines that passed sheet steel through a series of mills in a tandem train at a high speed. The process replaced the older and much slower methods. Operations began in 1924.

Manganese steel was manufactured in 1892 by the Taylor Iron and Steel Company in High Bridge, N.J.

Manganese steel for railroad tracks was manufactured August 28, 1894, by William Wharton, Jr. and Co., Inc., in High Bridge, N.J. The first rail frog with a cast manganese steel plate was installed at Fulton Street and Boerum Place, Brooklyn, N.Y.

Open-hearth furnace for the manufacture of steel by the Siemens-Martin process was built in 1868 by Frederick J. Slade for Cooper Hewitt & Company, owners of the New Jersey Steel & Iron Company, Trenton, N.J. The furnace was ready for operation in December, 1868. *(James Moore Swank—History of the Manufacture of Iron in All Ages)*

Ski slide (steel). *See* Ski jump (steel)

Steel was manufactured in May 1728 by Samuel Higley of Simsbury, Conn., and Joseph Dewey of Hebron, Conn. In May 1728 Higley employed three workmen in a "curious art, by which to convert, change and transmute common iron into good steel, sufficient for any use" and requested a ten-year monopoly from the state. *(Report of the United States Commissioner of Patents, 1850)*

The First

STEEL—*Continued*
Steel-frame building. *See under* Building

Steel mill to install an electrical machine was the Edgar Thomson Works of the Carnegie Steel Company, Braddock, Pa. A two-light arc machine, operated by belt drive from a line shaft, was installed in the blast furnace shop in 1882. (The Homestead Works of Carnegie Steel Company and other plants in the East also claim to have been first.) The first installation of electric-motor-driven rolls was made in the Edgar Thomson Works of the Carnegie Steel Company in No. 3 Mill in October 1905.

Vacuum-cast steel was poured July 2, 1957, by the Bethlehem Steel Corporation, Bethlehem, Pa., in the form of a 93,900-pound ingot, 78 inches in diameter. Vacuum-cast steel was melted in either an electric or open-hearth furnace and poured into ingots, its gases having been entrapped by vacuum-stream degassing with equipment designed by the F. J. Stokes Corporation, Philadelphia, Pa.

STEEL ANALYSIS LABORATORY was established in 1862 by William Franklin Durfee. He designed the machinery to test the Kelly process for making steel on a large scale and supervised the making of the first Bessemer steel in America at Wyandotte, Mich., by the Kelly-pneumatic process. *(Journal of the Iron and Steel Institute. Vol. 56. 1899)*

STEEL BOILER PLATE. *See* Boiler plates

STEEL BRIDGE. *See* Bridge: Steel arch bridge

STEEL-CUT NAILS. *See* Nails

STEEL DAM. *See* Dam

STEEL FISHING ROD. *See* Fishing rod

STEEL-FRAME BUILDING. *See* Building: Building of pressed structural steel

STEEL-HULL FERRYBOAT. *See* Ferryboat

STEEL HYDROPLANE. *See* Aviation—Airplane: Hydroplane of stainless steel

STEEL MAIL CAR. *See* Railroad car: Mail car (steel)

STEEL PASSENGER RAILROAD COACH. *See* Railroad car

STEEL PEN. *See* Pen

STEEL PIER. *See* Pier

STEEL POSTAL CAR. *See* Railroad car: Mail car (steel)

STEEL PROPELLER BLADE (hollow). *See* Aviation: Propeller blade of hollow steel

STEEL PULLMAN SLEEPING CAR. *See* Sleeping car: Pullman sleeping car made entirely of steel

The First

STEEL RAIL. *See* Railroad track: Railroad rails of steel

STEEL RAILWAY BRIDGE. *See* Bridge: Railroad all-steel bridge

STEEL SAILING VESSEL. *See* Ship

STEEL SCHOONER. *See* Ship: Schooner (seven-masted, steel)

STEEL SHAFT GOLF CLUB. *See* Golf clubs (or golf sticks)

STEEL SHOVEL. *See* Shovel

STEEPLE. *See* Building: Building with a high steeple

STEEL TRAPS. *See* Traps

STEEPLECHASE was held October 26, 1869, at Jerome Park, Westchester County, N.Y., by the American Jockey Club. Seven horses participated. The race was won by Oysterman, Jr., a five-year-old, owned by Colonel D. McDaniel. Between 15,000 and 20,000 spectators witnessed the inaugural race.

STELLAR SPECTRUM PHOTOGRAPH. *See* Photograph: Photograph of a stellar spectrum showing the dark lines

STEERING GEAR, AUTOMOBILE. *See* Automobile: Automobile with left-hand steering

STENOGRAPHY BOOK. *See* Shorthand book

STENOTYPE device for printing a legible text in the English alphabet at a high reporting speed was invented by John Celinergos Zachos of New York City, who received patent No. 175,892 on April 11, 1876, on a "typewriter and phonotypic notation." The type was fixed on eighteen shuttle bars, two or more of which might be simultaneously placed in position. The impression was given by a plunger common to all the bars.

STEREO TELECAST. *See* Television—Telecast

STEREOPHONIC SOUND PROGRAM BROADCAST BY SEPARATELY OWNED STATIONS. *See* Radio broadcast

STEREOSCOPE was invented in 1851 by Frederick and William Langenheim of Philadelphia, Pa. It had a hooded lens, a handle, and an adjustable card holder. Oliver Wendell Holmes invented a hand viewer and described it in an article, "The Stereoscope and the Stereograph," published in 1859 in the *Atlantic Monthly*. It was improved upon by Joseph L. Bates. Credit for the invention is often given to Holmes, despite the fact that an English version appeared about 1850. *(William Culp Darrah—Stereo Views, A History of Stereographs in America and Their Collection)*

STEREOTYPE
See also Laborsaving device approved by a labor organization

The First

Automatic plate-casting and finishing machine for stereotype printing was invented by Henry Alexander Wise Wood. It was called the Autoplate and was adopted by the New York *Herald* in 1900. This stereotyping machine greatly increased the speed at which newspapers could be printed. *(American Society of Mechanical Engineers—The Reorganization and Reconstruction of the Newspaper Printing Press. Feb. 7, 1929)*

Autoplate stereotype plate-making machine. *See* Laborsaving device approved by a labor organization

Curved stereotype plate was cast by Charles Craske in 1854 in New York City for a Hoe rotary press and used by the New York *Tribune*. On August 31, 1861, full pages of the *Tribune* were printed from curved plates. *(George Adolf Kubler—A Short History of Stereotyping)*

Stereotype printing attempt was made in 1745 in Philadelphia, Pa., by Benjamin Mecom, a nephew of Benjamin Franklin. He commenced casting plates for the New Testament but never finished the task. *(John Luther Ringwalt—Encyclopedia of Printing)*

Stereotyped book. *See under* Book

Stereotypers (successful) were David and George Bruce, who established the firm of D. & G. Bruce in New York City in 1813. They designed machinery and molds patterned after those in use in England and had them cast in New York City. The business remained in the family until 1895, when it was sold. *(Robert Francis Salade—Handbook of Electrotyping and Stereotyping)*

STERILAMP. *See* Electric lighting: Electric sterilamp

STERILIZATION
Sterilization legislation (state) that was optional, not punitive, was enacted April 10, 1976, by the state of Virginia. It sanctioned physicians performing a vasectomy, salpingectomy, or other surgical sterilization procedure upon any person under the age of 21, or over 21 and legally incompetent.

Sterilization Legislation was enacted by Indiana, March 9, 1907 (Indiana Chap. 215), for eugenic, punitive, and therapeutic reasons, and was entitled "an act to prevent the procreation of criminals, idiots, imbeciles and rapists." One hundred and twenty operations were performed under the law. The constitutionality of the law was challenged, and on May 11, 1921, the Supreme Court of Indiana, in the case of *Williams* vs. *Smith,* held it unconstitutional because it denied the appellee due process of law. A sterilization bill had been passed by the Pennsylvania legislature on March 21, 1905, but was vetoed by Governor Samuel

The First

Whitaker Pennypacker. *(Jacob Henry Landman—Human Sterlization)*

STETHOSCOPE
Electrical stethoscope (portable) to amplify the sounds of the human body was demonstrated to 500 doctors simultaneously by the Western Electric Company Incorporated, of New York City, on June 10, 1924, at the Municipal Pier, Chicago, Ill. It was developed by Western Electric in cooperation with Bell System engineers and Dr. Horatio Burt Williams, professor of physiology, Columbia University, New York City. The stethoscope was first marketed in October 1925. *(Western Electric News. November 1925)*

STEWARDESS, AIR. *See* Aviation: Air flight attendant (woman)

STOCK EXCHANGE. *See under* Brokerage

STOCK QUOTATION BOARD
Automatic electric stock quotation board was manufactured in 1929 by the Teleregister Corporation (later the Bunker-Ramo Corporation), Stamford, Conn., and placed in operation May 21, 1929, in the brokerage office of Sutro Bros. and Co., New York City. The board automatically shifted figures as changes were made. It showed open, high, low, and last prices of each stock listed.

Stock quotation boards were of slate and were manufactured by Mount and Robertson of New York City in 1889.

STOMACH WASHING with a tube or syringe was accomplished by Dr. Philip Syng Physick in 1800 in Philadelphia, Pa. His procedure is described in his "Account of a New Mode of Extracting Poisonous Substances from the Stomach," which appeared in the *Eclectic Report and Analytic Review,* Vol. 3, p. 111-13, 1813. *(Charles Caldwell—A Discourse Commemorative of Philip Syng Physick, M.D.)*

STONE BRIDGE. *See* Bridge

STONE CRUSHER
Stone breaking machine patent was granted April 13, 1831, to Benjamin F. Lodge and Ezekial T. Cox of Zanesville, Ohio.

Stone crusher of value was built by Eli Whitney Blake of New Haven, Conn., who obtained patent No. 20,542, June 15, 1858, on an "improvement in machines for crushing stones." Blake's stone crusher had upright convergent jaws, one fixed and one movable. The stones descended by gravity into pits and were sorted by screens. The device was first used in 1859 in Hartford, Conn., on a road construction job.

STONE PAVEMENT. *See under* Road

STORAGE BATTERY AUTOMOBILE. *See* Automobile: Electric storage battery automobile

The First

STORAGE BATTERY BOAT. *See* Motorboat: Storage battery motorboat

STORAGE TANK (gas). *See* Gas: Gas storage tank (waterless)

STORY, DETECTIVE. *See* Detective story

STOVE
See also Electric cooking experiment; Electric stove

Electronic range for domestic use was introduced at a press conference at the Hotel Pierre, New York City, on October 25, 1955, by the Tappan Stove Company, Mansfield, Ohio. A 220-volt electric current produced microwaves which cooked eggs in 22 seconds, bacon in 90 seconds, frozen broccoli in 4½ minutes, and a 5-pound roast in 30 minutes. The cost of the range was $1,200.

Stove for heating was a cast-iron wood-burning open box which stood out from the chimney and caused heat from its back and sides to be thrown into the room. The stove, invented in 1742 by Benjamin Franklin, was called the Pennsylvania fireplace. It is now known as the Franklin stove. Smoke escaped over the top of a flat chamber behind the fire, and passed downward between it and the real back of the stove, then into the chimney. Franklin would not patent his invention. The stoves were manufactured by Robert Grace, the master of Warwick furnace in Chester County, Pa. *(Benjamin Franklin—An Account of the New Invented Pennsylvania fire-places wherein their construction and manner of operation is particularly explained; their advantage above every other method of warming rooms demonstrated)*

STOVE PATENT was granted June 11, 1793, to Robert Haeterick of Pennsylvania. His name is spelled in various ways in the early records.

STOWAWAY, AERONAUTICAL. *See under* Aviation

STRATOLINER COMMERCIAL FLIGHT. *See under* Aviation—Flights

STRATOVISION. *See under* Television—Telecast:

STRAW HAT. *See* Hat

STRAW PAPER. *See* Paper

STRAWS (artificial) for drinking were made from paraffined manila paper rolled by hand by Marvin Chester Stone of Washington, D.C., in 1886. He obtained patent No. 375,962, January 3, 1888. Rye straws had been used previously, but they proved unsatisfactory as they were generally unclean and cracked. Artificial drinking straws were made by hand until 1905, when the first machine to manufacture them successfully was made by the Marvin C. Stone Estate.

The First

STREAMLINED ELECTRIC ENGINE. *See* Locomotive

STREAMLINED FERRYBOAT. *See* Ferryboat

STREAMLINED STEAM LOCOMOTIVE. *See* Locomotive

STREAMLINED STEAMSHIP. *See* Ship

STREAMLINED TRAIN. *See under* Railroad

STREETCAR
Aluminum streetcar in which the metal was used not only for the body and underframe but also for the trucks was placed in service December 2, 1926, by the Cleveland Railway Company. The total weight for the car was 30,300 pounds, of which 6,647 pounds were aluminum. The first use of aluminum in subway car construction occurred on October 27, 1904, when the Interborough Rapid Transit Company of New York City used aluminum in 300 subway motor cars and trailers for interior finish work, moldings, window panels, etc. *(Electric Railroad Journal. April 1930)*

Cable car was invented by Eleazer A. Gardner of Philadelphia, Pa., who obtained patent No. 19,-736, March 23, 1858, on an "improvement in tracks for city railways." An underground tunnel, having a series of pulleys inside, housed the cable.

Cable streetcar put into service in the world was August 1, 1873, on Clay Street Hill, San Francisco, Calif. The car was invented by Andrew Smith Hallidie, who obtained patent No. 110,971 on January 17, 1871, on an "endless-wire rope way." *(Edgar Myron Kahn—Cable Car Days in San Francisco)*

Double-deck streetcar was operated July 4, 1892, on a trial trip in San Diego, Calif. The upper deck, reached by a winding stairway at each end of the car, was on the roof, with longitudinal seats facing outward, accommodating 12 on each side, and roofed over by a canopy. There were no sides or enclosures on the upper deck other than a railing.

Electric cars commercially operated were those of the Baltimore and Hampden Line, a third-rail system which began operation on one line only on August 10, 1885, in Baltimore, Md. The line continued in service for more than a year. The first cars were run over the Hampden Branch of the Baltimore Union Passenger Railway Company, which later became a part of the United Railways and Electric Company of Baltimore, Md.

Electric streetcar successfully run with current generated by a stationary dynamo was invented by Stephen Dudley Field of New York City in 1874. In this system the current was carried by one of the rails to a wheel of the car, and thence to the motor. From this it flowed back through another wheel, which was insulated from the first one, to the other rail, and thence returned to the dynamo. Field filed a caveat on May 21, 1879, and obtained

The First

patent No. 229,991 on July 13, 1880, on "propelling railway cars by electro-magnetism." It covered his claim for an electric tramway motor, the current to be supplied by a stationary source of power and connected with the rails.

Gas-powered streetcar was No. 13 (later changed to No. 85), which was operated in 1873 in Providence, R.I., from the car barns to Olneyville Square. Henry Thompson was the conductor. It had a gas and air engine, compressed by separate pumps, designed by George B. Brayton of Boston, Mass., who obtained patent No. 125,166 on April 2, 1872, on "a pumping engine for condensing air and gas, and a reservoir for containing such agents."

Interurban streetcar line was established by Charles Lewis Henry, who organized the Union Traction Company, which ran its first car June 1, 1898, between Anderson, Ind., and Alexandria, Ind. The first conductor was Hadley Clifford.

Lightweight one-man streetcar was designed by Charles O. Birney and built by the American Car Company of St. Louis, Mo. The first one-man Birney cars were placed in operation in Fort Worth, Tex., November 1916. The safety features included a single front door for both entrance and exit, and a controller by means of which the power was thrown off, sand automatically applied to the tracks, and the brakes set when the operator failed to keep his hand in place. The door could not be opened or the step lowered until the brakes were set.

Municipally owned streetcars were operated December 28, 1912, in San Francisco, Calif. The Municipal Railway (an overhead trolley system) began operation with ten cars on Geary Street from Kearney Street to 33rd Avenue and Park. Thomas A. Cashin was superintendent. Mayor James Rolph, Jr., acted as motorman on the first car. *(Financial Report of the Geary Street Municipal Railway of San Francisco, Dec. 28, 1912–Dec. 31, 1913)*

Streetcar was the *John Mason,* a horse-drawn conveyance designed, constructed, and completed in 1832 by John Stephenson in Philadelphia, Pa., and placed in service in New York City by the New York and Harlem Railway. Named for a prominent New York banker who organized the railway company, the *John Mason* was equipped with iron wheels and drawn over iron rails laid in the center of the pavement. Lank O'Dell was the first driver. The car, which accommodated 30 passengers, was divided into three nonconnecting compartments with seats for 10 in each. The three doors opened outward. The first door bore on its panel the name *New York,* the second *Yorkville,* and the third *Harlaem.* The car made its first appearance in New York City November 14, 1832, when municipal officials took the first trip. Public transportation service began November 26, 1832.

The First

The tracks were laid along Fourth Avenue from Prince Street to 14th Street. The fare was 12½ cents. In November 1835 a double track running north to Yorkville was completed. (The *John Mason* was the first horse-drawn streetcar, but horses had been used earlier to pull trains on railroad track lines.)

Streetcar coin box. *See* Coin box

Streetcar company was the New York and Harlem Railway, Inc., New York City, incorporated April 25, 1831, "to construct a single or double railroad." It was capitalized for $350,000 and received a 30-year franchise December 22, 1831, from the Common Council. The first secretary was John Mason, who later became president.

Streetcar tracks that were tieless, soundless, and shockless were laid in New Orleans, La. The roadway was paved with eight inches of concrete base and three inches of wearing surface, the top of which was one and a half inches of the finest oil asphalt. The line was officially completed February 4, 1930.

Streetcars with clear-vision windows affording an unobstructed view of wide areas were placed in operation by the Pittsburgh Railways Company of Pittsburgh, Pa., in 1929. A new seating arrangement was introduced at the same time.

Trackless trolley system was built and placed in operation September 11, 1910, by Charles Mann between "Bungalow Land" in Laurel Canyon, Calif., and the terminal point of the Los Angeles Pacific Electric Railway Company, Los Angeles, Calif., a distance of a mile and a half. Two automobile buses were used. On top of the buses were trolley poles making contact with overhead wires. *(John Anderson Miller—Fares, Please)*

Transfers (printed) were invented by John Harry Stedman of Rochester, N.Y., who obtained U.S. patent No. 481,210 on August 23, 1892. They were 1⅞ by 2½ inches and were first used on October 31, 1892, in Rochester, N.Y.

STREET CLEANING MACHINE of importance was employed by Philadelphia, Pa., on December 15, 1854. It consisted of "a series of brooms on a cylinder about two feet six inches wide, attached to two endless chains, running over an upper and lower set of pulleys, which are suspended on a light frame of wrought iron behind a cart, the body of which is near the ground. As the cart wheels revolve, a rotary motion is given to the pulleys conveying the endless chains, and series of brooms attached to them; which being made to bear on the ground successively sweep the surface and carry the soil up an incline or carrier plate, over the top of which it is dropped into the cart." *(Philadelphia Public Ledger. Dec. 16, 1854)*

The First

STREET CLEANING SERVICE was instituted in 1757 by Benjamin Franklin in Philadelphia, Pa. He offered a bill to the Philadelphia Assembly and reported: "After some inquiry, I found a poor industrious man who was willing to undertake keeping the pavement clean by sweeping it twice a week, carrying off the dirt from before the neighbors' doors, for the sum of six pence per month, to be paid by each house."

STREET GASLIGHT. *See* Gas: Gaslights (street)

STREET LETTER BOX. *See under* Postal service

STREET PARADE. *See* Parade

STREPTOMYCIN was isolated from a culture of a soil microbe known as *Streptomyces griseus* by Dr. Selman Abraham Waksman and his students (Albert Schatz, Elizabeth Bugie, Doris Jones, and H. Christine Reilly) of the New Jersey Agricultural Experiment Station, Rutgers University, New Brunswick, N.J., in January 1944. It was first manufactured commercially by Merck & Co., Rahway, N.J., in September 1944. This antibiotic is active against both Gram-positive and Gram-negative bacteria as well as upon acidfast bacteria, of which the organism that causes tuberculosis is the most important. It is used to control certain diseases caused by Gram-negative bacteria as well as Gram-positive diseases that are resistant to penicillin.

STRIKE

Anti–sit-down-strike decision (federal) was rendered by the Supreme Court of the United States on February 27, 1939, in the case of National Labor Relations Board, petitioner, against Fansteel Metallurgical Corporation, North Chicago, Ill., whose employees were on strike from February 17 to February 26, 1937. Chief Justice Charles Evans Hughes wrote the opinion, Justices McReynolds, Butler, Stone and Roberts concurring, Justices Black and Reed dissenting.

Anti–sit-down-strike legislation (state) was Act No. 210, an act "prohibiting the conspiring of three or more persons unlawfully to occupy, hold and possess certain buildings against the will and without the consent of the lessee thereof," passed April 9, 1937, by Vermont. The bill was introduced by Senator Ernest Walter Dunklee of Windham, Vt., and provided for penalties of not more than two years' imprisonment or a $1,000 fine.

Baseball strike. *See* Baseball strike: Baseball strike

Helicopter to deliver across a picket line. *See under* Helicopter

Modern sit-down strike occurred in the packing plant of George A. Hormel and Company, Austin, Minn., on November 13, 1933, when striking employees seized control. The Industrial Commission of Minnesota, of which Niels Henriksen Debel was chairman, held mediation hearings

The First

November 16-18, 1933, and rendered a decision on December 8, 1933, affecting the specific issues involved. Various forms of stay-in strikes, slow-down strikes, and refusal-to-work strikes, however, had been attempted previously.

Strike took place in New York City in 1741 when the master bakers protested against municipal regulation of the price of bread. They were tried and convicted of unlawfully combining, but no sentence was passed. *(Selig Perlman—History of Trade Unionism in the United States)*

Strike in which federal troops were called in peacetime was that of railroad employees which began July 16, 1877. In response to requests for aid from several governors, including Henry Mason Mathews of West Virginia, John Lee Carroll of Maryland, and John Hartranft of Pennsylvania, President Rutherford Birchard Hayes called out federal troops. In eight days he received nine calls for assistance from governors. On January 29, 1834, President Andrew Jackson ordered troops to put down a "riotous assembly" among laborers on the Chesapeake and Ohio Canal.

Strike in which the militia was called occurred in Paterson, N.J., July 21, 1828, when the Godwin Guards of the national militia were required to keep peace during a strike brought about by the changing of dinner hours from 12 to 1 in the factories. The strikers were defeated but afterward the noon dinner hour was again established. *(Harry Lawrence Harris and John T. Hilton—History of the Second and Fifth Regiment)*

Strike in which women participated was that of the "female weavers" of Pawtucket, R.I., who went on strike in 1824 with the male workers. *(Florence Peterson—Strikes in the United States 1880–1936)*

Strike of postal employees was a wildcat strike of locals of the National Association of Letter Carriers that began in New York City on March 18, 1970, and spread to parts of New York, New Jersey, and Connecticut. On March 23, 1970, President Richard Milhous Nixon declared a state of national emergency and called out 30,000 troops (15,000 Army, Navy, and Marine Corps reservists from the New York City area; 12,000 members of the Army and Air National Guard in New York; and 2,500 men on active duty in New York) to handle the mail. The strike ended March 24, 1970.

Strike of women operatives occurred at the Dover Manufacturing Company, Dover, N.H., in 1828, when about 400 women went on strike against a wage cut and a ten-hour day in the needlework trades. *(Ruth Delzell—The Early History of Women Trade Unionists of America)*

Strike settlement mediated by the United States Department of Labor was the dispute of the Railway Clerks of the New York, New Haven and Hartford Railroad. Commissioners of conciliation

The First

had not yet been appointed, but the Secretary of Labor assigned the dispute to Glossbrenner Wallace William Hanger, chief statistician of the Bureau of Labor Statistics, who entered the case May 24, 1913, and effected a settlement June 2, 1913.

Strike to last longer than a year went into effect December 26, 1945, when Local 180 of the United Automobile Workers of America, C.I.O., struck the J. I. Case Manufacturing Company, Racine, Wis. (farm implements). On March 9, 1947, the workers voted 927-448 in favor of accepting the company offer of an increase of wages from 25 cents to 26 cents an hour.

Union strike benefit was authorized May 31, 1786, at the home of Henry Myers, Philadelphia, Pa. Twenty-six members of the Typographical Society in protest against a wage reduction agreed "that we will support such of our brethren as shall be thrown out of employment on account of their refusing to work for less than $6 per week." They won their demands. *(George A. Tracy—History of the Typographical Union)*

STROBORADIOGRAPH was made by General Electric's General Engineering Laboratory, Schenectady, N.Y., in cooperation with the Detroit Arsenal, Center Line, Mich., and the General Electric X-ray Department, Milwaukee, Wis., in 1956 and announced on August 14, 1956. Used with the X-ray betatron, operating at 5 million to 15 million volts, it could take still pictures of the inside of an engine operating at normal speed under load conditions. From still pictures spliced at graduated intervals, X-ray motion pictures of the complete cycle of an engine could be studied to detect flaws or improve design.

STRUCTURAL STEEL BUILDING. *See* Building: Building of pressed structural steel

STUDENTS' FEDERATION (international) was the Pan American Student League, founded in New York City in 1920 to promote inter-American understanding among the younger generation throughout the Americas. The first United States delegate to the International Council and first president of the council was Philip Leonard Green. The first secretary was J. Antonio Reyes of Peru.

STUDIO. *See* Motion picture studio

STUNT ACTOR. *See* Motion picture actor

SUBAQUEOUS HIGHWAY TUNNEL. *See* Tunnel

SUBMACHINE GUN. *See* Ordnance

SUBMARINE
  American ship sunk by a U-boat. *See under* World War II

The First

Atomic-powered submarine was the *Nautilus* SS(N) 571, built by the Electric Boat Company, a division of the General Dynamics Corporation, Groton, Conn., under the supervision of Captain Hyman George Rickover. President Harry S Truman participated in the keel-laying ceremony on June 14, 1952. The submarine, launched January 21, 1954, on the Thames River at Groton and christened by Mrs. Dwight David Eisenhower, was commissioned September 21, 1954, tested under nuclear power January 17, 1955, and completed April 22, 1955. Its crew consisted of 11 officers and 85 enlisted men. The first commander was Eugene Parks Wilkinson. The steam turbines were powered by a liquid-cooled atomic reactor. The *Nautilus* was 323¼ feet overall, 2,975 tons light, 3,200 tons standard, and 3,747 tons submerged.

Atomic-powered submarine built at a naval shipyard was the *Swordfish* (SSN-579), laid down January 25, 1956, and launched August 27, 1957, at the Portsmouth Naval Shipyard, Portsmouth, N.H. It was 268 feet long and had a 2,360-ton displacement. Commissioned September 15, 1958, its first officer was Commander Shannon Davenport Cramer, Jr.

Atomic-powered turbine-electric-drive submarine was the *Tullibee*, SSB(N) 597, 273 feet long, 2,000 tons light, 2,175 tons submerged, whose keel was laid May 26, 1958. It was launched April 27, 1960, at the Thames River plant of the General Dynamics Corporation's Electric Boat Company at Groton, Conn., and christened by Ann Davidson. The commanding officer was Commander Richard Edmund Jortberg. The vessel was commissioned at Groton November 9, 1960. It carried a crew of 60 men and 6 officers. All other submarines utilized reduction gears. The torpedo tubes of the *Tullibee* were located amidships rather than in the bow.

Ballistic missile submarine was the atomic-powered *George Washington*, SSB(N) 598, laid down November 7, 1957, launched June 9, 1959, and commissioned December 30, 1959, at Groton, Conn., on the Thames River. It was christened by Ellie Mae Anderson, wife of Robert Bernerd Anderson, Secretary of the Treasury. The cost of construction was approximately $110 million. The first commander was James Butler Osborn. The submarine was 380 feet long and had a 5,400-ton displacement light, 5,600 tons standard, and 6,700 tons submerged. It went on its patrol duty November 15, 1960, from Charleston, S.C., and returned January 21, 1961, having traveled 67 days underwater. It was equipped with 16 vertical Polaris missile tubes to be fired below the surface.

Cargo submarine to cross the Atlantic Ocean and the first to cross in time of war, was the German submarine *Deutschland*, which left Bremen, Germany, and after a 16-day voyage from the island of Heligoland, with a cargo of dyestuffs and

The First

SUBMARINE—*Continued*
chemicals worth $1 million, landed at Baltimore, Md., July 9, 1916. The submarine unloaded its cargo at Baltimore, left on August 1 with a supply of metal and rubber, and arrived in Germany on August 23, after running the British blockade. It was 315 feet long and had a 31-foot beam. Captain Paul Konig was in command. *(Paul Konig—Voyage of the "Deutschland")*

Diesel engine in a submarine. *See under* Engine

German submarine destroyed by a U.S. naval vessel. *See under* World War II

German submarine destroyed by an American aviator. *See under* World War II

Guided missile launched from a nuclear-powered submarine was a Regulus I launched March 25, 1960, from the *Halibut*, SSG (N) 587, off Oahu, Hawaii. The missile was guided over its simulated target on Lehua Island, 120 miles away, before landing, about 15 minutes after launching, at Bonham Air Force Base, ·Kauai, 20 miles beyond the target.

Japanese submarine sunk by an American ship at sea. *See under* World War II

Leaping submarine was the U.S.S. *Pickerel*, (SS-524), laid down February 8, 1944, at the Boston Naval Shipyard, Boston, Mass., and launched December 15, 1944. The submarine was christened and commissioned at the Portsmouth Shipyard, Portsmouth, N.H., on April 4, 1949. It was 311 feet 8 inches long, 27 feet 3 inches in breadth, with a 2,015-ton displacement. The submarine's first sea trials took place between April 4 and July 25, 1949. The first commanding officer was Commander Paul Richard Schratz. The *Pickerel* surfaced from a depth of 150 feet with a 48 degree up-angle during a routine training exercise off Oahu, Hawaii. Its bow seemed to leap up out of the water. It set a record by snorkeling from Hong Kong to Pearl Harbor, Honolulu, a distance of 5,200 miles, in 21 days (completely submerged from March 16, 1950, to April 5, 1950).

Naval vessels to sink an enemy submarine. *See under* Ship

Nuclear submarine named for a black was the *George Washington Carver* (SSBN 656), 425 feet long with a 7,000-ton displacement. The keel was laid August 24, 1964, and the ship launched August 14, 1965, by Marian Anderson at the Newport News Shipbuilding and Dry Dock Company, Newport News, Va. It was commissioned June 15, 1966. The first commanding officers were Captain Robert Duane Donavan (blue crew) and Lieutenant Commander Carl John Lidel (gold crew). The ship went on its first patrol December 12, 1966.

The First

Nuclear submarines launched simultaneously were the 2 nuclear submarines *Tecumseh* (SSBN 628) and *Flasher* (SSN 613), launched June 22, 1963, at the General Dynamics Corporation's Electric Boat Division at Groton, Conn., in the Thames River. The *Tecumseh*, 425 feet long, 7,000-ton displacement, was authorized, keel laid June 1, 1962, launched June 22, 1963, and commissioned May 29, 1964. The *Flasher* was authorized in 1960, keel laid April 14, 1961, launched June 22, 1963, and commissioned July 22, 1966. It was 292 feet long and displaced 4,060 tons. Its first officer was Commander Kenneth Monroe Carr.

Nuclear warhead fired from a Polaris submarine was fired May 6, 1962, from the U.S.S. *Ethan Allen*, submerged off Christmas Island in the Pacific test area. The missile sped skyward in a parabolic trajectory and then exploded. It carried a force estimated at 500,000 tons of TNT.

President to travel underwater in a submerged submarine. *See* President (U.S.)

Quadruple submarine launching was held January 27, 1944, at the Portsmouth Navy Yard, Portsmouth, N.H., when the *Razorback* (SS 394), the *Redfish* (AG SS 396), the *Ronquil* (SS 396), and the *Scabbard Fish* (SS 397) were floated from cradles in the new building basin into the Piscataqua River. They were respectively christened by Mrs. Henry F. D. Davis (wife of Captain Davis), Ruth Adair Roper (daughter of Captain Clifford H. Roper), Mrs. Charles M. Elder (wife of Captain Elder), and Ensign Nancy Jane Schetky.

Streamlined submarine of the U.S. Navy was the U.S.S. *Nautilus* (SS-168) built at the Navy Yard, Mare Island, Vallejo, Calif. The keel was laid May 10, 1927, and the ship was launched March 15, 1930, and commissioned July 1, 1930. Its length was 371 feet, extreme beam 33 feet 3 inches, mean draft 15 feet 9 inches, displacement 2,730 tons. It carried 2 six-inch 53-caliber guns and a complement of 88. On February 19, 1931, it was renamed *Nautilus*. (An atomic submarine with the same name was constructed later.)

Submarine accident occurred July 11, 1910, off Provincetown, Mass., when the *C4* (SS15) was rammed during maneuvers by the gunboat *Castine*, captained by Lieutenant Ralph A. Koch, with a crew of 80, and serving as a submarine tender. The *Castine* started for shore under her own power. The submarine, 105 feet long with a 275-ton displacement, carrying a crew of 15 under the command of Ensign Sloan Danenhaver, was beached to prevent sinking. A portion of the armor had been dented and a section of railing lost. No one was injured. The submarine had been launched June 17, 1909, as the *Bonita*, by the Fore River Shipbuilding Company, Quincy, Mass. It was commissioned November 23, 1909, with Lieutenant F. V. McNair in command. Renamed *C4* on

The First

November 17, 1911, it was decommissioned August 15, 1919.

Submarine built at a government shipyard was the *L-8* (SS-48), whose keel was laid February 24, 1915. It was launched April 23, 1917, at the Portsmouth Naval Shipyard, Portsmouth, N.H., and commissioned August 30, 1917. The ship was 165 feet long and had a 524-ton displacement. Lieutenant James Parker, Jr., was the first commanding officer.

Submarine built for use in war was the *American Turtle,* built in 1776 by David Bushnell of Saybrook, Conn. The vessel, which was large enough to accommodate one operator, had a 24-inch two-bladed wooden screw propeller, operated by hand, that enabled her to travel forward or in reverse at three knots. A crank operated the rudder aft. Water was admitted for descent and forced out with a hand pump for surfacing. Another screw, on the bottom, moved the submarine vertically. On September 7, 1776, Ezra Lee used the craft and attached a torpedo time bomb to the hull of Admiral Howe's flagship, the 64-gun *Eagle,* in New York harbor. An explosion resulted but no serious damage occurred, as the bomb drifted away from the ship. *(Connecticut Historical Society—Collections, Vol. 11)*

Submarine built on the Great Lakes was the *Peto* (SS-265), constructed from prefabricated parts by the Manitowoc Shipbuilding Company, Manitowoc, Wis. Authorized July 19, 1940, the ship was 312 feet long, with a displacement of 2,424 tons. The keel was laid June 18, 1941. It was launched sideways into the Manitowoc River on April 30, 1942, accepted November 21, 1942, by Commander Rudolph Frank Hans of the Ninth Naval District, and commissioned the next day.

Submarine captured and boarded on the high seas was the 740-ton German submarine U-505, which was attacked June 4, 1944, by airplanes and ships under the command of Captain Daniel Vincent Gallery of the aircraft carrier U.S.S. *Guadalcanal* and captured off Cape Blanco on the west coast of Africa between Cape Verde and the Canary Islands. The submarine was boarded by Lieutenant (j.g.) Albert Leroy David and eight crewmen from the destroyer U.S.S. *Pillsbury* (DE 133), commanded by George W. Cassleman. The *Guadalcanal* towed the U-505 for 1,700 miles across the Atlantic Ocean to Port Royal Bay, Bermuda, on June 19, 1944. *(Daniel Vincent Gallery—Twenty Million Tons Under The Sea)*

Submarine contract of the U.S. Navy for $150,-000 was awarded to the John P[hillip] Holland Torpedo Boat Company of New York City by Navy Secretary Hilary Abner Herbert on March 13, 1895. Construction was started at the Columbian Iron Works, Baltimore, Md. The keel was laid June 20, 1896, and the submarine launched August 7, 1897. The submarine, 85 feet 3 inches in length

The First

and 11 feet 6 inches in extreme breadth, with a displacement of 168 tons, was known as the *Plunger.* The project was abandoned and all expenses and advances returned to the government when the contract was canceled in April 1900. A new contract for another submarine was signed November 7, 1900.

Submarine crossing of the North Pole underwater was accomplished August 3, 1958, by the *Nautilus* under the command of Commander William Robert Anderson. The atomic-powered submarine, carrying 116 persons (14 officers, 98 crewmen, and 4 civilian scientists), traveled 8,146 miles at a speed of 20 knots. It left Pearl Harbor Hawaii, July 23, 1958; crossed the Pacific Ocean through the Bering Strait; surfaced and went under the ice cap at Point Barrow, Alaska, on August 1, 1958, at 11:15 P.M., E.D.T. Traveling 1,830 miles under the ice in 96 hours, it arrived under the North Pole August 3, 1958. The *Nautilus* then continued its voyage, reaching Iceland August 7, 1958. The expedition was designated "Northwest Passage."

Submarine disaster occurred March 25, 1915, when the F-4, commanded by Lieutenant Alfred L. Ede, sank with a loss of 21 men while approximately one and a half miles out of Honolulu Harbor, Hawaii.

Submarine expressly designed and built to fire guided missiles was the U.S.S. *Grayback,* ordered June 19, 1952, laid down July 1, 1954, launched July 2, 1957, and commissioned March 7, 1958, at Mare Island, Calif. The *Grayback,* designed to fire Regulus I and Regulus II missiles, was completed July 31, 1958. It was 322½ feet long, 1,740 tons light, 2,287 tons surface, and 3,638 tons submerged and carried a crew of 85 officers and men.

Submarine fitted with an internal combustion engine was the *Argonaut,* invented by Simon Lake and built by the Columbian Iron Works and Dry Dock Company of Baltimore, Md., in 1897. A working model had been built by Lake in 1894. He patented the engine on April 7, 1896 (No. 557,835), and the submarine vessel on April 20, 1897 (No. 581,213). The *Argonaut* was also the first submarine to salvage sunken objects of value. On December 16, 1897, a demonstration was given on the Patapsco River during which 22 representatives of newspapers made short descents ranging from an hour and a half to four hours.

Submarine jet propulsion device patent was obtained by Fritz Zwicky of Pasadena, Calif., who filed his application on October 23, 1944, and was granted patent No. 2,461,797 on February 15, 1949, on a "reaction propelled device for operation through water." The patent was assigned to the Aerojet Engineering Corporation, Azusa, Calif., which constructed, tested, and demonstrated the device in September 1943 in the company research laboratory at Pasadena, Calif.

The First

SUBMARINE—Continued

Submarine of the U.S. Navy christened by a President's wife was the U.S.S. *Nautilus* (SSN 571) launched January 21, 1954, at the shipyard of the Electric Boat Division of General Dynamics Corporation at Groton, Conn. The ship was christened by Mamie Geneva Doud Eisenhower.

Submarine powered by a liquid-metal-cooled atomic reactor was the U.S.S. *Seawolf,* SSN-575, ordered July 19, 1952, laid down September 15, 1953, and launched July 21, 1955, at Groton, Conn., under the sponsorship of Mrs. William Sterling Cole. The *Seawolf,* which was completed March 30, 1957, had a displacement of 3,260 tons light, 3,495 tons standard surface, and 4,110 tons submerged. It had a complement of 94. A prototype of the power plant was built by the General Electric Company at West Milton, N.Y. The first commanding officer was Richard Boyer Laning, U.S.N.

Submarine refloated was the U.S.S *Squalus* (SS-192), launched at Portsmouth, N.H., September 14, 1938. It foundered in 240 feet of water off Portsmouth on May 23, 1939, with a loss of 26 men. The ship was completely raised after a 113-day job and towed back to Portsmouth on September 13, 1939. On May 5, 1940, her name was changed to the U.S.S. *Sailfish.*

Submarine (submerged) broadcast. *See under* Radio broadcast

Submarine submerged for 2 weeks was the atomic submarine *Nautilus* (SSN-571), which left Groton, Conn., on August 19, 1957, and remained under water 14 days and 3½ hours, traveling 5,007 miles as part of NATO exercises in the North Atlantic under Commander William Robert Anderson. The submarine went to 180 miles of the North Pole (latitude 87°), spending 5½ days traveling 1,000 miles submerged under the Arctic pack. The maneuvers ended September 24, 1957, and the *Nautilus* returned to Groton on October 28, 1957.

Submarine that was practical and able to submerge was the *Holland No. 9,* built by the John P[hilip] Holland Torpedo Boat Company of New York City. Launched March 17, 1898, it submerged off Staten Island, remaining under water 1 hour 40 minutes. Its overall length was 53 feet 11 inches, its diameter 10 feet 3 inches; its equipment included a dynamite gun and one torpedo tube. The vessel was purchased by the U.S. Navy on April 11, 1900, for $150,000 (though the actual cost was greater) and placed in commission October 12, 1900.

Submarine to circumnavigate the world was the *Gudgeon* (SS 567), which sailed from Pearl Harbor, Hawaii, on July 8, 1957, visited Asian, African, and European ports, and returned to Hawaii February 21, 1958. In 228 days the ship traveled approximately 25,000 miles. The *Gudgeon* was 269 feet 2 inches long, had a complement of 83 and a

The First

2,050-ton displacement, and was launched June 11, 1952, at the Portsmouth Naval Shipyard, Portsmouth, N.H. It was commissioned Nov. 21, 1952.

Submarine to cross the Atlantic Ocean under its own power was the *E-1,* keel laid December 22, 1909, launched May 27, 1911, at the Fore River Shipbuilding Co., Quincy, Mass. It was commissioned February 14, 1912, and its first commander was Lieutenant Chester William Nimitz. The ship left Newport, R.I., on December 4, 1917, and arrived at Ponta Delgada, the Azores, to protect the islands from German attack by submarines. It returned to New London, Conn., on September 17, 1918. It was 135 feet 3 inches long and displaced 342 tons. On July 17, 1920, it was reclassified *SS 24.*

Submarine to cross the Atlantic Ocean within 9 days was the *Skate* (SSN–578), which left New London, Conn., on February 24, 1958, and arrived at Portland, England, on March 5, 1958, making the 3,161-mile trip in 8 days 11 hours. In 176 hours it traveled 2,828 miles, submerged until entering the English Channel, south of the tip of Conwall.

Submarine to have 2 complete crews was the U.S.S. *George Washington* (SSBN-598), commissioned December 30, 1959. The first crew, the blue crew under Commander James Butler Osborn, reported at Groton, Conn., in June 1959; the second crew, the gold crew under Commander John Lawrence From, Jr., reported in September 1959. While one crew is at sea operating the submarine, the other is ashore for recreation and refresher training. The 2 crews enable the submarine to remain on station for extended periods of time to take advantage of its nuclear power plant capabilities.

Submarine to make a submerged passage from the Atlantic to the Pacific via the North Pole (The Northwest Passage) was by the *Seadragon,* commanded by George P. Steele, 2nd, which sailed from Portsmouth, N.H., on August 1, 1960, cleared the ice pack September 3, 1960, and docked at Pearl Harbor, Hawaii, on September 14, 1960.

Submarine to make more than 13,000 dives was the U.S.S. *Sarda* (AGSS-488), 312 feet long with a 2,000 ton displacement, launched August 24, 1945, at Portsmouth Naval Shipyard, Portsmouth, N.H., commissioned April 19, 1946. The first officer was Commander Chester William Nimitz, Jr. The ship completed 13,851 dives and surfacings and served as a training ship at the Groton, Conn., submarine base. Stricken from the register May 30, 1964, it was sold for scrap in May of 1965.

Submarine to sink a Japanese ship was the U.S.S. *Swordfish* (SS 193), commanded by Lieutenant Chester Carl Smith, which torpedoed the 8,662-ton Japanese freighter *Atsutusan Maru* on December 16, 1941, off the coast of Indochina. The *Swordfish* was 311 feet long and displaced 2,350 tons. It was launched April 1, 1939, and commissioned July 22, 1939. (The ship hit a mine on its

The First

13th patrol in January 1945, near Okinawa; all aboard were lost.)

Submarine to sink a man-of-war in actual warfare was the *Hunley,* named after its designer. On the night of February 17, 1864, Lieutenant George Dixon of the Confederate *Hunley* succeeded in approaching the U.S.S. *Housatonic,* a new ship of 1,400 tons displacement, which was awash off Charleston, S.C., and sank it by exploding a torpedo under its bottom. The wave thrown up by the explosion swamped the submarine (because its forward hatch was open) and killed its crew. The submarine was built by [Horace L.] Hunley, McClintock & Watson in the shops of Parks & Lyons, Mobile, Ala., in 1863. The interior height of the vessel was 5 feet, its breadth 4 feet, its speed 4 knots. Its propeller was operated by eight men using hand power. There were no provisions for storage of air. *(John Thomas Scharf—History of the Confederate States Navy, from Its Organization to the Surrender of Its Last Vessel)*

Submarine to travel under ice for 12 days was the U.S.S. *Skate* (SSN-578), which logged 3,090 miles, surfacing 10 times. The submarine left New London, Conn., on March 4, 1959, traveled under the Arctic ice at the North Pole, surfacing through the ice on March 17, 1959. It was the first ship to surface at the North Pole.

Submarine to travel under the North Pole from the East was the U.S.S. *Skate* (SSN 578) built by the Electric Boat Division of General Dynamics Corp. The *Skate* took off from New London, Conn., on July 30, 1958, at 9:47 A.M. E.D.T. with a crew of 10 officers, 9 scientists and technicians, and 87 enlisted men. It passed between Iceland and Greenland and sent the message August 12, 1958: "North Geographic Pole August eleventh—now in polynya—about forty miles from pole—all well." The submarine, under Commander James Francis Calvert of Cleveland, Ohio, logged 12,000 miles of which 10,100 miles were submerged. The voyage ended at Boston, Mass., on September 22, 1958. *(James Calvert—Surface at the Pole, the Extraordinary Voyages of the U.S.S. Skate)*

Submarine (U.S.) destroyed in World War II was the *Sealion* (SS-195), keel laid June 20, 1938, launched May 25, 1939, at the Electric Boat Division of General Dynamics at Groton, Conn., and commissioned November 27, 1939. The ship, 311 feet long with a 2,350 ton displacement, was docked at Machina Wharf at the Navy Yard at Cavite, Philippine Islands, on December 10, 1941, when a group of 54 Japanese airplanes, in 2 groups of 27 each, dropped bombs putting the ship out of commission—4 men were lost. Since the closest repair facilities were at Pearl Harbor, Honolulu, the *Sealion* was towed out to sea on December 25, 1941, where it was exploded by 3 depth charges placed inside. Lieutenant Commander Richard G. Voge was the commanding officer.

The First

Submarine (U.S.) sunk by an enemy submarine was the *Corvina* (SS 226), of Task Force 72, length 311 feet 9 inches, breadth 27 feet 3 inches, draft 15 feet 3 inches, displacement 2,424 tons, launched May 9, 1943, at the Electric Boat Company, Groton, Conn. The ship was commissioned August 6, 1943. It left Pearl Harbor, Hawaii, on its first war patrol on November 4, 1943; refueled November 6, 1943, at Johnston Island; surfaced north of Guinea in Australian waters (Lat. 50° 50 N: Long. 151° 10 E); and was torpedoed south of Truk on November 16, 1943, by I-176, which fired 3 torpedoes, 2 of which hit. The ship, with a crew of 82, was presumed lost on December 23, 1943, and the loss announced March 14, 1944. Commander Roderick Shanahan Rooney was in command.

Submarine with a high-tensile-steel pressure hull was the U.S.S. *Balao* (SS-285), authorized December 23, 1941, keel laid June 26, 1942, launched October 27, 1942, at the Portsmouth Naval Shipyard, Portsmouth, N.H., and commissioned Feburary 4, 1943. The ship was 311 feet 8 inches long, 273 feet 3 inches in breadth, with a 2,424-ton displacement, The first commanding officer was Lieutenant Commander Richard H. Crane.

Submarines to rendezvous at the North Pole were the *Skate* (2,360 tons) of the Atlantic Fleet and the *Seadragon* (2,360 tons) of the Pacific Fleet, which surfaced August 2, 1962, at the North Pole through a small opening in the ice. The *Skate* (SSN 578) commander Joseph L. Skoog, Jr., of Seattle, Wash., left New London, Conn., on July 7, 1962, and returned August 28, 1962. The *Seadragon* (SSN 584) commander Charles D. Summitt of Nashville, Tenn., left Pearl Harbor, Hawaii, July 12, 1962, and arrived at Seattle, Wash., on August 27, 1962. The submarines met July 31, 1962. The successful mission was announced August 2, 1962.

Submarine with closed-circuit television. *See under* Television

Submarine with two nuclear reactors was the *Triton,* SSR(N) 586, built by the Electric Boat Company, Groton, Conn. The submarine was launched August 19, 1958, completed May 19, 1959, and commissioned November 10, 1959. It was 447 feet long, 37 feet wide, and had a draught of 25 feet. It displaced 5,650 tons light, 5,900 tons standard, and 7,750 tons submerged. It had a cruising range of 110,000 miles and a complement of 148 officers and crew. Its initial trip to sea was made September 28, 1959. The first captain was Edward Latimer Beach. The two water-cooled nuclear reactors were built by the General Electric Company. Each reactor provided current for a propeller.

Submerged circumnavigation of the earth was accomplished by the U.S.S. *Triton,* SSR(N) 586, which left New London, Conn., February 16, 1960,

The First

SUBMARINE—*Continued*

crossed the equator February 24, 1960, and completed the submerged navigation April 25, 1960, having traveled 41,500 miles in 84 days. It returned to New London on May 11, 1960. The hull of the submarine was submerged during the entire trip but the upper portion broached the surface twice. The nuclear-powered *Triton* was 447 feet long and had a 37-foot beam; it was 5,650 tons light, 5,900 tons standard, and 7,750 tons submerged. It carried a crew of 13 officers and 135 men and was commanded by Captain Edward Latimer Beach. The *Triton* was laid down May 21, 1956, launched August 19, 1958, and commissioned November 10, 1959.

Submerged submarine to fire a Polaris missile was the U.S.S. *George Washington* (SSBN-598), commanded by Commander James Butler Osborn, which submerged 90 feet about 30 miles off Cape Canaveral, Fla., on July 20, 1960, and fired a 28,500-pound Polaris missile at 1:39 P.M. and a second one at 4:32 P.M. The 28-foot two-stage rocket traveled 1,150 statute miles eastward in less than 14 minutes. News of the firing was sent to President Dwight David Eisenhower: "Polaris . . . from out of the deep to target. Perfect."

Telephone message from a submarine. *See* Radio telephone: Two-way radio conversation between a submerged submarine and another vessel

Underwater telecast from a submarine. *See under* Television—Telecast

SUBMARINE CABLE PLOW. *See* Plow

SUBMARINE-ESCAPE TRAINING TANK

Submarine-escape training tank was placed in operation August 15, 1930, at the U.S. Submarine Base, New London, Conn. It was a cylindrical "water tower" column 100 feet deep, with a spiral stairway winding around it and an abutting elevator shaft. Candidates entered the tank through locks at various depths, wearing the submarine-escape lung, and climbed up a rope, hand over hand, in order to slow down their ascent sufficiently to let their bodies become gradually adjusted to the decrease in pressure.

Women to take the submarine-escape test and receive certificates were Ensigns Eleanor MacDonald and Glenn Huckstep (Nurses Corps), U.S.N.R., who received certificates July 12, 1943, from Lieutenant George W. Albin, Jr., at the Submarine-Escape Training Tank, New London, Conn.

SUBMARINE "LUNG" was the result of the combined efforts of two naval officers, Lieutenant Charles Bowers Momsen and Chief Gunner Clarence Louis Tibbals, and a civilian, Frank M. Hobson, civil engineer of the Naval Bureau of Construction and Repairs. Momsen and Tibbals, who tested the device May 10, 1929, by escaping

The First

from it in depths of water as great as 206 feet, were rewarded with the Distinguished Service Cross. Hobson received a year's pay for his part in the invention, which consisted of an oxygen bag with a canister of soda lime and tubes similar to those of an army gas mask. The Navy put the invention to test under actual conditions on August 30, 1929, on the Thames River at New London, Conn. Twenty-six officers and men came out of the after hatch of the submerged submarine S-4.

SUBMARINE TELEGRAPH CABLE. *See* Cable

SUBWAY

Bank to operate a window in a subway station. *See under* Bank

Municipal subway, and the first shallow subway built under city streets for street railway transportation as distinguished from a deep tunnel, was the Tremont Street Subway, Boston, Mass., construction of which was begun on March 28, 1895. The section between Public Gardens and Park Street was opened for traffic September 1, 1897, and the section to North Station September 3, 1898. The subway was built by the City of Boston at a cost of $4,369,000 and leased to the Boston Elevated Railway at an annual rental of 4½ percent of construction cost.

Pneumatic subway was invented by Alfred Ely Beach and was known as the Beach Pneumatic Underground Railway of New York City. The company was incorporated for freight traffic on June 1, 1868, and for passenger traffic on May 3, 1869, with a capital stock of $5 million. The system was opened to the public on February 26, 1870. The tunnel was 312 feet long and ran from the west curb line of Broadway at Warren Street down the middle of Broadway to a point south of Murray Street. It consisted of a circular tube 9 feet in diameter built of iron plates for 60 feet on the curves and brick masonry the rest of the way. The cars, which were well upholstered, carried 22 persons. They were propelled by a rotary blower that drove a blast of air through the tunnel against the rear of the car, carrying it along "like a sailboat before the wind." *(James Walker—Fifty Years of Rapid Transit)*

Subway car with side doors was placed in service February 16, 1909, when 8 cars of the Interborough Rapid Transit of New York City left Lenox Avenue and 148th Street going south. The side doors, 4 feet from each end of the car, were opened and closed by a pneumatic-lever system. The cars cost $12,000 each. The doors were the invention of James McElroy of the Consolidated Car Heating Company.

Subway (rapid transit) was the Interborough Rapid Transit route in New York City from City Hall (Brooklyn Bridge), north under Lafayette Street, Fourth and Park avenues to Grand Central, west along 42nd Street to Times Square, then north on Broadway to 145th Street. The line was

The First

opened October 27, 1904, and at 7:00 P.M. 111,881 passengers paid a nickel each to ride for 26 minutes on the express train, 46 minutes on the local. Trains had run underground before 1904, but the Interborough Rapid Transit Company established the first rapid transit subway.

Train to run automatically without conductors or motormen was placed in operation January 4, 1962, between Grand Central station and Times Square station in the New York City subway system. The train carried a motorman who stood by without performing any duties—a safety measure demanded by the transport workers' union, then involved in a labor dispute with the New York City Transit Authority.

SUCTION VACUUM CLEANER. *See* Vacuum cleaner: Suction-type vacuum cleaner

SUFFRAGE

State to provide universal manhood suffrage without restriction as to property or wealth was Vermont. The state constitution agreed upon at a general convention held July 28, 1777, at Windsor, Vt., permitted all freemen (natural-born citizens over 21 years of age) to elect officers and be elected to office.

Suffrage for women. *See* Woman suffrage

SUGAR

Sugar and glucose from cornstarch were manufactured by the Union Sugar Company, New York City. The process was based on patent No. 42,727, dated May 10, 1864, for a "sugar produced from corn and beets." The patent was granted to Frederick W. Gossling and assigned to Gossling, Henry F. Briggs, and Leman Bradley of Buffalo, N.Y. Gossling also received patent No. 45,561 on December 20, 1864, for a new and improved compound sugar made by a combination of cane sugar or cane syrup with corn syrup.

Sugar beets were grown about 1830 at Ensfield, Pa., by the Beet Sugar Society of Philadelphia, of which James Donaldson was president. The first mill was the Northampton Beet Sugar Company, erected by David Lee Child in Northampton, Mass., in 1838 (incorporated March 10, 1837). In 1839, 1,300 pounds of sugar was produced from beets low in sucrose content. In 1839 the company received a $100 premium from the Massachusetts Agricultural Society and a silver medal at the Massachusetts Charitable Mechanics Association's exhibition. The factory did not operate after 1840. *(Franklin Stewart Harris—The Sugar Beet in America)*

Sugar cane was brought to Louisiana by Jesuit priests in 1751 from Hispaniola (Santo Domingo). It was used for making taffia, a kind of rum. Sugar was made from sugar cane in St. Bernard Parish, La., in 1791 by Antonio Méndez. The sugar industry started with the work of Étienne de Bore, who in 1794 planted cane and in 1795 harvested a crop

The First

of sugar which sold for $12,000. At his death, his wealth was estimated at $300,000, all from sugar. *(William Carter Stubs—Sugar Cane; Experiments in Cultivation. Bulletin of the Agricultural Experiment Station, Louisiana State University and A.&M. College. 2nd Ser., No. 66)*

Sugar cane 9-roll mill with common gearing and a single engine was built by the Fulton Iron Works Co., St. Louis, Mo., in 1892 for the Cora Plantation, operated by the New Iberville Planting Company, White Castle, La. It milled approximately 170 tons of cane in an 8-hour day.

Sugar refinery (practical) was opened in New Orleans, La., in 1791 by Antonio Méndez. Attempts had been made in 1759, 1764, 1765, and 1766, but because the exact crystallization point and the proper use of lime were not then known, the mills were unsuccessful and were abandoned. The first commercial mill began operation in New Orleans in 1795. *(Henry Rightor—Standard History of New Orleans, Louisiana)*

SULFANILAMIDE

Sulfanilamide was produced in December 1930 at the Jackson Laboratory of E. I. du Pont de Nemours & Company, Wilmington, Del., for use as a diazo component in an experimental disperse azo dye for cellulose acetate fibers. Acetanilide reacted with chlorosulfonic acid, and the reaction was followed by amidation and hydrolysis. Sulfanilamide was not used in medicine until about five years later.

Sulfanilamide as a treatment for infections of streptococcic origins was used in 1935 by Dr. Ashley Weech of Babies Hospital, New York City, but was not reported. Dr. Perrin Hamilton Long of Johns Hopkins Hospital, Baltimore, Md., obtained a sample from E. I. du Pont de Nemours & Company, Inc., on September 9, 1936, and a one-pound vial on November 9, 1936. Dr. Long and Eleanor Bliss reported on their use of the drug—in treating a seven-year-old child with erysipelas—to the Southern Medical Association, Baltimore, Md., on November 17, 1936. *(Journal of the American Medical Association. Vol. 108, No. 1. Jan. 2, 1937)*

SULFATE OF QUININE. *See* Quinine: Quinine sulfate

SULFUR DEPOSIT was discovered in the United States in 1869 in a salt dome in Calcasieu Parish, La. It was later developed as the Sulphur Dome of the Union Sulphur Company. Sulfur was first extracted from a well in the dome in October 1895 by Herman Frasch of Cleveland, Ohio. On October 20, 1891, he received patents No. 461,429 and 461,431 on "mining sulphur" and No. 461,430 on "an apparatus for mining sulphur." Sulfur was melted in the ground and pumped to the surface in a liquid state to congeal in bins or blocks.

The First

SULFUR MINE (offshore) was the Grand Isle offshore mine, 2,000 feet beneath the bottom of the Gulf of Mexico, about seven miles off the Louisiana coast. The mine was operated by means of a steel structure equipped with boilers, generators, and drilling rigs situated in 50 feet of water. The deposit was discovered by the Humble Oil and Refining Company and the mine built and operated by the Freeport Sulphur Company. The first sulfur was obtained on March 14, 1960.

SULFURIC ACID was produced by John Harrison in 1793 in a little shop at Third and Green streets, Philadelphia, Pa. At first the acid was concentrated in fragile glass retorts. Later, platinum containers were used instead. The business founded by Harrison, known as Harrison Brothers & Company, was purchased in 1917 by E. I. du Pont de Nemours & Company, Inc., of Wilmington, Del.

SUNDAY SCHOOL

Jewish Sunday School was established under the auspices of the Hebrew Sunday School Society of Philadelphia, Pa., organized March 4, 1838, by Rebecca Gratz for "the religious instruction and general improvement of children of the Jewish faith." The first meeting of the board of the society was held February 4, 1838. The Sunday school began with 50 pupils.

Protestant Sunday School was opened in Christ Church, Savannah, Ga., in 1736 by John Wesley and was under the leadership of Charles Delamotte. Before the Sunday evening services, Wesley instructed between 30 and 40 children and heard them recite their catechism. Prior to this, religious instruction had been given to children individually and in small groups which hardly merited the designation of "school." *(William Bacon Stevens—History of Georgia, Vol. 1. p. 341)*

SUPERINTENDENT OF DOCUMENTS. *See under* Government Printing Office

SUPREME COURT (state)

Associate justice (black) of a state supreme court was Jonathan Jasper Wright of Beaufort, S.C., who served as 1 of the 3 members of the court from February 2, 1870, to December 1, 1877.

Chief justice (woman) of a state supreme court was Lorna Elizabeth Lockwood of Douglas, Ariz., who was elected as an associate justice to the Arizona Supreme Court in 1961 and served to 1965. She was then elected as chief justice, serving from 1965 to 1975.

State Supreme Court composed entirely of women was the Special Supreme Court of Texas appointed by Governor Pat Morris Neff on January 8, 1925. When an application for writ of error in the case of *W. T. Johnson, et al.* vs. *J. M. Darr, et al.*, from El Paso County (a Woodmen of the World case) reached the Supreme Court of Texas, the three members thereof found themselves disqualified to consider it and immediately certified

The First

their disqualifications to the governor as required by law. Thereupon the governor appointed Hortense Ward of Houston as Special Chief Justice, and Hattie L. Henenberg of Dallas and Ruth Brazzil of Galveston as Special Associate Justices to hear and determine the cause of action. They were sworn in January 8, 1925. The case was finally decided by the Special Supreme Court on May 23, 1925, affirming the judgment of the Court of Civil Appeals.

SUPREME COURT (U.S.)

Associate Justice nominee to die before occupying his seat was Edwin McMasters Stanton, appointed by President Ulysses Simpson Grant on December 20, 1869. Stanton died December 24, 1869.

Associate Justice of the Supreme Court to become Chief Justice was Edward Douglass White, who was appointed Associate Justice March 12, 1894, and Chief Justice December 12, 1910. He took his seat December 19, 1910, and served until May 2, 1921, shortly before his death on May 19, 1921. However, White was not the first man who had served as an Associate Justice to be appointed Chief Justice. In 1795 President Washington appointed John Rutledge as Chief Justice, and Rutledge actually served during one session of the Court before the appointment was rejected by the Senate. Rutledge had been appointed as one of the original five Associate Justices in 1789, but had delayed taking his seat until 1790 and had resigned in 1791.

Associate Justice of the Supreme Court to participate in a television program was Hugo LaFayette Black, senior justice, who was interviewed in his home at Alexandria, Va., on December 3, 1968, for CBS News by Eric Sevareid and Martin Agronsky.

Associate Justice of the Supreme Court who had been a representative in Congress was Gabriel Duvall of Maryland, who served in the House of Representatives from November 11, 1794, to March 28, 1796, and as associate justice from February 3, 1812, to January 15, 1835.

Associate Justice of the Supreme Court who was a black was Thurgood Marshall of Maryland appointed June 13, 1967, by President Lyndon Baines Johnson, confirmed by the Senate 69-11 on August 30, 1967, and sworn in September 1, 1967, in a private ceremony in Justice Hugo Lafayette Black's office in the Supreme Court building. He was publicly sworn in at the opening ceremony of the new term on October 2, 1967, witnessed by the President. He was the 96th Justice.

Associate Justice of the Supreme Court who was Jewish was Louis Dembitz Brandeis, who was appointed on January 28, 1916, by President Woodrow Wilson. The nomination was confirmed by the Senate, June 1, 1916, and Bran-

The First

deis was sworn in June 3, 1916. *(Alpheus Thomas Mason—Brandeis, Lawyer and Judge in the Modern State)*

Black lawyer to practice before the Supreme Court. *See* Lawyer: Black lawyer to practice in the United States Supreme Court

Chief Justice of the Supreme Court was John Jay of New York, who was appointed by President George Washington on September 24, 1789. His appointment was confirmed on September 26, 1789, and he served until June 29, 1795. *(William Jay—Life of John Jay)*

Chief Justice of the Supreme Court who was Catholic was Roger Brooke Taney of Frederick, Md., who was appointed by President Andrew Jackson to succeed John Marshall and served from March 28, 1836, to his death on October 12, 1864. *(Bernard Christian Steiner—Life of Roger Brooke Taney)*

Chief Justice of the United States to administer the oath of office to his successor was Earl Warren, who swore in his successor, Warren Earl Burger, on June 23, 1969, in the chamber of the Supreme Court, Washington, D.C.

Chief Justice of the United States to serve in a presidential cabinet was John Marshall of Virginia, Chief Justice from February 4, 1801, to July 6, 1835. He served also as President John Adam's ad interim Secretary of State from February 4, 1801, to March 4, 1801, but accepted only the salary of the Chief Justice. Previously he had served as Secretary of State from May 13, 1800, entering on his duties June 6, 1800, and serving until February 4, 1801, when he was appointed to the Supreme Court.

Chief Justice of the United States who had been a representative in Congress was John Marshall of Virginia, who served in the House of Representatives from March 4, 1799, to June 7, 1800, and as Chief Justice from Febuary 4, 1801, to July 6, 1835, when he died.

Chief Justice whose nomination was not confirmed was John Rutledge, a Federalist, of South Carolina, who was appointed Chief Justice by President George Washington during the adjournment of Congress. He served at a salary of $4,000 a year from July 1, 1795, to December 15, 1795, on which date the Senate rejected the nomination. He presided at the August 1795 term. Rutledge had served as an Associate Justice from September 26, 1789, to March 5, 1791, at a salary of $3,500 a year and had resigned to become Chief Justice of South Carolina.

Clerk of the Supreme Court was John Tucker of Boston, Mass., appointed Febuary 3, 1790. It was required "that he reside and keep his office at the seat of the national government, and that he do not practice, either as an attorney or a counsellor

The First

in this court, while he shall continue to be clerk of the same."

Congressional act declared unconstitutional by the Supreme Court. *See under* Congress (U.S.)

Law secretary (black) of the Supreme Court was William Thaddeus Coleman, Jr., of Philadelphia, Pa., who served as secretary to Justice Felix Frankfurter from September 1, 1948 until August 31, 1949.

Lawyers admitted before the bar of the Supreme Court. *See under* Lawyer

Members of a family admitted simultaneously to practice in the Supreme Court of the United States were William Henry Faust, Mrs. William Henry Faust, and William Henry Faust, Jr., of Indianapolis, Ind., who were admitted March 1, 1940.

Page (black) was Charles Vernon Bush, who served from September 27, 1954, to July 13, 1957.

President to become a Chief Justice. *See under* President (U.S.)

Supreme Court first session began February 1, 1790, in the Royal Exchange Building, New York City, and was adjourned due to lack of a quorum. No cases were argued. The second session opened August 2, 1790.

Supreme Court justice impeachment proceedings. *See* Impeachment: Impeachment proceedings against a justice of the Supreme Court of the United States

Supreme Court justice who was nominated but who did not serve was Robert Hanson Harrison of Maryland, who was nominated by President George Washington on September 24, 1789, and whose appointment was confirmed by the Senate on September 26, 1789. Harrison declined the appointment on October 1, 1789. He also declined a later appointment as chancellor of Maryland.

Supreme Court nominee rejected was William Paterson of New Jersey, who was nominated February 20, 1793, by President George Washington. His name was sent to the Senate for approval on February 27, 1793. As the office was created during the term (1789-1790), Paterson was the senator from New Jersey; his name was withdrawn because of this technicality. On March 4, 1793, Washington renominated Paterson under a recess appointment, and he served from March 14, 1793, to September 9, 1806. *(Gertrude Sceery Wood—William Paterson of New Jersey)*

Supreme Court of the United States consisted of Chief Justice John Jay of New York (1789–1795), and Associate Justices John Rutledge of South Carolina (1789–1791), William Cushing of Massachusetts (1789–1810), James Wilson of Pennsylvania (1789–1798), John Blair of Virginia (1789–1796), and Robert Hanson Harrison of

The First

SUPREME COURT (U.S.)—*Continued*

Maryland (1789–1790). The appointments were made by President George Washington, September 24, and confirmed by the Senate on September 26, 1789. The Judiciary Act of 1789, which implemented the clause in the Constitution providing for the Supreme Court, was passed September 24, 1789 (1 Stat. L. 73). It provided for six members—a chief justice and five associate justices—four of whom were to constitute a quorum. The first session began February 1, 1790, in the Royal Exchange Building on Broad Street, New York City, and lasted ten days, terminating on February 10. Two sessions were held each year, beginning the first Monday of February and of August. Richard Wenman was the first crier of the Court, and John Tucker of Massachusetts, appointed February 3, 1790, was the first clerk.

Woman admitted to practice before the Supreme Court of the United States was Belva Ann Bennett Lockwood, who was admitted on March 3, 1879. The bill admitting women passed the House of Representatives February 21, 1878, and the Senate February 7, 1879. It was titled an "act to relieve certain legal disabilities of women" (20 Stat. L. 292) and was signed February 15, 1879, by President Rutherford Birchard Hayes. It provided that any women member of the bar of good moral character who had practiced for three years before a state supreme court was eligible for admittance to practice before the Supreme Court of the United States.

SUPREME COURT (U.S.) DECISION

Supreme Court commerce case. *See* Commerce case

Supreme Court decision was West (plaintiff) vs. Barnes, tried in the August 1791 term, which began Aug. 8. The motion was refused as "writs of error made by clerk of the circuit court for Rhode Island district to remove causes to this court from inferior courts, can regularly issue only from the clerk's office of court." No cases were argued during the first 4 terms of the court (Feb. 1790—Aug. 1790—Feb. 1791—Aug. 1791). *(Alexander James Dallas—Reports of Cases Ruled and Adjusted in the Several Courts of the United States)*

Supreme Court decision between states was the result of a bill in equity between New York and Connecticut in the term which began August 5, 1799. Chief Justice Oliver Ellsworth presided. The decision read: "As the state of New York was not a party to the suit, nor interested in the decision of these suits, an injunction ought not to issue." (4 Dallas 1). *(James Brown Scott—Judicial Settlement of Controversies Between States of the American Union)*

Supreme Court decision establishing the power of the United States as greater than that of the individual state was made February 20, 1809,

The First

when Chief Justice John Marshall rendered an opinion sustaining the federal power and ordered a mandamus issued to carry a previous decree into effect. Judge Richard Peters of the United States District Court of Pennsylvania had decreed that certain prize money be paid to a Mr. Olmstead of Connecticut for his capture of a British sloop during the Revolutionary War. The state of Pennsylvania refused to recognize Olmstead's claim or to award the prize money. As the state militia was called out to stop the United States marshal from serving his order, the United States marshal summoned a posse of 2,000 men, but delayed service in order to avoid bloodshed. The power of the federal government was later recognized. In the case of the United States versus Judge Peters (5 Cranch 1150), it was decided that the legislature of a state cannot annul the judgment or determine the jurisdiction of a United States court.

Supreme Court decision in a state boundary case was made in 1846 when Chief Justice Taney ruled that a bill "should be dismissed upon the ground that this court under the Constitution of the United States have not the power to try such a question between states, or redress a wrong, even if the wrong is proved to have been done." On March 16, 1832, Rhode Island, the complainant, had petitioned the Supreme Court to settle a boundary controversy with Massachusetts. (Reports United States Supreme Court 7 Peters 651; 11 Peters 226; 12 Peters 657; 12 Peters 755; 13 Peters 23; 14 Peters 210, 15 Peters 233; 4 Howard 591.) *(James Brown Scott—Judicial Settlement of Controversies Between States of the American Union)*

Supreme Court decision that a state law was unconstitutional was made March 16, 1810, in the case of Robert Fletcher of Amherst, N.H., who bought 13,000 acres of land for $3,000 on May 14, 1803, from John Peck of Boston, Mass., the court ruled that Georgia's rescinding act violated the contract clause of Article 1, Section 10, of the Federal Constitution. Chief Justice John Marshall decided that "the Union has a constitution, the supremacy of which all acknowledge, and which imposes limits to the legislation of the several states, which none claim a right to pass." *U.S. Reports, Vol. 10, [6 Cranch 87]: Error to the Circular Court for the District of Massachusetts in an Action of Covenant Brought by Fletcher against Peck)*

Supreme Court decision that reversed the decision of a state supreme court was rendered in 1813. The Virginia Court of Appeals in the case of *Fairfax's Devisee* vs. *Hunter's Lessee* held the confiscation of Lord Fairfax's estate by Virginia in the Revolutionary War illegal. A writ of error was obtained and the case was argued as *Martin* vs. *Hunter's Lessee.* The court in 1816 unanimously sustained the validity of the 25th section of Chapter 20 of the act of September 24, 1789 (1 Stat. L.

The First

73), which established the judicial system and established for all time the right of the Supreme Court to review the determinations of the highest state courts in cases involving the Constitution, and federal laws or treaties. *(Henry Wheaton— Reports of Cases Argued and Adjudged in the Supreme Court of the United States)*

Supreme Court decision to void an act of Congress (Act of September 24, 1789) was Marbury vs. Madison, in the Feburary 3, 1803, term. President John Adams appointed William Marbury justice of the peace. President Thomas Jefferson instructed Secretary of State James Madison not to deliver the commission. *(William Cranch—Reports of Cases Argued and Adjudged in the Supreme Court of the United States in August and December Terms 1801 and Feburary 1803)*

SURETY COMPANY. *See* Insurance

SURGEON. *See* Physician

SURGEON (army). *See* Army officer: Air surgeon; Army officer: Woman assistant army surgeon

SURGEON GENERAL (army). *See* Army officer

SURGEON GENERAL (navy). *See* Naval officer

SURGERY MANUAL. *See* Medical book

SURGICAL OPERATION
  Abdominal operation of the kind called ovariotomy, the surgical removal of an ovarian tumor, was performed by Dr. Ephraim McDowell upon Jane Todd Crawford on December 13, 1809, at Danville, Ky. The operation was performed without an anesthetic. She was 45 years of age at the time of the operation, and lived to be 78. *(Mary Thompson Young Valentine—Biography of Ephraim McDowell)*

Anesthesia. *See* Anesthesia

Appendicitis operation (appendectomy) was performed in Davenport, Iowa, January 4, 1885, by Dr. William West Grant, on Mary Gartside, aged 22. Dr. Grant was the first physician deliberately to open the abdomen and sever the appendix from the cecum, on a diagnosis of perforation of the appendix. The operation was the first successful appendectomy. The patient lived until 1919, when she died of a quite different illness. *(Colorado Medicine. August 1933)*

Artificial aortic valve was made by Dr. Charles Anthony Hufnagel of the Georgetown University Medical Center, Georgetown University Hospital, Washington, D.C., and successfully fitted on a 30-year-old patient on September 11, 1952. It was made of Flexiglas and contained a float three fourths of an inch in diameter that rose and slipped into one of three sockets in the side of the valve sleeve on the heart's upbeat, when blood was forced into the aorta.

The First

Cesarean operation (successful) was performed by Dr. Jessee Bennett, on his wife Elizabeth Hog Bennett, on January 14, 1794, in Edom, Kanawha Valley, Virginia. Bennett had asked Dr. Alexander Humphreys of Staunton, Va., to assist in performing the operation but because of the slight chance of success Humphreys had declined. Dr. Bennett performed the operation with the assistance of two blacks, who held the patient. She was placed on a table made of two planks laid on a couple of barrels and was given laudanum in lieu of an anesthetic *(Virginia Medical Monthly. Vol. 55, No. 10. January 1929)*

Epileptic case treated by elevation of the skull cap was demonstrated on November 2, 1933, by Dr. Karl Winfield Ney, professor of neurosurgery at the New York Medical College and Flower Hospital in New York City, before the members of the Eastern Homeopathic Medical Association and Clinical Congress held at the Flower Hospital. The top of the patient's skull was cut through almost all the way around, lifted slightly, and then replaced.

Gallstone operation was performed June 15, 1867, by Dr. John Stough Bobbs, "the father of cholecystotomy," in Indianapolis, Ind., on Mary E. Wiggins (Mrs. Z. Burnsworth) of McCordsville, Ind., and reported to the Indiana Medical Society, May 19–20, 1868. *(Lithotomy of the Gall Bladder. In Transactions of the Indiana State Medical Society, 1868)*

Heart operation for the relief of angina pectoris was performed February 13, 1935, by Dr. Claude Schaeffer Beck, associate professor of surgery at Western Reserve University, on a patient at the Lakeside Hospital, Cleveland, Ohio. Dr. Beck resected one of the pectoral (chest) muscles and fastened the cut end to the heart wall, to provide an additional source of blood for the heart. *(Annals of Surgery. Vol. 102. November 1935)*

Heart operation in which the deep-freezing technique was employed was a 58-minute operation performed September 2, 1952, by Dr. Floyd John Lewis, associate professor of surgery at the Medical School of the University of Minnesota, Minneapolis, Minn. The patient was a five-year-old girl, whose body temperature (except in her head) was reduced to 79 degrees. She recovered and left the hospital on the 11th post-operative day. *(Surgery. Vol. 33, No. 1)*

Heart operation in which the elective cardiac arrest technique was employed was performed in May 1956 on a 17-month-old boy at the Cleveland Clinic, Cleveland, Ohio, by Dr. Donald Brian Effler and a task force of 15 doctors and nurses. Potassium citrate arrested the heart beat, and the right ventricle was slit open, the blood being fed back into an artery in the chest by bypassing the heart.

The First

SURGICAL OPERATION—*Continued*

Kidney transplanting, from one human to another, was performed by Dr. Richard Harold Lawler of the Little Company of Mary Hospital, Chicago, Ill., on June 17, 1950, in a 45-minute operation witnessed by 40 visiting surgeons and doctors. Dr. James Ward West removed a healthy kidney from a woman who had died. Dr. Lawler transplanted the kidney in the renal pedicle of a patient from whom a polycystic left kidney had been removed.

Lobotomy (prefrontal), the cutting of nerve pathways in the frontal lobe of the brain, was performed by Doctors James Winston Watts and Walter Freeman on September 14, 1956, at the George Washington University Hospital, Washington, D.C., on a 63-year-old female patient. *(Walter Freeman and James Winston Watts—Psychosurgery)*

Lung removal was performed April 5, 1933, at the Barnes Hospital, St. Louis, Mo., by Dr. Evarts Ambrose Graham of St. Louis, who removed the left lung of Dr. Robert Gilmore, a Pittsburgh obstetrician. Seven ribs were also removed for the purpose of allowing the soft tissues of the chest wall to collapse against the bronchial stump and therefore to obliterate as much as possible of the pleural cavity.

Lung removal carried out according to preoperative plans was performed July 24, 1933, by Dr. William Francis Reinhoff, Jr., on Doris Yost, a three-year-old girl, at the Johns Hopkins Hospital, Baltimore, Md. She left the hospital September 13, 1933.

Lung tumor operation in which the patient was under hypnosis was performed on a 25-year-old woman at Cedars of Lebanon Hospital, Los Angeles, Calif., in January 1955. The hypnosis was performed by Dr. Milton Jacob Marmer, an anesthesiologist of Beverly Hills, Calif. The operation was reported at the 105th annual meeting of the American Medical Association at Chicago, Ill., on June 12, 1956.

Mastoid operation was performed June 15, 1859, at the Brooklyn City Hospital, Brooklyn, N.Y., by Dr. Joseph Chrisman Hutchison and described by him at the April 1865 meeting of the Medical Society of Kings County, Brooklyn. His report, entitled, "Otitis; Perforating of Mastoid Process with a Trephine," appeared in the *Transactions of the Medical Society of Kings County* (Vol. 2, No. 31, April 1865) and in the *Buffalo Medical and Surgical Journal* (Vol. 3, October 1865).

Mitral valve exposure (prolonged) in a human patient and corrective surgery were carried out on July 3, 1952, by Dr. Forest Dewey Dodrill at the Harper Hospital, Detroit, Mich., on a 41-year-old man. The Michigan Heart was used as a substitute for the lower left ventricle.

The First

Painless surgery operation. *See under* Anesthesia

Siamese twins separated successfully by surgery. *See under* Siamese twins

Skin grafting was suggested in 1847 by Dr. Frank Hastings Hamilton of Buffalo, N.Y. In 1854 he reported a case in which he had successfully grafted skin on a large raw surface of a man's leg injured by a heavy stone that had fallen on it. *(Howard Atwood Kelly and Walter Lincoln Burrage—Dictionary of American Medical Biography)*

Surgical operation classroom instruction telecast. *See under* Television—Telecast

Surgical operation on a bull to correct a sperm block was performed July 25, 1965, by Dr. James Hicks and Dr. Donald F. Walker at the Auburn University School of Veterinary Medicine, Auburn, Ala., on Linderis Evulse, a $176,000 Aberdeen-Angus bull. The bull, owned by the Black Watch Farms, Wappinger Falls, N.Y., was strapped on a hydraulic operating table for the operation.

Surgical operation telecast. *See under* Television—Telecast

Surgical operation under anesthesia. *See under* Anesthesia

Suture of the human heart (successful) was accomplished July 9, 1893, at the Provident Hospital, Chicago, Ill., on James Cornish, whose internal mammary artery had been damaged by a knife wound. Dr. Daniel Hale Williams sutured the pericardium. The operation, which was witnessed by six doctors, was not described until March 27, 1897, in the *Medical Record.*

SURPLUS RELIEF CORPORATION. *See* Federal Surplus Relief Corporation

SURVEY BOOK. *See* Coast survey book

SURVEY OF PUBLIC LANDS was authorized by the Ordinance of 1785, passed by the Continental Congress on May 20, 1785. The first surveys were made in the Seven Ranges in the Western Reserve. The Ordinance of 1785 provided for the division of all public lands into townships six miles square, numbered east and west from Primary Meridians and north and south from Base Lines. This rectangular system of surveying prevails throughout the United States except in the original 13 states and in Maine, Vermont, Kentucky, Tennessee, and West Virginia.

SURVEYOR was Thomas Hariot (Harriot), surveyor and historian of Sir Walter Raleigh's first colony, who landed in 1585 in Virginia. He remained a year under Sir Ralph Lane, the first governor, and returned to England in July 1586 with the fleet commanded by Sir Richard Grenville. He published his observations in London in 1588 as *A*

The First

Briefe and True Report of the New Found Land of Virginia, of the Commodities There Found and to be Raysed, As Well Merchantable, As Others for Victuall, Building and Other Necessarie Uses For Those That Are and Shalbe the Planters There. . . .

SUSPENDED ELEVATOR. See Elevator

SUSPENSION BRIDGE. See Bridge

SUTURE

Fiberglass sutures were used by Dr. Roy Philip Scholz of St. Louis, Mo., on July 19, 1939, in a mastoid operation. The caliber of the suture was that of #00 silk. It had a carrying strength of 7.4 pounds. *(American Journal of Surgery. Vol. 56. June 1942)*

Silk suture and ligatures, used in place of catgut in operations, were used in 1882 by Dr. William Stewart Halsted of Baltimore, Md. He advocated black silk and introduced its use in 1889 at the Johns Hopkins Hospital, Baltimore. *(Johns Hopkins Hospital Reports. March 1891. p. 306)*

Silver wire suture (in place of silk thread) was used by Dr. James Marion Sims of Montgomery, Ala., who reported his experiments in an article, "On the Treatment of Vesico-vaginal Fistula," in the *American Journal of the Medical Sciences,* January 1852. Sims had begun his experiments December 9, 1845. He performed a vesico-vaginal fistula operation on June 21, 1849. The suture was removed on the eighth day after the operation. *(American Journal of Surgery. Vol. 56. June 1942)*

SWEDENBORGIAN OR NEW CHURCH

German Swedenborgian Society was organized in Baltimore, Md., in 1855 by the Reverend Arthur Otto Brickman, a former Lutheran, who preached in both English and German.

Swedenborgian or New Church temple was erected at the southwest corner of Exeter and Baltimore streets, Baltimore, Md. in 1799. The brick structure was built with funds supplied by citizens of the community. The first church service was held Sunday, January 5, 1800. The New Church group in Baltimore was led by Robert Carter, a member of the Virginia Colonial Council, which began meeting in 1792. The first incorporated organization was formed in 1798. The first New Church ministers ordained in America were the Reverend Ralph Mather, formerly of England, and the Reverend John Hargrove, a former preacher of the Methodist Episcopal Church and the Baltimore City Registrar. Hargrove became the first pastor. The first General Convention met in Philadelphia, Pa., in 1817. Hargrove was chosen as the first president. *(John Ellis—The New Church)*

SWEDES arrived in America in 1638. Peter Minuit led an expedition that sailed from Gothenburg, Sweden, on November 20, 1637, in two Dutch vessels, *Kalmar Nyckel* (*The Key of Kalmar*) and *Vagel Grip* (*Bird Grip*), with Jan Hendricksen van

The First

de Waeter as skipper. The expedition landed in March 1638 at "The Rocks" on the Christina River (the site of Wilmington, Del.). Fort Christina was named by Minuit in honor of the Swedish queen. The Swedes brought out the Dutch interests, and in 1643 Johan Printz, the first Swedish governor, arrived.

SWEDISH MAGAZINE was *Skandinavia,* first published January 15, 1847, in New York City. Only eight issues of the magazine were published. *(Adolph Benson—Swedes in America 1638–1938)*

SWEET CRACKER. See Cracker

SWIMMER

American swimmer to cover a distance of 1,500 meters free style in less than 16 minutes was John Kinselta, age 17, at the Amateur Athletic Union's national outdoor swimming championship at the Los Angeles Swim Stadium on August 23, 1970, in 15 minutes 57.105 seconds.

American to swim the English Channel was Henry F. Sullivan of Lowell, Mass., who swam from Dover, England to Cape Gris-Nez, France, a distance of 56 miles, in 27 hours 23 minutes on August 5–6, 1923. Sullivan was the fourth man to swim the Channel.

American to swim the English Channel round trip was Ted Erikson of Chicago, Ill., 37 years old, who swam from St. Margaret's Bay, England, to the beach near Calais, France, in 14 hours 15 minutes on September 21, 1965. He stopped 3 minutes to receive a fresh coating of grease and returned in 15 hours 48 minutes, taking 30 hours 3 minutes for the round-trip swim.

American to swim the English Channel underwater was Fred Baldasare of Cocoa Beach, Fla., a frogman, who left Cap Gris-Nez, France at 1:00 P.M. on July 10, 1962 and arrived at Pegwell Bay, southwest of Ramsgate, England, about 8:15 A.M. on July 11, 1962, a little over 18 hours. He used aqualung equipment and received tanks of air from his helpers and was guided by a cage towed beneath the surface.

American woman to swim the English Channel. See under Woman

Swimmer to cover a distance of 100 meters free style in less than 1 minute was Johnny Weissmuller of the Illinois Athletic Club, whose time was 58 3/5 seconds on July 9, 1922, at the Neptune Beach Tank, Alameda, Calif.

Swimmer to cover a distance of 440 meters free style in less than 5 minutes was Johnny Weissmuller of the Illinois Athletic Club, who swam the distance on March 6, 1923, in the 75-foot Carnegie Pool, New Haven, Conn., in 4 minutes 57 seconds under the Athletic Association Union. He broke the old record of 5:08 minutes, achieving his 47th record.

The First

SWIMMER—*Continued*

Woman to swim the English Channel from both coasts. *See* Woman: American woman to swim the English Channel from both coasts

SWIMMING CHAMPIONSHIP (amateur open) meet was held on September 30, 1877, on the Harlem River by the New York Athletic Club.

SWIMMING POOL in the White House, Washington, D.C., was built by popular subscription. It was located in the west terrace of the mansion and was 50 feet long and 15 feet wide, with a depth ranging from 4 to 8 feet. The pool was lined with aquamarine terra-cotta and was a six-foot wainscot of pale green terra-cotta. The water was both filtered and sterilized. The pool was built under the direction of Lieutenant Colonel Ulysses Simpson Grant III, Director of Public Buildings, and was formally accepted by President Franklin Delano Roosevelt on June 2, 1933.

SWIMMING SCHOOL was opened July 23, 1827 in Boston, Mass. A boat beyond the Toll House conveyed the students to the Mill Dam, where the school was located. It was open from 5:30 A.M. to 7 A.M.; from 9 A.M. to 1 P.M.; and from 4 P.M. to 8 P.M. The method of instruction was described as follows: "A belt is placed about the bodies, under the arms, attached to a rope and pole, by which the head and body are kept in the proper position in the water, while the pupil is learning the use of his limbs."

SWITCHBACK RAILROAD. *See* Railroad

SWITCHBOARD, TELEPHONE. *See under* Telephone

SWORD SWALLOWER was Senaa Samma, "an Indian juggler from Madras and late from London," who performed at St. John's Hall, New York City, on November 11, 1817. Admission was $1, children half price. On November 25, 1817, Samma swallowed "a sword manufactured by Mr. William Pyle of New York as a substitute for the one lately stolen from him by some villain." *(Columbian, New York City. Nov. 26, 1817)*

SYMPHONY

Symphonic work by an American composer was the Symphony in C minor, Opus 23, by John Knowles Paine, presented in January 1876 in Boston, Mass., by Theodore Thomas and his orchestra.

Symphonic work to call for an airplane propeller was the *Ballet Mécanique,* by George Antheil, which he composed in 1922 at the age of 22. It was first presented in the United States April 10, 1927, at Carnegie Hall, New York City. The score called for player pianos and other mechanical contraptions, among them an airplane propeller. *(George Antheil—Bad Boy of Music)*

The First

Symphony on a black folk theme was the Symphony No. 1 (the Negro Folk Symphony), composed by the black conductor William Levi Dawson. It was first presented on November 14, 1934, by the Philadelphia Orchestra under the direction of Leopold Stokowski at the Academy of Music, Philadelphia, Pa.

SYMPHONY ORCHESTRA. *See* Orchestra

SYNCHROTRON

Synchrotron was constructed by the General Electric Research Laboratory, Schenectady, N.Y., by Dr. Herbert Chermside Pollock and Willem Fredrik Westendorp, and installed at the Radiation Laboratory, University of California, Berkeley, Calif., where it released its full energy on January 17, 1949. It was invented by Edwin Mattison McMillan of the university, weighed about 8 tons, had a betatron-type magnet and accelerated electrons that had negative charges.

SYNDICATE. *See* Newspaper syndicate

SYNOD

Synod was held in Cambridge, Mass. (formerly Newtown or Newe-Towne), in 1637. It condemned 82 erroneous opinions that had been propagated in New England.

Synod (ecumenical) was held at Cambridge, Mass., in 1646 and protracted its sessions by adjournments until 1648 when the Cambridge Platform was adopted. It was a platform of church discipline recommended to the General Court and to the churches. It was attended by 25 churchmen who discussed 80 subjects in an effort to reconcile Presbyterianism and Congregationalism.

SYNTHETIC DETERGENT. *See* Detergent

SYNTHETIC MICA. *See* Mica

SYNTHETIC RUBBER. *See* Rubber

SYNTHETIC RUBBER AUTOMOBILE TIRE. *See* Automobile tire

SYNTHETIC VITAMIN. *See* Vitamin

T

TABLOID. *See* Newspaper

TABULATING MACHINE was invented by Dr Herman Hollerith of New York City, who received patent No. 395,782, January 8, 1889, on a system of recording separate statistical items pertaining to the individual by means of holes, or combinations of holes, punched in cards, and then counting or tallying such statistical items either separately or in combination by means of electrical counters operated by electromagnets, the circuits being controlled by the perforated cards. The first extensive use of the electric tabulating system was

The First

in the compilation of the statistics of population for the 11th United States census in 1890.

TACONITE

Taconite project established for large-scale commercial production was the E. W. Davis Works at Silver Bay, Minn., built by the Reserve Mining Company, Duluth, Minn., and owned jointly by the Armco Steel Corporation and the Republic Steel Corporation. Full production began September 13, 1956. Taconite is a hard ferruginous rock containing 25 percent to 30 percent iron. The rock was crushed, ground, and processed by magnetic separation, and small pellets containing 62½ percent iron were produced. The processing plant began preliminary operations in the fall of 1955. Its capacity was rated at 3,750,000 tons of iron ore pellets annually.

Taconite production was undertaken in November 1919 by the Mesabi Iron Co., Babbitt, Minn. The first cargo was produced June 21, 1922, and the first cargo (5,076 tons) shipped October 1, 1922, to the Ford Motor Company, River Rouge, Mich.

TAFT-HARTLEY LAW. *See under* Labor relations

TALKING ANIMATED CARTOON. *See* Motion picture: Animated cartoon talking picture

TALKING BOOK for the blind was a collection of eight phonographs records of patriotic documents. The Declaration of Independence and the Constitution of the United States comprised four double-faced records, and Washington's Farewell Address to the Continental Army and letter to the Congress of the United States made up the other four. This collection, intended for reproduction on a specially designed phonograph, was issued in July 1934 by the American Foundation for the Blind, New York City.

TALKING HEADLIGHT. *See* Locomotive headlight

TALKING MOTION PICTURE. *See* Motion picture

TALLYHO. *See* Coaching

TANK (military). *See* Army armored tank; Ordnance

TANK CAR. *See* Railroad car: Glass-lined tank car

TANK CAR, OIL. *See under* Oil

TANK DISCHARGER, AIRPLANE. *See* Aviation: Airplane tank discharger

TANKER. *See* Ship

TANNER. *See* Leather: Leather tanning

TANNING (leather). *See under* Leather

The First

TAPE, ADHESIVE. *See* Adhesive and medicated plaster

TAPE, MASKING

Pressure-sensitive masking tape was invented by Richard Gurley Drew of St. Paul, Minn., who obtained U.S. Patent No. 1,760,820 on May 27, 1930. The tape was commercially marketed in 1926 by the Minnesota Mining and Manufacturing Company (3M), St. Paul, Minn. It is available in various widths and lengths and known as Scotch brand masking tape.

TAPE MEASURE PATENT was granted to Alvin J. Fellows of New Haven, Conn., July 14, 1868, No. 79,965. The tape measure was enclosed in a circular case with a spring click lock to hold the tape at any desired point.

TAPE RECORDER

Magnetic tape recorder was the Wireway, announced January 27, 1948, by the Wire Recording Corporation of America. It was a lightweight portable wire-recorder with a built-in oscillator. It retailed at $149.50.

Magnetic tape recorder (commercial) of sound and picture was manufactured by the Ampex Corporation, Redwood City, Calif., and demonstrated simultaneously in Redwood City and Chicago, Ill., on April 14, 1956. The tape, 2 inches wide, moved at a speed of 15 inches a second. A single 14-inch reel accommodated a 65-minute recording. The Columbia Broadcasting System purchased three of the video tape recorders at $75,000 each in 1956.

Tape-recording machine for mass production of tapes was announced January 26, 1949, by the Minnesota Mining and Manufacturing Company, St. Paul, Minn. The machine taped 48 hours of recorded music in 1 hour.

TAPE RECORDING

Presidential press conference recorded on tape. *See* President (U.S.): Presidential press conference recorded on tape

Radio broadcast from a tape recording was made by WQXR, Interstate Broadcasting Company, New York City, from 6:30 P.M. to 7 P.M. August 26, 1938, using Millertape, the invention of James Arthur Miller of the Miller Broadcasting System, New York City. A sapphire stylus engraved a 15-minute program on 1,000 feet of tape. Editing and cutting were possible on this sound tape transmission.

Video recording on magnetic tape of high definition was made on October 3, 1952, when the electronics division of Bing Crosby Enterprises, Inc., Los Angeles, Calif., using a Video Tape Recorder, recorded images on magnetic tape, rewound the tape, and immediately reproduced the picture through a standard television monitor tube. A one-inch tape with 12 tracks, 1 for sound and 11 for pictures, was used. The cost was one third that of photographic processes.

The First

TAPE RECORDING—*Continued*

Video recording on magnetic tape in color was the "Betty Feezor Show," recorded from 11:00 to 11:30 A.M. and shown from 1:00 to 1:30 P.M., on September 5, 1958, by WBTV, Charlotte, N.C.

Video recording on magnetic tape televised coast-to-coast was the Jonathan Winters show, televised 7:30–7:45 P.M. October 23, 1956, by WRCA-TV, New York City. The process was developed by the Radio Corporation of America for National Broadcasting Company television. Instead of film the system utilized instantaneous tape with pictures that could be played back immediately after recording. The telecast was shown in full compatible color and also in black-and-white.

TAPESTRY. *See* Carpeting: Carpeting (velvet)

TAPS (military signal) was played in its present form about the first week of July 1862. General Daniel Butterfield wrote the music on the back of a torn envelope he had been carrying around with him and whistled the tune to Oliver Willcox Norton, bugler and aide-de-camp of General Strong Vincent, commander of the 83rd Regiment Pennsylvania Volunteers of the Army of the Potomac. They were resting in camp at Harrison's Landing on the James River in Virginia, immediately after the seven days of fighting near Richmond. *(Julia Lorrilard Butterfield—A Biographical Memorial of General Daniel Butterfield)*

TARIFF

Import duty treaty. *See* Treaty: Treaty with a foreign nation to provide for mutual reduction of import duties

Narcotics tariff. *See under* Narcotics

Tariff commission was authorized June 7, 1882 (22 Stat. L. 64). Nine tariff commissioners at $10 a day and expenses were appointed from civil life to investigate tariff questions relating to agriculture, commerce, manufacturing, mining, and mercantile and industrial interests. The first chairman was John Lord.

Tariff commission woman chairman was Catherine May Bedell of Yakima, Wash. She was appointed chairman of the U. S. Tariff Commission by President Richard Milhous Nixon and sworn in July 12, 1971.

Tariff for protection rather than primarily for revenue was the "act to regulate the duties on imports and tonnage," passed April 27, 1816 (3 Stat. L. 310).

Tariff legislation passed by Congress after the adoption of the Constitution was the Tariff Act of July 4, 1789 (1 Stat. L. 24), an "act for laying a duty on goods, wares and merchandises imported into the United States," effective August 1, 1789. The main purpose was the collection of revenue, but protection was also extended to certain industries

The First

which the government wished to encourage, such as glass and earthenware. The act was signed by George Washington and was to continue in force until July 1796. It laid specific duties on some articles and ad valorem duties on others, equivalent to an 8½ percent ad valorem rate, with drawback, up to 1 percent of the duties on all articles exported within 12 months except distilled spirits other than brandy and geneva.

Tariff to prevent the importation of obscene literature and pictures was the Tariff Act of August 30, 1842 (5 Stat. L. 566), an "act to provide revenue from imports. . . . " Section 28 stated: "The importation of all indecent and obscene prints, paintings, lithographs, engravings and transparencies is hereby prohibited . . . and all invoices and packages whereof any such article shall compose a part are . . . liable . . . to be seized and forfeited . . . and the said articles shall be forthwith destroyed."

TARIFF REFUND. *See* Drawback legislation

TATTOO

Electric tattoo machine was employed by Samuel F. O'Reilly in 1875 on the Bowery, New York City. The electric tattoos were called "tattaugraphs." *(Albert Parry—Tattoo)*

Tattoo shop was opened in 1846 by Martin Hildebrandt at Oak Street between Oliver and James streets, New York City.

Tattooed man exhibited was James F. O'Connell, whose appearance at the Franklin Theatre, Chatham Square, New York City, on October 21, 1849, was advertised as follows in the New York *Herald:* "The manager has at an enormous expense engaged Mr. J. F. O'Connell, the wonderful 'Tattooed Man' who will go through a variety of performances peculiar to himself, and perfectly original."

TAURINE CLOTH. *See* Haircloth

TAX

See also Cigarette tax; Gasoline tax; School tax; and *see under* Tobacco

Bachelor tax was levied by Missouri which on December 20, 1820 (effective January 1, 1821) placed a $1 tax "on every unmarried free white male, above the age of 21 years and under 50 years." *(Missouri Territorial Laws, 1820. Chap 299. Vol. 1)*

Chain stores tax (state) was levied by Indiana (Chapter 207 of the acts of 1929). This statute commonly referred to as the Indiana Chain Store Tax Law, was signed March 16, 1929, by Governor Harry Leslie, and became effective July 1, 1929. Under the statute, owners were required to pay an annual license fee of $3 to operate a store in Indiana. The tax on 2 to 5 stores under the same management, supervision, or ownership was $10 for each additional store; on stores in excess of

The First

but not in excess of 10, $15 for each additional store; on stores in excess of 10 but not in excess of 20, $20 for each additional store; on all stores in excess of 20, $25 plus a 50-cent filing fee for each additional store. An amendment to this act (Chapter 271, Acts of 1933) was signed March 11, 1933, by Governor Paul Vories McNutt, requiring owners of stores in excess of 20 to pay $150 for each additional store.

Corporation tax was passed by act of Congress August 5, 1909 (36 Stat. L. 112). The act taxed all corporations with an income over $5,000. The law was passed prior to the adoption of the U.S. income tax amendment.

Excess profits tax was passed by act of Congress of March 3, 1917 (39 Stat. L. 1000), an "act to provide increased revenue to defray the expenses of the increased appropriation for the army and navy and the extension of fortifications." Under the act the profits of all corporations in excess of from 7 to 9 percent of the capital were taxed. The rates were progressive: 20 percent on excess profits up to 15 percent; 35 percent on the excess from 15 to 25 percent; 45 percent on the excess from 25 percent to 33 percent; and 60 percent on the excess above 33 percent. The act was repealed by section 214 of the Revenue Act of 1917, approved October 3, 1917 (40 Stat. L. 308).

Excise tax (federal) was enacted March 3, 1791. It was "an act repealing, after the last day of June next, the duties heretofore laid upon distilled spirits imported from abroad, and laying others in their stead; and also upon spirits distilled within the United States" (1 Stat. L. 199). It imposed a tax on distilled spirits from 11 cents to 30 cents a gallon in accordance with alcoholic content prior to removal from distilleries.

Federal income tax was imposed by the act of August 5, 1861 (12 Stat. L. 292), effective January 1, 1862, which imposed a 3 percent tax on incomes exceeding $800, to be paid prior to June 30, 1862. Income from federal and foreign bonds was assessed at other rates. The income tax lists were open to public inspection by "all persons who may apply to inspect the same." This was interpreted in such a way as to eliminate idle curiosity seekers. The tax was collected at a progressive rate based upon income. The tax was rescinded in 1872 with other Civil War taxes. An income tax law was passed August 27, 1894 (28 Stat. L. 553), as part of the tariff act, but it was declared unconstitutional. *(Joseph Jerome Klein—Federal Income Taxation)*

Federal tax levied directly upon the states was a direct pro rata tax upon the 16 states authorized by act of Congress of July 14, 1798 (1 Stat. L. 597), "an act to lay and collect a direct tax within the United States." It was levied upon dwellings, land, and slaves. The amount to be collected was $2 million, which was apportioned to the states in direct ratio to the population. The Constitution gives Congress "power to lay and collect taxes, duties, imposts and excises, to pay the debts and provide for the common defense and general welfare of the United States."

Income tax amendment to the Constitution (the 16th) was proposed to the legislatures of the several states by the 61st Congress on July 12, 1909, and was declared to have been ratified by a proclamation of Secretary of State Philander Chase Knox on February 25, 1913 (37 Stat. L. 1785). This amendment gave Congress power "to lay and collect taxes on incomes, from whatever source derived, without apportionment among the several states, and without regard to any census or enumeration." The income tax went into effect March 1, 1913.

Inheritance tax (colonial) was levied by Virginia in 1687 when the Colony of Virginia provided that the governor of the colony should collect a fee of a cask and 200 pounds of tobacco for impressing probates and letters testamentary or letters of administration with the public seal, without which they were invalid. *(William John Shultz—American Public Finance and Taxation)*

Inheritance tax (federal) was a part of the Internal Revenue Law of July 1, 1862 (12 Stat. L. 432), which assessed a tax on legacies and distributive shares of personal property.

Inheritance tax (state) was Chapter 72, "relating to collateral inheritance," passed by Pennsylvania on April 7, 1826, to become effective May 1, 1826. It was signed by Governor John Andrew Shulze. It established a 2.5 percent collateral inheritance tax. The surviving spouse, the parents, and the descendants of the decedent were exempted.

Internal revenue tax was imposed March 3, 1791 (1 Stat. L. 199), effective July 1, 1791. It levied taxes on distilled spirits and on carriages. Subsequent early modifications of the act of 1791 imposed taxes on retail dealers in distilled spirits, and on refined sugar, snuff, property sold at auction, snuff mills, legal instruments, and bonds. On July 9, 1798 (1 Stat. L. 584), a direct tax was placed on real estate. The receipts for the fiscal year 1792 from internal revenue netted the government $208,942.81.

Property tax law (colonial) was passed May 14, 1634, and signed by Governor William Bradford of the Massachusetts colony: "It is further ordered that in all rates and public charges, the towns shall have respect to levy each man according to his estate, and with consideration of all other his abilities, whatsoever, and not according to the number of persons."

Sales tax (state) was approved May 3, 1921, by West Virginia, to become effective July 1, 1921. The funds collected were used largely in place of

The First

TAX—*Continued*

funds from a tax on corporate net income. The rate was 1/5 of 1 percent on the gross income of banks, street railroads, telephones, telegraph, express, and electric light and power retailers, and 2/5 of 1 percent on timber, oil, coal, natural gas, and other minerals. Payments could be made to the state quarterly or annually. *(Robert Murray Haig and Carl Shoup—The Sales Tax in the American States)*

State university supported by a direct property tax. *See under* College

Tax on the American colonies without their consent was levied in 1672, when the British Parliament passed a law imposing a duty on sugar, tobacco, ginger, coconuts, indigo, logwood fustic, wool, and cotton.

TAX APPEALS BOARD MEMBER (woman). *See under* Woman

TAXICAB, ELECTRIC. *See under* Automobile

TAXIDERMY METHOD (sculptural) was devised by Carl Ethan Akeley in 1902. He mounted skins on specially constructed forms, lifelike and true in all details to the living animals. His first important work, "The Four Seasons," representing four groups of Virginia deer and their appropriate surroundings in spring, summer, autumn, and winter, was prepared for the Field Museum of Natural History, Chicago, Ill.

TEA SHRUB was planted at Middleton Barony, S.C., in 1802 by the French botanist Francois André Michaux.

TEACHERS' CONVENTION

Teachers' convention (national) was attended by representatives of state teachers' associations who met in the Hall of the Controllers of the Public Schools in Philadelphia, Pa., on August 26, 1857, and organized the National Teachers Association "to elevate the character and advance the interest of the profession of teaching and to promote the cause of popular education in the United States." John L. Enos was chairman and W. E. Sheldon secretary. At the convention held in Cleveland, Ohio, on August 15, 1870, the name was changed to the National Education Association.

Teachers' convention (state) was held in January 1831 at Utica, N.Y., and was advertised as the "State Convention of Teachers and Friends of Education."

TEACHERS' DEATH BENEFIT was in operation for a short time beginning in 1869 in New York City under the New York City Teachers Mutual Life Assurance Association. Upon the death of a member, the membership was required to contribute $1 to pay funeral expenses.

The First

TEACHERS' INSTITUTE was held at Hartford, Conn., in October 1839 when 26 men teachers attended a six-week course sponsored by Henry Barnard and received the "opportunity of critically reviewing the studies which they will be called upon to teach, with a full explanation of all the principles involved." Among the authorities who gave instruction were Charles Davies, higher mathematics, and Thomas Hopkins Gallaudet, composition and school government. *(Bernard Christian Steiner—Life of Henry Barnard)*

TEACHERS' PENSION FUND was set up in New York City under authority of Chapter 296, Laws of New York State, passed April 14, 1894, which provided for a public school teachers' retirement fund. The resources were to come from deductions made from the pay of the teachers because of absence. Regular salaries were not assessed.

TEACHERS' SICK BENEFIT FUNDS were established in 1887 in both New York City and Brooklyn. The two organizations were the New York City Teachers Mutual Benefit Association and the Brooklyn Aid Association. Dues based on salary were obtained from teachers. *(Frederick Albert Cleveland—Teachers' Pension Systems in the United States)*

TEACHERS' TRAINING SCHOOL. See Normal school

TEACHING CHAIR. *See* Education: Chair in education; Pedagogy chair: Pedagogy chair (permanent)

TEACHING METHODS BOOK was Christopher Dock's *Schul-ordnung; or A Simple and Thoroughly Prepared School-Management clearly setting forth not only in what manner children may best be taught in the branches usually given at school, but also how they may be well instructed in the knowledge of godliness.* The book was completed August 3, 1750, but not published until 20 years later. The preface was dated March 27, 1770. It was originally written in German and was printed by Christopher Saur in Germantown, Pa. *(Marian Groves Brumbaugh—Life and Work of Christopher Dock)*

TECHNICAL ANIMATED CARTOON. See Motion picture: Animated cartoon (technical)

TECHNICAL COLLEGE FOR WOMEN. See College

TECHNICAL INSTITUTE was the Gardiner Lyceum, Gardiner, Maine, founded by Robert Hallowell Gardiner in 1822 "for the purpose of giving to farmers and mechanics such a scientific education as would enable them to become skillful in their professions." Courses were offered in arithmetic, algebra, geometry, trigonometry, mensuration of surfaces and solids, bookkeeping, surveying, navigation, mechanics, hydrostatics, pneumatics, chemistry, natural philosophy and "the higher branches of mathematics and natural

The First

history." The first lecturer was Benjamin Hale. *(Society for the Promotion of Engineering Education—A Study of Technical Institutes. February 1931)*

TECHNICOLOR MOTION PICTURE. *See* Motion picture

TEE, GOLF. *See* Golf tee

TEETH. *See* Dentistry

TELAUTOGRAPH

Telautograph was invented by Elisha Gray of Highland Park, Ill., who obtained U.S. patent No. 386,815 on July 31, 1888, on a "telautograph" and No. 386,814 on the "art of telegraphy." He also obtained patent No. 491,347 February 7, 1893, on another telautograph and patent No. 491,346 on an "electro-mechanical movement."

TELECAST. *See* Television—Telecast

TELEGRAM

News dispatch telegram was "One o'clock. There has just been made a motion in the House to go into committee of the whole on the Oregon question. Rejected. Ayes 79—Nays 86." It was sent from Washington, D.C., to the Baltimore *Patriot,* Saturday afternoon, May 25, 1844.

Singing telegram was introduced by the Western Union Telegraph Company, New York City, July 28, 1933. The innovation, opposed by a company executive, proved popular with customers. Many telegrams were sung by messengers in person, but after 1950 all singing was done by telephone.

Telegram dispatched from an aerial station was sent from the balloon *Enterprise* on June 18, 1861, to President Abraham Lincoln by Professor Thaddeus Sobieski Coulincourt Lowe, who acknowledged his indebtedness "for the opportunity of demonstrating the availability of the science of aeronautics in the military service of the country." Lowe made his first official ascent July 24, 1861, and saw the movements of the Confederate troops after the battle of Manassas, Va. Again, he detected a Confederate maneuver to attack the troops of General Heintzelman, who were separated from the main force at Fair Oaks. And on May 24, 1862, he directed artillery fire from his balloon, the first use of a balloon for such a purpose.

Telegram inaugurating commercial service was sent May 24, 1844, by Professor Samuel Finley Breese Morse from the United States Supreme Court room in the Capitol, Washington, D.C., to Alfred Vail at the Mount Clare station of the Baltimore and Ohio Railroad Company, Baltimore, Md. Vail retransmitted it to Morse. The message, "What hath God wrought," was selected from the 23rd verse of the 23rd chapter of Numbers by Annie Ellsworth, daughter of the commissioner of Patents.

The First

Transcontinental telegram was sent October 24, 1861, by Stephen Johnson Field, Chief Justice of California, to President Abraham Lincoln. The Mayor of San Francisco, Calif., sent a message to Mayor Fernando Wood of New York City the next day.

TELEGRAPH

Army field telegraph used in warfare was employed May 24, 1862, in the Peninsula campaign during the Civil War. A wire several miles long extended from the headquarters of General George Brinton McClellan near Williamsport, Va., to an advance guard at Mechanicsville, Va., commanded by General George Stoneman, chief of cavalry in the Army of the Potomac. *(Military Affairs. Vol. 18, No. 4. Winter 1954)*

Duplex telegraph (practical) was invented by Thomas Alva Edison of Newark, N.J., who obtained patent No. 480,567 on August 9, 1892, in the United States and earlier patents in Britain, France, Italy, Austria-Hungary, and Russia. The telegraph was "to enable two operators to simultaneously send over one wire in one direction, by reversal of a battery current in one instance and increasing and decreasing the strength of the current in the other instance, and the connections are so arranged that the party at the receiving station can signal to the sender to repeat in case of inaccuracy."

Photographs sent over a city telegraph. *See under* Radio facsimile transmission

Semaphore telegraph system. *See* Semaphore telegraph system

Telegraph was constructed in 1827 by Harrison Gray Dyar, who operated a two-mile telegraph system at the racecourse at Long Island City, N.Y. Iron wire attached to glass insulators on wooden posts enabled the current to produce a red mark on litmus paper at the receiving station. The lapse of time between the sparks indicated the different letters. *(George Bartlett Prescott—History, Theory and Practice of the Electric Telegraph)*

Telegraph appropriation (federal) was made by Congress on March 3, 1843 (5 Stat. L. 618). A sum of $30,000 was appropriated "to test the practicability of establishing a system of electro-magnetic telegraphs by the United States."

Telegraph cable. *See* Cable

Telegraph call boxes were installed June 22, 1872, in Brooklyn, N.Y., by the American District Telegraph Company. Each metal box contained "a Seth Thomas clock movement supported upon a circular iron base . . . [with] two break wheels . . . attached to the clockwork, either of which could be brought into circuit by means of a switch." One wheel was notched for the even number and the other for the odd, the former indicating messenger and the latter fire. The idea was conceived by Edward A. Calahan, who ob-

The First

TELEGRAPH—*Continued*
tained patent No. 127,844 on June 11, 1872, and No. 129,526 on July 16, 1873. *(Telegraph and Telephone Age. Feb. 16, 1911)*

Telegraph code converter was the Trak Code Converter, made by CGS Laboratories, Inc., Stamford, Conn., and announced to the public in the October 1954 issue of *Wire and Radio Communications Magazine*. Incoming International Morse Code signals were converted by a teleprinter that recorded at speeds up to 600 words a minute. The converter, which cost $14,850, was housed in a relay rack 19 inches long and 54 inches high.

Telegraph company was the Magnetic Telegraph Company, incorporated February 4, 1847, under the laws of Maryland. The first meeting was held January 14, 1846. The first president was Amos Kendall. An office was erected at 10 Wall Street for the reception of messages. The rental for the New York office was $250 a year, Philadelphia $150, Baltimore $150, and Washington $50. At first messages were sent by pigeons across the Hudson River from Jersey City, N.J., to New York City; later a lead pipe, enclosing a covered wire saturated with pitch, was laid under the river. The rates from Baltimore to Washington were ten cents for the first ten words, and one cent for each additional word. The rates from New York to Washington were fifty cents for the first ten words and five cents for each additional word.

Telegraph convention (national) was held July 17, 1850, at the Telegraph Office, New York City. Henry O'Rielly was appointed president and L. W. Jerome secretary. *(American Telegraph Magazine. Vol. 1. April–May–June 1853)*

Telegraph (electromagnetic) was invented by Joseph Henry, who exhibited it in 1831 at the Albany Academy, Albany, N.Y. The device was 14 inches long. At each excitation of the electric magnet, one end of a compass rod or needle remained in contact with a limb of the soft iron core. Near the opposite end of the compass rod was a small stationary office bell. When the current was reversed, the compass rod moved back to the opposite limb of the electromagnet. Signals were transmitted by means of the electromagnet through more than a mile of wire. The invention was not put to practical use; it merely demonstrated the possibility of transmitting signals. *(William Bowers Taylor—An Historical Sketch of Henry's Contribution to the Electro-Magnetic Telegraph)*

Telegraph in railroading was used September 22, 1851, when Charles Minot, superintendent of the Erie Railroad, telegraphed 14 miles to Goshen, N.Y., to delay a train so that his train would not have to wait. Trains were run on the interval system.

The First

Telegraph line to the Pacific Coast was placed in operation October 24, 1861, when United States Supreme Court Justice Stephen Johnson Field of California sent the first message to President Abraham Lincoln. On October 25, 1861, telegrams were exchanged between Mayor Fernando Wood of New York City and Mayor H. F. Teschemacher of San Francisco, Calif. Rates during the first week were $1 a word between San Francisco and the Missouri River. Later the rates were reduced: ten words from San Francisco to New York cost $6, and each additional word 75 cents.

Telegraph station was opened in Washington, D.C., in 1844 under the direction of Samuel Finley Breese Morse. The station was located between Seventh and Eighth streets and E and F streets. *(National Intelligencer. May 22, 1844)*

Telegraph ticker to operate at high speed was installed November 1929 in the Bankers Club of America, 120 Broadway, New York City. It printed 500 characters a minute. It operated on only one transmitting wire, instead of two, as did the old tickers.

Telegraph ticker to print letters of the alphabet was patented by Royal Earl House of New York City, who obtained patent No. 4,464 on April 18, 1846, on a "magnetic letter printing telegraph." It printed 50 words a minute in Roman letters. The ticker was first publicly exhibited in 1844 at the American Institute Fair, New York City. It was extensively used for about ten years until superseded by new models.

Telegraph ticker used by a brokerage concern was installed December 29, 1867, in the office of David Groesbeck & Company, a member of the New York Stock Exchange, New York City, by the Gold and Stock Telegraph Company, New York City. A rental of $6 a week was charged for the service, which was operated by Daniel Drew. *(Edmund Clarence Stedman—The New York Stock Exchange)*

Telegraph ticker which successfully printed type was invented by David Edward Hughes of Louisville, Ky., who received patent No. 14,917 on May 20, 1856. He had sold his rights to the Commercial Company for $100,000 on November 1, 1855.

Telegraph wedding. *See under* Wedding

Telegraphic communication system in which dots and dashes represented letters was invented by Alfred Vail of Morristown, N.J., in September 1837. On January 8, 1838, the message "A patient waiter is no loser" was transmitted. On January 24, 1838, in a public demonstration given at New York University, New York City, the message "Attention the Universe. By Kingdom's Right Wheel" was transmitted through a circuit of ten miles. Previously, words had been assigned numbers, marks being acutely angulated lines like the letter

The First

V or V in reverse, which appeared on cylinders at the receiving station.

Woman telegrapher. *See under* Woman

TELEPHONE

Air-to-ground public telephone service began September 15, 1957, in the Chicago–Detroit area when about 20 airplanes were equipped for the two-way service. The rates varied from $1.50 to $4.25 for a 3-minute call, depending on the location of the airplane and the telephone on the ground.

Around-the-world telephone conversation was held on April 25, 1935, between Walter Sherman Gifford, president of the American Telephone Company, in his office in New York City, and T. G. Miller, a company vice president, who was in an office about 50 feet away. The call was routed by telephone (over 23,000 miles of wire) and radio through San Francisco, Java, Amsterdam, and London and back to New York.

Automatic telephone system patent was issued December 5, 1879 (No. 22,458), to Daniel Connolly of Philadelphia, Thomas A. Connolly of Washington, D.C., and Thomas J. McTighe of Pittsburgh, who had applied for a patent on September 10, 1879. The system employed a single-line wire, a battery of cells located at each telephone, and a dial switching mechanism for each line. The system could accommodate only a few lines and was not commercially applied.

Automatic telephone system (successful) was invented by Almon B. Strowger, who filed application for a patent March 12, 1889. During 1891 and 1892, 20 machines were made by the Union Model Works. In May 1892 Alexander E. Keith started the installation of the first automatic exchange at La Porte, Ind. This exchange was formally opened to the public November 3, 1892. The first exchange equipped with a rotating dial was an interior system in the City Hall of Milwaukee, Wis., which was installed during 1896. *(Harry Hughes Harrison—An Introduction to the Strowger System of Automatic Telephony)*

Coin telephone was invented by William Gray of Hartford, Conn., who received patent No. 408,-709 on August 13, 1889, on a "coin-controlled apparatus for telephones." He had filed his application August 13, 1888. The first machine in commercial use was installed in the Hartford Bank in 1889 under the supervision of Ellis Benjamin Baker, superintendent of the Southern New England Telephone Company. In 1891 Gray, with Amos Whitney and Francis Pratt, incorporated the Gray Telephone Pay Station Company (later the Gray Manufacturing Company) and installed the telephones in stores on a rental basis. The company rented out pay phones for 25 percent of the take. Ten percent of the take went to the place of business in which the telephones were in-

The First

stalled and 65 percent to the telephone company. *(J. Leigh Walsh—Pioneers in Telegraphy)*

Commercial telephone service on railroad trains for passengers was placed in operation August 15, 1947, simultaneously on the Baltimore and Ohio Railroad Company's *Royal Blue* and the Pennsylvania Railroad Company's *Congressional Limited* between New York City and Washington, D.C. Two-way telephone conversation was carried on in the same way as ordinary telephone calls.

Common battery (nonmultiple) switchboard was placed in operation January 9, 1894, in Lexington, Mass., by the New England Telephone and Telegraph Company.

Desk telephone, supplementing the wall telephone box, was used in 1886.

Dial telephone long-distance service began October 17, 1949, when Mark Sullivan, president of the Pacific Telephone and Telegraph Company, in New York City, dialed Oakland, Calif., and spoke to Dr. Oliver E. Buckley, president of the Bell Telephone Laboratories and Keith S. McHugh, president of the New York Telephone Company. It took less than 1 minute to complete the call.

Dial telephone service coast-to-coast without the aid of operators was commercially inaugurated November 10, 1951, with a conversation between Mayor M. Leslie Denning of Englewood, N.J., and Mayor Frank P. Osborn of Alameda, Calif. Three digits were added to the number to be dialed. Conversation took place 18 seconds after the dialing. Raymond J. Neiligan was the manager of the Englewood, N.J., exchange.

Hot line was installed August 30, 1962, between the White House, Washington, D.C., and the Kremlin, Moscow, Russia.

International telephone conversation was held July 1, 1881, when service was inaugurated by the National Bell Telephone Company of the State of Maine between Calais, Maine, and St. Stephen, N.B., Canada, two points separated by the St. Croix River, the international boundary line between the United States and Canada.

Interstate telephone call took place May 17, 1877, when a call was made from New Brunswick, N.J., to Dr. Alexander Graham Bell at Chickering Hall, New York City.

Long-distance telephone call was made March 27, 1884, by branch managers of the American Bell Telephone Company in Boston, Mass., and New York City. "The words were heard as perfectly as though the speakers were standing close by, while no extra effort was needed at the other end of the line to accomplish the result." *(Boston Journal. Mar. 27, 1884)*

Mobile long-distance car-to-car telephone conversation was made September 11, 1946, when a reporter on the Houston (Texas) *Post* telephoned

TELEPHONE—*Continued*

a reporter on the St. Louis (Mo.) *Globe Democrat.*

Mobile telephone commercial service was inaugurated June 17, 1946, by the Southwestern Bell Telephone Company, St. Louis, Mo. Installations were completed in the automobiles of two subscribers, the Monsanto Chemical Company and Henry L. Perkinson, a contractor. Conversation was possible with any Bell Telephone System or connecting company telephone.

Mobile telephone conversation overseas from a moving vehicle was made July 16, 1946, by Roger Pierce from St. Louis, Mo., to Honolulu, Hawaii.

Mobile telephone conversation with commercial equipment over commercial communication lines between an airplane in flight and a moving automobile was accomplished on October 9, 1947, by executives of the Hercules Powder Company, Wilmington, Del., from an airplane 2,000 feet in the air to an automobile about five miles west of Wilmington, Del., on the Lancaster Pike (Route 41).

Mobile telephone news dispatch transmitted from a moving car was sent May 15, 1946, by Richard Everett of the St. Louis (Mo.) *Star-Times.*

Mobile transatlantic telephone conversation between two telephone-equipped automobiles was made June 26, 1947, by United States Ambassador James Clement Dunn from Milan, Italy, to Vincent R. Impellitteri, president of the New York City Council, on the occasion of Marconi Day at the Milan Fair.

Multiple common battery switchboard was put in service in the fall of 1897 by the Ohio Valley Telephone Company in Louisville, Ky.

News dispatch by telephone was sent from Salem, Mass., February 12, 1877, to the Boston *Globe*, Boston, Mass., by Bell telephone. The *Globe* reported: "This special dispatch to the *Globe* has been transmitted by telephone in the presence of twenty people who have thus been witnesses to a feat never before attempted—the sending of news over the space of sixteen miles by the human voice."

Pay station telephone service began June 1, 1880, in the office of the Connecticut Telephone Company, Yale Bank Building, State and Chapel streets, New Haven, Conn. The toll was given to an attendant.

Photographs sent over a city telephone. *See under* Radio facsimile transmission

Picturephone service (commercial) was inaugurated June 24, 1964, in New York, Chicago, and Washington, D.C., when Lady Bird Johnson, wife of President Lyndon Baines Johnson, spoke in Washington, D.C., to Dr. Elizabeth A. Wood of the Bell Laboratories in New York City. The picturephone had 3 parts: a chassis containing the 4-3/8-

inch-wide and 5-3/4-inch-high screen, camera, and loudspeaker; a control unit; and power supply. It was possible to both hear and see the person talking. Service for the general public opened June 25, 1964. Rates for calls were $16 for the initial 3-minute period between New York and Washington, $21 between Washington and Chicago, and $27 between Chicago and New York.

Picturephone transcontinental call was made April 20, 1964, when William Leonard Laurence, science consultant to the New York World's Fair, New York City, spoke to Donald Shaffer, managing editor of the Anaheim, Calif., *Bulletin* at Disneyland, Anaheim, Calif. The set was about 12 inches across, 7 inches high, and 13 inches deep.

President to use a telephone. *See under* President (U.S.)

President who had used a telephone for campaigning. *See under* President (U.S.)

Radio telephone. *See* Radio telephone

Satellite (privately owned) telephone conversation was made July 10, 1962, at 7:28 P.M. EDT by Frederick Russell Kappel, board chairman of the American Telephone and Telegraph Company to Vice President Lyndon Baines Johnson in Washington, D.C., on the sixth orbit of the satellite Telstar 1. Kappel's voice went from Andover, Me., to the satellite, bounced back to Andover, and then was carried by land line to Washington, D.C. Johnson's voice was carried by land line to Andover.

Telecast over telephone wires. *See under* Television—Telecast

Telephone cable service (deep-sea) was established April 11, 1921 between Key West, Fla., and Havana, Cuba. It was officially opened by President Warren Gamaliel Harding. President Harding, at the Pan American Building, Washington, D.C., conversed with President Mario García Menocal of Cuba, at Havana.

Telephone company answering service was the Ohio Bell Telephone Co., which marketed a recording machine and offered service at $12.50 a month, plus a $15 installment fee. As many as twenty 30-second messages could be recorded on a cylinder, which could then be cleaned and used again. The service was offered to the public in March 1951.

Telephone concert. *See* Music: Long-distance telephone concert

Telephone concert transcontinental. *See* Radio telephone: Radio telephone concert transcontinental

Telephone conversation between someone on the ground and a person in a dirigible. *See* Radio telephone: Radio telephone conversation be-

The First

tween someone on the ground and a person in a dirigible

Telephone conversation (commercial) over a satellite was inaugurated over Early Bird I on June 28, 1965, between the United States and Europe with ceremonies in 6 countries. President Lyndon Baines Johnson was introduced by Joseph Vincent Charyk, president of COMSAT, Communications Satellite Corporation. Greetings were exchanged with Prime Minister Harold Wilson in London, German Chancellor Ludwig Erhard in Bonn, Swiss President Hans-Peter Tschudi in Berne, and French Minister of State Louis Jacquinot in Paris. Remarks of Carlo Russo, Italian Minister of Posts and Telecommunications, were read from Rome.

Telephone conversation (commercial) using electricity generated by the sun's rays took place October 4, 1955, at Americus, Ga., over the lines of the Southern Bell Telephone and Telegraph Company. The current was supplied by a solar battery developed by the Bell Telephone Laboratories. The aluminum housing of the battery, less than a yard square, contained 432 silicon cells cushioned in oil and covered with glass. The first call, over a distance of about 14 miles, was made to Gene Summerford by George Mathews, who said, "Hello, Gene. This is George Mathews. How many bales of cotton do I have in your warehouse?"

Telephone conversation over out-of-door wires (long distance) took place on October 9, 1876, between Alexander Graham Bell in Boston and Thomas Augustus Watson in Cambridge, Mass. The private telegraph wire of the Walworth Manufacturing Company from Boston to Cambridgeport, Mass., a distance of two miles, was used. Parallel accounts of the conversation as recorded by both Bell and Watson were published in the Boston *Advertiser,* October 19, 1876, in answer to the skeptics who did not believe that the telephone was as reliable as the telegraph. *(Thomas A. Watson—The Birth and Babyhood of the Telephone)*

Telephone conversation over the transoceanic telephone cable was held September 25, 1956, when Cleo Frank Craig, chairman of the board of the American Telegraph and Telephone Company in New York City, spoke to Dr. Charles Hill, Her Majesty's postmaster general, at Lancaster House, London, England. The cable, designed to carry 36 conversations at the same time, was the joint undertaking of the Bell System, the British Post Office (operator of the telephone service in Great Britain), and the Canadian Overseas Telecommunications Corporation. The first commercial service began with a conversation between Samuel H. Berlin of New York City and John Blackburn Batley of England. The rate was $12 for a three-minute call. The transatlantic cable—be-

The First

tween Clarenville, Newfoundland, and Oban, Scotland, a distance of about 2,250 miles—was laid by the *Monarch* from June 22, 1955, to September 26, 1955.

Telephone conversation to the moon. *See* Radio telephone: Telephone call to the moon

Telephone for domestic use was installed in April 1877 at the home of Charles Williams, Jr., of Somerville, Mass., at the corner of Arlington and Lincoln streets. Williams also had a telephone installed at the same time in his office at 109 Court Street, Boston, Mass.

Telephone message (distinguishable) was "Mr. Watson, come here, I want you," spoken into the telephone on March 10, 1876, by Alexander Graham Bell and received by Thomas Augustus Watson, on another floor in Bell's home at 5 Exeter Place, Boston, Mass.

Telephone message from a submarine underwater to shore was sent January 6, 1898, by the submarine inventor, Simon Lake, submerged at the bottom of the Patapsco River. Lake telephoned the mayor of Baltimore, Md., William Talbot Malster, at his office in the City Hall. Afterward, Lake called others in Washington, D.C., and New York City by telephone from his submarine. *(American Shipbuilder. Feb. 9, 1899)*

Telephone patent was No. 174,465, issued March 7, 1876, to Alexander Graham Bell of Salem, Mass. His application for an "improvement in telegraphy" was filed February 14, 1876. *(Catherine Dunlop Mackenzie—Alexander Graham Bell, the Man Who Contracted Space)*

Telephone recording devices were authorized by the Federal Communications Commission on June 30, 1948. They were required to have a tone-warning device producing a distinctive "beep" signal at regular intervals in order to let those taking part in the conversation know that their voices were being recorded. Recording devices had been used previously, however, by government and business.

Telephone service over the transpacific telephone cable took place June 18, 1964, when President Lyndon Baines Johnson in Washington, D.C., spoke to Premier Hayato Ikeda in Tokyo, Japan. The cable, with a capacity of 138 voice channels, stretched 5,300 nautical miles from Oahu, Hawaii, to Japan (via Midway, Wake, and Guam) and joined existing cables at Hawaii to the United States mainland, Canada, and Australia. Partners in the $80-million cable project were American Telephone and Telegraph Company, Kokusai Denshin Denwa Company, Ltd. (KDD) of Japan, the Hawaiian Telephone Company, and RCA Communications, Inc.

The First

TELEPHONE—*Continued*

Telephone switchboard or exchange was put in operation on May 17, 1877. It was located at 342 Washington Street, Boston, Mass., where Edwin Thomas Holmes was operating an electrical burglar alarm business. Holmes' office was connected by wire to a number of banks and similar institutions, and the telephones were placed in the offices of a few of his subscribers and connected to these wires. The first switchboard was connected with the telephones of six subscribers when the service began. It served as a telephone system by day and as a burglar alarm system at night. The telephones were connected only in the daytime. *(Herbert Newton Casson—History of the Telephone)*

Telephone switchboard or exchange (commercial) was installed on January 28, 1878, in New Haven, Conn., and served 21 subscribers. For the first six weeks the exchange was not operated at night. The first operator was George Willard Coy of New Haven. The first regularly employed boy operator was Louis Herrick Frost. "Ahoy-ahoy" was the first experimental shout, instead of "hello." *(Telephone Almanac—American Telephone and Telegraph Co.)*

Telephone switchboard or exchange for Chinese-American subscribers was established in 1894 by Loo Kum Shu in the Chinatown district of San Francisco, Calif. It was operated by three Chinese-American men who handled all the calls. The exchange is now the "China" central office of the Pacific Telephone and Telegraph Company and is located on Washington Street, east of Grant Avenue, San Francisco. The original number of subscribers was 100, a total which had increased by 1946 to over 2,000. At first all calls were made by name, but later the number system was adopted.

Telephone switchboard or exchange (multiple) was installed in Chicago, Ill., in January 1879.

Telephone switchboard with Braille markings and devices to enable the blind to operate it by touch and sound was designed by the Western Electric Company and installed by the New York Telephone Company on April 1, 1928, in the New York Institute for the Education of the Blind, the Bronx, New York City. The first operator was Frances Sievert, who held the position for over 25 years.

Telephone transatlantic wedding. *See* Wedding: Transatlantic telephone wedding

Telephone used by a railroad company was installed by the Pennsylvania Railroad Company. On May 21, 1877, Alexander Graham Bell sent his associate, Gardiner Greene Hubbard, and his mechanical expert, Thomas Augustus Watson, to Altoona, Pa., to give the telephone a trial test in the Pennsylvania Railroad Company shops. The

The First

demonstration was successful, and a permanent installation was made.

Telephone weather-forecasting service was inaugurated April 8, 1939, at New York City. A steel tape recorder, developed by the Bell Telephone Laboratories, was equipped to answer 30,000 inquiries a day based on reports obtained from the New York City Weather Bureau.

Telephone with push buttons instead of a rotary dial was the Touch-Tone Telephone with 10 push buttons, manufactured by the Western Electric Manufacturing and Supply Unit of the Bell System and placed in commercial service in Carnegie and Greensburg, Pa., on November 18, 1963, following marketing trials in Ohio and Pennsylvania. Service was offered at an extra charge on an optional basis.

Toll-line commercial telephone service was instituted on April 2, 1879, between Springfield, Mass., and Holyoke, Mass., by the District Telephone Company of New Haven, Conn. The distance was about 8 miles.

Transatlantic telephone service (commercial) was established between New York and London. It was inaugurated on January 7, 1927, when Walter Sherman Gifford, president of the American Telephone and Telegraph Company, in New York, talked to Sir George Evelyn Pemberton Murray, Secretary of the British Post Office, in London. Thirty-one commercial calls were made the first day. The charge was $75 for a three-minute conversation. The first private conversation was made by Adolph Simon Ochs, publisher of the New York *Times,* to Geoffrey Dawson, editor of the London *Times.* The messages were transmitted from Rocky Point, L.I., N.Y.

Transcontinental telephone demonstration was held January 25, 1915. On that date Alexander Graham Bell, calling from the offices of the American Telephone and Telegraph Company, New York City and using a model of the first telephone, again spoke the words "Mr. Watson, come here, I want you." Thomas Augustus Watson, in San Francisco, about 3,000 miles away, responded. Later, Mayor John Purroy Mitchel of New York City talked with Mayor James Rolph, Jr., of San Francisco. Commercial service was inaugurated April 7, 1915, the toll being $20.70 for the first three minutes and $6.75 for each minute thereafter.

Trimline telephone was placed in service by the Michigan Bell Telephone Company, Detroit, Mich., at Jackson, Mich., on October 21, 1963. It became commercially available throughout its territory on August 2, 1965, on an optional basis at a monthly charge of $1. The dial was mounted in the receiver midway between the mouth and the ear pieces, eliminating the need to reach for the base when dialing.

The First

Underground-cable long-distance telephone conversation was held February 26, 1914, between Boston, Mass., and Washington, D.C.

TELEPHONE DIRECTORY was issued February 21, 1878, by the New Haven District Telephone Company, New Haven, Conn. It listed about 50 names.

TELEPHONE OPERATOR

Woman telephone operator was Emma M. Nutt, who went to work for the Telephone Despatch Company, Boston, Mass., on September 1, 1878. Miss Nutt was hired by Edwin Thomas Holmes. Previously, operators had all been men.

TELESCOPE

Reflecting telescope was manufactured by Amasa Holcomb of Southwick, Mass., about 1826. The first one, made to order for John A. Fulton of Chillicothe, Ohio, was 14 feet long, with a 10-inch aperture and 6 eyepieces magnifying from 90 to 960 times. Telescopes were later made in four standard sizes. *(Elias Loomis—The Recent Progress of Astronomy, Especially the United States)*

Telescope lens 200 inches in diameter was molded by the Corning Glass Works, Corning, N.Y. On December 2, 1934, molten glass at 2,700 degrees Fahrenheit was poured into a ceramic mold, the construction of which had required several months. The temperature of the glass was lowered a degree or two a day during a period of 1 months; after this cooling period, the glass was removed to room temperature. The 20-ton disc was shipped on March 26, 1936, to the California Institute of Technology for grinding and polishing before installation in a telescope at the Mount Palomar Observatory, on Palomar Mountain, San Diego County, Calif. The lens was ground and polished over a period of 11 years and completed October 3, 1947. The first test pictures were taken in December 1947. The telescope and observatory were officially dedicated on June 3, 1948, at which time the instrument was named the Hale telescope in honor of the late Dr. George Ellery Hale, who had conceived and promoted it. The telescope was first used on February 1, 1949, to observe the constellation of Coma Berenices (area 7), near the north pole of the Milky Way, and objects 6 sextillion (6 billion trillion) miles away. *(David Oakes Woodbury—Glass Giant of Palomar)*

Telescope patent was No. 8,509, granted to Alvan Clark of Cambridge, Mass., November 11, 1851, for a combination of a glass and a sliding tube.

TELESCOPIC FISHING ROD. *See* Fishing rod

TELETYPE SERVICE

Teletype service (commercial) was inaugurated November 20, 1931, by the American Telegraph and Telephone Company. Messages typed on

The First

tape were transmitted automatically to a central office and retransmitted to their destinations. The charges were based on the time required to transmit each message, not on the number of words. On December 1, 1931, the teletype systems of the Postal Telegraph Company and the Western Union Telegraph Company cooperated in "Timed Wire Service" so that a patron of one service could transmit to a patron of the other service.

Teletypewriter system employed by a police department was opened by Governor John Stuchell Fisher of Pennsylvania and placed in service December 23, 1929, at central headquarters, Harrisburgh, Pa. It was connected to 95 cities and boroughs by 3,400 miles of telephone wires.

TELETYPESETTER

Teletypesetter was manufactured by the Teletypesetter Corporation, Chicago, Ill., and sold in October 1932 to a job printing plant in Detroit, Mich. The teletypesetter consisted of two units: a perforator for preparing a paper tape and an operating unit for attachment to either a Linotype or Intertype machine. As the tape was automatically fed into the operating unit, the keys of the line-casting machine were depressed and lines of type steadily produced at a speed impossible to match by manual operation.

Teletypesetter circuit operated by a news agency was established April 23, 1951, in Charlotte, N.C., by the Associated Press. The first message was "Greetings. This is the opening of the first teletypesetter circuit." Messages were sent by means of tape, which was perforated by machine and fed into a transmitter. At the receiving stations, a reperforating machine fed the tape into a monitor printer, which prepared the type for publication.

Teletypesetter installed in a school was placed on a Model 8 Linotype at the Empire State School of Printing, Ithaca, N.Y. The installation was made July 5, 1933, by the Teletypesetter Corporation, Chicago, Ill.

TELEVISION

See also

Television—Mobile unit	Television receiver
Television—Telecast	Television station
Television license	Television tube

College credit course in television was offered by the School of Speech, Marquette University, Milwaukee, Wis. The course, entitled "Introduction to Television," began in the fall of 1951. Fourteen students registered for instruction in programing, administrative duties, and coordination of writing, staging, directing, and acting. The course was conducted by Colby Lewis, assistant program manager of WTMJ-TV, Milwaukee.

The First

TELEVISION—*Continued*

Color television units to out sell black and white units did so in 1968, according to the Electronic Industries Association marketing service department, when 11.4 million units were sold of which 5.8 million were color and 5.5 million black and white.

Community television antenna system was placed in operation in December 1949 in Astoria, Oreg., by Le Roy Edward Parsons. There were three subscribers.

Electronic television system using the pickup device known as the Iconoscope, which displaced the mechanical system by means of motor-driven scanning disks, was invented by Vladimir Kosma Zworykin of Wilkinsburg, Pa., who obtained patent No. 2,141,059 on December 20, 1938. The patent covered 40 claims and was assigned to the Westinghouse Electric and Manufacturing Company, East Pittsburgh, Pa. Zworykin's application was filed December 29, 1923.

Municipal television film unit organized to produce films for presentation on commercial stations was established February 15, 1949, by the Municipal Broadcasting System of the City of New York. The first television supervisor was Clifford Evans.

Submarine with closed-circuit television was the *Tullibee,* SSB (N) 597, commissioned November 9, 1960. The keel was laid May 26, 1958, and the submarine launched April 27, 1960, at the Thames River plant of General Dynamic Corporation's Electric Boat division, Groton, Conn. The *Tullibee* was 273 feet long and had a displacement of 2,600 tons when submerged. It carried a crew of 60 men and 6 officers.

Television annual billing to exceed $6 billion was recorded in 1976: national network sales $2,-674,900,000; national nonnetwork sales $1,-922,600,000; local sales $1,431,900,000; total $6,029,400,000.

Television course in planning, writing, and producing television programs offered by a university began September 26, 1940, in evening sessions at New York University, New York City. The first instructor was Thomas H. Hutchinson of the National Broadcasting Company.

Television eyewitness allowed to testify in a federal court was Mrs. Sophie Eisenberg of Brooklyn, N.Y., who testified in United States Federal Court, New York City, before Judge Irving Robert Kaufman. On March 16, 1947, while viewing a hockey game between the Montreal Canadiens and the New York Rangers televised from Madison Square Garden, New York City, Mrs. Eisenberg saw Emile (Butch) Bouchard, captain of the Canadiens, hit Jonas Walvisch, a spectator from New York City. The spectator lost his $75,000 law-

The First

suit against the player, which was tried January 29, 1951.

Television industry profits to exceed those of radio were reported by the Federal Communications Commission on December 16, 1954, for the year 1953: television and networks, $68 million; radio and networks, $55 million.

Television news commentator who was black was Malvin Russell ("Mel") Goode of Pittsburgh, Pa., who was assigned on August 29, 1962, by WABC-TV to the United Nations staff, New York City.

TELEVISION—MOBILE UNIT

Mobile television unit for outdoor events consisted of two large motor vans containing television control apparatus and a microwave transmitter. The unit was completed by the RCA Manufacturing Company, Camden, N.J., and turned over to the National Broadcasting Company (W2XBT), New York City, on December 12, 1937. The telecasts were relayed by microwave to a tower transmitter in the Empire State Building, New York City, and rebroadcast from there.

Mobile television units (color) were placed in operation January 1, 1954, by the National Broadcasting Company's station WNBT, New York City. Two three-color mobile units with complete audio-video control were housed in an automobile van 35 feet long, 8 feet wide, and 10 feet 7 inches high.

TELEVISION—TELECAST

Academy of Motion Pictures Arts and Sciences annual awards telecast was made March 19, 1953, when pick-ups of the 25th award ceremony were made from New York City and Hollywood, Calif., and broadcast over 174 radio stations. Awards were made to Paramount Pictures for *The Greatest Show on Earth* (best picture), Gary Cooper (best actor) for his performance in *High Noon,* and Shirley Booth (best actress) for her performance in *Come Back, Little Sheba.* Many others received awards for their accomplishments in other specific categories.

Airplane telecast (network) was made by WRC-TV, Washington, D.C., from 9:40 A.M. to 11:25 A.M. on December 17, 1948, with a 20-watt transmitter from an Air Force C-47 airplane cruising over Washington, D.C., to an Air Force receiver in the Smithsonian Institution and from there relayed to a mobile unit and to the transmitter of WNBW at the Wardman Park Hotel, Washington, D.C. The occasion was the formal installation of the Wright brothers' airplane in the Smithsonian Institution. Previously television programs had been relayed by Westinghouse-Martin stratovision airplanes.

Art auction televised on a coast-to-coast circuit was held April 27, 1960, for the benefit of New York City's Museum of Modern Art's Thirtieth

The First

Anniversary Fund. It originated at the Parke-Bernet Galleries, New York City, and was seen in New York City, Chicago, Dallas, and Los Angeles through TNT Theatre Network Television.

Atomic bomb detonation from a captive balloon telecast was shown at 7:00 A.M. PDT, September 19, 1958. The balloon was 500 feet over Yucca Flat, Nev. The flash lasted only a second and was heard 30 miles away. It was the 112th shot since Alamogordo in 1945.

Atomic explosion telecast was made February 1, 1951, by KTLA, Los Angeles, Calif. A camera on Mount Wilson telecast a blast at Frenchman Flats, Nev., 300 miles away. The explosion was part of "Operation Ranger." It was the third by the Atomic Energy Commission and was shown on Channel 4, NBC network.

Atomic explosion telecast on a network was made April 22, 1952, from News Nob, Nev., by KTLA, Los Angeles, Calif. The image was relayed to the Atomic Energy Commission's station a quarter of a mile away; then 46 miles to Charleston Peak; 140 miles to another station; 125 miles to Mount San Antonio; and finally 23 miles to the KTLA transmitter on Mount Wilson. The explosion was part of "Operation Tumbler Snapper."

Auction of federal property to be televised was carried by closed circuit to six cities (Boston, Chicago, Columbus, New York, Philadelphia, and St. Louis) on October 7, 1959. Nine auctioneers conducted an eight-hour sale that brought $2,800,000 from the disposal of objects ranging from cartridge belts to cranes to Eisenhower jackets at the Philadelphia Naval Shipyard, the Air Force Depot at Shelby, Ohio, and the Army Engineer Depot at Granite City, Ill., from which the telecast emanated. More than 3,500 miles of coaxial cable were used.

Audience-participation telecast was a program of charades presented on August 7, 1941, by station WNBT, New York City.

Baseball game (collegiate) televised was the Columbia-Princeton game played May 17, 1939, at Baker Field, New York City. The game lasted ten innings and was won by Princeton, 2-1. It was telecast by station W2XBS, New York City. Bill Stern was the announcer, Burke Crotty the director, and Dick Pickard, the cameraman. Two mobile vans were used. The pictures were transmitted to the Empire State Building, New York City, and rebroadcast. The game was telecast from 4:00 P.M. to 6:15 P.M.

Baseball games (major-league) televised were two National League games played at Ebbets Field, Brooklyn, N.Y., August 26, 1939, between the Cincinnati Reds and the Brooklyn Dodgers. Station W2XBS, New York City, televised the

The First

games, using two cameras alternately, according to the play. Leo Durocher, manager of the Dodgers, William McKechnie, manager of the Reds, and several players appeared during the intermission of the double-header. Walter L. ("Red") Barber was the announcer.

Baseball games televised in color were the two games of a National League double-header played August 11, 1951, at Ebbets Field, Brooklyn, N.Y., between the Brooklyn Dodgers and the Boston Braves. The games were televised by WCBS-TV of the Columbia Broadcasting System. Walter Lanier (Red) Barber and Connie Desmond were the announcers. The Dodgers won the first game, 8-1, and the Braves the second game, 8-4.

Baseball major league night game telecast was played at the Atlanta Stadium, Atlanta, Ga., on May 30, 1966, from 7:00 P.M. to 9:45 P.M. and telecast by Channel 4. The National League Los Angeles Dodgers defeated the Atlanta Braves, 10-6.

Baseball World Series game televised was the opening game of the 1947 series, played on September 30, 1947, between the New York Yankees of the American League and the Brooklyn Dodgers of the National League at the Yankee Stadium, New York City. The game was transmitted to three stations (WABD, WCBS, WNBT) in New York City and to all the video outlets along the Eastern seaboard. The entire series was telecast under the joint sponsorship of the Ford Motor Company and the Gillette Safety Razor Company, at a cost of $65,000. The Yankees won the first game, 5-3, and the series, 4 games to 3. The play-by-play descriptions were given by Bob Edge, Bob Stanton, and Bill Slater.

Baseball World Series game televised in color was the opening game of the 1955 series, played on September 28, 1955, between the New York Yankees of the American League and the Brooklyn Dodgers of the National League at the Yankee Stadium, New York City. The game was televised by WRCA-TV. The Yankees won, 6–5. The series was won by Brooklyn, 4-3.

Basketball game to be televised was played February 28, 1940, at Madison Square Garden, and televised by station W2XBS, New York City. Fordham University played the University of Pittsburgh. Pittsburgh won the game, 50-37. A game between Georgetown University and New York University followed. New York University won, 50-27. Both games were televised.

Beauty contest (national) telecast was the Miss America Pageant, telecast September 11, 1954, by ABC from 10:30 P.M. to 12:00 P.M. from Convention Hall, Atlantic City, N.J. Bess Myerson and John (Charles) Daly narrated. Lee Ann Meriwether of San Francisco was named Miss America. Six cameras were used. Bert Parks was master of ceremonies.

Beauty contest telecast took place at 7:00 P.M. June 22, 1939, from Flushing Meadows, New York

The First

TELEVISION—TELECAST—*Continued*
City, during the New York World's Fair. The Fairest of the Fair contest was held on the Wild West Show and Rodeo platform in the amusement.

Bicycle race telecast was the 6-day bicycle race at Madison Square Garden, New York City, from May 15, 1939, to May 21, 1939. The telecast was shown by W2XBS, National Broadcasting Company (NBC), on May 20, 1939 from 8:30 P.M. to 9:00 P.M. and showed 10 teams in action. Only 8 of the 12 teams of riders completed the race. The starting gun was fired by Joe DiMaggio, Yankee center fielder; Bill Stern was the announcer. The race, 2,388 miles, was won by William Peden and Doug Peden, who scored 1,498 points in sprints; Killian and Thomas, 1,163 points; and Walthour and Crossley, 928 points.

Birth (human) to be televised (closed-circuit) was shown in color June 14, 1951, as part of the American Medical Association meeting at Atlantic City, N.J. Two thousand physicians and their families watched the birth of Michael Gallagher, who weighed 9 pounds 12 ounces.

Birth (human) to be televised for the public was shown December 2, 1952, by KOA, Denver, Colo., and televised over 49 stations of the National Broadcasting Company. Gordon Campbell Kerr, who weighed 5 pounds 7 ounces, was delivered by cesarian section in the hospital delivery room of the Colorado General Hospital of the University of Colorado Medical School, Denver. The parents were John R. Kerr and Lillian Kerr of Denver, Colo. The telecast was part of the "March of Medicine" program presented in conjunction with the annual clinical meeting of the American Medical Association.

Book review to be televised was Ernest Boyd's review on May 3, 1938, over station W2XBS, New York City, of Sidney Spencer's *The Greatest Show on Earth*. The program, which combined photographs and text to explain the economic problems of mankind, opened with a telecast of the reviewer and featured numerous pickups of photographs from the book.

Broadway play (current) to be telecast with its original cast was John Boynton Priestley's *When We Are Married*. It had been filmed in London, England, where a smaller set of scenery had been used. It was shown at the Lyceum Theatre, New York City, on December 25, 1939, and was telecast from 8:30 P.M. to 10:30 P.M. on Sunday, March 3, 1940, by W2XBS(NBC). The play featured John Charles Nugent, Alison Skipworth, Estelle Winwood, and Ann Andrews.

Cabinet meeting (staged) telecast was held May 14, 1950, at the Civic Opera House, Chicago, Ill., during a session of the Democratic National Convention and was entitled "Report to the American People." It was presided over by Vice President

The First

Alben William Barkley. Each cabinet member reported on the state of his department.

Cabinet session to be telecast and broadcast was recorded at the White House, Washington, D.C., on October 25, 1954. The telecast showed a special meeting assembled to hear the report of Secretary of State John Foster Dulles on agreements in regard to West Germany signed in Paris on October 23, 1954. All the members of President Dwight David Eisenhower's Cabinet were present. (Vice President Richard Milhous Nixon did not attend, however.) The report was broadcast and telecast over the ABC, NBC, and CBS radio and television networks.

Catholic mass (midnight) to be televised was transmitted December 24, 1948, from St. Patrick's Cathedral, New York City, by stations WNBT-TV, WJZ-TV, and WCBS-TV.

Catholic mass televised from a studio was celebrated June 10, 1953, by the Reverend Albert William Low, assistant superintendent of schools for the Roman Catholic Archdiocese, Boston, Mass., at an altar built in WBZ-TV, Boston. The telecast was permitted by the Most Reverend Richard James Cushing, archbishop of Boston.

Church service telecast was the candlelight service on December 24, 1946, at Grace Episcopal Church, Broadway at 10th Street, New York City telecast at 8:30 P.M. by WABD, on the New York-Philadelphia-Washington, D.C. network. The service was led by Rev. Louis W. Pitt; the choir of 50 men and boys, by the organist Ernest Mitchell.

Church service televised in sign language was conducted by the Reverend Floyd F. Possehl, who read the Scriptures and preached a sermon in sign language from St. Matthew's Lutheran Church for the Deaf, Jamaica, L.I., N.Y., on December 5, 1948 over WPIX-TV, New York City.

Circus telecast was a program featuring the Ringling Brothers and Barnum & Bailey circus. The three-hour show was televised April 25, 1940 from Madison Square Garden, New York City, by station W2XBS, New York City. Two cameras were used.

Color and black-and-white telecast to be sponsored was a program in the "Dragnet" series, presented December 24, 1953, by WNBT-TV, New York City, of the National Broadcasting Company. Jack Webb was featured as Detective Joe Friday and Ben Alexander as Detective Frank Smith.

Color coast-to-coast live telecast was transmitted November 3, 1953, from the Colonial Theatre, New York City, by WNBT-TV, New York City. The program, which starred Nanette Fabray, was sent in compatible color over the radio relay circuit system of the Bell Telephone Company and received by 14-inch receivers at Burbank, Calif.

The First

Color coast-to-coast telecast from the West Coast was made January 1, 1954, when the Tournament of Roses parade at Pasadena, Calif., was presented over the National Broadcasting Company network. The program was seen in color in 21 cities and in black and white in other cities. Don Ameche was the host and Roy Neal and James Wallington were the announcers.

Color commercial televised on a local show was commissioned on March 9, 1954, by Castro Decorators, Inc., New York City, in a contract with WNBT, New York City, for spot announcements. The first telecast was on August 6, 1954.

Color film (35 mm) telecast was a documentary prepared by the Leather Industries of America shown June 25, 1954, over Channel 4, NBC. It showed the various uses of leather. Previously, only 16 mm color film had been shown.

Color network telecast in compatible color was transmitted June 7, 1953, from Symphony Hall, Boston, Mass. It was seen in color in Washington, D.C., and in black-and-white elsewhere. The program was a puppet show, "St. George and the Dragon," featuring Kukla, Fran, and Ollie (Fran Allison and Burr Tillstrom), with Arthur Fiedler conducting the Boston Pops Orchestra. The operetta score was composed by John Fascinato.

Color program (commercial) was presented by 16 sponsors on June 25, 1951, at 4:35 P.M. by the Columbia Broadcasting System station in New York City and fed to Boston, Philadelphia, Baltimore, and Washington, D.C. Some of the performers were Arthur Godfrey, Faye Emerson, Sam Levenson, Robert Alda, Ed Sullivan, Isabel Bigley, and Garry Moore.

Color program (commercial) to be presented daily was Ivan T. Sanderson's "The World Is Yours," first seen on the Columbia Broadcasting System network over Channel 2 (W2CBS) on June 26, 1951, from 4:30 to 5:00 P.M. It depicted the earth's natural treasures.

Color program on coast-to-coast network commercial was the Colgate Palmolive *Colgate Comedy Hour* telecast Sunday, November 22, 1953, from the Colonial Theater, New York City, by WNBT-TV, New York City, on the National Broadcasting Company network from 8:00 P.M. to 9:00 P.M. It starred Donald O'Connor, Corinne Calvet, Ralph Bellamy, Dorothy Dandridge, and Sidney Miller.

Color telecast by a local station was presented December 18, 1953, by WPTZ-TV, Philadelphia, Pa. Color film clips of the Walt Disney Technicolor film *The Living Desert* were shown, and also a color commercial for Fels & Company's product Felso. The images were also visible in black and white.

The First

Color telecast on a closed-circuit local station was presented October 30, 1953, by WPTZ-TV, Philadelphia, Pa.

Color television demonstration of high-definition electronically scanned images was given for the press September 3, 1940, over station W2XAB of the Columbia Broadcasting System, New York City. The telecast was made from the high-power transmitter atop the Chrysler Building, New York City. It had a 343-line quality and used the 4.5 megacycle band, the same frequency required for ordinary black-and-white images. The images were received in black and white, but a color disk placed in front of the receiver tube enabled the audience at the station to view the pictures in color. The apparatus was invented by Dr. Peter Carl Goldmark, Columbia Broadcasting System's chief television engineer.

Color television demonstration (public) was given June 27, 1929, in the Bell Telephone Laboratories, New York City. Some of the objects shown in color were an American flag, a watermelon, and a bunch of roses. The images were of low definition and were mechanically scanned. The equipment demonstrated utilized three complete systems of photoelectric cells, amplifiers, and glow tubes. Each system had screens: red, blue, or green. A system of mirrors superposed the three monochromatic images to make one picture in color.

Commercial filmed by a camera operated by atomically generated electricity was produced at West Milton, N.Y., on July 18, 1955, and televised July 24, 1955, on the General Electric Summer Theatre. The three-minute commercial was produced by George Blake Enterprises, Inc., and supervised by Karl M. Fischer through Batten, Barton, Durstine and Osborne, Inc., New York City, for the General Electric Company. Nuclear energy generated the electricity produced at the West Milton power plant.

Commercial program telecast on a network was "Geographically Speaking," sponsored by Bristol-Myers Company and broadcast October 27, 1946, on WNBT (New York) and WPTZ (Philadelphia, Pa.).

Congressional opening session to be televised was the joint session of the 80th Congress that met on January 3, 1947. The proceedings were televised by the major networks.

Congressional session proceedings telecast were shown June 12, 1978, by the Associated Press for about 5 minutes. The Senate allowed a radio broadcast of the Panama Canal treaty debate. Closed circuit radio and television were beamed into offices of the House members to show the regular proceedings. Speaker Thomas Philip O'Neill, Jr., had designated Representative

The First

TELEVISION—TELECAST—*Continued*
James C. Wright, Jr., of Texas as Acting Secretary of the Senate for the day.

Congressional telecast and radio broadcast was authorized by the Senate on December 14, 1974, to permit the December 19, 1974, ceremonies for the inauguration of Nelson Aldrich Rockefeller as the 41st Vice President of the United States to be shown to the public.

Courtroom verdict telecast was that of March 14, 1964 (12:37 P.M. to 2:00 P.M.) from the Third Criminal District Court of Dallas County, Dallas, Tex. Jack Ruby (Jacob L. Rubenstein) was tried before Judge Joseph Brantley Brown for the murder (November 24, 1963) of Lee Harvey Oswald, alleged assassin of President John Fitzgerald Kennedy (November 22, 1963), and was sentenced to death in the electric chair for "murder with malice." The trial began March 4, 1964. The broadcast was pooled by the Columbia Broadcasting System, sent to New York City, and shared with the NBC and ABC networks.

Debate (nationally telecast) among candidates within a political party for the presidential nomination took place January 5, 1980, at Des Moines, Iowa, when 6 Republican candidate competitors faced each other in a 2-hour debate. There were 6 candidates: John Anderson of Illinois, Howard Baker, Jr., of Tennessee, George Bush of Texas, John Connally of Texas, Philip Crane of Illinois, and Robert Dole of Kansas. Ronald Reagan was absent. The confrontation was sponsored by the Des Moines *Register and Tribune.*

Demonstration of a telecast before a large audience took place May 23, 1927, before about 600 members of the American Institute of Electrical Engineers and the Institute of Radio Engineers in the Bell Telephone building, 55 Bethune Street, New York City. Switchboard operators on another floor were projected on a screen. L. S. O'Roarke explained the technical details of the telecast.

Demonstration of home reception of television was given in New York City on August 20, 1930, when a half-hour program broadcast from two stations was received on screens placed in a store in the Hotel Ansonia at Broadway and 73d Street, in the Hearst Building at Eighth Avenue and 57th Street, and in a residence at 98 Riverside Drive. On these screens appeared the images of performers talking and singing in the studios of the Jenkins W2XCR television station at Jersey City, N.J., and the de Forest W2XCD station at Passaic, N.J. The distance, approximately six miles, was the greatest over which pictures had been transmitted by television. Harry Hirschfeld, cartoonist, was master of ceremonies, introducing George Jessel, Arthur ("Bugs") Baer, Health Commissioner Shirley Wilmotte Wynne, Benny Rubin, Diana Seaby, and other entertainers. Sets had been installed in homes earlier, however. On January 13, 1928, the

The First

Radio Corporation of America and the General Electric Company installed three home sets in Schenectady, N.Y. The images were transmitted over a wavelength of 37.8 meters and the sound sent simultaneously over a wavelength of 379.5 meters. The picture was 1½ inches square. The television receiver's elements were a light source, a scanning device, and a synchronizing system.

Department store sales demonstrations (large-scale) were staged at Gimbel Brothers, Philadelphia, Pa., from October 24 to November 14, 1945, inclusive, with RCA-Victor equipment. A preview was held October 23, 1945. Approximately 25,000 people viewed the demonstrations at the auditorium and at 20 telesites scattered at strategic locations on the seven floors of the department store. Eleven daily demonstrations of about ten minutes each were given showing millinery, home furnishings, shoes, scarves, furs, nursery furniture, toys, curtains, interior decorating, and hair styling.

Dirigible telecast was made December 31, 1954, by the Camel News Caravan and showed the preparations for the telecast of the Tournament of Roses Parade, Pasadena, Calif., January 1, 1955, 12:15 P.M. to 1:45 P.M.

Drama series regularly scheduled was the *Kraft Television Theater* telecast on the National Broadcasting Company's network from May 7, 1947, to October 1, 1958, from 7:30 P.M. to 8:30 P.M. In the series' 11½-year run, 650 plays were presented; 5,236 sets were used; and 3,955 actors participated. The first drama was *Double Door,* starring John Baragrey.

Editorial opinion telecast on a network was voiced by Dr. Frank Stanton, president of the Columbia Broadcasting System, who made a 15-minute appeal on August 26, 1954, protesting the barring of radio and television from the hearings to censure Joseph Raymond McCarthy, representative in Congress from the state of Wisconsin.

Fashion show telecast was presented May 17, 1939, by WNBT-TV, New York City, in cooperation with the Swiss Fabric Group and the Ostrich Feather Group from the Ritz-Carlton Hotel, New York City. Renee Macready was the fashion coordinator.

Football game coast-to-coast telecast was made at Champaign-Urbana, Ill., on October 6, 1951 from 3:52 P.M. to 5:35 P.M. and telecast to 36 stations of the National Broadcasting Company's system. The Illini of the University of Illinois defeated the Badgers of the University of Wisconsin 14-10.

Football game (collegiate) sponsored was the night game played September 26, 1941, at the Owl's Stadium, Philadelphia, Pa., between Temple University and the University of Kansas. Temple won 31-9. The game was telecast by

The First

WPTZ-TV and was sponsored by the Atlantic Refining Company.

Football game (collegiate) to be televised was played at Randall's Island, New York City, September 30, 1939, between Fordham University and Waynesburg College and televised by station W2XBS, New York City. Fordham won, 34-7.

Football game (professional championship) telecast was shown January 15, 1967, from the Super Bowl, Los Angeles, Calif., when the National League Green Bay Packers defeated the American League Kansas City Chiefs 35-10. The telecast was pooled and shown by NBC-TV and CBS-TV.

Football game (professional) to be televised was transmitted on October 22, 1939, from Ebbets Field, Brooklyn, N.Y., by W2XBS of the National Broadcasting Company, New York City. The Brooklyn Dodgers defeated the Philadelphia Eagles, 23-14.

Football game televised in color on a network was transmitted September 29, 1951, by Channel 2 of the Columbia Broadcasting System from Franklin Field, Philadelphia, Pa. The Golden Bears of the University of California defeated the Quakers of the University of Pennsylvania, 35-0.

High-definition telecast was made June 29, 1936, by W2XBS from the Empire State Building, New York City, at the rate of 30 pictures per second with the 343-line screen. On July 7, 1936, David Sarnoff, president of the Radio Corporation of America, and Major General James Guthrie Harbord, chairman of the board of RCA, opened for invited guests a program in which Henry Hull, Graham McNamee, Ed Wynn, and members of the Water Lily Ensemble appeared as performers. A fashion show and a film were also presented.

Hockey game to be televised was played February 25, 1940, at Madison Square Garden, New York City, between the New York Rangers and the Montreal Canadiens and televised by W2XBS, New York City. The Rangers won, 6-2.

Horse race (Kentucky Derby) telecast in color was shown May 7, 1966, from Churchill Downs, Louisville, Ky., from 5:00 P.M. to 6:00 P.M. by Channel 2 WCBS-TV. The race, the 92nd consecutive running, was won by Michael J. Ford's Kauai King.

Horse-race telecast shown on a large screen in a theater was the Dwyer Stakes (1½ miles) at Aqueduct Race Track, won by Whirlaway, a 3-year old owned by Calumet Farms and ridden by Eddie Arcaro, on June 21, 1941. The race was telecast by W2XBS, New York City. It was shown on a 9-by-6½-foot rear-projection screen at the Rialto Theatre, 42nd Street, New York City, on equipment leased from Scophony Television, London, England.

The First

Husband and wife to broadcast a religious program were Dr. Norman Vincent Peale, minister of the Marble Collegiate Church, New York City, and Mrs. Ruth Peale, who on October 1, 1952, began a television series entitled "What's Your Trouble?" The program was produced by the Broadcasting and Film Commission of the National Council of the Churches of Christ in the United States and presented on the Columbia Broadcasting System.

Instruction (large-scale operation) telecast on a closed-circuit was offered in September 1956 to about 6,000 pupils in 8 public schools in Washington County, Md. The system was expanded in September 1963, when the 45 public schools in the county were linked to the television circuit. The Fund for the Advancement of Education and the Ford Foundation contributed about $200,000 a year to the project over a 5-year period. The Electronics Industries Association provided the equipment, a donation worth $300,000 made by 75 manufacturers.

International telecast took place October 15, 1951, from 10:45 A.M. to 11:15 A.M., when WWJ-TV, Detroit, Mich., had its mobile unit pick up the informal reception given Princess Elizabeth of Great Britain and Philip, Duke of Edinburgh, on Government Dock, Windsor, Canada. Budd Lynch was the announcer. The program was carried by the National Broadcasting Company and the American Broadcasting Company on Channel 4 and Channel 7. Princess Elizabeth became Elizabeth II, queen of Great Britain and Northern Ireland, on the death of her father George VI on February 6, 1952. Her coronation took place June 2, 1953.

Jewish temple services (complete) to be televised were shown November 4, 1951, from Temple Israel of the City of New York, by WPIX-TV, New York City. Rabbi William Franklin Rosenblum preached the sermon. Cantor Harold Orbach, of Temple Israel, New Rochelle, N.Y., conducted the musical portions. This service, as well as three others on successive Saturdays, was arranged by the Radio and Television Division of the American Jewish Committee.

King and queen to be televised were King George VI and Queen Elizabeth of Great Britain, who, on June 10, 1939, visited the New York World's Fair, New York City, during "British Week." They were pictured visiting the exhibits.

Laser-light-beam program telecast on a network (light amplification by stimulated emission of radiation) was Columbia Broadcasting System's *I've Got A Secret* telecast of May 14, 1963, from New York City. An electronic signal from a studio television camera was fed into a laser transmitter, carried across a 2-foot space on a light beam, picked up by a laser receiver, and transmitted via the studio control room over the national televi-

The First

TELEVISION—TELECAST—*Continued*
sion network. This laser communications system
was developed by Samuel M. Stone and Louis
Richard Bloom, General Telephone and Electronics Corporation scientists.

Live national commercial cablecast via satellite
was a game between the Birmingham Bulls and
the Edmonton Oilers of the World Hockey Association in Birmingham, Ala., transmitted via RCA
Satcom satellite on December 2, 1976. Edmonton
won 4-3.

**Live telecast from a noncontiguous foreign
country** was transmitted November 13, 1955, by
CMQ, Havana, Cuba. A five-minute aerial view of
Havana was televised from an airplane to CMQ
and thence relayed by airplanes to WIOD, Miami,
Fla., for telecasting on Dave Garroway's show
"Wide Wide World" on the National Broadcasting System network.

**Live television program seen simultaneously in
Europe and the United States.** *See* Television—
Telecast: Transoceanic television program

Medical intercity color telecast was shown
December 6-9, 1949, by WMAR-TV, Baltimore,
Md., from the John Hopkins Hospital, Baltimore,
over a closed circuit of the Columbia Broadcasting System to a clinical session of the American
Medical Association at the National Guard Armory, Washington, D.C. The telecast was arranged
by Georgetown University and George Washington University.

**Medical symposium televised coast to coast on
a closed circuit** was shown September 23, 1954, on
large-screen (11 by 14 feet) projection units in 23
cities by Box Office Television, Inc., through the
cooperation of the American College of Physicians and the Wyeth Laboratories, Philadelphia,
Pa. About 5,000 physicians at the Columbia
Auditorium, Louisville, Ky., viewed the telecast,
which originated in New York City. The postgraduate symposium dealt with hypertension.

Missing persons telecast was made October 3,
1943, by the Missing Persons Bureau of the Police
Department of the City of New York on W2XWV,
the DuMont station in New York City.

Motion picture (full-length) telecast was Alexander Korda's *The Return of the Scarlet Pimpernel*, a 1½-hour film shown by NBC on May 31,
1938, on a screen 7 by 10 inches. Preceding the
film, 5 actors produced a 20-minute play for children entitled *Sauce for the Gander*.

Motion picture premiere festivities to be televised were presented December 19, 1939, on
W2XBS of the National Broadcasting Company
on the occasion of the New York opening of *Gone
With the Wind*. Two cameras, one on the sidewalk outside the Capitol Theatre, New York City,
and the other in the lobby, recorded interviews
with celebrities. Ben Grauer was the master of

The First

ceremonies. The film, based on Margaret Mitchell's novel, was produced by David Oliver Selznick. It starred Clark Gable and Vivien Leigh.

Motion picture premiere performance to be televised was a presentation of a two-reel short *Patrolling the Ether*, which was televised April 10,
1944, simultaneously by WNBT of New York City,
WRGB of Schenectady, N.Y., and WPTZ of Philadelphia, Pa. The film depicted the wartime activities of the radio intelligence division of the
Federal Communications Commission in tracing
illegal and espionage radio transmitters. It was
produced by Metro-Goldwyn-Mayer and released
April 22, 1944, 12 days after its premiere on television.

Motion picture premiere performance to be televised (feature-length foreign film) was a presentation on WNBT, New York City, on January 1, 1948,
of *African Journey*, a French film featuring Victor
Francen and Harry Baur. English dialogue was
dubbed in on the sound track.

Motion picture premiere performance to be televised (major film) was a presentation of *The Constant Husband* by the National Broadcasting
Company on a coast-to-coast network from
WNBT-TV, New York City, on November 6, 1955.
The picture was a London Films production starring Rex Harrison and Margaret Leighton. It was
directed by Sir Alexander Korda.

Motion picture premiere telecast on 2 successive nights was *Vanished*, a 4-hour adaptation by
Dean Riesner of Fletcher Knebel's novel about
intrigue in Washington, a 2-part film, the first part
shown March 8, 1971, at 9:00 P.M., the second telecast on March 9, 1971, over Channel 4 of the National Broadcasting Company. The cast included
Richard Widmark, Robert Young, E. G. Marshall,
Skye Hubrey, and Tom Bosley.

Motion picture trailer to be televised was
shown September 20, 1946, on WNBT-TV, New
York City. It advertised a Columbia Pictures film
The Jolson Story.

Murder (actual) shown on television took place
at 12:20 P.M. on November 24, 1963, in the police
headquarters at Dallas, Tex. While pictures of Lee
Harvey Oswald, alleged assassin of President
John Fitzgerald Kennedy, were being televised for
news programs, Jack Ruby (Jacob L. Rubenstein)
fired a concealed pistol and killed Oswald, a
crime witnessed by millions of people.

Murder trial to be televised was the trial of
Harry Washburn, held December 5-9, 1955, in the
District Court, Waco, Tex., with Judge Drummond
William Bartlett presiding. The defense and
prosecution had agreed to the placing of one camera on a balcony, and the entire 25-hour proceedings were televised by KWTX-TV, Waco, as a
public service to the community. On December 10,
1955, Washburn was convicted of the automobile

The First

bomb slaying of his former mother-in-law, Mrs. Helen Harris Weaver, at San Angelo, Tex., and sentenced to life imprisonment. The jury was never shown the program.

Musical comedy (full-length) written especially for television was *The Boys from Boise,* produced by the Charles M. Storm Company for *Esquire* magazine on September 28, 1944, over WABD, New York City. The program was directed by Ray Nelson.

Musical comedy telecast (one-hour) was a performance of "Topsy and Eva—Television Edition," presented July 25, 1939, by W2XBS of National Broadcasting Company, New York City. The entertainers who appeared on the program were the Duncan sisters, Billy Kent, Florence Auer, Winfield Hoeney, Edwin Vail, the Southernaires, and the Chansonettes.

Newsreel telecast presented daily was the 20th Century-Fox Movietone News telecast, first presented on February 16, 1948, over the National Broadcasting Company's East Coast network. The program was sponsored by the R. J. Reynolds Tobacco Company.

Opera (complete) to be televised was presented December 23, 1943, by WRGB of the General Electric Company, Schenectady, N.Y. The presentation was Humperdinck's *Hansel and Gretel.*

Opera (complete) to be televised from the Metropolitan Opera House was Giuseppe Verdi's *Otello,* a three-and-a-half-hour performance on November 29, 1948, sponsored by the Texaco Company over WJZ-TV, New York City. It starred Licia Albanese, Ramon Vinay, Leonard Warren, Martha Lipton, John Garris, and Nicola Moscona and was conducted by Fritz Busch. Milton Cross was the commentator. The telecast was also seen at network outlets in Philadelphia, Pa., Baltimore, Md., Washington, D.C., and Boston, Mass.

Opera from the Metropolitan Opera House especially tailored and trimmed for television was Johann Strauss's *Die Fledermaus,* sung in English and telecast on *Omnibus* on Channel 2 from 4:30 P.M. to 6:00 P.M. on February 1, 1953. The cast included Lois Hunt, Charles Kullman, Brenda Lewis, and John Brownice.

Opera (major) televised in color was Bizet's *Carmen* presented October 31, 1953, by the NBC-TV Opera Theatre in compatible color in a one-hour program transmitted by WNBT-TV, New York City. It was sung in English. Vera Bryner was Carmen; Robert Rounseville, Don José; and Warren Galjour, Escamillo. Peter Herman Adler was the director.

Opera telecast was presented by members of the Metropolitan Opera Company, on March 10, 1940, over W2XBS, New York City. A condensed version of the first act of Ruggiero Leoncavallo's *I Pagliacci* was televised from a Radio City studio.

The First

Edward Johnson, general manager of the Metropolitan Opera Company, was the master of ceremonies, and Francis St. Leger conducted. In the cast were Armand Tokatyan (tenor), Hilda Burke (soprano), Richard Bonelli (baritone), George Cehanovsky (baritone), and Alessio de Paolis (tenor).

Opera written for television was *Amahl and the Night Visitors,* by Gian-Carlo Menotti, first televised December 24, 1951, by the National Broadcasting Company from WNBT, New York City. The program was sponsored by Hallmark Greeting Cards. Thomas Schippers was the conductor and Chet Allen, a 12-year-old boy soprano, the featured singer. The opera tells the story of the Three Wise Men and the miraculous cure of a crippled boy.

Opera written for television on commission for a commercial sponsor was *The Parrot,* presented by the Armstrong Cork Company of Lancaster, Pa., from WNBT, New York City, on March 24, 1953. Darrell Peter composed the score. The book, by Frank P. De Felitta, told the story of an eccentric old lady who willed her money to a parrot. The opera was directed by Garry Simpson. Six singers participated in the 23-minute show.

Operetta to be televised was Gilbert and Sullivan's *Pirates of Penzance,* presented June 20, 1939, from 8:30 to 9:30 P.M., by W2XBS, New York City. The program starred Margaret Daum and Ray Heatherton. Harold Sanford was the conductor.

Outdoor scenes to be televised were viewed in the offices of the Bell Telephone Laboratories, New York City, on July 12, 1928. Scenes enacted in the open air were almost as clear as those taken in specially designed studios.

Outer-space live telecast was made October 14, 1968, when Captain Walter Marty Schirra, Jr. (U.S. Navy), Major Donn Fulton Eisele (U.S. Air Force), and Major Ronnie Walter Cunningham (U.S. Marine Corps) showed views of the inside of the satellite and views through the windows of *Apollo VII. Apollo VII* was launched October 11, 1968, from launch complex 34 at Kennedy Space Center, Fla., at 11:03 A.M. E.D.T. and was recovered after a 260-hour 8-minute flight.

Outer-space live telecast from a manned spacecraft was transmitted at 3:01 P.M., December 22, 1968, from *Apollo VIII,* while it was 139,000 miles from earth, 31 hours 20 minutes after launching at Cape Kennedy, Fla. The earth appeared as a blurred ball of light. The crew consisted of Captain James Arthur Lovell, Jr. (U.S. Navy), Colonel Frank Borman (U.S. Air Force), and Major William Alison Anders (U.S. Air Force).

Outer-space telecast of pictures of the earth was transmitted August 14, 1959, when the paddlewheel satellite *Explorer 6* (launched August 7,

TELEVISION—TELECAST—*Continued*
1959) showed a 20,000-square-mile area. The total weight of the satellite, including the paddlewheels, was 142 pounds.

Passover services telecast were shown April 25, 1940, in New York City, by the National Broadcasting Company's studio set up as a dining room. Rabbi Saul Bezalel Applebaum of Central Synagogue, New York City, conducted the seder; Lazar Weiner directed the music and the Central Synagogue choir. There were 7 diners at the supper. The United Jewish Layman's Committee cooperated.

Pay program was a program entitled "Sunrise at Campobello," starring Ralph Bellamy, plus a Czechoslovakian presentation of William Shakespeare's *Midsummer Night's Dream,* telecast Friday, June 29, 1962, by WHCT-TV, Channel 18, Hartford, Conn., on ultrahigh frequency. Subscribers paid a $1 fee. No commercials were shown. Subscribers had decoders installed on their sets. The station operated under a test license granted on February 24, 1961, for 3 years by the Federal Communications Commission, effective when 2,000 paying customers signed up.

Pay television system was Phonovision, demonstrated January 1, 1951, by the Zenith Radio Corporation, Chicago, Ill., KS2KSBS, under authority of the Federal Communications Commission. A scrambled radio signal was transmitted for reception only by those with the "key signal" sent to their home sets by a telephone circuit. At 4 P.M., *April Showers,* with Jack Carson, was shown; at 7 P.M. *Welcome Stranger,* with Bing Crosby; and at 9 P.M. *Homecoming,* with Clark Gable and Lana Turner. A charge of $1 was made for each full-length feature program. During the first four weeks, 2,561 sales were made. The test was limited to 300 families chosen from 51,000 applicants by the National Opinion Research Council of the University of Chicago.

Pay television presentation of a motion picture shown simultaneously in theaters was a presentation of Paramount's *Forever Female,* starring William Holden, Ginger Rogers, and Paul Douglas, transmitted on November 28, 1953, to 70 Telemeter receiving sets in Palm Springs, Calif. The picture, directed by Pat Duggan, was based upon James Matthew Barrie's play *Rosalind.* It was presented simultaneously at the Plaza Theatre in Palm Springs. The telecast fee, $1.35, was placed in a coinbox attached to each set.

Pay television presentation of a sporting event was the closed-circuit coast-to-coast telecast of the Jersey Joe Walcott–Rocky Marciano fight at the Municipal Stadium, Philadelphia, Pa., on September 23, 1952. Marciano won the heavyweight title by a knockout in 43 seconds of the 13th round. The telecast was viewed by 40,379 persons in 49

theaters located in 31 cities. Ticket sales totaled $504,645.

Pay television presentation of an opera was a performance of *Carmen,* televised on a closed circuit December 11, 1952, from the Metropolitan Opera House, New York City. The opera was shown in 31 theaters located in 27 cities to a total audience of about 70,000. Prices for tickets ranged from $1.20 to $7.20. Fritz Reiner was the conductor. Richard Tucker starred as Don Jose, Nadine Conner as Micaela, Rise Stevens as Carmen, and Robert Merrill as Escamillo.

Phase-contrast cinemicrography film (American-made) telecast was a presentation of *The Birth of a Plant,* televised February 28, 1954, by KPIX-TV, San Francisco, Calif. The film process, which utilizes a system of optics that permits ordinarily invisible objects to be seen, was the invention of Colonel Arthur T. Brice of Ross, Calif., who produced the plant reproduction film under the supervision of Dr. Ralph Emerson, professor of botany, University of California, Berkeley, Calif.

Photograph telecast from an airplane was a photograph of Charles Augustus Lindbergh transmitted August 14, 1928, from an airplane above the Philadelphia, Pa., airport and received by WF1, the Strawbridge and Clothier store, Philadelphia, Pa. Tests were made in the afternoon by Robert Hewitt, using a 30-foot fishline hanging aerial.

Play telecast in color with its original cast was James Matthew Barrie's *Peter Pan* starring Mary Martin as Peter Pan and Cyril Ritchard as Captain Hook. The play was telecast March 7, 1955, from 7:30 to 9:30 P.M. by WRCA, Channel 4, New York City, on *Producer's Showcase.* It could also be seen in black and white on the National Broadcasting Company's network. The play had opened October 20, 1954, at the Winter Garden Theatre, New York City.

Play to be televised was *The Queen's Messenger,* by J. Hartley Manners, presented on September 11, 1928, by radio station WGY of the General Electric Company, Schenectady, N.Y. The telecast was under the direction of Mortimer Stewart, with Izetta Jewell (Mrs. Hugh Miller) and Maurice Randall as the principal performers, assisted by Joyce Evans and William J. Toniski. The performance went out on three wavelengths, the picture on 379.5 meters and 21.4 meters, and the voices on 31.96 meters. Several semicommercial 24-line receivers were set up in the WGY studios. Three cameras were used. The screen was 3 by 3 inches.

Play to be televised as a full-hour program was *The Donovan Affair,* by Owen Davis, presented June 29, 1939, by W2XBS, New York City, of the National Broadcasting Company. The cast included William Harrigan, Laura Baxter, Henry Wadsworth, Matt Briggs, and Horace Braham.

The First

Play to be televised with its original Broadway cast was Rachel Crothers's comedy *Susan and God,* presented on June 7, 1938, over W2XBS, operating on channels of 46.5 megacycles for the picture and 49.75 for sound. The play was produced by the Radio Corporation of America in cooperation with John Golden, the Broadway producer. Featured in the cast were Gertrude Lawrence, Paul McGrath, and Nancy Coleman, then playing in *Susan and God* at the Plymouth Theater, New York City. Exact replicas of the stage settings were built for the telecast from the National Broadcasting Company's studio in the RCA building, New York City.

Political campaign telecast was presented on October 11, 1932, when the Democratic National Committee broadcast a television show from the W2XAB studios of the Columbia Broadcasting System, 485 Madison Avenue, New York City. Some of the performers were Harriet Hoctor, Helen Morgan, Willis and Eugene Howard, and Tony Canzoneri. Harry Hershfield was the master of ceremonies.

Political convention telecast in color was the 29th Republican Convention held August 5th to 7th, 1968, at Miami Beach, Fla. The proceedings were broadcast starting at 9:30 A.M. by both the National Broadcasting Company and the Columbia Broadcasting System.

Political convention to be televised was the 22nd Republican Convention, June 24-29, 1940, in Philadelphia, Pa., at which Wendell Lewis Willkie of New York and Charles Linza McNary of Oregon were nominated for President and Vice President. The telecast was made by W2XBS of the National Broadcasting Company, New York City, 49.75 megacycles.

Pontifical Easter mass from Rome, Italy, telecast live was transmitted via satellite March 29, 1970, from the Basilica of St. Peter and heard on Channel 4. Pope Paul VI's Easter message *Urbi et Orbi* (For the City and the World) was heard in 11 European nations.

President to appear on television was Franklin Delano Roosevelt, who spoke at the Federal Building on the exposition grounds overlooking the Court of Peace at the opening session of the New York World's Fair, Flushing, L.I., on April 30, 1939, over WNBT of National Broadcasting Company, New York City. Two NBC mobile vans were used, one containing a transmitter and the other handling the pickup. Burke Crotty was the producer of the 3½-hour show. The show began with a view of the World's Fair Trylon and the Perisphere. The images were carried on 45.25 megacycles and the sound on 49.75 megacycles.

President to appear on television in color was Dwight David Eisenhower, colorcast while delivering the commencement address at the gradua-

The First

tion exercises of the United States Military Academy at West Point, N.Y., on June 7, 1955.

President to discuss state affairs with Cabinet members on television. *See* Cabinet of the United States: Cabinet conference telecast; Television—Telecast: Cabinet session to be televised

Presidential address televised from the White House was presented October 5, 1947, when President Harry S. Truman's speech about food conservation and the world food crisis was televised from Washington, D.C., and relayed to New York City, Philadelphia, and Schenectady. The President proposed meatless Tuesdays, and eggless and poultryless Thursdays.

Presidential candidate debate series on television. *See under* Presidential candidate

Presidential debate between an incumbent President and a candidate for the office was held September 23, 1976, when 3 networks pooled their efforts to telecast President Gerald Rudolph Ford and James Earl ("Jimmy") Carter, Democrat, discussing issues at the Walnut Street Theatre, Philadelphia, Pa. A second debate took place on October 6, 1976, from the Palace of Fine Arts Theatre, San Francisco, Calif. A third debate took place October 22, 1976, from the stage of Phi Beta Kappa Hall on the campus of the College of William and Mary, Williamsburg, Va. Each confrontation was 90 minutes long.

Presidential news conference filmed for television and newsreels was held January 19, 1955, in the treaty room of the State Department building, Washington, D.C. President Dwight David Eisenhower held a 33-minute conference. The film was cut to 28 minutes 25 seconds plus introductory and closing remarks, certain sections having been omitted. The television film was recorded by the National Broadcasting Company on a pooled basis with the Columbia Broadcasting System, the American Broadcasting System, and the DuMont Network. The cost was prorated.

Presidential news conference to be televised live was held January 25, 1961, in the auditorium of the State Department building, Washington, D.C. President John Fitzgerald Kennedy answered 31 questions in 38 minutes. The conference was also broadcast on radio. President Eisenhower's news conferences were filmed and recorded for use later the same day.

Presidential nomination notification ceremony to be televised by remote pickup was transmitted on Wednesday, August 22, 1928, from the New York State Assembly Chamber at Albany, where the Democratic candidate, Alfred Emanuel Smith, was notified of his nomination. The pictures were transmitted from Schenectady, N.Y., and relayed by short wave over 2XAF and 2XAD by the General Electric Company. This was the first remote televised pickup.

The First

TELEVISION—TELECAST—*Continued*

Prizefight heavyweight championship bout on large-screen television was the Joe Louis–Lee Savold championship fight at Madison Square Garden, New York City, on Friday, June 15, 1951. Louis won in the 6th round of the scheduled 15-round fight. The event was telecast by microwave of the American Telephone and Telegraph Company from Madison Square Garden to the Empire State Building, then by coaxial cable closed-circuit to 8 motion picture theaters in 6 cities: Chicago 2; Washington 2; Albany, Baltimore, Cleveland, and Pittsburgh.

Prizefight (heavyweight championship bout) telecast coast-to-coast was shown June 5, 1951, by the National Broadcasting Company. Jersey Joe Walcott (Arnold Raymond Cream) outpointed Ezzard Charles in a 15-round bout at the Municipal Stadium, Philadelphia, Pa.

Prizefight (heavyweight championship bout) to be televised was shown June 19, 1946, by WNBT-TV, New York City, and transmitted to Washington, D.C., by coaxial cable. Joe Louis defended his title against Billy Conn at the Yankee Stadium, New York City. Louis won by a knockout in the eighth round.

Prizefight in a "studio" was televised on September 1, 1954, from Philadelphia, Pa. Two 6-round bouts were substituted for a 15-round welterweight fight between Johnny Saxton of New York City and Kid Gavilan of Camaguey, Cuba, scheduled to take place at the Connie Mack Stadium but postponed because of illness. The televised fights were held at the Met, a small club with about 5,000 seats. No admission was charged. George Justine of Philadelphia defeated Ellwood Davis of Philadelphia, and Bobby Bell of Youngstown, Ohio, fought a draw with Ike Chestnut of New York City. Each fighter received $1,500.

Prizefight telecast shown on a large screen in a theater was the Billy Soos–Ken Overlin middleweight championship prizefight held at Madison Square Garden, New York City, on May 9, 1941. The fight was shown on a 15-by-20-foot screen at the New Yorker Theatre, New York City.

Prizefight (middle weight) televised coast-to-coast was the fight between Dave Sands, the British Empire champion, and Carl ("Bobo") Olson, held October 3, 1951, at the Stadium, Chicago, Ill., and televised by the Columbia Broadcasting System. Sands, an Australian who had achieved victory in 88 of his previous 98 fights, defeated Olson in the ten-round contest.

Prizefight televised in color was the Joe Giardello–Willie Troy fight held March 19, 1954, at Madison Square Garden, New York City, and televised by WNBT, New York City. Troy was

The First

knocked out in the seventh round of a scheduled ten-round fight.

Prizefight to be televised was the Lou Nova–Max Baer fight, shown June 1, 1939, by WNBT-TV, New York City, from the Yankee Stadium, New York City. Sam Taub was the announcer. Referee Frank Fullam halted the bout in the 11th round and awarded the decision to Nova. About 300 persons saw the telecast in the smoking room of the New Amsterdam Theatre, and about 20,000 saw it in stores and dealer display rooms.

Programs regularly televised were begun May 11, 1928, on a three-times-a-week schedule from the General Electric Station, WGY, Schenectady, N.Y. The image consisted of 24 scanning lines repeated 20 times a second.

Puppet show to be televised was a two-minute symbolic one-act play with puppet characters produced August 21, 1928, by WOR, Newark, N.J., a radio station then owned by L. Bamberger & Co. of Newark. In the play a character symbolizing "Creative Genius" produced an apparatus which brought forth "The Spirit of Television," a winged sprite holding a globe. Sight and sound were synchronized, the narrator and musical accompaniment being heard through earphones.

Religious services to be televised were produced March 24, 1940, by W2XBS, of the National Broadcasting Company, New York City. Reverend Dr. Samuel McCrea Cavert of the Federal Council of the Churches of Christ in America officiated at Protestant Easter services at 11:30 A.M. The Westminster Choir, directed by Dr. John Finley Williamson, provided the musical selections. At 12:30 Right Rev. Msgr. Fulton John Sheen of the Catholic University of America, Washington, D.C., officiated at a Roman Catholic Easter service with the Paulist Choristers directed by Father William Joseph Finn, C.S.P., in cooperation with the National Council of Catholic Men. Other Easter services were televised from the Hollywood Bowl, Hollywood, Calif., and from Central Park, New York City.

Rodeo telecast coast to coast was the 57th annual Fort Worth Rodeo, telecast at 3:00 P.M. from the Will Rogers Memorial Coliseum, Fort Worth, Tex., on January 31, 1953, by WNBT-TV (channel 4), New York City.

Sales meeting televised on a closed circuit was presented by the Bulova Watch Company on January 9, 1940, from WNBT-TV, New York City, and shown to convention delegates in a reception room. Milton Biow acted as the master of ceremonies for the 50-minute program, which featured moving pictures, visual charts, and sales presentations.

Satellite telecast from Europe was a 7-minute introduction by Jacques Henri Marette, French minister of communications, and a song entitled

The First

"La Chansonette," sung by Yves Montand (tape recorded), telecast at 7:35 P.M. EDT on July 11, 1962, from Pleumeur-Bodou in Brittany by Telstar 1. On the second orbit of Telstar, at 10:22 P.M. (3:22 A.M. British summer time), a program transmitted by the British General Post Office, Goonhilly Down, Cornwall, England, was transmitted exclusively over the Columbia Broadcasting System.

Satellite telecast live to Europe was transmitted by the American Broadcasting System, the National Broadcasting System, and the Columbia Broadcasting System by Telstar 1, on July 23, 1962, to the Eurovision network of 18 nations: Austria, Belgium, Denmark, Finland, France, West Germany, Ireland, Italy, Luxembourg, Monaco, the Netherlands, Norway, Portugal, Spain, Sweden, Switzerland, the United Kingdom, and Yugoslavia. The program was narrated in 7 languages and showed sequences picturing the Statue of Liberty, buffalo on the western plains, the Phillies-Cubs major league baseball game at Chicago, President John Fitzgerald Kennedy's news conference, the head of the Abraham Lincoln carving at Mount Rushmore, the Mormon Tabernacle Choir, astronaut Lieutenant Commander Walter Marty Schirra from Cape Canaveral, Fla., a small boy admiring an Indian chief, etc.

Senate proceedings telecast was the installation ceremony for Nelson Aldrich Rockefeller of New York as the 41st Vice President of the United States, sworn in December 19, 1974, in the Senate chamber, Washington, D.C., by Chief Justice Warren Earl Burger. He was selected by President Gerald Rudolph Ford on August 20, 1974, and confirmed by the Senate on December 19, 1974.

Serial daytime soap opera was *These Are My Children,* by Irna Phillips, telecast from Monday through Friday, January 31, 1949, to February 25, 1949, from 5:00 P.M. to 5:15 P.M., by NBC from Chicago, Ill.

Ship launching telecast was January 29, 1944, on WNBT, New York City, showing the launching of the 45,000-ton U.S.S. *Missouri* at the Brooklyn Navy Yard, East River, New York City. The ship was 880 feet long, with a 108-foot beam. It was christened by Mary Margaret Truman, daughter of Senator Harry S Truman, who was the principal speaker.

Ship-to-shore telecast was sent from the S.S. *President Roosevelt,* of the U.S. Lines, en route to Bermuda, when the ship was 102 miles at sea on May 11, 1940.

Simulcast presented regularly by a sponsor was the Lowell Thomas news commentary program sponsored by the Sun Oil Company, and first presented on February 21, 1940, on W2XBS-TV, New York City, and radio station WJZ, New York City, at 6:45 P.M.

The First

Speaker to address an organization by television was Dr. Peter Irving Wold, president of the Fortnightly Club, Schenectady, N.Y., who conducted a meeting of the club from the television station at the General Electric Laboratory on April 1, 1930. The members were assembled at the home of Dr. Ernst Fredrik Werner Alexanderson in Schenectady.

Split-screen image, showing two pictures from different points of origin side by side on the same kinescope picture tube, was exhibited December 8, 1948, by the National Broadcasting Company at the Television Broadcasters Association Clinic held at the Waldorf-Astoria Hotel, New York City. The telecast showed John Cameron Swayze, in New York City, interviewing Representative Karl Earl Mundt of South Dakota, in Washington, D.C.

Split-screen image (four-ways), showing four different scenes, was shown Tuesday, November 2, 1954, when four reporters, one each from New York City, Washington, Chicago, and Los Angeles, appeared on the same screen.

Sports event televised in color was the $15,000 Molly Pitcher Handicap, 1 1/16-mile race for three-year-olds and upward, run July 14, 1951, at the Monmouth Park Jockey Club, Oceanport, N.J. The seven-horse race was won by Marta. The jockey was Conn McCreary. The race was televised by the Columbia Broadcasting System.

Standard broadcast station to transmit a television image was Hugo Gernsback's station WRNY, Coytesville, N.J., which on August 13, 1928, transmitted a 1½-inch square image of the face of Mrs. John Geloso. The image was viewed at Philosophy Hall, New York University, New York City, by 500 persons. It was magnified by a lens to twice the size.

State dinner (U.S.) telecast was that from the Rose Garden of the White House, Washington, D.C., on July 7, 1976. The dinner in honor of Queen Elizabeth II of England and Prince Philip was attended by 224 guests.

State legislative hearing telecast was aired April 11, 1954, from 7:30 P.M. to 8:00 P.M. on WATV from Newark, N.J. Senator Malcolm Forbes' proposal to stop all new projects by the Port of New York Authority (later the Port Authority of New York and New Jersey) was voted upon and defeated by the Committee on Federal and Interstate Relations of the New Jersey senate.

Stereo telecast was made December 28, 1972, in a double-channel telecast over WNEW-TV and WNET, New York City, from 11:30 P.M. to midnight. The program was entitled "Two's Better Than One" and featured 4 playlets, *Boxes, Are You There?, What A Life,* and *The Yin and Yang of It.* Hosts were Bob Elliott on Channel 5 (where

TELEVISION—TELECAST—*Continued*

half the action took place) and Ray Goulding on Channel 13 (for the other half).

Stockholders' annual meeting televised on a closed circuit was the April 16, 1957, meeting of the American Machine and Foundry Company, televised in New York City and Chicago, Ill. Shareholders witnessed the proceedings in which they themselves participated on screens at the Blackstone Hotel, Chicago, and at the Hotel Sheraton-Astor, New York City. Executives in both cities were questioned by stockholders.

Stockholders' meetings televised coast-to-coast simultaneously were transmitted October 29, 1959, from Minneapolis, Minn., and from New York, Chicago, Los Angeles, San Francisco, Boston, and Buffalo. By means of a closed circuit, stockholders in each city were able to ask questions of two General Mills officials—Gerald S. Kennedy, chairman, and Charles Heffelfinger Bell, president—who presided at the meetings in New York City and Minneapolis, respectively.

Stratosphere telecast was made July 26, 1958, from the 17-story U.S. Navy plastic balloon Strato-Lab High III, at an altitude of 60,000 feet over Minnesota, by Commander Malcolm Ross and Commander Morton Lee Lewis. The pictures were received by KSTP-TV, St. Paul, Minn. They took off from an open-pit mine at Crosby, Minn., soared to 82,000 feet, and remained aloft 34 hours 29 minutes, establishing an endurance record. They landed at Jamestown, N.D.

Stratovision flight during which a television signal was transmitted was made April 30, 1948. It consisted of the test pattern of WMAR, Baltimore, Md. On a December 9, 1945, flight, only a frequency modulation sound signal was transmitted.

Stratovision flight public demonstration was made June 23, 1948 when at 8:55 P.M. an airplane flying 25,000 feet in the air in the vicinity of Pittsburgh, Pa., rebroadcast the television program of the Republican National Convention at Philadelphia, Pa., from WMAR-TV, in Baltimore, Md. Reception was obtained in nine states over an area 525 miles in diameter.

Stratovision flight test was made December 9, 1945, at Middle River, Md., under the direction of Charles Edward Nobles of the Westinghouse Electric Corporation, Baltimore, Md., in conjunction with the Glenn L. Martin Company. William Smith, a test pilot, flew an airplane in the stratosphere from which telecasts were made. A license to conduct experiments had been granted October 24, 1945, by the Federal Communications Commission.

Stratovision World Series telecast was made October 11, 1948, when the sixth game of the World Series between the Boston Braves of the National League and the Cleveland Indians of the

American League, played at Boston, Mass., was transmitted from a stratovision plane flying at 25,-000 feet over the Pittsburgh, Pa., area.

Surgical-operation classroom-instruction telecast was made March 21, 1939, at the Israel Zion Hospital, Brooklyn, N.Y., by the American Television Corporation and shown to students 500 feet away in another building of the hospital. A television camera and a microphone were above the operating table. The half-hour hernia operation was shown on closed circuit.

Surgical operation (major) on a closed circuit, performed in one building and transmitted to another was telecast September 11, 1947 at New York Hospital and viewed at the 33rd annual clinical congress of the American College of Surgeons at the Waldorf Hotel, New York City. Seven major operations were shown.

Surgical operation televised coast-to-coast was transmitted June 10, 1952, from the Wesley Memorial Hospital, Chicago, Ill., in connection with the 101st annual meeting of the American Medical Association at the Palmer House, Chicago, Ill. Shown on television was an 8-minute period during a 3½-hour duodenal ulcer operation performed on a 60-year-old man by Dr. Samuel Julian Fogelson. The program was sponsored by Smith, Kline and French Laboratories, Inc., and presented by the National Broadcasting Company.

Surgical operation televised on a closed circuit was shown February 27, 1947, at a meeting of the Johns Hopkins Medical and Surgical Association held at the Johns Hopkins Hospital, Baltimore, Md. The operation was one of four on the heart and one on the sympathetic nerve trunk along the vertebral column televised to ten receivers in four classrooms. The first two operations were performed by Dr. Alfred Blalock. *(Johns Hopkins Hospital. Bulletin. September 1947)*

Surgical operation televised on a closed circuit in color was presented on June 6, 1949, by the Columbia Broadcasting System. An appendectomy performed by Dr. David Bacharach Allman, surgical director of the Atlantic City Hospital, Atlantic City, N.J., was shown at the annual session of the American Medical Association convention at Atlantic City. The field sequential type of color television was shown by means of the equipment of the Smith, Kline and French Laboratories, Inc., made by the Zenith Radio Corporation and the Webster-Chicago Corporation. Ten television receivers, each with a tube 12 by 14 inches, were used.

Surgical operation televised on a coast-to-coast closed circuit in color was transmitted December 7, 1951, over a closed circuit of the Columbia Broadcasting System by KNXT-TV, Los Angeles, Calif. Dr. John Clifton Jones operated on the constricted aorta of Richard D. Russell, aged 20, of

The First

Pacoima, Calif., at the Los Angeles County Hospital, Los Angeles. Surgeons in New York questioned Dr. Jones while the operation was in progress. Neither the beginning nor the end of the operation was shown in the one-hour telecast.

Surgical operation televised on a local program for the general public was transmitted March 16, 1952, by WPTZ, Philadelphia, Pa. Dr. Isador Schwaner Ravdin, who performed a 2½-hour peptic ulcer operation at the University of Pennsylvania Hospital, Philadelphia, was observed in action for 10 minutes.

Symphonic concerts to be televised were transmitted March 20, 1948, by the Columbia Broadcasting System and the National Broadcasting Company. Eugene Ormandy at 5 P.M. conducted the Philadelphia Symphony Orchestra in a concert televised by WCAU-TV, Philadelphia, Pa., on CBS. Arturo Toscanini at 6:30 P.M. conducted the NBC Symphony Orchestra in an all-Wagner concert televised by WNBT, New York City.

Telecast images received in an airplane were sent on May 21, 1932, to a Western Air Express trimotor airplane in flight over Los Angeles, Calif. The images were transmitted by W6XAO of the Don Lee Broadcasting System, Los Angeles. A 150-watt transmitter on ultra-high frequency of 44.500 kilocycles under the direction of Harry R. Lubcke, director of television, transmitted at the rate of 15 pictures per second with the 80-line screen. The telecast, originating about ten miles away, was shown for five minutes on a screen eight inches in diameter.

Telecast (long-distance) received in an airplane was sent October 17, 1939, from W2XBS of the National Broadcasting Company, New York City. An airplane flying high above Washington, D.C., intercepted the ultra-short waves which came on a straight line from New York City.

Telecast of an object in motion was made June 13, 1925, from radio station NOF, Bellevue, D.C., and received at the laboratory of Charles Francis Jenkins, 1519 Connecticut Avenue, Washington, D.C., where it was viewed by Curtis Dwight Wilbur, Secretary of the Navy; George Kimball Burgess, director of the Bureau of Standards; Stephen Brooks Davis, acting Secretary of Commerce; and others. The apparatus used was Vision-by-Radio, invented by Jenkins. The image transmitted was a small model windmill with blades in motion.

Telecast of image and sound transmitted over any considerable distance was demonstrated April 7, 1927. Secretary of Commerce Herbert Clark Hoover, at 1208 H Street, Washington, D.C., read his speech into a telephone and was both seen and heard by a large group gathered in the auditorium of the Bell Telephone Laboratories, New York City. The picture was 2 by 3 inches, 18 images per second.

The First

Telecast originating live in three countries was presented on June 27, 1955, on the National Broadcasting Company's network program "Wide Wide World" under the sponsorship of the Ford Motor Company and the Radio Corporation of America. Pictures were shown of a fiesta-time bullfight in Tijuana, Mexico; the opening night of the Shakespeare Festival at Stratford, Ontario, Canada; and events in Washington, D.C.; Denver, Colo.; San Francisco, Calif.; and New York City.

Telecast produced for a tri-city gathering was accomplished December 8, 1939, when International Rotary leaders assembled at the General Electric Station, W2XB, Schenectady, N.Y., were seen and heard simultaneously at Rotary dinners in Albany, Troy, and Schenectady, N.Y.

Telecast (public) over telephone wires was a presentation of the bicycle races at Madison Square Garden, New York City, by the National Broadcasting Company on May 20, 1939. The images were transmitted from Madison Square Garden to the National Broadcasting Company studio at Radio City, New York City, via the Circle telephone exchange at Ninth Avenue and 50th Street. When the images were received at the studio over telephone wire, they were conveyed over a coaxial cable to the transmitter in the tower of the Empire State Building, from which they were telecast.

Telecast (public) over telephone wires using the narrow-band system (5 to 8 kc band width) was demonstrated March 20, 1957, by C. Raymond Kraus, general staff transmission engineer of the Bell Telephone Company of Pennsylvania at the Franklin Institute, Philadelphia, Pa. A 128-line picture, approximately 5 by 7 inches, was received over 3.2 miles of cable from the Franklin Institute, routing through 2 telephone central offices back to the Franklin Institute. This system enabled transmission on practically all pairs in a cable of over 1,000 pairs of conductors.

Telecast received from England was transmitted June 18, 1959, from London to Montreal, Canada, via cable and relayed by the Canadian Broadcasting Company to the National Broadcasting Company in New York City, from where it was sent out over the entire NBC network. The film showed the departure from London of Queen Elizabeth and Prince Philip to the St. Lawrence Seaway ceremonies. Motion Picture Facsimile process used in the telecast was developed by the BBC. Each frame required 8 seconds for transmission. The film was seen 2 hours and 21 minutes after the recording.

Telecast (transatlantic) transmitted regularly was sent February 6, February 10, and February 13, 1931, by W2XAW, Schenectady, N.Y., of the General Electric Company, on 17 meters using the 30-line 15-pictures-per-second German standard. The test was conducted by Dr. Ernst Fredrik

The First

TELEVISION—TELECAST—*Continued*
Werner Alexanderson. Geometrical pictures were transmitted and were so clearly received in Germany that drawings of them could be made (voice and sight).

Telecast transmitted by satellite from Japan was beamed over the satellite, *Relay II,* and showed Prime Minister Hayato Ikeda. It was viewed simultaneously on three national networks and rebroadcast on the *Today Show,* Wednesday, March 25, 1964, from 7:32 to 7:40 A.M.

Telecast transmitted by satellite to Japan a 15-minute news program beamed at 7:00 P.M. November 22, 1963, from the U.S. ground station in the Mohave Desert and relayed by *Relay I,* the communications satellite. The program was received by the Space Communications Laboratory (Ibaraki Orefecture) north of Tokyo, Japan, from 5:16 A.M. to 5:46 A.M. on November 23, 1963. ABC and NBC shared in producing the program, Japanese viewers saw scenic and cultural sequences and heard taped messages from Ryuji Takeuchi, Japanese Ambassador, and James Edwin Webb, director of the National Aeronautics and Space Administration.

Telecast transmitted to Canada was presented January 20, 1953, over a 66-mile microwave link between Buffalo, N.Y., and Toronto, Ontario. The lines of the American Telegraph and Telephone Company were linked with the Bell Telephone Company of Canada. The first live show, a "Studio One" play, was televised on CBLT, Toronto, by the Canadian Broadcasting System.

Telecast using coaxial cable was transmitted June 10, 1936, from Radio City, New York City, to the transmitter atop the Empire State Building, New York City, a distance of approximately 1½ miles. The first intercity telecast was transmitted October 5, 1936, from New York City to Philadelphia, Pa. The first coast-to-coast telecast was transmitted September 4, 1951, from New York City to San Francisco, Calif.

Television network demonstration (long-distance) was given February 1, 1940, when members of the Federal Communications Commission at General Electric station W2XB, Schenectady, N.Y., witnessed a program televised from New York City, approximately 130 miles distant. The program, which was received at a relay station on the 44-50 megacycle band by means of a rhombic antenna supported by four 128-foot towers, was rebroadcast to the Schenectady-Albany district.

Television theater. *See under* Theater

Television wedding. *See under* Wedding

Tennis game telecast was played on the roof of the Bell Telephone Company Laboratories, New York City, on July 12, 1928, and visible 3 floors below. The image was 2½ inches square. A 5-inch lens projected from behind a Nipkow disc 3 feet

The First

in diameter with 50 tiny holes 1/16th of an inch in diameter in the rim of the projector. Dr. Herbert Eugene Ives manipulated the controls. The photograph was taken in sunlight instead of glaring artificial lights.

Tennis tournament to be televised was the Eastern Grass Court championship matches which opened August 9, 1939, at the Westchester Country Club, Rye, N.Y. Station W2XBS, New York City, used a telescopic lens in addition to the iconoscope to obtain closeups of important points.

Tennis tournament to be televised in color was the Davis Cup match at the West Side Tennis Club, Forest Hills, N.Y., on August 26, 1955, between Australia and the United States. The match was televised by WNBT of the National Broadcasting Company.

Three-dimensional telecast was presented April 29, 1953, from KECA-TV, Los Angeles, Calif., by American Broadcasting–Paramount Theatres, Inc., to 70 newspaper and trade publishers attending the 31st annual convention of the National Association of Radio and Television Broadcasters. Special receivers were located on the 2nd floor of the Biltmore Hotel, Los Angeles, Calif. A live performance of *Space Patrol* and Lloyd Nolan's prologue to the motion picture *Bwana Devil* were seen in a 1-hour show through special sending and receiving equipment. Two offscreen images were shown simultaneously; they appeared blurred unless viewed through polaroid lenses.
See also Motion Picture—three-dimensional feature motion picture

Track meet (intercollegiate) to be televised was the 19th annual Intercollegiate A.A.A.A. track and field championship meet at Madison Square Garden, New York City, televised March 2, 1940, by W2XBS. Twenty-three colleges participated in the various events: dashes, runs, relays, high hurdles, shot put, pole vault, weight throwing, broad jumps, and high jumps. New York University won, with 27 points.

Transatlantic exchange of live television programs was held July 23, 1962, when a 20-minute program telecast via Telstar to 18 countries of Eurovision, showing the Statue of Liberty; a major league baseball game from Chicago (Phillies vs. Cubs); one of President John Fitzgerald Kennedy's news conferences; a buffalo roaming the western plains; the head of Lincoln at Mount Rushmore; Lieutenant Commander Walter Marty Schirra, Jr., at Cape Canaveral, Fla.; the Mormon Tabernacle choir in Custer National Park; etc. Three hours later, a 20-minute telecast was received from Europe, showing Big Ben and the House of Commons, London, England; reindeer in the Arctic circle; Swiss guards at the Sistine Chapel, Rome; the entrance to the Louvre; the Colosseum in Rome; a painting in the National Museum of Belgrade,

The First

Yugoslavia; fishermen in Sicily; etc. Telecast from the control center, RCA building, 30 Rockefeller Plaza, New York City, and produced by Ted Fetter of ABC, Fred W. Friendly of CBS, and Gerald Green of NBC, the program was entitled "America, July 23, 1962"

Transcontinental telecast by means of an orbiting satellite was accomplished April 24, 1962, when the Massachusetts Institute of Technology's Lincoln Laboratory field station at Camp Parks, Calif., transmitted to the two-year-old orbiting balloon Echo I waves that were bounced back to earth and received at Millstone Hill, Westford, Mass. The pictures were of poor quality but were recognizable.

Transcontinental telecast received on the East Coast was transmitted from the War Memorial Opera House, San Francisco, Calif., on September 4, 1951, at 10:30 P.M. by a pool of the four networks to 94 of the 107 television stations then in operation. The telecast was transmitted by microwave relays to Omaha, Neb., and then by coaxial cables to stations in the east, north, and south. Secretary of State Dean Acheson introduced President Harry S. Truman, who made an address from the War Memorial Opera House in conjunction with the signing of the Japanese Peace Treaty.

Transcontinental telecast received on the West Coast was the Columbia Broadcasting System program "Crusade for Freedom," transmitted from WCBS-TV, New York City, on September 23, 1951. General Lucius DuBignon Clay was chairman of the program.

Transoceanic television image was received February 8, 1928, at Hartsdale, N.Y., by Robert M. Hart, owner of shortwave station W2CVJ. The sound vision, a picture of Mrs. Mia Howe, was sent across the ocean from station 2 KZ, Purley, England, two kilowatt power, by John Logie Baird of the Baird Television Development Company of London, England, using short radio waves.

Transoceanic television program was transmitted July 10, 1962, from Andover, Maine, bounced off the 170-pound orbiting relay satellite Telstar, and received at various stations in Europe and the United States. The following day, July 11, a telecast from Pleumeur-Bodou, France, was received by means of the 380-ton horn-shaped antenna at Andover. The satellite was launched July 10, 1962, from Cape Canaveral, Fla.

Two-way demonstration of television in a theater was given April 9, 1930. On that date persons separated by a considerable distance were for the first time able to talk to and see each other as if they were on opposite sides of the same table. The two ends of the circuit were located in New York City, one in the auditorium of Bell Telephone Laboratories, 463 West Street, and the other at the American Telephone and Telegraph Company,

The First

195 Broadway. The images appeared on a foot-square screen.

Underwater telecast from a submarine was made April 10, 1947, from the U.S.S. *Trumpetfish* (SS-425) at the Brooklyn Navy Yard, New York City, by WNBT, New York City. It was relayed by coaxial cable to WTTG, Washington, D.C.; WPTZ, Philadelphia, Pa.; and WRGB, Schenectady, N.Y. Three cameras were installed in the submarine; another camera, on the dock, filmed the submarine as it submerged, conducted a simulated torpedo attack, and finally surfaced. It was submerged 15 minutes. Ray Forrest and Bob Stanton were the announcers.

Unscheduled event to be televised as it occurred was an outdoor scene of firemen answering an alarm on April 24, 1936, in Camden, N.J. It was shown in green tint, 5 by 7 inches, 24 pictures per second, 343-line screen; the pictures were taken by RCA-Victor engineers. On June 23, 1938, Ross Piasted of RCA-NBC recorded a woman as she fell or jumped from the 11th floor of the Time and Life Building, New York City. The telecast was not shown as the crew was on an experimental exercise. A W2XBT mobile television unit of NBC recorded a fire in an abandoned barracks on Ward's Island, N.Y., on November 15, 1938.

Variety talent show series of 1-hour programs was telecast May 9, 1946, by WNBT-TV, New York City, for Standard Brands on Thursday nights until March 6, 1947. The first episode, "The Hour Glass," starred Edgar Bergen, Paul Douglas, Joe Besser, and Evelyn Knight.

Variety talent show series with an all-black cast was "Happy Pappy," first televised on April 1, 1949 over WENR-TV, Chicago, Ill. The program featured Ray Grant as master of ceremonies, the Four Vagabonds, the Modern Modes, and guests.

Video recording on magnetic tape. *See under* Tape recording

Visible and oral communication by the deaf over distance. *See under* Deaf—Communication

Weather map telecast from a land sending station to a land receiving station was sent August 18, 1926, from radio station NAA, Arlington, Va., and received at the Weather Bureau Office, Washington, D.C. The demonstration was arranged by the Jenkins Laboratory, Washington, D.C. *(Monthly Weather Review. Vol. 54. October 1926)*

Weather map telecast to a transatlantic steamer was sent by the Radiomarine Corporation station, New York City, on June 20, 1930, to the S.S. *America* nearly 3,000 miles distant.

World live-television program was "Our World" shown June 25, 1967, via 4 satelites in 26 nations. The 2-hour production involved 10,000 technicians and 300 cameras in 14 countries on 5

The First

TELEVISION—TELECAST—*Continued*

continents. It opened with glimpses of births in Mexico, Canada, Denmark, and Japan and featured Leonard Bernstein and Van Cliburn rehearsing a Rachmaninoff concerto at Lincoln Center, New York City; the Beatles recording a song in London; a rehearsal of *Lohengrin* in Bayreuth, Germany; the making of a movie in Italy; and other presentations. The U.S. outlet was the National Educational Television (NET) network. The program cost about $5 million.

X-ray fluoroscopy television discussion was televised December 5, 1950, on the "Johns Hopkins Science Review" from WAAM, Baltimore, Md., over the DuMont Television Network. Dr. Russell Hedley Morgan, radiologist in chief of the Johns Hopkins Hospital, Baltimore, showed an X-ray fluoroscopic image of a patient with a chest wound. Dr. Paul Chesley Hodges in Chicago and Dr. Walter Sinnett in New York City viewed the closed-circuit telecast simultaneously in their respective cities and participated in the consultation.

TELEVISION AWARD

National Academy of Television Arts and Sciences award, the Emmy, was presented January 25, 1949, at the Hollywood Athletic Club, Los Angeles, Calif. Walter O'Keefe was the host. The recipients of the awards were *Pantomine Quiz Time*, KTLA, the most popular television program; Shirley Dinsdale and her puppet Judy Splinters, KTLA, the most outstanding television personality; "The Necklace" on *Your Show Time* series for the best film made for television; and to KTLA for outstanding overall achievements in 1948. Two other awards were given.

TELEVISION LICENSE

Commercial television licenses were granted to 10 stations, May 2, 1941, by the Federal Communications Commission, operations to begin on July 1, 1941. The first license, No. 1, was issued to W2XBS, NBC, which telecast from the Empire State Building using Channel 1. Four sponsors used the services: Lever Bros., for Spry; Proctor and Gamble, for Ivory Soap; the Sun Oil Company; and the Bulova Watch Company.

Construction permit for a commercial television station was granted June 17, 1941, to WNBT of the National Broadcasting Company, New York City, to operate on 50,000–56,000 kilocycles. A license to cover this construction permit was also granted June 17, 1941, effective July 1, 1941.

Television license was issued February 25, 1928, by the Federal Radio Commission to the [Charles Francis] Jenkins Laboratories for the operation of a television broadcast station at 1519 Connecticut Avenue, N.W., Washington, D.C., using the call letters W3XK. In 1929 the station was authorized to move its transmitter to a loca-

The First

tion between Silver Spring and Wheaton, Md. The station ceased to operate on October 31, 1932.

TELEVISION MAGAZINE

Television magazine was *Television, America's First Television Journal*, published June 1928 by the Television Publishing Company, New York City. It contained 32 pages plus cover and sold for 35 cents a copy.

TELEVISION NETWORK. *See under* Television station

TELEVISION RECEIVER

Coin-operated television receiver was the Tradio-Vision, manufactured by Tradio, Inc., Asbury Park, N.J., and publicly exhibited November 7, 1946, in New York City. The receiver, housed in a metal cabinet 16 inches high, 8 inches deep, and 9 inches wide, contained 20 tubes and a 5-inch cathode tube that reflected a 500-line image on a mirror on the lid. The apparatus was designed to operate upon insertion of a 25-cent piece.

Television receiver and transmitter operated by laser beam (light amplification by stimulated emission of radiation) was demonstrated February 20, 1963, by the General Telephone and Electronics Corporation, Bayside, L.I., N.Y. A laser device produces a narrow highly-intense beam of light that can be focused and directed over long distances.

Television receiver in a private railroad car was a 17-inch table model Motorola placed in service on November 16, 1955, in *Lynne*, the private railroad car of Warren Wentworth Brown, president of the Monon Railroad. En route from Chicago, Ill. to Rome, Georgia, it received stations broadcasting from Chicago, Indianapolis, Cincinnati; Rome and Atlanta, Ga.; and Chattanooga, Tenn.

Television receiver on a seagoing vessel permanently installed was placed on board the pilot boat *New Jersey* on November 20, 1947, by the Radio Corporation of America. Good signals from all 3 New York television stations were received off the Ambrose Light, 20 miles from New York City.

Television receiver on a ship was installed as an experiment on the United States Line *President Roosevelt* on May 11, 1940, when opening day ceremonies of the New York World's Fair were telecast by W2XBS, National Broadcasting Company, from the Empire State Building, New York City, and viewed while the liner was 102 miles away en route to Bermuda. On May 15, 1940, a distance record of 234 miles was established.

Television receiver to permit two audiences to see and hear two different programs at the same time was the Duoscopic, publicly demonstrated January 7, 1954, in New York City and Chicago, Ill., by the Allen B. Du Mont Laboratories, Inc. Two superimposed images were projected onto the screen by two cathode ray tubes set at right

The First

angles. The images were visible through polaroid glasses. Contrast controls were separate, and two separate systems were used to carry sounds through personalized earpieces. Each speaker could be turned off independently, and one image could be seen, if the viewer desired, as in standard sets. The listener could watch one picture on the screen and listen to another. It was announced for sale in a full-page advertisement January 21, 1954, in the New York *Times*.

Television receivers to project large images (up to 9 by 12 feet) were installed in April 1955 in seven of the Sheraton Hotels. The receivers, Fleetwood model FL-1001 Television Projectors built by the Fleetwood Corporation, Toledo, Ohio, were 4 feet high, 2 feet wide, and 3 feet deep and weighed 400 pounds. They were mounted on rubber-tired casters so that they could be moved easily. They were designed to show closed-circuit programs in ballrooms, conference rooms, and places of assembly.

TELEVISION STATION

All-color station to televise live local programs was WNBQ-TV, Channel 5, Chicago, Ill., which began operations on April 15, 1956. Three color studios were equipped with five color cameras and two color-film projector chains for 16 mm and 35 mm films. The station had begun operations on January 7, 1949, with black-and-white telecasts and had begun the conversion to color on November 3, 1955.

City to have two educational television channels was Pittsburgh, Pa. The Metropolitan Pittsburgh Educational Station was granted a permit to operate WQED, Channel 13, on May 13, 1953. The first community-supported educational television station, WQED, went on the air April 1, 1954. A second channel, WQEX, Channel 16, was granted on July 16, 1958.

Commercial television station west of the Mississippi River was KTLA, Hollywood, Calif., which began operations January 22, 1947, at 8:30 P.M., from a converted garage. Dick Lane was the announcer.

Illegal television station closed by the Federal Communications Commission was operated by the Tube Division of Sylvania Electric Products, Inc., at Emporium, Pa., and closed October 19, 1950. A station with a 90-foot tower on top of Whittemore Mountain had televised programs from WJAC-TV, Johnstown, Pa., without authorization.

Microwave television station was KTRE-TV, Lufkin, Tex., owned by the Forest Capital Broadcasting Company, which began operations August 1, 1955, on Channel 9 (very-high-frequency). Signals from KPRC-TV, Houston, Tex., Channel 2, were deflected to booster equipment at the bottom of a tower at Coldspring, 60 miles away. There the signals were amplified and sent to the

The First

next relay tower, at Carmona, 30 miles away, where they were again amplified and sent to Lufkin, 30 miles away. Richman Lewin was vice president and general manager of KTRE-TV.

Noncommercial educational television network was National Educational Television (NET), New York City, which interconnected 70 of its 100 independent affiliated educational stations for a live broadcast and analysis of President Lyndon Baines Johnson's State of the Union message on January 10, 1967. Regularly scheduled noncommercial network broadcasting began November 5, 1967, with the premiere of the Public Broadcast Laboratory over the NET network. NET began as a nonprofit Illinois corporation, the Educational Television and Radio Center, organized in 1952.

Noncommercial educational television station was KUHT (Channel 8), University of Houston, Houston, Tex., which broadcast test patterns May 12, 1953, and began programing May 25, 1953, from 5 P.M. to 9 P.M. five days a week over Channel 8, on very-high-frequency. The formal dedication ceremonies took place June 8, 1953. The station was licensed jointly by the University of Houston and the Houston Public School system on April 14, 1952. John Schwarzwalder was director.

Religious noncommercial television station was WYAR-TV (channel 27), Portsmouth, Va., which began operating October 1, 1961. It was founded by M. G. Robertson as the Christian Broadcasting Network, Inc. The station was on the air on Sunday from 1:00 P.M. to 6:00 P.M. and on weekdays from 7:00 P.M. to 10:00 P.M. (except Mondays).

Statewide and state-supported educational television network was officially opened August 9, 1956, by Governor James Elisha Folsom of Alabama. WAIQ, Andalusia, Ala. (Channel 2), was joined to WBIQ, Birmingham, Ala. (Channel 10), and WTIQ, Munford, Ala. (Channel 7), to reach 90 percent of the state of Alabama. Programs were supplied by the University of Alabama, Alabama Polytechnic Institute, and the Greater Birmingham Area Educational Television Association, Inc.

Television network sales to exceed those of radio was in 1952. The Federal Communications Commission announced on July 31, 1953, that television network sales amounted to $137,-700,000 while those of the 4 national radio organizations amounted to $102,100,000.

Television stations to share the same time and frequency were KSBW-TV, Salinas, Calif., and KMBY-TV, Monterey, Calif. On February 19, 1953, both stations were granted licenses. A protest was filed, but the licenses were declared valid on June 26, 1953, and both stations began telecasting officially on September 11, 1953, from the same transmitter atop Mount Toro, Calif. The hours were divided equally on alternate nights, each station transmitting alone on alternate Sundays.

The First

TELEVISION STATION—*Continued*

Ultra-high-frequency commercial television station was KPTV (Channel 27), Portland, Oreg., owned by the Empire Coil Company, which went on the air with its test pattern on September 18, 1952. It was operated under temporary permit until October 1, 1952, when commercial service began.

Ultra-high-frequency television station to operate on a regular daily basis was KC2XAK, Bridgeport, Conn., which began operating December 29, 1949, on 530 megacycles. Programs received via microwaves from WNBT, New York City, were rebroadcast on the ultra-high-frequency band. The transmitter, located on Success Hill, Stratford, Conn., was completed on November 15, 1949.

TELEVISION TUBE

Miniature tube was the "peanut tube," an N-type tube, 2 inches high and ⅝ inch in diameter, operated on a single dry cell. The tube was created by Howard W. Weinhart of Elizabeth, N.J., who filed his application July 14, 1919, and obtained patent 1,550,768 on August 25, 1925, on an "electric discharge device." The patent was assigned to the Western Electric Company, Inc., New York City.

Rectangular television tube (practical) was announced to the trade July 10, 1949, by the Kimble Glass Company, subsidiary of Owens-Illinois in Toledo, Ohio. The bulb faces of the tube were approximately 12 by 16 inches. The tube sold for approximately $12. The first deliveries were made October 1, 1949.

TELLURIUM. *See* Tungsten: Tungsten and tellurium

TEMPERANCE LAW (colonial) was signed

March 5, 1623, by Governor Sir Francis Wyatt of Virginia and 32 others. It provided that "the proclamations for swearing and drunkenness set out by the Governor and Counsell are confirmed by this assembly, and it is further ordered that the churchwardens shall be sworne to present them to the commanders of every plantation and that the forfeitures shall be collected by them to be for publique uses." *(William Waller Hening—Statutes at Large of Virginia, Vol. 1)*

TEMPERANCE SOCIETY

Anti-Saloon League was founded by Howard Hyde Russell and 15 members of the Oberlin Temperance Alliance who formed the Ohio Anti-Saloon League on May 24, 1893, in Oberlin, Ohio. The first meeting was held in the Oberlin College library building. The original purpose of the society was to force the Ohio saloons out of business and to preach the benefits of temperance. On June 23, 1893, the Anti-Saloon League of the District of Columbia was formed in Washington, D.C., with Major Samuel Hamilton Walker as the first president. The constitution was adopted July 7, 1893.

The First

Anti-Saloon League (national organization) was the Anti-Saloon League of America, formed December 17-18, 1895, at the Calvary Baptist Sunday School, Washington, D.C., by a coalition of the Anti-Saloon League of the District of Columbia, the Anti-Saloon League of Ohio, and 4? other local temperance organizations. The firs officers were Hiram Price, president; the Reverend Luther Barton Wilson, first vice president Archbishop John Ireland, second vice president James Lithgow Ewin, recording secretary; and F W. Walsh, treasurer.

Liquor reform movement. *See* Liquor reform movement

National temperance convention met at Philadelphia, Pa., May 24-27, 1833, with 440 delegate from 22 states in attendance.

Temperance organization (local) was formed in 1789 by the farmers of Litchfield County, Conn Their pledge read in part: "We do hereby associ ate and mutually agree that hereafter we wil carry on our business without the use of distille spirits as an article of refreshment, either for our selves or for those whom we employ; and that instead thereof, we will serve our workmen wit wholesome food and the common simple drinks o our production." *(Litchfield [Conn.] Enquirer Sept. 26, 1833)*

Temperance society (union) was the Union Temperate Society of Moreau and Northumber land, organized April 13, 1808, at a meeting i Saratoga Springs, N.Y., by Dr. Billy James Clark who became secretary. Sidney Berry was th president, Ichabod Hawley vice president, an Thomas Thompson treasurer. The member agreed not to drink, except at public dinner under a penalty of 25 cents for each offense an 50 cents for intoxication. Total abstinence wa not demanded until 1836. *(Jacob Hilton Durkee History of the World's Temperate Centennie Congress)*

Women's temperance society (national) wa the National Woman's Christian Temperanc Union organized in the Second Presbyteria Church, Cleveland, Ohio, November 18–20, 187 The society was incorporated March 1, 1883. Th first president was Mrs. Annie T. Wittenmyer o Philadelphia Pa., who served from November 1 1874, to October 29, 1879. At a convention in De troit, Mich., October 31–November 3, 1883, th World Woman's Christian Temperance Unic was organized. The first convention was hel November 10-11, 1891, in Boston, Mass.

Women's temperance society (state) was th New York Women's State Temperance Societ founded April 20, 1852, at a convention held i Rochester, N.Y., principally through the efforts Susan Brownell Anthony. Approximately 5C

The First

women attended. *(Standard Encyclopedia of the Alcohol Problem, Vol. 5)*

TEN-HOUR-DAY LAW. *See* Labor legislation

TENEMENT HOUSE. *See* Building

TENNESSEE VALLEY AUTHORITY CONTRACT. *See* Electrical contract

TENNIS

Court tennis was introduced in Boston, Mass., in 1876 by Hollis Hunnewell and Nathaniel Thayer, who built a court on Buckingham Street. Ted Hunt, an English professional, was in charge. The game is played with a curiously shaped racket on a court (usually enclosed) 110 feet long and 38 feet wide, with an elaborate layout. There are only about a dozen such courts in the United States.

Lawn tennis was introduced in March 1874 by Mary Ewing Outerbridge, who imported rackets and other equipment from Bermuda. It is said that customs officials were unable to determine under what section of the Tariff Act the equipment belonged, and after a week's indecision permitted it to enter duty-free. A court was laid out in 1874 at the Staten Island Cricket and Baseball Club, to which Miss Outerbridge's family belonged. The first players were members of the family. Within seven years tennis had become popular, and on May 21, 1881, her brother Eugenius H. Outerbridge organized the United States Lawn Tennis Association, to which 33 tennis clubs sent delegates. General Robert Shaw Oliver of the Albany Tennis Club was elected the first president. *(Malcolm Douglass Whitman—Tennis, Origin and Mysteries)*

TENNIS GAME

Tennis game telecast. *See under* Television—Telecast

TENNIS MATCH

Intercollegiate court tennis match was played May 4, 1954, at the Racquet and Tennis Club, New York City. Yale defeated Princeton 2-1: James Laughlin of Yale defeated Kenley Webster, Charles Watson of Yale defeated Gary Nash, and Dozier Gardner of Princeton defeated Robert Easton of Yale. On May 23, 1954, at Manhasset, Long Island, N.Y., Yale defeated Harvard 4-3 for the challenge bowl donated by James H. Van Alen.

Intercollegiate lawn tennis match was held June 8, 1883, at Hartford, Conn., on the grounds of Trinity College. Joseph Sill Clark of Philadelphia, Pa., won the singles. The doubles were won by Clark and Howard Augustus Taylor of New York City. The winners represented Harvard. A second series was held in the fall, played on September , 1883. Howard Augustus Taylor won the singles and the doubles teamed with R.E. Presbrey.

Lawn tennis champions who were brothers were Carr Baker Neel and Samuel R. Neel of Chicago, Ill., who on August 18, 1896, won the

The First

United States Lawn Tennis Association outdoor men's doubles championship at Newport Casino, Newport, R.I., defeating Robert D. Wrenn and M. G. Chace, 6-3, 1-6, 6-1, 3-6, 6-1.

Lawn tennis match (doubles) for the Davis Cup to exceed 100 games was played August 5, 1973, at North Little Rock, Ark. Stanley Roger ("Stan") Smith and Erik Van Dillen of the United States defeated Jaime Fillol and Patricio ("Pat") Cornejo of Chile: 7-9; 37-39; 8-6; 6-1; and 6-3; a total of 122 games. The American team was defeated by the Australian team (John Newcombe and Rod Laver) in the final round November 30-December 4, 1973, at Cleveland, Ohio.

Lawn tennis match (singles) for the Davis Cup to exceed 80 games was played August 31, 1970, at the Harold T. Clark Courts, Cleveland Heights, Ohio. Arthur Robert Ashe, Jr., of the United States defeated Christian Kuhnke of West Germany in the Challenge Round. Ashe won the five sets: 6-8; 10-12; 9-7; 13-11; 6-4; a total of 86 games.

Lawn tennis matches for the Davis Cup (international lawn tennis challenge trophy) were held at the Longwood Cricket Club, Brookline, Mass., August 8-10, 1900, under the auspices of the United States Lawn Tennis Association. The Davis Cup was first won by an American team consisting of Malcolm Douglass Whitman, Dwight Filley Davis, and Holcombe Ward, all of Harvard, who won 3 matches to none, 10 sets to one, and 76 games to 50 against England. The tournament called for 1 doubles and 4 singles matches. The United States won the first 3 matches (rain spoiled the other two) and was declared victorious. *(Stephen Wallis Merrihew—The Quest of the Davis Cup)*

Lawn tennis national championship matches were held at the Newport Casino, Newport, R.I., August 31, 1881, by the United States Lawn Tennis Association (USLTA), which introduced the first national uniform conditions. The singles match was won by Richard Dudley Sears, who defeated W. E. Glyn 6-0, 6-3, and 6-2. The doubles were won by Clarence Monroe Clark and Frederick W. Taylor.

Lawn tennis tournament of national scope was held September 1-4, 1880, at Camp Washington of the Staten Island Cricket Club, New Brighton, Staten Island, N.Y. Twenty-three entrants competed for the first prize, a silver cup valued at about $100, inscribed "The Champion Lawn Tennis Player of America." O. E. Woodhouse of England won.

National tennis tournament of the United States Lawn Tennis Association in which a black woman competed was held at the West Side Tennis Club, Forest Hills, N.Y. in August 1950. On August 29, 1950, Althea Gibson, a black player of New York City, was eliminated by Louise Brough of Beverly

The First

TENNIS MATCH—Continued

Hills Calif., the Wimbledon champion, who won 6–1, 3–6, 9–7.

Professional lawn tennis contest (international) was begun at the Newport Casino, Newport, R.I., on August 29, 1889. George Kerr, an Irish professional, defeated Thomas Pettit, 6-3, 6-1, 6-1. Pettit won 6-4, 2-6, 6-3, 6-4 on September 21, 1889, at Springfield, Mass. The third match was held at the Longwood Cricket Club, Brookline, Mass., on September 25, 1889, and Kerr won 6-3, 3-6, 6-4. *(American Lawn Tennis. Nov. 20, 1927)*

Tennis match broadcast. *See under* Radio Broadcast

Tennis tournament telecast. *See under* Television—Telecast

Women's national championship lawn tennis matches (United States Lawn Tennis Association) outdoors women's singles were held at the Philadelphia Cricket Club, Philadelphia, Pa., in 1887, and won by Ellen F. Hansell (Mrs. Allerdice), who defeated Laura Knight 6-1 and 6-0. The first women's doubles championship was played in 1890 and won by Ellen C. and Grace W. Roosevelt.

TENNIS PLAYER

Black tennis player to participate in a United States Indoor Lawn Tennis Association championship tournament was Dr. Reginald Weir of New York City, who won his first match on March 11, 1948, and was eliminated on March 13, 1948. The tournament was held in New York City.

Brother and sister to win national singles title championships in the same tournament were Clifford Richey of San Angelo, Tex., who defeated Frank Froehling of East Orange, N.J. (13-11; 6-1; and 6-3) on July 16, 1966, at the Town Hall Stadium, Milwaukee, Wis., for the National Clay Courts championship, and his sister, Nancy Richey, who won the women's title by defeating Stephanie De Fina of Hollywood, Fla. (6-3 and 6-2).

Lawn tennis champion to win four major titles, the "grand slam" of tennis, within a year was John Donald Budge of Oakland, Calif., who won the Australian title January 29, 1938, at Adelaide, Australia; the French title June 11, 1938, at Auteuil, France; the British title July 1, 1938, at Wimbledon, England; and the American title September 24, 1938, at Forest Hills, N.Y. *(John Donald Budge—Budge On Tennis)*

Tennis player to win 2 grand slams was Rodney George ("Rod") Laver of Australia, who defeated Tony Roche of Australia (7-9; 6-1; 6-2; 6-3) and won the United States Open at the West Side Tennis Club, Forest Hills, Queens, N.Y., on September 8, 1969. He won the Australian Open (6-3; 6-4; 7-5) defeating Andres Gimeno; the French Open (6-4; 6-3; 6-4) defeating Ken Rosewall; and

The First

the British Open (6-4; 5-7; 6-4; 6-4) defeating John Newcombe. Laver had won his first grand slam in 1962.

Woman tennis grand slam winner was Maureen ("Little Mo") Connolly (Mrs. Norman Brinker) of San Diego, Calif., who won the 4 major titles: the Australian title, at Kooyong, Melbourne, on January 17, 1953 (6-0; 6-1); the French title, at Roland Garros, Paris, on May 30, 1953 (6-1; 6-3); the English title, at Wimbledon, on July 4, 1953 (6-0; 6-0); and the United States title at Forest Hills, L.I., N.Y., on September 7, 1953 (6-1; 6-0).

TENNIS SOCIETY

Tennis society (national) was the United States Lawn Tennis Association, formed May 21, 1881, at the Fifth Avenue Hotel, New York City, by 34 clubs. It formulated the rules of play, standardized the height of the net and the size of the ball, and ruled on such matters as the service line and the size of the court. The first officers were Robert Shaw Oliver of the Albany Tennis Club, president; Samuel Campbell of the Orange Lawn Tennis Club, vice president; and Clarence Monroe Clark of the Young American Cricket Club, secretary and treasurer. In 1920 the name *United States Lawn Tennis Association* was adopted and in 1975 it was changed to United States Tennis Association (USTA).

TERMINAL, AIR. *See* Aviation—Airport: Air terminal (not located at an airport)

TERRA-COTTA. *See* Brick: Terra-cotta

TERRAMYCIN was publicly announced by Chas Pfizer & Co., Inc., Brooklyn, N.Y., in the January 27, 1950, issue of *Science* magazine. Terramycin, an antibiotic used in the treatment of some urinary tract infections and certain types of pneumonia and dysentery, was isolated from Indiana soil *(Science. Vol. 3, p 85. Jan. 27, 1950)*

TERRITORIAL EXPANSION

Acquisition of land by the federal government from various states took place between 1781 and 1802. New York was the first state to cede territory to the government (1781). Other states soon followed—Virginia in 1784, Massachusetts in 1785, Connecticut in 1786, and other states later. The ceded territory was established on July 13, 1787, as the Northwest Territory. Arthur St. Clair was appointed the first governor of this territory in October 1787. The first territorial legislature assembled on September 24, 1799. This territory was later formed into states, the first of which was Ohio, admitted to the Union February 19, 1803. *(Charles Moore—The Northwest Under Three Flags)*

Annexation of territory was the Louisiana Purchase, a tract of land bought from France on April 30, 1803, for $15 million. It covered 1,171,931 square miles and included the entire Mississippi Valley from the Mississippi River to the Rocky

The First

Mountains and from the Gulf of Mexico to Canada. This territory included the present states of Louisiana, Arkansas, Missouri, Iowa, North and South Dakota, Nebraska, Kansas, Oklahoma; part of Colorado and Wyoming; and most of Montana and Minnesota. The treaty was arranged by Robert R. Livingston, minister at Paris, and James Monroe, who had been sent by President Thomas Jefferson as a special envoy to assist Livingston. On November 30, 1803, Spain ceded its claims to the territory to France, and on December 20, 1803, France formally delivered the colony to the American representatives. *(James Alexander Robertson—Louisiana Under the Rule of Spain, France and the United States, 1785–1807)*

Island territory added to the United States was the Hawaiian Islands, which were formally annexed on August 12, 1898, at the request of the Hawaiian people. The treaty was signed June 16, 1897, by John Sherman, Secretary of State, for the United States. A joint congressional resolution to provide for the annexation was passed July 7, 1898 (30 Stat. L. 751). *(John Roy Musick—Hawaii: Our New Possession)*

Noncontiguous territory added to the United States was Alaska, which was purchased from Russia on June 20, 1867, for $7,200,000. General Lovell Harrison Rousseau, the first military governor of the territory, took formal possession of Alaska in October 1867.

Territory (U.S.) outside the continental limits of the United States was Midway Island in the North Pacific Ocean, claimed on August 28, 1867, by Captain William Reynolds (U.S. Navy) for the United States.

TETRAPLOID FLOWER. *See* Flowers

TEXAS PRESIDENT. *See* President of the Republic of Texas

TEXTBOOK printed in America was Thomas Dilworth's *A New Guide to the English Tongue*, a reader, speller, and grammar combined, published in London, England, in 1740 and reprinted by Franklin's press in 1747 in Philadelphia, Pa. It went through 26 editions before 1792. Dilworth was one of the first to provide word lists for spelling. Prior to this time, spelling had been taught incidentally with reading, the Bible being used as an advanced reader. *(Stuart Grayson Noble—The History of American Education)*

TEXTILE MACHINERY PATENT was granted February 14, 1794, on a carding and spinning machine, to James Davenport, who established the Globe Mills, Philadelphia, Pa.

TEXTILE SCHOOL

Textile school in a college was one of six departments of the Clemson Agricultural College, Clemson, S.C. It was established in 1899, six years after the opening of the college. The first textile graduates, five in number, received degrees in tex-

The First

tile engineering on June 6, 1904. The first director of the textile school was J. H. M. Beaty.

TEXTILE-WRAPPED DETONATING FUSE. *See* Fuse

THANKSGIVING DAY. *See* Holiday

THEATER

Baby show. *See* Baby show

Ballet. *See* Ballet

Brick theater. *See* Theater building (permanent)

Chinese theater was the theater of "Celestial John," on Telegraph Hill, fronting Dupont Street, San Francisco, Calif., which opened December 23, 1852. It consisted of one vast pit or parquet and had a seating capacity of 1,400. There were no tiers of boxes. No scenery was used.

Drama broadcast. *See under* Radio broadcast

Exhibition. *See* Fair

Flea circus. *See* Flea circus

Horse race on a stage in a theater. *See under* Horse race

Horse-race telecast shown in a theater. *See* Television—Telecast: Horse-race telecast shown on a large screen in a theater

Minstrel show. *See* Minstrel show troupe

Motion picture film exhibition in a theater. *See* Motion Picture: Motion picture film exhibition in a theater

Motion picture theater. *See* Motion picture theater

Municipal theater was the Academy of Music of Northampton, Mass., which was accepted by the City of Northampton as a gift from Edward Hutchinson Robbins Lyman on February 9, 1893. Visiting companies and traveling troupes offered their presentations there. The first stock company was that of Jessie Bonstelle and Bertram Harrison, who played from 1912 to 1917. *(Constance D'Arcy Mackay—Little Theatre in the United States)*

Municipally owned and operated summer theater-in-the-round was the Playhouse in the Park, Fairmount Park, Philadelphia, Pa., which opened June 30, 1951, with a performance of *Goodbye My Fancy* starring Conrad Nagel and Sylvia Sidney. Profits from performances went to the city. The theater was housed in a tent containing 1,072 seats encircling a stage 68½ feet in circumference.

Newsreel theater was the Embassy, on Broadway and 46th Street, New York City, which opened November 2, 1929.

Orchestra in a theater. *See under* Orchestra

Panorama show was *Jerusalem*, exhibited in 1790 at Lawrence Hyer's Tavern, 62 Chatham Street, New York City, "between the Gaol and the

THEATER—*Continued*
Tea Water Pump." It was open from ten in the morning until ten at night, and according to advertisements in the *Daily Advertiser*, the sight was "most brilliant by candlelight." *(George Clinton Densmore Odell—Annals of the New York Stage)*

Showboat or floating theater was a keel boat converted by Noah Miller Ludlow in 1817 at a cost of $200. It left Nashville, Tenn., October 20, 1817, and was used on the Cumberland, Ohio, and Mississippi rivers. The first dramatic pieces presented were David Garrick's *The Honeymoon* and *The Lying Valet*, which were performed November 15, 1817. *(Noah Miller Ludlow—Dramatic Life As I Found It)*

Showboat of importance was *The Floating Palace*, a flat scow with a superstructure which plied the Mississippi River in 1852. It was operated by Spalding and Rogers. The dress circle had 1,100 cane-bottom chairs, the family circle 500 cushioned settees, and the gallery 900 seats. It was heated by steam. *(Gleason's Pictorial Drawing Room Companion. Feb. 19, 1853)*

State-owned theater operated as an integral part of a state school system was the Washington State Theatre, authorized April 15, 1936, and sponsored by the Department of Public Instruction, State of Washington, in connection with the Seattle Repertory Playhouse, Seattle, Wash. The first play presented was William Shakespeare's *The Comedy of Errors*, produced November 2, 1936. Traveling troupes visited schools offering Shakespearian, classic, and significant modern plays. The first director of the theater was Burton Wakeley James.

State-owned theater dedicated to its own drama was the Playmakers Theatre, Chapel Hill, N.C., opened November 23, 1925. About 20 new full-length and one-act plays are presented annually by members of the four playwriting courses of the University of North Carolina.

Television theater to be licensed was the Massachusetts Television Institute, Boston, Mass., which opened July 13, 1938, with a 45-minute show witnessed by 200 people who had paid a 25-cent admission fee. Sound accompanied the black-and-white images appearing on a screen 9 by 12 inches. The show featured specialty acts—vocal, instrumental, and dance numbers—performed in a room above the auditorium and transmitted by wire.

Television theater demonstration took place May 22, 1930, at the RKO Proctor Theatre, Schenectady, N.Y. The theater orchestra was led by conductor John Gamble, who was not in the theater but in a laboratory a few miles away. The musicians followed Gamble's life-size television image, which was flashed on a six-foot screen. The projection was from the rear of the screen. Gamble listened to their music by telephone. Mer-

rill Trainer was the master of ceremonies. Other performers were Matilda Biglow Russ, soprano, and Frank Camadine, harmonica player. The demonstration was arranged by Dr. Ernst Fredrik Werner Alexanderson, consulting engineer of the General Electric Company and the Radio Corporation of America, to show the possibilities of television as a medium of theater entertainment. The telecast was made by the General Electric Company, Schenectady, N.Y., on a wavelength of 92 meters.

Television theater demonstration of a sports event on a full-size screen took place at the Paramount Theatre, New York City, on April 14, 1948 when a boxing match in Brooklyn, N.Y., was televised by WPIX-TV, New York City, on a special wavelength. The images were relayed from Brooklyn to the Daily News Building and thence to the Paramount Theatre.

Theater was built in 1718 by William Leving ston at Williamsburg, Va. It was 86½ feet long and 30 feet wide. He acquired the lots from the Trustees of Williamsburg on November 5, 1716 and in December 1716 contracted with Charles Stagg, dancing master, and Mary Stagg, his wife to act and teach others how to act in the play house he would erect for the acting of comedies drolls, and stage plays. In 1718 Governor Alex ander Spotswood entertained a number of guests at the theater.

Theater building (permanent) was the South wark Theatre, on South Street above Fourth Philadelphia, Pa., built by David Douglass, which opened November 21, 1766, with Lewis Hallam of the American Company in *The Gamester*. The walls and the first story were built of brick. The building was used as a hospital in the Revolutionary War and was partly destroyed by fire on May 9, 1821. *(John Fanning Watson—Annals of Phila delphia)*

Theater built and named for a living actress was the Ethel Barrymore Theatre, New York City opened December 20, 1928, with the performance of a translation of a Spanish play by Gregorio Martínez Sierra entitled *The Kingdom of God (Reino de Dios)*, in which she played Sister Gracia, the lead.

Theater designed solely for theatrical purpose was the New Theatre, corner of Church and Queen (Dock) streets, Charleston, S.C. It opened February 12, 1736, with George Farquhar's comedy *The Recruiting Officer*. It closed March 23 1736. The same play was produced by the Footlight Players on November 26, 1937, on the same site, in a new Dock Street Theatre.

Theater destroyed by fire was the Federal Street Theatre, Boston, Mass., which suffered $60,000 loss on February 2, 1798. It was 150 feet long, 62 feet wide, and 40 feet high. The opening performance had been on February 3, 1794.

The First

Theater lighted by electricity was the Bijou Theatre, 545 Washington Street, Boston, Mass., which was lighted by an Edison isolated plant on December 11, 1882. Six hundred and fifty lamps were used. The proscenium was surrounded with 192 lights, and 140 were used in the borders. Colliers' Standard Opera Company presented Gilbert and Sullivan's *Iolanthe, or the Peer and the Peri.* *(Boston Evening Transcript. Dec. 12, 1882)*

Theater lighted by gas was the Chatham Garden and Theatre, which was situated at what is now 80-90 Chatham Street, New York City. Gas lighting had been used previously in theaters, but as a novelty rather than as illumination. The New York *Post and Mirror* on May 9, 1825, stated that the whole theater was lighted by gas, "which sheds a clear soft light over the audience and stage." The illumination "elicited the loudest plaudits from all present."

Theater provided with scientific air distribution to furnish comfortable conditions throughout was the Metropolitan Theatre, Los Angeles, Calif., equipped in 1921 by the Carrier Engineering Corporation with a system to distribute air from various parts of the theater.

Theater school. *See* Theatrical school

Theater to employ women ushers was the Third Avenue Theatre, New York City, which opened August 30, 1884, with *49*, starring Mr. and Mrs. McKee Rankin. Young women wore white caps and aprons. The theater was redecorated during the summer recess. (New York *Herald*—Aug. 31, 1884)

Therapeutic theater to treat psychiatric cases by "psycho-dramatic shock treatment" was instituted by Dr. Jacob L. Moreno in Beacon, N.Y., in 1937. The treatment was designed to enable the psychiatric worker to achieve a clearer understanding of the patient's mental processes. None but interested participants and doctors were privileged to see the reenactment of cases. *(Jacob L. Moreno—Psychodrama)*

Vaudeville. *See* Vaudeville

Waxworks museum. *See* Waxworks museum

Wild West Show. *See* Wild West Show

THEATER HISTORY of importance was *A History of the American Theatre* by William Dunlap, published in 1832 in New York City by J. & J. Harper. It contained 430 pages.

THEATRICAL ADVANCE PUBLICITY MAN was Robert Upton, who left London in October 1750 for New York City to prepare the way for the Hallam Company. Instead, he joined the [Walter] Murray and [Thomas] Kean Company, then performing in New York City. *(George Overcash Seilhamer—History of the American Theatre)*

The First

THEATRICAL SCHOOL

Public high school to specialize in the performing field. *See* High school: Public high school to specialize in the performing field

Theater and dramatic criticism course to award a Ph.D. degree was established by the Department of Drama, Yale University, New Haven, Conn., on September 24, 1934. The first degrees were awarded to George Riley Kernodle, John Huber McDowell, and Virginia More Roediger on June 23, 1937. The normal minimum time required for the course was four full years of study and research. The first professor of the history of the drama was Allardyce Nicoll.

Theatrical school devoted exclusively to training for the professional stage was the Lyceum School of Acting in New York City, which was founded by Franklin Haven Sargent on October 1, 1884. It was renamed the American Academy of Dramatic Arts in 1890.

Theatrical school sponsored by an institution of higher learning in association with a professional theater was the Mohawk Drama Festival and Institute of the Theater, which offered its first courses on July 2, 1935, at Union College, Schenectady, N.Y. Seventy students enrolled in the intensive eight-week course covering history, theory, and practice. The director was Dr. Thomas Herbert Dickinson. Four plays were presented: *The Merry Wives of Windsor, Lysistrata, Rip Van Winkle,* and *Master of the Revels.* The course concluded August 24, 1935, when 25 certificates of meritorious achievement were awarded. The school was chartered by the Regents of the University of the State of New York in 1938.

THEME SONG. *See* Radio broadcast: Program theme song

THEOLOGICAL BIBLIOGRAPHY. *See* Bibliography: Bibliography of theological and biblical literature

THEOLOGICAL SCHOOL

Presbyterian theological seminary woman graduate was Emilie Grace Briggs, who received the Bachelor of Divinity degree on March 17, 1897, from the Union Theological Seminary, New York City.

Theological school was founded by the Dutch Reformed Church in 1784 with the appointment of Dr. John Henry Livingston of the Collegiate Church of New York City as professor of theology. In 1810 Livingston went to New Brunswick, N.J., under an agreement whereby the school was to share the campus of Queen's College (later Rutgers). The school, named the New Brunswick Theological Seminary, has been closely associated with the adjacent institution. The seminary campus today is surrounded by the buildings of Rutgers—The State University. The two institu-

The First

THEOLOGICAL SCHOOL—*Continued*
tions are not corporately connected, however, and have always retained separate identities.

Theological school black graduate to receive a degree was Theodore Sedgwick Wright, who was graduated from the Princeton Theological Seminary, Princeton, N.J., in 1818. He became a pastor in a Presbyterian church.

Theological school (major theological school) woman dean was Sallie McFague Teselle of Nashville, Tenn., who in 1971 was appointed to the faculty of Vanderbilt University and who became dean of the Divinity School, taking office June 1, 1975.

Theological school (nonsectarian) was the Divinity School of Harvard College, Cambridge, Mass., organized as a separate department in 1816, although the faculty of the Divinity School was not appointed until 1819. Six students graduated in 1817. Degrees were not conferred by the Divinity School until 1870. Theology had been taught since the opening of Harvard College.

Theological school to admit women as students was the Boston University School of Theology, Boston, Mass., formed March 30, 1871, when the Boston Theological Seminary united with Boston University. The first woman student matriculated on September 25, 1872. The first B.D. degree awarded to a woman was granted to Anna Oliver on June 7, 1876.

Theological school to present regular courses by scholars representing different denominations was the Boston Theological Seminary, Boston, Mass., which opened September 1867 with Catholic, Methodist, and Presbyterian professors, as well as members of other faiths.

THEOLOGICAL TREATISE of importance was *Vier kleine doch ungemeine und sehr nützliche Tractätlein,* by Francis Daniel Pastorius, published in 1690 in Germantown, Pa. It contained an outline of the saints, an account of the bishops and saints, and a review of the church councils and the bishops and patriarchs of Constantinople. *(Marion Dexter Learned—The Life of Francis Daniel Pastorius)*

THEOSOPHICAL SOCIETY was the American Theosophical Society, founded November 17, 1875, by Helena Petrovna Blavatsky and Colonel Henry Steele Olcott in New York City. The society later was incorporated in Adyar, Madras, India, the city which was made the international headquarters of the society. The national headquarters of the American section of the organization is now in Wheaton, Ill. Theosophy is not a religion but a "synthesis of the principles underlying all religions and science." Its object is to form a nucleus of the Universal Brotherhood of Humanity, without distinctions of race, creed, sex, caste, or color; to encourage the study of comparative religion, philosophy, and science; and to investigate the

The First

unexplained laws of nature and the powers latent in man. *(Theosophical Society in America— Inaugural Address)*

THERAPEUTIC THEATER. *See* Theater

THERAPEUTICS AND MATERIA MEDICA BOOK. *See* Medical book

THERAPY (occupational) COURSE. *See* Occupational therapy course

THERMIT used to break up ice jams was employed on February 24, 1925, when a 250,000-ton ice jam in the St. Lawrence River at Waddington, N.Y., was moved in a few hours after the reaction of three thermit charges of 90 pounds each. Thermit is a mixture of finely powdered aluminum metal and oxide of iron. When properly ignited, it reacts vigorously, generating very high temperatures and producing extremely hot liquid iron. This method of using Thermit in ice-breaking work was first applied by Howard Turner Barnes, Professor of Physics at McGill University, Montreal, Canada. *(Howard Turner Barnes—Ice Engineering)*

THERMONUCLEAR BOMB. *See* Atomic bomb: Atomic fusion (thermonuclear) bomb

THERMOSETTING PLASTIC. *See* Plastic

THESIS DIRECTORY was a broadside, "A List of Theses at the Commencement of Harvard College," published in 1642 by Stephen Day, Cambridge, Mass. No copy is known to exist. *(Sidney Arthur Kimber—The Story of an Old Press)*

THIRD-PARTY QUIDS. *See* Quids

THIRD-TERM PRESIDENT. *See* President (U.S.): President elected for a fourth term

THORIUM-URANIUM REACTOR. *See* Atomic reactor

THOROUGHBRED HORSE. *See* Horse

THREAD
Cotton thread was made in Pawtucket, R.I., in 1793 by Hannah Wilkinson (Mrs. Slater), who conceived the idea of twisting fine Surinam cotton yarn on spinning wheels. She manufactured No. 20 two-ply thread, which proved superior to the linen thread then in use.

Nontwisted sewing thread (and the first nontwisted nylon sewing thread) was made commercially available in February 1946 by Belding Hemingway Corticelli, Putnam, Conn. It was called Monocord and Nymo.

Silk thread was manufactured in 1819 at Mansfield, Conn., by Rodney Hanks and Horatio Hanks.

Silk thread on spools was produced in 1849 by General Merritt Heminway. Previous to this, silk thread had been sold in skeins. The spools at first contained 12 yards of thread, and later 50 and 100 yards. The factory in which this thread was manu

The First

factured was started in 1822 in Watertown, Conn., by Bishop & Heminway, incorporated in 1842 under the name of M. Heminway and Sons.

THREE-BALL BILLIARD MATCH. *See* Billiard match: Billiard three-ball match on a 6-by-12 carom table

THREE-CENT PIECE. *See* Money: Silver coins

THREE-DIMENSIONAL FEATURE MOTION PICTURE. *See* Motion picture

THREE-DIMENSIONAL NEWSPAPER ADVERTISEMENT. *See* Advertisement

THREE-ELEMENT VACUUM TUBE. *See* Radio tube

THREE-MOTOR AIRPLANE. *See* Aviation—Airplane

THREE-WIRE CENTRAL-STATION INCANDESCENT ELECTRIC LIGHTING PLANT. *See under* Electric company

THRESHER
  Threshing machine to employ steam was patented by John A. Pitts and Hiram Abial Pitts of Winthrop, Maine, who received patent No. 542 on December 29, 1837, on a "machine for threshing or cleaning grain." The machine separated grain from the straw and chaff.

THROAT CLINIC. *See* Medical clinic: Laryngology clinic

THROAT MICROPHONE. *See* Laryngophone

TICKER. *See* Telegraph: Telegraph ticker to operate at high speed

TICKER TAPE
  Ticker-tape shower occurred June 18, 1910, in New York City when former President Theodore Roosevelt returned on the S.S. *Kaiserin Auguste Victoria* from a 15-month hunting trip in Africa. He was greeted at the Battery by Mayor William Jay Gaynor and a delegation of Rough Riders and escorted up Broadway, where he was greeted by a shower of ticker tape.

TICKET AGENCY
  Theater-ticket agency office was open from 8:00 A.M. to 4:00 P.M. at Macoy and Herwig, Stationers, 112–114 Broadway, New York City. The agency advertised in the New York *Times* on September 9, 1866, that patrons could obtain reserved seats for theaters in New York and Brooklyn, and choice seats and tickets at all times and in advance, when required.

TICKET SPECULATORS plied their trade in New York City in September 1850. Prior to the first appearance of Jenny Lind at Castle Garden, September 11, 1850, Phineas Taylor Barnum auctioned the seats, charging 25 cents admission to the auction. The first ticket was sold to John Nicholas Genin for $225. One thousand tickets sold for $10,-41. Jenny Lind donated her share of the $17,864

The First

gross receipts of the first performance to New York charities. Premiums were exacted by those who sold their tickets. *(Rodman Gilder—The Battery)*

TICKETS
  Airplane commutation tickets. *See under* Aviation

  Rain check. *See* Baseball ticket: Baseball rain check

  TIE (cotton-bale metallic fastening). *See* Cotton-bale metallic tie

TIGHTROPE
  Tightrope crossing of Niagara Falls. *See* Niagara Falls: Person to cross Niagara Falls on a tightrope

  Tightrope walker to span 2 skyscrapers was Philippe Petit of Nemours, France, who walked across a tightrope at a height of 1,350 feet from 1 tower of the World Trade Center, New York City, to the 2nd tower at 7:15 A.M., on August 7, 1974. He was taken into custody by the police. His sentence was suspended on condition that he give a public demonstration of his skill under controlled conditions in Central Park, New York City.

  Woman tightrope performer was Madame Adolphe of Paris, who, accompanied by Monsieur Godau, appeared June 1, 1819, at the Anthony Street Theatre, New York City.

TIGHTS (circus) are believed to have been introduced in 1828 by Nelson Hower, a bareback rider in the Buckley and Wicks Show, as the result of a mishap. The performers wore short jackets, knee breeches and stockings, but Hower's costume failed to arrive and he appeared for the show in his long knit underwear. *(Billboard. Sept. 6, 1930)*

TILE
  Brick roofing tile was manufactured in 1735 by Hüster, a German tile maker in Montgomery County, Pa. *(W. G. Worcester—Geological Survey of Ohio)*

  Wall and floor tiles were manufactured in 1845 by Abraham Miller, 7th and Zane streets, Philadelphia, Pa. In 1810 he had succeeded Andrew Miller, who had conducted a pottery in Sugar Alley since 1791. *(Heinrich Ries and Henry Leighton—History of the Clay-working Industry in the United States)*

TIMBER DRY DOCK. *See* Dry dock

TIMBER TRESTLE PIER OF LATTICE CONSTRUCTION. *See under* Bridge

TIMBERLAND RESERVATION. *See* Forest reserve: Forest reserve (national)

TIME, STANDARD
  Standard time was suggested for the United States by Charles Ferdinand Dowd of Saratoga

The First

TIME, STANDARD—*Continued*

Springs, N.Y., in 1870 but was not adopted at the time. The question was again brought forward in 1879, but the change did not meet with popular approval. On the initiative of the American Railway Association in 1883, Standard Time was adopted in the United States. At noon on November 18, 1883, the telegraphic signals sent out daily from the Naval Observatory at Washington, D.C., were changed to the new system. The Uniform Time Act of 1966 (80 Stat. L. 107, April 13, 1966), effective April 1, 1967, divided the United States into 8 time zones: eastern, central, mountain, Pacific, Yukon, Alaska, Hawaii, and Bering. *(Charles North Dowd—Charles F. Dowd, A.M., PhD.: A Narrative of His Services in Originating and Promoting the System of Standard time)*

TIME LOCK. *See* Lock

TIME RECORDER

Autograph time recorder was patented by Benjamin Frederick Merritt of Newton, Mass., who received patent No. 375,087 on December 20, 1887. The recorder was manufactured by the Chicago Time Register Company, now a part of IBM Corporation.

Card time recorder was invented by Daniel M. Cooper of Rochester, N.Y., who received patent No. 528,223 on October 30, 1894. The pressing of a lever recorded the time on specially printed cards divided by horizontal lines into seven equal spaces for the days of the week. The recorder, known as the Rochester, was manufactured by the Willard and Frick Manufacturing Company.

Dial time recorder was invented in 1888 by Dr. Alexander Dey of Glasgow, Scotland, who obtained patent No. 411,586 on September 24, 1889. Employees' numbers appeared around the circumference of a large ring on the front of the machine. A pivoted pointer arm pressed into a guide hole printed the time opposite the number on a prepared sheet inside the machine. In 1893 Alexander Dey, with his two brothers, John and Robert, who operated a department store in Syracuse, N.Y., formed the Dey Patents Company of Syracuse, which later changed its name to the Dey Time Register Company.

Employees' time recorder was invented by Willard L. Bundy of Auburn, N.Y., who obtained patent No. 393,205 on November 20, 1888. A key bearing the workman's number inserted in the mechanism printed both the number and the time on a paper tape. Bundy formed the Bundy Manufacturing Company, which later became a division of IBM Corporation.

TIMER

Prizefight timed by automatic timer. *See under* Prizefight

TIMETABLE (railroad) was advertised in the Baltimore, Md., *American,* May 20, 1830, by the Baltimore and Ohio Railroad Company. It was

The First

announced that on May 24, 1830, passenger transportation would be effected between Baltimore, Md., and Ellicott's Mills, Md., and that a brigade of train coaches would leave the company's depot on Pratt Street, Baltimore, at 7 A.M., 11 A.M., and 4 P.M. and would return from Ellicott's Mills at 9 A.M., 1 P.M., and 6 P.M. The price for the 26-mile trip was 75 cents. Because of a shortage of cars, passengers were obliged to return in the same coach and had to book passage for the whole trip. When additional cars were available, passengers could use any car and engage passage for a shorter distance, if desired.

TIN CAN. *See under* Canning; Cans

TIN FACTORY, for the manufacture of black plate, as well as tin and terne plate, was established in 1874 by Rogers and Burchheld in Leechburg, Pa.

TINTYPE CAMERA. *See* Camera

TINWARE MANUFACTURERS

Successful tinware manufacturers were Lalance and Grosjean, who in 1860 established a factory at Woodhaven, L.I., N.Y., for the manufacture of deeper tinware, such as milk pans, wash bowls, and dishpans.

Tinware manufacturers are said to have been Edward and William Pattison, brothers who settled in Berlin, Conn., about 1740 and manufactured culinary vessels and household articles made of sheet tin. Exact data as to the extent of their manufacturing activities have not been definitely determined, but it is known that they peddled their wares from house to house. *(Timothy Dwight—Travels in New England and New York)*

TIRE. *See* Automobile tire; Bicycle tire

TIRE CHAIN. *See* Automobile tire chain

TISSUE (toilet). *See* Paper: Toilet paper

TISSUE BANK. *See under* Medicine

TITANIUM

Titanium mill for rolling and forging titanium was opened November 2, 1957, in Toronto, Ohio by the Titanium Metals Corporation of America owned by the National Lead Company and the Allegheny Ludlum Steel Corporation.

Titanium plant fully self-contained and fully integrated was opened June 1, 1951, in Henderson Nev., by the Titanium Metals Corporation of America. Titanium ore was converted at the plant to titanium sponge, which was melted and cast into ingots of titanium metal.

TITLE GUARANTY INSURANCE COMPANY *See under* Insurance

TOASTER. *See* Electric toaster

TOBACCO

Cigarette tax. *See* Cigarette tax

The First

Tobacco cultivation was undertaken at Jamestown, Va., in 1612 by John Rolfe, the husband of Pocahontas. Rolfe had arrived from England with 107 other settlers on May 13, 1607. Tobacco had been brought to England as early as 1565. *(Ralphe Hamor—A True Discourse of the present estate of Virginia and the successes of the Affaires there till the 18 of June 1614)*

Tobacco tax (colonial) was authorized October 3, 1632, by the Massachusetts Court of Assistants and General Court, which ruled in Boston "that no person shall take any tobacco publicly, under pain of punishment; also that everyone shall pay 1d. for every time he is convicted of taking tobacco in any place, and that any Assistant shall have power to receive evidence and give order for the levying of it, as also to give order for the levying of the officer's charge. This order to begin the tenth of November next." *(Nathaniel Bradstreet Shurtleff—Records of the Governor and Company of the Massachusetts Bay in New England)*

Tobacco tax for internal revenue was levied by an act of Congress of July 1, 1862 (12 Stat. L. 432), but did not go into effect until September 1, 1862. The first federal tax on tobacco was levied in 1794, but after two years it was abandoned. A similar attempt was made in 1812 and lasted until 1816, when the tax was repealed. *(Meyer Jacobstein—Tobacco Industry in the United States)*

TOILET PAPER. *See* Paper

TOKEN MONEY. *See* Money: Trade tokens

TOLL BRIDGE. *See* Bridge

TOLL COLLECTOR (automatic) was placed in service November 19, 1954, at the Union Toll Plaza (in the Newark–Irvington–Union area) on the Garden State Parkway of New Jersey. Two machines went into operation at the extreme right lane for each direction of traffic to provide the correct change. Coins were deposited in a wiremesh hopper. A green light flashed when the 25-cent toll was received, and an audible alarm sounded to signal evaders.

TOLL ROAD. *See* Road

"TOMMY GUN." *See* Ordnance: Submachine gun

TONG (Chinese secret society) organized was the Kwong Dock Tong of San Francisco, about 1870. The first tong war broke out in 1873 as a result of an attack made on Ming Long of the Kwong Dock Tong by Low Sing, a member of the Suey Sing Tong. The dispute arose in connection with the slave-girl traffic. At Ross Valley and Waverly Place, San Francisco, the two factions met by appointment and began shooting. Six members of the Kwong Dock Tong were wounded—three of the six died—and one of the Suey Sing Tong men was killed. *(Eng Ying Gong and Bruce Grant—Tong War)*

The First

TOOL FACTORY devoted exclusively to the manufacture of machinists' tools was established in 1838 by John H. Gage in the Water Street shop of the Nashua Manufacturing Company, Nashua, N.H. *(Edward Everett Parker—History of the City of Nashua, N.H.)*

TOOTHBRUSH with synthetic bristles was Dr. West's Miracle Tuft Toothbrush, made of Du Pont Exton, a product synthesized from elementary substances. The brush was introduced to the retail trade during September 1938.

TOOTHPICK MANUFACTURING MACHINE PATENT was No. 123,790, granted February 20, 1872, to Silas Noble and James P. Cooley of Granville, Mass. The machine made it possible for "a block of wood, with little waste, at one operation, [to] be cut up into toothpicks ready for use."

TORNADO

Tornado of which there is any record occurred at New Haven, Conn., June 10, 1682, about 2:30 P.M. It is believed there was a tornado off North Carolina on June 23, 1586. *(John Park Finley—Tornadoes)*

Tornado disaster (large-scale) occurred March 18, 1925, when 689 people died; 13,000 were injured; and $16-18 million worth of damage occurred in 3 hours in Indiana, Illinois, Kentucky, and Tennessee.

TORNADO AND FIRE INSURANCE FUND. *See* Insurance: Fire and tornado insurance fund (state)

TORPEDO

Airplane torpedo was invented by Bradley Allen Fiske of the U.S. Navy, who obtained patent No. 1,032,394, July 16, 1912, on a "method of and apparatus for delivering submarine torpedoes from airships." The torpedo, held rigidly in place, its bow pointing in the same direction as the airplane, was dropped under its own power. His patent application was made April 12, 1912.

Torpedo manufacturing station was established in 1869 on Goat Island, in Newport harbor, under the supervision of the Bureau of Ordnance of the Navy Department. The purpose of the station was to instruct naval officers in the manufacture of torpedoes. Commander Edmund O. Matthews was ordered on June 9, 1869, to report for duty and in September 1869 he took possession of Goat Island and commenced the erection of the necessary buildings. *(Records in Office of Naval Records and Library, Navy Department, Washington, D.C.)*

Torpedo mine attack in the Civil War was made July 7, 1861, by the Confederates at Acquia Creek on the Potomac. Two large casks, connected by a piece of manila rope about 25 fathoms long, and kept at surface by cork floats, were floated down the river in an attempt to destroy the *Pawnee*, commanded by Commander Stephen Clegg Rowan. The attempt failed. The first attack that de-

The First

TORPEDO—*Continued*

stroyed a war vessel was made in the Yazoo River, December 12, 1862, on the U.S. *Cairo*, an armored river gunboat of 512 tons, under the command of Lieutenant Commander Thomas Oliver Selfridge. A large demijohn placed in a wooden box was anchored in the channel and exploded by means of a friction fuse. The first Confederate loss was a torpedo boat destroyed February 17, 1864, off Charleston, S.C.

Torpedoes used for oil drilling. *See* Oil: Oil well drilled by torpedoes

Underwater torpedo operated by electric current was invented by Samuel Colt of Hartford, Conn., who wrote President John Tyler on June 19, 1841, that he could sink ships by mines. He sank the gunboat *Boxer* in New York harbor on July 4, 1842, and the 300-ton brig *Volta* on October 18, 1842. On April 13, 1843, in the presence of President Tyler and his Cabinet, General Winfield Scott, and other officials, Colt blew up a schooner on the Potomac River by an electric mine from a distance of five miles. His invention was a combination of Robert Fulton's stationary torpedo and Professor Robert Hare's galvanic current.

TORPEDO BOAT. *See* Ship

TOTALISATOR

Fully electronic, transistorized, data processing totalisator was the Westbury Tote used May 15, 1965, at Roosevelt Raceway, Westbury, L.I., N.Y.

Totalisator to record racetrack bets and odds was invented by Sir George Julius, an Australian engineer, and installed in 1931 by the American Totalisator Company, Inc., Baltimore, Md., at the Hialeah Race Track, Miami, Fla. It was known as "the totalizer" and "the Julius" and was first used January 14, 1932.

TOUR OF THE WORLD

Passenger to fly around the world on commercial airlines in less than 100 hours was Major Horace C. Boren of Dallas, Tex., who arrived at New York International Airport, Idlewild, N.Y., on June 25, 1953, having completed a world flight in 99 hours 16 minutes. Boren stopped at 19 airports on his 21,000-mile flight.

Tour of the world made by a woman traveling alone was made by Elizabeth Cochrane (Nellie Bly). She made the tour in 72 days 6 hours 11 minutes 14 seconds, as a stunt for the New York *World* in 1889–90. She left New York City, Thursday, November 14, 1889, sailed from Hoboken, N.J., on the *Augusta Victoria* for Southampton, went around the world, and returned to New York on the Chicago express January 25, 1890, spending 56 days, 12 hours and 41 minutes in actual travel. *(Nellie Bly—Around the World in 72 Days)*

TOURNAMENT OF ROSES, originally called the Battle of Flowers, was held January 1, 1890, at

The First

Pasadena, Calif., under the auspices of the Valley Hunt Club. In the afternoon, amateur sports contests were held. The first college football contest, held January 1, 1902, was a game between the University of Michigan and Stanford University. The University of Michigan won 49-0. Football games have been a regular annual event since January 1, 1916, when Washington State College defeated Brown University, 14-0. Since 1897 the tournament has been conducted by a nonprofit organization known as the Pasadena Tournament of Roses Association, Limited. *(Pasadena Tournament of Roses Association—Tournament of Roses)*

TOW ROPE (ski). *See under* Ski tow

TOWN

Town founded by a woman was Tangipahoa, La., settled in 1806 by Rhoda Holly Singleton Mixon accompanied by her daughters and slaves from South Carolina. Her grandchildren sold their property in 1869.

Town named for George Washington was the town of Forks of Tar River, N.C., which changed its name to Washington in 1775. The town was originally formed November 20, 1771, by James Bonner, who owned all the land on which it was situated. It was incorporated April 13, 1782. Washington, Wilkes County, Ga., incorporated January 23, 1780, was the first town incorporated under the name of Washington.

TOWN BALL

Baseball (town ball) team. *See under* Baseball team

TOYERY was opened September 24, 1932, at the New York University Community Center, New York City. The first director was Mrs. Ida Cash. At the toyery old toys were repaired for distribution to children.

TRACK. *See* Railroad track

TRACK MEET

College relay race was held by the New Jersey Athletic Club at Bayonne, N.J., on May 30, 1893, before 5,000 spectators. The 1-mile team race was won by Harvard in 3 minutes 25 2/5 seconds—3 seconds faster than the record. Princeton was second, Yale third. Four men constituted a team; each team member ran 440 yards.

Track meet (intercollegiate) was held in Saratoga, N.Y., July 20-21, 1876, under the auspices of the Intercollegiate Association of Amateur Athletes of America. The participating teams represented Bowdoin, City College of New York, Columbia, Dartmouth, University of Pennsylvania, Princeton, Wesleyan, Williams, and Yale. A silver cup was awarded annually to the winning team. Permanent possession of the trophy was granted to the college with the greatest number of victories over 14 years. The first meet was won by Princeton with 4 firsts and 4 seconds. The cup was given permanently to Harvard, which won 8 of the first 14 meets.

Track meet (intercollegiate) to be televised. *See under* Television—Telecast

Transcontinental race began March 4, 1928, at Los Angeles, Calif., and concluded at 8:19 P.M. May 26, 1928, at New York City, the last 20 miles within Madison Square Garden. There were 274 entrants in the 3,422.3-mile race for the $48,500 in prizes. The results were Andrew Payne of Claremore, Okla., first, $25,000, 573 hours 4 minutes 34 seconds; John Salo of Passaic, N.J., second, $10,-000, 588 hours 40 minutes 13 seconds; Philip Granville of Hamilton, Canada, third, $5,009, 613 hours 42 minutes 30 seconds.

TRACKLESS TROLLEY SYSTEM. *See under* Streetcar

TRACT SOCIETY
Tract society was the Massachusetts Society for Promoting Christian Knowledge, instituted in Boston, Mass., September 1, 1803, at the suggestion of Samuel Phillips and Professor D. Tappan.

Tract society (national) was the American Tract Society, organized May 11, 1825, in New York City. The first president was Sampson Vryling Stoddard and the first secretary the Reverend William Allen Hallock. The society, still in existence, was the outgrowth of a combination of about 50 large and small tract societies. The society is evangelical in principle, interdenominational in character, interracial in purpose, and international in scope. It was organized to minister to all classes and conditions of people, in many languages, through the medium of the printed page.

TRACTOR. *See* Automobile tractor

TRADE ASSOCIATION was the American Brass Association, which was organized in Naugatuck Valley, Conn., in February 1853. Headquarters were opened in Waterbury, Conn. Originally, in 1853, the object of the association was to regulate prices, but in 1856 it attempted to regulate production. The association ceased to function in 1869. Local associations had been formed earlier by various groups. *(William Gilbert Lathrop—The Brass Industry in Connecticut)*

TRADE COMMISSION, FEDERAL. *See* Federal Trade Commission

TRADE DOLLAR. *See* Money

TRADE JOURNAL. *See* Periodical

TRADE REGISTER was *Aitken's General American Register, and the Gentleman's and Tradesman's Complete Annual Account Book and Calendar for . . . 1773.* Printed by J. Crukshank for R. Aitken in Philadelphia, Pa., in 1772–73, it contained 110 unnumbered pages and included a calendar, an account book for the year, and space for

memoranda. Aitken's prefatory letter stated: "The intercourse and connection of the several colonies with each other is enlarging . . . so that it becomes a matter of some consequence to every inhabitant to be acquainted with the public offices and officers . . . in all the . . . provinces on the continent."

TRADE TOKENS. *See* Money

TRADEMARK LAWSUIT
Trademark controversy involving a newspaper was tried before Judge Nathan Sandford, chancellor of New York State, who decided on January 31, 1825, that the *National Advocate* of New York City was not entitled to an injunction to restrain the *New York National Advocate* in the case of *Thomas Snowden* vs. *Mordecai Manuel Noah, John D. Brown, and others. (Samuel M. Hopkins—Reports of Cases Argued and Determined in the Court of Chancery of the State of New York)*

TRADEMARK (U.S.) was registered under the act of July 8, 1870. During that year there were 121 registrations under the law, the first thereof (No. 1) under date of October 25, 1870, by the Averill Chemical Paint Company of New York City on a "trade-mark for liquid paint." This law was declared unconstitutional and void.
See also Cotton: Cotton goods to be trademarked

TRADING POST. *See* Fur trading post

TRADING SHIP. *See* Ship

TRADING STAMP was originated in 1891 by Thomas Alexander Sperry, who in 1896 organized the Sperry & Hutchinson Company of Bridgeport, Conn. The company was incorporated in 1900. *(Twenty-Fifth Anniversary—Sperry & Hutchinson Co.)*

TRAFFIC COURT, BICYCLE. *See* Bicycle traffic court

TRAFFIC LIGHT
Electric traffic signal lights were installed August 5, 1914, at Euclid Avenue and East 105th Street, Cleveland, Ohio, by the American Traffic Signal Company under the direction of Safety Director Alfred A. Benesch. Cross arms, 15 feet above the ground, were equipped with red and green lights and buzzers. Two long buzzes permitted Euclid Avenue traffic to proceed, and one long buzz, 105th Street traffic.

TRAFFIC LINES to designate lanes were painted in white on River Road, near Trenton, Wayne County, Mich., in the fall of 1911 under the direction of Edward Norris Hines (a road commissioner for Wayne County), who called his idea a "center line safety stripe." A machine was later developed that cut the painting cost.

TRAFFIC POLICE. *See* Police

The First

TRAFFIC REGULATION

One-way traffic regulation appears to have been issued in New York City on December 17, 1791, when a regulation incidental to a performance at the John Street Theatre requested that "Ladies and Gentlemen will order their Coachmen to take up and set down with their Horse Heads to the East River, to avoid Confusion."

Traffic law was passed June 27, 1652, by New Amsterdam (New York City): "The Director General and Council of New Netherland in order to prevent accidents do hereby ordain that no Wagons, Carts or Sleighs shall be run, rode or driven at a gallop within this city of New Amsterdam, that the drivers and conductors of all Wagons, Carts and Sleighs within this city (the Broad Highway alone excepted) shall walk by the Wagons, Carts or Sleighs and so take and lead the horses, on the penalty of two pounds Flemish for the first time, and for the second time double, and for the third time to be arbitrarily corrected therefor and in addition to be responsible for all damages which may arise therefrom." *(Minutes of the Common Council of the City of New York, 1675–1676)*

Traffic policemen. *See* Police: Traffic police squad

TRAFFIC REGULATION COURSE

Air traffic regulation course was endowed in 1934 by Godfrey Lowell Cabot, who created the James Jackson Cabot professorship of air traffic regulation and air transportation at Norwich University, Northfield, Vt. Lectures have been given at intervals since the establishment of the course.

Graduate course in traffic engineering and administration was established August 16, 1937, at Harvard University, Cambridge, Mass., under the direction of Miller McClintock.

Teacher training course in "Training Traffic Safety" was offered at the Pennsylvania State College during the 1936 summer session under the guidance of Amos Earl Neyhart, administrative head of the Institute of Public Safety, Pennsylvania State College, State College, Pa. This course included both classroom techniques and road instruction procedures.

TRAFFIC REGULATION PAMPHLET

Printed traffic regulations were *Rules For Driving.* The regulations, printed in a four-page pamphlet 3¼ by 6¼ inches in size, were put into effect October 30, 1903, by the New York City Police Department.

TRAILER BANK. *See* Bank

TRAILER CHURCH was St. Paul's Wayside Cathedral, which was placed in operation October 1, 1937, by the Diocese of Southern Ohio Protestant Episcopal Church under the direction of Bishop Henry Wise Hobson. It was designed by Norman R. Sturgis and built by the Aerocar Company, Detroit, Mich. The exterior was of sheet metal with a backing of Masonite painted gunmetal gray. The roof was covered with a silver-finish fabric. The church was equipped with a removable altar, an organ, an amplification unit, and sound moving-picture apparatus. It seated about 25 people.

TRAILER (motion pictures). *See* Television—Telecast: Motion picture trailer to be televised

TRAIN. *See* Railroad; Railroad car

TRAIN NEWSPAPER. *See* Newspaper: Newspaper printed on a train

TRAIN ROBBERY. *See* Railroad train robbery

TRAINER, AVIATION. *See* Aviation: Aviation trainer (jet)

TRAINING SCHOOL. *See under* Army School; Naval officers' training school; Police

TRAITOR to the American cause was William Demont (Dement) who, on February 29, 1776, was appointed adjutant in Colonel Robert Magraw's battalion. He notified the British of the position of Fort Washington, Mount Washington (now in New York City). Demont's act enabled Sir William Howe to conquer the fort on November 16, 1776. The British force of 8,900 men captured 2,818 officers and men, 43 guns, 2,800 muskets, etc. Demont, a member of the Fifth Pennsylvania Battalion, deserted on November 2, 1776, and gave his plans to Lieutenant General Earl Percy. *(Empire State Society of the Sons of the American Revolution—Fort Washington)*

TRAMPOLINE

Trampoline commercially manufactured was produced in 1937 by the Nissen Trampoline Company, Cedar Rapids, Iowa, founded by George P. Nissen and Paul F. Nissen. They were known as bouncing nets, bouncing tables, and rebound tumblers. The name was derived from the Spanish for diving board.

TRANSATLANTIC FLIGHT. *See* Aviation—Flights (transatlantic)

TRANSCONTINENTAL AIR MAIL. *See* Airmail service

TRANSCONTINENTAL AIR RACE. *See* Aviation—Races

TRANSCONTINENTAL FLIGHT. *See* Aviation—Flights (transcontinental)

TRANSCONTINENTAL HORSEBACK TRIP. *See* Woman: Woman horseback rider to make a solo transcontinental trip

TRANSCONTINENTAL TRIPS. *See under* Automobile transcontinental trip; Bicycle trip; Railroad excursion

TRANSCRIPTION (radio). *See* Radio broadcast: Recorded coast-to-coast broadcast

The First

TRANSFER PAPERS. *See* Decalcomanias

TRANSFERS (streetcar). *See* Streetcar: Transfers (printed)

TRANSISTOR

Junction transistor was invented by Dr. William Shockley of the Bell Telephone Laboratories, Murray Hill, N.J., and announced on July 5, 1951. He obtained patent No. 2,569,347 on September 25, 1951, on a "circuit element utilizing semiconductive material," which he assigned to the Bell Telephone Laboratories, Inc. It consisted of a tiny sandwich of germanium treated so that its alternate layers had different electrical properties. It occupied only about 1/400th of a cubic inch.

Phototransistor, a transistor operated by light rather than electric current, was invented by Dr. John Northrup Shive of the Bell Telephone Laboratories, Murray Hill, N.J., and announced on March 30, 1950. It was composed of a midget disk of germanium with only a single collector wire. Light focused on one side of the disk controlled the flow of current to the opposite side, the side to which the wire was attached.

Transistor was invented at the Bell Telephone Laboratories, Murray Hill, N.J., by Drs. John Bardeen and Walter Houser Brattain, and demonstrated on June 30, 1948. The essential element of the device was a tiny wafer of germanium, a semiconductor. Transistors occupy a fraction of the space required for vacuum tubes needed to do a comparable electronic task and operate on greatly reduced amounts of power.

Transistors produced commercially for a specific product were made in October 1951 by the Western Electric Company, Allentown, Pa., for long-distance dialing equipment of the Bell Telephone System. In 1948 experimental transistors had been manufactured and distributed to military and civilian engineering organizations for early circuit development work.

TRANSISTOR RADIO RECEIVER. *See* Radio receiver

TRANSISTORIZED HEARING AID. *See* Deaf—Hearing aid

TRANSOCEANIC NEWSPAPER. *See* Newspaper

TRANSPACIFIC FLIGHT. *See* Aviation—Flights (transpacific)

TRANSPARENT PAPER-STRIP PHOTOGRAPHIC FILM. *See* Photographic film

TRANSPARENT-TOP AUTOMOBILE. *See* Automobile

TRANSPORT AIRPLANE. *See* Aviation—Airplane

The First

TRANSPORTATION COORDINATION

Transportation coordination (federal) was undertaken by the act of June 16, 1933 (48 Stat. L. 211). Joseph Bartlett Eastman, a member of the Interstate Commerce Commission, was appointed coordinator June 16, 1933. His office was created the same day, by the enactment of the Emergency Railroad Transportation Act, "to relieve the existing national emergency in relation to interstate railroad transportation." *(Public Act No. 68.—73d Congress)*

TRANSPORTATION DEPARTMENT (U.S)

Transportation Department (U.S.) was authorized October 15, 1966, by the "act to establish a Department of Transportation" (80 Stat. L. 931), which became effective 90 days after the Secretary first took office. The first official day of existence for the Department of Transportation was April 1, 1967. The first secretary was Alan Stephenson Boyd of Florida, who received a recess appointment from President Lyndon Baines Johnson on November 6, 1966, and was sworn in January 16, 1967.

TRAPS

Steel animal traps commercially manufactured were made in 1855 by Sewell Newhouse of the Oneida Community, N.Y. He made them in eight different sizes, intended to trap animals ranging from the house rat to the grizzly bear, and sold them principally to Indians. Various types of traps had been made earlier by Newhouse and by others, but they had been devised for individual use and were not marketed. Newhouse was the author of *The Trapper's Guide: A Manual of Instructions for Capturing All Kinds of Fur-Bearing Animals and Curing Their Skins.*

TRAPSHOOTING

Clay pigeon target was invented by George Ligowsky of Cincinnati, Ohio, who obtained patent No. 231,919 on September 7, 1880, on a concave slotted "flying target."

Trapshooting intercollegiate association was the Intercollegiate Shooting Association, formed March 25, 1898, at the Fifth Avenue Hotel, New York City, by Columbia, Cornell, Harvard, Pennsylvania, Princeton, and Yale. The first officers were H. R. Lunt of Harvard, president; Oglesby Paul, secretary; and C. B. Spears, treasurer. The first meet was held at the New Haven Shooting Club, New Haven, Conn., on May 7, 1898. Clay pigeons were used.

TRAPSHOOTING TOURNAMENT

Trapshoot (Grand American) with clay targets was held at Interstate Park, Queens, L.I., New York, June 12, 1900, and won by Rolla O. (Pop) Heikes, of Dayton, Ohio, who scored 91 targets out of a possible 100 from a distance of 22 yards. There were 74 entries. Walter S. Beaver of Berwyn, Pa., was the first shooter to win the Grand American from the extreme distance of 25 yards.

TRAPSHOOTING TOURNAMENT—*Continued*
On August 25, 1933, he broke 99 out of 100 targets.

Trapshoot (Grand American) with live birds was held in March 1893 at Dexter Park, Jamaica, New York, with 21 entries. R. A. Welch won, and killed 23 out of 25 birds from 23 yards. *(Robert A. Welch, First Annual Grand American Handicap Program)*

TRAVELERS AID was instituted in 1851 when Bryan Mullanphy of St. Louis died and left approximately one third of his fortune of more than $1 million in a trust fund, to be administered by the City Council for the purpose of assisting, while they were in St. Louis, those who were "traveling to the west." In 1885 William Collins and Edward Prior, of the Society of Friends, paid the salary of the first employed worker among travelers. *(Travelers Aid Manual—National Association of Travelers Aid Societies)*

TRAVELERS AID SOCIETY
   Travelers Aid Society (national) was the National Association of Travelers Aid Societies, which developed from the Travelers Aid Society of the City of New York. The New York society, founded in 1904, cooperated in forming the National Travelers Aid Society in 1917. In May 1920 the name was changed from National Travelers Aid Society to National Association of Travelers Aid Societies and in 1923 articles of incorporation were secured under the new name. *(Travelers Aid Manual—National Association of Travelers Aid Societies)*

TRAVELER'S CHECKS. *See* Check

TRAVELING SIDEWALK. *See* Sidewalk (traveling)

TREADMILL was completed September 7, 1822 in a specially constructed building for the New York City Prison. By means of the treadmill, which was designed to be operated by 8 to 16 persons, 40 to 50 bushels of Indian corn were ground daily. The wheel was 5 feet 2 inches in diameter. The treadmill was placed in operation September 23, 1822, in a two-story building 60 feet in length and 30 feet wide, with a garret which served as a granary. Isaac Collins, one of the managers of the Society for the Prevention of Pauperism, and Stephen Greelet are credited with suggesting the treadmill to Stephen Allen, then mayor of New York. *(James Hardie—History of the Tread-Mill)*

TREASON
   American colonist hanged for treason was Jacob Leisler, who in 1689 led an insurrection against Governor Francis Nicholson of New York "for the preservation of the Protestant religion" and in behalf of the sovereigns William and Mary. Through trickery the aristocratic party regained power and in a manifestly unfair trial convicted Leisler of treason and on May 16, 1691, hanged

him from a scaffold erected in City Hall Park. *(Jared Sparks, Library of American Biography)*

Citizen of the United States to be tried for treason, convicted, and hanged was William Bruce Mumford, a retired gambler. During the Civil War, Captain Theodorus Bailey was sent by Admiral David Glasgow Farragut to New Orleans, La., where he hoisted the American flag over the mint on April 28, 1862. After the troops left, Mumford tore down the flag. On May 1, General Benjamin Franklin Butler arrived in New Orleans with 2,000 troops and took possession of the St. Charles Hotel. A crowd gathered in front of it, among them Mumford who boasted of his exploit in humbling the "old rag of the United States." Mumford was tried under the direction of the provost marshal of the district of New Orleans and hanged on June 7, 1862. *(James Parton—General Butler in New Orleans)*

Execution for treason in peacetime was the electrocution of Julius and Ethel Rosenberg, husband and wife, on June 19, 1953, at Sing Sing Prison, Ossining, N.Y. The Rosenbergs were the first native-born Americans executed for espionage by order of a civilian court. They were sentenced April 5, 1951, by Judge Irving Robert Kaufman of the United States District Court, Southern District.

Treason trial (colonial) was held May 7, 1634, when the Virginia Assembly heard complaints against Sir John Harvey, Governor of Virginia, who had assumed his duties March 24, 1630. Opposition to his rule increased and on April 28, 1635, he was accused of treason and thrust out of the government. Captain John West assumed the governorship until the wishes of the king could be ascertained. Harvey was returned to England, where his case was considered. On April 2, 1636, he returned to assume his post, which he held until November 1639.

TREASURY DEPARTMENT (U.S.)
   General Land Office (federal). *See under* Land Office

   Gold medallions issued by the Treasury Department under the American Arts Gold Medallion Act of March 8, 1977 (91 Stat. L. 19), to commemorate outstanding individuals in the American arts were placed on sale from June 16, 1980, to August 30, 1980. The price was based on the previous day's closing spot price of gold on the New York Commodity Exchange plus $12 an ounce, the cost of manufacturing and distribution. Two medallions were offered: the Marian Anderson Gold Medallion, limited to 1 million pieces, weighing one half troy ounce fine gold, and having a diameter of 1.08 inches; and the Grant Wood Gold Medallion, limited to a half million pieces, weighing one troy ounce of fine gold, and having a diameter of 1.26 inches.

The First

Register of the Treasury was Joseph Nourse, who served from September 12, 1789, to May 31, 1829.

Register of the Treasury who was a black was Blanche Kelso Bruce of Mississippi, who served from May 21, 1881, to June 7, 1885, and from December 3, 1897, to March 17, 1898.

Secretary of the Treasury was Alexander Hamilton of New York, who was appointed by President George Washington on September 11, 1789, and who served until February 1, 1795. *(Henry Jones Ford—Alexander Hamilton)*

Treasurer of the United States was Michael Hillegas, who held office from July 29, 1775, to September 11, 1789. On July 29, 1775, Hillegas and George Clymer were appointed joint treasurers of the United Colonies. On September 6, 1777, additional compensation was "allowed to Michael Hillegas, Esq., Treasurer of the United States, from the 6th day of August 1776 when Mr. Clymer resigned the office of joint treasurer" to become a delegate to the Continental Congress. Hillegas remained in office after the organization of the Treasury Department (September 2, 1789, (1 Stat. L. 65), until September 11, 1789, when Samuel Meredith assumed office. *(Emma St. Clair Whitney—Michael Hillegas, and His Descendants)*

Treasurer of the United States (black woman) was Azie Taylor Morton of Texas, who assumed her office on September 12, 1977. Her signature is on the $1, $5, and $10 bills.

Treasurer of the United States to sign currency with 2 names was Dorothy Andrews Elston, who was sworn in May 8, 1969. Her name appears on the Federal Reserve notes of the 1969 series first delivered on July 7, 1969. She married Walter Lawrence Kabis on September 17, 1970, and changed her name and signature to Dorothy Andrews Kabis, which appears on the bills delivered on December 4, 1970.

Treasury Department lifesaving medal. *See* Medal: Lifesaving medal

Treasury Department (U.S.) was organized September 2, 1789, by act of Congress (1 Stat. L. 65) under the Secretary of the Treasury. The Sub-Treasury Act of July 4, 1840 (5 Stat. L. 385), an "act to provide for the collection, safe-keeping, transfer and disbursement of the public revenue" provided for sub-treasuries in New York City, Boston, Charleston, and St. Louis, a mint in Philadelphia, and a branch mint in New Orleans. The first Sub-Treasury was established in 1846 in Wall Street, New York City, pursuant to the provisions of the act of August 4, 1846 (9 Stat. L. 59), an "act to provide for the better organization of the Treasury, and for the collection, safe-keeping, transfer, disbursement of the public revenue."

The First

Treasury surplus returned and apportioned among the several states was authorized by Section 13 of the act of June 23, 1836 (5 Stat. L. 55). Twenty-six states received a total of $28,-101,644.91, distributed in proportion to their respective representation in the Senate and House and given in three installments. This money was to remain on deposit until Congress directed otherwise, but no effort to secure its return has been made.

Woman assistant treasurer of the United States was Marion Glass Bannister, appointed July 26, 1933, by President Franklin Delano Roosevelt.

Woman treasurer of the United States was Georgia Neese Clark of Richland, Kan., nominated June 3, 1949 by President Harry S. Truman and confirmed June 9, 1949.

TREASURY NOTES. *See under* Bond

TREATY

Colonial treaty with the American Indians was a defensive alliance made April 1, 1621, on Strawberry Hill, Plymouth, Mass., between Massasoit, war chief of the Wampanoags, and the Pilgrims in behalf of King James I. The agreement in all its parts was kept by both parties for more than half a century. They promised not to "doe hurt" to one another. If a Wampanoag broke the law, he was sent to Plymouth for punishment; if a Pilgrim was the offender, he was sent to the Sowams. *(Henry William Elson—United States, Its Past and Present)*

International treaty for the protection of wild birds. *See* Bird legislation (international)

Status of Forces treaty was the March 27, 1941, Leased Naval and Air Bases Agreement between the United States and the United Kingdom. A similar treaty, the North Atlantic Status of Forces Treaty, became effective August 23, 1953.

Treaty between states after the Declaration of Independence was concluded between Georgia and South Carolina on May 20, 1777, at Dewitt's Corner, S.C. Under its provisions, the Cherokees retired behind a line running southwest from the straight part of Pickens County on the North to a point just below the mouth of the Tallulah at the western tip of the state.

Treaty between the United States Government and a nation with which it had been at war was the armistice with Great Britain. Preliminary articles of peace were signed November 30, 1782, in Paris, France. Hostilities ceased January 20, 1783. The treaty was proclaimed by the Continental Congress April 11, 1783. The definite treaty of peace was signed in Paris September 3, 1783, by David Hartley, plenipotentiary of Great Britain, and Benjamin Franklin and John Adams of the United States. The treaty was ratified and proclaimed January 14, 1784. *(Treaties, Conventions, International Acts, Protocols and Agreements Be-*

The First

TREATY—*Continued*
tween the United States of America and other Powers 1776–1909)

Treaty entered into by the United States was signed with France on February 6, 1778. The plenipotentiary of France was Conrad Alexandre Gérard; the United States plenipotentiaries were Benjamin Franklin, Silas Deane, and Arthur Lee. *(John Bassett Moore—History and Digest of International Arbitrations)*

Treaty entered into by the United States after the treaty of peace with Great Britain of September 3, 1783, was concluded with Prussia and signed at the Hague, September 10, 1785, by Benjamin Franklin, John Adams, and Thomas Jefferson for the United States. The treaty was ratified by Congress on May 17, 1786 (8 Stat. L. 84), and the ratifications exchanged in October 1786.

Treaty entered into by the United States with Indian tribes was a treaty with the Delaware Nation, signed September 17, 1778 (7 Stat. L. 13). The signers were Andrew and Thomas Lewis, Commissioners for and in behalf of the United States; and Captain White Eyes, Captain Pipe, and Captain John Kill Buck on behalf of the Delawares. This treaty, agreed upon at Fort Pitt (now Pittsburgh), contained the following provisions: (1) all offenses were to be mutually forgiven; (2) peace and friendship were to be perpetual; in case of war, each party was to assist the other; (3) the United States was to have free passage to forts and towns of former enemies, and such warriors as could be spared were to join the troops of the United States; (4) neither party was to inflict punishment without an impartial trial; (5) an agent was to be appointed by the United States to trade with the Delaware Nation; (6) the United States was to guarantee all territorial rights granted by former treaties and to allow a representative in Congress on certain conditions. *(Records in Office of Indian Affairs, U.S. Department of the Interior, Washington, D.C.)*

Treaty (federal) signed by a woman was the Charter of the United Nations, signed June 26, 1945, at San Francisco, Calif., by Virginia Crocheron Gildersleeve, a delegate to the United Nations Conference on International Organization.

Treaty rejected by the Senate of the United States was the pact with Colombia for suppressing the African slave trade, rejected February 22, 1825, by a vote of 40-0.

Treaty signed by a woman ambassador was the treaty of friendship, commerce, and navigation between the United States and Denmark, signed in Copenhagen, Denmark, on October 1, 1951, by Eugenie Anderson, United States ambassador to Denmark, and Ole Bjorn Kraft, Denmark's Minister of Foreign Affairs.

The First

Treaty violation occurred October 15, 1565. On that date Pedro Menéndez de Avilés, the Spanish navigator, captured French Huguenot settlers in Florida, who surrendered under a truce. Instead of granting them the customary amnesty which was expected, Menéndez put them to death. *(Francisco López de Mendoza Grajales—Memoir of the Happy Result and Prosperous Voyage of the Fleet commanded by the illustrious captain General Pedro Menéndez de Avilés which sailed from Cadiz on the morning of Thursday June 28th for the coast of Florida and arrived there on the 28th of August 1565)*

Treaty with a Far Eastern country was the Treaty of Amity and Commerce with Siam, concluded March 20, 1833 (the last day of the fourth month of the Siamese year 1194, called Pi-Marông-chat-tava-sôk, or the year of the Dragon). One copy was in Siamese, and one in English, with a Portuguese and a Chinese translation annexed. Edmund Roberts was the envoy of the United States. Ratifications were exchanged April 14, 1836, in Bangkok (the royal city of Sia-Yut'hia) and the treaty proclaimed June 24, 1837, by President Martin Van Buren.

Treaty with a foreign nation to provide for mutual reduction of import duties was the Convention with France, Regarding Claims and Regarding Duties on Wines and Cottons, signed in Paris, July 4, 1831 (8 Stat. L. 430). The ratifications were exchanged February 2, 1832, and proclaimed July 13, 1832 (1832 ch. 199) *(Treaties and Other International Acts of the United States of America, Vol. 3—U.S. Department of State, Washington, D.C.)*

Treaty with a South American country was the treaty or general convention of Peace, Amity, Navigation and Commerce which was signed at Bogotá, Colombia, October 3, 1824, between United States and the Republic of Colombia. (The Republic of Colombia then included Venezuela and Ecuador.) The treaty was submitted to the Senate on February 22, 1825, and ratified March 7, 1825. It was ratified by Colombia March 26, 1825. The treaty was proclaimed May 31, 1825. The plenipotentiaries who signed the treaty were Richard Clough Anderson, minister plenipotentiary of the United States to the Republic of Colombia, and Pedro Gual, Secretary of State and Foreign Relations of Colombia. *(Treaties and Other International Acts of the United States of America—U.S. Department of State, Washington, D.C.)*

TREATY ADVISORY BOARD was the Inter-Departmental Advisory Board on Reciprocity Treaties, established in July 1933, as a continuation and enlargement of a committee set up in March 1933 by arrangement between the heads of certain departments and other establishments of the government for the purpose of making studies more or

The First

less similar to those of the Advisory Board. Neither the board nor the committee which it succeeded was authorized by act of Congress. The duties of the board included the investigation of subjects suggested for inclusion in or regulation by treaties under contemplation or negotiation, the drafting of such treaties, and informal negotiations with foreign representatives or experts.

TREE, CHRISTMAS. *See* Christmas tree

TREE PATENT. *See* Patent: Fruit tree patent

TREE-PLANTING (federal). *See* Forest Service: Federal planting of forests

TREE SURGERY COURSE. *See* Forestry school: Forestry correspondence course

TRESTLE PIER, TIMBER. *See under* Bridge

TRIBAL CONSTITUTION, AMERICAN INDIAN. *See under* American Indians

TRIBUNAL (arbitration). *See* Arbitration: Arbitration tribunal

TRIFLUOROETHYL VINYL ETHER. *See* Anesthesia

TRIPLE CROWN. *See under* Horse; Jockey

TRIPLE PLAY (baseball). *See under* Baseball game

TROMBONE was used in the liturgical services conducted at the obsequies for a child whose remains were interred November 15, 1754, at Bethlehem, Pa. Trombones were used March 30, 1755 in the Easter services. *(William C. Reichel—Something About Trombones)*

TROPHY (aeronautical). *See* Aviation: Aeronautical trophy

TROTTER. *See* Horse

TROTTING COURSE. *See* Horse race

TROTTING FUTURITY. *See under* Horse race

TROTTING REGISTER. *See under* Horse register

TRUANCY legislation (state) was "an act to provide for the care and instruction of idle and truant children," enacted by New York on April 12, 1853 (Chapter 185). A $50 fine was levied against parents whose children between the ages of 5 and 15 were absent from school.

TRUCK, AUTOMOBILE. *See* Automobile truck

TRUCK-DRIVING TRAINING SCHOOL. *See* Automobile school

TRUSS BRIDGE. *See* Bridge: Iron-truss bridge

TRUST

Antitrust law (national), passed July 2, 1890 (26 Stat. L. 209), was an "act to protect trade and commerce against unlawful restraints and monopolies." Section One provided that "every contract combination in the form of trust or otherwise, or conspiracy, in restraint of trade or com-

The First

merce among the several states, or with foreign nations, is hereby declared to be illegal." The act is popularly known as the Sherman Act.

Antitrust law (state) was Act. No. 79, an act "to prevent monopolies in the transportation of freight, and to secure free and fair competition in the same," approved February 23, 1883, by Alabama. The first general law was Chapter 257, passed March 9, 1889, by Kansas "to declare unlawful trusts and combinations in restraint of trade and products, and to provide penalties therefor."

Blue-sky laws were passed by Kansas on March 10, 1911, "for the regulation and supervision of investment companies and providing penalties for the violation thereof." *(Chapter 133, Laws of 1911, Kansas)*

Cartel listed by that name was the Pacific Coast Gasolene Cartel. The cartel was an agreement entered into by companies selling 95 percent of the gasoline in the states of California, Washington, Oregon, Arizona, and Nevada, and the territories of Hawaii and Alaska. The agreement was approved by the Secretary of the Interior as oil administrator on February 13, 1934. A committee of seven persons was chosen to manage the activities of the cartel. The first chairman was Ralph Kenneth Davies of San Francisco, director of the Standard Oil Company of California, elected February 24, 1934. The government representative on the board was William Herbert Eaton. The cartel became effective March 1, 1934, but was abandoned before the end of the month.

Community trust. *See* Community trust

Investment trust. *See under* Brokerage

Manufacturers' price regulation agreement was signed by the coopers of New York City on December 17, 1679. The coopers agreed upon "ye Rate and Prizes of Caske, this is to Say, for euery Dry halfe Baril one shilling Six Pence. . . . " The agreement concluded: "And Wee, ye Under Written, Doo Joyntly and Seavorally Bind ourselves, that for Euery one that shall sell any cask Beefore mentioned under the Rate or Prizes aboue, Sd., that for euery Such Default ffiuety Shillinges he or they shall pay for vse of the poore, as Wittnes our hands, this 17th Day of December, 1679." Twenty-one coopers signed the agreement. Their action was condemned and they were brought to trial in the Council Chamber, January 8, 1680. The compact was annulled and the following verdict issued: "They are adjudged guilty, all that have signed the Contract, and are To pay each 50s, & either of them in publick employ to be dismist. The paym't to be to the Church or pious uses."

Trust was the salt trust organized November 10, 1817, by the salt manufacturers of Kanawha, W.Va. It went into active operation on the first day of January 1818, at the Kanawha Salt Compa-

The First

TRUST—*Continued*
ny. It was formed for the purpose of controlling the quantity of salt manufactured, the method of manufacture, the packing, and the production. The company disbanded January 1, 1822. *(Phil. Conley—West Virginia Encyclopedia)*

Trust company. *See under* Bank

Trust fund (educational). *See* Educational trust fund

TUBE
Collapsible tube was invented by John Rand who received patent No. 2,252 on September 11, 1841, on a "mode of preserving paints, and other fluids, by confining them in close metallic vessels so constructed as to collapse with slight pressure, and thus force out the paint or fluid confined therein through proper openings for that purpose." The tubes, molded of lead and used to hold oil colors, were provided with caps to keep them airtight.

Machine designed to produce collapsible tubes was built in 1873 at Philadelphia, Pa., under the direction of August Herman Wirz. Wirz had seen tube-making machines in operation when he was United States Commissioner at the Industrial Exposition in Vienna and had brought over the plans. The first machine-made tubes produced in the United States were used for cucumber jelly.

TUBE, ELECTRON. *See* Electron tube

TUBELESS AUTOMOBILE TIRE. *See* Automobile tire

TUBERCULOSIS CIRCULAR was issued in July 1889 by the New York City Department of Health through the efforts of Dr. Hermann Michael Biggs.

TUBERCULOSIS HOSPITAL. *See* Hospital

TUBERCULOSIS LABORATORY
Tuberculosis diagnostic community laboratory where specimens of sputum could be examined was authorized December 13, 1893, and opened by the New York City Department of Health under the direction of Dr. Hermann Michael Biggs. The laboratory administered sputum examinations, reporting and registration (compulsory by institutions, and voluntary by physicians), official supervision of isolation, terminal disinfection, provision of hospital facilities, and public education. *(American Review of Tuberculosis. July 1929)*

Tuberculosis research laboratory was the Saranac Laboratory, established in 1894 by Dr. Edward Livingston Trudeau in a room in his home at Saranac Lake, N.Y.

TUBERCULOSIS SANATORIUM. *See* Hospital

TUBERCULOSIS SCHOOL
Outdoor school for tubercular children was the Meeting Street School, Providence, R.I., opened January 27, 1908, as the Fresh Air School. A tem-

The First

porary teacher was appointed, but after three months Marie E. Powers was assigned to the school as teacher and principal. Dr. Ellen R. Stone was the superintendent. Twenty children were in the first class, which comprised grades one through eight. Hot lunches furnished by the school supplemented lunches brought by the children.

TUBERCULOSIS SOCIETY was the Pennsylvania Society for the Prevention of Tuberculosis, founded April 10, 1892, in Philadelphia, Pa., by Lawrence Francis Flick.

TUBERCULOSIS TEST (cattle). *See* Animals: Cattle tuberculosis test

TUBERCULOSIS VACCINE. *See* Vaccine

TUBULAR-PLATE GIRDER BRIDGE. *See* Bridge

TUFTED-PLASTIC CARPETING. *See* Carpeting: Carpeting of tufted plastic

TUGBOAT. *See* Ship

TULAREMIA. *See* Disease (distinctly American)

TUNG trees (*Aleurites fordii*) successfully grown for tung oil were planted in 1905 by the United States Plant Introduction Garden, Chico, Calif. The seeds had been forwarded by David Fairchild, chief of the Division of Plant Exploration and Introduction, United States Department of Agriculture, who had received them from L. S. Wilcox, United States consul general at Hankow, China.

TUNGSTEN
Ductile tungsten was produced in 1908 by Dr. William David Coolidge of the General Electric Company, Schenectady, N.Y., who used high temperatures to draw the tungsten into fine filaments for incandescent lamps. Coolidge reported his findings in the May 17, 1910, issue of the *Journal of the American Institute of Electrical Engineers* and obtained patent No. 1,082,933 on December 30, 1913, on "tungsten and method of making the same, for use as filaments of incandescent electric lamps."

Tungsten and tellurium were found in 1819 in a bismuth mine in Huntington, Conn. The mine was owned by Ephraim Lane. Tungsten, a ferruginous metal known to mineralogists as "wolfram," was found in the state of yellow oxide while tellurium was found in the metallic state. *(American Journal of Science. Vol. 1)*

TUNNEL
Freight delivery tunnel system was put into operation in Chicago, Ill., August 15, 1906, but the whole underground network was not completed until September 1, 1907. The completed system was placed in operation January 2, 1908. The original franchise was granted February 20, 1899, to the Illinois Telephone and Telegraph Company, and by an amendatory ordinance was extended to include mail delivery. This franchise was ac-

The First

quired by the Illinois Tunnel Company on July 20, 1903. A new franchise was given to the Chicago Tunnel Company on July 19, 1932.

Mining tunnel (large) was started as early as 1824 by the Lehigh Navigation Company. This was the Hacklebernie anthracite coal mine tunnel near Mauch Chunk, Pa. It was driven by hand with black powder. Work stopped in 1827, when 790 feet had been penetrated. The opening was 16 feet wide and 8 feet high. In 1846 work was resumed and the length extended to 2,000 feet. *(Henry Sturgis Drinker—Tunneling)*

Railroad tunnel was built in 1831 near Johnstown, Pa., by the Allegheny Portage Railroad, the first railroad to go west of the Allegheny Mountains. The tunnel, driven through slate, was 901 feet long, 25 feet wide, and 21 feet high. It was lined throughout with masonry 18 inches thick. Construction began on April 12, 1831, and was completed March 18, 1834. The segmented tunnel extended from Hollidaysburg, Pa., to Johnstown, Pa., a distance of 36 2/3 miles. The engineer was Solomon White Roberts. *(David William Brunton and John Allen Davis—Modern Tunneling)*

Subaqueous highway tunnel was the Washington Street Tunnel beneath the Chicago River, Chicago, Ill., authorized July 17, 1866, by the Board of Public Works. The total length of the tunnel and approaches was 1,520 feet. The contract price was $328,500, but the final cost was $512,709. The tunnel had two roadways, each 11 feet high and 13 feet wide, and a separate footway 10 feet high and 10 feet wide. Work was started November 30, 1866, and the tunnel completed in 1869. The tunnel was lowered in 1907 to provide a clear draft of 27 feet in the Chicago River. The tunnel was closed to automobile traffic until 1911.

Subaqueous railroad tunnel to a foreign country was the St. Clair Railway tunnel between Port Huron, Mich., and Sarnia, Ont., Canada, which was opened for freight traffic September 19, 1891, and for passenger traffic December 7, 1891. The tunnel has been equipped with electricity since May 17, 1908. It is still in use. Its length from portal to portal is 6,025 feet. The original cost was $2,700,000. It was designed and built under the supervision of Joseph Hobson, Chief Engineer of the Grand Trunk Railway, now the Canadian National Railways.

Triple-tube underwater roadway was the Lincoln Tunnel between New York City and Weehawken, N.J., begun September 25, 1952, and opened May 25, 1957, at 1:30 P.M. with ceremonies attended by Mayor Charles F. Krause, Jr. of Weehawken, N.J.; Governor Robert Baumle Meyner of New Jersey; Mayor Robert Ferdinand Wagner of New York City; and Governor William Averell Harriman of New York. Two tubes had been opened previously.

The First

Tunnel was built as part of the Schuylkill Navigation Company's canal above Auburn, Pa., at the Orwigsburg landing. Job Samson and Solomon Fudge were the contractors. Construction began in 1818, and the tunnel was opened to traffic in 1821. Cut through red shale, it was 20 feet wide, 18 feet high from the canal bottom, and 450 feet long. It was arched for about 75 feet inward from each portal. In 1834 it was shortened to half its length. It was shortened once more in 1845. In 1856 it was again shortened "until nothing remained but air." *(Gosta E. Sandstrom—Tunnels)*

Tunnel under the Hudson River was that of the Hudson and Manhattan Railroad System, going from Jersey City, N.J., to Morton Street, New York City. It was officially opened February 25, 1908. Two single-track tubes, approximately 5,700 feet long, with a minimum inside diameter of 15 feet 3 inches, were built under the river. *(Railroad Age Gazette. Vol. 47. 1909)*

Twin-tube subaqueous vehicular tunnel was the Holland Tunnel between New York City and Jersey City. Actual construction began October 12, 1920. The tunnel was opened November 12, 1927, by President Calvin Coolidge by signal from the presidential yacht *Mayflower* anchored in the Potomac River, off Washington, D.C. The first hour 20,000 people walked the 9,250 feet from shore to shore. It was opened for vehicular traffic on November 13, 1927. On April 21, 1930, all operation was turned over to the Port of New York Authority as agent for the states of New York and New Jersey. The tunnel consists of twin tubes 9,250 feet long. The part below the river is 5,480 feet in length. The tunnel accommodates 1,900 motor vehicles an hour. The air in the tubes is changed 42 times an hour, at the rate of 3,761,000 cubic feet a minute. The chief engineer was Clifford Milburn Holland. *(New York State Bridge and Tunnel Commission—The Holland Tunnel, the Underground Highway Which Joins a Continent to a City)*

Vehicular tunnel to a foreign country was the Detroit–Windsor tunnel under the Detroit River between Detroit, Mich., and Windsor, Ontario. It was 50 feet below the river, 5,135 feet from portal to portal, 2,200 feet of which were under water. The formal opening of the tunnel was on November 1, 1930; it was open to the public on November 2nd and opened for traffic November 3, 1930. It connects Canada with the United States and has a capacity of 1,000 motor cars per hour each way. (The Ambassador Bridge from Detroit to Canada was opened November 11, 1929. Ferries also ply between the two cities, adding a third mode of international travel between Detroit and Canadian border cities.)

Water supply tunnel. *See under* Water conduit

The First

TUNNEL—*Continued*
Wind tunnel. *See* Wind tunnel

TURBINE
See also Electric generator

Gas turbine to pump natural gas was installed by the Mississippi River Fuel Corporation of St. Louis, Mo., at Wilmar, Ark., on May 13, 1949. The unit was later moved to Bonne Terre, Mo., and placed in operation January 19, 1951.

Gas turbine used by an electrical utility company was a General Electric turbine placed in service July 29, 1949, in the Belle Isle station of the Oklahoma Gas and Electric Company, Oklahoma City, Okla. The unit attains full capacity in 17 minutes.

Steam turbine operated by a public utility to produce electricity was a 1,500-kilowatt steam turbine installed in April 1901 by the Hartford Electric Light Company, Hartford, Conn., at its Pearl Street Station. The turbine, manufactured by the Westinghouse Electric and Manufacturing Company, East Pittsburgh, Pa., began to generate electricity in October 1901.

Steam-turbine generator of large capacity for commercial service was a 5,000-kilowatt Curtis vertical-type turbine built by the General Electric Company, Schenectady, N.Y., for the Fiske Street station of the Commonwealth Edison Company, Chicago, Ill. The turbine required one-tenth the space of the reciprocating engine it replaced, weighed one-eighth as much, and cost only one-third as much. It operated with steam at 175 pounds per square inch at 375 degrees Fahrenheit and developed 6,700 h.p. It was factory-tested March 4, 1903, and placed in service on October 2, 1903.

Turbine successfully operated by waterpower was invented in 1844 by Uriah Atherton Boyden and installed in the cotton mills of the Appleton Company at Lowell, Mass. It was an improvement on the turbine waterwheel invented by the French engineer Fourneyron and utilized approximately 80 percent of the power expended.

TURBINE AUTOMOBILE. *See* Automobile: Gas-turbine automobile

TURBINE (gas) PROPELLER-DRIVEN AIRPLANE. *See* Aviation—Airplane: Gas-turbine propeller-driven airplane

TURBINE (mercury boiler). *See* Electric generator: Mercury-boiler turbine

TURBINE-PROPELLED OCEANGOING MERCHANT VESSEL. *See* Ship

TURBINE-PROPELLER LIGHT AIRPLANE. *See* Aviation—Airplane

TURBINE (wind). *See* Electric power plant: Wind turbine

The First

TURKISH BATH. *See under* Bathhouse

TURNPIKE. *See* Road

TURNSTILE (electric) with ratchet was used at the Philadelphia Centennial, Philadelphia, Pa., which opened May 10, 1876. When a person desired entrance, the attendant released the brake by foot pressure. The number of turns was registered on a machine in the central office.

TURRETED SHIP. *See* Ship

TUXEDO COAT. *See* Coat

TWENTY-CENT PIECE. *See* Money: Silver coins

TWINE. *See* Cotton twine factory

TWINE (paper) MACHINERY. *See* Paper-twine machinery

TWINS, SIAMESE. *See* Siamese twins

TWO-THIRDS RULE. *See under* Political convention

TYPE. *See* Dollar marks; Hebrew type

TYPE FOUNDRY
Type foundry in America was that belonging to Abel Buell, who cast his first font on April 1, 1769, at Killingworth, Conn. It is said that the statue of King George III which was torn down in New York was brought to Buell's foundry to be cast into type. *(Lawrence Counselman Wroth—Abel Buell of Connecticut)*

Type foundry to be permanently established in America was that of Christopher Sauer (or Sower) II, erected in Germantown, Pa., in 1771. The founding equipment was imported from Germany. *(Felix Reichmann—Christopher Sower, Sr., 1694–1758)*

TYPE SPECIMEN BOOK of an American type foundry is said to be that of [Archibald] Binny & [James] Ronaldson. It was printed in 1809 by Fry and Kammerer and titled *A Specimen of Metal Ornaments cast at the Letter Foundry of Binny & Ronaldson, Philadelphia.* Type sizes were not shown, but about 100 ornaments were illustrated. In 1812 Binny & Ronaldson published *A Specimen of Printing Types*, in which type faces were shown. *(Daniel Berkeley Updike—Printing Types)*

TYPESETTING MACHINE
Linotype machine was invented by Ottmar Mergenthaler of Baltimore, Md., who obtained patent No. 304,272 on August 26, 1884, on a "matrix making machine."

Linotype machine used commercially was a blower machine installed July 1, 1886, by the Mergenthaler Linotype Company in the New York *Tribune* printing plant and used to cast type for the July 3, 1886, newspaper. The machine had a keyboard assembling mechanism, a mechanism for casting a full line of type in a single bar, and a matrix lifting and distributing device. When the

The First

matrix was released from a vertical tube which resembled a pipe of an organ, it was carried by air blast along an inclined chute to its place in the assembling line of matrices.

Monotype machine for casting new type, letter by letter, from matrices which are used over and over, was invented by Tolbert Lanston of Washington, D.C., who received five patents, No. 364,521 to No. 364,525 inclusive, on June 7, 1887.

Photoengraving high-speed process for making halftones, line plates, or combination plates was developed by the Dow Chemical Company in cooperation with the American Newspaper Publishers Association Research Institute, Inc., Easton, Pa. By means of this process a machine could produce zinc or magnesium plates in about one fifth the conventional time. The first commercial machine was placed in operation in February 1954 by the *Patriot-Ledger,* Quincy, Mass.

Photographic type-composing machine was the Photon (Higonnet-Moyroud) machine, which was manufactured by Photon, Inc., under license from the Graphic Arts Research Foundation, Inc. in April 1953. The machine, operated from a standard typewriter keyboard at full electric-typewriter speed, delivers film negatives instead of type. The first book set by the Photon process was *The Wonderful World of Insects,* by Albro Tilton Gaul, offered for sale to the public on February 26, 1953, by Rinehart & Co., New York City. The first copy was presented to Dr. Karl Taylor Compton, chairman of the Corporation of the Massachusetts Institute of Technology, on February 5, 1953, by Dr. Vannevar Bush, a director of the Graphic Arts Research Foundation, Inc., Boston, Mass.

Typesetting machine that actually operated was a machine invented by Timothy Alden of New York City, who obtained patent No. 18,175 on September 15, 1857. The type was arranged in cells around the circumference of a horizontal wheel. As the wheel revolved, several receivers also started to rotate. The desired type was picked up and dropped in proper order in a line.

Typesetting machine patent was No. 2,139 issued June 22, 1841, to Adrien Delcambre and James Hadden Young of Lisle, France, on a "machine for setting type." The machine had keys like a piano, with push-type levers. The type fell by gravity.

Typesetting machine to dispense with metal type was the Intertype Fotosetter Photographic Line Composing Machine, manufactured by the Intertype Corporation, Brooklyn, N.Y., and installed at the plant of Stecher-Traung Lithograph Corporation, Rochester, N.Y., in 1949. The machine was exhibited at the Sixth Educational Graphic Arts Exposition held at the International Amphitheater, Chicago, Ill., on September 11, 1950.

The First

TYPEWRITER

Electric portable typewriter was manufactured by Smith-Corona, Inc., Syracuse, N.Y., announced October 9, 1956, and placed on sale February 4, 1957. It weighed about 19 pounds.

Portable typewriter was the Blickensderfer, which was patented April 12, 1892, by George C. Blickensderfer of Stamford, Conn. (patent No. 472,692).

Typewriter was patented July 23, 1829, by William Austin Burt of Mount Vernon, Mich., who received a patent on his invention of a "typographer." The first letter written on the machine was sent by John P. Sheldon, editor of the *Michigan Gazette,* Detroit, Mich., to Martin Van Buren, Secretary of State, on May 25, 1829. *(Horace Eldon Burt—William Austin Burt)*

Typewriter that successfully typed was a Chirographer, invented by Charles Thurber of Norwich, Conn., who received patent No. 3,228 on August 26, 1843. It was known as "Thurber's Patent Printer" and was proposed as an aid for the blind. The inking was effected by a roller. The machine lacked speed and did not meet with great success. *(The Weekly Mirror. Oct. 19, 1844)*

Typewriter that was practical was invented in 1867 by Christopher Latham Sholes, who also coined the word "type-writer." The machine was patented June 23, 1868 (No. 79,265), and was known commercially as The Type-Writer. This machine had a movable carriage, a lever for turning paper from line to line, and a converging type bar. The keyboard—similar to that of a piano—had two rows of black walnut keys with letters painted in white. The machine had all the letters in capitals, figures from 2 to 9, a comma, and a period. It was originally manufactured by E. Remington & Sons of Ilion, N.Y., under contract dated March 1, 1873. The first machine was completed September 12, 1873. A few years later they sold their typewriter business to Wyckoff, Seamans & Benedict, who afterward organized the Remington Typewriter Company. *(Herkimer County Historical Society—The Story of the Typewriter, 1873–1923)*

Typewriter to produce a line of writing visible as it was being typed was invented by Herman L. Wagner of Brooklyn, N.Y., who obtained patent No. 497,560 on May 16, 1893. This machine went through an experimental period with the Wagner Typewriter Company and then was sold to John T. Underwood, who had been associated with his father in the ribbon and carbon business of John Underwood & Company. The Underwood Typewriter Company, incorporated in March 1895, undertook the manufacture of Wagner's machine in New York City.

The First

TYPEWRITER RIBBON

Typewriter "copy" ribbon for manifold work was patented January 24, 1888, by Jacob L. Wortman of Philadelphia, Pa. The patent was No. 376,-764.

Typewriter ribbon patent was No. 349,026, which was granted September 14, 1886, to George K. Anderson of Memphis, Tenn.

TYPEWRITING PRIMER. *See* Primer

TYPEWRITING SCHOOL was opened by D. L. Scott-Browne at 737 Broadway, New York City, in 1878.

TYPEWRITTEN BOOK MANUSCRIPT was the manuscript of *The Adventures of Tom Sawyer,* by Mark Twain (Samuel Langhorne Clemens). It was typed on a Remington typewriter in 1875. *Life on The Mississippi* was also typewritten the same year. Mark Twain did not publicize these facts, as he did not want to write testimonials or explain the operation of the machine to inquirers. *(Herkimer County Historical Society—The Story of the Typewriter, 1873–1923)*

TYPHUS FEVER TREATISE. *See* Medical book

U

UKRAINIAN NEWSPAPER. *See* Newspaper

ULTRASONIC BURGLAR ALARM. *See* Burglar alarm: Burglar alarm operated by ultrasonic or radio' waves

UMBRELLA is believed to have been used in Windsor, Conn., in 1740. It produced a riot of merriment and derision, the neighbors parading after the user, carrying sieves balanced on broom handles.

UMPIRE. *See* Baseball umpire

UNCLE SAM CARTOON. *See* Cartoon

UNDERGROUND CITY SEWER. *See* Sewage: Underground comprehensive sewer system (city)

UNDERSEA PHOTOGRAPH. *See* Photograph

UNDERSEAS PARK (federal). *See* Park

UNDERWATER TORPEDO. *See* Torpedo

UNEMPLOYMENT INSURANCE. *See* Insurance

UNICAMERAL LEGISLATURE. *See* Legislature

UNIFORM. *See* Army uniform; Navy: Naval uniforms; Police: Police uniforms

UNION CATALOG OF BOOKS. *See* Library catalog

UNION DEPOT. *See* Railroad station: Union passenger station

The First

UNION LABEL. *See* Labor union label

UNION LABOR PARTY was formed February 22, 1887, when 300 delegates, including 10 women, attended the Industrial Labor Conference in Cincinnati, Ohio. A platform was adopted the following day. A nominating convention of 274 delegates from 25 states met at Cincinnati, Ohio, May 15-17, 1888, and nominated Alson Jenness Streeter of Illinois for President and Samuel Evans of Texas for Vice President. Evans refused the nomination and Charles E. Cunningham of Arkansas was selected. They received 146,935 votes in the election held November 6, 1888, in which Benjamin Harrison of Indiana, the Republican candidate, was elected President.

UNION PARTY was organized June 18, 1936. The first convention, held August 15, 1936, in Cleveland, Ohio, nominated William Lemke for President and Thomas Charles O'Brien for Vice President. The ticket was supported by liberals, the National Union of Social Justice, and Dr. Francis Everett Townsend of the Townsend organization, among others.

UNION REFORM PARTY held its first convention in Baltimore, Md., September 3, 1900. Seth Hockett Ellis of Ohio was nominated for President and Samuel T. Nicholson of Pennsylvania for Vice President. They received fewer than 6,000 votes as compared with 7,200,000 cast for William McKinley of Ohio, the Republican candidate, in the election of November 6, 1900. The platform had been adopted March 1, 1899, in Cincinnati, Ohio.

UNIT COMMENDATION DECORATION (U.S. Navy). *See* Medal

UNIT COST PLAN (college). *See under* College

UNIT RULE. *See under* Political convention

UNITARIAN CHURCH

Unitarian church building was erected in 1632 at the corner of Berkeley and Marlborough streets, Boston, Mass. It had mud walls and a thatched roof. The first pastors were John Wilson and John Cotton. Although 4 later churches were built, the last in 1867, the church is known as "The First Church in Boston." The Unitarian Church was founded by John Winthrop.

UNITARIAN CHURCH CONVENTION (national) assembled in New York City, April 5, 1865, at the call of the American Unitarian Association and elected Governor John Albion Andrew of Massachusetts as its president. The convention was attended by 379 lay delegates who represented 150 congregations. *(Joseph Henry Allen—A History of the Unitarian Movement Since the Reformation)*

UNITARIAN MINISTER

Unitarian minister was James Freeman, who was ordained minister by the congregation of

The First

King's Chapel, Boston, Mass., on November 18, 1787. The first church to adopt the Unitarian name was the Society of Unitarian Christians, Philadelphia, Pa., organized June 12, 1796, under the leadership of Joseph Priestley, LL.D. The first worship in a Unitarian church building took place February 14, 1813. *(Earl Morse Wilbur—Our Unitarian Heritage)*

Woman ordained to the Unitarian ministry was Celia C. Burleigh, who was given a parish in Brooklyn, Conn., October 5, 1871. *(George Willis Cooke—Unitarianism in America)*

UNITARIAN PRAYER BOOK was *A Liturgy, Collected Principally From the Book of Common Prayer, for the use of the first Episcopal Church in Boston; together with the Psalter or Psalms of David*, compiled by the Reverend James Freeman and printed in 1785 by Peter Edes of Boston, Mass., for King's Chapel, Boston.

UNITARIAN SOCIETY
National organization of the Unitarian churches of the United States and Canada was the American Unitarian Association, organized May 25, 1825, in the vestry of the Federal Street Church, Boston, Mass. The Reverend Aaron Bancroft, D.D., was the first president of the association, the Reverend Ezra Stiles Gannett, secretary, and Lewis Tappan, treasurer. The first anniversary was observed June 30, 1826, at Pantheon Hall, Boston.

Woman moderator of the Unitarian Church was Dr. Aurelia Henry Reinhardt, a member of the Oakland Unitarian Church, Oakland, Calif., who served as moderator of the Unitarian Churches of America from 1940 to 1942.

UNITED BRETHREN CHURCH. *See* Church of the United Brethren in Christ

UNITED CHRISTIAN PARTY was organized in Rock Island, Ill., and was devoted to the inculcation of religious and moral ideas as controlling forces in politics. The party held its first convention May 2, 1900, at which time Silas Comfort Swallow of Pennsylvania was nominated for President and John Granville Woolley of Illinois for Vice President. The candidates withdrew, and Jonah Fitz Randolph Leonard of Iowa was nominated for President and David H. Martin of Pennsylvania for Vice President. The party's popular vote in the election of November 6, 1900, was only 1,060, as compared with 7,200,000 cast for William McKinley, the Republican candidate.

UNITED CHURCH OF CHRIST
Minister (avowed homosexual) was Rev. William Johnson of the United Church of Christ, San Francisco, Calif., in 1972. His ordination was sanctioned April 30, 1972, by the Golden Gate Association by 62 of 96 votes at San Carlos, Calif. He

The First

was graduated from the Pacific School of Religion, Berkeley, Calif.

United Church of Christ ordination of a woman minister in which all the principal roles were filled by women was held September 17, 1972, at the United Church of Christ, Northfield, Conn., when Davida Foy Crabtree was ordained. The sermon was preached by Dr. Nelle Morton, Professor emeritus at Drew Theological Seminary; the charge by Rev. Emily Preston, minister of the Community Church in Deerfield Center, N.H.; the scriptures were read by Dr. Phyllis Trible, associate professor of Old Testament at Andover Newton Theological Seminary; and the ordination prayer by Rev. Barbara W. McCall, special assistant to the president of the United Church of Christ.

UNITED COLONIES OF NEW ENGLAND. *See* Colonial government: Colonial government union

UNITED LABOR PARTY was formed at Clarendon Hall, New York City, by secessionists from the Union Labor Party on January 6, 1887. At the party's first presidential nominating convention on May 15-17, 1888, at the Grand Opera House, Cincinnati, Ohio, Robert Hall Cowdrey of Illinois was nominated for President and William H. T. Wakefield of Kansas for Vice President. In the popular election held November 6, 1888, in which Benjamin Harrison, the Republican candidate, was elected President, Cowdrey received 2,818 votes.

UNITED NATIONS
General to command the forces of the United Nations in Korea. *See* Army Officer: General to command the forces of the United Nations in Korea

Veto by the United States in the Security Council of the United Nations, New York City was cast March 17, 1970, by Ambassador Charles Woodruff Yost, who rejected an African-Asian resolution to condemn Great Britain for not using force to overthrow the white minority government in Rhodesia. The Council consisted of 15 members (5 permanent and 10 elected for staggered 2-year terms). Great Britain also rejected the resolution, her 4th veto.

UNITED NATIONS CONFERENCE ON INTERNATIONAL ORGANIZATION was held in San Francisco, Calif., from April 25, 1945, to June 26, 1945, when the charter was signed. It was attended by representatives from 50 nations. The United Nations moved into temporary headquarters at Hunter College, New York City, on March 21, 1946; to Lake Success, N.Y., on August 16-19, 1946; and later to permanent headquarters in New York City.

UNITED NATIONS BLACK DELEGATE FROM THE UNITED STATES. *See* Diplomatic service:

UNITED NATIONS BLACK DELEGATE FROM THE UNITED STATES—*Continued*
Black delegate to the United Nations from the United States

UNITED STATES
See also specific bureaus and departments, e.g. Agriculture Bureau, Commerce Department, State Department, Veterans' Bureau

Nation to recognize the independence of the United States was France. A Treaty of Amity and Commerce and a Treaty of Alliance were signed by the United States and France in Paris on February 6, 1778. Benjamin Franklin, Silas Deane, and Arthur Lee represented the United States, and Conrad Alexandre Gerard, first secretary to Foreign Minister count Gravier de Vergennes, signed for France. These pacts were the first public agreements of the United States with a foreign power. The treaty was ratified by the Second Continental Congress at York, Pa., on May 4, 1778, and by France on July 16, 1778. Ratifications were exchanged in Paris on July 17, 1778, and the treaty declared in force. The treaty was abrogated on July 7, 1798, when Congress passed an act (1 Stat. L. 578) "to declare the treaties heretofore concluded with France no longer obligatory on the United States." *(Charles I. Bevans—Treaties and Other International Agreements of the United States of America, 1776–1949)*

"United States" as a name, instead of "United Colonies," was first authorized on September 9, 1776, by the Second Continental Congress: "That in all continental commissions and other instruments where heretofore the words, 'United Colonies' have been used, the style be altered, for the future, to the 'United States.' " The colonies were first definitely proclaimed to be united in a resolution adopted by the Second Continental Congress on June 7, 1775: "On motion, resolved, that Thursday, the 20th of July next, be observed throughout the Twelve United Colonies as a day of humiliation, fasting and prayer." Georgia not having sent delegates to the First and Second Continental Congresses, only 12 colonies were represented.

UNITED STATES AIR DEFENSE COMMAND. *See* Air Defense Command (U.S.)

UNITED STATES AMATEUR GOLF CHAMPION. *See* Golf champion: Golf champion (American-born)

UNITED STATES ARMY AIRPLANE. *See* Aviation—Airplane: Airplane purchased by the United States Government

UNITED STATES CAPITOL. *See* Capitol (U.S.)

UNITED STATES CIVIL AIR PATROL. *See* Civil Air Patrol (U.S.)

UNITED STATES CONSTITUTION. *See* Constitution of the United States

UNITED STATES EMPLOYMENT SERVICE. *See* Employment service

UNITED STATES FOREIGN SERVICE. *See* Diplomatic service

UNITED STATES GOLF ASSOCIATION. *See* Golf Club: Golf association (national)

UNITED STATES GOVERNMENT BUILDING. *See* Building: Building erected by the government in Washington, D.C.

UNITED STATES GOVERNMENT MAGAZINE. *See* Periodical: Magazine of the United States Government

UNITED STATES INFORMATION SERVICE. *See* Information Service (U.S.)

UNITED STATES LABOR ADVISORY BOARD. *See* Labor: Labor Advisory Board (federal)·

UNITED STATES MAP. *See* Map

UNITED STATES MORGAN HORSE FARM. *See* Horse: Horse farm operated by the United States Government

UNITED STATES NATIONAL AMATEUR GOLF CHAMPION. *See* Golf champion: Golf champion to win the United States National Amateur Tournament two years in succession

UNITED STATES NAVAL RESERVE BLACK FLIER. *See* Aviation—Pilot: Black flier of the United States Naval Reserve

UNITED STATES OPEN GOLF TOURNAMENT CHAMPION. *See* Golf champion: Golf champion (American-born professional) to win the United States Open Tournament

UNITED STATES SEAL. *See* Seal: Great Seal of the United States Government

UNITED STATES SHIPPING BOARD. *See* under Shipping

UNIVERSAL CHAPEL. *See* under Church

UNIVERSALIST CHURCH OF AMERICA (Independent Christian Church, Universalist) held its first meetings in 1774 but was not formally organized until January 1, 1779, when the articles of association were signed by 31 men and 30 women led by the Reverend John Murray. Reverend Murray, "father of the organized Universalist church," was made the first minister. A church built in Winthrop Sargent's garden, Water Street, Gloucester, Mass., was dedicated December 25, 1780. It contained 30 box pews. *(Richard Eddy—Universalism in America)*

UNIVERSITY. *See* College

UNKNOWN SOLDIER MEMORIAL. *See* Monument: Monument to the Unknown Soldier (national)

The First

USHER (woman). *See* Theater: Theater to employ women ushers

V

"V" MAIL. *See under* Postal service

VACATION FUND to send poor children to the country was established in 1847 by the Reverend William Augustus Muhlenberg, rector of the Church of the Holy Communion, New York City. *(Anne Ayres—Life and Work of W. A. Muhlenberg)*

VACCINATION for smallpox with cowpox, as originated in England by Dr. Edward Jenner, was introduced by Dr. Benjamin Waterhouse, Harvard professor of the theory and practice of medicine, Cambridge, Mass., who inoculated his son, Daniel Oliver Waterhouse, and 3 children and 3 servants, on July 8, 1800. Inoculation from human smallpox pustules had been introduced into America by Dr. Zabdiel Boylston of Boston, Mass. On June 26, 1721, Boylston inoculated his six-year-old son, Thomas, and two black servants. In 1721 and 1722 Boylston inoculated 247 individuals, the acceptance of inoculation due in large measure to the efforts of Cotton Mather, the Boston divine, who persistently advocated the practice. *(Benjamin Waterhouse—A Prospect of Exterminating the Small-pox; being the history of Variolae-Vaccine or Kine-pox, as it appeared in England with an account of a series of inoculations performed in Massachusetts)*

VACCINATION LEGISLATION
Vaccination legislation for American Indians was the act of May 5, 1832 (4 Stat. L. 514), "an act to provide the means of extending the benefits of vaccination, as a preventive of the smallpox, to the Indian tribes, and thereby, as far as possible, to save them from the destructive ravages of that disease." An appropriation of $12,000 was made. Physicians were paid $6 a day for their services.

Vaccination legislation (national) was the act of February 27, 1813 (2 Stat. L. 806), to encourage vaccination. It authorized the President to appoint a vaccine agent to furnish vaccine through the Post Office to any citizen of the United States who might apply for it. The act was repealed May 4, 1822 (3 Stat. L. 677). *(John Walter Kerr—Vaccination—U.S. Public Health Bulletin, No. 52)*

Vaccination legislation (state) was Chapter 116, "an act to diffuse the benefits of inoculation for the Cow-Pox," enacted March 6, 1810, by Massachusetts, which required "every town, district and plantation to choose "three or more suitable persons, whose duty it shall be to superintend the inoculation of the inhabitants . . . with the cowpox." The towns of Milton and Bedford offered

The First

free inoculations. A committee chosen July 8, 1809, authorized Dr. Amos Holbrook to charge a 25-cent fee for his services. He inoculated the entire population of Milton, 337, and pledged that the people "are for ever secure against Small Pox." *(Independent Chronicle, Boston, Mass. Dec. 25, 1809)*

VACCINE
Anthrax vaccine for humans was developed in 1948 by Dr. George Green Wright of the Biological Laboratory of the United States Army Chemical Laboratory.

Poliomyelitis vaccine was produced by Dr. Maurice Brodie, of New York City, in February 1933. The vaccine was obtained from the spinal cords of rare Indian monkeys that had been infected with poliomyelitis. The spinal cords were excised and an emulsion made of them. This emulsion was treated with formalin, which kills all viruses during the process of preparation.

Tuberculosis vaccine (effective) produced in this country was developed in 1928 by Dr. William Hallock Park, director of the research laboratory of the Health Department of New York City and professor of preventive medicine at New York University, New York City. The vaccine was manufactured at the research laboratories of the Department of Health and first used in January 1928. *(Wade Wright Oliver—The Man Who Lived for Tomorrow)*

Yellow fever vaccine for human immunization was developed by Drs. Wilbur Augustus Sawyer, Wray Devere Marr Lloyd, and Stuart Fordyce Kitchen and publicly announced April 28, 1932, at a meeting of the American Societies for Experimental Biology, Philadelphia, Pa. The work was sponsored by the Rockefeller Foundation. The first test vaccinations were made in May 1931. *(Journal of Experimental Medicine, Vol. 55, No. 6. June 1, 1932)*

VACCINE INSTITUTION for the propagation of the smallpox virus and free distribution of the vaccine to the poor was opened by Dr. James Smith in Baltimore, Md., on March 25, 1802. *(John Russel Quinan—Medical Annals of Baltimore from 1608 to 1880)*

VACUUM CLEANER
Motor-driven vacuum cleaner was invented by John S. Thurman of the General Compressed Air and Vacuum Machinery Company, St. Louis, Mo., who obtained patent No. 634,042 on October 3, 1899, on a "pneumatic carpet renovator." He obtained patents No. 663,943 on December 18, 1900; No. 665,983 on January 15, 1901; and No. 668,559 on December 10, 1901.

Suction-type vacuum cleaner was invented by Ives W. McGaffey of Chicago, Ill., who obtained patent No. 91,145, June 8, 1869, on a "sweeping

The First

VACUUM CLEANER—*Continued*
machine," a light hand-powered suction device for surface cleaning.

VACUUM TUBE. *See* Radio tube: Three-element vacuum tube

VALENTINE
Valentines commercially produced were manufactured in 1834 by Robert H. Elton, an engraver, who opened Elton & Company, in New York City, specializing in printing and publishing. Previously, valentines were handmade. *(Frank Staff—The Valentine and Its Origins)*

VALETERIA was made by the United States Hoffman Machinery Corporation and displayed September 19, 1951, in the lobby of the Bulkley Building, Cleveland, Ohio. The clothes-pressing device had a control unit equipped with a telephone and a series of lockers in which garments could be hung. It was designed to open doors, accept payments, and give correct change without any manual aid. It was based on the invention of Ross L. Timms of Akron, Ohio.

VANDERBILT CUP RACE. *See under* Automobile race

VAPOR LAMP. *See* Electric lighting: Sodium vapor lamps

VAPORIZED CHEMICAL FIRE EXTINGUISHER. *See* Fire extinguisher

VARIETY SHOW. *See* Vaudeville

VARNISH manufacturer to produce varnish exclusively was Christian Schrack, a carriage maker, who opened a shop in 1815 in Philadelphia, Pa. Furniture had previously been finished with shellac or oil. *(George Baugh Heckel—The Paint Industry)*

VASELINE. *See* Petroleum jelly

VAUDEVILLE originated in 1883 in Boston, Mass., when Benjamin Franklin Keith opened a small museum next to the old Adams House in Washington Street which he called the "Gaiety Museum." One of its principal attractions was "Baby Alice," a midget.

VAULT. *See* Safe deposit vault

VECTOLITE was manufactured by the General Electric Company in West Lynn, Mass., on February 27, 1935. Vectolite is a nonmetallic, lightweight, nonconducting magnetic material, a sintered combination of iron rust and cobalt oxide mixed in desired proportion in powdered form. It was known as "sintered oxide" until April 7, 1945, when the trade name was changed to Vectolite.

VEHICULAR TUNNEL. *See* Tunnel

VELOCIPEDE. *See* Bicycle: Bicycle velocipedes

The First

VELLUM BOOK. *See* Book

VELVET CARPETING. *See* Carpeting

VENDING MACHINE
Automatic liquid-dispensing vending machine patent was No. 309,219 issued December 16, 1884, to William Henry Fruen of Minneapolis, Minn. His application was filed January 28, 1884. When a coin was inserted in the slot, a uniform supply of liquid was released from a reservoir.

Newspaper vending machine to deliver a single copy of a newspaper with the insertion of the proper coins was the NewsVend, manufactured by the United Sound and Signal Company, Columbia, Pa., and leased on March 20, 1954, to the Chicago *Tribune,* the New York *Journal American,* the New York *Mirror,* the Philadelphia *Bulletin* and the Washington, D.C., *Times-Herald.* It had 30 compartments, each capable of holding any size paper or magazine up to 300 pages, and was available in any coin combination, returning pennies or nickels in change when required. All machines prior to this time unlocked the compartment and the customer could remove as many papers as he wanted.

Vending machine to operate automatically without the aid of plungers or indicators was produced by the Pulver Company, Inc., Rochester, N.Y., in 1897. The machine dispensed gum for a penny a package.

Vending machine (coin-operated) to dispense postage stamps was manufactured in 1892 by the United States Postage Stamp Delivery Company, Boston, Mass., of which Carroll Davidson Wright was president. It was a quartered-oak case 20 inches high, 9¾ inches wide, and 5⅝ inches deep. It delivered a capsule containing four cents' worth of stamps and a coupon upon insertion of a nickel. The coupon bore manufacturers' advertisements and was redeemable for one cent in purchases of a manufacturer's products at a ratio of one coupon to every ten cents in cash.

Vending machine law was ordinance No. 4,431 of Omaha, Neb., approved May 10, 1898, by Mayor Frank Edward Moores. All vending machines were subject to a $5 permit fee.

Vending machine to dispense live flowers was placed in the Grand Central Terminal, New York City, on October 20, 1961, by the Automated Flowers Company, Greenwich, Conn. It was 6 feet high, 3 feet wide, 2 feet deep, and was manufactured by Wittenborg of Denmark. It was a self-contained refrigerated unit that required no plumbing and operated on regular 110 volts and ordinary amperage.

Vending machine to sell from bulk was the Automatic Clerk, a wooden cabinet six feet high which dispensed hot peanuts in bags. The machine was equipped with a heater and a weighing device. It was invented in 1897 by T. S. Wheat

The First

:raft of Rush, Pa. *(New York Herald. Dec. 5, 1897)*

VENETIAN BLINDS

Venetian blind patent was granted to John Hampson of New Orleans, La., who obtained patent No. 2,223 on August 21, 1841, on a "manner of retaining in any desired position the slats of Venetian Blinds."

Venetian blinds are said to have been installed in 1761 in St. Peter's Church, Third and Pine streets, Philadelphia, Pa.

VESSEL. *See* Ship

VETERANS ADMINISTRATION

Army Corps veteran (woman) to receive a loan under the GI Bill of Rights. *See under* GI Bill of Rights

VETERANS' BUREAU was established under the act of August 9, 1921 (42 Stat. L. 147). The act provided that all forms of veterans' relief previously delegated to the Federal Board for Vocational Education, the U.S. Public Health Service, and the Bureau of War Risk Insurance should be delegated to one bureau to be known as the U.S. Veterans' Bureau and to be directly responsible to the President of the United States. The Veterans' Administration was created by Executive Order 398, dated July 21, 1930, under authorization of the act of Congress approved July 3, 1930 (46 Stat. . 1016).

VETERANS' DAY. *See* Holiday: Armistice Day

VETERANS' ORGANIZATION. *See* War veterans' society

VETERINARY CORPS, ARMY. *See* Army: Army veterinary corps

VETERINARY HOSPITAL

Municipal veterinary hospital was the Spay and Neuter Clinic of the Los Angeles City Department of Animal Regulation, Los Angeles, Calif.; general manager, Robert I. Rush. It opened on February 17, 1971. The cost for spaying was $17.50 and for neutering $11.50. The first head of the hospital was Walter E. Ziegler, D.V.M., chief of veterinary services.

Veterinary hospital was opened by Charles C. Grice in 1830 on Pearl Street, New York City. A fair beginning was made after much labor, patient waiting, and perseverance. After a few years, Grice moved to White Street, where he remained about 14 years; then he moved to his last residence, 122 Macdougal Street. Grice graduated from the Royal Veterinary College of England in 1826, and came to America in 1830. He was the first graduate of veterinary medicine to practice his profession in the United States. *(American Veterinary Review. Vol. 26, June 1902)*

VETERINARY SCHOOL

Veterinary college was the Boston Veterinary

The First

Institute, Boston, Mass., incorporated April 28, 1855. The first president was Daniel Denison Slade, M.D. Courses were given in anatomy, physiology, chemistry, pharmacy, the theory and practice of medicine and surgery, etc. *(American Veterinary Review. Vol. 1, No. 1. January 1877)*

Veterinary college of importance was the New York College of Veterinary Surgeons, New York City, incorporated April 6, 1857. It did not go into active operation until 1865. The course of study, which embraced comparative anatomy, was given in two sections of five months each. The tuition fee was $135, of which amount $5 was for matriculation fees, $100 for lecture fees, $5 for the dissecting room fee, and $25 for the diploma. The president of the school was Eben Mason. The school had professors of histology, anatomy, physiology, theory and practice, surgical pathology, and operative surgery. *(Annual Announcement of the New York College of Veterinary Surgeons, 1867–1868)*

Veterinary department of collegiate character in a university was the Department of Veterinary Science of Cornell University, Ithaca, N.Y., which offered courses by Professor James Law, October 7, 1868.

Veterinary school (state) was established May 23, 1879, by the Board of Trustees of Iowa State College at Ames, Iowa. Lectures were given on veterinary anatomy, physiology, materia medica, pathology, disease and treatment, surgery, sanitary science, and practice. The first class of the veterinary school graduated in 1880. In 1876 Dr. Milliken Stalker was granted the professorship of agriculture and veterinary science. The Iowa School was the first veterinary school in the United States to inaugurate a four-year course and the first to require as prerequisites for entrance a high school and college course. *(Charles Henry Stange —History of Veterinary Medicine at Iowa State College)*

VETO (presidential)

Legislation passed over a President's veto was S. 66 (28th Congress, 2nd session), "an act relating to revenue cutters and steamers." It provided that no revenue cutter could be built without prior appropriation. President John Tyler vetoed the bill on February 20, 1845, arguing that a contract for two revenue cutters had already been let, one to a firm in Richmond, Va., and another to a Pittsburgh, Pa., contractor. The bill was reconsidered by the Senate and House on March 3, 1845. The Senate passed it without debate over the veto, 41-1, and the House by a vote of 127-30. *(Benjamin Perley Poore—Veto Messages of the Presidents)*

Veto by a President of the United States was exercised by George Washington on April 5, 1792, when he vetoed a bill for the apportionment of representation. The House of Representatives

The First

VETO (presidential)—*Continued*
sustained the veto on April 6, 1792, by a vote of 28 yeas, 33 nays. *(Edward Campbell Mason—The Veto Power)*

Veto message read by a President in person was the veto of the Patman Bonus Bill (H.R. Bill No. 3896) read by President Franklin Delano Roosevelt, May 22, 1935, to a joint session of Congress, Washington, D.C. The Bonus Bill, introduced by Representative Wright Patman of Texas, provided for the immediate payment to veterans of the 1945 face value of their adjusted service certificates. Within an hour after the veto, the House voted to override the veto 322-98 (the original vote on the measure had been 318-90). The following day the Senate voted 54-40 to override the veto (the original vote had been 55-33). A two-thirds vote of both houses is necessary to override a veto.

VICE CONSUL (woman). *See* Diplomatic service: Woman vice consul

VICE PRESIDENT (U.S.)
American-Indian Vice President was Charles Curtis of Kansas, who served under President Herbert Clark Hoover from March 4, 1929, to March 4, 1933. *(Don Carlos Seitz—From Kaw Tepee to Capitol)*

Postage stamp issued by a foreign country to bear the likeness of a Vice President of the United States. *See* Postage stamp: Postage stamp to bear the likeness of a Vice President of the United States issued by a foreign country

Vice President appointed (not elected by popular vote) to become President of the United States was Gerald Rudolph Ford, who was sworn in Friday, August 9, 1974, at noon in the Oval Room of the White House, Washington, D.C., as the 38th President. He succeeded Richard Milhous Nixon, who had submitted his resignation the previous day.

Vice President arrested was Aaron Burr, accused of organizing an expedition to invade Mexico, arrested February 19, 1807, in Wakefield, Washington County, Ala., by Captain Edmund P. Gaines and held as a prisoner in Fort Stoddard, Ala. Nicholas Perkins, in charge of 8 soldiers, brought Burr to Richmond, Va., where he was taken before Chief Justice John Marshall, U.S. Circuit Court, on March 30, 1807; he was indicted for treason on June 24. The trial began August 3. Found not guilty of an "overt act" of treason, Burr was acquitted on September 1, 1807. He left the United States in 1808, went to Europe, and returned in May of 1812.

Vice President cremated was Nelson Aldrich Rockefeller, the 41st Vice President, who died in his townhouse in New York City on January 26, 1979. He was cremated January 27, 1979, and his ashes were buried in a small bronze urn on Janu-

The First

ary 29, 1979, in the private burial plot on his estate at Pocantico Hills, North Tarrytown, N.Y.

Vice President elected by the Senate was Richard Mentor Johnson, who was chosen by the Senate on February 8, 1837, as no candidate had received a majority of the electoral votes. He served from March 4, 1837, to March 4, 1841, as Vice President under Martin Van Buren. *(William Emmons—Authentic Biography of Col. Richard M. Johnson of Kentucky)*

Vice President sworn in on foreign soil was William Rufus de Vane King, a Democrat, the running mate of Franklin Pierce in the 1852 campaign. King took the oath of office March 4, 1853, in Havana, Cuba, where he had gone for his health. The oath was administered by William L. Sharkey, United States Consul in Havana. The privilege was extended to King by a special act of Congress (10 Stat. L. 180), March 2, 1853. King's term of office was of short duration; he died April 17, 1853, in Cahawba, Ala. *(U.S. Senate—Obituary Addresses. William R. King, 1853)*

Vice President to be nominated specifically for the vice presidency was George Clinton, who ran with Thomas Jefferson in the 1804 election. He served under Jefferson from 1805 to 1809, and under James Madison from 1809 to 1812. Prior to the ratification of the twelfth Amendment to the Constitution on September 24, 1804, the presidential candidate receiving the second-highest number of votes became Vice President.

Vice President to become President automatically on the death of a President was John Tyler, the tenth President. Tyler succeeded William Henry Harrison, who died on April 4, 1841. Harrison served from March 4, 1841, to April 4, 1841, and Tyler from April 4, 1841, to March 4, 1845. *(Oliver Perry Chitwood—John Tyler, Champion of the Old South)*

Vice President to die in office was George Clinton, who served under President Thomas Jefferson from March 4, 1805, to March 4, 1809, and under President James Madison from March 4, 1809, to April 20, 1812, when he died in Washington, D.C. William Harris Crawford acted as president pro tempore of the United States Senate for the unexpired portion of Clinton's term. *(Gouverneur Morris—Oration in Honor of the Memory of George Clinton)*

Vice President to have served in the House of Representatives was Elbridge Gerry of Massachusetts, who served as a representative from March 4, 1789, to March 3, 1793, and as Vice President from March 4, 1813, to November 23, 1814, when he died.

Vice President to leave the United States while the President was away was Vice President John Nance Garner, who sailed from Seattle, Wash., on October 16, 1936, for Japan on the *President Grant*

The First

while President Franklin Delano Roosevelt was aboard the U.S.S. *Houston* on vacation. Under the act of succession of January 19, 1886 (24 Stat. L. 2), Secretary of State Cordell Hull acted as President until the President's return. Technically the President was on United States soil, as he was on a naval vessel.

Vice President to marry in office was Alben William Barkley, who was married to Elizabeth Jane Rucker (widow of Carleton Sturtevant Hadley) on November 18, 1949, at St. John's Methodist Episcopal Church, St. Louis, Mo., by the Reverend Abea Godbold and Bishop Ivan Lee Holt, Methodist Bishop of Missouri. The ceremony was telecast.

Vice President to preside at a National Security Council meeting was Richard Milhous Nixon, who presided over the final session of a meeting held in Washington, D.C., on July 14, 1953. On August 13, 1953, he presided over an entire meeting.

Vice President to preside over a Cabinet meeting was Richard Milhous Nixon, who presided as chairman of a meeting held on July 22, 1955.

Vice President to resign before the expiration of his term of office was John Caldwell Calhoun, who served as Vice President under President John Quincy Adams from March 4, 1825, to March 4, 1829, and under President Andrew Jackson from March 4, 1829 to December 28, 1832, when he resigned. He had been elected senator from South Carolina on December 12, 1832, to fill the vacancy caused by the resignation of Robert Young Hayne. *(John Stilwell Jenkins—Life of John Caldwell Calhoun)*

Vice President to serve under two Presidents was George Clinton, who served under President Thomas Jefferson from March 4, 1805, to March 4, 1809, and under President James Madison from March 4, 1809, until his death on April 20, 1812 in Washington, D.C.

Vice presidential inauguration broadcast from the Senate. *See* Television—Telecast: Congressional telecast and radio broadcast

Vice President's flag. *See under* Flag

Vice President's widow to receive a pension was Lois I. Kimsey Marshall, widow of Thomas Riley Marshall, who died June 1, 1925. The act of January 25, 1929 (45 Stat. L. 2041), awarded her an annual allowance of $3,000 and instructed the Secretary of the Interior to place her name on the pension roll.

VICE PRESIDENTIAL CANDIDATE

Black vice presidential candidate was Frederick Douglass, nominated May 10, 1872, by the National Woman Suffrage Association convention, assembled at Apollo Hall, New York City, under the name of the National Radical Reform-

The First

ers. About 500 delegates attended from 26 states and 4 territories. The presidential nominee was Victoria Claflin Woodhull. *(Frederick Douglass—Life and Times of Frederick Douglass)*

Black woman vice presidential candidate was Charlotta A. Bass, nominated July 5, 1952, by the Progressive Party at their convention in the International Amphitheatre, Chicago, Ill.

Vice presidential candidate of a major political party to resign was Senator Thomas Francis Eagleton of Missouri, who was nominated July 13, 1972, at the Democratic National Convention held at Miami Beach, Fla. He submitted his resignation on August 1, 1972, and the National Democratic Committee nominated Robert Sargent Shriver of Maryland in his stead.

Vice presidential candidate (woman) to have her name placed in nomination at a major party convention was Lena Jones Springs (Mrs. Leroy Springs), national committee woman of Lancaster, S.C., who received the 18 votes of the South Carolina delegation to the Democratic Party convention on July 9, 1924, at New York City. Charles Wayland Bryan received the nomination, having obtained 739 of the 1097½ votes cast, 7 more than necessary for a choice.

Vice presidential nominee to decline nomination was John Langdon of New Hampshire. The congressional caucus of the Republican Party, which was held in Washington, D.C., May 12, 1812, nominated him as its vice presidential candidate. He received 64 of the 82 votes cast. James Madison, the presidential nominee, received 82 votes. Despite his nomination, Langdon declined to run, and a second caucus was held at which Elbridge Gerry was nominated. Gerry received 74 of the 77 votes for Vice President. *(Lawrence Shaw Mayo—John Langdon of New Hampshire)*

Vice presidential nominee to die before the meeting of the Electoral College was James Schoolcraft Sherman, candidate on the 1912 Republican ticket headed by William Howard Taft. He was Vice President from March 4, 1909, to October 12, 1912. In June 1912, he was renominated as the Republican vice presidential candidate. The notification speech was made August 21, 1912, at Utica, N.Y., by Senator George Sutherland of Utah. Sherman died on October 30, 1912, before the election. Nicholas Murray Butler was the substitute for whom the electoral college cast its Republican votes. *(James Schoolcraft Sherman—Speech Accepting the Republican Nomination for Vice President of the United States)*

VIDEO RECORDING ON MAGNETIC TAPE. *See* Tape recording

VIETNAM SERVICE MEDAL. *See* Medal

The First

VIETNAM WAR

American general killed in Vietnam by enemy fire was Major General Bruno Arthur Hochmuth, commander of the 3rd Marine Division, killed November 14, 1967, at Hué, Vietnam, when ground fire downed the helicopter in which he was a passenger. Two American pilots, an American crew chief, and a Vietnamese interpreter were also killed in the crash. *(New York Times. 1:8. Nov. 15, 1967)*

American general killed in Vietnam in an accident was Major General William Joseph Crumm (U.S. Air Force) of Scarsdale, N.Y., commander of the Strategic Air Command's 3rd Air Division on Guam, who was killed July 6, 1967, when two B-52 jet stratofortresses on a Guam to Vietnam bombing run to a target in South Vietnam collided in midair and crashed into the South China Sea, 35 miles off the Mekong Delta. He, with six others, was officially listed as dead on July 25, 1970.

General (American) to die in Vietnam was Brigadier General Alfred Judson Force Moody, commander of the U.S. Army 1st Air Cavalry Division, who died of a heart attack on March 20, 1967, at Saigon, South Vietnam.

General killed in action in Vietnam was Major General Robert F. Worley of Palm Desert, Calif., killed July 23, 1968, by ground fire while piloting a jet reconnaissance RF-4C Phantom Jet about 65 miles northwest of Danang. He was deputy commander of the 7th Air Force, Saigon, South Vietnam.

Pilot (American Navy) shot down and captured in North Vietnam was Lieutenant (junior grade) Everett Alvarez, Jr. (U.S. Navy), 26, of San Jose, Calif., aviator on the U.S.S. *Constellation,* who was shot down on August 5, 1964, and parachuted into the ocean. He was rescued and surrendered to a small Vietnamese boat crew and was confined in the Hon Gay naval base and later in the Hoa Lo prison. He was returned to the United States on February 13, 1973.

VILLAGE IMPROVEMENT SOCIETY with a continued existence was the Laurel Hill Association of Stockbridge, Mass., founded by Mary Gross Hopkins. Laurel Hill was presented to the town in 1834 by Theodore Sedgwick. The society was organized August 24, 1853, and incorporated September 5, 1853, "to improve and ornament the streets and public parts of Stockbridge, by planting and cultivating trees and doing such other acts as shall tend to improve and beautify the village." *(Frederick N. Evans—Town Improvement)*

VINEYARD (successful) was established on August 28, 1798, by John James Dufour on a tract of land consisting of about 630 acres situated 25 miles from Lexington, Ky. He called it "The First Vineyard." Dufour was one of the pioneer viticulturists and founder of Swiss vineyards in Ameri-

The First

ca. Attempts to establish vineyards had been made as early as 1619 in Virginia. *(Liberty Hyde Bailey—Sketch of the Evolution of Our Native Fruits)*

VINYL ETHER. *See* Anesthesia: Trifluoroethyl vinyl ether

VIRUS

Virus (human- or animal-infecting virus) to be crystallized was the poliomyelitis virus, which was crystallized by Dr. Carlton Everett Schwerdt of the Virus Laboratory, University of California Berkeley. The achievement was announced November 3, 1955, at the meeting of the National Academy of Sciences held at the California Institute of Technology, Pasadena.

Virus obtained in crystalline form was the tobacco mosaic virus crystallized by Dr. Wendell Meredith Stanley at the Rockefeller Institute for Medical Research, Princeton, N.J. The research was reported in *Science* magazine, June 28, 1935.

Virus separated into component parts, which on reconstruction yielded a material as effective as it was in its original form, was the tobacco virus which causes a disease in tobacco and many other plants. The research was performed by Drs. Heinz Ludwig Fraenkel-Conrat and Robley Cook Williams of the Virus Laboratory of the University of California at Berkeley early in 1955, and first reported on June 10, 1955.

VISIBLE SPEECH TRAINING. *See* Deaf—School: Oral instruction for the deaf

VISITING CELEBRITIES

Absolute monarch to visit the United States was King Prajadhipok of Siam. He arrived in New York City in April 1931, accompanied by his wife Queen Rambai Barni, and the royal entourage President Herbert Clark Hoover received him April 29, 1931. The visitors crossed into United States territory on April 19, 1931, at Portal, N.Dak. from Canada. The king had visited the United States when he was a prince, arriving September 22, 1924, in New York City from England.

Emperor of Japan to visit the continental United States was Emperor Hirohito of Japan, who landed, accompanied by his wife, at Patrick Henry Airport, Williamsburg, Va., on September 30 1975. (In 1971, he had touched Alaska on his way to Europe.)

European king buried in the United States was Peter Karageorgevich of Serbia (Serbian name Petar Karadjordjević) (patronymic name Peter Alexandrovich), who died November 4, 1970, in the Colorado General Hospital, Denver, Colo. and was buried at the Liberty Eastern Serbian Orthodox Monastery, Liberty, Ill. He became king October 11, 1934, fled his country in 1941, and headed the exiled Yugoslav government during World War II.

The First

King and Queen of Great Britain to visit the United States were King George VI and Queen Elizabeth, who crossed the international border at 10:39 P.M. on June 7, 1939, at the Suspension Bridge Station, Niagara Falls, N.Y. They visited New York City and Washington, D.C., and recrossed the border at 5:22 A.M. on June 12, 1939, bound for Halifax, Nova Scotia, whence they sailed June 15, 1939.

King (reigning) to visit the United States was David Kalakaua, King of the Sandwich Islands (Hawaii), elected February 12, 1874, by a vote of 39–6 to succeed William C. Lunalilo, who died February 3, 1874. He embarked November 17, 1874, on the U.S.S. *Benicia* and was received at the White House, Washington, D.C., by President Ulysses Simpson Grant on December 15, 1874. Congress tendered him a reception on December 18, 1874. He arranged for a treaty of reciprocity, which was concluded January 30, 1875, ratifications being exchanged in Washington, D.C., on June 3, 1875 (19 Stat. L. 625). He returned to his country on February 15, 1875, on the U.S.S. *Pensacola.*

Lecturer of royal blood to speak for personal profit. *See under* Lecturer

Pontiff who had visited the United States was Eugenio Pacelli (Pope Pius XII). He visited America while Papal Secretary of State, arriving October 8, 1936, and returned November 7, 1936. His headquarters were at Inisfada, which was the Long Island mansion of the Papal Duchess Genevieve Garvan Brady and later became a seminary of the Jesuit order.

Pontiff to visit the United States was Pope Paul VI, who arrived at Kennedy International Airport, New York City, on October 4, 1965, at 9:27 A.M. He went to St Patrick's Cathedral and Cardinal Spellman's residence at 11:44 A.M., conferred with President Lyndon Baines Johnson at the Waldorf Astoria Hotel at 1:40 P.M., addressed the General Assembly of the United Nations in French at 3:30 P.M., attended a public Mass at the Yankee Stadium at 8:20 P.M., visited the Vatican Pavilion at the New York World's Fair at 10:25 P.M., and returned to Rome the same day at 11:00 P.M. via the Alitalia jet liner. He was seen by about 1 million persons and by 100 million on television.

Pontiff to visit the White House, Washington, D.C., was His Holiness John Paul II (Karol Wojtyla, Cracow, Poland) who flew across the Atlantic in the *Shepherd 1,* landing in Boston, Mass., on October 1, 1979. In six days, he visited six cities: Boston, New York, Philadelphia; Urbandale, Iowa; Chicago, and Washington, D.C. On October 6, 1979, he returned to Rome from Andrews Air Force Base, the chief military airport of Washington, D.C.

The First

President of a black African country to visit the United States was President Edwin James Barclay of the Republic of Liberia, who addressed the U.S. Senate May 27, 1943, the day following his arrival. He was accompanied by the vice president, William Vacanarat Shadrach Tubman, president-elect, and was welcomed by President Franklin Delano Roosevelt. On October 14, 1943, President Elie Lescot of Haiti, former Minister to the United States, arrived for a brief visit.

Prince of Wales to visit the United States was Albert Edward (later King Edward VII), who left Plymouth, England, July 10, 1860, and arrived in Detroit, Mich., on September 20, 1860, from Hamilton, Ont., Canada. He was received by Moses Wisner, Governor of Michigan, and Mayor Christian Buhl of Detroit. He sailed from Portland, Maine, October 20, 1860. He traveled through Canada and the United States as Baron Renfrew. He became King of Great Britain and Ireland and Emperor of India on January 22, 1901. *(Kinahan Cornwallis—Royalty in the New World, or The Prince of Wales in America)*

Queen (reigning) to visit the United States was Queen Marie of Rumania, who arrived October 18, 1926, on the *Leviathan* at New York City and received a 21-gun salute from the fort at Governors Island. She was accompanied by Prince Nicholas and Princess Ileana. They returned November 24, 1926, on the *Berengaria.*

Queen to visit the United States was Queen Emma, widow of King Kamehameha IV, of the Sandwich Islands (Hawaii), who arrived August 8, 1866, in New York City from England on the Cunard *Java* and was received on August 14, 1866, by President Andrew Johnson and introduced to his official family. *(Gilson Willets—Inside History of the White House)*

VITAMIN

Synthetic vitamin was vitamin D commercially manufactured in 1927 by Mead, Johnson and Company, Evansville, Ind., and marketed in the spring of 1928. It was made by exposing a solution of ergosterol to ultraviolet light. *(Charles Everett Bell—Physiology of the Sterols, Including Vitamin D. In Physiological Reviews. Vol. 15, No. 1. January 1935)*

Synthetic vitamin K was made by Dr. Louis Frederick Fieser of the Harvard University Department of Chemistry, Cambridge, Mass., on August 1, 1939. A report was submitted to the September 10, 1939, meeting of the American Chemical Society in Boston, Mass.

Vitamin E, the anti-sterility vitamin, was first recognized by Dr. Herbert McLean Evans with Dr. Katherine Cott Bishop in 1922. Dr. Evans, Dr. Oliver Hudleston Emerson, and Gladys Anderson Emerson of the Institute for Experimental Biology of the University of California, Berkeley, were the

The First

VITAMIN—*Continued*
first to reduce it to a pure substance, alpha tocopherol. Announcement of the process was made at the American Chemical Society meeting at San Francisco, Calif., on August 20, 1935. This was published as "The Isolation from Wheat Germ Oil of an Alcohol, Alpha Tocopherol, Having the Properties of Vitamin E," by H. M. Evans, O. H. Emerson, and G. A. Emerson in the *Journal of Biological Chemistry* of February 1936. *(Science. 1922)*

VITROLITE was manufactured in 1907 in Parkersburg, W.Va., by the Meyercord-Carter Company. It was an opaque structural flat glass made originally in white. The first important installation was made in 1907 on the walls of the subway stations of the Interborough Rapid Transit System, New York City. About that time color was first utilized in firing-on colored designs for brewery signs, etc. In 1922 colors were added to the vitrolite itself by the introduction of coloring material into the sand, soda ash, lime, and other ingredients. The Meyercord-Carter Company was purchased in 1935 by the Libbey-Owens-Ford Glass Company.

VIVISECTION of animals to show the process of life was performed about 1855 by Dr. John Call Dalton. He introduced the methods of vivisection in classroom demonstrations. In 1859 he published his *Treatise on Human Physiology*, and in 1860 he became professor of physiology and microscopic anatomy at the Long Island College Hospital. *(James Joseph Walsh—History of Medicine in New York)*

VIVISECTION PLAY. *See* Play (drama): Antivivisection play

VIVISECTION SOCIETY. *See* Antivivisection society

VOCAL INSTRUCTION BOOK. *See* Music book

VOCATIONAL AGRICULTURAL SCHOOL. *See* Agricultural school

VOCATIONAL GUIDANCE CHAIR in an American university was established in 1914 by Indiana University, Bloomington. The first professor was Robert Josselyn Leonard, who served from June 1914 to April 1918.

VOCATIONAL HIGH SCHOOL FOR GIRLS. *See* High school

VOICE MECHANISM
Voice mechanism capable of creating the complex sounds of speech in an intelligible manner was Pedro, the Voder, designed by Homer Walter Dudley, Robert Richard Riesz, and Stanley Sylvester Alexander Watkins of the Bell Telephone Laboratories, New York City, and publicly exhibited June 5, 1938, at the Franklin Institute, Philadelphia, Pa.

The First

VOLCANO
Volcano eruption broadcast. *See under* Radio Broadcast

Volcano in eruption in America for which a date can be estimated occurred at Cinder Cone in the Lassen Peak district in California about 1694. On November 22, 1842, Mount St. Helens, and on November 13, 1843, Mount Rainier (Tacoma), both in the state of Washington, were in eruption. Professor George Davidson of the United States Coast Survey in 1843 and John Shertzer Hittell in 1858 saw Mount Baker, also in Washington, in eruption. *(Israel Cook Russell—Volcanoes of North America)*

VOLCANO IN A NATIONAL PARK. *See* Park: Park (national) containing an active volcano

VOLLEYBALL was developed in 1895 as a game by Physical Director William George Morgan of the Young Men's Christian Association, Holyoke, Mass. The game, at first called mintonette, was played with a basketball bladder over a rope. Later a lightweight leather-covered ball was adopted, and an eight-foot net substituted for the rope. Rules were local until 1900, when the Young Men's Christian Association Physical Directors' Association Volley Ball Committee developed standard rules. The first rules were published in the *Physical Education Magazine,* July 1896. *(Winged Acorn, November 1932)*

VOTE, ARMY. *See* Army vote

VOTERS' QUALIFICATIONS. *See* Literacy qualification for voting

VOTING. *See* Election; Election law

VOTING MACHINE
Electric vote recorder was patented by Thomas Alva Edison, then of Boston, Mass., who received patent No. 90,646, June 1, 1869, on an "electrographic vote recorder." By means of the device a legislator could register an "aye" or "no" vote by turning a switch to the right or to the left.

Electric vote recorder used by a legislative body was installed January 11, 1917, in the Wisconsin Assembly Chamber, Madison, Wis. Green and white signal lights opposite the name of each member showed how each legislator voted. It saved 99.5 percent of the time previously consumed in roll calls. A roll call could be recorded in 11 seconds. The acquisition was authorized by act approved July 29, 1915.

Presidential election in which votes were tallied electronically was that of November 3, 1964. The Coleman Vote Tally Systems were used in Hamilton County (Cincinnati), Ohio; Orange County (Santa Ana—Anaheim), Calif.; and Contra Costa (Martinez), Calif. They counted 600 ballots a minute. All data from each machine and counting center is automatically transmitted by wire to a central computer in the Registrar of Voters office

The First

where countywide returns are available as fast as votes are being counted.

Vote recorded by electronic means in the U.S. House of Representatives occurred January 23, 1973, when 331 members recorded their presence at a quorum call. Forty-four stations were located throughout the House Chamber. When a member placed a personalized plastic identification card in 1 of the vote stations to vote yea, nay, or present, a light indicating his presence appeared next to his name on the large display panels on the south wall above the Speaker's podium. The recorder, which cost $1,065,000, was designed by Dr. Frank B. Ryan, director of the House Information Systems.

Voting machine in the U.S. House of Representatives to record individual votes was used March 3, 1971, when 391 votes were cast (180 green cards for, and 211 red cards against, the Wright Patman amendment to delete an interest rate section of proposed debt-ceiling legislation). The name of the voter appeared on each card.

Voting machines for use in federal elections were approved by Congress, February 14, 1899 (30 Stat. L. 836). The bill was signed by President William McKinley, February 14, 1899. It provided that "all votes for representatives in Congress must be by written or printed ballot, or voting machines, the use of which has been duly authorized by the state."

Voting machines were authorized for use in New York State on March 15, 1892, by an act (Chapter 127) "to secure independence of voters at town meetings, secrecy of the ballot and provide for the use of Myers' automatic ballot cabinet." Later legislation extended the use of the machine to cities. The machines were first used on April 12, 1892, at Lockport, N.Y., where 3,271 votes were cast for mayor and other town officials. The machine was invented by Jacob H. Myers and manufactured by the American Ballot Machine Company, which was later absorbed by the Automatic Voting Machine Corporation of Jamestown, N.Y. *(T. David Zuckerman—The Voting Machine)*

VOTING MACHINE COMMISSION (state) was authorized by New York, Chapter 450, May 17, 1897, "an act relating to the use of voting machines," which provided that three commissioners should be appointed by the Governor, "one of whom shall be an expert in patent law and two of whom shall be mechanical experts." The term of the commissioners was five years. The first commissioners were Robert Henry Thurston, Philip Tell Dodge, and Palmer Chamberlaine Ricketts, appointed June 16, 1897. Ricketts declined and Harry de Berkeley Parsons was appointed June 18, 1897.

The First

VULCANIZED RUBBER. *See* Rubber

W

WAFFLE IRON PATENT was No. 94,093, issued August 24, 1869, to Cornelius Swarthout of Troy, N.Y.

WAGE LAW. *See* Labor legislation: Minimum wage law

WAGON, LUNCH. *See* Lunch wagon

WALK OF FAME was originated in the autumn of 1929 by Hamilton Holt, president of Rollins College, Winter Park, Fla., who gave the college 22 stones from the former homes, birthplaces, and resting places of world-famous men and women from all parts of the world. The stones were set between Carnegie Hall and Knowles Hall and along a walk leading past Carnegie Hall. They are of various sizes, shapes and textures, and follow no pattern. Some 700 stones have been placed, without any design, along both sides of the pathways.

WALKIE-TALKIE. *See* Radio telephone: Military portable

WALL TILE. *See* Tile: Wall and floor tiles

WALLPAPER
Wallpaper was manufactured in 1739 by Plunket Fleeson of Philadelphia, Pa. Wooden blocks stamped the design on sheets of paper which were joined together. A paintbrush was used to apply the color. In August 1739 Fleeson advertised in the *Pennsylvania Gazette* the sale of "bedticks, choice live geese feathers, blankets, as well as paperhangings." *(Nancy Vincent McClelland— Historic Wallpapers from Their Inception to the Introduction of Machinery)*

Wallpaper printing press. *See* Printing press: Printing press for printing "paper hangings"

WAR
See also

Civil War	War (Korean)
Revolutionary War	War (Mexican)
Spanish-American War	War (Quemoy)
War (colonial)	World War I
War (1812)	World War II
War (French Indo-china)	

Armed conflict between American Indians and whites occurred May 1539 in Clarke County, Ala., when Hernando de Soto in 9 hours of fighting killed about 11,000 American Indians. The Spanish loss was 70 killed and 900 wounded, including Hernando de Soto.

The First

WAR—*Continued*

Battle fought by United States troops, after the formation of the Union, was the Miami Expedition. On October 19, 1790, Colonel John Hardin, under Brigadier General Josiah Harmar, led 400 troops against 150 Indians in the territory of the United States, northwest of Ohio. Because of poor leadership, insufficient training, and unworkable guns, the attack culminated in a retreat. The force was composed principally of militia lacking the training of the federal troops. *(American State Papers. Military Affairs, Vol. I)*

Bloodshed in the New World caused by Europeans occurred in 1493 when Columbus and his men attempted to land in the dominion of Mayobanex (cacique of the Ciguaneyes of Haiti). Repulsed by the natives, the Europeans used force and wounded several of them.

Naval battle by white men in America took place April 23, 1635, when *The Cockatrice,* a pinnace commanded by Lieutenant Ratcliff Warren, attacked Captain Thomas Cornwallis' 2 pinnaces *(St. Helen* and *St. Margaret)* in the Little Pocomoke or Wicomoco River at St. Mary's, on the eastern shore of Maryland.

Rebellion against the federal government took place in 1786 when Daniel Shays organized an armed force in Massachusetts which threatened public order by overthrowing courts and committing other acts of violence. On December 5, 1786, the rebels seized Worcester. By February 1787, however, they were completely routed. The uprising was caused by economic discontent—the depreciation of paper money, the insistence of creditors on being paid in silver money, and the imprisonment of debtors.

WAR (colonial)

Bloodshed in the French and Indian War occurred May 28, 1754, on an isolated mountainside a few miles east of Uniontown, Pa. George Washington, at the head of several companies of Virginia militia, appeared on the Monongahela and overtook a French reconnoitering party from Fort Duquesne. Jumonville, the French commander, was slain and his force captured. *(Winthrop Sargent—History of Braddock's Campaign)*

Colonial warfare between England and France for the possession of North America occurred in 1613 at Mount Desert, Maine. Father Pierre Biard, Superior of Saint Sauveur, who sailed March 12, 1613, from France on the ship *Jonas,* established a French Jesuit settlement of colonists at Mount Desert. The settlement was attacked by an English expedition under the command of Captain Samuel Argall, whose aim was to suppress piracy and to defend England's title to the country founded on the discovery of the Cabots. A brief description of the conflict records that an English "vessel and forty soldiers landed at a place called Mount Desert in Nova Scotia, near St. John's River, or

The First

Tweed, possessed by the French; they killed some French, took away their guns and dismantled the Fort." *(A Description of the Province of New Albion, 1648)*

French and Indian War battle took place on July 3, 1754, at Fort Necessity, located on the Great Meadows, nine miles east of Uniontown, Pa. Lieutenant Colonel George Washington, commanding 400 Virginia and South Carolina provincial troops opposed the French commander Coulon de Villiers and his army of 1,600 French regulars, French Canadian militia, and Indians. *(Fort Necessity Memorial Association—A Young Colonel from Virginia and the Blow He Struck for American Independence in the Year 1754)*

Indian war of importance fought by English colonists took place on May 27, 1607, at which time about 200 Indians were repulsed by English settlers in Virginia under Captain Edward-Maria Wingfield. It is recorded that he "was shot clean through his beard" by an Indian. *(John Fiske—Old Virginia and Her Neighbors)*

Intercolonial war in America started September 20, 1565, when Pedro Menéndez de Avilés and 400 Spaniards proceeded overland to the St. Johns River, in Florida, and surprised and captured Fort Caroline (at St. John's Bluff, near the present site of Jacksonville) without the loss of a man. They had sailed from Cadiz, Spain, June 28, 1565, and arrived off the Florida coast August 28, 1565. The French, commanded by René Goulaine de Laudonnière, lost 140 men in the attack. Ground had been broken June 30, 1564, for Fort Caroline named for King Charles IX of France. After its capture, Menéndez changed the name to San Mateo. *(Florida Historical Association Quarterly Vol. 12, No. 2. October 1933)*

Marine engagement in battle took place on March 4, 1776, when Captain Samuel Nicholas and approximately 200 marines captured Fort Nassau in the Bahamas. Nicholas was assisted by 50 sailors under Lieutenant Thomas Weaver of the *Cabot.* The assault was a surprise attack and the fort was unprepared. It surrendered without conflict. Large military stores were captured—about 100 cannon, 15 mortars, 5,400 shells, 11,000 rounds of ammunition, etc.—and brought back to New London, Conn., on April 8, 1776. This naval expedition, which left the Delaware Capes on February 17, 1776, was under the command of Esek Hopkins of the *Alfred.*

WAR (1812)

British frigate captured by a single frigate was the *Macedonian,* 49 guns, under Captain John Surnam Garden, captured near Madeira on October 25, 1812, by the *United States,* 44 guns, under Captain Stephen Decatur. The *Macedonian* sustained a loss of 36 killed and 68 wounded, of whom 5 died of wounds; the *United States,* 6 killed and wounded. The captured *Macedonian* was taken

he First

nto New London, Conn., on December 4, 1812, nd later to the East River, New York City. *(Sam-el Putnam Waldo—Life and Character of Ste-hen Decatur)*

Defeat in history of a British squadron was rought about by Oliver Hazard Perry, American aval officer, in the War of 1812. In the beginning f the action of September 10, 1813, Perry's short-ange guns prevented success on his part, and his hip was battered to a hulk, with only a handful f capable men left. Perry went to a sister ship, the *Niagara,* renewed the fight, and had the satisfac-ion of seeing the British strike colors. This action ok place at Put-in Bay, Lake Erie. *(Charles Jud-on Dutton—Oliver Hazard Perry)*

Frigate action of importance in the War of 1812 ok place August 19, 1812, when the *Constitution,* ommanded by Captain Isaac Hull, met the Brit-h frigate *Guerrière,* commanded by Captain ames Richard Dacres. The *Constitution,* which as built in Boston, Mass., in 1797, rated as a 'igate of 1,576 tons, with an armament of 44 guns. he *Guerrière* was a 38-gun frigate. Within a quar-r of an hour the mizzenmast of the *Guerrière* as shot away, and its spars, sails, and rigging rn to shreds. The American loss was 14 killed nd wounded; the British, 79 killed and wounded. he contest was one-sided. On March 3, 1813, an ward of $50,000 was made by Congress (2 Stat. , 818), to Hull and the crew for the victory over ne *Guerrière.*

Naval battle took place May 16, 1811, in the tlantic Ocean off Sandy Hook, N.J., about 40 iles off Cape Cod, Mass., when the 18-gun sloop I.M. *Little Belt* (Captain A. B. Bingham) attacked ne 44-gun frigate *President* (Commodore John odgers), struck the mainmast and the foremast, it some rigging, and wounded one. The *President* plied, killing and wounding 20 of the crew of the *ittle Belt.* The *Little Belt,* a corvette, carried one er of guns and was rated at 20 guns; it had the ppearance of a frigate.

Naval battle after the U.S. declaration of war une 18, 1812) took place in the Atlantic Ocean ine 23, 1812, between the U.S.S. *President* (44 uns, Commodore John Rodgers) and H.M.S. *Belv-lera* (26-18 pounders, 2-9 pounders, and 14-32 rronades, Captain Richard Byron). The *Presi-ent* closed in for the telling shot but 1 of her guns xploded, killing and wounding 22 soldiers and ermitting the *Belvidera* to escape in the confu-ion. *(Charles Oscar Paullin—Commodore John odgers)*

President to face enemy gunfire while in office. ee President (U.S.): President to face enemy infire while in office

Prisoners in the War of 1812 were taken by ieutenant William Learned Marcy, who captured corps of Canadian militia at St. Regis, N.Y., on

The First

October 22–23, 1812. Their flag was the first trophy of the kind captured during the war.

War declaration was made by Congress on June 18, 1812 (2 Stat. L. 755), against the United King-dom of Great Britain and Ireland and the depen-dencies thereof. The following day, President James Madison issued a proclamation to that effect. The Treaty of Peace and Amity between His Britannic Majesty and the United States con-cluded at Ghent was signed on Christmas eve in 1814, ratified by the United States Senate on Feb-ruary 15, 1815, and proclaimed in effect by Presi-dent Madison on February 17.

WAR (French Indochina)
American civilian pilot wounded in Indochina was Paul Robert Holden of Greenleaf, Kan., who was wounded in the right thigh and arm by 37 mm. anti-aircraft shells over Dien Bien Phu on April 24, 1954. Holden was flying a C-119 Flying Boxcar for the Civil Air Transport to deliver supplies to the French. His copilot, Wallace Abbott Buford, of Kansas City, Kans., managed to land the plane safely in French territory. Buford was killed May 7, 1954, near Dien Bien Phu.

WAR (Korean)
American pilot to destroy an enemy airplane in the Korean War was First Lieutenant William G. Hudson of the 68th Fighter Squadron (all-weath-er), who shot down a YAK-9 on June 26, 1950, while flying an F-82 airplane over Kimpo to pro-vide cover for the evacuation of Kimpo.

American tank crew to cross the 38th Parallel in Korea was a patrol of the First Cavalry Division which crossed into the Kaesong Area, about 85 miles south of the Red capital of Pyongsang, at 3:14 P.M. on October 7, 1950. The crew members were Sergeant Homer Lee of Evansville, Ind.; Pri-vate First Class James Emerich of Sutton, W.Va.; Sergeant Walter Hill of Fairmont, N.Dak.; Ser-geant Charles Gissendanner of Autaughville, Ala.; and Corporal Clarence Johnson of Taylors-ville, N.C. South Korea was attacked by North Korea on June 25, 1950.

Korean War hero buried in Arlington National Cemetery, Arlington, Va., was Second Lieutenant Howell Garrone Thomas, Jr., of Washington, D.C., who served in Company L of the 21st Infantry Regiment. Thomas was buried August 14, 1950, with ceremonies attended by Secretary of the Army Frank Pace, Jr., Chief of Staff Joseph Lawton Collins; Major General Thomas Wade Herren, commander of the Washington Military District; two Korean embassy officials; and other federal representatives.

Marine corps jet ace. *See under* Marine Corps

Officer killed in action in the Korean War was Colonel Robert R. Martin of Toledo, Ohio, killed July 8, 1950, while leading a rocket and grenade attack against an enemy tank. He was awarded

The First

WAR (Korean)—*Continued*

the first Distinguished Service Cross of the Korean War, posthumously presented to his son, Robert, a cadet at the U.S. Military Academy.

Soldier killed in the Korean War was Private Kenneth Shadrick, 19, of Skin Fork, W.Va., a member of a bazooka squad, who was killed July 5, 1950, near Sojong, Korea, by a bullet fired from an enemy tank.

South Korean combat mission involving an exchange of fire occurred on June 27, 1950, between Communist forces and an F-80C aircraft from the Eighth Fighter-Bomber Group of the Fifth Air Force, which was based at Itazuke Air Base in southern Japan. A few visual reconnaissance missions had been flown June 26, 1950.

WAR (Mexican)

Mexican War shots were fired at La Rosia, Mexico, April 25, 1846. General Zachary Taylor sent Captain Seth Barton Thornton with a squadron of dragoons into enemy territory. Thornton and fifty cavalrymen were taken prisoners. Lieutenant George Thompson Mason was the first officer killed. *(George Lockhart Rives—The United States and Mexico)*

WAR (Quemoy)

American casualty of the Red Chinese bombardment of Quemoy, in Formosa Strait, was Army Specialist Third Class George W. Johnston of Springdale, Pa., who was wounded in the left arm September 3, 1958. Johnston was attached to the U.S. Military Assistance Advisory Group.

WAR BOND issued by the federal government, exclusive of the refunding of the Revolutionary War debts, was authorized on March 14, 1812, for the purchase of ordnance and equipment and the enlargement of the Army in preparation for the impending War of 1812. The amount authorized was $11 million. Bonds were issued to the amount of $8,134,700 and sold exclusively in the United States. *(William F. De Knight—History of the Currency of the Country and of the Loans of the United States from the Earliest Period to June 30, 1900)*

WAR COLLEGE. *See* Army school; Army war college; Naval war college

WAR CRIMINAL PROCEEDINGS were held in Washington, D.C., from August 23, 1865, to November 4, 1865. Captain Henry Wirz, superintendent of the Confederate prison at Andersonville, Ga., accused of conspiring to torture, injure, and murder federal prisoners, was tried under 13 separate specifications by a military commission presided over by General Lewis Wallace, U.S. Volunteers. Wirz was sentenced on November 6, 1865, to be hanged. The sentence was carried out November 10, 1865. He was buried in Mount Olivet Cemetery, Washington, D.C.

The First

WAR DEPARTMENT (U.S.)

See also National Defense Department (U.S.)

Aeronautical division. *See under* Aviation

War Department (U.S.) was authorized by an "act to establish an executive department to be denominated the Department of War," approved August 7, 1789 (1 Stat. L. 49). The department superseded a similar department established prior to the adoption of the Constitution. The act of 1789 authorized the appointment of a Secretary of War at a salary of $3,000 a year. The first Secretary was Henry Knox of Massachusetts, appointed by President Washington on September 11, 1789. The appointment was confirmed and Knox was commissioned. He entered on his duties on September 12, 1789. *(Lurton Dunham Ingersoll—History of the War Department of the United States)*

WAR LOAN. *See* Loan

WAR MAP. *See* Map

WAR ORPHANS EDUCATION LAW. *See under* Education

WAR PRISONER

Prisoner of War to head the Naval War College, Newport, R.I., was Vice Admiral James Bond Stockdale, who served as president from October 13, 1977, to August 22, 1979. He was graduated from the United States Naval Academy, Annapolis, Md., on June 5, 1946. While serving during the Vietnam War, he was forced to abandon his A-4 jet, parachuted, and was captured in North Vietnam. He endured 2,714 days of imprisonment, during which he was kept in solitary confinement for 3 years, suffering torture on numerous occasions. He was released on February 12, 1973, and on October 13, 1977, was promoted to the rank of vice admiral.

WAR RISK INSURANCE BUREAU. *See under* Insurance

WAR SHIPPING ADMINISTRATION

Mariner's medal. *See under* Medal

War Shipping Administration was established February 7, 1942, within the Office for Emergency Management of the Executive Office of the President by Executive Order No. 9054 issued by President Franklin Delano Roosevelt. The first administrator was Emory Scott Land, appointed February 9, 1942, to control the operation, purchase, charter requisition, and use of all oceangoing vessels under the flag or control of the United States, excluding Army, Navy, and Coast Guard, and inland transportation runs under control of the Office of Defense Transportation.

War Shipping Administration award was authorized by Vice Admiral Emory Scott Land, War Shipping Administration, on October 14, 1944. It was a dark green silk ribbon bar on which was mounted a silver sea horse.

The First

WAR SONG. *See under* Music

WAR VETERANS' COLLEGE. *See* College: College principally for war veterans

WAR VETERANS' SOCIETY

American Legion was organized in Paris, France, February 15-16, 1919, but the first caucus was not held until March 15, 1919. The adoption of the name was moved by Maurice Kirby Gordon of Madisonville, Ky. The legion was incorporated by act of Congress of September 16, 1919, "to uphold and defend the Constitution of the United States; to maintain law and order; to foster and perpetuate one hundred per cent Americanism; to preserve our memories of incidents in the Great War; to inculcate a sense of individual obligation to the community, state and nation; to safeguard and transmit to posterity the principles of justice, freedom and democracy; to consecrate and sanctify our comradeship by our devotion to mutual helpfulness." The first national convention was held in Minneapolis, Minn., November 10-12, 1919. *(Richard Seelye Jones—A History of the American Legion)*

Grand Army of the Republic post was established in Decatur, Illinois, on April 6, 1866. The organization was founded principally through the efforts of Dr. Benjamin Franklin Stephenson, surgeon, and the Reverend William J. Rutledge, chaplain, both of the 14th Illinois Infantry. The first state convention was held on July 12, 1866, in Springfield, Ill. At the first national convention, held November 20, 1866, in Indianapolis, Ind., Stephen Augustus Hurlbut was elected commander in chief.

Military Order of Foreign Wars was founded in New York City on December 27, 1894, by veterans and descendants of veterans of one or more of the five wars waged between the United States and foreign powers. Membership was restricted to commissioned officers and their lineal descendants. The National Commandery was instituted on March 11, 1896.

Society of the Cincinnati was instituted May 10, 1783, and organized May 13, 1783, when the constitution was completed, at the Verplanck house, near Fishkill, N.Y. Final organization was effected June 9, 1783, on which date New York and Massachusetts organized the first two of the 13 state societies. Membership was limited to officers who had served three years in the Continental army or who had been honorably discharged for disability. George Washington was elected the first president general in 1783; he remained in office until his death and was succeeded by Major General Alexander Hamilton. Major General Henry Knox was secretary general and Major General Alexander McDougall was treasurer general. The first general meeting was held May 7, 1784, in Philadelphia, Pa. The Society in France was organized January 7, 1784, in Paris. The name was derived from Lucius Quinctius Cincinnatus, the distinguished Roman who, called from the plow, "left all to save the republic." *(Alonzo Norton Lewis—Historical Sketches of the Venerable and Illustrious Order of the Cincinnati)*

Veterans of Foreign Wars of the United States, composed of Army, Navy, and Marine Corps veterans who served in time of war in theaters of operation, was formed August 18-20, 1913, in Denver, Colo. (under the temporary name of Army of the Philippines, Cuba and Puerto Rico) with Rice W. Means as the first commander in chief. It was an amalgamation of three separate groups: the American Veterans of Foreign Service (organized September 23, 1899, in Columbus, Ohio); the Army of the Philippines (organized December 12, 1899, in Denver as the Colorado Society of the Philippines); and the American Veterans of Foreign Service (organized September 10-12, 1903, in Altoona, Pa.). The society organized in Altoona was a combination of the Philippine War Veterans (organized October 13, 1901, in Pittsburgh, Pa.) and the American Veterans of the Philippines and China Wars (organized July 24, 1902, in Philadelphia, Pa.).

World War II veterans' society officially recognized by Congress was the American Veterans of World War II, chartered July 23, 1947. Eleven groups with a membership of about 1,700 amalgamated on December 12, 1944, in Kansas City, Mo. The first national commander was Elmo Woodrow Keel.

WARDEN. *See* Game warden

WAREHOUSE legislation was passed by Congress on August 6, 1846 (9 Stat. L. 53). This act permitted the storage of imported merchandise in warehouses owned or leased by the federal government, duty-free, the duty to be paid upon withdrawal of the merchandise within a specified time of not more than one year. The act of March 28, 1854 (10 Stat. L. 271), extended bonded storage privileges to private warehouses approved by the Secretary of the Treasury—warehouses having proper customs officers in charge or having joint custody with customs officers of all merchandise.

WARSHIP. *See* Ship

WARTIME CONSCRIPTION BILL. *See under* Conscription

WASHHOUSE AND PUBLIC BATHS. *See* Bathhouse: Public bath and washhouse

WASHING MACHINE

Complete, self-contained electric washing machine was a Thor machine, which was put on the market in 1907 by the Hurley Machine Company of Chicago, Ill. Patent No. 966,677 was granted August 9, 1910, to Alva J. Fisher of Chicago, Ill., on a "drive mechanism for washing machines."

The First

WASHING MACHINE—*Continued*

Rotary-motion washing machine was made in 1859 by Hamilton Erastus Smith of Philadelphia, Pa., who obtained patent No. 21,909, October 26, 1858. A crank, turned by hand, caused a perforated cylinder within a wooden shell to revolve. Smith continued to improve his machine and in 1863 secured patent protection on the first self-reversing-motion attachment to the machine.

Washing machine for public use was installed by J. F. Cantrell in a "washateria" in Fort Worth, Tex., on April 18, 1934. Four electric washing machines were rented by the hour to those who wished to do their laundry. Hot water and electricity were supplied, but users were obliged to furnish their own soap.

Washing machine patent was granted March 28, 1797, to Nathaniel Briggs of New Hampshire for an "improvement in washing cloaths."

WASHINGTON (town named for George Washington). *See under* Town

WASHINGTON COLLEGE (college named for George Washington). *See* College

WASHINGTON CORRESPONDENT. *See under* News correspondent

WASHINGTON MONUMENT. *See* Monument

WATCH. *See under* Clock

WATER

Cast-iron pipes used in a city waterworks. *See under* Iron

Community to fluoridate its municipal water in order to reduce tooth decay was Grand Rapids, Mich. Fluoridation started January 25, 1945, with the addition of one part of fluoride ion to each million parts of water passing through the water treatment plant.

Deep-bed pressure filtration system was built by Dravo-Doyle of Pittsburgh, Pa., for the Indiana Harbor Works, of the Youngstown Sheet and Tube Company, East Chicago, Ind., on Lake Michigan. Operation started in March 1968. The installation, designed to handle 60,000 gallons of water per minute from the hot-mill rolling operations of the 84" Hot Strip Mill, included 42 filters, each 16½ feet in diameter, using special sand as a media.

Heavy water, D_2O, was identified by Harold Clayton Urey in the autumn of 1931 and subsequently named deuterium. The first public scientific announcement of the discovery of the hydrogen atom of double weight was made at the Christmas meeting of the American Association for the Advancement of Science in New Orleans, La., December 29, 1931.

Irrigation legislation (federal). *See* Irrigation legislation (federal)

The First

Municipal water supply system was built in Boston, Mass., by the Water Works Company in 1652. A series of wooden pipes was used to convey the water from nearby springs to a central reservoir, which was only 12 feet square.

Seawater conversion plant (practical) was opened May 8, 1961, by the Office of Saline Water, U.S. Department of the Interior, at Freeport, Tex., and dedicated June 21, 1961, by President John Fitzgerald Kennedy, who pressed a switch installed in his office at Washington, D.C. The plant was set up to produce about a million gallons of water a day at a cost of $1 to $1.25 per 1,000 gallons.

Soda water. *See* Soda water

Track water tanks. *See* Railroad: Railroad to install track water tanks

Water pumping plant to supply water for municipal purposes was installed in Bethlehem, Pa., May 27, 1755. Water from a spring was pumped through wooden pipes into a 70-foot-high watertower. The pumping plant was constructed by Hans Christopher Christiansen. *(Joseph Mortimer Levering—History of Bethlehem, Pa.)*

WATER CONDUIT

Drinking water conduit placed underwater was built in 1848 by the Water Department of Boston, Mass. It was constructed on the shore, floated into place, and sunk into a prepared trench below the surface of the channel under Dover Street Bridge, Warren Avenue Bridge, Chelsea Street South Bridge, and Chelsea Street North Bridge. The wooden tunnels were approximately 4 feet 8½ inches in diameter and some 50 feet or more in length. Inside were laid cast-iron water pipes 20 inches in diameter to carry drinking water from Boston proper to the South Boston, Charlestown, and Chelsea sections of Boston. All these pipes were in use before 1852.

Water supply tunnel for a city was the Chicago Lake Tunnel, which extended 10,587 feet under Lake Michigan to an inlet crib. It was 5 feet in diameter. Ellis Sylvester Chesbrough was the city engineer at the time of construction. The work was contracted for October 28, 1863, by Dull and Gowan of Philadelphia, Pa., and cost $380,784.60. Construction was started March 17, 1864. The tunnel was completed December 6, 1866, but water was not let into it until March 25, 1867. The pumping station with the standpipe tower still stands at the intersection of Michigan Boulevard and Chicago Avenue, having escaped destruction during the fire of 1871. *(The Tunnels and Water System of Chicago)*

WATER CURES

Water cures were advocated by David Campbell, originator of the *Water Cure Journal*, who opened a water-cure resort in 1843 at 63 Barclay Street, New York City. Joel Shew, M.D., was the

The First

physician. Numerous physicians prescribed similar treatments at that time. *(Harry B. Weiss and Howard R. Kemple—The First American Water-Cure Craze)*

Periodical advocating water cures was the *Water Cure Journal*, devoted to the "proper explanation of hydropathy, or water cure, including bathing in its various forms, attention to diet, drink, air, exercise, cleanliness, and clothing, as affecting bodily and mental health." Edited by Joel Shew, M.D., and T. D. Pierson, M.D., this 16-page semimonthly was published in New York City on December 1, 1845, at $1 a copy.

WATER GAS PLANT. *See under* Gas

WATER PURIFICATION
Municipal filtration system for the bacterial purification of a water supply was the Lawrence Filter, Lawrence, Mass., designed by Hiram Francis Mills. It was an open filter of 2¾ acres and was completed in September 1893. Water from the Merrimack River was purified by slow sand filtration. *(Maurice B. Dorgan—History of Lawrence, Mass.)*

Water purification by filtration dates from 1870, when an English-type slow sand filter was built at Poughkeepsie, N.Y. The plans were prepared by James Pugh Kirkwood and the filter was erected in 1872-1873. *(George Chandler Whipple—History of Water Purification—American Society of Civil Engineers. Transactions, 1922)*

Water supply chemically treated with chlorine compounds for drinking water (on a practical scale) was the water supply of Jersey City, N.J., in 1908 under the supervision of George Arthur Johnson. The Jersey City Water Supply Company opened the Boonton reservoir September 26, 1908. *(George C. Bunker—The Use of Chlorine in Water Purification.* In *Journal of the American Medical Association. Jan. 5, 1929)*

WATER SKI ASSOCIATION (national) was the American Water Ski Association, formed in April 1939 at Trenton, N.J. The first president was Dan Hains of Bayville, N.Y.

WATER SKI TOURNAMENT (national) was held at Jones Beach State Park, Long Island, N.Y., on June 22, 1939. Bruce Parker of Garden City, N.Y., won the men's championship and Esther Yates of Amityville, N.Y., the women's championship. The events included the slalom, jumping, and trick riding.

WATER SKIER
Water skier to jump 100 feet was Warren Witherell of The Weirs, a northern suburb of Laconia, N.H., who jumped 106 feet at Laconia N.H., on August 15, 1954.

WATER VELOCIPEDE PATENT. *See* Bicycle patent

The First

WATERLESS GAS STORAGE TANK. *See* Gas: Gas storage tank (waterless)

WATERMARK was the single word "company," which was formed in the paper manufactured in 1690 by William Rittenhouse in his mill on Paper Mill Run or rivulet, Germantown, Pa. Afterwards he used several other watermarks to distinguish his paper. *(Mennonite Quarterly Review. Vol. 16, No. 2)*

WATERPOWER
Water power development grant was established in 1620 by Ferdinando Gorges on that part of the Piscataqua River known as the Newwichawanick River at South Berwick, Maine. Gorges obtained a grant from the English Crown which gave him the right to develop the territory lying between the 40th and 48th parallels north latitude, from sea to sea. The grant required him to develop waterpower. He constructed a log dam, erected a grist mill, and sent some of the meal to England as proof that he was conforming to the agreement in the charter. The waterpower has been in use ever since the grant to Gorges in 1620.

WATERPOWER CANAL. *See* Canal: Canal for creating waterpower

WAXWORKS MUSEUM was opened by James Wyatt in New York City in June 1749. The figures were imported from England and exhibited from June to December 1749 at the Sign of the Dolphin, Privateer, near the Work-House. Effigies were shown of George II and Frederick, Prince of Wales, "both dressed in Royal Robes . . . as when sitting in the Parliament House," the Duke of Cumberland "in his Regimentals," Miss Peggy [Woffington], "the present famous actress," nuns, friars, British and Hungarian-Bohemian royal personages, etc.

WEATHER BROADCAST. *See under* Radio broadcast

WEATHER BUREAU (U.S.)
Weather Bureau was authorized by act of Congress on February 9, 1870 (16 Stat. L. 369), which assigned meteorological duties to the Signal Corps of the War Department. The first weather observations were made November 1, 1870, from reports gathered by telegraph from 24 sources. Official forecasts were distributed by telegraph by the Division of Telegrams and Reports for the Benefit of Commerce and Agriculture, as well as by the Signal Corps. The first chief was Brigadier General Albert James Myer of the U.S. Army, who had been chief signal officer since 1860. Myer took over the direction of the weather service upon its organization and served until his death on August 24, 1880. The Weather Department was transferred to the Department of Agriculture on July 1, 1891, and the name changed to the Weather Bureau. In 1940 it came under the jurisdiction of the Department of Commerce and has since been re-

The First

WEATHER BUREAU (U.S.)—*Continued*
named The National Weather Service and transferred to the National Oceanic and Atmospheric Administration. *(William Babcock Hazen—History of the Signal Service)*

Weather Bureau woman employee was Dr. Joanne Simpson, who served from 1963 to 1973 as director of the Experimental Meteorology Branch in the National Hurricane and Experimental Meteorology Laboratory, Coral Gables, Fla.

WEATHER MAP (television). *See under* Television—Telecast

WEATHER-OBSERVATION SATELLITE. *See* Satellite

WEATHER OBSERVATIONS systematically recorded were made by Dr. John Lining of Charleston, S.C., who took daily observations at 6:30 A.M., 3 P.M., and 10 P.M. in January 1738. He recorded temperature, rainfall, atmospheric pressure, humidity, wind direction and force, and the state of the weather, and, as a physician, he studied the effect of the weather on the human body, communicating his reports to the Royal Society of London. *(Philosophical Transactions of the Royal Society of London, 1743)*

WEBBING, ELASTIC. *See* Elastic webbing

WEDDING
Airplane wedding took place on May 31, 1919, in a Handley-Paige bombing plane with two 12-cylinder motors. The plane was flying about 2,000 feet over Ellington Field, Houston, Tex. at the Flying Frolic air show. About 10,000 spectators were present at the field. Marjorie Dumont of Yorkville, Ind., and Lieutenant R. W. Meade of Cincinnati, Ohio, were married by Lieutenant J. E. Reese, chaplain, of Nevan, Ohio. The best man was C. R. Henriques, and the matron of honor was Laura Troy. The pilot of the bomber was Lieutenant E. W. Kilgore.

American woman married to a former king of Great Britain was Wallis Warfield Simpson of Baltimore, Md., who was married by the Reverend Robert Anderson Jardine on June 3, 1937, at Monts, France, to Edward Albert Christian George Andrew Patrick David, Duke of Windsor (the former Edward VIII). He acceded to the throne of Britain on January 20, 1936, and abdicated on December 11, 1936, without having been formally crowned. *(Robert Anderson Jardine—At Long Last)*

Balloon wedding took place October 19, 1874, in the 62,000-cubic-foot balloon *P. T. Barnum,* more than a mile above Cincinnati, Ohio. Reverend Howard B. Jeffries of the Church of Christ (Swedenborgian) married Mary Elizabeth Walsh, equestrian of Barnum's Great Roman Hippodrome, and Charles M. Colton. Washington Harrison Donaldson was the balloonist. The attendants were Anna Rosetta Yates and W. C. Coup. There

The First

were 7 people in the party. About 50,000 people assembled in Lincoln Park, Cincinnati, to witness the ascension and the marriage. The marriage was conceived as a publicity stunt for P. T. Barnum's Great Roman Hippodrome, which opened at the baseball grounds on October 13, 1874.

Double radio wedding took place December 22, 1922, at Grand Central Palace, New York City, in connection with the American Radio Exposition. The Reverend B. F. Saxon of the 61st Street Methodist Church, New York City, officiated at the ceremony uniting Margaret Girstner and Joseph Woorn of Brooklyn, N.Y., and Helen Koller and John Brunschweyler of New York City. Each couple was presented with $100. The ceremony, witnessed by 4,000 spectators, was broadcast by station WEAF, New York City.

Parachute wedding was performed August 25, 1940, at the World's Fair amusement area, New York City. The Reverend Homer Tomlinson of the Church of God, Jamaica, N.Y., performed the marriage ceremony for Arno Rudolphi and Ann Hayward, who sat side by side. The minister, the bride and groom, the best man, the maid of honor, and four musicians were all suspended in parachutes, about 50 feet in the air.

President married while in office. *See under* President (U.S.)

Silver wedding anniversary of a President in the White House. *See* President (U.S.): President to celebrate his silver wedding anniversary in the White House

Telegraph wedding took place at noon April 12, 1900, in Kansas City, Mo., when Rev. Albert H. Linder performed the 25-minute ceremony. The groom, Andrew M. Candell of Washington, D.C., was in Kansas City with two friends; the bride, Penelope Cundiff of Perkins, Okla., was in Mulhall, Okla., with her mother and sister. A direct wire conveyed the ceremony, a distance of approximately 200 miles.

Television wedding was held October 14, 1928, in the radio studio at Des Plaines, Ill. Cora Dennison and James Fowlkes of Kansas City, Mo., were married by the Reverend Gustave A. Klenle of St. Luke's Evangelical Church. The ceremony was telecast.

Transatlantic telephone wedding took place December 2, 1933, when Bertil Hjalmar Clason in Detroit, Mich., and Sigrid Sophia Margarete Carlson in Stockholm, Sweden, were married by Judge John Dennis Watts of the Wayne County Common Pleas Court in Detroit. The ceremony was relayed from Detroit through New York to a Maine radio station, whence it was sent to Scotland to be relayed through London to Stockholm.

The First

Vice President to marry in office. *See* Vice President (U.S.)

Wedding abroad of a soldier in the American Expeditionary Force was solemnized July 14, 1917, in London, England. The first war bride was Kate Lewis (Mrs. William Lewis).

Wedding broadcast was a ceremony performed June 15, 1920, in the First Presbyterian Church, Detroit, Mich., by Rev. C. E. Mieras, who received $10 for his services. The bride was Mabelle E. Ebert, the groom Seaman John R. Wichman, who was aboard the U.S.S. *Birmingham* in the Pacific Ocean. The marriage was authorized by Wayne County License No. 196125. Witnesses were Mrs. W. M. Stevens and Mrs C. R. Sholes, who served as the proxy. The ceremony was telephoned to the telegraph office, wired to the Great Lakes Naval Training Station, near Chicago, Ill., and wirelessed to the U.S.S. *Birmingham.*

Wedding in New England was that of Governor Edward Winslow and Susanna, the widow of William White, on May 12, 1621 (new style May 22, 1621). The Governor's first wife, Elizabeth Barker, whom he had married in Holland in 1618, died March 24, 1621. William White died February 21, 1621. *(William Franklin Atwood—The Pilgrim Story)*

Wedding in the United States Occupation Forces in Korea took place November 17, 1945, in the Immaculate Conception Cathedral, Seoul, Korea. First Lieutenant James Richardson Burrows of Oswego, S.C., attached to the 24th Corps Military Police, married Second Lieutenant Virginia Elizabeth Reynolds of Detroit, Mich., an army nurse. The ceremony was performed by Colonel Philip James Newman, Catholic chaplain of the 24th Corps.

Wedding in Virginia was that of Anne Burras, maid of Mistress Forrest, to John Laydon, in 1609. The maid and her mistress were the first women colonists in America, arriving in 1608. No women came over with the original Jamestown settlers in 1607.

White House wedding took place March 29, 1812, when Mrs. Lucy Payne Washington was married to Justice Thomas Todd of the United States Supreme Court. Mrs. Washington was a sister of Mrs. James Madison and the widow of George Steptoe Washington, a nephew of George Washington. *(National Intelligencer. March 31, 1812)*

White House wedding of a President was Grover Cleveland's marriage to his ward, Frances Folsom, June 2, 1886. Cleveland served as President of the United States from March 4, 1885, to March 4, 1889, and from March 4, 1893, to March 4, 1897.

The First

WEEVIL, COTTON-BOLL. *See* Cotton-boll weevil

WEIGHT LIFTER
Weight lifter to lift more than 6,000 pounds was Paul Anderson, age 22, who backlifted off the ground a table on which were heavy automobile parts and a safe full of lead totaling 6,270 pounds, in Toccoa, Ga., on June 17, 1957.

WEIGHTS AND MEASURES STANDARDIZATION
Act legalizing the employment of the metric system was approved July 28, 1866 (14 Stat. L. 339). The act provided that it "shall be lawful throughout the United States of America to employ the weights and measures of the metric system."

International Bureau of Weights and Measures was established by the International Metric Convention at Sèvres, France, on May 20, 1875. The bureau is maintained by assessed contributions of the signatory governments and is the repository for the International Prototype Meter, the International Prototype Kilogram, and secondary standards.

National organization to improve systems of weights, measures, and moneys was the American Metrological Society, formed December 30, 1873, at Columbia University, New York City, by Wolcott Gibbs, Frederick Augustus Porter Barnard, and Hubert Anson Newton. Samuel D. Tillman was corresponding secretary and Howard Potter, treasurer.

Standards bureau. *See* Standards Bureau (U.S.)

Weights and measures standardization was established by section 21 of the act of March 2, 1799 (1 Stat. L. 643), which required the surveyor of customs of each port to standardize his measures to comply with the customs clause requiring "all duties, imposts, and excises [to] be uniform throughout the United States."

WELDING
Aluminum-pipe welding machine (automatic) was a Mig (metal inert-gas) welder developed by the Reynolds Metal Company and the Air Reduction Company. A working model was tested in 1954 at White Point, Tex., and a completed model in 1957 at Corpus Christi, Tex., welding 2,880 feet of 4-inch pipe in a 4-hour period with no supplemental hand-welding needed at any point. A unit mounted on a tractor rotated around the pipe carrying a shielded electric arc. Inert gas was released to blanket the area being welded.

Welding by the electric process was invented by Professor Elihu Thomson of Lynn, Mass., who obtained patent No. 347,140 on August 10, 1886, on "an apparatus for electric welding." *(Franklin Institute Journal. Vol. 229. 1940)*

WELFARE SECRETARY (U.S.). *See* Cabinet (U.S.): Secretary of Health, Education, and Welfare

WELL, OIL. *See under* Oil

WELSH MAGAZINE was *Cymro Americaidd,* a semimonthly first published in 1832 in Welsh in New York City. J. A. Williams was the editor. Later, an English section was added.

WEST POINT. *See* Army school

WHALE
Killer whale born in captivity was a six-foot, 125-pound calf born February 28, 1977, at Marineland, Los Angeles, Calif. She was the offspring of Cork, a 16-year-old, eleven-ton killer whale.

Sperm whale was captured in 1711 at sea by a Nantucket, Mass., whaler. This was the beginning of an industry which in 1846 numbered over 700 whaling vessels.

WHALEBACK STEAMER. *See* Ship

WHALING
Whale-killing machine (electric) was patented by Dr. Albert Sonnenberg and Philip Rechten of Bremen, Germany, who obtained U.S. patent No. 8,843 on March 30, 1852.

Whaling expedition set sail from Nantucket, Mass., about 1715. Six sloops, of 30 to 40 tons burden each, returned with cargoes amounting to 600 barrels of oil and 11,000 pounds of bone, the total value of which was £1,100 sterling. There were whaling trips by single boats and it is possible that prior expeditions may have sailed, but early records of their activities have not been preserved. *(Alexander Starbuck—History of the American Whale Fishery)*

Whaling (systematic) was undertaken March 7, 1644, by Southampton, L.I., N.Y., which ordered the town divided into 4 wards of 11 persons each to attend to the driftwhales cast ashore. Two persons from each ward were employed to cut up the whales so that each and every inhabitant obtained an equal portion. A whaling franchise was granted a Mr. Whiting in 1647 for the waters between Stonington and Montauk Point. *(George Rogers Howell—The Early History of Southampton)*

WHEAT (shredded). *See* Breakfast food: Shredded wheat biscuits

WHEELCHAIR ATHLETICS
National wheelchair games were held June 1, 1957, at Adelphi College, Garden City, N.Y. Seventy-five paraplegics (paralyzed from the chest down) from Montreal (Canada), Ohio, Pennsylvania, and nearby states competed in team and individual events. Some of the winners were Tony Mucci, Pan American Jets, 60-yard dash; Al Slootsky, Jersey Wheelers, javelin throwing; Sol Welger, Pan American Jets, table tennis (singles); and Pierre Brousseau, Montreal Wheel Chair

Wonders, archery. Other events—such as shot putting, bowling, weight lifting, discus throwing, adapted swimming—were added in subsequent years.

WHIG PARTY held its first convention in Albany, N.Y., on February 3, 1836. William Henry Harrison of Ohio was unanimously nominated for President and Francis Granger of New York was designated as the candidate for Vice President. This was a state convention attended by delegates from 32 of the 52 counties. Ohio held a state convention in Columbus on February 22-23, 1836. In the election of November 8, 1836, Harrison received 73 electoral votes, compared with 170 electoral votes (762,000 popular votes) cast for Martin Van Buren, a Democrat, the successful candidate.

WHIPS were manufactured commercially in 1801 by Titus Pease in Little River (village), Westfield, and Thomas Rose, Mundale, Westfield, Mass. In 1808 Joseph Jokes of Westfield used hickory wood shafts and put a strip of horsehide at the end fastened to the stock by a "keeper." *(Clifton Johnson—Hampden County 1636–1936)*

WHIST ORGANIZATION of importance was the American Whist League, which convened at the Athenaeum, Milwaukee, Wis., April 14-17, 1891, in response to a call made by Cassius M. Paine, president of the Milwaukee Whist Club. Thirty-six clubs represented by 83 delegates standardized the rules and adopted a 61-section code. The first president was Eugene S. Elliott of the Milwaukee Whist Club, and Robert Frederick Foster of the Manhattan Club of New York City was secretary. *(John T. Mitchell—Duplicate Whist, Its Rules and Methods of Play)*

WHIST RULE BOOK was *The Whist Player's Hand Book, containing most of the maxims of the old school and several new ones exemplified by opposite cases; with a method of acquiring a knowledge of the principles on which they are grounded to which are added observations on short whist, also the games of Boston and euchre.* The book was written by Thomas Matthews and published in 1844 in Philadelphia, Pa., by Isaac M. Moss. It contained 96 pages, 75 of which were devoted to whist.

WHIST TOURNAMENT
Duplicate whist tournament was held April 15, 1891, in Milwaukee, Wis., by the American Whist League. Forty-eight delegates participated. Twelve tables were arranged in pairs, each with two teams of two players each. The eight players of each pair of tables changed positions after every deal. The medal winner was E. Price Townsend of the Hamilton Club, Philadelphia, Pa. The rules were substantially Cavendish with a few slight modifications to suit the American game.

The First

International whist tournament (world championship under the International Bridge League) was held June 13–20, 1937, at Budapest, Hungary. The American team, made up of Ely and Josephine Murphy Culbertson, Helen Martin Sobel (Mrs. Alexander M. Sobel), and Charles C. Vogelhofer, was defeated by Austria by 4,740 points in a 96-hand match.

WHISTLE, LOCOMOTIVE. *See* Locomotive steam whistle

WHITE HOUSE. *See under* Birth; Building; Gas; News correspondent; Swimming pool; Wedding

"WHITE HOUSE OF THE CONFEDERACY." *See under* Building

WHITE LEAD manufacturer was Samuel Wetherill of Philadelphia, Pa., who began production in 1789. The white lead was used primarily in paint and to some extent for medicinal purposes. *(William Henry Pulsifer—Notes for a History of Lead)*

WHITE RATS. *See* Actors' union

WHITE SETTLEMENT. *See* Colonist: Colonial white settlement (north of Florida)

WILD BIRD SANCTUARY. *See* Bird sanctuary

WILD WEST SHOW was prepared by William Frederick Cody, more familiarly known as "Buffalo Bill," and presented in North Platte, Neb., as part of a Fourth of July celebration in 1883. The following year, Cody commercialized the show and exhibited it in various parts of the United States. The first commercial showing was held in Omaha, Neb. Previously, exhibitions and contests, generally of local character, had been held, frequently on specific holidays or fair days.

WILDLIFE PROTECTION SOCIETY. *See* Game protection society

WILDLIFE REFUGE. *See* Bird reservation (national)

WILDLIFE RESTORATION PROJECT. *See* Game protection society

WIND TUNNEL

Full-scale wind tunnel for testing airplanes was placed in operation May 27, 1931, at the Langley Research Center of the National Advisory Committee for Aeronautics, Langley Field, Va. It was used to test airplanes to determine flying characteristics. The jet of air in the tunnel, 30 feet high and 60 feet wide, was moved by two propellers 35 feet 5 inches in diameter up to a speed of 110 m.p.h. Each propeller was driven by a 4,000 h.p. electric motor. In 1936 a new tunnel was constructed with air speed up to 600 m.p.h.

High-speed jet wind tunnel was completed June 29, 1929, at the Langley Field Laboratory of the National Advisory Committee for Aeronautics, Langley Field, Va. Preliminary design work was

The First

begun November 14, 1928. A wind speed of approximately 600 m.p.h. was attained, permitting the testing of airfoils at this speed. The tunnel has since been deactivated.

Propeller research tunnel was completed in the summer of 1927 at the Langley Field Laboratory of the National Advisory Committee for Aeronautics, Langley Field, Va. Preliminary work commenced April 28, 1925. The tunnel permitted the full-scale testing of engines and propellers, engine nacelles, wing combinations, and fuselages. It had an airstream 20 feet in diameter that traveled at speeds up to 110 m.p.h.

Wind tunnel of variable air density for testing airplanes was conceived by Dr. Max Michael Munk and completed in April 1923 at the Langley Field Laboratory of the National Advisory Committee for Aeronautics, Langley Field, Va. Air was compressed to 20 times its normal pressure and, by means of a propeller, moved past wing models at a speed as high as 80 m.p.h. By increasing the air pressure 20 times it was possible to obtain results equivalent to those that would be obtained if the model were 20 times the size.

WIND TURBINE. *See under* Electric power plant

WINDMILL

Windmill was erected in 1632 in Cambridge, Mass. As "it would not grind but with a westerly wind," it was moved in August 1632 to Copp's Hill (Boston Neck), Boston, Mass. *(John Winthrop—History of New England from 1630 to 1649)*

Windmill driven by rotor power was erected and tested in July 1933 in West Burlington, N.J., to determine the amount of rotor power needed to turn or spin the windmill and to measure the force. The first driving unit, a duralumin rotor 90 feet high and 22 feet wide, built like a cylinder, was revolved by a motor at 60 revolutions a minute. The combination of the turning and the wind produced the force tending to make the cylinder rotate along the ground. The principle involved was similar to that used by Anton Flettner in his rotor ship. Original plans were to have a series of cylinders mounted on 30-foot-gauge cars run around a circular track one-half mile in diameter. The rotor project was sponsored by the Madaras Rotor Power Corporation, Detroit, Mich., with the support of public utility companies.

WINDOW ENVELOPE. *See* Envelope

WINDOW GLASS. *See* Glass factory: Window glass factory

WINDOW SASH. *See* Sash: Wrought-iron window sash installation

WINDOWLESS FACTORY. *See* Factory

WINDOWLESS STRUCTURE. *See* Building: All-glass windowless structure

The First

WINGLESS AUTOGIRO. *See* Autogiro: Autogiro (wingless direct-control)

WINTER OLYMPIC GAMES. *See* Olympic games

WIRE
Barbed wire was made in 1873 by Joseph Farwell Glidden of De Kalb, Ill., who obtained patent No. 157,124 for this invention November 24, 1874. He filed his application October 27, 1873, and started manufacturing on November 1, 1873, in De Kalb, Ill. The barbs were cut from sheet metal and were inserted between two wires which were twisted considerably more than is the practice today. *(Wrought Iron Record. Vol. I, No. 4. Wrought Iron Research Association)*

Brass wire was manufactured in 1840 by Edwin Hodges of West Torrington, Conn., but was not commercially successful. In 1841 the Wolcottville Brass Company was founded with a capital investment of $56,000 and was the first to manufacture brass wire successfully. *(Samuel Orcutt—History of Torrington, Conn.)*

Legislation (state) requiring wires to be placed underground was enacted June 14, 1884 (chapter 534), by New York State. It required that "all telegraph, telephonic and electric light wires and cables in any incorporated city having a population of 500,000 or over . . . be placed under the surface of the streets, lanes and avenues." It also specified that telegraph poles be removed prior to November 1, 1885.

Piano wire was produced at the factory of Ichabod Washburn, Grove Street, Worcester, Mass., in 1850. This plant was later part of the Washburn and Moen Manufacturing Company, afterward absorbed by the American Steel and Wire Company.

Wire-cutting machine and automatic straightener was invented in 1866 by John Adt, who established a small plant in Wolcottville, Conn. Before this invention, wire had been straightened by being drawn between two corrugated wooden blocks or through holes in several wooden blocks. The cutting off was done by hand. Adt's machine did the work mechanically. The concern which he founded was absorbed in 1895 by the F. B. Shuster Company of New Haven, Conn.

Wire rope factory was erected in Saxonburg, Pa., in 1841 by John Augustus Roebling, who also had to create the machinery to make the rope. A small building was erected to house the machinery for splicing wire and winding it on large reels for running out. Separate strands, seven in number, were laid up and then twisted into the larger rope. The twisting machine was out in the open and operated by hand power. *(Hamilton Schuyler—The Roeblings)*

The First

Woven wire fence industry owes its creation to John Wallace Page, who in 1883 erected on his own farm in Lenawee County, Mich., a fence with horizontally and vertically interlaced wires. This type of fence found such demand among Page's neighbors that he opened a factory in Adrian, Mich.

WIRE BRIDGE. *See* Bridge

WIRE-DRAWING MACHINE, BRASS. *See* Brass wire drawing and tube-making machinery

WIRE GAUGE for standardizing the sizes of drawn wire, was a "V"-type gauge developed in 1849 by Ichabod Washburn of Worcester, Mass. It was used by the Washburn and Moen Manufacturing Company (afterward part of the American Steel and Wire Company) and was the foundation for the present steel wire gauge.

WIRE GLASS. *See* Glass

WIRE NAIL MACHINE. *See* Nail machine (wire)

WIRE SIEVE. *See* Sieves

WIRE RECORDER was invented in the late 1930s by Marvin Camras, a student at the Armour Institute of Technology, Chicago, Ill., who obtained U.S. patents No. 2,351,003 to 2,351,011 on June 13, 1944. The recorder was used experimentally in 1939 and in 1940. In 1941 several models were used by the U.S. Navy.

WIRELESS. *See* Radio broadcast; Radio receiver

WITCHCRAFT EXECUTION of record was that of Achsah Young of Massachusetts, who was hanged as a witch on May 27, 1647. *(Justin Winsor—Memorial History of Boston)*

WOLFRAM. *See* Tungsten: Tungsten and tellurium

WOMAN
See also under professions and other areas of activity, e.g., Astronaut, Aviation—Flights, Jockey, Rabbi, Representative (U.S.)

American-born woman to become a member of Parliament in Great Britain was Lady Astor, whose maiden name was Nancy Witcher Langhorne. She was elected to represent the Plymouth constituency. She took her oath as a member of the House of Commons on December 1, 1919. *(Nancy Witcher Langhorne Astor—My Two Countries)*

American woman to swim the English Channel (France to England) was Gertrude (Trudy) Ederle, who accomplished the feat on August 6, 1926. She swam from Gris-Nez, France, to Kingsdown (Dover), England in 14 hours 34 minutes.

American woman to swim the English Channel from both coasts was Florence Chadwick of San Diego, Calif., who on August 8, 1950, swam from Gris-Nez, France, to Dover, England, in 13 hours 28 minutes, and on September 10, 1951, from St.

The First

Margaret's Bay, near Dover to Sangatte, near Cap Gris-Nez, France, in 16 hours 22 minutes.

Bible translation by a woman. *See under* Bible

Heroine publicly rewarded was Hannah Duston. During an attack on Haverhill, Mass., on March 16, 1697, Indians killed her one-week-old baby by dashing it against a tree and captured her and Mary Neff, the child's nurse, as well as murdering or capturing 39 other persons and destroying 6 houses. The prisoners were brought to the Indian camp at which Samuel Leonardson, a young boy who had been captured on March 30, 1695, at Worcester, Mass., was held prisoner. Hannah Duston, on April 29, 1697, killed 10 Indians with a tomahawk, scalping them as proof of her deed. The Great and General Court of Massachusetts on June 8, 1697, voted "that Thomas Durstan [*sic*] in behalf of his wife shall be allowed and paid out of the publick treasury twenty-five pounds; and Mary Neff, the sum of twelve pounds ten shillings and the young man (named Samuel Lenerson [*sic*] concerned in the same action the like sum of twelve pounds ten shillings." *(George Wingate Chase—The History of Haverhill)*

Independant administrative agency of the federal government woman member. *See under* Interstate Commerce Commission

Monument to a woman financed by women. *See under* Monument

Nuclear commercial power plant licensed woman operator was Roberta A. Kankus, graduate of Rensselaer Polytechnic Institute, Troy, N.Y., who was licensed February 12, 1976, by the Nuclear Regulatory Commission, Washington, D.C. She was originally employed July 2, 1973, and underwent 14 months on-the-job training with the Philadelphia Electric Company's Peach Bottom Atomic power plant, 60 miles southwest of Philadelphia, Pa. Her title was engineer in the Generating Division.

White woman to become an American Indian chief was Harriet Maxwell Converse, who was made a chief of the Six Nations Tribe on September 18, 1891, at the Tonawanda Reservation, N.Y., in a ceremony known as the Condolence. In recognition of her services to the Indians she was given the name Ga-is-wa-noh, meaning "the watcher." In 1884, Mrs. Converse had been adopted as a member of the Seneca tribe in appreciation of her efforts in their behalf. *(American Scenic and Historic Preservation Society—10th Annual Report, 1905)*

Woman automotive engineer was Marie Luhring, draftsman for the International Motor Company, who received the Master of Engineering degree from Cooper Union, New York City, June , 1922. On April 9, 1920, she was elected an associate member of the Society of Automotive Engineers, becoming the first woman member. *(Journal*

The First

of the Society of Automotive Engineers. June 1920)

Woman clerk of a state supreme court was Grace F. Kaercher (later Mrs. Davis) of Ortonville, Minn., elected November 7, 1922. She was the first woman to be elected to a state office in Minnesota. She was reelected for four-year terms in 1926, 1930, 1938, and 1942. Her salary was $4,500 a year.

Woman congressional hearing witness was Elizabeth Cady Stanton, who addressed the District Committee of the United States Senate January 20, 1869, in a plea to save women of the District of Columbia from being debarred from voting. *(Carrie Chapman Catt and Nettie Rogers Shuler—Woman Suffrage and Politics)*

Woman coxswain of a men's collegiate varsity team was Sally Stearns, who led the shell of Rollins College, Winter Park, Fla., on May 27, 1936, against Marietta College and on June 1, 1936, against Manhattan College. The crew raced only twice in 1936, losing to Marietta by four lengths and winning from Manhattan by a half length.

Woman district attorney of the United States was Annette Abbott Adams, who served in the Northern California District from July 25, 1918, to June 26, 1920.

Woman director of the Voice of America was Mary Foley Bitterman, who was confirmed by the Senate February 28, 1980, and took office March 7, 1980, succeeding R. Peter Strauss.

Woman editor in chief of a law review was Mary Honor Donlon, who edited the November 1919, January 1920, and March 1920 issues of the *Cornell Law Quarterly* of the Cornell Law School, Ithaca, N.Y.

Woman federal regulatory agency chairman was Helen Delich Bentley (Mrs. William Roy Bentley), who was sworn in October 27, 1969, as chairman of the Federal Maritime Commission.

Woman granted a patent was Mary Kies of South Killingly, Conn., who obtained a patent on May 5, 1809, for "a new and useful improvement in weaving straw with silk or thread." *(George Larkin Clark—History of Connecticut)*

Woman hanged by the United States Government was Mary E. Surratt, convicted by a military commission of conspiracy in the assassination of President Abraham Lincoln at Ford's Theatre, Washington, D.C. on April 14, 1865. He died April 15, 1865. The trial by 9 army officers, Major General David Hunter presiding, began May 9, 1865. They deliberated June 29-30, 1865. A gallows was erected, and she was hanged Friday, July 7, 1865, with 3 male conspirators. Her guilt is still a subject of controversy. *(Guy. W. Moore—The Case of Mrs. Surratt, Her Controversial Trial and Execution in the Lincoln Assassination)*

The First

WOMAN—*Continued*

Woman horseback rider to make a solo transcontinental trip was Nan Jane Aspinwall, who left San Francisco, Calif., September 1, 1910, carrying a letter from Mayor Patrick Henry McCarthy to Mayor William Jay Gaynor of New York City. She covered 4,500 miles in 301 days, 108 of which were spent traveling. She arrived in New York City on July 8, 1911.

Woman humorist was Frances Miriam Berry Whitcher, who used the nom de plume "Frank" in 1846 in Joseph Clay Neal's *Saturday Gazette.* Her "Widow Bedott" papers, republished in book form in 1855, sold over 100,000 copies. *(Walter Blair—Native American Humor)*

Woman in the U.S. Marine Band. *See under* Marine Corps

Woman independent federal administrative agency chairman was Virginia Mae Brown of Pliny, W.Va., who became head of the Interstate Commerce Commission on January 1, 1969. She had been appointed to the commission by President Lyndon Baines Johnson and was sworn in May 25, 1964, at ceremonies in the White House. Chairmanship of the commission is generally rotated annually, based on the length of service.

Woman internal revenue collector was Mabel Gilmore Reinecke, who served from June 1, 1923, to March 31, 1929, as collector of Internal Revenue for the First District of Illinois. She was appointed by President Warren Gamaliel Harding.

Woman labor delegate to a national convention of the American Federation of Labor was Mary Burke, who represented the Retail Clerks' Union of Findlay, Ohio, at the convention held in Detroit, Mich., December 8-13, 1890.

Woman labor delegate to the British Trades Union was Sara Agnes McLaughlin Conboy, who was elected in 1920 as a fraternal delegate of the American Federation of Labor. She was the first woman organizer of the United Textile Workers of America.

Woman lobbyist of more than local influence was Dorothea Lynde Dix, who in the 1840s and 1850s championed the care of the indigent insane. On June 23, 1848, she presented a memorial to Congress for a grant of 5 million acres for "the relief and support of the indigent insane in the United States." By courtesy of Congress, a special alcove in the Capitol Library was set apart for her use, where she could converse with members. *(Francis Tiffany—Life of Dorothea Lynde Dix)*

Woman major political party chairman was Frances Jean Miles Westwood (Mrs. Richard Elwyn Westwood) of Utah, who was chosen as chairman of the Democratic National Committee to replace Lawrence ("Larry") Francis O'Brien on July 14, 1972, at Miami Beach, Fla.

The First

Woman moderator of the Unitarian Church. *See under* Unitarian society

Woman newspaper editor was Ann Franklin, Benjamin Franklin's sister-in-law, who became editor of the Newport *Mercury,* Newport, R.I., upon the death of her son, James Franklin, Jr., August 22, 1762. The first number had appeared June 12, 1758, under the editorship of the son. At his death, she took charge of the newspaper and printing plant. She edited the paper until her death, April 16, 1763. *(Newport Historical Society. Bulletin No. 65. April 1928)*

Woman of American descent to become a queen was Countess Geraldine Apponyi of Hungary (born August 6, 1915), who married King Zog (Ahmed Zogu) of Albania on April 27, 1938, at the Royal Palace, Tirana, Albania. The marriage was proclaimed by Heqmet Delvina, vice president of the Albanian Parliament. The countess was the daughter of Virginia Gladys Stewart, who married Count Julius Apponyi. *(Antoinette de Szinyei-Merse—Ten Years, Ten Months, Ten Days)*

Woman ordained a minister was the Reverend Antoinette Brown Blackwell, who was ordained September 15, 1853, at the Congregational Church, South Butler, N.Y. *(Harriot Kesia Hunt—Glances and Glimpses)*

Woman ordained to the Unitarian ministry. *See under* Unitarian minister

Woman passport division chief was Ruth Bielaski Shipley, appointed by Secretary of State Frank Billings Kellogg. She assumed office June 1, 1928.

Woman pilot in the Coast Guard. *See* Coast Guard: Woman pilot

Woman Presbyterian elder, as finally permitted by the General Assembly at Cincinnati, Ohio, on May 31, 1930, was Sarah E. Dickson of the Wauwatosa Presbyterian Church of Milwaukee, Wis., elected June 2, 1930. She served until January 1, 1934.

Woman presidential campaign comanager was Ruth Hanna McCormick Simms, daughter of Mark Hanna, who was made a comanager on December 2, 1939, of Thomas Edmund Dewey's campaign. J. Russel Sprague, Republican leader of Nassau County, N.Y., was the other comanager.

Woman printer was Dinah Nuthead of Annapolis, Md., who petitioned the Assembly on May 5, 1696, for license to print and carry on the printing trade of her deceased husband, William Nuthead. *(Lawrence Counselman Wroth—A History of Printing in Colonial Maryland 1686–1776)*

Woman prizefight referee (licensed). *See under* Prizefight referee

The First

Woman Republican national committee chairman was Mary Louise Smith of Iowa, elected September 16, 1974, at Washington, D.C.

Woman sculptor honored by membership in the National Academy of Design was Mary Evelyn Beatrice Longman, who was elected in 1919. Her first important work was a male statue, *Victory*, placed in Festival Hall at the 1904 St. Louis Exposition. For this statue she was awarded a silver medal.

Woman secretary of a national political party was Dorothy McElroy Vredenburgh of Alabama, who was appointed secretary of the Democratic National Committee on February 29, 1944, by chairman Robert Emmet Hannegan. She was secretary at the Democratic National Convention, July 19-21, 1944, in Chicago, Ill.

Woman secretary of a state senate was Fern Ale, who served as secretary of the Senate of Indiana, Indianapolis, during the session of 1927, beginning January 6 and adjourning March 7. She also served as secretary of the special meeting of the senate immediately following the regular adjournment of the legislature. This special meeting, called for the impeachment of a judge, lasted several days.

Woman secretary to a Vice President of the United States was Lola M. Williams, who served as secretary to Vice President Charles Curtis when he assumed office on March 4, 1929. Previously she had been his secretary five years while he was senator from Kansas.

Woman state budget commissioner was Jean Wetterau Wittich of Minneapolis, Minn. She served as budget commissioner of the state of Minnesota from March 16, 1931, to May 16, 1933.

Woman state committee chairman of a major political party was Mary Teresa Norton, who was elected Chairman of the Democratic State Committee of New Jersey at the state convention held in Trenton, May 22, 1934. Mrs. Norton was at the time of her election a member of the U.S. House of Representatives from the 13th District, New Jersey.

Woman state liquor board member was Jeanie Rumsey Sheppard, appointed April 12, 1933, by Governor Herbert Henry Lehman to New York's Alcoholic Beverage Control Board established to license, regulate, and control the sale of all alcoholic beverages.

Woman tax appeals board member was Annabel Matthews, whose appointment by President Herbert Clark Hoover was confirmed by the Senate on February 14, 1930. She served from February 18, 1930, to June 1, 1936.

Woman telegrapher was Sarah G. Bagley, who was in charge of the Lowell, Mass., office of the New York and Boston Magnetic Telegraph Association when the line opened February 21, 1846, between Boston and Lowell. *(James D. Reid—The Telegraph in America)*

Woman telephone operator. *See under* Telephone operator

Woman to compile a dictionary. *See* Dictionary: Dictionary compiled by a woman

Woman to have her name placed on the cornerstone of a United States Government building was Nellie Tayloe Ross, Director of the Mint. The building was the United States Depository, Fort Knox, Ky., completed during the early part of April 1936. No formal dedication ceremonies were held.

Woman to qualify in yard, freight, and passenger service. *See* Railroad: Railroad train operated exclusively by women

Woman to undergo astronaut tests was Jerrie Cobb of Oklahoma City, Okla., who passed a series of 75 examinations conducted February 15-21, 1960, at the Lovelace Foundation, Albuquerque, N.Mex. The tests were the same as those given to male astronauts. In August 1960 she underwent additional examinations, which included psychological, psychiatric, and isolation tests.

Woman to win 2 Pulitzer Prizes in history. *See under* Pulitzer Prize

Woman whose vote was recorded was the widow of Josiah Taft of Uxbridge, Mass., who in 1756 voted her approval of levying a town tax. She was granted this privilege because her son, Bazaleel, was a minor. *(Henry Chapin—Address Delivered at the Unitarian Church in Uxbridge, Mass., in 1864)*

Women eligible to enter the U.S. service academies were authorized by act of Congress of October 7, 1975 (89 Stat. L. 537), "to insure that female individuals shall be eligible for appointment and admission to the service academics beginning with appointments to such academy for the class beginning in calendar year 1976."

Women to become federal government employees were Sarah Waldrake and Rachael Summers, employed in 1795 by the Mint in Philadelphia, Pa., at 50 cents a day as adjusters to weigh gold coins.

Women ushers. *See* Theater: Theater to employ women ushers

WOMAN SUFFRAGE

Colony to grant suffrage to women was New Jersey. A new constitution, adopted on July 2, 1776, provided "that all the inhabitants of this Colony of full age who are worth 50 Pounds Proclamation money, with clear estate in the same, and have resided within the county in which they claim a vote for twelve months immediately preceding the election" were entitled to vote at

The First

WOMAN SUFFRAGE—*Continued*
the general election. In 1790 this was interpreted to mean both men and women, but on November 16, 1807, the General Assembly passed laws providing that only free white male citizens could exercise the franchise.

Convention (national) of women advocating woman suffrage was the National Woman's Rights Convention held at Brinley Hall, Worcester, Mass., October 23-24, 1850, "to consider the question of woman's rights, duties and relations." The convention was called to order by Sarah H. Earle of Worcester. The officers elected were Paulina W. Davis of Providence, R.I., president, and William H. Channing of Boston, Mass., and Sarah Tyndale of Philadelphia, Pa., vice presidents.

Convention of women advocating woman suffrage was held in the Wesleyan Chapel, Seneca Falls, N.Y., July 19-20, 1848. The convention was assembled through the initiative of Lucretia Mott and Elizabeth Cady Stanton. A Declaration of Sentiments was read and a series of resolutions adopted, one of them calling for woman suffrage. *(National American Woman Suffrage Association —Victory: How Women Won It)*

State to grant suffrage to women after the adoption of the United States Constitution was Wyoming, which became a state on July 10, 1890. Women had voted in Wyoming territory from the beginning. The first territorial legislature, which convened on October 12, 1869, had voted on December 10, 1869, to extend the vote to women. New Jersey women had the privilege of voting for a time under the constitution adopted July 2, 1776, but the constitutional provision was reinterpreted in 1807 as limiting the right to vote to free white male citizens. *(Carrie Chapman Catt and Nettie Rogers Shuler—Woman Suffrage and Politics)*

Woman suffrage advocate, better known as America's first feminist, was Margaret Brent, a niece of Lord Baltimore. She came to America in January 1638 and was the first woman of Maryland to own property in her own name. On June 24, 1647, she demanded a voice and vote for herself in the colonial assembly by virtue of her position as Governor Leonard Calvert's secretary. She was ejected from the meetings. She protested and demanded a "place and voyce." At the death of Calvert, she was his executor and became acting governor and presided over the General Assembly. She was refused a voice in the affairs of the government as "it would set a bad example to ye wives of ye colony." *(National Republic. May 1930)*

Woman suffrage amendment approved by Congress for submission to the states was passed by the House of Representatives May 21, 1919, and by the Senate on June 4, 1919. It was ratified by Illinois, Wisconsin, and Michigan on June 10,

The First

1919. Tennessee was the 36th state to ratify the amendment, on August 18, 1920, completing the necessary three quarters of the states to put the amendment into effect. On August 26, 1920, Secretary of State Bainbridge Colby signed the Proclamation of the Woman Suffrage Amendment to the Constitution, giving public notice that the 19th Amendment had been formally adopted, and was in effect. Woman suffrage amendments had been presented to Congress at intervals beginning in 1868 without success.

Woman suffrage association (international) was the International Woman Suffrage Alliance, which was organized in Washington, D.C., in February 1902 at a meeting of the National American Woman Suffrage Association. The first international convention of the Alliance was held in Berlin in 1904, in conjunction with the quinquennial convention of the International Council of Women.

Woman suffrage associations (national) stemmed from the American Equal Rights Association, which had been organized in 1866, when the 14th Amendment to the Constitution was up for ratification. The constitution of the association, adopted May 10, 1866, in New York City advocated the right of suffrage irrespective of race, color, or sex. Lucretia Mott was president and Susan Brownell Anthony secretary. In 1868 the American Equal Rights Association split over the question of equal suffrage for blacks, one faction forming the American Woman Suffrage Association led by Lucy Stone and Julia Ward Howe and the other forming the National Woman Suffrage Association led by Elizabeth Cady Stanton and Susan B. Anthony. Some 20 years later the two were reunited to form the National American Woman Suffrage Association.

Woman suffrage book was a reprint of *A Vindication of the Rights of Women, with Strictures on Political and Moral Subjects* by Mary Wollstonecraft Godwin, 276 pages, printed in 1792 in Philadelphia, Pa., by William Gibbons. The author's name was erroneously spelled "Woolstonecraft." Another edition, 340 pages, was published in Boston, Mass., by Peter Edes with a slight subtitle variation. The book was originally published in England in 1790 and was dedicated to Charles Maurice de Talleyrand-Périgord, formerly bishop of Autun.

WOMEN'S ARMY AUXILIARY CORPS. *See under* Army auxiliary corps

WOMEN'S AUXILIARY FERRYING SQUADRON
Women's Auxiliary Ferrying Squadron (WAFS) was established September 10, 1942, by the Air Transport Command. It consisted of women pilots with Civil Service status who ferried army aircraft to domestic airfields and overseas bases.

The First

WOMEN'S BUREAU (Labor Department). *See under* Labor Department (U.S.)

WOMEN'S CLUB

Chinese-American women's club incorporated was the Chinese Women's Association, Inc., New York City, organized March 29, 1932, and incorporated June 10, 1936. The first president was Theodora Chan Wang.

Jewish women's organization (national) was the National Council of Jewish Women formed in Chicago, Ill., in January 1894. The first president was Hannah Greenebaum Solomon and the first secretary was Sadie American.

Women's club was the Female Charitable Society of Wiscasset, Maine, which held its first meeting on November 18, 1805, at the home of "Tempe" Lee, wife of Judge Silas Lee, a member of Congress. Thirty women were present and were admitted as members. A total of $78 was subscribed. The first president was Sally Sayward Wood, Maine's first woman novelist. *(Daughters of the American Revolution Magazine. May 1920)*

Women's club federation was the General Federation of Women's Clubs organized March 20, 1890, at Madison Square Garden, New York City. The first convention was held April 23, 1890, and the constitution adopted April 24, 1890. The first officers were Charlotte Emerson Brown, president; Mary Wright Sewall, vice president; Phoebe Apperson Hearst, treasurer; Mary B. Temple, corresponding secretary; Jane Cunningham Croly ("Jennie June"), recording secretary; and Kate Tanett Woods, auditor. *(Jane Cunningham Croly— History of the Woman's Club Movement in America)*

Women's professional club was Sorosis, founded in New York City, March 21, 1868, by Jane Cunningham Croly ("Jennie June") and a few of her friends. The first officers were Alice Carey, president; Mrs. Croly, vice president; Kate Fields, corresponding secretary, and Charlotte Beebee Wilbour, treasurer and recording secretary. *(Jane Cunningham Croly—History of the Woman's Club Movement in America)*

Women's secret society was organized May 15, 1851, at Wesleyan College, Macon, Ga., as the Adelphean Society with 16 charter members whose motto was "We live for one another." The original founder was Eugenia Tucker Fitzgerald. The name was changed to Alpha Delta Phi Sorority in 1904, at which time the society had 60 active members and 3,000 alumnae. In 1913 it changed its name to the Alpha Delta Pi Sorority. *(The Adelphean of Alpha Delta Pi. Vol. 1, No. 1)*
See also Sorority

WOMEN'S COLLEGE. *See* College

The First

WOMEN'S HOSPITAL. *See* Hospital

WOMEN'S LABOR LEGISLATION. *See* Labor legislation: Women's equal employment legislation

WOMEN'S LABOR ORGANIZATION. *See under* Labor union

WOMEN'S RIGHTS CONVENTION. *See* Woman suffrage: Convention of women advocating woman suffrage

WOMEN'S STRIKE. *See* Strike

WOMEN'S WORLD'S FAIR. *See* Fair

WOOD DRY DOCK. *See* Dry dock: Timber dry dock

WOOD ENGRAVING. *See* Engraving

WOOD FIBER OR PULP PAPER. *See* Paper: Wood pulp and rag paper

WOODCUT. *See* Engraving

WOODEN MONEY. *See* Money

WOODEN RAILROAD BRIDGE. *See* Bridge

WOODEN TRACK (bicycle). *See* Bicycle racetrack of wood

WOOL

Fulling mill was established by John Pearson in Rowley, Mass., in 1643. It cleaned, felted, and shrank cloth until the desired consistency was obtained. The mill was operated by emigrants from Yorkshire, England.

Wool carding machine was built by John and Arthur Scholfield in Newburyport, Mass., and installed in a mill in Byfield, Mass., in 1793. It was 25 inches wide and had a single cylinder, 33 inches in diameter. It carried two workers and strippers, a fancy, and a 14-inch doffer cover with card clothing sheets. A fluted cylinder of 13 inches was arranged behind the doffer. *(Arthur Harrison Cole —The American Wool Manufacture)*

Worsted mill was established in 1695 in Boston, Mass., by John Cornish. The spinning was done by farmers, who called for clean top wool, from which the noil had been removed, and brought back spun worsted. An appraisal of Cornish's estate revealed "two pairs of combs, four looms and tackling, and two dye furnaces."

Worsted mill operated by waterpower and the first operated on a strictly commercial basis was the Hartford Woolen Manufactory, Hartford, Conn., which was organized on April 15, 1788. A capital of 1,250 pounds was raised by subscription in nearby towns, the largest contributor being Jeremiah Wadsworth. A bounty of one penny per pound was given for all yarn spun in the factory before June 1, 1789, as a means of encouraging the new industry. Waterpower had previously been used in fulling mills.

The First

WOOL, GLASS. *See* Glass wool

WORKERS' COMPENSATION. *See* Workmen's Compensation

WORKINGMEN'S PARTY. *See* Labor Party (political): Labor Party (state)

WORKMEN'S COMPENSATION

Workmen's compensation agreement was made January 26, 1695, by Captain William Kidd, commander of the *Adventure Galley* of 787 tons burden. One fourth of the booty captured was to be distributed among the crew. According to the agreement, "If any man should Loose a Leg or Arm in ye said service, he should have six hundred pieces of Eight, or six able slaves; if any man should loose a joynt on ye said service, he should have a hundred pieces of eight." *(Harold Tom Wilkins—Captain Kidd and His Skeleton Island)*

Workmen's compensation insurance. *See* Insurance: Workers' compensation insurance law

Workmen's compensation lawsuit involving the rights of an injured servant against his master was the case of *James Murray* vs. *South Carolina Railroad Company*, which was tried before Judge Belton O'Neall at the July Extra Term, 1838, of Barnwell County, S.C. The trial resulted in a verdict of $1,500 in favor of the plaintiff. The defendant appealed and the case was heard by the Court of Errors of South Carolina in Charleston in February 1841. The court reversed the decision and granted a new trial. The decision was written by Judge Josiah James Evans. *(McMullan Law Reports. Vol. I, p. 251)*

WORKS PROGRESS ADMINISTRATION

Works Progress Administration was created by Presidential Executive Order No. 7034, May 6, 1935, under the Emergency Relief Appropriation Act of 1935, approved April 8, 1935 (49 Stat. L. 115), to "provide relief, work relief and to increase employment by providing for useful projects." Harry Lloyd Hopkins, appointed May 6, 1935, was the first administrator.

Works Progress Administration Federal Art Project Gallery was officially opened December 28, 1935, in New York City "to provide an outlet for the showing of work by artists on the projects, and at the same time to enable the public and cooperating sponsors to see for themselves the results of the federal art program." A large part of the work exhibited was allocated to tax-free and tax-supported institutions which paid for the cost of the material used.

WORLD BANK. *See* Bank

WORLD FLIGHT. *See* Aviation—Flights (world)

WORLD SERIES BASEBALL GAME. *See* Baseball game

The First

WORLD TOUR BY A WOMAN TRAVELING ALONE. *See* Tour of the world

WORLD WAR I

Air combat of an American organization in World War I took place April 14, 1918. Alan Francis Winslow and Douglas Campbell shot down two German single-seaters almost directly over the Squadron Aerodrome at Toul, France.

Air squadron. *See under* Aviation

Airplane bombing raid by an American air unit. *See under* Aviation—Airplane bombing

American Army casualty in World War I was First Lieutenant Louis J. Genelba, Medical Corps, who received a shell wound July 14, 1917, while serving with the British Army at the front southwest of Arras, France. *(United States Battle Monuments Commission—American Armies and Battlefields in Europe)*

American Army division to cross the Rhine River into the American sector of the American Army of Occupation was the First Division, which passed over the pontoon bridge at Coblentz on the morning of December 13, 1918. Lieutenant Donald McClure, commanding officer of Company M, 18th Infantry, First Division, led the advance with his company of infantry. In daily marching order down the Moselle River from Luxembourg to the river's confluence with the Rhine, regiments, battalions, and companies rotated in the advance. On November 26, 1918, the American Army crossed the Moselle into Rhenish Prussia.

American Army soldiers killed in combat in World War I were Corporal James B. Gresham of Evansville, Ind., and Privates Thomas F. Enright of Pittsburgh, Pa., and Merle D. Hay of Glidden, Iowa, members of Company F, 16th Infantry, First Division. They met death when the Germans raided the 16th Infantry's trenches near Bathelémont, France, on the nights of November 2-3, 1917. On November 3, 1917, General Bordeaux of the French Army commended their heroism and sacrifice.

American Army soldiers killed in World War I were First Lieutenant William T. Fitzsimons of Kansas City, Mo., and enlisted men Rudolph Rubino, Jr., of the Bronx, New York City; Oscar Le Tugo of Boston, Mass.; and Leslie G. Woods of Streator, Ill., all of U.S. Army Base Hospital No. 5 then operating No. 11 General Hospital, British Expeditionary Force, Dannes-Camiers, France. They were killed at 11:00 P.M. September 4, 1917, when the hospital was bombed by a German airplane. *(Carlisle Barracks—In Memoriam: The Medical Department of the U.S. Army in the World War)*

American Army troopship in World War I torpedoed by the Germans was the S.S. *Tuscania* carrying 119 officers and 2,037 men. It was torpedoed and sunk, by the German Undersea Boat

The First

No. 77, February 15, 1918, off the north coast of Ireland, with a loss of 183 men.

American combatant casualty in World War I was Corporal Bouligny, serving in the French Army, who was shot through the knee November 15, 1914. Bouligny was wounded while attacking a German outpost installed at the cemetery surrounding the mausoleum erected to Napoleon's soldiers who fell at the battle of Craonne in 1814. Several combatants in the British Army came from Boston, Mass.

American combatant to die in World War I was Edward Mandell Stone of Chicago, Ill. He was wounded February 17, 1915, and he died February 27, 1915. Living in Paris, he enlisted in the French Foreign Legion and was assigned to the second regiment. He served at Champagne and in the Aisne until mortally wounded. He was posthumously awarded the Croix de Guerre and the Military Medal.

American division in the trenches in World War I and the first in battle was the First Division, which entered the line October 21, 1917, in the Lunéville sector, near Nancy, France. Each unit was attached to a corresponding French unit. *(Records in Adjutant General's Office, U.S. War Department. Washington, D.C.)*

American flag flown in World War I. *See under* Flag

American pilot shot down. *See under* Aviation —Pilot

American sailor to lose his life in World War I (before U.S. entry into the war) was John E. Eopolucci, who was killed when the steamship *Aztec* was torpedoed and sunk April 1, 1917. The sinking occurred five days before the War Risk Insurance Act went into effect.

American ship lost in World War I was the *William P. Frye,* a steel sailing vessel of 3,374 gross tons, built in 1901 and owned by Arthur Sewall & Company of Maine. She cleared from Seattle, Wash., November 4, 1914, bound for Queenstown, Falmouth, or Plymouth, for orders, with a cargo consisting solely of 186,950 bushels of wheat. She was sunk January 28, 1915, by the German cruiser *Prinz Eitel Friedrich. (Henry Ernest Dannack—Maine Book)*

American shot fired in World War I was fired at 6:05 A.M. October 23, 1917, by Battery C of the 6th Field Artillery, First Infantry Division. Sergeant Alexander L. Arch of South Bend, Ind., was in command of the crew that fired the shot. Corporal Robert E. Bralet is credited with having jerked the lanyard on a French 75-mm. gun at 6:10 A.M. to send the first shot by American infantry into a German trench a half-mile away.

American to sail to Europe to enlist in World War I was Denis Patrick Dowd, Jr., of Sea Cliff, Long Island, N.Y. He enlisted August 6, 1914,

The First

fought with the French Foreign Legion, was transferred to a line regiment when the battered legion was withdrawn, was wounded, and upon recovery was transferred to the Lafayette Escadrille. He died August 11, 1916, when his plane crashed in a nose dive at Buc, near Paris, the day before he was to fly to the front. His body lies in the Memorial Cemetery of the Lafayette Escadrille in the Parc du Villeneuve l'Étang near St. Cloud, France. *(James Norman Hall and Charles Bernard Nordhoff—The Lafayette Flying Corps)*

American troop contingent to arrive in France was Base Hospital 4, which sailed from New York City on May 8, 1917. The group arrived at Liverpool, England, on May 18, 1917, and at Rouen, France, on May 25, 1917.

American troops to land in England in World War I were members of a group of 40 regular army officers, 17 reserve officers, 2 marine corps officers, 67 enlisted men, 36 field clerks, 20 civilians, 3 interpreters, and 3 correspondents. The group left New York City May 28, 1917, on the *Baltic* and docked at Liverpool, England, June 8, 1917. After spending some days in consultation with British authorities, they reached Paris June 13, 1917. General John Joseph Pershing was in command.

American troops to land in France in World War I were the members of the First Division, 346 officers and 11,607 men, who sailed from America on June 14, 1917, on the S.S. *Tenadores,* and disembarked at St.-Nazaire, France, June 26, 1917. The first group to land was Company K, 28th Infantry. Major General William Luther Sibert was the commanding general of the First Division from June 8 to December 14, 1917. *(Henry Russell Miller —The First Division)*

Combat mission of all-American pilots ordered to battle by an all-American squadron commander was the 94th Aero Pursuit Squadron, the "Hat-in-the-Ring Squadron." Major John Huffer ordered Captain David Peterson, Lieutenant Reed Chambers, and Lieutenant Edward Vernon Rickenbacker on April 13, 1918, to a 2-hour patrol from Pont-à-Mousson to St. Mihiel at 6:00 A.M. on April 14, 1918. *(Edward Vernon Rickenbacker—Fighting the Flying Circus)*

German spy to receive a death sentence from the American forces during World War I was Lothar Witzke, alias Pablo Waberski. On Friday August 16, 1918, he was brought to Fort Sam Houston, where a court-martial found him guilty and sentenced him to be hanged. On November 2, 1918 the death sentence was approved by Major DeRosey Carroll Cabell, commanding officer. On November 11, 1918, the armistice was signed and President Wilson gave orders that Witzke was not to be executed until he personally reviewed the findings. On May 27, 1920, the President confirmed the sentence but commuted it to "confinement at hard labor for the term of his natural life." On

The First

WORLD WAR I—*Continued*
November 22, 1923, President Coolidge pardoned Witzke on the understanding that he leave the United States and never return. On November 29, 1923, Witzke sailed for Berlin.

Graduate of the U.S. Military Academy killed in action in World War I. *See* Army school: Graduate of the U.S. Military Academy killed in action

Marine regiment to land in Europe in World War I was the Fifth Regiment of Marines, commanded by Colonel Charles A. Doyen, which sailed from New York on board the *Henderson, De Kalb,* and *Hancock* on June 14, 1917. By July 2, 1917, the entire regiment had arrived at St.-Nazaire, France. President Woodrow Wilson's executive order of May 25, 1917, attached the Fifth Marine Regiment to the Army for service in France.

Naval ace in World War I. *See under* Aviation —Pilot

Naval enlisted man killed in World War I action was Osmond Kelly Ingram (gunners mate first class) of Pratt City, Ala., who was blown overboard on October 16, 1917, while throwing explosives overboard to save the destroyer U.S.S. *Cassin* (D.D.) on patrol duty. A torpedo fired by a German submarine from a distance of 5 miles hit the stern, put the engine out of commission, and wounded 5 other sailors.

Night-flying scout group. *See* Aviation: War night-flying scout group

Pilot to receive the Congressional Medal of Honor. *See under* Aviation—Pilot

Ship (American) attacked by a German submarine. *See under* Ship

Shot fired by the American Navy in World War I was fired on April 7, 1917, at Guam Island. Commander William Alden Hall, U.S.N., in command of a prize crew, left the U.S.S. *Supply* about 6:30 A.M. (Guam time) and proceeded to the port town of Piti with orders to follow the governor's aide, who had boarded the interned German cruiser *Cormorant* in Apra harbor under a flag of truce to demand its surrender. A German launch with a cutter in tow was sighted and a shot was fired across her bow by Corporal Michael B. Chickie, U.S.M.C. As the launch disregarded the warning, a second marine was ordered to fire. After several shots the launch hove to and was ordered to Piti to surrender to the authorities there. The Germans blew up their ship; 7 were killed and the rest were sent as prisoners to an army camp in Utah.

Shot fired by the American Navy in World War I against a known German submarine was fired on April 19, 1917, by the S.S. *Mongolia,* a merchant ship captained by Emery Rice. Lieutenant Bruce Richardson Ware, U.S.N., of Massachusetts, was in command of the naval gun crew aboard the

The First

ship. The submarine submerged, and the result of the shot could not be ascertained.

Shots to land on American soil in World War I were fired July 21, 1918, by the German submarine U-156 at the tugboat *Perth Amboy* and four barges loaded with stone off Nauset Bluffs, Orleans, Mass. About 70 or 80 shots were fired three miles offshore. A few shots landed at Meeting House Pond, Mass. *(Henry Johnson James—German Subs in Yankee Waters)*

United States declaration of war against Germany (World War I) was made on April 6, 1917, and against Austria-Hungary on December 7, 1917. The United States was the 13th country to declare war against the Central Powers.

WORLD WAR II
Admiral killed in action in World War II. *See under* Naval officer

Air attack on Germany itself by U.S. Army Air Forces was made January 27, 1943, by the 8th Air Force led by Brigadier General Haywood Shepherd Hansell, 3rd, of Washington, D.C., from bases in England against the German naval bases and docks at Wilhelmshaven and factories in Emden in northwest Germany. The American loss was 3 planes: 2 Liberators and 1 Flying Fortress; the German loss was 22 fighter airplanes and 3 bombers.

Air hero was Second Lieutenant George S Welch of Wilmington, Del., who during the attack on December 7, 1941, shot down four Japanese airplanes at Oahu, Hawaiian Islands. He was awarded the Distinguished Service Cross at Wheeler Field, Hawaii, on December 16, 1941, and was congratulated by President Franklin Delano Roosevelt at the White House, Washington, D.C. on May 25, 1942. In 33 months he shot down 18 enemy aircraft.

Aircraft carrier (American) sunk in World War II was the 33,000-ton *Lexington,* which was hit on May 8, 1942, in the Coral Sea by Japanese aircraft with 2 bombs and 2 aircraft torpedoes. About 92 percent of the normal complement of 1,899 men were saved. Rear Admiral Frederick Carl Sherman was the commander.

Airship (American) lost to enemy action was the K-74 a nonrigid blimp that while patrolling the east coast attacked a submarine submerged in the Caribbean on July 18, 1943. The airship was destroyed by gunfire and forced to alight on the water. All of the 11-man crew was saved with the exception of Isadore Stessel of Brooklyn, aviation machinist first class.

American air attack against the Japanese homeland was made April 18, 1942, by 16 B-25 airplanes of the 17th Bombardment Group, U.S. 8th Air Force, which took off from the U.S. *Hornet* under Colonel James Harold Doolittle and dropped bombs on Kobe, Yokohama, and Nagoya.

The First

American bombardier over German-occupied territory was Bernard L. Bell, who, while assigned to a British group, flew in a Boston bomber escorted by Spitfires in a raid over Hazebrouck, France, June 29, 1942.

American bombing mission in the Orient took place December 9, 1941, when B-17 airplanes of the 19th Bombardment Group attacked enemy ships off the east coast of Vigan, Luzon, Philippine Islands.

American bombing mission over enemy-occupied territory in Europe took place July 4, 1942, when six American crews manned A-20 Boston bombers of the Royal Air Force. They were accompanied by six British-manned Bostons in a daylight attack against Nazi airfields at Alkmaar, Haamstede, and Valkenburg, in the Netherlands. Enemy planes, installations, and personnel were gunned and bombed.

American destroyer torpedoed was the *Kearny*, under the command of Lieutenant Commander Anthony Leo Danis, which was attacked October 17, 1941, 350 miles southwest of Iceland. Eleven of the crew were killed, 2 were seriously wounded, and 8 sustained minor wounds. The *Kearny* arrived at Iceland on October 19, 1941.

American destroyer torpedoed and sunk while on convoy duty was the *Reuben James* (DD-245) off western Ireland, under the command of Lieutenant Commander Heywood Lane Edwards, on October 30, 1941. A torpedo fired by the German submarine U-562 hit the port side, exploded a magazine, and caused the destroyer to sink. About 115 of the crew of 160 were reported dead or missing.

American expeditionary force to land in Africa was the 41st Engineers General Service Regiment, which landed June 17, 1942, at Port Takoradi, Gold Coast, Africa. The first man to land was Private Napoleon Edward Taylor of Baltimore, Md., orderly of Major Charles S. Ward.

American expeditionary force to land on the European continent arrived January 26, 1942, in Ireland and was greeted by Sir Archibald Sinclair, British Air Minister. The first officer to land was Major General Russell Peter Hartle. The first enlisted man to land was Private Milburn Henke of Hutchinson, Minn.

American general captured by the Germans was Brigadier General Arthur William Vanaman of Millville, N.J., observer on an aerial bombing mission. He was reported missing in action on June 27, 1944, and ascertained to be a prisoner on September 16, 1944, according to announcement made October 14, 1944.

American general killed in World War II was Major General Herbert Arthur Dargue, killed December 12, 1941, in an airplane which crashed en route to the Pacific area.

The First

American general missing in action in World War II was Major General Clarence Leonard Tinker, missing in action off Midway, June 7, 1942, and declared dead June 7, 1943. He was posthumously awarded the Distinguished Service Medal on November 10, 1942.

American general wounded in action in World War II was Brigadier General Clinton Albert Pierce, commander of the 26th cavalry Philippine scouts, Fort Stotenburg, Philippine Islands, who was wounded February 4, 1942, at Bataan Peninsula while opposing the Japanese at Lingayen Gulf. He was subsequently held as a prisoner of war by the Japanese at Taiwan Camp, Formosa.

American naval counterattack against the Japanese was a naval surface engagement known as the Battle of Balikpapan (or, the Battle of the Makassar Strait), in the harbor of Balikpapan, East Borneo. The U.S. destroyers *John D. Ford* (DD-228), *Parrott* (DD-218), *Pope* (DD-225), and *Paul Jones* (DD-230), under command of Lieutenant Commander Paul H. Talbot (U.S. Navy), on February 23-24, 1942, at high speed, at night, sank a patrol craft, PC-37 (750 tons) and the transports *Tatsukami Maru* (7,064 tons), *Tsuruga Maru* (6,988 tons), *Kuretake Maru* (5,175 tons), and *Somanouri Maru* (3,519 tons).

American offensive in the Pacific area was undertaken August 7, 1942, at Guadalcanal, Solomon Islands, by the Marines under Lieutenant General Alexander Archer Vandergrift. The Marines landed in Floria, Gavutu, Guadalcanal, Tanambogo, and Tulagi, Solomon Islands. The overall commander was Vice Admiral Robert Lee Ghormley, South Pacific commander. *(Richard Tregaskis—Guadalcanal Diary)*

American pilot to shoot down a German fighter plane in World War II (a victory which was confirmed) was Second Lieutenant Sam F. Junkin of Natchez, Miss., who shot down a Focke-Wulf-190 ship over Dieppe, France, in a Commando-Ranger raid on August 19, 1942. Junkin was wounded and jumped from his disabled plane. He was picked up by a returning Commando barge. On the same date a similar plane was shot down by Frank A. Hill of the 31st Fighter Group, but it was listed as "probably destroyed," since observers did not see the plane hit the ground or explode in the air, or see the pilot bail out.

American ship sunk by a U-boat was the *Robin Moor*, 4,985 tons, operated by the Robin Line of New York, which sailed May 6, 1941, from New York City for Cape Town, South Africa, with 8 passengers and a crew of 38 under Captain Edward Myers. She was sunk May 21, 1941, in the South Atlantic, 400 miles south of the Cape Verde Islands and 900 miles due west of Monrovia, Liberia.

The First

WORLD WAR II—*Continued*

American territory occupied by the Japanese was the undefended island of Attu and the island of Kiska in the Western Aleutians, captured June 7, 1942. The capture was announced by the U.S. Navy on June 13, 1942. The islands were retaken by American forces May 1943.

American to land on French soil in World War II was Corporal Franklin M. Koons of Swea City, Iowa, one of the Rangers who accompanied Lieutenant Colonel Lord Lovat's Commandos on the Dieppe raid August 19, 1942. Koons destroyed a German 155 mm gun and was awarded the British Military Medal for "conspicuous gallantry and admirable leadership" on October 2, 1942.

Bombing on continental U.S. soil in World War II was made about 7:00 P.M. (PST) on Monday February 23, 1942, during President Franklin Delano Roosevelt's fireside war chat, by the Japanese submarine I-17, captained by Captain Kozo Nishino. The submarine, about a half-mile offshore, fired from 12 to 15 shots during 20 minutes at the Barnsdall Oil Refinery in Ellwood, Calif., about 12 miles west of Santa Barbara. No one was injured. One shell made a direct hit on the rigging and pumping equipment of an oil well, causing damage of about $500; other shells made crater holes, one of which was about 5 feet deep.

German ship captured in World War II by an American ship was the *Busko,* a 60-ton trawler, formerly Norwegian, which was captured at Mackenzie Bay, Greenland, on September 12, 1941, by the Coast Guard cutter *Northland,* captained by Commander Carl Christian von Paulsen. The *Busko* had entered U.S. waters without proper documentation and had radioed weather reports and other information to Germany. After being captured, the ship was sent under the escort of the Navy-manned U.S.S.*Bear* (Lieutenant Commander Joseph Gainard) to Commonwealth Pier, Boston, Mass., where her crew—20 men and 1 woman—was held without bail. *(Rex Ingraham—First Fleet)*

German submarine destroyed by an American pilot was the *U-656,* sunk off Cape Race, Newfoundland, on March 1, 1942, by Ensign William Tepuni, U.S. Naval Reserve, in a Lockhead-Hudson airplane of Squadron VP-82 based in Argentina.

German submarine sunk by a U.S. naval vessel was the *U-85,* sunk April 13-14, 1942, off Wimble Shoal, near Hatteras, N.C. by the destroyer *Roper* (DD-147) captained by Lieutenant Commander Hamilton Wilcox Howe.

Japanese airplane destroyed in World War II was a twin-engine bomber downed December 9, 1941, off Wake Island by a Grumman F4-F Wildcat fighter of the Marines.

The First

Japanese attack in World War II was made Sunday, December 7, 1941, against Pearl Harbor, Hawaii. The United States loss was 5 battleships, 3 destroyers, a minelayer, and a target vessel sunk, as well as many ships damaged. About 400 airplanes were destroyed. American casualties of the sneak attack totaled 2,117 killed, 1,272 wounded, and 960 missing.

Japanese balloon casualties occurred May 5, 1945, in the Bly-Lakeview area in Oregon, when Elsie Mitchell (Mrs. Archie Mitchell) and 5 children attempted to drag a Japanese balloon out of the woods. It exploded, killing all 6. On June 7, 1949, Congress awarded $5,000 to her husband as compensation for his loss (63 Stat. L. IIII), and $3,000 to the parents for the loss of each of the children: Edward Milian Engen, Jay Gifford, Ethel Jean Patzke, Richard Joe Patzke, and Sherman Shoemaker.

Japanese battleship sunk was the *Haruna,* sunk December 11, 1941, by the U.S. Air Forces off North Luzon in the Philippine Islands.

Japanese homeland bombardment by the U.S. Navy was made July 14, 1945, by the U.S. Pacific Fleet under the immediate tactical command of Rear Admiral John Franklin Shafroth. The battleships *Massachusetts, Indiana,* and *South Dakota,* the heavy cruisers *Chicago* and *Quincy,* and 9 destroyers bombed the iron works in the coast city of Kamaishi, Honshu, 275 miles northeast of Tokyo, Japan. Damage was inflicted on 342 airplanes, 4 ships, and 15 airfields.

Japanese submarine sunk by an American ship was the I-170 hit by a four-inch gun of the U.S.S. *Ward* on December 7, 1941, at Pearl Harbor, Hawaii.

Land victory without infantry was won June 11, 1943, when the Italian fortress on the island of Pantelleria in the Mediterranean Sea, about 70 miles southwest of Sicily, Italy, surrendered to the Northwest African Air Forces of the Anglo-American Air Command, which dropped 6,200 tons of bombs in over 5,000 sorties. The island was occupied 22 minutes after landing, Lieutenant General Carl Andrew Spaatz commanding.

Naval ace. *See under* Aviation—Pilot

Sea battle fought solely by air power was the Battle of the Coral Sea, which took place between U.S. Navy Task Force 17 and Vice Admiral Takeo Takagi's Japanese Carrier Striking Force, May 4-8, 1942. American planes took off from carriers 180 miles away from each other. The Japanese loss was 39 ships; the United States lost the aircraft carrier *Lexington* (CV-2).

Ship captain captured by a German U-boat crew was Henry Stephenson of Larchmont, N.Y., captain of the Grace Line's *Santa Rita,* who was removed from a lifeboat on July 9, 1942, about 500 miles south of Bermuda, while the lifeboat wa

The First

pulling away from its sinking vessel torpedoed after a U-boat attack. Stephenson was taken prisoner and was interned until repatriated February 1945, when he was 69 years old.

Warship convoy across the Atlantic Ocean was convoy HX-150, consisting of the destroyers *Dallas, Eberle, Ellis, Ericsson,* and *Upshur,* commanded by Captain Morton L. Deyo. The warships assumed charge on September 17, 1941, of 50 merchant ships that left Nova Scotia, Canada, on September 16, 1941.

WORLD WAR BABY. *See under* Births

WORSTED MILL. *See under* Wool

WOUND CHEVRON. *See* Army insignia

WOVEN-WIRE FENCE INDUSTRY. *See under* Wire

WRAPPING PAPER, PERFORATED. *See under* Paper

WRECKING CRANE. *See* Crane

WRENCH
Pipe or screw wrench (practical) was the Stillson wrench, invented by Daniel C. Stillson of Somerville, Mass., who obtained patent No. 184,993 on December 5, 1876. In 1869 Stillson had whittled a model out of wood.

Wrench patent was obtained August 17, 1835, by Solyman Merrick of Springfield, Mass.

WRESTLING
Intercollegiate wrestling association was formed April 7, 1905, at the University of Pennsylvania, Philadelphia, through the efforts of Leonard Mason, an instructor in gymnastics, who visited other eastern universities to seek members. The first tournament, held April 7, 1905, in the gymnasium of the University of Pennsylvania, was witnessed by over 1,000 spectators. Yale won, Columbia was second, Princeton third, and Pennsylvania fourth.

WRITER. *See* Author; Playwright (professional); Poet

WROUGHT IRON. *See under* Bridge; Building; Sash

X

X RAY
Fluoro-record reflector camera which made X-ray pictures in one-sixth the time previously required was announced November 18, 1950, by the Fairchild Camera & Instrument Corp., Jamaica, N.Y. The camera was used for gastrointestinal surveys.

The First

Photograph of a beam of 1-billion-volt X rays. *See under* Photograph

X-ray machine in the United States was exhibited January 18, 1896, at the Casino Chambers, New York City. Viewers were charged 25-cents admission to see the "Parisian sensation."

X-ray motion picture process by which pictures could be taken over a considerable period of time without danger of overexposing the patient to radiation was developed by Dr. Russell Hedley Morgan of Johns Hopkins Hospital, Baltimore, Md., and demonstrated on February 1, 1951.

X-ray motion pictures (successful) of the action of the human heart, stomach, diaphragm, lungs, etc., were made with an amateur motion picture camera set in front of a fluoroscopic screen by Drs. William Holmes Stewart, William Joseph Hoffman, and Francis Henshall Ghiselin, all of New York City. The pictures were exhibited October 2, 1937, at a convention of the American Roentgen Ray Society held in New York City.

X-ray of the entire body of a living person made by one exposure was taken by Dr. William James Morton of New York City in April 1897. The film was a coated single sheet 3 feet by 6 feet. The apparatus employed was a 12-inch induction coil whose primary was supplied from the 117-volt Edison current. At a revolution of the break wheel (the rate was 5,000 a minute), the coil afforded a free discharge of sparks across a 5-inch air gap. The Crookes tube employed was an ordinary focus tube; its vacuum at the start corresponded to a spark of 2 inches and gradually rose until at the end it corresponded to 8 inches. The distance of the tube from the sensitive film, made by the Eastman Kodak Company, Rochester, N.Y., was 4 feet 6 inches. The tube was run steadily for the first ten minutes; then the current was turned off several times a minute to allow it to cool. The total time consumed, including stoppages, was 30 minutes. The heavier regions of the body, such as the pelvis, spine, and thighs, were underexposed, while the thinner portions, such as the hands, were overexposed. (*Electrical Engineer. May 19, 1897*)

X-ray photograph was made January 12, 1896, by Dr. Henry Louis Smith, professor of physics and astronomy, Davidson College, Davidson, N.C. Smith obtained the hand of a corpse, fired a bullet into it, and then took a 15-minute exposure which, when developed, revealed the exact location of the bullet.

X-ray photograph of the entire body taken in a one-second exposure made under ordinary clinical conditions available to the average hospital or average radiographer, and the first in which a selective filter was used, was a full-length, full-size, one-piece radiograph of a living human body taken July 1, 1934, by Arthur Wolfram Fuchs of the

The First

X RAY—Continued

Eastman Kodak Company, Rochester, N.Y. The size of the film was 32 by 72 inches. The radiograph was exhibited by the Chicago Roentgen Society at the Century of Progress Exposition, Chicago, Ill.

X-ray photograph showing the complete arterial circulation in an adult individual was completed July 16, 1936, in Rochester, N.Y., by Dr. Edmond John Faris of the Wistar Institute of Anatomy and Biology, Philadelphia, Pa., and Arthur Wolfram Fuchs of the Medical Division, Eastman Kodak Company, Rochester, N.Y. A radio-opaque medium was injected into the arteries of a cadaver by Faris. Fuchs made several entire-body radiographs on film 32 by 72 inches, employing the following technical factors: 70 kilovolts, 10 milliamperes, 30 seconds of exposure at a distance of 12 feet. Ultra-speed X-ray intensifying screens, 32 by 72 inches, were also used in a large cassette made to accommodate the film and screen.

X-ray scanning system (commercial) to convert electronic information to visible X ray was the Pep-720 baggage X-ray system manufactured by the Princeton Electronic Products, Inc., New Brunswick, N.J. The first system installed and tested was ordered by the U.S. Army Picatinny Arsenal on August 9, 1971.

X-ray three-dimensional (stereo) fluoroscopic system was exhibited September 27, 1966, at the American Roentgen Ray Society at San Francisco, Calif., by the General Electric Company X ray Department of Milwaukee, Wis. (now called General Electric Medical Systems Division). The "stereo fluoricon" consisted of a single anode dual cathode X-ray tube, an image intensifier with polarizers, and a synchronized analyzer. The 3D image was observed through a viewing mirror without the use of special glasses. The first unit was installed at the University of Oregon Medical Center, Portland, Oreg., by Richard J. Kuhn on April 15, 1966. The development engineer was Joseph Quinn. It was primarily intended to be used in heart catherization. The selling price was $30,-000.

X-RAY FIELD HOSPITAL AUTOMOBILE. *See* Automobile: Field hospital automobile with X-ray equipment

Y

"Y" BRIDGE. *See* Bridge

YACHT. *See* Ship

YACHT, ICE. *See* Ice yacht

The First

YACHT CLUB was the New York Yacht Club, organized July 30, 1844, by four yachting enthusiasts in the cabin of John Cox Stevens' schooner *Gimcrack*. The first regular election of officers was held March 17, 1845, at which time Stevens was elected commodore, a post which he held until 1855. In 1846 a clubhouse was erected at the Elysian Fields, Hoboken, N.J. It was towed to Glen Cove, L.I., N.Y., in 1904 and officially reopened July 6, 1904. In 1848 the Secretary of the Navy allowed the vessels of the club—sloops and schooners—to proceed from port to port in the United States without entering or clearing at the Custom House, provided that they did not transport merchandise for pay (Act of August 7, 1848). The signal of the club was a pointed burgee, with a five-pointed white star in the center and two red stripes crossing on a field of blue. The Boston Yacht Club, founded in 1835, with Captain R. B. Forbes as commodore, was chiefly a fishing organization. It went out of existence in 1837. *(Charles A. Peverelly—Book of American Pastimes)*

YACHT RACE

Regatta of importance was held by the New York Yacht Club, New York City, July 16, 1845. The following contestants entered the competition: the *Cygnet*, 45 tons; the *Sybil*, 42 tons; the *Spray*, 37 tons; the *Newburg*, 33 tons; the *Minra*, 30 tons; the *Coquille*, 27 tons; the *Gimcrack*, 25 tons; the *Lancet*, 20 tons; and the *Ada*, 17 tons. The yachts raced in the waters of New York from Robbin's Reef to Bay Ridge, thence to Stapleton, thence to the Southwest Spit buoy, and then back to the starting point.

Yacht race across the Atlantic Ocean was held December 11, 1866. An agreement was entered into October 27, 1866, by which three contestants each put up a $30,000 purse, the winner to receive $90,000. The competing yachts were the *Henrietta*, 205 tons, owned by James Gordon Bennett, Jr.; the *Vesta*, 201 tons, owned by Pierre Lorillard; and the *Fleetwing*, 212 tons, owned by George Osgood. The *Henrietta* was the winner, making the trip in 13 days 22 hours from Sandy Hook, N.J., to Cowes, England. *(Charles A. Peverelly—Book of American Pastimes)*

Yacht race (international) was held August 22, 1851, under the auspices of the Royal Yacht Squadron around the Isle of Wight, a distance of 53 miles. The race was won by an American yacht, *America*, owned by a syndicate headed by Commodore John Cox Stevens of the New York Yacht Club. It was designed by George Steers and built by William Henry Brown of New York. It was 101 feet 9 inches over all, and 90 feet 3 inches at the waterline. It had a beam of 23 feet 11 inches. The foremast measured 79 feet 6 inches and the mainmast 81 feet. The total sail area was 5,263 square feet. It carried three sails: jib, foresail, and mainsail. It was planked with white oak and coppered below the water line. The *America* covered

The First

the course in 10 hours 37 minutes, defeating 14 other contestants. It received a trophy valued at 100 pounds sterling and known as the Queen's Cup, in honor of Queen Victoria. *(Herbert Lawrence Stone and Alfred Fullerton Loomis—Millions for Defense: A Pictorial History of the Races for the America's Cup)*

Yacht race (international) broadcast. *See under* Radio broadcast

"YANKEE DOODLE" verses were written in 1755 by Dr. Richard Shuckburgh, regimental surgeon of General Braddock, to accompany an ancient tune. The verses were written at Fort Crailo, Albany, N.Y., in derision of the "homely clad colonials," but later the song was taken up by the colonists themselves. The song was played at Yorktown at the surrender of Cornwallis. It was the first patriotic song to achieve national popularity. *(Burton Alva Konkle—Benjamin Chew)*

YARN (stretch). *See* Nylon: Nylon stretch yarn

YEAST

Compressed fresh yeast was introduced in 1868 by Charles Fleischmann, whose firm, Gaff, Fleischmann & Company, manufactured it in Riverside, near Cincinnati, Ohio.

Yeast preparation patent was No. 40,451, which was granted on November 3, 1863, to J. T. Alden of Cincinnati, Ohio, on "an improvement in the preparation of yeast."

YELLOW FEVER VACCINE. *See* Vaccine

YIDDISH NEWSPAPER. *See* Newspaper

YIDDISH PROFESSORSHIP was established on February 11, 1952, at Columbia University, New York City. The first incumbent was Uriel Weinreich, associate in Yiddish Language, Literature and Culture.

YOGURT

Yogurt dairy was the Colombo Dairy, Methuen, Mass., established in 1929 by Sarkis Colombosian. The first year about 3000-4000 quarts of yogurt were produced. At that time it was called *madzoon,* the Armenian name for yogurt.

YOUNG MEN'S CHRISTIAN ASSOCIATION

Young Men's Christian Association was organized on December 29, 1851, in Boston, Mass. (On December 9, 1851, a YMCA had been organized in Montreal, Canada.) The YMCA was patterned after a similar organization started in London on June 6, 1844. The first international convention was held in Boston, June 7, 1854. The first well-equipped gymnasium was opened in New York City in 1869, and in the same year the first separate boys' department was opened in Salem, Mass. *(Samuel Lowry—Historical Sketch of the Progress of the Young Men's Christian Associations in North America)*

The First

Young Men's Christian Association for black members was organized in Washington, D.C., in 1853 by Anthony Bowen and Jerome Johnson, who served respectively as president and secretary. The first paid secretary was William Alphaeus Hunton, a black, who received $800 a year for his services from the Norfolk, Va., YMCA in January 1888. *(Addie Waite Hunton—William Alphaeus Hunton)*

YOUNG MEN'S HEBREW ASSOCIATION was founded on March 22, 1874, in New York City. It was incorporated on September 15, 1875. The first president was Lewis May, who served from May 3, 1874, to February 15, 1876. The first building was opened October 10, 1874.

YOUNG WOMEN'S CHRISTIAN ASSOCIATION originated as a local organization in Boston, Mass., in 1866. The first president was Mrs. Henry Fowle Durant. In 1858 an organization called the Ladies Christian Association was formed in New York City, and a branch of this group was later called the YWCA. In 1871 the local eastern associations met in national convention in Hartford, Conn., and in 1886 a central group met in Lake Geneva, Wis. These two national organizations came together as the YWCA of the U.S. of A., of which the present National Board is the executive body. The first president of the national YWCA was Grace Hoadley Dodge of New York City, and the first convention of the present national organization was held in New York City December 5-6, 1906.

YOUNG WOMEN'S HEBREW ASSOCIATION was organized on February 6, 1902, in New York City. Mrs. Israel Unterberg was the founder and the first president. The first building used by the organization was at 1584 Lexington Avenue, New York City. *(Young Women's Hebrew Association —Annual Report 1903)*

YOUTH HOSTEL was opened December 27, 1934, in Northfield, Mass., as headquarters of the American Youth Hostels, Inc., incorporated March 15, 1934, in Hartford, Conn. The organization was the 18th group in the International Youth Hostels. Isabel and Monroe Smith were appointed directors of the American group. *(The Knapsack. November 1935)*

YOUTH'S LIBRARY. *See* Library

Z

ZINC

Underground mill for the separation of zinc and lead by the flotation process was completed in 1929 at the New Jersey Zinc Company's mine under Battle Mountain at Gilman, Colo. The mine was air-conditioned and fireproof and had its own

The First

ZINC—*Continued*
water system, an elevator, and 100 miles of steel track. Ore was hauled to a central point at the 450-foot level, where it was ground into small particles to enable the flotation milling process to separate the ore into zinc and lead concentrates.

Zinc was produced in 1835–1836 by John Hitz in the Arsenal at Washington, D.C. *(Heinrich Oscar Hofman—Metallurgy of Zinc and Cadmium)*

Zinc commercial production was undertaken at the Pennsylvania and Lehigh Zinc Company Mill, which was erected in Bethlehem, Pa., October 13, 1853, by Samuel Wetherill. The company was incorporated May 2, 1855. The zinc was obtained from calamine ores. *(Joseph Mortimer Levering—History of Bethlehem, Pa.)*

Zinc patent for the process of reducing zinc ore was No. 16,362, granted to Samuel Wetherill of Bethlehem, Pa., on January 6, 1857. On February 20, 1855, Wetherill received patent No. 12,418 for an apparatus for separating zinc white, and on November 13, 1855, patent No. 13,806 for the process of making zinc white. He patented a zinc white furnace on September 30, 1856 (No. 15,830). On January 7, 1868, he obtained patent No. 73,146 for the process of manufacturing white oxide of zinc.

Zinc sheet mill was erected in Bethlehem, Pa., and the first production begun in March 1865. *(Clifford Dyer Holley—Lead and Zinc in the United States)*

ZIONIST SOCIETY
Zionist national organization was the United American Zionists, formed October 22, 1897, in New York City by ten local societies. The first convention was held July 4, 1898, in New York City. Local Zionist societies, Chovevi (Hovevai) Zion or Hibat Zion (Love of Zion) groups, without political aims, had been formed as early as 1882 and had advocated Palestine colonization.

ZIP CODE. *See* Postal Service: Zone numbers

ZIPPER. *See* Fastening: Hookless fastening

ZITHER FACTORY
Zither factory was established by Franz Schwartzer in Washington, Mo., in 1866. In the first 20 years he sold about 3,000 zithers, ranging in price from $50 to $500. *(Eleanor B. MacClure—Early History of Washington, Mo.)*

ZOO
Twilight zoo was dedicated April 3, 1973, in Highland Park, Pittsburgh, Pa., by the Pittsburgh Zoological Society. The same degree of lighting prevailed day and night. It contained 6 ecological niches depicting both nocturnal and diurnal scenes, predator and prey, in groupings designed to reflect various areas of continents around the world.

The First

ZOOLOGICAL GARDEN
Barless zoological garden of naturalistic rock construction was started in 1915 at the City Park Zoo, Denver, Colo., and was completed in 1918 at a cost of $60,000. The materials used were colored concrete and steel. This "Mountain Habitat" was designed and supervised by Victor Borcherdt, the director of the zoo. This barless zoo was not a pit, the floors of the enclosures being on ground level or above the outside walkway.

Zoological garden was the Philadelphia Zoological Garden, Philadelphia, Pa., which was under the management of the Zoological Society of Philadelphia. The society was incorporated March 21, 1859. The garden was opened to the public July 1, 1874. Feature attractions were the bear pit and the lion house. *(Roger Conant—Official Illustrated Guide to the Philadelphia Zoological Garden)*

ZOOLOGICAL LABORATORY (U.S.)
Zoological laboratory (U.S.) for the study of human parasites was started August 16, 1902, by the Public Health Service simultaneously with the appointment of Dr. Charles Wardell Stiles as chief of the division of zoology at the Hygienic Laboratory (now the National Institutes of Health), Washington, D.C.

Zoological laboratory (U.S.) for the study of the parasites of livestock was opened August 1, 1886, in Washington, D.C., in the Bureau of Animal Industry of the Department of Agriculture. Dr. Cooper Curtice, the first person placed in charge of the work by the federal government, entered the service August 1, 1886. The appellation "zoological laboratory" was not applied, however, until June 3, 1891, when Dr. Charles Wardell Stiles was placed in charge, with Dr. Albert Hassall as his assistant. In 1901 the laboratory received the classification of a division. Dr. Brayton Howard Ransom was put in charge of the division June 1, 1903.

ZOOM LENS. *See* Lens: Lens to provide zoom effects

Index by Years

To obtain a complete account of the various items, the reader should consult the main body of the text. The **boldface** type shows the alphabetical heading under which each item may be found. If an item appears in the text under a general heading, the specific heading is noted below after the general heading.

1588

Map—map of a city—St. Augustine, Fla.

1602

Discovery—discovery of New England by an Englishman—B. Gosnold—landed—South Dartmouth, Mass.—May 15

1604

Colonist—colonial white settlement (north of Florida)—Calais, Me.

1607

Catholic Bishop—visited Florida
Colonial Government—colonial council in America—Jamestown, Va.—May 13
Colonist—English settlement in America—Jamestown, Va.—May 13
Holiday—Thanksgiving Day service—Phippsburg, Me.—Aug. 9
Protestant Episcopal Church—Protestant Episcopal Church—established—first Eucharist—May 9
Rebellion—rebellion (colonial)—led by George Kendall—Jamestown, Va.
Ship—prefabricated ship—launched—at entrance to Chesapeake Bay, Va.—May 18
Ship—ship built by the English in the American colonies—launched—Maine
Slander Proceedings—instituted—John Robinson—Jamestown, Va.—Sept. 17
War (colonial)—Indian war of importance fought by English colonists—Virginia—May 27

1608

Book—book written in America—author, Captain John Smith—published in England
Bottle—blown
Glass Bead—manufactured—Jamestown, Va.
Glass Factory—glass factory—established—Jamestown, Va.—Oct.
History—history of a colony—*A True Relation of ... Occurrences ... in Virginia*, by Th. Watson—published in London, England

1609

Animals—sheep—imported—Jamestown, Va.
Maize—Indian corn grown—Jamestown, Va.
Wedding—wedding in Virginia—Anne Burras and John Laydon

1610

Physician—doctor in the colony of Virginia—Lawrence Bohune—arrived

1611

Presbyterian Church—Presbyterian Church—established—Virginia

1612

Tobacco—tobacco—cultivation—Jamestown, Va.

1613

Navy—naval expedition (colonial)—Samuel Argal
War (colonial)—colonial warfare between England and France for the possession of North America

1614

Lottery—of importance—Virginia—June 26
Ship—decked ship—launched—New York—*Onrust*—A. Blok

1616

Epidemic—smallpox epidemic

1617

College—college proposed—Henrico, Va.

1618

Comet—comet recorded—November

1619

Blue Law—blue law—enacted—Virginia
Iron—iron works—erected—Falling Creek, Va.
Legislative Assembly—Jamestown, Va.—July 30
Slavery—slaves—introduced—Jamestown, Va.—Aug.

1620

Births—child born of English parents in New England—Peregrine White—born on *Mayflower* of Cape Cod harbor—Nov. 20
Congregational Church—Congregational Church founded—Plymouth, Mass.
Corn (maize)—corn (maize) found by British settlers—Provincetown, Mass.—Nov. 16
Lead—mined—Falling Creek, Va.
Physician—doctor in New England—Dr. Samuel Fuller—arrived—Mass.—Dec. 21
Water Power—water power development grant—South Berwick, Me.

1621

Duel—duel—E. Leister and E. Dotey—Plymouth Mass.—June 18
Furs—exported—Robert Cushman—Massachusetts—Dec. 13
Military Leader—Miles Standish—Massachusett
Sermon Printed (American)—delivered—Plymouth, Mass.—Robert Cushman—[published—Boston, Mass.—1724]
Treaty—colonial treaty with the Indians—Plymouth, Mass.—April 1
Wedding—wedding in New England—Edward Winslow and Susanna White—May 22

1622

American Indians—massacre of white people by American Indians—Jamestown, Va.—March 22

Potato—introduced—Jan.

Prohibition—prohibition enforcement officers—authorized—Virginia—June 21

1623

Breach of Promise Suit—Virginia—June 14

Leather—leather tanning—Plymouth, Mass.—Experience Miller

Liquor Reform Movement—New York City

Silk—silk culture—started

Temperance Law (colonial)—Virginia—March 5

1624

Animals — cows — imported — Massachusetts — March

Baptism—black child baptized in the English colonies—William Tucker—Jamestown, Va.

Blue Law—blue law regulating gambling—Virginia

1625

Road—road pavement—laid—Pemaquid, Me.

1626

Book—profane poetry translation prepared in the colonies to be published—Virginia

Forestry legislation—colonial forestry legislation—Mar. 29

1627

Oil—oil spring—recorded—Cuba, N.Y.—July 18

1628

Deportation—Thomas Morton—deported—June 9

Fur Trading Post—established—Augusta, Me.

Reformed Church (Dutch)—established—New York City—1628

Shoe—manufactured—Massachusetts—Thomas Beard

1629

Agriculture—crop limitation law—enacted—Virginia—Oct. 16

Apples—imported—John Winthrop

Brick Kiln—established—Salem, Mass.

Fishery (commercial)—established—Medford, Mass.—April 17

Game Law—game law (colonial)—enacted—Virginia—March 24

Horse—horses—imported

1630

Execution—execution in America—John Billington—hanged—Plymouth, Mass.—Sept. 30

Pork—introduced—Massachusetts—John Winthrop

Gambling Legislation (colonial)—enacted—Boston, Mass.—March 22

Popcorn—introduced

Salt—salt works—established—Virginia

1631

Election—accredited colonial election—Massachusetts—May 18

Fire Prevention Legislation—enacted—Cambridge, Mass.—March 17

Militia—militia—established—Boston, Mass.—April 12

1632

Pirate—Dixie Bull—looted Bristol, Me.

Road—highway legislation (colonial)—James City, Va.—Sept. 4

Tobacco—tobacco tax (colonial)—Massachusetts—enacted—Oct. 3

Unitarian Church—Unitarian church building—erected—Boston, Mass.

Windmill — windmill — erected — Cambridge, Mass.

1633

Building—brick building—New York City

School—school in America—New York City

1634

Bridge—bridge—erected—Dorchester, Mass.

Clubwoman—Anne Hutchinson—arrived—Boston, Mass.—Sept. 18

Educational Endowment—established—Virginia—Benjamin Syms

Tax—property tax law (colonial)—enacted—Massachusetts—May 14

Treason—treason trial (colonial)—Virginia—May 7

1635

Cod Liver Oil—described

Hurricane—recorded—Plymouth, Mass.—Aug. 15

Jury—grand jury—Newe Towne, Mass.—convened Sept. 1

Public School—public school with a continuous existence—established—Feb. 13

War—naval battle by white men in America—St. Mary's, Md.—April 23

1636

College—college—Harvard College—Cambridge, Mass.—established—Sept. 8

Insurance—government insurance—enacted—Plymouth Colony

Meat Packer—William Pynchon—warehouse—Springfield, Mass.

Pension—pension act—Massachusetts—Pilgrims

1637

Clubwoman—Anne Hutchinson—banished—Massachusetts—Nov. 17

Congregational Church—Congregational Church council—Cambridge, Mass.—Aug. 30

Conscription—colonial conscription legislation—enacted—Boston, Mass.—April 18

Prostitute—recorded

Quakers—Synod of Quakers—Cambridge, Mass.—Sept. 9-Oct. 2

Synod—synod—Cambridge, Mass.

1638

Almanac — almanac — published — Cambridge, Mass.

Cloth—cloth mill—John Pearson—Rowley, Mass.

Curfew Bell—introduced—New York City

Earthquake—earthquake description—Plymouth, Mass.—June 1

Military Organization—military organization—Ancient and Honorable Artillery Company—Boston, Mass.—chartered—March 13

Swedes—arrived—Delaware—March

1639

Agriculture—crop surplus destruction—Virginia—Jan. 6

Annulment—annulment by court decree—James Luxford—Boston, Mass.—Dec. 3

Autopsy—officially recorded autopsy—Salem, Mass.—Sept.

Baptist Church—Baptist Church—established—Providence, R.I.

Bookseller—of importance—Hezekiah Usher—Cambridge, Mass.

Canal—canal for creating water power—construction ordered—Dedham, Mass.—March 25

Constitution—constitution—"fundamental orders"—Connecticut—Jan. 14

Lawyer—lawyer disbarred—Thomas Lechford—Massachusetts—Sept. 3

Medical Legislation—medical law—Virginia—Oct. 21

Ordnance—gunpowder mill—Pecoit, Mass.—land grant—June 6

Post Office—post office (colonial)—established—Boston, Mass.—Nov. 5

Printing—document printed in America—*Oath of a Free Man*—Cambridge, Mass.—March

Printing Press—printing press—imported—Cambridge, Mass.—March

Public School—public school supported by direct taxation—established—May 20

1640

Author—woman author—Anne Bradstreet—poems published

Book—book (full-size)—published—Cambridge, Mass.

Election—election in defiance of the Royal Courts—Wethersfield, Conn.—April 11

Hebrew Type—used—Cambridge, Mass.

Lutheran Church—Lutheran pastor—Reorus Torkillus—landed—April 17

Music Book—hymnbook—published—Cambridge, Mass.

1641

Children's Book—published—*Milk for Babes*—Cambridge, Mass.

Fair—annual fair—authorized—New York City—Sept. 30

Patent—patent granted by the colonies—Massachusetts—Samuel Winslow

Potter—John Pride—Salem, Mass.

1642

City (incorporated)—Georgeana, Me.—March 1

College—college—Harvard College, Cambridge, Mass.—commencement—Sept. 23

Degrees (academic and honorary)—Bachelor Arts degree—conferred—Harvard College-Cambridge, Mass.—Sept. 23

Education—compulsory education law—enacte—Massachusetts—June 14

Labor Law—convict labor law—enacted—Mar 2

Thesis Directory—published—Cambridge, Mas

1643

Catholic Priest—native Catholic priest—join Jesuit order

Colonial Government—colonial governme union—organized—Boston, Mass.—May 10

Dictionary—American Indian-English dictiona—published

Divorce—divorce—to Anne Clarke—Bosto Mass.

Extradition—extradition—agreement—New Er land Confederation

Iron—iron works (successful)—constructed John Winthrop, Jr.

Spelling Book—spelling book—published—Ca bridge, Mass.

Wool—fulling mill—established—Rowley, Mas

1644

Branding Legislation—enacted—Connecticut Feb. 5

Legislature—legislature with two chambers Massachusetts—March 7

Whaling—whaling (systematic)—Southampto L.I., N.Y.—undertaken—March 7

1645

Brass and Iron Foundry—opened—Joseph Jenc—Lynn, Mass.

Lutheran Church—Lutheran Church building dedicated—Essington, Pa.—Sept. 4

School—endowed school—established—R bury, Mass.

School Committee—elected—Dorchester, Mas

1646

ounty—authorized—James City, Va.—Oct. 5

atent—machine patent—granted—Massachusetts—Joseph Jencks—March 6

ynod—synod (ecumenical)—opened—Cambridge, Mass.

1647

uarantine—quarantine legislation (colonial)—enacted—Massachusetts—March

ice—imported—Virginia

chool Legislation—school law (compulsory)—enacted—Nov. 11

itchcraft Execution—Achsah Young—Massachusetts—May 27

oman Suffrage—woman suffrage advocate—Margaret Brent—demanded vote—June 24

1648

bor Union—labor organization—authorized—Boston, Mass.—Oct. 18

tin Book—written in New England—published—London, England

wbook—compilation of colonial laws—published—Cambridge, Mass.

ynod—synod (ecumenical)—Cambridge, Mass.—adjourned

1649

ection Law—fraudulent election law (colonial)—enacted—Warwick, R.I.—May 22

edical Legislation—law to regulate the practice of medicine (colonial)—enacted—Massachusetts—May 3

issionary Society—missionary society (colonial)—chartered—July

ligious Liberty Act (colonial)—established—Maryland—April

1650

rporation—corporate body—Cambridge, Mass.—May 30

pedition—expedition—of Englishmen to cross the Allegheny Mountains—commenced—Aug. 27

n—exportation of iron

und (enclosure for animals)—authorized—Connecticut—May

1651

vigation Act—enacted

1652

ney—dies for coins in America—mint established—Boston, Mass.—May 27

very—law regulating slavery—enacted—Warwick, R.I.—May 18

ffic Regulation—traffic law—enacted—New York City—June 27

Water—municipal water supply system—built—Boston, Mass.

1654

Bridge—toll bridge—erected—Rowley, Mass.

Fire Engine—fire engine—manufactured—Lynn, Mass.—Joseph Jencks

Jews—Jew—arrived—New York City—Jacob Barsimson—Aug. 22

Orphanage — orphanage — established — New York City—June

1655

Jewish Congregation—Jewish Congregation—Shearith Israel—New York City—established

1656

Cemetery—Jewish burial plot—New York City

Jury—jury composed of women—Patuxent, Md.—Sept. 22

Physician—Jewish doctor—Jacob Lumbrozo—Maryland—Jan. 24

Quakers—Quakers to arrive in America—Massachusetts—July

1657

Autopsy—autopsy and verdict of a coroner's jury—recorded—Maryland—Sept. 24

College Student—college student to work his way through college—Z. Brigden

Jews—Jew to win all the rights and perform all the duties of citizenship—Asser Levy—April 20

Road—stone pavement—laid—New York City

Shoe Measuring Stick—introduced

1659

Fire Department—fire department established by municipal action—New York City

1660

American Indian Church—church for American Indians in New England—Natick, Mass.

Quakers—Quakers' annual meeting—Scituate, Mass.

1661

Bible—Bible in an American Indian language—John Eliot—New Testament—Cambridge, Mass.—translation finished

Medal—medals known to have been presented by the colonists to friendly American Indians—authorized—Virginia

School—evening school—established—New York City

1662

Book Auction—authorized—New York City—April 18

Lime—manufactured—Providence, R.I.—Jan. 27

Poet—American poet—Benjamin Tompson—graduated—Cambridge, Mass.

1663

Bible—Bible in an American Indian language—published—John Eliot
Book Binder—John Ratliffe—Massachusetts
Road—hard-surfaced road—Pahaquarry Mines, N.J., to Kingston, N.Y.—completed

1664

Citizenship—naturalization act—New York—March 12

1665

Book—book privately printed—*Communion of Churches*—Cambridge, Mass.
College Student—American Indian to graduate from college—Caleb Cheeshahteaumuck—Harvard College, Cambridge, Mass.
Horse Race—horse race—on a regular basis—Hempstead Plains, N.Y.
Play (drama)—play given by nonprofessional actors—Accomac (Accawmack), Va.—Aug. 27

1666

Brokerage—financial "corner"—New York City
Grammar—American Indian grammar—published—Cambridge, Mass.

1667

Cyclone—cyclone recorded—Jamestown, Va.—Aug. 27

1669

Engraving—engraving—woodcut—John Foster—April 22
History—history of New England—*New England's Memoriall*—published—Cambridge, Mass.
Primer—primer in an American Indian dialect—*Indian Primer*—published—Cambridge, Mass.
Rebellion—rebellion of colonists against the English—Marcus Jacobson—condemned—Dec. 20

1670

American Indians—American Indian preacher of Christianity—Hiacoomes—ordained—Aug. 22

1671

Baptist Church—Seventh Day Baptist Church—organized—Newport, R.I.

1672

Copyright Law—copyright law—passed—Massachusetts—May 15
Tax—tax on the American colonies without their consent

1673

Coal—coal—discovered—Louis Hennepin
Governor—native-born governor of New Englan —Josiah Winslow—elected
Postal Service—postal route—New York and Bos ton—service commenced—Jan. 22

1674

Horse Race—horse race prohibition legislation— Massachusetts

1675

American Indians—American Indian chief (wom an)—Queen Anne
Catholic Holy Orders—conferred—St. Augustin Fla.—Aug. 24
Corporation—commercial corporation—Ne York—Jan. 8

1676

Court-Martial—court-martial trial—Newport, R —Aug. 24
Fire—fire of serious consequence—Boston, Mas —Nov. 27
Insane Patient's Maintenance Act—Upland Cou Delaware County, Pa.
Prison—prison—constructed—Nantucket, Mass

1677

Map—map made in the United States publishe in a book—Boston, Mass.
Medical Book—medical pamphlet—published Boston, Mass.

1679

Ship—Great Lakes commercial vessel—*Le Gr fon*—sailed—Aug. 7
Trust—manufacturers' price regulation agre ment—New York City—Dec. 17

1680

Pottery—pottery—established—Burlington, N.J

1681

Shorthand Report—of a trial—St. John's, Md. Nov. 15

1682

Educational Trust Fund—created—Burlingt N.J.
Freemasons—Mason—arrived—John Skene Burlington, N.J.
Tornado—tornado of which there is any record New Haven, Conn.—June 10

1683

Architect—landscape architect—John R arrived—New York City—Dec. 19

Bible Concordance—Bible concordance published—Cambridge, Mass.

Labadist Community—established—Bohemia Manor, Md.

Mennonites — Mennonites — arrived — Philadelphia, Pa.—Oct. 6

Science Association—scientific society—Boston Philosophical Society founded

1685

Impeachment—impeachment—Nicolas More—Philadelphia, Pa.—June 2

1686

Church of England—Church of England organized in New England

1687

Knighthood—knighthood conferred on a native-born American—William Phips—June 28

Lawbook—lawbook—William Penn—published —Philadelphia, Pa.

Tax—inheritance tax (colonial)—Virginia

1688

Slavery—slavery protest—Philadelphia, Pa.—Feb. 18

1689

Newspaper—newspaper—broadside—published- —Cambridge, Mass.

Schoolbook—*New England Primer*—published— Boston, Mass.

1690

Indigo—planted—South Carolina

Loan—state loan—authorized—Massachusetts— Dec. 10

Money—paper money—issued—Massachusetts —Feb. 3

Newspaper—newspaper publisher—Benjamin Harris—*Publick Occurrances*—published— Boston, Mass.—Sept. 25

Paper Mill—built—William Rittenhouse—Philadelphia, Pa.

Play (drama)—play of note written by an American and acted in America—performed—Cambridge, Mass.

Theological Treatise—F. D. Pastorius—published —Philadelphia, Pa.

Watermark—William Rittenhouse—Philadelphia, Pa.

1691

Treason—American colonist hanged for treason —Jacob Leisler—hanged—New York City— May 16

1692

Advertisement—patent medicine advertisement—*Boston Almanack*

Degrees (academic and honorary)—Doctor of Sacred Theology degree—granted—Cambridge, Mass.—Sept. 5

Postal Service—parliamentary act to establish a post office

Postmaster—postmaster general (colonial)—Andrew Hamilton—appointed—April 4

1693

College—college charter granted by the crown— College of William and Mary—Feb. 8

College—college proposed—College of William and Mary—incorporated—Feb. 8

Police—police uniforms—authorized—New York City—July 8

1694

Ancient Mystical Order Rosae Crucis—established—Philadelphia, Pa.

College—college to receive a coat of arms from the College of Heralds—May 14

Lutheran Church—Lutheran services in English— Philadelphia, Pa.

Volcano—volcano in eruption in America for which a date can be established—California

1695

Wool—worsted mill—Boston, Mass.

Workmen's Compensation—workmen's compensation agreement—Jan. 26

1696

Book—book intended for circulation in the English colonies—printed

Woman—woman printer—Dinah Nuthead—Annapolis, Md.—petition—May 5

1697

Book Catalog—college book catalog—Harvard— printed by Bartholomew Green and John Allen —Boston, Mass.

Bridge—stone bridge—Germantown, Pa.

Fire Department—fire department to be paid— New York City

Woman—heroine—publicly rewarded—Hannah Duston—captured—Haverhill, Mass.

1698

Capitol—statehouse—Williamsburg, Va.

Library—library—established—Charleston, S.C.

Map—road map for public use—printed—John Tulley—Boston, Mass.

1699

Chimes—chimes and bells—manufactured—Benjamin Hanks—Plymouth, Mass.

1700

Organ—organs imported—Port Royal and Philadelphia, Pa.

1701

Engraving—engraving of any artistic merit—Thomas Emmes—published—Boston, Mass.

1703

Business Manual—*Young Secretary's Guide*—published—Boston, Mass.
Lutheran Church—Lutheran pastor ordained in America—Justus Falckner—ordained—Nov. 24

1704

Advertisement—advertisement—Boston, Mass.—*News-Letter*—May 1
Freemasons—Mason (native-born)—Jonathan Belcher
Newspaper—newspaper (successful)—Boston, Mass. *News-Letter*—April 17

1705

Book—miniature book—*A Wedding Ring*—published—Boston, Mass.
Copper Mine—worked—Granby, Conn.
Poem—poem (printed)—Boston, Mass.—Dec. 24
Presbyterian Presbytery—assembled—Philadelphia, Pa.

1706

Customhouse—Yorktown, Va.

1707

Artist—woman painter

1708

Mennonites—Mennonite church meetinghouse—built—Philadelphia, Pa.

1709

Copper Mine—company formed—Granby, Conn.
Grammar—Latin grammar textbook—published—Boston, Mass.
Hospital—insane detention home—erected—Philadelphia, Pa.

1710

Agricultural Book—agricultural book—*The Husbandman's Guide*—published—Boston, Mass.
Farrier's Guide—published—Boston, Mass.
Forest—community forest—Newington, N.H.
Iron—iron slitting mill—established—Milton, Mass.

1711

Whale—sperm whale—captured

1712

Calico—printery—established—Boston, Mass.

1713

Book Auction Catalog—book auction catalog—announced—May 18
Paleontology Report—prepared—Cotton Mathe

1714

Play (drama)—printed American play—*Androboros*—published—New York City
Ship—schooner built in America—launched—Gloucester, Mass.

1715

Book—Book of Common Prayer (in the Mohaw Indian language)—New York City
Indians—Indian league of nations—Tuscaror joined
Lighthouse—lighthouse authorized—Massach setts—July 23
Patent—English patent granted to a resident America—Thomas Masters—Nov. 25
Whaling—whaling expedition—sailed—Na tucket, Mass.

1716

Animals—lion—exhibited—Boston, Mass.—Nc 26
Lighthouse—lighthouse—erected—Little Bre ster Island, Mass.—Sept. 14
Theater—theater—land leased—William Levir ston—Nov. 5

1717

Book Auction Catalog—book auction print catalog—sale—July 2

1718

Theater—theater—built—Williamsburg, Va.

1719

Arithmetic—arithmetic—printed in the colonie
Aurora Borealis—recorded—Dec. 11
Jewish Book—Jewish book of Jewish authors published in America—*The Wars of the Je*—reprint of 3rd ed.—Samuel Kneeland a Nicholas Buttolph—Boston, Mass.
Potato—potato cultivation—Derry, N.H.

1720

American Indian School—American Ind school (permanent)—established—Willia burg, Va.

1721

Animals—camel imported—Boston, Mass.—vertised—Oct. 2

t Commission (public)—work ordered—Prince Georges County, Md.—Sept. 5

surance—fire insurance agent—John Copson—Philadelphia, Pa.—advertised—May 25

usic Book—music book printed with bars—published

usic Book—vocal instruction book—John Tufts—Boston, Mass.—published

ewspaper—newspaper editorial apology—*American Weekly Mercury*—published—April 20

accination for smallpox—inoculations introduced—Zabdiel Boylston—June 26

1722

t Commission (public)—work completed—Prince Georges County, Md.—Nov. 26

vinity Professor—E. Wigglesworth—appointed—Cambridge, Mass.—Jan. 24

1723

ptist Church—German Baptists—immersion—Philadelphia—Dec. 25

ok Catalog—printed library catalog in book form—Harvard College, Cambridge, Mass.—published—Boston, Mass.

dical Book—hydrotherapy book in English—*The Curiosities of Common Water*, by John Smith—reprinted—Philadelphia, Pa.

ysician—doctor to receive an honorary medical degree—Daniel Turner—Sept. 11

1724

ammar—English grammar by an American—Hugh Jones—published—London

vees—built—New Orleans, La.

mon Printed (American)—Robert Cushman—eprinted—Boston, Mass.

1725

erican Indians—scalping of American Indians y white men—New Hampshire—Feb. 20

urance Book—insurance proposal—*Ways and Means . . .*—published—Philadelphia, Pa.

rary—library building—used exclusively as a brary—Philadelphia, Pa.

1726

iography—bibliography of theological and blical literature—published—Boston, Mass.

k—book of folio size—*Compleat Body of ivinity . . .*—published—Boston, Mass.

1727

vent—convent—permanently established—ew Orleans, La.—mass offered—Aug. 9

ught—recorded—New England—April

raver—mezzotint—Peter Pelham

1728

Botanic Garden—John Bartram—Philadelphia, Pa.

German Book—German book printed in America—J. C. Beissel—published—Philadelphia, Pa.

Shorthand Book—published

Steel—steel—manufactured—Simsbury, Conn.

1729

Arithmetic—American arithmetic—Isaac Greenwood—published

Catholic Nuns—nun who professed her vows in the United States—Sister St. Stanislas Hachard—New Orleans, La.—vows—March 15

College—college to have a full faculty—William and Mary—Williamsburg, Va.

Engraving—mezzotint engraving of an American maritime print—William Burgis

Golf Clubs (or golf sticks)—golf clubs (or golf sticks)—mentioned

Jewish Congregation—Jewish congregation—foundation stones of synagogue—laid—Sept. 8

Newspaper—newspaper serial story—*Pennsylvania Gazette*

1730

Algebra Book—algebra book—*Arithmetic*—Pieter Venima—published—New York City

Bible Concordance—Welsh concordance of the Bible—published—Philadelphia, Pa.

Freemasons—Provincial grand master (Masonic)—Daniel Coxe—deputized—June 5

Hemp Exportation—to England

Horse—thoroughbred horse—imported—Bulle Rock

Jewish Congregation—Jewish congregation—synagogue consecrated—April 8

Quadrant—invented—Thomas Godfrey

1731

Catholic Nuns—nun who was born in the United States—Mary Turpin

Library—circulating library—formed—Philadelphia, Pa.—July 1

Medical Book—medical catalog—*A Short Treatise of the Virtues of Dr. Bateman's Pectoral Drops*—originally printed in London—reprinted—J. P. Zenger—New York City

Music—concert—Boston, Mass.—Dec. 30

Schwenkfelder—George Schultz—arrived—Philadelphia, Pa.

1732

Fishing Club—Schuylkill Fishing Company—founded—Philadelphia, Pa.

Librarian—librarian—to be paid for his service—Louis Timothee—hired—Nov. 14

Newspaper—German newspaper—*Philadelphische Zeitung*—published—May 6

Planetarium—planetarium or orrery—imported—Cambridge, Mass.

Play (drama)—play acted by professional players
—New York City—Dec. 6

1733

Animals—bear (white)—exhibited—Jan. 18
Communistic Society—communistic society—
J. C. Beissel—Lancaster, Pa.
Epidemic—influenza epidemic
Freemasons—Masonic lodge to work under a
regular charter—St. John's Lodge, Boston,
Mass.—established—July 30
Language Instruction—French instruction—Cam-
bridge, Mass.
Map—war map—published—New York City—
Dec. 24
Newspaper—political newspaper—*New York
Weekly Journal*—established—J. P. Zenger—
Nov. 5

1734

Advertisement—magician's advertisement—New
York City—March 18
Fencing Book—*A Compleat System on Fencing*
—published—Williamsburg, Va.
Fish Protection—fish legislation—New York City
—May 28
Masonic Book—*Constitutions of the Freemasons*
—published—Philadelphia, Pa.
Moravian—George Boehnisch—arrived—Sept. 22
Physician—American-born doctor—graduated
from a medical college abroad—William Bull—
Aug. 18
Slate—for roofing material—obtained—Delta,
Pa., and Cardiff, Md.

1735

Agricultural Experiment Station—agricultural ex-
periment farm—Savannah, Ga.
Book—translated classic published—Phila-
delphia, Pa.
Grammar—Hebrew grammar—*Grammar of the
Hebrew Tongue*—published—Boston, Mass.
Insurance—fire insurance company—organized
—Charleston, S.C.—subscriptions received—
Jan. 1
Logic Book—*Compendium Logicae*—published—
Boston, Mass.
Medical Society—medical society—Boston,
Mass.
Moravian Bishop—David Nitschmann—conse-
crated—Germany—March 13
Moravian Church—built—Savannah, Ga.
Opera—opera performed in America—Charles-
ton, S.C.—Feb. 18
Revival Meeting—of importance—Jonathan Ed-
wards
Silk—silk exportation—from Savannah, Ga.
Tile—brick roofing tile—manufactured—Mont-
gomery County, Pa.

1736

Medical Book—pleurisy book—*An Essay on th[e]
Pleurisy,* by John Tennent—printed by Willia[m]
Parks—Williamsburg, Va.
Medical Book—scarlet fever report—Willia[m]
Douglass—published—Boston, Mass.
Moravian Bishop—David Nitschmann—arrive[d]
—Georgia
Newspaper—newspaper published south of th[e]
Potomac River—*Virginia Gazette*—William[s]
burg, Va.—Aug. 5
Sunday School—Protestant Sunday school-
Christ Church—Savannah, Ga.
Theater—theater designed solely for theatric[al]
purposes—New Theatre—Charleston, S.C.
opened Feb. 12

1737

Greenhouse—erected—Andrew Faneuil—Bo[s]
ton, Mass.
Money—copper coins—minted—Granby, Conn[.]
Music Society—music society of importance [(musi]
cal)—Charleston, S.C.—organized

1738

Puppet Show—New York City—Feb. 12
Weather Observations—weather observatio[ns]
systematically recorded—John Lining[—]
Charleston, S.C.—Jan.

1739

Astronomer—astronomer of note in the Americ[an]
colonies—John Winthrop—sunspot observ[a]
tions—April 19
German Book—German book printed in Germ[an]
type in America—published—Philadelphia, [Pa.]
Iron—iron casting—Joseph Mallinson—Dusbo[ro]
Pa.
Slavery—insurrection of black slaves—So[uth]
Carolina
Wallpaper—wallpaper—manufactured—Philad[el]
phia, Pa.

1740

Bookplate—Nathaniel Hurd—Boston, Mass.
Marine Corps—Marine corps—organized—N[ew]
York
Organ—organ built in the U.S.—installed—Tri[ni]
ty Church—New York City
Orphanage—orphanage with a continuous ex[is]
tence—founded—Bethesda Home—Savann[ah]
Ga.
Tinware Manufacturers—tinware manufactur[ed]
—Berlin, Conn.
Umbrella—used—Windsor, Conn.

1741

Periodical—magazine published in Americ[a—]
American Magazine—Philadelphia, Pa.—F[eb.]
13
Strike—strike—New York City

1742

Cookbook — cookbook — published — Williamsburg, Va.

Moravian Easter Service—Bethlehem, Pa.

Music Book—German songbook published in America—*Ausbund, das ist*—Christoph Sauer—Germantown, Pa.

School—school for Protestant girls—established—Philadelphia, Pa.

Stove—stove—for heating—invented—Benjamin Franklin

1743

Advertisement—double-column advertisement—New York *Weekly Journal*—New York City—July 18

Automaton—automaton—imported from England—May 3

Bible—Bible printed in German—published—Philadelphia, Pa.

Fishing Treatise—published—Boston, Mass.

Periodical—sectarian magazine—*The Christian History*—published—Boston, Mass.—March 5

Planetarium—planetarium or orrery built in America—New Haven, Conn.

Religious Publication—religious journal—*The Christian History*—Boston, Mass.—March 5

Science Association—scientific society of importance—American Philosophical Society—organized

1744

Orchestra—symphony orchestra—Bethlehem, Pa.

1745

Carillon—carillon—installed—Old North Church—Boston, Mass.

Knighthood—knighthood conferred on a native-born American for military leadership—Sir William Pepperell—Sept. 23

Stereotype—stereotype printing—Benjamin Mecom—Philadelphia, Pa.

1746

College—college charter granted by a governor or acting governor with only the assent of his council—Princeton, N.J.—Oct. 22

Iron—rolling mill—established—Chester, Pa.

1747

Lawyers' Association (state)—New York Bar Association—formed

Textbook printed in America—Thomas Dilworth—*A New Guide to the English Tongue*—reprinted—Philadelphia, Pa.

1748

Candle Factory—Newport, R.I.

1748 (continued)

College—college charter granted by a governor or acting governor with only the assent of his council—first commencement—Nov. 9

Lutheran Church—Lutheran services in English—Lutheran synod—held—Aug. 26

1749

Academy—Academy and College of Philadelphia—founded

Electric Cooking Experiment—Benjamin Franklin—Philadelphia, Pa.

Lightning Rod—invented—Benjamin Franklin—Philadelphia, Pa.

Waxworks Museum—opened—James Wyatt—New York City—June

1750

Colonist—civilian settlement west of the Allegheny Mountains—Barbourville, Ky.—April 23

Medical Book—dissection essay—New York City

Opera—opera performed by a professional visiting troupe—*The Beggar's Opera*—New York City—Dec. 3

Orchestra—orchestra in a theater—New York City

Play (drama)—Shakespearean play—*King Richard III*—New York City—March 5

Teaching Methods Book—*Schul-ordnung*—completed—Aug. 3

Theatrical Advance Publicity Man—Robert Upton—arrived—New York City

1751

Academy—Academy and College of Philadelphia—Philadelphia, Pa.—opened—Aug. 13

Animals—monkey trained to perform—exhibited—New York City—Feb. 25

Cricket Tournament—cricket match—New York City—May 1

Grammar—Spanish grammar—*A Short Introduction to the Spanish Language,* by Garrat Noel—printed—New York City

Manual Training—school to offer courses in manual training—opened—Dec. 1

Play (drama)—benefit performance—New York City—Jan. 7

Sugar—sugarcane—imported—Louisiana

1752

Catholic Nuns—nun who was born in the United States—Mary Turpin—profession of faith—Jan. 31

Hospital—hospital in America—Pennsylvania Hospital—opened—Philadelphia, Pa.—Feb. 11

Insurance—fire insurance company to receive a charter—Philadelphia Contributionship for the Insurance of Houses—first policy—June 1

Lightning Demonstration—Benjamin Franklin—Philadelphia, Pa.—June 15

Orchestra—orchestra used in conjunction with an opera—*The Beggar's Opera*—Upper Marlborough, Md.

Philosophy Book—philosophy book (American)—*Elementa Philosophica*, by Samuel Johnson—printed by Benjamin Franklin and D. Hall—Philadelphia, Pa.

1753

Arbitration—colonial arbitration law—enacted—New Haven, Conn.—Oct. 11

Expedition—Arctic expedition to seek the northwest passage for the £20,000 reward—Charles Swaine—sailed—March

Medal—Copley Medal awarded to an American—Benjamin Franklin

Poet—black woman poet—Phillis Wheatley—born

Steam Engine—steam engine—imported—North Arlington, N.J.—Sept. 25

1754

Cartoon—newspaper cartoon—"Join or Die"—published—Philadelphia, Pa.—May 9

Clock—clock to strike the hours—constructed—Benjamin Banneker—Elkridge Landing, Md.

Congress (colonial)—colonial congress—Albany, N.Y.—June 19-July 11

Druggist—Jonathan Roberts—Philadelphia, Pa.—May

Language Instruction—German instruction—William Creamer—Philadelphia, Pa.

Trombone—used—Bethlehem, Pa.—Nov. 15

War (colonial)—bloodshed in the French and Indian War—Uniontown, Pa.—May 28

War (colonial)—French and Indian War battle—Fort Necessity, Pa.—July 3

1755

Animals—cattle exportation—Savannah, Ga.

Engraving—historical print engraved in America—printed—Boston, Mass.

Law School—law instruction in a college—King's College (Columbia University)—New York City

Meat—beef export—Savannah, Ga.

Steam Engine—steam engine—in service—March 12

Water—water pumping plant—municipal purposes—installed—Bethlehem, Pa.—May 27

"Yankee Doodle"—verses written—Richard Shuckburgh

1756

Spa—opened to public—Bath, Va.

Stagecoach Intercity Service—New York–Philadelphia, Pa.—Nov. 9

Woman—woman whose vote was recorded—Uxbridge, Mass.

1757

Academy—Academy and College of Philadelphia—Philadelphia, Pa.—graduation—May 17

Niagara Falls—utilization of Niagara Falls waterpower

Street Cleaning Service—instituted—Benjamin Franklin—Philadelphia, Pa.

1758

Holiday—Thanksgiving Day sermon—west of th Alleghenies—Charles Beatty—Pittsburgh, Pa —Nov. 26

Indian Reservation—Indian reservation (state)—established—New Jersey—Aug. 29

1759

Comb Factory—established—West Newbury Mass.

Freemasons—military Masonic lodge—Crow Point, N.Y.—April 13

Insurance—life insurance company—incorpora ed—Philadelphia, Pa.—Jan. 11

Music—musical instrument dealer—Michael Hi legas

Music—secular song—composed—Francis Hop kinson

Novel—novel (full-length)—*Theron, Paulinus an Aspasio*, by Joseph Bellamy—published—Bos ton, Mass.

1760

Agricultural Book—agricultural book distinctl American—published—Jared Eliot—Bosto Mass.

Chair—rocking chair—invented—Benjami Franklin

Medical Legislation—law to regulate the practic of medicine (actually enforced)—New Yo City—June 10

Methodist Church—Methodist preacher—Phili Embury—arrived—New York City—Aug. 11

1761

Bridge—pile bridge—constructed—York, Me.

Expedition—scientific expedition—John Wi throp

Insurance—life insurance company—first polic issued—May 22

Knighthood—knighthood conferred in America Jeffery Amherst—Staten Island, N.Y.—Oct. 2

Music Book—music book by a native American *Urania*—published—Philadelphia, Pa.

Slide Rule Book—*Subtensial Plain Trigonometr* by Thomas Abel—printed—Philadelphia, P

Venetian Blinds—venetian blinds—installed—S Peter's Church—Philadelphia, Pa.

1762

Caricature—published—Nathaniel Hurd—Bo ton, Mass.

Medical Instruction—anatomy lectures (scie tific)—William Shippen—Philadelphia, Pa.

Missionary Society—missionary society org nized in the U.S.—founded—Massachusetts

Woman—woman newspaper editor—Ann Franklin—Newport *Mercury*—Newport, R.I.—Aug. 22

1763

Prizefight—American to win distinction in the prize ring—Bill Richman—born—Aug. 5

Ship—steamboat—built—William Henry

1764

Cotton—cotton exported—Charleston, S.C.

Greenhouse—erected—James Beekman—New York City

Milestones—erected—Philadelphia, Pa.—May 15

Periodical—sectarian magazine (German)—*Ein Geistliches Magazien*—Christoph Saur (or Sower), editor—published—Germantown, Pa.

Railroad—inclined railway—erected—Lewiston, N.Y.

1765

Chocolate Mill—established—Dorchester, Mass.

College Literary Society—college literary society —Princeton, N.J.

Fire—fire in a mine—Pittsburgh, Pa.

Grammar—English grammar by an American published in America—Samuel Johnson—published—New York City

Medical Book—medical education book—*A Discourse Upon the Institution of Medical Schools in America,* by John Morgan—printed by William Bradford—Philadelphia, Pa.

Medical School—medical college—established—Philadelphia, Pa.—May 3

Stamp Act Repudiation—Frederick, Md.—Nov. 23

1766

Actor—matinee idol—John Henry—debut—Philadelphia, Pa.—Oct. 6

Church of the United Brethren in Christ—formed —Lancaster, Pa.—May 18

Fox Hunting Club—Gloucester Fox Hunting Club —organized—Philadelphia, Pa.—Oct. 29

Gem-cutting Machine—lapidary—invented—Abel Buell—Killingworth, Conn.

Jewish Book—Jewish prayer book—published in the United States—New York City

Theater—theater building (permanent)—opened —Philadelphia, Pa.—Nov. 21

1767

Libretto—published—*The Disappointment*—New York City

Medical Instruction—midwifery professor—Dr. J. V. B. Tennent—appointed—New York City

Music Book—music book printed from type—*The Psalms of David*—printed—New York City

Opera—opera (comic)—scheduled—Philadelphia, Pa.—April 20

President (U.S.)—President born posthumously—Andrew Jackson—March 15

1768

Arbitration—arbitration tribunal—New York City —May 3

Artist—artist successful in commercial art—Matthew Pratt

Botany Professor—Adam Kuhn—appointed—Philadelphia, Pa.

Chamber of Commerce—Chamber of Commerce (state)—formed—New York City—April 5

Cottonseed Oil—produced—Dr. Otto—Bethlehem, Pa.

Hospital—insane hospital (state)—Williamsburg, Va.—incorporated

Insurance—fire insurance company to receive a charter—Philadelphia, Pa.—Feb. 20

Medical School—medical college—College of Philadelphia—commencement—June 21

Methodist Church—Methodist chapel—Wesley Chapel—New York City—dedicated—Oct. 30

Music—patriotic American song—by John Dickinson—published—Boston, Mass.—July

Mustard—manufactured—Benjamin Jackson—Philadelphia, Pa.—advertised—Feb. 15

Physician—doctor to receive a Bachelor of Medicine degree—graduation—Philadelphia, Pa.—June 21

Sieve—sieve—produced—John Sellers—Philadelphia, Pa.

Spelling Reform Advocate—Benjamin Franklin—Philadelphia, Pa.

1769

Building—summer home—John Wentworth—Wolfeboro, N.H.

California Mission—dedicated—San Diego, Calif. —July 16

Chemistry Professor—chemistry professor—Benjamin Rush—Philadelphia, Pa.

Medical Book—medical ethics book—*A Discourse Upon the Duties of a Physician,* by Samuel Bard—printed by A. & J. Robertson—New York City

Medical Book—medical history—*A Medical Discourse,* by Peter Middleton—printed by Hugh Gaine—New York City

Piano—piano—John Harris—spinet described—Boston, Mass.—Sept. 18

Type Foundry—type foundry—Killingworth, Conn.—April 1

1770

Chamber of Commerce—Chamber of Commerce (state)—incorporated—New York City—March 13

Chemistry Textbook—chemistry text published—Benjamin Rush—Philadelphia, Pa.

College—college to confer medals as prizes—Williamsburg, Va.

Music Book—music composition book—*New England Psalm-Singer*—William Billings—Boston, Mass.

Physician—physician (Jewish) to head an insane asylum—John de Sequeyra—Williamsburg, Va.

Revolutionary War—American casualties—Boston, Mass.—March 5

Revolutionary War—attack on British soldiers—New York City—Jan. 18

Revolutionary War—martyr in the Revolutionary War—Christopher Snider—killed—Boston, Mass.—Feb. 22

Rhubarb—shipped from London, England, to Philadelphia, Pa.

Teaching Methods Book—*Schul-ordnung*—Christopher Dock—Germantown, Pa.

1771

Dwarf—exhibition advertised—Boston, Mass.—Aug. 22

Equestrian Exhibition—John Sharp—Boston, Mass.

Genealogy—genealogy—of American family—Ebenezer Watson—Hartford, Conn.

Type Foundry—type foundry to be permanently established in America—Christopher Sauer II—Germantown, Pa.

1772

Civil Government in America—Watauga Commonwealth—North Carolina and Tennessee

Medical Legislation—law to license the practice of medicine—New Jersey—Sept. 26

Protestant Church—Protestant church—west of Pennsylvania—Schoenbrunn, Ohio, communion service—June 9

Revolutionary War—naval attack—Providence, R.I.—June 9

Schoolhouse—west of the Allegheny Mountains—Schoenbrunn, Ohio—started—Dec. 22

Trade Register—*Aitken's General American Register*—Philadelphia, Pa.

1773

Baptist Church—Baptist church (black)—established—Silver Bluff, S.C.

Degrees (academic and honorary)—Doctor of Laws honorary degree—John Winthrop—Cambridge, Mass.

Execution—electrocution experiment—Benjamin Franklin

Hospital—insane hospital (state)—Williamsburg, Va.—opened—Oct. 12

Methodist Conference—Philadelphia, Pa.—July 16

Museum—public museum—organized—Charleston, S.C.—Jan. 12

Schoolhouse—west of the Allegheny Mountains—completed—Schoenbrunn, Ohio—July 29

1774

Business Publication—business publication—*South-Carolina Price-Current*—Charles Town, S.C.—first known copy July 30

College Student—Jewish college graduate—Isaa Abrahams—King's College (Columbia College New York City

Conscientious Objectors—landed—New Yor City—Aug. 6

Continental Congress—Continental Congress-assembled—Philadelphia, Pa.—Sept. 5

Continental Congress—Continental Congress t be opened with prayer—Philadelphia, Pa.-Sept. 7

Declaration of Independence—declaration of ir dependence—formally made—Carlisle, Pa.-July 12

Declaration of Rights—Philadelphia, Pa.—Oct. 1

Embargo Act—embargo act (Continental Co gress)—enacted—Oct. 14

Military Organization—military organizatio (anti-British)—organized—Philadelphia, Pa.-Nov. 17

Music—music printed in a magazine—Bosto Mass.—April

Novel—novel (pamphlet)—*A Pretty Story*, b Francis Hopkinson—printed—Williamsbur Va.

President of the Continental Congress—Peytc Randolph—elected—Philadelphia, Pa.—Sept.

Revolutionary War—incident in the Revolutio ary War—New Castle, N.H.—Major John Su livan—Dec. 13

Shaker Society—arrived—New York City—Au 6

Shovel—shovel (steel)—manufactured—Joh Ames—West Bridgewater, Mass.

Slavery—nonimportation of slaves act—enact —Rhode Island—June 13

1775

Abolition Society—organized—Philadelphia, P —April 14

Architecture Book—architectural book printed America—Philadelphia, Pa.

Army—army engineering department—Contine tal Army—authorized—June 16

Army Insignia—special insignia—authorized-Boston, Mass.—July 5

Army Officer—adjutant general—Horatio Gat —June 17

Army Officer—chief engineer—Richard Gridley-June 17

Army Officer—general (Continental Army)-George Washington—appointed—June 15

Army Officer—judge advocate—William Tudor July 29

Army Officer—major general—Artemas Ward-June 17

Army Officer—paymaster general—James Wa ren—June 27

Army Officer—quartermaster—Thomas Mifflin Aug. 14

Army Officer—surgeon general of the Continent Army—Benjamin Church—July 27

Ship—ship-of-the-line—*America*—authorized—Nov. 20

Ship—warship (American-built) to enter European waters—*Reprisal*—sailed—Dec. 4

Ship—warship captured by a commissioned officer of the U.S. Navy—*Edward*—captured by John Barry—April 17

Submarine—submarine built for use in war—*American Turtle*—built—Saybrook, Conn.

Traitor—to the American cause—William Demont—Nov. 2

United States—"United States" authorized—Sept. 9

War (colonial)—marine engagement in battle—Fort Nassau, Bahamas—March 4

Woman Suffrage—colony to grant suffrage to women—New Jersey—July 2

1777

Army—brevet conferred upon an American—Walter Stewart—Nov. 19

Army Officer—chaplain killed in action—John Rosbrugh—Trenton, N.J.—Jan. 2

Articles of Confederation—adopted—Philadelphia, Pa.—Nov. 15

Catholic Funeral—Catholic funeral attended by the U.S. Continental Congress—Philadelphia, Pa.—Sept. 17

Emancipation Act (state)—Vermont—July 2

Flag—American flag—formally adopted—Philadelphia, Pa.—June 14

Flag—American flag displayed on a man-of-war—Portsmouth Harbor, N.H.—July 4

Flag—American flag flown in battle—Cooch's Bridge, Del.—Sept. 3

Flag—American flag on the high seas—*Raleigh*—Sept. 4

Holiday—Thanksgiving Day celebration (nationwide, colonial)—Dec. 18

Loan—loan for war purposes—from France—received—June 4

Lottery—lottery held by the Continental Congress—Philadelphia, Pa.—April 10

Marine Corps—marine officer killed in service—John Fitzpatrick—April 6

Mine Barrage—David Bushnell—New London, Conn.—Aug.

Nails—nails—cold-cut—Jeremiah Wilkinson—Cumberland, R.I.

Price Regulation Legislation—price regulation law (colonial)—effective—Rhode Island—Jan. 8

Ship—ship-of-the-line—*America*—laid down—Portsmouth, N.H.—May

Ship—warship (American) captured overseas—*Lexington* (formerly *Wild Duck*)—surrendered—Sept. 20

Slavery—state to abolish slavery—Vermont—July 2

State—state to abolish both entail and primogeniture—Georgia—Feb. 5

Suffrage—state to provide universal manhood suffrage—Vermont—July 28

Treaty—treaty between states after the Declaration of Independence—Georgia and South Carolina—Dewitt's Corner, S.C.—May 20

1778

Arbitration—state arbitration law—Maryland—Dec. 15

Arsenal—Springfield, Mass.—April

Articles of Confederation—ratified—South Carolina—Feb. 5

Blockade—across Hudson River

Court-Martial—military court-martial—commenced—Cambridge, Mass.—Jan. 20

Diplomatic Service—minister plenipotentiary—to France—Benjamin Franklin—Sept. 14

Diplomatic Service—representative of a foreign country to the U.S.—C. A. Gérard—July

Flag—American flag saluted by a foreign nation—France—Feb. 14

Freemasons—Masonic grand lodge—organized—Williamsburg, Va.—Oct. 13

Music—war song—"Chester"—published—Boston, Mass.

Pharmacopoeia — pharmacopoeia — William Brown—published—Philadelphia, Pa.

Revolutionary War—conflict on equal terms between American regulars and British regulars—Freehold, N.J.—June 28

Secret Service—secret service (colonial)—organized—June

Treaty—treaty entered into by the United States—with France—Feb. 6

Treaty—treaty entered into by the United States with American Indian tribes—Sept. 17

United States—nation to recognize the independence of the United States—France—Feb. 6

1779

Army—Army engineering department—"Corps of Engineers"—established—March 11

Army Uniform—standardized—Oct.

College—elective system of study—Williamsburg, Va.

College—university legally designated as a university—University of Pennsylvania

Honor System—College of William and Mary—Williamsburg, Va.

Language Instruction—modern-language school—in a college—Williamsburg, Va.

Law School—law school in a college—Williamsburg, Va.

Medal—medal awarded by the Continental Congress to a foreigner—F. L. T. de Fleury—July 2

Military Drill Manual—military drill manual—published—Philadelphia, Pa.

Oyster Propagation—Rhode Island—June

Revolutionary War—bayonet charge in the Revolutionary War—Anthony Wayne—Stony Point, N.Y.—July 16

Universalist Church of America (Independent Christian Church Universalist)—organized—Jan. 1

Protestant Episcopal Bishop—Protestant Episcopal bishop—Samuel Seabury—consecrated—Nov. 14

Seed Business—established—Philadelphia, Pa.—Jan. 7

Ship—trading ship sent to China—*Empress of China*—Feb. 22

State—state denied admission into the Union—Franklin—formed, Aug. 23

State Department (U.S.)—State Department (U.S.) Secretary—John Jay—Dec. 21

Theological School—theological school—New York City

Treaty—treaty between the United States Government and a nation with which it had been at war—treaty with Great Britain—ratified and proclaimed—Jan. 14

War Veterans' Society—Society of the Cincinnati—general meeting—Philadelphia, Pa.—May 7

1785

Agricultural Society—agricultural society—Philadelphia Society for the Promotion of Agriculture—organized—March 1

Animals—mule—George Washington received jackasses from Spain—Oct. 26

Botany Book—botany book strictly American—printed—Philadelphia, Pa.

Church of England—Church of England—organized in New England—first minister ordained

College—state university chartered—Athens, Ga.—Jan. 27

Dentistry—porcelain teeth—introduced

Diplomatic Service—minister plenipotentiary—Thomas Jefferson—appointed—March 10

Diplomatic Service—minister to Great Britain—John Adams—June 1

Directory (city)—published—Philadelphia, Pa.—Oct. 1

Geographer of the United States—Thomas Hutchins—appointed—May 20

Land Grant—land grant to schools—by United States—May 20

Land Sale Ordinance (general)—enacted—May 20

Lens—eyeglass bifocals—invented—Benjamin Franklin

Marble Quarry—Dorset, Vt.

Methodist College—Cokesbury College, Abingdon, Md.—foundation sermon—June 5

Missionary—black missionary to the American Indians—John Marrant—ordained—May 15

Money—copper cents minted by a state—Vermont—June

Money—decimal system of money—with dollar as unit—adopted—July 6

Protestant Episcopal Catechism—Episcopal catechism—published—Philadelphia, Pa.

Road—toll road—commissioners appointed—Oct.

Ship—trading ship sent to China—returned—New York City—May 11

Survey of Public Lands—authorized—Continental Congress—May 20

Treaty—treaty entered into by the United State after the treaty of peace with Great Britain—Prussia—Sept. 10

Unitarian Prayer Book—published—Boston Mass.

1786

American Indian Reservation—American India reservation (federal)—established

Cotton Spinning Jenny—operated—Daniel Jack son—Providence, R.I.

Diplomatic Service—consul under the Department of State—Samuel Shaw—appointed—Jan 1

Golf Club—golf club—formed—Charleston, S.C.

Hospital—dispensary—Philadelphia Dispensary—April 12

Ice Cream—ice cream—commercially manufactured—Mr. Hall—New York City—advertise—June 8

Mineralogy Instruction—Rhode Island College—Providence, R.I.

Money—coin (state) to use "E Pluribus Unum"—New Jersey

Music Book—Lutheran hymnbook (German) published in America—H. M. Muhlenberg, comp.—*Erbauliche Lieder-Sammlung zum Gottesdienstlichten Gebrauch in den Vereinigte. Evangelisch-Lutherischen Gemeinen in Nord America*—published—Germantown, Pa.—Copyrighted, by Peter Leibert and Michael Bill meyer—Oct.2

Music Periodical—music magazine—*America Musical Magazine*—published—New Haven Conn.

Newspaper—newspaper published west of th Alleghenies—*Pittsburgh Gazette*—Pittsburgh Pa.—July 29

Spinning, Carding, and Roping Machines—manu factured—Bridgewater, Mass.

Strike—union strike benefit—authorized—Ma 31

War—rebellion against the federal government—Shays's Rebellion

1787

Clock—alarm clock—Levi Hutchins—Concord N.H.

Constitution of the United States—Constitutio (federal)—signed—Philadelphia, Pa.—Sept. 17

Constitution of the United States—Constitution of the United States was first published in a news paper—Philadelphia, Pa.—Sept. 19

Constitution of the United States—printed copie of the Constitution—proofs delivered to Consti tutional Convention—Aug. 6

Glass Factory—window-glass factory—chartere—Boston, Mass.

Lifesaving Stations for Distressed Mariners—Massachusetts

Methodist College—Cokesbury College—Abingdon, Md.—opened—Dec. 6

Money—Continental coin—copper Fugio—authorized—July 6

Music Book—secular songbook—A. Reinagle—published—Philadelphia, Pa.

Play (drama)—native American play successfully acted on a regular stage—Royall Tyler—*The Contrast*

Playwright—playwright (professional)—William Dunlap—comedy written

Prison Reform Society—formed—Philadelphia, Pa.—May 8

Ship—ship to carry the United States flag around the world—*Columbia*—sailed—Boston, Mass.—Sept. 30

Ship—steamboat to carry a man—John Fitch—Aug. 27

Slavery—law (federal) prohibiting slavery in a territory of the United States—Northwest Territory—enacted July 13

State—state to ratify the federal Constitution—Delaware—Dec. 7

Territorial Expansion—acquisition of land by the federal government

Unitarian Minister—Unitarian minister—James Freeman—Boston, Mass.—ordained—Nov. 18

1788

Algebra Book—algebra book by a native-born American—published—Newburyport, Mass.

Cloth—sailcloth factory—Boston, Mass.

Constitution of the United States—printed copies of the Constitution—Constitution ratified—June 21

Cotton—cotton goods to be trademarked—Beverly, Mass.—June 6

Cotton Mill—cotton mill—established—Beverly, Mass.

Dictionary—dictionary published in the United States—Worcester, Mass.

Dictionary—pocket dictionary published in the United States—William Perry—*Royal Standard English Dictionary*—Worcester, Mass.

Election—federal election in the United States—authorized—Sept. 13

Horse—horse (trotting horse)—imported—Philadelphia, Pa.

Music Book—secular songbook by a native American—published—Philadelphia, Pa.

Naval Officer—naval chaplain (Continental navy)—B. Parks—appointed—Oct. 28

Shaker Society—organized Shaker community—New Lebanon, N.Y.

Ship—ship built on the Pacific coast—*Northwest America*—begun—June 11

Ship—steamboat patent—Isaac Briggs—Georgia—Feb. 1

Wool—worsted mill operated by waterpower—Hartford, Conn.

1789

Army—army organization under the Constitution—act enacted, April 30

Army—medical corps—Richard Allison appointed surgeon—Sept. 29

Army Officer—commander-in-chief of the U.S. Army—Josiah Harmar—September

Attorney General—Attorney General—E. J. Randolph—Sept. 26

Attorney of the United States—Attorney General of the United States—Samuel Sherburne, Jr.—appointed—Sept. 26

Bibliography—bibliography of Americana in English—published

Book Publisher of denominational books—New York City—May

Cabinet of the United States—Cabinet—April 30

Catholic Diocese—established—Baltimore, Md.—April 6

Catholic Periodical—Catholic magazine—published—Boston, Mass.—April 23

College—Catholic college—Georgetown College—established—Washington, D.C.—Jan. 23

Comb—of ivory—manufactured—Centerbrook, Conn.

Comptroller—Comptroller of the United States Treasury—Nicholas Eveleigh—served—Sept. 11

Congress (U.S.)—Congress of the U.S.—New York City—March 4

Congress (U.S.)—congressional act—June 1

Congress (U.S.)—congressional act declared unconstitutional by the Supreme Court of the U.S.—Sept. 24

Congress (U.S.)—joint meeting of the Senate and the House of Representatives—April 6

Congress (U.S.)—House of Representatives—clerk of the House of Representatives—John Beckley—began service April 1

Congress (U.S.)—House of Representatives—chaplain of the House of Representatives—William Linn—began service May 1

Congress (U.S.)—House of Representatives—committee of the House of Representatives—appointed—April 2

Congress (U.S.)—House of Representatives—contested election—April 13

Congress (U.S.)—House of Representatives—House of Representatives—assembled—March 4

Congress (U.S.)—House of Representatives—sergeant at arms—Joseph Wheaton—began service April 8

Congress (U.S.)—House of Representatives—Speaker of the House—F. A. Muhlenberg

Congress (U.S.)—Senate—president pro tempore of the United States Senate—John Langdon—April 6

Congress (U.S.)—Senate—Senate—Senate meeting—New York City—March 4

Constitution of the United States—printed copies of the Constitution—Constitution declared in effect—March 4

Historical Society—historical society (state)—Massachusetts Historical Society—organized—Aug. 26

Ice Yacht—built—Oliver Booth—Poughkeepsie, N.Y.

Lawyer—lawyers admitted to the Supreme Court of the United States—Feb. 5

Medical Book—medical book for army medical use—published—New York City

Music—music publishers (exclusive)—Moller & Capron—Philadelphia, Pa.

Music—singing contest—Dorchester, Mass.

Naturalization Act—naturalization act—of the U.S. Government—March 26

Navy—naval protection—organized—Aug. 4

Patent—patent granted by the United States Government—Samuel Hopkins—July 31

Patent—patent law (national)—enacted—April 10

Physician—black doctor—James Derham—Philadelphia, Pa.

President (U.S.)—President who had been a senator—James Monroe—Nov. 9

Prison—prison to have individual cells—Philadelphia, Pa.

Refunding Act (federal)—approved—Aug. 4

Representative (U.S.)—representative to die—Theodore Bland—June 1

Senator (U.S.)—senator appointed by a governor—John Walker—Virginia—appointed—March 31

Ship—revenue cutter—*Massachusetts*—authorized—Aug. 4

Ship—ship to carry the U.S. flag around the world—*Columbia*—returned—Boston, Mass.—Aug. 9

State Department (U.S.)—State Department (U.S.) Secretary—Thomas Jefferson—took office—March 22

Supreme Court (U.S.)—clerk of the Supreme Court—John Tucker—appointed—Feb. 3

Supreme Court (U.S.)—Supreme Court first session—New York City—opened Feb. 1

Supreme Court (U.S.)—Supreme Court of the United States—first session—New York City—Feb. 1–10

Theater—panorama show—*Jerusalem*—New York City

War—battle fought by United States troops—Ohio—Oct. 19

1791

Academy—University of Pennsylvania—first trustees' meeting—Nov. 8

Army Officer—Chaplain of the U.S. Army—John Hurt—March 4

Attorney General—opinion by a U.S. Attorney General—decision—Aug. 21

Bank—Bank of the United States—chartered—Feb. 25

Bible—Bible in folio size to be illustrated—published—Worcester, Mass.

Carpet Factory—carpet mill—founded—Philadelphia, Pa.

Catholic Seminary—Catholic seminary—established—Baltimore, Md.—July 10

Coal—anthracite coal—discovered—Carbon County, Pa.

College—Catholic college—Georgetown College—opened—Washington, D.C.—Nov. 15

Congress (U.S.)—Senate—Senate special session—Philadelphia, Pa.—March 4

Constitutional Amendment (U.S.)—Constitutional amendments—"Bill of Rights"—Dec. 15

Corporation—corporate body chartered by a special act of Congress—Feb. 25

Countess—American woman to become a countess—Sarah Rumford

Dental Dispensary—dental dispensary—New York City—opened—Feb. 1

Export—export report—fiscal year ending Sept. 30

Internal Revenue Act—enacted—March 3

Lawbook—lawbook containing the federal laws of the United States of more than one session of Congress—published—New York City

Lawbook—lawbook containing the federal laws of the United States—published—Hartford, Conn.

Lighthouse—lighthouse built after American independence—contract for Cape Henry Lighthouse—March 31

Marble Building—of importance—Philadelphia, Pa.

Masonry—(for blacks)—Masonic Grand Lodge (not Free and Accepted Masons)—Boston, Mass.—organized—June 24

Music—orchestral song—published—Boston, Mass.

Naval Officer—naval officer commissioned—Hopley Yeaton—appointed—March 21

Patent—patent granted jointly to a father and son—Philadelphia, Pa.—Aug. 2

Patent—patentee to obtain more than one patent—Philadelphia, Pa.—March 11

Pile Driver—pile driver—patented—John Stone—Concord, Mass.—March 10

President (U.S.)—President to tour the country—to southern states—April 7

Representative (U.S.)—Jewish representative—Israel Jacobs—began service March 4

Ship—revenue cutter—*Massachusetts*—keel laid—Newburyport, Mass.

State—state admitted to the Union—Vermont—March 4

Sugar—sugar refinery—opened—New Orleans, La.

Supreme Court (U.S.) Decision—Supreme Court decision—West vs. Barnes—in August term

Tax—excise tax (federal)—enacted

Tax—internal revenue tax—imposed—March 3

Traffic Regulation—one-way traffic regulation—New York City—Dec. 17

1792

Agriculture Professor—Columbia College—New York City—July 9

Almanac—almanac with a continuous existence—*The Farmer's Almanac*—printed—Boston

Army Officer—paymaster—Caleb Swan—appointed—May 9

Bridge—bridge of importance—West Boston Bridge—construction begun July 15

Brokerage—stock exchange—predecessors—May 17

Building—building erected by the Government in Washington, D.C.—White House—cornerstone laid—Oct. 13

Building—building erected in the United States for public use—United States Mint—cornerstone laid—July 31

Chemists Society—chemical society—founded—Philadelphia, Pa.

Circus—circus—J. B. Ricketts—Philadelphia, Pa.

Congress of the United States—congressional investigation—March 27

Congressional Apportionment—authorized—April 14

Conscription—conscription—authorized—May 8

Cotton Gin—invented—Eli Whitney—Mulberry Grove, Ga.

Cracker Bakery—Newburyport, Mass.

Cremation—Charleston, S.C.—Dec. 8

Diplomatic Service—minister to Great Britain—Thomas Pinckney—minister plenipotentiary to Great Britain—Jan. 12

Glass Factory—window-glass factory—production began—Boston, Mass.

Health Board—health board (local)—Baltimore, Md.

Industrial Park—industrial park—Alexander Hamilton, sponsor—Paterson, N.J.—opened

Insurance—life insurance—Philadelphia, Pa.—organized—Dec. 10

Labor Union—craft labor union (local)—organized—Philadelphia, Pa.

Lighthouse—lighthouse built after American independence—completed—Cape Henry, Va.

Maternity Book—published—Philadelphia, Pa.

Medical Book—anatomy book—published Philadelphia, Pa.

Mint (U.S.)—mint (U.S.) director—David Rittenhouse—appointed—April 14

Mint (U.S.)—Mint of the United States—established—April 2

Money—coin (United States) to use "E Pluribus Unum"—authorized—April 2

Money—copper coins made by the United States Mint—authorized—April 2

Money—gold coinage—authorized—April 2

Money—gold price fixed by Congress—April 2

Money—half cent of the United States—authorized—April 2

Money—silver coins—authorized—April 2

Money—silver dollar—authorized—April 2

Money—silver half dimes—authorized—April 2

Monument—monument to Christopher Columbus—Baltimore, Md.—dedicated—Oct. 12

Postal Service—postal service act—established—Feb. 20

Postmaster—woman postmaster appointed after the adoption of the Constitution—Sarah De Crow—Hertford, N.C.—Sept. 27

Presidential Succession Act—enacted—March 1

Protestant Episcopal Bishop—Protestant Episcopal bishop consecrated in the United States—T. J. Claggett—New York City—Sept. 17

Road—macadam road—Lancaster Turnpike Railroad Company—chartered—April 9

Veto (presidential)—veto—by a President—George Washington—April 5

Woman Suffrage—woman suffrage book—*A Vindication of the Rights of Women*—published

1793

African Church—founded—Richard Allen—Philadelphia, Pa.

Alfalfa—description published—Wilmington, Del.

Animals—sheep (merino sheep)—William Foster—smuggled

Anthology (American)—published—Litchfield, Conn.

Balloon—Flights—balloon flight in which a presidential order was carried—Philadelphia, Pa.—Jan. 9

Bridge—bridge of importance—West Boston Bridge—opened Nov. 23

Broadcloth—produced—Pittsfield, Mass.

Canal—canal—built—South Hadley Falls, Mass.

Capitol (U.S.)—cornerstone laid—Sept. 18

Catholic Priest—Catholic priest ordained in the United States—S. T. Badin—May 25

Congress (U.S.)—Senate—contested election—Feb. 28

Deaf—School—lipreading was first referred to in print—Philadelphia, Pa.

Engraving—wood engraving made with an engraving tool—Alexander Anderson—New York City—June

"First Aid" Emergency Organization—Humane Society of Philadelphia—incorporated—Jan. 23

Money—metal purchased for coinage

Neutrality Proclamation—George Washington—April 22

Oiled Silk Patent—Ralph Hodgson—Lansingburg N.Y.—Feb. 1

Road—state road authorization—Kentucky—Dec. 14

Slavery—fugitive slave law (federal)—enacted—Feb. 12

Stove Patent—Robert Haeterick—June 11

Sulfuric Acid—produced—John Harrison—Philadelphia, Pa.

Supreme Court (U.S.)—Supreme Court nominee rejected—William Paterson—nominated, Feb. 20—name withdrawn—renamed, March 4—began service, March 14

Thread—cotton thread—made—Pawtucket, R.I.

Wool—wool carding machine—built—Newburyport, Mass.

1794

African Church—dedicated—Philadelphia, Pa.—July 29

Arsenal—national arsenal—Springfield, Mass.—April 2

Ball Bearing—commercial installation—Lancaster, Pa.—Oct. 30

Book—best-seller novel—published—Philadelphia, Pa.

Capital Punishment—death penalty was first abolished—Pennsylvania—April 22

College—nondenominational college—chartered—Knoxville, Tenn.—Sept. 10

Congress (U.S.)—Senate—contested election—case commenced—Feb. 20

Congress (U.S.)—Senate—Senate session to which the public was admitted—Feb. 11

Epidemic—medical record of an epidemic—Benjamin Rush—printed—Philadelphia, Pa.

Extradition—extradition treaty with a foreign country—Great Britain—Nov. 19

Flag Legislation—legislation authorizing changes in the American flag—enacted—Jan. 13

Glass Factory—glass factory west of the Allegheny Mountains—established—A. A. A. Gallatin

Historical Society—historical society (state)—Massachusetts Historical Society—incorporated—Feb. 19

Hotel—hotel built—City Hotel—New York City

Insurance—life insurance—Insurance Company of North America—Philadelphia, Pa.—chartered—April 14

Jewelers' Supply House—Nehemiah Dodge—Providence, R.I.

Money—deposit of silver for coinage—July 18

Money—silver dollar—coined—Philadelphia, Pa.

Naval Officer—naval officer to become a commodore—John Barry—appointed

Neutrality Regulation—enacted—June 5

Newspaper—French daily newspaper—*Courrier Français*—April 15

Opera—opera of a serious nature—*Tammany*—New York City—March 3

Presidential Commission—presidential commission—George Washington

Rivet—commercial production—J. G. Pierson—patent—March 23

Senator (U.S.)—senator appointed (not seated)—Kensey Johns of Delaware—seat denied, March 28

Ship—ship constructed by the federal government—*Chesapeake*—authorized—March 27

Ship—warship builder—Joshua Humphreys—appointed—June 28

Supreme Court (U.S.)—Associate Justice of the Supreme Court who had been a representative in Congress—Gabriel Duvall of Maryland—began service in Congress, Nov. 11

Surgical Operation—cesarean operation (successful)—Jessee Bennett—Edom, Va.—Jan. 14

Textile Machinery Patent—James Davenport—Philadelphia, Pa.—Feb. 14

1795

Belt Conveyor System—belt conveyor system—described—Oliver Evans—Philadelphia, Pa.

Book—book printed on American paper with American-made plates and bound in America—*Elegiac Sonnets*

Catholic Priest—Catholic priest to receive his full theological training in the U.S.—ordained bishop—March 18

College—college named after George Washington—Washington College, Tenn.—name changed—July 8

College—nondenominational college—Union College, Schenectady, N.Y.—chartered—Feb. 25

College—state university chartered—University of North Carolina opened—Feb. 13

Dental Dispensary—dental dispensary—City Dispensary—New York City—incorporated—April 8

Extradition—extradition treaty with a foreign country—Jay Treaty, with Great Britain—ratified by Senate, June 24—approved by the President, Oct. 28

Gazetteer—American gazetteer—Jedidiah Morse—published—Boston, Mass.

Grammar Instruction in a College—University of North Carolina—Chapel Hill, N.C.

Money—coin (United States) to use "E Pluribus Unum"—issued

Money—deposit of gold bullion—Feb. 12

Money—return of coins—gold eagles—July 31

Music Book—Lutheran hymnbook (English) created in America—J. C. Kunze—*A Hymn and Prayer Book for the Use of Such Lutheran Churches as Use the English Language*—printed—New York City

Ordnance — muskets — manufactured — Springfield Armory—Springfield, Mass.

Road—state road appropriation of a specific sum—Kentucky—Dec. 19

Steam Engine—steam engine that was practical—Oliver Evans—Philadelphia, Pa.

Supreme Court (U.S.)—Chief Justice whose nomination was not confirmed—John Rutledge

Woman—women to become federal government employees—Philadelphia, Pa.

1796

African Church—Bethel African Methodist Episcopal Church—incorporated—March 28

Animals—elephant—arrived—New York City—April 13

Bathhouse—steam baths for curing disease—Samuel Thomson

Bridge—suspension bridge—Westmoreland County, Pa.

Coast Survey Book—published—Newburyport, Mass.—March

Cookbook—cookbook of American authorship—published—Hartford, Conn.

Debt Legislation (federal)—enacted—May 28

Electoral College—Electoral vote cast contrary to instructions—Samuel Miles

Epidemiologist—Noah Webster—published report—New York City

Extradition—extradition treaty with a foreign country—Jay Treaty, with Great Britain—proclaimed Feb. 29

Game Law—game law (national)—approved—May 19

Gas—gaslights for display—introduced—Philadelphia, Pa.—Aug.

Hospital—dispensary—Philadelphia Dispensary —chartered—April 15

Land Grant—special land grant—May 17

Medical Book—pediatrics monograph—published—Charles Caldwell—Philadelphia, Pa.

Nail Cutting and Heading Machine—patented—George Chandler—Dec. 12

Newspaper—newspaper to appear on Sunday—Monitor—Baltimore, Md.—Dec. 18

Opera—opera by an American composer—The Archers—New York City—April 18

Passport—passport—recorded—State Department—July 8

Piano—piano patent—J. S. McLean—May 27

Pill—patented pills

Senator (U.S.)—senators-elect not seated—William Blount and William Cocke, of Tennessee—denied seats, May 9

Ship—ship from the Atlantic coast to anchor in a California port—Otter—arrived—Monterey, Calif.—Oct. 29

Supreme Court (U.S.)—Associate Justice of the Supreme Court who had been a representative in Congress—Gabriel Duvall of Maryland—congressional service ended March 28

Unitarian Minister—Unitarian minister—Society of Unitarian Christians organized—June 12

1797

Architecture Book—architectural book distinctly American—printed—Greenfield, Mass.

Army Officer—Judge Advocate of the U.S. Army —Campbell Smith—began service—March 3

Chemistry Laboratory Manual—James Woodhouse—published—Philadelphia, Pa.

Clock—clock patent—Eli Terry—Nov. 17

Congress (U.S.)—special session—May 15

Cryptography Chart—published—Philadelphia, Pa.

Dollar Marks—cast—Philadelphia, Pa.—Binny & Ronaldson

Impeachment—impeachment proceedings against a United States senator—William Blount—expelled—July 8

Medical Periodical—medical magazine—Medical Repository—New York—Aug. 8

Novel—American novel republished in England —Royall Tyler—The Algerine Captive

Plow—plow patent—Charles Newbold—June 26

President (U.S.)—President to reside in Washington, D.C.—John Adams—inaugurated

President (U.S.)—President whose son became President—John Adams—inaugurated

Presidential Election—presidential election in which more than one candidate declared—John Adams—elected

Representative (U.S.)—representative elected while serving a prison term—Matthew Lyon—began service March 4

Representative (U.S.)—representative to serve before his 25th birthday—W. C. C. Claiborne of Tennessee—began service March 4

Ship—frigate—United States—launched—Philadelphia, Pa.—May 10

Ship—ship to capture an enemy ship after the Revolution—Constellation—launched Sept. 7

Washing Machine—washing machine patent—Nathaniel Briggs—March 28

1798

Alien Discriminatory Law—enacted—July 6

Army Officer—lieutenant general—George Washington—appointed July 11

Author—author—professional—C. B. Brown—novel announced—April 28

Congress (U.S.)—House of Representatives—brawl—Philadelphia, Pa.—Jan. 30

Encyclopedia—encyclopedia—printed in the U.S —Philadelphia, Pa.

Hat—straw hats—made—Betsey Metcalf—Providence, R.I.

Hospital—marine hospital (U.S.)—authorized—July 16

Immigration—immigration act—enacted—June 25

Marine Corps—American Marines—under newly created Navy Department

Marine Corps—American Marines—United States Marine Corps—created—July 11

Marine Corps—marine band—authorized—July 11

Music Book—hymnbook with music—published —Boston, Mass.

Navy—Navy Department (U.S.)—established

Navy—navy yard—acquired—Portsmouth, N.H.

Navy—prize money awarded by the U.S. Navy—authorized—June 28

Navy—Secretary of the Navy—Benjamin Stoddert—May 21

Nullification Proceedings—Kentucky Resolutions

Nursing School—instruction for nurses—New York City

Nut and Bolt Machine—David Wilkinson—patent —Dec. 14

Pistol—government contract for pistols—authorized—May 4

Public Health—public health service (U.S.)—authorized—July 16

Screw—screw patent—David Wilkinson—patent —Dec. 14

Ship—Revenue cutter and Navy cooperation

Tax—federal tax levied directly upon the states—authorized—July 14

Theater—theater destroyed by fire—Boston, Mass.—Feb. 2

Vineyard (successful)—established—Lexington, Ky.—Aug. 28

1799

Astronomy—meteoric display—"shooting stars" —recorded—Nov. 12

Aviation—aeronautical patent—Moses McFarland—Oct. 28

Comb-cutting Machine—patented—April 12

Dry Dock—dry dock authorized for the United States Government—approved—Feb. 25

Educational Association—educational association (local)—Middletown, Conn.—organized— May

Election—printed ballot—authorized—Pennsylvania—Feb. 15

Forestry Legislation—federal forestry legislation —Feb. 25

Gold—gold nugget—found—Cabarrus County, N.C.

Ice—commercial transportation of ice—from New York City

Insurance—insurance regulation (state)—Massachusetts—Feb. 13

Labor Union—craft labor union contract—Philadelphia, Pa.

Language Instruction—Italian instruction in a college—Williamsburg, Va.

Musician—"Negro-song" popularizer—J. C. G. Graupner—Dec. 30

Naval Officer—naval chaplain—William Balch— commissioned—Oct. 30

Presidential Eulogy—delivered—Dec. 26

Quarantine—quarantine legislation (national)— enacted—Feb. 25

Seeding Machine Patent—Eliakim Spooner—Jan. 25

Semaphore Telegraph System—invented—J. Grout—Belchertown, Mass.

Ship—ship to capture an enemy ship after the Revolution—*Constellation* vs.*Insurgente*—Feb. 9

Supreme Court (U.S.)—Chief Justice of the United States who had been a representative in Congress—John Marshall of Virginia—congressional service began March 4

Supreme Court (U.S.) Decision—Supreme Court decision between states—New York and Connecticut—commenced—Aug. 5

Swedenborgian or New Church—Swedenborgian or New Church Temple—erected—Baltimore, Md.

Weights and Measures Standardization—weights and measures standardization—enacted— March 2

1800

Ax—manufacturing plant—erected—Johnstown, N.Y.

Bankruptcy Act—enacted—April 4

Bible—Greek Testament—printed—Worcester, Mass.

Book—book with color plates

Catholic Bishop—Catholic bishop consecrated in present U.S. limits—Leonard Neale—Baltimore, Md.—Dec. 7

Congress (U.S.)—House of Representatives— House of Representatives—first session— Washington, D.C.—Nov. 17

Congressional Caucus—congressional caucus— secretly held—Federalist Party

Evangelical Church—founded

Fireboat—fireboat—used—New York City

Land Grant—district land office—opened—Steubenville, Ohio—July 2

Library—Library of Congress—authorized—April 24

President (U.S.)—President's wife to frank mail— Martha Washington—authorization—April 3

Social Service Endowment—established—White-Williams Foundation—Philadelphia, Pa.

Stomach Washing—P. S. Physick—Philadelphia, Pa.

Supreme Court (U.S.)—Chief Justice of the United States who had been a representative in Congress—John Marshall of Virginia—congressional service ended June 7

Swedenborgian or New Church—Swedenborgian or New Church Temple—church service—Baltimore, Md.—Jan. 5

Vaccination for smallpox—Benjamin Waterhouse —Cambridge, Mass.—July 8

1801

Blowpipe—invented—Robert Hare—Philadelphia, Pa.

Booksellers' Association—American Company of Booksellers—organized—New York City—June 7

Bridge—suspension bridge—design patented— James Finley

Building—building erected by the U.S. Government in Washington, D.C.—first New Year's reception—Jan. 1

Cheese Factory—cheese factory cooperative— Cheshire, Mass.

Congress (U.S.)—Congress of the United States— assumed jurisdiction over the District of Columbia—Feb. 27

Cracker—hard water crackers—manufactured— Milton, Mass.

Dental Book—book on dentistry—R. C. Skinner— New York City

Dueling Legislation (state)—enacted—Tennessee —Nov. 10

Election Law—registration law (state)—enacted —Massachusetts—March 7

Governor—Jewish governor—David Emanuel— Georgia—March 3

Herbal Book—published—Samuel Stearns— *American Herbal*—Walpole, N.H.

Hospital—marine hospital (U.S.)—Norfolk Naval Hospital deeded to U.S.—April 20

Land Preemption Act (federal)—enacted—March 3

Naval Officer—naval surgeon of the U.S. Navy— George Balfour

Parliamentary Rules of Order—Thomas Jefferson —published—Washington, D.C.

President (U.S.)—President elected by the House of Representatives—Thomas Jefferson—Feb. 11

President (U.S.)—President inaugurated in the city of Washington—Thomas Jefferson—March 4

President (U.S.)—President to review the military forces—Thomas Jefferson—Washington, D.C. —July 4

President (U.S.)—President to review the U.S. Marine Band—John Adams—Jan. 1

Representative (U.S.)—representative appointed to a presidential Cabinet—James Madison—began service as secretary of state—May 2

Ship — yacht — constructed — *Jefferson* — Salem,

Supreme Court (U.S.)—Chief Justice of the United States who had been a representative in Congress—John Marshall of Virginia—began service as Chief Justice—Feb. 4

Supreme Court (U.S.)—Chief Justice of the United States to serve in a presidential cabinet—John Marshall—began term as Chief Justice Feb. 4—ad interim Secretary of State—Feb. 4-March 4

Whips—manufactured—Titus Pease—Westfield, Mass.

1802

Animals—leopard—exhibited—Boston, Mass.— Feb. 2

Animals—sheep (merino sheep)—imported

Army—engineer corps—established—March 16

Army School—army school—Military Academy of the United States—authorized—March 16

Army School—army school graduate (Jewish)—S. M. Levy—graduated—West Point, N.Y.—Oct. 11

Army School—army school graduates—commissioned—Oct. 12

Astronomer—astronomer to acquire fame after the Revolution—Nathaniel Bowditch

Book Fair—New York City—June 1

Brass—rolled—Abel Porter & Co.—Waterbury, Conn.

Button—gilt buttons to be commercially manufactured—Waterbury, Conn.

Chess Book—*Chess Made Easy*—published—Philadelphia, Pa.

Clock—banjo clock patent—Simon Willard—Boston, Mass.—Feb. 8

Fruit Culture Treatise—William Forsyth—published—Philadelphia, Pa.

Gymnastics Book—*Gymnastics for Youth*—published—Philadelphia, Pa.

Jewish Congregation—Jewish congregation (Ashkenazic)—founded—Philadelphia, Pa.—October 10

Land Grant—land subsidy for internal improvements—April 30

Lawbook—lawbook (text)—*Lex Mercatoria Americana*—published—New York City

Librarian—Librarian of Congress—John Beckley—appointed—Jan. 29

Library Catalog—catalog of the Library of Congress—published—Washington, D.C.

Periodical—comic magazine—*The Wasp*—Robert Rusticoat, editor—Harry Crosswell, publisher—Hudson, N.Y.—July 7

Social Service Endowment—White-Williams Foundation—incorporated—March 23

Tea Shrub—planted—Middleton, S.C.

Vaccine Institution—organized—Baltimore, Md. —March 25

1803

Apple Parer—invented—Moses Coats—Downington, Pa.—Feb. 14

Bird Banding—bird banding—J. J. Audubon—Montgomery County, Pa.

Botany Book—botany book (elementary work)—published—Philadelphia, Pa.

Camp Meeting—Logan County, Ky.

Evangelical Association Council—assembly—Bucks County, Pa.

History Instruction—school of modern history—College of William and Mary—Williamsburg, Va.

Impeachment—impeachment of a federal judge—John Pickering—trial—March 3

Land Grant—special land grant to a foreigner—enacted

Law Digest—*An Abridgement of the Laws*—published—Harrisburg, Pa.

Library—youth's library—Salisbury, Conn.—Jan.

Medical Book—gastroenterology treatise—published—Philadelphia, Pa.

Medical Book—hemophilia treatise—J. C. Otto—published—New York City

Mica—mica—mined—Grafton, N.H.

Reaper—reaper—patented—Richard French and J. F. Hawkins—May 17

Refrigerator—refrigerator—invented—Thomas Moore—Baltimore, Md.

Ship—steamboat with a twin-screw propeller—patented—John Stevens—Hoboken, N.J.—April 11

Supreme Court (U.S.) Decision—Supreme Court decision to void an act of Congress—Marbury vs. Madison—in the February term

Territorial Expansion—annexation of territory—Louisiana Purchase

Tract Society—tract society—Massachusetts Society for Promoting Christian Knowledge—instituted—Boston, Mass.—Sept. 1

1804

Agricultural Encyclopedia—*Domestic Encyclopedia*—published—Philadelphia, Pa.

American Indian Reservation—American Indian reservation (federal)—official notice of removal —act of March 26

Banana Importation—from Cuba

Book—book printed in the Indiana Territory

Bridge—pontoon bridge—Lynn, Mass.

Cemetery—congressional cemetery—Washington, D.C.

College—university founded by a federal land grant—Ohio University—chartered—Feb. 18

Congressional Caucus—congressional caucus (open, not secret)—Washington, D.C.—Feb. 29

Distilling Book—*American Distiller*—published —Philadelphia, Pa.

Expedition—expedition across the continent to the Pacific coast—Lewis and Clark—left—St. Louis, Mo.—May 14

Impeachment—impeachment of a federal judge— Joseph Pickering—impeached

Impeachment—impeachment proceedings against a Justice of the Supreme Court of the U.S.—Samuel Chase—Nov. 30

Insurance—insurance agency—Israel Whelan— New York City

Madstone—purchased—Benjamin Milam— Winona, Ill.

Marine Corps—commando raid—Stephen Decatur—Feb. 16

Pharmacist—pharmacist (woman)—Elizabeth Marshall—Philadelphia, Pa.

Political Convention—political nominating caucus attended by party leaders—Washington, D.C.—Feb. 25

Presidential Candidate—presidential candidate nominated at a caucus—Thomas Jefferson— Washington, D.C.—Feb. 25

Presidential Election—presidential election in which candidates had been nominated for the vice presidency—Nov. 6

Printer's Ink—successfully manufactured—C. E. Johnson—Philadelphia, Pa.

Quids—organized

Ship—steamboat with a twin-screw propeller— navigated—John Stevens

1805

Amphibious Vehicle—steam-operated amphibious vehicle—Oliver Evans—Philadelphia, Pa.— July

Art Organization—art organization—of importance—established—Philadelphia, Pa.—Dec. 26

Cryptography Book—published—Hartford, Conn.

Dry Dock—dry dock—constructed—Robert Fulton—Jersey City, N.J.

Expedition—expedition across the continent to the Pacific coast—reached mouth of Columbia River—Nov. 8

Flag—American flag flown over a fortress of the Old World—Tripoli—April 27

History—American history of importance written by a woman—M. O. Warren—published—Boston, Mass.

Ice—export of ice—to West Indies—Aug.

Magic Lantern—magic lantern book—*The Expositor*, by W. F. Pinchbeck—printed—Boston, Mass.

Prizefighter—American to win distinction in the prize ring—Bill Richmond—winner—July 8

Vice President (U.S.)—Vice President to be nominated—George Clinton—served—March 4

Women's Club—women's club—Female Charitable Society—Wiscasset, Me.—organized

1806

Art Organization—art organization—Pennsylvania Academy of Fine Arts—incorporated— March 28

Births—child born in the White House, Washington, D.C.—J. M. Randolph—Jan. 17

Cathedral—cathedral—cornerstone laid—Baltimore, Md.—July 7

Cider Mill—patented—I. Quintard—Stanfield, Conn.—April 5

Dictionary—American dictionary—*A Compendious Dictionary of the English Language*, by Noah Webster—published—New Haven, Conn.

Duel—duel in which a future President of the United States participated—Andrew Jackson— May 30

Expedition—expedition across the continent to the Pacific coast—returned to St. Louis, Mo.— Sept. 23

Gas—gaslights (street)—David Melville—Newport, R.I.

Horse—horse to trot 1 mile in less than 3 minutes —Yankey—New York City—June 10

Medical Book—dispensatory—*American Dispensatory*—published—Philadelphia, Pa.

Periodical—college magazine—*Literary Cabinet* —Yale—New Haven, Conn.—published—Nov. 15

Road—federal highway—Great National Pike— Cumberland, Md.—commenced

Senator (U.S.)—senator to serve in contravention to the age limit—Henry Clay of Kentucky—began service Nov. 19

Soap Manufacturer—soap manufacturer to render fats in his plant—William Colgate—New York City

Town—town founded by a woman—R. H. S. Mixon—Tangipahoa, La.

1807

Animals—sheep (Merino sheep) exhibition— Pittsfield, Mass.

Coast Survey—authorized—Feb. 10

College—college entrance requirement, other than Greek, Latin, and arithmetic—Harvard— Cambridge, Mass.

Deaf—School—instruction for the deaf—New York City

Embargo Act—enacted—Dec. 22

Evangelical Church—annual conference—Lebanon County, Pa.—Nov.

Evangelical Conference—Kleinfeltersville, Pa.—Nov. 15

Glass Factory—flint glass factory—successful—Pittsburgh, Pa.

Glue Factory (animal products)—established—Roger Upton—Boston, Mass.

Lifeboat—lifeboat—built—William Raymond—Nantucket, Mass.

Medical Book—obstetrics book—Samuel Bard—published—New York City

Meteorite—meteorite whose landing was recorded—fell at Weston (now Easton), Conn.—Dec. 14

Newspaper—Democratic newspaper—*Democratic Press*—published—Philadelphia, Pa.—March 27

Ship—steamboat to make regular trips—Robert Fulton—*Clermont*—trial trip—New York City—Aug. 7

Soda Water—soda water—prepared—Townsend Speakman—Philadelphia, Pa.

Vice President (U.S.)—Vice President arrested—Aaron Burr—Wakefield, Ala.—Feb. 19—indicted for treason, Richmond, Va.—June 24—trial began, Aug. 3

1808

Bible—Bible translated into English in America—copyrighted—Sept. 12

Bible Society—Bible society—organized—Philadelphia, Pa.—Dec. 12

Brushes—manufactured—Medford, Mass.

Catholic Diocese—became Archdiocese—Baltimore, Md.—April 8

Cheese—pineapple cheese—manufactured—Troy, Pa.

Coal—anthracite coal burned experimentally—Jesse Fell—Wilkes-Barre, Pa.—Feb. 11

College—university founded by a federal land grant—opened—Athens, Ohio—June 1

Duel—duel between representatives in Congress—Bladensburg, Md.

Law Periodical—law magazine—*American Law Journal*—published—Baltimore, Md.

Leather—leather-splitting machine—patented—Samuel Parker—Billerica, Mass.—July 9

Naval Officer—naval medical officer to write a book—Edward Cutbush—published—Philadelphia, Pa.

Orchestra—college orchestra—Harvard University—Cambridge, Mass.—formed—March 6

Pharmacopoeia—pharmacopoeia prepared by a medical association—published—Boston, Mass.

Play (drama)—play about an American Indian—by an American—J. N. Barker—*The Indian Princess*—produced—Philadelphia, Pa.—April 6

Religious Publication—religious review—*Herald of Gospel Liberty*—published—Portsmouth, N.H.—Sept. 1

Salt—salt well—west of the Allegheny Mountains—operated—Charlestown, W.Va.—Jan. 15

Temperance Society—temperance society (union)—organized—Saratoga Springs, N.Y.—April 13

1809

Catholic Periodical—Catholic magazine in English—issued—Detroit, Mich.—Aug. 31

Clock—watchmaker—Luther Goddard—Shrewsbury, Mass.

Cricket Club—cricket club—founded—Boston, Mass.

Dictionary—Hebrew dictionary—C. C. Moore—published—New York City

Disciples of Christ—church—organized—Washington, Pa.—Aug. 17

Geology Book—geology book—of importance—William Maclure—Philadelphia, Pa.

Gloves—commercial manufacture—Talmadge Edwards—Johnstown, N.Y.

Medical Book—typhus fever treatise—Elisha North—published—Philadelphia, Pa.

Pen—steel pen patent—Peregrine Williamson—Baltimore, Md.—Nov. 22

Periodical—magazine containing a fashion plate—*The Port Folio*—June

President (U.S.)—President born beyond the boundaries of the original 13 states—Abraham Lincoln—Hodgenville, Ky.—Feb. 12

Railroad—railroad for freight transportation—Thomas Leiper—Crum Creek, Pa. to Ridley Creek, Pa.

Railroad Track—railroad track (practical)—used—Philadelphia, Pa.—July 31

Ship—steamboat to make an ocean voyage—*Phoenix*—sailed—New York City to Philadelphia, Pa.—June 10

Supreme Court (U.S.) Decision—Supreme Court decision establishing the power of the United States—Feb. 20

Surgical Operation—abdominal operation—Ephraim McDowell—Danville, Ky.—Dec. 13

Type Specimen Book—showing ornaments—published—Philadelphia, Pa.

Vice President (U.S.)—Vice President to serve under two Presidents—George Clinton—second term—March 4

Woman—woman granted a patent—Mary Kies—South Killingly, Conn.—May 5

1810

Actor—English actor of note—G. F. Cooke—debut—New York City—Nov. 21

Agricultural Journal—agricultural journal—*Agricultural Museum*—published—Georgetown, D.C.—July 4

Auger (screw auger)—manufactured—Walter French—Seymour, Conn.

Carpet Factory—carpet mill to make ingrain carpets—Frederick City, Md.

Cheese—pineapple cheese—L. M. Norton—patent—April 17

Cigar Factory—of importance—West Suffield, Conn.

Colonist—colonists to reach the Pacific coast—left New York City—Sept. 6

Dictionary—military dictionary—William Duane—published—Philadelphia, Pa.

Fair—agricultural fair—Pittsfield, Mass.—Oct. 1

Glass Crystal Chandelier—Pittsburgh, Pa.

Horse Breeding Society—Massachusetts Society for Encouraging the Breed of Fine Horses—formed—Boston, Mass.—annual trials—Oct. 23

Insurance—black-owned insurance company—African Insurance Company of Philadelphia—organized

Insurance—fire insurance joint-stock company—American Fire Insurance Company—organized—Philadelphia, Pa.—Feb. 28

Irish Magazine—*The Shamrock*—published—New York City—Dec. 15

Leather—leather tanning by the "oil tan" method—Talmadge Edwards—Johnstown, N.Y.

Medical Book—pediatrics book—*The Maternal Physician*—published—Philadelphia, Pa.

Mineralogy Periodical—*American Mineralogical Journal*—published—New York City—Jan.

Missionary Society—foreign missionary society—organized—Bradford, Mass.—June 29

Orchestra—orchestra—founded—J. C. G. Graupner

Poem—poem by an American—to receive recognition at home and abroad—"Thanatopsis"—W. C. Bryant

Postal Service—mailbox locker—invented—Thomas Brown

Printing History—Isaiah Thomas—*History of Printing*—published—Worcester, Mass.

Screw—screw factory—established—Bellefonte, R.I.

Silk—silk mill—Mansfield, Conn.

Supreme Court (U.S.) Decision—Supreme Court decision that a state law was unconstitutional—Fletcher vs. Peck—March 16

Vaccination Legislation—vaccination legislation (state)—enacted—Massachusetts—March 6

1811

Boat Club—boat club—Knickerbocker Boat Club—New York City—organized

Colonist—colonists to reach the Pacific coast—April 12

Congress (U.S.)—Senate—Senate filibuster—Feb. 11

Conjurer—conjurer of note—Richard Potter—Boston, Mass.—performed in November

Conscience Fund—started

Disciples of Christ—church established—Brush Run, Pa.—May 4

Education Periodical—educational magazine—*Juvenile Mirror*—published—New York City

Export—exports from the United States to exceed the imports—fiscal year ending Sept. 30

Ferryboat—steam-propelled ferryboat—*Juliana*—Hoboken, N.J.–New York City—operation—Oct. 11

Hospital—naval hospital—authorized—Feb. 26

Masonic Magazine—*Free-Masons Magazine*—published—Philadelphia, Pa.—April

Medical Book—anatomy book (American)—Caspar Wistar—*A System of Anatomy*—published—Philadelphia, Pa.

News Agency—news agency—established—Boston, Mass.

Periodical—quarterly magazine—*American Review of History*—published—Philadelphia, Pa.—Jan.

Secession—secession first mentioned in Congress—Josiah Quincy—June 4

Senator (U.S.)—senator censured—Timothy Pickering of Massachusetts—Jan. 2

Ship—steamboat to sail down the Mississippi—*New Orleans*—from Pittsburgh, Pa.—arrived—New Orleans, La.—Oct. 1

War (1812)—naval battle—off Sandy Hook, N.J.—May 16

1812

Army School—army school graduate killed—in military action—George Ronan—Chicago, Ill.—Aug. 15

Bond—treasury notes (interest-bearing)—authorized—June 30

Bridge—"Y" bridge—authorized—Zanesville, Ohio—Jan. 21

Canning Book—François Appert—published—New York City

Coal—anthracite coal used commercially—Philadelphia, Pa.

Drug Mill—established—C. V. Hagner—Philadelphia, Pa.

Federal Foreign Aid Bill—enacted

File Manufacturing Machine—invented—Morris B. Belknap—Greenfield, Mass.

Flag—American flag over a schoolhouse—Colrain, Mass.—May

Historical Society—historical society (national)—American Antiquarian Society—Worcester, Mass.—incorporated—Oct. 24

History—comic history of the United States—J. K. Paulding—published—New York City

Land Office—General Land Office (federal)—established—April 25

Marine Corps—woman marine—Lucy Brewer—in battle—Aug. 19

Medical Book—hydrophobia book—James Thacher—*Observations on Hydrophobia*—published—Plymouth, Mass.

Medical Book—mental diseases book—*Medical Inquiries*—Benjamin Rush—published—Philadelphia, Pa.

Medical Book—psychiatry book—*Medical Inquiries and Observations Upon the Diseases of the Mind,* by Benjamin Rush—published—Philadelphia, Pa.—copyrighted Oct. 26

Mower (horsepower)—patented—Peter Gaillard—Lancaster, Pa.—Dec. 4

Pawnbroking Ordinance—enacted—New York City—July 13

Pencil Factory—William Monroe—Concord, Mass.—June

Political Convention—political nominating caucus—New York City—Sept. 15–16

Railroad Treatise—John Stevens—published— New York City

Russian Settlement—established—Cazadero, Calif.—March 15

School Superintendent—school superintendent (state)—Gideon Hawley—New York—appointed

Ship—naval vessel of the United States to display the American flag around Cape Horn—*Essex* —sailed—Oct. 27

Supreme Court (U.S.)—Associate Justice of the Supreme Court who had been a representative in Congress—Gabriel Duvall of Maryland—began service as Associate Justice, Feb. 3

Type Specimen Book—published—Binny & Ronaldson—Philadelphia, Pa.

Vice President (U.S.)—Vice President to die in office—George Clinton—died—April 20

Vice Presidential Candidate—vice presidential nominee to decline nomination—John Langdon —May 12

War (1812)—British frigate captured by a single frigate—*Macedonian* captured by *United States*—Oct. 25

War (1812)—frigate action of importance in the War of 1812—Aug. 19

War (1812)—naval battle after the U.S. declaration of war—*President* vs. *Belvidera*—June 23

War (1812)—prisoners in the War of 1812—captured—St. Regis, N.Y.—Oct. 22–23

War (1812)—war declaration—June 18

War Bond—issued by the federal government— authorized—March 14

Wedding—White House wedding—Todd-Washington—March 29

1813

Army Officer—surgeon general of the U.S. Army —James Tilton—June 11

Book—stereotyped book—published—New York City—June

Chemical Magazine—printed—Philadelphia, Pa.

Cotton Mill—cotton mill in the world in which the whole process of cotton manufacturing from spinning to weaving was carried on by power— Waltham, Mass.—incorporated—Feb. 23

Craps—introduced—New Orleans, La.

Diplomatic Service—Jewish diplomatic representative—M. M. Noah—Consul to Tunis

Factory Standardization of Production—contract —Middletown, Conn.—April 16

Flag—American flag flown in battle on the Pacific—*Essex*—docked—Valparaiso, Chile

Gas—gaslights (street)—patent—David Melville —March 18

Globe Factory—terrestrial and celestial globes— James Wilson—Bradford, Vt.

Haircloth—manufactured—Rahway, N.J.

Hospital—psychiatric hospital (private)—Philadelphia, Pa.—founded April 14

Medical Instruction—medical jurisprudence course—James Stringham—Columbia University—New York City

Postal Service—mail delivery by steamboats— authorized—Feb. 27

Religious Publication—religious weekly newspaper—*The Religious Remembrancer*—published —Philadelphia, Pa.—Sept. 4

Rubber—rubber patent—J. F. Hummel—Philadelphia, Pa.—April 29

School Superintendent—school superintendent (state)—Gideon Hawley—New York—served —Jan. 14

Ship—naval vessel of the United States to display the American flag around Cape Horn—arrived —Valparaiso, Chile—March 14

Stereotype — stereotypers — successful — New York City

Supreme Court (U.S.) Decision—Supreme Court decision that reversed the decision of a state supreme court

Vaccination Legislation—vaccination legislation (national)—enacted—Feb. 27

Vice President (U.S.)—Vice President to have served in the House of Representatives—Elbridge Gerry of Massachusetts—sworn in as Vice President—March 4

War (1812)—defeat in history of a British squadron—O. H. Perry—Sept. 10

1814

Bible—Hebrew Bible—*Biblia Hebraica*—published—Philadelphia, Pa.

Building—building in all-Gothic architecture— Trinity Episcopal Church—New Haven, Conn

College—school for the higher education of women—Middlebury, Vt.

Conscription—wartime conscription bill—passed by Senate—Dec. 9

Cottonseed Hulling Machine—patented—J. Lineback—Salem, N.C.—March 31

Freemasons—Knights Templar Grand Encampment—New York City—Jan. 22

Museum—museum especially constructed as a museum and art gallery—Baltimore, Md.—Aug 15

President (U.S.)—President to face enemy gunfire while in office—James Madison—Bladensburg Md.—Aug. 25

Saw (circular)—produced—Benjamin Cummins— Bentonsville, N.Y.

Secession—secession convention—Hartford Conn.—Dec. 15

Ship—steam-propelled frigate—*Demologos*— launched—New York City—Oct. 29

1815

Engraving—pamphlet produced from a steel plate engraving—Perkins' and Fairman's *Running Hand Stereographic Copies*—published— Charles Whipple—Newburyport, Mass.

Monument—monument to George Washington (city or state)—cornerstone laid—Baltimore, Md.—July 4

Music—music festival—Boston, Mass.—Feb. 16

Naval Officers' Training School—naval officers' training school—established—Boston, Mass.—Dec. 10

Peace Society—New York Peace Society—organized—New York City—Aug. 16

Railroad Charter—New Jersey—Feb. 6

Ship—steam-propelled frigate—*Demologos*—propelled by own steam—June 1

Ship—steamboat (double-decked)—*Washington*—keel laid—Wheeling, W.Va.—Sept. 10

Varnish manufacturer—exclusively—Christian Schrack—Philadelphia, Pa.

1816

American Language—book on Americanisms—John Pickering—published—Boston, Mass.

Army Officer—paymaster—Pay Department—organized—April 24

Bank—savings bank—Bank for Savings—New York City—conceived—Nov. 29

Bank—savings bank actually to receive money on deposit—Philadelphia Saving Fund Society—Philadelphia, Pa.—opened—Dec. 2

Bank—savings bank to become a corporation—Provident Institution for Savings—Boston, Mass.—chartered—Dec. 13

Bible Society—Bible society (national organization)—New York City—May 11

Boiler Plates—manufactured—Coatesville, Pa.

Bridge—iron-wire suspension bridge—Schuylkill River

Coast Survey Superintendent—F. R. Hassler—appointed—Aug. 3

Debt—public debt of the United States to exceed $100 million

Dry Dock Patent—John Adamson—Boston, Mass.—Dec. 13

Evangelical Church General Conference—Buffalo Valley, Pa.—Oct. 14–17

Gas—gas ordinance (city)—Baltimore, Md.—June 19

Methodist Episcopal Church—African Methodist Episcopal Church—established—Philadelphia, Pa.—April 9

Mineralogy Textbook—mineralogy textbook—*An Elementary Treatise on Mineralogy*, by Parker Cleaveland—published—Boston, Mass.

Pharmacopoeia—pharmacopoeia prepared by a hospital staff—published—New York City

Printing Press—printing press invented in America—G. E. Clymer—Columbian press—Philadelphia, Pa.

Ship—packet line—Black Ball Line—New York City–Liverpool, England

Ship—steamboat (double-decked)—arrived—New Orleans, La.—Oct. 7

Tariff—tariff for protection—enacted—April 27

Theological School—theological school (nonsectarian)—Harvard College—Cambridge, Mass.

1817

Bank—savings bank to become a corporation—opened—Feb. 19

Brokerage—stock exchange—New York Stock Exchange—new organization

Canal—canal of importance—Erie Canal—authorized—April 15

Conchology Report—published—Philadelphia, Pa.

Deaf—Church Service—prayers in the sign language of the deaf—Hartford, Conn.

Deaf—School—school for the deaf—permanent—Connecticut Asylum for the Education and Instruction of Deaf and Dumb Persons—Hartford, Conn.—opened—April 15

Diplomatic Service—Pan American delegates (American)—appointed—July

Evangelical Church Building—Evangelical Church—dedicated—New Berlin, Pa.—March 2

Game Law—game law (state)—Massachusetts

Gas—gas company—Gas Light Company—Baltimore, Md.—incorporated—Feb. 5

Hospital—eye infirmary—established—New London, Conn.

Iron—cast-iron pipes used in a city waterworks system—installed—Philadelphia, Pa.

Iron—iron mill to puddle and roll iron—Brownsville, Pa.—operated—Sept. 15

Law School—law school of collegiate rank—permanently organized—Harvard College School of Law—Cambridge, Mass.

Medical Book—therapeutics and materia medica book—Nathaniel Chapman—published—Philadelphia, Pa.

Newspaper—abolition newspaper—*Philanthropist*—published—Mount Pleasant, Ohio

Papermaking Machinery—papermaking machine (cylinder)—manufactured—Brandywine, Del.

Sword Swallower—Senaa Samma—New York City—Nov. 11

Theater—showboat—left Nashville, Tenn.—Oct. 20

Trust—trust—salt trust—organized—Nov. 10

1818

Army—medical corps—organized—April 14

Army Officer—Surgeon General of the U.S. Army—Joseph Lovell—began service—April 18

Cement—natural cement rock—discovered—Fayetteville, N.Y.

Chair Factory—established—Lambert Hitchcock—Riverton, Conn.

College—women's college (chartered)—college opened—Elizabeth Female Academy—Washington, Miss.—Nov.

Education Periodical—educational magazine to achieve success—*Academician*—published—New York City—Feb. 7

Flag Legislation—flag act—enacted—April 4

Geology Book—geology textbook—Amos Eaton—published—Leicester, Mass.

Horticultural Society—horticultural society—New York Horticultural Society—founded—New York City

Insurance—marine insurance law (state)—Massachusetts—enacted—Feb. 16

Medical Instruction—clinical instruction and bedside demonstration—introduced—A. H. Stevens—New York City

Medical Instruction—hygiene lectures—James Jackson—Harvard College—Cambridge, Mass.—Oct. 8

Melons—melons and cantaloupes—grown—Germantown, Pa.

Oil—oil well (flowing)—Martin Beatty—Monticello, Ky.

Oratorio—oratorio performance (complete)—*Messiah*—Boston, Mass.—Dec. 25

Pension—pensions paid by the United States Government—universal service pension act—enacted—March 18

Political Economy Course—college chair of political economy—Columbia University—New York City

Science Periodical—science magazine—*American Journal of Science*—published—New York City—July

Ship—steamboat built in America to cross the Atlantic ocean—*Savannah*—launched—New York City—Aug. 22

Ship—steamboat on the Great Lakes—*Walk-in-the-Water*—sailed—Buffalo, N.Y.—Oct. 10

Shoe Peg—invented—Joseph Walker—Hopkinton, Mass.

Theological School—theological school black graduate to receive a degree—T. S. Wright—Princeton Theological Seminary, Princeton, N.J.

Tunnel — tunnel — Auburn, Pa. — construction commenced

Engineering College—civil engineering course in a college—Norwich University—Northfield, Vt.—founded—Aug. 6

Fire Patrol—fire patrol—Philadelphia Society for the Protection of Movable Property in Time of Fire—organized—Philadelphia, Pa.

Geological Society (national)—American Geological Society—founded—New Haven, Conn.

Iron—angle iron—rolled—Samuel Leonard—Pittsburgh, Pa.

Lathe—patented—Thomas Blanchard—Middlebury, Conn.—Sept. 6

Leather—patent leather—tanned—Seth Boyden—Newark, N.J.

Lithograph—Bass Otis—published—Philadelphia, Pa.

Manual Training—industrial school—Fellenberg plan—Derby, Conn.

Methodist Church—Methodist missionary—Ebenezer Brown—New Orleans, La.

Military School—military school—Norwich, Vt.—founded—Aug. 6

Navy—naval legislation standardizing nomenclature for naval vessels—enacted—March 3

Odd Fellows Lodge—established—Baltimore Md.—April 26

Piracy Legislation—piracy legislation—enacted—March 3

Plow—plow with interchangeable parts—J. J Wood—Poplar Ridge, N.Y.—patented—Sept. 1

Ship—steamboat built in America to cross the Atlantic Ocean—*Savannah*—sailed—Savannah Ga.—May 22

Thread—silk thread—manufactured—Mansfield Conn.

Tightrope—woman tightrope performer—performance—New York City—June 1

Tungsten—tungsten and tellurium—found—Huntington, Conn.

1819

Agricultural "Board" (state)—authorized—New York—April 7

Agricultural Journal—agricultural journal to attain prominence—*American Farmer*—published—Baltimore, Md.—April 2

Aviation—Parachute—parachute jump from a balloon—New York City—Aug. 2

Bank—savings bank actually to receive money on deposit—chartered—Feb. 25

Bicycle—bicycle velocipedes—driven—New York City—May 21

Bicycle Patent—bicycle patent—W. K. Clarkson—New York City—June 26

Canal—canal of importance—first boat between Rome and Utica, N.Y.—Oct. 22

Canning—canning—introduced—Ezra Daggett

Church—mariners' church—New York City—chartered—April 13

College—women's college (chartered)—Elizabeth Female Academy—Washington, Miss.—chartered—Feb. 17

1820

Agricultural "Board" (state)—organized—New York—Jan. 20

Census—states to exceed 1 million in population—New York, Virginia, and Pennsylvania

Church—mariners' church—built—New York City—June 4

Cranberry Cultivation—Dennis, Mass.

Discovery—discovery of Antarctica—N. B. Palmer—Nov. 18

Felt Manufacturing Mechanical Process—invented—T. R. Williams

Granite—quarried—Quincy, Mass.

High School—high school—English Classical School—opened—Boston, Mass.—May

Hospital—eye hospital (permanent)—New York City—opened—Aug. 14

Library—mechanics' library—opened—New York City

Library—mercantile library—organized—New York City—Nov. 9

Lightship—Craney Island, Va.—July 14

Military School—military school—first class enrolled—Norwich, Vt.—Sept. 4

Periodical—antislavery magazine—*The Emancipator*—published—Jonesboro, Tenn.—April 30

Pharmacopoeia—pharmacopoeia (general)—published—Boston, Mass.—Dec. 15

Political Machine—Albany Regency

Tax—bachelor tax—Missouri—Dec. 20

1821

Actor—actor to receive curtain applause—Edmund Keene—Boston, Mass.

Cathedral—cathedral—Baltimore, Md.—dedicated—May 31

College Alumni Association—college alumni association—Williams College—Williamstown, Mass.—Sept.

Debtors' Prison—abolished—Kentucky—Dec. 17

Discovery—discovery of Antarctica—expedition returned—May 8

Fire Hose—of rubber-lined cotton web—patented—James Boyd—Boston, Mass.—May 30

Odd Fellows Lodge—grand lodges organized

Pharmacy College—pharmacy college—Philadelphia College of Apothecaries organized—Philadelphia, Pa.—Feb. 23

President (U.S.)—President inaugurated on March 5—James Monroe

State—state admitted to the Union west of the Mississippi River—Missouri—Aug. 10

Tunnel—tunnel—Auburn, Pa.—opened to traffic

1822

Bank—trust company—Farmer's Fire Insurance and Loan Company—New York City—incorporated—February 28

Building—building of fireproof construction—Charleston, S.C.

Dental Book—book on dentistry to become popular—J. F. Flagg—*The Family Dentist*—published—Boston, Mass.

Dentistry—patent for artificial teeth—C. M. Graham—New York City—March 9

Horticultural Society—horticultural society—New York Horticultural Society—New York City—incorporated—March 22

Hospital—eye hospital (permanent)—New York City—incorporated—March 29

Library—free public library—Juvenile Library—Dublin, N.H.

Printing Press—power or steam printing press—manufactured—Daniel Treadwell—Boston, Mass.

Printing Press—printing press for printing "paper hangings"—patented—Peter Force—Washington, D.C.—Aug. 22

Quinine—quinine—manufactured—Philadelphia, Pa.

Technical Institute—Gardiner Lyceum—Gardiner, Me.

Treadmill—completed—New York City—Sept. 7

1823

Birth Registration—birth registration law (state)—passed—Georgia—Dec. 19

Dictionary—rhyming dictionary—published—New York City

Diplomatic Service—ministers plenipotentiary to South and Central America—appointed—Jan. 27

Gymnasium—to offer systematic instruction—Round Hill School—Northampton, Mass.—opened—Oct. 1

Medical Book—medical jurisprudence treatise (authoritative)—T. R. Beck—published—Albany, N.Y.

Medical Book—ophthalmology book—George Frick—published—Baltimore, Md.

Medical Instruction—ophthalmology course (regular)—established—Baltimore, Md.

Medical School—naval medical school (unofficial)—authorized—Philadelphia, Pa.—May 19

Normal School—normal school established exclusively for the preparation of teachers—Concord Academy—Concord, Vt.—opened—March 11

Periodical—Jewish monthly magazine—*The Jew*—S. H. Jackson, editor—published—published—New York City—March

Quinine—quinine sulphate—manufactured commercially—New York City

Representative (U.S.)—Roman Catholic priest to serve in Congress—Gabriel Richard—Michigan Territory—took office—March 4

1824

American Indian School—Catholic school for American Indians—St. Regis Seminary—Florissant, Mo.—opened May 11

Britannia Ware—produced—Isaac Babbitt—Taunton, Mass.

College—college course without Greek or Latin—Hobart College—Geneva, N.Y.

Commerce Case—decided under the Constitution—Feb.

Convent—Catholic convent to admit black women as sisters—Loretto, Ky.—May

Engineering College—engineering college—Rensselaer School—Troy, N.Y.—founded—Nov. 5

Entomology Book (comprehensive)—*American Entomology*—published—Philadelphia, Pa.

Gas—natural gas used as an illuminant—Fredonia, N.Y.

Jewish Congregation—Jewish congregation (reform)—Reformed Society of Israelites—organized—Charleston, S.C.—Nov. 21

Locomotive—locomotive to pull a train—John Stevens—Hoboken, N.J.—Oct. 23

Political Convention—nominating convention (state)—assembled—Utica, N.Y.

President (U.S.)—President to receive fewer popular and electoral votes than an opponent—J. Q. Adams—elected—Nov. 2

Presidential Candidate—presidential candidate to receive the greatest number of popular and electoral votes yet fail of election—Andrew Jackson—Nov. 2

Presidential Popular Vote—Nov. 2

Prison—reformatory for juvenile delinquents under legislative control—New York City—incorporated—March 29

Prizefight—prizefight arena—Worcester, Mass.—first fight held Jan. 7

Representative (U.S.)—representative-elect refused a seat—John Bailey of Massachusetts—March 18

Strike—strike in which women participated—Pawtucket, R.I.

Treaty—treaty with a South American country—Colombia—signed—Oct. 3

Tunnel—mining tunnel (large)—commenced—Mauch Chunk, Pa.

1825

Annual—*Le Souvenir*—published—Philadelphia, Pa.

Archery Club—archery club—founded—United Bowmen—Philadelphia, Pa.

Art Organization—artists' society of importance —organized—New York City—Nov. 8

Atlas—issued by a state—South Carolina

Bottler of Mineral Water—E. M. Durand—Philadelphia, Pa.

Brick—fire brick—manufactured—Woodbridge, N.J.

Canal—canal of importance—Erie Canal—New York—opened—Oct. 26

Canning—canning—patent—Jan. 19

Collar—collar—made—Troy, N.Y.

Communistic Society—communistic nonreligious settlement—New Harmony, Ind.

Cutlery Shears—manufactured—R. Heinisch—Elizabethport, N.J.

Engineering College—engineering college—Rensselaer School—Troy, N.Y.—opened—Jan. 3

Fireworks Book—*A System of Pyrotechny*—published—Philadelphia, Pa.

Fraternity (Greek Letter)—social fraternity—Kappa Alpha—Schenectady, N.Y.—established—Nov. 26

Giant—theatrical attraction—New York City—exhibited—Oct. 6

Homeopathy—introduced—H. B. Gram—New York City

Horse Race—trotting course—established—Jamaica, N.Y.

Ink—ink—manufactured—Thaddeus Davids—New York City

Labor Union—women's labor organization—United Tailoresses Society—formed—New York City

Law Codification (state)—Louisiana—promulgated—June 13

Medical Book—homeopathic treatise—C. F. S. Hahnemann—published—New York City—Dec.

Music—secular song hit—composed—J. H. Hewitt—Greenville, S.C.

Opera—grand opera sung in English—*Der Frei schütz*—presented—New York City—March 2

Opera—opera (Italian)—*Il Barbiere di Siviglia*—produced—New York City—Nov. 29

Periodical—mechanics' magazine—*American Mechanics' Magazine*—published—New York City—Feb. 5

Pharmacy Magazine—*The Journal of the Philadelphia College of Pharmacy*—published—Philadelphia, Pa.—Dec.

Porcelain (hard)—successfully manufactured—W. E. Tucker—Philadelphia, Pa.

Postal Service—dead letter office—organized

President (U.S.)—President whose father had been President—J. Q. Adams—inaugurated

Prison—reformatory for juvenile delinquents under legislative control—New York City—opened—Jan. 1

School Tax—public school tax enacted by a state —Illinois—Jan. 15

Ship—iron vessel (sheet iron)—*Codorus*—tested —Nov. 14

Ship—tugboat (steam)—*Rufus King*—built—New York City

Theater—theater lighted by gas—Chatham Garden—New York City—newspaper account—May 9

Tract Society—tract society (national)—American Tract Society—organized—New York City —May 11

Trademark Lawsuit—trademark controversy involving a newspaper

Treaty—treaty rejected by the Senate of the United States—Feb. 22

Unitarian Church—national organization of the Unitarian Churches of the United States and Canada—organized—Boston, Mass.—May 25

1826

Actor—American actor to appear abroad—J. H. Hackett—New York City—professional appearance

Animals—rhinoceros—exhibited—New York City—Sept. 13

Arcade—cornerstone laid—Philadelphia, Pa.—May 3

Art Organization—artists' society of importance —National Academy of Design—authorized—Jan. 18

Belting—sold—Pliny Jewell—Hartford, Conn.

Button—cloth-covered button—made by hand—Easthampton, Mass.

College Student—college graduate (black)—E. A. Jones—Amherst College, Amherst, Mass.—Aug. 23

Conference—conference of American Republics —Panama—March 14

Engineering College—engineering college—Rensselaer School—Troy, N.Y.—incorporated—March 21

Engine—internal-combustion engine—patented—Samuel Morey—Orford, N.H.—April 1

Gymnastics Instruction—gymnastics instruction at a college—Harvard University—Cambridge, Mass.

High School—high school for girls—established—Boston, Mass.

Iron—iron castings (malleable)—produced—Newark, N.J.—July 4

Lyceum—organized—Josiah Holbrook—Millbury, Mass.—Oct.

Periodical—children's magazine with literary merit—*Juvenile Miscellany*—published—Boston, Mass.—Sept.

Printing Instruction—printing instruction—Robert Owen—New Harmony, Ind.

Railroad—railroad for freight transportation to celebrate its centenary—Granite Railway Company—Quincy, Mass.—road completed—Oct. 7

Railroad Technical Report—William Strickland—published—Philadelphia, Pa.

Reaper—reaper that actually worked—invented—Henry Ogle

Ship—warship to circumnavigate the globe— *Vincennes*—left—New York City—Aug. 31

Tax—inheritance tax (state)—Pennsylvania—effective—May 1

Telescope—reflecting telescope—manufactured—Amasa Holcomb—Southwick, Mass.

1827

Actor—American actor to appear abroad—J. H. Hackett—London, England—April 5

Anarchist—Josiah Warren—opened "time store"—Cincinnati, Ohio

Anti-Masonic Party—formed—New York

Ballet—ballet—presented—Bowery Theater—New York City—Feb. 7

Book—book (cloth-covered) commercially bound—C. A. W. Eaton—*Rome in the Nineteenth Century*—4th edition—New York City

Dry Dock—federal dry docks—authorized—March 28

Governor—brothers to serve simultaneously as governors of their respective states—Enoch Lincoln (Maine)—1827–1829—Levi Lincoln (Massachusetts)—1825–1834

Holiday—Mardi Gras of New Orleans, La.

Horticultural Society—horticultural society (permanent)—Pennsylvania Horticultural Society—organized—Philadelphia, Pa.—Nov. 24

Kindergarten—nursery school—established—New York City—Infant School Society—founded—May 23

Labor Union—union organization of trades in a city—Mechanics Union of Trade Associations—organized—Philadelphia, Pa.

Lottery—lottery legislation (national)—enacted—March 2

Monument—monument to George Washington—Boonsboro, Md.—July 4

Music—secular song hit—J. H. Hewitt—"The Minstrel's Return"—published—Boston, Mass.

Nautical School—nautical school—established—Nantucket, Mass.—May 29

Newspaper—black newspaper—*Freedom's Journal*—published—New York City—March 16

Newspaper—Spanish newspaper—*El Redactor*—published—New York City—July 1

Ordnance—gun (rifled)—Cyrus Alger—first perfect bronze cannon—made in Boston, Mass.

Printing Press—printing press invented in America that was practical and successful—Samuel Rust—Washington Press—New York City

Railroad—railroad for commercial transportation of passengers and freight—Baltimore and Ohio Railroad Company—incorporated—Feb. 28

Swimming School—opened—Boston, Mass.—July 23

Telegraph—telegraph—constructed—H. G. Dyar—New York City

1828

Belts of Leather—used in transmitting power—Paul Moody—Lowell, Mass.

Brake Patent—brake patent—Robert Turner—Ward, Mass.—Aug. 29

Electric Magnet—invented—Joseph Henry—Albany, N.Y.—June

Fair—manufacturers' fair—New York City—Oct. 24

Game Manufacturing Company—John McLoughlin—New York City

History—political history—Timothy Pitkin—published—New Haven, Conn.

Hotel—hotel to install bathrooms—Tremont House, Boston, Mass.—cornerstone laid—July 4

Labor Party (political)—labor party (state)—Workingmen's Party—organized—Philadelphia, Pa.—July

News Correspondent—Washington correspondent of importance—J. G. Bennett—New York *Enquirer*—Jan. 2

Newspaper—American Indian newspaper—*Cherokee Phoenix*—New Echota, Ga.—published—Feb. 21

Papermaking Machinery—papermaking machine (Fourdrinier) imported—Joseph Pickering—North Windham, Conn.—Jan.

Periodical—magazine for women—to continue publication for more than five years—*Ladies' Magazine*—published—Boston, Mass.

Railroad—railroad for commercial transportation of passengers and freight—Baltimore and Ohio Railroad Co.—construction began—July 4

Railroad—state-owned railroad—Philadelphia and Columbia Railway—authorized—March 24

Strike—strike in which the militia was called—Paterson, N.J.—July 21

Strike—strike of women operatives—Dover Manufacturing Company—Dover, N.H.

Tights (circus)—introduced—Nelson Hower

1829

Annunciator—used—Tremont House, Boston, Mass.—Oct. 16

Bank Legislation—bank legislation (state)—enacted—New York—April 2

Blind—school for the blind—incorporated—Boston, Mass.—March 2

Bridge—stone arch railroad bridge—Baltimore, Md.—inspection—Dec. 21

Catholic Nuns—Catholic nuns (black community) —founded—Baltimore, Md.—July 2

Catholic Provincial Council—Baltimore, Md.—Oct. 4

Coffee Mill Patent—James Carrington—Wallingford, Conn.—April 3

Collar Manufacturer—detachable collars—Ebenezer Brown—Troy, N.Y.

Cottonseed Oil Mill—established—Francis Follet —Petersburg, Va.

Dental Book—dental textbook—*A System of Dental Surgery*—published—New York City

Education Book—S. R. Hall—*Lectures to Teachers*—published—Boston, Mass.

Encyclopedia—American encyclopedia—*Encyclopedia Americana*—published—Philadelphia, Pa.

Fair—manufacturers' fair—American Institute in the City of New York—incorporated—May 2

File Factory—file factory (hand cutting)—Broadmeadow & Co.—Pittsburgh, Pa.

Genealogy—genealogical collective work—John Farmer—published—Lancaster, Mass.

High School Legislation—authorizing night classes—enacted—March 16

Hotel—hotel—first-class hotel—Tremont House —Boston, Mass.—opened—Oct. 16

Hotel—hotel to install bathrooms—Tremont House, Boston, Mass.—opened—Oct. 16

Labor Union—labor union to nominate its own political candidates and win an election—E. Ford—elected—New York State Assembly—Nov. 7

Library—library for seamen—inaugurated—American Seamen's Friend Society—New York City—March

Locomotive—locomotive for railroad use—*Stourbridge Lion*—in service—Carbondale-Honesdale, Pa.—Aug. 9

Manual Training—manual training institute—Fellenberg Manual Labor Institute—Greenfield, Mass.

Medical Book—pathology textbook—*A Treatise on Pathological Anatomy*—W. E. Horner—published—Philadelphia, Pa.

Ordnance—gun (revolving)—made—John Gill—Newberne, N.C.

Paper—straw paper—from straw and grass—made—G. A. Shryrock—Chambersburg, Pa.

Papermaking Machine—papermaking machine (Fourdrinier)—manufactured—South Windham, Conn.

Post Office—post office building (U.S.)—constructed—Newport, R.I.

Postmaster—Postmaster General of the United States to become a member of the President's Cabinet—W. T. Barry—April 6

President (U.S.)—President born posthumously—Andrew Jackson—inaugurated—March 4

Siamese Twins—Siamese twins—arrived—Boston, Mass.—Aug. 16

Spoils System—introduced—President Andrew Jackson—inaugurated—March 4

Sports Magazine—*American Turf Register*—published—Baltimore, Md.—Sept.

Typewriter—typewriter—patented—W. A. Burt —Mount Vernon, Mich.—July 23

1830

Adhesive and Medicated Plaster—adhesive and medicated plaster—used in treatment of fractures—S. D. Gross—Philadelphia, Pa.

Anti-Masonic Party—first national convention—Philadelphia, Pa.—Sept. 11

Balloon—Flights—balloon flight by a native-born American—C. F. Durant—New York City—Sept. 9

Bank—trust company—New York Life Insurance and Trust Company—chartered—March 9

Black—national convention for blacks—Philadelphia, Pa.—Sept. 15

Bookstore (antiquarian)—Boston, Mass.—established—July 10

Building—split-level buildings—Elfreth houses—built—Philadelphia, Pa.

Census—census in which the population of the United States exceeded 10 million

Census—census which included the deaf, dumb, and blind

Church of Jesus Christ of Latter-Day Saints—Church of Jesus Christ of Latter-Day Saints—organized—Manchester, N.Y.—April 6

Cooperative—consumers' cooperative society—organized—New York City

Education Association—educational association (national)—formed—Boston, Mass.—March 15–19

Etcher—of skill—William Dunlap

Fountain Pen Patent—D. Hyde—Reading, Pa.—May 20

Fraternity Catalog—Kappa Alpha Society—published—Schenectady, N.Y.

Geological Survey—geological survey (state)—begun—Massachusetts

Lighthouse—lighthouse fueled by natural gas—Barcelona Harbor, N.Y.—began operation

Locomotive—locomotive built in the U.S. to pull passengers—*Tom Thumb*—Baltimore, Md.—Aug. 28

Locomotive—race between a locomotive and a horse-drawn vehicle—Relay, Md. to Baltimore, Md.—Aug. 25

Marble Statuary Group—Horatio Greenough

Newspaper—penny daily newspaper—*The Cen* —Philadelphia, Pa.

Observatory—observatory (astronomical) connected with an institution of learning—Joseph Caldwell—Chapel Hill, N.C.

Observatory—observatory (national)—Washington, D.C.—Dec. 6

Parade—street parade held by a mystic society—Mobile, Ala.—Dec. 31

Pistol—pistol—with a revolving barrel—invented—Samuel Colt

Printing Press—power printing press capable of fine book work—patented—Isaac Adams—Boston, Mass.—Oct. 4

Railroad—interstate railroad—chartered—Petersburg Railroad

Railroad—railroad for commercial transportation of passengers and freight—Baltimore and Ohio Railroad Co.—passenger revenue received—Jan. 7

Railroad Car—double-deck railroad coaches—used—Baltimore, Md.

Railroad Station—railroad station—(passenger and freight)—erected—Baltimore, Md.

Railroad Track—railroad rails of "T" shape—invented—R. L. Stevens

Scale—platform scale—built—Thaddeus Fairbanks—St. Johnsbury, Vt.

Ship—warship to circumnavigate the globe—*Vincennes*—returned—New York City—June 8

Soap—cakes of soap of uniform weight and individually wrapped—manufactured—Jessie Oakley—Newburgh, N.Y.

Sugar—sugar beets—grown—Ensfield, Pa.

Timetable (railroad)—railroad timetable—advertised—Baltimore, Md.—May 20

Veterinary Hospital—veterinary hospital opened—C. C. Grice—New York City

1831

Agricultural Journal—agricultural journal written directly from practical experience—*Genesee Farmer and Gardener's Journal*—Rochester, N.Y.—first issue, Jan. 1

Animals—cattle (Guernsey cattle)—imported—Boston, Mass.

Anti-Masonic Party—presidential candidate nominated at convention—Baltimore, Md.—Sept. 26

Bank Robbery—New York City

Bedspring—bedspring manufacturing patent—Josiah French—Aug. 25

Brass Wire Drawing and Tube Making Machinery—imported—Waterbury, Conn.

Building and Loan Association—Oxford Provident Building Association—organized—Frankford, Pa.—Jan. 3

Cabinet (U.S.)—Cabinet member who was a Catholic—R. B. Taney—Attorney General

Chloroform—distilled—Samuel Guthrie—Sackets Harbor, N.Y.

Congress (U.S.)—Congress in which 1,000 bills were introduced

Congress (U.S.)—House of Representatives—Catholic chaplain—C. C. Pise—began service March 4

Curling Club—organized—Pontiac, Mich.

Electric Bell—invented—Joseph Henry

Glucose—from potato starch—Samuel Guthrie—Sackets Harbor, N.Y.

Locomotive—locomotive bid—advertised—Baltimore, Md.—Jan. 4

Locomotive—locomotive to burn coal (practical, American-made)—*York*—York, Pa.—Phineas Davis—Feb. 19

Locomotive Headlight—locomotive illumination—devised—Horatio Allen

Medical Book—hydrotherapy book (American)—*On Baths and Mineral Waters*, by John Bell—printed—Philadelphia, Pa.

Music Book—children's music book—*Juvenile Lyre*, by Lowell Mason—published—Boston, Mass.—copyrighted, Feb. 1

Periodical—trade journal—*Rail-road Advocate*—published—Rogersville, Tenn.—July 4

Play (drama)—play performed 1,000 times—*The Gladiator*—New York City—opened

Printing Press—cylinder printing press—made—R. Hoe & Co.—New York City

Railroad—railroad to carry troops—Baltimore and Ohio Railroad—to Sykesville, Md.—June 30

Railroad Car—car with a center aisle—*Columbus*—introduced—Baltimore, Md.—July 4

Railroad Passenger—railroad honeymoon trip—Charleston, S.C.–Hamburg, S.C.—Mr. & Mrs. H. L. Pierson—Jan. 15

Reaper—reaper that was practical—C. H. McCormick—Walnut Grove, Va.

Representative (U.S.)—representative who had been President—J. Q. Adams—began service March 4

Scale—platform scale—patented—June 30

Sculptor—sculptor (American) to obtain a federal commission—John Frazee—appropriation—March 2

Shipping—coastal shipping service—New York City–New Orleans, La.

Stone Crusher—stone breaking machine patent—B. F. Lodge and E. T. Cox—April 13

Streetcar—streetcar company—incorporated—New York City—April 25

Teachers' Convention—teachers' convention (state)—Utica, N.Y.—Jan.

Telegraph—telegraph (electromagnetic)—exhibited—Joseph Henry—Albany, N.Y.

Treaty—treaty with a foreign nation to provide for mutual reduction of import duties—with France—signed—July 4

Tunnel—railroad tunnel—built—Johnstown, Pa.

1832

"America" (song)—publicly sung—Boston, Mass.—July 4

American Indians—Indian Affairs Commissioner (U.S.)—Elbert Herring—appointed—July 10

Democratic National Convention—Baltimore, Md.—May 21-23

Education—chair in education—New York University—New York City

Epidemic—cholera epidemic

Guano—imported—from Peru

Horticultural Magazine—*Floral Magazine*—published—Philadelphia, Pa.—May

Hospital—hospital and asylum for blacks—Georgia Infirmary—chartered—Dec. 24

Knitting Machine (power)—operated—Cohoes, N.Y.

Locomotive—locomotive with a four-wheeled front truck—*Experiment*—tested—New York—Aug.

Museum—college art museum—founded—New Haven, Conn.

Park—park (national)—Hot Springs National Park—Arkansas—established as a reservation—April 20

Phrenologist—of importance—to visit the U.S.—J. G. Spurzheim—arrived—New York City—Aug. 6

Phrenology Book—*Outlines of Phrenology*—published—Boston, Mass.

Pin—machine for manufacturing pins—patented—J. I. Howe—Derby, Conn.—June 22

Political Convention—two-thirds rule—adopted—Baltimore, Md.—May 21

Political Platform (national)—adopted—Washington, D.C.—May 11

Presidential Candidate—presidential candidate nominated at a national convention—Andrew Jackson—Baltimore, Md.

Railroad Accident—Granite Railway—Quincy, Mass.—July 25

Rubber—rubber company—Roxbury, Mass.

School—school supported by local taxation—opened—St. Petersburg, Fla.—May 20

Sewing Machine—lock-stitch sewing machine—invented—Walter Hunt—New York City

Streetcar—streetcar—John Stephenson—service commenced—New York City—Nov. 26

Theater History—of importance—William Dunlap—*A History of the American Theatre*—published—New York City

Treaty—treaty with a foreign nation to provide for mutual reduction of import duties—France—proclaimed—July 13

Vaccination Legislation—vaccination legislation for American Indians—enacted—May 5

Vice President (U.S.)—Vice President to resign—J. C. Calhoun—resigned—Dec. 28

Welsh Magazine—*Cymro-Americaidd*—published—New York City

1833

Animals—cattle importation of purebred shorthorns—company organized—Chillicothe, Ohio—Nov. 2

Annunciator—patented—Seth Fuller—Boston, Mass.—Dec. 26

Antislavery book—L. M. F. Child—*An Appeal in Favor . . .* —published—Boston, Mass.

Army—cavalry unit—organized—Jefferson Barracks, Mo.—Aug.

Avocado—planted—Santa Barbara, Calif.

Book—book for the blind—*Gospel of St. Mark*—published—Philadelphia, Pa.

Book Jacket—used—New York City

Building—tenement house—built—New York City

Collar Factory—to produce shirts and collars—Troy, N.Y.

College—coeducational college—Oberlin Institute—opened—Dec. 3

Crime Prevention and Detection—interstate crime pact—signed—New York City—Sept. 16

Cutlery Factory—cutlery factory—of importance—Greenfield, Mass.

Dictionary—medical dictionary (complete)—*A Dictionary of Medical Science,* by Robley Dunglison—published—Philadelphia, Pa.

Dry Dock—national ship in a federal dry dock—*Delaware*—Portsmouth, Va.—June 17

Horse Register—pacing register—*American Race-Turf Register*—published—New York City

Hospital—hospital and asylum for blacks—Savannah, Ga.—organization meeting—Jan. 15

Library—free public library (town-supported)—Peterborough, N.H.—April 9

Locomotive Cowcatcher—used—Camden and Amboy Railroad—Bordentown, N.J.–Hightstown, N.J.

Medical Book—dispensatory (American)— *Dispensatory of the United States of America*—published—Philadelphia, Pa.

Medical Society—homeopathic medical society—Hahnemann Society—organized—Philadelphia, Pa.—April 10

Mormon Temple—cornerstone laid—Kirtland, Ohio—July 23

Music Instruction—musical pedagogy school—Boston Academy of Music—Boston, Mass.—founded—Jan. 8

Newsboy—Barney Flaherty—New York City—Sept. 4

Newspaper—penny daily newspaper—successful—New York *Sun*—appeared—Sept. 3

Ordnance—gun (revolving)—patent—D. G. Colburn—Canton Canal, N.Y.—June 29

Pensions Commissioner (U.S.)—J. L. Edwards—appointed—March 2

Physiologist—of note—William Beaumont—Plattsburg, N.Y.—observations published

President (U.S.)—President to ride on a railroad train—Andrew Jackson

Quakers—Quaker college—Haverford School—Haverford, Pa.—opened, Oct. 28

Rubber—rubber company—Roxbury India Rubber Co.—incorporated—Feb. 11

Safe (fireproof)—patented—C. A. Gayler—New York City—April 12

School—evening school (free, public)—New York City—opened

Ship—clipper ship—*Ann McKim*—launched—Baltimore, Md.

Soda Fountain—soda fountain patent—Jacob Ebert—Cadiz, Ohio—April 24

Temperance Society—national temperance convention—Philadelphia, Pa.—May 24-27

Treaty—treaty with a Far Eastern country—Siam —March 20

1834

Baseball Book—*The Book of Sports*—published— Boston, Mass.

Bellows—invented—J. R. Morrison—Springfield, Ohio—patented—Dec. 23

Boat Club—boat club association of amateur clubs—formed—New York City

Book Trade Magazine—book trade magazine— published—New York City—Jan. 1

Brass Kettles—made—Coe Brass Company—Torrington, Conn.

Cabinet (U.S.)—Cabinet appointee rejected by the Senate—R. B. Taney

College—coeducational college—Oberlin Collegiate Institute—first commencement—Oct. 29

Dental Society—dental society (local)—formed— New York City—Dec. 3

Dentistry—amalgam for filling teeth—introduced —New York City—Aug. 12

Diving Suit—(practical) for submarine diving— patented—Leonard Norcross—Dixfield, Me.— June 14

Dry Dock—federal dry docks—Norfolk, Va. dry dock—completed—March 15

Election—mayor elected by popular vote in a city —C. V. W. Lawrence—New York City—Apr. 8

Gas—gas meter (dry)—patented—James Bogardus—New York City—Oct. 17

Geological Survey—geological survey appropriation (U.S.)—authorized—June 28

Labor Paper—*The Man*—published—New York City—Feb. 18

Locomotive—locomotive with six or eight driving wheels—patented—Ross Winans—Oct. 1

Match—friction matches—manufactured commercially—Chicopee, Mass.

Medical Book—medical encyclopedia—*American Cyclopedia of Practical Medicine*—published—Philadelphia, Pa.

Methodist Church—Methodist missionary bishop —Francis Burns—sailed for Liberia

Money—gold price fixed by Congress—gold price raised—June 28

Opera—opera singer (American) to sing in an Italian opera in Italian—Julia Wheatley—New York City—Nov. 25

Ordnance—gun (rifled)—Cyrus Alger

Patent—black to obtain a patent—Henry Blair— Glenross, Md.—Oct. 14

Pharmacy—homeopathic pharmacy—J. G. Wesselhoeft—opened—Philadelphia, Pa.

Presidential Censure—Senate resolution—March 28

Presidential Protest—signed—Andrew Jackson— April 15

Railroad—state-owned railroad—Philadelphia and Columbia Railway—locomotive trip—Lancaster, Pa.–Columbia, Pa.—April 2

Refrigerator—ice-making machine—invented— Jacob Perkins

Sandpaper Patent—Isaac Fischer—Springfield, Vt.—June 14

Ship—iron vessel—*John Randolph*—built— Savannah, Ga.

Sieve—wire sieves—manufactured commercially —Georgetown, Conn.

Soda Water Machine Manufacturer—John Matthews—New York City

Tunnel—railroad tunnel—Hollidaysburg–Johnstown, Pa.—completed—March 18

Valentine—valentines commercially produced— R. H. Elton—New York City

1835

Bible—Bible for the blind in embossed form— New York City

Bowie Knife—invented—James Bowie

Bridge—cast-iron bridge—Brownsville, Pa.

Coke—used successfully as a blast-furnace fuel— Huntingdon County, Pa.

Egyptian Antiquities Collection—imported—M. I. Cohen—Baltimore, Md.

Fire—fire of great destructive force—New York City—Dec. 16

Fire Patrol—fire patrol to receive a salary—New York City

Flea Circus—opened—New York City—Jan.

Gardener's Manual—*Young Gardener's Assistant* —published—New York City

Governor—Catholic governor—E. D. White— Louisiana

Horseshoe Manufacturing Machine—patented— Henry Burden—Troy, N.Y.—Nov. 23

Insurance—mutual fire insurance company— Manufacturers' Mutual Fire Insurance Company—Providence, R.I.—incorporated—Oct. 31

Insurance—mutual life insurance company to be chartered—New England Mutual Life Insurance Company—Boston, Mass.—chartered— April 1

Laundry—laundry—established—Independence Starks—Troy, N.Y.

Lock—mortised lock—Blake Brothers—Westville, Conn.

Locomotive—locomotive with a cab—*Samuel D. Ingham*—built—Philadelphia, Pa.

Medical Periodical—homeopathic magazine— *American Journal of Homeopathia*—published —New York City—Feb.

Medical School—homeopathic school—North American Academy of the Homeopathic Healing Art—Allentown, Pa.—founded—April 10

Music Instruction—music school authorized to confer degrees—established—Salem, Conn.

Patent Commissioner—H. L. Ellsworth—appointed—June 15

Periodical—American Indian–language monthly—*Shawnee Sun*—Feb. 24

Police—state police—Texas Rangers—organized

President (U.S.)—President whose assassination was attempted—Andrew Jackson—Jan. 30

Railroad—railroad to run trains to Washington, D.C.—Baltimore and Ohio Railroad—July 1

Sculptor—sculptor (American) of merit—Hiram Powers

Soda Water—soda water commercially bottled— Philadelphia, Pa.—Elias Durand

Spoons—nickel-silver spoons—manufactured— Robert Wallace—Wallingford, Conn.

Wrench—wrench patent—Solyman Merrick— Springfield, Mass.—Aug. 17

Zinc—zinc—produced—Washington, D.C.

1836

Agricultural Seed Distribution (national)—H. L. Ellsworth

Animals—cattle (shorthorn) public auction sale— Chillicothe, Ohio—Oct. 29

Chemistry Laboratory—chemical laboratory for instruction in chemical analyses—Philadelphia, Pa.

Child Labor Law—child labor law to include educational provision—enacted—Massachusetts —April 16

College—college for women—Mount Holyoke Seminary—South Hadley, Mass.—chartered— Feb. 11

College—women's college (chartered)—Wesleyan College, Macon, Ga.

Colonist—women to cross the continent—crossed continental divide—South Pass, Wyo.—July 4

Congress (U.S.)—House of Representatives—gag rule—adopted—May 26

Cricket Tournament—cricket game played by a college team—Haverford College—Haverford, Pa.

Expedition—scientific expedition fitted out by the United States Government—authorized—May 14

Fastening—hooks and eyes—successfully manufactured—Waterbury, Conn.

Fuse—safety fuse—manufactured—Simsbury, Conn.

Match—match patent—phosphorus friction matches—A. D. Phillips—Springfield, Mass.—Oct. 24

Medical School—homeopathic school—North American Academy of the Homeopathic Healing Art—Allentown, Pa.—incorporated—June 17

Money—coins produced by steam power

Mormon Temple—Kirtland, Ohio—dedicated March 27

Naval Officer—naval officer to become an engineer—C. H. Haswell—commissioned—Feb. 19

Patent—numbering system for patents—introduced—July 13

Pistol—pistol—with a revolving barrel—patent— Samuel Colt—Feb. 25

Postage Stamp—adhesive stamps—local delivery service authorized—July 2

President of the Republic of Texas—Sam Houston —took oath—Columbia, Tex.—Oct. 22

Railroad Guide—railroad guide—*The Traveller's Guide . . .* —New York

School Superintendent—school superintendent (city)—R. W. Haskins—Buffalo, N.Y.

Ship—steamboat on the Pacific coast—*Beaver*— tested—Vancouver, Wash.—May 16

Sleeping Car—sleeping car—Harrisburg-Chambersburg, Pa.

Supreme Court (U.S.)—Chief Justice of the Supreme Court who was Catholic—R. B. Taney— appointed—March 28

Treasury Department (U.S.)—treasury surplus returned and apportioned among the several states—authorized—June 23

Whig Party—state convention—Albany, N.Y.— Feb. 3

1837

Blind—state school for the blind—opened— Columbus, Ohio—July 4

Carpet Loom—carpet power loom—patented—E. B. Bigelow—West Boylston, Mass.—April 20

Child Labor Law—child labor law to include educational provision—Massachusetts—effective —April 1

Clock—brass clock works—invented—Chauncey Jerome—Bristol, Conn.

Coal—anthracite coal used in smelting iron ore— Mauch Chunk, Pa.

College—city college—became municipal university—Charleston, S.C.

College—coeducational college—Oberlin Collegiate Institute—equal status granted to women— Sept. 6

College—college for women—Mount Holyoke Seminary opened—Nov. 8

Congress (U.S.)—Congress to contain members of political parties other than Federalist, Whig Republican, or Democrat—25th Congress— opened March 4

Education—state board of education—Massachusetts—established—April 30

Fluorspar—commercial mining—Trumbull, Conn

Locomotive Steam Whistle—used—*The San dusky*—Oct. 6

Music Instruction—music instruction (public school)—Hawes School—South Boston, Mass —Nov.

Periodical—magazine for the blind—*Student's Magazine*—published—Philadelphia, Pa.

Physiology Society—physiology society—American Physiological Society—organized—Boston Mass.—Feb. 11

Piano—piano frame of iron—Jonas Chickering— Boston, Mass.

Plow—steel plow with a steel moldboard—John Deere—tested—near Grand Detour, Ill.

Rubber—rubber patent of importance—Charles Goodyear—June 17

Silk—silk power loom—patented—William Crompton—Taunton, Mass.—Nov. 25

Telegraph—telegraphic communication system in which dots and dashes represented letters—invented—Alfred Vail—Morristown, N.J.—Sept.

Thresher—threshing machine to employ steam—patented—Dec. 29

Treaty—treaty with a Far Eastern country—proclaimed—June 24

Vice President (U.S.)—Vice President elected by the Senate—R. M. Johnson—Feb. 8

1838

Astronomical Observations Book—J. M. Gillis—*Astronomical Observations*—published—Washington, D.C.

Brake Patent—railroad brake patent—E. Morris—Bloomfield, N.J.—Sept. 19

Bridge—wooden railroad bridge of a purely truss type—built—Alberton, Md.

Bunting—manufactured—M. H. Simpson—Saxonville, Mass.

Caster—for furniture—patented—Blake—New Haven, Conn.—June 30

Clock—watch made by machinery—marketed—James and Henry Pitkin

College—city college—opened as municipal university—Charleston, S.C.—April 1

College—college for women—Mount Holyoke Seminary—graduation—Aug. 23

Embossing Press—built—B. Sheridan—New York City

Expedition—scientific expedition fitted out by the United States Government—started—Hampton Roads, Va.—Aug. 18

Free Lunch—free lunch—Pierre Maspero—New Orleans, La.

Hebrew Book—Hebrew spelling book—*The Hebrew Reader,* by Isaac Leeser—printed—Philadelphia, Pa.

History Instruction—ancient and modern history chair—Harvard College—Cambridge, Mass.

Music—music convention—Boston, Mass.—Aug. 16–25

Normal School—normal school instruction—Lafayette College—cornerstone laid—July 4

Patent—patent reissue—Julius Hatch—Great Bend, Pa.—Jan. 9

Periodical—black periodical—*The Mirror of Liberty*—David Ruggles—New York City—first issue in July

Phrenology Magazine—*American Phrenological Journal*—published—Nathan Allen—Philadelphia, Pa.—Oct.

Pin—pins manufactured with a solid head—Poughkeepsie, N.Y.

Prohibition—prohibition state—legislation enacted—Tennessee—Jan. 26

School—model school—opened—Lafayette College—Easton, Pa.—Oct. 31

Ship—steamboat service (regular) across the Atlantic Ocean—arrived New York City—April 23

Silk—silk dyers—Gurleyville, Conn.

Silver Mine—discovered—Lexington, N.C.

Steam Shovel—invented—W. S. Otis—Philadelphia, Pa.

Steamboat Inspection Service (U.S.)—established—July 7

Sugar—sugar beets—Northampton Beet Sugar Company—erected—Northampton, Mass.

Sunday School—Jewish Sunday School—organized—Hebrew Sunday School Society—Philadelphia, Pa.—March 4

Telegraph—telegraphic communication system in which dots and dashes represented letters—message sent—Jan. 8

Tool Factory—established—Nashua, N.H.—John H. Gage

Workmen's Compensation—workmen's compensation lawsuit—South Carolina—July

1839

Antislavery Party—convention—Warsaw, N.Y.—Nov. 13

Baseball Game—baseball—Abner Doubleday—Cooperstown, N.Y.

Building—building with a high steeple—commenced—New York City—Oct. 17

Cotton Twine Factory—Sloatsburg, N.Y.

Cranioscopy Book—*Crania Americana*—published—Philadelphia, Pa.

Dental Periodical—dental journal—*American Journal of Dental Science*—published—New York City—July

Dental School—dental college—Baltimore College of Dental Surgery—organized—Baltimore, Md.

Electrotype—electrotype—produced—New York City

Envelope Manufacturer—Mr. Pierson—New York City

Express Service—organized—W. F. Harnden—Boston, Mass.—Feb. 23

Fraternity (Greek Letter)—fraternity house—Kappa Alpha Society—Williams College—Williamstown, Mass.

Fraternity (Greek Letter)—fraternity west of the Alleghenies—Beta Theta Pi—Miami University—Oxford, Ohio—founded—Aug. 8

Horse—Percheron (horse)—importation—Moorestown, N.J.

Iron—iron blast furnace—anthracite coal—Pottsville, Pa.—furnace blown—Oct. 19

Law Dictionary (American)—John Bouvier—*A Law Dictionary*—published—Philadelphia, Pa.

Military School—state military school—Virginia Military Institute—Lexington, Va.—established—March 29

Normal School—normal school (state)—Normal School—Lexington, Mass.—opened—July 3

Photograph—celestial photograph—of the moon—J. W. Draper—New York City—Dec. 18

Photograph—photograph taken in the United States—daguerreotype

Photograph—photographs used in surveying—taken by Edward Anthony—delivered to Daniel Webster—submitted as evidence in boundary dispute (with Great Britain re Canadian border)

Political Convention—unit rule—adopted—Harrisburg, Pa.—Dec. 4

Printing Press—printing press operated by electricity—used—Thomas Davenport—New York City

Ship—iron vessel built of American iron—*De Rosset*—built—Baltimore, Md.

Statistical Society—of importance—American Statistical Association—Boston, Mass.—organized—Nov. 27

Steam Shovel—patented—W. S. Otis—Philadelphia, Pa.—Feb. 24

Teachers' Institute—Hartford, Conn.—Oct.

1840

Beer—lager beer—manufactured—John Wagner—Philadelphia, Pa.

Bowling Tournament—bowling match—New York City—Jan. 1

Bridge—cast-iron girder bridge—Erie Canal

Bridge—timber trestle pier of lattice construction—commenced—Shuman's Station, Pa.—June

Chiropodist—Nehemiah Kenison—Boston, Mass.

College—women's college (chartered)—Wesleyan College, Macon, Ga.—first class graduated—July 16

Dental School—dental college—Baltimore College of Dental Surgery—Baltimore, Md.—incorporated—Feb. 1

Dental Society—dental society of importance—American Society of Dental Surgeons—organized—New York City—Aug. 18

Dry Dock—timber dry dock—erected—Buffalo, N.Y.

Embalming Book—*History of Embalming*—published—Philadelphia, Pa.

Expedition—scientific expedition fitted out by the United States Government—saw Antarctic continent—Jan. 16

Graphite—commercial production—Ticonderoga, N.Y.

Gutta-percha—imported—New York City

Land Mines—used against Seminole Indians

Library—library building (university)—Columbia, S.C.—completed—May 6

Medical Clinic—college medical clinic—established—Willard Parker—New York City

Money—paper money issued by the American Indians—Oregon

Newspaper—line drawing of a current subject—New York *Sun*—New York City—Jan. 15

Nut and Bolt Factory—Marion, Conn.

Periodical—electricity journal—*The Electro-Magnetic and Mechanics Intelligencer*—published—New York City—Jan. 18

Periodical—factory workers' magazine—*The Lowell Offering*—published in October

Photograph—class photograph—S. F. B. Morse—Yale College, New Haven, Conn.—Aug. 18

Photographic Pamphlet—published—Boston Mass.

Photographic Patent—photographic patent—Alexander S. Wolcott—New York City—May 8

Photographic Studio—commercial photography studio—A. S. Wolcott and John Johnson—New York City—opened March 4

Photography—camera exposure scale—D. W Seager—published in March

Play (drama)—aquatic play—*The Pirate's Signal*—presented—New York City—July 4

Pump—independent single direct-acting steam power pump—invented—H. R. Worthington—New York City

Radio Impulse Transmission (wireless)—Joseph Henry—Princeton, N.J.—Dec.

Second Advent Believers General Conference—Boston, Mass.—Oct. 14–15

Seeding Machine (practical)—patented—Joseph Gibbens—Adrian, Mich.—Aug. 25

Treasury Department (U.S.)—Treasury Department (U.S.)—Sub-Treasury act—July 4

Wire—brass wire—manufactured—Edwin Hodges—West Torrington, Conn.

1841

Advertising Agency—V. B. Palmer—Philadelphia Pa.

Anesthesia—anesthetic—(general)—used—C. W Long—Jefferson, Ga.

Antislavery Party—Liberty Party national convention—New York City—May 12

Botanist—botanist—prominent landscape gardener—A. J. Downing

Brick—fire brick to withstand high heat—Mount Savage, Md.

Bridge—tubular-plate girder bridge—James Millholland

Business—commercial rating agency—Mercantile Agency—New York City—established—Aug. 1

Carpet Loom—carpet power loom to weave ingrain carpets—Lowell Manufacturing Company—Lowell, Mass.

Chair—recumbent chair patent—H. P. Kennedy—Philadelphia, Pa.

Congress (U.S.)—Senate—Senate filibuster (continuous)—began—Feb. 18

Cornstarch—cornstarch patent—O. Jones—March 22

Dental Book—orthodontia treatise—Solyman Brown—published—New York City

Dental Legislation—legislation (state) regarding dental surgery—enacted—Alabama—Dec. 31

Detective Story—to achieve popularity—E. A Poe—*Murders in the Rue Morgue*—published—Philadelphia, Pa.—April

Elastic Webbing—produced—Middletown, Conn

Fire Engine—steam fire engine—tested—P. R Hodge—New York City—March 27

Geodetic Survey—completed—Simeon Borden

Immigration—Japanese to enter the United States —Nakahama Manjiro—Fairhaven, Mass.

Life Preserver—life preserver of cork—patented —N. E. Guerin—New York City—Nov. 16

Newspaper Syndicate—syndication of newspaper material—M. Y. Beach—New York City— Dec. 7

Normal School—normal school instruction course given at a university—Middletown, Conn.— Dec. 1

Pin—machine "for sticking pins into paper"—patented—Samuel Slocum—Poughkeepsie, N.Y.— Sept. 30

President (U.S.)—President to die in Washington, D.C.—W. H. Harrison—April 4

President (U.S.)—President whose grandson became President—W. H. Harrison—served

Prizefight—prizefight (heavyweight) to last longer than 100 rounds—Tom Hyer vs. George McChester—Caldwell's Landing, N.Y.—Sept. 9

Senator (U.S.)—senator to receive a mileage allowance for a trip which he did not make— George Evans—March 4

Ship—iron vessel built for the U.S. Navy—*Michigan*—authorized—Sept. 9

Ship—steamboat engine built in America for a screw-propelled vessel—installed—*Vandalia* —launched—Dec. 1

Statistical Society—American Statistical Association—incorporated—Feb. 5

Torpedo—underwater torpedo operated by electric current—invented—Samuel Colt—Hartford, Conn.

Tube—collapsible tube—patented—John Rand

Typesetting Machine—typesetting machine patent—June 22

Venetian Blinds—venetian blind patent—John Hampson—New Orleans, La.—Aug. 21

Vice President (U.S.)—Vice President to become President automatically—John Tyler—April 4

Wire—wire rope factory—erected—J. A. Roebling —Saxonburg, Pa.

1842

Bridge—wire suspension bridge for general traffic —Schuylkill River—Jan. 2

Business School—business school—Eastman Commercial College—Rochester, N.Y.

Cable—cable—laid—S. F. B. Morse—New York Harbor

Child Labor Law—child labor law regulating hours of employment—Massachusetts—March 3

Coast Guard (U.S.)—Coast Guard commandant— appointed—Feb. 1

College—university on the Pacific coast—organized—Salem, Oreg.—Feb. 1

Cornstarch—starch made commercially from Indian corn—Thomas Kingsford—Jersey City, N.J.

Credit Protective Group—formed—New York City

Elevator—grain elevator operated by steam— Robert Dunbar—Buffalo, N.Y.

Expedition—scientific expedition fitted out by the United States Government—returned to New York City—June 10

Gold—gold discovered in California—San Fernando Mission

Insurance—mutual life insurance company to operate—Mutual Life Insurance Co.—New York City—chartered—April 12

Iron—hammered iron—Great Egg Harbor River, N.J.

Minstrel Show Troupe—performances—New York City

Narcotic—narcotic tariff—enacted—August 30

Naval Officer—naval officer condemned for mutiny—hanged—Dec. 1

Navy—Bureau of Medicine and Surgery—authorized—Aug. 31

Nut and Bolt Machine—patented—Micah Rugg— Aug. 31

Patent—design patent—George Bruce—New York City—Nov. 9

Periodical—illustrated weekly—*Brother Jonathan* —published—New York City—Jan. 1

Postage Stamp—adhesive stamps—issued—City Despatch Post—New York City—Feb. 15

Presidential Commission—President requested by Congress to justify the creation of a presidential committee—John Tyler—Feb. 7

Prizefight—prizefight fatality—Hastings, N.Y.— Sept. 13

Road—overland wagon road across the Rocky Mountains—Oregon Trail

Rubber—rubber shoe manufacturer—Leverett Candee—Hamden, Conn.

Sewing Machine—sewing machine patent—J. J. Greenough—Washington, D.C.—Feb. 21

State—state to repudiate a debt—Mississippi

Tariff—tariff to prevent the importation of obscene literature and pictures—enacted—Aug. 30

Volcano—volcano in eruption—reported—Washington—Nov. 22

1843

Almanac—patent medicine almanac—published —Batavia, N.Y.

Book Index—book index—published—New York City

Church—floating church—New York City

Colonial Government—government on the Pacific coast—Oregon—May 2

Diplomatic Service—consul to California—T. O. Larkin—appointed—May 1

Horse Race—futurity race—Nashville, Tenn.— Oct. 10

Horse Race—night harness race—Hoboken, N.J. —Oct. 5

Impeachment—impeachment proceedings attempt against a President of the United States— J. M. Botts against John Tyler—Jan. 10

Incubator (Eggs) Patent—N. E. Guerin—New York City—March 30

Insurance—mutual life insurance company to be chartered—organized for business—Dec. 1

Insurance—mutual life insurance company to operate—policy issued—Feb. 1

Medical Book—puerperal fever pamphlet—*The Contagiousness of Puerperal Fever*, by O. W. Holmes—published—April

Musician—orchestra leader to conduct without using a baton—G. J. Webb—Boston, Mass.

Paper—manila paper—patented—Hollingsworth —South Braintree, Mass.—Dec. 4

Periodical—American Jewish magazine (successful)—*The Occident and American Jewish Advocate*—Isaac Leeser, editor—published—Philadelphia, Pa.—first issue in April

Periodical—magazine published for mental patients—*Illuminator*—Philadelphia, Pa.—April 1

Photograph—photograph of a former President of the United States at his home—J. Q. Adams—Quincy, Mass.

Ship—frigate (American-built, steam-driven) to cross the Atlantic Ocean—*Missouri*—left Norfolk, Va.—Aug. 5

Ship—iron vessel built for the U.S. Navy—*Michigan*—launched—Dec. 5

Ship—naval vessel of the United States to sail around the Cape of Good Hope to the West Coast of the United States—*Constellation*—returned—Monterey Bay, Calif.—Sept. 15

Ship—warship with propelling machinery below the waterline—*Princeton*—launched—Dec. 10

Telegraph—telegraph appropriation (federal)—enacted—March 3

Typewriter—typewriter that successfully typed—patented—Charles Thurber—Norwich, Conn.—Aug. 26

1844

Anesthesia—anesthetic in dentistry—Horace Wells—Hartford, Conn.—Dec. 11

Book Review—book review editor—S. M. F. Ossoli—New York City—Dec.

Branding—branding punishment by a federal court—Jonathan Walker—Pensacola, Fla.—July 20

Coast Guard (U.S.)—Coast Guard commandant—first report submitted—Jan. 9

College—Masonic college—opened—Philadelphia, Mo.—May 12

Credit Report Book—prepared—S. P. Church—New York City

Game Protection Society—New York Sportsmen's Club—formed—New York City—May 20

Gas Engine—patented—Stuart Perry—New York City—May 25

Glass—stained figure glass—installed—Pelham Manor, N.Y.

Heating System—heating system (steam)—installed—Boston, Mass.

Insurance—mutual life insurance company to be chartered—first policy issued—Feb. 1

Iron—iron patent—S. Broadmeadow—Woodbridge, N.J.—Jan. 6

Lens—achromatic lenses—Cambridgeport, Mass —Alvan Clark

Naval Officer—captain in the U.S. Navy who wa Jewish—U. P. Levy—March 29

Pharmacy Professor—pharmacy professorship—Maryland College of Pharmacy—Baltimore Md.—appointed—April 24

Photograph—news photographs of distinction—studio opened—M. B. Brady—New York City

President (U.S.)—President married while i office—John Tyler—New York City—June 25

President (U.S.)—President who was a "dar horse" candidate—J. K. Polk—nominated—May 29

Presidential Candidate—presidential candidat assassinated—Joseph Smith—Carthage, Ill.—June 27

Printing Press—cylinder and flatbed combinatio printing press—manufactured—R. Hoe & Co.—New York City

Printing Press—printing press for polychromati printing—patented—T. F. Adams—Sept. 17

Psychiatric Association—formed—Oct. 16

Pump—independent single direct-acting stear power pump—patented—H. R. Worthington—July 24

Railroad Track—railroad rails of iron—rolled—Allegany County, Md.

Rowing—college to feature rowing—Yale—New Haven, Conn.

Rubber—vulcanized rubber—patented—Charle Goodyear—New York City—June 15

Seventh Day Adventist Church—Washingto Center, N.H.

Ship—iron steamship built for transatlantic se vice—*Bangor*—launched—Wilmington, Del.

Telegram—news dispatch telegram—Washing ton, D.C.–Baltimore, Md.—May 25

Telegram—telegram inaugurating commerci service—Washington, D.C.–Baltimore, Md.—May 24

Telegraph—telegraph station—opened—Wasł ington, D.C.

Turbine—turbine successfully operated by wat power—U. A. Boyden—Lowell, Mass.

Whist—whist rule book—*The Whist Player Handbook*—published—Philadelphia, Pa.

Yacht Club—New York Yacht Club—organized—New York City—July 30

1845

Adhesive and Medicated Plaster—adhesive ar medicated plaster patent—Jersey City, N.J.—March 26

Anesthesia—ether administered in childbirth—W. Long—Jefferson, Ga.—Dec. 27

Baseball Rules—baseball rule code—adopted Knickerbocker Club—New York City—Sept.

1847

Army Insignia—chevrons—authorized

Book Catalog—book catalog containing the combined tradelists of American publishers—compiled by A. V. Blake—published—Claremont, N.H.

Bread—bread from unbolted flour—introduced—Sylvester Graham

Bronze Statue (full-length)—Mount Auburn, Cambridge, Mass.—Ball Hughes

Capital Punishment—death penalty was first abolished—Michigan—effective—March 1

Chinese Students—arrived—New York City—April 12

Fertilizer (artificial)—developed—J. J. Mapes—Newark, N.J.

Insurance—health insurance company—Massachusetts Health Insurance Company—organized—Boston, Mass.—April 21

King—"king" to exercise the authority of king and high priest in the United States—J. J. Strang—settled in St. James, Beaver Islands, Mich.

Labor Law—ten-hour-day law—New Hampshire—July 9

Lighthouse—iron pile lighthouse built—Minot's Ledge, Mass.—commenced

Medical Instruction—pathology chair—established—Harvard University—Cambridge, Mass.

Medical Society—medical society (national)—of permanence—American Medical Association—organized—Philadelphia, Pa.—May 5

Newspaper—Norwegian—American newspaper—*Nordlyset*—Muskego, Wis.

Pile Driver—steam pile driver patent—awarded—James Nasmyth

Plow—plow for pulverizing the soil—patented—George Page—Washington, D.C.—August 7

Plow—steel plow with a steel moldboard—John Deere—manufacturing begun—Moline, Ill.

Postage Stamp—postage stamps issued by the Post Office Department—authorized—March 3

Printing Press—rotary-type printing press—patented—July 24

Prison—reformatory for boys (state)—Westborough, Mass.—authorized—April 9

Railroad Car—railroad coach—placed in service—May 19—Boston, Mass.

Railroad Guide—railroad guide that printed the time schedule—*United States Railroad and Ocean Steam Navigation Guide*—published—New York City

Rubber—rubber tire patent—R. W. Thomson—May 8

Senator (U.S.)—senator who served a term of less than 6 weeks—Pierre Soulé of Louisiana—Jan. 21-March 3

Ship—naval ship christened by a woman—*Germantown*—L. F. Watson—commissioned March 9

Ship—steamship passenger line between United States ports and Europe to fly the American flag—Ocean Steam and Navigation Company—New York City—service—June 1

Silver Plating Factory—Rogers Brothers—Hartford, Conn.

Surgical Operation—skin grafting—F. H. Hamilton—Buffalo, N.Y.

Swedish Magazine—*Skandinavia*—published—New York City—Jan. 15

Telegraph—telegraph company—Magnetic Telegraph Co.—incorporated—Feb. 4

Vacation Fund—established—W. A. Muhlenberg—New York City

1848

Arts and Science Society—woman elected to the American Academy of Arts and Sciences—Maria Mitchell—May 30

Baby Carriage—manufactured—Charles Burton—New York City

Bible—phonetic Bible—published—Philadelphia, Pa.

Bloomers—introduced—Seneca Falls, N.Y.—Jul 19

Building—building constructed wholly of cast iron—James Bogardus—New York City

Cable (telegraph)—submarine telegraph cable to be insulated with gutta-percha—Brooklyn, N.Y.—May

Chewing Gum—chewing gum—manufactured—Bangor, Me.

Child Labor Law—child labor law restricting the age of the worker—enacted—Pennsylvania—March 28

Dental Chair—patented—M. W. Hanchett—Syracuse, N.Y.—Aug. 15

Election—election day—uniformly observed—Nov. 7

Engineering Society—engineering society—of importance—Boston Society of Civil Engineers—Boston, Mass.—organized—April 26

Free Soil Party—National Free Soil Convention—organized—Buffalo, N.Y.—Aug. 9-10

Freemasons—Masonic lodge organized in the Indian Territory—Cherokee Lodge, Tahlequah, Okla.—chartered, Nov. 8

Gas—gaslight in the White House—Washington, D.C.—Dec. 29

Gold—gold discovered in California—Marshall discovery—Coloma, Calif.—Jan. 24

Ice Cream Freezer—patented—W. G. Young—Baltimore, Md.—May 30

Immigration—Chinese immigrants—arrived—San Francisco, Calif.

Macaroni Factory—Antoine Zerega—Brooklyn, N.Y.

Medical School—homeopathic college—Homeopathic Medical College—Philadelphia, Pa.—incorporated—April 8

Medical School—women's medical school—Boston Female Medical School—Boston, Mass.—organized—Nov. 1

Medical Society—women's medical society—organized—Boston, Mass.

Monument—monument to George Washington (national)—cornerstone laid—July 4

Periodical—comic weekly—*John Donkey*—published—Philadelphia, Pa.—Jan. 1

Periodical Index—published—W. F. Poole—New York City

Political Convention—national committee of a political organization—Baltimore, Md.—May 22–26

President of an African Country Born in the United States—J. J. Roberts—inaugurated—Liberia —Jan. 3

Pure Food Legislation—pure food and drug legislation (national)—enacted—June 26

Railroad—railroad to run west, out of Chicago— Chicago and North Western Railway—Oct. 25

School—school for the mentally retarded— opened—Massachusetts—Oct. 1

Science Association—scientific society (national organization)—American Association for the Advancement of Science—organized—Philadelphia, Pa.—Sept. 20

Senator (U.S.)—father and son senators at the same session—Henry Dodge and A. C. Dodge— Dec. 7

Ship—steamboat service (regular) to California via Cape Horn—left—New York City—Oct. 6

Shirt Factory—O. F. Winchester—Boston, Mass.

Shorthand Magazine—*American Phonographic Journal*—published—Philadelphia, Pa.

Spiritualist—J. D. Fox—Hydeville, N.Y.

Water Conduit—drinking-water conduit—built— Boston, Mass.

Woman Suffrage—convention of women advocating woman suffrage—Seneca Falls, N.Y.—July 19–20

1849

Army Officer—chaplain (Catholic) of the U.S. Army—served—Sept. 28

Bridge—twin covered-bridges—built—Peter Ent —Village Forks, Pa.

Business Economics Course—University of Louisiana—New Orleans, La.

Clock—watchmaker—American Horologe Company—Roxbury, Mass.—formed

Degrees (academic and honorary)—Doctor of Music degree—conferred—Georgetown University—Washington, D.C.—July 24

Disciples of Christ—general conference—Cincinnati, Ohio—Oct. 24

Drill—percussion rock drill—patented—J. J. Couch—March 27

Envelope—envelope machine patent—New York City—Jan. 23

Gas Mask—gas mask—patented—L. P. Haslett— Louisville, Ky.—June 12

Ice Skating Champion—skating champion (ice)— Charles June

Ice Skating Club—ice skating club—formed— Philadelphia, Pa.—Dec. 21

Interior Department (U.S.)—Interior Department Secretary—Thomas Ewing—appointed— March 8

Interior Department (U.S.)—Interior Department (U.S.)—created—March 3

Library Legislation—library law enacted by a state—New Hampshire—July 7

Medical School—homeopathic college—graduation—March 29

Melodeon Patent—C. Austin—Concord, N.H.— June 19

Money—double eagle coinage—authorized— March 3

Music—chamber music organization—Mendelssohn Quintette Club—Boston, Mass.—concert —Dec. 14

Music—saengerfest—Cincinnati, Ohio

Ordnance—cannon (breech loading)—patented— Benjamin Chambers—July 31

Periodical—Jewish weekly (German-American)— *Israels Herold*—Isidor Busch, editor—published—New York City—March 30-June 15

Periodical—Jewish weekly published in English— *The Asmonean*—New York City—Oct. 26

Photograph—photograph of a President (in office) —J. K. Polk—New York City—Feb. 14

Photography Book—photography book—*The History and Practice of the Art of Photography*, by H. H. Snelling—published—New York City

Physician—woman physician—Elizabeth Blackwell—graduated—Geneva, N.Y.—Jan. 23

Pin—safety pin—patented—Walter Hunt—New York City—April 10

Poultry Show—Boston, Mass.—Nov. 15–16

President (U.S.)—President who had received a patent—Abraham Lincoln—May 22

Railroad—railroad to run west of the Mississippi River—incorporated—March 12

Railroad Excursion—railroad excursion rates— Boston, Mass.

Senator (U.S.)—senator returned to the Senate after being defeated for the presidency—Henry Clay of Kentucky—March 4

Ship—steamboat service (regular) to California via Cape Horn—from New York City—arrived —San Francisco, Calif.—Feb. 28

Tattoo—tattooed man—J. F. O'Connell—exhibited

Thread—silk thread on spools—M. Heminway

Wire Gauge—developed—I. Washburn— Worcester, Mass.

1850

Adding Machine—adding machine to employ depressible keys—patented—D. D. Parmelee— New Paltz, N.Y.—Feb. 5

Aviation Book—aviation book—*A System of Aeronautics*, by John Wise—published—Philadelphia, Pa.

Billiard Book—*Billiards Without a Master*—published—New York City

Birds—sparrows—imported—Brooklyn, N.Y.

Catholic Bishop—native bishops of the South—ordained—Mobile, Ala.—Aug. 15

Clock—watch (eight-day)—manufactured—A. L. Dennison—Roxbury, Mass.

College Student—black woman college graduate—L. A. Stanton—Oberlin College, Oberlin, Ohio—Dec. 8

Cork Manufacturer—William King—Brooklyn, N.Y.

Cracker—meat biscuit—patented—Gail Borden—July 30

Desk with roll top—invented—Abner Cutler—Buffalo, N.Y.

Elevator—elevator—platform type—installed—Henry Waterman—New York City

Gas Mask—gas mask with a self-contained breathing apparatus—patented—B. J. Lane—Cambridge, Mass.—July 2

Hat—derby hat—manufactured—South Norwalk, Conn.

History Instruction—American history chair—established—University of Pennsylvania—Philadelphia, Pa.

Hospital—homeopathic hospital—Homeopathic Hospital of Pennsylvania—Philadelphia, Pa.—incorporated—Sept. 20

Ice Skating Club—ice skating club—formally organized—Philadelphia, Pa.—Jan. 4

Land Grant—railroad land grant of importance

Lighthouse—iron pile lighthouse—operated—Minot's Ledge, Mass.—Jan. 1

Magic Lantern—magic lantern slides (glass plate)—patented—F. Langenheim—Philadelphia, Pa.—Nov. 19

Medical School—women's medical school (still in existence as an independent institution)—organized—chartered in March—classes began Oct. 12

Mint (U.S.)—private mint authorized by the United States Government—Moffat Assay Office—Mount Ophir, Calif.

Money—double eagle coinage—double eagles coined

Museum—college museum—Charleston Museum—Charleston, S.C.—F. S. Holmes—elected curator—Nov. 25

Newspaper—German daily newspaper—New Yorker Staats-Zeitung—published—New York City—Jan. 26

Photograph—photograph of a star (other than the sun)—Vega—Cambridge, Mass.—July 17

Photography Magazine—photography magazine—Daguerreian Journal—published—New York City—Nov. 1

Railroad Car—private railroad car—used—Jenny Lind

School—school for the mentally retarded—incorporated—Boston, Mass.—April 4

State—state admitted to the Union on the Pacific Coast—California—Sept. 9

Telegraph—telegraph convention (national)—New York City—July 17

Ticket Speculators—New York City—Sept.

Wire—piano wire—manufactured—Ichabod Washburn—Worcester, Mass.

Woman Suffrage—convention (national) of women advocating woman suffrage—National Woman's Rights Convention—Worcester Mass.—Oct. 23–24

1851

Aviation—Airship—airship bombing—suggested—John Wise

Brass and Copper Seamless Tubes—manufactured—Somerville, Mass.

Brass Spinning—H. W. Hayden—Waterbury Conn.—Dec. 16

Cemetery—national cemeteries—Mexico City National Cemetery

Cheese Factory—cheese factory of consequence—Rome, N.Y.

College—college to prohibit discrimination because of race, religion, or color—Cooper Union—New York City—April 29

Deaf—Students' Magazine—magazine for deaf students—Deaf Mute Casket—published—Raleigh, N.C.

Engineering Society—engineering society—of importance—Boston Society of Civil Engineers—incorporated—April 24

Eye—artificial eyes—manufactured—Pierre Gougelman—New York City

Fire Alarm System (electric)—tested—Boston Mass.

Hat—soft felt hats for women—introduced—J. N Genin—New York City

Ice Cream—ice cream wholesale dealer—Jacob Fussel—Baltimore, Md.

Insurance—insurance board (state)—established—New Hampshire—July 1

Laundry—commercial power laundry—Oakland Calif.

Lock—lock ("clock")—patented—Linus Yale Newport, N.Y.—May 6

Locomotive—electric locomotive—trial trip—Washington, D.C.–Bladensburg, Md.—April 2

Medal—medal awarded to an American food producer—Gail Borden

Medical School—medical school based upon water-cure principles—American Hydropathic Institute—opened—New York City—March 15

Medical School—women's medical school (still in existence as an independent institution)—Women's Medical College—Philadelphia, Pa.—first class graduated—Dec. 30

Methodist Episcopal Church—Scandinavian Methodist Episcopal Church—organized—Cambridge, Wis.—April

Milk—condensed milk (commercial)—produced—Gail Borden—Brooklyn, N.Y.

Money—fifty-dollar gold pieces—minted—Moffat Assay Office—Mount Ophir, Calif.

Money—silver coins—three-cent piece authorized

Nail Machine (wire)—used—New York City

Horse—horse to trot 100 miles in less than 9 hours —Conqueror—Nov. 12

Horse Show—horse show—Upperville, Va.

Hospital—women's infirmary staffed by women physicians—New York Infirmary for Women and Children—incorporated—Dec. 13

Hygiene Instruction—physiology and hygiene courses—at a college—Antioch College—Yellow Springs, Ohio

Librarians' Convention—New York City—Sept. 15–17

Mechanics Textbook—*The Elements of Analytical Mechanics*—published—New York City

Medical School—medical summer school—Medical College of South Carolina—Columbia, S.C.

Money—gold coinage—three-dollar gold pieces authorized—Feb. 21

Monument—bronze equestrian statue—Andrew Jackson statue unveiled—Washington, D.C.— Jan. 8

Periodical—art magazine of merit—*The Illustrated Magazine of Art*—published—New York City—first issue in January

Pharmacy Society (national)—American Pharmaceutical Association—annual meeting— Boston, Mass.—Aug. 24

Postage Stamp—stamped envelopes (U.S.)—issued—June

Pottery—pottery to make sanitary ware—founded—Trenton, N.J.

Railroad—railroad merger—of importance—New York Central Railroad Company—May 17

Railroad Station—union passenger station— Union Station—Indianapolis, Ind.—opened— Sept. 20

Ship—yacht to circumnavigate the world—*North Star*—first voyage, from New York City—May 21—returned, Sept. 23

Trade Association—American Brass Association —organized

Truancy legislation (state)—enacted—New York —April 12

Vice President (U.S.)—Vice President sworn in on foreign soil—W. R. D. King—Havana, Cuba— March 4

Village Improvement Society—Laurel Hill Association—Stockbridge, Mass.—organized—Aug. 24

Water Cures—introduced—R. T. Trall—New York City—Nov. 1

Woman—woman ordained a minister—A. B. Blackwell—South Butler, N.Y.—Sept. 15

Young Men's Christian Association—Young Men's Christian Association for black members —organized—Washington, D.C.

Zinc—zinc commercial production—Bethlehem, Pa.—mill erected—Oct. 13

1854

Accordion Patent—Anthony Faas—Jan. 13

Agricultural School—agricultural college (state) to be chartered—Farmers High School of Pennsylvania—incorporated—April 13

Alfalfa—introduced—California

American Party—organized

Assay Office Building (federal)—erected—New York City

Baby Show—Springfield, Ohio—Oct. 5

Bank—clearinghouse—charter adopted—June 6

Billiard Match—billiard match—of importance— Syracuse, N.Y.—May 13

Blanket—blanket factory—Burleigh Blanket Mills —So. Berwick, Me.

Book—book (pamphlet) on vellum—published— Cambridge, Mass.

Bridge—railroad suspension bridge—completed —Niagara Falls, N.Y.

Building—building in which wrought-iron beams were used—New York City

Chair—folding theater chair—patented—A. H Allen—Boston, Mass.—Dec. 5

Chinese Students—college graduate—Yung Wing —Yale University—New Haven, Conn.—June 13

Collar—paper collar—patented—Walter Hunt— New York City—July 25

College—university for blacks—Chester County Pa.—chartered—April 29

Cricket Club—cricket club to own its own club house—Germantown, Pa.

Entomologist—federal entomologist—Townend Glover—commissioned—June 14

Entomologist—state entomologist—Asa Fitch— appointed—New York—May 4

Gazetteer—gazetteer of the world—*Lippincott's Pronouncing Gazetteer of the World*—published—Philadelphia, Pa.

Hospital—children's hospital—Nursery and Child's Hospital—established—New York City

Hospital—inebriates' asylum—United States Inebriate Asylum—organized—Binghamton, N.Y. —May 15

Immigration—Chinese labor immigration—William Kelly—Pittsburgh, Pa.

Manual Training—industrial school for girls—organized—Lancaster, Mass.

Oil—oil company—Pennsylvania Rock Oil Company—incorporated—Dec. 30

Ordnance—cannon (steel, breech loading, rifled) —J. R. Haskell

Ordnance—metal cartridge—patented—D. B Wesson—Springfield, Mass.—Aug. 8

Paper—wood-pulp and rag paper—manufactured —William Orr—Troy, N.Y.

Paper—wood-pulp paper—of basswood—exhibited—Buffalo, N.Y.—Dec. 26

Park—park land—purchased—Worcester, Mass —March

Physician—black doctor to become a member of a medical association—J. V. De Grasse—Massachusetts Medical Society

Publishing Society—Seventy-Six Society—organized—Philadelphia, Pa.—Sept. 5

Railroad Car—air-conditioned car—tested

Republican Party—Republican Party meeting (local)—Feb. 22

Sewing Machine—sewing machine to sew curving seams—patented—A. B. Wilson—Watertown, Conn.—Dec. 19

Sewing Machine—sewing machine to stitch buttonholes—patented—Charles Miller—St. Louis, Mo.—March 7

Ship—turreted frigate in the U.S. Navy—authorized—April 6

Sleeping Car—sleeping-car patent—H. B. Myer—Buffalo, N.Y.—Sept. 19

Sociology Treatise—Henry Hughes—published—Philadelphia, Pa.

Stereotype—curved stereotype plate—cast—Charles Craske—New York City

Street Cleaning Machine—used—Philadelphia, Pa.—Dec. 15

1855

Agricultural School—agricultural college (state) to be chartered—Farmers High School of Pennsylvania—reincorporated—Feb. 22

Agricultural School—agricultural college (state) to open—Agricultural College of Michigan—Lansing, Mich.—chartered—Feb. 12

American Party—national convention—Philadelphia, Pa.—June 5

Animals—camels imported for commercial purposes—congressional appropriation—March 3

Billiard Match—billiard three-ball match on a 6-by-12 carom table—San Francisco, Calif.—April 30

Bohemian American Church—opened—St. Louis, Mo.—April 20

Book Trade Magazine—successful book trade magazine—published—New York City—Sept. 1

Bridge—railroad suspension bridge—Niagara Falls—train crossed—March 8

Calliope—patented—J. C. Stoddard—Worcester, Mass.—Oct. 9

Carpeting—carpeting (velvet)—manufactured—John Johnson—Newark, N.J.

College—educational institution exclusively for women—Elmira Female College—opened

Court—court of claims—established—Feb. 24

Dentist—woman dentist—E. R. Jones—Danielson, Conn.

Dentistry—gold used for the filling of dental cavities

Dictionary—phonetic dictionary—published—Cincinnati, Ohio

Health Board—health board (state) to regulate quarantine—Louisiana

Hospital—Jewish hospital—Mount Sinai Hospital—New York City—received patients—June 5

Hospital—women's hospital—Woman's Hospital—New York City—opened—May 4

Jews—Jewish Rabbinical Conference—Cleveland, Ohio—Oct. 17

Lighthouse—lighted beacon on the Pacific coast—San Diego, Calif.

Oil—oil (kerosene)—from bituminous shale—patent—A. Gesner—March 27

Oil—oil refinery—S. M. Kier—Pittsburgh, Pa.

Ordnance—seacoast gun carriage—constructed

Poem—poem to win national acclaim—*Song of Hiawatha,* by H. W. Longfellow—printed Oct. 2—published—Boston, Mass.—Nov. 10

Postal Directory—published—Washington, D.C.

Postal Service—registration of letters—authorized—March 3

Printing Magazine (professional)—*Typographic Advertiser*—published—Philadelphia, Pa.—April

Railroad Union—organized—Baltimore, Md.—Nov. 6-10

Representative (U.S.)—representatives (brothers) to serve simultaneously—Washburn brothers—March 4

Sewing Machine—sewing machine motor patent—I. M. Singer—New York City—Oct. 9

Ship—dredge (seagoing hopper)—*General Moultrie*—built—New York City

Ship—turreted frigate in the U.S. Navy—*Roanoke*—launched—Norfolk, Va.—Dec. 13

Swedenborgian or New Church—German Swedenborgian Society—organized—Baltimore, Md.

Traps—steel animal traps—commercially manufactured—S. Newhouse—Oneida Community, N.Y.

Veterinary School—veterinary college—Boston Veterinary Institute—Boston, Mass.—incorporated—April 28

Vivisection—of animals—J. C. Dalton

Warehouse legislation—privileges extended to private warehouses—March 28

1856

Animals—camels imported for commercial purposes—Indianola, Tex.—May 14

Baseball Pitcher—baseball pitcher to pitch a perfect no-hit, no-run, no-walk World Series game—Don Larsen—Yankee Stadium, New York City—Oct. 8

Blotting Paper—manufactured—Joseph Parker & Son—New Haven, Conn.

Borax—discovered—Tuscan Springs, Calif.—Jan. 8

Bridge—railroad bridge across the Mississippi River—Rock Island, Ill.-Davenport, Iowa—completed—April 21

Camera—tintype camera—patented—H. L. Smith—Feb. 19

Cranberry Treatise—published—New York City

Dairy Legislation (state)—enacted—Massachusetts—May 30

Diplomatic Service—consul general—appointment authorized—Aug. 18

Fish Commission (state)—authorized—Massachusetts—May 16

Flag—American flag raised in Japan—flown—Sept. 4

Folding Machine—patented—Cyrus Chambers—Kennet Square, Pa.—Oct. 7

Governor—governor of a territory and a state—J. W. Geary—Kansas Territory

Governor—governor removed from office by a state supreme court—W. A. Barstow—Wisconsin—March 20

Horse Race—horse race on a stage in a theater—Old Broadway Theatre, New York City—Feb. 18

Milk—condensed milk (commercial)—patented—Gail Borden—Brooklyn, N.Y.—Aug. 19

Ordnance—machine gun—patented—Charles E. Barnes—Lowell, Mass.—July 8

Philology Chair—comparative philology chair—Lafayette College—Easton, Pa.

Pistol—revolver—self-cocking—invented—John Rider

Railroad Legislation—railroad legislation (state)—enacted—Georgia—March 5

Republican Party—Republican Party meeting (national)—Feb. 22—Pittsburgh, Pa.

Republican Party—Republican Party national convention—Philadelphia, Pa.—June 17

Screw—screw machine—patented—Cullen Whipple—Providence, R.I.—June 3

Sewage—underground comprehensive sewer system (city)—Chicago, Ill.

Telegraph—telegraph ticker which successfully printed type—patented—D. E. Hughes—Louisville, Ky.—May 20

1857

Agricultural School—agricultural college (state) to open—Agricultural College of Michigan—Lansing, Mich.—opened—May 13

Band—school band—formed—Thompson Island, Boston Harbor, Mass.

Bedspring—box spring—imported—New York City

Brick Machine—installed—Henry Martin—Hartford, Conn.

Bustle—patented—Alexander Douglas—New York City

Cable (Telegraph)—cable across the Atlantic Ocean was paid out—Aug. 6

Chess Champion—chess champion of the world (American-born)—P. C. Morphy—New York City

Chess Tournament—chess tournament of importance—New York City—Oct. 6

College—college to grant women absolutely equal rights—nonsectarian—Antioch College, Yellow Springs, Ohio—graduation—July 1

College—university for blacks—opened—Chester county, Pa.—Jan. 1

Deaf—School—institution in the world for the higher education of the deaf—National Deaf Mute College—Washington, D.C.—incorporated—Feb. 16

Elevator—elevator with completely enclosed car—installed—E. G. Otis—New York City

Fire Alarm System (electric)—patented—May 19

Gyroscope—gyroscopes (commercially manufactured)—Hartford, Conn.

Horse Race—American-bred horse to win a majo race abroad—Prioress—Newmarket, Englan—Oct. 13

Hospital—tuberculosis home for the care of con sumptives—Channing Home—Boston, Mass.—opened—May

Hospital—women's infirmary staffed by wome physicians—New York Infirmary for Wome and Children—New York City—opened—Ma 12

Lamp—oil lamp—developed

Literacy qualification for voting—enacted—Mas sachusetts—May 1

Medical Instruction—pediatrics professor—Abra ham Jacobi—lectured—New York City

Paper—toilet paper—manufactured—J. C. Gaye ty—New York City

Photograph—solar-eclipse photograph—Frede rick Langenheim—Philadelphia, Pa.—March 2

Postage Stamp—perforated postage stamps—used—Feb. 24

President (U.S.)—President who was a bachelo—James Buchanan—served

Scale—railway track scale—patented—Thad deus Fairbanks—St. Johnsbury, Vt.—Jan. 13

Sewage—sewage "dual system"—built—Brook lyn, N.Y.

Sewing Machine—chain-stitch single-thread sew ing machine (practical)—patented—J. E. A Gibbs—Mill Point, Va.—June 2

Ship—federal steamer named for a woman—Ha riet Lane—built—New York City

Ship—racing shell—The Harvard—built—Jame Mackay—Brooklyn, N.Y.

Teachers' Convention—teachers' convention (n tional)—Philadelphia, Pa.—Aug. 26

Typesetting Machine—typesetting machine—pa ented—Timothy Alden—New York City—Sep 15

Veterinary School—veterinary college of impo tance—New York College of Veterinary Su geons—New York City—incorporated—April

Zinc—zinc patent—Samuel Wetherill—Bet lehem, Pa.—Jan. 6

1858

Artics—patented—T. C. Wales—Dorcheste Mass.—Feb. 2

Baby Carriage Factory—Leominster, Mass.

Baseball Game—baseball series—July 20

Baseball Park—baseball park to charge admi sion—New York Fashion Race Track course—July 20

Baseball Rules—baseball rules—standardizir the game—passed—New York City—May

Burglar Alarm—burglar alarm—installed—Edw Holmes—Boston, Mass.—Feb. 21

Cable (Telegraph)—cable across the Atlan Ocean—completed—Aug. 5

Cable (Telegraph)—news dispatch by cable—published—New York City—Sun—Aug. 27

Chemistry Laboratory—chemical laboratory in a collegiate institution—Harvard University—Cambridge, Mass.

Cigar Band—cigar band of special interest—C. W. Field—New York City—Sept. 2

Citizenship—Japanese granted citizenship—Joseph Heco—June 30

Cotton-Bale Metallic Tie—patented—Frederick Cook—New Orleans, La.—March 2

Hospital—inebriates' asylum—cornerstone laid —Sept. 24

Medical Book—psychological medicine modern textbook—*A Manual of Psychological Medicine*, by J. C. Bucknill and D. H. Tuke—published—Philadelphia, Pa.

Medical School—medical college on the Pacific Coast—Medical Department of the University of the Pacific—opened—Santa Clara, Calif.

Pen—steel pens commercially produced—Richard Esterbrook—Camden, N.J.

Pencil—pencil with an attached eraser—patented —H. L. Lipman—Philadelphia, Pa.—March 30

Physician—doctor to receive a medal from Congress—F. H. Rose—authorized—May 11

Postal Service—overland mail service—to Pacific coast—Tipton, Mo.–San Francisco, Calif.—Sept. 15

Postal Service—street letter box—erected—Boston, Mass., and New York City—Aug. 2

Postal Service—street letter box—patented—Albert Potts—Philadelphia, Pa.—March 9

Sawmill—sawmill engine—portable—built—Zanesville, Ohio

Shoe Manufacturing Machine—patented—L. R. Blake—Abington, Mass.—July 6

Soda Fountain—ornamented soda fountain—produced—G. D. Dows—Lowell, Mass.

Stone Crusher—stone crusher—patented—E. W. Blake—New Haven, Conn.—June 15

Streetcar—cable car—patent—E. A. Gardner—Philadelphia, Pa.—March 23

Washing Machine—rotary-motion washing machine—patented—H. E. Smith—Philadelphia, Pa.—Oct. 26

Cricket Tournament—international cricket tournament—Hoboken, N.J.—Oct. 3–5

Electric Lighting—electric light—for household illumination—M. G. Farmer—Salem, Mass.—July

Electric Stove—electric range—invented—G. B. Simpson—Washington, D.C.

Elevator—elevator in a hotel—Fifth Avenue Hotel —New York City—Aug. 23

Escalator—escalator patent—Nathan Ames—Saugus, Mass.—Aug. 9

Fishing Line Factory—Henry Hall—New York City

Insurance—insurance department (state)—authorized—New York—April 15

Milk Inspectors—authorized—Massachusetts—April 6

Music—war song of the Confederate States "Dixie" sung—New York City—April 4

Niagara Falls—person to cross Niagara Falls on a tightrope—J. F. Gravelet (Émile Blondin)—June 30

Oil—oil well commercially productive—discovered—Titusville, Pa.—Aug. 27

Paper Bag Manufacturing Machine—paper bag manufacturing machine—patented—William Goodale—Clinton, Mass.—July 12

Periodical—gas magazine—*American Gas-Light Journal*—published—New York City—first issue, July 1

Public School—public school for Chinese-Americans—supported by a municipality—established—San Francisco, Calif.—Sept.

Rocket—rocket patent—Andrew Lanergan—Boston, Mass.—June 21

Sleeping Car—Pullman sleeping car—in service—Bloomington, Ill.–Chicago, Ill.—Sept. 1

Surgical Operation—mastoid operation—J. C. Hutchison—New York City—June 15

Washing Machine—rotary-motion washing machine—produced

Zoological Garden—zoological garden—Philadelphia Zoological Garden—Philadelphia, Pa. —society incorporated—March 21

1859

Agricultural School—agricultural college (state) to be chartered—Farmers High School of Pennsylvania—opened—Feb. 16

Balloon—Flights—balloon flight carrying mail—John Wise—Lafayette, Ind.—Aug. 17

Baseball Game—baseball series—spectators charged admission—New York—July 20

Baseball Game—intercollegiate baseball game—Pittsfield, Mass.—July 1

Billiard Match—billiard match to attain international prominence—Detroit, Mich.—April 12

Blind—school for the blind to adopt the Braille system—St. Louis, Mo.

Boat Race—intercollegiate regatta—Worcester, Mass.—July 26

Bridge—wrought-iron lattice-girder railroad bridge—Schenectady, N.Y.

1860

American Indian School—American Indian boarding school on a reservation—Yakima Reservation, Wash.—opened—November

Baseball Team—baseball team—Olympic Club—Philadelphia, Pa.

Baseball Team—baseball team to tour—Brooklyn Excelsiors—June 30

Billiard Match—intercollegiate billiard match—Worcester, Mass.—July 25

Business—department store to occupy a city block—A. T. Stewart & Co.—New York City—opened

Congress (U.S.)—House of Representatives—Jewish rabbi to open the House of Representatives with prayer—M. J. Raphall—Feb. 1

Constitutional Union Party—organized—Baltimore, Md.—May 9

Corkscrew Patent—M. L. Byrn—New York City—March 27

Electro-Therapeutic Book—*Electro-Physiology and Electro-Therapeutics*—published—Boston, Mass.

Fire Escapes for tenements—required—legislation—New York—April 17

Game Preserve—game preserve—J. D. Caton—Ottawa, Ill.

Government Printing Office—Government Printing Office—authorized—June 23

Hebrew Book—Hebrew book all in Hebrew—*Abne Yehoshua*—published—New York City

Hygiene Instruction—hygiene and physical education professorship—established—Amherst College—Amherst, Mass.

Insurance—nonforfeiture insurance policy—New York Life Insurance Company—New York City—Aug. 13

Japanese Ambassador—arrived—San Francisco, Calif.—March 9

Labor Law—eight-hour day—advocated

Medical Book—chiropody book—*Surgical and Practical Observations* . . . —I. Zacharie—published—New York City

Missionary Society—foreign missionary society organized by women—Boston, Mass.—Nov.

News Correspondent—woman news reporter at a political convention—M. A. R. Livermore—Republican National Convention—May 12–18

Newspaper—Czech-language newspaper—*Slovan Amerikansky*—published—Racine, Wis.—Jan. 1

Oil—oil refinery (commercial)—Oil Creek Valley, Pa.—June

Photograph—aerial photograph—taken—Boston, Mass.—Oct. 13

Police—traffic police squad—organized—New York City

Postal Service—Pony Express mail—St. Joseph, Mo.–Sacramento, Calif.—April 3

Secession—secession act—enacted—South Carolina—Dec. 20

Secret Service—Secret Service (federal)—authorized—June 23

Ship—steamboat built on the Pacific coast for the government—*Saginaw*—built—San Francisco, Calif.

Silver Mill—to treat silver ore successfully—formed—Virginia City, Nev.—March

Tinware Manufacturers—successful tinware manufacturers—Woodhaven, L.I., N.Y.

Visiting Celebrities—Prince of Wales—arrived—Detroit, Mich.—Sept. 20

1861

Army—law (state) conferring military privileges and duties on blacks—Tennessee—June 28

Army Balloon Corps—formed—Oct. 1

Army Secret Service Bureau—inaugurated

Bond—Confederate government bond—authorized—Feb. 28

Book Trade Magazine—book collectors' magazine—*The Philobiblion*—published—New York City

Building—"White House of the Confederacy"—occupied—Montgomery, Ala.—Feb. 18

Camp for Boys—Milford, Conn.—Aug.

Chromo—made

Civil War—act that marked the inauguration of the War of 1861–1865—firing upon *Star of the West*—Jan. 9

Civil War—attack in the Civil War—Fort Sumter, S.C.—April 12

Civil War—bloodshed in the Civil War—Baltimore, Md.—April 19

Civil War—call for Union troops in the Civil War—April 15

Civil War—Confederate forts to surrender—Fort Clark and Fort Hatteras—Hatteras Island, N.C.—Aug. 29

Civil War—Confederate general killed in the Civil War—R. S. Garnett—July 13

Civil War—Confederate officer killed in the Civil War—J. Q. Marr—Fairfax Court House, Va.—June 1

Civil War—naval attack—off Charleston, S.C.—April 12

Civil War—naval engagement in the Civil War—Pensacola, Fla.—Sept. 14

Civil War—naval officer (Union) killed in the Civil War—J. H. Ward—Mathias Point, Va.—June 27

Civil War—regiment to respond to President Abraham Lincoln's proclamation—April 16

Civil War—serious engagement in the Civil War—Bull Run Creek, Va.—July 21

Civil War—skirmish in the Civil War—Fairfax Court House, Va.—June 1

Civil War—Union soldier killed by enemy action in the Civil War—B. T. Brown—May 22

Congress of the Confederate States—House of Representatives under permanent constitution—assembled—Richmond, Va.—Feb. 18

Congress of the Confederate States—provisional session—Montgomery, Ala.—Feb. 4

Constitution of the Confederate States of America—adopted—March 11

Constitutional Amendment (U.S.)—proposed constitutional amendment to bear the signature of a President—Abraham Lincoln—March 2

Copyright Law—photographic copyright law—enacted March 2

Creamery—established—A. Slaughter—Wallkill, N.Y.

Degrees (academic and honorary)—Doctor of Philosophy degree—awarded—Yale University—New Haven, Conn.

Flag—Confederate States flag—adopted—Montgomery, Ala.—March 4

Fly Casting Tournament—fly casting tournament—Utica, N.Y.—June 18

Government Printing Office—Government Printing Office—began to function—March 4

Habeas Corpus—habeas corpus suspension order—May 3

Hospital—military hospital on the modern pavilion plan—Poolesville, Md.—Oct. 21

ce Yacht Club—formed—Poughkeepsie, N.Y.

nsurance—nonforfeiture insurance law (state)—Massachusetts—approved—April 10

Medal—Medal of Honor action—Apache Pass, Ariz.—Feb. 13–14

Medal—Medal of Honor awarded to a member of the Naval Service—authorized—Dec. 21

Medical Instruction—laryngology instruction—New York City

Medical Instruction—orthopedics chair—New York City

Money—Confederate coinage—minted—New Orleans, La.

Money—Confederate currency—authorized—Mobile, Ala.—March 9

Money—demand notes—authorized—July 17

Money—paper money issued by the government of the United States—authorized

Motion Picture—peep show machine—patented—S. D. Goodale—Cincinnati, Ohio—Feb. 5

Motion Picture—photographic attempt to show motion—Coleman Sellers—Philadelphia, Pa.—Feb. 5

Newspaper—newspaper published by soldiers in the field—*United States American Volunteer*—May 21

Normal School—normal school (state) at which students actually conducted classes—Oswego Training School for Primary Teachers—Oswego, N.Y.—established—May 1

Nursing School—school for nurses to award a diploma—Philadelphia, Pa.—chartered—March 22

Oil—oil well fire—Oil Creek, Pa.—April 17

Patent—patent issued by the Confederate States of America—J. J. Van Houten—Aug. 1

Petroleum—petroleum exported to Europe—Philadelphia, Pa.—shipment made Nov. 19

Postage Stamp—newspaper stamps—authorized Feb. 27

Postal Service—newspaper wrappers—authorized—Feb. 27

President (U.S.)—President to serve as an official of the Confederate States—John Tyler—delegate—Aug. 1

President of the Confederate States—Jefferson Davis—elected—Feb. 9

Road—divided highway—Savery's Avenue, Carver, Mass.—construction begun by William Savery

School—school for black freedmen—established—Fortress Monroe, Va.—Sept. 17

Seal—seals for raising funds—organization founded

Senator (U.S.)—senator in military uniform to address the Senate—E. D. Baker of Oregon—Aug. 11

Ship—balloon carrier—*Fanny*—used—Aug. 3

Ship—Confederate cruiser to raid Union commerce—*Sumter*—fitted out—New Orleans, La.

Ship—Union ship captured in the Civil War—*Fanny*—in Pimlico Sound (N.C.)—Oct. 1

Tax—federal income tax—law enacted—Aug. 5

Telegram—telegram dispatched from an aerial station—T. S. Lowe—June 18

Telegram—transcontinental telegram—Oct. 24

Telegraph—telegraph line to the Pacific coast—in operation—Oct. 24

Torpedo—torpedo mine—attack—Potomac River—July 7

1862

Agricultural Land Grant—bill signed by Abraham Lincoln—July 2

Agriculture Bureau—agriculture bureau—Commissioner of Agriculture—I. Newton—appointed—July 1

Agriculture Bureau—agriculture bureau scientific publication—published—Oct. 15

Army—law (federal) authorizing military service for blacks—signed—Abraham Lincoln—July 17

Army Ambulance Corps—army ambulance corps—established—Aug. 2

Army Officer—chaplain (Catholic) appointed by the President—June 13

Army Officer—chaplain (Jewish) of the U.S. Army—appointed—J. Frankel—Sept. 10

Baseball Park—baseball park (enclosed)—Brooklyn, N.Y.—opened—May 15

Brokerage—exchange to specialize in mining securities—San Francisco, Calif.—Sept. 11

Cathedral—Episcopal cathedral—begun—Faribault, Minn.

Cemetery—national cemeteries—authorized—July 17

Chinaware—chinaware for restaurant use

Civil War—conflict between ironclad vessels in the Civil War—Hampton Roads, Va.—March 9

Civil War—black regiment in the Civil War—organized—July-Aug.

Decalcomanias—imported

Emancipation Proclamation (preliminary)—Abraham Lincoln—Sept. 22

Engraving and Printing Bureau (U.S.)—Bureau of Engraving and Printing (U.S.)—operations commenced—Aug. 28

Execution—execution (federal) for slave trading—Nathaniel Gordon—New York City—Feb. 21

Football Club—football club—Oneida Football Club—Boston, Mass.—organized

Gymnastics Instruction—gymnastics instruction at a college for women—Mount Holyoke College—South Hadley, Mass.

Homestead Act—homestead act—enacted—May 20

Hospital—Army Field Hospital—Shiloh, Tenn.—established

Hospital—orthopedic hospital—Hospital for Ruptured and Crippled—society organized—New York City

Impeachment—impeachment proceedings against a state governor—Charles Robinson—Kansas—acquitted

Internal Revenue Commissioner—G. S. Boutwell—served—July 17

Land Mines—used in Civil War—May 3

Medal—Medal of Honor (Army)—authorized—July 12

Medal—Medal of Honor awarded to a Marine—John Mackie

Medical Clinic—children's clinic—established—New York City

Money—legal tender—authorized—Feb. 25

Money—paper money fractional currency—issued

Naval Officer—naval chaplain killed in action—J. L. Lenhart—March 8

Naval Officer—naval officer to become an admiral—D. G. Farragut—became rear admiral—July 16

Newspaper—newspaper printed on a train—T. A. Edison—*Weekly Herald*—Feb. 3

Oil—oil pipeline within the oil regions—laid—Oil Creek, Pa.

Ordnance—machine gun (rapid-fire)—patented—R. J. Gatling—Indianapolis, Ind.—Nov. 4

Ordnance—revolving gun turret—patented—T. R. Timby—July 8

Passport—passport fee—authorized—July 1

Patent—aerosol patent—J. D. Lynde—issued April 8

Polygamy Legislation (federal)—authorized—July 1

Postage Stamp—encased postage stamps—patented—John Gault—Aug. 12

Postal Service—railroad post office—tested—July 7

Presidential Executive Order to be numbered—Abraham Lincoln—Oct. 20

Ship—Confederate cruiser built in England—*Oneto*—left Liverpool, England—March 22

Ship—Confederate ship surrendered—*Planter*—seized by Robert Smalls—off Charleston Harbor, S. C.—May 12

Ship—hospital ship of the U.S. Navy—*Red Rover*—converted—Dec. 26

Ship—ironclad naval vessels—accepted—Jan. 15

Ship—ironclad turreted vessel in the U.S. Navy—*Monitor*—launched—Greenpoint, N.Y.—Jan. 30

Ship—ironclad warship for service at sea—*Galena*—launched—Mystic, Conn.—Feb. 14

Ship—warship sunk by an underwater torpedo mine—*Cairo*—built—Mound City, Ill.—commissioned Jan. 25—sunk near Vicksburg, Miss.—Dec. 12

Slavery—law abolishing slavery in the District of Columbia—enacted—April 16

Snowshoe—commercial production—A. M. Dunham—Norway, Me.

Stamp Catalog—A. C. Kline—Philadelphia, Pa.—published

Steel Analysis Laboratory—W. F. Durfee—Wyandotte, Mich.

Taps (military signal)—Daniel Butterfield—July

Tax—federal income tax—law effective—Jan. 1

Tax—inheritance tax (federal)—authorized—Jul 1

Telegraph—army field telegraph used in warfar—Mechanicsville, Va.—May 24

Tobacco—tobacco tax for internal revenue—au thorized—July 1

Torpedo—torpedo mine attack—to destroy wa vessel—Yazoo River—Dec. 12

Treason—citizen of the United States to be trie for treason, convicted, and hanged—W. I Mumford—New Orleans—hanged—June 7

1863

Amnesty—proclamation—Abraham Lincoln—Dec. 8

Army—Signal Corps—authorized—March 3

Army Insignia—corps badges systematically a signed to an entire army—adopted—March

Army Officer—chaplain (black) of the U.S. Arm—H. M. Turner—commissioned

Bank—national bank—under national bankin law—opened—June 29

Bank—national bank chartered—Philadelphi Pa.—June 20

Bank Legislation—national banking system—cre ated—Feb. 25

Bathhouse—Turkish bath—opened—New Yor City—Oct. 6

Book—book on vellum—published—Phil delphia, Pa.

Brokerage—stock exchange—name changed New York Stock Exchange

Catholic Church—Catholic parish church f blacks—Baltimore, Md.—purchased—Oct. 10

Charity Board (state)—Massachusetts—estab lished—April 29

Chenille Manufacturing Machine—patented—Jan. 13

Civil War—bloodshed north of the Mason-Dixo Line—June 30

Civil War—black regiment in the Civil War— federal service—Jan. 31

Comptroller—Comptroller of the Currency—l McCulloch—appointed—May 9

Congress (U.S.)—officer to preside over both the branches of Congress—March 4—House Representatives

Conscription—wartime conscription bill—passe—March 3

Cripples—private school for cripples—opened—New York City—May 1

Dock—state-owned docks—authorized—Cal fornia—April 24

Farmers' Institute—farmers' institute sponsore by a state—opened—Springfield, Mass.—Dec.

Fire Extinguisher Patent—Alanson Crane—Fo tress Monroe, Va.—Feb. 10

Habeas Corpus—habeas corpus suspension ord —proclamation suspending habeas corpus du ing military strife—Abraham Lincoln—Sept. 1

Holiday—Thanksgiving Day national proclam tion—Abraham Lincoln—Oct. 3

Homestead—awarded—Daniel Freeman—Beatrice, Neb.—Jan. 1

Hospital—orthopedic hospital—Hospital for the Ruptured and Crippled—New York City—opened—May 1

Insurance—accident insurance company—Travelers Insurance Company—Hartford, Conn.—chartered—June 17

Medal—Medal of Honor (Army)—authorized for commissioned officers—March 3

Medal—Medal of Honor (Army) earned by a black—W. H. Carney—for bravery in action at Fort Wagner, S.C.—July 18

Medal—Medal of Honor awarded to a member of the Naval Service—April 3

Medical Clinic—laryngology clinic—established—New York City—March

Money—gold certificates—authorized—March 3

Money—notes wholly engraved and printed at the Bureau of Engraving and Printing—Washington, D.C.—authorized—March 3

Monument—monument to commemorate the Civil War—dedicated—Kensington, Conn.—July 25

News Correspondent—news reporter tried as a spy—T. W. Knox—Young's Point, La.—Feb. 5

Newspaper—newspaper printed on wood-pulp paper—*Morning Journal*—Boston, Mass.—Jan. 15

Normal School—woman principal of a normal school—A. C. Brackett—St. Louis, Mo.—Jan. 5

Oil—oil pipeline within the oil regions—completed—Oil Creek, Pa.—Feb. 19

Paper Patterns—Ebenezer Butterick—Sterling, Mass.

Physician—woman surgeon—M. H. Thompson—graduated—New England Medical College—Boston, Mass.

Pill—compressed pills or tablets—commercially manufactured—Jacob Dunton—Philadelphia, Pa.

Postal Service—free city delivery of mail—authorized—March 3

Railroad Signal System—railroad signal system (manual block)—installed—Philadelphia, Pa.-Trenton, N.J.—Philadelphia and Trenton Railroad

Science Association—National Academy of Sciences—incorporated—March 3

Seal—seal of the Confederate States of America —authorized—April 30

Water Conduit—water supply tunnel for a city—contract—Chicago, Ill.—Oct. 28

Yeast—yeast preparation patent—J. T. Alden—Cincinnati, Ohio—Nov. 3

1864

Army Ambulance Corps—Army Ambulance Corps established by congressional action—authorized—March 11

Army Officer—woman assistant army surgeon—M. E. Walker—March 11

Army Vote—tabulated

Boiler Legislation—state boiler inspection law passed—Connecticut—July 9

Borax—commercial production—Borax Lake, Calif.

Business—chain store organization—Great American Tea Company—originated

Camel Race—Sacramento, Calif.—April 7

Canning—salmon cannery—Washington, Calif.

Catholic Church—Catholic parish church for blacks—dedicated—Baltimore, Md.—Feb. 21

Cigarette Tax—cigarette tax—federal—enacted —June 30

Circus—circus to feature an automobile as an attraction

Deaf—School—institution in the world for the higher education of the deaf—Columbia Institution for the Deaf—Washington, D.C.—authorized to confer degrees—April 8

Degrees (academic and honorary)—Law Degree of LL.M. (Master of Laws)—conferred—Columbia University—New York City—June 29

File Factory—file factory (machine cutting) to attain success—Nicholson File Company—Providence, R.I.—organized

Fine Arts Department—fine arts department in a college—School of Fine Arts—Yale University —New Haven, Conn.—established

Fish Hatchery—fish hatchery—to breed salmon—established—J. B. Johnson—New York City

Fraternity (Greek letter)—professional fraternity —Theta Xi—founded—Troy, N.Y.—April 29

Game Law—hunting license fee (state)—New York—April 30

Hall of Fame—hall of fame (national)—National Statuary Hall—Washington, D.C.—established —July 2

Insurance—accident insurance policy

Insurance—accident insurance policy (printed)—Travelers Insurance Company—Hartford, Conn.—issued—April 1

Knights of Pythias—founded—Washington, D.C. —J. H. Rathbone—Feb. 19

Medal—Medal of Honor awarded to a Jewish soldier—Leopold Karpeles—July 12

Mines School—opened—Columbia University—New York City—Nov. 15

Money—coin to use "In God We Trust"—authorized—April 22

Naval Officer—naval officer to become an admiral —D. G. Farragut—vice admiral—Dec. 13

Novel—novel by a black—*Clotelle*—published—Boston, Mass.

Oil—oil tank cars—introduced

Park—state park—Yosemite Valley park—granted by act of Congress

Periscope—invented—Thomas Doughty

Philatelic Magazine—philatelic magazine—*Stamp Collector's Record*—published—Albany, N.Y.—Dec. 15

Physician—black woman awarded a medical degree—Rebecca Lee—Boston, Mass.—March 1

Physician—ophthalmologist of note—Edward Delafield—became president of American Opthalmological Society

Postal Service—money order system—established—Nov. 1

Postal Service—railroad post office for the general distribution of mail—service commenced—Chicago, Ill.–Clinton, Iowa—Aug. 28

Railroad Track—railroad rails of steel—Altoona, Pa.–Pittsburgh, Pa.

Skate (all-metal)—marketed—E. H. Barney—Springfield, Mass.

Steel—Bessemer steel converter—used commercially—Eureka Iron and Steel Works—Wyandotte, Mich.

Submarine—submarine to sink a man-of-war—Hunley—Feb. 17

Sugar—sugar and glucose from cornstarch—patent—F. W. Gossling—May 10

Torpedo—torpedo mine attack—Confederate loss—near Charleston, S.C.—Feb. 17

Water Conduit—water supply tunnel for a city—construction started—Chicago, Ill.—March 17

1865

Advertising Legislation—outdoor advertising legislation (state)—New York—passed—March 28

Advertising Magazine—*Advertising Agency Circular*—published—New York City

Animals—cattle importation law (U.S.)—passed—Dec. 18

Architecture School—architectural school—of college rank—Massachusetts Institute of Technology—Boston, Mass.—opened—Feb. 20

Army Officer—major (black)—M. R. Delany—Feb. 8

Bank—freedmen's bank—chartered—March 3

Bank—national bank failure—Attica, N.Y.—April 14

Baseball Game—baseball game in which one team scored more than 100 runs—Philadelphia, Pa.—Oct. 1

Bathhouse—bathhouses owned and operated by a municipality—Boston, Mass.—built

Billiard Ball of composition material resembling ivory—patented—J. W. Hyatt—Oct. 10

Capitol (U.S.)—President's body to lie in state in the Capitol rotunda—Abraham Lincoln—Washington, D.C.—April 19-21

Coast Guard (U.S.)—coastguardsman (black)—M. A. Healy—appointed March 7

Coffee Percolator Patent—Dec. 26

Congress (U.S.)—House of Representatives—black preacher to deliver a sermon in the House of Representatives—H. H. Garnet—Feb. 12

Congressional Directory—authorized—Feb. 14

Cooperative—cooperative state law—enacted—Michigan—March 20

Cracker—cracker—manufactured—Albany, N.Y.

Dental Code of Ethics—proposed—Chicago, Ill.—July 28

Entomology Magazine—*Practical Entomologist*—published—Philadelphia, Pa.—Oct.

Freedmen's Bureau (U.S.)—authorized—March 3

Gas—natural gas corporation—organized—Fredonia, N.Y.

Ku Klux Klan—established—Pulaski, Tenn.

Lawyer—black lawyer to practice before the United States Supreme Court—J. S. Rock—admitted—Feb. 1

Linen Thread Factory (successful)—established—Paterson, N.J.

Medal—Medal of Honor winner to receive 2 awards—T. W. Custer—presented, May 3 and May 26

Medical Instruction—ophthalmology professor—Elkanah Williams—appointed—Cincinnati Ohio

Money—gold certificates—issued—Nov. 13

Naval Officer—judge advocate of the Navy—W E. Chandler—appointed—March 6

Newspaper—newspaper published at sea—*Atlantic Telegraph*—published—July 29

Nursing School—school for nurses to award a diploma—Philadelphia, Pa.—diploma awarded

Oil—oil pipeline of importance—completed—Pithole, Pa.—Oct. 9

Oil—oil well drilled by torpedoes—Titusville, Pa—Jan. 21

Postage Stamp—newspaper stamps—issued in September

Potato Chips—introduced

Premium—premiums given with merchandise—introduced—B. T. Babbitt

President (U.S.)—President to be assassinated—Abraham Lincoln—April 14

President (U.S.)—President to rest in state in the United States Capitol rotunda—Abraham Lincoln—April 19-21

Printing Press—printing press to use a continuous web or roll of paper—William Bullock—Pittsburgh, Pa.

Railroad—streamlined railroad train—patented—S. R. Calthorp—Roxbury, Mass.—Aug. 8

Railroad Track—railroad rails of Bessemer steel—Wyandotte, Mich.—May 24

Railroad Train Robbery—railroad train robbery of a disabled train—North Bend, Ohio—May

Safe Deposit Vault—opened—New York City—June 5

Sleeping Car—Pullman sleeping car that was comfortable—*The Pioneer*—built—Chicago, Ill.

Soap—soap in liquid form—patented—William Sheppard—New York City—Aug. 22

Social Science Society (national)—American Social Science Association—founded

Unitarian Church Convention (national)—assembled—New York City—April 5

War Criminal Proceedings—Henry Wirz—trial—Washington, D.C.—Aug. 23-Nov. 4

Woman—woman hanged by the United States Government—M. E. Surratt—Washington, D.C.—July 7

Zinc—zinc sheet mill—erected—Bethlehem, Pa

1866

Animals—fur-bearing animals—raised commercially—Oneida County, N.Y.

Army Officer—General of the U.S. Army—U. S. Grant—appointed—July 25

Automobile—steam automobile—invented—H. A. House—Bridgeport, Conn.

Baseball Pitcher—baseball pitcher—to curve a ball—W. A. Cummings

Bicycle—bicycle with a rotary crank—patented—Nov. 20

Births—sextuplets—born—Bushnell family—Chicago, Ill.—Sept. 8

Cans—can (tin) with a key opener—patented—J. Osterhoudt—New York City—Oct. 2

Civil Rights Legislation (federal)—civil rights legislation (federal)—enacted—April 9

College—university for blacks to establish undergraduate, graduate, and professional schools—Washington, D.C.—Nov. 20

Dentist—woman dentist to obtain a D.D.S. degree—from a dental college—L. B. Hobbs—graduated—Cincinnati, Ohio—Feb. 21

Dynamite—manufactured—San Francisco, Calif.

Election Law—fraudulent election law (state)—enacted—California—March 26

Elevator—elevator (suspended)—installed—St. James Hotel—New York City

Flag—American flag made of American bunting to fly over the Capitol, Washington, D.C.—hoisted—Feb. 24

Hat Blocking and Shaping Machine—patented—Yonkers, N.Y.—April 3

Health Board—health board (municipal) armed with sufficient powers—established—New York City—Feb. 26

Hotel—hotel with safe deposit boxes—New England Hotel, Boston, Mass.—installed

Humane Society—humane society—American Society for the Prevention of Cruelty to Animals—incorporated—New York City

Impregnation—impregnation (human) by means of artificial insemination—J. M. Sims

Insurance—boiler insurance company—Hartford Steam Boiler Inspection and Insurance Company—Hartford, Conn.—chartered—June

Insurance—insurance rate standardization—New York City—July 18

Irrigation Legislation (federal)—enacted—July 26

Labor Legislation—eight-hour day—unified action—Baltimore, Md.—Aug. 20

Lecture Series (endowed)—Union Theological Seminary—New York City

Legislator (state)—black representatives to sit in any state legislature—elected—Massachusetts

Medal—Medal of Honor awarded to a woman—M. E. Walker—Jan. 24

Money—nickel—coinage authorized—May 16

Monument—monument by a woman ordered by the U.S. Government—statue of Abraham Lincoln—authorized—Vinnie Ream—July 28

Naval Officer—naval officer to become an admiral—D. G. Farragut—appointed—July 25

Needles (machine-made)—Excelsior Needle Company—Wolcottville, Conn.—organized—March 2

Newspaper Index separately published—New York City

Oyster Cocktail—originated

Paleontology Chair—in a college—Yale University—New Haven, Conn.

Pencil—indelible pencil—patented—E. P. Clark—Northampton, Mass.—July 10

Play (drama)—burlesque show—of importance—Black Crook—opened—New York City—Sept. 12

Political Convention—black delegate to a national political convention—Frederick Douglass—Philadelphia, Pa.—Sept. 6

Postage Stamp—mourning stamp—issued—June 17

Railroad—cog railroad—Mount Washington, N.H.—construction began—May

Railroad Car—refrigerator car shipment of fresh fruit—Parker Earle

Railroad Train Robbery—railroad train robbery of a train en route—Jan. 6

Railroad Train Robbery—railroad train robbery of a train in motion

Roller Skating Rink—roller skating rink (public)—opened—Newport, R.I.

Root Beer—manufactured—C. E. Hires—Philadelphia, Pa.

Ship—side-wheeler transpacific steamer—Celestial Empire (later named China)—built by W. H. Webb—keel laid, Jan. 13—launched, Dec. 8

Ship—steam whaler—Pioneer—April 28

Soldiers' Home—soldiers' homes (national)—authorized—March 21

State—state readmitted to the Union—Tennessee—July 24

Ticket Agency—theater-ticket agency office—advertised—New York City—Sept. 9

Tunnel—subaqueous highway tunnel—Washington Street Tunnel—Chicago, Ill.—commenced—Nov. 30

Visiting Celebrities—queen to visit the United States—Queen Emma—Hawaii—arrived—New York City—Aug. 8

War Veterans' Society—Grand Army of the Republic—established—Decatur, Ill.—April 6

War Veterans' Society—Grand Army of the Republic—national convention—Indianapolis, Ind.—Nov. 20

War Veterans' Society—Grand Army of the Republic—state convention—Springfield, Ill.—July 12

Water Conduit—water supply tunnel for a city—Chicago Lake Tunnel—Chicago, Ill.—completed—Dec. 6

Weights and Measures Standardization—act legalizing the employment of the metric system—approved—July 28

Wire—wire-cutting machine and automatic straightener—invented—John Adt—Wolcottville, Conn.

Woman Suffrage—woman suffrage associations (national)—American Equal Rights Association—constitution adopted—New York City—May 10

Yacht Race—yacht race across the Atlantic Ocean—Dec. 11

Young Women's Christian Association—originated—Boston, Mass.

Zither Factory—zither factory—established—Franz Schwartzer—Washington, Mo.

1867

Agricultural Society—agricultural society of national importance—organized—Washington, D.C.—Dec. 4

Bank—national bank failure—receivership terminated—Attica, N.Y.—Jan. 2

Blanket—blanket robe and carriage lap robe business—successfully undertaken—Sanford, Me.

Brick—terra-cotta factory—successful—Louisville, Ky.

Cartridge Belt Patent—Anson Mills—Aug. 20

College—state university supported by a direct property tax—authorized—Michigan—March 15

College—university for blacks to establish undergraduate, graduate, and professional schools—incorporated—March 2

Deaf—School—oral school for the deaf (still existing)—Clarke School for the Deaf—Northampton, Mass.—founded

Dental Mallet—dental mallet—idea conceived—W. G. A. Bonwill—Philadelphia, Pa.—Feb. 27

Dental School—dental school permanently established by a university—Harvard School of Dental Medicine—Boston, Mass.—established—July 17

Education Department (U.S.)—Department of Education (U.S.)—authorized—March 2

Election Law—election law granting black males the right to vote—presidential veto overridden—Jan. 7-8

Elevated Railroad—elevated railroad—New York City—opened for traffic—July 2

Forest Service—forestry inquiry commission (state)—authorized—Wisconsin—March 23

Governor—governor of a territory and a state—J. W. Geary—served—Jan. 15

Greek Orthodox Church—Greek Orthodox church—Holy Trinity Church—New Orleans, La.—founded

Insurance—boiler insurance company—Hartford, Conn.—policy issued—Feb. 14

Insurance—insurance rate standardization—annual meeting—Feb. 20

Insurance—plate-glass insurance—United States Plate Glass Insurance Company—Philadelphia, Pa.—incorporated—April 12

Jewish College—Jewish college—Maimonides College—Philadelphia, Pa.—established—Oct.

Medical School—women's medical school (still in existence as an independent institution)—name changed to Women's Medical College of Pennsylvania

Motion Picture Machine—machine to show animated pictures—Zoëtrope—patented—W. E. Lincoln—Providence, R.I.—April 23

Paint—paint (ready-mixed)—patented—D. R. Averill—Newburg, Ohio—July 16

Periodical—fashion weekly—*Harper's Bazar*—M. L. Booth, editor—published—New York City—Nov. 2

Philatelic Society—philatelic society—New York Philatelic Society—organized—New York City—March 21

Railroad Car—refrigerator car patent—J. B. Sutherland—Detroit, Mich.—Nov. 26

Railroad Crossing Gate Patent—Boston, Mass.—Aug. 27

Railroad Signal System—railroad signal system (automatic electric block)—invented—T. S. Hall—Stamford, Conn.

Sawmill—band sawmill—operated—Hoffman Brothers—Fort Wayne, Ind.

Ship—side-wheeler transpacific steamer—*Celestial Empire* (later named *China*)—trial run, June 4—sailed for Panama and San Francisco, Calif.—July 1

Soldiers' Home—soldiers' homes (national)—opened

Surgical Operation—gallstone operation—J. S. Bobbs—Indianapolis, Ind.—June 15

Telegraph—telegraph ticker used by a brokerage concern—installed—New York City—Dec. 29

Territorial Expansion—noncontiguous territory—Alaska—acquired—June 20

Territorial Expansion—territory (U.S.) outside the continental limits of the United States—Midway Island—claimed by William Reynolds—Aug. 28

Theological School—theological school to present regular courses by scholars representing different denominations—Boston Theological Seminary—Boston, Mass.

Water Conduit—water supply tunnel for a city—Chicago, Ill.—operated—March 25

1868

Animals—cattle exportation to Great Britain

Baseball Team—women's baseball team—Peterboro, N.H.

Benevolent and Protective Order of Elks—founded—New York City—Feb. 16

Bicycle School—for velocipede riding—opened—New York City—Dec. 5

Business—department store—Zion's Co-Operative Mercantile Institution—Salt Lake City, Utah

Cattle Club—cattle club (Jersey cattle)—formed—Newport, R.I.—July

Cigarette Tax—cigarette tax—stamps on packages—legislation enacted—July 20

Commercial High School—commercial high school—established—Pittsburgh, Pa.—Aug.

Dyes—dyestuff full-scale plant—opened—Albany, N.Y.

Education Department (U.S.)—Department of Education (U.S.)—act abolished Department of Education and established Office of Education in the Department of the Interior

Elevator—elevator in an office building—installed—New York City

Farmers' Institute—farmers' institute sponsored by a college—Manhattan, Kan.—Nov. 14

Holiday—Decoration Day—celebration—May 30

Ice—commercial artificial-ice manufacturing plant—built—New Orleans, La.

Impeachment—impeachment proceedings against a President of the United States—Andrew Johnson—Feb. 24

Kindergarten—American kindergarten—opened—Boston, Mass.

Labor Legislation—eight-hour day for government laborers and mechanics—authorized—June 25

Lieutenant Governor—black lieutenant governor—O. J. Dunn—Louisiana—nominated Jan. 14—elected April 22

Medical Instruction—public hygiene professor—Thomas Bevan—appointed—Northwestern University—Chicago, Ill.

Medical Periodical—medical periodical devoted to diseases of women and children—*American Journal of Obstetrics*—published New York City—May

Motorcycle—motorcycle (steam-driven)—W. A. Austin—Winthrop, Mass.

Nickel Plating—patented—W. H. Remington—Boston, Mass.—Oct. 6

Parade—parade with float tableaus—Mobile, Ala.—Feb. 24

Philatelic Magazine—philatelic magazine (club organ)—*American Journal of Philately*—New York Philatelic Society—J. W. Scott, editor—published—New York City—March 1

Philatelic Society—philatelic society—New York Philatelic Society—constitution adopted—Jan. 19

Philological Society—national philological society—American Philological Association—organized—New York City—Nov. 13

Postal Service—letter carriers' uniforms—approved—Oct. 31

Postal Service—money order system—foreign service authorized—July 27

Postal Service—postage-canceling machine patent—March 17

Railroad Car—dining car—*Delmonico*—built

Sports—amateur indoor athletic games—New York City—Nov. 11

Sports—athletic club—New York Athletic Club—New York City—organized—Sept. 8

Steel—open hearth furnace—built—Trenton, N.J.

Subway—pneumatic subway—Beach Pneumatic Underground Railway—incorporated—June 1

Tape Measure Patent—A. J. Fellows—New Haven, Conn.—July 14

Typewriter—typewriter that was practical—patented—C. L. Sholes—June 23

Veterinary School—veterinary department of collegiate character—Cornell University—Ithaca, N.Y.—courses—Oct. 7

Women's Club—women's professional club—Sorosis—founded—New York City—March 21

Yeast—compressed fresh yeast—introduced—Cincinnati, Ohio

1869

Agricultural Society—agricultural society for dairymen—organized—Oct. 27

Air Brake—patented—George Westinghouse—April 13

American Indians—Indian Affairs Commissioner (U.S.) who was an American Indian—E. S. Parker—appointed—April 21

Baseball Team—baseball team to receive a regular salary—Cincinnati, Ohio

Bicycle Patent—water velocipede patent—Oct. 5

Blind—school for blind blacks—Raleigh, N.C.—opened—Jan. 4

Boat Race—international boat race—London, England—Aug. 27

Book Guide—book guide—*American Bookseller's Guide*—published—New York City—first issue Jan. 7

Brokerage—woman brokerage office owner—V. C. Woodhull—New York City

Building—apartment house with a modern layout—erected—New York City

Cathedral—Episcopal cathedral—Cathedral of Our Merciful Saviour—completed—Fairbault, Minn.

Cattle Club—cattle club (Jersey cattle)—annual meeting—New York City—April 5

Celluloid—patented—June 15

Chewing Gum—chewing gum patent—W. F. Semple—Dec. 28

College—state university to grant equal privileges to women—Indiana University—Bloomington, Ind.—S. P. Morrison—graduated

Congress (U.S.)—officer to preside over both of the branches of Congress—Schuyler Colfax—Senate—March 4

Dental Book—book on dental surgery—J. E. Garretson—*A Treatise on the Diseases and Surgery of the Mouth*—published—Philadelphia, Pa.

Dentistry—gold crown tooth—process described—W. N. Morrison—May

Diplomatic Service—black consul—E. D. C. Bassett—to Haiti—served—April 16

Drill—oil-drill offshore rig—T. F. Rowland—patented—May 4

Expedition—exploration of the Grand Canyon of the Colorado—J. W. Powell—May 24-Aug. 29

Foodstuffs Producer—H. J. Heinz—Sharpsburg, Pa.

Football Game—intercollegiate football contest—Rutgers-Princeton—New Brunswick, N.J.—Nov. 6

Health Board—health board (state)—Massachusetts—authorized—June 21

History Instruction—history seminar—University
of Michigan—Ann Arbor, Mich.

Holiday—Labor Day holiday—inaugurated—
Philadelphia, Pa.—Dec. 28

Horse Race—trotting futurity—New York City—
Oct. 12

Hotel—hotel for women—Women's Hotel, New
York City—ground broken Jan. 1

Insurance—fraternal group insurance—of consequence—Metropolitan Life Insurance Company
—New York City

Journalism Course—journalism course—Washington and Lee University—Lexington, Va.

Jute Culture—introduced

Kindergarten Manual—Edward Wiebé—Paradise
of Childhood—published—Springfield, Mass.

Labor—labor bureau (state)—Massachusetts Bureau of Statistics of Labor—authorized—June
23

Labor Union—labor organization to admit workmen other than craft workmen—Noble Order of
the Knights of Labor—organized—Philadelphia, Pa.—Dec. 9

Labor Union—women's labor organization (national)—convention—Lynn, Mass.—July 28

Law School—law school (university) to admit
women—St. Louis Law School—St. Louis, Mo.

Lawyer—woman lawyer—A. A. Mansfield—
Mount Pleasant, Iowa—June

Motion Picture Projector—motion picture projector patent—O. B. Brown—Malden, Mass.—Aug.
10

Naval Academy—Japanese midshipman in the
United States Naval Academy—Z. Z. Matzmulla—admitted—Dec. 8

Naval Officer—Surgeon General of the Navy—W.
M. Wood—appointed Chief of Medical Bureau
and Surgery—June 28

News Agency—financial news agency—Kiernan
Financial News Agency—established—New
York City

Philological Society—national philological society—American Philological Association—convention—Poughkeepsie, N.Y.—July 27

Photograph—photograph of a total solar eclipse—
Mount Pleasant, Iowa—August 7

Pipe—corncob pipe commercial manufacture—
Henry Tibbe—Washington, Mo.

Postage Stamp—flag (American) depicted on a
postage stamp—issued May 15

Postage Stamp—postage stamps depicting scenes
—issued—March 1

Postage Stamp—postage stamps to picture the
coat of arms of the United States—issued—
March 1

Postal Service—money order system—foreign
service agreement with Switzerland effective—
Sept. 1

Prizefight—international fight, with bare knuckles
—St. Louis, Mo.—June 15

Probation—probation legislation for juvenile delinquents—enacted—Massachusetts—June 23

Prohibition Party (national)—organized—Chicago, Ill.—Sept. 12

Railroad—municipal railroad—construction authorized—Ohio—May 4

Railroad—railroad to run west, out of Chicago—
last spike driven—Union Pacific—Promontory,
Utah—May 10

Railroad Commission (state)—established—Massachusetts—July 1

Ship—oil tanker—Charles

Snow-melting Apparatus—snow-melting apparatus—patented—N. H. Borgfeldt—New
York City—April 6

Steeplechase—New York City—Oct. 26

Sulfur Deposit—discovery—Calcasieu Parish, La.

Supreme Court (U.S.)—Associate Justice nominee
to die before occupying his seat—E. M. Stanton
—appointed, Dec. 20—died, Dec. 24

Teachers' Death Benefit—New York City

Torpedo—torpedo manufacturing station—Goat
Island, Va.

Vacuum Cleaner—suction-type vacuum cleaner
—patented—I. W. McGaffey—Chicago, Ill.—
June 8

Voting Machine—electric vote recorder—T. A.
Edison—Boston, Mass.—patented—June 1

Waffle Iron Patent—Cornelius Swarthout—Troy,
N.Y.—Aug. 24

Woman—woman congressional hearing witness
—E. C. Stanton—Jan. 20

Woman Suffrage—state to grant suffrage to
women—Wyoming Territory—Dec. 10

1870

Autopsy—autopsy by a woman physician on a
male corpse—Bethenia Owens-Adair—Roseburg, Oreg.

Baking Powder Manufacturer—B. T. Babbitt

Boardwalk—completed—Atlantic City, N.J.—
June 26

Brokerage—clearinghouse for stocks and bonds
—organized—Philadelphia, Pa.—Aug.

Canoe Club—New York Canoe Club—founded

Cartoon—Democratic cartoon—donkey emblem
used—New York City—Jan. 15

Cement—cement—imported

Check Protectors—manufactured

Coin Box—for streetcars—invented—T. L. Johnson—Louisville, Ky.

College—college summer school—Mount Union
College—Alliance, Ohio

Election Law—black man to vote under authority
of the Fifteenth Amendment—March 31

Entomology Professor—H. A. Hagen—Harvard
University—Cambridge, Mass.

Farmers' Institute—farmers' institute held by a
land grant agricultural college off its campus—
Iowa State College—Cedar Falls, Iowa—Dec
20

Gas—natural gas for manufacturing—used—
Olean, N.Y.—Tidioute, Pa.

Japanese Ambassador—Japanese legation—established—Washington, D.C.—Oct.

Judge—woman justice of the peace—E. H. Morris—South Pass City, Wyo.—appointed Feb. 17

Justice Department (U.S.)—authorized—June 22

Labor Union—labor organization to admit workmen other than craft workmen—Noble Order of the Knights of Labor—permitted membership—Oct. 20

Lawyer—woman lawyer graduated from a law school—A. H. Kepley—June 30

Medical Instruction—pediatrics professor—Abraham Jacobi—New York City

Motion Picture—animated photographic picture projection before a theater audience—Academy of Music—Philadelphia, Pa.—Feb. 5

Pension—pension to the widow of a President—Mary Lincoln—authorized—July 14

Petroleum Jelly—manufactured—R. A. Chesebrough

Philatelic Auction—philatelic auction—New York City—May 28

Premium—premiums given by publishers—*Christian Union*

Public Health—public health service (U.S.)—reorganization act—June 29

Railroad—railroad to install track water tanks—Pennsylvania Railroad

Railroad Excursion—railroad excursion (transcontinental) of an organization—Boston Board of Trade—left Boston, Mass. for San Francisco, Calif.—May 23

Railroad Signal System—railroad signal system (automatic electric block)—patented—T. S. Hall—Stamford, Conn.—June 7

Representative (U.S.)—black representative—J. R. Rainey—sworn in, Dec. 12

Road—brick pavement—laid—Charleston, W.Va.

Road—sheet asphalt pavement—laid—Newark, N.J.

Rubber—rubber company west of the Allegheny Mountains

Sand Blasting—patented—B. C. Tilghman—Oct. 18

School—black school (state)—Snowden School—Alexandria, Va.—authorized—July 11

Senator (U.S.)—black senator—H. R. Revels—Mississippi—sworn in—Feb. 25

Servite Church—Servite Church in America—established—Menasha, Wis.—Aug.

Soda Fountain—ornamented soda fountain—patent—G. D. Dows—Jan. 25

Solicitor General (U.S.)—Solicitor General of the United States—B. H. Bristow—appointed—Oct. 4

Sorority—sorority (women's Greek letter society)—Kappa Alpha Theta—founded—Greencastle, Ind.—Jan. 27

Subway—pneumatic subway—Beach Pneumatic Underground Railway—opened—Feb. 26

Supreme Court (state)—associate justice (black) of a state supreme court—J. J. Wright—South Carolina—began service, Feb. 2

Time, Standard—standard time—suggested—C. F. Dowd—Saratoga Springs, N.Y.

Tong (Chinese secret society)—Kwong Dock Tong—San Francisco, Calif.—organized

Trademark—registered—Oct. 25

Water Purification—water purification by filtration—Poughkeepsie, N.Y.

Weather Bureau (U.S.)—Weather Bureau authorized—Feb. 9

1871

Bandwagon—used—B. T. Babbitt

Baseball League—baseball league of importance—National Association of Base-Ball Players—organized—New York City—March 17

Baseball Player—professional baseball player—A. J. Reach

Benevolent and Protective Order of Elks—Grand Lodge incorporated—New York City—March 10

Carrousel—carrousel patent—Willhelm Schneider—Davenport, Iowa—July 25

Cement—cement—patent—D. O. Saylor—Allentown, Pa.—Sept. 26

Cigar Lighter Patent—M. F. Gale—New York City—Nov. 21

Civil Service—Civil Service Commission—authorized—March 3

College—college entrance "certified school plan"—introduced—Ann Arbor, Mich.—Sept.

College—land grant college for blacks—established—Rodney, Miss.

College President—woman college president—F. E. Willard—Feb.

Deaf—School—oral instruction for the deaf—Horace Mann School—Boston, Mass.

Fertilizer Law (state)—enacted—Delaware—March 16

Fish and Fisheries Commissioner—S. F. Baird—served—March 8

Fish Protection—fish protection office (federal)—authorized—Feb. 9

Forest Fire—forest fire of consequence—Peshtigo, Wis.—Oct. 8

Freemasons—Ancient Arabic Order of Nobles of the Mystic Shrine—established—New York City—June 16

Freemasons—Masonic lodge for blacks—Alpha Lodge—New Jersey—warrant granted—Jan. 19

Gas—municipal gas plant—acquired—Wheeling, W.Va.—June 23

Holiday—Saturday half holiday—inaugurated—George Westinghouse—Pittsburgh, Pa.

Horse Register—trotting register—J. H. Wallace—*American Trotting Register*—published—New York City

Impeachment—impeachment and removal from office of a state governor—W. W. Holden—North Carolina—March 22

Law School—law school (university) to admit women—St. Louis Law School—St. Louis, Mo.—woman graduate—June 15

Lifesaving Service—introduced—S. I. Kimball

Locomotive—narrow-gauge locomotive—used—Denver and Rio Grande Western Railroad Company—July 3

Map—relief map—made—E. E. Howell

Medical Book—neurology textbook—W. A. Hammond—*The Diseases of the Nervous System*—published—New York City

Medical Instruction—dermatology chair—J. C. White—Harvard University—Cambridge, Mass.

Medical Instruction—medical chemistry course (systematic)—E. S. Wood—Harvard Medical School, Cambridge, Mass.

Medical Society—woman physician admitted to the American Institute of Homeopathy—Philadelphia, Pa.—M. B. Jackson—accepted

Monument—monument by a woman ordered by the U.S. Government—unveiled—Washington, D.C.—Jan. 25

Newspaper—Hebrew newspaper—published—New York City

Oleomargarine—oleomargarine manufacturer (successful)—Alfred Paraf—New York City

Oleomargarine—oleomargarine patent—H. W. Bradley—Binghamton, N.Y.—Jan. 3

Oranges (seedless navel)—imported—from Brazil

Paper—corrugated paper—patented—A. L. Jones—New York City—Dec. 19

Paper—perforated wrapping paper—patented—Seth Wheeler—Albany, N.Y.—July 25

Political Economy Course—political economy chair—C. F. Dunbar—Harvard University—Cambridge, Mass.

Printing Press—rotary printing press—produced—R. Hoe & Co.—New York City

Rifle Association—rifle association (national)—organized—New York City—Nov. 24

Ship—iron sloop yacht—*Vindex*—built—Chester, Pa.

Sports—amateur outdoor athletic games—New York Athletic Club—New York City—Oct. 21

Streetcar—cable streetcar—patent—A. S. Hallidie—Jan. 17

Theological School—theological school to admit women—Boston University School of Theology—Boston, Mass.—formed—March 30

Unitarian Minister—woman ordained to the Unitarian ministry—C. C. Burleigh—Oct. 5

1872

Adding Machine—adding machine to print totals and subtotals—patented—E. D. Barbour—Boston, Mass.—Nov. 19

Air Brake—triple air brake—patented—George Westinghouse, Jr.—Schenectady, N.Y.—March 5

Baseball Player—black baseball player on a white team—J. W. Fowler—New Castle, Pa.

Bird Refuge—authorized by a state—Oakland, Calif.—Feb. 14

Book—book showing action photographs in action in sequence—*An Electro-Photographic Investigation of Consecutive Phases of Animal Movements,* by Eadweard Muybridge—begun

Burglar Alarm—burglar alarm system—installed—New York City

Business—mail-order house—A. M. Ward—Chicago, Ill.

Cigarette Manufacturing Machine—invented—A. H. Hook—New York City

Civil Service—Civil Service Commission—law on regulation of admissions effective—Jan. 1

Congress (U.S.)—House of Representatives—foreign clergyman to open the House of Representatives with prayer—Abraham de Sola—invocation—Jan. 9

Doughnut Cutter—patented—J. F. Blondel—Thomaston, Me.—July 9

Elevator—elevator patent, for a vertical-geared hydraulic electric elevator—C. W. Baldwin—Boston, Mass.—Feb. 20

Fish Hatchery—fish hatchery (federal)—established—Bucksport, Me.

Fraternity Magazine—fraternity journal—*Beta Theta Pi*—published—Alexandria, Va.—Dec. 15

Freemasons—Ancient Arabic Order of Nobles of the Mystic Shrine—Mecca temple—instituted—New York City—Sept. 26

Gas—pipeline (long-distance)—completed—Newton Wells–Titusville, Pa.—Aug. 1

Governor—black governor (acting)—P. B. S. Pinchback—Louisiana—Dec. 11

Holiday—Arbor Day—celebration—Nebraska—April 10

Labor Legislation—women's equal employment legislation—enacted—Illinois—March 22

Labor Party (political)—labor party (national)—Labor Reform Party—formed—Columbus, Ohio—Feb. 22

Lawyer—black woman lawyer—C. E. Ray—Washington, D.C.—April 23

Liberal Republican Party—convention—Cincinnati, Ohio—May 1

Lunch Wagon—introduced—Walter Scott—Providence, R.I.

Medical Book—hay fever book—Morrill Wyman—*Autumnal Catarrh*—published—New York City

Milk—dried milk patent—S. R. Percy—New York City—April 9

Mohair—commercial manufacture—Arlington Mills—Lawrence, Mass.

Naval Academy—black midshipman in the United States Naval Academy—J. H. Conyers—Sept. 21

Nurse—trained nurse—L. A. J. Richards—began instruction—Roxbury, Mass.—Sept. 1

Optometry Instruction—optometry school—Illinois College of Optometry—founded—Chicago, Ill.

Paper Bag Manufacturing Machine—square-bottom paper bag machinery—patented—L. C. Crowell

Park—park (national)—Yellowstone National Park—authorized—March 1

Patent List—*Official Gazette*—published—Washington, D.C.—Jan. 3

Pharmacy College—pharmacy college to make analytical chemistry a required course—Maryland College of Pharmacy—Baltimore, Md.—March 20

Photograph—photograph of a stellar spectrum showing the dark lines—Vega—Henry Draper—Hastings-on-Hudson, N.Y.

Photograph—photograph showing action (not moving pictures)—taken—Eadweard Muybridge—Palo Alto, Calif.

Post Office—Post Office Department of the United States—became executive department officially—act of June 8

Postal Service—mail fraud legislation—enacted—Washington, D.C.—June 8

Postal Service—postal fraud order—authorized—June 8

President (U.S.)—President born on Independence Day—Calvin Coolidge

Presidential Candidate—presidential candidate who was a Catholic—nominated—Charles O'Conor—Sept. 3

Presidential Candidate—woman presidential candidate—V. C. Woodhull—nominated—New York City—May 10

Prohibition Party (national)—national convention—Columbus, Ohio—Feb. 22

Railroad Apprentice School—established—Elkhart, Ind.

Science Periodical—science magazine (popular)—*Popular Science Monthly*—published—May

Ship—mine layer—used

Sprinkler—sprinkler system patent—P. W. Pratt—Abington, Mass.—Sept. 17

Streetcar—gas-powered streetcar—patented—April 2

Telegraph—telegraph call boxes—installed—Brooklyn, N.Y.—June 22

Toothpick Manufacturing Machine Patent—Silas Noble and J. P. Cooley—Feb. 20

Vice Presidential Candidate—black vice presidential candidate—Frederick Douglass—nominated—New York City—May 10

Water Purification—water purification by filtration—filter erected—Poughkeepsie, N.Y.

1873

Animals—cattle (Aberdeen-Angus) importation—George Grant—Victoria, Kan.

Army School—Army school graduate (black)—H. O. Flipper—admitted

Balloon—balloon Atlantic crossing attempt—Brooklyn, N.Y.—Oct. 6

Book Catalog—book catalog—*The Uniform Trade List Annual*—published—New York City

Brass Rod—drawn—Coe Brass Co.—Torrington, Conn.

Celluloid—celluloid trademark registered—Jan. 14

Degrees (academic and honorary)—Bachelor of Music degree—awarded—M. P. Lowrie—Adrian, Mich.—Dec. 23

Dentistry—patent for a gold crown—J. B. Beers—San Francisco, Calif.—Nov. 4

Earmuff—invented—Chester Greenwood—Farmington, Me.

Education—chair in education—established—University of Iowa—Iowa City, Iowa

Fine Arts Department—fine arts department in a college to grant degrees—College of Fine Arts—Syracuse University—Syracuse, N.Y.—established—June 24

Football Game—international football game—New Haven, Conn.—Dec. 6

Football Rules—formulated—New York City—Oct. 18

Free Lunch—free lunches to aid convalescents—N. Y. Diet Kitchen Association—opened—April 24

Gas—natural gas for manufacturing—used in iron working—Leechburg, Pa.

Hotel—fireproof hotel—Palmer House—Chicago, Ill.—opened

Kindergarten—public school kindergarten—authorized—St. Louis, Mo.—Aug. 26

Linoleum—linoleum—manufactured—American Linoleum Manufacturing Company—Richmond, S.I., N.Y.

Livestock Market Paper—*Drover's Journal*—published—Chicago, Ill.—Jan. 11

Medical School—coeducational medical school—Boston University School of Medicine—Boston, Mass.—founded

Medical Society—laryngological society (state)—organized—Oct.

Money—demonetization of silver—bimetallism abolished—Feb. 12

Money—trade dollar—authorized—Feb. 12

Newspaper—illustrated daily newspaper—New York City—*Daily Graphic*—published—March 4

Nurse—trained nurse—L. A. J. Richards—instruction concluded—Roxbury, Mass.—Sept. 1—began service—Bellevue Hospital, New York City—Oct. 1

Oratorio—oratorio by an American—J. K. Paine—*Oratorio of St. Peter*—performed—Portland, Me.—June 3

Patent Examiner—woman patent examiner—A. R. G. Nichols—Melrose, Mass.—July 1

Postage Stamp—departmental postage stamps—authorized—March 3

Postal Card—issued—May 1

Prison—prison built for women and managed exclusively by women—Indianapolis, Ind.

Railroad Coupler—patented—E. H. Janney—Alexandria, Va.—April 29

Representative (U.S.)—representative to serve 1 day—G. A. Sheridan of Louisiana—elected—Nov. 5

Rifle Association—rifle association (national)—shooting meet—April 25

Science School—natural science summer school—opened

Silo (of record)—constructed—F. L. Hatch—McHenry County, Ill.

Slicing Machine—patented—Anthony Iske—Lancaster, Pa.—Nov. 4

Streetcar—cable streetcar—in service—San Francisco, Calif.

Streetcar—gas-powered streetcar—operated—Providence, R.I.

Tube—machine designed to produce collapsible tubes—built—A. H. Wirz—Philadelphia, Pa.

Weights and Measures Standardization—national organization to improve systems of weights, measures, and moneys—American Metrological Society—formed—New York City—Dec. 30

Wire—barbed wire—manufactured—J. F. Glidden—De Kalb, Ill.

1874

Adhesive and Medicated Plaster—adhesive and medicated plaster with a rubber base—successfully manufactured—East Orange, N.J.

Agriculture Department (state)—state department of agriculture—created—Georgia—Feb. 28

Baseball Team—baseball teams to travel beyond the confines of the U.S.—exhibition—England—July 30

Bridge—steel arch bridge—St. Louis, Mo.—opened—July 4

Caliper (screw)—constructed—Ithaca, N.Y.

Cartoon—Republican cartoon—elephant emblem—used—New York City—Nov. 7

Chautauqua Organization—Fair Point, N.Y.—Aug. 4

Christmas Cards—engraved—Louis Prang—Roxbury, Mass.

Corset—manufactured as a health item—McGraw, N.Y.

Football Game—rugby contest (international)—Harvard-McGill—Cambridge, Mass.—May 14

Football Goalpost—football goalpost—used—Cambridge, Mass.—May 14

Gas—water gas plant—built—Phoenixville, Pa.

Greenback Party (or Independent Party)—organized—Indianapolis, Ind.—Nov. 25

Hospital Record—system—introduced—Bellevue Training School for Nurses—New York City

Ice Cream Soda—introduced—R. M. Green—Philadelphia, Pa.

Kidnapping—kidnapping for ransom—C. B. Ross—Germantown, Pa.—July 1

Labor Union Label—adopted—Cigar Makers' International Union—San Francisco, Calif.

Lock—time lock—manufactured—Sargent & Greenleaf—Rochester, N.Y.

Mechanical Engineering Laboratory for research work—Stevens Institute of Technology—Hoboken, N.J.

Medal—lifesaving medal—Treasury Department—authorized—June 20

Mint (U.S.)—coins minted for a foreign government—authorized—Jan. 29

Patent—label patent—issued—Pearl Hominy Company—Baltimore, Md.—Aug. 1

Physician—osteopathic physician—A. T. Still—Macon, Mo.

Physiology Laboratory—established—Sheffield Scientific School—Yale University—New Haven, Conn.

Play (drama)—musical with an American theme and original score—Evangeline, the Belle o. Acadia—opened in New York City—July 27

Railroad Signal System—railroad interlocking machine

Rifle Association—rifle tournament (international)—Creedmoor, L.I., N.Y.—Sept. 26

Socialist Labor Party of North America—formed—July 4

Sprinkler—sprinkler head—patented—H. S. Parmelee—New Haven, Conn.—Aug. 11

Streetcar—electric streetcar successfully run with current generated by a stationary dynamo—invented—S. D. Field—New York City

Temperance Society—women's temperance society (national)—National Woman's Christian Temperance Union—organized—Cleveland Ohio—Nov.

Tennis—lawn tennis—introduced—Staten Island, N.Y.—M. E. Outerbridge—March

Tin Factory—established—Rogers & Burchheld—Leechburg, Pa.

Visiting Celebrities—king (reigning) to visit the United States—David Kalakaua—Hawaii—received at Washington, D.C.—Dec. 15

Wire—barbed wire—patented—J. F. Glidden—De Kalb, Ill.—Nov. 24

Young Men's Hebrew Association—founded—March 22

Zoological Garden—zoological garden—Philadelphia Zoological Garden—open to public—Philadelphia, Pa.—July 1

1875

Advertising Magazine—issued as weekly—April 1

Agricultural Experiment Station—state agricultural experiment station—authorized—Connecticut—July 20

Animals—cattle importation law (U.S.)—cattle from Spain—excluded—July 31

Bankers' Association—national bankers' association—organized—May 24

Baseball Game—no-hit nine-inning baseball game—Philadelphia, Pa.—July 28

Baseball Game—no-run nine-inning baseball game—St. Louis, Mo.—May 11

Baseball Glove—worn—C. C. Waite

Bed—folding bed manufacture—Philadelphia, Pa.

Births—quintuplets—Watertown, Wis.—Feb. 13

Bowling Rule Standardization—New York City—Nov. 13

Cartoon—newspaper cartoon strip—Daily Graphic—New York City—Sept. 11

Cash Carrier System—patented—David Brown—July 13

Catholic Bishop—Catholic bishop (black)—consecrated

atholic Priest—Catholic priest to be elevated to the cardinalate—John McCloskey—investiture—April 27

oaching—introduced—D. A. Kane—New York City

oaching Club—formed—New York City—Dec. 3

ollege—intercontinental system of study—introduced—Boston, Mass.

ental Mallet—dental mallet—patented—W. G. A. Bonwill—Philadelphia, Pa.—Nov. 16

rill—dental drill (electric)—patented—G. F. Green

ynamo—dynamo for a direct-current outdoor lighting system—built—Cornell University—Ithaca, N.Y.

air—centennial celebration—Lexington and Concord, Mass.—April 19

ootball Uniform—football uniforms worn in a game—Yale vs. Harvard—New Haven, Conn.—Nov. 13

orestry Society—national forestry association—American Forestry Association—organized—Chicago, Ill.—Sept. 10

as—water gas production—patented—T. S. C. Lowe—Norristown, Pa.—Sept. 21

omestead Act—homestead act (desert)—enacted—March 3

orse Race—horse race (Kentucky Derby)—Louisville, Ky.—May 17

ospital—floating hospital—*Emma Abbott*—July 19

ospital—tuberculosis sanatorium (private)—Asheville, N.C.

wish College—Jewish college to train men for the rabbinate—Hebrew Union College—established—Cincinnati, Ohio—Oct. 3

eat—beef exported—shipped—New York City—Oct. 1

oney—silver coins—twenty-cent piece—authorized—March 3

onument—statue cast by the United States Government—contract awarded—Vinnie Ream—Jan. 28

usic Instruction—college music chair—established—Harvard University—Cambridge, Mass.—Aug. 30

autical School—nautical municipal school—opened—New York City—Jan. 11

at-crushing Machine—patented—A. J. Ehrrichson—Akron, Ohio—Nov. 30

resident (U.S.)—President to become a senator—Andrew Johnson—Tennessee—served—March 4

ailroad Car—parlor car—G. M. Pullman—in operation

epresentative (U.S.)—representative to serve 1 day—G. A. Sheridan of Louisiana—served March 3

enator (U.S.)—black senator to serve a full term—B. K. Bruce of Mississippi—began service, March 4

attoo—electric tattoo machine—New York City

heosophical Society—American Theosophical Society—founded—New York City—Nov. 17

Typewritten Book Manuscript—S. L. Clemens—*Adventures of Tom Sawyer*

Visiting Celebrities—king (reigning) to visit the United States—David Kalakaua—returned—Feb. 15

Weights and Measures Standardization—International Bureau of Weights and Measures—established—May 20

1876

Actors' Home—actors' home—Forrest Home—Philadelphia—opened Oct. 2

Agricultural Experiment Station—state agricultural experiment station—work began—Jan. 1

Animals—cattle exportation to Great Britain—large shipment—William Colwell—Boston, Mass.

Baseball Game—shutout game—Louisville, Ky.—April 25

Baseball League—National League—formed—Feb. 2

Baseball Player—baseball player to hit over .400—Ross Barnes

Baseball Player—baseball players to hit a home run—R. C. Barnes and C. W. Jones—Cincinnati, Ohio—May 2

Bible—Bible translation by a woman—J. E. Smith—published—Hartford, Conn.

Bridge—cantilever bridge—Kentucky River

Canning—sardine cannery—successful—Eastport, Me.

Carpet Loom—carpet power loom to weave Axminster carpets—Yonkers, N.Y.—invented

Carpet Sweeper—patented—M. R. Bissell—Grand Rapids, Mich.—Sept. 19

Cattle Club—cattle club (Guernsey cattle)—formed—Farmington, Conn.—March 1

Chemists Society—chemical society (national)—American Chemical Society—organized—New York City—April 20

Cigarette Manufacturing Machine—patented—A. H. Hook—New York City—Nov. 7

Clipper for Cutting Hair—manufactured—G. H. Coates—Worcester, Mass.

Clock—clock (one-day back-wind alarm clock)—Thomaston, Conn.

Coaching—first tallyho trip—New York City—May 1

Coaching Club—first meet—April 22

Coast Guard (U.S.)—Coast Guard officers' training school—New Bedford, Mass.—established—July 31

Cooking School—New York Cooking School—opened—New York City—Nov.

Crematory—crematory—Washington, Pa.

Degrees (academic and honorary)—Doctor of Philosophy degree awarded to a black—E. A. Bouchet—Yale University—New Haven, Conn.

Dictionary—Bohemian-American dictionary—published—Racine, Wis.

Ethical Culture Society—New York Society for Ethical Culture—founded—New York City—May

Fair—centennial exhibition—International Exhibition, Philadelphia, Pa.—May 10-Nov. 10

Football Club—intercollegiate football association—Springfield, Mass.—Nov. 23

Football Game—intercollegiate football championship

Forestry Legislation—federal forestry supervision —attempted—Aug. 15

Forestry Society—state forestry association—Minnesota—organized—St. Paul, Minn.—Jan. 12

Greenback Party (or Independent Party)—convention—Indianapolis, Ind.—May 17

Insurance—title guaranty insurance company—Philadelphia, Pa.—organized—March 31

Intercollegiate Athletic Association—organized—Saratoga, N.Y.—June

Kindergarten—free kindergarten—Florence Kindergarten—Florence, Mass.—opened—Jan. 3

Library Periodical—library periodical—*Library Journal*—published—New York City—First issue Sept. 30

Library Society—library association (national)—American Library Association—organized—Philadelphia, Pa.—Oct. 6

Medal—lifesaving medal—of Treasury Department—awarded—L. M. Clemons—June 19

Medical Book—dermatology treatise—L. A. Duhring—*Atlas of Skin Diseases*—published—Philadelphia, Pa.

Medical Society—woman physician elected a member of the American Medical Association —S. H. Stevenson

Mimeograph—patented—T. A. Edison—Menlo Park, N.J.—Aug. 8

Mint (U.S.)—coins minted for a foreign government—produced—Philadelphia, Pa.—during fiscal year ending June 30

Organ—electric organ—installed—New York City

Political Convention—presidential convention (national) addressed by a woman—S. A. Spencer—Cincinnati, Ohio—June 15

Polo—polo—introduced—J. G. Bennett—New York City

Polo Club—polo club—organized—New York City

Postage Stamp—public exhibition of postage stamps—Philadelphia, Pa.—May 10

Postage Stamp—stamped envelopes issued to commemorate an event—issued—Philadelphia, Pa.—May 10

Printing Press—high-speed newspaper printing and folding machine—installed—*Times*—Philadelphia, Pa.

Sewing Machine—sewing machine lamp holder—introduced

Ship—torpedo boat—worthy of the name—*Lightning*—built—Bristol, R.I.

Stenotype—patented—J. C. Zachos—New York City—April 11

Symphony—symphonic work by an American composer—J. K. Paine—presented—Boston, Mass.—Jan.

Telephone—telephone conversation over out-of door wires—Boston–Cambridge, Mass.—Oct.

Telephone—telephone message—distinguishabl ·—Boston, Mass.—March 10

Telephone—telephone patent—A. G. Bell—March 7

Tennis—court tennis—introduced—Hollis Hu newell—Boston, Mass.

Track Meet (intercollegiate)—track meet (inter collegiate)—Saratoga, N.Y.—July 20–21

Turnstile (electric)—used—Philadelphia, Pa.-May 10

Wrench—pipe or screw wrench (practical)—pa ented—D. C. Stillson—Somerville, Mass.—De 5

1877

Army School—army school graduate (black)—I O. Flipper—June 15

Bicycle Magazine—*American Bicycling Journal*-published—Boston, Mass.

Bridge—cantilever bridge—completed—Ker tucky River

Cabinet (U.S.)—Confederate to serve in the Cab net—D. M. Key—served—March 12

Cabinet (U.S.)—German-born Cabinet member-Carl Schurz—began service March 12

Carpet Loom—carpet power loom to weave A minster carpets—patented—Jan. 16

Catamaran—patented—N. G. Herreshoff—Prov dence, R.I.—April 10

Cattle Club—cattle club (Guernsey cattle)-American Guernsey Cattle Club—permaner organization—New York City—Feb. 7

Chemists Society—chemical society (national)-American Chemical Society—chartered—No 9

Chinese Language and Literature Lectureship—! W. Williams—Yale University—New Have Conn.

Cream Separator—centrifugal cream separatc patent—Sept. 25

Cricket Magazine—cricket magazine—*Th American Cricketer*—published—Philadelphi Pa.—June 28

Degrees (academic and honorary)—Doctor (Philosophy degree awarded to a woman—He en Magill—Boston University—Boston, Mass

Dog Show—of importance—New York City-May 8

Easter Egg Roll—Washington, D.C.—April 2

Heating System—heating system from a centr station—installed—Lockport, N.Y.

Holiday—Flag Day—remembrance—June 14

Humane Society—humane association nation organization—American Humane Associatic —organized—Cleveland, Ohio—Oct. 9

Lawyer—Japanese lawyer—Takeo Kikuchi—Bo ton University—Boston, Mass.—June 5

Library Society—library association (national)-annual convention—New York City—Sept. 4

ife Preserver—life preserver of cork approved by the Board of Supervising Inspectors—patented —David Kahnweiler—New York City—July 10

Monument—monument to an American poet— Fitz-Greene Halleck statue unveiled—New York City—May 15

Music—long-distance telephone concert—from Philadelphia, Pa.—heard in New York City— March 31

Newspaper—newspaper printed atop a mountain—*Among the Clouds*—Mount Washington, N.H.—first issue July 20

Nurse—district nurse—employed—New York City

Occupational Therapy Treatment—Training School for Nurses—Boston, Mass.—incorporated—March 16

Oleomargarine—oleomargarine legislation (state) —enacted—New York—June 5

Organ—color organ—patented—Bainbridge Bishop—New Russia, N.Y.—Jan. 16

Postage Stamp—stamp for balloon mail—used— Nashville, Tenn., to Gallatin, Tenn.—June 18

President (U.S.)—President to celebrate his silver wedding anniversary at the White House—R. B. Hayes—Dec. 31

Prison—reformatory (state) conducted for women —Reformatory Prison for Women—Sherborn, Mass.—opened—Nov. 7

Railroad—municipal railroad—Cincinnati Southern Railway—regular service—Cincinnati, Ohio–Somerset, Ky.—July 23

Railroad—railroad shipments of dressed beef (year-round, long-distance)—G. F. Swift— Chicago, Ill.

Royal Arcanum—founded—Boston, Mass.—June 23

Socialist Labor Party of North America—national convention—Newark, N.J.—Dec. 26

Strike—strike in which federal troops were called in peacetime—July 16

Swimming Championship (amateur open)—New York City—Sept. 30

Telephone—interstate telephone call—New Brunswick, N.J.–New York City—May 17

Telephone—news dispatch by telephone—*Globe* —Boston, Mass.—Feb. 12

Telephone—telephone for domestic use—installed—Somerville, Mass.—April

Telephone—telephone switchboard or exchange —Boston, Mass.—May 17

Telephone—telephone used by a railroad company—tried—Altoona, Pa.—May 21

1878

Aviation—Airship—dirigible—flight scheduled— July 3

Baseball Catcher's Mask—patented—F. W. Thayer—Feb. 12

Baseball Chest Protector—chest protector for catchers—invented by William Gray—used

Baseball Game—triple play unassisted—by player in organized baseball—Paul Hines—May 8

Bibliography Course—University of Michigan— Ann Arbor, Mich.

Bicycle Society—bicycle club—formed—Boston, Mass.—Feb. 11

Bridge—railroad all-steel bridge—Glasgow, Mo. —contract signed—Oct. 12

Chinese Embassy—Oct. 4

Copper Refinery Furnace—to use gaseous fuel— Ansonia, Conn.

Electric Company—electric company—Edison Electric Light Company—New York City—incorporated—Oct. 15

Electric Lighting—electric light in a store—installed—Philadelphia, Pa.—Dec. 26

Firehouse Pole—firehouse pole—New York City —installed, April 21

Fishes—goldfish industry

Fruit Spraying—Niagara County, N.Y.

Greenback Labor Party—organized—Toledo, Ohio—Feb. 22

Home Study Course—Chautauqua, N.Y.—organized—Aug. 10

Hotel—hotel for women—Women's Hotel, New York City—opened April 2

Humane Society—humane association national organization—American Humane Association —constitution adopted—Baltimore, Md.—Nov. 14

Lawyers' Association—lawyers' association (national)—American Bar Association—organized —Saratoga, N.Y.—Aug. 21

Lifesaving Service—lifesaving service—authorized—June 18

Medical Society—laryngological society (national)—American Laryngological Association —founded—Buffalo, N.Y.—June 3

Milk—milk delivery in glass bottles—Alexander Campbell—Brooklyn, N.Y.

Newspaper—college daily—*Yale News*—published—New Haven, Conn.—Jan. 28

Phonograph—phonograph—patented—T. A. Edison—Menlo Park, N.J.—Feb. 19

Pipe—corncob pipe commercial manufacture— Henry Tibbe—patent—July 9

President (U.S.)—President to use a telephone—J. A. Garfield—while in Congress

Probation—probation system, without restrictions as to age—established—Boston, Mass.

Soap—soap to float—manufactured—Cincinnati, Ohio

Telephone—telephone switchboard or exchange (commercial)—installed—New Haven, Conn.— Jan. 28

Telephone Directory—issued—New Haven, Conn.—Feb. 21

Telephone Operator—woman telephone operator —E. N. Nutt—Boston, Mass.—Sept. 1

Typewriting School—opened—New York City

1879

Air (compressed)—for tunnel construction— Hoboken, N.J.—New York City

American Indian School—American Indian school of prominence—Carlisle, Pa.—opened—Nov. 1

Archaeological Society—archaeological society (national)—founded—Boston, Mass.—May 10

Archery Club—archery association (national)—formed—Crawfordsville, Ind.—Jan. 23

Automobile Patent—filed—G. B. Selden—Rochester, N.Y.—May 8

Bottle—milk bottles—manufactured—L. P. Whiteman—Cumberland, Md.

Bridge—hanging railroad bridge—Canon City, Colo.—built

Bridge—railroad all-steel bridge—Glasgow bridge—opened

Business—five-cent store—opened—F. W. Woolworth—Utica, N.Y.—Feb. 22

Cash Carrier System—installed—Lowell, Mass.—Feb.

Cash Register—patented—J. J. Ritty—Dayton, Ohio—Nov. 4

Christian Science Church—M. B. Eddy—Boston, Mass.

Cream Separator—centrifugal cream separator—Boston, Mass.

Deaf—Hearing Aid—hearing aid of interest—Audiphone—patented—R. S. Rhodes—River Park, Ill.—Sept. 23

Electric Company—electric company organized to produce and sell electricity—California Electric Light Company, Inc.—San Francisco, Calif.

Electric Lighting—electric arc lights—used for street lighting—C. F. Brush—Cleveland, Ohio—April 29

Electric Lighting—electric incandescent lamp—of practical value—invented—T. A. Edison—Menlo Park, N.J.—Oct. 21

Geological Survey—geological survey director (U.S.)—Clarence King—confirmed—April 3

Ice Skating Rink—ice skating rink (indoor)—built—T. L. Rankin—New York City

Journalism Course—history of journalism course—University of Missouri—Columbia, Mo.

Labor Legislation—factory inspection law—enacted—Massachusetts—April 30

Labor Legislation—labor law prohibiting the employment of women—Illinois—effective—July 1

Library Society—library association (national)—American Library Association—incorporated—Dec. 10

Locomotive—locomotive to use oil fuel—*Young America*

Medical Society—laryngological society (national)—annual meeting—June 10

Pedagogy Chair—pedagogy chair (permanent)—University of Michigan—Ann Arbor, Mich.

Photograph—photograph taken by incandescent electric light—Menlo Park, N.J.—Dec.

Postage Stamp—postage-due stamps—authorized March 3—issued May 9 and Sept. 19

Saccharin—discovered—Baltimore, Md.

Senator (U.S.)—black senator to preside over the Senate—B. K. Bruce of Mississippi—Washington, D.C.—Feb. 15

Senator (U.S.)—senator to serve three states—James Shields—elected—Missouri—Jan. 22

Ship—fish hatching steamer (federal)—*Fishhaw*—authorized—March 3

Ship—steam whaler built as a whale boat—*Th Mary and Helen*—built—Bath, Me.

Ship—steamboat to employ electric lights—*Jear nette*

Sports—amateur athletic competition (interclub—New York City—Sept. 27

Supreme Court (U.S.)—woman admitted to prac tice before the Supreme Court of the Unite States—B. A. B. Lockwood—March 3

Telephone—automatic telephone system pater—Dec. 5

Telephone—telephone switchboard or exchang (multiple)—installed—Chicago, Ill.

Telephone—toll-line commercial telephone se vice—instituted—Springfield, Mass.-Holyok Mass.—April 2

Veterinary School—veterinary school (state)—Iowa State College—Ames, Iowa—May 23

1880

Archaeological Society—archaeological societ (national)—Archaeological Institute of Amer ca—annual meeting—Boston, Mass.—May 1

Bicycle Society—bicycle society (national organ zation)—formed—Newport, R.I.

Canoe Association—formed—Lake George, N.Y

Cattle Club—cattle club (Jersey cattle)—inco porated—May 25

Census—city to exceed 1 million in population-New York City

Census—state to exceed 5 million in population-New York

Croquet League—National Croquet League—formed—Feb. 12

Deaf—Hearing Aid—electrical hearing aid—bor conduction device patented—April 27

Electric Company—electric company—Edisc Electric Illuminating Company—incorporate—Dec. 17

Electric Lighting—electric incandescent lamp fa tory—Menlo Park, N.J.—Oct. 1

Electric Lighting—street lighting (electric) by municipality—in operation—March 31

Electric Power Plant—hydroelectric power pla (commercial)—Grand Rapids Electric Light a Power Co.—Grand Rapids, Mich.—organized March 22

Engineering Society—mechanical engineering n tional society—American Society of Mechar cal Engineers—founded—New York City—Fe 16

Engraving—halftone engraving—S. H. Horgan *Daily Graphic*—New York City—March 4

Flour Mill—flour rolling mill—patented—Jol Stevens—Neenah, Wis.—March 23

Greenback Labor Party—national convention Chicago, Ill.—June 9

Insurance—hail insurance—Tobacco Growers' Mutual Insurance Company—North Canaan, Conn.

Medical Book—bacteriology textbook—A. Magnin—*Bacteria*—published—Boston, Mass.

Medical Book—neurasthenia book—G. M. Beard—*A Practical Treatise on Nervous Exhaustion*—published—New York City

Medical Periodical—laryngology magazine—*Archives of Laryngology*—published—New York City

Newspaper—Italian newspaper—*Il Progresso Italo-Americano*—published—New York City—Sept.

Occupational Therapy Treatment—Adams Nervine Asylum—Boston, Mass.—patients admitted—April

Paint—paint prepared from standard formulas—manufactured—Cleveland, Ohio

Prizefighter—bareknuckle world heavyweight champion (American)—Paddy Ryan—won title near Colliers, W.Va.—June 1

Railroad—municipal railroad—freight service began—Feb. 21

Razor—safety razor—manufactured—Kampfe Brothers—New York City

Representative (U.S.)—representative in office elected President of the United States—J. A. Garfield of Ohio—Nov. 4

Salvation Army—landed—New York City—March 10

Sewage—separate system of sewage disposal—started—Memphis, Tenn.—Jan. 21

Ship—schooner (four-masted)—*William J. White*—launched—Bath, Me.—June

Ship—steamboat to employ electric lights successfully—*Columbia*—dynamo-operated

Steam Distribution Plant—New York Steam Corporation—New York City—formed

Telephone—pay station telephone service—New Haven, Conn.—June 1

Tennis Match—lawn tennis tournament of national scope—Staten Island, N.Y.—Sept. 1

Trapshooting—clay pigeon target—patented—G. Ligowsky—Cincinnati, Ohio—Sept. 7

1881

Air Brush Patent—L. L. Curtis—Cape Elizabeth, Me.—Oct. 25

American Red Cross—organized—Washington, D.C.—May 21

Architect—woman architect—L. B. Bethune—Buffalo, N.Y.

Business School—business collegiate school—Wharton School of Commerce and Finance—Philadelphia, Pa.—established

Catholic Student—pontifical college—M. A. Corrigan—became archbishop—March 4

Coast Guard (U.S.)—inland U.S. Coast Guard station—opened—Louisville, Ky.—Nov. 3

Cold Storage Plant—operated by mechanical refrigeration—Boston, Mass.

Cream Separator—continuous-flow centrifugal cream separator—used—Mahwah, N.J.

Dynamo—dynamo—successful—Jumbo—built—New York City

Electric Lighting—electric light from a power plant in a residence—installed—Fort Washington, N.Y.

Ferryboat—steel-hull ferryboat—*Lackawanna*—built—Newburgh, N.Y.

Fishing Magazine—*American Angler*—published—Philadelphia, Pa.—Oct. 15

Forestry School—forestry course in a university—University of Michigan—Ann Arbor, Mich.

Horse Race—American-bred horse to win the English Derby—Iroquois—June 1

Hotel—hotel to install electric lights—Prospect House—Blue Mountain Lake, N.Y.

Immigration—Chinese labor immigration act—proclaimed

Insurance—bonding company (exclusive)—American Surety Company—New York City—incorporated—Dec. 7

Labor Union—labor union of importance—American Federation of Labor—organized—Pittsburgh, Pa.

Locomotive—locomotive to attain a speed of more than 1 mile a minute—Pennsylvania—March 17

Locomotive Headlight—electric locomotive headlight—patented—L. G. Woolley—Mendon, Mich.—May 3

Loganberry—introduced—J. H. Logan—Santa Cruz, Calif.

Monument—statue cast by the United States Government—D. G. Farragut statue—accepted—April 25

Nursing School—training school for black nurses—Spelman Seminary—Atlanta, Ga.—founded

Photographic Film—roll film for cameras—patented—D. H. Houston—Cambria, Wis.—Oct. 11

Piano Player—piano player—patented—J. McTammany—Cambridge, Mass.—June 14

Piano Player—piano player (completely automatic)—patented—Oct. 4

Pier—ocean pier—built—G. W. Howard—Atlantic City, N.J.

Play (drama)—Greek play—*Oedipus Tyrannus*—produced—Harvard University—Cambridge, Mass.

Plumbing—state plumbing legislation—enacted—Illinois—May 30

President (U.S.)—President whose mother lived at the Executive Mansion—J. A. Garfield—served—March 4

Presidential Candidate—presidential candidate to campaign and make speeches in a foreign language—J. A. Garfield

Psychology Laboratory—established—Johns Hopkins University—Baltimore, Md.

Pure Food Legislation—pure food and drug legislation (state)—enacted—May 28

Quarantine—plant quarantine legislation (state)—enacted—California—March 4

Ship—schooner (five-masted)—*David Dows*—launched—Toledo, Ohio—April 21

Telephone—international telephone conversation—July 1

Tennis Match—lawn tennis national championship matches—Newport, R.I.—Aug. 31

Tennis Society—tennis society (national)—United States Lawn Tennis Association—formed—New York City—May 21

Treasury Department (U.S.)—Register of the Treasury who was a black—B. K. Bruce—began service, May 21

1882

Accountants' Society—accountants' society—organized—New York City—July 28

Army Officer—general to become a rear admiral—appointed—May 16

Baseball Team—professional-league baseball team to win three pennants in succession—Chicago, Ill.—Cubs

Bicycle Trip—bicycle trip of 100 miles sponsored by a club—Worcester to Boston, Mass.

Building—building shaped like an elephant—The Elephant—Atlantic City, N.J.

College—honors course—University of Michigan—Ann Arbor, Mich.

Cooperative—college cooperative store—Cambridge, Mass.—Feb. 28

Country Club—country club to remain in existence 80 years—formed—Brookline, Mass.—Sept. 13

Deaf—School—lipreading instruction for the deaf—S. W. Keeler—New York City

Degrees (academic and honorary)—Doctor of Philosophy degree awarded to a woman by a women's college—K. E. Morris—Northampton, Mass.

Dynamo—dynamo—New York City—tested July 5—in service Sept. 4

Electric Company—electric station (central) to supply light and power—Edison Electric Illuminating Company—New York City—opened—Sept. 4

Electric Fan—invented—S. S. Wheeler

Electric Flatiron—patented—H. W. Seely—New York City—June 6

Electric Power Plant—hydroelectric power plant—opened—Appleton, Wis.—Sept. 30

Electric Power Plant—municipally owned electric power plant—purchased—Fairfield, Iowa

Elevator—elevator with an electric light—Blue Mountain Lake, N.Y.—July 12

Flicker—patented—H. Van Hoevenbergh—Elizabeth, N.J.—May 16

Forestry Book—*Elements of Forestry,* by F. B. Hough—published—Cincinnati, Ohio

Forestry Society—national forestry association—American Forestry Congress and American Forestry Association—merged—June 29

Holiday—Labor Day holiday parade—New York City—Sept. 5

Hospital—hospital for the military and nava forces—authorized—June 30

Immigration—Chinese labor immigration act—enacted—May 6

Immigration—immigration head tax—authorize —Aug. 3

Knights of Columbus—chartered—Connecticut—March 29

Lacrosse Association (intercollegiate)—Interco legiate Lacrosse Association—organized-Princeton, N.J.—March 11

Library—library newspaper room—New buryport, Mass.—dedicated—April 28

Medical Instruction—state medicine and publi hygiene professorship—Northwestern Unive. sity—Chicago, Ill.

Milk—malted milk—invented—William Horlic —Racine, Wis.

Money—coins with a double mint mark—produ tion began—Carson City, Nev.

Naval Officer—naval attaché—F. E. Chadwick-served—Nov. 15

Newspaper—newspaper plant to install electric ty—New York *Times*—New York City—curre turned on, Sept. 4

Play (drama)—Hebrew professional acting troup —New York City—Aug. 12

Ski Club—ski club (local)—Nansen Ski Club-Berlin, N.H.

Steam Distribution Plant—first distribution fro central plant—March 3

Steel—steel mill to install an electrical machine-Braddock, Pa.

Suture—silk suture—used—W. S. Halsted—Ba timore, Md.

Tariff—tariff commission—authorized—June 7

Theater—theater lighted by electricity—Bijo Theatre—Boston, Mass.—Dec. 11

1883

Antivivisection Society—organized—Phil. delphia, Pa.—Feb. 23

Baseball Game—baseball game at night—Fo Wayne, Ind.—June 2

Baseball Player—baseball player to hit a hom run and a double in 1 inning—T. E. Burns-Chicago, Ill.—Sept. 6

Baseball Team—baseball team (major league) score 18 runs in 1 inning—Chicago White Sox-Chicago, Ill.—Sept. 6

Bible School—Missionary Training College—opened—New York City

Building—apartment house cooperative—Ne York City—incorporated March 28—ready f occupancy in September

Cigar Rolling Machine—patented—Oscar Har merstein—New York City—Feb. 27

Civil Service—civil service woman appointee—M. F. Hoyt—appointed

Coronation—coronation on what was to becom United States soil—King Kalakaua and Quee Kapiolani—Honolulu, Hawaiian Islands—Fe 12

1884

Milk—evaporated milk—patented—J. B. Meyenberg—Nov. 25

Monument—monument to George Washington (national)—Washington Monument—Washington, D.C.—completed—Dec. 6

Naval Academy—naval academy graduate to attain the rank of rear admiral—Edward Simpson

Naval War College—naval war college—established—Newport, R.I.—Oct. 6

Navigation Bureau (U.S.)—authorized—July 5

Newspaper Syndicate—newspaper syndicate to supply articles—S. S. McClure—New York City—Nov.

Parent-Teacher Association—parent-teacher association (local)—Froebel Society—Brooklyn, N.Y.—founded

Photograph—photograph of a lightning flash—W. C. Gurley—Marietta, Ohio—May 4

Photographic Film—transparent paper strip photographic film—patented—George Eastman—Rochester, N.Y.—Oct. 14

Police—police bureau of identification—established—Chicago, Ill.—Jan. 1

Political Convention—national nominating convention presided over by a black—J. R. Lynch—Chicago, Ill.—June 3

Press Clipping Bureau—Samuel Leavitt—New York City—April 15

Railroad—switchback railway—operated—Coney Island, N.Y.—June

Religious Hillside Shrine—built—New Ulm, Minn.

Roller Skate—ball-bearing skate patent—L. M. Richardson—Chicago, Ill.—Dec. 9

Telephone—long-distance telephone call—Boston–New York City—March 27

Theater—theater to employ women ushers—Third Avenue Theatre—New York City—Aug. 30

Theatrical School—theatrical school—Lyceum School of Acting—New York City—founded—Oct. 1

Typesetting Machine—linotype machine—patented—Ottmar Mergenthaler—Baltimore, Md.—Aug. 26

Vending Machine—automatic liquid-dispensing vending machine patent—W. H. Fruen of Minneapolis, Minn.—issued Dec. 16

Wire—legislation (state) requiring wires to be placed underground—New York State—enacted—June 14

1885

Bank—savings group—to teach children to save—organized—Long Island City, N.Y.

Bankers' Association—bankers' association formed by a state group—July 23

Baseball Batting and Fielding Cage—built—New Haven, Conn.

Baseball Team—baseball team (black professional)—organized—New York City

Biology—biology course (general) offered in a college—Bryn Mawr, Pa.

Bird Protection Agency (federal)—Economic Ornithology Division—July 1

Book—book showing action photographs in a tion in sequence—*An Electro-Photographic Investigation of Consecutive Phases of Anim Movements*, by Eadweard Muybridge—col pleted

Bookseller's Catalog—of first editions—Ne York City

Building—building known as a skyscraper—col pleted—Chicago, Ill.

Clock—watch movement to be electrically wou —Chicago, Ill.

College—graduate school for women—form opening—Bryn Mawr, Pa.—Oct. 23

College—state college for women—opened Columbus, Miss.—Oct. 22

Economics Association—American Economic A sociation—founded—Saratoga, N.Y.—Sept. 9

"First Aid" Instruction—Peekskill, N.Y.

Forest Reserve—forest reserve (state)—Ne York State Forest Preserve—designated—M 15

Forest Service—forest commission (state)—pe manent—authorized—California—March 3

Gas Commission (state)—authorized—Mass chusetts—June 11

History Instruction—history course (integrate in a women's college—Bryn Mawr College Bryn Mawr, Pa.

Hospital—tuberculosis sanatorium (modern) Saranac Lake, N.Y.—opened—Feb. 1

Index of Government Publications—published

Legislator (state)—black legislator (state)—B. Arnett—served—Ohio

Library Society—library society (local)—Ne York Library Club—formed—New York City

Medical Instruction—bacteriology lectures—H vard Medical School—Cambridge, Mass.

Monument—monument to George Washingt (national)—Washington, D.C.—dedicated Feb. 21

Motorboat—motorboat pleasure craft—manufa tured—New York City

Naval War College—naval war college—open —Sept. 3

Navigation Bureau (U.S.)—permanently org nized—July 1

Newspaper—newspaper daily railroad delive service—*Morning News*—Dallas, Tex.—Oct.

Newspaper—Yiddish daily newspaper—pu lished—*Yiddishes-Tageblatt*—New York Cit

Nurses' Society—nurses' society (local Philomena Society—organized—New Yc City—Nov. 24

Ordnance—cartridge-loading machinery—p ented—G. M. Peters—Xenia, Ohio—July 7

Photographic Film—motion picture film (comm cial)—manufactured—Rochester, N.Y.—Mar 26

Postal Card—postal card depicting other than Liberty head—issued, Aug. 24

Postal Service—special delivery service—auth ized—March 3

esident (U.S.)—President elected for two non-consecutive terms—Grover Cleveland—began first term

izefight—prizefight of importance under the Marquis of Queensberry rules—Cincinnati, Ohio—Aug. 29

otestant Episcopal Bishop—Protestant Episcopal bishop (black)—S. D. Ferguson—consecrated—New York City—June 24

mp—gasoline pump—manufactured—S. F. Bowser—Fort Wayne, Ind.

ailroad—piggyback railroad operation—Long Island Rail Road Company

estaurant—self-service restaurant—opened—New York City—Sept. 4

ale—coin-operated scale—invented by J. G. Sandeman and Percival Everitt—patented, July 28

reetcar—electric cars commercially operated—Baltimore, Md.—Aug. 10

rgical Operation—appendicitis operation (appendectomy)—performed—W. W. Grant—Davenport, Iowa—Jan. 4

1886

ccountants' Society—accountants' society to become a national organization—American Association of Public Accountants—formed—New York City—Dec. 22

ir Gun—wooden gun marketed—Markham Manufacturing Co.—Plymouth, Mich.—March

luminum—aluminum—C. M. Hall—invented process—Feb. 23

rbitration—State Board of Mediation and Arbitration—organized—New York State—June 1

utomobile Tractor—endless-chain tractor—patented—Charles Dinsmoor—Warren, Pa.—Nov. 2

utomobile Tractor—steam tractor—manufactured—San Leandro, Calif.

iblical Students Summer Conference—D. L. Moody—Northfield, Mass.—July 7

irds—ostrich farm—established—South Pasadena, Calif.

oat Race—fisherman's boat race—Boston, Mass.—May 1

rokerage—stock exchange at which more than a million shares were traded in one day—New York City—Dec. 15

atholic Priest—black Catholic priest—ordained to work in the U.S.—Augustus Tolton—ordained—April 24

oat—tuxedo coat—introduced—Tuxedo Park, N.Y.—Oct. 10

oursing Club—American Coursing Club—organized—Topeka, Kans.—July 9

arthquake—of consequence—Aug. 31

conomics Magazine—*Quarterly Journal of Economics*—published—Boston, Mass.—Oct.

lectric Power Plant—alternating-current power plant—operated—Great Barrington, Mass.—March 6

Electric Power Plant—alternating-current power plant commercially successful—built—Buffalo, N.Y.—Nov.

Football Team—football team to score more than 750 points in 1 season—Harvard College, Cambridge, Mass.

Forest Service—Forest Service (U.S.)—Division of Forestry—statutory recognition—June 30

Governor—gubernatorial election in which two brothers were the opposing candidates R. L. Taylor—A. A. Taylor—Tennessee—Nov. 2

Horse—horse whose total purses exceeded $100,000

Money—bill bearing the portrait of a woman—Martha Washington—Sept.

Monument—statue presented by a foreign country—Statue of Liberty—Liberty Island (Bedloe Island), N.Y.—unveiled—Oct. 28

Newspaper—newspaper association—American Newspaper Publishers Association—organized—Nov. 17

Newspaper—newspaper page set by linotype—*Daily Tribune*—New York City—July 3

Nurses' Magazine—*Nightingale*—published—New York City—March 6

Oleomargarine—oleomargarine legislation (federal)—enacted—Aug. 2

Phonograph—phonograph that was practical—patented—May 4

Physician—Hindu woman to receive a Doctor of Medicine degree—Anandibai Joshee—graduated—March 11

Playground—for children—Children's Mission—Boston, Mass.

Polo—international polo series—Newport, R.I.—England vs. U.S.—Aug. 25

Postage Stamp—special delivery stamp—on sale Aug. 4

Postal Service—special delivery service—extended to all free-delivery offices—Aug. 4

Scale—coin-operated weighing machine—Percival Everitt—patented—Feb. 9

Settlement House—University Settlement—established—New York City

Ship—battleship of importance—*Maine*—authorized—Aug. 3

Ship—torpedo boat of importance—*Cushing*—authorized—Aug. 3

Ski Club—ski club (local) that was active—Aurora Ski Club—Red Wing, Minn.—organized—Jan. 19

Social Register—published—New York City

Soup Company—Franco-American Soup Co.—organized—New York City

Telephone—desk telephone—used

Typesetting Machine—linotype machine used commercially—installed—*Tribune*—New York City—July 1

Typewriter Ribbon—typewriter ribbon patent—G. K. Anderson—Memphis, Tenn.—Sept. 14

Wedding—White House wedding of a President—Grover Cleveland—June 2

Welding—welding by the electric process—patented—Elihu Thomson—Lynn, Mass.—Aug. 10

Zoological Laboratory (U.S.)—zoological laboratory (U.S.) for the study of the parasites of livestock—opened—Washington, D.C.—Aug. 1'

1887

Accident Report—industrial accident reports—required—Massachusetts—Sept. 1

Accountants' Society—accountants' society to become a national organization—American Association of Public Accountants—incorporated—Aug. 20

Actor—actor to perform in 2 cities the same day—N. C. Goodwin—Boston and New York City—Feb. 10

Adding Machine—adding machine absolutely accurate at all times—patented—D. E. Felt—Chicago, Ill.—Oct. 11

Armor Plate Contract (U.S. Navy)—June 1

Bacteriology Laboratory—bacteriology laboratory—Brooklyn, N.Y.—incorporated—Feb. 21

Baseball Player—baseball player who was an American Indian—J. M. Toy—Cleveland team (American Association)

Baseball Ticket—baseball rain check—used by club manager C. A. Powell—New Orleans, La.

Bauxite—discovered—Floyd County, Ga.

Bicycle Rider—bicycle rider to go around the world—Thomas Stevens—returned—San Francisco, Calif.—Jan. 4

Book—book set by linotype—*Tribune Book of Open Air Sports*—published—New York City

Book—book showing action photographs in action in sequence—*An Electro-Photographic Investigation of Consecutive Phases of Animal Movements*, by Eadweard Muybridge—published—Philadelphia, Pa.

Brewery to remain in business for 200 years—Philadelphia, Pa.—incorporated

Building—steel-frame building—Tacoma Building—Chicago, Ill.—completed

College—college for women to affiliate with a university—New Orleans, La.

Diplomatic Service—Jewish ambassador—O. S. Straus—appointed—March 24

Esperanto—proposed—L. L. Zamenhof

Fishing Rod—of telescoping steel tubes—patented—Everett Horton—Bristol, Conn.—March 8

Game Warden (salaried game and fish warden)—authorized—Michigan—March 15

Holiday—Labor Day law (state)—enacted—Oregon—Feb. 21

Hospital—babies' hospital designed exclusively for infants—Babies Hospital of the City of New York—incorporated—June 23

Hospital—cancer hospital—opened—New York City—Dec. 7

Hospital—hospital for the military and naval forces—Army and Navy Hospital—Hot Springs, Ark.—opened—Jan. 17

Insurance—credit insurance—attempted—New York State

Insurance—mutual liability insurance company—American Mutual Liability Insurance Compan—Boston, Mass.—opened—Oct. 1

Interstate Commerce Act—enacted—Feb. 4

Kindergarten—kindergarten for the blind—estalished by Perkins Institution—opened—Ro bury, Mass.—May 2

Library Training (systematic)—introduced—C lumbia University—New York City—Jan. 5

Mayor—woman mayor—S. M. Salter—Argon Kan.—April 4

Newspaper—European edition of an Americ newspaper—*Herald*—Oct. 4

Newspaper—newspaper association—conve tion—Rochester, N.Y.—Feb.

Photographic Film—celluloid photographic film invented—H. W. Goodwin—Newark, N.J.

Physiology Society—physiological society (n tional organization)—American Physiologic Society—organized—New York City—Dec.

Postal Service—parcel post convention—neg tiated with Jamaica, B.W.I.—July 22

Printing Press—quadruple newspaper press constructed—New York City

Psychology Magazine—*American Journal of Ps chology*—published—Baltimore, Md.—Nov.

Railroad—daily railroad service to the Paci coast—established

Railroad—electrically lighted train—in service Pennsylvania Railroad Co.—June

Representative (U.S.)—Italo-American represe tative—F. B. Spinola of New York—began s vice March 4

Ship—navy vessel equipped to lay mines—*B timore*—keel laid—May 5

Silk—silk loom—of importance—Gem Silk Loc built—Worcester, Mass.

Ski Club—ski club (local) that was active—fi ski classic—Feb. 8

Softball—softball (indoor baseball game) played—Chicago, Ill.—Nov. 30

Teachers' Sick Benefit Funds—established—Ne York City

Tennis Match—women's national championsh lawn tennis matches—Philadelphia, Pa.

Time Recorder—autograph time recorder—p ented—B. F. Merritt—Newton, Mass.—Dec.

Typesetting Machine—monotype—patented—Lanston—Washington, D.C.—June 7

Union Labor Party—formed—Cincinnati, Ohio Feb. 22

1888

Adding Machine—adding machine successfu marketed—patented—Aug. 21

Agricultural School—vocational agricultu school—St. Paul, Minn.—established—Oct.

Air Gun—metal gun—manufactured

Aluminum—aluminum—commercial producti—Pittsburgh Reduction Company—Pittsbur Pa.

Arbitration—interstate carrier arbitration law enacted—Oct. 1

ank—bank for blacks operated by blacks—chartered—Richmond, Va.—March 2

ank—bank for blacks privately operated by blacks—organized—Washington, D.C.—Oct. 17

aseball Team—baseball teams to go on a world tour—Oct. 20

amera—roll-film camera—patented—George Eastman

ollege—papal seminary—Pontifical College Josephinum—established—Worthington, Ohio —Sept. 1

orporation Course—industrial corporation course—University of Nebraska—Lincoln, Neb.

ounty—county created by federal legislation—Latah County, Idaho—authorized May 14

rematory—crematory (state)—authorized—New York—May 21

oor (revolving)—patented—T. Van Kannel—Philadelphia, Pa.—Aug. 7

ection Law—Australian ballot system—adopted—Kentucky—Feb. 24

ectric Meter—patented—O. B. Shallenberger—Rochester, Pa.—Aug. 14

erryboat—double-deck ferryboat—launched—*Bergen*—Newburgh, N.Y.—Oct. 25

ealth Laboratory—health laboratory (municipal)—Providence, R.I.—established—Jan. 1

olding Company authorization (state)—enacted —New Jersey—April 4

otel—hotel transported—Brighton Beach Hotel, Brooklyn, N.Y.—April 3-July 29

cubator for Infants—constructed—New York City

ocomotive—electric freight locomotive—built—Pullman, Ill.—tested—May 1

ayor—woman mayor elected with an all-woman council—M. D. Lowman—Oskaloosa, Kans. —April

onument—monument to George Washington (national)—Washington, D.C.—opened to public—Oct. 9

otorboat—storage-battery motorboat—*Magnet* —built—Newark, N.J.

aval Officer—naval chaplain who was Catholic —C. H. Parks

en—ball-point pen patent—J. J. Loud—Weymouth, Mass.—Oct. 30

esidential Candidate—black presidential candidate nominated—Frederick Douglass—Chicago, Ill.—June 23

sychology Professor—J. M. Cattell—Philadelphia, Pa.

odeo—competition—Prescott, Ariz.—July 4

axophone—manufactured—Elkart, Ind.

eismograph—exhibited—Lick Observatory—Mount Hamilton, Calif.—June 1

hip—battleship of importance—*Maine*—keel laid—Oct. 17

hip—torpedo boat of importance—*Cushing* —keel laid—Bristol, Pa.

traws (artificial)—for drinking—patented—M. C. Stone—Washington, D.C.—Jan. 3

Telautograph—telautograph—invented—Elisha Gray—patented, July 31

Time Recorder—dial time recorder—invented—Alexander Dey

Time Recorder—employees' time recorder—patented—W. L. Bundy—Auburn, N.Y.—Nov. 20

Typewriter Ribbon—typewriter "copy" ribbon—patented—J. L. Wortman—Philadelphia, Pa.—Jan. 24

Union Labor Party—convention—Cincinnati, Ohio—May 15

United Labor Party—formed—Cincinnati, Ohio—May 16

1889

Agriculture Bureau—agriculture bureau—made an executive department—Feb. 9

Agriculture Department (U.S.)—Secretary of the Department of Agriculture—N. J. Colman—appointed—Feb. 13

Aluminum—aluminum—C. M. Hall—patented process—April 2

Bacteriology Laboratory—bacteriology laboratory—Hoagland Laboratory—New York City—opened—Feb.

Bank—bank for blacks operated by blacks—opened—Richmond, Va.—April 3

Bicycle—bicycle with a back-pedal brake—patented—Dec. 24

Bicycle Race—women's six-day bicycle race—Madison Square Garden, New York City—Feb. 11-16

Brokerage—investment trust—New York Stock Trust formed—April 11

Business School—business high school—authorized—Washington, D.C.—June 11

Clarinet—made of metal—patented—Aug. 27

Conference—Pan American Conference—Washington, D.C.—Oct. 2

Dam—dam disaster of great consequence—Johnstown, Pa.—May 31

Electric Power Plant—alternating-current hydroelectric power plant to operate over a long distance—June 2

Elevator—electric elevator successfully operated —installed—New York City

Fellowship—fellowship (graduate) awarded by a women's college—Bryn Mawr College—Bryn Mawr, Pa.—June 6

Football Dummy—used—New Haven, Conn.

Freemasons—Grotto—formed—Hamilton, N.Y.—Sept. 10

Golf Match—mixed foursome—Yonkers, N.Y.—March 30

High School—county high school—Dickinson County Community High School—opened—Chapman, Kan.

Historical Society—historical society (general)—American Historical Association—incorporated—Jan. 4

Holiday—national holiday—April 30

Library—children's department in a library—Minneapolis Public Library—Minneapolis, Minn.

Lithuanian Church—organized—Plymouth, Pa.—Oct. 27

Medical Clinic—medical clinic (general)—Johns Hopkins Medical School—Baltimore, Md.—opened—Oct.

Medical Instruction—bacteriology courses in a college—University of Michigan—Ann Arbor, Mich.—Jan.

Niagara Falls—utilization of Niagara Falls water-power (large-scale)—Cataract Construction Company incorporated—June 13

Novel Course—lecture course on the English novel—University of Pennsylvania—Philadelphia, Pa.

Photograph—photograph (taken in the U.S.) on which a meteor was found—Cambridge, Mass.—Aug. 10

Political Science Society—political and social science society (national)—American Academy of Political and Social Science—organized—Philadelphia, Pa.—Dec. 14

Railroad—daily railroad service to the Pacific coast—through service without a change—Nov. 17

Sanitary District—Chicago, Ill.—authorized—Nov. 5

Sewing Machine—electric sewing machine—manufactured—Singer Manufacturing Company—Elizabethport, N.J.

State—state named for a native-born American—Washington—admitted to Union—Nov. 11

State—states admitted to the Union simultaneously—North and South Dakota—Nov. 3

Stock Quotation Board—stock quotation boards—manufactured—New York City

Tabulating Machine—patented—Herman Hollerith—New York City—Jan. 8

Telephone—automatic telephone system (successful)—A. B. Strowger—patent application—March 12

Telephone—coin telephone—patented—William Gray—Aug. 13

Tennis Match—professional lawn tennis contest (international)—Newport, R.I.—Aug. 29

Time Recorder—dial time recorder—patented—A. Dey—Sept. 24

Tour of the World—tour of the world made by a woman traveling alone—E. Cochrane (Nellie Bly)—started—Nov. 14

Trust—antitrust law (state)—general law—enacted—Kansas—March 9

Tuberculosis Circular—issued—New York City—July

1890

Animal Husbandry—animal husbandry professor—J. A. Craig—University of Wisconsin—Madison, Wis.

Architect—woman architect—L. B. Bethune—elected to membership in American Institute of Architects—Sept. 15

Building—steel-frame residence—built—Brooklyn, N.Y.

Business School—business high school—opened—Washington, D.C.—Sept. 22

Button—buttons of freshwater pearl—Muscatine, Iowa

Census—census compiled by machines—June 1

Dairy School—of collegiate rank—University of Wisconsin—Madison, Wis.—Jan. 3

Dam—rock-filled dam—Castlewood, Colo.—opened—Nov.

Deaf—School—lipreading school for adults—established—New York City

Decalcomanias—manufactured—Thomas Burk—Philadelphia, Pa.

Election Law—corrupt election practices law (state)—New York State—enacted—April 4

Electric Transmission—alternating-current power transmission—Telluride, Colo.

Employment Service—state employment service—Ohio—April 28

Execution—electrocution of a human being—Auburn Prison—Auburn, N.Y.—Aug. 6

Football Game—Army-Navy football game—West Point, N.Y.—Nov. 29

Golf Course—golf course (nine holes)—completed—Newport, R.I.

Hammer (pneumatic)—invented—C. B. King—Detroit, Mich.

Leather—chrome tanned leather successfully marketed—R. H. Foerderer—Philadelphia, Pa.

Library Society—state library society—Albany, N.Y.

Meat Inspection Legislation (federal)—enacted—Aug. 30

Milk Tester—of value—invented—S. M. Babcock

Narcotics Legislation—narcotic regulation (federal)—enacted—Oct. 1

Navy—naval militia (state)—Massachusetts—organized—March 18

Niagara Falls—utilization of Niagara Falls water power (large-scale)—ground broken—Oct. 4

Opera—light opera presented in 2 cities on the same day by the same company—The Gondoliers—Francis Wilson's Company—New York City and Philadelphia—April 17

Pan American Union—established—Washington, D.C.—April 14

Paper—crepe paper—manufactured—Brooklyn, N.Y.

Polo Club—polo association (national)—U.S. Polo Association—formed—New York City—June 6

Prizefight—state legislation concerning prizefighting—Louisiana—enacted—May 12

Sewage—sewage disposal by chemical precipitation—Worcester, Mass.

Ship—battleship of importance—Maine—launched—Nov. 18

Ship—navy vessel equipped to lay mines—Baltimore—commissioned—Jan. 7

hip—torpedo boat of importance—*Cushing*—commissioned—Bristol, Pa.—April 22

hooting Gallery (mechanized)—invented—C. W. Parker—Abilene, Kan.

ingle Tax—single tax national conference—New York City—Sept. 1

our of the World—tour of the world made by a woman traveling alone—E. Cochrane (Nellie Bly)—returned—New York City—Jan. 25

ournament of Roses—Pasadena, Calif.—Jan. 1

rust—antitrust law (national)—enacted—July 2

Joman—woman labor delegate to a national convention—M. Burke—Detroit, Mich.—Dec. 8–13

Joman Suffrage—state to grant suffrage to women—Wyoming—July 10

omen's Club—women's club federation—General Federation of Women's Clubs—New York City—March 20

1891

nimal Industry Bureau (U.S.)—pathological division—established—April 1

utomobile—electric storage-battery automobile—designed—William Morrison

athhouse—public baths with showers—opened—New York City—Aug. 17

icycle Race—international six-day bicycle race—New York City—Oct. 18–24

icycle Tire—bicycle tire (pneumatic)—manufactured—New York City—April

illboard Standardization—Associated Bill Posters and Distributors of the U.S. and Canada—formed—Chicago, Ill.—July 15

arborundum—invented—E. G. Acheson—Monongahela City, Pa.

atholic Priest—black Catholic priest ordained in the United States—C. R. Uncles—Baltimore, Md.—Dec. 19

hair—steamer chair—introduced—New York City—H. Conried

heck—traveler's checks—devised—M. F. Berry

ongress (U.S.)—Congress to appropriate $1 billion—Washington, D.C.

opyright Law—international copyright agreement—enacted—March 4

orkboard Patent—J. T. Smith—New York City—July 14

orrespondence School—to achieve distinction—Scranton, Pa.—student enrolled—Oct. 16

iamond—diamonds in a meteorite—G. A. Koenig—June

xpedition—polar expedition of which a woman was a member—Peary Expedition—sailed—New York City—June 6

encing—fencing league (national)—Amateur Fencers League of America—organized—New York City—May 6

erryboat—double-deck ferryboat with propeller-type steel hull—*Hamburg*—built

ootball Book—*American Football*—Walter Camp—published—New York City

Football Game—indoor football game—New York City

Forest—national forest—Shoshone National Forest, Wyo.—established, March 30

Forest Management—professional scale—Asheville, N.C.

Forest Reserve—forest reserve (national)—Yellowstone Park Timberland Reserve—designated—March 30

Forest Service—federal planting of forests—Swan, Neb.

Fuller's Earth—discovered—Benton, Ark.

Gas—gas conservation legislation—Indiana—enacted March 2

Hospital—interracial hospital—Provident Hospital—Chicago, Ill.—opened—May 4

Immigration—immigration bureau superintendent—W. D. Owen—appointed—June 15

Jockey—jockey to win the Kentucky Derby 3 times—Isaac Murphy—Louisville, Ky.—(third time) May 13

Medical Periodical—optometry magazine—*The Optician*—published—New York City—Jan.

Museum—Semitic museum—Harvard University, Cambridge, Mass.—opened to public, May 13

Nautical School—nautical state school—established—Massachusetts—June 11

People's Party—organized—Cincinnati, Ohio—May 19

Phonograph Trade Magazine—*The Phonogram*—published—New York City—Jan.

Printing Press—sextuple printing press—installed—New York City

Prizefight—prizefight timed by automatic timer—Peter Jackson vs. J. J. Corbett—California Athletic Club, San Francisco, Calif.—May 21

Radio Patent of Importance—T. A. Edison—Dec. 29

Railroad Car—chapel car—*Evangel*—dedicated—May 23

Representative (U.S.)—representative elected by the Prohibitionists—Kittel Halvorson—began service—March 4

Research Institute—anatomy research institute—Wistar Institute of Anatomy and Biology—established—Philadelphia, Pa.—July 20

Road—law regarding state aid for roads—New Jersey—April 14

Scale—computing scales—manufactured—Dayton, Ohio—Computing Scale Company incorporated—March 20

Seal—state seal designed by a woman—E. S. Edwards—Idaho—approved, March 14

Ship—whaleback steamer to cross the Atlantic—*Charles W. Wetmore*—sailed—Duluth, Minn.—June 11

Ski Club—ski club association—Ishpeming, Mich.—Jan. 16

Temperance Society—women's temperance society (national)—World Woman's Christian Temperance Union—convention—Nov. 10

Trading Stamp—originated—T. A. Sperry

Tunnel—subaqueous railroad tunnel to a foreign country—Port Huron, Mich.–Sarnia, Ont., Canada—opened—Sept. 19

Whist—whist organization of importance—formed Milwaukee, Wis.—April 14

Whist Tournament—duplicate whist tournament —Milwaukee, Wis.

Woman—white woman to become an American Indian chief—H. M. Converse—Sept. 18

1892

Acetylene—acetylene—manufactured—T.   L. Willson—Spray, N.C.—May 4

Addressograph—invented—J. S. Duncan

Alligator Farm—established—Anastasia Island, Fla.

Animals—cattle tuberculosis test—Villa Nova, Pa.—March 3

Arabic Magazine—published—New York City

Attorney General—assistant attorney general (state) who was a woman—E. L. Knowles—Montana

Automobile Tire—pneumatic tire patent—Dec. 20

Automobile Tractor—gasoline tractor—manufactured

Bacteriology Laboratory—bacteriology diagnostic laboratory—as part of work of health department—New York City

Baseball Game—National League 20-inning baseball game—Cincinnati, Ohio—June 30

Baseball Player—baseball pinch hitter—played—Brooklyn, N.Y.—June 7

Baseball Player—baseball player to catch a ball dropped from the Washington Monument, Washington, D.C.—Aug. 29

Basketball—basketball—invented—J. Naismith

Basketball—basketball played at a women's college—Smith College—Northampton, Mass.

Basketball Rules—basketball rule book—published—Springfield, Mass.

Basketball Rules—basketball rules—Springfield, Mass.

Basketball Team—basketball team (college)—formed—Alliance, Ohio—Dec.

Bicycle Racer—bicyclist to ride a mile in less than 2 minutes from a standing start—John Johnson —Independence, Iowa—Sept. 22

Bicycle Tire—bicycle tire (cord)—patented—J. F. Palmer—Chicago, Ill.—June 7

Bottle Cap—crown cork—invented—W. Painter

Canal Locks made of concrete—Hennepin canal —Chicago–Rock Island, Ill.—excavation begun —July

Cheese—Liederkranz-brand cheese—produced—Monroe, N.Y.

College Self-Government Organization—Bryn Mawr, Pa.—chartered—Feb. 23

Cotton-Boll Weevil—introduced—Texas

Degrees (academic and honorary)—anthropology doctorate—conferred—Worcester,   Mass.—March 9

Electric Sign—electric sign (large)—installed New York City

Ferris Wheel—invented—G. W. G. Ferris

Football Game—football game at night—Man field, Pa.—Sept. 29

Glass—wire glass—patented—Frank Schuman-Philadelphia, Pa.—Sept. 20

Gold Leaf—in roll form—patented—W. H. Coe-Providence, R.I.—April 5

Hospital—tuberculosis hospital—National Jev ish Hospital—Denver, Colo.—cornerstone la —Oct. 9

Laundry—rough-dry laundry service—W. N Barnes—Philadelphia, Pa.

Library Loan—made by a state library to a cor munity—New York—Feb. 8

Locomotive—locomotive owned by an industri company—Whitinsville, Mass.—in servic May 11

Matches—book matches—patented

Medical Book—hydrotherapy book in Engli published originally in America—Simon B ruch—The Uses of Water—published—Detro Mich.

Medical Periodical—black medical journal Medical and Surgical Observer—published Jackson, Tenn.—Dec.

Medical School—osteopathy school—America School of Osteopathy—Kirksville, Mo.—incc porated—May 10

Money—commemorative coinage—authorized Aug. 5

Money—silver coins—Columbian half dollar a thorized—Aug. 5

Motion Picture "Studio"—built—West Orang N.J.

Physical Culture Department—University Chicago—Chicago, Ill.

Political Convention—political party nation delegates(women)—T. A. Jenkins and C. Carleton—Minneapolis, Minn.—June 7-10

Postal Card—paid-reply postal card—issued, O 25

Printing Press—web-fed four-color rotary printi press—used—Inter-Ocean—Chicago, Ill.

Prizefight—prizefight of importance under t Marquis of Queensberry rules—Sullivan-Cc bett—New Orleans, La.—Sept. 7

Psychology Society—psychological society (n tional organization)—American Psychologic Association—organized—Worcester, Mass. July 8

Public Speaking Department—in a university University of Michigan—Ann Arbor, Mich. Dec.

Radio Broadcast—radio broadcast demonstrati —N. B. Stubblefield

Research Institute—anatomy research institute incorporated—April 22

Road—concrete road—built—Bellefontaine, Oł

Ship—triple-screw cruiser—Columbia—launch —Philadelphia, Pa.—July 26

Single Tax—city to adopt the single tax for loc revenue purposes—Hyattsville, Md.—July

ociology Professor—A. W. Small—University of Chicago—Chicago, Ill.—Oct. 1

pring Winding Machine—built—Worcester, Mass.

teel—manganese steel—manufactured—Taylor Iron and Steel Co.—High Bridge, N.J.

treetcar—double-deck streetcar—operated—San Diego, Calif.—July 4

treetcar—transfers (printed)—patented—J. H. Stedman—Rochester, N.Y.

ugar—sugar cane 9-roll mill with common gearing and a single engine—built—St. Louis, Mo.

elegraph—duplex telegraph (practical)—patented—T. A. Edison—Newark, N.J.—Aug. 9

elephone—automatic telephone system (successful)—exchange opened—La Porte, Ind.—Nov. 3

uberculosis Society—tuberculosis society—Pennsylvania Society for the Prevention of Tuberculosis—founded—Philadelphia, Pa.—April 10

ypewriter—portable typewriter—patented—G. C. Blickensderfer—Stamford, Conn.—April 12

ending Machine—vending machine (coin-operated) to dispense postage stamps—manufactured—Boston, Mass.

oting Machine—voting machines authorized—New York—March 15

1893

ddressograph—manufactured—July 26

quarium—aquarium (inland saltwater)—Chicago, Ill.

utomobile—foreign automobile exhibited—Chicago, Ill.

viation—Expositions and Meets—air conference (international)—Chicago, Ill.—Aug. 1–4

viation—Magazine—aviation magazine—*Aeronautics*—published—New York City

cycle Racetrack of Wood—opened—San Francisco, Calif.—July 1

cycle Tire—bicycle tire (cord)—exhibited—Philadelphia Cycle Show—Philadelphia, Pa.—Feb.

rths—child born in the White House, Washington, D.C., the offspring of a President—Esther Cleveland—Sept. 9

owling Magazine—*Gut Holz*—published—New York City—Aug. 9

reakfast Food—shredded wheat biscuits—patented—Aug. 1

ridge—concrete arch highway bridge—erected—Philadelphia, Pa.

atholic Apostolic Delegate—arrived—Jan. 24

ollege—college extension courses—Chicago, Ill.—Jan. 1

ollege—university extension summer meeting—Philadelphia, Pa.—July 5

ollege Academic Costume Standardization—advocated—Albany, N.Y.—Dec.

iplomatic Service—ambassador—State Department reckoning—T. F. Bayard—to Great Britain—March 30

Electric Transmission—three-phase alternating high-frequency-current transmission—March

Fastening—hookless fastening—commercial manufacture—Meadville, Pa.

Ferris Wheel—erected—Chicago, Ill.

Glass Dress—of spun glass—manufactured

Golf Course—eighteen-hole golf course—opened—Wheaton, Ill.

Horse Race—horse race of 1,000 miles—from Chadron, Neb., to Chicago, Ill.—completed—June 27

Kapok—commercially introduced—Chicago, Ill.—May 1

Library—children's department in a library—Minneapolis Public Library—Minneapolis, Minn.—separate room

Locomotive—locomotive to attain the proved speed of 112.5 miles an hour—999—tested—May 10

Lynch Law (state)—enacted—Georgia—Dec. 20

Medical School—naval medical school—Brooklyn, N.Y.—opened—Aug. 1

Money—coin bearing the portrait of a foreign monarch—Isabella silver quarter—authorized—March 3

Money—silver coins—Columbian quarter dollar—authorized—March 3

Monument—monument to a woman financed by women—Fredericksburg, Va.—cornerstone laid—Oct. 21

Motion Picture—motion picture closeup—West Orange, N.J.—Feb. 2

Motion Picture—motion picture film exhibition—Brooklyn, N.Y.—May 9

Newspaper—newspaper color-page—*Recorder*—New York City—April 2

Newspaper—newspaper colored supplement—New York *World*—Nov. 19

Newspaper—newspaper Sunday comic section—published—New York *World*

Newspaper—newspaper with an illustrated color-page—*World*—New York City—May 21

Newspaper Premium—newspaper premiums—offered—New York *Recorder*—New York City—March 25

Nurses' Society—society for superintendents of nursing schools—formed—Chicago, Ill.—June 15–17

Patent—print patent—issued—H. J. Heinz Co.—Pittsburgh, Pa.—March 7

Photographic Patent—aerial photography patent—awarded—C. B. Adams

Police—police officer (woman) to be appointed—Marie Owen—Detroit, Mich.

Postage Stamp—commemorative postage stamps—issued—Columbia series—Jan. 2

Postage Stamp—one-dollar-valuation stamp—Isabella Pledging Her Jewels—issued—Washington, D.C.—Jan. 2

Postage Stamp—paintings depicted on postage stamps—on sale—Jan. 2

Postage Stamp—postage stamps to picture a woman—Columbian series—Jan. 2

Postal Service—rural free delivery appropriation

President (U.S.)—President elected for two non-consecutive terms—Grover Cleveland—began second term

Prizefight—prizefight of 110 rounds—Bowen vs. Burke—New Orleans, La.—April 6

Railroad Legislation—railroad legislation (federal)—Safety Appliance Act—enacted—March 2

Road—brick pavement on a rural road—Cleveland, Ohio

Road—federal road agency—established—March 3

Sidewalk (traveling)—sidewalk (traveling)—installed—Chicago, Ill.

Surgical Operation—suture of the human heart (successful)—D. H. Williams—Chicago, Ill.—July 9

Temperance Society—Anti-Saloon League—Ohio Anti-Saloon League—formed—Oberlin, Ohio—May 24

Theater—municipal theater—Academy of Music—Northampton, Mass.—Feb. 9

Track Meet—college relay race—Bayonne, N.J.—May 30

Trapshooting Tournament—trapshoot (Grand American) with live birds—Jamaica, N.Y.—March

Tuberculosis Laboratory—tuberculosis diagnostic community laboratory—authorized—New York City—Dec. 13

Typewriter—typewriter to produce a line of writing visible as it was being typed—patented—H. L. Wagner—Brooklyn, N.Y.—May 16

Water Purification—municipal filtration system—Lawrence, Mass.—Sept.

1894

Agricultural Appropriation—by a state—New York—May 12

Antitoxin Laboratory—established—New York City—Sept.

Baseball Player—baseball player to hit four home runs in one game—Bobby Lowe—Boston, Mass.—May 30

Bicycle Corps (military)—organized—Lake Geneva, Wis.

Bicycle Trip (world)—bicycle trip around the world by a woman—Annie Londonberry—started from Boston, Mass.—June 26

Building—caisson-foundation building—New York City—opened May 1

Carbide Factory—established—Spray, N.C.

Ceramics School—established—Ohio State University—Columbus, Ohio

Communion Cup—individual communion cups—Rochester, N.Y.—May

Copyright—motion picture film copyrighted—Fred Ott—Jan. 9

Cork—for steam pipe covering—manufactured—New York City

Dental Book—book on dental technics—T. E. Weeks—published—Chicago, Ill.

Dog License—dog license law (state)—New Yo —March 8

Employment Service—municipal employme office—authorized—Seattle, Wash.—March

Epidemic—poliomyelitis epidemic—Vermont June 17–Sept. 1

Fencing—intercollegiate fencing championsh competition—New York City—May 5

Football Team—midwestern football team to pla on the Pacific Coast—San Francisco, Calif. Dec. 25

Golf Club—golf association (national)—Unit States Golf Association—formed—New Yo City—Dec. 22

Golf Magazine—*Golfing*—published—W. L. Du ley

Golf Tournament—amateur golf tourname (unofficial)—Yonkers, N.Y.—Oct. 13

Golf Tournament—national championsh stroke-play golf match—Newport, R.I.—Sept

Health Laboratory—health laboratory (state) Providence, R.I.—Sept. 1

Holiday—Labor Day holiday (federal)—enact —June 28

Hospital—leper hospital—Louisiana Leper Hor —Carville, La.

Labor Legislation—labor discrimination la (state)—New Jersey—May 15

Magic Lantern—magic lantern feature show New York City—Oct. 9

Medal—Medal of Honor action—award made Jan. 21

Medical Book—pediatrics book of importance *The Care and Feeding of Children*—L. E. Holt published—New York City

Medical Periodical—osteopathy magazine—*Jo nal of Osteopathy*—Kirksville, Mo.—May

Medical School—osteopathy school—graduati —March 2

Monument—monument to a woman financed women—Fredericksburg, Va.—dedicated May 10

Motion Picture—motion picture of a staged p zefight—West Orange, N.J.—July

Motion Picture—peep show—using film—N York City—April 14

Motion Picture Actor—actor to have an exclusi contract—James Corbett

Museum—commercial museum—Philadelp Commercial Museum—organized—Philad phia, Pa.—June 15

Newspaper—Greek newspaper—*Atlantis*— sued—New York City—March 3

Nurses' Society—society for superintendents nursing schools—convention—New York C —Jan. 10

Physician—osteopath (woman)—J. H. Bolle graduated—Kirksville, Mo.—March 1

Public Health—medical system of inspection schoolchildren—Boston, Mass.

Pushball—game invented—M. G. Crane—Ne port, Mass.

Railroad—railroad to use an electric engine—B timore, Md.—Aug. 4

esearch Institute—anatomy research institute—building dedicated—May 21

hip—steel sailing vessel—*Dirigo*—launched—Bath, Me.—Feb. 3

hip—triple-screw cruiser—*Columbia*—commissioned—April 23

hip—warship built on inland waters—*Ericsson*—launched—Dubuque, Iowa—May 12

hoot-the-Chutes—built—Paul Boyton—Coney Island, N.Y.

teel—manganese steel for railroad tracks—High Bridge, N.J.—manufactured—Aug. 28

upreme Court (U.S.)—Associate Justice of the Supreme Court to become Chief Justice—E. D. White—appointed—March 12

eachers' Pension Fund—enacted—New York City—April 14

elephone—common battery (nonmultiple) switchboard—Lexington, Mass.—Jan. 9

elephone—telephone switchboard or exchange for Chinese-American subscribers—established—San Francisco, Calif.

ime Recorder—card time recorder—patented—D. M. Cooper—Rochester, N.Y.—Oct. 30

uberculosis Laboratory—tuberculosis research laboratory—established—Saranac Lake, N.Y.

Var Veterans' Society—Military Order of Foreign Wars—founded—New York City—Dec. 27

Vomen's Club—Jewish women's organization (national)—National Council of Jewish Women—formed—Chicago, Ill.—Jan.

1895

ir (liquid)—practical—C. E. Tripler—New York City

nimal Industry Bureau (U.S.)—dairy division—organized—July 1

utomobile—automobile regularly made for sale—Duryea Motor Wagon Co.—Springfield, Mass.

utomobile Catalog—Duryea Motor Wagon Co.—Springfield, Mass.

utomobile Club—American Motor League—organized—Chicago, Ill.—Nov.

utomobile Company—Duryea Motor Wagon Co.—Springfield, Mass.—incorporated—Sept. 21

utomobile Magazine—*The Horseless Age*—published—New York City—Nov.

utomobile Patent—G. B. Selden—Rochester, N.Y.—Nov. 5

utomobile Race—automobile race—Chicago, Ill. to Waukegan, Ill.—Nov. 28

utomobile Tire—pneumatic tire—manufactured—Hartford, Conn.

athhouse—legislation concerning public baths—New York—April 18

icycle Trip (world)—bicycle trip around the world by a married couple—started at Chicago—April 10

icycle Trip (world)—bicycle trip around the world by a woman—Annie Londonberry—completed at Boston, Mass.—Sept. 24

Bowling Tournament—bowling convention—New York City—Sept. 9

Bridge—rolling lift bridge—opened—Chicago, Ill.—Feb. 4

Building—building with an all-marble dome—Rhode Island State House—Providence, R.I.—ground broken Sept. 16

Cafeteria—opened—Chicago, Ill.

Canal Locks—of concrete—Hennepin canal—Rock Island, Ill.—opened—April 17

Cat Show—exhibition—Madison Square Garden, New York City—May 8-11

Catholic Apostolic Delegate—Francesco Satolli created cardinal—Nov. 29

Catholic Church—eucharistic congress of the Catholic Church—Francesco Satolli—Washington, D.C.—Oct. 2

Chiropractor—D. D. Palmer—Davenport, Iowa—treatment—Sept. 18

College—Catholic college for women—College of Notre Dame of Maryland—Baltimore, Md.—opened—Sept. 2

Degrees (academic and honorary)—Doctor of Science degree earned by a woman—C. W. Baldwin—Cornell University, Ithaca, N.Y.—June 20

Elevated Railroad—electric elevated railroad (permanent)—Chicago, Ill.—opened May 17

Enclave—enclave—Fairhope, Ala.—Jan. 5

Football Game—professional football game—Latrobe, Pa.—Sept. 3

Glass-blowing Machine—patented—M. J. Owens—Toledo, Ohio—Feb. 26

Glider—glider with cambered wings—invented—Octave Chanute—Miller's Station, Ill.

Golf Book—*Golf in America*—J. P. Lee—published—New York City—May 25

Golf Tournament—amateur golf tournament (official)—Newport, R.I.—Oct. 12

Golf Tournament—open championship (official)—Newport, R.I.—Oct. 4

Golf Tournament—women's tournament golf championship—Westbury, N.Y.—Nov.

Government Printing Office—Superintendent of Documents—authorized—Jan. 12

Manufacturers' Association—National Association of Manufacturers—organized—Cincinnati, Ohio—Jan. 22

Medical Legislation—chiropody law governing the study of chiropody—enacted—New York City

Medicine Ball—invented—R. J. Roberts—Boston, Mass.

Milk—milk pasteurized commercially—Bloomville, N.Y.

Monument—statue officially sanctioned by Rome—blessed—New Orleans, La.—Nov. 10

Motion Picture—motion picture on film shown on a screen—demonstrated—New York City—April 21

Niagara Falls—utilization of Niagara Falls water power (large-scale)—power transmitted commercially—Aug. 26

Normal School—teachers' training school (Jewish)—Gratz College—Philadelphia, Pa.—trustees elected—Feb. 17

Novel Course—course on the contemporary novel—W. L. Phelps—Yale University—New Haven, Conn.

Ordnance—shot tower—erected—Kings Mills, Ohio

Paper Twine machinery—patented—G. L. Brownell—Worcester, Mass.—Dec. 17

Pencil—paper pencil—patented—F. E. Blaisdell—Philadelphia, Pa.—Nov. 19

Postage Stamp—watermarked postage stamp—Benjamin Franklin—issued, April 29

Razor—safety razor to be successfully marketed—invented—K. C. Gillette

Ship—battleship of importance—*Maine*—commissioned—Sept. 17

Ship—ship to circumnavigate the world with but one in the crew—Joshua Slocum—sailed—Boston, Mass.—April 24

Submarine—submarine contract of the U.S. Navy—J. P. Holland—March 13

Subway—municipal subway—construction commenced—Boston, Mass.—March 28

Temperance Society—Anti-Saloon League (national organization)—Anti-Saloon League of America—formed—Washington, D.C.—Dec. 17–18

Volleyball—developed—W. G. Morgan—Holyoke, Mass.

1896

Accountancy Law (state)—enacted—New York—April 17

Accountant—certified public accountant—Frank Broaker—Dec. 1

Actors' Union—Actors' National Protective Union—chartered—Jan. 4

Automobile Accident—New York City—May 30

Automobile Race—automobile race on a track—Cranston, R.I.—Sept. 7

Aviation—Flights—airplane (heavier-than-air) to make any long sustained flight—under its own power—S. P. Langley—May 6

Basketball—basketball intercollegiate game—New Haven, Conn.—Dec. 10

Basketball Game—basketball intercollegiate five-man-team game—Iowa City, Iowa—Jan. 16

Bicycle Race—intercollegiate bicycle race—New York City

Book Review—book review newspaper supplement—published—New York City—Oct. 10

Building—building with an all-marble dome—Rhode Island State House—Providence, R.I.—cornerstone laid Oct. 15

Camouflage—treatise published—A. H. Thayer—New York City

Carrousel—carrousel with the jumping horse mechanism—invented—C. W. Parker—Leavenworth, Kan.

Carrousel—portable carrousel—manufactured—Abilene, Kan.

Chop Suey—concocted—New York City—Aug 29

College—Catholic college for women—College o Notre Dame of Maryland—Baltimore, Md.—in corporated—April 2

College—Finnish college—Suomi College, Har cock, Mich.—opened,·Sept. 8

Cricket Club—college cricket club team to tou England—July 17-31

Discus—discus throwing—Olympic Games—Athens, Greece

Election Law—absentee voting law (state)—Ver mont—enacted—Nov. 24

Electric Alternator—in parallel—installed—Har ford, Conn.

Electric Light Socket—with pull chain—patente —Harvey Hubbell—Bridgeport, Conn.—Aug. 1

Electric Power Plant—hydroelectric power plar to use a storage battery—Hartford, Conn.

Electric Power Plant—rotary-converter powe plant—opened—Chicago, Ill.—May 16

Electric Stove—electric stove—patented—W. ! Hadaway—New York City—June 30

Fastening—hookless fastening—patented—W. I Judson—Chicago, Ill.—March 31

Flashlight—manufactured—New York City

Football Game—indoor football game (large)— Chicago, Ill.—Nov. 26

Golf Tournament—amateur golf tournament c the United States Golf Association in which black contestant was entered—J. M. Shippen— Southampton, N.Y.—July 18

Golfer—woman to win the United States Wc men's Amateur Championship—Beatrice Hoy —Morristown, N.J.—Oct. 7-9

Health Ordinance prohibiting spitting—enacted- New York City—May 12

Hockey—professional hockey team—Portag Lake Hockey Club, Houghton, Mich.—formec

Hospital—cancer home for incurables (free)—es tablished—New York City—Sept. 15

Insurance—substandard life insurance policy— New York City—July 1

Match—book matches—manufactured—Barbe ton, Ohio

Medical Instruction—psychiatric institute—au thorized—May 12

Milk Sale Regulations—enacted—New York Cit

Motion Picture—motion picture film exhibition i a theater—New York City—April 23

Motion Picture—motion picture (successful) prc jected to a paying audience—New York City— April 23

Niagara Falls—utilization of Niagara Falls wate power (large-scale)—first power to Buffalc N.Y.—Nov. 15

Nurse—nurse employed by an industrial organ zation—Proctor, Vt.

Oil—offshore oil wells successfully drilled in th ocean—Summerland, Calif.

Olympic Games—Olympic competition winner— J. B. Connolly

Organists' Society—organists' society (nationa —American Guild of Organists—organized

Periodical—all-fiction pulp magazine—*Argosy*—published—Oct.

Physician—Chinese woman to receive a doctor of medicine degree—Mary Stone—Ann Arbor, Mich.—June 22

Postal Service—rural free delivery—established—West Virginia—Oct. 1

Postal Service—women railway postal clerks—Maude Olson and Mary Olson—Galva, Ill.

President (U.S.)—President who had used a telephone for campaiging—William McKinley—Canton, Ohio

Presidential Candidate—presidential candidate to ride in an automobile—W. J. Bryan—Decatur, Ill.

Prizefighter—American lightweight champion of the world—"Kid" Lavigne—won title June 1

Rowing—transatlantic trip by rowboat—George Harpo and Frank Samuelson—left—New York City—June 7

Sawmill—electrically driven sawmill—Folsom, Calif.

Silverites—national convention—St. Louis, Mo.—July 22

Single Tax—single tax political ticket—Delaware

Submarine—submarine contract of the U.S. Navy—*Plunger* keel laid—June 20

Telephone—automatic telephone system (successful)—rotating-type dial exchange opened—Milwaukee, Wis.

Tennis Match—lawn tennis champions who were brothers

Volleyball—rules published—*Physical Education Magazine*—July

War Veterans' Society—Military Order of Foreign Wars—National Commandery instituted—March 11

X Ray—X-ray machine—exhibited—New York City—Jan. 18

X Ray—X-ray photograph—taken—H. L. Smith—Davidson College—Davidson, N.C.

1897

Accountants' Society—accountants' society formed by a state group—New York State Society of Certified Public Accountants—formed—March 30

Automobile—electric taxicabs—introduced—New York City

Baseball Player—baseball player (major league) to hit in 44 consecutive games—W. H. Keeler—April 22-June 18

Book—best seller (nonfiction) other than a text or purely theological work—*In His Steps*—published

Breakfast Food—breakfast foods introduced—C. W. Post

College Alumni Association—college alumni association secretary (full-time paid position)—Ann Arbor, Mich.—June 30

Copyrights Register—copyrights registrar of the United States—Thorvald Solberg—took office—July 1

Country Day School—opened—Baltimore, Md.—Sept.

Fencing—fencing champion to win three titles in one year—C. G. Bothner—New York City—May 1

Fly Casting Tournament—cast to exceed 100 feet—R. C. Leonard—New York City—March 17

Fly Casting Tournament—indoor fly casting tournament—New York City—March 15-20

Football Game—football game between black colleges—Atlanta, Ga.—Jan. 1

Forestry Society—national forestry association—American Forestry Association—incorporated—Jan. 25

Golf Club—Intercollegiate Golf Association—tournament—Ardsley-on-Hudson, N.Y.—May 13-14

Handball—national championship match for amateurs—Jersey City, N.J.—Jan. 7-8

Hockey—professional hockey team—Portage Lake Hockey Club, Houghton, Mich.—formed

Holiday—Frontier Day—celebrated—Cheyenne, Wyo.—Sept. 23

Horse—horse to pace 1 mile in better than 2:00—Star Pointer—Readville, Mass.

Hospital—crippled children's hospital (state)—St. Paul, Minn.—authorized—April 23

Hospital—tuberculosis hospital (municipal) for consumptive poor—opened—Cincinnati, Ohio—July 8

Ice Cream Sundae—originated—Ithaca, N.Y.

Incinerator—established—St. Louis, Mo.

Initiative and Referendum—enacted—South Dakota—Jan. 27

Marathon Race (annual)—Hopkinton, Mass. to Boston, Mass.—April 19

Milk Station (municipal)—Rochester, N.Y.—established

Motion Picture—motion picture of a prizefight (heavyweight championship)—R. L. Fitzsimmons vs. J. J. Corbett—Carson City, Nev.—filmed March 17

Music Book—ragtime instruction book—*Rag-Time Instructor*—published—Ben Harney—New York City

News Correspondent—White House reporter—W. W. Price—Washington, D.C. *Star*—April 24

Parent-Teacher Association—parent-teacher association (national)—National Congress of Mothers—organized—Washington, D.C.—Feb. 17

Piano Player—piano player (completely automatic)—manufactured—Meriden, Conn.

Piano Player—pneumatic piano player—invented—E. S. Votey—Detroit, Mich.

Prizefight—open-air arena especially built for a prizefight—Carson City, Nev.

Rock Wool Factory—opened—Alexandria, Ind.—June 1

Senate (state)—woman state senator—M. H. Cannon—served—Jan. 11

Submarine—submarine contract of the U.S. Navy—*Plunger*—completed

Submarine—submarine fitted with an internal-combustion engine—*Argonaut*—Simon Lake—patent—Baltimore, Md.—April 20

Subway—municipal subway—first section opened—Sept. 3

Telephone—multiple common battery switchboard—Louisville, Ky.

Theological School—Presbyterian theological seminary woman graduate—E. G. Briggs—Union Theological Seminary, New York City—March 17

Vending Machine—vending machine—to operate automatically—Rochester, N.Y.

Vending Machine—vending machine to sell from bulk—invented—T. S. Wheatcraft—Rush, Pa.

Voting Machine Commission (state)—authorized—New York—May 17

X Ray—X ray of the entire body of a living person—New York City—April

Zionist Society—Zionist national organization—United American Zionists—formed—New York City—Oct. 22

1898

Advertisement—automobile advertisement

Advertising Law—advertising legislation (state)—enacted—New York—April 30

American Expeditionary Force—American Expeditionary Force—landed—Manila, P.I.—July 1

Automobile—armored car—designed—R. P. Davidson—Lake Geneva, Wis.—May

Automobile Driver—woman automobile driver—G. D. Mudge—drove a Waverly Electric

Automobile Truck—designed—Pittsburgh, Pa.

Balloon—balloon destroyed by enemy gun fire—Santiago, Cuba—July 1

Bicycle Trip (world)—bicycle trip around the world by a married couple—returned to Chicago—Dec. 1

Book Index—monthly cumulative index of books—published—Minneapolis, Minn.—Feb.

Cancer Laboratory—New York State Pathological Laboratory—established—Buffalo, N.Y.—May

Carrousel—carrousel with the jumping horse mechanism—completed—C. W. Parker

Dam—steel dam—built—Ashfork, Ariz.

Dental Corps (U.S. Army)—dentist officially employed in the U.S. Army—W. H. Ware

Engine—diesel engine built for commercial service—St. Louis, Mo.—Sept.

Envelope—envelope folding and gumming machine—patented—J. A. Sherman—Worcester, Mass.—Feb. 8

Foreign Service School—School of Comparative Jurisprudence and Diplomacy—George Washington University—Washington, D.C.—opened—Nov. 15

Forestry School—forestry school dealing exclusively with problems of forestry—Biltmore Forest School—Biltmore, N.C.—opened—Sept. 1

Forestry School—forestry school of collegiate character—established—Cornell University—Ithaca, N.Y.—Sept. 19

Geologist—woman graduate in geology—Lo Henry—Leland Stanford, Jr. University—Pal Alto, Calif.

Hospital—tuberculosis sanatorium (state)—Mas sachusetts Hospital for Consumptives an Tuberculosis Patients—Rutland, Mass.—com pleted—Sept. 23

Initiative and Referendum—South Dakota—amendment passed—Nov. 8

Insurance—automobile insurance policy—issue —Hartford, Conn.—Feb. 1

Library—county library—organized—Van Wer Ohio

Library Society—state librarians' society—Wash ington, D.C.—Nov. 16

Log Rolling (Birling) National Championship—Omaha, Neb.—Sept. 9

Loop-the-Loop Centrifugal Railway—patented—Edwin Prescott—Arlington, Mass.—Aug. 16

Medal—campaign medal—Dewey medal—au thorized—June 3

Mineral Segregation—demonstrated—F. E. E more

Newspaper—Arabic daily newspaper—*Al-Hod* —founded—Philadelphia, Pa.—Feb. 22

Optometry Society—optometry society (national —American Association of Opticians—orga nized—New York City—Oct. 10

Physiology Magazine—*American Journal o Physiology*—published—Boston, Mass.—Feb.

Pier—ocean pier of steel—Atlantic City, N.J.—opened—June 18

Play (drama)—musical comedy by a black fo black talent—*A Trip to Coontown*, by Bob Col and Billy Johnson—produced—New York Cit —April 4

Play (drama)—musical (full-length), written, pro duced, directed, and performed as a Broadwa (New York City) production—Bob Cole—*A Tri to Coontown*—opened April 4

Postcard—postcard—authorized May 19—in us July 1

Ship—ambulance ship—*Solace*—in service—April 14

Ship—battleship of importance—*Maine*—de stroyed—Feb. 15

Ship—ship to circumnavigate the world with bu one in the crew—Joshua Slocum—returned—Fairhaven, Mass.—July 3

Social Democracy of America Party—nationa convention—Chicago, Ill.—June 7

Social Democratic Party of America—formed

Spanish-American War—army officer killed i battle in the Spanish-American war—A. K. Ca pron—June 24

Spanish-American War—naval officer killed i the Spanish-American war—Worth Bagley—May 11

Spanish-American War—ship captured in th Spanish-American war—*Buena Ventura*—April 22

Spanish-American War—soldier killed in th Spanish-American war—G. B. Meek—May 11

1900

Advertisement—automobile advertisement—in a national magazine—March 31

Army War College—Army War College—maintenance appropriation—May 26

Astronomer—woman astronomer employed in the U.S. Naval Observatory—Washington, D.C.—July 20

Automobile Bus—automobile sightseeing bus—built—New York City

Automobile Race—fifty-mile automobile cross-country road race—between Springfield, L.I., N.Y., and Babylon, L.I., N.Y.—April 14

Automobile Show—New York City—Nov. 3-10

Baseball League—American League—formed—January 29

Bond—bonds payable specifically in U.S. gold coins—authorized—March 14

Bowling—duckpins—introduced—Baltimore, Md.—in Spring—first match—Union Hill, N.J.—July 18

Chiropractic School—opened—Davenport, Iowa

Corkboard (impregnated)—manufactured—Pittsburgh, Pa.

Cripples—kindergarten for crippled children—opened—Cleveland, Ohio

Cripples—public school for cripples—opened—Chicago, Ill.

Dam—needle-type dam—constructed—Louisa, Ky.

Dental Society—orthodontists' society—founded—St. Louis, Mo.—June

Escalator—escalator—manufactured—New York City

Industrial Research Laboratory—opened—Schenectady, N.Y.—Sept.

Laborsaving Device approved by a labor organization—Stereotypers' union

Medal—Medal of Honor (Army) earned by a black—W. H. Carney—issued May 23

Motorcycle—motorcycle (practical)—manufactured—Buffalo, N.Y.

Newspaper—Chinese daily newspaper—*Chung Sai Yat Po*—San Francisco, Calif.—Feb. 16

Olympic Games—American athlete to place in 4 events in 1 year—A. C. Kraenzlein—Paris, France

Piano Player—pneumatic piano player—patented—E. S. Votey—Detroit, Mich.—May 22

Political Convention—woman delegate to make a seconding speech—Elizabeth Cohn—Kansas City, Mo.—July 5

Postage Stamp—books of postage stamps—issued—April 16

Prizefight—championship heavyweight title won in the first round—Jeffries vs. Finnegan—Detroit, Mich.—April 6

Restaurant—penny restaurant—opened—New York City

Revolver Shooting Tournament (international)—Greenville, N.J.—June 16

Scale—automatic computing pendulum-type scales—patented—A. De Vilbiss—Toledo, Ohio—May 22

Ship—schooner (six-masted)—*George W. Well*—launched—Camden, Me.—July 1

Social-Democratic Party of America—convention—Rochester, N.Y.—Jan. 27

Socialist Party—formed—Indianapolis, Ind.—March 25

Stereotype—automatic plate-casting and finishing machine for stereotype printing—used—New York City

Tennis Match—lawn tennis matches for the Davis Cup—Brookline, Mass.—Aug. 8-10

Trapshooting Tournament—trapshoot (Grand American) with clay targets—Interstate Park, N.Y.—June 12

Union Reform Party—convention—Baltimore, Md.—Sept. 3

United Christian Party—organized—Rock Island, Ill.

Wedding—telegraph wedding—A. M. Candel and Penelope Cundiff—Kansas City, Mo.—April 12

1901

Architecture School—landscape architecture course for women—Groton, Mass.—Sept. 15

Army Nurse Corps (female)—superintendent appointed—D. H. Kinney—March 15

Army War College—Army War College—authorized—Nov. 27

Automobile—automobile to exceed the speed of a mile a minute—A. C. Bostwick—Brooklyn, N.Y.—Nov. 16

Automobile—shaft-driven automobile—constructed—Ardmore, Pa.

Automobile Hill-climbing Contest—Peekskill, N.Y.—Sept. 9

Automobile Legislation—state motorcar legislation—enacted—Conn.—May 21

Automobile License Plates—automobile license plates—law effective—N.Y.—April 25

Automobile Race—automobile race (long-distance)—New York City to Buffalo, N.Y.—Sept. 9-14

Aviation—Flights—airplane flight—Bridgeport, Conn.—Aug. 14

Baseball League—baseball league association—National Association of Professional Baseball Leagues—organized—Chicago, Ill.—Sept. 5

Baseball Player—black baseball player (American League)—Charles Grant (Charles Tokohama)

Bicycle Race—paired six-day bicycle race—New York City—Dec. 9-14

Bowling Tournament—bowling tournament sponsored by the American Bowling Congress—Chicago, Ill.—Jan. 8-11

Building—building with an all-marble dome—Rhode Island State House—Providence, R.I.—occupied Jan. 1

Woman Suffrage—woman suffrage association (international)—organized—Washington, D.C. —Feb.

Young Women's Hebrew Association—organized —New York City—Feb. 6

Zoological Laboratory (U.S.)—zoological laboratory (U.S.) for the study of parasites of man— Washington, D.C.—Aug. 16

1903

Animals—pronghorn antelope—bred and reared in captivity—born—Denver, Colo.

Architecture School—landscape architecture course for women—Groton, Mass.—certificates awarded—June 10

Army Officer—army chief of staff—S. B. M. Young —began service Aug. 15

Army War College—Army War College—cornerstone laid—Washington, D.C.—Feb. 21

Automobile Electric Self-Starter—automobile electric self-starter patent—C. J. Coleman— New York City—Nov. 24

Automobile School—automobile school—established—Y.M.C.A.—Boston, Mass.

Automobile Transcontinental Trip—transcontinental automobile trip—by a nonprofessional driver—H. N. Jackson—San Francisco to New York City—completed—July 26

Aviation—Airplane—airplane to receive national acclaim—Kitty Hawk, N.C.—Dec. 17

Bank—bank president (black woman)—M. L. Walker—Richmond, Va.—July 28

Baseball Game—shutout World Series game (nonsanctioned)—Pittsburgh Nationals-Boston Americans—Boston, Mass.—Oct. 2

Baseball Game—World Series baseball game— Pittsburgh Pirates vs. Boston Americans—Boston, Mass.—Oct. 1

Baseball Game—World Series home run—J. D. Sebring—Boston, Mass.—Oct. 1

Bird Reservation (national)—established—Pelican Island, Fla.—March 14

Boycott Law—enacted—Ala.—Sept. 26

Bridge—suspension bridge of importance having steel towers—New York City—Williamsburg Bridge—opened—Dec. 19

Cable (telegraph)—cable across the Pacific Ocean —completed—Jan. 1

Cable (telegraph)—cable across the Pacific Ocean between Honolulu, Midway, Guam, and Manila —completed—July 3

Camera—filmpack camera—introduced—Rochester, N.Y.

Commerce and Labor Department (U.S.)—authorized—Feb. 14

Fingerprinting—state prison to take fingerprints— Ossining, N.Y.—March 3

Horse—horse to trot a mile in less than two minutes—Lou Dillon—Readville, Mass.—Aug. 24

House of David—established—Benton Harbor, Mich.

Humane Society—humane association national organization—American Humane Association —incorporated—Nov. 12

Insurance—numerical system of insurance rating —New York Life Insurance Co.—New York City

Locker—public locker plant—established— Chico, Calif.

Motion Picture—motion picture with a plot—*The Great Train Robbery*—filmed—New Jersey

Motion Picture Actor—motion picture star—Max Aronson

Motorcycle Association—Federation of American Motorcyclists—organized—Manhattan Beach, N.Y.—Sept. 7

Motorcycle Hill-climbing Contest—Riverdale, N.Y.—May 30

Motorcycle Race—motorcycle distance race (hours)—G. N. Holden—Manhattan Beach, New York City—Sept. 5

Motorcycle Trip—motorcycle transcontinental trip—from San Francisco to New York City— completed—July 6

Multigraph—patented—H. C. Gammeter—Cleveland, Ohio—March 10

Museum—Semitic museum—Harvard University, Cambridge, Mass.—formally opened, Feb. 5

Nurse—nurses' registration law (state)—North Carolina—enacted—March 3

Opera—opera composed by a woman performed at the Metropolitan Opera House—New York City—E. M. Smyth—March 11

Political Science Society—political science association—American Political Science Association—founded—Dec. 30

Prizefighter—pugilist to win three world championships—Bob Fitzsimmons—Nov. 25

Radio Broadcast—transatlantic broadcast (non experimental)—from Cape Cod, Mass.—Jan. 1

Radio Distress Signal—radio distress (CQD) signal from an American ship—*Kroonland*

Radio Station—naval radio station—established —Navesink, N.J.

Railroad—railroad operated by an electric third rail system—Scranton, Pa.—May 25

Railroad Car—steel passenger railroad coach— completed—Altoona, Pa.

Traffic Regulation Pamphlet—printed traffic regulations—*Rules for Driving*—effective—Oct. 30 —New York City

Turbine—steam turbine generator of large capacity for commercial service—Chicago, Ill.—Oct.

1904

"American"—recommended as an adjective— Aug. 3

Animal Industry Bureau (U.S.)—animal husbandry federal appropriation—approved— April 23

Army War College—Army War College—first class convened—Nov. 1

Arts and Letters Society—arts and letters society (national)—founded—April 23

Automobile—automobile with a circulating lubrication system

Automobile Race—Vanderbilt Cup Race—Hicksville, N.Y.—Oct. 8

Automobile Tire Chain—patented—H. D. Weed—Canastota, N.Y.—Aug. 23

Automobile Trucking Service—automobile intercity trucking service—Oct. 29

Aviation—Airship—dirigible circular flight—T. S. Baldwin—Oakland, Calif.—Aug. 3

Bibliography Society (national)—Bibliographical Society of America—organized—St. Louis, Mo.—Oct. 18

Book—comic books—published—New York City

Border Patrol—border patrol officer—J. D. Milton—served

Buddhist Temple—established—Los Angeles, Calif.—July 15

Business—installment finance company—organized—Rochester, N.Y.—April 7

Carnegie Hero Fund Commission—established—March 12

College "Lettermen's Club"—established—Chicago, Ill.—Jan. 29

Electric Attachment Plug (separable)—patented—Harvey Hubbell—Bridgeport, Conn.—Nov. 8

Electric Motor—electric motor (interpole direct current)—invented—Mathias Pfatischer—Philadelphia, Pa.—patented Nov. 22

Fingerprinting—federal penitentiary fingerprinting—U.S. Penitentiary—Leavenworth, Kan.—Nov. 2

Fingerprinting—police department to adopt the fingerprinting system—St. Louis, Mo.—Oct. 28

Health Society—National Tuberculosis Association—organized—Atlantic City, N.J.—June 6

High School—vocational high school for girls—Boston, Mass.—opened—July

Hotel—hotel with individually controlled air conditioning and heating in every room—St. Regis, New York City—opened Sept. 4

Ice Cream Cone—ice cream cone—introduced—Louisiana Purchase Exposition—St. Louis, Mo.

Jai Alai—introduced—Louisiana Purchase Exposition—St. Louis, Mo.

Library—business library supported by taxes—Newark, N.J.

Locomotive—duplex compound locomotive (Mallet)—built—Schenectady, N.Y.

Monument—monument to the memory of the soldiers and sailors of the Spanish-American war—unveiled—Sept. 29

Motorboat Race—motorboat race under organized rules—New York City—June 23

Motorboating Magazine—motorboating magazine—*Motor Boat*—published—New York City—first issue April 10

Newspaper—Hungarian daily newspaper—published—Oct. 18

Olympic Games—black American athlete in the Olympic Games to place—G. C. Poage—St. Louis, Mo.—Aug. 31

Olympic Games—Olympic celebration—St. Louis, Mo.—May 14

Pharmacy Legislation (state)—enacted—New York—May 3

Phonograph Record—phonograph record of a stage performance by the original cast—recorded

Physician—surgeon to substitute radium treatment—Robert Abbe—report—June

Police—motorcycle police—A. L. Howe and Eugene Case—New York City—official status received Dec. 10

Postal Service—permit mail—authorized, April 28—in use, Oct. 1

Printing Press—rotogravure press—imported—Nov.

Radio Distress Signal—radio distress signal—CQD—established—Jan. 7

Rhodes Scholar—Rhodes scholars—appointed

Ski Club—ski club association—National Ski Association of America—formed—Ishpeming, Mich.—Feb. 21

Socialist Party—national convention—Indianapolis, Ind.—May 1

Stadium—cement stadium—Harvard Stadium—Cambridge, Mass.—completed

Streetcar—aluminum streetcar—aluminum used—Oct. 27

Subway—subway (rapid transit)—opened—New York City—Oct. 27

Travelers Aid Society—Travelers Aid Society (national)—Travelers Aid Society—formed—New York City

1905

Automobile Race—transcontinental automobile race (for a time record)—New York City to Portland, Oreg.—started—May 8

Aviation—Legislation—aviation legislation (state)—Tennessee enacted tax on aircraft

Balloon—balloon to land on a building—A. R. Knabenshoe—Toledo, Ohio—June 30

Baseball Game—American League 20-inning baseball game—Philadelphia–Boston—Boston, Mass.—July 4

Baseball Game—shutout World Series game—New York Nationals–Philadelphia Athletics—New York City—Oct. 13

Baseball Pitcher—baseball pitcher (World Series) with 3 shutout games—Christopher Mathewson—New York City—3rd game, Oct. 12

Bridge—aerial ferry—operated—Duluth, Minn.—April 9

Bridge—concrete cantilever bridge—Marion, Iowa

College—university to adopt the preceptorial system—Princeton, N.J.

Esperanto Club—Esperanto club—Esperanto Association—organized—Boston, Mass.—Feb. 16

Factory—air-conditioned factory—Gastonia, N.C.

Ferryboat—municipally owned ferryboats—operated—New York City—Oct. 25

Fingerprinting—international exchange of fingerprints—St. Louis, Mo.—July 6

Fire Extinguisher—using vaporized chemical—manufactured—Newark, N.J.

Forest Fire—forest fire lookout tower—Greenville, Me.—watchman service began—June 10

Forest Service—Forest Service (U.S.)—name changed—designated—March 3

Health Society—National Tuberculosis Association—national convention—Washington, D.C.—May 18-19

Helium—discovered as natural gas constituent

Library—book wagon—traveling library

Medal—Interstate Commerce Commission Medal of Honor—awarded—G. H. Poell—Grand Island, Neb.

Monument—statue of a woman in National Statuary Hall—Washington, D.C.—dedicated—Feb. 17

Motion Picture Theater—theater in the world devoted exclusively to the exhibition of motion pictures—Pittsburgh, Pa.—opened—June 19

Motorcycle—motorcycle (twin-cycle)—manufactured—Sprinfield, Mass.

Newspaper—Greek newspaper—*Atlantis*—daily—New York City—Jan. 3

Pharmacy Legislation (state)—New York—effective—Jan. 1

Plywood—Douglas fir plywood—commercial production—St. Johns, Oreg.

Punchboards—patented—C. A. Brewer—Chicago, Ill.—Jan. 17

Radio Facsimile Transmission—radio facsimile patent—C. D. Ehret—March 28

Railroad Car—mail car (steel)—exhibited—Washington, D.C.—May 4

Rotary Club—founded—Chicago, Ill.—Feb. 23

Sociology Society—sociological society (national)—American Sociological Society—organized—Baltimore, Md.—Dec.

Tung—trees planted—Chico, Calif.

Wrestling—intercollegiate wrestling association—formed—Philadelphia, Pa.—April 7

1906

Advertising Show (annual)—New York City—May 3

Archaeological Society—archaeological society (national)—Archaeological Institute of America—incorporated—May 26

Automobile Bus—bus with a double deck—imported

Automobile Tire—demountable tire-carrying rim—patent applied for—May 21

Aviation—Airship—woman airship passenger—M. P. Miller—Franklin, Pa.—Aug. 11

Balloon Race—balloon cup race—for James Gordon Bennett Aeronautic Cup—Sept. 30

Bank—bank open day and night—opened—New York City—May 1

Cabinet (U.S.)—Cabinet member who was Jewish—O. S. Straus—appointed—Dec. 12

College—technical college for women—Simmons College—Boston, Mass.—first graduation—June 13

Consumer Protection—consumer protection (federal law)—enacted June 13

Diamond—diamonds in actual rock—discovered Murfreesboro, Ark.—Aug. 1

Election Law—primary election (statewide)—Wisconsin—Sept. 4

Engineering Society—woman elected to the American Society of Civil Engineers—N. S. Blatch—March 6

Esperanto Magazine—*L'Amerika Esperantisto*—published—Oklahoma City, Okla.—Oct.

Fastening—hookless fastening for universal use—invented—Gideon Sundback—Hoboken, N.J.

Fraternity (Greek letter)—intercollegiate Greek-letter national fraternity for black men—Alpha Phi Alpha—Ithaca, N.Y.—formed—Dec. 4

Insurance—Employer's Liability Act (federal)—enacted—June 11

Japanese Ambassador—legation raised to embassy—Jan. 7

Medal—National Geographic Society gold medal—Hubbard medal—presented—R. E. Peary—Washington, D.C.—Dec. 15

Monument—national monument—established—Devils Tower, Wyo.—Sept. 24

Motion Picture—animated cartoon—*Humorous Phases of Funny Faces*—released

Nobel Prize—Nobel Prize—awarded to an American—Theodore Roosevelt

Nurse—nurse appointed to a university professorship—M. A. Nutting—Columbia University—New York City

Patent—airplane patent—Orville Wright and Wilbur Wright—May 22

Phonograph—phonograph with an enclosed horn in the cabinet—manufactured—Camden, N.J.—Aug. 22

Plastic—thermosetting manufactured plastic—developed—L. H. Baekeland—Yonkers, N.Y.

President of a South American Country Born in the United States—Galo Plaza Lasso—born—New York City—Feb. 17

President (U.S.)—President to visit a foreign country while President—Theodore Roosevelt—Panama—Nov. 14

Radio Broadcast—radio program broadcast—R. A. Fessenden—Dec. 24

Radio Distress Signal—radio distress signal—S O S—adopted—Nov. 22

Radio Receiver—radio receiver advertised—New York City—Jan. 13

Radio Tube—three-element vacuum tube—announced—Lee De Forest—New York City—Oct. 20

Ship—turbine-propelled oceangoing merchant vessel—*Governor Cobb*—launched—April 21

Sociology Society—sociological society (national)—American Sociological Society—annual meeting—Providence, R.I.—Dec. 27-29

Stamp—consular service fee stamps—authorized April 5—effective, June 30

Tunnel—freight delivery tunnel system—Chicago, Ill.—Aug. 15

Aviation—Passenger—airplane passenger (official)—passenger to fly—May 14

Aviation—Periodical—aviation magazine devoted primarily to airplanes—*Fly*—published—Philadelphia, Pa.

Aviation—School—correspondence school in aviation—International School of Aeronautics—opened—New York City—Jan. 1

Baseball Game—shutout double-header games—Brooklyn, N.Y.—Sept. 26

Baseball League—juvenile baseball league—Waynesburg, Pa.

Bible—Bibles in hotel rooms—Superior, Mont.—Oct.

Bowling Tournament—gold medal award to a perfect-score bowler—perfect scores obtained

Carbon Tetrachloride—C. E. Acker—introduced process

Child Hygiene Bureau—established—New York City—Aug.

Children's Welfare Congress (international)—Washington, D.C.—March 10-17

City Manager—Staunton, Va.—elected—April 2—office opened—April 15

Confectionery Machine—manufactured—Racine, Wis.

Credit Union Association—founded—Manchester, N.H.

Electric Lighting—electric indirect lighting demonstration—Chicago, Ill.—Oct.

Esperanto Club—Esperanto club (national organization)—organized—Chautauqua Lake, N.Y.—Sept. 7

Esperanto Course—carrying college credit—Clark University—Worcester, Mass.—Sept. 16

Federal Council of the Churches of Christ in America—organized—Philadelphia, Pa.—Dec. 2

Fireworks Legislation—fireworks legislation enacted by a large city—Cleveland, Ohio—July 18

Football Uniform—football uniform numerals—University of Pittsburgh—Pittsburgh, Pa.—Dec. 5

Forest—national forest in the southern states—Ocala National Forest, Fla.—Theodore Roosevelt proclaimed—Nov. 24

Health Department—county health department organized on a full-time basis—Jefferson County, Ky.—established Jan. 7

Holiday—Mother's Day—designated—Philadelphia, Pa.—May 10

Insurance—savings bank life insurance—Whitman, Mass.—policy—June 22

Insurance—workers' compensation insurance law (federal)—enacted—May 30

Intelligence Test—Binet-Simon test—used—Vineland, N.J.—Aug.

Journalism Course—journalism school—University of Missouri—Columbia, Mo.—Sept. 14

Motion Picture—presidential candidate shown in motion pictures—W. J. Bryan—filmed in Fairview, Neb.—July 10—shown in New York City—July 12

Naval Officer—admiral who was Jewish—Adolph Marix—July 4

Navy—naval nurses' corps—established—May 13

Newspaper—newspaper with an aviation section—*Inquirer*—Philadelphia, Pa.—June 7

Nursing School—university school of nursing—University of Minnesota—Minneapolis, Minn.—authorized—Oct. 1

Olympic Games—American athlete to win ten medals at the Olympic Games—Ray Ewry

Post Office—naval post office aboard a naval vessel—established—Aug. 20

Postage Stamp—postage stamps in coils—issued—Feb. 18

Postal Service—navy mail service—established—May 27

Price Regulation Legislation—price regulation law (state)—Louisiana—approved—July 2

Radio Distress Signal—radio distress signal—CQD—superseded by SOS—July

Radio Magazine—*Modern Electrics*—published—New York City—April

Radio Society—Wireless Association of America—formed—New York City

Ship—turbine-propelled ship of the U.S. Navy—*Chester*—commissioned

Ski Jump (steel)—built—Chippewa Falls, Wis.—Nov.

Sorority—black sorority—Alpha Kappa Alpha sorority—founded—Washington, D.C.—Jan. 15

Sousaphone—manufactured—Elkhart, Ind.

Tuberculosis School—outdoor school for tubercular children—opened—Providence, R.I.—Jan 27

Tungsten—ductile tungsten—produced—W. D Coolidge

Tunnel—freight delivery tunnel system—complete system in operation—Jan. 2

Tunnel—tunnel under the Hudson River—opened—New York City–Jersey City—Feb. 25

Water Purification—water supply chemically treated with chlorine compounds—Jersey City N.J.

1909

Army School—army school graduates (Chinese—Ying Shing Wen and Ting Chia Chen—were graduated June 11

Automobile—production of more than 100,00 passenger cars in one year

Automobile Race—transcontinental automobil race—left New York City—June 1

Automobile Transcontinental Trip—transconti nental automobile trip by a woman—left Nev York City—June 9—arrived San Francisco—Aug. 6

Aviation—Airplane—airplane purchased by th U.S. Government—accepted—Aug. 2

Aviation—Airplane—airplane sold commercial—Hammondsport, N.Y.

Aviation—Airplane—monoplane (American)—flown—Mineola, N.Y.—Dec. 9

Aviation—Flights—intercity airplane flight—B. D. Foulois—July 30

Aviation—Passenger—woman airplane passenger—flight—College Park, Md.—Oct. 27

Aviation—Pilot—Army pilot to solo—F. E. Humphreys—College Park, Md.—Oct. 26

Aviation—Races—airplane race won by an American in Europe—G. H. Curtiss—Aug.

Balloon Honeymoon—balloon honeymoon—R. N. Burnham and E. H. Waring—began, Woods Hole, Mass.—ended, Holbrook, Mass.—June 20

Balloon Race—dirigible balloon race—St. Louis, Mo.—Oct. 4-9

Bank—Christmas savings club—originated—Carlisle, Pa.

Baseball—cork-center baseball—patented—B. S. Shibe—June 15

Baseball Game—baseball game at night by a regular-league team—Grand Rapids, Mich.—July 8

Baseball Game—triple play unassisted in a modern major-league game—Neal Ball—Cleveland, Ohio—July 19

Bed—"concealed bed"—manufactured—San Francisco, Calif.

Bird Banding Society—formed—New York City—Dec. 8

Bowling Tournament—gold medal award to a perfect-score bowler—roll-off—Pittsburgh, Pa.—March 11

Bridge—double-deck bridge—of importance—opened—New York City—March 30

Building—apartment house to occupy a square city block—New York City—ready for occupancy Oct. 15

Child Delinquency law (state)—enacted—Colorado—April 28

City Planning Instruction—offered—Cambridge, Mass.

Continuation School—apprentice continuation school—established—Cincinnati, Ohio—Aug. 30

Court—domestic relations court—established—Buffalo, N.Y.

Credit Union Association—Manchester, N.H.—chartered—April 6

Credit Union Law—enacted—Massachusetts—May 21

Discovery—discovery of the North Pole—R. E. Peary—April 6

Election Law—preferential ballot system—Grand Junction, Colo.—Sept. 14

Electric Power Plant—hydroelectric power plant built by the federal government—Minidoka Dam, Idaho—first unit started, May 1

Engine—outboard motor (commercially successful)—developed—Ole Evinrude—Milwaukee, Wis.

Forestry School—forestry school to give scientific training in the care and preservation of trees—Davey Tree Expert Co.—incorporated—Feb. 9

Fraternity (Greek-letter)—interfraternity council—New York City—Nov. 17

High School—junior high school—Indianola Junior High School, Columbus, Ohio—opened Sept. 7

High School—junior high school system—authorized—Berkeley, Calif.—Dec. 21

Horseshoe Pitching Contest (international)—Bronson, Kan.

Hospital—tuberculosis preventorium for children—Lakewood, N.J.

Library Catalog—union catalog of books in a state library—Sacramento, Calif.

Medal—National Institute of Arts and Letters gold medal—awarded—Nov. 20

Money—coin bearing the portrait of a President

Motion Picture—colored motion pictures—exhibited—New York City—Dec. 11

Motion Picture Censorship—motion picture censorship board (national)—organized

Narcotics Legislation—narcotic prohibition act (federal)—enacted—Feb. 9

Nursing School—university school of nursing—established—March 1

Old Age Home for Pioneers—Prescott, Ariz.—authorized—March 10

Paint Spraying Device—commercially manufactured—De Vilbiss Co.—Toledo, Ohio

Plastic—thermosetting manufactured plastic—patented—L. H. Baekeland—Yonkers, N.Y.—Dec. 7

Postage Stamp—memorial stamp—issued—Feb. 12

Pressing Machine (steam-operated)—patent granted—A. J. Hoffman—July 13

Radio Distress Signal—radio SOS from an American ship—transmitted—Aug. 11

Research Institute—institute for research in nervous diseases—Neurological Institute—New York City—opened—Oct. 1

Road—concrete rural road—laid—Wayne County, Mich.

Ship—battleship to visit an inland city—Natchez, Miss.—May 20

Stadium—baseball stadium (fireproof)—Forbes Field, Pittsburgh, Pa.—opened—June 30

Subway—subway car with side doors—invented by James McElroy—in service—New York City—Feb. 16

Tax—corporation tax—enacted—Aug. 5

Tax—income tax amendment to the Constitution—proposed to states—July 12

1910

Air Rights Lease—New York Central Railroad Co.—New York City—Feb.

Automobile—automobile (gasoline-electric combination)—used

Automobile Racetrack—automobile speedway (board track)—Playa del Rey, Calif.—opened—April 7

Automobile Tire—cord tire—B. F. Goodrich Co.—Akron, Ohio

Aviation—airplane merchandise shipment—Dayton, Ohio to Columbus, Ohio—Nov. 7

Aviation—Airplane Bombing—airplane bombing experiment—Hammondsport, N.Y.—June 30

Aviation—Airport—airport municipal legislation —Modesto, Calif.—ratified—Sept. 14

Aviation—Expositions and Meets—aviation meet —Los Angeles, Calif.—Jan. 10-20

Aviation—Flights—airplane flight from a ship— Nov. 14

Aviation—Flights—airplane round trip—C. K. Hamilton—June 13

Aviation—Flights—airplane to carry 3 passengers —Mineola, N.Y.—Aug. 14

Aviation—Flights—airplane to exceed a mile in altitude—W. R. Brookins—Atlantic City, N.J.— July 9

Aviation—Flights—night flight—W. R. Brookins —Montgomery, Ala.—April 18

Aviation—Flights—over-water flight—G. H. Curtiss—Cleveland-Sandusky, Ohio—Aug. 31

Aviation—Flights (transatlantic)—transatlantic dirigible flight—left Atlantic City, N.J.—Oct. 15

Aviation—Pilot—aviator (American) to establish an altitude record—Louis Paulhan—Los Angeles, Calif.—Jan. 12

Aviation—Pilot—aviator to fire a gun from an airplane—J. E. Fickel—New York City—Aug. 20

Aviation—Pilot—woman aviator to make a public flight—B. S. Scott—Fort Wayne, Ind.—Oct. 23

Aviation—Races—airplane to race a train—May 29

Aviation—School—airplane flying school—Hammondsport, N.Y.—Sept.

Balloon Trophy—balloon trophy to a woman— Mrs. C. B. Harmon—Dayton, Ohio—Sept. 16

Bank—postal savings bank—authorized—June 25

Baseball—cork-center baseball—used in world series—Chicago, Ill.—Oct. 20

Boy Scouts of America—Boy Scouts of America— incorporated—Feb. 8

Bread—completely automatic bread plant— opened—Chicago, Ill.—July 1

Chiropody School—chiropody school of note— New York School of Chiropody—organized— New York City

Climatology Professor—R. De C. Ward—appointed—Cambridge, Mass.

Court—commerce court (U.S.)—established— June 18

Degrees (academic and honorary)—Master of Arts degree in aeronautics—G. C. Loening—Columbia University, New York City—June 1

Dental School—dental assistants' and nurses' course—Cincinnati, Ohio—Oct. 3

Disease (distinctly American)—recognized— Tulare County, Calif.

Esperanto Club—Esperanto Congress in the United States—Washington, D.C.—Aug. 14-20

Fine Arts Commission (federal)—fine arts commission (federal)—authorized—May 17

Golf Clubs (or golf sticks)—steel shaft for a golf club—patented—A. F. Knight—Schenectady, N.Y.—Nov. 22

Holiday—Father's Day—celebrated—Spokane, Wash.—June 19

Insect Electrocutor Patent—W. M. Frost—Spokane, Wash.—Nov. 8

Mayor—socialist mayor of a large city—Emil Seidel—Milwaukee, Wis.—began term in April

Medical Instruction—medical research chair— University of Pennsylvania—Philadelphia, Pa.

Mines Bureau (U.S.)—established—May 16

Motion Picture—newsreel—exhibited—Nov.

Opera—opera broadcast in part—New York City —Jan. 13

Opera—opera by an American composer performed at the Metropolitan Opera House of New York—March 18

Optometry Instruction—optics and optometry course—Columbia University—New York City

Pan American Union—name adopted—Aug. 11

Photostat—photographic copying machine—commercially manufactured—Rochester, N.Y.

Pinball Game—pinball game machine (toy)— manufactured—Detroit, Mich.

Police—police officer (woman) under civil service —A. S. Wells—appointed in Los Angeles, Calif. —Sept. 2

Postal Savings Stamps—issued—Dec. 22

President (U.S.)—President to fly—(ex-President Theodore Roosevelt—St. Louis, Mo.—Oct. 11

President (U.S.)—President to pitch a ball to open the baseball season—W. H. Taft—April 14

Prizefighter—black heavyweight champion of the world—Jack Johnson

Radio Broadcast—radio broadcast sent from an airplane—J. A. Macready—Sheepshead Bay, N.Y.—Aug. 27

Radio Broadcast—wireless message from an airship over the Atlantic Ocean—Walter Wellman, pilot—Jack Irwin, wireless operator—Oct. 15

Radio Contest—Philadelphia, Pa.—Feb. 23

Radio Distress Signal—radio distress signal resulting in an airship rescue—airship America rescued—Hatteras, N.C.—Oct. 18

Radio Legislation (national)—enacted—June 24

Radio Telephone—two-way radio in an automobile—New York City—March

Railroad Car—glass-lined tank car—for transporting milk—built—Rochester, N.Y.

Rayon—rayon—commercial production—Marcus Hook, Pa.—Dec. 19

Rotary Club—national organization—formed— Chicago, Ill.—Aug.

Stadium—school stadium—Tacoma, Wash.— dedicated—June 10

Streetcar—trackless trolley system—operated— Los Angeles, Calif.—Sept. 11

Submarine—submarine accident—Bonita (later named C4) rammed by gunboat Castine—off Provincetown, Mass.—July 11

Ticker Tape—ticker-tape shower—Theodore Roosevelt—New York City—June 18

Washing Machine—complete, self-contained electric washing machine—patented—A. Fisher—Aug. 9

Woman—woman horseback rider to make a solo transcontinental trip—left San Francisco, Calif., for New York City—Sept. 1

1911

Advertising Organization—to combat business abuses—formed—Dec.

Airmail Service—airmail pilot—E. L. Ovington—sworn in—Sept. 23

Army Officer—flight surgeon—J. P. Kelly—reported for duty—College Park, Md.—June 30

Attorney General—black assistant attorney general (U.S.)—W. H. Lewis—began service March 26

Automobile Electric Self-Starter—automobile electric self-starter applied commercially—Cadillac—May

Automobile Race—automobile race on a track (long-distance)—Indianapolis, Ind.—May 30

Automobile Transcontinental Trip—transcontinental automobile group tour—from Atlantic City, N.J.—concluded—Venice, Calif.—Aug. 13

Aviation—airplane rescue at sea—Jan. 30

Aviation—airplane rescue at sea effected by another airplane—Hugh Robinson—Aug. 14

Aviation—airplane to land on the White House lawn—H. N. Atwood—Washington, D.C.

Aviation—Airplane—hydroplane—that was successful—*Flying Fish*—flown—Jan. 26

Aviation—Airplane—naval airplane—delivered

Aviation—Airplane Bombing—airplane bombing experiment with explosives—Jan. 7-25

Aviation—Airplane Fatalities—airplane fatality in a solo military airplane—G. E. M. Kelly—San Antonio, Tex.—May 10

Aviation—Flights—airplane flight to the deck of a carrier—E. B. Ely—San Francisco, Calif.—Jan. 18

Aviation—Flights—airplane flight under a bridge—Lincoln Beachey—Niagara Falls, N.Y.—June 27

Aviation—Flights—hydroplane flight to and from a ship—Glenn Curtiss—Feb. 17

Aviation—Flights (transcontinental)—transcontinental airplane flight—left—Sheepshead Bay, N.Y.—C. P. Rodgers—Sept. 17

Aviation—Flights (transcontinental)—transcontinental airplane flight (eastbound)—left—Los Angeles, Calif.—Oct. 19

Aviation—Legislation—aviation legislation (state)—enacted—Connecticut—June 8

Aviation—License—pilot's license issued by the Aero Club of America—G. H. Curtiss—June 8

Aviation—License—woman pilot to pass the test of the Aero Club of America—Harriet Quimby—Aug. 1

Aviation—Races—intercity airplane race—New York City-Philadelphia, Pa.—Aug. 5

Bank—postal savings bank—initiated—Jan. 3

Baseball Player—"most valuable player" award (major league)—Frank Schulte and T. R. Cobb

Boy Scouts of America—boy scout uniformed troop—organized—Troy, N.Y.

Cable (telegram)—cable message sent around the world by commercial telegraph—from New York City—Aug. 20

Cemetery—federal cemetery in the U.S. to contain graves of both Union and Confederate soldiers—Springfield, Mo.—March 3

College—college foreign-language house—Deutsches Haus at Columbia University—New York City

Continuation School—continuation school established by state law—opened—Racine, Wis.—Nov. 3

Court—commerce court (U.S.)—opened—Feb. 15

Dental Corps (U.S. Army)—Dental Corps commissions—authorized—March 3

Electric Lighting—klieg light lighting unit—used

Farm Bureau—city department—established—Binghamton, N.Y.—March 20

Fingerprinting—fingerprint conviction—Thomas Jennings—Cook County, Ill.—Feb. 11

Golf Champion—golf champion (American-born professional) to win the United States Open Tournament—J. J. McDermott—Wheaton, Ill.—June 26

Gyro Compass—gyro compass installed on an American naval vessel—*Delaware*—tested—Aug. 28

Insurance—group insurance policy—New York City—June 1

Insurance—hail insurance law (state)—enacted—North Dakota—March 18

Insurance—workers' compensation insurance law (state)—enacted—Wisconsin—May 3

Library Society—woman to become president of the American Library Association—T. H. W. Elmendorf—May 24

Linoleum—linoleum machine (fully automatic)—installed—Kearny, N.J.

Locker—locker (coin vender)—patented—W. S. Farnsworth—Petaluma, Calif.

Mineral Segregation—commercial operation—Butte, Mont.

Motion Picture Censorship—motion picture censorship board (state)—enacted—Pennsylvania—June 19

Motorboat—motorboat to travel at a speed of more than 40 m.p.h.—Victor Emerson—Alexandria, Va.—May 27

Old Age Home for Pioneers—Prescott, Ariz.—opened—Feb. 6

Opera—opera singer to sing two major roles on the same day—Herman Jadlowker—Metropolitan Opera House—New York City—March 22

Photograph—photograph from an airplane—H. A. Erickson—Jan. 10

Postage Stamp—registry stamp—issued—Dec. 1

Printing Instruction—printing lecture course in a college—Cambridge, Mass.—Feb.

Radio Broadcast—transpacific conversation broadcast—received from Hokkaido Island, Japan, at San Francisco, Calif.—Oct. 6

Radio Car (military)—designed—R. P. Davidson—Lake Geneva, Wis.

Radio License—radio license—G. H. Lewis—Cincinnati, Ohio

Representative (U.S.)—representative to attend college after his term of office—G. A. Bartlett—University of Nevada, Reno, Nev.—enrolled, Aug. 18

Representative (U.S.)—Socialist representative—V. L. Berger—March 4

Ship—electrically propelled ship of the United States Navy—*Jupiter*—keel laid—Oct. 16

Shortening—shortening made by the hydrogenation process—introduced—Cincinnati, Ohio—Aug. 15

Squash Club—squash tennis organization (national)—formed—New York City—March 20

Squash Tournament—New York City—April 8-10

Traffic Lines—painted in white—Trenton, Mich.

Trust—blue-sky laws—Kansas—March 10

Woman—woman horseback rider to make a solo transcontinental trip—N. J. Aspinwall—arrived New York City—July 8

1912

Advertising Organization—investigation work commenced—March

Aviation—aeronautical elopement—Arthur Smith and Aimée Cour—Fort Wayne, Ind., to Hillsdale, Mich.—Oct. 26

Aviation—airplane takeoff from a hotel roof—Silas Christoferson—Portland, Oreg.

Aviation—Airplane—airplane outfitted with a machine gun—flown—College Park, Md.—May 7

Aviation—Airplane Fatalities—airplane fatality (woman)—Julia Clark—Springfield, Ill.—June 17

Aviation—Airplane Fatalities—airplane fatality (woman pilot with passenger)—Harriet Quimby—Dorchester Bay, Boston, Mass.—July 1

Aviation—Expositions and Meets—aeronautic international exposition—New York City—May 9-18

Aviation—Flights—airplane catapulted—Washington, D.C.—Nov. 12

Aviation—Flights—over-water round trip—to Catalina Island, Calif.—May 10

Aviation—Flights (transcontinental)—transcontinental airplane flight (eastbound)—R. G. Fowler—landed—Feb. 8

Aviation—Parachute—parachute jump from an airplane—Jefferson Barracks, Mo.—March 1

Aviation—Passenger—admiral in uniform to ride in an airplane—B. A. Fiske—New York City—May 10

Baseball Game—baseball game (major league) in which 1 team scored 24 runs—Philadelphia Athletics—Philadelphia, Pa.—May 18

Baseball Player—baseball player (major league) to steal 6 bases in 1 game—E. T. Collins, Sr.—St. Louis, Mo.—Sept. 11

Baseball Strike—baseball strike—Detroit Tigers—Shibe Park, Philadelphia, Pa.—May 18

Boy Scouts of America—Boy Scout to become an eagle scout—A. R. Eldred—Oceanside, N.Y.

Camp Fire Girls organization—formed—Lake Sebago, Me.—March 17

Chamber of Commerce—Chamber of Commerce of the United States of America—founded—Washington, D.C.

Children's Bureau (U.S.)—established—April 9

Church—church without theology, creed, or dogma—organized—Denver, Colo.

City Manager Plan—adopted—Sumter, S.C.—June

Civic Design Chair—established—Urbana, Ill.

Commerce Department (U.S.)—Foreign and Domestic Commerce Bureau—created—Aug. 23

Crepe—introduced—New York City

Dental Corps (U.S. Navy)—Dental Corps of the U.S. Navy—authorized—Aug. 12

Engine—diesel engine in a submarine—commissioned—Groton, Conn.—Feb. 14

Girl Scouts—organized—Savannah, Ga.—March 12

Horse Race—mutuel ticket to pay more than $1,000—Latonia track, Covington, Ky.—June 17

Insurance—group insurance contract of importance—Equitable Life Assurance Society—July 1

Labor Law—minimum-wage law—enacted—Massachusetts—June 4

Marine Corps—marine pilot—A. A. Cunningham—assigned—July 9

Medical Society—American College of Surgeons—incorporated—Nov. 25

Motion Picture—foreign feature film exhibited—New York City—July 12

Motion Picture—motion picture from an airplane—F. T. Coffin—New York City

Motion Picture Actor—stunt actor—F. R. Law

Motion Picture Censorship—motion picture censorship regulation (federal)—enacted—July 3

Music—community chorus—established—Rochester, N.Y.

Nobel Prize—Nobel Prize in medicine and physiology—Alexis Carrel

Nursing School—university school of nursing-graduation—June 13

Oceanography Institution—established—La Jolla, Calif.

Oil and Gas Production Course—Pittsburgh, Pa.

Police—woman detective—Isabella Goodwin—appointed—New York City

Postage Stamp—one-color one-size series of postage stamps—parcel post issue—first stamps in series issued Nov. 27

Postage Stamp—parcel post postage-due stamp—authorized, Aug. 24—issued, Nov. 27, Dec. 12, and 16

Postage Stamp—postage stamp to picture an airplane—issued—Dec. 16

Postal Service—parcel post service—authorized —Aug. 24

Progressive Party—national convention—Chicago, Ill.—Aug. 6

Quarantine—plant quarantine legislation (national)—enacted—Aug. 20

Radio License—experimental radio license—issued—Aug. 13

Representative (U.S.)—representative to serve 56 years—C. T. Hayden of Arizona—began service Feb. 19

Rotary Club—international association—formed —Duluth, Minn.—Aug.

Safety Congress—safety congress (national)— Milwaukee, Wis.—Sept. 30

Senator (U.S.)—senators collectively "elected by the people"—amendment enacted—June 12

Ship—battleship to use fuel oil exclusively— Nevada—laid down—Quincy, Mass.—Nov. 4

Ship—cruise ship to circumnavigate the world— left New York City—Feb. 6

Ship—electrically propelled ship of the U.S. Navy—Jupiter—launched—Aug. 24

Social Science Society (national)—National Institute of Social Sciences—organized

Streetcar—municipally owned streetcars—San Francisco, Calif.—Dec. 28

Torpedo—airplane torpedo—patented—B. A. Fiske—July 16

Vice Presidential Candidate—vice presidential nominee to die before the meeting of the electoral college—J. S. Sherman—Oct. 30

1913

Actors' Union—Actors' Equity Association—organized—May 26

Agriculture Department (U.S.)—Office of Markets —created—May 16

Arbitration—Federal Board of Mediation and Conciliation—authorized—March 4

Automobile—sedan-type automobile—publicly exhibited—New York City—Jan. 11

Automobile Service Station—drive-in service station—opened—Pittsburgh, Pa.—Dec. 1

Automobile Tire—demountable tire-carrying rim —patented—L. H. Perlman—New York City— Feb. 4

Aviation—gyroscope automatic stabilization— Hammondsport, N.Y.—Aug.

Aviation—Airplane—airplane in actual military operation—Augusta, Ga.

Aviation—Airplane Fatalities—airplane fatality (U.S. Navy)—W. D. Billingsley—off Kent Island, Md.—June 20

Aviation—Flights—airplane loop-the-loop—Lincoln Beachey—San Diego, Calif.—Nov. 18

Aviation—Parachute—parachute jump from an airplane by a woman—Georgia Broadwick— Los Angeles, Calif.—June 21

Aviation—School—aeronautical engineering course—Cambridge, Mass.

Bank—federal reserve system—act approved— Dec. 23

Birds—bird for which a definite crossing of the Atlantic has been recorded—banded—Eastern Egg Rock, Me.—July 3

Bowler—bowler to make a perfect score of 300 in an American Bowling Congress tournament— William Knox—Toledo, Ohio—March 10

Brick—brick insulating—manufactured—Lancaster, Pa.—June

Building—building higher than 750 feet in height —Woolworth Building—New York City— opened April 24

Civic Design Chair—professor appointed—C. M. Robinson—Urbana, Ill.—Sept. 1

College—college comprehensive senior examination program—adopted—Walla Walla, Wash. —May 26

Commerce Department (U.S.)—Commerce Department (U.S.)—established—March 4

Congress (U.S.)—Senate—whip—J. H. Lewis (Democrat)—appointed May 28

Court—conciliation tribunal for small claims—established—Cleveland, Ohio—March 15

Court—small debtors' court established by state law—authorized—Kansas—March 15

Crossword Puzzle—published—New York City— Dec. 21

Dental School—dental hygienists' course— Bridgeport, Conn.—A. C. Fones—started—Nov. 17

Dentist—dentist in the U.S. Navy to serve aboard a naval ship—H. E. Harvey—Solace—March 5

Dentist—dentist in the U.S. Navy to serve at an overseas base—J. L. Brown—Guam—April 27

Eye—eye conservation class—Boston, Mass.— April 3

Farm Bureau—state appropriation—New York— May 24

Fastening—hookless fastening for universal use— patented—Gideon Sundback—April 29

Foxhound Master (American)—in England—R. E. Strawbridge—May 1

Fuse—Cordeau-Bickford detonating fuse—introduced—Simsbury, Conn.

Gasoline—cracking process used to obtain gasoline from crude petroleum—W. M. Burton— Chicago, Ill.—Jan. 7

Goat Show (of milch goats)—Rochester, N.Y.— Sept. 15-27

Gyroscope—gyro stabilizer installed on an American naval vessel—Worden—April

Ice Loading Machinery—patent—April 22

Insurance—bonding law (state)—North Dakota— enacted—March 1

Labor Department (U.S.)—Labor Department (U.S.)—created

Labor Legislation—minimum-wage law—Massachusetts—effective—July 1

Mayor—woman mayor elected by a city west of the Rocky Mountains—Clara Munson—Warrenton, Oreg.—began term Jan. 6

Medical Legislation—chiropractic legislation (state)—Kansas—enacted March 18

Medical Society—American College of Surgeons —organized—Washington, D.C.—May 5

Medical Society—black member of the American College of Surgeons—D. H. Williams—admitted at Chicago, Ill.—Nov. 13

Medical Society—immunology society—American Association of Immunologists—organized—Minneapolis, Minn.—June 19

Monument—monument to a bird—Salt Lake City, Utah—Oct. 1

Motion Picture—animated cartoon (present technique)—*The Artist's Dream*—released

Motion Picture—serial motion picture—issued—Chicago, Ill.—Dec. 29

Motion Picture Projector—motion picture projector (portable)—produced—H. A. De Vry—Chicago, Ill.

Newspaper—newspaper 12-page advertising supplement—New York *Times*—New York City—Dec. 7

Occupational Therapy Course—Milwaukee, Wis.

Oil—oil and gas conservation legislation—Oklahoma—enacted May 17

Pension—pension plan—A.T.&T.—in effect Jan 1

Permalloy—developed—G. W. Elmen—New York City—June 7

Photograph—photographs taken under the sea—Chesapeake Bay, Va.

Postage Stamp—parcel post stamps—placed on sale—Jan. 1

Postage Stamp—postage stamp to picture an airplane—on sale—Jan. 1

Postal Service—parcel post service—started—Jan. 1

Public Defender's Office—created—Los Angeles, Calif.

Road—coast-to-coast paved road—Lincoln Highway—Lincoln Highway Association—formed

Rubber—synthetic rubber—manufactured—L. P. Kyrides and R. B. Earle—East Watertown, Mass.

Senator (U.S.)—senator elected by popular vote after the passage of the Seventeenth Amendment—A. O. Bacon—elected—Georgia—July 15—sworn in, July 28

Senator (U.S.)—senators collectively "elected by the people"—Seventeenth Amendment in effect—May 31

Strike—strike settlement—mediation settlement—June 2

Tax—income tax amendment to the Constitution—effective—March 1

Tungsten—ductile tungsten—patented—W. D. Coolidge—Dec. 30

War Veterans' Society—Veterans of Foreign Wars of the United States—formed—Denver, Colo.—Aug. 18-20

1914

Automobile Bus—bus with cross seats—New York City—double-deck buses—March 17

Automobile Tire—nonskid tire—patented April 14

Aviation—air service of the United States Army—created—July 18

Aviation—hydroplane commercial line service—St. Petersburg–Tampa, Fla.—Jan. 1

Aviation—Airplane—airplane with ailerons—patented—W. W. Christmas—May 5

Aviation—Airplane—hydroplane with a multiengine—christened—June 22

Aviation—School—airplane flying school operated by a woman—San Antonio, Tex.

Aviation—School—naval air training school—opened—Pensacola, Fla.—Dec. 1

Bank—bank established in a foreign country—Nov. 10

Bank—federal reserve system—formally opened—Nov. 16

Bird Banding—bird banding by federal authorities

Bridge (game)—auction bridge championship (duplicate)—Lake Placid, N.Y.—July 9

Community Trust—organized—Cleveland, Ohio—Jan. 2

Dental School—dental hygienists' course—graduation—June 5

Electric Transmission—substation with a rotary converter completely unattended—Detroit, Mich.

Federal Trade Commission—Federal Trade Commission—created—Sept. 26

Flag—American flag flown in World War I over a band of fighting Americans—Sept. 30

Forestry School—forestry correspondence course in tree surgery—Kent, Ohio

Holiday—Mother's Day—national recognition—May 12

Horseshoe Pitchers' Association (national)—organized—Kansas City, Kan.—May 16

Ice Skating Tournament—figure skating international championship tournament—New Haven Conn.—March 20

Insurance—War Risk Insurance Bureau—established—Sept. 2

Map—automobile road map—published—Pittsburgh, Pa.

Medical Society—women members of the American College of Surgeons—A. G. Bryant and F W. Duckering—June 22

Motion Picture—animated cartoon (present technique)—patent—J. R. Bray—August 11

Motion Picture—six-reel "feature"-length comedy—*Tillie's Punctured Romance*—released—Dec. 21

Motorcycle Race—motorcycle race (300 miles)—Dodge City, Kan.—July 4

Museum—industrial museum—New York City—incorporated—Feb. 26

Music Society—music society for the literary protection of composers and authors—American Society of Composers, Authors and Publishers—formed—New York City—Feb. 13

Newspaper—newspaper rotogravure sections

Newspaper Audit—newspaper circulation audit—Audit Bureau of Circulations—Chicago, Ill.—formed—Aug. 21

Nobel Prize—Nobel Prize in chemistry—T. W Richards

Organists' Society—organists' society (national)—convention—New York City—Dec. 29

Passport—passport photographs—required—Nov. 20

Police—woman chief of police—Dolly Spencer—Milford, Ohio

Postal Service—collection and delivery of mail in automobiles—government-owned—Oct. 19

Prison—organization of a prison—"community" groups—Auburn, N.Y.

Prohibition—prohibition vote—dry majority—Dec. 22

Public Defender's Office—W. J. Wood assumed duties—Los Angeles, Calif.

Railroad—railroad operated by the federal government—Alaska Railroad—acquisition authorized, March 12

Railroad Car—air-conditioned cars—built

Rocket—liquid-fuel rocket patent—R. H. Goddard—July 14

Ship—battleship to use fuel oil exclusively—*Nevada*—launched—Quincy, Mass.—July 11

Ship—steamboat to pass through the Panama Canal—*Alex La Valley*—Jan. 7

Skee-Ball Alley—built—Coney Island, N.Y.—April

Social Science Society (national)—annual meeting—New York City—March 20

Telephone—underground-cable long-distance telephone conversation—Boston, Mass.–Washington, D.C.—Feb. 26

Traffic Light—electric traffic signal lights—installed—Cleveland, Ohio—Aug. 5

Vocational Guidance Chair—Indiana University—Bloomington, Ind.

World War I—American combatant casualty in World War I—Corporal Bouligny—Nov. 15

World War I—American to sail to Europe to enlist in World War I—D. P. Dowd, Jr.—enlisted—Aug. 6

1915

Automobile—field hospital automobile with X-ray equipment—used—May

Automobile Bus—bus with a double-deck body and chassis made in the U.S.—New York City

Automobile Bus—bus with cross seats—single-deck buses—New York City—Aug. 27

Automobile Electric Self-Starter—automobile electric self-starter, applied commercially—patented—Aug. 17

Automobile Finance Company—organized—New York City—Feb.

Automobile Racetrack—automobile racetrack (asphalt-covered)—opened—Cranston, R.I.—Sept. 18

Aviation—Advisory Committee for Aeronautics (national)—approved—March 3

Aviation–Airship—airship of the U.S. Navy—contract—June 1

Chamber of Commerce—Junior Chamber of Commerce—organized—St. Louis, Mo.—Oct. 13

Chiropody School—chiropody school as a regular division of a university—opened—Philadelphia, Pa.—Sept. 20

Coast Guard (U.S.)—Coast Guard—created—Jan. 28

College—university for blacks (Catholic)—Xavier University—opened as a high school—Sept. 27

Dental Legislation—legislation (state) regarding dental hygienists—Connecticut—enacted—May 19

Dental Periodical—orthodontia magazine—published—St. Louis, Mo.—Jan.

Election Law—proportional representation election—Ashtabula, Ohio—Nov. 2

Federal Trade Commission—Federal Trade Commission—organized—March 16

Fingerprint Society—fingerprint society (international)—formed—Oakland, Calif.—Oct. 9

Girl Scouts—incorporated—June 10

Governor—Jewish governor—full term—Moses Alexander—served—Jan. 4

Horse Race—filly to win the Kentucky Derby—Louisville, Ky.—May 8

Horseshoe Pitchers' Association (national)—championship tournament—Kellerton, Iowa—Oct. 23

Medal—admiral to receive the Congressional Medal of Honor—F. F. Fletcher—award Dec. 4

Money—50-dollar gold pieces minted by the United States—San Francisco, Calif.—June 15

Motion Picture—motion picture to gross $50 million—*The Birth of a Nation*—shown in Los Angeles, Calif.—Feb. 8

Music Instruction—State Supervisor of Music—P. E. Beck—appointed—Pennsylvania—July 1

Navy—naval militia (state) to have a hydroplane—Illinois—*Alice*—christened in Chicago—May 22

Nobel Prize—Nobel Prize in chemistry—presented—T. W. Richards—Nov. 12

Ordnance—submachine gun—Auto-Ordnance Company—organized—J. T. Thompson

Protestant Church—Protestant church for lepers—dedicated—Carville, La.—June 14

Public Health—pellagra experiment—Jackson, Miss.—Joseph Goldberger—Feb. 4

Radio Telephone—radio telephone communication (one-way)—Montauk Point, N.Y.–Wilmington, Del.—April 4

Radio Telephone—transatlantic radio telephone message—Arlington, Va.–Paris, France—Oct. 21

Radio Telephone—transcontinental radio telephone demonstration—New York City–San Francisco—Sept. 29

Ship—battleship (major) built on the Pacific coast—*California*—authorized, March 3

Ship—ship (American) attacked by a German submarine—*Nantucket Chief*—torpedoed—May 1

Ship—warship propelled by electricity—*New Mexico*—keel laid—Oct. 14

Sound-absorbing Material—C. G. Muench—St. Paul, Minn.—patent—Sept. 14

Submarine—submarine built at a government shipyard—*L-8*—keel laid—Portsmouth Naval Shipyard, Portsmouth, N.H.—Feb. 24

Submarine—submarine disaster—Hawaii—March 25

Telephone—transcontinental telephone demonstration—New York City–San Francisco—Jan. 25

World War I—American combatant to die in World War I—E. M. Stone—Feb. 27

World War I—American ship lost in World War I—*William P. Frye*—sunk—Jan. 28

Zoological Garden—barless zoological garden of naturalistic rock construction—started—Denver, Colo.—City Park Zoo

1916

Army—Army Veterinary Corps—established

Army—Reserve Officers Training Corps—authorized—June 3

Army—Reserve Officers Training Corps Units—authorized—Oct. 21

Aviation—Coast Guard aviation unit—authorized—Aug. 29

Aviation—Airplane—airplane in actual military operation—Mexico—March

Aviation—Flights—airplane to fly a distance greater than 500 miles—Chicago, Ill.-Hornell, N.Y.—Ruth Law—Nov. 19

Aviation—Pilot—American pilot killed while a pilot in the Lafayette Escadrille—V. E. Chapman—June 23

Aviation—Pilot—American pilot shot down in World War I—H. C. Balsley—June 18

Bird Legislation (international)—Migratory Bird Treaty—signed—Aug. 16

Chess Champion—chess champion to play more than 100 games simultaneously—F. J. Marshall—Washington, D.C.—March 21

Child Labor Law—child labor law (federal)—enacted—Sept. 1

Corn—shipment of hybrid seed corn—Bloomington, Ill.—April 13

Dental Book—book for dental hygienists (text)—*Mouth Hygiene*—published

Farm Loan Board (federal)—authorized—July 17

Flag—President's flag—adopted—May 29

Golf Champion—golfer to win both the United States Open and the United States Amateur in the same year—Charles Evans, Jr.—June 30 (national open) and Sept. 9 (amateur)

Golf Tournament—Professional Golfers Association tournament—Siwanoy Golf Club—Mount Vernon, N.Y.—Oct. 14

Holiday—American Indian Day—observance—May 13

Hygiene Instruction—hygiene and public health school—established—Baltimore, Md.

Medal—arts and letters society (national) gold medal special award—C. W. Eliot—presented in New York City—Jan. 27

Medical Clinic—birth control clinic—opened—New York City—Oct. 16

Motion Picture—animated cartoon in color—produced—New York City

Motion Picture—animated cartoon (technical)—produced—New York City

Motion Picture—motion picture featuring a black actor—*Natural Born Gambler*—Bert Williams

Motion Picture—motion picture sex shocker—*A Daughter of the Gods*—Annette Kellerman—shown in New York City—Oct. 17

Motorcycle Trip—motorcycle transcontinental trip by women—completed—New York City–San Diego, Calif.—Sept. 12

Orchestra—municipal orchestra supported by taxes—Baltimore, Md.—first concert—Feb. 11

Park—park (national) containing an active volcano—Lassen Volcanic National Park—established—Aug. 9

Park—park (national) east of the Mississippi—Acadia National Park—established—July 8

Park Service (national)—created—Aug. 25

Radio Beacons—tested—Navesink Light Station—Atlantic Highlands, N.J.

Radio Telephone—radio telephone ship-to-shore conversation—May 6

Road—federal grant-in-aid to states for roads—enacted—July 11

Science Association—National Research Council—meeting—New York City—Sept. 20

Ship—battleship (major) built on the Pacific coast—*California*—keel laid, Oct. 25

Ship—battleship to use fuel oil exclusively—*Nevada*—commissioned—March 11

Shipping—United States Shipping Board—established—Sept. 7

Streetcar—lightweight one-man streetcar—built—St. Louis, Mo.

Submarine—cargo submarine to cross the Atlantic Ocean—*Deutschland*—landed—Baltimore, Md.—July 9

Supreme Court (U.S.)—associate justice of the Supreme Court who was Jewish—L. D. Brandeis—appointed—Jan. 28

Tournament of Roses—football game annual event

1917

Agricultural Soil Conference—Washington, D.C.—June 13-22

Air Force—air service (military) under one command—W. L. Kenly—effected Sept. 3

Army—gas regiment—authorized—Aug. 15

Army Balloon School—established—St. Louis, Mo.—April 6

Army Camp—army camp for training black officers—Des Moines, Iowa—June 15

Army Officer—American general to fly over enemy lines—W. L. Mitchell—April 24

Army Officer—regimental Jewish chaplain—commissioned—Nov. 15

Aviation—Airship—airship of the U.S. Navy—tested—Pensacola, Fla.—April

Aviation—Airship—airship of the U.S. Navy that was successful—tested—May 30

World War I—shot fired by the American Navy in World War I—April 7

World War I—shot fired by the American Navy in World War I against a known German submarine—*Mongolia*—April 19

World War I—United States declaration of war against Germany (World War I)—April 6

1918

Air Force—air force aviation unit—sailed, Cape May, N.J.—Jan. 9—landed, Ponta Delgada, Azores—Jan. 21

Airmail Service—airmail experimental route—Washington, D.C.-New York City—May 15

Airmail Service—airmail regular service—Aug. 12

Airmail Service—airmail regular service between New York and Chicago—began—Belmont Park, L.I.—Dec. 18

American Expeditionary Force—American Expeditionary Force Air Service chief—M. M. Patrick—appointed—May 29

American Indian Church—church organized by American Indians—El Reno, Okla.—incorporated—Oct. 10

Army—gas regiment—independent action against Germans—June 18

Army Insignia—service number—issued to an enlisted man—A. B. Crean—Feb. 28

Army Insignia—shoulder sleeve insignia—authorized—Oct. 19

Army Insignia—wound chevron—authorized

Army School—graduate of the U.S. Military Academy (West Point) killed in action in World War I—S. W. Hoover—March 1

Automobile—armored commercial car—used—Chicago, Ill.

Aviation—air squadron (complete)—crossed German lines—Aug. 7

Aviation—air squadron of the U.S. Army—assigned to front—April 8

Aviation—war night-flying scout group—went to front—Oct. 5

Aviation—Airplane—fighter airplane—tested—Garden City, N.Y.—Aug. 19

Aviation—Airplane—molded-plywood airplane—built—Garden City, N.Y.

Aviation—Airplane Bombing—airplane bombing raid by an American air unit—June 12

Aviation—Flights—airplane altitude flight to exceed 28,000 feet—R. W. Schroeder—Fairfield, Ohio—Sept. 18

Aviation—Pilot—American ace—Douglas Campbell—May 31

Aviation—Pilot—American ace of aces—first victory—April 29

Aviation—Pilot—Army pilot to win a victory—Feb. 5

Births—World War baby—born—June 7

Chaplains' School—Army school for chaplains—organized—Fort Monroe, Va.—Feb. 9

Chinaware—dishes (complete set) made in America for the Executive Mansion—delivered—July 31

Cooperatives Convention—Springfield, Ill.—Sept. 25-27

Daylight Saving—inaugurated—March 31

Employment Service—employment service (U.S.) inaugurated—Jan. 3

Judge—woman judge of a juvenile court—Kathryn Sellers—Washington, D.C.—appointed—Oct. 15

Lewisite—developed—Washington, D.C.—W. L. Lewis—Feb.

Locomotive Booster—used—New York Central R.R.—July

Marine Corps—woman marine reserve—O. M. Johnson, enrolled—Aug. 12

Medal—Croix de Guerre awarded to a black—Henry Johnson—May 24

Medal—Distinguished Service Cross (Army)—authorized—July 9

Medal—Distinguished Service Medal (Army)—authorized—July 9

Money—battleship depicted on a bill—$2 note issued by Federal Reserve Bank of Boston, Mass.

Newspaper—Pulitzer Prize award to a newspaper—New York *Times*—presented—New York City—June 5

Novel—novel to win the Pulitzer Prize in letters—*His Family*—award announced—June 3

Nursing School—Army School of Nursing—authorized—May 25

Ordnance—Army armored tank—used—Sept. 1

Passport—passport issued to a President of the United States in office—Woodrow Wilson—Nov. 27

Photograph—photograph showing air in motion—Washington, D.C.

Postage Stamp—airmail stamps—issued—May 13

Postage Stamp—offset-printed postage stamps—1-cent stamp issued—Dec. 24

President (U.S.)—President to visit a European country while President—Woodrow Wilson—sailed—Dec. 4

Prohibition—prohibition amendment to the Constitution—first state to ratify amendment—Mississippi—Jan. 8

Prohibition—prohibition law (national)—enacted—Nov. 21

Protestant Episcopal Bishop—black suffragan—T. Demby—appointed—Sept. 29

Railroad—government operation of railroads—Jan. 1

Rhodes Scholar—American Rhodes scholar to be killed in action—W. A. Fleet—May 18

Ship—concrete barge—*Socony 200*—launched—New York City—July 27

Ship—concrete seagoing ship—*Faith*—launched—Redwood City, Calif.—March 14

Ship—concrete ship built for the United States Shipping Board—*Atlantus*—launched—Dec.

Ship—Eagle boat—keel laid, May 7—launched—Detroit, Mich.—July 11—commissioned, Oct. 2

Ship—ship sunk by a submerged German submarine—*Frederick R. Kellogg*—12 miles north of Barnegat Light, N.J.—Aug. 13

Ship—warship propelled by electricity—*New Mexico*—commissioned—May 20

Submarine—submarine to cross the Atlantic Ocean under its own power—*E-1*—returned to New London, Conn.—Sept. 17

Woman—woman District Attorney of the United States—A. A. Adams—served—July 25

World War I—air combat of an American organization in World War I—Toul, France—April 14

World War I—American Army division to cross the Rhine River—Coblentz—Dec. 13

World War I—American Army troopship in World War I torpedoed by the Germans—*Tuscania*—Feb. 15

World War I—combat mission of all-American pilots ordered to battle by an all-American squadron commander—order given April 13—patrol flown April 14

World War I—German spy to receive a death sentence from the American forces during World War I—condemned—Aug. 16

World War I—shots to land on American soil—Orleans, Mass.—July 21

Zoological Garden—barless zoological garden of naturalistic rock construction—completed—Denver, Colo.

1919

Actors' Union—strike called—Aug. 7

Airmail Service—airmail service to a steamer at sea—Aug. 14

Airmail Service—airmail transcontinental service—first section opened—New York City to Cleveland—July 1

Airmail Service—international airmail—Seattle, Wash.-Victoria, B.C., Canada—March 3

Army Officer—General of the Armies of the U.S.—J. J. Pershing—confirmed—Sept. 4

Automobile—armored commercial car completely protected—construction started—Minneapolis, Minn.—March

Aviation—aeronautical stowaway—arrived July 6

Aviation—Airplane—three-motor airplane—flown—Garden City, N.Y.—July 24

Aviation—Airport—airport municipally owned—Tucson, Ariz.—Nov. 20

Aviation—Airship—airship (lighter-than-air)—arrived—New York City—July 6

Aviation—Airship—airship to land on a roof—Cleveland, Ohio.—May 23

Aviation—Flights—New York–Chicago nonstop flight—April 19

Aviation—Flights (transatlantic)—transatlantic hydroplane flight—left New York City—May 8

Aviation—Flights (transatlantic)—transatlantic nonstop flight from America—Alcock and Brown—left—June 14

Aviation—Parachute—parachute—"free parachute" jump—Dayton, Ohio—April 28

Aviation—Pilot—pilot to receive the Congressional Medal of Honor—posthumously presented—May 29

Aviation—Races—transcontinental air race—left San Francisco, Calif.—Oct. 8

Bank—bank with resources exceeding $1 billion—National City Bank, New York City—Nov. 17

Bank—state bank wholly owned and operated—established—Bismarck, N. Dak.—June 26—opened July 28

Biography Course—biography department—in a college—Northfield, Minn.

Book—book series of small-size paperbacks—Little Blue Books—published—Girard, Kans.

Caterpillar Club—Caterpillar Club member—John Boettner—July 21

College—fisheries college—College of Fisheries, Seattle, Wash.—established in March

College—university for blacks (Catholic)—Xavier University—normal-school diplomas awarded—June 20

Communist Labor Party of America—organized—Chicago, Ill.—Aug. 31

Communist Party of America—organized—Chicago, Ill.—Sept. 2

Congress (U.S.)—Senate—Senate cloture resolution—invoked—Nov. 15

Deaf—Association—national social organization for the hard of hearing—formed—New York City—Feb. 27

Federal Trade Commission—Federal Trade Commission trade practice conference—Omaha, Neb.—Oct. 3

Forest Service—forest service aerial patrol—established—June 1

Freemasons—Order of De Molay—founded—F. S. Land—Kansas City, Mo.

Gasoline Tax—gasoline tax (state)—Oregon—Feb. 25

Golfer—golfer to play 180 holes in 1 day—Edward Styles—Philadelphia, Pa.—July 11

Holiday—Armistice Day—celebrated—Nov. 11

Horse—horse to win the triple crown—Sir Barton

Horse Race—300-mile endurance run—Burlington, Vt., to Camp Devens, Mass.—Oct. 15

Insurance—aircraft liability and property damage insurance—Hartford, Conn.

Insurance—fire and tornado insurance fund (state)—North Dakota—in operation—July 1

Insurance—insurance service offered by a newspaper—*Star*—St. Louis, Mo.—April 14

Medal—Distinguished Service Medal awarded to a woman—Evangeline Booth

Medal—Distinguished Service Medal (Navy)—authorized—Feb. 4

Medal—Medal of Honor awarded in World War I—E. A. Janson—presented, May 21

Monument—monument to an insect—dedicated—Enterprise, Ala.—Dec. 11

Newspaper—illustrated tabloid—*Illustrated Daily News*—New York City—June 26

Novel—two-time winner of the Pulitzer Prize for a novel—Booth Tarkington—1918 award (first)—June 2

Periodical—photo-engraved magazine—*Literary Digest*—New York City—Oct. 25

Police—police airplane-arrest—simulated at Atlantic City, N.J.—May 6

Prison—prisoners (federal) employed in industry—Atlanta, Ga.—July 11

Prohibition—prohibition bureau (federal)—amendment enacted—Jan. 29

Prohibition—prohibition law (national)—Volstead Prohibition Act—enacted—Oct. 28

Radio Broadcast—submarine (submerged) broadcast—Oct. 5

Radio Telephone—two-way conversation between a submerged submarine and another vessel—Oct. 5

Ship—ambulance ship, designed and built as a hospital—*Relief*—launched—Dec. 23

Ship—battleship (major) built on the Pacific coast—*California*—launched, Nov. 20

Ship—concrete ship built for the United States Shipping Board—*Atlantus*—delivered—Nov. 11

Ship—destroyer of the U.S. Navy named for a Confederate officer—*Buchanan*—launched—Bath, Me.—Jan. 2—commissioned, Jan. 20

Ship—naval ship named for a dental officer—*Osborne*—launched—Squantum, Mass.—Dec. 29

Ship—naval ship named for an enlisted man—*Osmond Ingram*—launched—Quincy, Mass.—Feb. 23—commissioned—Boston, Mass.—June 28

Taconite—taconite production—Mesabi Iron Co., Babbitt, Minn.—undertaken in November

War Veterans' Society—American Legion—organized—Paris, France—Feb. 15-16

Wedding—airplane wedding—Houston, Texas—May 31

Woman—American-born woman to become a member of Parliament—in Great Britain—Lady Astor—Dec. 1

Woman—woman editor-in-chief of a law review—M. H. Donlon—*Cornell Law Quarterly*—Ithaca, N.Y.—Nov.

Woman—woman sculptor honored by membership in the National Academy of Design—M. E. B. Longman

Woman Suffrage—woman suffrage amendment approved by Congress—June 4

1920

Advertising School—established—Philadelphia

Airmail Service—airmail transcontinental service—combination airplane-railroad—Sept. 8

Airmail Service—international airmail—regular service under contract—commenced—Oct. 14

Arbitration—state arbitration law (modern)—passed—New York—April 19

Army Camp—Army Citizens' Military Training Camp—authorized—June 4

Army Officer—Chaplain (chief) of the U.S. Army—appointed—July 15

Army Officer—Chemical Warfare Chief—served—July 16

Army Officer—woman with rank corresponding to major—rank conferred—June 4

Army School—instructor nongraduate—C. H Hodges—West Point, N.Y.—assumed post Dec 14

Astronomer—astronomer to measure the size of a fixed star—Dec. 13

Astronomy—planet (asteroid) named for an American President—discovered—March

Automobile—armored commercial car completely protected—in service—St. Paul, Minn.—Feb 1

Aviation—Coast Guard air station—established—Morehead City, N.C.—March 24

Aviation—hydroplane commercial line service (international)—Key West, Fla.—Nov. 1

Aviation—Airplane—airplane used by a newspaper—Baltimore, Md.—Sept. 1

Aviation—Expositions and Meets—intercollegiate air meet—Mitchel Field, N.Y.—May 7

Aviation—Flights—New York–Alaska flight—left Mitchel Field, N.Y.—July 15

Aviation—Pilot—Naval ace in World War I—received Distinguished Service Medal

Baseball "Dictator"—K. M. Landis—elected—Nov. 12

Baseball Game—baseball game (major league) in which 14 runs were scored in 1 inning—Washington, D.C.—July 6

Baseball Game—baseball game (major league) to last longer than 25 innings—Boston Braves vs. Brooklyn Robins—Boston, Mass.—May 1

Baseball Game—triple play unassisted in a World Series—Cleveland, Ohio—Oct. 10

Baseball Game—World Series grand slam home run (American League)—E. J. Smith—Cleveland, Ohio—Oct. 10

Baseball Player—baseball player killed in a game—R. J. Chapman—New York City—Aug. 16

Cabinet (U.S.)—woman sub-Cabinet member—A. A. Adams—appointed—June 26

Census—census in which the population of the United States exceeded 100 million

Civil Service—woman Civil Service commissioner—H. H. Gardener—sworn in—Washington, D.C.

Curling Rink—indoor curling rink—opened—Brookline, Mass.—Dec. 19

Deaf—Association—national social organization for the hard of hearing—annual meeting—March 12

Dog Racetrack—imitation rabbit used—Emeryville, Calif.—opened—Feb. 22

Farmer Labor Party—organized—Chicago, Ill.—June 12

Football Club—football association (professional)—formed—Canton, Ohio—Sept. 17

Labor Department (U.S.)—Women's Bureau—permanently organized—June 5

Milk—acidophilus milk—devised—L. F. Rettger and Harry Cheplin—New Haven, Conn.

Newspaper—newspaper to operate a radio station—*News* (Detroit, Mich.)—WWJ began operating, Aug. 20

Monument—monument to the Unknown Soldier (national)—Unknown Soldier buried—Arlington, Va.—Nov. 11

Novel—Pulitzer Prize award to a woman for a novel—E. N. J. Wharton—announced—New York City—May 29

Nursing School—Army School of Nursing—graduation

Opera—opera broadcast in its entirety—*Martha*—Denver, Colo.—May 19

Opera—opera broadcast in its entirety by a professional cast—*Samson et Dalila*—Chicago, Ill.—Nov. 14

Postal Service—philatelic agency—in operation—Dec. 1

President (U.S.)—President to become Chief Justice of the United States—W. H. Taft—appointed—June 30

Prizefight—prizefight to gross $1 million—Jersey City, N.J.—July 2

Radio Beacons—placed in regular operation—May 1

Radio Broadcast—baseball game broadcast with a play-by-play description—Pittsburgh, Pa.—Aug. 5

Radio Broadcast—baseball world series broadcast—Oct. 5-13

Radio Broadcast—police broadcast—St. Louis, Mo.—Sept. 4

Radio Broadcast—prizefight (heavyweight championship) broadcast—Jersey City, N.J.—July 2

Radio Broadcast—religious service broadcast—Pittsburgh, Pa.—Jan. 2

Radio Broadcast—tennis match broadcast—Sewickley, Pa.—Aug. 4

Radio Broadcast—weather broadcasts—St. Louis, Mo.—April 26

Radio Church—New York City—Nov. 27

Radio Receiving Contest—radio receiving contest—B. G. Seutter, winner—New York City—Oct. 8

Radio Station—educational radio station licensed—WOI—Iowa State College of Agriculture and Mechanical Arts, Ames, Iowa—call letters granted, Nov. 21

Representative (U.S.)—representative (woman) to preside over the House of Representatives—A. M. Robertson—June 20

Sarrusophone—manufactured—Elkhart, Ind.

Ship—battleship (major) built on the Pacific coast—*California*—commissioned, Aug. 10

Tax—sales tax (state)—enacted—West Virginia—May 3

Telephone—telephone cable service (deep-sea)—opened—Key West, Fla.—April 11

Theater—theater provided with scientific air distribution—Los Angeles, Calif.

Veterans' Bureau—established—Aug. 9

1922

Aquatic Mammals—platypus (duckbill)—exhibited—New York City—July 15

Arbitration Association—arbitration associatio.—Arbitration Society of America—formed—New York City—May 15

Aviation—sermon from an airplane—B. W. May nard—April 16

Aviation—Airplane—airplane to land at the U.$ Capitol—L. B. Sperry—Washington, D.C.—March 23

Aviation—Flights—airplane to fly faster than th speed of 200 m.p.h.—L. J. Maitland—Oct. 14

Aviation—Flights (transcontinental)—transcont nental dirigible flight (nonrigid dirigible)—le Newport News, Va.—Sept. 14

Aviation—Parachute—pilot to bail out of a di abled airplane—H. R. Harris—Dayton, Ohio—Oct. 20

Aviation—Passenger—woman airplane passe ger (transcontinental)—left San Francisc Calif.—Oct. 5

Baseball Game—baseball game (major league) which 49 runs were made in a 9-inning game—Chicago, Ill.—Aug. 25

Blind—correspondence school for the blind offer instruction in the Braille system—Winne ka, Ill.—incorporated—Jan. 2

Business—shopping center in a suburban bus ness area—Kansas City, Mo.—master pl April 22—construction began in November

Carillon—carillon (modern)—blessed—Glouce ter, Mass.—July 2

Cartoon—cartoon awarded a Pulitzer Prize—M 21

Catholic Nuns (cloistered community)—found —Baltimore, Md.—April 24

Cornstone—produced—Ames, Iowa

Diplomatic Service—woman legation secretary Lucille Atcherson—appointed—Dec. 4

Electric Transmission—electric power line co mercial carrier—Utica, N.Y.—operation—D 6

Eskimo Pie—patented—C. K. Nelson—Onaw Iowa—Jan. 24

Golf Champion—golf champion to win the Unit States Open and the Professional—Gene Sa zen—Aug. 18

Golf Tournament—international golf match Southampton, N.Y.—Aug. 28-29

Helicopter—Flights—helicopter flight—Colle Park, Md.—June 16

Holiday—Navy Day—celebrated—Oct. 27

Hotel Administration College Course—Corn University—Ithaca, N.Y.

Judge—woman associate justice of a state preme court—F. E. Allen—Cleveland, Ohic Dec. 16

League of Nations representative (unofficial Grace Abbott—Oct. 13

Microfilm Machine—microfilm reading devic patented—B. A. Fiske—March 28

Motion Picture—Technicolor motion pictur released—New York City—Dec. 3

Novel—two-time winner of the Pulitzer Prize a novel—Booth Tarkington—1921 award (s ond)—May 21

Orchestra—radio orchestra—Detroit, Mich.—May 28

eritonitis—peritonitis preventive (successful)—used—H. L. Johnson—Boston, Mass.

etroleum—petroleum refining course—University of Pittsburgh—Pittsburgh, Pa.—W. F. Faragher

olo—intercollegiate indoor polo championship—Princeton-Yale—New York City—March 18

resident (U.S.)—President to broadcast by radio—W. G. Harding—Baltimore, Md.—June 14

resident (U.S.)—President to use a radio—W. G. Harding—set installed in White House—Feb. 8

adar—radar observations—Anacostia, D.C.—Sept. 27

adio Broadcast—advertising or commercial radio broadcast—New York City—Aug. 28

adio Broadcast—chain broadcast—New York City—Oct. 7

adio Broadcast—debate over the radio—Washington, D.C.—May 23

adio Broadcast—drama (full-length melodrama) broadcast—Schenectady, N.Y.—Aug. 3

adio Broadcast—election campaign using radio—H. S. New—Indiana—Oct. 27-Nov. 2

adio Broadcast—football game (collegiate) coast-to-coast broadcast—New York City

adio Broadcast—news program (daily)—New York City—Sept. 1

adio Broadcast—radio concert from an airplane—New York City—April 14

adio Conference—National Radio Conference—Washington, D.C.—Feb. 27

adio Facsimile Transmission—photograph sent by radio across the Atlantic from Europe—June 11

adio Facsimile Transmission—photographs sent over a city telephone—Washington, D.C.—Oct. 3

adio Receiving Contest—radio receiving contest in which a speed of more than 50 words a minute was recorded—T. R. McElroy—Boston, Mass.—May 7

adio Station—educational radio station licensed—WOI—Iowa State College of Agriculture and Mechanical Arts, Ames, Iowa—license granted, April 28

adio Telephone—radio telephone concert transcontinental—Schenectady, N.Y., to Oakland, Calif.—March 25

epresentative (U.S.)—mother elected to Congress—W. S. M. Huck of Illinois—elected, Nov. 7—began service, Nov. 20

enator (U.S.)—woman to occupy a seat in the Senate—R. L. Felton—appointed—Oct. 3

ip—cruise ship to circumnavigate the world—Laconia—New York City—start—Nov. 21

ipping—automatic steering gear—installed—April 7

kywriting—skywriting—Cyril Turner—New York City—Nov. 28

oybean Processing Plant—A. E. Staley—Decatur, Ill.

Steel—continuous-sheet steel mill—built—Ashland, Ky.

Swimmer—swimmer to cover a distance of 100 meters free style in less than 1 minute—Johnny Weissmuller—Alameda, Calif.—July 9

Taconite—taconite production—Mesabi Iron Co., Babbitt, Minn.—first cargo produced June 21—shipped to Ford Motor Company, River Rouge, Mich.—Oct. 1

Vitamin—vitamin E—recognized—Berkeley, Calif.

Wedding—double radio wedding—New York City—Dec. 22

Woman—woman automotive engineer—Marie Luhring—graduated—New York City—June 5

Woman—woman clerk of a state supreme court—G. F. Kaercher—elected—Nov. 7

1923

Animals—chinchilla farm—established—Los Angeles, Calif.—Feb. 22

Automobile Tire—balloon tire production—on regular basis—Akron, Ohio—April 5

Automobile Trucking Service—automobile trucking service—Baltimore, Chesapeake and Atlantic Railway—Jan. 8

Aviation—airways illumination—Aug. 21

Aviation—refueling attempt in midair—Coronado, Calif.—L. H. Smith and J. F. Richter—June 27

Aviation—Airship—dirigible (American-built rigid)—Lakehurst, N.J.—launched—Aug. 20

Aviation—Flights (transcontinental)—transcontinental nonstop flight—left New York City—May 2

Baseball Game—World Series baseball games to gross $1 million—New York City—Oct. 10-15

Baseball Player—baseball players paid more than $6,000 for winning the World Series—New York Yankees

Book—book (of size) completed entirely by one man—Dard Hunter—Chillicothe, Ohio

Business—shopping center in a suburban business area—Kansas City, Mo.—first tenant March 1923

Business History Chair—established—Cambridge, Mass.

Camera—motion picture camera (portable)—manufactured—Davenport, Iowa

Catholic Seminary—Catholic seminary for the education of black priests—opened—Bay St. Louis, Miss.—Sept. 16

College—"Junior Year Abroad"—Newark, Del.—first group tour—July 7

Dance Marathon—dance marathon—New York City—April 1

Dance Marathon—dance marathon to last longer than 200 hours—Bernie Brand—St. Louis, Mo.—June 1-10

Dental School—dental school of the U.S. Navy—opened Feb. 3

Electric Generator—mercury boiler turbine—Hartford, Conn.—Sept. 7

Electric Sign—neon-tube advertising sign—installed—New York City—July

Gasoline—ethyl gasoline—marketed—Dayton, Ohio—Feb. 2

Golf Champion—family to win more than one national championship in 1 year—Dexter Cummings—Bronxville, N.Y. (Intercollegiate championship)—June 30—Edith Cummings—Rye, N.Y. (National Women's Amateur championship)—Oct. 6

Hospital—cancer hospital (municipal)—New York City Cancer Institute—New York City—Aug. 1

Ink—ink paste—manufactured—Minneapolis, Minn.—Feb. 10

Language—legislation to establish the American language as an official language—Illinois—enacted June 19

Motion Picture—motion picture of an eclipse of the sun taken from an airplane—attempted—Santa Catalina, Calif.—Sept. 10

Motion Picture—sound motion picture featuring a black—*Snappy Tunes*—Noble Sissle and Eubie Blake

Motion Picture—sound-on-film motion picture—Lee De Forest—New York City

Newspaper—jointly published newspaper—issued—New York City—September

Newspaper—mimeographed daily newspaper—*Kellogg Daily Reminder*—published—Kellogg, Idaho—July 25

Parachute-Jumping Contest—parachute-jumping contest—Theodore Schieuming—Mitchel Field, N.Y.—Oct. 12

Pension—old-age pension laws (state)—enacted—Montana and Nevada—March 5

Postage Stamp—precanceled stamps printed on rotary presses—issued—April 21

President (U.S.)—President and President's wife to die during the term for which he had been elected—W. G. Harding—died—Aug. 2

President (U.S.)—President to visit Alaska and Canada while President—W. G. Harding

Radio Broadcast—chain broadcast—with repeater points—New York City and Boston, Mass.—Jan. 4

Radio Broadcast—congressional open-session broadcast—WRC, Washington, D.C.—Dec. 3

Radio Broadcast—presidential message to be broadcast—Calvin Coolidge—Dec. 6

Radio Broadcast—transatlantic broadcast of a voice—Pittsburgh, Pa.—Dec. 31

Radio Broadcast—transatlantic radio program from England—received, Nov. 25

Radio Facsimile Transmission—photograph sent overland by radio to a distant point—Anacostia, D.C., to Philadelphia, Pa.—March 3

Railroad—railroad operated by the federal government—Alaska Railroad—golden spike driven—W. G. Harding—Nenana, Alaska—July 15

Railroad—railroad to install gasoline-mechanical cars—Pennsylvania Railroad—Feb.

Railroad Signal System—railroad signal system of continuous cab signals—Pennsylvania Railroad—July 11

Representative (U.S.)—representative (woman) elected to serve in the place of her husband—M E. Nolan—California—began service Jan. 23

Smoke Screen—demonstrated—Cape Hatteras N.C.—Sept. 5

Swimmer—American to swim the English Channel—H. F. Sullivan—Aug. 5-6

Swimmer—swimmer to cover a distance of 44(meters free style in less than 5 minutes—Johnny Weissmuller—New Haven, Conn.—March 6

Wind Tunnel—wind tunnel of variable air density—Langley Field, Va.—April

Woman—woman internal revenue collector—M G. Reinecke—served—June 1

1924

Airmail Service—airmail transcontinenta through regular service—New York City–Sa Francisco—July 1

American Indians—citizenship statute for Ameri can Indians—enacted—June 2

Automobile Bus—bus operated by a railroad—company incorporated—July 23

Aviation—Airship—dirigible merchandise ship ment—arrived—Lakehurst, N.J.—Oct. 15

Aviation—Flights (transcontinental)—transconti nental airship voyage—left—Lakehurst, N.J.—Oct. 7

Aviation—Flights (transcontinental)—transconti nental flight within 24 hours—left—New Yor City—June 23

Aviation—Flights (world)—world flight—begun—Seattle, Wash.—April 6—completed—Sept. 2(

Baseball Player—baseball player (major leagu(to bat in 12 runs in a 9-inning game—J. L. Bo tomley—New York City—Sept. 16

Births—President of the United States to be bor in a hospital—Jimmy Carter—Plains, Ga.—Oc 1

Border Patrol—border patrol organization—e tablished—June 1

Bowler—bowler to roll two perfect games—Fran Caruana—Buffalo, N.Y.

Cellophane—manufactured—Buffalo, N.Y.

Chromium Plating process (commercial)—inven ed—New York City

Citizenship and Public Affairs School—opened—Syracuse, N.Y.—Oct. 3

Coast Guard Officer—rear admirals who we twins to serve at the same time—F. T. Kenn(and W. W. Kenner—commissioned Oct. 17

Corn Husking Championship Contest (nationa —Alleman, Iowa—Dec. 1

Crossword Puzzle Book—published—New Yo City—April 18

Degrees (academic and honorary)—Doctor of S cial Science degree—awarded—H. R. Jeter Chicago, Ill.

Diplomatic Service—Foreign Service of the Uni ed States—created—July 1

Execution—lethal-gas execution—Carson Ci Nev.—Feb. 8

Helium—helium plant of the United States—Bureau of Mines assumed charge—Fort Worth, Texas—July 1

Heresy Trial of a bishop—W. M. Brown—New Orleans, La.—Oct. 12

Hospital—Chinese-American hospital—opened —San Francisco, Calif.—April 18

Ice—dry ice—manufactured commercially—Long Island City, N.Y.

Insurance—automobile compulsory insurance act (state)—enacted—Massachusetts—May 1

Linoleum—embossed inlaid linoleum—introduced—Lancaster, Pa.

Motel—motel—Motel Inn, San Luis Obispo, Calif. —opened, Dec. 12

Motion Picture—motion picture of an eclipse of the sun taken from a dirigible—Montauk Point, L.I., N.Y.—Jan. 24

Museum—outdoor museum (or nature trail)—established—Tuxedo Park, N.Y.

Newspaper—composograph photograph in a newspaper—published—New York City—Nov. 25

Photoelectric Cell—photoelectric cell—demonstrated—New York City—Oct. 21

Photograph—photograph from an airplane at night—Rochester, N.Y.—Nov. 20

Photography—demonstration of rapid aerial photography—Fort Leavenworth, Kans.—Sept. 5

Play (drama)—full-length play by a black performed in New York City—*Appearances*—Garland Anderson—Oct. 13

Postage Stamp—fractional-denomination postage stamp—Harding stamp—issued—Washington, D.C.—March 19

Postage Stamp—special-handling stamps—authorized Feb. 28—issued—Washington, D.C.— April 11

Potato Chips—exclusive manufacturing plant— Albany, N.Y.

Psychology Society—psychological society (national organization)—American Psychological Association—incorporated—Jan. 2

Radio Broadcast—presidential inauguration— Calvin Coolidge—Washington, D.C.

Radio Broadcast—ship launching broadcast— Camden, N.J.—April 7

Radio Facsimile Transmission—photograph sent by radio across the continent—Washington, D.C.—March 4

Radio Facsimile Transmission—photograph sent by radio across the continent (commercial)— San Francisco, Calif.—April 18

Radio Facsimile Transmission—radio facsimile long-distance transmission of a medical subject —New York City—May 28

Radio Facsimile Transmission—transpacific and transcontinental facsimile transmission—May 6

Radio Station—radio station operating a 50-kilowatt transmitter—Schenectady, N.Y.—operated—July 29

Radio Telephone—radio telephone conversation between someone on the ground and a person in a dirigible—A. A. Kent and M. L. Kent– Philadelphia, Pa.—May 16

Railroad Car—coal cars with roller bearings— placed in service—Dec.

Representative (U.S.)—woman to serve 18 term in Congress—E. F. N. Rogers of Massachusett —began service Dec. 7

Road—road with a depressed trough—opened— Texas—Dec. 15

Road—route numbering system (nationwide)– adopted—March 2

Science Association—woman elected to the Na tional Academy of Sciences—F. R. Sabin– April 29

Ship—ship equipped with a masthead sea ancho age for a dirigible—Newport News, Va.—Au 15

Supreme Court (state)—state supreme court com posed entirely of women—Texas—appointe Jan. 8

Television—Telecast—telecast of an object i motion—Bellevue, D.C.—June 13

Television Tube—miniature tube—patented—I W. Weinhart—Elizabeth, N.J.—Aug. 25

Theater—state-owned theater dedicated to i own drama—Chapel Hill, N.C.—opened—No 23

Thermit—used to break up ice jams—Wadding ton, N.Y.—Feb. 24

Tornado—tornado disaster (large-scale)— linois, Indiana, Kentucky, and Tennessee— March 18

1926

Air Corps—Air Corps (U.S. Army)—establishe —July 2—F. T. Davison—sworn in as Assista Secretary of War for Aviation—July 16

Airmail Service—airmail contractor (domestic)– service—Pasco, Wash.-Elko, Nev.—April 6

Arbitration—federal arbitration law—effective– Jan. 1

Aviation—Airplane Bombing—airplane bombi in the United States—Williamson County, Ill.- Nov. 12

Aviation—Flights—North Pole flight—R. E. By —May 9

Aviation—Legislation—aviation legislation (n tional) dealing with the operation of civil a craft—passed—May 20

Baseball Game—World Series baseball game which 3 home runs were made in 1 game—Ne York Yankees vs. St. Louis Cardinals—S Louis, Mo.—G. H. Ruth—Oct. 6

Baseball Pitcher—baseball pitcher (major leagu to win 2 complete games in 1 day—E. H. Levs —Boston, Mass.—Aug. 28

Book Club—Book-of-the-Month Club—esta lished—New York City—April

Book Course—instruction—Winter Park, Fla. Sept. 22

1927

Balloon—Flights—balloon flight to exceed an altitude of 40,000 feet—ascended—Scott Field, Ill. —H. C. Gray—May 4

Boat Race—international lifeboat race—New York City—Sept. 7

Book—contract bridge laws book—*Laws of Contract Bridge*—published in New York City

Brick—lightweight brick—developed—Madison, Wis.

Building—housing cooperative sponsored by a labor union—Amalgamated Houses—New York City—opened Nov. 1

Business History Chair—N. S. B. Gras—appointed —Harvard University—Cambridge, Mass.

Check Photographing Device—commercial manufacture undertaken—May 1

Congress (U.S.)—Congress to enact over 1,000 laws—opened March 4

Electric Power Plant—hydroelectric power plant to use water pumped into a reservoir—Rocky River, Conn.

Electric Sign—electric sign flasher—patent—May 3

Engineering Society—woman elected to the American Society of Civil Engineers—Associate Member—Elsie Eaves—March 14

Flag—flag displayed from the right hand of the Statue of Liberty—in honor of an individual—June 13

Hotel—hotel to install radio reception—Hotel Statler—Boston, Mass.—May 10

Jewish College—Jewish college of liberal arts and sciences under Jewish auspices—Yeshiva College—New York City—cornerstone laid—May 1

King—king born in the United States—King Rama IX—Cambridge, Mass.—Dec. 5

Lecturer—lecturer of royal blood to speak for personal profit—Prince Vilhelm—arrived—New York City—Jan. 5

Medal—Distinguished Flying Cross (Air Corps)— presented—C. A. Lindbergh—June 11

Monument—monument to the American flag— dedicated—Pittsburgh, Pa.—June 14

Motion Picture Theater—theater built especially for the rear projection of motion pictures—rear-projection screen installed—New York City— March 11

Opera—opera broadcast over a national network from an American opera house—Chicago, Ill.— Jan. 21

Phonograph—phonograph with an automatic record changer—introduced—Camden, N.J.

Postage Stamp—postage stamp on which was inscribed the name of a living American—C. A. Lindbergh—sold—June 18

Postal Service—mailbox (drive-up)—installed— Houston, Tex.

Prizefight—prizefight to gross $2 million—Dempsey vs. Tunney—Chicago, Ill.—Sept. 22

Prohibition—prohibition bureau (federal)—authorized—March 3

Propaganda Course (college)—University of Chicago—Chicago, Ill.

Radio Broadcast—coast-to-coast football-game broadcast originating on the West coast—Alabama vs. Stanford—Rose Bowl game, Pasadena, Calif.—Jan. 1

Radio Broadcast—dinner broadcast round-the-world—Schenectady, N.Y.—April 20

Radio Commission (U.S.)—created—Feb. 23

Radio License—international broadcasting license—granted—Oct. 15

Radio Station—radio station operating a 100-kilowatt transmitter—Schenectady, N.Y.—Aug. 4

Radio Telephone—two-way radio conversation between a brakeman in a caboose of a moving freight train and an engineer in the cab of a locomotive—June 15

Railroad Car—Pullman train completely equipped with roller bearings—service began—May 21

Respirator (iron lung)—invented—Philip Drinker and L. A. Shaw

Snowmobile—snowmobile patent—C. J. E. Eliason of Sayner, Wis.—Nov. 22

Submarine—streamlined submarine of the U.S. Navy—*Nautilus*—keel laid—Aug. 2

Symphony—symphonic work to call for an airplane propeller—*Ballet Mécanique*—produced —New York City—April 10

Telephone—transatlantic telephone service (commercial)—Jan. 7

Television—Telecast—demonstration of a telecast before a large audience—L. S. O'Roarke— New York City—May 23

Television—Telecast—telecast of image and sound—April 7

Tunnel—twin-tube subaqueous vehicular tunnel —Holland Tunnel—opened—Nov. 13

Vitamin—synthetic vitamin—D—commercial manufacture—Evansville, Ind.

Wind Tunnel—propeller research tunnel—Langley Field, Va.—completed

Woman—woman secretary of a state senate— Fern Ale—Indiana—Jan. 6

1928

Airmail—dirigible to drop mail by parachute— *Graf Zeppelin*—Washington, D.C.—Oct. 15

Airmail Service—airmail service from ship to shore—Aug. 13

Army Armored Car Unit—organized

Autogiro—autogiro—C8 Mark II—arrived—Bryn Athyn, Pa.—Dec. 17—flown by H. F. Pitcairn— Dec. 19

Autogiro—Flights—autogiro flight—Willow Grove, Pa.—Dec. 19

Automobile Bus—coast-to-coast through bus line —New York City–Los Angeles, Calif.—Sept. 1

Aviation—airplane diesel engine—manufacture —Detroit, Mich.

Aviation—Airship—dirigible transfer of mail to train—June 15

Aviation—Passenger—woman airplane passenger to cross the Atlantic Ocean—Amelia Earhart—started—June 17

Aviation—Passenger—woman Zeppelin passenger (paying)—Clara Adams—started—Lakehurst, N.J.—Oct. 29

aseball Player—baseball player to score more than 4,000 hits—Ty Cobb

ook—book on cornstalk paper—printed—New York City—June

uilding—air-conditioned office building—San Antonio, Texas—opened—Jan. 1

aterpillar Club—father and son Caterpillar Club members—P. F. Collins—jumped—Nov. 19

ollege—university for blacks (Catholic)—Xavier University—degrees conferred—June 6

otton Picker (mechanical)—built—Weatherford, Texas

iathermy Machine—constructed—Schenectady, N.Y.

ectric Lighting—electric light bulb frosted on the inside—patented—Marvin Pipkin—Oct. 16

ectric Sign—electric sign flasher—New York City—operated—Nov. 6

thometer—patented—H. G. Dorsey—April 24

og Jumping Jubilee—Angels Camp, Calif.—May 19-20

wish College—Jewish college of liberal arts and sciences under Jewish auspices—New York City—chartered—March 29

dge—woman associate justice on the federal bench—G. R. Cline—appointed—May 4

comotive—diesel-electric freight locomotive—operated—New York Central—June

edical School—medical center devoted to teaching, treatment, and research—Columbia-Presbyterian Medical Center, New York City—opened March 6—formal dedication Oct. 12

odels' Training School—Chicago, Ill.—opened

otion Picture—animated cartoon talking picture—*Steamboat Willie*—exhibited—New York City—Sept. 19

otion Picture—talking picture whose footage exceeded 6,000 feet—*The Lights of New York*—released—July 21

agara Falls—person to go over Niagara Falls in a rubber ball—Jean Lussier—July 4

otography—film-developing machine (fully automatic)—patented—A. M. Josepho—New York City—Jan. 17

ysician—Capitol physician—G. W. Calver—Washington, D.C.—Dec. 8

stal Service—international dogsled mail—started—Lewiston, Me.—Dec. 20

dio Broadcast—presidential nomination ceremony broadcast—H. C. Hoover—Palo Alto, Calif.—Aug. 11

dio Facsimile Transmission—motion picture film transmitted by telephone wire—Chicago, Ill., to New York City—April 4

ilroad Car—rail detector car—tested—Beacon, N.Y.—June 13

ilroad Car—rail detector car in commercial service—Montpelier, Ohio—Nov. 15

spirator (iron lung)—improved model used—Children's Hospital—Boston, Mass.—Oct. 12

nner—transcontinental foot race—Los Angeles, Calif., to New York City—started March 4—completed May 26

Ship—cruise ship to circumnavigate the world—*Laconia*—returned to New York City—March 30

Ship—seatrain—built—Chester, Pa.

Skeet—college skeet tournament—Princeton, N.J.—Nov. 12

Squash Racquets Champion—woman to win the U.S.A. Women's Squash Racquets Singles championship—Greenwich, Conn.—Jan. 16-19

Telephone—telephone switchboard with Braille markings—New York City—April 1

Television—Telecast—outdoor scenes to be televised—New York City—July 12

Television—Telecast—photograph telecast from an airplane—Robert Hewitt—Philadelphia, Pa.—Aug. 14

Television—Telecast—play to be televised—*Queen's Messenger*—Schenectady, N.Y.—Sept. 11

Television—Telecast—presidential nomination notification ceremony to be televised—Aug. 22

Television—Telecast—programs regularly televised—Schenectady, N.Y.—May 11

Television—Telecast—puppet show to be televised—*Creative Genius*—Newark, N.J.—Aug. 21

Television—Telecast—standard broadcast station to transmit a television image—Coytesville, N.J.—Aug. 13

Television—Telecast—tennis game telecast—New York City—July 12

Television—Telecast—transoceanic television image—received—Hartsdale, N.Y.—Feb. 8

Television License—television license—issued—Washington, D.C.—Feb. 25

Television Magazine—television magazine—*Television*—published—New York City—in June

Theater—theater built and named for a living actress—Ethel Barrymore Theatre—New York City—opened Dec. 20

Track Meet—transcontinental race—began, Los Angeles, Calif.—March 4—concluded, New York City—May 26

Vaccine—tuberculosis vaccine—(effective)—produced—W. H. Park—New York City

Vitamin—synthetic vitamin—marketed

Wedding—television wedding—Des Plaines, Ill.—Oct. 14

Woman—woman passport division chief—R. B. Shipley—assumed office—June 1

1929

Airmail—airmail pickup from a steamer at sea—S.S. *Leviathan*—June 12

Airmail Service—airmail service between North and South America—May 14

Airmail Service—airplane mail pickup—demonstrated—Washington, D.C.—Oct. 1

Animals—dogs trained to guide the blind—The Seeing Eye incorporated—Jan. 9

Animals—reindeer—born—May 31

Autogiro—autogiro manufactured in the United States—Pitcairn-Cierva—completed Oct. 28

Autogiro—Flights—intercity autogiro flight—H. F. Pitcairn—Philadelphia, Pa., to Langley Field, Va.—May 13

Automobile—automobile (new-type gasoline-electric combination)—Aug. 30

Automobile Bus—bus night coach—in service—July

Aviation—air-rail passenger transcontinental daily service—began in New York City—June 14

Aviation—airplane commutation tickets—Newark–Boston—sold—May 1

Aviation—airplane "fly-it-yourself" system—Kansas City, Kan.—Sept. 15

Aviation—airplane high-speed tank to test airplanes—designed—Washington, D.C.

Aviation—airplane motion picture show—Oct. 8

Aviation—ambulance air service—organized—New York City—Oct. 21

Aviation—automatic pilot—tested—Trow Sebree—Oct. 8

Aviation—aviation trainer—sold—Binghamton, N.Y.

Aviation—Airport—airport hotel—opened—Oakland, Calif.—July 15

Aviation—Airship—dirigible made completely of metal—tested—Grosse Ile, Mich.

Aviation—Flights—airplane endurance flight exceeding 400 hours—St. Louis, Mo.—landed—July 30

Aviation—Flights—all-blind flight—J. H. Doolittle—Sept. 24

Aviation—Flights—South Pole flight—R. E. Byrd—Nov. 28

Aviation—License—glider pilot's license (honorary)—issued—Nov. 7

Aviation—Passenger—dirigible passenger transfer to an airplane—Cleveland, Ohio—Aug. 29

Aviation—Races—women's cross-country air derby—takeoff—Santa Monica, Calif.—Aug. 18 —completed—Cleveland, Ohio—Aug. 26

Aviation—School—high school aviation course—New York City—Sept.

Births—child born in an airplane—Miami, Fla.—Oct. 28

Bridge—bridge of flowers—Shelburne–Buckland, Mass.

Brokerage—curb exchange—to transact more business than the stock exchange—New York City—June 15

Brokerage—oceangoing brokerage office—opened—Aug. 15

Cabinet (U.S.)—Cabinet member convicted of a crime—A. B. Fall—Oct. 25

Codeball—played—Chicago, Ill.—May 11

Congress (U.S.)—Prime Minister of Great Britain to address the Congress of the United States—Ramsay MacDonald—Oct. 7

Congress (U.S.)—Senate—broadcast from the Senate chamber—Washington, D.C.—March 4

Congress (U.S.)—Senate—Senate hearing which women, other than members of Congress, were permitted on the floor—Washington, D.C.—Nov. 22

Congress (U.S.)—Senate—senatorial controversy in which no candidates were seated after a recount—Dec. 6

Discus—discus throw to exceed 160 feet—Eric Krenz—Palo Alto, Calif.—March 29

Envelope—airmail letter sheet—issued—Jan. 1

Farm Board (federal)—assembled—July 15

Fireworks Legislation—fireworks legislation (state)—enacted—Michigan—March 29

Fluorescent mineral exhibit—Philadelphia, Pa. April 26

Football Player—football player to score points in 1 game—Clark Hinkle—Lewisburg, Pa.—Nov. 28

Glider—Flights—glider flight in an America-built glider to last longer than 1 hour—W. Bowlus—Point Loma, Calif.—Dec. 11

Golf Course—midget golf course—Chattanooga, Tenn.

Horse Race—horse to win a $100,000 purse in one race—Whichone—Belmont Park, Elmont, N.Y. —Sept. 14

Hospital—community hospital—Elk City, Okla. organization meeting—Oct. 20

Humanist Society—established—Hollywood, Calif.—Jan. 13

Insurance—group hospital insurance plan effected—Dallas, Tex.—Dec. 21

Konel—metal alloy—announced—Pittsburgh, Pa. —Sept. 9

Marine Corps—marine pilot to fly over the Antarctic continent—A. U. Parker—took off from Little America, Dec. 5

Medical Instruction—History of Medicine Department—inaugurated—Baltimore, Md. Oct. 18

Medical Periodical—allergy magazine—Journal of Allergy—published—St. Louis, Mo.—Nov.

Money—paper money of the present small size issued—July 10

Motion Picture—black-oriented talking picture (all-talking, all-singing) by a major company—Hearts in Dixie—shown in New York City—Feb. 27

Motion Picture—talking picture entirely in color—On with the Show—exhibited—New York City —May 28

Motion Picture—talking picture in Esperanto—New York City—July 13

Motion Picture—talking picture taken outdoors (full-length)—In Old Arizona—released—Jan. 20

Motion Picture Actor—motion picture actors receive Oscars—May 16

Nudist Organization—American League Physical Culture—New York City—organized —Dec. 5

Radio Telephone—radio telephone ship-to-shore commercial service—inaugurated—Dec. 8

Glider—glider released from a dirigible—R. S. Barnaby—Lakehurst, N.J.—Jan. 31

Glider—glider towed across the continent—F. M. Hawks—landed—April 6

Glider—seaplane glider—Port Washington, L.I., N.Y.—March 15

Glider—Flights—glider flight indoors—St. Louis, Mo.—March 2

Golf Champion—golf champion to hold the four highest golf titles—R. T. Jones—Philadelphia, Pa.—Sept. 27

Grain Stabilization Corporation—authorized—Feb. 10

Jockey—jockey to win seven races in one day—Joseph Sylvester—Ravenna, Ohio

Labor Department (U.S.)—native-born Secretary of Labor—W. N. Doak—appointed—Dec. 9

Lutheran Church—American Lutheran Church—organized—Toledo, Ohio—Aug. 11

Medical Clinic—flying medical clinic—left U.S. for Panama City, Panama—Jan.

Medical Congress—Mental Hygiene International Congress—Washington, D.C.—May 4

Medical "Rogues' Gallery"—started—New York City—Jan.

Milking Platform (rotating)—Plainsboro, N.J.—Nov. 13

Mortuary—cooperative plan—Toledo, Ohio—Sept. 15

Motion Picture—motion picture of an eclipse of the sun taken from an airplane—Honey Lake, Calif.—April 28

Museum—maritime museum—established—Newport News, Va.—June 2

Museum—museum to install refrigerated vaults—Berkeley, Calif.—March

Music Periodical—music magazine published in Braille—Jan.

Nobel Prize—Nobel Prize in literature—awarded—Sinclair Lewis

Photograph—photograph in natural colors taken in the air—published—Sept.

Photography—photographic flashlight bulbs—patented—Sept. 23

Pinball Game—pinball game machine—manufactured—Chicago, Ill.

Planetarium—planetarium open to the public—Adler Planetarium—Chicago, Ill.—opened—May 10

Police—police bureau of criminal alien investigation—New York City—Dec. 23

Police—state police officers (women)—Lotta Caldwell and Mary Ramsdell—Massachusetts—appointed, April 18

President (U.S.)—President buried in the National Cemetery at Arlington, Va.—W. H. Taft—March 11

Prizefight—championship prizefight decided on a foul—Sharkey vs. Schmeling—New York City—June 12

Prizefighter—pugilist to win and lose a championship in the first round—Abraham ("Al") Singer—New York City—defeated Sammy Mandell, July 17—lost to Tony Canzoneri, Nov. 14

Radar—radar detection of airplanes—Anacostia, D.C.—June 24

Radio Broadcast—round-the-world broadcast—Schenectady, N.Y.—June 30

Radio Broadcast—ship-at-sea broadcast from a ocean liner—*Europa*—March 25

Radio Broadcast—zoo broadcast—C. W. Leiste—New York City—April 21

Radio Instruction—radio-advertising course—New York City—Sept. 28

Railroad Car—complete train of coal cars with roller bearings—in service—Jan.

Road—inter-American highway appropriation—March 26

Road—mosaic pavement—New Orleans, La.—completed—Feb. 4

Rubber—synthetic rubber (neoprene)—produced—April 10

Ship—air-conditioned ship—*Mariposa*—keel laid—Quincy, Mass.—May 17

Ship—diesel-engine passenger ship—*The City of New York*—tested on Delaware River—Jan. 1—left Brooklyn, N.Y., for Capetown, Union of South Africa—Feb. 1

Ship—rivetless cargo vessel—launched—Charleston, S.C.—Feb.

Sports Trophy—sports trophy for the outstanding amateur athlete of the year—James E. Sullivan Memorial Trophy—awarded—R. T. Jones—Dec. 16

Streetcar—streetcar tracks that were tieless, soundless, and shockless—New Orleans, La.—completed—Feb. 4

Submarine—streamlined submarine of the U.S. Navy—*Nautilus*—commissioned—Mare Island, Calif.—July 1

Submarine-Escape Training Tank—submarine escape training tank—New London, Conn.—operated—Aug. 15

Sulfanilamide—sulfanilamide—produced—Wilmington, Del.

Tape, Masking—pressure-sensitive adhesive masking tape—patented—R. G. Drew—May 2

Television—Telecast—demonstration of home reception of television—New York City—Aug. 20

Television—Telecast—speaker to address an organization by television—P. I. Wold—Schenectady, N.Y.—April 1

Television—Telecast—two-way demonstration of television in a theater—April 9

Television—Telecast—weather map telecast to transatlantic steamer—New York City—June 20

Theater—television theater demonstration—Schenectady, N.Y.—May 22

Tunnel—vehicular tunnel to a foreign country—Detroit, Mich.—opened—Nov. 3

Veterans' Bureau—Veterans' Administration authorized—July 3

Woman—woman Presbyterian elder—S. E. Dickson—Milwaukee, Wis.—June 2

Woman—woman tax appeals board member—Annabel Matthews—served—Feb. 18

1931

Animals—cattle (Africander cattle)—arrived—New York City—Dec. 11

Anthropology Laboratory—Santa Fe, N.M.—opened—Sept. 1

Athlete—athlete presented with the Associated Press Athlete of the Year award—J. L. Martin

Autogiro—autogiro licensed for commercial use—certified, April 2

Autogiro—autogiro manufactured with a closed cabin—flown—Philadelphia, Pa.—Oct. 21

Autogiro—autogiro of the U.S. Government—ordered from Pitcairn Aircraft Company, Inc.—Jan. 22—delivered June 1

Autogiro—autogiro to land and take off from a ship—XOP-1—built by Pitcairn Aircraft Company, Inc., Philadelphia—A. M. Pride—flown off Cape Henry, Va.—Sept. 23

Autogiro—autogiro to land on the White House lawn—J. G. Ray—Washington, D.C.—April 22

Autogiro—autogiro to land packages on a moving ship—April 30

Autogiro—autogiro used commercially—*Detroit News No. 2*—delivered to Detroit, Mich.—Feb. 12—demonstrated publicly Feb. 15

Autogiro—autogiro with side-by-side seating arrangement—tested—Philadelphia, Pa.—April 17

Autogiro—Flights—autogiro transcontinental flight made by a woman—Amelia Earhart—Newark, N.J., to Los Angeles, Calif.—takeoff May 29—landed June 7

Autogiro—Flights—transcontinental autogiro flight—J. M. Miller—arrived—May 28

Aviation—Flights—women to fly in excess of 120 hours—Evelyn Trout and E. M. Cooper—Glendale, Calif.—takeoff Jan. 4—landed Jan. 9

Automobile Tractor—diesel-powered tractor—manufactured—Peoria, Ill.

Aviation—airplane high-speed tank to test airplanes—completed—May

Aviation—Airplane—airplane (commercial) stabilized—built—New York City

Aviation—Flights (transpacific)—transpacific nonstop flight—landed—Wenatchee, Wash.—Oct. 5

Aviation—License—glider license awarded a woman—Maxine Dunlap—Feb. 5

Aviation—License—glider license Class "C"—R. S. Barnaby—Feb. 5

Aviation—Parachute—parachute jump from an autogiro—Caldwell, N.J.—Nov. 15

Aviation—Races—airplane race (of importance) in which both men and women were contestants—completed—Cleveland, Ohio—Aug. 31

Baha'i House of Worship—opened—Wilmette, Ill.—May 1

Baseball Pitcher—woman baseball pitcher—Chattanooga, Tenn.—April 1

Basketball Game—basketball game at a large commercial sports arena—Madison Square Garden, New York City—Jan. 19

Building—building higher than 1,250 feet—Empire State Building—New York City—dedicated May 1

Cable (telegraph)—coaxial cable—patented—Dec. 8

Church—General Council of Congregational and Christian Churches—Seattle, Wash.—June 25

City Planning Instruction—Master in City Planning degree conferred—June 18

Congress (U.S.)—House of Representatives—congressional committee headed by a woman—M. T. Norton—became chairman—Dec. 15

Elevator—dual elevator—installed—East Pittsburgh, Pa.

Glider—Flights—rocket glider flight—Atlantic City, N.J.—June 4

Hospital—community hospital—Elk City, Okla.—dedicated—Aug. 13

Medal—Air Mail Flyer's Medal of Honor—authorized—Feb. 14

Motion Picture—motion picture of a complete grand opera—*I Pagliacci*—Feb. 20

Motion Picture Theater—theater built especially for the rear projection of moving pictures—New York City—opened—March 14

National Anthem—"The Star-Spangled Banner"—officially designated—March 3

Nobel Prize—Nobel Peace Prize awarded an American woman—Jane Addams

Opera—opera broadcast in its entirety by the Metropolitan Opera Company—New York City—Dec. 25

Patent—plant patent—issued—H. F. Bosenberg—New Brunswick, N.J.—Aug. 18

Photoelectric Cell—photoelectric cell installed commercially—West Haven, Conn.—June 19

Photograph—infrared photograph—Rochester, N.Y.—Oct. 7

Play (drama)—musical play to win a Pulitzer Prize—*Of Thee I Sing*—opened—New York City—Dec. 26

Polo—polo game played outdoors at night—Baltimore, Md.—July 2

Postage Stamp—stamped envelopes with the identical design issued in various denominations—Washington Bicentennial envelopes—first stamps issued—Washington, D.C.—Jan.1

Price Regulation Legislation—resale price maintenance law (state)—California—enacted—May 8

Radio Broadcast—volcano eruption broadcast—Honolulu, Hawaii—Dec. 28

Railroad—air-conditioned train—installed—B.&O. R.R.—May 24

Rattlesnake Meat—canned—Arcadia, Fla.

Razor—electric dry shaver—manufactured—Stamford, Conn.

Rubber—synthetic rubber (neoprene)—commercial production—Deepwater, N.J.

Senate (U.S.)—woman elected to the Senate—H. O. W. Caraway—Arkansas—temporary appointment—Nov. 13

Ship—air-conditioned ship—*Mariposa*—launched—July 18

Ship—aircraft carrier—*Ranger*—keel laid—Newport News, Va.—Sept. 26

Ship—all-welded self-propelled seagoing petroleum carrier—*White Flash*—launched—Chester, Pa.—Sept. 10—in service, Sept. 14

Shuffleboard Championship—shuffleboard championship tournament—C. L. Bailey, winner—St. Petersburg, Fla.—March 27

Soilless Culture of Plants—private soilless garden—Berkeley, Calif.

Sports Trophy—sports trophy for the outstanding amateur athlete of the year—James E. Sullivan Memorial Trophy—presented to R. T. Jones—Chicago, Ill.—Feb.26

Teletype Service—teletype service (commercial)—begun—Nov. 20

Television—Telecast—telecast (transatlantic) transmitted regularly—E. F. W. Alexanderson—W2XAW, Schenectady, N.Y.—Feb. 6, 10, and 13

Totalisator—totalisator installed—Miami, Fla.

Visiting Celebrities—absolute monarch—to visit the U.S.—King Prajadhipok of Siam—April 19

Water—heavy water—identification publicly announced—H. C. Urey—New Orleans, La.—Dec. 29

Wind Tunnel—full-scale wind tunnel for testing airplanes—Langley Field, Va.—operated—May 27

Woman—woman state budget commissioner—J. W. Wittich—Minnesota—March 16

1932

Autogiro—autogiro to loop the loop publicly—demonstrated—Cleveland, Ohio—August 27

Autogiro—Flights—autogiro flight over an open sea—L. A. Yancey—takeoff, Key West, Fla.—Jan. 24

Aviation—Airport—airport manager (woman)—appointed—Port Bucyrus, Ohio—May 28

Aviation—Flights—all-blind solo flight by the U.S. Army—Dayton, Ohio—May 7

Aviation—Flights (transatlantic)—transatlantic solo flight by a woman—A. E. Putnam—landed—May 21

Aviation—Flights (transatlantic)—transatlantic solo westward flight—J. A. Mollison—landed—Aug. 19

Aviation—Flights (transcontinental)—transcontinental nonstop flight by a woman—A. E. Putnam—Aug. 24

Bank—savings bank with a half-billion-dollar deposit—New York City

Baseball Manager—baseball manager to win pennants in both leagues—J. V. McCarthy

Baseball Player—baseball player (major league) to make 9 hits in 1 game—J. H. Burnett—Cleveland, Ohio—July 10

Baseball Player—baseball player to hit four consecutive home runs in one game—Lou Gehrig—Philadelphia, Pa.—June 3

Bobsled Competition—four-man bob-team competition—Lake Placid, N.Y.—Feb. 14-15

Bobsled Competition—two-man bob-team competition—Lake Placid, N.Y.—Feb. 9-10

Bridge (game) Table—bridge table to shuffle and deal the cards by electricity—patented—Laurens Hammond—Chicago, Ill.—Nov. 29

Cooperative—cooperative operated entirely b women—Bethesda, Md.

Diplomatic Service—American legation in whic a woman assumed charge—F. E. Willis—Oc 12

Dogsled Race—dogsled race on an Olympi demonstration program—Lake Placid, N.Y.-Feb. 6-7

Electric Timer—electrical timing device—teste at Baker Field, New York City—May 14

Elevator—double-deck elevator—installed—Ne York City—Jan.

Federal Home Loan Bank Board—established-July 22

Gasoline Tax—gasoline tax (federal)—enacted-Washington, D.C.—June 6

Golfer—holes in one by a father and son—Wash ington, Ga.—Aug. 24

Greek College and Orphanage—dedicated—Ga tonia, N.C.—Sept. 18

Home Owners' Loan Corporation—Federal Hom Loan Bank Act—approved—July 22

Insurance—unemployment insurance act—by state—enacted—Wisconsin—Jan. 28

Jewish College—Jewish college of liberal arts an sciences under Jewish auspices—B. A. degree conferred—June 16

Light Beam Communication from a dirigible-Schenectady, N.Y.—May 19

Lightning (artificial)—demonstrated—Pittsfiel Mass.—June 10

Medal—National Geographic Society special go medal—presented—A. E. Putnam—June 21

Medal—platinum medal—presented to H. (Hoover—Dec. 1

Medical Clinic—ophthalmology clinic—opened-New York City—Sept.

Money—wooden money—issued—Tenin Wash.—Feb.

Olympic Games—winter Olympic Games comp tition—Lake Placid, N.Y.—began—Feb. 4

Opera—opera house municipally owned—Sa Francisco, Calif.—opened—Oct. 15

Opera—opera matinee at the Metropolitan Ope House—*Elektra*—New York City—Dec. 3

Patent—fruit tree patent—issued—Louisiana, M —Feb. 16

Photography—camera exposure meter—patente —W. N. Goodwin—Newark, N.J.—Feb. 21

Play (drama)—antivivisection play—*Wove Dreams*—presented—Philadelphia, Pa.—Oct.

Poet—black poet to be employed to teach creati writing—J. W. Johnson—Nashville, Tenn.—Ja

President (U.S.)—President to invite the Pres dent-elect—to discuss governmental problem —H. C. Hoover—Nov. 12

Presidential Candidate—presidential candida to fly to a political convention—F. D. Roosev Chicago, Ill.—July 2

Electrical Contract—by a city with the federal government—Tupelo, Mass.—signed—Nov. 11

Electrobasograph—exhibited publicly—Milwaukee, Wis.—June 12

Emergency Housing Corporation (U.S.)—authorized—Oct. 28

Employment Service—employment service (U.S.E.S.)—created—June 6

Enclave—municipal enclave of economic ground rent—Collierville, Tenn.—April 21

Farm Credit Administration (U.S.)—authorized—March 27

Federal Alcohol Control Administration—authorized—Dec. 4

Federal Deposit Insurance Corporation—created—June 16

Federal Emergency Relief Administration—created—May 12

Federal Savings and Loan Association—authorized—June 13

Federal Surplus Relief Corporation—incorporated—Oct. 4

Football Game—professional world championship football game—Chicago Bears vs. New York Giants—Chicago, Ill.—Dec. 17

Game Management Chair—established—University of Wisconsin—Madison, Wis.—Aug.

Glass—invisible glass installation—patent May 30

Governor—governor granted almost dictatorial power—P. V. McNutt—Indiana—Feb.

Holiday—Maritime Day—established—May 20

Home Owners' Loan Corporation—authorized—June 13

Industrial Recovery Act—code under the National Industrial Recovery Act—effective—July 17

Industrial Recovery Act—compliance board under the National Industrial Recovery Act—established—Oct. 26

Industrial Recovery Act—conviction under a National Industrial Recovery Code—New York City—Dec. 2

Industrial Recovery Act—Industrial Recovery Act (national)—enacted—June 16

Industrial Recovery Act—postage stamps commemorating the National Recovery Act—sold—Washington, D.C.—Aug. 15

Industrial Recovery Act—state to place all its employees under the blanket code of the National Recovery Act Code—West Virginia—July 27

Industry—Industrial Advisory Board (federal)—authorized—June 16

Kidnapping—death penalty for kidnapping—mandated—Kansas City, Mo.—July 27

Labor—Labor Advisory Board (federal)—authorized—June 16

Labor Department (U.S.)—woman Secretary of Labor—Frances Perkins—March 4

Labor Relations—Labor Board (national)—authorized—Aug. 5

Legislative Conference (interstate)—Washington, D.C.—Feb. 3

Legislator (state)—woman speaker of a stat house of representatives—M. D. Craig—Nort Dakota—elected—Jan. 3

Liquor Stores (state)—established—Pennsylvani —Nov. 29

Medal—Air Mail Flyer's Medal of Honor—pre sentation—Dec. 13

Mint (U.S.)—woman Director of the Mint—N. 1 Ross—May 3

Money—gold standard abrogation—enacted—June 5

Money—scrip money to be self-liquidating—i sued—Franklin, Ind.—March 8

Motion Picture Theater—drive-in motion pictur theater—Camden, N.J.—June 6

Narcotics—narcotics sanatorium (federal) fc drug addicts—cornerstone laid—Lexington, K —July 29

Narcotics Legislation—narcotics regulatio (state)—adopted—Nevada—March 10

National Emergency Council (U.S.)—authorize —Nov. 17

National Planning Board (U.S.)—organized—Ju 30

Newspaper—newspaper printed on pine-pulp p per—*Soperton News*—Soperton, Ga.—Marc 31

Opera—black prima donna of an opera compan —Caterina Jarboro—New York City—July 22

Poorhouse (state)—replaced by a state home—Delaware—state home dedicated—Oct. 11

Primer—typewriting primer—*Ted and Polly*—published—New York City

Public Works Administration (U.S.)—authorize —June 16

Radio Broadcast—drama broadcast from a reg lar stage—*Roses and Drums*—Sept. 24

Radio Broadcast—drama broadcast from a ship sea—July 1

Radio Broadcast—radio police system (two-wa three-way)—operated—Eastchester Townshi N.Y.—July 10

Radio Facsimile Transmission—facsimile broa cast in ultra-high frequencies—Milwauke Wis.—Dec. 19

Radio Telephone—military portable—Walki Talkie—built—Fort Monmouth, N.J.

Railroad—gasoline-driven, stainless-steel, a conditioned, pneumatic-tired, two-car train delivered—Dallas, Texas—Nov. 4

Science Advisory Board—authorized—July 31

Ship—aircraft carrier—*Ranger*—launched—Fe 25

Ship—steamship to cross the Atlantic Ocean less than 5 days—*Rex*—sailed from Gibralta Aug. 11—arrived off Ambrose Light, Aug. 16

Strike—modern sit-down strike—Austin, Minn.—Nov. 13

Surgical Operation—epileptic case treated by el vation of the skull cap—demonstrated—Ne York City—Nov. 2

Surgical Operation—lung removal—performed—St. Louis, Mo.—April 5

Surgical Operation—lung removal carried out according to preoperative plans—Baltimore, Md.—July 24

Swimming Pool in the White House—formally accepted—June 2

Telegram—singing telegram—introduced—New York City—July 28

Teletypesetter—teletypesetter installed in a school—Ithaca, N.Y.—July 5

Transportation Coordination—transportation coordination (federal)—June 16

Treasury Department (U.S.)—woman assistant treasurer of the United States—M. G. Bannister—appointed—July 26

Treaty Advisory Board—Inter-Departmental Advisory Board—established—July

Vaccine—poliomyelitis vaccine—produced—Maurice Brodie—New York City—Feb.

Wedding—transatlantic telephone wedding—Detroit, Mich.—Dec. 2

Windmill—windmill driven by rotor power—West Burlington, N.J.—tested—July

Woman—woman state liquor board member—J. R. Sheppard—New York—appointed—April 12

1934

Abrasive—boron carbide for commercial use—announced—Sept. 27

American Indians—American Indian tribal constitution—Indian Reorganization Act—June 18

Archivist of the United States—appointed—Oct. 10

Autogiro—autogiro (wingless direct control)—flown—Philadelphia, Pa.—Dec. 9

Automobile Driving Course—in a high school—State College, Pa.—Feb. 17

Aviation—floating seaplane ramp (municipally owned)—New York City—launched Aug. 15

Aviation—Flights—"airplane train"—New York City—Aug. 2

Aviation—Flights (transcontinental)—transcontinental commercial overnight transport service—inaugurated—Aug. 1

Aviation—Flights (transpacific)—Honolulu squadron flight—left San Francisco—Jan. 10

Aviation—Pilot—woman pilot to pilot an airmail transport—Helen Richey—Dec. 31

Bank—bank payments to depositors of a closed insured bank—East Peoria, Ill.—July 3

Bank—Export-Import Bank—Washington, D.C.—organized—Feb. 8

Bank Legislation—bank guaranty legislation—effective—Jan. 1

Bird Sanctuary—for wild birds—Drehersville, Pa.—Aug. 29

Birds—ptarmigan (Eskimo chicken)—hatched—Ithaca, N.Y.—July 24

Birds—snow goose—hatched—Denver, Colo.

Book—book bound with a preprinted offset cloth—*Portraits and Prayers*—published—New York City

Camera—aerial camera (nine-lens) for large-scale mapping—designed

Capital Punishment—capital punishment authorized by federal law—enacted—May 18

College—college silver diploma—Colorado School of Mines, Golden, Colo.—issued May 18

College—college to dispense with the system of credits, hours, points, grades, etc.—Olivet, Mich.—Oct. 1

Coral Reef Barrier—(copy)—of importance—installed—New York City—July

Electric Home and Farm Authority, Inc.—incorporated—Jan. 17

Electrical Contact—by a city with the federal government—effective—Feb. 7

Emergency Housing Corporation (U.S.)—Federal Housing Administration—created—June 27

Evangelical and Reformed Church—organized—Cleveland, Ohio—June 26

Factory—factories operated by the United States Government—in peacetime—Millville, Mass.—project started—June 4

Federal Communications Commission—Federal Communications Commission—created June 19

Federal Credit Union Act—authorized—June 26

Federal Deposit Insurance Corporation—effective—Jan. 1

Federal Savings and Loan Association—Federal Savings and Loan Insurance Corporation—created—June 27

Fingerprinting—community to fingerprint its citizens—Oskaloosa, Iowa—May 21

Football Game—all-star football game—Chicago, Ill.—Aug. 31

Football Game—professional football game in which 10 touchdowns were made—Philadelphia Eagles vs. Cincinnati Reds—Philadelphia, Pa.—Nov. 6

Free Port—legislation enacted—June 18

Holiday—Mother-in-Law Day—celebrated—Amarillo, Texas—March 5

Humanist Society—national assembly—New York City—Oct. 10-11

Information Service (U.S.)—opened—March 15

Judge—woman associate justice of the Circuit Court of Appeals—F. E. Allen—sworn in—April 9

Labor Relations—National Mediation Board—created—June 21

Legislature—unicameral legislature (state)—after the formation of the U.S.—Nebraska—Nov. 6

Liquor Stores (state)—Pennsylvania—opened—Jan. 2

Locomotive—streamlined steam locomotive—introduced—New York Central Lines—Dec. 14

Locomotive Headlight—talking headlight—installed—Schenectady—Nov. 6

Medal—National Geographic Society gold medal—A. M. Lindbergh—March 31

Motion Picture—motion picture of the sun—Pontiac, Mich.—June 19

National Union for Social Justice—founded—Royal Oak, Mich.—Nov.

Organ—pipeless organ—patented—Laurens Hammond—April 24

Periodical—sectarian magazine printed in roto-gravure—*Catholic Missions*—New York City—Oct. 1

Phonograph Record—instantaneous phonograph recording—Oct. 22

Physics—cyclotron—developed—E. O. Lawrence —Berkeley, Calif.

Physics—positron—recognized—C. D. Anderson —Pasadena, Calif.

Play (drama)—theatrical presentation sponsored by the federal government—*The Family Up-stairs*—New York City—Jan. 30

Police—police officer (woman) on the aerial force —Cora Sterling—Seattle, Wash.—appointed—July 13

Postage Stamp—dual-purpose postage stamp—is-sued—Chicago, Ill.—Aug. 30

Postage Stamp—imperforated ungummed sheet of postage stamps—issued—Feb. 10

Postage Stamp—seal of the United States on a postage stamp—issued—Chicago, Ill.—Aug. 30

President (U.S.)—President to broadcast from a foreign country—F. D. Roosevelt—Cartagena, Colombia—July 10

President (U.S.)—President to conduct ministerial services as commander-in-chief of the Navy—F. D. Roosevelt—off Key West, Fla.—April 1

President (U.S.)—President to go through the Panama Canal while President—F. D. Roose-velt—July 11

President (U.S.)—President to visit Hawaii while President—F. D. Roosevelt—July 25

President (U.S.)—President to visit South Ameri-ca while President—F. D. Roosevelt—Car-tagena, Colombia—July 10

President (U.S.)—President's wife to travel in an airplane to a foreign country—Eleanor Roose-velt—left Miami, Fla.—March 6—returned to United States—March 16

Radio Broadcast—musical comedy broadcast—with specially composed music—*The Gibson Family*—Sept. 15

Radio Broadcast—radio broadcast heard in both the Arctic and the Antarctic regions—effected —Sept. 23

Railroad—railroad train to run 1,000 miles non-stop—*Zephyr*—Denver, Colo., to Chicago, Ill.—May 26

Railroad—streamlined all-steel diesel-motor train —Nov. 11

Railroad—streamlined lightweight high-speed three-car passenger train—started—Omaha, Neb.—March 2

Railroad—streamlined Pullman train (six cars)—left Los Angeles, Calif.—Oct. 22

Revenue Stamp printed by the Post Office Depart-ment—"Federal duck stamp"—sold—Aug. 14

Road—highway planning surveys (nationwide)—authorized—June 18

Rocket—rocket to pass the sonic barrier—flown at Marine Park, Staten Island, N.Y.—Sept. 9

Rocket—rocket to reach a speed of 700 m.p.h.—launched—Marine Park, Staten Island, N.Y.—Sept. 9

Salvation Army—woman commander of the Sal vation Army—Elizabeth Booth—elected—Sept 3

Securities and Exchange Commission (U.S.)—cre ated—June 6

Servite Church—Marian Congress—held—Port land, Oreg.—Aug. 12-15

Ship—aircraft carrier—*Ranger*—formally deliv ered—June 4

Ship—streamlined steamship—*Arctees*—arrivec —Boston, Mass.—May 14

Ski Lift—ski tow (rope)—operated—Woodstock Vt.—Jan. 28

Soilless Culture of Plants—commercial produc tion of plants in water—Capitola, Calif.—Feb.

Stamp—hunting permit stamps (federal)—Migra tory Bird—issued

Symphony—symphony on a black folk theme—W. L. Dawson—Philadelphia, Pa.—Nov. 14

Talking Book—for the blind—issued—New York City—July

Telescope—telescope lens 200 inches in diamete —molding began—Corning, N.Y.—Dec. 2

Theatrical School—theater and dramatic criti cism course—to award a Ph.D. degree—Yale University—New Haven, Conn.—Sept. 24

Traffic Regulation Course—air traffic regulatior course—endowed—Northfield, Vt.

Trust—cartel—effective—March 1

Washing Machine—washing machine for publi use—installed—Fort Worth, Tex.—April 18

Woman—woman state committee chairman—M T. Norton—New Jersey—May 22

X Ray—X-ray photograph of the entire body taken in a one-second exposure—Rochester N.Y.—July 1

Youth Hostel—opened—Northfield, Mass.—Dec 27

1935

Airmail Service—autogiro mail delivery direct t a post office—Philadelphia, Pa.—May 25

Airmail Service—Pacific airmail flight—left Sar Francisco, Calif.—Nov. 22

Ambulance—incubator ambulance service—usec —Chicago, Ill.—March 21

American Indians—American Indian tribal con stitution—signed—Oct. 28

Artificial Heart—invented—New York City

Automobile—automobile to exceed the speed o 300 miles an hour—Sir Malcolm Campbell—Sept. 3

Automobile Legislation—federal motor carrie legislation—Interstate Commerce Act amend ment—Aug. 9

Automobile Truck—automobile truck completely streamlined—introduced—Cleveland, Ohio—Sept. 4

Aviation—Airplane—transport airplane designec especially for transoceanic service—left Sar Francisco, Calif.—April 16

Aviation—Flights—airplane flight with an auto slung beneath the fuselage—New York City—Feb. 11

Aviation—Flights—sky-train international round-trip flight—left Key West, Fla.—May 14

Aviation—Flights (transcontinental)—transcontinental nonstop east-west flight by a woman—Laura Ingalls—left New York City—July 10

Aviation—Parachute—parachute tower for training parachute jumpers—built—Hightstown, N.J.—April

Aviation—Pilot—woman pilot to fly solo across the Pacific Ocean—A. E. Putnam—left Honolulu—Jan. 11

Balloon—Flights—balloon flight to exceed an altitude of 70,000 feet—Rapid City, S.D.—Nov. 11

Bank—checkmaster plan—introduced—New York City—June 27

Baseball Game—baseball game at night by major league teams—Cincinnati, Ohio—May 24

Book—book on the game of bridge by a championship team—*The Four Aces System of Contract Bridge*—published—New York City

Bridge—bridge with open-mesh steel flooring—steel flooring patent—W. E. Irving—Feb. 12

Brokerage—woman stock exchange member (commodity exchange)—New York City—admitted—Sept. 3

Building—building with prefabricated walls of mosaic concrete—completed—Washington, D.C.—Feb.

Cans—beer in cans—placed on sale—Richmond, Va.—Jan. 24

Casein Fiber—produced—Washington, D.C.—Dec.

College—college classes to combat the influence of communism—instituted—Philadelphia, Pa.—Dec. 4

Crime Prevention and Detection—crime prevention commission for interstate cooperation—New Jersey—March 12

Crime Prevention and Detection—national conference on crime—Trenton, N.J.—Oct. 11-12

Electric Power Plant—hydroelectric power plant to produce a million kilowatts—dedicated—Sept. 30

Eye—identification system—announced—Atlantic City, N.J.—July 7

Ferryboat—streamlined ferryboat—*Kalakala*—in service—July 4

Glass—invisible glass installation—New York City—Sept.

Labor Relations—Labor Relations Act (national)—approved—July 5

Lie Detector—used in court—Portage, Wis.—Feb. 2

Lightning Observatory — erected — Pittsfield, Mass.

Locomotive—streamlined electric engine—tested—Jan. 28

Medal—woman to have her likeness on a medal issued by the United States Mint—N. T. Ross—issued—June

Medical Legislation—blood grouping test laws (state)—enacted—N.Y.—March 22

Medical Legislation—premature-baby health law—enacted—Chicago, Ill.—March 5

Medical School—medical college (Jewish sponsored)—Albert Einstein College of Medicine, Yeshiva University, New York City—instruction began Sept. 12

Microfilm—book series microfilmed—*A Short Title Catalogue of Books*—Ann Arbor, Mich.

Microfilm—newspaper to microfilm its past issues—New York *Times*—first issues received in November

Money—bill of $100,000 denomination—issued for use within Federal Reserve System—January

Money—bill to depict both the face and the reverse side of the Great Seal of the United States—issued—Dec. 18

Musician—woman conductor-composer—opera presented and conducted—Chicago, Ill.—Nov. 23

Narcotics—narcotics sanatorium (federal) for drug addicts—Lexington, Ky.—opened—May 29

Naval Officer—naval officer designated Commander, Aircraft Battle Force—H. V. Butler—appointed—March 5

News Correspondent—black news correspondent—J. A. Rogers—sailed for Ethiopia—Oct.

Parking Meter—parking meter (automatic)—installed—Oklahoma City, Okla.—July 16

Photograph—photograph showing the lateral curvature of the horizon—Nov. 11

Photograph—portrait (life-size) of a human in a newspaper—Larry Quinn—San Francisco, Calif.—Nov. 14

Police—police training school of the Federal Bureau of Investigation—initiated—Washington, D.C.—July 29

Public School—public school classes for epileptic children—Detroit, Mich.—Jan.

Radio Facsimile Transmission—press syndicate facsimile transmission direct to newspaper offices—Jan. 1

Radio Tube—radio tube—made of metal—Schenectady, N.Y.—announced—April 1

Representative (U.S.)—black representative (Democrat) to serve in Congress—A. W. Mitchell of Illinois—began service Jan. 3

Roller Skating—roller derby—opened—Chicago, Ill.—Aug. 13

Skeet—national skeet tournament—Indianapolis, Ind.—Aug. 31

Social Security Act (U.S.)—approved—Aug. 14

Soilless Culture of Plants—commercial hydroponicum (large)—established—Montebello, Calif.—Dec. 5

Spectrophotometer—patented—A. C. Hardy—Jan. 8

Sulfanilamide—sulfanilamide as a treatment for infections of streptococcic origins—used

Surgical Operation—heart operation for the relief of angina pectoris—performed—C. S. Beck—Cleveland, Ohio—Feb. 13

Telephone—around-the-world telephone conversation—New York City—April 25

Theatrical School—theatrical school sponsored by an institution of higher learning—Schenectady, N.Y.—July 2

Vectolite—manufactured—West Lynn, Mass.—Feb. 27

Veto (presidential)—veto message read by a President—May 22

Virus—virus obtained in crystalline form—Princeton, N.J.—reported—June 28

Works Progress Administration—Works Progress Administration—authorized—May 6

Works Progress Administration—Works Progress Administration Federal Art Project Gallery—opened—New York City—Dec. 28

1936

Airmail Service—rocket airmail flight—Greenwood Lake, N.Y.—Feb. 23

Alcohol—power alcohol plant—established—Atchison, Kan.—Oct. 2

Animals—giant panda—arrived—San Francisco, Calif.—Dec. 18

Art Course—art course—in true fresco painting—University, La.—Sept. 14

Automobile License (federal)—common carrier license—granted—Dec. 22

Automobile License (federal)—contract carrier license—issued—Dec. 29

Automobile Racer—automobile racer to win the Indianapolis 500 three times—Louis Meyer—Indianapolis, Ind.—third time May 30

Aviation—airplane tank discharger—patented—April 28

Aviation—Airplane—hydroplane of stainless steel—tested—Bristol, Pa.—Sept. 4

Aviation—Flights (transatlantic)—Atlantic Ocean regular commercial airship service—inaugurated—May 6

Aviation—Flights (transatlantic)—transatlantic round-trip flight from the United States—left—New York City—Sept. 2

Aviation—Races—airplane passenger race around the world—started—Lakehurst, N.J.—Sept. 30

Bicycle Traffic Court—instituted—Racine, Wis.—June 18

Bottle—screw-cap bottle with a pour lip—patented—May 5

Building—all-glass windowless structure—Toledo, Ohio—completed—Jan. 15

Camera—photofinish camera (electric-eye) installed at a racetrack—Hialeah, Fla.

Catholic Mass—Catholic mass in an airship over the ocean—May 7

Catholic Mass—Catholic mass in an airship over the ocean by an American priest—Aug. 6

Degrees (academic and honorary)—American awarded honorary degrees from three of England's universities—R. W. Bingham—third degree awarded—Nov. 21

Degrees (academic and honorary)—husband and wife awarded honorary degrees—Mr. and Mrs. J. N. Garner—Waco, Texas—Nov. 21

Electron Tube—described—St. Louis, Mo.—Jan.

Fingerprinting—high school to fingerprint its students—Watertown, S.D.—Oct. 19

Flag—Vice President's flag—established—Feb.

Football—football with a rubber covering—manufactured—Los Angeles, Calif.

Football Goalpost—football goalposts of collapsible folding metal—installed—New York City—June

Fuse—textile-wrapped detonating fuse—manufactured—Simsbury, Conn.

Gasoline—aviation gasoline—produced commercially—Paulsboro, N.J.—June 6

Hall of Fame—hall of fame (baseball)—election—Jan. 29

Insurance—group insurance policy for college students—Vassar College—Poughkeepsie, N.Y.—issued—Feb. 1

Isotope—radioactive isotope medicine—administered—Berkeley, Calif.—Dec. 24

Labor Legislation—40-hour-week law (federal)—approved—June 30

Lucite (polymethyl methacrylate) production (commercial)—Wilmington, Del.—May 21

Medical Congress—cancer institute (convention)—Madison, Wisc.—Sept. 7-8

Microfilm—newspaper to microfilm its current issues—New York Herald Tribune—Jan. 1

National Union for Social Justice—national convention—Cleveland, Ohio—Aug. 14

Old Age Colony—Millville, N.J.—dedicated—Oct. 23

Olympic Games—American athlete to win four medals in one year at the Olympic Games—Jesse Owens—Aug. 9

Olympic Games—Olympic Games basketball championship—Berlin, Germany—Aug. 14

Ordnance—semiautomatic rifle—adopted—U.S. Army—Jan. 9

Pension—pensions paid by the United States Government to workers in private industry—mailed—July 13

Periodical—magazine of the United States Government—Federal Register—issued—March 1

Physics—radioactive substance produced synthetically—radium E—Berkeley, Calif.—Feb.

Postage Stamp—sheet of postage stamps to contain more than one variety—sold—New York City—May 9

Presbyterian Church—Presbyterian Church of America—formed—Philadelphia, Pa.—June 11

Radio Station—radio station with 500,000-watt power—Pittsburgh, Pa.—June 12

School—school to have all classroom lights controlled by electric eyes—Hammondsport, N.Y.—Jan. 4

Soilless Culture of Plants—commercial hydroponicum built on the roof—Seattle, Wash.

Sponge—oxidized cellulose (sponge)—manufactured—W. O. Kenyon—Kingsport, Tenn.

elevision—Telecast—high-definition telecast—New York City—June 29

elevision—Telecast—telecast using coaxial cable—transmitted—June 10

elevision—Telecast—unscheduled event to be televised as it occurred—Camden, N.J.—April 24

heater—state-owned theater—Seattle, Wash.—authorized—April 15

raffic Regulation Course—teacher training course in Training Traffic Safety—State College, Pa.

Jnion Party—convention—Cleveland, Ohio—Aug. 15

ice President (U.S.)—Vice President to leave the United States while the President was away—J. N. Garner—sailed—Seattle, Wash.—Oct. 16

Visiting Celebrities—Pontiff—who had visited the U.S.—arrived as Papal Secretary of State—Oct. 8

Voman—woman coxswain of a men's collegiate varsity team—Sally Stearns—Winter Park, Fla.—May 27

Voman—woman to have her name placed on the cornerstone of a United States Government building—N. T. Ross—April

Vomen's Club—Chinese-American women's club incorporated—New York City—June 10

X Ray—X-ray photograph showing the complete arterial circulation—completed—Rochester, N.Y.—July 16

1937

Animals—okapi—imported—New York City—Aug. 4

Aquarium—aquarium for monsters of the deep—ground broken—Marineland, Fla.—May 15

Army Insignia—shoulder sleeve insignia issued to an independent air unit—authorized—July 20

Automobile—automobile-airplane combination—tested—Santa Monica, Calif.—Feb. 20

Automobile—License—common carrier license—effective—Jan. 21

Automobile License Plates—permanent license plates—Connecticut—issued—March 1

Aviation—physiological research laboratory of the U.S. Army Air Corps—Dayton, Ohio—completed—Jan. 1

Bicycle Racer—woman bicycle champion of the National Amateur Bicycle Association—Doris Kopsky—Sept. 4

Blood Bank—blood bank—established—Chicago, Ill.—March 15

Business—Keedoozle store—opened—Memphis, Tenn.—May 15

Church—children's church—dedicated—Milton, Mass.—Nov. 14

Codification Board (United States)—created—June 19

Congress (U.S.)—congressional session in air-conditioned Senate and House chambers—Washington, D.C.—Nov. 15

Congress (U.S.)—Senate—parliamentarian of the Senate—C. L. Watkins—appointed July 1

Electric Generator—hydrogen-cooled turbine generator—Dayton, Ohio—operated—Oct. 12

Electric Sign—animated-cartoon electric sign—New York City—displayed—April 28

Free Port—Stapleton, N.Y.—opened—Feb. 1

Game Preserve—game preserve appropriation (federal)—enacted—Sept. 2

Holiday—Flag Day—legal holiday—Pennsylvania—established—June 14

Insurance—group hospital-medical cooperative—Group Health Association—opened—Nov. 1

Jury—woman grand jury foreman—Newark, N.J.—April 6

Jury School—jury school—Newark, N.J.—opened—Jan 16

Lawyer—Japanese woman lawyer—K. E. Ohi—admitted—Illinois—June 10

Legislature—unicameral legislature (state)—first session—Jan. 5

Medical Clinic—contraceptive clinic (state)—opened—Raleigh, N.C.—March 15

Medical Congress—Fever Therapy International Conference—New York City—March 29-31

Monument—monument to a comic character—Popeye—Crystal City, Tex.—unveiled—March 26

Motion Picture—animated cartoon in color (Technicolor) of feature length with sound—exhibited—Dec. 21

Museum—costume museum—Museum of Costume Arts—New York City—incorporated—April 28

Newspaper—newspaper printed on pine-pulp paper in color—News—Dallas, Tex.—March 31

Newspaper—newspaper with perfumed advertising page—Daily News—Washington, D.C.—March 25

Newspaper—radio facsimile newspaper—transmitted—St. Paul, Minn.—Dec. 17

Nylon—nylon—patented—W. H. Carothers—Feb. 16

Orchestra—orchestra (symphony), full-size, devoted exclusively to radio broadcasting—NBC Symphony—New York City—formed, Nov. 13—debut, Dec. 25

Photographer—photographer to receive a John Simon Guggenheim Memorial Foundation award—Edward Weston—announced March 28

Pituitary Hormone—pituitary hormone isolated—announced—July 23

Plow—submarine cable plow—patented—Jan. 12

Postage Stamp—first-day special cancellation—Aug. 18

Postal Service—letter to encircle the world by commercial airmail—returned—New York City—May 25

President (U.S.)—President inaugurated on January 20—F. D. Roosevelt

President (U.S.)—President whose mother saw her son inaugurated President for a second term—F. D. Roosevelt—Jan. 20

Public School—public school opera studio—Los Angeles, Calif.—Oct.

Quadruplets to Complete a College Course—graduated—Baylor University—Waco, Tex.—May 31

Radio Broadcast—cooperative radio show—Hollywood, Calif.—Oct. 10

Radio Broadcast—news program (cooperative)—Washington, D.C.—Fulton Lewis—Nov.

Radio Broadcast—recorded coast-to-coast broadcast—May 6

Radio Broadcast—simultaneous broadcast on all 3 major networks—American National Red Cross relief fund benefit—New York City—Feb. 11

Radio License—frequency modulation (FM) construction permit granted—Paxton, Mass.—Aug.

Santa Claus School—opened—Albion, N.Y.—Sept. 27

Ship—seaplane tender designed and built for the U.S. Navy—authorized—July 30

Ship—ship permitted to enter port without stopping for quarantine procedure—*Cameronia* —New York City—Feb. 1

Ski Lift—aerial tramway—Franconia, N.H.—authorized June 17

Skywriting—skywriting at night—New York City—Sept. 18

Strike—anti-sit-down-strike legislation (state)—Vermont—enacted—April 9

Television—Mobile Unit—mobile television unit —New York City—Dec. 12

Theater—therapeutic theater—opened—Beacon, N.Y.

Traffic Regulation Course—graduate course in traffic engineering and administration—Cambridge, Mass.—established—Aug. 16

Trailer Church—operated—Ohio—Oct. 1

Trampoline—trampoline commercially manufactured—Cedar Rapids, Iowa

Wedding—American woman married to a former King of Great Britain—W. W. Simpson—June 3

Whist Tournament—international whist tournament—Budapest, Hungary—June 13-20

X ray—X-ray motion pictures (successful) of the action of the human heart—exhibited—New York City—Oct. 2

1938

Animal Breeding Society—artificial animal breeding cooperative society—organized—N.J.—May 16

Aquarium—aquarium for monsters of the deep—Marineland, Fla.—formal opening—June 23

Archival Course—Columbia University—New York City—Sept. 29

Athlete—two-time winner of the Associated Press Athlete of the Year award—J. D. Budge—Aug. 3 (for 1937)—Dec. 12 (for 1938)

Aviation—Airplane—fighter airplane carrying a cannon—tested—Dayton, Ohio—April 6

Aviation—Passenger—woman to fly entirely around the world by commercial heavier-than-air plane—started—June 4

Bank—national bank woman president—electe[d] —Limerick, Me.—Jan. 11

Baseball—baseball (yellow)—used—New Yor[k] City—April 27

Baseball Game—baseball game to attract mor[e] than 83,000 spectators—New York City—Ma[y] 30

Baseball Player—major-league baseball player t[o] pitch two successive no-hit no-run games—Johnny Vander Meer—June 11—June 15

Baseball Team—baseball team to win thre[e] World Series in succession—New York Yan[-] kees

Bridge—pontoon bridge of reinforced concrete—construction began—Seattle, Wash. Dec. 29

Building—building built inside a factory—floate[d] across Illinois River—Sept. 17

Building—building devoted entirely to highwa[y] traffic—ground broken—Saugatuck, Conn.—July 18

Cartoon School—production of animated car[-] toons—organized—New York City—Feb.

Casein Fiber—patented—Dec. 13

Catholic Beatification—Catholic beatification o[f] an American citizen (female)—Rome, Italy—Nov. 13

Chlorophyll—chlorophyll—patented—Benjamin Gruskin—June 14

Civil Aeronautics Authority (U.S.)—created—June 23

Degrees (academic and honorary)—degre[e] awarded a ventriloquist's dummy—Evansto[n] Ill.—Aug. 28

Electric Lighting—electric sterilamp—Bloomfiel[d] N.J.—introduced—March

Euthanasia Society—formed—New York City—Jan. 14

Federal Crop Insurance Corporation—authorize[d] —Feb. 16

Forest Service—aircraft owned by the Forest Ser[-] vice—operated—Oakland, Calif.—Aug. 17

Game Preserve—game preserve appropriatio[n] (federal)—approved—July 23

Gas Legislation—gas legislation (federal)—effec[-] tive June 21

Glass Wool—machinery patented—Oct. 11

Labor Legislation—labor law regulating fair labo[r] standards—enacted June 25

Library Chair—in a library school—New Yor[k] City—endowed—April 4

Medical Legislation—law (state) requiring mar[-] riage license applicants to undergo medica[l] tests—enacted—New York—April 12

Medical Legislation—law (state) requiring sero[-] logical blood tests of pregnant women—enact[-] ed—New York—March 18

Merchant Marine Academy—Merchant Marin[e] Cadet Corps (U.S.)—established—March 15

Newspaper—radio facsimile newspaper (daily)—*Post Dispatch*—St. Louis, Mo.—Dec. 7

Nobel Prize—Nobel Prize in literature to a woma[n] —awarded to P. S. Buck—Dec. 10

Nylon—nylon bristle filament production fo[r] toothbrushes—Arlington, N.J.—Feb. 24

Judge—woman judge (black)—J. M. Bolin—appointed—New York City—July 22

Locomotive—rack-rail diesel-electric locomotive—in service—July 16

Motion Picture—motion picture to gross more than $70 million—*Gone With the Wind*—premiere in Atlanta, Ga.—Dec. 15

Museum—museum devoted exclusively to papermaking—opened—Cambridge, Mass.—June 5

Newspaper—offset-printed daily newspaper—*World*—Opelousas, La.—operations began, Dec. 24

Nylon—nylon yarn manufacture (commercial)—Seaford, Del.—Dec. 15

Pinball Game—pinball legislation enacted by a major city prohibiting the machines—Atlanta, Ga.—effective—July 1

Postal Service—coin-operated mailbox—installed—New York City—May 17

President (U.S.)—President to hold an airplane pilot's license—D. D. Eisenhower—license issued

Public Buildings Administration—approved—April 3

Radar—battleship equipped with radar—*New York*—tested—Jan.

Radio Instruction—radio college course—offered—New York City

Railroad Car—train with fluorescent lights—in service—April 30

Ski School—indoor ski school—R. H. Johnson—opened—Boston, Mass.—Oct. 16

Snow Cruiser (automobile)—demonstrated—Chicago, Ill.—Oct. 22

Strike—anti-sit-down-strike decision (federal)—Feb. 27

Submarine—submarine refloated—*Squalus*—foundered—off Portsmouth, N.H.—May 23—raised, Sept. 13

Suture—fiberglass sutures—used—R. P. Scholz—St. Louis, Mo.—July 19

Telephone—telephone weather-forecasting service—inaugurated—New York City—April 8

Television—Telecast—baseball game (collegiate) televised—New York City—May 17

Television—Telecast—baseball games (major-league) televised—New York City—Aug. 26

Television—Telecast—beauty contest telecast—New York City—June 22

Television—Telecast—bicycle race telecast—New York City—May 20

Television—Telecast—fashion show telecast—New York City—May 17

Television—Telecast—football game (collegiate) to be televised—New York City—Sept. 30

Television—Telecast—football game (professional) to be televised—Brooklyn, N.Y.—Oct. 22

Television—Telecast—king and queen to be televised—New York City—June 10

Television—Telecast—motion picture premiere festivities to be televised—New York City—Dec. 19

Television—Telecast—musical comedy telecast (one-hour)—New York City—July 25

Television—Telecast—operetta to be televised—New York City—June 20

Television—Telecast—play to be televised as a full-hour program—New York City—June 29

Television—Telecast—President to appear on television—F. D. Roosevelt—April 30

Television—Telecast—prizefight to be televised—New York City—June 1

Television—Telecast—surgical-operation classroom-instruction telecast—Brooklyn, N.Y.—March 21

Television—Telecast—telecast (long-distance) received in an airplane—Oct. 17

Television—Telecast—telecast produced for a tri city gathering—Schenectady, N.Y.—Dec. 8

Television—Telecast—telecast (public) over telephone wires—New York City—May 20

Television—Telecast—tennis tournament to be televised—Rye, N.Y.—Aug. 9

Visiting Celebrities—King and Queen of Great Britain—arrived—Niagara Falls, N.Y.—June 7

Vitamin—synthetic vitamin K—produced—Cambridge, Mass.—Aug. 1

Water Ski Association (national)—American Water Ski Association—formed—Trenton, N.J.—April

Water Ski Tournament (national)—Jones Beach State Park, N.Y.—June 22

Woman—woman presidential campaign co manager—R. H. M. Simms—Dec. 2

1940

Air Defense Command (U.S.)—created—Feb. 26

Air Raid Shelter—air raid shelter—completed—Fleetwood, Pa.—Nov. 1

Aquatic Mammals—born in captivity—porpoise—Marineland, Fla.—Feb. 14

Archival Administration—American University—Washington, D.C.—training program offered—Sept. 25

Army Officer—brigadier-general (black)—B. O. Davis—appointed—Oct. 25

Army Parachute Troops—training started—July

Art Course—industrial camouflage course—Kansas City, Mo.—Oct. 15

Automobile Tire—synthetic rubber tire—exhibited—Akron, Ohio—June 5

Aviation—Airplane—naval patrol bomber—launched like a ship—*Mars*—keel laid—Baltimore, Md.—Aug. 22

Aviation—Airplane—plastic-bonded airplane—built—Van Nuys, Calif.—July

Aviation—Airport—airport (federally owned and operated)—cornerstone laid—Washington D.C.—Sept. 28

Aviation—Flights—all-blind distance flight by the U.S. Army—New York City–Langley Field, Va.—April 6

Aviation—Flights—stratoliner commercial flight—July 8

Aviation—License—Civil Aeronautics Administration—honorary license—to Orville Wright—Aug. 19

Television—Telecast—simulcast presented regularly by a sponsor—Lowell Thomas—New York City—Feb. 21

Television—Telecast—television network demonstration (long-distance)—New York City –Schenectady, N.Y.—Feb. 1

Television—Telecast—track meet (intercollegiate) to be televised—W2XBS—New York City —March 2

Television Receiver—television receiver on a ship —installed on *President Roosevelt*—May 11

Unitarian Church—woman moderator of the Unitarian Church—A. H. Reinhardt

Wedding—parachute wedding—New York City— Aug. 25

1941

Army Language School—courses begun—San Francisco, Calif.—Nov. 1

Army Officer—air surgeon of the War Department —D. N. W. Grant—appointed—Oct. 24

Automobile—plastic automobile—manufactured —Dearborn, Mich.—Aug.

Aviation—Airplane—naval patrol bomber— launched like a ship—*Mars*—christened—Baltimore, Md.—Nov. 8

Aviation—Airplane—plastic-bonded airplane— approved—April 5

Aviation—Airport—air terminal (not located at an airport)—opened—New York City—Jan. 27

Aviation—Airport—airport (federally owned and operated)—opened for traffic—Washington, D.C.—June 16

Aviation—Flights—airplane flight (commercially scheduled) over a single route linking four continents—started—New York City—Feb. 1

Aviation—Flights (world)—world flight by a commercial airplane—started—San Francisco, Calif.—Dec. 2

Aviation—Parachute—parachute fatality in the U.S. Army—F. S. Beard—Columbus, Ga.— March 6

Aviation—Pilot—American ace in World War II—B. D. Wagner

Aviation—Pilot—father and son commercial airline pilots—E. H. Lee and R. E. Lee—California —May 19

Aviation—Pilot—woman test pilot—Alma Heflin —Nov. 12

Baseball Player—baseball player to hit in more than 50 consecutive games—J. P. Di Maggio— 56th game on July 16

Blackout—blackout lighting demonstration— Lynn, Mass.—May 14

Brokerage—woman to sell securities on the floor of the New York Curb Exchange—Linda Darnell—Nov. 19

Building—building known as a Quonset hut— built—Greenwich, R.I.—Sept.

Business—department store to hold a public art auction—New York City—Nov. 14

Civil Air Patrol (U.S.)—organized—Dec. 1

Congress (U.S.)—Congress in session a full yea —third session 76th Congress—closed Jan. 3

Conscientious Objectors' Camp—opened—Rela Md.—May 15

Electric Generator—hydrogen-cooled turbine ge erator for outdoor installation—Glendale, Cal —operated—April 11

Electric Generator—wind turbine—Grandpa Knob, Vt.—operated—Oct. 19

Garage—municipally owned parking building Welch, W.Va.—opened Sept. 1

Glider—glider (all plywood-plastic)—San Fe nando, Calif.—mock-up test—Dec. 1

Helicopter—Flights—helicopter flight from wat —Stratford, Conn.—April 17

Helicopter—Flights—helicopter flight of one-ho duration—Stratford, Conn.—April 15

High Jumping Standards using electric eye dete tors—used—Schenectady, N.Y.—May 31

Insurance—health insurance clause in a lab contract—ILGWU—effective Aug. 25

Laryngophone—manufactured commercially New York City

Magnesium—magnesium commercially produce from seawater—extracted—Freeport, Tex.- Jan. 21

Medal—Order of the Purple Heart awarded to nurse—A. G. Fox

Medical Clinic—heredity clinic—Ann Arb Mich.—opened—Nov. 12

Motion Picture Professorship—motion pictu professorship—Robert Gessner appointed—e tablished at Washington Square College of Ar and Sciences, New York University—New Yo City—May 26

Naval Officer—admiral killed in action in Wor War II—I. C. Kidd—Dec. 7

Navy—naval task force assembled for foreign se vice—commanded by D. M. Le Breton—saile July 1

Navy "E" Award—navy "E" certificates meritorious service—awarded—July 25

Ordnance—automatic aircraft cannon—20 mm delivered—May 16

Ordnance—tank (heavy 60-ton)—presented Army Ordnance Department—Dec. 8

Paprika Mill—Dillon, S.C.—incorporated—Mar 25

Police—Army Military Police school—authoriz —Dec. 19

Postal Service—highway post office service—e tablished—Feb. 10

Price Regulation Legislation—price regulatic law (federal)—Office of Price Administratic and Civilian Supply—created—April 11

Radar—radar used to detect enemy airplanes Pearl Harbor, Hawaii—Dec. 7

Radio License—frequency modulation transm ter to receive a commercial license—W47NV Nashville, Tenn.—operations begun—March

Representative (U.S.)—representative (woma to vote twice against the entry of the Unit States into war—Jeannette Rankin—Dec. 8

Liquid Heat—system operated—Summit, N.J.—Jan. 7

Medal—American Academy of Arts and Letters-National Institute of Arts and Letters gold medal—awarded—C. E. Burchfield—New York City—May 8

Medal—Distinguished Service Cross awarded in enemy-occupied territory—presented by C. A. Spaatz to C. C. Kegelman—July 11

Medal—Distinguished Service Medal (Merchant Marine)—authorized—April 11

Medal—Legion of Merit Medal—authorized—July 20

Medal—Legion of Merit Medal awarded to a foreign national—presentation—Miami Beach, Fla.—Nov. 7

Medal—marines to win the Navy and Marine Corps Medal—N. C. S. Pearson and Gordon Miller—commended Sept. 21

Medal—Medal of Honor awarded in World War II—presented posthumously—A. R. Nininger—Feb. 10

Medal—Medal of Honor awarded to a Marine in World War II—G. H. Cannon—awarded March 14

Medal—Navy Cross awarded to a Coast Guard officer in World War II—M. D. Jester—June 4

Medal—Navy Cross 3-time winner—N. A. Gaylor—3rd presentation, Sept. 9

Medal—Presidential Unit Citation (Navy)—authorized—Feb. 6

Medal—Silver Star Army Medal awarded to a civilian—Vern Haugland—Oct. 3

Merchant Marine—Merchant Marine officer to hold the rank of rear admiral—A. B. Randall—commissioned—Feb. 1

Merchant Marine Academy—Merchant Marine Cadet Corps (U.S.)—first class started—Kings Point, N.Y.—Jan. 28

Naval Officer—black commissioned officer in the Naval Reserve—B. W. Robinson—commissioned—June 18

Naval Officer—engineer inspector (woman)—Jean Hales—appointed Aug. 24

Naval Officer—woman doctor in the WAVES—C. J. Gaskill—commissioned—Northampton, Mass.—Sept. 7

Naval Officer—woman naval inspector—Jean Hales—appointed—Aug. 24

Naval Officer—woman naval officer commissioned in the U.S. Naval Reserve—M. H. McAfee—inducted—Aug. 3

Naval Officer—women technicians in medicine assigned to the National Naval Medical Center—Kathryn Hyde and Dorothy Osborne—Bethesda, Md.—reported for duty—Nov. 13

Navy "E" Award—Army-Navy "E" awards—presented—Aug. 10

Navy "E" Award—Navy "E" certificates of meritorious service presented to an institution of higher learning—University of Wisconsin—Madison, Wis.—June 1

Ordnance—bazooka rocket gun—produced—Bridgeport, Conn.—June 14

Police—Army Military Police school—opened Fort Myer, Va.—Jan. 15

Postal Service—"V" mail film—dispatched—Ju 22

President (U.S.)—President to become a god ther to a member of the British royal family—D. Roosevelt—Aug. 4

President (U.S.)—President to broadcast in a f eign language—F. D. Roosevelt—Nov. 7

Price Regulation Legislation—price regulati law (federal)—enacted—Jan. 30

Pulitzer Prize—woman to win 2 Pulitzer prizes history—Margaret Leech—first award, May

Railroad Car—President's car—built

Saboteurs—saboteurs executed—6 electrocu —Washington, D.C.—Aug. 8

Ship—merchant ship of the United States cc manded by a black captain—*Booker T. Wa ington*—launched—Wilmington, Del.—Sept.

Ship—navy vessel constructed as a minelaye *Terror*—commissioned—July 15

Ship—ship completed in less than 2 weeks— *seph N. Teal*—Portland, Oreg.—trial run, Se 27

Ship—ship transported overland across Rocky Mountains—*Brennan*—assembled a launched as the *Bentinck*—Mare Island, Ca —Aug. 22

Ship—triple launching of Liberty ships—B timore, Md.—July 4

Submarine—submarine built on the Gr Lakes—*Peto*—launched—Manitowoc, Wis April 30

Submarine—submarine with a high tensile-st pressure hull—*Balao*—Portsmouth, N.H.—k laid, June 26—launched, Oct. 27

War Shipping Administration—War Shipping A ministration—established—Feb. 7

World War II—aircraft carrier (American) sunl World War II—*Lexington*—Coral Sea—Ma

World War II—American air attack against Japanese homeland—April 18

World War II—American bombardier over G man-occupied territory—B. L. Bell—June 29

World War II—American bombing mission o enemy-occupied territory in Europe—July 4

World War II—American expeditionary force land in Africa—June 17

World War II—American expeditionary force land on the European continent—arrived— land—Jan. 26

World War II—American general missing in tion in World War II—C. L. Tinker—June 7

World War II—American general wounded in tion in World War II—C. A. Pierce—Philipp Islands—Feb. 4

World War II—American naval counteratt against the Japanese—Battle of Balikpapa Feb. 23-24

World War II—American offensive in the Pac area—Guadalcanal, Solomon Islands—Aug

World War II—American pilot to shoot dow German fighter plane—S. F. Junkin—Aug. 1

Ship—warship named for a black—*Harmon*—laid down—Hingham, Mass.—April 12—assigned to United Kingdom, June 10—launched as *Aylmer,* July 10—transferred to Royal Navy Sept. 30

Submarine—submarine (U.S.) sunk by an enemy submarine—*Corvina*—Nov. 16—presumed lost, Dec. 23

Submarine—submarine with a high-tensile-steel pressure hull—*Balao*—commissioned—Feb. 4

Submarine-Escape Training Tank—women to take the submarine-escape test—certificates awarded—July 12

Television—Telecast—missing persons telecast —New York City—Oct. 3

Television—Telecast—opera (complete) to be televised—Schenectady, N.Y.—Dec. 23

Visiting Celebrities—President of a black African country—to visit the U.S.—Edwin Barclay of Liberia—arrived—May 26

World War II—air attack on Germany itself by U.S. Army Air Forces—H. S. Hansell, 3rd—Jan. 27

World War II—airship (American) lost to enemy action—K-74—July 18

World War II—land victory without infantry— Pantelleria, Sicily—June 11

1944

Army Officer—army officer to receive the three highest decorations—M. L. Britt—Distinguished Service Cross (3rd award)—presentation Dec. 7

Army Officer—generals to wear the five-star insignia—grade established—Dec. 14

Army Officer—woman officer in the Judge Advocate General's Department—P. L. Propp—May 3

Atomic Reactor—atomic reactor to produce plutonium—operated—Richland, Wash.

Aviation—Airplane—jet-propelled fighter plane —flown

Aviation—Airplane—rocket airplane (military)— flown—July 5

Births—quadruplets delivered by cesarean operation—Philadelphia, Pa.—Nov. 1

Business—retail store whose sales in 1 day exceeded $1 million—R. H. Macy Co.—New York City—Dec. 7

Caterpillar Club—father and son Caterpillar Club members—P. L. Collins—jumped—Feb. 11

Citizenship—Chinese granted citizenship—E. B. Kan—Chicago, Ill.—Jan. 18

Coast Guard Officer—Coast Guard Women's Reserve officer to serve overseas—Margaret Moon—assigned to Hawaii—Nov. 22

Cotton—cotton crop commercially produced entirely by machinery—Clarksdale, Miss.

Dentist—woman dentist in the U.S. Navy—S. G. Krout—Great Lakes, Ill.—began service June 1

Election Law—election law permitting persons 18 years of age or older to vote—Georgia—first used Nov. 7

Electric Power Plant—mobile electric power pla —delivered—Philadelphia, Pa.—Jan. 10

Eye—eye bank—New York City—opened May

Hockey Player—professional hockey player score 6 goals in 1 game—Syd Howe—Detro Mich.—Feb. 3

Horse Race—stakes race triple dead heat—Car Handicap—Belmont Park, Elmont, L.I., N.Y. June 10

Marine Corps—general (4 stars) of the Marines Thomas Holcomb—Jan. 1

Medal—Bronze Star—established—Feb. 4

Medal—Bronze Star presented to a woman—C. Cook—May

Medal—combat decoration—for army personn —authorized—Dec. 22

Medal—Distinguished Flying Cross awarded to nurse—A. E. Lutz—given posthumously, Dec.

Medal—Distinguished Service Medal (Arm awarded to a woman—O. C. Hobby—Dec. 3

Medal—Expert Infantryman's Badge—award —W. L. Bull—Fort Bragg, N.C.—March 29

Medal—Legion of Merit Medal awarded to Women's Army Corps member—W. B. Boyce Sept. 27

Medal—Legion of Merit Medal awarded to Women's Army Corps (WAC) member in t European Theater of Operations—A. M. Wils —awarded Oct. 20

Medal—Navy Unit Commendation decoration established—Dec. 20

Medal—soldier to win the three highest-ranki decorations—M. L. Britt

Naval Officer—captain in the U.S. Navy who w a woman—S. S. Dauser—Feb. 26

Naval Officer—naval officers to wear the five-st insignia—appointments ratified—Dec. 15

Naval Officer—woman physician in the Medic Corps Reserve of the U.S. Navy—Hulda Th lander—commissioned—April 19

News Correspondent—black news corresponde accredited to the White House—Harry McⲀ pin—Feb. 8

Newspaper—transoceanic newspaper—*Da Mail*—Jan. 5

President (U.S.)—President elected for a four term—F. D. Roosevelt

President (U.S.)—presidential airplane—deli ered

Quinine—synthetic quinine—produced—Ca bridge, Mass.—April 10

Serbian Orthodox Cathedral—Cathedral of ⵐ Sava—New York City—elevated—June 11

Ship—naval ship christened by a Marine Cor Women's Reserve member—*Bucyrus* launched—Richmond, Calif.—Oct. 31

Ship—naval ship christened by an Army officer *Colhoun*—launched—Seattle, Wash.—April —commissioned July 8

Ship—Victory ship launched—*United Victory* launched—Portland, Oreg.—Jan. 12

Stamp—revenue stamp of $10,000 denominati —issued

ate Department (U.S.)—State Department (U.S.) black official—R. J. Bunche—appointed—Jan. 4

reptomycin—manufactured commercially—Rahway, N.J.—Sept.

ibmarine—quadruple submarine launching—*Razorback, Redfish, Ronquil,* and *Scabbard Fish*—Portsmouth, N.H.—Jan. 27

ibmarine—submarine captured and boarded on the high seas—U-505—June 4

ielevision—Telecast—motion picture premiere performance to be televised—April 10

ielevision—Telecast—musical comedy (full-length) written especially for television—presented—New York City—Sept. 28

ielevision—Telecast—ship launching telecast—U.S.S. *Missouri*—New York City—Jan. 29

ar Shipping Administration—War Shipping Administration award—authorized by E. S. Land —Oct. 14

ire Recorder—patented—Marvin Camras—Chicago, Ill.—June 13

oman—woman secretary of a national political party—appointed—Feb. 29

orld War II—American general captured by the Germans—A. W. Vanaman—reported missing June 27—status as prisoner announced, Oct. 14

1945

ctor—actress elected to Congress—H. G. Douglas—began service Jan. 3

rmy Officer—general to be consecrated a bishop —Oct. 11

omic Bomb—atomic bomb explosion—Alamogordo Air Base, N.Mex.—July 16

omic Bomb—atomic bomb explosion over enemy territory—Hiroshima, Japan—Aug. 6

viation—Airplane—gas turbine propeller-driven airplane—tested—Feb. 11

viation—Airplane—jet-propelled landing on an aircraft carrier—Nov. 6

ink—world bank—International Bank for Reconstruction and Development—formed

cycle Racer—woman bicycle champion of the National Amateur Bicycle Association to win twice—M. M. Dietz—Aug. 18-19

isiness—"Food-O-Mat"—installed—Carlstadt, N.J.—May 24

ement—element 95—americium—announced—Nov. 16

ement—element 96—curium—announced—Nov. 16

ig—President's flag—48 stars—authorized—Oct. 25

Bill of Rights—Army Corps veteran (woman) to receive a loan under the GI Bill of Rights—E. M. Lutz—loan announced, Feb. 16

ll of Famer—Hall of Fame (university) black—B. T. Washington—selection announced Oct. 31

ckey Player—professional hockey player to score 50 goals in 1 season—J. H. M. Richard—50th goal in Boston, Mass.—March 18

Horse Race—racetrack at which more than $5 million was bet in one day—Belmont Park, Elmont, N.Y.—Sept. 22

Industrial and Labor Relations School—Ithaca, N.Y.—instruction began—Nov. 5

Judge—black judge of a customs court (U.S.)—I. C. Mollison—inducted—Nov. 3

Labor—labor antidiscrimination commission (state)—New York—appointed—July 1

Marine Corps—general (4 stars) of the Marines on active duty to become a full general—A. A. Vandegrift—date of rank March 21—appointed April 4

Medal—Medal of Freedom—established—July 6

Medal—Medal of Freedom awarded to a woman —Anna Rosenberg—Oct. 29

Medal—Medal of Honor awarded to a conscientious objector—Oct. 12

Medal—Navy Unit Commendation decoration—awarded—*Helena*—March 11

Medal—presidential citation to an entire division —March 15

Medal—Silver Star Medal awarded to a civilian by the U.S. Navy in World War II—approved—March 3

Microfilm—microfilm machine to project enlarged images on ceilings—manufactured—Ann Arbor, Mich.

Naval Officer—naval nurses' corps (woman member)—to receive the Distinguished Service Medal—S. S. Dauser—Dec. 14

Naval Officer—black nurse in the Navy Reserve Nurse Corps—P. M. Daley—sworn in—March 8

Navy—mobile dental office self-contained operating unit (U.S. Navy)—in operation Feb. 18

Opera—black to sing a white role with a white cast in an opera company—R. T. Duncan—New York City—Sept. 28

Postage Stamp—nonpictorial postage stamp—United Nations stamp—issued—San Francisco, Calif.—April 25

President (U.S.)—President to attend the swearing-in of an Associate Justice (H. H. Burton) of the Supreme Court—H. S. Truman—Washington, D.C.—Oct. 1

Radio Facsimile Transmission—color photoradio news photograph transmitted by radio for publication—Aug. 3

Radio Telephone—two-way-radio-equipped bus —in service—Sept. 8

Railroad Car—car with an observation dome—July 23

School—school completely irradiated with germicidal lamps—Cato, N.Y.—lamps installed—Jan. 3

Ship—naval ship (destroyer) christened by an enlisted woman Marine—*Basilone*—launched—Orange, Tex.—Dec. 21

Ship—ship to pass both ways through the Northwest Passage—*Northwind*—launched—San Pedro, Calif.—Feb. 25

Ship—warship named for a black—*Harmon*—returned by United Kingdom to United States—Nov. 5

Strike—strike to last longer than a year—J. I. Case Manufacturing Company, Racine, Wis.—strike began—Dec. 26

Submarine—submarine to make more than 13,000 dives—*Sarda*—launched—Portsmouth, N.H.—Aug. 24

Television—Telecast—department store sales demonstrations (large-scale)—Gimbel Bros.—Philadelphia, Pa.—Oct. 24

Television—Telecast—stratovision flight test—Middle River, Md.—Dec. 9

Treaty—treaty (federal) signed by a woman—Charter of the United Nations—San Francisco, Calif.—V. C. Gildersleeve—June 26

United Nations—Conference on International Organization of the UN—San Francisco, Calif.—April 25

Water—community to fluoridate its municipal water—Grand Rapids, Mich.—Jan. 25

Wedding—wedding in the United States Occupation Forces in Korea—Nov. 17

World War II—Japanese ballon casualties—Elsie Mitchell—Bly-Lakeview area, Oreg.—May 5, 1945

World War II—Japanese homeland bombardment by the U.S. Navy—Kamaishi, Honshu, Japan—July 14

1946

Airmail Service—helicopter airmail delivery—Bridgeport, Conn.—July 5

Airmail Service—helicopter airmail experimental tests—Burbank, Calif.—July 8

Airmail Service—jet-propelled airplane to transport mail—June 22

Atomic Bomb—atomic bomb dropped from an airplane over water—Bikini Lagoon—June 30

Atomic Bomb—atomic bomb underwater explosion—Bikini Atoll—July 24

Atomic Energy—atomic energy peacetime production—Clinton Laboratories, Chicago, Ill.—delivered—Barnard Free Skin and Cancer Hospital, St. Louis, Mo.—Aug. 2

Atomic Energy Commission—Atomic Energy Commission—established—Aug. 1

Aviation—Airplane—bomber with the Flying Wing design—flight—June 25

Aviation—Airplane—jet airplane to land on a ship—July 21

Aviation—Airplane—rocket plane—tested—Dec. 9

Aviation—Flights (transcontinental)—transcontinental round-trip airplane flight within one day—June 12

Bank—"autobank" complete service—Chicago, Ill.—Nov. 12

Baseball Game—baseball playoff series—Oct. 1

Baseball Game—night baseball World Series game—Red Socks-Cardinals—St. Louis, Mo.—Oct. 6

Blanket—electric (electronic) blanket—manufactured—Petersburg, Va.—Oct. 9

College—college principally for war veterans—Plattsburg, N.Y.—Sept. 16

Computer—electronic computer—completed—Philadelphia, Pa.

Evangelical United Brethren Church—formed—Johnstown, Pa.—Nov. 16

Glider—glider commercial freight service—Philadelphia, Pa.—April 24

Glider—powered soaring glider commercially licensed—*Dragonfly*—licensed—Oct. 15

Governor—black governor appointed by the President of the United States—W. H. Hastie—inaugurated—governor of Virgin Islands—M 7

Helicopter—helicopter commercially designed—tested—Bridgeport, Conn.—Feb. 16

Helicopter—helicopter licensed for commerce use—New York City—March 8

Helicopter—helicopter with a twin-engine—tested—St. Louis, Mo.—March

Medal—Medal of Honor awarded to a chaplain—Timothy O'Callahan—presented Jan. 23

Medal—Medal of Honor awarded to a Nisei—presented posthumously—March 13

Medal—soldier to receive seven decorations one time—L. M. Chilson—Dec. 6

Medical Clinic—cancer clinic (traveling)—established—Oklahoma City, Okla.—Feb. 14

Medicine—bone bank—established—New York City

Microfilm—microfilm machine to project enlarged images on ceilings—installed—Battle Creek Mich.—March 21

Money—coin bearing the portrait of black American—authorized—Aug. 7

Naval Officer—admiral (four stars) who did not attend the U.S. Naval Academy—Ben Morell—nominated June 7—confirmed June 11

Naval Officer—chaplain to win a Congressional Medal of Honor—J. T. O'Callahan—Jan. 23

Photograph—photograph of a beam of 1-billion volt X rays—Schenectady, N.Y.—Oct.

President (U.S.)—President to travel underwater in a captured enemy submarine—H. S. Truman—Key West, Fla.—Nov. 21

Prizefight—prizefight at which admission ticket sold at $100—New York City—June 19

Radar—radar signal to the moon—Belmar, N.J.—Jan. 10

Radio Facsimile Transmission—facsimile transmitted to a moving train—public demonstration—June 4

Rocket—rocket to attain a 100-mile altitude—White Sands Proving Grounds, N.M.—July

Saint (Catholic)—Saint (Catholic)—F. X. Cabrini—favorable vote, June 13—canonized, July

Ship—radar installation aboard a commercial carrier—installed—April 27

Sleeping Car—transcontinental through Pullman sleeping car service—began—March 30

Snow—artificial snow—produced from a natural cloud—Mount Greylock, Mass.—Nov. 13

now-melting Apparatus—snow-melting apparatus (practical) with pipe imbedded in the sidewalk—tested—New York City—Dec. 8

oldering Gun—soldering gun—invented by C. E. Weller—Easton, Pa.—patented—Aug. 13

ponge—oxidized cellulose (sponge) for medical and surgical use—marketed—June 5

ubmarine—submarine to make more than 13,000 dives—*Sarda*—commissioned—April 19

elephone—mobile long-distance car-to-car telephone conversation—Sept. 11

elephone—mobile telephone commercial service—began—St. Louis, Mo.—June 17

elephone—mobile telephone conversation overseas—July 16

elephone—mobile telephone news dispatch—from a moving car—St. Louis, Mo.—May 15

elevision—Telecast—church service telecast—Grace Episcopal church, New York City—Dec. 24

elevision—Telecast—commercial program telecast—"Geographically Speaking"—Oct. 27

elevision—Telecast—motion picture trailer to be televised—New York City—Sept. 20

elevision—Telecast—prizefight (heavyweight championship bout) to be televised—New York City—June 19

elevision—Telecast—variety talent-show series of 1-hour programs—WNBT-TV, New York City —May 9

elevision Receiver—coin-operated television receiver—exhibited—New York City—Nov. 7

hread—nontwisted sewing thread—manufactured—Putnam, Conn.

1947

ir Force—Air Force Secretary—W. S. Symington —sworn in—Washington, D.C.—Sept. 18

irmail Service—helicopter airmail and express service—began—Los Angeles, Calif.—Oct. 1

rmy—Reserve Officers Training Corps course in mountain and winter warfare—Norwich University—Northfield, Vt.—Oct. 3

rmy—Women's Army Medical Specialist Corps —authorized—April 16

rmy Officer—army officer to occupy both the nation's highest military post and the highest nonelective civilian post—Chief of Staff G. C. Marshall—became Secretary of State, Jan 21

rmy Officer—woman to be appointed a Regular Army officer (colonel)—F. A. Blanchfield—appointed—July 9

tomic Energy Commission—Atomic Energy Commission—confirmed—April 9

utomobile—automobile to exceed the speed of 400 miles an hour—John Cobb—Bonneville Salt Flats, Utah—Sept. 16

utomobile Tire—tubeless automobile tires—announced—Akron, Ohio—May 11

viation—Airplane—airplane with eight engines —tested—Long Beach, Calif.—Nov. 2

viation—Airplane—bomber (all-wing jet)—tested—Hawthorne, Calif.—Oct. 21

Aviation—Airplane—jet-propelled fighter plane (four-engine)—tested—Columbus, Ohio—Sept. 15

Aviation—Airplane—jet propulsion four-engine bomber—flown—March 6

Aviation—Airplane—transatlantic robot pilotless airplane—takeoff—Sept. 22

Aviation—Airplane—twin-engine pressurized airplane—flown—March 16

Aviation—Flights—airplane to fly faster than 600 m.p.h.—Albert Boyd—Muroc Air Field, Calif.— June 19

Aviation—Flights—airplane to fly faster than the speed of sound—Muroc, Calif.—Oct. 14

Aviation—Flights (world)—round-the-world civil air service—left New York City—June 17

Aviation—Pilot—woman pilot to fly an airplane faster than 300 m.p.h.—Maggie Hurlburt—Tampa, Fla.—March 16

Bank—world bank—International Bank for Reconstruction and Development—loan—May 9

Baseball Player—black major-league baseball player—Jackie Robinson—New York City— April 11

Camera—camera to take, develop, and print pictures on photographic paper—demonstrated— E. H. Land—New York City—Feb. 21

Christmas Carols Association (national)—organized—St. Louis, Mo.—Jan. 20

College President—woman college president of two colleges—Rosemary Park—Connecticut College for Women, New London, Conn.—inaugurated May 17 (first)

Defense Department (U.S.)—authorized July 26— formed Sept. 17

Forest Fire—forest fire drenched by artificial rain —Concord, N.H.—Oct. 29

Glass—photosensitive glass—publicly announced—Corning, N.Y.—June 1

Golf Champion—woman golfer (American-born) to win the British Women's Amateur Golf Tournament—B. D. Zaharias—June 12

Helicopter—helicopter to deliver material across a picket line—New Bedford, Mass.—March 9

Helicopter—helicopter with a fully servo-controlled intermeshing rotor—flown—Windsor Locks, Conn.

Helicopter—ramjet helicopter—tested—St. Louis, Mo.—May 5

Insurance—insurance policy to be illustrated—issued—Chicago, Ill.—April 8

Isotope—radioactive isotopes exported—arrived —Canberra, Australia—Sept. 11

Lens—lens to provide zoom effects—demonstrated—New York City—April 16

Medal—Agriculture Department distinguished service gold medal—awarded—Nov. 12

Medical Clinic—cancer prevention clinic for children—opened—New York City—Jan. 3

Microcard—book on microcards—*The Scholar and the Future of the Research Library*

National Security Council (U.S.)—National Security Council—established—Washington, D.C.—July 26

Naval Officer—black commissioned officer in the regular U.S. Navy—John Lee—March 15

Navy—air squadron of jets (U.S. Navy)—Quonset Point, R.I.—July 23

News Correspondent—black news correspondent admitted to the House of Representatives and Senate press gallery—P. L. Prattis—accredited —Feb. 3

Nobel Prize—husband and wife in the United States to receive a joint Nobel Prize—C. F. and G. T. Cori—St. Louis, Mo.—award announced —Oct. 23

Postmaster—postmaster general appointed from the ranks—J. M. Donaldson—appointed—Nov. 24

Radar—radar for commercial and private planes —demonstrated—Culver City, Calif.—May 1

Representative (U.S.)—representative who had a Medal of Honor and was graduated from the U.S. Naval Academy—W. W. Bradley of California—began term, Jan. 3

Representative (U.S.)—representative who had lost both legs in World War II—C. E. Potter of Michigan—began congressional service Aug. 26

Rocket—ballistic missile—fired—May 22

Ship—air-conditioned naval ship—*Newport News*—launched—Newport News, Va.— March 6

Ship—ship from which a long-range rocket was launched—*Midway*—Sept. 6

Strike—strike to last longer than a year—J. I. Case Manufacturing Company, Racine, Wis.—strike ended—March 9

Telephone—commercial telephone service on railroad trains for passengers—began—Aug. 15

Telephone—mobile telephone conversation with commercial equipment—between an airplane and a moving automobile—Oct. 9

Telephone—mobile transatlantic telephone conversation between two telephone-equipped automobiles—June 26

Telescope—telescope lens 200 inches in diameter —completed—Oct. 3

Television—Telecast—baseball World Series game televised—New York City—Sept. 30

Television—Telecast—congressional opening session to be televised—Washington, D.C.— Jan. 3

Television—Telecast—drama series regularly scheduled—*Kraft Television Theater*—began May 7

Television—Telecast—presidential address televised from the White House—H. S. Truman— Washington, D.C.—Oct. 5

Television—Telecast—surgical operation (major) on a closed circuit, performed in one building and transmitted to another—New York Hospital to Waldorf Hotel in N.Y.C.—Sept. 11

Television—Telecast—surgical operation televised on a closed circuit—Baltimore, Md.—Feb. 27

Television—Telecast—underwater telecast from a submarine—New York City—April 10

Television Receiver—television receiver on seagoing vessel permanently installed—*New Jersey*—Nov. 20

Television Station—commercial television station west of the Mississippi River—Hollywood Calif.—Jan. 22

War Veterans' Society—World War II veteran society officially recognized by Congress— American Veterans of World War II—chartered—July 23

1948

Air Force Officer—Judge Advocate General of the U.S. Air Force—R. C. Harmon—nominated- Sept. 8

Airmail Service—parcel post domestic air service —began—Sept. 1

Airmail Service—parcel post international air service—to Europe—began—March 15

Army Auxiliary Corps—woman to become member of the Women's Army Corps—V. N Bates—sworn in—Washington, D.C.—July 8

Army Officer—woman army officer—sworn in—M. A. Hallaren—Dec. 3

Aureomycin—aureomycin chlortetracycline- produced—Pearl River, N.Y.

Aviation—Airplane—airplane with a delta wing —Convair—first flight, Muroc, Calif.—Sept. 1

Aviation—Airplane—jet-propelled fighter plane (four-engine)—tested—Muroc, Calif.—March

Aviation—Flights—airplane to fly faster than the speed of sound which was piloted by a civilian —H. H. Hoover—Edwards Air Force Base Calif.—March 10

Aviation—Flights (transatlantic)—jet transatlantic flight west–east—from Mount Clemens Mich.—July 20

Baseball Player—baseball player to win the Most Valuable Player Award three times—Stan Musial—third time

Baseball Player—black player to hit a home run in a World Series—L. E. Doby—Cleveland, Ohio —Oct. 9

Betatron—mobile betatron—operated—White Oak, Md.—Nov. 12

Birth Registration—birth registration uniform system for the numbering of birth certificates—approved—Aug. 30

Building—house completely solar-heated—occupied—Dover, Mass.—Dec. 24

Cantor—school for cantors—opened—Oct. 16

Church—woman moderator of the General Council of Congregational and Christian Churches— Helen Kenyon—elected—June 17

Diplomatic Service—ambassador to Israel—J. McDonald—began service July 2

Economic Cooperation Administration (U.S.)— Economic Cooperation Administration—authorized—April 3

Aviation—Flights—airplane to carry 100,000 pounds—takeoff, Fort Worth, Tex.—April 15

Aviation—Flights—airplane to carry 300 passengers on one flight—*Caroline Mars*—Alameda to San Diego, Calif.—May 19

Aviation—Flights (world)—round-the-world nonstop airplane flight—completed—March 2

Aviation—License—cargo airlines licensed by the Civil Aeronautics Board—effective—June 24

Aviation—Pilot—black flier of the U.S. Naval Reserve—J. L. Brown—commissioned—April 15

Aviation—School—Air Force survival school—conducted

Ballet Instruction—university to offer ballet technique instruction—Texas Christian University, Fort Worth, Tex.

Baseball Player—"most valuable player" award (major league) to a black—J. R. Robinson—Nov. 18

Belt Conveyor System—belt conveyor more than four miles long—installed

Bicycle Rider—bicycle rider to cross the continent in less than three weeks—Eugene McPherson—trip completed—New York City—Sept. 21

Birth Registration—birth registration uniform system for the numbering of birth certificates—began—Jan. 1

Congress (U.S.)—House of Representatives—congressional standing committee headed by a black—W. L. Dawson—appointed—Jan. 18

Court-Martial—court-martial trial at which enlisted men were allowed to sit as members of the court—convened—Heidelberg, Germany—Feb. 1

Court-Martial—court-martial trial in the United States at which enlisted men were allowed to sit as members of the court—convened—Fort Bragg, N.C.—Feb. 3

Degrees (academic and honorary)—honorary degree awarded a black woman—by a southern white college—M. M. Bethune—Winter Park, Fla.—Feb. 21

Diplomatic Service—ambassador (woman)—Eugenie Anderson—nominated—Oct. 12

Diplomatic Service—woman ambassador from a foreign country—S. V. L. Pandit of India—received—May 12

Electric Lighting—streetlight of an automatic system—installed—New Milford, Conn.—March 2

Element—element 97—berkelium—identified

Fog Disposal Unit—accepted by test—Los Angeles, Calif.—March 29

Heliport—heliport commercial base—New York City—first flight, May 18

Holiday—Flag Day federal legislation—enacted —Aug. 3

Locomotive—gas turbine-electric locomotive—demonstrated—Erie, Pa.—June 16

Medal—Distinguished Service Medal (Coast Guard)—established Aug. 4

Microfilm—magazine on microfilm offered to subscribers—*Newsweek*—New York City—June 1

Mosque—of importance—cornerstone laid—Washington, D.C.—Jan. 11

Motion Picture Actor—husband and wife Oscar winners—Vivien Leigh (for 1939) and Sir Larence Olivier (for 1948)—March 24

Motion Picture Actor—motion picture actor and son to receive Oscars—Walter and John Huston—presented—March 24

Museum—museum devoted exclusively to atomic energy—opened—Oak Ridge, Tenn.—March

Naval Academy—black midshipman in the United States Naval Academy to graduate—W. Brown—June 3

Photograph—photograph of genes—announced Los Angeles, Calif.—Jan. 7

Planetarium—planetarium owned by a university—opened—Chapel Hill, N.C.—May 10

Postal Card—airmail postal card—issued, Jan.

Public Health—public health service (U.S.) assistant surgeon general (woman)—Lucile Petry appointed—June 7

Radio Station—radio station owned and operated by blacks—opened—Atlanta, Ga.—Oct. 3

Railroad Car—dining car (all-electric)—placed service—March 9

Railroad Car—passenger car (ACF-Talgo)—tested—March 3

Rocket—rocket to reach outer space—fired White Sands Proving Grounds, N.M.—Feb.

Senator(U.S.)—woman elected to serve in both the House of Representatives and the Senate M. C. Smith of Maine—began service in Senate Jan. 3

Ship—air-conditioned naval ship—*Newport News*—commissioned—Jan. 29

Submarine—leaping submarine—*Pickerel*—commissioned—Portsmouth, N.H.—April 4

Submarine—submarine jet propulsion device patent—Fritz Zwicky—Pasadena, Calif.—Feb. 1

Synchrotron—synchrotron—installed at Radiation Laboratory, University of California Berkeley—full energy released—Jan. 17

Tape Recorder—tape-recording machine for mass production of tapes—announced—Minnesota Mining and Manufacturing Company, St. Paul, Minn.—Jan. 26

Telephone—dial-telephone long distance service —New York City to Oakland, Calif.—Oct. 1

Telescope—telescope lens 200 inches in diameter—used—Feb. 1

Television—community television antenna system—used—Astoria, Oreg.

Television—municipal television film unit—established—New York City—Feb. 15

Television—Telecast—medical intracity color telecast—Johns Hopkins Hospital—Baltimore, Md.—Dec. 6-9

Television—Telecast—serial daytime soap opera—*These Are My Children*—telecast—Chicago, Ill.—Jan. 31–Feb. 25

Television—Telecast—surgical operation televised on a closed circuit in color—presented Atlantic City, N.J.—June 6

Television—Telecast—variety talent show series with an all-black cast—Chicago, Ill.—April

elevision Award—National Academy of Television Arts and Sciences award—presentation—Los Angeles, Calif.—Jan. 25

elevision Station—ultra-high-frequency television station to operate on a regular daily basis—Bridgeport, Conn.—Dec. 29

elevision Tube—rectangular television tube (practical)—announced—Toledo, Ohio—July 10

reasury Department (U.S.)—woman treasurer of the United States—G. N. Clark—confirmed June 9—sworn in June 21

urbine—gas turbine to pump natural gas—installed—Wilmar, Ark.—May 13

urbine—gas turbine used by an electrical utility company—in service—July 29

ice President (U.S.)—Vice President to marry in office—A. W. Barkley—Nov. 18

orld War II—Japanese ballon casualties—congressional award made

1950

rmy Officer—general to command the forces of the United Nations in Korea—Douglas MacArthur—began service July 4

viation—Flights (transatlantic)—jet passenger international trip—April 18

viation—Flights (transatlantic)—jet transatlantic nonstop flight east–west—D. C. Schilling—Sept. 22

viation—Pilot—pilot to down two enemy fighter airplanes in one day in Korea—R. E. Wayne—June 27

viation—Pilot—jet plane combat victor in the Korean War—R. J. Brown—Nov. 8

aseball Manager—baseball manager to guide the same club on three different occasions—Bucky Harris

asketball Player—National Basketball Association—black player—C. H. Cooper—played—Fort Wayne, Ind.—Nov. 1

asketball Team—basketball collegiate team to win the National Collegiate Athletic Association trophy—second win—March 28

ensus—census in which the population of the United States exceeded 100 million—over 150 million in 1950 census

vil Defense Director—P. J. Larsen—assumed office—March 1

oal—coal pipeline loops (experimental)—built—Library, Pa.—May 23

plomatic Service—black delegate to the United Nations from the United States—E. S. Sampson—appointed—Aug. 24

ement—element 94—Nobel Prize presented—Stockholm, Sweden—Dec. 10

ement—element 98—californium—announced—March 17

arbage Collection—city to discontinue garbage collection—Jasper, Ind.—Aug. 1

elicopter—helicopter rescue of an American pilot behind enemy lines—accomplished—Sept. 4

Hockey Player—black player in organized hockey—Arthur Dorrington—signed—Nov. 15

Insurance—baby-sitters' insurance policy—issued—St. Louis, Mo.—Jan. 26

Judge—black judge of a circuit court of appeals—W. H. Hastie—appointment confirmed—July 19

Legislator (state)—husband and wife simultaneously elected to both chambers of a state legislature—Oregon—Nov. 7

Marine Corps—Marine Corps jet ace—J. F. Bolt—Nov. 18

Medal—Agriculture Department distinguished service gold medal presented to a woman—L. M. Alexander—May 25

Medal—Distinguished Flying Cross in the Korean War—R. E. Wayne—July 14

Medal—Medal of Honor awarded in the Korean War—presented—Sept. 30

Medal—Order of the Purple Heart awarded in the Korean War—presented—Leroy Deans—July 8

Medical Society—woman member of the Association of American Physicians—H. B. Taussig—elected—Atlantic City, N.J.—May 3

Merchant Marine Academy—Merchant Marine Cadet Corps (U.S.)—B.S. degree awarded—Kings Point, N.Y.—June 21

Milk—concentrated milk—sold—Wilmington, Del.—Nov. 30

Naval Officer—woman medical officer assigned to a naval vessel—B. R. Walters—assigned—March 8

Nobel Prize—black American to win the Nobel Peace Prize—R. J. Bunche—Dec. 10

Nuclear Engineering College Course—Raleigh, N.C.—students enrolled—June 12

Poet—black woman to win the Pulitzer Prize for poetry—Gwendolyn Brooks—May 1

Postage Stamp—Jew depicted on a postage stamp—Samuel Gompers—issued—Washington, D.C.—Jan. 27

Radio Paging Service—instituted—New York City—Oct. 15

Radio Station—all-local network—formed—May 15

Surgical Operation—kidney transplanting—Chicago, Ill.—June 17

Television—Telecast—Cabinet meeting (staged) telecast—Chicago, Ill.—May 14

Television—Telecast—X-ray fluoroscopy television discussion—Baltimore, Md.—Dec. 5

Television Station—illegal television station—Emporium, Pa.—closed—Oct. 19

Tennis Match—national tennis tournament of the United States Lawn Tennis Association in which a black woman competed—Forest Hills, N.Y.

Terramycin—announced—Jan. 27

Transistor—phototransistor—invention announced—Murray Hill, N.J.—March 30

Typesetting Machine—typesetting machine to dispense with metal type—exhibited—Chicago, Ill.—Sept. 11

War (Korean)—American pilot to destroy an enemy airplane in the Korean War—W. G. Hudson—June 26

War (Korean)—American tank crew to cross the 38th Parallel in Korea—Oct. 7

War (Korean)—Korean War hero buried in Arlington National Cemetery—H. G. Thomas—Aug. 14

War (Korean)—officer killed in action in the Korean War—R. R. Martin—July 8

War (Korean)—soldier killed in the Korean War—Kenneth Shadrick—July 5

War (Korean)—South Korean combat mission—occurred—June 27

X ray—fluoro-record reflector camera—announced—Jamaica, N.Y.—Nov. 18

1951

Atomic Bomb—atomic bomb underground explosion—detonated—Frenchman Flat, Nev.—Nov. 29

Atomic Bomb—atomic explosion witnessed by troops—New Mexico—Nov. 1

Atomic Energy—electrical power from nuclear energy—obtained—Idaho Falls, Idaho

Atomic Energy Commission—Atomic Energy Commission Patent Compensation Board award—C. E. McClellan—Nov. 21

Atomic Reactor—atomic reactor in medical therapy—Brookhaven National Laboratory, Upton, L.I., N.Y.—began operation, Feb. 15

Automobile—right-hand-drive automobile for the delivery of mail—in service—Cincinnati, Ohio—Dec. 27

Aviation—air passenger-mile traffic volume to exceed first-class rail traffic volume—occurred

Aviation—Flights—jet passenger trip—made—Jan. 10

Aviation—Flights—North Pole flight in a single-engine airplane—C. F. Blair—May 29

Aviation—Flights—North Pole jet crossing—Sept. 20

Aviation—Pilot—American ace (jet)—James Jabara

Baseball Player—baseball rookie to hit a grand slam home run in the World Series—G. J. McDougald—New York City—Oct. 9

Basketball Game—all-star game of the National Basketball Association—Boston, Mass.—March 2

Battery—battery to convert radioactive energy into electrical energy—announced—P. E. Ohmart—Dec. 31

Coal—coal pipeline unit (demonstration)—Cadiz, Ohio—Nov. 1

Computer—electronic computer (commercial)—dedicated—Philadelphia, Pa.—June 14

Dacron—dacron men's suits—introduced—New York City—May 8

Flag—Air Force flag—approved—March 26

Football—football with a rubber covering used in a major collegiate game—Atlanta, Ga.—Oct. 13

Garage—completely automatic push-button-controlled garage—opened—Washington, D.C.—Dec. 5

Helicopter—gas-turbine helicopter (turborotor)—tested—Windsor Locks, Conn.—Dec. 10

Horse—horse to win $1 million in races—Citation—July 14

Hotel—hotel with all-foam-rubber mattresses, pillows, and furniture cushions—opened—Fort Worth, Tex.—Oct. 7

Jewish Congregation—Jewish congregation to call a woman to exercise a rabbi's function—Paula Ackerman—Meridian, Miss.—Jan. 26

Kenaf Fiber—planting of commercial importance—Belle Glade, Fla.

Medal—Air Force Medal of Honor for action in the Korean War—L. J. Sebille—presented—Riverside, Calif.—Aug. 24

Medal—Medal of Honor awarded to a marine in the Korean War—H. A. Commiskey—Aug. 1

Medal—Medal of Honor (posthumous) to a black in the Korean War—W. H. Thompson—presented June 21

Microscope—microscope for examining structure of materials—installed—Schenectady, N.Y.

Motion Picture—motion picture of the inside of a living heart (of a dog)—shown—New York City—Oct. 16

Newspaper Reporter—newspaper reporter to become a U.S. senator—Blair Moody—appointed April 23—sworn in April 25

Postage Stamp—United Nations postage stamp in U.S. denominations—first on sale, New York City—Oct. 24

President (U.S.)—presidential press conference recorded on tape—H. S. Truman—Washington, D.C.—Jan. 25

Rocket—air-to-air rocket—*Mighty Mouse*—placed in production

Rocket—rocket to intercept an airplane—White Sands Proving Grounds, N.M.—Nov. 27

Senator (U.S.)—senator to preside over a Senate session directly after being sworn in as a senator—Blair Moody of Michigan—April 25

Spy—peacetime death sentence for espionage—Julius Rosenberg and Ethel Rosenberg—New York City—guilty verdict, March 29—sentence imposed, April 5

Telephone—dial telephone service coast-to-coast without the aid of operators—commercial inaugurated—Nov. 10

Telephone—telephone company answering service—offered—Ohio Bell Telephone Co.

Teletypesetter—teletypesetter circuit operated by a news agency—established—Charlotte, N.C.—April 23

Television—college credit course in television offered—Marquette University—Milwaukee, Wis.

Television—television eyewitness allowed to testify in a federal court—Sophie Eisenberg—New York City

Television—Telecast—atomic explosion telecast—Feb. 1

Radio Station—seagoing radio broadcasting station—*Courier*—test broadcast—April 2

Railroad Car—"compartmentizer" freight cars—in service—Sept. 12

Representative (U.S.)—mother and son simultaneously elected to Congress—Ohio—Nov. 4

Ship—aircraft carrier to sail around Cape Horn—*Oriskany*—passed Cape Horn—June 29

Ship—aircraft carrier with an angle deck—*Forrestal*—laid down—July 14

Siamese Twins—Siamese twins to survive a separation operation and live for one year—born—Dec. 14—Cleveland, Ohio

Soda Water—sugar-free drink—NoCal—Hyman Kirsch—College Point, N.Y.

Submarine—atomic-powered submarine—*Nautilus*—keel laid—Groton, Conn.—June 14

Submarine—submarine expressly designed and built to fire guided missiles—*Grayback*—ordered—June 19

Submarine—submarine powered by a liquid-metal-cooled atomic reactor—*Seawolf*—ordered—July 19

Surgical Operation—artificial aortic valve—successfully fitted—Washington, D.C.—Sept. 11

Surgical Operation—heart operation in which the deep-freezing technique was employed—Minneapolis, Minn.—Sept. 2

Surgical Operation—mitral valve exposure (prolonged) in a human patient and corrective surgery—Detroit, Mich.—July 3

Tape Recording—video recording on magnetic tape—Los Angeles, Calif.—Oct. 3

Television—Telecast—atomic explosion telecast on a network—News Nob, Nev.—April 22

Television—Telecast—birth (human) to be televised for the public—Denver, Colo.—Dec. 2

Television—Telecast—husband and wife to broadcast a religious program—Dr. and Mrs. N. V. Peale—New York City—Oct. 1

Television—Telecast—pay television presentation of a sporting event—Philadelphia, Pa.—Sept. 23

Television—Telecast—pay television presentation of an opera—*Carmen*—New York City—Dec. 11

Television—Telecast—surgical operation televised coast-to-coast—Chicago, Ill.—June 10

Television—Telecast—surgical operation televised on a local program—Philadelphia, Pa.—March 16

Television Station—television network sales to exceed those of radio

Television Station—ultra-high-frequency commercial television station—Portland, Oreg.—Oct. 1

Vice Presidential Candidate—black woman vice presidential candidate—C. A. Bass—Progressive Party—nominated—Chicago, Ill.—July 5

Yiddish Professorship—established—Columbia University—New York City—Feb. 11

1953

Advertisement—three-dimensional newspape advertisement—*Daily Freeman*—Waukesh Wis.—June 12

Anesthesia—trifluorethyl vinyl ether—adminis tered—Chicago, Ill.—April 10

Army Officer—woman doctor commissioned i the regular Army—F. M. Adams—sworn in—March 11

Atomic Reactor—atomic reactor (large) to specif cally produce power—Idaho Falls, Idaho—be gan operation—May 31

Atomic Reactor—atomic reactor (privately ope ated)—Raleigh, N.C.—Sept. 5

Automobile—artmobile—tours began, Frede icksburg, Va.—October

Automobile—plastic-laminated fiberglass-bod sportscar—manufactured—Flint, Mich.—Jur 30

Automobile—transparent-top automobile—pr duction announced—Detroit, Mich.—Dec. 7

Automobile Bus—transcontinental no-chang bus service—began—Sept. 8

Aviation—airline to install rear-facing passeng seats—flight—June 1

Aviation—Flights—airplane to fly faster tha 1,300 m.p.h.—Scott Crossfield—Nov. 20

Aviation—Flights (transatlantic)—jet transatla tic nonstop flight west–east—April 7

Aviation—Flights (transcontinental)—transcon nental nonstop eastward scheduled service began—Oct. 19

Aviation—Flights (transcontinental)—transcon nental regularly scheduled two-way nonsto service—began—Nov. 29

Aviation—Pilot—naval ace in Korea—Guy Bo delon—fifth victory—July 17

Aviation—Pilot—woman to pilot an airplane fa er than the speed of sound—Jacqueline Coc ran—May 18

Baseball Team—baseball team to win five Wor Series in succession—N.Y. Yankees—Oct. 5

Boiler—carbon monoxide boiler—operated Houston, Tex.

Building—aluminum-faced building—Alc Building—Pittsburgh, Pa.—completed, Aug. 1 dedicated, Sept. 15

Building—building for telephone directory com lation and printing—dedicated—Des Plaine Ill.—April 30

Building—building with its roof supported by c bles—J. S. Dorton Arena, Raleigh, N.C.—co pleted and dedicated

Burglar Alarm—burglar alarm operated by ult sonic or radio waves—patented—Samuel B no—Oct. 13

Business—department store to sell apartments Philadelphia, Pa.—Jan. 13

Business—department store to sell insurance Chicago, Ill.—Sept. 29

Cabinet (U.S.)—Cabinet conference telecas Washington, D.C.—June 3

Cabinet (U.S.)—Secretary of Health, Education, and Welfare—O. C. Hobby—sworn in—April 11

Carpeting—carpeting of tufted plastic—offered for sale—La Fayette, Ga.—Jan. 4

Catholic Bishop—Catholic bishop (black) consecrated in the United States—J. O. Bowers—St. Louis, Miss.—April 22

Catholic Priest—Catholic cardinal whose see was west of the Rockies—J. F. McInytre—elevated —Jan. 12

Catholic Seminarians (black) to be ordained to the priesthood by a black bishop—St. Louis, Miss. —June 29

Censorship—state board of censorship on literature—authorized—Feb. 19

Congress (U.S.)—House of Representatives— Speaker of the House of Representatives to serve longer than 10 years—S. T. Rayburn— ended service Jan. 3

Degrees (academic and honorary)—Bachelor of Sacred Music degree—conferred—New York City—June 10

Dictionary—Mongolian-English English-Mongolian dictionary—published

Diplomatic Service—ambassador (woman) to a major nation—C. B. Luce—sworn in March 3

Diplomatic Service—woman career diplomat advanced to the rank of ambassador—F. E. Willis —sworn in—Aug. 10

Element—element 100—fermium—identified

Federal Security Agency—became Department of Health, Education, and Welfare—April 11

Fraternity (Greek-Letter)—scholastic fraternity chapter established at a university for blacks— Phi Beta Kappa—Fisk University—Nashville, Tenn.—April 4

Helicopter—helicopter fully operated by remote control—built—Windsor Locks, Conn.

Helicopter—helicopter passenger service—began —New York City—July 9

Hospital—hospital completely devoted to the study of the atom in the treatment of cancer— Argonne Cancer Research Hospital—Chicago, Ill.—opened—March 13

Hotel—hotel to establish a heliport—Fort Worth, Tex.—opened—May 20

Ice Skating Champion—American world figure skating champion—Tenley Albright—Feb. 15

Immigration—Japanese national to receive an immigration visa—Sozaburo Kujiraoka—Feb. 22

Jockey—jockey to ride 400 winners in one year— Willie Shoemaker

Library Society—Melvil Dewey medal—presented to R. R. Shaw—Los Angeles, Calif.— June 24

Locomotive—gas-turbine propane-fueled locomotive—in service—June 8

Medal—National Security Medal—established— Jan. 19

Medal—Navy-Marine Corps Medal for Heroism awarded to a woman—B. O. Barnwell—Aug. 7

Medal—Reserve Officers Association medal— presented—H. S. Truman—Jan. 15

Monument—national monument dedicated to a black American—G. W. Carver monument— dedicated—July 14

Motion Picture—animated three-dimensional cartoon in Technicolor (modern)—*Melody*—premiere—May 28

Motion Picture—three-dimensional feature motion picture—*Bwana Devil*—shown—New York City—Feb. 18

Motion Picture—three-dimensional feature motion picture in color—*The House of Wax*— shown—New York City—April 10

Motion Picture—three-dimensional feature motion picture produced and released by a major company—*Man in the Dark*—premiere—New York City—April 8

Naval Officer—naval officer to serve as chairman of the Joint Chiefs of Staff—A. W. Radford— began service Aug. 15

Navy—Podiatry Section of the Navy—established—Nov. 3

Nobel Prize—Nobel Prize for peace to a professional soldier—awarded to G. C. Marshall— Dec. 10

Oil—plastic pipeline to transport oil cross-country—Williston, Mont. (start of line)—in service, Oct. 19

Ordnance—atomic cannon—electronically fired —Frenchman Flat, Nev.—May 25

Pituitary Hormone—polypeptide hormone synthesized—announced

Railroad Car—observation cars (superdome)—in service—Jan. 1

Representative (U.S.)—mother and son simultaneously elected to Congress—Ohio—began service Jan. 3

Road—electronic highway system—demonstrated—Princeton, N.J.—June

Road—interchange structure of 4 levels—built— Los Angeles, Calif.—opened, Sept. 22

Senator (U.S.)—father whose 3 sons were senators—J. P. Kennedy—J. F. Kennedy sworn in on Jan. 3

Ship—woman to sail solo across the Atlantic Ocean—Ann Davidson—arrived—Miami, Fla. —Aug. 12

Siamese Twins—Siamese twins separated successfully by surgery—Sept. 17

Spy—peacetime death sentence for espionage— Julius Rosenberg and Ethel Rosenberg—electrocuted—Ossining, N.Y.—June 19

Submarine—submarine powered by a liquid-metal-cooled atomic reactor—*Seawolf*—laid down —Sept. 15

Television—Telecast—Academy of Motion Picture Arts and Sciences annual awards telecast —New York City and Hollywood, Calif.— March 19

Television—Telecast—Catholic mass televised from a studio—Boston, Mass.—June 10

Television—Telecast—color and black-and-white telecast to be sponsored—presented—Dec. 24

Television—Telecast—color coast-to-coast live telecast—New York City—Nov. 3

Television—Telecast—color network telecast in compatible color—Boston, Mass.—June 7

Television—Telecast—color program on coast-to-coast network commercial—New York City—Nov. 22

Television—Telecast—color telecast by a local station—Philadelphia, Pa.—Dec. 18

Television—Telecast—color telecast on a closed-circuit local station—Philadelphia, Pa.—Oct. 30

Television—Telecast—opera from the Metropolitan Opera House especially tailored and trimmed for television—*Die Fledermaus*—telecast—Feb. 1

Television—Telecast—opera (major) televised in color—*Carmen*—New York City—Oct. 31

Television—Telecast—opera written for television on commission for a commercial sponsor—New York City—March 24

Television—Telecast—pay television presentation of a motion picture shown simultaneously in theaters—Palm Springs, Calif.—Nov. 28

Television—Telecast—rodeo telecast coast to coast—Will Rogers Memorial Coliseum, Fort Worth, Tex.—Jan. 31

Television—Telecast—telecast transmitted to Canada—from Buffalo, N.Y.—Jan. 20

Television—Telecast—three-dimensional telecast—KECA-TV, Los Angeles, Calif.—April 29

Television Station—noncommercial educational television station—began programs—Houston, Tex.—May 25

Television Station—television network sales to exceed those of radio—FCC announced—July 31

Television Station—television stations to share the same time and frequency—Salinas and Monterey, Calif.—Sept. 11

Tennis Player—woman tennis grand slam winner—Maureen Connolly—Sept. 7

Tour of the World—passenger to fly around the world on commercial airlines in less than 100 hours—H. C. Boren—arrived—New York City—June 25

Treason—execution for treason in peacetime—Ossining, N.Y.—June 19

Typesetting Machine—photographic type-composing machine—Photon—manufactured

Vice President (U.S.)—Vice President to preside at a National Security Council meeting—R. M. Nixon—July 14

1954

Air Force Academy (U.S.)—Air Force Academy—authorized—April 1

Air Force Officer—brigadier general (black) in the Air Force—B. O. Davis—Oct. 27

Army—ballistic missile operational unit—completed training—Fort Bliss, Tex.

Army—helicopter battalion—formed—Fort Bragg, N.C.—April 1

Athlete—black to win the James E. Sullivan Memorial Trophy—M. G. Whitfield—Dec. 30

Automobile—gas-turbine automobile—exhibited—New York City—Jan. 21

Automobile Bus—gas-turbine bus—announced—Detroit, Mich.—June 10

Automobile School—truck-driving training school—Bedford, Pa.—graduation—July 31

Aviation—jet drone target missile—flown—Alamogordo, N.Mex.—April 23

Aviation—Airplane—jet transport commercial airplane built in the United States—tested—Renton, Wash.—July 15

Aviation—Flights—airship to exceed 200 hours in flight nonstop without refueling—takeoff, Lakehurst, N.J.—May 17

Aviation—Flights (world)—round-the-world flight over the North Pole on a regularly scheduled commercial air route—began—Nov. 15

Baseball Game—major-league game in which the majority of the players on one team were black—Brooklyn Dodgers—July 17

Battery—solar battery—announced—New York City—April 25

Bevatron—in operation—Berkeley, Calif.—Feb. 15

Bridge (game)—bridge hand in which each of the 4 players was dealt a perfect hand—Irene Motta—Cranston, R.I.—March 12

Cabinet (U.S.)—black sub-Cabinet member—J. E. Wilkins—appointed—March 4

Cabinet (U.S.)—secretary to the Cabinet and presidential assistant—M. M. Rabb—appointed—Nov. 22

Civil Defense—civil defense test (nationwide)—June 14

College—college for women under Jewish auspices—Stern College for Women—opened—New York City—Sept. 13

Court-Martial—court-martial trial of an officer for collaborating with his captors—Fort Sheridan, Ill.—Sept. 23

Electric Power Plant—atomic electric-generating station (full-scale)—ground breaking—Shippingport, Pa.—Sept. 6

Engraving and Printing Bureau (U.S.)—souvenir card of the Bureau of Engraving and Printing—issued—Philadelphia, Pa.—March 13

Execution—execution (federal) for the killing of a Federal Bureau of Investigation agent—Gerhard Puff—executed—Aug. 12

Garage—hydraulic lift parking device—installed—Washington, D.C.

Governor—governor to appoint two United States senators in one year for interim terms—Robert Crosby—Nebraska

Helicopter—twin gas-turbine helicopter (turbomotor)—flown—Bloomfield, Conn.—March 26

Heliport—military heliport—dedicated—Fort Eustis, Va.—Dec. 7

Horse Race—horse race in which the British Royal Silks participated—Laurel, Md.—Nov.

Immigration—refugee to arrive under the Refugee Relief Act of 1953—Jan. 1

Lieutenant Governor—woman lieutenant governor—C. N. Bailey—Vermont—elected Nov. 2

Medicine—tissue bank—Bethesda, Md.

Meteorite—meteorite known to have struck a woman—Sylacauga, Ala.—Nov. 30

Microbiology Laboratory—dedicated—New Brunswick, N.J.—June 7

National Security Council (U.S.)—National Security Council meeting held outside Washington, D.C.—Denver, Colo.—Sept. 13

Newspaper—newspaper printed on bagasse newsprint—*Daily World*—published—Opelousas, La.—Feb. 11

Nobel Prize—recipient of 2 full Nobel prizes—L. C. Pauling—first award (chemistry)—Dec. 10

Plastic—expandable polystyrene production (commercial)—Kobuta, Pa.

President (U.S.)—presidential airplane (turbocompound-powered)—christened—Nov. 24

Prison System—woman to direct a prison system—A. M. Kross—New York City—sworn in, Jan. 1

Protestant Church—Reformed Dutch Church black pastor—installed—New York City—Nov. 14

Radio Broadcast—editorial broadcast over a network—Frank Stanton—CBS network—Aug. 26

Radio Receiver—transistor radio receiver—manufactured—Indianapolis, Ind.

Radio Sextant—announced—Cedar Rapids, Iowa —July 14

Radio Station—black network—formed—Jan. 20

Railroad—railroad freight yard fully automatic—Gary, Ind.—Dec. 17

Rocket—rocket to exceed a 150-mile altitude—White Sands Proving Grounds, N.Mex.—May 24

Rocket Sled—rocket-driven sled on rails—tested —Alamogordo, N.Mex.—March 19

Senator (U.S.)—senator elected by a write-in vote —J. S. Thurmond—South Carolina—Nov. 2

Senator (U.S.)—woman senator to succeed a woman senator—H. H. Abel—elected—Nov. 2

Ship—aircraft carrier with an angle deck—*Forrestal*—launched—Newport News, Va.—Dec. 11

Ship—liquid-bulk-chemical carrier—*Marine Dow Chem*—first run, from Freeport, Tex.—arrived New York City—April 13

Shot Put—shot-put toss over 60 feet—Parry O'Brien—Los Angeles, Calif.—May 8

Sidewalk (traveling)—sidewalk (traveling) in a railroad station—Jersey City, N.J.—May 24

Submarine—atomic-powered submarine—*Nautilus*—launched—Groton, Conn.—Jan. 21

Submarine—submarine expressly designed and built to fire guided missiles—*Grayback*—laid down—Mare Island, Calif.—July 1

Submarine—submarine of the U.S. Navy christened by a President's wife—*Nautilus*—M. G. D. Eisenhower—Groton, Conn.—Jan. 21

Supreme Court (U.S.)—page (black)—C. V. Bush —began service, Sept. 27

Telegraph—telegraph code converter—announced—Stamford, Conn.

Television—television industry profits to exceed those of radio—reported Dec. 16

Television—Mobile Unit—mobile television units (color)—operated—New York City—Jan. 1

Television—Telecast—Cabinet session to be televised—Washington, D.C.—Oct. 25

Television—Telecast—color coast-to-coast telecast from the West Coast—Tournament of Roses—Pasadena, Calif.—Jan. 1

Television—Telecast—color commercial televised on a local show—commissioned—New York City—March 9

Television—Telecast—color film (35mm) telecast —June 25

Television—Telecast—dirigible telecast—Pasadena, Calif.—Dec. 31

Television—Telecast—editorial opinion telecast on a network—Frank Stanton—Aug. 26

Television—Telecast—medical symposium televised coast-to-coast on a closed circuit—New York City—Sept. 23

Television—Telecast—phase-contrast cinemicrography film (American-made) telecast—*The Birth of a Plant*—Feb. 28

Television—Telecast—prizefight in a "studio"—Philadelphia, Pa.—Sept. 1

Television—Telecast—prizefight televised in color—New York City—March 19

Television—Telecast—split-screen image (four ways)—shown—Nov. 2

Television—Telecast—state legislative hearing telecast—New Jersey—April 11

Television Receiver—television receiver to permit two audiences to see and hear two different programs at the same time—demonstrated—Jan. 7

Tennis Match—intercollegiate court tennis match —New York City—May 4

Toll Collector (automatic)—operated—Garden State Parkway, N.J.—Nov. 19

Typesetting Machine—photoengraving high-speed process for making halftones—used—Quincy, Mass.—Feb. 26

Vending Machine—newspaper vending machine to deliver a single copy—manufactured, Columbia, Pa.—leased, March 20

War (French Indochina)—American civilian pilot wounded in Indochina—P. R. Holden—April 24

Water Skier—water skier to jump 100 feet—Warren Witherell—Laconia, N.H.—Aug. 15

Welding—aluminum-pipe welding machine (automatic)—working model tested—White Point, Tex.

1955

Air Force Academy (U.S.)—Air Force Academy—temporary headquarters established—Denver, Colo.—July 11

Airmail Service—helicopter airmail and express service to carry passengers—began—Nov. 22

Aquatic Mammals—dugong—arrived—San Francisco, Calif.—Nov. 16

Army Officer—Army Medical Specialist Corps male officer—Sheldon Saffren—commissioned—Dec. 30

Army Officer—male nurse—E. L. T. Lyon—sworn in—Oct. 6

Atomic Reactor—atomic reactor patent—Enrico Fermi and Leo Szilard—May 17

Automobile—gas-turbine automobile operated on city streets—Detroit, Mich.—April 19

Automobile—sun-powered automobile—demonstrated—Chicago, Ill.—Aug. 31

Automobile Legislation—automobile seat belt safety legislation—enacted—Illinois—June 27

Aviation—Airplane—jet magnesium airplane—flown—June 11

Aviation—Flights—airplane to fly faster than 800 m.p.h.—H. A. Hanes—Palmdale, Calif.—Aug. 20

Aviation—Flights (transcontinental)—transcontinental round-trip solo flight between sunrise and sunset—J. M. Conroy—May 21

Aviation—Parachute—pilot to bail out of an airplane flying at supersonic speed—G. F. Smith—Feb. 26

Bank—bank to operate a window in a subway station for the convenience of subway riders—New York City—opened—Sept. 26

Battery—solar energy battery—shipment—June 1

Bridge (game) Player—father and son team to win a national contract bridge championship—Oswald Jacoby and James Jacoby—Miami Beach, Fla.—Dec. 1

Building—atom-bomb-resistant federal building—dedicated—Washington, D.C.—May 23

Building—solar-heated and radiation-cooled house—used—Tucson, Ariz.—Jan. 15

Cabinet (U.S.)—Cabinet session held at a place other than the seat of the United States Government—Gettysburg, Pa.—Nov. 22

Cantor—Jewish woman cantor—Betty Robbins—first service—Oceanside, N.Y.—Sept. 15

Cobra—king cobra snakes—born in captivity—New York City—July 4

Corporation—corporation to earn more than $1 billion in one year—Detroit, Mich.

Diamond—pilot plant for the actual production of artificial diamonds—production announced—Schenectady, N.Y.—Feb. 15

Drill—oil drill seagoing rig—placed in service—March 24

Electric Power Plant—electric power generated from atomic energy to be sold commercially—July 18

Electric Power Plant—electric power generated from atomic energy to illuminate an entire town—Arco, Ida.—July 17

Element—element 101—mendelevium—announced—April 30

Helicopter—aerocycle—purchased by U.S. Army—Dec. 29

Horse—forest horse—imported

Horse—trotter triple-crown winner—Scott Fros—(Hambletonian at Goshen, N.Y.) Aug. 3—(Yonkers Futurity in Yonkers, N.Y.) Sept. 1—(Kentucky Futurity in Lexington, Ky.) Oct 6

Jewish Congregation—Jewish mobile synagogu—operated—April 4

Lieutenant Governor—woman lieutenant gover nor—C. N. Bailey—sworn in Montpelier, Vt.—Jan 6

Medal—Medal of Honor awarded to a helicopte pilot—J. K. Koelsch—conferred posthumousl—April 8

Medical Society—woman president of a majo medical society—E. S. Moss—elected—Oct. 1

Methodist Church—black Methodist minister o an all-white congregation—S. P. Montgomery—Old Mystic, Conn.—Oct. 2

Motorboat—motorboat to travel at a speed c 216.2 m.p.h.—D. M. Campbell—Lake Mea Nev.—Nov. 16

Opera—black singer of the Metropolitan Opera—Marian Anderson—appeared—New York Cit—Jan. 7

Periodical—magazine to contain a phonograp record—Pageant—New York City—Oct. 10

Postage Stamp—certified-mail stamp—issued—Washington, D.C.—June 6

President (U.S.)—President telecast in color—D. D. Eisenhower—West Point, N.Y.—June 6—program on view, June 7

President (U.S.)—President to fly in a twin-en gined airplane—D. D. Eisenhower—June 3

Radar—offshore radar warning station—launched—May 20

Radio Broadcast—stereophonic sound progra broadcast by separately owned stations—pr sented—Nov. 5

Railroad Car—passenger car (ACF-Talgo for us in the United States)—completed—April 22

Railroad Car—remote-control railroad passenge car—between New Rochelle, N.Y., and Ry N.Y.—put in operation Dec. 1

School—air-conditioned public elementar school—opened—San Angelo, Tex.

Ship—guided missile cruiser—Boston—conver ed—Philadelphia, Pa.—Nov. 1

Ship—roll-on, roll-off carrier—Searoad—in se vice—Sept. 1

Ship—speedboat to exceed 200 miles an hour—M. Campbell—Nov. 16

Soldiers' Home—woman admitted to a soldier home—R. C. Jones—Washington, D.C.—Sept.—permanent admission granted, Sept. 16

State Department (U.S.)—woman acting assista Secretary of State—Florence Kirlin—Sept. 3

Stove—electronic range for domestic use—intr duced—New York City—Oct. 25

Submarine—submarine powered by a liquid-me al-cooled atomic reactor—Seawolf—launche—Groton, Conn.—July 21

Surgical Operation—lung tumor operation i which the patient was under hypnosis—pe formed—Los Angeles, Calif.

Motion Picture Actor—motion picture actress depicted on a postage stamp—Grace Kelly—stamps issued—April 19

Navy—naval expedition to the South Pole—G. J. Dufek—landed Oct. 31

Nobel Prize—Nobel Prize 2-time winner in the same category—John Bardeen—(first shared prize) Dec. 10

Postal Card—commemorative postal card—issued—New York City—May 4

Postal Card—Statue of Liberty depicted on a postal card—issued—New York City—Nov. 16

Presbyterian Church—woman ordained a minister in the Presbyterian Church—M. E. Towner—Syracuse, N.Y.—Oct. 24

Radio Receiver—radio receiver with an auxiliary silicon unit to convert the rays of the sun into electrical power—offered for sale—April 16

Railroad Car—freight car (Adapto Car)—in service—July 24

Railroad Car—passenger car (ACF-Talgo for use in the United States)—in service—Feb. 11

Railroad Signal Light—atomic-powered signal light—manufactured—Morristown, N.J.—November

Representative (U.S.)—representative of Asian ancestry—D. S. Saund—elected—Nov. 6

Representative (U.S.)—representative reelected after serving a prison term—T. J. Lane—reelected—Massachusetts—Nov. 6

Runner—runner to run a mile under four minutes —in the U.S.—Jim Bailey—Los Angeles, Calif. —May 5

Ship—atomic-powered merchant ship—Savannah—authorized—July 30

Ship—ballistic-missile test ship—Compass Island —acquired by U.S. Navy, March 29—tested at sea, Nov. 19—commissioned—New York City —Dec. 3

Ship—gyro-stabilized American liner—Mariposa —christened—Oct. 16

Ship—ship outfitted for hurricane research—Crawford—in service—July 3

Space Cabin—D. F. Smith—24 hours within cabin

Stroboradiograph — announced — Schenectady, N.Y.—Aug. 14

Submarine—atomic-powered submarine built at a naval shipyard—Swordfish—laid down—Portsmouth, N.H.—Jan. 25

Submarine—submerged circumnavigation of the earth—Triton—laid down—May 21

Surgical Operation—heart operation in which the elective-cardiac-arrest technique was employed—performed—Cleveland, Ohio

Surgical Operation—lobotomy (prefrontal)—performed—Washington, D.C.—Sept. 14

Taconite—taconite—large-scale commercial production—began—Sept. 13

Tape Recorder—magnetic tape recorder (commercial) of sound and picture—demonstrated—April 14

Tape Recording—video recording on magnetic tape televised coast-to-coast—presented—Oct. 23

Telephone—telephone conversation over the transoceanic telephone cable—Sept. 25

Television—Telecast—instruction (large-scale operation) telecast closed circuit—offered—Washington County, Md.—in September

Television Station—all-color station to televise live local programs—WNBQ-TV—Chicago, Ill —April 15

Television Station—statewide and state-supported educational television network—opened—Alabama—Aug. 9

1957

Air Force—air force class trained to fire intercontinental missiles—completed course—Hawthorne, Calif.—Dec. 17

Air Force Academy (U.S.)—Air Force Academy woman officer—N. M. McCracken—Denver Colo.—April 26

Air Force Officer—Air Force chairman of the Joint Chiefs of Staff—N. F. Twining—sworn in—Aug 15

Atomic Reactor—military nuclear power plant—dedicated—Fort Belvoir, Va.—April 29

Atomic Reactor—sodium reactor (experimental) —operated—April 25

Aviation—Flights (world)—jet round-the-world nonstop flight—completed—Jan. 18

Aviation—Parachute—parachute jump from an airplane from a 53,000-foot altitude—J. D. Nole —Del Rio, Tex.—Sept. 26

Aviation—Pilot—black airplane pilot on a scheduled passenger line—P. H. Young—began flights—Feb. 1

Balloon—Flights—balloon flight to exceed an altitude of 100,000 feet—D. G. Simons—Crosby Minn.—Aug. 19

Building—aluminum geodesic-dome civic center —Virginia Beach, Va.—opened May 15

Building—bronze and glass skyscraper—completed—New York City

Building—commercial building heated by the sun —completed—Albuquerque, N.Mex.—Aug. 1

Clock—electric watch—introduced—Lancaster Pa.—Jan. 3

Coal—commercial coal pipeline—placed in operation—June 4

Court-Martial—court-martial trial of an officer for collaborating with his captors—decision sustained—Feb. 8

Cryotrons—publicly reported—Cambridge, Mass —Feb. 6

Curling Championship (national)—held—Chicago, Ill.—March 28-30

Discovery—northwest passage—charted

Electric Power Plant—atomic electric-generating station (full-scale)—power generated—Shippingport, Pa.—Dec. 2

Element—element 102—nobelium—announced—July 9

Installment Sales Law—enacted—New York—April 17

Insurance—insurance company to exclusively insure the lives of animals—New York City—founded Aug. 1

Jockey—jockey to win more than $3 million in purses in 1 year—William Hartack, Jr.

Medal—recipient of the four highest decorations awarded by the United States—W. J. Donovan—fourth medal—April 4

Naval Officer—woman to preside as law officer—M. L. McDowell—appointed—Feb. 11

Newspaper—newspaper to insert an aluminum foil sheet—*Sentinel*—Milwaukee, Wis.—April 2

Playwright—playwright to win a Pulitzer Prize 4 times for drama—E. G. O'Neill—4th award, May 6

Postage Stamp—postage stamp in 3 colors printed in 1 passing of each sheet through the press—American flag stamp—issued—Washington, D.C.—July 4

President (U.S.)—President to fly in a helicopter—D. D. Eisenhower—July 12

Representative (U.S.)—representative of Asian ancestry—D. S. Saund—sworn in Jan. 3

Rocket—intermediate-range ballistic missile—fired—Cape Canaveral, Fla.—May 31

Rocket—rocket cone recovery—accomplished—Aug. 8

Rocket—rocket with an atomic warhead—fired—Yucca Flat, Nev.—July 19

Runner—runner (American) to run a mile in less than four minutes—Don Bowden—Stockton, Calif.—June 1

Senator (U.S.)—senator to filibuster for more than 24 hours—Strom Thurmond of South Carolina—Aug. 28-29

Ship—aircraft carrier (atomic-powered)—*Enterprise*—ordered—Aug. 16

Ship—atomic-powered cruiser—*Long Beach*—keel laid—Dec. 2

Ship—guided missile destroyer—*Dewey*—keel laid—Bath, Me.—Aug. 10

Ship—ship to circumnavigate the North American continent—*Spar*—completed Northwest Passage—Sept. 7

Ship—ship to transport fresh orange juice in stainless steel tanks—*Tropicana*—arrived—New York City—Feb. 19

Steel—vacuum-cast steel—poured—Bethlehem, Pa.—July 2

Submarine—atomic-powered submarine built at a naval shipyard—*Swordfish*—launched—Portsmouth, N.H.—Aug. 27

Submarine—ballistic missile submarine—*George Washington*—laid down—Groton, Conn.—Nov. 7

Submarine—submarine expressly designed and built to fire guided missiles—*Grayback*—launched—Mare Island, Calif.—July 2

Submarine—submarine powered by a liquid-metal-cooled atomic reactor—*Seawolf*—completed—March 30

Submarine—submarine submerged for 2 weeks (NATO exercises in North Atlantic)—*Nautilus*—left Groton, Conn.—Aug. 19—maneuvers ended Sept. 24—returned, Oct. 28

Submarine—submarine to circumnavigate the world—*Gudgeon*—left Pearl Harbor, Hawaii—July 8

Telephone—air-to-ground public telephone service—began—Sept. 15

Television—Telecast—stockholders' annual meeting televised on a closed circuit—April 16

Television—Telecast—telecast (public) over telephone wires using the narrow-band system—demonstrated by C. R. Kraus—Philadelphia, Pa.—March 20

Titanium—titanium mill—opened—Toronto, Ohio—Nov. 2

Tunnel—triple-tube underwater roadway—Lincoln Tunnel between New York City and Weehawken, N.J.—opened—May 25

Typewriter—electric portable typewriter—placed on sale—Syracuse, N.Y.—Feb. 4

Weight Lifter—weight lifter to lift more than 6,000 pounds—Paul Anderson—Toccoa, Ga.—June 17

Welding—aluminum-pipe welding machine (automatic)—completed model tested—Corpus Christi, Tex.

Wheelchair Athletics—national wheelchair games—Adelphi College, Garden City, N.Y.—June 1

1958

Air Force Academy (U.S.)—Air Force Academy—first cadets received—Colorado Springs, Colo.—Aug. 29

Atomic Reactor—thorium-uranium reactor (privately owned)—Buchanan, N.Y.—construction began—Jan. 28

Author—author to win a Pulitzer Prize in both fiction (1947) and poetry (1958)—R. P. Warren

Aviation—flight attendant (black woman)—R. C. Taylor—Ithaca, N.Y.—first flight—Feb. 11

Aviation—Flights—airplane endurance flight exceeding 1,200 hours—landed—Dallas, Tex.—Sept. 21

Aviation—Flights (transatlantic)—jet passenger commercial service—began—Oct. 4

Bridge—welded-aluminum girder-type highway bridge—completed—Urbandale, Iowa—Sept. 24

Brokerage—woman director of a stock exchange—M. G. Roebling—Oct. 28

Catholic Priest—prelate born in the United States named to the Roman Curia—S. A. Stritch—nominated March 1

College—college for women under Jewish auspices—Stern College for Women—New York City—first graduation June 19

Computer—solid-state electronic computer—developed—Philadelphia, Pa.

Electric Lighting—fluorescent lighting installed on every street in a city—Brookings, S. Dak.—project completed

Hockey Player—professional hockey player (black)—W. E. O'Ree—Jan. 18

Horse—Haflinger horse—imported—Aug. 18

Jockey—jockey to win the national riding championship four times—Willie Shoemaker—Dec. 31

Lens—bifocal contact lens—introduced—N. K. Wesley—Chicago, Ill.

Medal—Presidential Unit Citation award in peacetime—*Nautilus* crew—Aug. 8

Methodist Church—black minister with two white congregations—J. R. Washington—June 3

Molybdenum—molybdenum centrifugal casting —Albany, Oreg.—Nov. 4

Navy—atomic submarine division—formed— New London, Conn.—March 31

Navy—naval man to reenlist while under the North Pole—J. R. Sordelet—Aug. 3

Navy—task force to fight undersea craft—created —March 24

Newspaper—newspaper advertisement printed on aluminum foil—*Sentinel*—Milwaukee, Wis. —March 18

Pipeline—pipeline (interstate) to transport ethylene—in operation—Sept. 6

Postage Stamp—postage stamp to bear the likeness of a Vice President of the United States issued by a foreign country—Ecuador—R. M. Nixon—May 15

Presbyterian Church—moderator of the United Presbyterian Church—elected—Pittsburgh, Pa. —May 28

President (U.S.)—pension for Presidents—enacted—Aug. 25

Prizefighter—pugilist to win a world championship 5 times in the same weight division—Sugar Ray Robinson—(5th time) Chicago, Ill.—March 25

Radio Broadcast—outer space broadcast—D. D. Eisenhower—tape recording—Dec. 19

Rocket—rocket to intercept a low-flying airplane —fired—White Sands Proving Grounds, N.Mex.

Rocket—rocket to intercept a supersonic target missile—fired

Satellite—satellite placed in orbit—launched— Cape Canaveral, Fla.—Jan. 31

Ship—aircraft carrier (atomic-powered)—*Enterprise*—laid down—Newport News, Va.—Feb. 4

Ship—atomic-powered merchant ship—*Savannah*—keel laid—Camden, N.J.—May 22

Ship—guided missile destroyer—*Dewey*— launched—Bath, Me.—Nov. 30

Ship Motion Simulator—ship motion simulator— built and installed—Missile Testing Center, Cocoa Beach, Fla.

Sidewalk (traveling)—two-way moving walk—in service—Dallas, Tex.—Jan. 30

Space Agency (U.S.)—National Aeronautics and Space Administration—authorized July 29—organized Oct. 1

Submarine—automic-powered submarine built at a naval shipyard—*Swordfish*—commissioned —Sept. 15

Submarine—atomic-powered turbine-electric drive submarine—*Tullibee*—keel laid—Groton Conn.—May 26

Submarine—submarine crossing of the North Pole underwater—*Nautilus*—accomplished—Aug. 3

Submarine—submarine expressly designed and built to fire guided missiles—*Grayback*—commissioned—Mare Island, Calif.—March 7

Submarine—submarine to circumnavigate the world—*Gudgeon*—returned to Pearl Harbor Hawaii—Feb. 21

Submarine—submarine to cross the Atlantic Ocean within 9 days—*Skate*—left New London Conn.—Feb. 24—arrived at Portland, England —March 5

Submarine—submarine to travel under the North Pole from the East—*Skate*—left New London Conn.—July 30—in polynya Aug. 12—returned to Boston, Mass.—Sept. 22

Submarine—submarine with two nuclear reactors—*Triton*—launched—Groton, Conn.—Aug 19

Tape Recording—video recording in color on magnetic tape—presented—Charlotte, N.C.— Sept. 5

Television—Telecast—atomic bomb detonation from a captive balloon telecast—Yucca Flat Nev.—Sept. 19

Television—Telecast—stratosphere telecast— Strato-Lab High III—Malcolm Ross and M. L Lewis—takeoff from Crosby, Minn.—July 26— landing in Jamestown, N. Dak.—July 27

Television Station—city to have two educational television channels—Pittsburgh, Pa.—July 16

War (Quemoy)—American casualty of the Red Chinese bombardment of Quemoy—G. W Johnston—Sept. 3

1959

Air Force Academy (U.S.)—Air Force Academy— graduation—June 3

Airmail Service—missile mail (official)—landed —Jacksonville, Fla.—June 8

Astronaut—astronauts—National Aeronautic and Space Administration selection announced —April 7

Attorney General—state attorney general (woman)—A. X Alpern—commissioned—Harris burg, Pa.—Jan. 20

Automobile Racer—automobile racer to win $100,000 in a race—Roger Ward—Indianapolis Ind.—May 30

Aviation—Flights (transcontinental)—jet passenger commercial transcontinental service—began—Jan. 25

Aviation—Pilot—pilot to fly a million miles in jet airplane—M. C. Garlow—March 7

Baseball Game—World Series baseball game to draw more than 90,000 persons—Chicago White Sox vs. Los Angeles Dodgers—Los Angeles, Calif.—Oct. 6

owling Tournament—bowling match in which white balls were used on black lanes—Brooklyn, New York City—May 23

uilding—house with a built-in nuclear bomb shelter—exhibited—Pleasant Hills, Pa.—May 24

anal—St. Lawrence Seaway—opened—April 25

redit Card—nationally accepted bank-oriented credit card—originated—Bank of America, California

ictionary—medical slang dictionary—*Dictionary of Medical Slang and Related Esoteric Expressions*, by J. E. Schmidt—published—Springfield, Ill.

iplomatic Service—ambassador to Nepal—H. E. Stebbins—nomination approved—Sept. 9

ag—Navy Flag (official)—authorized—April 24

olfer—golfer to break 60 for 18 holes in a major tournament—S. J. Snead—White Sulphur Springs, W.Va.—May 16

olfer—golfer to play 24 hours continuously on a regulation course—J. J. Johnson—Abilene, Tex.—Oct. 14-15

twax—jetway—installed—International Airport, San Francisco, Calif.—July 29

edal—National Medal of Science—authorized—Aug. 25

lotion Picture—motion picture presented simultaneously in major cities throughout the world—*On the Beach*—Dec. 17

lotion Picture—motion picture with scent *Behind the Great Wall*—presented—New York City—Dec. 8

hotograph—photograph in color of the earth from outer space—missile launched—Cape Canaveral, Fla.—Dec. 1

hotograph—photographs in color of the heavens published in a magazine—*National Geographic Magazine*—Washington, D.C.—May issue

hotograph—ultraviolet pictures of the sun—White Sands, N.Mex.—March 13

ay (drama)—play written by a black woman to reach Broadway—*Raisin in the Sun*—opened in New York City—March 11

ostage Stamp—postage stamp of the United States having the same design as that of another country (Canada)—issued—June 26

adar—radar signal bounced off the sun—transmitted—Stanford, Calif.—April 7

epresentative (U.S.)—representative of Japanese ancestry elected to the House of Representatives—D. K. Inouye—July 28

ocket—animals fired into space and rescued from a rocket—launched—Cape Canaveral, Fla.—May 28

atellite—satellite to transmit photographs of the earth—launched—Cape Canaveral, Fla.—Aug. 7

enator (U.S.)—senator of Asian ancestry—H. L. Fong—elected—July 29

hip—atomic-powered cruiser—*Long Beach*—launched—Quincy, Mass.—July 14

hip—atomic-powered merchant ship—*Savannah*—christened—Camden, N.J.—July 21

Ship—guided missile destroyer—*Dewey*—commissioned—Bath, Me.—Dec. 7

Ship—ship to fire a Polaris missile—*Observation Island*—missile launched—Aug. 27

Ski Lift—tramway state legislation—New Hampshire—approved Sept. 17—effective Nov. 16

State—noncontiguous overseas state—Hawaii—admitted to the Union—Aug. 21

State—noncontiguous state—Alaska—admitted to the Union—Jan. 3

Submarine—ballistic missile submarine—*George Washington*—launched—Groton, Conn.—June 9

Submarine—submarine to have 2 complete crews—*George Washington*—Groton, Conn.—blue crew reported in June—gold crew in September—commissioned, Dec. 30

Submarine—submarine to travel under ice for 12 days—*Skate*—left New London, Conn.—March 4—traveled under Arctic ice at North Pole, surfacing March 17

Submarine—submarine with two nuclear reactors—*Triton*—commissioned—Nov. 10

Submarine—submerged circumnavigation of the earth—*Triton* commissioned—Nov. 10

Television—Telecast—auction of federal property to be televised—transmitted—Oct. 7

Television—Telecast—outer-space telecast of pictures of the earth—Aug. 14

Television—Telecast—stockholders' meetings televised coast-to-coast simultaneously—transmitted—Oct. 29

Television—Telecast—telecast received from England—transmitted—June 18

1960

Atomic Reactor—atomic reactor for research and development—placed in operation—Richland, Wash.—Nov. 25

Atomic Reactor—atomic reactor system to be patented—J. W. Flora—Canoga Park, Calif.—May 17

Atomic Reactor—commercial atomic energy reactor—Rowe, Mass.—power produced, Nov. 10

Basketball Player—basketball player (professional) to score more than 15,000 points—Dolph Schayes—Philadelphia, Pa.—Jan. 12

Bowler—bowler to win $10,000 in a tournament—Harry Smith—Omaha, Neb.—Jan. 15

Chlorophyll—chlorophyll "a"—synthesized—R. B. Woodward—Cambridge, Mass.—June 27

Clock—electronic wristwatch—placed on sale—New York City—Oct. 25

Computer—electronic computer to employ Thin-Film memory—announced—Dec. 9

Congress (U.S.)—Senate—election in which 2 women contested for the same Senate seat—M. C. Smith and L. M. Cormier—Maine—Nov. 8

Flag—American flag to orbit the earth—*Discoverer XIII*—launched, Aug. 10—recovered, Aug. 11—presented to D. D. Eisenhower, Aug. 15

Hockey Player—professional hockey player to reach a score of more than 1,000 points in a regular season—Gordon Howe—Nov. 27

Ice Skating Champion—national women's figure skating four-time winner—C. E. Heiss—fourth consecutive title—Seattle, Wash.—Jan. 29

Ice Skating Rink—ice skating rink (artificial) of Olympic size—Squaw Valley, Calif.—formally opened Feb. 18

Lasers—patent on lasers—A. L. Schawlow and C. H. Townes—March 22

Park—underseas park (federal)—Key Largo Coral Reef Preserve, Fla.—established—March 15

Photograph—photograph bounced off a satellite —beamed—Cedar Rapids, Iowa—Aug. 18

Photograph—photograph bounced off the moon—received—Washington, D.C.—Jan. 28

Police—parking-meter enforcement division—appointed by R. F. Wagner—New York City—June 1

Post Office—post office fully mechanized—opened—Providence, R.I.—Oct. 20

Postage Stamp—postage stamp issued jointly by 2 countries—Mexican Independence—issued—Los Angeles, Calif.—Sept. 16

Presidential Candidate—presidential candidate debate series on television—Nixon-Kennedy debates

Prizefighter—world heavyweight champion to regain his crown—Floyd Patterson—New York City—June 20

Pulitzer Prize—woman to win 2 Pulitzer prizes in history—Margaret Leech—2nd award, May 2

Radio Broadcast—solar power two-way radio coast-to-coast conversation—Fort Monmouth, N.J., and El Monte, Calif.—June 23

Representative (U.S.)—woman to serve 18 terms in Congress—E. F. N. Rogers of Massachusetts —ended service, Sept. 10

Satellite—communications satellite—launched—Cape Canaveral, Fla.—Aug. 12

Satellite—communications satellite successfully placed in orbit—launched, Cape Canaveral, Fla.—received and recorded message from D. D. Eisenhower through C. A. Herter to F. H. Boland—United Nations, New York City—Oct. 4

Satellite—multisatellite launching—Transit 2-A —launched—Cape Canaveral, Fla.—June 22

Satellite—navigational satellite—Transit 1-B—launched—Cape Canaveral, Fla.—April 13

Satellite—satellite placed in solar orbit—launched—Cape Canaveral, Fla.—March 11

Satellite—space capsule recovered from an orbiting satellite—located—Pacific Ocean—Aug. 11

Satellite—space capsule recovered in midair from an orbiting satellite—retrieved—Aug. 19

Satellite—surveillance satellite that was successful—Midas II—launched—Cape Canaveral, Fla.—May 24

Satellite—weather-observation satellite—Tiros 1 —launched—Cape Canaveral, Fla.—April 1

Senator (U.S.)—woman senator elected for a thir and a fourth term—M. C. Smith of Maine—elected to 3rd term

Ship—aircraft carrier (atomic-powered)—Ente prise—launched—Newport News, Va.—Sep 24

Stamp—motor boat stamps—required—April 1

Submarine—atomic-powered turbine-electri drive submarine—Tullibee—launched—Gr ton, Conn.—April 27

Submarine—ballistic missile submarine—Geor[Washington—on patrol duty—Nov. 15

Submarine—guided missile launched from a n clear-powered submarine—Halibut—March [

Submarine—submarine to make a submerge passage from the Atlantic to the Pacific via t North Pole—Seadragon—left Portsmouth, N.[—Aug. 1—cleared the ice pack Sept. 3—docke at Pearl Harbor, Hawaii—Sept. 14

Submarine—submerged circumnavigation of t earth—Triton—completed—April 25

Submarine—submerged submarine to fire a Pol ris missile—George Washington—July 20

Sulfur Mine (offshore)—Louisiana coast—sulf obtained—March 14

Television—submarine with closed-circuit telev sion—Tullibee—launched—Groton, Conn. April 27

Television—Telecast—art auction televised on coast-to-coast closed circuit—transmitted April 27

Woman—woman to undergo astronaut tests—Je rie Cobb—Albuquerque, N.Mex.—Feb. 15-21

1961

Air Raid Shelter—air raid community shelter completed—Boise, Idaho—July 1

Astronaut—astronaut (American) to be launche into space—A. B. Shepard, Jr.—Cape Canave al, Fla.—May 5

Astronaut—astronaut (American) to make suborbital flight twice—V. I. Grissom—fir takeoff—Cape Canaveral, Fla.—July 21

Astronaut—astronaut (black) selected for t manned orbiting laboratory program—E. Dwight, Jr.—March 31

Astronaut—space flight by an American a tronaut—Cape Canaveral, Fla.—A. B. Shepa —May 5

Attorney of the United States—United States [torney (black)—C. F. Poole—sworn in, S Francisco, Calif.—July 6

Aviation—Airplane—skyjack of a commerci American airplane—Antillo Ortiz—Marath(Fla.—May 1

Aviation—Flights—airplane to fly faster th 4,000 m.p.h.—Edwards Air Force Base, Calif. Robert White—Nov. 9

Aviation Company—airplane company to car 100 million passengers—American Airlines Dec. 28

Basketball Team—basketball team to score more than 10,000 points—Philadelphia Warriors—1961–1962 season

College President—woman college president of two colleges—Rosemary Park—Barnard College, New York City—inaugurated Nov. 15 (second)

Diplomatic Service—ambassador (woman) to a communist bloc nation—E. M. Anderson—presented credentials, Sofia, Bulgaria—Aug. 3

Discus—discus throw to exceed 200 feet—A. A. Oerter—Los Angeles, Calif.—May 18

Dock—containership facility—Elizabeth, N.J.—opened Aug. 15

Electric Power Plant—utility-operated plant for central heating and cooling—Hartford, Conn.—began operation June 25

Fair—world's fair that was financially successful—Seattle, Wash.—April 21–Oct. 21

Hammer Throw—hammer throw to exceed 231 feet—Harold Connolly—Palo Alto, Calif.—July 21

Hospital—children's hospital solely for research and treatment of catastrophic childhood diseases—St. Jude's Children's Research Hospital, Memphis, Tenn.—opened Feb. 4

Judge—black woman judge elected—E. S. Sampson—Chicago, Ill.—elected, Nov. 8—sworn in, Dec. 3

Labor Legislation—minimum wage law (city) for public contract work—New York City—effective Jan. 28

Marine Corps—marine officer to orbit the earth—J. H. Glenn—Feb. 20

Newspaper—newspaper reproduced commercially and regularly by radio facsimile—*Wall Street Journal* (San Francisco edition)—regular daily operation begun, May 28

Pole Vault—pole vault jump indoors over 16 feet—John Uelses—New York City—Feb. 2

Postage Stamp—Christmas-stamp regular issue—placed on sale—Pittsburgh, Pa.—Nov. 1

Postage Stamp—postage stamp issued on the date of the event it commemorated—Project Mercury commemorative—Feb. 20

President (U.S.)—President with a brother in the Senate—J. F. Kennedy—E. M. Kennedy—elected, Nov. 6

Protestant Episcopal Bishop—black to administer a diocese—J. M. Burgess—Boston, Mass.—elected Sept. 22—consecrated Dec. 9

Race Track—harness track to handle more than $3 million in bets in 1 night—Yonkers Raceway, Yonkers, N.Y.—topped that figure Nov. 30

Restaurant—revolving restaurant—The Top of the Needle, Seattle, Wash.—opened by remote control by J. F. Kennedy—from Palm Beach, Fla.—April 21

Rocket—launching silos for Atlas F missiles—built and turned over to Strategic Air Command—Sept. 13

Runner to run a mile indoors in less than 4 minutes—J. T. Beatty—Los Angeles, Calif.—Feb. 10

Satellite—American satellite to reach the moon—launched—Cape Canaveral, Fla.—April 23

Satellite—communications earth satellite t transmit telephone, television, teleprint, an facsimile signals—launched—Cape Canavera Fla.—Dec. 13

Satellite—geodetic satellite—*Anna 1B*—launche —Cape Canaveral, Fla.—Oct. 31

Satellite—international satellite—*Ariel 1* launched—Cape Canaveral, Fla.—April 26

Satellite—multisatellite launching (5 satellites 1 shot)—*Composite 1*—launched—Car Canaveral, Fla.—Jan. 24

Satellite—orbiting solar-observatory satellite—*OSO 1*—launched—Cape Canaveral, Fla.—March 7

Satellite—privately-owned satellite—*Telstar 1*—launched—Cape Canaveral, Fla.—July 10

Satellite—satellite to transmit date from Venus—*Mariner 2*—launched—Cape Canaveral, Fla.—Aug. 27—data transmitted, Dec. 14

Ship—dual sponsorship of a U.S. Navy ship—*Ha sey*—christened by Margaret Denham and Jai Halsey—San Francisco, Calif.—Jan. 15

Ship—FLIP ship—launched—Portland, Oreg.—June 22

Ship—guided-missile escort ship—*Brooke*—la down—Seattle, Wash.—Dec. 10

Ski Slope—ski slope indoors—Ski-Dek Center—opened—Buffalo, N.Y.—Jan. 17

Smog Chamber—smog chamber built by an indu trial organization for air pollution research General Motors Research Laboratories, Wa ren, Mich.—in operation in July

Stadium—domed, fully-enclosed sports arena Astrodome, Houston, Tex.—ground broke Jan. 3

Submarine—nuclear warhead fired from a Polar submarine—*Ethan Allen*—Christmas Island May 6

Submarine—submarines to rendezvous at t North Pole—*Skate* and *Seadragon*—met, July —successful mission announced, Aug. 2

Subway—train to run automatically without co ductors or motormen—New York City—Jan.

Swimmer—American to swim the English Cha nel underwater—Fred Baldasare—July 10-11

Telephone—hot line—The White House, Was ington, D.C., to the Kremlin, Moscow, Russia Aug. 30

Telephone—satellite (privately owned) telepho. conversation—F. R. Kappel to L. B. Johnson Andover, Me., via *Telstar 1* to Washington, D. —July 10

Television—television news commentator w. was black—M. R. Goode—assigned—Ne York City—Aug. 29

Television—Telecast—pay program—WHC TV, Hartford, Conn.—June 29

Television—Telecast—satellite telecast fro Europe—July 11

Television—Telecast—satellite telecast live Europe—July 23

elevision—Telecast—transatlantic exchange of live television programs—via Telstar—July 23

elevision—Telecast—transcontinental telecast by means of an orbiting satellite—Westford, Mass.—April 24

elevision—Telecast—transoceanic television program—Andover, Me.—July 10

1963

ir Force Academy (U.S.)—Air Force Academy graduates (black)—C. V. Bush and I. S. Payne, IV—were graduated June 5

mphibious Vehicle—Marsh screw amphibian—tested—Louisiana—March

nimals—gerenuk—born—Bronx Park Zoo, New York City—Sept. 30

rmy—armored division transported by airplanes to a foreign country—Texas to West Germany—Oct. 22

stronaut—astronaut (American) to orbit the earth on two trips—L. G. Cooper—first trip—*Faith 7*—Cape Canaveral, Fla.—May 15-16

stronaut—astronaut (American) to orbit the earth 22 times—L. G. Cooper—*Faith 7*—takeoff (Cape Canaveral, Fla.) May 15—landed (Pacific Ocean) May 16

tomic Reactor—plutonium-fueled nuclear reactor to produce useful amounts of electricity—Idaho Falls, Idaho—announced June 30

ank—major bank to lease personal property—Bank of America, San Francisco, Calif.—service instituted July 22

aseball Pitcher—baseball pitcher (major league) to strike out 300 or more batters in each of three seasons—Sanford Koufax—first season

aseball Player—"most valuable player" award (major league) to a black in the American League—Elston Howard—Nov. 7

aseball Team—baseball team to win more than 20 World Series—Yankees—New York City—21st series

rths—quintuplets to live more than 5 years—Fischer quintuplets—born in Aberdeen, S. Dak.—Sept. 14

idge (game) Player—bridge player to win more than 1,000 master points in 1 year—Oswald Jacoby—passed 1,000 mark at Edgewater Park, Miss.—Nov. 15

uilding—elliptical-shaped office building—Phoenix Mutual Building, Hartford, Conn.—completed in November

atholic Beatification—Catholic beatification of an American-born woman—E. A. B. Seton—March 17

atholic Beatification—Catholic beatification of an American citizen (male)—J. N. Neumann—Oct. 12

tizenship—honorary citizenship authorized by the U.S. Congress—Sir Winston Churchill—conferred by President John F. Kennedy—April

9

Electric Power Plant—cooling tower hyperbolic-shaped—Ashland, Ky.—in commercial service, Jan. 1

Golf Course—illuminated 9-hole regulation golf course—Tall Pines Golf Club, Sewell, N.J.—illuminated Aug. 23

Golfer—golfer to earn over $100,000 in one year—A. D. Palmer

Hall of Fame—Hall of Fame (football)—Canton, Ohio—first members selected Jan. 29—building dedicated Sept. 7

Hall of Famer—athlete enshrined in 2 halls of fame—Robert Hubbard—Canton, Ohio (professional football)—April 4

Labor Legislation—labor law prohibiting discrimination in the payment of wages because of sex—Equal Pay Act of 1963—enacted June 10

Labor Relations—National Labor Relations Board black member—Howard Jenkins, Jr.—sworn in at Washington, D.C.—Aug. 29

Leather Substitute—artificial leather shoe upper—Corfam—introduced to the press by E. I. Du Pont de Nemours Company—Oct. 2

Medal—Medal of Freedom awarded to a black woman—Marian Anderson—presented by L. B. Johnson—Washington, D.C.—Dec. 6

Medal—National Medal of Science—first presentation—Theodor von Karman—Feb. 17

Naval War College—black officers to attend the Naval War College—G. I. Thompson and S. L. Gravely, Jr.—Newport, R.I.—began studies Aug. 16

Nobel Prize—recipient of 2 full Nobel prizes—L. C. Pauling—second award (peace)—Dec. 10

Patent—patent on a "solar airplane vehicle"—E. G. Johnson—May 14

Photograph—photograph (authorized) of the Senate in session—taken, Sept. 24

Pole Vault—pole vault higher than 17 feet—John Pennel—Miami, Fla.—Aug. 24

Postage Stamp—fluorescent-coated (or -tagged) postage stamp—8-cent airmail—issued—Dayton, Ohio—Aug. 1

Postage Stamp—phosphorescent-impregnated postage stamp—issued—Nov. 2

Postage Stamp—President's wife depicted on a commemorative postage stamp—Eleanor Roosevelt—issued—Washington, D.C.—Oct. 11

Postal Card—international postal card—issued—New York City—Aug. 30

President (U.S.)—President to witness the firing of a Polaris missile—J. F. Kennedy—Cape Canaveral, Fla.—Nov. 16

Representative (U.S.)—representative sworn in before 8:00 A.M.—J. J. Pickle of Texas—elected, Dec. 17—sworn in, Dec. 24

Saint (Catholic)—saint (native-born Catholic)—E. A. B. Seton—beatified, March 17

Satellite—communications earth satellite to transmit telephone, television, teleprint, and facsimile signals—first test patterns transmitted, Jan. 3

Satellite—satellite fueled by liquid hydrogen successfully orbited—*Centaur II*—launched—Cape Canaveral, Fla.—Nov. 27

Satellite—synchronous satellite—*Syncom 2*—launched—Cape Canaveral, Fla.—July 26

Senator (U.S.)—father whose 3 sons were senators—J. P. Kennedy—E. M. Kennedy sworn in on Jan. 9

Ship—cargo ship fully automated and flying the American flag—*Mormacargo*—keel laid—Pascagoula, Miss.—April 22

Ship—guided-missile escort ship—*Brooke*—launched—Seattle, Wash.—July 19

Ship—naval ship designed to carry the DASH drone—*Belknap*—launched—Bath, Me.—July 19

Submarine—nuclear submarines launched simultaneously—*Flasher* and *Tecumseh*—Groton, Conn.—June 22

Telephone—telephone with push buttons—commercial service begun—Carnegie and Greensburg, Pa.—Nov. 18

Telephone—Trimline telephone—in service—Jackson, Mich.—Oct. 21

Television—Telecast—laser-light-beam program telecast on a network—*I've Got a Secret*—New York City—May 14

Television—Telecast—murder (actual) shown on television—L. H. Oswald killed by Jack Ruby—Dallas, Tex.—Nov. 24

Television—Telecast—telecast transmitted by satellite to Japan—via *Relay I*—news program beamed from U.S. ground station in Mohave Desert—Nov. 22—program received in Japan—Nov. 23

Television Receiver—television receiver and transmitter operated by laser beam—demonstrated—Bayside, N.Y.—Feb. 20

Weather Bureau (U.S.)—Weather Bureau woman employee—Joanne Simpson—began service—National Hurricane and Experimental Meteorology Laboratory, Coral Gables, Fla.

1964

Aquanaut—United States Navy divers to submerge 10 days—*Sealab 1*—off Hamilton, Bermuda—July 22-31

Astronaut—astronaut to die—T. C. Freeman—Houston, Tex.—Oct. 31

Atomic Energy Commission—Atomic Energy Commission woman member—M. I. Bunting—sworn in—June 29

Bridge (game) Player—bridge player to earn a lifetime total of 8,000 points—Oswald Jacoby—Oct. 15

Canonization—canonization of a saint in the United States—John Sergiev—New York City—Nov. 1

Catholic Mass—Catholic mass in English (full English mass)—celebrated in St. Louis, Mo.—Aug. 24

Catholic Mass—Catholic mass in English said fo a President—Holy Cross Cathedral, Bostor Mass.—Nov. 22

Coffee—freeze-dried coffee—marketed—Gener Foods, White Plains, N.Y.

College—liberal arts college for police and co rection officers established by a city—Colleg of Police Science, New York City—chartered June

Degrees (academic and honorary)—honorary d grees presented simultaneously to a Preside and his wife—L. B. Johnson and C. A. T. Johr son—Austin, Tex.—May 30

Diplomatic Service—woman to serve the Unite Nations as a permanent ambassador—M. Tree—sworn in Oct. 28

Economic Opportunity Office (U.S.)—Office Economic Opportunity—authorized—Aug. 20 first director, R. S. Shriver—sworn in—Oct.

Election—election in Washington, D.C.—May

Horse Race—harness driver (American) to sco 300 victories in 1 year—Bob Farrington—300 victory at Chicago, Ill.—Nov. 21

Interstate Commerce Commission—independe administrative agency of the federal gover ment woman member—V. M. Brown—appoir ed March 4—sworn in May 25

Leather Substitute—artificial leather shoe upp —Corfam—introduced in stores, Jan. 27

Lighthouse—lighthouse (atomic powered)—B timore Light, Baltimore Harbor, Md.—began c eration, May 20

Medal—Medal of Honor in the Vietnam war presented to R. H. Donlon—Dec. 5

Motion Picture Actor—black actor to win Oscar for best actor—Sidney Poitier—prese tation in Santa Monica, Calif.—April 13

Navy—all-nuclear task force voyage around t world without refueling—Task Force One Norfolk, Va.—departed, July 31—returned, O 3

Photograph—moon close-up photographs—*Rar er VII*—taken, July 31—received, NASA rece ing station, Mojave Desert, Calif.

Play (drama)—musical to run for more than 3,0 performances—*Fiddler on the Roof*—opened New York City—Sept. 22

Post Office—self-service post office—installed Wheaton, Md.—Oct. 17

Postage Stamp—brothers to be pictured on dividual postage stamps—J. F. Kennedy— cent blue-gray—issued May 29

Postal Card—street scene—issued—Washingt D.C.—Sept. 26

Presbyterian Church—moderator (black) of t United Presbyterian Church in the U.S.A.— G. Hawkins—assumed office—Oklahoma Ci Okla.—May 21

President (U.S.)—President to address the Sen —H. S Truman—Washington, D.C.—May 8

Presidential Candidate—woman presidential ca didate of a major political party—M. C. Smith nominated—San Francisco, Calif.—July 15

otestant Church—Protestant church formed by the amalgamation of 4 churches of different denominations—United Church of Schellsburg, Pa.—Nov. 22

ocket—American spacecraft to impact the moon—*Ranger VI*—launched—Cape Canaveral, Fla.—Jan. 30—impacted moon, Feb. 2

atellite—orbiting geophysical observatory—*OGO 1*—launched—Cape Kennedy, Fla.—Sept. 4

atellite—satellite to transmit a close-up photograph of Mars—*Mariner 4*—launched—Cape Kennedy, Fla.—Nov. 28

atellite—satellite to transmit lunar-surface close-up pictures—*Ranger VII*—launched—Cape Kennedy, Fla.—July 28—impacted moon, July 31

atellite—satellite with an electrostatic (ion) engine—*SERT 1*—launched—Wallops Island, Va.—July 20

atellite—weather satellite to provide high-resolution nighttime cloud-cover pictures—*Nimbus 1*—launched at Point Arguello, Calif.—Aug. 28—ceased operation Sept. 23

ip—cargo ship fully automated and flying the American flag—*Mormacargo*—launched—Pascagoula, Miss.—Jan. 25—first run (Pascagoula, Miss., to Boston, Mass.) Aug. 28—first transatlantic crossing Sept. 11

ip—nuclear ship named for a black—*George Washington Carver*—keel laid—Newport News, Va.—Aug. 24

ip—tanker (automated) under the U.S. flag—*Texaco Rhode Island*—launched—Sparrows Point, Baltimore, Md.—July 2

bmarine—nuclear submarine named for a black—*George Washington Carver*—keel laid—Newport News, Va.—Aug. 24

bmarine—submarine to make more than 13,000 dives—stricken from register, May 30

lephone—picturephone service (commercial)—New York City, Chicago, Washington, D.C.—inaugurated, June 24—service open to general public, June 25

lephone—picturephone transcontinental call—New York City to Anaheim, Calif.—April 20

lephone—telephone service over the transpacific telephone cable—Washington, D.C., to Tokyo, Japan—inaugurated, June 18

levision—Telecast—courtroom verdict telecast—Ruby trial—Dallas, Tex.—March 14

levision—Telecast—telecast transmitted by satellite from Japan—via *Relay II*—Hayato Ikeda—March 25

etnam War—pilot (American Navy) shot down and captured in North Vietnam—Everett Alvarez, Jr.—Aug. 5

oting Machine—presidential election in which votes were tallied electronically—Nov. 3

1965

ntenna—master skyscraper antenna—Empire State Building, New York City—erected

Astronaut—astronaut (American) to converse with an aquanaut—L. G. Cooper (*Gemini V*) and M. S. Carpenter (*Sealab II*)—off La Jolla, Calif.—Aug 29

Astronaut—astronaut (American) to make a suborbital flight twice—V. I. Grissom—second takeoff—Cape Kennedy, Fla.—March 23

Astronaut—astronaut (American) to maneuver outside a satellite—E. H. White—*Gemini IV*—launched—Cape Kennedy, Fla.—June 3

Astronaut—astronaut (American) to orbit the earth on two trips—L. G. Cooper—second trip—*Gemini V*—Cape Kennedy, Fla.—Aug. 21-29

Astronaut—astronauts (American) to orbit the earth 200 times—Frank Borman and J. A. Lovell, Jr.—*Gemini VII*—launched, Cape Kennedy, Fla.—Dec. 4—landed, Atlantic Ocean—Dec. 18

Astronaut—astronauts (American) to rendezvous in space—*Gemini VI* and *Gemini VII*—Dec. 15

Astronaut—two-man spaceflight (American) of 120 orbits—*Gemini V*—launched (Cape Kennedy, Fla.) Aug. 21—landed (Atlantic Ocean) Aug. 29

Astronaut—two-man spaceflight (American) of 62 orbits—*Gemini IV*—launched, Cape Kennedy, Fla.—June 3

Astronaut—two-man spaceflight (American) of 3 orbits—J. W. Young and V. I. Grissom—*Gemini III* ("Molly Brown")—launched, Cape Kennedy, Fla.—March 23

Automobile Driver—woman automobile driver to exceed the speed of 300 m.p.h.—L. A. R. Breedlove—Bonneville Salt Flats, Utah—Nov. 4

Baseball Pitcher—baseball pitcher (major league) to strike out 300 or more batters in each of 3 seasons—Sanford Koufax—second season

Baseball Pitcher—baseball pitcher to win 4 no-hitters—Sanford Koufax—4th game, Los Angeles, Calif.—Sept. 9

Baseball Player—baseball player to play all 9 positions in 1 game—B. D. Campaneris—Kansas City, Mo.—Sept. 8

Brokerage—American Stock Exchange women members—J. M. Walsh and P. K. S. Peterson—elected—New York City—Nov. 18

Cabinet (U.S.)—Cabinet meeting attended by a foreign national—Washington, D.C.—April 20

Catholic Bishop—black Catholic bishop who was American born—H. R. Perry—named auxiliary bishop, New Orleans, La.—Oct. 2

College—liberal arts college for police and corrections officers established by a city—College of Police Science, New York City—opened, Sept. 20—L. E. Reisman appointed president—Oct. 14

Congress (U.S.)—House of Representatives—black page of the House of Representatives—Frank Mitchell—appointed Aug. 14

Congress (U.S.)—Senate—black page of the Senate—L. W. Bradford—appointed April 13

Diplomatic Service—ambassador (black woman)—P. R. Harris—sworn in July 9

Horse Race—perfecta, or exacta—Monticello, N.Y.—June 30

Hotel—hotel (large) built over a pier—Flagship Hotel, Galveston, Tex.—opened June 30

Judge—chief justice (woman) of a state supreme court—L. E. Lockwood—Arizona—selected Jan. 8

Medal—Vietnam Service Medal—authorized—July 8

Medicare—health insurance federal plan—enacted—July 30

Money—coins bearing dates other than the year of issue—authorized July 23—issued at Philadelphia, Pa.—Nov. 1

Narcotics Legislation—narcotics prohibitory legislation (state)—Nevada—enacted March 19

Navy—navy man to reenlist while under water—B. L. Coffman—La Jolla, Calif.—Aug. 31

Oil—oil platform offshore with a radioisotone generator—Gulf of Mexico—in unattended operation in June

Photograph—planet close-up photograph—Mariner IV—July 14

Photography—camera multiple flashbulb device—Flashcubes—introduced, New York City—July 8

Presbyterian Church—woman ordained a minister in the Presbyterian Church in the United States (South)—Rachel Henderlite—ordained in Richmond, Va.—May 12

Radio Broadcast—underwater transatlantic radio conversation—La Jolla, Calif., to Cape Ferrat, France—Oct. 2

Radio Station—all-news radio station—WINS, New York City—April 19

Representative (U.S.)—Japanese-American woman representative—P. T. Mink of Hawaii—began service, Jan. 4

Satellite—multisatellite launching (8 satellites in 1 shot)—launched—Vandenberg Air Force Base, Calif.—March 9

Satellite—nuclear reactor in orbit—SNAP 10A—launched—Vandenberg Air Force Base, Calif.—April 3

Satellite—satellite to transmit a close-up photograph of Mars—Mariner 4—transmitted for 8.5 hours—July 14

Satellite—satellite to use a fuel cell—Gemini V—launched—Cape Kennedy, Fla.—Aug. 21

Satellite—satellite with a nuclear reactor to orbit the earth—Snapshot I—launched—Vandenberg Air Force Base, Calif.—April 3—reactor (SNAP 10A) in operation, April 3-May 16

Satellite—satellite with spring-folded wings to intercept bombardment of tiny meteoroids—Pegasus 1—launched—Cape Kennedy, Fla.—Feb. 16

School Legislation—school law (state) to end de facto segregation—enacted—Massachusetts—Aug. 18

Senator (U.S.)—father whose 3 sons were senators—J. P. Kennedy—R. F. Kennedy sworn in on Jan. 3

Ship—diesel-and-gas-turbine combined-propulsion plant in a major ship—Alexander Hamilton—launched—New Orleans, La.—Dec. 18

Ship—naval ship of the United States with a crew of mixed nationalities—Claude V. Ricketts (originally, William P. Biddle)—sailed on Caribbean cruise—Norfolk, Va.—Jan. 4

Ship—nuclear ship named for a black—George Washington Carver—launched—Newport News, Va.—Aug. 14

Shot-Put—shot-put to cover a distance of more than 70 feet—Randy Matson—College Station, Tex.,—May 8

Solicitor General (U.S.)—solicitor general of the United States who was a black—Thurgood Marshall—nominated, July 13—first case tried—Washington, D.C.—Oct. 13

Stadium—domed, fully-enclosed sports arena—Astrodome, Houston, Tex.—first baseball game, April 9—first football game, Sept. 11

Submarine—nuclear submarine named for a black—George Washington Carver—launched—Newport News, Va.—Aug. 14

Submarine—submarine to make more than 13,000 dives—sold for scrap in May

Supreme Court (state)—chief justice (woman) of a state supreme court—L. E. Lockwood—Arizona—elected

Surgical Operation—surgical operation on a baby to correct a sperm block—James Hicks and F. Walker—Auburn, Ala.—July 25

Swimmer—American to swim the English Channel round trip—Ted Erikson—Sept. 21

Telephone—telephone conversation (commercial) over a satellite—between the United States and Europe over Early Bird I—June 2

Telephone—Trimline telephone—commercially available—Michigan—Aug. 2

Totalisator—fully electronic, transistorized, data processing totalisator—in use—Westbury, L.I., N.Y.—May 15

Visiting Celebrities—pontiff to visit the United States—Pope Paul VI—arrived—New York City—Oct. 4

1966

Army Officer—sergeant major of the army—W. Wooldridge—sworn in July 11

Astronaut—astronaut (American civilian) to orbit the earth—N. A. Armstrong—Gemini VIII launched, Cape Kennedy, Fla.—March 16

Atomic Energy Commission—Atomic Energy Commission black member—S. M. Nabrit—began service Aug. 1

Aviation—Parachute—parachute jumper snagged in midair—C. M. Alexander—Georgetown, Del.—Aug. 29

Aviation—Pilot—ensign (woman) to fly solo—A. Gordon—Pensacola, Fla.—March 28

Baseball Pitcher—baseball pitcher (major league) to strike out 300 or more batters in each of 3 seasons—Sanford Koufax—Sept. 29 (third season)

Brokerage—New York Stock Exchange woman seat owner—Muriel Siebert—New York City—admitted Dec. 28

Diplomatic Service—ambassadors in service to wed—Ellsworth Bunker and C. C. Laise—Jan. 3

Fishing Reel—electric spinning reel—introduced—Chicago, Ill.—Aug. 15

Football Game—Super Bowl contest—Green Bay Packers vs. Kansas City Chiefs—Los Angeles, Calif.—Jan. 15

Golfer—golfer (woman) to play 150 holes continuously—Katherine Murphy—Bonsall, Calif.—June 19

Hospital—general hospital to adopt the Social Security account number as a numbering system for medical records—Altoona, Pa.—Jan. 20

Impregnation—legalization of artificial insemination for humans—D. F. Bartlett (signed bill)—Oklahoma—May 18

Jockey—jockey to win 7 consecutive races in 1 day—Leroy Moyers—Suffolk Downs, Boston, Mass.—July 4

Mayor—black mayor of a major city—C. B. Stokes—Cleveland, Ohio—elected Nov. 7—sworn in Nov. 13

Medicare—health insurance federal plan—first payments for skilled nursing facilities under extended care benefit provision—Jan. 2

Monastery—Zen Buddhist monastery—Tassajara Springs, Calif.—officially opened in July

Motel—horse motel—Wayne Biggs—Marshfield, Mo.—opened, June 10

Motorboat—motorboat to travel at a speed of more than 285 m.p.h.—Lee Taylor, Jr.—Lake Guntersville, Ala.—June 30

Museum—wine museum—Finger Lakes Wine Museum, Hammondsport, N.Y.—opened in July

Newspaper—large-type weekly—*New York Times Large Type Weekly*—published—New York City—March 6

Postage Stamp—brothers to be pictured on individual postage stamps—J. F. Kennedy—13-cent brown—issued May 29

Postage Stamp—gravure-printed postage stamp—The Biglin Brothers Racing—issued—Washington, D.C.—Nov. 2

Postage Stamp—stamp (U.S.) cancelled by a foreign country—Canadian federation commemorative—issued and cancelled—Montreal, Canada—May 25

Postage Stamp—stamped envelope (phosphor-coated, luminescent tag)—tagged—Washington, D.C.—Aug. 15

Postage Stamp—twin postage stamps—issued—Orlando, Fla.—Sept. 29

Postal Card—airmail postal card commemorative—issued—Charlotte Amalie, Virgin Islands (U.S.)—March 31

Public Defender—public defender (state)—Peter Murray—New Jersey—appointed June 20—term began July 1

Satellite—biosatellite (successful)—launched—Cape Kennedy, Fla.—Sept. 7

Satellite—satellite launched from another heavenly body—*Surveyor* 6—launched—Cape Kennedy, Fla.—Nov. 7

Satellite—satellite to transmit photographs of the full earth face—*Dodge*—launched—Cape Kennedy, Fla.—July 1

School—school for unmarried, pregnant, teen-age girls—opened—New York City—June 23

Senator (U.S.)—black senator elected by popular vote—E. W. Brooke of Massachusetts—took seat in Senate—Jan. 10

Ship—diesel-and-gas-turbine combined-propulsion plant in a major ship—*Alexander Hamilton*—commissioned, March 18

Shot-Put—shot-put to cover a distance of more than 71 feet—Randy Matson—College Station, Tex.—April 22

Supreme Court (U.S.)—Associate Justice of the Supreme Court who was a black—Thurgood Marshall—appointed, June 13—appointment confirmed, Aug. 30—sworn in (private ceremony), Sept. 1—publicly sworn in, Oct. 2

Television—Telecast—football game (professional championship) telecast—Green Bay Packers vs. Kansas City Chiefs—Los Angeles, Calif.—Jan. 15

Television—Telecast—world live-television program—"Our World"—June 25

Television Station—noncommercial education television network—New York City—first live broadcast Jan. 10—regularly scheduled non-commercial broadcasting began Nov. 5

Transportation Department (U.S.)—A. S. Boyd (first secretary)—sworn in Jan. 16—first official day, April 1

Vietnam War—American general killed in Vietnam by enemy fire—B. A. Hochmuth—Nov.

Vietnam War—American general killed in Vietnam in an accident—W. J. Crumm—July 6

Vietnam War—general (American) to die in Vietnam—A. J. F. Moody—March 20

1968

Ambulance—mobile coronary-care ambulance—St. Vincent's Hospital, New York City—October

Armenian Cathedral—consecrated—New York City—April 28

Army Officer—general (black) to lead an infantry brigade in combat—F. E. Davison—Vietnam—February

Army School—instructor (woman)—E. M. Lewis—West Point, N.Y.—began service Feb. 1

Astronaut—astronaut international rescue agreement—signed April 22—ratified Oct. 8—in force Dec. 3

Astronaut—astronauts (American) to land night—Frank Borman, J. A. Lovell, Jr., and W. A. Anders—*Apollo VIII*—landed, Pacific Ocean—Dec. 27

stronaut—astronauts (American) to orbit the earth—Frank Borman, J. A. Lovell, Jr., and W. A. Anders—*Apollo VIII*—launched, Cape Kennedy, Fla.—Dec. 21

stronaut—three-man spaceflight (American)—*Apollo VII*—launched, Cape Kennedy, Fla.—Oct. 11—landed, Atlantic Ocean—Oct. 22

aseball Game—night baseball game (major league) to last longer than 6 hours—Houston, Tex.—April 15

ook—book set into type completely by electronic composition—*The Long Short Cut,* by Andrew Garve—published in New York City—April

offee—freeze-dried coffee—available nationally

riminal—woman on the "ten most wanted" list —Ruth Eisemann-Schier

ustoms Bureau—Bureau of Customs receipts totaling over $3 billion

iplomatic Service—ambassador assassinated in office—J. G. Mein—Guatemala City, Guatemala —Aug. 27

iscus—discus hurler to win 4 gold medals in 4 consecutive Olympic Games—A. A. Oerter—Mexico City, Mex. (4th medal)—Oct. 14

ootball Game—professional football game attended by 80,000 spectators—Baltimore Colts vs. Cleveland Browns—Cleveland, Ohio—Dec. 29

olfer—golfer to earn over $200,000 in one year in regular tournaments—W. E. Casper

oliday—Monday holidays legislation (federal) —enacted—June 28

orse—pacer to win $1 million—Cardigan Bay—Freehold, N.J.—Sept. 14

edal—Medal of Honor in the Vietnam war awarded to a chaplain—A. J. Liteky—presented Nov. 19

edal—Medal of Honor to a Marine (black) in the Vietnam war—James Anderson, Jr.—presented Aug. 21

aturalization—naturalization ceremony in the White House—Washington, D.C.—Nov. 23

aval Officer—naval chaplain to win the silver star in Vietnam—R. M. Lyons—award presented April 18

ysician—captain (black) in the U.S. Navy Medical Corps—P. S. Green—commissioned July 12

olitical Convention—national nominating convention to propose blacks for the offices of both President and Vice President—Chicago, Ill.—C. E. Phillips nominated Aug. 28—Julian Bond nominated Aug. 29

ostage Stamp—native American pictured on a postage stamp—Chief Joseph—stamp on sale in Washington, D.C.—Nov. 4

ostage Stamp—postage stamp printed on the 9-color Huck press—multicolored Christmas stamp—issued—Washington, D.C.—Nov. 1

ostal Service—legislation permitting postage stamps of the United States to be illustrated in color—enacted June 20

Presidential Candidate—black presidential candidate proposed by a major political party—C. E. Phillips—Chicago, Ill.—Aug. 28

Presidential Candidate—presidential candidate assassinated while campaigning—R. F. Kennedy—Los Angeles, Calif.—June 6

Protestant Episcopal Bishop—Protestant Episcopal bishop consecrated in a Roman Catholic church—R. B. Appleyard—Pittsburgh, Pa.—Feb. 10

Representative (U.S.)—black representative (woman) to serve in Congress—S. A. S. Chisholm—elected—New York—Nov. 5

School—professional school for exclusively training potential circus clowns—established—Venice, Fla.—Sept. 1

Ship—naval ship to surrender in peacetime without a fight—*Pueblo*—Jan. 23

Ship—ship named for a Seabee—*Marvin Shields* —laid down—Seattle, Wash.—April 12

Supreme Court (U.S.)—Associate Justice of the Supreme Court to participate in a television program—H. L. Black—Alexandria, Va.—Dec. 3

Television—color television sets to outsell black and white units

Television—Telecast—outer-space live telecast—*Apollo VII*—Oct. 14

Television—Telecast—outer-space live telecast from a manned spacecraft—*Apollo VIII*—Dec. 22

Television—Telecast—political convention telecast in color—29th Republican National Convention—Miami Beach, Fla.—Aug. 5-7

Vietnam War—general killed in action in Vietnam—R. F. Worley—July 23

Water—deep-bed pressure filtration system—built—East Chicago, Ind.—in operation in March

1969

Airmail Service—rocket (steam-driven) to carry mail—launched—Las Curces, N.Mex.—May 24

Aquanaut—aquanaut to lose his life at work—B. L. Cannon—off San Clemente Island, Calif.—Feb. 17

Army War College—Army War College women graduates—F. V. Chaffin and S. R. Heinze—were graduated—Carlisle, Pa.—June 16

Astronaut—astronauts (American) in orbit to transfer from one spacecraft to another—R. L. Schweickart and J. A. McDivitt—March 6

Astronaut—astronauts (American) on the moon to retrieve an object—Charles Conrad, Jr., and A. L. Bean—Nov. 19

Astronaut—astronauts (American) to land on the moon—N. A. Armstrong and E. E. Aldrin, Jr.—July 20

Astronaut—astronauts (American) to remain one day on the moon—Charles Conrad and A. L. Bean—Nov. 19-20

884   FAMOUS FIRST FACTS

Astronaut—space-to-ground news conference telecast—Charles Conrad, A. L. Bean, and R. F. Gordon, Jr., in *Apollo XII* with G. P. Carr in Houston, Tex.—Nov. 23

Bank—bank to install an automatic teller—Chemical Bank—New York City—January

Baseball Pitcher—baseball pitcher (major league) to strike out 19 batters—S. N. Carlton—St. Louis, Mo.—Sept. 15

Brokerage—New York Stock Exchange black member—J. L. Searles, III—New York City—approved Feb. 13

Catholic Priest—deacon (married) ordained—M. G. Cole—Rochester, N.Y.—June 1

Criminal—woman on the "ten most wanted" list—Ruth Eisemann-Schier—arrested—Norman, Okla.—March 5—convicted in Decatur, Ga.—May 29

Electoral College—state law requiring presidential electors to cast their ballots for presidential and vice presidential candidates of the political party for which the electors were chosen—enacted—Maine—March 25

Electric Power Transmission—power line of 765,000 volts—Kentucky

element—element 194—rutherfordium—discovered at University of California Lawrence Radiation Laboratory, Berkeley, Calif.

Federal Maritime Commission—woman chairman of the Federal Maritime Commission—H. D. Bentley—began service Oct. 27

Football Player—football player to punt 98 yards—Steve O'Neal (New York Jets)—Denver, Colo.—Sept. 21

Hockey Player—professional hockey player to score more than 100 points in 1 season—Gordon Howe—1968/69 season

Horse Race—horse race pari-mutuel with an entire field of women jockeys—Suffolk Downs, Boston, Mass.—April 19

Jockey—jockey (woman) to ride in a pari-mutuel race on a flat track—Diane Crump—Hialeah, Fla.—Feb. 7

Jockey—jockey (woman) to ride 2 winners in 1 day—B. J. Rubin—Chester, W.Va.—March 8

Jockey—jockey (woman) to win on a regular pari-mutuel flat track—B. J. Rubin—Charles Town, W. Va.—Feb. 22

Medal—Distinguished Service Medals of the Army, Navy, and Air Force presented to one person at the same time—L. L. Lemnitzer—July 11

Medal—Meritorious Service Medal—established—Jan. 16

Medal—Presidential Citizen Medal—established by R. M. Nixon—Nov. 13

Medical Clinic—vasectomy outpatient service—Margaret Sanger Research Bureau—opened—New York City—Oct. 3

Medical School—women's medical school (still in existence as an independent institution)—male students admitted

Postage Stamp—coil multicolored postage stamp—issued—Chicago, Ill.—May 30

Postage Stamp—stamp to depict a living American—moon issue—N. A. Armstrong—issued—Washington, D.C.—Sept. 9

President (U.S.)—President to attend the launching of a manned spaceflight—R. M. Nixon—Cape Kennedy, Fla.—Nov. 14

Race Track—harness track to handle more than $300 million in bets in 1 year—Yonkers Raceway, Yonkers, N.Y.—topped that figure Dec.

Radio Telephone—telephone call to the moon—M. Nixon to N. A. Armstrong and E. E. Aldrin, Jr.—from Washington, D.C.—July 20

Representative (U.S.)—black representative (woman) to serve in Congress—S. A. S. Chisholm of New York—began service—Jan. 3

Rowing—transatlantic solo trip by rowboat—John Fairfax—left Canary Islands—Jan. 20—arrived Hollywood, Fla.—July 19

Sailing—woman to sail alone across the Pacific Ocean—S. S. Adams—left Yokohama, Japan—May 12—arrived San Diego, Calif.—July 25

Senator (U.S.)—senator to act in the movies—M. Dirksen of Illinois—*The Monitors*—film released, Oct. 9

Ship—commercial ship to conquer the Northwest Passage—*Manhattan*—left Chester, Pa.—Aug. 24

Ship—ship named for a Seabee—*Marvin Shields*—launched—Portland, Oreg.—November

Ship—ship to pass both ways through the Northwest Passage—*Northwind*

Supreme Court (U.S.)—Chief Justice of the United States to administer the oath of office to his successor—Earl Warren—June 23

Tennis Player—tennis player to win 2 grand slams—R. G. Laver—Sept. 8

Treasury Department (U.S.)—treasurer of the United States to sign currency with 2 names—D. A. Elston—sworn in, May 8

Woman—woman federal regulatory agency chairman—H. D. Bentley—sworn in—Oct. 27

Woman—woman independent federal administrative agency chairman—V. M. Brown—became head of Interstate Commerce Commission—Jan. 1

1970

Air Force Officer—Air Force general (woman)—M. Holm—nominated Dec. 12

Air Force Officer—nun in the Air Force Reserve—N. A. Eagan—became lieutenant May 5

Army Officer—generals who were brother and sister—E. P. Hoisington and P. M Hoisington—E. P. Hoisington sworn in June 11

Astronaut—astronaut (American) to become general—J. A. McDivitt—nominated Dec. 12

Astronaut—astronaut (American) to travel over 700 hours in space—J. A. Lovell, Jr.—fourth flight completed April 17

Bank—automated "tellerless" bank—Surety National Bank's Civic Center branch, Los Angeles, Calif.—opened April 27

ıseball Pitcher—baseball pitcher to hit a grand slam in a World Series game—D. A. McNally—Baltimore, Md.—Oct. 13

ıseball Player—baseball player (major league) to make 7 consecutive hits in 7 times at bat in the same game—C. D. Gutierrez—Cleveland, Ohio—June 21

ıauty Pageant—black contestant in the Miss America pageant—C. A. Browne—selected at Davenport, Iowa—June 13—contestant at Atlantic City, N.J.—Sept. 6

ıbinet (U.S.)—Cabinet member to serve in 4 different capacities—E. L. Richardson—sworn in as Secretary of Health, Education, and Welfare (first)—June 24

ınsus—census compiled in part from statistics obtained by mail—forms mailed April 1

ınsus—census in which the population of the United States exceeded 200 million

ıllege President—college president (black) of a major university predominantly white—C. R. Wharton, Jr.—Michigan State University, East Lansing, Mich.—assumed charge Jan. 2

vorce—"no fault" divorce law (state)—California—enacted July 6

ement—element 105—hahnium—discovered by Albert Ghiorso—University of California Lawrence Radiation Laboratory, Berkeley, Calif.—announced in Washington, D.C.—April 27

ıotball Player—woman football player (professional)—Patricia Palinkas—Orlando, Fla.—Aug. 15

eek Orthodox Church—Greek Orthodox Church bishop who had converted from the Roman Catholic Church—Paul de Ballester—New York City—March 15

ıckey Player—professional hockey player (defenseman) to score 100 points in 1 season—R. G. Orr—100th point in Boston, Mass.—Mar. 15

ıspital—ambulatory surgical facility independently operated—Surgicenter, Phoenix, Ariz.—opened Feb. 12

surance—no-fault automobile insurance law (state)—Massachusetts—enacted Aug. 13

ckey—jockey (woman) to ride in a Kentucky Derby—Diane Crump—Churchill Downs, Ky.—May 2

ıttery—lottery in which the top prize was $1 million—New York (state)—winner: George, Genevieve, and Glenn Ashton—Oct. 8

edical School—women's medical school (still in existence as an independent institution)—name changed to Medical College of Pennsylvania

ıysician—physician with a mobile medical office—H. C. Neals—Jersey City, N.J.—in service June 23

ıson System—woman to direct a state bureau of correction—Augusta, Me.—W. E. Murphy—July

ıpresentative (U.S.)—representative of Puerto Rican ancestry—Herman Badillo of New York—elected, Nov. 3

Secret Service—Executive Protective Service woman agent—P. F. Shantz—sworn in, Sept. 15

Sky Marshal—sky marshals—presidential directive, Oct. 28—first graduates, Dec. 23

Strike—strike of postal employees—New York City—March 18

Swimmer—American swimmer to cover a distance of 1,500 meters free style in less than 16 minutes—John Kinselta—Los Angeles, Calif.—Aug. 23

Television—Telecast—pontifical Easter mass—telecast—March 29

Tennis Match—lawn tennis match (singles) for the Davis Cup to exceed 80 games—A. R. Ashe, Jr. vs. Christian Kuhnke—Cleveland Heights, Ohio—Aug. 31

Treasury Department (U.S.)—treasurer of the United States to sign currency with 2 names—D. A. Kabis—new name on currency, Dec. 4

United Nations—veto by the United States in the Security Council of the United Nations—March 17

Visiting Celebrities—European king buried in the United States—Peter Karageorgevich—died—Denver, Colo.—Nov. 4

1971

Air Force Officer—Air Force general (woman)—J. M. Holm—commissioned July 16

Air Force Officer—military engineer (woman) in the Air Force—S. M. Ocobock—began service, Kelly Air Force Base, Tex.—April 8

Astronaut—astronaut (American) to become an admiral—A. B. Shepard, Jr.—date of rank—Dec. 1

Astronaut—astronauts (American) to ride a vehicle on another planet—D. R. Scott and J. B. Irwin—July 31

Automobile Racer—automobile racer to win over $200,000 in a race—Al Unser—Indianapolis, Ind.—May 29

Aviation—Airplane—skyjack that was successful—D. B. Cooper—Woodland, Wash.—Nov. 24

Brokerage—brokerage firm whose shares were traded by a major stock exchange—traded in New York City—July 27

College—college to offer courses to commuters in traveling railroad cars—Adelphi University—Oct. 18

College—college whose tuition fees were based on family income—Beloit College, Beloit, Wis.—plan adopted Oct. 11

Divorce—"no fault" divorce law (state)—California—effective Jan. 2

Election Law—federal legislation enabling persons 18 years of age or older to vote (26th Amendment)—passed by Senate March 10—by House of Representatives March 23—ratified by first state (Minnesota), March 23—enacted June 30—certified by President Nixon July 5

Envelope—commemorative envelope issued in 2 sizes by the U.S. Post Office Department—Milwaukee, Wis.—Aug. 21

Football Game—professional football game to last longer than 80 minutes—Miami Dolphins vs. Kansas City Chiefs—Kansas City, Mo.—Dec. 25

Holiday—Monday holidays legislation (federal)—effective—Jan. 1

Ice Skating Champion—ice skater to cover 100 miles in less than 6 hours—Kirt Barnes—Ann Arbor, Mich.—Feb. 26

Insurance—crime insurance federal policy—issued to William Early—Aug. 2

Litter Legislation—litter legislation (state)—Oregon—enacted July 2

Mayor—woman mayor of a city of over 200,000 population—P. S. Latting—Oklahoma City, Okla.—sworn in April 13

Microfiche—ultramicrofiche book collection of importance—*The Library of American Civilization*—first delivered to subscribers in July

Motorcyclist—woman professional motorcyclist—Kerry Kleid—licensed Aug. 22—debut, Mt. Peter moto-cross in New York state—Oct. 17

Patent Examiner—woman examiner-in-chief of the Patent Office and Trademark Office—Brereton Sturtevant—nominated July 2—appointment confirmed by Senate July 29—sworn in August 24

Postage Stamp—Christmas-stamp annual series depicting both a religious and nonreligious subject—issued—Washington, D.C.—Nov. 10

Prizefight—prizefight with a purse of $4.5 million—Frazier vs. Ali—New York City—March 8

Railroad—auto-train to transport passengers and their automobiles on the same train—service began—between Lorton, Pa., and Sanford, Fla.—Dec. 6

Representative (U.S.)—representative of Puerto Rican ancestry—Herman Badillo of New York—sworn in, Jan. 21

Road—road paved with glasphalt—completed—Omaha, Neb.—Aug. 6

Satellite—man-made object to orbit another planet—entered Martian orbit—Nov. 13

School—public school built in conjunction with an apartment house—opened—Bronx, New York City—Sept. 13

School—technical school for American Indians—Albuquerque, N. Mex.—dedicated, Aug. 21—opened, Sept. 16

Secret Service—Secret Service women agents—sworn in—Dec. 15

Sex Discrimination—state to ban sex discrimination—Washington—law enacted, May 17—effective, July 1

Ship—ship named for a Seabee—*Marvin Shields*—commissioned

Sky Marshal—sky marshals—first women graduates—April 9

Tariff—tariff commission woman chairman—C. M. Bedell—sworn in, July 12

Television—Telecast—motion picture premiere telecast on 2 successive nights—*Vanished*—March 8-9

Theological School—theological school (majo woman dean—S. M. Teselle—appointed faculty—Nashville, Tenn.

Veterinary Hospital—municipal veterinary hos tal—Spay and Neuter Clinic, Los Angeles, Cal —W. E. Ziegler—opened, Feb. 17

Voting Machine—voting machine in the U. House of Representatives to record individu votes—used—March 3

X ray—X-ray scanning system (commercial) convert electronic information to visible X r —manufactured—New Brunswick, N.J.—fir system installed and tested ordered by U Army Picatinny Arsenal, near Dover, N.J. Aug. 9

1972

Air Force Officer—Air Force Ace in Vietnam—S. Ritchie—Aug. 28

Astronaut—astronaut (American) to become general—J. A. McDivitt—promotion effecti March 1

Bank—bank to provide motion pictures for customers waiting in line to be served—Chem cal Bank—New York City—Dec. 22

Baseball Pitcher—baseball pitcher to retire mo than 40 batters in succession—Jim Barr—S Francisco, Calif., Aug. 23—St. Louis, Mo., A 29

Baseball Strike—baseball strike of serious cons quence—April 13

Brokerage—New York Stock Exchange black rector—J. H. Holland—elected—New York C —July 5

Brokerage—New York Stock Exchange wom governor—J. M. Kreps—elected—New Yo City—July 5

Business—corporation to have more than 3 m lion stockholders—American Telephone Telegraph Company—New York City—Oct.

College—college whose tuition fees were bas on family income—Beloit College, Beloit, W —effective Sept. 5

Electric Power—electric power using municip refuse as a boiler fuel—Union Electric Comp ny, St. Louis, Mo.—generated April 4

Geologist—geologist to reach the moon—H. Schmitt—Dec. 11

Horse Race—horse race with a purse of more th $1 million—All-American Futurity, Ruido N.Mex.—Sept. 4

Litter Legislation—litter legislation (state)—O gon—effective Oct. 1

Medical Clinic—acupuncture treatment center opened—New York City—July 12

Music—black to conduct the Metropolitan Ope House orchestra—Henry Lewis—New Yo City—Oct. 16

Naval Officer—admiral who was a black—S. Gravely, Jr.—date of rank July 1

Navy—women (other than nurses) assigned regular shipboard duty—R. E. Nelson—Aug. —Ann Kerr—Oct. 25

bel Prize—Nobel Prize 2-time winner in the same category—John Bardeen—(second shared prize) Dec. 10

ise Legislation—noise-control statewide comprehensive legislation—New Jersey—signed Jan. 24

lice—police training school women graduates of the Federal Bureau of Investigation—S. L. Roley and J. E. Pierce—Quantico, Va.—Oct. 25

lice—special agents (women) of the police training school of the Federal Bureau of Investigation Academy—Quantico, Va.—course completed, Sept. 11

litical Party—permanent chairman (woman) of a major political party—F. J. M. Westwood—elected at Miami Beach, Fla.—July 14

stage Stamp—block-of-four postage stamps combined in 1 design in which each stamp was an entity—Cape Hatteras National Seashore stamps—issued, Hatteras, N.C.—April 5

stal Card—pictorial postal card—issued—Boston, Mass.—June 29

bbi—woman rabbi—S. J. Priesand—ordained —Cincinnati, Ohio—June 3—appointed—New York City—Aug. 1

presentative (U.S.)—congressional candidate elected while "missing"—T. H. Boggs—elected —Louisiana—Nov. 7

ip—naval ship named for a black naval officer—*Jesse L. Brown*—launched—Westwego, La. —March 18

ip—navy ship with a male-female company— *Sanctuary* (originally, *Marine Owl*)—recommissioned—San Francisco, Calif.—Nov. 18

owmobile—snowmobile to exceed a speed of 125 m.p.h.—Yvon Duhamel—Boonville, N.Y.— Feb. 11

levision—Telecast—stereo telecast—New York City—Dec. 28

ited Church of Christ—minister (avowed homosexual)—William Johnson—ordination sanctioned—San Carlos, Calif.—April 30—first church, San Francisco, Calif.

ited Church of Christ—United Church of Christ ordination of a woman minister in which all the principal roles were filled by women—D. F. Crabtree—Northfield, Conn.—Sept. 17

ce Presidential Candidate—vice presidential candidate of a major political party to resign— T. F. Eagleton of Missouri—resigned—Aug. 1

1973

r Force Officer—Air Force chaplain (woman)— Lorraine Potter—appointed Sept. 26

r Force Officer—chief master sergeant (black) of the Air Force—T. N. Barnes—began service Oct. 1

tronaut—astronauts (American) to exceed 2,000 hours flight time—G. P. Carr, E. G. Gibson, and W. R. Pogue—*Skylab IV*—takeoff (Cape Canaveral) Nov. 16

Atomic Energy Commission—Atomic Energy Commission woman chairman—D. L. Ray— Feb. 6

Attorney General—attorney general (U.S.) to plead guilty to a criminal offense—R. G. Kleindienst—resigned April 30

Balloon—Flights—balloon flight powered by solar energy—Tracy Barnes—Statesville, N.C. —May 16

Building—building higher than 1,400 feet—Sears Building—Chicago, Ill.—topped out May 4

Building—"State House" located outside a state —Florida House—Washington, D.C.—opened Oct. 26

Cabinet (U.S.)—Cabinet member to serve in 4 different capacities—E. L. Richardson—sworn in as Attorney General (third)—May 25

Cabinet (U.S.)—Cabinet member to serve in 4 different capacities—E. L. Richardson—sworn in as Secretary of Defense (second)—Feb. 2

College—belly-dancing college course—University of Texas, Arlington, Tex.—August

College—college to offer athletic scholarships to women—University of Miami, Coral Gables, Fla.—scholarship awarded to Terry Williams— May 5

Copyright Register of the United States—woman Register of Copyrights—B. A. Ringer—appointed Nov. 19

Electoral College—electoral vote for a woman— cast for Theodora Nathan—R. L. MacBride— Jan. 6

Golfer—golfer to earn $100,000 in a contest—Miller Barber—Pinehurst, N.C.—Nov. 17

Information Service (U.S.)—woman to head an area office—Dorothy Dillon—in charge of Latin American activities—August

Jockey—jockey (woman) to win a major stakes race at a major track—Robyn Smith—Paumanauk Handicap, Aqueduct, L.I., N.Y.—March 1

Judge—woman trial judge of the U.S. Court of Claims—C. P. Murphy—sworn in Aug. 6

Marine Corps—woman in the U.S. Marine Band— Ruth Johnson—joined—May 17

Marine Corps—woman unit commander to direct 2,000 men—M. E. Bane—Camp Pendleton, Oceanside, Calif.—Dec. 10

Marshal—marshals of the United States (women) —sworn in Nov. 21

Medal—Presidential Citizen Medal—R. W. Clemente—first presentation (posthumous), May 14

Naval Officer—naval chaplain (woman)—F. D. Pohlman—sworn in—Newport, R.I.—July 2

Naval Officer—woman naval officer to hold a major navy command—R. L. Quigley—assumed command of Navy Service School, San Diego, Calif.—May 17

Photograph—comet photograph taken from space—*Skylab 3*—E. G. Gibson and G. P. Carr —Dec. 29

Physician—doctor to practice in space—J. P. Kerwin—*Skylab 2*—takeoff, May 25—landing, June 22

Pole Vault—pole vault indoors higher than 18 feet—Steve Smith—New York City—Jan. 26

Postage Stamp—printed matter on the reverse side of postage stamps—Postal People set—issued, April 30

Prison—woman prison guard in a maximum security prison for men—J. W. Stewart—Iowa State Penitentiary, Fort Madison, Iowa—appointed Feb. 1

Probate Legislation—probate law eliminating red tape—Wisconsin—enacted June 22—effective Oct. 1

Representative (U.S.)—representative to give birth while holding office—Y. B. Burke—Los Angeles, Calif.—Nov. 23

Road—state highway metric-distance-marker system—Ohio—erection begun, Feb. 12

Runner—runner (professional) to run a mile in less than 4 minutes—Jim Ryun—Detroit, Mich.—April 13

Ship—commercial crude-oil carrier—*Brooklyn*—christened, June 30—test trip, Oct. 22

Ship—ship to use coal-derived oil to power its engines—*Johnston*—test cruise from Philadelphia, Pa.—Nov. 15

Tennis Match—lawn tennis match (doubles) for the Davis Cup to exceed 100 games—Stan Smith and Erik Van Dillen vs. Jaime Fillol and Pat Cornejo—North Little Rock, Ark.—Aug. 5

Voting Machine—vote recorded by electronic means in the U.S. House of Representatives—Jan. 23

Zoo—twilight zoo—Highland Park, Pittsburgh, Pa.—dedicated—April 3

1974

American Indians—American Indian superintendent of a Bureau of Indian Affairs agency—Shirley Plume—appointed Jan. 24

Astronaut—astronauts (American) to exceed 2,000 hours flight time—G. P. Carr, E. G. Gibson, and W. R. Pogue—*Skylab IV*—landed, Feb. 8

Baseball Game—night baseball game (major league) to last longer than 7 hours—St. Louis Cardinals vs. New York Mets—New York City—Sept. 12

Book Catalog—state library to publish a master book catalog—Oregon State Library, Salem, Oreg.

Building—building higher than 1,400 feet—Sears Building—Chicago, Ill.—completed

Congress (U.S.)—Congressional Budget Office—authorized—July 12

Degrees (academic and honorary)—bachelor's degree awarded by a recognized institution without requiring a single college credit—N. E. France—University of the State of New York, Albany, N.Y.—Sept. 20

Governor—woman governor elected without succeeding her husband—R. G. O. T. Grasso—Connecticut—Nov. 5

Greek Orthodox Church—Greek Orthodox Archdiocesan Council women members announced Nov. 9

Jockey—jockey to win one hundred $100,000 stakes—Willie Shoemaker—Hot Springs, Ar—March 30

Lawyer's Association—lawyers' association (state) woman president—M. M. Lambert—New York—began service June 30

Legislator (state)—homosexual (avowed) elected to a state office—Elaine Noble—Boston, Mass—Nov. 5

Map—mosaic map of the contiguous 48 states from scenes transmitted from a satellite—assembled in November

Mayor—woman mayor of a major city—J. Hayes—San Jose, Calif.—elected Nov. 6

Merchant Marine Academy—women admitted the Merchant Marine Academy—Kings Point L.I., N.Y.—July

Naval Officer—naval chaplain (black woman) Vivian McFadden—sworn in—Atlanta, Ga. Sept. 8

Naval Officer—woman member of the Navy Hurricane Hunters—J. A. Neuffer—flew in storm—Sept. 1

Police—police officer (woman) killed in the line duty—G. A. Cobb—Washington, D.C.—Sept.

Police—woman employed at a high level within men's maximum security facility—Katheri Tripp—Thomaston, Me.—Sept. 11

Postage Stamp—pressure-sensitized-adhesive postage stamp—Dove of Peace—issued—New York City—Nov. 15

President (U.S.)—President to resign—R. M. Nixon—submitted resignation Aug. 8—resignation effective Aug. 9

Representative (U.S.)—grandmother to serve Congress—M. H. Fenwick—elected—New Jersey—Nov. 5

Senator (U.S.)—senator who was an astronaut—H. Glenn—elected—Ohio—Nov. 5

Television—Telecast—congressional telecast and radio broadcast—authorized by Senate—Washington, D.C.—Dec. 14—aired—Dec. 19

Television—Telecast—Senate proceedings telecast—vice presidential installation ceremony for N. A. Rockefeller—Washington, D.C.—Dec. 19

Tightrope Walker—tightrope walker to span skyscrapers—Philippe Petit—New York City Aug. 7

Vice President (U.S.)—Vice President appointed (not elected by popular vote) to become President—G. R. Ford—sworn in—Aug. 9

Woman—woman Republican national committee chairman—M. L. Smith—elected—Washington, D.C.—Sept. 16

1975

rmy Officer—mother and son to enlist simultaneously—Michael Fleming and Ethel Fleming—Merced, Calif.—Oct. 15

rmy Officer—woman to command an Armed Forces Examining and Entrance Station—M. V. Parker—Detroit, Mich.—May 31

stronaut—astronauts (American) to participate in an international spaceflight—T. P. Stafford and D. K. Slayton—*Apollo XVIII*—docked with *Soyuz XIX*—July 17

rd—whooping crane born in captivity—Laurel, Md.—May 28

owler—bowler to earn $100,000 in 1 year in tournaments—Earl Anthony—Battle Creek, Mich. —earnings reached $100,890 Oct. 27

oast Guard Academy—women students—admission authorized—Oct. 21

ollege—college commencement exercises within a prison—Jackson, Mich.—Jan. 20

ollege—educational hosteling network—Elderhostel—offered at New England College—Henniker, N.H.—June 8–14

ongress (U.S.)—Congressional Budget Office— G. A. M. Rivlin, director—began service Feb. 24

ourt—court in which the judge presided in a city other than the one (New York City) in which the lawyers appeared—Court of Claims, Washington, D.C.—Oct. 16

vorce—1 million divorces in 1 year

overnor—woman governor elected without succeeding her husband—R. G. O. T. Grasso—Connecticut—sworn in Jan. 8

dge—black chief justice of a federal court—J. B. Parsons—Illinois Supreme Court—April 18

nnel—hotel for dogs—Kennelworth—opened by Leo Wiener—New York City—Nov. 12

bor Relations—National Relations Board woman chairman—B. S. Murphy—appointed Jan. 8—sworn in Feb. 18

ysician—doctors' strike against long working hours in hospitals—New York City—March 17

le Vault—pole vault higher than 18.5 feet— Dave Roberts—Gainesville, Fla.—March 28

stage Stamp—postage stamps without a denomination—Christmas issue—Washington, D.C.—Oct. 14

presentative (U.S.)—grandmother to serve in Congress—M. H. Fenwick of New Jersey—began service Jan. 3

int (Catholic)—saint (native-born Catholic)—E. A. B. Seton—canonized, Sept. 14

x Discrimination—state that declared unconstitutional a ban against girls competing with boys in athletic events on a state basis—Pennsylvania—March 19

i Carousel—ski carousel—in service—Stratton Mountain, Vt.—November

adium—adjustable stadium—Aloha Stadium— Honolulu, Hawaii—dedicated, Sept. 12

eological School—theological school (major) woman dean—S. M. Teselle—took office— Nashville, Tenn.—June 1

Visiting Celebrities—emperor of Japan to visit the continental United States—Hirohito—arrived —Williamsburg, Va.—Sept. 30

Woman—women eligible to enter the U.S. service academies—authorized—Oct. 7

1976

Air Force Academy (U.S.)—women students—admitted—Colorado Springs, Colo.—June 28

Army Officer—general of the armies of the United States with the rank of 6 stars—George Washington—posthumous commission signed, Oct. 19

Army School—women cadets of the U.S. Military Academy (West Point)—accepted for admission, March 9—enrolled, July 7

Baseball Team—baseball team to win 30 pennants—New York Yankees

Blind—machine for reading printed matter aloud —Raymond Kurzweil—demonstrated, Jan. 13

Bridge—bridge named for a woman—Betsy Ross Bridge—Philadelphia, Pa.—Pennsauken, N.J.— opened April 30

Cabinet (U.S.)—Cabinet member to serve in 4 different capacities—E. L. Richardson—sworn in as Secretary of Commerce (fourth)—Feb. 2

Coast Guard Academy—women students—admitted—New London, Conn.—June 28

Diplomatic Service—ambassador (woman) to the Court of St. James—A. L. Armstrong—nominated Jan. 14—appointment confirmed Jan. 28— sworn in Feb. 10—presented credentials March 17

Euthanasia—"Right to Die" law—California— enacted Sept. 30

Geographical Society—geographical society director (woman)—S. K. Meyers—New York City —June 16

Hall of Famer—athlete enshrined in 2 halls of fame—Robert Hubbard—Cooperstown, N.Y. (baseball)—Aug. 9

Lottery—lottery (state regulated) in which 3 zeros made up the winning number—New Jersey— Sept. 13

Lottery—lottery to guarantee a minimum of $1,800,000—New Jersey—Jan. 27

Maritime School—woman graduate of a 4-year maritime school—D. B. Doane—Maine Maritime Academy, Castine, Me.—May 1

Medal—Defense Superior Service Medal—created Feb. 6

Naval Academy—women students—admitted— July 6

Nobel Prize—Nobel Prize winners all from one country in 5 categories—Dec. 10

Opera—opera at the Metropolitan Opera House, New York City, conducted by a woman—*La Traviata*—Sarah Caldwell—Jan. 13

Photograph—photographs taken on Mars—transmitted to Pasadena, Calif.—July 20

Postage Stamp—nurse (individual) depicted on a postage stamp—Clara Maass—issued—Belleville, N.J.—Aug. 18

Representative (U.S.)—Polish-American representative—B. A. Mikulski of Maryland—elected, Nov. 2

Representative (U.S.)—representatives to marry each other—M. E. Keys and Andrew Jacobs, Jr.—Topeka, Kans.—Jan. 3

School—underground school—Abo Elementary School—built—Artesia, N. Mex.

Ship—ambulance ship for first aid to boaters and pleasure craft—*Star of Life No. 1*—christened—Stamford, Conn.—April 2

Soccer—soccer game in which 12 points were scored by 1 player—Giorgio Chinaglia—Cosmos vs. Toros—New York City—Aug. 10

Softball—softball game of 365 innings—Monticello, N.Y.—Aug. 14-15

State Department (U.S.)—protocol chief (woman)—S. T. Black—began service, July 20

Sterilization—sterilization legislation (state) that was optional, not punitive—enacted—Virginia—April 10

Television—television annual billing to exceed $6 billion

Television—Telecast—live national commercial cablecast via satellite—via RCA Satcom—Birmingham Bulls vs. Edmonton Oilers—Birmingham, Ala.—Dec. 2

Television—Telecast—presidential debate between an incumbent President and a candidate for the office—G. R. Ford vs. Jimmy Carter—3 debates—Philadelphia, Pa., Sept. 23—San Francisco, Calif., Oct. 6—Williamsburg, Va., Oct. 22

Television—Telecast—state dinner (U.S.) telecast—Washington, D.C.—July 7

Woman—nuclear commercial power plant licensed woman operator—R. A. Kankus—licensed—Feb. 12

1977

Army Officer—Secretary of the Army (black)—C. L. Alexander, Jr.—named Jan. 18—sworn in Feb. 14

Attorney General—attorney general (U.S.) to be incarcerated—J. N. Mitchell—Maxwell Air Force Base, Ala.—June 21

Automobile Racer—automobile racer to win the Indianapolis 500 four times—A. J. Foyt, Jr.—Indianapolis, Ind.—fourth time May 29

Automobile Racer—woman driver to compete in the Indianapolis 500—Janet Guthrie—Indianapolis, Ind.—qualified May 22—raced May 29

Baseball Game—World Series baseball game in which a batter made 3 consecutive home runs in 1 game—R. M. Jackson—New York City—Oct. 18

Capital Punishment—lethal—drug execution authorized—Oklahoma—May 10

Civil Aeronautics Board—Civil Aeronautics Board woman member—E. E. Bailey—nominated by President Jimmy Carter—July 7—appointment confirmed July 28

Coast Guard (U.S.)—Coast Guard women to serve aboard ships (other than hospital ships)—B. Kelley and D. L. Wilson—assigned June 22

Coast Guard (U.S.)—woman airplane pilot in the Coast Guard—Janna Lambine—was graduated at Milton, Fla.—March 4

Department of Energy (U.S.)—Department of Energy—created Aug. 4—J. R. Schlesinger, first secretary—Aug. 5—formal opening Oct. 1

Golfer—golfer to break 60 in a Professional Golfers Association tour—A. L. Geiberger—Memphis, Tenn.—June 10

Horse Race—father and son harness drivers gross more than $1 million each in 1 season—Billy Haughton and Peter Haughton

Jockey—jockey to win more than $5 million purses in 1 year—Steve Cauthen—(winnings topped $5 million) Oct. 24

Judge—judge who had served time in prison—A. Young—Loomis, Calif.—began term of office Jan. 3

Judge—woman judge of the Surrogates Court—M. Lambert—elected—New York—Nov. 8

Lottery—daily state lotteries with the same winning daily number—New Jersey and Pennsylvania—Oct. 4

Medal—Defense Meritorious Service Medal—authorized Nov. 3

Medal—Humanitarian Service Medal—authorized Jan. 19

Medal—Medal of Freedom awarded to a husband and wife—Will Durant and Ariel Durant—announced Jan. 1—presented Jan. 10

Motion Picture Actor—motion picture performer (woman) to win the Life Achievement Award—Bette Davis—presentation at Beverly Hills, Calif.—March 1

Parade—parade in which all the marching music was supplied by transistor radio receivers—Streamwood, Ill.—July 4

Peace Corps—woman director of the Peace Corps—C. R. Payton—nominated Sept. 7

Photograph—color transparency (35mm) magnified 516 times—taken by Ernst Haas—exhibited—New York City—Feb. 22

Prizefight Referee—woman to judge a heavyweight championship fight—Eva Shain—Ali Shavers—New York City—Sept. 29

Protestant Episcopal Church—priests (husband and wife) ordained together—Michael Cobb and A. S. Coburn—Danbury, Conn.—Dec. 1

Radio Broadcast—presidential phone-in—Jimmy Carter—Walter Cronkite, moderator—Washington, D.C.—March 5

Road—border-to-border national highway—Interstate 75—dedicated—Dec. 22

Saint (Catholic)—American saint (male)—J. Neumann—canonized, June 19

Soccer—soccer game before 77,000 spectators—Cosmos vs. Strikers—East Rutherford, N.J.—Aug. 14

Treasury Department (U.S.)—gold medallions issued by the Treasury Department—authorized—March 8

easury Department (U.S.)—treasurer of the United States (black woman)—A. T. Morton—assumed office, Sept. 12

ar Prisoner—prisoner of war to head the Naval War College—J. B. Stockdale—began service as president—Newport, R.I.—Oct. 13

hale—killer whale born in captivity—Marine-land, Los Angeles, Calif.—Feb. 28

1978

chitect—woman graduate of the Webb Institute of Naval Architecture—Karen Hansen—Glen Cove, N.Y.—June 22

tronaut—astronauts (women)—selection announced—Jan. 16

iation—Airship—President's wife to pilot a dirigible—*America*—R. S. Carter—Aug. 18

llet—ballet transmitted by satellite—telecast over WNEW-TV—New York City—July 22

nk—bank with deposits exceeding $70 million —Bank of America National Trust and Savings Association, San Francisco, Calif.—Dec. 31

nk—bank with resources exceeding $90 million —Bank of America National Trust and Savings Association, San Francisco, Calif.—Dec. 31

urch of Jesus Christ of Latter-Day Saints— black ordained to the priesthood—Joseph Freeman, Jr.—Salt Lake City, Utah—June 11

ngress (U.S.)—House of Representatives—congressional committee bilingual report—March 28

deral Reserve System—Federal Reserve System Board of Governors member (woman)—N. H. Teeters—sworn in Sept. 18

otball Game—football game in which referees were permitted to use television instant replays —Philadelphia Eagles vs. Miami Dolphins—Canton, Ohio—July 29

rse—horse (thoroughbred) to defeat 2 triple-crown winners in the same race—Exceller—Elmont, N.Y.—Oct. 14

lge—woman judge of the Surrogates Court—M. M. Lambert—New York City—began term Jan.

nguage—plain language law—New York (state)—enacted May 31—effective Nov. 2

rine Corps—general (woman) in the Marine Corps—M. A. Brewer—nominated by President Jimmy Carter—April 6—sworn in May 11

ney—woman commemorated on a circulating U.S. coin—S. B. Anthony—coin authorized Oct. 10—issued at Philadelphia, Pa.—Dec. 13

vy—large-scale assignment of women (other than nurses) to sea duty—Nov. 1

wspaper—newspaper whose input was derived from a communications satellite—*Wall Street Journal*—dedication of new system, Nov. 20

n—pen with truly erasable ink—Eraser Mate— . A. Miller and Henry Peper, Jr.—patented— une 27

stage Stamp—postage stamp to honor a black woman—Harriet Tubman—issued—Washington, D.C.—Feb. 1

Postage Stamp—postage stamp (U.S.) issued in a foreign country prior to sale in the United States —Toronto, Canada, June 10—Washington, D.C., Aug. 26

Prizefight—prizefight to gross more than $5 million in sales—Ali vs. Spinks—New Orleans, La. —Sept. 15

Prizefighter—pugilist to win the heavyweight championship 3 times—Muhammad Ali—(3rd time) New Orleans, La.—Sept. 15

Slot Machine—slot-machine payoff of $275,000— James Schelich—Las Vegas, Nev.—Oct. 29

Television—Telecast—congressional session proceedings telecast—Washington, D.C.—June 12

1979

Automobile—rocket vehicle to break the sound barrier on land—Stan Barrett—Edwards Air Force Base, Calif.—Dec. 16

Automobile Racer—automobile racer to win the Daytona 500 six times—Richard Petty—Daytona, Fla.—(6th victory) Feb. 18

Book—book advance payment to exceed $3 million—*Princess Daisy,* by Judith Krantz—New York City—Sept. 12

Coal Mine—woman to die in a coal mine disaster —M. J. McCusker—Coalport, Pa.—Oct. 2

Coast Guard (U.S.)—woman to command a naval ship on regular patrol—S. I. Moritz—*Cape Current*—Straits of Florida—June 8

Coast Guard Officer—woman commander of a Coast Guard ship—Beverly Kelley—appointed, April 16

Golfer—golfer to shoot below his age—S. J. Snead —Coal City, Ill.—July 22

Judge—black woman judge of the U.S. Court of Appeals—A. L. Kearse—sworn in at New York City—June 27

Marine Corps—general (black) of the Marines—F. E. Petersen, Jr.—nominated Feb. 23

Money—woman commemorated on a circulating U.S. coin—S. B. Anthony—circulation begun July 1

Pen—pen with truly erasable ink—Eraser Mate— produced—Santa Monica, Calif.

Police—police training school Federal Bureau of Investigation field officer chief (black)—J. D. Glover—appointed to office in Milwaukee, Wis. —Feb. 16

Postage Stamp—brothers to be pictured on individual postage stamps—R. F. Kennedy—15-cent blue—issued Jan. 12

President (U.S.)—administration office of the President—authorized—Jan. 2

Railroad—railroad train operated exclusively by women—Port Washington, L.I., N.Y., to Pennsylvania station, New York City—in service, June 6

Runner—runner (woman) to run a marathon in less than 2.5 hours—Grete Waitz—New York City—Oct. 21

Runner—runner (woman) to run 1 mile in less than 4.5 minutes—Mary Decker—Philadelphia, Pa.—June 30

Vice President (U.S.)—Vice President cremated— N. A. Rockefeller—Jan. 27

Visiting Celebrities—pontiff to visit the White House—Pope John Paul II—arrived Boston, Mass.—Oct. 1—departed Washington, D.C. (for Rome)—Oct. 6

1980

Army School—Jewish woman graduate of the U.S. Military Academy (West Point)—Donna Maller—commissioned—June 4

Army School—woman cadet to receive a commission—Ms. Hollen—West Point, N.Y.—May 28

Automobile—front-wheel-drive subcompact American automobile—World Car—Ford Motor Company, Fort Wayne, Mich.—first car off assembly line, Aug. 11

Balloon—Flights—transcontinental nonstop balloon flight—M. L. Anderson and Kris Anderson —San Francisco, Calif., to Gaspé peninsula outside Matane, Que.—left May 8—landed May 11

Coast Guard Academy—women graduates—J. M. Butler—New London, Conn.—May 21

Horse Race—horse race for a purse of more than $1 million—Meadowland, East Rutherford, N.J. —July 18

Horse Race—horse race for a purse of more tha $2 million—Woodrow Wilson purse—East R therford, N.J.—Aug. 6

Methodist Church—bishop (woman)—M. S. Ma thews—elected—Dayton, Ohio—July 17—co secrated—Selinsgrove, Pa.—July 18

Ordance—tank with a turbine engine—XM (Abramstank)—rolled out—Lima, Ohio—Fe 28

Police—state police class of women—graduate at Sea Girt, N.J.—June 27

Rabbi—husband-and-wife rabbinical and ca torial team engaged by a synagogue—S. , Gertman and S. J. Sager—Cleveland, Ohio—b gan service, July 1

Secret Service—Secret Service female speci agent killed in the line of duty—J. Y. Cross—L Angeles, Calif.—June 4

Solar Power Plant—solar-cell power plant—de cated—Utah—June 7

Television—Telecast—debate (nationally tel cast) among candidates within a political par for the presidential nomination—Des Moine Iowa—Jan. 5

Treasury Department (U.S.)—gold medallions i sued by the Treasury Department—June 16

Woman—woman director of the Voice of Ame ca—M. F. Bitterman—appointment confirmed Feb. 28—took office—March 7

Index by Days of the Month

o obtain a complete account of the various items, the reader should consult the main body
the text. The **boldface** type shows the alphabetical heading under which each item may
e found. If an item appears in the text under a general heading, the specific heading is noted
elow after the general heading.

1927   **Insurance**—automobile compulsory insurance act (state)—effective—Massachusetts
1927   **Radio Broadcast**—coast-to-coast football-game broadcast originating on the West coast—Alabama vs. Stanford—Rose Bowl game, Pasadena, Calif.
1928   **Building**—air-conditioned office building—opened—San Antonio, Tex.
1931   **Postage Stamp**—stamped envelopes with the identical design issued in various denominations—Washington Bicentennial envelopes—first stamps issued—Washington, D.C.
1934   **Bank Legislation**—bank guaranty legislation—effective
1934   **Federal Deposit Insurance Corporation**—effective
1935   **Radio Facsimile Transmission**—press syndicate facsimile transmission direct to newspaper offices—Wirephoto
1936   **Microfilm**—newspaper to microfilm its current issues—New York *Herald Tribune*
1937   **Aviation**—physiological research laboratory of the U.S. Army Air Corps—completed—Dayton, Ohio
1939   **Flea Laboratory**—opened—San Francisco, Calif.
1944   **Marine Corps**—general (4 stars) of the Marines—Thomas Holcomb
1948   **Motion Picture**—newsreel in color—taken—Pasadena, Calif.
1948   **Television—Telecast**—motion picture premiere performance to be televised (feature-length foreign film)—New York City
1949   **Birth Registration**—birth registration uniform system for the numbering of birth certificates—system inaugurated
1951   **Television—Telecast**—pay television—Phonovision demonstrated—Chicago, Ill.
1953   **Railroad Car**—observation cars (super-dome)—in service
1954   **Immigration**—refugee to arrive under the Refugee Relief Act of 1953—Stamatoula Roumanis
1954   **Prison System**—woman to direct a prison system—A. M. Kross—New York City—sworn in
1954   **Television—Mobile Unit**—mobile television units (color)—WNBT, New York City
1954   **Television—Telecast**—color coast-to-coast telecast from the West Coast—Tournament of Roses—Pasadena, Calif.
1961   **Football Game**—American Football League's first championship game—Houston Oilers vs. Los Angeles Chargers—Houston, Tex.
1963   **Electric Power Plant**—cooling tower hyperbolic-shaped—Ashland, Ky.—in commercial service
1969   **Woman**—woman independent federal administrative agency chairman—V. M. Brown—Interstate Commerce Commission—became head

1971   **Holiday**—Monday holidays legislati (federal)—effective
1977   **Medal**—Medal of Freedom awarded to husband and wife—Will Durant and Ar Durant—announced
1978   **Judge**—woman judge of the Surrogat Court—M. M. Lambert—began term, Ne York City

JANUARY 2

1777   **Army Officer**—chaplain killed in action John Rosbrugh—Trenton, N.J.
1811   **Senator (U.S.)**—senator censured—Tim thy Pickering of Massachusetts
1828   **News Correspondent**—Washington corr spondent of importance—J. G. Bennett first articles
1842   **Bridge**—wire suspension bridge for gene traffic—opened—Fairmount, Pa.
1867   **Bank**—national bank failure—First N tional Bank of Attica, N.Y.—receiversh terminated
1893   **Postage Stamp**—commemorative posta stamps—issued
1893   **Postage Stamp**—one-dollar-valuation po age stamp—Isabella Pledging Her Jewels issued—Washington, D.C.
1893   **Postage Stamp**—paintings depicted postage stamps—on sale
1893   **Postage Stamp**—postage stamp to pictur woman—on sale
1908   **Tunnel**—freight delivery tunnel system completed—Chicago, Ill.
1910   **High School**—junior high school system opened—Berkeley, Calif.
1914   **Community Trust**—established—Clev land, Ohio
1918   **Army Insignia**—wound chevron—auth ized
1919   **Ship**—destroyer of the U.S. Navy nam for a Confederate officer—*Buchanar* launched—Bath, Me.
1921   **Radio Broadcast**—religious service broa cast—Pittsburgh, Pa.
1922   **Blind**—correspondence school for blind to offer instruction in the Braille s tem—incorporated—Winnetka, Ill.
1925   **Psychology Society**—psychology soci (national organization)—American P chological Association—incorporated
1934   **Liquor Stores (state)**—opened—Penns vania
1936   **Electron Tube**—described—St. Louis, M
1967   **Medicare**—health insurance federal plar first payments for skilled nursing facilit under extended care benefit provision
1970   **College President**—college presid (black) of a major university predomina ly white—C. R. Wharton, Jr.—Michig State University, East Lansing, Mich.— sumed charge
1971   **Divorce**—"no fault" divorce law (state California—effective

1889 Historical Society—historical society (general)—American Historical Association—first report published

1896 Actors' Union—Actors' National Protective Union—chartered

1915 Governor—Jewish governor—elected for a full term—served—Moses Alexander—Idaho

1923 Radio Broadcast—chain broadcast—with repeater points—WEAF and WNAC—New York City and Boston

1931 Aviation—Flights—women to fly in excess of 120 hours—Evelyn Trout and E. M. Cooper—Glendale, Calif.—takeoff

1936 School—school to have all classroom lights controlled by electric eyes—operated—Hammondsport, N.Y.

1939 College—woman dean of a graduate school—Frieda Wunderlich—elected—New York City

1944 State Department (U.S.)—State Department (U.S.) black official—R. J. Bunche—appointed

1953 Carpeting—carpeting of tufted plastic—offered for sale—La Fayette, Ga.

1962 Subway—train to run automatically without conductors or motormen—New York City

1965 Representative (U.S.)—Japanese-American woman representative—P. T. Mink of Hawaii—began service

1965 Ship—naval ship of the United States with a crew of mixed nationalities—*Claude V. Ricketts* (originally, *William P. Biddle*)—sailed on Caribbean cruise—Norfolk, Va.

JANUARY 5

1800 Swedenborgian or New Church—Swedenborgian or New Church Temple—service—Baltimore, Md.

1863 Normal School—woman principal of a normal school—A. C. Brackett—St. Louis, Mo.

1885 Railroad—piggyback railroad operation—Long Island Rail Road Company

1887 Library Training (systematic)—instruction—New York City

1895 Enclave—enclave—land purchased—Fairhope, Ala.

1903 Cable—cable across the Pacific Ocean—from San Francisco, Calif.—opened for public use

1925 Governor—woman governor of a state—N. T. Ross—assumed office—Wyoming

1927 Lecturer—lecturer of royal blood to speak for personal profit—Prince Vilhelm—arrived

1933 Bridge—bridge with piers sunk in the open sea—construction started—San Francisco, Calif.

1937 Legislature—unicameral legislature (state)—opened—Nebraska

1944 Newspaper—transoceanic newspaper—*Daily Mail*—issued

1948 Motion Picture—newsreel in color—exhibited

1980 Television—Telecast—debate (national telecast) among candidates within a political party for the presidential nomination—Des Moines, Iowa

JANUARY 6

1639 Agriculture—crop surplus destruction—ordered—Virginia

1844 Iron—iron patent—S. Broadmeadow

1857 Zinc—zinc patent—S. Wetherill

1866 Railroad Train Robbery—railroad train robbery of a train en route

1870 Labor Union—labor organization to admit workmen other than craft workmen—regular officers elected

1885 Legislator (state)—black legislator (state)—representing white constituency—B. W. Arnett—served—Ohio

1898 Telephone—telephone message from submarine underwater—Simon Lake—New York City

1913 Mayor—woman mayor elected by a city west of the Rocky Mountains—Clara Munson—Warrenton, Oreg.—began term

1927 Woman—woman secretary of a state senate—Fern Ale—served—Indiana

1930 Diesel Engine—diesel-engine automobile trip—completed—New York City

1942 Aviation—Flights (world)—world flight by a commercial airplane—*Pacific Clipper*—returned to New York City

1955 Lieutenant Governor—woman lieutenant governor—C. N. Bailey—sworn in—Montpelier, Vt.

1966 Catholic Bishop—black Catholic bishop who was American born—H. R. Perry—consecrated auxiliary bishop, New Orleans, La.

1973 Electoral College—electoral vote for woman—cast for Theodora Nathan—R. MacBride

JANUARY 7

1751 Play (drama)—benefit performance—New York City

1782 Bank—bank chartered by Congress—Bank of North America—Philadelphia, Pa.—opened for business

1784 Seed Business—organized—David Landreth—Philadelphia, Pa.

1784 War Veterans' Society—Society of the Cincinnati—Society in France—organized

1789 Congress (U.S.)—joint meeting of the Senate and the House of Representatives—election meeting

1817 Bank—Bank of the United States—second bank opened—Philadelphia, Pa.

1824 Prizefight—prizefight arena—Worcester, Mass.—first fight held

30 **Railroad**—railroad for commercial transportation of passengers and freight—Baltimore, Md.—passenger revenue obtained

67 **Election Law**—election law granting black males the right to vote—presidential veto overridden by Senate

69 **Book Guide**—book guide—*American Bookseller's Guide*—published—New York City—first issue

87 **Bicycle Rider**—bicycle rider to go around the world—returned to San Francisco, Calif.

90 **Ship**—navy vessel equipped to lay mines—*Baltimore*—commissioned

94 **Copyright**—motion picture film copyrighted—Frank Ott

97 **Handball**—national championship match for amateurs—Jersey City, N.J.

04 **Radio Distress Signal**—CQD signal—established

08 **Health Department**—county health department organized on a full-time basis—Jefferson County, Ky.—established

11 **Aviation—Airplane Bombing**—airplane bombing experiment with explosives—San Francisco, Calif.

13 **Gasoline**—cracking process used to obtain gasoline from crude petroleum—W. M. Burton—Chicago, Ill.

14 **Public Defender's Office**—W. J. Wood—assumed duties

14 **Ship**—steamboat to pass through the Panama Canal—craneboat—*Alex. La Valley*

24 **Postage Stamp**—precanceled stamps printed on rotary presses—one-cent precanceled stamps issued

27 **Telephone**—transatlantic telephone service—commercial—New York City and London, England

42 **Liquid Heat**—used—Summit, N.J.

49 **Photograph**—photograph of genes—Los Angeles, Calif.—announced

54 **Television Receiver**—television receiver to permit two audiences to see and hear two different programs at the same time

55 **Opera**—black singer of the Metropolitan Opera—Marian Anderson—New York City

JANUARY 8

75 **Corporation**—commercial corporation—New York City—incorporated

77 **Price Regulation Legislation**—price regulation law (colonial)—effective—Rhode Island

83 **Copyright Law**—copyright law (state)—enacted—Connecticut

33 **Music Instruction**—musical pedagogy school—Boston Academy of Music—founded—Boston, Mass.

38 **Telegraph**—telegraphic communication system in which dots and dashes represented letters—message transmitted

1853 **Monument**—bronze equestrian statue—unveiled—Washington, D.C.

1856 **Borax**—discovered—Tuscan Springs, Calif.

1867 **College**—university for blacks to establish undergraduate, graduate, and professional schools—C. B. Boynton elected president

1867 **Election Law**—election law granting black males the right to vote—presidential veto overridden by House of Representatives

1884 **Leather**—chrome tanning process—patented—Augustus Schultz

1889 **Tabulating Machine**—patented—Herman Hollerith

1901 **Bowling Tournament**—bowling tournament sponsored by the American Bowling Congress—Chicago, Ill.

1918 **Prohibition**—prohibition amendment to the Constitution—first state to ratify—Mississippi

1923 **Automobile Trucking Service**—automobile trucking service—by railroad motor coaches—inaugurated—Maryland

1925 **Supreme Court (state)**—state supreme court composed entirely of women—appointed—Texas

1935 **Spectrophotometer**—patented—A. C. Hardy—Wellesley, Mass.

1965 **Judge**—chief justice (woman) of a state supreme court—L. E. Lockwood—Arizona

1975 **Governor**—woman governor elected without succeeding her husband—R. G. O. T. Grasso—Connecticut—sworn in

1975 **Labor Relations**—National Labor Relations Board woman chairman—B. S. Murphy—appointed

JANUARY 9

1793 **Balloon—Flights**—balloon flight in which a presidential order was carried—ascended—Philadelphia, Pa.

1838 **Patent**—patent reissue—Julius Hatch—Great Bend, Pa.

1844 **Coast Guard (U.S.)**—Coast Guard commandant—A. V. Fraser—report submitted

1861 **Civil War**—act that marked the inauguration of the War of 1861–1865—*Star of the West* fired upon

1872 **Congress (U.S.)—House of Representatives**—foreign clergyman to open the House of Representatives with prayer—Abraham de Sola

1894 **Telephone**—common battery (nonmultiple) switchboard—operated—Lexington, Mass.

1918 **Air Force**—air force aviation unit—sailed—Cape May, N.J.

1929 **Animals**—dogs trained to guide the blind—Seeing Eye—Nashville, Tenn.—incorporated

1931 **Aviation—Flights**—women to fly in excess of 120 hours—Evelyn Trout and E. M. Cooper—Glendale, Calif.—landed

1936 **Ordnance**—semiautomatic rifle—adopted
—U.S. Army
1940 **Television—Telecast**—sales meeting televised—New York City
1963 **Senator (U.S.)**—father whose 3 sons were
senators—J. P. Kennedy—E. M. Kennedy
sworn in

JANUARY 10

1843 **Impeachment**—impeachment proceedings
attempt against a President of the United
States—J. M. Botts against John Tyler
1894 **Nurses' Society**—society for superintendents of nursing schools—American Society of Superintendents of Training Schools
for Nurses—national convention—New
York City
1910 **Aviation—Expositions and Meets**—aviation meet—Los Angeles, Calif.
1911 **Photograph**—photograph from an airplane
—San Diego, Calif.
1934 **Aviation—Flights (transpacific)**—Honolulu
squadron flight—left San Francisco, Calif.
1943 **President (U.S.)**—President to visit a foreign country in wartime—F. D. Roosevelt—
sailed from Miami to Trinidad
1944 **Electric Power Plant**—mobile electric
power plant—delivered—Philadelphia, Pa.
1946 **Radar**—radar signal to the moon—beamed
—Belmar, N.J.
1949 **Postal Card**—airmail postal card—issued
1951 **Aviation—Flights**—jet passenger trip—
Chicago–New York City
1955 **Radar**—offshore radar warning station—
keel laid
1967 **Senator (U.S.)**—black senator elected by
popular vote—E. W. Brooke of Massachusetts—took seat in Senate
1967 **Television Station**—noncommercial educational television network—New York City
—first live broadcast
1977 **Medal**—Medal of Freedom awarded to a
husband and wife—Will Durant and Ariel
Durant—presented in Washington, D.C.

JANUARY 11

1759 **Insurance**—life insurance company—
Philadelphia, Pa.—incorporated
1770 **Rhubarb**—shipped to the United States
from London, England
1860 **Insurance**—insurance department (state)
superintendent appointed
1873 **Livestock Market Paper**—published—
Chicago, Ill.
1875 **Nautical School**—nautical municipal
school—opened—New York City
1897 **Senate (state)**—woman state senator—
served—Utah—M. H. Cannon
1913 **Automobile**—sedan-type automobile—officially shown—New York City
1917 **Voting Machine**—electric vote-recorder
used by a legislative body—installed—
Madison, Wis.

1930 **Element**—element   87—francium—
nounced
1930 **Ship**—diesel-engine passenger ship—*T*
City of New York—tested on Delawa
River
1935 **Aviation—Pilot**—woman pilot to fly s
across the Pacific Ocean—start—Honol
—A. E. Putnam
1938 **Bank**—national bank woman presiden
F. E. Moulton—elected—Limerick, Me.
1949 **Mosque**—cornerstone laid—Islamic C
ter—Washington, D.C.

JANUARY 12

1773 **Museum**—public museum—organized
1792 **Diplomatic Service**—minister to Great B
ain—Thomas Pinckney—minister pleni
tentiary—appointed
1853 **College**—university on the Pacific Coas
Willamette University—incorporate
Salem, Oreg.
1876 **Forestry Society**—state forestry assoc
tion—Minnesota Forestry Association
organized
1895 **Government Printing Office**—Superinte
dent of Documents—authorized
1896 **X Ray**—X-ray photograph—H. L. Smith
Davidson, N.C.
1910 **Aviation—Pilot**—pilot (American) to
tablish an altitude record—Louis Paulh
—Los Angeles, Calif.
1924 **Science Association**—history of scien
society—organized—Boston, Mass.
1929 **Envelope**—airmail letter sheet—issued
1929 **Ship**—seatrain—service   inaugurate
New Orleans, La.–Havana, Cuba
1932 **Senator (U.S.)**—woman elected to the S
ate—H. O. W. Caraway—elected—Ark
sas
1937 **Plow**—submarine cable plow—patente
1942 **Medal**—Medal of Honor awarded in Wo
War II—A. R. Nininger
1944 **Ship**—Victory ship launched—*United V*
tory—launched—Portland, Oreg.
1953 **Catholic Priest**—Catholic Cardinal who
see was west of the Rockies—J. F. McInty
—elevated to the Sacred College of Car
nals
1960 **Basketball Player**—basketball pla
(professional) to score more than 15,
points—Dolph Schayes—Philadelphia, P
1979 **Postage Stamp**—brothers to be pictured
individual postage stamps—R. F. Kenne
—15-cent blue—issued

JANUARY 13

1794 **Flag Legislation**—legislation authoriz
changes—enacted
1854 **Accordion Patent**—Anthony Faas
1857 **Scale**—railway track scale—patented—
Fairbanks
1863 **Chenille Manufacturing Machine**—pate
ed—William Canter

6 **Ship**—side-wheeler transpacific steamer—*Celestial Empire* (later named *China*)—keel laid

6 **Radio Receiver**—radio receiver advertised—Hugo Gernsback—New York City

0 **Opera**—opera broadcast in part—from Metropolitan Opera—New York City

9 **Humanist Society**—established—Hollywood, Calif.

1 **Autogiro**—autogiro with side-by-side seating arrangement—design planned

2 **Automobile**—plastic automobile—construction patented—Henry Ford—Dearborn, Mich.

3 **Business**—department store to sell apartments—Gimbel Brothers—Philadelphia, Pa.

6 **Cabinet (U.S.)**—Cabinet member (black)—R. C. Weaver—nominated

6 **Blind**—machine for reading printed matter aloud—Raymond Kurzweil—demonstrated

6 **Opera**—opera at the Metropolitan Opera House, New York City, conducted by a woman—*La Traviata*—Sarah Caldwell

JANUARY 14

9 **Constitution**—constitution—fundamental orders—Hartford, Conn.

4 **Treaty**—treaty between the United States Government and a nation with which it had been at war—ratified and proclaimed

4 **Surgical Operation**—cesarean operation (successful)—Jessee Bennett—Edom, Va.

3 **School Superintendent**—school superintendent (state)—Gideon Hawley—New York—served

6 **Telegraph**—telegraph company—Magnetic Telegraph Company—formed

8 **Lieutenant Governor**—black lieutenant governor—O. J. Dunn—Louisiana—nominated

3 **Celluloid**—trademark registered

9 **Postal Service**—international dogsled mail—arrived—Montreal, Canada

2 **Totalisator**—totalisator used—Miami, Fla.

8 **Euthanasia Society**—National Society for the Legalization of Euthanasia—formed—New York City

3 **President (U.S.)**—President to fly in an airplane while in office—F. D. Roosevelt

6 **Diplomatic Service**—ambassador (woman) to the Court of St. James—A. L. Armstrong—nominated

JANUARY 15

2 **Mint (U.S.)**—Mint of the United States—proposed

5 **School Tax**—public school tax enacted by a state—Illinois

1 **Railroad Passenger**—railroad honeymoon trip—Charleston, S.C.–Hamburg, S.C.

1833 **Hospital**—Black hospital and asylum—Georgia Infirmary—organized—Savannah, Ga.

1840 **Newspaper**—line drawing of a current subject—New York *Sun*—New York City

1847 **Swedish Magazine**—*Skandinavia*—published—New York City

1862 **Ship**—ironclad naval vessels—accepted—St. Louis, Mo.

1863 **Newspaper**—newspaper printed on woodpulp paper—Boston *Morning Journal*—Boston, Mass.

1867 **Governor**—governor of a territory and a state—J. W. Geary—Pennsylvania

1870 **Cartoon**—Democratic cartoon—donkey emblem—published—New York City

1882 **Ski Club**—ski club (local)—Nansen Ski Club—Berlin, N.H.—formed

1892 **Basketball Rules**—basketball rules—published—Springfield, Mass.

1907 **Dentistry**—gold inlay—described—W. H. Taggart

1907 **Radio Tube**—three-element vacuum tube—patented—Lee De Forest

1908 **Sorority**—black sorority—Alpha Kappa Alpha Sorority—founded—Washington, D.C.

1936 **Building**—all-glass windowless structure—completed—Toledo, Ohio

1942 **Police**—Army Military Police school—opened in Fort Myer, Va.

1943 **Building**—building containing 6.5 million square feet of usable space—the Pentagon, Arlington, Va.—completed

1953 **Medal**—Reserve Officers Association medal—presented—H. S. Truman

1955 **Building**—solar-heated and radiation-cooled house—built—R. W. Bliss—Tucson, Ariz.—system in operation

1960 **Bowler**—bowler to win $10,000 in a tournament—Harry Smith—Omaha, Neb.

1962 **Ship**—dual sponsorship of a U.S. Navy ship—*Halsey*—christened by Margaret Denham and Jane Halsey—San Francisco, Calif.

1967 **Football Game**—Super Bowl contest—Green Bay Packers vs. Kansas City Chiefs—Los Angeles, Calif.

1967 **Television—Telecast**—football game (professional championship) telecast—Green Bay Packers vs. Kansas City Chiefs—Los Angeles, Calif.

JANUARY 16

1840 **Expedition**—scientific expedition fitted out by the United States Government—reached Antarctic

1866 **Skate (all-metal)**—screw-clamp skate—patented—E. H. Barney

1877 **Carpet Loom**—carpet power loom to weave Axminster carpets—patented—Halcyon Skinner

1877 **Organ**—color organ—patented—Bainbridge Bishop

1891 **Ski Club**—ski club association—tournament—Ishpeming, Mich.

1896 **Basketball Game**—basketball intercollegiate five-man-team game—Iowa City, Iowa

1919 **Medal**—Meritorious Service Medal—established

1919 **Prohibition**—prohibition amendment to the Constitution—ratified by 36th state—Nebraska

1920 **Prohibition**—prohibition amendment to the Constitution—Eighteenth Amendment effective

1920 **Prohibition**—prohibition bureau (federal) —prohibition amendment became effective

1936 **Camera**—photofinish camera (electric eye) installed at a racetrack—Hialeah, Fla.

1937 **Jury School**—jury school—opened— Newark, N.J.

1942 **Army Officer**—general appointed from civilian rank—W. S. Knudsen—appointed

1943 **Glider**—amphibious seaplane glider— flown—Philadelphia, Pa.

1957 **Aviation—Flights (world)**—jet round-the-world nonstop flight—takeoff—Merced, Calif.

1967 **Transportation Department (U.S.)**—transportation department (U.S.)—A. S. Boyd (first secretary)—sworn in

1978 **Astronaut**—astronauts (women)—selection announced

JANUARY 17

1806 **Births**—child born in the White House, Washington, D.C.—J. M. Randolph

1871 **Streetcar**—cable streetcar—patented—A. S. Hallidie—San Francisco, Calif.

1887 **Hospital**—hospital for the military and naval forces—Army and Navy Hospital— Hot Springs, Ark.—opened

1905 **Punchboards**—patented

1928 **Photography**—film-developing machine (fully automatic)—patented—A. M. Josepho

1934 **Electric Home and Farm Authority, Inc.**—incorporated—Delaware

1949 **Synchrotron**—synchrotron—installed at Radiation Laboratory, University of California, Berkeley—full energy released

1962 **Ski Slope**—ski slope indoors—Ski Dek Center—opened—Buffalo, N.Y.

JANUARY 18

1733 **Animals**—bear (white)—exhibited—Boston, Mass.

1770 **Revolutionary War**—attack on British soldiers—New York City

1826 **Art Organization**—artists' society of importance—New York Drawing Association committee formed for the National Academy of Design

1840 **Periodical**—electricity journal—publish —New York City

1890 **Sanitary District**—business meeting Chicago, Ill.

1896 **X Ray**—X-ray machine—exhibited—N York City

1911 **Aviation—Flights**—airplane flight to t deck of a carrier—E. B. Ely—San Franc co, Calif.

1934 **Information Service (U.S.)**—organized Washington, D.C.

1944 **Citizenship**—Chinese granted citizens —E. B. Kan—naturalized—Chicago, Ill.

1949 **Congress (U.S.)—House of Represen tives**—congressional standing committ headed by a black—W. L. Dawson

1957 **Aviation—Flights (world)**—jet round-tl world nonstop flight—landing—Riversi Calif.

1958 **Hockey Player**—professional hockey pl er (black)—W. E. O'Ree

1966 **Cabinet (U.S.)**—Cabinet member (black R. C. Weaver—sworn in

1977 **Army Officer**—Secretary of the Ar (black)—C. L. Alexander, Jr.—named

JANUARY 19

1825 **Canning**—canning—patent

1861 **Prison**—military prison of the Unit States on an island—Fort Jefferson, Fla garrisoned

1868 **Philatelic Society**—philatelic societ New York Philatelic Society—constituti adopted

1871 **Freemasons**—black Masonic lodge— pha lodge—New Jersey—warranted

1886 **Ski Club**—ski club (local) that was acti —Aurora Ski Club—Red Wing, Minn.— ganized

1903 **Radio Broadcast**—transatlantic broadc (not experimental)—Cape Cod, Mass.

1915 **Electric Sign**—neon-tube advertising s —patent awarded

1928 **Squash Racquets Champion**—woman win the U.S.A. Women's Squash Racqu Singles championship—E. R. Sears Greenwich, Conn.

1929 **Park**—park (national) east of the Miss sippi—name changed to Acadia Natio Park

1931 **Basketball Game**—basketball game a large commercial sports arena—Madis Square Garden, New York City

1953 **Medal**—National Security Medal—est lished

1955 **Television—Telecast**—presidential ne conference filmed for television and ne reels—Washington, D.C.

1977 **Medal**—Humanitarian Service Medal— thorized

JANUARY 20

'8 **Court-Martial**—military court-martial—Cambridge, Mass.

3 **Treaty**—treaty between the United States Government and a nation with which it had been at war—hostilities ceased—Great Britain

9 **Geology Book**—geology book—of importance—William Maclure—read before American Philosophical Society—Philadelphia, Pa.

0 **Agricultural "Board" (state)**—New York State board formed

9 **Woman**—woman congressional hearing witness—E. C. Stanton

5 **Railroad**—switchback railway—roller coaster patent—L. A. Thompson—Coney Island, N.Y.

9 **Ship**—destroyer of the U.S. Navy named for a Confederate officer—*Buchanan*—commissioned

9 **Motion Picture**—talking picture taken outdoors (full-length)—*In Old Arizona*—released

7 **President (U.S.)**—President inaugurated on Jan. 20—F. D. Roosevelt

7 **President (U.S.)**—President whose mother saw her son inaugurated President of the United States for a second term—F. D. Roosevelt

3 **Ship**—ship transported overland across the Rocky Mountains—*Brennan*—commissioned

7 **Christmas Carols Association (national)**—organized—St. Louis, Mo.

2 **Bullfight**—woman bullfighter (professional)—Patricia McCormick—debut

3 **Television—Telecast**—telecast transmitted to Canada—from Buffalo, N.Y.

4 **Radio Station**—black network—National Negro Network—formed

9 **Attorney General**—state attorney general (woman)—A. X Alpern—commissioned—Harrisburg, Pa.

6 **Medicare**—medicare identification card—presented to H. S. Truman—Independence, Mo.

7 **Hospital**—general hospital to adopt the Social Security account number as a numbering system for medical records—Altoona, Pa.

9 **Rowing**—transatlantic solo trip by rowboat—John Fairfax—left Canary Islands

5 **College**—college commencement exercises within a prison—Jackson, Mich.

JANUARY 21

7 **Medical Book**—medical pamphlet—published—Boston, Mass.

1 **Diplomatic Service**—consular officer detailed for duty in the Department of Foreign Affairs—Thomas Barclay—appointed

1789 **Novel**—American novel published in America—*Power of Sympathy*—advertised

1812 **Bridge**—"Y" bridge—authorized—Zanesville, Ohio

1847 **Senator (U.S.)**—senator who served a term of less than 6 weeks—Pierre Soule of Louisiana—began service

1853 **Envelope**—envelope folding machine—patented—R. L. Hawes

1865 **Oil**—oil well drilled by torpedoes

1880 **Sewage**—separate system of sewage disposal—started—Memphis, Tenn.

1894 **Medal**—Medal of Honor action—medal awarded to B. J. D. Irwin

1918 **Air Force**—air force aviation unit—landed—Ponta Delgada, Azores

1927 **Opera**—opera broadcast over a national network from an American opera house—Chicago, Ill.

1937 **Automobile License (federal)**—common carrier license—effective

1937 **Legislature**—unicameral legislature (state)—first appropriation bill—Nebraska

1941 **Magnesium**—magnesium commercial production—Freeport, Tex.

1947 **Army Officer**—army officer to occupy both the nation's highest military post and the highest nonelective civilian post—Chief of Staff G. C. Marshall—became Secretary of State

1954 **Automobile**—gas-turbine automobile—publicly introduced—New York City

1954 **Submarine**—atomic-powered submarine—*Nautilus*—launched—Groton, Conn.

1954 **Submarine**—submarine of the U.S. Navy christened by a President's wife—*Nautilus*—M. G. D. Eisenhower—Groton, Conn.

1961 **Cabinet (U.S.)**—Cabinet member who was a brother of a President—R. F. Kennedy—took office

1971 **Representative (U.S.)**—representative of Puerto Rican ancestry—Herman Badillo of New York—sworn in

JANUARY 22

1673 **Postal Service**—postal route—service began—Boston–New York City

1814 **Freemasons**—Knights Templar Grand Encampment—New York City

1879 **Senator (U.S.)**—senator to serve three states—James Shields—elected

1881 **Monument**—obelisk to be brought to the United States—erected on pedestal—New York City

1895 **Manufacturers' Association**—National Association of Manufacturers—organized—Cincinnati, Ohio

1931 **Autogiro**—autogiro of the U.S. Government—ordered from Pitcairn Aircraft Company, Inc.—Philadelphia, Pa.

1932 **Reconstruction Finance Corporation**—authorized

1947 Television Station—commercial television station west of the Mississippi River—Hollywood, Calif.

JANUARY 23

1780 Town—town incorporated under name of Washington—Washington, Ga.

1789 College—Catholic College—Georgetown College—established—Washington, D.C.

1793 "First Aid" Emergency Organization—Humane Society of Philadelphia—incorporated

1845 Election—election day—uniform observation authorized

1849 Envelope—envelope machine patent

1849 Physician—woman physician—Elizabeth Blackwell—graduated—Geneva, N.Y.

1879 Archery Club—archery association (national)—National Archery Association—formed—Crawfordsville, Ind.

1891 Hospital—interracial hospital—Provident Hospital—Chicago, Ill—incorporated

1907 Senator (U.S.)—American-Indian senator—Charles Curtis—served

1917 Shipping—United States Shipping Board—nominations of commissioners confirmed

1923 Representative (U.S.)—representative (woman) elected to serve in the place of her husband—M. E. Nolan—served

1946 Medal—Medal of Honor awarded to a chaplain—Timothy O'Callahan—presented

1946 Naval Officer—chaplain to win a Congressional Medal of Honor—awarded—J. T. O'-Callahan

1968 Ship—naval ship to surrender in peacetime without a fight—*Pueblo*

1973 Voting Machine—vote recorded by electronic means in the U.S. House of Representatives

JANUARY 24

1656 Physician—Jewish doctor—Jacob Lumbrozo—Maryland

1722 Divinity Professor—Edward Wigglesworth—appointed—Cambridge, Mass.

1838 Telegraph—telegraphic communication system in which dots and dashes represented letters—public demonstration

1848 Gold—gold discovered in California—J. W. Marshall—Coloma, Calif.

1866 Medal—Medal of Honor awarded to a woman—M. E. Walker

1888 Typewriter Ribbon—typewriter "copy" ribbon—patented—J. L. Wortman

1893 Catholic Apostolic Delegate—Francesco Satolli—arrived

1899 Rubber—rubber heel—Humphrey O'Sullivan—patent

1922 Eskimo Pie—C. K. Nelson—patent

1925 Motion Picture—motion picture of an eclipse of the sun taken from a dirigible—Montauk Point, L.I., N.Y.

1932 Autogiro—Flights—autogiro flight over open sea—L. A. Yancey—takeoff, K West, Fla.

1935 Cans—beer in cans—placed on sale Richmond, Va.

1944 Medal—soldier to win the three highe ranking decorations—M. L. Britt—heroi

1962 Satellite—multisatellite launching (5 sa lites in 1 shot)—*Composite 1*—launchee Cape Canaveral, Fla.

1972 Noise Legislation—noise-control statew comprehensive legislation—New Jerse signed

1974 American Indians—American Indian perintendent of a Bureau of Indian Affa agency—Shirley Plume—appointed

JANUARY 25

1799 Seeding Machine Patent—granted—E kim Spooner

1862 Ship—warship sunk by an underwater t pedo mine—*Cairo*—commissioned

1870 Soda Fountain—ornamented soda fount —patented—G. D. Dows

1871 Monument—monument by a woman dered by the United States Governmen Lincoln statue unveiled—Washington, [

1890 Tour of the World—tour of the world m by a woman traveling alone—Nellie Bl returned to New York City

1897 Accountants' Society—accountants' s ety formed by a state group—incorpora

1897 Forestry Society—national forestry as ciation—American Forestry Associatio incorporated

1897 Piano Player—pneumatic piano playe patent application

1901 Ship—schooner (seven-masted, steel contract signed

1907 Arts and Letters Society—woman elec to the National Institute of Arts and Lett —J. W. Howe

1915 Telephone—transcontinental telephe demonstration—New York City–San Fr cisco, Calif.

1929 Vice President (U.S.)—Vice Preside widow to receive a pension—L. I. K. M shall—authorized

1930 Medical Clinic—flying medical clini demonstration of operation—F. H. Alb

1945 Water—community to fluoridate municipal water—Grand Rapids, Mich.

1949 Television Award—National Academy Television Arts and Sciences award—▶ sentation—Los Angeles, Calif.

1951 President (U.S.)—presidential press c ference recorded on tape—H. S. Truma Washington, D.C.

1952 Headlight—automatic headlight contr Autronic Eye—Anderson, Ind.

1952 Railroad—railroad freight yard fully a matic—Gary, Ind.

1915   World War I—American ship lost in World War I—*William P. Frye* sunk

1916   Supreme Court (U.S.)—Associate Justice of the Supreme Court who was Jewish—L. D. Brandeis—appointed

1932   Insurance—unemployment insurance act —enacted—Wisconsin

1934   Ski Lift—ski tow (rope)—operated— Woodstock, Vt.

1935   Locomotive—streamlined electric engine— tested—Washington, D.C.–Philadelphia, Pa.

1942   Merchant Marine Academy—Merchant Marine Cadet Corps (U.S.)—first class started—Kings Point, N.Y.

1958   Atomic Reactor—thorium-uranium reactor (privately owned)—Buchanan, N.Y.—construction began

1960   Photograph—photograph bounced off the moon—received—Washington, D.C.

1962   Labor Legislation—minimum wage law (city) for public contract work—New York City—effective

1976   Diplomatic Service—ambassador (woman) to the Court of St. James—A. L. Armstrong —appointment confirmed

JANUARY 29

1802   Librarian—Librarian of Congress—John Beckley—appointed

1863   Brokerage—stock exchange—name changed to New York Stock Exchange

1874   Mint (U.S.)—coins minted for a foreign government—authorized

1874   Money—coins manufactured for a foreign government—authorized

1900   Baseball League—American League—organized—Philadelphia, Pa.

1904   College "Lettermen's Club"—established —Chicago, Ill.

1919   Prohibition—prohibition amendment to the Constitution—amendment proclaimed by Secretary of State

1919   Prohibition—prohibition bureau (federal) —prohibition amendment became part of the Constitution

1924   Ice Cream Cone—ice cream cone-rolling machine—patented—C. R. Taylor

1926   Lawyer—black woman lawyer to practice before the United States Supreme Court— V. N. Anderson—admitted

1936   Hall of Fame—hall of fame (baseball)— players elected—Cooperstown, N.Y.

1940   Flowers—tetraploid flower—publicly exhibited—New York City

1943   Marine Corps—woman marine major—R. C. Streeter—appointed

1944   Television—Telecast—ship launching telecast—U.S.S. *Missouri*—New York City

1949   Ship—air-conditioned naval ship—*Newport News*—commissioned

1951   Television—television eyewitness allow to testify in a federal court—New York C

1960   Ice Skating Champion—national wome figure skating four-time winner—C. Heiss—fourth consecutive title—Seatt Wash.

1963   Hall of Fame—Hall of Fame (football first members selected

1966   Stadium—domed, fully-enclosed spo arena—Astrodome, Houston, Tex.—fi polo game

JANUARY 30

1781   Articles of Confederation—adopted Maryland, last of the thirteen states

1798   Congress (U.S.)—House of Represen tives—brawl—Philadelphia, Pa.

1835   President (U.S.)—President whose assas nation was attempted—Andrew Jackson Washington, D.C.

1862   Ship—ironclad turreted vessel in the U Navy—*Monitor*—launched—Greenpoin N.Y.

1874   Mechanical Engineering Laboratory— research work—proposed—Stevens In tute of Technology

1884   Antivivisection Society—annual meetin Philadelphia, Pa.

1894   Hammer (pneumatic)—patented—C. King

1910   Automobile Racetrack—automob speedway (board track)—started—Los A geles, Calif.

1911   Aviation—airplane rescue at sea—J. A. McCurdy

1925   Science Association—History of Scie Society—incorporated

1934   Medal—National Geographic Society g medal—Hubbard Medal to a woman— M. Lindbergh—Washington, D.C.

1934   Play (drama)—theatrical presentati sponsored by the federal government—*7 Family Upstairs*—produced—New Y City

1942   Price Regulation Legislation—price regu tion law (federal)—enacted

1958   Sidewalk (traveling)—two-way mov walk—in service—Dallas, Tex.

1964   Rocket—American spacecraft to imp the moon—*Ranger VI*—launched—C Canaveral, Fla.

JANUARY 31

1825   Trademark Lawsuit—trademark cont versy involving a newspaper—tried

1863   Civil War—black regiment in the Civil W —First Regiment South Carolina vol teers—mustered into federal service

1871   Freemasons—black Masonic lodge— pha lodge—regular communication

1885   Labor—labor bureau (federal)—Comm sioner of Labor—C. D. Wright—appoint

920 **Newspaper**—Ukrainian daily newspaper—*Ukrainian Daily News*—New York City

930 **Glider**—glider released from a dirigible—piloted—Lakehurst, N.J.

949 **Television—Telecast**—serial daytime soap opera—*These Are My Children*—telecast began—Chicago, Ill.

953 **Television—Telecast**—rodeo telecast coast to coast—Will Rogers Memorial Stadium, Fort Worth, Tex.

958 **Satellite**—satellite placed in orbit—Explorer I—launched from Cape Canaveral, Fla.

961 **Naval Officer**—commander of a combat ship who was a black—S. L. Gravely

966 **Ship**—rocket-tracking ship—*Vanguard*—trials completed—off Boston, Mass.

FEBRUARY 1

788 **Ship**—steamboat patent—Georgia—Isaac Briggs and William Longstreet

790 **Supreme Court (U.S.)**—Supreme Court first session—New York City—opened

790 **Supreme Court (U.S.)**—Supreme Court of the United States—first session—New York City

791 **Dental Dispensary**—dental dispensary—opened—New York City

793 **Oiled-Silk Patent**—R. Hodgson

831 **Music Book**—children's music book—*Juvenile Lyre,* by Lowell Mason—copyrighted

840 **Dental School**—dental college—incorporated

842 **Coast Guard (U.S.)**—Coast Guard Commandant—A. V. Fraser—appointed

842 **College**—university on the Pacific Coast—trustees elected—Willamette University—Salem, Oreg.

843 **Insurance**—mutual life insurance company to operate—policy issued

844 **Insurance**—mutual life insurance company to be chartered—New England Mutual Life Insurance Company—first policy

860 **Congress (U.S.)—House of Representatives**—Jewish rabbi to open the House of Representatives with prayer—M. J. Raphall

864 **Mines School**—Thomas Egleston—professor of mines and metallurgy—appointed

865 **Lawyer**—black lawyer to practice before the United States Supreme Court—J. S. Rock

885 **Hospital**—tuberculosis sanatorium (modern) opened—Saranac Lake, N.Y.

898 **Insurance**—automobile insurance policy—issued—Travelers Insurance Company—Hartford, Conn.

904 **Radio Distress Signal**—radio distress signal—CQD signal—effective

906 **Prison**—penitentiary building (national)—completed—Federal Penitentiary—Leavenworth, Kan.

1907 **Horse**—horse farm operated by the United States Government—property deeded—Middlebury, Conn.

1911 **Fingerprinting**—fingerprint conviction—Thomas Jennings—recorded—Cook County, Ill.

1914 **Motion Picture Censorship**—motion picture censorship board (state)—censors appointed—Pennsylvania

1920 **Automobile**—armored commercial car completely protected—in service—St. Paul, Minn.

1930 **Ship**—diesel-engine passenger ship—*The City of New York*—left Brooklyn, N.Y., for Capetown, Union of South Africa

1936 **Insurance**—group insurance policy for college students—issued

1937 **Free Port**—opened—Stapleton, N.Y.

1937 **Ship**—ship permitted to enter port without stopping for quarantine procedure—*Cameronia*—New York City

1940 **Television—Telecast**—television network demonstration (long-distance)—New York City–Schenectady, N.Y.

1941 **Aviation—Flights**—airplane flight (commercially scheduled) over a single route linking four continents—left—New York City

1942 **Merchant Marine**—Merchant Marine officer to hold the rank of rear admiral—A. B. Randall—commissioned

1944 **Marine Corps**—woman marine major—R. C. Streeter—appointed colonel

1949 **Court-Martial**—court-martial trial at which enlisted men were allowed to sit as members of the court—Heidelberg, Germany

1949 **Telescope**—telescope lens 200 inches in diameter—used—Palomar Mountain, Calif.

1951 **Television—Telecast**—atomic explosion telecast—Los Angeles, Calif.

1951 **X Ray**—X-ray motion picture process by which pictures could be taken over a considerable period of time—demonstrated—Baltimore, Md.

1953 **Television—Telecast**—opera from the Metropolitan Opera House especially tailored and trimmed for television—*Die Fledermaus*—telecast

1957 **Aviation—Pilot**—black airplane pilot on a scheduled passenger line—P. H. Young

1966 **Naval Officer**—black captain in the U.S. Navy—T. D. Parham, Jr.

1968 **Army School**—instructor (woman)—E. M. Lewis—began service—West Point, N.Y.

1973 **Prison**—woman prison guard in a maximum security prison for men—J. W. Stewart—Iowa State Penitentiary, Fort Madison, Iowa—appointed

1978 **Postage Stamp**—postage stamp to honor a black woman—Harriet Tubman—issued—Washington, D.C.

FEBRUARY 2

1798 Theater—theater destroyed by fire—Federal Street Theatre—Boston, Mass.

1802 Animals — leopard — exhibited — Boston, Mass.

1832 Treaty—treaty with a foreign nation to provide for mutual reduction of import duties —ratifications exchanged with France

1834 College—coeducational college—Oberlin Collegiate Institute—Oberlin, Ohio—incorporated

1838 College—city college—Charleston, S.C.—president appointed

1843 Colonial Government—government on the Pacific Coast—committee appointed—Champoeg, Oreg.

1858 Artics—patented—T. C. Wales

1870 Supreme Court (state)—associate justice (black) of a state supreme court—J. J. Wright—South Carolina—began service

1876 Baseball League—National League—formed

1880 Electric Lighting—street lighting (electric) by a municipality—appropriation made—Wabash, Ind.

1892 Bottle Cap—crown cork—patented—William Painter

1893 Motion Picture—motion picture closeup—West Orange, N.J.

1901 Army Nurse Corps (female)—authorized

1901 Dental Corps (U.S. Army)—Dental Corps of the U.S. Army—authorized

1912 Motion Picture Actor—stunt actor—F. R. Law—jumped from Statue of Liberty

1923 Gasoline—ethyl gasoline—marketed—Dayton, Ohio

1929 Postal Service—international dogsled mail —returned from Montreal

1932 Reconstruction Finance Corporation—organized

1935 Lie Detector—tested—Portage, Wis.

1940 Dictionary—dictionary compiled by a woman—M. B. Picken—published—New York City

1962 Pole Vault—pole vault jump indoors over 16 feet—John Uelses—New York City

1964 Rocket—American spacecraft to impact the moon—*Ranger VI*

1973 Cabinet (U.S.)—Cabinet member to serve in 4 different capacities—E. L. Richardson —sworn in as Secretary of Defense (second)

1976 Cabinet (U.S.)—Cabinet member to serve in 4 different capacities—E. L. Richardson —sworn in as Secretary of Commerce (fourth)

FEBRUARY 3

1690 Money—paper money—issued—Massachusetts

1789 Cotton Mill—cotton mill—Beverly Cotton Manufactory — incorporated — Beverly, Mass.

1790 Supreme Court (U.S.)—clerk of the Supreme Court—John Tucker—appointed

1812 Supreme Court (U.S.)—Associate Justice of the Supreme Court who had been a representative in Congress—Gabriel Duvall of Maryland—began service as Associate Justice

1836 Whig Party—state convention—Albany, N.Y.

1860 Agriculture Bureau—Agriculture bureau—Superintendent of Agriculture under Department of Interior—T. G. Clemson—took office

1862 Newspaper—newspaper printed on a train —Port Huron, Mich.

1894 Ship—steel sailing vessel—*Dirigo*—launched—Bath, Me.

1923 Dental School—dental school of the U.S. Navy—opened

1933 Legislative Conference (interstate)—meeting—American Legislators' Association—Washington, D.C.

1944 Hockey Player—professional hockey player to score 6 goals in 1 game—Syd Howe—Detroit, Mich.

1947 News Correspondent—black news correspondent admitted to the House of Representatives and Senate press gallery—P. L. Prattis

1949 Court-martial—court-martial trial at which enlisted men were allowed to sit as members of the court—conviction

1949 Court-martial—court-martial trial in the United States at which enlisted men were allowed to sit as members of the court—convened—Fort Bragg, N.C.

FEBRUARY 4

1789 Congress (U.S.)—joint meeting of the Senate and the House of Representatives—presidential candidates elected—Continental Congress

1789 President (U.S.)—President to receive the unanimous vote of the presidential electors —George Washington

1801 Supreme Court (U.S.)—Chief Justice of the United States to serve in a presidential cabinet—John Marshall—Sectretary of State

1801 Supreme Court (U.S.)—Chief Justice of the United States who had been a representative in Congress—John Marshall of Virginia—began service as Chief Justice

1847 Telegraph—telegraph company—Magnetic Telegraph Company—incorporated

1861 Congress of the Confederate States—provisional session—Senate—Montgomery, Ala.

1887 Interstate Commerce Act—approved

1895 Bridge—rolling lift bridge—Van Buren Street bridge—Chicago, Ill.—opened

1913 Automobile Tire—demountable tire-carrying rim—patented—L. H. Perlman

1915 **Public Health**—pellagra experiment—Joseph Goldberger

1919 **Medal**—Distinguished Service Medal (Navy)—authorized

1930 **Road**—mosaic pavement—completed—New Orleans, La.

1930 **Streetcar**—streetcar tracks which were tieless, soundless, and shockless—completed—New Orleans, La.

1932 **Olympic Games**—winter Olympic Games competition—Lake Placid, N.Y.

1936 **Physics**—radioactive substance produced synthetically—radium E—produced—University of California—Berkeley, Calif.

1938 **Radio Facsimile Transmission**—radio facsimile broadcasting on the regular broadcast band—Des Moines, Iowa

1942 **World War II**—American general wounded in action in World War II—C. A. Pierce

1943 **Submarine**—submarine with a high-tensile-steel pressure hull—*Balao*—commissioned

1944 **Medal**—Bronze Star—established

1957 **Typewriter**—electric portable typewriter—on sale—Syracuse, N.Y.

1958 **Ship**—aircraft carrier (atomic-powered)—*Enterprise*—laid down—Newport News, Va.

1962 **Hospital**—children's hospital solely for research and treatment of catastrophic childhood diseases—St. Jude's Children's Research Hospital, Memphis, Tenn.—opened

FEBRUARY 5

644 **Branding Legislation**—enacted—Connecticut

777 **State**—state to abolish both entail and primogeniture—Georgia

778 **Articles of Confederation**—first state to ratify—South Carolina

790 **Lawyer**—lawyers admitted to the Supreme Court of the United States

817 **Gas**—gas company—incorporated—Baltimore, Md.

825 **Periodical**—mechanics' magazine—*American Mechanics' Magazine*—published—New York City

834 **Crime Prevention and Detection**—interstate crime pact—ratified by New York State

841 **Statistical Society**—American Statistical Society—incorporated

846 **Newspaper**—newspaper published on the Pacific Coast—*Oregon Spectator*—Oregon City, Oreg.

850 **Adding Machine**—adding machine to employ depressible keys—patented—D. D. Parmelee

861 **Motion Picture**—peep show machine—patented—S. D. Goodale

1861 **Motion Picture**—photographic attempt to show motion—patented—Coleman Sellers

1863 **News Correspondent**—news reporter tried as a spy—T. W. Knox—Young's Point, La.

1870 **Motion Picture**—animated photographic picture projection before a theater audience—H. R. Heyl

1901 **Loop-the-Loop Centrifugal Railway**—patent—Edwin Prescott—Arlington, Mass.

1903 **Museum**—Semitic museum—Harvard University, Cambridge, Mass.—formally opened

1918 **Aviation**—**Pilot**—Army pilot—to win victory—S. W. Thompson

1924 **President (U.S.)**—President buried in Washington, D.C.—Woodrow Wilson

1931 **Aviation**—**License**—glider license awarded a woman—M. Dunlap

1931 **Aviation**—**License**—glider license class "C"—National Aeronautic Association—awarded—R. S. Barnaby

1948 **Olympic Games**—figure skating Olympic champion (American)—Richard Button

1948 **Olympic Games**—woman slalom Olympic champion (American)—Gretchen Fraser

FEBRUARY 6

1778 **Treaty**—treaty entered into by the United States—France

1778 **United States**—nation to recognize the independence of the United States—France

1815 **Railroad Charter**—railroad charter—New Jersey

1857 **Postage Stamp**—perforated postage stamps—contract

1902 **Young Women's Hebrew Association**—organized—New York City

1911 **Old Age Home for Pioneers**—Prescott, Ariz.—opened

1912 **Ship**—cruise ship to circumnavigate the world—*Cleveland*—left New York City

1931 **Television**—**Telecast**—telecast (transatlantic) transmitted regularly—E. F. W. Alexanderson—W2XAW, Schenectady, N.Y.—first transmission

1932 **Dogsled Race**—dogsled race on an Olympic demonstration program—Lake Placid, N.Y.

1937 **Lawyer**—Japanese woman lawyer—K. E. Ohi—received LL.B. degree

1942 **Medal**—Presidential Unit Citation (Navy)—authorized

1956 **Building**—circular school building—opened—Kankakee, Ill.

1957 **Cryotrons**—publicly reported—D. A. Buck—Cambridge, Mass.

1973 **Atomic Energy Commission**—Atomic Energy Commission woman chairman—D. L. Ray

1976 **Medal**—Defense Superior Service Medal—created

FEBRUARY 7

1776 **Prison Reform Society**—organized for war prisoners—Philadelphia, Pa.

1818 **Education Periodical**—educational magazine to achieve success—*Academician*—published—New York City

1827 **Ballet**—ballet—presented—Bowery Theatre—New York City

1842 **Presidential Commission**—President requested by Congress to justify the creation of a presidential commission—John Tyler

1877 **Cattle Club**—cattle club (Guernsey cattle)—American Guernsey Cattle Club—permanent organization—New York City

1934 **Electrical Contract**—city with government—Tupelo, Miss.—effective

1936 **Flag**—Vice President's flag—established

1942 **War Shipping Administration**—War Shipping Administration—established

1969 **Jockey**—jockey (woman) to ride in a parimutual race on a flat track—Diane Crump—Hialeah, Fla.

FEBRUARY 8

1693 **College**—college charter granted by the Crown—Williamsburg, Va.

1693 **College**—college proposed—College of William and Mary—incorporated—Williamsburg, Va.

1802 **Clock**—banjo clock patent—Simon Willard

1837 **Vice President (U.S.)**—Vice President elected by the Senate—R. M. Johnson—chosen

1865 **Army Officer**—major (black)—M. R. Delany—commissioned

1887 **Ski Club**—ski club (local) that was active—Aurora Ski Club tournament—Red Wing, Minn.

1889 **Automobile Tractor**—steam tractor—delivered—San Leandro, Calif.

1892 **Library Loan**—made by a state library to a community—New York

1898 **Envelope**—envelope folding and gumming machine—patented—J. A. Sherman

1910 **Boy Scouts of America**—Boy Scouts of America—incorporated

1911 **Court**—commerce court (U.S.)—organized—Washington, D.C.

1912 **Aviation—Flights (transcontinental)**—transcontinental airplane flight (eastbound)—R. G. Fowler—landed—Jacksonville, Fla.

1915 **Motion Picture**—motion picture to gross $50 million—*The Birth of a Nation*—shown in Los Angeles, Calif.

1922 **President (U.S.)**—President to use a radio—W. G. Harding—set installed in White House

1924 **Execution**—lethal-gas execution—Carson City, Nev.

1924 **Radio Broadcast**—coast-to-coast hookup—J. J. Carty—Chicago, Ill.

1928 **Television—Telecast**—transoceanic television image—received—Hartsdale, N.Y.

1934 **Bank**—Export-Import Bank—organized

1944 **News Correspondent**—black news correspondent accredited to the White House—Harry McAlpin

1957 **Court-Martial**—court-martial trial of an officer for collaborating with his captors—decision sustained

1974 **Astronaut**—astronauts (American) to exceed 2,000 hours flight time—G. P. Carr, E. G. Gibson, and W. R. Pogue—*Skylab IV*—landed

FEBRUARY 9

1790 **Diplomatic Service**—consul under the Department of State—Samuel Shaw—nominated

1799 **Ship**—ship to capture an enemy ship after the Revolution—*Constellation* vs. *Insurgente*

1861 **President of the Confederate States**—Jefferson Davis—elected

1870 **Weather Bureau (U.S.)**—Weather Bureau—authorized

1871 **Fish Protection**—fish protection office (federal)—authorized

1886 **Scale**—coin-operated weighing machine—Percival Everitt—patented

1889 **Agriculture Bureau**—agriculture bureau—made an executive department in the federal government

1893 **Theater**—municipal theater—Academy of Music—Northampton, Mass.—accepted as a gift

1909 **Forestry School**—forestry school to give scientific training in the care and preservation of trees—Davey Tree Expert Company—Kent, Ohio—incorporated

1909 **Narcotics Legislation**—narcotics prohibition act (federal)—enacted

1918 **Chaplains' School**—Army school for chaplains—organized—Fort Monroe, Va.

1932 **Bobsled Competition**—two-man bob-team competition—Lake Placid, N.Y.

1941 **Aviation—Flights**—airplane flight (commercially scheduled) over a single route linking four continents—*Dixie Clipper* returned—New York City

1942 **War Shipping Administration**—War Shipping Administration—E. S. Land (first administrator)—appointed

FEBRUARY 10

1807 **Coast Survey**—authorized

1807 **Coast Survey Superintendent**—U.S. Survey—authorized

1830 **Railroad**—interstate railroad—Petersburg Railroad—chartered

1855 **Hospital**—women's hospital—constitution adopted—New York City

1863 **Fire Extinguisher Patent**—Alanson Crane

1887 **Actor**—actor to perform in 2 cities the same day—N. C. Goodwin—Boston and New York City

1923 **Ink**—ink paste—manufactured—Minneapolis, Minn.

1925 **Gas**—gas storage tank (waterless)—in service—Michigan City, Ind.

1930 **Grain Stabilization Corporation**—authorized

1932 **Ski Meet (international)**—Lake Placid, N.Y.

1934 **Postage Stamp**—imperforated ungummed sheet of postage stamps—issued—New York City

1935 **Locomotive**—streamlined electric engine—Pennsylvania Railroad Company—in passenger service

1941 **Postal Service**—highway post office service—route established—Washington, D.C.–Harrison, Va.

1942 **Medal**—Medal of Honor awarded in World War II—presented posthumously

1962 **Runner**—runner to run a mile indoors in less than 4 minutes—J. T. Beatty—Los Angeles, Calif.

1968 **Protestant Episcopal Bishop**—Protestant Episcopal bishop consecrated in a Roman Catholic church—R. B. Appleyard—Pittsburg, Pa.

FEBRUARY 11

1752 **Hospital**—hospital in America—opened—Philadelphia, Pa.

1794 **Congress (U.S.)—Senate**—Senate session to which the public was admitted—trial of A. A. A. Gallatin

1801 **President (U.S.)**—President elected by the House of Representatives—Thomas Jefferson—Washington, D.C.

1808 **Coal**—anthracite coal burned experimentally—Wilkes Barre, Pa.

1811 **Congress (U.S.)—Senate**—Senate filibuster

1833 **Rubber**—rubber company—Roxbury India Rubber Company—incorporated

1836 **College**—college for women—Mount Holyoke Seminary, South Hadley, Mass.—chartered

1837 **Physiology Society**—physiology society—American Physiological Society—organized—Boston, Mass.

1875 **College**—intercontinental system of study—introduced—Boston University—Boston, Mass.—reciprocal agreement

1878 **Bicycle Society**—bicycle club—Boston Bicycle Club—formed—Boston, Mass.

1901 **Dental Corps (U.S. Army)**—Dental Corps of the U.S. Army—contract—dental surgeons appointed

1916 **Orchestra**—municipal orchestra supported by taxes—Baltimore, Md.—first concert

1930 **Aviation—Airport**—airport to receive an A1-A rating—Pontiac, Mich.

1935 **Aviation—Flights**—airplane flight with an auto slung beneath the fuselage—Floyd Bennett Field, N.Y.

1937 **Radio Broadcast**—simultaneous broadcast on all 3 major networks—American National Red Cross relief fund—benefit New York City

1944 **Caterpillar Club**—father and son Caterpillar Club members—son jumped—Fairbanks, Alaska

1945 **Aviation—Airplane**—gas-turbine propeller-driven airplane—tested—Muroc, Calif.

1952 **Yiddish Professorship**—established—Columbia University—New York City

1954 **Newspaper**—newspaper printed on bagasse newsprint—*Daily World*—published

1956 **Railroad Car**—passenger car (ACF Talgo for use in the United States)—in service between Peoria, Ill., and Chicago, Ill.

1957 **Naval Officer**—woman to preside as law officer—Mary Lou McDowell

1958 **Aviation**—flight attendant (black woman)—R. C. Taylor—Ithaca, N.Y.–New York City

1972 **Snowmobile**—snowmobile to exceed a speed of 125 m.p.h.—Yvon Duhamel—Boonville, N.Y.

FEBRUARY 12

1736 **Theater**—theater designed solely for theatrical purposes—New Theatre—opened—Charleston, S.C.

1738 **Puppet Show**—New York City

1775 **President (U.S.)**—President whose wife was not born in the United States—J. Q. Adams

1793 **Slavery**—fugitive slave law (federal)—enacted

1795 **Money**—deposit of gold bullion

1809 **President (U.S.)**—President born beyond the boundaries of the original 13 states—Abraham Lincoln—Hodgenville, Ky.

1821 **Library**—mercantile library—opened—New York City

1855 **Agricultural School**—agricultural college (state) to open—Agricultural College of Michigan—Lansing, Mich.—incorporated

1865 **Congress (U.S.)—House of Representatives**—black preacher to deliver a sermon in the House of Representatives—H. H. Garnet

1873 **Assay Office Building (federal)**—under Bureau of Mint—authorized

1873 **Money**—demonetization of silver—bimetallism—abolished

1873 **Money**—silver coins—trade dollar authorized

1873 **Money**—trade dollar—authorized

1877 **Telephone**—news dispatch by telephone—from Salem, Mass., to Boston, Mass.

1878 **Baseball Catcher's Mask**—patented—F. W. Thayer

1880　**Croquet League**—National Croquet League —organized—Philadelphia, Pa.

1883　**Coronation**—coronation on what was to become United States soil—King Kalakaua and Queen Kapiolani—Honolulu, Hawaiian Islands

1899　**Bicycle Race**—international 6-day 2-man-team bicycle race—began—New York City

1908　**Automobile Race**—automobile race from New York to Paris—started

1909　**Postage Stamp**—memorial stamp—on sale

1924　**Radio Broadcast**—network sponsored broadcast—New York City

1924　**Radio Broadcast**—political speech by a President on radio—Calvin Coolidge—New York City

1925　**Arbitration**—federal arbitration law—enacted

1931　**Autogiro**—autogiro used commercially—*Detroit News No. 2*—delivered to Detroit, Mich.

1935　**Bridge**—bridge with open-mesh steel flooring—steel flooring patent—W. E. Irving

1943　**Marine Corps**—woman marine major—R. C. Streeter—sworn in

1970　**Hospital**—ambulatory surgical facility independently operated—Surgicenter, Phoenix, Ariz.—opened

1973　**Road**—state highway metric-distance-marker system—Ohio—erection begun

1976　**Woman**—nuclear commercial power plant licensed woman operator—R. A. Kankus—licensed

FEBRUARY 13

1635　**Public School**—public school with a continuous existence—Boston Public Latin School—established—Boston, Mass.

1741　**Periodical**—magazine published in America—*American Magazine*—published—Philadelphia, Pa.

1795　**College**—state university chartered—state university opened—University of North Carolina—Chapel Hill, N.C.

1799　**Insurance**—insurance regulation (state)—enacted—Massachusetts

1861　**Medal**—Medal of Honor action—Apache Pass, Ariz.

1875　**Births**—quintuplets—born—Watertown, Wis.

1889　**Agriculture Department (U.S.)**—Secretary of the Department of Agriculture—N. J. Colman—appointed

1914　**Music Society**—music society for the literary protection of composers and authors—formed—New York City

1934　**Bank**—Export-Import Bank—officers elected

1934　**Trust**—cartel—Pacific Coast Gasoline Cartel—approved

1935　**Surgical Operation**—heart operation for the relief of angina pectoris—C. S. Beck—Cleveland, Ohio

1943　**Marine Corps**—woman marine major—R. C. Streeter—began service as director of Marine Corps Women's Reserve

1969　**Brokerage**—New York Stock Exchange black member—J. L. Searles, III—New York City—approved

FEBRUARY 14

1778　**Flag**—American flag saluted by a foreign nation—France saluted the *Ranger*

1794　**Textile Machinery Patent**—James Davenport

1803　**Apple Parer**—patented—Moses Coats

1849　**Photograph**—photograph of a President (in office)—J. K. Polk—New York City

1862　**Ship**—ironclad warship for service at sea—*Galena*—launched—Mystic, Conn.

1865　**Congressional Directory**—publication authorized

1867　**Insurance**—boiler insurance company—policy issued—Hartford, Conn.

1872　**Bird Refuge**—authorized by a state—California

1883　**Labor Union**—labor union legalization (state)—New Jersey—enacted

1899　**Voting Machine**—voting machines for use in federal elections—approved

1903　**Commerce and Labor Department (U.S.)**—authorized

1907　**Foxhound Association**—Masters of Fox Hounds Association—formed—New York City

1912　**Engine**—diesel engine in a submarine—launched—Groton, Conn.

1931　**Medal**—Air Mail Flyer's Medal of Honor—authorized

1932　**Bobsled Competition**—four-man bob-team competition—Lake Placid, N.Y.

1940　**Aquatic Mammals**—porpoise—born in captivity—Marineland, Fla.

1946　**Medical Clinic**—cancer clinic (traveling)—established—Oklahoma City, Okla.

1961　**Element**—element 103—produced—Berkeley, Calif.

1977　**Army Officer**—Secretary of the Army (black)—C. L. Alexander, Jr.—sworn in

FEBRUARY 15

1768　**Mustard**—advertised—Benjamin Jackson—Philadelphia, Pa.

1799　**Election**—printed ballot—authorized—Pennsylvania

1842　**Postage Stamp**—adhesive stamps—used—City Despatch Post—New York City

1875　**Visiting Celebrities**—king (reigning) to visit the United States—David Kalakaua—returned

1879　**Senator (U.S.)**—black senator to preside over the Senate—B. K. Bruce of Mississippi—Washington, D.C.

1898　**Ship**—battleship of importance—*Maine*—destroyed by explosion—Havana harbor Cuba

1897 **Parent-Teacher Association**—parent-teacher association (national)—National Congress of Mothers—organized—Washington, D.C.

1899 **Bicycle Race**—international 6-day 2-man-team bicycle race—won by Miller and Waller—Madison Square Garden, New York City

1905 **Monument**—statue of a woman in National Statuary Hall—dedicated—F. E. Willard

1906 **President of a South American Country Born in the United States**—Galo Plaza Lasso—born—New York City

1911 **Aviation—Flights**—hydroplane flight to and from a ship—Glenn Curtiss—San Diego, Calif.

1913 **Labor Legislation**—minimum-wage law—enacted—Oregon

1915 **World War I**—American combatant to die in World War I—E. M. Stone—wounded

1934 **Automobile Driving Course**—State College, Pa.

1963 **Medal**——National Medal of Science—first presentation—Theodor von Karman

1969 **Aquanaut**—aquanaut to lose his life at work—B. L. Cannon—off San Clemente Island, Calif.

1971 **Veterinary Hospital**—municipal veterinary hospital—Spay and Neuter Clinic, Los Angeles, Calif.—W. E. Ziegler—opened

1972 **Astronaut**—astronaut (American) to become a general—J. A. McDivitt—date of rank

FEBRUARY 18

1688 **Slavery**—slavery protest—Germantown, Pa.

1735 **Opera**—opera performed—*Flora*—Charleston, S.C.

1804 **College**—university founded by a federal land grant—Ohio University—Athens, Ohio

1834 **Labor Paper**—*The Man*—published—New York City

1841 **Congress (U.S.)—Senate**—Senate filibuster (continuous)

1856 **American Party**—convention—Philadelphia, Pa.

1856 **Horse Race**—horse race on a stage in a theater—Old Broadway Theatre, New York City

1861 **Building**—"White House of the Confederacy"—used—Jefferson Davis—Montgomery, Ala.

1861 **Congress of the Confederate States**—House of Representatives—session—Richmond, Va.

1861 **President of the Confederate States**—Jefferson Davis—inducted—Montgomery, Ala.

1888 **Fish and Fisheries Commissioner**—salaried commissioner—M. McDonald—served

1908 **Postage Stamp**—postage stamps in coils—issued

1930 **Animals**—cow flown in an airplane—S Louis, Mo.

1930 **Astronomy**—planet—found beyond Neptune—Pluto

1930 **Woman**—woman tax appeals board member—Annabel Matthews

1943 **Congress (U.S.)**—woman private citizen address the House of Representatives an the Senate—Mme Chiang Kai-shek

1945 **Navy**—mobile dental office self-containe operating unit (U.S. Navy)—in operation

1953 **Motion Picture**—three-dimensional featur motion picture—*Bwana Devil*

1960 **Ice Skating Rink**—ice skating rink (artif cial) of Olympic size—Squaw Valley, Cali —formally opened

1975 **Labor Relations**—National Labor Relatior Board woman chairman—B. S. Murphy—sworn in

1979 **Automobile Racer**—automobile racer win the Daytona 500 six times—Richar Petty—Dayton, Fla.—6th victory

FEBRUARY 19

1794 **Historical Society**—historical societ (state)—Massachusetts Historical Socie —incorporated

1807 **Vice President (U.S.)**—Vice President a rested—Aaron Burr—Wakefield, Ala.

1817 **Bank**—savings bank to become a corpora tion—Provident Institution for Savings—Boston, Mass.—opened

1831 **Locomotive**—locomotive to burn coa (practical, American-made) tested—Yor Pa.

1836 **Naval Officer**—naval officer to become a engineer—C. H. Haswell—commissionec

1856 **Camera**—tintype camera—patented—H. Smith—Gambier, Ohio

1862 **Ship**—ironclad turreted vessel in the U. Navy — *Monitor* — completed — Gree point, L.I., N.Y.

1863 **Oil**—oil pipeline within the oil regions completed

1864 **Knights of Pythias**—founded—Washin ton, D.C.

1878 **Phonograph**—patented—T. A. Edison

1912 **Representative (U.S.)**—representative serve 56 years—C. T. Hayden of Arizona began service

1929 **Diathermy Machine**—used—Schenectad N.Y.

1953 **Censorship**—state board of censorship c literature—approved—Georgia

1953 **Television Station**—television stations share the same time and frequency—Sa nas, Calif., and Monterey, Calif.

1957 **Ship**—ship to transport fresh orange jui in stainless-steel tanks—*Tropicana* arrived—Whitestone, N.Y.

FEBRUARY 22

1630 **Popcorn**—introduced to English colonists

1770 **Revolutionary War**—martyr in the Revolutionary War—Boston, Mass.—Christopher Snider killed

1784 **Ship**—trading ship sent to China—*Empress of China*—sailed—New York City

1825 **Treaty**—treaty rejected by the Senate of the United States

1836 **Whig Party**—state convention—Columbus, Ohio

1854 **Republican Party**—Republican Party meeting (local)

1855 **Agricultural School**—agricultural college (state) to be chartered—Farmers High School of Pennsylvania—reincorporated

1856 **Republican Party**—Republican Party meeting (national)—Pittsburgh, Pa.

1872 **Labor Party (political)**—Labor Party (national)—Labor Reform Party—formed—Columbus, Ohio

1872 **Prohibition Party (national)**—national convention—Columbus, Ohio

1878 **Greenback Labor Party**—organized—Toledo, Ohio

1879 **Business**—five-cent store—opened—Utica, N.Y.

1881 **Monument**—obelisk to be brought to the United States—officially presented to New York City

1887 **Union Labor Party**—formed—Cincinnati, Ohio

1889 **State**—states admitted to the Union simultaneously—North and South Dakota

1890 **Monument**—monument to a woman financed by women—National Mary Washington Memorial Association—incorporated

1898 **Newspaper**—Arabic daily newspaper—*Al-Hoda*—published—Philadelphia, Pa.

1909 **Ship**—warship fleet to circumnavigate the globe—returned—Hampton Roads, Va.

1920 **Dog Racetrack**—to use imitation rabbit—opened—Emeryville, Calif.

1921 **Airmail Service**—airmail transcontinental flight—left San Francisco, Calif., for New York City

1923 **Animals**—chinchilla farm—established—Los Angeles, Calif.

1924 **Radio Broadcast**—President to broadcast from the White House—Calvin Coolidge—Washington, D.C.

1953 **Immigration**—Japanese national to receive an immigration visa—Sozaburo Kujiraoka

1966 **Motorboat Race**—motorboat race (ocean) under the Union of International Motorboating rules—Miami, Fla., to Bimini, Bahamas

1969 **Jockey**—jockey (woman) to win on a regular pari-mutuel flat track—B. J. Rubin—Charles Town, W.Va.

1977 **Photograph**—color transparency (35 mr magnified 516 times—taken by Ernst Ha —exhibited—New York City

FEBRUARY 23

1791 **Lifesaving Stations for Distressed Marine** —Humane Society of Massachusetts—i corporated

1813 **Cotton Mill**—cotton mill in the world which the whole process of cotton man facturing from spinning to weaving w carried on by power—Waltham, Mass.

1821 **Pharmacy College**—pharmacy college College of Apothecaries—organized Philadelphia, Pa.

1839 **Express Service**—organized—W. F. Har den—Boston, Mass.–New York City

1883 **Antivivisection Society**—American An Vivisection Society—organized—Phil delphia, Pa.

1883 **Trust**—antitrust law (state)—enacted—A abama

1886 **Aluminum**—aluminum—commercial pr cess invented—C. M. Hall

1892 **College Self-Government Organizati** —Bryn Mawr Self-Government Associ tion—chartered

1905 **Medal**—Interstate Commerce Commissi Medal of Honor—authorized

1905 **Rotary Club**—founded—Chicago, Ill.

1910 **Radio Contest**—Philadelphia, Pa.

1917 **Dental Society**—orthodontists' society American Society of Orthodontists—inc porated

1919 **Ship**—naval ship named for an enlist man—*Osmond Ingram*—launched—Qu cy, Mass.

1921 **Airmail Service**—airmail transcontinen flight—completed—New York City

1927 **Radio Commission (U.S.)**—created

1929 **Diathermy Machine**—first patient treat —Schenectady, N.Y.

1936 **Airmail Service**—rocket airmail fligh Greenwood Lake, N.Y.

1942 **Chaplains' School**—naval chaplai school—Norfolk, Va.

1942 **World War II**—American naval counter tack against the Japanese—Battle of Bal papan—began

1942 **World War II**—bombing on continen U.S. soil in World War II—Ellwood, Ca

1948 **Ship**—barge to transport liquid sulfur—service—Louisiana

1962 **Athlete**—black woman awarded the Jam E. Sullivan Memorial trophy—Wilma F dolph—New York City

1979 **Marine Corps**—general (black) of the M rines—F. E. Petersen, Jr.—nominated

FEBRUARY 24

1839 **Steam Shovel**—patented—W. S. Otis

1835 **Periodical**—American Indian–langua monthly—*Shawnee Sun*—published

1914 **Museum**—industrial museum—incorporated—New York City

1914 **Telephone**—underground-cable long-distance telephone conversation—Boston, Mass.–Washington, D.C.

1919 **Park**—park (national) east of the Mississippi—name changed to Lafayette National Park (later named Acadia National Park)

1931 **Sports Trophy**—sports trophy for the outstanding amateur athlete of the year—James E. Sullivan Memorial Trophy—presented to R. T. Jones—Chicago, Ill.

1935 **Ambulance**—incubator ambulance service —authorized—Chicago, Ill.

1938 **Radar**—passenger ship equipped with radar—*New York*

1940 **Air Defense Command (U.S.)**—created

1944 **Naval Officer**—captain in the U.S. Navy who was a woman—S. S. Dauser—appointed

1949 **Aviation—Flights (world)**—round-the-world nonstop airplane flight—takeoff—Fort Worth, Tex.

1953 **Typesetting Machine**—photographic type-composing machine—book set by the Photon process—*The Wonderful World of Insects*

1954 **Typesetting Machine**—photoengraving high-speed process for making halftones—in operation—Quincy, Mass.

1955 **Aviation—Parachute**—pilot to bail out of an airplane flying at supersonic speed—Los Angeles, Calif.

1971 **Ice Skating Champion**—ice skater to cover 100 miles in less than 6 hours—Kirt Barnes —Ann Arbor, Mich.

FEBRUARY 27

1729 **College**—college to have a full faculty—property transferred to the faculty—Williamsburg, Va.

1813 **Postal Service**—mail delivery by steamboats—authorized

1813 **Vaccination Legislation**—vaccination legislation (national)—enacted

1861 **Postal Service**—newspaper wrappers—authorized

1861 **Postage Stamp**—newspaper stamps—authorized

1867 **Dental Mallet**—dental mallet—idea conceived—W. G. A. Bonwill—Philadelphia, Pa.

1879 **Ship**—steamboat to employ electric lights—*Jeannette*—authorized

1883 **Cigar Rolling Machine**—practical—patented—Oscar Hammerstein

1897 **Initiative and Referendum**—passed—Senate—South Dakota

1915 **World War I**—American combatant to die in World War I—E. M. Stone

1919 **Deaf—Association**—national social organization for the hard of hearing—American Association for the Hard of Hearing formed—New York City

1922 **Radio Conference**—national radio conference—Washington, D.C.

1929 **Motion Picture**—black-oriented talking picture (all-talking, all-singing) by a major company—*Hearts in Dixie*—shown in New York City

1935 **Vectolite**—manufactured—West Lynn, Mass.

1939 **Strike**—anti–sit-down strike decision (federal)—U.S. Supreme Court

1947 **Television—Telecast**—surgical operation televised on a closed circuit—Baltimore, Md.

FEBRUARY 28

1794 **Congress (U.S.)—Senate**—contested election—election result voided

1810 **Insurance**—fire insurance joint-stock company—American Fire Insurance Company —organized—Philadelphia, Pa.

1820 **Library**—mechanics' library—constitution adopted—General Society of Mechanics and Tradesmen of the City of New York

1822 **Bank**—trust company—Farmer's Fire Insurance and Loan Company—New York City—incorporated

1827 **Railroad**—railroad for commercial transportation of passengers and freight—Baltimore and Ohio Railroad Company incorporated

1849 **Ship**—steamboat service (regular) to California via Cape Horn—*California*—arrive —San Francisco, Calif.

1861 **Confederate government bond**—authorized

1874 **Agriculture Department (state)**—state department of agriculture—created—Georgia

1882 **Cooperative**—college cooperative store—Harvard Co-operative Society—Cambridge, Mass.—constitution

1893 **Carborundum**—E. G. Acheson—patent granted

1918 **Army Insignia**—service number—issued an enlisted man—A. B. Crean

1925 **Postage Stamp**—special-handling stamp —authorized

1940 **Television—Telecast**—basketball game be televised—New York City

1952 **Basketball Player**—basketball player (collegiate) to score more than 1,000 points in 1 season—John O'Brien—reached 1, points in Seattle, Wash.

1954 **Television—Telecast**—phase-contrast cinemicrography film (American-made) telecast—*The Birth of a Plant*

1977 **Whale**—killer whale born in captivity—Marineland, Los Angeles, Calif.

30 **Ordnance**—tank with a turbine engine—XM-1 (Abrams tank)—rolled out—Lima, Ohio

30 **Woman**—woman director of the Voice of America—M. F. Bitterman—appointment confirmed

FEBRUARY 29

6 **Extradition**—extradition treaty with a foreign country—Jay Treaty, with Great Britain—proclaimed

4 **Congressional Caucus**—congressional caucus (open, not secret)—Washington, D.C.

0 **Motion Picture Actor**—black woman to win an Oscar—Hattie McDaniel—award presented

0 **Motion Picture Actor**—husband and wife Oscar winners—Vivien Leigh (for 1939)

4 **Woman**—woman secretary of a national political party—appointed

MARCH 1

2 **City (incorporated)**—Georgeana, Me.—incorporated

1 **Articles of Confederation**—formally announced

5 **Agricultural Society**—agricultural society—Philadelphia Society for the Promotion of Agriculture—organized

0 **Census**—census of the United States—authorized

2 **Presidential Succession Act**—enacted

6 **Actor**—American actor to appear abroad—J. H. Hackett—New York City debut

7 **Capital Punishment**—death penalty was first abolished—effective—Michigan

4 **Physician**—black woman awarded a medical degree—Rebecca Lee—Boston, Mass.

8 **Philatelic Magazine**—philatelic magazine (club organ)—*American Journal of Philately*—J. W. Scott, editor—published—New York City

9 **Postage Stamp**—postage stamps depicting scenes—on sale

9 **Postage Stamp**—postage stamp to picture the coat of arms of the United States—on sale

2 **Park**—park (national)—Yellowstone National Park—authorized

3 **Typewriter**—typewriter that was practical—contract to manufacture—Ilion, N.Y.

6 **Cattle Club**—cattle club (Guernsey cattle)—formed—Farmington, Conn.

3 **Index of Government Publications**—work assigned to B. P. Poore

3 **Temperance Society**—women's temperance society (national)—National Woman's Christian Temperance Union—organized—Cleveland, Ohio

4 **Physician**—osteopath (woman)—J. H. Bolles—graduated—Kirksville, Mo.

1899 **Union Reform Party**—platform adopted—Cincinnati, Ohio

1909 **Nursing School**—university school of nursing—established—Minneapolis, Minn.

1912 **Aviation—Parachute**—parachute jump from an airplane—Albert Berry—Jefferson Barracks, Mo.

1912 **Police**—woman detective—Isabella Goodwin—appointed—New York City

1913 **Insurance**—bonding law (state)—enacted—North Dakota

1913 **Tax**—income tax amendment to the Constitution—effective

1917 **Farm Loan Board (federal)**—federal land bank chartered

1918 **Army School**—graduate of the U.S. Military Academy (West Point) killed in action in World War I—S. W. Hoover

1937 **Automobile License Plates**—permanent license plates—effective—Connecticut

1940 **Supreme Court (U.S.)**—members of a family admitted simultaneously to practice in the Supreme Court of the United States—Faust family

1941 **Radio License**—frequency modulation transmitter to receive a commercial license—operation—Nashville, Tenn.

1942 **World War II**—German submarine destroyed by an American pilot—*U-656*—William Tepuni—off Cape Race, Newfoundland

1948 **Aviation—Airplane**—jet-propelled fighter plane (four-engine)—tested in flight—Muroc, Calif.

1950 **Civil Defense Director**—P. J. Larsen—assumed office

1958 **Catholic Priest**—prelate born in the United States named to the Roman Curia—S. A. Stritch—nominated

1972 **Astronaut**—astronaut (American) to become a general—J. A. McDivitt—promotion effective

1973 **Jockey**—jockey (woman) to win a major stakes race at a major track—Robyn Smith—Paumanauk Handicap, Aqueduct, L.I., N.Y.

1977 **Motion Picture Actor**—motion picture performer (woman) to win the Life Achievement Award—Bette Davis—presentation at Beverly Hills, Calif.

MARCH 2

1642 **Labor Law**—convict labor law—enacted—Virginia

1799 **Weights and Measures Standardization**—weights and measures standardization—enacted

1817 **Evangelical Church Building**—church dedicated—New Berlin, Pa.

1825 **Opera**—grand opera sung in English—*Der Freischutz*—New York City

1827 **Lottery**—lottery legislation (national)—enacted

1829 **Blind**—school for the blind—New England Asylum for the Blind—Boston, Mass.—incorporated

1831 **Sculptor**—sculptor (American) to obtain a federal commission—appropriation granted

1833 **Pensions Commissioner (U.S.)**—act authorizing appointment

1833 **Railroad**—state aid to railroads—authorized—Illinois

1858 **Cotton-Bale Metallic Tie**—patented—Frederick Cook

1861 **Constitutional Amendment (U.S.)**—proposed constitutional amendment to bear the signature of a President—Abraham Lincoln

1861 **Copyright Law**—photographic copyright law—enacted

1861 **Government Printing Office**—Government Printing Office—printing plant purchased—Washington, D.C.

1866 **Needles (machine-made)**—Excelsior Needle Company—incorporated

1867 **College**—university for blacks to establish undergraduate, graduate, and professional schools—Howard University—incorporated

1867 **Education Department (U.S.)**—Department of Education (U.S.)—created

1888 **Bank**—bank for blacks operated by blacks—Richmond, Va.—chartered

1891 **Gas**—gas conservation legislation—enacted—Indiana

1893 **Railroad Legislation**—railroad legislation (federal)—Safety Appliance Act—enacted

1894 **Medical School**—osteopathy school—Kirksville, Mo.—graduation

1899 **Naval Officer**—naval officer to become Admiral of the Navy—authorized

1901 **Forest Service**—Forest Service (U.S.)—Division of Forestry became Bureau of Forestry

1925 **Road**—route numbering system (nationwide)—adopted

1930 **Glider—Flights**—glider flight indoors—H. Kuchins—St. Louis, Mo.

1934 **Railroad**—streamlined lightweight high-speed three-car passenger train—operated—Union Pacific System

1940 **Television—Telecast**—track meet (intercollegiate) to be televised—New York City

1949 **Aviation—Flights (world)**—round-the-world nonstop airplane flight—completed—Fort Worth, Tex.

1949 **Electric Lighting**—streetlight of an automatic system—installed—New Milford, Conn.

1951 **Basketball Game**—all-star game of the National Basketball Association—Boston, Mass.

MARCH 3

1791 **Internal Revenue Act**—enacted

1791 **Tax**—excise tax (federal)—enacted

1791 **Tax**—internal revenue tax—imposed

1794 **Opera**—opera of a serious nature—*Tammany*—produced—New York City

1797 **Army Officer**—Judge Advocate of the U Army—Campbell Smith—began service

1801 **Governor** — Jewish governor — Dav Emanuel—Georgia—served

1801 **Land Preemption Act (federal)**—enacted

1803 **Impeachment**—impeachment of a federal judge—trial of John Pickering commenced

1803 **Land Grant**—special land grant to a foreigner—enacted

1813 **Army Officer**—surgeon general of the U Army—office established

1819 **Navy**—naval legislation standardizing nomenclature for naval vessels

1819 **Piracy Legislation**—piracy legislation enacted

1833 **Pensions Commissioner (U.S.)**—J. L. Edwards—served

1842 **Child Labor Law**—child labor law regulating hours of employment—approved Massachusetts

1843 **Telegraph**—telegraph appropriation (federal)—enacted

1845 **Lawbook**—law compilation of United States laws—authorized

1845 **Postal Service**—ocean mail contracts—authorized

1845 **Shipping**—ship subsidy—legislation

1845 **Veto (presidential)**—legislation passed over a President's veto—John Tyler

1847 **Postage Stamp**—postage stamps issued the Post Office Department—authorized

1847 **Senator (U.S.)**—senator who served a term of less than 6 weeks—Pierre Soule of Louisiana—term ended

1849 **Interior Department (U.S.)**—Interior Department (U.S.)—office authorized

1849 **Money**—double eagle coinage—authorized

1849 **Money**—gold coinage—double eagles and one-dollar gold pieces authorized

1851 **Money**—silver coins—three-cent pieces authorized

1853 **Assay Office Building (federal)**—authorized

1855 **Animals**—camels imported for commercial purposes—congressional appropriation

1855 **Court**—court of claims—judges appointed

1855 **Postal Service**—registration of letters—authorized

1863 **Army**—signal corps—authorized as separate branch of Army

1863 **Conscription**—wartime conscription bill enacted

1863 **Medal**—Medal of Honor (Army)—award authorized for officers

1863 **Money**—gold certificates—authorized

1863 **Money**—notes wholly engraved and printed at the Bureau of Engraving and Printing—authorized

1863 **Postal Service**—free city delivery of mail authorized

MARCH 4

1791 **Congress (U.S.)—Senate**—Senate special session

1791 **Representative (U.S.)**—Jewish representative—Israel Jacobs—served

1791 **State**—state admitted to the Union—after the Constitution—Vermont

1793 **Supreme Court (U.S.)**—Supreme Court nominee rejected—William Paterson—renamed under recess appointment

1797 **Representative (U.S.)**—representative elected while serving a prison term—Matthew Lyon—term began

1797 **Representative (U.S.)**—representative to serve before his 25th birthday—W. C. C. Claiborne of Tennessee—began service

1799 **Supreme Court (U.S.)**—Chief Justice of the United States who had been a representative in Congress—John Marshall of Virginia—congressional service began

1801 **President (U.S.)**—President inaugurated in the city of Washington—Thomas Jefferson

1809 **Vice President (U.S.)**—Vice President to serve under two presidents—George Clinton—began second term

1813 **Vice President (U.S.)**—Vice President to have served in the House of Representatives—Elbridge Gerry of Massachusetts—sworn in as Vice President

1823 **Representative (U.S.)**—Roman Catholic priest to serve in Congress—Gabriel Richard—Michigan Territory—term began

1826 **Railroad**—railroad for freight transportation to celebrate its centenary—Granite Railway Company—incorporated

1829 **Spoils System**—introduced—Andrew Jackson

1831 **Congress (U.S.)**—House of Representatives—Catholic chaplain—C. C. Pise—began service

1831 **Representative (U.S.)**—representative who had been a President of the United States—J. Q. Adams—served

1837 **Congress (U.S.)**—Congress to contain members of political parties other than Federalist, Whig, Republican, or Democrat—25th Congress—opened

1837 **Vice President (U.S.)**—Vice President elected by the Senate—R. M. Johnson—served

1838 **Sunday School**—Jewish Sunday school—organized—Philadelphia, Pa.

1840 **Photographic Studio**—commercial photography studio—A. S. Wolcott and John Johnson—New York City

1841 **Senator (U.S.)**—senator to receive a mileage allowance for a trip which he did not make—George Evans—served

1849 **Senator (U.S.)**—senator returned to the Senate after being defeated for the presidency—Henry Clay of Kentucky

1853 **Vice President (U.S.)**—Vice President sworn in on foreign soil—W. R. D. King—Havana, Cuba

1855 **Representative (U.S.)**—representati (brothers) to serve simultaneously—Wa burn brothers

1861 **Flag**—Confederate States flag—adopte Montgomery, Ala.

1861 **Government Printing Office**—Governm Printing Office—purchased printing pl began to function—Washington, D.C.

1863 **Congress (U.S.)**—officer to preside o both of the branches of Congress—Sch ler Colfax—served

1863 **Normal School**—normal school (state) which students actually conducted clas —Oswego, N.Y.—state appropriatio enacted

1873 **Newspaper**—illustrated daily news per—*Daily Graphic*—published—N York City

1875 **President (U.S.)**—President to becom senator—Andrew Johnson—served in t Senate

1875 **Senator (U.S.)**—black senator to serv full term—B. K. Bruce of Mississippi— gan service

1880 **Engraving**—halftone engraving—p lished—*Daily Graphic*—New York City

1881 **Catholic Student**—palladium conferre M. A. Corrigan

1881 **President (U.S.)**—President whose mo lived at the Executive Mansion—J. A. G field—inaugurated

1881 **Presidential Candidate**—presidential didate to campaign and make speeche a foreign language—J. A. Garfield—inau rated

1881 **Quarantine**—plant quarantine legisla (state)—enacted—California

1887 **Representative (U.S.)**—Italo-Ameri representative—F. B. Spinola of New Y —began service

1891 **Congress (U.S.)**—Congress to appropr $1 billion—Washington, D.C.

1891 **Copyright Law**—international copyr agreement—Platt-Simonds Copyright —enacted

1891 **Representative (U.S.)**—representa elected by the prohibitionists—Kittel vorson—served

1903 **Turbine**—steam-turbine generator of l capacity for commercial service—Chic Ill.—tested

1909 **Game Law Department (U.S.)**—game (state)—act prohibiting the transporta of game

1911 **Representative (U.S.)**—Socialist repre tative—V. L. Berger—served

1913 **Agriculture Department (U.S.)**—Offic Markets—created

1913 **Arbitration**—Federal Board of Media and Conciliation—authorized

1913 **Commerce Department (U.S.)**—Comm Department (U.S.)—established

Game Law—game law (state)—McLean law—regulating shooting of migratory birds—enacted

Labor Department (U.S.)—Labor Department (U.S.)—created

Agriculture Department (U.S.)—Office of Markets—changed to Bureau of Markets

Representative (U.S.)—representative (woman) elected—Jeannette Rankin—served

Park—park (national)—Hot Springs National Park—designated

Radio Broadcast—presidential inauguration—Calvin Coolidge—Washington, D.C.

Radio Facsimile Transmission—photograph sent by radio across the continent—Washington, D.C.

Congress (U.S.)—Congress to enact over 1,000 laws—opened

Runner-transcontinental foot race—to New York City—started Los Angeles, Calif.

Track Meet—transcontinental race—began, Los Angeles, Calif.

Congress (U.S.)—Senate—broadcast from the Senate chamber—Washington, D.C.

Representative (U.S.)—black representative from the North—O. S. De Priest—served

Vice President (U.S.)—American-Indian Vice President—Charles Curtis—served

Woman—woman secretary to a Vice President of the United States—L. M. Williams—served

Bowler—woman bowler to obtain a perfect score—Emma Fahning—Buffalo, N.Y.

Cabinet (U.S.)—father and son to occupy the same Cabinet posts—H. C. Wallace and H. A. Wallace—H. A. Wallace—served

Cabinet (U.S.)—full Cabinet sworn in at the same time and place—Washington, D.C.—F. D. Roosevelt

Cabinet (U.S.)—woman Cabinet member—Frances Perkins—served

Electoral College—electoral college members invited to a presidential inaugural—March 4

Labor Department (U.S.)—woman Secretary of Labor—Frances Perkins—served

Radio Station—seagoing radio broadcasting station—Courier—dedicated—Washington, D.C.

Cabinet (U.S.)—black sub-Cabinet member—J. E. Wilkins—appointed

Submarine—submarine to travel under ice for 12 days—Skate—left New London, Conn.

Interstate Commerce Commission—independent administrative agency of the federal government woman member—V. M. Brown—appointed

Coast Guard (U.S.)—woman airplane pilot in the Coast Guard—Janna Lambine—was graduated at Milton, Fla.

MARCH 5

1623 Temperance Law (colonial)—enacted—Virginia

1743 Periodical—sectarian magazine—The Christian History—published—Boston, Mass.

1743 Religious Publication—religious journal—Christian History—published—Boston, Mass.

1750 Play (drama)—Shakespearean play—King Richard III—presented—New York City

1770 Revolutionary War—American casualties—Boston, Mass.

1813 Flag—American flag flown in battle on the Pacific—Essex entered Pacific Ocean

1821 President (U.S.)—President inaugurated on March 5—James Monroe

1836 Pistol—pistol—Samuel Colt—company incorporated

1856 Railroad Legislation—railroad legislation (state)—enacted—Georgia

1866 Health Board—health board (municipal) armed with sufficient powers—meeting—New York City

1872 Air Brake—triple air brake patented—George Westinghouse

1880 Railroad—municipal railroad—through passenger trains—Cincinnati, Ohio–Chattanooga, Tenn.

1894 Employment Service—municipal employment office—opened—Seattle, Wash.

1913 Commerce and Labor Department (U.S.)—W. C. Redfield—became Secretary of Commerce

1913 Dentist—dentist in the U.S. Navy to serve aboard a naval ship—H. E. Harvey—Solace

1923 Pension—old-age pension laws (state)—enacted—Montana and Nevada

1924 Bowler—bowler to roll two perfect games—Frank Caruana—Buffalo, N.Y.

1934 Holiday—mother-in-law day—celebrated—Amarillo, Tex.

1935 Medical Legislation—premature-baby health law—enacted—Chicago, Ill.

1935 Naval Officer—naval officer designated Commander, Aircraft Battle Force—H. V. Butler

1958 Submarine—submarine to cross the Atlantic Ocean within 9 days—Skate—arrived at Portland, England

1969 Criminal—woman on the "ten most wanted" list—Ruth Eisemann-Schier—arrested—Norman, Okla.

1977 Radio Broadcast—presidential phone-in—Jimmy Carter—Walter Cronkite, moderator—Washington, D.C.

MARCH 6

1646 Patent—machine patent—Joseph Jencks—Massachusetts

1775 Freemasons—black Mason—initiated—Boston, Mass.

1808 Orchestra—college orchestra—founded—Cambridge, Mass.

1810 Vaccination Legislation—vaccination legislation (state)—enacted—Illinois

1865 Naval Officer—Judge Advocate of the Navy—W. E. Chandler—appointed

1886 Electric Power Plant—alternating-current power plant—Great Barrington, Mass.

1886 Nurses' Magazine—*The Nightingale*—published—New York City

1902 Census Bureau—Census Bureau permanent organization—authorized

1906 Engineering Society—woman elected to the American Society of Civil Engineers—N. S. Blatch

1923 Swimmer—swimmer to cover a distance of 440 meters free style in less than 5 minutes—Johnny Weissmuller—New Haven, Conn.

1928 Medical School—medical center devoted to teaching, treatment, and research—Columbia-Presbyterian Medical Center, New York City—opened

1934 President (U.S.)—President's wife to travel in an airplane to a foreign country—Eleanor Roosevelt—left Miami, Fla.

1941 Aviation—Parachute—parachute fatality in the U.S. Army—F. S. Beard—Columbus, Ga.

1941 Ship—aircraft carrier escort—*Long Island*—acquired

1947 Aviation—Airplane—jet-propulsion four-engine bomber—tested—Muroc, Calif.

1947 Ship—air-conditioned naval ship—*Newport News*—launched—Newport News, Va.

1966 Pole Vault—pole vault indoors higher than 17 feet—Bob Seagren—Albuquerque, N.Mex.

1967 Newspaper—large-type weekly—*New York Times Large Type Weekly*—published—New York City

1969 Astronaut—astronauts (American) in orbit to transfer from one spacecraft to another—R. L. Schweickart and J. A. McDivitt

MARCH 7

1644 Legislature—legislature with two chambers—established—Massachusetts

1644 Whaling—whaling (systematic)—Southampton, N.Y.

1801 Election Law—registration law (state)—enacted—Massachusetts

1825 Treaty—treaty with a South American country—Colombia—ratified

1854 Sewing Machine—sewing machine to stitch buttonholes—patented—Charles Miller

1865 Coast Guard (U.S.)—coastguardsman (black)—M. A. Healy—appointed

1876 Telephone—telephone patent—A. G. Bell

1893 Patent—print patent—H. J. Heinz Co.—Pittsburgh, Pa.

1911 Locker—locker (coin vendor)—patente W. S. Farnsworth

1955 Television—Telecast—play telecast color with its original cast—*Peter* —New York City

1958 Submarine—submarine expressly signed and built to fire guided missil *Grayback*—commissioned—Mare Isl Calif.

1959 Aviation—Pilot—pilot to fly a million m in a jet airplane—M. C. Garlow

1962 Satellite—orbiting solar-observatory s lite—OSO 1—launched—Cape Canav Fla.

1980 Woman—woman director of the Voic America—M. F. Bitterman—took offic

MARCH 8

1849 Interior Department (U.S.)—Interior partment secretary—Thomas Ewing pointed

1855 Bridge—railroad suspension brid Niagara Falls Suspension Bridge— crossed over

1862 Naval Officer—naval chaplain killed i tion—J. L. Lenhart

1871 Fish and Fisheries Commissioner (U.S.) F. Baird—served

1887 Fishing Rod—of telescoping steel tub patented—Everett Horton

1894 Dog License—dog license law (sta enacted—New York City

1917 Congress (U.S.)—Senate—Senate cl resolution—enacted

1933 Money—script money to be self-liquid —issued

1945 Naval Officer—black nurse in the Nav serve Corps—inducted—P. M. Da New York City

1946 Helicopter—helicopter licensed for mercial use—license granted to *Jou American*—New York City

1969 Jockey—jockey (woman) to ride 2 wi in 1 day—B. J. Rubin—Chester, W.V

1971 Prizefight—prizefight with a purse o million—Frazier vs. Ali—New York (

1971 Television—Telecast—motion pictur miere telecast on 2 successive nig *Vanished*—first part

1977 Treasury Department (U.S.)—gold lions issued by the Treasury Departm authorized

MARCH 9

1745 Carillon—carillon—shipped from En —to Boston, Mass.

1798 Naval Officer—naval surgeon of the Navy—George Balfour transferred to

1799 Pistol—government contract for pist Simeon North—Berlin, Conn.

1822 Dentistry—patent for artificial teeth— Graham

0 Bank—trust company—New York Life Insurance and Trust Company—chartered—New York City

1 Dental School—dental college—Baltimore College of Dental Surgery—Baltimore, Md.—degrees conferred

7 Ship—naval ship christened by a woman—*Germantown*—L. F. Watson—commissioned

8 Postal Service—street letter box—patented—Albert Potts

0 Japanese Ambassador—staff arrived—San Francisco, Calif.

1 Money—Confederate currency—authorized

2 Civil War—conflict between ironclad vessels in the Civil War—*Monitor* and *Merrimac*

2 Ordnance—revolving gun turret—*Monitor*—used

3 Bicycle Society—bicycle club—first meet—Boston, Mass.

3 Trust—antitrust law (state)—general law—enacted—Kansas

2 Degrees (academic and honorary)—anthropology doctorate—conferred—Worcester, Mass.

7 Sterilization Legislation—enacted—Indiana

7 Helicopter—helicopter to deliver material across a picket line—New Bedford, Mass.

7 Strike—strike to last longer than a year—J. I. Case Manufacturing Company, Racine, Wis.—strike ended

0 Railroad Car—dining car (all-electric)—in service between Chicago, Ill., and St. Louis, Mo.

4 Television—Telecast—color commercial televised on a local show

5 Satellite—multisatellite launching (8 satellites in 1 shot)—launched—Vandenberg Air Force Base, Calif.

4 Television—Telecast—motion picture premiere telecast on 2 successive nights—*Vanished*—second part

Army School—women cadets of the U.S. Military Academy (West Point)—accepted for admission

MARCH 10

Diplomatic Service—minister plenipotentiary—appointed after the Revolution—Thomas Jefferson

Pile Driver—pile driver—patented—John Stone

President (U.S.)—President who had received a patent—Abraham Lincoln made application

Dental School—dental school permanently established by a university—graduation—Cambridge, Mass.

Benevolent and Protective Order of Elks—Grand Lodge—incorporated

1876 Telephone—telephone message—A. G. Bell—Boston, Mass.

1880 Salvation Army—landed—New York City

1903 Multigraph—patented—H. C. Gammeter

1908 Children's Welfare Congress (international)—met—Washington, D.C.

1909 Old Age Home for Pioneers—approved—Arizona

1911 Trust—blue-sky laws—passed—Kansas

1913 Bowler—bowler to make a perfect score of 300 in an American Bowling Congress tournament—William Knox—Toledo, Ohio

1933 Narcotics Legislation—narcotics regulation (state)—adopted—Nevada

1940 Television—Telecast—opera telecast—New York City

1948 Aviation—Flights—airplane to fly faster than the speed of sound which was piloted by a civilian—H. H. Hoover—Edwards Air Force Base, Calif.

1961 Basketball Player—basketball player (professional) to score more than 3,000 points in 1 season—Wilt Chamberlain—reached 3,033 points in Ft. Wayne, Ind.

1967 Attorney General—attorney general (U.S.) whose father also served as attorney general—W. R. Clark—sworn in

1971 Election Law—federal legislation enabling persons 18 years of age or older to vote (26th Amendment)—passed by Senate

MARCH 11

1779 Army—Army Engineering Department—formal Corps of Engineers—established

1791 Patent—patentee to obtain more than one patent—Samuel Mulliken

1823 Normal School—normal school established exclusively for the preparation of teachers—Concord Academy—Concord, Vt.—opened

1852 Fair—industrial exposition—company chartered

1861 Constitution of the Confederate States of America—adopted—Montgomery, Ala.

1864 Army Ambulance Corps—Army Ambulance Corps established by congressional action

1864 Army Officer—woman assistant army surgeon—M. E. Walker

1882 Lacrosse Association (intercollegiate)—Intercollegiate Lacrosse Association—organized—Princeton, N.J.

1886 Physician—Hindu woman to receive a doctor of medicine degree—Anandibai Joshee—graduated

1896 War Veterans' Society—Military Order of Foreign Wars—National Commandery—instituted

1903 Opera—opera composed by a woman performed at the Metropolitan Opera House—*Der Wald*—New York City—E. M. Smyth

1909 Bowling Tournament—gold medal award to a perfect-score bowler—roll-off—Pittsburgh, Pa.

1916 Ship—battleship to use fuel oil exclusively—*Nevada*—commissioned

1927 Automobile Robbery—armored commercial car holdup—Pittsburgh, Pa.

1927 Motion Picture Theater—theater built especially for the rear projection of motion pictures—rear-projection screen used—New York City

1930 President (U.S.)—President buried in the National Cemetery at Arlington, Va.—W. H. Taft

1940 Photograph—cystoscopic photographs in color—publicly exhibited—Birmingham, Ala.

1945 Medal—navy unit commendation decoration—to ship—*Helena*—awarded

1948 Tennis Player—black tennis player to participate in a United States Indoor Lawn Tennis Association championship tournament—Reginald Weir—New York City

1953 Army Officer—woman doctor commissioned in the regular Army—F. M. Adams

1959 Play (drama)—play written by a black woman to reach Broadway—*Raisin in the Sun*—opened in New York City

1960 Satellite—satellite placed in solar orbit—Pioneer V (1960 Alpha)—launched—Cape Canaveral, Fla.

MARCH 12

1664 Citizenship—naturalization act—in the American colonies—enacted

1755 Steam Engine—steam engine—used—North Arlington, N.J.

1804 Impeachment—impeachment of a federal judge—John Pickering—impeached

1849 Railroad—railroad to run west of the Mississippi River—Pacific Railroad of Missouri—incorporated

1877 Cabinet (U.S.)—Confederate to serve in the Cabinet—D. M. Key—served

1877 Cabinet (U.S.)—German-born Cabinet member—Carl Schurz—began service

1884 College—state college for women—authorized—Mississippi

1889 Telephone—automatic telephone system (successful)—patent application

1894 Supreme Court (U.S.)—associate justice of the Supreme Court to become Chief Justice—E. D. White appointed justice

1904 Carnegie Hero Fund Commission—established—Andrew Carnegie

1912 Girl Scouts—founded—Savannah, Ga.

1914 Railroad—railroad operated by the federal government—Alaska Railroad—acquisition authorized

1920 Deaf—Association—national social organization for the hard of hearing—American Association for the Hard of Hearing—annual meeting

1923 Motion Picture—sound-on-film motion ture—demonstrated—for the press—de Forest—New York City

1925 Prison—prison (federal) exclusively women—Federal Industrial Institution Women—M. B. Harris, first superintend —Alderson, W.Va.—sworn in

1935 Crime Prevention and Detection—cri prevention commission for interstate co eration—joint resolution—enacted—N Jersey

1945 Labor—labor antidiscrimination comn sion (state)—commission authorize New York

1954 Bridge (game)—bridge hand in which e of the 4 players was dealt a perfect han Irene Motta—Cranston, R.I.

1966 Ship—guided-missile escort ship—*Bro* —commissioned

MARCH 13

1638 Military Organization—military organi tion—Ancient and Honorable Artill Company—chartered

1735 Moravian Bishop—David Nitschman consecrated at Berlin, Germany

1770 Chamber of Commerce—Chamber of C merce (state)—incorporated—New Yor

1790 Actor—actor of American birth—J Martin—appeared—Philadelphia, Pa.

1852 Cartoon—"Uncle Sam" cartoon—p lished—New York City

1868 Impeachment—impeachment proceedi against a President of the United State against Andrew Johnson—Washing D.C.

1877 Earmuff—patented—Chester Greenwo

1895 Submarine—submarine contract of United States Navy—*Plunger*—John P. F land Torpedo Boat Co.

1913 Motion Picture Censorship—motion ture censorship board (state)—approve Kansas

1930 Astronomy—planet—discovery of Plut announced

1942 Army Officer—woman with rank co sponding to colonel—J. O. Flikke

1943 Dental Corps (U.S. Navy)—admiral in Dental Corps (U.S. Navy)—A. G. Lyle pointed

1946 Medal—Medal of Honor awarded t Nisei—presented

1952 Chloromycetin—chloromycetin laborat —opened—Holland, Mich.

1953 Hospital—hospital completely devotec the study of the atom in the treatmen cancer—Argonne Cancer Research Ho tal—opened—Chicago, Ill.

1954 Engraving and Printing Bureau (U.S souvenir card of the Bureau of Engrav and Printing—issued—Philadelphia, Pa

1955 Building—atom-bomb-resistant fed building—occupied—Washington, D.C.

9 **Photograph**—ultraviolet pictures of the sun —White Sands, N.M.

MARCH 14

3 **Letter**—letter descriptive of America—dispatched

3 **Supreme Court (U.S.)**—Supreme Court nominee rejected—renamed—began service (renominated under recess appointment)

4 **Cotton Gin**—patented—Eli Whitney

2 **War Bond**—authorized

3 **Ship**—naval vessel of the United States to display the American flag around Cape Horn—arrived—Valparaiso, Chile

6 **Conference**—conference of American Republics—assembled at Panama

7 **Education Department (U.S.)**—Department of Education (U.S.)—Commissioner Henry Barnard—appointed

1 **Seal**—state seal designed by a woman—E. S. Edwards—Idaho—approved

0 **Bond**—bonds payable specifically in United States gold coins—authorized

3 **Bird Reservation (national)**—established—Sebastian, Fla.

7 **Bank**—national bank branch legally operated—chartered—Moss Point, Miss.

1 **Insurance**—workmen's compensation insurance law (state)—enacted—Washington

7 **Aviation—Airship**—airship of the United States Navy that was successful—F1—flight

8 **Ship**—concrete seagoing ship—*Faith*—launched—Redwood City, Calif.

7 **Engineering Society**—woman elected to the American Society of Civil Engineers—as associate member—Elsie Eaves

1 **Motion Picture Theater**—theater built especially for the rear projection of motion pictures—opened—New York City

6 **Periodical**—magazine of the United States Government—*Federal Register*—issued

2 **Medal**—Medal of Honor awarded to a Marine in World War II—G. H. Cannon

0 **Sulfur Mine (offshore)**—off Louisiana coast —sulfur obtained

2 **Basketball Player**—basketball player (professional) to score more than 4,000 points in 1 season—Wilt Chamberlain—reached 4,029 points in Chicago, Ill.

4 **Television—Telecast**—courtroom verdict telecast—Ruby trial—Dallas, Tex.

MARCH 15

9 **Catholic Nuns**—nun who professed her vows—New Orleans, La.

7 **President (U.S.)**—President born posthumously—Andrew Jackson—born—Union County, N.C.

2 **Russian Settlement**—established—Cazadero, Calif.

1830 **Education Association**—education association (national)—American Institute of Instruction—formed—Boston, Mass.

1834 **Dry Dock**—federal dry docks—Norfolk, Va.—dry dock completed

1851 **Medical School**—medical school based upon water-cure principles—American Hydropathic Institute—opened—New York City

1855 **Health Board**—health board (state) to regulate quarantine—Louisiana

1867 **College**—state university supported by a direct property tax—approved—Michigan

1875 **Catholic Priest**—Catholic priest to be elevated to the cardinalate—John McCloskey —preconized

1887 **Game Warden**—(salaried game and fish warden)—authorized—Michigan

1887 **Kindergarten**—kindergarten for the blind—authorized—Roxbury, Mass.

1892 **Voting Machine**—voting machines were authorized—New York

1897 **Fly Casting Tournament**—indoor fly casting tournament—New York City

1901 **Army Nurse Corps (female)**—Superintendent D. H. Kinney—appointed

1913 **Court**—conciliation tribunal for small claims—established—Cleveland, Ohio

1913 **Court**—small debtors' court established by state law—authorized—Kansas

1919 **War Veterans' Society**—American Legion —caucus—Paris, France

1927 **Radio Commission (U.S.)**—organization meeting

1930 **Glider**—seaplane glider—tested—Port Washington, N.Y.

1930 **Submarine**—streamlined submarine of the U.S. Navy—*Nautilus*—launched—Mare Island, Calif.

1934 **Information Service (U.S.)**—opened

1934 **Youth Hostel**—incorporated—Hartford, Conn.

1937 **Blood Bank**—blood bank—established—Chicago, Ill.

1937 **Medical Clinic**—contraceptive clinic (state)—opened—Raleigh, N.C.

1938 **Merchant Marine Academy**—Merchant Marine Cadet Corps (U.S.)—established—Kings Point, N.Y.

1945 **Medal**—presidential citation to an entire division—awarded

1947 **Naval Officer**—black commissioned officer in the regular U.S. Navy—John Lee—commissioned

1948 **Airmail Service**—parcel post international air service—inaugurated—to Europe

1960 **Park**—undersea park (federal)—Key Largo Coral Reef Preserve established—Key Largo, Fla.

1970 **Greek Orthodox Church**—Greek Orthodox Church bishop who had converted from the Roman Catholic Church—Paul de Ballester —New York City

1970 **Hockey Player**—professional hockey player (defenseman) to score 100 points in 1 season—R. G. Orr—100th point in Boston, Mass.

MARCH 16

1697 **Woman**—heroine—captured by Indians— Hannah Duston

1802 **Army**—engineer corps—established

1802 **Army School**—Army school—established —West Point, N.Y.

1810 **Supreme Court (U.S.) Decision**—Supreme Court decision that a state law was unconstitutional—Fletcher vs. Peck

1827 **Newspaper**—black newspaper—*Freedom's Journal*—published—New York City

1829 **High School Legislation**—high school legislation—enacted—Ohio

1871 **Fertilizer Law**—fertilizer law (state)— enacted—Delaware

1877 **Occupational Therapy Treatment**—training school—incorporated

1882 **American Red Cross**—ratification of international agreement by United States

1883 **Pharmacist**—pharmacist (woman graduate)—Susan Hayhurst—graduated

1885 **Bank**—savings group—started—Long Island City, N.Y.

1915 **Federal Trade Commission**—organized

1926 **Rocket**—liquid-fuel rocket flight—Auburn, Mass.

1929 **Tax**—chain stores tax (state)—authorized —Indiana

1931 **Woman**—woman state budget commissioner—J. W. Wittich—served—Minnesota

1934 **Revenue Stamp**—printed by the Post Office Department—authorized

1947 **Aviation—Airplane**—twin-engine pressurized airplane—tested—San Diego, Calif.

1947 **Aviation**—Pilot—woman pilot to fly an airplane faster than 300 m.p.h.—Margie Hurlburt—Tampa, Fla.

1952 **Television—Telecast**—surgical operation televised on a local program—Philadelphia, Pa.

1966 **Astronaut**—astronaut (American civilian) to orbit the earth—N. A. Armstrong— *Gemini VIII*—launched, Cape Kennedy, Fla.

1966 **Satellite**—manned docking of 2 spacecraft—*Gemini VIII*

MARCH 17

1631 **Fire Prevention Legislation**—enacted— Cambridge, Mass.

1845 **Yacht Club**—New York Yacht Club—regular election—New York City

1852 **Fair**—industrial exposition—directors elected—New York City

1854 **Park**—park land—purchased by a city— Worcester, Mass.

1861 **Money**—paper money issued by the G ernment of the United States—dema notes—made legal tender

1864 **Water Conduit**—water supply tunnel fc city—construction began—Chicago, Ill.

1868 **Postal Service**—postage-canceling r chine patent

1871 **Baseball League**—baseball league of portance—National Association of Ba Ball Players—organized

1881 **Locomotive**—locomotive to attain a spe of more than 1 mile a minute—Penn vania

1884 **Glider—Flights**—glider flight—J. J. Mc gomery—Otay, Calif.

1897 **Fly Casting Tournament**—cast to exc 100 feet—R. C. Leonard—New York Ci

1897 **Motion Picture**—motion picture of prizefight (heavyweight championship R. L. Fitzsimmons vs. J. J. Corbett—Car City, Nev.—filmed

1897 **Prizefight**—openair arena especially b for a prizefight—Carson City, Nev.—C bett-Fitzsimmons fight

1897 **Theological School**—Presbyterian theo ical seminary woman graduate—E. Briggs—Union Theological Seminary, N York City

1898 **Submarine**—submarine that was pract and able to submerge—*Holland No.* launched

1912 **Camp Fire Girls**—organization— nounced—Lake Sebago, Me.

1913 **Court**—conciliation tribunal for sn claims—Ohio—court opened

1914 **Automobile Bus**—bus with cross seat introduced

1917 **Bowling Tournament**—bowling tou ment for women—St. Louis, Mo.

1924 **Fireboat**—fireboat with two-way ra equipment—licensed—Boston, Mass.

1950 **Element**—element 98—announced

1959 **Submarine**—submarine to travel under for 12 days—*Skate*—surfaced through at North Pole

1963 **Catholic Beatification**—Catholic beatif tion of an American-born woman—E. A Seton

1963 **Saint (Catholic)**—saint (native-born Cat lic)—E. A. B. Seaton—beatified

1970 **United Nations**—veto by the United Sta in the Security Council of the United tions

1975 **Physician**—doctors' strike against I working hours in hospitals—New Y City

1976 **Diplomatic Service**—ambassador (won to the Court of St. James—A. L. Armstr —presented credentials

MARCH 18

1543 **Flood**—recorded—Mississippi River— nando de Soto

4 **Advertisement**—magician's advertisement —published—New York City

5 **Catholic Priest**—Catholic priest to receive his full theological training in the United States—D. A. Gallitzin—ordained bishop —Baltimore, Md.

3 **Gas**—gaslights (street)—David Melville— Newport, R.I.—patent

8 **Pension**—pensions paid by the United States Government—universal service pension

4 **Representative (U.S.)**—representative-elect refused a seat—John Bailey of Massachusetts

4 **Tunnel**—railroad tunnel—completed— Hollidaysburg-Johnstown, Pa.

0 **Navy**—naval militia (state)—Massachusetts Naval Battalion—organized

0 **Opera**—opera by an American composer performed at the Metropolitan Opera House of New York—*Pipe of Desire*—produced

1 **Insurance**—hail insurance law (state)— enacted—North Dakota

3 **Medical Legislation**—chiropractic legislation (state)—Kansas—enacted

2 **Polo**—intercollegiate indoor polo championship—Princeton-Yale—New York City

5 **Tornado**—tornado disaster (large-scale)— Illinois, Indiana, Kentucky, and Tennessee

1 **Razor**—electric dry shaver—manufactured —Stamford, Conn.

8 **Medical Legislation**—law (state) requiring serological blood tests of pregnant women —enacted—New York

5 **Hockey Player**—professional hockey player to score 50 goals in 1 season—J. H. M. Richard—50th goal in Boston, Mass.

8 **Birth Registration**—birth registration uniform system for the numbering of birth certificates

0 **Basketball Team**—basketball collegiate team to win the National Invitation Tournament and the National Collegiate Athletic Association trophy

2 **Lens**—plastic lens—for cataract patients— fitted—Philadelphia, Pa.

8 **Newspaper**—newspaper advertisement printed on aluminum foil—Milwaukee *Sentinel*

7 **Ship**—diesel-and-gas-turbine combined-propulsion plant in a major ship—*Alexander Hamilton*—commissioned

0 **Strike**—strike of postal employees—New York City

2 **Ship**—naval ship named for a black naval officer—*Jesse L. Brown*—launched—Westwego, La.

MARCH 19

1 **Bank Robbery**—bank robbery—New York City

1925 **Postage Stamp**—fractional-denomination postage stamp—Harding stamp—issued— Washington, D.C.

1948 **Labor Relations**—labor dispute in which the Taft-Hartley law was invoked—injunction issued

1949 **Museum**—museum devoted exclusively to atomic energy—opened—Oak Ridge, Tenn.

1953 **Television—Telecast**—Academy of Motion Picture Arts and Sciences annual awards telecast—New York City and Hollywood, Calif.

1954 **Rocket Sled**—rocket-driven sled on rails— tested—Alamogordo, N.Mex.

1954 **Television—Telecast**—prizefight televised in color—New York City

1965 **Narcotics Legislation**—narcotics prohibitory legislation (state)—Nevada—enacted

1975 **Sex Discrimination**—state that declared unconstitutional a ban against girls competing with boys in athletic events on a state basis—Pennsylvania

MARCH 20

1768 **Artist**—artist successful in commercial art —Matthew Pratt—sailed from Bristol, England

1833 **Treaty**—treaty with a Far Eastern country —concluded with Siam

1856 **Governor**—governor removed from office by a state supreme court—decision against W. A. Barstow

1865 **Cooperative**—cooperative state law— effective—Michigan

1872 **Pharmacy College**—pharmacy college to make analytical chemistry a required course—chair of analytical chemistry— Maryland College of Pharmacy—Baltimore, Md.

1886 **Electric Power Plant**—alternating-current power plant—commercial operation— Great Barrington, Mass.

1890 **Women's Club**—women's club federation —General Federation of Women's Clubs— organized—New York City

1891 **Scale**—computing scales—Computing Scale Company—Dayton, Ohio—incorporated

1899 **Execution**—execution of a woman by electrocution—M. M. Place—Ossining, N.Y.

1902 **Radio Telephone**—radio telephone marine demonstration—N. B. Stubblefield—*Bartholdi*

1911 **Farm Bureau**—Binghamton, N.Y.

1911 **Squash Club**—squash tennis organization (national)—National Squash Tennis Association—formed—New York City

1914 **Ice Skating Tournament**—figure skating international championship tournament— New Haven, Conn.

1925 **Diplomatic Service**—woman vice consul— P. H. Field—appointed

1930 **Diesel Engine**—diesel engine speed record (official)—Daytona Beach, Fla.

1948 **Radio Broadcast**—radio program simultaneously transmitted—over AM and FM stations, and telecast—NBC Symphony—New York City

1948 **Television—Telecast**—symphonic concerts to be televised—Philadelphia, Pa.

1954 **Vending Machine**—newspaper vending machine to deliver a single copy—manufactured, Columbia, Pa.—leased

1957 **Television—Telecast**—telecast (public) over telephone wires using the narrowband system—demonstrated by C. R. Kraus—Philadelphia, Pa.

1967 **Vietnam War**—general (American) to die in Vietnam—A. J. F. Moody

MARCH 21

1791 **Naval Officer**—naval officer commissioned—Hopley Yeaton

1791 **Navy**—naval protection—commissions granted to captains

1791 **Ship**—revenue cutter—officers appointed

1826 **Engineering College**—engineering college—Rensselaer School—Troy, N.Y.—incorporated

1850 **College**—coeducational college—Oberlin College—name adopted—Oberlin, Ohio

1856 **Governor**—governor removed from office by a state supreme court—W. A. Barstow—resigned

1859 **Zoological Garden**—zoological garden—Philadelphia Zoological Garden—incorporated

1866 **Soldiers' Home**—soldiers' homes (national)—authorized

1867 **Philatelic Society**—philatelic society—New York Philatelic Society—organized—New York City

1868 **Women's Club**—women's professional club—Sorosis—founded—New York City

1879 **Geological Survey**—geological survey director (U.S.)—Clarence King—nominated

1889 **Holiday**—national holiday—authorized for April 30, 1889

1905 **Sterilization Legislation**—passed by Pennsylvania but vetoed by governor

1916 **Chess Champion**—chess champion to play more than 100 games simultaneously—F. J. Marshall—Washington, D.C.

1917 **Naval Officer**—petty officer (woman)—Loretta Walsh—sworn in

1924 **Radio Broadcast**—foreign-language course broadcast—New York City

1933 **Aviation—Flights**—all-blind cross-country test—College Park, Md.

1935 **Ambulance**—incubator ambulance service—inaugurated—Chicago, Ill.

1939 **Television—Telecast**—surgical-operation classroom-instruction telecast—Brooklyn, N.Y.

1945 **Marine Corps**—general (4 stars) of the Marines on active duty to become a full general—A. A. Vandegrift—date of rank

1946 **Microfilm**—microfilm machine to project enlarged images on ceilings—installed Ann Arbor, Mich.

1946 **United Nations**—Conference on International Organization of the UN—temporary quarters established—New York City

MARCH 22

1622 **American Indians**—massacre of white people by American Indians—Jamestown,

1630 **Gambling Legislation (colonial)**—enacted—Boston, Mass.

1822 **Horticultural Society**—horticultural society—New York Horticultural Society—corporated

1841 **Cornstarch**—cornstarch patent—O. Jones

1861 **Nursing School**—school for nurses to award a diploma—School of Nursing Philadelphia, Pa.—incorporated

1862 **Ship**—Confederate cruiser built in England—sailed from England

1871 **Impeachment**—impeachment and removal from office of a state governor—W. Holden—North Carolina—impeached

1872 **Labor Legislation**—women's equal employment legislation—enacted—Illinois

1874 **Young Men's Hebrew Association**—founded—New York City

1880 **Electric Power Plant**—hydroelectric power plant (commercial)—organized—Grand Rapids, Mich.

1882 **Polygamy Legislation (federal)**—important legislation—enacted

1887 **Interstate Commerce Act**—commissioners appointed

1911 **Opera**—opera singer to sing two major roles on the same day—Herman Jadlowker—Metropolitan Opera House—New York City

1935 **Medical Legislation**—blood grouping laws (state)—enacted—New York

1948 **Radio Broadcast**—radio program simultaneously transmitted—over AM and stations, and telecast—commercial—*Voice of Firestone*—New York City

1960 **Lasers**—patent on lasers—A. L. Schawlow and C. H. Towne

MARCH 23

1794 **Rivet**—patent—J. G. Pierson

1802 **Social Service Endowment**—White-Williams Foundation—incorporated

1858 **Streetcar**—cable car—patented—E. Gardner—Philadelphia, Pa.

1861 **Government Printing Office**—Government Printing Office—J. D. Defrees—Superintendent of Public Printing—appointed

1867 **Forest Service**—forestry inquiry commission (state) authorized—Wisconsin

Flour Mill—flour rolling mill—patent—John Stevens—Neenah, Wis.

Automobile Racetrack—automobile speedway (board track)—trial race—Playa del Rey, Calif.

Aviation—Airplane—airplane to land at the U.S. Capitol—Washington, D.C.—L. B. Sperry

Evolution Law (state)—enacted—Tennessee

Astronaut—astronaut (American) to make a suborbital flight twice—V. I. Grissom—second takeoff—Cape Kennedy, Fla.

Astronaut—two-man spaceflight (American) of 3 orbits—J. W. Young and V. I. Grissom—*Gemini III* ("Molly Brown")—launched, Cape Kennedy, Fla.

Election Law—federal legislation enabling persons 18 years of age or older to vote (26th Amendment)—passed by House of Representatives—ratified by first state (Minnesota)

MARCH 24

Game Law—game law (colonial)—enacted—Virginia

Artist—American artist to win distinction—Benjamin West became president of Royal Academy of London

Railroad—state-owned railroad—Philadelphia and Columbia Railway—authorized

Insurance—hail insurance—company incorporated—North Canaan, Conn.

Diplomatic Service—Jewish ambassador—O. S. Straus—appointed

Aviation—Coast Guard air station—opened—Morehead City, N.C.

Radio Broadcast—radio broadcast from a moving train—WABC

Television—Telecast—religious services to be televised—New York City

Coast Guard (U.S.) Officer—vice admiral in the Coast Guard—appointed

Motion Picture Actor—husband and wife Oscar winners—Sir Laurence Olivier (for 1948)

Motion Picture Actor—motion picture actor and son to receive Oscars—John and Walter Huston—Hollywood, Calif.

Television—Telecast—opera written for television on commission for a commercial sponsor—New York City

Drill—oil drill seagoing rig—placed in service

Navy—task force to fight undersea craft—created

MARCH 25

Canal—canal for creating water power—Dedham, Mass.

1776 **Medal**—medal awarded by the Continental Congress—authorized for George Washington

1802 **Vaccine Institution**—opened—James Smith—Baltimore, Md.

1813 **Flag**—American flag flown in battle on the Pacific—*Essex*

1857 **Photograph**—solar-eclipse photograph—Frederick Langenheim—Philadelphia, Pa.

1867 **Water Conduit**—water supply tunnel for a city—Chicago, Ill.—water received

1890 **Navy**—naval militia (state)—formed—Massachusetts—companies formed

1893 **Newspaper Premium**—newspaper premiums—offered—New York *Recorder*—New York City

1898 **Trapshooting**—trapshooting intercollegiate association—formed—New York City

1900 **Socialist Party**—formed—Indianapolis, Ind.

1902 **Glass**—sheet-glass drawing machine—patented—I. W. Colburn

1915 **Submarine**—submarine disaster—Hawaii

1922 **Radio Telephone**—radio telephone concert transcontinental—Schenectady, N.Y., to Oakland, Calif.

1930 **Radio Broadcast**—ship-at-sea broadcast from an ocean liner—*Europa*

1937 **Newspaper**—newspaper with perfumed advertising page—*Daily News*—Washington, D.C.

1941 **Paprika Mill**—Dillon, S.C.—incorporated

1958 **Prizefighter**—pugilist to win a world championship 5 times in the same weight division—Sugar Ray Robinson—(5th time) Chicago, Ill.

1960 **Submarine**—guided missile launched from a nuclear-powered submarine—Regulus I

1964 **Television—Telecast**—telecast transmitted by satellite from Japan—via *Relay II*—Hayato Ikeda

1969 **Electoral College**—state law requiring presidential electors to cast their ballots for presidential and vice presidential candidates of the political party for which the electors were chosen—enacted—Maine

MARCH 26

1790 **Naturalization Act**—naturalization act—enacted

1804 **American Indian Reservation**—American Indian reservation (federal)—removal notice enacted

1819 **Bank**—savings bank—Bank for Savings in the City of New York—chartered

1845 **Adhesive and Medicated Plaster**—adhesive and medicated plaster patent

1845 **Lifeboat**—lifeboat (corrugated)—patented—Joseph Francis

1866 **Election Law**—fraudulent election law (state)—enacted—California

1885 **Photographic Film**—motion picture film (commercial)—manufactured—Rochester, N.Y.

1895 **Government Printing Office**—Superintendent of Documents—F. A. Crandall—served

1911 **Attorney General**—black assistant attorney general (U.S.)—W. H. Lewis—began service

1930 **Road**—inter-American highway appropriation

1936 **Telescope**—telescope lens 200 inches in diameter—shipped—Corning, N.Y.

1937 **Monument**—monument to a comic character—unveiled—Crystal City, Tex.

1943 **Medal**—Air Medal (U.S.) awarded to a woman—presented—E. S. Ott

1951 **Flag**—Air Force flag—approved

1954 **Helicopter**—twin gas-turbine helicopter (turborotor)—flown—Bloomfield, Conn.

1956 **Automobile Transcontinental Trip**—gas-turbine automobile to make a transcontinental trip—left New York City for Los Angeles, Calif.

MARCH 27

1770 **Teaching Methods Book**—preface dated—Christopher Dock

1792 **Congress (U.S.)**—congressional investigation—authorized

1794 **Ship**—ship constructed by the federal government—authorized—Gosport, Va.

1807 **Newspaper**—Democratic newspaper—published—Philadelphia, Pa.

1821 **Pharmacy College**—pharmacy college—Charles Marshall elected president—Philadelphia College of Pharmacy

1836 **Mormon Temple**—dedicated—Kirtland, Ohio

1841 **Fire Engine**—steam fire engine—tested—New York City

1849 **Drill (percussion rock drill)**—patent—J. J. Couch

1855 **Oil**—oil (kerosene)—patented—Abraham Gesner

1860 **Corkscrew Patent**—patented—M. L. Byrn

1863 **Cripples**—private school for cripples—New York Society for the Relief of the Ruptured and Crippled—incorporated

1867 **Normal School**—normal school (state) at which students actually conducted classes—Oswego, N.Y.—school acquired—New York State

1884 **Telephone**—long-distance telephone call—Boston, Mass.-New York City

1917 **Farm Loan Board (federal)**—federal land bank—chartered

1917 **Hockey**—hockey team (U.S.) to win the Stanley Cup—Seattle Metropolitans

1931 **Shuffleboard Championship**—shuffleboa championship tournament—C. L. Bai winner—St. Petersburg, Fla.

1933 **Farm Credit Administration (U.S.)**—thorized

1933 **Farm Loan Board (federal)**—transferre Farm Credit Administration

1941 **Treaty**—Status of Forces treaty

1955 **Jewish Congregation**—Jewish mobile sy gogue—dedicated

1961 **Computer**—mobile computer center—signment undertaken—Charlotte, N.C.

MARCH 28

1794 **Senator (U.S.)**—senator appointed seated)—Kensey Johns of Delaware—s denied

1796 **African Church**—Bethel African Metho Episcopal Church—Philadelphia, Pa.—corporated

1796 **Supreme Court (U.S.)**—Associate Justic the Supreme Court who had been a re sentative in Congress—Gabriel Duva Maryland—congressional service ende

1797 **Washing Machine**—washing machine ent—Nathaniel Briggs

1806 **Art Organization**—art organization—Pe sylvania Academy of Fine Arts—in porated

1827 **Dry Dock**—federal dry docks—author

1834 **Presidential Censure**—Senate resolu enacted—Washington, D.C.

1836 **Supreme Court (U.S.)**—Chief Justice of Supreme Court who was Catholic—R Taney—appointed

1848 **Child Labor Law**—child labor law rest ing the age of the worker—approve Pennsylvania

1854 **Warehouse**—warehouse legislatic privileges extended to private warehou

1865 **Advertising Legislation**—outdoor adve ing legislation (state)—enacted—N York

1883 **Building**—apartment house cooperativ New York City—incorporated

1895 **Subway**—municipal subway—const tion started—Boston, Mass.

1905 **Radio Facsimile Transmission**—radio simile patent—C. D. Ehret

1921 **Execution**—lethal-gas execution—aut ized—Nevada

1922 **Microfilm Machine**—microfilm reading vice—patented—B. A. Fiske

1937 **Photographer**—photographer to receiv John Simon Guggenheim Memorial Fe dation award—Edward Weston—nounced

1957 **Curling Championship (national)**—bega Chicago, Ill.

1966 **Aviation—Pilot**—ensign (woman) to solo—G. A. Gordon—Pensacola, Fla.

1975 **Pole Vault**—pole vault higher than 18.5 —Dave Roberts—Gainesville, Fla.

'8 **Congress (U.S.)**—House of Representatives—congressional committee bilingual report

MARCH 29

6 **Forestry Legislation**—colonial forestry legislation—enacted—Plymouth Colony, Mass.

6 **Road**—federal highway—Great National Pike—authorized

2 **Wedding**—White House wedding—Justice Thomas Todd

2 **Hospital**—eye hospital (permanent)—incorporated—New York Eye Infirmary

4 **Prison**—reformatory for juvenile delinquents under legislative control—incorporated

9 **Military School**—state military school—established—Lexington, Va.

4 **Naval Officer**—captain in the U.S. Navy who was Jewish—U. P. Levy

9 **Medical School**—homeopathic college—Homeopathic Medical College of Pennsylvania—graduation—Philadelphia, Pa.

2 **Labor Legislation**—labor law regulating the working hours of women—enacted—Ohio

2 **Knights of Columbus**—chartered

4 **Newspaper**—newspaper rotogravure sections

7 **Automobile**—automobile to exceed the speed of 200 miles an hour—Daytona Beach, Fla.

8 **Jewish College**—Jewish college of liberal arts and sciences under Jewish auspices—Yeshiva College—chartered—New York City

9 **Discus**—discus throw to exceed 160 feet—Eric Krenz—Palo Alto, Calif.

9 **Fireworks Legislation**—fireworks legislation (state)—enacted—Michigan

2 **Women's Club**—Chinese-American women's club incorporated—organized—New York City

7 **Medical Congress**—Fever Therapy International Conference—New York City

4 **Medal**—Expert Infantryman's Badge—awarded—Fort Bragg, N.C.

9 **Fog Disposal Unit**—accepted by test—Los Angeles, Calif.

1 **Spy**—peacetime death sentence for espionage—Julius Rosenberg and Ethel Rosenberg—guilty verdict—New York City

6 **Ship**—ballistic-missile test ship—*Compass Island*—acquired by U.S. Navy

0 **Television—Telecast**—pontifical Easter mass—telecast

MARCH 30

2 **Pharmacy College**—pharmacy college—Philadelphia College of Pharmacy—incorporated—Philadelphia, Pa.

1842 **Anesthesia**—anesthetic (general)—C. W. Long—operation performed—Jefferson, Ga.

1843 **Incubator (Eggs) Patent**—N. E. Guerin

1849 **Periodical**—Jewish weekly (German-American)—*Israels Herold*—Isidor Busch, editor—published—New York City

1852 **Whaling**—whale-killing machine (electric)—patented

1858 **Pencil**—pencil with an attached eraser—patented—H. L. Lipman

1871 **Theological School**—theological school to admit women—formed—Boston, Mass.

1880 **Electric Power Plant**—hydroelectric power plant (commercial)—incorporated—Grand Rapids, Mich.

1887 **Insurance**—mutual liability insurance company—American Mutual Liability Insurance Company—Boston, Mass.—incorporated

1887 **Kindergarten**—kindergarten for the blind—Roxbury, Mass.—incorporated

1889 **Golf Match**—mixed foursome—Yonkers, N.Y.

1891 **Forest**—national forest—Shoshone National Forest, Wyo.—established

1891 **Forest Reserve**—forest reserve (national)—Yellowstone Park Timberland Reserve—designated

1893 **Diplomatic Service**—ambassador—extraordinary and plenipotentiary—T. F. Bayard—appointed to Great Britain

1897 **Accountants' Society**—accountants' society formed by a state group—New York State Society of Certified Public Accountants—formed—New York City

1909 **Bridge**—double-deck bridge—Queensboro Bridge—New York City—opened to traffic

1923 **Ship**—cruise ship to circumnavigate the world—*Laconia*—returned—New York City

1930 **Glider**—glider towed across the continent—takeoff—F. M. Hawks—San Diego, Calif.

1946 **Sleeping Car**—transcontinental through Pullman sleeping car service—inaugurated—New York City–Los Angeles, Calif.

1950 **Transistor**—phototransistor—invention announced—Murray Hill, N.J.

1956 **Automobile Transcontinental Trip**—gas-turbine automobile to make a transcontinental trip—arrived in Los Angeles, Calif., from New York City

1957 **Submarine**—submarine powered by a liquid-metal-cooled atomic reactor—*Seawolf*—completed

1974 **Jockey**—jockey to win one hundred $100,-000 stakes—Willie Shoemaker—Hot Springs, Ark.

MARCH 31

1732 **Library**—circulating library—books ordered—Library Company of Philadelphia

1783 College—college named after George Washington—new charter received

1784 Map—map of the United States—engraved —advertised for sale

1790 Senator (U.S.)—senator appointed by a governor—John Walker—Virginia

1791 Lighthouse—lighthouse built after American independence—contract for Cape Henry Lighthouse—John McComb, Jr.

1812 Cemetery—congressional cemetery—deed recorded

1814 Cottonseed Hulling Machine—patented— John Lineback

1870 Election Law—black to vote under authority of the Fifteenth Amendment—Thomas Peterson-Mundy—Perth Amboy, N.J.

1876 Insurance—title guaranty insurance company—organized—Philadelphia, Pa.

1877 Music—long-distance-telephone concert— New York City

1880 Electric Lighting—street lighting (electric) by a municipality—installation made— Wabash, Ind.

1887 Interstate Commerce Act—commission organized

1896 Fastening—hookless fastening—patented —W. L. Judson

1900 Advertisement—automobile advertisement—national—Saturday Evening Post Philadelphia, Pa.

1918 Daylight Saving—in effect

1923 Dance Marathon—dance marathon—New York City—ended

1932 Bank—savings bank with a half-billion-dollar deposit—statement—Bowery Savings Bank—New York City

1933 Civilian Conservation Corps (U.S.)—authorized

1933 Newspaper—newspaper printed on pine-pulp paper—Soperton, Ga.

1934 Medal—National Geographic Society gold medal—awarded to a woman—A. M. Lindbergh—Washington, D.C.

1937 Newspaper—newspaper printed on pine-pulp paper in color—Dallas News

1956 Space Cabin—space cabin simulator—tested

1958 Navy—atomic submarine division—formed—New London, Conn.

1961 Astronaut—astronaut (black) selected for the manned orbiting laboratory program— E. J. Dwight, Jr.

1967 Postal Card—airmail postal card commemorative—issued—Charlotte Amalie, Virgin Islands (U.S.)

APRIL 1

1621 Treaty—colonial treaty with the Indians— Plymouth, Mass.

1769 Type Foundry—Abel Buell—Killingworth, Conn.

1789 Congress (U.S.)—House of Represen tives—clerk of the House of Represen tives—John Beckley—began service

1789 Congress (U.S.)—House of Represen tives—first quorum—New York City

1789 Congress (U.S.)—House of Represen tives—Speaker of the House—F. A. Muhlenberg

1826 Engine—internal-combustion engine—p ented—Samuel Morey—Orford, N.H.

1826 Railroad—railroad for freight transpor tion to celebrate its centenary—Quin Mass.—construction started

1827 Railroad—railroad for commercial tra portation of passengers and freight—stc offered

1835 Insurance—mutual life insurance compa to be chartered—New England Mutual L Insurance Company—Boston, Mass.

1837 Child Labor Law—child labor law to clude educational provision—effectiv Massachusetts

1838 College—city college—under munici control—opened—Charleston, S.C.

1840 Antislavery Party—nominations confirm

1843 Periodical—magazine published for men patients—Illuminator—Philadelphia, Pa

1853 Fire Department—fire department to paid a salary—established—Cincinn Ohio

1863 Conscription—wartime conscription bil enrollment required

1864 Insurance—accident insurance pol (printed)—Hartford, Conn.

1875 Advertising Magazine—Advertising Ag cy Circular—became a weekly

1885 Forest Service—forest commission (sta (permanent)—meeting—San Francis Calif.

1891 Animal Industry Bureau (U.S.)—patholc division—established

1894 Employment Service—municipal empl ment office—authorized—Seattle, Wash

1909 Narcotics Legislation—narcotics prohi tion act (federal)—effective

1913 Motion Picture Censorship—motion p ture censorship board (state)—Kansa act effective

1917 World War I—American sailor to lose life in World War I (before U.S. entry i the war)—J. E. Eopolucci

1923 Dance Marathon—dance marathon—l gan—New York City

1927 Aviation—Flights—airplane night sch uled passenger flight—left Boston, Mas

1928 Telephone—telephone switchboard w Braille markings—New York City

1930 Aviation—Flights—New York–Bermu flights—L. A. Yancey

1930 Television—Telecast—speaker to addr an organization by television—P. I. Wolc Schenectady, N.Y.

1931 Baseball Pitcher—woman baseball pitc —Jackie Mitchell—engaged

1973　**Zoo**—twilight zoo—Highland Park, Pittsburgh, Pa.—dedicated

APRIL 4

1692　**Postal Service**—parliamentary act to establish a post office—Andrew Hamilton—appointed postmaster

1692　**Postmaster**—postmaster general (colonial)—Andrew Hamilton—appointed

1800　**Bankruptcy Act**—enacted

1818　**Flag Legislation**—flag act—established

1818　**Ship**—steamboat on the Great Lakes—*Walk-in-the-Water* launched—Buffalo, N.Y.

1839　**Ship**—iron vessel built of American iron—*De Rosset*—registered—Baltimore, Md.

1841　**President (U.S.)**—President to die in Washington, D.C.—W. H. Harrison

1841　**Vice President (U.S.)**—Vice President to become President automatically—John Tyler

1850　**School**—school for the mentally retarded—incorporated—Boston, Mass.

1859　**Music**—war song of the Confederate States—"Dixie" sung—New York City

1870　**Sports**—athletic club—New York Athletic Club—New York City—incorporated

1873　**Pottery**—pottery to make sanitary ware—consolidated

1885　**Agriculture Department (U.S.)**—Secretary of the Department of Agriculture—N. J. Colman—served as Commissioner of Agriculture

1887　**Mayor**—woman mayor—S. M. Salter—elected

1888　**Holding Company**—holding company authorization (state)—enacted—New Jersey

1890　**Election Law**—corrupt election practices law (state)—enacted—New York State

1891　**Political Science Society**—political and social science society (national)—American Academy of Political and Social Science—incorporated

1898　**Play (drama)**—musical comedy by a black for black talent—*A Trip to Coontown,* by Bob Cole and Billy Johnson—produced—New York City

1898　**Play (drama)**—musical (full-length), written, produced, directed, and performed as a Broadway (New York City) production—Bob Cole—*A Trip to Coontown*—opened

1911　**Insurance**—workers' compensation insurance law (state)—legislation enacted—New Jersey

1913　**Motion Picture Censorship**—motion picture censorship board (state)—Pennsylvania—appropriation

1915　**Radio Telephone**—radio telephone communication (one-way)—Montauk Point, N.Y.–Wilmington, Del.

1928　**Radio Facsimile Transmission**—motion picture film transmitted by telephone wire—Chicago, Ill., to New York City

1933　**Aviation—Airship**—airship disaster res‑ ing in more than 70 deaths—*Akron* Barnegat Lightship, N.J.

1938　**Library Chair**—established—Colum‑ University—New York City

1943　**Ship**—naval ship with a plural name—*T Sullivans*—launched—San Francis Calif.

1945　**Marine Corps**—general (4 stars) of the M rines on active duty to become a full ger al—A. A. Vandegrift—appointed

1949　**Submarine**—leaping submarine—*Picke* —commissioned

1953　**Fraternity (Greek-Letter)**—scholastic f ternity chapter established at a univers for blacks—Phi Beta Kappa—Fisk Univ sity—Nashville, Tenn.

1955　**Jewish Congregation**—Jewish mobile sy gogue—in operation—North Carolina

1957　**Medal**—recipient of the four highest de rations awarded by the United States— J. Donovan

1963　**Hall of Famer**—athlete enshrined in 2 h of fame—Robert Hubbard—Canton, O (professional football)

1966　**Judge**—black woman judge of a federal c trict court—C. B. Motley—nominated A 4

1972　**Electric Power**—electric power us municipal refuse as a boiler fuel—gener ed, Union Electric Company, St. Louis, N

APRIL 5

1768　**Chamber of Commerce (state)**—formec New York City

1792　**Veto (presidential)**—veto by a Presiden George Washington

1806　**Cider Mill**—patented—I. Quintard—St field, Conn.

1827　**Actor**—American actor to appear abro —J. H. Hackett—London, England

1864　**File Factory**—file factory (machine cutti to attain success—machine patented— Nicholson—Providence, R.I.

1865　**Army Officer**—major (black)—M. R. De ny—ordered to Charleston, S.C.

1865　**Unitarian Church Convention (national** assembled—New York City

1869　**Cattle Club**—cattle club (Jersey cattle American Jersey Cattle Club—ann meeting—New York City

1887　**Interstate Commerce Act**—operatic began

1892　**Gold Leaf**—in roll form—patented—W. Coe—Providence, R.I.

1906　**Stamp**—consular service fee stamps— thorized

1909　**Research Institute**—institute for resea in nervous diseases—New York City— corporated

1923　**Automobile Tire**—balloon tire product —Firestone Tire and Rubber Compan Akron, Ohio

1910 Automobile Racetrack—automobile speedway (board track)—opened—Playa del Rey, Calif.

1913 Ship—electrically propelled ship of the United States Navy—*Jupiter*—commissioned

1917 World War I—shot fired by the American Navy in World War I—Guam

1922 Shipping—automatic steering gear—tested—*John D. Archibold*

1925 Radio Broadcast—ship launching broadcast—Camden, N.J.

1927 Television—Telecast—telecast of image and sound—transmitted—Washington, D.C.–New York City

1933 Bridge—bridge with open-mesh steel flooring—opened—Seattle, Wash.

1940 Postage Stamp—black American depicted upon a United States postage stamp—B. T. Washington

1953 Aviation—Flights (transatlantic)—jet transatlantic nonstop flight west–east—from Limestone, Me.

1959 Astronaut—astronauts—National Aeronautics and Space Administration selection announced

1959 Radar—radar signal bounced off the sun

APRIL 8

1730 Jewish Congregation—Jewish congregation—Shearith Israel—consecrated—New York City

1789 Congress (U.S.)—House of Representatives—sergeant at arms—Joseph Wheaton—began service

1795 Dental Dispensary—dental dispensary—City Dispensary—New York City—incorporated

1808 Catholic Diocese—raised to archdiocese—Baltimore, Md.

1834 Election—mayor elected by popular vote in a city—C. V. Lawrence—New York City

1848 Medical School—homeopathic college—Homeopathic Medical College of Pennsylvania—incorporated

1862 Patent—aerosol patent—J. D. Lynde—issued

1864 Knights of Pythias—grand lodge of District of Columbia—formed

1873 Oleomargarine—oleomargarine manufacturer (successful)—patent—A. Paraf—New York City

1898 Forestry School—forestry school of collegiate character—authorized

1911 Squash Tournament—squash tennis tournament—New York City

1918 Aviation—air squadron of the U.S. Army—assigned to front

1935 Works Progress Administration—Works Progress Administration—created

1939 Telephone—telephone weather-forecasting service—inaugurated—New York City

1947 Insurance—insurance policy to be illust? ed—Chicago, Ill.

1953 Motion Picture—three-dimensional feat? motion picture produced and released b? major company—New York City—*Mar? the Dark*

1955 Medal—Medal of Honor awarded to a h? copter pilot—J. K. Koelsch

1956 Church—universal chapel embracing e? faiths—Universalist Church of the Div? Paternity—New York City—dedicated

1971 Air Force Officer—military engineer (w? an) in the Air Force—S. M. Ocobock— gan service, Kelly Air Force Base, Tex?

APRIL 9

1792 Road—macadam road—turnpike comp? chartered

1816 Methodist Episcopal Church—Afri? Methodist Episcopal Church—establis? —Philadelphia, Pa.

1825 Prison—reformatory for juvenile de? quents under legislative control—five-y? appropriation enacted—New York

1833 Library—free public library (town-supp? ed)—established—Peterborough, N.H.

1847 Prison—reformatory for boys (state)— thorized—Westborough, Mass.

1866 Civil Rights Legislation (federal)—C? Rights legislation (federal)—enacted

1872 Milk—dried milk patent—S. R. Perc? New York City

1905 Bridge—aerial ferry—operated—Dul? Minn.

1912 Children's Bureau (U.S.)—establishe? Department of Commerce and Labor

1920 Woman—woman automotive enginee? Marie Luhring—associate member of S? ety of Automotive Engineers

1930 Television—Telecast—two-way dem? stration of television in a theater—N? York City

1934 Judge—woman associate justice of the? cuit court of appeals—F. E. Allen—sw? in

1937 Strike—anti–sit-down-strike legisla? (state)—Vermont

1947 Atomic Energy Commission—Atomic? ergy Commission—confirmed

1948 Economic Cooperation Administrat? (U.S.)—Economic Cooperation Admi? tration—Administrator P. G. Hoffma? sworn in

1963 Citizenship—honorary citizenship auth? ized by the U.S. Congress—Sir Wins? Churchill—conferred by President John? Kennedy

1965 Stadium—domed, fully-enclosed sp? arena—Astrodome, Houston, Tex.—f? baseball game

1971 Sky Marshal—sky marshals—first won graduates

APRIL 10

777 **Lottery**—lottery held by the Continental Congress—Philadelphia, Pa.

790 **Patent**—patent law (national)—enacted

816 **Bank**—Bank of the United States—second bank authorized

833 **Medical Society**—homeopathic medical society—Hahnemann Society—organized—Philadelphia, Pa.

835 **Medical School**—homeopathic school—North American Academy—founded—Allentown, Pa.

845 **Gingham Factory**—E. B. Bigelow—machinery patent

849 **Pin**—safety pin—patented—Walter Hunt—New York City

861 **Insurance**—nonforfeiture insurance law (state)—enacted—Massachusetts

866 **Humane Society**—humane society—American Society for the Prevention of Cruelty to Animals—incorporated

872 **Holiday**—Arbor Day celebration—Nebraska

877 **Catamaran**—patented—N. G. Herreshoff—Providence, R.I.

892 **Tuberculosis Society**—founded—Philadelphia, Pa.

895 **Bicycle Trip (world)**—bicycle trip around the world by a married couple—started at Chicago

904 **Motorboating Magazine**—motorboating magazine—*Motor Boat*—published—New York City—first issue

924 **Radio Broadcast**—circus broadcast—New York City

927 **Symphony**—symphonic work to call for an airplane propeller—*Ballet Mecanique*—produced—New York City

930 **Rubber**—synthetic rubber (neoprene)—produced

933 **Civilian Conservation Corps (U.S.)**—Camp Roosevelt established

933 **Constitutional Amendment (U.S.)**—constitutional amendment submitted to the states for repeal—first ratification—Michigan

944 **Quinine**—synthetic quinine—produced—Cambridge, Mass.

944 **Ship**—naval ship christened by an Army officer — *Colhoun* — launched — Seattle, Wash.

944 **Television—Telecast**—motion picture premiere performance to be televised—*Patrolling the Ether*

947 **Television—Telecast**—underwater telecast from a submarine—*Trumpetfish*—New York City

953 **Anesthesia**—trifluorethyl vinyl ether—administered—J. C. Krantz, Jr.—Chicago, Ill.

953 **Motion Picture**—three-dimensional feature motion picture in color—*The House of Wax*—New York City

1962 **Newspaper**—newspaper reproduced commercially and regularly by radio facsimile—*Wall Street Journal* (San Francisco edition)—experimental edition

1976 **Sterilization**—sterilization legislation (state) that was optional, not punitive—enacted—Virginia

APRIL 11

1640 **Election**—election in defiance of the Royal Courts—Wethersfield, Conn.

1783 **Treaty**—treaty between the United States Government and a nation with which it had been at war—proclaimed by Continental Congress

1789 **Newspaper**—political newspaper—*Gazette of the United States*—published—New York City

1803 **Ship**—steamboat with a twin-screw propeller—patented—New York

1816 **Methodist Episcopal Church**—African Methodist Episcopal church—Richard Allen ordained bishop

1831 **Building and Loan Association**—Oxford Provident Building Association—Philadelphia, Pa.—loan made

1876 **Stenotype**—patented—J. C. Zachos—New York City

1889 **Brokerage**—investment trust—New York Stock Trust formed

1921 **Cigarette Tax**—cigarette tax (state)—enacted—Iowa

1921 **Telephone**—telephone cable service (deepsea)—opened—Key West, Fla.

1925 **Postage Stamp**—special-handling stamps—issued—Washington, D.C.

1930 **Degrees (academic and honorary)**—Doctor of Military Science degree—awarded—J. J. Pershing—New York City

1941 **Electric Generator**—hydrogen-cooled turbine generator for outdoor installation—operated—Glendale, Calif.

1941 **Price Regulation Legislation**—price regulation law (federal)—Office of Price Administration and Civilian Supply—created

1942 **Medal**—Distinguished Service Medal (Merchant Marine)—authorized

1947 **Baseball Player**—black major-league baseball player—Jackie Robinson—New York City

1953 **Cabinet (U.S.)**—Secretary of Health, Education, and Welfare—O. C. Hobby—sworn in

1953 **Federal Security Agency**—changed to Department of Health, Education, and Welfare

1954 **Television—Telecast**—state legislative hearing telecast—New Jersey

APRIL 12

1631 **Militia** — militia — established — Boston, Mass.

1776   **Declaration of Independence (American)**—Declaration of Independence by a colony—Halifax, N.C.

1786   **Hospital**—dispensary—Philadelphia Dispensary—instituted

1799   **Comb-cutting Machine**—patented—Phineas Pratt—Connecticut

1811   **Colonist**—colonists to reach the Pacific Coast—landed—Cape Disappointment, Wash.

1824   **Law Codification (state)**—approved—Louisiana

1830   **Bank**—trust company—New York Life Insurance and Trust Company—New York City—organization meeting

1831   **Tunnel**—railroad tunnel—construction began—Hollidaysburg-Johnstown, Pa.

1833   **Safe (fireproof)**—patented—Charles A. Gayler—New York City

1842   **Insurance**—mutual life insurance company to operate—Mutual Life Insurance Company of New York—chartered—New York City

1847   **Chinese Students**—arrived—New York City

1853   **Bank**—trust company—United States Trust Company of New York—first exclusive trust company—incorporated

1853   **Truancy Legislation (state)**—enacted—New York

1859   **Billiard Match**—billiard match to attain international prominence—Detroit, Mich.

1861   **Civil War**—attack in the Civil War—Fort Sumter, S.C.

1861   **Civil War**—naval attack—off Charleston, S.C.

1861   **Seal**—seals for raising funds

1867   **Insurance**—plate-glass insurance—United States Plate Glass Insurance Company—Philadelphia, Pa.—incorporated

1877   **Baseball Catcher's Mask**—used in game—Lynn, Mass.

1892   **Typewriter**—portable typewriter—Blickensderfer—patented—Stamford, Conn.

1892   **Voting Machine**—voting machines were authorized—used—Lockport, N.Y.

1900   **Wedding**—telegraph wedding—A. M. Candell and Penelope Cundiff—Kansas City, Mo.

1918   **Aviation**—air squadron of the U.S. Army—first combat action

1926   **Senator (U.S.)**—senator unseated after a recount—S. W. Brookhart—Iowa

1933   **Diplomatic Service**—woman diplomat to represent the United States in the capacity of a Minister—R. B. Owen—appointed

1933   **Woman**—woman state liquor board member—J. R. Sheppard—appointed—New York State

1938   **Medical Legislation**—law (state) requiring marriage license applicants to undergo medical tests—enacted—New York State

1943   **Ship**—warship named for a black—*Harmon*—laid down—Hingham, Mass.

1966   **Baseball Umpire**—baseball umpire (major league) who was a black—E. L. Ashford—umpired, Washington, D.C.

1968   **Ship**—ship named for a Seabee—*Marvin Shields*—laid down—Seattle, Wash.

APRIL 13

1759   **Freemasons**—military Masonic lodge—formed—Crown Point, N.Y.

1782   **Town**—town named for George Washington—Washington, N.C.—incorporated

1796   **Animals**—elephant—arrived—New York City

1802   **Army**—engineer corps—Jonathan Williams—appointed

1808   **Temperance Society**—temperance society (union)—Union Temperate Society—organized—Saratoga Springs, N.Y.

1819   **Church**—mariners' church—New York Port Society—incorporated

1831   **Stone Crusher**—stone breaking machine patent—B.F. Lodge and E.T. Cox

1854   **Agricultural School**—agricultural college (state) to be chartered—Farmers High School of Pennsylvania—incorporated

1863   **Hospital**—orthopedic hospital—Hospital for Ruptured and Crippled—New York City—incorporated

1869   **Air Brake**—patented—George Westinghouse—Schenectady, N.Y.

1896   **Organists' Society**—organists' society (national)—American Guild of Organists—organized

1901   **Optometry Legislation (state)**—Minnesota

1904   **Border Patrol**—border patrol officer—J. D. Milton—served

1912   **Senator (U.S.)**—senators collectively "elected by the people"—legislation enacted—House of Representatives

1916   **Corn**—shipment of hybrid seed corn—sold—Jacobsburg, Ohio

1918   **World War I**—combat mission of all American pilots ordered to battle by an all American squadron commander

1920   **Civil Service**—woman Civil Service commissioner—H. H. Gardener—sworn in—Washington, D.C.

1940   **Pole Vaulter**—pole vaulter to clear the bar at 15 feet—Cornelius Warmerdam—Berkeley, Calif.

1942   **World War II**—German submarine sunk by a U.S. naval vessel—*U-85*—near Hatteras, N.C.

1954   **Ship**—liquid-bulk-chemical carrier—*Marine-Dow Chem*—first run, from Freeport, Tex.—arrived at New York City

1960   **Satellite**—navigational satellite—*Transit 1-B*—launched—Cape Canaveral, Fla.

1964   **Motion Picture Actor**—black actor to win an Oscar for best actor—Sidney Poitier—presentation in Santa Monica, Calif.

1949 **Aviation—Flights**—airplane to carry 100,000 pounds—takeoff, Fort Worth, Tex.

1949 **Aviation—Pilot**—black flier of the U.S. Naval Reserve—J. L. Brown—commissioned

1952 **Credit Card**—bank credit card—issued—Franklin National Bank, Franklin Square, N.Y.

1956 **Automobile**—free-piston automobile—announced—Detroit, Mich.

1956 **Television Station**—all-color station to televise live local programs—WNBQ-TV—Chicago, Ill.

1966 **X ray**—X ray three-dimensional (stereo) fluoroscopic system—first unit installed at University of Oregon Medical Center, Portland, Oreg.—R. J. Kuhn

1968 **Baseball Game**—night baseball game (major league) to last longer than 6 hours—Houston, Tex.

APRIL 16

1787 **Play (drama)**—native American play successfully acted on a regular stage—*The Contrast*—New York City

1813 **Factory Standardization of Production**—Simeon North—Middletown, Conn.

1836 **Child Labor Law**—child labor law to include educational provision—enacted—Massachusetts

1851 **Lighthouse**—iron pile lighthouse—Minot's Ledge, Mass.—swept away in storm

1861 **Civil War**—regiment to respond to President Abraham Lincoln's proclamation—Harrisburg, Pa.

1862 **Slavery**—law abolishing slavery in the District of Columbia—enacted

1863 **Ship**—turreted frigate in the U.S. Navy—*Roanoke*—transferred to U.S. Navy

1869 **Diplomatic Service**—black consul—E. D. C. Bassett—served

1900 **Postage Stamp**—books of postage stamps—issued

1922 **Aviation**—sermon from an airplane—B. W. Maynard

1926 **Book Club**—Book-of-the-Month Club—book selection—distributed—New York City

1935 **Aviation—Airplane**—transport airplane designed especially for transoceanic service—left San Francisco, Calif.

1940 **Baseball Game**—opening day no-hit major league baseball game—Cleveland Indians vs. Chicago White Sox—Chicago, Ill.

1943 **Physician**—physicians in the Medical Corps of the Army and Navy—authorized

1947 **Army**—Women's Army Medical Specialist Corps—authorized

1947 **Lens**—lens to provide zoom effects—demonstrated—New York City

1956 **Radio Receiver**—radio receiver with a auxiliary silicon unit to convert the rays o the sun into electrical power—Chicago, Il

1957 **Television—Telecast**—stockholders' annu al meeting televised on a closed circuit—New York City and Chicago, Ill.

1979 **Coast Guard Officer**—woman commande of a Coast Guard ship—Beverly Kelley—appointed

APRIL 17

1629 **Fishery (commercial)**—established—Med ford, Mass.

1629 **Horse** — horses — imported — Massach setts

1640 **Lutheran Church**—Lutheran pastor—Reorus Torkillus—arrived—Wilmingtor Del.

1704 **Newspaper**—newspaper (successful)—*News-Letter*—Boston, Mass.—published

1776 **Ship**—warship captured by a commis sioned officer of the U.S. Navy—*Edward*

1810 **Cheese**—pineapple cheese—patent—L. N Norton—Troy, Pa.

1844 **Printing Press**—cylinder and flatbed con bination printing press—patented—Rober Hoe

1860 **Fire Escapes for tenements**—required—legislation—New York

1861 **Oil**—oil well fire—Oil Creek, Pa.

1866 **Hospital**—Jewish hospital—name change to Mount Sinai Hospital

1890 **Opera**—light opera presented in 2 cities o the same day by the same company—*Th Gondoliers*—Francis Wilson's Company—New York City and Philadelphia

1895 **Canal Locks made of concrete**—Milan sec tion opened to traffic—Hennepin Canal

1896 **Accountancy Law (state)**—enacted—Ne York

1916 **Arts and Letters Society**—arts and letter society (national)—American Academy Arts and Letters—incorporated

1917 **Daylight Saving**—measure introduced i the U.S. Senate—W. M. Calder—defeate

1921 **Church**—church services aired from anoth er church—Pittsburgh, Pa.

1931 **Autogiro**—autogiro with side-by-side sea ing arrangement—tested—Philadelphia Pa.

1933 **Civilian Conservation Corps (U.S.)**—Cam Roosevelt—opened—Luray, Va.

1935 **Aviation—Airplane**—transport airplan designed especially for transoceanic se vice—Pan American Clipper—arrived—Pearl Harbor, Hawaii

1940 **Baseball Pitcher**—baseball pitcher to pitc a no-hitter on opening day—R. W. A. Felle —Chicago, Ill.

1941 **Helicopter—Flights**—helicopter flight fror water—I. I. Sikorsky—Stratford, Conn.

1837 **Carpet Loom**—carpet power loom—patented—E. B. Bigelow—West Boylston, Mass.

1852 **Temperance Society**—women's temperance society (state)—New York Women's State Temperance Society—founded—Rochester, N.Y.

1855 **Bohemian American Church**—opened—St. Louis, Mo.

1876 **Chemical Society**—chemical society (national)—American Chemical Society—organized—New York City

1899 **Election Law**—primary election law—enacted—Minnesota

1920 **Radio Broadcast**—speaker to address an organization by radio—W. C. Ketler—New Castle, Pa.

1926 **Radio Facsimile Transmission**—check sent by radio across the Atlantic Ocean—London–New York City

1927 **Radio Broadcast**—dinner broadcast around-the-world—Schenectady, N.Y.

1930 **Diplomatic Service**—chief executive–elect of a foreign country—to serve in a diplomatic position at Washington—E. O. Hererra of Colombia—arrived

1940 **Microscope**—electron microscope—demonstrated—Philadelphia, Pa.

1940 **Ship**—seaplane tender designed and built for the United States Navy—*Curtiss*—launched—Camden, N.J.

1964 **Telephone**—picturephone transcontinental call—New York City to Anaheim, Calif.

1965 **Cabinet (U.S.)**—Cabinet meeting attended by a foreign national—Washington, D.C.

APRIL 21

1712 **Calico**—printery　　　advertised—Boston, Mass.

1789 **Congress (U.S.)—Senate**—president pro tempore of the United States Senate—Vice President John Adams—took seat as president of the Senate—New York City

1847 **Insurance**—health insurance company—Massachusetts Health Insurance Company—Boston, Mass.—organized

1856 **Bridge**—railroad bridge across the Mississippi River—completed—Glasgow, Mo.

1857 **Bustle**—patented—Alexander Douglas

1869 **American Indians**—Indian Affairs Commissioner (U.S.) who was an Indian—E. S. Parker—appointed

1878 **Firehouse Pole**—firehouse pole—installed—New York City

1881 **Ship**—schooner　　　(five-masted)—*David Dows*—launched—Toledo, Ohio

1887 **Insurance**—mutual liability insurance company—American Mutual Liability Insurance Company—Boston, Mass.—organized

1895 **Motion Picture**—motion picture on film shown on a screen—exhibited—Woodville Latham—New York City

1899 **Chess Tournament**—intercollegiate transatlantic chess match by cable—New Yor City and London—began

1899 **Court**—juvenile court—authorized—Chcago, Ill.

1906 **Ship**—turbine-propelled oceangoing merchant vessel—*Governor Cobb*—launched

1923 **Postage Stamp**—precanceled stamp printed on rotary presses—issued

1930 **Radio Broadcast**—zoo broadcast—C. W Leister—New York City

1933 **Enclave**—municipal enclave of economi ground rent—authorized—Colliervill Tenn.

1937 **Dental Society**—orthodontists' society–American Society of Orthodontists—nam changed to American Association of O thodontists

1962 **Fair**—world's fair that was financially su cessful—Seattle, Wash.—opened

1962 **Restaurant**—revolving restaurant—Th Top of the Needle, Seattle, Wash.—opene by remote control by J. F. Kennedy—fro Palm Beach, Fla.

1966 **Medal**—Medal of Honor (posthumous) to black in the Vietnam war—M. L. Olive presented

APRIL 22

1669 **Engraving**—engraving—woodcut—made—John Foster

1793 **Circus**—circus—attended by Georg Washington—Philadelphia, Pa.

1793 **Neutrality Proclamation**—George Wasl ington

1794 **Capital Punishment**—death penalty fir abolished—except for first-degree murd —Pennsylvania

1856 **Bridge**—railroad bridge across the Missi sippi River—locomotive and passeng cars test trip—Rock Island, Ill.-Davenpor Iowa

1864 **Money**—coin to use "In God We Trust"- authorized

1868 **Lieutenant Governor**—black lieutena governor—O. J. Dunn—Louisiana—electe

1876 **Coaching Club**—first meet—New York Ci

1884 **Bicycle Rider**—bicycle rider to go arour the world—Thomas Stevens—left S Francisco, Calif.

1890 **Ship**—torpedo boat of importance—*Cus. ing*—commissioned—Bristol, Pa.

1892 **Research Institute**—anatomy research i stitute—Wistar Institute of Anatomy ar Biology—Philadelphia, Pa.—incorporate

1898 **Spanish-American War**—ship captured the Spanish-American War—*Buena Ve tura*

1913 **Ice Loading Machinery**—patent

1920 **Orchestra**—orchestra (American) to mal a European tour—Symphony Society New York—sailed

921 **Building**—building devoted entirely to highway traffic—Eno Foundation for Highway Traffic Control—incorporated

922 **Business**—shopping center in a suburban business area—Kansas City, Mo.—master plan

931 **Autogiro**—autogiro to land on the White House lawn—J. G. Ray—Washington, D.C.

940 **Radio Broadcast**—all-Chinese commercial radio broadcast—San Francisco, Calif.

944 **Television—Telecast**—motion picture premiere performance to be televised—*Patrolling the Ether*—released to theaters

952 **Television—Telecast**—atomic explosion telecast on a network—Los Angeles, Calif.

953 **Catholic Bishop**—Catholic bishop (black) consecrated in the United States—J. O. Bowers—Bay St. Louis, Miss.

955 **Railroad Car**—passenger car (ACF-Talgo) for use in the United States—completed

963 **Ship**—cargo ship fully automated and flying the American flag—*Mormacargo*—keel laid—Pascagoula, Miss.

967 **Shot-Put**—shot-put to cover a distance of more than 71 feet—Randy Matson—College Station, Tex.

968 **Astronaut**—astronaut international rescue agreement—signed

APRIL 23

635 **War**—naval battle by white men in America—St. Mary's, Md.

750 **Colonist**—civilian settlement west of the Allegheny Mountains—reached Barbourville, Ky.

789 **Catholic Periodical**—Catholic magazine—*Courier de Boston*—published—Boston, Mass.

789 **"Presidential Mansion"**—George Washington—New York City

821 **Pharmacy College**—pharmacy college—Samuel Jackson—appointed professor—Philadelphia, Pa.

827 **Railroad**—railroad for commercial transportation of passengers and freight—board of directors elected—Baltimore, Md.

838 **Ship**—steamboat service (regular) across the Atlantic—arrived—New York City

867 **Motion Picture Machine**—machine to show animated pictures—Zoetrope—patented—W. E. Lincoln—Providence, R.I.

872 **Lawyer**—black woman lawyer—C. E. Ray—Washington, D.C.

890 **Women's Club**—women's club federation—General Federation of Women's Clubs—convention

894 **Ship**—triple-screw cruiser—*Columbia*—commissioned

896 **Motion Picture**—motion picture film exhibition in a theater—New York City

896 **Motion Picture**—motion picture (successful) projected to a paying audience—New York City

1897 **Hospital**—crippled children's hospital (state)—authorized—St. Paul, Minn.

1899 **Movable Church**—service—Conanicut Island, R.I.

1904 **Animal Industry Bureau (U.S.)**—animal husbandry federal appropriation—approved

1904 **Arts and Letters Society**—arts and letters society (national)—American Academy of Arts and Letters—founded

1917 **Ship**—warship propelled by electricity—*New Mexico*—launched—New York City

1917 **Submarine**—submarine built at a government shipyard—*L-8*—launched—Portsmouth Naval Shipyard, Portsmouth, N.H.

1951 **Newspaper Reporter**—newspaper reporter to become a U.S. senator—Blair Moody—appointed

1951 **Teletypesetter**—teletypesetter circuit operated by a news agency—Charlotte, N.C.

1962 **Satellite**—American satellite to reach the moon—Ranger IV—launched—Cape Canaveral, Fla.

APRIL 24

1783 **College**—college named after George Washington—Washington College, Tennessee—chartered

1800 **Librarian**—librarian of Congress—authorized

1800 **Library**—Library of Congress—authorized

1816 **Army Officer**—paymaster—Pay Department—authorized

1827 **Railroad**—railroad for commercial transportation of passenger and freight—Baltimore and Ohio Railroad Company—organized

1833 **Soda Fountain**—soda fountain patent—Jacob Ebert—Cadiz, Ohio

1844 **Pharmacy Professor**—pharmacy professorship—David Stewart—appointed—Baltimore, Md.

1851 **Engineering Society**—engineering society—Boston Society of Civil Engineers—incorporated

1863 **Dock**—state-owned docks—authorized—California

1873 **Free Lunch**—free lunches to aid convalescents—New York Diet Kitchen Association—opened

1884 **Medical Society**—medical society for blacks—organized—Washington, D.C.

1886 **Catholic Priest**—black Catholic priest—Augustus Tolton—ordained

1890 **Women's Club**—women's club federation—constitution adopted—New York City

1895 **Ship**—ship to circumnavigate the world with but one in the crew—Joshua Slocum—sailed—Boston, Mass.

1897 **News Correspondent**—White House reporter—W. W. Price—Washington, D.C.

1908 Automobile Transcontinental Trip—transcontinental family automobile trip requiring only a month—Murdock family—left Los Angeles, Calif.

1913 Building—building higher than 750 feet in height—Woolworth Building—New York City—opened

1917 Army Officer—American general to fly over enemy lines—W. L. Mitchell

1917 Bank—joint stock land bank—chartered—Sioux City, Iowa

1917 Loan—liberty loan subscriptions—authorized

1922 Catholic Nuns (cloistered community)—Magdalen Sisters—Baltimore, Md.—founded

1928 Fathometer—patented—H. G. Dorsey

1934 Organ—pipeless organ—invented—Laurens Hammond—Chicago, Ill.

1936 Television—Telecast—unscheduled event to be televised as it occurred—Camden, N.J.

1946 Glider—glider commercial freight service —inaugurated—Philadelphia, Pa.

1954 War (French Indochina)—American civilian pilot wounded in Indochina

1956 Brokerage—visitor to open the New York Stock Exchange—Leonard Ross—New York City

1959 Flag—Navy flag (official)—authorized

1962 Television—Telecast—transcontinental telecast by means of an orbiting satellite—Westford, Mass.

APRIL 25

1812 Land Office—General Land Office (federal) —established

1831 Streetcar—streetcar company—New York and Harlem Railway—incorporated

1846 War (Mexican)—Mexican War shots—fired—La Rosia, Mexico

1860 Japanese Ambassador—arrived—Washington, D.C.

1865 Oil—oil well drilled by torpedoes—patent —E. A. L. Roberts—New York City

1873 Rifle Association—rifle association (national)—shooting meet

1876 Baseball Game—shutout game—Louisville, Ky.

1881 Monument—statue cast by the United States Government—Admiral D. G. Farragut—accepted by President Garfield

1882 Forestry Society—national forestry association—American Forestry Congress—held—Cincinnati, Ohio

1901 Automobile License Plates—automobile license plates—legislation enacted—New York

1908 Ship—turbine-propelled ship of the U.S. Navy—*Chester*—commissioned

1917 Loan—war loan made by the United States Government to a war ally—Great Britain

1928 Animals—dogs trained to guide the blind—Seeing Eye dog presented

1935 Telephone—around-the-world telephone conversation—New York City

1938 Ship—seaplane tender designed and built for the United States Navy—*Curtiss*—keel laid—Camden, N.J.

1939 Autogiro—autogiro patent—Juan de la Cierva—granted posthumously—assigned to Autogiro Company of America

1939 Federal Security Agency—established

1939 Federal Works Agency—authorized

1940 Television—Telecast—circus telecast—New York City

1940 Television—Telecast—Passover services telecast—New York City

1945 Postage Stamp—nonpictorial postage stamp—United Nations stamp—issued—San Francisco, Calif.

1945 United Nations—Conference on International Organization of the UN—San Francisco, Calif.

1951 Newspaper Reporter—newspaper reporter to become a U.S. senator—Blair Moody—sworn in

1951 Senator (U.S.)—senator to preside over a Senate session directly after being sworn in as a senator—Blair Moody of Michigan

1954 Battery—solar battery—announced—New York City

1957 Atomic Reactor—sodium reactor (experimental)—operated—Santa Susana Mountains, Calif.

1959 Canal—St. Lawrence Seaway—opened

1967 Abortion Legalization Law—signed—Colorado

APRIL 26

1790 Senator (U.S.)—senator appointed by a governor—John Walker—Virginia—seated

1819 Odd Fellows Lodge—established—Baltimore, Md.

1826 Engineering College—engineering college—Rensselaer School—Troy, N.Y.—graduation

1848 Engineering Society—Boston Society of Civil Engineers—organized—N.Y.C.

1921 Radio Broadcast—weather broadcasts—St. Louis, Mo.

1929 Fluorescent Mineral Exhibit—opened—Philadelphia, Pa.

1957 Air Force Academy (U.S.)—Air Force Academy woman officer—N. M. McCracken

1962 Satellite—international satellite—*Ariel I* —launched—Cape Canaveral, Fla.

APRIL 27

1805 Flag—American flag flown over a fortress of the Old World—Tripoli, Africa

1816 Tariff—tariff for protection—enacted

1875 Catholic Priest—Catholic priest to be elevated to the cardinalate—John McCloskey —investiture—New York City

1880 Deaf—Hearing Aid—electrical hearing aid —bone conduction device—patented

99 Hospital—tuberculosis hospital operated by the government—opened—Fort Stanton, N.Mex.

13 Dentist—dentist in the U.S. Navy to serve at an overseas base—J. L. Brown—Guam

38 Baseball—baseball (yellow)—used—Columbia-Fordham—New York City

38 Woman—woman of American descent to become a queen—Countess Geraldine Apponyi—married—King Zog of Albania

46 Ship—radar installation aboard a commercial carrier—New York City

60 Submarine—atomic-powered turbine electric-drive submarine—*Tullibee*—launched—Groton, Conn.

60 Television—submarine with closed-circuit television—*Tullibee*—launched—Groton, Conn.

60 Television—Telecast—art auction televised on a coast-to-coast closed circuit—New York City

70 Bank—automated "tellerless" bank—Surety National Bank's Civic Center branch, Los Angeles, Calif.—opened

70 Element—element 105—hahnium—discovered by Albert Ghiorso, University of California, Berkeley, Calif.—announced in Washington, D.C.

APRIL 28

98 Author—author whose livelihood was obtained exclusively by writing—C. B. Brown—book announced—New York City

55 Veterinary School—veterinary college—Boston Veterinary Institute—Boston, Mass.—incorporated

60 Japanese Ambassador—received by President Buchanan—Washington, D.C.

62 Treason—citizen of the United States to be tried for treason, convicted, and hanged—W. B. Mumford—New Orleans, La.

66 Ship—steam whaler—*Pioneer*

82 Library—library newspaper room—Newburyport, Mass.—dedicated

90 Employment Service—state employment service—created—Ohio

96 Addressograph—patented—J. S. Duncan—Sioux City, Iowa

98 Advertising Legislation—advertising legislation (state)—enacted

04 Postal Service—permit mail—authorized

09 Child Delinquency Law (state)—enacted—Colorado

19 Aviation—Parachute—parachute—jump with army parachute—L. L. R. Irving—Dayton, Ohio

22 Radio Station—educational radio station licensed—WOI—Iowa State College of Agriculture and Mechanical Arts, Ames, Iowa—license granted

25 Wind Tunnel—propeller research tunnel—Langley Field, Va.

1930 Motion Picture—motion picture of an eclipse of the sun taken from an airplane—Honey Lake, Calif.

1932 Vaccine—yellow fever vaccine for human immunization—announced

1936 Aviation—airplane tank discharger—patented—J. H. Hammond, Jr.—Gloucester, Mass.

1937 Electric Sign—animated-cartoon electric sign—displayed—Douglas Leigh—New York City

1937 Museum—costume museum—Museum of Costume Arts—New York City—incorporated

1939 Automobile—miniature automobile—Crosley—offered for sale

1968 Armenian Cathedral—consecrated—New York City

APRIL 29

1813 Rubber—rubber patent—J. F. Hummel—Philadelphia, Pa.

1851 College—college to prohibit discrimination because of race, religion, or color—Cooper Union—New York City

1851 Locomotive—electric locomotive—trial trip—Washington, D.C.

1854 College—university for blacks—Lincoln University—incorporated

1863 Charity Board (state)—authorized—Massachusetts

1864 Fraternity—professional fraternity—Theta Xi—Troy, N.Y.

1873 Railroad Coupler—railroad coupler—patented—E. H. Janney—Alexandria, Va.

1879 Electric Lighting—electric arc lights—used—Cleveland, Ohio

1895 Postage Stamp—watermarked postage stamp—Benjamin Franklin—issued

1898 Cancer Laboratory—appropriations—New York State

1913 Fastening—hookless fastening for universal use—patented—Gideon Sundback—Hoboken, N.J.

1918 Aviation—Pilot—American Ace of Aces—E. V. Rickenbacker—first victory—Toul, France

1921 Prison—prisoners (federal) employed in industry—wage system adopted—Atlanta, Ga.

1925 Science Association—woman elected to the National Academy of Sciences—F. R. Sabin—Baltimore, Md.

1931 Visiting Celebrities—absolute monarch—King Prajadhipok of Siam received by President Hoover—Washington, D.C.

1940 Sculpture—stainless-steel bas relief (large size)—A. P. building—unveiled—New York City

1942 Insurance—health insurance law (state)—Rhode Island—cash sickness compensation—approved

1943 **Civil Air Patrol (U.S.)**—transferred to War Department

1949 **Aviation—License**—cargo airlines licensed by the Civil Aeronautics Board

1953 **Television—Telecast**—three-dimensional telecast—KECA-TV, Los Angeles, Calif.

1957 **Atomic Reactor**—military nuclear power plant—dedicated—Fort Belvoir, Va.

APRIL 30

1778 **Blockade**—effected—West Point, N.Y.

1789 **Army**—army organization under the Constitution—act enacted

1789 **Cabinet (U.S.)**—Cabinet—appointed— George Washington

1789 **President (U.S.)**—President elected— George Washington—inaugurated

1798 **Marine Corps**—American Marines—transferred to Navy Department

1798 **Navy**—Navy Department (U.S.)—established

1798 **Navy**—navy yard—acquired—Portsmouth, N.H.

1802 **Land Grant**—land subsidy for internal improvements—granted

1803 **Territorial Expansion**—annexation of territory—Louisiana Purchase from France

1820 **Slavery**—antislavery magazine—*The Emancipator* — published — Jonesboro, Tenn.

1837 **Education**—state board of education—established—Massachusetts

1855 **Billiard Match**—billiard three-ball match on a 6-by-12 carom table—San Francisco, Calif.

1863 **Seal**—seal of the Confederate States of America—authorized

1864 **Game Law**—hunting license fee (state)— enacted—New York

1879 **Labor Legislation**—factory inspection law —enacted—Massachusetts

1883 **Electric Company**—three-wire central-station incandescent electric lighting plant— Sunbury, Pa.—incorporated

1888 **Naval Officer**—naval chaplain who was Catholic—C. H. Parks

1889 **Holiday**—national holiday—celebrated

1898 **Advertising Legislation**—advertising legislation (state)—enacted—New York

1913 **Court**—small debtors' court established by state law—effective—Kansas

1926 **Radio Facsimile Transmission**—photograph sent by radio across the Atlantic inaugurating commercial service—transmitted—London, England–New York City

1931 **Autogiro**—autogiro to land packages on a moving ship—New York City

1932 **Animals**—dogs trained to guide the blind— Seeing Eye—incorporated

1939 **Baseball Player**—baseball player to play in more than 2,100 consecutive games—H. L. Gehrig—2,130th game

1939 **Electric Power**—electric power generate by cosmic rays—Hayden Planetariu New York City

1939 **Railroad Car**—train with fluorescent ligh —St. Louis, Mo.–Kansas City, Mo.

1939 **Television—Telecast**—President to appea on television—F. D. Roosevelt

1940 **Prizefight Referee**—woman prizefight re eree (licensed)—Belle Martell—Van Nuy Calif.

1942 **Submarine**—submarine built on the Gre Lakes—*Peto*—launched—Manitowoc, W

1948 **Television—Telecast**—stratovision flight television signal transmitted

1953 **Building**—building for telephone directo compilation and printing—dedicated—D Plaines, Ill.

1955 **Element**—element 101-mendelevium—a nounced

1972 **United Church of Christ**—minist (avowed homosexual)—William Johns —ordination sanctioned—San Carlc Calif.

1973 **Attorney General**—attorney general (U.S to plead guilty to a criminal offense—R. Kleindienst—resigned

1973 **Postage Stamp**—printed matter on the r verse side of postage stamps—Postal Pe ple set—issued

1976 **Bridge**—bridge named for a woman—Bet Ross Bridge—Philadelphia, Pa.–Pennsau en, N.J.—opened

MAY 1

1704 **Advertisement** — advertisement — *Nev Letter*—Boston, Mass.—published

1751 **Cricket Tournament**—cricket match—Ne York City

1789 **Congress (U.S.)—House of Represent tives**—chaplain of the House of Represe tatives—William Linn—began service

1826 **Tax**—inheritance tax (state)—effective Pennsylvania

1840 **Blind**—state school for the blind—Ohio I stitution for the Blind—Superintende William Chapin—took office

1843 **Diplomatic Service**—consul to California appointed—T. O. Larkin

1857 **Literacy qualification for voting**—enact —Massachusetts

1861 **Normal School**—normal school (state) which students actually conducted class —Oswego Training School—Oswego, N —established

1863 **Cripples**—private school for cripples opened—New York City

1863 **Hospital**—orthopedic hospital—Hospi for Ruptured and Crippled—New York C —opened

1872 **Liberal Republican Party**—conventior Cincinnati, Ohio

1873 **Postal Card**—issued

76 **Coaching**—tallyho trip—New York City

83 **Sports**—sports trainer (professional)—Bob Rogers—engaged—New York City

84 **Building**—building known as a skyscraper —construction began—Chicago, Ill.

86 **Boat Race**—fisherman's boat race—Boston Light

88 **Locomotive**—electric freight locomotive— tested

93 **Kapok**—commercially introduced—Chicago, Ill.

94 **Building**—caisson-foundation building— opened—New York City

95 **Railroad**—railroad to use an electric engine—Baltimore and Ohio—for passenger service

97 **Fencing**—fencing champion to win three titles in one year—C. G. Bothner—New York City

99 **Hospital**—cancer home for incurables (free)—opened—New York City

03 **House of David**—established—Benton Harbor, Mich.

04 **Socialist Party**—national convention—Indianapolis, Ind.

06 **Bank**—bank open day and night—New York City

09 **Electric Power Plant**—hydroelectric power plant built by the federal government— Minidoka Dam, Idaho—first unit started

13 **Foxhound Master (American)**—R. E. Strawbridge—England

15 **Ship**—ship (American) attacked by a German submarine—*Nantucket Chief*—torpedoed

20 **Baseball Game**—baseball game (major league) to last longer than 25 innings—Boston Braves vs. Brooklyn Robins—Boston, Mass.

21 **Radio Beacons**—in regular service

25 **Insurance**—automobile compulsory insurance act (state)—approved—Massachusetts

26 **Christmas Tree**—National Christmas Tree —dedicated—General Grant National Park, Calif.

27 **Check Photographing Device**—commercial manufacture—Rochester, N.Y.

27 **Jewish College**—Jewish college of liberal arts and sciences under Jewish auspices— cornerstone laid

29 **Aviation**—airplane commutation tickets— placed on sale

31 **Baha'i House of Worship**—opened—Wilmette, Ill.

31 **Building**—building higher than 1,250 feet— Empire State Building—New York City— dedicated

43 **Postal Service**—zone numbers—put into use—Pittsburgh, Pa.

46 **Governor**—black governor appointed by the President of the United States—W. H. Hastie—appointed—U.S. Virgin Islands

1946 **Ship**—radar installation aboard a commercial carrier—*African Star*—in operation— New York City

1947 **Radar**—radar for commercial and private planes—demonstrated—Culver City, Calif.

1950 **Poet**—black woman to win the Pulitzer Prize for poetry—Gwendolyn Brooks

1961 **Aviation—Airplane**—skyjack of a commercial American airplane—Antillo Ortiz— Marathon, Fla.

1976 **Maritime School**—woman graduate of a 4-year maritime school—D. B. Doane— Maine Maritime Academy, Castine, Me.

MAY 2

1801 **Representative (U.S.)**—representative appointed to a presidential Cabinet—James Madison—began service as secretary of state

1829 **Fair**—manufacturers' fair—American Institute—New York City—incorporated

1843 **Colonial Government**—government on the Pacific coast—Champoeg, Oreg.

1855 **Zinc**—zinc commercial production—Pennsylvania and Lehigh Zinc Company—incorporated

1876 **Baseball Player**—baseball players to hit a home run—R. C. Barnes and C. W. Jones— Cincinnati, Ohio

1880 **Ship**—steamboat to employ electric lights successfully—*Columbia*—dynamo operated

1887 **Kindergarten**—kindergarten for the blind— Perkins Institution—Roxbury, Mass.— opened

1887 **Photographic Film**—celluloid photographic film—patent application—H. W. Goodwin

1900 **United Christian Party**—first convention

1917 **Baseball Game**—double no-hit nine-inning baseball game—major league—Chicago, Ill.

1917 **Loan**—liberty loan subscriptions—taken

1923 **Aviation—Flights (transcontinental)**— transcontinental nonstop flight—from Roosevelt Field, N.Y.

1926 **Radio Facsimile Transmission**—drawing sent by radio across the Atlantic—transmitted—London–New York City

1960 **Pulitzer Prize**—woman to win 2 Pulitzer prizes in history—Margaret Leech—2nd award

1970 **Jockey**—jockey (woman) to ride in a Kentucky Derby—Diane Crump—Churchill Downs, Ky.

MAY 3

1649 **Medical Legislation**—law to regulate the practice of medicine (colonial)—enacted— Massachusetts

1654 **Bridge**—toll bridge—erected—Rowley, Mass.

1743 **Automaton**—imported—New York City

1765 **Medical School**—medical college—established—Philadelphia, Pa.

1768 **Arbitration**—arbitration tribunal—established—New York City

1826 **Arcade**—cornerstone laid—Philadelphia, Pa.

1845 **Bridge**—iron-truss bridge—construction began—Pottstown, Pa.

1845 **Lawyer**—black lawyer formally admitted to the bar—M. B. Allen—Worcester, Mass.

1851 **Methodist Episcopal Church**—Scandinavian Methodist Episcopal Church—incorporated

1861 **Habeas Corpus**—habeas corpus suspension order—Abraham Lincoln

1862 **Land Mines**—land mines—used

1865 **Medal**—Medal of Honor winner to receive 2 awards—T. W. Custer—first presentation

1874 **Young Men's Hebrew Association**—Lewis May—served—New York City

1881 **Locomotive Headlight**—electric locomotive headlight—patented—L. G. Woolley—Mendon, Mich.

1904 **Pharmacy Legislation (state)**—requiring graduation—enacted—New York

1906 **Advertising Show (annual)**—New York City

1911 **Insurance**—workers' compensation insurance law (state)—enacted—Wisconsin

1913 **Motion Picture Censorship**—motion picture censorship board (state)—Ohio approved censorship

1921 **Tax**—sales tax (state)—approved—West Virginia

1923 **Aviation—Flights (transcontinental)**—transcontinental nonstop flight—O. G. Kelly and J. A. Macready—arrived—Coronado Beach, Calif.

1927 **Electric Sign**—electric sign flasher—F. E. J. Wilde—patent—Meadowmere Park, N.Y.

1933 **Mint (U.S.)**—woman director of the Mint—N. T. Ross—assumed office

1938 **Television—Telecast**—book review to be televised—New York City

1943 **Poet**—poet to win a Pulitzer Prize 4 times—Robert Frost—4th award

1944 **Army Officer**—woman officer in the Judge Advocate General's Department—P. L. Propp

1950 **Medical Society**—woman member of the Association of American Physicians—H. B. Taussig—elected—Atlantic City, N.J.

1952 **Aviation—Flights**—North Pole landing by an airplane at the geographic pole

1952 **Jockey**—jockey to win the Kentucky Derby 5 times—Eddie Arcaro

MAY 4

1776 **Ink**—invisible ink—Silas Deane—arrived in France as American agent

1780 **Arts and Science Society**—arts and science society (national)—American Academy of Arts and Sciences—incorporated

1798 **Pistol**—government contract for pistols—authorized—Simeon North

1811 **Disciples of Christ**—church established-Brush Run, Pa.

1845 **Bridge**—iron-truss bridge—completed-Pottstown, Pa.

1846 **Capital Punishment**—death penalty fir abolished—enacted—Michigan

1854 **Entomologist**—state entomologist—Ne York—Asa Fitch—appointed

1855 **Hospital**—women's hospital—opened-New York City

1869 **Drill**—oil-drill offshore rig—T. F. Rowlan —patented

1869 **Railroad**—municipal railroad—constru tion authorized—Ohio

1884 **Photograph**—photograph of a lightnir flash—W. C. Gurley—Marietta, Ohio

1886 **Phonograph**—phonograph that was prac cal—patented

1891 **Hospital**—interracial hospital—Provide Hospital—Chicago, Ill.—opened

1892 **Acetylene**—acetylene made—T. L. Willso —Spray, N.C.

1905 **Railroad Car**—mail car (steel)—exhibite —Washington, D.C.

1920 **Orchestra**—orchestra (American) to mak a European tour—concert—Paris, France

1927 **Balloon—Flights**—balloon flight to excee an altitude of 40,000 feet—ascended—Sco Field, Ill.—H. C. Gray

1928 **Judge**—woman associate justice on th federal bench—G. R. Cline—appointed

1930 **Medical Congress**—Mental Hygiene Inte national Congress—opened—Washingto D.C.

1933 **Agricultural Adjustment Administratio** —G. N. Peek—named administrator

1942 **Pulitzer Prize**—woman to win 2 Pulitz prizes in history—Margaret Leech—fir award

1942 **World War II**—sea battle fought entire by air power—Coral Sea

1954 **Tennis Match**—intercollegiate court tenn match—New York City

1956 **Postal Card**—commemorative postal car —issued—New York City

1973 **Building**—building higher than 1,400 feet-Sears Building—Chicago, Ill.—topped ou

MAY 5

1696 **Woman**—woman printer—Dinah Nuthea —license application—Annapolis, Md.

1809 **Woman**—woman granted a patent—Ma Kies—South Killingly, Conn.

1832 **Vaccination Legislation**—vaccinatio legislation for American Indians—enacte

1847 **Medical Society**—medical society (n tional)—American Medical Association-organized—Philadelphia, Pa.

1865 **Railroad Train Robbery**—railroad tra robbery of a disabled train—North Ben Ohio

1966 Television—Telecast—horse race (Kentucky Derby) telecast in color—Louisville, Ky.

MAY 8

1783 Salute (complimentary)—fired by Great Britain in honor of George Washington

1784 Hailstone Shower—hailstone shower of importance—Winnsborough, S.C.

1787 Prison Reform Society—formed—Philadelphia, Pa.

1792 Army Officer—paymaster—office authorized

1792 Conscription — conscription — authorized by Congress

1812 Federal Foreign Aid Bill—enacted

1816 Bible Society—Bible society (national organization)—American Bible Society—delegates met—New York City

1821 Discovery—discovery of Antarctica—expedition returned

1828 Peace Society—New York Peace Society joins American Peace Society

1840 Photographic Patent—photographic patent —A. S. Wolcott—New York City

1847 Rubber—rubber tire patent—R. W. Thomson—England

1848 School—school for the mentally retarded—created—Boston, Mass.

1877 Dog Show—of importance—New York City

1878 Baseball Game—triple play unassisted—Paul Hines—Providence, R.I.

1879 Automobile Patent—filed—G. B. Selden—Rochester, N.Y.

1895 Cat Show—exhibition—Madison Square Garden, New York City—opened

1905 Automobile Race—transcontinental automobile race (for a time record)—started —New York City

1915 Horse Race—filly to win the Kentucky Derby—Regret—Louisville, Ky.

1917 World War I—American troop contingent to arrive in France—sailed—New York City

1919 Aviation—Flights (transatlantic)—transatlantic hydroplane flight—left—New York City

1931 Price Regulation Legislation—resale price maintenance law (state)—approved—California

1939 Electric Starting Gate (racetrack)—used—Inglewood, Calif.

1942 Medal—American Academy of Arts and Letters-National Institute of Arts and Letters gold medal—awarded—C. E. Burchfield—New York City

1942 World War II—aircraft carrier (American) sunk in World War II—Lexington—Coral Sea

1951 Dacron—dacron men's suits—introduced —New York City

1952 Coal—coal hydrogenation chemicals pil plant (large)—opened—Institute, W.Va.

1954 Shot Put—shot put toss over 60 feet—Par O'Brien—Los Angeles, Calif.

1961 Medal—National Aeronautics and Spa Administration Distinguished Servi Medal—presented—A. B. Shepard Washington, D.C.

1961 Water—seawater conversion plant (prac cal)—Freeport, Tex.—opened

1964 President (U.S.)—President to address tl Senate—H. S. Truman—Washington, D.

1965 Shot-Put—shot-put to cover a distance more than 70 feet—Randy Matson—C lege Station, Tex.

1969 Treasury Department (U.S.)—treasurer the United States to sign currency with names—D. A. Elston—sworn in

1980 Balloon—Flights—transcontinental no stop balloon flight—takeoff, San Francisc Calif.

MAY 9

1607 Protestant Episcopal Church—Protesta Episcopal Church—established—Jame town, Va.

1754 Cartoon—newspaper cartoon—Penns, vania Gazette—Philadelphia, Pa.

1792 Army Officer—paymaster—Caleb Swan appointed

1796 Senator (U.S.)—senators-elect not seat —William Blount and William Cocke, Tennessee—denied seats

1825 Theater—theater lighted by gas—Ne York City—newspaper account

1860 Constitutional Union Party—organized Baltimore, Md.

1863 Bank Legislation—national banking sy tem—Comptroller of Currency—Hu McCulloch—served

1863 Comptroller—Comptroller of the Curren —Hugh McCulloch—began service

1879 Postage Stamp—postage-due stamps—fir stamps issued

1893 Motion Picture—motion picture film exi bition—T. A. Edison—Brooklyn, N.Y.

1912 Aviation—Exposition and Meets aeronautic international exposition—Ne York City

1913 Senator (U.S.)—senators "elected by t people"—amendment ratified by Wiscc sin, 36th state

1926 Aviation—Flights—North Pole flight—R. Byrd

1926 Ship—rotor ship—Baden-Baden—arriv —New York City

1932 Senator (U.S.)—woman senator to presi over the Senate—H. O. W. Caraway

1936 Aviation—Flights (transatlantic)—Atlan Ocean regular commercial airship s vice— Hindenburg — landed — Lakehur N.J.

1928 **Television—Telecast**—programs regularly televised—Schenectady, N.Y.

1929 **Codeball**—played—Chicago, Ill.

1940 **Television—Telecast**—ship-to-shore telecast—from S.S. *President Roosevelt*

1940 **Television Receiver**—television receiver on a ship—installed on *President Roosevelt*

1942 **Blackout**—blackout outdoor light control—Seattle, Wash.

1947 **Automobile Tire**—tubeless automobile tires—announced—Akron, Ohio

1960 **Submarine**—submerged circumnavigation of the earth—*Triton*—returned to New London, Conn.

1978 **Marine Corps**—general (woman) in the Marine Corps—M. A. Brewer—sworn in

1980 **Balloon—Flights**—Transcontinental nonstop balloon flight—landed outside Matane, Que., on Gaspe Peninsula

MAY 12

1812 **Vice Presidential Candidate**—vice presidential nominee to decline nomination—John Langdon

1831 **Bank Robbery**—bank robbery—Edward Smith—sentenced

1841 **Antislavery Party**—Liberty Party—national convention—New York City

1844 **College**—masonic college—opened—Philadelphia, Mo.

1857 **Hospital**—women's infirmary staffed by women physicians—hospital opened—New York City

1860 **News Correspondent**—woman news reporter at a political convention—M. A. R. Livermore—Chicago, Ill.

1862 **Ship**—Confederate ship surrendered—*Planter*—seized by Robert Smalls—off Charleston Harbor, S.C.

1873 **Postal Card**—first known cancellation

1890 **Prizefight**—state legalization concerning prizefighting—enacted—Louisiana

1894 **Agricultural Appropriation**—New York

1894 **Ship**—warship built on inland waters—*Ericsson*—launched—Dubuque, Iowa

1896 **Health Ordinance prohibiting spitting**—enacted—New York City

1896 **Medical Instruction**—psychiatric institute—authorized—New York

1908 **Radio Broadcast**—radio broadcast demonstration—N. B. Stubblefield—patent

1914 **Holiday**—Mother's Day—national recognition

1933 **Agricultural Adjustment Administration**—approved

1933 **Federal Emergency Relief Administration**—created

1949 **Diplomatic Service**—woman ambassador from a foreign country—S. V. L. Pandit—received

1953 **Television Station**—noncommercial educational television station—KUHT—Houston, Tex.

1965 **Presbyterian Church**—woman ordained minister in the Presbyterian Church in th United States (South)—Rachel Henderli —ordained in Richmond, Va.

1969 **Sailing**—woman to sail alone across th Pacific Ocean—S. S. Adams—left Yokoh ma, Japan

MAY 13

1607 **Colonial Government**—colonial council America—Jamestown, Va.

1607 **Colonist**—English settlement in Ameri (permanent)—arrived—Jamestown, Va.

1821 **Printing Press**—printing press invented America that was practical and success —patent—Samuel Rust—New York City

1829 **Peace Society**—American Peace Society annual meeting—New York City

1854 **Billiard Match**—billiard match—of impo tance—Syracuse, N.Y.

1857 **Agricultural School**—agricultural colle (state)—to open—Agricultural College Michigan—Lansing, Mich.—opened

1873 **Sewing Machine**—sewing machine lar holder—patented—M. N. Wolf—Avo Conn.

1891 **Jockey**—jockey to win the Kentucky Der 3 times—Isaac Murphy—Louisville, Ky.- third time

1891 **Museum**—Semitic museum—Harvard Un versity, Cambridge, Mass.—opened to pu lic

1897 **Golf Club**—intercollegiate golf associati tournament—Ardsley-on-Hudson, N.Y.

1908 **Navy**—naval nurses' corps—authorized

1916 **Holiday**—American Indian Day—obse vance

1918 **Postage Stamp**—airmail stamps—issued

1929 **Autogiro—Flights**—intercity autogiro flig —H. F. Pitcairn—Philadelphia, Pa., to Lan ley Field, Va.

1942 **Helicopter—Flights**—helicopter flig (cross country)—takeoff

1949 **Turbine**—gas turbine to pump natural g —installed—Wilmar, Ark.

1953 **Television Receiver**—city to have two ed cational television channels—Pittsburg Pa.

MAY 14

1634 **Tax**—property tax law (colonial)—Mass chusetts

1694 **College**—college to receive a coat of arm from the College of Heralds—William burg, Va.

1804 **Expedition**—expedition across the con nent to the Pacific coast—Lewis and Cla —left—St. Louis, Mo.

1836 **Expedition**—scientific expedition fitted o by the United States Government—autho ized

2 **College**—college to grant women absolutely equal rights with men—nonsectarian—Antioch College—Yellow Springs, Ohio—chartered

3 **Milk**—condensed milk (commercial)—Gail Borden—patent application

6 **Animals**—camels imported for commercial purposes—Indianola, Tex.

7 **Agricultural School**—agricultural college (state) to open—Agricultural College of Michigan—instruction offered

4 **Football Game**—rugby contest (international)—Cambridge, Mass.

4 **Football Goalpost**—football goalpost used —Cambridge, Mass.

8 **Petroleum Jelly**—Vaseline trademarked

4 **Anti-Monopoly Party**—formed—Chicago, Ill.

7 **Accident Report**—industrial accident reports required—Massachusetts

8 **County**—county created by federal legislation—Latah County, Idaho—authorized

4 **Olympic Games**—Olympic celebration—St. Louis, Mo.

8 **Aviation—Passenger**—airplane passenger (official)—first passenger to fly—C. W. Furnas—Fort Myer, Va.

1 **Judge**—woman judge to sentence a man to death—F. E. Allen—Cleveland, Ohio

9 **Airmail Service**—airmail service between North and South America—inaugurated—Miami, Fla.

1 **Autogiro—Flights**—transcontinental autogiro flights—J. M. Miller—started—Philadelphia, Pa.

2 **Electric Timer**—electrical timing device—tested at Baker Field, New York City

4 **Ship**—streamlined steamship—*Arctees*—arrived—Boston, Mass.

5 **Aviation—Flights**—sky-train international round-trip flight—left—Key West, Fla.

1 **Blackout**—blackout lighting demonstration —Lynn, Mass.

2 **Army Auxiliary Corps**—women's army auxiliary corps (WAAC)—authorized

9 **Aviation—Airplane**—airplane with a delta wing—Convair—delivered to the Air Force

0 **Television—Telecast**—Cabinet meeting (staged) telecast—Chicago, Ill.

3 **Patent**—patent on a "solar airplane vehicle"—E. G. Johnson

3 **Television — Telecast** — laser-light-beam program telecast on a network—*I've Got a Secret*—New York City

3 **Medal**—Presidential Citizen Medal—R. W. Clemente—first presentation (posthumous)

MAY 15

2 **Discovery**—discovery of New England by an Englishman—B. Gosnold

2 **Copyright Law**—copyright law—enacted—Massachusetts

4 **Milestones**—installed—Philadelphia, Pa.

1785 **Missionary**—black missionary to the American Indians—John Marrant—ordained

1797 **Congress (U.S.)**—special session

1851 **Women's Club**—women's secret society—Adelphean Society—organized—Macon, Ga.

1854 **Hospital**—inebriates' asylum—United States Inebriate Asylum—founded—Binghamton, N.Y.

1862 **Agriculture Bureau**—Agriculture Bureau made a separate entity

1862 **Baseball Park**—baseball park (enclosed)—Brooklyn, N.Y.—opened

1869 **Postage Stamp**—flag (American) depicted on a postage stamp—issued

1880 **Archaeological Society**—archaeological national society—Archaeological Institute of America—annual meeting—Boston, Mass.

1885 **Forest Reserve**—forest reserve (state)—New York State Forest Preserve—designated

1888 **Union Labor Party**—convention—Cincinnati, Ohio

1894 **Labor Legislation**—labor discrimination law (state)—enacted—New Jersey

1914 **Sound-absorbing Material**—production started—International Falls, Minn.

1917 **Army Balloon School**—graduation—St. Louis, Mo.

1917 **Librarians' Union**—Library Employes' Union affiliated with AFL—chartered

1918 **Airmail Service**—airmail experimental route—flown—Washington, D.C.–New York City

1918 **Ship**—ambulance ship designed and built as a hospital—*Relief*—frame erected

1919 **Airmail Service**—airmail transcontinental service—Cleveland, Ohio–Chicago, Ill.

1920 **Airmail Service**—airmail transcontinental service—Chicago, Ill.–Omaha, Neb.

1922 **Arbitration Association**—arbitration association—Arbitration Society of America—formed—New York City

1930 **Aviation**—flight attendant (woman)—Ellen Church

1933 **Congress (U.S.)—Senate**—loudspeaker—installed—Senate

1937 **Aquarium**—aquarium for monsters of the deep—ground broken—Marineland, Fla.

1937 **Business**—Keedoozle store—opened—Memphis, Tenn.

1938 **Post Office**—airplane post office—Washington, D.C.

1940 **Nylon**—nylon hose—placed on sale

1941 **Conscientious Objectors' Camp**—Relay Post Office, Md.

1942 **Army Auxiliary Corps**—women's army auxiliary corps (WAAC)—director—O. C. Hobby—appointed

1946 **Telephone**—mobile telephone news dispatch—St. Louis, Mo.

1950 **Radio Station**—all-local network

1952 **Jockey**—jockey to win 4,000 races—Johnny Longden—Inglewood, Calif.

1957 **Building**—aluminum geodesic-dome civic center—Virginia Beach, Va.—opened

1958 **Postage Stamp**—postage stamp to bear the likeness of a Vice President of the United States issued by a foreign country—Ecuador

1963 **Astronaut**—astronaut (American) to orbit the earth on two trips—L. G. Cooper—first takeoff—*Faith 7*—Cape Canavernal, Fla.

1963 **Astronaut**—astronaut (American) to orbit the earth 22 times—L. G. Cooper—*Faith 7* —takeoff, Cape Canaveral, Fla.

1965 **Totalisator**—fully electronic, transistorized, data processing totalisator—in use—Westbury, L.I., N.Y.

MAY 16

1691 **Treason**—American colonist hanged for treason—Jacob Leisler—New York City

1775 **State**—state constitution—adopted—Massachusetts

1811 **War (1812)**—naval battle—off Sandy Hook, N.J.

1825 **Horse Race**—trotting course—Screwdriver won main event

1856 **Fish Commission (state)**—authorized—Massachusetts

1866 **Money**—nickel—authorized

1882 **Army Officer**—general to become a rear admiral—S. P. Carter—appointed

1882 **Flicker**—Henry Van Hoevenbergh—Elizabeth, N.J.—patent

1888 **United Labor Party**—formed—Cincinnati, Ohio

1893 **Typewriter**—typewriter to produce a line of writing visible as it was being typed—patented—H. L. Wagner—Brooklyn, N.Y.

1895 **College Academic Costume Standardization**—assembled—New York City

1896 **Electric Power Plant**—rotary-converter power plant—operated—Chicago, Ill.

1903 **Motorcycle Trip**—motorcycle transcontinental trip—started—San Francisco, Calif.

1910 **Mines Bureau (U.S.)**—authorized

1913 **Agriculture Department (U.S.)**—Office of Markets—chief served—C. J. Brand

1914 **Horseshoe Pitchers Association (national)** —organized—Kansas City, Kan.

1925 **Radio Telephone**—radio telephone conversation between someone on the ground and a person in a dirigible—A. A. Kent and M. L. Kent—Philadelphia, Pa.

1929 **Motion Picture Actor**—motion picture actors to receive Oscars—Emil Jannings and Janet Gaynor—Hollywood, Calif.

1938 **Animal Breeding Society**—artificial animal breeding cooperative society—organized —New Jersey

1940 **Shovel**—two-handed shovel—used—Niagara Falls Bridge, N.Y.

1941 **Ordnance**—automatic aircraft cannon delivered—Elmira, N.Y.

1959 **Golfer**—golfer to break 60 for 18 holes in major tournament—S. J. Snead—White Sulphur Springs, W.Va.

1963 **Astronaut**—astronaut (American) to orbit the earth 22 times—L. G. Cooper—*Faith* —landed, Pacific Ocean

1973 **Balloon—Flights**—balloon flight power by solar energy—Tracy Barnes—Statesville, N.C.

MAY 17

1757 **Academy**—Academy and College of Philadelphia—seven men graduated

1786 **Treaty**—treaty entered into by the United States after the treaty of peace with Great Britain—with Prussia—ratified

1792 **Brokerage**—stock exchange—New York City

1796 **Land Grant**—special land grant

1796 **Medical Book**—pediatrics monograph presented—Philadelphia, Pa.

1803 **Reaper**—reaper patented

1853 **Railroad**—railroad merger—of importance—New York Central Railroad Co.

1875 **Horse Race**—horse race (Kentucky Derby) —Louisville, Ky.

1876 **Greenback Party**—convention—Indianapolis, Ind.

1877 **Telephone**—interstate telephone call New Brunswick, N.J.–New York City

1877 **Telephone**—telephone switchboard or exchange—operated—Boston, Mass.

1879 **Archaeological Society**—archaeological society (national)—constitution adopted Archaeological Institute of America

1895 **Elevated Railroad**—electric elevated railroad (permanent)—Chicago, Ill.—opened

1897 **Voting Machine Commission**—authorized —New York

1900 **Fine Arts Commission (federal)**—fine arts commission (federal)—authorized

1908 **Tunnel**—subaqueous railroad tunnel to foreign country—Port Huron, Mich.—operated by electricity

1912 **Ship**—cruise ship to circumnavigate world—arrived—Hamburg, Germany

1913 **Oil**—oil and gas conservation legislation Oklahoma—enacted

1918 **Aviation**—air squadron (complete)—first flight of De Havilland airplane in France

1920 **Ship**—naval ship named for a dental officer—*Osborne*—commissioned

1930 **Ship**—air-conditioned ship—*Mariposa* —keel laid—Quincy, Mass.

1939 **Postal Service**—coin-operated mailbox installed—New York City

1939 **Television—Telecast**—baseball game (collegiate) televised—Princeton-Columbia New York City

1939 **Television—Telecast**—fashion show telecast—New York City

1777 **Treaty**—treaty between states after the Declaration of Independence—Georgia and South Carolina—Dewitt's Corner, S.C.

1785 **Geographer of the United States**—Thomas Hutchins—appointment authority enacted

1785 **Land Grant**—land grant to schools—authorized

1785 **Land Sale Ordinance (general)**—enacted

1785 **Survey of Public Lands**—authorized

1830 **Fountain Pen Patent**—D. Hyde—Reading, Pa.

1830 **Timetable**—railroad timetable—advertised—Baltimore, Md.

1832 **School**—school supported by local taxation—opened—St. Petersburg, Fla.

1844 **Game Protection Society**—wildlife protection society—New York Sportsmen's Club —founded—New York City

1856 **Telegraph**—telegraph ticker that successfully printed type—patented—D. E. Hughes —Louisville, Ky.

1862 **Homestead Act**—homestead act—enacted

1865 **Lecture Series (endowed)**—Morse lectureship—Union Theological Seminary—New York City

1873 **Army School**—army school graduate (black)—H. O. Flipper—became cadet

1875 **Weights and Measures Standardization**— International Bureau of Weights and Measures—established

1899 **Automobile Speeding Arrest**—driver arrested for speeding—Jacob German—New York City

1899 **Physics**—national physics association— American Physical Society—formed—New York City

1904 **Carnegie Hero Fund Commission**—bylaws adopted

1909 **Ship**—battleship to visit an inland city— *Mississippi*—sailed to Natchez, Miss.

1918 **Ship**—warship propelled by electricity— *New Mexico*—commissioned

1925 **Chamber of Commerce**—Chamber of Commerce of the United States of America— headquarters dedicated—Washington, D.C.

1926 **Aviation—Legislation**—aviation legislation (national) dealing with the operation of civil aircraft—Air Commerce Act— enacted

1926 **Labor**—National Mediation Board—U.S. Board of Mediation—created

1927 **Aviation—Flights (transatlantic)**—transatlantic solo flight—takeoff—C. A. Lindbergh —New York City

1930 **Aviation—Flights**—airplane catapulted from a dirigible

1932 **Aviation—Flights (transatlantic)**—transatlantic solo flight by a woman—A. E. Putnam

1933 **Holiday**—Maritime Day—established— act of Congress

1939 **Airmail Service**—airmail transatlantic service—inaugurated

1939 **Aviation—Flights (transatlantic)**—Atlan Ocean scheduled air service—inaugur ed—*Yankee Clipper*

1939 **Television—Telecast**—bicycle race te cast—New York City

1939 **Television—Telecast**—telecast (pub over telephone wires—publicly display —New York City

1951 **Aviation—Pilot**—American ace (jet James Jabara

1953 **Hotel**—hotel to establish a heliport—F Worth, Tex.

1955 **Radar**—offshore radar warning statio launched

1956 **Atomic Bomb**—atomic fusion (thermo clear or hydrogen) bomb dropped from airplane—Bikini Atoll

1964 **Lighthouse**—lighthouse (atomic power —Baltimore Light, Baltimore Harbor, N —began operation

MAY 21

1819 **Bicycle**—bicycle velocipedes—used—N York City

1829 **Dry Dock**—federal dry docks—corn stone laid—Boston, Mass.

1832 **Democratic National Convention**—beg —Baltimore, Md.

1832 **Political Convention**—two-thirds rul enacted—Baltimore, Md.

1846 **Building**—building with a high steepl Trinity Church, New York City—dedica

1853 **Ship**—yacht to circumnavigate the worl *North Star*—first voyage began from N York City

1861 **Newspaper**—newspaper published by s diers in the field—*United States Americ Volunteer*—De Soto, Mo.

1863 **Seventh Day Adventist Church**—gene conference—organized

1877 **Telephone**—telephone used by a railr company—tested—Altoona, Pa.

1881 **American Red Cross**—organized—Wa ington, D.C.

1881 **Tennis Society**—tennis society (nation —United States Lawn Tennis Associat —formed—New York City

1881 **Treasury Department (U.S.)**—Register the Treasury who was a black—B. K. Br —began service

1888 **Crematory**—crematory (state)—authoriz —New York State

1891 **Prizefight**—prizefight timed by automa timer—Peter Jackson vs. J. J. Corbelt—C fornia Athletic Club, San Francisco, Ca

1893 **Newspaper**—newspaper with an illustr ed color-page—*World*—New York City

1894 **Research Institute**—anatomy research stitute—Wistar Institute of Anatomy a Biology—building dedicated—Philad phia, Pa.

1901 **Automobile Legislation**—state motor legislation—Connecticut

1919 Aviation—**Airship**—airship to land on a roof—Cleveland, Ohio

1922 **Radio Broadcast**—debate over the radio—WJH—Washington, D.C.

1925 **Court**—state supreme court composed entirely of women—case decided—Texas

1927 **Television—Telecast**—demonstration of a telecast before a large audience—L. S. O'-Roarke—New York City

1933 **Autogiro**—autogiro to tow a glider—J. M. Miller—Valley Stream, N.Y.

1939 **Submarine**—submarine refloated—*Squalus*—foundered—off Portsmouth, N.H.

1950 **Coal**—coal pipeline loops (experimental)—tested—Library, Pa.

1955 **Building**—atom-bomb-resistant federal building—dedicated—Washington, D.C.

1956 **Automaton**—automaton to operate by long-distance control—manufactured—Schenectady, N.Y.

1959 **Bowling Tournament**—bowling match in which white balls were used on black lanes—Brooklyn, New York City

MAY 24

1828 **Post Office**—post office building (U.S.)—authorized

1833 **Temperance Society**—national temperance convention—opened—Philadelphia, Pa.

1844 **Telegram**—telegram inaugurating commercial service—from Washington, D.C.

1862 **Telegraph**—army field telegraph used in warfare—Mechanicsville, Va.

1865 **Railroad Track**—railroad rails of Bessemer steel—rolled—Wyandotte, Mich.

1869 **Expedition**—exploration of the Grand Canyon of the Colorado—J. W. Powell

1870 **Railroad Excursion**—railroad excursion (transcontinental) of an organization—left Boston, Mass.

1873 **Postage Stamp**—departmental postage stamps used

1875 **Bankers' Association**—national bankers' association—American Bankers Association—organized

1879 **Geological Survey**—geological survey director (U.S.)—Clarence King—took office

1893 **Temperance Society**—Anti-Saloon League—Ohio Anti-Saloon League formed—Oberlin, Ohio

1899 **Garage** (public)—established—Boston, Mass.

1902 **Oil**—oil and gas magazine—*Oil Investors' Journal*—H. S. Reavis, founder and editor—published—Beaumont, Tex.

1911 **Library Society**—woman to become president of the American Library Association—T. H. W. Elmendorf

1913 **Farm Bureau**—appropriation—New York State

1913 **Strike**—strike settlement—mediated by United States Department of Labor

1918 **Medal**—Croix de Guerre awarded a bla[ck] American—Henry Johnson

1924 **Diplomatic Service**—Foreign Service of [the] United States—created

1931 **Railroad**—air-conditioned train—B[al]timore and Ohio Railroad Compan[y] Washington, D.C.–New York City

1935 **Baseball Game**—baseball game at night major-league teams—Cincinnati, Ohio

1935 **Spectrophotometer**—machine sold—Sc[he]nectady, N.Y.

1945 **Business**—Food-O-Mat installed—Ca[r]stadt, N.J.

1954 **Rocket**—rocket to exceed a 150-mile a[lti]tude—Viking XI—White Sands, N.Mex.

1954 **Sidewalk (traveling)**—sidewalk (traveli[ng] in a railroad station—Jersey City, N.J.

1959 **Building**—house with a built-in nucle[ar] bomb shelter—exhibited—Pleasant Hi[ll] Pa.

1960 **Satellite**—surveillance satellite that w[as] successful—*Midas II*—launched—Ca[pe] Canaveral, Fla.

1969 **Airmail Service**—rocket (steam-driven) carry mail—launched—Las Cruces, N.M[ex.]

MAY 25

1721 **Insurance**—fire insurance agent—Jo[hn] Copson—Philadelphia, Pa.—adverti[se]ment

1793 **Catholic Priest**—Catholic priest ordain[ed] in the United States—S. T. Badin—B[al]timore, Md.

1804 **Distilling Book**—*American Distiller*—pr[ef]ace dated—Bristol, Pa.

1825 **Unitarian Church**—national organizati[on] of the Unitarian Churches of the Uni[ted] States and Canada—organized—Bost[on] Mass.

1844 **Gas Engine**—patent—Stuart Perry—N[ew] York City

1844 **Telegram**—news dispatch telegram—fr[om] Washington, D.C.

1863 **Bank**—national bank—National Bank [of] Davenport—subscriptions opened[—] Davenport, Iowa

1880 **Cattle Club**—cattle club (Jersey cattle[)—] American Jersey Cattle Club—incorpor[at]ed

1895 **Golf Book**—golf book—*Golf in America[—]* published—New York City

1898 **American Expeditionary Force**—Americ[an] Expeditionary Force—sailed—San Fr[an]cisco, Calif.

1903 **Railroad**—railroad operated by an elect[ric] third-rail system—Scranton, Pa.

1917 **World War I**—American troop conting[ent] to land in France—arrived—Rouen, Fran[ce]

1918 **Nursing School**—Army School of Nurs[ing] —authorized

1926 **Catholic Church**—Catholic church rais[ed] to the dignity of a basilica—dedicated[—] Lackawanna, N.Y.

MAY 28

1734 Fish Protection—fish legislation—enacted—New York City

1754 War (colonial)—bloodshed in the French and Indian War—Uniontown, Pa.

1796 Debt Legislation (federal)—enacted—exemption from prison

1870 Philatelic Auction—philatelic auction—New York City

1879 Labor Legislation—labor law prohibiting the employment of women—enacted—Illinois

1881 Pure Food Legislation—pure food and drug legislation (state)—enacted—New York

1913 Congress (U.S.)—Senate—whip—J. H. Lewis (Democrat)—appointed

1917 World War I—American troops to land in England—left New York City

1922 Orchestra—radio orchestra—Detroit, Mich.

1924 Border Patrol—border patrol organization authorized

1925 Radio Facsimile Transmission—radio facsimile long-distance transmission of a medical subject—New York City

1929 Motion Picture—talking picture entirely in color—*On with the Show*—exhibited—New York City

1931 Autogiro—Flights—transcontinental autogiro flight—J. M. Miller—arrived—San Diego, Calif.—from Philadelphia, Pa.

1932 Aviation—Airport—airport manager (woman) appointed—Port Bucyrus, Ohio

1934 Bank—bank payments to depositors of a closed insured bank—East Peoria, Ill.—suspended business

1939 Degrees (academic and honorary)—Master of Hebrew Literature degree awarded a woman—H. H. Levinthal—New York City

1953 Motion Picture—animated three-dimensional cartoon in Technicolor (modern)—Walt Disney—premiere—Hollywood, Calif.

1958 Presbyterian Church—moderator of the United Presbyterian Church—elected—T. M. Taylor—Pittsburgh, Pa.

1959 Rocket—animals fired into space and rescued from a rocket

1962 Newspaper—newspaper reproduced commercially and regularly by radio facsimile—*Wall Street Journal* (San Francisco edition)—regular daily operation begun

1975 Bird—whooping crane born in captivity—Laurel, Md.

1980 Army School—woman cadet to receive a commission—Ms. Hollen—West Point, N.Y.

MAY 29

1827 Nautical School—established—Nantucket, Mass.

1844 President (U.S.)—President who was "dark horse" candidate—J. K. Polk—nominated—Baltimore, Md.

1883 Baseball Game—baseball game at night preliminary test—Fort Wayne, Ind.

1884 Animal Industry Bureau (U.S.)—Bureau Animal Industry—established

1909 Court—domestic relations court—authorized—New York

1910 Aviation—Races—airplane to race a train—G.H. Curtiss

1916 Flag—President's flag—adopted

1918 American Expeditionary Force—American Expeditionary Force Air Service chief—M. Patrick—appointed

1918 Aviation—Pilot—pilot to receive the Congressional Medal of Honor—presentation—Phoenix, Ariz.

1921 Novel—Pulitzer Prize award to a woman for a novel—E. N. J. Wharton—announced—New York City

1931 Autogiro—Flights—autogiro transcontinental flight made by a woman—Amelia Earhart—takeoff, Newark, N.J.

1933 Money—gold standard abrogation—authorized

1935 Narcotics—narcotics sanatorium (federal)—Lexington, Ky.—patients received

1951 Aviation—Flights—North Pole flight in single-engine airplane—C. F. Blair

1962 Baseball Coach—baseball coach (black) the major leagues—John O'Neil—hired—Chicago Cubs

1964 Postage Stamp—brothers to be pictured individual postage stamps—J. F. Kennedy—5-cent blue-gray—issued

1967 Postage Stamp—brothers to be pictured individual postage stamps—J. F. Kennedy—13-cent brown—issued

1969 Criminal—woman on the "ten most wanted" list—Ruth Eisemann-Schier—convicted in Decatur, Ga.

1971 Automobile Racer—automobile racer win over $200,000 in a race—Al Unser—Indianapolis, Ind.

1977 Automobile Racer—automobile racer win the Indianapolis 500 four times—A. Foyt, Jr.—Indianapolis, Ind.—fourth time

1977 Automobile Racer—woman driver to compete in the Indianapolis 500—Janet Guthrie—Indianapolis, Ind.

MAY 30

1650 Corporation—corporate body—chartered—Cambridge, Mass.

1806 Duel—duel in which a future President the United States participated—Andrew Jackson—Red River, Ky.

1821 Fire Hose—of rubber-lined cotton web patented—James Boyd—Boston, Mass.

1848 Arts and Science Society—woman elected to the American Academy of Arts and Sciences—Maria Mitchell

1819 Tightrope—woman tightrope performer—appearance—Mme Adolphe—New York City

1847 Postal Service—ocean mail contracts—service started

1847 Ship—steamship passenger line between United States ports and Europe to fly the American flag—*Washington*—sailed—New York City

1860 Army—signal corps—established

1861 Civil War—Confederate officer killed in the Civil War—J. Q. Marr—Fairfax Court House, Va.

1861 Civil War—skirmish in the Civil War—Fairfax Court House, Va.

1869 Voting Machine—electric vote recorder—patented—T. A. Edison—Boston, Mass.

1880 Prizefighter—bareknuckle world heavyweight champion (American)—Paddy Ryan—won title near Colliers, W.Va.

1880 Telephone—pay station telephone service—New Haven, Conn.

1881 Horse Race—American-bred horse to win the English Derby—Iroquois

1886 Arbitration—state board of mediation and arbitration—organized—New York State

1887 Armor-Plate Contract (U.S. Navy)—award—Bethlehem Iron Company—Bethlehem, Pa.

1887 Police—police bureau of identification—Bertillon system of identification used—Chicago, Ill.

1888 Seismograph—installed—Lick Observatory—Mount Hamilton, Calif.

1890 Census—census compiled by machines

1896 Prizefighter—American lightweight champion of the world—"Kid" Lavigne—won title

1897 Rock Wool Factory—opened—Alexandria, Ind.

1898 Streetcar—interurban streetcar line—Anderson, Ind.–Alexandra, Ind.

1901 Motorcycle—motorcycle with built-in gas engine—publicly demonstrated

1903 Zoological Laboratory (U.S.)—zoological laboratory (U.S.)—for the study of the parasites of livestock—B. H. Ransom put in charge of division

1909 Automobile Race—transcontinental automobile race—New York City–Seattle, Wash.—started

1910 Degrees (academic and honorary)—Master of Arts degree in aeronautics—G. C. Loening—Columbia University, New York City

1911 Insurance—group insurance policy—Equitable Life Assurance Company—New York City

1915 Aviation—Airship—airship of the United States Navy—DNI—purchase contract

1919 Forest Service—forest service aerial patrol—established—Department of Agriculture

1923 Woman—woman internal revenue collector—M. G. Reinecke—served

1924 Border Patrol—border patrol organizati—under Immigration and Naturalizati Service—established

1928 Woman—woman passport division chie R. B. Shipley—took office

1931 Autogiro—autogiro of the U.S. Governm —delivered to Anacostia station, Washi ton, D.C.

1933 Canal—Great Lakes to the Gulf waterw —tow left New Orleans, La.

1939 Television—Telecast—prizefight to be te vised—New York City—Lou Nova–M Baer

1942 Insurance—health insurance law (state effective—Rhode Island

1942 Navy "E" Award—Navy "E" certificate meritorious service presented to an insti tion of higher learning—University of W consin—Madison, Wis.

1944 Dentist—woman dentist in the U.S. Nav S. G. Krout—Great Lakes, Ill.—began s vice

1947 Glass—photosensitive glass—announc —Corning, N.Y.

1949 Microfilm—magazine on microfilm offe to subscribers—*Newsweek*—New Y City

1951 Titanium—titanium plant fully self-c tained and fully integrated—opened—H derson, Nev.

1953 Aviation—airline to install rear-facing p senger seats—first flight—Burbank, Ca New York City

1955 Battery—solar energy battery—shipm made—Chicago, Ill.

1957 Runner—runner (American) to run a m in less than four minutes—Don Bowde Stockton, Calif.

1957 Wheelchair Athletics—national whe chair games—Adelphi College, Gar City, N.Y.

1960 Police—parking-meter enforcement d sion—appointed by R. F. Wagner—N York City

1969 Catholic Priest—deacon (married) dained—M. G. Cole—Rochester, N.Y.

1975 Theological School—theological sch (major) woman dean—S. M. Teselle—t office—Nashville, Tenn.

JUNE 2

1685 Impeachment — impeachment — Nic More—Philadelphia, Pa.

1857 Sewing Machine—chain-stitch sing thread sewing machine (practical)—p ented—J. E. A. Gibbs—Mill Point, Va.

1883 Baseball Game—baseball game at nigh Fort Wayne, Ind.

1883 Elevated Railroad—electric elevated r road—Chicago, Ill.

1886 Wedding—White House wedding of President—Grover Cleveland—Fran Folsom

9 Electric Power Plant—alternating current hydroelectric power plant to operate over a long distance—supplied current—Portland, Oreg.

2 Initiative and Referendum—Oregon—authorized—constitutional amendment

9 Novel—two-time winner of the Pulitzer Prize for a novel—Booth Tarkington—1918 award (first)

4 American Indians—citizenship statute for American Indians—enacted

0 Births—child born on a vessel passing through the Panama Canal

0 Museum—maritime museum—Newport News, Va.

0 Woman—woman Presbyterian elder—S. E. Dickson—Cincinnati, Ohio—elected

3 Swimming Pool in the White House—accepted—Washington, D.C.

1 Ship—aircraft carrier escort—*Long Island*—commissioned

JUNE 3

0 President (U.S.)—President to reside in Washington, D.C.—John Adams

0 Library—mechanics' library—opened—New York City

3 Ship—clipper ship—*Ann McKim*—launched—Baltimore, Md.

6 Screw—screw machine—patent—Cullen Whipple—Providence, R.I.

1 Civil War—skirmish in the Civil War—Philippi, W.Va.

3 Oratorio—oratorio by an American—*Oratorio of St. Peter*—performed—Portland, Me.

8 Medical Society—laryngological society (national)—American Laryngological Association—founded—Buffalo, N.Y.

4 Political Convention—national nominating convention presided over by a black American—Chicago, Ill.

1 Zoological Laboratory (U.S.)—zoological laboratory (U.S.) for the study of the parasites of livestock—termed Zoological Laboratory—Washington, D.C.

8 Medal—"campaign medal"—"Dewey medal"—authorized

9 Movable Church—Chapel of the Transfiguration—consecrated—Conanicut Island, R.I.

3 Election Law—primary election (statewide)—enacted—Wisconsin

6 Army—Army Veterinary Corps—established

6 Army—Reserve Officers Training Corps—authorized

6 Supreme Court (U.S.)—associate justice of the Supreme Court who was Jewish—L. D. Brandeis—sworn in

8 Novel—novel to win the Pulitzer prize in letters—award announced—New York City

1921 Immigration—immigration quota act—effective

1925 Aviation—Airship—airship with an enclosed cabin—tested—Akron, Ohio

1932 Baseball Player—baseball player to hit four consecutive home runs in one game—Lou Gehrig—Philadelphia, Pa.

1937 Wedding—American woman married to a former king of Great Britain—W. W. Simpson—Monts, France

1940 Representative (U.S.)—woman elected to serve in both the House of Representatives and the Senate—M. C. Smith of Maine—began service in the House

1948 Telescope—telescope lens measuring 200 inches in diameter—officially dedicated—Mount Palomar, Calif.

1949 Naval Academy—black midshipman in the U.S. Naval Academy to graduate—W. A. Brown

1949 Treasury Department (U.S.)—woman treasurer of the United States—G. N. Clark—nominated

1953 Cabinet (U.S.)—Cabinet conference telecast—Washington, D.C.

1955 President (U.S.)—President to fly in a twin-engined airplane—D. D. Eisenhower

1958 Methodist Church—black minister with two white congregations—J. R. Washington—Newfield and West Newfield, Me.

1959 Air Force Academy (U.S.)—Air Force Academy—first class graduated—Colorado Springs, Colo.

1965 Astronaut—astronaut (American) to maneuver outside a satellite—E. H. White—*Gemini IV*—launched, Cape Kennedy, Fla.

1965 Astronaut—two-man spaceflight (American) of 62 orbits—*Gemini IV*—launched, Cape Kennedy, Fla.

1972 Rabbi—woman rabbi—S. J. Priesand—ordained—Cincinnati, Ohio

JUNE 4

1674 Horse Race—horse race prohibition legislation—Massachusetts

1777 Loan—loan for war purposes received—by a central government

1811 Secession—secession was first mentioned in Congress

1816 Ship—steamboat (double-decked)—*Washington*—launched—Wheeling, Va.

1820 Church—mariners' church—built—New York City

1833 Ship—clipper ship—*Ann McKim*—launched—Baltimore, Md.

1845 Opera—opera by an American composer (important)—*Leonora*—presented—Philadelphia, Pa.

1867 Ship—side-wheeler transpacific steamer—*Celestial Empire* (later named *China*)—trial run

1890 Employment Service—state employment service—office opened—Toledo, Ohio

1912 **Children's Bureau (U.S.)**—chief—J. C. Lathrop—appointed

1912 **Labor Legislation**—minimum-wage law—enacted—Massachusetts

1917 **Newspaper**—editorial award of a Pulitzer Prize in journalism and letters—New York *Tribune*—New York City

1917 **Newspaper Reporter**—newspaper reporter to receive a Pulitzer Prize for reporting—H. B. Swope—announced—New York City

1920 **Army Camp**—Army Citizens' Military Training Camp—camps authorized—National Defense Act—enacted

1920 **Army Officer**—chaplain (chief) of the United States Army—office—authorized

1920 **Army Officer**—woman with rank corresponding to major—J. C. Stimson—rank conferred

1931 **Glider**—**Flights**—rocket glider flight—W. G. Swan—Atlantic City, N.J.

1934 **Factory**—factories operated by the United States Government—project commenced—Millville, Mass.

1934 **Ship**—aircraft carrier—*Ranger*—delivered

1935 **Glass**—invisible-glass installation—patent

1938 **Aviation**—**Passenger**—woman to fly entirely around the world by commercial heavier-than-air plane—Marjorie Shuler—left Southampton, England

1942 **Medal**—Navy Cross awarded to a Coast Guard officer in World War II—M. D. Jester

1944 **Submarine**—submarine captured and boarded on the high seas—U-505

1946 **Radio Facsimile Transmission**—facsimile transmitted to a moving train—demonstrated—Baltimore, Md.–Washington, D.C.

1957 **Coal**—commercial coal pipeline—in operation—Eastlake, Ohio

1980 **Army School**—Jewish woman graduate of the U.S. Military Academy (West Point)—Donna Maller—commissioned

1980 **Secret Service**—Secret Service female special agent killed in the line of duty—J. Y. Cross—Los Angeles, Calif.

JUNE 5

1730 **Freemasons**—Provincial Grand Master (Masonic)—Daniel Coxe—deputized

1785 **Methodist College**—Cokesbury College—Abingdon, Md.—foundation sermon delivered

1794 **Neutrality Regulation**—enacted

1855 **American Party**—organized—Philadelphia, Pa.

1855 **Hospital**—Jewish hospital—Mount Sinai Hospital—opened—New York City

1865 **Safe Deposit Vault**—opened—New York City

1877 **Lawyer**—Japanese lawyer—Takeo Kikuchi—received LL.B. degree—Boston, Mass.

1877 **Oleomargarine**—oleomargarine legislati (state)—enacted—New York

1914 **Dental School**—dental hygienists' course Fones Clinic—Bridgeport, Conn.—grad⋅ tion

1918 **Newspaper**—Pulitzer Prize award to newspaper—New York *Times*—present —New York City

1920 **Labor Department (U.S.)**—women's bure —organized

1922 **Woman**—woman automotive engineer Marie Luhring—received M.E. degree New York City

1930 **Colorscope**—public demonstration—N⋅ York City

1933 **Money**—gold standard abrogation—ena ed

1938 **Voice Mechanism**—voice mechanism ⋅ pable of creating the complex sounds speech—exhibited—New York City

1939 **Museum**—museum devoted exclusively papermaking—opened—Cambridge Ma

1940 **Automobile Tire**—synthetic rubber tir⋅ exhibited—Akron, Ohio

1946 **Sponge**—oxidized cellulose (sponge) medical and surgical use—marketed—I troit, Mich.

1951 **Television**—**Telecast**—prizefight (hea weight championship bout) telecast co⋅ to-coast—Walcott vs. Charles—Ph⋅ delphia, Pa.

1952 **Prizefight Referee**—heavyweight-cha pionship-prizefight black referee—Z⋅ Clayton—Walcott vs. Charles—Ph⋅ delphia, Pa.

1963 **Air Force Academy (U.S.)**—Air Fo⋅ Academy graduates (black)—C. V. B⋅ and I. S. Payne, IV—were graduated

JUNE 6

1639 **Ordnance**—gunpowder mill—operate⋅ Edward Rawson—Pecoit, Mass.

1788 **Cotton**—cotton goods to be trademarke⋅ manufactured—Beverly, Mass.

1815 **Church of the United Brethren in Chris** conference of elected delegates—Mo Pleasant, Pa.

1829 **Horticultural Society**—horticultural s⋅ ety (permanent)—exhibition opened public

1833 **President (U.S.)**—President to ride o⋅ railroad train—Andrew Jackson

1854 **Bank**—clearinghouse—New York Clea⋅ House incorporated

1863 **Bank**—national bank—directors electe⋅ National Bank of Davenport, Iowa

1877 **Degrees (academic and honorary)**—Do⋅ of Philosophy degree awarded to a wom

1882 **Electric Flatiron**—patented—H. W. S⋅ —New York City

1889 **Fellowship**—fellowship (graduate) aw⋅ ed by a women's college—Bryn Mawr C lege—Bryn Mawr, Pa.

90 Polo Club—polo association (national)—United States Polo Association—formed—New York City

91 Expedition—polar expedition of which a woman was a member—Peary Expedition—sailed—New York City

04 Health Society—National Tuberculosis Association—organized—Atlantic City, N.J.

07 Jewish College—Jewish nonsectarian college—Dropsie College—chartered—Philadelphia, Pa.

25 City (Lilliputian city)—built—Springfield, Mo.

28 College—university for blacks (Catholic)—Xavier University—New Orleans, La.—degrees conferred

32 Gasoline Tax—gasoline tax (federal)

33 Employment Service—employment service (U.S.E.S.)—created

33 Motion Picture Theater—drive-in motion picture theater—opened—Camden, N.J.

34 Securities and Exchange Commission (U.S.)—created

36 Gasoline—aviation gasoline—produced—Paulsboro, N.J.

38 Recreational Ranching Course—degree conferred—University of Wyoming—Laramie, Wyo.

41 Ship—Navy vessel constructed as a minelayer — *Terror* — launched — Philadelphia, Pa.

42 Aviation — Parachute — nylon-parachute jump—Hartford, Conn.

49 Television—Telecast—surgical operation televised on a closed circuit in color—Atlantic City, N.J.

55 Postage Stamp—certified-mail stamp—issued—Washington, D.C.

55 President (U.S.)—President telecast in color—D. D. Eisenhower—West Point, N.Y.

56 Degrees (academic and honorary)—Master of Arts degree in Sacred Music—conferred—New York City

62 Air Force Academy (U.S.)—Air Force Academy graduate (American Indian)—Leo Johnson—was graduated

68 Presidential Candidate—presidential candidate assassinated while campaigning—R. F. Kennedy—Los Angeles, Calif.

79 Railroad—railroad train operated exclusively by women—Port Washington, L.I., N.Y., to Pennsylvania station, New York City—in service

JUNE 7

75 United States—"United States"—union proclaimed

80 Diplomatic Service—consuls of the United States appointed after the adoption of the Constitution

1800 Supreme Court (U.S.)—Chief Justice of the United States who had been a representative in Congress—John Marshall of Virginia—congressional service ended

1801 Booksellers' Association—American Company of Booksellers—organized—New York City

1854 Young Men's Christian Association—international convention—Boston, Mass.

1862 Treason—citizen of the United States to be tried for treason, convicted, and hanged—W. B. Mumford—hanged—New Orleans, La.

1870 Railroad Signal System—railroad signal system (automatic electric block)—patent—T. S. Hall—Stamford, Conn.

1876 Theological School—theological school to admit women—B. D. degree awarded—Boston, Mass.

1882 Tariff—tariff commission—authorized

1883 Tennis Match—intercollegiate lawn tennis match—Hartford, Conn.

1887 Typesetting Machine—monotype—patent—Tolbert Lanston—Washington, D.C.

1892 Baseball Player—baseball pinch hitter—J. J. Doyle—Brooklyn, N.Y.

1892 Bicycle Tire—bicycle tire (cord)—patent—J. F. Palmer—Chicago, Ill.

1892 Political Convention—political party national delegates (women)—T. A. Jenkins and C. G. Carleton—Minneapolis, Minn.—convention opened

1896 Rowing—transatlantic trip by rowboat—left—New York City

1898 Social Democracy of America—national convention—Chicago, Ill.

1905 Railroad Car—mail car (steel)—in service

1908 Newspaper—newspaper with an aviation section—*Inquirer*—Philadelphia, Pa.

1913 Permalloy—developed—G. W. Elmen—New York City

1918 Births—world war baby—born

1931 Autogiro—Flights—autogiro transcontinental flight made by a woman—Amelia Earhart—landed, Los Angeles, Calif.

1938 Television—Telecast—play to be televised with its original Broadway cast—*Susan and God*

1939 Visiting Celebrities—King and Queen of Great Britain—King George VI arrived—Niagara Falls, N.Y.

1942 World War II—American general missing in action in World War II—C. L. Tinker—Midway

1942 World War II—American territory occupied by the Japanese—Attu and Kiska, Alaska

1946 Naval Officer—admiral (four stars) who did not attend the U.S. Naval Academy—Ben Moreell—nominated

1949 Public Health—public health service (U.S.) assistant surgeon general (woman)—Lucile Petry—appointed

1949 World War II—Japanese balloon casualties—congressional award made

1953 Television—Telecast—color network telecast in compatible color

1954 Microbiology Laboratory—dedicated—New Brunswick, N.J.

1955 President (U.S.)—President telecast in color—D. D. Eisenhower—program on view

1955 Television—Telecast—President to appear on television in color—D. D. Eisenhower

1965 Astronant—two-man spaceflight (American) of 62 orbits—*Gemini IV*—landed, Atlantic Ocean

1980 Solar Power Plant—solar-cell power plant —dedicated—Utah

JUNE 8

1786 Ice Cream—ice cream—advertised—New York City

1830 Ship—warship to circumnavigate the globe—*Vincennes*—arrived—New York City

1869 Vacuum Cleaner—suction-type vacuum cleaner—patented—I. W. McGaffey—Chicago, Ill.

1872 Postal Card—authorized

1872 Post Office—Post Office Department of the United States—became executive department—act passed

1872 Postal Service—mail fraud legislation—enacted—Washington, D.C.

1872 Postal Service—postal fraud order—authorized

1911 Aviation—Legislation—aviation legislation (state)—enacted—Connecticut

1911 Aviation—License—pilot's license issued by the Aero Club of America—awarded—G. H. Curtiss

1917 World War I—American troops to land in England—arrived

1921 Hospital—leper hospital—reopened—Carville, La.

1940 Element—element 93—neptunium—discovery announced

1948 Marine Corps—black commissioned officer —J. E. Rudder

1953 Locomotive—gas-turbine propane-fueled locomotive

1959 Airmail Service—missile mail (official)—landed—Jacksonville, Fla.

1961 Baseball Team—baseball team to hit 4 consecutive runs in 1 inning—Cincinnati Reds —Cincinnati, Ohio

1966 Coast Guard Academy—black graduate—M. J. Smith, Jr.—New London, Conn.

1975 College—educational hosteling network—Elderhostel—offered at New England College—Henniker, N.H.

1979 Coast Guard (U.S.)—woman to command a naval ship on regular patrol—S. I. Moritz—*Cape Current*—Straits of Florida

JUNE 9

1628 Deportation—Thomas Morton—Plymou Colony

1772 Protestant Church—Protestant church west of Pennsylvania—communion servi —Schoenbrunn, Ohio

1772 Revolutionary War—naval attack—Pro dence, R.I.

1783 War Veterans' Society—Society of the C cinnati—organization effected

1790 Book—book entered for copyright—*T Philadelphia Spelling Book*—registerec Philadelphia, Pa.

1846 Senator (U.S.)—senator elected on an ɛ tislavery ticket—J. P. Hale—New Han shire

1880 Greenback Labor Party—national convɛ tion—Chicago, Ill.

1902 Restaurant—restaurant with an automɛ arrangement for vending food—openec Philadelphia, Pa.

1909 Automobile Transcontinental Trip—tra continental automobile trip by a womar left New York City for San Francisco, Ca

1925 Degrees (academic and honorary)—deg conferred by radio—University of Iowɛ Iowa City, Iowa

1943 Army Officer—army chaplain of Japanɛ ancestry—Masao Yamada—assigned camp Shelby, Miss.

1949 Treasury Department (U.S.)—woman trɛ surer of the United States—G. N. Clarl confirmed

1959 Submarine—ballistic missile submarinɛ *George Washington*—launched—Grot Conn.

JUNE 10

1682 Tornado—tornado of which there is ɛ record

1760 Medical Legislation—law to regulate practice of medicine (actually enforced New York City

1806 Horse—horse to trot 1 mile in less thaɪ minutes—Yankey—New York City

1809 Ship—steamboat to make an ocean vc age—*Phoenix*—sailed from New York C for Philadelphia, Pa.

1842 Expedition—scientific expedition fitted by the United States Government—Will expedition—returned to New York City

1851 Newspaper—French daily newspaper (s cessful)—*Courrier des Etats Unis*—p lished—New York City

1854 Naval Academy—naval academy (U.S. Annapolis, Md.—first graduation

1879 Medical Society—laryngological soci (national)—annual meeting

1884 Medal—Albert Medal presented to a tive-born American—J. B. Eads

1902 Envelope—envelope with an outlook window—patented—A. F. Callahaɪ Chicago, Ill.

1946 **Naval Officer**—admiral (four stars) who did not attend the U.S. Naval Academy—Ben Moreell—confirmed

1955 **Aviation—Airplane**—jet magnesium airplane—flown

1970 **Army Officer**—generals who were brother and sister—E. P. Hoisington and P. M. Hoisington—E. P. Hoisington sworn in

1978 **Church of Jesus Christ of Latter-Day Saints**—black ordained to the priesthood—Joseph Freeman, Jr.—Salt Lake City, Utah

1948 **Jockey**—jockey to win the triple crov twice—Belmont Park, Elmont, N.Y.

1950 **Nuclear Engineering College Course**—I leigh, N.C.—students enrolled

1953 **Advertisement**—three-dimensional nev paper advertisement—*Daily Freeman* Waukesha, Wis.

1956 **Flag**—Army flag (official)—established

1978 **Television—Telecast**—congressional si sion proceedings telecast—Washingt(D.C.

JUNE 12

1775 **Revolutionary War**—naval battle of the Revolution—*Margaretta*—Machias, Me.

1796 **Unitarian Minister**—Society of Unitarian Christians—organized—Philadelphia, Pa.

1800 **Navy**—navy yard—purchased—Portsmouth, N.H.

1845 **Colonial Government**—government on the Pacific Coast—Oregon—first governor—George Abernethy

1849 **Gas Mask**—gas mask—patented—L. P. Haslett—Louisville, Ky.

1880 **Monument**—obelisk to be brought to the United States—loaded at Alexandria, Egypt

1900 **Trapshooting Tournament**—trapshoot (Grand American) with clay targets—Interstate Park, N.Y.

1912 **Senator (U.S.)**—senators collectively "elected by the people"—Senate passed bill

1913 **Motion Picture**—animated cartoon (present technique)—*The Dachshund*—released

1918 **Aviation—Airplane Bombing**—airplane bombing raid by an American air unit

1920 **Farmer Labor Party**—organized—Chicago, Ill.

1929 **Airmail**—airmail pickup from a steamer at sea—S.S. *Leviathan*

1930 **Prizefight**—championship prizefight decided on a foul—Sharkey vs. Schmeling—New York City

1933 **Electrobasograph**—exhibited—R. P. Schwartz—Milwaukee, Wis.

1936 **Radio Station**—radio station with 500,000-watt power—Pittsburgh, Pa.

1939 **Degrees (academic and honorary)**—doctor of philosophy in accounting—degree conferred—J. W. McMahan—University of Illinois—Urbana, Ill.

1939 **Hall of Fame**—hall of fame (baseball)—dedicated—Cooperstown, N.Y.

1946 **Aviation—Flights (transcontinental)**—transcontinental round-trip airplane flight within one day—Shooting Star—March Field, Calif.-Andrews Field, Md.

1947 **Golf Champion**—woman golfer (American-born) to win the British Women's Amateur Golf tournament—B. D. Zaharias

JUNE 13

1774 **Slavery**—nonimportation of slaves ac enacted—Rhode Island

1825 **Law Codification (state)**—promulgated Louisiana

1854 **Chinese Students**—college graduate Yung Wing—Yale University, New Hav(Conn.

1862 **Army Officer**—chaplain (Catholic) ₴ pointed by the President—F. E. Boyle

1881 **Ship**—steamboat to employ elect lights—*Jeannette*—sank

1889 **Niagara Falls**—utilization of Niagara Fa waterpower (large-scale)—Cataract C(struction Company—incorporated

1890 **Freemasons**—Grotto—charter granted

1893 **Horse Race**—horse race of 1,000 miles started—Chadron, Neb.

1906 **College**—technical college for womer Simmons College—Boston, Mass.—cla graduated

1906 **Consumer Protection**—consumer prot« tion (federal law)—enacted

1910 **Aviation—Flights**—airplane round trip—one day between two cities—C. K. Han ton—New York City-Philadelphia, Pa.

1912 **Nursing School**—university school of nu ing—University of Minnesota—Minnea₽ lis, Minn.—class graduated

1913 **Public Defender's Office**—created—I Angeles, Calif.

1917 **Agricultural Soil Conference**—of imp tance—International Congress of S Science—Washington, D. C.

1925 **Television—Telecast**—telecast of an (ject in motion—Washington, D.C.

1927 **Flag**—flag displayed from the right hand the Statue of Liberty

1928 **Railroad Car**—rail detector car—testec Beacon, N.Y.

1933 **Electric Lighting**—sodium vapor lamps installed—Schenectady, N.Y.

1933 **Federal Savings and Loan Association** authorized

1933 **Home Owners' Loan Corporation**—auth ized

1937 **Whist Tournament**—international wh tournament—began in Budapest, Hunga

1940 **Aviation—License**—Civil Aeronautics ᴀ ministration honorary license—authoriz

42 **Army School**—army training school—to teach security troops—opened—Concord, Mass.

42 **Saboteurs**—saboteurs executed—4 landed at Amagansett, L.I., N.Y.

44 **Wire Recorder**—patented—Marvin Camras

66 **College**—liberal arts college for police and correction officers established by a city—College of Police Science, New York City—first graduation

67 **Supreme Court (U.S.)**—Associate Justice of the Supreme Court who was a black—Thurgood Marshall—appointed

70 **Beauty Pageant**—black contestant in the Miss America pageant—C. A. Browne—selected at Davenport, Iowa

JUNE 14

23 **Breach of Promise Suit**—instituted—Greville Pooley—Charles City County, Va.

42 **Education**—compulsory education law—Massachusetts

77 **Flag**—American flag—formally adopted—Philadelphia, Pa.

34 **Diving Suit**—(practical) for submarine diving—patented—Leonard Norcross—Dixfield, Me.

34 **Sandpaper Patent**—Isaac Fischer, Jr.—Springfield, Vt.

54 **Entomologist**—federal entomologist—Townend Glover—commissioned

81 **Piano Player**—piano player—patented—John McTammany, Jr.—Cambridge, Mass.

84 **Wire**—legislation (state) requiring wires to be placed underground—New York State

99 **College**—Catholic college for women—College of Notre Dame of Maryland—Baltimore, Md.—commencement

01 **Golf Tournament**—professional open championship—under rules of United States Golf Association—Hamilton, Mass.

15 **Protestant Church**—Protestant church for lepers—dedicated—Carville, La.

17 **Marine Corps**—marine regiment in France—left New York City

17 **World War I**—marine regiment to land in Europe in World War I—C. A. Doyen—sailed from New York City

19 **Aviation—Flights (transatlantic)**—transatlantic nonstop flight from America—John Alcock and A. W. Brown—started—St. John's, Newfoundland

22 **President (U.S.)**—President to broadcast by radio—W. G. Harding—Baltimore, Md.

27 **Monument**—monument to the American flag—dedicated—Pittsburgh, Pa.

29 **Aviation**—Air-rail passenger transcontinental daily service—began in New York City

37 **Holiday**—Flag Day—legal holiday—Pennsylvania

1938 **Chlorophyll**—chlorophyll—patented—Benjamin Gruskin

1942 **Ordnance**—bazooka rocket gun—produced—Bridgeport, Conn.

1951 **Computer**—electronic computer (commercial)—dedicated—Philadelphia, Pa.

1951 **Television—Telecast**—birth (human) to be televised (closed-circuit)

1952 **Submarine**—atomic-powered submarine—*Nautilus*—keel laid—Groton, Conn.

1954 **Civil defense**—civil defense test (nationwide)

JUNE 15

1752 **Lightning Demonstration**—Benjamin Franklin—Philadelphia, Pa.

1775 **Army Officer**—general (Continental Army)—George Washington

1785 **Money**—copper cents minted by a state—Vermont—authorized coinage

1835 **Patent Commissioner**—H. L. Ellsworth—appointed

1844 **Rubber**—vulcanized rubber—patented—Charles Goodyear—New York City

1858 **Stone Crusher**—of value—patent—E. W. Blake—New Haven, Conn.

1859 **Surgical Operation**—mastoid operation—performed—Brooklyn, N.Y.—J. C. Hutchison

1867 **Surgical Operation**—gallstone operation—J. S. Bobbs—Indianapolis, Ind.

1869 **Celluloid**—patent—J. W. and I. S. Hyatt—Albany, N.Y.

1869 **Prizefight**—international fight, with bare knuckles—Mike McCoole–Tom Allen—St. Louis, Mo.

1871 **Law School**—law school (university) to admit women—St. Louis Law School—P. W. Couzins—graduated—St. Louis, Mo.

1876 **Political Convention**—presidential convention (national) addressed by a woman—S. A. Spencer—Cincinnati, Ohio

1877 **Army School**—army school graduate (black)—H. O. Flipper—graduated

1891 **Immigration**—immigration bureau superintendent—W. D. Owen—appointment

1893 **Nurses' Society**—society for superintendents of nursing schools—American Society of Superintendents of Training Schools for Nurses—founded—Chicago, Ill.

1894 **Museum** — commercial museum — Philadelphia Commercial Museum—authorized

1901 **Dental Society**—orthodontists' society—American Society of Orthodontists—constitution adopted

1909 **Baseball**—cork-center baseball—patented—B. F. Shibe

1915 **Money**—$50 gold pieces minted by the United States—produced—San Francisco, Calif.

1917 **Army Camp**—army camp for training black officers—established—Fort Des Moines—Des Moines, Iowa

1917 **College**—university for blacks (Catholic)—diploma issued—New Orleans, La.

1920 **Wedding**—wedding broadcast—W. E. Ebert and J. R. Wichman—Detroit, Mich.

1927 **Radio Telephone**—two-way radio conversation between a brakeman in a caboose of a moving freight train and an engineer in the cab of a locomotive—Schenectady, N.Y.

1928 **Aviation—Airship**—dirigible transfer of mail to a train—effected—Belleville, Ill.

1929 **Brokerage**—curb exchange—to transact more business than the New York Stock Exchange—New York Curb

1938 **Baseball Player**—major-league baseball player to pitch two successive no-hit, no-run games—J. Vander Meer—New York City

1938 **Railroad Car**—car with fluorescent lighting—first fluorescent tail sign—used—*Twentieth Century Limited*

1951 **Television—Telecast**—prizefight (heavyweight championship bout) on large-screen television—Joe Louis vs. Lee Savold—Madison Square Garden, New York City

1966 **Ship**—nuclear ship named for a black—*George Washington Carver*—commissioned

1966 **Submarine**—nuclear submarine named for a black—*George Washington Carver*—commissioned

JUNE 16

1775 **Army**—Army engineering department—Continental Army—authorized

1775 **Army Officer**—Paymaster General—separate pay department established

1871 **Freemasons**—Ancient Arabic Order of Nobles of the Mystic Shrine—established—New York City

1890 **Historical Society**—historical society—American Historical Association—report submitted to Congress

1897 **Voting Machine Commission**—commissioners appointed

1900 **Revolver Shooting Tournament (international)**—Greenville, N.J.

1909 **Aviation—Airplane**—airplane sold commercially—G. H. Curtiss—Hammondsport, N.Y.

1921 **Nursing School**—army school of nursing—graduation—Washington, D.C.

1922 **Helicopter—Flights**—helicopter flight—of importance—H. A. Berliner—College Park, Md.

1932 **Jewish College**—Jewish college of liberal arts and sciences under Jewish auspices—B.A. degrees conferred—Yeshiva College—New York City

1933 **Bank Legislation**—bank guaranty legislation

1933 **Consumers' Advisory Board (U.S.)**—authorized

1933 **Consumers' Counsel (U.S.)**—authorized

1933 **Federal Deposit Insurance Corporation** created

1933 **Industrial Recovery Act**—code under t National Industrial Recovery Act—cott textile code—drawn up

1933 **Industrial Recovery Act**—industrial reco ery act (national)—enacted

1933 **Industry**—industrial advisory board (U. —authorized

1933 **Labor**—Labor Advisory Board (federal) authorized

1933 **Public Works Administration (U.S.)**—a thorized

1933 **Transportation Coordination**—transpor tion coordination (federal)—J. B. Eastm —appointed

1941 **Aviation—Airport**—airport (federa owned and operated)—opened—Washir ton, D.C.

1949 **Locomotive**—gas turbine-electric locom tive—demonstrated—Erie, Pa.

1969 **Army War College**—Army War Colle women graduated—F. V. Chaffin and S. Heinze—were graduated—Carlisle, Pa.

1976 **Geographical Society**—geographical so ety director (woman)—S. K. Myers—N York City

1980 **Treasury Department (U.S.)**—gold med lions issued by the Treasury Departmer

JUNE 17

1775 **Army Officer**—adjutant general—Hora Gates—selected

1775 **Army Officer**—chief engineer—Richa Gridley—served

1775 **Army Officer**—major general—Artem Ward—appointed

1833 **Dry Dock**—national ship in a federal d dock—*Delaware*—Portsmouth, Va.

1836 **Medical School**—homeopathic school North American Academy of the Home pathic Healing Art—Allentown, Pa chartered

1837 **Rubber**—rubber patent of importance Charles Goodyear—New York City

1856 **Republican Party**—Republican Party r tional convention—Philadelphia, Pa.

1863 **Insurance**—accident insurance company Travelers Insurance Company—Hartfo Conn.—chartered

1866 **Postage Stamp**—mourning stamp—issue

1894 **Epidemic**—poliomyelitis epidemic—R land, Vt.

1902 **Reclamation Service (federal)**—authoriz

1912 **Aviation—Airplane Fatalities**—airpla fatality (woman)—Julia Clark killed Springfield, Ill.

1912 **Horse Race**—mutuel ticket to pay mc than $1,000—Latonia track, Covington, I

1913 Medical Society—immunology society—American Association of Immunologists—organized—Minneapolis, Minn.

1923 Language—legislation to establish the American language as an official language—enacted in Illinois

1931 Photoelectric Cell—photoelectric cell installed commercially—West Haven, Conn.

1934 Archivist of the United States—national archives established

1934 Federal Communications Commission—created

1934 Motion Picture—motion picture of the sun—Pontiac, Mich.

1937 Codification Board (U.S.)—created—B. R. Kennedy—appointed director

1939 Aviation—Passenger—woman to fly entirely around the world by commercial heavier-than-air plane—trip completed—Marseilles, France

1939 Pinball Game—pinball legislation enacted by a major city prohibiting the machines—Atlanta, Ga.

1946 Prizefight—prizefight at which admission tickets sold at $100—Louis-Conn fight—New York City

1946 Television—Telecast—prizefight (heavyweight championship bout) to be televised—Louis-Conn Fight—New York City

1947 Aviation—Flights—airplane to fly faster than 600 m.p.h.—Albert Boyd—Muroc Air Field, Calif.

1952 Submarine—submarine expressly designed and built to fire guided missiles Grayback—ordered

1953 Spy—peacetime death sentence for espionage—Julius Rosenberg and Ethel Rosenberg—electrocuted—Ossining, N.Y.

1953 Treason—execution for treason in peacetime—Ossining, N.Y.

1956 Library Legislation—federal aid to libraries—enacted

1958 College—college for women under Jewish auspices—Stern College for Women—New York City—first graduation

1967 Golfer—golfer (woman) to play 150 holes continuously—Katherine Murphy—Bonsall, Calif.

1977 Saint (Catholic)—American saint (male)—J. N. Neumann—canonized

JUNE 20

1782 Seal—Great Seal of the United States Government—designed

1814 Ship—steam-propelled frigate—*Demologos*—keel laid

1819 Ship—steamboat built in America to cross the Atlantic Ocean—*Savannah*—arrived—Liverpool, England

1863 Bank—national bank chartered—National Bank of Philadelphia

1867 Territorial Expansion—noncontiguous territory—acquired—Alaska

1874 Medal—lifesaving medal—of Treasury Department—authorized

1894 Museum — commercial museum — Philadelphia Commercial Museum—first directors' meeting—Philadelphia, Pa.

1895 Degrees (academic and honorary)—Doctor of Science degree earned by a woman—W. Baldwin—Cornell University—Ithaca, N.Y.

1896 Submarine—submarine contract of the U.S. Navy—keel laid—*Plunger*

1907 Army War College—Army War College Washington, D.C.—opened

1909 Balloon Honeymoon—balloon honeymoon—R. N. Burnham and E. H. Waring—began Woods Hole, Mass.—ended, Holbrook Mass.

1913 Aviation—Airplane Fatalities—airplane fatality (U.S. Navy)—W. D. Billingsley—Kent Island, Md.

1919 College—university for blacks (Catholic) diplomas awarded for normal department—New Orleans, La.

1921 Representative (U.S.)—representative (woman) to preside over the House of Representatives—A. M. Robertson

1926 Catholic Church—Catholic eucharistic international congress in the United States Chicago, Ill.

1926 International Eucharistic Congress—America—Chicago, Ill.

1930 Television—Telecast—weather map telecast to a transatlantic steamer—*America*—New York City

1933 Labor—Labor Advisory Board (federal) organized

1939 Television—Telecast—operetta to be televised—presented—New York City

1960 Prizefighter—world heavyweight champion to regain his crown—Floyd Patterson—New York City

1967 Public Defender—public defender (state) Peter Murray—New Jersey—appointed

1968 Postal Service—legislation permitting postage stamps of the United States to be illustrated in color—enacted

JUNE 21

1622 Prohibition—prohibition enforcement officers—Virginia

1768 Medical School—medical college—commencement—College of Philadelphia

1768 Physician—doctor to receive a Bachelor Medicine degree—College of Philadelphia

1788 Constitution of the United States—printed copies of the Constitution—ratified

1834 Reaper—reaper that was practical—patented—C. H. McCormick

1859 Rocket—rocket patent—Andrew Lanergan—Boston, Mass.

1869 Health Board—health board (state)—authorized—Massachusetts

JUNE 23

1775 Book—book (American) made with American paper, ink, type—advertised—Philadelphia, Pa.

1812 War (1812)—naval battle after the U.S. declaration of war—*President* vs. *Belvidera*

1836 Treasury Department (U.S.)—treasury surplus returned and apportioned among the several states—authorized

1848 Woman—woman lobbyist—D. L. Dix—petition to Congress

1860 Government Printing Office—Government Printing Office—created independent office

1860 Secret Service—secret service (federal)—created

1868 Typewriter—typewriter that was practical—patented—C. L. Sholes

1869 Labor—labor bureau (state)—Massachusetts Bureau of Statistics of Labor—established

1869 Probation—probation legislation for juvenile delinquents—enacted—Massachusetts

1871 Gas—municipal gas plant—Wheeling, W.Va.—trustees appointed

1877 Royal Arcanum—founded—Boston, Mass.

1887 Hospital—babies' hospital designed exclusively for infants—New York City—incorporated

1888 Presidential Candidate—black presidential candidate nominated—Frederick Douglass—Chicago, Ill.

1899 Medal—Medal of Honor awarded to a black in the Spanish-American War—G. H. Wanton—issued

1904 Motorboat Race—motorboat race under organized rules—New York City

1916 Aviation—Pilot—American pilot killed while a pilot in the Lafayette Escadrille—V. E. Chapman

1924 Aviation—Flights (transcontinental)—transcontinental flight within 24 hours—R. L. Maugham

1926 Lipreading Tournament (national)—Philadelphia, Pa.

1937 Theatrical School—theater and dramatic criticism course—Ph.D. degree awarded—Yale University—New Haven, Conn.

1938 Aquarium—aquarium for monsters of the deep—Marineland—formal opening—St. Augustine, Fla.

1938 Civil Aeronautics Authority (U.S.)—created

1948 Television—Telecast—stratovision flight public demonstration—Pittsburgh, Pa.

1967 School—school for unmarried, pregnant, teen-age girls—opened—New York City

1969 Supreme Court (U.S.)—Chief Justice of the United States to administer the oath of office to his successor—Earl Warren

1970 Physician—physician with a mobile medical office—H. C. Neals—Jersey City, N.J.—in service

1980 Radio Broadcast—solar power two-wa[y] radio coast-to-coast conversation—F[ort] Monmouth, N.J., and El Monte, Calif.

JUNE 24

1579 Book—Book of Common Prayer—used[ ]San Francisco, Calif.

1579 Protestant Episcopal Church—Christi[an] religious service in English—on the Paci[fic] Coast—Francis Fletcher—San Francis[co] Calif.

1647 Woman Suffrage—woman suffrage adv[o]cate—Margaret Brent—demanded vote[ ]Maryland

1764 Artist—artist successful in commercial [art]—Matthew Pratt—sailed from Phil[a]delphia, Pa.

1783 Ship — ship-of-the-line — *America* sailed for France

1784 Balloon-Flights—balloon flight—Edwa[rd] Warren—Baltimore, Md.

1791 Masonry—black Masonic Grand Lod[ge] (not Free and Accepted Masons)—Prov[in]cial Grand Lodge—organized—Bost[on] Mass.

1795 Extradition—extradition treaty with a f[or]eign country—Jay Treaty, with Great Br[it]ain—ratified by Senate

1807 Vice President (U.S.)—Vice President [ar]rested—Aaron Burr—indicted for treas[on] Richmond, Va.

1833 Dry Dock—national ship in a federal d[ry] dock—*Constitution* at dry dock—Bost[on] Mass.

1834 Cabinet (U.S.)—Cabinet appointee reje[ct]ed by the Senate—R. B. Taney—nominat[ed]

1837 Treaty—treaty with a Far Eastern coun[try]—proclaimed

1873 Fine Arts Department—fine arts depa[rt]ment in a college to grant degrees—Colle[ge] of Fine Arts—Syracuse, N.Y.

1885 Protestant Episcopal Bishop—Protest[ant] Episcopal bishop (black)—S. D. Ferguson consecrated—New York City

1898 Spanish-American War—army offi[cer] killed in battle in the Spanish-Americ[an] war—A. K. Capron—killed—Las Gua[si]mas, Cuba

1898 Spanish-American War—Spanish-Ame[ri]can land engagement—Las Guasim[as] Cuba

1910 Radio Legislation (national)—Wirel[ess] Ship Act—enacted

1926 Catholic Church—Catholic eucharistic [in]ternational congress in the United State[s] adjourned to Mundelein, Ill.

1926 Navy—Navy Secretary of Aviation—off[ice] established

1930 Radar—radar detection of airplanes[ ]Anacostia, D.C.

1940 Television—Telecast—political conv[en]tion to be televised—Republican conv[en]tion—Philadelphia, Pa.

JUNE 27

1652 **Traffic Regulation**—traffic law—enacted—New Amsterdam

1775 **Army Officer**—paymaster general—James Warren—appointed

1776 **Army Execution**—Thomas Hickey—New York City

1844 **Presidential Candidate**—presidential candidate assassinated—Joseph Smith—Carthage, Ill.

1860 **Army**—signal corps—A. J. Myer appointed signal officer

1861 **Civil War**—naval officer (Union) killed in the Civil War—J. H. Ward—Mathias Point, Va.

1884 **Baseball Pitcher**—baseball pitcher to pitch three no-hit games—Larry Corcoran—third game

1884 **Labor**—labor bureau (federal)—authorized

1893 **Horse Race**—horse race of 1,000 miles—completed—Chicago, Ill.

1911 **Aviation—Flights**—airplane flight under a bridge—Lincoln Beachey—Niagara Falls, N.Y.

1917 **Daylight Saving**—legislation enacted

1921 **Comptroller General of the United States**—J. R. McCarl—appointed

1923 **Aviation**—refueling attempt in midair—L. H. Smith—Coronado, Calif.

1929 **Television — Telecast —** color television demonstration (public)—New York City

1934 **Emergency Housing Corporation (U.S.)**—Federal Housing Administration—created

1934 **Federal Savings and Loan Association**—Federal Savings and Loan Insurance Corporation—created

1935 **Bank**—checkmaster plan—introduced—New York City

1944 **World War II**—American general captured by the Germans—A. W. Vanaman—reported missing

1950 **Aviation—Pilot**—pilot to down two enemy fighter airplanes in one day in Korea—R. E. Wayne

1950 **War (Korean)**—South Korean combat mission—fire exchanged

1955 **Automobile Legislation**—automobile seat belt safety legislation—enacted—Illinois

1955 **Television—Telecast**—telecast originating live in three countries

1960 **Chlorophyll**—chlorophyll "a"—synthesized—R. B. Woodward—Cambridge, Mass.

1978 **Pen**—pen with truly erasable ink—Eraser Mate—F. A. Miller and Henry Peper, Jr.—patented

1979 **Judge**—black woman judge of the U.S. Court of Appeals—A. L. Kearse—sworn in at New York City

1980 **Police**—state police class of women—graduated at Sea Girt, N.J.

JUNE 28

1687 **Knighthood**—knighthood conferred on native-born American—William Phips—London, England

1778 **Revolutionary War**—conflict on equ terms between American regulars and Br ish regulars—Freehold, N.J.

1794 **Ship**—warship builder—Joshua Hu phreys—appointed

1798 **Navy**—prize money awarded by the U Navy—act

1832 **Epidemic**—cholera epidemic—case repo ed—New York City

1834 **Crime Prevention and Detection**—int state crime pact—ratified

1834 **Geological Survey**—geological survey a propriation (U.S.)—authorized

1845 **Newspaper**—newspaper with a full page woodcut engravings—*Weekly Herald* New York City

1861 **Army**—law (state) conferring milita privileges and duties on blacks—enacted Tennessee

1869 **Naval Officer**—Surgeon General of Navy—R. M. Wood—appointed

1877 **Cricket Magazine**—cricket magazine—*T American Cricketer*—published—Phi delphia, Pa.

1884 **Horse Race**—horse race (American Der —Chicago, Ill.

1894 **Holiday**—Labor Day holiday (federal) declared by act of Congress

1919 **Ship**—naval ship named for an enlist man—*Osmond Ingram*—commissioned Boston, Mass.

1925 **Caterpillar Club**—woman Caterpillar Cl member—Irene McFarland—jumped Cincinnati, Ohio

1927 **Aviation—Flights (transpacific)**—Calif nia–Hawaii flight—L. J. Maitland and A. Hegenberger—takeoff—Oakland, Calif.

1935 **Virus**—virus obtained in crystalline form reported

1938 **Ski Lift**—aerial tramway—Franconia, N —dedicated

1939 **Aviation—Flights (transatlantic)**—trans lantic regular commercial airplane serv —undertaken—left Port Washington, N.

1940 **Immigration**—alien registration—auth ized

1956 **Atomic Reactor**—nuclear reactor built private industrial research—Chicago, Ill in operation

1965 **Telephone**—telephone conversation (co mercial) over a satellite—between United States and Europe over *Early Bir*

1968 **Holiday**—Monday holidays legislat (federal)—enacted

1976 **Air Force Academy (U.S.)**—women s dents—admitted—Colorado Springs, Co

1976 **Coast Guard Academy**—women stude —New London, Conn.—admitted

JUNE 29

10 Missionary Society—foreign missionary society—American Board of Commissioners for Foreign Missions—organized—Bradford, Mass.

33 Ordnance—gun (revolving)—patented—D. G. Colburn—Canton Canal, N.Y.

37 Education—state board of education—Horace Mann—appointed commissioner—Massachusetts

50 Lighthouse—iron pile lighthouse—completed—Minot's Ledge, Mass.

53 Bank—national bank—National Bank of Davenport, Iowa—opened

54 Degrees (academic and honorary)—law degree of LL.M.—conferred—Columbia University—New York City

70 Public Health—public health service (U.S.)—reorganization act enacted

32 Forestry Society—national forestry association—merger of American Forestry Congress and American Forestry Association

25 Electric Lighting—electric light bulb frosted on the inside—patent application filed

27 Aviation—Airplane—airplane equipped with radio to cross the Atlantic Ocean—flight takeoff—Roosevelt Field, N.Y.

27 Aviation—Flights (transpacific)—California–Hawaii flight—concluded—L. J. Maitland and A. F. Hegenberger

29 Wind Tunnel—high-speed jet wind tunnel—completed—Langley Field, Va.

46 Television—Telecast—high definition telecast—W2XBS—New York City

39 Television—Telecast—play to be televised as a full-hour program—New York City

42 World War II—American bombardier over German occupied territory—B. L. Bell—raid—Hazebrouck, France

48 Airmail Service—parcel post domestic air service—authorized

48 Postal Service—parcel post domestic air service—authorized

52 Ship—aircraft carrier to sail around Cape Horn—*Oriskany*—passed Cape Horn

53 Catholic Seminarians (black) to be ordained to the priesthood by a black bishop—Bay St. Louis, Miss.

56 Education—war orphans education law—enacted

56 High Jump—over seven feet—Charles Dumas—Los Angeles, Calif.

61 Satellite—multisatellite launching (3 satellites in 1 shot)—*Omicron 1*—launched—Cape Canaveral, Fla.

61 Satellite—satellite with a nuclear power device—*Transit IV-A*—launched—Cape Canaveral, Fla.

62 Television—Telecast—pay program—WHCT-TV, Hartford, Conn.

64 Atomic Energy Commission—Atomic Energy Commission woman member—M. I. Bunting—sworn in

1972 Postal Card—pictorial postal card—issued—Boston, Mass.

JUNE 30

1812 Bond—treasury notes (interest-bearing)—authorized

1831 Railroad—railroad to carry troops—Baltimore and Ohio Railroad Company—to Sykes Mills, Md.

1831 Scale—platform scale—patented—T. Fairbanks—St. Johnsbury, Vt.

1838 Caster—for furniture—patented

1858 Citizenship—Japanese granted citizenship—Joseph Heco

1859 Niagara Falls—person to cross Niagara Falls on a tightrope—J. F. Gravelet

1860 Baseball Team—baseball team to tour—Excelsiors—left Albany, N.Y.

1863 Civil War—bloodshed north of the Mason-Dixon Line—Hanover, Pa.

1864 Cigarette Tax—cigarette tax—levied

1870 Lawyer—woman lawyer graduated from a law school—A. H. Kepley—graduated—Union College of Law—Chicago, Ill.

1879 Electric Company—electric company organized to provide and sell electricity—California Electric Light Company—organized—San Francisco, Calif.

1882 Hospital—hospital for the military and naval forces—appropriation authorized

1886 Forest Service (U.S.)—organized

1892 Baseball Game—National League 20-inning baseball game—Cincinnati, Ohio

1896 Electric Stove—patented—W. S. Hadaway—New York City

1897 College Alumni Association—college alumni association secretary (full-time paid position)—established—University of Michigan—Ann Arbor, Mich.

1898 American Expeditionary Force—American Expeditionary force—arrived—Manila, Philippines

1899 Bicycle Racer—bicycle racer—to attain mile-a-minute speed—C. M. Murphy—Farmingdale, N.Y.

1905 Balloon—balloon to land on a building—A. R. Knabenshoe—Toledo, Ohio

1906 Pure Food Law—pure food and drug legislation (national)—Federal Food and Drug Act—enacted

1906 Stamp—consular service fee stamps—effective

1909 Stadium—baseball stadium (fireproof)—Forbes Field, Pittsburgh, Pa.—opened

1910 Aviation—Airplane Bombing—airplane bombing experiment—G. H. Curtiss—Hammondsport, N.Y.

1911 Army Officer—flight surgeon—J. P. Kelly—reported for duty

1916 **Golf Champion**—golfer to win both the United States Open and the United States Amateur in the same year—Charles Evans, Jr.—Minneapolis, Minn. (U.S. Open)

1921 **President (U.S.)**—President to become Chief Justice of the United States—W. H. Taft—appointed

1923 **Golf Champion**—family to win more than one national championship in 1 year—Dexter Cummings—Bronxville, N.Y. (Intercollegiate championship)

1927 **Aviation—License**—pilot's license granted to a woman by the U.S. Department of Commerce—P. F. Omlie

1930 **Canonization**—canonization of North Americans

1930 **Radio Broadcast**—around-the-world broadcast—C. D. Wagoner—Schenectady, N.Y.

1934 **Securities and Exchange Commission (U.S.)**—five commissioners appointed

1936 **Labor Law**—40-hour-week law (federal)—enacted

1939 **Aviation—Flights (transatlantic)**—transatlantic regular commercial airplane service —plane landed—Marseilles, France

1946 **Atomic Bomb**—atomic bomb dropped from an airplane over water—Bikini Lagoon

1948 **Telephone**—telephone recording devices—authorized by Federal Communications Commission

1948 **Transistor** — transistor — demonstrated — Murray Hill, N.J.

1951 **Theater**—municipally owned and operated summer theater-in-the-round—Philadelphia, Pa.—opened

1953 **Automobile**—plastic laminated fiberglass-body sports car—manufactured—Flint, Mich.

1956 **Aviation**—airplane disaster involving more than 100 persons—Grand Canyon, Ariz.

1964 **Atomic Reactor**—plutonium-fueled nuclear reactor to produce useful amounts of electricity—Idaho Falls, Idaho—announced

1965 **Horse Race**—perfecta, or exacta—Monticello, N.Y.

1965 **Hotel**—hotel (large) built over a pier—Flagship Hotel, Galveston, Tex.—opened

1967 **Astronaut**—astronaut (black) to qualify for the training course—R. H. Lawrence—selected

1967 **Motorboat**—motorboat to travel at a speed of more than 285 m.p.h.—Lee Taylor, Jr.—Lake Guntersville, Ala.

1971 **Election Law**—federal legislation enabling persons 18 years of age or older to vote (26th Amendment)—enacted

1973 **Ship**—commercial crude-oil carrier—*Brooklyn*—christened

1974 **Lawyers' Association**—lawyers' association (state) woman president—M. M. Lambert—New York—began service

1979 **Runner**—runner (woman) to run 1 mile less than 4.5 minutes—Mary Decke Philadelphia, Pa.

JULY 1

1731 **Library**—circulating library—forme Philadelphia, Pa.

1791 **Tax**—internal revenue tax—effective

1795 **Supreme Court (U.S.)**—Chief Justice wh nomination was not confirmed—John R ledge—served

1827 **Newspaper**—Spanish newspaper—*El dactor*—published—New York City

1835 **Railroad**—railroad to run trains to Wa ington, D.C.—from Baltimore, Md.

1845 **Senator (U.S.)**—Jewish senator—D. Yulee—Florida

1847 **Postage Stamp**—postage stamps issued the Post Office Department

1851 **Insurance**—insurance board (state)—N Hampshire Insurance Department—est lished

1852 **Capitol (U.S.)**—body to lie in state in Capitol rotunda—Henry Clay—Washi ton, D.C.

1855 **Lighthouse**—iron pile lighthouse—c struction of new lighthouse begun— not's Ledge, Mass.

1855 **Postal Service**—registration of letters

1857 **College**—college to grant women absol ly equal rights—nonsectarian—Anti College—Yellow Springs, Ohio—grad tion

1859 **Baseball Game**—intercollegiate basel game — Amherst-Williams — Pittsfi Mass.

1859 **Periodical**—gas magazine—*American G Light Journal*—published—New York (—first issue

1862 **Internal Revenue Commissioner**—bur authorized

1862 **Passport**—passport fee—levied

1862 **Polygamy Legislation (federal)**—polyga legislation (federal)—enacted

1862 **Tax**—inheritance tax (federal)—enacte

1862 **Tobacco**—tobacco tax for internal reve —enacted

1863 **Postal Service**—free city delivery of ma in operation

1864 **Insurance**—accident insurance po (printed)—issued—Travelers Insura Company—Hartford, Conn.

1864 **Postal Service**—railroad post office for general distribution of mail—tested

1866 **Ship**—side-wheeler transpacific steame *Celestial Empire* (later named *China* sailed for Panama and San Francis Calif.

1869 **Railroad Commission (state)**—railr commission (state)—established—Mas chusetts

1870 **Justice Department (U.S.)**—department ganized

1939　**Pinball Game**—pinball legislation enacted by a major city prohibiting the machines—Atlanta, Ga.—effective

1940　**Army Parachute Troops**—training commenced

1941　**Navy**—naval task force assembled for foreign service—commanded by D. M. Le Breton—sailed

1941　**Television License**—commercial television license—W2XBS—New York City

1941　**Television License**—construction permit—effective

1945　**Labor**—labor antidiscrimination commission (state)—appointed—New York

1949　**Air Force Officer**—Air Force surgeon general—M. C. Grow

1952　**Narcotics**—narcotic sanatorium for minors—patients received—New York City

1954　**Submarine**—submarine expressly designed and built to fire guided missiles—*Grayback*—laid down—Mare Island, Calif.

1961　**Air Raid Shelter**—air raid community shelter—completed—Boise, Idaho

1966　**Medicare**—health insurance federal plan—first benefits paid

1967　**Public Defender**—public defender (state)—Peter Murray—New Jersey—term began

1967　**Satellite**—satellite to transmit colored photographs of the full earth face—*Dodge*—launched, Cape Kennedy, Fla.

1971　**Sex Discrimination**—state to ban sex discrimination—Washington—law effective

1972　**Naval Officer**—admiral who was a black—S. L. Gravely, Jr.—date of rank

1979　**Money**—woman commemorated on a circulating U.S. coin—S. B. Anthony—circulation begun

1980　**Rabbi**—husband-and-wife rabbinical and cantorial team engaged by a synagogue—S. A. Gertman and S. J. Sager—Cleveland, Ohio—began service

JULY 2

1717　**Book Auction Catalog**—book auction printed catalog—sale

1749　**Catholic Nuns**—nun who was born in the United States—Mary Turpin—began novitiate—New Orleans, La.

1776　**Woman Suffrage**—colony to grant suffrage to women—constitutional right—New Jersey

1777　**Emancipation Act (state)**—enacted—Vermont

1777　**Slavery**—state to abolish slavery—Vermont

1800　**Land Grant**—district land office—opened—Steubenville, Ohio

1829　**Catholic Nuns**—Catholic nuns (black community)—founded—Baltimore, Md.

1836　**Postage Stamp**—adhesive stamps—local delivery service—authorized

1842　**Ship**—iron vessel—John Randolph—enrolled

1850　**Gas Mask**—gas mask with a self-contain breathing apparatus—patented—B. J. L. —Cambridge, Mass.

1862　**Agricultural Land Grant**—signed—Ab ham Lincoln

1864　**Hall of Fame**—hall of fame (national)— tional Statuary Hall—authorized

1867　**Elevated Railroad**—elevated railroa opened for traffic—New York City

1890　**Trust**—antitrust law (national)—Shern act—enacted

1902　**College Academic Costume Standardi tion**—Bureau of Academic Costume— corporated

1908　**Price Regulation Legislation (state)**—en ed—Louisiana

1917　**Marine Corps**—marine regiment in Fra —arrived at St. Nazaire

1917　**Radio Telephone**—radio telephone c munication between the ground and an plane—Langley Field, Va.

1917　**World War I**—marine regiment to lan Europe in World War I—C. A. Doye arrived at St. Nazaire, France

1919　**Aviation**—aeronautical stowaway— East Fortune, Scotland

1919　**Aviation—Airship**—airship (lighter-th air)—left East Fortune, Scotland

1921　**Prizefight**—prizefight to gross $1 millio Dempsey-Carpentier fight—Jersey C N.J.

1921　**Radio Broadcast**—prizefight (heavywe championship) broadcast—Dempsey-C pentier fight—Jersey City, N.J.

1922　**Carillon**—carillon (modern)—blesse Gloucester, Mass.

1926　**Air Corps**—Air Corps (U.S. Army)—es lished

1926　**Medal**—Distinguished Flying Cross Corps)—authorized

1931　**Polo**—polo game played outdoors at n —Baltimore, Md.

1932　**Presidential Candidate**—presidential didate to fly to a political convention—I Roosevelt—Albany, N.Y.–Chicago, Ill.

1932　**Presidential Candidate**—presidential didate to make a speech of acceptance nominating convention—F. D. Rooseve Chicago, Ill.

1933　**Aviation—Flights (transatlantic)**—tran lantic foreign squadron flight to the Un States—left Orbetello, Italy

1934　**Securities and Exchange Commis (U.S.)**—meeting

1935　**Theatrical School**—theatrical school s sored by an institution of higher learni Union College—Schenectady, N.Y.

1940　**Bridge**—pontoon bridge of reinforced crete—Lake Washington Floating Brid Seattle, Wash.—dedicated

1943　**Aviation—Pilot**—black army pilot to d an Axis airplane—Charles Hall—Sicil

1948　**Diplomatic Service**—ambassador to Is —J. G. McDonald—began service

1874 Socialist Labor Party of North America—
      formed
1883 Electric Company—three-wire central-sta-
      tion incandescent electric lighting plant—
      operations started—Sunbury, Pa.
1883 Wild West Show—presented—North
      Platte, Neb.
1884 Bullfight—bullfight—Dodge City, Kan.
1888 Rodeo—competition—Prescott, Ariz.
1889 State—states admitted to the Union simul-
      taneously—constitutional conventions—
      North Dakota and South Dakota
1892 Streetcar—double-deck streetcar—oper-
      ated—San Diego, Calif.
1902 Motorcycle Endurance Run—motorcycle
      endurance run—Boston, Mass.–New York
      City
1902 Motorcycle Race—motorcycle race (250
      miles)—begun—Boston, Mass.
1903 Cable—cable across the Pacific Ocean be-
      tween Honolulu, Midway, Guam, and
      Manila—official message sent—President
      Theodore Roosevelt
1905 Baseball Game—American League 20-in-
      ning baseball game—Philadelphia–Boston,
      Mass.
1908 Aviation—aeronautical trophy—won—G.
      H. Curtiss—Hammondsport, N.Y.
1908 Naval Officer—admiral who was Jewish—
      Adolph Marix
1910 Prizefighter—black heavyweight champion
      of the world—Jack Johnson
1911 Insurance—workers' compensation insur-
      ance law (state)—New Jersey law became
      effective
1914 Motorcycle Race—motorcycle race (300
      miles)—Dodge City, Kan.
1917 Radio Telephone—radio telephone com-
      munication between the ground and an air-
      plane—received by an airplane
1917 Ship—ambulance ship, designed and built
      as a hospital—Relief—keel laid
1921 Cigarette Tax—cigarette tax (state)—effec-
      tive—Iowa
1928 Niagara Falls—person to go over Niagara
      Falls in a rubber ball—Jean Lussier
1935 Ferryboat—streamlined ferryboat—com-
      mercial operation—Kalakala—Houghton,
      Wash.
1942 Ship—triple launching of Liberty ships—
      Baltimore, Md.
1942 World War II—American bombing mission
      over enemy-occupied territory in Europe—
      Netherlands
1950 Army Officer—general to command the
      forces of the United Nations in Korea—
      Douglas MacArthur—began service
1952 Parachutist—parachutist to make 124
      jumps in one day—Neal Stewart—Grand
      Prairie, Tex.
1955 Cobra—king cobra snakes—born in cap-
      tivity—New York City

1957 Postage Stamp—postage stamp in 3 col
      printed in 1 passing of each sheet throu
      the press—American flag stamp—issue
      Washington, D.C.
1966 Freedom of Information Act—Freedom
      Information Act—approved
1967 Jockey—jockey to win 7 consecutive ra
      in 1 day—Leroy Moyers—Suffolk Dow
      Boston, Mass.
1977 Parade—parade in which all the march
      music was supplied by transistor radio
      ceivers—Streamwood, Ill.

JULY 5

1775 Army Insignia—special insignia—insti
      ed—Massachusetts
1776 Declaration of Independence (American
      Declaration of Independence was
      printed—John Dunlop—Philadelphia, P
1843 Colonial Government—government on
      Pacific Coast—committee of nine chose
      Champoeg, Oreg.
1882 Dynamo—dynamo—New York City—t
      ed
1884 Navigation Bureau (U.S.)—under Treas
      Department—authorized
1893 College—university extension sum
      meeting—Philadelphia, Pa.
1900 Political Convention—woman delegate
      make a seconding speech—Elizabeth C
      —Kansas City, Mo.
1902 Motorcycle Race—motorcycle race
      miles)—ended—New York City
1916 Motorcycle Trip—motorcycle transco
      nental trip by a woman—left—New Y
      City
1933 Teletypesetter—teletypesetter installe
      a school—Empire State School of Prin
      —Ithaca, N.Y.
1935 Labor Relations—Labor Relations Act
      tional)—approved
1944 Aviation—Airplane—rocket airplane (r
      tary)—flown—Hawthorne, Calif.
1946 Airmail Service—helicopter airmail de
      ery—Bridgeport, Conn.
1950 War (Korean)—soldier killed in the Kor
      War—Kenneth Shadrick
1951 Transistor—junction transistor—inven
      announced—Murray Hill, N.J.
1952 Vice Presidential Candidate—b
      woman vice presidential candidate—C
      Bass—Progressive Party—nominate
      Chicago, Ill.
1971 Election Law—federal legislation enab
      persons 18 years of age or older to
      (26th Amendment)—certified by Presi
      Nixon
1972 Brokerage—New York Stock Excha
      black director—J. H. Holland—electe
      New York City
1972 Brokerage—New York Stock Excha
      woman governor—J. M. Kreps—electe
      New York City

JULY 6

6 **Declaration of Independence (American)**—Declaration of Independence first published—Philadelphia, Pa.

5 **Money**—decimal system of money—adopted

7 **Money**—Continental coin—copper Fugio—authorized

3 **Alien Discriminatory Law**—enacted

3 **Railroad**—railroad merger—New York Central Railroad directors selected

3 **Shoe Manufacturing Machine**—patented—L. R. Blake—Abington, Mass.

9 **Automobile License Board**—authorized—Chicago, Ill.

8 **Motorcycle Trip**—motorcycle transcontinental trip—arrived—New York City

6 **Fingerprinting**—international exchange of fingerprints—St. Louis, Mo., and London, England

8 **Expedition**—polar expedition of which a woman was a member—Peary expedition—sailed

9 **Aviation**—aeronautical stowaway—William Ballantyne—arrived—Hazlehurst Field, L.I., N.Y.

9 **Aviation—Airship**—airship (lighter-than-air)—British dirigible R-34 arrived—Roosevelt Field, N.Y.

8 **Baseball Game**—baseball game (major league) in which 14 runs were scored in 1 inning—Washington, D.C.

Radio Facsimile Transmission—photograph sent by radio across the Atlantic—from New York City

Baseball Game—all-star baseball game (major league)—American League vs. National League—Chicago, Ill.

Baseball Player—baseball player to hit a home run in an All-Star game—Babe Ruth

Airmail Service—autogiro mail delivery regular service—Philadelphia, Pa.–Camden, N.J.

Medal—Medal of Freedom—established

Federal Communications Commission—federal communications commission woman member—F. B. Hennock—appointed

Attorney of the United States—United States attorney (black)—C. F. Poole—sworn in, San Francisco, Calif.

Vietnam War—American general killed in Vietnam in an accident—W. J. Crumm

Divorce—"no fault" divorce law (state)—California—enacted

Naval Academy—women students—admitted

JULY 7

Periodical—comic magazine—*The Wasp*—Robert Rusticoat, editor—Harry Crosswell, publisher—Hudson, N.Y.—first issue

1806 **Cathedral**—cathedral—cornerstone laid—Baltimore, Md.

1838 **Steamboat Inspection Service (U.S.)**—authorized

1849 **Library Legislation**—library law enacted by a state—New Hampshire

1861 **Torpedo**—torpedo mine—attack—Potomac River

1862 **Postal Service**—railroad post office—tested

1863 **Conscription**—wartime conscription bill—first draft call

1865 **Woman**—woman hanged by the United States Government—M. E. Surratt—Washington, D.C.

1885 **Ordnance**—cartridge-loading machinery—patented—G. M. Peters—Xenia, Ohio

1886 **Biblical Students Summer Conference**—organized—Mount Hermon School—Northfield, Mass.

1911 **Continuation School**—continuation school established by state law—Racine Continuation School—Racine, Wis.—authorized

1920 **Radio Compass**—on naval airplane—used—Norfolk, Va.

1923 **College**—junior year abroad—instituted—University of Delaware—Newark, Del.

1935 **Eyes**—identification system—presented—Atlantic City, N.J.

1946 **Saint (Catholic)**—Saint (Catholic)—F. X. Cabrini—canonized

1948 **Naval Officer**—women sworn into the regular U.S. Navy

1961 **Naval Officer**—naval line officer (woman) assigned to sea duty (MSTS)—C. I. Suneson—appointed

1976 **Army School**—women cadets of the U.S. Military Academy (West Point)—enrolled

1976 **Television—Telecast**—state dinner (U.S.) telecast—Washington, D.C.

1977 **Civil Aeronautics Board**—Civil Aeronautics Board woman member—E. E. Bailey—nominated by President Jimmy Carter

JULY 8

1524 **Kidnapping**—recorded in letter

1693 **Police**—police uniforms—authorized—New York City

1776 **Declaration of Independence (American)**—Declaration of Independence was first read publicly—Philadelphia, Pa.

1795 **College**—college named after George Washington—Washington, Tenn.—third charter

1796 **Passport**—passport—recorded in State Department

1797 **Impeachment**—impeachment proceedings against a United States senator—William Blount

1805 **Prizefighter**—American to win distinction in the prize ring—Bill Richman defeated Jack Holmes

1856 Ordnance—machine gun—patented—C. E. Barnes—Lowell, Mass.

1862 Ordnance—revolving gun turret—T. R. Timby—patent

1870 Trademark (U.S.)—registration authorized

1879 Ship—steamboat to employ electric lights—*Jeannette*—sailed—San Francisco, Calif.

1892 Psychology Society—psychology society (national organization)—American Psychological Association organized

1897 Hospital—tuberculosis hospital (municipal) for consumptive poor—Branch Hospital—opened—Cincinnati, Ohio

1899 Golf Champion—golf champion (American-born)—tournament—Lake Forest, Ill.

1909 Baseball Game—baseball game at night by a regular-league team—Grand Rapids, Mich.

1910 Aviation—Airport—airport municipal legislation—enacted—Modesto, Calif.

1911 Woman—woman horseback rider to make a solo transcontinental trip—N. J. Aspinwall—arrived in New York City from San Francisco, Calif.

1916 Park—park (national) east of the Mississippi—established—Mount Desert, Me.

1923 President (U.S.)—President to visit Alaska and Canada while President—W. G. Harding—visited—Alaska

1924 Olympic Games—black American athlete to win an individual event in the Olympic Games—W. D. Hubbard—at Colombes Stadium, Paris, France

1933 Public Works Administration (U.S.)—effective

1940 Aviation—Flights—stratoliner commercial flight—New York City–Burbank, Calif.

1944 Ship—naval ship christened by an Army officer—*Colhoun*—commissioned

1945 Radio   Telephone—two-way-radio-equipped bus—tested—Washington, D.C.

1946 Airmail Service—helicopter airmail experimental tests—Burbank, Calif.

1948 Army Auxiliary Corps—woman to become a member of the Women's Army Corps—sworn in—Washington, D.C.

1950 Medal—Order of the Purple Heart awarded in the Korean War—Leroy Deans

1950 War (Korean)—officer killed in action in the Korean War—R. R. Martin

1957 Submarine—submarine to circumnavigate the world—*Gudgeon*—left Pearl Harbor, Hawaii

1965 Medal—Vietnam Service Medal—authorized

1965 Photography—camera multiple flashbulb device—Flashcubes—introduced, New York City

JULY 9

1778 Articles of Confederation—formally engrossed

1792 Agriculture Professor—S. L. Mitchill—pointed—Columbia University—New Y[ork] City

1798 Tax—internal revenue tax—direct tax [on] real estate

1808 Leather—leather-splitting machine—p[at]ented—Samuel Parker—Billerica, Mass

1847 Labor   Legislation—ten-hour-day [law] enacted—New Hampshire

1864 Boiler Legislation—approved—Conne[cti]cut

1872 Doughnut Cutter—patented—J. F. Blon[dell] —Thomaston, Me.

1878 Pipe—corncob pipe commercial manuf[ac]ture—patent—Henry Tibbe—Washingt[on] Mo.

1886 Coursing Club—American Coursing C[lub] —organized—Topeka, Kans.

1893 Surgical Operation—suture of the hum[an] heart (successful)—D. H. William[s] Chicago, Ill.

1910 Aviation—Flights—airplane to fly hig[her] than 1 mile in altitude—W. R. Brookin[s] Atlantic City, N.J.

1912 Marine Corps—marine pilot—A. A. C[un]ningham—assigned—Annapolis, Md.

1914 Bridge (game)—auction bridge champi[on]ship (duplicate)—Lake Placid, N.Y.

1916 Submarine—cargo submarine to cross [the] Atlantic Ocean—landed—Baltimore, M[d.]

1918 Medal—Distinguished   Service   Cr[oss] (Army)—authorized

1918 Medal—Distinguished   Service   Me[dal] (Army)—authorized

1922 Swimmer—swimmer to cover a distanc[e of] 100 meters free style in less than 1 minut[e] Johnny Weissmuller—Alameda, Calif.

1924 Vice Presidential Candidate—vice pr[esi]dential candidate (woman) to have [her] name placed in nomination at a m[ajor] party convention—L. J. Springs of S[outh] Carolina—New York City

1933 Industrial Recovery Act—code under [the] National Industrial Recovery Act—[ap]proved

1942 World War II—ship captain captured [by] German U-boat crew—Henry Stephen[s]

1947 Army Officer—woman to be appointe[d a] regular army officer (colonel)—F. Blanchfield—appointed

1953 Helicopter—helicopter passenger ser[vice] —New York City

1957 Element—element   102—nobelium—[an]nounced

1965 Diplomatic Service—ambassador (b[lack] woman)—P. R. Harris—sworn in

JULY 10

1791 Catholic Seminary—Catholic semina[ry] established—Baltimore, Md.

1798 Ship—revenue cutter and navy coop[era]tion—under command of John Barry

Bookstore (antiquarian)—established—S. G. Drake—Boston, Mass.

American Indians—Indian Affairs Commissioner (U.S.)—E. Herring—appointed

Medal—Medal of Honor awarded to a marine—John Mackie

Pencil—indelible pencil—patented—E. P. Clark—Northampton, Mass.

Life Preserver—life preserver of cork—patented—David Kahnweiler—New York City

Woman Suffrage—state to grant suffrage to women—Wyoming—became state

Army War College—Army War College—S. B. M. Young—began service as first president

Ship—schooner (seven-masted, steel)—*Thomas W. Lawson*—launched—Quincy, Mass.

Motion Picture—presidential candidate shown in motion pictures—W. J. Bryant—filmed—Fairview, Neb.

Prison—prisoners (federal) employed in industry—authorized—Atlanta, Ga.

Money—paper money of the present small size—issued

Baseball Player—baseball player (major league) to make 9 hits in 1 game—J. H. Burnett—Cleveland, Ohio

Radio Broadcast—radio police system (two-way three-way)—operated—Eastchester Township, N.Y.

President (U.S.)—President to broadcast from a foreign country—F. D. Roosevelt—Cartagena, Colombia

President (U.S.)—President to visit South America while President—F. D. Roosevelt—Cartagena, Colombia

Aviation—Flight (transcontinental)—transcontinental nonstop east–west flight by a woman—Laura Ingalls—left—Brooklyn, N.Y.

Ship—warship named for a black—*Harmon*—launched as *Aylmer*

Television Tube—rectangular television tube (practical)—announced—Toledo, Ohio

Satellite—privately-owned satellite—*Telstar 1*—launched—Cape Canaveral, Fla.

Swimmer—American to swim the English Channel underwater—Fred Baldasare—began swim

Telephone—satellite (privately owned) telephone conversation—F. R. Kappel to L. B. Johnson—Andover, Me., via *Telstar 1* to Washington, D. C.

Television—Telecast—transoceanic television program—Andover, Me.

JULY 11

Army Officer—lieutenant general—George Washington—appointed

Marine Corps—American Marines—United States Marine Corps—created

1798 Marine Corps—marine band—authorized

1862 Secret Service—secret service (federal)—act extended to include counterfeiting

1863 Bank—national bank chartered—First National Bank of Philadelphia—opened for business—Philadelphia, Pa.

1870 School—school for blacks (state)—Snowden School—authorized—Alexandria, Va.

1883 Jewish College—Jewish college to train men for the rabbinate—graduation—Cincinnati, Ohio

1890 Library Society—state library society—organized

1910 Submarine—submarine accident—*Bonita* (later named *C-4*) rammed by gunboat *Castine*—off Provincetown, Mass.

1914 Ship—battleship to use fuel oil exclusively—*Nevada*—launched—Quincy, Mass.

1916 Road—federal grant-in-aid—act approved

1918 Ship—Eagle boat—launched—Detroit, Mich.

1919 Golfer—golfer to play 180 holes in 1 day—Edward Styles—Philadelphia, Pa.

1919 Prison—prisoners (federal) employed in industry—United States Penitentiary—Atlanta, Ga.

1919 Ship—electrically propelled ship of the United States Navy—*Jupiter*—conversion to aircraft carrier *Langley*—authorized

1923 Railroad Signal System—railroad signal system of continuous cab signals—installed—Sunbury, Pa.

1933 National Emergency Council (U.S.)—executive council established

1934 Federal Communications Commission—committee appointed

1934 President (U.S.)—President to go through the Panama Canal while President—F. D. Roosevelt

1940 Postal Service—highway post office service—approved

1942 Medal—Distinguished Service Cross awarded in enemy-occupied territory—presented by C. A. Spaatz to C. C. Kegelman

1955 Air Force Academy (U.S.)—Air Force Academy—temporary headquarters established—Denver, Colo.

1962 Swimmer—American to swim the English Channel underwater—Fred Baldasare—arrived in England from France

1962 Television—Telecast—satellite telecast from Europe

1966 Army Officer—sergeant major of the army—W. O. Wooldridge—sworn in

1969 Medal—Distinguished Service Medals of the Army, Navy, and Air Force presented to one person at the same time—L. L. Lemnitzer

JULY 12

1774 **Declaration of Independence (American)**—Declaration of Independence—Carlisle, Pa.

1859 **Paper Bag Manufacturing Machine**—patented—William Goodale—Clinton, Mass.

1862 **Medal**—Medal of Honor (Army)—authorized

1864 **Medal**—Medal of Honor awarded to a Jewish soldier—Leopold Karpeles—award authorized

1866 **War Veterans' Society**—Grand Army of the Republic—state convention—Springfield, Ill.

1882 **Elevator**—elevator with an electric light—installed—Blue Mountain Lake, N.Y.

1882 **Pier**—ocean pier—completed—Atlantic City, N.J.

1908 **Motion Picture**—presidential candidate shown in motion pictures—W. J. Bryan—shown in New York City

1909 **Tax**—income tax amendment to the Constitution—proposed to the states

1912 **Motion Picture**—foreign feature film exhibited—*Queen Elizabeth*—exhibited—New York City

1924 **Olympic Games**—American decathlon champion—H. M. Osborne—Paris, France

1926 **Navy**—Navy Secretary of Aviation—E. P. Warner—sworn in

1928 **Television—Telecast**—outdoor scenes to be televised—New York City

1928 **Television—Telecast**—tennis game telecast—New York City

1943 **Submarine-Escape Training Tank**—women to take the submarine-escape test—certificates awarded—New London, Conn.

1957 **President (U.S.)**—President to fly in a helicopter—D. D. Eisenhower—Washington, D.C.

1968 **Physician**—captain (black) in the U.S. Navy Medical Corps—P. S. Green

1971 **Tariff**—tariff commission woman chairman—C. M. Bedell—sworn in

1972 **Medical Clinic**—acupuncture treatment center—opened—New York City

1974 **Congress (U.S.)—Congressional Budget Office**—authorized

JULY 13

1787 **Slavery**—law (federal) prohibiting slavery in a territory of the United States—Northwest Territory—enacted

1787 **Territorial Expansion**—acquisition of land by the federal government—territory established

1812 **Pawnbroking Ordinance**—enacted—New York City

1832 **Treaty**—treaty with a foreign nation to provide for mutual reduction of import duties—with France—proclaimed

1836 **Patent**—numbering system for patents—adopted—patent No. 1 to John Ruggles—Thomaston, Me.

1861 **Civil War**—Confederate general killed the Civil War—R. S. Garnett—Corrio Ford, Va.

1875 **Cash Carrier System**—patented—Da Brown—Lebanon, N.J.

1880 **Streetcar**—electric streetcar successfu run with current generated by a station dynamo—patented—S. D. Field

1929 **Aviation—Flights**—airplane endura flight exceeding 400 hours—Dale Jack and Forest O'Brine—St. Louis, Mo takeoff

1929 **Motion Picture**—talking picture in peranto—New York City

1934 **Police**—police officer (woman) on the a al force—Cora Sterling—appointed—Se tle, Wash.

1936 **Pension**—pensions paid by the Uni States Government to workers in priv industry—mailed

1938 **Theater**—television theater—opene Massachusetts Television Institute—E ton, Mass.

1939 **Federal Security Agency**—administrato P. V. McNutt—took office

1950 **Naval Officer**—woman medical officer signed to a naval vessel—B. R. Walter

1965 **Solicitor General (U.S.)**—solicitor gen of the United States who was a blac Thurgood Marshall—nominated

JULY 14

1798 **Tax**—federal tax levied directly upon states—enacted

1820 **Lightship**—Craney Island, Va.

1832 **Narcotics Legislation**—narcotics tari opium exempted from duty

1853 **Fair**—industrial exposition—opened President Franklin Pierce—New York

1868 **Tape Measure Patent**—A. J. Fellows— Haven, Conn.

1870 **Pension**—pension to the widow of a Pr dent—authorized

1891 **Corkboard Patent**—J. T. Smith—Brook N.Y.

1911 **Aviation**—airplane to land on the W House lawn—H. N. Atwood—Washing D.C.

1914 **Rocket**—liquid fuel rocket patent—R Goddard—Worcester, Mass.

1917 **Wedding**—wedding abroad of a soldi the American Expeditionary Force— don, England

1917 **World War I**—American Army casual L. J. Genelba—Arras, France

1945 **World War II**—Japanese homeland b bardment by the U.S. Navy—Kama Honshu, Japan

1950 **Medal**—Distinguished Flying Cross in Korean War—R. E. Wayne

1951 **Horse**—horse to win $1 million in rac Citation—Inglewood, Calif.

51 **Television—Telecast**—sports event televised in color—Oceanport, N.J.

53 **Monument**—national monument dedicated to a black American—G. W. Carver—Newton County, Mo.

53 **Vice President (U.S.)**—Vice President to preside at a National Security Council meeting—R. M. Nixon

54 **Radio Sextant**—announced—Cedar Rapids, Iowa

59 **Ship**—atomic-powered cruiser—*Long Beach*—launched—Quincy, Mass.

65 **Photograph**—planet close-up photographs—*Mariner 4*

65 **Satellite**—satellite to transmit a close-up photograph of Mars—*Mariner 4*—transmitted for 8.5 hours

72 **Political Party**—permanent chairman (woman) of a major political party—F. J. M. Westwood—elected at Miami Beach, Fla.

JULY 15

2 **Bridge**—bridge of importance—West Boston Bridge—construction begun

1 **Billboard Standardization**—Associated Bill Posters and Distributors of the United States and Canada—formed—Chicago, Ill.

4 **Buddhist Temple**—established—Los Angeles, Calif.

3 **Senator (U.S.)**—senator elected by popular vote after the passage of the Seventeenth Amendment—A. O. Bacon—elected—Georgia

0 **Army Officer**—chaplain (chief) of the U.S. Army—J. T. Axton—appointed

0 **Aviation—Flights**—New York–Alaska flight—left New York City

2 **Aquatic Mammals**—platypus (duckbill)—exhibited—New York City

2 **Golf Champion**—golf champion to win the United States Open and the Professional—Gene Sarazen—won United States Open—Glencoe, Ill.

3 **Railroad**—railroad operated by the federal government—Alaska Railroad—golden spike driven—W. G. Harding—Nenana, Alaska

9 **Aviation—Airport**—airport hotel—opened—Oakland, Calif.

9 **Farm Board (federal)**—organization meeting

3 **Aviation—Flights (transatlantic)**—transatlantic foreign squadron flight to the United States—Italo Balbo—arrived—Chicago, Ill.

3 **Aviation—Flights (world)**—world solo airplane flight—W. H. Post—left—New York City

0 **Betatron**—operated—University of Illinois—Urbana, Ill.

2 **Ship**—Navy vessel constructed as a minelayer—*Terror*—commissioned

2 **Helicopter—Flights**—helicopter transatlantic flight—left for Germany

1954 **Aviation—Airplane**—jet transport commercial airplane built in the United States—tested—Renton, Wash.

1964 **Presidential Candidate**—woman presidential candidate of a major political party—M. C. Smith—nominated—San Francisco, Calif.

JULY 16

1769 **California Mission**—blessed—San Diego, Calif.

1773 **Methodist Conference**—Philadelphia, Pa.

1779 **Revolutionary War**—bayonet charge in the Revolutionary War—Anthony Wayne—Stony Point, N.Y.

1798 **Hospital**—marine hospital (U.S.)—authorized

1798 **Public Health**—Public Health Service (U.S.)—established

1840 **College**—women's college (chartered)—Wesleyan College—Macon, Ga.—first class graduated

1845 **Yacht Race**—regatta—of importance—New York Yacht Club—New York City

1862 **Naval Officer**—naval officer to become an admiral—D. G. Farragut—appointed rear admiral

1867 **Paint**—paint (ready-mixed)—patented—D. R. Averill—Newburg, Ohio

1877 **Strike**—strike in which federal troops were called in peacetime

1912 **Torpedo**—airplane torpedo—patented—B. A. Fiske

1920 **Army Officer**—chemical warfare chief—A. A. Fries—appointed

1920 **Radio Telephone**—radio telephone service (commercial)—inaugurated—Los Angeles–Santa Catalina Island, Calif.

1926 **Air Corps**—Air Corps (U.S. Army)—F. T. Davison—sworn in as Assistant Secretary of War for Aviation

1926 **Photograph**—photographs taken under the sea in natural colors—Tortugas, Fla.

1934 **Aviation**—floating seaplane ramp (municipally owned)—first passenger flight docked

1935 **Parking Meter**—parking meter (automatic)—installed—Oklahoma City, Okla.

1936 **X ray**—X-ray photograph showing the complete arterial circulation—completed—Rochester, N.Y.

1939 **Locomotive**—rack-rail diesel-electric locomotive—in service—Manitou and Pike's Peak Railway

1941 **Baseball Player**—baseball player to hit in more than 50 consecutive games—J. P. Di Maggio—56th game

1945 **Atomic Bomb**—atomic bomb explosion—Alamogordo, N.Mex.

1946 **Telephone**—mobile telephone conversation overseas—from a moving vehicle—St. Louis, Mo.–Honolulu

1958 **Television Station**—city to have two educational television channels—Pittsburgh,
Pa.—second channel granted

1966 **Tennis Player**—brother and sister to win
national singles title championships in the
same tournament—Clifford Richey and
Nancy Richey—Milwaukee, Wis.

1971 **Air Force Officer**—Air Force general (woman)—J. M. Holm—commissioned

JULY 17

1794 **African Church**—opened—Philadelphia,
Pa.

1839 **Britannia Ware**—patent—Isaac Babbitt—
Boston, Mass.

1850 **Photograph**—photograph of a star—Vega
—Cambridge, Mass.

1850 **Telegraph**—telegraph convention (national)—New York City

1861 **Money**—demand notes—authorized

1861 **Money**—paper money issued by the government of the United States—authorized

1862 **Army**—law (federal) authorizing military
service for blacks—signed

1862 **Cemetery**—national cemeteries—authorized

1862 **Internal Revenue Commissioner**—G. S.
Boutwell—served

1866 **Tunnel**—subaqueous highway tunnel—
Washington Street Tunnel—Chicago, Ill.—
construction authorized

1867 **Dental School**—dental school permanently
established by a university—Harvard
School of Dental Medicine—established—
Boston, Mass.

1896 **Cricket Club**—college cricket club team to
tour England—began competition

1904 **Carnegie Hero Fund Commission**—L. A.
Baumann, Jr.—heroic act—Wilkinsburg,
Pa.

1916 **Farm Loan Board (federal)**—Federal Farm
Loan Act—approved

1930 **Prizefighter**—pugilist to win and lose a
championship in the first round—Abraham
("Al") Singer—New York City—defeated
Sammy Mandell

1933 **Aviation—Flights (transcontinental)**—
transcontinental flight made by blacks in
their own plane—left Atlantic City, N.J.

1933 **Industrial Recovery Act**—code under the
National Industrial Recovery Act—effective

1953 **Aviation—Pilot**—naval ace in Korea—Guy
Bordelon

1954 **Baseball Game**—major league game in
which the majority of the players on one
team were blacks—Brooklyn Dodgers

1955 **Electric Power**—electric power generated
from atomic energy to illuminate an entire
town—Arco, Idaho

1962 **Aviation—Pilot**—pilot in an airplane
qualify as an astronaut—R. M. White

1975 **Astronaut**—astronauts (American) to p
ticipate in an international spaceflight—
P. Stafford and D. K. Slayton—*Apollo XV*
—docked with *Soyuz XIX*

1980 **Methodist Church**—bishop (woman)—
S. Matthews—elected—Dayton, Ohio

JULY 18

1627 **Oil**—oil spring—Cuba, N.Y.—described
letter

1743 **Advertisement**—double-column adverti
ment—New York *Weekly Journal*—N
York City

1775 **Revolutionary War**—Revolutionary W
volunteer detachment—arrived in Ca
bridge, Mass.

1794 **Money**—deposit of silver for coinage
Bank of Maryland

1846 **Road**—plank road—completed—Syracu
N.Y.

1853 **Railroad**—international railroad—tra
from Portland, Me., to Montreal, Cana

1863 **Medal**—Medal of Honor (Army) earned
a black—W. H. Carney—for bravery in
tion at Fort Wagner, S.C.

1866 **Insurance**—insurance rate standardizat
—effected—New York City

1896 **Golf Tournament**—amateur golf tour
ment of the United States Golf Associat
in which a black contestant was entere
J. M. Shippen—Southampton, N.Y.

1900 **Bowling**—duckpins—first match—Un
Hill, N.J.

1908 **Fireworks Legislation**—fireworks legi
tion enacted by a city—Cleveland, Oh

1914 **Aviation**—air service of the United Sta
Army—aviation section created

1938 **Building**—building devoted entirely
highway traffic—ground broken—Sau
tuck, Conn.

1940 **Helicopter**—helicopter (direct-lift-aircr
—flight—Stratford, Conn.

1943 **World War II**—airship (American) los
enemy action—K-74

1955 **Electric Power**—electric power genera
from atomic energy to be sold commerc
ly—West Milton, N.Y.

1955 **Television—Telecast**—commercial fil
by a camera operated by atomically ge
rated electricity—produced—West Mil
N.Y.

1962 **Aviation—Pilot**—pilot in an airplane
qualify as an astronaut—R. M. Whi
awarded astronaut wings

1980 **Horse Race**—horse race for a purse of m
than $1 million—Meadowland, East
therford, N.J.

1980 **Methodist Church**—bishop (woman)—
S. Matthews—consecrated—Selinsgr
Pa.

1921 Aviation—battleship sunk by an airplane —near Hampton Roads, Va.

1928 Motion Picture—talking picture whose footage exceeded 6,000 feet—*The Lights of New York*—released

1930 Veterans' Bureau—Veterans Administration—created

1934 Labor Relations—National Mediation Board—organized

1946 Aviation—Airplane—jet airplane to land on a ship—FD-I *Phantom*—on carrier *Franklin D. Roosevelt*—Cape Henry, Va.

1955 Submarine—submarine powered by a liquid-metal-cooled atomic reactor—*Seawolf* —launched—Groton, Conn.

1959 Ship—atomic-powered merchant ship— *Savannah*—christened—Camden, N.J.

1961 Astronaut—astronaut (American) to make a suborbital flight twice—V. I. Grissom— first takeoff—Cape Canaveral, Fla.

1962 Hammer Throw—hammer throw to exceed 231 feet—Harold Connolly—Palo Alto, Calif.

JULY 22

1887 Postal Service—parcel post convention— with Jamaica

1896 Silverites—national convention—St. Louis, Mo.

1932 Federal Home Loan Bank Board—established

1932 Home Owners' Loan Corporation—Federal Home Loan Bank Act—approved

1933 Aviation—Pilot—woman pilot to fly across the Atlantic Ocean east–west—A. J. Mollison—left—Pendine, Wales

1933 Aviation—Flights (world)—world solo airplane flight—W. H. Post returned—Floyd Bennett Field—New York City

1933 Opera—black prima donna of an opera company—Caterina Jarboro—*Aida*—New York City

1939 Judge—woman judge (black)—J. M. Bolin —appointed—New York City

1955 Vice President (U.S.)—Vice President to preside over a Cabinet meeting—R. M. Nixon—Washington, D.C.

1963 Bank—major bank to lease personal property—Bank of America, San Francisco, Calif.—service instituted

1964 Aquanaut—United States Navy divers to submerge 10 days—*Sealab 1*—off Hamilton, Bermuda—descended

1978 Ballet—ballet transmitted by satellite— telecast over WNEW-TV, New York City

1979 Golfer—golfer to shoot below his age—S. J. Snead—Coal City, Ill.

JULY 23

1715 Lighthouse—lighthouse—Little Brewster Island, Mass.—authorized

1827 Swimming School—opened—Boston, Mass.

1829 Typewriter—typewriter—patented—W. A. Burt—Mount Vernon, Mich.

1833 Mormon Temple—cornerstone laid—Ki land, Ohio

1877 Railroad—municipal railroad—service b gan—Cincinnati, Ohio

1880 Electric Power Plant—hydroelectric pow plant (commercial)—Grand Rapids Electr Light and Power Company—Grand Rapic Mich.—in operation

1885 Bankers' Association—bankers' associ tion formed by a state group—Texas Ban ers' Association—organized—Lampasa Texas

1921 Long Jump—broad jump to reach mc than 25 feet—E. O. Gourdin—Cambrid Mass.

1924 Automobile Bus—bus operated by a ra road—Spokane, Portland and Seat Transportation Company—incorporated

1933 Aviation—Pilot—woman pilot to fly acro the Atlantic Ocean east–west—A. J. Mo son—crash-landed—Stratford, Conn.

1937 Pituitary Hormone—pituitary hormone i lated—announced—Yale Univers School of Medicine—New Haven, Conn

1938 Game Preserve—game preserve appropr tion (federal)—state aid project approv —Utah

1945 Railroad Car—car with an observat dome

1947 Navy—air squadron of jets—Quon Point, R.I.

1947 War Veterans' Society—World War II v erans' society officially recognized by C gress—American Veterans of World W II—chartered

1962 Television—Telecast—satellite telec live to Europe

1962 Television—Telecast—transatlantic change of live television programs— Telstar

1965 Money—coins bearing dates other than year of issue—authorized

1968 Vietnam War—general killed in action Vietnam—R. F. Worley

JULY 24

1844 Pump—independent single direct-act steam power pump—patented—H. Worthington—New York City

1847 Printing Press—rotary type printing pr —patented—R. M. Hoe—New York Ci

1849 Degrees (academic and honorary)—do of music degree—conferred—Georgeto University—Washington, D.C.

1866 State—state readmitted to the Unio Tennessee

1919 Aviation—Airplane—three-motor airpl —flight—Garden City, N.Y.

1933 Surgical Operation—lung removal car out according to preoperative plans—W Reinhoff, Jr.—Baltimore, Md.

1934 Birds—ptarmigan (Eskimo chick hatched in captivity—Ithaca, N.Y.

1958 Television—Telecast—stratosphere tele-cast—Strato-Lab High III—Malcolm Ross and M. L. Lewis—landing in Jamestown, N. Dak.

1971 Brokerage—brokerage firm whose shares were traded by a major stock exchange—traded in New York City

JULY 28

1777 Suffrage—state to provide universal man-hood suffrage—Vermont—constitution adopted—Windsor, Vt.

1862 Postal Service—railroad post office—placed in operation—Hannibal and St. Jo-seph, Mo.

1865 Dental Code of Ethics—proposed—Ameri-can Dental Association—Chicago

1866 Monument—monument by a woman or-dered by the U.S. Government—authorized

1866 Weights and Measures Standardization—act legalizing the employment of the met-ric system—approved

1868 Education Department (U.S.)—Department of Education (U.S.)—Office of Education established

1869 Labor Union—women's labor organization (national)—Daughters of St. Crispin—con-vention—Lynn, Mass.

1875 Baseball Game—no-hit nine-inning base-ball game

1882 Accountants' Society—Institute of Ac-countants and Bookkeepers—organized—New York City

1885 Scale—coin-operated scale—invented by J. G. Sandeman and Percival Everitt—patent-ed

1903 Bank—bank president (black woman)—Saint Luke Penny Savings Bank—Rich-mond, Va.

1913 Senator (U.S.)—senator elected by popular vote after the passage of the Seventeenth Amendment—A. O. Bacon of Georgia—sworn in

1919 Bank—state bank wholly owned and oper-ated—opened—Bismarck, N. Dak.

1926 Catholic Church—Catholic church raised to the dignity of a basilica—Lackawanna, N.Y.

1933 Cotton—cotton acreage reduction payment—payment made

1933 Telegram—singing telegram—introduced—July 28

1942 Postal Service—coin-operated mailbox—patented—L. A. Thatcher—Stamford, Conn.

1959 Representative (U.S.)—representative of Japanese ancestry elected to the House of Representatives—D. K. Inouye

1964 Satellite—satellite to transmit lunar-sur-face close-up pictures—*Ranger VII*—launched—Cape Kennedy, Fla.

1977 Civil Aeronautics Board—Civil Aeron tics Board woman member—E. E. Baile appointment confirmed

JULY 29

1773 Schoolhouse—west of the Allegh mountains — completed — Schoenbru Ohio

1775 Army Officer—judge advocate—Will Tudor—served

1775 Treasury Department (U.S.)—Treasure the United States—Michael Hillega served

1786 Newspaper—newspaper published wes the Alleghenies—issued—*Pittsburgh zette*—Pittsburgh, Pa.

1794 African Church—Bethel African Metho Episcopal Church—opened—Philadelp Pa.

1847 Newspaper—Norwegian-American ne paper—*Nordlyset*—Muskego, Wis.

1865 Newspaper—newspaper published sea—*Atlantic Telegraph*—published

1870 Road—sheet asphalt pavement—laid—wark, N.J.

1888 Hotel—hotel transported—Brighton Be Hotel, Brooklyn, N.Y.—move complete

1899 Bicycle Race—motorcycle-paced bicy race—Manhattan Beach Track

1908 Price Regulation Legislation—price reg tion law (state)—effective—Louisiana

1933 Narcotics—narcotic sanatorium (fede for drug addicts—cornerstone laid—I ington, Ky.

1935 Police—police training school—of Fed Bureau of Investigation—initiated—W ington, D.C.

1943 Medal—Women's Army Corps Ser Medal—authorized

1949 Turbine—gas turbine used by an electr utility company—Oklahoma City, Okl

1952 Aviation—Flights (transpacific)—jet t spacific nonstop flight—Anchorage, A ka—Japan

1958 Space Agency (U.S.)—National Aeron tics and Space Administration—aut ized

1959 Jetway—jetway—installed—Internatio Airport, San Francisco, Calif.

1959 Senator (U.S.)—senator of Asian ance—Hiram Fong

1971 Patent Examiner—woman examine chief of the Patent Office and Tradem Office—appointment confirmed by Ser

1978 Football Game—football game in whic ferees were permitted to use televisior stant replays—Philadelphia Eagles Miami Dolphins—Canton, Ohio

JULY 30

1619 Legislative Assembly—Jamestown, Va

3 **Freemasons**—masonic lodge to work under a regular charter—St. John's lodge—established—Boston, Mass.

4 **Business Publication**—business publication—*South Carolina Price-Current*—Charles Town, S.C.—first known copy

4 **Yacht Club**—New York Yacht Club—organized

0 **Cracker**—meat biscuit—Gail Borden—patented

4 **Baseball Team**—baseball teams to travel beyond the confines of the United States—exhibition game—England

8 **Advertisement**—automobile advertisement—*Scientific American*

9 **Aviation—Airplane**—airplane purchased by the United States Government—tested—Dayton, Ohio

9 **Aviation—Flights**—intercity airplane flight—by a U.S. officer—B. D. Foulois—Fort Myer, Va.–Alexandria, Va.

9 **Aviation—Flights**—airplane endurance flight exceeding 400 hours—Dale Jackson and Forest O'Brine—St. Louis, Mo.—landed

3 **National Planning Board (U.S.)**—organized

7 **Ship**—seaplane tender designed and built for the United States Navy—*Curtiss*—authorized

6 **Rocket**—rocket to attain a 100-mile altitude—White Sands Proving Grounds, N.Mex.

6 **Motto of the United States**—"In God We Trust"—authorized

6 **Ship**—atomic-powered merchant ship—*Savannah*—authorized

8 **Submarine**—submarine to travel under the North Pole from the East—*Skate*—left New London, Conn.

5 **Medicare**—health insurance federal plan—enacted

JULY 31

9 **Patent**—patent granted by the United States Government—issued—Samuel Hopkins

2 **Building**—building erected in the United States for public use—cornerstone of mint—laid—Philadelphia, Pa.

2 **Mint (U.S.)**—Mint of the United States—cornerstone laid—Philadelphia, Pa.

5 **Money**—return of coins—to treasury

9 **Railroad Track**—railroad track (practical)—Philadelphia, Pa.

9 **Ordnance**—cannon (breech-loading)—patent—Benjamin Chambers

9 **Labor**—labor bureau (state)—Massachusetts Bureau of Statistics—H. K. Oliver—appointed chief

5 **Animals**—cattle importation law (U.S.)—prohibition enforced

1876 **Coast Guard (U.S.)**—Coast Guard officers' training school—established—New Bedford, Mass.

1888 **Telautograph** — telautograph — patented — Elisha Gray

1912 **Motion Picture Censorship**—motion picture censorship regulation (federal)—enacted

1918 **Chinaware**—dishes (complete set) made in America for the Executive Mansion—delivered—Washington, D.C.

1930 **Aviation—Airship**—dirigible landing and taking off from an oceangoing steamship—*Mayflower*—New York City

1933 **Science Advisory Board**—authorized

1953 **Television Station**—television network sales to exceed those of radio—FCC announced

1954 **Automobile School**—truck-driving training school—Bedford, Pa.—class graduated

1962 **Submarine**—submarines to rendezvous at the North Pole—*Skate* and *Seadragon*

1964 **Aquanaut**—United States Navy divers to submerge 10 days—*Sealab 1*—off Hamilton, Bermuda—surfaced

1964 **Navy**—all-nuclear task force voyage around the world without refueling—Task Force One—departed, Norfolk, Va.

1964 **Photograph**—moon close-up photographs—*Ranger VII*—taken

1964 **Satellite**—satellite to transmit lunar-surface close-up pictures—*Ranger VII*—impacted on moon

1971 **Astronaut**—astronauts (American) to ride a vehicle on another planet—D. R. Scott and J. B. Irwin

AUGUST 1

1776 **Jews**—Jew killed in the American Revolution—Francis Salvador—Seneca, S.C.

1787 **Constitution of the United States**—printed copies of the Constitution—proof sheets printed

1789 **Drawback Legislation**—tariff act—effective

1790 **Census**—census of the United States—enumeration

1841 **Business**—commercial rating agency—established—New York City

1842 **Postage Stamp**—adhesive stamps—City Despatch Post acquired by United States

1861 **Patent**—patent issued by the Confederate States of America—J. J. Van Houten

1861 **President (U.S.)**—President to serve as an official of the Confederate States—John Tyler—delegate

1872 **Gas**—pipeline (long-distance)—Newton Wells–Titusville, Pa.

1873 **Streetcar**—cable streetcar—operated—San Francisco, Calif.

1874 **Patent**—label patent—issued—Pearl Hominy Co.—Baltimore, Md.

1881 **Electric Power Plant**—hydroelectric power plant (commercial)—new station opened—Grand Rapids, Mich.

1886 **Zoological Laboratory (U.S.)**—zoological laboratory (U.S.) for the study of the parasites of livestock—opened—Washington, D.C.

1893 **Aviation—Expositions and Meets**—air conference (international)—Chicago, Ill.

1893 **Breakfast Food**—shredded wheat biscuits —patented

1893 **Medical School**—naval medical school—opened—Brooklyn, N.Y.

1906 **Diamond**—diamonds in actual rock—found—Murfreesboro, Ark.

1907 **Aviation**—aeronautical division of the United States War Department—authorized

1908 **Automobile Race**—automobile race New York–Paris, France

1908 **Insurance**—workers' compensation insurance law (federal)—effective

1911 **Aviation—License**—woman aviator to pass the test of the Aero Club of America—Harriet Quimby

1916 **Submarine**—cargo submarine to cross the Atlantic Ocean—*Deutschland*—returned

1923 **Hospital**—cancer hospital (municipal)—New York City Cancer Institute—New York City—dedicated

1930 **Electric Power Plant**—hydroelectric power plant (county-owned)—operated—Crisp County, Ga.

1930 **Photography**—photographic flashlight bulbs—manufactured—Schenectady, N.Y.

1933 **Poorhouse (state)**—superintendent—A. V. Gilliland—appointed

1934 **Aviation—Flights (transcontinental)**—transcontinental commercial overnight transport service—left Newark, N.J.

1939 **Vitamin**—synthetic vitamin K—made—L. F. Fieser—Cambridge, Mass.

1940 **Catholic Priest**—Catholic priest called to the Sacred Roman Rota—F. J. Brennan—appointed

1946 **Atomic Energy Commission**—Atomic Energy Commission—authorized

1950 **Garbage Collection**—city to discontinue garbage collection—Jasper, Ind.

1951 **Medal**—Medal of Honor awarded to a marine in the Korean War—presented—H. A. Commiskey

1953 **Building**—aluminum-faced building—Alcoa Building—completed—Pittsburgh, Pa.

1957 **Building**—commercial building heated by the sun—completed—Albuquerque, N.Mex.

1957 **Insurance**—insurance company to exclusively insure the lives of animals—New York City—founded

1960 **Submarine**—submarine to make a submerged passage from the Atlantic to the Pacific via the North Pole—*Seadragon* —left Portsmouth, N.H.

1963 **Postage Stamp**—fluorescent-coated (or tagged) postage stamp—8-cent airmail—issued—Dayton, Ohio

1966 **Atomic Energy Commission**—Atomic Energy Commission black member—S. M. Nabrit—began service

1972 **Rabbi**—woman rabbi—S. J. Priesand—appointed—New York City

1972 **Vice Presidential Candidate**—vice presidential candidate of a major political party to resign—T. F. Eagleton of Missouri—resigned

AUGUST 2

1776 **Declaration of Independence (American)**—Declaration of Independence was first ordered "to be fairly engrossed" on parchment—copy signed

1791 **Patent**—patent granted jointly to a father and son—Samuel Briggs, Sr. and Jr.—Philadelphia, Pa.

1819 **Aviation—Parachute**—parachute jump from a balloon—Charles Guille—New York City

1858 **Postal Service**—street letter box—erected —Boston, Mass., and New York City

1862 **Army Ambulance Corps**—established

1886 **Oleomargarine**—oleomargarine legislation (federal)—enacted

1909 **Aviation—Airplane**—airplane purchased by the United States Government—accepted

1923 **President (U.S.)**—President and President's wife to die during the term for which he had been elected—W. G. Harding and F. K. Harding

1927 **Submarine**—streamlined submarine of the U.S. Navy—*Nautilus*—keel laid—Mare Island, Calif.

1934 **Aviation—Flights**—"airplane train" started—Floyd Bennett Field, N.Y.

1946 **Atomic Energy**—atomic energy peacetime production—delivered—Barnard Free Skin and Cancer Hospital, St. Louis, Mo.

1958 **Aviation—Flights**—airplane endurance flight exceeding 1,200 hours—Jim Heth and Bill Burkhart—Dallas, Tex.—takeoff

1962 **Submarine**—submarines to rendezvous at the North Pole—*Skate* and *Seadragon* successful mission announced

1965 **Telephone**—Trimline telephone—commercially available—Michigan

1971 **Insurance**—crime insurance federal policy —issued to William Early

AUGUST 3

1750 **Teaching Methods Book**—completed—Germantown, Pa.

1807 **Vice President (U.S.)**—Vice President arrested—Aaron Burr—trial began—Richmond, Va.

1816 **Coast Survey Superintendent**—F. R. Hassler—appointed

52 **Boat Race**—intercollegiate boat race—Lake Winnepesaukee, N.H.

61 **Ship** — balloon carrier — *Fanny* — used — Fortress Monroe, Va.

80 **Canoe Association**—American Canoe Association—formed—Lake George, N.Y.

82 **Immigration**—immigration head tax—enacted

86 **Ship**—battleship of importance—*Maine*—authorized

86 **Ship**—torpedo boat of importance—*Cushing*—authorized

04 **"American"**—as an adjective—official—Secretary of State John Hay

04 **Aviation—Airship**—dirigible circular flight—T. S. Baldwin—Oakland, Calif.

22 **Radio Broadcast**—drama (full-length melodrama) broadcast—Schenectady, N.Y.

38 **Athlete**—two-time winner of the Associated Press Athlete of the Year award—J. D. Budge—first award

42 **Naval Officer**—woman naval officer commissioned in the U.S. Naval Reserve—M. H. McAfee—inducted

45 **Radio Facsimile Transmission**—color photoradio news photograph transmitted by radio for publication—received—Washington, D.C.

49 **Holiday**—Flag Day federal legislation—enacted

55 **Horse**—trotter triple-crown winner—Scott Frost—(Hambletonian) Goshen, N.Y.

58 **Navy**—naval man to reenlist while under the North Pole—J. R. Sordelet

58 **Submarine**—submarine crossing of the North Pole underwater—*Nautilus*

62 **Diplomatic Service**—ambassador (woman) to a communist bloc nation—E. M. Anderson—presented credentials, Sofia, Bulgaria

AUGUST 4

90 **Bonds**—bonds—of the United States Government—authorized

90 **Coast Guard (U.S.)**—Coast Guard—Revenue Cutter service organized

90 **Navy**—naval protection—Revenue Cutter service organized

90 **Refunding act (federal)**—approved

90 **Ship**—revenue cutter—*Massachusetts*—authorized

46 **Treasury Department (U.S.)**—treasury department (U.S.)—Sub-Treasury—authorized

74 **Chautauqua Organization**—formed—Fair Point, N.Y.

86 **Postal Service**—special delivery service—extended to all free delivery offices

86 **Postage Stamp**—special delivery stamp—on sale

94 **Railroad**—railroad to use an electric engine—for freight service

21 **Radio Broadcast**—tennis match broadcast—Sewickley, Pa.

1927 **Radio Station**—radio station operating a 100-kilowatt transmitter—2XAG—Schenectady, N.Y.

1930 **Bobsled Run**—North Elba, N.Y.—work begun

1937 **Animals**—okapi—imported—New York City

1942 **President (U.S.)**—President to become a godfather to a member of the British Royal Family—F. D. Roosevelt

1943 **Election Law**—election law permitting persons 18 years of age or older to vote—Georgia—constitutional amendment approved by popular vote

1943 **Medal**—Navy Expert Pistol Shot Medal awarded to a woman—awarded—Rosalie Thorne

1949 **Medal**—Distinguished Service Medal (Coast Guard)—established

1952 **Helicopter—Flights**—helicopter transatlantic flight—completed—Germany

1956 **Motorcycle Race**—motorcycle to exceed 200 miles an hour—Wilhelm Herz—Wendover, Utah

1977 **Department of Energy (U.S.)**—Department of Energy—created

AUGUST 5

1736 **Newspaper**—newspaper published south of the Potomac River—*Virginia Gazette*—Williamsburg, Va.

1763 **Prizefighter**—American to win distinction in the prize ring—Bill Richmond—born—Staten Island, N.Y.

1799 **Supreme Court (U.S.) Decision**—Supreme Court decision between states—term began—New York vs. Connecticut

1843 **Ship**—frigate (American-built, steam-driven) to cross the Atlantic Ocean—left Norfolk, Va.

1858 **Cable**—cable across the Atlantic Ocean completed

1861 **Tax**—federal income tax—law enacted

1870 **Knights of Pythias**—Supreme Lodge—incorporated

1892 **Money**—commemorative coinage—authorized

1892 **Money**—silver coins—Columbian half dollar—authorized

1909 **Tax**—corporation tax—enacted

1911 **Aviation—Races**—intercity airplane race—New York City–Philadelphia, Pa.

1914 **Traffic Light**—electric traffic signal lights—installed—Cleveland, Ohio

1921 **Cartoon**—cartoon awarded a Pulitzer prize—Rollin Kirby—New York City

1921 **Radio Broadcast**—baseball game broadcast with a play-by-play description—Pittsburgh, Pa.

1923 **Swimmer**—American to swim the English Channel—H. F. Sullivan

1926 **Motion Picture**—talking picture—presented—New York City

1933 **Labor Relations**—labor board (national)—authorized

1951 **Medal**—Air Force Medal of Honor for action in the Korean War—L. J. Sebille—killed in action

1964 **Vietnam War**—pilot (American Navy) shot down and captured in North Vietnam—Everett Alvarez, Jr.

1968 **Television—Telecast**—political convention telecast in color—29th Republican National Convention—opened—Miami Beach, Fla.

1973 **Tennis Match**—lawn tennis match (doubles) for the Davis Cup to exceed 100 games—Stan Smith and Erik Van Dillen vs. Jaime Fillol and Pat Cornejo—North Little Rock, Ark.

1977 **Department of Energy (U.S.)**—Department of Energy—J. R. Schlesinger, first secretary—appointed

AUGUST 6

1727 **Convent**—convent—permanently established—New Orleans, La.

1774 **Conscientious Objectors**—arrived—New York City

1774 **Shaker Society**—arrived—New York City

1787 **Constitution of the United States**—printed copies of the Constitution—proof sheets delivered to convention

1819 **Engineering College**—civil engineering course—Norwich University—Northfield, Vt.

1819 **Military School**—military school—American Literary, Scientific and Military Academy—Northfield, Vt.

1832 **Phrenologist**—J. G. Spurzheim—arrived—New York City

1846 **Warehouse**—warehouse legislation—enacted

1856 **Calliope**—marine exhibition—on tugboat *Union*

1857 **Cable**—cable across the Atlantic Ocean paid out

1890 **Execution**—electrocution of a human being—William Kemmler—Auburn, N.Y.

1909 **Automobile Transcontinental Trip**—transcontinental automobile trip by a woman—arrived in San Francisco from New York City

1912 **Progressive Party**—national convention—Chicago, Ill.

1914 **World War I**—American to sail to Europe to enlist in World War I—D. P. Dowd, Jr.—enlisted

1926 **Woman**—American woman to swim the English Channel—Gertrude Ederle

1936 **Catholic Mass**—Catholic mass in an airship over the ocean by an American priest—J. R. Cox

1942 **Congress (U.S.)**—reigning queen to address a joint session of Congress—Queen Wilhelmina of the Netherlands

1945 **Atomic Bomb**—atomic bomb explosion over enemy territory—Hiroshima, Japan

1971 **Road**—road paved with glasphalt—completed—Omaha, Neb.

1973 **Judge**—woman trial judge of the U.S. Court of Claims—C. P. Murphy—sworn in

1980 **Horse Race**—horse race for a purse of more than $2 million—Woodrow Wilson Purse—East Rutherford, N.J.

AUGUST 7

1679 **Ship**—Great Lakes commercial vessel—*Griffon*—first voyage

1782 **Medal**—Order of the Purple Heart—established—Newburgh, N.Y.

1789 **Lighthouse**—lighthouse built after American independence—authorized

1789 **War Department (U.S.)**—War Department (U.S.)—authorized

1807 **Ship**—steamboat to make regular trips—*Clermont*—tested

1847 **Plow**—plow for pulverizing the soil—patented—George Page—Washington, D.C.

1854 **Republican Party**—Republican Party meeting (local)—convention—Strong, Me.

1859 **Deaf—Church Service**—church service for the deaf—in St. Ann's Church for Deaf Mutes—New York City

1869 **Photograph**—photograph of a total solar eclipse—Mount Pleasant, Iowa

1888 **Door**—door (revolving)—patented—Theophilus Van Kannel—Philadelphia, Pa.

1897 **Submarine**—submarine contract of the U.S. Navy—*Plunger* launched

1916 **Farm Loan Board (federal)**—commission—G. W. Norris—served

1918 **Aviation**—air squadron (complete)—cross German lines

1919 **Actors' Union**—strike called

1930 **Diplomatic Service**—chief executive-elect of a foreign country—E. O. Herrera—sworn in as President of Colombia

1941 **Television—Telecast**—audience-participation telecast—New York City

1942 **World War II**—American offensive in the Pacific area—Guadalcanal

1953 **Medal**—Navy-Marine Corps Medal for Heroism awarded to a woman—B. O. Barwell

1959 **Satellite**—satellite to transmit photographs of the earth—Cape Canaveral, Fla.

1974 **Tightrope Walker**—tightrope walker to span 2 skyscrapers—Philippe Petit—New York City

AUGUST 8

1679 **Fire**—fire of serious consequence—Boston, Mass.

1786 **Money**—decimal system of money—standards established

1797 **Medical Periodical**—medical magazine—*Medical Repository*—New York City

1976 **Soccer**—soccer game in which 12 points were scored by 1 player—Giorgia Chinaglia—Cosmos vs. Toros—New York City

AUGUST 11

1760 **Methodist Church**—Methodist preacher—Philip Embury—arrived

1860 **Silver Mill**—ore crushed

1861 **Senator (U.S.)**—senator in military uniform to address the Senate—E. D. Baker of Oregon

1868 **Knights of Pythias**—Supreme Lodge convened—Washington, D.C.

1874 **Sprinkler**—sprinkler head—patented—H. S. Parmelee—New Haven, Conn.

1896 **Electric Light Socket**—with pull chain—patented—Harvey Hubbell—Bridgeport, Conn.

1906 **Aviation—Airship**—woman airship passenger—M. P. Miller—Franklin, Pa.

1909 **Radio Distress Signal**—radio SOS from an American ship—*Arapahoe*—received—Cape Hatteras, N.C.

1910 **Pan American Union**—Pan American Union—name adopted

1914 **Motion Picture**—animated cartoon (present technique)—patent—J. R. Bray

1924 **Motion Picture**—talking pictures of presidential candidates—taken—Washington, D.C.

1928 **Radio Broadcast**—presidential nomination ceremony broadcast—H. C. Hoover—Palo Alto, Calif.

1930 **Lutheran Church**—American Lutheran Church—organized—Toledo, Ohio

1933 **Ship**—steamship to cross the Atlantic Ocean in less than 5 days—*Rex*—sailed from Gibraltar

1943 **Horse Race**—harness race driver to win the Hambletonian four times—B. F. White

1951 **Television—Telecast**—baseball games televised in color—New York City—Brooklyn Dodgers–Boston Braves

1960 **Flag**—American flag to orbit the earth—*Discoverer XIII*—recovered

1960 **Satellite**—space capsule recovered from an orbiting satellite—Pacific Ocean

1972 **Navy**—women (other than nurses) assigned to regular shipboard duty—R. E. Nelson

1980 **Automobile**—front-wheel-drive subcompact American automobile—World Car—Ford Motor Company, Fort Wayne, Mich.—first car off assembly line

AUGUST 12

1585 **Letter**—letters written in English—in America—Ralph Lane

1834 **Dentistry**—amalgam for filling teeth—advertised—New York City

1851 **Sewing Machine**—sewing machine equipped with a rocking treadle or double treadle—patented—I. M. Singer—New York City

1862 **Postage Stamp**—encased postage stamp—patented—John Gault

1879 **Archery Club**—archery association (national)—tournament—Chicago, Ill.

1882 **Play (drama)**—Hebrew professional acting troupe—advertised—New York City

1898 **Territorial Expansion**—island territory—Hawaii—formally annexed

1912 **Dental Corps (U.S. Navy)**—Dental Corps the U.S. Navy—authorized

1912 **Motion Picture**—foreign feature film exhibited—commercially—*Queen Elizabeth*—New York City

1917 **College**—women's volunteer college unit serve overseas—Smith College Relief Unit—sailed

1918 **Airmail Service**—airmail regular service established—New York City

1918 **Marine Corps**—woman marine reserve—O. M. Johnson—enrolled

1918 **Ship**—concrete barge—*Socony 200*—commissioned—New York City

1923 **Camera**—motion picture camera (portable)—advertised

1931 **Aviation—License**—glider license class "C"—N.A.A. award to a woman—H. N Barnaby

1932 **Radio Telephone**—two-way conversation between a glider and the land—New York City

1934 **Servite Church**—Marian Congress—Portland, Oreg.

1953 **Ship**—woman to sail solo across the Atlantic Ocean—Ann Davidson—arrived—Miami, Fla.

1954 **Execution**—execution (federal) for the killing of a Federal Bureau of Investigation agent—Gerhard Puff

1958 **Submarine**—submarine to travel under the North Pole from the East—*Skate*—in polynya

1960 **Satellite**—communications satellite—launched—Cape Canaveral, Fla.

AUGUST 13

1587 **American Indians**—American Indian Protestant—Manteo

1751 **Academy**—Academy and College of Philadelphia—opened

1844 **College**—university on the Pacific Coast—Willamette University—Salem, Oreg.—opened

1860 **Insurance**—nonforfeiture insurance policy—New York Life Insurance Company—New York City

1872 **Gas**—water gas plant—patent—T. S. Lowe—Norristown, Pa.

1877 **Railroad**—municipal railroad—Cincinnati Southern Railway—freight service started

1930   **Submarine-Escape Training Tank**—submarine-escape training tank—used—New London, Conn.

1933   **Industrial Recovery Act**—postage stamps commemorating the National Recovery Act —sold—Washington, D.C.

1934   **Aviation**—floating seaplane ramp (municipally owned)—launched—Brooklyn, N.Y.

1936   **Union Party**—convention—Cleveland, Ohio

1937   **Automobile**—automobile-airplane combination—built—Santa Monica, Calif.

1947   **Telephone**—commercial telephone service on railroad trains for passengers—in operation—New York City to Washington, D.C.

1953   **Naval Officer**—naval officer to serve as chairman of the Joint Chiefs of Staff—A. W. Radford—began service

1954   **Water Skier**—water skier to jump 100 feet —Warren Witherell—Laconia, N.H.

1957   **Air Force Officer**—Air Force chairman of the Joint Chiefs of Staff—N. F. Twining— sworn in

1960   **Flag**—American flag to orbit the earth— presented to D. D. Eisenhower

1962   **Dock**—containership facility—Elizabeth, N.J.—opened

1967   **Fishing Reel**—electric spinning reel—introduced—Chicago, Ill.

1967   **Postage Stamp**—stamped envelope (phosphor-coated, luminescent tag)—tagged at Washington, D.C.

1970   **Football Player**—woman football player (professional)—Patricia Palinkas—Orlando, Fla.

1976   **Softball**—softball game of 365 innings— Monticello, N.Y.—game ended

AUGUST 16

1815   **Peace Society**—New York Peace Society— organized—New York City

1829   **Siamese Twins**—Siamese twins—Chang and Eng—arrived—Boston, Mass.

1838   **Music**—music convention—Boston, Mass.

1858   **Cable**—cable across the Atlantic Ocean completed—C. W. Field—Trinity Bay, Newfoundland—messages exchanged

1898   **Loop-the-Loop Centrifugal Railway**—patented—Edwin Prescott—Arlington, Mass.

1902   **Zoological Laboratory (U.S.)**—zoological laboratory (U.S.) for the study of parasites of man—chief—C. W. Stiles—appointed

1916   **Bird Legislation (international)**—Migratory Bird Treaty—signed

1918   **World War I**—German spy to receive a death sentence from the American forces during World War I—Lothar Witzke— found guilty

1920   **Baseball Player**—baseball player killed in a game—R. J. Chapman—New York City

1933   **Ship**—steamship to cross the Atlan Ocean in less than 5 days—*Rex*—arriv off Ambrose Light, N.J.

1937   **Traffic Regulation Course**—gradu course in traffic engineering and admin tration—established—Cambridge, Mass

1946   **United Nations**—Conference on Intern tional Organization—moved to Lake S cess, N.Y.

1957   **Ship**—aircraft carrier (atomic-powered *Enterprise*—ordered

1963   **Naval War College**—black officers to tend the Naval War College—G. I. Thom son and S. L. Gravely, Jr.—Newpc R.I.—began studies

AUGUST 17

1809   **Disciples of Christ**—organized—Washi ton, Pa.

1835   **Wrench**—wrench patent—Solyman M rick—Springfield, Mass.

1859   **Balloon—Flights**—balloon flight carry mail—left Lafayette, Ind.

1869   **Boat Race**—international boat race—L don, England

1891   **Bathhouse**—public baths with showers People's Bath—opened—New York City

1915   **Automobile Electric Self-Starter**—paten C. F. Kettering—Detroit, Mich.

1938   **Forest Service**—aircraft owned by the F est Service—in service—Oakland, Calif

1938   **Prizefighter**—pugilist to hold three titles multaneously—H. J. Armstrong

AUGUST 18

1587   **Births**—child born of English parents America—Virginia Dare—Roanoke Isla N.C.

1734   **Physician**—American-born doctor—grac ated abroad—William Bull—Leyden, Ne erlands

1838   **Expedition**—scientific expedition fitted by the United States Government—Charl Wilkes—left Hampton Roads, Va.

1840   **Dental Society**—dental society of impc tance—American Society of Dental S geons—organized—New York City

1840   **Photograph**—class photograph—S. F. Morse—Yale College, New Haven, Con

1856   **Diplomatic Service**—consul genera office established

1872   **Business**—mail-order house—A. M. Wa —catalog issued

1896   **Tennis Match**—lawn tennis champic who were brothers—National Lawn Ten Association

1908   **Navy**—naval nurses' corps—Superinte dent E. V. Hasson—began service

1911   **Representative (U.S.)**—representative attend college after his term of office— A. Bartlett—University of Nevada, Re Nev.—enrolled

13 **War Veterans' Society**—Veterans of Foreign Wars of the United States—formed—Denver, Colo.

17 **Radio Telephone**—radio telephone communication between the ground and an airplane—two-way communication—Langley Field, Va.

20 **Woman Suffrage**—woman suffrage amendment approved by Congress—ratification by Tennessee, 36th state

22 **Golf Champion**—golf champion to win the United States open and the Professional—Gene Sarazen—won Professional Golfers Tournament—Oakmont, Pa.

26 **Aviation—Airship**—dirigible made completely of metal—navy contract signed

26 **Television—Telecast**—weather map telecast—Arlington, Va.–Washington, D.C.

29 **Aviation—Races**—women's cross-country air derby—takeoff, Santa Monica, Calif.

31 **Patent**—plant patent—awarded—H. F. Bosenberg—New Brunswick, N.J.

32 **Aviation—Flights (transatlantic)**—transatlantic solo westward flight—J. A. Mollison—left Portmarnock, Ireland

37 **Postage Stamp**—first-day special cancellation

37 **Radio License**—frequency modulation (FM) construction permit—Yankee Network—Paxton, Mass.

45 **Bicycle Racer**—woman bicycle champion of the National Amateur Bicycle Association to win twice—M. M. Dietz—Chicago, Ill.

58 **Horse**—Haflinger horse—imported

60 **Photograph**—photograph bounced off a satellite—beamed—Cedar Rapids, Iowa

65 **School Legislation**—school law (state) to end de facto segregation—enacted—Massachusetts

76 **Postage Stamp**—nurse (individual) depicted on a postage stamp—Clara Maass—issued—Belleville, N.J.

78 **Aviation—Airship**—President's wife to pilot a dirigible—*America*—R. S. Carter

AUGUST 19

2 **Marine Corps**—woman marine—Lucy Brewer—served on *Constitution*

2 **War (1812)**—frigate action of importance in the War of 1812—*Constitution* and *Guerriere*

6 **Milk**—condensed milk (commercial) patented—Gail Borden—Brooklyn, N.Y.

8 **Aviation—Airplane**—fighter airplane—Kirkham fighter—tested—Garden City, N.Y.

9 **Aviation—Airship**—dirigible made completely of metal—tested—Grosse Ile, Mich.

2 **Aviation—Flights (transatlantic)**—transatlantic solo westward flight—J. A. Mollison—landed—New Brunswick, Canada

1940 **Aviation—License**—Civil Aeronautics Administration honorary license—awarded to Orville Wright

1942 **World War II**—American pilot to shoot down a German fighter plane—S. F. Junkin—Dieppe, France

1942 **World War II**—American to land on French soil in World War II—F. W. Koons—Dieppe, France

1957 **Balloon—Flights**—balloon flight to exceed an altitude of 100,000 feet—D. G. Simons—Crosby, Minn.

1957 **Submarine**—submarine submerged for 2 weeks (NATO exercises in North Atlantic)—*Nautilus*—left Groton, Conn.

1958 **Space Agency (U.S.)**—National Aeronautics and Space Administration—administrators appointed

1958 **Submarine**—submarine with two nuclear reactors—*Triton*—launched

1958 **Submarine**—submerged circumnavigation of the earth—*Triton*—launched

1960 **Satellite**—space capsule recovered from an orbiting satellite—Discoverer XIV (1960 Kappa)

AUGUST 20

1866 **Labor Legislation**—eight-hour day—advocated—unified action—Baltimore, Md.

1867 **Cartridge Belt Patent**—Anson Mills—Fort Bridger, Utah

1887 **Accountants' Society**—accountants' society to become a national organization—American Association of Public Accountants—incorporated

1908 **Post Office**—naval post office aboard a naval vessel—established—*Nebraska*

1910 **Aviation—Pilot**—pilot to fire a gun from an airplane—J. E. Fickel—Sheepshead Bay, N.Y.

1911 **Cable (telegram)**—cable message sent around the world by commercial telegraph—from New York City

1912 **Quarantine**—plant quarantine legislation (national)—enacted

1917 **Radio Telephone**—radio telephone communication between the ground and an airplane—conversation between two planes established

1920 **Newspaper**—newspaper to operate a radio station—*News* (Detroit, Mich.)—WWJ began operating

1920 **Radio Station**—commercial radio station—daily service—WWJ—Detroit, Mich.

1923 **Aviation—Airship**—dirigible (American-built rigid)—ZRI—launched—Lakehurst, N.J.

1930 **Television—Telecast**—demonstration of home reception of television—New York City

1948 **Birth Registration**—birth registration uniform system for the numbering of birth certificates

1955 **Aviation—Flights**—airplane to fly faster than the speed of 800 m.p.h.—H. A. Hanes —Palmdale, Calif.

1964 **Economic Opportunity Office (U.S.)** —Office of Economic Opportunity—authorized

AUGUST 21

1791 **Attorney General**—opinion by a U.S. Attorney General—Philadelphia, Pa.

1841 **Venetian Blinds**—venetian blind patent— John Hampson—New Orleans, La.

1862 **Money**—paper money fractional currency —issued

1878 **Lawyers' Association**—lawyers' association (national)—American Bar Association —organized—Saratoga, N.Y.

1888 **Adding Machine**—adding machine successfully marketed—patented—W. S. Burroughs—St. Louis, Mo.

1912 **Boy Scouts of America**—Boy Scout to become an eagle scout—A. R. Eldred— Oceanside, N.Y.

1914 **Newspaper Audit**—newspaper circulation audit—Audit Bureau of Circulations— formed—Chicago, Ill.

1923 **Aviation**—airways illumination—attempted

1928 **Television—Telecast**—puppet show to be televised—WOR—Newark, N.J.

1933 **Science Advisory Board**—first meeting

1959 **State**—noncontiguous overseas state—Hawaii—admitted

1965 **Astronaut**—astronaut (American) to orbit the earth on two trips L. G. Cooper—second takeoff—*Gemini V*—Cape Canaveral, Fla.

1965 **Astronaut**—two-man spaceflight (American) of 120 orbits—Gemini V—launched, Cape Kennedy, Fla.

1965 **Satellite**—satellite to use a fuel cell— *Gemini V*—launched—Cape Kennedy, Fla.

1968 **Medal**—Medal of Honor to a Marine (black) in the Vietnam war—James Anderson, Jr.—presented

1971 **Envelope**—commemorative issued in 2 sizes by the U.S. Post Office Department— Milwaukee, Wis.

1971 **School**—technical school for American Indians—dedicated Albuquerque, N. Mex.

AUGUST 22

1654 **Jews**—Jew—arrived—New Netherlands— Jacob Barsimson

1670 **American Indians**—American Indian preacher of Christianity—Hiacoomes—ordained

1762 **Woman**—woman newspaper editor—Ann Franklin—*Newport Mercury*—Newport, R.I.

1771 **Dwarf**—exhibited—Boston, Mass.

1818 **Ship**—steamboat built in America to cr the Atlantic Ocean—*Savannah*—launc

1822 **Printing Press**—printing press for prin "paper hangings"—(wallpaper)—paten —Peter Force—Washington, D.C.

1846 **Ship**—naval ship christened by a woma *Germantown*—L. F. Watson—Phila phia, Pa.

1851 **Yacht Race**—yacht race (internationa won by *America*

1865 **Soap**—soap in liquid form—patente William Sheppard—New York City

1902 **President (U.S.)**—President to ride in automobile—Theodore Roosevelt—H ford, Conn.

1906 **Phonograph**—phonograph with an closed horn in the cabinet—manufactu —Victor Victrola—Camden, N.J.

1909 **Aviation—Races**—airplane race won by American in Europe—G. H. Curtis Rheims, France

1928 **Television—Telecast**—presidential nc nation notification ceremony to be t vised—A. E. Smith—Albany, N.Y.

1939 **Cans**—disposable can for dispensing uids under pressure—J. S. Kahn—pater

1940 **Aviation—Airplane**—naval patrol bo er—*Mars*—keel laid—Baltimore, Md.

1942 **Ship**—ship transported overland acı the Rocky Mountains—*Brennan*—ass bled and launched as the *Bentinck*—M Island, Calif.

1971 **Motorcyclist**—woman motorcyclist— ry Kleid—licensed

AUGUST 23

1784 **State**—state denied admission into Union—Franklin—formed

1826 **College Student**—college graduate (bl —E. A. Jones—Amherst College, Amh Mass.

1838 **College**—college for women—Mount lyoke Seminary—South Hadley, Mas graduation

1853 **Bank** — clearinghouse — organizec New York City

1859 **Elevator**—elevator in a hotel—opene Fifth Avenue Hotel—New York City

1865 **War Criminal Proceedings**—Henry Wi trial

1892 **Streetcar**—transfers (printed)—J. H. S man—patented

1904 **Automobile Tire Chain**—patented—H Weed—Canastota, N.Y.

1912 **Commerce Department (U.S.)**—For and Domestic Commerce Bureau—crea

1916 **Submarine**—cargo submarine to cross Atlantic Ocean—*Deutschland*—retur to Germany—from Baltimore, Md.

1923 **Hospital**—cancer hospital (municipa New York City Cancer Institute— York City—patient admitted

5 Bank Legislation—bank guaranty legislation—insurance limited to $5000

6 Helicopter—Flights—transcontinental nonstop helicopter flight—San Diego, Calif.-Washington, D.C.

3 Golf Course—illuminated 9-hole regulation golf course—Tall Pines Golf Club, Sewell, N.J.—illuminated

3 Photograph—photograph taken from the moon of the earth—Lunar Orbiter 1—207 frames relayed back to earth

0 Swimmer—American swimmer to cover a distance of 1,500 meters free style in less than 16 minutes—John Kinselta—Los Angeles, Calif.

AUGUST 24

Catholic Holy Orders—conferred—St. Augustine, Fla.

Court-martial Trial—court-martial trial—Newport, R.I.

Education Association—education association (national)—constitution adopted

Pharmacy Society (national)—American Pharmaceutical Association—annual meeting—Boston, Mass.

Village Improvement Society—organized—Stockbridge, Mass.

Waffle Iron Patent—Cornelius Swarthout—Troy, N.Y.

Postal Card—postal card depicting other than the Liberty head—issued

Horse—horse to trot a mile in less than two minutes—Lou Dillon—Readville, Mass.

Postage Stamp—parcel post postage-due stamps—authorized

Ship—electrically propelled ship of the U.S. Navy—*Jupiter*—launched—Mare Island, Calif.

Aviation—Flights (transcontinental)—transcontinental nonstop flight by a woman—A. E. Putnam—left—Los Angeles, Calif.

Golfer—holes in one by a father and son—C. H. Calhoun, Sr. and Jr.—Washington, Ga.

Labor Relations—Labor Relations Act (national)—board appointed

Naval Officer—engineer inspector (woman)—Jean Hales—appointed

Naval Officer—woman naval inspector—Mrs. Jean Hales—appointed—Berkeley, Calif.

Submarine—submarine to make more than 13,000 dives—*Sarda*—launched—Portsmouth, N.H.

Diplomatic Service—black delegate to the United Nations from the United States—E. S. Sampson—appointed

1951 Medal—Air Force Medal of Honor for action in the Korean War—L. J. Sebille—medal presented posthumously—Riverside, Calif.

1959 Representative (U.S.)—representative of Japanese ancestry elected to the House of Representatives—D. K. Inouye—sworn in

1959 Senator (U.S.)—senator of Asian ancestry—Hiram Fong—sworn in

1963 Pole Vault—pole vault higher than 17 feet—John Pennel—Miami, Fla.

1964 Catholic Mass—Catholic mass in English (full English mass)—celebrated in St. Louis, Mo.

1964 Ship—nuclear ship named for a black—*George Washington Carver*—keel laid—Newport News, Va.

1964 Submarine—nuclear submarine named for a black—*George Washington Carver*—keel laid—Newport News, Va.

1969 Ship—commercial ship to conquer the Northwest Passage—*Manhattan*—left Chester, Pa.

1971 Patent Examiner—woman examiner-in-chief of the Patent Office and Trademark Office—sworn in

AUGUST 25

1814 President (U.S.)—President to face enemy gunfire while in office—James Madison—Bladensburg, Md.

1828 Labor Party (political)—labor party (state)—Workingmen's Party—convention—Philadelphia, Pa.

1830 Locomotive—race between a locomotive and a horse-drawn vehicle—Relay, Md.-Baltimore, Md.

1831 Bedspring—bedspring manufacturing patent—Josiah French

1840 Seeding Machine (practical)—patented—Joseph Gibbons—Adrian, Mich.

1843 Ship—frigate (American-built, steam-driven) to cross the Atlantic Ocean—arrived—Gibraltar

1886 Polo—international polo series—England vs. United States—Newport, R.I.

1902 Newspaper—Arabic daily newspaper—*Al-Hoda*—New York City

1916 Park Service (national)—National Park Service—authorized

1920 Aviation—Flights—New York–Alaska flight—arrived—Nome, Alaska

1922 Baseball Game—baseball game (major league) in which 49 runs were made in a 9-inning game—Chicago, Ill.

1924 Automobile Bus—bus operated by a railroad—highway operations began—Oregon and Washington

1925 Television Tube—miniature tube—patented—H. W. Weinhart, Elizabeth, N.J.

1940 Wedding—parachute wedding—New York City

1941 Insurance—health insurance clause in a labor contract—ILGWU—effective

1958 President (U.S.)—pension for Presidents—enacted

1959 Medal—National Medal of Science—authorized

AUGUST 26

1748 Lutheran Church—Lutheran services in English—synod held—Philadelphia, Pa.

1776 Pension—pension act of the Continental Congress

1790 Historical Society—historical society (state)—Massachusetts Historical Society —organized—Boston, Mass.

1843 Typewriter—typewriter that successfully typed—patented—Charles Thurber—Norwich, Conn.

1857 Teachers' Convention—teachers' convention (national)—National Teachers Association—organized—Philadelphia, Pa.

1858 Cable—news dispatch by cable—received —New York *Sun*

1873 Kindergarten—public school kindergarten —authorized—St. Louis, Mo.

1884 Typesetting Machine—linotype machine—patented—O. Mergenthaler—Baltimore, Md.

1890 Pan American Union—Pan American Union—W. E. Curtis appointed director

1895 Niagara Falls—utilization of Niagara Falls waterpower (large-scale)—power transmitted commercially

1920 Olympic Games—woman (American) to win an Olympic competition—Ethelda Bleibtrey

1920 Woman Suffrage—woman suffrage amendment approved by Congress—proclamation signed—Secretary of State Bainbridge Colby

1929 Aviation—Races—women's cross-country air derby—completed, Cleveland, Ohio

1938 Tape Recording—radio broadcast from a tape recording—WQXR—New York City

1939 Television—Telecast—baseball games (major-league) televised—Cincinnati Reds –Brooklyn Dodgers—New York City

1947 Representative (U.S.)—representative who had lost both legs in World War II—C. E. Potter of Michigan—began congressional service

1953 Medal—Medal of Honor awarded to a Nisei in the Korean War—H. H. Miyamura

1954 Radio Broadcast—editorial broadcast over a network—Frank Stanton—CBS network

1954 Television—Telecast—editorial opinion telecast on a network—Frank Stanton

1955 Television—Telecast—tennis tournament to be televised in color—Davis Cup matches—Forest Hills, N.Y.

AUGUST 27

1640 College—college—Henry Dunster—ser Harvard University—Cambridge, Mass as president

1650 Expedition—expedition—of Englishmen cross Allegheny Mountains

1665 Play (drama)—play given by nonprof sional actors—*Ye Bare and Ye Cubb*—p duced—Accawmack, Va.

1667 Cyclone—cyclone recorded—Jamesto Va.

1776 Land Grant—offered by Continental C gress to officers

1787 Ship—steamboat to carry a man—Jo Fitch—Delaware River

1856 Manual Training—industrial school girls—incorporated as a state institutio Lancaster, Mass.

1858 Cable—news dispatch by cable—p lished—New York *Sun*

1859 Oil—oil well commercially productiv discovered—Titusville, Pa.

1867 Railroad Crossing Gate Patent—pa awarded—Boston, Mass.

1867 Boat Race—international boat race—L don, England

1881 Pure Food Law—pure food and drug le lation (state)—effective—New York

1889 Clarinet—made exclusively of metal—p ented—C. G. Conn—Elkhart, Ind.

1894 Tax—federal income tax—declared und stitutional

1910 Radio Broadcast—radio broadcast s from an airplane—J. A. Macready

1915 Automobile Bus—bus with cross sea single-deck bus—New York City

1932 Autogiro—autogiro to loop the loop pub ly—J. M. Miller—Cleveland, Ohio

1957 Submarine—atomic-powered subma built at a naval shipyard—*Swordfis* launched—Portsmouth, N.H.

1959 Ship—ship to fire a Polaris missile—*Ob* *vation Island*

1962 Satellite—satellite to transmit data f Venus—*Mariner 2*—launched—Cape C averal, Fla.

1968 Diplomatic Service—ambassador ass sinated in office—J. G. Mein—Guatem City, Guatemala

AUGUST 28

1784 Ship—trading ship sent to China—*Emp* *of China*—arrived—Canton, China

1798 Vineyard (successful)—established—J Dufour—Lexington, Ky.

1830 Locomotive—locomotive built in the U ed States to pull passengers—*Tom Thu* —Baltimore, Md.

Music Instruction—music instruction (public schools)—appointment of teacher authorized

Engraving and Printing Bureau (U.S.)—Bureau of Engraving and Printing (U.S.)—operations began

Postal Service—railroad post office for the general distribution of mail—service tested—Chicago, Ill.-Clinton, Iowa

Territorial Expansion—territory (U.S.) outside the continental limits of the United States—Midway Island—claimed by William Reynolds

Steel—manganese steel for railroad tracks—manufactured—High Bridge, N.J.

Horse—horse to pace 1 mile in better than 2:00—Star Pointer—Readville, Mass.

Gyro Compass—gyro compass installed on an American naval vessel—*Delaware*—tested at sea

Actors' Union—Associated Actors and Artists of America—incorporated

Golf Tournament—international golf match—for Walker Cup—Southampton, N.Y.

Radio Broadcast—advertising or commercial radio broadcast—WEAF—New York City

Baseball Pitcher—pitcher (major league) to win 2 complete games in 1 day—E. H. Levsen—Boston, Mass.

Degrees (academic and honorary)—degree awarded a ventriloquist's dummy—Northwestern University—Evanston, Ill.

Satellite—weather satellite to provide high-resolution nightime cloud-cover pictures—*Nimbus 1*—launched at Point Arguello, Calif.

Ship—cargo ship fully automated and flying the America flag—*Mormacargo*—first run (Pascagoula, Miss., to Boston, Mass.)

Political Convention—national nominating convention to propose blacks for the offices of both President and Vice President—Chicago, Ill.—C. E. Phillips nominated

Presidential Candidate—black presidential candidate proposed by a major political party—E. E. Phillips—Chicago, Ill.

Air Force Officer—Air Force Ace in Vietnam—R. S. Ritchie

AUGUST 29

American Indian Reservation—American Indian reservation (state)—established—Indian Mills, N.J.

Newspaper—abolition newspaper—*Philanthropist*—published—Mount Pleasant, Ohio

Brake Patent—brake patent—Robert Turner—Ward, Mass.

Museum—college museum—curator authorized—Charleston, S.C.

1861 Civil War—Confederate forts to surrender—Fort Clark and Fort Hatteras—Hatteras Island, N.C.

1866 Railroad—cog railroad—public demonstration—Mount Washington, N.H.

1885 Prizefight—prizefight of importance under the Marquis of Queensberry rules—Cincinnati, Ohio

1889 Tennis Match—professional lawn tennis contest (international)—Newport Casino—Newport, R.I.

1892 Baseball Player—baseball player to catch a ball dropped from the Washington Monument—Billy ("Pop") Schriver—Washington, D.C.

1896 Chop Suey—concocted—New York City

1916 Aviation—Coast Guard aviation unit—authorized

1916 Ship—ambulance ship designed and built as a hospital—*Relief*—authorized

1920 Aviation—Flights—New York–Alaska flight—expedition left—Nome, Alaska

1929 Aviation—Passenger—dirigible passenger transfer to an airplane—A. W. Gorton—Cleveland, Ohio

1934 Bird Sanctuary—Hawk Mountain Sanctuary—Drehersville, Pa.—options received

1938 Building—building devoted entirely to highway traffic—cornerstone laid—Saugatuck, Conn.

1950 Tennis Match—national tennis tournament of the United States Lawn Tennis Association in which a black woman competed—Althea Gibson—Forest Hills, N.Y.

1952 Horse—two stable-mate trotters to break a world record the same day—Florican and Star's Pride—Du Quoin, Ill.

1957 Senator (U.S.)—senator to filibuster for more than 24 hours—Strom Thurmond of South Carolina—filibuster ended

1958 Air Force Academy (U.S.)—Air Force Academy—Colorado Springs, Colo.—received first Air Force cadets

1962 Television—television news commentator who was black—M. R. Goode—assigned—New York City

1963 Labor Relations—National Labor Relations Board black member—Howard Jenkins, Jr.—sworn in at Washington, D.C.

1965 Astronaut—astronaut (American) to converse with an aquanaut—L. G. Cooper *(Gemini V)* and M. S. Carpenter *(Sealab II)*—off La Jolla, Calif.

1965 Astronaut—two-man spacefight (American) of 120 orbits—*Gemini V*—landed, Atlantic Ocean

1966 Aviation—Parachute jumper snagged in midair—C. M. Alexander—Georgetown, Del.

1968 Political Convention—national nominating convention to propose blacks for offices of both President and Vice President—Chicago, Ill.—Julian Bond nominated

1972 **Baseball Pitcher**—pitcher to retire more than 40 batters in succession—Jim Barr—St. Louis, Mo.—reached record

AUGUST 30

1637 **Congregational Church**—Congregational Church council—Cambridge, Mass.

1842 **Narcotics Legislation**—narcotics tariff—enacted

1842 **Tariff**—tariff to prevent the importation of obscene literature and pictures—enacted

1875 **Music Instruction**—college music chair—established—Harvard University—Cambridge, Mass.

1884 **Theater**—theater to employ women ushers—Third Avenue Theatre—New York City

1890 **Meat Inspection Legislation (federal)**—enacted

1909 **Continuation School**—apprentice continuation school—established—Cincinnati, Ohio

1917 **Submarine**—submarine built at a government shipyard—*L-8*—commissioned

1926 **Horse Race**—harness horse race (Hambletonian) for three-year-olds—Syracuse, N.Y.

1929 **Automobile**—automobile (new-type gasoline-electric combination) delivered—E. H. R. Green—Schenectady, N.Y.

1929 **Submarine "Lung"**—tested—U.S. Navy

1931 **Aviation—Races**—airplane race (of importance) in which both men and women were contestants—Los Angeles, Calif.–Cleveland, Ohio

1934 **Postage Stamp**—dual-purpose postage stamp—issued—Chicago, Ill.

1934 **Postage Stamp**—seal of the United States on a postage stamp—issued—Chicago, Ill.

1961 **Judge**—black judge of a District Court (U.S.)—J. B. Parsons—confirmed

1962 **Telephone**—hot line—The White House, Washington, D.C., to the Kremlin, Moscow, Russia

1963 **Postal Card**—international postal card—issued—New York City

1966 **Judge**—black woman judge of a federal district court—C. B. Motley—appointment confirmed

1967 **Supreme Court (U.S.)**—Associate Justice of the Supreme Court who was a black—Thurgood Marshall—appointment confirmed

AUGUST 31

1809 **Catholic Periodical**—Catholic magazine in English—*Michigan Essay*—Detroit, Mich.

1826 **Ship**—warship to circumnavigate the globe—*Vincennes*—left—New York City

1842 **Navy**—Bureau of Medicine and Surgery—authorized

1842 **Nut and Bolt Machine**—Micah Rugg—patent

1852 **Postage Stamp**—stamped envelopes (U—authorized

1853 **Bank**—clearinghouse—plan presente New York City

1881 **Tennis Match**—lawn tennis national ch pionship matches—Newport, R.I.

1886 **Earthquake**—of importance—Charles S.C.

1904 **Olympic Games**—black American ath in the Olympic Games to place—G. C. age—St. Louis, Mo.

1910 **Aviation—Flights**—over-water flight—H. Curtiss—Cleveland–Sandusky, Ohi

1920 **Radio Broadcast**—election returns br cast—Detroit, Mich.

1920 **Radio Broadcast**—news program—Det Mich.

1934 **Football Game**—all-star football gam Chicago, Ill.

1935 **Skeet**—national skeet tournament–dianapolis, Ind.

1955 **Automobile**—sun-powered automobi demonstrated—Chicago, Ill.

1955 **Television Station**—microwave televi station—KTRE-TV—Lufkin, Tex.

1965 **Navy**—navy man to reenlist while u water—B. L. Coffman—La Jolla, Calif.

1970 **Tennis Match**—lawn tennis match (sing for the Davis Cup to exceed 80 games–R. Ash, Jr. vs. Christian Kuhnke—Cl land Heights, Ohio

SEPTEMBER 1

1635 **Jury**—grand jury—convened in N Towne, Mass.

1803 **Tract Society**—tract society—Ma chusetts Society for Promoting Chris Knowledge—instituted—Boston, Mass

1808 **Religious Publication**—religious revie *Herald of Gospel Liberty*—publish Portsmouth, N.H.

1819 **Plow**—plow with interchangeable par patented—J. J. Wood—Poplar Ridge, P

1836 **Colonist**—women to cross the contine reached Fort Walla Walla, Wash.

1855 **Book Trade Magazine**—successful t trade magazine—*American Publish Circular and Literary Gazette*—New Y City

1859 **Sleeping Car**—Pullman sleeping car service—Bloomington, Ill.–Chicago, Ill

1862 **Tobacco**—tobacco tax for internal rev —effective

1869 **Postal Service**—money order sys agreement effective—Switzerland

1872 **Nurse**—trained nurse—L. A. J. Richar instruction begun—Roxbury, Mass.

1873 **Nurse**—trained nurse—L. A. J. Richar instruction concluded—Roxbury, Mas

1878 **Telephone Operator**—woman telep operator—E. M. Nutt—Boston, Mass.

1880 **Tennis Match**—lawn tennis tourname national scope—Staten Island, N.Y.

7 **Accident Report**—industrial accident reports—law effective—Massachusetts

8 **College**—papal seminary—Pontifical College Josephinum—established—Worthington, Ohio

0 **Single Tax**—single tax national conference—New York City

4 **Health Laboratory**—health laboratory (state)—Providence, R.I.

7 **Subway**—municipal subway—opened for traffic—Boston, Mass.

8 **Forestry School**—forestry school dealing exclusively with problems of forestry—Biltmore Forest School—Biltmore, N.C.

7 **Court**—night court—opened—New York City

7 **Tunnel**—freight delivery tunnel system—completed—Chicago, Ill.

0 **Woman**—woman horseback rider to make a solo transcontinental trip—N. J. Aspinwall—left—San Francisco, Calif.

3 **Civic Design Chair**—C. M. Robinson served—Urbana, Ill.

5 **Bird Legislation (international)**—migratory bird treaty—ratified

5 **Child Labor Law**—child labor law (federal)—enacted

5 **Road**—federal grant-in-aid—project approved

7 **Child Labor Law**—child labor law (federal)—in force

0 **Communist Labor Party of America**—convention—Chicago, Ill.

0 **Aviation—Airplane**—airplane used by a newspaper—*Sun*—Baltimore, Md.

0 **Postal Service**—postage meter—approved

2 **Radio Broadcast**—news program (daily)—broadcast—New York City

4 **Navy**—Navy parachute school—Lakehurst, N.J.—opened

5 **Electric Lighting**—glass light bulb machine—patented—B. D. Chamberlin—Washington, D.C.

4 **Anthropology Laboratory**—opened—Sante Fe, N.Mex.

4 **Garage**—municipally owned parking building—Welch, W. Va.—opened

4 **Airmail Service**—parcel post domestic air service—began

4 **Postal Service**—parcel post domestic air service—begun

4 **Supreme Court (U.S.)**—law secretary (black) of the Supreme Court—W. T. Coleman—appointed

4 **Bicycle Rider**—bicycle rider to cross the continent in less than three weeks—Eugene McPherson—left Santa Monica, Calif.

4 **Television—Telecast**—prizefight in a "studio"—Philadelphia, Pa.

5. **Horse**—trotter triple-crown winner—Scott Frost—(Yonkers Futurity) Yonkers, N.Y.

5 **Ship**—roll-on, roll-off carrier—in service—Hyannis-Nantucket, Mass.

1967 **Supreme Court (U.S.)**—Associate Justice of the Supreme Court who was a black—Thurgood Marshall—sworn in (private ceremony)

1968 **School**—professional school for exclusively training potential circus clowns—established—Venice, Fla.

1974 **Naval Officer**—woman member of the Navy's Hurricane Hunters—J. A. Neuffer—flew into storm

SEPTEMBER 2

1775 **Ship**—warship regularly commissioned—*Hannah*—Marblehead, Mass.

1789 **Comptroller**—comptroller of the United States Treasury—office authorized

1789 **Treasury Department (U.S.)**—Treasury Department (U.S.)—organized

1858 **Cigar Band**—cigar band of special interest—C. W. Field—New York City

1884 **Electrical Show**—exhibition—Philadelphia, Pa.

1895 **College**—Catholic college for women—College of Notre Dame of Maryland—Baltimore, Md.—opened

1910 **Police**—police officer (woman) under civil service—A. S. Wells—appointed in Los Angeles, Calif.

1914 **Insurance**—war risk insurance bureau—established

1919 **Communist Labor Party of America**—name adopted

1919 **Communist Party of America**—formed—Chicago, Ill.

1930 **Aviation—Flights (transatlantic)**—transatlantic nonstop flight from Europe to the United States—Coste and Bellonte arrived—Valley Stream, N.Y.

1936 **Aviation—Flights (transatlantic)**—transatlantic round-trip flight from the United States—Richard Merrill and Harry Richman—left—New York City

1937 **Game Preserve**—game preserve appropriation (federal)—enacted

1938 **Railroad Car**—car with fluorescent lighting—in service—New York Central

1952 **Surgical Operation**—heart operation in which the deep freezing technique was employed—F. J. Lewis

1955 **Soldiers' Home**—woman admitted to a soldiers' home—R. C. Jones—Washington, D.C.

SEPTEMBER 3

1639 **Lawyer**—lawyer disbarred—Thomas Lechford—Massachusetts

1777 **Flag**—American flag flown in battle—Cooch's Bridge, Del.

1782 **Ship**—ship-of-the-line—*America*—presented to Louis XVI, king of France

1783 **Treaty**—treaty between the United States Government and a nation with which it had been at war—signed—Paris, France

1833 Newspaper—penny daily newspaper—New York *Sun*—published—successful

1872 Presidential Candidate—presidential candidate who was a Catholic—Charles O'Conor—nominated

1885 Naval War College—Naval War College—opened

1890 Single Tax—single tax national conference—platform adopted—New York City

1894 Golf Tournament—national championship stroke-play golf match—Newport, R.I.

1895 Football Game—professional football game—Latrobe, Pa.

1898 Subway—municipal subway—opened to North Station—Boston, Mass.

1900 Union Reform Party—convention—Baltimore, Md.

1917 Air Force—air service (military) under one command—W. L. Kenly—effected

1919 Army Officer—General of the Armies of the United States—rank authorized

1934 Salvation Army—woman commander of the Salvation Army—Elizabeth Booth

1935 Automobile—automobile to exceed the speed of 300 miles an hour—Sir Malcolm Campbell—Bonneville Salt Flats, Utah

1935 Brokerage—woman stock exchange member (commodity exchange)—admitted—New York Cocoa Exchange—New York City

1936 Aviation—Flights (transatlantic)—transatlantic round-trip flight from the United States—Richard Merrill and Harry Richman—arrived—Wales

1940 Ship—navy vessel constructed as a minelayer—*Terror*—keel laid—Philadelphia, Pa.

1940 Television—Telecast—color television demonstration of high-definition electronically scanned images—New York City

1955 State Department (U.S.)—woman acting assistant Secretary of State—Florence Kirlin

1958 War (Quemoy)—American casualty of the Red Chinese bombardment—G. W. Johnston

1960 Submarine—submarine to make a submerged passage from the Atlantic to the Pacific via the North Pole—*Seadragon*—cleared the ice pack

SEPTEMBER 4

1645 Lutheran Church—Lutheran Church building—dedicated—Essington, Pa.

1777 Flag—American flag on the high seas—*Raleigh*—encounter with a British vessel

1813 Religious Publication—religious weekly newspaper—*Religious Remembrancer*—published—Philadelphia, Pa.

1820 Military School—military school—first class—enrolled—Norwich, Vt.

1833 Newsboy—Barney Flaherty—New York City

1856 Flag—American flag raised in Japan flown

1877 Library Society—library association (national)—American Library Association annual convention—New York City

1882 Dynamo—dynamo—New York City—service

1882 Electric Company—electric station (central) to supply light and power—Edison Electric Illuminating Company—New York City

1882 Newspaper—newspaper plant to install electricity—New York *Times*—New York City—current turned on

1885 Restaurant—self-service restaurant—Exchange Buffet—opened—New York City

1888 Camera—roll-film camera—patented—George Eastman—Rochester, N.Y.

1904 Hotel—hotel with individually controlled air conditioning and heating in every room—St. Regis, New York City—opened

1906 Election Law—primary election (statewide)—Wisconsin

1908 Automobile Tire—nonskid tire—patent applied for

1917 World War I—American Army soldier killed in World War I—Dannes, France

1919 Army Officer—General of the Armies of the United States—J. J. Pershing confirmed

1921 Radio Broadcast—police broadcast—St. Louis, Mo.

1923 Aviation—Airship—dirigible (American built rigid)—ZR1—tested—Lakehurst, N.

1933 Aviation—Flights—airplane to fly faster than the speed of 300 m.p.h.—J. R. Wedell—Glenview, Ill.

1935 Automobile Truck—automobile truck completely streamlined—Cleveland, Ohio

1935 Labor Relations—Labor Relations Act (national)—National Labor Relations Board—first meeting

1936 Aviation—Airplane—hydroplane of stainless steel—*Sea Bird*—tested—Bristol, Pa.

1937 Bicycle Racer—woman bicycle champion of the National Amateur Bicycle Association—Doris Kopsky—Buffalo, N.Y.

1948 Airmail Service—parcel post international air service—inaugurated—to South America

1950 Helicopter—helicopter rescue of an American pilot behind enemy lines—Paul Van Boven

1951 Television—Telecast—telecast using coaxial cable—coast-to-coast transmission

1951 Television—Telecast—transcontinental telecast received on the East Coast—from San Francisco, Calif.

1964 Satellite—orbiting geophysical observatory—OGO 1—launched—Cape Kennedy, Fla.

1972 Horse Race—horse race with a purse of more than $1 million—All-American Futurity, Ruidoso, N.Mex.

SEPTEMBER 5

21 Art Commission (public)—order given—Gustavus Hesselius—Maryland

74 Continental Congress—Continental Congress—assembled—Philadelphia, Pa.

74 President of the Continental Congress—Peyton Randolph—Virginia—elected

76 Navy—naval uniforms (standardized)—adopted

36 President of the Republic of Texas—Sam Houston—elected

53 Village Improvement Society—Laurel Hill Association—Stockbridge, Mass.—incorporated

64 Publishing Society—Seventy-Six Society—organized—Philadelphia, Pa.

82 Holiday—Labor Day holiday parade—New York City

83 Civil Service—Civil Service woman appointee—M. F. Hoyt—appointed

85 Pump—gasoline pump—delivered—S. F. Bowser—Fort Wayne, Ind.

71 Baseball League—baseball league association—National Association of Professional Baseball Leagues—organized—Chicago, Ill.

03 Motorcycle Race—motorcycle distance race (4 hours)—G. N. Holden—Manhattan Beach, New York City

23 Smoke Screen—demonstrated—Cape Hatteras, N.C.

25 Animals—musk ox born in captivity—Bronx Zoo, New York City

25 Golf Champion—golf champion to win the United States National Amateur Tournament two years in succession—R. T. Jones

25 Photography—demonstration of rapid aerial photography—Fort Leavenworth, Kans.

34 Aviation—floating seaplane ramp (municipally owned)—dedicated—New York City

43 Aviation—airplane human pickup—Wilmington, Ohio

53 Atomic Reactor—atomic reactor (privately operated)—Raleigh, N.C.

58 Tape Recording—video recording on magnetic tape in color—Charlotte, N.C.

61 Hijack Legislation—hijack legislation (federal)—enacted

72 College—college whose tuition fees were based on family income—Beloit College, Beloit, Wis.—effective

SEPTEMBER 6

10 Colonist—colonists to reach the Pacific coast—left New York City

19 Lathe—patented—Thomas Blanchard—Middlebury, Conn.

37 College—coeducational college—Oberlin Collegiate Institute—Oberlin, Ohio—equal status to women

66 Political Convention—black delegate to a national political convention—Frederick Douglass—Philadelphia, Pa.

1882 Bicycle Trip—bicycle trip of 100 miles sponsored by a club—Worcester-Boston, Mass.—Boston Bicycle Club

1883 Baseball Player—baseball player to hit a home run and a double in 1 inning—T. E. Burns—Chicago, Ill.

1883 Baseball Team—baseball team (major league) to score 18 runs in 1 inning—Chicago White Sox—Chicago, Ill.

1892 Automobile Tractor—gasoline tractor—sold—John Froelich—Froelich, Iowa

1909 Expedition—polar expedition of which a woman was a member—North Pole discovery announced

1919 Actors' Union—strike settled

1920 Radio Broadcast—prizefight broadcast—WWJ—Detroit, Mich.

1947 Ship—ship from which a long-range rocket was launched—*Midway*

1954 Electric Power Plant—atomic electric generating station (full-scale)—ground breaking—Shippingport, Pa.

1958 Pipeline—pipeline (interstate) to transport ethylene—in operation—Orange, Tex.

1970 Beauty Pageant—black contestant in the Miss America pageant—C. A. Browne—Atlantic City, N.J.

SEPTEMBER 7

1724 Baptist Church—German Baptists—Coventry Congregation

1774 Continental Congress—Continental Congress to be opened with prayer—Philadelphia, Pa.

1776 Submarine—submarine built for use in war—*American Turtle*—attempt to sink *Eagle*

1797 Ship—ship to capture an enemy ship after the Revolution—*Constellation*—launched—Baltimore, Md.

1822 Treadmill—completed—New York City

1876 Piano Player—piano player—patent application—John McTammany—Cambridge, Mass.

1880 Trapshooting—clay pigeon target—patent—George Ligowsky—Cincinnati, Ohio

1888 Incubator for Infants—used—New York City

1892 Prizefight—prizefight of importance under the Marquis of Queensberry rules—Sullivan-Corbett—New Orleans, La.

1896 Automobile Race—automobile race on a track—Cranston, R.I.

1899 Automobile Parade—Newport, R.I.

1903 Motorcycle Association—Federation of American Motorcyclists—organized—Manhattan Beach, N.Y.

1908 Esperanto Club—Esperanto club (national organization) — organized — Chautauqua Lake, N.Y.

1909 High School—junior high school—Indianola Junior High School, Columbus, Ohio—opened

1916 **Shipping**—United States Shipping Board—authorized

1921 **Beauty Pageant**—beauty pageant (national)—Miss America pageant—Atlantic City, N.J.—began

1923 **Electric Generator**—mercury boiler turbine—installed—Hartford, Conn.

1927 **Boat Race**—international lifeboat race—New York City

1936 **Medical Congress**—cancer institute (convention)—Madison, Wis.

1942 **Naval Officer**—woman doctor in the WAVES—C. J. Gaskill—commissioned

1948 **Road**—synthetic rubber in an asphaltic concrete resurfacing mixture—Akron, Ohio

1953 **Tennis Player**—woman tennis grand slam winner—Maureen Connolly

1957 **Ship**—ship to circumnavigate the American continent—*Spar*—completed Northwest Passage

1963 **Hall of Fame**—Hall of Fame (football)—Canton, Ohio—building dedicated

1967 **Satellite**—biosatellite (successful)—launched—Cape Kennedy, Fla.

1977 **Peace Corps**—woman director of the Peace Corps—C. R. Payton—nominated

SEPTEMBER 8

1565 **Catholic Parish**—St. Augustine, Fla.

1565 **Colonist**—permanent white settlement—founded—St. Augustine, Fla.

1636 **College**—college—Harvard College—appropriation—Cambridge, Mass.

1729 **Jewish Congregation**—Jewish congregation—foundation stones laid—Shearith Israel—New York City

1866 **Births**—sextuplets—born—Bushnell family—Chicago, Ill.

1868 **Sports**—athletic club—organized—New York City

1879 **Ship**—steam whaler built as a whale boat—*Mary and Helen*—built—Bath, Me.—registered—New Bedford, Mass.

1896 **College**—Finnish college—Suomi College, Hancock, Mich.—opened

1920 **Airmail Service**—airmail transcontinental service—(combination airplane-railroad)—New York–San Francisco, Calif.

1939 **Autogiro**—autogiro rotary-wing aircraft fellowship—S. B. Sherwin—enrolled

1945 **Radio Telephone**—two-way-radio-equipped bus—in service—Washington, D.C.

1948 **Air Force Officer**—Judge Advocate General of the U.S. Air Force—R. C. Harmon—nominated

1953 **Automobile Bus**—transcontinental no-change bus service—instituted—New York City–San Francisco, Calif.

1965 **Baseball Player**—baseball player to play all 9 positions in 1 game—B. D. Campaneris—Kansas City, Mo.

1969 **Tennis Player**—tennis player to win grand slams—R. G. Laver

1974 **Naval Officer**—naval chaplain (black woman)—Vivian McFadden—sworn in—Atlanta, Ga.

SEPTEMBER 9

1637 **Quakers**—Synod of Quakers—Cambridge, Mass.—began

1753 **Steam Engine**—steam engine—Jos. Hornblower—arrived

1776 **United States**—*United States*—authorized

1830 **Balloon**—Flights—balloon flight by a native-born American—C. F. Durant—New York City

1833 **Dry Dock**—federal dry docks—Boston dock—delivery accepted

1841 **Prizefight**—prizefight (heavyweight) to longer than 100 rounds—Tom Hyer, George McChester—Caldwell's Landing, N.Y.

1841 **Ship**—iron vessel built for the United States Navy—*Michigan*—authorized

1850 **State**—state admitted to the union on Pacific Coast—California

1866 **Ticket Agency**—theater-ticket agency office—advertised—New York City

1885 **Economics Association**—American Economic Association—founded—Saratoga, N.Y.

1886 **Copyright Law**—international copyright agreement—convention at Berne, Switzerland

1893 **Births**—child born in the White House, Washington, D.C., the offspring of a President—Esther Cleveland—born

1895 **Bowling Rule Standardization**—convention—American Bowling Congress—New York City

1895 **Bowling Tournament**—bowling convention—of importance—American Bowling Congress—New York City

1898 **Log Rolling (Birling) National Championship**—Omaha, Neb.

1901 **Automobile Hill Climbing Contest**—Peekskill, N.Y.

1901 **Automobile Race**—automobile race (long distance)—New York City–Buffalo, N.Y.

1908 **Aviation**—Flights—airplane endurance flight exceeding one hour—Fort Myer, Va.

1908 **Aviation**—Passenger—airplane passenger (official)—F. P. Lahm—Fort Myer, Va.

1914 **Ship**—steamboat to pass through the Panama Canal—army transport—*Buford*

1916 **Golf Champion**—golfer to win both United States Open and the United States Amateur in the same year—Charles Evans Jr.—Philadelphia, Pa. (U.S. Amateur)

1929 **Konel**—announced—Pittsburgh, Pa.

1934 **Rocket**—rocket to pass the sonic barrier—flown at Marine Park, Staten Island, N.Y.

Rocket—rocket to reach a speed of 700 m.p.h.—launched—Marine Park, Staten Island, N.Y.

Medal—Navy Cross 3-time winner—N. A. Gaylor—3rd presentation

Diplomatic Service—ambassador to Nepal —H. E. Stebbins—confirmed

Baseball Pitcher—baseball pitcher to win 4 no-hitters—Sanford Koufax—4th game, Los Angeles, Calif.

Judge—black woman judge of a federal district court—C. B. Motley—sworn in

Postage Stamp—stamp to depict a living American—moon issue—N. A. Armstrong —issued—Washington, D.C.

SEPTEMBER 10

Treaty—treaty entered into by the United States after the treaty of peace—with Prussia—signed at The Hague

College—nondenominational college— Blount College—Knoxville, Tenn.—chartered

War (1812)—defeat in history of a British squadron—O. H. Perry

Ship—steamboat (double-decked)—*Washington*—keel laid—Wheeling, W.Va.

Army Officer—chaplain (Jewish) of the U.S. Army—Jacob Frankel—appointed

Forestry Society—national forestry association—American Forestry Association— organized—Chicago, Ill.

Historical Society—historical society (general)—American Historical Association— founded—Saratoga, N.Y.

Freemasons—Grotto—formal organization —Hamilton, N.Y.

Road—coast-to-coast paved road—Lincoln Highway—proclamation of opening

Motion Picture—motion picture of an eclipse of the sun taken from an airplane— Santa Catalina, Calif.

Ship—all-welded self-propelled seagoing petroleum carrier—*White Flash*— launched—Chester, Pa.

Aviation—Women's Auxiliary Ferrying Squadron—N. H. Love—appointed

Woman—American woman to swim the English Channel from both coasts—Florence Chadwick—England–France

Representative (U.S.)—woman to serve 18 terms in Congress—E. F. N. Rogers of Massachusetts—ended service

SEPTEMBER 11

Physician—doctor to receive an honorary medical degree—Daniel Turner—New Haven, Conn.

Comptroller—comptroller of the United States Treasury—Nicholas Eveleigh— served

1789 Internal Revenue Commissioner—Commissioner of the Revenue—Tench Coxe— served

1789 Treasury Department (U.S.)—Secretary of the Treasury—Alexander Hamilton—appointed

1789 War Department (U.S.)—War Department (U.S.)—Secretary—Henry Knox—appointed

1812 Russian Settlement—dedicated—Cazadero, Calif.

1830 Anti-Masonic Party—first national convention—Philadelphia, Pa.

1841 Tube—collapsible tube—patented—John Rand

1850 Railroad Car—private railroad car—Jenny Lind—appearance at Castle Garden—New York City

1850 Ticket Speculators—Jenny Lind—appearance at Castle Garden—New York City

1862 Brokerage—exchange to specialize in mining securities—San Francisco, Calif.

1875 Cartoon—newspaper cartoon strip—*Daily Graphic*—New York City

1883 Postal Service—mail chute-patented—J. G. Cutler—Rochester, N.Y.

1910 Streetcar—trackless trolley system—operated—Laurel Canyon, Calif.

1912 Baseball Player—player (major league) to steal 6 bases in 1 game—E. T. Collins, Sr.— St. Louis, Mo.

1928 Automobile Bus—coast-to-coast through bus line—operated—Los Angeles, Calif.– New York City

1928 Television—Telecast—play to be televised—*The Queen's Messenger*—Schenectady, N.Y.

1933 Federal Deposit Insurance Corporation— directors met

1946 Telephone—mobile long-distance car-to-car telephone conversation—Houston, Tex.–St. Louis, Mo.

1947 Isotope—radioactive isotopes exported— Oak Ridge, Tenn.—received at Canberra, Australia

1947 Television—Telecast—surgical operation (major) on a closed circuit, performed in one building and transmitted to another— New York Hospital to Waldorf Hotel in New York City

1948 Airmail Service—parcel post international air service—inaugurated—to Pacific area

1950 Typesetting Machine—typesetting machine to dispense with metal type—exhibited—Chicago, Ill.

1952 Surgical Operation—artificial aortic valve —C. A. Hufnagel—Washington, D.C.

1953 Television Station—television stations to share the same time and frequency—Salinas, Calif., and Monterey, Calif.

1964 Ship—cargo ship fully automated and flying the American flag—*Mormacargo*—first transatlantic crossing

1965 Stadium—domed, fully-enclosed sports arena—Astrodome, Houston, Tex.—first football game

1972 Police—special agents (women) of the police training school of the Federal Bureau of Investigation Academy—Quantico, Va.—course completed

1974 —Police—woman employed at a high level within a men's maximum security facility—Katherine Tripp—Thomaston, Me.

SEPTEMBER 12

1789 Treasury Department (U.S.)—Register of the Treasury—Joseph Nourse—began service

1789 War Department (U.S.)—War Department (U.S.)—Secretary—Henry Knox—served

1793 Health Board—health board (local)—quarantine imposed—Baltimore, Md.

1808 Bible—Bible translated into English in America—copyrighted

1866 Play (drama)—burlesque show—of importance—*The Black Crook*—New York City

1869 Prohibition Party (national)—organized—Chicago, Ill.

1873 Typewriter—typewriter that was practical—Sholes machine—completed—Ilion, N.Y.

1916 Motorcycle Trip—motorcycle transcontinental trip by a woman—arrived—San Diego, Calif.

1918 Ordnance—Army armored tank—used—St.-Mihiel, France

1935 Medical School—medical college (Jewish sponsored)—Albert Einstein College of Medicine, Yeshiva University, New York City—instruction began

1941 World War II—German ship captured in World War II—*Busko*—captured

1952 Railroad Car—"compartmentizer" freight cars—in service between Chicago, Ill., and San Francisco, Calif.

1956 Coal—commercial coal pipeline—completed—Eastlake, Ohio

1974 Baseball Game—night baseball game (major league) to last longer than 7 hours—St. Louis Cardinals vs. New York Mets—New York City

1975 Stadium—adjustable stadium—Aloha Stadium—Honolulu, Hawaii—dedicated

1977 Treasury Department (U.S.)—treasurer of the United States (black woman)—A. T. Morton—assumed office

1979 Book—book advance payment to exceed $3 million—*Princess Daisy;* by Judith Krantz—New York City

SEPTEMBER 13

1788 Election—federal election in the United States

1789 Loan—loan to the United States

1791 Academy—University of Pennsylva and College Academy and Charita School of Philadelphia—united

1814 National Anthem—"Star-Spangled B ner"—written—F. S. Key

1826 Animals — rhinoceros — exhibited — N York City

1842 Prizefight—prizefight fatality—Hasti N.Y.

1853 Bank—clearinghouse—plans adopted

1882 Country Club—country club to remai existence 80 years—Country Clu Brookline, Mass.—organized

1898 Photographic Film—celluloid photogra film—patent—H. W. Goodwin—New N.J.

1899 Automobile Fatality—H. H. Bliss—kille New York City

1925 College—university for blacks (Catholi Xavier University—New Orleans, L college department opened

1928 Railroad Car—rail detector car—dem strated—Poughkeepsie, N.Y.

1936 Aviation—Flights (transatlantic)—tran lantic round-trip flight—return trip—R ard Merrill and Harry Richma Southport, England

1938 Representative (U.S.)—woman represe tive who was not sworn in—E. H. Gas of South Carolina—began service

1939 Submarine—submarine refloated—*Sq lus*—raised and towed back to Portsmo N.H.

1948 High School—public high school to spec ize in the performing field—New York C

1948 Senator (U.S.)—woman senator elec without having previously served an pointed term—M. C. Smith—Maine

1954 College—college for women under Jew auspices—Stern College for Women—N York City—opened

1954 National Security Council (U.S.)—natic security council meeting held outs Washington, D.C.

1956 Taconite—taconite—large-scale comr cial project—Silver Bay, Minn.

1962 Rocket—launching silos for Atlas F n siles—built—turned over to Strategic Command

1966 Medal—Medal of Honor awarded to a S bee—M. G. Shields—presented pos mously

1971 School—public school built in conjunc with an apartment house—opened—Bro New York City

1976 Lottery—lottery (state regulated) in wl 3 zeros made up the winning number—N Jersey

SEPTEMBER 14

1716 Lighthouse — lighthouse — kindled — tle Brewster Island, Mass.

8 **Diplomatic Service**—minister plenipotentiary—Benjamin Franklin—elected

1 **Civil War**—naval engagement in the Civil War—Pensacola, Fla.—*Colorado* vs. *Judah*

5 **Typewriter Ribbon**—typewriter ribbon patent—G. K. Anderson—Memphis, Tenn.

2 **Bacteriology Laboratory**—bacteriology diagnostic laboratory—H. M. Biggs—served—New York City

8 **Journalism Course**—journalism school—University of Missouri—Columbia, Mo.

9 **Election Law**—preferential ballot system—charter adopted—Grand Junction, Colo.

0 **Aviation—Airport**—airport municipal legislation—ratified—Modesto, Calif.

5 **Sound-Absorbing Material**—patent—C. G. Muench—St. Paul, Minn.

2 **Aviation—Flights (transcontinental)**—transcontinental dirigible flight (nonrigid dirigible)—C2—left Newport News, Va.

9 **Horse Race**—horse to win a $100,000 purse in one race—Whichone—Belmont, N.Y.

1 **Ship**—all-welded self-propelled seagoing petroleum carrier—*White Flash*—in service

6 **Art Course**—art course—fresco painting—Louisiana State University—University, La.

3 **Submarine**—submarine refloated—*Squalus*—launched—Portsmouth, N.H.

0 **Conscription**—peacetime conscription bill—enacted

6 **Surgical Operation**—lobotomy (prefrontal)—J. W. Watts and Walter Freeman—Washington, D.C.

0 **Submarine**—submarine to make a submerged passage from the Atlantic to the Pacific via the North Pole—*Seadragon*—docked at Pearl Harbor, Hawaii

3 **Births**—quintuplets to live more than 5 years—Fischer quintuplets—born in Aberdeen, S. Dak.

3 **Horse**—pacer to win $1 million—Cardigan Bay—Freehold, N.J.

5 **Saint (Catholic)**—saint (native-born Catholic)—E. A. B. Seton—canonized

SEPTEMBER 15

7 **Catholic Funeral**—Catholic funeral attended by the U.S. Continental Congress—Tronson du Coudray—drowned

2 **Political Convention**—political nominating caucus—Democratic-Republican Party—New York City

7 **Iron**—iron mill to puddle and roll iron—in operation—Redstone Creek, Pa.

0 **Black**—national convention for blacks—Philadelphia, Pa.

3 **Ship**—naval vessel of the United States to sail around the Cape of Good Hope to the West Coast of the United States—anchored—Monterey Bay, Calif.—on return voyage

1847 **Labor Legislation**—ten-hour-day law—effective—New Hampshire

1853 **Librarians' Convention**—New York City

1853 **Woman**—woman ordained a minister—A. B. Blackwell—South Butler, N.Y.

1857 **Typesetting Machine**—typesetting machine—patented—Timothy Alden—New York City

1858 **Postal Service**—overland mail service—Tipton, Mo.–San Francisco, Calif.

1863 **Habeas Corpus**—habeas corpus suspension order—proclamation suspending habeas corpus during military strife—Abraham Lincoln

1890 **Architect**—woman architect—elected—American Institute of Architects—L. B. Bethune

1896 **Hospital**—cancer home for incurables (free)—established—New York City

1901 **Architectural School**—landscape architecture course for women—Groton, Mass.

1913 **Goat Show**—of importance—Rochester, N.Y.

1929 **Aviation**—airplane "fly-it-yourself" system—started—Kansas City, Kans.

1930 **Mortuary**—cooperative—opened—Toledo, Ohio

1934 **Radio Broadcast**—musical comedy broadcast—*The Gibson Family*—New York City

1939 **College**—woman dean of a graduate school—F. Wunderlich—took office—New York City

1947 **Aviation—Airplane**—jet-propelled fighter airplane (four-engine)—tested—Columbus, Ohio

1953 **Building**—aluminum-faced building—dedicated—Pittsburgh, Pa.

1953 **Submarine**—submarine powered by a liquid-metal-cooled atomic reactor—*Seawolf*—laid down

1955 **Cantor**—Jewish woman cantor—Betty Robbins—first service—Oceanside, N.Y.

1957 **Telephone**—air-to-ground public telephone service—Chicago–Detroit area

1958 **Submarine**—atomic-powered submarine built at a naval shipyard—*Swordfish*—commissioned

1969 **Baseball Pitcher**—baseball pitcher (major league) to strike out 19 batters—S. N. Carlton—St. Louis, Mo.

1970 **Secret Service**—Executive Protective Service woman agent—P. F. Shantz—sworn in

1978 **Prizefight**—prizefight to gross more than $5 million in sales—Ali vs. Spinks—New Orleans, La.

1978 **Prizefighter**—pugilist to win the heavyweight championship 3 times—Muhammad Ali—(3rd time) New Orleans, La.

SEPTEMBER 16

1782 **Seal**—Great Seal of the United States Government was impressed—Philadelphia, Pa.

1833 Crime Prevention and Detection—interstate crime pact—signed by New York and New Jersey

1895 Building—building with an all-marble dome—Rhode Island State House—Providence, R.I.—ground broken

1908 Esperanto Course—Esperanto course carrying college credit—Clark University, Worcester, Mass.

1910 Balloon Trophy—balloon trophy to a woman—Mrs. C. B. Harmon—Dayton, Ohio

1912 Quarantine—plant quarantine legislation (national)—white-pine blister rust quarantine effective

1918 Aviation—Flights—airplane altitude flight to exceed 28,000 feet—R. W. Schroeder—Fairfield, Ohio

1919 War Veterans' Society—American Legion —incorporated

1923 Catholic Seminary—Catholic seminary for the education of black priests—dedicated —Bay St. Louis, Miss.

1924 Baseball Player—baseball player (major league) to bat in 12 runs in a 9-inning game —J. L. Bottomley—New York City

1946 College—college principally for war veterans—opened—Plattsburg, N.Y.

1947 Automobile—automobile to exceed the speed of 400 m.p.h.—Bonneville, Utah

1955 Soldiers' Home—woman admitted to a soldiers' home—R. C. Jones—Washington, D.C.—permanent admission granted

1960 Postage Stamp—postage stamp issued jointly by 2 countries—Mexican Independence—issued—Los Angeles, Calif.

1971 School—technical school for American Indians—opened, Albuquerque, N.Mex.

1974 Woman—woman Republican national committee chairman—M. L. Smith—elected—Washington, D.C.

SEPTEMBER 17

1607 Slander Proceedings—instituted—Jamestown, Va.

1777 Catholic Funeral—Catholic funeral attended by the U.S. Continental Congress—Philadelphia, Pa.

1778 Treaty—treaty entered into by the United States with American Indian tribes—Delaware nations

1787 Constitution of the United States—Constitution (federal)—signed—Philadelphia, Pa.

1792 Protestant Episcopal Bishop—Protestant Episcopal bishop consecrated in the United States—T. J. Claggett—consecrated

1844 Printing Press—printing press for polychromatic printing—patented—T. F. Adams

1861 School—school for black freedmen—established—Fortress Monroe, Va.

1872 Sprinkler—sprinkler system patent—P. Pratt—Abington, Mass.

1895 Ship—battleship of importance—*Mair* commissioned

1901 Electric Lighting—mercury vapor lam patent—P. C. Hewitt—New York City

1908 Aviation—Airplane Fatalities—airp fatality—Fort Myer, Va.

1911 Aviation—Flights (transcontinenta transcontinental airplane flight—C. Rodgers—takeoff—Sheepshead Bay, N

1918 Submarine—submarine to cross the At tic Ocean under its own power—*E-1*- turned to New London, Conn.

1920 Football Club—football associa (professional)—formed—Canton, Ohio

1938 Building—building built inside a facto towed across Illinois River

1941 World War II—warship convoy across Atlantic Ocean—M. L. Deyo, comman —warships assumed charge of convoy

1942 Dental Corps (U.S. Army)—Army De Corps Major General—R. H. Mills

1947 Defense Department (U.S.)—J. V. Forre —sworn in

1953 Siamese Twins—Siamese twins separa successfully by surgery—operation formed

1959 Ski Lift—tramway state legislation—N Hampshire—approved

1961 Building—retractable-roof (large) buil —Civic Area and Exhibit Hall, Pittsb Pa.—dedicated

1972 United Church of Christ—United Churc Christ ordination of a woman ministe which all the principal roles were fillec women—D. F. Crabtree—Northfield, Cc

SEPTEMBER 18

1634 Clubwoman—Anne Hutchinson—arri —Boston, Mass.

1679 Ship—Great Lakes commercial vessel- *Griffon*—sank

1769 Piano—piano—John Harris—describec newspaper—Boston, Mass.

1793 Capitol (U.S.)—cornerstone laid—W; ington, D.C.

1883 Diplomatic Service—Korean embassy- ceived at Washington, D.C.

1891 Woman—white woman to become American Indian chief—Tonawa Reservation, N.Y.

1895 Chiropractor—D. D. Palmer—adjustn treatment

1901 Commission Form of Government—o; ated—Galveston, Tex.

1915 Automobile Racetrack—automobile ra track (asphalt-covered)—opened—C ston, R.I.

1918 Aviation—Flights—airplane altitude fl to exceed 28,000 feet—R. W. Schroed Fairfield, Ohio

Greek College and Orphanage—dedicated—Gastonia, N.C.

Skywriting—skywriting at night—exhibited—Andy Stinis—New York City

Air Force—Air Force Secretary—W. S. Symington—sworn in—Washington, D.C.

Defense Department (U.S.)—Secretary of the Navy and Secretary for Air—sworn in

Aviation—Airplane—airplane with a delta wing—Convair—first flight, Muroc, Calif.

Medical Society—woman president of a state medical society—L. S. Kent

Federal Reserve System—Federal Reserve System Board of Governors member (woman)—N. H. Teeters—sworn in

SEPTEMBER 19

Protestant Church—Protestant church—west of Pennsylvania—Schoenbrunn, Ohio

Constitution of the United States—Constitution of the United States was first published—in a newspaper—*Pennsylvania Packet and Daily Advertiser*—Philadelphia, Pa.

Brake Patent—railroad brake patent—Ephraim Morris—Bloomfield, N.J.

Sleeping Car—sleeping car patent—H. B. Myer—Buffalo, N.Y.

Carpet Sweeper—patent—M. R. Bissell—Grand Rapids, Mich.

Tunnel—subaqueous railroad tunnel to a foreign country—Port Huron, Mich.-Sarnia, Ont., Canada

Forestry School—forestry school of collegiate character—established—Cornell University—Ithaca, N.Y.

Aviation—airplane Diesel engine—tested—Detroit, Mich.

Motion Picture—animated-cartoon talking picture—*Steamboat Willie*—exhibited—New York City

Valeteria—displayed—Cleveland, Ohio

Television—Telecast—atomic bomb detonation from a captive balloon telecast—Yucca Flat, Nev.

SEPTEMBER 20

War (colonial)—intercolonial war—Fort Caroline, Fla.

Ship—warship (American) captured overseas—*Lexington*—(formerly *Wild Duck*)—surrendered

Science Association—scientific society (national organization)—American Association for the Advancement of Science—organized—Philadelphia, Pa.

Hospital—homeopathic hospital—Homeopathic Hospital of Pennsylvania—Philadelphia, Pa.—incorporated

Land Grant—railroad land grant of importance—authorized

Railroad Station—union passenger station—opened—Indianapolis, Ind.

1859 Electric Stove—electric range—patented—G. B. Simpson—Washington, D.C.

1860 Visiting Celebrities—Prince of Wales—arrived—Detroit, Mich.

1884 Equal Rights Party—formed—San Francisco, Calif.

1892 Glass — wire glass — patented — Frank Schuman—Philadelphia, Pa.

1915 Chiropody School—chiropody school as a regular division of a university—opened—Temple University—Philadelphia, Pa.

1916 Science Association—National Research Council—first meeting—New York City

1946 Television—Telecast—motion picture trailer to be televised—New York City

1951 Aviation—Flights—North Pole jet crossing—Fairbanks, Alaska

1965 College—liberal arts college for police and corrections officers established by a city—College of Police Science, New York City—opened

1974 Degrees (academic and honorary)—bachelor's degrees awarded by a recognized institution without requiring a single college credit—N. E. France—University of the State of New York, Albany, N.Y.

1974 Police—police officer (woman) killed in the line of duty—G. A. Cobb—Washington, D.C.

SEPTEMBER 21

1782 Bible—Bible printed in English—authorized by Congress

1784 Newspaper—daily newspaper—*Pennsylvania Packet and Daily Advertiser*—Philadelphia, Pa.

1872 Naval Academy—black midshipman in the United States Naval Academy—J. H. Conyers

1875 Gas—water gas production—patent—T. S. C. Lowe—Norristown, Pa.

1883 Engineering College—electrical engineering course—Cornell University—Ithaca, N.Y.

1895 Automobile Company—Duryea Motor Wagon Company—incorporated—Springfield, Mass.

1942 Medal—marines to win the Navy and Marine Corps Medal—N. C. S. Pearson and Gordon Miller—commended

1949 Bicycle Rider—bicycle rider to cross the continent in less than three weeks—Eugene McPherson—arrived—New York City

1954 Submarine—atomic-powered submarine—*Nautilus*—commissioned

1958 Aviation—Flights—airplane endurance flight exceeding 1,200 hours—Jim Heth and Bill Burkhart—landed—Dallas, Tex.

1965 Swimmer—American to swim the English Channel round trip—Ted Erikson

1969 Football Player—football player to punt 98 yards—Steve O'Neal (New York Jets) Denver, Colo.

SEPTEMBER 22

1656 Jury—jury composed of women—Patuxent, Md.

1734 Moravian—George Boehnisch—arrived

1789 Post Office—Post Office Department of the United States—established

1789 Postmaster—postmaster general of the United States—office authorized

1851 Telegraph—telegraph in railroading—Goshen, N.Y.

1862 Emancipation Proclamation (preliminary) —Abraham Lincoln

1890 Business School—business high school—opened—Washington, D.C.

1892 Bicycle Racer—bicyclist to ride a mile in less than 2 minutes from a standing start—John Johnson—Independence, Iowa

1926 Book Course—instruction—Rollins College—Winter Park, Fla.

1927 Prizefight—prizefight to gross $2 million—Dempsey vs. Tunney—Chicago, Ill.

1945 Horse Race—racetrack at which more than $5 million was bet in one day—Belmont Park, N.Y.

1947 Aviation—Airplane—transatlantic robot pilotless airplane—takeoff—Newfoundland

1950 Aviation—Flights (transatlantic)—jet transatlantic nonstop flight east–west—D. C. Schilling—to Limestone, Me.

1953 Road—interchange structure of 4 levels—built—Los Angeles, Calif.—opened

1958 Submarine—submarine to travel under the North Pole from the East—*Skate*—returned to Boston, Mass.

1962 Protestant Episcopal Bishop—black to administer a diocese—J. M. Burgess—Boston, Mass.—elected

1964 Play (drama)—musical to run for more than 3,000 performances—*Fiddler on the Roof*—opened in New York City

SEPTEMBER 23

1642 College—college—commencement exercises—Harvard College—Cambridge, Mass.

1642 Degrees (academic and honorary)—Bachelor of Arts degree—conferred—Harvard College—Cambridge, Mass.

1745 Knighthood—knighthood conferred on a native-born American for military leadership—Sir William Pepperell

1806 Expedition—expedition across the continent to the Pacific coast—returned to St. Louis, Mo.

1845 Baseball Rules—baseball rule code—adopted

1845 Baseball Team—baseball team—Knickerbocker Club—organized—New York City

1853 Ship—yacht to circumnavigate the world—*North Star*—returned to New York City

1879 Deaf—Hearing Aid—hearing aid of inte▮ —patented—R. S. Rhodes—River Park,

1885 Biology—biology course (general) offe▮ in a college—Bryn Mawr College—B▮ Mawr, Pa.

1897 Holiday—Frontier Day—celebratio▮ Cheyenne, Wyo.

1898 Hospital—tuberculosis sanatorium (sta▮ —completed—Rutland, Mass.

1911 Airmail Service—airmail pilot—E. L. ▮ ington—sworn in

1922 Aviation—Flights (transcontinental▮ transcontinental dirigible flight (nonri▮ dirigible)—landed—Arcadia, Calif.

1926 Prizefight—prizefight to attract 100,▮ spectators—Dempsey-Tunney figh▮ Philadelphia, Pa.

1930 Photography—photographic flashli▮ bulbs—patent

1931 Autogiro—autogiro to land and take ▮ from a ship—XOP-1—A. M. Pride—flo▮ off Cape Henry, Va.

1932 Baseball Manager—baseball manager ▮ win pennants in both leagues—J. ▮ McCarthy

1934 Radio Broadcast—radio broadcast he▮ in both the Arctic and the Antarctic regi▮ —Schenectady, N.Y.

1951 Television—Telecast—transcontinental ▮ lecast received on the West Coast—"C▮ sade for Freedom"

1952 Television—Telecast—pay television p▮ sentation of a sporting event—Ph▮ delphia, Pa.

1954 Court-martial—court-martial trial of ▮ officer for collaborating with his captor▮ Fort Sheridan, Ill.

1954 Television—Telecast—medical sympc▮ um televised coast-to-coast on a closed ▮ cuit—New York City

1964 Satellite—weather satellite to prov▮ high-resolution nighttime cloud-cover ▮ tures—*Nimbus 1*—ceased operation

1976 Television—Telecast—presidential deb▮ between an incumbent President and▮ candidate for the office—G. R. Ford ▮ Jimmy Carter—first debate—Philadelp▮ Pa.

SEPTEMBER 24

1657 Autopsy—autopsy and verdict of a co▮ ner's jury—recorded—Maryland

1789 Attorney General—Attorney General—▮ the United States—office created

1789 Congress (U.S.)—congressional act ▮ clared unconstitutional by the Supre▮ Court of the United States

1789 Justice Department (U.S.)—office of att▮ ney general created

1789 Supreme Court (U.S.)—Chief Justice of ▮ Supreme Court—John Jay—appointed

Supreme Court (U.S.)—Supreme Court justice who was nominated but who did not serve—R. H. Harrison

Supreme Court (U.S.)—Supreme Court of the United States—authorized

Hospital—inebriates' asylum—United States Inebriate Asylum—cornerstone laid—Binghamton, N.Y.

Time Recorder—dial time recorder—patented—Alexander Dey

Bicycle Trip (world)—bicycle trip around the world by a woman—Annie Londonberry—completed at Boston, Mass.

Monument—national monument—Devils Tower, Wyo.—established

College—university for blacks (Catholic)—two-year normal department—opened—New Orleans, La.

Aviation—Flights—all-blind flight—Lt. J. H. Doolittle—Mitchel Field, N.Y.

Toyery—opened—New York City

Radio Broadcast—drama broadcast from a regular stage—WABC—New York City

Theatrical School—theater and dramatic criticism course—established—Yale University—New Haven, Conn.

Tennis Player—lawn tennis champion to win four major titles—J. D. Budge—Forest Hills, N.Y.

Submarine—submarine submerged for 2 weeks (NATO exercises in North Atlantic)—maneuvers ended

Bridge—welded-aluminum girder-type highway bridge—completed—Urbandale, Iowa

Ship—aircraft carrier (atomic-powered)—*Enterprise*—launched

Photograph—photograph (authorized) of the Senate in session—taken, Washington, D.C.

SEPTEMBER 25

Newspaper—newspaper publisher—*Publick Occurrances*—issued—Benjamin Harris—Boston, Mass.

Steam Engine—steam engine—delivered—North Arlington, N.J.

Constitutional Amendment—constitutional amendments—submitted to the states

Presidential Election—presidential election in which candidates had been nominated for the vice presidency—Twelfth Amendment to Constitution

Cream Separator—centrifugal cream separator patent

Cooperatives Convention—Springfield, Ill.

Paleontology Course—micropaleontology course—Columbia University—New York City

Poorhouse (state)—opened—Smyrna, Del.

Archival Administration—complete course—School of Public Affairs—Washington, D.C.

1956 **Telephone**—telephone conversation over the transoceanic telephone cable

SEPTEMBER 26

1772 **Medical Legislation**—law to license the practice of medicine—New Jersey

1789 **Attorney General**—Attorney General of the United States—E. J. Randolph—appointed

1789 **Attorney of the United States**—Attorney of the United States—Samuel Sherburne, Jr.—appointed

1789 **Postmaster**—postmaster general of the United States—Samuel Osgood—appointed

1831 **Anti-Masonic Party**—convention—Baltimore, Md.

1831 **Play (drama)**—play performed 1,000 times—*The Gladiator*—New York City—opened

1871 **Cement**—patent—D. O. Saylor—Allentown, Pa.

1872 **Freemasons**—Ancient Arabic Order of Nobles of the Mystic Shrine—temple instituted—New York City

1874 **Rifle Tournament**—rifle tournament (international)—Creedmoor, N.Y.

1903 **Boycott Law**—enacted—Alabama

1908 **Baseball Game**—shutout double-header games—Brooklyn, N.Y.

1914 **Federal Trade Commission**—Federal Trade Commission—authorized

1931 **Ship**—aircraft carrier—*Ranger*—keel laid—Newport News, Va.

1940 **Television**—television course in planning, writing, and producing television programs offered by a university—New York University—begun

1941 **Television—Telecast**—football game (collegiate) sponsored—Temple University vs. University of Kansas—Philadelphia, Pa.

1943 **Ship**—naval ship named for a sailor killed at Pearl Harbor—*England*—launched—San Francisco, Calif.

1955 **Bank**—bank to operate a window in a subway station for the convenience of subway riders—New York City

1957 **Aviation—Parachute**—parachute jump from an airplane from a 53,000-foot altitude—J. D. Nole—Del Rio, Tex.

1960 **Presidential Candidate**—presidential candidate debate series on television—first Nixon-Kennedy debate—Chicago, Ill.

1962 **Baseball Player**—baseball player to steal more than 100 bases in a season—M. M. Wills—100th steal, Los Angeles, Calif.

1964 **Postal Card**—street scene—issued—Washington, D.C.

1973 **Air Force Officer**—Air Force chaplain (woman)—Lorraine Potter—appointed

SEPTEMBER 27

1792 **Postmaster**—woman postmaster appointed after the adoption of the Constitution—Sarah De Crow—Hertford, N.C.

1879 **Sports**—amateur athletic competition (interclub)—Mott Haven, N.Y.

1892 **Match**—"book matches"—patent—Joshua Pusey—Lima, Pa.

1915 **College**—university for blacks (Catholic)—Xavier University—New Orleans—opened as a high school

1922 **Radar**—radar observations—Anacostia, D.C.

1930 **Golf Champion**—golf champion to hold the four highest golf titles—R. T. Jones, Jr., won United States Amateur—Philadelphia, Pa.

1934 **Abrasive**—boron carbide—announced

1937 **Santa Claus School**—opened—Albion, N.Y.

1939 **Aviation—License**—airplane instructor's license—under C.A.A.—issued—A. J. Banks—Atlanta, Ga.

1941 **Ship**—Liberty ship—*Patrick Henry*—launched—Baltimore, Md.

1942 **Ship**—ship completed in less than 2 weeks—*Joseph N. Teal*—Portland, Oreg.—trial run

1944 **Medal**—Legion of Merit medal awarded to a Women's Army Corps member—presented—W. B. Boyce

1954 **Supreme Court (U.S.)**—page (black)—C. V. Bush—began service

1966 **X ray**—X ray three-dimensional (stereo) fluoroscopic system—Joseph Quinn, development engineer—exhibited—San Francisco, Calif.

SEPTEMBER 28

1542 **Discovery**—discovery of land on the United States Pacific coast—J. R. Cabrillo—landed—San Diego, Calif.

1800 **Fireboat**—fireboat—imported—New York City

1849 **Army Officer**—chaplain (Catholic) of the United States Army—S. H. Milley—served—Monterey, Calif.

1924 **Aviation—Flights (world)**—world flight—around-the-world flight completed—Seattle, Wash.

1930 **Radio Instruction**—radio-advertising course—in a college—instituted—New York City

1940 **Aviation—Airport**—airport (federally owned and operated)—cornerstone laid—Washington, D.C.

1944 **Television—Telecast**—musical comedy (full-length) written especially for television—*Boys from Boise*—presented—New York City

1945 **Opera**—black to sing a white role with a white cast in an opera company—R. T. Duncan—Washington, D.C.

1955 **Television—Telecast**—baseball World ries game televised in color—New Y City—New York Yankees–Brooklyn Do ers

SEPTEMBER 29

1784 **Freemasons**—black mason—warrant African Lodge

1789 **Army**—medical corps—Richard Alliso appointed surgeon

1789 **Pension**—pensions paid by the Uni States Government—authorized

1892 **Football Game**—football game at nigh Mansfield, Pa.

1904 **Monument**—monument to the memory the soldiers and sailors of the Span American War—Monroeville, Ohio

1915 **Radio Telephone**—transcontinental ra telephone demonstration—New York C

1918 **Protestant Episcopal Bishop**—black suff gan—E. T. Demby—appointed

1938 **Archival Course**—offered—Columbia U versity—New York City

1942 **Ship**—merchant ship of the United Sta commanded by a black captain—*Booke Washington*—launched—Wilmington, I

1951 **Television—Telecast**—football game te vised in color on a network—Philadelpl Pa.

1953 **Business**—department store to sell ins ance—Carson Pirie Scott & Co.—Chica Ill.

1966 **Baseball Pitcher**—baseball pitcher (ma league) to strikeout 300 or more batters each of 3 seasons—Sanford Koufax—th season

1967 **Postage Stamp**—twin postage stamps—sued—Orlando, Fla.

1977 **Prizefight Referee**—woman to judge heavyweight championship fight—I Shain—Ali vs. Shavers—New York Cit

SEPTEMBER 30

1630 **Execution**—execution in America—J Billington—Plymouth, Mass.

1641 **Fair**—annual fair—New Netherland New York City

1787 **Ship**—ship to carry the United States around the world—*Columbia*—saile Boston, Mass.

1791 **Export**—export report—by federal gove ment

1811 **Export**—exports from the United States exceed the imports

1841 **Pin**—machine "for sticking pins into per"—patented—Samuel Slocum—Pou keepsie, N.Y.

1876 **Library Periodical**—library periodical—brary Journal—published—New York C —first issue

1877 **Swimming Championship** (amateur op —New York City

2 **Electric Power Plant**—hydroelectric power plant—opened—Appleton, Wis.

2 **Rayon**—rayon patent

6 **Balloon Race**—balloon cup race—James Gordon Bennett Aeronautic Cup—Paris, France

9 **City Planning Instruction**—Harvard University—Cambridge, Mass.

2 **Safety Congress**—safety congress (national)—Cooperative Safety Congress—convention—Milwaukee, Wis.

4 **Flag**—American flag flown in World War I over a band of fighting Americans—Toulouse, France

5 **Electric Power Plant**—hydroelectric power plant to produce a million kilowatts—dedicated

6 **Aviation—Races**—airplane passenger race around the world—started—Lakehurst, N.J.

9 **Television—Telecast**—football game (collegiate) to be televised—New York City

3 **Merchant Marine Academy**—Merchant Marine Academy (U.S.)—dedicated—F. D. Roosevelt—Kings Point, N.Y.

3 **Ship**—warship named for a black—*Harmon*—transferred as *Aylmer* to Royal Navy

7 **Television—Telecast**—baseball World Series game televised—New York City—New York Yankees–Brooklyn Dodgers

0 **Medal**—Medal of Honor awarded in the Korean War—presented

3 **Animals** — gerenuk — born — Bronx Park Zoo, New York City

5 **Visiting Celebrities**—emperor of Japan to visit the continental United States—Hirohito—arrived—Williamsburg, Va.

6 **Euthanasia**—"Right to Die" law—enacted—California

OCTOBER 1

9 **Medal**—medal awarded by the Continental Congress to a foreigner—presentation made—F. L. T. de Fleury

5 **Directory (city)**—published—Philadelphia, Pa.

0 **Fair**—agricultural fair—Pittsfield, Mass.

1 **Ship**—steamboat to sail down the Mississippi—*New Orleans*—arrived—New Orleans, La.

3 **Gymnasium**—gymnasium to offer systematic instruction—Round Hill School—Northampton, Mass.—opened

4 **Locomotive**—locomotive with six or eight driving wheels—patented—Ross Winans

8 **School**—school for the mentally retarded—opened—Boston, Mass.

1 **Army Balloon Corps**—organized

1 **Ship**—Union ship captured in the Civil War—*Fanny*—in Pimlico Sound (N. C.)

1865 **Baseball Game**—baseball game in which one team scored more than 100 runs—Philadelphia, Pa.

1873 **Nurse**—trained nurse—L. A. J. Richards—began service—Bellevue Hospital, New York City

1875 **Agricultural Experiment Station**—state agricultural experiment station—appropriation—Connecticut

1875 **Meat**—beef exported—from New York City—to England

1880 **Electric Lighting**—electric incandescent lamp factory—Edison Lamp Works—Menlo Park, N.J.—opened

1883 **Bible School**—Missionary Training College—opened—New York City

1884 **Theatrical School**—theatrical school—exclusively for stage training—opened—New York City

1885 **Newspaper**—newspaper daily railroad delivery service—*Morning News*—Dallas, Tex.

1885 **Postal Service**—special delivery service—special delivery stamp issued

1887 **Insurance**—mutual liability insurance company—opened—Boston, Mass.

1888 **Arbitration**—interstate carrier arbitration law—enacted

1890 **Narcotics Legislation**—narcotics regulation (federal)—enacted

1892 **Sociology Professor**—A. W. Small—appointed professor—Chicago, Ill.

1896 **Postal Service**—rural free delivery—established

1903 **Baseball Game**—World Series baseball game—Pittsburgh Pirates vs. Boston Americans—Boston, Mass.

1904 **Library**—business library supported by taxes—Newark, N.J.

1904 **Postal Service**—permit mail—in use

1908 **Nursing School**—university school of nursing—as part of a university—Minneapolis, Minn.

1909 **Research Institute**—institute for research in nervous diseases—Neurological Institute of New York—New York City—opened

1911 **Insurance**—workers' compensation insurance law (state)—effective—Washington

1912 **Quarantine**—plant quarantine legislation (national)—effective

1913 **Monument**—monument to a bird—unveiled—Salt Lake City, Utah

1917 **Post Office**—open-air post office—opened—St. Petersburg, Fla.

1917 **Ship**—submarine chaser—*SC-1*—commissioned

1918 **Hygiene Instruction**—hygiene and public health school—Johns Hopkins University—Baltimore, Md.—opened

1922 Taconite—taconite production—Mesabi Iron Co., Babbitt, Minn.—first cargo shipped to Ford Motor Company, River Rouge, Mich.

1924 Births—President of the United States to be born in a hospital—Jimmy Carter—Plains, Ga.

1929 Airmail Service—airplane mail pickup—demonstrated—Washington, D.C.

1934 College—college to dispense with the system of credits, hours, points, grades, etc.—in operation—Olivet, Mich.

1934 Federal Credit Union Act—charter No. 1—Texarkana, Tex.

1934 Periodical—sectarian magazine printed in rotogravure—*Catholic Missions*—issued—New York City

1937 Trailer Church—operated

1940 Army Parachute Troops—battalion organized—Fort Benning, Ga.

1942 Aviation—Airplane—jet-propelled airplane—flown—Muroc, Calif.

1945 President (U.S.)—President to attend the swearing-in of an Associate Justice (H. H. Burton) of the Supreme Court—H. S. Truman—Washington, D.C.

1946 Baseball Game—baseball playoff series—St. Louis, Mo.

1947 Airmail Service—helicopter airmail and express service—Los Angeles, Calif.

1949 Television Tube—rectangular television tube (practical)—deliveries made

1951 Treaty—treaty signed by a woman ambassador—Eugenie Anderson

1952 Television—Telecast—husband and wife to broadcast a religious program—Dr. and Mrs. Norman Vincent Peale—New York City

1952 Television Station—ultra-high-frequency commercial television station—KPTV—Portland, Oreg.

1957 Installment Sales Law—effective—New York

1961 Baseball Player—baseball player (major league) to hit more than 60 home runs in 1 season—R. E. Maris—61st home run, New York City

1961 Television Station—religious noncommercial television station—WYAR-TV—began operating in Portsmouth, Va.

1972 Litter Legislation—litter legislation (state)—Oregon—effective

1973 Air Force Officer—chief master sergeant (black) of the Air Force—T. N. Barnes—began service

1973 Probate Legislation—probate law eliminating red tape—Wisconsin—effective

1977 Department of Energy (U.S.)—Department of Energy—formal opening

1979 Visiting Celebrities—pontiff to visit the White House—Pope John Paul II—arrived at Boston, Mass.

OCTOBER 2

1721 Animals—camel imported—Boston, Mass.—advertised

1786 Music Book—Lutheran hymnbook (German) published in America—H. M. Mühlenberg, comp.—*Erbauliche Lieder-Sammlung zum Gottesdienstlichsten Gebrauch in den Vereinigten Evangelisch-Lutherischen Gemeinen in Nord-America*—copyright—Peter Leibert and Michael Billmeyer

1831 Catholic Nuns—Catholic nuns (black community)—order approved

1866 Cans—can (tin) with a key opener—patented—J. Osterhoudt—New York City

1876 Actors' Home—actors' home—For. Home—Philadelphia—opened

1889 Conference—Pan American Conference opened—Washington, D.C.

1895 Catholic Church—eucharistic congress the Catholic Church—Francesco Satol Washington, D.C.

1903 Baseball Game—shutout World Se game (nonsanctioned)—Pittsburgh Nat als—Boston Americans—Boston, Mass.

1903 Turbine—steam turbine generator of la capacity for commercial service—ope —Chicago, Ill.

1936 Alcohol—power alcohol plant—power cohol sold—Atchison, Kan.

1937 X Ray—X-ray motion pictures (success of the action of the human heart—exhib —New York City

1943 Aviation—Airplane—rocket airplane (m tary)—tested as a glider

1955 Methodist Church—black Methodist mi ter of an all-white congregation—S. Montgomery—Old Mystic, Conn.

1956 Clock—clock to operate by atomic po —exhibited—New York City

1963 Leather Substitute—artificial leather s upper—Corfam—introduced to the pr by E. I. Du Pont de Nemours Company

1965 Catholic Bishop—black Catholic bis who was American born—H. R. Perr named auxiliary bishop, New Orleans,

1965 Radio Broadcast—underwater transat tic radio conversation—La Jolla, Calif. Cape Ferrat, France

1967 Supreme Court (U.S.)—Associate Justic the Supreme Court who was a blac Thurgood Marshall—publicly sworn in

1979 Coal Mine—woman to die in a coal m disaster—M. J. McCusker—Coalport, P

OCTOBER 3

1632 Tobacco—tobacco tax (colonial)—autl ized—Massachusetts

1789 Holiday—Thanksgiving Day—presiden proclamation issued

1805 Pharmacopoeia—pharmacopoeia (pared by a medical association)—autl ized—Boston, Mass.

1824 Engineering College—engineering coll —Rensselaer Polytechnic Institute—T N.Y.—founded

Treaty—treaty with a South American country—signed—Bogota, Colombia

Annual—published—Philadelphia, Pa.

Deaf—**Church Service**—church services for the deaf—New York City

Cricket Tournament—international cricket tournament—Hoboken, N.J.

Holiday—Thanksgiving Day national proclamation—Abraham Lincoln

Jewish College—Jewish college to train men for the rabbinate—Hebrew Union College—established—Cincinnati, Ohio

Blind—school for the blind—Perkins Asylum—Boston, Mass.—changed name

Hospital—tuberculosis sanatorium (state)—Massachusetts Hospital for Consumptives—Rutland, Mass.—opened

Vacuum Cleaner—motor-driven vacuum cleaner—patented—J. S. Thurman—St. Louis, Mo.

Dental School—dental assistants' and nurses' course—Ohio College of Dental Surgery—Cincinnati, Ohio

Federal Trade Commission—Federal Trade Commission trade practice conference—Omaha, Neb.

Radio Facsimile Transmission—photographs sent over a city telephone—transmitted—C. F. Jenkins—Washington, D.C.

Senator (U.S.)—woman to occupy a seat in the Senate—R. L. Felton—appointed—Georgia

Citizenship and Public Affairs School—opened—Syracuse, N.Y.

Medal—Silver Star Army Medal awarded to a civilian—Vern Haugland

Television—Telecast—missing persons telecast—New York City

Army—Reserve Officers Training Corps course in mountain and winter warfare—Norwich University—Northfield, Vt.

Telescope—telescope lens 200 inches in diameter—completed

Radio Station—radio station owned and operated by blacks—WERD—Atlanta, Ga.

Television—Telecast—prizefight (middleweight) televised coast-to-coast—Sands-Olson fight—Chicago, Ill.

Tape Recording—video recording on magnetic tape—Los Angeles, Calif.

Astronaut—astronaut (American) to orbit the earth six times—W. M. Schirra, Jr.—takeoff—*Sigma 7*—Cape Canaveral, Fla.

Navy—all-nuclear task force voyage around the world without refueling—returned, Norfork, Va.

Aviation—Flights—airplane to fly faster than 4,500 m.p.h.—W. J. Knight, pilot—Edwards Air Force Base, Calif.

Medical Clinic—vasectomy outpatient service—Margret Sanger Research Bureau—opened—New York City

OCTOBER 4

1810 Actor—English actor of note—G. F. Cooke—sailed to New York City—from Liverpool, England

1829 Catholic Provincial Council—convened—Baltimore, Md.

1830 Printing Press—power printing press capable of fine book work—patented—Isaac Adams—Boston, Mass.

1861 Ship—ironclad turreted vessel in the U.S. Navy—*Monitor*—contract signed

1870 Solicitor General (U.S.)—Solicitor General of the United States—B. H. Bristow—appointed

1878 Chinese Embassy—received—Washington, D.C.

1881 Cream Separator—continuous-flow centrifugal cream separator—patented—C. G. P. de Laval

1881 Piano Player—piano player (completely automatic)—patented

1887 Newspaper—European edition of an American newspaper—*Herald*

1890 Niagara Falls—utilization of Niagara Falls waterpower (large-scale)—ground broken

1895 Golf Tournament—open championship (official)—Newport, R.I.

1909 Balloon Race—dirigible balloon race—St. Louis, Mo.

1932 Play (drama)—antivivisection play—*Woven Dreams*—presented—Philadelphia, Pa.

1933 Federal Surplus Relief Corporation—incorporated—Delaware

1940 Birds—quetzal bird—imported—New York City

1955 Telephone—telephone conversation (commercial) using electricity generated by the sun's rays—Americus, Ga.

1958 Aviation—Flights (transatlantic)—jet passenger commercial service—New York City–London

1960 Satellite—communications satellite successfully placed in orbit—launched, Cape Canaveral, Fla.—received and recorded message from D. D. Eisenhower through C. A. Herter to F. H. Boland—United Nations, New York City

1961 Postage Stamp—postage stamp featuring a work of art in true color—on sale in Washington, D.C.

1965 Visiting Celebrities—pontiff to visit the United States—Pope Paul VI—arrived—New York City

1977 Lottery—daily state lotteries with the same winning daily number—New Jersey and Pennsylvania

OCTOBER 5

1646 Bounty—granted—Virginia

1843 Horse Race—night harness race—Hoboken, N.J.

1853 **College**—college to grant women absolutely equal rights—nonsectarian college of high rank—Antioch College—Yellow Springs, Ohio—opened

1853 **College**—woman college professor—R. M. Pennell—Antioch College—Yellow Springs, Ohio

1853 **Didactics Course**—didactics course in a college—Antioch College—Yellow Springs, Ohio—opened

1853 **Hygiene Instruction**—physiology and hygiene courses—offered—Antioch College—Yellow Springs, Ohio

1854 **Baby Show**—Springfield, Ohio

1869 **Bicycle Patent**—water velocipede patent—awarded—Columbus, Ohio

1871 **Unitarian Minister**—woman ordained to the Unitarian ministry—C. C. Burleigh—Brooklyn, Conn.

1881 **Immigration**—Chinese labor immigration act—ratifications proclaimed

1918 **Aviation**—war night-flying scout group—assigned to France

1919 **Radio Broadcast**—submarine (submerged) broadcast—U.S.S. *Nautilus*—Hudson River, N.Y.

1919 **Radio Telephone**—two-way radio conversation between a submerged submarine and another vessel—New York City

1921 **Baseball Player**—baseball players (brothers) to oppose each other in a World Series—R. W. Meusel and E. F. Meusel—New York City—first game

1921 **Radio Broadcast**—baseball World Series broadcast—New York City

1922 **Aviation—Passenger**—woman airplane passenger (transcontinental)—started—San Francisco, Calif.

1930 **Aviation—Flights (transcontinental)**—transcontinental airplane flight by a woman—Laura Ingalls—left Roosevelt Field, N.Y.

1931 **Aviation—Flights (transpacific)**—transpacific nonstop flight—landed at Wenatchee, Wash.—from Japan

1933 **Aviation**—airplane sleeping berths—introduced—Atlanta, Ga.-New York City

1936 **Television—Telecast**—telecast using coaxial cable—intercity telecast—Philadelphia, Pa.-New York City

1947 **Television—Telecast**—presidential address televised from the White House—H. S. Truman—Washington, D.C.

1953 **Baseball Team**—baseball team to win five World Series in succession—New York Yankees

OCTOBER 6

1683 **Mennonites**—Mennonites—arrived from Germany

1766 **Actor**—matinee idol—John Henry—American debut—Philadelphia, Pa.

1780 **Prison**—American imprisoned in Tower of London—Henry Laurens

1783 **Clock**—self-winding clock—patent plication—Benjamin Hanks—Litchfi Conn.

1825 **Giant**—Patrick Magee—exhibited—N York City

1837 **Locomotive Steam Whistle**—used—Pa son, N.J.

1848 **Ship**—steamboat service (regular) to C fornia via Cape Horn—*California*—sa —New York City

1852 **Pharmacy Society (national)**—Ameri Pharmaceutical Association—organize Philadelphia, Pa.

1857 **Chess Champion**—chess champion of world (American-born)—P. C. Morph New York City

1857 **Chess Tournament**—chess tournament importance—American Chess Congres New York City

1863 **Bathhouse**—Turkish bath—opene Brooklyn, N.Y.

1868 **Nickel Plating**—patent—W. H. Reming —Boston, Mass.

1873 **Balloon**—balloon Atlantic crossing tempt—*Daily Graphic*—Brooklyn, N.Y.

1876 **Library Society**—library association (tional)—American Library Associatio organized—Philadelphia, Pa.

1884 **Naval War College**—naval war colleg established—Newport, R.I.

1911 **Radio Broadcast**—transpacific conver tion broadcast—received from Hokka island, Japan, at San Francisco, Calif.

1917 **Employment Service**—Employment S vice (U.S.)—act approved

1923 **Golf Champion**—family to win more tl one national championship in 1 yea Edith Cummings—Rye, N.Y. (Natio Woman's Amateur championship)

1926 **Baseball Game**—World Series baset game in which 3 home runs were made 1 game—New York Yankees vs. St. Lo Cardinals—St. Louis, Mo.—G. H. Ruth

1946 **Baseball Game**—night baseball World ries game—Red Socks-Cardinals— Louis, Mo.

1951 **Television—Telecast**—football ga coast-to-coast telecast—Illini vs. Badg —Champaign-Urbana, Ill.

1955 **Army Officer**—male nurse—E. L. T. Lyor sworn in

1955 **Horse**—trotter triple-crown winner—Sc Frost—(Kentucky Futurity) Lexington, I

1959 **Baseball Game**—World Series baset game to draw more than 90,000 person Chicago White Sox vs. Los Angeles Do ers—Los Angeles, Calif.

1965 **Diplomatic Service**—ambassador (bla woman)—P. R. Harris—assumed duties Luxembourg

1915 Fingerprint Society—fingerprint society (international)—International Association for Criminal Identification—formed—Oakland, Calif.

1930 Aviation—Flights (transcontinental)—transcontinental flight by a woman—Laura Ingalls—left—Roosevelt Field, N.Y.

1938 Baseball Team—baseball team to win three World Series in succession—third series won

1946 Blanket—electric (electronic) blanket—manufactured—Petersburg, Va.

1947 Telephone—mobile telephone conversation—moving automobile to airplane—Wilmington, Del.

1948 Baseball Player—black baseball player to hit a home run in a World Series—L. E. Doby—Cleveland, Ohio

1951 Baseball Player—baseball rookie to hit a grand slam home run in the World Series—G. J. McDougald—New York City

1969 Senator (U.S.)—senator to act in the movies—E. M. Dirksen of Illinois—*The Monitors*—film released

OCTOBER 10

1802 Jewish Congregation—Jewish congregation (Ashkenazic)—Rodeph Shalom—Philadelphia, Pa.—founded

1818 Ship—steamboat on the Great Lakes—*Walk-in-the Water*—trip

1843 Horse Race—futurity race—Nashville, Tenn.

1845 Naval Academy—Naval Academy (U.S.)—officially opened—Annapolis, Md.

1857 Chess Tournament—American Chess Association—formed—New York City

1863 Catholic Church—Catholic parish church for blacks—purchased—Baltimore, Md.

1865 Billiard Ball—of composition material resembling ivory—patented—J. W. Hyatt

1874 Young Men's Hebrew Association—New York City—building opened

1886 Coat—tuxedo coat—introduced—Tuxedo Park, N.Y.

1896 Book Review—book review newspaper supplement—published—New York City

1898 Optometry Society—optometry society (national)—American Association of Opticians—organized—New York City

1918 American Indian Church—church organized by American Indians—First American Church—incorporated—El Reno, Okla.

1920 Baseball Game—triple play unassisted in a world series—Bill Wambsganss—Cleveland, Ohio

1920 Baseball Game—World Series grand slam home run (American League)—E. J. Smith—Cleveland, Ohio

1923 Aviation—Airship—dirigible (American-built rigid)—christened—Lakehurst, N.J.

1923 Baseball Game—World Series baseball games to gross $1 million—New York C

1933 Detergent—synthetic detergent—for ho use—marketed

1934 Archivist of the United States—R. D. Connor—appointed

1934 Humanist Society—Humanist National sembly—New York City

1937 Radio Broadcast—cooperative radio sh —Hollywood, Calif.

1967 Bowling—bowling automatic scorer—u in sanctioned league games—Chicago,

1978 Money—woman commemorated on a culation U.S. coin—S. B. Anthony—c authorized

OCTOBER 11

1753 Arbitration—colonial arbitration law enacted—New Haven, Conn.

1802 Army School—army school graduate West Point, N.Y.

1811 Ferryboat—steam-propelled ferryboa operated—Hoboken, N.J.–New York Ci

1853 Bank—clearinghouse—exchange open —New York City

1881 Photographic Film—roll film for camera patented—D. H. Houston—Cambria, W

1886 College—college for women to affili with a university—H. Sophie Newco Memorial College—New Orleans, La.

1887 Adding Machine—adding machine ab lutely accurate at all times—patent—D. Felt—Chicago, Ill.

1910 President (U.S.)—President to fly—The dore Roosevelt—St. Louis, Mo.

1919 Aviation—Races—transcontinental race—completed—San Francisco, Calif.

1924 Aviation—Flights (transcontinental) transcontinental airship voyage—*Shena doah*—arrived—San Diego, Calif.

1932 Television—Telecast—political campai telecast—New York City

1933 Poorhouse (state)—Smyrna, Del.—dedic ed

1935 Crime Prevention and Detection—nation conference on crime—Trenton, N.J.

1938 Glass Wool—patented—Newark, Ohio

1945 Army Officer—general to be consecrated bishop—W. R. Arnold—consecrated New York City

1948 Television—Telecast—stratovision Wor Series telecast—Boston, Mass.

1963 Postage Stamp—President's wife depict on a commemorative postage stamp—Ele nor Roosevelt—issued—Washington, D.

1968 Astronaut—three-man spaceflight (Ame can)—*Apollo VII*—launched, Cape Kenn dy, Fla.

1971 College—college whose tuition fees we based on family income—Beloit Colleg Beloit, Wis.—plan adopted

3 **Army Officer**—general of the armies of the United States with the rank of 6 stars—George Washington—posthumous appointment authorized by joint congressional resolution

OCTOBER 12

3 **Hospital**—insane hospital (state)—Williamsburg, Va.—opened

2 **Monument**—monument to Christopher Columbus—dedicated—Baltimore, Md.

4 **African Church**—received in full fellowship in Methodist Episcopal Church

2 **Army School**—army school graduate (Jewish)—Simon M. Levy—commissioned

2 **Army School**—army school graduates—commissioned

5 **Labor**—labor congress (national)—First Industrial Congress—convened—New York City

9 **Horse Race**—trotting futurity—New York City

6 **Bridge**—cantilever bridge—construction started

8 **Bridge**—railroad all-steel bridge—bridge contract signed

5 **Golf Tournament**—amateur golf tournament (official)—Newport, R.I.

5 **Baseball Pitcher**—baseball pitcher (World Series) with 3 shutout games—Christopher Mathewson—3rd game, New York City

0 **Tunnel**—twin-tube subaqueous vehicular tunnel—Holland tunnel—Jersey City, N.J.–New York City—construction began

3 **Parachute-Jumping Contest**—parachute-jumping contest—Theodore Schieuming—Mitchel Field, N.Y.

4 **Aviation—Airship**—dirigible merchandise equipment—left Germany

5 **Heresy Trial**—of a bishop—W. M. Brown—deposed—New Orleans, La.

8 **Medical School**—medical center devoted to teaching, treatment, and research—Columbia-Presbyterian Medical Center, New York City—formal dedication

8 **Respirator (iron lung)**—used at hospital—Boston, Mass.

2 **Diplomatic Service**—American legation in which a woman assumed charge—Stockholm, Sweden—F. E. Willis

7 **Electric Generator**—hydrogen-cooled turbine generator—used—Millers Ford station, Ohio

5 **Medal**—Medal of Honor awarded to a conscientious objector—D. T. Doss at Washington, D.C.

9 **Diplomatic Service**—ambassador (woman)—Eugenie Anderson

1963 **Catholic Beatification**—Catholic beatification of an American citizen (male)—J. N. Neumann

OCTOBER 13

1775 **Navy**—naval fleet—authorized

1778 **Freemasons**—Masonic Grand Lodge—organized—Williamsburg, Va.

1792 **Building**—building erected by the Government in Washington, D.C.—Executive Mansion—cornerstone laid

1843 **Jews**—Jewish fraternal society—B'nai B'rith—founded

1853 **Zinc**—zinc commercial production—Pennsylvania and Lehigh Zinc Company Mill—erected—Bethlehem, Pa.

1857 **Horse Race**—American-bred horse to win a major race abroad—Prioress—Newmarket, England

1860 **Photograph**—aerial photograph—Boston, Mass.

1894 **Golf Tournament**—amateur golf tournament (unofficial)—Yonkers, N.Y.

1905 **Baseball Game**—shutout World Series game—New York Nationals–Philadelphia Athletics—New York City

1915 **Chamber of Commerce**—junior chamber of commerce—organized—St. Louis, Mo.

1922 **League of Nations**—representative (unofficial)—Grace Abbott—appointed

1925 **Play (drama)**—full-length play by a black performed in New York City—*Appearances*—Garland Anderson

1939 **Aviation—License**—airplane instructor's license—under CAA—issued to a woman—E. P. Kilgore—San Bernardino, Calif.

1940 **Deaf—Communication**—visible and oral communication by the deaf over distance—accomplished—New York City

1951 **Football**—football with a rubber covering used in a major collegiate game—Atlanta, Ga.

1953 **Burglar Alarm**—burglar alarm operated by ultrasonic or radio waves—patented—Samuel Bagno—New York City

1955 **Medical Society**—woman president of a major medical society—E. S. Moss

1960 **Presidential Candidate**—presidential candidate debate series on television—third Nixon-Kennedy debate—New York City and Hollywood, Calif.

1965 **Solicitor General (U.S.)**—solicitor general of the United States who was a black—Thurgood Marshall—first case tried—Washington, D.C.

1970 **Baseball Pitcher**—baseball pitcher to hit a grand slam in a World Series game—D. A. McNally—Baltimore, Md.

1977 **War Prisoner**—prisoner of war to head the Naval War College—J. B. Stockdale—began service as president—Newport, R.I.

OCTOBER 14

1774 Declaration of Rights—enacted—Philadelphia, Pa.

1774 Embargo Act—embargo act (Continental Congress)—enacted

1816 Evangelical Church General Conference—convened—Buffalo Valley, Pa.

1834 Patent—black to obtain a patent—Henry Blair—Glenross, Md.

1840 Second Advent Believers—general conference—Boston, Mass.

1879 Ship—steamboat to employ electric lights—*Jeannette*—attempt to use electric lights

1884 Photographic Film—transparent paper-strip photographic film—patent—George Eastman—Rochester, N.Y.

1902 Arbitration—arbitration proceeding—court award made

1915 Ship—warship propelled by electricity—keel laid—*New Mexico*—New York City

1916 Golf Tournament—Professional Golfers Association tournament—Mount Vernon, N.Y.

1920 Radio Station—college radio station—WRUC—Union College, Schenectady, N.Y.—began operation

1922 Aviation—Flights—airplane to fly faster than 200 m.p.h.—L. J. Maitland

1928 Wedding—television wedding—Des Plaines, Ill.

1943 Ship—naval ship christened by a woman not a U.S. citizen—*Canberra*—commissioned

1944 War Shipping Administration—War Shipping Administration award—authorized by E. S. Land

1944 World War II—American general captured by the Germans—A. W. Vanaman—status as prisoner announced

1947 Aviation—Flights—airplane to fly faster than the speed of sound—Muroc, Calif.—C. E. Yeager

1959 Golfer—golfer to play 24 hours continuously on a regulation course—J. J. Johnson—Abilene, Tex.—began play

1968 Discus—discus hurler to win 4 gold medals in 4 consecutive Olympic Games—A. A. Oerter—Mexico City, Mex. (4th medal)

1968 Television—Telecast—outer-space live telecast—*Apollo VII*

1975 Postage Stamp—postage stamps without a denomination—Christmas issue—Washington, D.C.

1978 Horse—horse (thoroughbred) to defeat 2 triple-crown winners in the same race—Exceller—Elmont, N.Y.

OCTOBER 15

1565 Treaty—treaty violation—occurred—Florida

1725 Evangelical and Reformed Church—formed Church in the United States—organized—Montgomery County, Pa.

1789 President (U.S.)—President to tour country—George Washington—tour New England states

1840 Evangelical and Reformed Church—Evangelical Synod of North America—organized—Mehlville, Mo.

1862 Agriculture Bureau—agriculture bureau scientific publication—dated—Washington, D.C.

1878 Electric Company—electric company Edison Electric Light Company—New York City—incorporated

1881 Fishing Magazine—*American Angler*—Philadelphia, Pa.—published

1896 Building—building with an all-marble dome—Rhode Island State House—Providence, R.I.—cornerstone laid

1909 Building—apartment house to occupy square city block—New York City—ready for occupancy

1910 Aviation—Flights (transatlantic)—transatlantic dirigible flight—attempted—Walter Wellman

1910 Radio Broadcast—wireless message from an airship over the Atlantic Ocean—Walter Wellman, pilot—Jack Irwin, wireless operator

1917 Army Camp—army camp for training black officers—Fort Des Moines—Des Moines, Iowa—commissions granted

1918 Judge—woman judge of a juvenile court—Kathryn Sellers—appointed

1919 Horse Race—300-mile endurance run—start—Burlington, Vt.

1920 Radio Station—college radio station—WRUC—Union College, Schenectady, N.Y.—weekly program series begun

1924 Aviation—Airship—dirigible merchandise shipment—from Germany—landed—Lakehurst, N.J.

1927 Radio License—international broadcast license—issued—New York City

1928 Airmail—dirigible to drop mail by parachute—Washington, D.C.—*Graf Zeppelin*

1932 Opera—opera house municipally owned—opened—San Francisco, Calif.

1940 Art Course—industrial camouflage course—Kansas City, Mo.

1940 Conscription—peacetime conscription law—C. A. Dykstra—confirmed as director

1946 Glider—powered soaring glider commercially licensed—San Fernando, Calif.

1948 Naval Officer—woman doctor in the regular U.S. Navy—F. L. Willoughby

1950 Radio Paging Service—instituted—New York City

1951 Television—Telecast—international telecast—WWJ-TV, Detroit, Mich.

1959 Golfer—golfer to play 24 hours continuously on a regulation course—J. J. Johnson—Abilene, Tex.—ended play

1891 Bicycle Race—international six-day bicycle race—New York City

1904 Bibliography Society (national)—Bibliographical Society of America—organized—St. Louis, Mo.

1904 Newspaper—Hungarian daily newspaper—published—New York City

1910 Radio Distress Signal—radio distress signal resulting in an airship rescue—airship *America*—Hatteras, N.C.

1916 Road—federal grant-in-aid to states for roads—project approved

1919 Periodical—photoengraved magazine—*Literary Digest*—New York City

1926 Postage Stamp—sheet of souvenir postage stamps—Battle of White Plains commemorative—issued—New York City

1926 Visiting Celebrities—queen (reigning) to visit the United States—Queen Marie of Rumania—arrived—New York City

1929 Medical Instruction—History of Medicine Department—Johns Hopkins University—Baltimore, Md.

1930 Jockey—jockey to win seven races in one day—Joseph Sylvester—Ravenna, Ohio

1971 College—college to offer courses to commuters in traveling railroad cars—Adelphi University

1977 Baseball Game—World Series baseball game in which a batter made 3 consecutive home runs in 1 game—R. M. Jackson—New York City

OCTOBER 19

1790 War—battle fought by United States troops—Ohio

1839 Iron—iron blast furnace—using anthracite coal—Pottsville, Pa.

1911 Aviation—Flights (transcontinental)—transcontinental airplane flight (eastbound)—R. G. Fowler—left Los Angeles, Calif.

1914 Postal Service—collection and delivery of mail in automobiles—owned by the U.S. Government

1918 Army Insignia—shoulder sleeve insignia—"shoulder patch"—authorized

1919 Medal—Distinguished Service Medal awarded to a woman—Evangeline Booth

1926 Ordnance—semiautomatic rifle—patented—J. C. Garand

1936 Aviation—Races—airplane passenger race around the world—completed—Lakehurst, N.J.

1936 Fingerprinting—high school to fingerprint its students—Watertown, S.D.

1937 Soilless Culture of Plants—commercial hydroponicum (large)—Montebello, Calif.—company incorporated

1941 Electric Generator—wind turbine—for alternating current power plant—in service—Grandpa's Knob, Vt.

1950 Television Station—illegal television station—Johnstown, Pa.

1953 Aviation—Flights (transcontinenta transcontinental nonstop eastward sch uled service—Los Angeles, Calif.-N York City

1953 Oil—plastic pipeline to transport oil cr country—Williston Basin, Mont. (star line)—in service

1976 Army Officer—general of the armies of United States with the rank of 6 star George Washington—posthumous c mission signed

OCTOBER 20

1817 Theater—showboat—floating theater—Nashville, Tenn.

1846 College—college to grant women absol ly equal rights—Mount Union College liance, Ohio—founded

1852 Factory—steam-heated factory—sold auction—Burlington, Vt.

1860 Visiting Celebrities—Prince of Wales—Portland, Me.

1862 Presidential Executive Order—to be n bered—issued—Abraham Lincoln

1870 Labor Union—labor organization to ad workmen other than craft workmen ble Order of Knights of Labor

1883 Manual Training—manual training sch entirely financed by public taxes—aut ized—Baltimore, Md.

1888 Baseball Team—baseball teams to go world tour

1906 Radio Tube—three-element vacuum tub announced—Lee De Forest

1910 Baseball—cork-center baseball—used World Series—Chicago, Ill.

1916 Bird Legislation (international)—Migra Bird Treaty—ratified—Great Britain

1920 Aviation—Flights—New York-Ala flight—returned—Mitchel Field, N.Y.

1922 Aviation—Parachute—pilot to bail out disabled airplane—H. R. Harris—Day Ohio

1925 Compotype—patented—Clifton Chish—Cleveland, Ohio

1929 Hospital—community hospital—organi—Elk City, Okla.

1944 Medal—Legion of Merit Medal awarde a Women's Army Corps (WAC) membe the European Theater of Operations M. Wilson—awarded

1960 Post Office—post office fully mechanize opened—Providence, R.I.

1961 Vending Machine—vending machine dispense live flowers—installed at Gr Central Terminal, New York City

OCTOBER 21

1639 Medical Legislation—medical law—en ed—Virginia

1956 Tape Recording—video recording on magnetic tape televised coast-to-coast—Jonathan Winters show

OCTOBER 24

1812 Historical Society—historical society (national)—American Antiquarian Society—formed

1828 Fair—manufacturers' fair—New York City

1836 Match—match patent—A. D. Phillips—Springfield, Mass.

1849 Disciples of Christ—general convention—Cincinnati, Ohio

1861 Telegram—transcontinental telegram—San Francisco, Calif.–Washington, D.C.

1861 Telegraph—telegraph line to the Pacific coast—in operation

1876 Clock—clock (one-day back-wind alarm clock)—patented—S. E. Thomas—New York City

1878 Electric Company—electric company—Edison Electric Light Company—organized —New York City

1893 Niagara Falls—utilization of Niagara Falls waterpower (large-scale)—contract for equipment executed

1901 Niagara Falls—person to go over Niagara Falls in a barrel—A. E. Taylor

1908 Automobile Race—Vanderbilt cup race to be won by an American—G. H. Robertson —Motor Parkway, L.I., N.Y.

1917 Naval Officer—electrician (woman) in the Navy—A. P. Morrison—enlisted

1941 Army Officer—air surgeon of the War Department—D. N. W. Grant

1943 Medal—Distinguished Service Cross awarded to an animal—Chips—authorized

1945 Television—Telecast—department store sales demonstrations (large-scale)—Gimbel Brothers—Philadelphia, Pa.

1945 Television—Telecast—stratovision flight test—experimental license granted

1951 Postage Stamp—United Nations postage stamps in U.S. denominations—first on sale in New York City

1956 Presbyterian Church—woman ordained a minister in the Presbyterian Church—M. E. Towner—ordained—Syracuse, N.Y.

1977 Jockey—jockey to win more than $5 million in purses in 1 year—Steve Cauthen—winnings topped $5 million

OCTOBER 25

1761 Knighthood—knighthood conferred in America—presented to Jeffery Amherst—Staten Island, N.Y.

1812 War (1812)—British frigate captured by a single frigate—*Macedonian* captured by *United States*

1848 Railroad—railroad to run west out of Chicago

1870 Trademark—registered—Averill Chemi Paint Co.—New York City

1881 Air Brush Patent—L. L. Curtis—Cape Eli beth, Me.

1888 Ferryboat—double-deck ferryboa launched—Newburgh, N.Y.

1892 Postal Card—paid-reply postal card— sued

1905 Ferryboat—municipally owned ferrybo —operated—New York City

1916 Ship—battleship (major) built on the cific coast—*California*—keel laid

1924 Aviation—Flights (transcontinental transcontinental airship voyage—ret voyage—*Shenandoah*

1929 Cabinet (U.S.)—Cabinet member convic of a crime—A. B. Fall—found guilty

1930 Aviation—Flights (transcontinental transcontinental regularly schedu through air service—New York City– Angeles, Calif.

1940 Army Officer—brigadier general (black B. O. Davis—appointed

1945 Flag—President's flag—48 stars—auth ized—H. S. Truman

1954 Television—Telecast—Cabinet session be televised—Washington, D.C.

1955 Stove—electronic range for domestic us introduced—New York City

1960 Clock—electronic wristwatch—produc —New York City

1972 Navy—women (other than nurses) signed to regular shipboard duty—A Kerr

1972 Police—police training school wom graduates of the Federal Bureau of Inve gation—S. L. Roley and J. E. Pierce—Qu tico, Va.

OCTOBER 26

1785 Animals—mule—imported—Boston, Ma

1812 Medical Book—psychiatry book—*Medi Inquiries and Observations Upon the L eases of the Mind*, by Benjamin Rus copyrighted

1825 Canal—canal of importance—Erie Cana opened

1849 Periodical—Jewish weekly published English—*The Asmonean*—New York C

1858 Washing Machine—rotary-motion wash machine—patent—H. E. Smith—Ph delphia, Pa.

1869 Steeplechase—Jerome Park—New Y City

1909 Aviation—Pilot—army pilot to solo—F Humphreys—College Park, Md.

1912 Aviation—aeronautical elopement— thur Smith and Aimée Cour—Fort Way Ind., to Hillsdale, Mich.

1933 Industrial Recovery Act—complia board under the National Industrial Rec ery Act—established

56 **Ship**—gyro-stabilized American liner—*Mariposa*—maiden voyage

73 **Building**—"State House" located outside a state—Florida House—Washington, D.C.—opened

OCTOBER 27

30 **Astronomical Expedition**—observed eclipse—Boston, Mass.

12 **Ship**—naval vessel of the United States to display the American flag around Cape Horn—left Delaware capes

66 **Yacht Race**—yacht race across the Atlantic Ocean—agreement made

69 **Agricultural Society**—agricultural society for dairymen—Vermont Dairymen's Association—organized—Montpelier, Vt.

89 **Lithuanian Church**—organized—Plymouth, Pa.

04 **Streetcar**—aluminum streetcar—aluminum used in subway car construction

04 **Subway**—subway (rapid transit)—Interborough Rapid Transit—New York City

09 **Aviation—Passenger**—woman airplane passenger—College Park, Md.

18 **Ship**—Eagle boat—commissioned

20 **Radio License**—radio station licensed—Pittsburgh, Pa.

22 **Holiday**—Navy Day—celebrated

22 **Radio Broadcast**—election campaign using radio—H. S. New—Indiana—began use of radio in campaign

42 **Submarine**—submarine with a high-tensile-steel pressure hull—*Balao*—launched—Portsmouth, N.H.

46 **Television—Telecast**—commercial program telecast—"Geographically Speaking"

48 **Economic Cooperation Administration (U.S.)**—industrial guaranty contract of investment of American capital in ERP (European Recovery Program) countries

53 **Medal**—Medal of Honor awarded to a Nisei in the Korean War—presented—Washington, D.C.

54 **Army Officer**—brigadier general (black) in the Air Force—B. O. Davis, Jr.

69 **Federal Maritime Commission**—woman chairman of the Federal Maritime Commission—began service

69 **Woman**—woman federal regulatory agency chairman—H. D. Bentley—sworn in

75 **Bowler**—bowler to earn $100,000 in 1 year in tournaments—Earl Anthony—Battle Creek, Mich.—earnings reached $100,890

OCTOBER 28

88 **Naval Officer**—naval chaplain (Continental Navy)—Benjamin Parks—appointed

95 **Extradition**—extradition treaty with a foreign country—Jay Treaty, with Great Britain—approved by the President

99 **Aviation**—aeronautical patent—Moses McFarland

1833 **Quakers**—Quaker college—Haverford School, Haverford, Pa.—opened

1863 **Water Conduit**—water supply tunnel for a city—Chicago, Ill.—contract

1867 **Jewish College**—Jewish college—Maimonides College—opened

1886 **Monument**—statue presented by a foreign country—Statue of Liberty—New York harbor

1904 **Fingerprinting**—police department to adopt the fingerprinting system—St. Louis, Mo.

1919 **Prohibition**—prohibition law (national)—Volstead Act enacted

1922 **Radio Broadcast**—football game (collegiate) coast-to-coast broadcast—New York City

1927 **Aviation—Airport**—air passenger international station—opened—Key West, Fla.

1929 **Autogiro**—autogiro manufactured in the United States—Pitcairn-Cierva—completed

1929 **Births**—child born in an airplane—Miami, Fla.

1933 **Emergency Housing Corporation (U.S.)**—authorized

1935 **American Indians**—American Indian tribal constitution—signed—Washington, D.C.

1946 **Atomic Energy Commission**—Atomic Energy Commission—appointed

1957 **Submarine**—submarine submerged for 2 weeks (NATO exercises in North Atlantic)—*Nautilus*—returned to Groton, Conn.

1958 **Brokerage**—woman director of a stock exchange—M. G. Roebling

1964 **Diplomatic Service**—woman to serve the United Nations as a permanent ambassador—M. P. Tree—sworn in

1970 **Sky Marshal**—sky marshals—presidential directive—R. M. Nixon

OCTOBER 29

1766 **Fox Hunting Club**—preliminary meeting—Philadelphia, Pa.

1796 **Ship**—ship from the Atlantic coast to anchor in a California port—*Otter*—arrived—Monterey, Calif.

1814 **Ship**—steam-propelled frigate—*Demologos*—launched—New York City

1833 **Fraternity (Greek-letter)**—fraternity house—Kappa Alpha Society—Williamstown, Mass.—chapter founded

1834 **College**—coeducational college—Oberlin Collegiate Institute—Oberlin, Ohio—graduation

1836 **Animals**—cattle (shorthorn) public auction sale—Chillicothe, Ohio

1904 **Automobile Trucking Service**—automobile intercity trucking service—Colorado City, Colo.–Snyder, Tex.

1928 **Aviation—Passenger**—woman Zeppelin passenger (paying)—Clara Adams—sailed—Lakehurst, N.J.

1940 **Conscription**—peacetime conscription bill —drawing of numbers—Washington, D.C.

1945 **Medal**—Medal of Freedom awarded to a woman—Anna Rosenberg

1947 **Forest Fire**—forest fire drenched by artificial rain—Concord, N.H.

1959 **Television—Telecast**—stockholders' meetings televised coast-to-coast simultaneously

1978 **Slot Machine**—slot-machine payoff of $275,000—James Schelich—Las Vegas, Nev.

OCTOBER 30

1768 **Methodist Church**—Methodist chapel—dedicated—New York City

1794 **Ball Bearing**—commercial installation—Lancaster, Pa.

1799 **Naval Officer**—naval chaplain—William Balch—commissioned

1888 **Pen**—ball-point pen patent—J. J. Loud—Weymouth, Mass.

1894 **Time Recorder**—card time recorder—patented—D. M. Cooper—Rochester, N.Y.

1903 **Traffic Regulation Pamphlet**—printed traffic regulations—enacted—New York City

1912 **Vice Presidential Candidate**—vice presidential nominee to die before the meeting of the electoral college—J. S. Sherman—died

1917 **Naval Officer**—naval chaplain who was Jewish—David Goldberg

1941 **World War II**—American destroyer torpedoed and sunk while on convoy duty—*Reuben James*

1953 **Television—Telecast**—color telecast on a closed-circuit local station—Philadelphia, Pa.

OCTOBER 31

1777 **Holiday**—Thanksgiving Day celebration (nationwide, colonial)—committee appointed to draft recommendation

1835 **Insurance**—mutual fire insurance company —Manufacturers' Mutual Fire Insurance Company of Rhode Island—incorporated

1838 **School**—model school—opened—Lafayette College—Easton, Pa.

1868 **Postal Service**—letter carriers' uniforms approved

1883 **Temperance Society**—women's temperance society (national)—World Woman's Christian Temperance Union—organized

1892 **Streetcar**—transfers (printed)—used—Rochester, N.Y.

1944 **Ship**—naval ship christened by a Marine Corps Women's Reserve member—*Bucyrus*—launched—Richmond, Calif.

1945 **Hall of Famer**—Hall of Fame (university) black—B. T. Washington—selection announced

1952 **Atomic Bomb**—atomic fusion (thermo clear or hydrogen) bomb—detonate Marshall Islands

1953 **Television—Telecast**—opera (major) t vised in color—*Carmen*—New York C

1956 **Discovery**—American to land by air at South Pole—G. J. Dufek

1956 **Navy**—naval expedition to the South P —G. J. Dufek—landed

1962 **Satellite**—geodetic satellite—*Anna 1* launched—Cape Canaveral, Fla.

1964 **Astronaut**—astronaut to die—T. C. F man—Houston, Tex.

NOVEMBER 1

1776 **Lottery**—lottery held by the Continen Congress—lottery approved

1777 **Flag**—American flag saluted by a fore nation—*Ranger*—sailed for France

1778 **Holiday**—Thanksgiving Day celebrat (nationwide, colonial)—resolution acce ed

1781 **Bank**—bank chartered by Congress—Ba of North America—organized—Phi delphia, Pa.

1781 **Medical Society**—medical society (state Massachusetts Medical Society—inc porated—Boston, Mass.

1784 **Citizenship**—citizenship (colonial) c ferred by special grant—Maryland—s sion held

1848 **Medical School**—women's medical sch —Boston Female Medical School—or nized

1850 **Photography Magazine** — photograp magazine — *Daguerreian Journal* — pu lished — New York City

1853 **Water Cures**—introduced—R. T. Trall New York City

1864 **Postal Service**—money order system— tablished

1870 **Weather Bureau (U.S.)**—weather bureau observations made—War Department S nal Corps

1873 **Wire**—barbed wire—manufacturing beg —De Kalb, Ill.

1879 **Bridge**—railroad all-steel bridge—Gla gow, Mo.

1879 **American Indian School**—American In an School of prominence—opened—Ca lisle, Pa.

1895 **Automobile Club**—American Mot League—meeting—Chicago, Ill.

1901 **Ship**—schooner (seven-masted, steel) keel laid—Quincy, Mass.

1904 **Army War College**—Army War College first class—Washington, D.C.

1904 **Police**—police bureau of identification Henry fingerprinting system added Chicago, Ill.

1920 **Aviation**—hydroplane commercial line se vice (international)—Key West, Fla.

27 **Building**—housing cooperative sponsored by a labor union—Amalgamated Houses—New York City—opened

32 **Pump**—computer pump—marketed—Fort Wayne, Ind.

37 **Insurance**—group hospital-medical cooperative—Washington, D.C.

39 **Impregnation**—impregnation (artificial)—rabbit exhibited—New York City

40 **Air Raid Shelter**—air raid shelter—completed—Fleetwood, Pa.

41 **Army Language School**—began courses—San Francisco, Calif.

42 **Church of England**—American bishop to become bishop of a British Church of England—Spence Burton

44 **Births**—quadruplets delivered by cesarean operation—Philadelphia, Pa.

50 **Basketball Player**—National Basketball Association black player—C. H. Cooper—played—Fort Wayne, Ind.

51 **Atomic Bomb**—atomic explosion witnessed by troops—New Mexico

51 **Coal**—coal pipeline unit (demonstration)—in operation—Cadiz, Ohio

55 **Ship**—guided missile cruiser—*Boston*—converted—Philadelphia, Pa.

62 **Postage Stamp**—Christmas-stamp regular issue—placed on sale—Pittsburgh, Pa.

64 **Canonization**—canonization of a saint in the United States—John Sergiev—New York City

65 **Money**—coins bearing dates other than the year of issue—issued—Philadelphia, Pa.

68 **Postage Stamp**—postage stamp printed on the 9-color Huck press—multicolored Christmas stamp—issued—Washington, D.C.

78 **Navy**—large-scale assignment of women (other than nurses) to sea duty

NOVEMBER 2

76 **Traitor**—William Dement—deserted

24 **Presidential Candidate**—presidential candidate to receive the greatest number of popular and electoral votes and yet fail of election

24 **Presidential Popular Vote**—vote recorded

33 **Animals**—cattle importation of purebred shorthorns—Ohio Company for Importing English Cattle—organized—Chillicothe, Ohio

67 **Periodical**—fashion weekly—*Harper's Bazar*—M. L. Booth, editor—published—New York City

86 **Automobile Tractor**—endless-chain tractor —patent—Charles Dinsmoor—Warren, Pa.

86 **Governor**—gubernatorial election in which two brothers were the opposing candidates —R. L. Taylor and A. A. Taylor—Tennessee

04 **Fingerprinting**—federal penitentiary fingerprinting—Leavenworth, Kan.

1909 **Election Law**—preferential ballot system—election—Grand Junction, Colo.

1915 **Election Law**—proportional representation —Ashtabula, Ohio

1917 **World War I**—U.S. Army soldiers killed in combat—France

1918 **World War I**—German spy to receive a death sentence from the U.S. forces during World War I—death sentence confirmed

1929 **Theater**—newsreel theater—opened—New York City

1931 **Rubber**—synthetic rubber produced on a commercial scale—Wilmington, Del.

1933 **Surgical Operation**—epileptic case treated by elevation of the skull cap—demonstrated—New York City

1936 **Theater**—state-owned theater—performance of *The Comedy of Errors*—Seattle, Wash.

1945 **Industrial and Labor Relations School**—registration began

1947 **Aviation—Airplane**—airplane with eight engines—tested—Long Beach, Calif.

1948 **Senator (U.S.)**—senator to win a seat that had been occupied by his father and mother—Russell Long—elected—Louisiana

1954 **Lieutenant Governor**—woman lieutenant governor—C. N. Bailey—elected—Vermont

1954 **Senator (U.S.)**—senator elected by a write-in vote—J. S. Thurmond

1954 **Television—Telecast**—split-screen image (four ways)—shown

1957 **Titanium**—titanium mill—opened—Toronto, Ohio

1963 **Postage Stamp**—phosphorescent-impregnated postage stamp—issued

1967 **Postage Stamp**—gravure-printed postage stamp—The Biglin Brothers Racing—issued—Washington, D.C.

1976 **Representative (U.S.)**—Polish-American representative—B. A. Mikulski of Maryland—elected

1978 **Language**—plain language law—New York (state)—effective

NOVEMBER 3

1803 **Evangelical Association Council**—meeting —Bucks County, Pa.

1863 **Yeast**—yeast preparation patent—J. T. Alden—Cincinnati, Ohio

1881 **Coast Guard (U.S.)**—inland U.S. Coast Guard station—opened—Louisville, Ky.

1889 **State**—states admitted to the Union simultaneously—North and South Dakota

1892 **Telephone**—automatic telephone system (successful)—opened—La Porte, Ind.

1899 **Motion Picture**—motion picture of a real pugilistic encounter taken at night—Coney Island, N.Y.

1900 **Automobile Show**—New York City

1911 **Continuation School**—continuation school established by state law—opened—Racine, Wis.

1930 **Tunnel**—vehicular tunnel to a foreign country—Detroit, Mich.

1945 **Judge**—black judge of a customs court (U.S.)—I. C. Mollison—inducted—U.S. Customs Court—New York City

1952 **Bread**—frozen bread—marketed—Port Chester, N.Y.

1953 **Navy**—podiatry section of the Navy—established

1953 **Television—Telecast**—color coast-to-coast live telecast—New York City

1954 **Horse Race**—horse race in which the British Royal Silks participated—Laurel, Md.

1955 **Virus**—virus (human- or animal-infecting virus) to be crystallized—Berkeley, Calif.

1964 **Voting Machine**—presidential election in which votes were tallied electronically

1970 **Representative (U.S.)**—representative of Puerto Rican ancestry—Herman Badillo of New York—elected

1977 **Medal**—Defense Meritorious Service Medal—authorized

NOVEMBER 4

1780 **Diplomatic Service**—consul to die in service—William Palfrey—elected consul

1846 **Leg (artificial) patent**—B. F. Palmer—Meredith, N.H.

1862 **Ordnance**—machine gun (rapid-fire)—patent—R. J. Gatling—Indianapolis, Ind.

1873 **Dentistry**—patent for a gold crown—J. B. Beers—San Francisco, Calif.

1873 **Slicing Machine**—patent—Anthony Iske—Lancaster, Pa.

1879 **Cash Register**—patent—J. J. Ritty—Dayton, Ohio

1880 **Engineering Society**—mechanical engineering national society—American Society of Mechanical Engineers—annual meeting—New York City

1880 **Representative (U.S.)**—representative in office elected President of the United States—J. A. Garfield of Ohio

1912 **Ship**—battleship to use fuel oil exclusively—*Nevada*—laid down—Quincy, Mass.

1913 **Senator (U.S.)**—senators collectively "elected by the people"—election

1914 **World War I**—American ship lost in World War I—*William P. Frye*—cleared from—Seattle, Wash.

1924 **Governor**—woman governor of a state—N. T. Ross—elected governor—Wyoming

1927 **Aviation—Pilot**—pilot to die because of a lack of oxygen—H. C. Gray—balloon takeoff, Belleville, Ill.

1933 **Railroad**—gasoline-driven stainless-steel, air-conditioned, pneumatic-tired, two-car train—delivered—Dallas, Tex.

1939 **Automobile**—air-conditioned automobile —exhibited—Chicago, Ill.

1943 **Atomic Reactor**—graphite reactor with a sizeable power output—Oak Ridge, Tenn. —installed

1943 **Medal**—combat infantry badge—authorized

1951 **Television—Telecast**—Jewish temple services (complete) to be televised—New York City

1952 **Representative (U.S.)**—mother and son simultaneously elected to Congress—F. Bolton and O. P. Bolton

1958 **Molybdenum**—molybdenum centrifugal casting—Albany, Oreg.

1965 **Automobile Driver**—woman automobile driver to exceed the speed of 300 m.p.h.—A. R. Breedlove—Booneville Salt Flats Utah

1968 **Postage Stamp**—native American picture on a postage stamp—Chief Joseph—stamp on sale in Washington, D.C.

1970 **Visiting Celebrities**—European king buried in the United States—Peter Karageorgevich—died—Denver, Colo.

NOVEMBER 5

1639 **Post Office**—post office (colonial)—established—Massachusetts

1716 **Theater**—theater—land acquired—Williamsburg, Va.

1733 **Newspaper**—political newspaper—*New York Weekly Journal*—published—J. Zenger

1824 **Engineering College**—engineering college —Rensselaer School—Troy, N.Y.—founded

1852 **Engineering Society**—civil engineering national society—American Society of Civil Engineers—founded—New York City

1873 **Representative (U.S.)**—representative to serve 1 day—G. A. Sheridan of Louisiana—elected

1889 **Sanitary District**—Sanitary District—Chicago, Ill.—authorized

1895 **Automobile Patent**—G. B. Selden—Rochester, N.Y.

1911 **Aviation—Flights (transcontinental)**—transcontinental airplane flight—C. Rodgers—arrived—Pasadena, Calif.

1945 **Industrial and Labor Relations School** opened—Cornell University—Ithaca, N.Y.

1945 **Ship**—warship named for a black—*Harmon*—returned by United Kingdom to United States

1952 **Aviation — Airplane** — turbine-propeller light airplane—flown—Wichita, Kans.

1955 **Radio Broadcast**—stereophonic sound program broadcast by separately owned stations—Philadelphia, Pa., and Cleveland, Ohio

1967 **Television Station**—noncommercial educational television network—regularly scheduled noncommercial broadcast began

1968 **Representative (U.S.)**—black representative (woman) to serve in Congress—S. A. Chisholm—elected—New York

1967   **Satellite**—satellite launched from another heavenly body—*Surveyor 6*—launched—Cape Kennedy, Fla.

1972   **Representative (U.S.)**—congressional candidate elected while "missing"—T. H. Boggs—elected—Louisiana

NOVEMBER 8

1731   **Library**—circulating library—Library Company of Philadelphia—first meeting—Philadelphia, Pa.

1775   **Postal Service**—mail franking privilege—authorized

1791   **Academy**—meeting held—Philadelphia, Pa.

1805   **Expedition**—expedition across the continent to the Pacific coast—Lewis and Clark—reached Columbia River

1825   **Art Organization**—artists' society of importance—New York Drawing Association—organized—New York City

1837   **College**—college for women—Mount Holyoke Seminary—South Hadley, Mass.—opened

1848   **Freemasons**—masonic lodge organized in the Indian Territory—Cherokee Lodge, Tahlequah, Okla.—chartered

1864   **Army Vote**—election

1898   **Initiative and Referendum**—amendment submitted to state—South Dakota

1904   **Electric Attachment Plug (separable)**—patented—Harvey Hubbell—Bridgeport, Conn.

1910   **Insect Electrocutor Patent**—W. M. Frost—Spokane, Wash.

1926   **Ferryboat**—ferryboat built exclusively for motor vehicle transportation—in service—Weehawken, N.J.–New York City

1938   **Legislator (state)**—black woman state legislator—C. B. Fauset—elected—Philadelphia, Pa.

1941   **Aviation—Airplane**—naval patrol bomber—*Mars*—christened—Baltimore, Md.

1950   **Aviation—Pilot**—jet plane combat victor in the Korean War—R. J. Brown—over North Korea

1954   **Senator (U.S.)**—woman senator to succeed a woman senator—H. H. Abel

1960   **Congress (U.S.)**—Senate—election in which 2 women contested for the same Senate seat—M. C. Smith and L. M. Cormier—Maine

1962   **Judge**—black woman judge elected—E. S. Sampson—Chicago, Ill.

1966   **Baseball Player**—"most valuable player" in both major leagues—Frank Robinson—elected (American League)

1966   **Senator (U.S.)**—black senator elected by popular vote—E. W. Brooke—Massachusetts

1977   **Judge**—woman judge of the Surrogates Court—M. M. Lambert—New York—elected

NOVEMBER 9

1748   **College**—college charter granted by a governor or acting governor with only the consent of his council—first commencement—College of New Jersey—Princeton, N.J.

1756   **Stage Coach Intercity Service**—New York City–Philadelphia—inaugurated

1790   **President (U.S.)**—President who had been a senator—James Monroe—served—Virginia

1820   **Library**—mercantile library—organized—New York City

1821   **Pharmacy College**—pharmacy college—Philadelphia College of Apothecaries opened—Philadelphia, Pa.

1835   **Police**—state police—G. W. Davis authorized to raise 20 more Texas Rangers

1842   **Patent**—design patent—issued—George Bruce—New York City

1877   **Chemists Society**—chemical society (national)—American Chemical Society—incorporated

1911   **Electric Sign**—neon-tube advertising sign—George Claude—patent application

1930   **Aviation—Flights**—New York–Panama nonstop flight—R. W. Ammel

1933   **Civil Works Administration (U.S.)**—established

1943   **Medal**—Legion of Merit medal to a Coast guardsman in World War II—J. C. Cullen—New York City

1961   **Aviation—Flights**—airplane to fly faster than the speed of 4,000 m.p.h. —flown—Edwards Air Force Base, Calif.—Robert White

1974   **Greek Orthodox Church**—Greek Orthodox Archdiocesan Council women members announced

NOVEMBER 10

1775   **Marine Corps**—American marines—organized

1798   **Nullification Proceedings**—Kentucky Resolutions adopted—Lower House

1801   **Dueling Legislation (state)**—enacted—Knoxville, Tenn.

1814   **Conscription**—wartime conscription bill passed

1817   **Trust**—trust—organized—Kanawha, Va.

1855   **Poem**—poem to win national acclaim—*Song of Hiawatha*—H.W. Longfellow—published—Boston, Mass.

1865   **War Criminal Proceedings**—Henry Wirz—hanged

1868   **Knights of Pythias**—constitution adopted for Supreme Lodge—Wilmington, Del.

1891   **Temperance Society**—women's temperance society (national)—World Woman's Christian Temperance Union—convention—Boston, Mass.

95 **Monument**—statue officially sanctioned by Rome—blessed—New Orleans, La.

99 **Anesthesia**—spinal anesthesia report—Rudolph Matas—treated case—New Orleans, La.

44 **Bank**—bank established in a foreign country—Buenos Aires, Argentina

19 **War Veterans' Society**—American Legion —national convention—Minneapolis, Minn.

51 **Telephone**—dial telephone service coast-to-coast without the aid of operators—Englewood, N.J.–Alameda, Calif.

59 **Submarine**—submarine with two nuclear reactors—*Triton*—commissioned

59 **Submarine**—submerged circumnavigation of the earth—*Triton*—commissioned

60 **Atomic Reactor**—commercial atomic energy reactor—Rowe, Mass.—power produced

71 **Postage Stamp**—Christmas-stamp annual series depicting both a religious and nonreligious subject—issued—Washington, D.C.

NOVEMBER 11

47 **School Legislation**—school law (compulsory)—enacted—Massachusetts

44 **Supreme Court (U.S.)**—Associate Justice of the Supreme Court who had been a representative in Congress—Gabriel Duvall of Maryland—began service in Congress

47 **Sword Swallower** — exhibition — Senaa Samma—New York City

49 **Military School**—state military school—cadets mustered into service—Lexington, Va.

51 **Telescope**—telescope patent—Alvan Clark—Cambridge, Mass.

68 **Sports**—amateur indoor athletic games—New York City

49 **State**—state named for a native-born American—Washington—admitted to Union

19 **Holiday**—Armistice Day—celebrated

19 **Ship**—concrete ship built for the United States Shipping Board—*Atlantus*—delivered

10 **Aviation—Pilot**—naval ace in World War I—awarded Distinguished Service Medal —D. S. Ingalls

21 **Monument**—monument to the unknown soldier (national)—burial of unknown soldier—Arlington, Va.

25 **Cosmic Ray**—cosmic ray—discovery announced at Madison, Wis.

26 **Dance Course**—dance course with collegiate credit—University of Wisconsin—Madison, Wis.

43 **Electrical Contract**—by city with federal government—signed—Tupelo, Miss.

1934 **Railroad**—streamlined all-steel diesel motor train—Lincoln, Neb.–Kansas City, Mo.

1935 **Balloon—Flights**—balloon flight to exceed an altitude of 70,000 feet—O. A. Anderson and A. W. Stevens—Rapid City, S.Dak.

1935 **Photograph**—photograph showing the lateral curvature of the horizon—Rapid City, S.Dak.

NOVEMBER 12

1799 **Astronomy**—meteoric display—Florida

1843 **Jews**—Jewish fraternal society—B'nai B'rith—first lodge founded—New York City

1853 **Horse**—horse to trot 100 miles in less than 9 hours—Conqueror

1861 **Petroleum**—petroleum exported to Europe —shipped—Philadelphia, Pa.

1881 **Quarantine**—plant quarantine legislation (state)—rules and regulations issued—California

1885 **Library Society**—library society (local)—New York Library Club—general meeting —New York City

1903 **Humane Society**—humane association national organization—American Humane Association—incorporated

1911 **Aviation—Flights (transcontinental)**—transcontinental airplane flight—C. P. Rodgers—crashed—Compton, Calif.

1912 **Aviation—Flights**—airplane catapulted—Washington, D.C.

1915 **Nobel Prize**—Nobel Prize in Chemistry—T. W. Richards

1920 **"Baseball Dictator"**—K. M. Landis—elected

1921 **Conference**—conference of great powers—Conference on the Limitation of Armaments—Washington, D.C.

1926 **Aviation—Airplane Bombing**—airplane bombing in the United States—Williamson County, Ill.

1928 **Skeet**—college skeet tournament—Princeton, N.J.

1932 **President (U.S.)**—President to invite the President-elect for discussion—H. C. Hoover

1940 **Health Museum**—not connected with another museum—Cleveland Health Museum —opened—Cleveland, Ohio

1941 **Aviation—Pilot**—woman test pilot—Alma Heflin—Lock Haven, Pa.

1941 **Medical Clinic**—heredity clinic—opened—Ann Arbor, Mich.

1946 **Bank**—autobank complete service—Chicago, Ill.

1947 **Medal**—Agriculture Department distinguished service gold medal—awarded

1948 **Betatron**—mobile betatron—placed in service—White Oak, Md.

1038   FAMOUS FIRST FACTS

1966 **Photograph**—photograph of an eclipse of the sun taken from the atmosphere—satellite *Gemini XII*—J. A. Lovell, Jr., and E. E. Aldrin, Jr.

1975 **Kennel**—hotel for dogs—Kennelworth—opened by Leo Wiener—New York City

NOVEMBER 13

1749 **Academy**—Benjamin Franklin appointed president—Academy and College of Philadelphia

1798 **Nullification Proceedings**—Kentucky Resolutions—adopted—Upper House

1839 **Antislavery Party**—Liberty Party convention—Warsaw, N.Y.

1865 **Money**—gold certificates—issued

1868 **Philological Society**—national philological Association—organized—New York City

1875 **Bowling Rule Standardization**—undertaken—New York City

1875 **Football Uniform**—football uniforms worn in a game—Yale vs. Harvard—New Haven, Conn.

1913 **Medical Society**—black member of the American College of Surgeons—D. H. Williams—admitted at Chicago, Ill.

1913 **Medical Society**—American College of Surgeons—annual convocation—Chicago, Ill.

1927 **Tunnel**—twin-tube subaqueous vehicular tunnel—Holland tunnel—opened—Jersey City, N.J.-New York City

1930 **Milking Platform (rotating)**—housed—Plainsboro, N.J.

1931 **Senator (U.S.)**—woman elected to the Senate—H. O. W. Caraway—appointed—Arkansas

1933 **Strike**—modern sit-down strike—Austin, Minn.

1937 **Orchestra**—orchestra (symphony), full-size, devoted exclusively to radio broadcasting—NBC Symphony—New York City—formed

1938 **Catholic Beatification**—Catholic beatification of an American citizen (female)—Mother Frances Xavier Cabrini

1942 **Naval Officer**—women technicians in medicine assigned to the National Naval Medical Center—Kathryn Hyde and Dorothy Osborne—Bethesda, Md.—reported for duty

1945 **Radio Telephone**—two-way equipped bus—license granted to operate—Washington, D.C.

1946 **Snow**—artificial snow—produced—Mount Greylock, Mass.

1955 **Television—Telecast**—live telecast from a noncontiguous foreign country—Havana, Cuba

1967 **Mayor**—black mayor of a major city—C. B. Stokes—Cleveland, Ohio—sworn in

1969 **Medal**—Presidential Citizen Medal—established by R. M. Nixon

1971 **Satellite**—man-made object to orbit ano[ ]er planet—entered Martian orbit

NOVEMBER 14

1732 **Librarian**—librarian—Louis Timothee[ ] hired—Philadelphia, Pa.

1784 **Protestant Episcopal Bishop**—Protest[ ] Episcopal bishop—Samuel Seabury—c[ ]secrated

1825 **Ship**—iron vessel (sheet iron)—*Codorus*[ ] tested

1832 **Streetcar**—streetcar—used—New Y[ ] City

1868 **Farmers' Institute**—farmers' institute sp[ ]sored by a college—Manhattan, Kan.

1878 **Humane Society**—humane association [ ]tional organization—American Huma[ ] Association—constitution adopted

1889 **Tour of the World**—tour of the world ma[ ] by a woman traveling alone—Nellie Bl[ ] left New York City

1906 **President (U.S.)**—President to visit a f[ ]eign country—Theodore Roosevelt—Panama

1910 **Aviation—Flights**—airplane flight from[ ]ship—Eugene Ely

1921 **Opera**—opera broadcast in its entirety b[ ] professional cast (radio)—*Samson et D[ ]la*—Chicago, Ill.

1930 **Prizefighter**—pugilist to win and lose[ ] championship in the first round—Abrah[ ]("Al") Singer—New York City—lost [ ] Tony Canzoneri

1931 **Animals**—cattle (Africander cattle)—sh[ ]ment left Capetown, South Africa

1934 **Symphony**—symphony on a black f[ ]theme—presented—Philadelphia, Pa.

1935 **Photograph**—portrait (life-size) of a hum[ ]in a newspaper—Larry Quinn—San Fr[ ]cisco, Calif.

1937 **Church**—children's church—dedicate[ ]Milton, Mass.

1941 **Business**—department store to hold a p[ ]lic art auction—Gimbel Brothers—N[ ]York City

1954 **Protestant Church**—Reformed Du[ ]Church black pastor—New York City

1967 **Vietnam War**—American general killed [ ]Vietnam by enemy fire—B. A. Hochmu[ ]

1969 **President (U.S.)**—President to attend [ ]launching of a manned spaceflight—R.[ ]Nixon—Cape Kennedy, Fla.

NOVEMBER 15

1681 **Shorthand Report**—St. Johns, Md.

1777 **Articles of Confederation**—adopte[ ]Philadelphia, Pa.

1791 **College**—Catholic college—Georgeto[ ]College—opened—Washington, D.C.

1806 **Periodical**—college magazine—*Liter[ ]Cabinet*—published—New Haven, Con[ ]

7 **Evangelical Conference**—assembled—Kleinfeltersville, Pa.

9 **Poultry Show**—Boston, Mass.

0 **Lighthouse**—iron pile lighthouse—light operated—new lighthouse—Minot's Ledge, Mass.

4 **Mines School**—opened—Columbia University—New York City

2 **Naval Officer**—naval attache—F. E. Chadwick—sent to London, England

4 **Newspaper Syndicate**—newspaper syndicate to supply articles—S. S. McClure—New York City

6 **Niagara Falls**—utilization of Niagara Falls waterpower (large-scale)—power transmitted to Buffalo, N.Y.

8 **Foreign Service School**—School of Comparative Jurisprudence and Diplomacy—opened—George Washington University—Washington, D.C.

9 **Newspaper**—newspaper published at sea (radio news service)—*Trans-Atlantic Times* issued

4 **World War I**—American combatant casualty in World War I—France

7 **Army Officer**—regimental Jewish chaplain—E. C. Voorsanger—commissioned

9 **Congress (U.S.)—Senate**—Senate cloture resolution—invoked—Washington, D.C.

8 **Railroad Car**—rail detector car in commercial service—in service—Montpelier, Ohio

1 **Aviation—Parachute**—parachute jump from an autogiro—Frankie Hammond—Caldwell, N.J.

5 **Social Security Act (U.S.)**—unemployment compensation law—approved—Washington, D.C.

7 **Congress (U.S.)**—congressional session in air-conditioned Senate and House chambers—Washington, D.C.

0 **Conscription**—peacetime conscription bill—call for men

8 **Locomotive**—gas-turbine-electric locomotive—track-tested—Erie, Pa.

9 **Aviation**—aviation trainer (jet)—flight evaluation test

0 **Hockey Player**—black player in organized hockey—Arthur Dorrington—signed

4 **Aviation—Flights (world)**—round-the-world flight over the North Pole on a regularly scheduled commercial air route—Copenhagen, Denmark–Los Angeles, Calif.

0 **Submarine**—ballistic missile submarine—*George Washington*—on patrol duty

2 **College President**—woman college president of two colleges—Rosemary Park—inaugurated—Barnard College, New York City (second)

3 **Bridge (game) Player**—bridge player to win more than 1,000 master points in 1 year—Oswald Jacoby—passed 1,000 mark at Edgewater Park, Miss.

1973 **Ship**—ship to use coal-derived oil to power its engines—*Johnston*—test cruise from Philadelphia, Pa.

1974 **Postage Stamp**—pressure-sensitized-adhesive postage stamp—Dove of Peace—issued—New York City

NOVEMBER 16

1620 **Corn (maize)**—corn (maize) found by British settlers—Provincetown, Mass.

1676 **Prison**—prison—William Bunker—hired—Nantucket, Mass.

1776 **Flag**—American flag saluted by a foreigner—Johannes de Graeff—St. Eustatius, Dutch West Indies

1786 **Spinning, Carding, and Roping Machines**—compensation granted to manufacturers—Bridgewater, Mass.

1798 **Nullification Proceedings**—Kentucky Resolutions—approved by governor

1810 **Actor**—English actor of note—G. F. Cooke—arrived—New York City

1841 **Life Preserver**—life preserver of cork—patented—N. E. Guerin

1875 **Dental Mallet**—dental mallet patented—W. G. A. Bonwill—Philadelphia, Pa.

1898 **Library Society**—state librarians' society—Washington, D.C.

1901 **Automobile**—automobile to exceed the speed of a mile a minute—A. C. Bostwick—Brooklyn, N.Y.

1914 **Bank**—federal reserve system—in operation

1920 **Postal Service**—postage meter—officially set—Stamford, Conn.

1925 **Atheism Society**—of importance—American Association for the Advancement of Atheism—incorporated—New York

1943 **Submarine**—submarine (U.S.) sunk by an enemy submarine—*Corvina*

1945 **Element**—element 95—americium—announced

1945 **Element**—element 96—curium—announced

1945 **Jewish College**—Jewish college of liberal arts and sciences under Jewish auspices—became Yeshiva University—New York City

1946 **Evangelical United Brethren Church**—formed—Johnstown, Pa.

1955 **Aquatic Mammals**—dugong—arrived—San Francisco, Calif.

1955 **Motorboat**—motorboat to travel at a speed of 216.2 m.p.h.—D. M. Campbell—Lake Mead, Nev.

1955 **Ship**—speedboat to exceed 200 miles an hour—D. M. Campbell

1955 **Television Receiver**—television receiver in a private railroad car—Monon Railroad—Chicago, Ill., to Rome, Ga.

1956 **Postal Card**—Statue of Liberty depicted on a postal card—issued—New York City

1959 **Ski Lift**—tramway state legislation—New Hampshire—effective

1963 **President (U.S.)**—President to witness the firing of a Polaris missile—J. F. Kennedy—Cape Canaveral, Fla.

1973 **Astronaut**—astronauts (American) to exceed 2,000 hours flight time—G. P. Carr, E. G. Gibson, and W. R. Pogue—*Skylab IV*—takeoff, Cape Canaveral, Fla.

NOVEMBER 17

1637 **Clubwoman**—Anne Hutchinson—brought to trial—Cambridge, Mass.

1774 **Military Organization**—military organization (anti-British)—Light Horse of the City of Philadelphia—organized—Philadelphia, Pa.

1785 **Church of England**—Church of England organized in New England—James Freeman ordained

1797 **Clock**—clock patent—Eli Terry—East Windsor, Conn.

1800 **Congress (U.S.)**—Congress of the United States—first session—Washington, D.C.

1800 **Congress (U.S.)—House of Representatives**—House of Representatives—session in Washington, D.C.

1851 **Postage Stamp**—postage stamps depicting the American eagle—issued

1875 **Theosophical Society**—American Theosophical Society—founded—New York City

1880 **Immigration**—Chinese labor immigration act—treaty with China

1886 **Newspaper**—newspaper association—American Newspaper Publishers Association organized

1889 **Railroad**—daily railroad service to the Pacific coast—through service—Chicago, Ill.-Portland, Oreg.

1909 **Fraternity (Greek-letter)**—interfraternity council—meeting—New York City

1913 **Dental School**—dental hygienists' course—Fones Clinic—Bridgeport, Conn.

1917 **Ship**—naval vessels to sink an enemy submarine—*Fanning* and *Nicholson*

1919 **Bank**—bank with resources exceeding $1 billion—National City Bank, New York City

1933 **National Emergency Council (U.S.)**—authorized

1943 **Medal**—Soldier's Medal awarded to a Women's Army Corps member—presented—M. H. Maloney

1945 **Wedding**—wedding in the United States Occupation Forces in Korea

1949 **Aviation—Airplane**—airplane to carry 100 people on one flight across the Atlantic Ocean—*The Champ*—takeoff, Mobile, Ala.

1973 **Golfer**—golfer to earn $100,000 in a contest—Miller Barber—Pinehurst, N.C.

NOVEMBER 18

1787 **Unitarian Minister**—James Freeman—ordained—Boston, Mass.

1805 **Women's Club**—women's club—Female Charitable Society—Wiscasset, Me.

1820 **Discovery**—discovery of Antarctica—N. Palmer

1874 **Temperance Society**—women's temperance society (national)—National Woman's Christian Temperance Union organized—Cleveland, Ohio

1883 **Time (standard)**—adopted

1890 **Ship**—battleship of importance—*Maine* launched—New York City

1894 **Newspaper**—newspaper Sunday comic section—published—New York *World*

1899 **Hospital**—tuberculosis hospital operated by the government—patients received—Fort Stanton, N.Mex.

1913 **Aviation—Flights**—airplane loop-the-loop—Lincoln Beachey—San Diego, Calif.

1921 **Fencing**—international fencing championship competition—Washington, D.C.

1933 **Emergency Housing Corporation (U.S.)**—organized

1940 **Catholic Priest**—Catholic priest called the Sacred Roman Rota—F. J. Brennan took oath of office

1943 **Cabinet (U.S.)**—Cabinet officer to address a joint session of Congress—Cordell Hull

1943 **Diplomatic Service**—ambassador to Canada—Ray Atherton—nominated

1948 **Vice President (U.S.)**—Vice President marry in office—A. W. Barkley

1949 **Baseball Player**—"most valuable player" award (major league) to a black—J. R. Robinson

1950 **Marine Corps**—Marine Corps jet ace—J. Bolt

1950 **X Ray**—fluoro-record reflector camera—announced

1963 **Telephone**—telephone with push button—commercial service begun—Greensburg and Carnegie, Pa.

1965 **Brokerage**—American Stock Exchange women members—J. M. Walsh and P. K. Peterson—elected—New York City

1972 **Ship**—navy ship with a male-female company—*Sanctuary* (originally, *Marigold Owl*)—recommissioned—San Francisco, Calif.

NOVEMBER 19

1777 **Army**—brevet conferred upon an American—Walter Stewart—Continental Congress

1794 **Extradition**—extradition treaty with a foreign country—signed—Great Britain—London, England

1806 **Senator (U.S.)**—senator to serve in contravention to the age limit—Henry Clay of Kentucky—began service

2 **Historical Society**—historical society (national)—American Antiquarian Society—first meeting—Boston, Mass.

0 **Magic Lantern**—magic lantern slides (glass plate)—patent—Frederick Langenheim—Philadelphia, Pa.

1 **Petroleum**—petroleum exported to Europe—shipment made—Philadelphia, Pa.–London, England

2 **Adding Machine**—adding machine to print totals and subtotals—patented—E. D. Barbour—Boston, Mass.

3 **Newspaper**—newspaper colored supplement—issued—New York *World*

5 **Pencil**—paper pencil—patented—F. E. Blaisdell—Philadelphia, Pa.

6 **Aviation—Flights**—airplane to fly further than 500 miles—Chicago, Ill.–Hornell, N.Y.—Ruth Law

8 **Caterpillar Club**—father and son Caterpillar Club members—father jumped

1 **Brokerage**—woman to sell securities on the floor of the New York Curb Exchange—Linda Darnell

2 **Cemetery**—foreign service women interred in the Arlington National Cemetery—Arlington, Va.

4 **Toll Collector (automatic)**—Garden State Parkway, N.J.

6 **Ship**—ballistic-missile test ship—*Compass Island*—tested at sea

8 **Medal**—Medal of Honor in the Vietnam war awarded to a chaplain—A. J. Liteky—presented

9 **Astronaut**—astronauts (American) on the moon to retrieve an object—Charles Conrad, Jr., and A. L. Bean

9 **Astronaut**—astronauts (American) to remain one day on the moon—Charles Conrad and A. L. Bean—landed on the moon

3 **Copyright Register of the United States**—woman Register of Copyrights—B. A. Ringer—appointed

NOVEMBER 20

0 **Births**—child born of English parents in New England—Peregrine White—born on *Mayflower* off Cape Cod harbor

6 **Ship**—ship-of-the-line—*America*—authorized

9 **Constitutional Amendment (U.S.)**—constitutional amendments—first state to ratify—New Jersey

6 **Bicycle**—bicycle with a rotary crank—patented—Pierre Lallemont

6 **College**—university for blacks to establish undergraduate, graduate, and professional schools—Howard University—founded—Washington, D.C.

6 **War Veterans' Society**—Grand Army of the Republic—national convention—Indianapolis, Ind.

1888 **Time Recorder**—employees' time recorder—patented—W. L. Bundy—Auburn, N.Y.

1909 **Medal**—National Institute of Arts and Letters gold medal—awarded—posthumously—Augustus Saint-Gaudens

1914 **Passport**—passport photographs—required

1919 **Aviation—Airport**—airport municipally owned—Tucson, Ariz.

1919 **Ship**—battleship (major) built on the Pacific coast—*California*—launched

1922 **Representative (U.S.)**—mother elected to Congress—W. S. M. Huck of Illinois—began service

1925 **Photograph**—photograph from an airplane at night—Rochester, N.Y.

1931 **Teletype Service**—teletype service (commercial)—American Telegraph and Telephone Company

1947 **Television Receiver**—television receiver on a seagoing vessel permanently installed—*New Jersey*

1953 **Aviation—Flights**—airplane to fly faster than 1,300 m.p.h.—Scott Crossfield

1969 **Astronaut**—astronauts (American) to remain one day on the moon—Charles Conrad and A. L. Bean—took off from moon

1978 **Newspaper**—newspaper whose input was derived from a communications satellite—*Wall Street Journal*—dedication of new system

NOVEMBER 21

1766 **Theater**—theater building (permanent)—Southwark Theatre—Philadelphia,Pa.

1810 **Actor**—English actor of note—debut—G. F. Cooke—New York City

1824 **Jewish Congregation**—Jewish congregation (reform)—Charleston, S.C.

1871 **Cigar Lighter Patent**—M. F. Gale—New York City

1918 **Prohibition**—prohibition law (national)—enacted

1921 **Radio Station**—educational radio station licensed—WOI—Iowa State College of Agriculture and Mechanical Arts, Ames, Iowa—call letters granted

1922 **Senator (U.S.)**—woman to occupy a seat in the Senate—R. L. Felton—served

1922 **Ship**—cruise ship to circumnavigate the world—*Laconia*—left New York City

1933 **Commercial Policy Executive Committee**—organized

1933 **Diplomatic Service**—ambassador to the Union of Soviet Socialist Republics—W. C. Bullitt—served

1936 **Degrees (academic and honorary)**—American awarded honorary degrees from three of England's leading universities—R. W. Bingham—Oxford University

1936 **Degrees (academic and honorary)**—husband and wife awarded honorary degrees—Mr. and Mrs. J. N. Garner—Waco, Tex.

1938 **Radio Station**—municipal school-owned ultrahigh-frequency radio station—WBOE —Cleveland, Ohio

1942 **Submarine**—submarine built on the Great Lakes—*Peto*—accepted

1946 **President (U.S.)**—President to travel underwater in a captured enemy submarine—H. S. Truman—Key West, Fla.

1951 **Atomic Energy Commission**—Atomic Energy Commission Patent Compensation Board—award—C. E. McClellan

1952 **Postage Stamp**—postage stamp in two colors produced by the rotary process at the Bureau of Engraving and Printing—International Red Cross issue

1964 **Horse Race**—harness driver (American) to score 300 victories in 1 year—Bob Farrington—300th victory at Chicago, Ill.

1973 **Marshal**—marshals of the United States (women)—sworn in

NOVEMBER 22

1809 **Pen**—steel pen patent—Peregrine Williamson—Baltimore, Md.

1842 **Volcano**—volcano in eruption in America for which a date can be established—recorded—Lassen Peak, Calif.

1904 **Electric Motor**—electric motor (interpole direct current)—invented by Mathias Pfatischer—patented

1906 **Radio Distress Signal**—radio distress signal—SOS signal adopted

1910 **Golf Clubs**—steel shaft for a golf club—patented—A. F. Knight—Schenectady, N.Y.

1923 **World War I**—German spy to receive a death sentence from the American forces during World War I—pardon granted by President Coolidge

1924 **Football Game**—football game to attract 100,000 spectators—California vs. Stanford —Berkeley, Calif.

1927 **Snowmobile**—snowmobile patent—C. J. E. Eliason of Sayner, Wis.

1929 **Congress (U.S.)—Senate**—Senate hearing in which women, other than members of Congress, were permitted on the floor—Washington, D.C.

1930 **Football Game**—football game played in the United States to be broadcast in England—New Haven, Conn.

1932 **Pump**—computer pump—patented

1935 **Airmail Service**—Pacific airmail flight—*China Clipper*—left—San Francisco, Calif.

1943 **Marine Corps**—woman marine major—R. C. Streeter—advanced to lieutenant colonel

1943 **Medal**—Presidential Unit Citation (Army) —authorized

1944 **Coast Guard Officer**—Coast Guard Women's Reserve officer to serve overseas —Margaret Moon—assigned to Hawaii

1953 **Television—Telecast**—color program coast-to-coast network commercial—N York City

1955 **Airmail Service**—helicopter airmail express service to carry passengers—vice Los Angeles—Long Beach, Calif.

1954 **Cabinet (U.S.)**—secretary to the Cabi and presidential assistant—M. M. Rab appointed

1955 **Cabinet (U.S.)**—Cabinet session held place other than the seat of the Uni States Government—Gettysburg, Pa.

1961 **Baseball Player**—"most valuable play in both major leagues—Frank Robinso. elected (National League)

1963 **Television—Telecast**—telecast transr ted by satellite to Japan—via *Rela* —news program beamed from U.S. gro station in Mohave Desert

1964 **Catholic Mass**—Catholic mass in Engl said for a President—Holy Cross Cat dral, Boston, Mass.

1964 **Protestant Church**—Protestant chu formed by the amalgamation of 4 churc of different denominations—Uni Church of Schellsburg, Pa.

NOVEMBER 23

1765 **Stamp Act Repudiation**—Frederick, M

1792 **Bridge**—bridge of importance—West E ton Bridge—opened

1835 **Horseshoe Manufacturing Machine**—ented—Henry Burden—Troy, N.Y.

1848 **Medical Society**—women's medical s ety—organized—Boston, Mass.

1876 **Football Club**—intercollegiate football sociation—formed—Springfield, Mass.

1925 **Theater**—state-owned theater dedicate its own drama—opened—Chapel Hill, N

1935 **Musician**—woman conductor-compose to write and conduct an opera—Et Leginska—*Gale*—sung—Chicago, Ill.

1942 **Coast Guard (U.S.)**—Coast Guard V men's Reserve—SPARS—authorized

1948 **Lens**—lens to provide zoom effects—ented—F. G. Back

1963 **Television—Telecast**—telecast transn ted by satellite to Japan—via *Rela* —news program received in Japan

1968 **Naturalization**—naturalization ceremc in the White House—Washington, D.C

1969 **Astronaut**—space-to-ground news con ence telecast—Charles Conrad, A. L. Be and R. F. Gordon, Jr., in *Apollo XII* with P. Carr in Houston, Tex.

1973 **Representative (U.S.)**—representative give birth while holding office—Y. B. Bu —Los Angeles, Calif.

NOVEMBER 24

1703 **Lutheran Church**—Lutheran pastor dained in America—Justus Falckner

Horticultural Society—horticultural society (permanent)—Pennsylvania Horticultural Society—organized

Rifle Association—rifle association (national)—National Rifle Association—incorporated

Wire—barbed wire—patented—J. F. Glidden—De Kalb, Ill.

Nurses' Society—nurses' society (local)—Philomena Society—organized—New York City

Election Law—absentee voting law (state)—enacted—Vermont

Automobile Electric Self-Starter—automobile electric self-starter patent—C. J. Coleman—New York City

Forest—national forest in the southern states—Ocala National Forest, Fla.—Theodore Roosevelt proclaimed

Coast Guard (U.S.)—Coast Guard Women's Reserve—D. C. Stratton—assumed command

Postmaster—postmaster general appointed from the ranks—J. M. Donaldson

President (U.S.)—presidential airplane (turbo-compound-powered)

Television—Telecast—murder (actual) shown on television—L. H. Oswald killed by Jack Ruby—Dallas, Tex.

Aviation—Airplane—skyjack that was successful—D. B. Cooper—Woodland, Wash.

NOVEMBER 25

Patent—English patent granted to a resident of America—Thomas Masters

Opera—opera singer (American) to sing in an Italian opera in Italian—Julia Wheatley—New York City

Silk—silk power loom—patented—William Crompton—Taunton, Mass.

Museum—college museum—F. S. Holmes—elected curator

Greenback Party—Independent Party—organized—Indianapolis, Ind.

Milk—evaporated milk—patented—J. B. Meyenberg

Prizefighter—pugilist to win three world championships—R. P. (Bob) Fitzsimmons—light heavyweight championship won—San Francisco, Calif.

Medical Society—American College of Surgeons—incorporated—Springfield, Ill.

Radio Broadcast—football game (collegiate) broadcast—College Station, Tex.

Radio Broadcast—transatlantic radio program from England—received

Newspaper—composograph photograph in a newspaper—published—New York City

Atomic Reactor—atomic reactor for research and development—in operation—Richland, Wash.

NOVEMBER 26

1716 **Animals**—lion—exhibited—Boston, Mass.

1722 **Art Commission (public)**—Gustavus Hesselius—*The Last Supper*—painting hung

1758 **Holiday**—Thanksgiving Day sermon—west of the Alleghenies—delivered—Charles Beatty—Pittsburgh, Pa.

1789 **Holiday**—Thanksgiving Day—holiday—designated by presidential proclamation

1825 **Fraternity (Greek-letter)**—social fraternity—Kappa Alpha—established—Schenectady, N.Y.

1832 **Streetcar**—streetcar—service begun—New York City

1867 **Railroad Car**—refrigerator car patent—J. B. Sutherland—Detroit, Mich.

1896 **Football Game**—indoor football game (large)—Chicago, Ill.

NOVEMBER 27

1676 **Fire**—fire of serious consequence—Boston, Mass.

1779 **College**—university legally designated as a university—University of Pennsylvania

1820 **Library**—mercantile library—Mercantile Library Association of the City of New York—constitution adopted

1839 **Statistical Society**—of importance—American Statistical Association—organized—Boston, Mass.

1901 **Army War College**—Army War College—authorized—Washington, D.C.

1912 **Postage Stamp**—one-color one-size series of postage stamps—parcel post issue—first stamps in series issued

1912 **Postage Stamp**—parcel post postage-due stamps—1-cent stamp issued

1918 **Passport**—passport issued to a President of the United States in office—Woodrow Wilson

1921 **Radio Church**—Radio Church of America—New York City

1940 **Ship**—merchant ship formally blessed at a launching ceremony—*Rio Hudson*—Chester, Pa.

1951 **Rocket**—rocket to intercept an airplane—White Sands Proving Grounds, N.Mex.

1960 **Hockey Player**—professional hockey player to reach a score of more than 1,000 points in a regular season—Gordon Howe

1963 **Satellite**—satellite fueled by liquid hydrogen successfully orbited—*Centaur II*—launched—Cape Canaveral, Fla.

1966 **Football Game**—professional football game with 16 touchdowns—Washington Redskins vs. New York Giants—Washington, D.C.

NOVEMBER 28

1895 **Automobile Race**—automobile race—Chicago–Waukegan, Ill.

1922 **Skywriting**—skywriting—demonstrated—Cyril Turner—New York City

1929 **Aviation—Flights**—South Pole flight—takeoff—R. E. Byrd

1929 **Football Player**—football player to score 50 points in 1 game—Clark Hinkle—Lewisburg, Pa.

1953 **Television—Telecast**—pay television presentation of a motion picture shown simultaneously in theaters—Palm Springs, Calif.

1961 **Football Player**—black football player to win the Heisman Memorial Trophy—Ernest Davis—named

1964 **Satellite**—satellite to transmit a close-up photograph of Mars—*Mariner 4*—launched—Cape Kennedy, Fla.

1967 **Army Officer**—general who rose from draftee—K. L. Ware

NOVEMBER 29

1775 **Diplomatic Service**—foreign service committee—formed

1775 **Ink**—invisible ink—Committee of Secret Correspondence—formed

1816 **Bank**—savings bank—Bank for Savings in the City of New York—conceived—New York City

1825 **Opera**—opera (Italian)—*Il Barbiere di Siviglia*—performed—New York City

1890 **Football Game**—Army-Navy football game—West Point, N.Y.

1895 **Catholic Apostolic Delegate**—Francesco Satolli—appointed cardinal

1929 **Aviation—Flights**—South Pole flight—R. E. Byrd—flew over pole

1932 **Bridge (game) Table**—bridge table to shuffle and deal the cards by electricity—patented—Laurens Hammond—Chicago, Ill.

1933 **Liquor Stores (state)**—authorized—Pennsylvania

1948 **Television—Telecast**—opera (complete) to be televised from the Metropolitan Opera House—New York City

1951 **Atomic Bomb**—atomic bomb underground explosion—Frenchman Flat, Nev.

1953 **Aviation—Flights (transcontinental)**—transcontinental regularly scheduled two-way nonstop service—Los Angeles, Calif.-New York City

1961 **Satellite**—animal fired into space to orbit the earth—Enos—launched—Cape Canaveral, Fla.

NOVEMBER 30

1782 **Treaty**—treaty between the United States Government and a nation with which it had been at war—with Great Britain—preliminary articles signed

1803 **Territorial Expansion**—annexation of territory—Spain ceded Louisiana claims to France

1804 **Impeachment**—impeachment proceedi against a Justice of the Supreme Cour the United States—Samuel Chase

1866 **Tunnel**—subaqueous highway tunne work started—Chicago, Ill.

1875 **Oat-crushing Machine**—patented—A. Ehrrichson—Akron, Ohio

1886 **Electric Power Plant**—alternating-curr power plant commercially successful—erated—Buffalo, N.Y.

1887 **Softball**—softball (indoor baseball ga —played—Chicago, Ill.

1899 **Aluminum**—aluminum used commerci in a transmission conductor—Hartfc Conn.

1924 **Radio Facsimile Transmission**—ph(graph sent by radio across the Atlantic a public demonstration—received—N York City

1939 **President (U.S.)**—President to hold an plane pilot's license—D. D. Eisenhowe

1950 **Milk**—concentrated milk—sold—Wilm ton, Del.

1954 **Meteorite**—meteorite known to h struck a woman—Sylacauga, Ala.

1958 **Ship**—guided missile destroyer—*Dewe* launched—Bath, Me.

1962 **Race Track**—harness track to handle m than $3 million in bets in 1 night—Yonk Raceway, Yonkers, N.Y.—topped t figure

DECEMBER 1

1751 **Manual Training**—school to offer cour in manual training—opened—Tai County, Md.

1841 **Normal School**—normal school instruct course given at a university—Wesle University—Middletown, Conn.

1841 **Ship**—steamboat engine built in Amer for a screw-propelled vessel—*Vandali* launched

1842 **Naval Officer**—naval officer condem for mutiny—hanged

1843 **Insurance**—mutual life insurance comp: to be chartered—New England Life In: ance Company—Boston, Mass.—organi for business

1896 **Accountant**—C.P.A.'s conferred—N York

1898 **Bicycle Trip (world)**—bicycle trip aro the world by a married coupel—returne Chicago

1904 **Pressing Machine (steam-operated)**—r ent application—A. J. Hoffman

1909 **Bank**—Christmas savings club—paym made—Carlisle, Pa.

1911 **Postage Stamp**—registry stamp—issue(

1913 **Automobile Service Station**—drive-in vice station—opened—Pittsburgh, Pa.

1914 **Aviation—School**—naval air train school—opened—Pensacola, Fla.

Woman—American-born woman to become a member of Parliament (British)—Lady Astor—sworn in

Aviation—Airship—airship filled with helium gas—tested—Hampton Roads, Va.

Postal Service—philatelic agency—opened—Washington, D.C.

Corn Husking Championship Contest (national)—Alleman, Iowa

Aviation—Flights (transcontinental)—transcontinental airplane flight by a woman—Ruth Nichols—arrived—Burbank, Calif.

Medal—platinum medal—made by U.S. Mint—presented to President Hoover

Soilless Culture of Plants—commercial hydroponicum (large)—patent

Legislator (state)—black woman state legislator—assumed office—C. B. Fauset

Civil Air Patrol (U.S.)—organized

Glider—glider (all plywood-plastic)—tested—San Fernando, Calif.

Bridge (game) Player—father and son team to win a national contract bridge championship—Oswald Jacoby and James Jacoby—Miami Beach, Fla.

Railroad Car—remote-control railroad passenger car—between New Rochelle, N.Y., and Rye, N.Y.—put in operation

Brokerage—woman president of a major stock brokerage concern—J. P. Bay—New York City

Photograph—photograph in color of the earth from outer space—missile launched—Cape Canaveral, Fla.

Astronaut—astronaut (American) to become an admiral—A. B. Shepard, Jr.—date of rank

DECEMBER 2

Bank—savings bank actually to receive money on deposit—Philadelphia Savings Fund Society—Philadelphia, Pa.—opened

Railroad—railroad to run west of the Mississippi River—Pacific Railway of Missouri—test run

Federal Council of the Churches of Christ in America—organized—Philadelphia, Pa.

Streetcar—aluminum streetcar—service—Cleveland, Ohio

Industrial Recovery Act—conviction under a National Industrial Recovery Code—New York City

Wedding—transatlantic telephone wedding—Detroit, Mich.

Telescope—telescope lens 200 inches in diameter—molten glass poured—Corning, N.Y.

Woman—woman presidential campaign comanager—R. H. M. Simms

Aviation—Flights (world)—world flight by a commercial airplane—*Pacific Clipper*—left San Francisco, Calif.

1942 Atomic Energy—self-sustaining nuclear chain reaction demonstration—Chicago, Ill.

1952 Television—Telecast—birth (human) to be televised for the public—Denver, Colo.

1957 Electric Power Plant—atomic electric generating station (full-scale)—operated—Shippingport, Pa.

1957 Ship—atomic-powered cruiser—*Long Beach*—keel laid—Quincy, Mass.

1976 Television—Telecast—live national commercial cablecast via satellite—via RCA Satcom—Birmingham Bulls vs. Edmonton Oilers—Birmingham, Ala.

DECEMBER 3

1639 Annulment—annulment by court decree—James Luxford—Boston, Mass.

1750 Opera—opera performed by a professional visiting troupe—*The Beggar's Opera*—New York City

1825 Fraternity (Greek-letter)—social fraternity—Kappa Alpha—Schenectady, N.Y.—initiation

1833 College—coeducational college—Oberlin Collegiate Institute—Oberlin, Ohio—opened

1834 Dental Society—dental society (local)—Society of Surgeon-Dentists formed—New York City

1835 Insurance—mutual fire insurance company—policy issued—Manufacturers' Mutual Fire Insurance Company

1875 Coaching Club—formed—New York City

1922 Motion Picture—Technicolor motion picture film—successful—*Toll of the Sea*—released

1923 Radio Broadcast—congressional open-session broadcast—WRC, Washington, D.C.

1932 Opera—opera matinee at the Metropolitan Opera House—*Elektra*—New York City

1948 Army Officer—woman army officer—M. A. Hallaren—sworn in

1956 Ship—ballistic-missile test ship—*Compass Island*—commissioned—New York City

1962 Judge—black woman judge elected—E. S. Sampson—Chicago, Ill.—sworn in

1968 Astronaut—astronaut international rescue agreement—announced as in force by President Lyndon Baines Johnson

1968 Supreme Court (U.S.)—Associate Justice of the Supreme Court to participate in a television program—H. L. Black—Alexandria, Va.

DECEMBER 4

1776 Ship—warship (American-built) to enter European waters—*Reprisal*—sailed

1779 Law School—law school in a college—George Wythe appointed professor of law

1812 Mower (horsepower)—patented—Peter Gaillard—Lancaster, Pa.

1839 **Political Convention**—unit rule—adopted —Harrisburg, Pa.

1843 **Paper**—manila paper—patented—J. M. & L. Hollingsworth—South Braintree, Mass.

1867 **Agricultural Society**—agricultural society of national importance—National Grange of the Patrons of Husbandry—organized—Washington, D.C.

1875 **Intercollegiate Athletic Association**—organization meeting—Saratoga, N.Y.

1906 **Fraternity (Greek letter)**—intercollegiate Greek-letter national fraternity for black men—formed—Ithaca, N.Y.

1915 **Medal**—admiral to receive the Congressional Medal of Honor—F. F. Fletcher

1917 **Submarine**—submarine to cross the Atlantic Ocean under its own power—*E-1*—left Newport, R.I.

1918 **President (U.S.)**—President to visit a European country—Woodrow Wilson—left—Washington, D.C.

1918 **Ship**—concrete ship built for the United States Shipping Board—*Atlantus*—launched—Brunswick, Ga.

1921 **Aviation—Airship**—airship filled with helium gas—R. F. Wood (pilot)—round trip, Hampton Roads, Va.-Washington, D.C.

1922 **Diplomatic Service**—woman legation secretary—Lucille Atcherson—Columbus, Ohio—appointed

1933 **Federal Alcohol Control Administration**—authorized

1935 **College**—college classes to combat the influence of communism—instituted—St. Joseph's College—Philadelphia, Pa.

1942 **Citizenship**—citizenship granted to an alien on foreign soil—conferred—Panama Canal Zone

1961 **Medal**—Armed Forces Expeditionary Medal—established—J. F. Kennedy

1965 **Astronaut**—astronauts (American) to orbit the earth 200 times—Frank Borman and J. A. Lovell, Jr.—*Gemini VII*—launched, Cape Kennedy, Fla.

1970 **Treasury Department (U.S.)**—treasurer of the United States to sign currency with 2 names—D. A. Kabis—notes issued with new name

DECEMBER 5

1776 **Fraternity (Greek-letter)**—scholastic fraternity—Phi Beta Kappa—founded—Williamsburg, Va.

1782 **President (U.S.)**—President born a citizen of the United States—Martin Van Buren—Kinderhook, N.Y.

1786 **War**—rebellion against the federal government—Daniel Shays—Worcester, Mass.

1831 **Congress (U.S.)**—Congress in which 1,000 bills were introduced

1843 **Ship**—iron vessel built for the United States Navy—*Michigan* launched—Pittsburgh, Pa.

1846 **Cellulose Nitrate Patent**—C. F. Schoenb
1854 **Chair**—folding theater chair—patente A. H. Allen—Boston, Mass.

1868 **Bicycle School**—velocipede ridin opened—New York City

1876 **Wrench**—pipe or screw wrench (practi —patented—D. C. Stillson—Somervi Mass.

1879 **Telephone**—automatic telephone sys patent—Daniel Connolly—Philadelp Pa.

1905 **Medal**—Interstate Commerce Commiss Medal of Honor—awarded—G. H. Poe Grand Island, Neb.

1906 **Young Women's Christian Associatio** national convention—New York City

1908 **Football Uniform**—football uniform merals—used—University of Pittsburg Pittsburgh, Pa.

1927 **King**—king born in the United State Rama IX of Thailand

1929 **Marine Corps**—marine pilot to fly over Antarctic continent—A. U. Parker— off from Little America

1929 **Nudist Organization**—American Lea for Physical Culture—organized— York City

1933 **Constitutional Amendment (U.S.)**—co tutional amendment submitted to the st for repeal—amendment ratified

1935 **Soilless Culture of Plants**—commercial droponicum (large)—established—N tebello, Calif.

1948 **Television—Telecast**—church service vised in sign language—Jamaica, N.Y.

1950 **Television—Telecast**—X-ray fluorosc television discussion—Baltimore, Md.

1951 **Garage**—completely automatic push-ton-controlled garage—Washington, —opened

1955 **Television—Telecast**—murder trial to televised—Waco, Tex.

1964 **Medal**—Medal of Honor in the Viet war—presented to R. H. Donlon

DECEMBER 6

1732 **Play (drama)**—play acted by professi players—*The Recruiting Officer—* York City

1787 **Methodist College**—opened—Cokes College—Abingdon, Md.

1787 **State**—state to ratify the federal Cons tion—Delaware

1790 **Congress (U.S.)**—Congress of the Ur States—first session in Philadelphia,

1825 **Conference**—conference of Amer Republics—appointment of deleg confirmed

1830 **Observatory**—observatory (national)— tablished—Washington, D.C.

1866 **Water Conduit**—water supply tunnel city—completed—Chicago, Ill.

Football Game—international football game—New Haven, Conn.

Crematory—crematory—incineration—Baron de Palm—Washington, Pa.

Monument—monument to George Washington (national)—aluminum tip set—Washington, D.C.

Postage Stamp—American woman whose likeness appeared on a U.S. stamp—Martha Washington

Electric Transmission—electric power line commercial carrier—operated—Utica, N.Y.

Radio Broadcast—presidential message to be broadcast—Calvin Coolidge—Washington, D.C.

Congress (U.S.)—Senate—senatorial controversy in which no candidates were seated after a recount

Airmail Service—Pacific airmail flight—*China Clipper*—return—San Francisco, Calif.

Medal—soldier to receive seven decorations at once—L. M. Chilson

Television—Telecast—medical intracity color telecast—Johns Hopkins Hospital—Baltimore, Md.

Football Player—black football player to win the Heisman Memorial Trophy—Ernest Davis—presentation

Medal—Medal of Freedom awarded to a black woman—Marian Anderson—presented by L. B. Johnson—Washington, D.C.

Medal—Medal of Honor in the Vietnam war awarded to a Marine—R. E. O'Malley—presented in Austin, Tex.

Railroad—auto-train to transport passengers and their automobiles on the same train—between Lorton, Pa., and Sanford, Fla.—service began

DECEMBER 7

State—state to ratify the federal Constitution—signed—Delaware

Catholic Bishop—Catholic bishop consecrated in present U.S. limits—Leonard Neale—Baltimore, Md.

Newspaper Syndicate—syndication of newspaper material—M. Y. Beach—New York City

Senator (U.S.)—father and son senators at the same session—Henry Dodge and A. C. Dodge

Insurance—bonding company (exclusive)—American Surety Company—New York City—incorporated

Hospital—cancer hospital—opened for patients—New York City

Congress (U.S.)—Congress to appropriate $1 billion—session opened—Washington, D.C.

Tunnel—subaqueous railroad tunnel to a foreign country—opened for passenger traffic—Port Huron, Mich.

1903 Radio Distress Signal—radio distress signal (CQD) from an American ship—*Kroonland*

1909 Plastic—thermosetting manufactured plastic—patented—L. H. Baekeland—Yonkers, N.Y.

1913 Newspaper—newspaper 12-page advertising supplement—New York *Times*—New York City

1916 Bird Legislation (international)—international treaty for the protection of wild birds—ratifications exchanged—United States and Great Britain

1917 World War I—United States declaration of war against Germany (World War I)—declaration against Austria-Hungary

1925 Representative (U.S.)—woman to serve 18 terms in Congress—E. F. N. Rogers of Massachusetts—began service

1926 Refrigerator—gas refrigerator (household)—patented

1932 Ship—gyro-stabilized vessel to cross the Atlantic Ocean—*Conte di Savoia*—arrived—New York City

1938 Newspaper—radio facsimile newspaper daily—St. Louis *Post-Dispatch*

1939 Aviation—Passenger—woman flown in a U.S. Army plane from one country to another—left Mitchel Field, N.Y.

1941 Naval Officer—admiral killed in action in World War II—I. C. Kidd—Pearl Harbor, Hawaii

1941 Radar—radar used to detect enemy airplanes—Pearl Harbor, Hawaii

1941 World War II—air hero—G. S. Welch

1941 World War II—Japanese attack in World War II

1941 World War II—Japanese submarine sunk by an American ship—*Ward*

1942 Coast Guard (U.S.)—Coast Guard Women's Reserve—SPARS—first recruit—D. E. L. Tuttle

1944 Army Officer—army officer to receive the three highest decorations—M. L. Britt—Distinguished Service Cross (3rd award)—presentation

1944 Business—retail store whose sales in 1 day exceeded $1 million—R. H. Macy Co.—New York City

1951 Television—Telecast—surgical operation televised on a coast-to-coast closed circuit in color—Los Angeles, Calif.

1953 Automobile—transparent-top automobile—Sun Valley—manufactured—Detroit, Mich.

1954 Heliport—military heliport—dedicated

1959 Ship—guided missile destroyer—*Dewey*—commissioned—Bath, Me.

DECEMBER 8

1792 Cremation—Henry Laurens—died

1850 **College Student**—black woman college graduate—L. A. Stanton—Oberlin College, Oberlin, Ohio

1863 **Amnesty**—proclamation—Abraham Lincoln

1863 **Farmers' Institute**—farmers' institute sponsored by a state—Springfield, Mass.

1866 **Ship**—side-wheeler transpacific steamer—*Celestial Empire* (later named *China*)—launched

1869 **Naval Academy (U.S.)**—Japanese midshipman in the United States Naval Academy—Z. Z. Matzmulla—admitted

1886 **Labor Union**—labor union of importance—adopted name American Federation of Labor

1890 **Woman**—woman labor delegate to a national convention—of the American Federation of Labor—Mary Burke—Detroit, Mich.

1909 **Bird Banding Society**—bird banding society—American Bird Banding Association—formed—New York City

1916 **Bird Legislation (international)**—Migratory Bird Treaty—proclaimed

1928 **Physician**—Capitol physician—G. W. Calver

1929 **Radio Telephone**—radio telephone ship-to-shore commercial service—New York City

1931 **Cable**—coaxial cable—patented

1939 **Television—Telecast**—telecast produced for a tri-city gathering—Schenectady, N.Y.

1940 **Radio Broadcast**—football game championship (professional) broadcast on a network—Washington Redskins vs. Chicago Bears—Washington, D.C.

1941 **Ordnance**—tank (heavy 60-ton)—delivered—Eddystone, Pa.

1941 **Representative (U.S.)**—representative (woman) to vote twice against the entry of the United States into war—Jeannette Rankin

1941 **Ship**—ship (American) to surrender to the Japanese—*Wake*—at Shanghai, China

1946 **Snow-melting Apparatus**—snow-melting apparatus (practical) with pipe imbedded in the sidewalk—tested—New York City

1948 **Television—Telecast**—split-screen image—exhibited—New York City

1959 **Motion Picture**—motion picture with scent—*Behind the Great Wall*—presented—New York City

1961 **Naval Officer**—naval line officer (woman) assigned to sea duty (MSTS)—C. I. Suneson—reported for duty, Oakland, Calif.

1969 **Race Track**—harness track to handle more than $300 million in bets in 1 year—Yonkers Raceway, Yonkers, N.Y.—topped that figure

DECEMBER 9

1621 **Sermon Printed (American)**—Robert Cushman—Plymouth, Mass.

1814 **Conscription**—wartime conscription bil approved by House of Representative but not enacted into law

1845 **Suture**—silver wire suture—J. M. Sim experimented—Montgomery, Ala.

1869 **Labor Union**—labor organization to ad workmen other than craft workmen—ble Order of the Knights of Labor—foun —Philadelphia, Pa.

1884 **Roller Skate**—ball-bearing skate pater L. M. Richardson—Chicago, Ill.

1901 **Bicycle Race**—paired six-day bicycle r —New York City

1907 **Seal**—Christmas seals of the modern v ety sold to raise funds to fight tubercul —Wilmington, Del.

1909 **Aviation—Airplane**—monoplane (Am can)—flown—Mineola, N.Y.

1912 **Postage Stamp**—parcel post postage- stamps—2-cent stamp issued

1930 **Labor Department (U.S.)**—native-b Secretary of Labor—W. N. Doak—swor

1934 **Autogiro**—autogiro (wingless direct c trol)—flown—Philadelphia, Pa.

1939 **Aviation—Passenger**—woman flown i U.S. Army plane from one country to an er—arrived—Santiago, Chile

1940 **Radio Advertising**—radio advertising c tract for frequency modulation broadc. —signed—New York City

1941 **World War II**—American bombing mis in the Orient—Vigan, Philippines

1941 **World War II**—Japanese airplane stroyed—off Wake Island

1945 **Television—Telecast**—stratovision f test—Middle River, Md.

1960 **Computer**—electronic computer to emj Thin-Film memory—announced

1962 **Protestant Episcopal Bishop**—black to minister a diocese—J. M. Burgess—Bos Mass.—consecrated

DECEMBER 10

1672 **Postal Service**—postal route—announ

1690 **Loan**—state loan—authorized—Ma chusetts

1792 **Insurance**—life insurance—Insura Company of North America—organize Philadelphia, Pa.

1815 **Naval Officers' Training School**—n officers' training school—establishe Boston, Mass.

1843 **Ship**—warship with propelling machi below the waterline—*Princete* launched—Philadelphia, Pa.

1869 **Woman Suffrage**—state to grant suffra; women—vote extended to women by ritorial legislature—Wyoming

1879 **Library Society**—library association tional)—American Library Associati incorporated

Baseball Team—baseball teams to go on a world tour—first game abroad—Auckland, New Zealand

Basketball—basketball intercollegiate game—New Haven, Conn.

Hospital—tuberculosis hospital—National Jewish Hospital—Denver, Colo.—opened

Police—motorcycle police—A. L. Howe and Eugene Case—New York City—official status received

Nobel Prize—Nobel Peace Prize awarded an American woman—Jane Addams

Nobel Prize—Nobel Prize in literature to a woman—awarded to P. S. Buck

Civil Air Patrol (U.S.)—national commander J. F. Curry—appointed

Submarine—submarine (U.S.) destroyed in World War II—*Sealion*—Cavite, Philippine Islands

Ship—naval ship named for a sailor killed at Pearl Harbor—*England*—commissioned

Aviation—Airplane—rocket plane—tested —Muroc, Calif.

Nobel Prize—black to win the Nobel Peace Prize—R. J. Bunche

Element—element 94—Nobel Prize—presented—Stockholm, Sweden

Helicopter—gas-turbine helicopter (turborotor)—tested—Windsor Locks, Conn.

Nobel Prize—Nobel Prize for peace to a professional soldier—awarded to G. C. Marshall

Nobel Prize—recipient of 2 full Nobel prizes—L. C. Pauling—first award (chemistry)

Nobel Prize—Nobel Prize 2-time winner in the same category—John Bardeen—first shared prize

Ship—guided-missile escort ship—*Brooke* —laid down—Seattle, Wash.

Nobel Prize—recipient of 2 full Nobel prizes—L. C. Pauling—second award (peace)

Nobel Prize—Nobel Prize 2-time winner in the same category—John Bardeen—second shared prize

Marine Corps—woman unit commander to direct 2,000 men—M. E. Bane—Camp Pendleton, Oceanside, Calif.

Nobel Prize—Nobel Prize winners all from one country in 5 categories

DECEMBER 11

Aurora Borealis—recorded

Statistical Society—American Statistical Association—constitution adopted—Boston, Mass.

Anesthesia—anesthetic in dentistry—Horace Wells—extraction

Yacht Race—yacht race across the Atlantic Ocean

Governor—black governor (acting)—P. B. S. Pinchback—Louisiana

1882 **Theater**—theater lighted by electricity—Bijou Theater—Boston, Mass.

1901 **Radio Broadcast**—transatlantic radio signal—Guglielmo Marconi—England to Newfoundland

1909 **Motion Picture**—colored motion pictures—exhibited—New York City

1919 **Monument**—monument to an insect—dedicated—Enterprise, Ala.

1929 **Glider**—Flights—glider flight in an American-built glider to last longer than 1 hour—W. H. Bowlus—Point Loma, Calif.

1931 **Animals**—cattle (Africander cattle)—arrived—New York City

1941 **World War II**—Japanese battleship sunk—*Haruna*—off North Luzon, P.I.

1952 **Television—Telecast**—pay television presentation of an opera—*Carmen*—New York City

1954 **Ship**—aircraft carrier with an angle deck—*Forrestal*—launched—Newport News, Va.

1972 **Geologist**—geologist to reach the moon—H. H. Schmitt

DECEMBER 12

1796 **Nail Cutting and Heading Machine**—patented—G. Chandler—Maryland

1808 **Bible Society**—Bible society—Bible Society of Philadelphia—organized

1862 **Ship**—warship sunk by an underwater torpedo mine—*Cairo*—sunk near Vicksburg, Miss.

1862 **Torpedo**—torpedo mine attack—Civil War —against war vessel—Yazoo River—*Cairo*

1870 **Representative (U.S.)**—black representative—J. H. Rainey—sworn in

1889 **Sanitary District**—Chicago, Ill.—special election

1893 **Photographic Patent**—aerial photography patent—C. B. Adams

1899 **Golf Tee**—patented—G. F. Grant—Boston, Mass.

1902 **Multigraph**—commercial manufacture—Cleveland, Ohio

1906 **Cabinet (U.S.)**—Cabinet member who was Jewish—O. S. Straus—appointed

1912 **Postage Stamp**—parcel post postage-due stamps—10-cent stamp issued

1925 **Motel**—motel—Motel Inn—opened, San Luis Obispo, Calif.

1937 **Television Mobile Unit**—mobile television unit—New York City

1938 **Athlete**—two-time winner of the Associated Press Athlete of the Year award—J. D. Budge—second award

1941 **Aviation—Pilot**—American ace in World War II—B. D. Wagner—attacked Japanese planes

1941 **World War II**—American general killed in World War II—H. A. Dargue

1961 **Satellite**—satellite in orbit built by private citizens—*Discoverer XXXVI*—launched—Vandenberg Air Force Base, Calif.

1970 **Air Force Officer**—Air Force general (woman)—J. M. Holm—nominated

1970 **Astronaut**—astronaut (American) to become a general—J. A. McDivitt—nominated

DECEMBER 13

1621 **Furs**—exported—Boston, Mass.

1766 **Fox Hunting Club**—Gloucester Fox Hunting Club—meeting

1774 **Revolutionary War**—incident in the Revolutionary War—New Castle, N.H.

1809 **Surgical Operation**—abdominal operation—performed—Danville, Ky.

1816 **Bank**—savings bank to become a corporation—Provident Institution for Savings—Boston, Mass.—chartered

1816 **Dry Dock Patent**—issued—John Adamson—Boston, Mass.

1853 **Hospital**—women's infirmary staffed by women physicians—New York Infirmary—incorporated

1855 **Ship**—turreted frigate in the U.S. Navy—*Roanoke*—launched

1864 **Naval Officer**—naval officer to become an admiral—D. G. Farragut advanced to vice admiral

1879 **Ship**—fish hatching steamer (federal)—*Fishhawk*—launched

1893 **Tuberculosis Laboratory**—tuberculosis diagnostic community laboratory—authorized—New York City

1918 **President (U.S.)**—President to visit a European country—Woodrow Wilson—arrived—Brest, France

1918 **World War I**—U.S. Army division to cross the Rhine River—First Division

1920 **Astronomer**—astronomer to measure the size of a fixed star—A. A. Michelson—Mount Wilson, Calif.

1933 **Medal**—Air Mail Flyer's Medal of Honor—presented—M. B. Freeburg

1938 **Casein Fiber**—patented

1962 **Satellite**—communications earth satellite to transmit telephone, television, teleprint, and facsimile signals—launched—Cape Canaveral, Fla.

1978 **Money**—woman commemorated on a circulating U.S. coin—S. B. Anthony—coin issued

DECEMBER 14

1793 **Road**—state road authorization—Kentucky

1798 **Nut and Bolt Machine**—nut and bolt machine—patented—David Wilkinson

1798 **Screw**—screw patent—David Wilkinson

1807 **Meteorite**—meteorite whose landing was recorded—fell at Weston (now Easton), Conn.

1849 **Music**—chamber music organization—concert—Boston, Mass.

1889 **Political Science Society**—political and social science society (national)—American Academy of Political and Social Science organized—Philadelphia, Pa.

1902 **Cable**—cable across the Pacific Ocean paid out

1920 **Army School**—instructor nongraduate—H. Hodges—West Point, N.Y.—assured post

1934 **Locomotive**—streamlined steam locomotive—introduced—Albany, N.Y.

1944 **Army Officer**—generals to wear the star insignia—grade approved

1944 **Naval Officer**—naval officers to wear five-star insignia—grade approved

1945 **Naval Officer**—naval nurses' corps (woman a member)—S. S. Dauser—received tinguished Service Medal

1952 **Siamese Twins**—Siamese twins to survive a separation operation and live for year—born

1962 **Satellite**—satellite to transmit data from Venus—data transmitted

1966 **Satellite** — biosatellite — launched—Cape Kennedy, Fla.

1974 **Television—Telecast**—congressional telecast and radio broadcast—authorized—Senate—Washington, D.C.

DECEMBER 15

1778 **Arbitration**—state arbitration law—enacted—Maryland

1791 **Constitutional Amendment (U.S.)**—constitutional amendments—declared in force

1792 **Insurance**—life insurance—first policy—Insurance Company of North America—Philadelphia, Pa.

1810 **Irish Magazine**—*The Shamrock*—published—New York City

1814 **Secession**—secession convention—Hartford, Conn.

1820 **Pharmacopoeia**—pharmacopoeia (general)—published—Boston, Mass.

1854 **Street Cleaning Machine**—used—Philadelphia, Pa.

1864 **Philatelic Magazine**—philatelic magazine—*Stamp Collector's Record*—published—Albany, N.Y.

1872 **Fraternity Magazine**—fraternity journal—*Beta Theta Pi*—published—Alexandria, Va.

1874 **Visiting Celebrities**—king (reigning) to visit the United States—David Kalakaua of Hawaii—received by U.S. Grant

1886 **Brokerage**—stock exchange at which more than a million shares were traded in a day—New York City

1906 **Medal**—National Geographic Society medal—Hubbard Medal presented—R. Peary—Washington, D.C.

1925 **Road**—road with a depressed trough opened to traffic—Texas

1839   **Photograph**—celestial photograph—J. W. Draper—New York City

1862   **Hospital**—orthopedic hospital—New York Society for the Relief of the Ruptured and Crippled—organized—New York City

1865   **Animals**—cattle importation law (U.S.)—enacted

1917   **Prohibition**—prohibition amendment to the Constitution—submitted to the states

1918   **Airmail Service**—airmail regular service between New York and Chicago—began—Belmont Park, L.I.

1920   **Postage Stamp**—postage stamps without the words *United States* or the initials *U.S.* —Pilgrim Tercentenary issue—on sale—Provincetown and Plymouth, Mass.

1924   **Radio Broadcast**—auction of livestock broadcast—Chicago, Ill.

1930   **Autogiro Flights**—autogiro solo flight by a woman—Amelia Earhart—Willow Grove, Pa.

1935   **Money**—bill to depict both the face and the reverse side of the Great Seal of the United States—issued

1936   **Animals**—giant panda—arrived—San Francisco, Calif.

1953   **Television—Telecast**—color telecast by a local station—WPTZ-TV—Philadelphia, Pa.

1965   **Astronaut**—astronauts (American) to orbit the earth 200 times—Frank Borman and J. A. Lovell, Jr.—*Gemini VII*—landed, Atlantic Ocean

1965   **Ship**—diesel-and-gas-turbine combined-propulsion plant in a major ship—*Alexander Hamilton*—launched—New Orleans, La.

DECEMBER 19

1620   **Colonist**—English settlement in America (permanent)—left Blackwell, England

1683   **Architect**—landscape architect—John Reid—arrived

1795   **Road**—state road appropriation of a specific sum—enacted—Kentucky

1799   **Forestry Legislation**—federal forestry legislation—land purchased—Grover's Island, Ga.

1823   **Birth Registration**—birth registration law (state)—enacted—Georgia

1854   **Sewing Machine**—sewing machine to sew curving seams—patented—A. B. Wilson—Watertown, Conn.

1871   **Paper**—corrugated paper—patented—A. L. Jones—New York City

1877   **Cattle Club**—cattle club (Guernsey cattle)—American Guernsey Cattle Club—annual meeting

1891   **Catholic Priest**—black Catholic priest ordained in the United States—C. R. Uncles—Baltimore, Md.

1903   **Bridge**—suspension bridge of importance having steel towers—opened—New York City

1910   **Rayon**—rayon—commercially produce American Viscose Company—Mar Hook, Pa.

1910   **Supreme Court (U.S.)**—Associate Justic the Supreme Court to become Chief Jus —E. D. White—took seat as Chief Just

1920   **Curling Rink**—indoor curling rink—Co try Club—Brookline, Mass.

1927   **Aviation**—air control municipal boar formed—San Diego, Calif.

1928   **Autogiro—Flights**—autogiro flight—\ low Grove, Pa.

1930   **Autogiro**—pilot to carry a passenger— elia Earhart—Willow Grove, Pa.

1933   **Electric Home and Farm Authority, In** authorized

1933   **Radio Facsimile Transmission**—facsir broadcast in ultrahigh frequencies—\ waukee, Wis.

1939   **Television—Telecast**—motion picture miere festivities to be televised—? York City

1941   **Police**—Army Military Police school— thorized

1958   **Radio Broadcast**—outer-space broad —tape recording broadcast from rock D. D. Eisenhower

1974   **Television—Telecast**—congressional cast and radio broadcast—aired—W. ington, D.C.

1974   **Television—Telecast**—Senate proceed telecast—vice presidential installa ceremony for N. A. Rockefeller—Wash ton, D.C.

DECEMBER 20

1669   **Rebellion**—rebellion of colonists aga the English—Marcus Jacobson— demned for insurrection

1780   **Conscientious Objectors**—released f prison—Albany, N.Y.

1790   **Cotton Mill**—cotton mill to spin cot yarn successfully—started—Samuel Sl. —Pawtucket, R.I.

1803   **Territorial Expansion**—annexation of te tory—France ceded Louisiana territory

1820   **Tax**—bachelor tax—levied—Missouri

1837   **College**—city college—College of Char ton—became municipal universi Charleston, S.C.

1860   **Secession**—secession act—enacte South Carolina

1864   **Postal Service**—railroad post office for general distribution of mail—G. B. A strong—appointed general superintend

1869   **Supreme Court (U.S.)**—Associate Jus nominee to die before occupying his se E. M. Stanton—appointed

1870   **Farmers' Institute**—farmers' institute l by a land grant agricultural college of campus—Cedar Falls, Iowa

Impeachment—impeachment and removal from office of a state governor—proceedings against W. W. Holden—North Carolina

Electric Lighting—electric incandescent lamp—demonstration—Menlo Park, N.J.

Electric Company—electric company—president chosen—Edison Electric Illuminating Company

Time Recorder—autograph time recorder —patented—B. F. Merritt—Newton, Mass.

Automobile Tire—pneumatic tire patent—Syracuse, N.Y.

Lynch Law (state)—enacted—Georgia

Postal Service—international dogsled mail —left—Lewiston, Me.

Theater—theater built and named for a living actress—Ethel Barrymore Theatre—opened—New York City

Television—electronic television system—patented—V. K. Zworykin—Wilkinsburg, Pa.

Medal—navy unit commendation decoration—established

Atomic Energy—electric power from nuclear energy—100,000 watts—Idaho Falls, Idaho

Ship—aircraft carrier (atomic powered)—Enterprise—completed

DECEMBER 21

Physician—doctor in New England—Samuel Fuller—arrived

State Department (U.S.)—State Department (U.S.) Secretary—John Jay—served

Bridge—stone-arch railroad bridge—Carrollton viaduct—Baltimore, Md.—opened

Ice Skating Club—ice skating club formed —Philadelphia, Pa.

Medal—Medal of Honor awarded to a member of the Naval Service—authorized

High School—junior high school system—authorized—Berkeley, Calif.

Fingerprinting—fingerprint conviction—Thomas Jennings—upheld—Illinois

Crossword Puzzle—published—New York World

Motion Picture—six-reel feature-length comedy—Tillie's Punctured Romance—released

Insurance—group hospital insurance plan —Dallas, Tex.

Blood Bank—blood serum (human, dried) —prepared

Motion Picture—animated cartoon in color (Technicolor) of feature length with sound —exhibited

Ship—naval ship (destroyer) christened by an enlisted woman Marine—Basilone—launched—Orange, Tex.

1968 Astronaut—astronauts (American) to orbit the earth—Frank Borman, J. A. Lovell, Jr., and W. A. Anders—Apollo VIII—launched, Cape Kennedy, Fla.

DECEMBER 22

1772 Schoolhouse—west of the Allegheny Mountains—started—Schoenbrunn, Ohio

1775 Naval Officer—commander in chief of the Continental Navy—Esek Hopkins—served

1775 Navy—naval fleet—Continental Navy organized

1807 Embargo Act—enacted

1831 Streetcar—streetcar company—New York and Harlem Railway—franchise received

1877 Bicycle Magazine—American Bicycling Journal—published—Boston, Mass.

1885 Railroad—switchback railway—patent—L. A. Thompson—Coney Island, N.Y.

1886 Accountants' Society—accountants' society to become a national organization—American Association of Public Accountants—formed—New York City

1894 Golf Club—golf association (national)—United States Golf Association—formed—New York City

1910 Postal Savings Stamps—issued

1914 Prohibition—prohibition vote—showing dry majority in House of Representatives

1920 Radio Broadcast—prizefight broadcast from the ringside—New York City

1922 Wedding—double radio wedding—New York City

1936 Automobile License (federal)—common carrier license—granted—Rodger's Motor Lines—Scranton, Pa.

1943 Arts and Letters Society—black member of the National Institute of Arts and Letters—W. E. B. Du Bois—elected

1944 Medal—combat decoration—for army personnel—authorized

1956 Animals—gorilla born in captivity—Colo—Columbus, Ohio

1968 Television—Telecast—outer-space live telecast from a manned spacecraft—Apollo VIII

1972 Bank—bank to provide motion pictures for its customers waiting in line to be served—Chemical Bank—New York City

1977 Road—border-to-border national highway —Interstate 75—dedicated

DECEMBER 23

1776 Loan—loan for war purposes—authorized

1780 Diplomatic Service—consul to die in service—left Wilmington, Del.

1834 Bellows—patented—J. R. Morrison—Springfield, Ohio

1852 Theater—Chinese theater—"Celestial John" opened—San Francisco, Calif.

1873 Degrees (academic and honorary)—Bachelor of Music degree—awarded—M. P. Lowrie

1907 **Railroad Car**—steel passenger railroad coach—all-steel car completed—Altoona, Pa.

1913 **Bank**—bank established in a foreign country—Federal Reserve Act approved

1913 **Bank**—federal reserve system—Federal Reserve Act—approved

1919 **Ship**—ambulance ship, designed and built as a hospital—*Relief*—launched

1929 **Teletype Service**—teletypewriter system employed by a police department—in service—central headquarters, Harrisburg, Pa.

1930 **Police**—police bureau of criminal alien investigation—organized—New York City

1941 **Submarine**—submarine with a high-tensile-steel pressure hull—*Balao*—authorized

1943 **Submarine**—submarine (U.S.) sunk by an enemy submarine—*Corvina*—presumed lost

1943 **Television—Telecast**—opera (complete) to be televised—*Hansel and Gretel*

1970 **Sky Marshal**—sky marshals—first graduates

DECEMBER 24

1705 **Poem**—poem (printed)—Boston, Mass.

1733 **Map**—war map—published—*New York Weekly Journal*

1784 **Methodist Church**—Methodist bishop—Francis Asbury—elected—Baltimore, Md.

1832 **Hospital**—black hospital and asylum—Georgia Infirmary—Savannah, Ga.—incorporated

1869 **Supreme Court (U.S.)**—Associate Justice nominee to die before occupying his seat—E. M. Stanton—died

1889 **Bicycle**—bicycle with a back-pedal brake—patented

1906 **Radio Broadcast**—radio program broadcast—R. A. Fessenden—Bryant Rock, Mass.

1918 **Postage Stamp**—offset-printed postage stamps—1-cent stamp—issued

1936 **Isotope**—radioactive isotope medicine—administered—Berkeley, Calif.

1939 **Newspaper**—offset-printed daily newspaper—*World*—Opelousas, La.—began operations

1946 **Television—Telecast**—church service telecast—Grace Episcopal church, New York City

1948 **Building**—house completely solar-heated—occupied—Dover, Mass.

1948 **Television—Telecast**—Catholic mass (midnight) to be televised—New York City

1951 **Television—Telecast**—opera written for television—*Amahl and the Night Visitors*—New York City

1953 **Television—Telecast**—color and black-and-white telecast to be sponsored—"Dragnet"

1963 **Representative** (U.S.)—representa sworn in before 8:00 A.M.—J. J. Pickl Texas

DECEMBER 25

1723 **Baptist Church**—German Baptists— immersion—Philadelphia, Pa.

1780 **Universalist Church of America**—ch dedicated—Gloucester, Mass.

1818 **Oratorio**—oratorio performance (c plete)—*Messiah*—Boston, Mass.

1894 **Football Team**—midwestern football t to play on the Pacific Coast—San Fran co, Calif.

1917 **Play (drama)**—drama to win a Puli prize—*Why Marry?*—opened—New \ City

1930 **Bobsled Run**—Lake Placid, N.Y.—ope public

1931 **Opera**—opera broadcast in its entirety dio) by the Metropolitan Opera Con ny—*Hansel and Gretel*—New York Ci

1937 **Orchestra**—orchestra (symphony), size, devoted exclusively to radio bro casting—NBC Symphony—New York —debut

1971 **Football Game**—professional foot game to last longer than 80 minute Miami Dolphins vs. Kansas City Chief

DECEMBER 26

1799 **Presidential Eulogy**—Henry Lee

1805 **Art Organization**—art organization—P sylvania Academy of Fine Arts establi —Philadelphia, Pa.

1833 **Annunciator**—patented—Seth Full Boston, Mass.

1854 **Paper**—wood pulp paper—exhibited Beardsley—Buffalo, N.Y.

1862 **Ship**—hospital ship of the U.S. Navy— *Rover*—converted into a hospital ship

1865 **Coffee Percolator Patent**—J. H. Nas Franklin, Mass.

1877 **Socialist Labor Party of North Ameri** national convention—Newark, N.J.

1878 **Electric Lighting**—electric light in a sto installed—Philadelphia, Pa.

1917 **Railroad**—government operation of roads—proclamation made—Wood Wilson

1931 **Play (drama)**—musical play to win a Pu er prize—*Of Thee I Sing*—opened— York City

1945 **Strike**—strike to last longer than a yea I. Case Manufacturing Company, Ra Wis.—strike began

DECEMBER 27

1845 **Anesthesia**—ether administered in c birth—C. W. Long—Jefferson, Ga.

1892 **Psychology Society**—psychology soc

1873 **Weights and Measures Standardization—**national organization to improve systems of weights, measures, and moneys—American Metrological Society—formed—New York City

1887 **Physiology Society—**physiology society national organization—American Physiological Society—formed—New York City

1903 **Political Science Society—**political science association—American Political Science Association—founded—New Orleans, La.

1913 **Crepe—**Crepe Georgette trademark—registered

1913 **Tungsten—**ductile tungsten—patented—W. D. Coolidge—Schenectady, N.Y.

1941 **Ship—**Liberty ship—*Patrick Henry*—delivered—Baltimore, Md.

1954 **Athlete—**black to win the James E. Sullivan Memorial Trophy—M. G. Whitfield

1955 **Army Officer—**Army Medical Specialist Corps male officer—Sheldon Saffren—commissioned

1959 **Submarine—**ballistic missile submarine—*George Washington*—commissioned—Groton, Conn.

1959 **Submarine—**submarine to have 2 complete crews—*George Washington*—commissioned

DECEMBER 31

1776 **Price Regulation Legislation—**price regulation law (colonial)—enacted—Rhode Island

1800 **Book—**book with color plates—*The City of Philadelphia* — published — Philadelphia, Pa.

1830 **Parade—**street parade held by a mystic society—Mobile, Ala.

1841 **Dental Legislation—**legislation (state) garding dental surgery—enacted—bama

1877 **President (U.S.)—**President to celebrate silver wedding anniversary at the W House—R. B. Hayes

1879 **Electric Lighting—**electric incandesc lamp—public demonstration—Menlo P N.J.

1923 **Radio Broadcast—**transatlantic broad of a voice—KDKA—Pittsburgh, Pa.

1934 **Aviation—Pilot—**woman pilot to pilot airmail transport—Helen Richey

1944 **Medal—**Distinguished Service Me (Army) awarded to a woman—O. C. Hol

1948 **Senator (U.S.)—**senator to win a seat had been occupied by his father and m er—Russell Long

1951 **Battery—**battery to convert radioactive ergy into electrical energy—announce P. E. Ohmart

1953 **Jockey—**jockey to ride 400 winners in year—Willie Shoemaker

1954 **Television—Telecast—**dirigible telecas Pasadena, Calif.

1955 **Corporation—**corporation to earn m than $1 billion in one year

1961 **Football Game—**football game to gros million—Green Bay Packers vs. New Y Giants—Green Bay, Wis.

1978 **Bank—**bank with deposits exceeding million—Bank of America National T and Savings Association, San Francis Calif.

1978 **Bank—**bank with resources exceeding million—Bank of America National T and Savings Association, San Francis Calif.

Index to Personal Names

obtain a complete account of the various items, the reader should consult the main body
the text. The **boldface** type shows the alphabetical heading under which each item may
found. If an item appears in the text under a general heading, the specific heading is noted
low after the general heading. The individuals listed in this index are associated in some
y with the events described; they are not necessarily the persons referred to in the
adings.

Adams, John—**Treaty**—treaty between the United States Government and a nation with which it had been at war

Adams, John—**Treaty**—treaty entered into by the United States after the treaty of peace with Great Britain

Adams, John Quincy—**Photograph**—photograph of a former President of the United States at his home

Adams, John Quincy—**President (U.S.)**—President to receive fewer popular votes and electoral votes than an opponent

Adams, John Quincy—**President (U.S.)**—President to translate a German book

Adams, John Quincy—**President (U.S.)**—President whose father had been President

Adams, Mrs. John Quincy—**President (U.S.)**—President whose wife was not born in the United States

Adams, John Quincy—**Representative (U.S.)**—representative who had been a President of the United States

Adams, Joseph Alexander—**Electrotype**—electrotype

Adams, Julius—**Sewage**—sewage "dual system"

Adams, L. S.—**Airmail**—airmail pickup from a steamer at sea

Adams, Nathan—**Federal Home Loan Bank Board**

Adams, Samuel—**Holiday**—Thanksgiving Day celebration (nationwide, colonial)

Adams, Samuel—**Medical Society**—medical society (state)

Adams, Sharon Sites—**Sailing**—woman to sail alone across the Pacific Ocean

Adams, Thomas F.—**Printing Press**—printing press for polychromatic printing

Adams, William Francis—**Ship**—diesel-and-gas-turbine combined-propulsion plant in a major ship

Adamson, John—**Dry Dock Patent**

Adcock, Joe—**Baseball Team**—baseball team to hit 4 consecutive runs in 1 inning

Addams, Jane—**Nobel Prize**—Nobel Peace Prize awarded an American woman

Ader, Barbara—**Horse Race**—horse race parimutuel with an entire field of women jockeys

Adler, Cyrus—**Jewish College**—Jewish nonsectarian college

Adler, Felix—**Ethical Culture Society**

Adler, Max—**Planetarium**—planetarium open to the public

Adler, Peter Herman—**Television—Telecast**—opera (major) televised in color

Adt, John—**Wire**—wire cutting machine and automatic straightener

Affel, Herman A.—**Cable**—coaxial cable

Agassiz, Louis—**Science School**—natural science summer school

Agronsky, Martin—**Supreme Court (U.S.)**—Associate Justice of the Supreme Court to participate in a television program (CBS News interviewer)

Aidala, Arthur—**Prizefight**—prizefight with a purse of $4.5 million (judge)

Aiken, George David—**Presidential Candidate**—woman presidential candidate of a major political party

Aitken, Jane—**Bible**—Bible translated in English in America

Aitken, R.—**Trade Register**

Aitken, Robert—**Bible**—Bible printed in English

Aitken, Robert—**Military Drill Manual**—military drill manual devoted to field strategy

Aitken, Robert—**Money**—$50 gold pieces minted by the United States

Akeley, Carl Ethan—**Taxidermy Method (scultural)**

Akin, Irwin—**Curling Championship (national)**

Akin, William B.—**Map**—automobile road map

Albanese, Licia—**Television—Telecast**—opera (complete) to be televised from the Metropolitan Opera House

Albee, Fred Houdlett—**Medical Clinic**—flying medical clinic

Albin, A.—**Aviation—Flights**—airplane to carry passengers

Albright, Charlene—**Navy**—large-scale assignment of women (other than nurses) to sea duty

Albright, Horace Marden—**Park Service (national)**

Albright, Jacob—**Evangelical Association Council**

Albright, Jacob—**Evangelical Church**

Albright, Jacob—**Evangelical Conference**

Albright, Tenley—**Ice Skating Champion**—American world figure skating champion

Albrizio, Conrad—**Art Course**—art course

Alcock, John—**Aviation—Flights (transatlantic)**—transatlantic nonstop flight from America

Alcott, William Andrus—**Physiology Society**—physiology society

Alda, Robert—**Television—Telecast**—color program (commercial)

Alden, J. T.—**Yeast**—yeast preparation patent

Alden, Timothy—**Typesetting Machine**—typesetting machine

Alden, William Livingston—**Canoe Association**

Aldrin, Edwin Eugene, Jr.—**Astronaut**—astronauts (American) to land on the moon

Aldrin, Edwin Eugene, Jr.—**Photograph**—photograph of an eclipse of the sun taken from the atmosphere

Aldrin, Edwin Eugene, Jr.—**Radio Telephone**—telephone call to the moon

Ale, Fern—**Woman**—woman secretary of a state senate

Aleichem, Sholom—**Play (drama)**—musical to run for more than 3,000 performances

Alexander, Ben—**Television—Telecast**—color and black-and-white telecast to be sponsored

Alexander, Charles M.—**Aviation—Parachute**—parachute jumper snagged in midair

Alexander, Clifford Leopold, Jr.—**Army Officer**—Secretary of the Army (black)

Alexander, Harry Louis—**Medical Periodical**—allergy magazine

Alexander, Lucy Maclay—**Medal**—Agriculture Department distinguished service gold medal presented to a woman

Anders, William Alison—**Television—Telecast**—outer-space live telecast from a manned spacecraft

Anderson, Alexander—**Engraving**—wood engraving made with an engraving tool

Anderson, Broncho Billy. *See* Aronson, Max

Anderson, Carl David—**Physics**—positron

Anderson, Charles Alfred—**Aviation—Flights (transcontinental)**—transcontinental flight made by blacks in their own plane

Anderson, Ellie Mae—**Submarine**—ballistic missile submarine

Anderson, Eugenie—**Diplomatic Service**—ambassador (woman)

Anderson, Eugenie Moore (Mrs. John Pierce Anderson)—**Diplomatic Service**—ambassador (woman) to a communist bloc nation

Anderson, Eugenie—**Treaty**—treaty signed by a woman ambassador

Anderson, G. M. *See* Aronson, Max

Anderson, Garland—**Play (drama)**—full-length play by a black performed in New York City

Anderson, George K.—**Typewriter Ribbon**—typewriter ribbon patent

Anderson, Humphrey Stevenson—**Baseball Game**—intercollegiate baseball game

Anderson, James—**Newspaper**—newspaper published at sea

Anderson, James, Jr.—**Medal**—Medal of Honor to a Marine (black) in the Vietnam war

Anderson, John—**Television—Telecast**—debate (nationally telecast) among candidates within a political party for the presidential nomination

Anderson, Kris—**Balloon—Flights**—transcontinental nonstop balloon flight

Anderson, Laurie B.—**Secret Service**—Secret Service women agents

Anderson, Lester E.—**Aquanaut**—United States Navy divers to submerge 10 days

Anderson, Louis Francis—**College**—dean of men

Anderson, Marian—**Medal**—Medal of Freedom awarded to a black woman

Anderson, Marian—**Opera**—black singer of the Metropolitan Opera

Anderson, Marian—**Submarine**—nuclear submarine named for a black (christened ship)

Anderson, Marian—**Treasury Department (U.S.)**—gold medallions issued by the Treasury Department

Anderson, Mary—**Labor Department (U.S.)**—Women's Bureau

Anderson, Max. *See* Aronson, Max

Anderson, Maxie Leroy—**Ballon—Flights**—transcontinental nonstop balloon flight

Anderson, Orvil A.—**Balloon—Flights**—balloon flight to exceed an altitude of 70,000 feet

Anderson, Paul—**Weight Lifter**—weight lifter to lift more than 6,000 pounds

Anderson, Richard Clough—**Conference**—conference of American republics

Anderson, Richard Clough—**Diplomatic Service**—ministers plenipotentiary to South and Central America

Anderson, Richard Clough—**Treaty**—treaty w a South American country

Anderson, Robert—**Civil War**—act that mark the inauguration of the War of 1861–65

Anderson, William Robert—**Submarine**—subm rine submerged for 2 weeks

Anderson, Violette Neatly—**Lawyer**—bla woman lawyer to practice before the Unit States Supreme Court

Anderson, William Robert—**Submarine**—subm rine crossing of the North Pole underwater

Anderson, Willie—**Golf Tournament**—prof sional open championship

Andrew, John Albion—**Unitarian Church Conve tion (national)**

Andrews, Ann—**Television—Telecast**—curre Broadway play to be telecast with its origir cast

Andrews, Ebenezer T.—**Gazetteer**—Americ gazetteer

Andrews, Jedidiah—**Presbyterian Presbytery**

Andrews, William—**Book**—Book of Comm Prayer (in the Mohawk Indian language)

Angell, James Rowland—**Radio Broadcast**—d ner broadcast around the world

Angle, Edward Hartley—**Dental Society**—orth dontists' society

Anne, queen of the Pamunkey tribe of Virginia **American Indians**—American Indian ch (woman)

Anson, Adrian Constantine—**Baseball Team** professional league baseball team to win thr pennants in succession

Antheil, George—**Symphony**—symphonic wo to call for an airplane propeller

Anther, Georg—**Opera**—opera composed by woman performed at the Metropolitan Ope House

Anthony, Earl—**Bowler**—bowler to earn $100,0 in 1 year in tournaments

Anthony, Edward—**Photograph**—photograp used in surveying

Anthony, Susan Brownell—**Money**—wom commemorated on a circulating U.S. coin

Anthony, Susan Brownell—**Temperance Socie** —women's temperance society (state)

Anthony, Susan Brownell—**Woman Suffrage** woman suffrage associations (national)

Anthony, William Arnold—**Dynamo**—dynar for a direct-current outdoor lighting system

Apache Ben—**American Indian Church**—chur organized by American Indians

Appert, François—**Canning Book**

Applebaum, Saul Bezalel—**Television—Teleca** —Passover services telecast (rabbi who cc ducted seder)

Appleton, Edward—**Railroad Commission (stat**

Appleton, Nathan—**Cotton Mill**—cotton mill the world in which the whole process of cott manufacturing from spinning to weaving w carried on by power

Appleton, Nathaniel Walker—**Medical Society** medical society (state)

ird, Spencer Fullerton—**Fish and Fisheries Commissioner**

ird, Spencer Fullerton—**Fish Protection**—fish protection office (federal)

ker, Belle—**Radio Broadcast**—radio broadcast from a moving train of a regular program on a national network

ker, Bernard Nadel—**Shipping**—United States Shipping Board

ker, Edward Dickinson—**Senator (U.S.)**—senator in military uniform to address the Senate

ker, Elisha—**Dental Periodical**—dental journal

ker, Ellis Benjamin—**Telephone**—coin telephone

ker, Eugene Voy—**Football Game**—intercollegiate football championship

ker, Howard, Jr.—**Television—Telecast**—debate (nationally telecast) among candidates within a political party for the presidential nomination

ker, Newton Diehl—**Medal**—Distinguished Service Medal awarded to a woman

ker, Newton Diehl—**Nursing School**—Army school of nursing

ker, Richard—**Monastery**—Zen Buddhist monastery

ker, Richard Freligh—**Photograph**—photograph of genes

ker, Sara Josephine—**Child Hygiene Bureau**

ker, Sue A.—**Secret Service**—Secret Service women agents

ker, Thomas M.—**Health Department**—county health department organized on a full-time basis

laca, R.—**Postage Stamp**—paintings depicted on postage stamps

lbo, Italo—**Aviation—Flights (transatlantic)**—transatlantic foreign squadron flight to the United States

lch, Emily Greene—**Fellowship**—fellowship (graduate) awarded by a women's college

lch, William—**Naval Officer**—naval chaplain

lchen, Bernt—**Aviation—Airplane**—airplane equipped with radio to cross the Atlantic Ocean

lchen, Bernt—**Aviation—Flights**—South Pole flight

lcom, Homer Gage—**Building**—building higher than 1,250 feet

ldasare, Fred—**Swimmer**—American to swim the English Channel underwater

ldwin, Caroline Willard—**Degrees (academic and honorary)**—Doctor of Science degree earned by a woman

ldwin, Cyrus W.—**Elevator**—elevator patent, for a vertical-geared hydraulic electric elevator

ldwin, David J.—**Freemasons**—Masonic lodge organized in the Indian Territory

ldwin, James Fowle—**Engineering Society**—engineering society

ldwin, John—**Abolition Society**

ldwin, Loammi—**Dry Dock**—federal dry docks

ldwin, Luke—**Rubber**—rubber company

ldwin, Simeon Eben—**Aviation—Legislation**—aviation legislation (state)

Baldwin, Simeon Eben—**Lawyers' Association**—lawyers' association (national)

Baldwin, Thomas Scott—**Aviation—Airship**—dirigible balloon contracted for by the United States Government

Baldwin, Thomas Scott—**Aviation—Airship**—dirigible circular flight

Balfour, George—**Naval Officer**—naval surgeon of the U.S. Navy

Ball, Cornelius ("Neal")—**Baseball Game**—triple play unassisted in a modern major-league game

Ball, Sarah B.—**Library**—business library supported by taxes

Ballantyne, William—**Aviation**—aeronautical stowaway

Ballenger, Edgar Garrison—**Photograph**—cystoscopic photographs in color

Ballentine, John Jennings—**Ship**—ship from which a long-range rocket was launched

Ballester, Paul de—**Greek Orthodox Church**—Greek Orthodox Church bishop who had converted from the Roman Catholic Church

Balley, Jacqueline P.—**Marshal**—marshals of the United States (women)

Balsley, H. Clyde—**Aviation—Pilot**—American pilot shot down in World War I

Bancroft, Aaron—**Historical Society**—historical society (national)

Bancroft, Aaron—**Unitarian Church**—national organization of the Unitarian Churches of the United States and Canada

Bancroft, George—**Gymnasium**—gymnasium to offer systematic instruction

Bancroft, Jane M.—**Fellowship**—resident fellowship for women awarded by a women's college

Bancroft, Priscilla—**Births**—sextuplets

Bandmann, Julius—**Dynamite**

Bane, Mary E.—**Marine Corps**—woman unit commander to direct 2,000 men

Banks, Arthur J.—**Aviation—License**—airplane instructor's license

Banky, Vilma—**Radio Facsimile Transmission**—motion picture film transmitted by telephone wire

Banneker, Benjamin—**Clock**—clock to strike the hours

Bannister, Marion Glass—**Treasury Department (U.S.)**—woman assistant treasurer of the United States

Banvard, John—**Chromo**

Baptist, John—**Boat Club**—boat club

Baragrey, John—**Television—Telecast**—drama series regularly scheduled

Barber, Charles E.—**Money**—commemorative coinage

Barber, Miller—**Golfer**—golfer to earn $100,000 in a contest

Barber, "Red" (Walter Lanier Barber)—**Radio Broadcast**—football game championship (professional) broadcast on a network

Barber, "Red" (Walter Lanier Barber)—**Television—Telecast**—baseball games televised in color

Beard, Thomas—**Shoe**

Beardsley, John—**Paper**—wood-pulp paper

Beasy, Peter—**Curling Championship (national)**

Beatty, Charles—**Fire**—fire in a mine

Beatty, Charles—**Holiday**—Thanksgiving Day sermon

Beatty, James Tully ("Jim")—**Runner**—runner to run a mile indoors in less than 4 minutes

Beatty, Martin—**Oil**—oil well (flowing)

Beaty, J. H. M.—**Textile School**—textile school in a college

Beaumont, William—**Physiologist**

Beaver, Walter S.—**Trapshooting Tournament**—trapshoot (Grand American) with clay targets

Beck, Charles—**Gymnasium**—to offer systematic instruction

Beck, Claude Schaeffer—**Surgical Operation**—heart operation for the relief of angina pectoris

Beck, Clifford Keith—**Nuclear Engineering College Course**

Beck, Dorothy Wright Miller (Mrs. Thomas Hambly Beck)—**Ship**—Victory ship launched

Beck, Paul Eugene—**Music Instruction**—state supervisor of music

Beck, Paul N.—**Aviation—School**—airplane flying school

Beck, Theodoric Romeyn—**Medical Book**—medical jurisprudence treatise (authoritative)

Beck, Mrs. Thomas Hambly. *See* Beck, Dorothy Wright Miller

Becker, Peter—**Baptist Church**—German Baptists

Becker, Samuel—**Evangelical Conference**

Becket, Welton—**Building**—circular office building

Beckley, John James—**Congress (U.S.)—House of Representatives**—House of Representatives

Beckley, John James—**Congress (U.S.)—House of Representatives**—clerk of the House of Representatives

Beckley, John—**Librarian**—Librarian of Congress

Beckwith, G.—**Ferryboat**—double-deck ferryboat

Bedell, Catherine May—**Tariff**—tariff commission woman chairman

Beebe, Richard—**Ordnance**—muskets

Beecher, Henry Ward—**Premium**—premiums given by publishers

Beekman, James—**Greenhouse**

Beers, Alanson—**Colonial Government**—government on the Pacific Coast

Beers, John B.—**Dentistry**—patent for a gold crown

Beissel, Johann Conrad—**Communistic Society**—communistic society

Beissel, Johann Conrad—**German Book**—German book printed in America

Belcher, Jonathan—**Freemasons**—Mason (native-born)

Belfer, Ben William—**Degrees (academic and honorary)**—Master of Arts degree in Sacred Music

Belkin, Saul—**College**—college for women under Jewish auspices

Belknap, Jeremy—**Historical Society**—historical society (state)

Belknap, Morris B.—**File Manufacturing Mach**

Belknap, William Worth—**Fair**—centennial c bration

Bell, Alexander Graham—**Deaf—School**—oral struction for the deaf

Bell, Alexander Graham—**Phonograph**—pho graph that was practical

Bell, Alexander Graham—**Telephone**—inters telephone call

Bell, Alexander Graham—**Telephone**—teleph conversation over out-of-door wires

Bell, Alexander Graham—**Telephone**—teleph message

Bell, Alexander Graham—**Telephone**—teleph patent

Bell, Alexander Graham—**Telephone**—teleph used by a railroad company

Bell, Alexander Graham—**Telephone**—transc tinental telephone demonstration

Bell, Bernard L.—**World War II**—American b bardier over German occupied territory

Bell, Bobby—**Television—Telecast**—prizefigh a "studio"

Bell, Charles Heffelfinger—**Television—Tele** —stockholders' meetings televised coast coast simultaneously

Bell, Chichester—**Phonograph**—phonograph was practical

Bell, John—**Constitutional Union Party**

Bell, John—**Medical Book**—hydrotherapy b (American)

Bell, Robert—**Architecture Book**—architect book printed in America

Bell, Robert Mowry—**Esperanto Course**—peranto course carrying college credit

Bellamy, Joseph—**Novel**—novel (full-length)

Bellamy, Ralph—**Television—Telecast**—c program on coast-to-coast network commer

Bellamy, Ralph—**Television—Telecast**—pay gram

Bellew, Frank Henry Temple—**Cartoon**—"U Sam" cartoon

Bellinger, Patrick Nelson Lynch—**Aviation**—g scope automatic stabilization

Bellingham, Samuel—**Degrees (academic honorary)**—Bachelor of Arts degree

Bellini, Carlo—**Language Instruction**—Italia struction in a college

Bellonte, Maurice—**Aviation—Flights (transa tic)**—transatlantic nonstop flight from Europ the United States

Bellow, Saul—**Nobel Prize**—Nobel Prize win all from one country in 5 categories

Bellows, Henry Adams—**Radio Commis (U.S.)**

Belmont, Raymond—**Polo**—international pol ries

Belshe, Thomas—**President (U.S.)**—preside. airplane (turbo-compound-powered)

Benedict, William Pershing—**Aviation—Fligh** North Pole landing by an airplane at the graphic pole

Benedict, Zadoc—**Hat Factory**

Biard, Pierre—**War (colonial)**—colonial warfare between Great Britain and France for the possession of the United States

Biardot, Alphonse—**Soup Company**

Biardot, Ernest—**Soup Company**

Biardot, Octave—**Soup Company**

Bibb, William Wyatt—**Money**—coin bearing the portrait of a living person

Bickford, William—**Fuse**—safety fuse

Biddle, Nicholas—**Flag**—American flag saluted by a foreigner

Biddle, Nicholas—**Navy**—naval fleet

Bidwell, George R.—**Bicycle Tire**—bicycle tire (pneumatic)

Biedenbach, Charles Louis—**High School**—junior high school system

Bigelow, Charles D.—**Shoe Pegging Machine**

Bigelow, Erastus Brigham—**Carpet Loom**—carpet power loom

Bigelow, Erastus Brigham—**Carpet Loom**—carpet power loom to weave ingrain carpet

Bigelow, Erastus Brigham—**Gingham Factory**

Bigelow, Timothy—**Historical Society**—historical society (national)

Biggs, Hermann Michael—**Bacteriology Laboratory**—bacteriology diagnostic laboratory

Biggs, Hermann Michael—**Tuberculosis Circular**

Biggs, Hermann Michael—**Tuberculosis Laboratory**—tuberculosis diagnostic community laboratory

Biggs, John—**Judge**—black judge of a circuit court of appeals

Biggs, John F.—**Federal Crop Insurance Corporation**

Biggs, Wayne—**Motel**—horse motel

Bigley, Isabel—**Television—Telecast**—color program (commercial)

Billings, Frank—**Hospital**—interracial hospital

Billings, William—**Music**—war song

Billings, William—**Music Book**—music composition book

Billingsley, William Devotie—**Aviation—Airplane Fatalities**—airplane fatality (U.S. Navy)

Billington, George—**Bank**—savings bank actually to receive money on deposit

Billington, John—**Execution**—execution in America

Billmeyer, Michael—**Music Book**—Lutheran hymnbook (German) published in America

Bingham, A. B.—**War (1812)**—naval battle

Bingham, Caleb—**Library**—youth's library

Bingham, Robert Worth—**Degrees (academic and honorary)**—American awarded honorary degrees from three of England's leading universities

Bingham, William—**Road**—macadam road

Binney, Horace—**Horticultural Society**—horticultural society (permanent)

Binney, Horace—**Library**—mechanics' library

Binns, John—**Newspaper**—democratic newspaper

Binny, Archibald—**Dollar Marks**

Binny, Archibald—**Type Specimen Book**

Biow, Milton—**Television—Telecast**—sales me ing televised

Bird, Robert Montgomery—**Play (drama)**—p performed 1,000 times

Birdsong, George Purnell—**Aviation—Flig (transatlantic)**—jet transatlantic nonstop fli west–east

Birney, Alice McLellan—**Parent-Teacher Asso tion**—parent-teacher association (national)

Birney, Charles O.—**Streetcar**—lightweight o man streetcar

Birney, James Gillespie—**Antislavery Party**

Bishop, Bainbridge—**Organ**—color organ

Bishop, David Wolfe—**Automobile Race**—tomobile race (long-distance)

Bishop, Katherine Cott—**Vitamin**—vitamin E

Bishop, Max Frederick—**Baseball Game**—ba ball game in which there were two triple-ste

Bishop, Nathaniel Holmes—**Canoe Associatio**

Bishop, Samuel—**Money**—copper cents min by a state

Bispham, David—**Opera**—opera composed b woman performed at the Metropolitan Op House

Bissell, Daniel—**Medal**—Order of the Pur Heart

Bissell, Emily Perkins—**Seal**—Christmas seal the modern variety sold to raise funds to f tuberculosis

Bissell, George Henry—**Oil**—oil company

Bissell, Melville Reuben—**Carpet Sweeper**

Bittencourt, Amaro Soares—**Medal**—Legion Merit Medal awarded to a foreign national

Bitterman, Mary Foley—**Woman**—woman di tor of the Voice of America

Black, Alexander—**Magic Lantern**—magic tern feature show

Black, Frank Swett—**Forestry School**—fore school of collegiate character

Black, Hugo LaFayette—**Supreme Court (U.S** Associate Justice of the Supreme Court to ticipate in a television program

Black, J. W.—**Photograph**—aerial photograph

Black, James—**Prohibition Party** (national)

Black, Robert Glennwood—**Navy**—atomic s marine division

Black, Shirley Temple—**State Department (U** —protocol chief (woman)

Black, William Henry—**Animals**—cattle (A cander cattle)

Blackfan, Joseph H.—**Civil Service**—Civil Ser Commission

Blackford, Isaac—**Court**—court of claims

Blackton, James Stuart—**Motion Picture**—anir ed cartoon

Blackwell, Antoinette Brown—**Woman**—wo ordained a minister

Blackwell, Edward—**Fencing Book**

Blackwell, Elizabeth—**Hospital**—women's i mary staffed by women physicians

Blackwell, Elizabeth—**Physician**—woman ph cian

Blackwell, Emily—**Hospital**—women's infirm staffed by women physicians

Boger, Frederick—**Optometry Society**—optometry society (national)

Boggs, Corinne Claiborne ("Lindy")—**Representative (U.S.)**—congressional candidate elected while "missing" (elected in his stead)

Boggs, Thomas Hale—**Representative (U.S.)**—congressional candidate elected while "missing"

Bohne, William—**Optometry Society**—optometry society (national)

Bohune, Lawrence—**Physician**—doctor in the colony of Virginia

Boland, Frederick Henry—**Satellite**—communications satellite successfully placed in orbit

Bolin, Jane Matilda—**Judge**—woman judge (black)

Bolívar, Simón—**Conference**—conference of American Republics

Bolles, Frank—**Cooperative**—college cooperative store

Bolles, Jenette Hubbard—**Medical Periodical**—osteopathy magazine

Bolles, Jenette Hubbard—**Physician**—osteopath (woman)

Bolling, William—**Deaf—School**—oral school for the deaf (still existing)

Bolster, Calvin—**Aviation—Passenger**—dirigible passenger transfer to an airplane

Bolt, John F.—**Marine Corps**—Marine Corps jet ace

Bolter, James—**Insurance**—accident insurance policy

Bolton, Elmer K.—**Rubber**—synthetic rubber produced on a commercial scale

Bolton, Frances Payne—**Representative (U.S.)**—mother and son simultaneously elected to Congress

Bolton, John—**Glass**—stained figure glass

Bolton, Oliver Payne—**Representative (U.S.)**—mother and son simultaneously elected to Congress

Bolton, William Jay—**Glass**—stained figure glass

Bonaparte, Charles Joseph—**College**—Catholic college for women

Bond, Julian—**Political Convention**—national nominating convention to propose blacks for the offices of both President and Vice President

Bond, Thomas—**Hospital**—hospital in America

Bond, William Cranch—**Photograph**—photograph of a star

Bonelli, Richard—**Opera**—opera broadcast over a national network from an American opera house

Bonelli, Richard—**Television—Telecast**—opera telecast

Bonner, James—**Town**—town named for George Washington

Bonstelle, Jessie—**Theater**—municipal theater

Bonwill, William Gibson Arlington—**Dental Mallet**—dental mallet

Bonzano, John—**International Eucharistic Congress**—in America

Booth, Elizabeth—**Salvation Army**—woman commander of the Salvation Army

Booth, Evangeline—**Medal**—Distinguished S vice Medal awarded to a woman

Booth, James Curtis—**Chemistry Laborator** chemical laboratory

Booth, Mary Louise—**Periodical**—fashion wee

Booth, Oliver—**Ice Yacht**

Booth, Shirley—**Television—Telecast**—Acade of Motion Picture Arts and Sciences ann awards telecast

Booth, William—**Salvation Army**

Borcherdt, Victor—**Zoological Garden**—bar zoological garden of naturalistic rock constr tion

Bordelon, Guy—**Aviation—Pilot**—naval ace Korea

Borden, Gail—**Cracker**—meat biscuit

Borden, Gail—**Medal**—medal awarded to American food producer

Borden, Gail—**Milk**—condensed milk (comr cial)

Borden, Joseph Emley—**Baseball Game**—no nine-inning baseball game

Borden, Joseph Emley—**Baseball League**— tional League

Borden, Simeon—**Geodetic Survey**

Boren, Horace C.—**Tour of the World**—passer to fly around the world on commercial airl in less than 100 hours

Borgfeldt, Nicholas H.—**Snow-melting Appar** —snow-melting apparatus

Borman, Frank—**Astronaut**—astronauts (An can) to land at night

Borman, Frank—**Astronaut**—astronauts (An can) to orbit the earth

Borman, Frank—**Astronaut**—astronauts (An can) to orbit the earth 200 times

Borman, Frank—**Astronaut**—astronauts (An can) to rendezvous in space *(Gemini VII)*

Borman, Frank—**Television—Telecast**—o space live telecast from a manned spacec

Borsch, Henry—**Optometry Society**—optom society (national)

Bosenberg, Henry F.—**Patent**—plant patent

Bosley, Tom—**Television—Telecast**—motion ture premiere telecast on 2 successive nig

Bostwick, A. C.—**Automobile**—automobile to ceed the speed of a mile a minute

Boswell, William—**Censorship**—state boar censorship on literature

Botetourt, Lord—**College**—college to confer r als as prizes

Bottomley, James Le Roy—**Baseball Play** baseball player (major league) to bat in 12 in a 9-inning game

Botts, John Minor—**Impeachment**—impeachr proceedings attempt against a President o United States

Bouchard, Emile—**Television**—television eye ness allowed to testify in a federal court

Bouchet, Edward Alexander—**Degrees (acad and honorary)**—Doctor of Philosophy de awarded to a black

Bouck, Zeh—**Aviation—Flights**—New York-muda flight

Bradford, William—**Tax**—property tax law (colonial)

Bradley, Basil G.—**Medal**—Distinguished Flying Cross

Bradley, Henry W.—**Oleomargarine**—oleomargarine patent

Bradley, Omar Nelson—**Army Officer**—woman army officer

Bradley, Willis Winter, Jr.—**Representative (U.S.)**—representative who had a Medal of Honor and was graduated from the U.S. Naval Academy

Bradstreet, Anne Dudley—**Author**—woman author

Brady, Mathew B.—**Money**—coin bearing the portrait of a President

Brady, Mathew B.—**Photograph**—news photographs of distinction

Brady, Mathew B.—**Photograph**—photograph of a President (in office)

Bragg, Walter Lawrence—**Interstate Commerce Act**

Braham, Horace—**Television—Telecast**—play to be televised as a full-hour program

Braidwood, John—**Deaf—School**—oral school for the deaf (still existing)

Brainard, John—**American Indian Reservation**—American Indian reservation (state)

Brallier, John K.—**Football Game**—professional football game

Brand, Bernie—**Dance Marathon**—dance marathon to last longer than 200 hours

Brand, Charles John—**Agriculture Department (U.S.)**—Office of Markets

Brand, Vance Devoe—**Astronaut**—astronauts (American) to participate in an international spaceflight (command module pilot)

Brandeis, Louis Dembitz—**Insurance**—savings bank life insurance

Brandeis, Louis Dembitz—**Supreme Court (U.S.)**—associate justice of the Supreme Court who was Jewish

Brantley, William Theophilus—**College**—city college

Branzell, Karin—**Opera**—opera matinee at the Metropolitan Opera House

Brattain, Walter Houser—**Transistor**—transistor

Brattle, William—**Degrees (academic and honorary)**—Doctor of Sacred Theology degree

Brattle, William—**Logic Book**

Bray, John Randolph—**Motion Picture**—animated cartoon (present technique)

Bray, Thomas—**Library**—library

Brayton, George B.—**Streetcar**—gas-powered streetcar

Brazzil, Ruth—**Supreme Court (state)**—state supreme court composed entirely of women

Brearley, William Henry—**Newspaper**—newspaper association

Brébeuf, Jean de. *See* De Brébeuf, Jean

Breckinridge, John—**Nullification Proceedings**

Breedlove, Lee Ann Roberts—**Automobile Driver**—woman automobile driver to exceed the speed of 300 m.p.h.

Breese, Edmund—**Play (drama)**—drama to wi[n] Pulitzer Prize

Breese, James Lawrence—**Aviation—Flig[ht] (transatlantic)**—transatlantic hydroplane fli[ght]

Brehant de Galinée, René de—**Oil**—oil spring

Brehm, George O.—**Soilless Culture of Plant[s]** commercial hydroponicum built on the roo[f]

Breill, Frank ("Pop")—**Bowling Tournamen[t]** bowling tournament sponsored by the Am[eri]can Bowling Congress

Breitbart, Charles H.—**Medical Legislatio[n]** blood grouping test laws (state)

Brennan, Francis (James)—**Catholic Pries[t]** Catholic priest called to the Sacred Roman R[ota]

Brenner, Victor David—**Money**—coin bearing portrait of a President

Brenon, Herbert—**Motion Picture**—motion pic[ture] sex shocker (director)

Brent, Margaret—**Woman Suffrage**—wo[man] suffrage advocate

Brent, Theodore—**Shipping**—United States S[hip]ping Board

Bres, Elizabeth W.—**Navy**—large-scale assi[gn]ment of women (other than nurses) to sea d[uty]

Brewer, Catherine E.—**College**—women's coll[ege] chartered

Brewer, Charles A.—**Punchboards**

Brewer, Joseph—**College**—college to dispe[nse] with the system of credits, hours, points, gra[des] etc.

Brewer, Lucy—**Marine Corps**—woman marin[e]

Brewer, Margaret Ann—**Marine Corps**—gen[eral] (woman) in the Marine Corps

Brewster, Nathaniel—**Degrees (academic honorary)**—Bachelor of Arts degree

Brewster, Sackford—**Expedition**—expedition

Brewster, William—**Congregational Church**

Brice, Arthur T.—**Television—Telecast**—ph[ase] contrast cinemicrography film (Ameri[can] made) telecast

Brickman, Arthur Otto—**Swedenborgian or N[ew] Church**—German Swedenborgian Society

Bridgeman, Thomas—**Gardener's Manual**

Bridgers, Frank Hillman—**Building**—commer[cial] building heated by the sun

Bridges, Marshall—**Baseball Team**—base[ball] team to hit 4 consecutive runs in 1 inning

Bridges, Robert—**Iron**—iron works (successf[ul]

Brigden, Zechariah—**College Student**—col[lege] student to work his way through college

Briggs, Emilie Grace—**Theological School**—P[res]byterian theological seminary woman grad[uate]

Briggs, Emily Edson—**News Corresponde[nt]** woman news correspondent accredited to [the] White House

Briggs, Isaac—**Ship**—steamboat patent

Briggs, Matt—**Television—Telecast**—play t[o] televised as a full-hour program

Briggs, Nathaniel—**Washing Machine**—was[hing] machine patent

Briggs, Samuel, Jr.—**Patent**—patent granted j[oint]ly to a father and son

Briggs, Samuel, Sr.—**Patent**—patent granted j[oint]ly to a father and son

Brown, Samuel Robbins—**College**—educational institution exclusively for women

Brown, Saul—**Jewish Congregation**—Jewish congregation

Brown, Solyman—**Dental Book**—orthodontia treatise

Brown, Solyman—**Dental Periodical**—dental journal

Brown, Solyman—**Dental Society**—dental society (local)

Brown, Thomas—**Postal Service**—mailbox locker

Brown, Virginia Mae (Mrs. James V. Brown)—**Interstate Commerce Commission**—independent administrative agency of the federal government woman member

Brown, Virginia Mae—**Woman**—woman independent federal administrative agency chairman

Brown, W. R.—**Horse Race**—300-mile endurance run

Brown, Warren Wentworth—**Television Receiver**—television receiver in a private railroad car

Brown, Wesley Anthony—**Naval Academy**—black midshipman in the U.S. Naval Academy to graduate

Brown, William—**Medal**—Order of the Purple Heart

Brown, William—**Pharmacopoeia**—pharmacopoeia

Brown, William Henry—**Yacht Race**—yacht race (international)

Brown, William Hill—**Novel**—American novel published in America

Brown, William Montgomery—**Heresy Trial of a bishop**

Brown, William Wells—**Novel**—novel by a black

Browne, Cheryl Adrenne—**Beauty Pageant**—black contestant in the Miss America pageant

Browne, Joseph—**Medical Book**—medical book for army medical use

Browne, William W.—**Bank**—bank for blacks operated by blacks

Brownell, George Loomis—**Paper Twine Machinery**

Brownell, Herbert—**Cabinet (U.S.)**—Cabinet conference telecast

Brownice, John—**Television—Telecast**—opera from the Metropolitan Opera House especially tailored and trimmed for television

Brownie, Leon—**Shooting Gallery (mechanized)**

Bruce, Archibald—**Mineralogy Periodical**

Bruce, Blanche Kelso—**Senator (U.S.)**—black senator to preside over the Senate

Bruce, Blanche Kelso—**Senator (U.S.)**—black senator to serve a full term

Bruce, Blanche Kelso—**Treasury Department (U.S.)**—Register of the Treasury who was a black

Bruce, David—**Stereotype**—stereotypers

Bruce, George—**Patent**—design patent

Bruce, George—**Stereotype**—stereotypers

Bruce, Nigel—**Motion Picture**—three-dimensional feature motion picture

Bruce, Philip Alexander—**Play (drama)**—p given by nonprofessional actors

Brucker, Wilber Marion—**Atomic Reactor**—n tary nuclear power plant

Brucker, Wilber Marion—**Flag**—Army flag (cial)

Brundin, Ernest Walfrid—**Soilless Culture Plants**—commercial hydroponicum (large)

Brunel, Isambard Kingdom—**Ship**—steamb service (regular) across the Atlantic

Brunner, Edward—**College**—university for bla (Catholic)

Brunschweyler, John—**Wedding**—double ra wedding

Brush, Charles Francis—**Electric Lighting**—e tric arc lights

Bryan, Hiram—**Horse Race**—night harness ra

Bryan, Otis Frank—**Aviation—Flights (transco nental)**—transcontinental commercial o night transport service

Bryan, William—**Cooperative**—consumers' cc erative society

Bryan, William Jennings—**Motion Picture**—pr dential candidate shown in motion picture

Bryan, William Jennings—**Presidential Candic**—presidential candidate to ride in an auto bile

Bryan, William Jennings—**Silverites**

Bryant, Alice Gertrude—**Medical Societ** women members of the American College Surgeons

Bryant, Charles—**Petroleum**—Petroleum exp ed to Europe

Bryant, Gridley—**Railroad**—railroad for fre transportation to celebrate its centenary

Bryant, Ralph Clement—**Forestry School**— estry school of collegiate character

Bryant, William Cullen—**Poem**—poem by American to receive recognition at home abroad

Bryner, Vera—**Television—Telecast**—opera (jor) televised in color

Buchanan, Franklin—**Naval Academy**—Na Academy (U.S.)

Buchanan, Franklin—**Ship**—destroyer of the Navy named for a Confederate officer

Buchanan, Franklin—**Ship**—naval ship ch tened by a woman (first captain)

Buchanan, James—**Cable (telegraph)**—ca across the Atlantic Ocean completed

Buchanan, James—**Copyright Law**—photogra copyright law (signed by)

Buchanan, James—**President (U.S.)**—Presi who was a bachelor

Bucher, Lloyd Mark—**Ship**—naval ship to sur der in peacetime without a fight (commande ship)

Buck, Dudley Allen—**Cryotrons**—publicly rep ed

Buck, John Kill—**Treaty**—treaty entered into the United States with American Indian tr

Buck, Pearl Sydenstricker—**Nobel Prize**—N Prize in literature to a woman

Buck, Solon Justus—**Archival Course**

cke, Mr.—**Legislative Assembly**

ckley, Oliver E.—**Telephone**—dial-telephone
ong distance service

ckner, Simon Bolivar—**Election Law**—Australi-
n ballot system

cknill, John Charles—**Medical Book**—psycho-
ogical medicine modern textbook

dge, Don (John Donald Budge)—**Athlete**—two-
ime winner of the Associated Press Athlete of
he Year award

dge, Don (John Donald Budge)—**Tennis Player**
—lawn tennis champion to win four major titles

ll, Abel—**Gem-cutting Machine**

ll, Abel—**Money**—Continental coin

ll, Abel—**Type Foundry**—type foundry

falo Bill. *See* Cody, William Frederick

ord, Wallace Abbott—**War (French Indo-
hina)**—American civilian pilot wounded in In-
ochina

ie, Elizabeth—**Streptomycin**

keley, Morgan Gardner—**Baseball League**—
National League

kley, John—**Degrees (academic and honorary)**
—Bachelor of Arts degree

l, C. M.—**Squash Club**—squash tennis organi-
ation (national)

l, Dixie—**Pirate**

l, Lucius—**Library**—mercantile library

l, Walter L.—**Medal**—Expert Infantryman's
adge

l, William—**Physician**—American-born doctor

l, William—**Slavery**—insurrection of black
aves

l, William Tillinghast—**Hospital**—cancer hos-
ital

ard, William Hannum Grubb—**Radio Com-
ission (U.S.)**

itt, William Christian—**Diplomatic Service**—
mbassador to the Union of Soviet Socialist
epublics

lock, William—**Printing Press**—printing press
o use a continuous web or roll of paper

che, Ralph Johnson—**Nobel Prize**—black
merican to win the Nobel Peace Prize

che, Ralph Johnson—**State Department (U.S.)**
—State Department (U.S.) black official

dy, Willard L.—**Time Recorder**—employees'
me recorder

ker, Chang and Eng—**Siamese Twins**

ker, Ellsworth—**Diplomatic Service**—ambas-
adors in service to wed

ker, Frank Forest—**High School**—junior high
chool system

ker, William—**Prison**—prison

ting, Mary Ingraham—**Atomic Energy Com-
ission**—Atomic Energy Commission woman
ember

anelli, (Albert) Prosper—**Crossword Puzzle
ook**

ba, Alexander—**Lithuanian Church**

bank, Asa—**College Alumni Association**—col-
ge alumni association

chard, Anson W.—**Arbitration Association**—
rbitration association

Burchfield, Charles Ephraim—**Medal**—American
Academy of Arts and Letters–National Institute
of Arts and Letters gold medal

Burden, Henry—**Horseshoe Manufacturing Machine**

Burger, Ernest Peter—**Saboteurs**—saboteurs executed (sentenced for life)

Burger, Warren Earl—**Supreme Court (U.S.)**—
Chief Justice of the United States to administer
the oath of office to his successor

Burger, Warren Earl—**Television—Telecast**—
Senate proceedings telecast

Burgess, Charles Frederick—**Brick**—lightweight
brick

Burgess, Dorothy—**Motion Picture**—talking picture taken outdoors (full-length)

Burgess, George Kimball—**Television—Telecast**
—telecast of an object in motion

Burgess, John Melville—**Protestant Episcopal
Bishop**—black to administer a diocese

Burgis, William—**Engraving**—mezzotint engraving of an American maritime print

Burgoyne, John—**Holiday**—Thanksgiving Day
celebration (nationwide, colonial)

Burke, Hilda—**Television—Telecast**—opera telecast

Burke, John—**Insurance**—hail insurance law
(state)

Burke, John—**Money**—battleship depicted on a
bill

Burke, John—**Prizefight**—prizefight of 110 rounds

Burke, Mary—**Woman**—woman labor delegate to
a national convention

Burke, Thomas—**Decalcomanias**

Burke, Yvonne Braithwaite (Mrs. William
Burke)—**Representative (U.S.)**—representative
to give birth while holding office

Burkhart, Bill—**Aviation—Flights**—airplane endurance flight exceeding 1,200 hours

Burleigh, Celia C.—**Unitarian Minister**—woman
ordained to the Unitarian ministry

Burleigh, John H.—**Blanket**—blanket factory

Burnet, William—**Golf Clubs (or golf sticks)**—golf
clubs (or golf sticks)

Burnett, David Gouverneur—**President of the
Republic of Texas**

Burnett, Edward—**Cream Separator**—centrifugal
cream separator

Burnett, John Henderson—**Baseball Player**—
baseball player (major league) to make 9 hits in
1 game

Burnett, Peter Hardeman—**State**—state admitted
to the Union on the Pacific Coast

Burnham, Roger Noble—**Balloon Honeymoon**—
balloon honeymoon

Burnham, Mrs. Walter—**Bridge**—bridge of flowers

Burns, Dick—**Baseball Team**—baseball team (major league) to score 18 runs in 1 inning

Burns, Francis—**Methodist Church**—Methodist
missionary bishop

Burns, Thomas Everett ("Tommy")—**Baseball
Player**—baseball player to hit a home run and
a double in 1 inning

Burnside, Ambrose Everett—**Rifle Association**—rifle association (national)

Burnstine, David—**Book**—book on the game of bridge by a championship team

Burnsworth, Z.—**Surgical Operation**—gallstone operation

Burpee, David—**Flowers**—tetraploid flower

Burr, Aaron—**Secret Service**—secret service (colonial)

Burr, Aaron—**Vice President (U.S.)**—Vice President arrested

Burras, Anne—**Wedding**—wedding in Virginia

Burroughs, Edward—**Road**—law regarding state aid for roads

Burroughs, William Seward—**Adding Machine**—adding machine successfully marketed

Burrows, James Richardson—**Wedding**—wedding in the United States Occupation Forces in Korea

Burrows, William Ward—**Marine Corps**—American marines

Burt, Henry M.—**Newspaper**—newspaper printed atop a mountain

Burt, John—**Boat Club**—boat club

Burt, William Austin—**Typewriter**—typewriter

Burton, Charles—**Baby Carriage**

Burton, Charles Emerson—**Church**—General Council of Congregational and Christian Churches

Burton, Harold Hitz—**President (U.S.)**—President (H. S. Truman) to attend the swearing-in of an Associate Justice of the Supreme Court

Burton, Spence—**Church of England**—American bishop to become bishop of a British Church of England

Burton, William M.—**Gasoline**—cracking process used to obtain gasoline from crude petroleum

Busch, Adolphus—**Engine**—diesel engine built for commercial service

Busch, Fritz—**Television—Telecast**—opera (complete) to be televised from the Metropolitan Opera House

Busch, Isidor—**Periodical**—Jewish weekly (German-American)

Bush, Charles Vernon—**Air Force Academy (U.S.)**—Air Force Academy graduates (black)

Bush, Charles Vernon—**Supreme Court (U.S.)**—page (black)

Bush, George Herbert Walker—**Television—Telecast**—debate (nationally telecast) among candidates within a political party for the presidential nomination

Bush, Leonard Franklin—**Medicine**—bone bank

Bush, Vannevar—**Typesetting Machine**—photographic type-composing machine

Bushnell, Alberto—**Births**—sextuplets

Bushnell, Alice Elizabeth—**Births**—sextuplets

Bushnell, Alincia L.—**Births**—sextuplets

Bushnell, Cornelius Scranton—**Ship**—ironclad warship for service at sea

Bushnell, David—**Mine Barrage**

Bushnell, David—**Submarine**—submarine built for use in war

Bushnell, Edward W.—**Ice Skating Club**—skating club

Bushnell, H. L.—**Ship**—ironclad warship for vice at sea

Bushnell, James—**Births**—sextuplets

Bushnell, Jennie A.—**Births**—sextuplets

Bushnell, Laberto—**Births**—sextuplets

Bushnell, Lucy—**Births**—sextuplets

Bushnell, Norberto—**Births**—sextuplets

Bute, George H.—**Medical Society**—homeopa medical society

Butler, Benjamin Franklin—**Anti-Monopoly Pa**

Butler, Benjamin Franklin—**Civil War**—Confe ate forts to surrender

Butler, Benjamin Franklin—**Crime Prevention Detection**—interstate crime pact

Butler, Benjamin Franklin—**Treason**—citizer the United States to be tried for treason, c victed, and hanged

Butler, Henry Varnum—**Naval Officer**—na officer designated Commander, Aircraft Ba Force

Butler, Jean Marie—**Coast Guard Academ** women graduates

Butler, John—**Stagecoach Intercity Service**

Butler, John Washington—**Evolution Law (sta**

Butler, Nicholas Murray—**College**—college eign-language house

Butler, Nicholas Murray—**Nobel Prize**—N Peace Prize awarded an American woman

Butler, Nicholas Murray—**Novel**—novel to the Pulitzer Prize in letters

Butler, William Orlando—**Political Conventio** national committee of a political organizat

Butterfield, Daniel—**Taps (military signal)**

Butterick, Ebenezer—**Paper Patterns**

Buttolph, Nicholas—**Book**—miniature book

Button, Richard—**Olympic Games**—figure ska Olympic champion (American)

Buzennokami, Niimi—**Japanese Ambassador**

Byers, Jack—**Horse Race**—horse race wit purse of more than $1 million

Byrd, Andrew D.—**Court-martial**—court-ma trial at which enlisted men were allowed t as members of the court

Byrd, Richard Evelyn—**Aviation—Airplane**— plane equipped with radio to cross the Atla Ocean

Byrd, Richard Evelyn—**Aviation—Flights**—N Pole flight

Byrd, Richard Evelyn—**Aviation—Flights**—S Pole flight

Byrd, Richard Evelyn—**Radio Broadcast**—r broadcast heard in both the Arctic and the tarctic regions

Byrn, M. L.—**Corkscrew Patent**

Byrne, Ethel—**Medical Clinic**—birth control cl

Byron, Richard—**War (1812)**—naval battle a the U.S. declaration of war

C

ot, George—**Navy**—Secretary of the Navy

ot, Godfrey Lowell—**Traffic Regulation ourse**—air traffic regulation course

rillo, Juan Rodríguez—**Discovery**—discovery f land on the United States Pacific coast

rini, Frances Xavier—**Catholic Beatification**—atholic beatification of an American citizen emale)

rini, Frances Xavier—**Saint (Catholic)**—Saint Catholic)—canonized—July 7, 1946

ore, Leon Joseph—**Baseball Game**—baseball me (major league) to last longer than 25 in-ngs

ly, Hamilton Perkins—**Helium**—helium

ill, William Thomas—**Noise Legislation**—oise-control state-wide comprehensive legis-tion

le, Adolph—**Pinball Game**—pinball game ma-aine (toy)

nes, George—**Lawbook**—lawbook (text)

ahan, Edward A.—**Telegraph**—telegraph call oxes

der, William Musgrave—**Daylight Saving**

lerón, Gabriel Díaz Vara—**Catholic Holy Or-ers**

dwell, Charles—**Medical Book**—pediatrics onograph

dwell, Eunice—**College**—college for women

dwell, Goldie—**Motion Picture**—serial motion cture with installments longer than one reel

dwell, Harry Howard—**Fingerprint Society**—gerprint society (international)

dwell, James—**Revolutionary War**—American sualities

dwell, John Edward—**Catholic Seminary**—atholic seminary

well, Joseph—**Observatory**—observatory stronomical) connected with an institution of arning

dwell, Lotta—**Police**—state police officers omen)

dwell, Orestes Hampton—**Radio Commission** J.S.)

dwell, Sarah—**Opera**—opera at the Metropoli-n Opera House, New York City, conducted by woman

oun, Charles H., Sr.—**Golfer**—holes in one by father and son

oun, Charles H., Jr.—**Golfer**—holes in one by father and son

oun, John Caldwell—**Money**—Confederate rrency

oun, John Caldwell—**Vice President (U.S.)** Vice President to resign

ahan, Americus F.—**Envelope**—envelope ith an outlook or window

ahan, George—**Heliport**—heliport commer-al base

Calle, Paul—**Postage Stamp**—twin postage stamps

Callsen, Peter—**Ship**—rotor ship

Calthorp, Samuel R.—**Railroad**—streamlined rail-road train

Calver, George Wehnes—**Physician**—Capitol physician

Calverly, Edmund—**Court-martial Trial**—court-martial trial

Calvert, James Francis—**Submarine**—submarine to travel under the North Pole from the East

Calvet, Corinne—**Television—Telecast**—color program on coast-to-coast network commercial

Camadine, Frank—**Theater**—television theater demonstration

Cameron, Simon—**Spoils System**

Camp, Sol—**Horse**—trotter triple-crown winner

Camp, Walter Chauncey—**Football Book**

Campanella, Roy—**Baseball Game**—major-league game in which the majority of the play-ers on one team were blacks

Campaneris, Blanco Dagoberto ("Bert")—**Base-ball Player**—baseball player to play all 9 posi-tions in 1 game

Campanini, Italo—**Opera**—opera at the Met-ropolitan Opera House

Campanius, Johannes—**Book**—book intended for circulation in the English colonies

Campanius, Johannes—**Lutheran Church**—Luth-eran church building

Campbell, Alexander—**Disciples of Christ**

Campbell, Alexander—**Milk**—milk delivery in glass bottles

Campbell, David—**Physiology Society**—physiolo-gy society

Campbell, Donald Malcolm—**Motorboat**—motor-boat to travel at a speed of 216.2 m.p.h.

Campbell, Donald Malcolm—**Ship**—speedboat to exceed 200 miles an hour

Campbell, Douglas—**Aviation—Pilot**—American ace

Campbell, Douglas—**World War I**—air combat of an American organization in World War I

Campbell, Francis J.—**Radio Station**—college radio station

Campbell, George Washington—**Duel**—duel be-tween representatives in Congress

Campbell, James—**Building**—apartment house cooperative

Campbell, John—**Newspaper**—newspaper (suc-cessful)

Campbell, Malcolm—**Automobile**—automobile to exceed the speed of 300 miles an hour

Campbell, Samuel—**Tennis Society**—tennis soci-ety (national)

Campbell, Thomas—**Disciples of Christ**

Camras, Marvin—**Wire Recorder**

Canby, Edward—**Scale**—computing scales

Canby, Henry Seidel—**Book Club**—Book-of-the-Month Club

Candee, Leverett—**Rubber**—rubber shoe manu-facturer

Candell, Andrew M.—**Wedding**—telegraph wed-ding

nautical division of the United States War Department

Chandler, Charles deForest—**Aviation—Airplane** —airplane outfitted with a machine gun

Chandler, George—**Nail Cutting and Heading Machine**

Chandler, Lloyd Horwitz—**Radio Telephone**—radio telephone ship-to-shore conversation

Chandler, William Eaton—**Naval Officer**—Judge Advocate of the Navy

Chaney, James Eugene—**Air Defense Command (U.S.)**

Chang—**Siamese Twins**—Siamese twins

Channing, William Francis—**Fire Alarm System (electric)**

Channing, William H.—**Woman Suffrage**—convention (national) of women advocating woman suffrage

Chanute, Octave—**Aviation—Expositions and Meets**—air conference (international)

Chanute, Octave—**Glider**—glider with cambered wings

Chao Chung Ting, Samuel—**Nobel Prize**—Nobel Prize winners all from one country in 5 categories

Chapin, Charles Value—**Health Laboratory**—health laboratory (municipal)

Chapin, Charles ˙ Willard—**Disease (distinctly American)**

Chapin, Daniel M.—**Match**—friction matches

Chapin, Daryl M.—**Battery**—solar battery

Chapin, William—**Blind**—state school for the blind

Chaplin, Charles—**Motion Picture**—six-reel feature-length comedy

Chapman, Mathias Farrell—**Animals**—chinchilla farm

Chapman, Nathaniel—**Medical Book**—therapeutics and materia medica book

Chapman, R. A.—**Fish Commission (state)**

Chapman, Raymond ("Ray") Johnson—**Baseball Player**—baseball player killed in a game

Chapman, Victor Emmanuel—**Aviation—Pilot**—American aviator killed while a pilot in the Lafayette Escadrille

Charles, Ezzard (Arnold Raymond Cream) — **Prizefight Referee** — heavyweight championship-prizefight black referee

Charles, Ezzard (Arnold Raymond Cream)—**Television—Telecast**—prizefight (heavyweight championship bout) telecast coast-to-coast

Charlo, Martin—**American Indians**—American Indian tribal constitution

Charyk, Joseph Vincent—**Telephone**—telephone conversation (commercial) over a satellite

Chase, Charles M.—**Forest Service**—forest commission (state)

Chase, John Paul—**Capital Punishment**—capital punishment authorized by federal law

Chase, Salmon Portland—**Impeachment**—impeachment proceedings against a President of the United States

Chase, Salmon Portland—**Money**—coin to use "In God We Trust"

Chase, Samuel—**Impeachment**—impeachm proceedings against a Justice of the Supre Court of the United States

Cheeshahteaumuck, Caleb—**College Studer** American Indian to graduate from college

Cheever, Ezekiel—**Grammar**—Latin gramɪ textbook

Chen, Ting Chia—**Army School**—army sch graduates (Chinese)

Cheney, Edwin Fox—**Medal**—Distinguished ! vice Medal (Merchant Marine)

Chenoweth, William B.—**Automobile Truck Service**—automobile intercity trucking serv

Cheplin, Harry—**Milk**—acidophilus milk

Chermayeff, Ivan—**Postage Stamp**—stamp (L cancelled by a foreign country

Chesbrough, Ellis Sylvester—**Water Condu** water supply tunnel for a city

Chesebrough, Robert Augustus—**Petroleum Jɪ**

Chestnut, Ike—**Television—Telecast**—prizef in a "studio"

Chew, Colby—**Colonist**—civilian settlement ʋ of the Allegheny Mountains

Chew, Ng Poon—**Newspaper**—Chinese dɪ newspaper

Chiang Kai-shek, Mme—**Congress (U.S.)**—w an private citizen to address the House of ɪ resentatives and the Senate

Chick, Tong—**Play (drama)**—Chinese theatɪ performance

Chickering, Charles—**Postage Stamp**—posɪ stamp issued jointly by 2 countries

Chickering, Jonas—**Piano**—piano frame of ir

Chickie, Michael B.—**World War I**—shot fireɪ the American Navy in World War I

Child, David Lee—**Sugar**—sugar beets

Child, Lydia Maria Francis—**Antislavery boɪ**

Child, Lydia Maria Francis—**Periodical**—dren's magazine with literary merit

Childs, Francis—**Lawbook**—lawbook contaɪ the federal laws of the United States of ɪ than one session of Congress

Chilson, Llewellyn M.—**Medal**—soldier to rec seven decorations at one time

Chilstrom, Kenneth Oscar—**Airmail Service** ɪropelled airplane to transport mail

ɪnaglia, Giorgio—**Soccer**—soccer game ʋhich 12 points were scored by 1 player

Chipman, Norton Parker—**Holiday**—Decora Day

Chisholm, Clifton—**Compotype**

Chisholm, John Julian—**Medical School**—meɪ summer school

Chisholm, Shirley Anita St. Hill—**Representɪ (U.S.)**—black representative (woman) to sɪ in Congress

Chittenden, Russell Henry—**Physiology Laboɪ** ry

Chittenden, Thomas—**State**—state admitteɪ the Union

Choate, Joseph Hodges—**Federal Alcohol Coɪ Administration**

Chomette, Germaine—**Motion Picture**—taɪ picture in Esperanto

Claypoole, David C.—**Newspaper**—daily newspaper

Clayton, Henry Holm—**Balloon Race**—balloon cup race

Clayton, Joshua—**Senator (U.S.)**—senator (Kensey Johns) appointed (not seated)

Clayton, Powell—**Political Convention**—national nominating convention presided over by a black

Clayton, Zack—**Prizefight Referee**—heavyweight-championship-prizefight black referee

Cleaveland, Parker—**Mineralogy Textbook**—mineralogy textbook

Clemens, Samuel Langhorne—**Arts and Letters Society**—arts and letters society (national)

Clemens, Samuel Langhorne—**Typewritten Book Manuscript**

Clement, L. M.—**Radio Telephone**—radio telephone communication between the ground and an airplane

Clemente, Roberto Walker—**Medal**—Presidential Citizen Medal

Clemons, Lucian M.—**Medal**—lifesaving medal

Clemson, Thomas Green—**Agriculture Bureau**—agriculture bureau

Clerc, Laurent—**Deaf**—**School**—school for the deaf

Cleveland, Clement—**Hospital**—cancer hospital

Cleveland, Esther—**Births**—child born in the White House, Washington, D.C., the offspring of a President

Cleveland, Frances Folsom—**Births**—child born in the White House, Washington, D.C., the offspring of a President

Cleveland, Grover—**Agriculture Department (U.S.)**—Secretary of the Department of Agriculture

Cleveland, Grover—**Births**—child born in the White House, Washington, D.C., the offspring of a President

Cleveland, Grover—**Interstate Commerce Act**

Cleveland, Grover—**President (U.S.)**—President elected for two nonconsecutive terms

Cleveland, Grover—**President (U.S.)**—President to visit a foreign country while President

Cleveland, Grover—**Wedding**—White House wedding of a President

Cliburn, Van—**Television**—**Telecast**—world live-television program

Clifford, Hadley—**Streetcar**—interurban streetcar line

Cline, Genevieve Rose—**Judge**—woman associate justice on the federal bench

Clinton, De Witt—**Freemasons**—Knights Templar Grand Encampment

Clinton, De Witt—**Political Convention**—nominating convention (state)

Clinton, De Witt—**Political Convention**—political nominating caucus

Clinton, George—**Congressional Caucus**—congressional caucus (open, not secret)

Clinton, George—**Political Convention**—political nominating caucus attended by party leaders

Clinton, George—**Presidential Candidate**—presidential candidate nominated at a caucus

Clinton, George—**Presidential Election**—presidential election in which candidates had be nominated for the vice presidency

Clinton, George—**Salute (complimentary)**

Clinton, George—**Vice President (U.S.)**—V President to be nominated

Clinton, George—**Vice President (U.S.)**—V President to die in office

Clinton, George—**Vice President (U.S.)**—V President to serve under two Presidents

Clinton, Sir Henry—**Revolutionary War**—conf on equal terms between American regulars a British regulars

Clippinger, Arthur Raymond—**Evangelical Uni Brethren Church**

Clymer, George—**Art Organization**—art organi tion

Clymer, George—**Treasury Department (U.S** Treasurer of the United States

Clymer, George E.—**Printing Press**—print press invented in America

Coates, George Henry—**Clipper for Cutting H**

Coats, Moses—**Apple Parer**

Cobb, Gail A.—**Police**—police officer (wom killed in the line of duty

Cobb, Jerrie—**Woman**—woman to undergo tronaut tests

Cobb, John Nathan—**College**—fisheries colleg

Cobb, John Rhodes—**Automobile**—automobil exceed the speed of 400 miles an hour

Cobb, Ty (Tyrus Raymond Cobb)—**Baseball P** er—"most valuable player" award (Ameri League)

Cobb, Ty (Tyrus Raymond Cobb)—**Baseball P** er—baseball player to score more than 4 hits

Cobb, Ty (Tyrus Raymond Cobb)—**Base Strike**—baseball strike

Cobb, Ty (Tyrus Raymond Cobb)—**Hall of F** —hall of fame (baseball)

Cobb, William G.—**Automobile**—sun-powe automobile

Cobbett, William—**Fruit Culture Treatise**

Coburn, Ann Struthers—**Protestant Episco Church**—priests (husband and wife) ordai together

Coburn, Michael—**Protestant Episcopal Churc** priests (husband and wife) ordained togeth

Cochran, Jacqueline—**Aviation**—**Pilot**—wom to pilot an airplane faster than the spee sound

Cochrane, Elizabeth—**Tour of the World**—tou the world made by a woman traveling alo

Cochrane, Gordon Stanley ("Mickey")—**Base Game**—baseball game in which there were triple-steals

Cocke, William—**Senator (U.S.)**—senators-e not seated

Code, William Edward—**Codeball**

Cody, William Frederick—**Wild West Show**

Coe, Israel—**Brass Kettles**

Coe, Walter Hamilton—**Gold Leaf**

fin, Frank Trenholm—**Motion Picture**—motion picture from an airplane

fin, James Henry—**Manual Training**—manual training institute

fin, William—**Nautical School**—nautical school

man, Billie L.—**Navy**—navy man to reenlist while under water

swell, John Green—**Gymnasium**—to offer systematic instruction

swell, Mason Fitch—**Deaf—School**—school for the deaf

en, Charles Joseph—**Normal School**—teachers' training school (Jewish)

en, Mendes I.—**Egyptian Antiquities Collection**

n, Elizabeth—**Political Convention**—woman delegate to make a seconding speech

t, Stanton—**Settlement House**

e, Thomas—**Methodist Church**—Methodist bishop

aw, Emerson—**Methodist Church**—bishop (woman)

burn, David G.—**Ordnance**—gun (revolving)

burn, Irving Wightman—**Glass**—sheet glass drawing machine

den, Cadwallader David—**Prison**—reformatory for juvenile delinquents under legislative control

den, Jane—**Botanist**—woman botanist

e, Bob—**Play (drama)**—musical comedy by a lack for black talent

e, Bob—**Play (drama)**—musical (full-length), written, produced, directed, and performed as a roadway (New York City) production

e, Michael George—**Catholic Priest**—deacon (married) ordained

e, Nelson—**Newspaper**—newspaper published by soldiers in the field

e, Mrs. William Sterling—**Submarine**—submarine powered by a liquid-metal-cooled atomic reactor

man, Clyde Jay—**Automobile Electric Self-Starter**—automobile electric self-starter patent

man, Edward—**Book**—book for the blind

man, James V.—**Forest Service**—forest commission (state)

man, Nancy—**Television—Telecast**—play to e televised with its original Broadway cast

man, Reese Clinton—**Photograph**—cystoscopic photographs in color

man, William—**Insurance**—black-owned insurance company

man, William Thaddeus—**Supreme Court (U.S.)**—law secretary (black) of the Supreme Court

ax, Schuyler—**Congress (U.S.)**—officer to preside over both of the branches of Congress

gate, William—**Soap Manufacturer**—to render ts in his plant

oun, Edmund Ross—**Ship**—naval ship christened by an Army officer

es, Christopher—**Map**—road map

Collier, Robert Joseph—**Aviation—Expositions and Meets**—aeronautic international exposition

Collins, Archie Frederick—**Radio Distress Signal**—radio distress signal resulting in an airship rescue

Collins, Edward Trowbridge ("Cocky"), Sr.—**Baseball Player**—baseball player (major league) to steal 6 bases in 1 game

Collins, Isaac—**Treadmill**

Collins, Joseph Lawton—**Atomic Bomb**—atomic bomb underground explosion

Collins, Joseph Lawton—**Ordnance**—atomic cannon

Collins, Joseph Lawton—**War (Korean)**—Korean War hero buried in Arlington cemetery

Collins, Morgan A.—**Police**—police officer (woman) to be appointed

Collins, Paul Fisk—**Caterpillar Club**—father and son Caterpillar Club members

Collins, Thomas—**State**—state to ratify the federal Constitution

Collins, William—**Travelers Aid**

Colman, Benjamin—**Play (drama)**—play of note written by an American and acted in America

Colman, Norman Jay—**Agriculture Department (U.S.)**—Secretary of the Department of Agriculture

Colombosian, Sarkis—**Yogurt**—yogurt dairy

Colt, Samuel—**Cable**—cable

Colt, Samuel—**Pistol**—pistol

Colt, Samuel—**Torpedo**—underwater torpedo operated by electric current

Colton, Walter—**Newspaper**—newspaper published on the Pacific Coast

Columbus, Christopher—**Letter**—letter descriptive of America

Columbus, Christopher—**Monument**—monument to Christopher Columbus

Columbus, Christopher—**War**—bloodshed in the New World

Colver, William Byron—**Federal Trade Commission**—federal trade commission trade practice conference

Colwell, Stephen—**Iron**—hammered iron

Colwell, William—**Animals**—cattle exportation to Great Britain

Colyer, William—**Ship**—dredge (seagoing hopper)

Comfort, George Fisk—**Fine Arts Department**—fine arts department in a college to grant degrees

Commiskey, Henry Alfred—**Medal**—Medal of Honor awarded to a marine in the Korean War

Compson, Betty—**Motion Picture**—talking picture entirely in color

Compton, Arthur Holly—**Air Force Academy (U.S.)**—Air Force Academy

Compton, Karl Taylor—**Science Advisory Board**

Compton, Karl Taylor—**Typesetting Machine**—photographic type-composing machine

Comstock, Andrew—**Bible**—phonetic Bible

Comyn, W. Leslie—**Ship**—concrete seagoing ship

Conboy, Sara Agnes McLaughlin—**Woman**—woman labor delegate to the British Trades Union

Coney, William Devoe—**Aviation—Flights (transcontinental)**—transcontinental flight in 24 hours' flying time

Conn, Billy—**Prizefight**—prizefight at which admission tickets sold at $100

Conn, Billy—**Television—Telecast**—prizefight (heavyweight championship bout) to be televised

Conn, Charles Gerard—**Clarinet**

Conn, Charles Gerard—**Sarrusophone**

Conn, Charles Gerard—**Saxophone**

Connally, Charles M.—**Boy Scouts of America**—Boy Scout uniformed troop

Connally, John—**Television—Telecast**—debate (nationally telecast) among candidates within a political party for the presidential nomination

Conner, Nadine—**Television—Telecast**—pay television presentation of an opera

Connolly, Daniel—**Telephone**—automatic telephone system patent

Connolly, Harold—**Hammer Throw**—hammer throw to exceed 231 feet

Connolly, James Brendan—**Olympic Games**—Olympic competition winner

Connolly, Maureen ("Little Mo")—**Tennis Player**—woman tennis grand slam winner

Connolly, Thomas A.—**Telephone**—automatic telephone system patent

Connor, Robert Digges Wimberly—**Archivist of the United States**

Conrad, Charles, Jr. ("Pete")—**Astronaut**—astronauts (American) on the moon to retrieve an object

Conrad, Charles, Jr. ("Pete")—**Astronaut**—astronauts (American) to remain one day on the moon

Conrad, Charles, Jr. ("Pete")—**Astronaut**—space-to-ground news conference telecast

Conrad, Charles, Jr. ("Pete")—**Astronaut**—two-man spaceflight (American) of 120 orbits

Conrad, Charles, Jr. ("Pete")—**Physician**—doctor to practice in space

Conrad, Charles, Jr. ("Pete")—**Satellite**—satellite to use a fuel cell

Conradt, George M.—**Carpet Factory**—carpet mill to make ingrain carpets

Conreid, Heinrich—**Chair**—steamer chair

Conroy, John M.—**Aviation—Flights (transcontinental)**—transcontinental round-trip solo flight between sunrise and sunset

Contini, Ludovico—**Opera**—opera at the Metropolitan Opera House

Converse, Frederick Shepherd—**Opera**—opera by an American composer performed at the Metropolitan Opera House of New York

Converse, Harriet Maxwell—**Woman**—white woman to become an American Indian chief

Converse, James C.—**Railroad Commission (state)**

Conway, Phip—**Skeet**—national skeet tournament

Conwell, Christopher Columbus—**Newspap**⋅—penny daily newspaper

Conyers, James Henry—**Naval Academy—b**⋅—midshipman in the United States Naval Aca⋅my

Coody, Joseph—**Freemasons**—Masonic lodge⋅ganized in the Indian Territory

Cook, Cordelia E.—**Medal**—Bronze Star ⋅sented to a woman

Cook, Frederick—**Cotton-Bale Metallic Tie**

Cook, S. M.—**High School**—county high scho⋅

Cooke, George Frederick—**Actor**—English a⋅ of note

Cooke, Josiah Parsons—**Chemistry Laborato**⋅ chemical laboratory in a collegiate institut⋅

Cooke, William D.—**Deaf—Students' Magazin**⋅ magazine for deaf students

Coolbaugh, Melville Fuller—**College**—college⋅ver diploma

Cooley, James P.—**Toothpick Manufacturing** ⋅chine Patent

Cooley, Lyman Edgar—**Sanitary District**

Cooley, Thomas McIntyre—**Interstate Comm**⋅ Act

Coolidge, Calvin—**Money**—coin bearing the ⋅trait of a living President

Coolidge, Calvin—**Motion Picture**—talking ⋅tures of presidential candidates

Coolidge, Calvin—**President (U.S.)**—Presi⋅ born on Independence Day

Coolidge, Calvin—**Radio Broadcast**—netw⋅ broadcast received on the Pacific Coast

Coolidge, Calvin—**Radio Broadcast**—poli⋅ convention broadcast

Coolidge, Calvin—**Radio Broadcast**—poli⋅ speech by a President on radio

Coolidge, Calvin—**Radio Broadcast**—Presiden⋅ broadcast from the White House

Coolidge, Calvin—**Radio Broadcast**—presiden⋅ inauguration

Coolidge, Calvin—**Radio Broadcast**—presiden⋅ message to be broadcast

Coolidge, Calvin—**Radio Facsimile Transmis**⋅—photograph sent by radio across the co⋅nent

Coolidge, Mrs. Calvin—**Fair**—Woman's W⋅ Fair

Coolidge, William David—**Tungsten**—du⋅ tungsten

Cooney, Frank Buckley—**Ink**—ink paste

Coons, Wilbur K.—**Baseball League**—Natic⋅ League

Coontz, Robert Edward—**Radio Facsimile Tr**⋅mission—transpacific and transcontinental ⋅simile transmission

Cooper, Charles Henry—**Basketball Player**—⋅tional Basketball Association black player⋅

Cooper, D. B.—**Aviation—Airplane**—skyjack ⋅was successful

Cooper, Daniel M.—**Time Recorder**—card tim⋅ corder

Cooper, Edna May—**Aviation—Flights**—wo⋅ to fly in excess of 120 hours

Coxe, Daniel—**Freemasons**—Provincial Grand Master (Masonic)

Coxe, Daniel—**Pottery**—pottery

Coxe, John Redman—**Medical Book**—dispensatory

Coxe, Tench—**Internal Revenue Commissioner**

Coy, George Willard—**Telephone**—telephone switchboard or exchange (commercial)

Crabb, Benjamin—**Candle Factory**

Crabtree, Davida Foy—**United Church of Christ** —United Church of Christ ordination of a woman minister in which all the principal roles were filled by women

Cracker, William—**Boat Club**—boat club

Cradock, Matthewe—**Horse**—horses

Craig, Cleo Frank—**Telephone**—telephone conversation over the transoceanic telephone cable

Craig, Daniel Frank—**Army Field Range**

Craig, John Alexander—**Animal Husbandry**—animal husbandry professor

Craig, Minnie Davenport—**Legislator (state)**— woman speaker of a state house of representatives

Craik, James—**Army**—medical corps

Cramer, Shannon Davenport, Jr.—**Submarine**— atomic-powered submarine built at a naval shipyard

Cramer, Stuart W.—**Factory**—air-conditioned factory

Crandall, F. A.—**Government Printing Office**—Superintendent of Documents

Crane, Alanson—**Fire Extinguisher Patent**

Crane, James—**Health Board**—health board (municipal) armed with sufficient powers for all emergencies

Crane, M. G.—**Pushball**

Crane, Philip—**Television—Telecast**—debate (nationally telecast) among candidates within a political party for the presidential nomination

Crane, Richard H.—**Submarine**—submarine with a high-tensile-steel pressure hull

Craske, Charles—**Stereotype**—curved stereotype plate

Crawford, Mr.—**Monument**—monument to a woman financed by women

Crawford, Alexander—**Arsenal**

Crawford, Alexander—**Ordnance**—muskets

Crawford, Jane Todd—**Surgical Operation**—abdominal operation

Crawford, Jim—**Postage Stamp**—Christmas-stamp regular issue

Crawford, William Harris—**President (U.S.)**— President to receive fewer popular and electoral votes than an opponent

Crayton, John—**Court-martial**—court-martial trial

Cream, Arnold Raymond. *See* Charles, Ezzard

Creamer, William—**Language Instruction**—German instruction

Crean, A. B.—**Army Insignia**—service number issued to an enlisted man

Cresson, Ezra Townsend—**Entomology Magazine**

Creswell, John Angel James—**Bank**—postal savings bank

Creswell, John Angel James—**Post Office**—P Office Department of the United States

Crissy, Myron Sidney—**Aviation—Airpl** **Bombing**—airplane bombing experiment w explosives

Crivelli, Manuel—**Opera**—opera (Italian)

Croasdale, William T.—**Single Tax**—single national conference

Crocker, Edwin S.—**Diplomatic Service**—Am can legation in which a woman assumed cha

Crocker, Hans—**Forest Service**—forestry inq commission (state)

Crocker, Sewell K.—**Automobile Transco** **nental Trip**—transcontinental automobile t

Crockett, Linda L.—**Navy**—large-scale ass ment of women (other than nurses) to sea d

Croezens, Anna Claas—**Book Auction**

Croly, Jane Cunningham—**Women's Clu** women's club federation

Croly, Jane Cunningham—**Women's Clu** women's professional club

Crompton, William—**Silk**—silk power loom

Cromwell, Samuel—**Naval Officer**—naval off condemned for mutiny

Cronkite, Walter—**Radio Broadcast**—presiden phone-in

Crosby, Alpheus Benning—**Hospital**—milit hospital on the modern pavilion plan

Crosby, Bing—**Television—Telecast**—pay tel sion

Crosby, Harry—**Aviation—Airplane**—rocket plane (military)

Crosby, Robert—**Governor**—governor to app two United States senators in one year for terim terms

Crosland, Alan—**Motion Picture**—talking pic

Crosland, Alan—**Motion Picture**—talking pic entirely in color

Crosley, Powell, Jr.—**Automobile**—miniature tomobile

Cross, Andrew Jay—**Optometry Instruction**— tics and optometry courses

Cross, Julie Yvonne—**Secret Service**—Secret vice female special agent killed in the lin duty

Cross, Milton—**Television—Telecast**—op (complete) to be televised from the Metrop tan Opera House

Cross, Robert—**Insurance**—life insurance com ny

Cross, Thaddeus M. B.—**Medical Book**—neur gy textbook

Crossfield, Scott—**Aviation—Flights**—airplan fly faster than 1,300 m.p.h.

Crossman, William—**Britannia Ware**

Crosswell, Harry—**Periodical**—comic magazi

Crothers, Rachel—**Television—Telecast**—pla be televised with its original Broadway ca

Crotty, Burke—**Television—Telecast**—basel game (collegiate) televised

Crotty, Burke—**Television—Telecast**—Presid to appear on television

well, Luther Childs—**Paper Bag Manufacturing Machine**—square-bottom paper bag machinery

wley, Jim—**Prizefight**—championship prizefight decided on a foul (referee)

wley, John G.—**Ship**—schooner (six-masted)

wninshield, George—**Ship**—yacht

wninshield, Jacob—**Animals**—elephant

ger, John—**Chamber of Commerce**—chamber f commerce (state)

kshank, Joseph—**Botany Book**—botany book trictly American

kshank, Joseph—**Trade Register**

mm, William Joseph—**Vietnam War**—American general killed in Vietnam in an accident

mp, Diane—**Horse Race**—horse race pari-mutuel with an entire field of women jockeys

mp, Diane—**Jockey**—jockey (woman) to ride n a Kentucky Derby

mp, Diane—**Jockey**—jockey (woman) to ride n a pari-mutuel race on a flat track

mrine, Clarence E.—**Aviation—Flights**—New ork–Alaska flight

er, George Edward—**Aviation**—air-rail passenger transcontinental daily service

bertson, Ely—**Whist Tournament**—international whist tournament

bertson, Josephine Murphy—**Whist Tournament**—international whist tournament

l, Dan B.—**Court**—conciliation tribunal for mall claims

len, John Cornelius—**Medal**—Legion of Merit medal to a Coastguardsman in World War II

len, John Cornelius—**Saboteurs**—saboteurs xecuted (discovered 4 Long Island saboteurs)

ley, Langley B.—**Ship**—iron vessel built of merican iron

lum, Elizabeth Hamilton—**Hospital**—cancer ospital

ver, H. Paul—**Airmail Service**—airmail experimental route

mmings, Alma—**Dance Marathon**—dance marathon

mmings, Dexter—**Golf Champion**—family to win more than one national championship in 1 ear

mmings, Edith—**Golf Champion**—family to win ore than one national championship in 1 year

mmings, Irving—**Motion Picture**—talking picture taken outdoors (full-length)

mmings, Thomas Seir—**Art Organization**—arts' society of importance

mmings, Walter Joseph—**Federal Deposit Insurance Corporation**

mmings, William Arthur ("Candy")—**Baseball itcher**—baseball pitcher

mmins, Albert Baird—**Radio Broadcast**—conressional open-session broadcast

mmins, Benjamin—**Saw** (circular)

mmins, Clessie Lyle—**Diesel Engine**—diesel-ngine automobile trip

mmins, Clessie Lyle—**Diesel Engine**—diesel-ngine speed record (official)

Cundiff, Penelope—**Wedding**—telegraph wedding

Cunningham, Alfred Austell—**Marine Corps**—marine pilot

Cunningham, Charles E.—**Union Labor Party**

Cunningham, Harold A.—**Radio Telephone**—radio telephone ship-to-shore commercial service

Cunningham, Ronnie Walter—**Astronaut**—three-man spaceflight (American)

Cunningham, Ronnie Walter—**Television—Telecast**—outer-space live telecast

Curry, Duncan F.—**Baseball Team**—baseball team

Curry, John Francis—**Civil Air Patrol (U.S.)**

Curtice, Cooper—**Zoological Laboratory (U.S.)**—zoological laboratory (U.S.) for the study of the parasites of livestock

Curtis, Augustus Darwin—**Electric Lighting**—electric indirect lighting demonstration

Curtis, Austen M.—**Radio Telephone**—transatlantic radio telephone message

Curtis, Charles—**Congress (U.S.)—Senate**—broadcast from the Senate chamber

Curtis, Charles—**Senator (U.S.)**—American Indian senator

Curtis, Charles—**Vice President (U.S.)**—American Indian Vice President

Curtis, Charles—**Woman**—woman secretary to a Vice President of the United States

Curtis, George—**Bank**—clearinghouse

Curtis, George William—**Civil Service**—Civil Service Commission

Curtis, George William—**Political Convention**—nominating convention presided over by a black

Curtis, John—**Chewing Gum**—chewing gum

Curtis, Joseph—**Prison**—reformatory for juvenile delinquents under legislative control

Curtis, Leslie L.—**Air Brush Patent**

Curtis, William Eleroy—**Pan American Union**

Curtiss, Glenn Hammond—**Aviation**—aeronautical trophy

Curtiss, Glenn Hammond—**Aviation—Airplane**—airplane sold commercially

Curtiss, Glenn Hammond—**Aviation—Airplane**—hydroplane

Curtiss, Glenn Hammond—**Aviation—Airplane Bombing**—airplane bombing experiment

Curtiss, Glenn Hammond—**Aviation—Expositions and Meets**—aviation meet

Curtiss, Glenn Hammond—**Aviation—Flights**—hydroplane flight to and from a ship

Curtiss, Glenn Hammond—**Aviation—Flights**—over-water flight

Curtiss, Glenn Hammond—**Aviation—License**—pilot's license issued by the Aero Club of America

Curtiss, Glenn Hammond—**Aviation—Races**—airplane race won by an American in Europe

Curtiss, Glenn Hammond—**Aviation—Races**—airplane to race a train

Curtiss, Glenn Hammond—**Aviation—School**—airplane flying school

Curtiss, Glenn Hammond—**Motorcycle Hill-climbing Contest**

Cushing, Jack—**Motion Picture**—motion picture of a staged prizefight

Cushing, Richard James, cardinal—**Catholic Mass** —Catholic mass in English said for a President

Cushing, Richard James, cardinal—**Television— Telecast**—Catholic mass televised from a studio

Cushing, William—**Supreme Court (U.S.)**—Supreme Court of the United States

Cushman, Robert—**Furs**

Cushman, Robert—**Sermon Printed** (American)

Custer, Thomas W.—**Medal**—Medal of Honor winner to receive 2 awards

Cutbush, Clara F.—**Fireworks Book**

Cutbush, Edward—**Naval Officer**—naval medical officer to write a book

Cutbush, James—**Fireworks Book**

Cutler, Abner—**Desk with roll top**

Cutler, James Goold—**Postal Service**—mail chute

Cutler, Manasseh—**Botanic Scientific Expedition**

D

Dacres, James Richard—**War (1812)**—frigate action of importance in the War of 1812

Dafydd Harry—**Bible Concordance**—Welsh concordance of the Bible

Daggett, Ezra—**Canning**—canning

Daguerre, Louis Jacques Mandé—**Photograph**— photograph taken in the United States

Dailey, Charles W.—**American Indian Church**— church organized by American Indians

Daimler, Gottlieb—**Automobile**—foreign automobile exhibited

Dale, Richard—**Ship**—ship constructed by the federal government

Daley, Phyllis Mae—**Naval Officer**—black nurse in the Navy Reserve Nurse Corps

Dalton, Edward Barry—**Ambulance**—hospital ambulance service

Dalton, John Call—**Vivisection**

D'Alvarez, Marguerite—**Opera**—opera broadcast in its entirety by a professional cast

Damon, Monsieur—**Billiard Match**—billiard three-ball match on a 6-by-12 carom table

Damrosch, Walter Johannes—**Orchestra**—orchestra (American) to make a European tour

Dana, John Cotton—**Library**—business library supported by taxes

Dancer, Stanley—**Horse**—pacer to win $1 million

Dandridge, Dorothy—**Television—Telecast**—color program on coast-to-coast network commercial

Dane, Nathan—**Slavery**—law (federal) prohibiting slavery in a territory of the United States

Danenhower, Sloan—**Submarine**—submarine accident

Danford, Samuel—**Corporation**—corporate body

Danford, Thomas—**Corporation**—corporate body

Danforth, William Henry—**Christmas Carols Association (national)**

Daniel, Anthony—**Canonization**—canoniza[ ] of North Americans

Daniels, Josephus—**Radio Telephone**—radio t[ ] phone ship-to-shore conversation

Danis, Anthony Leo—**World War II**—Ameri[ ] destroyer torpedoed

Dannenberg, Nathan Baron—**Freemasons**—[ ] sonic lodge organized in the Indian Territo[ ]

Darby, William—**Play (drama)**—play given [ ] nonprofessional actors

Darche, L.—**Nurses' Society**—society for supe[ ] tendents of nursing schools

Dare, Virginia—**Births**—child born of English [ ] ents in America

Dare, Virginia—**Postage Stamp**—first-day spe[ ] cancellation

Dargue, Herbert Arthur—**World War II**—Am[ ] can general killed in World War II

Darley, Felix Octavius Carr—**Periodical**—co[ ] weekly

Darling, Jay Norwood—**Revenue Stamp prin[ ] by the Post Office Department**

Darnell, Linda—**Brokerage**—woman to [ ] securities on the floor of the New York C[ ] Exchange

Darrach, William—**Medical School**—med[ ] center devoted to teaching, treatment, and[ ] search

Dasch, George John—**Saboteurs**—saboteurs e[ ] cuted (sentenced to 30 years)

Daum, Margaret—**Television—Telecast**—ope[ ] ta to be televised

Dauser, Sue Sophia—**Naval Officer**—captair[ ] the U.S. Navy who was a woman

Dauser, Sue Sophia—**Naval Officer**—na[ ] nurses' corps (woman member)

Davenport, James—**Textile Machinery Patent[ ]**

Davenport, Thomas—**Periodical**—electrical je[ ] nal

Davenport, Thomas—**Printing Press**—prin[ ] press operated by electricity

Daventry, Monica M.—**Cemetery**—foreign [ ] vicewomen interred in the Arlington Natie[ ] Cemetery

Davey, John—**Forestry School**—forestry schoo[ ] give scientific training in the care and prese[ ] tion of trees

David, Albert Leroy—**Submarine**—subma[ ] captured and boarded on the high seas

Davids, Thaddeus—**Ink**—ink

Davidson, Ann—**Ship**—woman to sail solo acr[ ] the Atlantic Ocean

Davidson, Ann—**Submarine**—atomic-powe[ ] turbine electric-drive submarine

Davidson, George—**Volcano**—volcano in e[ ] tion—Mt. Baker, Wash.

Davidson, James Ole—**Election Law**—prim[ ] election (statewide)

Davidson, Royal Page—**Automobile**—armo[ ] car

Davidson, Royal Page—**Automobile**—field ho[ ] tal automobile with X-ray equipment

Davidson, Royal Page—**Bicycle Corps (milita[ ]**

Davidson, Royal Page—**Radio Car (military)**

De Blauw, John—**Airmail Service**—helicopter airmail and express service

DeBlois, Thomas A.—**Navy**—naval militia (state)

De Bow, James Dunwoody Brownson—**Business Economics Course**

De Brébeuf, Jean — Canonization — canonization of North Americans

Debrett, J.—**Bibliography**—bibliography of Americana in English

Debs, Eugene Victor—**Social Democratic Party of America**

Debs, Eugene Victor—**Socialist Party**

Decatur, Stephen—**Marine Corps**—commando raid

Decatur, Stephen—**Navy**—prize money awarded by the United States Navy

Decatur, Stephen—**War (1812)**—British frigate captured by a single frigate

Decker, John Wright—**Dairy School**

Decker, Mary—**Runner**—runner (woman) to run 1 mile in less than 4.5 minutes

De Crow, Sarah—**Postmaster**—woman postmaster appointed after the adoption of the Constitution

Deere, John—**Plow**—steel plow with a steel moldboard

Deere, John—**Steel**—cast steel for plows

De Felitta, Frank P.—**Television—Telecast**—opera written for television on commission for a commercial sponsor

Defoe, Daniel—**Newspaper**—newspaper serial story

De Forest, Lee—**Motion Picture**—sound motion picture featuring a black

De Forest, Lee—**Motion Picture**—sound on film motion picture

De Forest, Lee—**Motion Picture**—talking pictures of presidential candidates

De Forest, Lee—**Radio Broadcast**—singer to broadcast

De Forest, Lee—**Radio Microphone** (carbon)

De Forest, Lee—**Radio Society**

De Forest, Lee—**Radio Tube**—three-element vacuum tube

Defrees, John Dougherty—**Government Printing Office**—Government Printing Office

De Gersdorff, George Bruns—**Stadium**—cement stadium

Degrain, Antonio Muñoz—**Postage Stamp**—one-dollar-valuation postage stamp

De Grasse, John Vancerlle—**Physician**—black doctor to become a member of a medical association

De Havilland, Olivia—**Motion Picture**—motion picture to gross more than $70 million

Delafield, Edward—**Hospital**—eye hospital (permanent)

Delafield, Edward—**Physician**—ophthalmologist of note

Delamotte, Charles—**Sunday School**—Protestant Sunday school

Delano, Columbus—**Fair**—centennial celebration

Delano, Frederic Adrian—**National Planning Board (U.S.)**

De Lanoy, William C.—**Insurance**—war risk insurance bureau

Delany, Martin Robinson—**Army Officer**—ma (black)

Delaplace, William—**Revolutionary War**—m ary action

cambre, Adrien—**Typesetting Machine**—ty setting machine patent

Delk, Edward Buehler—**Business**—shopping c ter in a suburban business area

De Long, George Washington—**Nautical Scho** nautical municipal school

De Long, George Washington—**Ship**—steamb to employ electric lights

Del Puente, Giuseppe—**Opera**—opera at the M ropolitan Opera House

De Luce, Nathaniel—**Opera**—opera (Italian)

De May, Philip—**Automobile Transcontine Trip**—transcontinental family automobile requiring only a month

Demby, Edward Thomas—**Protestant Episc Bishop**—black suffragan

Deming, William Champion—**Incubator for fants**

Demont (Dement), William—**Traitor to the Am can cause**

Dempsey, Jack (William Harrison Dempsey)— **zefight**—prizefight to attract 100,000 specta

Dempsey, Jack—**Prizefight**—prizefight to gros million

Dempsey, Jack—**Radio Broadcast**—prizef broadcast

Dempsey, Jack—**Radio Broadcast**—prize (heavyweight championship) broadcast

Dempsey, Jack—**Prizefight**—prizefight to gros million

Denby, Mrs. Edwin—**Aviation—Airship**—di ble (American-built rigid)

Denham, Margaret—**Ship**—dual sponsorship U.S. Navy ship

Denman, James—**Public School**—public sc for Chinese-Americans

Denman, William—**Shipping**—United St Shipping Board

Denn, Eileen—**Railroad**—railroad train oper exclusively by women

Dennet, William—**Navy**—navy yard

Denney, Oswald Evans—**Hospital**—leper ho tal

Denning, M. Leslie—**Telephone**—dial teleph service coast-to-coast without the aid of op tors

Dennison, Aaron Lufkin—**Clock**—watch (e day)

Dennison, Cora—**Wedding**—television wedd

Dennison, Warren Hathaway—**Church**—Ge Council of Congregational and Chris Churches

Denny, Jack—**Radio Broadcast**—radio broad from a moving train, of a regular program national network

De Paolis, Alessio—**Television—Telecast**—op telecast

Dinsmoor, Charles—**Automobile Tractor**—endless-chain tractor

Dirksen, Everett McKinley—**Senator (U.S.)**—senator to act in the movies

Disney, Walt—**Motion Picture**—animated cartoon in color (Technicolor) of feature length with sound

Disney, Walt—**Motion Picture**—animated cartoon talking picture

Disney, Walt—**Motion Picture**—animated three-dimensional cartoon in Technicolor (modern)

Disturnell, J.—**Railroad Guide**—railroad guide

Dittenhoefer, Isaac—**Jews**—Jewish fraternal society

Dix, Dorothea Lynde—**Woman**—woman lobbyist

Dix, John Adams—**Political Machine**

Dixon, Alice Crossland—**Ship**—naval ship christened by a woman not a U.S. citizen

Dixon, Brandt Van Blarcom—**College**—college for women to affiliate with a university

Dixon, Emmet—**Congress of the Confederate States**

Dixon, George—**Submarine**—submarine to sink a man-of-war

Dixon, James—**Air Force Officer**—Air Force general (woman) commissioned

Dixon, Thomas—**Boat Club**—boat club

Dixon, Thomas—**Motion Picture**—motion picture to gross $50 million

Dixwell, Epes Sargent—**Football Club**—football club

Doak, Samuel—**College**—college named after George Washington

Doak, William Nuckles—**Labor Department (U.S.)**—native-born Secretary of Labor

Doane, Deborah B.—**Maritime School**—woman graduate of a 4-year maritime school

Dobson, J.—**Cranioscopy Book**

Dobson, Judah—**Embalming Book**

Dobson, Thomas—**Bible**—Hebrew Bible

Dobson, Thomas—**Encyclopedia**—encyclopedia

Dobson, Thomas—**Medical Book**—anatomy book

Dobson, Thomas—**Medical Book**—anatomy book (American)

Dobson, Thomas—**Medical Book**—dispensatory

Dobson, Thomas—**Music Book**—secular songbook by a native American

Doby, Lawrence Eugene ("Larry")—**Baseball Player**—black baseball player to hit a home run in a World Series

Dock, Christopher—**Teaching Methods Book**

Dod, Daniel—**Ship**—steamboat built in America to cross the Atlantic Ocean

Dodd, Mrs. John Bruce—**Holiday**—Father's Day

Dodge, Augustus Caesar—**Senator (U.S.)**—father and son senators at the same session

Dodge, David Low—**Peace Society**

Dodge, Grace Hoadley—**Young Women's Christian Association**

Dodge, Henry—**Army**—cavalry unit

Dodge, Henry—**Senator (U.S.)**—father and son senators at the same session

Dodge, Homer Levi—**Army**—Reserve Offic Training Corps course in mountain and wir warfare

Dodge, Nehemiah—**Jewelers' Supply House**

Dodge, Philip Tell—**Voting Machine Commiss (state)**

Dodrill, Forest Dewey—**Surgical Operation**—tral valve exposure (prolonged) in a human tient

Doering, William von Eggers—**Quinine**—synth ic quinine

Doggett, John—**Railroad Guide**—railroad gu that printed the time schedule

Doheny, Edward Laurence—**Cabinet (U.S** Cabinet member convicted of a crime

Dolan, Thomas P.—**Manufacturers' Associati**

Dole, Robert—**Television**—**Telecast**—debate (tionally telecast) among candidates withi political party for the presidential nominat

Dollenberg, Fred Paul—**Glider**—glider comm cial freight service

Dollier de Casson, François—**Oil**—oil spring

Dolph, William B.—**Radio Broadcast**—news gram (cooperative)

Donahue, Peter M.—**Ship**—steamboat built on Pacific coast for the government

Donald, John A.—**Shipping**—United States S ping Board

Donald, Mrs. W. F.—**Holiday**—Mother-in-L Day

Donaldson, James—**Sugar**—sugar beets

Donaldson, Jesse Monroe—**Postmaster**—p master general appointed from the ranks

Donaldson, Washington Harrison—**Balloon**— loon Atlantic crossing attempt

Donaldson, Washington Harrison—**Weddin** balloon wedding

Donavan, Robert Duane—**Submarine**—nucl submarine named for a black (blue crew c mander)

Donelson, Andrew Jackson—**American Party**

Donlon, Mary Honor—**Woman**—woman edito chief of a law review

Donlon, Roger Hugh—**Medal**—Medal of Hono the Vietnam war

Donovan, Florence F.—**Arbitration**—state bo of mediation and arbitration

Donovan, William Joseph—**Medal**—recipien the four highest decorations awarded by United States

Doolittle, Amos—**Music Periodical**—music ma zine

Doolittle, James Harold—**Aviation Compan** airplane company to carry 100 million pas gers (American Airlines presentation)

Doolittle, James Harold—**Aviation**—**Flights**— blind flight

Doolittle, James Harold—**Aviation**—**Fli** **(transcontinental)**—transcontinental one-: flight

Doolittle, James Harold—**World War II**—Am can air attack against the Japanese homel:

Doolittle, Sylvester—**Ship**—steamboat en; built in America for a screw-propelled ves

Dufek, George John—**Discovery**—American to land by air at the South Pole

Dufek, George John—**Navy**—naval expedition to the South Pole

Duffield, Howard—**Organ School**

Dufour, John James—**Vineyard** (successful)

Dufriche, Eugene—**Opera**—opera composed by a woman performed at the Metropolitan Opera House

Duggan, Pat—**Television—Telecast**—pay television presentation of a motion picture shown simultaneously in theaters

Duggar, Benjamin Minge—**Aureomycin**—aureomycin chlortetracycline

Duhamel, Yvon—**Snowmobile**—snowmobile to exceed a speed of 125 m.p.h.

Duhring, Louis Adolphus—**Medical Book**—dermatology treatise

Dulany, Richard Hunter—**Horse Show**

Dulty, George—**Soda Fountain**—soda fountain patent

Dumas, Charles—**High Jump**

Dumont, Marjorie—**Wedding**—airplane wedding

Dunant, Jean Henri—**American Red Cross**

Dunbar, Charles Franklin—**Political Economy Course**—political economy chair

Dunbar, Edward Lucian—**Spring Manufacturer**

Dunbar, Robert—**Elevator**—grain elevator operated by steam

Duncan, Donald B.—**Ship**—aircraft carrier escort

Duncan, Joseph Smith—**Addressograph**

Duncan, Robert Todd—**Opera**—black to sing a white role with a white cast in an opera company

Dunglison, Robley—**Dictionary**—medical dictionary (complete)

Dunham, Alanson Millen—**Snowshoe**

Dunham, Isaac—**Lighthouse**—iron pile lighthouse

Dunham, Otis Emerson—**Animals**—reindeer

Dunklee, Ernest Walter—**Strike**—anti–sit-down-strike legislation (state)

Dunlap, John—**Constitution of the United States**—Constitution of the United States first published in a newspaper

Dunlap, John—**Newspaper**—daily newspaper

Dunlap, Maxine—**Aviation—License**—glider license awarded a woman

Dunlap, William—**Etcher**

Dunlap, William—**Opera**—opera by an American composer

Dunlap, William—**Playwright**—playwright (professional)

Dunlap, William—**Theater History**

Dunlop, John—**Declaration of Independence (American)**—Declaration of Independence first printed

Dunn, James Clement—**Telephone**—mobile transatlantic telephone conversation between two telephone-equipped automobiles

Dunn, Nathan—**Book**—book for the blind

Dunn, Oscar James—**Lieutenant Governor**—black lieutenant governor

Dunn, Willie—**Golf Tournament**—open championship (official)

Dunne, Mona—**Navy**—naval militia (state) have a hydroplane

Dunster, Henry—**College**—college

Dunster, Henry—**Corporation**—corporate boc

Dunster, Henry—**Missionary Society**—miss ary society (colonial)

Dunton, Jacob—**Pill**—compressed pills or tab

Du Pont, E. Paul, Jr.—**Aviation—Flights**—s train international round-trip flight

Durand, Elias—**Soda Water**—soda water c mercially bottled

Durand, Elie Magloire—**Bottler of Mineral W**

Durant, Ariel—**Medal**—Medal of Freedom aw ed to a husband and wife

Durant, Charles Ferson—**Balloon—Flights**— loon flight by a native-born American

Durant, Mrs. Henry Fowle—**Young Wom Christian Association**

Durant, Howard M.—**Hotel**—hotel to install e tric lights

Durant, Will—**Medal**—Medal of Freedom aw ed to a husband and wife

Durell, William—**Engraving**—wood engra made with an engraving tool

Durfee, William Franklin—**Copper Refinery** nace

Durfee, William Franklin—**Steel**—Bessemer s converter

Durfee, William Franklin—**Steel Analysis Lab** tory

Durocher, Leo—**Television—Telecast**—base games (major-league) televised

Duryea, Charles Edgar—**Automobile**—auto bile regularly made for sale

Duryea, Charles Edgar—**Automobile Club**

Duryea, Charles Edgar—**Aviation—Expositi and Meets**—air conference (international)

Duryea, James Franklin—**Automobile Race**— tomobile race

Dusenbury, William C.—**Credit Protective Gr**

Duston, Hannah—**Woman**—heroine

Duvall, Gabriel—**Supreme Court (U.S.)**—Ass ate Justice of the Supreme Court who had b a representative in Congress

du Vigneaud, Vincent—**Pituitary Hormone**—p peptide hormone synthesized

Dwight, Edmund—**Normal School**—nor school (state)

Dwight, Edward Joseph, Jr.—**Astronaut**— tronaut (black) selected for the manned orbi laboratory program

Dwight, John—**Baking Soda**

Dwyer, Michael—**Horse**—horse whose t purses exceeded $100,000

Dwyer, Philip—**Horse**—horse whose total pu exceeded $100,000

Dyan, Hubert—**Censorship**—state board of sorship on literature

Dyar, Harrison Gray—**Telegraph**—telegraph

Dykstra, Clarence Addison—**Conscriptio** peacetime conscription bill

Dykstra, Clarence Addison—**Navy "E" Aw**—Navy "E" certificates of meritorious ser presented to an institution of higher learni

E

ls, James Buchanan—**Bridge**—steel-arch
ridge

ls, James Buchanan—**Medal**—Albert medal
resented to a native-born American

ls, James Buchanan—**Ship**—ironclad naval
essels

an, Edward F.—**Bobsled Competition**—four-
an bob-team competition

an, Michael—**Handball national champion-
hip match for amateurs**

an, Nancy Ann—**Air Force Officer**—nun in the
ir Force Reserve

le, Frank—**American Indian Church**—church
rganized by American Indians

leton, Thomas Francis—**Vice Presidential
andidate**—vice presidential candidate of a
ajor political party to resign

ins, Thomas—**Postage Stamp**—gravure-
rinted postage stamp

es, Joseph—**Fuse**—safety fuse

nes, A. G.—**Locker**—public locker plant

nes, Wilberforce—**Bibliography Society** (na-
ional)

hart, Amelia (Amelia Earhart Putnam)—**Au-
ogiro**—pilot to carry a passenger

hart, Amelia (Amelia Earhart Putnam)—**Au-
ogiro**—**Flights**—autogiro solo flight by a
voman

hart, Amelia (Amelia Earhart Putnam)—**Au-
ogiro**—**Flights**—autogiro transcontinental
light made by a woman

hart, Amelia (Amelia Earhart Putnam)—**Avia-
ion**—**Flights (transatlantic)**—transatlantic solo
ight by a woman

hart, Amelia (Amelia Earhart Putnam)—**Avia-
ion**—**Flights (transcontinental)**—transconti-
ental nonstop flight by a woman

hart, Amelia (Amelia Earhart Putnam)—**Avia-
ion**—**Passenger**—woman airplane passenger
cross the Atlantic Ocean

hart, Amelia (Amelia Earhart Putnam)—**Avia-
ion**—**Pilot**—woman pilot to fly solo across the
acific Ocean

hart, Amelia (Amelia Earhart Putnam)—
Medal—National Geographic Society special
old medal

l, George H.—**Philatelic Society**—philatelic so-
iety

le, Parker—**Railroad Car**—refrigerator car
hipment of fresh fruit

le, Richard Blair—**Rubber**—synthetic rubber

le, Sarah H.—**Woman Suffrage**—convention
national) of women advocating woman suffr-
ge

ly, A. R.—**Ship**—naval ship christened by a
voman not a U.S. citizen (placed in command)

ly, Penny Ann—**Horse Race**—horse race pari-
utuel with an entire field of women jockeys

Early, William—**Insurance**—crime insurance federal policy

Eastman, George—**Camera**—roll-film camera

Eastman, George—**Photographic Film**—transparent paper-strip photographic film

Eastman, George Washington—**Business School**
—business school

Eastman, Joseph Bartlett—**Transportation Coordination**—transportation coordination (federal)

Eastman, Lucius Root—**Arbitration Association**—
arbitration association

Eastman, Timothy C.—**Meat**—beef exported

Easton, Robert—**Tennis Match**—intercollegiate
court tennis match

Eastwick, Andrew—**Locomotive**—locomotive
with a cab

Eastwood, B.—**Cranberry Treatise**

Eaton, Amos—**Engineering College**—engineering
college

Eaton, Amos—**Geology Book**—geology textbook

Eaton, Charlotte Anne Waldie—**Book**—book
(cloth-covered) commercially bound

Eaton, Marson M.—**Newspaper**—mimeographed
daily newspaper

Eaton, Nathaniel—**College**—college

Eaton, Samuel—**Corporation**—corporate body

Eaton, William Herbert—**Trust**—cartel

Eaves, Elsie—**Engineering Society**—woman elected to the American Society of Civil Engineers

Ebert, Jacob—**Soda Fountain**—Soda fountain patent

Ebert, Mabelle E.—**Wedding**—wedding broadcast

Eckener, Hugo—**Aviation**—Atlantic Ocean regular commercial airship service

Eckert, J. Presper—**Computer**—electronic computer

Eddy, Mary Baker—**Christian Science Church**

Ede, Alfred L.—**Submarine**—submarine disaster

Ederle, Gertrude—**Woman**—American woman to
swim the English Channel

Edes, Peter—**Woman Suffrage**—woman suffrage
book

Edgar, Patrick Nisbett—**Horse Register**—pacing
register

Edge, Bob—**Television**—**Telecast**—baseball
World Series game televised

Edgerton, James Clark—**Airmail Service**—airmail
experimental route

Edgerton, James Clark—**Radio Facsimile Transmission**—photographs sent over a city telephone

Edison, Thomas Alva—**Electric Company**—three-
wire central-station incandescent electric lighting plant

Edison, Thomas Alva—**Electric Lighting**—electric
incandescent lamp

Edison, Thomas Alva—**Mimeograph**

Edison, Thomas Alva—**Motion Picture**—motion
picture film exhibition in a theater

Edison, Thomas Alva—**Motion Picture**—motion
picture film exposition

Edison, Thomas Alva—**Motion Picture**—motion picture (successful) projected to a paying audience

Edison, Thomas Alva—**Motion Picture**—peep show

Edison, Thomas Alva—**Newspaper**—newspaper printed on a train

Edison, Thomas Alva—**Phonograph**—phonograph

Edison, Thomas Alva—**Radio Patent of importance**

Edison, Thomas Alva—**Voting Machine**—electric vote recorder

Edmunds, George Franklin—**Polygamy Legislation (federal)**

Edson, Susan Ann—**Physician**—woman appointed "personal physician to the President"

Edward VII, King of Great Britain—**Radio Broadcast**—transatlantic broadcast (not experimental)

Edward VII—**Visiting Celebrities**—Prince of Wales

Edward VIII (Duke of Windsor—**Wedding**—American woman married to a former King of Great Britain

Edwards, Emma Sarah—**Seal**—state seal designed by a woman

Edwards, Heywood Lane—**World War II**—American destroyer torpedoed and sunk while on convoy duty

Edwards, James—**Births**—sextuplets

Edwards, James L.—**Pensions Commissioner (U.S.)**

Edwards, Jonathan—**Revival Meeting**

Edwards, Julian—**Phonograph Record**—phonograph record of a stage performance by the original cast

Edwards, Philip—**Newspaper**—newspaper to appear on Sunday

Edwards, Robert H.—**Opera**—opera broadcast in its entirety

Edwards, Talmadge—**Gloves**

Edwards, Talmadge—**Leather**—leather tanning by the "oil tan" method

Effler, Donald Brian—**Surgical Operation**—heart operation in which the elective cardiac arrest technique was employed

Egberts, Egbert—**Knitting Machine (power)**

Egleston, Thomas—**Mines School**

Ehret, Cornelius D.—**Radio Facsimile Transmission**—radio facsimile patent

Ehrrichson, Asmus J.—**Oat-crushing Machine**

Eichbaum, William Peter—**Glass Crystal Chandelier**

Eickemeyer, Rudolph—**Hat Blocking and Shaping Machine**

Eisele, Donn Fulton—**Astronaut**—three-man spaceflight (American)

Eisele, Donn Fulton—**Television—Telecast**—outer-space live telecast

Eisemann-Schier, Ruth—**Criminal**—woman on the "ten most wanted" list

Eisenberg, Sophie—**Television—Telecast**—television eyewitness allowed to testify in a federal court

Eisenhower, Dwight David—**Air Force Officer**—Air Force chairman of the Joint Chiefs of Staff

Eisenhower, Dwight David—**Airmail Service**—missile mail (official)

Eisenhower, Dwight David—**Army Officer**—generals to wear the five-star insignia

Eisenhower, Dwight David—**Building**—atomic bomb-resistant federal building

Eisenhower, Dwight David—**Cabinet (U.S.)**—Cabinet conference telecast

Eisenhower, Dwight David—**Cabinet (U.S.)**—black sub-Cabinet member

Eisenhower, Dwight David—**Cabinet (U.S.)**—secretary to the Cabinet and presidential assistant (appointed by)

Eisenhower, Dwight David—**Canal**—St. Lawrence Seaway

Eisenhower, Dwight David—**Electric Power Plant**—atomic electric generating station (full-scale)

Eisenhower, Dwight David—**Flag**—Navy flag (official)

Eisenhower, Dwight David—**Medal**—Medal of Honor awarded to a Nisei in the Korean War

Eisenhower, Dwight David—**Medal**—presidential citation to an entire division

Eisenhower, Dwight David—**Motto of the United States**

Eisenhower, Dwight David—**Photograph**—photograph bounced off a satellite

Eisenhower, Dwight David—**President (U.S.)**—President telecast in color

Eisenhower, Dwight David—**President (U.S.)**—President to fly in a helicopter

Eisenhower, Dwight David—**President (U.S.)**—President to fly in a twin-engined airplane

Eisenhower, Dwight David—**President (U.S.)**—President to hold an airplane pilot's license

Eisenhower, Dwight David—**Radio Broadcast**—outer-space broadcast

Eisenhower, Dwight David—**Satellite**—communication satellite successfully placed in orbit

Eisenhower, Dwight David—**State**—noncontiguous overseas state

Eisenhower, Dwight David—**State**—noncontiguous state

Eisenhower, Dwight David—**Television—Telecast**—Cabinet session to be televised

Eisenhower, Dwight David—**Television—Telecast**—President to appear on television in color

Eisenhower, Dwight David—**Television—Telecast**—presidential news conference filmed television and newsreels

Eisenhower, Mamie Geneva Doud—**Ship**—atomic-powered merchant ship

Eisenhower, Mamie Geneva Doud—**Submarine**—atomic-powered submarine

Eisenhower, Mamie Geneva Doud—**Submarine**—submarine of the U.S. Navy christened by President's wife

Ekins, Herbert Roslyn—**Aviation—Races**—plane passenger race around the world

Jacob E.—**Insurance**—insurance board tate)

ed, Arthur Rose—**Boy Scouts of America** -boy scout to become an eagle scout

idge, A.—**Ship**—yacht to circumnavigate the orld

r, John—**Ship**—iron vessel (sheet-iron)

son, Carl J. E.—**Snowmobile**—snowmobile atent

t, Benjamin—**Grammar**—Latin grammar text- ook

t, Charles William—**Medal**—arts and letters ociety (national) gold medal special award

t, Jared—**Agricultural Book**—agricultural ook distinctly American

t, John—**Bible**—Bible in an American Indian nguage

t, John—**Book**—book privately printed

t, John—**Grammar**—American Indian gram- ar

t, John—**American Indian Church**—church for merican Indians in New England

t, John—**American Indians**—American Indian reacher of Christianity

t, John—**Missionary Society**—missionary so- ety (colonial)

t, John—**Primer**—primer in an American Indi- n dialect

t, Samuel Atkins—**Music Instruction**—musi- al pedagogy school

abeth II, queen of Great Britain—**Canal**—St. awrence Seaway

abeth II, queen of Great Britain—**Television**— **elecast**—international telecast

abeth II, queen of Great Britain—**Television**— **elecast**—state dinner (U.S.) telecast

abeth II, queen of Great Britain—**Television**— **elecast**—telecast received from England

abeth, consort of George VI, King of Great ritain—**Television—Telecast**—king and queen be televised

abeth, consort of George VI—**Visiting Celebri- es**—King and Queen of Great Britain

es, Harry—**Bicycle Race**—motorcycle-paced icycle race

t, Charles—**Bridge**—railroad suspension ridge

t, Charles—**Bridge**—wire suspension bridge r general traffic

cott, Andrew—**Astronomy**—meteoric display

cott, Edward Beach—**Automobile License oard**

ot, Eugene S.—**Whist**—whist organization

ott, Bob—**Television—Telecast**—stereo tele- ast (host)

ott, Ezekiel Brown—**Civil Service**—Civil Ser- ice Commission

s, Richard Gailard—**Ship**—Liberty ship

s, Seth Hockett—**Union Reform Party**

naker, Amos—**Anti-Masonic Party**

trom, Marvin—**Football Game**—professional otball game in which 10 touchdowns were ade

Ellsworth, Annie—**Telegram**—telegram inaugu- rating commercial service

Ellsworth, Henry Leavitt—**Agricultural Seed Dis- tribution (national)**

Ellsworth, Henry Leavitt—**Patent Commissioner**

Ellsworth, Oliver—**Congress (U.S.)—Senate**— Senate

Ellsworth, Oliver—**Supreme Court (U.S.) Decision** —Supreme Court decision between states

Ellyson, Theodore Gordon—**Aviation—Airplane** —naval airplane

Ellyson, Theodore Gordon—**Aviation—Flights**— airplane catapulted

Elman, Mischa—**Motion Picture**—talking picture

Elmen, Gustaf Waldemar—**Permalloy**

Elmer, Lucius Quintius Cincinnatus—**Crime Pre- vention and Detection**—interstate crime pact

Elmore, Francis Edward—**Mineral Segregation**

Elsberg, Louis—**Medical Clinic**—laryngology clin- ic

Elsberg, Louis—**Medical Instruction**—laryngology instruction

Elsberg, Louis—**Medical Periodical**—laryngology magazine

Elsberg, Louis—**Medical Society**—laryngology so- ciety (national)

Elston, Dorothy Andrews. *See* Kabis, D. A. E.

Elton, Robert H.—**Valentine**—valentines com- mercially produced

Ely, Eugene Burton—**Aviation—Flights**—airplane flight to the deck of a carrier

Ely, Euguene Burton—**Aviation—Flights**—air- plane flight from a ship

Ely, Eugene Burton—**Aviation—Races**—intercity airplane race

Ely, William H. J.—**Old Age Colony**

Emanuel, David—**Governor**—Jewish governor

Embree, Elihu—**Slavery**—antislavery magazine

Embury, Philip—**Methodist Church**—Methodist chapel

Embury, Philip—**Methodist Church**—Methodist preacher

Embury, Philip—**Methodist Church**—Methodist Society in America

Emerich, Charles Rulf—**Football Game**—Army- Navy football game

Emerich, James—**War (Korean)**—American tank crew to cross the 38th Parallel in Korea

Emerson, Faye—**Television—Telecast**—color program (commercial)

Emerson, Gladys Anderson—**Vitamin**—vitamin E

Emerson, H. D.—**Automobile Club**

Emerson, Oliver Hudleston—**Vitamin**—vitamin E

Emerson, Ralph—**Television—Telecast**—phase- contrast cinemicrography film (American- made) telecast

Emerson, Victor—**Motorboat**—motorboat to trav- el at a speed of 40 m.p.h. (builder-owner)

Emma, Queen (Hawaii)—**Visiting Celebrities**— queen to visit the United States

Emmes, Thomas—**Engraving**—engraving of any artistic merit

Emmett, Daniel Decatur—**Ministrel Show Troupe**

Emmett, Daniel Decatur—**Music**—war song of the Confederate States

End, George Kenneth—**Rattlesnake Meat**

Endicott, John—**Apples**

Eng—**Siamese Twins**—Siamese twins

Engel, Arthur Bright—**Coast Guard Officer**—rear admirals who were twins nominated at the same time

Engel, Benjamin Franklin—**Coast Guard Officer** —rear admirals who were twins nominated at the same time

Engen, Edward Milian—**World War II**—Japanese balloon casualties

England, John Charles—**Ship**—naval ship named for a sailor killed at Pearl Harbor

English, Joseph E.—**Aviation—Flights**—New York –Alaska flight

English, Thomas Dunn—**Periodical**—comic weekly

Enos, John L.—**Teachers' Convention**—teachers' convention (national)

Enright, Thomas F.—**World War I**—U.S. Army soldiers killed in combat

Ensel, Edward—**Glass Factory**—flint glass factory

Ent, Peter—**Bridge**—twin covered-bridges

Eopolucci, John E.—**World War I**—American sailor to lose his life in World War I before U.S. entry into the war

Eppes, Marion H.—**Aviation—Flights**—airship to exceed 200 hours in flight nonstop without refueling

Erbslöh, Oscar—**Balloon Race**—balloon cup race

Erdmann, Bertha—**Nursing School**—university school of nursing

Erhard, Ludwig—**Telephone**—telephone conversation (commercial) over a satellite

Erickson, B. A.—**Aviation—Flights**—airplane to carry 100,000 pounds

Erickson, H. A.—**Photograph**—photograph from an airplane

Ericson, John—**Automobile License Board**

Ericsson, John—**Ship**—ironclad turreted vessel in the U.S. Navy

Ericsson, John—**Ship**—steamboat engine built in America for a screw-propelled vessel

Ericsson, John—**Ship**—warship with propelling machinery below the waterline

Erikson, Olaf—**Baseball Game**—baseball game (major league) in which 14 runs were scored in 1 inning

Erikson, Ted—**Swimmer**—American to swim the English Channel roundtrip

Ermoyan, Suren H.—**Postal Card**—international postal card

Ernst, Harold Clarence—**Medical Instruction**—bacteriology lectures

Eshleman, Von Russel—**Radar**—radar signal bounced off the sun

Espenschied, Lloyd—**Cable**—coaxial cable

Espitallier, Lieutenant Colonel—**Aviation—School**—correspondence school in aviation

Esterbrook, Richard—**Pen**—steel pen commercially produced

Eustis, Mrs. Harrison—**Animals**—dogs traine guide the blind

Evans, Ms.—**Gymnastics Instruction**—gymn tics instruction at a college for women

Evans, Charles ("Chick"), Jr.—**Golf Champio** golfer to win both the United States Open the United States Amateur in the same yea

Evans, Clifford—**Television—Telecast**—mun pal television film unit

Evans, David—**Croquet League**

Evans, George—**Senator (U.S.)**—senator to ceive a mileage allowance for a trip that he not make

Evans, George Henry—**Labor Paper**

Evans, Herbert McLean—**Vitamin**—vitamin F

Evans, Josiah—**Ice Skating Club**—ice skating c

Evans, Josiah James—**Workmen's Compensa** —workmen's compensation lawsuit

Evans, Joyce—**Television—Telecast**—play to televised

Evans, Michael Patrick—**Police**—police burea identification

Evans, Oliver—**Belt Conveyor System**—belt c veyor system

Evans, Oliver—**Flour Mill**—flour mill

Evans, Oliver—**Steam Engine**—steam engine was practical

Evans, Oliver—**Amphibious Vehicle**—steam erated amphibious vehicle

Evans, Robley Dunglison—**Ship**—warship flee circumnavigate the globe

Evans, Rudolph Martin—**Federal Crop Insura Corporation**

Evans, Samuel—**Union Labor Party**

Evarts, William Maxwell—**Monument**—obe to be brought to the United States

Eveleigh, Nichols—**Comptroller**—comptroller the United States Treasury

Everett, Mr.—**Bed**—folding bed manufacture

Everett, Edward—**Constitutional Union Party**

Everett, Richard—**Telephone**—mobile teleph news dispatch

Everitt, Percival—**Scale**—coin-operated scale

Everitt, Percival—**Scale**—coin-operated weigh machine

Evers, Luke J.—**Catholic Mass**—Catholic mass night workers

Evinrude, Ole—**Engine**—outboard motor (c mercially successful)

Evinrude, Ole—**Engine**—outboard twin-cylin motor (light)

Ewin, James Lithgow—**Temperance Societ** Anti-Saloon League (national organization)

Ewing, James—**Railroad Charter**

Ewing, Thomas—**Interior Department (U.S.)**– terior Department Secretary

Ewry, Ray—**Olympic Games**—American ath to win ten prizes at the Olympic Games

Eyck, Jan van—**Postage Stamp**—postage sta printed on the 9-color Huck press

Eyer, Abraham—**Evangelical Church Gen Conference**

F

s, Anthony—**Accordion Patent**

ray, Nanette—**Television—Telecast**—color oast-to-coast live telecast

lberg, Constantine—**Saccharin**

ning, Emma—**Bowler**—woman bowler to obain a perfect score

n, Sarah Lee—**Information Service (U.S.)**

rbanks, Erastus—**Scale**—platform scale

rbanks, Richard—**Post Office**—post office olonial)

rbanks, Thaddeus—**Scale**—platform scale

rbanks, Thaddeus—**Scale**—railway track cale

child, David—**Tung**

child, Le Roy—**Freemasons**—Grotto

child, Schell—**Prizefighter**—bareknuckle vorld heavyweight champion (American)

rfax, John—**Rowing**—transatlantic solo trip by owboat

rfax, Thomas, 6th Baron Fairfax—**Spa**

rman, Gideon—**Engraving**—pamphlet produced from a steel plate engraving

ckner, Justus—**Lutheran Church**—Lutheran astor ordained in America

k, Joshua ben Mordecai ha-Cohen—**Hebrew ook**—Hebrew book all in Hebrew

kner, Roland Post—**Political Science Society** –political and social science society (national)

l, Albert Bacon—**Cabinet (U.S.)**—Cabinet member convicted of a crime

fani, Amintore—**Cabinet (U.S.)**—Cabinet meeting attended by a foreign national

agher, Warren Fred—**Petroleum**—petroleum efining course

is, Edmond John—**X Ray**—X-ray photograph howing the complete arterial circulation

ley, James Aloysius—**Industrial Recovery Act** –postage stamps commemorating the National Recovery Act

mer, John—**Genealogy**—genealogical collecive work

mer, Moses Gerrish—**Electric Lighting**—elecric light

mer, Moses Gerrish—**Fire Alarm System (electic)**

mer, Robert—**Expedition**—expedition

nham, Ivan Richard—**Pump**—computer pump

nsworth, Willis S.—**Locker**—locker (coin ender)

quhar, George—**Play (drama)**—play acted by rofessional players

quhar, George—**Theater**—theater designed olely for theatrical purposes

r, John—**Quinine**—quinine

ragut, David Glasgow—**Naval Officer**—naval fficer to become an admiral

Farragut, David Glasgow—**Treason**—citizen of the United States to be tried for treason, convicted, and hanged

Farrar, Eugenia H.—**Radio Broadcast**—singer to broadcast

Farrington, Bob—**Horse Race**—harness driver (American) to score 300 victories in 1 year

Farrington, Wallace Rider—**Radio Facsimile Transmission**—transpacific and transcontinental facsimile transmission

Fascinato, John—**Television—Telecast**—color network telecast in compatible color

Faur, William—**Marine Corps**—marine band

Fauset, Crystal Bird—**Legislator (state)**—black woman state legislator

Faust family—**Supreme Court (U.S.)**—members of a family admitted simultaneously to practice in the Supreme Court of the United States

Fauvel-Gouraud, François—**Photographic Pamphlet**

Fayssoux, Peter—**Museum**—public museum

Featherstonhaugh, George William—**Geological Survey**—geological survey appropriation (U.S.)

Fechner, Robert—**Civilian Conservation Corps (U.S.)**

Feezor, Betty—**Tape Recording**—video recording on magnetic tape in color

Fehrenbach, John—**Hospital**—tuberculosis hospital (municipal) for consumptive poor

Feld, Irvin—**School**—professional school for exclusively training potential circus clowns

Fell, Jesse—**Coal**—anthracite coal burned experimentally

Feller, Robert William Andrew ("Rapid Robert," "Bob")—**Baseball Game**—opening day no-hit major league baseball game

Feller, Robert William Andrew ("Rapid Robert," "Bob")—**Baseball Pitcher**—baseball pitcher to pitch a no-hitter on opening day

Fellowes, Cornelius—**Horse Show**—horse show of national scope

Fellows, Alvin J.—**Tape Measure Patent**

Felt, Dorr Eugene—**Adding Machine**—adding machine absolutely accurate at all times

Feltham, Jocelyn—**Revolutionary War**—military action

Felton, Rebecca Latimer—**Senator (U.S.)**—woman to occupy a seat in the Senate

Fendall, Josias—**Shorthand Report**

Fenger, Christian—**Hospital**—interracial hospital

Fenno, John—**Newspaper**—political newspaper

Fenoaltea, Sergio—**Cabinet (U.S.)**—Cabinet meeting attended by a foreign national

Fenwick, Joseph—**Diplomatic Service**—consuls of the United States appointed after the adoption of the Constitution

Fenwick, Millicent Hammond—**Representative (U.S.)**—grandmother to serve in Congress

Ferebee, Thomas W.—**Atomic Bomb**—explosion over enemy territory

Ferentinos, Paisios—**Greek Orthodox Church**— Greek Orthodox church

Ferguson, Homer Lenoir—**Museum**—maritime museum

Ferguson, Mrs. Homer Lenoir—**Ship**—air-conditioned naval ship

Ferguson, Samuel David—**Protestant Episcopal Bishop**—Protestant Episcopal bishop (black)

Fermi, Enrico—**Atomic Reactor**—atomic reactor patent

Fernald, Walter Elmore—**School**—school for the mentally retarded

Fernow, Bernhard Eduard—**Forest Service**—Forest Service (U.S.)

Fernow, Bernhard Eduard—**Forestry School**—forestry school of collegiate character

Ferris, George Washington Gale—**Ferris Wheel**

Ferris, Hattie—**Baseball Team**—women's baseball team

Ferry, Elisha Peyre—**State**—state named for a native-born American (first governor)

Fessenden, Reginald Aubrey—**Radio Broadcast**—radio program broadcast

Fetchit, Stephen ("Stepin' ")—**Motion Picture**—black-oriented talking picture (all-talking, all-singing) by a major company

Fetter, Ted—**Television—Telecast**—transatlantic exchange of live television programs

Few, William—**Congress (U.S.)—Senate**—Senate

Few, William—**Hospital**—eye hospital (permanent)

Fickel, Jacob Earl—**Aviation—Pilot**—pilot to fire a gun from an airplane

Fiedler, Arthur—**Television—Telecast**—color network telecast in compatible color

Field, Ben—**Sleeping Car**—Pullman sleeping car

Field, Cyrus West—**Cable**—cable across the Atlantic Ocean was completed

Field, Cyrus West—**Cigar Band**—cigar band of special interest

Field, James Gaven—**People's Party**

Field, Pattie Hockaday—**Diplomatic Service**—woman vice consul

Field, Stephen Dudley—**Streetcar**—electric streetcar successfully run with current generated by a stationary dynamo

Field, Stephen Johnson—**Telegram**—transcontinental telegram

Field, Stephen Johnson—**Telegraph**—telegraph line to the Pacific coast

Fields, Kate—**Women's Club**—women's professional club

Fieser, Louis Frederick—**Vitamin**—synthetic vitamin K

Fillmore, Millard—**American Party**

Fillol, Jaime—**Tennis Match**—lawn tennis match (doubles) for the Davis Cup to exceed 100 games

Finch, William Bolton—**Ship**—warship to circumnavigate the globe

Findley, Paul—**Congress (U.S.)—House of Representatives**—black page of the House of Representatives (appointed by)

Fink, Colin Garfield—**Chromium Plating Process (commercial)**

Finletter, Thomas Knight—**Air Force**—Air Force Secretary

Finley, James—**Bridge**—suspension bridge

Finn, William Joseph—**Television—Telecas**—religious services to be televised

Finnegan, John ("Jack")—**Prizefight**—champ ship heavyweight title won in the first rou

Finney, John Miller Turpin—**Medical Socie**—American College of Surgeons

Firmstone, William—**Coke**

Firth, Abraham—**Humane Society**—humane sociation national organization

Fischer, Andrew J.—**Births**—quintuplets to more than 5 years

Fischer, Isaac—**Sandpaper Patent**

Fischer, James Andrew—**Births**—quintuplets live more than 5 years

Fischer, Karl M.—**Television—Telecast**—c mercial filmed by a camera operated by ato cally generated electricity

Fischer, Louis R.—**Frog Jumping Jubilee**

Fischer, Mary Ann—**Births**—quintuplets to more than 5 years

Fischer, Mary Catherine—**Births**—quintuplet live more than 5 years

Fischer, Mary Magdalen—**Births**—quintuplet live more than 5 years

Fischer, Mary Margaret—**Births**—quintuplets live more than 5 years

Fisher, Alva J.—**Washing Machine**—compl self-contained electric washing machine

Fisher, Anna L.—**Astronaut**—astronauts (wom

Fisher, Carl—**Postal Service**—postage cance machine patent

Fisher, Carl Graham—**Road**—coast-to-c paved road

Fisher, John Dix—**Blind**—school for the blind

Fisher, John Stuchell—**Congress (U.S.)—Sena**—senatorial controversy in which no candida were seated after a recount

Fisher, John Stuchell—**Teletype Service**—t typewriter system employed by a police dep ment

Fisher, Mary—**Quakers**—Quakers to arrive America

Fiske, Bradley Allen—**Aviation—Passenger**—miral in uniform to ride in an airplane

Fiske, Bradley Allen—**Microfilm**—microfilm re ing device

Fiske, Bradley Allen—**Torpedo**—airplane torp

Fiske, Daniel Willard—**Chess Tourname**—chess tournament of importance

Fiske, Willard—**Journalism Course**—journa course

Fiske, William L.—**Bobsled Competition**—f man bob-team competition

Fitch, Asa—**Entomologist**—state entomologis

Fitch, Howard W.—**Ship**—navy vessel constr ed as a mine layer

Fitch, John—**Ship**—steamboat to carry a man

Fitch, Samuel Sheldon—**Dental Book**—de textbook

Fitzgerald, Eugenia Tucker—**Women's Clu**—women's secret society

Fitzpatrick, John—**Marine Corps**—marine off killed in service

Ford, Robert—**Aviation**—**Flights (world)**—world flight by a commercial airplane

Forman, Sands W.—**Forest Service**—forest commission (state)

Forney, Matthias Nace—**Aviation**—**Periodical**—aviation magazine

Forrest, Edwin—**Play (drama)**—play performed 1,000 times

Forrest, Nathan Bedford—**Ku Klux Klan**

Forrest, Ray—**Television**—**Telecast**—underwater telecast from a submarine

Forrestal, James Vincent—**Defense Department (U.S.)**

Forrestal, Mrs. James Vincent—**Ship**—aircraft carrier with an angle deck

Forsyth, Ann J.—**Normal School**—woman principal of a normal school

Forsyth, William—**Fruit Culture Treatise**

Forsythe, Albert Ernest—**Aviation**—**Flights (transcontinental)**—transcontinental flight made by blacks in their own plane

Fort, Franklin William—**Federal Home Loan Bank Board**

Fort, Franklin—**Home Owners Loan Corporation**

Fortesque, George K.—**Play (drama)**—musical with an American theme and original score

Foster, George G.—**Periodical**—comic weekly

Foster, George Gale—**Business**—installment finance company

Foster, John—**Disciples of Christ**

Foster, John—**Engraving**—engraving

Foster, John—**Map**—map made in the United States published in a book

Foster, John—**Poet**—American poet

Foster, John Gibbons—**Aviation**—**Flights**—North Pole jet crossing

Foster, M. G.—**Deaf**—**Hearing Aid**—electrical hearing aid

Foster, Robert Frederick—**Whist**—whist organization

Foster, Thomas Jefferson—**Correspondence School**

Foster, William—**Animals**—sheep (Merino sheep)

Foulois, Benjamin Delahauf—**Aviation**—**Flights**—intercity airplane flight

Fourdrinier, Henry—**Papermaking Machinery**—papermaking machine (Fourdrinier) imported

Fourdrinier, Sealy—**Papermaking Machinery**—papermaking machine (Fourdrinier) imported

Fowler, George Ryerson—**First Aid Instruction**—first aid instruction

Fowler, John W. ("Bud")—**Baseball Player**—black baseball player (major league)

Fowler, Robert Grant—**Aviation**—**Flights (transcontinental)**—transcontinental airplane flight (eastbound)

Fowlkes, James—**Wedding**—television wedding

Fox, Annie G.—**Medal**—Order of the Purple Heart award to a nurse

Fox, Chastity—**College**—belly-dancing college course

Fox, Edward—**Insurance**—fire insurance joint-stock company

Fox, John D.—**Spiritualist**

Fox, Joseph—**Brass and Copper Seamless Tul**

Fox, Philip—**Planetarium**—planetarium open the public

Fox, William—**Motion Picture**—black-orien talking picture (all-talking, all-singing) by major company

Foyt, Anthony Joseph, Jr.—**Automobile Race** automobile racer to win the Indianapolis : four times

Fraenkel-Conrat, Heinz Ludwig—**Virus**—vi separated into component parts

France, Nicholas E.—**Degrees (academic and h orary)**—bachelor's degree awarded by a rec nized institution without requiring a sin college credit

Francen, Victor—**Television**—**Telecast**—mot picture premiere performance to be televis (feature-length foreign film)

Frances, Mary—**College**—university for bla (Catholic)

Franchessin, Jacques Antoine de—**Army**—bre

Francis I, King of France—**Kidnapping**—kidn ping

Francis, Edward—**Disease (distinctly Americ**

Francis, James Bichens—**Sprinkler**—sprinkler

Francis, Joseph—**Lifeboat**—lifeboat (corrugate

Francis, Tench—**Bank**—bank chartered by C gress

Frank, Glenn—**Medical Congress**—cancer in tute (convention)

Frank, Morris S.—**Animals**—dogs trained to gu the blind

Frank, Walter H.—**Medal**—Medal of Ho awarded in World War II

Franke, Mrs. William Birrell—**Ship**—aircraft c rier (atomic-powered)

Frankel, Jacob—**Army Officer**—chaplain (Jewi of the United States Army

Frankenberg, J.—**Aviation**—airplane motion p ture show

Franklin, Ann—**Woman**—woman newspaper e tor

Franklin, Benjamin—**Academy**

Franklin, Benjamin—**Book**—translated clas published

Franklin, Benjamin—**Cartoon**—newspaper c toon

Franklin, Benjamin—**Chair**—rocking chair

Franklin, Benjamin—**Chess Book**

Franklin, Benjamin—**Diplomatic Service**—fore service committee

Franklin, Benjamin—**Diplomatic Service**—mir ter plenipotentiary

Franklin, Benjamin—**Electric Cooking Exp** ment

Franklin, Benjamin—**Execution**—electrocut experiment

Franklin, Benjamin—**Hospital**—hospital America

Franklin, Benjamin—**Insurance**—fire insurar company to receive a charter

Franklin, Benjamin—**Lens**—eyeglass bifocals

Franklin, Benjamin—**Library**—circulating libra

Franklin, Benjamin—**Lightning Demonstration**

G

Goodlin, Chalmers ("Slick")—**Aviation—Airplane**—rocket plane

Goodman, Louis—**Airmail Service**—rocket airmail flight

Goodnow, Frank Johnson—**Political Science Society**—political science association

Goodrich, Annie Warburton—**Nursing School**—army school of nursing

Goodrich, Benjamin Franklin—**Rubber**—rubber company west of the Allegheny Mountains

Goodrich, J. Z.—**Republican Party**—Republican Party meeting (national)

Goodrich, John—**Money**—copper cents minted by a state

Goodrich, Joseph—**Building**—monolithic concrete building

Goodsell, N.—**Agricultural Journal**—agricultural journal written directly from practical experience

Goodwin, George—**Lawbook**—lawbook containing the federal laws of the United States

Goodwin, George—**Periodical**—children's magazine

Goodwin, George W.—**Ship**—steel sailing vessel

Goodwin, Hannibal Williston—**Photographic Film**—celluloid photographic film

Goodwin, Isabella—**Police**—woman detective

Goodwin, J. Cheever—**Play (drama)**—musical with an American theme and original score

Goodwin, Nathaniel Carr—**Actor**—actor to perform in 2 cities the same day

Goodwin, Nathaniel Carr—**Play (drama)**—drama to win a Pulitzer Prize

Goodwin, William Nelson—**Photography**—camera exposure meter

Goodyear, Charles—**Rubber**—rubber patent of importance

Goodyear, Charles—**Rubber**—vulcanized rubber

Gordon, Gale Ann—**Aviation—Pilot**—ensign (woman) to fly solo

Gordon, Hugh—**Aviation—Flights (world)**—round-the-world civil air service

Gordon, Louis—**Aviation—Passenger**—woman airplane passenger to cross the Atlantic Ocean

Gordon, Maurice Kirby—**War Veterans' Society**—American Legion

Gordon, Nathaniel—**Execution**—execution (federal) for slave trading

Gordon, Richard F., Jr.—**Astronaut**—space-to-ground news conference telecast

Gordon, Samuel George—**Fluorescent Mineral Exhibit**

Gore, Sammy—**Revolutionary War**—martyr in the Revolutionary War

Gorges, Ferdinando—**City (incorporated)**

Gorges, Ferdinando—**Waterpower**—waterpower development grant

Gorham, Nathaniel—**Land Office**

Gorman, Margaret—**Beauty Pageant**—beauty pageant (national)

Gorrie, John—**Refrigerator**—mechanical refrigerator patent

Gorringe, Henry Honeychurch—**Monument**—obelisk to be brought to the United States

Gorsuch, Robert Bennett—**Engineering Socie**—civil engineering national society

Gorton, Adolphus W.—**Aviation—Passeng**—dirigible passenger transfer to an airplane

Gosnold, Bartholomew—**Colonial Governme**—colonial council in America

Gosnold, Bartholomew—**Colonist**—English tlement in America (permanent)

Gosnold, Bartholomew—**Discovery**—disco of New England by an Englishman

Goss, Joe—**Prizefighter**—bareknuckle w heavyweight champion (American)

Gossling, Frederick W.—**Sugar**—sugar and cose from cornstarch

Gottlieb, Michael T.—**Book**—book on the gam bridge by a championship team

Gottschalk, Louis Moreau—**Musician**—musi (native-born American) to achieve Euroj fame

Gougelman, Pierre—**Eye**—artificial eyes

Goulaine de Laudonnière, René. See Laudonn René Goulaine de

Gould, Helen Miller—**Hall of Fame**—hall of 1 (university)

Gould, Stephen Philip—**Casein Fiber**

Goulding, Ray—**Television—Telecast**—st telecast (host)

Gounder, Howard Moyer—**Air Raid Shelter**—raid shelter

Gounod, Charles François—**Opera**—opera at Metropolitan Opera House

Goupil, René—**Canonization**—canonization North Americans

Govern, S. K.—**Baseball Team**—baseball 1 (black professional)

Gourdin, Edward O.—**Long Jump**—broad jum reach more than 25 feet

Grace, Robert—**Stove**—stove

Grace, William Joseph—**Ambulance**—me coronary-care ambulance

Grace, William Russell—**Monument**—obelis be brought to the United States

Graeff, Johannes de—**Flag**—American flag s ed by a foreigner

Grafton, H.—**Philatelic Society**—philatelic 1 ety

Graham, Charles M.—**Dentistry**—patent for a cial teeth

Graham, Evarts Ambrose—**Surgical Oper**—lung removal

Graham, John—**Diplomatic Service**—Pan Ai can delegates (American)

Graham, Lew—**Radio Broadcast**—circus br cast

Graham, Sylvester—**Bread**—bread made fror bolted flour

Graham, William J.—**Insurance**—group insur policy

Grajales, Martín Francisco López de Mendo **Catholic Parish**

Gram, Hans—**Music**—orchestral song

Gram, Hans Birch—**Homeopathy**—homeopa

Gram, Hans Birch—**Medical Book**—homeop treatise

Green, Philip Leonard—**Periodical**—Spanish magazine published by students

Green, Philip Leonard—**Students' Federation (international)**

Green, Robert M.—**Ice Cream Soda**

Green, Roy M.—**Federal Crop Insurance Corporation**

Green, S.—**History**—History of New England

Green, Samuel—**Bible**—Bible in an American Indian language

Green, Samuel—**Children's Book**

Green, Samuel—**Newspaper**—newspaper

Green, T.—**Book**—miniature book

Green, Theodore Francis—**Army Exclusion Law**

Green, Timothy—**Fishing Treatise**

Green, Timothy—**Religious Publication**—religious journal

Green, William—**Aviation**—automatic pilot

Greenberg, Henry ("Hank")—**Hall of Famer** —Hall of Fame (baseball) Jewish player

Greene, Jacob Lyman—**President (U.S.)**—President to ride in an automobile

Greene, John S.—**Photostat**—photographic copying machine

Greenleaf, Halbert—**Lock**—time lock

Greenough, Horatio—**Marble Statuary Group**

Greenough, John James—**Sewing Machine**—sewing machine patent

Greenwood, Chester—**Earmuff**

Greenwood, Edith—**Medal**—soldier's medal awarded to a woman

Greenwood, Isaac—**Arithmetic**—American arithmetic

Greenwood, John—**Dentistry**—porcelain teeth

Greenwood, John—**Drill**—dental drill

Greenwood, Miles—**Fire Department**—fire department to be paid a salary

Greer, James Richard—**Radio Facsimile**—radio facsimile long-distance transmission of a medical subject

Gregory, Samuel—**Medical School**—women's medical school

Gregory, Samuel—**Medical Society**—women's medical society

Greig, Alexander M.—**Postage Stamp**—adhesive stamps

Grenville, William Wyndham, Baron Grenville— **Extradition**—extradition treaty with a foreign country

Gresham, James B.—**World War I**—U.S. Army soldiers killed in combat

Grice, Charles C.—**Veterinary Hospital**—veterinary hospital

Gridley, Jeremy—**Freemasons**—military Masonic lodge

Gridley, Richard—**Army**—Army Engineering Department

Gridley, Richard—**Army Officer**—chief engineer

Gries, John Matthew—**Federal Home Loan Bank Board**

Griffin, Lloyd Dean—**Aviation**—**Flights (transatlantic)**—jet transatlantic nonstop flight west–east

Griffith, David Wark—**Motion Picture**—m(picture to gross $50 million

Griffith, Robert E.—**Archery Club**—archery

Griffith, Samuel P.—**Archery Club**—archery

Griffiths, Hall McAllister—**Presbyterian Chur** Presbyterian Church of America

Griffitts, Samuel Powel—**Pharmacy Professo**

Grilley, Henry—**Button**—pewter or block tin tons

Grilley, Samuel—**Button**—pewter or block buttons

Grilley, Silas—**Button**—pewter or block tin tons

Grissom, Virgil Ivan—**Astronaut**—astronaut

Grissom, Virgil Ivan—**Astronaut**—astron (American) to die in a spacecraft

Grissom, Virgil Ivan—**Astronaut**—astro (American) to make a suborbital flight tw

Grissom, Virgil Ivan—**Astronaut**—two-spaceflight (American) of 3 orbits

Griswold, Roger—**Congress (U.S.)**—**House Representatives**—brawl

Gross, Samuel David—**Adhesive and Medic Plaster**—adhesive and medicated plaster

Grosvenor, Gilbert—**Medal**—National Geogr ic Society gold medal

Grosvenor, Melville Bell—**Photograph**—pʰ graph in natural colors taken in the air

Grote, Augustus Radcliffe—**Entomology M** zine

Grotecloss, Harriet Elizabeth—**Fellowship**—lowship awarded a woman

Grout, Jonathan—**Semaphore Telegraph Sys**

Grover, Edwin Osgood—**Book Course**

Groves, Ernest Rutherford—**Marriage Cours**

Groves, John—**Aviation**—**Airport**—airport (fe ally owned and operated)

Grow, Malcolm Cummings—**Air Force O** —Air Force surgeon general

Gruskin, Benjamin—**Chlorophyll**—chlorophy

Gual, Pedro—**Treaty**—treaty with a South A can country

Guerin, Eric—**Horse Race**—stakes race t dead heat

Guerin, Napoleon E.—**Incubator (Eggs) Pate**

Guerin, Napoleon E.—**Life Preserver**—life server of cork

Guggenheim, H. Robert—**Automobile Ra** transcontinental automobile race

Guille, Charles—**Aviation**—**Parachute**—p chute jump from a balloon

Guilmant, Alexandre—**Organ School**

Gulick, Mrs. Luther Halsey—**Camp Fire Organization**

Gummere, William Stryker—**Football Game** tercollegiate football contest

Gumbert, Addison Courtney ("Ad")—**Bas Game**—National League 20-inning bas game

Gumper, Jake D.—**Pump**—gasoline pump

Gunn, Frederick William—**Camp for Boys**

Gunnells, Leonard Blake—**Birth Registrati** birth registration uniform system for the bering of birth certificates

er, Thomas—**Carillon**—carillon

ey, W. C.—**Photograph**—photograph of a
htning flash

rie, Janet—**Automobile Racer**—woman
ver to compete in the Indianapolis 500

rie, Samuel—**Chloroform**

rie, Samuel—**Glucose**

errez, Cesar Dario ("Cocoa")—**Baseball Play-**
-baseball player (major league) to make 7
nsecutive hits in 7 times at bat in the same
ne

t, Arnold—**Lecture Series (endowed)**

n, Mary—**Fellowship**—resident fellowship
women awarded by a women's college

H

, Mack—**American Indian Church**—church
anized by American Indians

, Ernst—**Photograph**—color transparency
mm) magnified 516 times

, Robert—**Book Club**—Book-of-the-Month
b

e, J. M. F.—**Motion Picture**—motion pictures
an eclipse of the sun taken from an airplane

is, Dunbar Ferdinand—**Lacrosse Association**
tercollegiate)

rsham, James—**Orphanage**—orphanage
th a continuous existence

ard, Sister St. Stanislas—**Catholic Nuns**
un who professed her vows

elton, Thomas—**Lime**

ett, Charles—**Opera**—opera broadcast over
national network from an American opera
use

ett, James Henry—**Actor**—American actor
appear abroad

way, William S.—**Electric Stove**—electric
ve

nwater, Harry—**Radio Station**—radio sta-
n operating a 100-kilowatt transmitter

ey, John—**Quadrant**

ey, William Aaron—**Blind**—correspondence
ool for the blind to offer instruction in the
aille system

ner, Ralph—**Primer**—typewriting primer

erick, Robert—**Stove Patent**

n, Hermann August—**Entomology Professor**

er, Charles V.—**Drug Mill**

enmann, Christian Friedrich Samuel—**Medi-**
Book—homeopathic treatise

s, Dan—**Water Ski Association (national)**

nson, Walter C.—**Softball**—softball (indoor
eball game)

s, George—**Football Game**—all-star football
ne

eman, Emanuel—**Book**—book series of
all-size paperbacks

Benjamin—**Technical Institute**

George Ellery—**Telescope**—telescope lens
inches in diameter

Hale, H. S.—**Bed**—folding bed manufacture

Hale, John Parker—**Senator (U.S.)**—senator elected on an antislavery ticket

Hale, Sarah Josepha—**Periodical**—magazine for
women

Hale, Mrs. Stephen—**Flag**—American flag over a
schoolhouse

Hales, Jean—**Naval Officer**—engineer inspector
(woman)

Hall, Mr.—**Ice Cream**—ice cream

Hall, Charles—**Aviation—Pilot**—black army pilot
to down an Axis airplane

Hall, Charles Bingley—**Bankers' Association**—
national bankers' association

Hall, Charles Corydon—**Rock Wool Factory**

Hall, Charles Martin—**Aluminum**—aluminum

Hall, Cyrenius—**Postage Stamp**—native American pictured on a postage stamp

Hall, D.—**Philosophy Book**—philosophy book
(American)

Hall, Glenn—**Opera**—opera by an American composer performed at the Metropolitan Opera
House of New York

Hall, Granville Stanley—**Psychology Society**—
psychology society (national organization)

Hall, Granville Stanley—**Psychology Laboratory**

Hall, Granville Stanley—**Psychology Magazine**

Hall, Henry—**Book**—book set by linotype

Hall, Henry—**Cranberry Cultivation**

Hall, Henry—**Fishing Line Factory**

Hall, John Elihu—**Law Periodical**

Hall, Joseph—**Newspaper**—newspaper published
west of the Alleghenies

Hall, Juanita—**Radio Station**—black network

Hall, Prince—**Masonry**—Negro Masonic Grand
Lodge (not Free and Accepted Masons)

Hall, Samuel Read—**Education Book**

Hall, Samuel Read—**Normal School**—normal
school established exclusively for the preparation of teachers

Hall, Thomas S.—**Railroad Signal System**—railroad signal system (automatic electric block)

Hall, William Alden—**World War I**—shot fired by
the U.S. Navy in World War I

Hallam, Lewis—**Play (drama)**—native American
play successfully acted on a regular stage

Hallam, Lewis—**Theater**—theater building (permanent)

Hallaren, Mary Agnes—**Army Officer**—woman
army officer

Halleck, Fitz-Greene—**Monument**—monument to
an American poet

Hallidie, Andrew Smith—**Streetcar**—cable streetcar

Hallock, William—**Physics**—national physics association

Hallock, William Allen—**Tract Society**—tract society (national)

Halsey, Francis Whiting—**Book Review**—book
review newspaper supplement

Halsey, Jane—**Ship**—dual sponsorship of a U.S.
Navy ship

Halsey, Lewis Benjamin—**Milk**—milk pasteurized commercially

Halsey, William Frederick ("Bull")—**Ship**—dual sponsorship of a U.S. Navy ship

Halsted, William Stewart—**Suture**—silk suture

Halvey, Nina—**Play (drama)**—antivivisection play

Halvorson, Kittel—**Representative (U.S.)**—representative elected by the prohibitionists

Hambrick, George Okie—**Helicopter—Flights**—helicopter transatlantic flight

Hamilton, Alexander—**Bank**—Bank of the United States

Hamilton, Alexander—**Cabinet (U.S.)**—cabinet

Hamilton, Alexander—**Congressional Caucus**—congressional caucus

Hamilton, Alexander—**Industrial Park**—industrial park

Hamilton, Alexander—**Loan**—loan to the United States

Hamilton, Alexander—**Mint (U.S.)**—Mint of the United States

Hamilton, Alexander—**Newspaper**—political newspaper

Hamilton, Alexander—**Treasury Department (U.S.)**—Secretary of the Treasury

Hamilton, Alexander—**War Veterans' Society**—Society of the Cincinnati

Hamilton, Andrew—**Postal Service**—parliamentary act to establish a post office

Hamilton, Andrew—**Postmaster**—postmaster general (colonial)

Hamilton, Charles Keeney—**Aviation—Expositions and Meets**—aviation meet

Hamilton, Charles Keeney—**Aviation—Flights**—airplane round trip

Hamilton, Frank Hastings—**Surgical Operation**—skin graft

Hamilton, James—**Insurance**—fire insurance company to receive a charter

Hamilton, John—**College**—college charter granted by a governor or acting governor with only the assent of his council

Hamilton, Samuel—**Postal Service**—Pony Express mail

Hamilton, Mrs. William—**Holiday**—Navy Day

Hammerstein, Oscar—**Cigar Rolling Machine**

Hammond, Elisha—**Library**—library building (university)

Hammond, Frankie—**Aviation—Parachute**—parachute jump from an autogiro

Hammond, Graeme M.—**Fencing**—fencing league (national)

Hammond, John—**Park**—park land

Hammond, John Hays—**Aviation**—airplane tank discharger

Hammond, Laurens—**Bridge (game) Table**

Hammond, Laurens—**Organ**—pipeless organ

Hammond, William Alexander—**Medical Book**—neurology textbook

Hampson, John—**Venetian Blinds**—venetian blind patent

Hampton, John—**Presbyterian Presbytery**

Hance, William A.—**Bicycle**—bicycle with a back-pedal brake

Hancher, Virgil Melvin—**Air Force Aca** (U.S.)—Air Force Academy

Hanchett, Henry Granger—**Organists' Soci** organists' society (national)

Hanchett, M. Waldo—**Dental Chair**

Hancock, George W.—**Softball**—softball (ir baseball game)

Hancock, John—**Declaration of Independ (American)**—Declaration of Independ signed

Hancock, John—**Medical Society**—medical ety (state)

Hancock, John—**State**—state constitution

Hancock, Thomas—**Bibliography**—bibliogr of theological and biblical literature

Hand, Jennie—**Baseball Team**—women's ball team

Hand, Thomas J.—**Cattle Club**—cattle club sey cattle)

Handy, William Christopher—**Musician**—poser of jazz music

Hanes, Horace Albert—**Aviation—Flights** plane to fly faster than 800 m.p.h.

Haney, David Jacob—**Aviation—Flights** Pole jet crossing

Hanger, Glossbrenner Wallace William—**S** —strike settlement

Hanks, Benjamin—**Chimes**

Hanks, Benjamin—**Clock**—self-winding clo

Hanks, Horatio—**Silk Mill**—silk mill

Hanks, Horatio—**Thread**—silk thread

Hanks, Rodney—**Silk Mill**—silk mill

Hanks, Rodney—**Thread**—silk thread

Hannah, John Alfred—**Air Force Academy** —Air Force Academy

Hannan, John—**Chocolate Mill**

Hannegan, Robert Emmet—**Radio Facs Transmission**—facsimile transmitted to a ing train

Hans, Rudolph Frank—**Submarine**—subm built on the Great Lakes

Hansberry, Lorraine—**Play (drama)**—play w by a black woman to reach Broadway

Hansell, Ellen F.—**Tennis Match**—women' tional championship lawn tennis matches

Hansell, Haywood Shepherd, 3rd—**World W** —air attack on Germany itself by U.S. Arm Forces

Hansen, Edmund H.—**Radio Facsimile Tran sion**—photograph sent by radio across th lantic from Europe

Hansen, Karen—**Architect**—woman gradua the Webb Institute of Naval Architecture

Hansen, Wilbur—**Bicycle Traffic Court**

Hanson, Homer ("Swede")—**Football Ga** professional football game in which 10 t downs were made

Hanson, John—**Seal**—Great Seal of the U States Government was impressed

Hapgood, Andrew S.—**Canning**—salmon ca

Harbo, George—**Rowing**—transatlantic tri rowboat

Harrison, Benjamin—**Forest Reserve**—forest reserve (national)

Harrison, Benjamin—**State**—states admitted to the Union simultaneously

Harrison, Bertram—**Theater**—municipal theater

Harrison, Earl Grant—**Immigration**—alien registration

Harrison, John—**Sulfuric Acid**

Harrison, Joseph—**Naval Officer**—naval doctor

Harrison, Rex—**Television—Telecast**—motion picture premiere performance to be televised (major film)

Harrison, Richard—**Lawyer**—lawyers admitted to the Supreme Court of the United States

Harrison, Robert Hanson—**Supreme Court (U.S.)**—Supreme Court justice who was nominated but who did not serve

Harrison, Robert Hanson—**Supreme Court (U.S.)**—Supreme Court of the United States

Harrison, Wallace Kirkman—**Building**—elliptical-shaped building

Harrison, William Henry—**Political Convention**—unit rule

Harrison, William Henry—**President (U.S.)**—President to die in Washington, D.C.

Harrision, William Henry—**President (U.S.)**—President whose grandson became president

Harrison, William Henry—**Whig Party**

Harroun, Ray—**Automobile Race**—automobile race on a track (long-distance)

Hart, Edwin Giles—**Citron**

Hart, Robert M.—**Television—Telecast**—transoceanic television image

Hartack, William ("Bill"), Jr.—**Jockey**—jockey to win more than $3 million in purses in 1 year

Hartford, George Huntington—**Business**—chain store organization

Hartle, Russell Peter—**World War II**—American expeditionary force to land on the European continent

Hartley, David—**Treaty**—treaty between the U.S. Government and a nation with which it had been at war

Hartly, Thomas—**Lawyer**—lawyers admitted to the Supreme Court of the United States

Hartranft, John—**Strike**—strike in which federal troops were called in peacetime

Harts, Rutherford B.—**Photograph**—photograph showing air in motion

Hartsfield, William Berry—**Pinball Game**—pinball legislation enacted by a major city prohibiting the machines

Hartshorn, Orville Nelson—**College**—college to grant women absolutely equal rights with men

Hartshorne, Richard—**Crime Prevention and Detection**—crime prevention commission for interstate cooperation

Hartswick, F. Gregory—**Crossword Puzzle Book**

Hartwell, John A.—**Football Game**—indoor football game

Harvard, John—**College**—college

Harvey, Bernard George—**Element**—element 99

Harvey, Bernard George—**Element**—element 101

Harvey, Charles T.—**Elevated Railroad**—ele[vated] railroad

Harvey, George Brinton McClellan—**Esp[eranto] Club**—Esperanto club (national organiza[tion])

Harvey, Harry Edward—**Dentist**—dentist [in] U.S. Navy to serve aboard a naval ship

Harvey, John—**Salt**—salt works

Harvey, John—**Treason**—treason trial (colo[nial])

Haskell, Ella Louise Knowles—**Attorney Ge[neral]**—assistant attorney general (state) who [was a] woman

Haskell, Emma—**Cripples**—public school fo[r] crip[ples]

Haskell, James Richards—**Ordnance**—c[annon] (steel, breech-loading, rifled)

Haskin, Dewitt Clinton—**Air (compressed)**

Haskins, Charles Waldo—**Accountancy** (state)

Haskins, Charles Waldo—**Accountants' S[ociety]**—accountants' society formed by a state

Haskins, Roswell Willson—**School Super[inten]dent**—school superintendent (city)

Haslett, Lewis Phectic—**Gas Mask**—gas m[ask]

Hassall, Albert—**Zoological Laboratory (U.S.)**—zoological laboratory (U.S.) for the study [of] parasites of livestock

Hassler, Ferdinand Rudolph—**Coast Surve[y] [Su]perintendent**

Hasson, Esther Voorhees—**Navy**—naval n[urse] corps

Hastie, William Henry—**Governor**—black [gover]nor appointed by the President of the U[nited] States

Hastie, William Henry—**Judge**—black judg[e] circuit court of appeals

Hastings, Ernest—**Magic Lantern**—magic la[ntern] feature show

Haswell, Charles Haynes—**Naval Officer**—[naval] officer to become an engineer

Hatch, Charles P.—**Oil**—oil tank cars

Hatch, Fred L.—**Silo**

Hatch, Julius—**Patent**—patent reissue

Hathway, Isaac Scott—**Money**—coin beari[ng] portrait of a black

Hatton, Anne Julia Kemble—**Opera**—oper[a of] serious nature

Haubner, Theodore D.—**Radio Distress Si[gnal]**—radio SOS from an American ship

Haubold, R. O.—**Fencing**—fencing leagu[e (na]tional)

Haugh, Daniel (Howe)—**Military Organiza[tion]**—military organization

Haughland, Vern—**Medal**—Silver Star Medal awarded to a civilian

Haughton, Billy—**Horse Race**—father an[d son] harness drivers to gross more than $1 m[illion] each in 1 season

Haughton, Peter—**Horse Race**—father an[d son] harness drivers to gross more than $1 m[illion] each in 1 season

Hauser, Joseph John ("Unser Choe")—**Ba[seball] Player**—baseball player to hit 60 home r[uns in] 2 different seasons

Henderson, James Arnold—**Animal Breeding Society**—artificial animal breeding cooperative

Henderson, John Brooks—**Political Convention**—national nominating convention presided over by a black

Henderson, Lawrence Joseph—**Science Association**—history of science society

Hendricks, Connie—**Horse Race**—horse race pari-mutuel with an entire field of women jockeys

Hendricks, Gerhard—**Slavery**—slavery protest

Hendrix, Eugene Russell—**Federal Council of the Churches of Christ in America**

Henenberg, Hattie L.—**Supreme Court (state)**—state supreme court composed entirely of women

Henke, Milburn—**World War II**—American expeditionary force to land on the European continent

Henley, David—**Court-martial**—military court-martial

Hennepin, Louis—**Coal**—coal

Hennock, Frieda Barkin—**Federal Communications Commission**—Federal Communications Commission woman member

Henriques, C. R.—**Wedding**—airplane wedding

Henriques, J. A.—**Coast Guard (U.S.)**—Coast Guard officers' training school

Henry, Charles Lewis—**Streetcar**—interurban streetcar line

Henry, Frederick F.—**Medal**—Medal of Honor awarded in the Korean War

Henry, John—**Actor**—matinee idol

Henry, John—**Play (drama)**—native American play successfully acted on a regular stage

Henry, Joseph—**Electric Bell**

Henry, Joseph—**Electric Magnet**

Henry, Joseph—**Radio Impulse Transmission (wireless)**

Henry, Joseph—**Telegraph**—telegraph (electromagnetic)

Henry, Lou (Mrs. Herbert Clark Hoover)—**Geologist**—woman graduate in geology

Henry, William—**Ship**—steamboat

Henry, William Elmer—**Library Society**—state librarians' society

Hensley, William Nicholas—**Radio Broadcast**—radio broadcast (two-way) from an airplane

Henson, Matthew Alexander—**Discovery**—discovery of the North Pole

Herbert, F. Hugh—**Motion Picture**—talking picture whose footage exceeded 6,000 feet

Herbert, H. L.—**Polo Club**—polo association (national)

Herbert, Henry William—**Author**—sports writer

Herbert, Hilary Abner—**Submarine**—submarine contract of the U.S. Navy

Herbert, Xavier—**Hospital**—hospital in America

Herbertson, John—**Bridge**—cast-iron bridge

Hererra, Enrique Olaya—**Diplomatic Service**—chief executive-elect of a foreign country

Hering, Constantine—**Medical School**—homeopathic school

Hering, Constantine—**Medical Society**—ho pathic medical society

Herman, Peter—**Radio Broadcast**—prize broadcast from the ringside

Herndon, Hugh—**Aviation—Flights (transpa** —transpacific nonstop flight

Herren, Thomas Wade—**War (Korean)**—Kc War hero buried in Arlington cemetery

Herrera, Pete—**Horse Race**—horse race wi purse of more than $1 million

Herreshoff, John Brown—**Ship**—torpedo boa

Herreshoff, Nathanael Greene—**Catamaran**

Herreshoff, Nathanael Greene—**Ship**—tor boat

Herring, Elbert—**American Indians**—In Affairs Commissioner

Herrington, Carl D.—**Helicopter—Flights**—t continental nonstop helicopter flight

Hersey, Henry Blanchard—**Balloon Race**—loon cup race

Hershfield, Harry—**Television—Telecast**—p cal campaign telecast

Herskovitz, Anatol—**Motion Picture**—motior ture of the inside of a living heart (of a d

Herter, Christian Archibald—**Satellite**—munications satellite successfully place orbit

Hertz, Alfred—**Opera**—opera composed b woman performed at the Metropolitan O House

Herz, Wilhelm—**Motorcycle Race**—motorcyc exceed 200 miles an hour

Hessel, John—**Radio Telephone**—military p ble

Hesselius, Gustavus—**Art Commission (pub**

Heth, Jim—**Aviation—Flights**—airplane er ance flight exceeding 1,200 hours

Hetzel, Henry W.—**Motion Picture**—talking ture in Esperanto

Hewitt, James—**Opera**—opera of a serious na

Hewitt, John Hill—**Music**—secular song hit

Hewitt, Peter Cooper—**Electric Lighting**—cury vapor lamp

Hewitt, Robert—**Television—Telecast**—p graph telecast from an airplane

Heyl, Henry Renno—**Motion Picture**—anim photographic picture projection before a ater audience

Heyward, Thomas—**Museum**—public museu

Hiacoomes—**American Indians**—American an preacher of Christianity

Hiawatha—**American Indians**—league of A can Indian nations

Hibbard, Frederick Cleveland—**Monument**—ue to commemorate literary characters

Hickey, Deirdre—**Railroad**—railroad train c ated exclusively by women

Hickey, Thomas—**Army Execution**

Hicks, Hassel T.—**Garage**—municipally ov parking building

Hicks, James—**Surgical Operation**—surgica eration on a bull to correct a sperm block

Hicks, Xen—**Judge**—woman associate justic the Circuit Court of Appeals

Hoey, James Alexander Finnell—**Citizenship**—citizenship granted to an alien on foreign soil

Hoffman, Adon J.—**Pressing Machine (steam-operated)**

Hoffman, Charles F., pseud. *See* Janson, E. A.

Hoffman, David—**Law School**—law school of collegiate rank

Hoffman, Edward L.—**Aviation—Parachute**—parachute

Hoffman, Harold Giles—**Crime Prevention and Detection**—crime prevention commission for interstate cooperation

Hoffman, Jacob Rosecrans—**Sawmill**—band sawmill

Hoffman, Paul Gray—**Economic Cooperation Administration (U.S.)**—Economic Cooperation Administration

Hoffman, William Joseph—**X Ray**—X-ray moving pictures (successful) of the action of the human heart

Hofmannsthal, Hugo von—**Opera**—opera matinee at the Metropolitan Opera House

Hoge, David—**Land Grant**—district land office

Hoisington, Elizabeth Paschel—**Army Officer**—generals who were brother and sister

Hoisington, Perry Milo—**Army Officer**—generals who were brother and sister

Holbrook, Amos—**Vaccination Legislation**—vaccination legislation (state)

Holbrook, Josiah—**Lyceum**

Holbrook, Josiah—**Manual Training**—industrial school

Holcomb, Amasa—**Photograph**—photograph taken in the United States

Holcomb, Amasa—**Telescope**—reflecting telescope

Holcomb, Thomas—**Marine Corps**—general (4 stars) of the Marines

Holden, George N.—**Motorcycle Race**—motorcycle distance race (4 hours)

Holden, Paul Robert—**War (French Indochina)**—American civilian pilot wounded in Indochina

Holden, William—**Television—Telecast**—pay television presentation of a motion picture shown simultaneously in theaters

Holden, William Woods—**Impeachment**—impeachment and removal from office of a state governor

Holland, Andrew M.—**Motion Picture**—peep show

Holland, Clifford Milburn—**Tunnel**—twin-tube subaqueous vehicular tunnel

Holland, Jerome Heartwell—**Brokerage**—New York Stock Exchange black director

Holland, John Philip—**Submarine**—submarine contract of the United States Navy

Holland, John Philip—**Submarine**—submarine that was practical and able to submerge

Hollen, Ms.—**Army School**—woman cadet to receive a commission

Hollerith, Herman—**Tabulating Machine**

Holley, Alexander Lyman—**Engineering Society**—mechanical engineering national society

Hollingshead, Richard Milton—**Motion P** Theater—drive-in motion picture theater

Hollingsworth, John Mark—**Paper**—manila

Hollingsworth, Lyman—**Paper**—manila pap

Hollis, Thomas—**Planetarium**—planetariu orrery

Holly, Birdsall—**Heating System**—heating s from a central station

Holly, George N.—**Motorcycle Race**—motor race (250 miles) (winner)

Holm, Hanya—**Copyright**—choreographic copyrighted

Holm, Jeanne Marjorie—**Air Force Officer** Force general (woman)

Holman, Francis—**Stagecoach Intercity Ser**

Holman, Nat—**Basketball Team**—basketba legiate team to win the National Invi Tournament and the National Collegiate letic Association trophy

Holmes, Edwin Thomas—**Burglar Alarm**—b alarm

Holmes, Edwin Thomas—**Telephone**—tele switchboard or exchange

Holmes, Edwin Thomas—**Telephone Opera** woman telephone operator

Holmes, Francis Simmons—**Museum**—c museum

Holmes, Israel—**Brass Wire Drawing and Making Machinery**

Holmes, Joseph Austin—**Mines Bureau (U.**

Holmes, Oliver Wendell—**Medical Book**—peral fever pamphlet

Holmes, Oliver Wendell—**Stereoscope**

Holmes, Oliver Wendell—**Stereoscope**—s scope (hand viewer, not patented)

Holt, Mr.—**Puppet Show**

Holt, Benjamin—**Oratorio**—oratorio perforr (complete)

Holt, Hamilton—**Book Course**

Holt, Hamilton—**College**—"Unit Cost Plan'

Holt, Hamilton—**Walk of Fame**

Holt, Harold G.—**Army Armored Car Unit**

Holt, J.—**Grammar**—English grammar b American published in America

Holt, John—**Jewish Book**—Jewish prayer b published in the United States

Holt, John—**Medical Book**—surgery manua

Holt, Lewis B.—**Medal**—Agriculture Depar distinguished service gold medal

Holt, Luther Emmett—**Medical Book**—pedi book of importance

Holyoke, Edward Augustus—**Medical Soci** medical society (state)

Homer, Louise—**Opera**—opera by an Am composer performed at the Metropolitan (House of New York

Hone, John—**Hospital**—eye hospital (perma

Hook, Albert H.—**Cigarette Manufacturin;** chine

Hooker, John Worthington—**Hygiene Instr** —hygiene and physical education prof ship

Hooper, Elihu Morgan—**Hospital**—leper ho

er, Herbert Clark—**Congress (U.S.)**—Senate
broadcast from the Senate chamber

er, Herbert Clark—**Medal**—National Geographic Society special gold medal

er, Herbert Clark—**Medal**—platinum medal

er, Herbert Clark—**President (U.S.)**—President to invite the President-elect

er, Herbert Clark—**Radio Broadcast**—presidential nomination ceremony broadcast

er, Herbert Clark—**Radio Conference**—national radio conference

er, Herbert Clark—**Radio Facsimile Transmission**—photograph sent overland by radio to distant point

er, Herbert Clark—**Television**—Telecast—cast of image and sound

er, Herbert Clark—**Visiting Celebrities**—absolute monarch

er, Herbert Henry—**Aviation**—Flights—airplane to fly faster than the speed of sound that is piloted by a civilian

er, Mrs. Herbert Clark—**Geologist**—woman graduate in geology

er, Stewart Whiting—**Army School**—graduate of the U.S. Military Academy (West Point) killed in action in World War I

ins, B. B.—**Bible Society**—Bible society

ins, Esek—**Naval Officer**—commander in chief of the Continental Navy

ins, Esek—**Navy**—naval fleet

ins, Esek—**War (colonial)**—marine engagement in battle

ins, Harry Lloyd—**Civil Works Administration (U.S.)**

ins, Harry Lloyd—**Federal Emergency Relief** ministration

ins, Harry Lloyd—**Federal Surplus Relief** rporation

ins, Harry Lloyd—**Works Progress Administration**—Works Progress Administration

ins, John Burroughs—**Navy**—naval fleet

ins, Joseph—**Money**—copper cents minted a state

ins, Mary Gross—**Village Improvement Society**

ins, Samuel—**Patent**—patent granted by the United States Government

ins, Stephen—**Corn (maize)**—corn (maize) nd by British settlers

inson, Francis—**Music**—secular song

inson, Francis—**Music Book**—secular song-ok by a native American

inson, Francis—**Musician**—composer (native-born American)

inson, Francis—**Novel**—novel (pamphlet)

an, Stephen Henry—**Engraving**—halftone graving

ck, William—**Milk**—malted milk

blower, Josiah—**Steam Engine**—steam engine

er, William Edmonds—**Medical Book**—pathology textbook

sby, Joseph Allan—**Automobile Club**

Horrocks, Jeremiah—**Building and Loan Association**

Horton, Everett—**Fishing Rod of telescoping steel tubes**

Hosford, Mary—**College**—coeducational college

Hoskin, E. William—**Newspaper**—French daily newspaper (successful)

Hoskins, Timo—**Insurance**—insurance board (state)

Hosmer, Bradley Clark—**Air Force Academy (U.S.)**—Air Force Academy

Hosmer, Mrs. Craig—**Ship**—atomic-powered cruiser

Houdry, Eugene—**Gasoline**—aviation gasoline

Hough, Franklin Benjamin—**Forestry Book**—*Elements of Forestry*

Hough, Franklin Benjamin—**Forestry Legislation**—federal forestry supervision

House, Henry Alonzo—**Automobile**—steam automobile

House, James A.—**Automobile**—steam automobile

House, Royal Earl—**Telegraph**—telegraph ticker to print letters of the alphabet

Houston, Abner—**Locomotive**—locomotive with a cab

Houston, David Franklin—**Road**—federal grant-in-aid

Houston, David Henderson—**Photographic Film**—roll film for cameras

Houston, Sam—**President of the Republic of Texas**

Howard, Charles Willis—**Santa Claus School**

Howard, Elston—**Baseball Player**—"most valuable player" award (major league) to a black in the American League

Howard, Eugene—**Television**—Telecast—political campaign telecast

Howard, George W.—**Pier**—ocean pier

Howard, John Eager—**Monument**—monument to George Washington (city or state)

Howard, Leslie—**Motion Picture**—motion picture to gross more than $70 million

Howard, Oliver Otis—**Freedmen's Bureau (U.S.)**

Howard, Philip—**Play (drama)**—play given by nonprofessional actors

Howard, Willie—**Television**—Telecast—political campaign telecast

Howe, Anthony L.—**Police**—motorcycle police

Howe, Frederic Clemson—**Consumers' Counsel (U.S.)**

Howe, Gene—**Holiday**—Mother-in-Law Day

Howe, Gordon ("Gordie")—**Hockey Player**—professional hockey player to reach a score of more than 1,000 points in a regular season

Howe, Gordon ("Gordie")—**Hockey Player**—professional hockey player to score more than 100 points in 1 season

Howe, Hamilton Wilcox—**World War II**—German submarine sunk by a U.S. naval vessel

Howe, John Ireland—**Pin**—machine for manufacturing pins

Howe, Julia Ward—**Arts and Letters Society**—woman elected to the American Academy of Arts and Letters

Howe, Julia Ward—**Arts and Letters Society**—woman elected to the National Institute of Arts and Letters

Howe, Mia—**Television—Telecast**—transoceanic television image

Howe, Richard—**Flag**—American flag flown in battle

Howe, Samuel Gridley—**Blind**—school for the blind

Howe, Samuel Gridley—**School**—school for the mentally retarded

Howe, Syd—**Hockey Player**—professional hockey player to score 6 goals in 1 game

Howell, Edwin Eugene—**Map**—relief map

Howell, Thomas—**Fireboat**—fireboat

Howells, William Dean—**Arts and Letters Society**—arts and letters society (national)

Hower, Nelson—**Tights (circus)**

Howick, Tom—**Insurance**—health insurance law (state)

Hoxie, Vinnie Ream. *See* Ream, Vinnie

Hoxsey, Archibald—**President (U.S.)**—President to fly

Hoyt, John Wesley—**Hygiene Instruction**—physiology and hygiene courses

Hoyt, Mary Frances—**Civil Service**—Civil Service woman appointee

Hoyt, Wayland—**Railroad Car**—chapel car

Hruska, Roman Lee—**Governor**—governor to appoint two United States senators in one year for interim terms

Hubbard, Amos H.—**Papermaking Machinery**—papermaking machine (Fourdrinier)

Hubbard, Edward—**Airmail Service**—international airmail

Hubbard, Gardiner Greene—**Telephone**—telephone used by a railroad company

Hubbard, Henry Griswold—**Elastic Webbing**

Hubbard, Robert ("Cal")—**Hall of Famer**—athlete enshrined in 2 halls of fame

Hubbard, Samuel D.—**Elastic Webbing**

Hubbard, William—**Degrees (academic and honorary)**—Bachelor of Arts degree

Hubbard, William—**Map**—map made in the United States published in a book

Hubbard, William DeHart—**Olympic Games**—black American athlete to win an individual event in the Olympic Games

Hubbell, Harvey—**Electric Attachment Plug (separable)**

Hubbell, Harvey—**Electric Light Socket with pull chain**

Huber, Alice—**Hospital**—cancer home for incurables (free)

Huber, Frederick R.—**Orchestra**—municipal orchestra supported by taxes

Hubrey, Skye—**Television—Telecast**—motion picture premiere telecast on 2 successive nights

Huck, Winnifred Sprague Mason—**Representative (U.S.)**—mother elected to Congress

Huckstep, Glenn—**Submarine-Escape Tra**[nk]—**Tank**—women to take the submarine-e[scape] test

Huddleson, John W.—**Diamond**—diamond i[n ac]tual rock

Hudson, Barzillai—**Lawbook**—lawbook co[ntain]ing the federal laws of the United States

Hudson, Barzillai—**Periodical**—children's [maga]zine

Hudson, William G.—**War (Korean)**—Ame[rican] pilot to destroy an enemy airplane in th[e Ko]rean War

Huebner, George John—**Automobile Trans**[conti]**nental Trip**—gas-turbine automobile to m[ake] transcontinental trip

Huffner, John—**World War I**—combat missi[on by] all-American pilots ordered to battle by a[n] American squadron commander

Hufnagel, Charles Anthony—**Surgical Ope**[ration]—artificial aortic valve

Hufschmidt, Holly A.—**Secret Service**—S[ecret] Service women agents

Huggins, Miller J.—**Baseball Game**—World S[eries] baseball games to gross $1 million

Hughes, Ball—**Bronze Statue**

Hughes, Charles Evans—**Conference**—c[onfer]ence of great powers

Hughes, Charles Evans—**Radio Facsimile T**[rans]**mission**—photograph sent by radio acros[s the] Atlantic as a public demonstration

Hughes, Charles Evans—**Strike**—anti-sit-d[own] strike decision (federal)

Hughes, David Edward—**Telegraph**—tele[graph] ticker that successfully printed type

Hughes, Henry—**Sociology Treatise**

Hughes, Howard—**Aviation—Airplane**—air[plane] with eight engines

Hughes, Howard—**Radar**—radar for comm[ercial] and private planes

Hughes, John—**Colonist**—civilian settlement of the Allegheny Mountains

Huling, Marcus—**Oil**—oil well (flowing)

Hull, Amos Gerald—**Medical Periodical**—h[omeo]pathic magazine

Hull, Cordell—**Cabinet (U.S.)**—Cabinet offi[cer to] address a joint session of Congress

Hull, Henry—**Television—Telecast**—high-d[efini]tion telecast

Hull, Isaac—**War (1812)**—frigate action of i[mpor]tance in the War of 1812

Hull, John—**Money**—dies for coins in Ame[rica]

Humbert, Augustus—**Mint (U.S.)**—private [mint] authorized by the United States Governm[ent]

Hume, Edgar Erskine—**Medal**—Order of th[e Pur]ple Heart awarded in the Korean War

Hume, George W.—**Canning**—salmon cann[ery]

Hume, William—**Canning**—salmon cannery

Hummel, Jacob Frederick—**Rubber**—rubbe[r d]ent

Humperdinck, Engelbert—**Opera**—opera b[road]cast in its entirety by the Metropolitan [Opera] Company

Humphrey, George Magoffin—**Cabinet (U**[.S.)]—Cabinet conference telecast

I

J

Jefferson, Thomas—**Embargo Act**

Jefferson, Thomas—**Mint (U.S.)**—Mint of the United States

Jefferson, Thomas—**Parliamentary Rules of Order**

Jefferson, Thomas—**Patent**—patent granted by the United States Government

Jefferson, Thomas—**Patent**—patent law (national)

Jefferson, Thomas—**Political Convention**—political nominating caucus attended by party leaders

Jefferson, Thomas—**Postal Card**—postal card depicting other than the Liberty head

Jefferson, Thomas—**President (U.S.)**—President elected by the House of Representatives

Jefferson, Thomas—**President (U.S.)**—President inaugurated in the city of Washington

Jefferson, Thomas—**President (U.S.)**—President to review the military forces

Jefferson, Thomas—**Presidential Candidate**—presidential candidate nominated at a caucus

Jefferson, Thomas—**Presidential Election**—presidential election in which candidates had been nominated for the vice presidency

Jefferson, Thomas—**State Department (U.S.)**—State Department (U.S.) Secretary

Jefferson, Thomas—**Supreme Court (U.S.) Decision**—Supreme Court decision to void an act of Congress

Jefferson, Thomas—**Territorial Expansion**—annexation of territory

Jefferson, Thomas—**Treaty**—treaty entered into by the United States after the treaty of peace with Great Britain

Jeffries, Jim (James Jackson Jeffries)—**Motion Picture**—motion picture of a real pugilistic encounter taken at night

Jeffries, Jim (James Jackson Jeffries) —**Prizefight**—championship heavyweight title won in the first round

Jeffries, Jim (James Jackson Jeffries)—**Prizefighter**—black heavyweight champion of the world

Jellison, A. C.—**Bowling Tournament**—gold medal award to a perfect-score bowler

Jencks (Jenckes, Jenkes, Jenks), Joseph—**Brass and Iron Foundry**

Jencks, Joseph—**Fire Engine**—fire engine

Jencks, Joseph—**Money**—dies for coins in America

Jencks, Joseph—**Patent**—machine patent

Jenkins, Charles Francis—**Radio Facsimile Transmission**—photographs sent over a city telephone

Jenkins, Charles Francis—**Television—Telecast**—telecast of an object in motion

Jenkins, Charles Francis—**Television License**—television license

Jenkins, Howard, Jr.—**Labor Relations**—National Labor Relations Board black member

Jenkins, Therese A.—**Political Convention**—political party national delegates (women)

Jenney, William Le Baron—**Building**—building known as a skyscraper

Jenner, Edward—**Vaccination for smallpox**

Jennings, Hugh ("Hughie") Ambrose—**Base****Game**—baseball game (major league) in w 1 team scored 24 runs

Jennings, Hugh ("Hughie") Ambrose—**Base****Strike**—baseball strike

Jennings, Thomas—**Fingerprinting**—finger conviction

Jernigin, J. D. ("Duke")—**Glider**—glider to across the continent

Jerome, Chauncy—**Clock**—brass clock work

Jervis, John Bloomfield—**Locomotive**—loco tive with a four-wheeled front truck

Jessel, George—**Radio Broadcast**—coopera radio show

Jessel, George—**Television—Telecast**—der stration of home reception of television

Jester, Maurice D.—**Medal**—Navy Cross awa to a Coast Guard officer in World War II

Jeter, Helen Rankin—**Degrees (academic and)****orary)**—Doctor of Social Science degree

Jewell, Izetta—**Television—Telecast**—play t televised

Jewell, Pliny—**Belting**

Jewett, Charles Coffin—**Librarians' Conventi**

Jewett, John P.—**Medical Society**—wom medical society

Jogues, Isaac—**Canonization**—canonization North Americans

Johansson, Ingemar—**Prizefighter**—world he weight champion to regain his crown (Patte defeated Johansson)

John, Augustus—**Radio Facsimile Transmissi** drawing sent by radio across the Atlantic

John of Cronstadt, Father (John Sergiev)—**Can****zation**—canonization of a saint in the Ur States

John Paul II, pope (Karol Wojtyla)—**Visiting (****brities**—pontiff to visit the White House

Johns, Kensey—**Senator (U.S.)**—senator app ed (not seated)

Johnson, Andrew—**Election Law**—election granting black males the right to vote (ve bill)

Johnson, Andrew—**Impeachment**—impeachr proceedings against a President of the Ur States

Johnson, Andrew—**Labor Legislation**—eight-l day for government laborers and mechani

Johnson, Andrew—**President (U.S.)**—Preside become a senator

Johnson, Billy—**Play (drama)**—musical con by a black for black talent

Johnson, Billy—**Play (drama)**—musical (length), written, produced, directed, and formed as a Broadway (New York City) pro tion

Johnson, Byron Bancroft ("Ban")—**Bas****League**—American league

Johnson, Byron Bancroft ("Ban")—**Baseball S** —baseball strike

Johnson, Charles Eneu—**Printer's Ink**

Johnson, Clarence—**War (Korean)**—Amer tank crew to cross the 38th Parallel in Ko

son, Clarence L.—**Aviation**—**Airplane**—jet-opelled fighter plane

son, Claudia Alta ("Lady Bird") Taylor—**Degrees (academic and honorary)**—honorary degrees presented simultaneously to a President and his wife

son, Claudia Alta ("Lady Bird") Taylor—**Telephone**—picturephone service (commercial)

son, Eads—**Ferryboat**—ferryboat built exclusively for motor vehicle transportation

son, Edward—**Gas**—gas ordinance (city)

son, Edward—**Television**—**Telecast**—opera telecast

son, Elmer G.—**Patent**—patent on a "solar airplane vehicle"

son, George Arthur—**Water Purification**—water supply chemically treated with chlorine compounds

son, George Washington—**Croquet League**

son, Henry—**Medal**—Croix de Guerre awarded to a black American

son, Henry—**Ship**—warship (American) captured overseas

son, Herbert Lester—**Peritonitis**—peritonitis preventive (successful)

son, Hiram Warren—**Progressive Party**

son, Hugh Samuel—**Industrial Recovery Act**—compliance board under the National Industrial Recovery Act

son, Hugh Samuel—**Industrial Recovery Act**—industrial recovery act (national)

son, Hugh Samuel—**Industrial Recovery Act**—postage stamps commemorating the National Recovery Act

son, Jack—**Prizefighter**—black heavyweight champion of the world

son, James B.—**Fish Hatchery**—fish hatchery

son, James J.—**Golfer**—golfer to play 24 hours continuously on a regulation course

son, James Weldon—**Poet**—black poet to be employed to teach creative writing

son, Jerome—**Young Men's Christian Association**—Young Men's Christian Association (or black members)

son, John—**Bicycle Racer**—bicyclist to ride a mile in less than 2 minutes from a standing start

son, John—**Carpeting**—carpeting (velvet)

son, John—**Photographic Studio**—commercial photography studio

son, Kathryn Kuntz—**Ship**—naval ship christened by an Army officer

son, Leo—**Air Force Academy (U.S.)**—Air Force Academy graduate (American Indian)

son, Lewis Jerome—**Stadium**—cement stadium

son, Louisa Catherine. *See* Adams, Mrs. John Quincy

son, Lyndon Baines—**Astronaut**—astronaut international rescue agreement

son, Lyndon Baines—**Cabinet (U.S.)**—Cabinet meeting attended by a foreign national

son, Lyndon Baines—**Cabinet (U.S.)**—Cabinet member (black)—nominated by

Johnson, Lyndon Baines—**Degrees (academic and honorary)**—honorary degrees presented simultaneously to a President and his wife

Johnson, Lyndon Baines—**Medal**—Vietnam Service Medal authorized

Johnson, Lyndon Baines—**Solicitor General (U.S.)**—solicitor general of the United States who was a black (named by)

Johnson, Lyndon Baines—**Telephone**—satellite (privately owned) telephone conversation

Johnson, Lyndon Baines—**Telephone**—telephone conversation (commercial) over a satellite

Johnson, Lyndon Baines—**Telephone**—telephone service over the transpacific telephone cable

Johnson, Lyndon Baines—**Television Station**—noncommercial educational television network

Johnson, M.—**History**—History of New England

Johnson, Marmaduke—**Bible**—Bible in an American Indian language

Johnson, Marmaduke—**Book**—book privately printed

Johnson, Marmaduke—**Grammar**—American Indian grammar

Johnson, Marmaduke—**Primer**—primer in an American Indian dialect

Johnson, Mordecai Wyatt—**College**—university for blacks to establish undergraduate, graduate, and professional schools

Johnson, Morris—**Ship**—roll-on, roll-off carrier

Johnson, Neils—**Helicopter**—helicopter passenger service

Johnson, Opha May—**Marine Corps**—woman marine reserve

Johnson, Philip—**Building**—bronze and glass skyscraper

Johnson, Richard Mentor—**Vice President (U.S.)**—Vice President elected by the Senate

Johnson, Robert H.—**Ski School**—indoor ski school

Johnson, Robert Wood—**Adhesive and Medicated Plaster**—adhesive and medicated plaster with a rubber base

Johnson, Roswell Hill—**Oil and Gas Production Course**

Johnson, Roy Lee—**Ship**—aircraft carrier with an angle deck

Johnson, Rudy F.—**Court-martial**—court-martial trial in the United States at which enlisted men were allowed to sit as members of the court

Johnson, Ruth—**Marine Corps**—woman in the U.S. Marine Band

Johnson, Samuel—**Grammar**—English grammar by an American published in America

Johnson, Samuel—**Philosophy Book**—philosophy book (American)

Johnson, Thomas Loftin—**Coin Box**

Johnson, Walter—**Hall of Fame**—hall of fame (baseball)

Johnson, William—**United Church of Christ**—minister (avowed homosexual)

Johnson, William H.—**City (Lilliputian)**

Johnson, William Samuel—**Congress (U.S.)**—**Senate**—Senate

Johnson, William Samuel—**Diplomatic Service**—foreign service committee

Johnson, Woolsey—**Medical Society**—laryngological society (state)

Johnston, George W.—**War (Quemoy)**—American casualty of the Red Chinese bombardment of Quemoy

Johnston, Henrietta—**Artist**—woman painter

Johnston, Henrietta—**Pastelist**

Johnston, Joseph Eccleston—**Civil War**—serious engagement in the Civil War

Johnston, Thomas—**Engraving**—historical print engraved in America

Jokes, Joseph—**Whips**

Jon, Gee—**Execution**—lethal gas execution

Jonas, Karel—**Dictionary**—Bohemian-American dictionary

Joncaire, Chabert—**Niagara Falls**—utilization of Niagara Falls waterpower

Jones, Albert L.—**Paper**—corrugated paper

Jones, Alice—**Newspaper**—composograph photograph in a newspaper

Jones, Billy—**Radio Broadcast**—program theme song

Jones, Charles Wesley ("Baby")—**Baseball Player**—baseball players to hit a home run

Jones, Doris—**Streptomycin**

Jones, Edward A.—**College Student**—college graduate (black)

Jones, Emeline Roberts—**Dentist**—woman dentist

Jones, George William—**Farmers' Institute**—farmers' institute held by a land grant agricultural college off its campus

Jones, H. S.—**Basketball Team**—basketball team (college)

Jones, Henry—**Jews**—Jewish fraternal society

Jones, Hugh—**Grammar**—English grammar by an American

Jones, James I.—**Hospital**—eye hospital (permanent)

Jones, John—**Medical Book**—surgery manual

Jones, John Clifton—**Television—Telecast**—surgical operation televised on a coast-to-coast closed circuit in color

Jones, John Paul—**Flag**—American flag displayed on a man-of-war

Jones, John Paul—**Flag**—American flag saluted by a foreign nation

Jones, John Paul—**Ship**—ship-of-the-line

Jones, Orlando—**Cornstarch**—cornstarch patent

Jones, Pauline L.—**Library Society**—state librarians' society

Jones, Regina C.—**Soldiers' Home**—woman admitted to a soldiers' home

Jones, Richard Watson—**College**—state college for women

Jones, Robert J.—**Postage Stamp**—native American pictured on a postage stamp

Jones, Robert Tyre (Bobby)—**Golf Champion**—golf champion to hold the four highest golf titles

Jones, Robert Tyre (Bobby)—**Golf Cham**—golf champion to win the United States tional Amateur Tournament two year succession

Jones, Robert Tyre (Bobby)—**Sports Trop** sports trophy for the outstanding amateur lete of the year

Jones, Ruel B.—**Lunch Wagon**

Jones, William—**Insurance**—fire insurance stock company

Jones, William H.—**Ice Skating Club**—ice sk club

Jordan, Cicely—**Breach of Promise Suit**

Jortberg, Richard Edmund—**Submarine**—at powered turbine electric-drive submarine

Joseph, chief of the Nez Perce—**Postage S**—native American pictured on a postage s

Josepho, Anatol M.—**Photography**—film dev ing machine

Josephus, Flavius—**Jewish Book**—Jewish bo Jewish authorship published in America

Joshee, Anandibai—**Physician**—Hindu wom receive a Doctor of Medicine degree

Joubert de la Muraille, Jacques Hector Nicho **Catholic Nuns**—Catholic nuns (black comr ty)

Joyce, Mike—**Runner**—transcontinental foot

Judson, Whitcomb L.—**Fastening**—hookless tening

Juett, Howard W.—**Automobile License (fed**—contract carrier license

Julius, Sir George—**Totalisator**—totalisator

Jump, William Ashby—**Medal**—Agriculture partment distinguished service gold meda

June, Charles—**Ice Skating Champion**—sk champion (ice)

June, Harold Irving—**Aviation—Flights**—S Pole flight

Junkin, George—**Normal School**—normal s instruction offered by a college

Junkin, George—**School**—model school

Junkin, Sam F.—**World War II**—American p shoot down a German fighter plane

Jurgensen, Walter Herman—**Legislature**—cameral legislature (state)

Justine, George—**Television—Telecast** zefight in a "studio"

K

Kabis, Dorothy Andrews Elston—**Treasury partment (U.S.)**—treasurer of the United to sign currency with 2 names

Kaercher, Grace—**Woman**—woman clerk state supreme court

Kahn, Julian Seth—**Cans**—disposable can fo pensing liquids under pressure

Kahnweiler, David—**Life Preserver**—life pre er of cork

kaua, David, king of the Sandwich Islands
[awaii)—**Coronation**—coronation on what
as to become United States soil

kaua, David, king of the Sandwich Islands
[awaii)—**Visiting Celebrities**—king (reigning)
visit the United States

sch, Isidor—**Jews**—Jewish Rabbinical Con-
rence

nus, Herbert Thomas—**Motion Picture**—
chnicolor motion picture film

Edward Bing—**Citizenship**—Chinese grant-
citizenship

e, Delancey Astor—**Coaching**

e, Elisha Kent—**Expedition**—Arctic expedi-
n

kus, Roberta A.—**Woman**—nuclear commer-
al power plant licensed woman power operator

ouse, Edna Beecham—**Births**—quintuplets

ouse, Edward Cole—**Births**—quintuplets

rowitz, Adrian—**Motion Picture**—motion
cture of the inside of a living heart (of a dog)

olani, queen—**Coronation**—coronation on
nat was to become United States soil

pel, Frederick Russell—**Telephone**—satellite
rivately owned) telephone conversation

pel, Gertrude—**Opera**—opera matinee at the
etropolitan Opera House

georgevich, Peter. *See* Peter I, king of Serbia

nan, Theodor von—**Medal**—National Medal
Science

eles, Leopold—**Medal**—Medal of Honor
varded to a Jewish soldier

man, George Simon—**Play (drama)**—musical
ay to win a Pulitzer Prize

man, Irving Robert—**Spy**—peacetime death
ntence for espionage (judge)

man, Irving Robert—**Television**—television
ewitness allowed to testify in a federal court

man, Irving Robert—**Treason**—execution for
eason in peacetime

n, Abraham Eli—**Building**—housing coop-
ative sponsored by a labor union

a, Thomas—**Opera**—opera performed by a
ofessional visiting troupe

a, Thomas—**Play (drama)**—Shakespearean
ay

a, Thomas—**Theatrical Advance Publicity**
an

se, Amalya Lyle—**Judge**—black woman
dge of the U.S. Court of Appeals

ne, Robert—**Military Organization**—military
ganization

, Elmo Woodrow—**War Veterans' Society**—
orld War II veterans' society officially recog-
ed by Congress

er, Leonarde—**Lie Detector**

er, Sarah Warren—**Deaf**—**School**—lipread-
g instruction for the deaf

er, William Henry ("Wee Willie")—**Baseball**
yer—baseball player (major league) to hit in
consecutive games

a, F.—**Aviation**—**Flights**—airplane to carry
0,000 pounds

Keene, Edmund—**Actor**—actor to receive curtain
applause

Keene, Foxhall—**Automobile**—automobile to exceed the speed of a mile a minute

Keene, Foxhall P.—**Polo**—international polo series

Keep, John—**Book Jacket**—(designer)

Keep, Nathan Cooley—**Dental School**—dental
school permanently established by a university

Kegelman, Charles C.—**Medal**—Distinguished
Service Cross awarded in enemy-occupied territory

Keim, Elwood—**Aviation**—**Flights**—"airplane
train"

Keim, Elwood—**Aviation**—**Flights**—sky-train international round-trip flight

Keim, Jacob—**Boardwalk**

Keimer, S.—**Insurance Book**—insurance proposal

Keimer, S.—**Shorthand Book**

Keimer, Samuel—**Bible Concordance**—Welsh
concordance of the Bible

Keimer, Samuel—**Newspaper**—newspaper serial
story

Keith, A. E.—**Telephone**—automatic telephone
system (successful)

Keith, Benjamin Franklin—**Vaudeville**

Keller, Frances—**Arbitration Association**—arbitration association

Keller, Franklin J.—**High School**—public high
school to specialize in the performing field

Keller, Kaufman Thuma—**Air Force Academy
(U.S.)**—Air Force Academy

Kellerman, Annette—**Motion Picture**—motion
picture sex shocker

Kelley, Beverly Gwin—**Coast Guard (U.S.)**—
Coast Guard women to serve aboard ships (other than hospital ships)

Kelley, Beverly Gwin—**Coast Guard Officer**—
woman commander of a Coast Guard ship

Kelley, George B.—**Fraternity (Greek letter)**—intercollegiate Greek-letter national fraternity for
black men

Kelley, John F.—**Aviation**—**Periodical**—aviation
magazine devoted primarily to airplanes

Kelley, Oliver Hudson—**Agricultural Society**—
agricultural society of national importance

Kellogg, Albert—**Forest Service**—forest Commission (state)

Kellogg, Frank Billings—**Woman**—woman passport division chief

Kellogg, Mary Fletcher—**College**—coeducational
college

Kelly, Gene—**Ballet**—ballet transmitted by satellite

Kelly, George E. Maurice—**Aviation**—**Airplane
Fatalities**—airplane fatality in a solo military
airplane

Kelly, Grace—**Motion Picture Actor**—motion picture actress depicted on a postage stamp

Kelly, John M.—**Aviation**—**Airplane**—airplane to
carry 100 people on one flight across the Atlantic Ocean

Kelly, John Patrick—**Army Officer**—flight surgeon

Kelly, Oakley G.—**Aviation—Flights (transcontinental)**—transcontinental nonstop flight

Kelly, William—**Immigration**—Chinese labor immigration

Kelpius, Magister—**Ancient Mystical Order Rosae Crucis**

Kelsey, Benjamin—**Aviation—Flights**—all-blind flight

Kemmler, William—**Execution**—electrocution of a human being

Kemper, W. H.—**Court**—small debtors' court established by state law

Kempon, G. S.—**Radio Broadcast**—transatlantic radio signal

Kendall, Amos—**Telegraph**—telegraph company

Kendall, George—**Colonial Government**—colonial council in America

Kendall, George—**Rebellion (colonial)**

Kendrick, Captain—**Ship**—ship to carry the United States flag around the world

Kenison, Nehemiah—**Chiropodist**

Kenly, William Lacy—**Air Force**—air service (military) under one command

Kennedy, Bernard Reilly—**Codification Board (United States)**

Kennedy, Edward Moore—**President (U.S.)**—President with a brother in the Senate

Kennedy, Edward Moore—**Senator (U.S.)**—father whose 3 sons were senators

Kennedy, Gerald S.—**Television—Telecast**—stockholders' meetings televised coast-to-coast simultaneously

Kennedy, Henry Peres—**Chair**—recumbent chair patent

Kennedy, John Fitzgerald—**Air Force Officer**—Air Force general (woman) nominated

Kennedy, John Fitzgerald—**Cabinet (U.S.)**—cabinet member who was a brother of a President

Kennedy, John Fitzgerald—**Catholic Mass**—Catholic mass in English said for a President

Kennedy, John Fitzgerald—**Fair**—world's fair that was financially successful

Kennedy, John Fitzgerald—**Hijack Legislation**—hijack legislation (federal)

Kennedy, John Fitzgerald—**Medal**—Armed Forces Expeditionary Medal

Kennedy, John Fitzgerald—**Medal**—National Aeronautics and Space Administration Distinguished Service Medal

Kennedy, John Fitzgerald—**Postage Stamp**—brothers to be pictured on individual postage stamps

Kennedy, John Fitzgerald—**President (U.S.)**—President to witness the firing of a Polaris missile

Kennedy, John Fitzgerald—**President (U.S.)**—President with a brother in the Senate

Kennedy, John Fitzgerald—**Presidential Candidate**—presidential candidate debate series on television

Kennedy, John Fitzgerald—**Restaurant**—revolving restaurant (opened by remote control)

Kennedy, John Fitzgerald—**Senator (U.S.)**—father whose 3 sons were senators

Kennedy, John Fitzgerald—**Television—Tele**—courtroom verdict telecast

Kennedy, John Fitzgerald—**Television—Tele**—presidential news conference to be telev live

Kennedy, John Fitzgerald—**Water**—seaw conversion plant (practical)

Kennedy, Joseph Patrick—**Senator (U.S.)**—fa whose 3 sons were senators

Kennedy, Robert Francis—**Cabinet (U.S.)**—C net member who was a brother of a Presi

Kennedy, Robert Francis—**Postage Star** brothers to be pictured on individual pos stamps

Kennedy, Robert Francis—**Presidential Candi** —presidential candidate assassinated v campaigning

Kennedy, Robert Francis—**Senator (U.S.)**—fa whose 3 sons were senators

Kennedy, W. Ashton—**Chiropody Sch** chiropody school as a regular division of a versity

Kenner, Frank Terry—**Coast Guard Officer**— admirals who were twins to serve at the s time

Kenner, William Wilson—**Coast Guard O** —rear admirals who were twins to serve a same time

Kensett, Thomas—**Canning**—canning

Kent, Arthur Atwater—**Radio Telephone**— phone conversation between someone o ground and a person in a dirigible

Kent, Billy—**Television—Telecast**—musical edy telecast (one-hour)

Kent, Leslie Swigart—**Medical Society**—wc president of a state medical society

Kent, Mabel Lucas (Mrs. Arthur Atwater Ke **Radio Telephone**—radio telephone conv tion between someone on the ground and a son in a dirigible

Kenyon, David B.—**Firehouse Pole**—fireh pole

Kenyon, Helen—**Church**—woman moderat the General Council of Congregational Christian Churches

Kenyon, William Orlin—**Sponge**—oxidized lulose (sponge)

Kephart, Calvin Ira—**Radio Broadcast**—de over the radio

Kepley, Ada H.—**Lawyer**—woman lawyer gr ated from a law school

Kepner, William E.—**Aviation—Airship**—d ble made completely of metal

Kern, Mrs. Lou J.—**Physician**—osteopath (v an)

Kernodle, George Riley—**Theatrical School**— ater and dramatic criticism course

Kerns, James N.—**Baseball League**—bas league of importance

Kerr, Ann—**Navy**—women (other than nurses signed to regular shipboard duty

Kerr, George—**Tennis Match**—professional tennis contest (international)

Kirsch, Hyman—**Soda Water**—sugar-free soft drink

Kissinger, Henry Alfred—**President (U.S.)**—President to resign

Kisters, Gerry—**Medal**—Medal of Honor awarded to a soldier who already had received a Distinguished Service Cross

Kitchen, Stuart Fordyce—**Vaccine**—yellow fever vaccine for human immunization

Kizer, Noble—**Football Game**—all-star football game

Kleid, Kerry—**Motorcyclist**—woman professional motorcyclist

Kleindienst, Richard Gordon—**Attorney General**—attorney general (U.S.) to plead guilty to a criminal offense

Klemm, Johann Gottlob—**Organ**—organ built in the United States

Klenle, Gustave A.—**Wedding**—television wedding

Kliegl, Anton Tiberius—**Electric Lighting**—klieg light lighting unit

Kliegl, John Hugh—**Electric Lighting**—klieg light lighting unit

Kline, A. C.—**Stamp Catalog**

Knabenshoe, A. Roy—**Balloon**—balloon to land on a building

Knapp, James Henry—**Hat**—derby hat

Knapp, Joseph Gillett—**Forest Service**—forestry inquiry commission (state)

Knebel, Fletcher—**Television—Telecast**—motion picture premiere telecast on 2 successive nights (author of original novel)

Kneeland, Samuel—**Fishing Treatise**

Kneeland, Samuel—**Periodical**—sectarian magazine

Kneeland, Samuel—**Religious Publication**—religious journal

Knight, Alonzo P. ("Lon")—**Baseball League**—National League

Knight, Arthur F.—**Golf Clubs (or golf sticks)**—steel shaft for a golf club

Knight, Evelyn—**Television—Telecast**—variety talent-show series of 1-hour programs

Knight, Frederick Irving—**Medical Periodical**—laryngology magazine

Knight, James—**Cripples**—private school for cripples

Knight, James—**Hospital**—orthopedic hospital

Knight, Jonathan—**Medical Society**—medical society (national)

Knight, William J. ("Pete")—**Aviation—Flights**—airplane to fly faster than 4,500 m.p.h.

Knowles, Asa Smallidge—**College**—college principally for war veterans

Knowlton, Martin P.—**College**—educational hosteling network

Knox, Clarence Moore—**Aviation—Legislation**—aviation legislation (state)

Knox, Henry—**Cabinet (U.S.)**—Cabinet

Knox, Henry—**Patent**—patent law (national)

Knox, Henry—**War Department (U.S.)**—War Department (U.S.)

Knox, Henry—**War Veterans' Society**—Society the Cincinnati

Knox, Thomas Wallace—**News Corresponde**—news reporter tried as a spy

Knox, William—**Bowler**—bowler to make a pe fect score of 300 in an American Bowling Co gress tournament

Knox, William—**Diplomatic Service**—consuls the United States appointed after the adopti of the Constitution

Knudsen, William Signius—**Army Officer**—gene al appointed from civilian rank

Knyphausen, Wilhelm, Baron von—**Flag**—Ame can flag flown in battle

Koch, Ralph A.—**Submarine**—submarine ac dent

Koelsch, John Kelvin—**Medal**—Medal of Hon awarded to a helicopter pilot

Koenig, Alfred J.—**Radio Facsimile Transmissi**—transpacific and transcontinental facsim transmission

Koenig, George Augustus—**Diamond**—diamon in a meteorite

Koester, Heinrich Bernhard—**Lutheran Church** Lutheran services in English

Koester, Mrs. M.—**Bowling Tournament**—bow ing tournament for women

Kogel, Marcus David—**Medical School**—medic college (Jewish sponsored)

Kolb, Lawrence—**Narcotics**—narcotics sanato um (federal) for drug addicts

Kolb, Robert—**Army**—helicopter battalion

Koller, Helen—**Wedding**—double radio weddi

König, Paul—**Submarine**—cargo submarine cross the Atlantic Ocean

Koons, Franklin M.—**World War II**—American land on French soil in World War II

Koos-ta-ta, Paul—**American Indians**—America Indian tribal constitution

Kopsky, Doris—**Bicycle Racer**—woman bicyc champion of the National Amateur Bicycle A sociation

Korda, Alexander—**Television—Telecast**—m tion picture premiere performance to be tel vised (major film)

Korda, Alexander—**Television—Telecast**—m tion picture (full-length) telecast

Korizek, Frank—**Newspaper**—Czech-langua newspaper

Korn, Arthur—**Radio Facsimile Transmission** photograph sent by radio across the Atlan from Europe

Koufax, Sanford ("Sandy")—**Baseball Pitcher** baseball pitcher (major league) to strike out 3 or more batters in each of 3 seasons

Koufax, Sanford ("Sandy")—**Baseball Pitcher** baseball pitcher to win 4 no-hitters

Kraenzlein, Alvin C.—**Olympic Games**—Ame can athlete to place in 4 events in 1 year

Krafft, Michael—**Parade**—street parade held by mystic society

Krafft, Michael August—**Distilling Book**

Kramer, John Franklin—**Prohibition**—prohibiti bureau (federal)

amer, Stanley—**Motion Picture**—motion picture presented simultaneously in major cities throughout the world

antz, John Christian—**Anesthesia**—trifluoroethyl vinyl ether

antz, Judith—**Book**—book advance payment to exceed $3 million

atz, Daniel Griswold—**Protestant Church**—Protestant church formed by the amalgamation of 4 churches of different denominations

aus, C. Raymond—**Television**—**Telecast**—telecast (public) over telephone wires using the narrow-band system

ause, Charles F., Jr.—**Tunnel**—triple-tube underwater roadway

auskopf, Joseph—**Jewish College**—Jewish college to train men for the rabbinate

ebs, George—**Aviation**—**Airplane**—jet-propulsion four-engine bomber

enz, Eric—**Discus**—discus throw to exceed 160 feet

eps, Juanita Morris—**Brokerage**—New York Stock Exchange woman governor

eusi, John—**Phonograph**—phonograph

igbaum, William Lutz—**Army Camp**—army camp for "limited service"

oss, Anna Moscowitz—**Prison System**—woman to direct a prison system

out, Sara Gdulin—**Dentist**—woman dentist in the U.S. Navy

ueger, Otto E.—**Orchestra**—radio orchestra

basov, Valery Nikolayevich—**Astronaut**—astronauts (American) to participate in an international spaceflight

chins, Harry—**Glider**—**Flights**—glider flight indoors

hn, Adam—**Botany Professor**

hn, Richard J.—**X Ray**—X-ray three-dimensional (stereo) fluoroscopic system

hnke, Christian—**Tennis Match**—lawn tennis match (singles) for the Davis Cup to exceed 80 games

jiraoka, Sozaburo—**Immigration**—Japanese national to receive an immigration visa

llman, Charles—**Television**—**Telecast**—opera from the Metropolitan Opera House especially tailored and trimmed for television

mp, Herman Guy—**Industrial Recovery Act**—state to place all its employees under the blanket code of the National Recovery Act Code

ndla, John—**Basketball Game**—all-star game of the National Basketball Association (West team coach)

ntzig, Robert—**Court**—court in which the judge presided in a city other than the one in which the lawyers appeared

nze, Johann Christoff—**Music Book**—Lutheran hymnbook (English) created in America

nzi, Abraham—**Quinine**—quinine

rtz, Gerald N.—**Postal Card**—street scene

rzweil, Raymond—**Blind**—machine for reading printed matter aloud

skof, Ivan Alexandrovich—**Russian Settlement**

Kyrides, Lucas Petrou—**Rubber**—synthetic rubber

L

Labadie, Jean de—**Labadist Community**

Lablache, Louise—**Opera**—opera at the Metropolitan Opera House

La Farge, John—**Arts and Letters Society**—arts and letters society (national)

Lafayette, Marquis de—**Citizenship**—citizenship (colonial) conferred by special grant

Lafayette, Marquis de—**Land Grant**—special land grant to a foreigner

Lafferty, James V.—**Building**—building shaped like an elephant

La Follette, Philip—**Insurance**—unemployment insurance act

La Follette, Robert Marion—**Motion Picture**—talking pictures of presidential candidates

Lagan, M. D.—**Hospital**—leper hospital

Lahm, Frank Purdy—**Aviation**—**Airplane**—airplane purchased by the United States Government

Lahm, Frank Purdy—**Aviation**—**Pilot**—Army pilot to solo

Lahm, Frank Purdy—**Aviation**—**Passenger**—airplane passenger (official)

Lahm, Frank Purdy—**Balloon Race**—balloon cup race

Laird, John—**Ship**—iron vessel

Laise, Carol Clendening—**Diplomatic Service**—ambassadors in service to wed

Lake, Simon—**Submarine**—submarine fitted with an internal-combustion engine

Lake, Simon—**Telephone**—telephone message from a submarine underwater

Lalande, John—**Canonization**—canonization of North Americans

Lalemant, Gabriel—**Canonization**—canonization of North Americans

Lallemont, Pierre—**Bicycle**—bicycle with a rotary crank

Lamar, Gazaway Bugg—**Ship**—iron vessel

Lamar, Mirabeau Buonaparte—**President of the Republic of Texas**

Lamb, John—**Employment Service**—municipal employment office

Lamb, William Frederick—**Building**—building higher than 1,250 feet

Lambert, Albert Bond—**Army Balloon School**

Lambert, Marie Macri—**Judge**—woman judge of the Surrogates Court

Lambert, Marie Macri—**Lawyers' Association**—lawyers' association (state) woman president

Lambine, Janna—**Coast Guard (U.S.)**—woman airplane pilot in the Coast Guard

Lambrecht, John Osgo—**Ship**—aircraft carrier to sail around Cape Horn

La Mountain, John—**Ship**—balloon carrier

Lamson, Eleanor Annie—**Astronomer**—woman astronomer employed in the United States Naval Observatory

Land, Edwin Herbert—**Camera**—camera to take, develop, and print pictures on photographic paper

Land, Emory Scott—**War Shipping Administration**—War Shipping Administration award

Land, Emory Scott—**War Shipping Administration**—War Shipping Administration (first administrator)

Land, Frank Sherman—**Freemasons**—Order of De Molay

Landis, Cullen—**Motion Picture**—talking picture whose footage exceeded 6,000 feet

Landis, James McCauley—**Securities and Exchange Commission (U.S.)**

Landis, Kenesaw Mountain—**Baseball Dictator**

Landis, Merkel—**Bank**—Christmas savings club

Landreth, David—**Seed Business**

Lane, Benjamin J.—**Gas Mask**—gas mask with a self-contained breathing apparatus

Lane, Dick—**Television Station**—commercial television station west of the Mississippi River

Lane, Ephraim—**Tungsten**—tungsten and tellurium

Lane, Ralph—**Letter**—letters written in English

Lane, Thomas Joseph—**Representative (U.S.)**—representative reelected after serving a prison term

Lane, William Coolidge—**Bibliography Society** (national)

Lanergan, Andrew—**Rocket**—rocket patent

Langan, Jack—**Prizefight**—prizefight arena

Langdon, John—**Congress (U.S.)—Senate**—president pro tempore of the United States Senate

Langdon, John—**Congress (U.S.)—Senate**—Senate

Langdon, John—**Navy**—naval fleet

Langdon, John—**Ship**—ship-of-the-line (shipyard owner)

Langdon, John—**Vice Presidential Candidate**—vice presidential nominee to decline nomination

Langdon, Kay Louise—**Naval Officer**—women sworn into the regular U.S. Navy

Langenheim, Frederick—**Magic Lantern**—magic lantern slides (glass-plate)

Langenheim, Frederick—**Photograph**—photograph to gain world fame

Langenheim, Frederick—**Photograph**—solar-eclipse photograph

Langenheim, Frederick—**Stereoscope**—stereoscope

Langenheim, William—**Photograph**—photograph to gain world fame

Langenheim, William—**Stereoscope**—stereoscope

Langer, Jerry—**Motorboat Race**—motorboat race (ocean) under the Union of International Motorboating rules

Langford, Nathaniel Pitt—**Park**—park (national)

Langhorne, Nancy Witcher. *See* Astor, Nancy Witcher Langhorne

Langley, Samuel Pierpont—**Aviation—Expe**[...] **tions and Meets**—air conference (internation[...]

Langley, Samuel Pierpont—**Aviation—Flight**[...] airplane (heavier-than-air) to make any l[...] sustained flight

Langloiserie, Louis—**Language Instructio**[...] French instruction

Laning, Richard Boyer—**Submarine**—submar[...] powered by a liquid-metal-cooled atomic re[...] tor

Lansdowne, Zachary—**Aviation—Airship**—d[...] gible (American-built rigid)

Lansdowne, Zachary—**Aviation—Flights (tra**[...] **continental)**—transcontinental airship voya[...]

Lanston, Tolbert—**Typesetting Machine**—mo[...] type

Lapchick, Joe—**Basketball Game**—all-star ga[...] of the National Basketball Association (E[...] team coach)

Lapham, Increase Allen—**Forest Service**—f[...] estry inquiry commission (state)

La Porte, Arthur Earl—**Airmail Service**—airm[...] transatlantic service

La Porte, Arthur Earl—**Aviation—Flights (trans**[...] **lantic)**—Atlantic Ocean scheduled air servi[...]

Larkin, Thomas Oliver—**Diplomatic Service**[...] consul to California

Larsen, Don—**Baseball Pitcher**—baseball pitc[...] to pitch a perfect no-hit, no-run, no-walk Wo[...] Series game

Larsen, Paul J.—**Civil Defense Director**

Larsh, Almon E.—**Element**—element 103

La Salle, Robert Cavelier, Sieur de—**Ship**—Gr[...] Lakes commercial vessel

Lasswell, Harold Dwight—**Propaganda Cou**[...] **(college)**

Latham, Woodville—**Motion Picture**—motion p[...] ture on film shown on a screen

Lathrop, Julia Clifford—**Children's Bureau (U.**[...]

Lathrop, Mary Florence—**Lawyer**—woman la[...] yer to become a member of the American [...] Association

Lathrop, Rose Hawthorne—**Hospital**—can[...] home for incurables (free)

Latimer, Robert M.—**Element**—element 103

La Tour, Sieur le Blond de—**Levees**

Latrobe, Benjamin Henry—**Bridge**—wooden ra[...] road bridge of a purely truss type

Latta, Alexander Bonner—**Fire Engine**—fire [...] gine that was practical

Latting, Patience Sewell—**Mayor**—woman may[...] of a city of over 200,000 population

Lauber, Harold—**Curling Championship (**[...] **tional)**

Lauber, Louis—**Curling Championship (nation**[...]

Laudonnière, René Goulaine de—**War (coloni**[...] —intercolonial war

Laughlin, James—**Tennis Match**—intercollegia[...] court tennis match

Laurence, William Leonard—**Telephone**—p[...] turephone transcontinental call

Laurens, Henry—**Colonial Government**—in[...] pendent government in any of the Americ[...] colonies

Lehmann, Ernest August—**Aviation—Flights (transatlantic)**—Atlantic Ocean regular commercial airship service

Leibert, Peter—**Music Book**—Lutheran hymnbook (German) published in America

Leigh, Douglas—**Electric Sign**—animated-cartoon electric sign

Leigh, Lewis—**Silk**—silk dyers

Leigh, Vivien—**Motion Picture Actor**—husband and wife Oscar winners

Leigh, Vivien—**Motion Picture**—motion picture to gross more than $70 million

Leigh, Vivien—**Television—Telecast**—motion picture premiere festivities to be televised

Leighton, Margaret—**Television—Telecast**—motion picture premiere performance to be televised (major film)

Leiper, Thomas—**Railroad**—railroad for freight transportation

Leiserson, William Morris—**Labor Relations**—National Mediation Board

Leisler, Jacob—**Treason**—American colonist hanged for treason

Leister, Claude Willard—**Radio Broadcast**—zoo broadcast

Leister, Edward—**Duel**—duel

Leivas, Juan—**Rodeo**

Lembke, Charles—**Optometry Society**—optometry society (national)

Lemke, William—**National Union for Social Justice**

Lemke, William—**Union Party**

Lemnitzer, Lymon Louis—**Medal**—Distinguished Service Medals of the Army, Navy, and Air Force presented to one person at the same time

LeMoyne, Francis Julius—**Anti-Slavery Party**

LeMoyne, Francis Julius—**Crematory**—crematory

Le Moyne de Morgues, Jacques de—**Artist**

Lena, Antonio—**Ship**—gyro-stabilized vessel to cross the Atlantic Ocean

Lenhart, John L.—**Naval Officer**—naval chaplain killed in action

Lennebacker, George—**Fly Casting Tournament**—fly casting tournament

Lenox, Walter Scott—**Chinaware**—dishes (complete set) made in America for the Executive Mansion

Lentsch, Carl G. O.—**Cream Separator**—centrifugal cream separator patent

Leon, Jerome Louis—**Narcotics**—narcotics sanatorium for minors

Leonard, Gardner Cotrell—**College Academic Costume Standardization**

Leonard, Jonah Fitz Randolph—**United Christian Party**

Leonard, Johnny—**Baseball Game**—all-star baseball game (major league)

Leonard Michael—**Motion Picture**—motion picture of a staged prizefight

Leonard, R. C.—**Fly Casting Tournament**—cast to exceed 100 feet

Leonard, Robert Josselyn—**Vocational Guidance Chair**

Leonard, Samuel—**Iron**—angle iron

Leonardson, Samuel—**Woman**—heroine

Leone, Mrs. Nicholas Charles. *See* Petry, Luci

Leonhardt, Elmer C.—**Aviation—Passenge**r woman airplane passenger (transcontinent a

Leonov, Aleksei Arkhipovich—**Astronaut**—tronauts (American) to participate in an int national spaceflight

Leopold, Aldo—**Game Management Chair**

Lerena, Juan José de—**Newspaper**—Span newspaper

Leslie, Harry—**Tax**—chain stores tax (state)

Lester, John—**Cricket Club**—college cricket cl team to tour England

Le Tourneau, Robert Gilmour—**Building**—bu ing built inside a factory

Le Tugo, Oscar—**World War I**—American Ar soldiers killed in World War I

Levadoux, Michael—**Catholic Seminary**—Cat lic seminary

Leveaux, Edward H.—**Piano Player**—piano pl er (completely automatic)

Levenson, Sam—**Television—Telecast**—co program (commercial)

Leventhal, M. H.—**Radio Church**

Leverett, John—**Degrees (academic and honora**—Doctor of Sacred Theology degree

Levin, Isaac—**Hospital**—cancer hospital (mun pal)

Levingston, William—**Theater**—theater

Levinthal, Helen Hadassah—**Degrees (acade**and honorary)—Master of Hebrew Literat degree

Levsen, Emil Henry ("Dutch")—**Baseball Pitc**—baseball pitcher (major league) to win 2 cc plete games in 1 day

Levy, Asser—**Jews**—Jew to win all the rights a perform all the duties of American citizens

Levy, Bert ("Yank")—**Army School**—army tra ing school

Levy, Louis—**Airmail Service**—autogiro n delivery direct to a post office

Levy, Simon Magruder—**Army School**—ar school graduate (Jewish)

Levy, Simon Magruder—**Army School**—ar school graduates

Levy, Uriah Phillips—**Naval Officer**—captain the U.S. Navy who was Jewish

Lewi, Maurice J.—**Chiropody School**—chiropo school of note

Lewin, Richman—**Television Station**—crowave television station

Lewis, Andrew—**Treaty**—treaty entered into the United States with American Indian tri

Lewis, Brenda—**Television—Telecast**—op from the Metropolitan Opera House especi tailored and trimmed for television

Lewis, Colby—**Television**—college credit cou in television

Lewis, Elizabeth Matthew—**Army School**—structor (woman)

Lewis, Floyd John—**Surgical Operation**—he operation in which the deep freezing techni was employed

Linder, Albert H.—**Wedding**—telegraph wedding (minister)

Linderman, Henry—**Assay Office Building (federal)**

Lindley, Jacob—**College**—university founded by a federal land grant

Lindsay, Mary Harrison (Mrs. John Vliet Lindsay)—**Ship**—commercial crude-oil carrier

Lineback, John—**Cottonseed Hulling Machine**

Lining, John—**Weather Observations**

Link, Edwin Albert—**Aviation**—aviation trainer

Linn, William—**Congress (U.S.)—House of Representatives**—chaplain of the House of Representatives

Lipman, Hyman L.—**Pencil**—pencil with an attached eraser

Lipowsky, Henry—**Bohemian American Church**

Lipscomb, William Nunn, Jr.—**Nobel Prize**—Nobel Prize winners all from one country in 5 categories

Lipsner, Ben B.—**Airmail Service**—airmail regular service

Lipton, Martha—**Television—Telecast**—opera (complete) to be televised from the Metropolitan Opera House

Lipton, Thomas—**Radio Telephone**—radio telephone ship-to-shore commercial service

Lisbon, Isaac—**Motion Picture Theater**—theater in the world devoted exclusively to the exhibition of motion pictures

Lislet, L. Moreau—**Law Codification** (state)

Litchfield, Paul Weeks—**Aviation—Airship**—dirigible landing and taking off from an oceangoing steamship

Liteky, Angelo Joseph—**Medal**—Medal of Honor in the Vietnam war awarded to a chaplain

Little, Arthur D.—**Rayon**—rayon patent

Little, Charles C.—**Lawbook**—law compilation of United States laws

Litvinov, Maksim Maksimovich—**Diplomatic Service**—ambassador to the Union of Soviet Socialist Republics

Livermore, Mary Ashton Rice—**News Correspondent**—woman news reporter at a political convention

Livingood, John Jacob—**Physics**—radioactive substance produced synthetically

Livingston, Edward—**Law Codification** (state)

Livingston, John Henry—**Theological School**—theological school

Livingston, Milton Stanley—**Physics**—cyclotron

Livingston, Robert R.—**Territorial Expansion**—annexation of territory

Lloyd, James—**Bridge**—stone-arch railroad bridge

Lloyd, Wray Devere Marr—**Vaccine**—yellow fever vaccine for human immunization

Llywellin, John—**Shorthand Report**

Lobsiger, Lydia—**Federal Deposit Insurance Corporation**

Lockard, Joseph L.—**Radar**—radar used to detect enemy airplanes

Locke, Alain Le Roy—**Rhodes Scholar**—black to win a Rhodes scholarship

Lockwood, Belva Ann Bennett—**Equal Rig**l **Party**

Lockwood, Belva Ann Bennett—**Supreme Co** **(U.S.)**—woman admitted to practice before t Supreme Court of the United States

Lockwood, Lorna Elizabeth—**Judge**—chief just (woman) of a state supreme court

Lockwood, Lorna Elizabeth—**Supreme Co** **(state)**—chief justice (woman) of a state preme court

Lodge, Benjamin F.—**Stone Crusher**—sto breaking machine patent

Lodge, Henry Cabot—**Conference**—conference great powers

Lodge, Henry Cabot—**Political Convention—**tional nominating convention presided over a black

Loening, Grover Cleveland—**Degrees (academ and honorary)**—Master of Arts degree aeronautics

Logan, James—**Book**—translated classic p lished

Logan, James—**Library**—library building

Logan, James Harvey—**Loganberry**

Logan, William—**Library**—library building

Lombe, Thomas—**Silk**—silk exportation

Londonberry, Annie—**Bicycle Trip (world)**—bi cle trip around the world by a woman

Long, Craig—**Presbyterian Church**—Presbyter Church of America

Long, Crawford Williamson—**Anesthesia**—an thetic (general)

Long, Crawford Williamson—**Anesthesia**—et administered in childbirth

Long, Cyril Norman Hugh—**Pituitary Hormon** pituitary hormone (isolated)

Long, Isaac—**Church of the United Brethren Christ**

Long, James—**Aviation—Flights**—New Yo Alaska flight

Long, James G.—**Aviation—Flights**—airplane carry 300 passengers on one flight

Long, Perrin Hamilton—**Sulfanilamide**—s fanilamide as a treatment for infections streptococcic origins

Long, Russell—**Senator (U.S.)**—senator to wi seat that had been occupied by his father a mother

Longden, Johnny—**Jockey**—jockey to win 4, races

Longfellow, Henry Wadsworth—**Play (drama** musical with an American theme and origi score

Longfellow, Henry Wadsworth—**Poem**—poem win national acclaim

Longley, William Harding—**Photograph**—pho graphs taken under the sea in natural color

Longman, Mary Evelyn Beatrice—**Woma** woman sculptor honored by membership in National Academy of Design

"Longshore, Squire"—**Locomotive**—locomot with a cab

Longstreet, William—**Ship**—steamboat patent

Lutter, Grover Cleveland—**Bicycle Traffic Court**

Lutz, Aleda E.—**Medal**—Distinguished Flying Cross awarded to a nurse

Lutz, Elizabeth M.—**GI Bill of Rights**—Army Corps veteran (woman) to receive a loan under the GI Bill of Rights

Lutz, Frank Eugene—**Museum**—outdoor museum (or nature trail)

Lutz, Isaac C.—**Monument**—monument to George Washington

Luxford, James—**Annulment**—annulment by court decree

Lykins, Johnston—**Periodical**—American Indian-language monthly

Lyle, Alexander Gordon—**Dental Corps (U.S. Navy)**—admiral in the dental corps (U.S. Navy)

Lyle, Benjamin—**Hospital**—tuberculosis hospital (municipal) for consumptive poor

Lyle, Ethel Hedgeman—**Sorority**—black sorority

Lyman, Edward Hutchinson Robbins—**Theater**—municipal theater

Lyman, William—**Iron**—iron blast furnace

Lynch, Budd—**Television—Telecast**—international telecast (announcer)

Lynch, Joe—**Radio Broadcast**—prizefight broadcast from the ringside

Lynch, John Roy—**Political Convention**—national nominating convention presided over by a black

Lynde, John D.—**Patent**—aerosol patent

Lynk, Vandahurst—**Medical Periodical**—black medical journal

Lyon, Edward L. T.—**Army Officer**—male nurse

Lyon, Frank Farrington—**Soilless Culture of Plants**—commercial hydroponicum (large)

Lyon, James—**Music Book**—music book by a native American

Lyon, Mary—**College**—college for women

Lyon, Matthew—**Congress (U.S.)—House of Representatives**—brawl

Lyon, Robert—**Periodical**—Jewish weekly published in English

Lyons, Richard M.—**Naval Officer**—naval chaplain to win the silver star in Vietnam

Lytton, George—**Prizefight**—prizefight to gross $2 million (judge)

M

Maas, J. C. W.—**Postal Service**—postage canceling machine patent

Maass, Clara—**Postage Stamp**—nurse (individual) depicted on a postage stamp

Mabie, Hamilton Wright—**Social Science Society (national)**

McAdoo, William Gibbs—**Railroad**—government operation of railroads

McAfee, Henry H.—**Forestry Society**—national forestry association

McAfee, Mildred Helen—**Naval Officer**—wom naval officer commissioned in the U.S. Nav Reserve

McAlister, Hill—**Enclave**—municipal enclave economic ground rent

MacAllan, Jack—**Farriers' Course in a College**

McAllister, James W.—**Entomology Magazine**

McAllister, Ralph C.—**College Alumni Assoc tion**—college alumni association secreta (full-time paid position)

McAlpin, Harry—**News Correspondent**—bla news correspondent accredited to the Wh House

McAnnally, David R.—**Journalism Course**—h tory of journalism course

McArdle, Joseph—**Actors' Home**—actors' hom

MacArthur, Arthur—**Governor**—governor moved from office by a state supreme court

MacArthur, Douglas—**Army Officer**—general command the forces of the United Nations Korea

MacArthur, Douglas—**Army Officer**—generals wear the five-star insignia

MacArthur, Douglas—**Medal**—Silver Star Arr Medal awarded to a civilian

Macatee, Charles—**Aviation—Flights (transcor nental)**—jet passenger commercial transcor nental service

MacBride, Roger L.—**Electoral College**—electo vote for a woman

McBride, John—**Employment Service**—state e ployment service

McCabe, Lorenzo Dow—**President (U.S.)**—Pre dent to celebrate his silver wedding anniv sary at the White House

McCaffery, Dominick F.—**Prizefight**—prizefight importance under the Marquis of Queensber rules

McCall, Barbara W.—**United Church of Christ** United Church of Christ ordination of a wom minister in which all the principal roles we filled by women

McCarl, John Raymond—**Comptroller General the United States**

McCarthy, George Lewis—**Check Photographi Device**

McCarthy, Joseph Vincent—**Baseball Manager** baseball manager to win pennants in bc leagues

McCarthy, William—**Airmail Service**—airm pilot

McChester, George ("Country McChester")—**P zefight**—prizefight (heavyweight) to last long than 100 rounds

McCleary, Dave—**Horse**—horse to pace 1 mile better than 2:00

McClellan, Cyril Elwin—**Atomic Energy Comm sion**—Atomic Energy Commission Patent Co pensation Board—award

McClellan, George Brinton—**Army Ambulan Corps**—Army ambulance corps

McClellan, George Brinton—**Telegraph**—Arr field telegraph used in warfare

cClellan, George Brinton (mayor)—**Automobile Race**—transcontinental automobile race

cClintock, Miller—**Traffic Regulation Course**—graduate course in traffic engineering and administration

cCloskey, John—**Catholic Priest**—Catholic priest to be elevated to the cardinalate

cCloskey, Victor S.—**Postage Stamp**—nonpictorial postage stamp

cClure, Donald—**World War I**—American Army division to cross the Rhine River

cClure, Samuel Sidney—**Newspaper Syndicate**—newspaper syndicate to supply articles

cComb, John—**Lighthouse**—lighthouse built after American independence

cConnell, Ambrose Moses ("Amby")—**Baseball Game**—triple play unassisted in a modern major league game

cConnell, Joseph Christopher—**Aviation—Pilot**—American ace (triple-jet) in Korea

cConnell, Matthew—**Brokerage**—stock exchange

cCoole, Mike—**Prizefight**—international fight, with bare knuckles

cCord, Frank C.—**Aviation—Airship**—airship disaster resulting in more than 70 deaths

cCormick, Charles H.—**Pharmacy College**—pharmacy college

cCormick, Cyrus Hall—**Reaper**—reaper that was practical

cCormick, Macushla M.—**Navy**—large-scale assignment of women (other than nurses) to sea duty

cCormick, Patricia—**Bullfight**—woman bullfighter (professional)

cCormick, Robert Rutherford—**Newspaper**—illustrated tabloid

cCoy, George Walter—**Disease (distinctly American)**

cCoy, Michael Norman Wright—**Aviation—Flights (transatlantic)**—jet transatlantic nonstop flight west–east

cCoy, Tom—**Prizefight**—prizefight fatality

acCracken, Henry Mitchell—**Hall of Fame**—hall of fame (university)

cCracken, Naomi M.—**Air Force Academy**—Air Force Academy woman officer

acCracken, William Patterson—**Aviation—License**—pilot's license issued by the U.S. Department of Commerce

cCreary, Conn—**Television—Telecast**—sports event televised in color

cCulloch, Hugh—**Bank Legislation**—national banking system

cCulloch, Hugh—**Comptroller**—comptroller of the Currency

cCullough, W. T.—**Garage** (public)

cCurdy, John Alexander Douglas—**Aviation**—airplane rescue at sea

cCusker, Marilyn J.—**Coal Mine**—woman to die in a coal mine disaster

cDaniel, Carl B.—**Aviation—Flights**—all-blind distance flight by the United States Army

McDaniel, Hattie—**Motion Picture**—motion picture to gross more than $70 million

McDaniel, Hattie—**Motion Picture Actor**—black woman to win an Oscar

McDermott, John J.—**Golf Champion**—golf champion (American-born professional) to win the United States Open Tournament

McDermott, John J.—**Marathon Race (annual)**

McDivitt, James Alton—**Astronaut**—astronauts (American) in orbit to transfer from one spacecraft to another

McDivitt, James Alton—**Astronaut**—astronaut (American) to become a general

McDivitt, James Alton—**Astronaut**—astronaut (American) to maneuver outside a satellite (command pilot)

McDivitt, James Alton—**Astronaut**—two-man spaceflight (American) of 62 orbits

MacDonald, Allan—**Ship**—concrete seagoing ship

Macdonald, Charles Blair—**Golf Course**—18-hole golf course

Macdonald, Charles Blair—**Golf Tournament**—amateur golf tournament (official)

Macdonald, Charles Blair—**Golf Tournament**—amateur golf tournament (unofficial)

Macdonald, Charles Blair—**Golf Tournament**—national championship stroke-play golf match

MacDonald, Eleanor—**Submarine-Escape Training Tank**—women to take the submarine-escape test

McDonald, Harold Paul—**Photograph**—cystoscopic photographs in color

McDonald, J. B.—**Automobile**—electric storage battery automobile

McDonald, James Grover—**Diplomatic Service**—ambassador to Israel

McDonald, Marshall—**Aquarium**—aquarium (inland saltwater)

McDonald, Marshall—**Fish and Fisheries Commissioner**

MacDonald, Ramsay—**Congress (U.S.)**—Prime Minister of Great Britain to address the Congress of the United States

MacDonald, Wilson—**Monument**—monument to an American poet

Macdonough, H.—**Opera**—light opera presented in 2 cities on the same day by the same company

McDougald, Gilbert James ("Gil")—**Baseball Player**—baseball rookie to hit a grand slam home run in the World Series

McDougall, Alexander—**War Veterans' Society**—Society of the Cincinnati

McDougall, Walt—**Newspaper**—newspaper with an illustrated color-page

MacDowell, Edward—**Arts and Letters Society**—arts and letters society (national)

McDowell, Ephraim—**Surgical Operation**—abdominal operation

McDowell, Irvin—**Civil War**—serious engagement in the Civil War

McDowell, John Huber—**Theatrical School**—theater and dramatic criticism course

McDowell, Mary Lou—**Naval Officer**—woman to preside as law officer

McEachern, Archie—**Bicycle Race**—paired six-day bicycle race

McElroy, James—**Subway**—subway car with side doors (inventor)

McElroy, Mary—**Kidnapping**—death penalty for kidnapping

McElroy, Theodore R.—**Radio Receiving Contest** —radio receiving contest in which a speed of more than 50 words a minute was recorded

McEntire, George W.—**Aviation—Flights (transcontinental)**—transcontinental dirigible flight (nonrigid dirigible)

Macfadden, Bernarr—**Restaurant**—penny restaurant

McFadden, Vivian—**Naval Officer**—naval chaplain (black woman)

McFarland, David Ford—**Helium**—helium

McFarland, Irene—**Caterpillar Club**—woman Caterpillar Club member

McFarland, Moses—**Aviation**—aeronautical patent

McFatrick, James D.—**Optometry Instruction**—optometry school

McGaffey, Ives W.—**Vacuum Cleaner**—suction-type vacuum cleaner

McGay, James—**Game Protection Society**

M'Geary, James—**Camp Meeting**

McGee, Anita Newcomb—**Army Nurse Corps (female)**

McGee, John—**Camp Meeting**

McGee, Walter H.—**Kidnapping**—death penalty for kidnapping

McGee, William—**Camp Meeting**

McGinley, Timothy S.—**Baseball League**—National League

McGinnis, Knefler—**Aviation—Flights (transpacific)**—Honolulu squadron flight

McGinnity, Joseph Jerome ("Iron Man")—**Baseball Game**—shutout World Series game

McGivney, Michael Joseph—**Knights of Columbus**

McGovern, Vincent Howard—**Helicopter— Flights**—helicopter transatlantic flight

McGowan, John—**Civil War**—act that marked the inauguration of the War of 1861–65

MacGrath, Harold—**Motion Picture**—serial motion picture

McGrath, Paul—**Television—Telecast**—play to be televised with its original Broadway cast

McGraw, John Joseph—**Baseball Game**—all-star baseball game (major league)

McGraw, John Joseph—**Baseball Game**—World Series baseball games to gross $1 million

McGraw, John Joseph—**Bowling**—duckpins

McHugh, Keith S.—**Telephone**—dial-telephone long distance service

McIlrath, H. Darwin—**Bicycle Trip (world)**—bicycle trip around the world by a married couple

McIntyre, James Francis—**Catholic Priest**— Catholic cardinal whose see was west of the Rockies

McIntyre, Roberta L.—**Navy**—large-scale assi ment of women (other than nurses) to sea d

Mack, Cornelius McGillicuddy ("Connie")—**Ba ball Game**—all-star baseball game (ma league)

Mackall, R. Covington—**Dental School**—den college

Mackay, Clarence Hungerford—**Cable**—ca across the Pacific Ocean between Honoli Midway, Guam, and Manila

Mackay, James—**Ship**—racing shell

McKean, Thomas—**Declaration of Independer (American)**—Declaration of Independence fi ordered "to be fairly engrossed on parchme

McKean, Thomas—**President (U.S.)**—Presid elected

McKechnie, William—**Television—Telecas** baseball games (major-league) telecast

McKenzie, John—**Free Port**

Mackie, John—**Medal**—Medal of Honor awar to a marine

McKim, Isaac—**Ship**—clipper ship

McKinley, Ashley C.—**Aviation—Flights—So** Pole flight

McKinley, William—**President (U.S.)**—Presid who had used a telephone for campaigning

McKinley, William—**Voting Machine**—voting r chines for use in federal elections

McLaughlin, Frank—**Automobile Service Stat** —drive-in service station

McLaurin, John Lowndes—**Senator (U.S.)**—se tors censured

Maclay, William—**Congress (U.S.)—Senat** Senate

McLean, Edith Eleanor—**Incubator for Infants**

McLean, James—**Insurance**—insurance r standardization

McLean, James Sylvanus—**Piano**—piano pate

McLean, John—**Eye**—eye bank

McLean, John—**History Instruction**—ancient a modern history chair

McLoughlin, John—**Game Manufacturing Com** ny

Maclure, William—**Geological Society (nation**

Maclure, William—**Geology Book**—geology bc

McMahan, John Wood—**Degrees (academic a honorary)**—Doctor of Philosophy in Account degree

McManus, Frederick Richard—**Catholic Mas** Catholic mass in English (full English mass

McMath, Robert Reynolds—**Motion Picture—** tion picture of the sun

McMillan, Edwin Mattison—**Element**—elem 93

McMillan, Edwin Mattison—**Element**—elem 94

McMillan, Edwin Mattison—**Synchrotron**—s chrotron (inventor)

McNair, Alexander—**State**—state admitted to Union west of the Mississippi River

McNair, F. V.—**Submarine**—submarine accid

McNair, Lesley James—**Medal**—Expert Infant man's Badge

Marchal, Wilma Juanita—**Naval Officer**—women sworn into the regular U.S. Navy

Marciano, Rocky—**Television**—**Telecast**—pay television presentation of a sporting event

Marcley, Walter John—**Hospital**—tuberculosis sanatorium (state)

Marconi, Guglielmo—**Newspaper**—newspaper published at sea (radio news service)

Marconi, Guglielmo—**Radio Broadcast**—transatlantic radio signal

Marcy, William Learned—**Political Machine**

Marcy, William Learned—**War (1812)**—prisoners in the War of 1812

Marechal, Ambrose—**Cathedral**—cathedral

Marette, Jacques Henri—**Television**—**Telecast**—satellite telecast from Europe

Marie, queen of Rumania—**Visiting Celebrities**—queen (reigning) to visit the United States

Mario, Queena—**Opera**—opera broadcast in its entirety by the Metropolitan Opera Company

Maris, Roger Eugene—**Baseball Player**—baseball player (major league) to hit more than 60 home runs in 1 season

Marix, Adolph—**Naval Officer**—admiral who was Jewish

Mark—**Baptism**—baptism

Markham, James E.—**Patent**—fruit tree patent

Marmer, Milton Jacob—**Surgical Operation**—lung tumor operation in which the patient was under hypnosis

Marr, John Quincy—**Civil War**—Confederate officer killed in the Civil War

Marrant, John—**Missionary**—black missionary to the American Indians

Marsh, Othniel Charles—**Paleontology Chair**

Marsh, Sylvester—**Railroad**—cog railroad

Marshall, Albert T.—**Refrigerator**—household refrigerating machine patent

Marshall, Albert Ware—**Motion Picture**—motion picture of an eclipse of the sun taken from an airplane

Marshall, Charles—**Pharmacy College**—pharmacy college

Marshall, Clinton S.—**Spring Winding Machine**

Marshall, E. G.—**Television**—**Telecast**—motion picture premiere telecast on 2 successive nights

Marshall, Elizabeth—**Pharmacist**—pharmacist (woman)

Marshall, Frank James—**Chess Champion**—chess champion to play more than 100 games simultaneously

Marshall, George Catlett—**Army Officer**—army officer to occupy both the nation's highest military post and the highest nonelective civilian post

Marshall, George Catlett—**Army Officer**—generals to wear the five-star insignia

Marshall, George Catlett—**Medal**—Distinguished Service Medal (Army) awarded to a woman

Marshall, George Catlett—**Nobel Prize**—Nobel Prize for peace to a professional soldier

Marshall, Humphry—**Botany Book**—botany book strictly American

Marshall, James Wilson—**Gold**—gold discove[r] in California

Marshall, John—**Commerce Case**

Marshall, John—**Supreme Court (U.S.)**—Ch[ief] Justice of the United States to serve in a pre[si]dential cabinet

Marshall, John—**Supreme Court (U.S.)**—Ch[ief] Justice of the United States who had bee[n] representative in Congress

Marshall, John—**Supreme Court (U.S.)**—Supre[me] Court decision that a state law was unconsti[tu]tional

Marshall, John—**Supreme Court (U.S.) Decis**[ion] —Supreme Court decision establishing power of the United States

Marshall, John—**Vice President (U.S.)**—V[ice] President arrested (judge)

Marshall, John Sayre—**Dental Corps (U.S. Arm**[y)] —Dental Corps of the U.S. Army

Marshall, Lois I. Kimsey—**Vice President (U**[.S.)] —Vice President's widow to receive a pens[ion]

Marshall, Maggie—**Baseball Team**—wome[n] baseball team

Marshall, Roy Kenneth—**Planetarium**—planet[ari]um owned by a university

Marshall, Thomas Riley—**Vice President (U**[.S.)] —Vice President's widow to receive a pens[ion]

Marshall, Thurgood—**Solicitor General (U.S.**[)]— solicitor general of the United States who w[as] a black

Marshall, Thurgood—**Supreme Court (U.S.)**—[As]sociate Justice of the Supreme Court who w[as] a black

Marston, Sarah H.—**Missionary Society**—fore[ign] missionary society organized by women

Martell, Charles Bowling—**Ship**—guided mis[sile] cruiser

Martell, Belle—**Prizefight Referee**—woman [pri]zefight referee (licensed)

Martin, Charles—**Photograph**—photogra[ph] taken under the sea in natural colors

Martin, David H.—**United Christian Party**

Martin, Edwin—**Play (drama)**—play given [by] nonprofessional actors

Martin, Glenn Luther—**Aviation**—**Flights**—o[ver] water round-trip flight

Martin, Henry—**Brick Machine**

Martin, Henry Newell—**Physiology Societ**[y]— physiology society (national organization)

Martin, John—**Actor**—actor of American birt[h]

Martin, John—**Colonial Government**—colo[nial] council in America

Martin, John Leonard ("Pepper")—**Athlete**—[ath]lete presented with the Associated Press A[th]lete of the Year award

Martin, Joseph—**Ship**—clipper ship

Martin, Keith—**Art Course**—industrial cam[ou]flage course

Martin, Mary—**Television**—**Telecast**—play t[ele]cast in color with its original cast

Martin, Riccardo—**Opera**—opera by an Ameri[can] composer performed at the Metropolitan Op[era] House of New York

artin, Robert R.—**War (Korean)**—officer killed
n action in the Korean War

artin, Roosevelt ("Pepper," "The Wild Hoss of
he Osage")—**Baseball Game**—all-star baseball
game (major league)

artin, Truman J.—**Insurance**—automobile insurance policy

artin, William—**Bicycle Race**—international
six-day bicycle race

artinelli, Giovanni—**Motion Picture**—talking
picture

ary, John—**Grammar**—French grammar

ason, Eben—**Veterinary School**—veterinary
college of importance

ason, Edith—**Opera**—opera broadcast over a
national network from an American opera
house

ason, Ellen H. B.—**Missionary Society**—foreign
missionary society organized by women

ason, George Thompson—**War (Mexican)**—
Mexican war shots

ason, John—**Streetcar**—streetcar company

ason, Leonard—**Wrestling**—intercollegiate
wrestling association

ason, Lowell—**Music Book**—children's music
book

ason, Lowell—**Music Instruction**—music instruction (public school)

ason, Lowell—**Music Instruction**—musical
pedagogy school

ason, William Ernest—**Representative (U.S.)**—
father and daughter to serve in the same Congress

aspero, Pierre—**Free Lunch**—free lunch

assasoit—**Treaty**—colonial treaty with the
American Indians

assey, John—**Fox Hunting Club**

asters, Thomas—**Patent**—English patent granted to a resident of America

atas, Rudolph—**Anesthesia**—spinal anesthesia
report

atchett, Charles Horatio—**Socialist Labor Party
of North America**

atesic, Edward—**Football Game**—professional
football game in which 10 touchdowns were
made

atheny, William A.—**Aviation—Flights**—all-
blind distance flight by the United States Army

ather, Cotton—**Bibliography**—bibliography of
theological and biblical literature

ather, Cotton—**Paleontology Report**

ather, Increase—**Degrees (academic and honorary)**—doctor of sacred theology degree

ather, Ralph—**Swedenborgian or New Church**
—Swedenborgian or New Church temple

ather, Samuel—**Corporation**—corporate body

ather, Stephen Tyng—**Park Service (national)**

athews, Eddie—**Baseball Team**—baseball team
to hit 4 consecutive runs in 1 inning

athews, George—**Telephone**—telephone conversation (commercial) using electricity generated by the sun's rays

athews, Henry Mason—**Strike**—strike in which
federal troops were called in peacetime

Mathews, James—**Farmers' Institute**—farmers'
institute held by a land grant agricultural college off its campus

Mathewson, Christopher ("Christy")—**Baseball
Pitcher**—baseball pitcher (World Series) with 3
shutout games

Mathewson, Christy—**Hall of Fame**—hall of fame
(baseball)

Matlack, Charles F.—**Medical Society**—homeopathic medical society

Matson, Randy—**Shot-Put**—shot-put to cover a
distance of more than 70 feet

Matson, Randy—**Shot-Put**—shot-put to cover a
distance of more than 71 feet

Matthews, Annabel—**Woman**—woman tax appeals board member

Matthews, Clarence—**Football Game**—football
game between black colleges

Matthews, Edmund O.—**Torpedo**—torpedo
manufacturing station

Matthews, John—**Soda Water Machine Manufacturer**

Matthews, Marjorie Swank—**Methodist Church**—
bishop (woman)

Matthews, Thomas—**Whist**—whist rule book

Matzmulla, Zun Zow—**Naval Academy**—Japanese midshipman in the United States Naval
Academy

Mauchly, John W.—**Computer**—electronic computer

Maugham, Russell Lowell—**Aviation—Flights
(transcontinental)**—transcontinental flight
within 24 hours

Maury, James—**Diplomatic Service**—consuls of
the United States appointed after the adoption
of the Constitution

Mauver, William—**Radio Society**

Maverick, Samuel—**Revolutionary War**—American casualties

Maxim, Hiram Percy—**Automobile Club**

Maxwell, George—**Music Society**—music society
for the literary protection of composers and authors

Maxwell, George Holmes—**Citizenship and Public Affairs School**

Maxwell, Stephen—**Locomotive**—locomotive
with a cab

Maxwell, William—**Flag**—American flag flown in
battle

May, Lewis—**Young Men's Hebrew Association**

Mayer, Louis Burt—**Radio Facsimile Transmission**—photograph sent by radio across the continent (commercial)

Mayhew, Thomas—**American Indians**—American Indian preacher of Christianity

Maynard, Belvin W.—**Aviation**—sermon from an
airplane

Maynard, Belvin W.—**Aviation—Races**—transcontinental air race

Maynard, Belvin W.—**Radio Broadcast**—radio
concert from an airplane

Maynard, Lambert—**Hotel**—hotel with safe
deposit boxes

Mayor, Bruce—**Court**—court in which the judge presided in a city other than the one in which the lawyers appeared

Mays, Carl William ("Willie")—**Baseball Player**—baseball player (R. J. Chapman) killed in a game

Meach, A.—**Nautical School**—nautical school

Meade, R. W.—**Wedding**—airplane wedding

Means, Rice W.—**War Veterans' Society**—Veterans of Foreign Wars of the United States

Mecom, Benjamin—**Stereotype**—stereotype printing

Medill, Joseph—**Civil Service**—Civil Service Commission

Meek, A. B.—**Chess Tournament**—chess tournament

Meek, George Burton—**Spanish-American War**—soldier killed in the Spanish-American war

Meek, Howard Bagnall—**Hotel Administration College Course**

Meeker, Jotham—**Periodical**—American Indian-language monthly

Mein, John—**Music**—patriotic American song

Mein, John Gordon—**Diplomatic Service**—ambassador assassinated in office

Mellette, Arthur Calvin—**State**—states admitted to the Union simultaneously

Melville, David—**Gas**—gaslights (street)

Menches, Charles E.—**Ice Cream Cone**—ice cream cone

Mendez, Antonio—**Sugar**—sugar cane

Mendez, Antonio—**Sugar**—sugar refinery

Menéndez de Avilés, Pedro—**Catholic Parish**

Menéndez de Avilés, Pedro—**Colonist**—permanent white settlement

Menéndez de Avilés, Pedro—**Treaty**—treaty violation

Menéndez de Avilés, Pedro—**War (colonial)**—intercolonial war

Menocal, Mario García—**Telephone**—telephone cable service (deep-sea)

Menotti, Gian-Carlo—**Television—Telecast**—opera written for television

Mercante, Arthur—**Prizefight**—prizefight with a purse of $4.5 million (referee)

Meredith, Samuel—**Treasury Department (U.S.)**—Treasurer of the United States

Mergenthaler, Ottmar—**Typesetting Machine**—linotype machine

Merriam, Charles Edward—**National Planning Board (U.S.)**

Merrick, Solyman—**Wrench**—wrench patent

Merrill, Richard—**Aviation—Flights (transatlantic)**—transatlantic round-trip flight from the United States

Merrill, Robert—**Television—Telecast**—pay television presentation of an opera

Merritt, Benjamin Frederick—**Time Recorder**—autograph time recorder

Merritt, Ernest—**Physics**—national physics association

Merritt, Wesley—**American Expeditionary Force**—American Expeditionary Force

Merryman, John—**Habeas Corpus**—habeas c pus suspension order

Merwin, M. T.—**Elevator**—elevator with an el tric light

Meserole, B. J.—**Game Protection Society**

Metcalf, Betsey (Mrs. Baker)—**Hat**—straw ha

Meusel, Emil Frederick ("Irish")—**Baseball Pla**—baseball players (brothers) to oppose e other in a World Series

Meusel, Robert William ("Bob," "Long Bob"—**Baseball Player**—baseball players (brothers oppose each other in a World Series

Meyenberg, John B.—**Milk**—evaporated milk

Meyer, Karl Friedrich—**Flea Laboratory**

Meyer, Louis—**Automobile Racer**—automo racer to win the Indianapolis 500 three tim

Meyner, Robert Baumle—**Tunnel**—triple-tube derwater roadway

Michaux, François André—**Tea Shrub**

Michell, Jonathan—**Corporation**—corporate b

Michelson, Albert Abraham—**Astronomer**—tronomer to measure the size of a fixed sta

Michelson, Albert Abraham—**Nobel Prize**—bel Prize in physics

Michelson, Albert Abraham—**Physics**—natio physics association

Michie, Dennis—**Football Game**—Army-N football game

Middleton, Peter—**Medical Book**—dissect essay

Middleton, Peter—**Medical Book**—medical tory

Middleton, William Shainline—**Medical Congr**—cancer institute (convention)

Midgley, Thomas—**Gasoline**—ethyl gasoline

Mieras, C. E.—**Wedding**—wedding broadc (minister)

Mies van der Rohe, Ludwig—**Building**—bro and glass skyscraper

Mifflin, Thomas—**Army Officer**—quartermast

Mikulski, Barbara Ann—**Representative (U.S**—Polish-American representative

Milam, Benjamin—**Madstone**

Miles, Samuel—**Electoral College**—electoral v cast contrary to instruction

Miles, Sherman—**Army School**—army train school

Miles, Vincent Morgan—**Social Security**—(U.S.)

Miles, William Porcher—**Flag**—Confede States flag

Miley, William Maynadier—**Army Parach Troops**

Millard, M. V. B.—**Ship**—steam whaler built a whaleboat

Miller, Abraham—**Tile**—wall and floor tiles

Miller, Charles—**Bicycle Race**—internatio 6-day 2-man-team bicycle race

Miller, Charles—**Bicycle Race**—motorcy paced bicycle race

Miller, Charles—**Sewing Machine**—sewing chine to stitch buttonholes

Miller, Charles J. S.—**Aviation—Airship**—wor airship passenger

Mitchell, Samuel Augustus—**Entomology Book (comprehensive)**

Mitchell, Samuel Weir—**Physiology Society**—physiology society (national organization)

Mitchell, Virne Beatrice (Jackie)—**Baseball Pitcher**—woman baseball pitcher

Mitchell, Wesley Clair—**National Planning Board (U.S.)**

Mitchell, William Lendrum ("Billy")—**Army Officer**—American general to fly over enemy lines

Mitchill, Samuel Latham—**Agriculture Professor**

Mitchill, Samuel Latham—**Medical Periodical**—medical magazine

Mitchill, Samuel Latham—**Pharmacopoeia**—pharmacopoeia prepared by a hospital staff

Miyamura, Hiroshi Hershey—**Medal**—Medal of Honor awarded to a Nisei in the Korean War

Moedy, Henry—**Book Auction**

Moffat, John L.—**Mint (U.S.)**—private mint authorized by the United States Government

Mixon, Rhoda Holly Singleton—**Town**—town founded by a woman

Moffett, James Andrew—**Emergency Housing Corporation (U.S.)**

Moffett, William Adger—**Aviation—Airship**—airship disaster resulting in more than 70 deaths

Mokarzel, Naoum Anthony—**Newspaper**—Arabic daily newspaper

Moley, Raymond—**Community Trust**

Molis, William—**Button**—buttons of freshwater pearl

Moller, John C.—**Music**—music publishers (exclusive)

Mollison, Amy Johnson—**Aviation—Pilot**—woman pilot to fly across the Atlantic Ocean east-west

Mollison, Irvin Charles—**Judge**—black judge of a customs court (U.S.)

Mollison, James Allan—**Aviation—Flights (transatlantic)**—transatlantic solo westward flight

Momsen, Charles Bowers—**Submarine "Lung"**

Mondésir, John Edward de—**Catholic Seminary**—Catholic seminary

Monis, Judah—**Grammar**—Hebrew grammar

Monroe, G. W.—**High School**—junior high school system

Monroe, James—**Diplomatic Service**—ministers plenipotentiary to South and Central America

Monroe, James—**Diplomatic Service**—Pan American delegates (American)

Monroe, James—**Hospital**—marine hospital (U.S.)

Monroe, James—**President (U.S.)**—President inaugurated on March 5

Monroe, James—**President (U.S.)**—President who had been a senator

Monroe, James—**Quids**

Monroe, James—**Territorial Expansion**—annexation of territory

Monroe, William—**Pencil Factory**

Montague, Hannah Lord—**Collar**—collar

Montague, Orlando—**Collar Factory**

Montand, Yves—**Television—Telecast**—satellite telecast from Europe

Montesino, Antonio—**Catholic Mass**—Catholic mass

Montgomery, Alexander—**Periodical**—art magazine of merit

Montgomery, Bernard Law—**President (U.S.)** presidential airplane (turbo-compound-powered)

Montgomery, John—**Declaration of Independence (American)**—Declaration of Independence

Montgomery, John Joseph—**Glider—Flights**—glider flight

Montgomery, Richard—**Revolutionary War**—British flag capture

Montgomery, Simon Peter—**Methodist Church** black Methodist minister of an all-white congregation

Montresor, John—**Railroad**—inclined railway

Monts, Sieur de (Pierre du Guast)—**Colony** colonial white settlement (north of Florida

Moody, Alfred Judson Force—**Vietnam War** general (American) to die in Vietnam

Moody, (Arthur Edson) Blair—**Newspaper reporter**—newspaper reporter to become a senator

Moody, (Arthur Edson) Blair—**Senator (U.S.)** senator to preside over a Senate session directly after being sworn in as a senator

Moody, Dwight Lyman—**Biblical Students Summer Conference**

Moody, Paul—**Belts of Leather**

Moody, Paul—**Cotton Mill**—cotton mill in world in which the whole process of cotton manufacturing from spinning to weaving carried on by power

Moon, Margaret—**Coast Guard Officer**—Coast Guard Women's Reserve officer to serve overseas

Moore, Abigail—**College**—college for women

Moore, Arthur Harry—**Old Age Colony**

Moore, Charles N.—**American Indian Church** church organized by American Indians

Moore, Clement Clarke—**Dictionary**—Hebrew dictionary

Moore, Garry—**Television—Telecast**—color program (commercial)

Moore, Harold W.—**Helicopter—Flights**—helicopter transatlantic flight

Moore, James—**Revolutionary War**—naval battle of the Revolution

Moore, John M.—**Periodical**—illustrated weekly

Moore, Nelson Augustus—**Monument**—monument to commemorate the Civil War

Moore, Thomas—**Refrigerator**—refrigerator

Moore, Victor—**Play (drama)**—musical play to win a Pulitzer Prize

Moores, Frank Edward—**Vending Machine** vending machine law

Moorman, Charles—**Judge**—woman associate justice of the circuit court of appeals

More, Nicolas—**Impeachment**—impeachment

Moreell, Ben—**Naval Officer**—admiral (four star) who did not attend the U.S. Naval Academy

Morton, George Arthur—**Electron Tube**

Morton, Julius Sterling—**Holiday**—Arbor Day

Morton, Ladislaus—**Microscope**—electron microscope

Morton, Levi Parsons—**Accountancy Law (state)**

Morton, Nathaniel—**History**—history of New England

Morton, Nelle—**United Church of Christ**—United Church of Christ ordination of a woman minister in which all the principal roles were filled by women

Morton, Samuel George—**Cranioscopy Book**—published

Morton, Sarah Wentworth Apthorp—**Novel**—American novel published in America

Morton, Thomas—**Cod Liver Oil**

Morton, Thomas—**Deportation**

Morton, Thomas George—**Anti-Vivisection Society**

Morton, William James—**X Ray**—X ray of the entire body of a living person

Moscona, Nicola—**Television—Telecast**—opera (complete) to be televised from the Metropolitan Opera House

Mosconi, Willie—**Billiards**—billiard player to win a match in the first inning

Mosher, Jesse Montgomery—**Hospital**—psychiatric ward

Mosher, William Eugene—**Citizenship and Public Affairs School**

Moskovics, Fred Evans—**Automobile Racetrack**—automobile speedway (board track)

Moss, Emma Sadler—**Medical Society**—woman president of a major medical society

Moss, Isaac M.—**Whist**—whist rule book

Mostel, Zero—**Play (drama)**—musical to run for more than 3,000 performances

Motley, Constance Baker—**Judge**—black woman judge of a federal district court

Mott, John—**Money**—trade tokens

Mott, Lucretia—**Woman Suffrage**—convention of women advocating woman suffrage

Mott, Lucretia—**Woman Suffrage**—woman suffrage associations (national)

Mott, William—**Money**—trade tokens

Motta, Irene—**Bridge (game)**—bridge hand in which each of the 4 players was dealt a perfect hand

Moulton, Frances Estelle—**Bank**—national bank woman president

Mouton, Carolyn Anne—**Siamese Twins**—Siamese twins separated successfully by surgery

Mouton, Catherine Anne—**Siamese Twins**—Siamese twins separated successfully by surgery

Moyers, Leroy—**Jockey**—jockey to win 7 consecutive races in 1 day

Mucci, Tony—**Wheelchair Athletics**—national wheelchair games

Mudd, Stuart—**Blood Bank**—blood serum (human, dried)

Mudge, Genevra Delphine—**Automobile Driver**—woman automobile driver

Muench, Carl Gebhard—**Sound-absorbing Material**

Muhlenberg, Frederick Augustus Conrad—**Congress (U.S.)—House of Representatives** House of Representatives

Muhlenberg, Frederick Augustus Conrad—**Congress (U.S.)—House of Representatives** Speaker of the House

Muhlenberg, Henry Melchior—**Lutheran Church** —Lutheran services in English

Muhlenberg, Henry Melchior—**Music Book** Lutheran hymnbook (German) published America

Muhlenberg, William Augustus—**Vacation Fund**

Mühlmann, Adolph—**Opera**—opera composed a woman performed at the Metropolitan Opera House

Mullane, Anthony John ("Tony")—**Baseball Game**—National League 20-inning baseball game

Mullanphy, Bryan—**Travelers Aid**

Mulliken, Samuel—**Patent**—patentee to obtain more than one patent

Mulzac, Hugh Nathanial—**Ship**—merchant ship of the U.S. commanded by a black captain

Mumford, Stephen—**Baptist Church**—Seventh Day Baptist Church

Mumford, William Bruce—**Treason**—citizen of the United States to be tried for treason, convicted, and hanged

Mundt, Karl Earl—**Television—Telecast**—split screen image

Munemori, Nawa—**Medal**—Medal of Honor awarded to a Nisei

Munemori, Sadao S.—**Medal**—Medal of Honor awarded to a Nisei

Munk, Max Michael—**Wind Tunnel**—wind tunnel of variable air density

Munro, Douglas Albert—**Medal**—Medal of Honor to a Coast Guardsman killed in action in World War II

Munro, Mrs. James—**Coast Guard (U.S.)**—mother of a coastguardsman killed in action to join SPARS

Munroe, C. Kirk—**Bicycle Society**—bicycle society (national organization)

Munsey, Frank Andrew—**Periodical**—all-fiction pulp magazine

Munson, Clara—**Mayor**—woman mayor elected by a city west of the Rocky Mountains

Munters, Georg—**Refrigerator**—gas refrigerator (household)

Muraille, Jacques Hector Nicholas Joubert de *See* Joubert de la Muraille, Jacques Hector Nicholas

Muratore, Lucien—**Opera**—opera broadcast in entirety by a professional cast

Murdock, Jacob M.—**Automobile Transcontinental Trip**—transcontinental family automobile trip requiring only a month

Murphy, Betty Southard—**Labor Relations**—National Labor Relations Board woman chairman

Murphy, Charles Minthorn—**Bicycle Racer**—bicycle racer

Murphy, Charles W.—**Employment Service**—state employment service

N

Neiligan, Raymond J.—**Telephone**—dial telephone service coast-to-coast without the aid of operators

Neilson, Martha—**School**—school for unmarried, pregnant, teen-age girls

Nelson, C. Alexander—**Library Society**—library society (local)

Nelson, Christian K.—**Eskimo Pie**

Nelson, Erik Henning—**Aviation—Flights**—New York–Alaska flight

Nelson, Erik Henning—**Aviation—Flights (world)** —world flight

Nelson, Murray—**Sanitary District**

Nelson, Ray—**Television—Telecast**—musical comedy (full-length) written especially for television

Nelson, Rosemary Elaine—**Navy**—women (other than nurses) assigned to regular shipboard duty

Nerinck, Charles—**Convent**—Catholic convent to admit black women as sisters

Nesbitt, John Maxwell—**Insurance**—life insurance

Neuberger, Maurine Brown—**Congress (U.S.)— Senate**—Senate session in which 2 women were seated

Neuberger, Maurine Brown—**Legislator (state)**— husband and wife simultaneously elected to both chambers of a state legislature

Neuberger, Richard Lewis—**Legislator (state)**— husband and wife simultaneously elected to both chambers of a state legislature

Neuffer Judith Ann ("Judy")—**Naval Officer**— woman member of the Navy's Hurricane Hunters

Neumann, Gustav Adolf—**Newspaper**—German daily newspaper

Neumann, John Nepomucene—**Catholic Beatification**—Catholic beatification of an American citizen (male)

Neumann, John Nepomucene—**Saint (Catholic)**— American saint (male)

New, Harry Stewart—**Radio Broadcast**—election campaign using radio

Newbold, Charles—**Plow**—plow patent

Newcombe, Don—**Baseball Game**—major-league game in which the majority of the players on one team were blacks

Newcombe, Henry—**Expedition**—expedition

Newcombe, John—**Tennis Player**—tennis player to win 2 grand slams (defeated in British Open)

Newell, William Allan—**Medical Legislation** —law (state) requiring serological blood tests of pregnant women

Newhouse, Sewell—**Traps**—steel animal traps

Newlands, Francis Griffith—**Silverites**

Newman, Philip James—**Wedding**—wedding in the United States Occupation Forces in Korea

Newman, Samuel—**Bible Concordance**—Bible concordance

Newman, William—**Shoe Measuring Stick**

Newport, Christopher—**Colonial Government**— colonial council in America

Newport, Christopher—**Colonist**—English settlement in America (permanent)

Newton, Hubert Anson—**Weights and Measu Standardization**—national organization to prove systems of weights, measures, moneys

Newton, John Thomas—**Ship**—frigate (Americ built, steam-driven) to cross the Atlantic Oc

Newton, Maurice—**Airmail Service**—air regular service

Newton, Mortimer W.—**Insurance**—health in ance law (state)

Ney, Karl Winfield—**Surgical Operation**—epi tic case treated by elevation of the skull c

Neyhart, Amos Earl—**Automobile Driving Cou**

Neyhart, Amos Earl—**Traffic Regulation Cou** —teacher training course in "Training Tr Safety"

Ng, Yee Y.—**Hospital**—Chinese-American ho tal

Nicholas, prince of Rumania—**Visiting Celebri** —queen (reigning) to visit the United Stat

Nicholas, Samuel—**Marine Corps**—American rines

Nicholas, Samuel—**War (Colonial)**—marine gagement in battle

Nichols, Anna R. G.—**Patent Examiner**—wo patent examiner

Nichols, Jesse Clyde—**Business**—shopping ce in a suburban business area

Nichols, Mary S.—**Medical School**—med school based upon water-cure principles

Nichols, Philip—**Court**—court in which the ju presided in a city other than the one in w the lawyers appeared

Nichols, Thomas L.—**Medical School**—med school based upon water-cure principles

Nichols, William—**Animals**—lion

Nicholson, Charles Ambrose—**Aviation—Fli** —airplane catapulted from a dirigible

Nicholson, Francis—**Capitol**

Nicholson, Francis—**Treason**—American colc hanged for treason

Nicholson, L. A.—**Stadium**—school stadium

Nicholson, Reginald Fairfax—**Ship**—battle built on the Pacific coast

Nicholson, Samuel T.—**Union Reform Party**

Nicholson, William—**Conchology Report**

Nicholson, William—**File Factory**—file fac (machine cutting) to attain success

Nicola, Lewis—**Engineering Book**

Nicoll, Allardyce—**Theatrical School**—the and dramatic criticism course

Nicolls, Richard—**Horse Race**—horse race

Nikander, Juho Kustra—**College**—Finnish co

Nilsson, Christine—**Opera**—opera at the ropolitan Opera House

Nimitz, Chester William—**Naval Officer**—n officers to wear the five-star insignia

Nimitz, Chester William—**Submarine**—sub rine to cross the Atlantic Ocean under its power

Nimitz, Chester William, Jr.—**Submarine**— marine to make more than 13,000 dives

Nininger, Alexander Ramsey ("Sandy")—**M** —Medal of Honor awarded in World Wa

O

Oakman, Wheeler—**Motion Picture**—talking picture whose footage exceeded 6,000 feet   .

Oaks, Orion O.—**Liquid Heat**

O'Bannon, Presley Neville—**Flag**—American flag flown over a fortress of the Old World

Oboler, Arch—**Motion Picture**—three-dimensional feature motion picture

O'Brien, Edmond—**Motion Picture**—three-dimensional feature motion picture produced and released by a major company

O'Brien, Jay—**Bobsled Competition**—four-man bob-team competition

O'Brien, Jeremiah—**Revolutionary War**—naval battle of the Revolution

O'Brien, Joe—**Horse**—trotter triple-crown winner

O'Brien, John—**Basketball Player**—basketball player (collegiate) to score more than 1,000 points in 1 season

O'Brien, John—**Revolutionary War**—naval battle of the Revolution

O'Brien, Parry—**Shot Put**—shot-put toss over 60 feet

O'Brien, Thomas Charles—**National Union for Social Justice**

O'Brien, Thomas Charles—**Union Party**

O'Brien, William—**Bicycle Race**—woman's six-day bicycle race (manager of race)

O'Brine, Forest—**Aviation—Flights**—airplane endurance flight exceeding 400 hours

O'Callahan, Joseph Timothy—**Medal**—Medal of Honor awarded to chaplain

O'Callahan, Joseph Timothy—**Naval Officer**—chaplain to win a Congressional Medal of Honor

Ocobock, Susanne M.—**Air Force Officer**—military engineer (woman) in the Air Force

O'Connell, James F.—**Tattoo**—tattooed man

O'Connor, B. F.—**Fencing**—fencing league (national)

O'Connor, Donald—**Television—Telecast**—color program on coast-to-coast network commercial

O'Connor, James Francis Thaddeus—**Federal Deposit Insurance Corporation**

O'Connor, W. Scott—**Fencing**—fencing league (national)

O'Conor, Charles—**Presidential Candidate**—presidential candidate who was a Catholic

Odlum, Mrs. Floyd Bostwick. *See* Cochran, Jacqueline

O'Donnell, Bertha—**Deaf—Communication**—visible and oral communication by the deaf over distance

O'Donnell, Gladys—**Aviation—Races**—women's cross-country air derby

Oelrichs, Mrs. Hermann—**Automobile Parade**

Oerter, Alfred A. ("Al")—**Discus**—discus hurler to win 4 gold medals in 4 consecutive Olympic Games

Oerter, Alfred A. ("Al")—**Discus**—discus throw to exceed 200 feet

Oeschger, Joseph Carl—**Baseball Game**—baseball game (major league) to last longer than 25 innings

Ofeldt, F. W.—**Motorboat**—motorboat plea: craft

Ogden, Aaron—**Commerce Case**

Ogle, Henry—**Reaper**—reaper that actu: worked

Ogle, Samuel—**Horse**—thoroughbred horse

Oglethorpe, James Edward—**Moravian Churc**

O'Hare, Edward Henry—**Aviation—Pilot**—n: ace in World War II

O'Hern, Michael W.—**Kidnapping**—death pe ty for kidnapping

Ohi, K. Elizabeth—**Lawyer**—Japanese wo: lawyer

Ohmart, Philip Edwin—**Battery**—battery to (vert radioactive energy into electrical ener

O'Keefe, Walter—**Television Award**—Natic Academy of Television Arts and Scier award

Oland, Warner—**Motion Picture**—talking pic

Olcott, Henry Steele—**Theosophical Society**

Old, Archie J., Jr.—**Army**—armored divi: transported by airplanes to a foreign coun

Old, Archie J.—**Aviation—Flights (world)**—around-the-world nonstop flight

Olds, Robin—**Aviation—Flights (transcc nental)**—transcontinental round-trip airp: flight within one day

O'Leary, Dan—**Baseball Team**—baseball t: (major league) to score 18 runs in 1 inning

Olive, Milton Lee—**Medal**—Medal of H< (posthumous) awarded to a black in the V nam war

Oliver, Anna—**Theological School**—theolog school to admit women

Oliver, Henry Kemble—**Labor**—labor bur (state)

Oliver, Robert Shaw—**Tennis**—lawn tennis

Oliver, Robert Shaw—**Tennis Society**—tennis ciety (national)

Oliver, Robert T.—**Dental Corps (U.S. Arm** Dental Corps of the U.S. Army

Olivier, Sir Laurence—**Motion Picture Act(** husband and wife Oscar winners

Olson, Carl ("Bobo")—**Television—Teleca:** prizefight (middleweight) televised coas coast

Olson, John—**Fuller's Earth**

Olson, Mary—**Postal Service**—women rail: postal clerks

Olson, Maude—**Postal Service**—women rail: postal clerks

O'Malley, Robert Emmett—**Medal**—Medal Honor in the Vietnam war awarded to a Ma:

O'Meara, Jack—**Aviation—Flights**—"airp: train"

O'Meara, Jack—**Aviation—Flights**—sky-train ternational round-trip flight

O'Meara, Jack—**Radio Telephone**—two-way (versation between a glider and the land

Omlie, Phoebe Fairgrave—**Aviation—Licen:** pilot's license granted to a woman by the Dept. of Commerce

P

Pacheco, Mr.—**Automaton**—automaton

Packard, Sophia Booker—**Nursing School**—training school for black nurses

Padilla, Juan de—**Martyr**—Christian martyr on U.S. soil

Page, Albert B.—**Diathermy Machine**

Page, Charles Grafton—**Locomotive**—electric locomotive

Page, George—**Plow**—plow for pulverizing the soil

Page, James—**Ice Skating Club**—ice skating club

Page, John Wallace—**Wire**—woven wire fence industry

Page, Joseph—**Planetarium**—planetarium or orrery

Paget, Percy Wright—**Radio Broadcast**—transatlantic radio signal

Paine, Cassius M.—**Whist**—whist organization

Paine, John Knowles—**Music Instruction**—college music chair

Paine, John Knowles—**Oratorio**—oratorio by an American

Paine, John Knowles—**Symphony**—symphonic work by an American composer

Painter, William—**Bottle Cap**

Palfrey, William—**Diplomatic Service**—consul to die in service

Palinkas, Patricia—**Football Player**—woman football player (professional)

Palisan, Johann—**Astronomy**—planet (asteroid) named for an American President

Palm, Joseph Henry Louis de, Baron—**Crematory**—crematory

Palmer, Mr.—**Baptist Church**—Baptist church (black)

Palmer, Arnold Daniel—**Golfer**—golfer to earn over $100,000 in one year

Palmer, Benjamin F.—**Leg (artificial) patent**

Palmer, Daniel David—**Chiropractic School**

Palmer, Daniel David—**Chiropractor**

Palmer, John F.—**Bicycle Tire**—bicycle tire (cord)

Palmer, John McAuley—**Labor Legislation**—women's equal employment legislation

Palmer, Nathaniel Brown—**Discovery**—discovery of Antarctica

Palmer, Potter—**Hotel**—fireproof hotel

Palmer, Volney B.—**Advertising Agency**

Palmerton, John—**Boat Club**—boat club

Palmerton, Thomas—**Boat Club**—boat club

Pandit, Shrimati Vijaya Lakshmi—**Diplomatic Service**—woman ambassador from a foreign country

Pangborn, Clyde—**Aviation—Flights (transpacific)**—transpacific nonstop flight

Pappas, Katharine—**Greek Orthodox Church**—Greek Orthodox Archdiocesan Council women members

Paraf, Alfred—**Oleomargarine**—oleomargarine manufacturer (successful)

Pardee, Charles Laban—**Heresy Trial**

Parham, Thomas David, Jr.—**Naval Officer**—black captain in the U.S. Navy

Park, James Alan—**Insurance Treatise**

Park, Jesse K.—**Envelope**—envelope machine ent

Park, Rosemary—**College President**—woman lege president of two colleges

Park, Roswell—**Cancer Laboratory**

Park, Thomas—**Library**—library building (un sity)

Park, William Hallock—**Antitoxin Laborator**

Park, William Hallock—**Vaccine**—tubercu vaccine

Parker, Dr.—**Madstone**

Parker, Alton U.—**Marine Corps**—marine pil fly over the Antarctic continent

Parker, Benjamin Clarke Cutler—**Church**—f ing church

Parker, Bruce—**Water Ski Tournament (natio**

Parker, Charles Wallace—**Carrousel**—carro with the jumping horse mechanism

Parker, Charles Wallace—**Shooting Gal (mechanized)**

Parker, Ely Samuel—**American Indians—In** Affairs Commissioner (U.S.) who was American Indian

Parker, James—**Crime Prevention and Detec** —interstate crime pact

Parker, James—**Grammar**—Spanish gram (printer)

Parker, James—**Music Book**—music book pri from type

Parker, James, Jr.—**Submarine**—submarine at a government shipyard (first comman officer)

Parker, Joel—**Labor Party (political)**—labor p (national)

Parker, John—**Revolutionary War**—armed flict in the Revolutionary War

Parker, Joseph—**Blotting Paper**

Parker, Mattie V.—**Army Officer**—woman to c mand an Armed Forces Examining and trance Station

Parker, Samuel—**Leather**—leather-splitting chine

Parker, Willard—**Health Board**—health b (municipal) armed with sufficient powers fc emergencies.

Parker, Willard—**Medical Clinic**—college m cal clinic

Parker, William T.—**Carrousel**—carrousel the jumping horse mechanism

Parks, Benjamin—**Naval Officer**—naval chap (Continental Navy)

Parks, Charles Henry—**Naval Officer**—n chaplain who was Catholic

Parks, William—**Cookbook**—cookbook

Parks, William—**Fencing Book**

Parks, William—**Medical Book**—pleurisy bo

Parks, William—**Newspaper**—newspaper lished south of the Potomac River

Parmelee, DuBois D.—**Adding Machine**—ad machine to employ depressible keys

Parmelee, Henry S.—**Sprinkler**—sprinkler he

Parmelee, Philip—**Aviation**—airplane merc dise shipment

Pearson, Leonard—**Animals**—cattle tuberculosis test

Pearson, Norman C. S.—**Medal**—marines to win the Navy and Marine Corps Medal

Pearson, Theodore—**Cracker Bakery**

Peary, Josephine—**Expedition**—polar expedition of which a woman was a member

Peary, Robert Edwin—**Discovery**—discovery of the North Pole

Peary, Robert Edwin—**Medal**—National Geographic Society gold medal

Pease, Daniel Chapin—**Photograph**—photograph of genes

Pease, Francis Gladheim—**Astronomer**—astronomer to measure the size of a fixed star

Pease, Titus—**Whips**

Peawa, William—**American Indian Church**—church organized by American Indians

Peay, Austin—**Evolution Law (state)**

Peck, Frederick M.—**Rifle Association**—rifle association (national)

Peck, Gregory—**Motion Picture**—motion picture presented simultaneously in major cities throughout the world

Peck, John—**Supreme Court (U.S.) Decision**—Supreme Court decision that a state law was unconstitutional

Pecker, James—**Medical Society**—medical society (state)

Peden, Doug—**Television—Telecast**—bicycle race telecast

Peden, William—**Television—Telecast**—bicycle race telecast

Peek, George Nelson—**Agricultural Adjustment Administration**

Peek, George Nelson—**Bank**—Export-Import Bank

Peek, George Nelson—**Commercial Policy Executive Committee**

Peer, Lyle Hudson Bennett—**High Jumping Standards using electric eye detectors**

Peirce, Isaac—**Chemistry Magazine**

Peirce, William—**Almanac**—almanac

Pelham, Peter—**Engraver**

Pelham, Peter—**Music**—concert

Pelham, Richard—**Minstrel Show Troupe**

Pellicier, Anthony Domenic Ambrose—**Catholic Bishop**—native bishops of the South

Pemberton, Bennett—**Road**—state road authorization

Pendergast, William Wirt—**Agricultural School**—vocational agricultural school

Penington, Henry—**Publishing Society**

Penman, Edward—**Golf Club**—golf club

Penn, William—**Lawbook**

Penn, William—**Mennonites**—Mennonites

Pennant, Elias—**Expedition**—expedition

Pennel, John—**Pole Vault**—pole vault higher than 17 feet

Pennell, Rebecca Mann—**College**—woman college professor

Pennell, Rebecca Mann—**Didactics Course**—didactics course in a college

Pennell, Rebecca Mann—**Hygiene Instructi**‹ physiology and hygiene courses

Penniman, Anson W.—**Blind**—state school fo‹ blind

Pennock, Cyril—**Military School**—military sc‹

Pennypacker, Samuel Whitaker—**Steriliza Legislation**

Peper, Henry, Jr.—**Pen**—pen with truly eras‹ ink

Pepperell, William—**Knighthood**—knighth‹ conferred on a native-born American for ‹ tary leadership

Peratis, Christine—**Greek Orthodox Chur**‹ Greek Orthodox Archdiocesan Council wo‹ members

Percy, Samuel R.—**Milk**—dried milk patent

Perham, Josiah—**Railroad Excursion**—rail‹ excursion rates

Perinault, Joseph—**Catholic Seminary**—Catl‹ seminary

Perkings, Jay—**Health Laboratory**—health lab‹ tory (state)

Perkins, Anthony—**Motion Picture**—motion ‹ ture presented simultaneously in major c‹ throughout the world

Perkins, Frances (Mrs. Paul Caldwell Wilso‹ **Cabinet (U.S.)**—woman Cabinet member

Perkins, Frances (Mrs. Paul Caldwell Wilso‹ **Labor Department (U.S.)**—woman Secreta‹ Labor

Perkins, Jacob—**Engraving**—pamphlet prod‹ from a steel plate engraving

Perkins, Jacob—**Refrigerator**—ice-making ‹ chine

Perkins, Nicholas—**Vice President (U.S.)**—‹ President arrested

Perkins, Thomas Handasyd—**Blind**—schoo‹ the blind

Perkins, Thomas Handasyd—**Railroad**—rail‹ for freight transportation to celebrate its c‹ nary

Perkinson, Henry L.—**Telephone**—mobile ‹ phone commercial service

Perky, Henry D.—**Breakfast Food**—shre‹ wheat biscuits

Perlman, Louis Henry—**Automobile Tire**—‹ mountable tire-carrying rim

Perrine, Henry—**Avocado**

Perry, Benjamin—**Iron**—iron blast furnace

Perry, Harold Robert—**Catholic Bishop**—b‹ Catholic bishop who was American born

Perry, Marmaduke—**Autopsy**—officially reco‹ autopsy

Perry, Michael—**Music Book**—hymnbook ‹ music

Perry, Nathaniel—**Physiology Society**—phys‹ gy society

Perry, Oliver Hazard—**War (1812)**—defeat in‹ tory of a British squadron

Perry, Stuart—**Gas Engine**

Perry, William—**Dictionary**—dictionary ‹ lished in the United States

Perry, William—**Dictionary**—pocket dictiona‹

Pickering, Joseph—**Papermaking Machinery**—papermaking machine (Fourdrinier) imported

Pickering, Thomas—**Passport**—passport

Pickering, Timothy—**Senator (U.S.)**—senator censured

Picket, Albert—**Education Periodical**—educational magazine

Picket, Albert—**Education Periodical**—educational magazine to achieve success

Picket, John W.—**Education Periodical**—educational magazine

Picket, John W.—**Education Periodical**—educational magazine to achieve success

Pickle, James Jarrell ("Jake")—**Representative (U.S.)**—representative sworn in before 8:00 A.M.

Pierce, Bradford K.—**Manual Training**—industrial school for girls

Pierce, Clinton Albert—**World War II**—American general wounded in action in World War II

Pierce, Cyrus—**Normal School**—normal school (state)

Pierce, Franklin—**Court**—court of claims

Pierce, Franklin—**Fair**—industrial exposition

Pierce, George Foster—**College**—women's college chartered

Pierce, Hugh Franklin—**Airmail Service**—rocket airmail flight

Pierce, Joanne E.—**Police**—police training school women graduates of the Federal Bureau of Investigation

Pierce, R.—**Schoolbook**

Pierce, Roger—**Telephone**—mobile telephone conversation overseas

Pierson, Mr.—**Envelope Manufacturer**

Pierson, Henry L.—**Railroad Passenger**—railroad honeymoon trip

Pierson, Josiah Gilbert—**Rivet**

Pierson, Warren Lee—**Bank**—Export-Import Bank

Pietersen, Evert—**School**—evening school

Pike, Nicholas—**Algebra Book**—algebra book by a native-born American

Pike, Nicholas—**Birds**—sparrows

Pike, Sumner Tucker—**Atomic Energy Commission**—Atomic Energy Commission

Pilling, Samuel—**Building and Loan Association**

Pillsbury, Moody Adams—**Animals**—cattle (Guernsey cattle)

Pin, Chen Lan—**Chinese Embassy**

Pinchback, Pinckney Benton Stewart—**Governor**—black governor (acting)

Pinchbeck, William Federick—**Magic Lantern**—magic lantern book

Pinchot, Gifford—**Liquor Stores (state)**

Pinchot, Gifford—**Radio Facsimile Transmission**—photograph sent overland by radio to a distant point

Pinckney, Charles Cotesworth—**Museum**—public museum

Pinckney, Thomas—**Diplomatic Service**—minister to Great Britain

Pincus, Gregory—**Impregnation**—impregnation (artificial)

Pinkerton, Allan—**Army Secret Service Bureau**

Pintard, John Marsden—**Diplomatic Servi**—consuls of the United States appointed afte adoption of the Constitution

Pinto, Isaac—**Jewish Book**—Jewish prayer published in the United States

Pipe, Captain—**Treaty**—treaty entered into b United States with American Indian tribe

Pipestem, George—**American Indian Chu**—church organized by American Indians

Pipkin, Marvin—**Electric Lighting**—electric bulb frosted on the inside

Piquet, La Motte—**Flag**—American flag sa by a foreign nation

Pise, Charles Constantine—**Congress (U.** **House of Representatives**—Catholic chap

Pitcairn, Harold Frederick—**Autogiro**—autog

Pitcairn, Harold Frederick—**Autogiro**—**Fligh** autogiro flight

Pitcairn, Harold Frederick—**Autogiro**—**Figh** intercity autogiro flight

Pitcairn, John—**Revolutionary War**—armed flict in the Revolutionary war

Pitkin, Henry—**Clock**—watch made by ma ery

Pitkin, James—**Clock**—watch made by machi

Pitkin, Timothy—**History**—political history

Pitt, Louis W.—**Television**—**Telecast**—ch service telecast

Pitts, Hiram Abial—**Thresher**—threshing mac to employ steam

Pitts, John A.—**Thresher**—threshing machin employ steam

Pius VI, Pope—**Catholic Bishop**—Catholic bi appointed to serve in the United States

Pius XI, Pope—**Radio Facsimile Transmissi** photograph sent by radio across the Atl from Europe

Pius XII, Pope—**Visiting Celebrities**—pontiff

Place, Martha M.—**Execution**—execution woman by electrocution

Plant, Joseph Theophilus Kirk—**Knights of Py**

Platen, Baltzar Carl von—**Refrigerator**—ga frigerator (household)

Platt, Sarah M.—**Normal School**—woman pr pal of a normal school

Plaza Lasso, Galo—**President of a South An** **can Country Born in the United States**

Plimpton, James Leonard—**Roller Skating Ri** roller skating rink (public)

Plume, Shirley—**American Indians**—America dian superintendent of a Bureau of In Affairs agency

Plunkett, Charles—**Opera**—light opera prese in 2 cities on the same day by the same cor ny

Poage, George C.—**Olympic Games**—b American athlete in the Olympic Game place

Poe, Edgar Allan—**Detective Story**

Poell, George H.—**Medal**—Interstate Comm Commission Medal of Honor

Pogue, William Reid—**Astronaut**—astron (American) to exceed 2,000 hours flight tir

Pratt, Matthew—**Artist**—artist successful in commercial art

Pratt, Philip W.—**Sprinkler**—sprinkler system patent

Pratt, Phineas—**Comb-cutting Machine**

Pratt, Richard Henry—**American Indian School**—American Indian school of prominence

Pratt, Roberta—**Medical Clinic**—contraceptive clinic (state)

Prattis, Percival L.—**News Correspondent**—black news correspondent admitted to the House of Representatives and Senate press gallery

Pray, James Sturgis—**City Planning Instruction**

Prentiss, John W.—**Squash Club**—squash tennis organization (national)

Prentiss, John W.—**Squash Tournament**

Presbrey, R. E.—**Tennis Match**—intercollegiate lawn tennis match

Prescott, Benjamin—**Canal**—canal

Prescott, Edwin—**Loop-the-Loop Centrifugal Railway**

Preston, Charles E.—**Movable Church**

Preston, David—**Ballet Instruction**—university to offer ballet technique instruction

Preston, Emily—**United Church of Christ**—United Church of Christ ordination of a woman minister in which all the principal roles were filled by women

Preston, Thomas—**Revolutionary War**—American casualties (acquitted in trial)

Price, Henry—**Freemasons**—Masonic lodge to work under a regular charter

Price, Hiram—**Temperance Society**—Anti-Saloon League (national organization)

Price, Robert M.—**Helicopter—Flights**—transcontinental nonstop helicopter flight

Price, Vincent—**Motion Picture**—three-dimensional feature motion picture in color

Price, William W. (Bill)—**News Correspondent**—White House reporter

Pride, Alfred Melville—**Autogiro**—autogiro to land and take off from a ship

Pride, John—**Potter**

Priesand, Sally Jane—**Rabbi**—woman rabbi

Priestley, Joseph—**Unitarian Minister**—Unitarian minister

Prince, Harold—**Play (drama)**—musical to run for more than 3,000 performances

Prince, N. A.—**Hospital**—inebriates' asylum

Prince, Thomas—**Periodical**—sectarian magazine

Prince, Thomas—**Religious Publication**—religious journal

Prior, Edward—**Travelers Aid**

Procter, William—**Pharmacy Society (national)**

Propp, Phyllis Ladora—**Army Officer**—woman officer in the Judge Advocate General's Department

Prountis, Lila—**Greek Orthodox Church**—Greek Orthodox Archdiocesan Council women members

Puett, Clay—**Electric Starting Gate** (racetrack)

Puff, Gerhard—**Execution**—execution (federal) for the killing of a Federal Bureau of Investigation agent

Pugh, David—**Gas**—gas company

Pullman, George Mortimer—**Railroad Car**—p. car

Pullman, George Mortimer—**Sleeping Car**—man sleeping car

Pullman, George Mortimer—**Sleeping Car**—man sleeping car that was comfortable

Pulsifer, Alden William—**Postal Service**—i national dogsled mail

Purcell, Dr.—**Golf Club**—golf club

Purcell, William—**Arbitration**—state boar mediation and arbitration

Purnell, Benjamin—**House of David**

Purvines, M. L.—**Federal Crop Insurance Corp tion**

Pusey, Joshua—**Match**—"book matches"

Putnam, Amelia Earhart—**Aviation—Fli (transatlantic)**—transatlantic solo flight l woman

Putnam, Amelia Earhart—**Aviation—Fli (transcontinental)**—transcontinental non flight by a woman

Putnam, Amelia Earhart—**Aviation—Passeng** woman airplane passenger to cross the Atla Ocean

Putnam, Amelia Earhart—**Aviation—Pilot**—w an pilot to fly solo across the Pacific Ocea

Putnam, Amelia Earhart—**Medal**—National (graphic Society special gold medal

Putnam, George Palmer—**Book Trade Maga** —successful book trade magazine

Putnam, George Palmer—**Periodical Index**

Putnam, Herbert—**Bibliography Society (natio**

Putnam, Palmer Cosslet—**Electric Gener** —wind turbine

Pynchon, William—**Meat Packer**

Q

Quadequina—**Popcorn**

Quanpen (Sowagonish)—**Court-martial Tri** court-martial trial

Quigley, Robin Lindsay—**Naval Officer**—wo naval officer to hold a major navy comma

Quimby, Harriet—**Aviation—Airplane Fatal** —airplane fatality (woman pilot with pas ger)

Quimby, Harriet—**Aviation—License**—wo pilot to pass the test of the Aero Club of An ca

Quincy, Josiah—**Secession**—secession was mentioned in Congress

Quincy, Josiah, Jr.—**Revolutionary War**—An can casualties (defense lawyer in trial)

Quinn, Joseph—**X ray**—X-ray three-dimensi (stereo) fluoroscopic system (development e neer)

Quinn, Larry—**Photograph**—portrait (life-size a human in a newspaper

Ray, Dixy Lee—**Atomic Energy Commission**—Atomic Energy Commission woman chairman

Ray, James Garrett—**Airmail Service**—autogiro mail delivery direct to a post office

Ray, James Garrett—**Autogiro**—autogiro to land on the White House lawn

Ray, James Garrett—**Autogiro**—autogiro to land packages on a moving ship

Ray, Nat—**Horse Race**—harness horse race (Hambletonian) for three-year-olds

Rayburn, Samuel Taliaferro ("Sam")—**Congress (U.S.)—House of Representatives**—Speaker of the House of Representatives to serve longer than 10 years

Raymond, Eleanor—**Building**—house completely solar-heated

Raymond, Julius—**Hospital**—Jewish hospital

Raymond, William—**Lifeboat**—lifeboat

Rea, Henry B.—**Horse Race**—harness horse race (Hambletonian) for three-year-olds

Reach, Alfred James—**Baseball Player**—professional baseball player

Read, Albert Cushing—**Aviation—Flights (transatlantic)**—transatlantic hydroplane flight

Read, Daniel—**Music Periodical**—music magazine

Read, George—**Senator (U.S.)**—senator (Kensey Johns) appointed (not seated)

Reading, Oliver Scott—**Camera**—aerial camera (nine-lens) for large-scale mapping

Ream, Vinnie (Mrs. Richard Leveridge Hoxie)—**Monument**—monument by a woman ordered by the U.S. Government

Ream, Vinnie (Mrs. Richard Leveridge Hoxie)—**Monument**—statue cast by the U.S. Government

Reavis, Holland S.—**Oil**—oil and gas magazine

Recht, Bill—**Prizefight**—prizefight with a purse of $4.5 million (judge)

Rechten, Philip—**Whaling**—whale-killing machine (electric)

Reckenzaun, Anthony—**Motorboat**—storage-battery motorboat

Reckenzaun, Frederick—**Motorboat**—storage-battery motorboat

Reddington, George—**Alligator Farm**

Redfield, William Charles—**Science Association**—scientific society (national organization)

Redfield, William Cox—**Commerce and Labor Department (U.S.)**

Redfield, William Cox—**Commerce Department (U.S.)**—Commerce Department (U.S.)

Redgrave, Gilbert Richard—**Microfilm**—book series microfilmed

Redpath, James—**Novel**—novel by a black

Reece, Ernest James—**Library Chair**

Reed, Wallace Allison—**Hospital**—ambulatory surgical facility independently operated

Reed, William Bradford—**History Instruction**—American history chair

Reeder, Alner—**Railroad Charter**

Reese, J. E.—**Wedding**—airplane wedding

Reese, James—**Slate**

Reese, Warren Snyder—**Lens**—plastic lens

Reese, William—**Slate**

Reeve, Tapping—**Law School**—law school

Reeves, Frank Daniel—**Election**—election Washington, D.C.

Regal, Betty—**Play (drama)**—burlesque show

Reichers, Lou—**Aviation—Flights**—airplane fl with an auto slung beneath the fuselage

Reid, John—**Architect**—landscape architect

Reid, John—**Golf Match**—mixed foursome

Reid, John—**Radio Telephone**—military porta

Reid, Mrs. John G.—**Golf Match**—mixed fourso

Reilly, H. Christine—**Streptomycin**

Reinagle, Alexander—**Music Book**—secu songbook

Reinecke, Mabel Gilmore—**Woman**—woman ternal revenue collector

Reiner, Fritz—**Television—Telecast**—pay tel sion presentation of an opera

Reinhardt, Aurelia Henry—**Unitarian Churc** woman moderator of the Unitarian Church

Reisman, Leonard E.—**College**—liberal arts lege for police and correction officers est lished by a city

Remington, Frederic—**Postage Stamp**—post stamp featuring a work of art in true color

Remington, William H.—**Nickel Plating**

Remsen, Ira—**Saccharin**

Renick, Felix—**Animals**—cattle importation purebred shorthorns

Renick, Felix—**Animals**—cattle (shorthorn) p lic auction sale

Reno, John—**Railroad Train Robbery**—railr train robbery of a train in motion

Reno, Simeon—**Railroad Train Robbery**—railr train robbery of a train in motion

Renoe, A. J.—**Fingerprint Society**—fingerprint ciety (international)

Renwick, James—**Brick**—terra-cotta

Respess, J. S.—**Horse Race**—mutuel ticket to more than $1,000

Ressegue, H.—**Animals**—fur-bearing animals

Rettger, Leo Frederick—**Milk**—acidophilus m

Reulbach, Edward Marvin ("Big Ed")—**Basel Game**—shutout double-header games

Reuss-Belce, Luisa—**Opera**—opera composed a woman performed at the Metropolitan Op House

Revel, Bernard—**Jewish College**—Jewish coll of liberal arts and sciences under Jewish a pices

Revels, Hiram Rhodes—**Senator (U.S.)**—bl senator

Revere, Paul—**Engraving**—engraving to achi popularity

Reyburn, Robert—**Medical Society**—black m cal society

Reyes, J. Antonio—**Students' Federation (inte tional)**

Reymert, James De Noon—**Newspaper**—Nor gian-American newspaper

Reynolds, Arthur Rowley—**Automobile Lice Board**

Rintoul, Norman—**Aviation**—airplane human pickup

Riotte, C. C.—**Motorboat Race**—motorboat race under organized rules

Ritchard, Cyril—**Television—Telecast**—play telecast in color with its original cast

Ritchie, Richard Stephen—**Air Force Officer**—Air Force Ace in Vietnam

Rittenhouse, David—**Building**—building erected in the United States for public use

Rittenhouse, David—**Mint (U.S.)**—Mint (U.S.) director

Rittenhouse, William—**Mennonites**—Mennonite church meetinghouse

Rittenhouse, William—**Paper Mill**

Rittenhouse, William—**Watermark**

Ritty, James J. (Jake)—**Cash Register**

Ritty, John—**Cash Register**

Rivlin, Georgianna Alice Mitchell—**Congress (U.S.)**—Congressional Budget Office

Roach, Elizabeth—**College**—women's college (chartered)

Roane, Archibald—**Dueling Legislation (state)**

Robb, Al—**Electric Power Plant**—municipally owned electric power plant

Robb, Lotus—**Play (drama)**—drama to win a Pulitzer Prize

Robbins, Betty (Mrs. Sheldon Robbins)—**Cantor**—Jewish woman cantor

Robbins, Jerome—**Play (drama)**—musical to run for more than 3,000 performances

Roberdeau, Daniel—**Holiday**—Thanksgiving Day celebration (nationwide, colonial)

Robert, Nicholas Louis—**Papermaking Machinery**—papermaking machine (Fourdrinier) imported

Robert, René—**Ship**—Great Lakes commercial vessel

Roberts, Dave—**Pole Vault**—pole vault higher than 18.5 feet

Roberts, Edmund—**Treaty**—treaty with a Far Eastern country

Roberts, Edward A. L.—**Oil**—oil well drilled by torpedoes

Roberts, Enoch—**Insurance**—boiler insurance company

Roberts, Jonathan—**Druggist**

Roberts, Joseph Jenkins—**President of an African Country Born in the United States**

Roberts, Montague—**Automobile Race**—automobile race New York–Paris

Roberts, Robert Jeffries—**Medicine Ball**

Roberts, Solomon White—**Tunnel**—railroad tunnel

Robertson, Alice Mary—**Representative (U.S.)**—representative (woman) to preside over the House of Representatives

Robertson, Charles—**Civil Government in America**

Robertson, Doris Roberta—**Naval Officer**—woman sworn into the regular U.S. Navy

Robertson, George H.—**Automobile Race**—Vanderbilt Cup Race to be won by an American

Robertson, Gilbert, Jr.—**Arbitration**—state board of mediation and arbitration

Robertson, James—**Civil Government in Amer**
ica

Robertson, M. G.—**Television Station**—religi noncommercial television station

Robeson, George Maxwell—**Fair**—centen celebration

Robeson, George Maxwell—**Monument**—sta cast by the United States Government

Robich, Robert—**Paprika Mill**

Robinson, Bernard Whitfield—**Naval Office** black commissioned officer in the Naval serve

Robinson, Charles—**Impeachment**—impea ment proceedings against a state governor

Robinson, Charles Mulford—**Civic Design Ch**

Robinson, Douglas—**Polo Club**—polo associa (national)

Robinson, Frank—**Baseball Player**—"most v able player" in both major leagues

Robinson, George—**Glass Factory**—flint glass tory

Robinson, George Dexter—**Gas Commiss (state)**

Robinson, Henry—**Ship**—schooner built America

Robinson, Hugh—**Aviation**—airplane rescue sea effected by another airplane

Robinson, Hugh—**Aviation—Races**—intercity plane race

Robinson, Jack Roosevelt ("Jackie")—**Base Game**—major-league game in which the maj ty of the players on one team were blacks

Robinson, Jack Roosevelt ("Jackie")—**Base Player**—black major-league baseball playe

Robinson, Jack Roosevelt ("Jackie")—**Base Player**—"most valuable player" award (m league) to a black

Robinson, John—**Slander Proceedings**

Robinson, Morris—**Insurance**—mutual life in ance company to operate

Robinson, Sugar Ray (*originally*, Walker Smit **Prizefighter**—pugilist to win a world champ ship 5 times in the same weight division

Robinson, Wilbert—**Bowling**—duckpins

Robinson, William E.—**Radio Broadcast**—r police system (two-way three-way)

Roche d'Allison, Joseph de la—**Oil**—oil sprir

Roche, Tony—**Tennis Player**—tennis playe win 2 grand slams (defeated in U.S. Open)

Rock, John S.—**Lawyer**—black lawyer to prac before the United States Supreme Court

Rockefeller, Nelson Aldrich—**Television—T cast**—congressional telecast and radio br cast

Rockefeller, Nelson Aldrich—**Television—T cast**—Senate proceedings telecast

Rockefeller, Nelson Aldrich—**Vice Presi (U.S.)**—Vice President cremated

Rockenbach, Samuel Dickerson—**Ordna** —Army armored tank

Rockwell, Alphonse David—**Execution**—elec cution of a human being

Rodd, Herbert Charles—**Aviation—Flights (tr atlantic)**—transatlantic hydroplane flight

Roosevelt, Franklin Delano—**President (U.S.)**—President elected for a fourth term

Roosevelt, Franklin Delano—**President (U.S.)**—President inaugurated on January 20

Roosevelt, Franklin Delano—**President (U.S.)**—President to become a godfather to a member of the British royal family

Roosevelt, Franklin Delano—**President (U.S.)**—President to broadcast from a foreign country

Roosevelt, Franklin Delano—**President (U.S.)**—President to broadcast in a foreign language

Roosevelt, Franklin Delano—**President (U.S.)**—President to conduct ministerial services as commander-in-chief of the Navy

Roosevelt, Franklin Delano—**President (U.S.)**—President to fly in an airplane while in office

Roosevelt, Franklin Delano—**President (U.S.)**—President to go through the Panama Canal

Roosevelt, Franklin Delano—**President (U.S.)**—President to invite the President-elect

Roosevelt, Franklin Delano—**President (U.S.)**—President to visit a foreign country in wartime

Roosevelt, Franklin Delano—**President (U.S.)**—President to visit Hawaii while President

Roosevelt, Franklin Delano—**President (U.S.)**—President to visit South America while President

Roosevelt, Franklin Delano—**President (U.S.)**—President whose mother saw her son inaugurated President of the United States for a second term

Roosevelt, Franklin Delano—**Presidential Candidate**—presidential candidate to fly to a political convention

Roosevelt, Franklin Delano—**Presidential Candidate**—presidential candidate to make a speech of acceptance at a nominating convention

Roosevelt, Franklin Delano—**Public Works Administration**

Roosevelt, Franklin Delano—**Securities and Exchange Commission (U.S.)**

Roosevelt, Franklin Delano—**Television—Telecast**—President to appear on television

Roosevelt, Franklin Delano—**Veto (presidential)**—veto message read by a President

Roosevelt, Grace—**Tennis Match**—women's national championship lawn tennis matches

Roosevelt, Hilborne Lewis—**Organ**—electric organ

Roosevelt, Isaac—**Dental Dispensary**—dental dispensary

Roosevelt, Nicholas J.—**Ship**—steamboat to sail down the Mississippi

Roosevelt, Sarah Delano—**President (U.S.)**—President whose mother saw her son inaugurated President of the United States for a second term

Roosevelt, Theodore—**Cabinet (U.S.)**—Cabinet member who was Jewish

Roosevelt, Theodore—**Cable**—cable across the Pacific Ocean between Honolulu, Midway, Guam, and Manila

Roosevelt, Theodore—**Children's Welfare Congress (international)**

Roosevelt, Theodore—**Election Law**—corr election practices law (state)

Roosevelt, Theodore—**Forest**—national forest the southern states

Roosevelt, Theodore—**Forest Service**—Fore Service (U.S.)

Roosevelt, Theodore—**Medal**—National G graphic Society gold medal

Roosevelt, Theodore—**Monument**—natio monument

Roosevelt, Theodore—**Nobel Prize**—Nobel Pr

Roosevelt, Theodore—**Political Convention**—tional nominating convention presided over a black

Roosevelt, Theodore—**President (U.S.)**—Pr dent to fly

Roosevelt, Theodore—**President (U.S.)**—Pr dent to ride in an automobile

Roosevelt, Theodore—**President (U.S.)**—Pr dent to visit a foreign country while Presid

Roosevelt, Theodore—**Progressive Party**

Roosevelt, Theodore—**Radio Broadcast**—tran lantic broadcast (not experimental)

Roosevelt, Theodore—**Ticker Tape**—ticker-t shower

Root, Elihu—**Conference**—conference of gr powers

Root, Harriet Maria—**Information Service (U ed States)

Rosbrugh, John—**Army Officer**—chaplain kille action

Rose, Frederick Henry—**Physician**—doctor to ceive a medal from Congress

Rose, James McKinley, Jr.—**Insurance**—crime surance federal policy

Rose, Mauri—**Automobile**—gas-turbine auto bile

Rose, Thomas—**Whips**

Rosenberg, Anna—**Medal**—Medal of Freed awarded to a woman

Rosenberg, Ethel—**Spy**—peacetime death s tence for espionage

Rosenberg, Ethel—**Treason**—execution for t son in peacetime

Rosenberg, Julius—**Spy**—peacetime death s tence for espionage

Rosenberg, Julius—**Treason**—execution for t son in peacetime

Rosenblum, William Franklin—**Television—T cast**—Jewish temple services (complete) to televised

Rosewall, Ken—**Tennis Player**—tennis playe win 2 grand slams (defeated in French Op

Ross, Betsy—**Bridge**—bridge named for a wor

Ross, Betsy—**Flag**—American flag

Ross, Charles Brewster—**Kidnapping**—kidr ping for ransom

Ross, George—**Flag**—American flag

Ross, John—**Health Board**—health board (loc

Ross, Leonard—**Brokerage**—visitor to open New York Stock Exchange

Ross, Malcolm—**Television—Telecast**—str sphere telecast

s, Nellie Tayloe—**Governor**—woman gover-
or of a state

s, Nellie Tayloe—**Medal**—woman to have her
keness on a medal issued by the United States
lint

s, Nellie Tayloe—**Mint (U.S.)**—woman direc-
r of the mint

s, Nellie Tayloe—**Woman**—woman to have
er name placed on the cornerstone of a United
tates Government building

s, William Potter—**Freemasons**—Masonic
dge organized in the Indian Territory

si, G. Bernard—**Element**—element 99

sini, Gioacchino Antonio—**Opera**—opera
talian)

h, Murray—**Motion Picture**—talking picture
hose footage exceeded 6,000 feet

hwell, Al—**Bowling Tournament**—gold medal
ward to a perfect-score bowler

ge, Leon J. D.—**Radio Broadcast**—solar power
vo-way-radio coast-to-coast conversation

gement, Philip (Felipe de Rojamón)—**Autopsy**
-autopsy

manis, Stamatoula—**Immigration**—refugee to
rive under the Refugee Relief Act of 1953

nseville, Robert—**Television—Telecast**—op-
a (major) televised in color

sseau, Lovell Harrison—**Territorial Expan-
on**—noncontiguous territory

van, Stephen Clegg—**Torpedo**—torpedo mine

ell, George Presbury—**Advertising Magazine**

vland, Henry Augustus—**Physics**—national
hysics association

vland, Thomas F.—**Drill**—oil-drill offshore rig

vson, Susanna Haswell—**Book**—best-seller
ovel

all, Kenneth Claiborne—**Army Officer**—wom-
n army officer

all, Kenneth Claiborne—**Defense Department**
J.S.)

ce, G. Irwin—**Coursing Club**—American
oursing Club

ce, Robert—**Ski Tow**—ski tow (rope)

in, Barbara Jo—**Jockey**—jockey (woman) to
de 2 winners in 1 day

in, Barbara Jo—**Jockey**—jockey (woman) to
in on a regular pari-mutuel flat track

in, Benny—**Television—Telecast**—demon-
ration of home reception of television

ino, Rudolph, Jr.—**World War I**—American
rmy soldiers killed in World War I

lee, George—**Federal Trade Commission**—
deral Trade Commission

y, Jack (Jacob L. Rubinstein)—**Television**—
elecast—courtroom verdict telecast

y, Jack (Jacob L. Rubinstein)—**Television**—
elecast—murder (actual) shown on television

ker, Charles W.—**Medal**—Distinguished Fly-
g Cross

ker, Elizabeth Jane—**Vice President (U.S.)**
Vice President to marry in office

d, Caroline Mary—**College**—coeducational
llege

Rudder, John Earl—**Marines**—black commissioned officer

Rudolph, Wilma (Wilma Glodean Rudolph
Ward)—**Athlete**—black woman awarded the
James E. Sullivan Memorial trophy

Rudolphi, Arno—**Wedding**—parachute wedding

Ruffin, Edmund—**Civil War**—attack in the Civil
War

Ruffner, David—**Salt**—salt well

Ruffner, Joseph—**Salt**—salt well

Rugg, Micah—**Nut and Bolt Factory**

Ruggles, David—**Periodical**—black periodical

Ruggles, John—**Patent**—numbering system for
patents

Ruggles, Joseph—**Stadium**—cement stadium

Rumford, Sarah Thompson, Countess of—**Countess**—American woman to become a countess

Rumsey, Mrs. Charles Cary—**Consumers' Advisory Board (U.S.)**

Rumsey, James—**Motorboat**—motorboat

Rush, Benjamin—**Chemistry Professor**—chemistry professor

Rush, Benjamin—**Chemistry Textbook**—chemistry text

Rush, Benjamin—**Epidemic**—medical record of an
epidemic

Rush, Benjamin—**Medical Book**—mental diseases book

Rush, Benjamin—**Medical Book**—psychiatry
book

Rush, James—**Boat Club**—boat club

Rush, Robert I.—**Veterinary Hospital**—municipal
veterinary hospital

Rusk, (David) Dean—**Astronaut**—astronaut international rescue agreement

Russ, Matilda Biglow—**Theater**—television theater demonstration

Russell, George Lucius—**Naval Officer**—women
sworn into the regular U.S. Navy

Russell, Howard Hyde—**Temperance Society**—
Anti-Saloon League

Russell, John—**Prohibition Party (national)**

Russell, John Henry—**Civil War**—naval engagement in the Civil War

Russell, Richard D.—**Television—Telecast**—surgical operation televised on a coast-to-coast
closed circuit in color

Russell, Samuel—**Elastic Webbing**

Russo, Carlo—**Telephone**—telephone conversation (commercial) over a satellite

Russwurm, John Brown—**Newspaper**—black
newspaper

Rust, John Daniel—**Cotton Picker (mechanical)**

Rust, Samuel—**Printing Press**—printing press invented in America that was practical and successful

Rusticoat, Robert ("Rusty-Turncoat")—**Periodical**
—comic magazine

Ruth, George Herman ("Babe")—**Baseball Game**
—all-star baseball game (major league)

Ruth, George Herman ("Babe")—**Baseball Game**
—World Series baseball game in which 3 home
runs were made in 1 game

Ruth, George Herman ("Babe")—**Baseball Player**—baseball player to hit a home run in an all-star game

Ruth, George Herman ("Babe")—**Hall of Fame**—hall of fame (baseball)

Rutledge, John—**Colonial Government**—independent government in any of the American colonies

Rutledge, John—**Supreme Court (U.S.)**—Associate Justice of the Supreme Court to become Chief Justice

Rutledge, John—**Supreme Court (U.S.)**—Chief Justice whose nomination was not confirmed

Rutledge, John—**Supreme Court (U.S.)**—Supreme Court of the United States

Rutledge, William J.—**War Veterans' Society**—Grand Army of the Republic

Ryan, Frank B.—**Voting Machine**—vote recorded by electronic means in the U.S. House of Representatives (designer)

Ryan, Harriet—**Hospital**—tuberculosis home for the care of consumptives

Ryan, Harry—**Football Game**—professional football game

Ryan, Paddy—**Prizefighter**—bareknuckle world heavyweight champion (American)

Rynder, Isaiah—**Horse Race**—trotting futurity

Ryskind, Morrie—**Play (drama)**—musical play to win a Pulitzer Prize

Ryun, Jim—**Runner**—runner (professional) to run a mile in less than 4 minutes

S

Sabin, Florence Rena—**College**—woman professor at a first class medical school

Sabin, Florence Rena—**Science Association**—woman elected to the National Academy of Sciences

Sadove, Max Samuel—**Anesthesia**—trifluoroethyl vinyl ether

Saffren, Sheldon—**Army Officer**—army medical specialist corps male officer

Sager, Lester W.—**Play (drama)**—full-length play by a black performed in New York City (producer)

Sager, Sarah Jean—**Rabbi**—husband-and-wife rabbinical and cantorial team engaged by a synagogue

St. Clair, Arthur—**Congress (U.S.)**—congressional investigation

St. Clair, Arthur—**Territorial Expansion**—acquisition of land by the federal government

Saint-Gaudens, Augustus—**Arts and Letters Society**—arts and letters society (national)

Saint-Gaudens, Augustus—**Medal**—National Institute of Arts and Letters gold medal

St. Goddard, Emile—**Dogsled Race**—dogsled race on an Olympic demonstration program

St. John, William Pope—**Silverites**

St. Leger, Francis—**Television—Telecast**—o[ ] telecast

Salmon, Daniel Elmer—**Animal Industry Bu[r]** **(U.S.)**—Bureau of Animal Industry

Salo, John—**Track Meet**—transcontinental ra[ ]

Salo, John—**Runner**—transcontinental foot ra[ ]

Salter, Susanna Medora—**Mayor**—woman ma[ ]

Saltonstall, Dudley—**Navy**—naval fleet

Saltonstall, Henry—**Degrees (academic and** **orary)**—Bachelor of Arts degree

Salvador, Francis—**Jews**—Jew killed in American Revolution

Samma, Senaa—**Sword Swallower**

Sampson, Edith Spurlock—**Diplomatic Servi[c]**—black delegate to the United Nations from United States

Sampson, Edith Spurlock—**Judge**—black wo[ ] judge elected

Samson, Job—**Tunnel**—tunnel

Samuelson, Frank—**Rowing**—transatlantic by row boat

Sandeman, John Glas—**Scale**—coin-opera[ ] scale

Sanders, Homer—**Bowling Tournament**—[ ] medal award to a perfect-score bowler

Sanders, Jared Young—**Price Regulation Leg[ ]** **tion**—price regulation law (state)

Sanders, Millard F.—**Horse**—horse to trot a [ ] in less than two minutes

Sanders, Nathaniel—**Road**—state road author[ ] tion

Sanderson, Ivan T.—**Television—Telecast**—c[ ] program (commercial) to be presented dail[ ]

Sanderson, Lawson H.—**Medal**—Distinguis[ ] Flying Cross

Sandford, Nathan—**Trademark Lawsuit**—tr[ ] mark controversy involving a newspaper

Sands, Charles E.—**Golf Tournament**—ama[ ] golf tournament (official)

Sands, Dave—**Television—Telecast**—prize [ ] (middleweight) televised coast-to-coast

Sandys, George—**Book**—profane poetry tran[ ] tion prepared in the colonies to be publish[ ]

Sanford, Elias Benjamin—**Federal Council of** **Churches of Christ in America**

Sanford, Harold—**Television—Telecast**—ope[ ] ta to be televised

Sanger, Margaret—**Medical Clinic**—birth cor[ ] clinic

Santschi, Tom—**Motion Picture**—serial mo[ ] picture with installments longer than one [ ]

Sarasohn, Kasriel Hersch—**Newspaper**—Yid[ ] daily newspaper

Sarazen, Gene—**Golf Champion**—golf cham[ ] to win the United States Open and the Pro[ ] sional

Sargeant, John—**Conference**—conference [ ] American republics

Sargent, Edith—**Public School**—public sc[ ] classes for epileptic children

Sargent, Franklin Haven—**Theatrical Scho[ ]** theatrical school

Sargent, Francis Williams—**Insurance**—no-f[ ] automobile insurance law (state)

Shecut, W. H.—**Adhesive and Medicated Plaster**—adhesive and medicated plaster patent

Sheehan, Joseph Eastman—**Medical Instruction**—plastic surgery professor

Sheen, Fulton John—**Television—Telecast**—religious services to be televised

Sheffield, George St. John—**Billiard Match**—intercollegiate billiard match

Sheldon, Charles Monroe—**Book**—best seller (nonfiction) other than a text or purely theological work

Sheldon, Edward Austin—**Normal School**—normal school (state) at which students actually conducted classes

Sheldon, Harold Horton—**Colorscope**

Sheldon, John P.—**Typewriter**—typewriter

Sheldon, W. E.—**Teachers' Convention**—teachers' convention (national)

Shepard, Alan Bartlett, Jr.—**Astronaut**—astronaut (American) to be launched into space

Shepard, Alan Bartlett, Jr.—**Astronaut**—astronaut (American) to become an admiral

Shepard, Alan Bartlett, Jr.—**Astronaut**—astronauts

Shepard, Alan Bartlett, Jr.—**Astronaut**—space flight by an American astronaut

Shepard, Alan Bartlett, Jr.—**Medal**—National Aeronautics and Space Administration distinguished service medal

Shepard, Charles H.—**Bathhouse**—Turkish bath

Shepard, Mr.—**Congregational Church**—Congregational Church council

Shepard, Mrs. Finley Johnson—**Hall of Fame**—hall of fame (university)

Shepherd, Lemuel Cornick—**Medal**—Navy-Marine Corps Medal for Heroism awarded to a woman

Sheppard, Jeanie Ramsey—**Woman**—woman state liquor board member

Sheppard, William—**Soap**—soap in liquid form

Sherburne, Samuel—**Attorney of the United States**—Attorney of the United States

Sheridan, Bernard—**Embossing Press**

Sheridan, George Augustus—**Representative (U.S.)**—representative to serve 1 day

Sherman, Frederick Carl—**World War II**—aircraft carrier (American) sunk in World War II

Sherman, James Schoolcraft—**Vice Presidential Candidate**—vice presidential nominee to die before the meeting of the electoral college

Sherman, John—**Territorial Expansion**—island territory

Sherman, John Ames—**Envelope**—envelope folding and gumming machine

Sherwin, Samuel B.—**Autogiro**—autogiro rotary-wing aircraft fellowship

Shibe, Benjamin F.—**Baseball**—cork-center baseball

Shield, Lansing Peter—**Business**—Food-O-Mat

Shields, James—**Senator (U.S.)**—senator to serve three states

Shields, Marvin Glen—**Medal**—Medal of Honor awarded to a Seabee

Shields, Marvin Glen—**Ship**—ship named Seabee

Shilders, J.—**Labadist Community**

Shipley, Ruth Bielaski—**Woman**—woman port division chief

Shippee, Amasa—**Flag**—American flag ov schoolhouse

Shippee, Lois—**Flag**—American flag ov schoolhouse

Shippee, Rhoda—**Flag**—American flag ov schoolhouse

Shippen, John M.—**Golf Tournament**—am golf tournament of the United States Golf ciation in which a black contestant was en

Shippen, William—**Medical Instruction**—a my lectures (scientific)

Shippen, William—**Medical School**—medica lege

Shireman, Eugene Curtis—**Fish Hatch** goldfish hatchery

Shive, John Northrup—**Transistor**—phototra tor

Shockley, William—**Transistor**—junction tra tor

Shoemaker, Sherman—**World War II**—Japa balloon casualties

Shoemaker, Thomas Buckman—**Citizens** citizenship granted to an alien on foreign

Shoemaker, Willie—**Jockey**—jockey to rid winners in one year

Shoemaker, Willie—**Jockey**—jockey to win hundred $100,000 stakes

Shoemaker, Willie—**Jockey**—jockey to wi national riding championship four times

Sholes, Christopher Latham—**Typewriter**—writer that was practical

Shook, Frederic W.—**Aviation—Flights (t pacific)**—jet transpacific nonstop flight

Short, Shirley—**Airmail Service**—airmail distance night service

Shotwell, Luman W.—**American Indians**—A can Indian tribal constitution

Shotwell, William—**Haircloth**

Shoukletovich, Doushan Jefta—**Serbian Orth Cathedral**

Shreeve, Herbert E.—**Radio Telephone**—tra lantic radio telephone message

Shreve, Henry Miller—**Ship**—steamboat (do decked)

Shriver, Robert Sargent, Jr.—**Economic Opp nity Office (U.S.)**—Office of Economic Opp nity

Shryrock, George Augustus—**Paper**—straw p

Shu, Loo Kum—**Telephone**—telephone sw board or exchange for Chinese-American scribers

Shuckburgh, Richard—**"Yankee Doodle"**

Shuler, Marjorie—**Aviation—Passenger**—wo to fly entirely around the world by comme heavier-than-air plane

Shulze, John Andrew—**Tax**—inheritance (state)

Shunk, Francis Rawn—**Child Labor Law**—labor law restricting the age of the worke

er, George—**Automobile Race**—automobile
e New York–Paris

, Nevil—**Motion Picture**—motion picture
sented simultaneously in major cities
oughout the world

t, William Luther—**World War I**—American
ops to land in France

ll, Joseph S.—**Insurance**—title guaranty in-
ance company

y, Sylvia—**Theater**—municipally owned
operated summer theater-in-the-round

rt, Muriel ("Mickie")—**Brokerage**—New
k Stock Exchange woman seat owner

rt, Frances—**Telephone**—telephone switch-
ard with Braille markings

Hong Yong—**Diplomatic Service**—Korean
bassy

land, Torbjørn—**Element**—element 103

sky, Igor Ivan—**Helicopter**—helicopter (di-
t-lift aircraft)

sky, Igor Ivan—**Helicopter**—**Flights**—heli-
ter flight (cross-country)

sky, Igor Ivan—**Helicopter**—**Flights**—heli-
ter flight from water

sky, Igor Ivan—**Helicopter**—**Flights**—heli-
ter flight of one-hour duration

an, Benjamin—**Chemistry Professor**—
fessorship of applied chemistry

an, Benjamin—**Science Periodical**—science
gazine

, George—**Motion Picture**—motion picture
a real pugilistic encounter taken at night

ons, Aloysius Harry ("Al")—**Baseball Game**
aseball game in which there were two triple-
als

ons, Amelia—**Cookbook**—cookbook of
erican authorship

ons, John—**College**—technical college for
men

s, Ruth Hanna McCormick—**Woman**—
man presidential campaign comanager

, Carleton—**Eye**—identification system

, Irving B.—**Periodical**—Spanish magazine
lished by students

, Rene—**Aviation**—airplane rescue at sea
cted by another airplane

, William—**Pharmacy College**—pharmacy
ege to make analytical chemistry a required
rse

ds, Frank Herbert—**Newspaper**—editorial
ard of a Pulitzer Prize in journalism and let-

s, Charles Caspar—**Judge**—woman associ-
justice of the Circuit Court of Appeals

s, David Goodman—**Balloon**—**Flights**—
loon flight to exceed an altitude of 100,000
t

son, Albert Benjamin—**Bible School**

son, Edward—**Naval Academy**—naval
demy graduate to attain the rank of rear
miral

son, Garry—**Television**—**Telecast**—opera
tten for television on commission for a com-
rcial sponsor

Simpson, George B.—**Electric Stove**—electric
range

Simpson, Joanne—**Weather Bureau (U.S.)**—
Weather Bureau woman employee

Simpson, Michael Hodge—**Bunting**

Simpson, Michael Hodge—**Library**—library
newspaper room

Simpson, Wallis Warfield—**Wedding**—American
woman married to a former King of Great Britain

Simpson, William—**Root Beer**

Sims, James Marion—**Hospital**—women's hospital

Sims, James Marion—**Impregnation**—impregnation (human) by means of artificial insemination

Sims, James Marion—**Suture**—silver wire suture

Sims, Julia Isabelle—**Jury**—woman grand jury
foreman

Sims, William Sowden—**Ship**—battleship to use
fuel oil exclusively

Simson, Sampson—**Hospital**—Jewish hospital

Sinclair, Richard L.—**Garage**—completely automatic push-button-controlled garage

Singer, Abraham ("Al")—**Prizefighter**—pugilist to
win and lose a championship in the first round

Singer, Isaac Merritt—**Sewing Machine**—sewing
machine equipped with a rocking treadle or
double treadle

Singer, Isaac Merritt—**Sewing Machine**—sewing
machine manufacturer

Singer, Isaac Merritt—**Sewing Machine**—sewing
machine motor—patent

Sinnett, Walter—**Television**—**Telecast**—X-ray
fluoroscopy television discussion

Sinnock, John Ray—**Medal**—woman to have her
likeness on a medal issued by the United States
Mint

Skeldon, Joseph—**Ship**—schooner (five-masted)

Sirhan, Sirhan Bishara—**Presidential Candidate**—
presidential candidate assassinated while campaigning

Sissle, Noble—**Motion Picture**—sound motion
picture featuring a black

Skelton, Byron—**Court**—court in which the judge
presided in a city other than the one in which
the lawyers appeared

Skene (Skeen) John—**Freemasons**—Mason

Skinner, Frederick Henry—**Museum**—maritime
museum

Skinner, Halcyon—**Carpet Loom**—carpet power
loom to weave Axminster carpets

Skinner, John Stuart—**Agricultural Journal**—
agricultural journal to attain prominence

Skinner, John Stuart—**Sports Magazine**

Skinner, Richard Cort—**Dental Book**—book on
dentistry

Skipwith, Fulwar—**Diplomatic Service**—consuls
of the United States appointed after the adoption of the Constitution

Skipworth, Alison—**Television**—**Telecast**—current Broadway play to be telecast with its original cast

Skoog, Joseph L., Jr.—**Submarine**—submarines to rendezvous at the North Pole

Slack, Leslie—**Ship**—ship to fire a Polaris missile

Slade, Daniel Denison—**Veterinary School**—veterinary college

Slade, Frederick J.—**Steel**—open-hearth furnace

Slate, Thomas Benton—**Ice**—dry ice

Slater, Bill—**Television—Telecast**—baseball World Series game televised

Slater, Ellis—**President (U.S.)**—presidential airplane (turbo-compound-powered)

Slater, Samuel—**Cotton Mill**—cotton mill to spin cotton yarn successfully

Slaughter, Alanson—**Creamery**

Slaughter, Louis N.—**Single Tax**—single tax political ticket

Slayter, Games—**Glass Wool**

Slayton, Donald Kent ("Duke")—**Astronaut**—astronauts

Slayton, Donald Kent ("Duke")—**Astronaut**—astronauts (American) to participate in an international spaceflight

Slifer, Eli—**Civil War**—regiment to respond to President Abraham Lincoln's proclamation

Sloane, Paul—**Motion Picture**—black-oriented talking picture (all-talking, all-singing) by a major company

Sloat, Jacob—**Cotton Twine Factory**

Slocum, Joshua—**Ship**—ship to circumnavigate the world with but one in the crew

Slocum, Samuel—**Pin**—machine for sticking pins into paper

Slocum, Samuel—**Pin**—pins manufactured with a solid head

Slootsky, Al—**Wheelchair Athletics**—national wheelchair games

Slowe, Lucy—**Sorority**—black sorority

Small, Albion Woodbury—**Sociology Professor**

Small, Elisha—**Naval Officer**—naval officer condemned for mutiny

Smalley, Daniel S.—**Dictionary**—phonetic dictionary

Smalls, Robert—**Ship**—Confederate ship surrendered

Smith, Alex—**Golf Tournament**—professional open championship

Smith, Alfred Emanuel—**Arbitration**—state arbitration law (modern)

Smith, Alfred Emanuel—**Building**—building higher than 1,250 feet

Smith, Alfred Emanuel—**Television—Telecast**—presidential nomination notification ceremony to be televised

Smith, Arthur—**Automobile Fatality**

Smith, Arthur Roy—**Aviation**—aeronautical elopement

Smith, C. James—**Automobile Race**—transcontinental automobile race

Smith, Campbell—**Army Officer**—judge advocate of the U.S. Army

Smith, Charles—**Atheism Society**

Smith, Charles—**Papermaking Machinery**—papermaking machine (Fourdrinier)

Smith, Charles Louis—**Police**—police c (woman) on the aerial force

Smith, Charles Shaler—**Bridge**—cantilever b

Smith, Charles Shaler—**Bridge**—hanging rai bridge

Smith, Charles Sprague—**Motion Picture Ce ship**—motion picture censorship board tional)

Smith, Charlotte—**Book**—book printed on A can paper with American-made plates bound in America

Smith, Chester Carl—**Submarine**—submarii sink a Japanese ship

Smith, Dalton F.—**Space Cabin**

Smith, Daniel B.—**Library**—mechanics' libra

Smith, Daniel B.—**Pharmacy Magazine**

Smith, Daniel B.—**Pharmacy Society (natio**

Smith, Dean C.—**Airmail Service**—airmail distance night service

Smith, Donald Ellsworth—**Recreational Ran Course**

Smith, Edward—**Bank Robbery**—bank robb

Smith, Edward H.—**Radio Broadcast**—d (full-length melodrama) broadcast

Smith, Edwin Seymour—**Labor Relations**—I Relations Act (national)

Smith, Elias—**Religious Publication**—religio view

Smith, Elihu Hubbard—**Anthology** (Americ

Smith, Elihu Hubbard—**Medical Periodi** medical magazine

Smith, Elmer John—**Baseball Game**—Worl ries grand slam home run (American Lea

Smith, Francis Henney—**Military School**— military school

Smith, G. Albert—**Motion Picture**—colored tion pictures

Smith, G. L.—**Horse Race**—stakes race triple heat

Smith, George—**Billiard Match**—billiard ma

Smith, George Franklin—**Aviation**—Parach pilot to bail out of an airplane flying at s sonic speed

Smith, Gerrit—**Organists' Society**—organist ciety (national)

Smith, Hamilton Erastus—**Washing Machine** tary-motion washing machine

Smith, Hamilton Lamphere—**Camera**—ti camera

Smith, Harry—**Bowler**—bowler to win $10,0 a tournament

Smith, Helen L.—**Eye**—eye conservation cl

Smith, Henry Louis—**X ray**—X-ray photogr

Smith, Henry Tomlinson—**Dental School**—d assistants' and nurses' course

Smith, Hugh—**Maternity Book**

Smith, Hyrum—**Mormon Temple**

Smith, Isabel—**Youth Hostel**

Smith, J. Worthington—**College**—Masonic cc

Smith, James—**Vaccine Institution**

Smith, James F.—**Bridge**—timber trestle pi lattice construction

Smith, James Webster—**Army School**— school graduate (black)

Snowden, Thomas—**Trademark Lawsuit**—trademark controversy involving a newspaper

Sobel, Helen Martin—**Whist Tournament**—international whist tournament

Sobrero, Aquiles Jose—**Medical Clinic**—vasectomy outpatient service

Sola, Abraham de—**Congress (U.S.)—House of Representatives**—foreign clergyman to open the House of Representatives with prayer

Solberg, Thorvald—**Copyrights Register**—Copyrights registrar of the United States

Soley, John Codman—**Navy**—naval militia (state)

Solis-Cohen, Jacob—**Medical Periodical**—laryngology magazine

Solomon, Hannah Greenebaum—**Women's Club**—Jewish women's organization (national)

Sonnenberg, Albert—**Whaling**—whale-killing machine (electric)

Sordelet, James Robert—**Navy**—naval man to reenlist while under the North Pole

Sothell, Seth—**Indigo**

Soto, Hernando de—**Discovery**—discovery of the Mississippi River by a European

Souder, Frank A.—**Pier**—ocean pier of steel

Soulé, Pierre—**Senator (U.S.)**—senator who served a term of less than 6 weeks

Sousa, John Philip—**Sousaphone**

Southworth, Effie A.—**Fellowship**—resident fellowship for women awarded by a women's college

Southworth, Albert Sands—**Photograph**—photograph of a former President of the United States at his home

Southworth, Evelyn—**Congress (U.S.)—Senate**—Senate session in which women, other than members of Congress, were permitted on the floor

Sower, Christoph. *See* Sauer, Christoph

Spaatz, Carl Andrew—**Air Force Academy (U.S.)**—Air Force Academy

Spaatz, Carl Andrew—**World War II**—land victory without infantry

Spafford, George—**Papermaking Machinery**—papermaking machine (Fourdrinier)

Spafford, George—**Papermaking Machinery**—papermaking machine (Fourdrinier) imported

Spalding, Albert Goodwill—**Baseball Chest Protector**—chest protector for catchers

Spalding, Albert Goodwill—**Baseball Game**—shutout game

Spalding, Eliza Hart—**Colonist**—women to cross the continent

Spalding, Lyman—**Pharmacopoeia**—pharmacopoeia (general)

Spangenberg, August Gottlieb—**Moravian Church**

Sparkes, Leonora—**Opera**—opera by an American composer performed at the Metropolitan Opera House of New York

Sparks, Frank—**Railroad Train Robbery**—railroad train robbery of a train in motion

Sparks, Jared—**History Instruction**—ancient and modern history chair

Speakman, Townsend—**Soda Water**—soda water

Spears, C. B.—**Trapshooting**—trapshooting collegiate association

Spencer, Dolly—**Police**—woman chief of po

Spencer, Philip—**Naval Officer**—naval office demned for mutiny

Spencer, Sara Andrews—**Political Conven**t presidential convention (national) addr by a woman

Sperry, Charles Stillman—**Ship**—warship fl circumnavigate the globe

Sperry, Elmer Ambrose—**Gyroscope**—gyros stabilizer

Sperry, Elmer Ambrose—**Railroad Car**—ra tector car

Sperry, Lawrence B.—**Aviation**—gyroscope matic stabilization

Sperry, Lawrence Burst—**Aviation—Airpl**l airplane to land at the U.S. Capitol

Sperry, Thomas Alexander—**Trading Stam**p

Spicer, George—**Horse**—horse to trot 100 mi less than 9 hours

Spicer, George—**Horse Race**—night harness

Spiedel, Robert C.—**Heliport**—military heli

Spiegler, Caesar—**Aviation—Airship**—dirig

Spinks, Leon—**Prizefight**—prizefight to more than $5 million in sales

Spinola, Francis Barretto—**Representative**—Italo-American representative

Spofford, F. A.—**Bicycle Patent**—water v pede patent

Spooner, Eliakim—**Seeding Machine Paten**t

Spotswood, Alexander—**Theater**—theater

Sprague, J. Russel—**Woman**—woman pres tial campaign comanager

Sprague, William Peter—**Carpet Factory**—c mill

Springs, Lena Jonas (Mrs. Leroy Springs)—**Presidential Candidate**—vice presidentia didate (woman) to have her name plac nomination at a major party convention

Springs, Tom—**Prizefight**—prizefight arena

Spurrier, John—**Alfalfa**

Spurzheim, Johann Gaspar—**Phrenologist**

Spurzheim, Johann Gaspar—**Phrenology Bo**

Squires, Tilloah—**Librarians' Union**

Stack, Robert—**Motion Picture**—three-d sional feature motion picture

Stackpole, William—**Billiard Match**—in legiate billiard match

Stafford, Thomas Patten—**Astronaut**—astro (American) to participate in an interna spaceflight

Stafford, Thomas Patten—**Astronaut**—astro (American) to rendezvous in space (G VI)

Stafford, Ward—**Church**—Mariners' church

Stagg, Amos Alonzo—**College "Lettermen's**

Stagg, Amos Alonzo—**Football Dummy**

Stagg, Amos Alonzo—**Physical Culture D**e ment

Stagg, Charles—**Theater**—theater

Stagg, Mary—**Theater**—theater

Stevens, John—**Locomotive**—locomotive to pull a train

Stevens, John—**Railroad Charter**

Stevens, John—**Railroad Treatise**

Stevens, John—**Ship**—steamboat to make an ocean voyage

Stevens, John—**Ship**—steamboat with a twin-screw propeller

Stevens, John Cox—**Yacht Club**

Stevens, John Cox—**Yacht Race**—yacht race (international)

Stevens, Leo—**Aviation**—**Airship**—woman airship passenger

Stevens, P. F.—**Civil War**—act that marked the inauguration of the War of 1861–65

Stevens, Rise—**Television**—**Telecast**—pay television presentation of an opera

Stevens, Robert—**Ordnance**—atomic cannon

Stevens, Robert Livingston—**Ferryboat**—steam-propelled ferryboat

Stevens, Robert Livingston—**Railroad Track**—railroad rails of T shape

Stevens, Robert Livingston—**Ship**—steamboat to make an ocean voyage

Stevens, Thomas—**Bicycle Rider**—bicycle rider to go around the world

Stevens, Uriah Smith—**Labor Union**—labor organization to admit workmen other than craft workmen

Stevenson, Sarah Hackett—**Medical Society**—woman physician elected a member of the American Medical Association

Steward, Roger—**Ship**—commercial ship to conquer the Northwest Passage

Stewart, Ada—**Nurse**—nurse employed by an industrial organization

Stewart, Alexander Turney—**Business**—department store to occupy a city block

Stewart, Alexander Turney—**Hotel**—hotel for women

Stewart, David—**Pharmacy Professor**—pharmacy professorship

Stewart, Joan Wyatt—**Prison**—woman prison guard in a maximum security prison for men

Stewart, Mortimer—**Television**—**Telecast**—play to be televised

Stewart, Neal—**Parachutist**—parachutist to make 124 jumps in one day

Stewart, Philip Battell—**Baseball Batting and Fielding Cage**

Stewart, Pinckney Benton—**Representative (U.S.)**—representative to serve 1 day (contested election)

Stewart, Walter—**Army**—brevet conferred upon an American

Stewart, William Holmes—**X Ray**—X-ray moving pictures (successful) of the action of the human heart

Stiles, Charles Wardell—**Zoological Laboratory (U.S.)**—zoological laboratory (U.S.) for the study of the parasites of livestock

Stiles, Charles Wardell—**Zoological Laboratory (U.S.)**—zoological laboratory (U.S.) for the study of parasites of man

Still, Andrew Taylor—**Medical School**—oste thy school

Still, Andrew Taylor—**Physician**—osteopa physician

Stillman, Alfred—**Squash Club**—squash te organization (national)

Stillman, Alfred—**Squash Tournament**—sq tennis tournament

Stillman, George F.—**Automobile Tire**—pneu ic tire patent

Stillson, Daniel C.—**Wrench**—pipe or s(wrench (practical)

Stimson, Henry Lewis—**Army Auxiliary Cor** Women's Army Auxiliary Corps (WAAC)

Stimson, Henry Lewis—**Conscription**—peace conscription bill

Stimson, Henry Lewis—**Medal**—Distingui! Service Medal (Army) awarded to a wom

Stimson, Henry Lewis—**President (U.S.)**—p dential airplane

Stimson, Julia Catherine—**Army Officer**—wo with rank corresponding to major

Stinis, Andy—**Skywriting**—skywriting at ni<

Stinson, Emma Beavers—**Aviation**—**School**– plane flying school operated by a woman

Stockdale, James Bond—**War Prisoner**—pris of war to head the Naval War College

Stockton, Robert Field—**Ship**—warship with pelling machinery below the waterline

Stockton, Samuel Witham—**Agricultural So** —agricultural society

Stoddard, Joshua C.—**Calliope**

Stoddard, Lawrence B.—**Golf Tournament**—teur golf tournament (unofficial)

Stoddard, Sampson Vryling—**Tract Socie** tract society (national)

Stoddert, Benjamin—**Navy**—Secretary of Navy

Stokes, Carl Burton—**Mayor**—black mayor major city

Stokowski, Leopold—**Symphony**—symphon a black folk theme

Stone, A. P.—**Republican Party**—Repub Party meeting (national)

Stone, Charles Pomeroy—**Hospital**—military pital on the modern pavilion plan

Stone, Edward Mandell—**World War I**—A can combatant to die in World War I

Stone, Ellen R.—**Tuberculosis School**—ou school for tubercular children

Stone, Elmer Fowler—**Aviation**—**Flights (tra lantic)**—transatlantic hydroplane flight

Stone, John—**Pile Driver**—pile driver

Stone, John—**Radio Society**

Stone, John Osgood—**Health Board**—h board (municipal) armed with sufficient po

Stone, Marvin Chester—**Straws** (artificial drinking

Stone, Mary (Shih Mai-yu)—**Physician**—Ch woman to receive a Doctor of Medicine d

Stone, Roy—**Road**—federal road agency

Stone, Samuel M.—**Television**—**Telecast**—l light-beam program telecast on a network

Sullivan, Madison Abel—**Ship**—naval vessel with a plural name

Sullivan, Mark—**Telephone**—dial-telephone long distance service

Sullivan, Philip—**Capital Punishment**—capital punishment authorized by federal law

Sullivan, Robert Oliver Daniel—**Aviation—Flights (transatlantic)**—transatlantic regular commercial airplane service

Sullivan, Robert Oliver Daniel—**Aviation—Pilot**—pilot to fly 100 times across the Atlantic Ocean

Sully, Thomas—**Archery Club**—archery club

Sulzberger, David—**Normal School**—teachers' training school (Jewish)

Summerfield, Arthur Ellsworth—**Airmail Service**—missile mail (official)

Summerford, Gene—**Telephone**—telephone conversation (commercial) using electricity generated by the sun's rays

Summers, Rachael—**Woman**—women to become federal government employees

Summitt, Charles D.—**Submarine**—submarines to rendezvous at the North Pole

Sumner, Miss—**Oratorio**—oratorio performance (complete)

Sumner, G. W.—**Ship**—triple-screw cruiser

Sundback, Gideon—**Fastening**—hookless fastening for universal use

Suneson, Charlene Ida—**Naval Officer**—naval line officer (woman) assigned to sea duty (MSTS)

Surratt, Mary E.—**Woman**—woman hanged by the United States Government

Surratt, Mary E.—**Woman**—woman hanged by the United States Government

Sutherland, J. B.—**Railroad Car**—refrigerator car patent

Sutter, John Augustus—**Gold**—gold discovered in California

Sutter, John Augustus—**Russian Settlement**

Suzuki, Shunryu—**Monastery**—Zen Buddhist monastery

Swaine, Charles—**Expedition**—arctic expedition to seek the Northwest Passage, for the £20,000 reward

Swaine, John—**Lawbook**—lawbook containing the federal laws of the United States of more than one session of Congress

Swallow, Silas Comfort—**United Christian Party**

Swan, Abraham—**Architecture Book**—architecture book printed in America

Swan, Caleb—**Army Officer**—paymaster

Swan, William G.—**Glider**—**Flights**—rocket glider flight

Swarthout, Cornelius—**Waffle Iron Patent**

Swarts, Gardner Taber—**Health Laboratory**—health laboratory (municipal)

Swarts, Gardner Taber—**Health Laboratory**—health laboratory (state)

Swayze, John Cameron—**Television**—**Telecast**—split-screen image

Sweeney, Michael Francis—**Automobile**—armored commercial car completely protected

Sweet, John Edson—**Caliper** (screw)

Swift, Gustavus Franklin—**Railroad**—rail shipments of dressed beef (year-round long tance)

Swift, John Barnard—**Medical Society**—me society (state)

Swift, Joseph Gardner—**Army School**—school graduates

Swift, William Henry—**Lighthouse**—iron lighthouse

Swinburn, John—**Boat Club**—boat club

Swinnerton, James—**Book**—comic books

Swinton, George R.—**Old Age Colony**

Swope, Herbert Bayard—**Newspaper Repor** newspaper reporter to receive a Pulitzer l

Swords, J.—**Railroad Treatise**

Swords, T.—**Railroad Treatise**

Syer, Robert D'Oyly—**Bank**—major bank to l personal property

Sykes, Eugene Octave—**Federal Communica Commission**

Sykes, Eugene Octave—**Radio Commission (**

Syle, Henry Winter—**Deaf**—**Church Service** dained deaf clergyman

Sylvester, Joseph—**Jockey**—jockey to win s races in one day

Symington, William Stuart—**Air Force**—Air l Secretary

Symington, William Stuart—**Defense Depart** (U.S.)

Symmes (Syms), Benjamin—**Educational En ment**

Symmes, John Cleves—**Land Preemption (federal)**

Sze, Wilbur Carl—**Marine Corps**—marine o of Chinese descent

Szilard, Leo—**Atomic Reactor**—atomic re patent

T

Taft, Mrs. Josiah—**Woman**—woman whose was recorded

Taft, William Howard—**Attorney General**— assistant attorney general (U.S.) appointe

Taft, William Howard—**Bank**—postal sa bank

Taft, William Howard—**Cable**—cable acros Pacific Ocean between Honolulu, Mic Guam, and Manila

Taft, William Howard—**Chamber of Com** —Chamber of Commerce of the United S of America

Taft, William Howard—**Naval Officer**—ad who was Jewish

Taft, William Howard—**President (U.S.)**—. dent buried in the National Cemetery at A ton, Va.

Taft, William Howard—**President (U.S.)**— dent to become Chief Justice of the U States

Tepuni, William—**World War II**—German submarine destroyed by an American pilot

Terrillion, Beverly—**Railroad**—railroad train operated exclusively by women

Terry, Eli—**Clock**—clock patent

Terry, Silas Burnham—**Spring Manufacturer**

Teschemacher, H. F.—**Telegraph**—telegraph line to the Pacific Coast

Teselle, Sallie McFague—**Theological School**—theological school (major) woman dean

Tessier, John Mary—**Catholic Seminary**—Catholic seminary

Testa, Tuesee—**Horse Race**—horse race parimutuel with an entire field of women jockeys

Thach, John Smith—**Navy**—task force to fight undersea craft

Thacher, James—**Medical Book**—hydrophobia book

Thacher, Thomas—**Medical Book**—medical pamphlet

Thaden, Louise McPhetridge—**Aviation—Races**—women's cross-country air derby

Thatcher, Linden A.—**Postal Service**—coin-operated mailbox

Thayer, Abbott Henderson—**Camouflage**

Thayer, Frederick Winthrop—**Baseball Catcher's Mask**

Thayer, Nathaniel—**Tennis**—court tennis

Thelander, Hulda—**Naval officer**—woman physician in the Medical Corps Reserve of the U.S. Navy

Thiess, Ruth Hammond—**Opera**—opera broadcast in its entirety

Thiry, John Henry—**Bank**—savings group

Thistlewaite, John Richmond—**Newspaper**—offset-printed daily newspaper

Thomas, Mr.—**Library**—book wagon

Thomas, Allan M.—**Incubator for Infants**

Thomas, B. F.—**Dam**—needle-type dam

Thomas, Danny—**Hospital**—children's hospital solely for research and treatment of catastrophic childhood diseases

Thomas, Evylyn—**Automobile Accident**

Thomas, Frank—**Baseball Team**—baseball team to hit 4 consecutive runs in 1 inning

Thomas, Howell Garrone—**War (Korean)**—Korean War hero buried in Arlington Cemetery

Thomas, Isaiah—**Bible**—Bible in folio size to be illustrated

Thomas, Isaiah (Isaias)—**Bible**—Greek testament

Thomas, Isaiah—**Book**—book printed on American paper with American-made plates and bound in America

Thomas, Isaiah—**Dictionary**—agricultural dictionary

Thomas, Isaiah—**Dictionary**—dictionary published in the United States

Thomas, Isaiah—**Dictionary**—pocket dictionary

Thomas, Isaiah—**Gazetteer**—American gazetteer

Thomas, Isaiah—**Historical Society**—historical society (national)

Thomas, Isaiah—**Music**—music printed in a magazine

Thomas, Isaiah—**Printing History**

Thomas, James Joshua—**Protestant Church**—formed Dutch Church black pastor

Thomas, John H.—**Glass Wool**

Thomas, Lowell—**Television—Telecast**—si̇ cast presented regularly by a sponsor

Thomas, Martha Carey—**College**—"Dean of faculty"

Thomas, Philip E.—**Railroad**—railroad for c mercial transportation of passengers freight

Thomas, Robert Bailey—**Almanac**—alma with a continuous existence

Thomas, Theodore—**Symphony**—symph work by an American composer

Thompson, Bradbury—**Postage Stamp**—Ch mas-stamp annual series depicting both a gious and nonreligious subject

Thompson, Frank Adoniram—**Chiropody Sc**—chiropody school as a regular division university

Thompson, Frank P.—**Baseball Team**—base team (black professional)

Thompson, George F.—**Radio Broadcast**—r̅ program (daily)

Thompson, George Irwin—**Naval War Colle** black officers to attend the Naval War Co͏

Thompson, George Kramer—**Building**—cais foundation building

Thompson, George W.—**Benevolent and Pr҉ tive Order of Elks**

Thompson, Henry—**Streetcar**—gas-pow streetcars

Thompson, John—**Railroad**—railroad for fr̅ transportation

Thompson, John—**Stagecoach Intercity Servi̇**

Thompson, John Taliaferro—**Ordnance**—su͏ chine gun

Thompson, La Marcus Adna—**Railroad**—sw back railway

Thompson, Mary Harris—**Physician**—wo͏ surgeon

Thompson, Maurice—**Archery Club**—archer͏ sociation (national)

Thompson, Robert E.—**Aquanaut**—United S Navy divers to submerge 10 days

Thompson, Sarah. *See* Rumford, Sarah The͏ son, Countess of

Thompson, Stanley Gerald—**Element**—ele͏ 97

Thompson, Stanley Gerald—**Element**—ele͏ 98

Thompson, Stanley Gerald—**Element**—ele͏ 99

Thompson, Stanley Gerald—**Element**—ele͏ 101

Thompson, Stephen W.—**Aviation—Pilot**—́ pilot

Thompson, Thomas—**Flag**—American flag o high seas

Thompson, Thomas—**Temperance Society**—̇ perance society (union)

Thompson, W. H.—**Phonograph Record**—ph graph record of a stage performance b͏ original cast

Towner, Margaret Ellen—**Presbyterian Church**—woman ordained a minister in the Presbyterian Church

Townes, Charles Hard—**Lasers**—patent on lasers

Townsend, E. Price—**Whist Tournament**—duplicate whist tournament

Toy, James Madison ("Jim")—**Baseball Player**—baseball player who was an American Indian

Toy, John D.—**Atlas**

Toy, John D.—**Medical Book**—ophthalmology book

Tracy, Susan Edith—**Occupational Therapy Treatment**

Trainer, Merrill—**Theater**—television theater demonstration

Trall, Russell Thacher—**Water Cures**

Tranchepain, Marie—**Convent**—convent

Travell, Janet Graeme—**Physician**—woman appointed "personal physician to the President"

Treadwell, Daniel—**Printing Press**—power or steam printing press

Tree, Marietta Peabody—**Diplomatic Service**—woman to serve the United Nations as a permanent ambassador

Tresse, Thomas—**Paper Mill**

Triaca, Albert C.—**Aviation—School**—correspondence school in aviation

Trible, Phyllis—**United Church of Christ**—United Church of Christ ordination of a woman minister in which all the principal roles were filled by women

Trik, Carl A.—**Bridge**—concrete-arch highway bridge

Tripler, Charles Eastman—**Air (liquid)**

Tripler, Charles Stuart—**Hospital**—military hospital on the modern pavilion plan

Tripp, Katherine—**Police**—woman employed at a high level within a men's maximum security facility

Tristam, Augustus ("Gus")—**Railroad Train Robbery**—railroad train robbery of a train en route

Tronson du Coudray, Philippe Charles Jean Baptiste—**Catholic Funeral**—Catholic funeral attended by the U.S. Continental Congress

Troost, Gerardt—**Pharmacy College**—pharmacy college

Trout, Evelyn ("Bobby")—**Aviation—Flights**—women to fly in excess of 120 hours

Troxel, Dorothy A.—**Dictionary**—Mongolian-English, English-Mongolian dictionary

Troy, Laura—**Wedding**—airplane wedding

Troy, Willie—**Television—Telecast**—prizefight televised in color

Troyanovsky, Alexander Antonovich—**Diplomatic Service**—ambassador to the Union of Soviet Socialist Republics

Trudeau, Edward Livingston—**Health Society**

Trudeau, Edward Livingston—**Hospital**—tuberculosis sanatorium (modern)

Trudeau, Edward Livingston—**Tuberculosis Laboratory**—tuberculosis research laboratory

Trueblood, Thomas Clarkson—**Public Speaking Department**

Truman, Harry S.—**Air Force Officer**—judge vocate general of the U.S. Air Force

Truman, Harry S.—**Diplomatic Service**—wo ambassador from a foreign country

Truman, Harry S.—**Flag**—President's flag

Truman, Harry S.—**Governor**—black gove appointed by the President of the United St

Truman, Harry S.—**Holiday**—Flag Day fe legislation

Truman, Harry S.—**Labor Relations**—labor pute in which the Taft-Hartley law was inv

Truman, Harry S.—**Medal**—Medal of Freed

Truman, Harry S.—**Medal**—Medal of H awarded in the Korean War

Truman, Harry S.—**Medal**—Reserve Officers sociation medal

Truman, Harry S.—**Medicare**—medicare ide cation card

Truman, Harry S.—**Money**—coin bearing the trait of a black American

Truman, Harry S.—**Postmaster**—postmaster eral appointed from the ranks

Truman, Harry S.—**President (U.S.)**—Preside address the Senate

Truman, Harry S.—**President (U.S.)**—Preside attend the swearing-in of an Associate Ju (H.H. Burton) of the Supreme Court

Truman, Harry S.—**President (U.S.)**—Preside travel underwater in a captured enemy su rine

Truman, Harry S.—**President (U.S.)**—preside press conference recorded on tape

Truman, Harry S.—**Submarine**—atomic-pow submarine

Truman, Harry S.—**Television—Telecast**—p dential address televised from the White H

Truman, Harry S.—**Television—Telecast**—t continental telecast received on the East C

Truman, Mary Margaret—**Television—Tel** —ship launching telecast

Trumbull, Earl—**Bridge**—cast-iron girder bri

Truscott, Lucian—**Medal**—Distinguished Se Cross awarded to an animal

Truxton, Thomas—**Ship**—ship to capture enemy ship after the Revolution

Tschudi, Hans-Peter—**Telephone**—telep conversation (commercial) over a satellit

Tubman, Harriet—**Postage Stamp**—pos stamp to honor a black woman

Tucker, John—**Supreme Court (U.S.)**—clerk o Supreme Court

Tucker, John—**Supreme Court (U.S.)**—Sup Court of the United States

Tucker, Richard—**Television—Telecast**—television presentation of an opera

Tucker, Stephen D.—**Printing Press**—rotary p ing press

Tucker, Tommy—**Radio Broadcast**—cooper radio show

Tucker, William—**Baptism**—black child bap in the English colonies

Tucker, William Ellis—**Porcelain (hard)**

Tudor, Frederick—**Ice**—export of ice

Tudor, William—**Army Officer**—judge advo

U

V

Vail, Edwin—**Television**—**Telecast**—musical comedy telecast (one-hour)

Vaili, Mario—**Motion Picture**—motion picture of a complete grand opera

Vallentine, Edward—**Silk**—silk dyers

Vanaman, Arthur William—**World War II**— American general captured by the Germans

Van Bokkelen, Libertius—**Military School**— church military school

Van Boven, Paul—**Helicopter**—helicopter rescue of an American pilot behind enemy lines

Van Buren, Adelina—**Motorcycle Trip**—motorcycle transcontinental trip by women

Van Buren, Augusta—**Motorcycle Trip**—motorcycle transcontinental trip by women

Van Buren, Martin—**Free Soil Party**

Van Buren, Martin—**Political Convention**—two-thirds rule

Van Buren, Martin—**Political Machine**

Van Buren, Martin—**President (U.S.)**—President born a citizen of the United States

Van Buren, Martin—**Presidential Candidate**—presidential candidate nominated at a national convention

Van Buren, Martin—**Treaty**—treaty with a Far Eastern country

Vance, Claire K.—**Airmail Service**—airmail regular transcontinental through-service

Van Dam, Anthony—**Chamber of Commerce**—chamber of commerce (state)

Vandegrift, Alexander Archer—**Marine Corps**—general (4 stars) of the Marines on active duty to become a full general

Van Deman, Mrs. Ralph Henry—**Aviation**—**Passenger**—woman airplane passenger

Vandenberg, Hoyt Sanford—**Flag**—Air Force flag

Vandenberg, Hoyt Sanford—**Medal**—Air Force Medal of Honor for action in the Korean War

Vanderbilt, Alfred Gwynn—**Jockey**—jockey (woman) to win a major stakes race at a major track (owner of the winning horse)

Vanderbilt, Cornelius—**Ship**—yacht to circumnavigate the world

Vanderbilt, Cornelius—**Ship**—yacht to circumnavigate the world (owner)

Vanderbilt, George Washington—**Forest Management**

Vanderbilt, Harold Stirling—**Book**—book on the game of bridge by a championship team

Vanderbilt, William Henry—**Monument**—obelisk to be brought to the United States

Vandergrift, Alexander Archer—**World War II**—American offensive in the Pacific area

Vander Meer, Johnny—**Baseball Player**—major league baseball player to pitch two successive no-hit no-run games

Vanderlyn, John—**Postage Stamp**—paintings depicted on postage stamps

Van de Waeter, Jan Hendricksen—**Swedes**

Van Dillen, Erik—**Tennis Match**—lawn tennis match (doubles) for the Davis Cup to exceed 100 games

Van Dusen, John—**Insurance**—plate-glass insurance

Van Etten, Edwin Jan—**Radio Broadcast**—religious service broadcast

Van Gieson, Ira—**Medical Instruction**—Psyc tric Institute

Van Houten, James J.—**Patent**—patent issued the Confederate States of America

Van Hulsteyn, J. C.—**Orchestra**—municipal chestra supported by taxes

Van Kannel, Theophilus—**Door**—door (revolv

Vanni-Marcoux—**Opera**—opera broadcast ov national network from an American op house

Van Quickenborne, Father—**American In School**—Catholic school for American Ind

Van Reypen, William Knickerbocker—**Ship**—bulance ship

Van Sant, Samuel Rinnah—**Optometry Legi tion**

Van Sleet, William—**Balloon Honeymoon**—l loon honeymoon (pilot)

Van Syckel, Samuel—**Oil**—oil pipeline of imp tance

Van Twiller, Wouter—**Building**—brick buildi

Van Vechten, Carl—**Book**—book bound wit preprinted offset cloth

Van Winckle, H. A.—**Wedding**—wedding bro cast

Vare, William Scott—**Congress (U.S.)**—Sena senatorial controversy in which no candid were seated after a recount

VASKEN I, supreme patriarch and catholico all Armenians—**Armenian Cathedral**

Vaughan, Henry G.—**Foxhound Association**

Vaughan, Victor Clarence—**Medical Instructio** bacteriology courses in a college

Vaughn, Jim—**Baseball Game**—double no nine-inning baseball game

Veatch, John A.—**Borax**

Venima, Pieter—**Algebra Book**—algebra boo

Vening-Meinesz, Felix Andries—**Astronom** woman astronomer employed in the U.S. N Observatory

Vernon, Ambrose White—**Biography Course**—ography department

Vernon, Fortesque—**Astronomy Expedition**

Verplanck, Gulian Crommelin—**Election**—ma elected by popular vote in a city

Verrazano, Giovanni da—**Kidnapping**—kidn ping

Vianesi, Augusto—**Opera**—opera at the N ropolitan Opera House

Vicente, Manuel de Populo—**Opera**—opera (l ian)

Victoria, Queen of Great Britain—**Cable (t graph)**—cable across the Atlantic Ocean c pleted

Viets, Simeon—**Cigar Factory**

Vilhelm, Prince of Sweden—**Lecturer**—lecture royal blood to speak for personal profit

Villiers, Coulon de—**War (colonial)**—French Indian War battle

Vinay, Ramon—**Television**—**Telecast**—op (complete) to be televised from the Metrop tan Opera House

cent, Ambrose—**Book Auction Catalog**—book
uction catalog

cent, George Edgar—**Radio Broadcast**—diner broadcast around-the-world

cent, John Heyl—**Chautauqua Organization**

er, D. D. ("Jimmy")—**Airmail Service**—heli-
opter airmail delivery

son, Frederick Moore—**Air Force**—Air Force
ecretary

son, Frederick Moore—**Defense Department**
J.S.)

ian, Charles A. S.—**Benevolent and Protective**
•rder of Elks

sto, Solon John—**Newspaper**—Greek newspa-
er

•e, Richard G.—**Submarine**—submarine (U.S.)
estroyed in World War II

elhofer, Charles C.—**Whist Tournament**—in-
•rnational whist tournament

k, Douglas—**Postage Stamp**—phosphores-
•nt-impregnated postage stamps

a Braun, Wernher—**Rocket**—rocket to reach
uter space

a Hagen, Victor Wolfgang—**Birds**—quetzal
ird

•rsanger, Elkan Cohen—**Army Officer**—regi-
ental Jewish chaplain

stman, P.—**Labadist Community**

burg, R. J.—**Radio Distress Signal**—radio SOS
om an American ship

ey, Edwin S.—**Piano Player**—pneumatic piano
ayer

denburgh, Dorothy McElroy—**Woman**—wom-
a secretary of a national political party

eland, Jeanette—**Radio Broadcast**—radio con-
•rt from an airplane

W

ddell, George Edward ("Rube")—**Baseball**
ame—American League 20-inning baseball
ame

de, John—**Ship**—iron vessel

de, Leigh—**Aviation—Flights (world)**—world
ght

dleigh, George Henry—**Nautical School**—
utical municipal school

dsworth, Henry—**Television—Telecast**—play
• be televised as a full-hour program

dsworth, James Wolcott—**Congress (U.S.)**—
enate—Republican whip

dsworth, Jeremiah—**Wool**—worsted mill op-
ated by water power

dsworth, W. Austin—**Foxhound Association**

esche, Russell Randolph—**Coast Guard (U.S.)**
fficer—vice admiral in the Coast Guard

gner, Boyd David—**Aviation—Pilot**—Ameri-
•n Ace in World War II

gner, Charles F. ("Honus")—**Baseball Game**
-triple play unassisted in a modern major
ague game

Wagner, Charles F. ("Honus")—**Hall of Fame**
—hall of fame (baseball)

Wagner, Clinton—**Medical Society**—laryngological society (state)

Wagner, Herman L.—**Typewriter**—typewriter to
produce a line of writing visible as it was being
typed

Wagner, John—**Beer**—lager beer

Wagner, Robert Ferdinand—**Labor Relations**—
Labor Board (national)

Wagner, Robert Ferdinand—**Police**—parking-meter enforcement division

Wagner, Robert Ferdinand—**Tunnel**—triple-tube
underwater roadway

Wagoner, Clyde Decker—**Radio Broadcast**—
around the world broadcast

Wait, William E.—**Labor**—labor congress (national)

Waite, Charles C.—**Baseball Glove**

Waitz, Grete—**Runner**—runner (woman) to run a
marathon in less than 2.5 hours

Wakefield, William H. T.—**United Labor Party**

Waksman, Selman Abraham—**Microbiology**
Laboratory

Waksman, Selman Abraham—**Streptomycin**

Walcott, Joe ("Jersey Joe") (Arnold Raymond
Cream)—**Prizefight Referee**—heavyweight-
championship-prizefight black referee

Walcott, Joe ("Jersey Joe") (Arnold Raymond
Cream)—**Television—Telecast**—pay television
presentation of a sporting event

Walcott, Joe ("Jersey Joe") (Arnold Raymond
Cream) — **Television — Telecast** — prizefight
(heavyweight championship bout) telecast
coast-to-coast

Waldauer, Abe D.—**Enclave**—municipal enclave
of economic ground rent

Walden, Henry W.—**Aviation—Airplane**—monoplane (American)

Waldrake, Sarah—**Woman**—women to become
federal government employees

Waldseemüller, Martin H.—**"America"**

Waldseemüller, Martin H.—**Map**—globular map
published showing the Western Hemisphere

Wales, Thomas Crane—**Artics**

Walker, Aldace Freeman—**Interstate Commerce**
Act

Walker, Charles Duy—**Fraternity Magazine**—fraternity journal

Walker, D. A.—**Civil Service**—Civil Service Commission

Walker, Donald F.—**Surgical Operation**—surgical
operation on a bull to correct a sperm block

Walker, Edwin Garrison—**Legislator (state)**—
black representatives to sit in any legislature

Walker, Francis Amasa—**Economics Association**

Walker, Frank Comerford—**National Emergency**
Council (U.S.)

Walker, George Herbert—**Golf Tournament**—international golf match

Walker, John—**Dictionary**—rhyming dictionary

Walker, John—**Senator (U.S.)**—senator appointed
by a governor

Walker, John (John Pearson)—**Fingerprinting**—international exchange of fingerprints

Walker, Jonathan—**Branding**—branding punishment by a federal court

Walker, Joseph—**Shoe Peg**

Walker, Maggie Lena—**Bank**—bank president (black woman)

Walker, Mary Edwards—**Army Officer**—woman assistant army surgeon

Walker, Mary Edwards—**Medal**—Medal of Honor awarded to a woman

Walker, May—**Librarians' Union**

Walker, Moses Fleetwood—**Baseball Player**—black baseball player in the American Association

Walker, Samuel Hamilton—**Temperance Society**—Anti-Saloon League

Walker, Thomas—**Colonist**—civilian settlement west of the Allegheny Mountains

Walker, William—**Land Office**

Walker, William H.—**Rayon**—rayon patent

Wallace, Henry—**Postal Service**—Pony Express mail

Wallace, Henry Agard—**Cabinet (U.S.)**—father and son to occupy the same Cabinet posts

Wallace, Henry Agard—**Federal Surplus Relief Corporation**

Wallace, Mrs. Henry Agard—**Ship**—Liberty ship

Wallace, Henry Cantwell—**Cabinet (U.S.)**—father and son to occupy the same Cabinet posts

Wallace, John Hankins—**Horse Register**—trotting register

Wallace, Lewis—**War Criminal Proceedings**

Wallace, Robert—**Spoons**—nickel silver spoons

Waller, Frank—**Bicycle Race**—international 6-day 2-man-team bicycle race

Waller, Frank—**Bicycle Race**—motorcycle-paced bicycle race

Waller, William—**Stagecoach Intercity Service**

Wallington, James—**Television—Telecast**—color coast-to-coast telecast from the West Coast

Walmesley, Charles—**Catholic Bishop**—Catholic bishop appointed to serve in the United States

Walsh, F. W.—**Temperance Society**—Anti-Saloon League (national organization)

Walsh, Julia Montgomery—**Brokerage**—American Stock Exchange women members

Walsh, Loretta—**Naval Officer**—petty officer (woman)

Walsh, Raoul—**Motion Picture**—talking picture taken outdoors (full-length)

Walsh, Robert—**Periodical**—quarterly magazine

Walter, Eugene—**Motion Picture**—black-oriented talking picture (all-talking, all-singing) by a major company

Walter, Eugene—**Radio Broadcast**—drama (full-length melodrama) broadcast

Walter, John—**Evangelical Association Council**

Walter, Thomas—**Music Book**—music book printed with bars

Walters, Bernice Rosenthal—**Naval Officer**—woman medical officer assigned to a naval vessel

Walters, Robert Levi—**Ship**—guided-missile cort ship

Walters, Walt—**Motorboat Race**—motorl race (ocean) under the Union of Internati Motorboating rules

Walthall, Henry—**Motion Picture**—motion ture to gross $50 million

Walthour, Robert—**Bicycle Race**—paired six-bicycle race

Walvisch, Jonas—**Television**—television eye ness allowed to testify in a federal court

Walworth, James Jones—**Heating System**—h ing system (steam)

Wambsganss, Bill (William Wambsgans **Baseball Game**—triple play unassisted World Series

Wanamaker, John—**Electric Lighting**—ele light in a store

Wanamaker, Rodman—**Aviation—Airplane**—droplane with a multi-engine

Wang, Theodora Chan—**Women's Club**—nese-American women's club incorporated

Wanton, George Henry—**Medal**—Medal of Ho awarded to a black in the Spanish-Ameri War

Warbasse, James Peter—**Cooperatives Con** tion

Ward, Aaron Montgomery—**Business**—mail der house

Ward, Artemas—**Army Officer**—major gener

Ward, August—**Cattle Club**—cattle club (Gu sey cattle)

Ward, Charles S.—**World War II**—American peditionary force to land in Africa

Ward, Donald Gordon—**Radio Facsimile Tr** mission—photograph sent by radio across Atlantic as a public demonstration

Ward, Edward—**Aviation**—Aeronautical L sion of the United States War Department

Ward, Henry Dana—**Second Advent Belie** General Conference

Ward, Holcombe—**Tennis Match**—lawn te matches for the Davis Cup

Ward, Hortense—**Supreme Court (state)**—s supreme court composed entirely of wome

Ward, James Harmon—**Civil War**—naval of (Union) killed in the Civil War

Ward, Lester Frank—**Sociological Society**—s ological society (national)

Ward, Richard Jay—**Radio Church**

Ward, Roger—**Automobile Racer**—automo racer to win $100,000 in a race

Ward, Robert De Courcy—**Climatology Profe**

Warder, John Aston—**Forestry Society**—nati forestry association

Ware, Bruce Richardson—**World War I**—fired by the American Navy in World W against a known German submarine

Ware, Keith L.—**Army Officer**—general who from draftee

Ware, W. H.—**Dental Corps (U.S. Army)**—de officially employed in the U.S. Army

Ware, William Robert—**Architecture School**—chitectural school

Washington, George—**Revolutionary War**—conflict on equal terms between American regulars and British regulars

Washington, George—**Salute (complimentary)**

Washington, George—**State**—state named for a native-born American

Washington, George—**State Department (U.S.)**—State Department (U.S.) Secretary

Washington, George—**Supreme Court (U.S.)**—Chief Justice of the Supreme Court

Washington, George—**Supreme Court (U.S.)**—Supreme Court justice who was nominated but who did not serve

Washington, George—**Supreme Court (U.S.)**—Supreme Court of the United States

Washington, George—**Tariff**—tariff legislation

Washington, George—**Town**—town named for George Washington

Washington, George—**Veto (presidential)**—veto

Washington, George—**War (colonial)**—bloodshed in the French and Indian War

Washington, George—**War (colonial)**—French and Indian War battle

Washington, George—**War Veterans' Society**—Society of the Cincinnati

Washington, Joseph Reed—**Methodist Church**—black minister with two white congregations

Washington, Lucy Payne—**Wedding**—White House wedding

Washington, Martha—**Money**—bill bearing the portrait of a woman

Washington, Martha—**Postage Stamp**—American woman whose likeness appeared on a U.S. stamp

Washington, Martha—**Postage Stamp**—postage stamp to picture a woman

Washington, Martha—**Postal Service**—mail franking privilege

Washington, Martha—**President (U.S.)**—President's wife to frank mail

Washington, Mary Ball—**Monument**—monument to a woman financed by women

Waterhouse, Benjamin—**Mineralogy Instruction**

Waterhouse, Benjamin—**Vaccination for smallpox with cowpox**

Waterhouse, Daniel Oliver—**Vaccination for smallpox with cowpox**

Waterman, Fred—**Baseball Team**—baseball team to receive a regular salary

Waterman, Henry—**Elevator**—elevator

Waterman, Lewis Edson—**Fountain Pen**

Waters, Ethel—**Motion Picture**—talking picture entirely in color

Watkins, Charles Lee—**Congress (U.S.)—Senate**—parliamentarian of the Senate

Watkins, Stanley Sylvester Alexander—**Voice Mechanism**—voice mechanism capable of creating the complex sounds of speech

Watkins, Travis E.—**Medal**—Medal of Honor awarded in the Korean War

Watkinson, Cornelius—**Play (drama)**—play given by nonprofessional actors

Watson, Charles—**Philatelic Society**—philatelic society

Watson, Charles—**Tennis Match**—intercolleg court tennis match

Watson, Cornelius S.—**Envelope**—envelope chine patent

Watson, Ebenezer—**Genealogy**—genealogy

Watson, Elkanah—**Animals**—sheep (Mer sheep)

Watson, Elkanah—**Fair**—agricultural fair

Watson, Lavinia Fanning—**Ship**—naval s christened by a woman

Watson, Ruth P.—**Cemetery**—foreign serv women interred in Arlington National Cer tery

Watson, Th., pseud. See Smith, John (captain

Watson, Thomas, pseud. See Smith, John (c tain)

Watson, Thomas Augustus—**Telephone**—t phone conversation over out-of-door wires

Watson, Thomas Augustus—**Telephone**—t phone message

Watson, Thomas Augustus—**Telephone**—t phone used by a railroad company

Watson, Thomas Augustus—**Telephone**—tra continental telephone demonstration

Watson, Thomas Edward—**Postal Service**—r free delivery appropriation

Watterston, George—**Librarian**—Librarian Congress

Watts, James Winston—**Surgical Operatio** lobotomy (prefrontal)

Watts, John—**Book**—stereotyped book

Watts, John Dennis—**Wedding**—transatla telephone wedding

Wayland, Francis—**Education Association**—e cation association (national)

Wayland, Julius Augustus—**Social Democrac America**

Waymack, William Wesley—**Atomic Ene Commission**—Atomic Energy Commission

Wayne, Anthony—**Revolutionary War**—bayo charge in the Revolutionary War

Wayne, Robert Earl—**Aviation—Pilot**—pilo down two enemy fighter airplanes in one da Korea

Wayne, Robert Earl—**Helicopter**—helicopter cue of an American pilot behind enemy lir

Wayne, Robert Earl—**Medal**—Distinguished ing Cross in the Korean War

Weaver, James Baird—**Greenback Labor Par**

Weaver, James Baird—**People's Party**

Weaver, Robert Clifton—**Cabinet (U.S.)**—Cab member (black)

Weaver, Thomas—**War (colonial)**—marine gagement in battle

Webb, B. B.—**Radio Telephone**—transatla radio telephone message

Webb, George James—**Music Instruction**—m cal pedagogy school

Webb, George James—**Musician**—orchestra le er to conduct without using a baton

Webb, Gerald Bertram—**Medical Society**— munology society

Webb, Jack—**Television—Telecast**—color black-and-white telecast to be sponsored

West, James Ward—**Surgical Operation**—kidney transplant

West, John—**Treason**—treason trial (colonial)

Westendorf, Willem Fredrik—**Synchrotron**—synchrotron

Westinghouse, George—**Air Brake**

Westinghouse, George—**Holiday**—Saturday half holiday

Weston, David M.—**Cream Separator**—centrifugal cream separator

Weston, Edward—**Photographer**—photographer to receive a John Simon Memorial Foundation award

Weston, Frank William—**Bicycle Magazine**

Westwood, Frances Jean Miles—**Political Party**—permanent chairman (woman) of a major political party

Wetherill, Charles Mayer—**Agriculture Bureau**—agriculture bureau scientific publication

Wetherill, Samuel—**Cloth**—jeans, fustians, everlastings, and coatings

Wetherill, Samuel—**White Lead manufacturer**

Wetherill, Samuel—**Zinc**—zinc commercial production

Wetherill, Samuel—**Zinc**—zinc patent

Wetmore, Alexander—**Bird Banding**—bird banding by federal authorities

Wev, Oscar Cottman Buckingham—**Radio Station**—seagoing radio broadcasting station

Wharton, Clifton Reginald, Jr.—**College President**—college president (black) of a major university predominantly white

Wharton, Edith Newbold Jones—**Novel**—Pulitzer Prize award to a woman for a novel

Wharton, Joseph—**Business School**—business collegiate school

Wharton, Thomas—**Milestones**

Wheatcraft, T. S.—**Vending Machine**—vending machine to sell from bulk

Wheatland, Henry—**Fish Commission** (state)

Wheatley, Julia—**Opera**—opera singer (American) to sing in an Italian opera in Italian

Wheatley, Phillis—**Poet**—black woman poet

Wheaton, Joseph—**Congress (U.S.)—House of Representatives**—sergeant at arms

Wheeler, E. G.—**Railroad Car**—chapel car

Wheeler, Frederick—**Seventh Day Adventist Church**

Wheeler, Schuyler Skaats—**Electric Fan**

Wheeler, Seth—**Paper**—perforated wrapping paper

Whelan, Israel—**Insurance**—insurance agency

Whipple—**Photograph**—photograph of a star (other than the sun)

Whipple, Abraham—**Navy**—naval fleet

Whipple, Abraham—**Revolutionary War**—naval attack

Whipple, Charles—**Engraving**—pamphlet produced from a steel plate engraving

Whipple, Cullen—**Screw**—screw machine

Whitaker, Alexander—**Presbyterian Church**—Presbyterian Church

Whitcher, Frances Miriam Berry—**Woman**—woman humorist

White, Master—**Oratorio**—oratorio performa (complete)

White, Abraham—**Pituitary Hormone**—pitui hormone isolated

White, Andrew—**Engineering College**—electi engineering course

White, Andrew—**Radio Receiving Contest**—r receiving contest (presented award)

White, Andrew Dickson—**Historical Socie** historical society (general)

White, Arthur M.—**Automobile Race**—auto bile race

White, Benjamin Franklin—**Horse Race**—har horse race (Hambletonian) for three-year-

White, Benjamin Franklin—**Horse Race**—har race driver to win the Hambletonian four ti

White, Canvas—**Cement**—natural cement ro

White, Caroline Earle—**Antivivisection Socie**

White, David—**Fraternity**—social fraternity

White, E. F.—**Aviation**—**Flights**—New Y Chicago nonstop flight

White, Edward Douglass—**Governor**—Catl governor

White, Edward Douglass—**Supreme Court (l**—Associate Justice of the Supreme Cou become Chief Justice

White, Edward H.—**Aviation**—**Airship**—dirig transfer of mail to a train

White, Edward Higgins, II—**Astronaut**—tronaut (American) to maneuver outside a tellite

White, Edward Higgins, II—**Astronaut**—tronauts (American) to die in a spacecraft

White, Edward Higgins, II—**Astronaut**—two-i spaceflight (American) of 62 orbits

White, J. Andrew—**Radio Broadcast**—prizel (heavyweight championship) broadcast

White, James Clarke—**Medical Instruction**—matology chair

White, John—**Artist**—English artist

White, John Barber—**Shipping**—United St Shipping Board

White, Joseph N.—**Billiard Match**—billiard ma

White, Josiah—**Bridge**—iron-wire suspen bridge

White, Peregrine—**Births**—child born of Eng parents in New England

White, Robert Michael—**Aviation**—**Flights**—plane to fly faster than 4,000 m.p.h.

White, Robert Michael—**Aviation**—**Pilot**—pilc an airplane to qualify as an astronaut

White, Samuel—**Psychiatric Association**

White, Susanna—**Wedding**—wedding in M England

White, William—**Bible Society**—Bible societ

White, William—**Hospital**—dispensary

White, William—**Prison Reform Society**

White, William Alanson—**Medical Congres** mental hygiene international congress

White, William Allen—**Book Club**—Book-of-Month Club

White, William W.—**Republican Party**—Repu can Party meeting (national)

ite Crane, Sidney—**American Indian Church**
-church organized by American Indians

ite Eyes, Captain—**Treaty**—treaty entered
to by the United States with American Indian
ibes

itefield, George—**Orphanage**—orphanage
ith a continuous existence

itehead, Gustave—**Aviation—Flights**—air-
ane flight

itehill, Clarence—**Opera**—opera by an Ameri-
n composer performed at the Metropolitan
pera House of New York

iteman, Louis Porter—**Bottle**—milk bottles

itfield, Malvin Greston—**Athlete**—black to
in the James E. Sullivan Memorial Trophy

iting, A. H.—**Automobile Race**—automobile
ce on a track

itlock, William—**Minstrel Show Troupe**

itman, Malcolm Douglass—**Tennis Match**
-lawn tennis matches for the Davis Cup

itman, Narcissa Prentiss—**Colonist**—women
cross the continent

tney, Amos—**Telephone**—coin telephone

tney, Eli—**Cotton Gin**

tney, F. C.—**Phonograph Record**—phono-
aph record of a stage performance by the
iginal cast

tney, Flora Payne—**Free Lunch**—free lunches
aid convalescents

tney, Harry Payne—**Horse Race**—filly to win
e Kentucky Derby

tney, Harry Payne—**Horse Race**—horse to
in a $100,000 purse in one race

tney, William Dwight—**Philological Society**—
ational philological society

tney, Willis Rodney—**Diathermy Machine**

tney, Willis Rodney—**Industrial Research**
aboratory

ton, James Morris—**Degrees (academic and
onorary)**—Doctor of Philosophy degree

ttier, Earle Ovando—**Casein Fiber**

ttlesey, Oramel—**Music Instruction**—music
hool authorized to confer degrees

hman, John R.—**Wedding**—wedding broad-
ast

kes, Lambert—**Ship**—warship (American-
ilt) to enter European waters

mark, Richard—**Television—Telecast**—mo-
n picture premiere telecast on 2 successive
ghts

be, Edward—**Kindergarten Manual**

land, Christoph Martin—**President (U.S.)**—
esident to translate a German Book (author of
e original book)

ner, Leo—**Kennel**—hotel for dogs

gins, Leonard A.—**Aviation—License**—glider
lot's license

gins, Mary E.—**Surgical Operation**—gallstone
eration

glesworth, Edward—**Divinity Professor**

le, Milford—**Automobile Race**—transconti-
ntal automobile race (for a time record)

Wignell, Thomas—**Play (drama)**—native American play successfully acted on a regular stage

Wilbour, Charlotte Beebee—**Women's Club**—
women's professional club

Wilbur, Curtis Dwight—**Television—Telecast**—
telecast of an object in motion

Wilbur, James H.—**American Indian School**—
American Indian boarding school on a reservation

Wilcox, John W.—**Electrotype**—electrotype
manufacturing

Wilcox, L. S.—**Tung**

Wilde, Francis E. J.—**Electric Sign**—electric sign
flasher

Wildey, Thomas—**Odd Fellows Lodge**

Wildman, Ernest Atkins—**Conscientious Objectors' Camp**

Wiley, David—**Agricultural Journal**—agricultural
journal

Wiley, Herbert Victor—**Glider**—glider released
from a dirigible

Wilhelmina, Queen of the Netherlands—**Congress (U.S.)**—reigning queen to address a joint
session of Congress

Wilke, Hubert—**Opera**—light opera presented in
2 cities on the same day by the same company

Wilkes, Charles—**Expedition**—scientific expedition fitted out by the United States Government

Wilkins, James Ernest—**Cabinet (U.S.)**—black
sub-Cabinet member

Wilkinson, David—**Nut and Bolt Machine**

Wilkinson, David—**Screw**—screw patent

Wilkinson, Eugene Parks—**Navy**—atomic submarine division

Wilkinson, Eugene Parks—**Submarine**—atomic-
powered submarine

Wilkinson, Hannah—**Thread**—cotton thread

Wilkinson, Jeremiah—**Nails**—nails

Willard, Charles Foster—**Aviation—Expositions
and Meets**—aviation meet

Willard, Charles Foster—**Aviation—Flights**—airplane to carry 3 passengers

Willard, Emma Hart—**College**—school for the
higher education of women

Willard, Frances Elizabeth—**College President**—
woman college president

Willard, Frances Elizabeth—**Monument**—statue
of a woman in National Statuary Hall

Willard, Harry—**Aviation—Flights**—airplane to
carry 3 passengers

Willard, Samuel—**Book**—book of folio size

Willard, Simon—**Clock**—banjo clock patent

Willard, William A. P.—**Aviation—Airplane
Fatalities**—airplane fatality (woman pilot with
passenger)

Willerup, Christian B.—**Methodist Episcopal
Church**—Scandinavian Methodist Episcopal
Church

Willets, Edward—**Animals**—monkey trained to
perform

Willets, Gilson—**Motion Picture**—serial motion
picture

Williams, Bert—**Motion Picture**—motion picture
featuring a black actor

Williams, Charles—**Railroad**—railroad to run west of the Mississippi River

Williams, Charles—**Telephone**—telephone for domestic use

Williams, Daniel Hale—**Hospital**—interracial hospital

Williams, Daniel Hale—**Medical Society**—black member of the American College of Surgeons

Williams, Daniel Hale—**Surgical Operation**—suture of the human heart (successful)

Williams, Edwin Debbell ("Deb")—**Baseball Game**—baseball game in which there were two triple-steals

Williams, Elkanah—**Medical Instruction**—ophthalmology professor

Williams, Ella C.—**Fellowship**—resident fellowship for women awarded by a women's college

Williams, Harvey—**Radio Contest**

Williams, Henry J.—**Publishing Society**

Williams, Horatio Burt—**Stethoscope**—electrical stethoscope (portable)

Williams, Isaac—**Neutrality Regulation**

Williams, J. A.—**Welsh Magazine**

Williams, Jesse—**Cheese Factory**—cheese factory of consequence

Williams, Jesse Lynch—**Play (drama)**—drama to win a Pulitzer Prize

Williams, John—**Medal**—Medal of Honor awarded to a member of the Naval Service

Williams, John Foster—**Ship**—revenue cutter

Williams, Jonathan—**Army**—engineer corps

Williams, Jonathan—**Army School**—army school

Williams, Joseph Ricketson—**Agricultural School**—agricultural college (state) to open

Williams, Kathlyn—**Motion Picture**—serial motion picture with installments longer than one reel

Williams, Lola M.—**Woman**—woman secretary to a Vice President of the United States

Williams, Richard F.—**Hospital**—black hospital and asylum

Williams, Robley Cook—**Virus**—virus separated into component parts

Williams, Roger—**Baptist Church**—Baptist Church

Williams, Roger—**Dictionary**—American Indian–English dictionary

Williams, Samuel—**Astronomy Expedition**

Williams, Samuel Wells—**Chinese Language and Literature Lectureship**

Williams, Sydney Augustus—**Insurance**—mutual liability insurance company

Williams, Terry—**College**—college to offer athletic scholarships to women

Williams, Thomas Robinson—**Felt**—manufacturing mechanical process

Williams, Thomas W.—**Ship**—steam whaler

Williams, Walter—**Journalism Course**—journalism school

Williamson, James De Long—**Community Trust**

Williamson, John Ernest—**Photograph**—photographs taken under the sea

Williamson, John Finley—**Television—Telecast**—religious services to be televised

Williamson, Peregrine—**Pen**—steel pen pate

Williamson, Walter—**Medical School**—ho pathic college

Willich, Anthony Florian Madinger—**Agricul Encyclopedia**

Willing, Thomas—**Bank**—bank chartered by gress

Willingham, Harris Emanuel—**Federal Al Control Administration**

Willis, Frances Elizabeth—**Diplomatic Serv** American legation in which a woman assu charge

Willis, Frances Elizabeth—**Diplomatic Serv** woman career diplomat advanced to the ra ambassador

Willis, Nathaniel Parker—**Periodical**—illust weekly

Willis, Sophia—**Flag**—American flag ov schoolhouse

Williston, Samuel—**Button**—cloth-covered tons

Willkie, Wendell Lewis—**Television—Telec** political convention to be televised

Willoughby, Frances Lois—**Naval Officer**—v an doctor in the regular U.S. Navy

Wills, Maurice Morning ("Maury")—**Bas Player**—baseball player to steal more tha bases in a season

Willson, Thomas Leopold—**Acetylene**—a lene

Willson, Thomas Leopold—**Carbide Factory**

Wilmot, David—**Republican Party**—Repub party meeting (national)

Wilmoth, A. David—**Health Department**—c health department organized on a full basis

Wilson, Allen Benjamin—**Sewing Machine**— ing machine to sew curving seams

Wilson, Anna M.—**Medal**—Legion of Merit M awarded to a Women's Army Corps (V member in the European Theater of Opera

Wilson, Brenda—**Horse Race**—horse race mutuel with an entire field of women joc

Wilson, Carrie—**Labor Union**—women's organization (national)

Wilson, Charles Erwin—**Ordnance**—atomic non

Wilson, Darius—**Royal Arcanum**

Wilson, Debra Lee—**Coast Guard (U.S.)**—C Guard women to serve aboard ships (other hospital ships)

Wilson, Edmund Beecher—**Biology**—bi course (general) offered in a college

Wilson, Francis—**Opera**—light opera pres in 2 cities on the same day by the same co ny

Wilson, G. R.—**Ship**—naval ship christened Army officer (first commander)

Wilson, Harold—**Telephone**—telephone co sation (commercial) over a satellite

Wilson, Henry—**Army**—law (federal) author military service for blacks

Wilson, J. F.—**Railroad Crossing Gate Pate**

Wilson, James—**Globe Factory**

Wistar, Isaac Jones—**Research Institute**—anatomy research institute

Wister, William—**Cricket Club**—cricket club to own its own clubhouse

Witherell, Warren—**Water Skier**—water skier to jump 100 feet

Withers, C. Clark—**Radio Broadcast**—submarine (submerged) broadcast

Withers, C. Clark—**Radio Telephone**—two-way radio conversation between a submerged submarine and another vessel

Witherspoon, Herbert—**Opera**—opera by an American composer performed at the Metropolitan Opera House of New York

Witsell, Edward Fuller—**Army Officer**—woman army officer

Wittenmyer, Annie T.—**Temperance Society**—women's temperance society (national)

Wittich, Jean Wetterau—**Woman**—woman state budget commissioner

Witzke, Lothar—**World War I**—German spy to receive a death sentence from the American forces during World War I

Wolber, Joseph Gustave—**Crime Prevention and Detection**—crime prevention commission for interstate cooperation

Wolcott, Alexander S.—**Photographic Patent**

Wolcott, Alexander S.—**Photographic Studio**—commercial photography studio

Wold, Peter Irving—**Television—Telecast**—speaker to address an organization by television

Wolf, Ludwig Martin Nicolaus—**Sewing Machine**—sewing machine lamp holder

Wolfe, Richard—**Church**—church without theology, creed, or dogma

Wolff, Julius—**Canning**—sardine cannery

Wolfson, Arthur M.—**Degrees (academic and honorary)**—Master of Arts degree in Sacred Music

Woll, Frederic Albert—**Optometry Instruction**—optics and optometry courses

Wollstonecraft, Mary—**Woman Suffrage**—woman suffrage book

Wolman, Leo—**Labor**—Labor Advisory Board (U.S.)

Wood, Abraham—**Expedition**—expedition

Wood, Charles Raymond—**Helicopter**—ramjet helicopter

Wood, Edward Stickney—**Medical Instruction**—medical chemistry course (systematic)

Wood, Elizabeth A.—**Telephone**—picturephone service (commercial)

Wood, Fernando—**Telegram**—transcontinental telegram

Wood, Fernando—**Telegraph**—telegraph line to the Pacific Coast

Wood, George Bacon—**Medical Book**—dispensatory (American)

Wood, Harold L.—**Discovery**—Northwest Passage

Wood, Henry Alexander Wise—**Laborsaving Device**

Wood, Henry Alexander Wise—**Stereotype**—tomatic plate-casting and finishing machine stereotype printing

Wood, John—**Printing Press**—rotogravure pre

Wood, John Jethro—**Plow**—plow with in changeable parts

Wood, Peter Grant—**Treasury Department (L**—gold medallions issued by the Treasury partment

Wood, R. F.—**Aviation—Airship**—airship fi with helium gas

Wood, Sally Sayward—**Women's Club**—men's club

Wood, Stuart—**Political Science Society**—po cal and social science society (national)

Wood, Walton J.—**Public Defenders' Office**

Wood, William M.—**Navy**—naval militia (st

Wood, William Maxwell—**Naval Officer**—geon General of the Navy

Woodbridge, Benjamin—**Degrees (academic honorary)**—Bachelor of Arts degree

Woodbridge, Timothy—**Physician**—doctor to ceive an honorary medical degree

Woodbridge, William—**Education Associati** education association (local)

Woodhouse, James—**Chemistry Labora Manual**

Woodhouse, James—**Chemists Society**—ch cal society

Woodhull, Victoria Claflin—**Brokerage**—wo brokerage office owner

Woodhull, Victoria Claflin—**Equal Rights Pa**

Woodhull, Victoria Claflin—**Presidential Ca date**—woman presidential candidate

Woods, Kate Tanett—**Women's Club**—wom club federation

Woods, Leslie G.—**World War I**—U.S. Army diers killed in combat

Woods, Persis C.—**College**—college for wom

Woods, William—**Steel**—cast steel for plow

Woodward, Artemas—**Brushes**

Woodward, George B.—**Bicycle Society**—bic club

Woodward, John Blackburne—**Rifle Associa**—rifle association (national)

Woodward, Robert Burns—**Chlorophyll**—ch phyll "a"

Woodward, Robert Burns—**Quinine**—synth quinine

Woodward, Samuel B.—**Psychiatric Associa**

Woodworth, John Maynard—**Public Heal** Public Health Service (U.S.)

Wooldridge, William O.—**Army Officer**—geant major of the army

Woolfolk, Marie—**Sorority**—black sorority

Woolley, John Granville—**United Christian P**

Woolley, Leonidas G.—**Locomotive Headlig** electric locomotive headlight

Woolman, Mary Schenck—**School**—trade sc for girls

Woolworth, Frank Winfield—**Business**—five-store

Woorn, Joseph—**Wedding**—double radio v ding

Y

Z

Geographical Index

To obtain a complete account of the various items, the reader should consult the main body of the text. The **boldface** type shows the alphabetical heading under which each item may be found. If an item appears in the text under a general heading, the specific heading is noted below after the general heading.

ALASKA

State—noncontiguous state—admitted—Jan. 3, 1959

Attu

World War II—American territory occupied by the Japanese—June 7, 1942

Fairbanks

Aviation—Flights—North Pole jet crossing—Sept. 20, 1951

Kiska

World War II—American territory occupied by the Japanese—June 7, 1942

Metlakahtla

President (U.S.)—President to visit Alaska and Canada while President—W. G. Harding—July 8, 1923

Nenana

Railroad—railroad operated by the federal government—Alaska Railroad—golden spike driven—W. G. Harding—July 15, 1923

ARIZONA

Judge—chief justice (woman) of a state supreme court—L. E. Lockwood—selected, Jan. 8, 1965
Supreme Court (state)—chief justice (woman) of a state supreme court—L. E. Lockwood—elected 1965

Apache Pass

Medal—Medal of Honor action—B. J. D. Irwin—Feb. 13, 1861

Ashfork

Dam—steel dam—built—1898

Canon Diablo

Diamond—diamonds in a meteorite—found—June 1891

Flagstaff

Astronomy—planet—found beyond Neptune Feb. 18, 1930

Grand Canyon

Aviation—airplane disaster involving more than 100 persons—June 30, 1956

Phoenix

Aviation—Pilot—pilot to receive the Congressional Medal of Honor—posthumous award—May 29, 1919

Hospital—ambulatory surgical facility independently operated—Surgicenter—opened Feb. 1970

Prescott

Old Age Home for Pioneers—approved—M 10, 1909
Rodeo—July 4, 1888

Tucson

Aviation—Airport—airport municipally own Nov. 20, 1919
Building—solar-heated and radiation-co house—built—R. W. Bliss—Jan. 15, 1955

ARKANSAS

Park—park (national)—Hot Springs Nati Park—March 4, 1921
Protestant Episcopal Bishop—black suffrag Rev. E. T. Demby—appointed—Sept. 29, 1
Senator (U.S.)—woman elected to the Senate O. W. Caraway—Jan. 12, 1932

Benton

Fuller's Earth—discovered—1891

Fayetteville

Army—Reserve Officers Training Corps Un authorized—Oct. 21, 1916

Hot Springs

Hospital—hospital for the military and r forces—opened—Jan. 17, 1887
Jockey—jockey to win one hundred $10 stakes—Willie Shoemaker—March 30, 19

Little Rock

Tennis Match—lawn tennis match (doubles the Davis Cup to exceed 100 games— Smith and Erik Van Dillen vs. Jaime Fillo Pat Cornejo—Aug. 5, 1973

Murfreesboro

Diamond—diamond in actual rock—discove Aug. 1, 1906

Wilmar

Turbine—gas turbine to pump natural gas stalled—May 13, 1949

CALIFORNIA

Alfalfa—introduced—1854
Aviation—Pilot—father and son commercia line pilots—E. H. Lee and R. E. Lee—Ma 1941
Credit Card—nationally accepted bank-ori credit card—originated—Bank of Amer 1959

rce—"no fault" divorce law (state)—enacted
ly 6, 1970—effective Jan. 2, 1971

;—state-owned docks—authorized—April
, 1863

tion Law—fraudulent election law (state)—
acted—March 26, 1866

anasia—"Right to Die" law—enacted Sept.
, 1976

st Service—forest commission (state)—per-
anent—authorized—March 3, 1885

estead Act—homestead act (desert)—enact-
—March 3, 1875

er Cocktail—originated—1866

—park (national) containing an active vol-
no—established—Aug. 9, 1916

—state park—Yosemite Valley park—1865

Regulation Legislation—resale price
aintenance law (state)—"Fair Trade Act"—
proved—May 8, 1931

fight Referee—woman prizefight referee (lic-
sed)—Belle Martell—April 30, 1940

rantine—plant quarantine legislation (state)
enacted—March 4, 1881

esentative (U.S.)—representative of Asian
cestry—D. S. Saund—elected—Nov. 6, 1956

esentative (U.S.)—representative (woman)
ected to serve in the place of her husband—
n. 23, 1923

—state admitted to the Union on the Pacific
ast—Sept. 9, 1850

ano—eruption—recorded—1694

an—woman district attorney of the United
ates—A. A. Adams—served—July 25, 1918

Alameda

tion—Flights—airplane to carry 300 passen-
rs on one flight—*Caroline Mars*—takeoff May
, 1949

mmer—swimmer to cover a distance of 100
eters free style in less than 1 minute—Johnny
eissmuller—July 9, 1922

phone—dial telephone service coast-to-coast
thout the aid of operators—to Englewood,
J.—Nov. 10, 1951

Anaheim

phone—picturephone transcontinental call—
om New York City—April 20, 1964

Angels Camp, Calaveras County

Jumping Jubilee—May 19-20, 1928

Arcadia

tion—Flights (transcontinental)—transconti-
ntal dirigible flight (nonrigid dirigible)—from
ewport News, Va.—Sept. 23, 1922

Bakersfield

ation—Airport—airport county owned—Kern
ounty Airport—developed 1925

Berkeley

Aviation—Airship—airship disaster—May 23, 1908

Bevatron—in operation—Feb. 15, 1954

Element—element 93—neptunium—discovery announced—June 8, 1940

Element—element 94—plutonium—discovered—1940

Element—element 96—curium—discovered—1944

Element—element 97—berkelium—identified—Dec. 1949

Element—element 98—californium identified and produced—Jan. 1950

Element—element 99—einsteinium—identified—Dec. 1952

Element—element 101—mendelevium—discovered—Feb. 1955

Element—element 103—produced—Feb. 14, 1961

Element—element 104—rutherfordium—discovered at University of California Lawrence Radiation Laboratory—1969

Element—element 105—hahnium—discovered by Albert Ghiorso—University of California Lawrence Radiation Laboratory—1970

Football Game—football game to attract 100,000 spectators—California vs. Stanford—Nov. 22, 1924

High School—junior high school system authorized—Dec. 21, 1909

Isotope—radioactive isotope medicine—administered—Dec. 24, 1936

Museum—museum to install refrigerated vaults—March 1930

Naval Officer—woman naval inspector—Jean Hales—appointed—Aug. 24, 1942

Physics—cyclotron—developed—E. O. Lawrence—1934

Physics—radioactive substance produced synthetically—Feb. 4, 1936

Pole Vaulter—pole vaulter to clear the bar at 15 feet—Cornelius Warmerdam—April 13, 1940

Soilless Culture of Plants—private soilless garden—W. F. Gericke—1931

Synchrotron—synchrotron—invented by E. M. McMillan—installed at Radiation Laboratory, University of California—full energy released Jan. 17, 1949

Virus—virus (human- or animal-infecting virus) to be crystallized—poliomyelitis virus—C. E. Schwerdt

Virus—virus separated into component parts—reported—June 10, 1955

Vitamin—vitamin E—recognized—1922

Beverly Hills

Motion Picture Actor—motion picture performer (woman) to win the Life Achievement Award—Bette Davis—March 1, 1977

CALIFORNIA—*Continued*

Bonsall

Golfer—golfer (woman) to play 150 holes continuously—Katherine Murphy—June 19, 1967

Burbank

Airmail Service—helicopter airmail experimental tests—July 8, 1946

Aviation—airline to install rear-facing passenger seats—to New York City—June 1, 1953

Aviation—Airplane—jet-propelled fighter plane —U.S. Army Air Forces—flight—Jan. 1944

Aviation—Flights—stratoliner commercial flight —to New York City—July 8, 1940

Aviation—Flights (transcontinental)—transcontinental nonstop east–west flight by a woman— landed—July 11, 1935

Television—Telecast—color coast-to-coast live telecast—from New York City—Nov. 3, 1953

Camp Parks

Television—Telecast—transcontinental telecast by means of an orbiting satellite—transmission —April 24, 1962

Canoga Park

Atomic Reactor—atomic reactor system to be patented—J. W. Flora—May 17, 1960

Satellite—nuclear reactor in orbit—*SNAP 10A*— developed at Atomic International division of North American Aviation, Inc.

Capitola

Soilless Culture of Plants—commercial production of plants in water—Feb. 1934

Catalina Island

See Santa Catalina Island

Cazadero

Russian Settlement—established—March 15, 1812

Chico

Locker—public locker plant—established—A. G. Eames—1903

Tung—trees successfully grown—planted—1905

Coloma

Gold—gold discovered in California—of importance—Jan. 24, 1848

Coronado

Aviation—refueling attempt in midair—June 27, 1923

Aviation—Flights (transcontinental)—transcontinental nonstop flight—from New York City— landed—May 3, 1923

Culver City

Aviation—Airplane—airplane with eight en —Hughes Flying Boat—built—1947

Radar—radar for commercial and private p —demonstrated—May 1, 1947

Edwards Air Force Base

See also under Muroc

Automobile—rocket vehicle to break the s barrier on land—Stan Barrett—Dec. 16, 1

Aviation—Flights—airplane to fly faster 4,500 m.p.h.—W. J. Knight, pilot—Oct. 3, 1

Aviation—Flights—airplane to fly faster 4,000 m.p.h.—Robert White—Nov. 9, 1961

Aviation—Flights—airplane to fly faster tha speed of sound that was piloted by a civili H. H. Hoover—March 10, 1948

Aviation—Pilot—pilot in an airplane to quali an astronaut—R. M. White—takeoff Jul 1962

El Monte

Radio Broadcast—solar power two-way-r coast-to-coast conversation—to Fort I mouth, N.J.—June 23, 1960

El Segundo

Astronaut—astronaut (black) selected for manned orbiting laboratory program—I Dwight, Jr.—March 31, 1961

Astronaut—astronaut (black) to qualify fo training course—R. H. Lawrence—sele June 30, 1967

Ellwood

World War II—bombing on continental U.S. in World War II—Barnsdall Oil Refinery— 23, 1942

Emeryville

Dog Racetrack—opened—Feb. 22, 1920

Folsom

Sawmill—electrically driven sawmill—ope successfully—1896

General Grant National Park

Christmas Tree—Nation's Christmas Tree— cated—May 1, 1926

Glendale

Aviation—Flights—women to fly in excess o hours—Evelyn Trout and E. M. Cooper—tal Jan. 4—landed Jan. 9, 1931

Aviation—Flights (transcontinental)—transc nental airplane flight by a woman—arr from New York City—Oct. 9, 1930

Electric Generator—hydrogen-cooled turbine erator for outdoor installation—operat April 11, 1941

CALIFORNIA—Los Angeles—*Continued*

Aviation—Parachute—pilot to bail out of an airplane flying at supersonic speed—G. F. Smith—Feb. 26, 1955

Aviation—Pilot—pilot (American) to establish an altitude record—Louis Paulhan—Jan. 12, 1910

Aviation—Races—airplane race (of importance) in which both men and women were contestants—commenced—Aug. 30, 1931

Bank—automated "tellerless" bank—Surety National Bank's Civic Center branch—opened April 27, 1970

Baseball Game—World Series baseball game to draw more than 90,000 persons—Chicago White Sox vs. Los Angeles Dodgers—Oct. 6, 1959

Baseball Pitcher—baseball pitcher to win 4 no-hitters—Sanford Koufax—4th game, Los Angeles, Calif.—Sept. 9, 1965

Baseball Player—baseball player to steal more than 100 bases in a season—M. M. Wills—100th steal, Sept. 26, 1962

Buddhist Temple—established—July 15, 1904

Building—circular office building—dedicated—April 6, 1956

Catholic Priest—Catholic cardinal whose see was west of the Rockies—J. F. McIntyre—elevated—Jan. 12, 1953

Discus—discus throw to exceed 200 feet—A. A. Oerter—May 18, 1962

Fog Disposal Unit—accepted by test—March 29, 1949

Football—football with a rubber covering—manufactured—March 1936

Football Game—Super Bowl contest—Green Bay Packers vs. Kansas City Chiefs—Jan. 15, 1967

High Jump—over seven feet—Charles Dumas—June 29, 1956

Humanist Society—established—Jan. 13, 1929

Library Society—Melvil Dewey medal—presented to R. R. Shaw—June 24, 1953

Motion Picture—animated cartoon in color (Technicolor) of feature length with sound—exhibited—Dec. 21, 1937

Motion Picture—animated cartoon talking picture—produced—1928

Motion Picture—animated three-dimensional cartoon in Technicolor (modern)—premiere—May 28, 1953

Motion Picture—motion picture to gross $50 million—*The Birth of a Nation*—shown Feb. 8, 1915

Motion Picture Actor—black woman to win an Oscar—Feb. 29, 1940

Motion Picture Actor—motion picture actor and son to receive Oscars—John and Walter Huston—March 24, 1949

Motion Picture Actor—motion picture actors to receive Oscars—May 16, 1929

Motion Picture Theater—motion picture theater—opened—April 2, 1902

Photograph—photograph of genes—announced—Jan. 7, 1949

Police—police officer (woman) under civil service—A. S. Wells—appointed, Sept. 2, 1910

Postage Stamp—postage stamp issued joint[ ] 2 countries—Mexican Independence—issu[ ] Sept. 16, 1960

Presidential Candidate—presidential cand[ ] assassinated while campaigning—R. F. Ke[ ] dy—June 6, 1968

Presidential Candidate—presidential cand[ ] debate series on television—third de[ ] Kennedy in New York City and Nixon in H[ ] wood—Oct. 13, 1960

Public Defender's Office—created—June 13, [ ]

Public School—public school opera stu[ ] opened—Oct. 1937

Radio Broadcast—cooperative radio show—[ ] 10, 1937

Radio Broadcast—network broadcast receiv[ ] the Pacific Coast—Oct. 23, 1924

Radio Telephone—radio telephone service ([ ] mercial)—July 16, 1920

Railroad—streamlined Pullman train (six ca[ ] to New York City—Oct. 22, 1934

Railroad Car—air-conditioned cars—instal[ ] to Chicago—1914

Representative (U.S.)—representative to [ ] birth while holding office—Y. B. Burke—[ ] 23, 1973

Road—interchange structure of 4 levels—op[ ] Sept. 22, 1953

Runner—runner to run a mile indoors in less [ ] 4 minutes—J. T. Beatty—Feb. 10, 1962

Runner—runner to run a mile under four mi[ ] —Jim Bailey—May 5, 1956

Runner—transcontinental foot race—to [ ] York City—started, March 4, 1928

Secret Service—Secret Service female sp[ ] agent killed in the line of duty—J. Y. Cro[ ] June 4, 1980

Ship—gyro-stabilized American liner—*Mari*[ ] —sailed—Oct. 26, 1956

Shot Put—shot-put toss over 60 feet—Parry C[ ] en—May 8, 1954

Sleeping Car—transcontinental through Pul[ ] sleeping car service—to New York C[ ] inaugurated—March 30, 1946

Streetcar—trackless trolley system—operat[ ] Sept. 11, 1910

Surgical Operation—lung tumor operatio[ ] which the patient was under hypnosis—[ ] 1955

Swimmer—American swimmer to cover a [ ] tance of 1,500 meters free style in less tha[ ] minutes—John Kinselta—Aug. 23, 1970

Tape Recording—video recording on mag[ ] tape—Oct. 3, 1952

Television—Telecast—Academy of Motion [ ] ture Arts and Sciences annual awards tele[ ] —March 19, 1953

Television—Telecast—atomic explosion tele[ ] —Feb. 1, 1951

Television—Telecast—football game (profes[ ] al championship) telecast—Green Bay Pac[ ] vs. Kansas City Chiefs—Jan. 15, 1967

Television—Telecast—split-screen image ([ ] ways)—shown—Nov. 2, 1954

vision—Telecast—stockholders' meetings
evised coast-to-coast simultaneously—Oct.
1959
vision—Telecast—surgical operation tele-
·ed on a coast-to-coast closed circuit in color
Dec. 7, 1951
vision—Telecast—telecast images received
an airplane—May 21, 1932
vision—Telecast—three-dimensional tele-
st—KECA-TV—April 29, 1953
vision Award—National Academy of Televi-
·n Arts and Sciences award—presentation—
1. 25, 1949
vision Station—commercial television station
·st of the Mississippi River—Jan. 22, 1947
·ter—theater provided with scientific air dis-
bution—1921
k Meet—transcontinental race—began,
arch 4, 1928
rinary Hospital—municipal veterinary hospi-
—Spay and Neuter Clinic—W. E. Ziegler—
ened, Feb. 17, 1971
le—killer whale born in captivity—Marine-
ad—Feb. 28, 1977

Mare Island

—battleship (major) built on the Pacific
ast—*California*—keel laid, Oct. 25, 1916—
anched, Nov. 20, 1919—commissioned, Aug.
, 1921
—electrically propelled ship of the U.S. Navy
launched—Aug. 24, 1912
—ship transported overland across the
cky Mountains—*Brennan*—assembled and
anched as the *Bentinck*—Aug. 22, 1942
narine—streamlined submarine of the U.S.
·vy—*Nautilus*—launched—March 15, 1930
narine—submarine expressly designed and
ilt to fire guided missiles—*Grayback*—
anched—July 2, 1957

Martinez

ng Machine—presidential election in which
tes were tallied electronically—Nov. 3, 1964

Merced

y Officer—mother and son to enlist simulta-
ously—Michael Fleming and Ethel Fleming—
:t. 15, 1975
tion—Flights (world)—jet around-the-world
nstop flight—Jan. 1957

Modesto

tion—Airport—airport municipal legislation
·atified—Sept. 14, 1910

Mojave Desert

·ograph—moon close-up photographs—*Rang-
VII*—taken July 31, 1964—received at NASA
ceiving station

Montebello

Soilless Culture of Plants—commercial hydroponicum (large)—established—Dec. 5, 1935

Monterey

Army Officer—chaplain (Catholic) of the U.S.
Army—S. H. Milley—served—Sept. 28, 1849
Newspaper—newspaper published on the Pacific
coast—*Californian*—Aug. 15, 1846
Ship—naval vessel of the United States to sail
around the Cape of Good Hope to the West
Coast of the United States—arrived—Sept. 15,
1843
Ship—ship from the Atlantic coast to anchor in a
California port—*Otter*—Oct. 29, 1796
Television Station—television stations to share
the same time and frequency—KMBY-TV and
KSBW-TV (Salinas)—Sept. 11, 1953

Mount Hamilton

Motion Picture—motion picture of the planets—
Oct. 1926
Seismograph—exhibited—June 1, 1888

Mount Ophir

Mint (U.S.)—private mint authorized by the United States Government—built—1850
Money—$50 gold pieces—minted—Feb. 20, 1851

Mount Wilson

Astronomer—astronomer to measure the size of a
fixed star—F. G. Pease—Dec. 13, 1920

Muroc

See also under Edwards Air Force Base
Aviation—Airplane—airplane with a delta wing
—Convair—first flight, Sept. 18, 1948
Aviation—Airplane—bomber with the Flying
Wing design—landed—June 25, 1946
Aviation—Airplane—gas-turbine propeller-driv-
en airplane—tested—Feb. 11, 1945
Aviation—Airplane—jet-propelled airplane—
flown—Oct. 1, 1942
Aviation—Airplane—jet-propulsion four-engine
bomber—flown—March 6, 1947
Aviation—Flights—airplane to fly faster than 600
m.p.h.—Albert Boyd—June 19, 1947
Aviation—Flights—airplane to fly faster than
1,300 m.p.h.—Scott Crossfield—Nov. 20, 1953
Aviation—Flights—airplane to fly faster than the
speed of sound—C. E. Yeager—Oct. 14, 1947

Newport Bay

Aviation—Flights—over-water round-trip flight—
to Santa Catalina Island—May 10, 1912

Oakland

Aviation—Airport—airport hotel—opened—July
15, 1929

CALIFORNIA—Oakland—*Continued*

Aviation—Airship—dirigible circular flight—T. S. Baldwin—Aug. 3, 1904

Aviation—Flights (transpacific)—California–Hawaii flight—June 28, 1927

Aviation—Pilot—woman pilot to fly solo across the Pacific Ocean—A. E. Putnam—arrived—Jan. 12, 1935

Bird Refuge—authorized by a state—Feb. 14, 1872

Fingerprint Society—fingerprint society (international)—formed—Oct. 9, 1915

Forest Service—aircraft owned by the Forest Service—in service—Aug. 17, 1938

Laundry—commercial power laundry—1851

Naval Officer—naval line officer (woman) assigned to sea duty (MSTS)—C. I. Suneson—reported for duty, December 8, 1961

Radio Telephone—radio telephone concert transcontinental—from Schenectady, N.Y.—March 25, 1922

Telephone—dial-telephone long distance service —from New York City—Oct. 17, 1949

Unitarian Church—woman moderator of the Unitarian Church—A. H. Reinhardt—1940

Oceanside

Marine Corps—woman unit commander to direct 2,000 men—M. E. Bane—Camp Pendleton—Dec. 10, 1973

Otay

Glider—Flights—glider flight—J. J. Montgomery—March 17, 1884

Palm Springs

Television—Telecast—pay television presentation of a motion picture shown simultaneously in theaters—Nov. 28, 1953

Palmdale

Aviation—Flights—airplane to fly faster than 800 m.p.h.—H. A. Hanes—Aug. 20, 1955

Palo Alto

Discus—discus throw to exceed 160 feet—Eric Krenz—March 29, 1929

Geologist—woman graduate in geology—Lou Henry—1898

Hammer Throw—hammer throw to exceed 231 feet—Harold Connolly—July 21, 1962

Photograph—photograph showing action (not motion pictures)—Eadweard Muybridge—1872

Radio Broadcast—presidential nomination ceremony broadcast—H. C. Hoover—Aug. 11, 1928

Palomar Mountain

Telescope—telescope lens 200 inches in diameter —installed—1947

Pasadena

Cosmic Ray—discovered—R. A. Millikan—

Motion Picture—newsreel in color—taken— 1, 1948

Photograph—photographs taken on Mars— mitted via radio telescope in Spain—Ju 1976

Physics—positron—recognized—C. D. And —1934

Radio Broadcast—coast-to-coast football broadcast originating on the West coast—bama vs. Stanford—Rose Bowl game—J 1927

Submarine—submarine jet-propulsion devic ent—Fritz Zwicky—Feb. 15, 1949

Television—Telecast—color coast-to-coast cast from the West Coast—Tourname Roses—Jan. 1, 1954

Television—Telecast—dirigible telecast— 31, 1954

Tournament of Roses—Jan. 1, 1890

Virus—virus (human- or animal-infecting vir be crystallized—poliomyelitis virus nounced—Nov. 3, 1955

Petaluma

Locker—locker (coin vendor)—patented— Farnsworth—March 7, 1911

Playa Del Rey

See under Los Angeles

Point Arguello

Satellite—weather satellite to provide high lution nighttime cloud-cover pictures—N 1—launched at Western Test Range—Au 1964

Point Loma

Glider—Flights—glider flight in an Ame built glider to last longer than 1 hour— Bowlus—Dec. 11, 1929

Redwood City

Ship—concrete seagoing ship—*Faith*—laur —March 14, 1918

Tape Recorder—magnetic tape recorder mercial) of sound and picture—demonstra April 14, 1956

Richmond

Ship—naval ship christened by a Marine (Women's Reserve member—*Bucy* launched, Oct. 31, 1944

Riverside

Aviation—Flights (transcontinental)—trans nental round-trip airplane flight within on —to Andrews Field, Md.—June 13, 1946

CALIFORNIA—San Francisco—*Continued*

Automobile Transcontinental Trip—transcontinental automobile trip—by a nonprofessional driver—started—May 23, 1903

Automobile Transcontinental Trip—transcontinental automobile trip by a woman—arrived—Aug. 6, 1909

Aviation—flight attendant (woman)—May 15, 1930

Aviation—Airplane—transport airplane designed especially for transoceanic service—flight—to Hawaii—April 16, 1935

Aviation—Airplane Bombing—airplane bombing experiment with explosives—Jan. 7, 1911

Aviation—Flights—airplane flight to the deck of a carrier—E. B. Ely—Jan. 18, 1911

Aviation—Flights (transcontinental)—transcontinental flight within 24 hours—landed—June 23, 1924

Aviation—Flights (transpacific)—Honolulu squadron flight—Jan. 10, 1934

Aviation—Flights (world)—world flight by a commercial airplane—left—Dec. 2, 1941

Aviation—Passenger—woman airplane passenger (transcontinental)—left—Oct. 5, 1922

Aviation—Races—transcontinental air race—Oct. 8, 1919

Balloon—Flights—transcontinental nonstop balloon flight—M. L. Anderson and Kris Anderson—takeoff May 8, 1980

Bank—bank with deposits exceeding $70 million—Bank of America National Trust and Savings Association—Dec. 31, 1978

Bank—bank with resources exceeding $90 million—Bank of America National Trust and Savings Association—Dec. 31, 1978

Bank—major bank to lease personal property—Bank of America—service instituted July 22, 1963

Bed—"concealed bed"—manufactured—1909

Bicycle Racetrack of Wood—opened—July 1, 1893

Bicycle Rider—bicycle rider to go around the world—Thomas Stevens—started—April 22, 1884

Billiard Match—billiard three-ball match on a 6-by-12 carom table—April 30, 1855

Book—Book of Common Prayer—used—June 24, 1579

Bridge—bridge with piers sunk in the open sea—commenced—Jan. 5, 1933

Brokerage—exchange to specialize in mining securities—Sept. 11, 1862

Cable—cable across the Pacific Ocean—completed—Jan. 1, 1903

Chinese Embassy—landed—July 25, 1878

Dentistry—patent for a gold crown—J. B. Beer—Nov. 4, 1873

Dock—state-owned docks—Board of State Harbor Commissioners meeting—Nov. 4, 1863

Dynamite—manufactured—1866

Electric Company—electric company organized to produce and sell electricity—June 30, 1879

Equal Rights Party—formed—Sept. 20, 1884

Flea Laboratory—opened—Jan. 1, 1939

Football Team—midwestern football team to on the Pacific Coast—Univ. of Chicago—Dec. 25, 1894

Forest Service—forest commission (state)—manent)—meeting—April 1, 1885

Hospital—Chinese-American hospital—op—April 18, 1925

Immigration—Chinese immigrants—arriv 1848

Japanese Ambassador—arrived—March 9, 1

Jetway—jetway—installed—International port—July 29, 1959

Labor Union Label—adopted—Cigar Maker ternational Union—1874

Law School—law school where the faculty w years of age or over—Hastings College o Law—policy started 1940—policy firm 194

Money—$50 gold pieces minted by the U States—coined—June 15, 1915

Motorcycle Trip—motorcycle transcontin trip—to New York City—left—May 16, 19

Naval Officer—woman physician in the Me Corps Reserve of the U.S. Navy—Hulda lander—commissioned—April 19, 1944

Newspaper—Chinese daily newspaper—lished—Feb. 16, 1900

Opera—opera house municipally own opened—Oct. 15, 1932

Photograph—portrait (life-size) of a human newspaper—Larry Quinn—Nov. 14, 1935

Play (drama)—Chinese theatrical performan Oct. 18, 1852

Postage Stamp—nonpictorial postage sta United Nations stamp—issued, April 25, 1

Postal Service—overland mail service—to Ti Mo.—Sept. 15, 1858

President (U.S.)—President and President's to die during the term for which he had elected—W. G. Harding—Aug. 2, 1923

Presidential Candidate—woman presidential didate of a major political party—M. C. Sm nominated, July 15, 1964

Prizefight—prizefight timed by automatic tin Peter Jackson vs. J. J. Corbett—California letic Club—May 21, 1891

Prizefighter—pugilist to win three world cl pionships—Bob Fitzsimmons—won th Nov. 25, 1903

Public School—public school for Chinese-A cans—opened—Sept. 1859

Radio Broadcast—all-Chinese commercial program—April 22, 1940

Radio Broadcast—transpacific convers broadcast—received from Hokkaido islan pan—Oct. 6, 1911

Radio Facsimile Transmission—photograph by radio across the continent (commercial New York City—April 18, 1925

Railroad Car—"compartmentizer" freight ca in service—Sept. 12, 1952

Railroad Excursion—railroad excursion (t continental) of an organization—from Bos arrived—May 31, 1870

CALIFORNIA—Santa Monica—*Continued*

Pen—pen with truly erasable ink—Eraser Mate—produced—1979

President (U.S.)—presidential airplane—built—1944

Santa Susana Mountains

Atomic Reactor—sodium reactor (experimental)—operated—April 25, 1957

South Pasadena

Birds—ostrich farm—established—1886

Squaw Valley

Ice Skating Rink—ice skating rink (artificial) of Olympic size—formally opened Feb. 18, 1960

Stanford

Radar—radar signal bounced off the sun—April 7, 1959

Stockton

Runner—runner (American) to run a mile in less than four minutes—Don Bowden—June 1, 1957

Summerland

Oil—offshore oil wells successfully drilled in the ocean—1896

Tassajara Springs

Monastery—Zen Buddhist monastery—officially opened July 1967

Tulare County

Disease (distinctly American)—tularemia—recognized—1910

Tuscan Springs

Borax—discovered—Jan. 8, 1856

Van Nuys

Aviation—Airplane—plastic bonded airplane—built—July 1940

Woman—woman prizefight referee (licensed)—Belle Martell—April 30, 1940

Vandenberg Air Force Base

Flag—American flag to orbit the earth—*Discoverer XIII*—launched—Aug. 10, 1960

Satellite—multisatellite launching (8 satellites in 1 shot)—launched, March 9, 1965

Satellite—nuclear reactor in orbit—*SNAP 10A*—launched, April 3, 1965

Satellite—satellite in orbit built by private citizens—*Discoverer XXXVI*—launched, Dec. 12, 1961

Satellite—satellite with a nuclear reactor to c the earth—*Snapshot I*—launched, April 3,

Venice

Automobile Transcontinental Trip—transc nental automobile group tour—conclude Aug. 13, 1911

Washington

Canning—salmon cannery—erected—1864

COLORADO

Abortion Legalization Law—signed—April 1967

Child Delinquency Law (state)—passed— 28, 1909

Expedition—exploration of the Grand Canyo the Colorado—J. W. Powell—May 24, 186

Canon City

Bridge—hanging railroad bridge—built—187

Castlewood

Dam—rock-filled dam—opened—Nov. 1890

Colorado City

Automobile Trucking Service—automobile i city trucking service—to Snyder, Texas— 29, 1904

Colorado Springs

Air Force Academy (U.S.)—Air Force Acader cadets received—Aug. 29, 1958

Air Force Academy (U.S.)—Air Force Acad graduate (American Indian)—Leo Johns was graduated June 6, 1962

Air Force Academy (U.S.)—Air Force Acad graduates (black)—C. V. Bush and I. S. Pa IV—were graduated June 5, 1963

Air Force Academy (U.S.)—women students- mitted—June 28, 1976

Denver

Air Force Academy (U.S.)—Air Force Acade temporary headquarters—July 11, 1955

Air Force Academy (U.S.)—Air Force Acad woman officer—N. M. McCracken—Apr 1957

Animals—pronghorn antelope—bred and re in captivity—1903

Birds—snow goose—bred and hatched in ca ty—1934

Church—church without theology, creed, or ma—organized—1912

Football Player—football player to punt 98 y —Steve O'Neal (New York Jets)—Sept. 21,

Hospital—tuberculosis hospital—nonsectar opened—Dec. 10, 1899

onal Security Council (U.S.)—national securi-
council meeting held outside Washington,
,C.—Sept. 13, 1954

ra—opera broadcast in its entirety—*Martha*
May 19, 1921

road—railroad train to run 1,000 miles non-
op—*Zephyr*—to Chicago, Ill.—May 26, 1934

vision—Telecast—birth (human) to be tele-
sed for the public—G. C. Kerr—Dec. 2, 1952

ting Celebrities—European king buried in the
nited States—Peter Karageorgevich—died—
ov. 4, 1970

Veterans' Society—Veterans of Foreign
'ars of the United States—organized—Aug.
, 1913

logical Garden—barless zoological garden of
turalistic rock construction—completed—
18

Gilman

—underground mill for the separation of zinc
d lead—completed—1929

Golden

ege—college   silver   diploma—Colorado
hool of Mines—issued May 18, 1934

Grand Junction

tion Law—preferential ballot system—first
ction—Nov. 2, 1909

Telluride

ric Transmission—alternating current power
nsmission—installation—1890

CONNECTICUT

tration—colonial arbitration law—enacted—
53

mobile Legislation—state motorcar legisla-
n—May 21, 1901

mobile License Plates—permanent license
tes—March 1, 1937

tion—Legislation—aviation   legislation
ate)—June 8, 1911

r Legislation—approved—July 9, 1864

ding Legislation—enacted—Feb. 5, 1644

stitution—constitution—"fundamental   or-
rs"—passed—Jan. 14, 1639

right Law—copyright law (state)—passed—
n. 8, 1783

al Legislation—legislation (state) regarding
ntal hygienists—approved—May 19, 1915

adition—extradition—established—New En-
nd Confederation—1643

rnor—woman governor elected without suc-
eding her husband—R. G. O. T. Grasso—
cted, Nov. 5, 1974—sworn in, Jan. 8, 1975

d (enclosure for animals)—authorized—May
50

Supreme Court (U.S.) Decision—Supreme Court
decision between states—Connecticut vs. New
York—commenced—Aug. 5, 1799

Ansonia

Bicycle—bicycle with a rotary crank—demonstrated—1866

Copper Refinery Furnace—to use gaseous fuel—
1878

Avon

Sewing Machine—sewing machine lamp holder—
patented—L. M. N. Wolf—May 13, 1873

Berlin

Tinware Manufacturers—Pattison brothers—1740

Bloomfield

Helicopter—helicopter fully operated by remote
control—built—1953

Helicopter—helicopter with a fully servo-controlled intermeshing rotor—built—1947

Helicopter—twin gas-turbine helicopter (turborotor)—flown—March 26, 1954

Bridgeport

Airmail Service—helicopter airmail delivery—
July 5, 1946

Automobile—steam automobile—H. A. House—
1866

Aviation—Flights—airplane   flight—Gustave
Whitehead—Aug. 14, 1901

Dental School—dental hygienists' course—commenced—Nov. 17, 1913

Electric Attachment Plug (separable)—patented
—Harvey Hubbell—Nov. 8, 1904

Electric Light Socket with pull chain—patented—
Harvey Hubbell—Aug. 11, 1896

Helicopter—helicopter commercially designed—
initial flight—Feb. 16, 1946

Ordnance—bazooka   rocket   gun—produced—
June 14, 1942

Phonograph Record—long-playing microgroove
records—manufactured—1948

Television Station—ultra-high-frequency television station to operate on a regular daily basis
—KC2XAK—Dec. 29, 1949

Trading Stamp—originated—T. A. Sperry—1891

Bristol

Clock—brass clock works—invented—1837

Fishing Rod of telescoping steel tubes—patented
—Everett Horton—March 8, 1887

Spring Manufacturer—E. L. Dunbar—1845

Brooklyn

Unitarian Minister—woman ordained to the Unitarian ministry—C. C. Burleigh—parish—Oct.
5, 1871

CONNECTICUT—*Continued*

Centerbrook

Comb—ivory comb—manufactured—1789

Danbury

Hat Factory—established—Zadoc Benedict—1780

Protestant Episcopal Church—priests (husband and wife) ordained together—Michael Coburn and A. S. Coburn—Dec. 17, 1977

Danielson

Dentist—woman dentist—E. R. Jones—began practice—May 1855

Derby

Animals—sheep (merino sheep)—imported—1802

Manual Training—industrial school—Josiah Holbrook—1819

Pin—machine for manufacturing pins—patented—J. I. Howe—June 22, 1832

East Windsor

Clock—clock patent—Eli Terry—Nov. 17, 1797

Easton

Meteorite—meteorite whose landing was recorded—Dec. 14, 1807

Farmington

Cattle Club—cattle club (Guernsey cattle)—formed—March 1, 1876

Georgetown

Sieve—wire sieves—manufactured—1834

Granby

Copper Mine—company chartered—1709

Money—copper coins—1737

Greenwich

Squash Racquets Champion—woman to win the U.S.A. Women's Squash Racquets Singles championship—E. R. Sears—Jan. 19, 1928

Groton

Engine—diesel engine in a submarine—submarines commissioned—Feb. 14, 1912

Submarine—atomic-powered submarine—*Nautilus*—launched—Jan. 21, 1954

Submarine—atomic-powered turbine electric-drive submarine—*Tullibee*—launched—April 27, 1960

Submarine—ballistic missile submarine—*George Washington*—launched—June 9, 1959

Submarine—nuclear submarines launched simultaneously—*Flasher* and *Tecumseh*—June 1963

Submarine—submarine of the U.S. Navy christened by a President's wife—*Nautilus*—M D. Eisenhower—Jan. 21, 1954

Submarine—submarine powered by a liquid metal-cooled atomic reactor—*Seawolf*—launc—July 21, 1955

Submarine—submarine to have 2 complete crews—*George Washington*—blue crew reported in June—gold crew in September—ship commissioned, Dec. 30, 1959

Submarine—submarine to make more than 13 dives—served as training ship at submarine base

Submarine—submarine with two nuclear reactors—*Triton*—launched—Aug. 19, 1958

Television—submarine with closed-circuit television—*Tullibee*—launched—April 27, 1960

Gurleyville

Silk—silk dyers—1838

Hamden

Rubber—rubber shoes manufacturer—Leve Candee—1842

Hartford

Aluminum—aluminum used commercially transmission conductor—Nov. 30, 1899

Anesthesia—anesthetic in dentistry—used—race Wells—Dec. 11, 1844

Automobile Tire—pneumatic tire—manufact—1895

Aviation—Parachute—nylon parachute jun June 6, 1942

Baseball Chest Protector—chest protector catchers—invented by William Gray—1878

Belting—manufactured—1826

Bible—Bible translation by a woman—J. E. S—published—1876

Bicycle Manufacturer—bicycle factory—established—1877

Brick Machine—installed—1857

Building—elliptical-shaped office buildi Phoenix Mutual Building—completed Nov ber 1963

Clock—watch made by machinery—1838

Cookbook—cookbook of American authorsh published—1796

Cryptography Book—published—1805

Deaf—Church Service—prayers in the sign guage of the deaf—1817

Deaf—School—school for the deaf—Connec Asylum—opened—April 15, 1817

Electric Alternator—successfully operated in allel—installed—1896

Electric Generator—mercury boiler turbi placed in service—Sept. 7, 1923

tric Power Generator—steam-turbine electric
nerator—in operation, October 1901

tric Power Plant—hydroelectric power plant
use a storage battery—1896

tric Power Plant—utility-operated plant for
ntral heating and cooling—began operation
ne 25, 1962

tric Transmission—three-phase alternating
gh-frequency-current transmission—oper-
ed—March 1893

ealogy—genealogy—of American family—
blished—1771

oscope—gyroscopes—commercially manu-
ctured—June 1857

rance—accident insurance company—charted—June 17, 1863

rance—accident insurance policy—issued—
64

rance—accident insurance policy (printed)—
ued—April 1, 1864

rance—aircraft liability and property damage
surance—1919

rance—automobile insurance policy—Feb. 1,
98

rance—boiler insurance company—charted—June 1866

book—lawbook containing the federal laws
the United States—published—1791

dical—children's magazine—*Children's*
agazine—published—Jan. 1789

dent (U.S.)—President to ride in an automo-
e—Theodore Roosevelt—Aug. 22, 1902

ssion—secession convention—Dec. 15, 1814

r Plating Factory—successful—Rogers
others—1847

hers' Institute—Oct. 1839

phone—coin telephone—patented—William
ay—Aug. 13, 1889

vision—Telecast—pay program—WHCT-TV
une 29, 1962

is Match—intercollegiate lawn tennis match
une 7, 1883

edo—underwater torpedo operated by elec-
c current—invented—Samuel Colt—1841

ne—steam turbine—installed—April 1901

l—worsted mill operated by waterpower—
ganized—April 15, 1788

Huntington

sten—tungsten and tellurium—found—1819

Ivoryton

b-cutting Machine—patented—April 12, 1799

Kensington

ument—monument to commemorate the
vil War—dedicated—July 25, 1863

Killingworth

-cutting Machine—lapidary—invented—
el Buell—1766

Type Foundry—type foundry—Abel Buell—April
1, 1769

Lakeville

Cutlery Factory—cutlery factory for the manufacture of pocket cutlery—1845

Litchfield

Anthology (American)—published—1793

Clock—self-winding clock—1783

Law Reports—published—1789

Law School—law school—opened—Judge Tapping Reeve—1784

Temperance Society—temperance organization
(local)—formed—1789

Mansfield

Silk Mill—silk mill—erected—1810

Thread—silk thread—manufactured—1819

Marion

Nut and Bolt Factory—established—1840

Meriden

Piano Player—piano player (completely automatic)—manufactured—Feb. 1897

Middlebury

Lathe—profile lathe patent—Thomas Blanchard
—Sept. 6, 1819

Middletown

Agricultural Experiment Station—state agricultural experiment station—approved—July 20,
1875

Education Association—education association
(local)—organized—May 1799

Elastic Webbing—produced—Russell Manufacturing Co.—1841

Factory Standardization of Production—interchangeable parts contract with U.S. government—April 16, 1813

Normal School—normal school instruction course
given at a university—Dec. 1, 1841

Milford

Camp for Boys—established—Aug. 1861

Mystic

Ship—ironclad warship for service at sea—*Galena*—launched—Feb. 14, 1862

Naugatuck

Trade Association—American Brass Association
—organized—Feb. 1853

CONNECTICUT—*Continued*

New Haven

Baseball Batting and Fielding Cage—built—1885

Basketball—basketball intercollegiate game—Dec. 10, 1896

Bicycle—bicycle with a rotary crank—demonstrated—1866

Blotting Paper—manufactured—1856

Building—building in all-Gothic architecture—Trinity Episcopal Church—designed—1814

Caster—for furniture—patented—June 30, 1838

Chemistry Professor—professorship of applied chemistry—granted—Yale University—1846

Chinese Language and Literature Lectureship—Yale University—1877

Chinese Students—college graduate—Yung Wing—Yale University—1854

Confectionery Machine—lollipop machine—used—1908

Degrees (academic and honorary)—Doctor of Philosophy degree—awarded—Yale University—1861

Degrees (academic and honorary)—Doctor of Philosophy degree awarded to a black—Yale University—1876

Dictionary—American dictionary—*A Compendious Dictionary of the English Language,* by Noah Webster—published 1806

Extradition—extradition—New England Confederation—1643

Fine Arts Department—fine arts department in a college—School of Fine Arts—established—1864

Football Dummy—improvised by A. A. Stagg—1889

Football Game—football game played in the United States to be broadcast in England—Nov. 22, 1930

Football Game—intercollegiate football championship—1876

Football Game—international football game—Yale—Dec. 6, 1873

Football Uniform—football uniforms worn in a game—Yale vs. Harvard—Nov. 13, 1875

Geography—printed—1784

Geological Society (national)—founded—1819

Glider—amphibious seaplane glider—manufactured—1943

History—political history—Timothy Pitkin—published—1828

Ice Skating Tournament—figure skating international championship tournament—March 20, 1914

Knights of Columbus—founded—Jan. 16, 1882

Map—map of the United States—engraved—Abel Buell—1783

Milk—acidophilus milk—devised—1920

Money—Continental coin—manufactured—1787

Museum—college art museum—Trumbull Art Gallery of Yale University—founded—1832

Music Periodical—*American Musical Magazine*—published—May 1786

Newspaper—college daily—*Yale News*—lished—Jan. 28, 1878

Novel Course—course on the contemporary n—W. L. Phelps—1895

Paleontology Chair—in a college—establish 1866

Periodical—college magazine—*Literary Cal*—published—Nov. 15, 1806

Photograph—class photograph—S. F. B. Mor Yale College—Aug. 18, 1840

Physician—doctor to receive an honorary me degree—Daniel Turner—Sept. 11, 1723

Physiology Laboratory—established—1874

Pituitary Hormone—pituitary hormone isolat announced—July 23, 1937

Planetarium—planetarium or orrery buil America—Thomas Clap—1743

Rowing—college to feature rowing—1844

Sprinkler—sprinkler head—patented—H. S. melee—Aug. 11, 1874

Stone Crusher—patented—E. W. Blake—Jun 1858

Swimmer—swimmer to cover a distance of meters free style in less than 5 minutes—Jo Weissmuller—March 6, 1923

Tape Measure Patent—patented—A. J. Fello July 14, 1868

Telephone—pay station telephone service—1, 1880

Telephone—telephone switchboard or exch (commercial)—installed—Jan. 28, 1878

Telephone Directory—issued—Feb. 21, 1878

Theatrical School—theater and dramatic cism course—to award a Ph.D.—establish Sept. 24, 1934

Tornado—tornado of which there is any recc June 10, 1682

Trapshooting—trapshooting intercollegiate a ciation—meet held—May 7, 1898

New London

Coast Guard Academy—black graduate—N Smith, Jr.—June 8, 1966

Coast Guard Academy—women graduates—Butler—May 21, 1980

Coast Guard Academy—women students mitted June 28, 1976

College President—woman college preside two colleges—Rosemary Park—Connec College for Women—inaugurated (first) 17, 1947

Hospital—eye infirmary—established—E North—1817

Mine Barrage—David Bushnell—Aug. 1777

Navy—atomic submarine division—form March 31, 1958

Ship—steam whaler—*Pioneer*—converted b W. Williams—1865

Submarine—submarine to cross the Atl Ocean under its own power—*E-1*—retu Sept. 17, 1918

marine—submarine to cross the Atlantic cean within 9 days—*Skate*—left, Feb. 24, 1958
marine—submarine to travel under ice for 12 ys—*Skate*—left, March 4, 1959
marine—submarine to travel under the North le from the East—*Skate*—left, July 30, 1958
marine—submarines to rendezvous at the rth Pole—*Skate*—left July 7—returned Aug. , 1962
marine-Escape Training Tank—in operation Aug. 15, 1930
marine-Escape Training Tank—women to ke the submarine-escape test—certified—July , 1943

New Milford

tric Lighting—streetlight of an automatic sys- m—installed—March 2, 1949

North Canaan

rance—hail insurance—on growing tobacco ops—1880

North Windham

rmaking Machinery—papermaking machine ourdrinier) imported—installed—Jan. 1828

Northfield

ed Church of Christ—United Church of Christ dination of a woman minister in which all the ncipal roles were filled by women—D. F. abtree—Sept. 17, 1972

Norwich

writer—typewriter that successfully typed— tented—Charles Thurber—Aug. 26, 1843

Old Mystic

odist Church—black Methodist minister of all-white congregation—S. P. Montgomery— t. 2, 1955

Putnam

ad—nontwisted sewing thread—manufac- ed—1946

Riverton

r Factory—Lambert Hitchcock—established 818

Rocky River

ric Power Plant—hydroelectric power plant use water pumped into a reservoir—Con- cticut Light and Power Co.—1927

Salem

c Instruction—music school authorized to nfer degrees—established—Oramel Whitt- ey—1835

Salisbury

Library—youth's library—established—Jan. 1803

Saugatuck

Building—building devoted entirely to highway traffic—completed—July 1, 1939

Saybrook

Submarine—submarine for use in war—*American Turtle*—built—David Bushnell—1776

Seymour

Auger (screw auger)—manufactured—Walter French—1810

Simsbury

Fuse—Cordeau-Bickford detonating fuse—introduced—1913
Fuse—safety fuse—manufactured—1836
Fuse—textile-wrapped detonating fuse—manufactured—1936
Steel—steel—manufactured—Samuel Higley— May 1728

South Killingly

Woman—woman granted a patent—Mary Kies— May 5, 1809

South Norwalk

Hat—derby hat—manufactured—1850

South Windham

Papermaking Machinery—papermaking machine (Fourdrinier)—manufactured—1829

Stamford

Crane—crane—manufactured—1883
Postal Service—coin-operated mailbox—patented—L. A. Thatcher—July 28, 1942
Postal Service—postage meter—officially set— Nov. 16, 1920
Railroad Signal System—railroad signal system (automatic electric block)—patented—T. S. Hall—June 7, 1870
Razor—electric dry shaver—manufactured— March 18, 1931
Ship—ambulance ship for first aid to boaters and pleasure craft—*Star of Life No. 1*—christened, April 2, 1976
Shoe Measuring Stick—introduced—1657
Telegraph—telegraph code converter—announced—Oct. 1854
Typewriter—portable typewriter—patented—G. C. Blickensderfer—April 12, 1892

Stanfield

Cider Mill—patented—Isaac Quintard—April 5, 1806

CONNECTICUT—*Continued*

Stonington

Discovery—discovery of Antarctica—July 25, 1820—expedition sailed

Stratford

Aviation—Flights (transatlantic)—transatlantic solo westward flight—J. A. Mollison—July 23, 1933

Aviation—Pilot—woman pilot to fly across the Atlantic Ocean east–west—A. J. Mollison—crashed—July 23, 1933

Helicopter—helicopter (direct-lift aircraft)—constructed—Oct. 1939

Helicopter—Flights—helicopter flight (cross-country)—May 13, 1942

Helicopter—Flights—helicopter flight from water —April 17, 1941

Helicopter—Flights—helicopter flight of one-hour duration—April 15, 1941

Suffield

See West Suffield

Tariffville

Aluminum—aluminum used commercially in a transmission conductor—Hartford Electric Light Co.—Nov. 30, 1899

Thomaston

Clock—clock (one-day back-wind alarm clock)—in metal case—1876

Torrington (Wolcottville)

Brass Kettles—made—Coe Brass Co.—1834
Brass Rod—drawn—Coe Brass Co.—1873
Brass Spinning—process used—1851
Milk—condensed milk (commercial)—condensery established—1856
Needles (machine-made)—manufactured—1866
Wire—wire-cutting machine and automatic straightener—invented—1866

Trumbull

Fluorspar—commercial mining—1837

Wallingford

Coffee Mill Patent—James Carrington—April 3, 1829
Spoons—nickel silver spoons—manufactured—Robert Wallace—1835

Waterbury

Brass—rolled—Abel Porter & Co.—1802
Brass Spinning—patented—H. W. Hayden—Dec. 16, 1851
Brass Wire Drawing and Tube-making Machinery —imported—1831

Button—gilt buttons to be commercially manu tured—Abel Porter & Co.—1802
Button—pewter or block tin buttons—man tured—1790
Fastening—hooks and eyes—successfully m factured—1836
Postage Stamp—encased postage stamps— duced by Scovill Button Works

Watertown

Sewing Machine—sewing machine to sew ing seams—patented—A. B. Wilson—Dec 1854
Thread—silk thread on spools—Merritt He way—1849

West Haven

Photoelectric Cell—photoelectric cell inst commercially—June 19, 1931

West Suffield

Cigar Factory—of importance—establish Simeon Viets—1810

West Torrington

Wire—brass   wire—manufactured—E Hodges—1840

Weston

See under Easton

Westville

Lock—mortised lock—introduced—Blake Br 1835

Wethersfield

Election—election in defiance of the Royal C —April 11, 1640

Windsor

Umbrella—used—1740

Windsor Locks

Helicopter—gas-turbine helicopter (turborot tested—Dec. 10, 1951
Helicopter—helicopter fully operated by re control—flown—July 1953
Helicopter—helicopter with a fully servo trolled intermeshing rotor—flown—Jan. 1

Wolcottville

See Torrington and West Torrington

DELAWARE

Electric Home and Farm Authority—incorpo —Jan. 17, 1934
Fertilizer Law (state)—enacted—March 16,
Poorhouse (state)—replaced by state ho closed—Dec. 1933

llion—rebellion of colonists against the
glish—Marcus Jacobson—condemned—Dec.
1669

e Tax—single tax political ticket—formed—
t. 1896

—state to ratify the federal Constitution—
. 7, 1787

Brandywine

making Machinery—papermaking machine
linder)—manufactured—Thomas Gilpen—
g. 1817

Cooch's Bridge

-American flag flown in battle—Sept. 3, 1777

Fort Christina

ran Church—Lutheran pastor—Reorus Tor-
us—arrived—April 17, 1640

Georgetown

ion—Parachute—parachute jumper snagged
midair—C. M. Alexander—Aug. 29, 1966

Newark

ge—"Junior Year Abroad"—instituted—
versity of Delaware—July 7, 1923

Seaford

—nylon yarn manufacture (commercial)—
mmenced—Dec. 15, 1939

Wilmington

e (polymethyl methacrylate) Production
mmercial)—May 21, 1936

-concentrated milk—sold—Nov. 30, 1950

—nylon—patented—W. H. Carothers—
. 16, 1937

Telephone—radio telephone communica-
(one-way)—from Montauk Point, N.Y.—
il 4, 1915

er—synthetic rubber produced on a com-
rcial scale—Nov. 2, 1931

-Christmas seals of the modern variety, sold
aise funds to fight tuberculosis—designed—
. Bissell—sold—Dec. 9, 1907

-iron steamship built for transatlantic ser-
e—Bangor—launched—May 1844

-merchant ship of the U.S. commanded by a
ck captain—Booker T. Washington—
nched—Sept. 29, 1942

nilamide—sulfanilamide—produced—Dec.
0

es—landed—1638

hone—mobile telephone conversation with
mmercial equipment—automobile to an air-
ne—Oct. 9, 1947

DISTRICT OF COLUMBIA

Slavery—law abolishing slavery in the District of
Columbia—enacted April 16, 1862

Anacostia

See under Washington

Georgetown

See under Washington

Washington

Agricultural Journal—agricultural journal—issued—July 4, 1810

Agricultural Society—agricultural society of national importance—organized—Dec. 4, 1867

Agricultural Soil Conference—June 13, 1917

Agriculture Bureau—agriculture bureau scientific
publication—issued—Oct. 15, 1862

Air Force—Air Force Secretary—W. S. Symington
—sworn in—Sept. 18, 1947

Air Force Officer—Air Force chairman of the Joint
Chiefs of Staff—N. F. Twining—sworn in—Aug.
15, 1957

Air Force Officer—Air Force general (woman)—J.
M. Holm—commissioned July 16, 1971

Air Force Officer—brigadier general (black) in the
Air Force—B. O. Davis, Jr.—appointed—Oct.
27, 1954

Airmail—dirigible to drop mail by parachute—
Graf Zeppelin—Oct. 15, 1928

Airmail Service—airmail experimental route—to
New York City and Philadelphia—May 15, 1918

Airmail Service—airplane mail pickup—demonstrated—Oct. 1, 1929

Almanac—almanac bibliography—published—
1907

American Indians—American Indian tribal constitution—signed—Oct. 28, 1935

American Red Cross—organized—Clara Barton
—May 21, 1881

Archival Administration—course offered—Sept.
25, 1940

Army Auxiliary Corps—woman to become a
member of the Women's Army Corps—sworn
in—July 8, 1948

Army Officer—chaplain (Catholic) appointed by
the President—June 13, 1862

Army Officer—chaplain (black) of the U.S. Army
—H. M. Turner—commissioned—1863

Army War College—Army War College—cornerstone laid—Feb. 21, 1903

Astronomer—woman astronomer employed in
the U.S. Naval Observatory—E. A. Lamson—
July 20, 1900

Astronomical Observations Book—published—
1838

Autogiro—autogiro of the U.S. Government—
delivered to Anacostia Station—June 1, 1931

Autogiro—autogiro to land on the White House
lawn—J. G. Ray—April 22, 1931

Aviation—airplane high-speed tank to test airplanes—completed—May 1931

DISTRICT OF COLUMBIA—Washington
—*Continued*

Aviation—airplane to land on the White House lawn—H. N. Atwood—July 14, 1911

Aviation—Airplane—airplane to land at the U.S. Capitol—L. B. Sperry—March 23, 1922

Aviation—Airport—airport (federally owned and operated)—Washington National Airport—opened—June 16, 1941

Aviation—Airship—airship filled with helium gas —R. F. Wood—round trip from Hampton Roads, Va.—Dec. 4, 1921

Aviation—Flights—airplane catapulted—successfully—Nov. 12, 1912

Aviation—License—glider license class "C"—first woman—H. M. Barnaby—Aug. 12, 1931

Aviation—Pilot—woman pilot to pilot an airmail transport—Helen Richey—to Detroit, Mich.—Dec. 31, 1934

Bank—bank for blacks privately operated by blacks—organized—Oct. 17, 1888

Bank—Export-Import bank—organized—Feb. 8, 1934

Bank—Freedmen's bank—Freedman's Savings and Trust Co.—chartered—March 3, 1865

Baseball Game—baseball game (major league) in which 14 runs were scored in 1 inning—July 6, 1920

Baseball Player—baseball player to catch a ball dropped from the Washington Monument—Aug. 29, 1892

Baseball Umpire—baseball umpire (major-league) to wear eyeglasses—E. A. Rommel—April 18, 1956

Baseball Umpire—baseball umpire (major league) who was a black—E. L. Ashford—officiated, April 12, 1966

Bird Legislation (international)—Migratory Bird Treaty—signed—Aug. 16, 1916

Births—child born in the White House, Washington, D.C.—Jan. 17, 1806

Births—child born in the White House, Washington, D.C., the offspring of a President—Sept. 9, 1893

Boy Scouts of America—Boy Scouts of America—incorporated—Feb. 8, 1910

Building—atom-bomb-resistant federal building —dedicated—May 23, 1955

Building—building erected by the government in Washington, D.C.—Executive Mansion—cornerstone laid—Oct. 13, 1792

Building—building with prefabricated walls of mosaic concrete—completed—Feb. 1935

Building—"State House" located outside a state —Florida House—opened Oct. 26, 1973

Business School—business high school—opened —Sept. 22, 1890

Cabinet (U.S.)—black sub-Cabinet member—J. E. Wilkins—sworn in—March 18, 1954

Cabinet (U.S.)—Cabinet conference telecast—June 3, 1953

Cabinet (U.S.)—Cabinet meeting attended by a foreign national—April 20, 1965

Cabinet (U.S.)—Cabinet member convicted crime—A. B. Fall—Oct. 25, 1929

Cabinet (U.S.)—full Cabinet sworn in at the time and place—March 4, 1933

Cabinet (U.S.)—Secretary of Health, Educ and Welfare—O. C. Hobby—sworn in— 11, 1953

Capitol (U.S.)—body to lie in state in the C rotunda—Henry Clay—July 1, 1852

Capitol (U.S.)—cornerstone laid—Sept. 18,

Capitol (U.S.)—President's body to lie in st the Capitol rotunda—Abraham Lincoln— 19-21, 1865

Casein Fiber—patented—Dec. 13, 1938

Catholic Apostolic Delegate—perman arrived—Jan. 24, 1893

Catholic Church—eucharistic congress o Catholic Church—Francesco Satolli—O 1895

Cemetery—congressional cemetery—1804

Cemetery—national cemeteries—authoriz July 17, 1862

Chamber of Commerce—Chamber of Comr of the United States of America—headqua dedicated—May 20, 1925

Chess Champion—chess champion to play than 100 games simultaneously—F. J. Mar —March 21, 1916

Children's Welfare Congress (internation March 10-17, 1908

Chinaware—dishes (complete set) mad America for the Executive Mansion—deli —July 31, 1918

Chinese Embassy—Oct. 4, 1878

Civil Service—woman Civil Service commis er—H. H. Gardener—sworn in—April 13,

College—Catholic college—Georgetown C —opened—Nov. 15, 1791

College—university for blacks to establish u graduate, graduate, and professional scho Howard University—founded—Nov. 20, 1

Conference—conference of great powers— 12, 1921

Conference—Pan American Conference—op —Oct. 2, 1889

Congress (U.S.)—congressional session in conditioned Senate and House chamb Nov. 15, 1937

Congress (U.S.)—Prime Minister of England dress the Congress of the United States— say MacDonald—Oct. 7, 1929

Congress (U.S.)—reigning queen to addre joint session of Congress—Queen Wilhel —Aug. 6, 1942

Congress (U.S.)—woman private citizen t dress the House of Representatives an Senate—Mme. Chiang Kai-Shek—Feb. 18,

Congress (U.S.)—House of Representati black preacher to deliver a sermon in the F of Representatives—Feb. 12, 1865

Congress (U.S.)—House of Representati House of Representatives—first sessio Washington—Nov. 17, 1800

DISTRICT OF COLUMBIA—Washington
—Continued

Medal—National Geographic Society gold medal —Hubbard medal—presented—R. E. Peary— Dec. 15, 1906

Medal—National Geographic Society special gold medal—presented—A. E. Putnam—June 21, 1932

Medal—Navy-Marine Corps Medal for Heroism awarded to a woman—awarded—B. O. Barnwell—Aug. 7, 1953

Medal—Reserve Officers Association medal presented—H. S. Truman—Jan. 15, 1953

Medal—soldier to receive seven decorations at one time—L. M. Chilson—Dec. 6, 1946

Medical Congress—Mental Hygiene International Congress—opened—May 4, 1930

Medical Society—American College of Surgeons —organized—May 5, 1913

Medical Society—black medical society—organized—April 24, 1884

Microfilm—microfilm reading device—patented —B. A. Fiske—March 28, 1922

Money—bill of $100,000 denomination—issued for use within Federal Reserve System—January 1935

Monument—bronze equestrian statue—unveiled —Jan. 8, 1853

Monument—monument by a woman ordered by the U.S. Government—July 28, 1866

Monument—monument to George Washington (national)—capstone set—Dec. 6, 1884

Monument—statue cast by the U.S. Government —accepted—April 25, 1881

Monument—statue of a woman in National Statuary Hall—dedicated—Feb. 17, 1905

Mosque—Islamic Center—cornerstone laid—Jan. 11, 1949

Motion Picture—talking pictures of presidential candidates—taken—Aug. 11, 1924

Naturalization—naturalization ceremony in the White House—Nov. 23, 1968

Naval Officer—chaplain to win a Congressional Medal of Honor—J. T. O'Callahan—presentation—Jan. 23, 1946

News Correspondent—black news correspondent accredited to the White House—Harry McAlpin—Feb. 8, 1944

News Correspondent—black news correspondent admitted to the House of Representatives and Senate press gallery—P. L. Prattis—accredited Feb. 3, 1947

News Correspondent—White House reporter— W. W. Price—employed—April 24, 1897

Newspaper—newspaper with perfumed advertising page—issued—March 25, 1937

Nursing School—Army School of Nursing—authorized—May 25, 1918

Observatory—observatory (national)—established—Dec. 6, 1830

Pan American Union—established—April 14, 1890

Parent-Teacher Association—parent-teacher association (national)—organized—Feb. 17, 1897

Parliamentary Rules of Order—printed—18●

Periodical—magazine of the United States ernment—issued—March 14, 1936

Photograph—photograph bounced off the mo received—Jan. 28, 1960

Photograph—photograph showing air in moti 1918

Photograph—photographs in color of the hea published in a magazine—*National Geogr Magazine*—May 1959 issue

Physician—Capitol physician—G. W. Cal● Dec. 8, 1928

Plow—plow for pulverizing the soil—paten● George Page—Aug. 7, 1847

Police—police officer (woman) killed in the li duty—G. A. Cobb—Sept. 20, 1974

Police—police training school of the Federa reau of Investigation—initiated—July 29,

Political Convention—political nomin caucus attended by party leaders—Feb. 25.

Political Platform (national)—adopted—Ma 1832

Post Office—airplane post office—dedica● May 15, 1938

Postage Stamp—certified-mail stamp—is. June 6, 1955

Postage Stamp—Christmas-stamp annual s depicting both a religious and nonreligious ject—issued, Nov. 10, 1971

Postage Stamp—flag series honoring cour overrun by Axis forces—issued June 22, 1

Postage Stamp—fractional-denomination po stamp—Harding stamp—issued, March 19,

Postage Stamp—gravure-printed postage sta● The Biglin Brothers Racing—issued, No● 1967

Postage Stamp—Jew depicted on a postage s —Samuel Gompers—issued, Jan. 27, 1950

Postage Stamp—native American pictured postage stamp—Chief Joseph—stamp on Nov. 4, 1968

Postage Stamp—one-dollar-valuation po● stamp—Queen Isabella Pledging Her Jew● issued, Jan. 2, 1893

Postage Stamp—postage stamp featuring a ● of art in true color—on sale, Oct. 4, 1961

Postage Stamp—postage stamp in 3 colors pr in 1 passing of each sheet through the pr● American flag stamp—issued, July 4, 1957

Postage Stamp—postage stamp in two colors duced by the rotary process at the Bure● Engraving and Printing—1952

Postage Stamp—postage stamp on which w● scribed the name of a living American—is —June 18, 1927

Postage Stamp—postage stamp printed on ● color Huck press—multicolored Chris● stamp—issued, Nov. 1, 1968

Postage Stamp—postage stamp to honor a ● woman—Harriet Tubman—issued, Feb. 1,

Postage Stamp—postage stamps in coils—is —Feb. 18, 1908

DISTRICT OF COLUMBIA—Washington
—Continued

Radio Telephone—telephone call to the moon—R. M. Nixon to N. A. Armstrong and E. E. Aldrin, Jr.—July 20, 1969

Radio Telephone—two-way radio equipped bus in service—Sept. 8, 1945

Railroad—air-conditioned train—installed—May 24, 1931

Railroad—railroad to run trains to Washington, D.C.—trial trip—July 1, 1835

Saboteurs—saboteurs executed—6 electrocuted—Aug. 8, 1942

Senator (U.S.)—black senator to preside over the Senate—B. K. Bruce of Mississippi—Feb. 15, 1879

Sewing Machine—sewing machine patent—J. J. Greenough—Feb. 21, 1842

Soldiers' Home—woman admitted to a soldiers' home—R. C. Jones—Sept. 2—permanent admission granted, Sept. 16, 1955

Solicitor General (U.S.)—solicitor general of the United States who was a black—Thurgood Marshall—first case tried—Oct. 13, 1965

Sorority—black sorority—Alpha Kappa Alpha—founded—Jan. 15, 1908

Supreme Court (U.S.)—black page of the Supreme Court—C. V. Bush—served—Sept. 27, 1954

Surgical Operation—artificial aortic valve—C. A. Hufnagel—fitted—Sept. 11, 1952

Surgical Operation—lobotomy (prefrontal)—Drs. J. W. Watts and Walter Freeman—Sept. 14, 1956

Swimming Pool in the White House—formally accepted—June 2, 1933

Telegram—news dispatch telegram—to Baltimore, Md.—May 25, 1844

Telegram—telegram inaugurating commercial service—May 24, 1844

Telegraph—telegraph appropriation (federal)—March 3, 1843

Telegraph—telegraph station—opened—1844

Telephone—commercial telephone service on railroad trains for passengers—in operation—Aug. 15, 1947

Telephone—hot line—to Moscow, Russia—Aug. 30, 1962

Telephone—picturephone service (commercial)—to Chicago, Ill., and New York City—inaugurated, June 24, 1964

Telephone—satellite (privately owned) telephone conversation—L. B. Johnson from F. R. Kappel—from Andover, Me. via *Telestar 1*—July 10, 1962

Telephone—telephone conversation (commercial) over a satellite—to Europe via *Early Bird I*—June 28, 1965

Telephone—telephone service over the transpacific telephone cable—to Tokyo, Japan—June 18, 1964

Telephone—underground cable long-distance telephone conversation—to Boston, Mass.—Feb. 26, 1914

Television—Telecast—airplane telecast work)—Dec. 17, 1948

Television—Telecast—Cabinet session to be vised—Oct. 25, 1954

Television—Telecast—congressional ope session to be televised—Jan. 3, 1947

Television—Telecast—congressional session ceedings telecast—June 12, 1978

Television—Telecast—congressional tele and radio broadcast—authorized by Se Dec. 14—aired, Dec. 19, 1974

Television—Telecast—medical intercity telecast—from Johns Hopkins Hospital, timore, Md.—Dec. 6, 1949

Television—Telecast—presidential address vised from the White House—H. S. Trum Oct. 5, 1947

Television—Telecast—presidential news co ence filmed for television and newsreels—19, 1955

Television—Telecast—presidential news co ence to be televised live—J. F. Kennedy—25, 1961

Television—Telecast—prizefight (heavyw championship bout) to be televised—rece —Louis-Conn fight—June 19, 1946

Television—Telecast—Senate proceedings cast—vice presidential installation ceren for N. A. Rockefeller—Dec. 19, 1974

Television—Telecast—split-screen image ways)—shown—Nov. 2, 1954

Television—Telecast—state dinner (U.S.) tele —July 7, 1976

Television—Telecast—telecast (long-dista received in an airplane—Oct. 17, 1939

Television—Telecast—telecast of an objec motion—June 13, 1925

Television—Telecast—weather map telecast ceived—Aug. 18, 1926

Television License—television license—issu Feb. 25, 1928

Temperance Society—Anti-Saloon League tional organization)—formed—Dec. 17–18,

Time, Standard—standard time—adopted—18, 1883

Typesetting Machine—monotype—patent Tolbert Lanston—June 7, 1887

Veto (presidential)—veto message read President—May 22, 1935

Vice President (U.S.)—Vice President appo (not elected by popular vote) to become P dent—G. R. Ford—sworn in—Oval Room o White House—Aug. 9, 1974

Vice President (U.S.)—Vice President to d office—George Clinton—April 20, 1812

Vice President (U.S.)—Vice President to pre at a National Security Council meeting—Nixon—July 14, 1953

Vice Presidential Candidate—vice preside nominee to decline nomination—John Lan —May 12, 1812

Visiting Celebrities—king (reigning) to visi United States—David Kalakaua of Haw Dec. 15, 1874

FLORIDA—Cape Canaveral (Cape Kennedy)— *Continued*

Astronaut—space flight by an American astronaut—A. B. Shepard—May 5, 1961

Astronaut—three-man spaceflight (American)— *Apollo VII*—launched—Oct. 11, 1968

Astronaut—two-man spaceflight (American) of 3 orbits—J. W. Young and V. I. Grissom—*Gemini III* ("Molly Brown")—launched, March 23, 1965

Astronaut—two-man spaceflight (American) of 62 orbits—*Gemini IV*—launched, June 3, 1965

Astronaut—two-man spaceflight (American) of 120 orbits—*Gemini V*—launched, Aug. 21, 1965

Photograph—photograph in color of the earth from outer space—Dec. 1, 1959

President (U.S.)—President to attend the launching of a manned spaceflight—R. M. Nixon—Nov. 14, 1969

President (U.S.)—President to witness the firing of a Polaris missile—J. F. Kennedy—Nov. 16, 1963

Rocket—American spacecraft to impact the moon—*Ranger VI*—launched, Jan. 30, 1964

Rocket—intermediate-range ballistic missile—Jupiter—fired—May 31, 1957

Rocket—rocket cone recovery—Aug. 8, 1957

Satellite—American satellite to reach the moon— *Ranger IV*—launched—April 23, 1962

Satellite—animal fired into space to orbit the earth—Enos—launched, Nov. 29, 1961

Satellite—biosatellite—launched, Dec. 14, 1966

Satellite—biosatellite (successful)—launched, Sept. 7, 1967

Satellite—communications earth satellite to transmit telephone, television, teleprint, and facsimile signals—launched, Dec. 13, 1962

Satellite—communications satellite—launched—Aug. 12, 1960

Satellite—communications satellite successfully placed in orbit—launched, Oct. 4, 1960

Satellite—geodetic satellite—*Anna 1B*—launched, Oct.31, 1962

Satellite—international satellite—*Ariel 1*—launched, April 26, 1962

Satellite—manned docking of 2 spacecraft— *Gemini VIII*—launched, March 16, 1966

Satellite—multisatellite launching—*Transit 2-A* —launched, June 22, 1960

Satellite—multisatellite launching (3 satellites in 1 shot)—*Omicron 1*—launched, June 29, 1961

Satellite—multisatellite launching (5 satellites in 1 shot)—*Composite 1*—launched, Jan. 24, 1962

Satellite—navigational satellite—*Transit 1-B*—launched, April 13, 1960

Satellite—orbiting geophysical observatory— *OGO 1*—launched—Sept. 4, 1964

Satellite—orbiting solar—observatory satellite— *OSO 1*—launched, March 7, 1962

Satellite—privately-owned satellite—*Telstar 1*—launched, July 10, 1962

Satellite—satellite fueled by liquid hydrogen successfully orbited—*Centaur II*—launched, Nov. 27, 1963

Satellite—satellite launched from another enly body—*Surveyor 6*—launched, Nov. 7

Satellite—satellite placed in orbit—*Explo* —Jan. 31, 1958

Satellite—satellite placed in solar orbit—*Pi V*—launched—March 11, 1960

Satellite—satellite to transmit a close-up p graph of Mars—*Mariner 4*—launched, No 1964

Satellite—satellite to transmit colored p graphs of the full earth face—*Do* launched, July 1, 1967

Satellite—satellite to transmit data from Ver *Mariner 2*—launched, Aug. 27, 1962

Satellite—satellite to transmit lunar-orbit p graphs—*Lunar Orbiter 1*—launched, Au 1966

Satellite—satellite to transmit lunar-su close-up pictures—*Ranger VII*—launched. 28, 1964

Satellite—satellite to transmit photographs earth—Aug. 7, 1959

Satellite—satellite to use a fuel cell—*Gem* —launched, Aug. 21, 1965

Satellite—satellite with a nuclear power dev *Transit IV-A*—launched at Atlantic M Range—June 29, 1961

Satellite—satellite with spring-folded wings tercept bombardment of tiny meteoro *Pegasus 1*—launched, Feb. 16, 1965

Satellite—surveillance satellite that was suc ful—*Midas II*—launched, May 24, 1960

Satellite—synchronous satellite—*Syncom* launched, July 26, 1963

Satellite—weather-observation satellite—*T* —launched, April 1, 1960

Ship—ship to transport fresh orange jui stainless-steel tanks—Feb. 16, 1957

Submarine—submerged submarine to fire a ris missile—*George Washington*—July 20,

Television—Telecast—transoceanic telev program—satellite launched—July 10, 196

Cape Kennedy

See under Cape Canaveral, above named July 21, 1972)

Cocoa Beach

Ship Motion Simulator—ship motion simula built and installed at Missile Testing Cen 1958

Coral Gables

College—college to offer athletic scholarshi women—University of Miami—first recip Terry Williams—May 5, 1973

Weather Bureau(U.S.)—Weather Bureau w employee—Joanne Simpson—National F cane and Experimental Meteorology Labo ry—1963–1973

Daytona Beach

tomobile—automobile to exceed the speed of
00 miles an hour—H. O. Segrave—March 29,
927

tomobile Racer—automobile racer to win the
)aytona 500 six times—Richard Petty—sixth
ictory Feb. 18, 1979

sel Engine—diesel-engine speed record (offi-
ial)—C. L. Cummins—March 20, 1930

Fort Caroline

ths—white child of French Protestant parent-
ge—born—1565

r (colonial)—intercolonial war—commenced
—Sept. 20, 1565

Fort Jefferson

son—military prison of the United States on an
sland—construction started—1846

Gainesville

e Vault—pole vault higher than 18.5 feet—
)ave Roberts—March 28, 1975

Hialeah

nera—photo-finish camera (electric-eye) in-
talled at a racetrack—Jan. 16, 1936

key—jockey (woman) to ride in a pari-mutuel
ace on a flat track—Diane Crump—Feb. 7, 1969

Hollywood

ving—transatlantic solo trip by rowboat—
ohn Fairfax—arrived, July 19

Jacksonville

mail Service—missile mail (official)—landed
—June 8, 1959

ation—Flights (transcontinental)—transconti-
ental airplane flight (eastbound)—R. G. Fowl-
r—landed—Feb. 8, 1912

ation—Flights (transcontinental)—transconti-
ental flight in 24 hours' flying time—from San
)iego—landed—Feb. 24, 1921

oteurs—saboteurs executed— 4 landed—
onte Vedra Beach—June 17, 1942

Key Largo

k—underseas park (federal)—Key Largo Coral
eef Preserve—established—March 15, 1960

Key West

togiro—Flights—autogiro flight over an open
ea—L. A. Yancey—takeoff Jan. 24, 1932

ation—airplane rescue at sea—J. A. D.
1cCurdy—Jan. 30, 1911

ation—hydroplane commercial line service
nternational)—established—Nov. 1, 1920

ation—Airport—air passenger international
tation—opened—Oct. 28, 1927

Aviation—Flights—sky-train international round-
trip flight—started—May 14, 1935

President (U.S.)—President to conduct ministerial
services as commander-in-chief of the Navy—
F. D. Roosevelt—April 1, 1934

President (U.S.)—President to travel underwater
in a captured enemy submarine—H. S. Truman
—Nov. 21, 1946

Telephone—telephone cable service (deep-sea)—
established—April 11, 1921

Aviation—Legislation—aviation legislation (municipal)—enacted in August 1908

Marathon

Aviation—Airplane—skyjack of a commercial
American airplane—Antillo Ortiz—May 1, 1961

Marineland

Aquarium—aquarium for monsters of the deep—
opened—June 23, 1938

Aquatic Mammals—porpoise—born in captivity
—Feb. 14, 1940

Miami

Airmail Service—airmail service between North
and South America—May 14, 1929

Births—child born in an airplane—Oct. 28, 1929

Federal Savings and Loan Association—created
—Aug. 8, 1933

Greyhound Racing Association—formed—March
3, 1926

Motorboat Race—motorboat race (ocean) under
the Union of International Motorboating rules
—to Bimini, Bahamas—Feb. 22, 1966

Pole Vault—pole vault higher than 17 feet—John
Pennel—Aug. 24, 1963

President (U.S.)—president to fly in an airplane
while in office—F. D. Roosevelt—Jan. 14, 1943

President (U.S.)—President's wife to travel in an
airplane to a foreign country—Eleanor Roosevelt—left, March 6, 1934

Ship—woman to sail solo across the Atlantic
Ocean—Ann Davidson—arrived—Aug. 12,
1953

Television—Telecast—live telecast from a noncontiguous foreign country—received Nov. 13,
1955

Totalisator—totalisator used—Jan. 14, 1932

Miami Beach

Bridge (game) Player—father and son team to win
a national contract bridge championship—Oswald Jacoby and James Jacoby—Dec. 1, 1955

Medal—Legion of Merit Medal awarded to a foreign national—presentation—Nov. 7, 1942

Political Party—permanent chairman (woman) of
a major political party—F. J. M. Westwood—
elected, July 14, 1972

Television—Telecast—political convention telecast in color—29th Republican National Convention—Aug. 5-7, 1968

FLORIDA—*Continued*

Milton

Coast Guard (U.S.)—woman airplane pilot in the Coast Guard—Janna Lambine—was graduated on March 4, 1977

Orlando

Football Player—woman football player (professional)—Patricia Palinkas—Aug. 15, 1970
Naval Officer—naval chaplain (woman)—F. D. Pohlman—assigned to Naval Training Center
Postage Stamp—twin postage stamps—issued, Sept. 29, 1967

Palm Beach

Restaurant—revolving restaurant—The Top of the Needle, Seattle, Wash.—opened by remote control by J. F. Kennedy—April 21, 1962

Pelican Island

Bird Reservation (national)—established—March 14, 1903

Pensacola

Aviation—Airship—airship of the U.S. Navy—flown—April 1917
Aviation—Pilot—ensign (woman) to fly solo—G. A. Gordon—March 28, 1966
Aviation—School—naval air training school—opened—Dec. 1, 1914
Branding—branding punishment by a federal court—Jonathan Walker—July 20, 1844
Civil War—naval engagement in the Civil War—Sept. 14, 1861

Port Canaveral

See under Cape Canaveral

St. Augustine

Billiards—billiards—introduced—1565
Catholic Bishop—Catholic bishop—to exercise episcopal functions—1607
Catholic Holy Orders—conferred—Aug. 24, 1675
Catholic Parish—founded—Sept. 8, 1565
Catholic Priest—native Catholic priest—born—1620
Catholic Settlement—1565
Colonist—permanent white settlement—Sept. 8, 1565
Map—map of a city—engraved—1588

St. Marks

Ship—vessel built by Europeans in America—1528

St. Petersburg

Aviation—hydroplane commercial line service—Jan. 1, 1914

Post Office

Post Office—open-air post office—opened—1, 1917
School—school supported by local taxatic opened, May 20, 1832
Shuffleboard Championship—shuffleboard ch pionship tournament—C. L. Bailey, winn March 27, 1931

San Mateo

War (colonial)—intercolonial war—commer —Sept. 20, 1565

Sanford

Railroad—auto-train to transport passengers their automobiles on the same train—to from Lorton, Va.—service began, Dec. 6, 1

Tampa

Aviation—hydroplane commercial line servi Jan. 1, 1914
Aviation—Pilot—woman pilot to fly an airp. faster than 300 m.p.h.—Margie Hurlbu March 16, 1947
Medal—Medal of Honor awarded in World II—presented posthumously—Feb. 10, 1942
School—professional school for exclusively tr ing potential circus clowns—Irvin Feld—es lished, Sept. 1, 1968

Winter Park

Book Course—Rollins College—1926
College—"Unit Cost Plan"—Rollins Colle; Sept. 1933
Degrees (academic and honorary)—honorary gree awarded a black woman—M. M. Beth —Feb. 21, 1949
Walk of Fame—Rollins College—1929
Woman—woman coxswain of a men's colleg varsity team—Sally Stearns—May 27, 193(

GEORGIA

Agriculture Department (state)—state departn of agriculture—created—Feb. 28, 1874
Birth Registration—birth registration law (st —enacted—Dec. 19, 1823
Censorship—state board of censorship on lit ture—act approved—Feb. 19, 1953
Election Law—election law permitting person years of age or older to vote—enacted, Mar(1943—constitutional amendment approvec popular vote, Aug. 4, 1943—first used, No 1944
Governor—Jewish governor—David Emanu March 3, 1801
Lynch Law (state)—enacted—Dec. 20, 1893
Moravian Bishop—David Nitschmann—arri —1736
Railroad Legislation—railroad legislation (st —enacted—March 5, 1856

GEORGIA—*Continued*

Savannah

Agricultural Experiment Station—agricultural experiment farm—1735
Animals—cattle exportation—1755
Girl Scouts—founded—March 12, 1912
Hospital—black hospital and asylum—chartered —Dec. 24, 1832
Meat—beef export—1755
Moravian Church—built—1735
Orphanage—orphanage with a continuous existence—1740
Ship—iron vessel—*John Randolph*—1834
Ship—steamboat built in America to cross the Atlantic Ocean—sailed—May 22, 1819
Silk—silk exportation—1735
Sunday School—Protestant Sunday school—established—John Wesley—1736

Soperton

Newspaper—newspaper printed on pine-pulp paper—*Soperton News*—published—March 31, 1933

Toccoa

Weight Lifter—weight lifter to lift more than 6,000 pounds—Paul Anderson—June 17, 1957

Washington

Golfer—holes in one by a father and son—C. H. Calhoun, Sr. and Jr.—Aug. 24, 1932
Town—town incorporated under the name of Washington—Jan. 23, 1780

GUAM

Dentist—dentist in the U.S. Navy to serve at an overseas base—J. L. Brown—April 27, 1913

HAWAII

Representative   (U.S.)—Japanese-American woman representative—P. T. Mink—elected, November 1964
Representative (U.S.)—representative of Japanese ancestry elected to the House of Representatives—D. K. Inouye—July 28, 1959
Senator (U.S.)—Senator of Asian ancestry—H. L. Fong—elected—July 29, 1959
State—noncontiguous overseas state—admitted —Aug. 21, 1959

Hilo

President (U.S.)—President to visit Hawaii while President—F. D. Roosevelt—landed—July 25, 1934

Honolulu

Coronation—coronation on what was to become United States soil—King Kalakaua and Queen Kapiolani—Feb. 12, 1883

Radio Broadcast—volcano eruption broadcas Dec. 28, 1931
Stadium—adjustable stadium—Aloha Stadiu dedicated, Sept. 12, 1975

Maalaea, Maui

Coast Guard Officer—woman commander o Coast Guard ship—Beverly Kelley—appoin April 16, 1979

Pearl Harbor

Submarine—submarine to circumnavigate world—*Gudgeon*—left July 8, 1957—returr Feb. 21, 1958
Submarine—submarine to make a submer passage from the Atlantic to the Pacific via North Pole—*Seadragon*—docked on Sept. 1960
Submarine—submarines to rendezvous at North Pole—*Seadragon*—left July 12, 1962

IDAHO

County—county created by federal legislatio Latah County—authorized May 14, 1888
Electric Power Plant—hydroelectric power p built by the federal government—Minid Dam—first unit started, May 1, 1909
Governor—Jewish governor—elected for full t —Moses Alexander—Jan. 4, 1915
Seal—state seal designed by a woman—E. S. wards—approved, March 14, 1891

Arco

Electric Power Plant—electric power genera from atomic energy to illuminate an entire t —July 17, 1955

Boise

Air Raid Shelter—air raid community shelt completed—July 1, 1961

Idaho Falls

Atomic Energy—electric power from nuclear ergy—100,000 watts power—Dec. 20, 1951
Atomic Reactor—atomic reactor (large) to spe cally produce power—began operation—N 31, 1953
Atomic Reactor—plutonium-fueled nuclear r tor to produce useful amounts of electrici announced June 30, 1963

Kellogg

Newspaper—mimeographed daily newspap July 25, 1923

ILLINOIS

Automobile Legislation—automobile seat safety legislation—enacted—June 27, 1955

ILLINOIS—Chicago—*Continued*

Baseball Game—all-star baseball game (major league)—American League vs. National League —July 6, 1933

Baseball Game—baseball game (major league) in which 49 runs were made in a 9-inning game— Aug. 25, 1922

Baseball Game—double no-hit nine-inning baseball game—May 2, 1917

Baseball Game—opening day no-hit major league baseball game—Cleveland Indians vs. Chicago White Sox—April 16, 1940

Baseball Game—World Series baseball game to last longer than 9 innings—Chicago Cubs vs. Detroit Tigers—Oct. 8, 1907

Baseball League—baseball league association— National Association of Professional Baseball Leagues—organized—Sept. 5, 1901

Baseball Pitcher—baseball pitcher to pitch a no-hitter on opening day—Cleveland Indians vs. Chicago White Sox—R. W. A. Feller—April 17, 1940

Baseball Player—baseball player to hit a home run and a double in 1 inning—T. E. Burns—Sept. 6, 1883

Baseball Player—baseball player to hit a home run in an all-star game—Babe Ruth—July 6, 1933

Baseball Team—baseball team (major league) to score 18 runs in 1 inning—Chicago White Sox— Sept. 6, 1883

Baseball Team—professional league baseball team to win three pennants in succession—1882

Basketball Player—basketball player (professional) to score more than 4,000 points in 1 season— Wilt Chamberlain—reached 4,029 points— March 14, 1962

Battery—solar energy battery—sold—June 1, 1955

Bicycle Racer—woman bicycle champion of the National Amateur Bicycle Association to win twice—M. M. Dietz—Aug. 19, 1945

Bicycle Tire—bicycle tire (cord)—patented—J. F. Palmer—June 7, 1892

Bicycle Trip (world)—bicycle trip around the world by a married couple—Dr. and Mrs. H. D. McIlrath—started April 10, 1895—returned Dec. 1, 1898

Billboard Standardization—association formed— July 15, 1891

Births—sextuplets—born—Bushnell family— Sept. 8, 1866

Blood Bank—blood bank—established—March 15, 1937

Bowling—bowling automatic scorer—installed— September 1967—first used in sanctioned league games Oct. 10, 1967

Bowling Tournament—bowling tournament sponsored by the American Bowling Congress—Jan. 8, 1901

Bread—completely automatic bread plant— opened—July 1, 1910

Bridge—rolling lift bridge—opened—Feb. 4, 1895

Bridge (game) Table—manufactured—patented— Laurens Hammond—Nov. 29, 1932

Building—building higher than 1,400 feet—S(**Building**—topped out May 4, 1973

Building—building known as a skyscraper— struction started—May 1, 1884

Building—steel-frame building—Tacoma B(ing—completed—1887

Business—department store to sell insuran(Carson Pirie Scott & Co.—Sept. 29, 1953

Business—mail-order house—established—1

Cafeteria—opened—1895

Canal—Great Lakes to the Gulf waterw(opened—June 21, 1933

Canal Locks made of concrete—Hennepin c —to Rock Island, Ill.—section opened—(17, 1895

Caterpillar Club—Caterpillar Club memb(crashed—July 21, 1919

Catholic Church—Catholic eucharistic int(tional congress in the United States—Jun(1926

Citizenship—Chinese granted citizenship—r ralized—Jan. 18, 1944

Clock—watch movement to be electrically w(—1885

Codeball—played—May 11, 1929

College—college extension courses—Jan. 1,

College "Lettermen's Club"—established— 29, 1904

Communist Labor Party of America—organiz(Aug. 31, 1919

Communist Party of America—organized—(2, 1919

Court—juvenile court—opened—July 1, 1899

Cripples—public school for cripples—open(1900

Curling Championship (national)—March 30,

Deaf—Bone Bank—national temporal bone (center for ear research—established—Jan.

Degrees (academic and honorary)—Doctor o cial Science degree—H. R. Jeter—1924

Dental Book—book on dental technics—of (—published—1894

Dental Code of Ethics—proposed—Ame(Dental Assn.—July 28, 1865

Electric Lighting—electric indirect lig(demonstration—Oct. 1908

Electric Power Plant—rotary converter p(plant—operated—May 16, 1896

Elevated Railroad—electric elevated railro(June 2, 1883

Elevated Railroad—electric elevated rail (permanent)—opened May 17, 1895

Envelope—envelope with an outlook or win —patented—A. F. Callahan—June 10, 190

Fair—Woman's World Fair—April 18–25, 19

Farmer Labor Party—organized—June 12, 19

Fastening—hookless fastening—patented—V Judson—March 31, 1896

Ferris Wheel—exhibited—1893

Fishing Reel—electric spinning reel—introd(Aug. 15, 1967

Football Game—all-star football game—Au(1934

ILLINOIS—Chicago—*Continued*

Presidential Candidate—black presidential candidate proposed by a major political party—C. E. Phillips—Aug. 28, 1968

Presidential Candidate—presidential candidate debate series on television—first debate—Sept. 26, 1960

Presidential Candidate—presidential candidate to fly to a political convention—from Albany, N.Y.—F. D. Roosevelt—July 2, 1932

Presidential Candidate—presidential candidate to make a speech of acceptance at a nominating convention—F. D. Roosevelt—July 2, 1932

Printing—Press—web-fed four-color rotary printing press—operated—*Inter-Ocean*—1892

Prizefight—prizefight to gross $2 million—Dempsey vs. Tunney—Sept. 22, 1927

Prizefighter—pugilist to win a world championship 5 times in the same weight division—Sugar Ray Robinson—(5th time) March 25, 1958

Progressive Party—national convention—Aug. 6, 1912

Prohibition Party (national)—organized—Sept. 12, 1869

Propaganda Course (college)—University of Chicago—1927

Punchboards—patented—Jan. 17, 1905

Radio Broadcast—auction of livestock broadcast—Dec. 18, 1924

Radio Broadcast—coast-to-coast hookup—J. J. Carty—Feb. 8, 1924

Radio Facsimile Transmission—motion picture film transmitted by telephone wire—to New York City—April 4, 1928

Radio Receiver—radio receiver with an auxiliary silicon unit to convert the rays of the sun into electrical power—April 16, 1956

Railroad—daily railroad service to the Pacific Coast—to Portland, Oreg.—through service without change—Nov. 17, 1889

Railroad—electrically lighted train—*Pennsylvania Limited*—service to New York—June 1887

Railroad—railroad shipments of dressed beef (year-round long-distance)—G. F. Swift—1877

Railroad—railroad to run west out of Chicago—C.N.W.—Oct. 25, 1848

Railroad—railroad train to run 1,000 miles nonstop—from Denver, Colo.—May 26, 1934

Railroad Car—air-conditioned cars—service to Los Angeles—A.T.&S.F.—1914

Railroad Car—"compartmentizer" freight cars—in service to San Francisco, Calif.—Sept. 12, 1952

Railroad Car—dining car—operated—1868

Railroad Car—dining car (all-electric)—in service between Chicago and St. Louis, Mo.—March 9, 1949

Railroad Car—observation cars (super-dome)—built—1952

Railroad Car—passenger car (ACF-Talgo for use in the United States)—in service to Peoria, Ill.—Feb. 11, 1956

Railroad Car—Pullman train completely equip with roller bearings—to St. Paul, Minn.—21, 1927

Railroad Car—refrigerator car shipment of f fruit—Parker Earle—1872

Railroad Track—railroad rails of Bessemer s—made—May 24, 1865

Representative (U.S.)—black representative the North—O. B. De Priest

Roller Skate—ball-bearing skate patent—L. Richardson—Dec. 9, 1884

Roller Skating—roller derby—opened—Aug 1935

Rotary Club—organized—Feb. 23, 1905

Sanitary District—authorized—Nov. 5, 1889

Sewage—underground comprehensive sewer tem (city)—grid pattern—1856

Sidewalk (traveling)—sidewalk (traveling)—

Sleeping Car—Pullman sleeping car—servic Bloomington—Sept. 1, 1859

Sleeping Car—Pullman sleeping car that comfortable—built—1865

Snow Cruiser (automobile)—operated—Oct 1939

Social Democracy of America Party—nati convention—June 7, 1898

Sociology Professor—A. W. Small—appoint Oct. 1, 1892

Softball—softball (indoor baseball gam played—Nov. 30, 1887

Sports Trophy—sports trophy for the outstan amateur athlete of the year—James E. Sull Memorial Trophy—presented to R. T. Jone the Medinah Athletic Club—Feb. 26, 1931

Stethoscope—electrical stethoscope (portab exhibited—June 10, 1924

Surgical Operation—kidney transplanting—17, 1950

Surgical Operation—suture of the human h (successful)—D. H. Williams—July 9, 1893

Tape Recorder—magnetic tape recorder (c mercial) of sound and picture—demonstrat April 14, 1956

Taxidermy Method (sculptural)—devised—C Akeley—1902

Telephone—air-to-ground public telephone vice—Chicago–Detroit area—Sept. 15, 195

Telephone—picturephone service (commerci to New York City and Washington, D. inaugurated, June 24, 1964

Telephone—telephone switchboard or exch (multiple)—Jan. 1879

Teletypesetter—teletypesetter—manufacture 1932

Television—Telecast—Cabinet meeting (sta telecast—May 14, 1950

Television—Telecast—pay television—Phon sion—demonstrated—Jan. 1, 1951

Television—Telecast—prizefight (middlewe televised coast-to-coast—Sands-Olson—O 1951

Television—Telecast—serial daytime soap era—*These Are My Children*—telecast—Ja –Feb. 25, 1949

ision—Telecast—split-screen image (four
ys)—shown—Nov. 2, 1954

ision—Telecast—stockholders'   annual
eting televised on a closed circuit—April 16,
7

ision—Telecast—stockholders'   meetings
vised coast-to-coast simultaneously—Oct.
1959

ision—Telecast—surgical operation tele-
ed coast-to-coast—June 10, 1952

ision—Telecast—variety talent show series
h an all-black cast—April 1, 1949

ision Receiver—television receiver in a pri-
e railroad car—Monon Railroad to Rome,
,—Nov. 16, 1955

ision Station—all-color station to televise
local programs—WNBQ-TV—April 15,
6

el—freight delivery tunnel system—Aug. 15,
6

el—subaqueous highway tunnel—com-
nced—Nov. 30, 1866

ine—steam turbine generator of large capaci-
for commercial service—Oct. 2, 1903

setting Machine—typesetting machine to
pense with metal type—exhibited—Sept. 11,
0

um Cleaner—suction-type vacuum cleaner
atented—June 8, 1869

Presidential Candidate—black woman vice
sidential candidate—C. A. Bass—Progres-
e Party—nominated—July 5, 1952

ing Machine—complete self-contained elec-
: washing machine—1907

r Conduit—water supply tunnel for a city—
npleted—Dec. 6, 1866

Recorder—patented—Marvin Camras—
e 13, 1944

en's Club—Jewish women's organization
tional)—National Council of Jewish Women
ormed—Jan. 1894

Coal City

r—golfer to shoot below his age—S. J. Snead
Quad Cities Open—July 22, 1979

Decatur

dential Candidate—presidential candidate
ride in an automobile—W. J. Bryan—1896

ean Processing Plant—commercially suc-
sful—1922

Veterans' Society—Grand Army of the
public—established—April 6, 1866

De Kalb

—barbed wire—patented—J. F. Glidden—
v. 24, 1874

Des Plaines

ling—building for telephone directory compi-
ion and printing—dedicated—April 30, 1953

ding—television wedding—Oct. 14, 1928

Du Quoin

Horse—two stable-mate trotters to break a world
record the same day—Florican and Star's Pride
—Aug. 29, 1952

East Peoria

See also Peoria

Bank—bank payments to depositors of a closed
insured bank—July 3, 1934

Building—building built inside a factory—Sept.
17, 1938

East St. Louis

Bridge—steel arch bridge—Eads bridge—built—
to St. Louis—opened—July 4, 1874

Evanston

College President—woman college president—
Feb. 1871

Degrees (academic and honorary)—degree
awarded a ventriloquist's dummy—Aug. 28,
1938

Fort Chicago

See also Chicago

Army School—army school graduate killed—in
military action—George Ronan—Aug. 15, 1812

Fort Sheridan

Court-martial—court-martial trial of an officer for
collaborating with his captors—Sept. 23, 1954

Freeport

Bicycle—bicycle with a back-pedal brake—patented—Dec. 24, 1889

Galva

Postal Service—women railway postal clerks—
Maude Olson and Mary Olson—1896

Glencoe

Bottle—screw-cap bottle with a pour lip—patented—E. A. Ravenscroft—May 5, 1936

Golf Champion—golf champion to win the United
States Open and the Professional—Gene Sarazen

Glenview

Aviation—Flights—airplane to fly faster than 300
m.p.h.—J. R. Wedell—Sept. 4, 1933

Grand Detour

Plow—steel plow with a steel moldboard—John
Deere—tested—1837

Great Lakes

Dentist—woman dentist in the U.S. Navy—S. G.
Krout—began service June 1, 1944

ILLINOIS—*Continued*

Highland Park

Telautograph—telautograph—invented—Elisha Gray—1888

Kankakee

Building—circular school building—opened—Feb. 6, 1956

Lake Forest

Golf Champion—golf champion (American-born)—H. M. Harriman—won U.S. Amateur Golf Championship—July 8, 1899

La Salle

Coal—coal—discovered nearby—Louis Hennepin—1673

Lemont

Element—element 102—nobelium—announced—Argonne National Laboratory—July 9, 1957

Liberty

Visiting Celebrities—European king buried in the United States—Peter Karageorgevich—buried, Liberty Eastern Serbian Orthodox Monastery

McHenry County

Silo (of record)—constructed—F. L. Hatch—1873

Miller's Station

Glider—glider with cambered wings—invented—Octave Chanute—1895

Moline

Plow—steel plow with a steel moldboard—John Deere—manufacturing begun—1847

Morrison

Lock—time lock—installed in bank—May 1874

Mound Ctiy

Ship—warship sunk by an underwater torpedo mine—Cairo—built

Mundelein

Catholic Church—Catholic eucharistic international congress in the United States—adjourned to—June 24, 1926

North Chicago

Bottle—screw-cap bottle with a pour lip—manufactured—1936

Ottawa

Coal—coal—discovered nearby—Louis Hennepin—1673

Game Preserve—game preserve—establish 1860

Peoria

See also East Peoria

Automobile—armored car—manufactured—

Automobile Tractor—diesel-powered tra commercial manufacture—1931

Railroad Car—passenger car (ACF-Talgo f in the United States)—in service to Ch Ill.—Feb. 11, 1956

Pullman

Locomotive—electric freight locomotive—t 1888

Sleeping Car—Pullman sleeping car made e ly of steel—manufactured—1907

Quincy

Catholic Priest—black Catholic priest—ord to work in U.S.—April 24, 1886

River Park

Deaf—Hearing Aid—hearing aid of interest ented—R. S. Rhodes—Sept. 23, 1879

Rock Island

Bridge—railroad bridge across the Missi River—completed—to Davenport, Iowa— 21, 1856

Canal Locks made of concrete—Hennepin —to Chicago, Ill.—section opened—Ap 1895

United Christian Party—first convention—N 1900

Scott Field

Balloon—Flights—balloon flight to exceed a tude of 40,000 feet—ascended—H. C. G May 4, 1927

Spring Grove

Horse—Haflinger horse—imported—Aug. 1958

Springfield

Aviation—Airplane Fatalities—airplane fa (woman)—Julia Clark—killed—June 17, 1

Cooperatives Convention—Sept. 25, 1918

Dictionary—medical slang dictionary—*L nary of Medical Slang and Related Esoter pressions,* by J. E. Schmidt—published 1

Medical Society—American College of Sur —incorporated—Nov. 25, 1912

President (U.S.)—President who had recei patent—Abraham Lincoln—May 22, 1849

War Veterans' Society—Grand Army o Republic—first state convention—July 12

INDIANA—Fort Wayne—*Continued*

Basketball Player—National Basketball Association black player—C. H. Cooper—played—Nov. 1, 1950

Pump—computer pump—sold—Nov. 1, 1932

Pump—gasoline pump—installed—Sept. 5, 1885

Sawmill—band sawmill—operated—1867

Franklin

Money—scrip money to be self-liquidating—issued—March 8, 1933

Gary

Railroad—railroad freight yard fully automatic—in operation—Jan. 25, 1952

Greencastle

Sorority—sorority—Kappa Alpha Theta—Jan. 27, 1870

Indianapolis

Automobile Race—automobile race on a track (long-distance)—May 30, 1911

Automobile Racer—automobile racer to win $100,000 in a race—Roger Ward—May 30, 1959

Automobile Racer—automobile racer to win over $200,000 in a race—Al Unser—May 29, 1971

Automobile Racer—automobile racer to win the Indianapolis 500 three times—Louis Meyer—third time May 30, 1936

Automobile Racer—automobile racer to win the Indianapolis 500 four times—A. J. Foyt, Jr.—fourth time May 29, 1977

Automobile Racer—woman driver to compete in the Indianapolis 500—Janet Guthrie—qualified May 22—raced May 29, 1977

Greenback Party—organized—Nov. 25, 1874

Naval Officer—black commissioned officer in the regular U.S. Navy—John Lee—March 15, 1947

Ordnance—machine gun (rapid-fire)—patented—Nov. 4, 1862

Prison—prison built for women and managed exclusively by women—Oct. 8, 1873

Radio Receiver—transistor radio receiver—manufactured—1954

Railroad Station—union passenger station—opened—Sept. 20, 1853

Socialist Party—formed—March 25, 1900

Surgical Operation—gallstone operation—Dr. J. S. Bobbs—June 15, 1867

War Veterans' Society—Grand Army of the Republic—national convention—Nov. 20, 1866

Woman—woman secretary of a state senate—Fern Ale—Jan. 6, 1927

Jasper

Garbage Collection—city to discontinue garbage collection—Aug. 1, 1950

Lafayette

Balloon—Flights—balloon flight carrying r John Wise—started—Aug. 17, 1859

La Porte

Telephone—automatic telephone system cessful)—installed—1892

Martinsville

Fish Hatchery—goldfish hatchery—succes operated—1899

Michigan City

Gas—gas storage tank (waterless)—placed i vice—Feb. 10, 1925

New Harmony

Communistic Society—communistic nonrel settlement—1825

Printing Instruction—printing instruction—R Owen—1826

Richmond

Automobile—miniature automobile mar tured in the United States—Crosley—o for sale—April 28, 1939

South Bend

Automobile—automobile-airplane combir —delivery received—Aug. 15, 1937

Wabash

Electric Lighting—streetlighting (electric) municipality—March 31, 1880

IOWA

Cigarette Tax—cigarette tax (state)—Apr 1921

Senator (U.S.)—father and son senators at session—Henry Dodge of Wisconsin and Dodge of Iowa—Dec. 7, 1848–Feb. 22, 18

Alleman

Corn Husking Championship Contest (nat —Dec. 1, 1924

Ames

Cornstone—Maizolith—made—1922

Radio Station—educational radio station lic —WOI—Iowa State College of Agricultur Mechanical Arts—call letters granted, No 1921—license granted, April 28, 1922

Veterinary School—veterinary school (state tablished—May 23, 1879

Cedar Falls

ers' Institute—farmers' institute held by a
d grant agricultural college off its campus—
Iowa State College—Dec. 20, 1870

Cedar Rapids

graph—photograph bounced off a satellite
eamed—Aug. 18, 1960
Sextant—announced—July 14, 1954
poline—trampoline commercially manufac-
ed—Nissen Trampoline Company—1937

Davenport

—national bank—opened—under law of
3—June 29, 1863
y Pageant—black contestant in the Miss
erica pageant—C. A. Browne—selected—
e 13, 1970
e—railroad bridge across the Mississippi
er—to Rock Island, Ill.—completed—April
1856
ra—motion picture camera (portable)—
ıufactured—1923
usel—carrousel patent—July 25, 1871
practic School—opened—1900
practor—D. D. Palmer—adjustment treat-
ıt—Sept. 18, 1895
cal Operation—appendicitis operation (ap-
dectomy)—Jan. 4, 1885

Des Moines

Auxiliary Corps—Women's Army Auxili-
Corps (WAAC) training course—July 20,
2
Camp—army camp for training black offic-
—June 15, 1917
nobile—electric storage battery automobile
uilt—1891
Facsimile Transmission—radio facsimile
adcasting on the regular broadcasting band
eb. 4, 1938
ision—Telecast—debate (nationally tele-
t) among candidates within a political party
the presidential nomination—Jan. 5, 1980

Dubuque

—warship built on inland waters—*Ericsson*
aunched—May 12, 1894

Fairfield

ic Power Plant—municipally owned electric
ver plant—purchased—1882

Fort Madison

—woman prison guard in a maximum
urity prison for men—J. W. Stewart—Iowa
te Penitentiary—appointed, Feb. 1, 1973

Froelich

Automobile Tractor—gasoline tractor—manufactured—1892

Independence

Bicycle Racer—bicyclist to ride a mile in less than
2 minutes from a standing start—John Johnson
—Sept. 22, 1892

Iowa City

Basketball Game—basketball intercollegiate five-
man-team game—Jan. 16, 1896
Degrees (academic and honorary)—degree conferred by radio—June 9, 1925
Education—chair in education—permanently established—1873

Kellerton

Horseshoe Pitchers' Association (national)—
championship tournament—Oct. 23, 1915

Marion

Bridge—concrete cantilever bridge—erected—
1905

Mount Pleasant

Lawyer—woman lawyer—admitted to practice—
A. A. Mansfield—June 1869
Photograph—photograph of a total solar eclipse—
E. C. Pickering—Aug. 7, 1869

Muscatine

Button—buttons of freshwater pearl—1890

Onawa

Eskimo Pie—patented—C. K. Nelson—Jan. 24,
1922

Oskaloosa

Fingerprinting—community to fingerprint its citizens—May 21, 1934

Sioux City

Addressograph—invented—J. S. Duncan—1892
Bank—joint stock land bank—chartered—April
24, 1917

Urbandale

Bridge—welded-aluminum girder-type highway
bridge—completed—Sept. 24, 1958

KANSAS

Impeachment—impeachment proceedings
against a state governor—acquittal—1862
Medical Legislation—chiropractic legislation
(state)—enacted March 18, 1913
Periodical—American Indian-language monthly
—printed—Feb. 24, 1835

KANSAS—*Continued*

Trust—antitrust law (state)—general—enacted—March 9, 1889

Trust—blue-sky laws—enacted—March 10, 1911

Abilene

Carrousel—portable carrousel—manufactured—1896

Shooting Gallery (mechanized)—invented—C. W. Parker—1890

Argonia

Mayor—woman mayor—S. M. Salter—April 4, 1887

Atchison

Alcohol—power alcohol plant—established—Oct. 2, 1936

Bronson

Horseshoe Pitching Contest (International)—1909

Dexter

Helium—helium—discovered as a constituent of natural gas—1905

Chapman

High School—county high school—Dickinson County Community High School—opened—Sept. 1889

Dodge City

Bullfight—bullfight—July 4, 1884

Motorcycle Race—motorcycle race (300 miles)—July 4, 1914

Fort Riley

Army Officer—brigadier general (black)—appointed—Oct. 25, 1940

Garden City

Aviation—air-rail passenger transcontinental service—plane service from Cleveland—June 14, 1929

Girard

Book—book series of small-size paperbacks—Little Blue Books—published—1919

Kansas City

Aviation—airplane "fly-it-yourself" system—Fairfax Airport—Sept. 15, 1929

Horseshoe Pitchers' Association (National)—formed—May 16, 1914

Leavenworth

Carrousel—carrousel with the jumping mechanism—manufactured—1896

Fingerprinting—federal penitentiary finger ing—United States Penitentiary—Nov. 2

Photography—demonstration of rapid aeri tography—Sept. 5, 1925

Prison—penitentiary building (national)- pleted—Feb. 1, 1906

Lyon

Martyr—Christian martyr on U.S. soil—J Padilla—killed, 1542

Manhattan

Farmers' Institute—farmers' institute spo by a college—held—Nov. 14, 1868

Oskaloosa

Mayor—woman mayor elected with an al an council—M. D. Lowman—April 1888

Salina

Rocket—launching silos for Atlas F missile sitioned underground around the city

Topeka

Coursing Club—American Coursing Club- nized—July 9, 1886

Court—small debtors' court established b law—1913

Represenative (U.S.)—representatives to each other—M. E. Keys and Andrew Jr.—Jan. 3, 1976

Victoria

Animals—cattle (Aberdeen-Angus) impo —1873

Wichita

Aviation—Airplane—turbine-propeller lig plane—flown—Nov. 5, 1952

Railroad Car—freight car (Adapto Car)— vice to St. Louis, Mo.—July 24, 1956

KENTUCKY

Debtors' Prison—abolished by legislation 17, 1821

Election Law—Australian ballot system— ed for Louisville—Feb. 24, 1888

Electric Power Transmission—power line c 000 volts—1969

Nullification Proceedings—approved—No 1798

Road—state road appropriation of a specif —Dec. 19, 1795

Road—state road authorization—Dec. 14,

do—tornado disaster (large-scale)—March
1925

Ashland

c Power Plant—cooling tower hyperbolic-
ed—in commerical service, Jan. 1, 1963
—continuous sheet steel mill—built—1922

Barbourville

st—civilian settlement west of the Alleghe-
Mountains—April 23, 1750

Calvert City

ene—acetylene chemical products full-
e commercial plant—completed—1956

Churchill Downs

See under Louisville

Covington

Race—mutuel ticket to pay more than $1,-
—Latonia track—June 17, 1912

Danville

e—university west of the Allegheny Moun-
s—chartered—1783
al Operation—abdominal operation—
iotomy—Dr. E. McDowell—Dec. 13, 1809

Fort Knox

n—woman to have her name placed on the
erstone of a United States government
ling—N. T. Ross—April 1936

Harrison's Mills

duel in which a future President of the
ed States participated—May 30, 1806

Harrodsburg

—cantilever bridge—construction started
t. 12, 1876

Hodgenville

ent (U.S.)—President born beyond the
daries of the original thirteen states—
ham Lincoln—Feb. 12, 1809

Jefferson County

Department—county health department
nized on a full-time basis—established Jan.
08

Lexington

—trotter triple-crown winner—Scott Frost
entucky Futurity) Oct. 6, 1955
ics—narcotics sanatorium (federal) for
addicts—opened—May 29, 1935

Logan County

Camp Meeting—1803

Loretto

Convent—Catholic convent to admit black
women as sisters—May 1824

Louisa

Dam—needle-type dam—constructed—1900

Louisville

Baseball Game—shutout game—Chicago–Louis-
ville—April 25, 1876
Brick—terra-cotta factory—to be successful—
1867
Coast Guard (U.S.)—inland U.S. Coast Guard station—opened—Nov. 3, 1881
Coin Box—for streetcars—invented—T. L. John-
son—1870
Encyclopedia—braille encyclopedia for the
blind—*World Book Encyclopedia*—issued
1961-1972
Gas Mask—gas mask—resembling modern type
—patented—L. P. Haslett—June 12, 1849
Horse Race—filly to win the Kentucky Derby—
May 8, 1915
Horse Race—horse race (Kentucky Derby)—May
17, 1875
Jockey—jockey to win the Kentucky Derby 3
times—Isaac Murphy—(third time) May 13,
1891
Jockey—jockey to win the Kentucky Derby 4
times—Eddie Arcaro
Jockey—jockey (woman) to ride in a Kentucky
Derby—Diane Crump—May 2, 1970
Medal—Air Medal (U.S.) awarded to a woman—
presentation—March 26, 1943
Presidential Candidate—presidential candidate
who was a Catholic—Charles O'Conor—nomi-
nated—Sept. 3, 1872
Telegraph—telegraph ticker that successfully
printed type—patented—D. E. Hughes—May
20, 1856
Telephone—multiple common battery switchboard—in service—1897
Television—Telecast—horse race (Kentucky
Derby) telecast in color—May 7, 1966

Ludlow

Railroad—municipal railroad—from Cincinnati—
service—July 23, 1877

Somerset

Railroad—municipal railroad—from Cincinnati—
service—July 23, 1877

LOUISIANA

Amphibious Vehicle—Marsh screw amphibian—
tested—March 1963

LOUISIANA—*Continued*

Governor—black governor (acting)—P. B. S. Pinchback—Dec. 11, 1872

Governor—Catholic governor—E. D. White—1835

Health Board—health board (state) to regulate quarantine

Law Codification (state)—promulgated—June 13, 1825

Lieutenant Governor—black lieutenant governor—O. J. Dunn—nominated Jan. 14—elected April 22, 1868

Price Regulation Legislation—price regulation law (state)—approved—July 2, 1908

Prizefight—state legislation concerning prizefighting—May 12, 1890

Representative (U.S.)—congressional candidate elected while "missing"—T. H. Boggs—elected, Nov. 7, 1972

Representative (U.S.)—representative to serve 1 day—G. A. Sheridan—elected, Nov. 5, 1873

Senator (U.S.)—Senator to win a seat which had been occupied by his father and mother—Russell Long—elected—Nov. 2, 1948

Ship—barge to transport liquid sulfur—in service, Feb. 23, 1948

Sugar—sugar cane—imported—1751

Sulfur Mine (offshore)—Louisiana coast—March 14, 1960

Calcasieu Parish

Sulfur Deposit—discovered—1869

Carville

Hospital—leper hospital—founded—1894

Protestant Church—Protestant church for lepers—dedicated—June 14, 1915

Lake Charles

Pipeline—pipeline (interstate) to transport ethylene—in operation—to Orange, Texas—Sept. 6, 1958

New Orleans

Anesthesia—spinal anesthesia report—Rudolph Matas—1900

Baseball Ticket—baseball rain check—used by club manager C. A. Powell—1887

Business Economics Course—Tulane University—1849

Catholic Bishop—black Catholic bishop who was American born—H. R. Perry—consecrated auxiliary bishop, Jan. 6, 1966

Catholic Nuns—nun who professed her vows in the United States—March 15, 1729

Catholic Nuns—nun who was born in the United States—novitiate—July 2, 1749

College—college for women to affiliate with a university—established—Oct. 11, 1886

College—university for blacks (Catholic)—Xavier University—college department opened—Sept. 13, 1925

Convent—convent—opened—Aug. 6, 1727

Cotton-Bale Metallic Tie—patented—Mar 1858

Craps—introduced—1813

Free Lunch—free lunch—Pierre Maspero—

Greek Orthodox Church—Greek Ort church—founded—1867

Heresy Trial of a bishop—Oct. 12, 1925

Holiday—Mardi Gras of New Orleans, La.-

Ice—commercial artificial-ice manufac plant—built—1868

Levees—on Mississippi River—built—1724

Methodist Church—Methodist mission Ebenezer Brown—1819

Money—Confederate coinage—1861

Monument—statue officially sanctioned by—blessed—Nov. 10, 1895

Political Science Society—political science ciation—founded—Dec. 30, 1903

Prizefight—prizefight of importance unde Marquis of Queensberry rules—Sept. 7,

Prizefight—prizefight of 110 rounds—Bow Burke—April 6, 1893

Prizefight—prizefight to gross more than $ lion in sales—Ali vs. Spinks—Sept. 15, 1

Prizefight—pugilist to win the heavyweight pionship 3 times—Muhammad Ali—(3rd Sept. 15, 1978

Road—mosaic pavement—completed—Fe 1930

Ship—Confederate cruiser to raid Union merce—fitted out—1861

Ship—diesel-and-gas-turbine combined-p sion plant in a major ship—*Alexander I ton*—launched, Dec. 18, 1965

Ship—steamboat (double-decked)—*Wash* —arrived—Oct. 7, 1816

Ship—steamboat to sail down the Mississi *New Orleans*—arrived—Oct. 1, 1811

Ship—submarine chaser—*SC-1*—built at Station

Shipping—coastal shipping service—T. L voss—1831

Siamese Twins—Siamese twins separate cessfully by surgery—Sept. 17, 1953

Streetcar—streetcar tracks which were t soundless, and shockless—1930

Sugar—sugar refinery—practical—1791

Treason—citizen of the United States to b for treason, convicted, and hanged— Mumford—hanged—June 7, 1862

Venetian Blinds—venetian blind patent- Hampson—Aug. 21, 1841

Water—heavy water—discovery annou Dec. 29, 1931

Opelousas

Newspaper—newspaper printed on b newsprint—*Daily World*—published Fe 1954

Newspaper—offset-printed daily newsp *World*—operations began, Dec. 24, 1939

Tangipahoa

—town founded by a woman—R. H. S. Mix-
-1806

University

:ourse—art course—true fresco painting
rse—Louisiana State University—Sept. 14,
￼

Westwego

-naval ship named for a black naval offic-
Jesse L. Brown—launched, March 18, 1972

White Castle

—sugar cane 9-roll mill with common gear-
and a single engine—in operation at Cora
tation

Young's Point

Correspondent—news reporter tried as a
-T. W. Knox—Feb. 5, 1863

MAINE

—child born of European parents on Ameri-
soil—Snorro—1007

ess (U.S.)—Senate—election in which 2
en contested for the same Senate seat—M.
mith and L. M. Cormier—Nov. 8, 1960

ral College—state law requiring presiden-
:lectors to cast their ballots for presidential
vice presidential candidates of the political
y for which the electors were chosen—
ted March 25, 1969

1or—brothers to serve simultaneously as
·rnors of their respective states—Levi Lin-
(Massachusetts) and Enoch Lincoln

entative (U.S.)—representatives (brothers)
erve simultaneously—Washburn brothers
arch 4, 1855–Jan. 1, 1861

r (U.S.)—woman senator elected for a third
a fourth term—M. C. Smith—1960 and 1966,
ectively

r (U.S.)—woman senator elected without
ng previously served an appointed term—
·. Smith—Sept. 13, 1948

ship built by the English in the American
1ies—launched—1607

Andover

one—satellite (privately owned) telephone
ersation—F. R. Kappel to L. B. Johnson—
elstar 1 to Washington, D.C.—July 10, 1962

ion—Telecast—transoceanic television
·am—July 10, 1962

Augusta

ading Post—established—1628

System—woman to direct a state bureau of
·ction—W. E. Murphy—July 1970

Bangor

Chewing Gum—manufactured—1848

Bar Harbor

Radio Facsimile Transmission—photograph sent
by radio across the Atlantic from Europe—received—June 11, 1922

Bath

Ship—destroyer of the U.S. Navy named for a
Confederate officer—*Buchanan*—launched,
Jan. 2, 1919

Ship—guided missile destroyer—*Dewey*

Ship—naval ship designed to carry the DASH
drone—*Belknap*—launched, July 19, 1963

Ship—schooner (four-masted)—*William J. White*
—launched—June 1880

Ship—steam whaler built as a whaleboat—*The
Mary and Helen*—built—1879

Ship—steel sailing vessel—*Dirigo*—launched—
Feb. 3, 1894

Ship—turbine-propelled ship of the U.S. Navy—
Chester

Bristol

Pirate—on the Atlantic Seaboard—Dixie Bull—
looted—1632

Bucksport

Electric Power Plant—floating electric power
plant—*Jacona*—in operation November 1930-
March 1931

Fish Hatchery (federal)—established—1872

Calais

Colonist—colonial white settlement (north of
Florida)—founded—1604

Telephone—international telephone conversation—to St. Stephen—July 1, 1881

Camden

Ship—schooner (six-masted)—launched—July 1,
1900

Cape Elizabeth

Air Brush Patent—L. L. Curtis—Oct. 25, 1881

Cape Porpoise

Discovery—discovery of New England by an Englishman—Bartholomew Gosnold—landed—
May 15, 1602

Castine

Maritime School—woman graduate of a 4-year
maritime school—D. B. Doane—May 1, 1976

MAINE—*Continued*

Dixfield

Diving Suit (practical) for submarine diving—patented—Leonard Norcross—June 14, 1834

Eastern Egg Rock

Birds—bird for which a definite crossing of the Atlantic has been recorded—banded—July 3, 1913

Eastport

Canning—sardine cannery—1876

Farmington

Earmuff—patented—Chester   Greenwood—March 13, 1877

Gardiner

Technical Institute—Gardiner Lyceum—founded —1822

Greenville

Forest Fire—forest fire lookout tower—service began—June 10, 1905

Lake Sebago

Camp Fire Girls Organization—announced—March 17, 1912

Lewiston

Postal Service—international dogsled mail—left —Dec. 20, 1928

Limerick

Bank—national bank woman president—elected —Jan. 11, 1938

Limestone

Aviation—Flights (transatlantic)—jet transatlantic nonstop flight east–west—D. C. Schilling—Sept. 22, 1950

Aviation—Flights (transatlantic)—jet transatlantic nonstop flight west–east—April 7, 1953

Machias

Revolutionary War—naval battle of the Revolution—*Unity* and *Margaretta*—June 12, 1775

Mount Desert

Park—park (national) east of the Mississippi—established—July 8, 1916

War (colonial)—colonial warfare between England and France for the possession of North America—took place—1613

Newfield

Methodist Church—black minister with two congregations—J. R. Washington—June 3

Norway

Snowshoe—commercial production—A. M. ham, Jr.—1862

Orono

Army—Reserve Officers Training Corps U authorized—Oct. 21, 1916

Pemaquid

Road—road pavement—laid—1625

Phippsburg

Holiday—Thanksgiving Day service—A 1607

Portland

Brokerage—stock order from a Zeppeli ceived—Aug. 8, 1930

Catholic Bishop—Catholic bishop (black) secrated—1875

Oratorio—oratorio by an American—perf —June 3, 1873

Railroad—international railroad—to Mont service—July 18, 1853

Sanford

Blanket—blanket robe and carriage lap rob ness—successfully undertaken—1867

South Berwick

Blanket—blanket factory—Burleigh Blanke —1854

Waterpower—waterpower development g established—1620

Thomaston

Doughnut Cutter—patented—J. F. Blondel 9, 1872

Police—woman employed at a high level w men's maximum security facility—Ka Tripp—Maine State Prison—Sept. 11, 19

Togus

Soldiers' Home—soldiers' homes (natic Eastern Home—authorized—March 21,

West Newfield

Methodist Church—black minister with two congregations—J. R. Washington—June

Winthrop

Oilcloth Factory—successful—established

Thresher—threshing machines to employ s patented—Dec. 29, 1837

MARYLAND—Baltimore—*Continued*

Health Board—health board (local)—appointed—1792

Humane Society—humane association national organization—American Humane Association —constitution adopted—Nov. 14, 1878

Hygiene Instruction—hygiene and public health school—established—1916

Ice Cream—ice cream wholesale dealer—Jacob Fussel—1851

Ice Cream Freezer—patented—W. G. Young—May 30, 1848

Labor Legislation—eight-hour day—uniform action—Aug. 20, 1866

Law Periodical—*American Law Journal*—published—1808

Lighthouse—lighthouse (atomic powered)—Baltimore Light, Baltimore Harbor—began operation, May 20, 1964

Locomotive—locomotive bid—solicited—Jan. 4, 1831

Locomotive—locomotive built in the United States to pull passengers—*Tom Thumb*—test—Aug. 28, 1830

Locomotive—race between a locomotive and a horse-drawn vehicle—to Relay, Md.—Aug. 25, 1830

Manual Training—manual training school entirely financed by public taxes—established—1884

Medical Book—aviation medicine book—*Aviation Medicine*—published—1926

Medical Book—ophthalmology book—published —1823

Medical Clinic—medical clinic (general)—of importance—Johns Hopkins—opened—Oct. 1889

Medical Instruction—History of Medicine Department—Johns Hopkins University—Oct. 18, 1929

Medical Instruction—ophthalmology course (regular)—Ophthalmic Clinic—established—1823

Medical Instruction—pathology chair—modern pathology chair—W. H. Welch—Johns Hopkins University—1883

Methodist Church—Methodist Bishop—Francis Asbury—appointed—1784

Monument—monument to Christopher Columbus —dedicated—Oct. 12, 1792

Monument—monument to George Washington (city or state)—cornerstone laid—July 4, 1815

Museum—museum especially constructed as a museum and art gallery—Aug. 15, 1814

Newspaper—newspaper to appear on Sunday—*Monitor*—Dec. 18, 1796

Odd Fellows Lodge—established—April 26, 1819

Orchestra—municipal orchestra supported by taxes—first concert—Feb. 11, 1916

Patent—label patent—issued—Aug. 1, 1874

Pen—steel pen patent—Peregrine Williamson—Nov. 22, 1809

Pharmacy College—pharmacy college to make analytical chemistry a required course—Maryland College of Pharmacy—March 20, 1872

Pharmacy Professor—pharmacy professorship—David Stewart—April 24, 1844

Political Convention—national committee political organization—formed—May 22, 1

Political Convention—two-thirds rule—ado —May 21, 1832

Polo—polo game played outdoors at night—Ju 1931

Postmaster—woman postmaster (colonial)-K. Goddard—1775

President (U.S.)—President to broadcast by r —W. G. Harding—June 14, 1922

President (U.S.)—President to ride on a rail train—Andrew Jackson—June 6, 1833

Psychology   Laboratory—established—Je Hopkins—1881

Psychology Magazine—*American Journal of chology*—published—Nov. 1887

Radio Facsimile Transmission—facsimile tr mitted to a moving train—public demonstra —June 4, 1946

Railroad—railroad for commercial transport: of passengers and freight—construction b —July 4, 1828

Railroad—railroad to run trains to Washin; D.C.—Baltimore and Ohio Railroad Co.—Ju 1835

Railroad—railroad to use an electric engine— timore tunnel—Aug. 4, 1894

Railroad Car—car with a center aisle—*Columbus*—July 4, 1831

Railroad Car—double-deck railroad coach used—to Ellicott's Mills—Aug. 1830

Railroad Station—railroad station—passe and freight—erected—1830

Railroad   Union—organized—November 1855

Refrigerator—refrigerator—invented—Thom Moore—1803

Saccharin—discovered—Constantine Fahlbe 1879

Satellite—satellite with a nuclear power dev: *Transit IV-A*—Snap battery built by M Company

Science Association—woman elected to the tional Academy of Sciences—F. R. Sab April 29, 1925

Ship—clipper ship—*Ann McKim*—launch June 4, 1833

Ship—iron vessel built of American iron *Rosset*—registered—April 4, 1839

Ship—Liberty ship—*Patrick Henry*—launch Sept. 27, 1941

Ship—ship to capture an enemy ship afte Revolution—*Constellation*—launched—Se 1797

Ship—tanker (automated) under the U.S. fl *Texaco Rhode Island*—built—Sparrows] —launched July 2, 1964

Ship—triple ship launching of Liberty ships– 4, 1942

Sociology   Society—sociological society tional)—American Sociological Society— nized—Dec. 1905

Sports Magazine—*American Turf Register Sporting Magazine*—published—Sept. 182

etcar—electric cars commercially operated—
4g. 10, 1885

4narine—cargo submarine to cross the Atlan-
Ocean—*Deutschland*—landed—July 9, 1916

4narine—submarine fitted with an internal-
4mbustion engine—*Argonaut*—patented—Si-
4n Lake—1897

4ical Operation—lung removal carried out ac-
4rding to preoperative plans—W. F. Rienhoff
4uly 24, 1933

4re—silk suture—used—W. S. Halsted—1882

4denborgian or New Church—German Swe-
4nborgian Society—organized—1855

4denborgian or New Church—Swedenborgian
New Church Temple—erected—1799

4gram—news dispatch telegram—from Wash-
4ton, D.C.—May 25, 1844

4gram—telegram inaugurating commercial
4rvice—from Washington, D.C.—May 24, 1844

4ohone—telephone message from a submarine
4derwater—Jan. 6, 1898

4vision—Telecast—medical intercity color
4ecast—Johns Hopkins Hospital—to Wash-
4ton, D.C.—Dec. 6, 1949

4vision—Telecast—stratovision flight—televi-
4n signal transmitted—April 30, 1948

4vision—Telecast—surgical operation tele-
4ed on a closed circuit—Feb. 27, 1947

4vision—Telecast—X-ray fluoroscopy televi-
4n discussion—Dec. 5, 1950

4table (railroad)—railroad timetable—adver-
4ed—May 20, 1830

4setting Machine—linotype machine—pat-
4ted—O. Mergenthaler—Aug. 26, 1884

4n Reform Party—convention—Sept. 3, 1900

4ine Institution—opened—James Smith—
4rch 25, 1802

4y—X-ray motion picture process by which
4tures could be taken over a considerable pe-
4d of time—Feb. 1, 1951

Beltsville

4o Broadcast—radio broadcast from a moving
4in, of a regular program on a national net-
4rk—pickup—March 27, 1932

Bethesda

4erative—cooperative operated entirely by
4men—incorporated—Aug. 1932

4cine—tissue bank—1954

4l Officer—women technicians in medicine
4igned to the National Naval Medical Center
4athryn Hyde and Dorothy Osborne—report-
for duty—Nov. 13, 1942

4o Station—all-local network—May 15, 1950

Bladensburg

4—duel between representatives in Congress
4808

4motive—electric locomotive—trial trip—
4m Washington, D.C.—April 29, 1851

President (U.S.)—President to face enemy gunfire while in office—James Madison—Aug. 25, 1814

Bohemia Manor

Labadist Community—established—1683

Bolton Depot

Bridge—tubular-plate girder bridge—built—1841

Boonsboro

Monument—monument to George Washington—July 4, 1827

Cambridge

Automobile Trucking Service—automobile trucking service—by railroad—to Salisbury and Tyaskin, Md.—Jan. 8, 1923

Cardiff

Slate—for roofing material—1734

Catonsville

Military School—church military school—founded—1845

College Park

Army Officer—flight surgeon—J. P. Kelly—reported for duty—June 30, 1911

Aviation—Airplane—airplane outfitted with a machine gun—flown—May 7, 1912

Aviation—Flights—all-blind cross-country test—to Newark, N.J.—March 21, 1933

Aviation—Passenger—woman airplane passenger—Oct. 27, 1909

Aviation—Pilot—Army pilot to solo—F. E. Humphreys—Oct. 26, 1909

Helicopter—Flights—helicopter flight—of importance—June 16, 1922

Cumberland

Bottle—milk bottles—manufactured—L. P. Whiteman—1879

Road—federal highway—Cumberland road—to Vandalia, Ill.—appropriation—March 29, 1806

Elkridge Landing

Clock—clock to strike the hours—constructed—Benjamin Banneker—1754

Ellicott Mills (now Ellicott City)

President (U.S.)—President to ride on a railroad train—Andrew Jackson—June 6, 1833

Railroad Car—double-deck railroad coaches—to Baltimore, Md.

Elysville

See under Alberton

MARYLAND—*Continued*

Fort George G. Meade

Army Armored Car Unit—organized—1928

Frederick

Carpet Factory—carpet mill to make ingrain carpets—established—1810

Stamp Act Repudiation—Nov. 23, 1765

Supreme Court (U.S.)—Chief Justice of the Supreme Court who was Catholic—R. B. Taney—appointed—March 28, 1836

Glenross

Patent—black to obtain a patent—Henry Blair—Oct. 14, 1834

Hagerstown

Library—book wagon—service—April 1905

Hyattsville

Map—mosaic map of the contiguous 48 states from scenes transmitted from a satellite—assembled, November 1974

Single Tax—city to adopt the single tax for local revenue purposes—July 1892

Kent Island

Aviation—Airplane Fatalities—airplane fatality (U.S. Navy)—W. D. Billingsley—June 20, 1913

Laurel

Bird—whooping crane born in captivity—May 28, 1975

Horse Race—horse race in which the British Royal Silks participated—Nov. 3, 1954

Radio Broadcast—radio broadcast from a moving train, of a regular program on a national network—pickup—March 27, 1932

Middle River

Television—Telecast—stratovision flight test—Dec. 9, 1945

Mount Savage

Brick—fire brick to withstand high heat—manufactured—1841

Railroad Track—railroad rails of iron—rolled 1844—inverted "U" type rolled 1845

Patuxent

Jury—jury composed of women—ordered—Sept. 22, 1656

Poolesville

Hospital—military hospital on the modern pavilion plan—Oct. 21, 1861

Prince Georges County

Art Commission (public)—contract placed—5, 1721

Relay

Conscientious Objectors' Camp—opened—15, 1941

Locomotive—race between a locomotive a horse-drawn vehicle—from Baltimore—25, 1830

St. Johns

Shorthand Report—Nov. 15, 1681

War—naval battle by white men in Amer April 23, 1635

Salisbury

Automobile Trucking Service—automobile t ing service—by railroad—to Cambridge Tyaskin, Md.—Jan. 8, 1923

Silver Spring

Radio Station—all-local network—May 15,

Somerset

Ordnance—semiautomatic rifle—patented—Garand—Oct. 19, 1926

Sykesville

Railroad—railroad to carry troops—B.&O.—30, 1831

Talbot County

Manual Training—school to offer cours manual training—opened—Dec. 1, 1751

Tyaskin

Automobile Trucking Service—automobile t ing service—by railroad—to Cambridge Salisbury, Md.—Jan. 8, 1923

Upper Marlborough (Marlboro)

Orchestra—orchestra used in conjunction wi opera—1752

Washington County

Television—Telecast—instruction (large-operation) telecast closed circuit—offered tember 1956

Wheaton

Post Office—self-service post office—inst Oct. 17, 1964

White Oak

Betatron—mobile betatron—operated—No 1948

MASSACHUSETTS

lent Report—industrial accident reports—
uired—Sept. 1, 1887

als—cows—imported—March 1624

es—imported—John Winthrop—1629

Insignia—special insignia—authorized—
y 5, 1775

nobile License Plates—plastic license plate
s—issued—Dec. 15, 1942

ion—aeronautical patent—Moses McFar-
d—Oct. 28, 1799

**—child born of English parents in New Eng-
d—Peregrine White—born on *Mayflower* off
e Cod harbor—Nov. 20, 1620

ty Board (state)—established—April 29,
3

Labor Law—child labor law regulating
rs of employment—March 3, 1842

Labor Law—child labor law to include edu-
ional provision—effective—April 1, 1837

right Law—copyright law—May 15, 1672

t Union Law—approved—May 21, 1909

Legislation (state)—May 30, 1856

ition—compulsory education law—June 14,
2

ition—compulsory school attendance law
te)—May 18, 1852

ition—state board of education—estab-
ed—April 30, 1837

on—accredited colonial election—May 18,
1

on Law—registration law (state)—March 7,
1

mic—smallpox epidemic—of importance—
6

dition—scientific expedition—outfitted—
1

dition—extradition—New England Confed-
tion—1643

Commission (state)—authorized—May 16,
6

try Legislation—colonial forestry legislation
larch 29, 1626

**—imported—1630

**—exported—Robert Cushman—Dec. 1621

Law—game law (state)—1817

Commission (state)—legislation approved—
e 11, 1885

gical Survey—geological survey (state)—
0–1833

rnor—brothers to serve simultaneously as
ernors of their respective states—Levi Lin-
1 and Enoch Lincoln (Maine)

h Board—health board (state)—approved—
e 21, 1869

**—horses—imported—April 17, 1629

Race—horse race prohibition legislation—
e 4, 1674

cane—recorded—Aug. 15, 1635

nce—automobile compulsory insurance act
te)—effective—Jan. 1, 1927

nce—government insurance—1636

Insurance—insurance regulation (state)—legislation—Feb. 13, 1799

Insurance—marine insurance law (state)—approved—Feb. 16, 1818

Insurance—no-fault automobile insurance law
(state)—enacted Aug. 13, 1970—effective Jan. 1,
1971

Insurance—nonforfeiture insurance law (state)—
approved—April 10, 1861

Insurance—savings bank life insurance—approved—June 26, 1907

Labor—labor bureau (state)—approved—June 23,
1869

Labor Legislation—factory inspection law—April
30, 1879

Labor Legislation—minimum wage law—June 4,
1912

Lawyer—lawyer disbarred—Thomas Lechford—
Sept. 3, 1639

Legislature—legislature with two chambers—
March 1644

Lifesaving Stations for Distressed Mariners—established—1787

Literacy qualification for voting—amendment—
May 1, 1857

Loan—state loan—authorized—Dec. 10, 1690

Medical Legislation—law to regulate the practice
of medicine (colonial)—enacted—May 3, 1649

Military Leader—of Puritans—Miles Standish—
1621

Milk Inspectors—authorized—April 6, 1859

Missionary Society—missionary society organized in the United States—1762

Money—paper money—issued—1690

Nautical School—nautical state school—established—June 11, 1891

Patent—machine patent—granted—Joseph
Jencks—March 6, 1646

Patent—patent granted by the colonies—Samuel
Winslow—1641

Physician—black doctor to become a member of
a medical association—J. V. De Grasse—1854

Physician—doctor in New England—Samuel
Fuller—arrived—Dec. 21, 1620

Police—state police officers (women)—Lotta
Caldwell and Mary Ramsdell—appointed,
April 18, 1930

Post Office—post office (colonial)—established—
Nov. 5, 1639

Probation—probation legislation for juvenile delinquents—enacted—June 23, 1869

Quakers—Quakers to arrive in America—July
1656

Quarantine—quarantine legislation (colonial)—
March 1647

Railroad Commission (state)—established—July
1, 1869

Representative (U.S.)—representative reelected
after serving a prison term—T. J. Lane—reelected, Nov. 6, 1956

School Legislation—school law (compulsory)—
enacted—Nov. 11, 1647

School Legislation—school law (state) to end de
facto segregation—enacted—Aug. 18, 1965

MASSACHUSETTS—*Continued*

Senator(U.S.)—black senator elected by popular vote—E. W. Brooke—Nov. 8, 1966
State—state constitution—adopted—May 16, 1775
Tax—property tax law (colonial)—enacted—May 14, 1634
Tobacco—tobacco tax (colonial)—authorized—Oct. 3, 1632
Vaccination Legislation—vaccination legislation (state)—enacted—March 6, 1810
Witchcraft Execution—Achsah Young—May 27, 1647

Abington

Shoe Manufacturing Machine—patented—L. R. Blake—July 6, 1858
Sprinkler—sprinkler system patent—P. W. Pratt —Sept. 17, 1872

Amherst

College Student—college graduate (black)—E. A. Jones—Amherst College—Aug. 23, 1826
Hygiene Instruction—hygiene and physical education professorship—established—1860

Arlington

Loop-the-Loop Centrifugal Railway—patented— Edwin Prescott—Aug. 16, 1898

Auburn

Brake Patent—brake patent—Robert Turner— Aug. 29, 1828
Rocket—liquid-fuel rocket flight—March 16, 1926

Belchertown

Semaphore Telegraph System—invented—Jonathan Grout—1799

Beverly

Cotton—cotton goods to be trademarked—June 6, 1788
Cotton Mill—established—Beverly Cotton Manufactory—1788

Billerica

Leather—leather-splitting machine—patented— Samuel Parker—July 9, 1808

Boston

Actor—actor to perform in 2 cities the same day— N. C. Goodwin—Feb. 10, 1887
Actor—actor to receive curtain applause—Edmund Keene—1821
Adding Machine—adding machine to print totals and subtotals—patented—Nov. 19, 1872
Advertisement—advertisement—*News-Letter*— May 1–8, 1704

Advertisement—patent medicine advertise —published—*Boston Almanack*—1692
Agricultural Book—agricultural book—*The bandman's Guide*—published—1710
Agricultural Book—agricultural book disti American—published—1760
Almanac—almanac with a continuous tence—*The Farmer's Almanac*—printed—
Almanac—nautical almanac—published— 29, 1782
"America" (the song)—publicly sung—July 4
American Language—book on Americanis published—1816
Anesthesia—painless surgery demonstrat Oct. 16, 1846
Animals—bear (white)—exhibited—Jan. 18
Animals—camel imported—advertised—O 1721
Animals—cattle (Guernsey cattle)—impor 1831
Animals—leopard—exhibited—Feb. 2, 1802
Animals—lion—exhibited—Nov. 26, 1716
Animals—mule—imported—Oct. 26, 1785
Annulment—annulment by court decree—] Luxford—Dec. 3, 1639
Annunciator—patented—Dec. 26, 1833
Antislavery Book—L. M. F. Child—publis 1833
Archaeological Society—archaeological s (national)—founded—May 10, 1879
Architecture School—architectural scho collegiate rank—Massachusetts Institu Technology—established—Feb. 20, 1865
Arithmetic—American arithmetic—by a n born American—published—1729
Arithmetic—arithmetic—printed—1719
Artist—American artist of importance—J. S. ley
Arts and Science Society—arts and science ety (national)—chartered—May 4, 1780
Automobile School—automobile school—e lished—1903
Aviation—airplane commutation ticke Newark, N.J.—May 1, 1929
Aviation—Airplane Fatalities—airplane fa (woman pilot with passenger)—Harriet (by—Dorchester Bay—July 1, 1912
Aviation—Flights—airplane night schedulec senger flight—left—April 1, 1927
Bank—savings bank to become a corpora chartered—Dec. 13, 1816
Baseball Book—published—1834
Baseball Game—American League 20-i baseball game—Philadelphia-Boston—Ju 1905
Baseball Game—baseball game (major leag last longer than 25 innings—Boston Brav Brooklyn Robins—May 1, 1920
Baseball Game—shutout World Series (nonsanctioned)—Pittsburgh Nationals-B Americans—Oct. 2, 1903
Baseball Game—World Series baseball ga Pittsburgh Pirates (National League) vs. B Americans—Oct. 1, 1903

MASSACHUSETTS —Boston—*Continued*

Eye—eye conservation class—Thornton Street School—opened—April 3, 1913

Farrier's Guide—*The Husband-Man's Guide*—published—1710

Fire—fire of serious consequence—Nov. 27, 1676

Fire Alarm System (electric)—patented—May 19, 1857

Fire Hose of rubber-lined cotton web—patented—May 30, 1821

Fireboat—fireboat with two-way radio equipment—1925

Fishing Treatise—published—1743

Football Club—football club—Oneida Football Club—organized—1862

Freemasons—black Mason—initiated—March 6, 1775

Freemasons—Mason (native-born)—Jonathan Belcher

Freemasons—Masonic lodge to work under a regular charter—St. John's Lodge—established—July 30, 1733

Gambling Legislation (colonial)—passed—March 22, 1630

Garage—garage (public)—established—May 24, 1899

Gazetteer—American gazetteer—compiled—Jedidiah Morse—1795

Glass Factory—window glass factory—Boston Crown Glass Company—1792

Glue Factory (animal products)—established—Roger Upton—1807

Golf Tee—patented—Dec. 12, 1899

Grammar—French grammar—John Mary—published—1784

Grammar—Hebrew grammar—Judah Monis—published—1735

Grammar—Latin grammar textbook—Ezekiel Cheever—published—1709

Greenhouse—erected—Andrew Faneuil—1737

Heating System—heating system (steam)—installed—1844

High School—high school—English Classical School—opened—May 1820

High School—high school for girls—established—1826

High School—vocational high school for girls—opened—July 1904

Historical Society—historical society (state)—Massachusetts Historical Society—organized—Aug. 26, 1790

History—American history of importance written by a woman—published—M. O. Warren—1805

Hockey Player—professional hockey player (defenseman) to score 100 points in 1 season—R. G. Orr—100th point on March 15, 1970

Hockey Player—professional hockey player to score 50 goals in 1 season—J. H. M. Richard—50th goal, March 18, 1945

Horse Breeding Society—Massachusetts Society for Encouraging the Breed of Fine Horses—formed—1810

Horse Race—horse race pari-mutuel with a tire field of women jockeys—Suffolk Dow April 19, 1969

Hospital—tuberculosis home for the care of sumptives—Channing Home—opened—1857

Hotel—hotel—Tremont House—opened—Oc 1829

Hotel—hotel to install bathrooms—Tre House—opened—Oct. 16, 1829

Hotel—hotel to install radio reception—I Statler—May 10, 1927

Hotel—hotel with safe deposit boxes—New land Hotel—1866

Hygiene Instruction—School Department of giene—established—1907

Ice—export of ice—to Martinique—Aug. 18

Insurance—health insurance company—nized—April 21, 1847

Insurance—mutual liability insurance compa organized—April 21, 1887

Insurance—mutual life insurance company chartered—April 1, 1835

Jewish Book—Jewish book of Jewish autho published in America—*The Wars of the* by Flavius Josephus—reprint of 3rd ed.— uel Kneeland and Nicholas Buttolph—171

Jockey—jockey to win 7 consecutive races day—Leroy Moyers—July 4, 1967

Kindergarten—American kindergarten—186

Labor Union—labor organization—shoemak Oct. 18, 1648

Lawyer—Japanese lawyer—graduated—Jun 1877

Legislator (state)—black representatives to any state legislature—1866

Legislator (state)—homosexual (avowed) el to a state office—Elaine Noble—Nov. 5, 1

Lighthouse—lighthouse—in operation—Sep 1716

Logic Book—published—1735

Magic Lantern—magic lantern book—*The positor*, by W. F. Pinchbeck—printed 180

Map—map made in the United States publi in a book—1677

Map—road map for public use—published—

Marathon Race (annual)—April 19, 1897

Masonry—black Masonic Grand Lodge (not and Accepted Masons)—organized—Jun 1791

Medical Book—bacteriology textbook—lished—1880

Medical Book—medical pamphlet—treatis smallpox—published—Jan. 21, 1677

Medical Book—scarlet fever report—Wi Douglass—published—1736

Medical Instruction—medical chemistry c (systematic)—Harvard Medical School—1

Medical School—coeducational medical sch Boston University School of Medicine—1

Medical School—women's medical school— ton Female Medical School—organized— 1, 1848

Medical Society—medical society—founded

MASSACHUSETTS—Boston—*Continued*

Postal Card—pictorial postal card—issued, June 29, 1972

Postal Service—postal route—to New York City —Jan. 22, 1673

Postal Service—street letter box—erected—Aug. 2, 1858

Poultry Show—Public Garden—Nov. 15-16, 1849

Printing Press—power or steam printing press— made—1822

Printing Press—power printing press capable of fine book work—patented—Oct. 4, 1830

Probation—probation system, without restrictions as to age—established—1878

Protestant Episcopal Bishop—black to administer a diocese—J. M. Burgess—elected Sept. 22— consecrated Dec. 9, 1962

Public Health—medical system of inspection of schoolchildren—1894

Public School—public school with a continuous existence—Boston Public Latin School—established—Feb. 13, 1635

Radio Receiving Contest—radio receiving contest in which a speed of more than 50 words a minute was recorded—T. R. McElroy—May 7, 1922

Railroad Car—railroad coach—placed in service —May 19, 1847

Railroad Crossing Gate Patent—Aug. 27, 1867

Railroad Excursion—railroad excursion rates— originated—1849

Railroad Excursion—railroad excursion (transcontinental) of an organization—left—May 23, 1870

Rayon—rayon patent—Sept. 30, 1902

Religious Publication—religious journal—*Christian History*—March 5, 1743

Respirator (iron lung)—used—Oct. 12, 1928

Revolutionary War—American casualties— March 5, 1770

Revolutionary War—martyr in the Revolutionary War—Christopher Snider—killed—Feb. 22, 1770

Rocket—rocket patent—Andrew Lanergan—June 21, 1859

Royal Arcanum—founded—June 23, 1877

Schoolbook—printed—1689

Science Association—history of science society— organized—Jan. 12, 1924

Science Association—scientific society—Boston Philosophical Society—founded—1683

Second Advent Believers General Conference —Oct. 14-15, 1840

Sermon Printed (American)—reprinted—1724

Sewing Machine—sewing machine manufacturer —I. M. Singer—1851

Ship—naval ship named for an enlisted man— *Osmond Ingram*—commissioned, June 28, 1919

Ship—naval vessel of the United States to sail around the Cape of Good Hope to the west coast of the United States—*Constellation*—left —Dec. 1840

Ship—rocket-tracking ship—*Vanguard*—t completed in Atlantic Ocean—Jan. 31, 196

Ship—ship to carry the United States flag arc the world—*Columbia*—sailed—Sept. 30, 1?

Ship—ship to circumnavigate the world with one in the crew—*Spray*—sailed—April 24,

Ship—streamlined steamship—to arrive in United States—May 14, 1934

Shirt Factory—of importance—O. F. Winche —established—1848

Siamese Twins—Chang and Eng—arrived—, 16, 1829

Ski School—indoor ski school—R. H. Johns opened, Oct. 16, 1939

Statistical Society—American Statistical A ciation—formed—Nov. 27, 1839

Submarine—submarine to travel under the N Pole from the East—*Skate*—returned, Sept 1958

Subway—municipal subway—construc started—March 28, 1895

Swimming School—opened—July 23, 1827

Symphony—symphonic work by an Amer composer—J. K. Paine—Jan. 1876

Telephone—long-distance telephone call New York City—March 27, 1884

Telephone—news dispatch by telephone—to *Globe*—Feb. 12, 1877

Telephone—telephone conversation over ou door wires—to Cambridge—Oct. 9, 1876

Telephone—telephone message—distinguish —March 10, 1876

Telephone—telephone switchboard or excha —May 17, 1877

Telephone—underground cable long-dista telephone conversation—to Washington, —Feb. 26, 1914

Telephone Operator—woman telephone oper —E. M. Nutt—Sept. 1, 1878

Television—Telecast—Catholic mass telev from a studio—WBZ-TV—June 10, 1953

Television—Telecast—color network telecas compatible color—June 7, 1953

Television—Telecast—stockholders' mee televised coast-to-coast simultaneously— 29, 1959

Television—Telecast—stratovision World S telecast—Oct. 11, 1948

Tennis—court tennis—introduced—Hollis I newell—1876

Theater—television theater—licensed—ope —July 13, 1938

Theater—theater destroyed by fire—Fed Street Theater—Feb. 2, 1798

Theater—theater lighted by electricity—B Theater—Dec. 11, 1882

Theological School—theological school to a women—Boston University School of Theo —formed—March 30, 1871

Theological School—theological school to pre regular courses by scholars representing di ent denominations—Boston Theological S nary—opened—Sept. 1867

t Society—tract society—formed—Sept. 1,
03

arian Church—national organization of the
nitarian Churches of the United States and
anada—American Unitarian Association—
ganized—May 25, 1825

arian Church—Unitarian church building—
ected—1632

arian Minister—Unitarian minister—James
reeman—ordained—Nov. 18, 1787

arian Prayer Book—*A Liturgy*—published—
85

deville—originated—1883

ding Machine—vending machine (coin-oper-
ed) to dispense postage stamps—manufac-
red—1892

rinary School—veterinary college—Boston
eterinary Institute—incorporated—April 28,
55

ing Celebrities—pontiff to visit the White
ouse—Pope John Paul II—arrived Oct. 1, 1979

ng Machine—electric vote recorder—patent-
—T. A. Edison—June 1, 1869

er—municipal water supply system—built—
52

er Conduit—drinking water conduit—built—
48

l—worsted mill—established—John Cornish
1695

ng Men's Christian Association—Young
en's Christian Association—organized—Dec.
, 1851

ng Women's Christian Association—orga-
zed—1866

Bradford

sionary Society—foreign missionary society
organized—June 29, 1810

Braintree

Quincy

Brant Rock

io Broadcast—radio program broadcast—
ec. 24, 1906

Bridgewater

ning, Carding, and Roping Machines—manu-
ctured—1786

Brockton

igerator—household refrigerating machine
tent—A. T. Marshall—Aug. 8, 1899

Brookline

ntry Club—country club to remain in exis-
nce 80 years—organized—Sept. 13, 1882

ing Rink—indoor curling rink—opened—Dec.
, 1920

nis Match—lawn tennis matches for the Davis
up—Aug. 8–10, 1900

Buckland

Bridge—bridge of flowers—to Shelburne, Mass.—
1929

Byfield

Wool—wool carding machine—installed—1793

Cambridge

Almanac—by William Peirce—1639

Astronomer—astronomer of note in the American
colonies—observations made—April 19, 1739

Astronomy Expedition—left—Oct. 9, 1780

Aviation—School—aeronautical   engineering
course—complete college course—1913

Baseball Catcher's Mask—manufactured—1876

Bible—Bible in an American Indian language—
translation—1661

Bible Concordance—Bible concordance—published—1683

Blind—machine for reading printed matter aloud
—Raymond Kurzweil—demonstrated Jan. 13,
1976

Book—book (full-size)—published—July 1640

Book—book (pamphlet) on vellum—published—
1854

Book—book privately printed—1665

Bookseller—of importance—Hezekiah Usher—
1639

Bronze Statue—full-length statue—1847

Business History Chair—established—1923

Camera—nonelectronic device for observing in
total darkness—announced—Feb. 15, 1956

Chemistry Laboratory—chemical laboratory in a
collegiate institution—1858

Children's Book—published—1641

Chlorophyll—chlorophyll "a"—synthesized—R.
B. Woodward—June 27, 1960

City Planning Instruction—offered—1909

Climatology Professor—appointed—1910

College—college—established—Sept. 8, 1636

College—college entrance requirement, other
than Greek, Latin, and arithmetic—1807

College Student—American Indian to graduate
from college—Caleb Cheeshahteaumuck—Harvard College—1665

College Student—college student to work his way
through college—Zechariah Brigden—1657

Congregational Church—Congregational Church
council—met—Aug. 30, 1637

Cooperative—college cooperative store—Feb. 28,
1882

Corporation—corporate body—Harvard chartered—May 30, 1650

Court-martial—military   court-martial—commenced—Jan. 20, 1778

Cryotrons—publicly reported—D. A. Buck—Feb.
6, 1957

Degrees (academic and honorary)—Bachelor of
Arts degree—conferred—Harvard College—
Sept. 23, 1642

MASSACHUSETTS—Cambridge—*Continued*

Degrees (academic and honorary)—Doctor of Laws honorary degree—Harvard—July 21, 1773

Degrees (academic and honorary)—Doctor of Sacred Theology degree—Harvard—Increase Mather—Sept. 5, 1692

Degrees (academic and honorary)—honorary degree granted George Washington—Harvard—April 3, 1776

Divinity Professor—E. Wigglesworth—appointed —Jan. 24, 1722

Entomology Professor—H. A. Hagen—1870

Fire Prevention Legislation—enacted—March 17, 1631

Football Game—rugby contest (international)—with McGill University—May 14, 1874

Football Goalpost—football goalpost—used—May 14, 1874

Football Team—football team to score more than 750 points in 1 season—Harvard College

Gas Mask—gas mask with a self-contained breathing apparatus—patented—B. J. Lane—July 2, 1850

Grammar—American Indian grammar—John Eliot—published—1666

Gymnastics Instruction—gymnastics instruction at a college—1826

Hebrew Type—used—1640

History—History of New England—published—1669

History Instruction—ancient and modern history chair—1838

Impregnation—impregnation (artificial)—Nov. 1939

Jury—grand jury—convened Sept. 1, 1635

King—king born in the United States—Rama IX of Thailand—Dec. 5, 1927

Language Instruction—French instruction—1733

Lawbook—compilation of colonial laws—published—1648

Law School—law school of collegiate rank—Harvard College School of Law—opened—1817

Long Jump—broad jump to reach more than 25 feet—E. O. Gourdin—July 23, 1921

Medical Instruction—bacteriology lectures—H. C. Ernst—1885

Medical Instruction—dermatology chair—Dr. J. C. White—1871

Medical Instruction—hygiene lectures—Dr. J. Jackson—1818

Medical Instruction—pathology chair—J. B. S. Jackson—1847

Museum—museum devoted exclusively to paper-making—opened—June 5, 1939

Museum—Semitic museum—Harvard University —opened to public, May 13, 1891—formally opened, Feb. 5, 1903

Music Book—hymnbook—published—1640

Music Instruction—college music chair—established—Aug. 30, 1875

Naval Officer—black commissioned officer in the Naval Reserve—B. W. Robinson—commissioned—June 18, 1942

Newspaper—newspaper—Samuel Green—16

Nobel Prize—Nobel Prize in chemistry—T. Richards—1914

Orchestra—college orchestra—founded—M 6, 1808

Photograph—photograph of a star (other than sun)—July 17, 1850

Photograph—photograph (taken in the Un States) on which a meteor was found—Aug 1889

Piano Player—piano player—patented— McTammany, Jr.—June 14, 1881

Planetarium—planetarium or orrery—import 1732

Play (drama)—Greek play—produced—*Oed Tyrannus*—May 1881

Play (drama)—play of note written by an Am can and acted in America—*Gustavus Va* presented—1690

Political Economy Course—political econom chair—C. F. Dunbar—1871

Primer—primer in an American Indian diale *Indian Primer*—published—1669

Printing—document printed in America—"(of a Free Man"—March 1639

Printing Instruction—printing lecture course college—Feb. 1911

Printing Press—printing press—operated—M 1639

Quakers—Synod of Quakers—Sept. 9–Oct. 2,

Quinine—synthetic quinine—produced—/ 10, 1944

Revolutionary War—Revolutionary War vc teer detachment—arrived, July 18, 1775

Spelling Book—spelling book printed—Ste Day—1643

Stadium—cement stadium—completed—190

Synod—synod—1637

Synod—synod (ecumenical)—1646–1648

Telephone—telephone conversation over ou door wires—Oct. 9, 1876

Telescope—telescope patent—Alvan Cla Nov. 11, 1851

Theological School—theological school (nor tarian)—organized—1816

Thesis Directory—published—Stephen D 1642

Traffic Regulation Course—graduate cours traffic engineering and administration— 16, 1937

Vitamin—synthetic vitamin K—made—Dr. Fieser—Aug. 1, 1939

Windmill—erected—1632

Cambridgeport

Lens—achromatic lenses—made—1844

Camp Devens

Horse Race—300-mile endurance run—from lington, Vt.—Oct. 15, 1919

MASSACHUSETTS—Greenfield—*Continued*

Manual Training—manual training institute—opened—1829

Groton

Architecture School—landscape architecture course for women—certificates awarded—June 10, 1903

Hamilton

Golf Tournament—professional open championship—June 14, 1901

Haverhill

Woman—heroine—publicly rewarded—Hannah Duston—1697

Hingham

Ship—warship named for a black—*Harmon*—laid down, April 12, 1943

Holbrook

Balloon Honeymoon—balloon honeymoon—ended June 20, 1909

Holyoke

Telephone—toll-line commercial telephone service—instituted—April 2, 1879
Volleyball—developed—W. G. Morgan—1895

Hopkinton

Marathon Race (annual)—to Boston—April 19, 1897
Ship—roll-on roll-off carrier—in service—to Nantucket—Sept. 1, 1955
Shoe Peg—invented—Joseph Walker—1818

Ipswich

Botanic Scientific Expedition—started—July 19, 1784

Lancaster

Genealogy—genealogical collective work—published—1829
Manual Training—industrial school for girls—incorporated—Aug. 27, 1856

Lawrence

Mohair—commercially manufactured—Arlington Mills—1872
Water Purification—municipal filtration system—completed—Sept. 1893

Leicester

Geology Book—geology textbook—published—1818

Leominster

Baby Carriage Factory—F. W. & F. A. Whitn 1858

Lexington

Fair—centennial celebration—April 19, 1875
Normal School—normal school (state)—op —July 3, 1839
Revolutionary War—armed conflict in the F lutionary War—April 19, 1775
Telephone—common battery (nonmul switchboard—operated—Jan. 9, 1894

Little Brewster Island

Lighthouse—lighthouse—built—1716

Lowell

Belts of Leather—for transmitting power—1
Carpet Loom—carpet power loom—used—Lc Manufacturing Co.
Carpet Loom—carpet power loom to weav grain carpets—1841
Cash Carrier System—installed—Feb. 1879
Ordnance—machine gun—patented—C. Barnes—July 8, 1856
Periodical—factory workers' magazine—*Lowell Offering*—published—October 184
Rubber—rubber heel—manufactured—pat Jan. 24, 1899
Soda Fountain—ornamented soda founta manufactured—1858
Sprinkler—sprinkler—installation—1852
Turbine—turbine successfully operated by v power—1844
Woman—woman telegrapher—S. G. Bagl Feb. 21, 1846

Lynn

Baseball Catcher's Mask—used—April 12, 1
Blackout—blackout lighting demonstrati May 14, 1941
Brass and Iron Foundry—Joseph Jencks—16
Bridge—pontoon bridge—1804
Fire Engine—constructed—Joseph Jencks—1
Iron—exportation of iron—1650
Labor Union—women's labor organization tional)—convention—July 28, 1869
Money—dies for coins in America—made seph Jencks—1652
Welding—welding by the electric process— ented—Elihu Thomson—Aug. 10, 1886

Malden

Clock—clock to operate by atomic pow Atomicron manufactured
Motion Picture Projector—motion picture pr tor patent—O. B. Brown—Aug. 10, 1869

Marblehead

—warship regularly commissioned—*Hannah*
—Sept. 2, 1775

Mare Mount

ortation—Thomas Morton—June 9, 1628

Martha's Vineyard

erican Indians—American Indian preacher of
hristianity—ordained—Aug. 22, 1670

Medfield

hes—manufactured—Artemas Woodward—
08

Medford

ery (commercial)—established—1629

Meeting House Pond

ld War I—shots to land on American soil—
ly 21, 1918

Melrose

nt Examiner—woman patent examiner—A.
G. Nichols—served—July 1, 1873

Methuen

urt—yogurt dairy—established—Sarkis
olombosian—1929

Millbury

um—organized—Oct. 1826

Millville

ory—factories operated by the United States
overnment—project commenced—June 4,
34

Milton

ge—bridge erected—to Dorchester—1634
rch—children's church—dedicated—Nov. 14,
37
ker—hard water crackers—manufactured—
01
—iron slitting mill—established—1710

Minot's Ledge

thouse—iron pile lighthouse—completed—
n. 1, 1850

Mount Greylock

w—artificial snow—produced—Nov. 13, 1946

Nantucket

oat—lifeboat—built—1807
tical School—nautical school—established—
ay 29, 1827

Prison—prison—constructed—1676
Ship—roll-on roll-off carrier—in service—to Hyannis, Mass.—Sept. 1, 1955
Whale—sperm whale—captured—1711
Whaling—whaling expedition—started—c. 1715

Natick

American Indian Church—church for American Indians in New England—established—1600

New Bedford

Coast Guard (U.S.)—Coast Guard officers' training school—established—July 31, 1876
Helicopter—helicopter to deliver material across a picket line—March 9, 1947

Newburyport

Algebra Book—algebra book by a native-born American—published—1788
Astronomer—astronomer to acquire fame after the Revolution—Nathaniel Bowditch—1802
Coast Survey Book—published—March 1796
Cracker Bakery—Theodore Pearson—1792
Engraving—pamphlet produced from a steel plate engraving—Perkins' and Fairman's *Running Hand Stereographic Copies*—published—Charles Whipple—1815
Library—library newspaper room—dedicated—April 28, 1882
Ship—revenue cutter—*Massachusetts*—keel laid—1791
Wool—wool carding machine—built—1793

Newport

Pushball—invented—M. G. Crane—1894

Newton

Time Recorder—autograph time recorder—B. F. Merritt—Dec. 20, 1887

Newtowne (Newe-Towne)

See Cambridge

North Beverly

Animals—reindeer—born—May 31, 1929

Northampton

Basketball—basketball played at a women's college—Smith College—1892
College—women's volunteer college unit to serve overseas—Smith College Relief Unit—1917
Deaf—School—oral school for the deaf (still existing)—Clarke School for the Deaf—founded—1867
Degrees (academic and honorary)—Doctor of Philosophy degree awarded to a woman by a women's college—K. E. Morris—June 21, 1882
Gymnasium—gymnasium to offer systematic instruction—Round Hill School—opened—Oct. 1, 1823

MASSACHUSETTS—Northampton—*Continued*

Naval Officer—woman doctor in the WAVES—C. J. Gaskill—commissioned Sept. 7, 1942
Pencil—indelible pencil—patented—E. P. Clark—July 10, 1866
Sugar—sugar beets—factory—D. L. Child—erected—1838
Theater—municipal theater—Academy of Music —Feb. 9, 1893

Northfield

Biblical Students Summer Conference—organized—July 7, 1886
Youth Hostel—opened—Dec. 27, 1934

Orleans

World War I—shots to land on American soil— fired at tugs near Nauset Bluffs—July 21, 1918

Paxton

Radio License—frequency modulation (FM) construction permit—WIXOJ—Aug. 18, 1937

Pecoit

Ordnance—gunpowder mill—operated—1639

Penikese Island

Science School—natural science summer school —opened—1873

Pittsfield

Animals—sheep (Merino sheep) exhibition—1807
Baseball Game—intercollegiate baseball game— Amherst vs. Williams—July 1, 1859
Broadcloth—produced—1793
Fair—agricultural fair—Oct. 1, 1810
Lightning (artificial)—demonstrated—June 10, 1932
Lightning Observatory—erected—General Electric Company—1935

Plymouth

Chimes—chimes and bells manufactured—Benjamin Hanks
Congregational Church—Congregational Church —founded—1620
Duel—duel—recorded—June 18, 1621
Earthquake—earthquake description—June 1, 1638
Execution—execution in America—John Billington—hanged—Sept. 30, 1630
Furs—exported—Robert Cushman—Dec. 13, 1621
Governor—native-born governor of New England —Josiah Winslow—elected—1673
Leather—leather tanning—first tanner—Experience Miller—1623
Medical Book—hydrophobia book—*Observations on Hydrophobia*—published—1812
Pension—pension act—1636

Physician—doctor in New England—Sar Fuller—arrived—Dec. 21, 1620
Postage Stamp—postage stamps without words *United States* or the initials *U.S.*—Pil Tercentenary issue—on sale, Dec. 18, 1920
Representative (U.S.)—representative who been a President of the United States— Adams—began service March 4, 1831
Sermon Printed (American)—delivered—De 1621
Treaty—colonial treaty with the Indians—Ap 1621

Provincetown

Postage Stamp—postage stamps without words *United States* or the initials *U.S.*—Pil Tercentenary issue—on sale, Dec. 18, 1920
Submarine—submarine accident—*Bonita* (l named *C-4*) rammed offshore by gunboat *tine*—July 11, 1910

Quincy

Granite—quarried—1820
Photograph—photograph of a former Preside the United States at his home—J. Q. Ada 1843
Radar—offshore radar warning station—bu 1955
Radio Broadcast—transatlantic radio pro from England—received, Nov. 25, 1923
Railroad—railroad—for freight transportatio celebrate its centenary—Granite Railway C road completed—Oct. 7, 1826
Railroad Accident—railroad accident—July 1832
School—school to operate on the one-class room basis—established—1846
Ship—air-conditioned ship—*Mariposa*—keel —May 17, 1930
Ship—atomic-powered cruiser—*Long Bea* launched—July 14, 1959
Ship—battleship to use fuel oil exclusive *Nevada*—laid down, Nov. 4, 1912—laun July 11, 1914
Ship—naval ship christened by a woman r U.S. citizen—*Canberra*—launched, Apri 1943
Ship—naval ship named for an enlisted m *Osmond Ingram*—launched, Feb. 23, 1919
Ship—rocket-tracking ship—*Vanguard*—with new body
Ship—schooner (seven-masted, steel)—*Tho W. Lawson*—launched—July 10, 1902
Typesetting Machine—photoengraving speed process for making halftones—in o tion—Feb. 26, 1954

Readville

Horse—horse to pace 1 mile in better than 2 Star Pointer—Aug. 28, 1897

MASSACHUSETTS—Springfield—*Continued*

Football Club—intercollegiate football association—formed—Nov. 23, 1876
Kindergarten Manual—*The Paradise of Childhood*—published—1869
Match—match patent—phosphorous friction matches—A. D. Phillips—Oct. 24, 1836
Meat Packer—William Pynchon—1636
Motorcycle—motorcycle (twin-cycle)—manufactured—1905
Motorcycle—motorcycle with built-in gas engine—manufactured—1901
Ordnance—metal cartridge—patented—D. B. Wesson—Aug. 8, 1854
Ordnance—muskets—made—Springfield Armory—1795
Skate (all-metal)—marketed—E. H. Barney—1864
Telephone—toll-line commercial telephone service—instituted—April 2, 1879
Wrench—wrench patent—Solyman Merrick—Aug. 17, 1835

Squantum

Ship—naval ship named for a dental officer—*Osborne*—launched, Dec. 29, 1919

Sterling

Paper Patterns—manufactured—Ebenezer Butterick—1863

Stockbridge

Village Improvement Society—with a continued existence—formed—Aug. 24, 1853

Taunton

Britannia Ware—manufactured—1824
Silk—silk power loom—patented—William Crompton—Nov. 25, 1837

Thompson Island

Band—school band—formed—1857

Uxbridge

Woman—woman whose vote was recorded—1756

Waltham

Coal Oil Factory—to manufacture coal oil from coal tar—1853
Cotton Mill—cotton mill in the world in which the whole process of cotton manufacturing from spinning to weaving was carried on by power—incorporated—Feb. 23, 1813

Ward

See under Auburn

Ware

Bedspring—bedspring manufacturing patent siah French—Aug. 25, 1831

Watertown

See under Cambridge

Waverly

Baseball Catcher's Mask—patented—F. W. T er—Feb. 12, 1878

Wellesley

Spectrophotometer—patented—A. C. Har Jan. 8, 1935

West Boylston

Carpet Loom—carpet power loom—patente B. Bigelow—April 20, 1837

West Bridgewater

Shovel—shovel (steel)—manufactured— Ames—1774

West Lynn

Vectolite—manufactured—Feb. 27, 1935

West Newbury

Comb Factory—1759

Westborough

Prison—reformatory for boys (state)—autho —April 9, 1847

Westfield

Whips—manufactured commercially—1801

Westford

Television—Telecast—transcontinental tel by means of an orbiting satellite—receiv April 24, 1962

Westover Air Force Base

Helicopter—Flights—helicopter transat flight—left for Germany—July 15, 1952

Weymouth

Pen—ball-point pen patent—J. J. Loud—Oc 1888

Whitinsville

Locomotive—locomotive owned by an indu company—in service, May 11, 1892

Whitman

Insurance—savings bank life insurance—ba establish department—June 18, 1908

Williamstown

ge Alumni Association—college alumni as-
iation—formed—Williams College—Sept.
1

rnity (Greek letter)—fraternity house—oc-
ied—1839

Winthrop

rcycle—motorcycle (steam-driven)—invent-
—W. A. Austin—1868

Woods Hole

on Honeymoon—ballon honeymoon—begun
e 20, 1909

—ship outfitted for hurricane research—
wford—July 3, 1956

Worcester

ive—manufactured—1934

—Bible in folio size to be illustrated—pub-
ed—1791

—Greek testament—printed—1800

le Trip—bicycle trip of 100 miles sponsored
a club—to Boston—Sept. 6, 1882

rd Match—intercollegiate billiard match—
25, 1860

Race—intercollegiate regatta—July 26, 1859

—book printed on American paper with
erican-made plates and bound in America—
giac Sonnets and Other Poems—1795

pe—patented—Oct. 9, 1855

er for Cutting Hair—manufactured—G. H.
tes—1876

es (academic and honorary)—anthropology
torate—Clark University—March 9, 1892

nary—agricultural dictionary—The New
land Farmer—published—1790

nary—dictionary published in the United
es—published—1788

nary—pocket dictionary—Royal Standard
lish Dictionary—published—1788

ope—envelope folding and gumming ma-
e—patented—J. A. Sherman—Feb. 8, 1898

ope—envelope folding machine—practical
atented—R. L. Hawes—Jan. 21, 1853

anto Course—Esperanto course carrying
ege credit—Clark University—Sept. 16, 1908

aphy School—Clark University—opened—

ical Society—historical society (national)—
erican Antiquarian Society—incorporated
ct. 24, 1812

er—black lawyer formally admitted to the
—M. B. Allen—passed examination—May
45

Twine Machinery—patented—G. L. Brow-
—Dec. 17, 1895

-park land—purchased by a city—March
854

g History—Isaiah Thomas—published—

Prizefight—prizefight arena—first fight held—Jan.
7, 1824

Psychology Society—psychology society (national organization)—American Psychological
Association—organized—July 8, 1892

Rocket—liquid-fuel rocket patent—R. H. Goddard
—July 14, 1914

Sewage—sewage disposal by chemical precipitation—1890

Silk—silk loom—of importance—Gem Silk Loom
—built—1887

Spring Winding Machine—built—1892

War—rebellion against the federal government—
Daniel Shays—1786

Wire—piano wire—produced—1850

Wire Gauge—developed—1849

Woman Suffrage—convention (national) of
women advocating woman suffrage—Oct. 23–
24, 1850

MICHIGAN

Capital Punishment—death penalty first abolished—March 1, 1847

Cooperative—cooperative state law—effective—
March 20, 1865

Fireworks Legislation—fireworks legislation
(state)—enacted—March 29, 1929

Telephone—Trimline telephone—commercially
available—Aug. 2, 1965

Woman Suffrage—woman suffrage amendment
approved by Congress—ratified—June 10, 1919

Adrian

Degrees (academic and honorary)—Bachelor of
Music degree—awarded M. P. Lowrie—Dec. 23,
1873

Seeding Machine (practical)—patented—Joseph
Gibbons—Aug. 25, 1840

Wire—woven wire fence industry—factory—J.
W. Page—1883

Ann Arbor

Bibliography Course—University of Michigan—
1878

College—college entrance "certified school plan"
—introduced—Sept. 1871

College—honors course—University of Michigan
—Sept. 1882

College—state university supported by a direct
property tax—approved—March 15, 1867

College Alumni Association—college alumni association secretary (full-time paid position)—
established—June 30, 1897

Forestry School—forestry course in a university—
established—1881

History Instruction—history seminar—University
of Michigan—1869

Ice Skating Champion—ice skater to cover 100
miles in less than 6 hours—Kirt Barnes—Feb.
26, 1971

Medical Clinic—heredity clinic—opened—Nov.
12, 1941

MICHIGAN—Ann Arbor—*Continued*

Medical Instruction—bacteriology courses in a college—Jan. 1889

Microfilm—book series microfilmed—microfilmed—1935

Microfilm—microfilm machine to project enlarged images on ceilings—1945

Microfilm—microfilms of U.S. Government publications or documents—April 1952

Pedagogy Chair—pedagogy chair (permanent)—established—1879

Physician—Chinese woman to receive a Doctor of Medicine degree—Mary Stone—June 22, 1896

Public Speaking Department—established—1892

Battle Creek

Bowler—bowler to earn $100,000 in 1 year in tournaments—Earl Anthony—earnings reached $100,890 on Oct. 27, 1975

Microfilm—microfilm machine to project enlarged images on ceilings—installed—March 21, 1946

Bay City

Crane—wrecking crane—built—1883

Beaver Islands

King—"king" to exercise the authority of king and high priest in the United States—J. J. Strang—settled in St. James

Benton Harbor

House of David—established—May 1, 1903

Dearborn

Automobile—plastic automobile—manufactured —Aug. 1941

Detroit

Army Officer—woman to command an Armed Forces Examining and Entrance Station—M. V. Parker—May 31, 1975

Autogiro—autogiro used commercially—*Detroit News No. 2*—delivered Feb. 12, 1931

Automobile—automobile with left-hand steering —manufactured—1907

Automobile—free-piston automobile—announced—April 15, 1956

Automobile—gas-turbine automobile operated on city streets—April 19, 1955

Automobile—production of more than one million passenger cars of one make in one year—Chevrolet—1949

Automobile—sedan type automobile

Automobile—transparent-top automobile—Sun Valley—manufactured—Dec. 7, 1953

Automobile Bus—gas-turbine bus—announced—June 10, 1954

Automobile Electric Self-Starter—automobile electric self-starter applied commercially—May 1911

Aviation—airplane diesel engine—1928

Aviation—Airplane—airplane owned by a company—*Stanolind*—first flight, to Chica May 21, 1927

Aviation—Airship—dirigible made complete metal—tested—Aug. 19, 1929

Aviation—Pilot—woman pilot to pilot an a transport—from Washington, D.C.—lanc Dec. 31, 1934

Billiard Match—billiard match to attain in tional prominence—April 12, 1859

Catholic Periodical—Catholic magazine English—issued Aug. 31, 1809

Corporation—corporation to earn more tha billion in one year—General Motors—195

Electric Transmission—substation with a r converter completely unattended—April

Hammer (pneumatic)—patented—C. B. K Jan. 30, 1894

Hockey Player—professional hockey play reach a score of more than 1,000 points regular season—Gordon Howe—reached points Nov. 27, 1960

Hockey Player—professional hockey play score 6 goals in 1 game—Syd Howe—F 1944

Medical Book—hydrotherapy book in E published originally in America—publisl 1892

Newspaper—newspaper association—Ame Newspaper Publishers Association—orga —1886

Newspaper—newspaper printed on a tr *Weekly Herald*—Feb. 3, 1862

Newspaper—newspaper to operate a radi tion—*News* (Detroit, Mich.)—WWJ bega erating, Aug. 20, 1920

Orchestra—radio orchestra—May 28, 1922

Piano Player—pneumatic piano player—pat —E. S. Votey—May 22, 1900

Pinball Game—pinball game machine (manufactured—1910

Police—police officer (woman) to be appoin 1893

Prizefight—championship heavyweight title in the first round—Jeffries vs. Finnegan— 6, 1900

Public School—public school classes for epi children—organized—Jan. 1935

Radio Broadcast—election returns broadc Aug. 31, 1920

Radio Broadcast—news program—Aug. 31,

Radio Broadcast—prizefight broadcast—Se 1920

Radio Station—commercial radio station— service—WWJ—Aug. 20, 1920

Railroad Car—refrigerator car patent—aw —J. B. Sutherland—Nov. 26, 1867

Runner—runner (professional) to run a m less than 4 minutes—Jim Ryun—April 13

Ship—Eagle boat—keel laid, May 7—laur July 11, 1918

Sponge—oxidized cellulose (sponge) for m and surgical use—marketed—June 5, 194

;ical **Operation**—mitral valve exposure (pro-
nged) in a human patient and corrective sur-
ry—July 3, 1952

phone—air-to-ground public telephone ser-
ce—Chicago–Detroit area—Sept. 15, 1957

vision—Telecast—international telecast—
WJ-TV—Oct. 15, 1951

ler Church—St. Paul's Wayside Cathedral—
operation—Oct. 1, 1937

nel—vehicular tunnel to a foreign country—
ened—Nov. 3, 1930

ting Celebrities—Prince of Wales—Albert Ed-
ard—arrived—Sept. 20, 1860

lding—transatlantic telephone wedding—
c. 2, 1933

lding—wedding broadcast—M. E. Ebert and J.
Wichman—June 15, 1920

nan—woman labor delegate to a national
nvention—of the AFL—Mary Burke—Dec. 8,
90

East Lansing

ge President—college president (black) of a
ajor university predominantly white—C. R.
harton, Jr.—Michigan State University—as-
med charge Jan. 2, 1970

lers' Course in a College—Michigan State
ollege—1930

Flint

mobile—plastic laminated fiberglass-body
orts car—manufactured—June 30, 1953

Fort Wayne

mobile—front-wheel-drive subcompact
nerican automobile—World Car—Ford
otor Company—first car off assembly line—
g. 11, 1980

Grand Rapids

ball Game—baseball game at night by a
gular league team—July 8, 1909

et Sweeper—practical—M. R. Bissell—1876

tric Power Plant—hydroelectric power plant
ommercial)—organized—March 22, 1880

e Warden (salaried game and fish warden)
W. A. Smith—1887

er—community to fluoridate its municipal
ter—Jan. 25, 1945

Grosse Ile

tion—Airship—dirigible made completely of
tal—tested—Aug. 19, 1929

Hancock

ge—Finnish college—Suomi College—
ened Sept. 8, 1896

Hillsdale

Aviation—aeronautical elopement—Arthur
Smith and Aimée Cour—from Fort Wayne, Ind.
—Oct. 26, 1912

Holland

Chloromycetin—chloromycetin laboratory—
March 13, 1952

Houghton

Hockey—professional hockey team—Portage
Lake Hockey Club—formed, 1896/1897—
became professional 1903

Ishpeming

Ski Club—ski club association—meeting—Jan.
16, 1891

Jackson

College—college commencement exercises within a prison—Jan. 20, 1975

Telephone—Trimline telephone—in service—
Oct. 21, 1963

Kalamazoo

Drill—dental drill (electric)—patented—G. F.
Green—Jan. 26, 1875

Lansing

Agricultural School—agricultural college (state)
to open—Agricultural College of Michigan—
May 13, 1857

Mendon

Locomotive Headlight—electric locomotive headlight—patented—May 3, 1881

Mount Clemens

Aviation—Flights—airplane to fly faster than 200
m.p.h.—L. J. Maitland—Oct. 14, 1922

Aviation—Flights (transatlantic)—jet transatlantic flight west–east—to Odiham, England—July
20, 1948

Mount Vernon

Typewriter—typewriter—patented—W. A. Burt
—July 23, 1829

Olivet

College—college to dispense with the system of
credits, hours, points, grades, etc.—Olivet College—Oct. 1, 1934

Plymouth

Air Gun—wooden gun marketed—Markham
Manufacturing Co.—March 1886—metal gun
manufactured, 1888

MICHIGAN—*Continued*

Pontiac

Aviation—Airport—airport to receive an AI-A rating—Feb. 11, 1930

Curling Club—organized—1831–32

Motion Picture—motion picture of the sun—June 19, 1934

Port Huron

Newspaper—newspaper printed on a train—*Weekly Herald*—Feb. 3, 1862

Tunnel—subaqueous railroad tunnel to a foreign country—opened—Sept. 19, 1891

River Rouge

Taconite—taconite production—Mesabi Iron Co., Babbitt, Minn.—first cargo shipped to Ford Motor Company—Oct. 1

Royal Oak

National Union for Social Justice—formed—Nov. 1934

Warren

Smog Chamber—smog chamber built by an industrial organization for air pollution research—General Motors Research Laboratories—in operation, July 1962

Wayne County

Road—concrete rural road—laid—1909

Traffic Lines—painted—1911

Wyandotte

Steel—Bessemer steel converter—erected—1864

Steel Analysis Laboratory—established—W. F. Durfee—1862

MINNESOTA

Election Law—federal legislation enabling persons 18 years of age or older to vote—first state to ratify (26th Amendment)—March 23, 1971

Election Law—primary election law—enacted—April 20, 1899

Optometry Legislation—state—enacted—April 13, 1901

Austin

Strike—modern sit-down strike—G. A. Hormel & Co.—Nov. 13, 1933

Babbitt

Taconite—taconite production—Mesabi Iron Co.—undertaken November 1919—first cargo produced June 21, 1922

Crosby

Balloon—Flights—balloon flight to exceed an tude of 100,000 feet—D. G. Simons—Aug 1957

Television—Telecast—stratosphere teleca Strato-Lab High III—Malcolm Ross and N Lewis—takeoff, July 26, 1958

Duluth

Bridge—aerial ferry—opened—April 9, 1905

Canal—St. Lawrence Seaway—opened—, 25, 1959

Ship—whaleback steamer to cross the Atlan sailed—June 11, 1891

Faribault

Cathedral—Episcopal cathedral—Cathedra Our Merciful Saviour—completed—1869

Minneapolis

Automobile—armored commercial car comp ly protected—construction commenc March 1919

Book Index—monthly cumulative index of b —published—Feb. 1898

Electric Toaster—electric toaster—housel type—marketed—June 1926

Golf Champion—golfer to win both the U: States Open and the United States Amate the same year—Charles Evans, Jr.—U.S. C —June 30, 1916

Ink—ink paste—patented—F. B. Cooney—Ja 1924

Library—children's department in a libra Minneapolis Public Library

Medical Society—immunology society— nized—June 19, 1913

Nursing School—university school of nursi authorized—Oct. 1, 1908

Political Convention—political party nat delegates (women)—T. A. Jenkins and C Carleton—June 7-10, 1892

Railroad Car—chapel car—*Evangel*—servic

Railroad Car—Pullman train completely equi with roller bearings—May 21, 1927

Surgical Operation—heart operation in whic deep-freezing technique was employed— 2, 1952

Television—Telecast—stockholders' mee televised coast-to-coast simultaneously— 29, 1959

Vending Machine—automatic liquid-dispe vending machine patent—W. H. Fruen—is Dec. 16, 1884

War Veterans' Society—American Legion—national convention—Nov. 10, 1919

Woman—woman state budget commissione W. Wittich—served—March 16, 1931

Minnesota Point

ge—aerial ferry—opened—April 9, 1905

New Ulm

ious Hillside Shrine—"The Way of the oss"—built—1884

Northfield

raphy Course—biography department—rleton College—1919

Ortonville

an—woman clerk of a state supreme court—F. Kaercher—elected—Nov. 7, 1922

Red Wing

lub—ski club (local) that was active—Auro-Ski Club—organized—Jan. 19, 1886

St. Paul

ultural School—vocational agricultural ool—opened—Oct. 18, 1888

y—Reserve Officers Training Corps Units—thorized—Oct. 21, 1916

mobile—armored commercial car complete-protected—in service—Feb. 1, 1920

phane—cellophane transparent tape—in-nted—R. G. Drew

puter—electronic computer to employ Thin-m Memory—announced—Dec. 9, 1960

stry Society—state forestry association—or-nized—Jan. 12, 1876

ital—crippled children's hospital (state)—thorized—April 23, 1897

spaper—radio facsimile newspaper—KSTP Dec. 17, 1937

oad Car—chapel car—*Evangel*—services

oad Car—Pullman train completely equipped th roller bearings—May 21, 1927

d-absorbing Material—rigid insulating board patented—Sept. 14, 1915

, Masking—pressure-sensitive adhesive sking tape—Scotch tape—commercially rketed—1926

Recorder—tape-recording machine for mass duction of tapes announced—Minnesota ning and Manufacturing Company—Jan. 26, 49

Silver Bay

nite—taconite—large-scale commercial ject

MISSISSIPPI

tor (U.S.)—black senator—H. R. Revels—cted—Jan. 20, 1870

State—state to repudiate a debt—1842

Bay St. Louis

Catholic Bishop—Catholic bishop (black) conse-crated in the United States—J. O. Bowers—Apr. 22, 1953

Catholic Seminarians (black) to be ordained to the priesthood by a black bishop—June 29, 1953

Catholic Seminary—Catholic seminary for the education of black priests—Sept. 16, 1923

Camp Shelby

Army Officer—army chaplain of Japanese ances-try—Masao Yamada—assigned June 9

Clarksdale

Cotton—cotton crop commercially produced en-tirely by machinery—1944

Columbus

College—state college for women—established—March 12, 1884

Holiday—Decoration Day—celebrated—May 30, 1868

Edgewater Park

Bridge (game) Player—bridge player to win more than 1,000 master points in 1 year—Oswald Jacoby—passed 1,000 mark Nov. 15, 1963

Jackson

Public Health—pellagra experiment—of note—Joseph Goldberger—test—Feb. 4, 1915

Meridian

Jewish Congregation—Jewish congregation to call a woman to exercise a rabbi's function—Jan. 26, 1951

Moss Point

Bank—national bank branch legally operated—chartered—March 14, 1907

Natchez

Ship—battleship to visit an inland city—*Missis-sippi*—May 20, 1909

Pascagoula

Ship—cargo ship fully automated and flying the American flag—*Mormacargo*—keel laid, April 22, 1963—launched, Jan. 25, 1964

Rodney

College—land grant college for blacks—estab-lished—1871

MISSISSIPPI—*Continued*

Tupelo

Electrical Contract—with federal government—signed—Nov. 11, 1933

Vicksburg

Ship—warship sunk by an underwater torpedo mine—*Cairo*—Dec. 12, 1862

Washington

College—women's college chartered—Elizabeth Female Academy—Feb. 17, 1819

MISSOURI

Dentistry—gold crown tooth—process described —May 1869

Senator (U.S.)—senator to serve three states—James Shields

State—state admitted to the Union west of the Mississippi River—Aug. 10, 1821

Tax—bachelor tax—effective—Jan. 1, 1821

Arcadia

Railroad Excursion—railroad excursion (mystery)—from St. Louis—May 21, 1932

Columbia

Journalism Course—history of journalism course —University of Missouri—1879

Journalism Course—journalism school—University of Missouri—opened—Sept. 14, 1908

Crystal City

Sash—wrought-iron window sash installation—Pittsburgh Plate Glass Co.—1929

De Soto

Newspaper—newspaper published by soldiers in the field—*United States American Volunteer* —May 21, 1861

Florissant

American Indian School—Catholic school for American Indians—St. Regis Seminary—opened May 11, 1824

Glasgow

Bridge—railroad all-steel bridge—in service—Nov. 1, 1879

Hannibal

Monument—statue to commemorate literary characters—erected—May 27, 1926

Postal Service—railroad post office—mail car built—1862

Independence

Medicare—medicare identification card—sented to H. S. Truman—Jan. 20, 1966

Jefferson Barracks

Army—cavalry unit—Regiment of Dragoons ganized—August 1833

Aviation—Parachute—parachute jump from airplane—March 1, 1912

Kansas City

Art Course—industrial camouflage course—sas City Art Institute—Oct. 15, 1940

Baseball Player—baseball player to play all sitions in 1 game—B. D. Campaneris—Se 1965

Business—shopping center in a suburban ness area—master plan April 22, 1922—struction began in November 1922—first te March 1923

Football Game—professional football gam last longer than 80 minutes—Miami Dolp vs. Kansas City Chiefs—Dec. 25, 1971

Freemasons—Order of De Molay—found 1919

Kidnapping—death penalty for kidnapping-posed—July 27, 1933

Newspaper—newspaper rotogravure sectio published—*Star*—March 29, 1914

Political Convention—woman delegate to ma seconding speech—Elizabeth Cohn—Jul 1900

Railroad—streamlined all-steel diesel-motor —Nov. 11, 1934

Railroad Car—train with fluorescent lights—St. Louis, Mo.—April 30, 1939

War Veterans' Society—World War II vete society officially recognized by Congre amalgamation of 11 groups—Dec. 12, 1944

Wedding—telegraph wedding—A. M. Ca and Penelope Cundiff—April 12, 1900

Kirksville

Medical Periodical—osteopathy magazine—*nal of Osteopathy*—published—May 1894

Medical School—osteopathy school—char —May 10, 1892

Physician—osteopath (woman)—J. H. Boll graduated—March 1, 1894

Louisiana

Patent—fruit tree patent—J. E. Markham—16, 1932

Macon

Physician—osteopathic physician—A. T. S treatment—June 22, 1874

MISSOURI—St. Louis—*Continued*

Olympic Games—black American athlete in the Olympic Games to place—G. C. Poage—at Third Olympiad—Aug. 31, 1904

Olympic Games—Olympic celebration—May 14, 1904

President (U.S.)—President to fly—Theodore Roosevelt—Oct. 11, 1910

Prizefight—international fight, with bare knuckles —June 15, 1869

Radio Broadcast—police broadcast—WIL—Sept. 4, 1921

Radio Broadcast—weather broadcasts—WEW— April 26, 1921

Railroad—railroad to run west of the Mississippi River—Pacific Railway of Missouri—incorporated—March 12, 1849

Railroad Car—dining car (all-electric)—in service to Chicago, Ill.—March 9, 1949

Railroad Car—freight car (Adapto Car)—in service to Wichita, Kan.—July 24, 1956

Railroad Car—train with fluorescent lights—to Kansas City—April 30, 1939

Railroad Excursion—railroad excursion (mystery)—to Arcadia, Mo.—May 21, 1932

Sash—wrought-iron window sash installation—constructed—1929

Sewing Machine—sewing machine to stitch buttonholes—patented—Charles Miller—March 7, 1854

Ship—ironclad naval vessels—accepted—Jan. 15, 1862

Silverites—first national convention—July 22, 1896

Streetcar—lightweight one-man streetcar—built

Sugar—sugar cane 9-roll mill with common gearing and a single engine—built—1892

Surgical Operation—lung removal—performed— April 5, 1933

Suture—fiberglass-sutures—used—mastoid operation—July 19, 1939

Telephone—mobile telephone commercial service—inaugurated—June 17, 1946

Telephone—mobile telephone conversation overseas—July 16, 1946

Telephone—mobile telephone news dispatch— May 15, 1946

Travelers Aid—instituted—1851

Vacuum Cleaner—motor-driven vacuum cleaner —patented—J. S. Thurman—Oct. 3, 1899

Vice President (U.S.)—Vice President to marry in office—A. W. Barkley

Springfield

Cemetery—federal cemetery in the United States to contain graves of both Union and Confederate soldiers—March 3, 1911

City (Lilliputian city)—built—June 6, 1925

Tipton

Postal Service—overland mail service—Butterfield stage lines—to San Francisco—Sept. 15, 1858

Washington

Pipe—corncob pipe commercial manufact Henry Tibbe—1869

Zither Factory—zither factory—establis Franz Schwartzer—1866

Westport Landing

Road—overland wagon road across the F Mountains—to Vancouver, Wash.—1842

MONTANA

Attorney General—assistant attorney ge (state) who was a woman—E. L. K. Hasl 1892

Pension—old age pension laws (state)—Mai 1923

Representative (U.S.)—representative (wo elected—Jeannette Rankin—March 4, 191

Representative (U.S.)—representative (wo to vote twice against the entry of the U.S war—Jeannette Rankin

Butte

Mineral Segregation—by flotation—comme operation—J. M. Hyde—1911

Superior

Bible—Bibles in hotel rooms—Oct. 1908

Williston Basin

Oil—plastic pipeline to transport oil cross-e try—start of line—in service, Oct. 19, 195

NEBRASKA

Forest Service—federal planting of trees—1

Governor—governor to appoint two United S senators in one year for interim terms—R Crosby—1954

Holiday—Arbor Day—celebration—April 1872

Legislature—unicameral legislature (sta adopted—Nov. 6, 1934

Beatrice

Homestead—taken—Jan. 1, 1863

Chadron

Horse Race—horse race of 1,000 miles—to C go—started—June 13, 1893

Fairview

Motion Picture—presidential candidate shov motion pictures—W. J. Bryant—filmed Jul 1908

Grand Island

Medal—Interstate Commerce Commission M of Honor—awarded—G. H. Poell—Dec. 5,

Lincoln

ration Course—industrial corporation
·se—University of Nebraska—1888
ad—streamlined all-steel diesel-motor train
Kansas City, Mo.—Nov. 11, 1934

North Platte

West Show—prepared and exhibited—July
483

Omaha

r—bowler to win $10,000 in a tournament—
·y Smith—Jan. 15, 1960
l Trade Commission—Federal Trade Com-
·ion trade practice conference—Oct. 3, 1919
olling (Birling) National Championship—
t. 9, 1898
ad—streamlined lightweight high-speed
·e-car passenger train—operated—March 2,
·
·road paved with glasphalt—completed,
· 6, 1971
ng Machine—vending machine law—enact-
·May 10, 1898

NEVADA

·ics Legislation—narcotics prohibitory
·lation (state)—enacted March 19, 1965
·ics Legislation—narcotics regulation
·e)—adopted—March 10, 1933
n—old age pension laws (state)—March 5,
·

Boulder City

c Power Plant—hydroelectric power plant
·oduce a million kilowatts—June 1943

Carson City

·ion—lethal-gas execution—Gee Jon—Feb.
·24
·—coins with a double mint mark—pro-
·d by U.S. Mint—1882-1884
· Picture—motion picture of a prizefight
·vyweight championship)—R. L. Fitzsim-
·s vs. J. J. Corbett—filmed March 17, 1897
·ght—open-air arena especially built for a
·fight—1897

Elko

·l Service—airmail contractor (domestic)—
·e operation to Pasco, Wash.—April 6, 1926

Frenchman Flat

c Bomb—atomic bomb underground explo-
·—detonated—Nov. 29, 1951
·nce—atomic cannon—electronically fired
·ay 25, 1953

Henderson

Titanium—titanium plant fully self-contained and
fully integrated—opened—June 1, 1951

Lake Mead

Motorboat—motorboat to travel at a speed of
216.2 m.p.h.—D. M. Campbell—Nov. 16, 1955
Ship—speedboat to exceed 200 miles an hour—
Bluebird—Nov. 16, 1955

Las Vegas

Locomotive—gas turbine propane-fueled locomo-
tive—in service—June 8, 1953
Slot Machine—slot-machine payoff of $275,000—
James Schelich—Oct. 29, 1978

News Nob

Television—Telecast—atomic explosion telecast
on a network—April 22, 1952

Reno

Prizefighter—black heavyweight champion of the
world—Jack Johnson—July 4, 1910
Representative (U.S.)—representative to attend
college after his term of office—G. A. Bartlett—
University of Nevada—enrolled, Aug. 18, 1911

Virginia City

Silver Mill—to treat silver ore successfully—
opened—Aug. 11, 1860

Yucca Flat

Rocket—rocket with an atomic warhead—fired—
July 19, 1957
Television—Telecast—atomic bomb detonation
from a captive balloon telecast—Sept. 19, 1958

NEW HAMPSHIRE

American Indians—scalping of American Indians
by white men—Feb. 20, 1725
Attorney of the United States —Attorney General
of the United States—Samuel Sherburne, Jr.—
appointed—Sept. 26, 1789
Insurance—insurance board (state)—established
—July 1, 1851
Labor Legislation—ten-hour-day law—enacted—
July 9, 1847
Library Legislation—library law enacted by a
state—July 7, 1849
Naval Officer—naval officer commissioned—
Hopley Yeaton—March 21, 1791
Senator (U.S.)—senator elected on an antislavery
ticket—J. P. Hale—June 9, 1846
Ski Lift—tramway state legislation—approved
Sept. 17—effective Nov. 16, 1959

NEW HAMPSHIRE—*Continued*

Washing Machine—washing machine patent—Nathaniel Briggs—March 28, 1797

Berlin

Ski Club—ski club (local)—Nansen Ski Club—formed—Jan. 15, 1882

Claremont

Book Catalog—book catalog containing the combined tradelists of American publishers—published—1847

Concord

Clock—alarm clock—made—Levi Hutchins—1787

Forest Fire—forest fire drenched by artificial rain—Oct. 29, 1947

Melodeon Patent—C. Austin—June 19, 1849

Derry

Potato—potato cultivation—1719

Dover

Strike—strike of women operatives—1828

Dublin

Library—free public library—1822

Franconia

Ski Lift—aerial tramway—dedicated June 28, 1938

Goodrich Falls

Skimobile—invented—George Morton—1937

Grafton

Mica—mica—obtained—Ruggles mine—1803

Henniker

College—educational hosteling network—Elderhostel—offered at New England College—June 8, 1975

Laconia

Water Skier—water skier to jump 100 feet—Warren Witherell—The Weirs—Aug. 15, 1954

Lake Winnepesaukee

Animals—cattle (Guernsey cattle)—imported—1831

Boat Race—intercollegiate boat race—Aug. 3, 1852

Manchester

Credit Union Association—founded—Dec. 16, 1908

Meredith

Leg (artificial) Patent—B. F. Palmer—Nov. 4

Mount Washington

Newspaper—newspaper printed atop a ɪ tain—*Among the Clouds*—published issue July 20, 1977

Railroad—cog railroad—demonstrated—Aι 1866

Nashua

Tool Factory—machinists' tools—1838

New Castle

Revolutionary War—incident in the Revol ary War—Dec. 13, 1774

Newington

Forest—community forest—1710

North Conway

Skimobile—in operation—Dec. 27, 1938

Orford

Engine—internal combustion engine—S Morey—patented—April 1, 1826

Peterborough

Baseball Team—women's baseball team—

Library—free public library (town-suppor April 9, 1833

Portsmouth

Flag—American flag displayed on a man-ϲ —July 4, 1777

Navy—navy yard—purchased—June 12, 18

Religious Publication—religious review—ƀ *of Gospel Liberty*—published—Sept. 1, 1

Ship—ship-of-the-line—*America*—laid dϲ May 1777

Submarine—atomic-powered submarine bˀ a naval shipyard—*Swordfish*—laid dowɪ 25, 1956—launched, Aug. 27, 1957

Submarine—leaping submarine—*Pickerel*— missioned—April 4, 1949

Submarine—quadruple submarine launcƗ *Razorback, Redfish, Ronquil,* and *Scaᵃ Fish*—Jan. 27, 1944

Submarine—submarine built at a goverɪ shipyard—*L-8*—Portsmouth Naval Shipᵧ keel laid, Feb. 24, 1915—launched, Aᴘ 1917

Submarine—submarine refloated—*Squ* launched, Sept. 14, 1938—foundered, M 1939—raised, Sept. 13, 1939

Submarine—submarine to make a subɴ passage from the Atlantic to the Pacific ᴠ North Pole—*Seadragon*—left, Aug. 1, 19ϲ

Submarine—submarine to make more than dives—*Sarda*—launched, Aug. 24, 1945

arine—submarine with a high-tensile-steel
ssure hull—*Balao*—keel laid, June 26—
nched, October 27, 1942

Troy

et—horse   blankets—manufactured—
omas Goodall—1852

Walpole

al Book—*The American Herbal*—published
801
—American novel republished in England
riginally published—1797

Washington Center

th Day Adventist Church—1844

Wolfeboro

ing—summer home—John Wentworth—
9

NEW JERSEY

al Breeding Society—artificial animal
eding cooperative society—organized—
y 16, 1938
e Prevention and Detection—crime preven-
n commission for interstate cooperation—
rch 12, 1935
ing Company authorization (state)—enacted
April 4, 1888
ance—workers' compensation insurance
v (state)—passed, April 4, 1911—effective,
y 4, 1911
r Legislation—labor discrimination law
te)—enacted—May 15, 1894
r Union—labor union legalization (state)—
cted—Feb. 14, 1883
ry—daily state lotteries with the same win-
g daily number—Oct. 4, 1977
ry—lottery (state regulated) in which 3
oes made up the winning number—Sept. 13,
6
ry—lottery to guarantee a minimum of
800,000—Jan. 27, 1976
cal Legislation—law to license the practice
medicine—enacted—Sept. 26, 1772
on Picture—motion picture with a plot—*The
eat Train Robbery*—filmed—1903
e Legislation—noise-control statewide com-
hensive legislation—signed Jan. 24, 1972
—piano patent—J. S. McLean—May 27, 1796
c Defender—public defender (state)—Peter
rray—appointed June 20—term began July 1,
7
oad Charter—granted—Feb. 6, 1815
er—reaper—patent—May 17, 1803
esentative (U.S.)—grandmother to serve in
ngress—M. H. Fenwick—elected, Nov. 5,
4
—law regarding state aid for roads—enact-
—April 14, 1891

Television—Telecast—state legislative hearing
telecast—April 11, 1954
Toll Collector (automatic)—Graden State Parkway—Nov. 19, 1954
Woman Suffrage—colony to grant suffrage to
women—constitution adopted—July 2, 1776

Arlington

Nylon—nylon bristle filament production for
toothbrushes—Feb. 24, 1938

Athenia

Animals—sheep (karakul fur sheep)—quarantined—1908

Atlantic City

Automobile Transcontinental Trip—transconti-
nental automobile group tour—commenced—
June 26, 1911
Aviation—Flights—airplane to fly higher than 1
mile in altitude—W. R. Brookins—July 9, 1910
Aviation—Flights (transatlantic)—transatlantic
dirigible flight—attempted—Oct. 15, 1910
Aviation—Flights (transcontinental)—transconti-
nental flight made by blacks in their own plane
—left—July 17, 1933
Beauty Pageant—beauty pageant (national)—
Miss America pageant—Sept. 7-8, 1921
Beauty Pageant—black contestant in the Miss
America pageant—C. A. Browne—contestant
representing Iowa—Sept. 6-12, 1970
Boardwalk—completed—June 26, 1870
Building—building shaped like an elephant—the
Elephant—1882
Glider—Flights—rocket glider flight—successful
—June 4, 1931
Health Society—National Tuberculosis Associa-
tion—organized—June 6, 1904
Hockey Player—black player in organized hock-
ey—Arthur Dorrington—Nov. 15, 1950
Medical Society—woman member of the Associa-
tion of American Physicians—H. B. Taussig—
elected—May 3, 1950
Pier—ocean pier—built—Howard's pier—1881
Pier—ocean pier of steel—opened—June 18, 1898
Police—police airplane-arrest—simulated—May
6, 1919
Television—Telecast—birth (human) to be tele-
vised (closed-circuit)—June 14, 1951
Television—Telecast—surgical operation televised on a closed circuit in color—June 6, 1949

Atlantic Highlands

Radio Beacons—installed—fog signals—tests—
1916

Barnegat Light

Aviation—Airship—airship disaster resulting in
more than 70 deaths—*Akron*—April 4, 1933

NEW JERSEY—Barnegat Light—*Continued*

Ship—ship sunk by a submerged German submarine—*Frederick R. Kellogg*—12 miles north of Barnegat Light—Aug. 13, 1918

Bayonne

Radio Broadcast—radio police system (two-way three-way)—construction permit application—Oct. 7, 1932
Track Meet—college relay race—May 30, 1893

Belleville

Postage Stamp—nurse (individual) depicted on a postage stamp—Clara Maass—issued, Aug. 18, 1976

Belmar

Radar—radar signal to the moon—Jan. 10, 1946

Beverly

Birds—partridge propagation—encouraged 1790

Bloomfield

Brake Patent—railroad brake patent—Ephraim Morris—Sept. 19, 1838
Electric Lighting—electric sterilamp—introduced —March 1938

Bordentown

Locomotive Cowcatcher—used—to Hightstown—1833

Bound Brook

Railroad Signal System—railroad signal system of interlocking signal apparatus operated by compressed air—installed—1883

Burlington

Educational Trust Fund—created—1682
Freemasons—Mason—to arrive in America—John Skene—1682
Plow—plow patent—Charles Newbold—June 26, 1797
Pottery—pottery—Daniel Coxe—1680
Windmill—windmill driven by rotor power—tested—July 1933

Caldwell

Aviation—Parachute—parachute jump from an autogiro—Nov. 15, 1931

Caldwell Township

Mica—synthetic mica—May 17, 1956

Camden

Airmail Service—autogiro mail delivery regular service—from Philadelphia—July 6, 1939

Ferryboat—ferryboat built exclusively for m vehicle transportation—1926
Microscope—electron microscope—invented K. Zworykin—1940
Motion Picture Theater—drive-in motion pi theater—opened—June 6, 1933
Pen—steel pens commercially produced—*P* ard Esterbrook—1858
Phonograph—phonograph with an autor record changer—introduced—March 1927
Phonograph—phonograph with an enclosed in the cabinet—Aug. 22, 1906
Phonograph Record—phonograph record stage performance by the original cast—1
Radio Broadcast—ship launching broadc April 7, 1925
Television—Telecast—unscheduled event t televised as it occurred—April 24, 1936
Television Mobile Unit—mobile television u manufactured—1937

Camp Kilmer

Helicopter—aerocycle—tested

Cape May

Air Force—air force aviation unit—sailed Ja 1918

Carlstadt

Business—Food-O-Mat—May 24, 1945

Coytesville

Television—Telecast—standard broadcast tion to transmit a television image—WR*P* Aug. 13, 1928

Deepwater

Rubber—synthetic rubber (neoprene)—prod commercially—1931

Dover

X ray—X-ray scanning system (commercia convert electronic information to visible *X* —first system installed and tested orderec U.S. Army Picatinny Arsenal

East Orange

Adhesive and Medicated Plaster—adhesive medicated plaster with a rubber base—18

East Rutherford

Horse Race—horse race for a purse of more $2 million—Woodrow Wilson purse—Au 1980
Soccer—soccer game before 77,000 spectatc Cosmos vs. Strikers—Aug. 14, 1977

Edgewater

boat—ferryboat built exclusively for motor
icle transportation—in service—Nov. 8,
5

Elizabeth

—containership facility—opened Aug. 15,
2
r—patented—Henry Van Hoevenbergh—
y 16, 1882
sion Tube—miniature tube—patented—H.
Weinhart—Aug. 25, 1925

Elizabethport

ry Shears—manufactured—1825
ig Machine—electric sewing machine—
iufactured—1889

Englewood

hone—dial telephone service coast-to-coast
iout the aid of operators—Nov. 10, 1951

Fort Lee

—submarine telegraph cable that was prac-
l—Ezra Cornell—1845

Fort Monmouth

Broadcast—solar power two-way-radio
st-to-coast conversation—to El Monte,
if.—June 23, 1960
Telephone—military portable—Walkie-
kie—constructed—1933
ite—communications satellite successfully
ed in orbit—message sent by D. D. Eisen-
ier through C. A. Herter to F. H. Boland

Freehold

—pacer to win $1 million—Cardigan Bay—
t. 14, 1968
utionary War—conflict on equal terms be-
en American regulars and British regulars—
er Gen. George Washington and Sir Henry
ton, respectively—June 28, 1778

Greenville

ver Shooting Tournament (international)
ne 16, 1900

Hadley Field

on—Flights—airplane night scheduled pas-
ier flight—to Boston—April 1, 1927

High Bridge

–manganese steel—manufactured—1892
–manganese steel for railroad tracks—
iufactured—Aug. 28, 1894

Hightstown

Aviation—Parachute—parachute tower for training parachute jumpers—built—April 1935
Locomotive Cowcatcher—used—to Bordentown
—1833

Hoboken

Air (compressed)—for tunnel construction—1879
Baseball Game—baseball game under the code—
June 19, 1846
Cricket Tournament—international cricket tour-
nament—Oct. 3, 1859
Engineering Society—mechanical engineering na-
tional society—organization meeting—April 7,
1880
Fastening—hookless fastening for universal use—
invented—1906
Ferryboat—double-deck ferryboat with the pro-
peller-type steel hull—to New York City—1891
Ferryboat—steam-propelled ferryboat—to New
York City—Oct. 11, 1811
Ferryboat—steel-hull ferryboat—operated to
New York City—1881
Horse Race—night harness race—Beacon Track
—Oct. 5, 1843
Locomotive—locomotive to pull a train—built—
John Stevens—Oct. 23, 1824
Mechanical Engineering Laboratory for Research
Work—established—1874
Radio Station—seagoing radio broadcasting sta-
tion—Courier—commissioned—Feb. 15, 1952
Ship—steamboat to make an ocean voyage—
Phoenix—built
Ship—steamboat with a twin-screw propeller—
built—1803

Holmdel

Satellite—communications satellite—message received from Goldstone, Calif.

Indian Mills

American Indian Reservation—American Indian
reservation (state)—established—Aug. 29, 1758

Jersey City

Adhesive and Medicated Plaster—adhesive and
medicated plaster patent—March 26, 1845
Cornstarch—starch made commercially from Indian corn—Thomas Kingsford—1842
Dry Dock—dry dock—constructed—Robert Fulton—1805
Handball National Championship Match for Amateurs—Jan. 7, 1897
Physician—physician with a mobile medical
office—H. C. Neals—in service, June 23, 1970
Prizefight—prizefight to gross $1 million—Demp-
sey-Carpentier—July 2, 1921
Radio Broadcast—prizefight (heavyweight championship) broadcast—July 2, 1921
Sidewalk (Traveling)—sidewalk (traveling) in a
railroad station—May 24, 1954

NEW JERSEY—Jersey City—*Continued*

Tunnel—tunnel under the Hudson River—to New York City—opened—Feb. 25, 1908
Tunnel—twin-tube subaqueous vehicular tunnel —Holland tunnel—opened—Nov. 13, 1927
Water Purification—water supply chemically treated with chlorine compounds—1908

Kearny

Linoleum—linoleum machine (fully automatic)—installed—1911

Keyport

Airmail—airmail pickup from a steamer at sea—S.S. *Leviathan*—June 12, 1929

Lakehurst

Aviation—Airship—dirigible (American-built rigid)—tested—Sept. 4, 1923
Aviation—Airship—dirigible merchandise shipment—arrived—Oct. 15, 1924
Aviation—Flights—airship to exceed 200 hours in flight nonstop without refueling—takeoff May 17, 1954
Aviation—Flights (transatlantic)—Atlantic Ocean regular commercial airship service—*Hindenburg*—arrived—May 9, 1936
Aviation—Flights (transcontinental)—transcontinental airship voyage—commenced—Oct. 7, 1924
Aviation—Passenger—woman Zeppelin passenger (paying)—Oct. 29, 1928
Aviation—Races—airplane passenger race around the world—start—Sept. 30, 1936
Glider—glider released from a dirigible—Jan. 31, 1930
Navy—Navy parachute school—opened Sept. 1, 1924

Lakewood

Hospital—tuberculosis preventorium for children —established—1909

Lebanon

Cash Carrier System—patented—David Brown—July 13, 1875

Lynn

Money—dies for coins in America—Joseph Jencks—1652

Mahwah

Cream Separator—continuous-flow centrifugal cream separator—installed—1881

Menlo Park

Electric Lighting—electric incandescent lamp—invented—T. A. Edison—Oct. 21, 1879

Electric Lighting—electric incandescent lam tory—Edison Lamp Works—opened—O 1880
Mimeograph—patented—T. A. Edison—A 1876
Phonograph—phonograph—patented—T. A son—Feb. 19, 1878
Photograph—photograph taken by incande electric light—Dec. 1879
Radio Patent of importance—T. A. Edison- 29, 1891

Millville

Old Age Colony—dedicated—Oct. 23, 1936

Moorestown

Horse—Percheron (horse) importation—183

Morristown

Golfer—woman to win the United States men's Amateur Championship—Beatrice —Oct. 7-9, 1896
Railroad Signal Light—atomic-powered light—manufactured—November 1956
Telegraph—telegraphic communication sys which dots and dashes represented letter vented—Alfred Vail—Sept. 1837

Murray Hill

Transistor—junction transistor—inventior nounced—July 5, 1951
Transistor—phototransistor—invention nounced—March 30, 1950
Transistor—transistor—demonstrated—Jun 1948

Navesink

Radio Station—naval radio station—estab —1903

New Brunswick

Football Game—intercollegiate football con Nov. 6, 1869
Microbiology Laboratory—dedicated—Ju 1954
Patent—plant patent—H. F. Bosenberg—A 1931
Radio Facsimile Transmission—photograp by radio across the Atlantic—transmit England—July 6, 1924
Telephone—interstate telephone call—to York City—May 17, 1877
X ray—X-ray scanning system (commerc convert electronic information to visible —manufactured

Newark

Autogiro—Flights—autogiro transconti flight made by a woman—Amelia Ear takeoff May 29, 1931

Virus—virus obtained in crystalline form—reported—June 28, 1935

Rahway

Haircloth—manufactured—1813
Streptomycin—commercially manufactured—Sept. 1944

Ridgewood

Cable (telegraph)—coaxial cable—patented—Dec. 8, 1931
Plow—submarine cable plow—patented—Jan. 12, 1937

Sandy Hook

Radio Broadcast—yacht race broadcast—Oct. 16, 1899

Sea Girt

Police—state police class of women—graduated, June 27, 1980

Sewell

Golf Course—illuminated 9-hole regulation golf course—Tall Pines Golf Club—illuminated Aug. 23, 1963

Summit

Liquid Heat—system operated—Jan. 7, 1942

Trenton

Army Officer—chaplain killed in action—John Rosbrugh—Jan. 2, 1777
Building—building in which wrought-iron beams were used—rolled—1854
Chinaware—chinaware for restaurant use—made—1862
Crime Prevention and Detection—national conference on crime—Oct. 11–12, 1935
Freemasons—black Masonic lodge—Alpha Lodge of New Jersey—warrant granted—Jan. 19, 1871
Pottery—pottery to make sanitary ware—founded—1853
Steel—open hearth furnace—built—1868
Water Ski Association (national)—American Water Ski Association—formed—April 1939
Woman—woman state committee chairman—M. T. Norton—elected—May 22, 1934

Tuckerton

Brokerage—stock order from a Zeppelin—message picked up—Aug. 8, 1930

Union Hill

Bowling—duckpins—first match—July 18, 1900

Vineland

Intelligence Test—introduced—Aug. 1908

Weehawken

Ferryboat—ferryboat built exclusively for vehicle transportation—in service—N(1926
Tunnel—triple-tube underwater roadway coln Tunnel to New York City—opened M 1957

West Burlington

See under Burlington

West Orange

Motion Picture—motion picture closeup—F 1893
Motion Picture—motion picture of a stage zefight—July 1894
Motion Picture "Studio"—erected—1892

Woodbridge

Brick—fire brick—manufactured—1825
Iron—iron patent—S. Broadmeadow—Jan. ?

NEW MEXICO

Atomic Bomb—atomic explosion witness(troops—Nov. 1, 1951

Alamogordo

Atomic Bomb—atomic bomb explosion—J(1945
Aviation—jet drone target missile—flown— 23, 1954
Rocket Sled—rocket-driven sled on rails— —March 19, 1954

Albuquerque

Building—commercial building heated by t? —Aug. 1, 1957
Pole Vault—pole vault indoors higher than 1 —Bob Seagren—March 6, 1966
School—technical school for American Ind? dedicated, Aug. 21—opened, Sept. 16, 19
Woman—woman to undergo astronaut tests rie Cobb—Feb. 15, 1960

Artesia

School—underground school—Abo Elem(School—built 1976

Fort Stanton

Hospital—tuberculosis hospital operated ? government—opened—April 27, 1899

Las Cruces

Airmail Service—rocket (steam-driven) to mail—launched—May 24, 1969

Ruidoso

Race—horse race with a purse of more than million—All-American Futurity—Sept. 4, 2

Santa Fe

opology Laboratory—opened—Sept. 1, 1931

White Sands Proving Grounds

graph—ultraviolet pictures of the sun—rch 13, 1959

et—ballistic missile—fired—May 22, 1947

et—rocket to attain a 100-mile altitude—July 1946

et—rocket to exceed a 150-mile altitude—ing XI—May 24, 1954

et—rocket to intercept a low-flying airplane—May 1958

et—rocket to intercept an airplane—Nov. 27, 1

et—rocket to reach outer space—Feb. 24, 9

NEW YORK

untancy Law (state)—April 17, 1896

rtising Law—advertising legislation (state)—April 30, 1898

rtising Law—outdoor advertising legislation te)—March 28, 1865

ultural Appropriation—for state extension ning—May 12, 1894

ultural "Board" (state)—organized—Jan. 20, 0

ration—state arbitration law (modern)—ril 19, 1920

ration—State Board of Mediation and Arbi-ion—organized—June 1, 1886

nobile License Plates—automobile license tes—required by law—April 25, 1901

nobile Race—Vanderbilt Cup Race to be n by an American—G. H. Robertson—Oct. 1908

Legislation—bank legislation (state)—cted—April 2, 1829

all Park—baseball park to charge admis-n—New York Fashion Race Track course—r 20, 1858

ouse—legislation concerning public baths—sed—April 18, 1895

is—state to exceed 5 million in population—0

is—states to exceed 1 million in population 820

atory—crematory (state)—authorized—y 21, 1888

icense—dog license law (state)—enacted—rch 8, 1894

on—federal election in the United States—horized—Sept. 13, 1788

on Law—corrupt election practices law te)—enacted—April 4, 1890

Entomologist—state entomologist—Asa Fitch—appointed—May 4, 1854

Farm Bureau—state assistance—appropriation enacted—May 24, 1913

Fire Escapes—for tenements—required by law—April 17, 1860

Forest Reserve—forest reserve (state)—designated—May 15, 1885

Game Law—hunting license fee (state)—law enacted—April 30, 1864

Installment Sales Law—enacted—April 17, 1957

Insurance—credit insurance—attempted—1887

Insurance—insurance department (state)—authorized—April 15, 1859

Judge—woman judge of the Surrogates Court—elected—Nov. 8, 1977

Labor—labor antidiscrimination commission (state)—appointed—July 1, 1945

Labor Union—labor union to nominate its own political candidates—Mechanics Union—1784

Labor Union—labor union to nominate its own political candidates and win an election—Ebenezer Ford—elected—Nov. 7, 1829

Language—plain language law—enacted, May 31 —effective, Nov. 2, 1978

Lawyers' Association—lawyers' association (state) woman president—M. M. Lambert—June 30, 1974–June 30, 1976

Library Loan—made by a state library to a community—Feb. 8, 1892

Lottery—lottery in which the top prize was $1 million—winners: George, Genevieve, and Glenn Ashton—Oct. 8, 1970

Medical Legislation—blood grouping test laws (state)—enacted—March 22, 1935

Medical Legislation—law (state) requiring marriage license applicants to undergo medical tests—enacted—April 12, 1938

Medical Legislation—law (state) requiring serological blood tests of pregnant women—enacted—March 18, 1938

Missionary—black missionary—John Marrant—ordained—May 15, 1785

Motorcyclist—woman professional motorcyclist —Kerry Kleid—debut at Mt. Peter moto-cross (6 miles north of Greenwood Lake)—Oct. 17, 1971

Oleomargarine—oleomargarine legislation (state) —enacted—June 5, 1877

Pharmacy Legislation (state)—enacted—May 3, 1904

Pure Food Law—pure food and drug legislation (state)—enacted—May 28, 1881

Railroad—railroad merger—of importance—May 17, 1853

Representative (U.S.)—black representative (woman) to serve in Congress—S. A. S. Chisholm—elected—Nov. 5, 1968

Representative (U.S.)—Italo-American representative—F. B. Spinola—elected, November 1886

Representative (U.S.)—representative of Puerto Rican ancestry—Herman Badillo—elected, Nov. 3, 1970

NEW YORK— *Continued*

School Superintendent—school superintendent (state)—Gideon Hawley—served—Jan. 14, 1813

Supreme Court (U.S.) Decision—Supreme Court decision between states—action commenced—Aug. 5, 1799

Territorial Expansion—acquisition of land by the federal government—New York ceded land—1781

Trademark Lawsuit—trademark controversy involving a newspaper—decision—Jan. 31, 1825

Traitor to the American Cause—William Demont —Nov. 2, 1776

Treason—American colonist hanged for treason —Jacob Leisler—May 16, 1691

Truancy Legislation (state)—enacted—April 12, 1853

Voting Machine—voting machines authorized— March 15, 1892

Voting Machine Commission (state)—authorized —May 17, 1897

Wire—legislation (state) requiring wires to be placed underground—enacted—June 14, 1884

Woman—woman state liquor board member—J. R. Sheppard—appointed—April 12, 1933

Albany

Aviation—Races—airplane to race a train—G. H. Curtiss—May 29, 1910

Baseball Team—baseball team to tour—played— July 1860

Canal—canal of importance—to Buffalo, N.Y.— opened—Oct. 26, 1825

Celluloid—patented—June 15, 1869

College Academic Costume Standardization —May 16, 1895

Congress (colonial)—colonial congress—June 19-July 11, 1754

Cracker—cracker (sweet)—manufactured—1865

Degrees (academic and honorary)—bachelor's degree awarded by a recognized institution without requiring a single college credit—N. E. France—University of the State of New York—Sept. 20, 1974

Dyes—dyestuff full-scale plant—opened—1868

Electric Magnet—invented—Joseph Henry—June 1828

Hospital—psychiatric ward—associated with a general hospital—opened—1901

Library Society—state library society—formed— July 11, 1890

Locomotive—locomotive to attain the proved speed of 112.5 miles an hour

Locomotive—streamlined steam locomotive—introduced—Dec. 14, 1934

Medical Book—medical jurisprudence treatise (authoritative)—published—1823

Paleontology Report—based on Albany discovery—prepared—1713

Paper—perforated wrapping paper—patented— Seth Wheeler—July 25, 1871

Philatelic Magazine—philatelic magaz*Stamp Collector's Record*—published—D₍ 1864

Political Machine—well organized—Alban gency—1820

Potato Chips—manufacturing plant—1925

Presidential Candidate—presidential can₍ to fly to a political convention—F.D. Roo₍ —to Chicago—July 2, 1932

Presidential Candidate—presidential can₍ to make a speech of acceptance at a nomir convention—F. D. Roosevelt—Chicago—▌ 1932

Telegraph—telegraph (electromagnetic)—₍ ited—Joseph Henry—1831

Television—Telecast—presidential nomi₍ notification ceremony to be televised— Smith—Aug. 22, 1928

Whig Party—convention—Feb. 3, 1836

"Yankee Doodle"—written—Richard Shuck —1755

Albion

Santa Claus School—opened—C. W. How Sept. 27, 1937

Amangasett

Saboteurs—saboteurs executed—4 landed 13, 1942

Ardsley-on-Hudson

Golf Club—intercollegiate golf association—nament—May 13–14, 1897

Ashville

Fire Department—fire department compos₍ tirely of women—Feb. 1943

Attica

Bank—national bank failure—April 14, 18₍

Auburn

Execution—electrocution of a human being—liam Kemmler—Aug. 6, 1890

Prison—organization of a prison—into "c₍ nity" groups—1914

Time Recorder—employees' time recorder ented—W. L. Bundy—Nov. 20, 1888

Auriesville

Catholic Beatification—Catholic beatificat₍ an American Indian—May 9, 1939

Babylon

mobile Race—fifty-mile automobile cross-
untry road race—from Springfield, L.I., N.Y.,
l return—April 14, 1900

Barcelona Harbor

house—lighthouse fueled by natural gas—in
·ration, 1830–1859

Batavia

nac—patent medicine almanac—published
843

Bayside

ision Receiver—television receiver and
1smitter operated by laser beam—demon-
ted—Feb. 20, 1963

Beacon

ad Car—rail detector car—tested—June 13,
8

er—therapeutic theater—"psychodramatic
ck treatment"—1937

Bedloe Island

See under Liberty Island

Belmont Park

See under Elmont

Bentonsville

(circular)—manufactured—c. 1814

Binghamton

ion—aviation trainer—used in a school—
9

ion—aviation trainer (jet)—completed—
9

Bureau—established—March 20, 1911
tal—inebriates' asylum—organized—May
1854

nargarine—oleomargarine patent—H. W.
dley—Jan. 3, 1871

Bloomville

—milk pasteurized commercially—1895

Blue Mountain Lake

tor—elevator with an electric light—in-
led—July 12, 1882
—hotel to install electric lights—1881

Boonville

mobile—snowmobile to exceed a speed of
m.p.h.—Yvon Duhamel—Feb. 11, 1972

Bronx

See under New York City

Bronxville

Golf Champion—family to win more than one national championship in 1 year—Dexter Cummings—June 30, 1923 (intercollegiate
championship)

Brooklyn

See under New York City

Buchanan

Atomic Reactor—thorium-uranium reactor (privately owned)—construction began—Jan. 28,
1958

Buffalo

Almanac—patent medicine almanac—issued—
1843
Architect—woman architect—L. B. Bethune—
opened office—1881
Automobile Race—automobile race (long-dis-
tance)—completed—Sept. 14, 1901
Aviation—Airplane—rocket plane—built—1946
Bicycle Racer—woman bicycle champion of the
National Amateur Bicycle Association—Doris
Kopsky—Sept. 4, 1937
Bowler—bowler to roll two perfect games—Frank
Caruana—March 5, 1924
Bowler—woman bowler to obtain a perfect score
—Emma Fahning—March 4, 1930
Canal—canal of importance—to Albany—opened
—Oct. 26, 1825
Cancer Laboratory—established—University of
Buffalo—May 1898
Cellophane — cellophane — manufactured — Du
Pont Cellophane Co.—1924
Court—domestic relations court—established—
1909
Desk—with roll top—invented—c. 1850
Dry Dock—timber dry dock—erected—1840
Electric Power Plant—alternating-current power
plant commercially successful—built—Nov.
1886
Elevator—grain elevator operated by steam—
built—1842
Free Soil Party—organized—Aug. 9, 1848
Herd Book—*American Herd Book*—published—
1846
Library Society—woman to become president of
the American Library Association—T. H. W.
Elmendorf—served—May 24, 1911
Medical Society—laryngological society (na-
tional)—American Laryngological Association
—founded—June 3, 1878
Microscope—microscope for examining structure
of materials—built—American Optical Compa-
ny—1951
Motorcycle—motorcycle (practical)—E. R.
Thomas Motor Co.—1900

NEW YORK—Buffalo—*Continued*

Paper—wood-pulp paper—basswood—John Beardsley—exhibited—Dec. 26, 1854

School Superintendent—school superintendent (city)—R. W. Haskins—appointed—1836

Ship—steamboat on the Great Lakes—launched —April 4, 1818

Ski Slope—ski slope indoors—Ski-Dek Center— opened, Jan. 17, 1962

Sleeping Car—sleeping car patent—H. B. Myer— Sept. 19, 1854

Surgical Operation—skin grafting—suggested—F. H. Hamilton—1847

Television—Telecast—stockholders' meetings televised coast-to-coast simultaneously—Oct. 29, 1959

Television—Telecast—telecast transmitted to Canada—Jan. 20, 1953

Caldwell's Landing

Prizefight—prizefight (heavyweight) to last longer than 100 rounds—Tom Hyer vs. George McChester—Sept. 9, 1841

Canastota

Automobile Tire Chain—patented—H. D. Weed— Aug. 23, 1904

Cato

School—school completely irradiated with germicidal lamps—installed—Jan. 3, 1945

Chautauqua

See also Fair Point

Esperanto Club—Esperanto club (national organization)—formed—Sept. 7, 1908

Home Study Course—serious nature—Aug. 10, 1878

Cohoes

Knitting Machine (power)—operated—1832

College Point

Soda Water—sugar-free soft drink—NoCal—Hyman Kirsch—1952

Coney Island

See under New York City

Cooperstown

Baseball Game—baseball—played—1839

Hall of Fame—hall of fame (baseball)—dedicated —June 12, 1939

Hall of Famer—athlete enshrined in 2 halls of fame—Robert Hubbard—baseball Hall of Fame —Aug. 9, 1976

Corning

Glass—photosensitive glass—manufactu Nov. 1937

Telescope—telescope lens 200 inches in dia —molded—Dec. 2, 1934

Creedmoor

Rifle Association—rifle association (nation shooting meet—April 25, 1873

Rifle Association—rifle tournament (interna al)—Sept. 26, 1874

Crown Point

Freemasons—military Masonic lodge—form April 13, 1759

Cuba

Oil—oil spring—recorded—1627

Dexter Park

See under New York City

Eastchester Township

Radio Broadcast—radio police system (two three-way)—placed in operation—July 10,

Elizabethport

Cracker—meat biscuit—patented—Gail Bo Jr.—July 30, 1850

Elmira

College—educational institution exclusivel women—opened—1855

Ordnance—automatic aircraft cannon—man tured for U.S. Army—May 16, 1941

Elmont

Airmail Service—airmail regular service bet New York and Chicago—began Dec. 18,

Horse—horse (thoroughbred) to defeat 2 t crown winners in the same race—Exce Oct. 14, 1978

Horse—horse to win a the triple crown—Sir ton—Belmont Park—1919

Horse Race—horse to win a $100,000 purse i race—Whichone—Belmont Park—Sept. 1929

Horse Race—racetrack at which more tha million was bet in one day—Belmont P Sept. 22, 1945

Horse Race—stakes race triple dead heat—C Handicap—Belmont Park—June 10, 1944

Elmsford

Cocktail—introduced—1776

Deaf—Hearing Aid—transistorized hearing offered for sale—Dec. 29, 1952

Fair Point

See also Chautauqua

utauqua Organization—organized—Aug. 4,
74

Farmingdale

cle Racer—to attain the speed of a mile a
nute—C. M. Murphy—June 30, 1899

Fayetteville

ent—natural cement rock—discovered—
18

Fishkill

Veterans' Society—Society of the Cincinnati
instituted—May 10, 1783

Floyd Bennett Field

See under New York City

Forest Hills

See under New York City

Fort Washington

See under New York City

Frankfort

ge—cast-iron girder bridge—built—1840

Franklin Square

it Card—bank credit card—Franklin Na-
nal Bank—issued April 15, 1952

Fredonia

—natural gas corporation—organized—1865
—natural gas used as an illuminant—1824

Garden City

ail Service—airmail pilot—E. L. Ovington—
Mineola, L.I.—Sept. 23, 1911
tion—Airplane—airplane (commercial) sta-
ized—built—1931
tion—Airplane—fighter airplane—Kirkham
ghter—tested—Aug. 19, 1918
tion—Airplane—molded plywood airplane—
histling Bill—built—1918
o Broadcast—transatlantic radio program
m England—received, Nov. 25, 1923
elchair Athletics—national wheelchair
mes—Adelphi College—June 1, 1957

Geneva

ge—college course without Greek or Latin—
tablished—1824
ician—woman physician—Elizabeth Black-
ll—graduated—Jan. 23, 1849

Glen Cove

Architect—woman graduate of the Webb Institute
of Naval Architecture—Karen Hansen—June
22, 1978

Goshen

Horse—trotter triple-crown winner—Scott Frost
—(Hambletonian) Aug. 3, 1955
Telegraph—telegraph in railroading—used—
Sept. 22, 1851

Governors Island

Army Officer—male nurse—E. L. Lyon—sworn in
—Oct. 6, 1955
Court-martial—court-martial trial in the United
States at which enlisted men were allowed to
sit as members of the court—Feb. 3, 1949

Greenpoint

See under New York City

Greenwood Lake

Airmail Service—rocket airmail flight—Feb. 23,
1936

Hamilton

Freemasons—Grotto—formal organization—
Sept. 10, 1889
Freemasons—Grotto—Veiled Prophets—institut-
ed—June 13, 1890

Hammondsport

Aviation—gyroscope automatic stabilization—
demonstrated—Aug. 1913
Aviation—Airplane—airplane sold commercially
—June 16, 1909
Aviation—Airplane—hydroplane with a multi-en-
gine—christened—June 22, 1914
Aviation—Airplane—naval airplane—tested—
1911
Aviation—Airplane Bombing—airplane bombing
experiment—G. H. Curtiss—June 30, 1910
Aviation—School—airplane flying school—
opened—Sept. 1910
Museum—wine museum—Finger Lakes Wine
Museum—opened July 1967
School—school to have all classroom lights con-
trolled by electric eyes—lights in operation—
Jan. 4. 1936

Harlem

See under New York City

Hartsdale

Television—Telecast—transoceanic television
image—received—Feb. 8, 1928

NEW YORK—*Continued*

Hastings

Prizefight—prizefight fatality—Sept. 13, 1842

Hastings-on-Hudson

Photograph—photograph of a stellar spectrum showing the dark lines—1872

Hempstead Plains

Horse Race—horse race—on regular basis—1665

Hicksville

Automobile Race—Vanderbilt Cup Race—Oct. 8, 1904

Hornell

Aviation—Flights—airplane to fly further than 500 miles—from Chicago, Ill.—Ruth Law—Nov. 19, 1916

Hudson

Periodical—comic magazine—*The Wasp*—published—July 7, 1802

Hydeville

Spiritualist—J. D. Fox—1848

Ilion

Computer—solid-state electronic computer—built—1958
Pistol—revolver—self-cocking—manufactured—1856
Typewriter—typewriter that was practical—patented—C. L. Sholes—June 23, 1868

Ithaca

Aviation—flight attendant (black woman)—R. C. Taylor—to New York City—Feb. 11, 1958
Birds—ptarmigan (Eskimo chicken)—hatched—July 24, 1934
Caliper (screw)—constructed—J. E. Sweet—1874
Degrees (academic and honorary)—Doctor of Science degree earned by a woman—C. W. Baldwin—Cornell University—June 20, 1895
Dynamo—dynamo for a direct-current outdoor lighting system—built—1875
Engineering College—electrical engineering course—established—Sept. 21, 1883
Fellowship—fellowship awarded a woman—granted—H. E. Grotecloss—June 19, 1884
Forestry School—forestry school of collegiate character—established—Sept. 19, 1898
Fraternity (Greek letter)—intercollegiate Greek-letter national fraternity for black men—Alpha Phi Alpha—formed, Dec. 4, 1906
Hotel Administration College Course—offered—1922
Ice Cream Sundae—originated—1897

Industrial and Labor Relations School—open Nov. 2, 1945
Teletypesetter—teletypesetter installed in school—July 5, 1933
Veterinary School—veterinary department of legiate character—opened—Oct. 7, 1868
Woman—woman editor in chief of a law revie M. H. Donlon—Nov. 1919

Jamaica

See under New York City

Johnstown

Ax—manufacturing plant—erected—1800
Gloves—commercial manufacture—1809
Leather—leather tanning by the "oil tan" me —originated—Talmadge Edwards—1810

Karner

Locomotive—streamlined steam locomotive-troduced—Dec. 14, 1934

Kinderhook

President (U.S.)—President born a citizen of United States—Martin Van Buren—Dec. 5,

Kings Point

Merchant Marine Academy—Merchant Ma Academy (U.S.)—dedicated—F. D. Roosev Sept. 30, 1943
Merchant Marine Academy—Merchant Ma Cadet Corps (U.S.)—established—March 1938
Merchant Marine Academy—women were ad ted to the Merchant Marine Academy—1974

Kingston

Road—hard-surfaced road—from Pahaqu Mines, N.J.—completed 1663

La Guardia Field

See under New York City

Lackawanna

Catholic Church—Catholic church raised to dignity of a basilica—dedicated—May 25,

Lake George

Canoe Association—American Canoe Asse tion—formed—Aug. 3, 1880

Lake Placid

Bobsled Competition—four-man bob-team petition—Feb. 14–15, 1932
Bobsled Competition—two-man bob-team petition—Feb. 9–10, 1932
Bridge (game)—auction bridge championship plicate)—July 9, 1914

sled Race—dogsled race on an Olympic
monstration program—Feb. 6–7, 1932
mpic Games—Winter Olympic Games compe-
ion—opened—Feb. 4, 1932
Meet (international)—of importance—Feb.
3, 1932

Lansingburgh

d Silk Patent—Ralph Hodgson—Feb. 1, 1793

Lewiston

oad—inclined railway—erected—1764

Liberty Island

ument—statue presented by a foreign coun-
—Statue of Liberty—unveiled—Oct. 28, 1886
on Picture Actor—stunt actor—F. R. Law—
rachute jump—Feb. 2, 1912

Lockport

ing System—heating system from a central
tion—installed—Birdsall Holly—1877
ng Machine—voting machines authorized for
e—machines used—April 12, 1892

Locust Grove

—trailer bank—opened—May 26, 1956

McGraw

et—health corset—manufactured—July 1874

Manchester

ch of Jesus Christ of Latter-Day Saints—
urch of Jesus Christ of Latter-Day Saints—
ganized—April 6, 1830

Mineola

tion—Flights—airplane to carry 3 passengers
Aug. 14, 1910
tion—Passenger—woman airplane passen-
r (transcontinental)—Lillian Gatlin—landed
Oct. 8, 1922

Mitchel Air Force Base

chute-Jumping Contest—parachute-jumping
ntest—Theodore Schieuming—Oct. 12, 1923

Monroe

se—Liederkranz-brand cheese—produced—
2

Montauk Point

on Picture—motion picture of an eclipse of
sun taken from a dirigible—Jan. 24, 1925
o Telephone—radio telephone communica-
n (one-way)—to Wilmington, Del.—April 4,
5

Monticello

Horse Race—perfecta or exacta—June 30, 1965
Softball—softball game of 365 innings—Aug. 14–
15, 1976

Mount Lebanon

See under New Lebanon

Mount Vernon

Golf Tournament—Professional Golfers Association tournament—Siwanoy Golf Club—Oct. 14,
1916

New Lebanon

Shaker Society—organized community—established—1788

New Paltz

Adding Machine—adding machine to employ depressible keys—patented—D. D. Parmelee—
Feb. 5, 1850

New Rochelle

Railroad Car—remote control railroad passenger
car—to and from Rye, N.Y.—Dec. 1, 1955

New Russia

Organ—color organ—patented—Bainbridge Bishop—Jan. 16, 1877

New York City

Abrasive—boron carbide—announced—Sept. 27,
1934
Accountant—C.P.A.—licensed—Dec. 1, 1896
Accountants' Society—accountants' society—or-
ganized—July 28, 1882
Accountants' Society—accountants' society
formed by a state group—organized—March 30,
1897
Accountants' Society—accountants' society to
become a national organization—formed—Dec.
22, 1886
Actor—actor to perform in 2 cities the same day—
N. C. Goodwin—Feb. 10, 1887
Actor—English actor of note—arrived—Nov. 16,
1810
Actors' Union—chartered—Jan. 4, 1896
Advertisement—automobile advertisement—July
30, 1898
Advertisement—double-column advertisement—
New York *Weekly Journal*—July 18, 1743
Advertisement—magician's advertisement—
March 18, 1734
Advertising Magazine—published—1865
Advertising Organization—to combat business
abuses—organized—December 1911
Advertising Show (annual)—May 3, 1906
Agriculture Professor—appointed—July 9, 1792

NEW YORK—New York City—*Continued*

Air (compressed)—for tunnel construction—used 1879

Air (liquid)—practical production—1895

Air Defense Command (U.S.)—created—Feb. 26, 1940

Air Rights Lease—Feb. 1910

Airmail Service—airmail experimental route—May 15, 1918

Airmail Service—airmail long-distance night service—established—July 1, 1925

Airmail Service—airmail regular service—established—Aug. 12, 1918

Airmail Service—airmail regular transcontinental through-service—to San Francisco—July 1, 1924

Airmail Service—airmail service from ship to shore—inaugurated—Aug. 13, 1928

Airmail Service—airmail service to a steamer at sea—Aug. 14, 1919

Airmail Service—airmail transcontinental flight—Feb. 22, 1921

Airmail Service—airmail transcontinental service (combination airplane-railroad)—to San Francisco—Sept. 8, 1920

Algebra Book—algebra book—published—1730

Ambulance—mobile coronary-care ambulance—St. Vincent's Hospital—October 1968

Animals—cattle (Africander cattle)—arrived—Dec. 11, 1931

Animals—elephant—arrived—April 13, 1796

Animals—gerenuk—born—Bronx Park Zoo—Sept. 30, 1963

Animals—monkey trained to perform—exhibited—Feb. 25, 1751

Animals—musk ox born in captivity—Bronx Zoo—Sept. 5, 1925

Animals—okapi—imported—August 4, 1937

Animals—rhinoceros—exhibited—Sept. 13, 1826

Animals—sheep (Karakul fur sheep)—imported—1908

Antenna—master skyscraper antenna—Empire State Building—erected 1965

Antislavery Party—national convention—May 12, 1841

Antitoxin Laboratory—established—Sept. 1894

Aquatic Mammals—platypus (duckbill)—exhibited—July 15, 1922

Arabic Magazine—*Star of America*—published—1892

Arbitration—arbitration tribunal—established—May 3, 1768

Arbitration Association—arbitration association —Arbitration Society of America, Inc.—formed —May 15, 1922

Architect—landscape architect—John Reid—arrived—Dec. 19, 1683

Archival Course—Columbia University—Sept. 29, 1938

Armenian Cathedral—consecrated—April 28, 1968

Army Execution—Thomas Hickey—June 27, 1776

Art Organization—artists' society of importance —organized—Nov. 8, 1825

Artificial Heart—invented—1935

Arts and Letters Society—arts and letters soc (national) founded—April 23, 1904

Arts and Letters Society—black member of National Institute of Arts and Letters—W. Du Bois—elected

Arts and Letters Society—woman elected to American Academy of Arts and Letters—Howe—Jan. 28, 1908

Assay Office Building (federal)—erected—18

Atheism Society—atheism society of import —organized—Oct. 1925

Athlete—black woman awarded the James E. livan Memorial trophy—Wilma Rudolph—23, 1962

Author—author—professional—C. B. Brown

Autogiro—autogiro rotary wing aircraft fe ship—New York University—Sept. 8, 1939

Autogiro—autogiro to land packages on a mo ship—April 30, 1931

Automaton—imported—May 3, 1743

Automobile—automobile to exceed the speed mile a minute—Nov. 16, 1901

Automobile—electric taxicabs—1897

Automobile—gas-turbine automobile—pub introduced—Jan. 21, 1954

Automobile—sedan-type automobile—pub exhibited—Jan. 11, 1913

Automobile Accident—May 30, 1896

Automobile Bus—automobile sightseeing b built—1900

Automobile Bus—bus with a double deck—

Automobile Bus—bus with a double-deck and chassis made in the United States—1

Automobile Bus—bus with cross seats—M 17, 1914

Automobile Bus—coast-to-coast through bus —from Los Angeles—1928

Automobile Bus—transcontinental no-ch bus service—instituted—to San Franc Calif.—Sept. 8, 1953

Automobile Driver—woman automobile driv G. D. Mudge—1898

Automobile Electric Self-Starter—autom electric self-starter patent—Nov. 24, 1903

Automobile Fatality—H. H. Bliss—Sept. 13,

Automobile Finance Company—organized—1915

Automobile Magazine—*The Horseless A* published—Nov. 1895

Automobile Race—automobile race from York to Paris—left—Feb. 12, 1908

Automobile Race—automobile race (long tance)—to Buffalo—Sept. 9–14, 1901

Automobile Race—transcontinental autom race—left—June 1, 1909

Automobile Race—transcontinental autom race (for a time record)—May 8, 1905

Automobile Show—Madison Square Gard Nov. 3, 1900

Automobile Speeding Arrest—driver arreste speeding—Jacob German—May 20, 1899

Automobile Tire—demountable tire-carrying —patented—Feb. 4, 1913

NEW YORK—New York City—*Continued*

Aviation—Pilot—pilot to fly 100 times across the Atlantic Ocean—R. O. D. Sullivan—Dec. 28, 1942

Aviation—Races—airplane to race a train—G. H. Curtiss—May 29, 1910

Aviation—Races—intercity airplane race—to Philadelphia—August 5, 1911

Aviation—School—correspondence school in aviation—International School of Aeronautics —opened Jan. 1, 1908

Aviation—School—high school aviation course— Sept. 1929

Baby Carriage—manufactured—Charles Burton —1848

Bacteriology Laboratory—bacteriology diagnostic laboratory of health department—1892

Bacteriology Laboratory—bacteriology laboratory—incorporated—Feb. 21, 1887

Baking Soda—manufactured—1846

Ballet—ballet—presented—Bowery Theatre— Feb. 7, 1827

Ballet—ballet transmitted by satellite—telecast over WNEW-TV—July 22, 1978

Balloon—balloon Atlantic crossing attempt—Oct. 6, 1873

Balloon—Flights—balloon flight by a native-born American—Sept. 9, 1830

Bank—bank established in a foreign country—by National City Bank—Nov. 10, 1914

Bank—bank open day and night—opened—May 1, 1906

Bank—bank to install an automatic teller— Chemical Bank—January 1969

Bank—bank to operate a window in a subway station for the convenience of subway riders— opened—Sept. 26, 1955

Bank—bank to provide motion pictures for its customers waiting in line to be served—Chemical Bank—Dec. 22, 1972

Bank—bank with resources exceeding $1 billion —National City Bank—Nov. 17, 1919

Bank—checkmaster plan—introduced—June 27, 1935

Bank—clearinghouse—New York Clearing House organized—Aug. 23, 1853

Bank—savings bank—conceived—Nov. 29, 1816

Bank—savings bank with a half-billion-dollar deposit—March 31, 1932

Bank—savings group—to teach children—March 16, 1885

Bank—trust company—Farmer's Fire Insurance and Loan Co.—incorporated Feb. 28, 1822

Bank Robbery—bank robbery—City Bank— March 19, 1831

Baseball—baseball (yellow)—used—April 27, 1938

Baseball Game—baseball game to attract more than 83,000 spectators—May 30, 1938

Baseball Game—baseball series—July 20, 1858

Baseball Game—night baseball game (major league) to last longer than 7 hours—St. Louis Cardinals vs. New York Mets—Sept. 12, 1974

Baseball Game—shutout double-header gam Chicago Cubs vs. Brooklyn Superbas—W ington Park, Brooklyn—Sept. 26, 1908

Baseball Game—shutout World Series gan New York Nationals–Philadelphia Athleti Oct. 13, 1905

Baseball Game—World Series baseball an championship—Oct. 23-24-25, 1884

Baseball Game—World Series baseball gan which a batter made 3 consecutive home in 1 game—Yankees vs. Dodgers—R. M. son—Oct. 18, 1977

Baseball Game—World Series baseball gam gross $1 million—Oct. 10-15, 1923

Baseball Game—World Series grand slam h run (National League)—C. J. Hiller—Oct. 8,

Baseball League—baseball league of import —National Association of Base-Ball playe organized—March 17, 1871

Baseball Park—baseball park (enclose opened—May 15, 1862

Baseball Pitcher—baseball pitcher—to cur ball—Arthur Cummings—1866

Baseball Pitcher—baseball pitcher (World Se with 3 shutout games—Christopher Mathev —3rd game, Oct. 12, 1905

Baseball Pitcher—baseball pitcher to pitch a fect no-hit, no-run, no-walk World Series g —Don Larsen—Oct. 8, 1956

Baseball Player—baseball pinch hitter—us June 7, 1892

Baseball Player—baseball player killed in a g —R. J. Chapman—Aug. 16, 1920

Baseball Player—baseball player (major lea to bat in 12 runs in a 9-inning game—J. L. tomley—St. Louis Cardinals vs. Brooklyn ins—Sept. 16, 1924

Baseball Player—baseball player (major lea to hit more than 60 home runs in 1 seasor E. Maris—61st home run, Oct. 1, 1961

Baseball Player—baseball players (brother oppose each other in a World Series—R Meusel and E. F. Meusel—Oct. 5 first game Oct. 13, 1921 (last game)

Baseball Player—baseball rookie to hit a g slam home run in the World Series— McDougald—Oct. 9, 1951

Baseball Player—black major league bas player—Jackie Robinson—played—April 1947

Baseball Player—major-league baseball play pitch two successive no-hit no-run games— 11, 1938—June 15, 1938

Baseball Player—"most valuable player"a (major league) to a black in the Ame League—Elston Howard—Nov. 7, 1963

Baseball Rules—baseball rules—standardiz —National Baseball Assn.—May 1858

Baseball Team—baseball team—Knickerb Club—organized—Sept. 23, 1845

Baseball Team—baseball team (black profes al)—organized—1885

Baseball Team—baseball team to tour—Bro team—left for Albany—June 30, 1860

ball Team—baseball team to win five World
ries in succession—New York Yankees—
t. 5, 1953

ball Team—baseball team to win more than
World Series—21st series 1963

ball Team—baseball team to win three
orld Series in succession—New York Yan-
es—1936, 1937, 1938

etball—basketball collegiate team to win the
tional Invitation Tournament and the Na-
nal Collegiate Athletic Association trophy—
rch 28, 1950

etball Game—basketball game at a large
nmercial sports arena—Madison Square
rden—Jan. 19, 1931

iouse—public bath- and washhouse—
ened—Jan. 1, 1852

iouse—public baths with showers—opened
\ug. 17, 1891

iouse—Turkish bath opened—Oct. 6, 1863

ry—solar battery—announced—April 25,
·4

pring—box spring—imported—1857

volent Protective Order of Elks—organized
'eb. 16, 1868

—Bible for the blind in embossed form—is-
·d—1835

School—Missionary Training College—
ened—Oct. 1, 1883

Society—Bible society (national organiza-
n)—American Bible Society—formed—May
816

le—bicycle velocipedes—imported—1819

le Patent—W. K. Clarkson, Jr.—June 26, 1819

le Race—intercollegiate bicycle race—May
1896

le Race—international six-day bicycle race
)ct. 18, 1891

le Race—international 6-day 2-man-team bile race—Madison Square Garden—Feb. 12–
1899

le Race—motorcycle-paced bicycle race—
/ 29, 1899

le Race—paired six-day bicycle race—Dec.
4, 1901

le Race—women's six-day bicycle race—
, 6–11, 1896

le School—opened—Dec. 5, 1868

le Rider—bicycle rider to cross the continent
less than 5 weeks—Eugene McPherson—
ived—Sept. 21, 1949

le Tire—bicycle tire (pneumatic)—manufac-
ed—April 1891

rd Ball of composition material resembling
ry—patented—Oct. 10, 1865

rd Book—Billiards Without a Master—pub-
ed—1850

3anding Society—formed—Dec. 8, 1909

—quetzal bird—imported—Oct. 4, 1940

—sparrows—imported—1850

Club—boat club—Knickerbocker Boat Club
rganized—1811

Club—boat club association of amateur
os—1834

Boat Race—international lifeboat race—Sept. 7,
1927

Book—book advance payment to exceed $3 mil-
lion—Princess Daisy, by Judith Krantz—Sept.
12, 1979

Book—book bound with a preprinted offset
cloth—Portraits and Prayers—published—Nov.
7, 1934

Book—book (cloth-covered) commercially bound
—C. A. W. Eaton—Rome in the Nineteenth Century—4th edition—1827

Book—Book of Common Prayer (in the Mohawk
Indian language)—published—1715

Book—book on cornstalk paper—printed—June
1928

Book—book on the game of bridge by a championship team—The Four Aces System of Contract Bridge—published—1935

Book—book set by linotype—published—1887

Book—book set into type completely by electronic composition—The Long Short Cut, by Andrew Garve—published—1968

Book—book showing action photographs in action in sequence—An Electric-Photographic
Investigation of Consecutive Phases of Animal
Movements, by Eadweard Muybridge—plates
printed

Book—comic books—published—1904

Book—contract bridge laws book—Laws of Contract Bridge—published 1927

Book—stereotyped book—stereotyped—June
1813

Book Auction—authorized—April 18, 1662

Book Catalog—book catalog—The Uniform
Trade List Annual—published—1873

Book Club—Book-of-the-Month Club—formed—
April 1926

Book Fair—June 1, 1802

Book Guide—book guide—American Bookseller's Guide—published—first issue Jan. 7, 1869

Book Index—American Book Circular—published—1843

Book Jacket—used—1833

Book Publisher of denominational books—organized—May 1789

Book Review—book review editor—Margaret
Fuller—appointed—Dec. 1844

Book Review—book review newspaper supplement—published—Oct. 10, 1896

Book Trade Magazine—book collectors' magazine—The Philobiblion—published—1861

Book Trade Magazine—book trade magazine—
issued—Jan. 1, 1834

Book Trade Magazine—successful book trade
magazine—weekly—issued—Sept. 1, 1855

Booksellers' Association—American Company of
Booksellers—organized—June 7, 1801

Booksellers' Catalog—published—Leon & Brother
—1885

Bottle—milk bottles—used—1879

Bowling Magazine—Gut Holz—issued—Aug. 9,
1893

Bowling Rule Standardization—National Bowling
Assn.—Nov. 13, 1875

NEW YORK—New York City—*Continued*

Bowling Tournament—bowling convention—of importance—Sept. 9, 1895

Bowling Tournament—bowling match—Jan. 1, 1840

Bowling Tournament—bowling match in which white balls were used on black lanes—Brooklyn—May 23, 1959

Brick—terra-cotta—manufactured—1853

Bridge—double-deck bridge—of importance— Queensboro Bridge opened—March 30, 1909

Bridge—suspension bridge of importance having steel towers—Williamsburg Bridge—opened— Dec. 19, 1903

Brokerage—American Stock Exchange women members—J. M. Walsh and P. K. S. Peterson— elected Nov. 18, 1965

Brokerage—brokerage firm whose shares were traded by a major stock exchange—traded on July 27, 1971

Brokerage—curb exchange—to transact more business in a day than the Stock Exchange— June 15, 1929

Brokerage—financial "corner"—1666

Brokerage—investment trust—New York Stock Trust organized—April 1, 1889

Brokerage—New York Stock Exchange black director—J. H. Holland—elected July 5, 1972

Brokerage—New York Stock Exchange black member—J. L. Searles, III—approved Feb. 13, 1969

Brokerage—New York Stock Exchange woman governor—J. M. Kreps—elected July 5, 1972

Brokerage—New York Stock Exchange woman seat owner—Muriel Siebert—admitted, Dec. 28, 1967

Brokerage—oceangoing brokerage office—*Ile de France*—Aug. 15, 1929

Brokerage—stock exchange—New York Stock Exchange—May 17, 1792

Brokerage—stock exchange at which more than a million shares were traded in one day—Dec. 15, 1886

Brokerage—visitor to open the New York Stock Exchange—Leonard Ross—April 24, 1956

Brokerage—woman brokerage office owner— offices opened—1869

Brokerage—woman director of a stock exchange —M. G. Roebling—Oct. 28, 1958

Brokerage—woman president of a major stock brokerage concern—J. P. Bay—Dec. 1, 1956

Brokerage—woman stock exchange member (commodity exchange)—admitted—Sept. 3, 1935

Brokerage—woman to sell securities on the floor of the New York Curb Exchange—Nov. 19, 1941

Building—apartment house cooperative—incorporated March 28, 1883—opened September 1883

Building—apartment house to occupy a sq city block—ready for occupancy Oct. 15,

Building—apartment house with a modern la —erected—1869

Building—brick building—erected—1633

Building—bronze and glass skyscraper— pleted—Nov. 1957

Building—building constructed wholly of iron—May 1848

Building—building higher than 750 feet in h —Woolworth Building—opened April 24,

Building—building higher than 1,250 feet—En State Building—dedicated May 1, 1931

Building—building in which wrought-iron be were used—1854

Building—building with a high steeple—ded ed—May 21, 1846

Building—housing cooperative sponsored labor union—Amalgamated Houses—op Nov. 1, 1927

Building—steel-frame residence—built—189

Building—tenement house—built—1833

Burglar Alarm—burglar alarm operated by sonic or radio waves—patented—Samuel no—Oct. 13, 1953

Burglar Alarm—burglar alarm system—187

Business—chain store organization—1857

Business—commercial rating agency—e lished—Aug. 1, 1841

Business—corporation to have more than 3 lion stockholders—American Telephon Telegraph Company—Oct. 17, 1972

Business—department store to hold a publi auction—Nov. 14–15, 1941

Business—department store to occupy a block—A. T. Stewart & Co.—opened 186C

Business—retail store whose sales in 1 day ceeded $1 million—R. H. Macy Co.—De 1944

Bustle—patented—Alexander Douglas—Apr 1857

Cabinet (U.S.)—Cabinet—appointed—1789–

Cable (telegram)—cable message sent aroun world by commercial telegraph—Aug. 20,

—cable—submarine telegraph cable—S. Morse—Oct. 18, 1842

Cable (telegraph)—news dispatch by cable— York *Sun*—Aug. 26, 1858

Cable (telegraph)—submarine telegraph that was practical—Ezra Cornell—1845

Cable (telegraph)—submarine telegraph cal be insulated with gutta-percha—May 184

Camera—aerial camera (nine-lens) for large- mapping—built—1935

Camera—camera to take, develop, and prin tures on photographic paper—demonstra E. H. Land—Feb. 21, 1947

Camouflage—scientific paper published— 1896

Cancer Research Fund—established—New Cancer Hospital—1902

Canning—introduced—Ezra Daggett—1819

Canning Book—published—1812

Canoe Club—New York Canoe Club—1870

nization—canonization of a saint in the Unit-
States—John Sergiev—Nov. 1, 1964

—can (tin) with a key opener—patented—
t. 2, 1866

or—school for cantors—Hebrew Union
ool of Education and Sacred Music—
ned—Oct. 16, 1948

on—cartoon awarded a Pulitzer Prize—Rol-
Kirby—Aug. 5, 1921

on—Democratic cartoon—Jan. 15, 1870

on—newspaper cartoon strip—*Daily Graph-*
-Sept. 11, 1875

on—Republican cartoon—Nov. 7, 1874

on—Uncle Sam cartoon—published—*Lan-*
1—March 13, 1852

on School—organized—Feb. 1938

how—exhibition—Madison Square Garden
1ay 8–11, 1895

lic Mass—Catholic mass for night workers
1ay 5, 1901

lic Priest—Catholic priest to be elevated to
cardinalate—John McCloskey—April 27,
5

Club (Guernsey cattle)—permanent organi-
ion formed—Feb. 7, 1877

tery—Jewish burial plot—established—
6

is—city to exceed a million in population—
0

—steamer chair—introduced—1891

ber of Commerce—chamber of commerce
te)—formed—April 5, 1768

ists Society—chemical society (national)—
anized—April 20, 1876

lle Manufacturing Machine—patented—
. 13, 1863

Champion—chess champion of the world
nerican-born)—Paul Charles Morphy—Oct.
857

Tournament—chess tournament of impor-
ce—Oct. 6, 1857

Tournament—intercollegiate transatlantic
ss match by cable—April 21–22, 1899

Hygiene Bureau—Aug. 1908

se Students—arrived—April 12, 1847

pody School—chiropody school of note—or-
ized—1910

Suey—concocted—August 29, 1896

nium Plating Process (commercial)—invent-
–1924

no—John Banvard—1861

h—floating church—built—1843

h—Mariners' church—built—June 4, 1820

h—universal chapel embracing eight faiths
Jniversalist Church of the Divine Paternity—
icated—April 8, 1956

Band—cigar band of special interest—C. W.
ld—Sept. 2, 1858

Lighter Patent—Nov. 21, 1871

Rolling Machine—practical—patented—
. 27, 1883

ette Manufacturing Machine—invented—
2

Clock—clock to operate by atomic power—
Atomicron—exhibited—Oct. 2, 1956

Clock—electronic wristwatch—produced—Oct.
25, 1960

Coaching—tallyho trip—May 1, 1876

Coaching Club—formed—Dec. 3, 1875

Cobra—King cobra snakes—born in captivity—
July 4, 1955

Collar—paper collar—patented July 25, 1854

College—college for women under Jewish auspices—Stern College for Women—opened Sept.
13, 1954—first graduation June 19, 1958

College—college foreign-language house—Deutsches Haus at Columbia University—1911

College—college to prohibit discrimination because of race, religion, or color—Cooper Union
—April 29, 1851

College—liberal arts college for police and corrections officers established by a city—College
of Police Science—opened Sept. 20, 1965—first
graduation June 13, 1966

College—woman dean of a graduate school—
Frieda Wunderlich—elected—Jan. 4, 1939

College President—woman college president of
two colleges—Rosemary Park—Barnard College—inaugurated Nov. 15, 1962 (second)

College Student—Jewish college graduate—Issac
Abrahams—King's College (Columbia College)
—1774

Colonist—colonists to reach the Pacific coast—
left New York City—Sept. 6, 1810

Colorscope—public demonstration—June 5, 1930

Congress (U.S.)—Congress of the United States—
March 4, 1789

Congress (U.S.)—congressional act—June 1, 1789

Congress (U.S.)—joint meeting of the Senate and
the House of Representatives—April 6, 1789

Congress (U.S.)—House of Representatives—
committee of the House of Representatives—
appointed—April 2, 1789

Congress (U.S.)—House of Representatives—contested election—April 18, 1789

Congress (U.S.)—House of Representatives—
House of Representatives—meeting—March 4,
1789

Congress (U.S.)—House of Representatives—
House of Representatives—quorum assembled
—April 1, 1789

Congress (U.S.)—Senate—Senate—meeting—
March 4, 1789

Congress (U.S.)—Senate—Senate—quorum assembled—April 6, 1789

Conscientious Objectors—arrived August 6, 1774

Cooking School—New York Cooking School—
Nov. 1876

Cooperative—consumers' cooperative society—
organized—1830

Copyright—choreographic score copyrighted—
Hanya Holm—Feb. 25, 1952

Coral Reef Barrier—exhibition completed—July
1934

Cork—for steam pipe covering—manufactured—
1894

Cork Manufacturer—1850

NEW YORK—New York City—*Continued*

Corkboard Patent—John T. Smith—July 14, 1891
Corkscrew Patent—M. L. Byrn—March 27, 1860
Corporation—commercial corporation—New York Fishing Co.—Jan. 8, 1675
Court—court in which the judge presided in a city (Washington, D.C.) other than the one in which the lawyers appeared—Court of Claims, Washington, D.C.—Oct. 16, 1975
Court—night court—opened—Sept. 1, 1907
Cranberry Treatise—published—1856
Credit Protective Group—formed—1842
Credit Report Book—published—1844
Crepe—imported—1912
Cricket Tournament—cricket match—May 1, 1751
Crime—interstate crime pact—signed—Sept. 16, 1833
Cripples—private school for cripples—opened—May 1, 1863
Crossword Puzzle—published—Dec. 21, 1913
Crossword Puzzle Book—published—April 18, 1924
Curfew Bell—introduced—Wilhelm Kieft—1638
Dacron—Dacron men's suits—introduced—May 8, 1951
Dance Marathon—dance marathon—began March 30, 1923
Deaf—Association—national social organization for the hard of hearing—formed—Feb. 27, 1919
Deaf—Church Service—church services for the deaf—Thomas Gallaudet—Oct. 3, 1852
Deaf—Communication—visible and oral communication by the deaf over distance—by television—Oct. 13, 1940
Deaf—School—instruction for the deaf—John Stanford—1807
Deaf—School—lipreading instruction for the deaf—S. W. Keeler—1882
Deaf—School—lipreading school for girls—established—L. E. Warren—1890
Degrees (academic and honorary)—Bachelor of Sacred Music degree—conferred—June 10, 1953
Degrees (academic and honorary)—Doctor of Military Science degree—J. J. Pershing—April 11, 1930
Degrees (academic and honorary)—law degree of LL.M. (Master of Laws)—conferred by Columbia University—June 29, 1864
Degrees (academic and honorary)—Master of Arts degree in aeronautics—G. C. Loening—Columbia University—June 1, 1910
Degrees (academic and honorary)—Master of Arts degree in Sacred Music—conferred—June 6, 1956
Degrees (academic and honorary)—Master of Hebrew Literature degree awarded a woman—H. H. Levinthal—May 28, 1939
Dental Book—book on dentistry—strictly American—R. C. Skinner—published—1801
Dental Book—dental textbook—*A System of Dental Surgery*—published—1829
Dental Book—orthodontia treatise—Solyman Brown—published—1841

Dental Dispensary—dental dispensary—City pensary for the Medical Relief of the P opened—Feb. 1, 1791
Dental Periodical—dental journal—*Ame Journal of Dental Science*—published—18
Dental Society—dental society (local)—So of Surgeon-Dentists—formed—Dec. 3, 183
Dental Society—dental society of importa American Society of Dental Surgeons—nized—Aug. 18, 1840
Dentistry—amalgam for filling teeth—introd —advertised—Aug. 12, 1834
Dentistry—gold inlay—described—Jan. 15,
Dentistry—patent for artificial teeth—C. M. ham—March 9, 1822
Dictionary—dictionary compiled by a wom published—Feb. 2, 1940
Dictionary—Hebrew dictionary—publish 1809
Dictionary—rhyming dictionary—publish 1823
Diesel Engine—diesel-engine automobile from Indianapolis—arrived—Jan. 6, 1930
Diplomatic Service—black delegate to the U Nations from the U.S.—E. S. Sampson pointed—August 24, 1950
Dog Show—of importance—May 8, 1877
Drill—dental drill—invented—John Green —1790
Dynamo—that was successful—built—1881
Education—chair in education—temporary—
Education Periodical—educational magaz *Juvenile Mirror or Educational Magazine*— lished—1811
Education Periodical—educational magazi achieve success—published—Feb. 7, 1818
Election—mayor elected by popular vote in —C. V. W. Lawrence—April 8, 1834
Electric Company—electric company—E Electric Light Co.—organized—Oct. 24, 18
Electric Company—electric station (centra supply light and power—opened—Sept. 4,
Electric Flatiron—patented—H. W. Seely—J 1882
Electric Lighting—electric light from a p plant in a residence—installed—c. Dec. 1
Electric Lighting—klieg light lighting unit—us 1911
Electric Lighting—mercury vapor lamp—pate —P. C. Hewitt—Sept. 17, 1901
Electric Power—electric power generated by mic rays—Hayden Planetarium—April 30,
Electric Sign—animated-cartoon electric s displayed—April 28, 1937
Electric Sign—electric sign flasher—opera Nov. 6, 1928
Electric Sign—electric sign (large)—instal June 1892
Electric Sign—neon-tube advertising sign stalled—July 1923
Electric Stove—electric stove—patented— Hadaway, Jr.—June 30, 1896

NEW YORK—New York City—Continued

Free Port—opened—Stapleton, Staten Island, N.Y.—Feb. 1, 1937

Freemasons—Ancient Arabic Order of Nobles of the Mystic Shrine—established—June 16, 1871

Freemasons—Knights Templar Grand Encampment—Jan. 22, 1814

Game Manufacturing Company—organized by J. McLoughlin—1828

Game Protection Society—formed—May 20, 1844

Gardener's Manual—Thomas Bridgeman—published—1835

Gas—gas meter (dry)—patented—James Bogardus—Oct. 17, 1834

Gas Engine—patented—S. Perry—May 25, 1844

Geographical Society—geographical society director (woman)—S. K. Myers—June 16, 1976

Giant—exhibited—Oct. 6, 1825

Glass—invisible-glass installation—Sept. 1935

Glider—glider towed across the continent—landed—April 6, 1930

Golf Book—J. P. Lee—published—May 25, 1895

Golf Club—golf association (national)—United States Golf Assn.—formed—Dec. 22, 1894

Golf Clubs (or golf sticks)—golf clubs (or golf sticks)—described—1729

Golf Magazine—Golfing—published—1894

Grammar—English grammar by an American published in America—Samuel Johnson—1765

Grammer—Spanish grammer—A Short Introduction to the Spanish Language, by Garrat Noel—printed—1751

Greek Orthodox Church—Greek Orthodox Church bishop who had converted from the Roman Catholic Church—Paul de Ballester—March 15, 1970

Greenhouse—erected—James Beekman—1764

Gutta-percha—imported—1840

Gyroscope—gyro stabilizer installed on an American naval vessel—April 1913

Gyroscope—gyroscopic stabilizer—E. A. Sperry and H. L. Tanner—patented—Aug. 14, 1917

Hall of Fame—Hall of Fame (university)—dedicated—May 30, 1901

Hall of Famer—Hall of Fame (university) black—B. T. Washington—selection announced Oct. 31, 1945

Hat—soft felt hats for women—introduced—J. N. Genin—1851

Health Board—health board (municipal) armed with sufficient powers—authorized—Feb. 26, 1866

Health Instruction in connection with the schools—undertaken—Oct. 1902

Health Ordinance prohibiting spitting—on the sidewalks—passed—May 12, 1896

Hebrew Book—Hebrew book all in Hebrew—published—1860

Helicopter—helicopter licensed for commercial use—March 8, 1946

Helicopter—helicopter passenger service—July 9, 1953

Heliport—heliport commercial base—first
May 18, 1949

High School—public high school to speciali
the performing field—Sept. 13, 1948

History—comic history of the United Sta
published—1812

Holiday—Labor Day holiday parade—Sep
1882

Homeopathy—introduced—H. B. Gram—18
Horse—horse to trot 1 mile in less than 3 mi
—Yankey—June 10, 1806

Horse Race—horse race on a stage in a thea
Old Broadway Theatre—Feb. 18, 1856

Horse Race—trotting course—establish
Jamaica—1825

Horse Race—trotting futurity—Oct. 12, 1869

Horse Register—pacing register—Ame
Race-Turf Register—published 1833

Horse Register—trotting register—Ame
Trotting Register—published—1871

Horse Show—horse show of national scope—
22–26, 1883

Horticultural Society—horticultural soci
New York Horticultural Society—found
1818

Hospital—babies' hospital designed exclus
for infants—chartered—June 23, 1887

Hospital—cancer home for incurables (free)
tablished—Sept. 15, 1896

Hospital—cancer hospital—New York Ca
Hospital—opened for patients—Dec. 7, 18

Hospital—cancer hospital (municipal)—dec
ed—Aug. 1, 1923

Hospital—children's hospital—Nursery
Child's Hospital—established—1854

Hospital—eye hospital (permanent)—New
Eye Infirmary—opened—Aug. 14, 1820

Hospital—floating hospital—trial trip—July
1875

Hospital—Jewish hospital—Mount Sinai Hos
—incorporated—1852

Hospital—orthopedic hospital—Hospital fo
Ruptured and Crippled—opened—May 1,

Hospital—women's hospital—Woman's Hos
—opened—May 4, 1855

Hospital—women's infirmary staffed by wc
physicians—New York Infirmary for We
and Children—incorporated—Dec. 13, 185

Hospital Record—system introduced—Bell
Training School for Nurses—1874

Hotel—hotel built—City Hotel—1794

Hotel—hotel for women—Women's Ho
opened April 2, 1878

Hotel—hotel transported—Brighton Beach H
Brooklyn—April 3–July 29, 1888

Hotel—hotel with individually controlled air
ditioning and heating in every room—St.
—opened Sept. 4, 1904

Humane Society—humane society—Ame
Society for the Prevention of Cruelty to Ani
—incorporated—April 10, 1866

Hydrotherapy Chair—Simon Baruch—appo
—1907

-commercial transportation of ice—to arleston, S.C.—1799

-dry ice—commercial manufacture—1925

:ream—ice cream—commercial manufacture advertised—June 8, 1786

kating Rink—ice skating rink (indoor)—built 1879

igration—refugee to arrive under the Refugee lief Act of 1953—Stamatoula Roumanis— 1, 1954

egnation—impregnation (human) by means artificial insemination—Dr. J. M. Sims—1866

ator (Eggs) Patent—awarded—N. E. Guerin March 30, 1843

ator for Infants—used—Sept. 7, 1888

strial Recovery Act—conviction under a Na-nal Industrial Recovery Code—Dec. 2, 1933

-ink—commercial manufacture—1825

ance—bonding company (exclusive)—com-nced operations—April 15, 1884

ance—fraternal group insurance—of conse-ence—issued—1869

ance—group insurance contract of impor-nce—July 1, 1912

ance—group insurance policy—June 1, 1911

ance—insurance agency—opened—Israel helan—1804

ance—insurance company to exclusively in-e the lives of animals—founded Aug. 1, 1957

ance—insurance rate standardization—ected—July 18, 1866

ance—mutual life insurance company to op-te—chartered—April 12, 1842

ance—nonforfeiture insurance policy—is-d—Aug. 13, 1860

ance—numerical system of insurance rating 903

ance—substandard life insurance policy—ued—July 1, 1896

Magazine—The Shamrock or Hibernian ronicle—published—Dec. 15, 1810

h Book—Jewish prayer book published in United States—1766

h College—Jewish college of liberal arts and ences under Jewish auspices—Yeshiva Col-e—chartered—March 29, 1928

h Congregation—Jewish congregation—earith Israel—established—1655

—Jew—landed—August 22, 1654

—Jew to win all the rights and perform all the ties of citizenship—April 20, 1657

—Jewish fraternal society—B'nai B'rith—nded—Oct. 13, 1843

ey—jockey (woman) to win a major stakes e at a major track—Robyn Smith—Aqueduct cetrack—March 1, 1973

—black judge of a customs court (U.S.)—orn in—Nov. 3, 1945

—black woman judge of a federal district rt—C. B. Motley—sworn in Sept. 9, 1966

—black woman judge of the U.S. Court of peals—A. L. Kearse—sworn in June 27, 1979

—woman associate justice on the federal nch—G. R. Cline—appointed—May 4, 1928

—woman judge (black)—J. M. Bolin—ap-nted—July 22, 1939

Judge—woman judge of the Surrogates Court—began term Jan. 1, 1978

Kennel—hotel for dogs—Kennelworth—opened by Leo Wiener—Nov. 12, 1975

Kindergarten—nursery school—established—1827

Knighthood—knighthood conferred in America—Oct. 25, 1761

Labor—labor congress (national)—Oct. 12, 1845

Labor Legislation—minimum wage law (city) for public contract work—approved Dec. 29, 1961—effective Jan. 28, 1962

Labor Paper—The Man—published—Feb. 18, 1834

Labor Union—women's labor organization—formed—1825

Laryngophone—throat microphone—manufac-tured—1941

Law School—law instruction in a college—King's College—1755

Lawbook—lawbook containing the federal laws of the United States—published—1791

Lawbook—lawbook (text)—published—1802

Lawbook—law compilation of federal session laws—published—1789

Lawyers' Association—lawyers' association (state)—New York Bar Assn.—formed—1747

Leather—chrome tanning process—for tanning hides—patented—Jan. 8, 1884

Lecture Series (endowed)—presented—Union Theological Seminary—1866

Lecturer—lecturer of royal blood to speak for per-sonal profit—Prince Vilhelm of Sweden—arrived—Jan. 5, 1927

Lens—contact lenses—imported—1924

Lens—lens to provide zoom effects—patented—F. G. Back—Nov. 23, 1948

Librarians' Convention—Sept. 15, 1853

Librarians' Union—American Federation of Labor affiliate—chartered—May 15, 1917

Library—library for seamen—inaugurated—March 1829

Library—mechanics' library—opened—1820

Library—mercantile library—organized—Nov. 9, 1820

Library Chair—established—Columbia Universi-ty—April 4, 1938

Library Periodical—library periodical—Library Journal—published—first issue Sept. 30, 1876

Library Society—library society (local)—New York Library Club—formed—June 18, 1885

Library Training (systematic)—courses—Co-lumbia University—Jan. 5, 1887

Libretto—libretto—The Disappointment—pub-lished—1767

Life Preserver—life preserver of cork—patented—N. E. Guerin—Nov. 16, 1841

Life Preserver—life preserver of cork approved by the Board of Supervising Inspectors—patented—David Kahnweiler—July 10, 1877

Lifeboat—lifeboat (corrugated)—patented—Jo-seph Francis—March 26, 1845

NEW YORK—New York City—*Continued*

Linoleum—linoleum—manufactured—1873

Liquor Reform Movement—1623

Locomotive—diesel-electric locomotive—in service—Dec. 17, 1924

Loop-the-Loop Centrifugal Railway—installed—Coney Island—1900

Macaroni Factory—established—Antoine Zerega—1848

Magic Lantern—magic lantern feature show—Oct. 9, 1894

Map—road map—published—1789

Map—war map—published—Dec. 24, 1733

Marine Corps—Marine corps—organized—1740

Marine Corps—marine regiment in France—left for France, June 14, 1917

Meat—beef exported—to England—Oct. 1, 1875

Mechanics Textbook—*The Elements of Analytical Mechanics*—published—1853

Medal—American Academy of Arts and Letters-National Institute of Arts and Letters gold medal—awarded—C. E. Burchfield—May 8, 1942

Medal—arts and letters society (national) gold medal special award—C. W. Eliot—presented Jan. 27, 1916

Medal—Legion of Merit medal to a Coastguardsman in World War II—J. C. Cullen—Nov. 9, 1943

Medical Book—bronchitis treatise—Horace Green—published—1846

Medical Book—chiropody book—Issachar Zacharie—published—1860

Medical Book—croup report (printed)—Richard Bayley—published—1781

Medical Book—dissection essay—1750

Medical Book—hay fever book—Morrill Wyman—published—1872

Medical Book—hemophilia treatise—published—1803

Medical Book—homeopathic treatise—C. F. S. Hahnemann—published—1825

Medical Book—medical book for army medical use—published—1790

Medical Book—medical catalog—*A Short Treatise of the Virtues of Dr. Bateman's Pectoral Drops*—reprinted—J. P. Zenger—1731

Medical Book—medical ethics book—*A Discourse Upon the Duties of a Physician,* by Samuel Bard—printed by A.&J. Robertson—1769

Medical Book—medical history—*A Medical Discourse,* by Peter Middleton—printed by Hugh Gaine—1769

Medical Book—neurasthenia book—G. M. Beard—published—1880

Medical Book—neurology textbook—W. A. Hammond—published—1871

Medical Book—obstetrics book—Samuel Bard—published—1807

Medical Book—pediatrics book of importance—L. E. Holt—published—1894

Medical Book—surgery manual—John Jones—published—1775

Medical Clinic—acupuncture treatment cen opened—July 12, 1972

Medical Clinic—birth control clinic—oper Oct. 16, 1916

Medical Clinic—cancer prevention clinic for dren—opened—Jan. 3, 1947

Medical Clinic—children's clinic—establisł 1862

Medical Clinic—college medical clinic—e lished—1840

Medical Clinic—laryngology clinic—establ —March 1863

Medical Clinic—ophthalmology clinic–Avenue Hospital—Sept. 1932

Medical Clinic—vasectomy outpatient serv Margaret Sanger Research Bureau—oper Oct. 3, 1969

Medical Congress—Fever Therapy Internat Conference—March 29, 1937

Medical Instruction—clinical instruction and side demonstration—A. H. Stevens—1818

Medical Instruction—laryngology instruct University of the City of New York—Loui berg—1861

Medical Instruction—medical jurispruc course—James Stringham—1813

Medical Instruction—midwifery professor–B. Tennent—1767

Medical Instruction—orthopedics chair—e lished—Bellevue Hospital Medical Coll 1861

Medical Instruction—pediatrics professor–A ham Jacobi—1870

Medical Instruction—plastic surgery profes J. E. Sheehan—1926

Medical Instruction—Psychiatric Institute thorized—May 12, 1896

Medical Legislation—chiropody law gove the study of chiropody—passed—1895

Medical Legislation—law to regulate the pra of medicine (actually enforced)—June 10,

Medical Periodical—homeopathic magaz *American Journal of Homeopathia*—publ —1835

Medical Periodical—laryngology magazine–chives of Laryngology—published—1880

Medical Periodical—medical magazine—*Me Repository*—published—Aug. 8, 1797

Medical Periodical—medical periodical dev to diseases of women and children—*Ame Journal of Obstetrics*—published—May 1

Medical Periodical—optometry magazine–*Optician*—published—Jan. 1891

Medical "Rogues' Gallery"—started—Jan. 1

Medical School—medical center devote teaching, treatment, and research—Colu Presbyterian Medical Center—opened Ma —formal dedication Oct. 12, 1928

Medical School—medical college (Jewish sored)—Albert Einstein College of Med Yeshiva University—instruction began Sep 1935

cal School—medical school based upon wa-
-cure principles—American Hydropathic In-
ute—opened March 15, 1851

cal School—naval medical school—opened
Aug. 1, 1893

cal Society—laryngological society (state)—
anized—October 1873

cine—bone bank—established—April 1946

odist Church—Methodist chapel dedicated
Oct. 30, 1768

odist Church—Methodist preacher—Philip
bury—arrived—Aug. 11, 1760

odist Church—Methodist Society in America
Philip Embury and Barbara Heck—organized
6

ofilm—magazine on microfilm offered to sub-
ibers—Newsweek—June 1, 1949

ofilm—newspaper to microfilm its current is-
es—New York Herald Tribune—Jan. 1, 1936

ofilm—newspaper to microfilm its past issues
New York Times—Nov. 1935

—condensed milk (commercial)—patent
nted—Gail Borden—Aug. 19, 1856

—dried milk patent—S. R. Percy—April 9,
'2

—milk delivery in glass bottles—Alexander
mpbell—1878

Sale Regulations—enacted—1896

ralogy Periodical—American Mineralogical
rnal—published—Jan. 1810

s School—Columbia University—opened—
v. 15, 1864

trel Show Troupe—organized—D. D. Emmett
842–1843

ey—trade tokens—issued—1789

ument—monument to an American poet—
z-Greene Halleck—unveiled—May 15, 1877

ument—obelisk to be brought to the United
ites—arrived—July 20, 1880

on Picture—animated cartoon in color—pro-
ced—1916

on Picture—animated cartoon (present tech-
ue)—released—June 12, 1913

on Picture—animated cartoon talking picture
exhibited—Sept. 19, 1928

on Picture—animated cartoon (technical)—
duced—1916

on Picture—black-oriented talking picture
l-talking, all-singing) by a major company—
arts in Dixie—shown Feb. 27, 1929

on Picture—colored motion pictures—exhib-
d—Dec. 11, 1909

on Picture—foreign feature film exhibited—
y 12, 1912

on Picture—motion picture film exhibition—
y 9, 1893

on Picture—motion picture film exhibition in
heater—April 23, 1896

on Picture—motion picture for training sol-
rs—produced—1917

on Picture—motion picture from an airplane
. T. Coffin—Feb. 16, 1912

on Picture—motion picture of a complete
nd opera—I Pagliacci—Feb. 20, 1931

Motion Picture—motion picture of a real pugilistic
encounter taken at night—Jeffries-Sharkey fight
—Nov. 3, 1899

Motion Picture—motion picture of the inside of a
living heart (of a dog)—shown—Oct. 16, 1951

Motion Picture—motion picture on film shown on
a screen—exhibited—April 21, 1895

Motion Picture—motion picture presented simultaneously in major cities throughout the
world—On the Beach—Dec. 17, 1959

Motion Picture—motion picture sex shocker—A
Daughter of the Gods—Annette Kellerman—
shown Oct. 17, 1916

Motion Picture—motion picture (successful) projected to a paying audience—April 23, 1896

Motion Picture—motion picture with scent—Behind The Great Wall—presented—Dec. 8, 1959

Motion Picture—peep show—exhibition—April
14, 1894

Motion Picture—presidential candidate shown in
motion pictures—W. J. Bryan—shown July 12,
1908

Motion Picture—sound-on-film motion picture—
demonstrated—Lee De Forest—March 12, 1923

Motion Picture—talking picture—presented—
Aug. 5, 1926

Motion Picture—talking picture entirely in color—
On with the Show—exhibited—May 28, 1929

Motion Picture—talking picture in Esperanto—
exhibited—July 13, 1929

Motion Picture—talking picture of more than
6,000 feet—exhibited—July 6, 1928

Motion Picture—Technicolor motion picture—
released—Dec. 3, 1922

Motion Picture—three-dimensional feature motion picture in color—The House of Wax—April
10, 1953

Motion Picture—three-dimensional feature motion picture produced and released by a major
company—Man in the Dark—April 8, 1953

Motion Picture Censorship—motion picture censorship board (national)—organized—March
1909

Motion Picture Professorship—motion picture
professorship—Robert Gessner appointed—established at Washington Square College of Arts
and Sciences, New York University—May 26,
1941

Motion Picture Theater—theater built especially
for the rear projection of motion pictures—
Trans-Lux Theatre—opened—March 14, 1931

Motorboat—motorboat pleasure craft—produced
—F. W. Ofeldt—1885

Motorboat Race—motorboat race under organized rules—June 23–24, 1904

Motorboating Magazine—motorboating magazine—Motor Boat—published—first issue April
10, 1904

Motorcycle Association—Federation of American
Motorcyclists—organized—Sept. 7, 1903

Motorcycle Endurance Run—from Boston—July
4–5, 1902

Motorcycle Hill-climbing Contest—May 30, 1903

NEW YORK—New York City—*Continued*

Motorcycle Race—motorcycle distance race (4 hours)—G. N. Holden—Manhattan Beach—Sept. 5, 1903

Motorcycle Race—motorcycle race (250 miles)—ended—July 5, 1902

Motorcycle Trip—motorcycle transcontinental trip—from San Francisco, Calif.—completed—July 6, 1903

Motorcycle Trip—motorcycle transcontinental trip by a woman—commenced—July 5, 1916

Museum—children's museum—opened in Brooklyn—Dec. 16, 1899

Museum—costume museum—Museum of Costume Arts—incorporated—April 28, 1937

Museum—industrial museum—incorporated—Feb. 26, 1914

Music—black to conduct the Metropolitan Opera House orchestra—Henry Lewis—Oct. 16, 1972

Music—long-distance telephone concert—from Philadelphia—March 31, 1877

Music—war song of the Confederate States "Dixie"—sung—April 4, 1859

Music Book—Lutheran hymnbook (English) created in America—J. C. Kunze—*A Hymn and Prayer Book 'for the Use of Such Lutheran Churches as Use the English Language*—printed—1795

Music Book—music book printed from type—*The Psalms of David*—printed—1767

Music Book—ragtime instruction book—published—1897

Music Society—musical society for the literary protection of composers and authors—ASCAP—formed—Feb. 13, 1914

Nail Machine (wire)—built—1851

Narcotics—narcotics sanatorium for minors—opened—July 1, 1952

Nautical School—nautical municipal school—opened—Jan. 11, 1875

Naval Officer—black nurse in the Navy Reserve Nurse Corps—sworn in—March 8, 1945

News Agency—financial news agency—established—J. J. Kiernan—1869

News Correspondent—Washington correspondent of importance—J. G. Bennett—New York *Enquirer*—Jan. 2, 1828

Newsboy—Barney Flaherty—New York *Sun*—Sept. 4, 1833

Newspaper—black newspaper—*Freedom's Journal*—published—March 16, 1827

Newspaper—composograph photograph in a newspaper—Nov. 25, 1925

Newspaper—editorial award of a Pulitzer Prize in journalism and letters—New York *Tribune*—June 4, 1917

Newspaper—French daily newspaper (successful)—*Courrier des États Unis*—published—June 10, 1851

Newspaper—German daily newspaper—*New Yorker Staats-Zeitung*—published—Jan. 26, 1850

Newspaper—Greek newspaper—*Atlantis*—lished—March 3, 1894

Newspaper—Hebrew newspaper—publish 1871

Newspaper—Hungarian daily newspa *Amerikai Magyar Népszava*—published—18, 1904

Newspaper—illustrated daily newspaper— *Graphic*—published—March 4, 1873

Newspaper—illustrated tabloid—*Illust. Daily News*—published—June 26, 1919

Newspaper—Italian newspaper—*Il Prog. Italo-Americano*—published—Sept. 1880

Newspaper—jointly published newspape sued—September 1923

Newspaper—large-type weekly—*New Times Large Type Weekly*—published—N 6, 1967

Newspaper—line drawing of a current subj New York *Sun*—Jan. 15, 1840

Newspaper—newspaper color-page—*Recor* April 2, 1893

Newspaper—newspaper colored supplem *World*—published—Nov. 19, 1893

Newspaper—newspaper page set by linoty *Daily Tribune*—July 3, 1886

Newspaper—newspaper plant to install elec ty—New York *Times*—current turned on, 4, 1882

Newspaper—newspaper rotogravure sectic published—*Times*—March 29, 1914

Newspaper—newspaper Sunday comic sect published—*World*—1893

Newspaper—newspaper 12-page advertising plement—New York *Times*—Dec. 7, 1913

Newspaper—newspaper with a full page of v cut engravings—*Weekly Herald*—June 28,

Newspaper—newspaper with an illustrated or-page—*World*—May 21, 1893

Newspaper—penny daily newspaper—suc ful—*Sun*—Sept. 3, 1833

Newspaper—political newspaper—*Gazette* United States—published—April 11, 1789

Newspaper—Pulitzer Prize award to a news —New York *Times*—presented at Colu University—June 5, 1918

Newspaper—Spanish newspaper—*El Redac* published—July 1, 1827

Newspaper—transoceanic newspaper— *Mail*—Jan. 5, 1944

Newspaper—Ukrainian daily newspaper ranian *Daily News*—published—Jan. 31,

Newspaper—Yiddish daily newspaper— dishes-Tageblatt—published—1885

Newspaper Index—newspaper index separ published—1866

Newspaper Premium—newspaper premiu offered—New York *Recorder*—March 25,

Newspaper Reporter—newspaper reporter ceive a Pulitzer Prize for reporting—H Swope—announced at Columbia Univers June 4, 1917

Newspaper Syndicate—newspaper syndica supply articles—S. S. McClure—Nov. 8, 1

NEW YORK—New York City—*Continued*

Periodical—Jewish weekly (German-American)—*Israels Herold*—Isidor Busch, editor—published—March 30–June 15, 1849

Periodical—Jewish weekly published in English—*The Asmonean*—Oct. 26, 1849

Periodical—magazine containing a fashion plate—*The Port Folio*—June 1809

Periodical—magazine to contain a phonograph record—*Pageant*—Nov. 1955

Periodical—mechanics' magazine—*American Mechanics' Magazine*—published—Feb. 5, 1825 –Feb. 11, 1826

Periodical—photoengraved magazine—*Literary Digest*—published—Oct. 18, 1919

Periodical—sectarian magazine printed in rotogravure—*Catholic Missions*—published—Oct. 1, 1934

Periodical—Spanish magazine published by students—*El Estudiante Comercial*—published—1917

Periodical Index—W. F. Poole—published—1848

Permalloy—developed—G. W. Elmen—June 7, 1913

Petroleum Jelly—manufactured—1870

Pharmacopoeia—pharmacopoeia prepared by a hospital staff—published—1816

Philatelic Auction—philatelic auction—May 28, 1870

Philatelic Magazine—philatelic magazine (club organ)—*American Journal of Philately*—J. W. Scott, editor—published—March 1, 1868

Philatelic Society—philatelic society—New York Philatelic Society—organized—March 21, 1867 —constitution adopted—Jan. 19, 1868

Philological Society—national philological society—American Philological Association—organized—Nov. 13, 1868

Phonograph Trade Magazine—*The Phonogram*—published—Jan. 1891

Photoelectric Cell—photoelectric cell—publicly demonstrated—Oct. 21, 1925

Photograph—celestial photograph—of the moon —Dec. 18, 1839

Photograph—color transparency (35 mm) magnified 516 times—taken by Ernest Haas—exhibited—Feb. 22–March 28, 1977

Photograph—news photographs of distinction—Mathew B. Brady—studio opened—1844

Photograph—photograph of a President (in office) —J. K. Polk—Feb. 14, 1849

Photograph—photograph taken in the United States—Aug. 19, 1839

Photographic Patent—photographic patent—A. S. Wolcott—May 8, 1840

Photographic Studio—commercial photography studio—A. S. Wolcott and John Johnson—opened March 4, 1840

Photography—camera multiple flashbulb device —Flashcubes—introduced July 8, 1965

Photography—film developing machine-automatic—patented—A. M. Josepho—Ja 1928

Photography Book—photography book—*Th tory and Practice of the Art of Photograp.* H. H. Snelling—published—1849

Photography Magazine—photography zine—*Daguerreian Journal*—published– 1, 1850

Physician—doctors' strike against long w hours in hospitals—March 17, 1975

Physician—ophthalmologist of note—E Delafield—1864

Physics—national physics association—*f* can Physical Society—formed—May 20,

Physiology Society—physiology society (na organization)—American Physiological S —organized—Dec. 30, 1887

Pin—safety pin—patented—Walter Hunt– 10, 1849

Pituitary Hormone—polypeptide hormone thesized—1953

Play (drama)—aquatic play—*The Pirate's* —July 4, 1840

Play (drama)—benefit performance—Jan. 7

Play (drama)—burlesque show—of importa *The Black Crook*—Sept. 12, 1866

Play (drama)—drama to win a Pulitzer F opened—Dec. 25, 1917

Play (drama)—full-length play by a blac formed in New York City—*Appearances*-land Anderson—Oct. 13, 1925

Play (drama)—Hebrew professional acting —performed—Aug. 12, 1882

Play (drama)—musical comedy by a bla black talent—*A Trip to Coontown*, by Bo and Billy Johnson—produced April 4, 18

Play (drama)—musical (full-length), writte duced, directed, and performed as a Broa production—Bob Cole—*A Trip to Coont* opened April 4, 1898

Play (drama)—musical play to win a P Prize—*Of Thee I Sing*—opened—Dec. 26

Play (drama)—musical to run for more thar performances—*Fiddler on the Roof*—o Sept. 22, 1964

Play (drama)—musical with an American and an original score—*Evangeline, the B Acadia*—opened at Niblo's Theatre—Ju 1874

Play (drama)—native American play succes acted on a regular stage—*The Contrast*–16, 1787

Play (drama)—play acted by professional ers—*The Recruiting Officer*—Dec. 6, 173

Play (drama)—play performed 1,000 times *Gladiator*—opened—Sept. 26, 1831

Play (drama)—play written by a black wor reach Broadway—*Raisin in the Sun*—ope Ethel Barrymore Theatre—March 11, 195

Play (drama)—printed American play *droboros*—printed—1714

Play (drama)—Shakespearean play—*King ard III*—March 5, 1750

NEW YORK—New York City—*Continued*

Prizefight—pugilist to win and lose a championship in the first round—Abraham ("Al") Singer—defeated Sammy Mandell, July 17—lost to Tony Canzoneri, Nov. 14, 1930

Prizefighter—world heavyweight champion to regain his crown—Floyd Patterson—June 20, 1960

Protestant Church—Reformed Dutch Church black pastor—J. J. Thomas

Protestant Episcopal Bishop—Protestant Episcopal bishop consecrated in the United States—T. J. Claggett—Sept. 17, 1792

Protestant Episcopal Bishop—Protestant Episcopal bishop (black)—S. D. Ferguson—consecrated—June 24, 1885

Pump—independent single direct-acting steam power pump—patented—H. R. Worthington—July 24, 1844

Puppet Show—Feb. 12, 1738

Quinine—quinine sulfate—manufactured—1823

Rabbi—woman rabbi—S. J. Priesand—appointed, Aug. 1, 1972

Radio Advertising—radio advertising contract for frequency modulation broadcasts—Dec. 9, 1940

Radio Broadcast—advertising or commercial radio broadcast—WEAF—Aug. 28, 1922

Radio Broadcast—chain broadcast—Polo Grounds—from Newark, N.J.—Oct. 7, 1922

Radio Broadcast—circus broadcast—April 10, 1924

Radio Broadcast—drama broadcast from a regular stage—WABC—Sept. 24, 1933

Radio Broadcast—football game (collegiate) coast-to-coast broadcast—Oct. 28, 1922

Radio Broadcast—foreign language course broadcast—WJZ—March 21, 1924

Radio Broadcast—network-sponsored broadcast—Feb. 12, 1924

Radio Broadcast—news program (daily)—Sept. 1, 1922

Radio Broadcast—political speech by a President on radio—Calvin Coolidge—Feb. 12, 1924

Radio Broadcast—prizefight broadcast from the ringside—Dec. 22, 1920

Radio Broadcast—radio broadcast sent from an airplane—J. A. Macready—Sheepshead Bay, N.Y.—Aug. 27, 1910

Radio Broadcast—radio broadcast (two-way) from an airplane—Aug. 14, 1924

Radio Broadcast—radio concert from an airplane—April 14, 1922

Radio Broadcast—radio program simultaneously transmitted—over AM and FM stations and telecast—March 20, 1948

Radio Broadcast—recorded coast-to-coast broadcast—*Hindenburg* explosion—May 6, 1937

Radio Broadcast—ship-at-sea broadcast from an ocean liner—*Europa*—March 25, 1930

Radio Broadcast—simultaneous broadcast on all 3 major networks—American National Red Cross relief fund benefit—Feb. 11, 1937

Radio Broadcast—singer to broadcast—E. H. Farrar—Dec. 16, 1907

Radio Broadcast—transatlantic radio messa the regular westward service—Oct. 17, 1⁹

Radio Broadcast—zoo broadcast—C. W. L —April 21, 1930

Radio Church—established—Nov. 27, 1921

Radio Distress Signal—radio SOS from an A can ship—*Arapahoe*—Aug. 11, 1909

Radio Facsimile Transmission—check se radio across the Atlantic Ocean—against ers Trust Co.—April 20, 1926

Radio Facsimile Transmission—drawing se radio across the Atlantic—transmitted—N 1926

Radio Facsimile Transmission—motion p film transmitted by telephone wire—Chicago, Ill.—April 4, 1928

Radio Facsimile Transmission—photograph by radio across the Atlantic—July 6, 192⁴

Radio Facsimile Transmission—photograph by radio across the Atlantic as a public de stration—Nov. 30, 1924

Radio Facsimile Transmission—photograph by radio across the Atlantic inaugurating mercial service—April 30, 1926

Radio Facsimile Transmission—photograph by radio across the continent (commerc from San Francisco, Calif.—April 18, 192⁹

Radio Facsimile Transmission—radio facs long-distance transmission of a medical su —May 28, 1925

Radio Facsimile Transmission—transpacifi transcontinental facsimile transmission— 6, 1925

Radio Instruction—radio-advertising cou City College of New York—Sept. 28, 193⁶

Radio Instruction—radio college course— York University—Sept. 1939

Radio License—international broadcastin cense—Experimenter Publishing Compa Oct. 15, 1927

Radio Magazine—*Modern Electrics*—publis April 1908

Radio Microphone (carbon)—used—Lee De est—1907

Radio Paging Service—instituted—Oct. 15,

Radio Receiver—radio receiver advertised sale—Jan. 13, 1906

Radio Receiving Contest—radio receiving cc —B.G. Seutter, winner—Oct. 8, 1921

Radio Society—Wireless Association of Am —formed—Nov. 1908

Radio Station—all-news radio station—W first all-news broadcast, April 19, 1965

Radio Telephone—radio telephone ship-to- commercial service—Dec. 8, 1929

Radio Telephone—transcontinental radio phone demonstration—to Arlington, Va.— 29, 1915

Radio Telephone—two-way conversation tween a glider and the land—Aug. 12, 19

Radio Telephone—two-way radio convers between a submerged submarine and an vessel—Oct. 5, 1919

NEW YORK—New York City—*Continued*

Ship—federal steamer named for a woman—*Harriet Lane*—built—1857

Ship—gyro-stabilized vessel to cross the Atlantic Ocean—*Conte di Savoia*—arrived—Dec. 7, 1932

Ship—ironclad turreted vessel in the U.S. Navy—*Monitor*—launched—Jan. 30, 1862

Ship—liquid-bulk-chemical carrier—*Marine-Dow Chem*—first run, from Freeport, Tex.—arrived, April 13, 1954

Ship—packet line—Black Ball Line—to Liverpool—1816

Ship—racing shell—*The Harvard*—built—James Mackay—1857

Ship—radar installation aboard a commercial carrier—*African Star*—April 27, 1946

Ship—rotor ship—*Baden-Baden*—arrived—May 9, 1926

Ship—ship permitted to enter port without stopping for quarantine procedure—*Cameronia*—arrived—Feb. 1, 1937

Ship—ship to transport fresh orange juice in stainless steel tanks—*Tropicana*—arrived—Feb. 19, 1957

Ship—steam-propelled   frigate—*Demologos*—launched—Oct. 29, 1814

Ship—steamboat built in America to cross the Atlantic Ocean—*Savannah*—launched—Aug. 22, 1818

Ship—steamboat service (regular) across the Atlantic—arrived—April 23, 1838

Ship—steamboat to make an ocean voyage—to Philadelphia—June 10, 1809

Ship—steamboat to make regular trips—*Clermont*—trial trip—Aug. 7, 1807

Ship—steamship passenger line between United States ports and Europe to fly the American flag—sailed—June 1, 1847

Ship—steamship to cross the Atlantic Ocean in less than 5 days—*Rex*—arrived at entrance to harbor, Aug. 16, 1933

Ship—trading ship sent to China—*Empress of China*—left—Feb. 22, 1784

Ship—tugboat (steam)—*Rufus King*—built—1825

Ship—warship propelled by electricity—*New Mexico*—launched—April 23, 1917

Ship—warship to circumnavigate the globe—*Vincennes*—left—Aug. 31, 1826

Ship—yacht to circumnavigate the world—*North Star*—first voyage—left, May 21—returned Sept. 23, 1853

Shipping—coastal shipping service—established—T. L. Servoss—to New Orleans—1831

Shoe Pegging Machine—operated—C. D. Bigelow—1852

Shoot-the-Chutes—built—Paul Boyton—1894

Single Tax—single tax national conference—assembled—Sept. 1, 1890

Skee Ball Alley—built—1914

Skywriting—skywriting—Nov. 28, 1922

Skywriting—skywriting at night—Sept. 18, 1937

Sleeping Car—transcontinental through Pu sleeping car service—to Los Angeles, C March 30, 1946

Snow-melting   Apparatus—snow-melting paratus—patented—N. H. Borgfeldt—A 1869

Snow-melting   Apparatus—snow-melting paratus (practical) with pipe imbedded sidewalk—tested—Dec. 8, 1946

Soap—soap in liquid form—patented—W Sheppard—Aug. 22, 1865

Soap Manufacturer—to render fats in his p William Colgate—1806

Soccer—soccer game in which 12 points scored by 1 player—Giorgio Chinaglia mos vs. Toros—Yankee Stadium—Aug. 1C

Social Register—*Society List and Club Re* —published—1886

Social Science Society (national)—America cial Science Association—founded—186!

Soda Water Machine Manufacturer—John thews—1834

Soup Company—Franco-American Food Co ganized—Nov. 1886

Sports—amateur athletic competition (inte —Sept. 27, 1879

Sports—amateur indoor athletic games—N 1868

Sports—amateur outdoor athletic games— 21, 1871

Sports—athletic club—New York Athletic C organized—Sept. 8, 1868

Sports—cross-country   championships—N 1883

Sports—sports trainer (professional)—Bo gers—May 1, 1883

Sports Book—of importance—*The Sports Companion*—published—1783

Spy—peacetime death sentence for espion Julius Rosenberg and Ethel Rosenberg— verdict, March 29—sentence imposed, A 1951

Squash Club—squash tennis organizatior tional)—formed—March 20, 1911

Squash Tournament—April 8–10, 1911

Stagecoach Intercity Service—to Philadel Nov. 9, 1756

State Department (U.S.)—State Department —established—July 27, 1789

State Department (U.S.)—State Department Secretary—Thomas Jefferson—March 22

Steam Distribution Plant—formed—July 26

Steam Engine—steam engine—imported—S 1753

Steeplechase—Jerome Park—Oct. 26, 1869

Stenotype—patented—J. C. Zachos—Apr 1876

Stereotype—automatic plate-casting and ing machine for stereotype printing—inv —H. A. W. Wood—1900

Stereotype—curved stereotype plate— Charles Craske—1854

Stereotype—stereotypers—successful—D. Bruce—1813

NEW YORK—New York City—*Continued*

Television—television news commentator who was black—M. R. Goode—assigned—Aug. 29, 1962

Television—**Mobile Unit**—mobile television unit —delivered—Dec. 12, 1937

Television—**Mobile Unit**—mobile television units (color)—WNBT—Jan. 1, 1954

Television—**Telecast**—Academy of Motion Picture Arts and Sciences annual awards telecast —March 19, 1953

Television—**Telecast**—art auction televised on a coast-to-coast circuit—April 27, 1960

Television—**Telecast**—audience participation telecast—Aug. 7, 1941

Television—**Telecast**—baseball game (collegiate) telecast—May 17, 1939

Television—**Telecast**—baseball games (major-league) televised—Aug. 26, 1939

Television—**Telecast**—baseball games televised in color—Aug. 11, 1951

Television—**Telecast**—baseball World Series game televised—Sept. 30, 1947

Television—**Telecast**—baseball World Series game televised in color—Sept. 28, 1955

Television—**Telecast**—basketball game to be televised—Feb. 28, 1940

Television—**Telecast**—beauty contest telecast— June 22, 1939

Television—**Telecast**—bicycle race telecast— May 20, 1939

Television—**Telecast**—book review to be televised—May 3, 1938

Television—**Telecast**—Catholic mass (midnight) to be televised—Dec. 24, 1948

Television—**Telecast**—church service telecast— Grace Episcopal church—Dec. 24, 1946

Television—**Telecast**—church service televised in sign language—Dec. 5, 1948

Television—**Telecast**—circus telecast—April 25, 1940

Television—**Telecast**—color and black-and-white telecast to be sponsored—Dec. 24, 1953

Television—**Telecast**—color coast-to-coast live telecast—to Burbank, Calif.—Nov. 3, 1953

Television—**Telecast**—color commercial televised on a local show—commissioned—March 9, 1954

Television—**Telecast**—color program (commercial)—June 25, 1951

Television—**Telecast**—color program on coast-to-coast network commercial—WNBT-TV—Nov. 22, 1953

Television—**Telecast**—color television demonstration of high-definition electronically scanned images—Sept. 3, 1940

Television—**Telecast**—color television demonstration (public)—June 27, 1929

Television—**Telecast**—commercial program telecast—"Geographically Speaking"—Oct. 27, 1946

Television—**Telecast**—current Broadway play to be telecast with its original cast—*When We Are Married*—March 3, 1940

Television—**Telecast**—demonstration of a cast before a large audience—L. S. O'Roa May 23, 1927

Television—**Telecast**—demonstration of reception of television—Aug. 20, 1930

Television—**Telecast**—fashion show tele May 17, 1939

Television—**Telecast**—football game (colle to be telecast—Sept. 30, 1939

Television—**Telecast**—football game (profe al) to be televised—Oct. 22, 1939

Television—**Telecast**—high-definition tele June 29, 1936

Television—**Telecast**—hockey game to be vised—Feb. 25, 1940

Television—**Telecast**—horse-race telecast s on a large screen in a theater—Dwyer Sta Rialto Theatre—June 21, 1941

Television—**Telecast**—husband and wi broadcast a religious program—Dr. and M V. Peale—Oct. 1, 1952

Television—**Telecast**—Jewish temple se (complete) to be televised—Nov. 4, 1951

Television—**Telecast**—king and queen to be vised—June 10, 1939

Television—**Telecast**—laser-light-beam pro telecast on a network—*I've Got a Secret*— 14, 1963

Television—**Telecast**—medical symposium vised coast-to-coast on a closed circuit— 23, 1954

Television—**Telecast**—missing persons te —Oct. 3, 1943

Television—**Telecast**—motion picture pre festivities to be televised—Dec. 19, 1939

Television—**Telecast**—motion picture pre performance to be televised—April 10, 1

Television—**Telecast**—motion picture pre performance to be televised (feature-leng eign film)—Jan. 1, 1948

Television—**Telecast**—motion picture pre performance to be televised (major film)— 6, 1955

Television—**Telecast**—motion picture trail be televised—Sept. 20, 1946

Television—**Telecast**—musical comedy length) written especially for television— 28, 1944

Television—**Telecast**—musical comedy te (one-hour)—July 25, 1939

Television—**Telecast**—newsreel telecast sented daily—Feb. 16, 1948

Television—**Telecast**—opera (complete) televised from the Metropolitan Opera Ho Nov. 29, 1948

Television—**Telecast**—opera (major) televi color—*Carmen*—Oct. 31, 1953

Television—**Telecast**—opera telecast—Mar 1940

Television—**Telecast**—opera written for sion—*Amahl and the Night Visitors*—De 1951

NEW YORK—New York City—*Continued*

Tennis Player—black tennis player to participate in a U.S. indoor Lawn Tennis Association championship tournament—Reginald Weir—March 11, 1948

Tennis Society—tennis society (national)—United States Lawn Tennis Association—formed—May 21, 1881

Terramycin—announced—Jan. 27, 1950

Theater—newsreel theater—Nov. 2, 1929

Theater—panorama show—1790

Theater—television theater demonstration of a sports event on a full-size screen—April 14, 1948

Theater—theater built and named for a living actress—Ethel Barrymore Theatre—opened Dec. 20, 1928

Theater—theater lighted by gas—Chatham Garden—May 8, 1825

Theater—theater to employ women ushers—Third Avenue Theatre—Aug. 30, 1884

Theater History—of importance—published—William Dunlap—*History of the American Theatre*—1832

Theatrical Advance Publicity Man—Robert Upton—1750

Theatrical School—devoted exclusively to training for the professional stage—founded—Oct. 1, 1884

Theological School—Presbyterian theological seminary woman graduate—E. G. Briggs—Union Theological Seminary—March 17, 1897

Theological School—theological school—founded—1784

Theosophical Society—American Theosophical Society—founded—Nov. 17, 1875

Ticker Tape—ticker-tape shower—Theodore Roosevelt—June 18, 1910

Ticket Agency—theater-ticket agency office—advertised—Sept. 9, 1866

Ticket Speculators—operated—Sept. 1850

Tightrope—woman tightrope performer—performance—June 1, 1819

Tightrope Walker—tightrope walker to span 2 skyscrapers—Philippe Petit—Aug. 7, 1974

Tinware Manufacturers—successful tinware manufacturers—factory opened—Woodhaven—1860

Tour of the World—passenger to fly around the world on commercial airlines in less than 100 hours—H. C. Boren—landed—June 25, 1953

Tour of the World—tour of the world made by a woman traveling alone—Nelly Bly—left—Nov. 14, 1889

Toyery—opened—Sept. 24, 1932

Track Meet—transcontinental race—concluded, May 26, 1928

Tract Society—tract society (national)—American Tract Society—organized—May 11, 1825

Trademark (U.S.)—registered—Oct. 25, 1870

Traffic Regulation—one-way traffic regulation—Dec. 17, 1791

Traffic Regulation—traffic law—enacted—J 27, 1652

Traffic Regulation Pamphlet—printed traffic re lations—issued—Oct. 30, 1903

Traitor to the American Cause—William Dem —Nov. 2, 1776

Trapshooting—trapshooting intercollegiate a ciation—formed—March 25, 1898

Trapshooting Tournament—trapshoot (Gr American) with clay targets—June 12, 1900

Trapshooting Tournament—trapshoot (Gr American) with live birds—March 1893

Travelers Aid Society—Travelers Aid Soc (national)—founded—1904

Treadmill—used—New York City Prison—S 7, 1822

Treason—American colonist hanged for trea —Jacob Leisler—May 16, 1691

Trust—manufacturers' price regulation ag ment—coopers—Dec. 17, 1679

Tuberculosis Circular—issued—July 1889

Tuberculosis Laboratory—tuberculosis diagr tic community laboratory—authorized—I 13, 1893

Tunnel—triple-tube underwater roadway—I coln Tunnel to Weehawken, N.J.—opened N 25, 1957

Tunnel—tunnel under the Hudson River—ope officially—Feb. 25, 1908

Tunnel—twin-tube subaqueous vehicular tur —Holland Tunnel—opened—Nov. 13, 1927

Typesetting Machine—linotype machine u commercially—installed—July 1, 1886

Typesetting Machine—photographic type-c posing machine—book set by the Photon cess—*The Wonderful World of Insects*—19

Typesetting Machine—typesetting machin practical—patented—Timothy Alden—S 15, 1857

Typewriter—typewriter to produce a line of v ing visible as it was being typed—patente May 16, 1893

Typewriting School—opened—1878

Unitarian Church Convention (national)—ass bled—April 5, 1865

United Nations—veto by the United States in Security Council of the United Nations—Ma 17, 1970

Vacation Fund—established—1847

Vaccine—poliomyelitis vaccine—produce Feb. 1933

Vaccine—tuberculosis vaccine—effective— veloped—1928

Valentine—valentines commercially produce R. H. Elton—1834

Vending Machine—vending machine to dispe live flowers—installed at Grand Central Ter nal—Oct. 20, 1961

Veterinary Hospital—veterinary hospital ope —C. C. Grice—1830

Veterinary School—veterinary college of imp tance—incorporated—April 6, 1857

Vice Presidential Candidate—black vice pr dential candidate—nominated—May 10, 18

Newburgh

Newport

Newton Creek

Niagara County

Niagara Falls

NEW YORK—Niagara Falls—Continued

Photograph—photograph to gain world fame—taken—July 1845

Shovel—two-handed shovel—used—May 16, 1940

Visiting Celebrities—King and Queen of Great Britain—arrived—June 7, 1939

Nieuw Amsterdam

See New York City

North Elba

Bobsled Run—of international specifications—opened—Dec. 25, 1930

North Tarrytown

Vice President (U.S.)—Vice President cremated—N. A. Rockefeller—ashes buried on estate—Jan. 29, 1979

Oceanside

Boy Scouts of America—boy scout to become an eagle scout—A. R. Eldred—Aug. 21, 1912

Cantor—Jewish woman cantor—Betty Robbins—first service—Sept. 15, 1955

Olean

Gas—natural gas for manufacturing—used—1870

Oneida Community

Traps—steel animal traps—commercially manufactured—Sewell Newhouse—1855

Oneida County

Animals—fur-bearing animals—raised commercially—1866

Ossining

Execution—execution (federal) for the killing of a Federal Bureau of Investigation agent—Gerhard Puff—Aug. 12, 1954

Execution—execution of a woman by electrocution—M. M. Place—March 20, 1899

Fingerprinting—state prison to take fingerprints—Sing Sing Prison—March 3, 1903

Spy—peacetime death sentence for espionage—Julius Rosenberg and Ethel Rosenberg—electrocuted, June 19, 1953

Treason—execution for treason in peacetime—June 19, 1953

Oswego

Normal School—normal school (state) at which students actually conducted classes—established—May 1, 1861

Ship—steamboat engine built in America for a screw-propelled vessel—Vandalia—ship enrolled—April 14, 1842

Oyster Bay

Cable—cable across the Pacific Ocean betw Honolulu, Midway, Guam, and Manila—offi message sent—July 4, 1903

Pearl River

Aureomycin—aureomycin chlorotetracyclin released—1948

Catgut—catgut substitute for medical use—I on—produced in April 1966

Peekskill

Automobile Hill Climbing Contest—Sept. 9, 1

First Aid Instruction—given—1885

Pelham Manor

Glass—stained figure glass—manufactured—1

Plattsburg

College—college principally for war veterar opened—Sept. 16, 1946

Physiologist—of note—William Beaumont—port published—1833

Poplar Ridge

Plow—plow with interchangeable parts—pat ed—J. J. Wood—Sept. 1, 1819

Port Chester

Bread—frozen bread—marketed—Nov. 3, 19

Port Washington

Airmail Service—airmail transatlantic servi inaugurated—left, May 20, 1939

Aviation—Flights (transatlantic)—Atlantic Oc scheduled air service—left—May 20, 1939

Aviation—Flights (transatlantic)—transatla regular commercial airplane service—le June 28, 1939

Aviation—Passenger—woman to fly enti around the world by commercial heavier-tl air plane—last lap—June 17, 1939

Glider—seaplane glider—flight—March 15, 1

Railroad—railroad train operated exclusively women—to Pennsylvania station, New Y City—in service, June 6, 1979

Poughkeepsie

Ice Yacht—built—Oliver Booth—1790

Ice Yacht Club—organized—1861

Insurance—group insurance policy for col students—Feb. 1, 1936

Philological Society—national philological s ety—American Philological Association— vention—July 27, 1869

Pin—machine "for sticking pins into paper"—ented—Samuel Slocum—Sept. 30, 1841

Pin—pins manufactured with a solid head—S uel Slocum—1838

road Car—rail detector car—demonstrated—
pt. 13, 1928
er Purification—water purification by filtra-
on—1870

Queens

See under New York City

Riverdale

See under New York City

Rochester

cultural Journal—agricultural journal written
rectly from practical experience—*Genesee
rmer and Gardener's Journal*—first issue, Jan.
1831
mobile Patent—G. B. Selden—May 8, 1879
ness—installment finance company—meet-
—April 7, 1904
ness School—business school—opened—
42
era—filmpack camera—introduced 1903
era—roll-film camera—announced—George
stman—June 1888
olic Priest—deacon (married) ordained—M.
Cole—June 1, 1969
k Photographing Device—patented—Feb. 25,
30
k Protectors—manufactured—1870
munion Cup—individual communion cups—
roduced—May 1894
robasograph—invented—R. P. Schwartz
33
Show—(of milch goats)—Sept. 15–27, 1913
—time lock—manufactured—Sargent &
eenleaf—1874
Station (municipal)—established—1897
c—community chorus—established—1912
spaper—newspaper association—conven-
n—Feb. 16, 1887
ograph—infrared photograph—taken—Oct.
1931
ograph—photograph from an airplane at
ht—taken—Nov. 20, 1925
ographic Film—motion picture film (commer-
l)—manufactured—March 26, 1885
ographic Film—transparent paper-strip
otographic film—patented—George Eastman
Oct. 14, 1884
ostat—photographic copying machine—com-
rcially manufactured—1910
l Service—mail chute—patented—J. G. Cut-
—Sept. 11, 1883
dential Candidate—black presidential candi-
te nominated—Frederick Douglass—June 23,
38
oad Car—glass-lined tank car—built—1910
l-Democratic Party of America—convention
an. 27, 1900
tcar—transfers (printed)—used—Oct. 31,
2
erance Society—women's temperance soci-
(state)—founded—April 20, 1852

Time Recorder—card time recorder—patented—
D. M. Cooper—Oct. 30, 1894
Vending Machine—vending machine—automati-
cally operated—produced—1897
X Ray—X-ray photograph of the entire body
taken in a one-second exposure—A. W. Fuchs
—July 1, 1934
X Ray—X-ray photograph showing the complete
arterial circulation—completed—July 16, 1936

Rome

Cheese Factory—cheese factory of consequence
—established—1851

Roosevelt Field

See under Garden City

Rye

Golf Champion—family to win more than one national championship in 1 year—Edith Cummings—Oct. 6, 1923 (National Women's
Amateur championship)
Railroad Car—remote-control railroad passenger
car—to and from New Rochelle, N.Y.—Dec. 1,
1955
Television—Telecast—tennis tournament to be
televised—Aug. 9, 1939

Sackets Harbor

Chloroform—distilled—Samuel Guthrie—1831
Glucose—from potato starch—refined—Samuel
Guthrie—1831

St. Regis

War (1812)—prisoners in the War of 1812—captured—Oct. 22–23, 1812

Saranac Lake

Hospital—tuberculosis sanatorium (modern)—
opened—Feb. 1, 1885
Tuberculosis Laboratory—tuberculosis research
laboratory—established—1894

Saratoga Springs

Bankers' Association—national bankers' associa-
tion—convention—July 20, 1875
Economics Association—American Economic As-
sociation—founded—Sept. 9, 1885
Historical Society—historical society (general)—
American Historical Association—founded—
Sept. 10, 1884
Intercollegiate Athletic Association—organized—
June 1876
Lawyers' Association—lawyers' association (na-
tional)—American Bar Association—organized
—Aug. 21, 1878
Temperance Society—temperance society (union)
—Union Temperate Society—organized—April
13, 1808
Time, Standard—standard time—suggested—C.
F. Dowd—1870

NEW YORK—Saratoga Springs—*Continued*

Track Meet—track meet (intercollegiate)—July 20-21, 1876

Schenectady

Air Brake—patented—George Westinghouse, Jr. —April 13, 1869

Airmail Service—jet-propelled airplane to transport mail—June 22, 1946

Automaton—automaton to operate by long-distance control—announced—May 23, 1956

Automobile—automobile (new-type gasoline-electric combination)—delivered—Aug. 30, 1929

Automobile License Plates—plastic license plate tabs—manufactured—1942

Bridge—wrought-iron lattice girder railroad bridge—1859

Diamond—pilot plant for the actual production of artificial diamonds—production announced—Feb. 15, 1955

Diathermy Machine—practical—manufactured—Dec. 1928

Electric Lighting—sodium vapor lamps—installed —June 13, 1933

Electric Power Plant—mobile electric power plant —delivered—Jan. 10, 1944

Fraternity (Greek-letter)—social fraternity—Kappa Alpha—established—Nov. 26, 1825

Fraternity Catalog—published—1830

Golf Clubs (or golf sticks)—steel shaft for a golf club—patented—A. F. Knight—Nov. 22, 1910

High Jumping Standards—using electric eye detectors—used—May 31, 1941

Industrial Research Laboratory—opened—Sept. 1900

Light Beam Communication—from a dirigible—May 19, 1932

Locomotive—duplex compound locomotive (Mallet)—built—1904

Locomotive—rack-rail diesel-electric locomotive —built—1939

Locomotive Headlight—talking headlight—installed—Nov. 6, 1934

Microscope—microscope for examining structure of materials—installed—Sept. 1951

Photograph—photograph of a beam of 1-billion-volt X rays—made—Oct. 1946

Photography—photographic flashlight bulbs—manufactured—1930

Radio Broadcast—dinner broadcast around the world—April 20, 1927

Radio Broadcast—drama (full-length melodrama) broadcast—Aug. 3, 1922

Radio Broadcast—radio broadcast heard in both the Arctic and the Antarctic regions—Sept. 23, 1934

Radio Broadcast—around-the-world broadcast W2XAD—June 30, 1930

Radio Station—college radio station—WRUC—Union College—began operation, Oct. 14—weekly program series began, Oct. 15, 1920

Radio Station—radio station operating a 50-k watt transmitter—2XAG—in operation—29, 1925

Radio Station—radio station operating a 100-k watt transmitter—2XAG—Aug. 4, 1927

Radio Telephone—radio telephone concert tr continental—to Oakland, Calif—March 25, 1

Radio Telephone—two-way radio conversa between a brakeman in a caboose of a mo freight train and an engineer in the cab locomotive—demonstrated—June 15, 1927

Radio Tube—radio tube—of metal—annou —April 1, 1935

Ship—radar installation aboard a comme carrier—General Electric Co.—April 27, 19

Stroboradiograph—announced—Aug. 14, 195

Synchrotron—synchrotron—constructed by F Pollock and W. F. Westendorf—at Gen Electric Research Laboratory

Television—Telecast—motion picture prem performance to be televised—April 10, 194

Television—Telecast—opera (complete) to televised—presented—Dec. 23, 1943

Television—Telecast—play to be televised—*Queen's Messenger*—Sept. 11, 1928

Television—Telecast—presidential nomina notification ceremony to be televised—Aug 1928

Television—Telecast—programs regularly vised—WGY—May 11, 1928

Television—Telecast—speaker to address organization by television—April 1, 1930

Television—Telecast—telecast produced for city gathering—Dec. 8, 1939

Television—Telecast—telecast (transatla transmitted regularly—E. F. W. Alexande —Feb. 6, 10, and 13, 1931

Television—Telecast—television network onstration (long-distance)—Feb. 1, 1940

Theater—television theater demonstration—22, 1930

Theatrical School—theatrical school spons by an institution of higher learning—cours July 2, 1935

Tungsten—ductile tungsten—produced—W Coolidge—1908

Seneca Falls

Bloomers—introduced—July 19, 1848

Woman Suffrage—convention of women adv ing woman suffrage—July 19-20, 1848

Sheepshead Bay

See under New York City

Sloatsburg

Cotton Twine Factory—Jacob Sloat—1839

South Butler

Woman—woman ordained a minister—A Blackwell—Sept. 15, 1853

NEW YORK—*Continued*

Watertown

Breakfast Food—shredded wheat biscuits—patented—Aug. 1, 1893

Watervliet

Conscientious Objectors—settled—1776
Shaker Society—Shaker "Family"—formed—1776

West Milton

Electric Power—electric power generated from atomic energy to be sold commercially—July 18, 1955
Television—**Telecast**—commercial filmed by a camera operated by atomically generated electricity—televised—July 24, 1955

West Point

Army School—army school—Military Academy of the United States—established—March 16, 1802
Army School—army school graduate (black)—H. O. Flipper—June 1877
Army School—army school graduate (Jewish)—S. M. Levy—Oct. 11, 1802
Army School—army school graduates—Oct. 11, 1802
Army School—army school graduates (Chinese)—Ying Shing Wen and Ting Chia Chen—were graduated June 11, 1909
Army School—instructor nongraduate—C. H. Hodges—assumed post Dec. 14, 1920
Army School—instructor (woman)—E. M. Lewis—began service Feb. 1, 1968
Army School—Jewish woman graduate of the U.S. Military Academy—Donna Maller—commissioned—June 4, 1980
Army School—woman cadet to receive a commission—Ms. Hollen—May 28, 1980
Army School—women cadets of the U.S. Military Academy—enrolled July 7, 1976
Blockade—across Hudson River—April 30, 1778
Football Game—Army-Navy football game—Nov. 29, 1890
President (U.S.)—President telecast in color—D. D. Eisenhower—June 6, 1955
Television—**Telecast**—President to appear on television in color—D. D. Eisenhower—June 7, 1955

Westbury

Golf Tournament—women's tournament golf championship—Nov. 1895
Totalisator—fully electronic, transistorized, data processing totalisator—in use—Roosevelt Raceway—May 15, 1965

White Plains

Coffee—freeze-dried coffee—marketed by Ge al Foods—1964

Whitestone

See under New York City

Woodhaven

See under New York City

Yonkers

Carpet Loom—carpet power loom to weave minster carpets—invented—Halcyon Ski —1876
Golf Match—mixed foursome—St. Andrews Club—March 30, 1889
Golf Tournament—amateur golf tournar (unofficial)—Oct. 13, 1894
Hat Blocking and Shaping Machine—patent April 3, 1866
Horse—trotter triple-crown winner—Scott —(Yonkers Futurity) Sept. 1, 1955
Horse Race—harness race driver to win the bletonian four times—B. F. White—Aug 1943
Plastic—thermosetting artificial plastic—de oped—L. H. Baekeland—1906
Race Track—harness track to handle more $3 million in bets in 1 night—Yonkers Race —topped that figure Nov. 30, 1962
Race Track—harness track to handle more $300 million in bets in 1 year—Yonkers R way—topped that figure Dec. 8, 1969

NORTH CAROLINA

Civil Government in America—Watauga (monwealth—May 1772
Impeachment—impeachment and removal office of a state governor—W. W. Hold March 22, 1871
Nurse—nurses' registration law (state)—Mar 1903
President (U.S.)—President born posthumou Andrew Jackson—March 15, 1767
State—state denied admission into the Uni Franklin (seceded from North Carolir formed, Aug. 23, 1784

Asheville

Forest Management—professional scale—18
Hospital—tuberculosis sanatorium (priva opened—1875

Biltmore

Forestry School—forestry school dealing e sively with problems of forestry—Biltmore est School—opened—Sept. 1, 1898

NORTH CAROLINA—Raleigh—*Continued*

Blind—school for blind blacks—opened—Jan. 4, 1869
Building—building with its roof supported by cables—J. S. Dorton Arena—completed and dedicated 1953
Deaf—Students' Magazine—magazine for deaf students—*Deaf Mute Casket*—published—1851
Medical Clinic—contraceptive clinic (state)—opened—March 15, 1937
Nuclear Engineering College Course—students enrolled—June 12, 1950

Roanoke Island

Births—child born of English parents in America—Virginia Dare—Aug. 18, 1587

Salem

Cottonseed Hulling Machine—patented—John Lineback—March 31, 1814

Spray

Acetylene—acetylene manufactured—T. L. Willson—May 4, 1892
Carbide Factory—established—1894

Statesville

Balloon—Flights—balloon flight powered by solar energy—Tracy Barnes—May 16, 1973

Washington

Town—town named for George Washington—1775

NORTH DAKOTA

Insurance—bonding law (state)—enacted—March 1, 1913
Insurance—fire and tornado insurance fund (state)—July 1, 1919
Insurance—hail insurance law (state)—enacted—March 18, 1911
Legislator (state)—woman speaker of a state house of representatives—Jan. 3, 1933
State—states admitted to the Union simultaneously—North and South Dakota—Nov. 3, 1889

Bismarck

Bank—state bank wholly owned and operated—established June 26—opened July 28, 1919

Fort Yates

American Indians—American Indian superintendent of a Bureau of Indian Affairs agency—Shirly Plume—appointed Jan. 24, 1974

Jamestown

Television—Telecast—stratosphere telec Strato-Lab High III—Malcolm Ross and Lewis—landing, July 27, 1958

Portal

Visiting Celebrities—absolute monarch—Prajadhipok of Siam—arrived in United ! —April 19, 1931

NORTHWEST TERRITORY

Slavery—law (federal) prohibiting slavery territory of the United States—enacted Ju 1787

OHIO

Employment Service—state employment s —authorized—April 28, 1890
High School Legislation—authorizing classes—March 16, 1829
Judge—woman associate justice of a sta preme court—F. E. Allen—elected—De 1922
Labor Legislation—labor law regulating the ing hours of women—March 29, 1852
Land Grant—land subsidy for internal im ments—April 30, 1802
Legislator (state)—black legislator (state)— 1885
Representative (U.S.)—representative in elected President of the United States— Garfield—Nov. 4, 1880
Road—state highway metric-distance-m system—Interstate 71 between Cincinna Columbus—erection begun, Feb. 12, 1973
Senator (U.S.)—senator who was an astrona H. Glenn—elected—Nov. 5, 1974
Telephone—telephone company answering vice—March 1951
Territorial Expansion—acquisition of land l federal government—Northwest Territory tablished—July 13, 1787
War—battle fought by United States troop ter formation of Union—Oct. 19, 1790

Akron

Automobile Police Patrol Wagon—opera 1899
Automobile Tire—balloon tire production—duced—April 5, 1923
Automobile Tire—clincher tire—manufactu 1899
Automobile Tire—cord tire—manufactu 1910
Automobile Tire—nonskid tire—patented—14, 1914
Automobile Tire—synthetic-rubber tire—m ed—June 5, 1940
Automobile Tire—tubeless automobile tires nounced—May 11, 1947

on—Airship—airship of the U.S. Navy that
successful—May 30, 1917
on—Airship—airship to land on a roof—
: off—May 23, 1919
on—Airship—airship with an enclosed cab-
flight—June 3, 1925
on—Airship—dirigible for private commer-
operation—built 1930
on—License—glider   pilot's   license—
rded—Oct. 7, 1930
onveyor System—belt conveyor more than
miles long—manufactured
e Tire—bicycle tire (cord)—manufactured
F. Goodrich Co.—1892
ushing Machine—patented—Nov. 30, 1875
—synthetic rubber in asphaltic concrete
rfacing mixture—Sept. 7, 1948
r—rubber company west of the Allegheny
ntains—established—1870

Alliance

tball Team—basketball team (college)—
ed—1892
e—college summer school—Mount Union
ege—1870
e—college to grant women absolutely
l rights—Mount Union College—founded
ct. 20, 1846

Ashtabula

n Law—proportional representation elec-
—Nov. 2, 1915

Athens

e—university founded by a federal land
t—Ohio University—opened—June 1, 1808

Barberton

—"book matches"—made—1896

Bellefontaine

—concrete road—1892

Cadiz

coal pipeline unit (demonstration)—in op-
on—Nov. 1, 1951
commercial coal pipeline—in operation—
4, 1957

Canton

ll Club—football association (profession-
-formed—Sept. 17, 1920
ll Game—football game in which referees
e permitted to use television instant replays
iladelphia Eagles vs. Miami Dolphins—
29, 1978
f Fame—Hall of Fame (football)—building
cated, Sept. 7, 1963

Hall of Famer—athlete enshrined in 2 halls of
fame—Robert Hubbard—professional football
Hall Of Fame—April 4, 1963
President (U.S.)—President who had used a telephone for campaigning—William McKinley—
1896

Chillicothe

Animals—cattle importation of purebred shor-
thorns—1834
Animals—cattle (shorthorn) public auction sale—
Oct. 29, 1836
Book—book (of size) completed entirely by one
man—Dard Hunter—1923

Cincinnati

Ambulance—hospital ambulance service
Anarchist—Josiah   Warren—"time   store"—
opened—1827
Astronomy Magazine—*Sidereal Messenger*—
published—July 1846
Automobile—right-hand-drive automobile for the
delivery of mail—in service—Dec. 27, 1951
Baseball Game—baseball game at night by major-
league teams—played—May 24, 1935
Baseball Game—National League 20-inning baseball game—Cincinnati–Chicago—June 30, 1892
Baseball Player—baseball players to hit a home
run—R. C. Barnes and C. W. Jones—May 2, 1876
Baseball Player—major-league baseball player to
pitch two successive no-hit no-run games—first
game—June 11, 1938
Baseball Team—baseball team to hit 4 consecutive runs in 1 inning—Cincinnati Reds—June 8,
1961
Baseball Team—baseball team to receive a regular salary—1869
Battery—battery to convert radioactive energy
into electrical energy—announced—P. E. Ohmart—Dec. 31, 1951
Caterpillar Club—woman Caterpillar Club member—Irene McFarland—June 28, 1925
Continuation School—apprentice continuation
school—established—Aug. 30, 1909
Dental School—dental assistants' and nurses'
course—Oct. 3, 1910
Dentist—woman dentist to obtain a D.D.S. degree
—graduated—Feb. 21, 1866
Detergent—synthetic detergent—for home use—
marketed—Oct. 10, 1933
Dictionary—phonetic   dictionary—published—
1855
Fire Department—fire department to be paid a
salary—April 1, 1853
Fire Engine—fire engine that was practical—tested—Jan. 1, 1853
Forestry Book—*Elements of Forestry*, by F. B.
Hough—published—1882
Hospital—tuberculosis hospital (municipal) for
consumptive poor—opened—July 8, 1897
Jewish College—Jewish college to train men for
the rabbinate—Hebrew Union College—estab-
lished—Oct. 3, 1875

OHIO—Cincinnati—*Continued*

Liberal Republican Party—convention—May 1, 1872

Manufacturers' Association—national organization—formed—Jan. 22, 1895

Medical Instruction—ophthalmology professor—Elkanah Williams—1865

Motion Picture—peep show machine—patented—S. D. Goodale—Feb. 5, 1861

Music—saengerfest—1849

People's Party—organized—May 19, 1891

Political Convention—presidential convention (national) addressed by a woman—S. A. Spencer—June 15, 1876

Prizefight—prizefight of importance under the Marquis of Queensberry rules—Aug. 29, 1885

Rabbi—woman rabbi—S. J. Priesand—ordained, June 3, 1972

Radio License—radio license—G. H. Lewis—1911

Railroad—municipal railroad—service commenced—July 23, 1877

Railroad Car—chapel car—*Evangel*—dedicated—May 23, 1891

Shortening—shortening made by the hydrogenation process—Aug. 15, 1911

Soap—soap to float—manufactured—1878

Trapshooting—clay pigeon target—patented—George Ligowsky—Sept. 7, 1880

Union Labor Party—formed—Feb. 22, 1887—nominating convention—May 15–17, 1888

Union Reform Party—platform adopted—March 1, 1899

United Labor Party—organized—May 16, 1888

Voting Machine—presidential election in which votes were tallied electronically—Nov. 3, 1964

Woman—woman Presbyterian elder—permission granted—May 31, 1930

Yeast—compressed fresh yeast—introduced—Charles Fleischmann—1868

Yeast—yeast preparation patent—J. T. Alden—Nov. 3, 1863

Cleveland

Advertisement—automobile advertisement—Winton Motor Car Co.—July 30, 1898

Autogiro—autogiro to loop the loop publicly—Aug. 27, 1932

Automobile Mail Wagon—constructed—1899

Automobile Truck—automobile truck completely streamlined—Sept. 4, 1935

Aviation—air-rail passenger transcontinental service—June 14, 1929

Aviation—automatic pilot—tested—Oct. 8, 1929

Aviation—Airship—airship to land on a roof—Hotel Statler—May 23, 1919

Aviation—Flights—over-water flight—G. H. Curtiss—Aug. 31, 1910

Aviation—Passenger—dirigible passenger transfer to an airplane—August 29, 1929

Aviation—Races—airplane race (of importance) in which both men and women were contestants—from Los Angeles, Calif.—Aug. 30, 1931

Aviation—Races—women's cross-countr[y] derby—completed Aug. 26, 1929

Baseball Game—baseball game in which were two triple-steals—July 25, 1930

Baseball Game—triple play unassisted in a Series—Oct. 10, 1920

Baseball Game—triple play unassisted in a[n east]ern major-league game—Neal Ball—Ju[ly] 1909

Baseball Game—World Series grand slam [home] run (American League)—E. J. Smith—O[ct.] 1920

Baseball Player—baseball player (major l[eague] to make 9 hits in 1 game—J. H. Burnett—J[uly] 1932

Baseball Player—baseball player (major l[eague] to make 7 consecutive hits in 7 times at [bat in] the same game—C. D. Gutierrez—June 2[1]

Baseball Player—baseball player who w[as an] American Indian—J. M. Toy—Clevelan[d] (American Association)

Baseball Player—black baseball player t[o hit a] home run in a World Series—L. E. Dob[y—Oct.] 9, 1948

Community Trust—Cleveland Foundatio[n es]tablished—Jan. 2, 1914

Compotype—patented—Oct. 20, 1925

Court—conciliation tribunal for small claim[s es]tablished—March 15, 1913

Cripples—kindergarten for crippled chil[dren] opened—1900

Electric Lighting—electric arc lights—for [use in] streetlighting—April 29, 1879

Evangelical and Reformed Church—organ[ized] June 26, 1934

Fireworks Legislation—fireworks legi[slation] enacted by a large city—July 18, 1908

Football Game—professional football ga[me at]tended by 80,000 spectators—Baltimore[s] vs. Cleveland Browns—Dec. 29, 1968

Health Museum—Cleveland Health Mus[eum] opened—Nov. 12, 1940

Humane Society—humane association n[ational] organization—American Humane Asso[c.] —organized—Oct. 9, 1877

Ice Cream Cone—ice cream cone-rolling m[achine] —patented—C. R. Taylor—Jan. 29, 1924

Jews—Jewish Rabbinical Conference—O[rganized] 1855

Judge—woman judge to sentence a man to [death] —F. E. Allen—May 14, 1921

Mayor—black mayor of a major city—[C. B.] Stokes—elected Nov. 7—sworn in Nov. 1[3, 1967]

Multigraph—patented—H. C. Gammeter—[Nov.] 10, 1903

National Union for Social Justice—nation[al con]vention—Aug. 14, 1936

Newspaper—newspaper rotogravure s[ection] published—*Plain Dealer*—March 29, 191[4]

Ordnance—submachine gun—invented—[J. T.] Thompson—1915

Paint—paint prepared from standard form[ula—] 1880

OHIO—*Continued*

Kirtland

Mormon Temple—dedicated—March 27, 1836

Lima

Ordnance—tank with a turbine engine—XM-1 (Abrams tank)—rolled out—Feb. 28, 1980

Mansfield

Stove—electronic range for domestic use—manufactured—1955

Marblehead

Medal—lifesaving medal—awarded by Treasury Dept.—to L. M. Clemons—June 19, 1876

Marietta

Photograph—photograph of a lightning flash—W. C. Gurley—May 4, 1884

Marion

President (U.S.)—President and President's wife to die during the term for which he had been elected—Mrs. W. G. Harding died—Nov. 21, 1924

Milford

Police—woman chief of police—Dolly Spencer— 1914

Monroeville

Monument—monument to the memory of the soldiers and sailors of the Spanish-American War —unveiled—Sept. 29, 1904

Montpelier

Railroad Car—rail detector car in commercial service—Nov. 15, 1928

Mount Pleasant

Newspaper—abolition newspaper—*Philanthropist*—published—Aug. 29, 1817

Mount Vernon

Chewing Gum—chewing gum patent—W. F. Semple—Dec. 28, 1869

Nela Park

Electric Lighting—electric light bulb frosted on the inside—patented—Marvin Pipkin—Oct. 16, 1928

Newark

Glass Wool—patented—Oct. 11, 1938

North Bend

Railroad Train Robbery—railroad train r of a disabled train—May 5, 1865

Oberlin

Black—black woman college graduate— Stanton—Oberlin College—Dec. 8, 1850
College—coeducational college—opened 3, 1833
College Student—black woman college gr —L. A. Stanton—Oberlin College—Dec.
Temperance Society—Anti-Saloon Le founded—May 24, 1893

Oxford

Fraternity (Greek-letter)—fraternity west Alleghenies—founded—Aug. 8, 1839

Port Bucyrus

Aviation—Airport—airport manager (wo appointed—May 28, 1932

Ravenna

Jockey—jockey to win seven races in one Joseph Sylvester—Oct. 18, 1930

Riverside

See Cincinnati

Sandusky

Aviation—Flights—over-water flight—G. tiss—Aug. 31, 1910

Schoenbrunn

Protestant Church—west of Pennsylvania munion service—June 9, 1772
Schoolhouse—west of the Allegheny mo —completed—July 29, 1773

Solon

Skeet—national skeet tournament—Aug.

Springfield

Baby Show—Oct. 5, 1854
Bellows—invented—J. B. Morrison—p Dec. 23, 1834

Steubenville

Land Grant—district land office—opened 1800

Toledo

Aviation—propeller blade of hollow steel factured—June 1942

n—balloon to land on a building—A. R. benshoe—June 30, 1905

ill Player—black baseball player—M. F. ker—1884

r—bowler to make a perfect score of 300 in American Bowling Congress tournament— iam Knox—March 10, 1913

ig—all-glass windowless structure—com- d—Jan. 15, 1936

yment Service—state employment service fice opened—June 4, 1890

Blowing Machine—patented—M. J. Owens b. 26, 1895

Dress of spun glass—manufactured—1893 ack Labor Party—organized—Feb. 22,

an Church—American Lutheran Church— nized—Aug. 11, 1930

ry—cooperative—Sept. 15, 1930

praying Device—employed—1909

-automatic computing pendulum-type es—patented—Allen De Vilbiss—May 22,

schooner (five-masted)—*David Dows*— hed—April 21, 1881

ion Receiver—television receivers to ct large images—built—1955

ion Tube—rectangular television tube tical)—announced—July 10, 1949

Toronto

m—titanium mill—opened—Nov. 2, 1957

Van Wert

—county library—successfully conducted anized—1898

Wilmington

n—airplane human pickup—Sept. 5, 1943

Worthington

—papal seminary—Pontifical College hinum—established Sept. 1, 1888

Xenia

ce—cartridge-loading machinery—pat- —G. M. Peters—July 7, 1885

Yellow Springs

—college to grant women absolutely rights with men—nonsectarian—Antioch ge—opened—Oct. 5, 1853

—woman college professor—accorded privileges as men professors—appointed tioch College—Sept. 1852

Literary Society—college literary society ucational)—founded—1853

cs Course—didactics course in a college— ch College—1853

e Instruction—physiology and hygiene es—Antioch College—Oct. 5, 1853

Zanesville

Bridge—"Y" bridge—authorized—Jan. 21, 1812

Sawmill—sawmill engine—portable—construct- ed—1858

OKLAHOMA

Capital Punishment—lethal-drug executions au- thorized—May 10, 1977

Impregnation—legalization of artificial insemina- tion for humans—D. F. Bartlett—bill signed, May 18, 1967

Oil—oil and gas conservation legislation—enact- ed May 17, 1913

El Reno

American Indian Church—church organized by American Indians—incorporated—Oct. 10, 1918

Elk City

Hospital—community hospital—dedicated—Aug. 13, 1931

Norman

Criminal—woman on the "ten most wanted" list —Ruth Eisemann-Schier—arrested March 5, 1969

Oklahoma City

Esperanto Magazine—published—Oct. 1906

Mayor—woman mayor of a city of over 200,000 population—P. S. Latting—sworn in April 13, 1971

Medical Clinic—cancer clinic (traveling)—estab- lished—Feb. 14, 1946

Parking Meter—parking meter (automatic)—in- stalled—July 16, 1935

Presbyterian Church—moderator (black) of the United Presbyterian Church in the U.S.A.—E. G. Hawkins—assumed office, May 21, 1964

Turbine—gas turbine used by an electrical utility company—in service—July 29, 1949

Tahlequah

Freemasons—Masonic lodge organized in the In- dian Territory—Cherokee Lodge—chartered, Nov. 8, 1848

Tonkawa

Medical Clinic—cancer clinic (traveling)— opened—1946

OREGON

Gasoline Tax—gasoline tax (state)—Feb. 25, 1919

Holiday—Labor Day law (state)—state holiday— enacted—Feb. 21, 1887

Labor Legislation—minimum wage law—commis- sion authorized—Feb. 17, 1913

Legislator (state)—husband and wife simulta- neously elected to both chambers of a state legislature—Nov. 7, 1950

OREGON—*Continued*

Litter Legislation—litter legislation (state)—enacted July 2, 1971—effective Oct. 1, 1972

Money—paper money issued by the American Indians—c.1840

Albany

Molybdenum—molybdenum centrifugal casting —Nov. 4, 1958

Astoria

Television—community television antenna system—Dec. 1949

Bly-Lakeview area

World War II—Japanese balloon casualties— May 5, 1945

Champoeg

Colonial Government—government on the Pacific Coast—authorized—May 2, 1843

Medford

Medical Society—woman president of a state medical society—L. S. Kent—elected—Sept. 18, 1948

Oregon City

Newspaper—newspaper published on the Pacific Coast—*Oregon Spectator*—Feb. 5, 1846

Portland

Automobile Bus—bus operated by a railroad—service—Aug. 25, 1924

Automobile Race—transcontinental automobile race (for a time record)—from New York City—arrived—June 21, 1905

Aviation—airplane takeoff from a hotel roof—Silas Christoferson—June 11, 1912

Electric Power Plant—alternating-current hydroelectric power plant to operate over a long distance—current from Willamette Falls, Oreg.—June 2, 1889

Radio Broadcast—network broadcast received on the Pacific Coast—Oct. 23, 1924

Railroad—daily railroad service to the Pacific Coast—through service without a change—Nov. 17, 1889

Servite Church—Marian Congress—Aug. 12, 1934

Ship—FLIP ship—launched, June 22, 1962

Ship—ship completed in less than 2 weeks—*Joseph N. Teal*—trial run, Sept. 27, 1942

Ship—steamboat to employ electric lights successfully—to San Francisco—May 2, 1880

Ship—Victory ship launched—*United Victory*—launched, Jan. 12, 1944

Television Station—ultra-high-frequency commercial television station—KPTV—regular commercial service—Oct. 1, 1952

X Ray—X-ray three-dimensional (stereo) scopic system—first unit installed at Uni of Oregon Medical Center—R. J. Kuhn— 15, 1966

Roseburg

Autopsy—autopsy by a woman physicia male corpse—Bethenia Owens-Adair—1

St. Johns

Plywood—Douglas fir plywood—commerc duction—1905

Salem

Book Catalog—state library to publish a book catalog—1974

College—university on the Pacific Coast lamette University—organized—Feb. 1,

Warrenton

Mayor—woman mayor elected by a city the Rocky Mountains—Clara Munson— term Jan. 6, 1913

Willamette Falls

Electric Power Plant—alternating-current electric power plant to operate over a lo tance—supplied current to Portland, (June 2, 1889

PENNSYLVANIA

Bible—Bible translated into English in Am copyrighted—Sept. 12, 1808

Census—states to exceed 1 million in pop —1820

Child Labor Law—child labor law restrict age of the worker—approved—March 2

College—university for blacks—chartered 29, 1854

Election—printed ballot—authorized—Fe 1799

Governor—governor of a territory and a s W. Geary

Holiday—Flag Day—as a legal holiday— ized—May 7, 1937

Liquor Stores (state)—opened—Jan. 2, 193

Locomotive—locomotive to attain a sp more than 1 mile a minute—built and 1881

Lottery—daily state lotteries with the sam ning daily number—Oct. 4, 1977

Moravian—George Boehnich—arrived—S 1734

Motion Picture Censorship—motion pictu sorship board (state)—June 19, 1911

Music Instruction—State Supervisor of Mu E. Beck—appointed—July 1, 1915

Patent—English patent granted to a resi America—issued—Nov. 25, 1715

Railroad—state-owned railroad—opened 2, 1834

PENNSYLVANIA—*Continued*

Carlisle

American Indian School—American Indian school of prominence—opened—Nov. 1, 1879

Army War College—Army War College women graduates—F. V. Chaffin and S. R. Heinze—were graduated June 16, 1969

Bank—Christmas savings club—in operation—Dec. 1, 1909

Declaration of Independence (American)—Declaration of Independence—July 12, 1774

Carnegie

Telephone—telephone with push buttons—commercial service begun—to and from Greensburg, Pa.—Nov. 18, 1963

Chambersburg

Paper—straw paper—manufactured—1829

Sleeping Car—sleeping car—to Harrisburg, Pa.—1836

Chester

Iron—rolling mill—established—1746

Ship—all-welded self-propelled seagoing petroleum carrier—*White Flash*—launched, Sept. 10, 1931

Ship—commercial ship to conquer the Northwest Passage—*Manhattan*—left Aug. 24, 1969

Ship—iron sloop yacht—*Vindex*—built—1871

Ship—merchant ship formally blessed at a launching ceremony—Nov. 27, 1940

Ship—seatrain—built—1928

Ship—steamboat to employ electric lights successfully—*Columbia*—built

Chester County

Stove—stove—Pennsylvania fireplace—manufactured—1742

Coalport

Coal Mine—woman to die in a coal mine disaster—M. J. McCusker—Oct. 2, 1979

Coatesville

Boiler Plates—manufactured—1816

Columbia

Vending Machine—newspaper vending machine to deliver a single copy—manufactured and leased—March 20, 1954

Connellsville

Iron—iron mill to puddle and roll iron—operated—Sept. 15, 1817

Creighton

Glass—plate glass produced on a large s 1883

Crum Creek

Railroad—railroad for freight transportati Ridley Creek—1809

Delaware County

Insane Patient's Maintenance Act—1676

Delta

Slate—used for roofing material—obtained

Downington

Apple Parer—invented—Moses Coats—F 1803

Drehersville

Bird Sanctuary—established—Aug. 29, 19

Dusboro

Iron—iron casting—Joseph Mallinson—17

East Pittsburgh

Elevator—dual elevator—placed in service

Easton

Civil Rights Chair—established—Lafayet lege

Normal School—normal school instructio fayette College—cornerstone laid—July

Philology Chair—comparative philology Lafayette College—1856

School—model school—opened—Oct. 31,

Soldering Gun—soldering gun—invented b Weller

Eddystone

Ordnance—tank (heavy 60-ton)—built—1§

Emporium

Television Station—illegal television sta closed—Oct. 19, 1950

Ensfield

Sugar—sugar beets—grown—c.1830

Ephrata

Communistic Society—communistic so 1733

Erie

Locomotive—gas turbine–electric locom track-tested—Nov. 15, 1948

Essington

Lutheran Church—Lutheran Church bui dedicated—Sept. 4, 1645

PENNSYLVANIA—*Continued*

Leechburg

Gas—natural gas for manufacturing—in iron and puddle mill furnaces—1873

Tin Factory—to manufacture black plate, tin, and terne plate—1874

Lewisburg

Football Player—football player to score 50 points in 1 game—Clark Hinkle—Nov. 28, 1929

Lewiston

Railroad Signal System—railroad signal system of continuous cab signals—July 11, 1923

Library

Coal—coal pipeline loops (experimental)—built —May 23, 1950

Mansfield

Football Game—football game at night—Sept. 29, 1892

Marcus Hook

Rayon—rayon—production—Dec. 19, 1910

Mauch Chunk

Coal—anthracite coal used in smelting iron ore— 1837

Tunnel—mining tunnel (large)—commenced— 1824

Meadville

Fastening—hookless fastening—manufactured— 1893

Monongahela City

Carborundum—invented—E. G. Acheson—1891

Montgomery County

Bird Banding—bird banding—1803

Tile—brick roofing tile—manufactured—1735

Montoursville

Photography—camera multiple flashbulb device —Flashcubes—made by Sylvania Electric Company

New Berlin

Evangelical Church Building—dedicated—March 2, 1817

New Castle

Baseball Player—black baseball player on a white team—J. W. Fowler—1872

New Geneva

Glass Factory—glass factory west of the Al ny mountains—established—1794

Newton Wells

Gas—pipeline (long-distance)—for natural to Titusville, Pa.—completed—Aug. 1, 18

Norristown

Gas—water gas production—patented—T. Lowe—Sept. 21, 1875

Oakmont

Golf Champion—golf champion to win the U States Open and the Professional—Gene zen—Professional Golfers' Tournament– 18, 1922

Oil Creek

Oil—oil pipeline of importance—comple Oct. 9, 1865

Oil—oil pipeline within the oil regions—to er, Pa.—1862

Oil—oil refinery (commercial)—erected– 1860

Orwigsburg

Tunnel—tunnel—opened to traffic—1821

Philadelphia

Abolition Society—formed—April 14, 1775

Academy—founded—Benjamin Franklin—:

Accordion Patent—issued—Anthony Faas 13, 1854

Actor—matinee idol—John Henry—Am debut—1766

Actors' Home—actors' home—Forrest H opened Oct. 2, 1876

Adhesive and Medicated Plaster—adhesiv medicated plaster—used in the treatm fractures—reported—1830

Advertisement—automobile advertisement national magazine—March 31, 1900

Advertising Agency—V. B. Palmer—ope 1841

Advertising School—established—1920

African Church—founded—Richard Allen–

Agricultural Encyclopedia—published—18C

Agricultural Society—agricultural society— delphia Society for the Promotion of Agric —formed—March 1, 1785

Airmail Service—airmail experimental r May 15, 1918

Airmail Service—autogiro mail delivery dir a post office—May 25, 1935

Airmail Service—autogiro mail delivery r service—July 6, 1939

American Party—national convention—Ju 1855

Botany Professor—Adam Kuhn—Philadelphia College—1768
Bottler of Mineral Water—E. M. Durand
Brewery to remain in business for 200 years—established—1687
Bridge—bridge named for a woman—Betsy Ross Bridge—to Pennsauken, N.J.—opened, April 30, 1976
Bridge—concrete arch highway bridge—erected—1893
Bridge—iron-wire suspension bridge—opened—June 1816
Bridge—stone bridge—1697
Brokerage—clearinghouse for stocks and bonds—organized—Aug. 1870
Building—building erected in the United States for public use—cornerstone laid—July 31, 1792
Building—split-level buildings—Elfreth houses—built—1830
Business—department store to sell apartments—Gimbel Bros.—Jan. 13, 1953
Business School—business collegiate school—Wharton School of Commerce and Finance—established—1881
Carpet Factory—carpet mill—founded—1791
Cartoon—newspaper cartoon—"Join or Die"—May 9, 1754
Catholic Funeral—Catholic funeral attended by the U.S. Continental Congress—Sept. 17, 1777
Chair—recumbent chair patent—H. P. Kennedy—May 22, 1841
Chemistry Laboratory—established—1836
Chemistry Laboratory Manual—published—1797
Chemistry Magazine—printed—1813
Chemistry Professor—chemistry professor—Benjamin Rush—lectured—1769
Chemistry Textbook—chemistry text published—1770
Chemists Society—chemical society—founded—1792
Chess Book—*Chess Made Easy*—published—1802
Chiropody School—chiropody school as a regular division of a university—opened—Sept. 20, 1915
Circus—circus—Ricketts' Circus—1792
Cloth—jeans, fustians, everlastings, and coatings—manufactured
Coal—anthracite coal used commercially—1812
College—college classes to combat the influence of communism—instituted—Dec. 4, 1935
College—university extension summer meeting—July 5, 1893
College—university legally designated as a university—University of Pennsylvania—Nov. 27, 1779
Computer—electronic computer—built—1946
Computer—electronic computer (commercial)—dedicated—June 14, 1951
Computer—solid-state electronic computer—developed—1958
Conchology Report—published—1817
Congress (U.S.)—special session—May 15, 1797

Congress (U.S.)—Senate—senate special s—March 4, 1791
Constitution of the United States—Const (federal)—signed—Sept. 17, 1787
Constitution of the United States—Constitu the United States was first published in a paper—Sept. 19, 1787
Continental Congress—Continental Cong assembled—Sept. 5, 1774
Continental Congress—Continental Congr be opened with prayer—Sept. 7, 1774
Cranioscopy Book—*Crania Americana*—lished—1839
Cricket Club—cricket club to own its own house—1854
Cricket Magazine—cricket magazine *American Cricketer*—published—June 2
Croquet League—National Croquet Leagu ganized—Feb. 12, 1880
Cryptography Chart—published—1797
Deaf—Church Service—ordained deaf cler—1883
Deaf—School—lipreading was first referre print—report—1793
Decalcomanias—commercial production—
Declaration of Independence (American)—ration of Independence first ordered "to b ly engrossed on parchment"—July 19, 17
Declaration of Independence (American)—ration of Independence first printed—Joh lop—July 5, 1776
Declaration of Independence (American)—ration of Independence first published—1776
Declaration of Independence (American)—ration of Independence first read publicly 8, 1776
Declaration of Independence (American)—ration of Independence signed first—by Hancock—July 4, 1776
Declaration of Rights—passed—First Conti Congress—Oct. 14, 1774
Dental Book—book for dental hygienists (published—1916
Dental Book—book on dental surgery—pub—1869
Dental Mallet—dental mallet—patented—A. Bonwill—Nov. 16, 1875
Detective Story—to achieve popularity-lished—April 1841
Dictionary—medical dictionary (comple *Dictionary of Medical Science*, by Robley glison—published—1833
Dictionary—military dictionary—publis 1810
Directory (city)—published—Oct. 1, 1785
Distilling Book—published—1804
Dollar Marks—to be made in type—cast—
Door (revolving)—patented—Theophilus Kannel—Aug. 7, 1888
Drug Mill—established—C. V. Hagner—18
Druggist—Jonathan Roberts—May 1754
Electric Cooking Experiment—Benjamin Fr—1749

PENNSYLVANIA—Philadelphia—*Continued*

Opera—opera by an American composer (important)—*Leonora*—performed—June 4, 1845

Opera—opera (comic)—*The Disappointment*—scheduled—April 20, 1767

Organ—organs imported—1700

Organists' Society—organists' society (national)—branch chapter formed—June 10, 1902

Paper Mill—built—1690

Patent—patent granted jointly to a father and son—Aug. 2, 1791

Patent—patentee to obtain more than one patent—Samuel Mulliken—March 11, 1791

Pencil—paper pencil—patented—F. E. Blaisdell—Nov. 19, 1895

Pencil—pencil with an attached eraser—patented—March 30, 1858

Periodical—American Jewish magazine (successful)—*The Occident and American Jewish Advocate*—Isaac Leeser, editor—published—first issue April 1843

Periodical—comic weekly—*John Donkey*—published—Jan. 1, 1848

Periodical—magazine containing a fashion plate—*The Port Folio*—June 1809

Periodical—magazine for the blind—*Student's Magazine*—published—Jan. 1837

Periodical—magazine published for mental patients—*Illuminator*—April 1, 1843

Periodical—magazine published in America—*American Magazine*—published—Feb. 13, 1741

Periodical—quarterly magazine—*American Review of History*—published—Jan. 1811

Periodical—sectarian magazine (German)—*Ein Geistliches Magazien*—Christoph Saur (or Sower), editor—published—1764-1771

Petroleum—petroleum exported to Europe—boat chartered—Nov. 12, 1861

Pharmacist—pharmacist (woman)—Elizabeth Marshall—1804

Pharmacist—pharmacist (woman graduate)—Susan Hayhurst—graduated—March 16, 1883

Pharmacopoeia — pharmacopoeia — William Brown—published—1778

Pharmacy—homeopathic pharmacy—J. G. Wesselhoeft—opened—1834

Pharmacy College—pharmacy college—Philadelphia College of Apothecaries—organized—Feb. 23, 1821

Pharmacy Magazine—*Journal of the Philadelphia College of Pharmacy*—published—Dec. 1825

Pharmacy Professor—pharmacy professor—S. P. Griffitts—1789

Pharmacy Society (national)—American Pharmaceutical Association—organized—Oct. 6, 1852

Philosophy Book—philosophy book (American)—*Elementa Philosophica*, by Samuel Johnson—printed by Benjamin Franklin and D. Hall—1752

Photograph—solar-eclipse photograph—Frederick Langenheim—March 25, 1857

Phrenology Magazine—*American Phrenolo Journal*—published—Oct. 1838

Physician—black doctor—James Derham

Physician—doctor to receive a Bachelor of N cine degree—John Archer—graduated— 21, 1768

Physician—Hindu woman to receive a Doct Medicine degree—Anandibai Joshee—gr ated—March 11, 1886

Pill—compressed pills or tablets—commerc manufactured—1863

Play (drama)—antivivisection play—*W Dreams*—produced—Oct. 4, 1932

Play (drama)—play about an American Indi *The Indian Princess*—produced—April 6,

Political Convention—black delegate to a tional political convention—Frederick glass—Sept. 6, 1866

Political Science Society—political and s science society (national)—American Ac my of Political and Social Science—organ —Dec. 14, 1889

Porcelain (hard)—manufactured successfu W. E. Tucker—1825

Postage Stamp—public exhibition of pos stamps—May 10, 1876

Postage Stamp—stamped envelopes issue commemorate an event—printed—May 1876

Postal Service—street letter box—patented- bert Potts—March 9, 1858

Presbyterian Church—Presbyterian Churc America—formed—June 11, 1936

Presbyterian General Assembly—meeting— 22, 1789

Presbyterian Presbytery—assembled—1705

Presidential Candidate—presidential candi (Republican) renominated after a defeat— Dewey—June 24, 1948

Printer's Ink—manufactured—C. E. Johns 1804

Printing Magazine (professional)—*Typogra Advertiser*—published—April 1855

Printing Press—high-speed newspaper pri and folding machine—installed—1876

Printing Press—printing press for polychrom printing—patented—T. F. Adams—Sept. 1844

Printing Press—printing press invented in Ar ca—G. E. Clymer—1816

Printing Press—rotogravure press—import 1904

Prison—prison to have individual cells—sy introduced—1790

Prison Reform Society—formed—May 8, 178

Prizefight—prizefight to attract 100,000 specta —Dempsey-Tunney fight—Sept. 23, 1926

Prizefight Referee—heavyweight-champion prizefight black referee—Zack Clayton—V cott-vs. Charles—June 5, 1952

Protestant Episcopal Catechism—Episcopal c chism—published—1785

Psychiatric Association—formed—Oct. 16, 1

Psychology Professor—J. M. Cattell—1888

PENNSYLVANIA—Philadelphia—*Continued*

Teachers' Convention—teachers' convention (national)—Aug. 26, 1857

Teaching Methods Book—*Schul-ordnung*—published—1770

Telephone—automatic telephone system patent—Dec. 5, 1879

Television—Telecast—color telecast by a local station—WPTZ-TV—Dec. 18, 1953

Television—Telecast—color telecast on a closed-circuit local station—WPTZ-TV—Oct. 30, 1953

Television—Telecast—commercial program telecast—"Geographically Speaking"—Oct. 27, 1946

Television—Telecast—department store sales demonstrations (large-scale)—Gimbel Bros.—Oct. 24, 1945

Television—Telecast—football game (collegiate) sponsored—Temple University vs. University of Kansas—Sept. 26, 1941

Television—Telecast—football game televised in color on a network—Sept. 29, 1951

Television—Telecast—motion picture premiere performance to be televised—WPTZ—April 10, 1944

Television—Telecast—pay television presentation of a sporting event—Walcott-Marciano fight—Sept. 23, 1952

Television—Telecast—photograph telecast from an airplane—Robert Hewitt—Aug. 14, 1928

Television—Telecast—political convention to be televised—June 24, 1940

Television—Telecast—presidential debate between an incumbent President and a candidate for the office—G. R. Ford vs. Jimmy Carter—first debate—Sept. 23, 1976

Television—Telecast—prizefight (heavyweight championship bout) telecast coast-to-coast—Walcott vs. Charles—Municipal Stadium—June 5, 1951

Television—Telecast—prizefight in a "studio"—televised—Sept. 1, 1954

Television—Telecast—surgical operation televised on a local program—March 16, 1952

Television—Telecast—symphonic concerts to be televised—March 20, 1948

Television—Telecast—telecast (public) over telephone wires using the narrow-band system—demonstrated by C. R. Kraus—March 20, 1957

Television—Telecast—telecast using coaxial cable—intercity telecast to New York City—Oct. 5, 1936

Temperance Society—national temperance convention—May 24–27, 1833

Tennis Match—women's national championship lawn tennis matches—1887

Textbook printed in America—*A New Guide to the English Tongue*—reprinted—1747

Textile Machinery Patent—James Davenport—Feb. 14, 1794

Theater—municipally owned and operated summer theater-in-the-round—opened—June 30, 1951

Theater—theater building (permanent)—So wark Theatre—opened—Nov. 21, 1766

Theological Treatise—of importance—publi —1690

Tile—wall and floor tiles—manufactured—1

Trade Register—*Aitken's General American ister*—published—1773

Tube—machine designed to produce collap tubes—built—1873

Tuberculosis Society—tuberculosis socie Pennsylvania Society for the Prevention Tuberculosis—founded—April 10, 1892

Turnstile (electric)—used—May 10, 1876

Type Foundry—type foundry to be permane established in America—Christopher Sa erected—1771

Type Specimen Book—published—Binny & naldson—1812

Typewriter Ribbon—typewriter "copy" ribb patented—Jan. 24, 1888

Vaccine—yellow fever vaccine for human im nization—announced—April 28, 1932

Varnish Manufacturer—Christian Schrack—

Venetian Blinds—venetian blinds—install 1761

Wallpaper — wallpaper — manufactured Plunkett Fleeson—1739

War Veterans' Society—Society of the Cincin —general meeting—May 7, 1784

Washing Machine—rotary-motion washing chine—patented—H. E. Smith—Oct. 26, 18

Watermark—in paper—William Rittenhou 1690

Whist—whist rule book—*The Whist Pla Hand Book*—published—1844

White Lead Manufacturer—Samuel Wether 1789

Woman—women to become federal governm employees—1795

Woman Suffrage—woman suffrage book—*A dication of the Rights of Women*—publishe 1792

Wrestling—intercollegiate wrestling associa —formed—April 7, 1905

Zoological Garden—opened to public—Jul 1874

Phoenixville

Gas—water gas plant—built—1874

Pithole

Oil—oil pipeline of importance—completed 9, 1865

Pittsburgh

Aluminum—aluminum—commercial produc —Nov. 1888

Automobile Robbery—armored commercial holdup—March 11, 1927

Automobile Service Station—drive-in service tion—opened—Dec. 1, 1913

Automobile Truck—built—1898

ation—automatic pilot—tested—from Cleveland, Ohio—Oct. 8, 1929

vling Tournament—gold medal award to a erfect-score bowler—roll-off—March 11, 1909

ge—wire-cable suspension aqueduct bridge -completed—May 1845

ding—aluminum-faced building—Alcoa uilding—completed—Aug. 1, 1953

ding—retractable-roof (large) building—Civic rea and Exhibit Hall—dedicated Sept. 17, 1961

rch—church services aired from another urch—April 17, 1921

mercial High School—commercial high hool—established—1868

tric Meter—commercial production—Aug. 388

Factory (hand cutting)—established—1829 —fire in a mine—recorded—1765

ball Uniform—football uniform numerals— sed—Dec. 5, 1908

ss Crystal Chandelier—1810

ss Factory—flint glass factory—successful— 307

iday—Saturday half holiday—introduced— ine 1871

iday—Thanksgiving Day sermon—west of the lleghenies—Nov. 26, 1758

Loading Machinery—operated—May 1917

nigration—Chinese labor immigration—Wiliam Kelly—1854

—angle iron—rolled—Samuel Leonard—1819

el—discovery announced—Sept. 9, 1929

or Union—labor union of importance—organized—1881

p—automobile road map—published—1914

nument—monument to the American flag— edicated—June 14, 1927

tion Picture Theater—theater in the world devoted exclusively to the exhibition of motion ictures—Nickelodeon—opened—June 19, 1905

vs Correspondent—black news correspondent –J. A. Rogers—assigned to Ethiopia—Oct. 1935

vspaper—newspaper published west of the lleghenies—Pittsburgh Gazette—July 29, 1786

—oil refinery—S. M. Kier—1855

and Gas Production Course—in a college— 912

ent—print patent—H. J. Heinz Co.—March 7, 893

roleum—petroleum refining course—collegite grade—1922–23

tage Stamp—Christmas-stamp regular issue— laced on sale, Nov. 1, 1962

tal Service—zone numbers—put into use, May , 1943

sbyterian Church—Moderator of the United resbyterian Church—elected—T. M. Taylor— Aay 28, 1958

nting Press—printing press to use a continuous veb or roll of paper—Bullock Press—manufacured—1865

testant Episcopal Bishop—Protestant Episcoal bishop consecrated in a Roman Catholic hurch—R. B. Appleyard—Feb. 10, 1968

Radio Broadcast—baseball game broadcast with a play-by-play description—Aug. 5, 1921

Radio Broadcast—religious service broadcast— Jan. 2, 1921

Radio Broadcast—transatlantic broadcast of a voice—KDKA—Dec. 31, 1923

Radio License—radio station licensed—Oct. 27, 1920

Radio Station—radio station with 500,000-watt power—June 12, 1936

Railroad—railroad to install track water tanks— 1870

Railroad Car—mail car (steel)—built

Republican Party—Republican Party meeting (national)—Feb. 22, 1856

Ship—iron vessel built for the U.S. Navy—*Michigan*—sections built—1842

Ship—steamboat to sail down the Mississippi— *New Orleans*—sailed—Sept. 1811

Stadium—baseball stadium (fireproof)—Forbes Field—opened, June 30, 1909

Steel—cast steel for plows—1846

Streetcar—streetcars with clear-vision windows —in operation—1929

Television—Telecast—stratovision flight public demonstration—June 23, 1948

Television Station—city to have two educational television channels—permit for second channel granted on July 16, 1958

Treaty—treaty entered into by the United States with American Indian tribes—Sept. 17, 1778

Zoo—twilight zoo—Highland Park—dedicated— April 3, 1973

Pleasant Hills

Building—house with a built-in nuclear bomb shelter—exhibited—May 24, 1959

Plumer

Oil—oil pipeline within oil regions—from Oil Creek, Pa.—1862

Plymouth

Lithuanian Church—St. Casimir's Lithuanian Church—organized—Oct. 27, 1889

Port Royal

Organ—organs imported—Episcopal Church— 1700

Pottstown

Bridge—iron-truss bridge—trusses constructed— March 1845

Pottsville

Iron—iron blast furnace—used anthracite successfully—blown—Oct. 19, 1839

Reading

Civil War—regiment to respond to President Lincoln's proclamation—Ringgold Light Artillery

PENNSYLVANIA—Reading—*Continued*

Fountain Pen Patent—D. Hyde—May 20, 1830

Ridley Creek

Railroad—railroad for freight transportation—to Crum Creek, Pa.—1809

Rochester

Electric Meter—patented—O. B. Shallenberger—Aug. 14, 1888

Glass—cut glass—manufactured from pressed blanks—1902

Radio Facsimile Transmission—radio facsimile patent—C. D. Ehret—March 28, 1905

Rouseville

Oil—oil well fire—April 17, 1861

Rush

Vending Machine—vending machine to sell from bulk—invented—T. S. Wheatcraft—1897

Saxonburg

Wire—wire rope factory—erected—J. A. Roebling —1841

Schellsburg

Protestant Church—Protestant church formed by the amalgamation of 4 churches of different denominations—United Church of Schellsburg, Pa—Nov. 22, 1964

Scranton

Automobile License (federal)—common carrier license—license issued to Rodger's Motor Lines —Dec. 22, 1936

Correspondence School—student enrolled—1891

Railroad—railroad operated by an electric third-rail system—operated—May 25, 1903

Selinsgrove

Methodist Church—bishop (woman)—M. S. Matthews—consecrated—July 18, 1980

Sewickley

Radio Broadcast—tennis match broadcast—Aug. 4, 1921

Sharpsburg

Foodstuffs Producer—to achieve great commercial success—H. J. Heinz—opened factory— 1869

Shippingport

Electric Power Plant—atomic electric generating station (full-scale)—power generated—Dec. 2, 1957

Shuman's Station

Bridge—timber trestle pier of lattice construc —started—June 1840

South Bethlehem

Armor Plate Contract (U.S. Navy)—award June 1, 1887

State College

Agricultural School—agricultural college (s to be chartered—opened—Feb. 16, 1859

Automobile Driving Course—State College School—Feb. 1934

Traffic Regulation Course—teacher trai course in "Training Traffic Safety"—Penr vania State College—1936

Sunbury

Electric Company—three-wire central-statio candescent electric lighting plant—operate July 4, 1883

Railroad Signal System—railroad signal sys of continuous cab signals—installation— 11, 1923

Tidioute

Gas—natural gas for manufacturing—1870

Titusville

Gas—pipeline (long-distance)—to Newton W Pa.—completed—Aug. 1, 1872

Oil—oil well commercially productive—dis ered—Aug. 27, 1859

Oil—oil well drilled by torpedoes—Jan. 21, 1

Troy

Cheese—pineapple cheese—made—1808

Union County

Evangelical Church General Conference—Oct. 17, 1816

Uniontown

War (colonial)—bloodshed in the French and dian War—May 28, 1754

Villa Nova

Animals—cattle tuberculosis test—March 3, 1

Village Forks

Bridge—twin covered-bridges—built—Peter —1849

Warren

Automobile Tractor—endless-chain tractor— ented—Nov. 2, 1886

Washington

ratory—crematory—erected—1876

ples of Christ—organized—Aug. 17, 1809

Waynesburg

ball League—juvenile baseball league—
rmed—1908

Westmoreland County

ge—suspension bridge—James Finley—1796

Wildwood

, Mine—coal mine designed for 100 percent
echanical operation—opened—Oct. 1930

Wilkes-Barre

—anthracite coal burned experimentally—
b. 11, 1808

Wilkinsburg

vision—electronic television system—pat-
ted—V. K. Zworykin—Dec. 20, 1938

Willow Grove

ogiro—autogiro licensed for commercial use
built by Pitcairn Aircraft Company, Inc.—cer-
ied, April 2, 1931

ogiro—pilot to carry a passenger—Amelia
arhart—Dec. 19, 1930

ogiro—Flights—autogiro flight—Pitcairn Field
Dec. 19, 1928

ogiro—Flights—autogiro solo flight by a wom-
—Amelia Earhart—Dec. 18, 1930

York

omotive—locomotive to burn coal (practical,
merican-made)—built—Phineas Davis—test-
l—Feb. 19, 1831

—iron vessel (sheet iron)—*Codorus*—built

PHILIPPINE ISLANDS

Cavite

marine—submarine (U.S.) destroyed in World
ar II—*Sealion*—1941

Luzon

rld War II—Japanese battleship sunk—*Haru-
a*—Dec. 11, 1941

RHODE ISLAND

ny Exclusion Law—enacted—May 5, 1908

urance—health insurance law (state)—effec-
ve—May 10, 1942

and Bolt Machine—nut and bolt machine—
atented—Dec. 14, 1798

ter Propagation—state—June 1779

Screw—screw patent—granted—Dec. 14, 1798

Bellefonte

Screw—screw factory—established—1810

Bristol

Ship—torpedo boat—*Lightning*—built—J. B. Herreshoff—1876

Conanicut Island

Movable Church—consecrated—June 3, 1899

Cranston

Automobile Race—automobile race on a track—
Sept. 7, 1896

Automobile Racetrack—automobile racetrack
(asphalt-covered)—opened—Sept. 18, 1915

Bridge (game)—bridge hand in which each of the
4 players was dealt a perfect hand—Irene Motta—March 12, 1954

Cumberland

Nails—cold-cut—manufactured—Jeremiah Wilkinson—1777

Goat Island

Torpedo—torpedo manufacturing station—established—1869

Greenwich

Building—building known as a Quonset hut—
built—Sept. 1941

Newport

Automobile Parade—Sept. 7, 1899

Baptist Church—Seventh Day Baptist Church—
organized—1671

Bicycle Society—bicycle society (national organization)—formed—May 31, 1880

Candle Factory—established—1748

Cattle Club—cattle club (Jersey cattle)—formed—
July 1868

Court-martial—court-martial trial—Aug. 24, 1676

Felt Manufacturing Mechanical Process—invented—T. R. Williams—1820

Gas—gaslights (street)—installed—1806

Golf Course—golf course (nine holes)—completed—1890

Golf Tournament—amateur golf tournament (official)—Oct. 12, 1895

Golf Tournament—national championship
stroke-play golf match—Sept. 3-4, 1894

Golf Tournament—open championship (official)
—Oct. 4, 1895

Naval Officer—naval chaplain (woman)—F. D.
Pohlman—sworn in—July 2, 1973

Naval War College—black officers to attend the
Naval War College—G. I. Thompson and S. L.
Gravely, Jr.—began studies Aug. 16, 1963

RHODE ISLAND—Newport—Continued

Naval War College—naval war college—opened —Sept. 1885

Polo—international polo series—England vs. America—Aug. 25, 1886

Post Office—post office building (U.S.)—built— 1829

Roller Skating Rink—roller skating rink (public) —opened—1866

Slavery—nonimportation of slaves act—enacted —June 13, 1774

Submarine—submarine to cross the Atlantic Ocean under its own power—E-1—left, Dec. 4, 1917

Tennis Match—lawn tennis champions who were brothers—won—Aug. 18, 1896

Tennis Match—lawn tennis national championship matches—Aug. 31, 1881

Tennis Match—professional lawn tennis contest (international)—Aug. 29, 1889

War Prisoner—prisoner of war to head the Naval War College—J. B. Stockdale—served as president—Oct. 13, 1977–Aug. 22, 1979

Woman—woman newspaper editor—Ann Franklin—Newport *Mercury*—Aug. 22, 1762

Pawtucket

Cotton Mill—cotton mill to spin cotton yarn successfully—1790

Strike—strike in which women participated— 1824

Thread—cotton thread—made—Hannah Wilkinson—1793

Providence

Baptist Church—Baptist Church—established— 1639

Baseball Game—triple play unassisted—May 8, 1878

Building—building with an all-marble dome— Rhode Island State House—ground broken Sept. 16, 1895—cornerstone laid Oct. 15, 1896— occupied Jan. 1, 1901

Catamaran—patented—N. G. Herreshoff—April 10, 1877

Cotton Spinning Jenny—operated—1786

File Factory—file factory (machine cutting) to attain success—Nicholson File Co.—organized— 1864

Gold Leaf—in roll form—patented—W. H. Coe— April 5, 1892

Hat—straw hats—produced—June 1798

Health Laboratory—health laboratory (municipal)—established—Jan. 1, 1888

Health Laboratory—health laboratory (state)— established—Sept. 1, 1894

Insurance—mutual fire insurance company—incorporated—Oct. 31, 1835

Jewelers' Supply House—established—Nehemiah Dodge—1794

Lime—manufactured—Jan. 27, 1662

Lunch Wagon—introduced—1872

Mineralogy Instruction—Rhode Island Colle: 1786

Motion Picture Machine—machine to show mated pictures—patented—April 23, 1867

Price Regulation Legislation—price regula law (colonial)—effective—Jan. 8, 1777

Revolutionary War—naval attack—June 9, 1

Screw—screw machine—to manufacture poi screws—patented—Cullen Whipple—June 1856

Sociology Society—sociological society tional)—first annual meeting—Dec. 27, 190

Streetcar—gas-powered streetcar—operate 1873

Tuberculosis School—outdoor school for tube lar children—opened—Jan. 27, 1908

Quonset Point

Navy—air squadron of jets (U.S. Navy)—July 1947

Warwick

Election Law—fraudulent election law (color —enacted—May 22, 1649

Post Office—post office fully mechanize opened—Oct. 20, 1960

Slavery—law regulating slavery—prohibit law—enacted—May 18, 1652

SOUTH CAROLINA

Civil War—black regiment in the Civil War— ganized—July 1862

Indigo—planted—c.1690

Naval Academy—black midshipman in the Naval Academy—J. H. Conyers—appointe 1872

Secession—secession act—Dec. 20, 1860

Senator (U.S.)—senator elected by a write-in —J. S. Thurmond—elected—Nov. 2, 1954

Slavery—insurrection of black slaves—1739

Supreme Court (state)—associate justice (bla of a state supreme court—J. J. Wright—be service, Feb. 2, 1870

Treaty—treaty between states after the Decla tion of Independence—Georgia and So Carolina—Dewitt's Corner, S.C.—May 20, 1

Workmen's Compensation—workmen's comp sation lawsuit—trial—July 1838

Chapin

Road—cotton fabric used on a road—to Prosp ty, S.C.—1926

Charleston (Charles-Towne)

Army—Reserve Officers Training Corps Uni authorized—Oct. 21, 1916

Building—building of fireproof constructio 1822

Business Publication—business publicatio *South-Carolina Price-Current*—first kno copy July 30, 1774

SOUTH DAKOTA—Rapid City—*Continued*

Photograph—photograph showing the lateral curvature of the horizon—balloon takeoff—Nov. 11, 1935

Watertown

Fingerprinting—high school to fingerprint its students—Watertown Senior High School—Oct. 19, 1936

White Lake

Photograph—photograph showing the lateral curvature of the horizon—balloon landed—Nov. 11, 1935

TENNESSEE

Army—law (state) conferring military privileges and duties on blacks—enacted—June 28, 1861

Civil Government in America—Watauga Commonwealth—May 1772

Dueling Legislation (state)—enacted—Nov. 10, 1801

Evolution Law (state)—enacted—March 23, 1925

Governor—gubernatorial election in which two brothers were the opposing candidates—R. L. Taylor and A. A. Taylor—Nov. 2, 1886

President (U.S.)—President to become a senator —Andrew Johnson—1875

Prohibition—prohibition state—legislation enacted—Jan. 26, 1838

State—state readmitted to the Union—July 24, 1866

Tornado—tornado disaster (large-scale)—March 18, 1925

Chattanooga

Baseball Player—woman baseball pitcher—engaged by organized male team—April 1, 1931

Golf Course—midget golf course—1929

Clinton

Element—element 95—americium—formed

Collierville

Enclave—municipal enclave of economic ground rent—authorized—April 21, 1933

Gallatin

Postage Stamp—stamp for balloon mail—from Nashville, Tenn.—June 18, 1877

Jackson

Medical Periodical—black medical journal— *Medical and Surgical Observer*—published— 1892

Jonesboro

Periodical—antislavery magazine—*The E*‌ *cipator*—published—April 30, 1820

Kingsport

Sponge—oxidized cellulose (sponge)—man‌ tured—1936

Knoxville

College—nondenominational college—B‌ College—chartered—Sept. 10, 1794

Memphis

Business—Keedoozle store—opened—May 1937

Golfer—golfer to break 60 in a Professional (ers Association tour—A. L. Geiberger—D‌ Thomas Memphis Open—June 10, 1977

Hospital—children's hospital solely for rese and treatment of catastrophic childhood eases—St. Jude's Children's Research Hos —opened Feb. 4, 1962

Sewage—separate system of sewage dispo‌ started—Jan. 21, 1880

Typewriter Ribbon—typewriter ribbon pate G. K. Anderson—Sept. 14, 1886

Nashville

Animals—dogs trained to guide the blind—t‌ —1928

Fraternity (Greek-letter)—scholastic frate chapter established at a university for blac Phi Beta Kappa—Fisk University—April 4,

Horse Race—futurity race—Oct. 10, 1843

Poet—black poet to be employed to teach cre writing—J. W. Johnson—Jan. 1932

Postage Stamp—stamp for balloon mail—to latin, Tenn.—June 18, 1877

Radio License—frequency modulation tran ter to receive a commercial license—W47‌ operated—March 1, 1941

Theater—showboat—floating theater— menced tour—Oct. 20, 1817

Theological School—theological school (m‌ woman dean—S. M. Teselle—appointe faculty 1971—took office as dean June 1,

Oak Ridge

Atomic Reactor—graphite reactor with a siz‌ power output—installed Nov. 4, 1943

Isotope—radioactive isotopes exported-‌ duced—1947

Museum—museum devoted exclusively to a‌ energy—opened—March 19, 1949

Pulaski

Ku Klux Klan—organized—1865

Rogersville

dical—trade journal—*Rail-road Advocate*—
blished—July 4, 1831

Shiloh

ital—Army Field Hospital—established—
ril 1862

Washington College

ge—college named after George Washington
Washington College—July 8, 1795

TEXAS

e Knife—invented—1835
n-Boll Weevil—introduced—1892
e—state police—Texas Rangers—organized
835
esentative (U.S.)—representative sworn in
ore 8:00 A.M.—elected, Dec. 17, 1963
eme Court (state)—state supreme court com-
sed entirely of women—appointed—Jan. 8,
5

Abilene

r—golfer to play 24 hours continuously on a
ulation course—J. J. Johnson—Oct. 14–15,
9

Amarillo

ay—Mother-in-Law   Day—celebrated—
rch 5, 1934

Arlington

ge—belly-dancing college course—Universi-
of Texas—August 1973

Austin

—armored division transported by air-
nes to a foreign country—to West Germany
ct. 22, 1963
es (academic and honorary)—honorary de-
es presented simultaneously to a President
his wife—L. B. Johnson and C. A. T. John-
—May 30, 1964
l—Medal of Honor in the Vietnam War
arded to a Marine—R. E. O'Malley—pre-
ted Dec. 6, 1966

Beaumont

–oil drill seagoing rig—built—1955
oil and gas magazine—*Oil Investors' Journal*
. S. Reavis, founder and editor—published
May 24, 1902

Belton

—road with a depressed trough—opened to
fic—Dec. 5, 1925

College Station

Army—Reserve Officers Training Corps Units—
authorized—Oct. 21, 1916

Radio Broadcast—football game (collegiate)
broadcast—Nov. 25, 1920

Shot-Put—shot-put to cover a distance of more
than 70 feet—Randy Matson—Southwest Conference trackmeet—May 8, 1965

Shot-Put—shot-put to cover a distance of more
than 71 feet—Randy Matson—April 22, 1967

Columbia

President of the Republic of Texas—Sam Houston
—oath of office—Oct. 22, 1836

Corpus Christi

Welding—aluminum-pipe welding machine (automatic)—completed model tested—1957

Crystal City

Monument—monument to a comic character—
Popeye statue—unveiled—March 26, 1937

Dallas

Aviation—Flights—airplane endurance flight exceeding 1,200 hours—Jim Heth and Bill Burkhart
—began—Aug. 2, 1958

Insurance—group hospital insurance plan—Baylor University Hospital—Dec. 21, 1929

Newspaper—newspaper daily railroad delivery
service—*Morning News*—Oct. 1, 1885

Newspaper—newspaper printed on pine-pulp
paper in color—*News*—March 31, 1937

Photograph—photograph bounced off a satellite
—received—Aug. 18, 1960

Radio Station—municipal radio station—1920

Sidewalk (traveling)—two-way moving walk—in
service—Jan. 30, 1958

Television—Telecast—courtroom verdict telecast
—Ruby trial—March 14, 1964

Television—Telecast—murder (actual) shown on
television—L. H. Oswald killed by Jack Ruby—
Nov. 24, 1963

Del Rio

Aviation—Parachute—parachute jump from an
airplane from a 53,000-foot altitude—J. D. Nole
—Sept. 26, 1957

Floydada

Federal Crop Insurance Corporation—first indemnity payment—April 14, 1939

Fort Bliss

Army—ballistic missile operational unit—completed training—Nov. 1954

TEXAS—*Continued*

Fort Sam Houston

World War I—German spy to receive a death sentence from the American forces during World War I—sentenced—Aug. 16, 1918

Fort Worth

Aviation—Flights—airplane to carry 100,000 pounds—takeoff April 15, 1949

Aviation—Flights (world)—round-the-world non-stop airplane flight—completed—March 2, 1949

Ballet Instruction—university to offer ballet technique instruction—Texas Christian University—1949

Helium—helium plant of the United States—completed—April 1921

Helium—helium plants (experimental)—erected—1917

Hotel—hotel to establish a heliport—May 20, 1953

Hotel—hotel with all-foam-rubber mattresses, pillows, and furniture cushions—Oct. 7, 1951

Railroad—gasoline-driven, stainless-steel, air-conditioned, pneumatic-tired, two-car train—in service—to Texarkana, Tex.—1933

Streetcar—lightweight one-man streetcar—placed in operation—Nov. 1916

Television—Telecast—rodeo telecast coast to coast—Will Rogers Memorial Coliseum—Jan. 31, 1953

Washing Machine—washing machine for public use—"washateria"—introduced—April 18, 1934

Freeport

Magnesium—magnesium commercially produced from seawater—extracted—Jan. 21, 1941

Ship—liquid-bulk-chemical carrier—*Marine-Dow Chem*—first run, to New York City

Water—seawater conversion plant (practical)—opened—May 8, 1961

Galveston

Commission Form of Government—inaugurated—Sept. 18, 1901

Hotel—hotel (large) built over a pier—Flagship Hotel—opened June 30, 1965

Newspaper—newspaper delivery train—to Houston—1883

Grand Prairie

Parachutist—parachutist to make 124 jumps in one day—Neal Stewart—July 4, 1952

Holliday

Animals—sheep (Karakul fur sheep)—imported—1908

Houston

Astronaut—astronaut (American) to die—Freeman—Oct. 31, 1964

Astronaut—space-to-ground news confer telecast—Charles Conrad, A. L. Bean, and Gordon, Jr., in *Apollo XII* with G. P. Carr—23, 1969

Baseball Game—night baseball game (r league) to last longer than 6 hours—New Mets vs. Houston Astros—April 15, 1968

Boiler—carbon monoxide boiler—in operat Nov. 1953

Football Game—American Football League' championship game—Houston Oilers vs Angeles Chargers—Jan. 1, 1961

Newspaper—newspaper delivery train—Galveston—1883

Postal Service—mailbox (drive-up)—instal July 1927

Stadium—domed, fully-enclosed sports are Astrodome—ground broken, Jan. 3, 1962—baseball game, April 9, 1965—first fo game, Sept. 11, 1965—first polo game, Ja 1966

Telephone—mobile long-distance car-to-car phone conversation—to St. Louis, Mo.—11, 1946

Television Station—noncommercial educa television station—KUHT—May 12, 1953

Wedding—airplane wedding—May 31, 1919

Indianola

Animals—camels imported for commercial poses—May 14, 1856

Kelly Air Force Base

Air Force Officer—military engineer (woma the Air Force—S. M. Ocobock—began se April 8, 1971

Kingsville

Animals—cattle (Africander cattle)—impor March 14, 1932

Lampasas

Bankers' Association—bankers' associ formed by a state group—July 23, 1885

Lufkin

Television Station—microwave television s —KTRE-TV—Aug. 31, 1955

Nueces County

Cotton—cotton acreage reduction paymen ceived—July 28, 1933

Orange

Pipeline—pipeline (interstate) to transport ene—in operation—Sept. 6, 1958

—naval ship (destroyer) christened by an ented woman Marine—*Basilone*—launched,
c. 21, 1945

Panhandle

ral Crop Insurance Corporation—first ap-
cation made—M. L. Purvines—May 18, 1938

Petrolia

m—helium plants (experimental)—erected
917

Randolph Air Force Base

e Cabin—used—1956

San Angelo

ol—air-conditioned public elementary
ool—Oct. 1955

San Antonio

ion—Airplane Fatalities—airplane fatality
a solo military plane—G. E. M. Kelly—May
1911

ion—School—airplane flying school oper-
d by a woman—1914

ing—air-conditioned office building—
ned—Jan. 1, 1928

Snyder

nobile Trucking Service—automobile inter-
trucking service—to Colorado City, Colo.—
. 29, 1904

Temple

—road with a depressed trough—opened—
. 15, 1925

Texarkana

al Credit Union Act—charter No. 1—granted
934

ad—gasoline-driven, stainless-steel, air-
ditioned, pneumatic-tired, two-car train—in
vice—to Fort Worth, Tex.—1933

Texas City

ion—Airplane—airplane in actual military
ration—Army Aviation School—1913

Waco

es (academic and honorary)—husband and
e awarded honorary degrees—Vice Presi-
t and Mrs. J. N. Garner—Nov. 21, 1936

uplets to Complete a College Course—Keys
ers—graduated—May 31, 1937

ision—Telecast—murder trial to be tele-
d—Dec. 5, 1955

Weatherford

Cotton Picker (mechanical)—built—J. D. Rust—
1928

White Point

Welding—aluminum-pipe welding machine (automatic)—working model tested—1954

UTAH

Game Preserve—game preserve appropriation
(federal)—state aid project approved—July 23,
1938

Motion Picture—talking picture taken outdoors
(full-length)—*In Old Arizona*

Senate (state)—woman state senator—M. H. Cannon—served—Jan. 11, 1897

Solar Power Plant—solar-cell power plant—dedicated, June 7, 1980

Bonneville Salt Flats

Automobile—automobile to exceed the speed of
300 miles an hour—Sir Malcolm Campbell—
Sept. 3, 1935

Automobile—automobile to exceed the speed of
400 miles an hour—John Cobb—Sept. 16, 1947

Automobile Driver—woman automobile driver to
exceed the speed of 300 m.p.h.—L. A. R. Breedlove—Nov. 4, 1965

Fort Bridger

Cartridge Belt patent—Anson Mills—Aug. 20,
1867

Salt Lake City

Business—department store—Zion's Cooperative
Mercantile Institution—1868

Church of Jesus Christ of Latter-Day Saints—
black ordained to the priesthood—Joseph Freeman, Jr.—June 11, 1978

Monument—monument to a bird—sea gull monument—unveiled—Oct. 1, 1913

Wendover

Motorcycle Race—motorcycle to exceed 200
miles an hour—Wilhelm Herz—Aug. 4, 1956

VERMONT

Election Law—absentee voting law (state)—
enacted—Nov. 24, 1896

Emancipation Act (state)—enacted—July 2, 1777

Lieutenant Governor—woman lieutenant governor—C. N. Bailey—elected Nov. 2, 1954

Money—copper cents minted by a state—authorized—June 1785

Patent—patent granted by the United States government—to Samuel Hopkins—July 31, 1790

Representative (U.S.)—representative elected
while serving a prison term—Matthew Lyon

Seeding Machine Patent—Eliakim Spooner—Jan.
25, 1799

VERMONT—*Continued*

Slavery—state to abolish slavery—July 2, 1777
State—state admitted to the Union—after the ratification of the Constitution—March 4, 1791
Strike—anti–sit-down-strike 'legislation (state)—enacted—April 9, 1937

Bradford

Globe Factory—to manufacture terrestrial and celestial globes—1813

Burlington

Factory—steam-heated factory—Burlington Woolen Company—1846
Horse Race—300-mile endurance run—to Camp Devens, Mass.—held—Oct. 15, 1919

Concord

Normal School—normal school established exclusively for the preparation of teachers—Concord Academy—opened—March 11, 1823

Dorset

Marble Quarry—operated—Isaac Underhill—1785

Grandpa's Knob

Electric Generator—wind turbine—to generate energy for an alternating-current power system—operated—Oct. 19, 1941

Middlebury

College—school for the higher education of women—Emma Willard—1814
Horse—horse farm operated by the United States government—established—1907

Montpelier

Agricultural Society—agricultural society for dairymen—organized—Oct. 27, 1869
Lieutenant Governor—woman lieutenant governor—C. N. Bailey—sworn in Jan. 6, 1955

Northfield

Army—Reserve Officers Training Corps course in mountain and winter warfare—Norwich University—announced—Oct. 3, 1947
Traffic Regulation Course—air traffic regulation course—endowed—1934

Norwich

Engineering College—civil engineering course—Norwich University—1819
Military School—military school—American Literary, Scientific and Military Academy—founded—Aug. 6, 1819

Plymouth

President (U.S.)—President born on Independence Day—Calvin Coolidge—July 4, 1872

Proctor

Nurse—nurse employed by an industrial organization—Ada Stewart—1896

Randolph

Horse—Morgan horse—foaled—1789

Rutland

Epidemic—poliomyelitis epidemic—June 17,

St. Johnsbury

Scale—platform scale—built—Thaddeus banks—1830
Scale—railway track scale—patented—Jan 1857

Springfield

Sandpaper Patent—Isaac Fischer—June 14,

Stratton Mountain

Ski Carousel—ski carousel—in service—November 1975

Wallingford

Epidemic—poliomyelitis epidemic—June 17,

Windsor

Suffrage—state to provide universal man suffrage—constitution enacted—July 28, 1

Woodstock

Ski Lift—ski tow (rope)—in operation—Jan 1934

VIRGIN ISLANDS (U.S.)

Charlotte Amalie

Postal Card—airmail postal card commemor—issued, March 31, 1967

VIRGINIA

Agriculture—crop limitation law—enacted—16, 1629
Agriculture—crop surplus destruction—or—Jan. 6, 1639
American Indians—American Indian chief (—an)—Queen Anne—c.1675–1715
Artist—English artist—John White—arriv 1585
Beer—brewed—Roanoke Colony—1587
Blue Law—blue law—enacted—1619
Blue Law—blue law regulating gambling—
Census—states to exceed 1 million in popul—1820

VIRGINIA—Fairfax—*Continued*

Civil War—skirmish in the Civil War—June 1, 1861

Falling Creek

Iron—iron works—erected—1619
Lead—mined and smelted—1620

Falls Church

Radio Station—all-local network—May 15, 1950

Fort Belvoir

Atomic Reactor—military nuclear power plant—dedicated—April 29, 1957

Fort Eustis

Heliport—military heliport—dedicated—Dec. 7, 1954

Fort Henry

Expedition—expedition—of Englishmen—to cross Allegheny Mountains—started—Aug. 27, 1650

Fort (Fortress) Monroe

Chaplains' School—army school for chaplains—Feb. 9, 1918
Fire Extinguisher Patent—Alanson Crane—Feb. 10, 1863
School—black school for freedmen—established—Sept. 17, 1861
Ship—balloon carrier—observed military positions—Aug. 3, 1861

Fort Myer

Aviation—Airplane Fatalities—airplane fatality—T. E. Selfridge—Sept. 17, 1908
Aviation—Airship—dirigible balloon contracted for by the U.S. government—demonstrated—Aug. 1908
Aviation—Flights—airplane endurance flight exceeding one hour—Sept. 9, 1908
Aviation—Flights—intercity airplane flight—to Alexandria, Va.—July 30, 1909
Aviation—Passenger—airplane passenger (official)—Sept. 9, 1908
Police—Army Military Police school—opened, Jan. 15, 1942

Fredericksburg

Automobile—artmobile—tours began—October 1953
Monument—monument to a woman financed by women—dedicated—May 10, 1894

Gosport

Ship—ship constructed by the federal government—1794

Hampton

Educational Endowment—Benjamin Syms—

Hampton Roads

Aviation—battleship sunk by an airplane—21, 1921
Aviation—Airship—airship filled with heliu—tested, Dec. 1, 1921—R. F. Wood (p round trip to Washington, D.C.—Dec. 4,
Aviation—Flights—airplane flight from a s Eugene Ely—takeoff—Nov. 14, 1910
Civil War—conflict between ironclad vess the Civil War—*Merrimac* and *Monitor*—N 9, 1862
Expedition—scientific expedition fitted out I United States Government—sailed—Au 1838
Ordnance—revolving gun turret—*Monitor* gagement—March 9, 1862
Radio Telephone—radio telephone ship-to conversation—May 6, 1916
Ship—warship fleet to circumnavigate the —returned—Feb. 22, 1909

Harrisonburg

Postal Service—Highway Post Office Serv route to Washington, D.C.—established 10, 1941

Harrison's Landing

Taps (military signal)—played—July 1862

James City

Bounty—authorized—Oct. 5, 1646
Road—highway legislation (colonial)—pas Sept. 4, 1632

Jamestown

American Indians—massacre by Americar ans of white people—March 22, 1622
Animals—sheep—imported—1609
Baptism—black child baptized in the E colonies—William Tucker—1624
Bottle—bottle—blown—1608
Colonial Government—colonial council in / ca—May 13, 1607
Colonist—English settlement in America (p nent)—May 13, 1607
Cyclone—cyclone recorded—Aug. 27, 1667
Glass Bead—manufactured—1608
Glass Factory—glass factory—established 1608
Legislative Assembly—July 30, 1619
Maize—Indian corn—planting—1609
Rebellion (colonial)—George Kendall—160
Slander Proceedings—John Robinson—Se 1607
Slavery—slaves—introduced—Aug. 1619
Tobacco—tobacco—cultivated—1612

VIRGINIA—*Continued*

Richmond

Automobile—artmobile—conceived and designed by Virginia Museum of Fine Arts—1953

Bank—bank for blacks operated by blacks—opened—April 3, 1889

Bank—bank president (black woman)—M. L. Walker—July 28, 1903

Cans—beer in cans—placed on sale—Jan. 24, 1935

Congress of the Confederate States—under permanent constitution—meeting—Feb. 18, 1861

Presbyterian Church—woman ordained a minister in the Presbyterian Church in the United States (South)—Rachel Henderlite—ordained, May 12, 1965

Vice President (U.S.)—Vice President arrested—indicted for treason June 24—trial began Aug. 3—acquitted Sept. 1, 1807

Roanoke

Locomotive—locomotive (super-giant)—operated—Jan. 27, 1948

Snicker's Gap

Road—toll road—to Alexandria, Va.—1785

Staunton

City Manager—elected—April 2, 1908

Upperville

Horse Show—Upperville Colt and Horse Show—1853

Virginia Beach

Building—aluminum geodesic-dome civic center—opened May 15, 1957

Wallops Island

Satellite—satellite placed in orbit by an all-solid-propellant rocket—launched—Feb. 16, 1961

Satellite—satellite with an electrostatic (ion) engine—*SERT 1*—launched, July 20, 1964

Walnut Grove

Reaper—reaper that was practical—C. H. McCormick—1831

Wheeling

See Wheeling, W.Va.

Williamsburg

American Indian School—American Indian school (permanent)—established—1720

Capitol—erected—1698

College—college charter granted by the Crown—Feb. 8, 1693

College—college proposed—William and Mar[ ] 1617

College—college to confer medals as prizes—1[ ]

College—college to have a full faculty—Will[ ] and Mary

College—college to receive a coat of arms fr[ ] the College of Heralds—William and Mar[ ] May 14, 1694

College—elective system of study—introduce[ ] 1779

Cook Book—*Compleat Housewife*—publishe[ ] 1742

Fencing Book—*Compleat System of Fencin[ ]* published—1734

Fraternity (Greek-letter)—scholastic fraternit[ ] Phi Beta Kappa—founded—Dec. 5, 1776

Freemasons—Masonic Grand Lodge—organi[ ] —Oct. 13, 1778

Grammar—English grammar by an America[ ] Hugh Jones

History Instruction—school of modern histor[ ] 1803

Honor System—of conducting examinations—[ ] troduced—1779

Hospital—insane hospital (state)—opened—[ ] 12, 1773

Language Instruction—modern language schoo[ ] in a college—1779

Medical Book—pleurisy book—*An Essay on Pleurisy*, by John Tennent—printed by Willi[ ] Parks—1736

Newspaper—newspaper published south of Potomac River—*Virginia Gazette*—publishe[ ] Aug. 5, 1736

Novel—novel (pamphlet)—*A Pretty Story*, Francis Hopkinson—printed—1774

Physician—physician (Jewish) to head an ins[ ] asylum—John de Sequeyra—1770

Political Economy Course—political econo[ ] course—1784

Theater—theater—built—1718

Visiting Celebrities—emperor of Japan to visit continental United States—Hirohito—arriv[ ] Sept. 30, 1975

Yorktown

Customhouse—1706

WASHINGTON

Insurance—workers' compensation insura[ ] law (state)—passed—March 14, 1911

Sex Discrimination—state to ban sex discrim[ ] tion—law enacted, May 17—effective, Jul[ ] 1971

State—state named for a native-born America[ ] admitted to Union, Nov. 11, 1889

Bremerton

Ferryboat—streamlined ferryboat—commer[ ] service to Seattle, Wash.—July 4, 1935

WASHINGTON—*Continued*

Woodland

Aviation—Airplane—skyjack that was successful
—D. B. Cooper—Nov. 24, 1971

Yakima County

American Indian School—American Indian
boarding school on a reservation—Yakima
Agency Boarding School—opened—1860

WEST VIRGINIA

Industrial Recovery Act—state to place all its em-
ployees under the blanket code of the National
Recovery Act Code—July 27, 1933
Tax—sales tax (state)—effective—July 1, 1921

Alderson

Prison—prison (federal) exclusively for women—
Federal Industrial Institution for Women—
opened 1926

Berkeley Springs

Spa—opened to the public—1756

Charles Town

Postal Service—rural free delivery—Oct. 1, 1896

Charleston

Jockey—jockey (woman) to win on a regular pari-
mutuel flat track—B. J. Rubin—Feb. 22, 1969
Road—brick pavement—1870
Salt—salt well—west of Alleghenies—1808

Chester

Jockey—jockey (woman) to ride 2 winners in 1
day—B. J. Rubin—March 8, 1969

Colliers

Prizefighter—bareknuckle world heavyweight
champion (American)—Paddy Ryan—won title, June 1, 1880

Fetterman

Civil War—Union soldier killed by enemy action
in the Civil War—B. T. Brown—May 22, 1861

Halltown

Postal Service—rural free delivery—Oct. 1, 1896

Institute

Coal—coal hydrogenation chemicals pilot plant
(large)—opened—May 8, 1952

Kanawha

Trust—trust—organized—Nov. 10, 1817

Mullens

Locomotive—locomotive (super-giant)—place
service—Jan. 27, 1948

Parkersburg

Vitrolite—manufactured—1907

Uvilla

Postal Service—rural free delivery—Oct. 1,

Welch

Garage—municipally owned parking buildi
opened Sept. 1, 1941

Wheeling

Gas—municipal gas plant—acquired—1871
Nails—steel-cut nails—manufactured—1883
Ship—steamboat (double-decked)—*Washin*
—launched—June 4, 1816
Soda Fountain—soda fountain patent—grant
April 24, 1833

White Sulphur Springs

Golfer—golfer to break 60 for 18 holes in a m
tournament—S. J. Snead—May 16, 1959

WISCONSIN

Election Law—primary election (statewid
Sept. 4, 1906
Forest Service—forestry inquiry commis
(state)—authorized—March 23, 1867
Governor—governor removed from office t
state supreme court—W. A. Barstow—185
Insurance—unemployment insurance act—
28, 1932
Insurance—workers' compensation insura
law (state)—effective—May 3, 1911
Probate Legislation—probate law eliminating
tape—enacted June 22—effective Oct. 1, 1
Representative (U.S.)—Socialist representati
V. L. Berger—1911–1913
Senator (U.S.)—father and son senators at
same session—Henry Dodge of Wisconsin
A. C. Dodge of Iowa—Dec. 7, 1848–Feb. 22,
Woman Suffrage—woman suffrage amend
approved by Congress—ratified—June 10,

Appleton

Electric Power Plant—hydroelectric power p
—opened—Sept. 30, 1882

Beloit

College—college whose tuition fees were b
on family income—Beloit College—plan ad
ed Oct. 11, 1971—effective Sept. 5, 1972

WISCONSIN—*Continued*

Peshtigo

Forest Fire—forest fire of consequence—Oct. 8, 1871

Portage

Lie Detector—Keeler Polygraph—tested—Feb. 2, 1935

Racine

Bicycle Traffic Court—held—June 18, 1936

Confectionery Machine—for making "suckers"—manufactured—1908

Continuation School—continuation school established by state law—opened—Nov. 3, 1911

Dictionary—Bohemian-American dictionary—published—1876

Milk—malted milk—invented—William Horlick —1882

Newspaper—Czech-language newspaper—*Slovan Amerikansky*—published—Jan. 1, 1860

Strike—strike to last longer than a year—J. I. Case Manufacturing Company—Dec. 26, 1945–March 9, 1947

Ripon

Republican Party—Republican Party meeting (local)—name "Republican" suggested—March 20, 1854

Watertown

Births—quintuplets—Feb. 13, 1875

Waukesha

Advertisement—three-dimensional newspa advertisement—*Daily Freeman*—June 12, 1

WYOMING

Forest—national forest—Shoshone National est—established, March 30, 1891

Governor—woman governor of a state—N Ross—Jan. 5, 1925

Woman Suffrage—state to grant suffrage women—July 10, 1890

Cheyenne

Aviation—flight attendant (woman)—flight fi San Francisco—May 15, 1930

Holiday—Frontier Day—celebrated—Sept. 1897

Devils Tower National Monument

Monument—national monument—establishe Sept. 24, 1906

Laramie

Recreational Ranching Course—in a college— degree awarded—June 6, 1938

South Pass City

Judge—woman justice of the peace—E. H. Mc —appointed Feb. 17, 1870

Yellowstone National Park

Park—park (national)—authorized—March 1872